WHO'S WHO
IN OPERA

AN INTERNATIONAL
BIOGRAPHICAL DIRECTORY
OF SINGERS, CONDUCTORS,
DIRECTORS, DESIGNERS,
AND ADMINISTRATORS.
ALSO INCLUDING PROFILES
OF 101 OPERA COMPANIES

MARIA F. RICH
EDITOR

ARNO PRESS

A NEW YORK TIMES COMPANY

NEW YORK • 1976

ARNO Press, Inc. New York 10017

Manufactured in the United States of America

Library of Congress Cataloging in Publication Data
Main entry under title:

Who's who in opera.

(Arno Press who's who series)
1.   Opera—Biography—Dictionaries.   2.   Opera—
Directories.   I.   Series.
ML102.06W5   782.1'092'2   [B]   75-7963
ISBN 0-405-06652-X

Contents

Foreword

A few days after his appointment as general manager of the Metropolitan Opera, Goeran Gentele was asked what he thought an opera house should be. His reply was one word, "Alive".

This is an alive book about an alive art. Nothing like it has ever been undertaken before. That it will be a must for professionals and libraries is obvious. It will also give boundless information and pleasure to opera-lovers in all categories.

Where else will you find that Salvador Novoa sings something besides *Bomarzo*, that Reri Grist began as a child performer on Broadway, the budgets of Salzburg and Tel Aviv, the season setups of Helsinki and Prague, that Warsaw has a subscription of forty-eight per cent of capacity?

There are over 2,300 listings from Abbado to Zylis-Gara in the biographical section and the particulars on 101 opera companies in 25 countries.

The nearest we have ever come to this in completeness is *Annals of Opera* by Alfred Loewenberg, published in 1943.

Freddie Loewenberg, as his friend John Gutman called him, was headed toward a career in philosophy but was seduced by the lyric muse. According to *Grove's Dictionary*, he attended "every operatic performance to which he could gain access" and patiently began to assemble details "of every opera ever written about which he could obtain information".

The Nazi terror drove him into exile in 1935. He drew a small pension of a few pounds from a refugee relief organization and was the house guest of Victor Gollancz in London. The British Museum proved a gold mine of new sources and he worked there every day until the closing bell. He would then gather his papers and stop for his black coffee at the Gutmans' nearby.

The editor of *Who's Who in Opera* can lay claim to no such dramatic circumstances. Her labors nevertheless are extraordinary, exhaustive, and indispensable. For the last ten years Mrs. Rich has been editor of the *Central Opera Service Bulletin*, an invaluable quarterly covering with miraculous conciseness the entire field. Central Opera Service, of which she is the director, is an arm of the Metropolitan Opera National Council and is a unique clearinghouse of information on opera. It can tell a regional company, of which there are more than 700 in the United States, anything from where to get the orchestral parts of *Tristan* to renting a backdrop for *Traviata*.

The thanks of the entire operatic community around the world must go to Arno Press, a *New York Times* company, for undertaking and financing this monumental work.

Franz Liszt said "The theatre is a madhouse; the opera is the ward for the incurables". But it's a glorious madness.

Come join the club!

Francis Robinson
Assistant Manager, Metropolitan Opera

Preface

WHO'S WHO IN OPERA is being published in response to a need expressed by librarians, musicologists, opera administrators, performers and writers. It is a reference source on the professional activities and personal data of currently active operatic artists and on international operatic trends.

The tasks faced in the preparation of this volume were: to establish objective criteria for selection of artists to be included; to determine which artists met these criteria; to design questionnaires which would elicit the desired information; to reach eligible artists and secure a high degree of response; to sort, verify and edit the information received; to account for artists who did not reply.

To assist the editor in policy decisions, the publisher invited distinguished directors from eight of the world's leading opera companies to form an Advisory Panel. The members of the Advisory Panel are listed on page ii.

It was the publisher's desire to include living artists from opera companies in all countries with an active operatic program and to have the representation of individual countries reflect the degree of their operatic activity. To this end the members of the Advisory Panel selected 144 opera companies and festivals in 33 countries from an initial list of 225 opera companies prepared by the editor. The final choice included 24 companies from the Federal Republic of Germany and 15 from Italy. The United States, where there were more than 6,500 operatic performances during the 1974-75 season, is also well represented. A full listing of the selected companies is to be found on page 675.

Eligibility of artists was based on their engagements with one or more of these major companies, insuring international representation and professional standing among the artists included.

The following requirements were established: Since the beginning of the 1971-72 season: singers must have sung at least five major roles with one or more of the designated companies; conductors must have conducted at least five different operas with one or more of the designated companies; stage directors/producers must have staged at least two new opera productions with one or more of the designated companies; designers must have designed sets, costumes or lighting for at least two new opera productions with one or more of the designated companies. Administrators must have been in key administrative positions with any of the designated companies after the beginning of the 1971-72 season.

Unfortunately, these criteria exclude some important living singers who have retired or are no longer singing leading roles in major opera houses. However, their complete repertoire is mainly of historical interest and many of them are discussed in other books.

The latter is also true of composers. Thanks to three Central Opera Service Directories of Contemporary Operas published in 1967, 1969 and 1975 listing over 3,500 operas written since 1950, the output of contemporary composers all over the world is well documented. Therefore, *Who's Who in Opera* does not include composers or librettists.

In order to determine which operas and roles to include, the editor undertook a survey of the international operatic repertoire of the last four seasons. It disclosed that more than 800 operas had been performed, excluding operettas and light opera. The number of operas chosen for listing in the questionnaires was 465 written by 169 composers. The number of roles included in the questionnaires was 1,771 (517 soprano, 269 mezzo/contralto, 452 tenor, 533 baritone/bass). Members of each voice category received the appropriate forms listing relevant roles.

Conductors, stage directors and designers received forms listing opera titles. Artists were invited to make additions whenever necessary. Inclusion of these was subject to editorial review. The decision concerning what constitutes a major role was based on detailed research of scores, musical literature, union designation, company contracts and polled expert opinion. Length of role was not necessarily a deciding factor and no attempt was made to designate one role in each vocal category for each opera.

Next came the task of distributing to the eligible artists the eight different forms: soprano, mezzo-soprano/contralto, tenor, baritone/bass, conductor, stage director/producer, designer, administrator. Since, until the publication of this book, no lists of such artists existed, a variety of different channels had to be used.

Of primary importance were the major opera companies selected by the Advisory Panel. Forms were sent to companies and festivals in 133 cities on all five continents. The letters of transmission accompanying the questionnaires were in four different languages: English, French, German, and Italian. Forms also went to more than 250 artists' managers in 38 countries for distribution to their eligible artists.

Arrangements were made with various trade unions in the United States and abroad for distribution of forms to their members (The American Guild of Musical Artists, American Federation of Musicians, Genossenschaft Deutscher Bühnen-Angehörigen, Syndicat Français des Artistes-interprètes, Syndicat Français des Artistes-musiciens, British Actors' Equity).

The assistance of cultural attachés in the United States and of Ministries of Culture in the various countries was also enlisted. The members of the Advisory Panel were of invaluable aid and support.

To facilitate the return of questionnaires from European countries, the office of Feffer and Simons in Weesp, The Netherlands, was designated to receive mail and forward it to Arno Press in New York.

Dr. Luigi Oldani, European representative of the Metropolitan Opera, kindly assisted in contacting Italian artists. For their convenience and to insure accuracy, he translated all questionnaires into Italian and reversed the process before returning the replies. Thanks to his broad knowledge, efficiency and thoroughness, there is a wide representation of Italian artists in *Who's Who in Opera*. Similarly, Dr. Pavel Ekstein of the National Opera in Prague, kindly assisted Czech artists in the completion of their forms. Questionnaires were translated into Russian and replies back into English by Metropolitan Opera baritone and language coach George Cehanovsky in order that Russian artists might complete the forms in their native tongue.

In order to make *Who's Who in Opera* complete as well as authoritative, the editorial staff prepared a list of eligible major international artists whose inclusion was deemed essential. Biographical information on the limited number who did not return their questionnaires was obtained by research in existing literature, company records, newspaper files, archives of the Central Opera Service, and particularly those of the Lincoln Center Library for the Performing Arts in New York.

The biographical section of *Who's Who in Opera* contains 2,350 entries: 497 sopranos, 197 mezzo-sopranos and contraltos, 351 tenors, 508 baritones and basses, 287 conductors, 188 stage directors, 187 designers, and 135 administrators, not including among the latter those conductors and stage directors who also hold administrative positions. The book includes 1,814 opera titles and more than 6,000 roles, all performed by the biographees.

Who's Who in Opera presents more than one-quarter of a million facts. While dates and places of world premieres have been verified, it was not possible to check all information submitted. Special care has been taken to observe correct spelling throughout *Who's Who in Opera*, not only for opera titles, but particularly for roles whose spelling often varies from one reference book to another. For details see Repertoire section in Guidelines to Biographical Entries, page xiv.

Most of the biographical information is current as of the 1974-75 season. Wherever possible, artists were sent a rough proof and, where time permitted, changes called to our attention were made.

In the course of the work on *Who's Who in Opera* it became apparent that there was a need for basic information on major opera companies and festivals, presented on a comparable basis. It was therefore decided to expand this volume to include profiles of major international opera companies. A questionnaire was prepared and distributed to the 144 companies and festivals selected by the Advisory Panel. Of these, 101 responded in time for inclusion. These data are found in the opera company section.

The reader's indulgence is sought for any typographical errors which have eluded the best efforts to eliminate them. We hope that errata will be called to our attention so that we may make corrections for subsequent printings.

ACKNOWLEDGMENTS

This book could not have been undertaken or completed without the help of hundreds of members of the operatic community around the world. Leading administrators from more than 125 companies in 38 countries were involved, as well as hundreds of agents and artists. Unfortunately, for reasons of space they cannot all be mentioned here. However, recognition must be given to Dr. Luigi Oldani (Milan), Wolfgang Stoll of the Robert Schultz Agentur (Munich), Paul Rainer and Henri de la Grange (Paris), Jean Williams (London), and Thea Dispeker, Edgar Kneedler, Michael Ries and Tony Russo (New York).

The inestimable work of the Advisory Panel has been mentioned earlier. They helped to chart the course we all followed.

Making a most significant contribution to *Who's Who in Opera* were its three assistant editors, Robert D. Daniels, Frank Merkling and Paul Reif. They brought to their work a high degree of professionalism and diligence combined with consummate knowledge of the material. Responsible for the smooth organization of the tens of thousands of forms and the thousands of replies received were Patrice Glickman and Jeanne Kemp. Karl Kraus's resourcefulness and perseverance were much in evidence in tracking down artists and information.

Giving us initial encouragement and serving as an informal board of advisors whose judgment and experience helped facilitate our work were Sir Rudolf Bing, Jean Bowen, Raymond Ericson, George Jellinek, Warren Michon, Francis Robinson, Harold C. Schonberg, Susan Sommer and Clara Steuermann.

A special word of gratitude to Maestro Martin Rich, conductor at the Metropolitan Opera, who served *Who's Who In Opera* as minister without portfolio. His great knowledge of the operatic repertoire and his keen insight were invaluable.

Finally, we acknowledge the role of Mr. Clive Barnes, a man of many arts, who was instrumental in the decision to undertake this work.

Stanley R. Greenfield, *Director*
Maria F. Rich, *Editor*

Guidelines to Biographical Entries

Alphabetizing

All biographical entries are in alphabetical order in accordance with the letter-by-letter method. MAC precedes MC and both appear in their appropriate places among names beginning with M. DE, VAN and VON are also alphabetized using the letter-by-letter method.

Alphabetizing in the company section is by country. Within each country, companies are arranged in alphabetical order by city.

Abbreviations

Abbreviations will be found on page xvii. The book follows contemporary style trends in omitting all periods after abbreviations.

Personalia

Personal data were requested but not required for completion of questionnaires or for eligibility. Birth date or year is omitted if unknown or not supplied by the biographee; the country of birth is listed as it was known at that time, e g, "Germany" prior to 1945.

Marital status and private address are listed if submitted by the respondent. (An interesting fact brought to light was the many marriages between operatic performers.)

Nationality indicates citizenship and not origin.

Education

Only professional training is listed under "Studied". Degrees are not mentioned since titles and requirements vary among different countries. Listed first is the school(s), followed by the specific teacher at that institute, then by the city. In case of a singer's private instructions, the voice teacher is listed first, followed by the coach and the drama teacher, in that order. For conductors, teachers are listed in the following order: conducting, composition, instrument(s). It is self-evident that conductors studied conducting and singers studied voice. Therefore only related subjects are specifically mentioned.

Performing artists who also teach at present have this information included under "Teaches" towards the end of their entry, and "Affiliated with" if they are members of a faculty. Previous teaching positions are listed under "Previous occupations" only if they preceded the present career or position.

Debut

Debuts are presented as submitted and were not restricted to major roles or to the designated opera companies.

Previous occupations; Previous positions

Under "Previous occupations" only those unrelated to the present career were acceptable. "Music student" did not qualify as an entry but studies in a different field did, and we find many operatic artists who have completed studies in an unrelated profession.

"Previous positions" were restricted to administrative ones, applicable to administrators, conductors or stage directors who now occupy or have occupied administrative posts.

Awards

The name or title of the award is succeeded by the awarding institution or individual and, wherever known, the year it was awarded.

Related professional activities

For each of the categories of professionals featured in *Who's Who in Opera,* special questions were included to elicit information on related professional activities: recital and concert work for opera singers; symphonic, administrative or compositional involvement for conductors; dramatic theatre, film or television affiliation, opera administration, or writing, designing or singing for stage directors; work in architecture, painting, sculpting, illustration, fashion or interior design for set or costume designers. A listing of museum and gallery exhibits is also part of the designers' entries.

Opera companies

The listing of major companies where an artist performed is limited to the 144 designated organizations shown on page 675. They are arranged in alphabetical order by country, followed by cities within each country. Names of companies or theatres are included only where more than one has been selected from the same city. In these cases names are listed in brief for identification purposes only.

Repertoire

One of the unique features of *Who's Who in Opera* is the inclusion of artists' repertoire. By limiting it to performances with the major designated companies, a degree of proficiency in roles listed is assured, while the total repertoire will include roles studied only or performed under workshop conditions.

Special attention and research by the editorial staff was devoted to correct spelling of opera titles and particularly of operatic roles. Those of Italian, German, French and English language operas appear in the original, all others are translated into English, with the rare exception of an opera better known in a second language, e g, *Pique Dame*. Operas by Italian composers originally written to a French libretto are always referred to in French. To retain clarity and uniformity throughout the book, roles and titles are always listed in the same language and do not reflect the language of the actual performance.

Capitalization in opera titles follows the style of the individual language. All articles are deleted from the beginning of opera titles.

Operas and roles in the biographical entries are grouped by composers who appear in alphabetical order. Operas or eligible roles added by individual artists follow the initial listing preceded by "Also". All opera titles are in italics; in singers' entries they follow the roles in parentheses (). In the case of a title role, the name of the opera is not repeated. The only exceptions to this rule occur under "World premieres". Two roles in one opera are connected by an ampersand (&) followed by the opera title, while the same character in two or more operas is listed only once followed by the opera titles in a single parenthetical expression ().

An asterisk (*) identifies roles sung or operas conducted/staged/ designed with the aforementioned companies during the four seasons of 1971-72 to 1974-75. (See eligibility requirements described in Preface.)

Several entries have no asterisks and would seem not to fulfill the prescribed requirements. However, only those were accepted where it was evident from the date of the debut that all or most performances took place during the last four seasons. Of over 2,900 returns, 2,350 were found eligible.

A dagger (†) indicates operas staged *and* designed. For double dagger (‡) see below.

Recordings, Film, Television

Complete roles recorded by singers and complete operas recorded by conductors are marked by a double dagger (‡). Recording companies for whom the artist recorded are listed following the repertoire. All performances of complete works on film or television are listed under that heading and, wherever available, include information on the film and television company.

World premieres

Because of its special significance, participation in world premieres is mentioned separately with information on date and place which has been verified. Roles or operas listed under this heading are not repeated under repertoire. Participation in world premieres and debuts is not restricted to the designated companies.

Artists' agents

Where an artist is represented by one or more agents or managers, a code designation is used to identify the agent. The management's name and address may be found in the Directory of International Artists' Agents arranged by country on page 679. Names and addresses of artists' consultants are listed for Italy, where a law prohibits the establishment of artists' managers.

The Editor

Guide to Abbreviations

ABC	American Broadcasting Company
abt	about
Acad	Academy, Académie, academic
Accad	Accademia
accmp	accompanist, accompaniment
Acct	Accountant
act	acting
AD	Anno Domini
addr	address
Adm	Administration, administrator, administrative
Adv	Advisor, advisory
advt	advertisement, advertising
aff	affiliate, affiliated
AGIS	Associazione Generale Italiana dello Spectacolo
AGMA	American Guild of Musical Artists
Agy	Agency
AK	Alaska, USA
Akad	Akademie
AL	Alabama, USA
Alta	Alberta, Canada
Amer	America, American
ANELS	Associazione Nazionale Ente Lirici e Sinfonici
ANTA	American National Theater & Academy
Apr	April
AR	Arkansas, USA
ARCM	Associate of the Royal College of Music
ARG	Argentina
art	artist, artistic
AS	Austrian Shillings
ASCAP	American Society of Composers, Authors & Publishers
ASID	American Society of Interior Designers
As Li Co	Associazone Lirico Compagnia
Assn	Association, Associazione
Assoc	Associate(s)
Asst	Assistant
Aud	Auditions

aud	audience
audt	auditorium
AUS	Austria
AUSTRL	Australia
Aug	August
Ave	Avenue
avg	average
Awd(s)	Award(s)
AZ	Arizona, USA
B	Bachelor
b	bei
BA	Bachelor of Arts
BAA	Bachelor of Arts Administration
bar	baritone
BASF	Badische Anilin & Soda Fabrik (tapes & records)
BBC	British Broadcasting Corporation
BC	British Columbia, Canada
Bd	Board
BED	Bachelor of Education
BEL	Belgium
BFA	Bachelor of Fine Arts
B Fr	Belgian Franc
bk	book
Bldg	Building
Blvd	Boulevard
BM	Bachelor of Music
BRA	Brazil
Brdc	Broadcasting
BS	Bachelor of Science
bs	bass
bs b	bass-baritone
BUL	Bulgaria
busn	business
CA	California, USA
CAN	Canada
cap	capacity
Capt	Captain
CBC	Canadian Broadcasting Corporation

CBE	Commander of the British [
CBS	Columbia Broadcasting Sy
Cert	Certificate, Certified
Chefdram	Chefdramaturg
Chmn	Chairman
chr	chorus
cit	citation
Cnt	Center
Cntry	Country
Cnty	County
CO	Colorado, USA
Co(s)	Company(ies)
Coll	College
Collab	Collaborator
Commdr	Commander
Commen	Commendatore
Commss	Commission
Commtt	Committee
comp	composer, composition
Compt	Competition
Conc	Concours, Concorso
conct	concert
cond	conductor, conducting
Conf	Conference
Cong	Congress
constr	construction
Consv	Conservatory
Cont	Contest
contmp	contemporary
contr	contralto
Coord	Coordinator
Corp	Corporation, corporate
COS	Central Opera Service
Counc	Council
Cresc	Crescent
CRI	Composers Recordings Incorporated
CSR	Republic of Czechoslovakia
CSSR	Socialist Republic of Czechoslovakia
cst	costume(s)
CT	Connecticut, USA
Cult	Culture, cultural
CZE	Czechoslovakia
DAR	Daughters of the American Revolution
darst	darstellende
DC	District of Columbia, USA
DE	Delaware, USA
Dec	December
DEN	Denmark
Dept	Department
designt	designate
Devlp	Development
D f	Dutch florin
DFA	Doctor of Fine Arts
DG(G)	Deutsche Grammophon (Gesellschaft)
DHL	Doctor of Humanities and Letters
dial	dialogue
diff	different
Din	Yugoslavian Dinar

..	Diploma
Dir	Director
Dist	District
Distng	Distinguished
Div	Division
DL	Doctor of Humane Letters
DM	Deutsche Mark
DM	Doctor of Music
dnc	dancer, dancing
Dram	Dramaturg, dramatic
Dr Med	Doctor of Medicine
dsgn	designer, designing, design
ds sc/cst/lt	designer of scenery/ costumes/lights
E	East
Ed	Editor, edit
educt	educator, education, educational
elct	electric
elctrn	electronic
elem	elementary
EMI	Electric & Musical Industries
engr	engineer
ens	ensemble
Esq	Esquire
est	estimated
exec	executive
f	für, for
FBA	Fellow of the British Academy
fclt	faculty
fdr	founder
Feb	February
Fed	Federation
fed	federal
Fest	Festival
FIN	Finland
Fin	Finance, financial
finl	finalist
FL	Florida, USA
Fllshp	Fellowship
FMK	Finnish Mark
Fndt	Foundation
form	former, formerly
Found	Founder
Fr	Frau
FRA	France
Frankfurt/M	Frankfurt am Main
Frankfurt/O	Frankfurt an der Oder
Freiburg/Br	Freiburg im Breisgau
Fr Ger/FRG	Federal Republic of Germany
Frl	Fräulein
Fr	French Franc
FRSA	Fellow of Royal Society of the Arts
G/g	Gasse
GA	Georgia, USA
Gal	Gallery
Gdns	Gardens
Gen	General
Gen Mus Dir/GMD	Generalmusikdirektor
Ger DR/GDR	German Democratic Republic
Ger Dr M	East German Mark

GmbH	Gesellschaft mit beschrenkter Haftung	M	Monsieur
Gov	Governor, governing	MA	Massachusetts, USA
grad	graduate	Ma	Maestra
GRE	Greece	MAA	Master of Arts Administration
gvnmt	government	maj	major
		Man	Manitoba, Canada
HDAL	Honorary Doctor of Arts and Letters	Mar	March
HDM	Honorary Doctor of Music	MBE	Member of the British Empire
Hgts	Heights	M B Rockf Fund	Martha Baird Rockefeller Fund for Music
HH	Hansestadt Hamburg	MD	Maryland, USA
HI	Hawaii, USA	Mdl	Medal, Medallion
HM	Her/His Majesty	ME	Maine, USA
HMV	His Master's Voice	mech	mechanic, mechanical
HOL	Holland	Mem	Memorial
Hon	Honorary, honors, Honorable	mem	member
HRH	Her (His) Royal Highness	Merc	Mercury Records
HS	High School	Met	Metropolitan Opera
HUN	Hungary	Met Op Ntl Counc Aud	Metropolitan Opera National Council Auditions
Hun fl	Hungarian florin	MEX	Mexico
		MFA	Master of Fine Arts
IA	Iowa, USA	MGM	Metro-Goldwyn-Mayer (records)
ID	Idaho, USA	Mgmt	Management
IIE	Institute of International Education	MI	Michigan, USA
IL	Illinois, USA	Min	Minister, Ministry
IMZ	Internationales Musik Zentrum	MM	Master of Music
IN	Indiana, USA	MME	Master of Music Education
Inc	Incorporated	Mme	Madame
incl	including, inclusive	MN	Minnesota, USA
indv	individual	Mng	Manager
Insp	Inspector	MO	Missouri, USA
Inst	Institute, Institution	Mo	Maestro
instrm	instrument	MS	Mississippi, USA
Int	Intendant	ms	mezzo-soprano
Intl	International	MT	Montana, USA
ISR	Israel	Munc	Municipal
ITA	Italy	Mus	Music, Musical
ITI	International Theatre Institute	mus com	musical comedy
		muscl	musicologist
Jan	January	muscn	musician
JPN	Japan	Musm	Museum
Jr	Junior		
Jul	July	N	North
Jun	June	n/a	not available
		NATS	National Association of Teachers of Singing
Kcs	Czech Krona	NB	New Brunswick, Canada
Kmsg	Kammersänger(in)	NBC	National Broadcasting Company
Konsv	Konservatorium	NC	North Carolina, USA
Kr	Swedish Krona	ND	North Dakota, USA
Krs	Kreis	NDR	Norddeutscher Rundfunk
KS	Kansas, USA	NE	Nebraska, USA
KY	Kentucky, USA	NEA	National Endowment for the Arts
		NEAH	National Endowment for the Arts and the Humanities
L	Italian Lire		
LA	Louisiana, USA	NET	National Educational Television
La	Lane	NF	Newfoundland, Canada
lab	laboratory	NFMC	National Federation of Music Clubs
lect	lecture, lecturer		
Libr	Library	NH	New Hampshire, USA
LRAM	Licentiate of the Royal Academy of Music	NHK	Nippon Hoso Kyokai/Japanese Broadcasting Corporation
lt	light, lighting		
Ltd	Limited	NJ	New Jersey, USA
Lyr	Lyric		

N Kr	Norwegian Krona	**QC**	Queen's Counsellor
NM	New Mexico, USA		
NO	Nieder Oesterreich	**r**	rue
No	Number	**RAI**	Radio Italiano
NOI	National Opera Institute	**RCA**	Radio Corporation of America
NOR	Norway	**RCM**	Royal College of Music
Nov	November	**rcrdg**	recording
NPT	National Preis Träger(in)	**Rd**	Road
NS	Nova Scotia, Canada	**Rdfk**	Rundfunk
NSW	New South Wales, Australia	**reconstr**	reconstructed
Ntl	National	**recpt**	recipient, receipt
NV	Nevada, USA	**recptst**	receptionist
NY	New York, USA	**reg**	regional
		Rep	Republic
O	Ohio, USA	**rep**	repertoire
OBE	Order of the British Empire	**Repres**	Representative
occas	occasional	**repty**	repertory
occup	occupation	**Res**	Residence, resident
Oct	October	**ret**	retired
off	office, official	**rev**	revised
OISTT	Organization of Scenographers and Theater Technicians	**RI**	Rhode Island, USA
		RIAS	Radio in the American Sector, Berlin
OK	Oklahoma, USA		
Ont	Ontario, Canada	**RJO**	Radio Jugend Orchester
Op	Opera	**RL**	Romanian Lei
OR	Oregon, USA	**Rt Hon**	Right Honorable
orch	orchestra, orchestration		
Ord	Order of . . .	**S**	South; also San, Santa
ORF	Oesterreichischer Rundfunk	**SAF**	South Africa
orgn	organize, organization	**Sask**	Saskatchewan, Canada
orig	original	**SC**	South Carolina, USA
ORTF	Organisation de Radio et Télévision Française	**Scand**	Scandinavian
		Schl	School
		Schlshp	Scholarship
P	Spanish Peseta	**Sch M**	School of Music
p	British pence	**scn**	scenery
PBS	Public Broadcasting System	**SD**	South Dakota, USA
Pde	Parade	**SDR**	Süddeutscher Rundfunk
PEI	Prince Edward Island, Canada	**seat cap**	seating capacity
perf	performing, performs	**secy**	secretary
pf(s)	performance(s)	**Sep**	September
PhD	Doctor of Philosophy	**S Fr**	Swiss Franc
Phil	Philharmonic	**Sig**	Signore
Pk	Park	**Siga**	Signora
Pkwy	Parkway	**Socy**	Society
Pl	Place	**sop**	soprano
POB	Post Office Box	**SOR**	Südostdeutscher Rundfunk
POL	Poland	**SPA**	Spain
POR	Portugal	**spec**	special, specializes
PQ	Province of Quebec, Canada	**Spiell**	Spielleiter
PR	Public Relations; also Puerto Rico, USA	**spons**	sponsored
		Sq	Square
prem	premiere	**Sr**	Senior
Pres	President	**St**	Street; Saint
prev	previous	**Staatl**	Staatliche
prgm	program	**Städt**	Städtische
princ	principal	**stand**	standard
prod(s)	production(s), producer	**St Dir/st dir**	Stage Director
Prof	Professor	**stg(d)**	stage(d)
prof	professional	**stipd**	stipend
PS	Public School	**Str**	Strasse
Pt	Point	**Svc**	Service
publ	public	**Stud**	Studies
Pza	Piazza	**Svrint**	Sovrintendente

SWE	Sweden		**VEN**	Venezuela
SWI	Switzerland		**Verein**	Vereinte(r)
symph	symphony		**vers**	version
			VP	Vice President
t b a	to be announced		**VT**	Vermont, USA
tchr	teacher			
tech	technical; technician		**W**	West
tel	telephone		**WA**	State of Washington, USA
temp	temporary		**WDR**	Westdeutscher Rundfunk
ten	tenor		**WI**	Wisconsin, USA
thtr	theater		**win**	winner
TN	Tennessee, USA		**wkshp**	workshop
transl	translate, translator, translation		**wld prem**	world premiere
Treas	Treasurer, Treasury		**wmn**	woman, women
trng	training		**WW II**	World War II
TV	Television		**WY**	Wyoming, USA
TX	Texas, USA			
			Y	Japanese Yen
u	útja		**yr**	year
UCLA	University of California at Los Angeles		**yng**	young
			YUG	Yugoslavia
UK	United Kingdom			
Univ	University		**ZDF**	Zweites Deutsches Fernsehen
USA	United States of America; or United Scenic Artists		**ZI**	Polish Zloti
USC	University of Southern California			
USITT	United States Institute of Theatre Technology			
USSR	Union of Socialist Soviet Republics			

V Via
VA Virginia, USA
var various, varied, variety
Vc Vice

SYMBOLS:

*roles sung, operas conducted, staged or designed during the four seasons ending 1974-75.

‡roles or operas recorded in their entirety.

†operas staged *and* designed.

[†] deceased [after August 1975].

Biographical Entries

A

ABBADO, CLAUDIO. Conductor of opera and symphony. Italian. Music Dir & Resident Cond, Teatro alla Scala, Milan since 1969. Also Princ Cond, Phil Orch, Vienna 1971-, Res Cond, La Scala Orch, Milan; Princ Guest Cond, London Symph. Born 26 Jun 1933, Milan. Wife Gabriella. Three children. Studied: Giuseppe Verdi Consv, Milan; Acad of Music, H Swarowsky, Vienna; incl piano. **Operatic debut:** *Love for Three Oranges,* Teatro Comunale Trieste 1959. Symphonic debut: Orch Filarmonica Trieste 1958. Awards: First Prize, Koussevitzky Compt, Tanglewood, MA 1958 & Mitropoulos Compt, New York 1963; intl recording prizes; Mozart-Medaille, Vienna 1973.

Conducted with major companies in AUS: Salzburg Fest, Vienna Staatsoper; CZE: Prague National; FR GER: Berlin Deutsche Oper, Munich Staatsoper; HOL: Amsterdam; ITA: Florence Maggio & Comunale, Milan La Scala, Rome Opera, Trieste, Venice; UK: Edinburgh Fest, London Royal; USA: New York Met. **Operas with these companies incl** BELLINI: *Capuleti ed i Montecchi;* BERG: *Wozzeck;* DONIZETTI: *Lucia, Maria Stuarda;* MOZART: *Nozze di Figaro;* PROKOFIEV: *Fiery Angel, Love for Three Oranges★;* ROSSINI: *Barbiere di Siviglia★‡, Cenerentola, Italiana in Algeri★;* STRAVINSKY: *Oedipus Rex★;* VERDI: *Aida, Ballo, Don Carlo★, Macbeth, Simon Boccanegra★.* **World premieres:** MANZONI: *Atomtod* Piccola Scala, Milan 1965; NONO: *Al gran sole carico d'amore* La Scala, Milan 1975. Recorded for DG, Decca. Film—Unitel Munich: *Barbiere di Siviglia.* Conducted major orch in Europe, USA/Canada & Asia. **Res:** Milan, Italy. Mgmt: CAM/USA.

ABRAMS, RICHARD. Stages/produces opera & film and is an author. American. Born 13 Jan 1942, Cincinnati, O. Wife Nancy, occupation writer. Studied: Indiana Univ; Cincinnati, Hamburg, Cologne; incl music, piano, recorder. Operatic training as asst stage dir at New York City Opera, Metropolitan Opera. Previous occupation: coll lecturer, radio announcer, speechwriter. Awards: Chicago Lyric Stage Dir Compt 1964.

Directed/produced opera for major companies in USA: Baltimore, New Orleans, NY Met & City Opera, San Diego. **Operas staged with these cos** BELLINI: *Sonnambula★;* BORODIN: *Prince Igor;* DONIZETTI: *Elisir★;* HUMPERDINCK: *Hänsel und Gretel;* MOORE: *Ballad of Baby Doe;* MOZART: *Entführung aus dem Serail;* OFFENBACH: *Contes d'Hoffmann★;* PUCCINI: *Bohème, Butterfly;* SAINT-SAENS: *Samson et Dalila★;* STRAUSS, R: *Rosenkavalier★;* TCHAIKOVSKY: *Pique Dame★;* VERDI: *Ballo in maschera★;* WAGNER: *Meistersinger★, Parsifal★, Walküre★, Siegfried★, Götterdämmerung★, Tristan und Isolde★;* WEBER: *Freischütz.* Teaches. **Res:** 325 Riverside Dr, New York, USA.

ADAM, THEO SIEGFRIED. Bass-baritone. German. Resident mem: Staatsoper, Berlin. Born 1 Aug 1926, Dresden, Germany. Wife Eleonore. Two children. Studied: Rudolf Dittrich, Dresden. **Debut:** Eremit (*Freischütz*) State Opera, Dresden, Ger DR 1949.

Sang with major companies in ARG: Buenos Aires; AUS: Salzburg Fest, Vienna Staatsoper; CZE: Prague National; FIN: Helsinki; FRA: Paris; FR GER: Bayreuth Fest, Cologne, Düsseldorf-Duisburg, Frankfurt, Hamburg, Mannheim, Munich Staatsoper, Stuttgart, Wiesbaden; GER DR: Berlin Staatsoper, Dresden, Leipzig; HUN: Budapest; ITA: Rome Teatro dell'Opera; POL: Warsaw Teatr Wielki; POR: Lisbon; SWE: Stockholm; SWI: Geneva; UK: Edinburgh Fest, London Royal Opera; USSR: Moscow Bolshoi; USA: Chicago, New York Met, San Francisco Opera. **Roles with these companies incl** d'ALBERT: Tommaso (*Tiefland*); BEETHOVEN: Don Pizarro★ & Rocco (*Fidelio*); BERG: Wozzeck★; HANDEL: King of Scotland (*Ariodante*), Giulio Cesare★; MOZART: Don Alfonso★ (*Così fan tutte*), Leporello & Don Giovanni★ (*Don Giovanni*), Conte Almaviva★ & Figaro (*Nozze di Figaro*), Sarastro (*Zauberflöte*); MUSSORGSKY: Boris★ & Pimen (*Boris Godunov*), Dosifei (*Khovanshchina*); PUCCINI: Scarpia★ (*Tosca*); STRAUSS, R: La Roche★ (*Capriccio*), Orest★ (*Elektra*), Barak★ (*Frau ohne Schatten*), Baron Ochs★ (*Rosenkavalier*), Jochanaan (*Salome*), Sir Morosus★ (*Schweigsame Frau*); STRAVINSKY: Creon (*Oedipus Rex*); VERDI: Ramfis (*Aida*), Philip II★ & Grande Inquisitore (*Don Carlo*), Pardre Guardiano (*Forza del destino*), Banquo (*Macbeth*), Zaccaria (*Nabucco*); WAGNER: Holländer★, König Heinrich★ (*Lohengrin*), Hans Sachs★ & Pogner (*Meistersinger*), Amfortas★ (*Parsifal*), Wotan (*Rheingold★, Walküre★*), Wanderer★ (*Siegfried*), Fasolt (*Rheingold*), Hunding (*Walküre*), Landgraf★ (*Tannhäuser*), König Marke★ (*Tristan und Isolde*). **World**

premieres: DESSAU: Einstein, Staatsoper Berlin, Ger DR 1974. Recorded for: EMI, Ariola, Eurodisc, Eterna, Polydor. Video/Film: (*Fidelio*). **Res:** Schillerstr 13, Dresden, Ger DR. Mgmt: MAA/USA; HLB/FRA; SLZ/FRG.

ADANI, MARIELLA; née Laura Adani. Lyric soprano (lirico leggiero). Italian. Born 17 Dec 1934, Parma, Italy. Husband Giorgio Tadeo, occupation opera singer. Two children. Studied: Consv Parma; Mo Campogalliani; Scuola Scala. **Debut:** Barbarina (*Nozze di Figaro*) La Scala Milan 1955.

Sang with major companies in ARG: Buenos Aires; AUS: Salzburg Fest, Vienna Staatsoper; FRA: Aix-en-Provence Fest, Paris, Toulouse; GRE: Athens Fest; FR GER: Berlin Deutsche Oper, Cologne, Hamburg, Mannheim, Munich Staatsoper, Wiesbaden; HOL: Amsterdam; ISR: Tel Aviv; ITA: Bologna, Florence Maggio & Comunale, Genoa, Milan La Scala, Naples, Palermo, Parma, Rome Opera & Caracalla, Trieste, Turin, Venice; MEX: Mexico City; MON: Monte Carlo; POR: Lisbon; SPA: Barcelona; SWI: Geneva, Zurich; UK: Edinburgh Fest, Glyndebourne Fest; USA: Chicago. **Roles with these companies incl** BIZET: Micaëla (*Carmen*); CIMAROSA: Carolina (*Matrimonio segreto*); DONIZETTI: Serafina (*Campanello*), Norina★ (*Don Pasquale*), Adina★ (*Elisir*), Linda di Chamounix, Rita★; GALUPPI: Eugenia (*Filosofo di campagna*); GLUCK: Amor (*Orfeo ed Euridice*); HAYDN: Clarissa (*Mondo della luna*); HUMPERDINCK: Gretel; JANACEK: Vixen (*Cunning Little Vixen*); MENOTTI: Amelia (*Amelia al ballo*), Laetitia (*Old Maid and the Thief*); MONTEVERDI: Clorinda (*Combattimento di Tancredi*); MOZART: Despina★ (*Così fan tutte*), Zerlina (*Don Giovanni*), Serpetta★ (*Finta giardiniera*), Susanna★ & Cherubino (*Nozze di Figaro*); PAISIELLO: Rosina (*Barbiere di Siviglia*); PERGOLESI: Lucrezia (*Frate 'nnamorato*), Lauretta (*Maestro di musica*), Serpina★‡ (*Serva padrona*); PUCCINI: Musetta★‡ (*Bohème*), Lauretta (*Gianni Schicchi*), Magda & Lisette (*Rondine*); ROSSINI: Fanny★ (*Cambiale di matrimonio*), Ninetta (*Gazza ladra*), Giulia (*Scala di seta*), Sofia★ (*Signor Bruschino*), Fiorilla (*Turco in Italia*); STRAUSS, J: Adele★ (*Fledermaus*); VERDI: Nannetta (*Falstaff*); WOLF-FERRARI: Rosaura (*Donne curiose*), Maliella (*Gioielli della Madonna*), Lucieta★ (*Quattro rusteghi*), Susanna (*Segreto di Susanna*). Also CIMAROSA: (*Astuzie femminili*); SALIERI: (*Grotta di Trofonio*); PERGOLESI: (*Livietta e Tracollo*); DONIZETTI: (*Betly*); PICCINNI: (*Buona figliola*); ROTA: (*Cappello di paglia*); STEFFANI: (*Tassilone*). Recorded for: RCA. Video—RAI TV: (*Astuzie femminili*). Gives recitals. Appears with symphony orchestra. **Res:** Copernico 59, Milan, Italy.

ADLER, KURT HERBERT. American. Gen Dir, San Francisco Opera Assn, War Memorial Opera House, Van Ness Ave, San Francisco, CA 94102; also of S F Spring Opera, Western Opera Theater, Merola Opera Program, Brown Bag Opera, all in San Francisco. In charge of overall adm matters, art policy, mus matters & finances. Is also an opera & symphony conductor. Born 2 Apr 1905, Vienna, Austria. Wife Nancy. Two children. Studied: Vienna Consv, Franz Schmidt, A Wunderer; Acad

of Music, Eugen Zador, Vienna. Plays the piano. Previous occupations: accompanist, lecturer. Form positions: res cond, Josefstädtertheater, Vienna 1925-28; var opera houses Germany & Italy 1928-34; Volksoper, Vienna 1934-36; asst to Toscanini, Salzburg 1936; res cond, Opera Co of Chicago 1938-43. Started with present company in 1943 as chorus master & cond; in present position since 1953. World premieres at theaters under his management: DELLO JOIO: *Blood Moon* San Francisco Opera 1961.

Conducted with major companies in AUS: Vienna Volksoper; ITA: Naples; USA: Chicago, San Francisco Opera. **Operas with these companies incl** BEETHOVEN: *Fidelio;* BIZET: *Carmen;* DONIZETTI: *Lucia;* FLOTOW: *Martha;* GOUNOD: *Faust;* HUMPERDINCK: *Hänsel und Gretel;* LEONCAVALLO: *Pagliacci;* MASCAGNI: *Cavalleria rusticana;* MASSENET: *Manon;* MOZART: *Così fan tutte, Don Giovanni★, Nozze di Figaro, Zauberflöte★;* PUCCINI: *Bohème★, Butterfly★, Suor Angelica, Tosca;* ROSSINI: *Barbiere di Siviglia;* STRAUSS, J: *Fledermaus;* VERDI: *Aida, Ballo in maschera, Forza del destino, Rigoletto, Traviata★, Trovatore★;* WAGNER: *Meistersinger, Walküre;* WEBER: *Freischütz.* Awards: State decorations from Italy, Germany, Austria. Initiated major policy changes including expansion of company from five-week to eleven-1/2-week season & adding subsidiary companies: Spring Opera—4 five-week res seasons at S F Curran Theatre; Western Opera Theater—touring comp with young American artists; Merola Training Program—six-week summer training for singers; Brown Bag Opera—noontime opera concerts. Introduced many foreign singers in American debuts. Trustee, Natl Opera Institute; Vice Pres, OPERA America; Prof Commtt COS; Mem Intl Club of Op Dirs. Teaches at San Francisco Opera, master classes. **Res:** 2058 Vallejo St, San Francisco, CA, USA.

ADLER, PETER HERMAN. Conductor of opera and symphony; operatic stage director. American. Dir & Resident Cond, Juilliard American Opera Center, New York 1973- . Born 2 Dec 1899, Jablonec, Czechoslovakia. Divorced. Studied: Consv Prague, CSR; incl violin, piano, timpani. **Operatic debut:** *Lohengrin* Brno Opera, CSR 1925. Symphonic debut: Symph of Kiev, USSR 1933. Awards: var awds for NBC TV Opera. Previous adm positions in opera: Mus Dir, Brno Opera, CSR 1925-27; Teplice Opera, CSR 1927-29; Bremen Opera, Germany 1929-32; Mus & Art Dir, NBC Opera, New York 1949-59; NET Opera 1969-73.

Conducted with major companies in CZE: Brno; USA: Baltimore, New York Met. **Operas with these companies incl** PUCCINI: *Manon Lescaut★;* STRAUSS, R: *Rosenkavalier;* VERDI: *Aida, Ballo in maschera★, Otello, Rigoletto.* Also WEILL: *Down in the Valley‡.* **World premieres:** MENOTTI: *Maria Golovin* Brussels 1958; DELLO JOIO: *St Joan/Trial at Rouen* 1956; FOSS: *Griffelkin* 1955; MARTINU: *Marriage* 1953, all at NBC Opera; BEESON: *My Heart's in the Highlands* 1970; PASATIERI: *Trial of Mary Lincoln* 1972, both at NET Opera. Recorded for RCA. Video—NBC TV 1949-59: *Così fan tutte; Nozze di Figaro; Don Giovanni; Entführung; Bar-*

biere; Traviata; Rigoletto; Macbeth; Bohème; Butterfly; Tosca; Gianni Schicchi; Tabarro; Suor Angelica; Salome; Rosenkavalier; Ariadne auf Naxos; War and Peace; NET TV 1969-73; From the House of the Dead; Queen of Spades*; Nightingale*. Conducted major orch in Europe, USA/Canada. Previous positions as Mus Dir with major orch: Kharkov Symph USSR 1933-35; Kiev Symph USSR 1935-37; Baltimore Symph, USA 1959-69. Teaches at Juilliard School, New York. Res: New York, NY, USA. Mgmt: CAM/USA.

ADOLBERT, BELA; né Turpinszky. Heldentenor. Hungarian. Resident mem: Hungarian State Opera, Budapest. Born 10 Dec 1933, Leva, Czechoslovakia. Wife Agnes Gippert. Two children. Studied: Alexander Sved, Jozsef Reti. Debut: Sid (Albert Herring) Hungarian State Opera 1959. Previous occupations: solicitor. Awards: First Prize, Liszt Awd.
Sang with major companies in FR GER: Kassel; HUN: Budapest. Roles with these companies incl JANACEK: Laca* (Jenufa); WAGNER: Erik (Fliegende Holländer), Walther* (Meistersinger), Siegmund* (Walküre), Siegfried (Siegfried*, Götterdämmerung*). Gives recitals. Appears with symphony orchestra. Res: Nepköztarsaság u 56, 1062 Budapest, Hungary. Mgmt: ITK/HUN; LSM/UK.

AF MALMBORG, GUNILLA EVA; née Plym-Forshell. Dramatic soprano. Swedish. Resident mem: Royal Opera, Stockholm. Born 26 Feb 1933, Luleå. Husband Lars, occupation Studienleiter, conductor. Three children. Studied: Royal Acad of Music, Ove Meyer Leegard, Stockholm. Debut: Marzelline (Fidelio) Royal Opera Co, Stockholm 1960. Awards: Kristina Nilsson and Set Svanholm Awds.
Sang with major companies in CAN: Vancouver; DEN: Copenhagen; FIN: Helsinki; FRA: Bordeaux, Nancy; FR GER: Kiel, Munich, Cologne; HUN: Budapest; ITA: Genoa, Naples, Trieste, Venice; MON: Monte Carlo; NOR: Oslo; SWE: Drottningholm Fest, Stockholm; UK: Glyndebourne Fest. Roles with these companies incl BEETHOVEN: Marzelline (Fidelio); BIET: Micaëla (Carmen); BRITTEN: Lady Billows* (Albert Herring); MASCAGNI: Santuzza (Cavalleria rusticana); MOZART: Donna Anna (Don Giovanni), Contessa* (Nozze di Figaro); OFFENBACH: Antonia* & Giulietta* (Contes d'Hoffmann); PUCCINI: Tosca*, Turandot*; STRAUSS, R: Kaiserin* (Frau ohne Schatten), Salome*; TCHAIKOVSKY: Tatiana (Eugene Onegin), Lisa* (Pique Dame); VERDI: Aida*, Amelia (Ballo in maschera), Elisabetta (Don Carlo), Alice Ford (Falstaff), Lady Macbeth, Abigaille (Nabucco); WAGNER: Elsa* & Ortrud* (Lohengrin), Sieglinde (Walküre), Brünnhilde (Walküre*, Siegfried*, Götterdämmerung*), Gutrune* (Götterdämmerung), Elisabeth (Tannhäuser), Isolde*. Mgmt: SVE/SWE; SLZ/FRG.

AHLSTEDT, DOUGLAS. Lyric tenor. American. Resident mem: Metropolitan Opera, New York. Born 16 Mar 1945, Jamestown, NY. Wife Linda, occupation music teacher. Studied: State Univ of NY, Fredonia; Eastman School of Music, Josephine Antoine, Rochester, NY. Debut: Don Ra-

miro (Cenerentola) Western Opera Theater, San Francisco 1971. Awards: First Prize & Met Contract Winner, Met Op Ntl Counc Aud 1973.
Sang with major companies in USA: New York Met, San Francisco Spring Opera. Roles with these companies incl BRITTEN: Male Chorus* (Rape of Lucretia), Peter Quint* (Turn of the Screw); STRAUSS, R: Ein Sänger* (Rosenkavalier); VERDI: Fenton*(Falstaff); ROSSINI: Almaviva (Barbiere di Siviglia). Appears with symphony orchestra. Res: 415 Deerwood Rd, Fort Lee, NJ 07024, USA.

AHNSJÖ, CLAES HÅKAN. Lyric tenor. Swedish. Resident mem: Bayerische Staatsoper, Munich. Born 1 Aug 1942, Stockholm. Wife Helena Jungwirth, occupation opera singer. Two children. Studied: Erik Saedén, Esther Ruhrseitz, Stockholm; Hanno Blaschke, Munich. Debut: Tamino (Zauberflöte) Royal Opera, Stockholm 1969.
Sang with major companies in FRA: Nancy; FR GER: Cologne, Frankfurt, Hamburg, Munich Staatsoper, Saarbrücken, Stuttgart; SWE: Drottningholm Fest, Stockholm. Roles with these companies incl BRITTEN: Albert Herring*; DONIZETTI: Ernesto* (Don Pasquale); HAYDN: Cecco (Mondo della luna); HENZE: Des Grieux* (Boulevard Solitude); MASSENET: Des Grieux* (Manon); MOZART: Ferrando* (Così fan tutte), Don Ottavio* (Don Giovanni), Belmonte* (Entführung), Idamante* (Idomeneo), Tamino* (Zauberflöte); ORFF: Tenor solo* (Carmina burana); PUCCINI: Rinuccio* (Gianni Schicchi); ROSSINI: Almaviva* (Barbiere di Siviglia), Giocondo* (Pietra del paragone); STRAUSS, R: Ein Sänger* (Rosenkavalier); STRAVINSKY: Tom Rakewell* (Rake's Progress); VERDI: Fenton* (Falstaff), Duca di Mantova* (Rigoletto); WAGNER: David* (Meistersinger), Walther v d Vogelweide* (Tannhäuser). Also HANDEL: Silvio* (Pastor fido); PERGOLESI: Ascanio (Frate 'nnamorato). World premieres: WERLE: King Gustavus & Prince Charles (Tintomara) Royal Opera, Stockholm 1973. Gives recitals. Appears with symphony orchestra. Res: Josef Danzer Str 2, D8033 Planegg-Munich, FR Ger. Mgmt: SLZ/FRG.

ALAUPOVIC, TUGOMIR. Bass-baritone & character baritone. Yugoslavian. Resident mem: Croatian Natl Opera, Zagreb; Stadttheater Klagenfurt, Austria. Born 26 Dec 1925, Zemun. Wife Durda, occupation med lab worker. Two children. Studied: Prof Louis Kaderabek, Prague; Prof Zlatko Sir, Zagreb. Debut: Graf Homonay (Zigeunerbaron) Komedija, Zagreb 1953. Awards: First Prize, Music Acad, Zagreb.
Sang with major companies in AUS: Graz; CZE: Prague Smetana; FRA: Paris; GRE: Athens Fest; FR GER: Mannheim, Stuttgart, Wiesbaden; GER DR: Berlin Komische Oper; HOL: Amsterdam; ITA: Bologna, Genoa, Naples, Trieste; SWI: Geneva; YUG: Dubrovnik, Zagreb, Belgrade. Roles with these companies incl BRITTEN: Bottom (Midsummer Night), Captain Balstrode (Peter Grimes); DONIZETTI: Dulcamara* (Elisir); GAY/Britten: Lockit* (Beggar's Opera); GOTOVAC: Sima* (Ero der Schelm); HAYDN: Eclittico (Mondo della luna); IBERT: Boniface

(*Angélique*); MARTINU: Hans (*Comedy on the Bridge*); MOZART: Guglielmo (*Così fan tutte*), Allazim (*Zaïde*), Papageno (*Zauberflöte*); MUSSORGSKY: Varlaam (*Boris Godunov*); PERGOLESI: Uberto (*Serva padrona*); PUCCINI: Gianni Schicchi, Sharpless (*Butterfly*), Lescaut (*Manon Lescaut*), Michele (*Tabarro*); PURCELL: Aeneas; ROSSINI: Figaro & Dott Bartolo (*Barbiere di Siviglia*), Don Magnifico (*Cenerentola*), Signor Bruschino; STRAVINSKY: Creon (*Oedipus Rex*); VERDI: Ford (*Falstaff*), Germont (*Traviata*), Conte di Luna (*Trovatore*); WAGNER: Beckmesser★ (*Meistersinger*). **World premieres: ODAK:** (*Majka Margarita*) 1957; DEVCIC: (*Witch of Labin*) 1957; SULEK: (*Coriolanus*) 1958, (*Tempest*) 1969; all at Croat Ntl Opera, Zagreb. Video/Film: (*Serva padrona*); (*Maestro di cappella*); (*Serafina*). Gives recitals. Appears with symphony orchestra. Teaches voice. Coaches repertoire. On faculty of Music School Lisinski, Zagreb. **Res:** Gunduliceva ul, Zagreb, Yugoslavia.

ALBANESE, CECILIA; née Nuñez. Coloratura soprano. Italian/Venezuelan. Born 26 Nov 1937, Caracas, Venezuela. Husband Gaetano, occupation publicity agent. Two children. Studied: Consv G Verdi, Milan; Mo Ettore Campogalliani, Ma Magda Piccarolo. **Debut:** Gilda (*Rigoletto*) Reggio Emilia, Italy. Awards: First Prize Conc Maria Canals, Macerata; Winner Intl Singing Cont, Vercelli & Parma.

Sang with major companies in FR GER: Hamburg; ITA: Naples; SPA: Barcelona, Majorca; UK: Cardiff Welsh, Glasgow Scottish; USA: New York City Opera. **Roles with these companies incl** BELLINI: Amina★(*Sonnambula*); DONIZETTI: Norina★(*Don Pasquale*), Adina★ (*Elisir*), Lucia★; MENOTTI: Monica (*Medium*); MOZART: Königin der Nacht★ (*Zauberflöte*); OFFENBACH: Olympia★ (*Contes d'Hoffmann*); PUCCINI: Musetta★ (*Bohème*); ROSSINI: Rosina★ (*Barbiere di Siviglia*); VERDI: Nannetta★ (*Falstaff*), Gilda★ (*Rigoletto*), Violetta★ (*Traviata*). Gives recitals. Appears with symphony orchestra. **Res:** V Don Gnocchi 12, Milan, Italy. Mgmt: SLA/UK.

ALBERTS, EUNICE DOROTHY. Contralto. American. Resident mem: Opera Co of Boston. Born Boston, USA. Husband Dean Nicholson, occupation attorney. Three daughters. Studied: Cleora Wood & Rosalie Miller, Boston; New England Consv, dramatics, Boris Goldovsky, Boston; two yrs with Madrigal Group, cond Nadia Boulanger, Paris. **Debut:** Suzuki (*Butterfly*) New York City Opera 1951. Awards: Hon Mem Sigma Alpha Iota Mus Sorority.

Sang with major companies in USA: Boston, Chicago, Cincinnati, Houston, Kansas City, Kentucky, New Orleans, New York City Opera, Washington DC. **Roles with these companies incl** BERG: Gräfin Geschwitz (*Lulu*); BERLIOZ: Cassandre & Anna★ (*Troyens*); BIZET: Carmen; BRITTEN: Mrs Herring★ (*Albert Herring*), Lucretia (*Rape of Lucretia*); CHARPENTIER: Mère★ (*Louise*); DEBUSSY: Geneviève (*Pelléas et Mélisande*); FALLA: Abuela★ (*Vida breve*); FOSS: Lulu (*Jumping Frog of Calaveras County*); GLUCK: Orfeo; HANDEL: Giulio Cesare; HUMPERDINCK: Hexe (*Hänsel und Gre-*

tel); MENOTTI: Miss Todd (*Old Maid and the Thief*); MOORE: Augusta Tabor (*Ballad of Baby Doe*); MUSSORGSKY: Marina (*Boris Godunov*); PUCCINI: Suzuki★ (*Butterfly*), Frugola (*Tabarro*); RAVEL: L'Enfant (*Enfant et les sortilèges*); SCHOENBERG: Die Kranke (*Moses and Aron*); STRAVINSKY: La mère (*Mavra*), Jocasta (*Oedipus Rex*), Baba the Turk★ (*Rake's Progress*); TCHAIKOVSKY: La Comtesse (*Pique Dame*); VAUGHAN WILLIAMS: Maurya★ (*Riders to the Sea*); VERDI: Amneris★ (*Aida*), Ulrica (*Ballo in maschera*), Dame Quickly★ (*Falstaff*); WAGNER: Magdalene (*Meistersinger*), Erda (*Rheingold*), Brangäne (*Tristan und Isolde*). Also PROKOFIEV: Akhrosimova★ (*War and Peace*); GIORDANO: Madelon (*Andrea Chénier*). **World premieres:** WARD: Rebecca Nurse‡ (*Crucible*) New York City Opera 1961. Recorded for: CRI. Video/Film — WNET: Dryade (*Ariadne auf Naxos*). Gives recitals. Appears with symphony orchestra. Teaches voice. On faculty of Boston Univ, MA. **Res:** 7 Sherburne Rd, Lexington, MA, USA. Mgmt: DBA/USA.

ALBRECHT, GEORGE ALEXANDER. Conductor of opera and symphony. German. Gen Mus Dir, Niedersächsische Staatstheater, Hannover. Born 15 Feb 1935, Bremen, Germany. Divorced. Two children. Studied: Hermann Grevesmühl, Paul van Kempen, Prof Maria Landes-Hindemith; incl violin, piano and voice. Operatic training as repetiteur & asst cond at Theater am Goetheplatz, Bremen. **Operatic debut:** Theater am Goetheplatz, Bremen. Symphonic debut: Siena, Italy.

Conducted with major companies in FRA: Paris; GRE: Athens Fest; FR GER: Dortmund, Hamburg, Hannover, Munich Staatsoper, Nürnberg, Stuttgart; GER DR: Dresden; ITA: Bologna, Parma, Trieste, Turin, Venice; POL: Warsaw; YUG: Belgrade. **Operas with these companies incl** BEETHOVEN: *Fidelio;* BERG: *Wozzeck;* BIZET: *Carmen;* BRITTEN: *Owen Wingrave;* CAVALLI: *Calisto;* DONIZETTI: *Lucia;* EGK: *Verlobung in San Domingo;* GLUCK: *Alceste;* HANDEL: *Ariodante;* HENZE: *Elegy for Young Lovers, Junge Lord;* JANACEK: *Jenufa;* LORTZING: *Waffenschmied, Wildschütz;* MARSCHNER: *Hans Heiling;* MOZART: *Così fan tutte, Don Giovanni, Entführung aus dem Serail, Nozze di Figaro, Zauberflöte;* MUSSORGSKY: *Boris Godunov;* OFFENBACH: *Contes d'Hoffmann;* ORFF: *Antigonae, Kluge;* PFITZNER: *Palestrina;* PUCCINI: *Bohème, Butterfly, Tosca;* SMETANA: *Bartered Bride;* STRAUSS, R: *Arabella, Ariadne auf Naxos, Daphne, Elektra, Rosenkavalier, Schweigsame Frau;* TCHAIKOVSKY: *Eugene Onegin;* VERDI: *Aida, Ballo in maschera, Falstaff, Forza del destino, Otello, Rigoletto, Traviata, Trovatore;* WAGNER: *Fliegende Holländer, Lohengrin, Meistersinger, Rheingold, Walküre, Siegfried, Götterdämmerung, Tannhäuser, Tristan und Isolde;* WEBER: *Freischütz, Oberon.* Also MARTINU: *Julietta;* FORTNER: *Bluthochzeit;* HENZE: *Ende einer Welt.* **World premieres:** HOLTERDORF: *Alexander* Bremen, 1960. Recorded for RAI Rome & Turin. Conducted major orch in Europe. **Res:** Berkowitzweg 2, Hannover, Germany. Mgmt: CMV/FRA.

ALBRECHT, GERD. Conductor of opera and symphony. German. Music Dir & Resident Cond, Deutsche Oper Berlin, FR Ger. Born 1934, Kiel, Germany. Studied: Musikhochschule Hamburg. Operatic training as repetiteur at Württembergische Staatsoper, Stuttgart till 1961. Previous adm positions in opera: Gen Mus Dir, Lübeck 1963-66 and Kassel 1966-72.
  Conducted with major companies in AUS: Vienna Staatsoper; BEL: Brussels; FR GER: Berlin Deutsche Oper, Kassel, Munich Staatsoper, Stuttgart; ITA: Venice; et al. Operas with these companies incl BEETHOVEN: *Fidelio;* BERG: *Wozzeck;* BORODIN: *Prince Igor;* BRITTEN: *Death in Venice;* FORTNER: *Elisabeth Tudor;* GLUCK: *Armide;* MOZART: *Don Giovanni;* STRAUSS, R: *Elektra;* TCHAIKOVSKY: *Eugene Onegin;* WAGNER: *Meistersinger, Rheingold, Walküre, Siegfried, Götterdämmerung, Tannhäuser;* WOLF: *Corregidor‡;* et al. World premieres: STROE: *The Nobel Prize Will Not Be Awarded* Kassel 1972. Recorded for EMI. Res: Berlin, FR Ger.

ALDREDGE, THEONI; née Theoni Vachliotis. Costume designer for opera, theater, film, television. Greek. Resident designer at New York Shakespeare Fest. Born Salonica, Greece. Husband Tom Aldredge, occupation actor. Studied: Goodman Mem Theatre, Chicago. Operatic debut: *Don Rodrigo* New York City Opera 1966. Theater debut: Studebaker Theatre, Chicago 1956. Previous occupation: costume design instructor. Awards: Acad Awd "Oscar" 1975; American Fashion Inst Awd; British Socy, Film & TV Arts Awd.
  Designed for major companies in USA: New York City Opera, Washington DC. Operas designed for these companies incl DELIUS: *Village Romeo and Juliet⋆;* GINASTERA: *Don Rodrigo;* KORNGOLD: *Tote Stadt⋆;* MOZART: *Idomeneo⋆;* STRAUSS, J: *Fledermaus⋆.* Operatic world premieres: GINASTERA: *Beatrix Cenci* Washington Opera Socy 1971. Exhibitions of costumes. Res: New York, NY, USA. Mgmt: WMA/USA.

ALEKSANDRIC, ZORAN. Lyric baritone. Yugoslavian. Resident mem: Belgrade Opera. Born 10 Jun 1941, Belgrade. Wife Mirjana, occupation student. Studied: Music School Stankovic, Prof B Cvejic; Stanoje Jankovic. Debut: Valentin (*Faust*) Belgrade Opera 1972. Previous occupations: economist. Awards: First Prize Compt Belgrade Mus Schools.
  Sang with major companies in YUG: Belgrade. Roles with these companies incl MASSENET: Albert⋆ (*Werther*); ORFF: Solo⋆ (*Carmina burana*); PUCCINI: Sharpless⋆ (*Butterfly*); VERDI: Renato⋆ (*Ballo in maschera*), Rodrigo⋆ (*Don Carlo*), Germont⋆ (*Traviata*). Also GOUNOD: Valentin⋆ (*Faust*). Gives recitals. Appears with symphony orchestra. Res: Borisa Kidrica 16, Belgrade, Yugoslavia.

ALESSANDRO, VICTOR. Conductor of opera and symphony. American. Art Dir & Res Cond, San

Antonio Grand Opera, TX, USA. Mus Dir, San Antonio Symph since 1951. Born 27 Nov 1915, Waco, TX. Wife Ruth Drisko. Two children. Studied: Eastman School of Music, Rochester, NY; Mozarteum Acad, Salzburg; Accad Santa Cecilia, Rome. Awards: Hon DM Univ of Rochester & Southwestern Univ; LHD So Methodist Univ; Alice M Ditson Awd, Columbia Univ; Ntl Music Council Awd.
  Conducted with major companies in USA: New York City Opera, San Antonio, San Francisco Spring Opera. Operas with these companies incl BEETHOVEN: *Fidelio;* BERNSTEIN: *Trouble in Tahiti;* BIZET: *Carmen, Pêcheurs de perles;* DELIBES: *Lakmé;* DONIZETTI: *Elisir, Fille du régiment, Lucia;* FLOTOW: *Martha;* FLOYD: *Markheim, Susannah;* GOUNOD: *Faust, Roméo et Juliette;* HUMPERDINCK: *Hänsel und Gretel;* LEONCAVALLO: *Pagliacci;* MASCAGNI: *Cavalleria rusticana;* MASSENET: *Manon;* MENOTTI: *Amahl;* MONTEMEZZI: *Amore dei tre re;* MOZART: *Così fan tutte, Don Giovanni, Nozze di Figaro;* MUSSORGSKY: *Boris Godunov;* OFFENBACH: *Contes d'Hoffmann;* ORFF: *Carmina burana;* PONCHIELLI: *Gioconda;* POULENC: *Voix humaine;* PUCCINI: *Bohème, Gianni Schicchi, Butterfly, Manon Lescaut, Rondine, Tosca, Turandot;* RIMSKY-KORSAKOV: *Coq d'or;* ROSSINI: *Barbiere di Siviglia;* SAINT-SAENS: *Samson et Dalila;* SMETANA: *Bartered Bride;* STRAUSS, J: *Fledermaus;* STRAUSS, R: *Elektra, Rosenkavalier, Salome;* VERDI: *Aida, Ballo in maschera, Don Carlo, Nabucco, Otello, Rigoletto, Traviata, Trovatore;* WAGNER: *Lohengrin, Meistersinger, Tannhäuser, Tristan und Isolde.* Conducted major orch in Europe, USA/Canada. Previous positions as Mus Dir with major orch: Oklahoma City Symph 1938-51. Res: 711 Garraty, San Antonio, TX 78209, USA. Mgmt: CAM/USA.

ALEXANDER, CARLOS. Dramatic baritone; stage director; composer. American. Resident mem: Württembergische Staatsoper, Stuttgart. Born 15 Oct 1915, Utica, NY, USA. Wife Cynthia. One son. Studied: Alma Schadow, Berlin; Anna Bahr-Mildenburg, Berlin; Friedrich Schorr, Lothar Wallerstein, New York. Debut as singer: Conte di Luna (*Trovatore*) Scranton, PA, USA 1940; debut as stage dir: (*Fledermaus*) Pittsburgh Opera 1944. Previous adm position: Art Dir, Utah Opera Theater, Salt Lake City 1952-54. Awards: Kammersänger, Ministry of Culture.
  Sang with major companies in ARG: Buenos Aires; AUS: Vienna Staatsoper & Volksoper; BEL: Brussels; CAN: Montreal/Quebec; DEN: Copenhagen; FRA: Lyon, Paris; GRE: Athens Fest; FR GER: Bayreuth Fest, Berlin Deutsche Oper, Cologne, Düsseldorf-Duisburg, Frankfurt, Hamburg, Hannover, Karlsruhe, Krefeld, Munich Staatsoper, Stuttgart, Wuppertal; ITA: Florence Maggio & Comunale; MEX: Mexico City; SWI: Basel, Geneva, Zurich; UK: Edinburgh Fest, Glyndebourne Fest; USA: Baltimore, Boston, Chicago, Cincinnati, Fort Worth, Hartford, New York City Opera, Pittsburgh. Roles with these companies incl BEETHOVEN: Don Pizarro⋆ & Rocco (*Fidelio*); BERG: Dr Schön⋆ (*Lulu*); BIZET: Escamillo (*Carmen*); BORODIN: Galitzky (*Prince*

Igor); BUSONI: Doktor Faust; DALLAPIC-
COLA: Prigioniero★; EINEM: George Danton
(*Dantons Tod*); GAY: Mr Peachum★ (*Beggar's
Opera*); GIORDANO: Carlo Gérard (*Andrea
Chénier*); GOUNOD: Méphistophélès (*Faust*);
HENZE: Mittenhofer (*Elegy for Young Lovers*);
JANACEK: Gorianchikov & Shishkov (*From the
House of the Dead*), Jaroslav Prus (*Makropoulos
Affair*); LEONCAVALLO: Tonio (*Pagliacci*);
MASCAGNI: Alfio (*Cavalleria rusticana*); ME-
NOTTI: Husband (*Amelia al ballo*), Bob (*Old
Maid and the Thief*); MOZART: Don Alfonso
(*Così fan tutte*), Don Giovanni, Osmin (*Entfüh-
rung aus dem Serail*), Conte Almaviva (*Nozze di
Figaro*), Sarastro (*Zauberflöte*); OFFENBACH:
Coppélius etc (*Contes d'Hoffmann*); ORFF:
Kreon‡ (*Antigonae*); PENDERECKI: Grandier★
(*Teufel von Loudun*); PROKOFIEV: Ruprecht
(*Fiery Angel*); PUCCINI: Colline (*Bohème*),
Schicchi, Sharpless (*Butterfly*), Lescaut (*Manon
Lescaut*), Michele (*Tabarro*), Scarpia (*Tosca*);
PURCELL: Oswald (*King Arthur*); ROSSINI:
Bartolo & Basilio (*Barbiere di Siviglia*);
SCHOENBERG: Moses★; STRAUSS, R: Man-
dryka (*Arabella*), Musiklehrer (*Ariadne auf
Naxos*), La Roche (*Capriccio*), Orest (*Elektra*),
Barak (*Frau ohne Schatten*), Jochanaan★ (*Sa-
lome*); STRAVINSKY: Nick Shadow (*Rake's
Progress*); THOMAS: Lothario (*Mignon*);
VERDI: Amonasro & Ramfis (*Aida*), Philip II
(*Don Carlo*), Don Carlo (*Forza del destino*), Mac-
beth, Iago (*Otello*), Rigoletto, Simon Boccanegra,
Conte di Luna (*Trovatore*); WAGNER: Hollän-
der, Telramund & König Heinrich (*Lohengrin*),
Beckmesser (*Meistersinger*), Amfortas (*Parsifal*),
Wotan (*Rheingold, Walküre*), Wanderer (*Sieg-
fried*), Gunther★ (*Götterdämmerung*), Wolfram &
Landgraf (*Tannhäuser*), Kurwenal (*Tristan*);
WOLF-FERRARI: Conte Gil (*Segreto di Su-
sanna*). Also PFITZNER: Borromeo (*Palestrina*);
CIKKER: Nechludoff (*Resurrection*); BRITTEN:
Collatinus (*Rape of Lucretia*); HINDEMITH:
Keppler (*Harmonie der Welt*); ORFF: Messenger
(*Oedipus*). **World premieres:** RONNEFELD: Sal-
vatore (*Die Ameise*) Düsseldorf 1961; ORFF:
Prometheus, Stuttgart 1968. Recorded for: DG.
Video/Film: La Roche (*Capriccio*); Nechludoff
(*Resurrection*); Dr Schön (*Lulu*). Gives recitals.
Appears with symphony orchestra. Teaches voice.
Coaches repertoire. On faculty of Mozarteum,
Salzburg. **Directed at major companies in** CAN:
Toronto; FR GER: Düsseldorf-Duisburg, Stutt-
gart; USA: Chicago, New Orleans, Pittsburgh,
Santa Fe. **Operas staged with these companies incl**
d'ALBERT: *Tiefland;* BEETHOVEN: *Fidelio★;*
BIZET: *Carmen;* BRITTEN: *Rape of Lucretia;*
DONIZETTI: *Elisir;* HUMPERDINCK: *Hänsel
und Gretel;* LEONCAVALLO: *Pagliacci;* MA-
SCAGNI: *Cavalleria rusticana;* MENOTTI:
*Amahl, Amelia al ballo, Consul, Medium, Old
Maid and the Thief, Telephone;* MOZART: *Don
Giovanni, Entführung aus dem Serail, Nozze di
Figaro, Zauberflöte;* OFFENBACH: *Contes
d'Hoffmann;* PUCCINI: *Bohème, Gianni
Schicchi, Butterfly★, Suor Angelica, Tabarro,
Tosca;* STRAUSS, J: *Fledermaus;* STRAUSS, R:
Arabella, Ariadne auf Naxos, Salome★; VERDI:
Trovatore; WAGNER: *Fliegende Holländer★, Lo-
hengrin, Tristan und Isolde.* **Res:** Ahornstr 4A,
Stuttgart, FR Ger.

ALEXANDER, JOHN Lyric tenor. American.
Resident mem: Metropolitan Opera, New York.
Born Meridian, MS, USA. Wife Sue, occupation
pianist. One daughter. Studied: Consv of Music,
Cincinnati Univ, O, USA; Robert Weede. **Debut:**
Faust, Cincinnati Summer Opera 1952.
    Sang with major companies in AUS: Vienna
Volksoper; CAN: Montreal/Quebec, Vancouver;
USA: Baltimore, Boston, Chicago, Cincinnati,
Dallas, Fort Worth, Hartford, Houston, Miami,
Milwaukee Florentine, New Orleans, New York
Met & City Opera, Pittsburgh, San Antonio, San
Diego, San Francisco Opera, Seattle, Washington
DC. **Roles with these companies incl** BARBER:
Anatol (*Vanessa*); BEETHOVEN: Florestan (*Fi-
delio*); BELLINI: Pollione (*Norma*), Lord Arthur
(*Puritani*), Elvino (*Sonnambula*); BERLIOZ:
Faust (*Damnation de Faust*); BIZET: Don José
(*Carmen*); BLACHER: Romeo; BOITO: Faust
(*Mefistofele*); CHARPENTIER: Julien (*Louise*);
CILEA: Maurizio (*A. Lecouvreur*); DONI-
ZETTI: Riccardo (*Anna Bolena*), Ernesto (*Don
Pasquale*), Nemorino (*Elisir*), Tonio (*Fille du régi-
ment*), Edgardo (*Lucia*), Gennaro (*Lucrezia Bor-
gia*), Leicester (*Maria Stuarda*), Roberto
Devereux; FLOTOW: Lionel (*Martha*); GOU-
NOD: Faust, Roméo; KORNGOLD: Paul (*Tote
Stadt*); LEONCAVALLO: Canio (*Pagliacci*);
MASCAGNI: Turiddu (*Cavalleria rusticana*);
MASSENET: Des Grieux (*Manon*), Werther;
MOZART: Ferrando (*Così fan tutte*), Don Ot-
tavio (*Don Giovanni*), Tamino (*Zauberflöte*); OF-
FENBACH: Hoffmann; PONCHIELLI: Enzo
(*Gioconda*); PUCCINI: Rodolfo (*Bohème*), Dick
Johnson (*Fanciulla del West*), Pinkerton (*But-
terfly*), Des Grieux (*Manon Lescaut*), Ruggero
(*Rondine*), Cavaradossi (*Tosca*), Calaf (*Turandot*);
ROSSINI: Almaviva (*Barbiere di Siviglia*), Lin-
doro (*Italiana in Algeri*); SAINT-SAENS: Sam-
son; STRAUSS, J: Eisenstein (*Fledermaus*);
STRAUSS, R: Bacchus (*Ariadne auf Naxos*), Ein
Sänger (*Rosenkavalier*); VERDI: Radames (*Aida*),
Riccardo (*Ballo in maschera*), Don Carlo, Ernani,
Don Alvaro (*Forza del destino*), Rodolfo (*Luisa
Miller*), Duca di Mantova (*Rigoletto*), Manrico
(*Trovatore*); WAGNER: Erik (*Fliegende Hollän-
der*), Lohengrin, Walther (*Meistersinger*), Loge
(*Rheingold*). Recorded for: London. Appears with
symphony orchestra. Teaches voice. On faculty of
Univ of Cincinnati College-Consv of Music, O,
USA. **Res:** Manhasset, NY, USA. **Mgmt:**
CAM/USA; AIM/UK.

ALLEN, BETTY; née Elizabeth Louise Allen. Dramatic mezzo-soprano. American. Resident mem:
New York City Opera. Born 17 Mar 1930, Campbell, O. Husband R Edward Lee III, occupation
exec dir, settlement house. Two children. Studied:
Hartford School of Music, CT; Sarah Peck More,
Paul Ulanowsky, Zinka Milanov, New York. **De-
but:** Jocasta (*Oedipus Rex*) Teatro Colón, Buenos
Aires 1964. Awards: Hon DL Wittenberg Univ,
1971.
    Sang with major companies in ARG: Buenos
Aires; MEX: Mexico City; USA: Boston, Hous-
ton, Kansas City, New York City Opera, San
Francisco Opera & Spring Opera, Santa Fe, Wash-
ington DC. **Roles with these companies incl** BIZET:
Carmen; DEBUSSY: Geneviève★ (*Pelléas et
Mélisande*); FALLA: Abuela★ (*Vida breve*);

GLUCK: Clytemnestre (*Iphigénie en Aulide*); HANDEL: Medoro (*Orlando furioso*); JOPLIN: Mother★ (*Treemonisha*); MOZART: Sesto & Annio (*Clemenza di Tito*), Dorabella (*Così fan tutte*); POULENC: Mère Marie (*Dialogues des Carmélites*); PUCCINI: Suzuki (*Butterfly*), Frugola★ (*Tabarro*); REIMANN: Pythia★ (*Melusine*); ROSSINI: Zaida (*Turco in Italia*); STRAVINSKY: Jocasta★ (*Oedipus Rex*), Baba the Turk★ (*Rake's Progress*); THOMSON: St Teresa II (*Four Saints in Three Acts*), Anne (*Mother of Us All*); VERDI: Ulrica★ (*Ballo in maschera*), Dame Quickly★ (*Falstaff*), Azucena★ (*Trovatore*); WAGNER: Erda (*Rheingold, Siegfried*), Brangäne★ (*Tristan und Isolde*). Gives recitals. Appears with symphony orchestra. Teaches voice. Coaches repertoire. On faculty of Manhattan School of Music. **Res:** New York, NY, USA. Mgmt: CAM/USA; MFZ/FIN.

ALLEN, THOMAS. Lyric Baritone. British. Resident member: Royal Opera, London. Born 10 Sep 1944, Seaham Harbour, Durham, UK. Wife Margaret. One child. Studied: Royal Coll of Music, Hervey Alan, London. **Debut:** Figaro (*Nozze di Figaro*) Welsh National Opera, Cardiff 1969. Awards: Queen's Prize for Commonwealth Singers, Royal Coll of Music; Gulbenkian Fllshp, London.

Sang with major companies in UK: Aldeburgh Fest, Cardiff Welsh, Glyndebourne Fest, London Royal Opera. **Roles with these companies incl** BRITTEN: Billy Budd★, Demetrius★ (*Midsummer Night*); DONIZETTI: Belcore★ (*Elisir*); MOZART: Guglielmo★ (*Così fan tutte*), Conte Almaviva★ & Figaro★ (*Nozze di Figaro*), Papageno★ (*Zauberflöte*); ROSSINI: Figaro★ (*Barbiere di Siviglia*). Also PURCELL: King Arthur★; VERDI: Paolo★ (*Simon Boccanegra*); BRITTEN: Sid★ (*Albert Herring*); GOUNOD: Valentin★ (*Faust*). **World premieres:** MUSGRAVE: The Count (*Voice of Ariadne*) English Opera Group, Aldeburgh & London 1974. Recorded for: EMI; Philips. Video—BBC TV: Figaro (*Nozze di Figaro*). Gives recitals. Appears with symphony orchestra. **Res:** 4 Sydney Rd, London W 13, UK. Mgmt: CST/UK; SHA/USA.

ALLERS, FRANZ. Conductor of opera and symphony. American. Principal Cond, Theater am Gärtnerplatz, Munich. Born 6 Aug 1905, Carlsbad, Czechoslovakia. Wife Janne Furch, occupation author. One child. Studied: Prague Consv; Berlin Staatl Hochschule für Musik; incl violin, piano, flute. Plays the piano. Operatic training as repetiteur & asst cond at Wuppertal Opera, Germany 1926-33; Wagner Fest, Bayreuth 1927; Wagner Fest, Paris 1929. **Operatic debut:** *Zar und Zimmermann* Wuppertal Opera 1927. Symphonic debut: Radio Symphony, Prague 1935. Awards: Antoinette Perry Awd, Amer Theatre Wing 1957 & 1961. Previous adm positions in opera: Opernchef, Municipal Opera, Aussig, CSR 1933-38.

Conducted with major companies in FR GER: Cologne, Düsseldorf-Duisburg, Hamburg, Munich Staatsoper & Gärtnerplatz, Stuttgart, Wuppertal; HOL: Amsterdam; POR: Lisbon; SWI: Geneva; USA: New York Met & City Opera. **Operas with these companies incl** d'ALBERT: *Tiefland*★; BEETHOVEN: *Fidelio;* BIZET: *Carmen*★;

DONIZETTI: *Don Pasquale, Lucia*★; DVORAK: *Rusalka*★; FLOTOW: *Martha;* GERSHWIN: *Porgy and Bess*★; GIORDANO: *Andrea Chénier;* GOUNOD: *Faust;* HINDEMITH: *Cardillac;* HUMPERDINCK: *Hänsel und Gretel*★; JANACEK: *Katya Kabanova;* LEONCAVALLO: *Pagliacci*★; LORTZING: *Zar und Zimmermann*★; MASCAGNI: *Cavalleria rusticana*★; MOZART: *Don Giovanni, Entführung aus dem Serail, Nozze di Figaro;* OFFENBACH: *Contes d'Hoffmann, Périchole*★; PUCCINI: *Bohème, Gianni Schicchi, Butterfly, Manon Lescaut, Tosca, Turandot;* ROSSINI: *Barbiere di Siviglia;* SMETANA: *Bartered Bride*★; STRAUSS, J: *Fledermaus*★; STRAUSS, R: *Rosenkavalier;* VERDI: *Aida, Ballo in maschera, Falstaff, Otello, Rigoletto, Traviata;* WAGNER: *Lohengrin, Meistersinger, Rheingold, Walküre, Siegfried, Götterdämmerung, Tristan und Isolde.* Recorded for RCA. Video—ARD TV: *Zar und Zimmermann;* Vienna TV: *Segreto di Susanna;* Michael Meyerberg Prod: *Hänsel und Gretel.* Conducted major orchestras in Europe, USA/Canada, Central/So America, Asia. Mgmt: CAM/USA; SRN/HOL.

ALLMAN, ROBERT. Dramatic baritone. Australian. Resident mem: Australian Opera, Sydney. Born 8 Jun 1929, Melbourne. Married. Two children. Studied: Australian Ntl Theatre Opera School, Melbourne; Marjorie Smith, Sydney; Dominique Modesti, Paris. **Debut:** Sharpless (*Butterfly*) Victorian Ntl Opera Co, Melbourne.

Sang with major companies in AUSTRL: Sydney; AUS: Vienna Volksoper; FRA: Strasbourg; FR GER: Berlin Deutsche Oper, Cologne, Darmstadt, Düsseldorf-Duisburg, Essen, Frankfurt, Hamburg, Hannover, Kassel, Mannheim, Munich Staatsoper, Stuttgart, Wiesbaden, Wuppertal; S AFR: Johannesburg; SWI: Zurich; UK: London Royal & English National; USA: Houston, New Orleans. **Roles with these companies incl** BEETHOVEN: Don Pizarro★ (*Fidelio*); BIZET: Escamillo (*Carmen*); BUSONI: Matteo (*Arlecchino*); DONIZETTI: Belcore (*Elisir*), Enrico (*Lucia*); LEONCAVALLO: Tonio★ (*Pagliacci*); MASCAGNI: Alfio (*Cavalleria rusticana*); MOZART: Don Alfonso (*Così fan tutte*), Conte Almaviva (*Nozze di Figaro*); OFFENBACH: Coppélius etc★ (*Contes d'Hoffmann*); PUCCINI: Marcello (*Bohème*), Gianni Schicchi, Lescaut (*Manon Lescaut*), Michele★ (*Tabarro*), Scarpia★ (*Tosca*); STRAUSS, R: Musiklehrer (*Ariadne auf Naxos*), Jochanaan★ (*Salome*); TCHAIKOVSKY: Eugene Onegin; VERDI: Amonasro★ (*Aida*), Renato★ (*Ballo in maschera*), Rodrigo (*Don Carlo*), Don Carlo★ (*Forza del destino*), Macbeth, Nabucco★, Iago★ (*Otello*), Rigoletto★, Simon Boccanegra★, Germont (*Traviata*), Conte di Luna (*Trovatore*); WAGNER: Amfortas (*Parsifal*), Wolfram★ (*Tannhäuser*); WEILL: Trinity Moses★ (*Aufstieg und Fall der Stadt Mahagonny*). Also GOUNOD: Valentin (*Faust*). Gives recitals. Appears with symphony orchestra. Teaches voice. **Res:** 66 Screen St, Frankston, Victoria, Australia.

ALTMAN, KAREN. Soprano. American. Resident mem: Deutsche Oper am Rhein, Düsseldorf-Duisburg. Born McDonald, PA. Studied: Juilliard School of Music; Metropolitan Opera Studio, New

York. **Debut:** Pamina (*Zauberflöte*) Frankfurt/M 1970.

Sang with major companies in FRA: Bordeaux; FR GER: Düsseldorf-Duisburg, Frankfurt; USA: Cincinnati, Kansas City, New York City Opera; et al. **Roles with these companies incl** MASSENET: Salomé (*Hérodiade*); MOZART: Donna Elvira (*Don Giovanni*), Konstanze (*Entführung aus dem Serail*); PUCCINI: Mimi (*Bohème*); ROSSINI: Rosina (*Barbiere di Siviglia*), Comtesse Adèle (*Comte Ory*); VERDI: Violetta (*Traviata*); WAGNER: Gutrune (*Götterdämmerung*); et al. **World premieres:** BERNSTEIN: Sop solo (*Mass*) Kennedy Center, Washington DC 1971. Appears with symphony orchestra. Mgmt: DSP/USA.

ALTMEYER, JEANNINE THERESA. Dramatic soprano (*jugendlich dramatische*). American. Resident mem: Zurich Opera. Born 2 May 1948, Pasadena, CA, USA. Single. Studied: Betty Olssen, Fullerton, CA; Martial Singher, Lotte Lehmann, Santa Barbara, CA; George London, Washington DC. **Debut:** Voce dal cielo (*Don Carlo*) Metropolitan Op 1971. Awards: Met Op Ntl Counc Aud, Contract First Prize, 1970; WGN Opera Aud; Ntl Opera Inst Grant.

Sang with major companies in AUS: Salzburg Fest; FR GER: Cologne, Düsseldorf-Duisburg, Frankfurt, Hamburg, Stuttgart; SWI: Zurich; USA: Chicago. **Roles with these companies incl** STRAUSS, R: Gräfin★ (*Capriccio*); WAGNER: Elsa★ (*Lohengrin*), Eva★ (*Meistersinger*), Gutrune★ (*Götterdämmerung*), Elisabeth★ (*Tannhäuser*); WEBER: Agathe★ (*Freischütz*). Gives recitals. Appears with symphony orchestra. **Res:** 8740 Herrliberg, Zurich, Switzerland. Mgmt: CAM/USA; JUC/SWI.

ALVA, LUIGI ERNESTO. Lyric tenor. Peruvian. Born 10 Apr 1927, Lima, Peru. Wife Anna Maria Zanetti. Two children. Studied: Rosa Mercedes de Morales, Lima; Emilio Ghirardini, Ettore Campogalliani, Milan. **Debut:** Beppe (*Pagliacci*) Lima, Peru 1951. Previous occupations: cadet, Peruvian Naval Acad; clerk Intl Petroleum Co, Lima. Awards: Orden del Merito, Orden del Sol, Peruvian Gvnmt; Viotti d'oro, Vercelli, Italy; Medaglia d'oro, Società del Giardino, Milan; Medaglia d'oro dei Concerti, Mantua, Italy.

Sang with major companies in ARG: Buenos Aires; AUSTRL: Sydney; AUS: Bregenz Fest, Salzburg Fest, Vienna Staatsoper; BEL: Brussels; BUL: Sofia; DEN: Copenhagen; FRA: Aix-en-Provence Fest, Orange Fest, Strasbourg; GRE: Athens Fest; FR GER: Berlin Deutsche Oper, Hamburg, Munich Staatsoper, Wiesbaden; HOL: Amsterdam; ISR: Tel Aviv; ITA: Florence Maggio Musicale & Comunale, Genoa, Milan La Scala, Naples, Palermo, Rome Teatro dell'Opera, Trieste, Turin, Venice; MEX: Mexico City; MON: Monte Carlo; POR: Lisbon; S AFR: Johannesburg; SWE: Stockholm; SWI: Geneva; UK: Edinburgh Fest, Glyndebourne Fest, London Royal Opera; USSR: Moscow Bolshoi; USA: Baltimore, Boston, Chicago, Dallas, Fort Worth, New Orleans, New York Met, Philadelphia Grand, Pittsburgh, Seattle, Washington DC; YUG: Dubrovnik. **Roles with these companies incl** BELLINI: Elvino★ (*Sonnambula*); BRITTEN: Peter Quint (*Turn of the Screw*); CAVALLI: Egisto★; CIMA-

ROSA: Paolino★‡ (*Matrimonio segreto*); DONIZETTI: Ernesto★ (*Don Pasquale*), Nemorino★‡ (*Elisir*), Tonio★ (*Fille du régiment*), Beppo (*Rita*); FALLA: Maese Pedro (*Retablo de Maese Pedro*); GLUCK: Paride; GOUNOD: Siebel (*Faust*); HANDEL: Oronte‡ (*Alcina*), Xerxes; HAYDN: Eclittico (*Mondo della luna*), Lindoro (*Fedeltà premiata*); LEONCAVALLO: Beppe (*Pagliacci*); MASSENET: Nicias (*Thaïs*), Werther; MONTEVERDI: Testo‡ (*Combattimento di Tancredi*); MOZART: Sesto (*Clemenza di Tito*), Ferrando★‡ (*Così fan tutte*), Don Ottavio★‡ (*Don Giovanni*), Belmonte (*Entführung aus dem Serail*), Idamante (*Idomeneo*), Alessandro‡ (*Re pastore*), Tamino (*Zauberflöte*); ROSSINI: Almaviva★‡ (*Barbiere di Siviglia*), Don Ramiro★ (*Cenerentola*), Lindoro★‡ (*Italiana in Algeri*), Dorvil (*Scala di seta*), Florville (*Signor Bruschino*), Narciso (*Turco in Italia*); ROUSSEAU: Colin (*Devin du village*); STRAUSS, R: Bacchus (*Ariadne auf Naxos*), Ein Sänger (*Rosenkavalier*); VERDI: Fenton★‡ (*Falstaff*), Alfredo★ (*Traviata*); WOLF-FERRARI: Filipeto (*Quattro rusteghi*). **World premieres:** CHAILLY: Fidanzato (*La domanda di matrimonio*) La Scala, Milan 1957; MALIPIERO: (*La donna è mobile*) La Scala, Milan 1957. Recorded for: EMI, Decca, DG, Ricordi, RCA, Philips. Video/Film: (*Barbiere di Siviglia*); (*Così fan tutte*); (*Don Pasquale*). Gives recitals. Appears with symphony orchestra. **Res:** V Moscova 46/3, Milan, Italy.

ALVARES, EDUARDO. Tenor. Brazilian. Born 10 Jun 1947, Rio de Janeiro, Brazil. Single. Studied: Pina Monaco, Rio de Janeiro; Mo Luigi Ricci, Rome; Fr Dr Sittner, Vienna. **Debut:** Don José (*Carmen*) Stadttheater Linz 1970.

Sang with major companies in AUS: Vienna Staatsoper; BRA: Rio de Janeiro; FRA: Nancy; FR GER: Bielefeld, Cologne, Düsseldorf-Duisburg, Frankfurt, Munich Staatsoper, Stuttgart; GER DR: Dresden; ITA: Spoleto Fest, Venice. **Roles with these companies incl** BIZET: Don José★ (*Carmen*); CILEA: Maurizio★ (*A. Lecouvreur*); DONIZETTI: Edgardo★ (*Lucia*); PUCCINI: Rodolfo★ (*Bohème*); Pinkerton★ (*Butterfly*), Cavaradossi★ (*Tosca*); STRAUSS, J: Alfred★ (*Fledermaus*); STRAUSS, R: Ein Sänger★ (*Rosenkavalier*); TCHAIKOVSKY: Lenski★ (*Eugene Onegin*); VERDI: Riccardo★ (*Ballo in maschera*), Don Carlo★, Don Alvaro★ (*Forza del destino*), Rodolfo★ (*Luisa Miller*), Duca di Mantova★ (*Rigoletto*). Also VERDI: Macduff (*Macbeth*). Appears with symphony orchestra. **Res:** rua Prudente de Moraes 709, Rio de Janeiro, Brazil. Mgmt: DSP/USA.

AMARA, LUCINE; née Lucine Tockqui Armaganian. Spinto. American. Resident mem: Metropolitan Opera, New York. Born 1 Mar 1927, Hartford, CT, USA. Divorced. Studied: Stella Eisner-Eyn, San Francisco; Music Acad of the West, Santa Barbara, CA; Univ of Southern California, Los Angeles. **Debut:** Celestial Voice (*Don Carlo*) Metropolitan Opera 1950. Previous occupations: typist-receptionist, bank teller. Awards: First Prize, Atwater Kent Awd 1948; Hon Mem Sigma Alpha Iota 1954.

Sang with major companies in AUS: Vienna

Staatsoper; CAN: Toronto; FR GER: Stuttgart; ITA: Rome Caracalla; MEX: Mexico City; SWE: Stockholm; UK: Edinburgh Fest, Glyndebourne Fest; USSR: Tbilisi; USA: Boston, Cincinnati, Hartford, Houston, Miami, New Orleans, New York Met, Philadelphia Lyric, Pittsburgh, San Diego, San Francisco Opera, Seattle. **Roles with these companies incl** BIZET: Micaëla★ (*Carmen*); BRITTEN: Lady Billows (*Albert Herring*), Ellen Orford★ (*Peter Grimes*); GIORDANO: Maddalena★ (*Andrea Chénier*); GLUCK: Euridice; GOUNOD: Marguerite (*Faust*); LEONCAVALLO: Nedda★‡ (*Pagliacci*); MOZART: Fiordiligi (*Così fan tutte*), Donna Elvira★ (*Don Giovanni*), Contessa★ (*Nozze di Figaro*), Pamina (*Zauberflöte*); OFFENBACH: Antonia★ (*Contes d'Hoffmann*); PUCCINI: Mimi★ (*Bohème*), Lauretta (*Gianni Schicchi*), Cio-Cio-San★ (*Butterfly*), Manon Lescaut★, Giorgetta★ (*Tabarro*), Tosca★, Liù★ (*Turandot*); STRAUSS, R: Ariadne: TCHAIKOVSKY: Tatiana (*Eugene Onegin*); VERDI: Aida★, Donna Elvira (*Ernani*), Alice Ford★ (*Falstaff*), Leonora★ (*Forza del destino*), Luisa Miller, Desdemona★ (*Otello*), Amelia (*Simon Boccanegra*), Leonora★ (*Trovatore*); WAGNER: Elsa‡ (*Lohengrin*), Eva★ (*Meistersinger*). Recorded for: Angel, RCA, Columbia. Gives recitals. Appears with symphony orchestra. **Res:** San Francisco, CA, USA. Mgmt: RIV/USA.

AMBROZIAK, DELFINA. Lyric soprano. Polish. Resident mem: Grand Theatre, Lódz. Born 21 Mar 1939, Rowne, Poland. Husband Tadeusz Kopacki, occupation singer. One child. Studied: Consv Lódz, Poland; Vacance Musicali, Venice, Italy. **Debut:** Lakmé, Lódz Opera 1962. Awards: First Prize Munich Intl Compt 1962; Gold Cross of Merit, Polish State Council.

Sang with major companies in AUS: Salzburg Fest; BEL: Brussels; CZE: Brno, Prague National & Smetana Theaters; FR GER: Cologne, Dortmund, Düsseldorf-Duisburg, Munich Staatsoper; GER DR: Dresden, Leipzig; HUN: Budapest; ITA: Palermo; MEX: Mexico City; POL: Lódz, Warsaw; SWE: Stockholm; USSR: Kiev, Moscow Bolshoi, Tbilisi; YUG: Belgrade. **Roles with these companies incl** AUBER: Zerlina★ (*Fra Diavolo*); BEETHOVEN: Marzelline★ (*Fidelio*); BIZET: Micaëla★ (*Carmen*); DELIBES: Lakmé★; GOUNOD: Marguerite★ (*Faust*); HANDEL: Galatea★; LEONCAVALLO: Nedda★ (*Pagliacci*); MASSENET: Manon★; MENOTTI: Amelia★ (*Amelia al ballo*); MONTEVERDI: Euridice★ (*Orfeo*); MOZART: Fiordiligi★ (*Così fan tutte*), Donna Anna & Donna Elvira★ & Zerlina★ (*Don Giovanni*), Contessa (*Nozze di Figaro*), Pamina★ (*Zauberflöte*); OFFENBACH: Antonia★ & Giulietta★ (*Contes d'Hoffmann*); ORFF: Solo★ (*Carmina burana*); PERGOLESI: Serpina★ (*Serva padrona*); PUCCINI: Mimi★ (*Bohème*), Liù★ (*Turandot*); ROSSINI: Rosina★ (*Barbiere di Siviglia*); SMETANA: Marinka★ (*The Kiss*); STRAUSS, J: Adele★ (*Fledermaus*); VERDI: Gilda★ (*Rigoletto*), Violetta★ (*Traviata*); WOLF-FERRARI: Susanna★ (*Segreto di Susanna*). **Res:** Swierczewskiego 4, Lódz, Poland. Mgmt: WLS/USA.

AMEDEO, EDY LETIZIA. Lyric soprano. Italian. Born 12 Feb 1935, Turin, Italy. Married. Studied:

Consv G Verdi, Turin, Renza Ferrari. **Debut:** Suor Angelica, Teatro Nuovo, Milan 1957. Awards: First Prizes, Conc Puccini RAI 1959, RAI New Voices 1953, Castrocaro Terme and Montichiari/Brescia.

Sang with major companies in AUS: Bregenz Fest, Vienna Staatsoper; BEL: Brussels; CZE: Brno, Prague National; FRA: Aix-en-Provence Fest, Bordeaux, Marseille, Nancy, Nice, Paris, Rouen, Strasbourg, Toulouse; GRE: Athens National & Fest; FR GER: Bayreuth Fest, Berlin Deutsche Oper, Frankfurt, Hamburg, Karlsruhe, Wiesbaden; GER DR: Berlin Komische Oper & Staatsoper; HOL: Amsterdam; HUN: Budapest; ITA: Bologna, Florence Comunale, Genoa, Milan La Scala, Naples, Palermo, Parma, Rome Opera & Caracalla, Trieste, Turin, Venice; MON: Monte Carlo; POR: Lisbon; SPA: Barcelona, Majorca; SWI: Geneva; UK: London Royal & English National; USA: Chicago, Hartford, New York City Opera; YUG: Dubrovnik. **Roles with these companies incl** BELLINI: Agnese★ (*Beatrice di Tenda*); BIZET: Micaëla★ (*Carmen*), Léila★ (*Pêcheurs de perles*); CATALANI: Wally★; DONIZETTI: Anna Bolena★, Maria Stuarda★; GIORDANO: Maddalena★ (*Andrea Chénier*), Fedora★; GOUNOD: Marguerite★ (*Faust*), Juliette★; LEONCAVALLO: Nedda★ (*Pagliacci*); MASCAGNI: Suzel★ (*Amico Fritz*), Carmela★ (*Silvano*); MASSENET: Manon★; MENOTTI: Monica★ (*Medium*); MEYERBEER: Marguerite de Valois★ (*Huguenots*); MONTEVERDI: Poppea★ (*Incoronazione di Poppea*); PUCCINI: Mimi★ (*Bohème*), Minnie★ (*Fanciulla del West*), Lauretta★ (*Gianni Schicchi*), Cio-Cio-San★ (*Butterfly*), Manon Lescaut★, Magda★ & Lisette★ (*Rondine*), Suor Angelica★, Giorgetta★ (*Tabarro*), Tosca★, Liù★ (*Turandot*), Anna★ (*Villi*); ROSSINI: Desdemona★ (*Otello*); VERDI: Lucrezia Contarini★ (*Due Foscari*), Alice Ford★ (*Falstaff*), Luisa Miller★, Desdemona★ (*Otello*), Amelia★ (*Simon Boccanegra*), Violetta★ (*Traviata*), Leonora★ (*Trovatore*); WOLF-FERRARI: Lucieta★ (*Quattro rusteghi*); ZANDONAI: Francesca da Rimini, Giulietta★. **Res:** V Momigliano 2, Milan, Italy or V Gramsei 39, 10055 Condove/Turin, Italy.

AMES, RICHARD; né Herbert Edward Abrams. Heldentenor & character tenor. American. Resident mem: Vereinigte Bühnen, Graz, Austria. Born 20 Aug 1937, Cleveland, O, USA. Wife Ingeborg, occupation priv secy. One child. Studied: Kmsg Max Lorenz, Munich; Prof Franz Schuch-Tovini, Vienna; Mario Basiola, Milan. **Debut:** Siegmund (*Walküre*) Staatstheater Oldenburg 1968. Awards: M B Rockefeller Fund Awd; John Hay Whitney Awd.

Sang with major companies in AUS: Graz; BEL: Brussels; FR GER: Dortmund, Kassel, Mannheim, Wuppertal; SPA: Majorca; SWI: Basel; USA: Boston, New Orleans, Philadelphia Grand. **Roles with these companies incl** BEETHOVEN: Florestan★ (*Fidelio*); BERG: Hauptmann★ (*Wozzeck*); EINEM: Bürgermeister★ (*Besuch der alten Dame*); LEONCAVALLO: Canio★ (*Pagliacci*); PENDERECKI: de Laubardemont★ (*Teufel von Loudun*); PFITZNER: Palestrina★; RIMSKY-KORSAKOV: Grishka Kouterma★ (*Invisible City of Kitezh*); STRAUSS, R: Aegisth★ (*Elektra*), Herodes★ (*Salome*); VERDI: Otello★; WAGNER: Erik★ (*Fliegende Holländer*), Lohengrin★, Loge★ (*Rheingold*), Siegmund★ (*Walküre*), Mime★ (*Siegfried*); WEBER: Max★ (*Freischütz*). World premieres: WEISHAPPEL: Basileus (*Lederköpfe*) Graz Opera 1970; SCHWERTSIK: Shi Huang-ti (*Lange Weg zur grossen Mauer*) Lucerne Opera 1975. Video—ORF TV: Basileus (*Lederköpfe*). Res: Uhlandg 18, A 8010 Graz, Austria. Mgmt: LLF/USA; TAS/AUS.

ANDERSON, SYLVIA. Mezzo-soprano. American. Born Denver, CO, USA. Husband Matthias Kuntzsch, occupation Gen Mus Dir & cond, Lübeck, FR Ger. Two children. Studied: Eastman School of Music, Anna Kaskas, Rochester, NY; Hochschule für Musik, Ellen Bosenius, Cologne. Debut: Feodor (*Boris Godunov*) Cologne Opera 1962. Awards: Hon DM MacMurray Coll, Jacksonville, IL; Fulbright Schlshp to Germany; Rockefeller Scholar; First Prize Intl Music Cont, Geneva.
   Sang with major companies in AUS: Salzburg Fest, Vienna Volksoper; BEL: Brussels; GRE: Athens Fest; FR GER: Bayreuth Fest, Bielefeld, Bonn, Cologne, Dortmund, Düsseldorf-Duisburg, Essen, Frankfurt, Hamburg, Mannheim, Saarbrücken, Stuttgart; HOL: Amsterdam; ITA: Trieste; SPA: Barcelona; SWI: Zurich; USA: Baltimore, New York Met & City Opera, Portland, San Francisco Opera, Santa Fe, Washington DC. Roles with these companies incl AUBER: Pamela (*Fra Diavolo*); BIZET: Carmen★; BORODIN: Kontchakovna (*Prince Igor*); BRITTEN: Hermia (*Midsummer Night*); DONIZETTI: Giovanna★ (*Anna Bolena*); GLUCK: Orfeo; GOUNOD: Siebel (*Faust*); HUMPERDINCK: Hänsel; MOZART: Dorabella★ (*Così fan tutte*), Cherubino (*Nozze di Figaro*); PUCCINI: Suzuki (*Butterfly*); ROSSINI: Rosina (*Barbiere di Siviglia*), Angelina (*Cenerentola*); STRAUSS, J: Prinz Orlovsky (*Fledermaus*); STRAUSS, R: Komponist★ (*Ariadne auf Naxos*), Octavian★ (*Rosenkavalier*); STRAVINSKY: Baba the Turk (*Rake's Progress*); VERDI: Eboli★ (*Don Carlo*), Preziosilla (*Forza del destino*); WAGNER: Magdalene (*Meistersinger*), Fricka (*Rheingold*★, *Walküre*★), Brangäne★ (*Tristan und Isolde*); WEINBERGER: Königin (*Schwanda*). Also ORFF: Antigonae★; PURCELL: Dido★; GNECCHI: Cassandra★; KRENEK: Klytemnestra★ (*Life of Orest*); VERDI: Meg Page (*Falstaff*), Fenena (*Nabucco*); TRAETTA: Ismene (*Antigone*). World premieres: SEARLE: Ophelia (*Hamlet*) Hamburg Opera 1968. Gives recitals. Appears with symphony orchestra. Coaches repertoire. Res: Blüchereiche 31, 2401 Lübeck-Ratekau, FR Ger. Mgmt: SLZ/FRG; DSP/USA.

ANDERSSON, LAILA ELISABETH. Lyric & dramatic soprano. Swedish. Resident mem: Royal Opera, Stockholm. Born 30 Mar 1941, Lösen, Sweden. Widowed. Studied: Sylvia Mang-Bocenberg, Ragnar Hultén, Isobel Ghasal-Öhman, Hjördis Schymberg, Stockholm. Debut: Susanna (*Nozze di Figaro*) Royal Opera, Stockholm 1965. Awards: Kristina Nilsson stipd; Edwin Ruudes Fndt; Statens Stora Arbetsstipd.
   Sang with major companies in DEN: Copenhagen; FIN: Helsinki; FR GER: Wiesbaden; NOR:

Oslo; SWE: Drottningholm Fest, Stockholm; UK: Edinburgh Fest. Roles with these companies incl BEETHOVEN: Marzelline (*Fidelio*); BIZET: Micaëla (*Carmen*); GLUCK: Euridice; HANDEL: Alcina★; JANACEK: Jenufa★; MOZART: Fiordiligi & Despina (*Così fan tutte*), Donna Elvira★ (*Don Giovanni*), Konstanze (*Entführung aus dem Serail*), Susanna (*Nozze di Figaro*), Pamina & Königin der Nacht (*Zauberflöte*); OFFENBACH: Antonia (*Contes d'Hoffmann*); PUCCINI: Mimi & Musetta★ (*Bohème*), Cio-Cio-San★ (*Butterfly*); ROSSINI: Mathilde (*Guillaume Tell*); STRAUSS, J: Rosalinde★ (*Fledermaus*); STRAUSS, R: Danae★ (*Liebe der Danae*), Sophie (*Rosenkavalier*); VERDI: Alice Ford★ (*Falstaff*), Gilda★ (*Rigoletto*), Violetta★ (*Traviata*), Leonora★ (*Trovatore*); WAGNER: Gutrune★ (*Götterdämmerung*). Also HANDEL: Erato & Amarilli★ (*Pastor fido*); VOGLER: Ebba Brahe★ (*Gustaf Adolf and Ebba Brahe*); BERWALD: Aline (*Drottningen av Golconda*). World premieres: BLOMDAHL: Nora (*Herr von Hancken*) Royal Opera Stockholm 1965; BUCHT: Margrete (*Tronkkävarna*) Royal Opera Stockholm 1966; KARKOFF: Tamar (*Gränskibbutzen*) Royal Opera Stockholm 1975. Gives recitals. Appears with symphony orchestra. Res: Box 16094, 10322 Stockholm 16, Sweden.

ANDERSSON, PER ÅKE. Conductor of opera and symphony. Swedish. Resident Cond, Norwegian Opera, Oslo. Born 3 Nov 1935, Norrköping, Sweden. Wife Irma Urrila, occupation singer. Studied: Music Acad, Stockholm, Tor Mann, Eric Ericson, Herbert Blomstedt; incl piano, violin, organ and voice. Operatic training as repetiteur & asst cond at Royal Opera, Stockholm, 1961-69. Symphonic debut: Helsingborg Orch, Sweden 1962.
   Conducted with major companies in NOR: Oslo; SWE: Stockholm. Operas with these companies incl BRITTEN: *Rape of Lucretia*★; DALLAPICCOLA: *Prigioniero*★; GLUCK: *Iphigénie en Tauride*★; LEONCAVALLO: *Pagliacci*★; MOZART: *Così fan tutte*★, *Don Giovanni*★, *Entführung aus dem Serail*, *Nozze di Figaro*★, *Zauberflöte*★; OFFENBACH: *Contes d'Hoffmann*; PUCCINI: *Bohème*, *Gianni Schicchi*★, *Butterfly*★, *Tabarro*★; ROSSINI: *Barbiere di Siviglia*★, *Cambiale di matrimonio*★, *Cenerentola*★, *Guillaume Tell*; SMETANA: *Bartered Bride*; STRAUSS, J: *Fledermaus*; STRAVINSKY: *Oedipus Rex*★; VERDI: *Don Carlo*★, *Rigoletto*★; WAGNER: *Fliegende Holländer*. Also BERWALD: *Drottningen av Golconda*. World premieres: BOLDEMANN: *Svart är vitt* Stockholm Royal Opera 1965; JOHNSEN: *Svein og Maria* Norwegian Opera 1973. Video—Norwegian TV: *Cenerentola*. Teaches at Statens Opera Klasse, Oslo. Res: Enebakkveien 164, Oslo, Norway.

ANDOR, EVA. Lyric soprano. Hungarian. Resident mem: State Opera, Budapest. Born 15 Dec 1939, Budapest. Married. Studied: Franz Liszt Acad of Music, Budapest; Frau Prof Freiwald-Lange, Berlin, Ger DR. Awards: First Prize Munich Singing Compt; Zoltán Kodály Grant, Hungarian Gvnmt.
   Sang with major companies in GER DR: Berlin Staatsoper; HUN: Budapest; ROM: Bucharest;

UK: Edinburgh Fest. **Roles with these companies incl** BEETHOVEN: Marzelline★ (*Fidelio*); BIZET: Micaëla★ (*Carmen*); GLUCK: Euridice★ (*Orfeo ed Euridice*); GOUNOD: Marguerite (*Faust*); LEONCAVALLO: Nedda (*Pagliacci*); MOZART: Zerlina★ (*Don Giovanni*), Blondchen★ (*Entführung aus den Serail*), Susanna (*Nozze di Figaro*), Pamina★ (*Zauberflöte*); PUCCINI: Mimi (*Bohème*), Cio-Cio-San (*Butterfly*), Manon Lescaut; STRAUSS, R: Sophie★ (*Rosenkavalier*); VERDI: Nannetta★ (*Falstaff*); WAGNER: Eva★ (*Meistersinger*); WOLF-FERRARI: Lucieta (*Quattro rusteghi*). Gives recitals. Appears with symphony orchestra. **Res:** Budapest, Hungary. Mgmt: ITK/HUN; LSM/UK.

ANDREW, MILLA EUGENIA. Spinto. Canadian. Born Vancouver, BC, Canada. Husband Seva Koyander, occupation architect. Two children. Studied: Royal Consv of Music, Toronto; Mo Georges Cunelli, Mme Madeline Finden, London. **Debut:** Cio-Cio-San (*Butterfly*) Sadler's Wells, London 1964.
Sang with major companies in BEL: Brussels; CAN: Toronto, Vancouver; POR: Lisbon; SPA: Barcelona; UK: Aldeburgh Fest, Cardiff Welsh, Glasgow Scottish, Glyndebourne Fest, London Royal & English National; USA: Santa Fe. **Roles with these companies incl** BELLINI: Norma★; BRITTEN: Lady Billows (*Albert Herring*), Penelope★ (*Gloriana*), Governess & Miss Jessel★ (*Turn of the Screw*); CILEA: Adriana Lecouvreur; DONIZETTI: Anna Bolena, Lucrezia Borgia, Maria Stuarda; HINDEMITH: Ursula (*Mathis der Maler*); JANACEK: Jenufa; MASSENET: Fanny (*Sappho*); MAYR: Medea (*Medea in Corinto*); MENOTTI: Magda Sorel (*Consul*); MOZART: Donna Anna★ & Donna Elvira (*Don Giovanni*), Contessa (*Nozze di Figaro*); PUCCINI: Musetta (*Bohème*), Cio-Cio-San★ (*Butterfly*), Manon Lescaut, Giorgetta (*Tabarro*), Tosca★; STRAUSS, J: Rosalinde★ (*Fledermaus*); TCHAIKOVSKY: Tatiana (*Eugene Onegin*), Lisa (*Pique Dame*); VERDI: Aida★, Amelia (*Ballo in maschera*), Elisabetta (*Don Carlo*), Donna Elvira (*Ernani*), Leonora★ (*Forza del destino*), Lady Macbeth, Abigaille★ (*Nabucco*), Leonora★ (*Trovatore*); WAGNER: Senta (*Fliegende Holländer*). Gives recitals. Appears with symphony orchestra. **Res:** 27 Melville Rd, London, UK. Mgmt: MIN/UK; LOM/USA.

ANDREYEVA, ELEONORA EVGENIEVNA. Lyric mezzo-soprano. Russian. Resident mem: Bolshoi Theater, Moscow. Born 27 Jan 1930, Vitebsk. Divorced. Husband Dubrovskiy, occupation tenor, Stanislavski Theater, Moscow. One son. Studied: Gnesin Musical Pedagog Inst, P L Trochina, Moscow. **Debut:** Elena (*Vespri siciliani*) Stanislavski Theater, Moscow 1958. Awards: Grand Prix, Paris and Gold Medal, Japan.
Sang with major companies in BUL: Sofia; USSR: Moscow Bolshoi & Stanislavski. **Roles with these companies incl** BORODIN: Jaroslavna (*Prince Igor*); DARGOMIJSKY: Natasha (*Rusalka*); PUCCINI: Tosca; RIMSKY-KORSAKOV: Fevronia (*Invisible City of Kitezh*); SHOSTAKOVICH: Katerina Ismailova★; TCHAIKOVSKY: Maria (*Mazeppa*); VERDI: Elisabetta★ (*Don Carlo*). Recorded for: Melodiya.

Gives recitals. Appears with symphony orchestra. **Res:** dom 8, kv 17, ul Bakuninskaya, Moscow, USSR. Mgmt: SOY/USSR.

ANELLO, JOHN-DAVID. Conductor of opera and symphony. American. Art Dir, Founder & Resident Cond, Florentine Opera Co, Milwaukee, WI 1932-75. Also resident cond, Summer Series, Milwaukee Symph Orch 1968- . Born Milwaukee, WI, USA. Wife Josephine, occupation cultural activities asst. Two children. Studied: Wisconsin Consv of Music, Univ of Wisconsin; Artur Rodzinski, Otto Semper, Foca di Leo, G Balestrieri; incl piano & voice. **Operatic debut:** *Traviata* Florentine Opera, Milwaukee 1950. Symphonic debut: Milwaukee Orch, Williams Bay, WI 1952. Previous occupations: instructor, Milwaukee PS. Awards: Congress Record USA; Gov's Awd, WI; Mayor's Awd, Milwaukee; NFMC; Ntl Assn of Counties, Washington, DC. Previous adm positions in opera: Milw Op Theatre 1948-52, Ntl Op Fest 1948-49, Jackson, MI, Op Co 1950-52, and Intl Friendship Gdns, Michigan City 1951-52.
Conducted with major companies in USA: Milwaukee Florentine. **Operas with these companies incl** BELLINI: *Norma;* BIZET: *Carmen★;* DELIBES: *Lakmé;* DONIZETTI: *Don Pasquale★, Elisir★, Lucia★;* FLOTOW: *Martha;* GERSHWIN: *Porgy and Bess;* GOUNOD: *Faust★, Roméo et Juliette★;* HUMPERDINCK: *Hänsel und Gretel★;* LEONCAVALLO: *Pagliacci★;* MASCAGNI: *Cavalleria rusticana★;* MENOTTI: *Old Maid and the Thief, Telephone;* MOZART: *Così fan tutte★, Don Giovanni;* OFFENBACH: *Contes d'Hoffmann★, Périchole;* PUCCINI: *Bohème★, Butterfly★, Manon Lescaut★, Tosca★, Turandot★;* ROSSINI: *Barbiere di Siviglia★, Otello;* SAINT-SAENS: *Samson et Dalila;* SMETANA: *Bartered Bride;* STRAUSS, J: *Fledermaus★;* STRAUSS, R: *Salome;* VERDI: *Aida★, Ernani, Forza del destino, Rigoletto★, Traviata★, Trovatore★;* WAGNER: *Lohengrin★, Tannhäuser.* Video—WTMJ TV Milwaukee: *Aida, Martha, Contes d'Hoffmann.* **Res:** 2004 E Edgewood Ave, Milwaukee, WI 53211, USA. Mgmt: NAP/USA.

ANGERVO, HELJÄ. Mezzo-soprano. Finnish. Resident mem: Staatsoper, Hamburg; Finnish National Opera, Helsinki. Born Helsinki, Finland. Husband Antero Karttunen, occupation with Finnish Broadcasting Corp. Studied: Sibelius Acad, Helsinki. **Debut:** Dorabella (*Così fan tutte*) Finnish National Opera 1964. Awards: Winner mezzo & alto div 's Hertogenbosch Compt 1967; Second Prize, Vocal Compt Rio de Janeiro 1969; Diploma & spec awd, Tchaikovsky Compt, Moscow 1970.
Sang with major companies in AUS: Salzburg Fest; FIN: Helsinki; FR GER: Bayreuth Fest, Hamburg. **Roles with these companies incl** BARTOK: Judith★ (*Bluebeard's Castle*); BIZET: Carmen★; EĠK: Babekan★ (*Verlobung in San Domingo*); GLUCK: Orfeo★; HAYDN: Lisetta★ (*Mondo della luna*); MONTEVERDI: Ottavia★ (*Incoronazione di Poppea*); MOZART: Dorabella★ (*Così fan tutte*), Cherubino (*Nozze di Figaro*); STRAUSS, R: Octavian★ (*Rosenkavalier*); STRAVINSKY: Jocasta★ (*Oedipus Rex*); TCHAIKOVSKY: Olga★ (*Eugene Onegin*);

VERDI: Eboli★ (*Don Carlo*), Preziosilla★ (*Forza del destino*), Azucena★ (*Trovatore*). Also VERDI: Fenena (*Nabucco*). Gives recitals. Appears with symphony orchestra. **Res:** Helsinki, Finland. Mgmt: SFM/USA.

ANGOT, JEAN. Lyric baritone, now dramatic tenor. French. Resident mem: Opéra de Paris. Born 20 Jun 1932, Thury Harcourt, Calvados, France. Wife Chantal Lemasson, occupation secy. One child. **Debut:** Amonasro (*Aida*) Théâtre des Arts, Rouen 1959. Previous occupations: prof of voice. Awards: First Prize in Opera, First Prize Opéra Comique, First Prize in Voice, Consv Ntl Supérieur de Paris.

Sang with major companies in BEL: Liège; FRA: Bordeaux, Lyon, Marseille, Nancy, Nice, Paris, Rouen, Strasbourg, Toulouse; HOL: Amsterdam; MON: Monte Carlo; POR: Lisbon; SWI: Geneva; USA: Chicago. **Roles with these companies incl** BECAUD: Sean★ (*Opéra d'Aran*); BEETHOVEN: Don Pizarro★ (*Fidelio*); BERLIOZ: Méphistophélès (*Damnation de Faust*); BIZET: Escamillo (*Carmen*), Zurga (*Pêcheurs de perles*); DALLAPICCOLA: Ulisse, Riviere & Robineau (*Volo di notte*); DONIZETTI: Dott Malatesta★ (*Don Pasquale*); GLUCK: Oreste & Thoas (*Iphigénie en Tauride*); GOUNOD: Ourrias★ (*Mireille*); HENZE: Mittenhofer (*Elegy for Young Lovers*); MARTINU: Hans★ (*Comedy on the Bridge*); MASSENET: Hérode (*Hérodiade*), Albert (*Werther*); MILHAUD: David; OFFENBACH: Don Andres (*Périchole*); PROKOFIEV: Mr Astley (*Gambler*); PUCCINI: Marcello (*Bohème*), Sharpless (*Butterfly*), Scarpia (*Tosca*); RAMEAU: Pollux; RAVEL: Ramiro (*Heure espagnole*); SAINT-SAENS: Grand prêtre (*Samson et Dalila*); VERDI: Amonasro (*Aida*), Renato (*Ballo in maschera*), Rigoletto, Germont (*Traviata*), Conte di Luna (*Trovatore*). Video—ORTF: Sid (*Albert Herring*). Appears with symphony orchestra. Mgmt: IMR/FRA.

ANGUELAKOVA, CRISTINA BORISSOVA. Dramatic mezzo-soprano. Bulgarian. Born 29 Oct 1944, Isperich, Bulgaria. Single. Studied: Consv Sofia, Sima Ivanova, Bulgaria; Gina Cigna, Renato Pastorino, Centro di Perfez, Milan. **Debut:** Amastris (*Xerxes*) National Opera Sofia 1967. Awards: First Prize, Golden Medal, Intl Conc Sofia 1973; First Prize, Intl Conc Treviso 1972.

Sang with major companies in BUL: Sofia; ITA: Milan La Scala, Palermo, Venice. **Roles with these companies incl** BRITTEN: Mrs Herring (*Albert Herring*); HANDEL: Amastris (*Xerxes*); PUCCINI: Principessa★ (*Suor Angelica*); STRAVINSKY: Jocasta★ (*Oedipus Rex*); TCHAIKOVSKY: Olga★ (*Eugene Onegin*); VERDI: Amneris★ (*Aida*), Ulrica★ (*Ballo in maschera*), Federica‡ (*Luisa Miller*), Azucena★ (*Trovatore*). Also GLUCK: Haine (*Armide*); PROKOFIEV: Helene (*War and Peace*); both on records only. Video—RAI TV: Madelon (*Andrea Chénier*). Gives recitals. Appears with symphony orchestra. **Res:** V Scopie 24, Choumen, Bulgaria. Mgmt: BAA/BUL.

ANNALS, MICHAEL. Scenic and costume designer for opera, theater, film & television. British.

Born 21 Apr 1938, Harrow. Single. Studied: Hornsey Coll of Art, London.

Designed for major companies in UK: Glyndebourne Fest, London Royal. **Operas designed for these companies incl** EINEM: *Besuch der alten Dame*★; PUCCINI: *Tabarro*★; STRAUSS, R: *Ariadne auf Naxos*★. **Res:** 12 Wellington Court, Shelton St, London WC 2, UK.

ANNOVAZZI, NAPOLEONE. Conductor of opera and symphony; composer; also operatic stage director. Italian. Artistic Dir & Resident Cond, Dublin Grand Opera Society, Rep of Ireland. Born 14 Aug 1907, Florence. Studied: Profs Frugatta, Scarlino, Ravanello and Agostini, Venice and Milan; also piano, organ & cello. Plays the piano. Operatic training as repetiteur, asst cond & chorus master at var opera comps. **Operatic debut:** *Lohengrin* Merano, Italy 1926. Symphonic debut: National Orch of Riga, Latvia 1934. Awards: Commenda al Merito, Republic of Italy, and Board of Education, Portugal. Previous adm positions in opera: Artistic Dir, Gran Teatro del Liceo, Barcelona, Spain 1947-51.

Conducted with major companies in AUS: Graz, Vienna Staatsoper & Volksoper; BEL: Brussels; BUL: Sofia; DEN: Copenhagen; FR GER: Cologne, Düsseldorf-Duisburg, Hamburg, Munich Staatsoper, Nürnberg, Saarbrücken, Wiesbaden; HOL: Amsterdam; ITA: Bologna, Naples, Palermo, Parma, Rome Opera & Caracalla, Trieste; MEX: Mexico City; NOR: Oslo; POL: Lodz; POR: Lisbon; ROM: Bucharest; SPA: Barcelona; USA: New York City Opera; YUG: Zagreb. **Operas with these companies incl** d'ALBERT: *Tiefland*; AUBER: *Fra Diavolo*; BEETHOVEN: *Fidelio*; BELLINI: *Beatrice di Tenda, Norma, Puritani, Sonnambula*; BERLIOZ: *Damnation de Faust*; BIZET: *Carmen*‡, *Pêcheurs de perles*; BOITO: *Mefistofele*★; BORODIN: *Prince Igor*; BRITTEN: *Rape of Lucretia*; CATALANI: *Wally*; CHARPENTIER: *Louise*; CILEA: *A. Lecouvreur*★‡; CIMAROSA: *Matrimonio segreto*★‡; DEBUSSY: *Enfant prodigue*; DELIBES: *Lakmé*; DONIZETTI: *Anna Bolena, Campanello, Don Pasquale*★, *Elisir*★, *Favorite*★, *Fille du régiment, Linda di Chamounix, Lucia*★, *Rita*; FALLA: *Retablo de Maese Pedro, Vida breve*; FLOTOW: *Martha*; GALUPPI: *Filosofo di campagna*; GIORDANO: *Andrea Chénier*★‡, *Fedora*; GLUCK: *Orfeo ed Euridice*; GOLDMARK: *Königin von Saba*; GOMES: *Guarany*; GOUNOD: *Faust*‡, *Roméo et Juliette*; GRANADOS: *Goyescas*; HALEVY: *Juive*; HANDEL: *Acis and Galatea, Giulio Cesare*; HUMPERDINCK: *Hänsel und Gretel*; LALO: *Roi d'Ys*; LEONCAVALLO: *Pagliacci*★; MASCAGNI: *Amico Fritz*★, *Cavalleria rusticana*★, *Silvano, Piccolo Marat*; MASSENET: *Don Quichotte, Manon*★‡, *Thaïs, Werther*★‡; MENOTTI: *Amahl, Medium, Telephone*; MEYERBEER: *Africaine, Huguenots*; MONTEMEZZI: *Amore dei tre re*; MONTEVERDI: *Combattimento di Tancredi*; MOZART: *Così fan tutte, Don Giovanni, Entführung aus dem Serail, Nozze di Figaro, Oca del Cairo*; MUSSORGSKY: *Boris Godunov, Fair at Sorochinsk, Khovanshchina*; OFFENBACH: *Contes d'Hoffmann*★‡; ORFF: *Carmina burana*★‡; PAISIELLO: *Barbiere di Siviglia*; PERGOLESI: *Frate 'nnamorato, Maestro di musica,*

Serva padrona; PONCHIELLI: *Gioconda;* PUC-CINI: *Bohème*★‡, Fanciulla del West★, Gianni Schicchi★‡, Butterfly★‡, Manon Lescaut★‡, Ron-dine★, Suor Angelica★, Tabarro★, Tosca★‡, Turan-dot★‡;* PURCELL: *Dido and Aeneas;* RAVEL: *Heure espagnole;* RIMSKY-KORSAKOV: *Invis-ible City of Kitezh, Sadko;* ROSSINI: *Barbiere di Siviglia*★‡, Cambiale di matrimonio, Ceneren-tola★‡, Guillaume Tell, Italiana in Algeri, Scala di seta, Signor Bruschino;* SAINT-SAENS: *Samson et Dalila*★‡;* SCARLATTI: *Trionfo dell'onore;* SMETANA: *Bartered Bride;* STRAUSS, J: *Fledermaus;* STRAUSS, R: *Ariadne auf Naxos, Frau ohne Schatten, Rosenkavalier*★‡, Salome;* STRAVINSKY: *Mavra, Oedipus Rex, Rossignol;* TCHAIKOVSKY: *Eugene Onegin*★‡, Pique Dame★;* THOMAS: *Hamlet, Mignon*★‡;* VERDI: *Aida*★‡, Ballo in maschera*★‡, Don Carlo★, Er-nani★, Falstaff★, Forza del destino★, Lombardi, Luisa Miller, Macbeth*★‡, Nabucco*★‡, Otello*★‡, Rigoletto★, Simon Boccanegra*★‡, Traviata*★‡, Trovatore*★‡, Vespri;* WAGNER: *Fliegende Holländer, Lohengrin*★‡, Meistersinger, Parsifal, Rienzi, Rheingold, Walküre, Siegfried, Tannhäu-ser*★‡, Tristan und Isolde;* WEBER: *Freischütz;* WOLF-FERRARI: *Donne curiose, Gioielli della Madonna, Quattro rusteghi, Segreto di Susanna;* ZANDONAI: *Francesca da Rimini*★‡, Giulietta e Romeo, Cavalieri di Ekebù.* Also CIMAROSA: *Giannina e Bernardone;* PAISIELLO: *Scuffiara;* ZANDONAI: *Conchita;* RESPIGHI: *Fiamma, Maria Egiziaca;* WOLF-FERRARI: *Campiello;* CATALANI: *Loreley;* MASCAGNI: *Iris, Lodo-letta;* CILEA: *Arlesiana;* VICTORY: *Music Hath Mischief.* Recorded for Ars et Litera, Saga. Conducted major orch in Europe. Previous posi-tions as Mus Dir with major orch: Orch Radio Nacional, Madrid; Orch Municipal, Valencia; Orch da Camera, Barcelona. **Operas composed:** *Lampada* Cagliari 1931; *Burle del Pievano Arlotto,* no pfs. **Res:** V Colleferro 16, Rome, Italy.

ANTHONY, CHARLES; né Calogero Anthony Ca-ruso. Lyric tenor. American. Resident mem: Met-ropolitan Opera, New York. Born 15 Jul 1929, New Orleans, LA. Wife Eleanor. Three children. Studied: Loyola Univ, Dorothy Hulse, New Or-leans; Kathryn Long Course, Met Opera; Ric-cardo Picozzi, Giuseppe Ruisi, Italy. **Debut:** Simpleton (*Boris Godunov*) Metropolitan Opera 1954. Awards: First Prize, Met Op Aud 1952.

Sang with major companies in USA: Boston, Cincinnati, Dallas, Miami, New Orleans, New York Met, Pittsburgh, Santa Fe, Washington DC. **Roles with these companies incl** DELIBES: Gérald (*Lakmé*); DONIZETTI: Ernesto (*Don Pasquale*), Nemorino (*Elisir*); MOZART: Ferrando (*Così fan tutte*), Don Ottavio (*Don Giovanni*); PUCCINI: Rodolfo (*Bohème*), Rinuccio (*Gianni Schicchi*), Pinkerton (*Butterfly*); ROSSINI: Almaviva (*Bar-biere di Siviglia*), Don Ramiro (*Cenerentola*); STRAUSS, R: Matteo (*Arabella*), Ein Sänger (*Ro-senkavalier*); VERDI: Fenton (*Falstaff*), Alfredo (*Traviata*); WAGNER: David (*Meistersinger*). Gives recitals. Appears with symphony orchestra.

ANTOINE, ANNE-MARIE. Dramatic soprano. Belgian. Resident mem: Städtische Bühnen, Co-logne. Born 17 Oct 1944, Brussels. Single. Studied: Consv Royal de Musique, Mme Rochat, Brussels.

Debut: Elsa (*Lohengrin*) Opéra Royal Anvers, Bel-gium 1970. Awards: Prize for Excellence in Voice and Opera, Consv Brussels 1969; Prix Fernand Anceau, Prix Roteux, Prix Kufferath Guide, 1968; Prix du Brabant 1966.

Sang with major companies in AUS: Vienna Staatsoper; BEL: Brussels, Liège; CZE: Prague National & Smetana; FR GER: Cologne, Düssel-dorf-Duisburg, Kassel, Wiesbaden; ITA: Milan La Scala; SPA: Barcelona; SWI: Geneva. **Roles with these companies incl** BARTOK: Judith★ (*Blue-beard's Castle*); FALLA: Salud (*Vida breve*); GIORDANO: Maddalena★ (*Andrea Chénier*); MASCAGNI: Santuzza★ (*Cavalleria rusticana*); MOZART: Donna Anna★ (*Don Giovanni*), Contessa★ (*Nozze di Figaro*); PUCCINI: Manon Lescaut★; VERDI: Aida★, Amelia★ (*Ballo in ma-schera*), Elisabetta★ (*Don Carlo*), Abigaille★ (*Na-bucco*), Amelia★ (*Simon Boccanegra*); WAGNER: Senta★ (*Fliegende Holländer*), Elsa★ (*Lohengrin*), Sieglinde★ (*Walküre*), Venus★ (*Tann-häuser*); WEBER: Agathe★ (*Freischütz*). Also d'ALBERT: Marta (*Tiefland*); BOITO: Elena (*Mefistofele*). Gives recitals. Appears with sym-phony orchestra. **Res:** Ave Selliers de Moranville 3, 2830 Rijmenam (Malines), Belgium. Mgmt: SLZ/FRG; VLD/AUS.

ANTOINE, BERNADETTE. Lyric soprano. French. Born 8 Mar 1940, Nancy, France. Hus-band Arnaud, occupation painter. Studied: Consv de Nancy; Consv National Supérieur, Paris. **De-but:** Musetta (*Bohème*) Théâtre Région Parisienne 1967. Previous occupations: literature stud Nancy Univ; piano stud. Awards: First Prize in Voice and Lyric Art, Paris Consv; First Prize for Inter-pretation of French Songs.

Sang with major companies in BEL: Brussels, Liège; FRA: Bordeaux, Lyon, Marseille, Nancy, Paris, Rouen, Strasbourg, Toulouse; FR GER: Hamburg; POR: Lisbon; SWI: Geneva. **Roles with these companies incl** BERLIOZ: Teresa (*Ben-venuto Cellini*); BIZET: Micaëla★ (*Carmen*); BOIELDIEU: Anna (*Dame blanche*); BRIT-TEN: Governess (*Turn of the Screw*); DE-BUSSY: Mélisande; GLUCK: Euridice; GOUNOD: Marguerite (*Faust*); MASSENET: Manon; MOZART: Despina (*Così fan tutte*), Donna Elvira★ (*Don Giovanni*), Contessa (*Nozze di Figaro*); OFFENBACH: Giulietta (*Contes d'Hoffmann*); PERGOLESI: Serpina (*Serva pa-drona*); POULENC: Blanche (*Dialogues des Car-mélites*); PROKOFIEV: Louisa (*Duenna*); PUCCINI: Mimi & Musetta (*Bohème*); RAMEAU: Aricie (*Hippolyte et Aricie*); RAVEL: Concepcion★ (*Heure espagnole*); STRAUSS, J: Rosalinde (*Fledermaus*). Also CAVALLI: Sicle (*Ormindo*); LECOCQ: Mlle Lange (*Fille de Mme Angot*); MILHAUD: Eurydice (*Malheurs d'Orphée*). **World premieres:** SEMENOFF: Elvire (*Don Juan ou L'amour de la géométrie*) ORTF, Paris 1972; PREY: Marquise de Merteuil (*Liai-sons dangereuses*) Opéra du Rhin, Strasbourg 1974. Gives recitals. Appears with symphony or-chestra. **Res:** 38 rue Eugène Carrière, Paris 18, France. Mgmt: IMR/FRA.

AOYAMA, YOSHIO. Stages/produces opera, the-ater, film & television. Japanese. Born Tokyo.

Studied: Gakushuin School, Tokyo; Acad Dr Shiko Tsoubouch, Japan.

Directed/produced opera for major companies in JPN: Tokyo Fujiwara & Niki Kai; USA: Chicago, New York Met; et al. Operas staged with these companies incl MASSENET: *Werther;* PUCCINI: *Bohème, Butterfly, Turandot;* VERDI: *Traviata;* WAGNER: *Tannhäuser;* et al.

APPEL, WOLF WILLY. Dramatic tenor & character tenor. German. Resident mem: Deutsche Oper, Berlin. Born 1 May 1942, Senftenberg, Germany. Wife Eva. Seven children. Studied: Hochschule für Musik, Prof Walter Hauck, Berlin, FR Ger. Debut: David (*Meistersinger*) Städtische Bühnen, Essen 1964.

Sang with major companies in AUS: Salzburg Fest; BEL: Brussels; DEN: Copenhagen; FIN: Helsinki; FRA: Lyon, Marseille, Nancy; FR GER: Bayreuth Fest, Berlin Deutsche Oper, Bonn, Cologne, Dortmund, Düsseldorf-Duisburg, Essen, Hamburg, Hannover, Kiel, Krefeld, Mannheim, Wuppertal; GER DR: Berlin Staatsoper; ITA: Florence Maggio, Milan La Scala, Naples, Trieste; POL: Warsaw; SWE: Stockholm; SWI: Geneva; UK: Edinburgh Fest; USSR: Moscow Bolshoi; USA: San Francisco Opera. Roles with these companies incl BRITTEN: Albert Herring; HUMPERDINCK: Hexe (*Hänsel und Gretel*); JANACEK: Laca (*Jenufa*); LEONCAVALLO: Canio (*Pagliacci*); LORTZING: Peter Ivanov (*Zar und Zimmermann*); MOZART: Pedrillo (*Entführung aus dem Serail*); ORFF: Solo (*Carmina burana*); SMETANA: Wenzel (*Bartered Bride*); STRAUSS, R: Aegisth (*Elektra*), Herodes (*Salome*); TCHAIKOVSKY: Gherman (*Pique Dame*); WAGNER: David (*Meistersinger*), Loge (*Rheingold*), Mime (*Rheingold, Siegfried*), Walther v d Vogelweide (*Tannhäuser*); WEILL: Jim Mahoney (*Aufstieg und Fall der Stadt Mahagonny*); WOLF-FERRARI: Filipeto (*Quattro rusteghi*). Teaches voice. Mgmt: SLZ/FRG.

ARAGALL, GIACOMO; né Jaime Aragall y Garriga. Lyric tenor. Spanish. Born 6 Jun 1939, Barcelona. Wife Luisa Sabirón. Two sons. Studied: Francisco Puig, Barcelona; Waldimiro Badiali, Milan. Debut: Gastone (*Gerusalemme*) Teatro la Fenice, Venice 1963. Awards: Medallia de oro, Teatro del Liceo, Barcelona; Bellini d'oro, Catania; Prize Piemonte, Teatro Regio, Turin.

Sang with major companies in ARG: Buenos Aires; AUS: Vienna Staatsoper & Volksoper; CAN: Montreal/Quebec; CZE: Prague National; DEN: Copenhagen; FRA: Marseille, Nice, Paris, Rouen; GRE: Athens National & Fest; FR GER: Berlin Deutsche Oper, Frankfurt, Hamburg, Hannover, Mannheim, Munich Staatsoper, Stuttgart, Wiesbaden; HOL: Amsterdam; HUN: Budapest; ITA: Bologna, Florence Maggio & Comunale, Genoa, Milan La Scala, Naples, Palermo, Parma, Rome Opera, Trieste, Turin, Venice, Verona Arena; MON: Monte Carlo; POR: Lisbon; SPA: Barcelona, Majorca; SWI: Geneva, Zurich; UK: Edinburgh Fest, London Royal; USA: New York Met, Philadelphia Lyric, San Francisco Opera. Roles with these companies incl CILEA: Maurizio⋆ (*A. Lecouvreur*); DONIZETTI: Gerardo⋆ (*Caterina Cornaro*), Nemorino⋆ (*Elisir*), Fernand⋆ (*Favorite*), Edgardo⋆ (*Lucia*), Gennaro (*Lucrezia Borgia*); GOUNOD: Faust⋆, Roméo⋆; HINDEMITH: Apprentice (*Cardillac*); MASCAGNI: Fritz (*Amico Fritz*); MASSENET: Roland⋆‡ (*Esclarmonde*), Des Grieux⋆ (*Manon*), Werther⋆; PUCCINI: Rodolfo⋆ (*Bohème*), Pinkerton⋆ (*Butterfly*), Cavaradossi⋆ (*Tosca*); VERDI: Oronte (*Lombardi*), Duca di Mantova⋆ (*Rigoletto*), Alfredo⋆‡ (*Traviata*). Also BELLINI/Abbado: Romeo (*Capuleti ed i Montecchi*). Recorded for: Decca. Gives recitals. Appears with symphony orchestra. Res: Barcelona, Spain. Mgmt: LOM/USA.

ARDOYNO, DOLORES. American. Gen Mng, Opera/South. Mississippi Inter-Collegiate Opera Guild, Jackson State Univ, MS 39217. In charge of adm matters & finances. Born 23 Sep 1921, Mobile, AL. Husband Donald Dorr, occupation art dir, writer. Studied: Webster Coll, St Louis; St Louis Univ, MO; Loyola Univ, Los Angeles. Previous positions, primarily adm & theatrical: Dir PR, New Orleans Opera 1968-71; Mng, Summer Pops Orch 1960-1966; own public relations service 1960-68; Dir, Radio/TV Div, Whitlock Swigart, Evans 1957-60; Publicity Dir, Petit Théâtre 1955-58; all New Orleans; Asst Prod Coord, ABC Western Div, Los Angeles, 1950-54. Started with present company Jan 1971 as PR Dir; in present position since Jun 1971. World premieres at theaters under her management: STILL: *Bayou Legend* Jackson, MS 1974. Initiated major policy changes including expansion of season to year-round operation; increase in budget; ending all-black casting; initiating policy of mounting new operas, if possible by living black composers. Res: 822 Governor Nicholls, New Orleans, LA 70116, USA.

ARENA, MAURIZIO. Conductor of opera and symphony. Italian. Born 13 Mar 1935, Messina. Wife Teresa. Two children. Studied: Mo Mannino, Mo Ferrara, Palermo and Perugia; also piano & violin. Plays the piano. Operatic training as repetiteur & asst cond at Teatro Massimo, Palermo 1960-64. Operatic debut: Teatro Massimo, Palermo 1963. Symphonic debut: AIDEM Orch, Florence 1966. Awards: Antonello da Messina Awd.

Conducted with major companies in BEL: Brussels; BUL: Sofia; FRA: Lyon, Paris; ITA: Bologna, Genoa, Milan La Scala, Naples, Palermo, Parma, Rome Opera & Caracalla, Trieste, Venice; USA: Chicago; YUG: Dubrovnik. Operas with these companies incl BARTOK: *Bluebeard's Castle;* BELLINI: *Puritani⋆;* BERG: *Wozzeck;* BOITO: *Mefistofele;* DONIZETTI: *Campanello, Don Pasquale, Elisir⋆, Favorite, Lucia⋆;* LEONCAVALLO: *Pagliacci⋆;* MASCAGNI: *Amico Fritz⋆, Cavalleria rusticana⋆;* MENOTTI: *Amahl⋆, Saint of Bleecker Street;* MONTEMEZZI: *Amore dei tre re⋆;* ORFF: *Carmina burana;* PUCCINI: *Bohème⋆, Fanciulla del West, Gianni Schicchi, Butterfly⋆, Manon Lescaut⋆, Suor Angelica, Tabarro, Tosca⋆, Turandot;* ROSSINI: *Barbiere di Siviglia, Cenerentola, Signor Bruschino;* VERDI: *Aida⋆, Ballo in maschera⋆, Forza del destino, Macbeth, Rigoletto⋆, Traviata⋆, Trovatore.* Also ROSSINI: *Donna del lago;* RUBINSTEIN: *Demon;* ALFANO: *Cyrano de Bergerac;* ROTA: *Cappello di paglia di Firenze,*

Visita meravigliosa; ZANDONAI: *Cavalieri di Ekebù;* FERRARI: *Lord Savile;* FIUME: *Tamburo di panno;* MANNINO: *Luisella;* VERDI: *Oberto.* **World premieres:** MUSCO: *Il Gattopardo* Teatro Massimo, Palermo 1967. Conducted major orch in Europe. **Res:** V Trionfale 13720, Rome, Italy. Mgmt: IMR/FRA.

ARGENTO, MANFREDI RUGGERO. Conductor of opera and symphony. Italian. Resident Cond, Teatro alla Scala, Milan. Born 20 Apr 1924, Buenos Aires. Divorced. Studied: Consv Municipal Manuel de Falla, Buenos Aires; incl piano, bassoon and voice. Plays the piano. Operatic training as repetiteur, assi cond & chorus master at Teatro Colón, Buenos Aires; Madrid, Lisbon, Italy. **Operatic debut:** *Traviata* Teatro Colón 1956. Symphonic debut: Phil Orch, Buenos Aires 1955.

Conducted with major companies in ARG: Buenos Aires; FRA: Paris; ITA: Milan La Scala; POR: Lisbon. **Operas with these companies incl** AUBER: *Muette de Portici;* BELLINI: *Norma;* BIZET: *Carmen;* BRITTEN: *Rape of Lucretia;* CIMAROSA: *Matrimonio segreto;* DEBUSSY: *Enfant prodigue;* DONIZETTI: *Lucia, Rita;* FALLA: *Retablo de Maese Pedro, Vida breve;* GALUPPI: *Filosofo di campagna;* GAY/Britten: *Beggar's Opera;* GLUCK: *Orfeo ed Euridice;* GRANADOS: *Goyescas;* HANDEL: *Xerxes;* HUMPERDINCK: *Hänsel und Gretel;* IBERT: *Angélique;* LEONCAVALLO: *Pagliacci;* MASCAGNI: *Cavalleria rusticana;* MASSENET: *Jongleur de Notre Dame, Manon, Thaïs, Werther;* MENOTTI: *Amahl, Amelia al ballo, Consul, Medium, Telephone;* MILHAUD: *Christophe Colomb;* MONTEVERDI: *Combattimento di Tancredi, Incoronazione di Poppea;* MOZART: *Così fan tutte, Don Giovanni, Finta giardiniera, Nozze di Figaro, Zauberflöte;* ORFF: *Carmina burana;* PAISIELLO: *Barbiere di Siviglia;* PERGOLESI: *Maestro di musica, Serva padrona;* POULENC: *Voix humaine;* PUCCINI: *Bohème, Gianni Schicchi, Butterfly, Manon Lescaut, Suor Angelica, Tabarro, Tosca;* ROSSINI: *Barbiere di Siviglia, Cambiale di matrimonio, Cenerentola;* STRAUSS, J: *Fledermaus;* STRAVINSKY: *Oedipus Rex;* VERDI: *Ballo in maschera, Forza del destino, Macbeth, Otello, Rigoletto, Simon Boccanegra, Traviata, Trovatore;* WOLF-FERRARI: *Donne curiose, Segreto di Susanna.* Conducted major orch in Europe, Cent/S America. Teaches at Opera School, Teatro Colón; Consv Municipal, Buenos Aires. **Res:** V Fiori Oscuri 7, Milan, Italy. Mgmt: CDA/ARG.

ARIÉ, RAFFAELE. Bass-baritone & bass. Italian. Born 22 Aug 1922, Sofia, Bulgaria. Wife Elisabeth Geiger. Studied: Consv Sofia, violin & voice; Riccardo Stracciari, Apollo Granforte, Carlo Tagliabue, Italy. **Debut:** King of Spades (*Love for Three Oranges*) La Scala, Milan 1948. Previous occupations: medical student. Awards: Italian "Oscar" for opera; Ben Gurion Prize, Israel; First Prize Voice Compt, Bulgaria; First Prize Conc Intl, Geneva.

Sang with major companies in ARG: Buenos Aires; AUS: Bregenz Fest, Salzburg Fest, Vienna Staatsoper; BUL: Sofia; FRA: Aix-en-Provence Fest, Lyon, Marseille, Nice, Paris, Rouen, Strasbourg; GRE: Athens National & Fest; FR

GER: Hamburg, Stuttgart, Wiesbaden; HOL: Amsterdam; ISR: Tel Aviv; ITA: Bologna, Florence Maggio & Comunale, Genoa, Milan La Scala, Naples, Palermo, Parma, Rome Opera & Caracalla, Trieste, Turin, Venice, Verona Arena; MEX: Mexico City; MON: Monte Carlo; NOR: Oslo; POR: Lisbon; SWI: Geneva, Zurich; UK: Edinburgh Fest, Glyndebourne Fest; USA: Chicago, New Orleans, New York City Opera, Philadelphia Grand & Lyric. **Roles with these companies incl** BARTOK: Bluebeard; BEETHOVEN: Rocco (*Fidelio*); BELLINI: Oroveso (*Norma*), Sir George★ (*Puritani*), Rodolfo★ (*Sonnambula*); BERLIOZ: Méphisthophélès (*Damnation de Faust*); BOITO: Mefistofele★; BORODIN: Prince Igor & Galitzky (*Prince Igor*); DEBUSSY: Arkel★ (*Pelléas et Mélisande*); DONIZETTI: Don Pasquale★, Dulcamara (*Elisir*), Baldassare★ (*Favorite*), Antonio (*Linda di Chamounix*), Talbot★ (*Maria Stuarda*); GLINKA: Ivan (*Life for the Tsar*); GOUNOD: Méphisthophélès★ (*Faust*); HALEVY: Brogny (*Juive*); HANDEL: Polyphemus (*Acis and Galatea*); HINDEMITH: Cardillac; MASSENET: Don Quichotte; MOZART: Publio (*Clemenza di Tito*), Leporello (*Don Giovanni*), Osmin (*Entführung aus dem Serail*), Conte Almaviva (*Nozze di Figaro*), Osmin (*Zaïde*), Sarastro (*Zauberflöte*); MUSSORGSKY: Boris & Varlaam & Pimen (*Boris Godunov*), Ivan Khovansky★ & Dosifei★ (*Khovanshchina*); PROKOFIEV: General★ (*Gambler*); PUCCINI: Colline (*Bohème*); ROSSINI: Don Basilio★ (*Barbiere di Siviglia*), Don Magnifico (*Cenerentola*), Mustafà (*Italiana in Algeri*), Moïse; SMETANA: Kezal (*Bartered Bride*); THOMAS: Lothario (*Mignon*); VERDI: Ramfis★ (*Aida*), Attila★, Philip II & Grande Inquisitore (*Don Carlo*), Silva★ (*Ernani*), Padre Guardiano (*Forza del destino*), Conte Walter★ (*Luisa Miller*), Zaccaria (*Nabucco*), Fiesco★ (*Simon Boccanegra*), Procida (*Vespri*); WAGNER: König Heinrich (*Lohengrin*), Fafner (*Rheingold, Siegfried*), König Marke (*Tristan und Isolde*); WEBER: Kaspar (*Freischütz*). Also GALUPPI: Ercole (*Ercole amante*); SUTERMEISTER: Marmeladoff (*Raskolnikov*); NABOKOV: Rasputin (*Death of Rasputin*). **World premieres:** STRAVINSKY: Trulove (*Rake's Progress*) Venice 1951. Recorded for: Decca, RCA, Pathé-Marconi. Gives recitals. Appears with symphony orchestra. Teaches voice. Coaches repertoire. **Res:** Largo Murani 2, Milan, Italy.

ARKHIPOVA, IRINA; née Veloshkina. Dramatic mezzo-soprano. Russian. Resident mem: Bolshoi Theater, Moscow. Born 2 Jan 1925, Moscow. Husband Vladislav Piavko, occupation singer. One child. Studied: Nadejda Malisheva, Leonid Savranski, Moscow. **Debut:** Lyoubacha (*Tsar's Bride*) Sverdlovsk 1954. Previous occupations: architect. Awards: First Prize, Compt of Warsaw Festival 1955.

Sang with major companies in ARG: Buenos Aires; AUS: Vienna Staatsoper; CAN: Montreal/Quebec; CZE: Brno, Prague National & Smetana; FIN: Helsinki; FRA: Bordeaux, Lyon, Marseille, Nancy, Orange Fest, Paris, Rouen; FR GER: Berlin Deutsche Oper, Wiesbaden; GER DR: Berlin Komische Oper & Staatsoper, Dresden; HUN: Budapest; ITA: Milan La Scala, Naples, Rome Opera; POL: Lodz, Warsaw; ROM:

Bucharest; UK: London Royal; USSR: Kiev, Leningrad Kirov, Moscow Bolshoi, Tbilisi; USA: San Francisco Opera; YUG: Belgrade. **Roles with these companies incl** BIZET: Carmen★‡; DUKAS: Nourrice★ (*Ariane et Barbe Bleue*); JANACEK: Kostelnicka★ (*Jenufa*); MASSENET: Charlotte★ (*Werther*); MUSSORGSKY: Marina★ (*Boris Godunov*), Marfa★‡ (*Khovanshchina*); PROKOFIEV: Helene★ (*War and Peace*); RIMSKY-KORSAKOV: Lyoubacha★‡ (*Tsar's Bride*); TCHAIKOVSKY: Pauline★‡ (*Pique Dame*); VERDI: Amneris★ (*Aida*), Ulrica★ (*Ballo in maschera*), Eboli★ (*Don Carlo*), Azucena★ (*Trovatore*). Also TCHAIKOVSKY: Lyubov (*Mazeppa*). **World premieres:** KHOLMINOV: Komissar (*Optimistic Tragedy*) 1967; SHCHEDRIN: Varvara (*Not Only Love*) 1964; KHRENNIKOV: Nilovna (*Mother*) 1957; all at Bolshoi Theater. Recorded for: Melodiya. Gives recitals. Appears with symphony orchestra. **Res:** Nejolonovi 7 kv 16, Moscow, USSR. Mgmt: GOS/USSR.

ARMSTRONG, KARAN. Lirico spinto. American. Born Havre, MT, USA. Husband Dana Tefkin, occupation mngt consultant. Studied: Mme & Dr Fritz Zweig, Los Angeles; Dr Dean Verhines, Los Angeles; Aldo Di Tullio, New York; Alberta Masiello, New York. **Debut:** Musetta (*Bohème*) San Francisco Spring Opera 1966. Awards: First Place Met Op Ntl Counc Aud 1966, 3 yr Met contract; First Place San Francisco Op Aud 1965, 1 yr contract.

Sang with major companies in FRA: Strasbourg; USA: Baltimore, Cincinnati, Fort Worth, Hartford, Houston, Lake George, Memphis, Milwaukee Florentine, New York Met & City Opera, Omaha, Portland, San Antonio, San Diego, San Francisco Spring, Santa Fe. **Roles with these companies incl** BIZET: Micaëla★ (*Carmen*); DONIZETTI: Norina★ (*Don Pasquale*), Adina★ (*Elisir*); FLOYD: Susannah★ & Marguerite★ (*Faust*), Juliette; HANDEL: Morgana★ (*Alcina*); HAYDN: Vespina (*Infedeltà delusa*); LEONCAVALLO: Nedda★ (*Pagliacci*); MOORE: Baby Doe; MOZART: Blondchen★ (*Entführung aus dem Serail*), Mme Herz★ (*Schauspieldirektor*), Susanna (*Nozze di Figaro*); OFFENBACH: Olympia★ & Antonia★ & Giulietta★ (*Contes d'Hoffmann*); PUCCINI: Mimi★ & Musetta (*Bohème*), Cio-Cio-San (*Butterfly*), Lisette (*Rondine*), Tosca★; RAVEL: Concepcion (*Heure espagnole*); RIMSKY-KORSAKOV: Reine de Schemakan★ (*Coq d'or*); ROSSINI: Rosina (*Barbiere di Siviglia*), Elvira (*Italiana in Algeri*); SALIERI: Eleonora★ (*Prima la musica*); STRAUSS, J: Rosalinde★ (*Fledermaus*); STRAUSS, R: Salome★; VERDI: Violetta★ (*Traviata*). Gives recitals. Appears with symphony orchestra. **Res:** Los Angeles. Mgmt: CAM/USA; AIM/UK.

ARMSTRONG, RICHARD. Conductor of opera and symphony. British. Mus Dir & Principal Cond, Welsh National Opera, Cardiff, UK 1973-. Also Mus Dir, Welsh Phil, Cardiff. Born 7 Jan 1943, Leicester, UK. Single. Studied: Corpus Christi College, Cambridge, UK; incl piano. Plays the piano. Operatic training as repetiteur at Royal Opera, Covent Garden, London 1966-68. **Operatic debut:** *Nozze di Figaro* Welsh National Opera

1969. Symphonic debut: Welsh Phil, Swansea 1971.

Conducted with major companies in SPA: Barcelona; UK: Welsh National; USA: Philadelphia Lyric. **Operas with these companies incl** BEETHOVEN: *Fidelio;* BERG: *Lulu★, Wozzeck;* BIZET: *Carmen, Pêcheurs de perles;* BRITTEN: *Albert Herring★, Billy Budd★;* DONIZETTI: *Elisir★;* GLUCK: *Orfeo ed Euridice;* HAYDN: *Infedeltà delusa;* JANACEK: *Jenufa★;* MOZART: *Così fan tutte, Entführung aus dem Serail, Idomeneo★, Nozze di Figaro★, Zauberflöte★;* MUSSORGSKY: *Boris Godunov★;* PUCCINI: *Bohème★, Butterfly★, Manon Lescaut★, Turandot★;* ROSSINI: *Barbiere di Siviglia★;* STRAUSS, J: *Fledermaus;* TIPPETT: *Midsummer Marriage;* VERDI: *Aida★, Don Carlo★, Falstaff★, Macbeth, Nabucco★, Otello★, Rigoletto★, Simon Boccanegra★, Traviata★, Trovatore★;* WAGNER: *Fliegende Holländer★.* **World premieres:** HODDINOTT: *Beach of Falesa* Welsh National Opera 1974. **Res:** Cardiff, UK. Mgmt: CST/UK; BAR/USA.

ARMSTRONG, SHEILA ANN. Lyric soprano. British. Born 1942, Ashington/Northumberland, UK. Studied: Newcastle; Royal Acad of Music, London; Flora Neilson, J E Hutchinson, Frederick Jackson. **Debut:** Belinda (*Dido and Aeneas*) Glyndebourne Fest 1966. Awards: Kathleen Ferrier Memorial Awd; Mozart Prize, Royal Acad of Music, London.

Sang with major companies in UK: Glasgow Scottish, Glyndebourne Fest, London Royal & English National; et al. **Roles with these companies incl** BEETHOVEN: Marzelline (*Fidelio*); DONIZETTI: Norina (*Don Pasquale*); MOZART: Zerlina (*Don Giovanni*), Zaïde, Pamina (*Zauberflöte*); ROSSINI: Fiorilla (*Turco in Italia*); STRAUSS, J: Rosalinde (*Fledermaus*); STRAUSS, R: Sophie (*Rosenkavalier*); VERDI: Nannetta (*Falstaff*); et al. Also HANDEL: Delilah (*Samson*). Recorded for: DG, Angel. Video/Film—BBC TV: Rosalinde (*Fledermaus*). Gives recitals. Appears with symphony orchestra. **Res:** London, UK. Mgmt: CAM/USA.

ARONSON, BORIS. Scenic and costume designer for opera & theater. Is a lighting designer; also a painter, sculptor, fashion designer & illustrator. American. Born 15 Oct 1899, Kiev, Russia. Wife Lisa Jalowetz. One son. Studied: State Art School, Kiev; School of Theater, Alexandra Exter, Kiev; Hermann Struch, Berlin; School of Modern Painting, Ilya Mashkov, Moscow; other studies in France. **Operatic debut:** *Mourning Becomes Electra* Metropolitan Opera, New York 1967. Theater debut: Unser Theater, Bronx, NY 1924. Awards: Guggenheim Fllshp 1950; Amer Th Wing Awds 1950, 51; Tony Awds 1956,67,69,71,72.

Designed for major companies in USA: New York Met. **Operas designed for these companies incl** BEETHOVEN: *Fidelio.* **Operatic world premieres:** LEVY: *Mourning Becomes Electra* Metropolitan Opera, New York 1967. Exhibitions of paintings & sculptures, Babcock Gal 1938, New Art Circle 1941, Nierendorf Gal 1945, Saidenberg Gal 1962, B Schaefer Gal 1958, all in New York; Art Inst of Chicago 1934; Storm King Art Center, Mountainville, NY 1963; Whitney Museum, New

York 1935; Musm of Mod Art, New York 1947. Teaches at Pratt Inst, New York. **Res:** 729 Route 9W, Nyack, NY, USA. Mgmt: AWS/USA.

ARROYO, MARTINA. Spinto. American. Born 2 Feb, New York. Husband Emilio Poggioni, occupation violist. Studied: Mme Marinka Gurewich, New York; Mo Martin Rich, coach, New York; Hunter Coll Opera Workshop, Josef Turnau, Rose Landver, New York; Kathryn Long Course, Met Opera. **Debut:** 1st Corifea (*Assassinio nella cattedrale*) Carnegie Hall, New York 1958. Previous occupations: social case worker for Welfare Dept of NY State; schoolteacher for City of New York.

Sang with major companies in ARG: Buenos Aires; AUS: Vienna Staatsoper; CZE: Prague National; FRA: Bordeaux, Paris; FR GER: Berlin Deutsche Oper, Cologne, Düsseldorf-Duisburg, Frankfurt, Hamburg, Kassel, Kiel, Krefeld, Mannheim, Munich Staatsoper, Stuttgart, Wiesbaden; ITA: Milan La Scala, Rome Opera, Turin, Verona Arena; POL: Warsaw; SWI: Zurich; UK: London Royal Opera; USA: Cincinnati, Hartford, Houston, Memphis, Miami, New York Met, Philadelphia Lyric, San Francisco Opera; YUG: Zagreb, Belgrade. **Roles with these companies incl** MASCAGNI: Santuzza★ (*Cavalleria rusticana*); MEYERBEER: Selika (*Africaine*), Valentine‡ (*Huguenots*); MOZART: Donna Anna★‡, Donna Elvira‡ (*Don Giovanni*); PUCCINI: Cio-Cio-San★ (*Butterfly*); Liù (*Turandot*); VERDI: Aida★, Amelia★‡ (*Ballo in maschera*), Elisabetta★ (*Don Carlo*), Donna Elvira★ (*Ernani*), Leonora★‡ (*Forza del destino*), Lady Macbeth★ (*Macbeth*), Amelia★ (*Simon Boccanegra*), Leonora★ (*Trovatore*), Elena★‡ (*Vespri*); WAGNER: Elsa (*Lohengrin*); WEBER: Agathe (*Freischütz*), Rezia (*Oberon*). Recorded for: EMI/Angel, London/Decca, RCA, Philips, DG. Gives recitals. Appears with symphony orchestra. **Res:** New York, NY, USA. Mgmt: DSP/USA; SLA/UK.

ARUHN, BRITT MARIE. Coloratura soprano. Swedish. Resident mem: Royal Opera, Stockholm. Born 11 Nov 1943, Motala, Sweden. Single. Studied: Royal Acad of Music, Stockholm. **Debut:** Olympia (*Contes d'Hoffmann*) Royal Opera, Stockholm 1974. Awards: Jenny Lind, Kristina Nilsson Schlshps.

Sang with major companies in SWE: Drottningholm Fest, Stockholm. **Roles with these companies incl** DONIZETTI: Norina★ (*Don Pasquale*), Adina★ (*Elisir*); OFFENBACH: Olympia★ (*Contes d'Hoffmann*); PUCCINI: Musetta★ (*Bohème*); STRAUSS, R: Zerbinetta★ (*Ariadne auf Naxos*); VERDI: Gilda★ (*Rigoletto*). Also ROTA: Helena★ (*Cappello di paglia di Firenze*). **World premieres:** LUNDQUIST: Maria (*Second of Eternity*) Royal Opera, Stockholm 1974. Recorded for: Sonab. Video/Film—Swed TV: Erste Dame (*Zauberflöte*). Gives recitals. Appears with symphony orchestra. Mgmt: KBL/SWE.

ARUNDELL, DENNIS DREW. Stages/produces opera, theater, film & television; is also an actor, author, conductor, composer & translator of opera libretti. British. Born 22 Jul 1898, Finchley, UK. Single. Studied: St John's Coll, Cambridge, UK; incl music, piano & voice. **Operatic debut:** ROO-

THAM: *Two Sisters* Cambridge 1922. Previous occupation: opera singer; lecturer Cambridge; leading actor at London's West End theaters; taught Royal Coll of Music, London & No Coll of Music, Manchester. Awards: Fellow St John's Coll, Cambridge & Royal Coll of Music, London. Previous adm positions in opera; Chief Prod, Sadler's Wells, London 1946-63.

Directed/produced opera for major companies in FIN: Helsinki Finnish; UK: Scottish, London English National. **Operas staged with these companies incl** AUBER: *Fra Diavolo*; BIZET: *Carmen*; BRITTEN: *Peter Grimes*; CIMAROSA: *Matrimonio segreto*; DEBUSSY: *Enfant prodigue, Pelléas et Mélisande*; DONIZETTI: *Don Pasquale★*; GLUCK: *Orfeo ed Euridice*; GOUNOD: *Faust*; HOLST: *Savitri*; HUMPERDINCK: *Hänsel und Gretel★*; JANACEK: *Katya Kabanova*; LEONCAVALLO: *Pagliacci*; MASCAGNI: *Cavalleria rusticana*; MASSENET: *Don Quichotte, Werther*; MENOTTI: *Amahl★, Consul, Medium*; MONTEVERDI: *Combattimento di Tancredi★*; MOZART: *Così fan tutte, Don Giovanni, Nozze di Figaro*; PERGOLESI: *Maestro di musica, Serva padrona*; PUCCINI: *Gianni Schicchi, Butterfly, Suor Angelica, Tabarro, Tosca*; PURCELL: *Dido and Aeneas, King Arthur*; STRAVINSKY: *Oedipus Rex, Rake's Progress*; VAUGHAN WILLIAMS: *Hugh the Drover, Pilgrim's Progress*; WAGNER: *Fliegende Holländer*; WALTON: *Bear*; WEINBERGER: *Schwanda*; WOLF-FERRARI: *Quattro rusteghi, Segreto di Susanna*. Also LOCKE: *Cupid and Death*; STRAVINSKY: *Histoire du soldat*; HANDEL: *Semele*; HOLST: *Wandering Scholar*; PURCELL: *Fairy Queen, Dioclesian*; VAUGHAN WILLIAMS: *Hugh the Drover*. **Operatic world premieres:** LLOYD: *John Socman* Manchester 1951; DELIUS: *Irmelin* Oxford 1953; MACONCHY: *Sofa* Camden Fest, London 1967. Operatic Video/Film—*Contes d'Hoffmann*. **Opera libretti:** translated numerous opera libretti into English. Composed: *Ghost of Abel* and *A Midsummer Night's Dream*. **Res:** 11 Lloyd Sq, London WC1, UK.

ARVIDSON, JERKER BENGT. Bass-baritone. Swedish. Resident mem: Royal Opera, Stockholm. Born 13 Nov 1939, Gnarp, Sweden. Wife Inga Lill. Three children. Studied: Arne Sunnegårdh, Bertil Düring. **Debut:** Monterone (*Rigoletto*) Norway Opera, Oslo 1970. Previous occupations: postman.

Sang with major companies in SWE: Drottningholm Fest, Stockholm. **Roles with these companies incl** BIZET: Escamillo★ (*Carmen*); DONIZETTI: Belcore★ (*Elisir*); MOZART: Don Giovanni★; OFFENBACH: Coppélius etc★ (*Contes d'Hoffmann*); STRAUSS, R: Barak★ (*Frau ohne Schatten*); VERDI: Ramfis★ (*Aida*), Conte di Luna★ (*Trovatore*); WAGNER: Amfortas★ (*Parsifal*), Wotan★ (*Rheingold*), Wanderer★ (*Siegfried*). Also PERGOLESI: Tracollo★. Gives recitals. Appears with symphony orchestra. Mgmt: KBL/SWE; SLZ/FRG.

ASKER, BJÖRN. Dramatic baritone. Swedish. Resident mem: Royal Opera, Stockholm. Born 23 Sep 1941, Stockholm. Wife Anne-Marie, occupation teacher. Two children. Studied: Royal Acad of

Music, Stockholm. **Debut:** Peter (*Resan*) Royal Opera, Stockholm 1970.

Sang with major companies in FIN: Helsinki; ISR: Tel Aviv; SWE: Drottningholm Fest. **Roles with these companies incl** MOZART: Don Giovanni*; PUCCINI: Marcello* (*Bohème*); ROSSINI: Figaro* (*Barbiere di Siviglia*); TCHAIKOVSKY: Yeletsky* (*Pique Dame*); VERDI: Ford* (*Falstaff*); WAGNER: Telramund* (*Lohengrin*), Alberich (*Rheingold*, *Götterdämmerung*). **World premieres:** HALLBERG: Carl (*Evakueringen*) Royal Opera, Stockholm 1969; WERLE: Count Essen (*Tintomara*) Royal Opera, Stockholm 1973. Recorded for: EMI. Gives recitals. Appears with symphony orchestra. Mgmt: KBL/SWE.

ASMUS, RUTH MARIA. Dramatic mezzo-soprano (Jugendlich-dramatisch). German. Resident mem: Opernhaus, Leipzig. Born 30 Mar 1934, Halle/Saale, Germany. Divorced. Two children. Studied: Vocal & Dance Ensemble of FDGB, Weimar/Thüringen, Ger DR; Musikhochschule Weimar, Egon Förster. **Debut:** Mercedès (*Carmen*) Städt Theater, Magdeburg, Ger DR 1957. Previous occupations: electrical worker at Stahlwalzwerk, Riesa, Ger DR. Awards: Kammersängerin, Ministry for Culture, Ger DR 1973; Erich Weinert Médaille, Art Prize of Ger DR Gvnmt.

Sang with major companies in GER DR: Berlin Komische Oper & Staatsoper; POL: Lodz. **Roles with these companies incl** AUBER: Pamela* (*Fra Diavolo*); BERG: Gräfin Geschwitz (*Lulu*); BIZET: Carmen*; BRITTEN: Nancy (*Albert Herring*); FLOTOW: Nancy (*Martha*); GOUNOD: Siebel* (*Faust*); HUMPERDINCK: Hänsel*; MEYERBEER: Urbain (*Huguenots*); MOZART: Dorabella* (*Così fan tutte*), Ramiro (*Finta giardiniera*), Cherubino* (*Nozze di Figaro*); OFFENBACH: Nicklausse (*Contes d'Hoffmann*); PROKOFIEV: Blanche (*Gambler*); TCHAIKOVSKY: Olga (*Eugene Onegin*); VERDI: Preziosilla (*Forza del destino*); WEBER: Fatime (*Oberon*); WEILL: Leocadia Begbick (*Aufstieg und Fall der Stadt Mahagonny*). Also PROKOFIEV: Renata (*Fiery Angel*); TCHAIKOVSKY: Johanna (*Maid of Orleans*); GERSHWIN: Bess; HANDEL: Achilles (*Deidamia*); OFFENBACH: Boulette (*Barbe Bleue*). **World premieres:** MATTHUS: Marjutka (*Letzte Schuss*) Opernhaus Leipzig 1968. Video/Film−Ger DR TV: Achilles (*Deidamia*). Gives recitals. Appears with symphony orchestra. **Res:** Funkenburgstr 14, Leipzig, Ger DR.

ATHERTON, DAVID. Conductor of opera and symphony; composer. British. Resident Cond, Royal Opera, Covent Garden, London. Born 3 Jan 1944, Blackpool, UK. Wife Ann Gianetta. One daughter. Studied: Cambridge Univ, UK; incl piano, clarinet and voice. Plays the piano and other keyboard instrm. Operatic training as repetiteur at Covent Garden, London 1967-68. **Operatic debut:** *Trovatore* Covent Garden, London 1968. Symphonic debut: Royal Phil Orch, London 1968. Awards: Ntl Acad of Rec Arts & Sciences 1973; Conductor of Year, Gt Britain Composers' Guild 1971.

Conducted with major companies in BEL: Brussels; FRA: Paris; FR GER: Berlin Fest, Frankfurt, Saarbrücken, Stuttgart, Wiesbaden; HOL: Amsterdam; ISR: Tel Aviv; ITA: Florence Maggio, Milan La Scala, Rome, Turin, Venice; POR: Lisbon; SPA: Barcelona; UK: Aldeburgh Fest, Welsh National, Edinburgh Fest, London Royal. **Operas with these companies incl** BERLIOZ: Béatrice et Bénédict*; BIZET: Carmen*, Pêcheurs de perles*; BRITTEN: Albert Herring*, Peter Grimes*; MONTEVERDI: Combattimento di Tancredi*; MOZART: Don Giovanni; PUCCINI: Bohème*, Tosca*; ROSSINI: Barbiere di Siviglia*; STRAUSS, R: Ariadne auf Naxos; TCHAIKOVSKY: Eugene Onegin*; TIPPETT: King Priam*; VERDI: Aida*, Rigoletto*, Trovatore; WEBER: Oberon. Also STRAVINSKY: Renard*; DONIZETTI: Giovedi grasso; ROSSINI: Inganno felice; GOEHR: Naboth's Vineyard; BARBER: Hand of Bridge; WEILL: Kleine Mahagonny*; CROSSE: Purgatory; GERHARD: Duenna*. **World premieres:** BIRTWISTLE: Punch and Judy Aldeburgh Fest 1968; CROSSE: Grace of Todd Aldeburgh Fest 1969; HAMILTON: Pharsalia Edinburgh Fest 1969; HENZE: The River London Royal Opera 1976. Conducted major orch in Europe, USA/Canada, Asia. Previous positions as Mus Dir with major orch: London Sinfonietta 1968-73. **Res:** London, UK. Mgmt: HLT/UK.

ATLANTOV, VLADIMIR. Lyric & dramatic tenor. Russian. Born Leningrad, USSR. Studied: Spec Music School for Children, piano, violin, cello; Leningrad Consv, Prof Bolotina; Mo Barra, Italy. Previous occupation: choral director. Awards: First Prize, Intl Tchaikovsky Compt 1966; Winner Vocal Contests Sofia & Montreal 1967; Natl Glinka Vocal Cont.

Sang with major companies in AUS: Vienna Staatsoper; FRA: Marseille; FR GER: Berlin Deutsche Oper, Wiesbaden; GER DR: Berlin Staatsoper; ITA: Milan La Scala; USSR: Leningrad Kirov, Moscow Bolshoi; et al. **Roles with these companies incl** BIZET: Don José (*Carmen*); LEONCAVALLO: Canio (*Pagliacci*); MUSSORGSKY: Dimitri & Grigori (*Boris Godunov*); PUCCINI: Rodolfo (*Bohème*), Pinkerton (*Butterfly*), Des Grieux (*Manon Lescaut*), Cavaradossi (*Tosca*); TCHAIKOVSKY: Lenski (*Eugene Onegin*), Gherman (*Pique Dame*); VERDI: Riccardo (*Ballo in maschera*), Don Carlo, Don Alvaro (*Forza del destino*), Otello, Alfredo (*Traviata*); et al. Film−DARGOMIZHSKY: Don Juan (*Stone Guest*). Mgmt: MAA/USA.

AUGÉR, ARLEEN. Lyric coloratura soprano. American. Resident mem: Staatsoper, Vienna. Born 13 Sep 1939, Los Angeles. Husband Dr Wolfgang Fahrenholtz, occupation musicologist. Studied: Mo Ralph Errolle, Chicago. **Debut:** Königin der Nacht (*Zauberflöte*) Staatsoper, Vienna 1967. Previous occupations: elem school teacher. Awards: L'Orphée d'or, Mozart Interpretation; Grand Prix du Disque; twice Wiener Flötenuhr; annual awd best Mahler record; Max Reinhardt Medal, Salzburg Fest.

Sang with major companies in AUS: Bregenz Fest, Salzburg Fest, Vienna Staatsoper & Volksoper; FRA: Aix-en-Provence Fest, Orange Fest; FR GER: Cologne, Düsseldorf-Duisburg, Frankfurt, Hamburg, Munich Staatsoper, Stuttgart; ITA:

Milan La Scala; SWI: Zurich; USA: New York City Opera. **Roles with these companies incl** CIMAROSA: Carolina★ (*Matrimonio segreto*); DEBUSSY: Mélisande★; DONIZETTI: Serafina★ (*Campanello*), Marie★ (*Fille du régiment*); HAYDN: Sandrina (*Infedeltà delusa*); MOZART: Konstanze★‡ (*Entführung aus dem Serail*), Giunia★‡ (*Lucio Silla*), Sifare★ & Aspasia (*Mitridate*), Elisa★‡ (*Re pastore*), Pamina (*Zauberflöte*), Königin der Nacht★ (*Zauberflöte*); OFFENBACH: Olympia★ (*Contes d'Hoffmann*); REIMANN: Melusine★; VERDI: Gilda★ (*Rigoletto*). Also HANDEL: Almirena‡ (*Rinaldo*). **World premieres:** WEISHAPPEL: Alma (*König Nicolo*) Vienna Volksoper 1972. Recorded for: CBS, Eurodisc, Decca, Westminster, Polydor, RCA, BASF, Philips, VEB-East Germany. Video/Film: (*Zauberflöte*). Gives recitals. Appears with symphony orchestra. Teaches voice. Coaches repertoire. On faculty of Mozarteum Salzburg, Austria. **Res:** Florianig 7/3, A-1080 Vienna, Austria. Mgmt: OOC/FRA.

AUGUSTIN, VIRPI. Dramatic mezzo-soprano. Finnish. Resident mem: Badische Staatstheater, Karlsruhe, FR Ger. Born 19 Sep 1942, Vihti, Finland. Husband T K Ritvala, occupation mngt consultant. One child. Studied: Sibelius Acad, Jolanda di Maria Petris, Aune Antti, Helsinki; Luigi Ricci, Rome. **Debut:** Eboli (*Don Carlo*) Finnish National Opera, Helsinki 1971. **Sang with major companies in** FIN: Helsinki; FR GER: Karlsruhe. **Roles with these companies incl** BIZET: Carmen★; GLUCK: Clytemnestre★ (*Iphigénie en Aulide*); LORTZING: Gräfin Eberbach★ (*Wildschütz*); OFFENBACH: Giulietta★ (*Contes d'Hoffmann*); PUCCINI: Suzuki★ (*Butterfly*); VERDI: Eboli★ (*Don Carlo*). Also CAVALLI: Delfa★ (*Giasone e Medea*). Gives recitals. Appears with symphony orchestra. Teaches voice. Coaches repertoire. **Res:** Oskelantie 5 c 22, Helsinki, Finland. Mgmt: MFZ/FIN; SLZ/FRG.

AUSTIN, ANSON WILLIAM. Lyric tenor. Australian. Resident mem: Australian Opera, Sydney. Born 9 Jul 1940, Dunedin, New Zealand. Wife Ruth, occupation schoolteacher. Two children. Studied: Clifton Cook, Christchurch, New Zealand; Jani Strasser, London. **Debut:** Rodolfo (*Bohème*) Australian Opera, Sydney 1970. Previous occupations: civil engineer. **Sang with major companies in** AUSTRL: Sydney; UK: Glyndebourne Fest. **Roles with these companies incl** DONIZETTI: Nemorino★ (*Elisir*); MOZART: Ferrando★ (*Così fan tutte*), Don Ottavio★ (*Don Giovanni*), Tamino★ (*Zauberflöte*); PUCCINI: Rodolfo★ (*Bohème*), Rinuccio★ (*Gianni Schicchi*); ROSSINI: Almaviva★ (*Barbiere di Siviglia*); STRAUSS, R: Ein Sänger★ (*Rosenkavalier*). Gives recitals. Appears with symphony orchestra. **Res:** Sydney, Australia. Mgmt: AIM/UK.

AUVRAY, JEAN-CLAUDE. Stages/produces opera & television. Also designs sets, costumes & stagelighting. French. Resident Stage Dir, Opéra de Paris. Born 14 May 1942, Saint-Lô. Single. Studied: as asst to Vilar, Ponnelle, Strehler, Chereau, Enriquez; also music and violin. Operatic training as asst stage dir at opera comps in Rome, Milan,

Naples, Buenos Aires. **Operatic debut:** *Norma* Opéra de Nice 1972. Previous occupation: chemist. Awards: Awd Best Opera Production in France 1974, Toulouse.

Directed/produced opera for major companies in FRA: Aix-en-Provence Fest, Nancy, Nice, Toulouse; USA: New York City Opera. **Operas staged for these companies incl** BELLINI: *Norma★;* DONIZETTI: *Maria Stuarda;* GOUNOD: *Faust★;* LALO: *Roi d'Ys★;* MASSENET: *Don Quichotte★, Manon★;* MOZART: *Così fan tutte, Nozze di Figaro★;* MUSSORGSKY: *Boris Godunov;* OFFENBACH: *Contes d'Hoffmann★;* PENDERECKI: *Teufel von Loudun★;* PUCCINI: *Turandot;* ROSSINI: *Barbiere di Siviglia★, Cenerentola, Elisabetta Regina;* VERDI: *Forza del destino★, Nabucco, Otello, Trovatore★;* ZANDONAI: *Francesca da Rimini★.* Mgmt: CMW/FRA; SLA/UK.

AXARLIS, STELLA. Dramatic soprano. German. Resident mem: Deutsche Oper am Rhein, Düsseldorf-Duisburg.

Sang with major companies in AUSTRL: Sydney; AUS: Vienna Staatsoper; FR GER: Düsseldorf-Duisburg, Hamburg, Kassel; UK: London Royal; et al. **Roles with these companies incl** BEETHOVEN: Leonore (*Fidelio*); GIORDANO: Maddalena (*Andrea Chénier*); JANACEK: Jenufa, Katya Kabanova; MASCAGNI: Santuzza (*Cavalleria rusticana*); MASSENET: Manon; MUSSORGSKY: Marina (*Boris Godunov*); PUCCINI: Cio-Cio-San (*Butterfly*), Tosca; STRAUSS, R: Ariadne (*Ariadne auf Naxos*), Marschallin (*Rosenkavalier*); TCHAIKOVSKY: Tatiana (*Eugene Onegin*); VERDI: Aida, Elisabetta (*Don Carlo*), Leonora (*Forza del destino*), Lady Macbeth; WAGNER: Senta (*Fliegende Holländer*), Sieglinde (*Walküre*), Gutrune (*Götterdämmerung*), Venus (*Tannhäuser*); et al. Also d'ALBERT: Marta (*Tiefland*). Mgmt: CAM/USA.

AZARMI, NASSRIN. Lyric-coloratura soprano. Iranian. Resident mem: Deutsche Oper am Rhein, Düsseldorf. Born 5 Jan 1949, Brujderd, Iran. Single. Studied: Teheran Consv of Music, Mme Fachere Saba; Fr Margarethe Düren-Herrmann, Cologne. **Debut:** Despina (*Così fan tutte*) Teheran Opera 1967.

Sang with major companies in AUS: Vienna Volksoper; FR GER: Düsseldorf-Duisburg Oper am Rhein; USA: San Francisco Opera. **Roles with these companies incl** BIZET: Micaëla (*Carmen*); CAVALIERI: Anima beata★ (*Rappresentazione*); DONIZETTI: Adina★ (*Elisir*); GLUCK: Amor (*Orfeo ed Euridice*); MOZART: Despina (*Così fan tutte*), Zerlina★ (*Don Giovanni*), Konstanze★ & Blondchen★ (*Entführung aus dem Serail*), Aspasia★ (*Mitridate, re di Ponto*), Susanna★ (*Nozze di Figaro*), Pamina & Königin der Nacht (*Zauberflöte*); NICOLAI: Frau Fluth★ (*Lustigen Weiber*); OFFENBACH: Olympia★ (*Contes d'Hoffmann*); ORFF: Solo (*Carmina burana*); PUCCINI: Lauretta (*Gianni Schicchi*); ROSSINI: Elvira★ (*Italiana in Algeri*); STRAUSS, R: Fiakermilli★ (*Arabella*), Aminta★ (*Schweigsame Frau*); VERDI: Nannetta★ (*Falstaff*), Gilda (*Rigoletto*); WEBER: Fatima (*Abu Hassan*). Also ROSSINI: Clorinda★ (*Cenerentola*). Gives recitals. Appears with symphony orchestra. **Res:** Arnoldstr 23, 4 Düsseldorf 30, FR Ger. Mgmt: SLG/FRG; RAB/AUS.

AZUMA, ATSUKO. Lyric soprano. Japanese. Born 11 Dec 1939, Osaka, Japan. Husband Eiji Nitahara, occupation sculptor. One child. Studied: Tokyo Univ of Arts, Mrs Fumiko Yotsuya; Consv Arrigo Boito, Giulia Tess, Prof Ettore Campogalliani, Parma, Italy. **Debut:** Suzel (*Amico Fritz*) Teatro Municipale di Reggio Emilia, Italy 1963.

Sang with major companies in ARG: Buenos Aires; AUS: Vienna Staatsoper; BEL: Liège; CZE: Prague National; DEN: Copenhagen; FRA: Bordeaux, Lyon, Marseille, Nancy, Nice, Strasbourg, Toulouse; FR GER: Berlin Deutsche Oper, Bielefeld, Hamburg, Munich Staatsoper; GER DR: Berlin Staatsoper, Dresden, Leipzig; HUN: Budapest; ITA: Genoa, Naples, Parma, Venice; JPN: Tokyo Fujiwara; MON: Monte Carlo; POR: Lisbon; SPA: Barcelona Teatro del Liceo; USA: Boston, Cincinnati, Fort Worth, Miami, New York Met, Portland, Washington DC; YUG: Belgrade. **Roles with these companies incl** BIZET: Micaëla (*Carmen*); DONIZETTI: Norina★ (*Don Pasquale*); LEONCAVALLO: Nedda (*Pagliacci*); MASCAGNI: Suzel (*Amico Fritz*); MOZART: Zerlina (*Don Giovanni*), Susanna (*Nozze di Figaro*), Pamina (*Zauberflöte*); PUCCINI: Mimì★ (*Bohème*), Cio-Cio-San★ (*Butterfly*), Suor Angelica, Liù★ (*Turandot*); VERDI: Violetta (*Traviata*). Also MASCAGNI: Iris; DAN: Tsu (*Yuzuru*). **World premieres:** LUDWIG: Frau (*Rashomon*) Städt Bühnen, Augsburg 1972. Video/Film: Cio-Cio-San. Gives recitals. Appears with symphony orchestra. **Res:** V Zenalc 13, Milan 20123, Italy. Mgmt: JAR/JPN; DSP/USA.

AZZOLINI, ACLY CARLO. Stages/produces opera, theater & film. Also designs sets & stagelighting and is an actor & writer. Italian. Born 7 Sep 1913, Palestrina/Rome. Wife Fernanda Cadoni, occupation singer. Two children. Studied: Accad S Cecilia, Teatro dell'Opera, Rome; also music, piano, violin and voice. Operatic training as asst stage dir with Carro di Tespi Lirico Nazionale, tours of Italy 1935-38. **Operatic debut:** *Cavalleria rusticana* Teatro la Fenice, Venice 1939. Theater debut: Rome 1948. Previous occupation: swimmer, dancer, actor, elemen school teacher. Awards: Second Place, Ital Swimming Championship Jrs; Gold Medal for recording, Rome, Macerata, Rovigo, Taormina & Cori; Cavaliere

Ufficiale, Rep of Italy. Previous adm positions in opera: Gen Stage Mng, Teatro Carlo Felice, Genoa 1938-40.

Directed/produced opera for major companies in BEL: Brussels; BRA: Rio de Janeiro; DEN: Copenhagen; FRA: Lyon, Paris; FR GER: Frankfurt, Munich Staatsoper, Wiesbaden; ITA: Bologna, Genoa, Naples, Rome Opera & Caracalla, Trieste, Venice; SPA: Barcelona; SWI: Basel, Zurich; UK: Scottish; YUG: Dubrovnik. **Operas staged with these companies incl** AUBER: *Fra Diavolo;* BEETHOVEN: *Fidelio;* BELLINI: *Norma★†, Puritani★†, Sonnambula★†;* BERLIOZ: *Damnation de Faust;* BIZET: *Carmen★†, Pêcheurs de perles★†;* BOITO: *Mefistofele;* BORODIN: *Prince Igor†;* BUSONI: *Arlecchino;* CATALANI: *Wally;* CILEA: *A. Lecouvreur★;* CIMAROSA: *Matrimonio segreto★†;* DONIZETTI: *Campanello★†, Don Pasquale★†, Elisir★†, Favorite, Lucia★†, Rita★;* FALLA: *Retablo de Maese Pedro, Vida breve;* GALUPPI: *Filosofo di campagna;* GIORDANO: *Andrea Chénier★†, Fedora★;* GLUCK: *Orfeo ed Euridice;* GOUNOD: *Faust, Roméo et Juliette;* LECOCQ: *Fille de Madame Angot;* LEONCAVALLO: *Pagliacci★†;* MASCAGNI: *Amico Fritz★, Cavalleria rusticana★†;* MASSENET: *Manon★, Werther;* MENOTTI: *Amelia al ballo, Medium★†, Telephone★;* MERCADANTE: *Vestale★†;* MONTEVERDI: *Combattimento di Tancredi, Favola d'Orfeo;* MOZART: *Così fan tutte, Don Giovanni★†, Nozze di Figaro†;* MUSSORGSKY: *Boris Godunov, Khovanshchina;* PERGOLESI: *Maestro di musica★, Serva padrona★;* PONCHIELLI: *Gioconda★;* POULENC: *Dialogues des Carmélites;* PUCCINI: *Bohème★, Fanciulla del West, Gianni Schicchi, Butterfly★, Manon Lescaut, Suor Angelica★†, Tosca★, Turandot★†;* ROSSINI: *Barbiere di Siviglia, Cambiale di matrimonio★, Cenerentola, Guillaume Tell★†, Signor Bruschino★;* SAINT-SAENS: *Samson et Dalila;* STRAUSS, R: *Elektra;* VERDI: *Aida★†, Ballo in maschera★, Don Carlo★, Ernani★, Falstaff★, Forza del destino, Macbeth, Nabucco★, Rigoletto★†, Simon Boccanegra★, Traviata★†, Trovatore★;* WAGNER: *Lohengrin★†, Meistersinger;* WOLF-FERRARI: *Donne curiose, Quattro rusteghi★, Segreto di Susanna★.* Also PIZZETTI: *Straniero;* FIORAVANTI: *Cantatrici villane;* ROSSELLINI: *Sguardo dal ponte;* LIVIABELLA: *Antigone.* **Operatic world premieres:** ALFANO: *Dott Antonio* Teatro dell'Opera, Rome 1950; ALLEGRA: *Romulus* Teatro San Carlo, Naples 1954. Teaches. **Res:** V Livorno 66, 00162 Rome, Italy.

B

BABAK, RENATA. Dramatic mezzo-soprano. Ukrainian/Russian. Born Charkev, USSR. Divorced. One child. Studied: Leningrad Consv, Prof Msuanskaja; Kiev Consv, Prof Evtoushenko. **Debut:** Carmen, Bolshoi Theater, Moscow, USSR 1963.

Sang with major companies in FIN: Helsinki; GER DR: Berlin Komische Oper, Leipzig; HUN: Budapest; ITA: Milan La Scala; POL: Warsaw; USSR: Kiev, Leningrad Kirov, Moscow Bolshoi, Tbilisi. **Roles with these companies incl** BIZET: Carmen; BORODIN: Kontchakovna (*Prince Igor*); BRITTEN: Hermia (*Midsummer Night*); DONIZETTI: Léonore (*Favorite*); GLINKA: Ratmir (*Ruslan and Ludmilla*); GLUCK: Orfeo; GOUNOD: Siebel (*Faust*); MASSENET: Charlotte (*Werther*); MEYERBEER: Urbain (*Huguenots*); MOZART: Cherubino (*Nozze di Figaro*); MUSSORGSKY: Marina (*Boris Godunov*), Marfa (*Khovanshchina*); PONCHIELLI: Laura (*Gioconda*); RIMSKY-KORSAKOV: Ljuba (*Sadko*), Lyoubacha (*Tsar's Bride*); ROSSINI: Rosina (*Barbiere di Siviglia*); SAINT-SAENS: Dalila; TCHAIKOVSKY: Olga (*Eugene Onegin*), Comtesse & Pauline (*Pique Dame*); VERDI: Amneris (*Aida*), Eboli (*Don Carlo*), Azucena (*Trovatore*); WAGNER: Ortrud (*Lohengrin*). Also MASCAGNI: Santuzza (*Cavalleria rusticana*); WAGNER: Senta (*Fliegende Holländer*); TCHAIKOVSKY: Lubov (*Mazeppa*). Appears with symphony orchestra. Teaches voice. Coaches repertoire. **Res:** 2109 Broadway, New York, NY 10023, USA. Mgmt: NAP/USA.

BABER, DAVID M. American. Mng Dir, Opera Society of Washington, J F Kennedy Center, Washington, DC 20566, 1974- . In charge of adm matters & finances; is also a lyric baritone. Born 24 Oct 1945, Montgomery, WV. Single. Studied: West Virginia Univ, Morgantown; Morris Harvey Coll, Charleston, WV. Previous occupation: concert artist. Form positions, primarily adm: Exec Dir, OPERA America, Washington DC 1972-74. Initiated major changes including the founding of new programs and the expansion of OPERA America as its first executive director. Mem of OPERA America committee on gvnmt support. **Res:** Washington, DC, USA.

BÄCKMAN, ILKKA OLAVI. Stages/produces opera & theater. Finnish. Resident Stage Dir, Finnish National Opera, Helsinki. Born 26 Nov 1945, Virrat, Finland. Wife Anja Aulikki, occupation administrator. One child. Studied: Drama Studio, Tampere Univ, Finland. Operatic training as asst stage dir at Finnish Ntl Opera, Helsinki 1970-71. **Operatic debut:** *Tabarro* Finnish Ntl Opera 1972. Theater debut: City Theater, Oulu, Finland 1974. **Directed/produced opera for major companies in** FIN: Helsinki. **Operas staged for these companies incl** BRITTEN: *Midsummer Night*; GOUNOD: *Faust;* PASATIERI: *Divina*; POULENC: *Voix humaine*; PUCCINI: *Tabarro*; SHOSTAKO-VICH: *Nose;* VERDI: *Ballo in maschera*, *Rigoletto*. Also MADETOJA: *Pohjalaisia;* HAUPT: *Puppe.* **Operatic world premieres:** RAUTA-WAARA: *Apollo and Marsyas* Finnish Ntl Opera 1973. **Res:** Siimakuja 14, 00720 Helsinki 72, Finland.

BACQUIER, GABRIEL (Augustin Raymond Théodore Louis). Bass-baritone. French. Born 17 May 1924, Béziers, France. Wife Mauricette Bénard. Two children. Studied: Consv Ntl de Musique, Paris. **Debut:** Figaro (*Barbiere di Siviglia*) Théâtre Royal de la Monnaie, Brussels 1953. Previous occupations: publicity officer. Awards: Chevalier de la Légion d'Honneur; Chevalier de l'Ordre Ntl du Mérite; Vermeil Medal, City of Paris; 1st Prizes in Voice and Opera, Consv.

Sang with major companies in ARG: Buenos Aires; AUS: Vienna Staatsoper; BEL: Brussels, Liège; CAN: Montreal/Quebec; FRA: Aix-en-Provence Fest, Bordeaux, Lyon, Marseille, Nancy, Nice, Paris, Rouen, Strasbourg, Toulouse; FR GER: Berlin Deutsche Oper, Hamburg; HOL: Amsterdam; ITA: Florence Maggio, Genoa, Milan La Scala, Naples, Rome Opera & Caracalla, Turin, Venice; MON: Monte Carlo; POR: Lisbon; SPA: Barcelona; SWI: Geneva; UK: Glyndebourne Fest, London Royal; USA: Boston, Chicago, Dallas, Hartford, Miami, New York Met, Philadelphia Grand, San Francisco Opera, Seattle. **Roles with these companies incl** BELLINI: Sir Richard (*Puritani*); BERLIOZ: Méphistophélès (*Damnation de Faust*); BIZET: Escamillo (*Carmen*), Zurga (*Pêcheurs de perles*); BORODIN: Prince Igor; CHARPENTIER: Père (*Louise*); DEBUSSY: Golaud (*Pelléas et Mélisande*); DELIBES: Nilakantha (*Lakmé*); DONIZETTI: Dott Malatesta & Don Pasquale (*Don Pasquale*), Dulcamara (*Elisir*), Alfonse (*Favorite*), Sulpice (*Fille du régiment*); GLUCK: Agamemnon (*Iphigénie en Aulide*),

Oreste & Thoas (*Iphigénie en Tauride*); GOU-
NOD: Ourrias & Ramon (*Mireille*); MASCA-
GNI: Alfio (*Cavalleria rusticana*); MASSENET:
Sancho (*Don Quichotte*), Hérode (*Hérodiade*),
Boniface (*Jongleur de Notre Dame*), Lescaut (*Ma-
non*), Des Grieux (*Portrait de Manon*), Athanaël
(*Thaïs*), Albert (*Werther*); MENOTTI: Husband
(*Amelia al ballo*); MEYERBEER: Comte de St
Bris (*Huguenots*); MOZART: Don Alfonso (*Così
fan tutte*), Leporello & Don Giovanni (*Don Gio-
vanni*), Conte Almaviva & Figaro (*Nozze di Fi-
garo*); OFFENBACH: Coppélius, etc (*Contes
d'Hoffmann*); PUCCINI: Colline (*Bohème*),
Gianni Schicchi, Sharpless (*Butterfly*), Michele
(*Tabarro*), Scarpia (*Tosca*); RAVEL: Ramiro
(*Heure espagnole*); ROSSINI: Dott Bartolo (*Bar-
biere di Siviglia*), Guillaume Tell; SAINT-
SAENS: Grand prêtre (*Samson et Dalila*);
TCHAIKOVSKY: Eugene Onegin; VERDI: Rodrigo (*Don Carlo*), Falstaff, Fra Melitone (*Forza
del destino*), Iago (*Otello*), Rigoletto, Simon Boc-
canegra, Germont (*Traviata*); WAGNER: Wolf-
ram (*Tannhäuser*). Also GLUCK: Orphée★;
GOUNOD: Mercutio (*Roméo et Juliette*); POU-
LENC: Marquis de la Force (*Dialogues des Car-
mélites*); RAVEL: (*Enfant et les sortilèges*);
THIRIET: Veredigne (*Histoire du docteur*).
World premieres: MENOTTI: Abdul (*Dernier
sauvage*) Opéra Comique, Paris 1963. Video/Film:
Comte des Grieux (*Manon*), Coppélius, etc
(*Contes d'Hoffmann*). Gives recitals. Appears
with symphony orchestra. **Res:** 141 rue de Rome,
17 Paris, France. Mgmt: GLZ/FRA; CAM/USA;
ASK/UK.

BADER, HANS-DIETER. Dramatic tenor. Ger-
man. Resident mem: Niedersächsisches
Staatstheater, Hannover. Born 16 Feb 1938, Stutt-
gart. Wife Ursula Wolters. Studied: Prof Rudolf
Gehrung; Frl Weglein, piano, theory; Frl Siegel,
language, Stuttgart. **Debut:** Arturo (*Lucia*)
Württembergisches Staatstheater, Baden 1960.
Previous occupations: builder.
   Sang with major companies in AUS: Vienna
Volksoper; FRA: Strasbourg; FR GER: Berlin
Deutsche Oper, Bielefeld, Darmstadt, Düsseldorf-
Duisburg, Essen, Frankfurt, Hamburg, Hannover,
Karlsruhe, Kassel, Mannheim, Nürnberg, Stutt-
gart, Wuppertal; SWI: Basel. **Roles with these com-
panies incl** AUBER: Fra Diavolo★; BERG:
Tambourmajor (*Wozzeck*); BIZET: Don José★
(*Carmen*); BUSONI: Mephisto (*Doktor Faust*);
CHERUBINI: Giasone (*Medea*); DONIZETTI:
Edgardo★ (*Lucia*); DVORAK: Prince★ (*Rusalka*);
FLOTOW: Lionel★ (*Martha*); GLUCK: Achille
(*Iphigénie en Aulide*); GOUNOD: Faust★; HIN-
DEMITH: Apprentice (*Cardillac*); JANACEK:
Mazal (*Excursions of Mr Broucek*); LEON-
CAVALLO: Canio★ (*Pagliacci*); MASCAGNI:
Turiddu★ (*Cavalleria rusticana*); MOZART:
Ferrando (*Così fan tutte*); OFFENBACH: Hoff-
mann★; PUCCINI: Rodolfo★ (*Bohème*), Pinkerton
(*Butterfly*), Cavaradossi (*Tosca*); SMETANA:
Hans★ (*Bartered Bride*); STRAUSS, J: Alfred
(*Fledermaus*); STRAUSS, R: Bacchus★ (*Ariadne
auf Naxos*), Flamand★ (*Capriccio*), Aegisth (*Elek-
tra*); Ein Sänger★ (*Rosenkavalier*); TCHAIKOV-
SKY: Gherman★ (*Pique Dame*); VERDI:
Radames★ (*Aida*), Riccardo★ (*Ballo in maschera*),
Don Carlo★, Ismaele (*Nabucco*), Duca di Man-

tova★ (*Rigoletto*), Gabriele★ (*Simon Boccanegra*),
Manrico★ (*Trovatore*); WAGNER: Erik★
(*Fliegende Holländer*), Lohengrin★, Loge★ (*Rhein-
gold*); WEBER: Max★ (*Freischütz*). **World pre-
mieres:** MEYEROWITZ: Pfarrer Arnison
(*Doppelgängerin*) Niedersächsisches Staatsthea-
ter, Hannover 1967; MIHALOVICI: Eusebe
(*Zwillinge*) Braunschweig 1963. Gives recitals.
Appears with symphony orchestra. **Res:** Schäfer-
weg 20, 3012 Langenhagen, FR Ger. Mgmt:
PAS/FRG; SLZ/FRG; HUS/FRG

BAGLIONI, BRUNA; née Costantini. Dramatic
mezzo-soprano. Italian. Born 8 Apr 1947,
Frascati/Rome. Husband Mario, occupation busi-
nessman. Studied: Prof Gina Maria Rebori, Mo
Walter Cataldi-Tassoni, Rome. **Debut:** Maddalena
(*Rigoletto*) Spoleto Fest 1970.
   Sang with major companies in ITA: Bologna,
Milan La Scala, Naples, Parma, Rome Opera &
Caracalla, Spoleto Fest, Trieste, Venice; USSR:
Moscow Bolshoi. **Roles with these companies incl**
BELLINI: Adalgisa★ (*Norma*); CILEA: Prin-
cesse de Bouillon★ (*A. Lecouvreur*); DONI-
ZETTI: Léonore★ (*Favorite*); MASSENET:
Charlotte★ (*Werther*); MUSSORGSKY: Marina★
(*Boris Godunov*); PONCHIELLI: Laura★ & La
Cieca★ (*Gioconda*); SPONTINI: High Priestess★
(*Vestale*); VERDI: Amneris★ (*Aida*), Ulrica★
(*Ballo in maschera*), Azucena★ (*Trovatore*). Gives
recitals. Appears with symphony orchestra. **Res:** V
Luciano-Manara 9, Frascati/Rome, Italy.

BAILEY, NORMAN STANLEY. Dramatic bari-
tone. British. Born 23 Mar 1933, Birmingham, UK.
Wife Doreen, occupation personal secy. Three
children. Studied: Prof Georg Gruber, Graham-
stown, South Africa; Vienna State Acad, Prof Adolf
Vogel; Mo Francesco Carrino, Düsseldorf; Prof
Clemens Kaiser-Breme, London & Essen. **Debut:**
Tobias Mill (*Cambiale di matrimonio*) Vienna
Chamber Opera 1959.
   Sang with major companies in BEL: Brussels;
CAN: Toronto; FIN: Helsinki; FRA: Paris,
Strasbourg; FR GER: Bayreuth Fest, Bielefeld,
Cologne, Düsseldorf-Duisburg, Essen, Frankfurt,
Hamburg, Hannover, Karlsruhe, Kiel, Munich
Staatsoper, Saarbrücken, Stuttgart, Wuppertal;
HOL: Amsterdam; ITA: Milan La Scala; S AFR:
Johannesburg; SWI: Zurich; UK: Cardiff
Welsh, Glasgow Scottish, London Royal &
Eng Natl; USA: Miami, New York City Op.
Roles with these cos incl BEETHOVEN: Don
Pizarro (*Fidelio*); BERG: Dr Schön (*Lulu*);
BIZET: Escamillo (*Carmen*); BRITTEN: Cap-
tain Balstrode★ (*Peter Grimes*); DALLA-
PICCOLA: Prigioniero; DEBUSSY: Golaud
(*Pelléas et Mélisande*); EINEM: George
Danton (*Dantons Tod*); HAYDN: Buonafede
(*Mondo della luna*); HINDEMITH: Cardil-
lac; LORTZING: Graf v Liebenau
(*Waffenschmied*); MASCAGNI: Alfio (*Cavalleria
rusticana*); MOZART: Figaro (*Nozze di Figaro*);
OFFENBACH: Coppélius etc★ (*Contes
d'Hoffmann*); PROKOFIEV: Michael★ (*War and
Peace*); PUCCINI: Sharpless (*Butterfly*), Scarpia
(*Tosca*); ROSSINI: Tobias Mill (*Cambiale di ma-
trimonio*); SAINT-SAENS: Grand prêtre (*Sam-
son et Dalila*); STRAUSS, R: Musiklehrer
(*Ariadne auf Naxos*), Orest★ (*Elektra*), Jochanaan★

(*Salome*); STRAVINSKY: Creon (*Oedipus Rex*); TCHAIKOVSKY: Eugene Onegin; VERDI: Renato★ (*Ballo in maschera*), Ford★ (*Falstaff*), Nabucco, Rigoletto, Simon Boccanegra, Germont★ (*Traviata*), Conte di Luna★ (*Trovatore*); WAGNER: Holländer★, Hans Sachs★ (*Meistersinger*), Amfortas★ (*Parsifal*), Wotan (*Rheingold★, Walküre★*), Wanderer★ (*Siegfried*), Gunther (*Götterdämmerung*), Wolfram (*Tannhäuser*), Kurwenal★ (*Tristan und Isolde*). Recorded for: EMI, Decca. Video–BBC TV: Ford (*Falstaff*); Germont (*Traviata*). Gives recitals. Appears with symphony orchestra. **Res:** 63 Kimbolton Rd, Bedford, UK. Mgmt: GOR/UK; CSA/USA.

BAINBRIDGE, ELIZABETH. Dramatic mezzo-soprano & contralto. British. Resident mem: Royal Opera, London. Born 28 Mar 1936, UK. Single. Studied: Guildhall School of Music & Drama, London; Norman Walker. **Debut:** Dritte Dame (*Zauberflöte*) Glyndebourne Fest 1963. **Sang with major companies in** FRA: Bordeaux; UK: Aldeburgh Fest, Cardiff Welsh, Glasgow Scottish, Glyndebourne Fest, London Royal Opera & English National. **Roles with these companies incl** BERLIOZ: Anna★ (*Troyens*); BRITTEN: Hippolita★ (*Midsummer Night*), Auntie★ (*Peter Grimes*); PUCCINI: Suzuki★ (*Butterfly*), Frugola (*Tabarro*); SMETANA: Hata (*Bartered Bride*); VERDI: Amneris★ (*Aida*), Ulrica★ (*Ballo in maschera*), Dame Quickly★ (*Falstaff*), Azucena (*Trovatore*); WAGNER: Erda (*Rheingold★, Siegfried★*). Recorded for: EMI, Decca, RCA, Philips. Gives recitals. Appears with symphony orchestra. **Res:** London, UK. Mgmt: SLA/UK; CMW/FRA.

BAIRD, EDWARD ALLEN. Bass-baritone. American. Resident mem: Fort Worth Opera, TX. Born 18 Mar 1933, Kansas City, KA, USA. Wife Shirley. One child. Studied: Univ of Missouri/Kansas City, Hardin Van Deursen; Univ of Mich, Chase Baromeo, Ralph Herbert, Josef Blatt, Ann Arbor; Boris Goldovsky summer wrkshp, USA. **Debut:** Dr Grenvil (*Traviata*) Fort Worth Opera, TX 1963. Awards: DM Arts degree for vocal perf, Univ of Michigan; Reg Finalist, Met Op Aud; Best Supporting Actor Awd, Casa Mañana Summer Musicals, Fort Worth, TX 1971. **Sang with major companies in** USA: Fort Worth, Houston, Kansas City, New Orleans, San Diego. **Roles with these companies incl** BARBER: Doctor (*Vanessa*); DEBUSSY: Arkel (*Pelléas et Mélisande*); DONIZETTI: Don Pasquale; MOZART: Leporello (*Don Giovanni*), Figaro (*Nozze di Figaro*); PUCCINI: Colline (*Bohème*); ROSSINI: Dott Bartolo & Don Basilio (*Barbiere di Siviglia*), Don Magnifico (*Cenerentola*). Also MOZART: Masetto & Commendatore (*Don Giovanni*), Sprecher (*Zauberflöte*). **World premieres:** ADLER: Uncle Billy (*Outcasts of Poker Flat*) No Texas Univ, Denton 1962; Obadiah & Esau (*Wrestler*) Dallas, TX 1972; SMITH: Mandarin (*Shepherdess and Chimney Sweep*) Fort Worth Opera 1966. Gives recitals. Appears with symphony orchestra. Teaches voice. Coaches repertoire. On faculty of No Texas State Univ, Denton, TX. **Res:** 2602 Woodhaven Dr, Denton, TX, USA.

BAKER, ALAN. Lyric baritone. American. Resident member: New York City Opera. Born Kansas City, MO. Single. Studied: Juilliard School, Sergius Kagen, Mack Harrell, New York; Stuttgart Hochschule für Musik, Alfred Paulus, Hermann Reutter, FR Ger. **Debut:** Dandini (*Cenerentola*) Turnau Opera, Woodstock, NY 1959.
Sang with major companies in USA: Boston, Kentucky, New York City Opera, Philadelphia Grand & Lyric, St Paul. **Roles with these companies incl** BARTOK: Bluebeard; CIMAROSA: Count Robinson (*Matrimonio segreto*); DEBUSSY: Siméon (*Enfant prodigue*); DONIZETTI: Enrico (*Campanello*), Dott Malatesta★ (*Don Pasquale*); FALLA: Don Quixote★ (*Retablo de Maese Pedro*); GLUCK: Agamemnon (*Iphigénie en Aulide*), Oreste (*Iphigénie en Tauride*), Orfeo★; GOUNOD: Valentin★ (*Faust*); HUMPERDINCK: Peter★ (*Hänsel und Gretel*); MASSENET: Lescaut (*Manon*), Des Grieux (*Portrait de Manon*); MENOTTI: Husband (*Amelia al ballo*); MONTEVERDI: Ottone★ (*Incoronazione di Poppea*); MOZART: Don Alfonso★ (*Così fan tutte*), Don Giovanni, Conte Almaviva★ (*Nozze di Figaro*); ORFF: Solo★ (*Carmina burana*); PUCCINI: Marcello★ (*Bohème*), Sharpless★ (*Butterfly*), Michele (*Tabarro*); PURCELL: Aeneas★ (*Dido and Aeneas*); ROSSINI: Figaro★ (*Barbiere di Siviglia*), Dandini★ (*Cenerentola*), Geronio★ (*Turco in Italia*); STRAVINSKY: Nick Shadow★ (*Rake's Progress*); VERDI: Germont★ (*Traviata*); WAGNER: Wolfram (*Tannhäuser*). **World premieres:** LADERMAN: Angel (*Sarah*) CBS TV 1958; Clown (*Goodbye to the Clown*) Turnau Opera, NY 1960; AMRAM: Max (*Final Ingredient*) ABC TV 1965. Recorded for: Decca. Gives recitals. Appears with symphony orchestra. **Res:** New York, NY, USA. Mgmt: SFM/USA.

BAKER, JANET. Dramatic mezzo-soprano. British. Born 21 Aug 1933, York, UK. Husband Keith Shelley, occupation concert manager. Studied: Helen Isepp, Meriel St Clair, London; Lotte Lehmann master class, Wigmore Hall, London; Mozarteum Salzburg. **Debut:** Dido (*Dido and Aeneas*) English Op Group, Aldeburgh Fest 1962. Previous occupations: bank employee. Awards: Kathleen Ferrier Memorial Prize 1956; Queen's Prize 1959; grant from Arts Council 1960; CBE, HM Queen Elizabeth II, 1971; HDM Birmingham, Hull, Leicester, London & Oxford Univs.
Sang with major companies in UK: Aldeburgh Fest, Edinburgh Fest, Glasgow Scottish, Glyndebourne Fest, London Royal & English National. **Roles with these companies incl** BERLIOZ: Marguerite (*Damnation de Faust*), Didon (*Troyens*); BRITTEN: Nancy (*Albert Herring*), Hermia (*Midsummer Night*), Lucretia★ (*Rape of Lucretia*); CAVALLI: Diana★ (*Calisto*); DONIZETTI: Maria Stuarda; GAY/Britten: Polly (*Beggar's Opera*); HANDEL: Ariodante★, Orlando (*Orlando furioso*); MONTEVERDI: Poppea (*Incoronazione di Poppea*), Penelope‡ (*Ritorno d'Ulisse*); MOZART: Vitellia (*Clemenza di Tito*), Dorabella (*Così fan tutte*); STRAUSS, R: Komponist (*Ariadne*), Octavian (*Rosenkavalier*). Also HOLST: Savitri★. **World premieres:** BRITTEN: Kate Julian (*Owen Wingrave*) BBC prod 1971. Recorded for: Phonogram, CBS, Decca, EMI. Video–BBC TV: (*Owen Wingrave*); Andronico (*Tamerlano*); Diana (*Calisto*); Penelope (*Ritorno*

d'Ulisse). Gives recitals. Appears with symphony orchestra. Mgmt: HUR/USA; IBB/UK.

BAKKER, MARCO; né Jacob Marinus Bakker. Lyric baritone. Dutch. Born 8 Feb 1938, Beverwijk, Holland. Wife Patricia Anne Madden, occupation singer. One child. Studied: Amsterdam Consv, Coby Riemers; Ruth Horna, Amsterdam; Prof Hans Hotter, Munich; Otakar Kraus, London. **Debut:** MONTEVERDI: Orfeo, Holland Festival 1967. Awards: First Prize, Vocal Cont 's Hertogenbosch; Second Prize, Vocal Cont Munich; First Prize, Vocal Cont Rio de Janeiro.

Sang with major companies in BEL: Brussels; HOL: Amsterdam; UK: Glasgow Scottish, Glyndebourne Fest. **Roles with these companies incl** BELLINI: Ernesto★ (*Pirata*); BIZET: Zurga★ (*Pêcheurs de perles*); DONIZETTI: Belcore & Dulcamara (*Elisir*); GOUNOD: Méphistophélès★ (*Faust*); HANDEL: Giulio Cesare★; LORTZING: Peter I★ & Van Bett (*Zar und Zimmermann*); MONTEVERDI: Orfeo; MOZART: Guglielmo & Don Alfonso (*Così fan tutte*), Leporello & Don Giovanni (*Don Giovanni*), Conte Almaviva & Figaro★ (*Nozze di Figaro*), Papageno (*Zauberflöte*); MUSSORGSKY: Boris Godunov & Pimen (*Boris Godunov*); ORFF: Solo★ (*Carmina burana*); PUCCINI: Marcello (*Bohème*), Sharpless (*Butterfly*); ROSSINI: Signor Bruschino; STRAUSS, R: Robert Storch★ (*Intermezzo*); TCHAIKOVSKY: Eugene Onegin; VERDI: Germont (*Traviata*). **World premieres:** DE LEEUW: Student (*De droom*) Holland Fest, Amsterdam 1965. Gives recitals. Appears with symphony orchestra. **Res:** Jan v Scorelpark 5, Schoorl, Holland. Mgmt: ALF/HOL; AIM/UK.

BAKOCEVIC, RADMILA; née Radmila Vasovic. Dramatic soprano. Yugoslavian. Resident mem: Belgrade Opera. Born 6 Jan 1933, Guca, Yugoslavia. Husband Aleksandar, occupation lawyer. One child. Studied: Acad of Music, Prof Nikola Cvejic, Belgrade; School of the Teatro alla Scala, Milan. **Debut:** Mimi (*Bohème*) Belgrade Opera 1955. Awards: Second Prize, Intl Compt of Young Artists, Belgrade 1958; Grand Prix, Geneva 1962 and Liège, Belgium 1964; Targa d'oro, Brescia, Italy 1972-73.

Sang with major companies in ARG: Buenos Aires; AUS: Vienna Staatsoper; BUL: Sofia; DEN: Copenhagen; FRA: Bordeaux, Paris; GRE: Athens National & Fest; FR GER: Berlin Deutsche Oper, Düsseldorf-Duisburg, Frankfurt, Hamburg, Wiesbaden; GER DR: Berlin Staatsoper; HUN: Budapest; ITA: Florence Comunale, Genoa, Milan La Scala, Naples, Palermo, Parma, Rome Opera & Caracalla, Trieste, Turin, Venice; MEX: Mexico City; POL: Warsaw Teatr Wielki; POR: Lisbon; ROM: Bucharest; SPA: Barcelona Teatro del Liceo; SWI: Geneva; UK: London Royal; USSR: Kiev, Leningrad Kirov, Moscow Bolshoi, Tbilisi; USA: New York Met, Philadelphia Lyric, San Francisco Opera; YUG: Dubrovnik, Zagreb, Belgrade. **Roles with these companies incl** BELLINI: Beatrice di Tenda★, Norma★; BORODIN: Jaroslavna★; CILEA: Adriana Lecouvreur; DONIZETTI: Elisabetta (*Roberto Devereux*); GLINKA: Antonida (*Life for the Tsar*); GOUNOD: Marguerite★ (*Faust*); MONTEVERDI: Poppea (*Incoronazione di Pop-*

pea); MOZART: Cherubino (*Nozze di Figaro*); OFFENBACH: Giulietta (*Contes d'Hoffmann*); PROKOFIEV: Pauline (*Gambler*), Natasha (*War and Peace*); PUCCINI: Mimi★ (*Bohème*), Minnie★ (*Fanciulla del West*), Cio-Cio-San★ (*Butterfly*), Manon Lescaut★, Tosca★; RIMSKY-KORSAKOV: Olga (*Maid of Pskov*); SMETANA: Marie (*Bartered Bride*), Mlada (*Dalibor*); STRAUSS, R: Salome★; TCHAIKOVSKY: Tatiana★ (*Eugene Onegin*), Iolanthe, Lisa (*Pique Dame*); VERDI: Aida★, Amelia★ (*Ballo in maschera*), Elisabetta★ (*Don Carlo*), Donna Elvira★ (*Ernani*), Leonora (*Forza del destino*), Desdemona★ (*Otello*), Amelia (*Simon Boccanegra*), Violetta★ (*Traviata*), Leonora★ (*Trovatore*); WAGNER: Elisabeth (*Tannhäuser*). Recorded for: MGM. Gives recitals. Appears with symphony orchestra. **Res:** Ul Ivana Milutinovica 77, Belgrade, Yugoslavia.

BALDANI, RUZA; née Pospis. Lyric & dramatic mezzo-soprano. Yugoslavian. Born 25 Jul 1942, Varazdin. Husband Jovan, occupation univ teacher. Two children. Studied: Prof Ankica Opolski, Varazdin; Prof Marija Borcic, Zagreb; Kmsg Georgine von Milinkovic, Munich. **Debut:** Kontchakovna (*Prince Igor*) Zagreb Opera 1961.

Sang with major companies in AUS: Graz, Salzburg Fest, Vienna Staatsoper; BUL: Sofia; CAN: Ottawa, Toronto; GRE: Athens Fest; FR GER: Cologne, Dortmund, Hamburg, Munich Staatsoper, Wiesbaden; HUN: Budapest; ITA: Genoa, Milan La Scala, Naples, Rome Opera; SPA: Barcelona; UK: Edinburgh Fest; USSR: Leningrad Kirov; USA: Chicago, Houston, Kansas City, New Orleans, New York Met, San Francisco Opera; YUG: Dubrovnik, Zagreb, Belgrade. **Roles with these companies incl** BIZET: Carmen★; BORODIN: Kontchakovna★ (*Prince Igor*); BRITTEN: Hippolita (*Midsummer Night*); DEBUSSY: Geneviève (*Pelléas et Mélisande*); GLUCK: Orfeo★ (*Orfeo ed Euridice*); MUSSORGSKY: Marina★‡ (*Boris Godunov*), Marfa★ (*Khovanshchina*); PONCHIELLI: La Cieca★ (*Gioconda*); PUCCINI: Suzuki (*Butterfly*); ROSSINI: Sinaïde (*Moïse*); SAINT-SAENS: Dalila★; SPONTINI: High Priestess★‡ (*Vestale*); TCHAIKOVSKY: Olga (*Eugene Onegin*); VERDI: Amneris★ (*Aida*), Ulrica★ (*Ballo in maschera*), Azucena★ (*Trovatore*); WAGNER: Erda (*Rheingold★, Siegfried★*), Fricka (*Rheingold★, Walküre★*), Brangäne (*Tristan und Isolde*). Also BOITO: Rubria★ (*Nerone*). Gives recitals. Appears with symphony orchestra. **Res:** Jurjevska 27, Zagreb, Yugoslavia. Mgmt: SLZ/FRG.

BALDWIN, MARCIA. Lyric coloratura mezzo-soprano & jugendlich dramatisch soprano. American. Resident mem: Metropolitan Opera, New York. Born 5 Nov 1939, Milford, NE. Single. Studied: Northwestern Univ, Evanston, IL; Marinka Gurewich, New York; Hunter Coll Op Wkshp, Rose Landver, Ludwig Donath, New York. **Debut:** Mercedès (*Carmen*) Santa Fe Opera, NM 1961. Awards: Rockefeller Fndt Grant; Ford Fllwshp; Winner Intl Music Compt, Munich.

Sang with major companies in USA: Cincinnati, Fort Worth, Lake George, New York Met, Philadelphia Lyric, San Francisco Spring Opera. **Roles with these companies incl** BRITTEN: Mrs Herring

(*Albert Herring*), Hermia (*Midsummer Night*); GOUNOD: Siebel★ (*Faust*); HUMPERDINCK: Hänsel★; MOZART: Cherubino (*Nozze di Figaro*); PUCCINI: Suzuki★ (*Butterfly*); ROSSINI: Isabella (*Italiana in Algeri*); STRAUSS, R: Komponist (*Ariadne auf Naxos*), Octavian (*Rosenkavalier*); WAGNER: Magdalene★ (*Meistersinger*); WARD: Elizabeth Proctor (*Crucible*). Also GOUNOD: Stephano★ (*Roméo et Juliette*); TCHAIKOVSKY: Lisa (*Pique Dame*); ROSSINI: Desdemona (*Otello*); GIORDANO: Madelon (*Andrea Chénier*). **World premieres:** AMRAM: Viola (*Twelfth Night*) Lake George Opera, NY 1968. Recorded for: DG. Gives recitals. Appears with symphony orchestra. Teaches voice. **Res:** 115 W 11 St, New York, USA. Mgmt: SMN/USA.

BALK, HOWARD WESLEY. Stages/produces opera & theater and is an author. American. Art Dir & Resident Stage Dir, Minnesota Opera Co, Minneapolis. Born 31 Oct 1932, St Paul, MN. Wife Barbara J, occupation singer. Studied: Yale Drama School; incl voice. **Operatic debut:** *Rape of Lucretia* New Haven Opera Socy, CT 1964. Previous occupation: teacher.
Directed/produced opera for major companies in USA: Houston, Kansas City, Lake George, Minneapolis, New York City Opera, San Francisco Spring Opera, Santa Fe, Washington DC. **Operas staged with these companies incl** BRITTEN: *Albert Herring★, Midsummer Night;* HAYDN: *Mondo della luna;* MILHAUD: *Abandon d'Ariane, Délivrance de Thésée, Enlèvement d'Europe;* MOZART: *Così fan tutte★, Don Giovanni★, Entführung aus dem Serail, Nozze di Figaro★, Zauberflöte★;* ORFF: *Kluge★;* PUCCINI: *Gianni Schicchi★;* ROSSINI: *Barbiere di Siviglia★;* SATIE: *Socrate;* THOMSON: *Mother of Us All;* WEILL: *Dreigroschenoper★.* Also BIRTWISTLE: *Punch and Judy;* EGK: *17 Tage und 4 Minuten.* **Operatic world premieres:** STOKES: *Horspfal* 1968; MARSHALL: *Oedipus and the Sphinx* 1969, *Business of Good Government* 1970; GESSNER: *Faust Counter Faust* 1971; BRUNELLE/HUCKABY: *Newest Opera in the World* 1974; SUSA: *Transformations* 1973; KAPLAN/BLACKWOOD/LEWIN: *Gulliver* 1975; all at Minnesota Opera Co. **Opera libretti:** MARSHALL: *Oedipus and the Sphinx;* GESSNER: *Faust Counter Faust;* BRUNELLE: *Newest Opera in the World.* Teaches at Univ of Minnesota, Minneapolis. **Res:** 2630 Irving So, Minneapolis, MN, USA.

BALKWILL, BRYAN. Conductor of opera and symphony; composer. British. Wife Susan. Two children. Studied: Royal Acad of Music, London; incl piano, violin. Operatic training as repetiteur, asst cond & chorus master at New London Opera Co, London 1947-49; Glyndebourne Fest 1950-60; under Busch, Gui, Beecham. **Operatic debut:** *Rigoletto* New London Opera Co 1947. Symphonic debut: Royal Phil, London 1957. Previous adm positions in opera: Mus Dir, Welsh Ntl Opera, Cardiff 1963-67; Mus Dir, Sadler's Wells, London 1966-69.
Conducted with major companies in BUL: Sofia; CAN: Montreal/Quebec, Toronto, Vancouver; UK: Aldeburgh Fest, Welsh National, Edinburgh Fest, Glyndebourne Fest, London Royal &

English National. **Operas with these companies incl** BEETHOVEN: *Fidelio;* BELLINI: *Norma, Puritani, Sonnambula;* BIZET: *Carmen★, Jolie Fille de Perth;* BOIELDIEU: *Dame blanche;* BRITTEN: *Albert Herring★, Billy Budd★, Gloriana, Midsummer Night, Peter Grimes, Rape of Lucretia, Turn of the Screw;* CIMAROSA: *Matrimonio segreto;* DONIZETTI: *Anna Bolena, Don Pasquale, Elisir★, Fille du régiment, Lucia★;* FLOTOW: *Martha;* GLUCK: *Alceste, Iphigénie en Tauride, Orfeo ed Euridice;* GOUNOD: *Faust, Mireille;* HANDEL: *Alcina;* HUMPERDINCK: *Hänsel und Gretel;* LEONCAVALLO: *Pagliacci★;* LORTZING: *Wildschütz;* MASCAGNI: *Cavalleria rusticana;* MASSENET: *Manon★, Werther;* MENOTTI: *Amahl, Consul, Medium;* MOZART: *Così fan tutte★, Don Giovanni, Entführung aus dem Serail★, Idomeneo★, Nozze di Figaro★, Zauberflöte★;* OFFENBACH: *Contes d'Hoffmann★;* PUCCINI: *Bohème★, Gianni Schicchi, Butterfly★, Manon Lescaut, Tabarro★, Tosca★;* ROSSINI: *Barbiere di Siviglia★, Cenerentola, Comte Ory★, Gazza ladra★, Guillaume Tell, Italiana in Algeri★, Moïse;* SAINT-SAENS: *Samson et Dalila;* SMETANA: *Bartered Bride, Dalibor;* STRAUSS, J: *Fledermaus★;* STRAUSS, R: *Ariadne auf Naxos, Capriccio, Rosenkavalier;* STRAVINSKY: *Oedipus Rex, Rake's Progress;* TCHAIKOVSKY: *Eugene Onegin, Pique Dame;* TIPPETT: *King Priam;* VAUGHAN WILLIAMS: *Riders to the Sea;* VERDI: *Aida, Ballo in maschera, Don Carlo, Due Foscari, Ernani, Falstaff, Forza del destino★, Lombardi, Macbeth, Nabucco, Otello, Rigoletto★, Simon Boccanegra, Traviata★, Trovatore;* WAGNER: *Fliegende Holländer★, Lohengrin, Meistersinger, Walküre;* WEBER: *Freischütz;* WOLF-FERRARI: *Segreto di Susanna.* Also PUCCINI: *Edgar★.* **World premieres:** BENNETT: *Penny for a Song* Sadler's Wells, London 1967. Video—BBC: *Otello, Traviata, Medium, Amahl.* Conducted major orchestras in Europe, USA/Canada, Africa. **Res:** 19 Lingfield Rd, Wimbledon, London SW19 4QD, UK. Mgmt: AIM/UK.

BALTSA, AGNES. Lyric coloratura mezzo-soprano. Greek. Resident mem: Deutsche Oper, Berlin; Staatsoper, Vienna. Born 19 Nov 1944, Lefkas, Greece. Husband Missenhardt, occupation opera singer. Studied: Nunuka Fragia-Spiliopulos, Athens; Dr Henny Schöner, Munich; Prof Herbert Champain, Frankfurt. **Debut:** Cherubino (*Nozze di Figaro*) Frankfurt 1968. Awards: Winner Georges Enesco Compt, Bucharest 1964; Highest Awd Conserv Athens 1964; Maria Callas stipd, Athens 1965.
Sang with major companies in AUS: Salzburg Fest, Vienna Staatsoper; FR GER: Berlin Deutsche Oper, Düsseldorf-Duisburg, Frankfurt, Hamburg, Munich Staatsoper; HOL: Amsterdam; ITA: Trieste; SPA: Barcelona; SWI: Zurich; USA: Houston; YUG: Zagreb, Belgrade. **Roles with these companies incl** BIZET: Carmen★; BORODIN: Kontchakovna★ (*Prince Igor*); CHERUBINI: Neris★ (*Medea*); GLUCK: Orfeo★; HUMPERDINCK: Hänsel★; MOZART: Sesto★ (*Clemenza di Tito*), Dorabella★ (*Così fan tutte*), Cherubino★ (*Nozze di Figaro*); ROSSINI: Rosina★ (*Barbiere di Siviglia*), Angelina★ (*Cene-*

rentola), Isabella (*Italiana in Algeri*); STRAUSS, J: Prinz Orlovsky★ (*Fledermaus*); STRAUSS, R: Komponist★ (*Ariadne auf Naxos*), Octavian★ (*Rosenkavalier*); TCHAIKOVSKY: Olga★ (*Eugene Onegin*). Also WOLF: Frasquita (*Corregidor*); MERCADANTE: Bianca (*Giuramento*); MOZART: Bastien. Recorded for: EMI. Gives recitals. Appears with symphony orchestra. Teaches voice. Coaches repertoire. **Res:** Georgin Sografu 25, Athens, Greece. Mgmt: JUC/SWI; MAA/USA.

BAMBI, GILBERTO. Italian. Adm Dir, Teatro Comunale/Maggio Musicale Fiorentino, 15 V Solferino, Florence, Italy. In charge of adm matters. Born 1 Feb 1925, Florence. Wife Lidia Castiglioni. One child. Studied: Istituto Tecnico, Florence. Started with present company 1945 as clerk; in present position since 1967.

BAN, VIOREL. Bass. Romanian. Resident mem: Romanian Opera, Bucharest. Born 21 Jan 1920, Arad. Wife Petra, occupation professor. Studied: Consv, Prof Constantin Stroescu, Bucharest. **Debut:** Sparafucile (*Rigoletto*) Romanian Opera 1950. Previous occupations: studied physics & chemistry.
Sang with major companies in GER DR: Berlin Staatsoper; ROM: Bucharest. **Roles with these companies incl** BEETHOVEN: Rocco★ (*Fidelio*); DEBUSSY: Arkel★ (*Pelléas et Mélisande*); GLINKA: Ivan (*Life for the Tsar*); GOUNOD: Méphistophélès (*Faust*); MOZART: Figaro (*Nozze di Figaro*), Sarastro★ (*Zauberflöte*); MUSSORGSKY: Pimen★ (*Boris Godunov*); PROKOFIEV: Mendoza (*Duenna*); PUCCINI: Colline★ (*Bohème*); ROSSINI: Don Basilio (*Barbiere di Siviglia*); WAGNER: Pogner (*Meistersinger*). Also BORODIN: Kontchak★ (*Prince Igor*); ENESCU: High Priest★ (*Oedipe*). **World premieres:** TRAILESCU: Damian (*Balcescu*) 1974; DUMITRESCU: Batto (*Decebal*) 1969; both at Romanian Opera. Recorded for: Electrecord. Teaches voice. Coaches repertoire. On faculty of Consv Ciprian Porumbescu, Bucharest. **Res:** Bucharest 6, Romania. Mgmt: RIA/ROM.

BAÑUELAS, ROBERTO. Lyric & dramatic baritone. Mexican. Resident mem: Deutsche Oper Berlin. Born 20 Jan 1931, Camargo, Mexico. Wife Hortensia Cervantes, occupation opera singer. Two children. Studied: Consv Nacional de Musica and Acad de la Opera de Bellas Artes, Mexico City. **Debut:** Marcello (*Bohème*) Opera Nacional de Bellas Artes, Mexico 1958. Awards: Diploma, Union Mexicana de Criticos de Teatro y Musica; etc.
Sang with major companies in BUL: Sofia; CZE: Prague National; FR GER: Berlin Deutsche Oper, Cologne, Frankfurt, Hamburg, Mannheim, Munich Staatsoper, Saarbrücken, Stuttgart; MEX: Mexico City; USA: New York City Opera. **Roles with these companies incl** BIZET: Escamillo (*Carmen*), Zurga (*Pêcheurs de perles*); DEBUSSY: Siméon (*Enfant prodigue*), Golaud (*Pelléas et Mélisande*); DELIBES: Nilakantha (*Lakmé*); DONIZETTI: Enrico★ (*Lucia*), Nottingham (*Roberto Devereux*); GINASTERA: Silvio de Narni (*Bomarzo*); GIORDANO: Carlo Gérard (*Andrea Chénier*); LEONCAVALLO: Tonio★ (*Pagliacci*); MASCA-

GNI: Alfio (*Cavalleria rusticana*); MASSENET: Lescaut (*Manon*); MOZART: Guglielmo (*Così fan tutte*), Conte Almaviva★ & Figaro (*Nozze di Figaro*), Papageno (*Zauberflöte*); ORFF: Solo (*Carmina burana*); PERGOLESI: Tracolino (*Maestro di musica*); PUCCINI: Marcello★ (*Bohème*), Sharpless★ (*Butterfly*), Lescaut (*Manon Lescaut*), Scarpia★ (*Tosca*); ROSSINI: Figaro (*Barbiere di Siviglia*); STRAUSS, R: Orest (*Elektra*); STRAVINSKY: Creon (*Oedipus Rex*), Empereur de Chine (*Rossignol*); VERDI: Amonasro★ (*Aida*), Renato★ (*Ballo in maschera*), Rodrigo (*Don Carlo*), Ford & Falstaff (*Falstaff*), Don Carlo★ (*Forza del destino*), Iago (*Otello*), Rigoletto★, Germont★ (*Traviata*), Conte di Luna★ (*Trovatore*).

BARBIER, GUY. Conductor of opera and symphony; composer; & operatic stage director. Belgian. Music Dir, Orchestre Mozart de Belgique. Born 10 Jun 1924, Namur, Belgium. Wife Floris-Nicole, occupation ballet teacher. Two children. Studied: Acad of Music, Vienna, Hans Swarowsky; incl piano & violin. **Operatic debut:** *Faust* Opéra de Lyon, France 1967. Symphonic debut: Orch Ntl de Belgique, Namur, Belgium 1956. Previous occupations: violinist and composer. Awards: Grand Prix Acad Charles Cros, Paris 1955; Lion d'or de Venise, Critics Awd 1964.
Conducted with major companies in BEL: Brussels, Liège; CAN: Montreal/Quebec; FRA: Bordeaux, Lyon, Paris; GRE: Athens Fest; FR GER: Berlin Deutsche Oper, Munich Staatsoper; GER DR: Leipzig; ISR: Tel Aviv; ITA: Palermo, Turin; MEX: Mexico City; MON: Monte Carlo; SPA: Barcelona; UK: London English National. **Operas with these companies incl** BIZET: *Pêcheurs de perles★;* BRITTEN: *Rape of Lucretia★;* CIMAROSA: *Matrimonio segreto;* DELIBES: *Lakmé;* DONIZETTI: *Lucia★;* GLINKA: *Life for the Tsar★;* GOUNOD: *Faust, Mireille;* HUMPERDINCK: *Hänsel und Gretel★;* LECOCQ: *Fille de Madame Angot★;* PUCCINI: *Bohème, Butterfly★;* RAVEL: *Heure espagnole;* ROSSINI: *Barbiere di Siviglia★;* SAINT-SAENS: *Samson et Dalila;* STRAUSS, J: *Fledermaus★;* VERDI: *Aida★, Traviata.* **World premieres:** BARBIER: *Gulliver ou Le doyen fou* National Opera, Brussels 1967. Conducted major orch in Europe, Canada, Cent/S America & Asia. **Operas composed:** *Gulliver* see above. Teaches at Consv Royal de Liège, Belgium. **Res:** Ave Léopold 58A, Rixensart, Belgium. Mgmt: GAR/BEL.

BARBIERI, FEDORA. Mezzo-soprano & contralto. Italian. Born 4 Jun 1920, Trieste, Italy. Husband Luigi Barlozzetti. Two children. Studied: Consv Trieste, Mo Luigi Toffolo; Centro Avviamento Teatro Lirico, Florence. **Debut:** Fidalma (*Matrimonio segreto*) Florence 1940. Awards: Citation, Republic of Italy.
Sang with major companies in ARG: Buenos Aires; AUS: Salzburg Fest, Vienna Staatsoper; BEL: Brussels; BRA: Rio de Janeiro; BUL: Sofia; CAN: Montreal/Quebec; CZE: Prague National; FRA: Aix-en-Provence Fest, Bordeaux, Marseille, Nice, Paris; FR GER: Berlin Deutsche Oper, Bonn, Cologne, Dortmund, Düsseldorf-Duisburg, Essen, Frankfurt, Hamburg, Karlsruhe, Kassel, Munich Staatsoper, Nürnberg, Saarbrücken, Stutt-

gart, Wiesbaden, Wuppertal; GER DR: Berlin Staatsoper, Dresden; HOL: Amsterdam; HUN: Budapest; ITA: Bologna, Florence Maggio & Comunale, Genoa, Milan, Naples, Palermo, Parma, Rome Opera & Caracalla, Trieste, Turin, Venice, Verona; MON: Monte Carlo; POL: Warsaw; POR: Lisbon; SPA: Barcelona, Canary Isl Las Palmas Fest; SWI: Geneva; UK: Edinburgh Fest, London Royal; USA: Baltimore, Boston, Hartford, New Orleans, New York Metropolitan, Philadelphia Grand & Lyric, San Francisco Opera. **Roles with these companies incl** BELLINI: Adalgisa (*Norma*); BIZET: Carmen; BORODIN: Kontchakovna (*Prince Igor*); CHERUBINI: Neris (*Medea*); CILEA: Princesse de Bouillon (*A. Lecouvreur*); CIMAROSA: Fidalma (*Matrimonio segreto*); DONIZETTI: Léonore‡ (*Favorite*), Pierrot‡ (*Linda di Chamounix*); GLUCK: Orfeo; HANDEL: Cornelia (*Giulio Cesare*); HENZE: Agave & Beroe (*Bassariden*), Baronin von Grünwiesel (*Junge Lord*); MONTEVERDI: Orfeo, Penelope (*Ritorno d'Ulisse*); MUSSORGSKY: Marina (*Boris Godunov*), Marfa (*Khovanshchina*); PONCHIELLI: Laura‡ & La Cieca★ (*Gioconda*); PUCCINI: Principessa‡ (*Suor Angelica*); ROSSINI: Angelina (*Cenerentola*), Isabella (*Italiana in Algeri*); SAINT-SAENS: Dalila; STRAVINSKY: Mère (*Mavra*), Jocasta★ (*Oedipus Rex*); VERDI: Amneris‡ (*Aida*), Ulrica★‡ (*Ballo in maschera*), Eboli (*Don Carlo*), Dame Quickly★‡ (*Falstaff*), Preziosilla (*Forza del destino*), Azucena★‡ (*Trovatore*); WAGNER: Ortrud (*Lohengrin*), Brangäne (*Tristan und Isolde*); WOLF-FERRARI: Margarita★ (*Quattro rusteghi*). Also PERGOLESI: Giustina (*Flaminio*); VERDI: Fenena (*Nabucco*); MASCAGNI: Santuzza (*Cavalleria rusticana*); DONIZETTI: Zaida (*Don Sebastiano*); HANDEL: Dejanira (*Eracle*); ZANDONAI: Comandante (*Cavalieri di Ekebu*); PIZZETTI: Clitennestra (*Ifigenia*), Debora (*Debora e Jaele*), Candia (*Figlia di Jorio*); VLAD: Mamma (*Storia di una mamma*). **World premieres:** ALFANO: Dariola (*Don Giovanni Mañara*) Maggio M, Florence 1943; TESTI: Celestina, Maggio M, Florence 1963; ROSSELLINI: Governante (*Linguaggio dei fiori*) La Scala, Milan 1963; CHAILLY: Lizaveta (*Idiota*) Rome 1970; PORRINO: Anfissa (*Esculapio al neon*) Cagliari 1972. Recorded for: His Master's Voice, RCA Victor, Cetra, Philips. Video/Film: Angelina (*Cenerentola*). Gives recitals. Appears with symphony orchestra. **Res:** Viale Belfiore 9, Florence, Italy 50144.

BARDON, HENRY; né Jindrich Bardon. Scenic designer for opera, theater, television. Is a lighting designer; also a painter & interior decorator. Stateless. Born 19 Jun 1923, Cesky Tesin, Czechoslovakia. Widowed. Wife Stephanie Bidmead, occupation actress (deceased). Two sons. Studied: Dundee Art Coll, Perth Theatre, Scotland; Shakespeare Mem Theatre, Stratford-on-Avon, UK. **Operatic debut:** *Suor Angelica* Covent Garden, London 1964. Theater debut: Royal Shakespeare Co, Stratford, UK 1961. Previous occupation: musician; plays violin, cello, guitar.

Designed for major companies in AUSTRL: Sydney; AUS: Vienna Volksoper; HOL: Amsterdam; POR: Lisbon; SWE: Drottningholm Fest, Stockholm; UK: Aldeburgh Fest, Scottish, Glynde-

bourne Fest, London Royal; USA: Dallas, Miami. **Operas designed for these companies incl** DONIZETTI: *Lucia, Lucrezia Borgia;* GLUCK: *Iphigénie en Tauride;* HANDEL: *Acis and Galatea;* HENZE: *Elegy for Young Lovers;* MASSENET: *Werther;* MOZART: *Così fan tutte, Schauspieldirektor, Nozze di Figaro;* PUCCINI: *Bohème, Suor Angelica;* ROSSINI: *Guillaume Tell;* STRAUSS, R: *Rosenkavalier;* VERDI: *Rigoletto.* Also PURCELL: *Fairy Queen.* Exhibitions of stage designs & paintings London, New York 1965, 1967, 1969. **Res:** 16 Meredyth Rd, London SW 13, UK. Mgmt: DLZ/UK.

BAREZA, NIKSA. Conductor of opera and symphony; composer. Yugoslavian. Resident Cond, Croatian National Opera, Zagreb. Born 31 Mar 1936, Split. Wife Dubravka, occupation musician. Two children. Studied: Acad of Music, Milan Sachs, Lovro v Matacic, Zagreb; Mozarteum, Hermann Scherchen, Salzburg; incl piano. Plays the piano. Operatic training as repetiteur, asst cond & chorus master at Croat Ntl Op, Zagreb 1957-59. **Operatic debut:** *Ballo in maschera* Zagreb 1959. Symphonic debut: Symph Orch, Belgrade 1957. Awards: Hon mention in *Vjesnik* and *Vecernji* for best pfs. Previous adm positions in opera: Opera Dir, Croat Ntl Theater, Zagreb 1965-74.

Conducted at major companies in AUS: Bregenz Fest, Graz, Vienna Staatsoper; FRA: Bordeaux, Paris; GRE: Athens Fest; FR GER: Cologne, Hamburg, Mannheim, Munich Staatsoper, Stuttgart, Wiesbaden; GER DR: Berlin Staatsoper; ITA: Trieste, Turin, Venice; NOR: Oslo; SWI: Geneva; USSR: Leningrad Kirov; YUG: Dubrovnik, Zagreb, Belgrade. **Operas with these companies incl** BEETHOVEN: Fidelio★; BERLIOZ: *Damnation de Faust★;* BIZET: *Carmen★;* BORODIN: *Prince Igor★;* BRITTEN: *Midsummer Night;* CALDARA: *Dafne★;* DEBUSSY: *Pelléas et Mélisande;* DONIZETTI: *Lucia★;* GIORDANO: *Andrea Chénier;* GLUCK: *Orfeo ed Euridice;* GOTOVAC: *Ero der Schelm★;* GOUNOD: *Faust;* HINDEMITH: *Hin und zurück;* KELEMEN: *Belagerungszustand★;* LEONCAVALLO: *Pagliacci★;* MARTINU: *Comedy on the Bridge;* MASCAGNI: *Cavalleria rusticana★;* MASSENET: *Werther★;* MONTEVERDI: *Combattimento di Tancredi★;* MOZART: *Mitridate re di Ponto, Nozze di Figaro★, Zaïde, Zauberflöte★;* MUSSORGSKY: *Boris Godunov, Khovanshchina★;* ORFF: *Carmina burana, Kluge;* PERGOLESI: *Serva padrona★;* PONCHIELLI: *Gioconda★;* PROKOFIEV: *Duenna, Love for Three Oranges★;* PUCCINI: *Bohème★, Butterfly★, Tosca★;* ROSSINI: *Barbiere di Siviglia;* SALIERI: *Prima la musica★;* SHOSTAKOVICH: *Katerina Ismailova;* SMETANA: *Bartered Bride★;* STRAUSS, J: *Fledermaus;* STRAUSS, R: *Arabella★;* STRAVINSKY: *Rake's Progress;* TCHAIKOVSKY: *Eugene Onegin;* VERDI: *Aida★, Ballo in maschera★, Don Carlo★, Lombardi★, Rigoletto★, Traviata★, Trovatore★;* WAGNER: *Fliegende Holländer★, Meistersinger★.* Also RIMSKY-KORSAKOV: *Mlada;* KELEMEN: *Neue Mieter;* LISINSKI: *Porin;* SUTERMEISTER: *Serafine;* WOLF-FERRARI: *Campiello.* **World premieres:** BRKANOVIC: *Matija Gubec* Croat Ntl Opera, Zagreb 1974. Video—Zagreb TV: *Ballo in ma-*

schera, Serafine. Conducted major orch in Europe. **Res:** Gunduliceva 38, Zagreb, Yugoslavia. **Mgmt:** CDK/YUG; SLZ/FRG.

BARHAM, PATRICIA LYNN; née Howatt. Lyric coloratura soprano. American. Resident mem: Vereinigte Bühnen, Graz, Austria. Born 8 Aug 1941, Chicago. Studied: Curtis Inst of Music, Martial Singher, Philadelphia; Elisabeth Parham, CA; Franz Schuch-Tovini, Vienna, Austria. **Debut;** Angelina (*Sud*) Opéra Municipal de Marseille 1965.
Sang with major companies in AUS: Graz, Vienna Volksoper; FRA: Marseille, Strasbourg. **Roles with these companies incl** GLUCK: Amor★ (*Orfeo ed Euridice*); LORTZING: Gretchen★ (*Wildschütz*); MOZART: Zerlina★ (*Don Giovanni*), Blondchen★ (*Entführung aus dem Serail*), Susanna★ (*Nozze di Figaro*); NICOLAI: Aennchen★ (*Lustigen Weiber*); OFFENBACH: Olympia★ (*Contes d'Hoffmann*); PERGOLESI: Serpina★ (*Serva padrona*); ROSSINI: Ninetta★ (*Gazza ladra*); STRAUSS, J: Adele★ (*Fledermaus*); VERDI: Nannetta (*Falstaff*). **World premieres:** COE: Angelina (*Sud*) Marseille 1965. Gives recitals. Appears with symphony orchestra. **Res:** Steyrerg 9c, Graz, Austria. **Mgmt:** RAB/AUS.

BARKER, JOHN EDGAR. Conductor of opera and symphony; composer. British. Head of Music Staff & Resident Cond, English National Opera, London till fall 1975; followed by same position Royal Opera, Covent Garden. Born 23 Sep 1931, London. Single. Studied: Royal Coll of Music, Richard Austin, London; Mozarteum, Lovro von Matacic, Salzburg; incl piano, viola, clarinet and voice. Plays the piano. Operatic training as repetiteur, asst cond & chorus master at Sadler's Wells Opera, London 1959-74; English National Opera 1974-75. **Operatic debut:** *Pagliacci* Touring Opera, Wolverhampton, UK 1958. Symphonic debut: Radio Eireann Symph Orch, Dublin 1969. Previous occupations: schoolteacher. Awards: ARCM, GRSM, Royal Coll of Music, London.
Conducted with major companies in UK: London English National. **Operas with these companies incl** GLUCK: *Orfeo ed Euridice;* HUMPERDINCK: *Hänsel und Gretel;* LEONCAVALLO: *Pagliacci★;* MASCAGNI: *Cavalleria rusticana★;* MOZART: *Nozze di Figaro★, Zauberflöte;* PUCCINI: *Butterfly★;* ROSSINI: *Barbiere di Siviglia, Cenerentola, Comte Ory, Gazza ladra;* SAINT-SAENS: *Samson et Dalila;* SMETANA: *Bartered Bride;* STRAUSS, J: *Fledermaus★;* STRAVINSKY: *Oedipus Rex★, Rake's Progress;* VERDI: *Ballo in maschera★, Ernani, Forza del destino★, Traviata★;* WAGNER: *Fliegende Holländer★, Rheingold★, Walküre★, Siegfried★, Götterdämmerung;* WEBER: *Freischütz.* Also WILLIAMSON: *Violins of St Jacques.* **World premieres:** WILLIAMSON: *Lucky Peter's Journey* Sadler's Wells, London 1969. **Res:** 16 Elm Tree Ave, Esher-Surrey, London, UK.

BARKER, JOYCE. Dramatic soprano. South African. Born 6 Jun 1937, Mooi River, S Africa. Husband Harold Elwyn Dyer, occupation fashion buyer. Two children. Studied: Royal Acad of Music, Olive Groves, London; Borishka Gerer, London; Mario Basiola, Sr, Milan; Frederick Dalberg,

Capetown, S Africa. **Debut:** Elena (*Mefistofele*) Welsh National Opera 1958. Awards: first recpt Kathleen Ferrier Schlshp Royal Philharm Socy; Gold Medal Intl Voice Compt, Toulouse, France; Brit Arts Counc Awd; four major prizes Royal Acad, London; Intl Schlshp Assc Board of Royal Schools of Music, UK.
Sang with major companies in FRA: Strasbourg; S AFR: Johannesburg; UK: Cardiff Welsh, Glyndebourne Fest, London Royal Opera; USA: New York City Opera, Santa Fe, Seattle. **Roles with these companies incl** OFFENBACH: Giulietta (*Contes d'Hoffmann*); PUCCINI: Giorgetta (*Tabarro*), Turandot★; VERDI: Aida★, Amelia★ (*Ballo in maschera*), Elisabetta★ (*Don Carlo*), Giselda (*Lombardi*), Lady Macbeth★, Abigaille (*Nabucco*), Leonora (*Trovatore*); WAGNER: Senta★ (*Fliegende Holländer*). Video/Film: Elisabetta (*Don Carlo*). Gives recitals. Appears with symphony orchestra. Teaches voice. Coaches repertoire. **Res:** Johannesburg, S Africa. **Mgmt:** AIM/UK.

BARLOG, BOLESLAW STANISLAUS. Stages/produces opera, theater & film. German. Resident Stage Dir for theater in Berlin. Born 28 Mar 1906, Breslau. Wife Herta. **Operatic debut:** Deutsche Oper Berlin & Staatsoper, Hamburg 1964. Theater debut: Schlossparktheater, Berlin 1945. Previous occupation: theater asst since 1930, film since 1939. Awards: Kunstpreis der Stadt Berlin; Ernst Reuter Silver Medal; Max Reinhardt Ring; Grosses Bundesverdienstkreuz mit Stern; Ordre National de l'Art et des Lettres; Karl Kraus Tabatière, Akad der Künste, Berlin.
Directed/produced opera for major companies in AUS: Vienna; FR GER: Berlin Deutsche Oper, Hamburg, Hannover, Munich, Stuttgart. **Operas staged with these companies incl** CIMAROSA: *Matrimonio segreto;* LORTZING: *Wildschütz;* MOZART: *Don Giovanni★, Entführung aus dem Serail;* NICOLAI: *Lustigen Weiber;* PUCCINI: *Bohème, Manon Lescaut, Tosca★;* STRAUSS, R: *Salome;* TCHAIKOVSKY: *Eugene Onegin;* VERDI: *Rigoletto.* Previous leading positions with major theater companies: Generalintendant, Schiller- and Schlossparktheater Berlin 1945-72. **Res:** Spindelmühler Weg 7, Berlin 45, FR Ger.

BARLOW, KLARA; née Alma Claire Williams. Dramatic soprano. American. Resident mem: Metropolitan Opera, New York. Born 28 Jul 1928, Brooklyn, New York. Divorced. Two children. Studied: Cecile Jacobson, New York. **Debut:** Venus (*Tannhäuser*) Stadttheater Bern 1962. Previous occupations: secy, saleswoman, recept, model.
Sang with major companies in AUS: Vienna Staatsoper; CAN: Toronto; DEN: Copenhagen; FRA: Nancy, Strasbourg, Toulouse; FR GER: Berlin Deutsche Oper, Bielefeld, Bonn, Cologne, Dortmund, Düsseldorf-Duisburg, Essen, Hamburg, Hannover, Kassel, Kiel, Munich Staatsoper, Nürnberg, Saarbrücken, Stuttgart, Wiesbaden; GER DR: Berlin Komische Oper, Dresden; HUN: Budapest; ITA: Bologna, Genoa, Milan La Scala, Spoleto Fest, Trieste; MEX: Mexico City; SWI: Zurich; UK: Glasgow Scottish; USA: Houston, Memphis, New York Met, Philadelphia Grand, Portland, San Diego, Seattle. **Roles with**

these companies incl BEETHOVEN: Leonore★ (*Fidelio*); BELLINI: Norma (*Norma*); JANACEK: Jenufa; MOZART: Donna Anna★ (*Don Giovanni*); MUSSORGSKY: Marina★ (*Boris Godunov*); OFFENBACH: Giulietta (*Contes d'Hoffmann*); PROKOFIEV: Fata Morgana★ (*Love for Three Oranges*); PUCCINI: Tosca★; STRAUSS, R: Arabella, Ariadne, Elektra★, Salome★; VERDI: Aida★, Amelia (*Ballo in maschera*), Elisabetta (*Don Carlo*), Abigaille★ (*Nabucco*), Amelia (*Simon Boccanegra*), Leonora (*Trovatore*); WAGNER: Senta★ (*Fliegende Holländer*), Elsa★ (*Lohengrin*), Brünnhilde (*Walküre★, Siegfried★, Götterdämmerung★*), Elisabeth★ & Venus★ (*Tannhäuser*), Isolde★; WEBER: Agathe (*Freischütz*). Film—Komische Oper Berlin: Donna Anna (*Don Giovanni*); CBC TV Montreal: Salome. Gives recitals. Appears with symphony orchestra. Teaches voice. Coaches repertoire & dramatics. **Res:** New York, NY, USA.

BARRAUD, DANY; née Danielle-Jeanne Barraud. Dramatic soprano. French. Born 24 Oct 1940, Charlieu, France. Single. Studied: Consv Russe Serge Rachmaninoff, Abby Richard Chereau, acting; Ecole Normale de Musique, Paris. **Debut:** Mathilde (*Guillaume Tell*) TRP Paris 1965. Previous occupations: IBM computer prgr secy. Awards: Prize for Excellence, Consv Serge Rachmaninoff; Golden Voice Prize Dupore, Ecole Normale, Paris.

Sang with major companies in BEL: Brussels; FRA: Bordeaux, Lyon, Marseille, Paris, Toulouse; SWI: Geneva. **Roles with these companies incl** BARTOK: Judith★ (*Bluebeard's Castle*); BERG: Marie★ (*Wozzeck*); BERLIOZ: Marguerite★ (*Damnation de Faust*); BIZET: Micaëla (*Carmen*); BRITTEN: Female Chorus★ (*Rape of Lucretia*); DALLAPICCOLA: Mrs Fabian★ (*Volo di notte*); GLUCK: Euridice★; GOUNOD: Marguerite★ (*Faust*); JANACEK: Jenufa; LEONCAVALLO: Nedda★ (*Pagliacci*); MENOTTI: Magda Sorel★ (*Consul*), Maria Golovin; OFFENBACH: Antonia & Giulietta (*Contes d'Hoffmann*); ORFF: Solo (*Carmina burana*); POULENC: Mme Lidoine★ (*Dialogues des Carmélites*); PUCCINI: Mimi★ & Musetta★ (*Bohème*); ROSSINI: Mathilde (*Guillaume Tell*); VERDI: Alice Ford★ (*Falstaff*), Desdemona (*Otello*); WAGNER: Sieglinde★ (*Walküre*), Elisabeth★ (*Tannhäuser*); WEILL: Jenny★ (*Aufstieg und Fall der Stadt Mahagonny*), Jenny★ (*Dreigroschenoper*). Also MENOTTI: Annina (*Saint of Bleecker Street*); SCHOENBERG: sopr role (*Glückliche Hand*). World premieres: KOSMA: Cosima (*Les Hussards*) Lyon 1969; PREY: Clio (*Jonas*) Lyon 1969; BENTOIU: Reine (*Hamlet*) Marseille 1974; DUHAMEL: 1ᵉʳ Oiseau (*L'Opéra des Oiseaux*) Lyon 1971. Recorded for: ORTF. **Res:** 75 Blvd Ornand 75018, Paris, and 241 Ave du Prado 13008, Marseille, France.

BARRAULT, JEAN-LOUIS. Stages/produces opera, theater & film; is also an actor. French. Born 8 Sep 1910, Le Vésinet, France. Wife Madeleine Renaud, occupation actress. Studied: Collège Cleaptal; Atelier Dramatic School & Theater, Paris. Awards: Officer of the Légion d'Honneur.

Directed/produced opera for major companies in FRA: Paris; FR GER: Berlin Deutsche Oper,

Cologne; ITA: Milan La Scala, Rome Opera; USA: New York Met; et al. **Operas staged with these companies incl** BIZET: *Carmen;* GOUNOD: *Faust;* MOZART: *Don Giovanni;* et al. Also OFFENBACH: *Vie parisienne*. Previous leading positions with major theater companies: Prod Dir, Comédie Française, Paris 1940-46; Dir, Odéon/ Théâtre de France, Paris 1959-68; Dir, Théâtre des Nations, Paris 1965-67.

BARRERA, GIULIA; née Julia A DeCurtis. Dramatic soprano. American. Born 28 Apr 1942, Brooklyn, NY. Husband Michael, occupation pharmacist. Studied: Mo Dick Marzollo, New York. **Debut:** Aida, New York City Opera 1963. Previous occupations: studied Span literature.

Sang with major companies in CAN: Montreal/Quebec; DEN: Copenhagen; FR GER: Nürnberg; ITA: Parma, Rome Opera; SPA: Barcelona; UK: Cardiff Welsh; USA: Baltimore, Kentucky, Newark, New Orleans, New York City Opera, Philadelphia Grand, Pittsburgh, Portland, San Francisco Spring Opera, Seattle, Washington DC. **Roles with these companies incl** BIZET: Micaëla (*Carmen*); DALLAPICCOLA: Madre★‡ (*Prigioniero*); LEONCAVALLO: Nedda (*Pagliacci*); MASCAGNI: Santuzza★ (*Cavalleria rusticana*); MENOTTI: Magda Sorel (*Consul*); MONTEVERDI: Euridice (*Favola d'Orfeo*); MOZART: Donna Anna★ (*Don Giovanni*); PUCCINI: Manon Lescaut, Tosca★, Turandot★; VERDI: Aida★, Amelia★ (*Ballo in maschera*), Elisabetta★ (*Don Carlo*), Leonora★ (*Trovatore*); WAGNER: Sieglinde★ (*Walküre*), Venus★ (*Tannhäuser*).

BARSTOW, JOSEPHINE. Spinto. British. Born 27 Sep 1940, Sheffield. Husband Ande Anderson, occupation opera director. Studied: London Opera Centre, Dame Eva Turner, Andrew Field. **Debut:** Mimi (*Bohème*) Opera For All, London 1964. Previous occupations: English teacher.

Sang with major companies in FRA: Aix-en-Provence Fest; SWI: Geneva; UK: Aldeburgh Fest, Cardiff Welsh, Glyndebourne Fest, London Royal & English National. **Roles with these companies incl** BRITTEN: Helena★ (*Midsummer Night*); JANACEK: Emilia Marty★ (*Makropoulos Affair*); MOZART: Fiordiligi (*Così fan tutte*), Elettra★ (*Idomeneo*), Contessa★ & Cherubino (*Nozze di Figaro*); OFFENBACH: Olympia★ & Antonia★ & Giulietta★ (*Contes d'Hoffmann*); PENDERECKI: Jeanne★ (*Teufel von Loudun*); PROKOFIEV: Natasha★ (*War and Peace*); PUCCINI: Mimi★ & Musetta (*Bohème*); PURCELL: Emmeline★ (*King Arthur*); SCHOENBERG: Woman★ (*Erwartung*); STRAUSS, R: Octavian★ (*Rosenkavalier*); TCHAIKOVSKY: Iolanthe; VERDI: Elisabetta★ (*Don Carlo*), Alice Ford★ (*Falstaff*), Lady Macbeth★, Amelia★ (*Simon Boccanegra*), Violetta★ (*Traviata*). Also HENZE: Autonoe★ (*Bassariden*); MOZART: Idamante★ (*Idomeneo*); HANDEL: Nitocris★ (*Belshazzar*). **World premieres:** TIPPETT: Denise‡ (*Knot Garden*) Royal Opera, London 1970; CROSSE: Marguerite (*Story of Vasco*) English National Opera, London 1974. Recorded for: Philips. Gives recitals. Appears with symphony orchestra. **Res:** London, UK. Mgmt: CST/UK.

BÁRTFAI, ÉVA; née Kovács. Dramatic coloratura soprano. Hungarian. Resident mem: Vereinigte Bühnen, Graz, Austria. Born 31 Aug 1945, Budapest. Studied: Prof Márta Onody-Kiss, Budapest. **Debut:** Königin der Nacht (*Zauberflöte*) Graz 1973. Previous occupations: seamstress & fashion designer.

Sang with major companies in AUS: Graz. **Roles with these companies incl** DONIZETTI: Lucia★; MOZART: Donna Anna★ (*Don Giovanni*), Konstanze★ (*Entführung aus dem Serail*), Königin der Nacht★ (*Zauberflöte*); NICOLAI: Frau Fluth★ (*Lustigen Weiber*); OFFENBACH: Antonia★ & Olympia (*Hoffmann*); PUCCINI: Cio-Cio-San★ (*Butterfly*). Gives recitals. Appears with symphony orchestra. **Res:** R Wagnerg 33, Graz, Austria. Mgmt: ITK/HUN.

BARTH, RUODI. Scenic and costume designer for opera, theater, television; specl in sets. Is a lighting designer; also a painter & poster designer. Swiss. Resident designer, Opera Houses Düsseldorf & Darmstadt. Born 19 Jun 1921, Basel. Wife Monica. Two children. Studied: Basel Acad. **Operatic debut:** sets & cost, Basel Stadttheater 1951. Theater debut: Theater Comedie, Basel 1950. Awards: many diplomas for best Swiss posters.

Designed for major companies in AUS: Vienna Volksoper; FRA: Strasbourg; FR GER: Darmstadt, Düsseldorf-Duisburg, Hamburg, Kassel, Munich Staatsoper & Gärtnerplatz, Nürnberg, Stuttgart, Wiesbaden; HOL: Amsterdam; ITA: Palermo; SWI: Basel, Zurich. **Operas designed for these companies incl** AUBER: *Fra Diavolo*; BEETHOVEN: *Fidelio★*; BERLIOZ: *Damnation de Faust★*; BRITTEN: *Billy Budd, Peter Grimes*; BUSONI: *Doktor Faust*; CAVALLI: *Ormindo★*; CORNELIUS: *Barbier von Bagdad*; DESSAU: *Verurteilung des Lukullus★*; DONIZETTI: *Don Pasquale, Elisir, Lucia*; DVORAK: *Rusalka★*; GLUCK: *Iphigénie en Aulide*; GOUNOD: *Faust★*; HANDEL: *Alcina, Deidamia*; HENZE: *Junge Lord★*; HINDEMITH: *Mathis der Maler*; IBERT: *Angélique*; JANACEK: *Cunning Little Vixen★, Excursions of Mr Broucek★, From the House of the Dead, Katya Kabanova★, Makropoulos Affair★*; KELEMEN: *Belagerungszustand★*; LORTZING: *Wildschütz★*; MASSENET: *Manon*; MENOTTI: *Medium, Saint of Bleecker Street, Telephone*; MILHAUD: *Pauvre matelot*; MOZART: *Così fan tutte, Don Giovanni★, Entführung aus dem Serail, Finta giardiniera, Schauspieldirektor, Mitridate, re di Ponto★, Nozze di Figaro, Zauberflöte*; NICOLAI: *Lustigen Weiber*; OFFENBACH: *Périchole*; ORFF: *Carmina burana★, Kluge★*; PERGOLESI: *Serva padrona*; POULENC: *Mamelles de Tirésias★*; PROKOFIEV: *Love for Three Oranges*; PUCCINI: *Gianni Schicchi, Tosca★, Turandot*; RAVEL: *Heure espagnole*; ROSSINI: *Barbiere di Siviglia, Signor Bruschino*; SCHOENBERG: *Moses und Aron*; SHOSTAKOVICH: *Nose★*; STRAUSS, J: *Fledermaus*; STRAUSS, R: *Elektra, Frau ohne Schatten★, Rosenkavalier, Salome*; STRAVINSKY: *Oedipus Rex★, Rossignol★*; TCHAIKOVSKY: *Eugene Onegin, Pique Dame*; THOMAS: *Mignon*; VERDI: *Don Carlo, Simon Boccanegra, Traviata*; WEBER: *Freischütz*; WEILL: *Aufstieg und Fall der Stadt Mahagonny*;

WOLF: *Corregidor*; WOLF-FERRARI: *Donne curiose, Quattro rusteghi, Segreto di Susanna.* Also MARTINU: *Julietta*; LORTZING: *Undine*; FALLA: *Vida breve.* **Operatic world premieres:** VOGT: *Stadt hinter dem Strom* Wiesbaden. Exhibitions of stage designs, paintings & graphics Basel, Wiesbaden, New York, Düsseldorf, Zurich; museum shows in Munich, Darmstadt. **Res:** Am Hermertsberg 10, 6101 Seeheim, FR Ger.

BARTOLETTI, BRUNO. Conductor of opera and symphony. Italian. Artistic Director & Resident Cond, Lyric Opera of Chicago, USA. Born 10 Jun 1926, Sesto Fiorentino, Italy. Wife Rosanna. Two children. Studied: Consv Florence; incl flute & piano. Plays the flute. Operatic training as repetiteur & asst cond at Teatro Comunale, Florence 1948-53. **Operatic debut:** *Rigoletto* Teatro Comunale, Florence 1953. Symphonic debut: Maggio Musicale Fiorentino 1954.

Conducted with major cos in ARG: Buenos Aires; FRA: Aix-en-Provence, Orange; HUN: Budapest; ITA: Bologna, Florence Maggio & Comunale, Genoa, Milan La Scala, Naples, Palermo, Rome Opera & Caracalla, Trieste, Turin, Venice; POR: Lisbon; SWI: Geneva; UK: London Royal; USA: Chicago, San Francisco Opera. **Operas with these companies incl** BARTOK: *Bluebeard's Castle*; BELLINI: *Capuleti ed i Montecchi★, Norma, Sonnambula*; BERG: *Lulu, Wozzeck★*; BIZET: *Djamileh*; BRITTEN: *Billy Budd, Peter Grimes★*; CIMAROSA: *Matrimonio segreto*; DALLAPICCOLA: *Prigioniero, Volo di notte★*; DESSAU: *Verurteilung des Lukullus*; DONIZETTI: *Don Pasquale★, Elisir, Favorite, Linda di Chamounix★, Lucia★, Maria di Rohan, Maria Stuarda★, Roberto Devereux★*; DUKAS: *Ariane et Barbe Bleue*; EINEM: *Dantons Tod*; FALLA: *Vida breve*; GIORDANO: *Andrea Chénier★, Fedora*; GLUCK: *Cadi dupé*; LEONCAVALLO: *Pagliacci*; MASCAGNI: *Cavalleria rusticana*; MENOTTI: *Amahl, Amelia al ballo*; MONTEVERDI: *Incoronazione di Poppea*; MUSSORGSKY: *Boris Godunov, Khovanshchina*; OFFENBACH: *Contes d'Hoffmann*; PERAGALLO: *Gita in campagna*; PERGOLESI: *Frate 'nnamorato, Serva padrona*; PONCHIELLI: *Gioconda★*; POULENC: *Voix humaine*; PROKOFIEV: *Fiery Angel★, Gambler★*; PUCCINI: *Bohème★, Gianni Schicchi, Butterfly★, Manon Lescaut★‡, Suor Angelica★‡, Tabarro, Tosca★*; RAVEL: *Enfant et les sortilèges, Heure espagnole*; ROSSINI: *Barbiere di Siviglia‡, Cambiale di matrimonio★, Cenerentola, Gazza ladra, Guillaume Tell, Moïse★, Scala di seta*; SCHOENBERG: *Erwartung*; SHOSTAKOVICH: *Nose*; STRAUSS, R: *Elektra, Salome*; STRAVINSKY: *Oedipus Rex, Rake★*; VERDI: *Aida, Attila, Ballo in maschera‡, Don Carlo★, Due Foscari, Falstaff★, Forza del destino, Giovanna d'Arco, Luisa Miller, Macbeth, Nabucco, Otello, Rigoletto, Simon Boccanegra★, Traviata, Trovatore*; WAGNER: *Lohengrin★*; WEBER: *Abu Hassan*; WOLF-FERRARI: *Quattro rusteghi.* **World premieres:** GINASTERA: *Don Rodrigo* Teatro Colón, Buenos Aires 1964. Recorded for DG, RCA, EMI, Decca. Video—RAI TV: *Fedora, Andrea Chénier, Sonnambula.* Danish TV: *Heure espagnole, Enfant et les sortilèges, Prigioniero.*

Conducted major orch in Europe. **Res:** V San Marco Vecchio 16, Florence, Italy.

BASIOLA, MARIO. Lyric baritone. Italian. Born 1 Sep 1935, Highland Park, IL, USA. Wife Aslaug. One child. Studied: Mario Basiola, Sr (father); Cntr di Avviamento, Teatro la Fenice, Venice. **Debut:** Belcore (*Elisir*) Teatro la Fenice, Venice 1961. Previous occupations: studied law.

Sang with major companies in AUS: Vienna Staatsoper; FR GER: Stuttgart; ITA: Bologna, Florence Comunale, Genoa, Milan La Scala, Naples, Palermo, Parma, Rome Opera, Spoleto Fest, Trieste, Turin, Venice; POR: Lisbon; USA: Dallas, Hawaii, Philadelphia Lyric; YUG: Zagreb, Belgrade. **Roles with these companies incl** BERG: Wozzeck★; BIBALO: Augusto★ (*Lächeln am Fusse der Leiter*); CILEA: Michonnet★ (*A. Lecouvreur*); DALLAPICCOLA: Prigioniero★, Riviere★ (*Volo di notte*); DONIZETTI: Dott Malatesta★ (*Don Pasquale*), Belcore (*Elisir*), Enrico (*Lucia*); GALUPPI: Don Tritemio (*Filosofo di campagna*); GIORDANO: De Siriex (*Fedora*); HAYDN: Nanni (*Infedeltà delusa*); MASSENET: Lescaut (*Manon*), Albert (*Werther*); MOZART: Guglielmo (*Così fan tutte*), Conte Almaviva & Figaro (*Nozze di Figaro*); PAISIELLO: Figaro★ (*Barbiere di Siviglia*), Ashmed★ (*Re Teodoro in Venezia*); PENDERECKI: Grandier (*Teufel von Loudun*); PUCCINI: Marcello (*Bohème*), Jack Rance (*Fanciulla del West*), Sharpless★ (*Butterfly*), Lescaut (*Manon Lescaut*); ROSSINI: Figaro (*Barbiere di Siviglia*), Slook (*Cambiale di matrimonio*), Dandini (*Cenerentola*), Macrobio (*Pietra del paragone*), Gaudenzio (*Signor Bruschino*); VERDI: Amonasro (*Aida*), Ford (*Falstaff*), Fra Melitone (*Forza del destino*), Germont (*Traviata*).

BASTIN, JULES ARMAND. Bass-baritone & basso-buffo. Belgian. Born 18 Aug 1933, Pont. Wife Marie-José Beaujean, occupation professor. Three children. Studied: Consv Royal de Musique, Prof Frederic Anspach, Brussels. **Debut:** MONTEVERDI: Caronte (*Orfeo*) Théâtre Royal de la Monnaie, Brussels 1960. Previous occupations: prof in French & history. Awards: First Prize, Intl Singing Compt, Munich 1963; First Prize and Best Singer, 's Hertogenbosch, Holland 1962.

Sang with major companies in BEL: Brussels, Liège; FRA: Bordeaux, Lyon, Nancy, Nice, Paris, Rouen, Strasbourg; FR GER: Bonn; HOL: Amsterdam; ITA: Milan La Scala; ROM: Bucharest; SWI: Geneva; UK: London Royal. **Roles with these companies incl** BEETHOVEN: Rocco★ (*Fidelio*); BERLIOZ: Balducci★‡ (*Benvenuto Cellini*), Méphistophélès★‡ (*Damnation de Faust*); CHARPENTIER: Père★ (*Louise*); CIMAROSA: Geronimo★ (*Matrimonio segreto*); DEBUSSY: Arkel★ (*Pelléas et Mélisande*); DELIBES: Nilakantha★ (*Lakmé*); DONIZETTI: Don Pasquale; GLUCK: Thoas (*Iphigénie en Tauride*); GOUNOD: Ramon★ (*Mireille*); JANACEK: Harasta (*Cunning Little Vixen*); MARTIN: Marc (*Vin herbé*); MASSENET: Phanuel★ (*Hérodiade*); MOZART: Leporello (*Don Giovanni*), Osmin★ (*Entführung aus dem Serail*), Sarastro (*Zauberflöte*); MUSSORGSKY: Pimen★ (*Boris Godunov*); OFFENBACH: Coppélius etc (*Contes d'Hoffmann*), Don Andres★ (*Périchole*); PER-

GOLESI: Uberto★ (*Serva padrona*); PUCCINI: Colline (*Bohème*); ROSSINI: Dott Bartolo★ & Don Basilio★ (*Barbiere di Siviglia*); SMETANA: Kezal★ (*Bartered Bride*); STRAUSS, R: Baron Ochs★ (*Rosenkavalier*); STRAVINSKY: Creon★ & Tiresias★ (*Oedipus Rex*), Empereur de Chine★ (*Rossignol*); VERDI: Ramfis★ (*Aida*), Philip II★ & Grande Inquisitore★ (*Don Carlo*), Falstaff★, Padre Guardiano★ (*Forza del destino*), Banquo★ (*Macbeth*); WAGNER: Daland (*Fliegende Holländer*), König Heinrich★ (*Lohengrin*), Gurnemanz (*Parsifal*), Wotan (*Walküre*), Fasolt★ (*Rheingold*), Landgraf (*Tannhäuser*), König Marke (*Tristan und Isolde*). Also MARTIN: Trinculo (*Sturm*); POUSSEUR: Solo (*Votre Faust*); SEMENOFF: Godfruno (*Sire Halewyn*). Recorded for: Philips. Gives recitals. Appears with symphony orchestra. Teaches voice. On faculty of Consv de Musique, Brussels. **Res:** Av Solvay 16, La Hulpe, Belgium. Mgmt: GLZ/FRA.

BAUDO, SERGE PAUL. Conductor of opera and symphony; composer. French. Mus Dir & Cond, Orchestre de Lyon. Born 16 Jul 1927, Marseille. Wife Madeleine Reties. Two children. Studied: Consv de Paris; incl piano, percussion. Plays the piano, percussion. Operatic training as orchestra member at Opéra de Paris, 1949-57. **Operatic debut:** La Scala Milan 1962. Symphonic debut: Orch National, Paris 1952. Previous occupations: orch mem of Opéra and Orch de la Société des Concerts. Awards: Chevalier des Arts et des Lettres, Ordre du Mérite. Previous adm positions in opera: Mus Dir, Opéra de Lyon 1969-71.

Conducted with major companies in AUS: Vienna Staatsoper; FRA: Aix-en-Provence Fest, Lyon, Marseille, Orange Fest, Paris; FR GER: Berlin Deutsche Oper; ITA: Bologna, Genoa, Milan La Scala, Naples, Trieste; MON: Monte Carlo; POR: Lisbon; SWI: Geneva; USA: New York Met. **Operas with these companies incl** BECAUD: *Opéra d'Aran*; BERG: *Wozzeck*; BERLIOZ: *Damnation de Faust*; BIZET: *Carmen*; BOIELDIEU: *Dame blanche*; CHERUBINI: *Medea*; DEBUSSY: *Enfant prodigue, Pelléas et Mélisande*; FALLA: *Retablo de Maese Pedro, Vida breve*; GOUNOD: *Faust*; MASSENET: *Manon, Werther*; MENOTTI: *Dernier sauvage*; MILHAUD: *Pauvre matelot*; MOZART: *Così fan tutte, Don Giovanni, Entführung aus dem Serail, Zauberflöte*; OFFENBACH: *Contes d'Hoffmann, Périchole*; PAISIELLO: *Barbiere di Siviglia*; POULENC: *Dialogues des Carmélites*; PUCCINI: *Butterfly, Tosca*; ROSSINI: *Barbiere di Siviglia*; SAINT-SAENS: *Samson et Dalila*; SHOSTAKOVICH: *Katerina Ismailova*; STRAUSS, R: *Ariadne auf Naxos*; STRAVINSKY: *Rake's Progress*; VERDI: *Ballo in maschera, Don Carlo, Falstaff, Rigoletto*. Also MILHAUD: *Bolivar*. **World premieres:** MILHAUD: *Mère coupable* Opera Geneva 1966; BARRAUD: *Lavinia* Aix-en-Provence Fest 1961. Conducted major orch in Europe, USA/Canada, Cent/S America, Asia. **Res:** 23 rue Fontaine, 75009 Paris, France. Mgmt: KSG/FRA.

BAUER-ECSY, LENI. Scenic and costume designer for opera & theater. Austrian.

Designed opera for major companies in ARG: Buenos Aires; AUS: Salzburg Fest, Vienna

Staatsoper & Volksoper; FR GER: Berlin Deutsche Oper, Essen, Hamburg, Munich Staatsoper, Saarbrücken, Stuttgart; USA: San Francisco Opera; et al. **Operas designed for these companies incl** BERG: *Wozzeck;* BIZET: *Carmen;* DALLA-PICCOLA: *Prigioniero;* DONIZETTI: *Don Pasquale, Lucia;* JANACEK: *From the House of the Dead, Jenufa, Makropoulos Affair;* LORTZING: *Wildschütz;* MOZART: *Così fan tutte, Nozze di Figaro;* MUSSORGSKY: *Boris Godunov;* PENDERECKI: *Teufel von Loudun;* PUCCINI: *Turandot;* RAVEL: *Heure espagnole;* ROSSINI: *Barbiere di Siviglia;* SCHOENBERG: *Moses und Aron;* SCHULLER: *Visitation;* SMETANA: *Bartered Bride;* STRAUSS, R: *Arabella, Elektra, Rosenkavalier, Schweigsame Frau;* STRAVINSKY: *Oedipus Rex;* VERDI: *Don Carlo, Falstaff, Forza del destino;* WAGNER: *Tristan und Isolde;* et al. Also BENNETT: *Penny for a Song.*

BAUERNFEIND, WINFRIED. Stages/produces opera & television. Also designs stage-lighting and is an author. German. Head Stage Dir, Deutsche Oper Berlin, FR Ger. Born 26 Jan 1935, Bielefeld. Single. Studied: Hochschule für Musik, Prof Carl Ebert, G R Sellner, Berlin; incl music & piano. Operatic training as asst stage dir at Deutsche Oper Berlin. **Operatic debut:** *Hin und zurück* Théâtre des Nations, Paris 1961.

Directed/produced opera for major companies in BEL: Brussels; DEN: Copenhagen; FR GER: Berlin Deutsche Oper, Essen, Frankfurt, Kassel, Kiel, Krefeld, Wuppertal. **Operas staged for these companies incl** BUSONI: *Arlecchino;* CAVALLI: *Calisto*;* EGK: *Irische Legende*;* GLUCK: *Orfeo ed Euridice;* HENZE: *Junge Lord;* JANA-CEK: *Excursions of Mr Broucek;* LEONCAVALLO: *Pagliacci*;* MENOTTI: *Amahl;* MOZART: *Clemenza di Tito*, Così fan tutte, Nozze di Figaro, Zauberflöte;* ORFF: *Kluge;* PFITZNER: *Palestrina;* PUCCINI: *Bohème*;* RAVEL: *Heure espagnole;* ROSSINI: *Barbiere di Siviglia;* SEARLE: *Hamlet;* SHOSTAKOVICH: *Katerina Ismailova*;* SME-TANA: *Bartered Bride;* STRAUSS, R: *Arabella*, Ariadne auf Naxos;* STRAVINSKY: *Mavra;* TCHAIKOVSKY: *Eugene Onegin;* VERDI: *Forza del destino, Trovatore;* YUN: *Traum des Liu-Tung.* Also BLACHER: *Preussisches Märchen*;* PAISIELLO: *Don Chisciotte*;* HARTMANN: *Simplicius Simplicissimus;* MI-HALOVICI: *Krapp's Last Tape.* **Operatic world premieres:** NABOKOV: *Love's Labour's Lost,* Deutsche Oper in Brussels 1973; KESSLER: *Nationale Feiertage* Deutsche Oper Berlin 1970. Operatic Video—Freies Berlin TV: *Preussisches Märchen.* **Opera libretti:** YUN: *Traum des Liu-Tung* Deutsche Oper Berlin 1967. Teaches at Hochschule für Musik, Berlin; Mozarteum, Salzburg. **Res:** Reichstr 97b, Berlin 19, FR Ger.

BAUER-THEUSSL, FRANZ FERDINAND; né Bauer. Conductor of opera and symphony. Austrian. Gen Mus Dir, Volksoper, Vienna. Born 25 Sep 1928, Zillingdorf, Austria. Wife Herta. One child. Studied: Staatsakad für Musik, Vienna, incl piano, cembalo, trumpet. Plays the piano. Operatic training as asst cond at Salzburg Fest 1953-57. **Operatic debut:** *Contes d'Hoffmann* Landestheater Salzburg 1953. Symphonic debut: Mozarteum

Orch, Salzburg 1954. Previous occupations: pianist, intl prizes Geneva & London. Awards: Hon Prof, Austrian Gvnmt; Grosses Ehrenzeichen, Austrian Republic. Previous adm positions in opera: Mus Dir Netherlands Opera, Amsterdam 1960-64; Resident Cond Volksoper, Vienna 1957-.

Conducted with major companies in AUS: Bregenz Fest, Graz, Salzburg Fest, Vienna Volksoper; FRA: Aix-en-Provence Fest, Paris; FR GER: Hamburg, Saarbrücken; HOL: Amsterdam; MON: Monte Carlo; NOR: Oslo; SWE: Stockholm. **Operas with these companies incl** ADAM: *Postillon de Lonjumeau;* d'ALBERT: *Tiefland;* AUBER: *Fra Diavolo;* BIZET: *Carmen*;* BORODIN: *Prince Igor;* CORNELIUS: *Barbier von Bagdad;* DONIZETTI: *Don Pasquale*, Elisir, Fille du régiment*, Lucia;* DVORAK: *Rusalka;* EGK: *Zaubergeige;* FLOTOW: *Martha;* GOTOVAC: *Ero der Schelm;* GOUNOD: *Faust;* HUMPERDINCK: *Hänsel und Gretel;* LORTZING: *Waffenschmied, Wildschütz*, Zar und Zimmermann*;* MASCAGNI: *Cavalleria rusticana;* MENOTTI: *Consul;* MONIUSZKO: *Halka;* MOZART: *Così fan tutte, Don Giovanni, Entführung aus dem Serail, Nozze di Figaro, Zauberflöte*;* NICOLAI: *Lustigen Weiber*;* OF-FENBACH: *Contes d'Hoffmann*;* ORFF: *Kluge*, Mond*;* PUCCINI: *Bohème*, Gianni Schicchi*, Butterfly*, Tabarro*, Tosca, Turandot;* ROSSINI: *Barbiere di Siviglia, Comte Ory;* SME-TANA: *Bartered Bride*;* STRAUSS, J: *Fledermaus*;* STRAUSS, R: *Ariadne auf Naxos, Rosenkavalier, Salome;* TCHAIKOVSKY: *Eugene Onegin, Pique Dame;* VERDI: *Aida, Ballo in maschera, Don Carlo, Forza del destino, Nabucco, Otello, Rigoletto*, Traviata, Trovatore;* WAGNER: *Fliegende Holländer, Lohengrin, Rheingold, Walküre, Tannhäuser;* WEBER: *Freischütz.* Also BRESGEN: *Brüderlein Hund.* **World premieres:** WOLPERT: *Eingebildete Kranke* Volksoper, Vienna 1975. Recorded for Ariola. Video—Austrian TV: *Consul.* Conducted major orch in Europe. **Res:** Leopold Risterg 5/5/30, Vienna, Austria.

BAUMVOLL, ESTHER LEVY; née Esther Levy. Lyric coloratura soprano. Israeli. Resident mem: Israel National Opera, Tel Aviv. Born 22 Jun 1937, Tel Aviv. Husband Zefania. One child. Studied: Nora Vecsler, Dr Hilel Pincus; School of Music, Tel Aviv; Manhattan School of Music, New York. **Debut:** Périchole, Israel National Opera 1961. Previous occupations: classical ballet dancer; service in Army. Awards: Buckstein Prize, Ntl Newspaper Critics of Israel; First Prize Voice Compt American Israel Cultural Fndt.

Sang with major companies in ISR: Tel Aviv. **Roles with these companies incl** BIZET: Micaëla* (*Carmen*), Léila* (*Pêcheurs de perles*); DELIBES: Lakmé*; DONIZETTI: Norina* (*Don Pasquale*), Adina* (*Elisir*), Lucia*; GOUNOD: Juliette*; LEONCAVALLO: Nedda* (*Pagliacci*); MO-ZART; Zerlina (*Don Giovanni*), Contessa* (*Nozze di Figaro*); OFFENBACH: Olympia* & Antonia* (*Contes d'Hoffmann*), Périchole; PUC-CINI: Mimi* & Musetta (*Bohème*), Lauretta (*Gianni Schicchi*), Liù (*Turandot*); ROSSINI: Rosina* (*Barbiere di Siviglia*); SMETANA: Marie* (*Bartered Bride*); STRAUSS, J: Rosalinde* (*Fledermaus*); VERDI: Gilda* (*Rigoletto*), Violetta★ (*Traviata*). Gives recitals. Appears with symphony orchestra. **Res:** 2 Hazanchanim, Givatayim, Israel.

BAUSTIAN, ROBERT F. Conductor of opera and symphony. American. Resident Cond & Head of Music Staff, Santa Fe Opera, NM. Also Resident Cond, Oberlin Orchestra, O. Born 4 Jun 1921, Storm Lake, IA, USA. Single. Studied: Eastman School of Music, Rochester, NY; Zurich Consv, Switzerland; incl piano. Operatic training as repetiteur & asst cond at Municipal Opera, Zurich 1948-53; Hessian State Opera, Wiesbaden, FR Ger 1953-57. **Operatic debut:** *Consul* original company, Boston 1950. Symphonic debut: Swiss Radio, Zurich 1953.

Conducted with major companies in FRA: Lyon; FR GER: Frankfurt, Hamburg, Kiel, Wiesbaden; SPA: Barcelona; SWI: Zurich; USA: New York City Opera, Santa Fe. **Operas with these companies** incl BIZET: *Carmen;* BRITTEN: *Rape of Lucretia;* DEBUSSY: *Pelléas et Mélisande★;* DONIZETTI: *Elisir, Lucia;* FALLA: *Vida breve★;* GLUCK: *Orfeo ed Euridice;* HENZE: *Boulevard Solitude, König Hirsch/Re Cervo;* HUMPERDINCK: *Hänsel und Gretel;* IBERT: *Angélique;* JANACEK: *Cunning Little Vixen★;* LORTZING: *Waffenschmied, Zar und Zimmermann;* MARTINU: *Comedy on the Bridge;* MENOTTI: *Consul;* MOORE: *Ballad of Baby Doe;* MOZART: *Così fan tutte★, Don Giovanni, Entführung aus dem Serail, Nozze di Figaro★, Zauberflöte★;* POULENC: *Dialogues des Carmélites;* PUCCINI: *Butterfly★, Tosca;* PURCELL: *Dido and Aeneas;* RAVEL: *Enfant et les sortilèges★;* ROSSINI: *Barbiere di Siviglia, Cenerentola;* STRAUSS, R: *Arabella;* STRAVINSKY: *Mavra, Perséphone, Rossignol★;* TCHAIKOVSKY: *Eugene Onegin;* VERDI: *Aida, Falstaff, Nabucco, Rigoletto, Traviata;* WAGNER: *Rheingold.* Also SUTERMEISTER: *Schwarze Spinne;* HONNEGGER: *Jeanne d'Arc au bûcher;* LEVY: *Tower;* SCHOENBERG: *Jakobsleiter;* VOGT: *Stadt hinter dem Strom.* **World premieres:** MOORE: *Carry Nation,* Univ of Kansas, Lawrence 1966. Conducted major orch in USA/Canada. Teaches at Oberlin Coll Consv of Music. **Res:** 139 N Prospect, Oberlin, O 44074, USA.

BAYARD, CAROL ANN. Spinto. American. Born 22 Jun 1934, Glens Falls, NY, USA. Husband Thomas Booth, occupation conductor, pianist, composer. One child. **Debut:** Micaëla (*Carmen*) New York City Opera 1964. Previous occupations: cellist. Awards: Hunter Coll Opera Workshop Schlshp, New York.

Sang with major companies in USA: Fort Worth, Houston, Kentucky, Lake George, New Orleans, New York City Opera, Philadelphia Lyric, San Francisco Spring, Seattle. **Roles with these companies** incl BIZET: Micaëla (*Carmen*); GOUNOD: Marguerite★ (*Faust*); LEONCAVALLO: Nedda★ (*Pagliacci*); MASSENET: Manon; MOZART: Fiordiligi (*Così fan tutte*), Donna Anna★ (*Don Giovanni*), Contessa★ (*Nozze di Figaro*); OFFENBACH: Antonia★ (*Contes d'Hoffmann*); PUCCINI: Mimi & Musetta★ (*Bohème*), Giorgetta★ (*Tabarro*); STRAUSS, J: Adele & Rosalinde★ (*Fledermaus*); VERDI: Alice Ford★

(*Falstaff*), Violetta (*Traviata*). Also MEYEROWITZ: Esther. **World premieres:** FLOYD: Curley's Wife (*Of Mice and Men*) Seattle Opera 1970. Gives recitals. Appears with symphony orchestra. Teaches voice. **Res:** 884 West End Ave, New York, NY, USA.

BAZUKY, MAYA; née Maria Johanna Michel. Dramatic mezzo-soprano. Dutch/American. Born 15 Jul 1932, The Hague, Holland. Husband Manu N Thacker, occupation engineer, businessman. Studied: Royal Coll of Music, Nelly Vertrgt, Frans Vroons, Wolf-Dieter Ludwig, The Hague. **Debut:** Amneris (*Aida*) Stadttheater Bern, Switzerland 1967. Awards: Noëmie Perugia Awd 1961.

Sang with major companies in ITA: Milan La Scala, Naples, Palermo; SWI: Geneva. **Roles with these companies incl** BIZET: Carmen; TCHAIKOVSKY: Comtesse★ (*Pique Dame*); VERDI: Amneris★ (*Aida*), Eboli★ (*Don Carlo*), Azucena★ (*Trovatore*); WAGNER: Ortrud★ (*Lohengrin*), Erda (*Rheingold, Siegfried*), Fricka (*Rheingold★, Walküre★*); WEBER: Eglantine★ (*Euryanthe*). Gives recitals. Appears with symphony orchestra. **Res:** Van Eycklei 17, Antwerp, Belgium.

BEATTIE, HERBERT. Bass. American. Born 23 Aug 1926, Chicago. Married. Five children. Studied: American Consv of Music, John C Wilcox, Chicago; Josef Krips, Buffalo, NY. **Debut:** Baron Douphol (*Traviata*) New York City Opera 1958. Previous occupations: radio announcer; prof of music.

Sang with major companies in BEL: Brussels; CAN: Vancouver; HOL: Amsterdam; USA: Baltimore, Boston, Fort Worth, Kentucky, Miami, Milwaukee Florentine, New Orleans, New York City Opera, Pittsburgh, St Paul, San Antonio, San Francisco Opera & Spring Opera, Washington DC. **Roles with these companies incl** BERG: Doktor (*Wozzeck*); BERLIOZ: Méphistophélès (*Damnation de Faust*); DONIZETTI: Don Pasquale★, Dulcamara★ (*Elisir*), Sulpice (*Fille du régiment*); HINDEMITH: Mathis; MOZART: Don Alfonso★ (*Così fan tutte*), Leporello★ (*Don Giovanni*), Osmin★ (*Entführung aus dem Serail*), Sarastro★ (*Zauberflöte*); MUSSORGSKY: Boris & Varlaam & Pimen (*Boris Godunov*); OFFENBACH: Coppélius etc★ (*Contes d'Hoffmann*); PROKOFIEV: King of Clubs★ (*Love for Three Oranges*); PUCCINI: Colline (*Bohème*); ROSSINI: Dott Bartolo★ (*Barbiere di Siviglia*), Mustafà★ (*Italiana in Algeri*); SMETANA: Kezal (*Bartered Bride*); STRAUSS, R: Sir Morosus (*Schweigsame Frau*); VERDI: Ramfis (*Aida*), Fra Melitone (*Forza del destino*), Banquo (*Macbeth*); WAGNER: König Heinrich (*Lohengrin*), Landgraf (*Tannhäuser*). Also EGK: Bürgermeister (*Revisor*); CAVALLI: Erimante★ (*Erismena*); MONTEVERDI: Seneca (*Incoronazione di Poppea*). **World premieres:** BEESON: Andrew Borden (*Lizzie Borden*) New York City Opera 1965. Recorded for: Columbia, Desto, Cambridge. Video/Film — NET TV: Andrew Borden (*Lizzie Borden*); (*Rossignol*). Gives recitals. Appears with symphony orchestra. Teaches voice. Coaches repertoire. On faculty of Hofstra Univ, Hempstead, NY. Form Dir Colorado Op Fest 1970-75. **Res:** 159 Landing Rd, Glen Cove, NY 11542, USA. Mgmt: LLF/USA.

BECAR, LUCIA; née Tudose. Dramatic soprano, spinto. Romanian. Resident mem: Romanian Opera, Bucharest. Born 24 Sep 1938, Tecuci. Husband Paraschiv, occupation economist. One child. Studied: Consv, Profs Ana Talmaceanu, Petre Stefanescu-Goanga, Viorel Ban, Bucharest. **Debut:** Leonora (*Trovatore*) Romanian Opera 1968.

Sang with major companies in ROM: Bucharest. **Roles with these companies incl** GOUNOD: Marguerite (*Faust*); LEONCAVALLO: Nedda (*Pagliacci*); MASCAGNI: Santuzza★ (*Cavalleria rusticana*); PUCCINI: Mimi & Musetta (*Bohème*), Tosca★, Liù★ (*Turandot*); VERDI: Amelia★ (*Ballo in maschera*), Leonora★ (*Trovatore*); WAGNER: Elsa & Ortrud★ (*Lohengrin*), Venus★ (*Tannhäuser*). **Res:** 16 Remus St, Bucharest 4, Romania. Mgmt: RIA/ROM.

BECERRIL, ANTHONY RAYMOND. Baritone. American. Born 8 Feb 1945, Flagstaff, AZ, USA. Single. Studied: Robert Lawrence, Felix Popper, New York; Mo Nicolosi, Rome. **Debut:** Silvio (*Pagliacci*) Salmaggi Opera, New York 1967. Awards: Dram Musical Comedy Schlshp, AMDA.

Sang with major companies in AUS: Vienna Staatsoper & Volksoper; USA: New York City Opera, Philadelphia Lyric. **Roles with these companies incl** BIZET: Escamillo★ (*Carmen*); DONIZETTI: Dott Malatesta★ (*Don Pasquale*), Belcore★ (*Elisir*), Enrico★ (*Lucia*); LEONCAVALLO: Silvio★ (*Pagliacci*); MASCAGNI: Rabbi David (*Amico Fritz*); MASSENET: Albert★ (*Werther*); PUCCINI: Marcello★ (*Bohème*), Sharpless★ (*Butterfly*), Lescaut★ (*Manon Lescaut*); ROSSINI: Figaro★ (*Barbiere di Siviglia*); VERDI: Renato★ (*Ballo in maschera*), Germont★ (*Traviata*), Conte di Luna★ (*Trovatore*); WAGNER: Wolfram★ (*Tannhäuser*). Also GOUNOD: Valentin (*Faust*); MOZART: Masetto★ (*Don Giovanni*). Gives recitals. Appears with symphony orchestra. Teaches voice. **Res:** 312 W 48 St, New York, NY 10036, USA. Mgmt: NAP/USA; DST/USA.

BECHER, GIANRICO FEDERICO. Stages/produces opera. Also designs sets, costumes & stagelighting. Italian. Born 25 Sep 1917, Genoa. Wife Anna Granzarolo. Studied: Accademia, incl music. Operatic training as asst stage dir at Teatro alla Scala, Milan 1953-54. **Operatic debut:** *Rigoletto* Teatro Verdi, Trieste 1965. Previous occupation: studied architecture.

Directed/produced opera for major companies in BUL: Sofia; ITA: Florence Comunale, Genoa, Naples, Parma, Rome Opera, Trieste, Turin, Venice, Verona Arena; SPA: Barcelona. **Operas staged for these companies incl** BELLINI: *Puritani*★†, *Sonnambula*†; BIZET: *Carmen*†; BOITO: *Mefistofele*; DONIZETTI: *Elisir*†, *Favorite*, *Lucia*★†, *Lucrezia Borgia*★†; FALLA: *Retablo de Maese Pedro*†; GALUPPI: *Filosofo di campagna*†; GIORDANO: *Andrea Chénier*†; MASCAGNI: *Amico Fritz*†; MASSENET: *Manon*, *Werther*; MENOTTI: *Saint of Bleecker Street*; PONCHIELLI: *Gioconda*★†; PUCCINI: *Bohème*†, *Fanciulla del West*★†, *Butterfly*★†, *Tosca*†, *Turandot*★†; ROSSINI: *Barbiere di Siviglia*, *Comte Ory*†, *Turco in Italia*; VERDI: *Aida*†, *Ballo in maschera*★†, *Ernani*†, *Falstaff*†, *Forza del destino*†, *Nabucco*†, *Otello*†, *Rigoletto*★†, *Simon*

Boccanegra★†, *Trovatore*†; ZANDONAI: *Giulietta e Romeo*†. **Res:** San Marco 1858, Venice, Italy.

BECKE, FRANZ GERHARD. Austrian. Head of Art Adm, Deutsche Oper am Rhein, Düsseldorf-Duisburg, FR Ger 1973-79. In charge of adm matters. Born 2 Nov 1937, Vienna. Wife Renate. Two children. Studied: Teachers Training Coll, Vienna; Univ, Vienna; Consv, Nürnberg. Plays the piano. Previous occupations: teacher, singer, actor, stage director in Austria & FR Ger 1960-69. Form positions, primarily musical: Head of Art Adm, Bielefeld Opera 1970-73. **Res:** Windvogt 27, D4044 Kaarst, FR Ger.

BECKER, ANDREAS FRED. Bass-baritone. German. Resident mem: Opernhaus, Dortmund. Born 13 May 1940, Berlin. Wife Regina. Studied: Städtisches Konsv, Kmsg Eugen v Kovatsy, Berlin, FR Ger. **Debut:** Landgraf (*Tannhäuser*) Opernhaus, Osnabrück 1966. Previous occupations: advertising consultant. Awards: Third Prize, Voice Cont Assn of German Music Educators, Berlin.

Sang with major companies in FR GER: Bielefeld, Dortmund, Essen, Krefeld. **Roles with these companies incl** ADAM: Bijou (*Postillon de Longjumeau*); d'ALBERT: Tommaso (*Tiefland*); BEETHOVEN: Don Pizarro★ & Rocco (*Fidelio*); BERG: Doktor★ (*Wozzeck*); BIZET: Escamillo (*Carmen*); GOUNOD: Méphistophélès (*Faust*); HANDEL: Ptolemy★ (*Giulio Cesare*); LORTZING: Stadinger★ (*Waffenschmied*); MOZART: Don Alfonso★ (*Così fan tutte*), Osmin (*Entführung aus dem Serail*), Sarastro★ (*Zauberflöte*); PUCCINI: Colline★ (*Bohème*); SMETANA: Kezal★ (*Bartered Bride*); VERDI: Philip II★ (*Don Carlo*), Padre Guardiano (*Forza del destino*), Zaccaria★ (*Nabucco*); WAGNER: Fasolt★ (*Rheingold*), Hunding★ (*Walküre*), Landgraf (*Tannhäuser*), König Marke★ (*Tristan und Isolde*); WEBER: Kaspar★ (*Freischütz*); WOLF-FERRARI: Lunardo (*Quattro rusteghi*). Also DVORAK: Wassermann (*Rusalka*); BRITTEN: Collatinus (*Rape of Lucretia*). Teaches voice. On faculty of Pädagogische Hochschule. **Res:** Lindemannstr 46, Dortmund, FR Ger. Mgmt: ARM/FRG; SMN/USA.

BECKER, HERBERT. Heldentenor. German. Resident mem: Städtische Bühnen, Hannover. Born 17 May 1933, Oberhausen, Germany. Wife Anneliese Dobberdin, occupation opera singer. Two children. Studied: Folkwangschule, Essen; Dr Unold, Mannheim, FR Ger; Dr Müller, Milan. **Debut:** Radames (*Aida*) Städtische Bühnen, Gelsenkirchen, FR Ger 1963. Previous occupations: locksmith. Awards: Schlshp City of Gelsenkirchen, FR Ger.

Sang with major companies in AUS: Graz, Salzburg Fest, Vienna Staatsoper; FRA: Lyon, Marseille, Toulouse; FR GER: Bielefeld, Bonn, Cologne, Dortmund, Düsseldorf-Duisburg, Essen, Frankfurt, Hannover, Karlsruhe, Krefeld, Wuppertal; ITA: Milan La Scala, Trieste; SPA: Barcelona, Majorca; SWI: Zurich; USA: Portland, Seattle. **Roles with these companies incl** BEETHOVEN: Florestan★ (*Fidelio*); FLOTOW: Lionel (*Martha*); HANDEL: Sextus★ (*Giulio Cesare*); HINDEMITH: Albrecht v Brandenberg★ (*Mathis* *der Maler*); LEONCAVALLO: Canio★ (*Pagliacci*); MOZART: Don Ottavio (*Don Giovanni*); OFFENBACH: Hoffmann; PUCCINI: Pinkerton★ (*Butterfly*), Cavaradossi★ (*Tosca*); STRAUSS, R: Bacchus★ (*Ariadne auf Naxos*), Aegisth★ (*Elektra*), VERDI: Radames★ (*Aida*), Don Carlo★, Ismaele★ (*Nabucco*), Duca di Mantova★ (*Rigoletto*), Alfredo★ (*Traviata*), Manrico★ (*Trovatore*); WAGNER: Erik★ (*Fliegende Holländer*), Lohengrin★, Parsifal★, Siegmund★ (*Walküre*), Siegfried (*Siegfried★*, *Götterdämmerung★*), Tannhäuser★, Tristan★; WEBER: Max (*Freischütz*). Gives recitals. Appears with symphony orchestra. Teaches voice. **Res:** Muscheid-Westerwald, FR Ger. Mgmt: SLZ/FRG; VLD/AUS.

BECKMANN, JUDITH; née Reed. Lyric soprano. American. Resident mem: Staatsoper, Hamburg; Staatsoper, Vienna. Born 10 May 1935, Jamestown, ND, USA. Husband Irving, occupation pianist, coach, conductor. Two children. Studied: UCLA, Occidental Coll, Los Angeles; Mme Lotte Lehmann, Santa Barbara, CA; Henny Wolff, Hamburg; Prof Franziska Martienssen-Lohmann, Düsseldorf. **Debut:** Fiordiligi (*Così fan tutte*) Staatstheater, Braunschweig 1962. Awards: Winner San Francisco Op Aud 1961; Fulbright Schlshp 1961; Phi Beta Kappa, Occidental Coll.

Sang with major companies in AUS: Vienna Staatsoper & Volksoper; BEL: Brussels; FRA: Nancy; FR GER: Berlin Deutsche Oper, Bonn, Cologne, Darmstadt, Dortmund, Düsseldorf-Duisburg, Essen, Frankfurt, Hamburg, Hannover, Karlsruhe, Kassel, Mannheim, Munich Staatsoper, Stuttgart, Wiesbaden; GER DR: Berlin Staatsoper; HOL: Amsterdam; ITA: Florence Maggio, Venice; SWI: Geneva; UK: London Royal; USA: San Francisco Opera. Roles with these cos incl BEETHOVEN: Marzelline (*Fidelio*); BIZET: Micaëla★ (*Carmen*); DEBUSSY: Mélisande; GLUCK: Euridice★; GOUNOD: Marguerite★ (*Faust*); HANDEL: Achille★ (*Deidamia*); HUMPERDINCK: Gretel; LEONCAVALLO: Nedda★ (*Pagliacci*); LORTZING: Baronin Freimann★ (*Wildschütz*); MENOTTI: Mother (*Amahl*), Lucy (*Telephone*); MONTEVERDI: Clorinda (*Combattimento di Tancredi*), Euridice (*Favola d'Orfeo*); MOORE: Lola (*Gallantry*); MOZART: Servilia (*Clemenza di Tito*), Fiordiligi★ (*Così fan tutte*), Donna Anna★ & Donna Elvira★ (*Don Giovanni*), Konstanze (*Entführung aus dem Serail*), Ilia★ (*Idomeneo*), Mlle Silberklang (*Schauspieldirektor*), Contessa★ (*Nozze di Figaro*), Pamina★ (*Zauberflöte*); OFFENBACH: Antonia★ (*Contes d'Hoffmann*); ORFF: Solo★ (*Carmina burana*); PUCCINI: Mimi★ (*Bohème*); SMETANA: Marie★ (*Bartered Bride*); STRAUSS, R: Arabella★ & Zdenka (*Arabella*), Gräfin★ (*Capriccio*); TCHAIKOVSKY: Tatiana★ (*Eugene Onegin*); VERDI: Elisabetta (*Don Carlo*), Alice Ford (*Falstaff*), Gilda (*Rigoletto*), Violetta★ (*Traviata*); WAGNER: Eva★ (*Meistersinger*); WEBER: Euryanthe★, Agathe★ (*Freischütz*). Also FORTNER: Braut (*Bluthochzeit*); KLEBE: Schlange (*Märchen von der schönen Lilie*). Gives recitals. Appears with symphony orchestra. Teaches voice. Coaches repertoire. On faculty of Hochschule für Musik, Hamburg. **Res:** Höppnerallee 6, 2057 Wen-

torf/Hamburg, FR Ger. Mgmt: SLZ/FRG; SLA/UK; RAB/AUS.

BEDFORD, STEUART JOHN RUDOLF. Conductor of opera and symphony. British. Art Dir & Resident Cond, English Music Theatre, London 1974-. Born 31 Jul 1939, London. Wife Norma Burrowes, occupation singer. Studied: Royal Acad of Music, London; incl piano, organ. Plays the piano. Operatic training as repetiteur, assistant conductor at Glyndebourne Festival 1965-67; English Opera Group, Aldeburgh & London 1967-73. **Operatic debut:** *Beggar's Opera* Sadler's Wells, London 1967. Symphonic debut; Oxford Chamber Orch 1964. Awards: FRCO; FRAM; BA Oxon; Medal, Worshipful Co of Musicians; organ schlshp.

Conducted with major companies in BEL: Brussels; CAN: Montreal; DEN: Copenhagen Royal; SWI: Geneva; UK: Aldeburgh Fest, Welsh National, Edinburgh Fest, London Royal; USA: New York Met, San Francisco Opera. **Operas with these companies incl** BRITTEN: *Albert Herring★, Burning Fiery Furnace★, Curlew River★, Death in Venice★‡, Midsummer Night★, Owen Wingrave★, Prodigal Son★, Rape of Lucretia★, Turn of the Screw★*; CAVALLI: *Erismena★*; DONIZETTI: *Linda di Chamounix★*; GAY/Britten: *Beggar's Opera★*; HOLST: *Savitri★*; JANACEK: *Cunning Little Vixen★*; MENOTTI: *Consul★*; MONTEVERDI: *Incoronazione di Poppea★*; MOZART: *Così fan tutte★, Idomeneo★, Nozze di Figaro★, Zauberflöte★*; POULENC: *Mamelles de Tirésias★*; PURCELL: *Dido and Aeneas★, King Arthur★*; ROSSINI: *Barbiere di Siviglia★*; VAUGHAN WILLIAMS: *Riders to the Sea★*. Also HOLST: *Wandering Scholar★*; DONIZETTI: *Belisario★, Torquato Tasso★*. World premieres: BRITTEN: *Death in Venice* English Opera Group, Aldeburgh Fest 1973. Recorded for Decca, EMI. Conducted major orch in Europe, USA/Canada. **Res:** 56 Rochester Rd, NW1 9JG London, UK. Mgmt: HPL/UK.

BEGG, HEATHER. Mezzo-soprano. British. Resident mem: Royal Opera, London. Born Nelson, New Zealand. Husband William Joseph King, occupation supervisor, workshop for the disabled. Studied: St Mary's Music Coll, Dame Sister Mary Leo, Auckland, New Zealand; Consv of Music, Sydney; Ntl School of Opera, Joan Cross & Anne Wood, London; Florence Wiese-Norberg, London. **Debut:** Azucena (*Trovatore*) Ntl Opera of Australia 1954. Previous occupations: draftswoman Lands & Survey Dept, Auckland. Awards: New Zealand Gvnmt Music Bursary for Overseas Study, Ntl Artist of NZ 1956; Winner Sydney Sun Aria Contest, Australia 1955; Countess of Munster Music Schlshp 1959.

Sang with major companies in AUSTRL: Sydney; FRA: Bordeaux, Orange Fest; UK: Edinburgh, London Royal Opera & English National; USA: Chicago. **Roles with these companies incl** BERLIOZ: Anna★‡ (*Troyens*); GLUCK: Orfeo; MUSSORGSKY: Marina★ (*Boris Godunov*); PROKOFIEV: Clarissa (*Love for Three Oranges*); PUCCINI: Suzuki (*Butterfly*), Frugola (*Tabarro*); ROSSINI: Angelina (*Cenerentola*);

SAINT-SAENS: Dalila; STRAUSS, J: Prinz Orlovsky★ (*Fledermaus*); STRAUSS, R: Herodias (*Salome*); STRAVINSKY: Baba the Turk (*Rake's Progress*); TCHAIKOVSKY: Mme Larina (*Eugene Onegin*); VERDI: Azucena (*Trovatore*); WAGNER: Waltraute★ (*Götterdämmerung*). Also ROSSINI: Ragonde (*Comte Ory*); BRITTEN: Mrs Sedley★ (*Peter Grimes*); JANACEK: Grandmother Buryja★ (*Jenufa*). Recorded for: EMI, Philips. Video/Film—Granada TV: Juno (*Orpheus in the Underworld*); Orange Fest: Inez (*Trovatore*). Gives recitals. Appears with symphony orchestra. **Res:** London, UK. Mgmt: AIM/UK.

BEHLENDORF, DIETER. Bass-baritone. German. Resident mem: Opernhaus Dortmund. Born 21 Apr 1930, Rostock, Germany. Wife Margarete, occupation pianist. Three children. Studied: Nordwestdeutsche Musikakad, Prof Fred Husler, Detmold. **Debut:** Dott Bartolo (*Nozze di Figaro*) Detmold 1954.

Sang with major companies in FRA: Bordeaux; FR GER: Berlin Deutsche Oper, Bielefeld, Bonn, Dortmund, Düsseldorf-Duisburg, Essen, Kassel, Nürnberg, Wuppertal. **Roles with these companies incl** BARTOK: Bluebeard★; BEETHOVEN: Rocco (*Fidelio*); BERG: Wozzeck & Doktor★ (*Wozzeck*); BIZET: Escamillo★ (*Carmen*); CORNELIUS: Abul Hassan (*Barbier von Bagdad*); DONIZETTI: Don Pasquale★; FLOTOW: Plunkett (*Martha*); GOUNOD: Méphistophélès★ (*Faust*); LORTZING: Baculus★ (*Wildschütz*), Van Bett★ (*Zar und Zimmermann*); MOZART: Don Alfonso★ (*Così fan tutte*), Leporello★ (*Don Giovanni*), Osmin (*Entführung aus dem Serail*), Figaro (*Nozze di Figaro*), Papageno★ (*Zauberflöte*); NICOLAI: Falstaff (*Lustigen Weiber*); PERGOLESI: Uberto (*Serva padrona*); ROSSINI: Dott Bartolo★ (*Barbiere di Siviglia*); SMETANA: Kezal★ (*Bartered Bride*); VERDI: Grande Inquisitore★ (*Don Carlo*), Fra Melitone (*Forza del destino*); WAGNER: Beckmesser (*Meistersinger*), Alberich★ (*Rheingold*); WEBER: Kaspar★ (*Freischütz*). Also LIEBERMANN: Arnolphe (*Schule der Frauen*). Video/Film: Figaro (*Nozze di Figaro*). Appears with symphony orchestra. **Res:** Zur Haar 15, 5758 Fröndenberg-Langschede, FR Ger.

BEHR, ANDREAS. German. Asst to Gen Mgr, Oper der Stadt Köln, Offenbachplatz, Cologne 5, FR Ger 1975- . In charge of adm matters & art policy, and is architecture consultant. Born 6 May 1947, Berlin, FR Ger. Single. Studied: Handelsschule, Stuttgart. Plays the cello. Previous occupations: Officer, W German Army 1966-68; studied banking & industrial mngt 1968-70. Form positions, primarily adm & musical: Adm Asst, Staatstheater Oldenburg, FR Ger 1971-73; Asst to Gen Mgr, Nationaltheater Mannheim 1973-75. Mem of Building Committee as consultant for new Heilbronn Stadttheater. **Res:** Am alten Posthof 2-4, 5 Cologne, FR Ger.

BEHR, JAN. Conductor of opera and symphony. American. Resident Cond, Metropolitan Opera, New York. Born 1 Apr 1911, Krnov, Czechoslovakia. Wife Elizabeth. One daughter. Studied: Acad of Music, Prague, George Szell, Franz Langer; incl piano, violin, bassoon and voice. Plays the piano. Operatic training as repetiteur & asst cond at German Opera House, Prague 1933-38. **Operatic debut:** *Traviata* Opera House Prague 1936. Symphonic debut: Orch National, Brussels 1946.

Conducted with major companies in USA: Cincinnati, New York Met. **Operas with these companies incl** CILEA: *A. Lecouvreur;* DONIZETTI: *Don Pasquale★, Elisir★;* GOUNOD: *Faust;* MASSENET: *Werther★;* PUCCINI: *Bohème★, Fanciulla del West, Butterfly★, Tosca★;* ROSSINI: *Barbiere di Siviglia★;* STRAUSS, J: *Fledermaus★;* VERDI: *Ballo in maschera★, Forza del destino★, Rigoletto, Traviata, Trovatore★.* Conducted major orch in Europe. Teaches. **Res:** 514 West End Ave, New York, NY, USA.

BEHRENS, HILDEGARD. Lyric & dramatic soprano. German. Resident mem: Deutsche Oper am Rhein, Düsseldorf-Duisburg; Oper, Frankfurt/M. Born Oldenburg, Germany. Studied: Music Consv, Freiburg. **Debut:** Freiburg, FR Ger 1971. Previous occupations: studied law.

Sang with major companies in AUS: Vienna Staatsoper; FR GER: Düsseldorf-Duisburg, Frankfurt; POR: Lisbon; et al. **Roles with these companies incl** BERG: Marie (*Wozzeck*); JANACEK: Katya Kabanova; MOZART: Fiordiligi (*Così fan tutte*), Contessa (*Nozze di Figaro*); PUCCINI: Musetta (*Bohème*), Giorgetta (*Tabarro*); WAGNER: Elsa (*Lohengrin*), Eva (*Meistersinger*), Gutrune (*Götterdämmerung*), Elisabeth (*Tannhäuser*); WEBER: Agathe (*Freischütz*); et al. Also KELEMEN: Victoria (*Belagerungszustand*). Gives recitals. Appears with symphony orchestra.

BEIRER, HANS. Heldentenor. Austrian. Resident mem: Deutsche Oper, Berlin; Staatsoper, Vienna. Born 23 Jun 1916, Wiener-Neustadt, Austria. Wife Terry. Studied: Staatsakad Wien, Tino Patiera; Paul Neuhaus, Vienna. **Debut:** Hans (*Bartered Bride*) Linz Opera 1938. Previous occupations: studied medicine, Univ Vienna. Awards: Ehrenmitglied Deutsche Oper, Berlin; Kammersänger, Berlin; Kammersänger, Austria; Bundesverdienstkreuz First Class, FR Ger; Grosses Bundersverdienstkreuz am Bande, FR Ger.

Sang with major companies in ARG: Buenos Aires; AUSTRL: Sydney; AUS: Bregenz Fest, Salzburg Fest, Vienna Staatsoper; BEL: Brussels; DEN: Copenhagen; FRA: Bordeaux, Lyon, Marseille, Nice, Paris, Rouen, Toulouse; FR GER: Bayreuth Fest, Berlin Deutsche Oper, Cologne, Frankfurt, Hamburg Staatsoper, Mannheim, Munich Staatsoper; ITA: Bologna, Genoa, Milan La Scala, Naples, Rome Teatro dell'Opera & Caracalla, Venice; POR: Lisbon; SPA: Barcelona; SWI: Basel, Geneva, Zurich; UK: Edinburgh Fest, London Royal Opera; USA: New York City Opera, Washington DC. **Roles with these companies incl** d'ALBERT: Pedro (*Tiefland*); BEETHOVEN: Florestan★ (*Fidelio*); BERG: Tambourmajor★ (*Wozzeck*); BIZET: Don José (*Carmen*); FLOTOW: Lionel (*Martha*); GIORDANO: Andrea Chénier; GOUNOD: Faust; LEONCAVALLO: Canio★ (*Pagliacci*); MASCAGNI: Turiddu (*Cavalleria rusticana*); MASSENET: Des Grieux (*Manon*); MEYERBEER: Vasco da Gama (*Africaine*); MOZART: Don Ottavio (*Don Giovanni*), Belmonte (*Entführung aus dem Serail*);

OFFENBACH: Hoffmann; PUCCINI: Rodolfo (*Bohème*), Pinkerton (*Butterfly*); ROSSINI: Almaviva (*Barbiere di Siviglia*); SAINT-SAENS: Samson*; SMETANA: Hans (*Bartered Bride*); STRAUSS, J: Eisenstein & Alfred* (*Fledermaus*); STRAUSS, R: Bacchus (*Ariadne auf Naxos*), Aegisth* (*Elektra*), Midas (*Liebe der Danae*), Herodes (*Salome*); VERDI: Radames (*Aida*), Otello*, Duca di Mantova (*Rigoletto*); WAGNER: Erik* (*Fliegende Holländer*), Walther* (*Meistersinger*), Parsifal*, Siegmund* (*Walküre*), Siegfried (*Siegfried*, *Götterdämmerung*), Tannhäuser* & Walther v d Vogelweide* (*Tannhäuser*), Tristan*. **World premieres:** BLACHER: Junger Mann (*Die Flut*) Berlin 1946; EGK: Ulysses (*Circe*) Berlin 1948; ZILLIG: Achilles (*Troilus und Cressida*) Berlin 1957; EINEM: Bürgermeister (*Besuch der alten Dame*) Vienna Staatsoper 1971. Recorded for: Eur Phonoclub. Gives recitals. Appears with symphony orchestra. Teaches voice. Coaches repertoire. **Res:** Mahlerstr 13, Vienna 1010, Austria. Mgmt: TRY/AUS.

BÉJART, MAURICE; né Berger. Stages/produces opera, theater; is also a dancer & choreographer. French. Art Dir, Opéra National, Théâtre de la Monnaie, Brussels, Belgium. Born 1 Jan 1927, Marseille. Studied: École de l'Opéra, Leo Staats, Lubov Egorova, Marseille; Vera Volkova, London. Theater debut: choreographed ballet Stockholm 1950. Previous adm positions in opera: Founder/Dir, Ballet du XXᵉ siècle, Brussels 1960.
  Directed/produced opera for major companies in AUS: Salzburg Fest; BEL: Brussels; FRA: Paris; et al. **Operas staged with these companies incl** BERLIOZ: *Damnation de Faust;* VERDI: *Traviata;* and numerous ballets.

BÉKÉS, ANDRÁS. Stages/produces opera, theater, film & television. Hungarian. Resident Stage Dir, State Opera House, Budapest. Born 23 Mar 1927, Debrecen. Wife Eva Gaal, occupation solo dancer. One child. Studied: Acad of Dramatic Art, Budapest, incl music and violin. Operatic training as asst stage dir at Ntl Theater, Szeged, Hungary 1958-60. **Operatic debut:** *Martha* Csokonai Theater, Debrecen 1957. Theater debut: Acad of Dram Art, Budapest 1949. Previous occupation: press photographer. Awards: Merited Artist, Hungarian People's Republic.
  Dir/prod opera for major companies in FR GER: Wuppertal; HUN: Budapest. **Operas staged for these companies incl** BEETHOVEN: *Fidelio;* BIZET: *Djamileh;* DONIZETTI: *Campanello*, Elisir*, Rita;* ERKEL: *Bánk Bán;* FLOTOW: *Martha;* GLINKA: *Life for the Tsar;* GOUNOD: *Faust;* HANDEL: *Rodelinda;* JANACEK: *Jenufa*;* KODALY: *Háry János;* LEONCAVALLO: *Pagliacci;* MASCAGNI: *Cavalleria rusticana;* MOZART: *Don Giovanni*;* MUSSORGSKY: *Khovanshchina*;* OFFENBACH: *Mariage aux lanternes;* ORFF: *Kluge;* PROKOFIEV: *Love for Three Oranges*;* PUCCINI: *Bohème, Gianni Schicchi*, Butterfly*, Tabarro, Tosca;* RAVEL: *Heure espagnole;* RIMSKY-KORSAKOV: *Coq d'or;* ROSSINI: *Barbiere di Siviglia, Cenerentola;* STRAUSS, J: *Fledermaus;* STRAUSS, R: *Elektra*;* VERDI: *Ballo in maschera*, Forza del destino*, Nabucco, Otello, Rigoletto, Traviata;* WAGNER: *Lohengrin,*

Rheingold, Walküre, Götterdämmerung, Tannhäuser, Tristan und Isolde*.* Operatic Video–TV Budapest: *Häuslicher Krieg.* Teaches at Acad of Dram Art, Budapest. **Res:** Budapest, Hungary. Mgmt: ITK/HUN.

BELL, JOHN HERBERT. Conductor of opera and symphony. British. Resident Cond, Vereinigte Städtische Bühnen, Krefeld-Mönchengladbach, FR Ger. Also Resident Cond, Niederrheinische Sinfoniker, Krefeld. Born 21 Dec 1926, London. Wife Ursula. Four children. Studied: Cambridge Univ; Guildhall School of Music, London; Hochschule für Musik, Munich; incl piano, organ, harpsichord, viola. Plays the piano, harpsichord. Operatic training as repetiteur, asst cond & chorus master at Carl Rosa Opera Co, UK 1953-58; Kaiserslautern, FR Ger 1959-64. **Operatic debut:** *Barbiere di Siviglia,* Carl Rosa Opera 1954. Symphonic debut: Symph Orch Münster/Westfalen, FR Ger 1961. Previous occupations: army service 3 yrs. Awards: Sawyer Prize, Royal Coll of Organists 1947.
  Conducted with major companies in FR GER: Karlsruhe, Krefeld. **Operas with these companies incl** BERG: *Wozzeck*;* BIZET: *Carmen;* DONIZETTI: *Elisir;* HUMPERDINCK: *Hänsel und Gretel;* LEONCAVALLO: *Pagliacci;* LORTZING: *Waffenschmied*, Wildschütz*, Zar und Zimmermann;* MASCAGNI: *Cavalleria rusticana*;* MASSENET: *Don Quichotte;* MOZART: *Così fan tutte, Don Giovanni, Entführung aus dem Serail, Zauberflöte;* MUSSORGSKY: *Khovanshchina;* OFFENBACH: *Contes d'Hoffmann*;* PUCCINI: *Bohème*, Butterfly, Tosca*, Turandot;* RAVEL: *Heure espagnole;* ROSSINI: *Barbiere di Siviglia;* STRAUSS, R: *Arabella*, Elektra*, Rosenkavalier, Salome*;* VERDI: *Aida*, Falstaff, Forza del destino, Rigoletto, Traviata*, Trovatore;* WAGNER: *Fliegende Holländer*, Liebesverbot, Tannhäuser;* WEBER: *Freischütz*.* Conducted major orch in Europe. **Res:** Krefeld, FR Ger. Mgmt: PAS/FRG.

BELLAMENTE, ALAN JOHN. American. Gen Mng, Milwaukee Florentine Opera Co, 750 N Lincoln Memorial Dr, Milwaukee, WI. In charge of adm matters, art policy & finances. Born 15 Feb 1937, Floral Park, NY. Single. Studied: Long Island Univ, Brookville, NY. Previous occupations: Audio-Visual Dir, Post Coll, Brookville. Background primarily adm. Started with present company in 1969 as Bus Mng, in present position since Jun 1973. Initiated major policy changes including increase in length of season, hiring of guest conductors, professional chorus master. **Res:** 750 N Lincoln Memorial Dr, Milwaukee, WI, USA.

BELLING, SUSAN. Coloratura soprano. American. Born New York. Studied: Manhattan School of Music; Chatham Square Music School, New York. **Debut:** Blondchen (*Entführung aus dem Serail*) San Francisco Spring Opera 1968. Awards: Rockefeller Fndt Grant; W M Sullivan Fndt Grant; Met Op Ntl Counc Aud finalist; US Represent Tchaikovsky Compt, Moscow 1966; Winner Ntl Arts & Letters Club; Winner Singers Club Awd; Schlshp Met Studio.
  Sang with major companies in USA: Fort Worth, Miami, New York Met, San Francisco Spring Op-

era, Santa Fe. **Roles with these companies incl** BI-ZET: Léila★ (*Pêcheurs de perles*); DONIZETTI: Norina (*Don Pasquale*), Adina (*Elisir*); MASSE-NET: Sophie★ (*Werther*); MENOTTI: Monica★ (*Medium*); MILHAUD: Europe★ (*Enlèvement d'Europe*); MONTEVERDI: Euridice★ (*Favola d'Orfeo*); MOZART: Despina★ (*Così fan tutte*), Zerlina★ (*Don Giovanni*), Blondchen★ (*Entführung aus dem Serail*), Ilia★ (*Idomeneo*), Mme Herz★ (*Schauspieldirektor*), Susanna★ (*Nozze di Figaro*), Elisa★ (*Re pastore*); OFFENBACH: Olympia (*Contes d'Hoffmann*); ORFF: Solo★ (*Carmina burana*); PUCCINI: Lisette (*Rondine*); REI-MANN: Melusine★; ROSSINI: Rosina★ (*Barbiere di Siviglia*); STRAUSS: Zdenka★ (*Arabella*), Zerbinetta★ (*Ariadne auf Naxos*); STRA-VINSKY: Parasha★‡ (*Mavra*). Recorded for: Columbia. Gives recitals. Appears with symphony orchestra. **Res:** 230 Central Park W, New York, NY 10024, USA. Mgmt: DSP/USA.

BELLUGI, PIERO. Conductor of opera and symphony; composer. Italian. Resident Cond, Orch Sinfonica RAI, Turin. Born 14 Jul 1924, Florence. Studied: L Dallapiccola, Florence; Van Kempen, I Markevitch, R Kubelik, L Bernstein; also violin. **Conducted with major companies in** AUS: Bregenz Fest; ITA: Milan La Scala, Trieste, Venice; et al. **Operas with these companies incl** BELLINI: *Capuleti ed i Montecchi;* DONIZETTI: *Don Pasquale;* PENDERECKI: *Teufel von Loudun;* SCHOENBERG: *Glückliche Hand;* VERDI: *Giorno di regno, Luisa Miller; et al.* Also GAZZANIGA: *Convitato di pietra;* ROSSINI: *Donna del lago;* PIZZETTI: *Assassinio nella cattedrale.* Conducted major orch in Europe, USA/Canada. Previous positions as Mus Dir with major orch: Symph Orch, Portland, OR, USA 1959-61.

BENCE, MARGARETHE; née Gretchen Anne Bence. Dramatic mezzo-soprano. American. Resident mem: Bayerische Staatsoper, Munich. Born 13 Aug 1930, Kingston, NY, USA. Single. Studied: Prof Mielsch-Nied, Res Fischer, Elinor Junker-Giesen, Stuttgart. **Debut:** Erste Magd (*Elektra*) Staatsoper, Stuttgart 1954.

Sang with major cos in AUS: Salzburg, Vienna Staatsoper; BRA: Rio de Janeiro; FRA: Paris, Strasbourg; GRE: Athens Fest; FR GER: Bayreuth Fest, Berlin Deutsche Oper, Hamburg, Hannover, Karlsruhe, Mannheim, Munich Staatsoper, Munich Gärtnerplatz, Stuttgart; ITA: Bologna, Naples, Rome Opera; POR: Lisbon; ROM: Bucharest; SWI: Basel; USA: San Francisco Opera. **Roles with these companies incl** BIZET: Carmen; BRITTEN: Mrs Herring★ (*Albert Herring*); GAY/Britten: Mrs Peachum★ (*Beggar's Opera*); GLUCK: Orfeo; HANDEL: Cornelia (*Giulio Cesare*), Amastris (*Xerxes*); HUMPERDINCK: Hexe★ (*Hänsel und Gretel*); MONTEVERDI: Penelope (*Ritorno d'Ulisse*); NICOLAI: Frau Reich (*Lustigen Weiber*); SMETANA: Hata★‡ (*Bartered Bride*); STRAUSS, J: Prinz Orlovsky (*Fledermaus*); STRAUSS, R: Klytämnestra★ (*Elektra*), Octavian (*Rosenkavalier*); VERDI: Amneris (*Aida*), Ulrica (*Ballo in maschera*), Dame Quickly★ (*Falstaff*), Azucena★ (*Trovatore*); WAGNER: Erda (*Rheingold, Siegfried*), Fricka (*Rheingold, Walküre*), Waltraute (*Götterdämmerung*). Also FORTNER: Magd (*Bluthochzeit*). **World**

premieres: EGK: Babekan (*Verlobung in San Domingo*) Munich 1963; REUTTER: Panthea (*Tod des Empedocles*) Schwetzingen Fest 1966. Recorded for: Ariola. Appears with symphony orchestra. Coaches repertoire. On faculty of Hochschule für Musik, Stuttgart. **Res:** Stolzingstr 10, Munich, FR Ger.

BENDER, HEINRICH. Conductor of opera and symphony, & composer. German. Principal Cond, Bayerische Staatsoper, Munich, FR Ger; since 1959. Born 11 May 1925, Saarbrücken, Germany. Wife Meye. Two children. Studied: Mendelssohn Acad, Heinz Bongartz, Leipzig; Mus Acad Berlin, Felix Lederer; incl piano, violin, timpani & voice. Plays the piano. Operatic training as repetiteur & asst cond at Stadttheater Saarbrücken 1946-47; Landestheater Coburg 1949-57; Stadttheater Hagen/Westf 1958-59. **Operatic debut:** *Carmen* Landestheater Coburg, FR Ger 1950. Symphonic debut: Orch of Coburg, Bavaria 1955.

Conducted with major companies in AUS: Vienna Staatsoper; CAN: Ottawa, Toronto; FRA: Lyon, Paris; FR GER: Düsseldorf-Duisburg, Krefeld, Munich Staatsoper, Nürnberg, Saarbrücken, Stuttgart, Wiesbaden; GER DR: Dresden; ITA: Trieste; POR: Lisbon. **Operas with these companies incl** BEETHOVEN: *Fidelio★;* BERG: *Lulu★;* BIZET: *Carmen, Djamileh;* CIMAROSA: *Matrimonio segreto★;* DONIZETTI: *Anna Bolena, Convenienze/Viva la Mamma★, Don Pasquale★, Lucia, Rita;* EGK: *Verlobung in San Domingo;* GIORDANO: *Andrea Chénier;* GOUNOD: *Faust;* HANDEL: *Giulio Cesare;* HENZE: *Boulevard Solitude★, Elegy for Young Lovers;* HINDEMITH: *Mathis der Maler;* HUMPERDINCK: *Hänsel und Gretel★;* JANACEK: *Jenufa★;* LEONCAVALLO: *Pagliacci;* LORTZING: *Waffenschmied, Wildschütz, Zar und Zimmermann;* MASCAGNI: *Cavalleria rusticana;* MEYERBEER: *Africaine;* MOZART: *Così fan tutte★, Don Giovanni★, Entführung aus dem Serail★, Finta giardiniera, Nozze di Figaro, Zauberflöte★;* MUSSORGSKY: *Boris Godunov★;* NICOLAI: *Lustigen Weiber;* ORFF: *Carmina burana★;* PUCCINI: *Bohème★, Gianni Schicchi, Butterfly★, Suor Angelica, Tabarro, Tosca★, Turandot★;* RAVEL: *Heure espagnole;* ROSSINI: *Barbiere di Siviglia★, Cenerentola, Pietra del paragone, Turco in Italia;* SMETANA: *Bartered Bride★;* STRAUSS, J: *Fledermaus;* STRAUSS, R: *Ariadne auf Naxos★, Elektra, Rosenkavalier, Salome★;* TCHAIKOVSKY: *Eugene Onegin;* VERDI: *Aida★, Ballo in maschera★, Don Carlo★, Falstaff, Forza del destino★, Macbeth, Nabucco, Otello★, Rigoletto★, Simon Boccanegra★, Traviata, Trovatore★;* WAGNER: *Fliegende Holländer★, Lohengrin, Meistersinger, Rheingold, Walküre★, Siegfried★, Götterdämmerung★, Tannhäuser, Tristan und Isolde;* WEBER: *Abu Hassan, Freischütz, Oberon;* WEINBERGER: *Schwanda;* ZIMMERMANN: *Soldaten.* Also HEGER: *Bettler Namenlos;* HARTMANN: *Simplicius Simplicissimus;* EGK: *Columbus, Peer Gynt, Revisor;* KRENEK: *Karl V;* ORFF: *Oedipus der Tyrann, Trionfo di Afrodite, Catulli carmina.* **World premieres:** HENZE: *Elegy for Young Lovers* Bavarian State Opera in Schwetzingen, FR Ger 1961. Video/Film—TV: *Doktor und Apotheker; Pélerins de la Mecque.* Conducted major orch in Europe.

Teaches at Studio Bavarian State Opera, Munich.
Res: Munich, FR Ger.

BENELLI, UGO. Lyric tenor. Italian. Born 20 Jan
1935, Genoa, Italy. Wife Angelamaria Patrone.
Two children. Studied: Scuolo di Perfez, La Scala,
Mo Giulio Confalonieri, Milan. **Debut:** Fenton
(*Falstaff*) Barcelona 1960. Awards: Golden Bar-
que, Genoa 1969; TZ Golden Rose, Munich 1972.
Sang with major companies in ARG: Buenos
Aires; AUS: Vienna Staatsoper; BEL: Brussels;
FRA: Aix-en-Provence, Paris, Strasbourg; GRE:
Athens National; FR GER: Bonn, Dortmund,
Düsseldorf-Duisburg, Frankfurt, Munich Opera,
Stuttgart, Wiesbaden; ISR: Tel Aviv; ITA: Bo-
logna, Florence Comunale, Genoa, Milan La
Scala, Naples, Palermo, Parma, Rome Opera, Tri-
este, Turin, Venice; MEX: Mexico City; POR:
Lisbon; SPA: Barcelona; SWI: Geneva, Zurich;
UK: Edinburgh Fest, Glyndebourne Fest, London
Royal Opera; USSR: Moscow Bolshoi; USA: Cin-
cinnati, Dallas, Kansas City, San Francisco Opera.
Roles with these companies incl AUBER: Fra Dia-
volo★; BELLINI: Elvino★ (*Sonnambula*); BIZET:
Nadir (*Pêcheurs de perles*); BUSONI: Leandro
(*Arlecchino*); CAVALLI: Ormindo★; CIMA-
ROSA: Paolino (*Matrimonio segreto*); DONI-
ZETTI: Ernesto★ (*Don Pasquale*), Nemorino★
(*Elisir*), Tonio★ (*Fille du régiment*), Beppe (*Rita*);
HAYDN: Nancio★ (*Infedeltà delusa*), Ernesto★
(*Mondo della luna*); MASCAGNI: Fritz (*Amico
Fritz*); MASSENET: Des Grieux (*Manon*), Wer-
ther; MONTEVERDI: Orfeo; MOZART:
Ferrando★ (*Così fan tutte*), Don Ottavio★ (*Don
Giovanni*), Belfiore★ (*Finta giardiniera*); PAI-
SIELLO: Almaviva (*Barbiere di Siviglia*); PUC-
CINI: Rinuccio★ (*Gianni Schicchi*), Ruggero★
(*Rondine*); ROSSINI: Almaviva★ (*Barbiere di Si-
viglia*), Edward Milfort★ (*Cambiale di matrimo-
nio*), Don Ramiro★ (*Cenerentola*), Comte Ory,
Giannetto (*Gazza ladra*), Lindoro★ (*Italiana in
Algeri*), Rodrigo (*Otello*), Giocondo (*Pietra del
paragone*), Florville (*Signor Bruschino*), Narciso
(*Turco in Italia*); STRAUSS, R: Ein Sänger (*Ro-
senkavalier*); VERDI: Fenton★ (*Falstaff*),
Edoardo (*Giorno di regno*); WOLF-FERRARI:
Florindo (*Donne curiose*), Gennaro (*Gioielli della
Madonna*), Filipeto★ (*Quattro rusteghi*). Also BU-
SONI: (*Brautwahl*); ROSSINI: Norfolk★ (*Elisa-
betta Regina*). Recorded for: RCA, Decca, DG,
Philips, Cetra, Amadeo. Video/Film: (*Fille du
régiment*); (*Fra Diavolo*); (*Cenerentola*);
(*Schicchi*); (*Don Pasquale*); (*Cappello di paglia di
Firenze*). Res: Antonio Cecchi 1, Genoa, Italy.
Mgmt: SLZ/FRG.

BENI, GIMI; né James J Beni. Bass-baritone &
basso-buffo. American. Born Philadelphia, USA.
Single. Studied: Acad of Vocal Arts, Clytie
Mundy, Philadelphia; Stuart Ross, Julia Drobner,
New York; American Theatre Wing, New York.
Debut: Don Pasquale, Rome Opera 1955. Previous
occupations: stenographer, salesman. Awards:
Fulbright Schlshp to Italy, and renewal.
Sang with major companies in ISR: Tel Aviv;
ITA: Rome Opera; USA: Baltimore, Boston, Dal-
las, Fort Worth, Hawaii, Houston, Lake George,
New Orleans, St Paul, San Diego, San Francisco
Spring Opera, Santa Fe, Seattle, Washington DC.
Roles with these companies incl BERLIOZ: Bal-

ducci★ (*Benvenuto Cellini*); CHARPENTIER:
Père (*Louise*); CIMAROSA: Geronimo (*Matri-
monio segreto*); DONIZETTI: Don Pasquale★,
Dulcamara★ (*Elisir*); HOIBY: Rev Winemiller★
(*Summer and Smoke*); MENOTTI: Maharaja
(*Dernier sauvage*); MOZART: Don Alfonso★
(*Così fan tutte*), Leporello★ (*Don Giovanni*), Os-
min (*Entführung aus dem Serail*), Podestà★ (*Finta
giardiniera*); MUSSORGSKY: Varlaam (*Boris
Godunov*); NICOLAI: Falstaff (*Lustigen Weiber*);
OFFENBACH: Don Andres★ (*Périchole*); PER-
GOLESI: Uberto★ (*Serva padrona*); PUCCINI:
Gianni Schicchi, Sharpless★ (*Butterfly*); ROS-
SINI: Dott Bartolo★ (*Barbiere di Siviglia*), Ge-
ronio (*Turco in Italia*); SMETANA: Kezal★
(*Bartered Bride*); STRAVINSKY: Creon (*Oedi-
pus Rex*), Empereur de Chine★ (*Rossignol*);
VERDI: Fra Melitone (*Forza del destino*);
WEILL: Mr Peachum★ (*Dreigroschenoper*). Also
PUCCINI: Sacristan★ (*Tosca*); MASSENET:
Comte des Grieux★ (*Manon*); MOZART: Spre-
cher★ (*Zauberflöte*); PROKOFIEV: Rostov★
(*War and Peace*); ROSSINI: Taddeo★ (*Italiana in
Algeri*). World premieres: HOIBY: Papa Gonzalez
(*Summer and Smoke*) St Paul Opera, MN 1971.
Gives recitals. Appears with symphony orchestra.
Teaches voice. Stages opera as guest artist-in-res,
var coll & univ. Res: Fort Lee, NJ, USA. Mgmt:
SCO/USA.

BENNETT, SHARON KAY. Coloratura soprano.
American. Resident mem: Staatsoper, Hamburg.
Born West Jefferson, O, USA. Divorced. Studied:
Eastman School of Music, Rochester, NY; Anna
Hamlin, Otto Guth, New York. **Debut:** Lauretta
(*Gianni Schicchi*) Opera Under the Stars, Roches-
ter, NY.
Sang with major companies in FR GER: Frank-
furt, Hamburg, Karlsruhe, Nürnberg, Stuttgart;
USA: St Paul. Roles with these companies incl
DONIZETTI: Lucia★; GLUCK: Amor★ (*Orfeo
ed Euridice*); HUMPERDINCK: Gretel★; LOR-
TZING: Gretchen★ (*Wildschütz*); MENOTTI:
Emily★ (*Globolinks*); MOZART: Despina★ (*Così
fan tutte*), Zerlina★ (*Don Giovanni*), Blondchen★
(*Entführung aus dem Serail*); OFFENBACH:
Olympia★ (*Contes d'Hoffmann*); STRAUSS, R:
Fiakermilli★ (*Arabella*); VERDI: Nannetta★ (*Fal-
staff*), Gilda★ (*Rigoletto*). Also: ROSSINI: Clo-
rinda★ (*Cenerentola*); HAYDN: Nerina★ (*Fedeltà
premiata*). Video/Film: Gilda (*Rigoletto*); Norina
(*Don Pasquale*). Gives recitals. Appears with sym-
phony orchestra. Res: 2 Hamburg 36, FR Ger.
Mgmt: HPL/UK.

BENNINGSEN, LILIAN. Dramatic mezzo-so-
prano. Austrian. Resident mem: Bayerische
Staatsoper, Munich. Born 17 Jul, Vienna. Husband
Hans Reischl, occupation singer. Studied: Prof
Rado, Vienna; Anna Bahr-Mildenburg. **Debut:**
Bostana (*Barbier von Bagdad*) Landestheater Salz-
burg 1948. Awards: Bayerische Kammersängerin;
Bavarian Order of Merit; First Prize Vocal Compt
Vienna 1946.
Sang with major companies in BEL: Brussels;
FIN: Helsinki; FRA: Lyon, Strasbourg; GRE:
Athens Fest; FR GER: Berlin Deutsche Oper,
Cologne, Düsseldorf-Duisburg, Frankfurt, Ham-
burg, Hannover, Karlsruhe, Munich Staatsoper &
Gärtnerplatz, Nürnberg, Stuttgart, Wiesbaden;

GER DR: Dresden; HOL: Amsterdam; ITA: Florence Maggio, Naples; POR: Lisbon; SWI: Zurich; UK: Edinburgh Festival, London Royal. **Roles with these companies incl** AUBER: Pamela (*Fra Diavolo*); BERG: Gräfin Geschwitz★ (*Lulu*); BIZET: Carmen; BORODIN: Kontchakovna (*Prince Igor*); BRITTEN: Mrs Herring★ (*Albert Herring*); CHARPENTIER: Mère (*Louise*); CIMAROSA: Fidalma★ (*Matrimonio segreto*); DVORAK: Jezibaba (*Rusalka*); HANDEL: Amastris★ (*Xerxes*); HENZE: Baronin von Grünwiesel★ (*Junge Lord*); HUMPERDINCK: Hänsel & Hexe★ (*Hänsel und Gretel*); MOZART: Sesto (*Clemenza di Tito*), Dorabella (*Così fan tutte*); MUSSORGSKY: Marfa (*Khovanshchina*); NICOLAI: Frau Reich (*Lustigen Weiber*); POULENC: Prioresse (*Dialogues des Carmélites*); PUCCINI: Suzuki (*Butterfly*), Frugola (*Tabarro*); SMETANA: Hata★ (*Bartered Bride*); STRAUSS, R: Komponist (*Ariadne auf Naxos*), Klytämnestra★ (*Elektra*), Amme★ (*Frau ohne Schatten*), Octavian (*Rosenkavalier*), Herodias★ (*Salome*); STRAVINSKY: Jocasta (*Oedipus Rex*), Baba the Turk★ (*Rake's Progress*); TCHAIKOVSKY: Comtesse (*Pique Dame*); VERDI: Amneris★ (*Aida*), Ulrica★ (*Ballo in maschera*), Eboli★ (*Don Carlo*), Dame Quickly★ (*Falstaff*), Preziosilla (*Forza del destino*), Azucena (*Trovatore*); WAGNER: Magdalene (*Meistersinger*), Erda (*Siegfried*), Fricka (*Rheingold, Walküre★*), Waltraute (*Götterdämmerung*). Also HANDEL: Achilles (*Deidamia*), Hera (*Semele*); JANACEK: Burya★ (*Jenufa*); MENOTTI: Magda Sorel (*Consul*). **World premieres:** HENZE: Carolina (*Elegy for Young Lovers*) Schwetzingen 1961. Recorded for: Teldec, DG. Appears with symphony orchestra. **Res:** Würmstr 19, 8031 Stockdorf b München, FR Ger.

BENOIS, NICOLA. Scenic and costume designer for opera, theater, television. Is a lighting designer, stage director; also a painter, illustrator & architect. Italian. Born 2 May 1901, St Petersburg (Leningrad), Russia. Wife Disma De Cecco, occupation opera singer. One child. Studied: with father Alessandro Benois, St Petersburg; Profs Oreste Allegri, Kardovsky, Jakovlevi; Accad Belle Arti, St Petersburg. Prof training: State Theater, Leningrad. **Operatic debut:** sets & cost, *Khovanshchina* La Scala, Milan 1925-26. Theater debut: State Acad Maryinsky, Leningrad, USSR 1923. Awards: Hon Commend, Italy 1938; Gold Medal, City of Milan, Prize Luigi Illica 1971. Prev positions in opera: Chief set & cost designer La Scala, Milan 1937-70.

Designed for major companies in ARG: Buenos Aires; AUS: Salzburg Fest, Vienna Staatsoper; BRA: Rio de Janeiro; BUL: Sofia; CZE: Brno, Prague National; FRA: Paris; FR GER: Berlin Deutsche Oper, Hamburg, Munich Staatsoper; GER DR: Dresden; ITA: Florence Maggio & Comunale, Milan La Scala, Naples, Palermo, Parma, Rome Opera & Caracalla, Trieste, Turin, Venice, Verona Arena; MON: Monte Carlo; SPA: Barcelona; SWE: Stockholm; SWI: Geneva, Zurich; USSR: Leningrad Kirov, Moscow Bolshoi; USA: Chicago, New York Met. **Operas designed for these cos incl** BELLINI: *Norma, Puritani;* BIZET: *Carmen;* BOITO: *Mefistofele;* BORODIN: *Prince Igor;* BRITTEN: *Midsummer Night;*

CATALANI: *Wally;* CILEA: *Adriana Lecouvreur;* DEBUSSY: *Pelléas et Mélisande;* DONIZETTI: *Anna Bolena, Caterina Cornaro★, Favorite, Lucia, Lucrezia Borgia, Maria Stuarda, Roberto Devereux;* FALLA: *Retablo de Maese Pedro;* GIORDANO: *Andrea Chénier, Fedora;* GLINKA: *Life for the Tsar, Ruslan and Ludmilla;* GLUCK: *Iphigénie en Aulide, Iphigénie en Tauride, Orfeo ed Euridice;* GOUNOD: *Faust;* HONEGGER: *Antigone;* HUMPERDINCK: *Hänsel und Gretel;* LEONCAVALLO: *Pagliacci;* MASCAGNI: *Cavalleria rusticana;* MASSENET: *Manon;* MEYERBEER: *Africaine, Huguenots;* MOZART: *Don Giovanni;* MUSSORGSKY: *Boris Godunov★, Fair at Sorochinsk, Khovanshchina;* PONCHIELLI: *Gioconda;* PROKOFIEV: *Love for Three Oranges;* PUCCINI: *Bohème★, Fanciulla del West★, Gianni Schicchi★, Manon Lescaut, Suor Angelica★, Tabarro★, Tosca★, Turandot;* RIMSKY-KORSAKOV: *Coq d'Or, Maid of Pskov, Invisible City of Kitezh, Sadko;* ROSSINI: *Guillaume Tell, Moïse, Semiramide, Assedio di Corinto★;* SAINT-SAENS: *Samson et Dalila;* STRAUSS, R: *Elektra, Salome;* STRAVINSKY: *Oedipus Rex, Perséphone;* SUTERMEISTER: *Raskolnikoff;* TCHAIKOVSKY: *Pique Dame;* VERDI: *Aida, Aroldo/Stiffelio★, Ballo in maschera, Don Carlo, Ernani, Falstaff, Forza del destino★, Luisa Miller, Macbeth, Nabucco, Otello, Rigoletto, Simon Boccanegra, Traviata, Trovatore, Vespri;* WAGNER: *Meistersinger, Parsifal, Rienzi, Rheingold, Walküre, Siegfried, Götterdämmerung, Tannhäuser, Tristan und Isolde;* WEBER: *Freischütz, Oberon;* ZANDONAI: *Giulietta e Romeo.* Also HONEGGER: *Jeanne d'Arc au bûcher;* PIZZETTI: *Fedra;* EGK: *Revisor;* ALFANO: *Risurrezione;* MONTEVERDI: *Ballo delle ingrate.* **Operatic world premieres:** MILHAUD: *David* 1955; FALLA: *Atlantida* 1961; both at La Scala, Milan; RESPIGHI: *Campana sommersa* Opera Reale, Rome 1927-28. Operatic Video—RAI Milan: *Manon.* Exhibitions of stage designs, paintings & graphics Galleria Scopinic, Milan 1938; Gal Ranzini, Milan 1947; Villa Olmo, Como 1955; Museum T Scala 1970; Museum G Verdi, Busseto 1957; etc. **Res:** Piazza Maria Adelaide 2, Milan, Italy.

BEN-SCHACHAR, MORDECAI ENRIC; né Maximilian Enric Stern. Lyric baritone. Israeli. Resident mem: Israel National Opera, Tel Aviv. Born 18 Feb 1926, Craiova, Romania. Wife Hana. Three children. Studied: Consv Shulamith, Tel Aviv, Israel; Acad of Vocal Arts, Philadelphia. **Debut:** Escamillo (*Carmen*) Israel Opera 1951. Previous occupations: accountant, actor. Awards: Kinor David Awd, Israeli newspaper *Yedioth Aharonot.*

Sang with major companies in ISR: Tel Aviv; SWI: Zurich; USA: Philadelphia Grand Opera. **Roles with these companies incl** BIZET: Escamillo★ (*Carmen*); DONIZETTI: Belcore (*Elisir*); MASCAGNI: Alfio★ (*Cavalleria rusticana*); OFFENBACH: Dappertutto★ (*Contes d'Hoffmann*); PUCCINI: Marcello (*Bohème*), Sharpless★ (*Butterfly*); ROSSINI: Figaro★ (*Barbiere di Siviglia*); SAINT-SAENS: Grand prêtre (*Samson et Dalila*); VERDI: Amonasro (*Aida*), Germont★ (*Traviata*). Also GOUNOD: Valentin (*Faust*). Gives recitals. Appears with symphony orchestra. Teaches voice. **Res:** 105 Sokolov St, Tel Aviv, Israel.

BENZI, ROBERTO. Conductor of opera and symphony; composer. French/Italian. Mus Dir, Orchestre de Bordeaux-Aquitaine, Bordeaux, France 1973- . Born 12 Dec 1937, Marseille. Wife Jane Rhodes, occupation soprano. Studied: André Cluytens and Fernand Lamy, Paris; incl piano, violin. **Operatic debut:** *Barbiere di Siviglia* Marseille 1954. Symphonic debut: Bayonne, France 1948. Awards: Chevalier de la Légion d'Honneur; Chevalier de l'Ordre National du Mérite, French Gvnmt.

Conducted with major companies in BEL: Brussels, Liège; BUL: Sofia; CZE: Prague National; FRA: Bordeaux, Lyon, Marseille, Nancy, Nice, Paris, Toulouse; HOL: Amsterdam; ITA: Trieste; SWI: Geneva; USA: New York Met. **Operas with these companies incl** BIZET: *Carmen*; GOUNOD: *Faust*; MASSENET: *Werther;* MOZART: *Entführung aus dem Serail*; OFFENBACH: *Périchole;* PUCCINI: *Tosca;* ROSSINI: *Barbiere di Siviglia*; THOMAS: *Mignon*; VERDI: *Aida, Ballo in maschera*, *Traviata, Trovatore*. Also CHABRIER: *Etoile*. Conducted major orch in Europe, USA/Canada, Cent/S America, Asia, Africa. Teaches. **Res:** 15 rue Général Cordonnier, 92200 Neuilly-sur-Seine, France. Mgmt: CAM/USA; IBK/HOL.

BERBERIAN, ARA. Bass. American. Resident mem: New York City Opera. Born Detroit, MI, USA. Wife Virginia. Three children. Studied: Dr Kenneth Westerman, Ann Arbor, MI; Themy Georgi, Washington, DC; Beverley Johnson, New York. **Debut:** Don Magnifico (*Cenerentola*) Turnau Opera, New York 1958. Previous occupations: attorney at law, real estate, insurance.

Sang with major companies in CAN: Ottawa; USA: Baltimore, Cincinnati, Hartford, Houston, Milwaukee Florentine, New Orleans, New York City Opera, Philadelphia Grand Opera, Pittsburgh, San Antonio, San Francisco Opera & Spring Opera. **Roles with these companies incl** BARTOK: Bluebeard; BEETHOVEN: Rocco (*Fidelio*); BERLIOZ: Narbal (*Troyens*); BRITTEN: Chorus leader (*Curlew River*); DEBUSSY: Arkel★ (*Pelléas et Mélisande*); DONIZETTI: Talbot★ (*Maria Stuarda*); GOUNOD: Méphistophélès (*Faust*); MENOTTI: Don Marco★ (*Saint of Bleecker Street*); MOZART: Don Alfonso★ (*Così fan tutte*), Osmin (*Entführung aus dem Serail*); MUSSORGSKY: Pimen★ (*Boris Godunov*); PONCHIELLI: Alvise (*Gioconda*); PUCCINI: Colline★ (*Bohème*); ROSSINI: Don Basilio★ (*Barbiere di Siviglia*); STRAVINSKY: Creon (*Oedipus Rex*); VERDI: Ramfis★ (*Aida*), Grande Inquisitore (*Don Carlo*); WAGNER: Daland★ (*Fliegende Holländer*). König Heinrich★ (*Lohengrin*), Pogner★ (*Meistersinger*), Fafner (*Rheingold, Siegfried*), König Marke★ (*Tristan und Isolde*). Also DONIZETTI: Raimondo (*Lucia*). Video/Film—CBS TV: Abraham (*Sarah*), Galileo (*Galileo*); Uriah (*And David Wept*). Gives recitals. Appears with symphony orchestra. Teaches voice. **Res:** Southfield, MI, USA. Mgmt: BAR/USA.

BERBIÉ, JANE. Dramatic mezzo-soprano. French. Resident mem: Opéra, Paris.

Sang with major companies in AUS: Salzburg Fest; FRA: Aix-en-Provence Fest, Paris, Strasbourg; ITA: Milan La Scala; SPA: Barcelona; UK: London Royal; USA: San Francisco Opera; et al. **Roles with these companies incl** BERLIOZ: Ascanio‡ (*Benvenuto Cellini*); DONIZETTI: Maffio Orsini‡ (*Lucrezia Borgia*); MOZART: Dorabella (*Così fan tutte*), Zerlina (*Don Giovanni*), Cherubino (*Nozze di Figaro*); ROSSINI: Rosina (*Barbiere di Siviglia*); et al. Also MOZART: Despina (*Così fan tutte*); BOIELDIEU: Jenny (*Dame blanche*); RAVEL: Concepcion (*Heure espagnole*). Recorded for: Philips, Decca.

BERESFORD, HUGH. Heldentenor, form baritone. British.

Sang with major companies in AUS: Vienna Staatsoper; FR GER: Bayreuth Fest, Cologne, Düsseldorf-Duisburg, Hamburg, Hannover, Karlsruhe, Wuppertal; UK: Glyndebourne Fest, London Royal & English National; et al. **Roles with these companies incl** BEETHOVEN: Florestan (*Fidelio*); PUCCINI: Dick Johnson (*Fanciulla del West*); VERDI: Aroldo (*Aroldo/Stiffelio*), Don Alvaro (*Forza del destino*), Otello; WAGNER: Erik (*Fliegende Holländer*), Siegmund (*Walküre*), Tannhäuser; et al. Also STRAUSS, R: Mandryka (*Arabella*). Appears with symphony orchestra.

BERETOVAC, BRANKA. Lyric soprano. Yugoslavian. Resident mem: Croatian National Opera, Zagreb. Born 17 Jun 1944, Zagreb. Widowed. One child. Studied: Prof Zlatko Sir, Zagreb. **Debut:** Jelena (*N Subric Zrinjski*) Croat Ntl Op, Zagreb 1964. Awards: Vatroslav Lisinski Awd; Milka Ternina Awd; Fed Counc of Youths of Yugoslavia Awd.

Sang with major companies in FR GER: Bonn; YUG: Dubrovnik, Zagreb, Belgrade. **Roles with these companies incl** BEETHOVEN: Marzelline (*Fidelio*); BIZET: Micaëla (*Carmen*); DONIZETTI: Adina (*Elisir*); GLUCK: Euridice; MOZART: Ilia (*Idomeneo*), Contessa (*Nozze di Figaro*), Pamina (*Zauberflöte*); PUCCINI: Mimi★ (*Bohème*); SMETANA: Marie (*Bartered Bride*); STRAUSS, J: Adele (*Fledermaus*); STRAUSS, R: Arabella. Video—RTV Zagreb: Pamina (*Zauberflöte*). Gives recitals. Appears with symphony orchestra. Teaches voice. Coaches repertoire. On faculty of Acad of Music, Zagreb. **Res:** Gunduliceva 6, Zagreb, Yugoslavia.

BERGANZA, TERESA; née Vargas. Coloratura mezzo-soprano. Spanish. Born 16 Mar 1935, Madrid. Husband Felix Lavilla, occupation pianist. Three children. Studied: with father; Consv Madrid, Miss Rodriguez Aragon. **Debut:** Dorabella (*Così fan tutte*) Aix-en-Provence Fest, France 1957. Awards: Isabel la Católica, Span Gvnmt; Grand Prix Acad Charles Croos, three times; Gold Medal for best Rossini singer.

Sang with major companies in ARG: Buenos Aires; AUS: Salzburg Fest, Vienna Staatsoper; FIN: Helsinki; FRA: Aix-en-Provence Fest, Paris; HOL: Amsterdam; ISR: Tel Aviv; ITA: Bologna, Florence Maggio & Comunale, Genoa, Milan La Scala, Naples, Palermo, Rome Opera, Turin, Venice; MEX: Mexico City; NOR: Oslo;

SPA: Barcelona; SWE: Stockholm; SWI: Geneva, Zurich; UK: Edinburgh Fest, Glyndebourne Fest, London Royal; USA: Chicago, Dallas, Miami, New York Met, Philadelphia Grand, San Francisco Opera. **Roles with these companies incl** BELLINI: Romeo (*Capuleti ed i Montecchi*); CHERUBINI: Neris (*Medea*); FALLA: Salud (*Vida breve*); GLUCK: Orfeo; HANDEL: Ruggiero‡ (*Alcina*), Giulio Cesare; MASSENET: Dulcinée (*Don Quichotte*), Charlotte (*Werther*); MOZART: Sesto‡ (*Clemenza di Tito*), Dorabella‡ (*Così fan tutte*), Cherubino‡ (*Nozze di Figaro*); ROSSINI: Rosina‡ (*Barbiere di Siviglia*), Angelina‡ (*Cenerentola*), Isolier (*Comte Ory*), Isabella‡ (*Italiana in Algeri*), Arsace (*Semiramide*); THOMAS: Mignon. Also PURCELL: Dido; CESTI: Orontea; MONTEVERDI: Ottavia (*Incoronazione di Poppea*). Recorded for: Decca, EMI, DG. Video—Japan TV and UNITEL: Rosina (*Barbiere di Siviglia*). Gives recitals. Appears with symphony orchestra. **Res:** Gaztambide 26, Madrid 15, Spain. Mgmt: VIT/SPA.

BERGELL, AARON. Lirico spinto tenor. American. Born 13 Nov 1943, Bayonne, NJ, USA. Wife Helene, occupation language teacher. Three children. Studied: NY Univ, BS in Music Ed, Raymond Buckingham, Carolina Segrera, New York; American Opera Center, Juilliard School, New York. **Debut:** Rodolfo (*Bohème*) Israel Opera, Tel Aviv 1971. Previous occupations: retail buyer and salesman. Awards: Sullivan Fndt Winner 1973; American Opera Center Schlshp.

Sang with major companies in FR GER: Munich Gärtnerplatz, Wiesbaden; ISR: Tel Aviv; USA: Philadelphia Lyric, San Francisco Spring Opera. **Roles with these companies incl** BIZET: Don José★ (*Carmen*), Nadir★ (*Pêcheurs de perles*); DONIZETTI: Nemorino★ (*Elisir*), Edgardo★ (*Lucia*); GOUNOD: Faust★; MASCAGNI: Turiddu★ (*Cavalleria rusticana*); PUCCINI: Rodolfo★ (*Bohème*), Pinkerton★ (*Butterfly*), Cavaradossi★ (*Tosca*); VERDI: Duca di Mantova (*Rigoletto*), Alfredo (*Traviata*). Gives recitals. Appears with symphony orchestra. **Res:** 32 Wellesley Rd, Upper Montclair, NJ, USA. Mgmt: NAP/USA.

BERGER-TUNA, HELMUT. Bass & basso-buffo. Austrian. Resident mem: Opernhaus, Graz. Born 7 May 1942, Vienna. Wife Elfriede. One son. Studied: Franz Schuch-Tovini, Vienna. **Debut:** Lodovico (*Otello*) Landestheater Linz, Austria 1969. Previous occupations: electrotech eng.

Sang with major companies in AUS: Graz; FR GER: Frankfurt, Karlsruhe; NOR: Oslo; SPA: Barcelona, Majorca. **Roles with these companies incl** BEETHOVEN: Rocco★ (*Fidelio*); BERG: Doktor (*Wozzeck*); DONIZETTI: Don Pasquale★‡; LORTZING: Baculus (*Wildschütz*); MOZART: Publio★ (*Clemenza di Tito*), Leporello (*Don Giovanni*), Osmin★‡ (*Entführung aus dem Serail*), Sarastro★‡ (*Zauberflöte*); NICOLAI: Falstaff (*Lustigen Weiber*); PERGOLESI: Marcaniello (*Frate 'nnamorato*); ROSSINI: Dott Bartolo (*Barbiere di Siviglia*), Podestà (*Gazza ladra*); SMETANA: Kezal (*Bartered Bride*); VERDI: Ramfis (*Aida*); WAGNER: Daland★ (*Fliegende Holländer*), Fafner (*Rheingold, Siegfried*). Also STRAUSS, R: Geisterbote★ (*Frau ohne Schatten*). Video/Film—BASF Munich:

Syndham (*Zar und Zimmermann*). Gives recitals. Appears with symphony orchestra. **Res:** Richard Wagner Gasse 33, A-8010 Graz, Austria. Mgmt: RAB/AUS.

BERGONZI, CARLO. Spinto tenor; began as baritone. Italian. Born 13 Jul 1924, Vidalenzo/Parma. Wife Adele. Studied: Consv Arrigo Boito, Parma. **Debut:** as baritone: Figaro (*Barbiere di Siviglia*) Lecce 1948; as tenor: Andrea Chénier, Teatro Petruzelli, Bari 1951. Awards: Commendatore, Rep of Italy; Disco d'Oro.

Sang with major companies in ARG: Buenos Aires; AUS: Vienna Staatsoper; FRA: Paris; FR GER: Hamburg, Munich Staatsoper; ITA: Milan La Scala, Naples, Rome Opera & Caracalla, Verona Arena; POR: Lisbon; SPA: Barcelona; UK: London Royal; USA: Chicago, New York Met, Philadelphia Grand & Lyric; et al. **Roles with these companies incl** BELLINI: Pollione (*Norma*); BIZET: Don José (*Carmen*); DONIZETTI: Nemorino‡ (*Elisir*), Edgardo (*Lucia*); GIORDANO: Andrea Chénier; LEONCAVALLO: Canio‡ (*Pagliacci*); PONCHIELLI: Enzo‡ (*Gioconda*); PUCCINI: Rodolfo‡ (*Bohème*), Pinkerton‡ (*Butterfly*), Des Grieux (*Manon Lescaut*), Cavaradossi‡ (*Tosca*); VERDI: Radames‡ (*Aida*), Foresto‡ (*Attila*), Riccardo‡ (*Ballo in maschera*), Don Carlo‡, Jacopo Foscari (*Due Foscari*), Ernani‡, Don Alvaro‡ (*Forza del destino*), Carlo (*Giovanna d'Arco*), Rodolfo‡ (*Luisa Miller*), Duca di Mantova‡ (*Rigoletto*), Gabriele‡ (*Simon Boccanegra*), Alfredo‡ (*Traviata*), Manrico‡ (*Trovatore*); et al. Recorded for: Philips, RCA, London, DG, Cetra.

BERINI, BIANCA. Lyric & dramatic mezzo-soprano. Italian. Born Trieste, Italy. Single. **Debut:** Suzuki (*Butterfly*) Teatro Nuovo, Milan.

Sang with major companies in AUS: Vienna Staatsoper; BEL: Brussels; FRA: Marseille, Nice, Toulouse; FR GER: Berlin Deutsche Oper, Cologne, Hamburg; GER DR: Berlin Staatsoper; HOL: Amsterdam; ITA: Genoa, Milan La Scala, Naples, Rome Opera, Trieste, Turin, Venice; MEX: Mexico City; POR: Lisbon; SPA: Barcelona, Majorca; SWI: Basel, Zurich; UK: London Royal; USA: Dallas, Hartford, Milwaukee Florentine, New Orleans, Philadelphia Lyric, Pittsburgh. **Roles with these companies incl** BELLINI: Adalgisa★ (*Norma*); BIZET: Carmen★; CILEA: Princesse de Bouillon★ (*A. Lecouvreur*); DONIZETTI: Giovanna★ (*Anna Bolena*), Léonore★ (*Favorite*), Elisabetta★ (*Maria Stuarda*), Sara★ (*Roberto Devereux*); MASSENET: Charlotte★ (*Werther*); MENOTTI: Donato's Mother★ (*Maria Golovin*); PONCHIELLI: Laura★ (*Gioconda*); PUCCINI: Suzuki★ (*Butterfly*); SAINT-SAENS: Dalila★; VERDI: Amneris★ (*Aida*), Ulrica★ (*Ballo in maschera*), Eboli★ (*Don Carlo*), Preziosilla★ (*Forza del destino*), Azucena★ (*Trovatore*); WAGNER: Ortrud★ (*Lohengrin*). Also MASCAGNI: Santuzza★ (*Cavalleria rusticana*). Appears with symphony orchestra. Teaches voice. On faculty of Consv Trieste. **Res:** Vignoli 30, 20146 Milan, Italy. Mgmt: CAM/USA; CAB/SPA; SLA/UK; VLD/AUS.

BERMAN, KAREL. Bass-baritone. Czechoslovakian. Resident mem: National Theater,

Prague. Born 14 Apr 1919, Jindrichuv Hradec, CSR. Wife Hana Böhmova, occupation opera singer. One child. Studied: Prof Egon Fuchs, Prague; Apollo Granforte, Milan. **Debut:** The Burgrave (*Jakobin*) Opera Opava 1946. Awards: Artist of Merit, Gvnmt Awd; Gold Medal, Ministry of Culture.

Sang with major companies in CZE: Prague National & Smetana; FIN: Helsinki; FR GER: Wiesbaden; GER DR: Berlin Komische Oper, Leipzig; HOL: Amsterdam; ITA: Bologna, Parma, Venice; SWI: Geneva; UK: Edinburgh Fest. **Roles with these companies incl** BEETHOVEN: Rocco★ (*Fidelio*); BERG: Doktor (*Wozzeck*); BERLIOZ: Méphistophélès (*Damnation de Faust*); DONIZETTI: Don Pasquale; DVORAK: Marbuel (*Devil and Kate*); GOUNOD: Méphistophélès (*Faust*); JANACEK: Forester★ (*Cunning Little Vixen*), Sacristan‡ (*Excursions of Mr Broucek*), Dikoy★ (*Katya Kabanova*), Dr Kolenaty (*Makropoulos Affair*); MASSENET: Sancho (*Don Quichotte*); MOZART: Leporello★ (*Don Giovanni*), Osmin (*Entführung aus dem Serail*), Figaro (*Nozze di Figaro*), Papageno & Sarastro (*Zauberflöte*); MUSSORGSKY: Boris Godunov; PERGOLESI: Uberto (*Serva padrona*); PROKOFIEV: Mendoza (*Duenna*); ROSSINI: Dott Bartolo★ (*Barbiere di Siviglia*), Mustafà (*Italiana in Algeri*), Signor Bruschino; SHOSTAKOVICH: Boris (*Katerina Ismailova*); SMETANA: Kezal★ (*Bartered Bride*), Rarach‡ (*Devil's Wall*), Janus (*The Kiss*), Premysl‡ (*Libuse*), Peter (*Two Widows*); STRAVINSKY: Nick Shadow (*Rake's Progress*); VERDI: Philip II (*Don Carlo*), Falstaff; WAGNER: König Heinrich (*Lohengrin*), Beckmesser (*Meistersinger*), Alberich★ (*Rheingold, Siegfried, Götterdämmerung*); WEBER: Kaspar (*Freischütz*). Also SMETANA: Bonifac★ (*Secret*); DVORAK: Wassermann★ (*Rusalka*); BORODIN: Kontchak (*Prince Igor*); PUCCINI: Timur★ (*Turandot*); JEREMIAS: Smerdakoff★ (*Brothers Karamazov*); FOERSTER: Shylock (*Merchant of Venice*); AUBER: Pietro (*Muette de Portici*); MARTINU: Bedron (*Comedy on the Bridge*). **World premieres:** CIKKER: President (*Resurrection*) National Theater, Prague 1962; SUCHON: High Priest (*Svatopluk*) Prague 1960; PAUER: Argan (*Malade imaginaire*) Prague 1970. Recorded for: Supraphon. Gives recitals. Appears with symphony orchestra. Teaches voice. Coaches repertoire. On faculty of Acad of Music, Prague. **Res:** Prague, Czechoslovakia. **Mgmt:** PRG/CZE.

BERNARD, ANNABELLE. Lyric & dramatic soprano. American. Resident mem: Deutsche Oper Berlin, FR Ger. Born New Orleans, LA. Husband Karl Ernst Mercker, occupation opera singer. Studied: Boston Consv. **Debut:** Susanna (*Nozze di Figaro*) Boston. Awards: Kammersängerin; Rundfunkpreis, Munich 1961.

Sang with major companies in AUS: Salzburg Fest, Vienna Staatsoper; FR GER: Berlin Deutsche Oper, Cologne, Hamburg, Mannheim, Munich Staatsoper, Stuttgart; GER DR: Berlin Staatsoper; et al. **Roles with these companies incl** MOZART: Vitellia (*Clemenza di Tito*), Elettra (*Idomeneo*); PUCCINI: Cio-Cio-San (*Butterfly*), Liù (*Turandot*); TCHAIKOVSKY: Tatiana (*Eugene Onegin*), Lisa (*Pique Dame*); VERDI: Aida,

Elisabetta (*Don Carlo*), Leonora (*Forza del destino*), Leonora (*Trovatore*); et al. **Res:** Trabener Str 32 A, Berlin 33, FR Ger.

BERNARDI, MARIO. Conductor of opera and symphony. Canadian. Dir of Music & Resident Cond, National Arts Centre, Ottawa. Also Music Dir, National Arts Centre Orch, Ottawa. Born 20 Aug 1930, Kirkland Lake, Ont, Can. Wife Mona Kelly, occupation singer. One child. Studied: in Italy, Canada, Austria; incl piano and organ. Plays the piano. Operatic training as repetiteur, asst cond & chorus master at Canadian Opera Co, Toronto 1953-58; Sadler's Wells Opera, London 1963-64. **Operatic debut:** *Hänsel und Gretel* Canadian Op Co, Toronto 1956. Symphonic debut: Toronto Symph 1957. Awards: Companion of the Order of Canada; Confed of Canada Medal 1967; HDM Ottawa Univ and Laurentian Univ. Previous adm positions in opera: Music Dir Sadler's Wells Opera, London 1966-69.

Conducted with major companies in CAN: Montreal/Quebec, Ottawa, Toronto, Vancouver; UK: Aldeburgh Fest, London English National; USA: New York City Opera, San Francisco Opera. **Operas with these companies incl** BIZET: *Carmen*; BRITTEN: *Albert Herring★, Gloriana, Rape of Lucretia, Turn of the Screw★*; DELIUS: *Village Romeo and Juliet★*; DONIZETTI: *Campanello, Don Pasquale*; HANDEL: *Acis and Galatea*; HUMPERDINCK: *Hänsel und Gretel‡*; LEONCAVALLO: *Pagliacci*; MARTINU: *Comedy on the Bridge*; MENOTTI: *Amahl, Consul*; MOZART: *Così fan tutte★, Don Giovanni★, Entführung aus dem Serail★, Schauspieldirektor, Nozze di Figaro★, Zauberflöte★*; PERGOLESI: *Serva padrona*; PUCCINI: *Bohème★, Gianni Schicchi, Butterfly, Tosca*; PURCELL: *Dido and Aeneas*; ROSSINI: *Barbiere di Siviglia, Comte Ory★, Italiana in Algeri*; STRAUSS, R: *Rosenkavalier★*; STRAVINSKY: *Mavra*; TCHAIKOVSKY: *Pique Dame*; VERDI: *Aida, Ballo in maschera, Otello, Rigoletto, Traviata★*; WAGNER: *Fliegende Holländer*. Recorded for EMI. Video—CBC TV: *Hänsel und Gretel*. Conducted major orch in Europe, USA/Canada. **Res:** Ottawa, Ont, Canada. **Mgmt:** CAM/USA.

BERNET, DIETFRIED. Conductor of opera and symphony; composer. Austrian. Gen Mus Dir, Städt Bühnen, Mainz; Resident Cond, Volksoper, Vienna. Also Mus Dir, Städtisches Orchester, Mainz. Born 14 May 1940, Vienna. Wife Anca Monica Pandelea, occupation pianist. Studied: Acad of Music, Vienna; Hans Swarowsky; Dimitri Mitropoulos; incl piano, violin and voice. Operatic training as repetiteur, asst cond & chorus master at Volksoper, Vienna 1963-64. **Operatic debut:** *Feuersnot* Volksoper, Vienna 1964. Symphonic debut: N Ö Tonkünstler Orch, Vienna 1958. Awards: First Prize, Liverpool Intl Cond Compt 1962.

Conducted with major companies in AUS: Salzburg, Vienna Staatsoper & Volksoper; FR GER: Cologne, Frankfurt, Hamburg, Munich, Stuttgart; ITA: Spoleto Fest, Trieste. **Operas with these companies incl** d'ALBERT: *Tiefland★;* AUBER: *Fra Diavolo★;* BARTOK: *Bluebeard's Castle★;* BEETHOVEN: *Fidelio★;* BERG: *Lulu,*

Wozzeck; BERLIOZ: *Damnation de Faust★;* BIZET: *Carmen★;* CILEA: *A. Lecouvreur;* CIMAROSA: *Matrimonio segreto;* CORNELIUS: *Barbier von Bagdad★;* DONIZETTI: *Don Pasquale, Lucia★;* DVORAK: *Rusalka;* EGK: *Zaubergeige;* EINEM: *Dantons Tod;* FLOTOW: *Martha★;* GLUCK: *Orfeo ed Euridice★;* GOUNOD: *Faust;* HUMPERDINCK: *Hänsel und Gretel★;* JANACEK: *Excursions of Mr Broucek;* KODALY: *Háry János;* KORNGOLD: *Tote Stadt;* LEONCAVALLO: *Pagliacci;* LORTZING: *Waffenschmied, Wildschütz, Zar und Zimmermann★;* MASCAGNI: *Cavalleria rusticana;* MASSENET: *Werther★;* MONIUSZKO: *Halka;* MOZART: *Così fan tutte★, Don Giovanni, Entführung aus dem Serail★, Nozze di Figaro★, Zauberflöte★;* NICOLAI: *Lustigen Weiber★;* OFFENBACH: *Contes d'Hoffmann★, Périchole;* ORFF: *Kluge, Mond;* PERGOLESI: *Serva padrona;* PUCCINI: *Bohème★, Gianni Schicchi, Butterfly★, Suor Angelica, Tabarro, Tosca, Turandot;* RAVEL: *Enfant et les sortilèges, Heure espagnole;* ROSSINI: *Barbiere di Siviglia, Comte Ory;* SMETANA: *Bartered Bride★;* STRAUSS, J: *Fledermaus★;* STRAUSS, R: *Arabella★, Ariadne auf Naxos★, Intermezzo, Rosenkavalier★, Salome;* STRAVINSKY: *Rossignol★;* TCHAIKOVSKY: *Pique Dame★;* VERDI: *Aida★, Ballo in maschera★, Don Carlo★, Forza del destino★, Nabucco, Otello★, Rigoletto, Traviata★, Trovatore;* WAGNER: *Fliegende Holländer★, Lohengrin★, Tannhäuser★, Tristan und Isolde★;* WEBER: *Freischütz★.* **World premieres:** SALMHOFER: *Dreikönig* Volksoper, Vienna 1970. Conducted major orch in Europe, USA/Canada, Asia. Teaches. Mgmt: JUC/SWI; CAM/USA.

BERNSTEIN, LEONARD. Conductor of opera and symphony; composer. American. Laureate Conductor for life, New York Philharmonic. Born 25 Aug 1918, Lawrence, MA, USA. Wife Felicia Montealegre, occupation actress. One son, two daughters. Studied: Curtis Inst, Fritz Reiner; Berkshire Music Center, Serge Koussevitzky; incl piano with Helen Coates, Heinrich Gebhard, Isabella Vengerova. Plays the piano. **Operatic debut:** *Medea* La Scala, Milan 1953. Symphonic debut: New York Philharmonic 1943. Awards: 11 honorary degrees and numerous awds.

Conducted with major companies in AUS: Vienna Staatsoper; ITA: Milan La Scala; USA: New York Met. **Operas with these companies incl** BEETHOVEN: *Fidelio★;* BELLINI: *Sonnambula;* BERNSTEIN: *Trouble in Tahiti★;* BIZET: *Carmen★;* BRITTEN: *Peter Grimes;* CHERUBINI: *Medea;* MASCAGNI: *Cavalleria rusticana★;* PUCCINI: *Bohème;* STRAUSS, R: *Rosenkavalier★;* VERDI: *Falstaff.* Recorded for Decca, London, Columbia. Conducted major orch in Europe, USA/Canada, Cent/S America, Asia, Australia. Prev positions as Mus Dir with major orch: New York City Symphony 1945-48; New York Philharmonic 1958-69. **Operas composed:** *Trouble in Tahiti* 1952. **Res:** New York, NY, USA. Mgmt: KRT/USA.

BERRY, WALTER. Bass-baritone. Austrian. Resident mem: Vienna Staatsoper. Born 8 Apr, Vienna. Wife Brigitte. One son, from prev marriage. Studied: Vienna Schl of Engr; Vienna Acad

of Music. **Debut:** Bass Solo (*Jeanne d'Arc*), Vienna Staatsoper 1950. Previous occupations: played jazz piano for American troops in Vienna, sang popular American songs with group called "Melody Boys". Awards: Kammersänger, Austrian Gvnmt 1962; Austrian Order for Arts and Sciences First Class, 1968; Order for Arts and Sciences, Swedish Gvnmt 1965.

Sang with major companies in ARG: Buenos Aires; AUS: Salzburg Fest, Vienna Staatsoper & Volksoper; FRA: Aix-en-Provence Fest, Paris Opéra, Orange Fest; FR GER: Berlin Deutsche Oper, Cologne, Hamburg, Munich; GER DR: Dresden; ITA: Milan La Scala; POR: Lisbon; SWE: Stockholm; USA: Chicago, New York Met. **Roles with these companies incl** BEETHOVEN: Don Pizarro★‡ (*Fidelio*); BERG: Wozzeck★; BIZET: Escamillo★ (*Carmen*); HUMPERDINCK: Spielmann★‡ (*Königskinder*); MASCAGNI: Alfio (*Cavalleria rusticana*); MOZART: Guglielmo★‡ & Don Alfonso★ (*Così fan tutte*), Leporello★‡ (*Don Giovanni*), Figaro★‡ (*Nozze di Figaro*), Papageno★‡ (*Zauberflöte*); PUCCINI: Scarpia★ (*Tosca*); SMETANA: Kezal★ (*Bartered Bride*); STRAUSS, R: Musiklehrer★ (*Ariadne auf Naxos*), Olivier★ (*Capriccio*), Barak★ (*Frau ohne Schatten*), Baron Ochs★‡ (*Rosenkavalier*); VERDI: Amonasro★ (*Aida*); WAGNER: Telramund★ (*Lohengrin*), Amfortas★ (*Parsifal*), Alberich (*Rheingold*), Wotan★ (*Walküre*), Kurwenal★‡ (*Tristan und Isolde*); WEBER: Kaspar★‡ (*Freischütz*). Recorded for: CBS, Electrola, Philips, Decca, EMI, Polydor, Angel, Seraphim. Video/Film Bavarian TV: Kezal (*Bartered Bride*); film: (*Così fan tutte*); (*Don Giovanni*); (*Tosca*); (*Wildschütz*). Gives recitals. Appears with symphony orchestra. **Res:** Lucerne, Switzerland. Mgmt: FLD/USA; JUC/SWI.

BERTHOLD, CHARLOTTE. Mezzo-soprano. Swiss. Resident mem: Bayerische Staatsoper, Munich; Opernhaus Zurich.

Sang with major companies in FRA: Strasbourg; FR GER: Hamburg, Munich Staatsoper, Stuttgart; ITA: Venice; SWI: Zurich; UK: London Royal; USA: Chicago; et al. **Roles with these companies incl** MOZART: Dorabella (*Così fan tutte*), Cherubino (*Nozze di Figaro*); STRAUSS, R: Clairon (*Capriccio*), Octavian (*Rosenkavalier*); WAGNER: Venus (*Tannhäuser*); et al. Recorded for: RCA. Appears with symphony orchestra. **Res:** Churer Str 32, 8808 Pfäffikon, Switzerland.

BERTINI, GARY. Conductor of opera and symphony; composer. Israeli. Resident Cond, Israel Chamber Opera, Tel Aviv. Also Music Dir, Israel Chamber Orch, Tel Aviv. Born 1 May 1927, Brizewo, USSR. Wife Rosette. Two children. Studied: Consv Ntl Supérieur de Musique, Paris; Univ de Paris, Sorbonne; Consv Verdi, Milan; Music Training Coll, Tel Aviv; incl violin, piano and voice. **Operatic debut:** *Medium* Israel Chamber Opera, Tel Aviv 1965. Symphonic debut: Israel Phil Orch, Tel Aviv 1956. Awards: Cavaliere del Ordine del Merito, Italian Republic.

Conducted with major companies in FRA: Paris; FR GER: Hamburg; ISR: Tel Aviv; UK: Scottish. **Operas with these companies incl** BIZET: *Docteur Miracle;* BRITTEN: *Billy Budd★;* DUKAS: *Ariane et Barbe Bleue★;* FALLA: *Retablo de Maese Pedro★;* GLUCK: *Orfeo ed Euridice;*

MENOTTI: *Consul*★, *Medium;* MOZART: *Clemenza di Tito*★, *Così fan tutte*★, *Nozze di Figaro*★; MUSSORGSKY: *Boris Godunov;* PERGOLESI: *Serva padrona;* PURCELL: *Dido and Aeneas;* RAVEL: *Enfant et les sortilèges*★; ROSSINI: *Barbiere di Siviglia*★; SCHOENBERG: *Moses und Aron*★. **World premieres:** TAL: *Ashmedai* Hamburg Staatsoper 1971; *Masada 967* Israel Fest Opera, Jerusalem 1973. Conducted major orch in Europe, USA/Canada, Austrl. Teaches at Israel Acad of Music, Tel Aviv Univ. **Res:** Tel Aviv, Israel. Mgmt: SRN/HOL.

BERTOLA, GIULIO. Conductor of opera and symphony; composer. Italian. Music Dir & Resident Cond, RAI Radiotelevisione Italiana Orch, Milan. Born 30 Apr 1921, Murano/Venezia. Wife Elisabella. Two children. Studied: Consv of Venice B Marcello, G F Malipiero; incl piano & violin. Operatic training as asst cond & chorus master at Teatro la Fenice, Venice 1946. **Operatic debut:** *Rigoletto* Venice 1948. Symphonic debut: RAI TV Orch Milan 1959. Awards: Medaglia d'oro 1972; Commendatore Ordine Rep of Italy.

Conducted with major companies in ITA: Milan La Scala, Palermo, Venice, Verona Arena. **Operas with these companies incl** DONIZETTI: *Lucia;* MASCAGNI: *Cavalleria rusticana;* MENOTTI: *Consul;* ORFF: *Carmina burana;* PUCCINI: *Butterfly*★, *Tosca;* ROSSELLINI: *Annonce faite à Marie*★; ROSSINI: *Barbiere di Siviglia;* VERDI: *Ernani*★, *Traviata*★. Recorded for G Ricordi. Video/Film—TV: *Cavalleria rusticana.* Conducted major orch in Europe. Teaches at Consv, Milan. **Res:** V G da Procida 7, Milan, Italy.

BERTOLINO, MARIO ERCOLE. Bass-baritone & basso-buffo. American. Born 10 Sep 1934, Palermo, Italy. Wife Constance, occupation fashion designer. One child. Studied: Consv di Musica V Bellini, Palermo; Consv di Musica G Verdi, Milan; Mario Basiola, Milan; Giuseppe Danise, New York. **Debut:** Marcello (*Bohème*) Teatro Nuovo, Milan 1955. Awards: First Place, Intl Voice Cont, Assoc Lirica Concertistica Ital, Milan 1955.

Sang with major companies in ARG: Buenos Aires; CAN: Vancouver; FRA: Lyon; FR GER: Munich Staatsoper; GER DR: Berlin Komische; ITA: Milan La Scala, Palermo, Rome Opera; MEX: Mexico City; USA: Boston, Cincinnati, Hartford, Hawaii, Milwaukee Florentine; New York City Opera, Philadelphia Grand & Lyric, Pittsburgh, San Antonio, Washington DC. **Roles with these companies incl** d'ALBERT: Sebastiano (*Tiefland*); BELLINI: Oroveso (*Norma*); BIZET: Escamillo (*Carmen*); DONIZETTI: Pasquale★, Belcore & Dulcamara★ (*Elisir*), Enrico & Raimondo (*Lucia*); GIORDANO: Carlo Gérard (*Andrea Chénier*); MASCAGNI: Alfio (*Cavalleria rusticana*); MASSENET: Lescaut (*Manon*); PONCHIELLI: Barnaba (*Gioconda*); PUCCINI: Marcello (*Bohème*), Sharpless (*Butterfly*), Lescaut (*Manon Lescaut*), Scarpia (*Tosca*); ROSSINI: Dott Bartolo (*Barbiere di Siviglia*); VERDI: Amonasro★ (*Aida*), Renato (*Ballo in maschera*), Don Carlo & Fra Melitone (*Forza del destino*), Macbeth, Iago (*Otello*), Rigoletto, Germont (*Traviata*), Conte di Luna (*Trovatore*). Also GOUNOD: Valentin★ (*Faust*); ROTA: Bopertius★ (*Cappello di paglia di Firenze*). Gives recitals. Appears with

symphony orchestra. **Res:** 99-44 67 Rd, Forest Hills, NY, USA. Mgmt: HUR/USA.

BESCH, ANTHONY JOHN ELWYN. Stages/produces opera & theater. British. Born 5 Feb 1924, London. Single. Operatic training as asst stage dir at Glyndebourne Fest, Sussex 1951-55. **Operatic debut:** *Idomeneo* Oxford Univ Opera Club 1947. Theater debut: Oxford Univ Dramatic Socy 1947.

Directed/produced opera for major companies in ARG: Buenos Aires; BEL: Brussels; CAN: Ottawa, Toronto; FR GER: Berlin Deutsche Oper; HOL: Amsterdam; S AFR: Johannesburg; UK: Aldeburgh Fest, Welsh National, Edinburgh Fest, Scottish, Glyndebourne Fest, London Royal; USA: Lake George, New York City Opera, San Francisco Opera, Washington DC. **Operas staged with these companies incl** BIZET: *Carmen, Docteur Miracle, Pêcheurs de perles, Don Procopio;* BOIELDIEU: *Dame blanche;* BRITTEN: *Albert Herring, Death in Venice*★, *Turn of the Screw*★; CAVALLI: *Ormindo;* CHARPENTIER: *Louise*★; CIMAROSA: *Matrimonio segreto;* DALLAPICCOLA: *Prigioniero;* DONIZETTI: *Campanello, Don Pasquale*★, *Favorite, Rita;* FALLA: *Retablo de Maese Pedro;* FLOTOW: *Martha;* GAY/Britten: *Beggar's Opera;* GIORDANO: *Andrea Chénier;* GLUCK: *Alceste*★; GOUNOD: *Faust, Mireille;* HANDEL: *Alcina, Rodelinda;* HAYDN: *Infedeltà delusa;* HOLST: *Savitri;* LALO: *Roi d'Ys;* LORTZING: *Wildschütz;* LUTYENS: *Time Off? Not a Ghost of a Chance*★; MASCAGNI: *Cavalleria rusticana;* MENOTTI: *Medium, Telephone;* MONTEVERDI: *Incoronazione di Poppea*★; MOZART: *Clemenza di Tito*★, *Così fan tutte, Don Giovanni*★, *Entführung aus dem Serail*★, *Schauspieldirektor, Nozze di Figaro, Zauberflöte*★; NICOLAI: *Lustigen Weiber;* OFFENBACH: *Périchole;* POULENC: *Mamelles de Tirésias, Voix humaine;* PUCCINI: *Butterfly, Manon Lescaut, Rondine*★, *Suor Angelica, Tosca;* PURCELL: *Dido and Aeneas;* RAVEL: *Enfant et les sortilèges, Heure espagnole;* ROSSINI: *Comte Ory, Gazza ladra, Italiana in Algeri, Otello, Turco in Italia;* SEARLE: *Hamlet;* SHOSTAKOVICH: *Nose;* STRAUSS, R: *Ariadne auf Naxos, Rosenkavalier*★; STRAVINSKY: *Rake's Progress;* TCHAIKOVSKY: *Pique Dame;* VERDI: *Attila, Forza del destino, Otello, Vespri;* WAGNER: *Tannhäuser;* WEBER: *Oberon*★. Also EGK: *Revisor;* BERKELEY: *Castaway;* GARDNER: *Visitors;* BENJAMIN: *Tale of Two Cities.* **Operatic world premieres:** BIRTWISTLE: *Punch and Judy* Aldeburgh Fest 1968; LUTYENS: *Time Off?/Infidelio* New Opera Comp, London 1972; HAMILTON: *Catiline Conspiracy* Scottish Opera 1974. Teaches at London Opera Centre. **Res:** London, UK. Mgmt: AIM/UK.

BEST, RICHARD WARNER. Basso-buffo. American. Resident mem: Metropolitan Opera, New York. Born 22 Apr 1935, Chicago. Single. Studied: Lola Fletcher, Hermanus Baer, Chicago; Audrey Langford, London; Margaret Harshaw, New York. **Debut:** Bonze (*Butterfly*) Santa Fe Opera 1959. Previous occupations: prof organist & accompanist. Awards: Rockefeller Fndt Grant; Best Male Singer Chicagoland Music Fest, IL.

BETLEY

Sang with major companies in HOL: Amsterdam; USA: Chicago, New York Met, Philadelphia Lyric, San Francisco Spring, Santa Fe, Seattle. **Roles with these companies incl** DONIZETTI: Don Pasquale★; EGK: Cuperus (*Zaubergeige*); MOZART: Don Alfonso★(*Così fan tutte*); STRAUSS, R: Baron Ochs★(*Rosenkavalier*). Also MOZART: Dott Bartolo★ (*Nozze di Figaro*); PUCCINI: Sacristan★ (*Tosca*). Gives recitals. Appears with symphony orchestra. Teaches voice. Coaches repertoire. On faculty of Am Inst of Musical Studies, Graz, Austria. **Res:** 84 Riverside Dr, New York, NY, USA.

BETLEY, BOZENA. Spinto. Polish. Resident mem: Grand Theater, Warsaw. Born 19 Nov 1940, Dabrowa, Poland. Husband Gregor Sieradzki, occupation painter. One child. Studied: Asst Prof Maria Boyar-Przemieniecka, Warsaw; School of Music, voice & flute, Warsaw. **Debut:** Aida, Bydgoszcz Opera, Poland 1970. Previous occupations: flutist, operetta company orchestra, Warsaw. Awards: Second Prize Intl Singing Compt Toulouse, 1970.
Sang with major companies in ITA: Palermo; POL: Lodz, Warsaw; UK: Glyndebourne Fest. **Roles with these companies incl** BIZET: Micaëla★ (*Carmen*), Léila★ (*Pêcheurs de perles*); GLUCK: Euridice★; LEONCAVALLO: Nedda★ (*Pagliacci*); MOZART: Fiordiligi★ (*Così fan tutte*), Donna Anna★ (*Don Giovanni*), Ilia★ (*Idomeneo*), Mlle Silberklang★ (*Schauspieldirektor*), Pamina★ (*Zauberflöte*); ORFF: Solo★ (*Carmina burana*); VERDI: Elisabetta★ (*Don Carlo*), Alice Ford★ (*Falstaff*), Violetta★(*Traviata*); WAGNER: Elisabeth★ (*Tannhäuser*). **World premieres:** RUDZINSKI: Jagno (*Peasants*) Warsaw 1974. Video/Film—BBC TV: Ilia (*Idomeneo*). Gives recitals. Appears with symphony orchestra. **Res:** Korczynska 11 apt 5, Warsaw, Poland. **Mgmt:** PAG/POL.

BEVACQUA, ANTONIO. Lyric tenor. Italian. Born 17 Sep 1941, Messina. Wife Maria Costa, occupation teacher. Two children. Studied: Raffaele Tenaglia, Milan. **Debut:** Tamino (*Zauberflöte*) Parma Opera 1972-73. Previous occupations: industrial consultant. Awards: Winner, Compt of Spoleto 1970-71.
Sang with major companies in FRA: Marseille; ITA: Bologna, Palermo, Parma, Rome Opera, Trieste. **Roles with these companies incl** MOZART: Pedrillo★ (*Entführung aus dem Serail*), Tamino★ (*Zauberflöte*); PUCCINI: Rinuccio★ (*Gianni Schicchi*); ROSSINI: Almaviva★ (*Barbiere di Siviglia*), Dorvil★ (*Scala di seta*); VERDI: Fenton★ (*Falstaff*), Duca di Mantova★ (*Rigoletto*). Video—RAI TV: Sposo (*Trionfo di Afrodite*). **Res:** Forze Armate 28, Milan, Italy.

BEZETTI, VICTORIA; née Frincu. Lyric coloratura soprano. Romanian. Resident mem: Romanian Opera, Bucharest. Born 11 Mar 1937, Constanta. Husband Mircea, occupation music edit, TV. One child. Studied: Consv, Prof Viorel Ban, Bucharest. **Debut:** Gilda (*Rigoletto*) Musical Theater, Galati 1964.
Sang with major companies in BUL: Sofia; FIN: Helsinki; GER DR: Berlin Staatsoper; ROM: Bucharest; YUG: Belgrade. **Roles with these com-**

panies incl BEETHOVEN: Marzelline★ (*Fidelio*); BIZET: Micaëla★ (*Carmen*); DONIZETTI: Lucia★; MOZART: Zerlina★ (*Don Giovanni*), Konstanze★ (*Entführung aus dem Serail*), Pamina★ (*Zauberflöte*); OFFENBACH: Antonia★ (*Contes d'Hoffmann*); PUCCINI: Mimi★ (*Bohème*), Lauretta★ (*Gianni Schicchi*); STRAUSS, R: Sophie★ (*Rosenkavalier*); VERDI: Oscar★ (*Ballo in maschera*), Nannetta (*Falstaff*), Gilda★ (*Rigoletto*), Violetta★ (*Traviata*); WEBER: Aennchen (*Freischütz*). Also on records only MOZART: Vitellia (*Clemenza di Tito*). **World premieres:** TRAILESCU: Florica (*Balcescu*) Romanian Opera 1974. Video/Film: Violetta (*Traviata*). Gives recitals. Appears with symphony orchestra. **Res:** 2 Bucsanesti St, Bucharest 7, Romania. **Mgmt:** RIA/ROM.

BIBL, RUDOLF. Conductor of opera and symphony, & composer. Austrian. Resident Cond, Volksoper, Vienna. Born 4 May 1929, Vienna. Divorced. Studied: Acad of Music, Profs Stella Wang, H Swarowsky, M Zallinger, Josef Marx, Vienna; incl piano, clarinet & voice. Plays the piano. Operatic training as repetiteur at Opernhaus Graz, Austria. **Operatic debut:** *Lustigen Weiber* Opernhaus Innsbruck, Austria 1952. Symphonic debut: Wiener Tonkünstler Orch 1968.
Conducted with major companies in AUS: Graz, Vienna Volksoper; BUL: Sofia; FRA: Bordeaux, Strasbourg; ITA: Trieste, Turin; MON: Monte Carlo. **Operas with these companies incl** BELLINI: *Norma★*; DEBUSSY: *Pelléas et Mélisande*; GERSHWIN: *Porgy and Bess*; HANDEL: *Giulio Cesare*; HINDEMITH: *Mathis der Maler*; LORTZING: *Wildschütz, Zar und Zimmermann*; MENOTTI: *Medium*; MOZART: *Così fan tutte, Finta giardiniera, Nozze di Figaro*; NICOLAI: *Lustigen Weiber★*; OFFENBACH: *Périchole*; PUCCINI: *Gianni Schicchi, Butterfly, Tosca*; ROSSINI: *Barbiere di Siviglia*; STRAUSS, J: *Fledermaus★*; STRAUSS, R: *Arabella, Ariadne auf Naxos, Rosenkavalier★, Salome*; STRAVINSKY: *Rake's Progress*; VERDI: *Aida, Don Carlo, Nabucco★, Traviata*; WEILL: *Dreigroschenoper*. Also KIENZL: *Evangelimann★*. Conducted major orch in Europe. **Res:** Vienna, Austria.

BIBLE, FRANCES L. Dramatic mezzo-soprano. American. Resident mem: New York City Opera. Born 26 Jan, Sackets Harbor, NY, USA. Single. Studied: Inst of Musical Art; Juilliard Graduate School, New York; Queena Mario. **Debut:** Cherubino (*Nozze di Figaro*) New York City Opera 1948. Awards: Woman of the Year, *Mademoiselle* magazine 1950; Alice Breen Memorial Prize and Fllshp, Juilliard School.
Sang with major companies in AUS: Vienna Staatsoper; CAN: Vancouver; FR GER: Karlsruhe; UK: Glyndebourne Festival; USA: Baltimore, Cincinnati, Dallas, Fort Worth, Hawaii, Houston, Kansas City, Lake George, Miami, Minneapolis, New Orleans, New York City Opera, Philadelphia Grand & Lyric, Pittsburgh, San Antonio, San Francisco Opera & Spring Opera, Seattle, Washington DC. **Roles with these companies incl** AUBER: Pamela (*Fra Diavolo*); BELLINI: Adalgisa (*Norma*); BERG: Gräfin Geschwitz★(*Lulu*); BERLIOZ: Marguerite (*Damnation de Faust*); BERNSTEIN: Dinah (*Trouble*

in Tahiti); BIZET: Djamileh; BRITTEN: Oberon & Hermia (*Midsummer Night*), Lucretia (*Rape of Lucretia*); CHARPENTIER: Mère★ (*Louise*); CHERUBINI: Neris★ (*Medea*); DEBUSSY: Geneviève★ (*Pelléas et Mélisande*); FLOTOW: Nancy (*Martha*); GLUCK: Orfeo; GOUNOD: Siebel (*Faust*); HANDEL: Cornelia★ & Sextus (*Giulio Cesare*); HUMPERDINCK: Hänsel; MONTEVERDI: Ottavia★‡ (*Incoronazione di Poppea*); MOORE: Augusta Tabor‡ (*Baby Doe*); MOZART: Sesto (*Clemenza di Tito*), Dorabella★ (*Così fan tutte*), Cherubino★ (*Nozze di Figaro*); MUSSORGSKY: Marina (*Boris Godunov*); PONCHIELLI: Laura (*Gioconda*); PROKOFIEV: Smeraldina & Clarissa (*Love for Three Oranges*); PUCCINI: Suzuki (*Butterfly*), Principessa (*Suor Angelica*); ROSSINI: Angelina★ (*Cenerentola*); STRAUSS, J: Prinz Orlovsky (*Fledermaus*); STRAUSS, R: Octavian★ (*Rosenkavalier*), Herodias★ (*Salome*); STRAVINSKY: Jocasta (*Oedipus Rex*); TCHAIKOVSKY: Mme Larina (*Eugene Onegin*); THOMAS: Mignon; VERDI: Amneris (*Aida*), Preziosilla (*Forza del destino*); WAGNER: Magdalene (*Meistersinger*); WARD: Elizabeth Proctor‡ (*Crucible*); WEBER: Eglantine★ (*Euryanthe*). Also ROSSELLINI: Marta (*Guerra*); ROSSINI: Desdemona (*Otello*). **World premieres:** MOORE: Augusta (*Ballad of Baby Doe*) Central City Opera 1956; WARD: Elizabeth Proctor (*Crucible*) New York City Opera 1961. Gives recitals. Appears with symphony orchestra. Teaches voice. Coaches repertoire. On faculty of Rice Univ, Houston, TX. **Res:** 2225 Bolsover, Houston, TX 77005, USA. Mgmt: RMG/USA.

BICKERSTAFF, ROBERT. Dramatic baritone. Australian. Born Sydney, Australia. Single. Studied: NSW Consv, Lyndon Jones, Sydney; Melbourne Univ Consv, Henry Portnoj, Australia; Rachmaninov Consv, Dominique Modesti, Paris. **Debut:** Thoas (*Iphigénie en Tauride*) Opéra de Marseille 1962. Previous occupations: insurance surveyor, manufacturer agent. Awards: Melbourne *Sun* Aria Schlshp, Melbourne newspaper; Shell Aria Compt, Canberra; South Austral Gvnmt Schlshp Awd, Adelaide; ABC Vocal Compt, Victoria, Australia.

Sang with major companies in BEL: Liège; FRA: Bordeaux, Marseille, Nice; UK: Cardiff Welsh, London Royal & English National; USA: Pittsburgh. **Roles with these companies incl** BECAUD: Sean (*Opéra d'Aran*); BIZET: Escamillo★ (*Carmen*), Zurga (*Pêcheurs de perles*); DONIZETTI: Enrico★ (*Lucia*); GLUCK: Thoas★ (*Iphigénie en Tauride*); LEONCAVALLO: Tonio (*Pagliacci*); MASSENET: Hérode (*Hérodiade*); MOZART: Conte Almaviva (*Nozze di Figaro*); PUCCINI: Marcello★ (*Bohème*), Sharpless (*Butterfly*); SAINT-SAENS: Grand prêtre (*Samson et Dalila*); TCHAIKOVSKY: Yeletsky★ (*Pique Dame*); VERDI: Amonasro★ (*Aida*), Ezio (*Attila*), Renato (*Ballo in maschera*), Rodrigo (*Don Carlo*), Don Carlo (*Forza del destino*), Conte di Luna★ (*Trovatore*); WAGNER: Holländer★. Gives recitals. Appears with symphony orchestra. Teaches voice. Coaches repertoire. On faculty of Royal Acad of Music, London, UK. **Res:** 3 Hook La, Welling/Kent, UK.

BICZYCKI, JAN-PAUL. Stages/produces opera, theater & television. Also designs stage-lighting and is an actor & author. Polish/German. Born 20 Jun 1931, Biczyce, Poland. Wife Roma Ligocka, occupation painter, designer. Two children. Studied: Acad of Theater, Erwin Axer, Alexander Bardini, Korzeniewski, Warsaw; Univ of Warsaw, Jan Kott; incl music, piano & oboe. **Operatic debut:** *Don Quichotte* State Opera, Krakow 1962. Theater debut: Barn/Stodola, Warsaw 1958.

Directed/produced opera for major companies in AUS: Graz, Salzburg Fest; DEN: Copenhagen; FR GER: Bielefeld, Bonn, Darmstadt, Dortmund, Kassel, Kiel, Munich Staatsoper & Gärtnerplatz; POL: Warsaw; USSR: Kiev. **Operas staged with these companies incl** BIZET: *Carmen★;* BORODIN: *Prince Igor;* DONIZETTI: *Don Pasquale★;* DVORAK: *Rusalka;* GAY/Britten: *Beggar's Opera;* GLUCK: *Orfeo ed Euridice;* JANACEK: *From the House of the Dead, Jenufa;* LEONCAVALLO: *Pagliacci;* MASCAGNI: *Cavalleria rusticana;* MASSENET: *Don Quichotte★, Manon;* MONIUSZKO: *Halka;* MOZART: *Così fan tutte★, Zauberflöte;* MUSSORGSKY: *Boris Godunov, Khovanshchina;* OFFENBACH: *Contes d'Hoffmann, Périchole;* PUCCINI: *Tosca, Turandot;* RAVEL: *Heure espagnole;* RIMSKY-KORSAKOV: *Coq d'or, Sadko, Tsar's Bride;* ROSSINI: *Barbiere di Siviglia;* SHOSTAKOVICH: *Katerina Ismailova★;* SMETANA: *Bartered Bride;* TCHAIKOVSKY: *Eugene Onegin, Maid of Orleans;* VERDI: *Macbeth, Traviata;* WEILL: *Dreigroschenoper.* Also KAGEL: *Sur scène★;* HAUBENSTOCK-RAMATI: *Spiel★.* **Operatic world premieres:** ENGELMANN: *Revue* Bonn Opera House 1973; NIEHAUS: *Maldoror* Kiel Opera 1970. Previous leading positions with major theater companies: Art Dir & Adm, Comedia, Warsaw 1963-65. Teaches at Univ of Munich; Otto Falckenberg Schule, Munich. **Res:** Lehárweg 5, 8012 Ottobrunn, FR Ger. Mgmt: SLZ/FRG; ALF/HOL.

BING, SIR RUDOLF. British. Former Gen Mng, Metropolitan Opera, New York 1950-72; in charge of overall adm & art matters. Consultant, Columbia Artists Management Inc, 165 W 57 St, New York, NY 10019, USA; in charge of Columbia Artists' Series of Stars and Special Projects. Born 9 Jan 1902, Vienna. Wife Nina. Additional prev positions, primarily administrative & musical: Art Adm, State Opera Darmstadt, Germany 1928-30; Art Adm, Charlottenburg Opera, Germany 1930-33; Gen Mng, Glyndebourne Opera, UK 1934-49 except WW II yrs; Gen Mng, Edinburgh Fest, UK 1947-49. In present position since 1974. World premieres at theaters under his management: BARBER: *Vanessa* 1958, *Antony and Cleopatra* 1966; LEVY: *Mourning Becomes Electra* 1967; all at Metropolitan Opera. Awards: Knight Commander of Brit Empire, Queen Elizabeth II; Chevalier of the Legion of Honor, Pres of French Rep; Grand Officer of the Order of Merit, Rep of Italy; Grand Silver Medal of Honor, Rep of Austria; Commander's Cross of the Order of Merit, FR Ger; Hon DHL: New York Univ, Temple Univ, Dickenson Coll, Wagner Coll, Jacksonville Univ. Author of *5,000 Nights at The Opera.* **Res:** Essex House, New York, NY 10019, USA.

BINI, CARLO; né Carlo Bifone. Lyric tenor. Italian. Wife Margaret Elizabeth Bailey. Studied: Consv di Musica San Pietro a Maiella, Naples; Mo Mino Campanino, Italy. **Debut:** Pinkerton (*Butterfly*) San Carlo, Naples 1969. Awards: Vesuvio d'Argento, Premio Musicale Napolitano 1970; Premio Artistico Noce d'Oro, Lecco 1972.

Sang with major companies in BEL: Brussels; BRA: Rio de Janeiro; FRA: Marseille, Paris, Rouen, Toulouse; FR GER: Berlin Deutsche Oper, Düsseldorf-Duisburg, Hamburg, Hannover, Munich Staatsoper, Stuttgart; ITA: Naples, Rome Opera, Trieste, Turin; SPA: Canary Isl Las Palmas Festival; USA: New York City Opera, Washington DC. **Roles with these companies incl** AUBER: Fra Diavolo★; BERG: Tambourmajor★ (*Wozzeck*); BIZET: Don José★ (*Carmen*); CHARPENTIER: Julien★ (*Louise*); CILEA: Maurizio★ (*A. Lecouvreur*); DONIZETTI: Fernand (*Favorite*), Edgardo★ (*Lucia*); OFFENBACH: Hoffmann★; PONCHIELLI: Enzo (*Gioconda*); PUCCINI: Rodolfo★ (*Bohème*), Pinkerton★ (*Butterfly*), Des Grieux★ (*Manon Lescaut*), Cavaradossi★ (*Tosca*); STRAUSS, J: Eisenstein & Alfred (*Fledermaus*); VERDI: Radames★ (*Aida*), Riccardo★ (*Ballo in maschera*), Fenton★ (*Falstaff*), Don Alvaro★ (*Forza del destino*), Duca di Mantova★ (*Rigoletto*), Alfredo★ (*Traviata*), Arrigo★ (*Vespri*); ZANDONAI: Romeo★. Also DALLAPICCOLA: Demodoco & Tiresia (*Ulisse*). **World premieres:** NAPOLI: Dubrowski (*Dubrowski II*) San Carlo, Naples 1973; PORRINO: Rovello (*Esculapeo al neon*) Cagliari, Sardinia, Italy 1972. **Res:** V Orazio 167, Naples, Italy. Mgmt: CAM/USA; SLZ/FRG.

BISHOP, ADELAIDE. Stages/produces opera, was an opera singer. American. Born New York. Husband Bertram H Schur, occupation attorney. One child. Studied: Louis Polanski, Luigi Rossini, Rose Landver, Paul Breisach etc, New York; including piano and voice. Operatic training as performer at New York City Opera 1948-60.

Directed/produced opera for major companies in USA: Kansas City, Lake George, St Paul. **Operas staged with these companies incl** BARTOK: *Bluebeard's Castle;* BIZET: *Carmen★;* BRITTEN: *Rape of Lucretia★;* DONIZETTI: *Don Pasquale;* HOIBY: *Summer and Smoke★;* HUMPERDINCK: *Hänsel und Gretel;* MASSENET: *Manon★;* MENOTTI: *Amahl, Medium, Old Maid and the Thief, Telephone;* MOZART: *Così fan tutte, Nozze di Figaro;* NICOLAI: *Lustigen Weiber;* PUCCINI: *Bohème, Gianni Schicchi★;* ROSSINI: *Barbiere di Siviglia, Turco in Italia★;* SCHOENBERG: *Erwartung;* SMETANA: *Bartered Bride;* STRAUSS, R: *Ariadne auf Naxos★;* VERDI: *Rigoletto, Traviata;* WARD: *Crucible★;* WOLF-FERRARI: *Quattro rusteghi.* **Operatic world premieres:** AMRAM: *Twelfth Night* Lake George Fest, NY 1968. Teaches at School for the Arts, Boston Univ, MA. **Res:** Bethesda, MD, USA.

BISKUP, RENATE MARIA. Lyric mezzo-soprano. German. Resident mem: Staatsoper Dresden, Ger DR. Born 6 Mar 1939, Freital. Husband Thomas Kästner, occupation actor. One child. Studied: Carl Maria v Weber Hochschule für Musik, Dresden; Prof Herbert Winkler, Prof Dagmar Freiwald-

Lange. **Debut:** Emilia (*Otello*) Opernhaus Magdeburg, Ger DR 1963.

Sang with major companies in FR GER: Wiesbaden: GER DR: Dresden; USSR: Leningrad Kirov. **Roles with these cos incl** BIZET: Carmen★; HUMPERDINCK: Hänsel★; MOZART: Dorabella★ (*Così fan tutte*), Cherubino★ (*Nozze di Figaro*); NICOLAI: Frau Reich (*Lustigen Weiber*); PROKOFIEV: Clarissa★ (*Love for Three Oranges*); VERDI: Preziosilla (*Forza del destino*); WEBER: Puck (*Oberon*). Also MUSSORGSKY: Feodor (*Boris Godunov*). **World premieres:** KUNAD: Giulimette (*Maître Pathelin*) Staatsoper Dresden 1969; ZIMMERMANN: Frau Rosinke (*Levins Mühle*) Staatsoper Dresden 1973. Gives recitals. Coaches repertoire. **Res:** Bergbahnstr 1, 8051 Dresden, Ger DR. Mgmt: KDR/GDR.

BISSON, IVES. Lyric baritone. French. Born 31 May 1936, Mostaganem, Algiers. Married. Two children. Studied: Consv Ntl de Musique, Mme Gilly-Musy, Louis Noguera, Paris. **Debut:** Albert (*Werther*) Opéra de Nice 1962. Previous occupations: sang in music hall and variety shows. Awards: First Prize in Voice and Opera, Consv Ntl of Paris.

Sang with major companies in AUS: Vienna Staatsoper; BEL: Brussels, Liège; FRA: Aix-en-Provence Fest, Bordeaux, Lyon, Marseille, Nancy, Nice, Paris, Rouen, Strasbourg, Toulouse; HOL: Amsterdam; MON: Monte Carlo; POR: Lisbon; SPA: Barcelona; SWI: Geneva. **Roles with these companies incl** BERLIOZ: Choroebus (*Troyens*); BIZET: Escamillo★ (*Carmen*), Zurga★ (*Pêcheurs de perles*); DONIZETTI: Enrico (*Lucia*); GLUCK: Oreste★ & Thoas★ (*Iphigénie en Tauride*); GOUNOD: Ourrias (*Mireille*); MASCAGNI: Alfio★ (*Cavalleria rusticana*); MASSENET: Lescaut★ (*Manon*), Des Grieux★ (*Portrait de Manon*), Albert★ (*Werther*); PROKOFIEV: Prince Andrei★ (*War and Peace*); PUCCINI: Marcello★ (*Bohème*), Sharpless★ (*Butterfly*), Lescaut★ (*Manon Lescaut*); RAVEL: Ramiro★ (*Heure espagnole*); ROSSINI: Figaro★ (*Barbiere di Siviglia*), Robert (*Comte Ory*); TCHAIKOVSKY: Yeletsky★ (*Pique Dame*); THOMAS: Hamlet. Also GOUNOD: Mercutio (*Roméo et Juliette*); GLUCK: Orphée; ROSSINI: Paccuvio (*Pietra del paragone*); MILHAUD: Orphée (*Malheurs d'Orphée*). Video/Film: (*Manon*); (*Fledermaus*). Appears with symphony orchestra. Teaches voice. **Res:** 36 rue Ballu, Paris FS 009, France. Mgmt: IMR/FRA.

BISSON, NAPOLEON. Dramatic baritone & basso-buffo. Canadian. Widowed. Four children.

Sang with major companies in CAN: Montreal/Quebec, Ottawa, Toronto, Vancouver; UK: London Royal Opera & English National; USA: Dallas, New Orleans, Pittsburgh. **Roles with these companies incl** DONIZETTI: Don Pasquale★, Sulpice★ (*Fille du régiment*); LEONCAVALLO: Tonio★ (*Pagliacci*); MASCAGNI: Alfio★ (*Cavalleria rusticana*); PAISIELLO: Bartolo★ (*Barbiere di Siviglia*); PUCCINI: Gianni Schicchi★, Michele★ (*Tabarro*); ROSSINI: Dott Bartolo★ (*Barbiere di Siviglia*); SAINT-SAENS: Grand prêtre★ (*Samson et Dalila*); VERDI: Amonasro (*Aida*), Rigoletto; WAGNER: Alberich (*Rheingold*). Also PUCCINI: Sacristan★ (*Tosca*); RIM-

SKY-KORSAKOV: Polkan★ (*Coq d'or*); ROSSINI: Taddeo (*Italiana in Algeri*). Video/Film: (*Heure espagnole*). Appears with symphony orchestra. **Res:** Montreal, PQ, Canada. Mgmt: SAM/USA.

BJONER, INGRID. Dramatic soprano. Norwegian. Born Kråkstad, Norway. Husband Thomas R Pierpoint, occupation Dir, Boeing Co, USA. Studied: Gudrun Boellemose, Oslo; Prof Paul Lohmann, Wiesbaden, FR Ger; Prof Ellen Repp, New York. **Debut:** Donna Anna (*Don Giovanni*) Norwegian Opera Oslo 1957. Previous occupations: pharmacist, grad Oslo Univ 1951. Awards: Order of St Olav First Class, King of Norway; Bavarian Order of Merit, Bavarian Senate; Kammersängerin, Bavarian Senate, Munich.

Sang with major companies in ARG: Buenos Aires; AUS: Salzburg Fest, Vienna Staatsoper; BEL: Brussels; CAN: Montreal/Quebec; CZE: Prague National; DEN: Copenhagen; FRA: Paris; FR GER: Bayreuth Fest, Berlin Deutsche Oper, Bielefeld, Bonn, Cologne, Dortmund, Düsseldorf-Duisburg, Essen, Frankfurt, Hamburg, Hannover, Karlsruhe, Kassel, Kiel, Mannheim, Munich Staatsoper, Nürnberg, Saarbrücken, Stuttgart, Wiesbaden, Wuppertal; ITA: Milan La Scala, Naples, Rome Opera, Turin; NOR: Oslo; POR: Lisbon; SPA: Barcelona; SWE: Drottningholm Fest, Stockholm; SWI: Zurich; UK: Edinburgh Fest, London Royal; USA: Fort Worth, Hartford, Memphis, Miami, New Orleans, New York Met, Philadelphia Lyric, San Antonio, San Francisco Opera, Seattle. **Roles with these companies incl** BEETHOVEN: Leonore★ (*Fidelio*); BIZET: Micaëla (*Carmen*); BUSONI: Herzogin (*Doktor Faust*); GLUCK: Alceste★, Armide, Iphigénie★ (*Iphigénie en Tauride*); HANDEL: Rodelinda; JANACEK: Jenufa; MARTIN: Iseut (*Vin herbé*); MEYERBEER: Selika (*Africaine*); MONTEVERDI: Poppea (*Incoronazione di Poppea*); MOZART: Vitellia (*Clemenza di Tito*), Fiordiligi (*Così fan tutte*), Donna Anna★ (*Don Giovanni*), Contessa (*Nozze di Figaro*), Pamina (*Zauberflöte*); PONCHIELLI: Gioconda★; PUCCINI: Tosca★, Turandot★; STRAUSS, R: Helena (*Aegyptische Helena*), Ariadne★ (*Ariadne auf Naxos*), Gräfin★ (*Capriccio*), Daphne★, Chrysothemis★ (*Elektra*), Kaiserin★‡ (*Frau ohne Schatten*), Marschallin★ (*Rosenkavalier*), Salome★; VERDI: Aida★, Amelia★ (*Ballo in maschera*), Elisabetta★ (*Don Carlo*), Leonora★ (*Forza del destino*), Desdemona★ (*Otello*); WAGNER: Senta★ (*Fliegende Holländer*), Elsa★ (*Lohengrin*), Eva★ (*Meistersinger*), Sieglinde (*Walküre*), Brünnhilde (*Walküre★, Siegfried★, Götterdämmerung★*), Elisabeth★ (*Tannhäuser*), Isolde★; WEBER: Euryanthe, Agathe (*Freischütz*), Rezia★ (*Oberon*). Recorded for: DGG, EMI, Eurodisc. Gives recitals. Appears with symphony orchestra. **Res:** Gregers Grams vei 33, Oslo 3, Norway. Mgmt: SLZ/FRG; CAM/USA.

BJÖRLING, ROLF. Lyric & dramatic tenor. Swedish. Resident mem: Royal Opera, Stockholm. Born 25 Dec 1928, Jönköping, Sweden. Three children. Studied: Royal Acad of Music, Stockholm; Dimitri Onofrei, San Francisco. **Debut:** Pinkerton (*Butterfly*) Royal Opera, Stockholm 1962. Previous

occupations: salesman. Awards: Metropolitan Opera schlshp.

Sang with major companies in DEN: Copenhagen; FIN: Helsinki; FR GER: Berlin Deutsche Oper, Hamburg, Munich Staatsoper; NOR: Oslo; SWE: Drottningholm Fest; USA: San Francisco Spring Opera. **Roles with these companies incl** BEETHOVEN: Florestan (*Fidelio*); BIZET: Don José★ (*Carmen*); EINEM: Hérault de Séchelles (*Dantons Tod*); LEONCAVALLO: Canio★ (*Pagliacci*); PUCCINI: Rodolfo★ (*Bohème*), Pinkerton★ (*Butterfly*), Cavaradossi★ (*Tosca*), Calaf★ (*Turandot*); SMETANA: Hans (*Bartered Bride*); STRAUSS, J: Alfred★ (*Fledermaus*); STRAUSS, R: Ein Sänger★ (*Rosenkavalier*); VERDI: Radames★ (*Aida*), Don Carlo★, Ismaele★ (*Nabucco*), Duca di Mantova★ (*Rigoletto*), Alfredo★ (*Traviata*), Manrico★ (*Trovatore*). Gives recitals. Appears with symphony orchestra. Teaches voice. Mgmt: ULF/SWE; JRM/USA.

BJÖRNSSON, SIGURD. Lyric tenor. Icelandic. Resident mem: Opera House, Graz; Gärtnerplatztheater, Munich. Born 19 Mar 1932, Hafnarfjördur, Iceland. Wife Sieglinde, occupation opera singer. Two children. Studied: Staatliche Hochschule für Musik, Prof Gerhard Hüsch, Prof Hanno Blaschke, Munich. **Debut:** Lord Arthur (*Lucia*) Staatsoper Stuttgart 1962. Previous occupations: studied violin. Awards: Second Prize 's Hertogenbosch Compt, Holland 1960.

Sang with major companies in AUS: Bregenz Fest, Graz, Vienna Volksoper; GRE: Athens Fest; FR GER: Berlin Deutsche Oper, Darmstadt, Frankfurt, Hamburg, Kassel, Munich Staatsoper & Gärtnerplatz, Stuttgart, Wuppertal; SWI: Zurich. **Roles with these companies incl** FLOTOW: Lionel★ (*Martha*); LORTZING: Baron Kronthal★ (*Wildschütz*); MOZART: Tito★ (*Clemenza di Tito*), Ferrando★ (*Così fan tutte*), Don Ottavio★ (*Don Giovanni*), Belmonte★ (*Entführung aus dem Serail*), Tamino★ (*Zauberflöte*); NICOLAI: Fenton★ (*Lustigen Weiber*); ORFF: Erzähler★ (*Mond*); PUCCINI: Rinuccio★ (*Gianni Schicchi*); ROSSINI: Almaviva★ (*Barbiere di Siviglia*), Gianetto★ (*Gazza ladra*); STRAUSS, J: Eisenstein★ & Alfred★ (*Fledermaus*); STRAUSS, R: Ein Sänger★ (*Rosenkavalier*); VERDI: Fenton★ (*Falstaff*); ZIMMERMANN: Desportes★ (*Soldaten*). Gives recitals. Appears with symphony orchestra. **Res:** Ursbergerstr 21, Munich, FR Ger. Mgmt: PAS/FRG; TAS/AUS.

BLACHUT, BENO. Lyric & dramatic tenor. Czechoslovakian. Resident mem: National Theater, Prague. Born 14 Jun 1913, Ostrava, CSR. Wife Anna. Two children. Studied: Prague Consv, Prof Louis Kaderábek. **Debut:** Hans (*Bartered Bride*) Olomouc Opera, CSSR 1938. Previous occupations: worker in Vítkovice ironworks. Awards: Ntl Artist, Pres of CSSR; twice Laureate of the State Awd, Gvnmt of Republic.

Sang with major companies in AUS: Vienna Staatsoper; BEL: Brussels; BUL: Sofia; CZE: Brno, Prague National; FIN: Helsinki; FR GER: Bielefeld, Wiesbaden; GER DR: Berlin Komische Oper; HOL: Amsterdam; ITA: Venice; POL: Warsaw; UK: Edinburgh Fest; USSR: Moscow Bolshoi. **Roles with these companies incl** BEETHO-

VEN: Florestan (*Fidelio*); BIZET: Don José (*Carmen*); BORODIN: Vladimir (*Prince Igor*); BRITTEN: Albert Herring; DONIZETTI: Ernesto (*Don Pasquale*); DVORAK: Jirka★ (*Devil and Kate*), Prince (*Rusalka*); GLINKA: Finn (*Ruslan and Ludmilla*); GOUNOD: Faust; HANDEL: Acis; HUMPERDINCK: Königssohn; JANACEK: Broucek★‡ (*Excursions of Mr Broucek*), Alyei★ (*From the House of the Dead*), Laca★ (*Jenufa*), Boris★‡ (*Katya Kabanova*), Albert Gregor (*Makropoulos Affair*); LEONCAVALLO: Canio (*Pagliacci*); MOZART: Ferrando (*Così fan tutte*), Belmonte (*Entführung aus dem Serail*); MUSSORGSKY: Dimitri (*Boris Godunov*), Andrei Khovansky (*Khovanshchina*); PROKOFIEV: Pierre (*War and Peace*); PUCCINI: Rodolfo (*Bohème*), Cavaradossi (*Tosca*); SMETANA: Hans★ (*Bartered Bride*), Dalibor★‡, Lukas★‡ (*The Kiss*), Stalav★ (*Libuse*), Vitek (*Secret*), Heinrich (*Two Widows*); STRAUSS, R: Aegisth (*Elektra*), Ein Sänger (*Rosenkavalier*); STRAVINSKY: Vasili (*Mavra*); SUCHON: Andrew (*Whirlpool*); TCHAIKOVSKY: Lenski (*Eugene Onegin*), Gherman (*Pique Dame*); THOMAS: Wilhelm Meister (*Mignon*); VERDI: Radames (*Aida*), Ismaele★ (*Nabucco*), Otello, Alfredo (*Traviata*); WAGNER: Erik (*Fliegende Holländer*), Walther (*Meistersinger*). Also DVORAK: Benda★ (*Jakobin*), Dimitrij; FIBICH: Ctirad (*Sárka*), Don Juan (*Hedy*); KOVAROVIC: Kozina (*Dog Heads*); LORTZING: Chateauneuf (*Zar und Zimmermann*). World premieres: PAUER: Thomas Diafoirus (*Malade imaginaire*) National Theater, Prague 1970. Recorded for Supraphon. Gives recitals. Appears with symphony orchestra. **Res:** Havelská 29, Prague 1, CSSR. Mgmt: PRG/CZE.

BLACKBURN, HAROLD. Bass. British. Resident mem: English National Opera, London. Born 21 Apr 1925, Hamilton, Scotland, UK. Wife Joyce Gartside. Two children. Studied: Carl Rosa Opera; Engl Opera Group. **Debut:** Ferrando (*Trovatore*) Carl Rosa Opera 1947. Previous occupations: wagon builder.

Sang with major companies in UK: Aldeburgh Fest, Cardiff Welsh, Edinburgh Fest, Glasgow Scottish, London English National. **Roles with these companies incl** BEETHOVEN: Rocco (*Fidelio*); BRITTEN: Chorus leader (*Curlew River*); DONIZETTI: Don Pistacchio (*Campanello*), Don Pasquale★; FLOTOW: Plunkett (*Martha*); GAY/Britten: Mr Peachum (*Beggar's Opera*); MASSENET: Des Grieux★ (*Portrait de Manon*); MOZART: Leporello★ (*Don Giovanni*), Osmin (*Entführung aus dem Serail*), Sarastro (*Zauberflöte*); PENDERECKI: Barré★ (*Teufel von Loudun*); PUCCINI: Colline (*Bohème*); RIMSKY-KORSAKOV: Roi Dodon (*Coq d'or*); ROSSINI: Don Basilio★ (*Barbiere di Siviglia*), Podestà (*Gazza ladra*), Mustafà★ (*Italiana in Algeri*); SMETANA: Kezal (*Bartered Bride*); STRAUSS, R: Baron Ochs (*Rosenkavalier*); STRAVINSKY: Tiresias (*Oedipus Rex*); VERDI: Grande Inquisitore (*Don Carlo*); WAGNER: Daland (*Fliegende Holländer*), Fasolt★ (*Rheingold*), Hunding★ (*Walküre*). World premieres: BENNETT: (*Mines of Sulphur*) Sadler's Wells 1965; (*Penny for a Song*) Sadler's Wells 1967. Recorded for: EMI. Gives recitals. Appears with symphony orchestra.

Teaches voice. **Res:** London, UK. Mgmt: IBB/UK.

BLACKHAM, JOYCE. Mezzo-soprano, form lyric soprano. British. Resident mem: English National Opera, London. Born 1 Jan 1934, Rotherham/Yorkshire, UK. Husband Peter Glossop, occupation opera singer. Studied: Guildhall School, Joseph Hislop, London.

Sang with major companies in FR GER: Berlin Deutsche Oper; NOR: Oslo; UK: London Royal Opera Covent Garden & English National Opera; USA: Fort Worth, New York City Opera; et al. **Roles with these companies incl** DONIZETTI: Norina (*Don Pasquale*); MASSENET: Anita (*Navarraise*); MOZART: Cherubino (*Nozze di Figaro*); PUCCINI: Mimi (*Bohème*), Cio-Cio-San (*Butterfly*); ROSSINI: Rosina (*Barbiere di Siviglia*); VERDI: Leonora (*Trovatore*); et al. Also BIZET: Carmen; MOZART: Dorabella (*Così fan tutte*). **Res:** 11 The Bishop's Ave, Kenlade/London N2, UK.

BLACKWELL, DEREK; né James Derek Blackwell. Lyric & dramatic tenor. British. Born Barnsley, UK. Wife Margaret. One child. Studied: Leeds Coll of Music, Victor Helliwell, UK. **Debut:** First Prisoner (*Fidelio*) Scottish Opera, Glasgow 1970. Previous occupations: in family business as gen bldg contractor.

Sang with major companies in UK: Cardiff Welsh, Edinburgh Fest, Glasgow Scottish, London Royal. **Roles with these companies incl** BEETHOVEN: Florestan (*Fidelio*); BIZET: Nadir★ (*Pêcheurs de perles*); DONIZETTI: Nemorino★ (*Elisir*); FLOTOW: Lionel★ (*Martha*); MOZART: Don Ottavio★ (*Don Giovanni*); PUCCINI: Pinkerton★ (*Butterfly*); STRAUSS, R: Ein Sänger★ (*Rosenkavalier*); VERDI: Radames (*Aida*), Rodolfo (*Luisa Miller*), Ismaele★ (*Nabucco*), Alfredo★ (*Traviata*); WAGNER: Erik★ (*Fliegende Holländer*), Walther v d Vogelweide★ (*Tannhäuser*). Recorded for: Philips, EMI. Gives recitals. Appears with symphony orchestra. Teaches voice. On faculty of Yorkshire Coll of Music, Leeds. **Res:** 130 New Rd, Staincross/Barnsley, UK. Mgmt: GBN/UK.

BLACKWOOD, FREDA. Costume designer for opera, theater. Scottish. Born 17 Nov 1943, Kilmarnock. Single. Studied: Glasgow School of Art. **Operatic debut:** *David and Bathsheba* Opera da Camera, Newcastle Fest, UK 1969. Theater debut: Palace Theatre, Watford, UK 1968. Awards: schlshp, Glasgow School of Art.

Designed for major companies in UK: Welsh National, London Royal & English National. **Operas designed for these companies incl** BARTOK: *Bluebeard's Castle*★; BERG: *Lulu*★; MOZART: *Così fan tutte*★; WAGNER: *Rheingold*★. Operatic Video — Dutch TV: *Down by the Greenwood Side; Change the World.* **Res:** London, UK. Mgmt: HPL/UK.

BLANC, ERNEST. Lyric baritone. French. Born 1 Nov 1923, Sanary s/mer. Wife Elyane. One child. Studied: Consv de Toulon. **Debut:** Tonio (*Pagliacci*) Opéra de Marseille 1950. Previous occupations: mechanic. Awards: First Prize in Voice, Consv de Toulon 1950.

Sang with major companies in ARG: Buenos Aires; AUS: Salzburg Fest; BEL: Brussels, Liège; BRA: Rio de Janeiro; FRA: Bordeaux, Lyon, Marseille, Nancy, Nice, Orange Fest, Paris, Rouen, Strasbourg, Toulouse; FR GER: Bayreuth Fest, Berlin Deutsche Oper, Dortmund; HOL: Amsterdam; ISR: Tel Aviv; ITA: Florence Maggio, Milan La Scala, Naples; MON: Monte Carlo; POR: Lisbon; SPA: Barcelona; SWI: Geneva; UK: Edinburgh Fest, Glyndebourne Fest, London Royal; USA: Chicago, New York City Opera, Philadelphia Lyric. Roles with these companies incl BELLINI: Sir Richard (*Puritani*); BERLIOZ: Méphistophélès (*Damnation de Faust*); BIZET: Escamillo★ (*Carmen*), Zurga★ (*Pêcheurs de perles*); DONIZETTI: Alfonse (*Favorite*), Enrico (*Lucia*); GIORDANO: Carlo Gérard★ (*Andrea Chénier*); GOUNOD: Ourrias (*Mireille*); LEONCAVALLO: Tonio★ (*Pagliacci*); MASCAGNI: Alfio (*Cavalleria rusticana*); MASSENET: Hérode★ (*Hérodiade*), Albert (*Werther*); MOZART: Don Giovanni, Conte Almaviva (*Nozze di Figaro*); PUCCINI: Scarpia (*Tosca*); SAINT-SAENS: Grand prêtre★ (*Samson et Dalila*); TCHAIKOVSKY: Eugene Onegin★; VERDI: Amonasro★ (*Aida*), Renato★ (*Ballo in maschera*), Rodrigo (*Don Carlo*), Rigoletto★, Germont★ (*Traviata*), Conte di Luna★ (*Trovatore*); WAGNER: Holländer★, Telramund (*Lohengrin*), Amfortas (*Parsifal*), Wolfram (*Tannhäuser*). Recorded for: Pathé-Marconi, His Master's Voice. Mgmt: IMR/FRA.

BLANC, JONNY. Lyric & dramatic tenor. Swedish. Resident mem: Royal Opera, Stockholm; Norwegian Opera, Oslo. Born 10 Jul 1939, Lessebo, Sweden. Wife Lillemor, occupation ballet dancer. Studied: Royal Acad of Music, Käthe Sundström, Stockholm. **Debut:** Dimitri (*Boris Godunov*) Royal Opera, Stockholm 1967. Awards: Kristina Nilsson, Jussi Björling Schlshps.
Sang with major companies in DEN: Copenhagen; FIN: Helsinki; FR GER: Frankfurt, Hannover; NOR: Oslo; POR: Lisbon; SWE: Drottningholm Fest; USA: Miami. Roles with these companies incl BEETHOVEN: Florestan★ (*Fidelio*); BIZET: Don José★ (*Carmen*); JANACEK: Steva★ (*Jenufa*); MUSSORGSKY: Vassily Golitsin (*Khovanshchina*); PUCCINI: Pinkerton (*Butterfly*), Cavaradossi★ (*Tosca*); STRAUSS, J: Eisenstein★ (*Fledermaus*); TCHAIKOVSKY: Gherman★ (*Pique Dame*); VERDI: Riccardo★ (*Ballo in maschera*), Don Carlo★; WAGNER: Siegmund (*Walküre*); WEILL: Jim Mahoney★ (*Aufstieg und Fall der Stadt Mahagonny*). **World premieres:** BRAEIN: Martin (*Anne Pedersdotter*) Oslo Opera 1971. Gives recitals. Appears with symphony orchestra. Mgmt: KBL/SWE; DSP/USA.

BLANCHARD, BARBARA. Dramatic soprano. American. Resident mem: Theater am Gärtnerplatz, Munich. Born 24 Jan 1939, Mexico DF, Mexico. Husband Pierre C Hohenberg, occupation physicist. Studied: Pierre Bernac, Paris; John Brownlee, Uta Graf, Thomas LoMonaco, New York.
Sang with major companies in FR GER: Munich Gärtnerplatz; USA: New York City Opera. Roles with these companies incl DONIZETTI: Lucia★;

GIORDANO: Maddalena (*Andrea Chénier*); MASCAGNI: Santuzza★ (*Cavalleria rusticana*); OFFENBACH: Giulietta★ (*Contes d'Hoffmann*); PUCCINI: Lauretta★ (*Gianni Schicchi*); RAVEL: Concepcion (*Heure espagnole*); RIMSKY-KORSAKOV: Coq d'or. Gives recitals. Appears with symphony orchestra. Res: Mauerkircherstr 6, 8 Munich 80, FR Ger.

BLANKE, EDELTRAUD. Dramatic soprano. German. Resident mem: Nationaltheater Mannheim, FR Ger; Staatsoper Berlin; Ger DR. Born 17 Jul 1939, Berlin, Germany. Husband Frank Düsterwald, occupation musician. One child. Studied: Hochschule für Musik, Berlin; Prof Margarethe Bärwinkel, Germany. **Debut:** Arabella, Stadttheater Münster, FR Ger 1965-66.
Sang with major companies in FRA: Bordeaux; FR GER: Cologne, Dortmund, Düsseldorf-Duisburg, Frankfurt, Hannover, Kassel, Kiel, Mannheim, Nürnberg, Wiesbaden; GER DR: Berlin Staatsoper. Roles with these companies incl BRITTEN: Penelope (*Gloriana*); CHARPENTIER: Louise; EINEM: Lucille (*Dantons Tod*); FALLA: Salud (*Vida breve*); GLUCK: Euridice; GOUNOD: Marguerite (*Faust*); HINDEMITH: Tochter (*Cardillac*); LORTZING: Baronin Freimann (*Wildschütz*); MASCAGNI: Santuzza★ (*Cavalleria rusticana*); MOZART: Fiordiligi (*Così fan tutte*), Donna Elvira★ (*Don Giovanni*), Contessa★ (*Nozze di Figaro*), Pamina (*Zauberflöte*); OFFENBACH: Giulietta (*Contes d'Hoffmann*); PUCCINI: Mimi (*Bohème*), Cio-Cio-San (*Butterfly*), Manon★ (*Manon Lescaut*), Tosca★; STRAUSS, J: Rosalinde★ (*Fledermaus*); STRAUSS, R: Arabella★, Daphne★, Marschallin★ (*Rosenkavalier*); VERDI: Amelia (*Ballo in maschera*), Elisabetta★ (*Don Carlo*), Alice Ford★ (*Falstaff*), Desdemona★ (*Otello*), Leonora★ (*Trovatore*); WAGNER: Senta★ (*Fliegende Holländer*), Elsa★ (*Lohengrin*), Eva★ (*Meistersinger*), Elisabeth★ (*Tannhäuser*); WEBER: Agathe★ (*Freischütz*). Gives recitals. Appears with symphony orchestra. Res: Halberstädterstr 4/5, Berlin 31, FR Ger. Mgmt: SMD/FRG.

BLANKENHEIM, TONI. Bass-baritone. German. Resident mem: Staatsoper, Hamburg. Born 12 Dec 1922, Cologne. Wife Brigitte. One child. Studied: Prof Paul Lohmann, Frankfurt; Prof Res Fischer, Stuttgart; Prof Dietger Jacob, Cologne-Hamburg. **Debut:** Figaro (*Nozze di Figaro*) Städtische Bühnen, Frankfurt/Main 1947.
Sang with major companies in AUS: Vienna Volksoper; BEL: Brussels, Liège; CAN: Montreal/Quebec; DEN: Copenhagen; FRA: Bordeaux, Lyon, Marseille, Nancy, Nice, Paris, Rouen, Toulouse; FR GER: Bayreuth Fest, Berlin Deutsche Oper, Cologne, Darmstadt, Düsseldorf-Duisburg, Frankfurt, Hamburg, Hannover, Kassel, Kiel, Krefeld, Munich Staatsoper, Stuttgart, Wuppertal; GER DR: Berlin Staatsoper, Leipzig; HOL: Amsterdam; ISR: Tel Aviv; ITA: Bologna, Florence Maggio & Comunale, Milan La Scala, Naples, Spoleto Fest, Venice; MEX: Mexico City; SPA: Barcelona; SWE: Stockholm; UK: Edinburgh Fest, London English National; USA: New York Met, San Francisco Opera; YUG: Zagreb. Roles with these companies incl BEETHOVEN: Don Pizarro (*Fidelio*); BERG: Dr Schön★

(*Lulu*), Wozzeck★; BIZET: Escamillo (*Carmen*); DALLAPICCOLA: Riviere (*Volo di notte*); DONIZETTI: Don Pasquale; FLOTOW: Plunkett (*Martha*); FORTNER: Don Perlimplin; GOEHR: Arden★ (*Arden muss sterben*); HANDEL: Garibald (*Rodelinda*); HINDEMITH: Lorenz v Pommersfelden (*Mathis der Maler*); LORTZING: Baculus★ (*Wildschütz*), Van Bett (*Zar und Zimmermann*); MASSENET: Don Quichotte, Lescaut (*Manon*); MOZART: Don Alfonso (*Così fan tutte*), Leporello (*Don Giovanni*), Nardo (*Finta giardiniera*), Figaro (*Nozze di Figaro*); MUSSORGSKY: Varlaam (*Boris Godunov*); ORFF: König (*Kluge*), Bauer (*Mond*); PROKOFIEV: King of Clubs (*Love for Three Oranges*); PUCCINI: Scarpia (*Tosca*); ROSSINI: Dott Bartolo★ (*Barbiere di Siviglia*), Macrobio (*Pietra del paragone*), Geronio (*Turco in Italia*); SCHOENBERG: Mann (*Glückliche Hand*); STRAUSS, R: Musiklehrer★ (*Ariadne auf Naxos*), La Roche (*Capriccio*), Orest (*Elektra*), Baron Ochs (*Rosenkavalier*); STRAVINSKY: Nick Shadow (*Rake's Progress*); VERDI: Egberto (*Aroldo/Stiffelio*), Grande Inquisitore (*Don Carlo*), Fra Melitone (*Forza del destino*); WAGNER: Beckmesser★ (*Meistersinger*), Alberich (*Rheingold★, Götterdämmerung★*); WEILL: Trinity Moses (*Aufstieg und Fall der Stadt Mahagonny*); WOLF-FERRARI: Pantalone (*Donne curiose*). Recorded for: DG. **Res:** Steenbargkoppel 21, 2 Hamburg 65, FR Ger.

BLANKENSHIP, WILLIAM LEONARD. Lyric tenor. American. Resident mem: Staatsoper, Vienna. Born 7 Mar 1928. Gatesville, TX, USA. Wife Barbara. Four children. Studied: Mary McCormic, N Texas Univ, Denton, TX; Mack Harrell, Juilliard School, New York; Sergei Radamsky, Karl Heinz Tuttner, Vienna. **Debut:** Narraboth (*Salome*) Fort Worth Opera, TX 1954. Awards: Disting Alumni N Texas Univ 1971; Mary Garden Awd 1955.

Sang with major companies in AUS: Bregenz Fest, Graz, Vienna Staatsoper & Volksoper; BEL: Brussels; BRA: Rio de Janeiro; CAN: Montreal/Quebec; FRA: Aix-en-Provence Fest, Toulouse; FR GER: Berlin Deutsche Oper, Frankfurt, Hamburg, Hannover, Kassel, Mannheim, Munich Staatsoper, Stuttgart; HOL: Amsterdam; HUN: Budapest; MON: Monte Carlo; SPA: Barcelona; SWI: Zurich; USSR: Moscow Bolshoi; USA: Fort Worth, Houston, San Diego, Santa Fe. **Roles with these companies incl** BERG: Maler (*Lulu*); BRITTEN: Male Chorus (*Rape of Lucretia*); CIMAROSA: Paolino (*Matrimonio segreto*); CORNELIUS: Nureddin (*Barbier von Bagdad*); DONIZETTI: Ernesto (*Don Pasquale*), Edgardo (*Lucia*); EINEM: Camille Desmoulins (*Dantons Tod*); FLOTOW: Lionel (*Martha*); GLUCK: Pylade (*Iphigénie en Tauride*); MILHAUD: Matelot (*Pauvre matelot*); MOZART: Ferrando (*Così fan tutte*), Don Ottavio (*Don Giovanni*), Belmonte (*Entführung aus dem Serail*), Graf Belfiore (*Finta giardiniera*), Idamante (*Idomeneo*), Tamino (*Zauberflöte*); NICOLAI: Fenton (*Lustigen Weiber*); OFFENBACH: Hoffmann; ORFF: Solo (*Carmina burana*); PUCCINI: Rodolfo (*Bohème*), Pinkerton (*Butterfly*), Luigi (*Tabarro*); ROSSINI: Almaviva (*Barbiere di Siviglia*); SMETANA: Hans (*Bartered Bride*); STRAUSS, R: Menelaus

(*Aegyptische Helena*), Matteo (*Arabella*), Flamand (*Capriccio*), Leukippos (*Daphne*), Ein Sänger (*Rosenkavalier*), Henry Morosus (*Schweigsame Frau*); STRAVINSKY: Tom Rakewell (*Rake's Progress*); TCHAIKOVSKY: Lenski (*Eugene Onegin*); VERDI: Fenton (*Falstaff*), Duca di Mantova (*Rigoletto*), Alfredo (*Traviata*); WAGNER: Walther v d Vogelweide (*Tannhäuser*). Gives recitals. Appears with symphony orchestra. Teaches voice. On faculty of American Inst of Musical Studies, Dallas, TX/Graz, Austria. **Res:** Lehárg 3a/14, 1060 Vienna, Austria. Mgmt: RAB/AUS.

BLANZAT, ANNE-MARIE. Lyric soprano. French. Born 24 Nov 1944, Neuilly, France. Husband Jacques Plas, occupation professor. Studied: Jacques Jouineau; Maîtrise de Radio-France. **Debut:** Micaëla (*Carmen*) Mulhouse, France 1965. Awards: Oscar for Lyric Theater 1974, Ntl Confed of the Assns for the Defense of the Lyric Theater, France.

Sang with major companies in BEL: Brussels; FRA: Bordeaux, Lyon, Marseille, Nancy, Rouen, Strasbourg; ITA: Naples, Palermo; POR: Lisbon; SWI: Basel, Geneva; UK: Glyndebourne Fest. **Roles with these companies incl** BEETHOVEN: Marzelline★ (*Fidelio*); BIZET: Micaëla★ (*Carmen*), Lauretta (*Docteur Miracle*), Léila (*Pêcheurs de perles*); CIMAROSA: Carolina★ (*Matrimonio segreto*); DEBUSSY: Mélisande★; GAY/Britten: Lucy★ (*Beggar's Opera*); GOUNOD: Juliette★; HAYDN: Sandrina★ (*Infedeltà delusa*); HUMPERDINCK: Gretel; MARTIN: Iseut★ (*Vin herbé*); MASSENET: Sophie★ (*Werther*); MOZART: Pamina★ (*Zauberflöte*); OFFENBACH: Antonia (*Contes d'Hoffmann*); ORFF: Solo★ (*Carmina burana*); POULENC: Blanche (*Dialogues des Carmélites*); PUCCINI: Lisette (*Rondine*); RABAUD: Fille de Sultan★ (*Mârouf*); STRAVINSKY: Anne Trulove (*Rake's Progress*); VERDI: Nannetta★ (*Falstaff*). Also RAMEAU: Clarine & Thalie (*Platée*); TOMASI: Kalidassa (*Ulysse*). **World premieres:** BONDON: Estelle (*Nuit foudroyée*) Metz 1968; KOSMA: Elisa (*Les Hussards*) Lyon 1969; PREY: Cecile (*Les liaisons dangereuses*) Opéra du Rhin, Strasbourg 1974. Video/Film: Sandrina (*Infedeltà delusa*). Appears with symphony orchestra. **Res:** 100 rue du Chemin Vert, Paris 75011, France. Mgmt: IMR/FRA.

BLATAS, ARBIT; né Nicolai Arbit Blatas. Scenic and costume designer for opera. Is a lighting designer; also a painter, sculptor & lithographer. American. Born 19 Nov 1910, Kaunas, Lithuania. Wife Regina Resnik, occupation opera singer & stage dir. One daughter. Studied: painting, sculpture. **Operatic debut:** *Carmen* Staatsoper Hamburg 1971. Awards: Order Mérite de France; Commander Arts, Sciences & Letters of France.

Designed for major companies in CAN: Vancouver; FRA: Strasbourg; FR GER: Hamburg; ITA: Venice; POL: Warsaw; POR: Lisbon. **Operas designed for these companies incl** BIZET: *Carmen★*; MENOTTI: *Medium★*; STRAUSS, R: *Elektra★, Salome★*; TCHAIKOVSKY: *Pique Dame★*; VERDI: *Falstaff★*; WALTON: *Bear★*; WEILL: *Mahagonny★*. Operatic TV: *Carmen*. Exhibitions of paintings and sculptures in princ gal New York, Paris, London, Lausanne, etc; in perm coll of Metropolitan Museum, Whitney Museum, New York; Orangerie, Paris; etc. **Res:** 50 W 56th St, New York, USA.

BLEGEN, JUDITH EYER. Lyric coloratura soprano. American. Resident mem: Metropolitan Opera, New York. Born 27 Apr, Missoula, MO, USA. Divorced. One son. Studied: Curtis Inst of Music, Philadelphia; Music Acad of the West, Santa Barbara, CA, USA. **Debut:** Olympia (*Contes d'Hoffmann*) Nürnberg 1965. Awards: Fulbright Schlshp 1964.

Sang with major companies in AUS: Salzburg Fest, Vienna Staatsoper & Volksoper; FR GER: Nürnberg; SWI: Geneva; UK: London Royal; USA: Chicago, Miami, New York Met, San Francisco Opera, Santa Fe. **Roles with these companies incl** AUBER: Zerlina (*Fra Diavolo*); BEETHOVEN: Marzelline★‡ (*Fidelio*); DEBUSSY: Mélisande★; DONIZETTI: Norina (*Don Pasquale*), Adina★ (*Elisir*); GLUCK: Amor★ (*Orfeo ed Euridice*); GOUNOD: Juliette★; LORTZING: Marie (*Waffenschmied*), Marie (*Zar und Zimmermann*); MASSENET: Manon, Sophie★ (*Werther*); MENOTTI: Emily (*Globolinks*), Monica★‡ (*Medium*), Laetitia★‡ (*Old Maid and the Thief*); MOZART: Despina★ (*Così fan tutte*), Zerlina★ (*Don Giovanni*), Blondchen★ (*Entführung aus dem Serail*), Susanna★ (*Nozze di Figaro*), Aminta (*Re pastore*); NICOLAI: Aennchen★ (*Lustigen Weiber*); OFFENBACH: Olympia (*Contes d'Hoffmann*); ORFF: Solo★‡ (*Carmina burana*); PAISIELLO: Rosina (*Barbiere di Siviglia*); PUCCINI: Musetta‡ (*Bohème*), Lauretta★ (*Gianni Schicchi*); ROSSINI: Rosina (*Barbiere di Siviglia*); STRAUSS, J: Adele★ (*Fledermaus*); STRAUSS, R: Zerbinetta (*Ariadne auf Naxos*), Sophie★ (*Rosenkavalier*); STRAVINSKY: Rossignol; VERDI: Nannetta★ (*Falstaff*); WEBER: Aennchen★ (*Freischütz*). Recorded for: RCA, Columbia, Mercury. Video—Bavaria TV: Blondchen (*Entführung aus dem Serail*); ZDF: Amor (*Orfeo ed Euridice*). Gives recitals. Appears with symphony orchestra. **Res:** New York, NY, USA. Mgmt: DSP/USA; RAB/AUS.

BLESER, ROBERT L A. Conductor of opera and symphony. Belgian. Resident Cond, Centre Lyrique de Wallonie, Liège. Born 20 Feb 1928, Bressoux, Belgium. Divorced. Studied: Consv de Liège; incl piano, organ. Plays the piano. Operatic training as repetiteur, asst cond & chorus master at Théâtre Royal, Liège. **Operatic debut:** Théâtre Royal, Liège 1959.

Conducted with major companies in BEL: Liège; ROM: Bucharest. **Operas with these companies incl** ADAM: *Si j'étais roi★;* BECAUD: *Opéra d'Aran★;* GIORDANO: *Andrea Chénier★;* GOUNOD: *Faust★, Mireille★;* LECOCQ: *Fille de Madame Angot★;* LEONCAVALLO: *Pagliacci★;* OFFENBACH: *Contes d'Hoffmann★;* POULENC: *Dialogues des Carmélites★;* PROKOFIEV: *Love for Three Oranges★;* PUCCINI: *Fanciulla del West★, Butterfly★, Manon Lescaut★, Suor Angelica★, Tosca★;* RAVEL: *Enfant et les sortilèges★;* STRAUSS, J: *Fledermaus★;* STRAUSS, R: *Rosenkavalier★;* TCHAIKOVSKY: *Eugene Onegin★;* VERDI: *Nabucco★,*

Otello★, Traviata★. Teaches at Acad Grétry, Liège. **Res:** 6 rue St Hubert, Liège, Belgium.

BLINKHOF, JAN. Dramatic tenor. Dutch. Resident mem: Amsterdam Opera. Born 10 Jul 1940, Leyden, Holland. Divorced. Studied: Riemerma, Amsterdam; Josef Metternich, Cologne; Luigi Ricci, Rome. **Debut:** Arturo (*Lucia*) Amsterdam Opera 1971. Previous occupations: salesman.

Sang with major companies in HOL: Amsterdam. **Roles with these companies incl** BERG: Tambourmajor★ (*Wozzeck*); BRITTEN: Male Chorus★ (*Rape of Lucretia*); JANACEK: Boris★ (*Katya Kabanova*); PROKOFIEV: Alexis★ (*Gambler*); PUCCINI: Cavaradossi★ (*Tosca*); VERDI: Ismaele★ (*Nabucco*). Also HENZE: Wilhelm (*Junge Lord*). **World premieres:** DE KRUYF: Magistrate (*Spinoza*) Amsterdam/Hague 1971; KOX: James Vane (*Dorian Gray*) Amsterdam 1974. **Res:** Weegbreestr 76, Soert, Holland.

BLISS, ANTHONY ADDISON. American. Exec Dir, Metropolitan Opera, Lincoln Center, New York, NY 10023. In charge of administrative matters. Also Mem, Bd of Dir, Metropolitan Opera Assn New York 1949- . Born 19 Apr 1913, New York. Wife Sally Brayley, occupation form dancer, Dir Joffrey II Ballet Co. Six children. Studied: Harvard Univ, Cambridge, BA 1936; Univ of Virginia Law School, Charlotteville, LLB 1940. Previous occupations: lawyer, mem of Milbank, Tweed, Hadley & McCloy. Form positions, primarily administrative: Pres, Metropolitan Opera Assn 1956-67; Chmn of the Bd, City Center Joffrey Ballet New York 1970- ; Dir, Lincoln Center, New York 1961-67. Started with present company 1949 & on Bd of Dir; in present position since 1974. Initiated major policy changes including: as president initiated planning and actual move to L.C. in 1966 and expansion of season to full employment. Mem of music and dance panels, Ntl Endowment for the Arts, Chmn of the Ntl Corp Fund for Dance, Dir of NY Foundation of the Arts, form mem Ntl Council on the Arts, NEA, and Bd of Ntl Opera Inst. **Res:** Oyster Bay, New York, USA.

BLUM, THOMAS; né Tamás Blum. Conductor of opera and symphony. Hungarian. Resident Cond, Opernhaus Zurich. Born 19 Jun 1927, Budapest. Wife Josepfa B, occupation chemical engineer. One child. Studied: Janos Ferencsik, Budapest; Cons de Lausanne, Paul Kletzki, Switzerland; incl piano. Plays the piano. Operatic training as repetiteur & asst cond at Budapest Opera 1945-49; Opera, Debrecen 1949-53. **Operatic debut:** *Così fan tutte* Budapest Opera 1950. Symphonic debut: Radio Orch, Budapest 1950. Awards: F Liszt Prize, 1956 and 1963, Hungarian State Gvnmt. Previous adm positions in opera: Mus Dir, Municipal Theater, Debrecen 1953-58.

Conducted with major companies in CAN: Toronto; HUN: Budapest; ITA: Bologna Comunale, Turin; SWI: Zurich. **Operas with these companies incl** BARTOK: *Bluebeard's Castle★;* BEETHOVEN: *Fidelio★;* BIZET: *Carmen, Djamileh;* BRITTEN: *Albert Herring, Midsummer Night;* CIMAROSA: *Matrimonio segreto;* DALLAPICCOLA: *Volo di notte;* DEBUSSY: *Enfant prodigue, Pelléas et Mélisande★;* DONIZETTI:

Campanello★, Don Pasquale, Elisir★, Rita★; ER-
KEL: *Bánk Bán;* FLOTOW: *Martha;*
GAY/Britten: *Beggar's Opera;* GLUCK: *Cadi
dupé, Iphigénie en Aulide, Orfeo ed Euridice;*
HANDEL: *Rodelinda;* IBERT: *Angélique;* KO-
DALY: *Háry János;* LEONCAVALLO: *Pa-
gliacci★;* MASCAGNI: *Cavalleria rusticana;*
MONTEVERDI: *Incoronazione di Poppea★;*
MOZART: *Così fan tutte, Don Giovanni, Entfüh-
rung aus dem Serail★, Nozze di Figaro★, Schau-
spieldirektor, Zauberflöte★;* MUSSORGSKY:
Boris Godunov; NICOLAI: *Lustigen Weiber;*
OFFENBACH: *Contes d'Hoffmann, Périchole,
Mariage aux lanternes;* PERGOLESI: *Serva pa-
drona;* PUCCINI: *Bohème★, Fanciulla del West,
Gianni Schicchi, Butterfly, Manon Lescaut, Suor
Angelica, Tabarro, Tosca★;* PURCELL: *Dido and
Aeneas;* RAVEL: *Enfant et les sortilèges★, Heure
espagnole★;* ROSSINI: *Barbiere di Siviglia★,
Cenerentola, Comte Ory, Signor Bruschino;*
SHOSTAKOVICH: *Katerina Ismailova;* SME-
TANA: *Bartered Bride;* STRAUSS, J:
Fledermaus; STRAVINSKY: *Oedipus Rex;*
TCHAIKOVSKY: *Eugene Onegin, Pique Dame;*
VERDI: *Aida, Ballo in maschera, Don Carlo,
Ernani, Falstaff★, Forza del destino, Otello, Simon
Boccanegra★, Traviata, Trovatore★;* WEBER:
Abu Hassan; WEILL: *Aufstieg und Fall der Stadt
Mahagonny, Dreigroschenoper‡.* **World pre-
mieres:** KOSMA: *Un amour électronique* Buda-
pest Opera 1966; PETROVICS: *C'est la guerre‡*
Budapest Opera 1962. Video—Hungarian TV:
various TV music-theater pieces. Teaches at Intl
Opernstudio, Zurich. **Res:** Im Walder 28, 8702
Zollikon, Switzerland.

BLYLODS, HILLEVI. Lyric soprano. Swedish.
Resident mem: Royal Opera, Stockholm. Married.
Studied: Royal Acad of Music, Stockholm; Prof
Arne Sunnergärder. **Debut:** Contessa (*Nozze di
Figaro*) Royal Opera Stockholm 1969.
Sang with major companies in SWE: Stockholm.
Roles with these companies incl: BIZET: Micaëla★
(*Carmen*); GLUCK: Euridice★; HANDEL: Mor-
gana★ (*Alcina*); MOZART: Fiordiligi★ (*Così fan
tutte*), Donna Anna★ (*Don Giovanni*), Contessa★
(*Nozze di Figaro*), Pamina★ (*Zauberflöte*);
STRAUSS, R: Sophie★ (*Rosenkavalier*). Gives re-
citals. Appears with symphony orchestra.

BOCCA, LAURA ANGELA. Dramatic mezzo-so-
prano & contralto. Italian. Born 21 Oct 1931,
Alessandria, Italy. Husband Luciano Scati. Stud-
ied: Consv di Parma, E Campogalliani, Ferrari
Siliotti. **Debut:** Maddalena (*Rigoletto*) Opera Co-
munale, Treviso 1966. Awards: First Prize Conc
di Bologna; Winner Conc di Mantua; First Prize
Studio of the Consv, Parma.
Sang with major companies in BEL: Brussels;
FRA: Paris; FR GER: Essen, Frankfurt, Ham-
burg, Kiel; ITA: Bologna, Genoa, Milan La Scala,
Naples, Parma, Trieste, Turin. **Roles with these
companies incl** BELLINI: Adalgisa (*Norma*);
DALLAPICCOLA: Circe★ (*Ulisse*); MASCA-
GNI: Beppe (*Amico Fritz*); PONCHIELLI: La
Cieca★ (*Gioconda*); PUCCINI: Suzuki (*But-
terfly*), Principessa (*Suor Angelica*); STRA-
VINSKY: Baba the Turk★ (*Rake's Progress*);
VERDI: Preziosilla★ (*Forza del destino*), Federica

(*Luisa Miller*). Also MASCAGNI: Zanetto★. **Res:**
V Righi 29, Alessandria, Italy.

BOCCACCINI, WALTER. Italian. Gen Coord &
Chief of Staff, Teatro Comunale/Maggio Musicale
Fiorentino, 15 V Solferino, Florence, Italy. In
charge of adm matters; is also stage dir/prod. Born
1 May 1927, Florence. Wife Maria Adelaide Ghi-
nozzi, occupation prof of literature. Two children.
Studied: Liceo Classico G Galilei, Florence. Pre-
vious positions, primarily theatrical: Stage Dir,
Teatro Verdi, Trieste; Teatro alla Scala, Milan;
Teatro Regio, Turin; Teatro Comunale, Bologna;
Teatro Comunale, Florence; and different fest in
Spain. Started with present company 1947 as stage
dir; in present position since 1967.

BOCZKOWSKI, WOJCIECH. Polish. Gen Dir,
Teatr Wielki/Grand Theater, Plac Dabrowskiego,
Lódz 1974- . In charge of adm matters & finances.
Born 26 May 1933, Dabrowa/Czarna. Wife, occu-
pation biologist. One child. Studied: Univ Lódz.
Background primarily administrative & theatrical.
World premieres at theaters under his manage-
ment: TWARDOWSKI: *Lord Jim* Lódz Grand
Theater 1975. Awards: Medal of 30th Anniv Pol-
ish Rep, Polish Gvnmt; Medal of Honor, City of
Lódz; Order of Polonia Restituta, Polish Gvnmt;
Cultural Medal of Activities, Polish Ministry of
Culture & Art. **Res:** Plac Wolnosci 5/11, Lódz,
Poland.

BODE, HANNELORE. Lyric & dramatic soprano.
German. Resident mem: Deutsche Oper am
Rhein, Düsseldorf; Staatsoper, Vienna.
Sang with major companies in AUS: Vienna
Staatsoper; FR GER: Bayreuth Fest, Düsseldorf-
Duisburg, Hamburg, Hannover, Mannheim, Stutt-
gart; et al. **Roles with these companies incl** BEET-
HOVEN: Leonore (*Fidelio*); MOZART:
Fiordiligi (*Così fan tutte*), Pamina (*Zauberflöte*);
WAGNER: Senta (*Fliegende Holländer*), Elsa
(*Lohengrin*), Eva (*Meistersinger*), Gutrune (*Göt-
terdämmerung*); WEBER: Agathe (*Freischütz*);
et al.

BOERLAGE, FRANS; né Theodoor Frans Boerlage. Stages/produces opera, theater & television
and is an actor and author. Dutch. Resident Stage
Dir, Opera Wkshp, Univ So California, Los Angeles. Born 1 Oct 1926, Bussum, Netherlands.
Single. Studied: Webber Douglas School of Singing
and Dram Art, London, incl voice. Operatic training as asst stage dir at Netherlands Opera, Amster-
dam 1953-57. **Operatic debut:** *Hänsel und Gretel*
Netherlands Opera 1955. Theater debut: TV play,
Hilversum, Holland 1963. Previous occupation:
law student. Awards: Margaret Rutherford Medal
for Acting, Webber Douglas School 1953. Pre-
vious adm positions in opera: Acting Art Dir,
Netherlands Opera summer 1960.
Directed/produced opera for major companies in
BRA: Rio de Janeiro; HOL: Amsterdam; POL:
Lodz; S AFR: Johannesburg; SPA: Barcelona;
USA: Fort Worth, Hawaii, Milwaukee Florentine,
Portland, San Antonio, Seattle. **Operas staged for
these companies incl** BARTOK: *Bluebeard's
Castle;* BIZET: *Carmen;* BRITTEN: *Rape of*

Lucretia; DONIZETTI: *Campanello★, Don Pasquale★, Elisir, Fille du régiment★, Lucia★;* FALLA: *Retablo de Maese Pedro;* FLOTOW: *Martha;* GLUCK: *Orfeo ed Euridice;* GOUNOD: *Faust★;* HUMPERDINCK: *Hänsel und Gretel;* LEONCAVALLO: *Pagliacci★;* MASCAGNI: *Cavalleria rusticana;* MASSENET: *Werther;* MENOTTI: *Amahl★, Medium, Old Maid and the Thief★, Telephone★;* MILHAUD: *Abandon d'Ariane★, Délivrance de Thésée★, Enlèvement d'Europe★;* MOZART: *Così fan tutte★, Entführung aus dem Serail★, Schauspieldirektor;* PERGOLESI: *Maestro di musica★;* PUCCINI: *Gianni Schicchi★, Butterfly★, Manon Lescaut★, Suor Angelica, Tabarro, Tosca★;* PURCELL: *Dido and Aeneas;* ROSSINI: *Barbiere di Siviglia, Italiana in Algeri;* STRAUSS, J: *Fledermaus;* STRAUSS, R: *Salome★;* VERDI: *Aida★, Aroldo/Stiffelio, Forza del destino, Otello★, Rigoletto★, Traviata★;* WAGNER: *Fliegende Holländer★, Meistersinger★;* WEBER: *Freischütz★;* WOLF-FERRARI: *Quattro rusteghi★, Segreto di Susanna.* Also de LEEUW: *Droom;* MOZART: *Bastien und Bastienne;* de BANFIELD: *Alissa;* BLACHER: *Flut;* TOCH: *Edgar and Emily★.* Operatic Video—AVRO TV, Hilversum: *Droom.* **Opera libretti:** RODRIGUES: *Visiteurs du soir.* Teaches at Univ So Cal, Los Angeles, Assoc Prof. Mgmt: SOF/USA.

BOESE, URSULA. Contralto. German. Resident mem: Staatsoper Hamburg. Born 27 Jul 1933, Hamburg. Divorced. Studied: Hochschule für Musik, Profs Wolf and Jacob, Hamburg. **Debut:** Norn (*Götterdämmerung*) Bayreuther Fest 1958. Awards: Kammersängerin, Hamburg 1969.

Sang with major companies in ARG: Buenos Aires; AUS: Graz, Vienna Staatsoper & Volksoper; FRA: Paris; FR GER: Bayreuth Fest, Berlin Deutsche Oper, Düsseldorf-Duisburg, Frankfurt, Hamburg, Stuttgart; ITA: Genoa, Milan La Scala, Rome Opera, Turin, Venice; POR: Lisbon; SPA: Barcelona; UK: Edinburgh Fest, London Royal; USA: Chicago. **Roles with these companies incl** DEBUSSY: Geneviève★ (*Pelléas et Mélisande*); GLUCK: Orfeo★; HANDEL: Cornelia★ (*Giulio Cesare*), Rinaldo, Hadwig (*Rodelinda*); MUSSORGSKY: Marfa (*Khovanshchina*); SMETANA: Hata (*Bartered Bride*); STRAUSS, R: Klytämnestra (*Elektra*); STRAVINSKY: Jocasta★ (*Oedipus Rex*); VERDI: Ulrica★ (*Ballo in maschera*); WAGNER: Magdalene★ (*Meistersinger*), Erda (*Rheingold★, Siegfried★*), Fricka (*Rheingold★, Walküre★*), Waltraute★ (*Götterdämmerung*). **World premieres:** GOEHR: Mrs Bradshaw (*Arden muss sterben*) Hamburg Staatsoper 1967. Recorded for: DG. Video—Hamburg TV: Magdalene (*Meistersinger*). Gives recitals. Appears with symphony orchestra. **Res:** Schönsberg 4, Hamburg 68, FR Ger.

BOGARD, CAROLE CHRISTINE; neé Geistweit. Lyric soprano. American. Born 25 Jun 1936, Cincinnati, O, USA. Husband Charles Paine Fisher, occupation electronic engineer. One child. Studied: Univ of California, Berkeley; Mrs Amy C McMurray. **Debut:** Despina (*Così fan tutte*) San Francisco Opera 1965.

Sang with major companies in BEL: Brussels; HOL: Amsterdam; USA: Boston, Cincinnati, San

Francisco Spring. **Roles with these companies incl** BIZET: Micaëla★ (*Carmen*); CAVALLI: Aldimira★‡ (*Erismena*); HANDEL: Dalinda‡ (*Ariodante*); MONTEVERDI: Poppea★‡; MOZART: Despina★ (*Così fan tutte*), Violante★ (*Finta giardiniera*), Susanna★ & Cherubino★ (*Nozze di Figaro*); RAMEAU: Aricie; STRAVINSKY: Anne Trulove★ (*Rake's Progress*); VERDI: Nannetta★ (*Falstaff*). Also HANDEL: Asteria (*Tamerlano*), Dorinda (*Orlando furioso*). **World premieres:** PASATIERI: (*Trial of Mary Lincoln*), NET Opera, New York 1972. Recorded for: RCA, Vox, Cambridge. Video/Film—NET TV: (*Trial of Mary Lincoln*). Gives recitals. Appears with symphony orchestra. **Res:** Boston, USA. Mgmt: DSP/USA.

BOGHOSSIAN, LEVON. Bass-baritone. Argentinean. Resident mem: Teatro Colón, Buenos Aires. Born 10 Oct 1930, Beirut, Lebanon. Single. Studied: Primavera de Sivieri, Enrique Sivieri, Buenos Aires. **Debut:** Prince Igor, Yerevan, USSR 1959.

Sang with major companies in ARG: Buenos Aires; BRA: Rio de Janeiro. **Roles with these companies incl** BIZET: Escamillo (*Carmen*); BORODIN: Prince Igor; GOUNOD: Méphistophélès (*Faust*); MUSSORGSKY: Boris Godunov, Dosifei (*Khovanshchina*); PUCCINI: Colline (*Bohème*), Michele (*Tabarro*), Scarpia (*Tosca*); VERDI: Zaccaria (*Nabucco*). Also BELLINI: Lorenzo (*Capuleti ed i Montecchi*). Gives recitals. Appears with symphony orchestra. **Res:** Uriburu 1253, Buenos Aires, Argentina.

BOGIANCKINO, MASSIMO. Italian. Art Dir, Ente autonomo Teatro Comunale/Maggio Musicale Fiorentino, 15 V Solferino, Florence, Italy since 1974. In charge of mus, dram & tech matters & art policy; is also a musicologist. Born 10 Nov 1922, Rome. Wife Judith Matthias. Studied: Univ Rome and Accad S Cecilia, Rome; PhD. Plays the piano. Previous occupations: prof at Carnegie Inst, Pittsburgh USA; Consv Rossini, Pesaro; Consv S Cecilia, Rome; Univ of Perugia. Form positions, primarily musical & theatrical: Dir, *Enciclopedia dello Spettacolo*, Italy; Art Dir, Accad Filarmonica, Rome; Teatro dell'Opera, Rome; Fest of Two Worlds, Spoleto; Accad S Cecilia, Rome; Teatro alla Scala, Milan. Awards: Great Cross, FR Ger. Mem of Accad Filarmonica Rome; SIMC, Italy; Italian Socy of Musicology. Board mem of: Consv S Cecilia, Rome; Amici della Musica, Perugia; Società Aquilana dei Concerti, L'Aquila; Teatro Lirico Sperimentale, Spoleto. **Res:** 15 Corso Italia, Florence, Italy.

BOHÁCOVÁ, MARTA: née Leinweberová. Lyric coloratura soprano. Czechoslovakian. Resident mem: National Theater Prague. Born 8 May 1936, Brno. Husband Josef Boháč, occupation musician, composer. Studied: Premysl Koci, Prague; Anna Korinska, Bratislava; Franz Schuch-Tovini, Vienna; Gina Cigna, Palermo, Italy. **Debut:** Königin der Nacht (*Zauberflöte*) National Theater Prague 1967. Previous occupations: teacher.

Sang with major companies in BUL: Sofia; CZE: Brno, Prague National & Smetana Theaters; FR GER: Wiesbaden; GER DR: Berlin Staatsoper; ITA: Parma; SWI: Basel; USSR: Moscow. **Roles with these companies incl** BIZET: Micaëla★ (*Car-*

men); DONIZETTI: Norina★ (*Don Pasquale*); GLUCK: Euridice; GOUNOD: Marguerite★ (*Faust*); HANDEL: Galatea; MOZART: Zerlina★ (*Don Giovanni*), Blondchen (*Entführung aus dem Serail*), Susanna★ (*Nozze di Figaro*), Königin der Nacht (*Zauberflöte*); OFFENBACH: Olympia (*Contes d'Hoffmann*); ORFF: Solo★ (*Carmina burana*); PUCCINI: Musetta★ (*Bohème*), Liù★ (*Turandot*); ROSSINI: Rosina★ (*Barbiere di Siviglia*); SMETANA: Carla★ (*Two Widows*); STRAUSS, R: Fiakermilli★ (*Arabella*); VERDI: Oscar★ (*Ballo in maschera*), Gilda★ (*Rigoletto*), Violetta★ (*Traviata*). Also FIBICH: Svatava (*Sárka*). **World premieres:** JIRASEK: Popova (*The Bear*) The Disk, Prague 1965. Recorded for: Panton, Supraphon. Video/Film: Marguerite (*Faust*); Katuska (*Devil's Wall*); Norina (*Don Pasquale*); Mirandolina; Rosina (*Barbiere di Siviglia*); Pamina (*Zauberflöte*); Nedda (*Pagliacci*). Gives recitals. Appears with symphony orchestra. Teaches voice. Coaches repertoire. On faculty of Consv Prague. **Res:** Ustavni 130, Prague, CSSR. Mgmt: PRG/CZE.

BOHANEC, MIRJANA. Lyric coloratura soprano. Yugoslavian. Resident mem: National Theater, Rijeka. Born Zagreb. Divorced. Studied: Prof N Pirnat, I Lhotka-Kalinski, Z Dundenac-Gavella. **Debut:** Solo (*Carmina burana*) 1967. Previous occupations: on editorial staff, station RTV, Zagreb. Awards: Conc Toulouse, France; V Lisinski Awd, Music Acad Zagreb. **Sang with major companies in** AUS: Vienna Volksoper; YUG: Dubrovnik, Zagreb, Belgrade. **Roles with these companies incl** DONIZETTI: Adina★ (*Elisir*); GAY/Britten: Lucy★ (*Beggar's Opera*); HUMPERDINCK: Gretel; LEONCAVALLO: Nedda (*Pagliacci*); MOZART: Zerlina (*Don Giovanni*), Blondchen★ (*Entführung aus dem Serail*), Susanna (*Nozze di Figaro*); PUCCINI: Musetta (*Bohème*); STRAUSS, J: Adele (*Fledermaus*); STRAUSS, R: Zdenka (*Arabella*); VERDI: Oscar★ (*Ballo in maschera*), Gilda (*Rigoletto*); WEBER: Aennchen (*Freischütz*). Video/Film: Lucy (*Beggar's Opera*). Gives recitals. Appears with symphony orchestra. Teaches voice. Coaches repertoire. On faculty of Acad of Music, Zagreb. **Res:** Gunduliceva 8, Zagreb, Yugoslavia. Mgmt: CDK/YUG.

BÖHM, KARL. Conductor of opera and symphony. Austrian. Österreichischer Generalmusikdirektor. Born 28 Aug 1894, Graz. Wife Thea. One son. Studied: Eusebius Mandyczewski; also piano. Operatic training as asst cond. **Operatic debut:** *Trompeter von Säkkingen* Graz 1917. Previous occupations: Ph D in Law, Univ of Graz. Awards: the only Austrian Generalmusikdirektor; hon mem Vienna Phil; hon citizen Salzburg and Vienna; Brahms Medal, Bruckner Medal; etc. Previous adm positions in opera: Dir, Darmstadt Opera 1927-31; Staatsoper Hamburg 1931-34; Dresden Opera 1934-38; Staatsoper Vienna 1943-45 and 1955-56.
Conducted with major companies in ARG: Buenos Aires; AUS: Graz, Salzburg Fest, Vienna Staatsoper; FRA: Aix-en-Provence Fest, Orange Fest, Paris; FR GER: Bayreuth Fest, Berlin Deutsche Oper, Darmstadt, Hamburg, Hannover, Munich Staatsoper; GER DR: Dresden; ITA: Milan La Scala, Naples; UK: London Royal; USA: Chicago, New York Met. **Operas with these companies incl** BEETHOVEN: *Fidelio*★‡; BERG: *Lulu*★‡, *Wozzeck*★‡; BIZET: *Carmen;* HANDEL: *Giulio Cesare;* LEONCAVALLO: *Pagliacci;* LORTZING: *Zar und Zimmermann;* MASCAGNI: *Cavalleria rusticana;* MOZART: *Così fan tutte*★‡, *Don Giovanni*★‡, *Entführung aus dem Serail*★‡, *Nozze di Figaro*★‡, *Zauberflöte*★‡; NICOLAI: *Lustigen Weiber;* STRAUSS, R: *Ariadne auf Naxos*★‡, *Capriccio*★‡, *Daphne*★‡, *Elektra*★‡, *Frau ohne Schatten*★‡, *Rosenkavalier*★‡, *Salome*★‡; VERDI: *Macbeth*‡, *Otello;* WAGNER: *Fliegende Holländer*★‡, *Lohengrin, Meistersinger, Rheingold*★‡, *Walküre*★‡, *Siegfried*★‡, *Götterdämmerung*★‡, *Tristan und Isolde*★‡; WEBER: *Freischütz*★‡. **World premieres:** STRAUSS, R: *Schweigsame Frau* Dresden Opera 1935. Recorded for BASF, Richmond, Angel, Epic, Urania, Philips, DG, Vox. Video—UNITEL: *Così fan tutte, Fledermaus.* Conducted major orch in Europe, USA/Canada, Cent/S America, Asia. Previous positions as Mus Dir with major orch: Vienna Phil; Berlin Phil. Mgmt: FLD/USA.

BÖHM, KARL-WALTER. Heldentenor. German. Resident mem: Nationaltheater, Mannheim; Gärtnerplatztheater, Munich. Born 6 Jun 1938, Nürnberg, Germany. Married. Two children. Studied: Prof Paul Mangold, Prof Lilo Mangold, Berlin. **Debut:** Radames (*Aida*) Aachen, FR Ger 1969-70. Previous occupations: insurance mgr.
Sang with major companies in ARG: Buenos Aires; AUS: Graz, Salzburg Fest, Vienna Staatsoper; FRA: Nancy; FR GER: Berlin Deutsche Oper, Cologne, Essen, Kiel, Mannheim, Munich Gärtnerplatz, Nürnberg, Saarbrücken; ROM: Bucharest; SPA: Barcelona; USA: Milwaukee Florentine, Portland. **Roles with these companies incl** d'ALBERT: Pedro★ (*Tiefland*); BEETHOVEN: Florestan★ (*Fidelio*); BIZET: Don José★ (*Carmen*); EGK: Christoph★ (*Verlobung in San Domingo*); GERSHWIN: Sportin' Life★ (*Porgy and Bess*); LEONCAVALLO: Canio★ (*Pagliacci*); PUCCINI: Cavaradossi★ (*Tosca*); ROSSINI: Arnold★ (*Guillaume Tell*); SMETANA: Hans (*Bartered Bride*); STRAUSS, R: Matteo★ (*Arabella*); TCHAIKOVSKY: Lenski★ (*Eugene Onegin*), Gherman★ (*Pique Dame*); VERDI: Radames★ (*Aida*), Don Carlo★, Otello★, Manrico★ (*Trovatore*); WAGNER: Erik★ (*Fliegende Holländer*), Lohengrin★, Walther★ (*Meistersinger*), Parsifal★, Rienzi★. Siegmund+ (*Walküre*), Siegfried (*Siegfried, Götterdämmerung*), Tristan★; WEBER: Max★ (*Freischütz*). Also LORTZING: Hugo★ (*Undine*). Gives recitals. Appears with symphony orchestra. Teaches voice. **Res:** Klenest 32, Munich, FR Ger.

BÖHME, KURT. Bass. German. Resident mem: Bayerische Staatsoper, Munich; Vienna Staatsoper. Born 5 May 1908, Dresden. Studied: Dresden Consv, Dr Kluge. **Debut:** Kaspar (*Freischütz*) Dresden Staatsoper 1930.
Sang with major companies in ARG: Buenos Aires; AUS: Salzburg Fest, Vienna Staatsoper; DEN: Copenhagen; FRA: Nice, Paris; GRE: Athens National; FR GER: Bayreuth Fest, Bielefeld, Munich Staatsoper & Gärtnerplatz; GER

DR: Dresden; HUN: Budapest; ITA: Florence Comunale, Milan La Scala, Naples, Rome Opera; MON: Monte Carlo; POR: Lisbon; SPA: Barcelona; SWE: Stockholm; SWI: Zurich; UK: London Royal; USA: New York Met, San Francisco Opera; et al. **Roles with these companies incl** LORTZING: Stadinger‡ (*Waffenschmied*); MOZART: Leporello‡ (*Don Giovanni*), Osmin‡ (*Entführung aus dem Serail*), Sarastro‡ (*Zauberflöte*); SMETANA: Kezal‡ (*Bartered Bride*); STRAUSS, R: Baron Ochs‡ (*Rosenkavalier*), Sir Morosus (*Schweigsame Frau*); WAGNER: König Heinrich‡ (*Lohengrin*), Pogner (*Meistersinger*), Fafner (*Rheingold‡, Siegfried‡*); et al. Also MOZART: Commendatore (*Don Giovanni*). **World premieres:** LIEBERMANN: (*Penelope*) 1954; EGK: (*Irische Legende*) 1955; both at Salzburg Fest. Recorded for: London, Urania, DG, Philips, Columbia, Ariola, HMV. Appears with symphony orchestra.

BOIREAU, GÉRARD. Stages/produces opera. Also designs stage-lighting and is a singer & actor. French. Gen Dir & Resident Stage Dir, Grand Théâtre de Bordeaux. Born 10 Jul 1919, Bordeaux. Wife Rolande Riffaud, occupation opera singer. One child. Studied: Consv National de Musique, Bordeaux, incl music, piano & voice. Operatic training as asst stage dir at Opéra d'Avignon 1965-70. **Operatic debut:** Grand Théâtre de Bordeaux 1970. Previous occupation: singer, comedian. Awards: Chevalier de l'Encouragement; Officier de l'Encouragement; Chevalier des Arts et Lettres; Adm de la Chambre Syndicate; Président de l'ADANA. Previous adm positions in opera: Comissaire Gen, Fest Musical de Bordeaux 1973; Opéra de Liège, Belgium 2 yrs; Dir, Opéra d'Avignon 1965-70; Grand Casino de Vichy, 5 yrs. **Directed/produced opera for major companies in** BEL: Brussels, Liège; CAN: Montreal/Quebec; FRA: Bordeaux, Lyon, Marseille, Nancy, Nice, Orange Fest, Paris, Rouen, Toulouse. **Operas staged for these companies incl** BECAUD: *Opéra d'Aran★;* BEETHOVEN: *Fidelio★†;* BERLIOZ: *Damnation de Faust★†;* BIZET: *Carmen★, Pêcheurs de perles;* DELIBES: *Lakmé;* DONIZETTI: *Don Pasquale★†, Elisir★†, Lucia;* GERSHWIN: *Porgy and Bess;* GIORDANO: *Andrea Chénier★;* GOUNOD: *Faust★†, Mireille, Roméo;* HALEVY: *Juive;* LECOCQ: *Fille de Madame Angot;* LEONCAVALLO: *Pagliacci;* MASCAGNI: *Cavalleria rusticana;* MASSENET: *Hérodiade, Manon, Werther;* MOZART: *Così fan tutte★†, Don Giovanni, Entführung aus dem Serail★†, Nozze di Figaro★†, Zauberflöte;* MUSSORGSKY: *Boris Godunov★†;* OFFENBACH: *Contes d'Hoffmann★†;* POULENC: *Dialogues des Carmélites;* PUCCINI: *Bohème★†, Gianni Schicchi, Butterfly, Manon Lescaut★, Suor Angelica, Tabarro, Tosca★, Turandot★†;* RAVEL: *Heure espagnole;* ROSSINI: *Barbiere di Siviglia★;* STRAUSS, J: *Fledermaus★;* STRAUSS, R: *Rosenkavalier★†;* VERDI: *Aida★†, Ballo in maschera★, Don Carlo★, Forza del destino, Nabucco★†, Rigoletto, Traviata, Trovatore★;* WAGNER: *Lohengrin, Tannhäuser.* Also BRITTEN: *Little Sweep†;* DUCASSE: *Orphée.* **Operatic world premieres:** DAMASE: *Eurydice* Opéra de Bordeaux 1972. **Res:** Bordeaux, France.

BOJAR, JERZY. Polish. Tech Dir, Teatr Wielki/Grand Theater, Moliera St 2 d12, Warsaw. In charge of tech matters. Born 26 Nov 1933, Warsaw. Wife Zubelewicz, occupation prof of music. One child. Studied: electronics eng, Politech School, Warsaw. Previous positions, primarily theatrical: Inst of Theater Projects 1956-60; Opera House, Lódz 1956-65; tech consultant: Opera House Bydgoszcz 1970-75; Opera House Poznan 1973-75: Opera House Krakow 1973-75; Opera House Gdansk 1974-75. Started with present company 1960 as elct inspector, in present position since 1970. World premieres at theaters during his employment: RUDZINSKI: *Peasants* Warsaw 1974. Awards: Silver Cross of Merit 1955, Gold Cross of Merit 1960, Badge of Merit for Cult Activity 1974. Mem of OISTT, Poland, Vice Pres of Polish dept; Projects Office, BPBO, Warsaw. **Res:** 00-076 Moliera 2/12, Warsaw.

BOKY, COLETTE; née Giroux. Coloratura soprano. Canadian. Resident mem: Metropolitan Opera, New York. Born 4 Jun 1935, Montreal. Single. One child. Studied: Consv de Musique et d'Art Dramatique de la Provence de Québec, Montreal. **Debut:** Königin der Nacht (*Zauberflöte*) Metropolitan Opera 1967. Previous occupations: modeling. Awards: Le Prix d'Europe, Acad de Musique de Québec; Conc Intl d'Exécution Musicale de Genève; Woman of the Year 1973, Gvnmt of Quebec.

Sang with major companies in AUS: Salzburg Fest, Vienna Volksoper; CAN: Montreal/Quebec, Ottawa, Toronto; FRA: Bordeaux, Paris; FR Ger: Munich Gärtnerplatz; SWI: Geneva; USA: Boston, Hartford Conn Opera, Memphis, Miami, New Orleans, New York Metropolitan Opera, Pittsburgh, San Francisco Opera. **Roles with these companies incl** ADAM: Madeleine (*Postillon de Lonjumeau*); BEETHOVEN: Marzelline (*Fidelio*); BIZET: Micaëla (*Carmen*); DELIBES: Lakmé; DONIZETTI: Norina (*Don Pasquale*), Adina (*Elisir*), Lucia★; GLUCK: Amor★ (*Orfeo ed Euridice*); GOUNOD: Marguerite★ (*Faust*), Baucis★ (*Philémon et Baucis*), Juliette; LORTZING: Baronin Freimann (*Wildschütz*), Marie (*Zar und Zimmermann*); MASSENET: Manon★, Sophie (*Werther*); MENOTTI: Lucy (*Telephone*); MOZART: Despina (*Così fan tutte*), Zerlina (*Don Giovanni*), Konstanze & Blondchen (*Entführung aus dem Serail*), Violante (*Finta giardiniera*), Pamina★ & Königin der Nacht★ (*Zauberflöte*); OFFENBACH: Olympia★ & Antonia & Giulietta (*Contes d'Hoffmann*), Périchole★; ORFF: Solo (*Carmina burana*); PUCCINI: Mimi & Musetta★ (*Bohème*); RAVEL: Concepcion (*Heure espagnole*); ROSSINI: Rosina★ (*Barbiere di Siviglia*), Giulia (*Scala di seta*); STRAUSS, R: Zerbinetta (*Ariadne auf Naxos*), Sophie (*Rosenkavalier*); STRAVINSKY: Rossignol; THOMAS: Philine (*Mignon*); VERDI: Oscar (*Ballo in maschera*), Gilda★ (*Rigoletto*), Violetta (*Traviata*); WEBER: Aennchen★ (*Freischütz*); WOLF-FERRARI: Lucieta★ (*Quattro rusteghi*). Recorded for: DG. Video/Film—CBC TV: Violetta (*Traviata*); Concepcion (*Heure espagnole*); Gilda (*Rigoletto*); Soprano (*Carmina burana*); Frau Fluth (*Lustigen Weiber*). Gives recitals. Appears with symphony orchestra. **Res:** 10819 rue Waverly, Montreal, Que, Canada. **Mgmt:** CST/UK; SAM/USA.

BOMHARD, MORITZ VON. Conductor of opera and symphony; composer; operatic stage director & designer of sets & costumes. American. Gen & Art Dir, cond, st dir & des, Kentucky Opera Assn, Louisville, KY, USA. Born 19 Jun 1908, Berlin. Wife Charme, occupation singer, voice teacher. Studied: Consv Leipzig; Juilliard Graduate School; Columbia Univ; incl piano, cello. Plays the cello. **Operatic debut:** *Così fan tutte* New York Lyric Stage 1948; as designer *Don Pasquale* N Y Lyric 1946; as dir *Nozze di Figaro* Kentucky Opera 1948. Symphonic debut: RIAS Orch, Berlin 1954. Previous occupations: studied law; paints. Awards: G Martinelli Awd, Bellarmine Coll; Hon PhD Ursuline Coll; Man of the Year, Downtown Salute of the Arts, Advert Club of Louisville.

Conducted with major companies in FR GER: Hamburg, Kassel; USA: Kentucky, Memphis, New York City Opera. **Operas conducted, directed & designed as indicated with these companies incl** BARBER: *Vanessa* d s/c; BIZET: *Carmen*★d s/c; BRITTEN: *Albert Herring* d, *Rape of Lucretia* d s/c; DONIZETTI: *Don Pasquale*★d s/c, *Elisir* d, *Lucia*; FLOYD: *Susannah*★d s; GLUCK: *Orfeo ed Euridice* d s/c; GOUNOD: *Faust*★d s/c, *Roméo et Juliette* d s/c; HOIBY: *Beatrice*; HUMPERDINCK: *Hänsel und Gretel* d s/c; JANACEK: *Jenufa*★d s, *Katya Kabanova*★d s; LEONCAVALLO: *Pagliacci* d; MASSENET: *Manon* d s; MENOTTI: *Amahl* d s, *Medium* d s/c, *Old Maid and the Thief* d s/c, *Telephone* d s/c; MONTEVERDI: *Combattimento di Tancredi* d s/c, *Incoronazione di Poppea* d s/c; MOZART: *Così fan tutte*★d s/c, *Don Giovanni* d s/c, *Entführung aus dem Serail*★d s/c, *Schauspieldirektor*, *Nozze di Figaro*★d s/c, *Zauberflöte* d s/c; MUSSORGSKY: *Boris Godunov*; NICOLAI: *Lustigen Weiber* d; OFFENBACH: *Contes d'Hoffmann* d; ORFF: *Carmina burana*★d, *Kluge* d s/c; PERGOLESI: *Serva padrona* d s/c; POULENC: *Dialogues des Carmélites* d s; PUCCINI: *Bohème*★d s/c, *Gianni Schicchi* d s/c, *Butterfly* d s/c, *Tabarro*★d s, *Tosca* s/c only, *Turandot* s/c; RAVEL: *Heure espagnole* d s/c; ROSSINI: *Barbiere di Siviglia*★d s/c; SMETANA: *Bartered Bride* d s/c; STRAUSS, J: *Fledermaus*★d s/c; STRAUSS, R: *Ariadne auf Naxos* d s/c, *Salome*★d; STRAVINSKY: *Oedipus Rex* d s/c; VERDI: *Aida*★d s/c, *Ballo in maschera* d s/c, *Macbeth* d s/c, *Otello*★d s, *Rigoletto* d s/c, *Traviata*★d s/c, *Trovatore* d s/c; WAGNER: *Fliegende Holländer*★d. **World premieres:** cond, dir & designed: ANTHEIL: *Wish* 1955; MOHAUPT: *Double Trouble* 1954; GLANVILLE-HICKS: *Transposed Heads* 1954; LIEBERMANN: *School for Wives* 1955; NABOKOV: *Holy Devil* 1958; HOIBY: *Beatrice* 1959; all in Louisville. Recorded for Louisville Orch Recds. Video/Film: *Beatrice*. Conducted major orch in Europe, USA/Canada. Teaches at Univ of Louisville. Res: 1725 Cherokee Terrace, Louisville, KY 40205, USA.

BONANOME, FRANCO. Lyric tenor. Italian. Born 24 Feb 1938, Rome. Studied: Mo Gavino A Canu, Liceo Artistico, Rome. **Debut:** Nemorino (*Elisir*) 1961.

Sang with major companies in FRA: Marseille; ITA: Naples, Palermo, Rome Opera & Caracalla; S AFR: Johannesburg; SPA: Barcelona, Majorca.

Roles with these companies incl BERG: Tambourmajor★ (*Wozzeck*); BIZET: Don José★ (*Carmen*); BOITO: Faust★ (*Mefistofele*); BRITTEN: Male Chorus★ (*Rape of Lucretia*); CILEA: Maurizio★ (*A. Lecouvreur*); CIMAROSA: Paolino (*Matrimonio segreto*); DONIZETTI: Ernesto★ (*Don Pasquale*), Nemorino★ (*Elisir*), Fernand (*Favorite*), Edgardo★ (*Lucia*); GOUNOD: Faust; MASCAGNI: Fritz★ (*Amico Fritz*); MASSENET: Des Grieux★ (*Manon*), Werther★; OFFENBACH: Hoffmann★; PONCHIELLI: Enzo★ (*Gioconda*); PUCCINI: Rodolfo★ (*Bohème*), Pinkerton★ (*Butterfly*), Des Grieux★ (*Manon Lescaut*), Cavaradossi★ (*Tosca*); ROSSINI: Almaviva (*Barbiere di Siviglia*), Don Ramiro (*Cenerentola*); STRAUSS, R: Ein Sänger (*Rosenkavalier*); VERDI: Riccardo★ (*Ballo in maschera*), Don Alvaro★ (*Forza del destino*), Ismaele★ (*Nabucco*), Duca di Mantova★ (*Rigoletto*), Alfredo★ (*Traviata*).

BONAVOLONTÀ, NINO GIOACCHINO. Conductor of opera and symphony; composer; operatic stage director. Italian. Art Dir & Resident Cond, Teatro di Tradizione/Ente Concerti, Sardinia. Born 4 Jun 1920, Rome. Wife Giuseppina. Three children. Studied: Consv S Cecilia, Petrassi, Rome; Mozarteum Salzburg, Zecchi, von Karajan; incl piano, organ and voice. Plays the piano. Operatic training as asst cond. **Operatic debut:** *Suor Angelica* & *Pagliacci* Florence 1957. Symphonic debut: Sinfonica di Roma 1945. Previous occupations: Dir, Consv of Music, Colombia 1951-57. Awards: Commendatore della Repubblica Italiana 1953.

Conducted with major companies in AUS: Salzburg Fest; BRA: Rio de Janeiro; BUL: Sofia; CZE: Brno; DEN: Copenhagen; FR GER: Berlin Deutsche Oper, Bielefeld, Dortmund, Düsseldorf-Duisburg, Essen, Karlsruhe, Saarbrücken; HOL: Amsterdam; ITA: Bologna, Milan La Scala, Naples, Palermo, Rome Opera & Caracalla, Turin; ROM: Bucharest; SWI: Geneva; USSR: Kiev, Leningrad Kirov, Moscow Stanislavski, Tbilisi. **Operas with these companies incl** BELLINI: *Norma;* BIZET: *Carmen;* CAVALIERI: *Rappresentazione;* CILEA: *A. Lecouvreur;* CIMAROSA: *Matrimonio segreto;* DONIZETTI: *Campanello, Don Pasquale, Elisir, Favorite, Lucia, Rita, Roberto Devereux;* GALUPPI: *Filosofo di campagna;* GIORDANO: *Andrea Chénier, Fedora;* HUMPERDINCK: *Hänsel und Gretel;* LEONCAVALLO: *Bohème★, Pagliacci;* MASCAGNI: *Amico Fritz★;* MENOTTI: *Amelia al ballo, Medium, Old Maid and the Thief★, Telephone;* PAISIELLO: *Barbiere di Siviglia;* PERGOLESI: *Maestro di musica, Serva padrona★;* PUCCINI: *Bohème, Gianni Schicchi, Butterfly★, Manon Lescaut, Rondine★, Suor Angelica, Tabarro, Tosca, Turandot;* ROSSINI: *Barbiere di Siviglia, Cambiale di matrimonio, Cenerentola, Italiana in Algeri;* VERDI: *Aida, Ballo in maschera, Don Carlo, Nabucco, Rigoletto, Simon Boccanegra, Traviata, Trovatore;* WOLF-FERRARI: *Segreto di Susanna★.* Also BETTARINI: *Ritorno;* GABRIEL: *Jura;* DONATI: *Corradino Losvevo†;* LANGELLA: *Assunta Spina†;* PETRASSI: *Cordovano.* Recorded for RAI, ORTF. Conducted major orch in Europe, Cent/S America. Previous positions as Mus Dir with major orch; Dir, Orch and Chorus, Ibagué & Manizales, Colombia 1951-57. Teaches at Consv di Musica S Cecilia, Rome. **Res:** V Muzio Clementi 70, Rome, Italy. Mgmt: IMR/FRA.

BONAZZI, ELAINE. Lyric coloratura mezzo-soprano. American. Born Endicott, NY, USA. Husband Jerome Carrington, occupation cellist, performer & teacher. One child. Studied: Eastman School of Music, Rochester, NY; Hunter College Opera Dept, New York; Aldo di Tullio. **Debut:** Meg Page (*Falstaff*) Santa Fe Opera 1959. Awards: Eastman School of Music, Distinguished Alumni Achiev Awd; Sullivan Fndt Grant.

Sang with major companies in CAN: Vancouver; ITA: Spoleto Fest; MEX: Mexico City; USA: Boston, Cincinnati, Dallas, Houston, New York City Opera, Pittsburgh, San Antonio, Santa Fe, Seattle, Washington DC; YUG: Belgrade. **Roles with these companies incl** AUBER: Pamela (*Fra Diavolo*); BERG: Gräfin Geschwitz★ (*Lulu*); BERNSTEIN: Dinah★ (*Trouble in Tahiti*); BIZET: Carmen; BRITTEN: Lucretia (*Rape of Lucretia*); CHARPENTIER: Mère★ (*Louise*); DEBUSSY: Geneviève★ (*Pelléas et Mélisande*); DONIZETTI: Marquise de Birkenfeld★ (*Fille du régiment*); GOUNOD: Siebel (*Faust*); HUMPERDINCK: Hänsel & Hexe★ (*Hänsel und Gretel*); MENOTTI: Secretary (*Consul*), Mme Flora (*Medium*), Miss Todd (*Old Maid and the Thief*); MOORE: Augusta Tabor (*Ballad of Baby Doe*); MOZART: Dorabella (*Così fan tutte*), Cherubino★ (*Nozze di Figaro*); PASATIERI: Mary Lincoln★ (*Trial of Mary Lincoln*); PUCCINI: Suzuki★ (*Butterfly*), Principessa★ (*Suor Angelica*), Frugola★ (*Tabarro*); STRAUSS, J: Prinz Orlovsky★ (*Fledermaus*); STRAUSS, R: Clairon (*Capriccio*), Herodias (*Salome*); STRAVINSKY: Mère (*Mavra*), Jocasta (*Oedipus Rex*), Baba the Turk (*Rake's Progress*); TCHAIKOVSKY: Olga (*Eugene Onegin*), Comtesse (*Pique Dame*); VERDI: Preziosilla (*Forza del destino*); WEILL: Leocadia Begbick (*Aufstieg und Fall der Stadt Mahagonny*). Also BARBER: Baroness (*Vanessa*); BLITZSTEIN: Regina; DONIZETTI: Smeton‡ (*Anna Bolena*); HINDEMITH: Frau Pick‡ (*Neues vom Tage*); MONTEVERDI: Messaggera★ (*Orfeo*), Arnalta★ (*Incoronazione di Poppea*); STEFFANI: Gismonda★‡ (*Tassilone*); PURCELL: Sorceress (*Dido & Aeneas*); ROSSINI: Ragonde★ (*Comte Ory*); OHANA: Phèdre★ (*Syllabaire pour Phèdre*). **World premieres:** ROREM: Christine (*Miss Julie*) New York City Opera 1965; VILLA LOBOS: La Vieja (*Yerma*) Santa Fe Opera 1971; CHAVEZ: Elissa (*El amor propiciado*) Opera Intl Mexico City 1963; RAUSCHER: Joan (*Joan of Arc at Rheims*) Cincinnati 1968; LaMONTAINE: Tebell (*Novellis, Novellis*) Opera Soc of Washington 1961. Recorded for: Columbia, Vanguard. Video — NET TV: Mary Lincoln; NBC TV: Spy (*Labyrinth*); ABC TV: Woman (*Final Ingredient*); Old One (*Thief and the Hangman*); Blind Woman (*Break of Day*). Gives recitals. Appears with symphony orchestra. Teaches voice. On faculty of Peabody Consv, Baltimore, MD. **Res:** New York, NY, USA. Mgmt: DSP/USA.

BONCOMPAGNI, ELIO. Conductor of opera and symphony. Italian. Resident Cond, Opéra National, Brussels. Born 8 May 1933, Caprese Michelangelo, Italy. Wife Vittoria Serafin. Studied: Tullio Serafin, Franco Ferrara; incl violin. **Operatic debut:** *Don Carlo* Teatro Comunale, Bologna 1962. Symphonic debut: RAI Orch, Milan 1961. Awards: Mitropoulos Prize; RAI Intl Compt; NRU Hilversum, Holland.

Conducted with major companies in BEL: Brussels; BRA: Rio de Janeiro; FRA: Paris; FR GER: Berlin Deutsche Oper, Bielefeld, Dortmund, Frankfurt; ITA: Bologna, Florence Maggio, Milan La Scala, Naples, Palermo, Rome Opera & Caracalla, Trieste, Turin, Venice; POL: Warsaw; POR: Lisbon; SPA: Barcelona; SWI: Zurich. **Operas with these companies incl** BIZET: *Carmen;* CILEA: *A. Lecouvreur;* DONIZETTI: *Caterina Cornaro, Elisir★, Lucia;* HUMPERDINCK: *Hänsel und Gretel;* LEONCAVALLO: *Pagliacci;* MOZART: *Don Giovanni★, Zauberflöte;* PERGOLESI: *Serva padrona;* PUCCINI: *Bohème★, Gianni Schicchi, Tabarro, Tosca, Turandot;* ROSSINI: *Barbiere di Siviglia, Cenerentola, Italiana in Algeri;* VERDI: *Aida★, Don Carlo★, Forza del destino, Rigoletto, Traviata, Trovatore★;* WAGNER: *Lohengrin.* Also ALFANO: *Risurrezione★;* LEONCAVALLO: *Zingari;* GIORDANO: *Cena delle beffe★;* DE BELLIS: *Maria Stuart★;* CASELLA: *Favola d'Orfeo★.* **World premieres:** LIVIABELLA: *Canto di Natale* Teatro Comunale, Bologna 1966. Conducted major orch in Europe. Teaches. **Res:** V Francesco Coletti 39, Rome, Italy. Mgmt: IMR/FRA.

BONDINO, RUGGERO; né Guerrino Bondino. Lirico spinto tenor. Italian. Born 14 Dec 1930, Pavia di Udine, Italy. Wife Diana Edge, occupation livestock breeder. Studied: Bruno Carmassi, Milan; Luigi Ricci, Rome. **Debut:** Faust, Teatro Nuovo, Milan 1957. Previous occupations: football player.

Sang with major companies in AUS: Graz, Vienna Staatsoper; BRA: Rio de Janeiro; CAN: Toronto; DEN: Copenhagen; FRA: Marseille, Nancy, Toulouse; FR GER: Cologne, Frankfurt, Hannover, Mannheim, Stuttgart, Wiesbaden; HOL: Amsterdam; ITA: Bologna, Florence Comunale, Genoa, Milan La Scala, Naples, Palermo, Parma, Rome Teatro dell'Opera & Caracalla, Trieste, Venice, Verona Arena; MON: Monte Carlo; NOR: Oslo; POR: Lisbon; SPA: Barcelona Liceo; SWI: Basel, Geneva; UK: Cardiff Welsh, Glasgow Scottish; YUG: Belgrade. **Roles with these companies incl** BELLINI: Elvino (*Sonnambula*); BERLIOZ: Faust‡ (*Damnation de Faust*); BOITO: Faust★ (*Mefistofele*); CILEA: Maurizio★ (*A. Lecouvreur*); DONIZETTI: Fernand (*Favorite*), Edgardo (*Lucia*), Roberto Devereux‡; FALLA: Paco (*Vida breve*); GIORDANO: Loris Ipanov★ (*Fedora*); GOUNOD: Faust; MENOTTI: Lover★ (*Amelia al ballo*); PUCCINI: Rodolfo★‡ (*Bohème*), Pinkerton★‡ (*Butterfly*), Ruggero★ (*Rondine*), Cavaradossi★‡ (*Tosca*); RIMSKY-KORSAKOV: Toucha (*Maid of Pskov*); VERDI: Foresto‡ (*Attila*), Riccardo★ (*Ballo in maschera*), Don Carlo★, Ernani‡, Ismaele (*Nabucco*), Duca di Mantova★ (*Rigoletto*), Gabriele★ (*Simon Boccanegra*), Alfredo★ (*Traviata*), Arrigo (*Vespri*); ZANDONAI: Paolo★‡ (*Francesca da Rimini*). Also TCHAIKOVSKY: Andrei (*Mazeppa*); VERDI: Macduff (*Macbeth*); ALFANO: Dimitri (*Risurrezione*); SMAREGLIA: Lorenzo (*Nozze*

59

istriane), Re Stelio (*Falena*); ROSSELLINI: Fritz (*Guerra*). **World premieres:** ROSSELLINI: Rodolfo (*Sguardo dal ponte*) Rome Opera 1961; PIZZETTI: Oreste (*Clitennestra*) La Scala, Milan 1965. Video—Germany, Japan, Brazil, Belgium: Rodolfo (*Bohème*); Cavaradossi (*Tosca*); Pinkerton (*Butterfly*). **Res:** Udine, Italy or PO Box 27, 6932 Breganzona, Switzerland.

BONHOMME, JEAN ROBERT. Lirico spinto tenor. Canadian. Born 14 Feb 1937, Ottawa, Ont, Canada. Wife Judith. Two daughters. Studied: Consv de PQ, Raoul Jobin, Montreal; Royal Consv of Music, George Lambert, Toronto; Univ of Toronto, Dr Herman Geiger-Torel; Ma Maria Carpi, Geneva; Mo Luigi Ricci, Rome. **Debut:** Pinkerton (*Butterfly*) Sadler's Wells, London 1965. Previous occupations: pre-med and law studies. Awards: First Prize CBC Talent Fest, 1964.

Sang with major companies in CAN: Montreal/Quebec, Ottawa, Toronto, Vancouver; FRA: Marseille, Paris; HOL: Amsterdam; HUN: Budapest; MON: Monte Carlo; S AFR: Johannesburg; UK: London Royal & English National; USA: Hartford, Houston, New Orleans, Pittsburgh, Santa Fe. **Roles with these companies incl** BERLIOZ: Bénédict, Aeneas★ (*Troyens*); BIZET: Don José★ (*Carmen*); FALLA: Paco (*Vida breve*); GLUCK: Pylade★ (*Iphigénie en Tauride*); GOUNOD: Faust★; MASCAGNI: Turiddu★ (*Cavalleria rusticana*); MASSENET: Jean le Baptiste★ (*Hérodiade*), Des Grieux (*Manon*); MILHAUD: Matelot (*Pauvre matelot*); PUCCINI: Rodolfo (*Bohème*), Pinkerton (*Butterfly*), Luigi★ (*Tabarro*), Cavaradossi★ (*Tosca*); STRAUSS, R: Ein Sänger (*Rosenkavalier*); VERDI: Radames (*Aida*), Riccardo (*Ballo in maschera*), Don Carlo★, Alfredo (*Traviata*), Arrigo (*Vespri*); WAGNER: Erik★ (*Fliegende Holländer*). Recorded for: EMI, London. Gives recitals. **Res:** 20 Redenda Cres, Ottawa, Canada. Mgmt: GOR/UK; SAM/USA.

BONISOLLI, FRANCO. Lyric tenor. Italian. Resident mem: Staatsoper, Vienna. Born Rovereto, Italy. Wife Sally. **Debut:** Ruggero (*Rondine*) Teatro Lirico Sperimentale, Spoleto.

Sang with major companies in AUS: Vienna Staatsoper; FRA: Bordeaux, Lyon, Toulouse; HOL: Amsterdam; ITA: Milan La Scala, Rome Opera, Spoleto Fest, Turin; SPA: Barcelona; UK: Glasgow Scottish; USA: Dallas, New York Met, Philadelphia Lyric, San Antonio, San Francisco Opera; et al. **Roles with these companies incl** BERLIOZ: Benvenuto Cellini; DONIZETTI: Nemorino (*Elisir*); GOUNOD: Faust; MASCAGNI: Fritz (*Amico Fritz*); MASSENET: Des Grieux (*Manon*); MENOTTI: Michele (*Saint of Bleecker Street*); PUCCINI: Rodolfo (*Bohème*), Pinkerton (*Butterfly*); ROSSINI: Almaviva (*Barbiere di Siviglia*), Otello; VERDI: Don Alvaro (*Forza del destino*), Duca di Mantova (*Rigoletto*), Alfredo (*Traviata*); et al. Also ROSSINI: Giacomo (*Donna del lago*), Cleomene (*Assedio di Corinto*); CHERUBINI: Anacréon. **World premieres:** ROTA: Aladino (*Lampada di Aladino*) Naples 1968; MANNINO: (*Luisella*) Palermo 1969. Video/Film: Alfredo (*Traviata*).

BONYNGE, RICHARD. Conductor of opera; researches and edits opera scores. Australian. Resident Cond, Metropolitan Opera, New York; Art Dir, Vancouver Opera Co, Canada. Also Music Dir designate, Australian Opera, Sydney 1976-Born 29 Sep 1930, Sydney. Wife Joan Sutherland, occupation opera singer. One son. Studied: Sydney Consv of Music, Lindley Evans; Herber Fryer, London; incl piano. Plays the piano. **Operatic debut:** *Faust* Vancouver Opera 1963. Previous occupations: concert pianist.

Conducted with major companies in ARG: Buenos Aires; AUSTRL: Sydney; AUS: Vienna Staatsoper; CAN: Vancouver; FRA: Paris; FR GER: Hamburg; HOL: Amsterdam; ITA: Florence Maggio & Comunale, Milan La Scala; POR: Lisbon; UK: Edinburgh Fest, London Royal & English National; USA: Boston, Chicago, Hartford, Houston, Miami, New York Met, Philadelphia Lyric, San Diego, San Francisco Opera, Seattle; et al. **Operas with these companies incl** BELLINI: *Beatrice di Tenda‡, Norma‡, Puritani‡, Sonnambula‡*; DELIBES: *Lakmé*; DONIZETTI: *Elisir‡, Favorite‡, Fille du régiment‡, Lucia‡, Lucrezia Borgia, Maria Stuarda‡*; GLUCK: *Orfeo ed Euridice*; GOUNOD: *Faust‡*; HANDEL: *Alcina‡, Giulio Cesare, Rodelinda*; MASSENET: *Esclarmonde*; MEYERBEER: *Huguenots‡*; MOZART: *Don Giovanni‡, Nozze di Figaro*; OFFENBACH: *Contes d'Hoffmann‡*; ROSSINI: *Barbiere di Siviglia, Semiramide‡*; STRAUSS, J: *Fledermaus*; VERDI: *Rigoletto‡, Traviata, Trovatore*; et al. Also MASSENET: *Thérèse*; HAYDN: *Orfeo ed Euridice*. Recorded for London, RCA, Decca. Video/Film: *Barbiere, Fille du régiment, Périchole, Mignon, Rigoletto, Traviata, Lucia, Faust*; spec series *Who's Afraid of Opera?* Conducted major orch in Europe, USA/Canada, Austrl. **Res:** Montreux, Switzerland. Mgmt: COL/USA.

BOOTH, PHILIP SAFFERY EVANS. Bass. American. Resident mem: Metropolitan Opera, New York. Born 6 May 1942, Washington, DC. Wife Sandra Bush, occupation opera singer. One child. Studied: Eastman School of Music, Julius Huehn, Rochester, NY; Todd Duncan, Washington, DC; Daniel Ferro, New York. **Debut:** King of Scotland (*Ariodante*) Kennedy Center opening, Washington, DC 1971. Previous occupations: soloist, US Army chorus. Awards: Met Op Ntl Counc Aud, Gramma Fisher Awd; Kansas City Lyric Awd 1970; Ntl Op Inst Awd 1972-73.

Sang with major companies in USA: Cincinnati, Houston, Lake George, New York Met, San Diego, San Francisco & Spring Opera. **Roles with these companies incl** HANDEL: King of Scotland★ (*Ariodante*); MOZART: Osmin★ (*Entführung aus dem Serail*); MUSSORGSKY: Pimen★ (*Boris Godunov*); PUCCINI: Colline★ (*Bohème*); ROSSINI: Don Basilio★ (*Barbiere di Siviglia*); VERDI: Ramfis★ (*Aida*); WAGNER: Fasolt★ (*Rheingold*), Fafner (*Rheingold★, Siegfried★*). Also POUND: (*Testament de Villon*)‡. **World premieres:** MOLLICONE: Stranger (*Young Goodman Brown*) Lake George Fest (wkshp) 1970. Recorded for: Fantasy Records. Gives recitals. Appears with symphony orchestra. **Res:** Leonia, NJ, USA. Mgmt: CAM/USA.

BORDÁS, GYÖRGY. Bass-baritone. Hungarian. Resident mem: Hungarian State Opera, Budapest.

Born 30 Jun 1938, Budapest. Wife Dr Mária Lukács, occupation dentist. Studied: Consv of Music, Anna Renée, Szeged, Hungary; F Liszt Music Acad, Prof Endre Rösler, Prof Dr Jenö Sipos, Budapest. **Debut:** Ben (*Telephone*) Hungarian State Opera, Budapest 1964. Previous occupations: trumpeter in symph orch.

Sang with major companies in HUN: Budapest. **Roles with these companies incl** BEETHOVEN: Don Pizarro (*Fidelio*); BIZET: Escamillo★ (*Carmen*); BRITTEN: Bottom (*Midsummer Night*); DONIZETTI: Don Pistacchio (*Campanello*), Don Pasquale, Dulcamara (*Elisir*), Enrico (*Lucia*); HANDEL: Garibald (*Rodelinda*); KODALY: Háry János★; LEONCAVALLO: Tonio★ (*Pagliacci*); MASCAGNI: Alfio (*Cavalleria rusticana*); MOZART: Guglielmo (*Così fan tutte*), Leporello (*Don Giovanni*), Figaro★ (*Nozze di Figaro*), Papageno★ (*Zauberflöte*); PERGOLESI: Uberto★ (*Serva padrona*); PUCCINI: Gianni Schicchi★, Sharpless (*Butterfly*), Lescaut★ (*Manon Lescaut*); ROSSINI: Dott Bartolo (*Barbiere di Siviglia*), Dandini (*Cenerentola*); VERDI: Amonasro (*Aida*), Fra Melitone‡ (*Forza del destino*); WAGNER: Beckmesser★ (*Meistersinger*), Alberich (*Rheingold★, Götterdämmerung★*). Also ERKEL: Tiborc (*Bánk Bán*). Recorded for: Hungaroton. Video/Film: (*The Woman and the Devil*). Gives recitals. Appears with symphony orchestra. Teaches voice. Coaches repertoire. **Res:** Luther utca 4-6, Budapest 1087, Hungary.

BORGONOVO, OTELLO. Lyric baritone. Italian. Born 19 Jun 1928, Genoa, Italy. Wife Silvana Zanolli, occup op singer, soprano. Studied: Riccardo Stracciari, Domenico Malatesta, Tomaso Jappelli, and Scuola del Teatro alla Scala. **Debut:** Germont (*Traviata*) Teatro Castello Sforza, Milan 1953. Previous occupations: chemical asst. Awards: Puccini Gold Medal, Opera Comp of Bombay, India; Puccini Silver Medal, Teatro Treviso.

Sang with major companies in ARG: Buenos Aires; AUSTRL: Sydney; AUS: Salzburg Fest; BEL: Brussels; CAN: Montreal/Quebec; FRA: Marseille, Nancy, Nice, Paris; FR GER: Bielefeld, Berlin, Bonn, Cologne, Darmstadt, Dortmund, Düsseldorf, Essen, Frankfurt, Hamburg, Hannover, Karlsruhe, Kassel, Mannheim, Munich Staatsoper, Nürnberg; ITA: Bologna, Florence Comunale, Genoa, Milan La Scala, Naples, Palermo, Parma, Rome, Trieste, Turin, Venice, Verona Arena; MON: Monte Carlo; POL: Warsaw; POR: Lisbon; SPA: Barcelona, Las Palmas Fest; SWI: Geneva, Zurich; UK: Cardiff Welsh, Edinburgh Fest, Glasgow Scottish. **Roles with these companies incl** ADAM DE LA HALLE: Chevalier (*Robin et Marion*); BIZET: Escamillo (*Carmen*), Zurga (*Pêcheurs de perles*); BUSONI: Matteo (*Arlecchino*); CILEA: Michonnet (*A. Lecouvreur*); CIMAROSA: Geronimo (*Matrimonio segreto*); DALLAPICCOLA: Prigioniero, Riviere & Robineau (*Volo di notte*), Job★; DONIZETTI: Dott Malatesta (*Don Pasquale*), Belcore (*Elisir*), Alfonse‡ (*Favorite*), Enrico (*Lucia*), Gasparo★ (*Rita*); GIORDANO: De Siriex (*Fedora*); LEONCAVALLO: Tonio (*Pagliacci*); MASCAGNI: Rabbi David (*Amico Fritz*), Alfio (*Cavalleria rusticana*); MASSENET: Lescaut (*Manon*), Athanaël (*Thaïs*), Albert (*Werther*); MENOTTI:

Husband (*Amelia al ballo*); MONTEVERDI: Orfeo; MOZART: Guglielmo (*Così fan tutte*), Leporello★ (*Don Giovanni*), Nardo★ (*Finta giardiniera*), Conte Almaviva (*Nozze di Figaro*), Papageno (*Zauberflöte*); PAISIELLO: Bartolo (*Barbiere di Siviglia*); PERGOLESI: Marcaniello (*Frate 'nnamorato*), Uberto (*Serva padrona*); PUCCINI: Marcello★ (*Bohème*), Jack Rance★ (*Fanciulla del West*), Gianni Schicchi, Sharpless (*Butterfly*), Lescaut (*Manon Lescaut*), Michele (*Tabarro*), Scarpia (*Tosca*); ROSSINI: Figaro & Dott Bartolo★ (*Barbiere di Siviglia*), Slook (*Cambiale di matrimonio*), Dandini (*Cenerentola*), Gaudenzio (*Signor Bruschino*); STRAVINSKY: Creon (*Oedipus Rex*); VERDI: Renato (*Ballo in maschera*), Ford (*Falstaff*), Fra Melitone (*Forza del destino*), Iago (*Otello*), Rigoletto,· Conte di Luna (*Trovatore*); WAGNER: Telramund★ (*Lohengrin*); WOLF-FERRARI: Conte Gil (*Segreto di Susanna*). **World premieres:** NAPOLI: Barone (*Barone avaro*) Teatro San Carlo, Naples 1970; ROTA: Emilio (*Cappello di paglia di Firenze*) Teatro Massimo, Palermo 1955; VIOZZI: Lamadonnin (*Elisabetta*) Teatro Verdi, Trieste 1971; CHAILLY: Giandomenico (*Procedura penale*) Teatro Festival, Como 1959; Mayer (*Vassilievic*) Teatro Comunale, Genoa 1967. Recorded for: Columbia, Cetra, Philips, Fonit, Angelicum, Tecniphon. Video/Film: (*Adriana Lecouvreur*), (*Geloso schernito*), (*Cappello di paglia*), (*Speziale*), (*Maestro di cappella*). Gives recitals. Appears with symphony orchestra. **Res:** V J Kennedy 7, Cologno Monzese/Milan, Italy.

BORISOVA, GALINA ILINICHNA. Dramatic mezzo-soprano. Russian. Resident mem: Bolshoi Theater, Moscow. Born 22 Apr 1941, Moscow. Husband Makarov-Miranov, occupation engineer. Studied: Moscow State Consv, Prof F S Petrova; Olga Borisova; Nemirovich-Danchenko. **Debut:** Otrok (*Invisible City of Kitezh*) Bolshoi Theater.

Sang with major companies in BUL: Sofia; HUN: Budapest; USSR: Moscow Bolshoi. **Roles with these companies incl** BIZET: Carmen★; BORODIN: Kontchakovna (*Prince Igor*); BRITTEN: Hermia & Hippolita (*Midsummer Night*); GLINKA: Naina‡ & Ratmir★ (*Ruslan and Ludmilla*); GLUCK: Orfeo; GOUNOD: Siebel (*Faust*); MOZART: Cherubino (*Nozze di Figaro*); MUSSORGSKY: Marina★ (*Boris Godunov*), Marfa★ (*Khovanshchina*); PROKOFIEV: Blanche★ (*Gambler*), Helene★ (*War and Peace*); PUCCINI: Suzuki‡ (*Butterfly*), Badessa & Principessa (*Suor Angelica*); RIMSKY-KORSAKOV: Hanna (*May Night*), Ljuba (*Sadko*), Lyoubacha★ (*Tsar's Bride*); TCHAIKOVSKY: Olga (*Eugene Onegin*), Comtesse‡ (*Pique Dame*); VERDI: Amneris★ (*Aida*), Ulrica (*Ballo in maschera*), Eboli★ (*Don Carlo*), Azucena★ (*Trovatore*). Recorded for: Melodiya. TV — Pauline (*Pique Dame*), Hippolita (*Midsummer Night*). Gives recitals. Appears with symphony orchestra. **Res:** 4a, kv 77 ul Chernyakhovskogo, Moscow, USSR. Mgmt: GOS/USSR.

BORKH, INGE; née Simon. Dramatic soprano. Swiss. Born 26 May 1921, Mannheim, Germany. Husband Kmsg Alexander Welitsch, occupation singer. Studied: Mo Moratti, Milan; Mrs Simon (mother); Alexander Welitsch (husband). **Debut:**

Pamina (*Zauberflöte*) Stadttheater Lucerne, Switzerland 1941. Previous occupations: actress, 2 yrs. Awards: Bayerische Kammersängerin, Bavarian Senate 1963; Reinhardt Ring 1973; Grand Prix du Disque 1961.

Sang with major companies in ARG: Buenos Aires; AUS: Salzburg Fest, Vienna Staatsoper; BEL: Brussels; BRA: Rio de Janeiro; FRA: Bordeaux, Lyon, Nice, Paris, Strasbourg, Toulouse; GRE: Athens Fest; FR GER: Bayreuth Fest, Berlin Deutsche Oper, Bielefeld, Cologne, Frankfurt, Hamburg, Hannover, Munich Staatsoper, Saarbrücken, Stuttgart, Wiesbaden; ITA: Florence Maggio, Milan La Scala, Naples, Palermo, Rome Opera & Caracalla, Trieste, Turin, Venice; MON: Monte Carlo; POR: Lisbon; ROM: Bucharest; SPA: Barcelona; SWE: Stockholm; SWI: Basel, Geneva, Zurich; UK: Edinburgh Fest, London Royal; USA: Chicago, Cincinnati, Houston, New Orleans, New York Met, San Francisco Opera, Washington DC. **Roles with these companies incl** BARTOK: Judith (*Bluebeard's Castle*); BEETHOVEN: Leonore (*Fidelio*); BERG: Marie (*Wozzeck*); BRITTEN: Elizabeth (*Gloriana*); CATALANI: Wally; CHERUBINI: Medea; DVORAK: Kate (*Devil and Kate*); GIORDANO: Maddalena (*Andrea Chénier*); GLUCK: Alceste, Iphigénie (*Iphigénie en Aulide*); GOUNOD: Marguerite (*Faust*); JANACEK: Jenufa; MASCAGNI: Santuzza (*Cavalleria rusticana*); MENOTTI: Magda Sorel (*Consul*); MEYERBEER: Valentine (*Huguenots*); MOZART: Donna Anna (*Don Giovanni*), Contessa (*Nozze di Figaro*), Pamina (*Zauberflöte*); OFFENBACH: Giulietta (*Contes d'Hoffmann*); ORFF: Antigonae; PUCCINI: Tosca, Turandot; SHOSTAKOVICH: Katerina Ismailova; SMETANA: Marie (*Bartered Bride*); STRAUSS, R: Helena (*Aegyptische Helena*), Komponist (*Ariadne auf Naxos*), Elektra, Salome; VERDI: Aida, Amelia (*Ballo in maschera*), Leonora (*Forza del destino*), Lady Macbeth, Leonora (*Trovatore*); WAGNER: Senta (*Fliegende Holländer*), Elsa (*Lohengrin*), Sieglinde (*Walküre*), Brünnhilde (*Siegfried*); WEBER: Rezia (*Oberon*); WEINBERGER: Dorota (*Schwanda*). Also STRAUSS, R: Färberin (*Frau ohne Schatten*); RESPIGHI: (*Fiamma*); WEBER: Eglantine (*Euryanthe*). **World premieres:** EGK: Cathleen (*Irische Legende*) Salzburg Fest 1955; TALMA: Alkeste (*Alkestiade*) Oper Frankfurt 1962; TAL: Queen (*Ashmedai*) Staatsoper Hamburg 1971. Recorded for: DG, Decca. **Res:** CH 9405 Wienacht, Switzerland.

BORSÓ, UMBERTO. Dramatic tenor. Italian. Born 3 Apr 1923, La Spezia, Italy. Married. Studied: Wera Amerighi Rutili, Melchiorre Luise. **Debut:** Don Alvaro (*Forza del destino*) Teatro Sperimentale, Spoleto 1952. Previous occupations: accountant.

Sang with major companies in AUSTRL: Sydney; AUS: Salzburg Fest, Vienna Staatsoper; BEL: Brussels; FIN: Helsinki; FRA: Bordeaux, Marseille; GRE: Athens National; FR GER: Berlin Deutsche Oper, Cologne, Frankfurt, Hamburg, Mannheim, Wiesbaden; GER DR: Berlin Staatsoper; HOL: Amsterdam; HUN: Budapest; ITA: Bologna, Florence Maggio & Comunale, Genoa, Milan La Scala, Naples, Palermo, Parma, Rome Opera & Caracalla, Trieste, Turin, Venice, Verona

Arena; MEX: Mexico City; NOR: Oslo; POR: Lisbon; SPA: Barcelona; SWI: Zurich; UK: London Royal; USSR: Moscow Bolshoi; USA: Boston, Hartford, Miami, New Orleans, New York Met, Philadelphia Grand & Lyric, Pittsburgh; YUG: Zagreb, Belgrade. **Roles with these companies incl** BELLINI: Pollione★ (*Norma*), Gualtiero (*Pirata*); BIZET: Don José★ (*Carmen*); CATALANI: Giuseppe Hagenbach (*Wally*); CILEA: Maurizio (*A. Lecouvreur*); DONIZETTI: Edgardo★ (*Lucia*); GIORDANO: Andrea Chénier★, Loris Ipanov (*Fedora*); GOUNOD: Roméo★; LEONCAVALLO: Canio★ (*Pagliacci*); MASCAGNI: Turiddu★ (*Cavalleria rusticana*); PONCHIELLI: Enzo★ (*Gioconda*); PUCCINI: Rodolfo (*Bohème*), Dick Johnson★ (*Fanciulla del West*), Pinkerton (*Butterfly*), Des Grieux★ (*Manon Lescaut*), Cavaradossi★ (*Tosca*), Calaf★ (*Turandot*); ROSSINI: Arnold (*Guillaume Tell*), Aménophis (*Moïse*); SAINT-SAENS: Samson★; VERDI: Radames★ (*Aida*), Riccardo★ (*Ballo in maschera*), Don Carlo★, Ernani, Don Alvaro★ (*Forza del destino*), Otello★, Duca di Mantova (*Rigoletto*), Gabriele (*Simon Boccanegra*), Alfredo (*Traviata*), Manrico★ (*Trovatore*); WAGNER: Lohengrin, Rienzi. Also RESPIGHI: Enrico (*Campana sommersa*); MASCAGNI: Piccolo Marat, Osaka (*Iris*), Flammen (*Lodoletta*); ROCCA: Imar (*Monte Ivnor*). **World premieres:** CANONICA: Giasone (*Medea*) Opera Rome 1953; SULEK: Ferdinando (*Tempest*) Narodno Kazaliste, Zagreb, Yugoslavia 1969. Recorded for: Remington. Teaches voice. **Res:** Rome, Italy. Mgmt: LLF/USA.

BOSABALIAN, LUISA ANAÏS; née Yeghiayan. Spinto. French. Born 24 Mar 1936, Marseille, France. Single. Studied: Mo Ruffo, Mo Perrazzi, Mo Ferrari, Milan. **Debut:** Micaëla (*Carmen*) Théâtre Royal, Brussels 1962. Awards: Mem Légion d'Honneur, France; First Prize Queen Elisabeth Compt, Brussels; Prize Compt for Verdi Voices, Busseto, Italy; Silver Medal for Young Singers, Reggio Emilia, Italy.

Sang with major companies in AUS: Vienna Staatsoper; BEL: Brussels; BRA: Rio de Janeiro; CZE: Prague Smetana; DEN: Copenhagen; FRA: Aix-en-Provence Fest, Bordeaux, Lyon, Marseille, Nancy, Nice, Paris, Strasbourg; FR GER: Berlin Deutsche Oper, Bonn, Cologne, Düsseldorf-Duisburg, Frankfurt, Hamburg, Munich Staatsoper, Saarbrücken, Stuttgart; HOL: Amsterdam; ITA: Bologna, Florence Comunale, Genoa, Milan La Scala, Palermo, Trieste; NOR: Oslo; POR: Lisbon; SWE: Drottningholm Fest, Stockholm, SWI: Zurich; UK: Edinburgh Fest, Glasgow Scottish Opera Co, Glyndebourne Festival, London Royal Opera. **Roles with these companies incl** BIZET: Micaëla (*Carmen*); GOUNOD: Marguerite (*Faust*); JANACEK: Jenufa★; MOZART: Donna Anna★ & Donna Elvira★ (*Don Giovanni*), Contessa★ (*Nozze di Figaro*); OFFENBACH: Antonia★ & Giulietta★ (*Contes d'Hoffmann*); PUCCINI: Mimi★ (*Bohème*), Cio-Cio-San★ (*Butterfly*), Manon Lescaut, Liù★ (*Turandot*); RAMEAU: Phèdre★ (*Hippolyte et Aricie*); ROSSINI: Mathilde (*Guillaume Tell*); VERDI: Amelia★ (*Ballo in maschera*), Alice Ford★ (*Falstaff*), Desdemona★ (*Otello*), Leonora★ (*Trovatore*), Elena★ (*Vespri*). Gives recitals. Appears with symphony orchestra. **Res:** Leostr 99, 4 Düsseldorf 11, FR Ger. **Mgmt:** GOR/UK.

BOSQUET, THIERRY F. Scenic and costume designer for opera, theater & film. Is a stage director; also a painter & fashion designer. Belgian. Born 4 May 1937, Brussels. Single. Studied: Ecole Ntl Supérieur d'Architecture et des Arts Décoratifs, Hermann Classon, Brussels. **Operatic debut:** Théâtre Royal de la Monnaie, Brussels 1957. Theater debut: Théâtre Volant, Brussels 1955.

Designed for major companies in BEL: Brussels, Liège; FRA: Lyon, Paris; FR GER: Cologne, Munich Staatsoper; HOL: Amsterdam; ITA: Palermo, Rome Opera; UK: Scottish. **Operas designed for these companies incl** BIZET: *Carmen;* DEBUSSY: *Pelléas et Mélisande★;* DONIZETTI: *Don Pasquale★;* GIORDANO: *Andrea Chénier;* HUMPERDINCK: *Hänsel und Gretel;* MARTINU: *Comedy on the Bridge;* MASSENET: *Manon;* MONTEVERDI: *Favola d'Orfeo, Incoronazione di Poppea;* MOZART: *Così fan tutte★, Don Giovanni★, Entführung aus dem Serail★, Nozze di Figaro★, Zauberflöte★;* RABAUD: *Mârouf;* RAVEL: *Heure espagnole;* ROSSINI: *Barbiere di Siviglia, Comte Ory;* STRAUSS, J: *Fledermaus;* STRAUSS, R: *Arabella, Ariadne auf Naxos, Frau ohne Schatten★, Rosenkavalier★, Salome★;* VERDI: *Aida★, Ballo in maschera★, Don Carlo★, Otello★, Rigoletto★, Traviata★, Trovatore★.* Also RAMEAU: *Platée.* Exhibitions of stage designs & paintings Exposition Intl Brussels 1958; Foyer of the Théâtre Royal de la Monnaie, Brussels 1973. **Res:** rue de Percke 161, B 1180 Brussels, Belgium.

BOTEZ, MICHAELA CRISTINA. Mezzo-soprano & contralto. Romanian. Resident mem: Romanian Opera, Bucharest. Born 22 Jun 1932, Piatra Neamt. Single. Studied: Consv, Prof Petre Stefanescu-Goanga, Bucharest; Profs Giulia Tess and Ricci, Milan. **Debut:** ENESCU: Sphinx (*Oedipe*) Romanian Opera 1957. Awards: Winner Vercelli, Italy 1957; Second Prize, Moscow 1957.

Sang with major companies in BUL: Sofia; ROM: Bucharest. **Roles with these companies incl** BRITTEN: Mrs Herring★ (*Albert Herring*); CILEA: Princesse de Bouillon‡ (*A. Lecouvreur*); PUCCINI: Suzuki★ (*Butterfly*); TCHAIKOVSKY: Comtesse (*Pique Dame*); VERDI: Amneris★ (*Aida*), Ulrica★ (*Ballo in maschera*), Eboli★ (*Don Carlo*), Dame Quickly (*Falstaff*), Azucena★ (*Trovatore*); WAGNER: Ortud★ (*Lohengrin*). Also on records only PONCHIELLI: Laura & La Cieca (*Gioconda*). **World premieres:** DUMITRESCU: Mother (*Girl with Carnations*) 1959; BRATU: Mother (*Right for Love*) 1975; both at Romanian Opera, Bucharest. Video/Film: Ulrica (*Ballo in maschera*). Gives recitals. Appears with symphony orchestra. **Res:** 2 Aviator Caranda Intr, Bucharest 7, Romania. **Mgmt:** RIA/ROM.

BOTTAZZO, PIETRO SILVANO. Light lyric tenor. Italian. Born 5 Dec 1934, Padua, Italy. Wife Lynne, occupation singer. One child. Studied: Consv B Marcello, Venice; Prof Cecilia Sacchetti. **Debut:** Wilhelm Meister (*Mignon*) Milan 1959.

Sang with major companies in AUS: Bregenz Fest, Salzburg Fest; DEN: Copenhagen; FRA: Aix-en-Provence Fest, Bordeaux; FR GER: Ber-

lin Deutsche Oper, Bonn, Cologne, Düsseldorf-Duisburg, Frankfurt, Munich Staatsoper, Wiesbaden; HOL: Amsterdam; ISR: Tel Aviv; ITA: Bologna, Florence Maggio & Comunale, Genoa, Milan La Scala, Naples, Palermo, Parma, Rome Opera, Spoleto Fest, Trieste, Venice; MON: Monte Carlo; NOR: Oslo; POR: Lisbon; SPA: Barcelona; SWE: Drottningholm Fest, Stockholm; SWI: Basel, Zurich; UK: Edinburgh Fest, Glyndebourne Fest; USA: Chicago, Miami, New York Met, Philadelphia Lyric, San Francisco Opera; YUG: Dubrovnik. **Roles with these companies incl** BELLINI: Orombello★ (*Beatrice di Tenda*), Lord Arthur★ (*Puritani*), Elvino★ (*Sonnambula*); BIZET: Nadir (*Pêcheurs de perles*); CIMAROSA: Paolino (*Matrimonio segreto*); DONIZETTI: Ernesto★ (*Don Pasquale*), Nemorino★ (*Elisir*), Tonio (*Fille du régiment*); HAYDN: Fileno (*Fedeltà premiata*); MOZART: Tito (*Clemenza di Tito*), Ferrando★ (*Così fan tutte*), Don Ottavio★ (*Don Giovanni*), Belmonte★ (*Entführung aus dem Serail*), Tamino★ (*Zauberflöte*); ORFF: Solo★ (*Carmina burana*); PAISIELLO: Almaviva★ (*Barbiere di Siviglia*); PUCCINI: Rinuccio★ (*Gianni Schicchi*); ROSSINI: Almaviva★ (*Barbiere di Siviglia*), Edward Milfort★ (*Cambiale di matrimonio*), Don Ramiro★ (*Cenerentola*), Comte Ory, Leicester (*Elisabetta Regina*), Gianetto★ (*Gazza ladra*), Lindoro (*Italiana in Algeri*), Rodrigo★ (*Otello*), Dorvil★ (*Scala di seta*), Idreno★ (*Semiramide*), Florville★ (*Signor Bruschino*), Narciso★ (*Turco in Italiana*); VERDI: Fenton (*Falstaff*); WAGNER: Adriano (*Rienzi*); WOLF-FERRARI: Florindo★ (*Donne curiose*), Filipeto★ (*Quattro rusteghi*). Also ROSSINI: Corradino (*Matilde di Shabran*), Rinaldo (*Armida*), (*Equivoco stravagante*), Roderigo (*Inganno felice*), Giacomo V (*Donna del lago*), (*Occasione fa il ladro*), (*Gazza ladra*). Gives recitals. Appears with symphony orchestra. Teaches voice. On faculty of Consv of Venice. **Res:** V Luzzati 14, Vicenza, Italy.

BOULEZ, PIERRE LOUIS JOSEPH. Conductor of opera and symphony; composer. French. Music Dir, New York Phil, USA, 1971-77. Born 26 Mar 1925, Montbrison/Loire, France. Single. Studied: Paris Consv with Messiaen; René Leibowitz; incl piano. **Operatic debut:** *Wozzeck* Paris Opéra 1963. Symphonic debut: Südwestfunk Orch, Baden-Baden, FR Ger 1958. Previous occupations: studied engineering. Previous adm positions: Mus Dir, Barrault/Renaud Theatre, Paris 1946-56; Founder & Dir, Domaine Musical Concerts 1953.

Conducted with major companies in FRA: Paris; FR GER: Bayreuth Fest, Frankfurt; UK: London Royal. **Operas with these companies incl** BERG: *Wozzeck‡;* DEBUSSY: *Pelléas et Mélisande‡;* WAGNER: *Parsifal‡, Tristan und Isolde.* Recorded for DG, CBS. Previous positions as Mus Dir with major orch: Mus Dir, BBC Orch, London 1971-75; Principal Cond, Cleveland Orch 1968-73. **Res:** Baden-Baden, FR Ger. **Mgmt:** IWL/UK.

BOWMAN, JAMES THOMAS. Countertenor. British. Born 6 Nov 1941, Oxford. Single. Studied: F E de Rentz; Lucie Manen. **Debut:** Oberon (*Midsummer Night's Dream*) Covent Garden Op 1967. Previous occupations: teacher.

Sang with major companies in BEL: Brussels;

DEN: Copenhagen; FRA: Orange Fest, Strasbourg; HOL: Amsterdam; POR: Lisbon; SWE: Drottningholm Fest; UK: Aldeburgh Fest, Edinburgh Fest, Glyndebourne Fest, London Royal & English National; USA: San Francisco Opera, Santa Fe, Washington DC. **Roles with these companies incl** CAVALLI: Lidio (*Egisto*); HANDEL: Ruggiero (*Alcina*), Polinesso (*Ariodante*), Giulio Cesare, Ottone, David‡ (*Saul*); ORFF: Solo (*Carmina burana*); RAMEAU: Pygmalion. **World premieres:** BRITTEN: Voice of Apollo (*Death in Venice*) Aldeburgh 1973; MAXWELL-DAVIES: Priest-Confessor (*Taverner*) London Royal 1974.

BOZIC, WOLFGANG. Conductor of opera and symphony. Austrian. Coordinator/Principal Cond, Vereinigte Bühnen, Graz, Austria. Also Resident Cond, Phil Orch, Graz. Born 9 Nov 1947, Graz. Divorced. Three children. Studied: Carlo Zecchi, Franco Ferrara; incl piano, clarinet and voice. Plays the piano. Operatic training as repetiteur at Graz Opera 1970-73; as asst cond 1972-75. **Operatic debut:** *Wildschütz* Graz Opera 1972. Symphonic debut: Pro Arte Orch, Graz 1973.
Conducted with major companies in AUS: Graz. **Operas with these companies incl** BIZET: *Carmen*★; BRITTEN: *Death in Venice*★; GOUNOD: *Faust*★; LORTZING: *Wildschütz*★; MOZART: *Clemenza di Tito*★, *Entführung aus dem Serail*★, *Nozze di Figaro*★; NICOLAI: *Lustigen Weiber*★; PONCHIELLI: *Gioconda*★; PUCCINI: *Gianni Schicchi*★, *Tabarro*★; ROSSINI: *Barbiere di Siviglia*★, *Gazza ladra*★. Also GEISSLER: *Zerbrochene Krug*. Teaches at Musikhochschule, Graz. **Res:** Schillerstr 29, Graz, Austria.

BRAITHWAITE, NICHOLAS. Conductor of opera and symphony. British. Born 26 Aug 1939, London. Single. Studied: Royal Acad, London; Bayreuth Master Classes; Akad für Musik, Vienna; incl trombone. Plays the trombone. **Operatic debut:** *Don Pasquale* Welsh Ntl Opera, Cardiff, UK 1966. Symphonic debut: BBC Scottish Symph Orch, Glasgow 1966. Awards: Associate, Royal Acad of Music, London.
Conducted with major companies in FR GER: Hamburg; UK: Welsh National, London Royal & English National. **Operas with these companies incl** BIZET: *Carmen*★; DONIZETTI: *Don Pasquale;* LEONCAVALLO: *Pagliacci*★; MASCAGNI: *Cavalleria rusticana*★; OFFENBACH: *Contes d'Hoffmann;* PENDERECKI: *Teufel von Loudun*★; PUCCINI: *Bohème*★, *Tosca;* VERDI: *Aida*★, *Ballo in maschera*★, *Don Carlo*★, *Nabucco*, *Traviata*★, *Trovatore*★; WAGNER: *Lohengrin*★, *Rheingold*★, *Walküre*★, *Siegfried*★, *Götterdämmerung*★, *Tannhäuser*★. Video—BBC TV: *Amahl*. Conducted major orch in Europe. **Res:** 42 Muswell Ave, N10, London, UK. Mgmt: SLA/UK.

BRAND, ROBERT. Lighting designer for opera, theater. American. Resident designer, San Francisco Opera. Born 9 Apr 1934, Stanford, CA, USA. Wife Joan, occupation secy. Two children. Studied: Stanford Univ, CA. **Operatic debut:** *Butterfly* Opera Co of Boston 1964. Theater debut: Off Broadway, New York 1957.
Designed for major companies in USA: Baltimore, Boston, Hartford, Houston, Miami, Milwau-

kee Florentine, Philadelphia Grand & Lyric, San Antonio, San Francisco Opera. **Operas designed for these companies incl** BELLINI: *Capuleti ed i Montecchi*, *Norma*★, *Pirata*, *Puritani;* BIZET: *Carmen*★; BRITTEN: *Albert Herring*, *Peter Grimes*★; DELIBES: *Lakmé;* DONIZETTI: *Don Pasquale*, *Elisir*★, *Favorite*★, *Fille du régiment*★, *Lucia*★, *Maria Stuarda*★; EINEM: *Besuch der alten Dame*★; FLOYD: *Susannah*★; GIORDANO: *Andrea Chénier*★; GOUNOD: *Faust*, *Roméo et Juliette;* LEONCAVALLO: *Pagliacci;* MASCAGNI: *Cavalleria rusticana*★; MASSENET: *Esclarmonde*★, *Manon*★, *Thaïs*★; MENOTTI: *Saint of Bleecker Street*★; MEYERBEER: *Africaine*★; MOZART: *Così fan tutte*★, *Don Giovanni*★, *Entführung aus dem Serail*★, *Schauspieldirektor*★, *Nozze di Figaro*★; MUSSORGSKY: *Boris Godunov;* OFFENBACH: *Contes d'Hoffmann;* PUCCINI: *Bohème*★, *Butterfly*★, *Manon Lescaut*★, *Rondine*★, *Tabarro*★, *Tosca*★; ROSSINI: *Barbiere di Siviglia;* SAINT-SAENS: *Samson et Dalila;* STRAUSS, J: *Fledermaus*★; STRAUSS, R: *Elektra*, *Salome;* VAUGHAN WILLIAMS: *Hugh the Drover*★; VERDI: *Aida*★, *Ballo in maschera*★, *Don Carlo*★, *Forza del destino*, *Luisa Miller*★, *Nabucco*, *Otello*★, *Rigoletto*★, *Traviata*★, *Trovatore*★; WAGNER: *Meistersinger*, *Parsifal*★, *Tannhäuser*, *Tristan und Isolde*★; WARD: *Crucible*★; WEILL: *Dreigroschenoper*★. Also ROSSELLINI: *Guerra*, *Sguardo dal ponte*. **Res:** 505 West End Ave, New York, NY 10024, USA.

BRANDT, BARBARA JEAN. Spinto. American. Resident mem: Minnesota Opera Co, Minneapolis. Born 18 Feb 1942, Battle Creek, MI, USA. Husband Dr H Wesley Balk, occupation Art Dir, Minnesota Opera Co. Studied: Michigan State Univ, Gean Greenwell, Ann Arbor; Oren Brown, New York; Thelma Halverson, Minneapolis, MI; Opera Acting Studio. **Debut:** Socrate, Minnesota Opera Co, Minneapolis 1966-67. Previous occupations: voice teacher, PS music teacher.
Sang with major companies in USA: Houston, Kansas City, Lake George, Minneapolis, San Francisco Spring. **Roles with these companies incl** BRITTEN: Lady Billows★ (*Albert Herring*); HAYDN: Clarissa (*Mondo della luna*); MILHAUD: Ariane (*Abandon d'Ariane*), Europe (*Enlèvement d'Europe*); MONTEVERDI: Clorinda★ (*Combattimento di Tancredi*), Poppea; MOZART: Fiordiligi (*Così fan tutte*), Donna Elvira★ (*Don Giovanni*), Contessa★ (*Nozze di Figaro*), Pamina★ (*Zauberflöte*); ORFF: Kluge; THOMSON: Saint Teresa I★ (*Four Saints in Three Acts*); WEILL: Jenny★ (*Dreigroschenoper*). **World premieres:** BRUNELLE: Lois (*Newest Opera in the World*) 1973-74; ARGENTO: Lady with a Hatbox (*Postcard from Morocco*) 1971-72; GESSNER: Margherita (*Faust Counter Faust*) 1970-71; MARSHALL: Sphinx (*Oedipus and the Sphinx*) 1969-70; BOESING: Birdwoman (*Wanderer*) 1969-70; SUSA: Ann Sexton (*Transformations*) 1972-73; all above with Minnesota Opera Co. Recorded for: Desto. Gives recitals. Appears with symphony orchestra. Teaches voice. **Res:** 2630 Irving Ave So, Minneapolis, MI, USA.

BRANISTEANU, HORIANA. Lyric soprano. Romanian. Resident mem: Deutsche Oper am Rhein,

Düsseldorf-Duisburg. Born 18 Oct 1942, Galati, Romania, Married. Studied: Consv Ciprian Porumbescu, Arta Florescu, Bucharest; Elsa Chioreanu, Constantin Stroescu. **Debut:** Violetta (*Traviata*) Bucharest 1972. Awards: First Prize, Intl Vocal Compt, 's Hertogenbosch, Holland; Second Prize, Intl Compt Francisco Vinas, Barcelona; Third Prize, Intl Compt Enrico Caruso, Rio de Janeiro, also prize for best voice, Brazil.

Sang with major companies in AUS: Graz; FR GER: Düsseldorf-Duisburg, Frankfurt; HOL: Amsterdam; ROM: Bucharest. **Roles with these companies incl** BELLINI: Giulietta★ (*Capuleti ed i Montecchi*); BIZET: Micaëla (*Carmen*); DONIZETTI: Lucia★, Rita★; FLOTOW: Lady Harriet★ (*Martha*); GLINKA: Antonida★ (*Life for the Tsar*); MONTEVERDI: Poppea★ (*Incoronazione di Poppea*); MOZART: Fiordiligi★ (*Così fan tutte*), Donna Anna★ (*Don Giovanni*), Konstanze★ (*Entführung aus dem Serail*), Pamina★ (*Zauberflöte*); PUCCINI: Mimi★ (*Bohème*); ROSSINI: Anaï★ (*Moïse*), Fiorilla★ (*Turco in Italia*); TCHAIKOVSKY: Tatiana★ (*Eugene Onegin*); VERDI: Amelia★ (*Ballo in maschera*), Desdemona★ (*Otello*), Gilda★ (*Rigoletto*), Violetta★ (*Traviata*), Leonora★ (*Trovatore*). Also WOLF-FERRARI: Mariana★ (*Quattro rusteghi*). Gives recitals. Appears with symphony orchestra. Teaches voice. Coaches repertoire. Mgmt: RIA/ROM; SLZ/FRG.

BRASAOLA, AULO. Italian. Dir of Prod, Teatro Regio, Piazza Castello 215, 10124 Turin 1972- . In charge of tech matters and is a designer. Born 29 Apr 1915, Casale Monferrato/Alessandria, Italy. Wife Maria Colombo. Two children. Studied: Istituto Industriale, sceno tecnico, Novara. Previous occupations: worked for theater scenery design and supply company. Background primarily theatrical. Mem of Istituto Moderno di Cultura Artistica. **Res:** V Lagrange 7, Turin, Italy.

BRAUN, GUSTL; née Augusta-Johanna Braun. Contralto. German. Resident mem: Bühnen der Landeshauptstadt Kiel. Born 31 Aug 1931, Beckstein, Baden, Germany. Divorced. One child. Studied: Hochschule für Musik und Theater, Mannheim; Prof Dürr, Hannover; Prof Dietger Jacob, Hamburg and Cologne. **Debut:** Frau Reich (*Lustigen Weiber*) Musiktheater, Gelsenkirchen 1961. Previous occupations: businesswoman.

Sang with major companies in FR GER: Bielefeld, Dortmund, Essen, Kiel. **Roles with these companies incl** AUBER: Pamela★ (*Fra Diavolo*); DEBUSSY: Geneviève★ (*Pelléas et Mélisande*); FLOTOW: Nancy (*Martha*); GLUCK: Orfeo★; HUMPERDINCK: Hexe★ (*Hänsel und Gretel*); LORTZING: Gräfin Eberbach★ (*Wildschütz*); MOZART: Dorabella (*Così fan tutte*); NICOLAI: Frau Reich (*Lustigen Weiber*); OFFENBACH: Nicklausse (*Contes d'Hoffmann*); PERGOLESI: Cardella★ (*Frate 'nnamorato*); PUCCINI: Suzuki★ (*Butterfly*); SMETANA: Hata★ (*Bartered Bride*); VERDI: Ulrica★ (*Ballo in maschera*), Dame Quickly (*Falstaff*), Preziosilla★ (*Forza del destino*); WAGNER: Erda★ (*Rheingold*), Fricka (*Walküre*). Also TCHAIKOVSKY: Ljuboff (*Mazeppa*). **World premieres:** AUBER/ HONOLKA: Duchess of Marlborough (*Glas Wasser*) Kiel Opera 1975. Gives recitals. Appears

with symphony orchestra. **Res:** Sylter Bogen 24, 23 Kiel, FR Ger. Mgmt: PAS/FRG.

BRAUN, VICTOR CONRAD. Dramatic baritone. Canadian. Resident mem: Bayerische Staatsoper, Munich.

Sang with major companies in AUS: Salzburg Fest; CAN: Toronto, Vancouver; FR GER: Cologne, Düsseldorf-Duisburg, Hamburg, Munich Staatsoper, Stuttgart; UK: London Royal; USA: San Francisco Spring Opera; et al. **Roles with these companies incl** BIZET: Escamillo (*Carmen*); DEBUSSY: Golaud (*Pelléas et Mélisande*); DONIZETTI: Enrico (*Lucia*); MOZART: Guglielmo (*Così fan tutte*), Don Giovanni, Conte Almaviva (*Nozze di Figaro*); PUCCINI: Marcello (*Bohème*), Sharpless (*Butterfly*), Lescaut (*Manon Lescaut*); SEARLE: Hamlet; STRAUSS, R: Graf (*Capriccio*); TCHAIKOVSKY: Eugene Onegin; VERDI: Renato (*Ballo in maschera*), Rodrigo (*Don Carlo*), Ford (*Falstaff*), Rigoletto, Germont (*Traviata*), Conte di Luna (*Trovatore*); WAGNER: Wolfram‡ (*Tannhäuser*); et al. Recorded for: Decca.

BRAZDA, JAN. Scenic and costume designer for opera, theater & ballet. Is a lighting designer; also a painter, sculptor, architect & stained glass artist. Swedish. Born 4 Dec 1917, Vatican City. Wife Luci. One son. Studied: Acad of Fine Arts, Prague. **Operatic debut:** Royal Opera House Covent Garden, London 1955. Theater debut: ballet at Royal Opera, Stockholm 1952. Awards: Grand Prize, Triennale, Milan; Prize, 27th Biennale, Venice; ITI Prize, Novy Sad 1974.

Designed for major companies in DEN: Copenhagen; FIN: Helsinki; FR GER: Munich Staatsoper; SWE: Stockholm; UK: London Royal; USSR: Moscow Bolshoi; USA: Chicago. **Operas designed for these companies incl** JANACEK: *Jenufa★*; PUCCINI: *Butterfly★*; SMETANA: *Bartered Bride★*; STRAUSS, R: *Elektra★*; WAGNER: *Parsifal★, Rheingold★, Walküre, Siegfried★, Götterdämmerung★*. **Operatic world premieres:** LUNDQUIST: *Sekund av Evighet* Royal Opera, Stockholm 1974. Exhibitions of stage designs, paintings & light projections var cities in Europe. Teaches at Inst of Dramatic Art, Stockholm. **Res:** Rindögatan 44, Stockholm, Sweden.

BRECKNOCK, JOHN LEIGHTON. Lyric tenor. British. Born 29 Nov 1937, Derby, UK. Wife Lore Lina Maria. One child. Studied: Birmingham School of Music, Fredric Sharp; Denis Dowling. **Debut:** Alfred (*Fledermaus*) Sadler's Wells Opera London 1966. Previous occupations: engineer.

Sang with major companies in CAN: Ottawa; UK: Glasgow Scottish, Glyndebourne Fest, London Royal & English National; USA: Houston. **Roles with these companies incl** DONIZETTI: Edgardo★ (*Lucia*), Gennaro★ (*Lucrezia Borgia*); MOZART: Ferrando★ (*Così fan tutte*), Don Ottavio★ (*Don Giovanni*), Belmonte★ (*Entführung aus dem Serail*), Tamino★ (*Zauberflöte*); PETRASSI: Inventore★ (*Morte dell'aria*); PROKOFIEV: Anatole★ (*War and Peace*); ROSSINI: Almaviva★ (*Barbiere di Siviglia*), Don Ramiro★ (*Cenerentola*), Comte Ory★; STRAUSS, J: Alfred (*Fledermaus*); VERDI: Fenton★ (*Falstaff*). Also HANDEL: Jupiter (*Semele*). **World premieres:** CROSSE: Vasco

(*Story of Vasco*) Sadler's Wells 1974. Video/Film: Alfredo (*Traviata*), Duca (*Rigoletto*), Edgardo (*Lucia*). Gives recitals. Appears with symphony orchestra. **Res:** 153 Prince George Ave, London N14, UK. Mgmt: MIN/UK; CMW/FRA; CSA/USA.

BREGNI, PAOLO. Scenic and costume designer for opera, theater, television; specl in sets. Is also a sculptor & architect. Italian. Born 11 Nov 1937, Milan. Wife Rosalba Leotta, occupation biologist. Two children. Studied: Accad di Scenografia, Milan; Prof Arch Tito B Varisco. Prof training: var theaters. **Operatic debut:** sets, cost, *Traviata* Teatro la Fenice, Venice 1966. Theater debut: Montevideo, Uruguay 1962. Previous occupation: studied architecture; potter, sculptor.

Designed for major companies in GER DR: Berlin Komische Oper; ITA: Florence Comunale, Genoa, Milan La Scala, Parma, Trieste, Turin, Venice; SPA: Barcelona; USA: San Francisco Opera. **Operas designed for these companies incl** DESSAU: *Verurteilung des Lukullus*⋆; GIORDANO: *Fedora;* GOUNOD: *Faust;* LEONCAVALLO: *Pagliacci;* MASCAGNI: *Cavalleria rusticana;* MASSENET: *Portrait de Manon*⋆; MONTEVERDI: *Combattimento di Tancredi, Incoronazione di Poppea*⋆; MOZART: *Nozze di Figaro*⋆; PUCCINI: *Bohème, Tabarro*⋆, *Tosca;* ROSSINI: *Barbiere di Siviglia;* VERDI: *Attila*⋆, *Traviata.* Also VLAD: *Storia di una mamma;* PETRASSI: *Cordovano;* CHABRIER: *Education manquée;* BUGAMELLI: *Fontana.* **Operatic world premieres:** WEBER/Maler: *Drei Pintos* Teatro Regio, Turin 1975. Exhibitions of stage designs & maquettes Palazzo delle Prigioni, Venice; Palazzo Reale, Naples 1969. **Res:** V Dandini 8, Rome, Italy.

BRENCKE, DIETER. Bass & character bass. German. Resident mem: Badische Staatsoper, Karlsruhe. Born 22 Feb 1938, Lengerich, Westfalen, FR Ger. Wife Ruth, occupation teacher. Studied: Folkwanghochschule, Clemens Kaiser-Breme, Essen; Konsv Dortmund, Rudolf Watzke. **Debut:** Leporello (*Don Giovanni*) Landestheater Coburg, FR Ger 1970.

Sang with major companies in FR GER: Karlsruhe. **Roles with these companies incl** CIMAROSA: Geronimo (*Matrimonio segreto*); DONIZETTI: Don Pasquale⋆; LORTZING: Baculus⋆ (*Wildschütz*), Van Bett⋆ (*Zar und Zimmermann*); MOZART: Leporello⋆ (*Don Giovanni*), Osmin⋆ (*Entführung aus dem Serail*), Sarastro⋆ (*Zauberflöte*); PERGOLESI: Uberto (*Serva padrona*); PUCCINI: Colline⋆ (*Bohème*); SMETANA: Kezal⋆ (*Bartered Bride*); VERDI: Fra Melitone⋆ (*Forza del destino*), Zaccaria⋆ (*Nabucco*); WAGNER: Daland⋆ (*Fliegende Holländer*), Fasolt⋆ (*Rheingold*), Hunding⋆ *Walküre*). Also BRAUNFELS: Ratefreund⋆ (*Vögel*); BRITTEN: Noye⋆ (*Noye's Fludde*); HAYDN: Melibeo⋆ (*Fedeltà premiata*). Gives recitals. Appears with symphony orchestra. **Res:** Fridtjof-Nansen-Str 3, 75 Karlsruhe 41, FR Ger. Mgmt: SLZ/FRG.

BRENDEL, WOLFGANG. Lyric baritone. German. Resident mem: Bayerische Staatsoper, Munich. Born Wiesbaden. **Debut:** Kaiserslautern.

Sang with major companies in AUS: Vienna Staatsoper; FR GER: Düsseldorf-Duisburg, Hamburg, Karlsruhe, Munich Staatsoper; USA: New York Met; et al. **Roles with these companies incl** DEBUSSY: Pelléas; MOZART: Don Giovanni, Conte Almaviva (*Nozze di Figaro*), Papageno (*Zauberflöte*); ROSSINI: Figaro (*Barbiere di Siviglia*); TCHAIKOVSKY: Eugene Onegin; VERDI: Rodrigo (*Don Carlo*); WAGNER: Wolfram (*Tannhäuser*); et al. Also BERLIOZ: Fieramosca (*Benvenuto Cellini*). Mgmt: CAM/USA.

BRENNEIS, GERD. Heldentenor. Austrian. Resident mem: Deutsche Oper, Berlin; Hamburg Staatsoper.

Sang with major companies in AUS: Vienna Staatsoper; CAN: Montreal/Quebec, Toronto; FR GER: Bayreuth Fest, Berlin Deutsche Oper, Düsseldorf-Duisburg, Essen, Hamburg, Stuttgart; et al. **Roles with these companies incl** BIZET: Don José (*Carmen*); GIORDANO: Andrea Chénier; MOZART: Idomeneo; PUCCINI: Des Grieux (*Manon Lescaut*); STRAUSS, R: Bacchus (*Ariadne auf Naxos*); VERDI: Manrico (*Trovatore*); WAGNER: Erik (*Fliegende Holländer*), Lohengrin, Walther (*Meistersinger*), Siegmund (*Walküre*), Walther v d Vogelweide (*Tannhäuser*); WEBER: Max (*Freischütz*); et al. Also VERDI: Macduff (*Macbeth*).

BRENNER, PETER; né Felsenstein. Stages/ produces opera. Austrian. Oberspielleiter der Oper & Resident Stage Dir, Theater der Freien Hansestadt Bremen, FR Ger since 1973. Born 8 May 1930, Freiburg, Germany. Wife Cató Brink. Studied: Staatsakad für Musik und darst Kunst, Vienna, incl music, violin, piano and voice. Operatic training as asst stage dir at Deutsche Oper am Rhein, Düsseldorf 1965-69, Salzburg Fest, Austria, 1966. **Operatic debut:** *Fledermaus* PACT, Johannesburg, S Afr 1966. Previous occupation: lawyer, actor, singer, head of opera school Staatliche Musikhochschule Freiburg. Awards: DL, Univ Vienna.

Directed/produced opera for major companies in FR GER: Bielefeld, Hamburg, Kassel, Mannheim, Munich Staatsoper, Wiesbaden, Wuppertal; S AFR: Johannesburg; USA: Portland. **Operas staged for these companies incl** BEETHOVEN: *Fidelio;* BIZET: *Carmen;* CIMAROSA: *Matrimonio segreto*⋆; DESSAU: *Verurteilung des Lukullus*⋆; GIORDANO: *Andrea Chénier*⋆; LORTZING: *Wildschütz*⋆, *Zar und Zimmermann;* MOZART: *Don Giovanni*⋆, *Idomeneo*⋆, *Zauberflöte;* PERGOLESI: *Frate 'nnamorato*⋆; PUCCINI: *Bohème*⋆, *Butterfly*⋆; ROSSINI: *Cenerentola*⋆, *Turco in Italia*⋆; STRAUSS, J: *Fledermaus;* STRAUSS, R: *Ariadne auf Naxos*⋆; STRAVINSKY: *Mavra*⋆, *Oedipus Rex*⋆; VERDI: *Aida, Don Carlo*⋆, *Simon Boccanegra;* WAGNER: *Tannhäuser*⋆, *Tristan und Isolde*⋆. **Operatic world premieres:** SANDLOFF: *Traum unter dem Galgen* Freiburg 1971. Previous leading positions with major theater companies: Oberspielleiter der Oper, Städtische Bühnen Freiburg, FR Ger 1969-73. **Opera libretti:** *Traum unter dem Galgen,* see prem. **Res:** Auf dem Esch 29, 2807 Achim-Uphusen, FR Ger.

BREUL, ELISABETH. Lyric soprano. German DR. Resident mem: Opernhaus, Leipzig; Staatsoper, Dresden. Born 25 Aug 1936, Gera, Germany. Husband Dr Karl-Heinz Viertel, occupation musicologist. One child. Studied: Marta-Luise Fink, Gera; Hochschule für Musik, Prof G Intrau, Dresden. **Debut:** Tatiana (*Eugene Onegin*) Opernhaus, Leipzig 1960. Awards: Kammersängerin 1965; Art Prize, Gvnmt Ger DR 1968; Critics' Prize Berlin Biennale 1969; Ntl Prize, Gvnmt Ger DR 1970; Critics' Prize *Berliner Zeitung* 1970; Robert Schumann Prize, City of Zwickau 1973.

Sang with major companies in BEL: Brussels; CZE: Brno; FR GER: Wiesbaden; GER DR: Berlin Komische Oper & Staatsoper, Dresden, Leipzig; HUN: Budapest; ITA: Genoa; POL: Lodz. **Roles with these companies incl** BEETHOVEN: Marzelline∗‡ (*Fidelio*); BIZET: Micaëla∗ (*Carmen*), Lauretta‡ (*Docteur Miracle*); DVORAK: Rusalka∗; GLUCK: Euridice; GOTOVAC: Djula (*Ero der Schelm*); GOUNOD: Marguerite (*Faust*); HANDEL: Galatea, Deidamia∗, Romilda∗ (*Xerxes*); HINDEMITH: Tochter des Cardillac; JANACEK: Malinka‡ (*Excursions of Mr Broucek*), Jenufa; MOZART: Fiordiligi∗ (*Così fan tutte*), Donna Anna∗ & Donna Elvira∗ (*Don Giovanni*), Violante (*Finta giardiniera*), Contessa∗ & Susanna∗ (*Nozze di Figaro*), Pamina∗ (*Zauberflöte*); OFFENBACH: Antonia∗ (*Contes d'Hoffmann*); PROKOFIEV: Pauline∗ (*Gambler*), Natasha (*War and Peace*); PUCCINI: Mimi∗ (*Bohème*), Cio-Cio-San∗ (*Butterfly*), Manon Lescaut∗, Tosca, Liù∗‡ (*Turandot*); PURCELL: Dido; SMETANA: Marie∗ (*Bartered Bride*); STRAUSS, R: Zdenka∗ (*Arabella*); TCHAIKOVSKY: Tatiana∗ (*Eugene Onegin*), Lisa (*Pique Dame*); VERDI: Desdemona∗ (*Otello*); WEBER: Agathe∗ (*Freischütz*). Video—TV of Ger DR: Titania (*Fairy Queen*). Gives recitals. Appears with symphony orchestra. Teaches voice. Mgmt: KDR/GDR.

BREWER, BRUCE. Lyric tenor. American. Born 12 Oct 1944, San Antonio, Texas, USA. Wife Joyce Castle, occupation opera singer, mezzo-soprano. Studied: Univ of Texas, Austin, Josephine Lucchese, San Antonio, TX; Richard Bonynge, bel canto interpr, London & New York; Nadia Boulanger, French song interpr, Paris; Rosalyn Tureck, Bach interpr, New York. **Debut:** Don Ottavio (*Don Giovanni*) San Antonio Opera 1970. Awards: prizewinner Conc Intl d'Art Vocal, Montreal 1967; NFMC Schlshp.

Sang with major companies in FRA: Aix-en-Provence Fest, Toulouse; FR GER: Berlin Deutsche Oper, Düsseldorf-Duisburg; ITA: Spoleto Fest; USA: Boston, San Antonio, San Francisco Opera, Washington DC. **Roles with these companies incl** BELLINI: Lord Arthur∗ (*Puritani*); DONIZETTI: Nemorino∗ (*Elisir*); GLUCK: Renaud∗ (*Armide*); MOZART: Ferrando∗ (*Così fan tutte*), Don Ottavio∗ (*Don Giovanni*), Belfiore (*Finta giardiniera*); ORFF: Solo∗ (*Carmina burana*); ROSSINI: Almaviva∗ (*Barbiere di Siviglia*), Don Ramiro∗ (*Cenerentola*), Rodrigo∗ (*Otello*). Also CAMPRA: Orfeo (*Carnaval de Venise*); STRAUSS, R: Ital Sänger (*Capriccio*); DONIZETTI: Roberto (*Torquato Tasso*). **World premieres:** KOHS: Robinson (*Amerika*) Western Opera Theater, San Francisco 1970. Recorded for: CBS, RCA, VOX. Video—

Eurovision: Orfeo (*Carnaval de Venise*). Gives recitals. Appears with symphony orchestra. Teaches voice. Coaches repertoire. **Res:** 3923 N 5 St, Arlington, VA, USA. Mgmt: GLZ/FRA.

BRILIOTH, HELGE A A. Heldentenor. Swedish. Resident mem: Royal Opera, Stockholm. Born 7 May 1931, Lund, Sweden. Wife Maj-Britt, occupation teacher. Five children. Studied: Prof Arne Sunnegardh, Stockholm & Salzburg; Accad di S Cecilia, Mo Giorgio Favaretto, Rome; Prof C Kaiser-Breme, Essen, FR Ger. **Debut:** PAISIELLO: Dott Bartolo (*Barbiere di Siviglia*) Drottningholm Court Theater 1959. Previous occupations: organist.

Sang with major companies in AUS: Salzburg Fest, Vienna Staatsoper; CAN: Montreal/Quebec; DEN: Copenhagen; FIN: Helsinki; FRA: Orange Fest, Paris, Toulouse; FR GER: Bayreuth Fest, Berlin Deutsche Oper, Bielefeld, Düsseldorf-Duisburg, Hannover, Munich Staatsoper, Nürnberg, Wiesbaden; GER DR: Berlin Staatsoper; HUN: Budapest; ITA: Milan La Scala, Rome Opera; POL: Warsaw; SPA: Barcelona; SWE: Drottningholm Fest, Stockholm; SWI: Basel; UK: Glyndebourne Fest, London Royal Opera; USA: New York Met, Pittsburgh, Washington DC. **Roles with these companies incl** BEETHOVEN: Florestan∗ (*Fidelio*); BERLIOZ: Faust∗ (*Damnation de Faust*); BIZET: Don José (*Carmen*); STRAUSS, R: Bacchus∗ (*Ariadne auf Naxos*), Aegisth∗ (*Elektra*), Kaiser (*Frau ohne Schatten*); VERDI: Radames (*Aida*), Otello; WAGNER: Lohengrin∗, Parsifal∗, Siegmund∗ (*Walküre*), Siegfried (*Siegfried∗, Götterdämmerung∗‡*), Tristan∗. Also CAVALLI: Scipio Africanus∗. Recorded for: DG. Gives recitals. Appears with symphony orchestra. Teaches voice. Coaches repertoire. **Res:** Odengatan 22, 11351 Stockholm, Sweden. Mgmt: DSP/USA.

BRITTON, DONALD. American. Business Mng, Lyric Opera of Chicago & The Opera School of Chicago, 20 No Wacker Dr, Chicago, IL 60606, USA since 1972. In charge of finances. Born 8 Oct 1937, Philadelphia, PA. Wife Susan Marchant, occupation writer. Two children. Studied: Haverford Coll, PA. Previous occupations: actor in films, TV & stage. Form positions, primarily administrative: Distr Mng, Trans-Lux Theatres, New York 1962-65; Mng Dir, Meadow Brook Theatre, Detroit, MI 1966-70; Exec Dir, UPSTAGE: Detroit Inc, 1971-72. **Res:** 232 E Walton Pl, Chicago, IL, USA.

BROCK, KARL. Dramatic tenor. American. Born 17 Jun 1930, Great Bend, KS, USA. Single. Studied: Paul Althouse, Alice Nichols coach, Rose Landver dramatics, New York. **Debut:** Tamino (*Zauberflöte*) Basel Opera 1957.

Sang with major companies in FR GER: Bonn, Essen, Hannover, Kassel, Wiesbaden; MON: Monte Carlo; SWI: Basel; USA: St Paul. **Roles with these companies incl** d'ALBERT: Pedro (*Tiefland*); BEETHOVEN: Florestan (*Fidelio*); BERG: Tambourmajor (*Wozzeck*); BIZET: Don José (*Carmen*); BRITTEN: Albert Herring, Male Chorus∗ (*Rape of Lucretia*), Peter Quint (*Turn of the Screw*); CORNELIUS: Nureddin (*Barbier von*

Bagdad); DONIZETTI: Ernesto (*Don Pasquale*); EGK: Christoph★ (*Verlobung in San Domingo*); HANDEL: Sextus (*Giulio Cesare*); LEONCAVALLO: Canio (*Pagliacci*); MENOTTI: Michele (*Saint of Bleecker Street*); MOZART: Ferrando (*Così fan tutte*), Don Ottavio (*Don Giovanni*), Belmonte & Pedrillo (*Entführung aus dem Serail*), Idomeneo, Tamino (*Zauberflöte*); NICOLAI: Fenton (*Lustigen Weiber*); OFFENBACH: Hoffmann; PERGOLESI: Lamberto (*Maestro di musica*); PUCCINI: Rodolfo (*Bohème*), Rinuccio (*Gianni Schicchi*), Pinkerton (*Butterfly*), Luigi (*Tabarro*); SMETANA: Hans (*Bartered Bride*); STRAUSS, R: Matteo (*Arabella*), Bacchus★ (*Ariadne auf Naxos*), Ein Sänger (*Rosenkavalier*); TCHAIKOVSKY: Lenski (*Eugene Onegin*); VERDI: Riccardo (*Ballo in maschera*), Fenton (*Falstaff*); WAGNER: Lohengrin. Also WARD: Judge Danforth & Rev Parris★ (*Crucible*); EGK: Der Revisor. Video–NBC TV: Grumio (*Taming of the Shrew*). Gives recitals. Teaches voice. Coaches repertoire. Also stages opera. On faculty of Univ of Wisconsin, Oshkosh, USA. **Res:** 416 E Irving Ave, Oshkosh, WI, USA.

BRONSON, MICHAEL. American. Technical and Business Adm, Metropolitan Opera, Lincoln Center, New York 10023, USA 1972- . In charge of tech and business matters. Born 23 Aug 1938, New York. Wife Doris, occupation teacher. Two children. Studied: City Coll of New York, NY. Previous occupations: Stage Mng & theater tech, summer theater and Off Broadway. Form positions, primarily theatrical: technician, Green Mansions Theatre, Warrensburg, NY 1952-57 and Prod Stage Mng 1957-61; Stage Mng, Metropolitan Opera Studio, New York 1961-63; Asst Tech Adm, Metropolitan Opera, NY 1963-72. Mem of OPERA America, & treasurer. **Res:** 40 W 77 St, New York, NY, USA.

BROOK, PETER. Stages/produces opera & theater; is also a composer. British. Born 21 Mar 1925, London. Wife Natasha Parry. Studied: Gresham School, Magdalen Coll Oxford, UK. Theater debut: The Torch Theatre, London 1943. Awards: CBE, Commander of the British Empire. Previous adm positions in opera: Dir of Prod, Covent Garden, London. **Directed/produced opera for major companies in** UK: London Royal; USA: New York Met; et al. **Operas staged with these companies incl** GOUNOD: *Faust;* MOZART: *Nozze di Figaro;* MUSSORGSKY: *Boris Godunov;* STRAUSS, R: *Salome;* TCHAIKOVSKY: *Eugene Onegin;* et al.

BROOKS, GARNET JAMES. Lyric tenor. Canadian. Resident mem: Opera Bern, Switzerland. Born 4 Sep 1936, London, Ont, Canada. Wife Delores, occupation nutritionist. Two children. Studied: Univ of Toronto; Merola Opera Training Prgr & Western Opera, San Francisco; Glyndebourne Opera, UK. **Debut:** Pinkerton (*Butterfly*) Canadian Opera Co, Toronto. **Sang with major companies in** CAN: Ottawa, Toronto; UK: Glyndebourne Fest. **Roles with these companies incl** BRITTEN: Albert Herring, Misael (*Burning Fiery Furnace*), Younger Son (*Prodigal Son*); DONIZETTI: Ernesto (*Don Pasquale*),

Nemorino (*Elisir*), Beppo (*Rita*); HANDEL: Acis, Xerxes; MAYR: Giasone (*Medea in Corinto*); MOZART: Ferrando (*Così fan tutte*), Don Ottavio (*Don Giovanni*), Belmonte (*Entführung aus dem Serail*), Tamino (*Zauberflöte*); PERGOLESI: Lamberto (*Maestro di musica*); PUCCINI: Rodolfo (*Bohème*), Rinuccio (*Gianni Schicchi*), Pinkerton (*Butterfly*); ROSSINI: Almaviva (*Barbiere di Siviglia*); STRAUSS, R: Ein Sänger (*Rosenkavalier*), Narraboth (*Salome*); TCHAIKOVSKY: Lenski (*Eugene Onegin*); VERDI: Alfredo (*Traviata*). Also MAYR: Ageus (*Medea in Corinto*). **World premieres:** WILSON: Everyman (*Summoning of Everyman*) Halifax, Canada 1973. Gives recitals. Appears with symphony orchestra. **Res:** Wiesenstr 16, 3072 Ostermundigen, Bern, Switzerland. Mgmt: DSP/USA.

BROOKS, PATRICIA ANNE. Lyric soprano. American. Resident mem: New York City Opera. Born 7 Nov, New York. Husband Theodore D Mann, occupation prod & dir Circle-in-the-Square Theatres, New York. Two sons. Studied: E Brooks (mother), Margaret Harshaw, USA; Daniel Ferro, Luigi Ricci, Rome. **Debut:** Musetta (*Bohème*) New York City Opera 1963. Previous occupations: actress, dancer, worked in musical comedy, folk singer. Awards: Rockefeller Fndt Study Grant.
Sang with major companies in USA: Chicago, Hartford, Houston, Lake George, Memphis, New Orleans, New York City Opera, Philadelphia Grand, Santa Fe. **Roles with these companies incl** BELLINI: Adalgisa (*Norma*); BERG: Lulu; DEBUSSY: Mélisande★; DONIZETTI: Norina (*Don Pasquale*), Adina (*Elisir*), Lucia★; GOUNOD: Marguerite★ (*Faust*); HENZE: Manon (*Boulevard Solitude*); LEONCAVALLO: Nedda★ (*Pagliacci*); MASSENET: Manon★; MOZART: Fiordiligi★ & Despina (*Così fan tutte*), Donna Elvira★ & Zerlina (*Don Giovanni*), Konstanze & Blondchen (*Entführung aus dem Serail*), Susanna (*Nozze di Figaro*); OFFENBACH: Olympia & Antonia★ (*Contes d'Hoffmann*); ORFF: Solo★ (*Carmina burana*); PUCCINI: Mimi★ & Musetta (*Bohème*), Lauretta★ (*Gianni Schicchi*), Lisette★ (*Rondine*); ROSSINI: Rosina (*Barbiere di Siviglia*); STRAUSS, J: Adele (*Fledermaus*); STRAUSS, R: Zerbinetta★ (*Ariadne auf Naxos*), Sophie (*Rosenkavalier*); STRAVINSKY: Rossignol; VERDI: Gilda★ (*Rigoletto*), Violetta★ (*Traviata*). **World premieres:** HOIBY: Governess (*Natalia Petrovna*) 1964; WARD: Abigail (*Crucible*) 1961, both New York City Opera. Recorded for: CRI. Gives recitals. Appears with symphony orchestra. **Res:** New York, NY, USA. Mgmt: CAM/USA.

BROWN, DEAN; né Dean Edgar Brown III. Scenic and costume designer for opera, theater; specl in costumes. American. Resident designer, Cincinnati Opera, O, and designer at Harlequin Dinner Theatre. Born 4 Sep 1940, Washington, DC. Single. Studied: Carnegie Inst of Tech (now Carnegie-Mellon Univ) Pittsburgh; New York Univ. **Operatic debut:** *Bohème* Syracuse Symph, NY 1965. Theater debut: White Barn Theatre, Irwin, PA 1963. Previous occupation: teacher.
Designed for major companies in USA: Cincinnati, Kentucky, Memphis, Omaha. **Operas designed**

for these companies incl BIZET: *Carmen;* GOU-
NOD: *Faust;* HUMPERDINCK: *Hänsel und
Gretel*;* MENOTTI: *Amelia al ballo;* MOZART:
Nozze di Figaro; OFFENBACH: *Contes
d'Hoffmann;* PUCCINI: *Bohème*, Gianni
Schicchi*, Butterfly, Suor Angelica*, Tabarro*,
Tosca;* ROSSINI: *Barbiere di Siviglia;* VERDI:
Otello, Traviata. **Res:** 260 E 10th St, New York,
USA.

BROWN, WILLIAM ALBERT. Lyric tenor. Amer-
ican. Born 29 Mar 1938, Jackson, MS, USA. Wife
Marian T, occupation music instructor. One child.
Studied: Indiana Univ, Charles Kullman, Paul
Matthen, Bloomington; Carolyn Long, Washing-
ton, DC; Peabody Consv, Alice Duschak, Balti-
more, USA. **Debut:** Rodolfo (*Bohème*) No Virginia
Opera Co 1962. Previous occupations: jazz
trumpeter. Awards: Sullivan Fndt Grant; *High
Fidelity* Magazine Awd; Outstanding Educators of
America Awd; Personalities of the South Awd.
   Sang with major companies in USA: Baltimore,
Jackson, Lake George, New York City Opera,
Washington DC. Roles with these companies incl
BRITTEN: Lysander* (*Midsummer Night*); BU-
SONI: Calaf (*Turandot*); DONIZETTI: Ernesto*
(*Don Pasquale*); GERSHWIN: Sportin' Life*
(*Porgy and Bess*); GOUNOD: Faust*, Roméo*;
HAYDN: Nancio* (*Infedeltà delusa*); MOZART:
Don Ottavio* (*Don Giovanni*), Belmonte*
(*Entführung aus dem Serail*); NICOLAI: Fenton*
(*Lustigen Weiber*); PUCCINI: Rinuccio* (*Gianni
Schicchi*); ROSSINI: Almaviva* (*Barbiere di Si-
viglia*), Otello*; VERDI: Alfredo* (*Traviata*).
World premieres: AMRAM: Feste (*Twelfth Night*)
Lake George Fest 1968; WEISGALL: Lt Jean
l'Aiglon (*Nine Rivers from Jordan*) New York
City Opera 1968; BERLINSKI: Son (*Job*) Wash-
ington, DC 1971-72. Video—ABC TV: Angel
(*Shephardes Playe*). Gives recitals. Appears with
symphony orchestra. Teaches voice. Coaches rep-
ertoire. On faculty of Univ of N Florida, Jacksonville, USA. **Res:** 8865 Yorkshire Crt, Jacksonville,
FL, USA. Mgmt: TOR/USA.

BRUNO, JOANNA MARY. Lyric soprano. Ameri-
can. Born Orange, NJ, USA. Single. Studied:
Katherine Eastment, Nutley, NJ, USA; Juilliard
School, New York; Jennie Tourel, New York;
Luigi Ricci, Rome; Ellen Faull, New York. **Debut:**
Monica (*Medium*) Spoleto Fest Italy, 1969.
Awards: Minna Kauffmann Ruud Awd 1968; Out-
standing Young Woman of America; Natl Arts
Club Awd 1968; M B Rockefeller Fund Grant
1970; Liederkranz Fndt Schlshp concert 1968;
Met Op Ntl Counc Aud Reg Finl 1969.
   Sang with major companies in FRA: Paris;
HOL: Amsterdam; ITA: Spoleto Fest, Trieste;
UK: Glasgow; USA: Chicago, Fort Worth, Ha-
waii, Houston, New York City Opera, Santa Fe;
YUG: Zagreb. Roles with these companies incl
BIZET: Micaëla* (*Carmen*); MENOTTI: Sar-
dule* (*Dernier sauvage*), Monica* (*Medium*); MO-
ZART: Despina (*Così fan tutte*), Susanna* (*Nozze
di Figaro*), Pamina* (*Zauberflöte*); PUCCINI:
Mimì* & Musetta* (*Bohème*), Cio-Cio-San* (*But-
terfly*); STRAVINSKY: Anne Trulove* (*Rake's
Progress*); VERDI: Nannetta* (*Falstaff*). Also
RAVEL: Princesse (*Enfant et les sortilèges*).

World premieres: MENOTTI: Cora (*Most Important Man*) New York City Opera 1971. Gives
recitals. Appears with symphony orchestra.
Teaches voice. **Res:** West Orange, NJ, USA.
Mgmt: CAM/USA; AIM/UK.

BRUNS, HEINER. German. Intendant, Bühnen der
Stadt Bielefeld, 3 Brunnenstr, D 48 Bielefeld, FR
Ger; and Dir, Theater am Alten Markt. In charge
of adm, mus, dram matters, art policy & finances;
and is also a stage dir/prod. Born 12 Aug 1935,
Düsseldorf, Germany. Single. Studied: Univs Cologne, Munich and Zurich. Previous positions primarily theatrical: Asst Dir, Ruhrfestspiele
Recklinghausen, FR Ger 1957; Schauspielhaus
Zurich 1957-58; Landestheater Darmstadt, FR
Ger 1958-60; Chefdramaturg, Bühnen Hansestadt
Lübeck 1960-62; Städtische Bühnen Freiburg
1962-68; Adm Dir, Bühnen Hansestadt Lübeck
1968-70; Adm Dir, Bühnen der Stadt Essen 1970-
71; Int & Dir, Stadttheater Pforzheim 1971-75; all
FR Ger. In present position since 1975. **Res:** Bielefeld, FR Ger.

BRUNVOLL, GUNNAR ARNE. Norwegian. Gen
Mng, Norwegian National Opera/Den Norske Opera, Storgaten 23 c, Oslo 1. In charge of adm
matters, art policy, mus & dram matters, tech &
finances. Born 6 Jun 1924, Jar near Oslo. Wife
Solveig. Three children. Previous occupations:
fighter pilot, WW II; impresario, concert agent.
Form positions, primarily adm: Dir, Norsk Operaselskap, Oslo 1950-58. Started with present company in 1958 as Dir, in present position since 1973.
World premieres at theaters under his management: JOHNSEN: *Legenden om Svein og Maria*
Oslo 1973. Initiated major policy changes including touring in Norway, cooperating with local
orchestras and choruses; tours in Europe and
USA; expanded budget from 1 million Norwegian
kroner to 31 million. Mem of Bd of De Norske
Teatres Forening, Norsk Teaterlederforening,
Nordisk Teaterlederrad, Nordiske Operasceners
Forening.

BRUSCANTINI, SESTO. Dramatic baritone,
started as bass. Italian. Born 10 Dec 1919, Civi-
tanova, Italy. Married. Studied: Luigi Ricci, Rome.
Debut: Geronimo (*Matrimonio segreto*) La Scala,
Milan 1948-49. Previous occupations: Doctor of
Law, Macerata Univ, 1946; poetry editor Rome
newspaper 1947. Awards: Winner RAI Compt
1948.
   Sang with major companies in ARG: Buenos
Aires; AUSTRL: Sydney; AUS: Bregenz Fest,
Salzburg Fest, Vienna Staatsoper; BEL: Brussels;
CZE: Prague National; FRA: Bordeaux, Mar-
seille, Paris; FR GER: Karlsruhe, Wiesbaden;
HOL: Amsterdam; ISR: Tel Aviv; ITA: Bologna,
Florence Maggio & Comunale, Genoa, Milan La
Scala, Naples, Palermo, Parma, Rome Opera, Tri-
este, Turin, Venice; MEX: Mexico City; MON:
Monte Carlo; POR: Lisbon; SPA: Barcelona, Ma-
jorca; SWE: Drottningholm Fest; SWI: Geneva;
UK: Edinburgh Fest, Glasgow Scottish, Glynde-
bourne Fest, London Royal; USA: Chicago, Dal-
las Civic Opera, Miami, San Francisco Opera,
Washington DC; YUG: Dubrovnik. **Roles with
these companies incl** BEETHOVEN: Rocco (*Fi-

delio); BELLINI: Sir Richard & Sir George (*Puritani*), Rodolfo (*Sonnambula*); BIZET: Escamillo (*Carmen*), Zurga‡ (*Pêcheurs de perles*); CILEA: Michonnet (*A. Lecouvreur*); CIMAROSA: Count Robinson★ & Geronimo‡ (*Matrimonio segreto*); DONIZETTI: Enrico & Don Pistacchio‡ (*Campanello*), Dott Malatesta★ & Don Pasquale‡ (*Don Pasquale*), Belcore & Dulcamara‡ (*Elisir*), Alfonse★ & Baldassare (*Favorite*), Sulpice‡ (*Fille du régiment*), Enrico (*Lucia*); GALUPPI: Don Tritemio (*Filosofo di campagna*); HANDEL: King of Scotland (*Ariodante*); MASCAGNI: Alfio (*Cavalleria rusticana*); MASSENET: Lescaut (*Manon*), Athanaël (*Thaïs*), Albert (*Werther*); MOZART: Guglielmo★ & Don Alfonso‡ (*Così fan tutte*), Leporello & Don Giovanni (*Don Giovanni*), Nardo (*Finta giardiniera*), Conte Almaviva★ & Figaro★ (*Nozze di Figaro*), Papageno (*Zauberflöte*); OFFENBACH: Coppélius etc★ (*Contes d'Hoffmann*); ORFF: Solo (*Carmina burana*), König (*Kluge*); PAISIELLO: Figaro★ (*Barbiere di Siviglia*), Teodoro (*Re Teodoro in Venezia*); PERGOLESI: Uberto‡ (*Serva padrona*); PUCCINI: Colline & Marcello (*Bohème*), Gianni Schicchi, Sharpless (*Butterfly*), Lescaut (*Manon Lescaut*), Scarpia★ (*Tosca*); ROSSINI: Figaro★‡ (*Barbiere di Siviglia*), Slook (*Cambiale di matrimonio*), Dandini★‡ (*Cenerentola*), Robert (*Comte Ory*), Signor Bruschino‡, Sultan Selim (*Turco in Italia*); SMETANA: Kezal (*Bartered Bride*); TCHAIKOVSKY: Yeletsky (*Pique Dame*); VERDI: Renato (*Ballo in maschera*), Rodrigo (*Don Carlo*), Ford & Falstaff★ (*Falstaff*), Fra Melitone (*Forza del destino*), Barone (*Giorno di regno*), Miller★ (*Luisa Miller*), Massimiliano Moor (*Masnadieri*), Iago (*Otello*), Rigoletto, Simon Boccanegra★, Germont★‡ (*Traviata*), Conte di Luna (*Trovatore*); WEBER: Kaspar (*Freischütz*); WOLF-FERRARI: Ottavio (*Donne curiose*), Conte Gil (*Segreto di Susanna*). Also WEBER: (*Drei Pintos*)★; MALIPIERO: (*Asino d'oro*); ROSSINI: Taddeo (*Italiana in Algeri*); CAVALLI: Lidio (*Egisto*). Recorded for: RCA, Columbia, Cetra, Ricordi, Decca, BASF. Video/Film: Dandini (*Cenerentola*). Teaches voice. Coaches repertoire. **Res**: Rome, Italy. **Mgmt**: CST/UK.

BRUSON, RENATO. Dramatic baritone. Italian. Born 13 Jan 1936, Granze/Padua, Italy. Wife Concettina Tegano, occupation costume designer. Studied: Consv Pollini, Elena Fava Ceriati, Padua. **Debut**: Conte di Luna (*Trovatore*) Teatro Sperimentale, Spoleto 1961.

Sang with major companies in BEL: Brussels; DEN: Copenhagen; FRA: Paris; FR GER: Bonn, Frankfurt, Hamburg, Munich Staatsoper, Wiesbaden; HOL: Amsterdam; HUN: Budapest; ITA: Bologna, Florence Comunale, Genoa, Milan La Scala, Naples, Palermo Massimo, Parma, Rome Teatro dell'Opera & Caracalla, Trieste, Turin, Venice, Verona; MON: Monte Carlo; ROM: Bucharest; SPA: Barcelona; UK: Edinburgh Fest, London Royal Opera; USA: Chicago, New York Met, San Francisco Opera. **Roles with these companies incl** BELLINI: Filippo (*Beatrice di Tenda*), Sir Richard★ (*Puritani*); BERLIOZ: Méphistophélès (*Damnation du Faust*); BIZET: Escamillo (*Carmen*), Zurga (*Pêcheurs de perles*); DONIZETTI: Lusignano (*Caterina Cornaro*), Alfonse★ (*Favorite*), Antonio (*Linda di Chamounix*),

Enrico★ (*Lucia*), Chevreuse (*Maria di Rohan*); GLUCK: Ubalde (*Armide*); HANDEL: Giulio Cesare; MASCAGNI: Alfio (*Cavalleria rusticana*); MASSENET: Lescaut (*Manon*), Athanaël (*Thaïs*); MOZART: Guglielmo (*Così fan tutte*), Conte Almaviva (*Nozze di Figaro*); PONCHIELLI: Barnaba (*Gioconda*); PUCCINI: Marcello (*Bohème*), Lescaut (*Manon Lescaut*), Scarpia (*Tosca*); ROSSINI: Figaro (*Barbiere di Siviglia*), Tobias Mill (*Cambiale di matrimonio*), Guillaume Tell; SAINT-SAENS: Grand prêtre (*Samson et Dalila*); SPONTINI: Cinna (*Vestale*); STRAUSS, R: Jochanaan (*Salome*); STRAVINSKY: Creon (*Oedipus Rex*); TCHAIKOVSKY: Eugene Onegin★; THOMAS: Hamlet; VERDI: Amonasro (*Aida*), Ezio (*Attila*), Renato★ (*Ballo in maschera*), Rodrigo★ (*Don Carlo*), Francesco Foscari★ (*Due Foscari*), Don Carlo (*Ernani*), Don Carlo★ (*Forza del destino*), Miller (*Luisa Miller*), Macbeth★, Massimiliano Moor (*Masnadieri*), Nabucco, Iago (*Otello*), Rigoletto★, Simon Boccanegra★, Germont★ (*Traviata*), Conte di Luna★ (*Trovatore*), Monforte (*Vespri*); WAGNER: Telramund (*Lohengrin*), Wolfram (*Tannhäuser*). Also DONIZETTI: Belisario, Conte di Vergy (*Gemma di Vergy*); VERDI: Seid (*Corsaro*); SACCHINI: Oedipe (*Oedipe à Colone*); de BANFIELD: Giovane (*Alissa*). Gives recitals. Appears with symphony orchestra. **Res**: Viale Somalia 18, Rome, Italy.

BRYN-JONES, DELME. Baritone. British. Born 29 Mar, Brynamman, Wales, UK. Wife Carolyn. Two children. Studied: Redvers Llewellyn; Guildhall School of Music, London; Acad of Music, Vienna. **Debut**: MACONCHY: Edward (*The Sofa*) New Opera Co, London 1959. Previous occupations: ten yrs with GB Ntl Coal Board, building & maintenance. Awards: Druid of Gorsedd of Bards, Royal Ntl Eisteddfod of Wales.

Sang with major companies in AUS: Vienna Staatsoper; FR GER: Mannheim; UK: Aldeburgh Festival, Cardiff Welsh, Edinburgh Fest, Glasgow Scottish, Glyndebourne Fest, London Royal; USA: Fort Worth, San Francisco Opera & Spring Opera. **Roles with these companies incl** BEETHOVEN: Don Pizarro (*Fidelio*); BERLIOZ: Méphistophélès (*Damnation du Faust*), Choroebus★ (*Troyens*); BIZET: Zurga★ (*Pêcheurs de perles*); BRITTEN: Demetrius (*Midsummer Night*); CILEA: Michonnet (*A. Lecouvreur*); DONIZETTI: Dott Malatesta (*Don Pasquale*), Enrico★ (*Lucia*); GAY/Britten: Mr Peachum (*Beggar's Opera*); GIORDANO: Carlo Gérard (*Andrea Chénier*); GLUCK: Hercule★ (*Alceste*); HENZE: Pentheus (*Bassariden*); MASCAGNI: Alfio★ (*Cavalleria rusticana*); MOZART: Guglielmo (*Così fan tutte*), Conte Almaviva★ (*Nozze di Figaro*), Osmin★ (*Zaïde*), Papageno★ (*Zauberflöte*); PUCCINI: Marcello★ (*Bohème*), Sharpless★ (*Butterfly*), Lescaut (*Manon Lescaut*), Michele (*Tabarro*), Guglielmo Wulf (*Villi*); STRAVINSKY: Nick Shadow (*Rake's Progress*); VERDI: Amonasro★ (*Aida*), Renato★ (*Ballo in maschera*), Ford★ (*Falstaff*), Macbeth★, Nabucco★, Iago★ (*Otello*), Rigoletto★, Simon Boccanegra★, Germont (*Traviata*); WEBER: Omar (*Abu Hassan*), Kaspar (*Freischütz*). **World premieres**: HODDINOTT: Wiltshire (*Beach at Falesa*) Welsh National Opera 1974; JONES: The

Sheriff (*Knife*) New Opera Co, London 1963. Recorded for: Decca. Gives recitals. Appears with symphony orchestra. **Res:** London & Wales, UK. Mgmt: GBN/UK; COL/USA.

BRYSON, EVELYN MARY. British. Comp Mgr, Scottish Opera, 39 Elmbank Crescent, Glasgow G2 4PT, Scotland. In charge of overall adm matters. Born 25 Jun 1939, Kilmarnock, Scotland. Single. Studied: music & English, Glasgow Univ, Scotland. Plays the piano, organ. Previous occupation: teacher of English in Norway. Started with present company 1967 as Assist to Gen Admin, in present position since 1971. **Res:** 3 Rosslyn Ter, G12 9NB, Glasgow, Scotland, UK.

BUBENIK, KVETOSLAV. Scenic and costume designer for opera, theater, film, television. Is a lighting designer, stage director; also a painter, sculptor & graphics designer. Czechoslovakian. Resident designer, National Theater, Prague. Born 29 May 1922, Kostelec na Hané, CSR. Wife Helena, occupation artist. Studied: School of Art, Zlin, Profs Makovsky, Wiesner, Hoffman, Sládek; Acad of Applied Arts, Prague, Profs Strnadel, Svolinsky, Kaplicky. **Operatic debut:** sets & cost, *Bohème* National Theater, Prague 1952. Theater debut: Divadlo Statniho Filmu, Prague 1950. Awards: Medal for Excellent Work 1968; Merited Artist of CSSR 1975.

Designed for major companies in ARG: Buenos Aires; AUS: Bregenz Fest, Vienna Volksoper; BUL: Sofia; CZE: Brno, Prague National & Smetana; FRA: Aix-en-Provence Fest; GRE: Athens Fest; FR GER: Wiesbaden; GER DR: Berlin Komische Oper; ITA: Bologna, Florence Maggio & Comunale, Milan La Scala, Naples, Parma, Rome Caracalla, Venice; SWI: Geneva. **Operas designed for these companies incl** ADAM: *Postillon de Lonjumeau;* ADAM DE LA HALLE: *Robin et Marion;* AUBER: *Fra Diavolo, Muette de Portici;* BEETHOVEN: *Fidelio★;* BELLINI: *Capuleti ed i Montecchi;* BIZET: *Carmen;* BORODIN: *Prince Igor;* CALDARA: *Dafne;* CHARPENTIER: *Louise;* CORNELIUS: *Barbier von Bagdad;* DESSAU: *Lanzelot;* DONIZETTI: *Don Pasquale, Maria Stuarda;* DVORAK: *Devil and Kate, Rusalka;* GLUCK: *Iphigénie en Tauride;* GOUNOD: *Faust;* HANDEL: *Acis and Galatea;* JANACEK: *From the House of the Dead, Jenufa;* KURKA: *Good Soldier Schweik;* LEONCAVALLO: *Pagliacci;* LORTZING: *Zar und Zimmermann;* MARTINU: *Comedy on the Bridge, Griechische Passion;* MASCAGNI: *Cavalleria rusticana;* MASSENET: *Don Quichotte, Manon;* MILHAUD: *Médée;* MONIUSZKO: *Halka;* MONTEVERDI: *Ritorno d'Ulisse;* MOZART: *Clemenza di Tito, Così fan tutte, Don Giovanni, Entführung aus dem Serail, Schauspieldirektor, Nozze di Figaro, Zauberflöte;* MUSSORGSKY: *Boris Godunov;* OFFENBACH: *Contes d'Hoffmann;* PIPKOV: *Antigonae;* PUCCINI: *Bohème, Gianni Schicchi, Butterfly, Manon Lescaut, Tosca, Turandot;* RACHMANINOFF: *Miserly Knight;* RIMSKY-KORSAKOV: *Coq d'or, Maid of Pskov, Invisible City of Kitezh;* ROSSINI: *Barbiere di Siviglia, Otello;* SMETANA: *Bartered Bride, Dalibor, Devil's Wall, The Kiss★, Libuse, Secret, Two Widows;* STRAUSS, J: *Fledermaus;* STRAUSS, R: *Arabella★, Elektra, Rosenkavalier, Salome;* TCHAIKOVSKY: *Eugene Onegin, Pique Dame★;* VERDI: *Aida, Ballo in maschera, Don Carlo, Falstaff, Nabucco, Rigoletto, Simon Boccanegra, Traviata, Trovatore;* WAGNER: *Lohengrin, Tannhäuser;* WEBER: *Freischütz;* VRANICKY: *Oberon.* Also FIBICH: *Sárka;* JEREMIAS: *Brothers Karamazov.* **Operatic world premieres:** PAUER: *Malade imaginaire* Nat Th, Prague 1970. Operatic TV: *Martha, Two Widows, The Kiss, Libuse.* Exhibitions of stage designs, paintings & graphics: abt 20 throughout Europe. Teaches at art schools, Prague. **Res:** Smecky 25, Prague, CSSR.

BUCIUCEANU, IULIA. Lyric & dramatic mezzo-soprano; contralto. Romanian. Resident mem: Romanian Opera, Bucharest. Born 25 Jun 1934, Tigina, USSR. Husband George Constantin, occupation actor. One child. Studied: Consv, Profs Petre Stefanescu-Goanga, Elena Costescu-Duca, Bucharest. **Debut:** Kneagina (*Rusalka*) Romanian Opera 1960. Awards: Silver Medal, Spring in Prague 1959; Gold Medal, Vienna 1959, Helsinki 1960 and Sofia 1961; Grand Prix, Toulouse 1961.

Sang with major companies in BUL: Sofia; FRA: Toulouse; FR GER: Berlin Deutsche Oper; GER DR: Berlin Staatsoper, Dresden, Leipzig; ROM: Bucharest; USSR: Kiev, Leningrad Kirov, Moscow Bolshoi, Tbilisi. **Roles with these companies incl** BIZET: Carmen★; BORODIN: Kontchakovna★ (*Prince Igor*); MASSENET: Charlotte★ (*Werther*); MOZART: Cherubino (*Nozze di Figaro*); MUSSORGSKY: Marina (*Boris Godunov*); PONCHIELLI: La Cieca (*Gioconda*); PROKOFIEV: Duenna; PUCCINI: Suzuki (*Butterfly*); SAINT-SAENS: Dalila; STRAUSS, J: Prinz Orlovsky★ (*Fledermaus*); TCHAIKOVSKY: Mme Larina★ & Olga★ (*Eugene Onegin*), Comtesse★ (*Pique Dame*); VERDI: Amneris★ (*Aida*), Ulrica★ (*Ballo in maschera*), Eboli★ (*Don Carlo*), Dame Quickly★ (*Falstaff*), Azucena★ (*Trovatore*); WAGNER: Magdalene★ (*Meistersinger*), Fricka★ (*Walküre*), Venus★ (*Tannhäuser*). Also BENTOIU: (*Hamlet*). **World premieres:** BARBERIS: (*Sunset*) 1967; DUMITRESCU: (*Ion Voda the Cruel*) 1956, (*Decebal*) 1969; all in Bucharest. Gives recitals. Appears with symphony orchestra. Teaches voice. Coaches repertoire. **Res:** 16 Schitu Darvari St, Bucharest 2, Romania. Mgmt: RIA/ROM.

BUCKLEY, EMERSON. Conductor of opera and symphony; operatic administrator. American. Art Dir & Resident Cond, Greater Miami Opera Assn & Florida Family Opera, USA 1973-. Also Cond & Mus Dir, Ft Lauderdale Symph Orch, FL 1963-. Born 14 Apr 1916, New York. Wife Mary Henderson, occupation Prof of Voice, Univ of Miami. Two sons. Studied: Columbia & Denver Univs; Daniel Gegory Mason, Douglas Moore, Chalmers Clifton, Hans Weise, Paul Henry Lang, Giorgio Polacco, Henry Cowell, Quincy Porter, Walter Piston; incl piano, violin & voice. Operatic training as repetiteur, asst cond & chorus master at Columbia Grand Op, New York; San Carlo, Hippodrome; other touring opera cos. **Operatic debut:** *Rigoletto* Columbia Grand Op, New York 1936. Symphonic debut: Fed New York City Symph Orch, WPA, New York 1937. Awards: Chevalier de l'Ordre des Arts et des Lettres, France; Amer Patriot Awd, State of FL; Colorado Ambassador's Sash, State of CO; Alice Ditson Cond Awd, Columbia; Gold Chair, Central City, CO. Previous adm positions in opera: Mus Dir, Greater Miami Opera Assn 1950-73; Mus Dir, Central City Opera Fest, CO 1956-69; Mus Dir, Puerto Rico Opera Fest, San Juan 1954-58; Mus Dir, WOR Brdcg, New York 1945-54; Mus Dir, Empire State Fest, Ellenville, NY 1955.

Conducted with major companies in CAN: Montreal/Quebec; USA: Baltimore, Chicago, Cincinnati, Hartford, Houston, Miami, Milwaukee Florentine, New Orleans, New York City Opera, Philadelphia Lyric, San Francisco Opera, Seattle. **Operas with these companies incl** BERLIOZ: *Béatrice et Bénédict;* BIZET: *Carmen*, *Pêcheurs de perles*; BOITO: *Mefistofele;* BRITTEN: *Rape of Lucretia;* DELIBES: *Lakmé;* DONIZETTI: *Don Pasquale*, *Elisir*, *Fille du régiment*, *Lucia*, *Rita*; FLOTOW: *Martha*; FLOYD: *Of Mice and Men*; GIORDANO: *Andrea Chénier*; GOUNOD: *Faust, Mireille, Roméo et Juliette*; HUMPERDINCK: *Hänsel und Gretel;* LEONCAVALLO: *Pagliacci;* MASCAGNI: *Amico Fritz, Cavalleria rusticana;* MASSENET: *Hérodiade, Manon, Thaïs*, *Werther*; MENOTTI: *Telephone;* MOZART: *Così fan tutte, Don Giovanni, Nozze di Figaro, Zauberflöte;* MUSSORGSKY: *Boris Godunov;* OFFENBACH: *Contes d'Hoffmann, Périchole*; PONCHIELLI: *Gioconda;* PUCCINI: *Bohème*, *Fanciulla del West*, *Gianni Schicchi*, *Butterfly, Manon Lescaut*, *Rondine, Tosca*, *Turandot, Villi;* ROSSINI: *Barbiere di Siviglia*, *Italiana in Algeri;* SAINT-SAENS: *Samson et Dalila;* SMETANA: *Bartered Bride;* STRAUSS, J: *Fledermaus;* THOMAS: *Hamlet, Mignon;* VERDI: *Aida*, *Ballo in maschera*, *Don Carlo*, *Ernani*, *Forza del destino*, *Otello*, *Rigoletto*, *Traviata, Trovatore*; WOLF-FERRARI: *Segreto di Susanna.* Also MOORE: *Wings of the Dove;* ARGENTO: *Boor;* WARD: *He Who Gets Slapped.* **World premieres:** MOORE: *Ballad of Baby Doe* Central City Opera Fest 1956; *Gallantry* Columbia Univ, New York 1958; WARD: *Crucible* New York City Opera 1961; MOROSS: *Gentlemen, Be Seated!* New York City Opera 1963; WARD: *Lady from Colorado* Central City Fest 1964. Recorded for MGM, Heliodor, CRI. Conducted major orch in USA/Canada. **Res:** 19640 NE 20 Ave, N Miami Beach, FL 33179, USA. **Mgmt:** BAR/USA.

BUCKLEY, ROBERT ALLEN. American. Mng & Dir of Operations, Houston Grand Opera Assn, 615 Louisiana, Houston, TX 77002, 1973-77; also Texas Opera Theatre. In charge of adm matters, tech & finances. Born 27 Mar 1949, New York. Single. Studied: Univ of Oklahoma, Norman. Previous positions, primarily theatrical: Asst Gen Mng, Minnesota Opera, Minneapolis 1971-73; Prod Coord, Baltimore Opera 1970-71; St Mng/prod, Santa Fe Opera 1970, '71; St Mng, Central City Opera, CO 1969, '70; lt dsgn, Minnesota Opera 1971-73; lt dsgn, Univ of Oklahoma Music Theatre 1968-70. World premieres at theaters during his employment: FLOYD: *Bilby's Doll* Houston 1976; PASATIERI: *Seagull* Houston 1974; SUSA: *Transformations* Minneapolis

1973. Initiated major policy changes assisting Gen Mng David Gockley; personally designed new data processing system to encompass financial, subscription, fund-raising records; established Houston's own scenic studios. Mem of OPERA America Consortium Commtt; OPERA America AGMA dialogue commtt; USITT Admin Presentation Commtt. **Res:** Houston, TX, USA.

BUKOVAC, PAULA. Dramatic soprano. Yugoslavian. Resident mem: Staatstheater Braunschweig. Born 29 Jun 1935, Zagreb, Yugoslavia. Divorced. One son. Studied: Prof Fritz Lunzer, Zagreb. **Debut:** Antonia & Giulietta (*Contes d'Hoffmann*) Saarbrücken 1960. Previous occupations: folk singer & folk dancer.

Sang with major companies in AUS: Vienna Volksoper; FR GER: Berlin Deutsche Oper, Bonn, Cologne, Düsseldorf-Duisburg, Hamburg, Hannover, Karlsruhe, Krefeld, Mannheim, Munich Staatsoper, Saarbrücken, Stuttgart; ITA: Milan La Scala, Venice. **Roles with these companies incl** BEETHOVEN: Leonore (*Fidelio*); BERG: Marie (*Wozzeck*); BIZET: Carmen‡; BORODIN: Jaroslavna* (*Prince Igor*); CIKKER: (*Resurrection*); GIORDANO: Maddalena* (*Andrea Chénier*); HINDEMITH: Tochter des Cardillac*; HUMPERDINCK: Hänsel*‡ & Hexe (*Hänsel und Gretel*); JANACEK: Kostelnicka (*Jenufa*), Katya Kabanova*; MASCAGNI: Santuzza* (*Cavalleria rusticana*); MEYERBEER: Selika* (*Africaine*); OFFENBACH: Antonia* & Giulietta* (*Contes d'Hoffmann*); PUCCINI: Minnie (*Fanciulla del West*), Cio-Cio-San* (*Butterfly*), Manon Lescaut*, Tosca*, Turandot; SHOSTAKOVICH: Katerina Ismailova; STRAUSS, R: Arabella*, Elektra & Chrysothemis* (*Elektra*), Octavian* (*Rosenkavalier*), Salome*‡; TCHAIKOVSKY: Lisa (*Pique Dame*); VERDI: Aida*, Eboli & Elisabetta (*Don Carlo*), Leonora* (*Forza del destino*), Lady Macbeth*, Abigaille (*Nabucco*), Amelia* (*Simon Boccanegra*), Leonora* (*Trovatore*); WAGNER: Senta (*Fliegende Holländer*), Sieglinde (*Walküre*), Venus* (*Tannhäuser*). **World premieres:** EDER: Teresa (*Der Kardinal*) Landestheater Linz, Austria 1965. Teaches voice.

BULLARD, GENE; né Milton Eugene Bullard. Lyric tenor. American. Born 26 Oct 1937, Bessemer, AL, USA. Single. Studied: Raymond J D Buckingham, New York. **Debut:** Duca di Mantova (*Rigoletto*) Baltimore Civic Opera 1964. Previous occupations: advertising, stock exchange, bartender.

Sang with major companies in AUS: Vienna Staatsoper; SPA: Barcelona; USA: Baltimore, Cincinnati, Fort Worth, Hawaii, Houston, Kansas City, Kentucky, Miami, New Orleans, New York City Opera, Philadelphia Lyric, San Diego, San Francisco Spring Opera, Seattle. **Roles with these companies incl** BERLIOZ: Faust (*Damnation de Faust*); BIZET: Don José (*Carmen*); DELIBES: Gérald (*Lakmé*); DONIZETTI: Riccardo* (*Anna Bolena*), Nemorino* (*Elisir*), Tonio* (*Fille du régiment*), Edgardo* (*Lucia*), Leicester* (*Maria Stuarda*); FALLA: Paco* (*Vida breve*); GOUNOD: Faust*, Roméo*; HALEVY: Léopold* (*Juive*); MASSENET: Des Grieux (*Manon*); MOZART: Don Ottavio* (*Don Giovanni*), Belmonte

(*Entführung aus dem Serail*), Tamino (*Zauberflöte*); MUSSORGSKY: Dimitri★ (*Boris Godunov*); ORFF: Solo (*Carmina burana*); PUCCINI: Rodolfo★ (*Bohème*), Pinkerton (*Butterfly*), Cavaradossi (*Tosca*), Calaf (*Turandot*); ROSSINI: Almaviva (*Barbiere di Siviglia*), Edward Milfort (*Cambiale di matrimonio*), Don Ramiro (*Cenerentola*); STRAUSS, J: Eisenstein & Alfred (*Fledermaus*); VERDI: Radames★ (*Aida*), Riccardo★ (*Ballo in maschera*), Duca di Mantova★ (*Rigoletto*), Alfredo★ (*Traviata*). Gives recitals. Appears with symphony orchestra. **Res:** New York, NY, USA. Mgmt: HJH/USA.

BUMBRY, GRACE MELZIA: neé Grace Ann Bumbry. Dramatic soprano & mezzo-soprano. American. Resident mem: Metropolitan Opera, New York. Born 4 Jan, St Louis, MO, USA. Divorced. Studied: Music Acad of the West, Lotte Lehmann, Santa Barbara, CA; Northwestern Univ, Evanston, IL; Boston Univ, MA, USA. **Debut:** Amneris (*Aida*) Paris Opera 1960. Awards: Met Aud of the Air; Kimber Foundation Awd, San Francisco; Natl Marian Anderson Awd; John Jay Whitney Foundation.
Sang with major companies in ARG: Buenos Aires; AUS: Salzburg Fest, Vienna Staatsoper; BEL: Brussels; CAN: Toronto; FIN: Helsinki; FRA: Bordeaux, Lyon, Orange Fest, Paris; GRE: Athens Fest; FR GER: Bayreuth Fest, Berlin Deutsche Oper, Frankfurt, Hamburg, Mannheim, Munich Staatsoper, Wiesbaden; HUN: Budapest; ITA: Bologna, Florence Maggio, Milan La Scala, Rome, Verona Arena; POR: Lisbon; SPA: Barcelona; SWE: Stockholm; SWI: Basel; UK: London Royal Opera; USA: Chicago, Dallas, Memphis, Newark, New York Metropolitan, Philadelphia Lyric, San Francisco Opera; YUG: Belgrade. **Roles with these companies incl** BIZET: Carmen★‡; DUKAS: Ariane‡ (*Ariane et Barbe Bleue*); FALLA: Salud (*Vida breve*); GLUCK: Alceste, Orfeo★‡; HONEGGER: Antigone★; JANACEK: Jenufa★; MASCAGNI: Santuzza★ (*Cavalleria rusticana*); MONTEVERDI: Poppea; PONCHIELLI: Gioconda★; PUCCINI: Tosca★; SMETANA: Hata (*Bartered Bride*); STRAUSS, R: Salome★; TCHAIKOVSKY: Olga★ (*Eugene Onegin*); VERDI: Aida★, Amelia★ (*Ballo in maschera*), Elisabetta (*Don Carlo*), Elvira★ (*Ernani*), Lady Macbeth★, Amneris★‡ (*Aida*), Ulrica (*Ballo in maschera*), Eboli★‡ (*Don Carlo*), Azucena★ (*Trovatore*); WAGNER: Elisabeth★‡ & Venus★ (*Tannhäuser*), Ortrud (*Lohengrin*), Fricka (*Walküre*). Recorded for: Angel, London, Philips, Westminster, DG, RCA. Video/Film: Carmen. Gives recitals. Appears with symphony orchestra. **Res:** Lugano, Switzerland. Mgmt: BAR/USA; CST/UK.

BUNGER, REID. Bass-baritone. American. Resident mem: Vienna Staatsoper. Born 6 Mar 1935, Chicago. Wife Bette, occupation teacher. Two children. Studied: Tex Christian Univ, Ft Worth, TX. **Debut:** Moralès (*Carmen*) Vienna Staatsoper 1966. Previous occupations: US Army officer; schoolteacher. Awards: Fulbright Schlshp 1965; Rockefeller Fndt Grant 1967.
Sang with major companies in AUS: Graz, Vienna Staatsoper; CAN: Montreal/Quebec; FR GER: Bayreuth, Essen; GER DR: Leipzig; SWI:

Basel. **Roles with these companies incl** BEETHOVEN: Don Pizarro★ (*Fidelio*); EINEM: Priest (*Prozess*); MASCAGNI: Alfio★ (*Cavalleria rusticana*); ORFF: Solo★ (*Carmina burana*); SCHOENBERG: Der Mann★ (*Glückliche Hand*); STRAUSS, R: Jochanaan★ (*Salome*); VERDI: Grande Inquisitore★ (*Don Carlo*), Fra Melitone★ (*Forza del destino*), Fiesco★ (*Simon Boccanegra*); WAGNER: Holländer★, Sachs (*Meistersinger*), Klingsor (*Parsifal*); SMETANA: König Vladislav (*Dalibor*). Gives recitals. Appears with symphony orchestra. Teaches voice. Coaches repertoire. **Res:** Kaasgrabeng 58, Vienna, Austria. Mgmt: TAS/AUS; HJH/USA.

BURGESS, GARY ELLSWORTH. Lyric tenor. American. Resident mem: San Francisco Opera; Greek National Opera, Athens. Born 31 May 1938, Devonshire, Bermuda. Divorced. Studied: Indiana Univ, Margaret Harshaw, Bloomington, IN; Curtis Inst of Music, Dino Yannopoulos, Margaret Harshaw, Philadelphia. **Debut:** Male Chorus (*Rape of Lucretia*) Kentucky Opera 1969. Previous occupations: music teacher at Jr HS.
Sang with major companies in GRE: Athens National; USA: Jackson Opera/South, Kentucky, Philadelphia Lyric, San Francisco Opera. **Roles with these companies incl** BRITTEN: Male Chorus★ (*Rape of Lucretia*); DONIZETTI: Edgardo★ (*Lucia*); MASCAGNI: Turiddu★ (*Cavalleria rusticana*); PUCCINI: Rodolfo★ (*Bohème*), Rinuccio★ (*Gianni Schicchi*), Pinkerton★ (*Butterfly*), Cavaradossi★ (*Tosca*); ROSSINI: Giocondo★ (*Pietra del paragone*); STRAUSS, R: Bacchus★ (*Ariadne auf Naxos*); STRAVINSKY: Tom Rakewell★ (*Rake's Progress*); VERDI: Riccardo★ (*Ballo in maschera*), Fenton★ (*Falstaff*), Alfredo★ (*Traviata*); WAGNER: Erik★ (*Fliegende Holländer*). Gives recitals. Appears with symphony orchestra. **Res:** Philadelphia, USA. Mgmt: LLF/USA.

BURLES, CHARLES. Lirico spinto tenor. French. Born 21 Jun 1936, Marseille, France. Wife Davin, occupation hospital nurse. Three children. Studied: Leon Cazauran, M Mercadel, Marseille. **Debut:** Almaviva (*Barbiere di Siviglia*) Toulon 1958. Previous occupations: decorator, commercial artist. Awards: Orphée d'or, Acad Disque Lyrique 1971, 1973, 1974; Croix de Commandeur du Mérite.
Sang with major companies in FRA: Bordeaux, Lyon, Marseille, Nancy, Nice, Paris, Rouen, Strasbourg, Toulouse; ITA: Turin, Venice. **Roles with these companies incl** ADAM: Chapelou★ (*Postillon de Lonjumeau*), Zephoris★ (*Si j'étais roi*); BELLINI: Lord Arthur★ (*Puritani*); BIZET: Nadir★ (*Pêcheurs de perles*); BOIELDIEU: George Brown★ (*Dame blanche*); CIMAROSA: Paolino★ (*Matrimonio segreto*); DELIBES: Gérald★ (*Lakmé*); DONIZETTI: Ernesto★ (*Don Pasquale*); FALLA: Paco (*Vida breve*); GOUNOD: Vincent★ (*Mireille*); HALEVY: Léopold (*Juive*); LECOCQ: Pomponnet (*Fille de Madame Angot*); MASSENET: Jean★ (*Jongleur de Notre Dame*); MOZART: Belmonte★ (*Entführung aus dem Serail*); PUCCINI: Rodolfo★ (*Bohème*); ROSSINI: Almaviva★ (*Barbiere di Siviglia*), Comte Ory; STRAUSS, J: Alfred★ (*Fledermaus*); THOMAS: Wilhelm Meister (*Mignon*). Also RAMEAU: Zoroastre (*Paladins*); VIVALDI:

(*Fida ninfa*). **World premieres:** ROSSELLINI: Jacques (*L'annonce faite à Marie*) Opéra Comique, Paris 1970; AUBIN: Martin Zapater (*Goya*) Lille, France 1974. Recorded for: EMI, Pathé-Marconi. Video/Film—ORTF: (*Paladins*); Jacques (*Annonce faite à Marie*); var operas by Chabrier. **Res:** 5 rue Felix Eboué, Marseille 13002, France.

BURNS, ALAN RAYMOND. Stages/produces opera, theater, film & television. Also designs stage lighting and is an author. American. Born 27 Apr 1936, New York. Wife Winifred, occupation singer. One child. Studied: Centre Lyrique Intl, Dr Herbert Graf, Lotfi Mansouri, Dino Yannopoulos, Geneva; incl music, piano and voice. Operatic training as asst stage dir at Grand Théâtre, Geneva 1969-70. **Operatic debut:** *Tosca* Seattle Opera, WA 1972. Theater debut: TV film, Talent Assoc, New York 1963. Awards: Ford Fndt internship grant for Centre Lyrique, Geneva 1969; Ntl Opera Inst grant as adm intern at New York City & Met Operas 1973-74.

Directed/produced opera for major companies in USA: Newark, New York City Opera, Seattle. **Operas staged for these companies incl** DONI-ZETTI: *Lucia;* HUMPERDINCK: *Hänsel und Gretel;* MASSENET: *Manon;* MOZART: *Entführung aus dem Serail*★, *Nozze di Figaro, Zauberflöte;* PUCCINI: *Bohème, Tosca*★; STRAUSS, J: *Fledermaus*★. Operatic Video—TV Albany, NY: *Hänsel und Gretel.* Teaches. **Res:** 190 Washington St, Hempstead, NY 11550, USA.

BURROWES, NORMA ELIZABETH. Lyric coloratura soprano. British. Born 24 Apr 1944, Bangor/Co Down, UK. Husband Steuart Bedford, occupation conductor. Studied: Queen's Univ, Belfast; Royal Acad of Music, Flora Nielsen, Rupert Bruce-Lockhart, London. **Debut:** Zerlina (*Don Giovanni*) Glyndebourne 1970. Awards: Order of Worshipful Company of Musicians; recital diploma, Royal Acad of Music, London.

Sang with major companies in AUS: Salzburg Fest; HOL: Amsterdam; SWE: Drottningholm Fest; UK: Aldeburgh Fest, Glyndebourne Fest, London Royal & English National. **Roles with these companies incl** JANACEK: Vixen★ (*Cunning Little Vixen*); MOZART: Zerlina★ (*Don Giovanni*), Blondchen★ (*Entführung aus dem Serail*), Ilia★ (*Idomeneo*), Susanna★ (*Nozze di Figaro*), Elisa★ (*Re pastore*); POULENC: Thérèse★ (*Mamelles de Tirésias*); PUCCINI: Lisette★ (*Rondine*); ROSSINI: Fiorilla★ (*Turco in Italia*); STRAUSS, R: Fiakermilli★ (*Arabella*), Sophie★ (*Rosenkavalier*); VERDI: Oscar★ (*Ballo in maschera*). Recorded for: Decca, EMI. Video/Film: Susanna (*Nozze di Figaro*), Nannetta (*Falstaff*), Lauretta (*Gianni Schicchi*). Gives recitals. Appears with symphony orchestra. **Res:** 56 Rochester Rd, London NW1, London, UK. **Mgmt:** HPL/UK; CAM/USA.

BURROWS, STUART. Lyric tenor. British. Born 7 Feb 1933, Pontypridd, Wales. Wife Enid. Two children. Studied: Trinity Coll, Carmarthen. **Debut:** Ismaele (*Nabucco*) Welsh National Opera 1963. Previous occupations: schoolteacher.

Sang with major companies in FRA: Aix-en-Provence, Nice, Orange Fest, Paris; GRE: Athens Fest; FR GER: Mannheim; UK: Cardiff Welsh, London Royal; USA: Boston, Houston, New York Met, San Francisco Opera, Santa Fe. **Roles with these companies incl** BELLINI: Elvino★ (*Sonnambula*); BERLIOZ: Bénédict★, Faust★‡ (*Damnation de Faust*); DONIZETTI: Riccardo‡ (*Anna Bolena*), Ernesto★ (*Don Pasquale*), Nemorino★ (*Elisir*), Edgardo★ (*Lucia*), Leicester★‡ (*Maria Stuarda*); GOUNOD: Faust★; HANDEL: Acis★; MASSENET: Des Grieux★ (*Manon*); MOZART: Don Ottavio★‡ (*Don Giovanni*), Belmonte★ (*Entführung aus dem Serail*), Idamante★ & Idomeneo★ (*Idomeneo*), Tamino★‡ (*Zauberflöte*); OFFENBACH: Hoffmann★‡; PAISIELLO: Almaviva★ (*Barbiere di Siviglia*); PUCCINI: Rodolfo★ (*Bohème*), Des Grieux★ (*Manon Lescaut*); ROSSINI: Almaviva★ (*Barbiere di Siviglia*); SMETANA: Wenzel (*Bartered Bride*); STRAUSS, R: Ein Sänger★ (*Rosenkavalier*); STRAVINSKY: Oedipus★, Pêcheur★ (*Rossignol*); TCHAIKOVSKY: Lenski★‡ (*Eugene Onegin*); VAUGHAN WILLIAMS: Hugh (*Hugh the Drover*); VERDI: Fenton (*Falstaff*), Ismaele (*Nabucco*), Duca di Mantova (*Rigoletto*), Alfredo (*Traviata*). Recorded for: Decca-London, RCA, EMI, DG. Video/Film: Faust, Rodolfo (*Bohème*), Duca (*Rigoletto*). Gives recitals. Appears with symphony orchestra. **Res:** St Fagans Dr, Cardiff, Wales, UK. **Mgmt:** AIM/UK.

BURY, JOHN. Scenic and costume designer for opera, theater & film. Is a lighting designer; also a theater consultant. British. Head of Design, National Theater of Great Britain. Born 27 Jan 1925, Aberystwyth, Wales. Wife Elizabeth, occupation designer. Four children. **Operatic debut:** *Moses und Aron* Royal Opera, Covent Garden 1965. Theater debut: Theatre Workshop, London 1950.

Designed opera for major companies in UK: Glyndebourne Fest, London Royal. **Operas designed for these companies incl** CAVALLI: *Calisto;* MONTEVERDI: *Ritorno d'Ulisse;* MOZART: *Nozze di Figaro, Zauberflöte;* ROSSINI: *Pietra del paragone;* WAGNER: *Tristan und Isolde.* Exhibitions of stage designs. Teaches at art schools. **Res:** 14 Woodlands Rd, London, UK.

BUSINGER, TONI. Scenic and costume designer for opera, theater & television. Is a lighting designer; also a painter & illustrator. Swiss. Born 6 Jun 1934, Wettingen. Single. Prof training: personal asst to Teo Otto, Schauspielhaus Zurich 1956-60. **Operatic debut:** *Otello* Stadttheater Freiburg/Br, FR Ger 1960. Theater debut: Schauspielhaus Zurich 1957. Previous occupation: studied literature, art, science at Univ Zurich. Previous adm positions in opera: head of supplies, Stadttheater Freiburg 1960-62; chief scenic designer, Staatsoper Hamburg 1973-75.

Designed for major companies in AUS: Bregenz, Salzburg Fest, Vienna Staatsoper; FRA: Nancy, Paris, Strasbourg; FR GER: Cologne, Düsseldorf-Duisburg, Frankfurt, Hamburg, Krefeld, Munich Staatsoper, Nürnberg, Stuttgart; HOL: Amsterdam; S AFR: Johannesburg; SWI: Geneva, Zurich; USA: Miami, San Francisco Opera; YUG: Zagreb. **Operas designed for these companies incl** BARTOK: *Bluebeard's Castle;* BEETHOVEN: *Fidelio;* BERG: *Wozzeck*★; BERLIOZ: *Béatrice* *et Bénédict;* BIZET: *Carmen★;* CHERUBINI: *Medea;* DONIZETTI: *Don Pasquale, Fille du régiment★, Lucia;* FLOTOW: *Martha;* FORTNER: *Elisabeth Tudor★;* GLUCK: *Alceste, Orfeo ed Euridice;* GOUNOD: *Faust;* HANDEL: *Giulio Cesare;* HINDEMITH: *Cardillac;* JANACEK: *Jenufa;* LEONCAVALLO: *Pagliacci;* LORTZING: *Wildschütz★;* MASCAGNI: *Cavalleria rusticana;* MONTEVERDI: *Incoronazione di Poppea★;* MOZART: *Così fan tutte★, Don Giovanni★, Entführung aus dem Serail★, Finta giardiniera, Nozze di Figaro★, Zauberflöte★;* OFFENBACH: *Contes d'Hoffmann;* ORFF: *Bernauerin★;* PERGOLESI: *Frate 'nnamorato★;* PUCCINI: *Bohème★, Fanciulla del West, Butterfly, Tosca★;* ROSSINI: *Barbiere di Siviglia, Cenerentola★, Italiana in Algeri;* SEARLE: *Hamlet;* SMETANA: *Bartered Bride;* STRAUSS, R: *Arabella★, Capriccio★, Elektra★, Rosenkavalier★, Salome★;* TCHAIKOVSKY: *Eugene Onegin★;* VERDI: *Don Carlo★, Ernani★, Rigoletto, Traviata★;* WAGNER: *Fliegende Holländer★, Tannhäuser★, Tristan und Isolde.* Also FORTNER: *Bluthochzeit;* HANDEL: *Jephtha;* HARTMANN: *Simplicius Simplicissimus;* PURCELL: *Fairy Queen★;* WOLF-FERRARI: *Vedova scaltra★;* MARTIN: *Sturm★.* **Operatic world premieres:** SEARLE: *Hamlet* Staatsoper, Hamburg 1968; RUBIN: *Kleider machen Leute* Volksoper, Vienna 1973. Exhibitions in Helsinki and at Savonlinna Fest 1974; at museums in Zurich, Baden-Baden, Prague, Biennale Venice and São Paulo. **Res:** Bifangstr 72, CH-5430 Wettingen, Switzerland.

BUSTOS, GERMÁN EDUARDO. Lyric tenor. Chilean. Born 26 Feb 1938, Chillán, Chile. Studied: Gustavo Selva; Consv Nacional de Chile, Federico Heinlein; Acad of Vocal Arts, Nicola Moscona, Philadelphia, USA. **Debut:** Cassio (*Otello*) Teatro Municipal de Santiago, Chile 1969. Previous occupations: advertising exec; communic specialist with US Agcy for Intl Develp; art dir of two major magazines in Santiago. Awards: Whelen Awd, Acad of Vocal Arts, Philadelphia 1970; Special Awd Phila Lyric Opera 1971.

Sang with major companies in ISR: Tel Aviv; USA: Hartford, Philadelphia Lyric. **Roles with these companies incl** DONIZETTI: Tonio★ (*Fille du régiment*); GOUNOD: Faust★; PUCCINI: Rinuccio★ (*Gianni Schicchi*); ROSSINI: Almaviva★ (*Barbiere di Siviglia*); VERDI: Duca di Mantova★ (*Rigoletto*), Alfredo★ (*Traviata*). Teaches voice. On faculty of Acad of Vocal Arts, Philadelphia. **Res:** Philadelphia, PA, USA. Mgmt: SMN/USA.

BUTLER, HENRY WILLIS. Stages/produces opera, theater & television and is an actor and author. American. Born 3 May, Eureka, KS. Single. Operatic training as asst stage dir to Menotti, Broadway prod of *Consul.* **Operatic debut:** *Butterfly* NBC TV, New York 1953. Theater debut: Phoenix Theatre, New York. Previous occupation: actor.

Directed/produced opera for major companies in CAN: Montreal/Quebec, Vancouver; USA: Kentucky, New York Met. **Operas staged for these companies incl** BELLINI: *Sonnambula;* BERG: *Wozzeck★;* BIZET: *Carmen;* CAVALLI: *Calisto★;* DONIZETTI: *Don Pasquale, Elisir★, Lucia★;* GOUNOD: *Faust;* MENOTTI: *Amahl,*

Consul, Medium, Old Maid and the Thief, Saint of Bleecker Street, Telephone; MOORE: *Ballad of Baby Doe;* MOZART: *Così fan tutte, Don Giovanni, Nozze di Figaro;* PASATIERI: *Divina;* POULENC: *Dialogues des Carmélites;* PUCCINI: *Fanciulla del West, Butterfly, Tosca;* RAVEL: *Heure espagnole;* ROSSINI: *Barbiere di Siviglia, Cenerentola;* STRAVINSKY: *Oedipus Rex, Rake's Progress;* TCHAIKOVSKY: *Eugene Onegin, Pique Dame★;* THOMSON: *Mother of Us All;* VERDI: *Ballo in maschera★, Ernani, Rigoletto, Traviata;* WAGNER: *Lohengrin.* **Operatic world premieres:** PASATIERI: *Trial of Mary Lincoln* NET TV, New York 1972. Operatic Video—NET TV: *Mary Lincoln.* **Opera libretti:** LEVY: *Mourning Becomes Electra* Met Opera 1967. **Res:** 56 Irving Pl, New York 10003, USA.

BUTLIN, ROGER JOHN. Scenic and costume designer for opera, theater; specl in sets. Is also a lecturer. British. Born 1 Jun 1935, Stafford. Wife Joanna, occupation writer. Three children. Studied: West of England Coll of Art, Bristol; Southampton Univ, Inst of Education; all in textile design and education. Prof training: Sadler's Wells Opera, London 1967-68. **Operatic debut:** sets, *Simon Boccanegra* 1970; cost, *Billy Budd* 1972; both at Welsh National Opera, Cardiff. Theater debut: Greenwich Theatre, London 1969. Previous occupation: teacher, Cheltenham Coll. Awards: Design Schlshp. Arts Counc of Great Britain; nominated by *Variety* for best design, Apollo Theatre London.

Designed opera for major companies in AUSTRL: Sydney; SPA: Barcelona Liceo; SWI: Zurich; UK: Welsh National, Scottish, Glyndebourne Fest. **Operas designed for these companies incl** BIZET: *Carmen★;* BRITTEN: *Albert Herring★, Billy Budd★;* MONTEVERDI: *Incoronazione di Poppea★;* MOZART: *Idomeneo★, Zauberflöte★;* ROSSINI: *Barbiere di Siviglia★;* VERDI: *Rigoletto★, Simon Boccanegra★.* Exhibitions of stage designs Wright-Hepburn Gallery, London 1969; Glyndebourne, UK. Teaches at Univ Coll, Goldsmith Coll, Central School of Art & Design, London. **Res:** 20 Circus St, Greenwich/London SE10, UK.

BUTTINO, ALFRED NICHOLAS. American. Business Mng, Lake George Opera Festival, Box 471, Glens Falls, NY 12801, USA. In charge of adm matters & finances. Additional adm positions: assoc prof, Adirondack Community Coll, Glens Falls, NY. Born 22 Nov 1938, Philadelphia, PA. Wife Sandra Ann, occupation assoc prof. Six children. Studied: Siena Coll and State Univ of NY, Albany. Plays the guitar. Previous occupations: prof of economics and business. Started with present company 1967 as accountant, in present position since 1969. World premieres at theaters under his management: AMRAM: *Twelfth Night* 1968; BERNARDO: *The Child* 1974; both Lake George Opera Fest, Glens Falls. **Res:** 10601 Terry Dr, South Glens Falls, NY, USA.

BUZEA, ION. Dramatic tenor. Romanian. Born 14 Aug 1934, Cluj, Romania. Single. Studied: Lya Pop, Romania; Luigi Ricci, Italy. **Debut:** Alfredo (*Traviata*) Cluj Opera 1960. Previous occupations: stud geology & natur sciences. Awards: First

Prize, Enesco Fest, Bucharest; Third Prize, Conc de Chant, Toulouse.

Sang with major companies in AUS: Vienna Staatsoper & Volksoper; BEL: Liège; BUL: Sofia; CZE: Brno, Prague National & Smetana; FRA: Bordeaux, Nice; GRE: Athens Fest; FR GER: Berlin Deutsche Oper, Cologne, Frankfurt, Hamburg, Munich Staatsoper, Stuttgart, Wiesbaden; HOL: Amsterdam; HUN: Budapest; ROM: Bucharest; SWI: Basel, Zurich; UK: London Royal; USA: Boston, Cincinnati, Dallas, Houston, New Orleans, New York Met; YUG: Zagreb, Belgrade. **Roles with these companies incl** d'ALBERT: Pedro* (*Tiefland*); AUBER: Frà Diavolo*; BIZET: Don José* (*Carmen*); BOITO: Faust* (*Mefistofele*); CILEA: Maurizio* (*A. Lecouvreur*); DONIZETTI: Edgardo* (*Lucia*); DVORAK: Prince (*Rusalka*); JANACEK: Boris* (*Katya Kabanova*); LEONCAVALLO: Canio* (*Pagliacci*); MASCAGNI: Turiddu* (*Cavalleria rusticana*); MASSENET: Werther; MUSSORGSKY: Dimitri (*Boris Godunov*); PUCCINI: Rodolfo* (*Bohème*), Dick Johnson* (*Fanciulla del West*), Pinkerton* (*Butterfly*), Des Grieux* (*Manon Lescaut*), Luigi* (*Tabarro*), Cavaradossi* (*Tosca*), Calaf* (*Turandot*); SMETANA: Hans (*Bartered Bride*); STRAUSS, R: Bacchus* (*Ariadne auf Naxos*); VERDI: Radames* (*Aida*), Riccardo* (*Ballo in maschera*), Don Carlo*, Ernani*, Don Alvaro* (*Forza del destino*), Ismaele (*Nabucco*), Duca di Mantova* (*Rigoletto*), Alfredo* (*Traviata*), Manrico* (*Trovatore*); WAGNER: Lohengrin, Walther v d Vogelweide (*Tannhäuser*); WOLF-FERRARI: Filipeto (*Quattro rusteghi*). Recorded for: Electrecord. Gives recitals. Appears with symphony orchestra. **Res:** Zurich, Switzerland.

BYBEE, ARIEL. Lyric soprano. American. Born 9 Jan 1943, Reno, NV, USA. Husband John N McBaine, occupation lawyer. Studied: Merola Opera Prgr, San Francisco; Music Acad of the West, Martial Singher, Santa Barbara, CA; Brigham Young Univ, Kurt Weinzinger, Blanche Christensen, Provo, UT; Univ of So California, William Vennard, Seth Riggs, Los Angeles. **Debut:** Anna (*Nabucco*) San Francisco 1970. Previous occupations: PS teacher. Awards: Reg Winner Met Op Ntl Counc Aud; Ntl Winner San Francisco Op Aud.

Sang with major companies in USA: San Francisco Opera & Spring Opera. **Roles with these companies incl** BRITTEN: Governess* & Miss Jessel* (*Turn of the Screw*); DONIZETTI: Prima Donna* (*Convenienze/Viva la Mamma*); PUCCINI: Musetta* (*Bohème*); WEILL: Jenny* (*Aufstieg und Fall der Stadt Mahagonny*). Also BIZET: Carmen*. Gives recitals. Appears with symphony orchestra. **Res:** 44 W 62 St, New York, NY, USA.

BYERS, REGINALD SYDNEY. Lyric & spinto tenor. Australian. Resident mem: Australian Opera, Sydney. Born 5 Dec 1934, Sydney. Wife Alison. Two children. Studied: Sydney Consv, Fred Foscley; Margerita Mayer, Kufstein, Austria. **Debut:** Cavaradossi (*Tosca*) Australian Opera, Sydney. Previous occupations: clerk with Austral Navy; businessman. Awards: Tenor Championship of Sydney.

Sang with major companies in AUSTRL: Sydney; UK: Glasgow Scottish; USA: New York City Opera. **Roles with these companies incl** DONIZETTI: Ernesto* (*Don Pasquale*); GOUNOD: Faust*; JANACEK: Steva* (*Jenufa*); MASCAGNI: Turiddu* (*Cavalleria rusticana*); PUCCINI: Rodolfo* (*Bohème*), Dick Johnson* (*Fanciulla del West*), Pinkerton* (*Butterfly*), Luigi* (*Tabarro*), Calaf* (*Turandot*); STRAUSS, J: Alfred* (*Fledermaus*); STRAUSS, R: Bacchus* (*Ariadne auf Naxos*); VERDI: Radames* (*Aida*), Riccardo* (*Ballo in maschera*), Don Carlo*, Fenton* (*Falstaff*), Ismaele* (*Nabucco*), Gabriele* (*Simon Boccanegra*), Alfredo* (*Traviata*). Gives recitals. Coaches repertoire. **Res:** Sydney, Australia. Mgmt: SLA/UK.

C

CABALLÉ, MONTSERRAT FOLCH. Lyric soprano. Spanish. Born 12 Apr 1933, Barcelona. Husband Bernabé Martí, occupation opera singer, tenor. Two children. Studied: Eugenie Keminy, Conchita Badia, Napoleone Annovazzi, all in Barcelona. **Debut:** Mimi (*Bohème*) Basel, Switzerland 1956. Awards: numerous intl awds.

Sang with major companies in ARG: Buenos Aires; AUS: Vienna Staatsoper; BRA: Rio de Janeiro; CAN: Vancouver; FRA: Aix-en-Provence Fest, Marseille, Nice, Orange Fest, Paris; FR GER: Berlin Deutsche Oper, Bonn, Cologne, Dortmund, Düsseldorf-Duisburg, Frankfurt, Hamburg, Hannover, Munich Staatsoper, Stuttgart; HUN: Budapest; ITA: Florence Maggio & Comunale, Milan La Scala, Naples, Rome Opera, Trieste, Venice, Verona Arena; MEX: Mexico City; POR: Lisbon; SPA: Barcelona; SWI: Basel, Geneva, Zurich; UK: Edinburgh Fest, Glyndebourne Fest, London Royal; USSR: Moscow Bolshoi; USA: Cincinnati, Dallas, Hartford, Houston, Miami, New York Met, Philadelphia Grand & Lyric, Pittsburgh, San Antonio, San Diego, San Francisco Opera, Santa Fe, Seattle, Washington DC. **Roles with these companies incl** BELLINI: Norma∗‡, Imogene∗‡ (*Pirata*), Alaide∗‡ (*Straniera*); BOITO: Margherita∗‡ (*Mefistofele*); CILEA: Adriana Lecouvreur∗‡; DONIZETTI: Anna Bolena∗, Caterina Cornaro∗, Lucrezia Borgia∗‡, Maria Stuarda∗, Elisabetta∗‡ (*Roberto Devereux*); FALLA: Salud (*Vida breve*); GIORDANO: Maddalena∗ (*Andrea Chénier*); GOUNOD: Marguerite∗ (*Faust*); LEONCAVALLO: Nedda∗‡ (*Pagliacci*); MASSENET: Manon∗; MOZART: Fiordiligi‡ (*Così fan tutte*), Donna Anna∗ & Donna Elvira∗ (*Don Giovanni*), Contessa∗ (*Nozze di Figaro*); PUCCINI: Mimi∗‡ (*Bohème*), Cio-Cio-San∗‡ (*Butterfly*), Manon Lescaut∗‡, Tosca∗, Liù∗‡ (*Turandot*); ROSSINI: Elisabetta Regina∗‡, Mathilde∗‡ (*Guillaume Tell*); STRAUSS, R: Arabella, Ariadne (*Ariadne auf Naxos*), Marschallin (*Rosenkavalier*), Salome∗‡; VERDI: Aida∗‡, Amelia∗‡ (*Ballo in maschera*), Elisabetta∗‡ (*Don Carlo*), Donna Elvira (*Ernani*), Giovanna d'Arco‡, Luisa Miller∗‡, Amelia∗‡ (*Masnadieri*), Desdemona∗ (*Otello*), Violetta∗‡ (*Traviata*), Leonora∗ (*Trovatore*), Elena∗ (*Vespri*); WAGNER: Elisabeth (*Tannhäuser*). Also DONIZETTI: Gemma di Vergy. Recorded for: His Master's Voice, Philips, DG, EMI, London, Columbia, RCA. Video/Film: Leonora (*Trovatore*), Norma,

Aida. **Res:** Infanta Carlota 15/17, Barcelona, Spain. Mgmt: CAB/SPA.

CAHILL, TERESA. Lyric soprano. British. Resident mem: Royal Opera, London. Born 30 Jul 1944, Maidenhead, Berkshire, UK. Husband John A Kiernander, occupation chartered accountant. Studied: Guildhall School of Music, London; London Opera Centre, Vera Rozsa, London. **Debut:** Rosina (*Barbiere di Siviglia*) Phoenix Opera, London 1967. Awards: Peter Stuyvesant Schlshp; John Christie Prize, Glyndebourne; Silver Medal Worshipful Co of Musicians.

Sang with major companies in UK: Aldeburgh Fest, Cardiff Welsh, Glasgow Scottish, London Royal Opera; USA: Santa Fe. **Roles with these companies incl** BIZET: Micaëla (*Carmen*); MOZART: Servilia∗ (*Clemenza di Tito*), Fiordiligi∗ (*Così fan tutte*), Donna Elvira∗ & Zerlina∗ (*Don Giovanni*); STRAUSS, R: Sophie∗ (*Rosenkavalier*); TCHAIKOVSKY: Iolanthe∗. Also BRITTEN: Miss Wordsworth∗ (*Albert Herring*). Recorded for: EMI, Argo. Gives recitals. Appears with symphony orchestra. **Res:** London, UK. Mgmt: IWL/UK.

CALDWELL, SARAH. Conductor of opera and symphony, operatic stage director/producer and administrator. American. Art Dir & Founder, Resident Cond & Prod, Opera Company of Boston, form Opera Group of Boston, 172 Newbury St, Boston, MA 02116; also Opera New England, form Eastern Opera Consortium. Founded original company in 1957. Born 1928, Maryville, MO, USA. Single. Studied: Hendrix Coll, Conway, AR, USA; New England Consv of Music, Richard Burgin, Boston; incl violin. Operatic training: asst to Boris Goldovsky. **Operatic debut as dir:** *Rake's Progress* Boston Univ Opera Wkshp 1953; **as cond:** Opera Group of Boston, MA 1957. Symphonic debut: Am Symph Orch, New York 1974. Previous occupations: studied psychology. Awards: Hon DM, Harvard Univ, Simmons Coll Boston, Bates Coll & Bowdoin Coll, ME 1975; Rodgers and Hammerstein Awd; etc. Previous adm positions in opera: Dir, Am Ntl Opera Co, touring comp of Opera Co of Boston 1967-68; Dir, Boston Univ Opera Wkshp 1953-57.

Conducted and/or directed with major companies in USA: Boston, Dallas, Houston, New York Met

& City Opera. **Operas conducted († indicates also directed) with these companies incl** BEETHOVEN: *Fidelio*★†; BELLINI: *Capuleti ed i Montecchi*★†, *Norma*†; BERLIOZ: *Benvenuto Cellini*★†, *Troyens*★†; BIZET: *Carmen*†; CHARPENTIER: *Louise*†; DONIZETTI: *Elisir*†, *Fille du régiment*★†, *Lucrezia Borgia*†; GAY/Britten: *Beggar's Opera*†; HAYDN: *Mondo della luna*†; KURKA: *Good Soldier Schweik*†; MASSENET: *Don Quichotte*★†; MOZART: *Così fan tutte*★†, *Don Giovanni*†, *Entführung aus dem Serail*†, *Finta giardiniera*†, *Nozze di Figaro*†, *Zauberflöte*†; OFFENBACH: *Contes d'Hoffmann*; PROKOFIEV: *War and Peace*★†; PUCCINI: *Bohème*†, *Fanciulla del West*★†, *Butterfly*★†, *Tosca*†; ROSSINI: *Barbiere di Siviglia*★†; SMETANA: *Bartered Bride*★†; THOMAS: *Mignon*★; VERDI: *Don Carlo*★†, *Falstaff*★†, *Rigoletto*†, *Traviata*★†; WAGNER: *Fliegende Holländer*†; WEILL: *Aufstieg und Fall der Stadt Mahagonny*★†. **Operas only directed with these companies incl** BARTOK: *Bluebeard's Castle*; BELLINI: *Puritani*; BERG: *Lulu*; GOUNOD: *Faust*; HENZE: *Junge Lord*; HUMPERDINCK: *Hänsel und Gretel*; MASSENET: *Manon*; ORFF: *Kluge*; PUCCINI: *Tabarro*; ROSSINI: *Semiramide*; SCHOENBERG: *Moses und Aron*; STRAUSS, J: *Fledermaus*; STRAUSS, R: *Ariadne auf Naxos*; STRAVINSKY: *Rake's Progress*; VERDI: *Macbeth, Otello*; WAGNER: *Meistersinger*. Also NONO: *Intolleranza*†; RAMEAU: *Hippolyte et Aricie*†; SESSIONS: *Montezuma*★†. **World premieres dir:** MIDDLETON: *Command Performance* 1961; SCHULLER: *Fisherman and his Wife* 1970; both Op Co of Boston. Conducted major orch in USA/Canada. Translated numerous operas, some in collaboration with B Goldovsky. Mem of Massachusetts Counc on the Arts; Prof Committee Central Op Service; OPERA America. **Res:** Boston, MA, USA. **Mgmt:** VIN/USA.

CALEB, FRANK. American. Asst Mng/Dir of Development, Lyric Opera of Chicago, 20 No Wacker Dr, Chicago, IL 60606, USA since 1973. In charge of finc. Born 13 Sep 1940, Fort Smith, AR. Wife Victoria, occupation student. Two children. Studied: Yale Univ, New Haven, CT. Plays the piano. Previous occupations: asst to Headmaster, Cushing Acad, Ashburnham, MA. Form positions, primarily administrative & musical: Fund Raising Consultant, Ravinia Fest, Chicago 1970-72; Gen Mng, Duluth Symph Assn, MI 1972-73. Initiated major policy changes including record-setting fund drive in 1974 for Lyric Opera Chicago. Mem of St Paul Opera, Dir; Yale School of Music, Chmn Midwestern Region; Evanston Art Center, Vice Pres; Chicago Theatre of the Deaf, Dir. **Res:** 739 Forest Ave, Evanston, IL, USA.

CALÈS, CLAUDE; né Jean-Claude Calestrémé. Lyric & dramatic baritone. French. Born 20 Apr 1934, Villeneuve. Wife Michèle Claverie, occupation lyric coloratura soprano. One child. Studied: Consv de Bordeaux, Marthe Nestoulous; Consv of Paris & of Madrid, Jean Claverie. **Debut:** Zurga (*Pêcheurs de perles*) Opéra de Rennes, France 1961. Previous occupations: studied philosophy. Awards: First Prize in Voice and Opera, Consv of Paris; Grand Prize Caruso Golden Voice; 2 First

Prizes Acad du Disque; Grand Prize Acad Charles Cros.

Sang with major companies in BEL: Liège; FRA: Bordeaux, Lyon, Marseille, Nancy, Nice, Paris, Rouen, Strasbourg, Toulouse; ITA: Palermo. **Roles with these companies incl** BERLIOZ: Choroebus (*Troyens*); BIZET: Escamillo★ (*Carmen*), Splendiano★ (*Djamileh*), Zurga★ (*Pêcheurs de perles*); DONIZETTI: Dott Malatesta★ (*Don Pasquale*), Belcore★ (*Elisir*); GLUCK: Oreste (*Iphigénie en Tauride*), Orphée; GOUNOD: Ourrias★ (*Mireille*); MASCAGNI: Alfio★ (*Cavalleria rusticana*); MASSENET: Albert★ (*Werther*); MENOTTI: John Sorel★ (*Consul*); MEYERBEER: Comte de Nevers★ (*Huguenots*); MOZART: Guglielmo★ (*Così fan tutte*), Conte Almaviva★ (*Nozze di Figaro*); PUCCINI: Marcello★ (*Bohème*), Sharpless★ (*Butterfly*); ROSSINI: Figaro★ (*Barbiere di Siviglia*), Robert★ (*Comte Ory*); ROUSSEAU: Devin★ (*Devin du village*); SAINT-SAENS: Grand prêtre★ (*Samson et Dalila*); VERDI: Renato★ (*Ballo in maschera*), Ford (*Falstaff*), Rigoletto. Also BECAUD: Mickey★ (*Opéra d'Aran*); DAMASE: Julien★ (*Colombe*); MILHAUD: Orphée (*Malheurs d'Orphée*); RAMEAU: Ali (*Indes galantes*); de BANFIELD: Giovane★ (*Alissa*); BRITTEN: Tarquinius★ (*Rape of Lucretia*); POULENC: Directeur★ (*Mamelles de Tirésias*); GOUNOD: Valentin (*Faust*); DAMASE: Ambassadeur (*Madame de*). **World premieres:** DAMASE: Orphée (*Eurydice*) Bordeaux Opera 1972; AUBIN: Goya, Lille Opera 1974. Recorded for: HMV, Pathé-Marconi, Decca-London, RCA, Guilde Internationale. Video/Film: Ambassadeur (*Madame de*). Gives recitals. Appears with symphony orchestra. Teaches voice. **Res:** rue de la Paix 19, 92270 Bois-Colombes, France. **Mgmt:** BCP/FRA.

CALLAWAY, PAUL. Conductor of opera. American. Resident Cond, Lake George Opera Fest, Glens Falls, NY. Born 16 Aug 1909, Atlanta, IL, USA. Single. Plays the organ and piano. **Operatic debut:** Opera Socy of Washington, DC, 1956. Previous occupations: Organist and Choirmaster, Washington Cathedral 1939- . Awards: Hon DM Westminster Coll, Fulton, MO, & Washington Coll, Chestertown, MD. Previous adm positions in opera: Mus Dir, Opera Socy of Washington, DC, 1957-67.

Conducted with major companies in USA: Lake George, Washington DC. **Operas with these companies incl** BARBER: *Vanessa;* BEETHOVEN: *Fidelio;* BERLIOZ: *Béatrice et Bénédict;* BIZET: *Carmen;* CAVALLI: *Ormindo;* DEBUSSY: *Pelléas et Mélisande;* DELIUS: *Koanga*★, *Village Romeo and Juliet*★; GOUNOD: *Faust;* HAYDN: *Infedeltà delusa;* MASSENET: *Werther;* MENOTTI: *Maria Golovin, Old Maid and the Thief;* MONTEVERDI: *Favola d'Orfeo, Incoronazione di Poppea*★; MOZART: *Così fan tutte, Don Giovanni, Entführung aus dem Serail, Idomeneo, Nozze di Figaro, Zauberflöte;* PASATIERI: *Black Widow*★; PUCCINI: *Bohème, Gianni Schicchi, Butterfly, Tosca;* RAVEL: *Enfant et les sortilèges, Heure espagnole;* ROSSINI: *Barbiere di Siviglia, Otello;* STRAUSS, J: *Fledermaus*★; STRAUSS, R: *Ariadne auf Naxos;* STRAVINSKY: *Rake's Progress;* TCHAIKOVSKY: *Pique Dame;* VERDI: *Falstaff, Otello, Traviata;*

WARD: *Crucible*★. **World premieres:** BER-NARDO: *Child* Lake George Fest, Albany, NY 1974; AMRAM: *Twelfth Night,* Lake George Fest 1968. **Res:** 2230 Decatur Pl NW, Washington DC, USA.

CAMANI, ADRIANA. Dramatic mezzo-soprano. Italian. Born 27 Mar 1936, Padua, Italy. Single. Studied: Consv C Pollini, Padua; Mo P Montanari, Ma Sara Sforni Corti. **Debut:** Nutrice (*Incoronazione di Poppea*) Teatro San Carlo, Naples 1968. Awards: Conc Intl G Verdi, Parma; Voci Verdiane di Busseto.
Sang with major companies in ITA: Genoa, Milan La Scala, Naples, Trieste, Turin, Venice, Verona Arena. **Roles with these companies incl** PONCHIELLI: La Cieca★ (*Gioconda*); PUC-CINI: Suzuki★ (*Butterfly*), Badessa★ & Principessa (*Suor Angelica*), Frugola★ (*Tabarro*); STRAVINSKY: Mère★ (*Mavra*); VERDI: Ulrica (*Ballo in maschera*), Eboli (*Don Carlo*); WAG-NER: Erda (*Siegfried*), Waltraute (*Götterdämmerung*); WOLF-FERRARI: Margarita (*Quattro rusteghi*); ZANDONAI: Samaritana (*Francesca da Rimini*). Also GIORDANO: Madelon (*Andrea Chénier*); MASCAGNI: Madre (*Silvano*); DAL-LAPICCOLA: Baldad (*Job*); TESTI: Vassilissa (*Albergo dei poveri*). **World premieres:** INGO: Santa (*Nunziatella*) Teatro Regio, Turin 1971. Appears with symphony orchestra. **Res:** V E Petrella 9, Milan, Italy.

CAMPANELLA, BRUNO CARMELO. Conductor of opera and symphony; composer. Italian. Born 6 Jan 1943, Bari. Wife Rosalia. Two children. Studied: Luigi Dallapiccola & Piero Bellugi, Florence; incl piano & viola. Plays the piano. Operatic training as asst cond at Spoleto Fest 1967. **Operatic debut:** *Furioso all'isola di San Domingo,* Spoleto Fest 1967. Symphonic debut: Symph Orch of Vera Cruz, Mexico 1968.
Conducted with major companies in ISR: Tel Aviv; ITA: Bologna, Florence Maggio & Comunale, Milan La Scala, Naples, Palermo, Spoleto Fest, Trieste, Venice; MEX: Mexico City. **Operas with these companies incl** DALLAPICCOLA: *Prigioniero*★; DONIZETTI: *Don Pasquale*★; FALLA: *Retablo de Maese Pedro*★; MENOTTI: *Medium*★‡; PUCCINI: *Gianni Schicchi*★; ROS-SINI: *Cambiale di matrimonio*★, *Signor Bruschino*‡. Also DONIZETTI: *Furioso all'isola di San Domingo*★; STRAVINSKY: *Histoire du soldat.* Video—Spoleto Fest TV: *Medium, Retablo di Maese Pedro.* Conducted major orch in Europe. Teaches at Florence Consv. **Res:** V Cinque Giornate 31, Florence, Italy.

CAMPBELL, PATTON. Scenic and costume designer for opera, theater, film; specl in costumes. Is also a teacher. American. Resident designer, New York City Opera. Born 10 Sep 1926, Omaha, NE. Single. Studied: Yale Drama School, Donald Oenslager, Frank Bevan, CT. Prof training: Cape Playhouse, Dennis, MA 1948-50. **Operatic debut:** cost, *Ballad of Baby Doe* Central City Opera, CO 1956. Theater debut: Plymouth Theater, New York 1955. Previous occupation: instructor Barnard Coll, NY Univ; assoc prof Columbia Univ. Previous adm positions in opera: resident designer, Santa Fe Opera, NM 1957-59.

Designed for major companies in USA: Kansas City, New York City Opera, Santa Fe. **Operas designed for these companies incl** BERNSTEIN: *Trouble in Tahiti;* DONIZETTI: *Anna Bolena;* FLOYD: *Susannah*★; JANACEK: *Katya Kabanova, Makropoulos Affair*★; MOZART: *Così fan tutte, Entführung aus dem Serail;* PUCCINI: *Bohème, Gianni Schicchi, Butterfly, Tabarro, Tosca;* ROSSINI: *Barbiere di Siviglia, Cenerentola;* STRAUSS, J: *Fledermaus;* STRAUSS, R: *Ariadne auL Naxos, Capriccio, Rosenkavalier;* STRAVINSKY: *Rake's Progress;* VERDI: *Falstaff, Traviata.* Also MOORE: *Carry Nation;* EGK: *Revisor.* **Operatic world premieres:** FLOYD: *Wuthering Heights* Santa Fe Op, NM 1958; MOORE: *Wings of the Dove* 1961, HOIBY: *Natalia Petrovna* 1964, BEESON: *Lizzie Borden* 1964, ROREM: *Miss Julie* 1965, all at New York City Opera; MOORE: *Ballad of Baby Doe* 1956, WARD: *Lady from Colorado* 1964, both at Central City Op, CO; SCHULLER: *Fisherman and His Wife* Op Co of Boston 1970; BEE-SON: *Captain Jinks of the Horse Marines* Kansas City Lyric, MO 1975. Operatic Video—NET TV: *Lizzie Borden, Fisherman and His Wife.* Exhibitions of stage designs Wright-Hepburn Gal 1968; Lincoln Center Libr, New York 1970 & 1975. Teaches at State Univ of New York. **Res:** 46 W 95th St, New York, USA.

CAMPORA, GUISEPPE. Lyric tenor. Italian. Born 30 Sep 1925, Tortona, Italy. Wife France. One child. Studied: Mo Magenta, Genoa, Italy. **Debut:** Rodolfo (*Bohème*) Bari Opera, Italy 1952.
Sang with major companies in ARG: Buenos Aires; AUS: Bregenz Fest; BEL: Brussels; BRA: Rio de Janeiro; CAN: Toronto, Vancouver; FRA: Paris; FR GER: Hamburg; HOL: Amsterdam; ITA: Bologna, Florence Maggio & Comunale, Genoa, Milan La Scala, Naples, Palermo, Parma, Rome Opera & Caracalla, Trieste, Turin, Venice, Verona Arena; MEX: Mexico City; MON: Monte Carlo; ROM: Bucharest; S AFR: Johannesburg; SPA: Barcelona; SWI: Geneva, Zurich; UK: Glasgow Scottish; USA: Baltimore, Cincinnati, Hartford, Miami, Newark, New Orleans, New York Met & City Opera, Philadelphia Grand & Lyric, Pittsburgh, Portland, San Antonio, San Francisco Opera. **Roles with these companies incl** AUBER: Fra Diavolo★; BELLINI: Orombello (*Beatrice di Tenda*), Tebaldo (*Capuleti ed i Montecchi*), Elvino (*Sonnambula*); BIZET: Don José (*Carmen*), Nadir (*Pêcheurs de perles*); BOITO: Faust (*Mefistofele*); CILEA: Maurizio (*A. Lecouvreur*); DONIZETTI: Gerardo (*Caterina Cornaro*),˜Nemorino★ (*Elisir*), Fernand (*Favorite*), Edgardo★ (*Lucia*), Gennaro (*Lucrezia Borgia*); FLOTOW: Lionel (*Martha*); GIORDANO: Loris Ipanov★ (*Fedora*); GOUNOD: Faust, Roméo; HENZE: Lord Barrat (*Junge Lord*); LALO: Mylio (*Roi d'Ys*); MASCAGNI: Fritz (*Amico Fritz*), Turiddu (*Cavalleria rusticana*); MASSENET: Des Grieux★ (*Manon*), Werther; MONTEMEZZI: Avito (*Amore dei tre re*); MUS-SORGSKY: Gritzko (*Fair at Sorochinsk*); NI-COLAI: Fenton (*Lustigen Weiber*); OFFENBACH: Hoffmann, Paquillo (*Périchole*); PONCHIELLI: Enzo‡ (*Gioconda*); PUCCINI: Rodolfo (*Bohème*), Rinuccio (*Gianni Schicchi*), Pinkerton★‡ (*Butterfly*), Ruggero (*Rondine*), Luigi

(*Tabarro*), Cavaradossi★‡ (*Tosca*), Calaf (*Turandot*); ROSSINI: Almaviva (*Barbiere di Siviglia*), Leicester (*Elisabetta Regina*); STRAUSS, J: Alfred★ (*Fledermaus*); THOMAS: Wilhelm Meister (*Mignon*); VERDI: Radames (*Aida*), Riccardo (*Ballo in maschera*), Fenton (*Falstaff*), Don Alvaro‡ (*Forza del destino*), Rodolfo (*Luisa Miller*), Duca di Mantova (*Rigoletto*); Gabriele‡ (*Simon Boccanegra*), Alfredo★ (*Traviata*); WEBER: Hüon (*Oberon*); ZANDONAI: Paolo (*Francesca da Rimini*), Romeo. Also CILEA: Federico (*Arlesiana*); LEONCAVALLO: Milio‡ (*Zazà*); MASCAGNI: Flammen (*Lodoletta*); ZANDONAI: Matteo‡ (*Conchita*). World premieres: ROCCA: Boris (*Uragano*) La Scala, Milan 1952. Recorded for: Decca, Angel, Cetra, Urania. Video/Film: Radames (*Aida*); Pinkerton (*Butterfly*); Enzo (*Gioconda*). Gives recitals. Appears with symphony orchestra. **Res:** V G Bosco 19, Tortona, Italy. Mgmt: HUR/USA.

CANGALOVIC, MIROSLAV MIHAIL. Bass. Yugoslavian. Resident mem: Opera Belgrade. Born 3 Mar 1921, Glamoc, Yugoslavia. Wife Dusanka, occupation stage director/producer. One child. **Debut:** Pimen (*Boris Godunov*) Opera Belgrade 1946. Previous occupations: journalist.
Sang with major companies in ARG: Buenos Aires; AUS: Vienna Staatsoper; BEL: Brussels; BUL: Sofia; CAN: Montreal/Quebec, Toronto; CZE: Brno, Prague Smetana; DEN: Copenhagen; FIN: Helsinki; FRA: Bordeaux, Marseille, Nice, Paris, Rouen; GRE: Athens National Opera & Festival; FR GER: Wiesbaden; GER DR: Berlin Staatsoper, Leipzig; HOL: Amsterdam; HUN: Budapest; ITA: Florence Maggio Musicale & Comunale, Genoa, Milan La Scala, Naples, Palermo, Rome Teatro dell'Opera, Turin, Venice; MON: Monte Carlo; NOR: Oslo; POL: Warsaw; POR: Lisbon; ROM: Bucharest; SPA: Barcelona; SWI: Basel, Geneva, Zurich, Lausanne; UK: Edinburgh Fest; USSR: Kiev, Leningrad Kirov, Moscow Bolshoi, Tbilisi; USA: Chicago; YUG: Dubrovnik, Zagreb, Belgrade. **Roles with these companies incl** BARTOK: Bluebeard; BEETHOVEN: Rocco (*Fidelio*); BORODIN: Kontchak & Galitzky★ (*Prince Igor*); CHERUBINI: Creon (*Medea*); DONIZETTI: Dott Dulcamara (*Elisir*); FALLA: Don Quixote (*Retablo de Maese Pedro*), Tio Sarvaor (*Vida breve*); GERSHWIN: Porgy; GLINKA: Ivan (*Life for the Tsar*); GOUNOD: Méphistophélès (*Faust*); HANDEL: Giulio Cesare; JANACEK: Dikoy (*Katya Kabanova*); MASSENET: Don Quichotte, Lescaut (*Manon*); MOZART: Leporello (*Don Giovanni*), Figaro (*Nozze di Figaro*), Sarastro (*Zauberflöte*); MUSSORGSKY: Boris★ 3 vers & Varlaam & Pimen (*Boris Godunov*), Tcherevik (*Fair at Sorochinsk*), Dosifei (*Khovanshchina*); NICOLAI: Falstaff (*Lustigen Weiber*); OFFENBACH: Coppélius etc (*Contes d'Hoffmann*); PUCCINI: Colline (*Bohème*), Gianni Schicchi; RIMSKY-KORSAKOV: Tsar Ivan (*Maid of Pskov*); ROSSINI: Don Basilio (*Barbiere di Siviglia*); SHOSTAKOVICH: Boris★ (*Katerina Ismailova*); SMETANA: Kezal (*Bartered Bride*); STRAVINSKY: Tiresias★ (*Oedipus Rex*); VERDI: Philip II & Grande Inquisitore (*Don Carlo*), Silva (*Ernani*), Padre Guardiano (*Forza del destino*), Fiesco (*Simon Boccanegra*). Also TCHAIKOVSKY:

Kotchubay (*Mazeppa*). Recorded for: Decca. Gives recitals. Appears with symphony orchestra. **Res:** Belgrade, Yugoslavia. Mgmt: YGC/YUG.

CANNARILE, ANTONIETTA. Lyric soprano. Italian. Widowed. Studied: Maria Miracolo, Milan. **Debut:** Mimi (*Bohème*) Teatro Comunale, Piacenza 1966. Awards: Golden Plaque, Grand Theater Brescia 1969.
Sang with major companies in FR GER: Munich Staatsoper, Stuttgart; HUN: Budapest; ITA: Bologna, Florence Maggio & Comunale, Naples, Rome Opera & Caracalla, Turin, Verona Arena; SPA: Barcelona; YUG: Belgrade. **Roles with these companies incl** BIZET: Micaëla★ (*Carmen*); BOITO: Margherita (*Mefistofele*); CILEA: Adriana Lecouvreur★; GOUNOD: Marguerite★ (*Faust*); LEONCAVALLO: Nedda★ (*Pagliacci*); MASSENET: Manon★; PUCCINI: Mimi★ (*Bohème*), Suor Angelica★, Tosca★, Liù★ (*Turandot*); VERDI: Alice Ford★ (*Falstaff*), Desdemona★ (*Otello*), Amelia★ (*Simon Boccanegra*), Violetta★ (*Traviata*). **Res:** V Tuscolana 58, Rome, Italy.

CANNE-MEIJER, CORA. Lyric coloratura mezzosoprano. Dutch. Born Amsterdam, Holland. Husband Patriasz G, occupation antiquarian. One child. Studied: Consv Amsterdam, Jan Keizer; Ré Koster, N Perugia, Paris; Alfred Jerger, Vienna. **Debut:** Cherubino (*Nozze di Figaro*) Netherlands Opera, Amsterdam 1953. Awards: Knight in the Order of Oranie-Nassau, HM Queen Juliana, 1973.
Sang with major companies in AUS: Salzburg Fest, Vienna Staatsoper; BEL: Brussels; FRA: Bordeaux, Lyon, Marseille, Nancy, Nice, Rouen, Strasbourg; FR GER: Berlin Deutsche Oper, Frankfurt, Hamburg; HOL: Amsterdam; MON: Monte Carlo; POR: Lisbon; SPA: Barcelona; SWI: Geneva, Zurich; UK: Glyndebourne Fest. **Roles with these companies incl** AUBER: Pamela (*Fra Diavolo*); BARTOK: Judith (*Bluebeard's Castle*); BENNETT: Rosalind★ (*Mines of Sulphur*); BERNSTEIN: Dinah (*Trouble in Tahiti*); BIZET: Carmen★; BORODIN: Kontchakovna (*Prince Igor*); BRITTEN: Hermia (*Midsummer Night*); DEBUSSY: Geneviève★ (*Pelléas et Mélisande*); DONIZETTI: Maffio Orsini (*Lucrezia Borgia*); FLOTOW: Nancy (*Martha*); GLUCK: Orfeo; GOUNOD: Siebel (*Faust*), Taven (*Mireille*); HAYDN: Lisetta (*Mondo della luna*); HUMPERDINCK: Hänsel; MARTINU: Katerina (*Griechische Passion*); MASSENET: Dulcinée★ (*Don Quichotte*), Charlotte★ (*Werther*); MOZART: Dorabella★ (*Così fan tutte*), Cherubino (*Nozze di Figaro*); MUSSORGSKY: Marina★ (*Boris Godunov*), Khivria (*Fair at Sorochinsk*); POULENC: Prioresse★ (*Dialogues des Carmélites*); PUCCINI: Suzuki (*Butterfly*), Frugola (*Tabarro*); ROSSINI: Rosina (*Barbiere di Siviglia*), Isolier‡ (*Comte Ory*), Isabella (*Italiana in Algeri*); SAINT-SAENS: Dalila; STRAUSS, J: Prinz Orlovsky (*Fledermaus*); STRAUSS, R: Komponist (*Ariadne auf Naxos*), Clairon★ (*Capriccio*), Octavian★ (*Rosenkavalier*); STRAVINSKY: Baba the Turk★ (*Rake's Progress*); TCHAIKOVSKY: Olga (*Eugene Onegin*); THOMAS: Mignon; VERDI: Amneris (*Aida*), Ulrica (*Ballo in maschera*), Eboli★ (*Don Carlo*), Preziosilla (*Forza del*

destino); WOLF-FERRARI: Margarita (*Quattro rusteghi*). Also RAVEL: Concepcion★ (*Heure espagnole*); HANDEL: Hunolf★ (*Rodelinda*); DE LEEUW: Zienster (*De droom*). **World premieres:** MARTIN: Nérine (*M de Pourceaugnac*) Geneva Opera/Amsterdam 1963; MILHAUD: Suzanne (*La mère coupable*) Geneva 1966; SAGUER: Mariana (*Mariana Pineda*) Marseille Opera 1970; DAMASE: Mrs Montgomery (*L'Héritière*) Nancy Opera 1974. Recorded for: RCA. Video/Film: Carmen; Rosina (*Barbiere di Siviglia*); Dinah (*Trouble in Tahiti*). Gives recitals. Appears with symphony orchestra. Teaches voice. Coaches repertoire. On faculty of Sweelinck Consv, Amsterdam. **Res:** Weteringstraat 48, Amsterdam, Holland. Mgmt: RAP/FRA.

CAPECCHI, RENATO. Bass-baritone. Italian. Born 6 Nov 1923, Cairo, Egypt. Wife Jeannette Rigaud. Two children. Studied: Ubaldo Carrozzi, Milan. **Debut:** Amonsaro (*Aida*) Teatro Comunale, Reggio Emilia, Italy 1949. Awards: Accademia Tiberina, Rome.

Sang with major companies in AUS: Salzburg Fest, Vienna Volksoper; BEL: Brussels; CAN: Montreal/Quebec; FRA: Aix-en-Provence Fest, Bordeaux, Lyon, Paris, Strasbourg, Toulouse; FR GER: Berlin Deutsche Oper, Munich Staatsoper, Saarbrücken, Stuttgart, Wiesbaden; GER DR: Berlin Staatsoper; HOL: Amsterdam; ISR: Tel Aviv; ITA: Bologna, Florence Maggio & Comunale, Genoa, Milan La Scala, Naples, Palermo, Rome Opera, Trieste, Turin, Venice, Verona Arena; MON: Monte Carlo; POR: Lisbon; SPA: Barcelona; SWE: Drottningholm Fest; SWI: Geneva, Zurich; UK: Edinburgh Fest, London Royal Opera; USSR: Moscow Bolshoi; USA: Chicago, Dallas, Fort Worth, New Orleans, New York Met, Philadelphia Lyric, San Antonio, San Francisco Opera. **Roles with these companies incl** BELLINI: Sir Richard‡ (*Puritani*); BERG: Wozzeck; BERLIOZ: Méphistophélès (*Damnation de Faust*); BIZET: Escamillo (*Carmen*); BORODIN: (*Prince Igor*); CILEA: Michonnet (*A. Lecouvreur*); CIMAROSA: Count Robinson & Geronimo (*Matrimonio segreto*); DEBUSSY: Golaud (*Pelléas et Mélisande*); DONIZETTI: Enrico‡ (*Campanello*), Agata (*Convenienze*), Dott Malatesta & Don Pasquale‡ (*Don Pasquale*), Belcore‡ & Dott Dulcamara‡ (*Elisir*), Sulpice★ (*Fille du régiment*), Marquis & Antonio (*Linda di Chamounix*), Enrico (*Lucia*), Gasparo★ (*Rita*); GALUPPI: Don Tritemio (*Filosofo di campagna*); GIORDANO: De Siriex (*Fedora*); HENZE: Tartaglia (*König Hirsch/Re Cervo*); HINDEMITH: Cardillac; IBERT: Boniface (*Angélique*); MASSENET: Lescaut (*Manon*), Des Grieux‡ (*Portrait de Manon*), Albert (*Werther*); MENOTTI: Husband (*Amelia al ballo*); MONTEMEZZI: Manfredo‡ (*Amore dei tre re*); MONTEVERDI: Orfeo; MOZART: Guglielmo & Don Alfonso★ (*Così fan tutte*), Leporello & Don Giovanni (*Don Giovanni*), Conte Almaviva & Figaro‡ (*Nozze di Figaro*), Papageno (*Zauberflöte*); OFFENBACH: Coppélius etc (*Contes d'Hoffmann*); ORFF: Solo (*Carmina burana*); PAISIELLO: Figaro & Bartolo★‡ (*Barbiere di Siviglia*); PERGOLESI: Marcaniello (*Frate 'nnamorato*), Uberto★‡ (*Serva padrona*); PROKOFIEV: Prince Andrei & Vassili Denisov & Ilya

(*War and Peace*); PUCCINI: Marcello‡ (*Bohème*), Gianni Schicchi, Sharpless (*Butterfly*), Lescaut (*Manon Lescaut*), Michele (*Tabarro*), Scarpia (*Tosca*); ROSSINI: Figaro‡ & Dott Bartolo★‡ (*Barbiere di Siviglia*), Tobias Mill & Slook★ (*Cambiale di Matrimonio*), Dandini★ (*Cenerentola*), Robert (*Comte Ory*), Macrobio (*Pietra del paragone*), Assur (*Semiramide*), Bruschino★ & Gaudenzio‡ (*Signor Bruschino*), Geronio (*Turco in Italia*); ROUSSEAU: Le Devin (*Devin du village*); SHOSTAKOVICH: Platon Kusmich Kovalioff★ (*The Nose*); STRAUSS, R: Robert Storch (*Intermezzo*); TCHAIKOVSKY: Yeletsky (*Pique Dame*); VERDI: Amonasro (*Aida*), Ford & Falstaff (*Falstaff*), Fra Melitone (*Forza del destino*), Barone‡ (*Giorno di regno*), Iago (*Otello*), Rigoletto‡, Germont (*Traviata*); WAGNER: Beckmesser (*Meistersinger*); WOLF-FERRARI: Conte Gil (*Segreto di Susanna*); ZANDONAI: Gianciotti (*Francesca da Rimini*). **World premieres:** GHEDINI: Billy Budd, Fest Venezia 1949; TOSATTI: (*Giudizio Universale*) La Scala, Milan 1955; MALIPIERO: (*Donna è mobile*) Piccola Scala 1957; CHAILLY: (*Domanda di matrimonio*) Piccola Scala, Milan 1957. Recorded for: EMI, Decca, DG, Columbia, Philips, Ricordi, Cetra. Gives recitals. Appears with symphony orchestra. Teaches voice. Coaches repertoire. On faculty of NOS Opera Studio, Amsterdam; Paris Opera Studio. **Res:** V Stradella 7, Milan, Italy. Mgmt: CSA/USA.

CAPECE MINUTOLO, IRMA. Spinto soprano. Italian. Born 6 Aug 1940, Naples. Single. Studied: Toti Dal Monte & Maria Caniglia, Rome. **Debut:** Mimi (*Bohème*) Opera House, Vicenza 1965. Previous occupations: tennis and classical dance. Awards: Grand Gold Medal, Verdi, Brescia & Giordano, Rome.

Sang with major companies in FRA: Strasbourg; FR GER: Frankfurt; ITA: Florence Comunale, Milan La Scala, Naples, Palermo, Parma, Rome Opera, Turin, Venice; MON: Monte Carlo; SWI: Basel. **Roles with these companies incl** BIZET: Micaëla (*Carmen*); BOITO: Margherita (*Mefistofele*); CILEA: Adriana Lecouvreur; GLUCK: Euridice; GOUNOD: Marguerite (*Faust*); LEONCAVALLO: Nedda (*Pagliacci*); MASSENET: Thaïs; PUCCINI: Mimi (*Bohème*), Lauretta (*Gianni Schicchi*), Suor Angelica, Liù (*Turandot*); VERDI: Desdemona (*Otello*), Leonora (*Trovatore*). Also MALIPIERO: (*Torneo notturno*); GIORDANO: (*Cena delle beffe*), (*Mese mariano*). **World premieres:** MILELLA: Caterina (*Una storia d'altri tempi*) Teatro Petruzzelli, Bari 1972. Gives recitals. Appears with symphony orchestra. **Res:** Val Gardena 3, Rome, Italy.

CAPELL, MANFRED. Dramatic baritone. German. Resident mem: Ulmer Theater, Ulm FR Ger. Born Lübeck, Germany. Wife Maria, occupation dancer. Two children. Studied: Prof Kosubek, Berlin; Sidney Dietch, New York; Prof Jaro Prohaska, Berlin; Inge Borkh. **Debut:** Alfio & Tonio (*Cavalleria rusticana & Pagliacci*) Osnabrück Opera 1960. Previous occupations: actor. Awards: First Prize GYA Meistersinger Cont, Nürnberg 1954; Mrs Whelen Awd, Acad of Vocal Arts, Philadelphia, USA.

Sang with major companies in FRA: Nice; FR GER: Bielefeld, Cologne, Dortmund, Düsseldorf, Essen, Krefeld, Nürnberg, Wuppertal; SPA: Barcelona. **Roles with these cos incl** BEETHOVEN: Don Pizarro★ (*Fidelio*); BIZET: Escamillo★ (*Carmen*); CIMAROSA: Count Robinson (*Matrimonio segreto*); DONIZETTI: Belcore★ (*Elisir*), Enrico (*Lucia*); GLUCK: Thoas (*Iphigénie en Tauride*); HENZE: Mittenhofer★ (*Elegy for Young Lovers*); JANACEK: Forester (*Cunning Little Vixen*); LEONCAVALLO: Tonio★ (*Pagliacci*); LORTZING: Graf Eberbach★ (*Wildschütz*), Peter I★ (*Zar und Zimmermann*); MASCAGNI: Alfio★ (*Cavalleria rusticana*); MENOTTI: Husband (*Amelia al ballo*); MOZART: Don Alfonso★ (*Così fan tutte*), Don Giovanni★, Conte Almaviva★ & Figaro★ (*Nozze di Figaro*); MUSSORGSKY: Ivan Khovansky★ (*Khovanshchina*); OFFENBACH: Coppélius etc★ (*Contes d'Hoffmann*); ORFF: Solo★ (*Carmina burana*), König (*Kluge*); PERGOLESI: Tracolino (*Maestro di musica*), Uberto (*Serva padrona*); PUCCINI: Marcello★ (*Bohème*), Jack Rance★ (*Fanciulla del West*), Gianni Schicchi, Sharpless (*Butterfly*), Lescaut★ (*Manon Lescaut*), Scarpia★ (*Tosca*); RAVEL: Ramiro (*Heure espagnole*); ROSSINI: Don Basilio (*Barbiere di Siviglia*); STRAUSS, R: Mandryka★ (*Arabella*), Musiklehrer★ (*Ariadne auf Naxos*), Jochanaan★ (*Salome*); TCHAIKOVSKY: Eugene Onegin, Yeletsky★ (*Pique Dame*); VERDI: Amonasro★ (*Aida*), Renato (*Ballo in maschera*), Rodrigo & Grande Inquisitore (*Don Carlo*), Don Carlo★ (*Forza del destino*), Nabucco, Iago★ (*Otello*), Rigoletto★, Germont★ (*Traviata*), Conte di Luna★ (*Trovatore*); WAGNER: Holländer★, Wolfram (*Tannhäuser*). Also STRAUSS, R: Faninal (*Rosenkavalier*); MONIUSZKO: Miecznik (*Haunted Castle*); BRITTEN: Oberon (*Midsummer Night*); ZAFRED: Hamlet; PERGOLESI: Tracollo. **World premieres:** SCHWERTSIK: Orakelleser (*Lange Weg zur grossen Mauer*) Ulmer Theater 1975; KRENEK: Bannadonna (*Bell Tower*) Univ of Ill, Urbana, USA 1957. Gives recitals. Appears with symphony orchestra. Teaches voice. **Res:** Silcherstr 1, D-7919 Tiefenbach, FR Ger. **Mgmt:** PAS/FRG.

CAPLAT, MORAN VICTOR HINGSTON. British. Gen Adm, Glyndebourne Festival Opera and Glyndebourne Touring Opera, Lewes, Sussex, UK. In charge of overall adm matters, art policy, mus, dram & tech matters & finances. Born 1 Oct 1916, Herne Bay, Kent. Wife Diana M. Three children. Studied: Royal Acad of Dram Art, London. Previous occupations: actor; Lt Comman, Royal Navy. Started with present company in 1945 as Asst to Gen Mng, in present position since 1948. World premieres at theaters under his management: BRITTEN: *Albert Herring* 1947; HENZE: *Elegy for Young Lovers* 1961; MAW: *Rising of the Moon* 1970, all at Glyndebourne. Awards: Commander of the British Empire. Initiated major policy changes including continuous development and expansion of the Festival, its ancillary activities and plant; expansion of repertory to include var operas in first productions in UK. Mem of Theatre Mngt Assoc; London Opera Centre.

CAPOBIANCO, TITO. Stages/produces opera, theater, film & television. Also designs sets & stage-lighting. American. Resident Stage Dir, New York City Opera; Art Dir designate, San Diego Opera, CA; Gen Dir, Las Palmas Fest, Canary Isl. Born 28 Aug 1931, La Plata, Argentina. Wife Elena Denda, occupation choreographer. Two children. Studied: theater; also music, piano, organ and voice. Operatic training as asst stage dir at Teatro Argentino, La Plata 1950-53; Teatro Colón, Buenos Aires. **Operatic debut:** *Aida* Teatro Argentino, La Plata 1953. Theater debut: State Co, Buenos Aires 1954. Previous occupation: univ prof, Chile. Awards: Mem & Dir Council for the Arts, Argentina; one of Ten Best Talents in Argentina 1968; Hon Citizen of Baltimore, New Orleans & Miami, USA. Previous adm positions in opera: Art Dir, Cincinnati Opera, O 5 yrs; Tech Dir, Teatro Colón 3 yrs; Gen Dir, Chile Opera Co 4 yrs; Gen Dir, La Plata 3 yrs.

Directed/produced opera for major companies in ARG: Buenos Aires†; AUSTRL: Sydney; FRA: Paris; FR GER: Berlin Deutsche Oper, Hamburg; HOL: Amsterdam; ITA: Spoleto Fest; MEX: Mexico City; SPA: Canary Isl Las Palmas Fest; USA: Baltimore, Cincinnati, Dallas, Fort Worth, Hartford, Houston, Milwaukee Florentine, New Orleans, New York City Opera, Philadelphia Grand & Lyric, Pittsburgh, San Antonio, San Diego, San Francisco Opera, Washington DC. **Operas staged for these companies incl** BARTOK: *Bluebeard's Castle*†; BELLINI: *Norma★, Puritani★, Sonnambula*; BIZET: *Carmen★*; BOITO: *Mefistofele★*; CILEA: *Adriana Lecouvreur*; CIMAROSA: *Matrimonio segreto*; DALLAPICCOLA: *Volo di notte*†; DONIZETTI: *Anna Bolena★, Campanello, Convenienze/Viva la Mamma★, Don Pasquale, Elisir, Fille du régiment, Lucia★, Lucrezia Borgia★, Maria Stuarda★, Rita, Roberto Devereux★*; DVORAK: *Rusalka★*; GALUPPI: *Filosofo di campagna*; GINASTERA: *Don Rodrigo★*; GIORDANO: *Andrea Chénier*; GOUNOD: *Faust*†, *Roméo et Juliette*; HANDEL: *Ariodante★, Giulio Cesare, Rodelinda★*; HINDEMITH: *Hin und zurück*; HONEGGER: *Antigone★*; HUMPERDINCK: *Hänsel und Gretel*; LEONCAVALLO: *Pagliacci★*†; MASCAGNI: *Cavalleria rusticana★*†; MASSENET: *Manon★, Thaïs★, Werther★*†; MENOTTI: *Consul, Medium, Saint of Bleecker Street, Telephone*; MONTEVERDI: *Incoronazione di Poppea*; MOZART: *Clemenza di Tito, Così fan tutte★*†, *Don Giovanni, Idomeneo★, Nozze di Figaro, Schauspieldirektor★*†, MUSSORGSKY: *Boris Godunov★*; OFFENBACH: *Contes d'Hoffmann★*; ORFF: *Carmina burana, Kluge*; PERGOLESI: *Serva padrona*; PONCHIELLI: *Gioconda*; POULENC: *Voix humaine★*; PROKOFIEV: *Love for Three Oranges★*; PUCCINI: *Bohème★, Gianni Schicchi, Butterfly*†, *Manon Lescaut, Suor Angelica, Tabarro, Tosca★*†, *Turandot★*†; RIMSKY-KORSAKOV: *Coq d'or*; ROSSINI: *Barbiere di Siviglia, Cenerentola*†, *Italiana in Algeri*†, *Signor Bruschino*; SAINT-SAENS: *Samson et Dalila*; SCARLATTI: *Trionfo dell'onore*†; SCHOENBERG: *Erwartung*†; STRAUSS, J: *Fledermaus*†; STRAUSS, R: *Salome*†; STRAVINSKY: *Mavra*†, *Rake's Progress*†; THOMAS: *Hamlet*; VERDI: *Aida★, Attila★, Ballo in maschera★, Don*

Carlo★, *Falstaff*★, *Forza del destino*†, *Macbeth*★†, *Nabucco*†, *Otello*★†, *Rigoletto*★†, *Simon Boccanegra*★, *Traviata*★†, *Trovatore*★†; WAGNER: *Fliegende Holländer*†, *Lohengrin*, *Meistersinger*†, *Tannhäuser*. Also CASTRO: *Proserpina y Extranjero;* GIANNINI: *Servant of Two Masters;* MERCADANTE: *Giuramento;* de BANFIELD: *Lord Byron's Love Letter.* **Operatic world premieres** GINASTERA: *Bomarzo* Washington, DC, Op Socy 1967. Operatic Video—Argent TV: *Tosca, Traviata.* Previous leading positions with major theater companies: Prod/Dir, National Co, Buenos Aires 1959-61. Teaches at Philadelphia Mus Acad. **Res:** San Diego, CA, USA. **Mgmt:** SSR/USA.

CAPPELLI, CARLO ALBERTO. Italian. Gen Int, Ente Autonomo Lirico Arena di Verona, Piazza Bra' 28, Verona, Italy. In charge of admin & art matters & finances. Born 23 Mar 1907, Rocca S Casciano/Bologna, Italy. Studied: accounting, commerce and economics. Previous occupations: editor. In present position since 1971. Awards: Grande Ufficiale Ordine al Merito, Rep of Italy. **Res:** V Orsoni 13, Bologna, Italy.

CAPPUCCILLI, PIERO. Dramatic baritone. Italian. Born 9 Nov 1929, Trieste, Italy. Wife Graziella. Three children. **Debut:** Tonio (*Pagliacci*) Teatro Nuovo, Milan 1957. Previous occupations: studied architecture.
Sang with major companies in ARG: Buenos Aires; AUS: Salzburg Fest, Vienna Staatsoper; BEL: Brussels; BRA: Rio de Janeiro; CAN: Montreal/Quebec; DEN: Copenhagen; FRA: Bordeaux, Nancy, Paris, Toulouse; GRE: Athens National; FR GER: Berlin Deutsche Oper, Düsseldorf-Duisburg, Frankfurt, Hannover, Munich Staatsoper, Stuttgart; HUN: Budapest; ITA: Bologna, Florence Maggio & Comunale, Genoa, Milan La Scala, Naples, Palermo, Parma, Rome Opera & Caracalla, Trieste, Turin, Venice, Verona Arena; POR: Lisbon; S AFR: Johannesburg; SPA: Barcelona; SWI: Zurich; UK: Edinburgh Fest, London Royal; USSR: Moscow Bolshoi; USA: Chicago, Miami, New York Met; YUG: Belgrade. **Roles with these companies incl** BELLINI: Ernesto★ (*Pirata*), Sir Richard★ (*Puritani*); CATALANI: Vincenzo Gellner★ (*Wally*); DONIZETTI: Alfonse★ (*Favorite*), Enrico★ (*Lucia*), Nottingham★ (*Roberto Devereux*); GIORDANO: Carlo Gérard★ (*Andrea Chénier*); LEONCAVALLO: Tonio★ (*Pagliacci*); MASCAGNI: Alfio (*Cavalleria rusticana*); PONCHIELLI: Barnaba★ (*Gioconda*); PUCCINI: Marcello (*Bohème*), Sharpless (*Butterfly*), Michele (*Tabarro*), Scarpia (*Tosca*); ROSSINI: Figaro★ (*Barbiere di Siviglia*); VERDI: Amonasro★ (*Aida*), Ezio (*Attila*), Renato★ (*Ballo in maschera*), Rodrigo★ (*Don Carlo*), Francesco Foscari★ (*Due Foscari*), Don Carlo★ (*Ernani*), Ford (*Falstaff*), Don Carlo★ (*Forza del destino*), Miller (*Luisa Miller*), Macbeth, Nabucco★, Iago★ (*Otello*), Rigoletto★, Simon Boccanegra★, Germont★ (*Traviata*), Conte di Luna★ (*Trovatore*), Monforte★ (*Vespri*). **Mgmt:** GOR/UK.

CARD, JUNE. Lyric coloratura soprano. American. Resident mem: Bayerische Staatsoper, Munich; Städtische Bühnen, Frankfurt. Born 10 Apr 1942, Dunkirk, NY, USA. Husband Manfred Lütgenhorst, occupation journalist. Studied: Mrs May Browner, New York. **Debut:** Valencienne (*Lustige Witwe*) New York City Opera. Previous occupations: typist, waitress, English teacher, salesgirl, journalist. Awards: Bayerische Kammersängerin, Bavarian State Senate.
Sang with major companies in AUS: Vienna Staatsoper; BEL: Brussels; FR GER: Berlin Deutsche Oper, Cologne, Düsseldorf-Duisburg, Frankfurt, Hamburg, Munich Staatsoper & Gärtnerplatz, Nürnberg, Stuttgart; SWI: Geneva; USA: Kansas City, New York City Opera. **Roles with these companies incl** ADAM: Madeleine (*Postillon de Lonjumeau*); BEETHOVEN: Marzelline (*Fidelio*); BERG: Lulu; BIZET: Micaëla★ (*Carmen*); CHARPENTIER: Louise; GOUNOD: Marguerite★ (*Faust*), Juliette; HALEVY: Eudoxie★ (*Juive*); HENZE: Luise (*Junge Lord*); JANACEK: Vixen★ (*Cunning Little Vixen*), Katya Kabanova; LEONCAVALLO: Nedda★ (*Pagliacci*); MASSENET: Manon★; MENOTTI: Monica (*Medium*); MONTEVERDI: Poppea (*Incoronazione di Poppea*); MOZART: Fiordiligi (*Così fan tutte*), Donna Anna & Donna Elvira★ & Zerlina (*Don Giovanni*), Konstanze (*Entführung aus dem Serail*), Susanna (*Nozze di Figaro*), Zaïde, Pamina & Königin der Nacht (*Zauberflöte*); OFFENBACH: Olympia★ & Antonia★ & Giulietta★ (*Contes d'Hoffmann*); PROKOFIEV: Renata (*Fiery Angel*); PUCCINI: Mimi★ & Musetta★ (*Bohème*), Cio-Cio-San (*Butterfly*), Magda (*Rondine*), Liù (*Turandot*), Anna (*Villi*); ROSSINI: Rosina (*Barbiere di Siviglia*); SHOSTAKOVICH: Katerina Ismailova; STRAUSS, J: Adele & Rosalinde (*Fledermaus*); STRAUSS, R: Zdenka & Fiakermilli (*Arabella*); STRAVINSKY: Anne Trulove (*Rake's Progress*); TCHAIKOVSKY: Lisa (*Pique Dame*); VERDI: Oscar (*Ballo in maschera*), Alice Ford★ & Nannetta (*Falstaff*), Gilda (*Rigoletto*), Violetta★ (*Traviata*); WEBER: Aennchen (*Freischütz*); WEILL: Jenny★ (*Aufstieg und Fall der Stadt Mahagonny*). Also CHERUBINI: Creusa (*Medea*); KORNGOLD: Laura (*Ring des Polykrates*); SCHOENBERG: Frau★ (*Von heute auf morgen*); HENZE: Autonoe★ (*Bassariden*); HARTMANN: Simplicius Simplicissimus★. Video/Film: Zaïde. Gives recitals. Appears with symphony orchestra. **Res:** Arabellastr 5, 8 Munich 81, FR Ger. **Mgmt:** SLZ/FRG.

CARDEN, JOAN MARALYN. Lyric soprano. Australian. Resident mem: Australian Opera, Sydney. Born 9 Oct, Melbourne. Married. Two daughters. Studied: Thea Phillips, Henry Portnoj, Melbourne; Vida Harford, London; London Opera Centre. **Debut:** Liù (*Turandot*) Australian Opera 1971. Previous occupations: secy. Awards: prizewinner Munich Intl Music Compt 1967; Stuyvesant Schlshp for London Opera Centre 1967.
Sang with major companies in AUSTRL: Sydney; UK: London Royal. **Roles with these companies incl** GOUNOD: Marguerite★ (*Faust*); MOZART: Fiordiligi (*Così fan tutte*); Donna Elvira★ (*Don Giovanni*), Contessa★ (*Nozze di Figaro*), Pamina (*Zauberflöte*); OFFENBACH: Olympia★ & Antonia★ & Giulietta★ (*Contes d'Hoffmann*); PROKOFIEV: Natasha★ (*War and Peace*); VERDI: Gilda★ (*Rigoletto*), Amelia

(*Simon Boccanegra*). Also MACONCHY: Shepherd's Wife (*Three Strangers*); ORFF: Solo (*Catulli carmina, Carmina burana*). **World prem:** WISHART: Tomoe (*Captive*) BBC Radio 1969. Appears with symphony orchestra. **Res:** 16 Mercer Rd, Armadale 3143 Victoria, Melbourne, Australia. Mgmt: ASK/UK.

CAREY, THOMAS. Lyric baritone. American. Born 29 Dec 1937, Bennettsville, SC, USA. Wife Carol Brice, occupation singer, professor. Studied: Henry Street Music School, New York; Stuttgart Hochschule für Musik, FR Ger; Rose Bampton, Lola Urbach, Hans Hotter, Rupert Gundlach. **Debut:** Germont (*Traviata*) Amsterdam Opera 1964. Awards: John Hay Whitney Schlshp; M B Rockefeller Fund Grant; Intl Compts: Brussels, Munich, 's Hertogenbosch; Marian Anderson Awd.

Sang with major companies in AUS: Salzburg Fest; BEL: Liège; DEN: Copenhagen; FRA: Bordeaux, Lyon, Marseille, Nice, Paris, Rouen, Strasbourg, Toulouse; GRE: Athens Fest; FR GER: Berlin Deutsche Oper, Bielefeld, Cologne, Darmstadt, Dortmund, Düsseldorf-Duisburg, Essen, Frankfurt, Hamburg, Hannover, Karlsruhe, Kassel, Krefeld, Munich Staatsoper, Nürnberg, Saarbrücken, Stuttgart, Wuppertal; GER DR: Berlin Staatsoper, Leipzig; HOL: Amsterdam; ITA: Spoleto Fest, Venice; POR: Lisbon; SWE: Stockholm; SWI: Basel; UK: London Royal Opera; USA: Boston, Memphis, New Orleans; YUG: Dubrovnik, Zagreb, Belgrade. **Roles with these companies incl** BIZET: Escamillo (*Carmen*); DONIZETTI: Dott Malatesta (*Don Pasquale*), Belcore (*Elisir*), Enrico (*Lucia*); GERSHWIN: Porgy★; GLUCK: Oreste (*Iphigénie en Tauride*); HANDEL: Giulio Cesare; LEONCAVALLO: Tonio (*Pagliacci*); MENOTTI: Bob (*Old Maid and the Thief*); MONTEVERDI: Orfeo; MOZART: Figaro (*Nozze di Figaro*), Papageno (*Zauberflöte*); ORFF: Solo★ (*Carmina burana*); PUCCINI: Marcello (*Bohème*), Sharpless (*Butterfly*); RAMEAU: Pollux & Jupiter (*Castor et Pollux*); ROSSINI: Figaro (*Barbiere di Siviglia*); TCHAIKOVSKY: Eugene Onegin; VERDI: Amonasro (*Aida*), Renato (*Ballo in maschera*), Ford & Falstaff (*Falstaff*), Rigoletto, Simon Boccanegra, Germont (*Traviata*), Conte di Luna (*Trovatore*); WAGNER: Wolfram (*Tannhäuser*); WOLF-FERRARI: Lunardo (*Quattro rusteghi*). **World premieres:** TIPPETT: Mel (*Knot Garden*) Royal Opera, London 1970. Recorded for: Philips. Gives recitals. Appears with symphony orchestra. Teaches voice. Coaches repertoire. On faculty of Oklahoma Univ, Norman, OK, USA. **Res:** 801 Jona Kay Terrace, Norman, OK, USA. Mgmt: AOD/USA; IBB/UK.

CARIAGA, MARVELLEE; née Moody. Dramatic mezzo-soprano. American. Born 11 Aug, Los Angeles. Husband Daniel P, occupation dance ed, *Los Angeles Times*. Two children. Studied: Ernest St John Metz, Los Angeles. **Debut:** Hexe (*Hänsel und Gretel*) Los Angeles Guild Opera 1965.

Sang with major companies in CAN: Vancouver; USA: San Diego, San Francisco Opera, Seattle. **Roles with these companies incl** ROSSINI: Semiramide★; WAGNER: Fricka (*Rheingold★, Walküre★*), Waltraute★ (*Götterdämmerung*), Brünnhilde★ (*Siegfried*). Also PUCCINI: Zita★

(*Gianni Schicchi*). **World premieres:** HENDERSON: Medea, San Diego Opera 1972, altern cast. Gives recitals. Appears with symphony orchestra. **Res:** 4350 Lime Ave, Long Beach, CA, USA. Mgmt: CAM/USA.

CARINI, NINA; née Josefina Scalisi. Dramatic soprano. Argentinean. Resident mem: Teatro Colón, Buenos Aires. Born 25 Oct 1932, Buenos Aires. Single. Studied: Lidya Kindermann, Kirsten Flagstad. **Debut:** Santuzza (*Cavalleria rusticana*) Teatro Colón 1955. Awards: Special Citation, Music Day, Municipality of Buenos Aires.

Sang with major companies in ARG: Buenos Aires; BRA: Rio de Janeiro. **Roles with these companies incl** MASCAGNI: Santuzza★ (*Cavalleria rusticana*); MENOTTI: Magda Sorel★ (*Consul*); MOZART: Contessa (*Nozze di Figaro*); MUSSORGSKY: Marina (*Boris Godunov*); PUCCINI: Suor Angelica, Tosca, Anna (*Villi*); VERDI: Aida★, Lady Macbeth, Abigaille (*Nabucco*), Amelia (*Simon Boccanegra*), Leonora★ (*Trovatore*); WAGNER: Venus (*Tannhäuser*). Also BOERO: Mercedes (*Tucuman*); ARIZAGA: Palas (*Prometeo 45*); CHAILLY: Condesa Mautitzia (*Procedura penale*). Video—TV Argentina: Santuzza (*Cavalleria rusticana*); Leonora (*Trovatore*). Gives recitals. Appears with symphony orchestra. **Res:** Buenos Aires, Argentina.

CARLSON, LENUS JESSE. Lyric baritone. American. Resident mem: Metropolitan Opera, New York. Born 11 Feb 1945, Jamestown, ND. Wife Linda Jones, occupation opera coach, accompanist. Studied: Moorehead State Coll, Dwayne Jorgenson, MN; Juilliard School, Oren Brown, New York; Central City Opera Apprentice Prgrm, CO; Tanglewood Opera Theatre Wkshp, MA. **Debut:** Demetrius (*Midsummer Night*) Center Opera, Minneapolis 1967.

Sang with major companies in HOL: Amsterdam; UK: Edinburgh Fest, Glasgow Scottish; USA: Boston, Dallas, Houston, Minneapolis, New York Met, Philadelphia Lyric, San Antonio, Washington DC. **Roles with these companies incl** BIZET: Escamillo★ (*Carmen*); BRITTEN: Demetrius★ (*Midsummer Night*); DONIZETTI: Enrico★ (*Campanello*), Dott Malatesta (*Don Pasquale*); GOUNOD: Mercutio★ (*Faust*); MASSENET: Lescaut★ (*Manon*); MENOTTI: John Sorel (*Consul*); MOZART: Guglielmo (*Così fan tutte*), Don Giovanni, Conte Almaviva★ (*Nozze di Figaro*), Papageno★ (*Zauberflöte*); PROKOFIEV: Prince Andrei Bolkonsky★ (*War and Peace*); PUCCINI: Marcello★ (*Bohème*), Sharpless (*Butterfly*), Michele★ (*Tabarro*); PURCELL: Aeneas★; ROSSINI: Figaro★ (*Barbiere di Siviglia*); STRAVINSKY: Nick Shadow★ (*Rake's Progress*); TCHAIKOVSKY: Eugene Onegin★; VERDI: Ford (*Falstaff*). **World premieres:** ORR: Archie Weir (*Hermiston*) Scottish Op 1975; THOMSON: Thomas Moore (*Lord Byron*) 1972; FARBERMAN: Buzz (*The Losers*) 1971; OVERTON: Preacher (*Huckleberry Finn*) 1971, last three at Juilliard Am Opera Center, New York. Gives recitals. Appears with symphony orchestra. **Res:** 782 West End Ave, New York, NY, USA. Mgmt: CAM/USA; AIM/UK.

CARLYLE, JOAN. Lyric soprano. British. Born 6 Apr 1933, Cheshire, UK.

Sang with major companies in AUS: Vienna Staatsoper; FR GER: Munich Staatsoper; ITA: Milan La Scala; UK: London Royal & English National; et al. **Roles with these companies incl** CILEA: Adriana Lecouvreur; STRAUSS, R: Arabella; STRAVINSKY: Parasha‡ (*Mavra*); TIPPETT: Jennifer‡ (*Midsummer Marriage*); VERDI: Oscar (*Ballo in maschera*), Elisabetta (*Don Carlo*), Desdemona (*Otello*); et al. Recorded for: Philips. **Res:** 44 Abbey Rd, St John's Wood, London NW 8, UK. Mgmt: CST/UK.

CARMELI, BORIS. Bass. Italian. Studied: Mo Fornarini, Mo Giovanni Binetti, Milan; Mo Melocchi, Pesaro; Ma Maria Cascioli, Rome. **Debut:** Colline (*Bohème*) Arena Faenza, Bologna 1956.

Sang with major companies in AUS: Salzburg Fest; BEL: Brussels; BRA: Rio de Janeiro; FRA: Bordeaux, Marseille, Nice, Rouen, Strasbourg; FR GER: Cologne, Hamburg, Munich Staatsoper; HOL: Amsterdam; ITA: Bologna, Florence Maggio & Comunale, Genoa, Milan La Scala, Naples, Palermo, Parma, Rome Opera, Turin, Venice; MEX: Mexico City; S AFR: Johannesburg; SWI: Geneva; USA: Boston, New Orleans, Philadelphia Lyric, San Francisco Opera; YUG: Dubrovnik. **Roles with these companies incl** BARTOK: Bluebeard★; BELLINI: Oroveso (*Norma*), Rodolfo (*Sonnambula*); BERLIOZ: Narbal (*Troyens*); BORODIN: Galitzky & Kontchak (*Prince Igor*); DALLAPICCOLA: Robineau (*Volo di notte*); DEBUSSY: Arkel (*Pelléas et Mélisande*); DONIZETTI: Baldassare (*Favorite*); GAY: Mr Peachum (*Beggar's Opera*); GLUCK: Thoas (*Iphigénie en Tauride*); GOUNOD: Méphistophélès (*Faust*); HANDEL: Polyphemus (*Acis and Galatea*); MARTIN: Marc (*Vin herbé*); MEYERBEER: Marcel (*Huguenots*), Comte Oberthal (*Prophète*); MILHAUD: Agenor (*Enlèvement d'Europe*); MOZART: Sarastro★ (*Zauberflöte*); MUSSORGSKY: Pimen★ (*Boris Godunov*), Dosifei (*Khovanshchina*); PONCHIELLI: Alvise (*Gioconda*); PUCCINI: Colline (*Bohème*); RIMSKY-KORSAKOV: Juri Vsevolodovic (*Invisible City of Kitezh*); ROSSINI: Don Basilio (*Barbiere di Siviglia*), Dormont (*Scala di seta*); STRAVINSKY: Creon★ & Tiresias★ (*Oedipus Rex*); VERDI: Ramfis (*Aida*), Philip II & Grande Inquisitore (*Don Carlo*), Padre Guardiano (*Forza del destino*), Conte Walter★ (*Luisa Miller*), Banquo★ (*Macbeth*), Zaccaria (*Nabucco*). Also RAMEAU: Plutone (*Hippolyte et Aricie*); PETRASSI: Cannizares (*Cordovano*); MANZONI: Cardinale (*Atomtod*); PIZZETTI: (*Straniero*). **World premieres:** ORFF: Anachoret (*De temporum fine comedia*) Salzburg Fest 1973; BARTOLOZZI: Vegliardo (*Tutto ciò che accade ti riguarda*) Florence Maggio Musicale 1972; CHAILLY: (*Idiota*) Teatro dell'Opera, Rome 1970; ALLEGRA: Arne (*Portrait*) Milan 1968; COE: (*South*) Marseille Opéra 1965. Recorded for: Polydor, DG, Decca. Video/Film—RAI-TV: Timur (*Turandot*); Italian film: (*Scala di seta*). Gives recitals. Appears with symphony orchestra. **Res:** V dei Fienaroli 8, Rome, Italy. Mgmt: DSP/USA.

CARMONA, NORBERTO. Dramatic baritone. Argentinean. Resident mem: Teatro Colón, Buenos Aires. Born 22 May 1925, Mendoza Ciudad. Wife Giselle Oitana, occupation exec secy. One son. Studied: Marcelo Urizar, Jerome Haine, Julio Perceval. **Debut:** Germont (*Traviata*) Teatro Colón 1955.

Sang with major companies in ARG: Buenos Aires; BEL: Brussels, Liège; BRA: Rio de Janeiro; FRA: Aix-en-Provence Fest, Bordeaux, Lyon, Marseille, Nancy, Nice, Paris, Strasbourg, Toulouse; HOL: Amsterdam; ISR: Tel Aviv; ITA: Bologna, Florence Maggio, Milan La Scala, Naples; MEX: Mexico City; MON: Monte Carlo; SPA: Barcelona; SWI: Geneva, Zurich. **Roles with these companies incl** BEETHOVEN: Don Pizarro★ (*Fidelio*); BIZET: Escamillo★ (*Carmen*); DONIZETTI: Belcore★ (*Elisir*); GIORDANO: Carlo Gérard★ (*Andrea Chénier*); LEONCAVALLO: Tonio★ (*Pagliacci*); MASCAGNI: Alfio★ (*Cavalleria rusticana*); MOZART: Don Giovanni★, Conte Almaviva★ & Figaro★ (*Nozze di Figaro*); ORFF: Solo★ (*Carmina burana*); PONCHIELLI: Barnaba★ (*Gioconda*); PUCCINI: Marcello★ (*Bohème*), Sharpless★ (*Butterfly*), Michele★ (*Tabarro*), Scarpia★ (*Tosca*); ROSSINI: Figaro★ (*Barbiere di Siviglia*), Slook★ (*Cambiale di matrimonio*); SHOSTAKOVICH: Boris★ (*Katerina Ismailova*); VERDI: Amonasro★ (*Aida*), Falstaff★, Macbeth★, Rigoletto★, Simon Boccanegra★, Germont★ (*Traviata*), Conte di Luna★ (*Trovatore*). Gives recitals. Appears with symphony orchestra. Teaches voice. Coaches repertoire. On faculty of Inst del Teatro Colón. **Res:** Combate de los Pozos 59-2-14, Buenos Aires, Argentina.

CAROLLO, ANTONINO. Italian. Dir of Scenic Prod, Teatro Massimo, Piazza Giuseppe Verdi, Palermo. Born 4 Jul 1935, Palermo. Wife Tommasa Cusimano, occupation Dr of biology. One child. Studied: Univ Palermo. Plays the piano. **Res:** Piazza R Strauss 10, 90144 Palermo, Italy.

CARRERAS, JOSÉ. Lyric tenor. Spanish. **Debut:** Gennaro (*Lucrezia Borgia*) Teatro del Liceo, Barcelona 1970. Previous occupations: chemistry student. Awards: Verdi Compt, Parma 1971; Palcoscenico d'oro, Italy.

Sang with major companies in ARG: Buenos Aires; AUS: Vienna Staatsoper; BEL: Brussels; CZE: Prague National; FRA: Aix-en-Provence Fest, Marseille, Nice, Paris, Toulouse; FR GER: Berlin Deutsche Oper, Frankfurt, Hamburg, Karlsruhe, Munich Staatsoper, Stuttgart; HUN: Budapest; ITA: Florence Maggio Musicale & Teatro Comunale, Milan La Scala, Parma, Trieste, Turin; SPA: Barcelona; SWI: Geneva, Zurich; UK: London Royal Opera; USA: Chicago, Dallas, New York Met & City Opera, Philadelphia Lyric, San Francisco Opera. **Roles with these companies incl** BELLINI: Orombello (*Beatrice di Tenda*), Tebaldo (*Capuleti ed i Montecchi*); BOITO: Faust★ (*Mefistofele*); CILEA: Maurizio★ (*A. Lecouvreur*); DONIZETTI: Gerardo★ (*Caterina Cornaro*), Nemorino★ (*Elisir*), Edgardo★ (*Lucia*), Gennaro★ (*Lucrezia Borgia*), Riccardo★ (*Maria di Rohan*), Leicester★ (*Maria Stuarda*), Roberto Devereux★; GOUNOD: Faust★, Roméo★; MASSENET: Des Grieux★ (*Manon*), Nicias★ (*Thaïs*), Werther★; MEYERBEER: Vasco da Gama★ (*Africaine*); OFFENBACH: Hoffmann★; PONCHIELLI: Enzo★ (*Gioconda*); PUCCINI:

Rodolfo★ (*Bohème*), Rinuccio★ (*Gianni Schicchi*), Pinkerton★ (*Butterfly*), Cavaradossi★ (*Tosca*); ROSSINI: Leicester★ (*Elisabetta Regina*), Giocondo★ (*Pietra del paragone*); VERDI: Aroldo★ (*Aroldo/Stiffelio*), Riccardo★ (*Ballo in maschera*), Don Carlo★, Fenton★ (*Falstaff*), Edoardo★ (*Giorno di regno*), Arvino★ (*Lombardi*), Rodolfo★ (*Luisa Miller*), Ismaele★ (*Nabucco*), Duca di Mantova★ (*Rigoletto*), Gabriele★ (*Simon Boccanegra*), Alfredo★ (*Traviata*). Recorded for: Philips, RCA, Vanguard. Gives recitals. Appears with symphony orchestra. Coaches repertoire. Affiliated with Barcelona Consv. Mgmt: CAM/USA.

CARRON, ELISABETH; née Elisabetta Caradonna. Spinto. American. Born 12 Feb, USA. Husband Marte Previti, occupation chemical engineer. Two children. Studied: Mrs Rodney Saylor; Mr Rodney Saylor, piano. **Debut:** Cio-Cio-San (*Butterfly*) New York City Opera.
   Sang with major companies in MEX: Mexico City; USA: Cincinnati, Dallas, Houston, New Orleans, New York City Opera, Philadelphia Grand & Lyric, Pittsburgh, St Paul, San Francisco Spring. **Roles with these companies incl** BIZET: Micaëla (*Carmen*); CHERUBINI: Medea; DEBUSSY: Lia (*Enfant prodigue*); DONIZETTI: Norina (*Don Pasquale*); MOZART: Zerlina (*Don Giovanni*), Konstanze (*Entführung aus dem Serail*), Ilia (*Idomeneo*), Susanna (*Nozze di Figaro*); ORFF: Solo (*Carmina burana*); PUCCINI: Mimi & Musetta (*Bohème*), Cio-Cio-San (*Butterfly*), Suor Angelica, Liù (*Turandot*); STRAUSS, R: Aithra (*Aegyptische Helena*), Zerbinetta (*Ariadne auf Naxos*), Daphne, Salome; VERDI: Violetta (*Traviata*). Also BLITZSTEIN: Birdie (*Regina*). Recorded for: Columbia, RCA. Gives recitals. Appears with symphony orchestra. Teaches voice. Coaches repertoire. Mgmt: NAP/USA.

CARSON, CLARICE. Dramatic soprano. Canadian. Born Montreal. Husband Philon Ktsanes. Two children. Studied: Pauline Donalda, Jacqueline Richard, Montreal; Julia Drobner, New York. **Debut:** Mother (*Amahl*) Montreal Opera 1962.
   Sang with major companies in CAN: Montreal/Quebec, Vancouver; FRA: Rouen; HOL: Amsterdam; ISR: Tel Aviv; SPA: Barcelona; UK: Glasgow Scottish; USA: Cincinnati, Fort Worth, Dallas Civic, Houston, New York Metropolitan & City Opera, San Francisco Opera. **Roles with these companies incl** BERLIOZ: Cassandre (*Troyens*); BIZET: Micaëla (*Carmen*); BOITO: Margherita (*Mefistofele*); BRITTEN: Female Chorus (*Rape of Lucretia*); GOUNOD: Siebel & Marguerite (*Faust*); MENOTTI: Magda (*Consul*), Monica (*Medium*); MOZART: Donna Anna (*Don Giovanni*), Konstanze (*Entführung aus dem Serail*), Contessa (*Nozze di Figaro*), Pamina (*Zauberflöte*); PUCCINI: Mimi & Musetta (*Bohème*), Cio-Cio-San (*Butterfly*), Suor Angelica, Tosca, Liù (*Turandot*); STRAUSS, R: Salome; VERDI: Aida, Amelia (*Ballo in maschera*), Elisabetta (*Don Carlo*), Donna Elvira (*Ernani*), Alice Ford (*Falstaff*), Leonora (*Forza del destino*), Desdemona (*Otello*), Violetta (*Traviata*), Leonora (*Trovatore*); et al. Also MOZART: Auretta (*Oca del Cairo*); OFFENBACH: Denise (*Mariage aux lanternes*). Gives recitals. Appears with symphony orchestra. Mgmt: CAM/USA.

CASALS MANTOVANI, MARGHERITA; née Margarita Elias Casals. Dramatic soprano. Italian. Born 10 Jan 1928, Barcelona, Spain. Husband Ivo Mantovani, occupation opera singer. One son. Studied: Consv Barcelona, Maria Gonzales, Spain; Mo Giacomo Armani, Giulia Tess, Ivan del Manto, Italy. **Debut:** Siebel (*Faust*) Opera House, Seville, Spain 1948. Awards: Winner Conc As Li Co, Milan.
   Sang with major companies in AUS: Vienna Staatsoper; BUL: Sofia; CZE: Prague National; FRA: Bordeaux; GER DR: Leipzig; ITA: Bologna, Florence Maggio & Comunale, Genoa, Milan La Scala, Naples, Parma, Rome Opera & Caracalla, Turin, Venice, Verona Arena; POR: Lisbon; SPA: Barcelona; SWI: Zurich. **Roles with these companies incl** BOITO: Margherita/Elena★ (*Mefistofele*); DALLAPICCOLA: Madre★ (*Prigioniero*); FALLA: Salud (*Vida breve*); GOUNOD: Marguerite (*Faust*); JANACEK: Jenufa & Kostelnicka★ (*Jenufa*); MASCAGNI: Santuzza (*Cavalleria rusticana*); MONTEVERDI: Poppea (*Incoronazione di Poppea*); PUCCINI: Turandot; VERDI: Aida, Amelia★ (*Ballo in maschera*), Leonora (*Forza del destino*), Leonora (*Trovatore*). Gives recitals. Teaches voice. **Res:** V Flli Zoia 105, Milan, Italy.

CASAPIETRA-KEGEL, CELESTINA. Lyric soprano. Italian. Resident mem: Deutsche Staatsoper Berlin, Ger DR. Born 23 Aug 1939, Genoa. Husband Herbert Kegel, occupation conductor. One child. Studied: Consvs of Genoa, Milan; Profs Mario Vasquez d'Acuno, Gina Cigna. **Debut:** MASCAGNI: Matilde (*Silvano*) Teatro Nuovo, Milan 1963. Previous occupations: pianist. Awards: Kammersängerin, Deutsche Staatsoper Berlin.
   Sang with major companies in AUS: Graz, Vienna Staatsoper; BUL: Sofia; CZE: Prague National & Smetana; DEN: Copenhagen; FIN: Helsinki; FRA: Lyon, Nancy, Paris; GER DR: Berlin Staatsoper, Dresden, Leipzig; ITA: Bologna, Florence Maggio & Comunale, Genoa, Milan La Scala, Naples, Palermo, Parma, Turin, Venice; MON: Monte Carlo; POR: Lisbon; ROM: Bucharest; SWE: Drottningholm Fest, Stockholm; USSR: Moscow Bolshoi; USA: Chicago. **Roles with these companies incl** BIZET: Micaëla (*Carmen*); BOITO: Margherita (*Mefistofele*); GIORDANO: Maddalena (*Andrea Chénier*); GOUNOD: Marguerite (*Faust*); HANDEL: Cleopatra★ (*Giulio Cesare*); LEONCAVALLO: Nedda (*Pagliacci*); MASSENET: Manon; MOZART: Fiordiligi★ (*Così fan tutte*), Donna Anna★ (*Don Giovanni*), Contessa★ (*Nozze di Figaro*), Pamina (*Zauberflöte*); ORFF: Solo★ (*Carmina burana*); PUCCINI: Mimi★ (*Bohème*), Lauretta (*Gianni Schicchi*), Manon Lescaut★, Suor Angelica, Liù★ (*Turandot*); ROSSINI: Mathilde (*Guillaume Tell*), Anaï (*Moïse*); STRAUSS, J: Rosalinde (*Fledermaus*); STRAUSS, R: Arabella, Gräfin (*Capriccio*), Daphne; TCHAIKOVSKY: Tatiana (*Eugene Onegin*), Lisa (*Pique Dame*); VERDI: Alice Ford★ (*Falstaff*), Luisa Miller, Desdemona★ (*Otello*), Amelia (*Simon Boccanegra*), Violetta★ (*Traviata*); WAGNER: Elsa★ (*Lohengrin*), Eva★ (*Meistersinger*); WEBER: Agathe★ (*Freischütz*); ZANDONAI: Francesca da Rimini★. Recorded for: Eterna. Video/Film: Maddalena (*Andrea Chénier*). Gives recitals. Appears with symphony

orchestra. **Res:** Argo Allee 10b, Berlin, Ger DR. **Mgmt:** SLZ/FRG; BAL/FRG.

CASARINI, GIANFRANCO. Bass. Italian. Born 10 Jun 1940, Bologna, Italy. Wife Fiammetta, occupation businesswoman. One son. Studied: Mo Messina, Mo Brambarov, Mo Siliotti, Mo Muller; Accad Chigiana, Siena. **Debut:** Re (*Aida*) 1967. Awards: First Prize, Ntl Compt ENAL 1965.

Sang with major companies in DEN: Copenhagen; FRA: Lyon, Nice, Orange Fest; FR GER: Hamburg; HUN: Budapest; ITA: Bologna, Florence Maggio & Comunale, Genoa, Milan La Scala, Naples, Palermo, Trieste, Turin, Venice, Verona Arena; YUG: Zagreb. **Roles with these companies incl** BELLINI: Capellio★ (*Capuleti ed i Montecchi*), Oroveso★ (*Norma*), Sir George★ (*Puritani*), Rodolfo★ (*Sonnambula*); DONIZETTI: Alfonse★ (*Favorite*), Alfonso d'Este★ (*Lucrezia Borgia*); MEYERBEER: Don Pedro★ (*Africaine*); PONCHIELLI: Alvise★ (*Gioconda*); PUCCINI: Colline★ (*Bohème*); ROSSINI: Don Basilio★ (*Barbiere di Siviglia*), Moïse★; VERDI: Ramfis★ (*Aida*), Grande Inquisitore★ (*Don Carlo*), Silva★ (*Ernani*), Padre Guardiano★ (*Forza del destino*), Zaccaria★ (*Nabucco*); WAGNER: König Heinrich★ (*Lohengrin*). Gives recitals. **Res:** Meravigli 7, Milan, Italy. **Mgmt:** EUR/FRG.

CASEI, NEDDA; née Nedda-Jane Casey. Lyric & dramatic mezzo-soprano. American. Resident mem Metropolitan Opera, New York. Born 9 Sep 1935, Baltimore, MD, USA. Husband John A Wiles, occupation bass-baritone and voice teacher. Studied: William P Herman, New York; Dick Marzollo, coach, New York; Salzburg Mozarteum, Austria; Vittorio Piccinini, Milan. **Debut:** Maddalena (*Rigoletto*) Théâtre Royal de la Monnaie, Brussels 1960. Awards: Outstanding Young Singers Awd, New Orleans Opera 1959; M B Rockefeller Fund Awd 1962 & 1963.

Sang with major companies in AUS: Salzburg Fest; BEL: Brussels; CAN: Vancouver; CZE: Brno, Prague National; FRA: Strasbourg; GER DR: Leipzig; ITA: Genoa, Naples, Parma, Trieste; SPA: Barcelona; SWI: Basel; USA: Boston, Chicago, Cincinnati, Hartford, Houston, Miami, New Orleans, New York Met, Philadelphia Grand, San Diego. **Roles with these companies incl** BELLINI: Adalgisa (*Norma*); BIZET: Carmen★; DEBUSSY: Geneviève (*Pelléas et Mélisande*); DONIZETTI: Léonore (*Favorite*); GLUCK: Orfeo; HUMPERDINCK: Hänsel; MASSENET: Dulcinée★ (*Don Quichotte*), Charlotte (*Werther*); MEYERBEER: Urbain (*Huguenots*); MONTEVERDI: Poppea★ (*Incoronazione di Poppea*); MOZART: Dorabella (*Così fan tutte*), Cherubino (*Nozze di Figaro*); MUSSORGSKY: Marina★ (*Boris Godunov*); OFFENBACH: Giulietta (*Contes d'Hoffmann*); PONCHIELLI: Laura & La Cieca (*Gioconda*); PUCCINI: Suzuki★ (*Butterfly*); ROSSINI: Rosina★ (*Barbiere di Siviglia*), Angelina (*Cenerentola*), Isabella★ (*Italiana in Algeri*); SAINT-SAENS: Dalila; STRAUSS, J: Prinz Orlovsky★ (*Fledermaus*); STRAUSS, R: Komponist (*Ariadne auf Naxos*), Octavian (*Rosenkavalier*); STRAVINSKY: Jocasta (*Oedipus Rex*); TCHAIKOVSKY: Pauline (*Pique Dame*); VERDI: Amneris★ (*Aida*), Preziosilla★ (*Forza del destino*), Azucena★ (*Trovatore*). Also LEON-

CAVALLO: Musetta‡ (*Bohème*); HANDEL: Silvio (*Pastor fido*); PERGOLESI: Lucrezia (*Frate 'nnamorato*). Recorded for: Cetra, Everest, Concert Hall, Nonesuch, Supraphon. Gives recitals. Appears with symphony orchestra. Coaches repertoire. **Res:** New York, NY, USA.

CASELLATO, RENZO. Lyric tenor. Italian. Born 18 Oct 1936, Adria, Italy. Wife Luigina Pizzo. Two children. Studied: Consv Benedetto Marcello, Venice; Ma Maria Carbone. **Debut:** Nemorino (*Elisir*) Parma Opera 1963. Awards: Silver Prize, RAI 1964.

Sang with major companies in ARG: Buenos Aires; AUS: Vienna Staatsoper; BRA: Rio de Janeiro; DEN: Copenhagen; FRA: Marseille, Nice, Paris, Toulouse; ITA: Bologna, Florence Maggio & Comunale, Genoa, Milan La Scala, Naples, Palermo, Parma, Rome Opera, Trieste, Turin, Venice; MON: Monte Carlo; POR: Lisbon; USSR: Moscow Bolshoi; USA: Chicago, Dallas; YUG: Belgrade. **Roles with these companies incl** BELLINI: Orombello (*Beatrice di Tenda*), Tebaldo★ (*Capuleti ed i Montecchi*), Elvino (*Sonnambula*); BIZET: Nadir (*Pêcheurs de perles*); BOITO: Faust (*Mefistofele*); CIMAROSA: Paolino★ (*Matrimonio segreto*); DONIZETTI: Ernesto★ (*Don Pasquale*), Nemorino★ (*Elisir*), Edgardo (*Lucia*); HANDEL: Acis; MASSENET: Werther; MOZART: Tito★ (*Clemenza di Tito*), Ferrando★ (*Così fan tutte*), Idamante & Idomeneo (*Idomeneo*), Tamino (*Zauberflöte*); PAISIELLO: Almaviva★ (*Barbiere di Siviglia*); PUCCINI: Rinuccio★ (*Gianni Schicchi*); ROSSINI: Almaviva★ (*Barbiere di Siviglia*), Don Ramiro★ (*Cenerentola*), Lindoro (*Italiana in Algeri*), Giocondo (*Pietra del paragone*); VERDI: Fenton★ (*Falstaff*), Alfredo★ (*Traviata*). Appears with symphony orchestra. **Res:** V Chilla 3, Adria, Italy.

CASELLATO LAMBERTI, GIORGIO; né Giorgio Casellato. Tenor. Italian. Born 9 Jul 1938, Adria/Rovigo, Italy. Wife Teresa Martens. One child. Studied: Mo Campogalliani, Mantua, Italy. **Debut:** Arrigo (*Vespri*) Rome Opera 1964. Previous occupations: accountant.

Sang with major companies in AUS: Vienna Staatsoper; BEL: Brussels; BUL: Sofia; FIN: Helsinki; FRA: Paris; FR GER: Berlin Deutsche Oper, Cologne, Frankfurt, Hamburg, Munich Staatsoper; GER DR: Berlin Staatsoper; HOL: Amsterdam; HUN: Budapest; ITA: Bologna, Florence Maggio & Comunale, Genoa, Milan La Scala, Naples, Palermo, Parma, Rome Opera & Caracalla, Trieste, Turin, Venice, Verona Arena; ROM: Bucharest; SWI: Basel; USA: Baltimore, Chicago, Hartford, Milwaukee Florentine, New York Met & City Opera, Philadelphia Grand; YUG: Zagreb. **Roles with these companies incl** d'ALBERT: Pedro (*Tiefland*); BELLINI: Orombello (*Beatrice di Tenda*), Tebaldo★ (*Capuleti ed i Montecchi*), Pollione★ (*Norma*); BIZET: Don José★ (*Carmen*); BOITO: Faust★ (*Mefistofele*); CHERUBINI: Giasone★ (*Medea*); CILEA: Maurizio★ (*A. Lecouvreur*); DONIZETTI: Edgardo (*Lucia*), Leicester★ (*Maria Stuarda*); GLINKA: Bogdan (*Life for the Tsar*); GLUCK: Admetos★ (*Alceste*); MASCAGNI: Turiddu (*Cavalleria rusticana*); PONCHIELLI: Enzo★ (*Gioconda*);

CASONI

PUCCINI: Rodolfo★ (*Bohème*), Dick Johnson★ (*Fanciulla del West*), Pinkerton★ (*Butterfly*), Des Grieux★ (*Manon Lescaut*), Luigi★ (*Tabarro*), Cavaradossi★ (*Tosca*), Calaf★ (*Turandot*); ROSSINI: Aménophis (*Moïse*); SPONTINI: Fernand Cortez★, Licinio★ (*Vestale*); STRAUSS, R: Bacchus (*Ariadne auf Naxos*), Ein Sänger (*Rosenkavalier*); STRAVINSKY: Vasili★ (*Mavra*), Oedipus Rex★; TCHAIKOVSKY: Gherman★ (*Pique Dame*); VERDI: Radames★ (*Aida*), Foresto★ (*Attila*), Riccardo★ (*Ballo in maschera*), Corrado★ (*Corsaro*), Don Carlo★, Jacopo Foscari★ (*Due Foscari*), Ernani★, Don Alvaro★ (*Forza del destino*), Oronte★ (*Lombardi*), Rodolfo★ (*Luisa Miller*), Carlo★ (*Masnadieri*), Ismaele★ (*Nabucco*), Duca di Mantova★ (*Rigoletto*), Gabriele★ (*Simon Boccanegra*), Alfredo★ (*Traviata*), Manrico★ (*Trovatore*), Arrigo★ (*Vespri*); WAGNER: Erik★ (*Fliegende Holländer*), Lohengrin, Tannhäuser. World premieres: ZAFRED: (*Wallenstein*) Rome Opera 1965. Res: 12 Boetsenberg, 3044 Haasrode (Leuven), Belgium. Mgmt: CAM/USA.

CASONI, BIANCA MARIA. Lyric coloratura mezzo-soprano. Italian. Born Milan, Italy. Married. Studied: Bruna Jona, Mercedes Llopart, Milan. Also piano studies. Debut: Mercedès (*Carmen*) Advanced Theater School, Giovani Cantanti Lirici, Italy 1956. Awards: Golden Rose Awd of Garda; Gold Medal, Parma; Golden Stage Awd, Mantua; Golden Pentagram; Winner Conc of Radiofonico 1958; Winner Conc of La Scala School.
Sang with major companies in AUS: Bregenz Fest, Salzburg Fest; BRA: Rio de Janeiro; DEN: Copenhagen; FRA: Aix-en-Provence Fest; FR GER: Berlin Deutsche Oper, Wiesbaden; HOL: Amsterdam; HUN: Budapest; ISR: Tel Aviv; ITA: Bologna, Florence Comunale, Genoa, Milan La Scala, Naples, Palermo, Parma, Rome Opera, Spoleto Fest, Trieste, Turin, Venice; MEX: Mexico City; MON: Monte Carlo; SPA: Barcelona; SWI: Geneva; UK: Edinburgh Fest, Glyndebourne Fest; USA: Dallas, Kansas City, New York Met, Philadelphia Lyric; YUG: Dubrovnik, Belgrade. Roles with these companies incl BARTOK: Judith (*Bluebeard's Castle*); BELLINI: Adalgisa (*Norma*); BERLIOZ: Marguerite (*Damnation de Faust*); BRITTEN: Hermia (*Midsummer Night*); CHERUBINI: Neris (*Medea*); CIMAROSA: Fidalma (*Matrimonio segreto*); DONIZETTI: Giovanna (*Anna Bolena*), Mme Rosa (*Campanello*), Léonore (*Favorite*), Pierrot (*Linda di Chamounix*), Maffio Orsini (*Lucrezia Borgia*); GLUCK: Orfeo; GOUNOD: Siebel (*Faust*); HANDEL: Cornelia (*Giulio Cesare*); HAYDN: Lisetta (*Mondo della luna*); HUMPERDINCK: Hänsel; MASCAGNI: Beppe (*Amico Fritz*); MASSENET: Charlotte (*Werther*); MONTEVERDI: Poppea (*Incoronazione di Poppea*); MOZART: Dorabella (*Così fan tutte*), Cherubino (*Nozze di Figaro*); MUSSORGSKY: Marina (*Boris Godunov*); PONCHIELLI: Laura (*Gioconda*); ROSSINI: Rosina★ (*Barbiere di Siviglia*), Angelina★ (*Cenerentola*), ·Isabella★ (*Italiana in Algeri*), Sinaïde★ (*Moïse*), Marchesina Clarice★ (*Pietra del paragone*); SPONTINI: High Priestess★ (*Vestale*); STRAVINSKY: Jocasta (*Oedipus Rex*); THOMAS: Mignon★: VERDI: Preziosilla‡ (*Forza del destino*); WOLF-

FERRARI: Beatrice (*Donne curiose*). Gives recitals. Appears with symphony orchestra. Res: Milan, Italy.

CASSEL, WALTER JOHN. Dramatic baritone. American. Resident mem: Metropolitan Opera, New York. Born 15 May 1920, Council Bluffs, IA, USA. Wife Gail Manners, occupation form soprano. Two children. Studied: Council Bluffs, IA; Frank LaForge, New York. Debut: Brétigny (*Manon*) Metropolitan Opera 1944.
Sang with major companies in AUS: Vienna Staatsoper; CAN: Ottawa, Toronto, Vancouver; FR GER: Düsseldorf-Duisburg; ITA: Palermo; MEX: Mexico City; SPA: Barcelona; USA: Baltimore, Cincinnati, Fort Worth, Hartford, Houston, Miami, Milwaukee Florentine Opera, New Orleans, New York Met & City Opera, Philadelphia Lyric, Pittsburgh, San Antonio, Seattle. Roles with these companies incl BEETHOVEN: Don Pizarro (*Fidelio*); BIZET: Escamillo (*Carmen*); GIORDANO: Carlo Gérard (*Andrea Chénier*); LEONCAVALLO: Tonio (*Pagliacci*); MASCAGNI: Alfio★ (*Cavalleria rusticana*); MENOTTI: Husband (*Amelia al ballo*), Abdul★ (*Dernier sauvage*); MOZART: Don Giovanni, Conte Almaviva (*Nozze di Figaro*); OFFENBACH: Coppélius etc (*Contes d'Hoffmann*); PUCCINI: Jack Rance (*Fanciulla del West*), Gianni Schicchi★, Scarpia★ (*Tosca*); RAVEL: Ramiro (*Heure espagnole*); STRAUSS, R: Mandryka (*Arabella*), Orest (*Elektra*), Barak (*Frau ohne Schatten*), Jochanaan★ (*Salome*); VERDI: Amonasro (*Aida*), Renato (*Ballo in maschera*), Ford (*Falstaff*), Don Carlo (*Forza del destino*), Rigoletto, Germont (*Traviata*); WAGNER: Holländer★, Telramund★ (*Lohengrin*), Amfortas (*Parsifal*), Wotan★ (*Rheingold*), Wanderer★ (*Siegfried*), Gunther★ (*Götterdämmerung*), Wolfram (*Tannhäuser*), Kurwenal★ (*Tristan und Isolde*). World premieres: MOORE: Horace Tabor (*Ballad of Baby Doe*) Central City Fest, CO 1956; GIANNINI: Petruchio (*Taming of the Shrew*) New York City Opera 1958. Recorded for: MGM. Gives recitals. Appears with symphony orchestra. Teaches voice. Coaches repertoire. On faculty of Indiana Univ, Bloomington, USA. Res: Bloomington, IN, USA. Mgmt: SAM/USA.

CASSILLY, RICHARD. Heldentenor. American. Resident mem: Staatsoper, Hamburg. Born 14 Dec 1927, Washington DC, USA. Wife Helen Koliopulos. Seven children. Studied: Peabody Consv, Baltimore, MD, USA; Hans Heinz, New York. Debut: Michele (*Saint of Bleecker Street*) Broadway Co, New York 1955. Awards: Voice of Achievement, 2 prizes, Peabody Consv, Baltimore; Kammersänger, Hamburg.
Sang with major companies in AUS: Vienna Staatsoper; CAN: Montreal/Quebec, Toronto, Vancouver; FRA: Bordeaux, Orange Fest, Paris; FR GER: Berlin Deutsche Oper, Düsseldorf-Duisburg, Hamburg, Karlsruhe, Munich Staatsoper, Saarbrücken; ITA: Milan La Scala, Turin; MEX: Mexico City; SPA: Barcelona, Las Palmas Fest; SWI: Geneva, Zurich; UK: Edinburgh Fest, London Royal Opera; USA: Baltimore, Boston, Chicago, Cincinnati, Fort Worth, Houston, Milwaukee Florentine, New Orleans, New York Met & City Opera, Philadelphia Grand & Lyric, Pitts-

burgh, St Paul, San Antonio, San Diego, San Francisco Opera & Spring Opera, Santa Fe, Seattle. **Roles with these companies incl** BEETHOVEN: Florestan (*Fidelio, Leonore*); BELLINI: Orombello (*Beatrice di Tenda*), Tebaldo (*Capuleti ed i Montecchi*), Pollione (*Norma*); BERG: Tambourmajor★(*Wozzeck*); BERLIOZ: Aeneas (*Troyens*); BIZET: Don José★ (*Carmen*); BRITTEN: Albert Herring, Peter Grimes, Peter Quint (*Turn of the Screw*); DALLAPICCOLA: Jailer/Inquisitor (*Prigioniero*); DONIZETTI: Riccardo (*Anna Bolena*); EINEM: Bürgermeister★ (*Besuch der alten Dame*); FALLA: Paco (*Vida breve*); FLOYD: Sam Polk (*Susannah*); GLUCK: Achille (*Iphigénie en Tauride*); GOUNOD: Faust, Roméo; HINDEMITH: Albrecht v Brandenberg★ (*Mathis der Maler*); JANACEK: Luka★ (*From the House of the Dead*), Laca★ (*Jenufa*); LEONCAVALLO: Canio★ (*Pagliacci*); MENOTTI: Michele (*Saint of Bleecker Street*); MUSSORGSKY: Dimitri (*Boris Godunov*); PUCCINI: Dick Johnson (*Fanciulla del West*), Pinkerton (*Butterfly*), Cavaradossi★ (*Tosca*), Calaf★ (*Turandot*); SAINT-SAENS: Samson; SCHOENBERG: Aron★ (*Moses und Aron*); SHOSTAKOVICH: Sergei (*Katerina Ismailova*); STRAUSS, R: Aegisth★(*Elektra*), Herodes★(*Salome*); STRAVINSKY: Oedipus Rex; SUTERMEISTER: Raskolnikoff; VERDI: Radames★ (*Aida*), Don Alvaro (*Forza del destino*), Otello★, Manrico★(*Trovatore*), Macduff (*Macbeth*); WAGNER: Erik★ (*Fliegende Holländer*), Lohengrin★, Walther (*Meistersinger*), Parsifal, Siegmund★ (*Walküre*), Tannhäuser★, Tristan★; WEBER: Max★(*Freischütz*). Also SCHULLER: Pulisi (*Visitation*); MARTIN: Ferdinand (*Sturm*); TCHAIKOVSKY: Vakula (*Golden Slippers*). **World premieres:** BUCCI: German Soldier (*Tale for a Deaf Ear*) 1st prof N Y City Opera 1958; STEFFENS: Mog Edwards (*Unter dem Milchwald*) Staatsoper, Hamburg 1973; WEISGALL: (*The Tenor*) Baltimore, MD 1952. Recorded for: Columbia, Westminster, EMI, DG. Video/Film: Otello; Walther (*Meistersinger*); Florestan (*Fidelio*); Tambourmajor (*Wozzeck*). Appears with symphony orchestra. **Res:** Hamburg, FR Ger. Mgmt: HUR/USA; ASK/UK.

CASSINELLA, RICARDO. Lyric tenor. Argentinean. Resident mem: Teatro Colón, Buenos Aires. Born 27 Feb 1936, Buenos Aires. Wife Marie Louise Koolmoes, occupation dancer. Three children. Studied: Inst of Art, Teatro Colón, Anatolio Kabanciw, Aldo Bonifanti. **Debut:** Aménophis (*Moïse*) Bern, Switzerland. **Sang with major companies in** ARG: Buenos Aires; BEL: Brussels; FRA: Lyon, Toulouse; ROM: Bucharest; UK: Glyndebourne Fest. **Roles with these companies incl** ADAM: Zephoris★ (*Si j'étais roi*); DELIBES: Gérald★ (*Lakmé*); DONIZETTI: Nemorino★ (*Elisir*), Beppo★ (*Rita*); MOZART: Ferrando★ (*Così fan tutte*), Don Ottavio★ (*Don Giovanni*), Tamino★ (*Zauberflöte*); PAISIELLO: Almaviva (*Barbiere di Siviglia*); ROSSINI: Almaviva★ (*Barbiere di Siviglia*), Aménophis★ (*Moïse*); STRAUSS, R: Ein Sänger★ (*Rosenkavalier*); WEILL: Fatty★ (*Aufstieg und Fall der Stadt Mahagonny*). Also LIEBERMANN: Demoptolemos (*Penelope*). Recorded

for: Decca, Philips, EMI, ABC. Gives recitals. Appears with symphony orchestra. **Res:** Lavalle 1171, Buenos Aires, Argentina. Mgmt: CDA/ARG; IMR/FRA.

CASTEL, NICO. Character tenor. American. Resident mem: Metropolitan Opera, New York. Born 1 Aug 1931, Lisbon, Portugal. Wife Nancy, occupation airline employee. One child. Studied: Carmen Hurtado, Caracas, Venezuela; Mercedes Llopart, Milan; Julia Drobner, New York. **Debut:** Fenton (*Falstaff*) Santa Fe 1958. Previous occupations: sales repres in Latin America. Awards: Joy-in-Singing, Town Hall Awd Recital 1958.

Sang with major companies in ITA: Florence Maggio & Comunale, Spoleto Fest; POR: Lisbon; USA: Baltimore, Cincinnati, Fort Worth, Hartford, Houston, Lake George, Newark, New Orleans, New York Met & City Opera, Philadelphia Grand & Lyric, San Antonio, San Diego, Santa Fe, Washington DC. **Roles with these companies incl** BERG: Hauptmann★ (*Wozzeck*); HUMPERDINCK: Hexe★ (*Hänsel*); MENOTTI: Magician (*Consul*); MOZART: Ferrando (*Così fan tutte*), Pedrillo (*Entführung aus dem Serail*); MUSSORGSKY: Shuisky (*Boris Godunov*); STRAUSS, J: Prinz Orlovsky★ & Eisenstein★ (*Fledermaus*); WAGNER: David★ (*Meistersinger*). Also over 100 smaller character roles. Recorded for: ABC-Dunhill, RCA. Gives recitals. Appears with symphony orchestra. Teaches voice. Coaches repertoire. **Res:** 170 West End Ave, New York, NY 10023, USA. Mgmt: LLF/USA.

CASTLE, JOYCE; née Lillian Joyce Malicky. Lyric mezzo-soprano. American. Born 17 Jan 1944, Beaumont, TX, USA. Husband Bruce Brewer, occupation opera singer, tenor. Studied: Univ of Kansas, Reinhold Schmid, USA; Eastman School of Music, Julius Huehn, Rochester, NY; Otto Guth, coaching, New York; Harry Garland, New York. **Debut:** Siebel (*Faust*) San Francisco Opera 1970.

Sang with major companies in USA: Houston, Philadelphia Lyric, San Antonio, San Francisco Opera, Washington DC. **Roles with these companies incl** GOUNOD: Siebel★ (*Faust*); MENOTTI: Mme Flora★ (*Medium*); WARD: Elizabeth Proctor★ (*Crucible*); WEILL: Leocadia Begbick★ (*Aufstieg und Fall der Stadt Mahagonny*). Also WEILL: Jenny★ & Mrs Peachum★ (*Dreigroschenoper*); PUCCINI: Zita★ (*Gianni Schicchi*); MASCAGNI: Lola★ (*Cavalleria rusticana*). **World premieres:** KOHS: Brunelda (*Amerika*) Western Opera Theater 1970. Video—NET TV: Jenny (*Dreigroschenoper*). Gives recitals. Appears with symphony orchestra. Teaches voice. Coaches repertoire. **Res:** 3923 N 5 St, Arlington, VA 22203, USA. Mgmt: RAP/FRA.

CATALDI-TASSONI, WALTER. Stages/produces opera. Also conducts opera. American. Born 12 Mar 1921, Milan. Divorced. One daughter. Studied: with father Mo Corace Cataldi-Tassoni, Rome & Milan; also piano, violin & voice. **Operatic debut:** *Trovatore* Mantua, Italy. Previous occupation: operatic cond & coach; accomp for recitals.

Directed/produced opera for major companies in BRA: Rio de Janeiro; ITA: Genoa, Rome Opera; SPA: Barcelona, Majorca. Operas staged with these companies incl BELLINI: *Norma, Puritani;* BIZET: *Carmen;* DONIZETTI: *Elisir*, *Lucia*; GIORDANO: *Andrea Chénier*; GOUNOD: *Faust*; LEONCAVALLO: *Pagliacci;* MASCAGNI: *Cavalleria rusticana;* PONCHIELLI: *Gioconda;* PUCCINI: *Bohème*, *Butterfly, Tosca*; VERDI: *Aida*, *Ballo in maschera, Forza del destino*, *Otello*, *Rigoletto*, *Traviata*; WAGNER: *Fliegende Holländer*. Also MASCAGNI: *Iris*. Teaches privately.

CATHCART, ALLEN. Heldentenor. American. Resident mem: Städtische Oper, Frankfurt. Born 2 Aug 1938, Baltimore, MD, USA. Wife Hiltrud Eisele, occupation opera singer. Two children. Studied: Univ of California, Jan Popper, Los Angeles; Boris Goldovsky, New York. **Debut:** Guglielmo (*Così fan tutte*) Metropolitan Opera Studio 1961.

Sang with major companies in BEL: Brussels; FRA: Lyon; FR GER: Cologne, Darmstadt, Frankfurt, Kiel, Saarbrücken, Stuttgart; ITA: Rome Opera; POR: Lisbon; SWI: Zurich; UK: Cardiff Welsh; USA: Kansas City, Lake George, Seattle. Roles with these companies incl d'ALBERT: Pedro★ (*Tiefland*); BEETHOVEN: Florestan★ (*Fidelio*); BERG: Tambourmajor★ (*Wozzeck*); BIZET: Don José★ (*Carmen*); FLOYD: Lennie★ (*Of Mice and Men*); HINDEMITH: Soldier★ (*Cardillac*); JANACEK: Laca★ (*Jenufa*), Boris★ (*Katya Kabanova*); MASCAGNI: Turiddu★ (*Cavalleria rusticana*); MAYR: Giasone★‡ (*Medea in Corinto*); MUSSORGSKY: Andrei Khovansky & Vassily Golitsin (*Khovanshchina*); OFFENBACH: Hoffmann★; PUCCINI: Pinkerton (*Butterfly*), Cavaradossi★ (*Tosca*); STRAUSS, R: Aegisth★ (*Elektra*), Kaiser★ (*Frau ohne Schatten*); VERDI: Alfredo (*Traviata*); WAGNER: Lohengrin★, Walther★ (*Meistersinger*), Siegfried★ (*Götterdämmerung*). Recorded for: Vanguard. Gives recitals. Appears with symphony orchestra. Teaches voice. **Res:** Gartenstr 7, Königstein, FR Ger. Mgmt: SLZ/FRG.

CATTINI, UMBERTO. Conductor of opera and symphony; composer. Italian. Born 14 Nov 1922, Verona. Studied: Milan Consv, Mo Paribeni, Mo Votto; incl violin. **Operatic debut:** *Combattimento di Tancredi* Verona 1943. Awards: Grand Prix du Disque 1961; Zenatello Prize, Arena di Verona 1968; Commendatore della Rep Italiana. Previous adm positions in opera: Mus Dir, Württembergische Staatsoper, Stuttgart.

Conducted with major companies in AUS: Salzburg Fest; ITA: Bologna, Florence Maggio & Comunale, Genoa, Milan La Scala, Naples, Palermo, Rome Opera & Caracalla, Turin, Venice, Verona Arena. Operas with these companies incl ADAM DE LA HALLE: *Robin et Marion;* BELLINI: *Norma, Sonnambula;* BIZET: *Carmen;* BOITO: *Mefistofele;* CILEA: *A. Lecouvreur*; CIMAROSA: *Matrimonio segreto*; DEBUSSY: *Enfant prodigue*; DONIZETTI: *Campanello*, *Don Pasquale*, *Elisir*, *Lucia*, *Rita*; FALLA: *Retablo de Maese Pedro*; GALUPPI: *Filosofo di campagna*; GIORDANO: *Andrea Chénier*;

GLUCK: *Armide*; LEONCAVALLO: *Pagliacci*; MASCAGNI: *Amico Fritz*, *Cavalleria rusticana*; MASSENET: *Manon*; MENOTTI: *Telephone*; MONTEVERDI: *Combattimento di Tancredi*; MOZART: *Finta giardiniera*, *Schauspieldirektor*; ORFF: *Carmina burana*; PERGOLESI: *Serva padrona*; POULENC: *Voix humaine*; PUCCINI: *Bohème*, *Gianni Schicchi*, *Butterfly*, *Manon Lescaut*, *Suor Angelica*, *Tabarro*, *Tosca*; ROSSINI: *Barbiere di Siviglia*, *Cambiale di matrimonio*, *Comte Ory*, *Signor Bruschino*; VERDI: *Ballo in maschera*, *Nabucco*, *Rigoletto*, *Traviata*, *Trovatore*; WOLF-FERRARI: *Segreto di Susanna*. Also SALIERI: *Grotto di Trofonio, Falstaff;* MOZART: *Finta semplice*. Recorded for Cetra. Conducted major orch in Europe, USA/Canada. Previous positions as Mus Dir with major orch: Orch Sinf di Verona; Orch dell'Angelicum, Milan. Teaches at Consv Verdi, Milan, Prof. **Res:** V Varanini 29a, Milan, Italy.

CAVA, CARLO. Bass. Italian. Born 16 Aug 1928, Ascoli Piceno. Wife Carolina Piro. Studied: in Rome. **Debut:** Mustafà (*Italiana in Algeri*) Spoleto Fest 1955. Previous occupations: studied pharmacology, Univ Rome. Awards: Recording Prize, Mar de la Plata.

Sang with major companies in AUS: Salzburg Fest, Vienna Staatsoper; BEL: Brussels; BRA: Rio de Janeiro; DEN: Copenhagen; FRA: Paris; FR GER: Berlin Deutsche Oper, Cologne, Frankfurt, Hamburg, Munich Staatsoper, Wiesbaden; GER DR: Berlin Komische Oper; HOL: Amsterdam; HUN: Budapest; ITA: Bologna, Florence Maggio & Comunale, Genoa, Milan La Scala, Naples, Palermo, Parma, Rome Opera & Caracalla, Trieste, Turin, Venice, Verona Arena; NOR: Oslo; SPA: Barcelona; UK: Glyndebourne Fest; YUG: Dubrovnik, Zagreb. Roles with these companies incl BEETHOVEN: Rocco★ (*Fidelio*); BELLINI: Oroveso★, Sir George★ (*Puritani*), Rodolfo★ (*Sonnambula*); BOITO: Mefistofele★; BRITTEN: Theseus (*Midsummer Night*); CHERUBINI: Creon (*Medea*); CIMAROSA: Geronimo★ (*Matrimonio segreto*); DONIZETTI: Henry VIII★ (*Anna Bolena*), Dulcamara (*Elisir*); GOUNOD: Méphistophélès (*Faust*); HANDEL: Giulio Cesare★; HINDEMITH; Professor (*Hin und zurück*); MOZART: Conte Almaviva★ (*Nozze di Figaro*), Sarastro★ (*Zauberflöte*); MUSSORGSKY: Boris★ & Pimen (*Boris Godunov*), Dosifei★ (*Khovanshchina*); PENDERECKI: Barré★ (*Teufel von Loudun*); PONCHIELLI: Alvise★ (*Gioconda*); PUCCINI: Colline (*Bohème*); ROSSINI: Don Basilio★‡ (*Barbiere di Siviglia*), Podestà★ (*Gazza ladra*), Moïse; SPONTINI: Pontifex Maximus★ (*Vestale*); VERDI: Ramfis★ (*Aida*), Attila★, Philip II★ & Grande Inquisitore★ (*Don Carlo*), Silva★ (*Ernani*), Padre Guardiano★ (*Forza del destino*), Conte Walter★ (*Luisa Miller*), Banquo (*Macbeth*), Massimiliano Moor (*Masnadieri*), Zaccaria★‡ (*Nabucco*), Fiesco★ (*Simon Boccanegra*), Procida★ (*Vespri*); WAGNER: König Heinrich★ (*Lohengrin*), Pogner (*Meistersinger*), Landgraf (*Tannhäuser*). Recorded for: Decca, DG, EMI. Video/Film: (*Luisa Miller*); (*Elisir d'amore*); (*Barbiere*). **Res:** Castagneti 46, Ascoli Piceno, Italy.

CAVANIGLIA, FERNANDO. Italian. Asst to the Artistic Director, Teatro dell'Opera, Piazza Beniamino Gigli, Rome, Italy. In charge of art policy & mus matters, and is also a cond. Additional administrative positions: Prof, Consv S Pietro a Maiella, Naples. Born 12 Nov 1920, Bari, Italy. Wife Valentina Fanella. Two children. Studied: Consv S Pietro a Maiella, Naples. Plays the piano. Previous positions primarily musical. Started with present company 1950 as assoc cond, in present position since 1966. Awards: Campidoglio Prize. Res: V della Brianza 4, Rome, Italy.

CECCATO, ALDO. Conductor of opera and symphony. Italian. Mus Dir, Detroit Symph Orch, MI, USA 1973- ; and Mus Dir, Hamburg Phil, FR Ger 1975- . Born 18 Feb 1934, Italy. Wife Eliana. Two children. Studied: Verdi Consv, Milan; S Celibidache, Siena; Hochschule für Musik, Berlin; incl piano, violin and voice. Plays the piano. **Operatic debut:** *Don Giovanni* Teatro Nuovo, Milan 1963. Symphonic debut: Angelicum, Milan 1963. Previous occupations: concert pianist.
   Conducted with major companies in FRA: Paris; ITA: Bologna, Florence Maggio & Comunale, Milan La Scala, Naples, Parma, Venice; UK: Edinburgh Fest, Glyndebourne Fest, London Royal; USA: Chicago. **Operas with these companies incl** BELLINI: *Puritani;* BUSONI: *Arlecchino;* FALLA: *Vida breve;* LEONCAVALLO: *Pagliacci;* MOZART: *Don Giovanni, Nozze di Figaro;* PUCCINI: *Bohème*★, *Gianni Schicchi, Turandot;* RAVEL: *Enfant et les sortilèges*★; ROSSINI: *Barbiere di Siviglia, Comte Ory;* STRAUSS, R: *Ariadne auf Naxos*★; VERDI: *Ballo in maschera, Due Foscari, Falstaff*★, *Otello*★, *Simon Boccanegra*★, *Traviata*★‡. Also BUSONI: *Brautwahl;* DONIZETTI: *Maria Stuarda* on records; MONTEVERDI: *Ballo delle ingrate;* ROSSINI: *Equivoco stravagante.* Recorded for Angel, ABC. Conducted major orch in Europe, USA/Canada, Cent/S America, Asia. **Res:** V A Corti 28, Milan, Italy. Mgmt: HPL/UK; JUD/USA.

CECCHELE, GIANFRANCO. Lirico-spinto tenor. Italian. Born 25 Jun 1940, Galliera Veneta, Italy. Wife Antonietta Tecla. Five children. Studied: Marcello del Monaco, Treviso. **Debut:** Mico Angiú (*La Zolfara*) Catania, Sicily, Italy 1964.
   Sang with major companies in AUS: Vienna Staatsoper; BEL: Brussels; BUL: Sofia; CAN: Montreal/Quebec; FRA: Marseille, Nice, Paris; GRE: Athens Fest; FR GER: Hamburg, Munich Staatsoper; HUN: Budapest; ITA: Bologna, Florence Maggio Musicale & Comunale, Genoa, Milan La Scala, Naples, Palermo, Parma, Rome Teatro dell'Opera & Caracalla, Trieste, Turin, Venice, Verona Arena; MON: Monte Carlo; SPA: Barcelona, Majorca; UK: London Royal Opera; USA: Chicago, Philadelphia Lyric. **Roles with these companies incl** BELLINI: Pollione★ (*Norma*); GIORDANO: Andrea Chénier★; LEONCAVALLO: Canio★ (*Pagliacci*); MASCAGNI: Turiddu★ (*Cavalleria rusticana*); PONCHIELLI: Enzo★ (*Gioconda*); PUCCINI: Dick Johnson★ (*Fanciulla del West*), Pinkerton★ (*Butterfly*), Des Grieux★ (*Manon Lescaut*), Cavaradossi★ (*Tosca*), Calaf★‡ (*Turandot*); VERDI: Radames★ (*Aida*), Aroldo★ &

Godvino★ (*Aroldo/Stiffelio*), Foresto★‡ (*Attila*), Don Carlo★ Ernani★, Don Alvaro★ (*Forza del destino*), Carlo★ (*Masnadieri*), Ismaele★ (*Nabucco*), Gabriele★ (*Simon Boccanegra*), Arrigo★‡ (*Vespri*); WAGNER: Rienzi. Also VERDI: Arrigo‡ (*Battaglia di Legnano*), Zamoro★‡ (*Alzira*); CATALANI: (*Loreley*); MULE: Mico Angiú (*La Zolfara*). **World premieres:** ZAFRED: 1st tenor (*Wallenstein*) Teatro dell'Opera, Rome 1965. Recorded for: RAI, Rome. Video/Film: (*Turandot*), (*Cavalleria rusticana*). Appears with symphony orchestra. **Res:** Galliera Veneta, Padua, Italy. Mgmt: MAU/USA.

CEDERLÖF, ROLF TORE. Bass. Swedish. Resident mem: Royal Opera, Stockholm. Born 22 Sep 1937, Stockholm. Wife Majottie, occupation singer. One child. Studied: Royal Acad of Mus, Prof Ragnar Hultén, Stockholm. **Debut:** Rocco (*Fidelio*) Royal Opera, Stockholm 1970.
   Sang with major companies in ISR: Tel Aviv; SWE: Drottningholm Fest, Stockholm. **Roles with these companies incl** BEETHOVEN: Rocco★ (*Fidelio*); MOZART: Leporello★ (*Don Giovanni*), Osmin★ (*Entführung aus dem Serail*); PUCCINI: Colline★(*Bohème*); ROSSINI: Dott Bartolo★(*Barbiere di Siviglia*); VERDI: Ramfis★ (*Aida*); WAGNER: Fafner★ (*Rheingold*), Hunding★ (*Walküre*). Also ROSENBERG: Kalabass★ (*Hus med dubbel ingång*). Gives recitals. Appears with symphony orchestra.

CERVENA, SONA. Contralto. Czechoslovakian. Res mem: Städtische Bühnen, Frankfurt. Born Prague. Studied: R Rosner, Prague; L Wegener-Salmonova, acting, Prague. **Debut:** Carmen, Pilsen, Czechoslovakia. Awards: Laureat of Singing Compt, Prague and Warsaw; Kammersängerin, State Opera, Berlin 1961.
   Sang with major companies in AUS: Salzburg Fest, Vienna Staatsoper; BEL: Brussels; CZE: Brno, Prague National & Smetana; FRA: Orange Fest, Rouen; FR GER: Bayreuth Fest, Berlin Deutsche Oper, Cologne, Düsseldorf-Duisburg, Essen, Frankfurt, Hamburg, Munich Staatsoper & Gärtnerplatz, Nürnberg, Stuttgart, Wiesbaden; GER DR: Berlin Komische Oper & Staatsoper; HOL: Amsterdam; ITA: Milan La Scala, Palermo; POR: Lisbon; SPA: Barcelona; SWI: Geneva, Zurich Opernhaus; UK: Edinburgh Fest, Glasgow Scottish, Glyndebourne Fest; USA: Chicago, San Diego, San Francisco Opera, Seattle. **Roles with these companies incl** BERG: Gräfin Geschwitz★‡ (*Lulu*); BIZET: Carmen★‡; BORODIN: Kontchakovna (*Prince Igor*); DEBUSSY: Geneviève★ (*Pelléas et Mélisande*); DVORAK: Jezibaba (*Rusalka*); GLUCK: Orfeo; HANDEL: Ariodante; HENZE: Carolina★‡ (*Elegy for Young Lovers*), Baron von Grünweisel★ (*Junge Lord*); JANACEK: Kabanikha★‡ (*Katya Kabanova*); MENOTTI: Mme Flora★ (*Medium*); MONTEVERDI: Poppea (*Incoronazione di Poppea*); MOZART: Sesto (*Clemenza di Tito*), Dorabella (*Così fan tutte*), Cherubino (*Nozze di Figaro*); MUSSORGSKY: Marfa (*Khovanshchina*); NICOLAI: Frau Reich (*Lustigen Weiber*); PROKOFIEV: Grandmother★ (*Gambler*), Clarissa★ (*Love for Three Oranges*); PUCCINI: Suzuki (*Butterfly*); SMETANA: Hata (*Bartered*

Bride), Roza (*Secret*); STRAUSS, J: Prinz Orlovsky★ (*Fledermaus*); STRAUSS, R: Clairon (*Capriccio*), Klytämnestra★ (*Elektra*), Octavian (*Rosenkavalier*), Herodias★ (*Salome*); STRAVINSKY: Baba the Turk★ (*Rake's Progress*); TCHAIKOVSKY: Olga (*Eugene Onegin*), Comtesse (*Pique Dame*); VERDI: Amneris (*Aida*), Ulrica (*Ballo in maschera*), Dame Quickly★ (*Falstaff*), Azucena (*Trovatore*); WAGNER: Magdalene (*Meistersinger*), Erda (*Rheingold, Siegfried*), Fricka (*Rheingold, Walküre*), Brangäne (*Tristan und Isolde*); WEILL: Leocadia Begbick (*Aufstieg und Fall der Stadt Mahagonny*). Also WAGNER-REGENY: Bergkönigin (*Bergwerk zu Falun*). Recorded for: Eterna, Helidor. **Res:** Rosenstr 58, 6078 Neu Isenburg, FR Ger.

CERVO, ELDA. Lyric soprano. Italian. Born 8 Dec 1933, Lecce. Single. One child. Studied: Consv Rossini, Pesaro; Ma Raggi-Valentini. **Debut:** Cio-Cio-San (*Butterfly*) CIERAL Cooperativa Emiliana, Italy. Awards: Third Prize Conc Intl, Munich 1960; First Prize, Intl Petrassi Compt, Fano/Pesaro 1962; Second Prize, Conc R Emilia, Busseto, & Macerata.

Sang with major companies in ITA: Bologna, Naples, Parma, Venice. **Roles with these companies incl** BIZET: Micaëla (*Carmen*); DALLAPICCOLA: Madre★ (*Prigioniero*); GALUPPI: Eugenia★ (*Filosofo di campagna*); LEONCAVALLO: Nedda★ (*Pagliacci*); PUCCINI: Mimi (*Bohème*), Cio-Cio-San★ (*Butterfly*), Liù (*Turandot*); ROSSINI: Anaï★ (*Moïse*); VERDI: Giulietta‡ (*Giorno di regno*), Leonora (*Trovatore*). Also VERDI: Giulietta (*Finto Stanislao*). **World premieres:** SQUADRONI: Lisa (*Calandrino*) Teatro Pergolesi, Iesi 1969. **Res:** V Frassinago 21, Bologna, Italy.

CHAILLY, LUCIANO. Italian. Art Dir, Ente Autonomo Lirico Arena di Verona, Piazza Bra' 28, Verona, Italy. In charge of art policy & musical matters; he is also a composer. Born 19 Jan 1920, Ferrara, Italy. Studied: Literature at Univ of Bologna; also composition & violin. Plays the violin and piano. Previous positions primarily musical. Composed the following operas: *Sogno—ma forse no; Riva delle sirti; Vassiliev; Markheim; Mantello; Idiota; Era proibita; Una Domanda di matrimonio; Canto del cigno;* etc. (See COS Directories.) **Res:** V Bianca Maria 17, 20122 Milan.

CHAILLY, RICCARDO. Conductor of opera and symphony. Italian. Born 20 Feb 1953, Milan. Wife Anahi Carfi, occupation first violin, La Scala, Milan. Studied: Consv G Verdi, Milan; Accad Chigiana, Prof Franco Ferrara, Siena; incl piano. **Operatic debut:** *Werther* As Li Co, Milan 1973. Symphonic debut: Pomeriggi Musicali, Milan 1972. Previous occupations: Asst Cond, symph concts at Teatro alla Scala, Milan. Awards: Diploma di Merito, Accad Chigiana; Medal F Alfano, Turin 1975.

Conducted with major companies in ITA: Bologna, Milan La Scala, Palermo, Spoleto Fest, Turin; USA: Chicago. **Operas with these companies incl** MASSENET: *Werther★;* PERGOLESI: *Serva padrona★;* PUCCINI: *Butterfly★;* ROSSINI: *Turco in Italia★;* STRAVINSKY: *Rake's Progress★*. Also LORENZINI: *Quattro per cin-*

que; VERDI: *Oberto*. Conducted major orch in Europe. **Res:** Viale Premuda 7, Milan, Italy.

CHALMERS, BRUCE ABERNETHY. British. Adm Dir, Canadian Opera Co/Canadian Opera Assn, 35 Front St E, Toronto, Canada. In charge of adm matters & finances. Born 3 May 1915, Turriff, Scotland. Wife Sarah Djana. Four children. Studied: Edinburgh Univ, Scotland; Inns of Court Law School, London. Previous positions primarily adm: barrister; Asst Secy, Edinburgh Univ; Secy & Registrar, Univ of Southampton; Vc Pres & Dir, Bristol Aeroplane Co of Canada. Started with present company 1972 as Bus Adm, in present position since 1973. Initiated major policy changes including development of new warehouse and workshop facilities, supposed to be the largest and most modern in Canada. Advocates closer cooperation between the seven Canadian opera companies. Mem of Bd of Dir, Canadian Opera Assn; Bd of Dir, Coordinated Arts Services, Toronto. **Res:** Linden St, Toronto, Canada. After 1/76 Gen Mng Portland Opera, OR, USA.

CHAMBERS, MARTIN. Lyric tenor. Canadian. Resident mem: Hessisches Staatstheater, Kassel. Born 27 Sep 1944, Victoria, BC, Canada. Wife Elinor, occupation pianist. One child. Studied: French Tickner, Univ of BC, Vancouver, Canada; Kmsg Richard Holm, Hermann Reutter, Erich Bohner, Munich. **Debut:** SOLER: Prince (*Cosa rara*) Vienna Chamber Opera 1971. Awards: Canada Counc Awd 1969; Centennial Fest Grant 1966.

Sang with major companies in FR GER: Dortmund, Kassel. **Roles with these companies incl** CIMAROSA: Paolino★ (*Matrimonio segreto*); MOZART: Idamante★ (*Idomeneo*), Tamino★ (*Zauberflöte*); PAISIELLO: Almaviva★ (*Barbiere di Siviglia*); ROSSINI: Giannetto★ (*Gazza ladra*). Also STRAUSS, R: Narraboth (*Salome*)★. **World premieres:** TURNER: Rev McDonald (*The Brideship*) CBC Radio, Canada 1967. Gives recitals. Appears with symphony orchestra. Coaches repertoire. On faculty of Univ of Western Ont, Dir Opera School, London, Canada. **Res:** Kassel, FR Ger, and London, Ont, Canada. **Mgmt:** SLZ/FRG; TAS/AUS.

CHAPIN, SCHUYLER GARRISON. American. Arts Administrator. Born 13 Feb 1923, New York. Wife Elizabeth Steinway. Four sons. Studied: Millbrook School; Longy School of Music, Cambridge, MA. Plays the piano. Previous positions, primarily administrative: Agent, Columbia Artists Mngmt 1954-59; Dir, Columbia Masterworks; Vice Pres, Columbia Records; Vice Pres Programming, Lincoln Center; Exec Dir, Amberson Productions; Gen Mng, Metropolitan Opera Assoc. New York 1972-75. Awards: Hon DHL, Hobart and Wm Smith Coll 1974 & New York Univ 1974; Emmy Awd, CBS TV 1971. Initiated major policy changes including addition of Mini Met, new company designed for small or chamber operas but due to finances able to produce only one season. Mem of National Opera Inst, Dir. **Res:** 901 Lexington Ave, New York, NY 10021, USA.

CHAPMAN, JANICE LESLEY; née Hearne. Dramatic soprano. Australian. Born 10 Jan 1938, Adelaide, Australia. Husband John P, occupation school music specialist. Two children. Studied: Elder Consv of Music, Arnold Matters, Adelaide; Royal Coll of Music, London Opera Centre, Ruth Packer, London. **Debut:** Contessa (*Nozze di Figaro*) Sadler's Wells Opera 1965. Previous occupations: secy. Awards: Melbourne *Sun* Aria, Australia 1961; Kathleen Ferrier Prize, Royal Phil Socy, London.

Sang with major companies in BEL: Liège; FR GER: Hamburg; SWI: Geneva; UK: Aldeburgh Fest, Cardiff Welsh, Glasgow Scottish, London Royal & English National. **Roles with these companies incl** BRITTEN: Lady Billows★ (*Albert Herring*), Mrs Julian★ (*Owen Wingrave*), Ellen Orford★ (*Peter Grimes*), Miss Jessel & Mrs Grose★ (*Turn of the Screw*); MOZART: Donna Anna (*Don Giovanni*), Elettra (*Idomeneo*), Contessa★ (*Nozze di Figaro*); PROKOFIEV: Fata Morgana★ (*Love for Three Oranges*); VERDI: Aida★, Leonora★ (*Forza del destino*), Abigaille★ (*Nabucco*); WAGNER: Sieglinde★ (*Walküre*); WEBER: Agathe (*Freischütz*). **World premieres:** BRITTEN: Mrs Julian (*Owen Wingrave*) Covent Garden stage prem 1973. Gives recitals. Appears with symphony orchestra. **Res:** 76 Pollards Hill N, London SW16, UK. Mgmt: MIN/UK; ASK/UK.

CHAPMAN, WILLIAM. Dramatic baritone. American. Born 30 Apr, Los Angeles. Wife Irene, occupation singer, singing teacher. Two children. Studied: Univ of So California, William de Mille, Los Angeles; Edward Lippi, Leon Ceppapro, Los Angeles; Raymond Smolover, New York. **Debut:** Macbeth, New York City Opera 1957. Previous occupations: movie actor, Paramount.

Sang with major companies in CAN: Montreal/Quebec; ITA: Spoleto Fest; USA: Hawaii, Milwaukee Florentine Opera, New York City Opera. **Roles with these companies incl** BIZET: Escamillo★ (*Carmen*), BOITO: Mefistofele★; BORODIN: Galitzky (*Prince Igor*); FLOYD: Olin Blitch★ (*Susannah*); GOUNOD: Méphistophélès★ (*Faust*); LEONCAVALLO: Tonio (*Pagliacci*); MASCAGNI: Alfio★ (*Cavalleria rusticana*); MENOTTI: Bob (*Old Maid and the Thief*); MOORE: Horace Tabor (*Baby Doe*); MOZART: Conte Almaviva & Figaro (*Nozze di Figaro*); OFFENBACH: Coppélius★ etc (*Contes d'Hoffmann*); PUCCINI: Marcello (*Bohème*), Jack Rance (*Fanciulla del West*), Sharpless (*Butterfly*), Michele (*Tabarro*), Scarpia (*Tosca*); SHOSTAKOVICH: Boris (*Katerina Ismailova*); STRAUSS, R: Jochanaan (*Salome*); VERDI: Amonasro★ (*Aida*), Macbeth; WAGNER: Daland (*Fliegende Holländer*). Also BRITTEN: Tarquinius (*Rape of Lucretia*); BORODIN: Kontchak (*Prince Igor*). **World premieres:** MENOTTI: The Prisoner (*Maria Golovin*) Brussels World's Fair 1958; BUCCI: Tracy (*Tale for a Deaf Ear*) Berkshire Fest, MA, USA 1957. Recorded for: RCA. Gives recitals. Appears with symphony orchestra. Teaches voice. On faculty of US Intl Univ, San Diego, CA, USA. **Res:** Van Nuys, CA, USA. Mgmt: HJH/USA.

CHARD, GEOFFREY WILLIAM. Dramatic baritone. Australian. Resident mem: English National Opera, London. Born 9 Aug 1930, Sydney. Wife Margaret Elizabeth. One child. Studied: Consv of Music, Sydney, NSW, Australia. **Debut:** Dancaire (*Carmen*) National Opera of NSW 1951. Previous occupations: secy, accountant.

Sang with major companies in AUSTRL: Sydney; UK: Aldeburgh Fest, Cardiff Welsh, Edinburgh Fest, Glyndebourne Fest, English National. **Roles with these companies incl** BERLIOZ: Méphistophélès (*Damnation de Faust*); BIZET: Escamillo★ (*Carmen*), Zurga (*Pêcheurs de perles*); DONIZETTI: Belcore & Dott Dulcamara (*Elisir*), Enrico (*Lucia*); FLOTOW: Plunkett (*Martha*); GLINKA: Ruslan; GLUCK: Agamemnon (*Iphigénie en Aulide*), Oreste (*Iphigénie en Tauride*); JANACEK: Jaroslav Prus★ (*Makropoulos Affair*); LEONCAVALLO: Tonio (*Pagliacci*); MASCAGNI: Alfio (*Cavalleria rusticana*); MASSENET: Lescaut (*Manon*); MENOTTI: Bob (*Old Maid and the Thief*); MOZART: Guglielmo & Don Alfonso★ (*Così fan tutte*), Don Giovanni★, Conte Almaviva★ & Figaro (*Nozze di Figaro*), Papageno (*Zauberflöte*); OFFENBACH: Coppélius etc★ (*Contes d'Hoffmann*); ORFF: Solo (*Carmina burana*); PENDERECKI: Grandier★ (*Teufel von Loudun*); PUCCINI: Marcello★ (*Bohème*), Gianni Schicchi, Sharpless★ (*Butterfly*), Scarpia (*Tosca*); ROSSINI: Figaro (*Barbiere di Siviglia*), Robert★ (*Comte Ory*); SHOSTAKOVICH: Platon Kusmich Kovalioff★ (*The Nose*); TCHAIKOVSKY: Yeletsky (*Pique Dame*); THOMAS: Hamlet; VERDI: Amonasro (*Aida*), Renato (*Ballo in maschera*), Ford (*Falstaff*), Don Carlo (*Forza del destino*), Macbeth, Nabucco, Iago (*Otello*), Rigoletto, Germont★ (*Traviata*), Conte di Luna (*Trovatore*); WAGNER: Gunther (*Götterdämmerung*); WEBER: Lysiart (*Euryanthe*); WOLF-FERRARI: Conte Gil (*Segreto di Susanna*). Also BRITTEN: Tarquinius (*Rape of Lucretia*); DONIZETTI: Cecil (*Maria Stuarda*); STRAUSS, R: Harlekin (*Ariadne auf Naxos*), Faninal (*Rosenkavalier*). **World premieres:** BERKELEY: Odysseus (*Castaway*) English Opera, Aldeburgh 1967; BIRTWISTLE: Choregos (*Punch and Judy*) English Opera, Aldeburgh 1968; WILLIAMSON: Lawyer (*Growing Castle*) Sadler's Wells Opera 1968; Peter (*Lucky Peter's Journey*) Sadler's Wells Opera 1969. Gives recitals. Appears with symphony orchestra. **Res:** 21 Regal Way, Harrow/London, UK.

CHARLENT, GERTIE. Coloratura soprano. German. Resident mem: Staatstheater, Darmstadt. Born 12 Jan, Kassel, Germany. Husband Manfred Mützel, occupation Intendant, Theater der Stadt Trier. **Debut:** Fiordiligi (*Così fan tutte*) Staatstheater Kassel.

Sang with major companies in AUS: Graz, Salzburg Fest; FR GER: Bielefeld, Bonn, Cologne, Darmstadt, Dortmund, Düsseldorf-Duisburg, Essen, Frankfurt, Hamburg, Hannover, Karlsruhe, Kassel, Krefeld, Mannheim, Munich Staatsoper, Nürnberg, Saarbrücken, Stuttgart, Wiesbaden, Wuppertal; HOL: Amsterdam Netherlands Opera; ITA: Rome, Venice; SWI: Basel, Zurich. **Roles with these companies incl** ADAM: Neméa (*Si j'étais roi*); AUBER: Zerlina (*Fra Diavolo*); BEETHOVEN: Marzelline (*Fidelio*); BERG: Lulu★; CIMAROSA: Carolina (*Matrimonio segreto*); DONIZETTI: Norina★ (*Don Pasquale*); FLOTOW: Lady Harriet★ (*Martha*); FORTNER: Belisa★ (*Don Perlimplin*); GLUCK: Amor (*Orfeo* *ed Euridice)*; HANDEL: Deidamia; HAYDN: Sandrina (*Infedeltà delusa*); HINDEMITH: Helene (*Hin und zurück*); LEONCAVALLO: Nedda (*Pagliacci*); LORTZING: Gretchen & Baronin Freimann (*Wildschütz*); MENOTTI: Lucy (*Telephone*); MILHAUD: Ariane (*Abandon d'Ariane*), Europe (*Enlèvement d'Europe*); MOZART: Fiordiligi & Despina (*Così fan tutte*), Zerlina (*Don Giovanni*), Konstanze★ & Blondchen★ (*Entführung aus dem Serail*), Violante (*Finta giardiniera*), Susanna (*Nozze di Figaro*), Zaïde, Königin der Nacht★ (*Zauberflöte*); NICOLAI: Frau Fluth (*Lustigen Weiber*); OFFENBACH: Olympia★ (*Contes d'Hoffmann*); ORFF: Solo★ (*Carmina burana*); PERGOLESI: Serpina (*Serva padrona*); PUCCINI: Musetta★ (*Bohème*), Lauretta (*Gianni Schicchi*); ROSSINI: Rosina★ (*Barbiere di Siviglia*); STRAUSS, J: Adele★ & Rosalinde★ (*Fledermaus*); STRAUSS, R: Fiakermilli★ (*Arabella*), Zerbinetta★ (*Ariadne auf Naxos*), Sophie★ (*Rosenkavalier*); STRAVINSKY: Rossignol★; THOMAS: Philine★ (*Mignon*); VERDI: Oscar★ (*Ballo in maschera*), Alice Ford & Nannetta (*Falstaff*), Gilda★ (*Rigoletto*), Violetta★ (*Traviata*); WEBER: Aennchen (*Freischütz*); WOLF-FERRARI: Rosaura★ (*Donne curiose*). Also DESSAU: Königin (*Verurteilung des Lukullus*); NONO: Sopran (*Al gran sole carico d'amore*); BLOMDAHL: Blind Poetess (*Aniara*). **World premieres**: LIGETI: Soprano I & II (*Aventures/Nouvelles aventures*) Staatsoper Stuttgart 1966. Recorded for: Wergo, Fox, Hör zu. Video/Film: *Aventures/Nouvelles aventures*. Teaches voice. **Res**: Karlstr 63A, 61 Darmstadt, FR Ger. Mgmt: SLZ/FRG.

CHARRY, MICHAEL RONALD. Conductor of opera and symphony. American. Born 28 Aug 1933, New York. Wife Jane Thoms, occupation teacher. Two children. Studied: Oberlin Consv of Music, O; Juilliard School of Music, Jean Morel, Frederic Cohen, Frederic Waldman; Domaine School, Pierre Monteux, Hancock, ME; Hochschule für Musik, Hans Schmidt-Isserstedt, Hamburg; Cleveland Orch, George Szell 1961-72. Incl piano, Arthur Dann, Rosalyn Tureck; oboe, Lois Wann. Plays the piano. **Operatic debut**: *Gianni Schicchi* Lake Erie Opera Theater, Cleveland, O 1964. Symphonic debut: Cleveland Orch 1962. Awards: Kulas Fndt apprentice cond, Cleveland Orch 1961-65; Fulbright Schlshp for Germany 1956-57; M B Rockefeller Fund grant 1975. Previous adm positions in opera: Assoc Mus Dir, Lake Erie Opera Theater, Cleveland 1964-70.

Conducted with major companies in USA: Kansas City, Lake George, San Francisco Spring Opera, Santa Fe. **Operas with these companies incl** DONIZETTI: *Don Pasquale★;* MOZART: *Nozze di Figaro★, Zauberflöte★;* OFFENBACH: *Périchole★;* PUCCINI: *Butterfly★, Tosca★;* STRAVINSKY: *Rake's Progress★;* VERDI: *Traviata★*. Conducted major orch in Europe, USA/Canada, Cent/S America. **Res**: Westport, CT, USA. Mgmt: TOR/USA.

CHASE, RONALD. Scenic designer and still & film projections for opera, theater; is also a painter, sculptor, visual artist & film producer. American. Born 29 Dec 1934, Seminole, OK. Single. Studied: Bard Coll, New York. **Operatic debut**: *Turn of the*

Screw Washington Opera Socy, DC 1969. Awards: SECA Awd, San Francisco Museum of Art; var film fest awds.

Designed opera for major companies in USA: Houston, New York City Opera, Seattle, Washington DC; et al. **Operas designed for these companies incl** BERG: *Lulu;* BRITTEN: *Turn of the Screw;* DELIUS: *Koanga, Village Romeo and Juliet;* GINASTERA: *Beatrix Cenci;* KORNGOLD: *Tote Stadt;* et al. Exhibitions of paintings & sculptures Triangle Gallery, San Francisco & New York; maj museums of fine art in Boston, Philadelphia, San Francisco, Montreal, Toronto and Vancouver BC. **Res**: 136 The Embarcadero, San Francisco, CA 94105, USA.

CHAUVET, GUY-JACQUES. Heldentenor. French. Born 2 Oct 1933, Montluçon, France. Married. Two children. Studied: Consv de Tarbes, Hautes Pyrénées, France; Prof Bernard Gaillour. **Debut**: Faust (*Damnation de Faust*) Opéra de Paris 1959. Awards: Lauréat du Conc Intl, Toulouse; Voix d'Or de la France 1959; Chevalier des Arts et Lettres; Chevalier dans l'Ordre National du Mérite Français.

Sang with major companies in ARG: Buenos Aires; BEL: Brussels, Liège; FRA: Aix-en-Provence Fest, Bordeaux, Lyon, Marseille, Nancy, Nice, Orange Fest, Paris, Rouen, Strasbourg, Toulouse; GRE: Athens Fest; FR GER: Frankfurt, Hamburg, Mannheim, Munich Staatsoper & Gärtnerplatz, Stuttgart; HOL: Amsterdam; ISR: Tel Aviv; ITA: Florence Maggio, Milan La Scala, Naples, Palermo, Turin, Verona Arena; MON: Monte Carlo; POR: Lisbon; SWI: Geneva; UK: London Royal; USA: Chicago, New York Met, San Francisco Opera. **Roles with these companies incl** BEETHOVEN: Florestan (*Fidelio*); BERG: Tambourmajor (*Wozzeck*); BERLIOZ: Faust (*Damnation de Faust*), Aeneas (*Troyens*); BIZET: Don José (*Carmen*); CHERUBINI: Giasone (*Medea*); GLUCK: Pylade (*Iphigénie en Tauride*); GOUNOD: Faust; LEONCAVALLO: Canio (*Pagliacci*); MASSENET: Jean le Baptiste (*Hérodiade*), Werther; PUCCINI: Cavaradossi (*Tosca*), Calaf (*Turandot*); SAINT-SAENS: Samson; VERDI: Radames (*Aida*), Don Carlo; WAGNER: Erik (*Fliegende Holländer*), Lohengrin, Parsifal, Siegmund (*Walküre*), Siegfried (*Siegfried*). **World premieres**: GRUENENWALD: (*Sardanapale*) Opéra de Monte Carlo 1960-61. **Res**: 20 Rue de la Solidarité, Epinay-sur-Seine 93.800, France. Mgmt: IMR/FRA.

CHEVALIER, GEORGES. Stages/produces opera. Also designs stage-lighting and is a singer. French. Scenic Dir & Stage Mng, Centre Lyrique de Wallonie, Liège & Verviers, Belgium. Born 20 Mar 1934, Angers, France. Wife Marie-Thérèse Fenasse, occupation form ballet dancer. Two children. Studied: Consv National, Nantes; also studied music & voice. Operatic training as asst to Gérard Boireau, Théâtre de Bordeaux. **Operatic debut**: Opéra de Rennes, France 1969. Previous occupation: composer, baritone. Form adm positions: Stage Dir, Théâtre Rennes, Théâtre Avignon; Stage Mng, Aix-en-Provence Fest, Casino de Vichy. Started with present company in 1969 as St Dir, in present position since 1974.

Directed/produced opera for major companies in BEL: Brussels, Liège; FRA: Aix-en-Provence Fest, Bordeaux, Marseille, Nancy, Nice, Orange Fest, Rouen, Toulouse. **Operas staged with these companies incl** ADAM: *Postillon de Lonjumeau;* BECAUD: *Opéra d'Aran*★; BIZET: *Carmen*★, *Pêcheurs de perles*★; DELIBES: *Lakmé*★; GOUNOD: *Faust*★, *Mireille*★; LECOCQ: *Fille de Madame Angot*★; LEONCAVALLO: *Pagliacci*★; MASCAGNI: *Cavalleria rusticana*★; MASSENET: *Jongleur de Notre Dame*★, *Manon*★, *Werther*★; POULENC: *Voix humaine*★; PUCCINI: *Bohème*★, *Butterfly*★, *Tosca*★; ROSSINI: *Barbiere di Siviglia*★; STRAUSS, J: *Fledermaus*★; VERDI: *Otello*★, *Rigoletto*★, *Traviata*★; WAGNER: *Fliegende Holländer.* Also TOMASI: *Silence de la mer.* **Operatic world premieres:** ARRIEU: *Clavier pour un autre* Opéra d'Avignon, France 1971; FRANCY: *Chevaliers de la Table Ronde* Verviers 1976. **Res:** 10 rue Tivoli, 4821 Andrimont, Belgium. **Mgmt:** DAU/FRA.

CHIARA, MARIA; née Maria-Rita Chiara. Lyric soprano. Italian. Born 24 Nov 1942, Oderzo/Treviso, Italy. Husband Antonio Cassinelli, occupation voice teacher & coach. Studied: Antonio Cassinelli; Consv Musicale Benedetto Marcello, Venice; Ma Maria Carbone, Italy. **Debut:** Desdemona (*Otello*) La Fenice, Venice 1966. Awards: FIALSET-Targa per la migliore interpretazione di Butterfly 1970.
Sang with major companies in AUS: Vienna Staatsoper; BEL: Brussels; CAN: Toronto; FRA: Nice; GRE: Athens National; FR GER: Berlin Deutsche Oper, Bonn, Cologne, Hamburg, Mannheim, Munich Staatsoper, Stuttgart, Wiesbaden; HOL: Amsterdam; HUN: Budapest; ITA: Bologna, Florence Maggio & Comunale, Genoa, Milan La Scala, Naples, Parma, Rome Opera & Caracalla, Trieste, Venice, Verona Arena; MON: Monte Carlo; SWI: Geneva, Zurich; UK: London Royal. **Roles with these companies incl** BIZET: Micaëla★ (*Carmen*); BOITO: Margherita★ (*Mefistofele*), CILEA: Adriana Lecouvreur; DONIZETTI: Anna Bolena★; GIORDANO: Maddalena★ (*Andrea Chénier*); GOUNOD: Marguerite★ (*Faust*); HENZE: Luise★ (*Junge Lord*); MASCAGNI: Suzel★ (*Amico Fritz*); MASSENET: Manon★; MOZART: Fiordiligi★ (*Così fan tutte*), Donna Anna★ (*Don Giovanni*), Contessa★ (*Nozze di Figaro*); PUCCINI: Mimi★ (*Bohème*), Cio-Cio-San★ (*Butterfly*), Manon Lescaut★, Suor Angelica★, Tosca★, Liù★ (*Turandot*); ROSSINI: Mathilde★ (*Guillaume Tell*), Desdemona★ (*Otello*); VERDI: Aida★, Alice Ford★ (*Falstaff*), Leonora★ (*Forza del destino*), Desdemona★ (*Otello*), Amelia★ (*Simon Boccanegra*), Violetta★ (*Traviata*), Leonora★ (*Trovatore*), Elena★ (*Vespri*); WAGNER: Elsa★ (*Lohengrin*); ZANDONAI: Francesca da Rimini★, Giulietta★ Recorded for: Decca, Eurodisc, Ariola. **Mgmt:** GOR/UK.

CHOOKASIAN, LILI. Dramatic mezzo-soprano & contralto. American. Resident mem: Metropolitan Opera, New York. Born Chicago, IL, USA. Husband George Gavejian, occupation realtor. Three children. Studied: Philip Manuel, Chicago; Ludwig Donath, New York; Armen Boyajian, Paterson, NJ, USA. **Debut:** La Cieca (*Gioconda*) Metropoli-

tan Opera 1962. Previous occupations: voice teacher Northwestern Univ, Evanston, IL. Awards: Sullivan Fndt Grant.
Sang with major companies in ARG: Buenos Aires; AUS: Salzburg Fest; CAN: Toronto; FR GER: Bayreuth Fest, Hamburg; ITA: Florence Comunale, Spoleto Fest, Turin; MEX: Mexico City; SPA: Barcelona; USA: Baltimore, Chicago, Cincinnati, Dallas, Fort Worth, Houston, Miami, New York Met & City Opera, Philadelphia Lyric, Portland, San Francisco Opera, Washington DC. **Roles with these companies incl** BRITTEN: Auntie★ (*Peter Grimes*); DEBUSSY: Geneviève★ (*Pelléas et Mélisande*); DONIZETTI: Sara (*Roberto Devereux*); MENOTTI: Maharani (*Dernier sauvage*), Mme Flora (*Medium*); PONCHIELLI: La Cieca★ (*Gioconda*); PUCCINI: Principessa (*Suor Angelica*), Frugola (*Tabarro*); STRAVINSKY: Jocasta (*Oedipus Rex*); VERDI: Amneris★ (*Aida*), Ulrica★ (*Ballo in maschera*), Dame Quickly★ (*Falstaff*), Azucena★ (*Trovatore*); WAGNER: Erda (*Rheingold*★, *Siegfried*★), Waltraute★ (*Götterdämmerung*), Brangäne (*Tristan und Isolde*). Recorded for: DG. Gives recitals. Appears with symphony orchestra. Coaches repertoire. **Mgmt:** DSP/USA.

CHOSET, FRANKLIN. Conductor of opera and symphony; operatic stage director. American. Resident Cond, Israel National Opera, Tel Aviv. Born 15 Feb 1934, New York. Wife Malka Mevorach, occupation pianist. Two children. Studied: New England Consv, Boris Goldovsky, Boston; incl piano, viola and voice. Plays the piano. Operatic training as repetiteur, asst cond & chorus master at Goldovsky Opera Theater; various community and workshop groups. **Operatic debut:** *Barbiere di Siviglia* Goldovsky Opera Theater, Boston 1954. Symphonic debut: US Seventh Army Symph Orch, Stuttgart 1958. Previous occupations: coaching, lecturing. Awards: Key to City of New York for NYC Opera cond debut 1974.
Conducted with major companies in ISR: Tel Aviv; USA: New York City Opera. **Operas with these companies incl** BIZET: *Carmen*★; DELIBES: *Lakmé*★; DONIZETTI: *Don Pasquale*★, *Elisir*★, *Lucia*★; GIORDANO: *Andrea Chénier*★; GOLDMARK: *Königin von Saba*★; GOUNOD: *Faust*★, *Roméo et Juliette*★; HUMPERDINCK: *Hänsel und Gretel*★; LEONCAVALLO: *Pagliacci*★; MASCAGNI: *Amico Fritz*★, *Cavalleria rusticana*★; MENOTTI: *Old Maid and the Thief, Telephone*‡; MOZART: *Così fan tutte, Don Giovanni. Nozze di Figaro*★, *Schauspieldirektor*★; OFFENBACH: *Contes d'Hoffmann*★; PERGOLESI: *Serva padrona;* PONCHIELLI: *Gioconda;* PUCCINI: *Bohème*★, *Butterfly*★, *Manon Lescaut, Tosca*★, *Turandot;* ROSSINI: *Barbiere di Siviglia*★; SAINT-SAENS: *Samson et Dalila*★; STRAUSS, J: *Fledermaus*★; VERDI: *Aida*★, *Ballo in maschera, Don Carlo, Falstaff, Forza del destino, Nabucco*★, *Otello*★, *Rigoletto*★, *Traviata*★, *Trovatore*★. Also HINDEMITH: *Wir bauen eine Stadt*★. Recorded for Israel Broadcasting. Conducted major orch in Europe, USA/Canada, Asia. Teaches conducting. Also worked as translator and editor of orch scores. **Res:** 91/15 Derech Eshkol Kiron (Kiryat Ono), Tel Aviv, Israel.

CHRISTESEN, ROBERT CURRIER. Baritone. American. Resident mem: Staatsoper, Frankfurt/Main & Dortmund, FR Ger. Born 15 Feb 1943, Washington, DC, USA. Wife Miroslava, Russian-English interpreter. Studied: Manhattan School of Music, Daniel Ferro, George Schick, New York; Aspen School of Music, Aksel Schiotz, Jennie Tourel, CO; Univ of Wisconsin, David Astor, Madison, USA; Hans Hotter, Munich; Pierre Bernac, Paris. **Debut:** Henrik (*Maskarade*) St Paul Opera 1972. Previous occupations: Ibero-American studies, Scandinavian grad studies. Awards: Marshall Schlshp Fellow, Danish Gvnmt 1971; First Prize Intl Singing Compts Prague, Paris, Holland, Toulouse; Second Prize Munich, Geneva, Salzburg; First Prize, Concert Artists Guild, New York 1971.
    Sang with major companies in BRA: Rio de Janeiro; CZE: Brno, Prague Smetana; DEN: Copenhagen; FRA: Toulouse; FR GER: Dortmund, Frankfurt; GER DR: Berlin Komische Oper & Staatsoper; HOL: Amsterdam; HUN: Budapest; POL: Warsaw; USA: St Paul. **Roles with these companies incl** DONIZETTI: Gasparo (*Rita*); FALLA: Don Quixote (*Retablo de Maese Pedro*); HENZE: Lescaut (*Boulevard Solitude*); LORTZING: Graf Eberbach (*Wildschütz*); MENOTTI: Bob (*Old Maid and the Thief*); MOZART: Don Giovanni, Conte Almaviva (*Nozze di Figaro*); ORFF: Solo (*Carmina burana*); PAISIELLO: Teodoro (*Re Teodoro in Venezia*); PUCCINI: Marcello (*Bohème*); RAVEL: Ramiro (*Heure espagnole*); ROSSINI: Figaro (*Barbiere di Siviglia*); SMETANA: Tomas (*The Kiss*); STRAUSS, R: Jochanaan (*Salome*); TCHAIKOVSKY: Eugene Onegin, Yeletsky (*Pique Dame*); VERDI: Ezio (*Attila*), Rodrigo (*Don Carlo*), Ford (*Falstaff*), Germont (*Traviata*), Conte di Luna (*Trovatore*); WARD: John Proctor (*Crucible*); WEBER: Kaspar (*Freischütz*). **Res:** Frankfurt, FR Ger.

CHRISTIAN, HANS. Dramatic baritone. Austrian. Resident mem: Staatsoper, Vienna. Born 4 Oct 1929, Vienna. Wife Dr Monika. One child. Studied: Tino Pattiera, Paul Schoeffler, Ludwig Weber, Vienna. **Debut:** St Just (*Dantons Tod*) Vienna Fest 1963. Previous occupations: actor, TV announcer.
    Sang with major companies in AUS: Salzburg Fest, Vienna Staatsoper; FRA: Strasbourg; FR GER: Munich Staatsoper, Wiesbaden; ITA: Turin, Venice; USSR: Moscow Bolshoi; YUG: Zagreb. **Roles with these companies incl** BEETHOVEN: Don Pizarro★ (*Fidelio*); BIZET: Escamillo★ (*Carmen*); EINEM: St Just★ (*Dantons Tod*); MARTIN: Marc★ (*Vin herbé*); MOZART: Conte Almaviva★ (*Nozze di Figaro*); OFFENBACH: Coppélius, etc★ (*Contes d'Hoffmann*); PUCCINI: Sharpless★ (*Butterfly*), Scarpia★ (*Tosca*). Gives recitals. Appears with symphony orchestra. Teaches voice. **Res:** Spiegelg 19, 1010 Vienna, Austria.

CHRISTIE, NAN; née Agnes Stevenson Christie. Lyric coloratura soprano. Scottish. Resident mem: Scottish Opera, Glasgow. Born 6 Mar 1948, Irvine, UK. Husband Andrew S Hendrie, occupation musician. Studied: Royal Scottish Acad of Music, Miss W Busfield, Glasgow; S Duncan, Ayr; London Opera Centre, Mme Vera Rozsa. **Debut:**

Flora (*Turn of the Screw*) Scottish Opera 1970. Awards: Prizewinner Compt 's Hertogenbosch 1971; Countess of Munster Awd; Peter Stuyvesant Schlshp; James Caird Travelling Schlshp.
    Sang with major companies in BEL: Brussels; UK: Edinburgh Fest, Glasgow Scottish, London Royal. **Roles with these companies incl** BRITTEN: Tytania★ (*Midsummer Night*), Flora★ (*Turn of the Screw*); MOZART: Susanna★ (*Nozze di Figaro*); PUCCINI: Musetta★ (*Bohème*), Lauretta★ (*Gianni Schicchi*). **World premieres:** PURSER: Juliette (*Undertaker*) Scottish Opera, Edinburgh 1969; HAMILTON: Galla (*Catiline Conspiracy*) Scottish Opera, Glasgow 1974. Gives recitals. Appears with symphony orchestra. **Res:** London, UK. Mgmt: AIM/UK.

CHRISTOFF, BORIS. Bass. Bulgarian. Born 18 May 1919, Sofia. Wife Franca de Rensis. Studied: Riccardo Stracciari, Rome; Mozarteum, Salzburg. **Debut:** Colline (*Bohème*) La Fenice, Venice 1946. Previous occupations: studied law; magistrate, City of Sofia; cavalry officer. Awards: Commander, Ital Rep; Order St Peter & St Paul, Brazil; Hon Mem Opéra & Acad of Paris; Sonning Prize, Copenhagen; Awd Acad Française and Acad Charles Cros, Paris; Edison Prize; Nat Acad of Arts & Sciences, USA.
    Sang with major companies in ARG: Buenos Aires; AUS: Salzburg Fest, Vienna Staatsoper; BRA: Rio de Janeiro; DEN: Copenhagen; FRA: Aix-en-Provence Fest, Lyon, Orange Fest, Paris; FR GER: Frankfurt, Hamburg, Wiesbaden; HOL: Amsterdam; HUN: Budapest; ITA: Florence Maggio, Milan La Scala, Naples, Palermo, Parma, Rome Opera & Caracalla, Turin, Venice, Verona Arena; MON: Monte Carlo; POR: Lisbon; SPA: Barcelona; SWI: Geneva; UK: Aldeburgh Fest, Edinburgh Fest, London Royal; USA: Chicago Lyric, San Francisco Opera. **Roles with these companies incl** BEETHOVEN: Don Pizarro & Rocco (*Fidelio*); BELLINI: Oroveso (*Norma*); BOITO: Mefistofele; BORODIN: Galitzky (*Prince Igor*); GLINKA: Ivan (*Life for the Tsar*), Farlaf & Svietozar (*Ruslan and Ludmilla*); GLUCK: Agamemnon (*Iphigénie en Aulide*); GOUNOD: Méphistophélès‡ (*Faust*); HANDEL: Giulio Cesare; MUSSORGSKY: Boris & Varlaam & Pimen (*Boris Godunov*), Dosifei (*Khovanshchina*); RIMSKY-KORSAKOV: Tsar Ivan (*Maid of Pskov*); ROSSINI: Don Basilio (*Barbiere di Siviglia*), Moïse‡; VERDI: Attila, Philip II‡ (*Don Carlo*), Padre Guardiano (*Forza del destino*), Simon Boccanegra & Fiesco‡ (*Simon Boccanegra*), Procida (*Vespri*); WAGNER: König Heinrich (*Lohengrin*), Hagen (*Götterdämmerung*), Landgraf (*Tannhäuser*), König Marke (*Tristan und Isolde*); WEBER: Kaspar (*Freischütz*). Also MONTEVERDI: Seneca (*Incoronazione di Poppea*); TCHAIKOVSKY: Kotchubey (*Mazeppa*); RACHMANINOFF: Aleko; BORODIN: Kontchak (*Prince Igor*). Recorded for Angel. **Res:** Rome, Italy.

CHRISTOPHER, RUSSELL LEWIS. Lyric baritone. American. Resident mem: Metropolitan Opera, New York. Born 12 Mar 1930, Grand Rapids, MI, USA. Wife Gail Eldredge, occupation exec secy. One child. Studied: Frank Goodwin, Grand Rapids, MI; Univ of Michigan, Dr Philip Duey,

Ann Arbor; Raymond McDermott, New York. **Debut:** Emperor (*Turandot*) New York City Opera 1959. Previous occupations: mailroom boy, music librarian, NBC Network; sales clerk, music store. Awards: Winner, Met Op Ntl Counc Aud, Met contract 1963; American Opera Aud, Cincinnati Summer Opera; M B Rockefeller Fund Awd.

Sang with major companies in CAN: Toronto, Vancouver; USA: Baltimore, Hartford, Newark, New York Met & City Opera, Philadelphia Grand & Lyric, San Francisco Opera. **Roles with these companies incl** DONIZETTI: Enrico★ (*Lucia*); LEONCAVALLO: Tonio (*Pagliacci*); ORFF: Solo (*Carmina burana*); PUCCINI: Marcello (*Bohème*), Sharpless★ (*Butterfly*), Lescaut★ (*Manon Lescaut*); VERDI: Ford★ (*Falstaff*), Germont (*Traviata*). Also MOZART: Masetto★ (*Don Giovanni*); WAGNER: Alberich★ (*Siegfried*). Recorded for: DG. Gives recitals. Appears with symphony orchestra. **Res:** 314 W 77 St, New York, NY, USA. Mgmt: SMN/USA.

CHRYST, DOROTHEA; née Dorli-Maria Schüler. Lyric coloratura soprano. German. Resident mem: Theater am Gärtnerplatz, Munich. Born 12 Aug 1940, Halberstadt/Harz, Germany. Husband Werner Mayer, occupation producer. Studied: Gernot-Heindl, Prof Glettenberg, Fr Metternich. **Debut:** Aennchen (*Lustigen Weiber*) Theater am Gärtnerplatz, Munich 1964.

Sang with major companies in AUS: Bregenz Fest, Vienna Staatsoper & Volksoper; BEL: Brussels; FR GER: Cologne, Dortmund, Düsseldorf-Duisburg, Frankfurt, Hamburg, Hannover, Kassel, Munich Staatsoper & Gärtnerplatz, Nürnberg, Stuttgart; SWI: Basel. **Roles with these companies incl** AUBER: Zerlina★ (*Fra Diavolo*); DELIBES: Javotte (*Roi l'a dit*); DONIZETTI: Norina★ (*Don Pasquale*); JANACEK: Vixen★ (*Cunning Little Vixen*); LEONCAVALLO: Nedda★ (*Pagliacci*); LORTZING: Marie★ (*Waffenschmied*), Gretchen (*Wildschütz*), Marie★ (*Zar und Zimmermann*); MOZART: Despina★ (*Così fan tutte*), Blondchen (*Entführung aus dem Serail*), Mme Herz & Mlle Silberklang★ (*Schauspieldirektor*); NICOLAI: Frau Fluth★ & Aennchen (*Lustigen Weiber*); OFFENBACH: Olympia★ (*Contes d'Hoffmann*); RIMSKY-KORSAKOV: Coq d'or; ROSSINI: Rosina (*Barbiere di Siviglia*); ROUSSEL: Noémi (*Testament de la Tante Caroline*); STRAUSS, J: Adele★ (*Fledermaus*); STRAUSS, R: Zdenka (*Arabella*); VERDI: Oscar (*Ballo in maschera*); WEBER: Aennchen (*Freischütz*). Also KILLMAYER: Yolimba★. Gives recitals. Appears with symphony orchestra. **Res:** Waxensteinstr 40, 8 Munich 70, FR Ger.

CIAFFI RICAGNO, LUISELLA. Lyric mezzo-soprano. Italian. Born 28 Dec 1933, Turin, Italy. Husband Franco Ricagno, occupation chief sound eng, RAI. Two children. Studied: Turin Consv; Accad Chigiana, Siena; Accad S Cecilia, Rome. Awards: First Prize, Accad Chigiana 1955; First Prize, Rassegna Nazionale 1956; Awd Accad S Cecilia, Rome 1956.

Sang with major companies in FRA: Strasbourg; ITA: Bologna, Florence Comunale, Genoa, Milan La Scala, Palermo, Spoleto Fest, Turin, Venice. **Roles with these companies incl** CIMAROSA: Fi-

dalma★ (*Matrimonio segreto*); FOSS: Lulu (*Jumping Frog*); MARTIN: Mère d'Iseut (*Vin herbé*); MONTEVERDI: Poppea★ (*Incoronazione di Poppea*); MOZART: Dorabella (*Così fan tutte*); PROKOFIEV: Duenna; STRAVINSKY: Mère (*Mavra*). Also VERDI: Fenena★ (*Nabucco*); MONTEVERDI: Ottavia★ (*Incoronazione di Poppea*); GIORDANO: Madelon★ (*Andrea Chénier*); PETRASSI: Ortigosa★ (*Cordovano*); MARTIN: Anna (*Mystère de la nativité*); EATON: Deianira (*Heracles*). **World premieres:** RENOSTO: Mago (*Camera degli sposi*) Piccola Scala, Milan 1972; NONO: Fourth soprano (*Al gran sole carico d'amore*) Teatro Lirico, Milan 1975. Recorded for: Angelicum. Video – RAI TV: (*Otello*). Gives recitals. Appears with symphony orchestra. Teaches voice. Coaches repertoire. On faculty of Consv G Verdi, Turin. **Res:** C Rosselli 87, Turin, Italy.

CIHELNIKOVA, MARTA. Lyric soprano. Czechoslovakian. Resident mem: National Theater, Prague. Born 4 Oct 1942, Prague. Husband Zdenek Jankovsky, occupation opera singer. Studied: Prof B Chlabalaova, Prof Prexlerova, Prague. **Debut:** Marguerite (*Faust*) Banska Bystrica, CSSR.

Sang with major companies in CZE: Prague National; YUG: Belgrade. **Roles with these companies incl** DVORAK: Rusalka★; JANACEK: Jenufa★, Katya Kabanova★; SMETANA: Marie★ (*Bartered Bride*), Hedvika★ (*Devil's Wall*), Vendulka★ (*The Kiss*); SUCHON: Katrena★ (*Whirlpool*); TCHAIKOVSKY: Tatiana★ (*Eugene Onegin*). Gives recitals. Appears with symphony orchestra. **Res:** Pod trati 1914, 150 00 Prague-Smichov, CSSR. Mgmt: PRG/CZE.

CILLARIO, CARLO FELICE. Conductor of opera and symphony. Italian. Widowed. Two children. Studied: Consv G B Martini, Mo Consolini & Materassi, Bologna; Odessa Consv, Mo Cerniatinsky, USSR; incl violin, piano. Plays the violin. **Operatic debut:** Barbiere di Siviglia Odessa Op Co, USSR 1942. Symphonic debut: Phil Orch Bucharest, Romania 1943. Previous occupations: violin soloist. Awards: Violin Paganini Prize, Ital Ministry 1935; winner, Cond Compt Buenos Aires 1957.

Conducted with major companies in ARG: Buenos Aires; AUSTRL: Sydney; AUS: Vienna Staatsoper; BRA: Rio de Janeiro; BUL: Sofia; FRA: Marseille, Paris; FR GER: Hamburg, Munich Staatsoper, Wiesbaden; ITA: Bologna, Florence Maggio, Genoa, Milan La Scala, Naples, Palermo, Parma, Rome Opera & Caracalla, Trieste, Turin, Venice, Verona Arena; MEX: Mexico City; POR: Lisbon; ROM: Bucharest; SPA: Barcelona; SWE: Stockholm; SWI: Zurich; UK: Glyndebourne Fest, London Royal; USA: Boston, Chicago, Dallas, Memphis, Minneapolis, New York Met, San Francisco Opera; YUG: Zagreb, Belgrade. **Operas with these companies incl** BARTOK: *Bluebeard's Castle;* BELLINI: *Norma★‡, Pirata, Puritani, Sonnambula★;* BIZET: *Carmen, Pêcheurs de perles‡;* BOITO: *Mefistofele;* CIMAROSA: *Matrimonio segreto;* DALLAPICCOLA: *Prigioniero;* DEBUSSY: *Pelléas et Mélisande;* DELIBES: *Lakmé;* DONIZETTI: *Anna Bolena★, Caterina Cornaro★, Don Pasquale, Elisir, Favorite★, Lucia★, Maria Stuarda★, Rita, Roberto De-*

vereux*; FALLA: *Vida breve;* GLUCK: *Orfeo ed Euridice;* GOUNOD: *Faust;* HANDEL: *Acis and Galatea, Giulio Cesare;* HAYDN: *Infedeltà delusa;* HUMPERDINCK: *Hänsel und Gretel;* JANACEK: *Cunning Little Vixen**; LEONCAVALLO: *Pagliacci**; MASCAGNI: *Cavalleria rusticana**; MASSENET: *Manon, Werther;* MENOTTI: *Amelia al ballo, Consul**; MONTEVERDI: *Favola d'Orfeo;* MOZART: *Così fan tutte, Don Giovanni**, *Lucio Silla*‡, *Nozze di Figaro, Zauberflöte;* MUSSORGSKY: *Boris Godunov;* PERGOLESI: *Frate 'nnamorato, Serva padrona;* PONCHIELLI: *Gioconda;* PUCCINI: *Bohème**, *Gianni Schicchi, Butterfly**, *Manon Lescaut, Suor Angelica, Tabarro, Tosca**, *Turandot;* PURCELL: *Dido and Aeneas;* RAVEL: *Heure espagnole;* ROSSINI: *Barbiere di Siviglia, Cenerentola, Guillaume Tell;* SCHOENBERG: *Erwartung;* STRAVINSKY: *Mavra, Oedipus Rex;* TCHAIKOVSKY: *Eugene Onegin, Pique Dame;* VERDI: *Aida**, *Ballo in maschera**, *Don Carlo**, *Falstaff, Forza del destino, Giovanna d'Arco, Lombardi**, *Macbeth**, *Nabucco, Otello, Rigoletto**, *Simon Boccanegra, Traviata**, *Trovatore**; WAGNER: *Fliegende Holländer**, *Lohengrin, Tannhäuser;* WEBER: *Freischütz:* WOLF-FERRARI: *Segreto di Susanna.* Also ZANDONAI: *Conchita;* WOLF-FERRARI: *Campiello;* MOZART: *Ascanio in Alba;* PUCCINI: *Edgar**. Recorded for RCA, London, Angelicum-Milan, Harmonia Mundi-Paris. Video/Film—Glyndebourne TV: *Elisir d'amore;* Rome film: *Lucia.* Conducted major orch in Europe, USA/Canada, Cent/S America, Austrl. Mgmt: GOR/UK.

CIONI, RENATO. Lyric tenor. Italian. Born 15 Apr 1929, Portoferraio. Wife Loretta Carletti. Three children. Studied: Consv Cherubini, Florence. **Debut:** Edgardo (*Lucia*) 1953. Awards: Commendatore al Merito della Repubblica Italiana.

Sang with major companies in ARG: Buenos Aires; AUS: Graz, Salzburg Fest, Vienna Staatsoper; BEL: Liège; BRA: Rio de Janeiro; CAN: Montreal/Quebec, Vancouver; CZE: Prague National; DEN: Copenhagen; FRA: Bordeaux, Lyon, Nice, Paris, Strasbourg; FR GER: Berlin Deutsche Oper, Frankfurt, Hamburg, Hannover, Karlsruhe, Mannheim, Munich Staatsoper, Stuttgart, Wiesbaden; HOL: Amsterdam; HUN: Budapest; ITA: Bologna, Florence Maggio & Comunale, Genoa, Milan La Scala, Naples, Palermo, Parma, Rome Opera & Caracalla, Spoleto Fest, Trieste, Turin, Venice, Verona Arena; MON: Monte Carlo; POR: Lisbon; ROM: Bucharest; SPA: Barcelona, Majorca; SWI: Basel, Geneva, Zurich; UK: Edinburgh Fest, Glasgow Scottish, London Royal; USA: Baltimore, Boston, Chicago Lyric, Dallas, Houston Grand, Memphis, Miami, New Orleans, New York Met, Philadelphia Lyric, Pittsburgh, San Antonio, San Diego, San Francisco Opera, Seattle, Washington DC; YUG: Zagreb, Belgrade. **Roles with these companies incl** BELLINI: Orombello (*Beatrice di Tenda*), Pollione* (*Norma*), Elvino (*Sonnambula*), Arturo* (*Straniera*); BUSONI: Calaf (*Turandot*); DONIZETTI: Lord Riccardo (*Anna Bolena*), Nemorino (*Elisir*), Tonio (*Fille du régiment*), Edgardo* (*Lucia*), Gennaro (*Lucrezia Borgia*); JANACEK: Laca* (*Jenufa*); MASCAGNI: Tu-

riddu (*Cavalleria rusticana*); PONCHIELLI: Enzo* (*Gioconda*); PUCCINI: Rodolfo* (*Bohème*), Pinkerton* (*Butterfly*), Des Grieux* (*Manon Lescaut*), Cavaradossi* (*Tosca*); VERDI: Riccardo* (*Ballo in maschera*), Don Carlo, Jacopo Foscari* (*Due Foscari*), Ernani*, Rodolfo* (*Luisa Miller*), Carlo* (*Masnadieri*), Ismaele* (*Nabucco*), Duca di Mantova* (*Rigoletto*), Gabriele* (*Simon Boccanegra*), Alfredo* (*Traviata*); ZANDONAI: Paolo (*Francesca da Rimini*). Also MENOTTI: Doctor* (*Most Important Man*). Recorded for: Decca. Video/Film: Pinkerton (*Butterfly*). **Res:** V XX Settembre, Portoferraio/Livorno, Italy.

CITTANTI, EDUARDO. Bass-baritone. Argentinean. Resident mem: Teatro Colón, Buenos Aires. Born 26 Nov 1926, Buenos Aires. Wife Maria Pia Girolla, occupation opera singer. One son. Studied: Isabel Marengo, O Albanese, Raggi Valentini, M Stabile. **Debut:** Amonasro (*Aida*) Teatro Marconi 1950. Awards: Becado de la Comision Nacional de Cultura 1949.

Sang with major companies in ARG: Buenos Aires; BRA: Rio de Janeiro; CZE: Prague Smetana; FRA: Bordeaux, Marseille, Nice, Paris; FR GER: Berlin Deutsche Oper, Bonn, Cologne, Düsseldorf-Duisburg, Frankfurt, Munich Staatsoper & Gärtnerplatz, Nürnberg, Saarbrücken, Stuttgart; GER DR: Leipzig; HOL: Amsterdam; ISR: Tel Aviv; ITA: Bologna, Florence Maggio & Comunale, Genoa, Milan La Scala, Naples, Palermo, Parma, Rome Opera & Caracalla, Trieste, Turin, Venice; POR: Lisbon; SPA: Barcelona; SWI: Basel, Zurich. **Roles with these companies incl** BELLINI: Oroveso (*Norma*); BIZET: Escamillo (*Carmen*); DONIZETTI: Enrico (*Lucia*); FLOTOW: Plunkett (*Martha*); GIORDANO: Carlo Gérard (*Andrea Chénier*); LEONCAVALLO: Tonio (*Pagliacci*); MASCAGNI: Alfio* (*Cavalleria rusticana*); PONCHIELLI: Barnaba & Alvise (*Gioconda*); PUCCINI: Colline & Marcello (*Bohème*), Jack Rance (*Fanciulla del West*), Scarpia (*Tosca*); ROSSINI: Don Basilio (*Barbiere di Siviglia*), Guillaume Tell: VERDI: Ramfis (*Aida*), Renato (*Ballo in maschera*), Philip II (*Don Carlo*), Silva (*Ernani*), Don Carlo & Padre Guardiano (*Forza del destino*), Banquo (*Macbeth*), Nabucco & Zaccaria (*Nabucco*), Rigoletto, Germont (*Traviata*), Conte di Luna (*Trovatore*); WAGNER: Telramund (*Lohengrin*). Also BOERO: Liborio (*Matrero*); GAITO: Rocamora (*Sangre de las guitarras*); ROGATIS: Mateo (*Novia del hereje*); VERDI: (*Finto Stanislao*); VILLOUD: Tucma (*Oro del Inca*). Gives recitals. Appears with symphony orchestra. On faculty of Liceo Rossini, Pesaro, Italy. **Res:** E Frias 263, Buenos Aires, Argentina.

CLAVELL, RICHARD J. American. Dir of Finance, Metropolitan Opera Assoc, Lincoln Center, New York, NY 10023, 1974- . Born 6 Jan 1932, Bristol, UK. Single. Studied: New York Univ, Business School; Hofstra Univ, Hempstead, NY. Previous occupations: Business Mng, Corp for Public Broadcasting; Audit Mng, Price Waterhouse & Co. Background primarily administrative. **Res:** New York, NY, USA.

CLAVERIE, MICHÈLE. Coloratura soprano. French. Born 5 Jun 1939, Boulogne/Seine. Husband Claude Calès, occupation baritone. One child. Studied: Consv Ntl Supérieur de Paris. **Debut:** Olympia (*Contes d'Hoffmann*) Opéra Comique, Paris 1965. Previous occupations: univ degree in philosophy & piano. Awards: First Prize in Voice/Opéra Comique, Consv Ntl Paris 1969; Grand Prize Acad du Disque 1969.

Sang with major companies in BEL: Brussels, Liège; FRA: Bordeaux, Marseille, Nice, Paris, Rouen, Toulouse. **Roles with these companies incl** BIZET: Léila★ (*Pêcheurs de perles*); CIMAROSA: Carolina★ (*Matrimonio segreto*); DONIZETTI: Norina★ (*Don Pasquale*); GLUCK: Amor★ (*Orfeo ed Euridice*); GOUNOD: Juliette★; MASSENET: Manon★, Sophie★ (*Werther*); MOZART: Despina★ (*Così fan tutte*), Zerlina★ (*Don Giovanni*), Blondchen★ (*Entführung aus dem Serail*), Susanna★ (*Nozze di Figaro*); OFFENBACH: Olympia & Antonia★ (*Contes d'Hoffmann*); ROSSINI: Rosina★ (*Barbiere di Siviglia*), Comtesse Adèle (*Comte Ory*); STRAUSS, J: Adele★ (*Fledermaus*); THOMAS: Philine (*Mignon*); VERDI: Oscar★ (*Ballo in maschera*), Gilda (*Rigoletto*). Also SAUGUET: Marianne★ (*Caprices de Marianne*); POULENC: Constance★ (*Dialogues des Carmélites*). Recorded for: RCA. Video/Film: Lakmé. Gives recitals. Appears with symphony orchestra. **Res:** rue de la Paix 19, 92270 Bois-Colombes, France. Mgmt: BCP/FRA.

CLEMENTS, JOY; née Joyce Marie Albrecht. Soprano. American. Born Dayton, O, USA. Husband Lewis, occupation insurance agent. Two children. Studied: Marinka Gurewich, New York; Univ of Miami, Coral Gables, FL; Acad of Vocal Arts, Philadelphia. **Debut:** Musetta (*Bohème*) Opera of Greater Miami 1956.

Sang with major companies in CAN: Vancouver; ISR: Tel Aviv; USA: Baltimore, Cincinnati, Fort Worth, Hawaii, Houston, Memphis, Miami, Milwaukee Florentine, New York Met & City Opera, Omaha, Philadelphia Lyric, Pittsburgh, St Paul, San Diego. **Roles with these companies incl** BEETHOVEN: Marzelline (*Fidelio*); BIZET: Micaëla (*Carmen*); DONIZETTI: Norina (*Don Pasquale*), Adina (*Elisir*); FLOTOW: Lady Harriet (*Martha*); FLOYD: Susannah; GERSHWIN: Bess; GLUCK: Amor (*Orfeo ed Euridice*); GOUNOD: Marguerite (*Faust*), Juliette; HUMPERDINCK: Gretel; MASSENET: Manon, Sophie (*Werther*); MENOTTI: Sardula (*Dernier sauvage*), Monica (*Medium*), Lucy (*Telephone*); MOZART: Despina (*Così fan tutte*), Mme Herz (*Schauspieldirektor*), Susanna (*Nozze di Figaro*), Pamina (*Zauberflöte*); OFFENBACH: Olympia & Antonia (*Contes d'Hoffmann*); PUCCINI: Mimi & Musetta (*Bohème*), Lauretta (*Gianni Schicchi*), Lisette (*Rondine*); RIMSKY-KORSAKOV: Reine de Schemakan (*Coq d'or*); ROSSINI: Rosina (*Barbiere di Siviglia*); STRAUSS, J: Adele & Rosalinde (*Fledermaus*); STRAUSS, R: Zdenka (*Arabella*); VERDI: Oscar (*Ballo in maschera*), Gilda (*Rigoletto*), Violetta (*Traviata*); WARD: Abigail (*Crucible*); WOLF-FERRARI: Susanna (*Segreto di Susanna*). **World premieres:** WARD: Mary Warren (*Crucible*) New York City Opera 1961. Gives recitals. Appears with symphony orchestra. Teaches voice. Coaches repertoire. **Res:** Lakeshore Dr E, Stockholm, NJ, USA. Mgmt: LLF/USA.

CLEVA, MARIA ANGELA. Lyric soprano. American. Resident mem: Nationaltheater, Mannheim. Born New York. Single. Studied: Giuseppe Danise; Manhattan School of Music, New York. **Debut:** Suzel (*Amico Fritz*) Teatro Coccia, Novara, Italy 1962.

Sang with major companies in AUS: Graz; CAN: Vancouver; FR GER: Cologne, Dortmund, Frankfurt, Hannover, Kiel, Mannheim, Nürnberg, Stuttgart, Wiesbaden; ITA: Palermo, Trieste; USA: Cincinnati, Hartford, Newark, Philadelphia Grand & Lyric. **Roles with these companies incl** AUBER: Zerlina (*Fra Diavolo*); BEETHOVEN: Marzelline (*Fidelio*); BIZET: Micaëla★ (*Carmen*), Léila (*Pêcheurs de perles*); BRITTEN: Ellen Orford (*Peter Grimes*); CORNELIUS: Margiana (*Barbier von Bagdad*); DONIZETTI: Norina★ (*Don Pasquale*), Adina★ (*Elisir*); DVORAK: Rusalka★; FLOTOW: Lady Harriet (*Martha*); GLUCK: Euridice; GOUNOD: Marguerite (*Faust*); LEONCAVALLO: Nedda★ (*Pagliacci*); MASCAGNI: Suzel (*Amico Fritz*); MASSENET: Manon, Sophie (*Werther*); MENOTTI: Lucy (*Telephone*); MOZART: Despina (*Così fan tutte*), Zerlina★ (*Don Giovanni*), Susanna★ (*Nozze di Figaro*), Pamina (*Zauberflöte*); NICOLAI: Aennchen★ (*Lustigen Weiber*); OFFENBACH: Antonia★ (*Contes d'Hoffmann*); ORFF: Kluge; PERGOLESI: Serpina (*Serva padrona*); PUCCINI: Mimi★ & Musetta (*Bohème*), Lauretta (*Gianni Schicchi*), Cio-Cio-San★ (*Butterfly*), Liù (*Turandot*); SMETANA: Marie★ (*Bartered Bride*); STRAUSS, R: Sophie★ (*Rosenkavalier*); STRAVINSKY: Anne Trulove (*Rake's Progress*); VERDI: Nannetta (*Falstaff*), Gilda★ (*Rigoletto*), Violetta★ (*Traviata*); WOLF-FERRARI: Susanna (*Segreto di Susanna*). Also MILHAUD: Florestine (*Mère coupable*) Stadttheater Kiel 1969-70. Gives recitals. Appears with symphony orchestra. **Res:** FR Ger. Mgmt: HUR/USA; SMD/FRG.

COATS, GORDON TELFER. American. Gen Mng, Hawaii Opera Theatre and Honolulu Symphony Orchestra, 1000 Bishop St, Honolulu, Hawaii 96813, 1974- . In charge of overall adm matters. Born 11 Apr 1930, Fort Wayne, IN. Divorced. Three children. Studied: Michigan State Univ, East Lansing. Plays the tuba. Prev occupations: PS music teacher; univ adm. Form positions, primarily adm & musical: Gen Mng, Toledo Symph, 1969-74; Asst Mng, Cincinnati Symph, 1966-69; Sales Rep, Columbia Artists Mngt, New York 1965-66; Tour Arts Coord, Michigan St Univ 1960-65. Mem of Bd of Dir of Children's Opera Chorus, Opera Players Hawaii; Adv, Ensemble Players' Guild. **Res:** 1684 Ala Moana, Honolulu, HI 96815, USA.

COCHRAN, WILLIAM. Dramatic & Heldentenor. American. Resident mem: Städtische Oper, Frankfurt; Staatsoper, Vienna. Born Arlington, VA. Studied: Wesleyan Univ, CT; Curtis Inst of Music, Martial Singher, Philadelphia. Awards: Lauritz Melchior Heldentenor Fndt Awd 1969; Winner Met Op Ntl Counc Aud 1968.

Sang with major companies in AUS: Graz, Vienna Staatsoper; FR GER: Düsseldorf-Duisburg, Frankfurt, Hamburg, Munich Staatsoper; ITA: Rome Opera; UK: London Royal; USA:

Cincinnati, Fort Worth, Houston, New York Met, San Francisco Opera; et al. **Roles with these companies incl** BIZET: Don José (*Carmen*); BUSONI: Mephisto‡ (*Doktor Faust*); JANACEK: Laca (*Jenufa*); OFFENBACH: Hoffmann; PUCCINI: Cavaradossi (*Tosca*); SAINT-SAENS: Samson; STRAUSS, R: Bacchus (*Ariadne auf Naxos*); WAGNER: Erik (*Fliegende Holländer*), Lohengrin, Walther (*Meistersinger*), Parsifal, Rienzi, Siegmund (*Walküre*); WEBER: Max (*Freischütz*); et al. Also MUSSORGSKY: Dimitri (*Boris Godunov*). Recorded for: DG, Angel, Philips. Appears with symphony orchestra. **Res:** Wilhelm Meister Str 3, 638 Bad Homburg, FR Ger. Mgmt: DSP/USA.

CODREANU, PETRE. Romanian. Gen Mng, Romanian Opera, 70-72 Gh Gheorghiu-Dej Blvd, Bucharest 6, Romania. In charge of admin, mus & dramatic matters; art policy; techn & finances, and is also a musicologist. Born 16 Nov 1933, Dediulesti-Buzau, Romania. Wife Elena, occupation translator. Three children. Studied: Consv Ciprian Porumbescu, Bucharest. Plays the violin & viola. Previous occupations: Documentarist Composer's Union; Editor with music magazine; Councilman in State Commtt for Culture and Art; Gen Insp Cultural Council. Previous positions primarily musical: Deputy Art Mng, Romanian Opera, Bucharest 1966-71; Mng, State Operetta Theater, Bucharest 1971-75. In present position since 1975. World premieres at theaters under his management: BENTOIU: *Amorul Doctor* 1964; PROFETA: *Prince and Pauper* 1967; BARBERIS: *Apus de soare* 1967; DUMITRESCU: *Decebal* 1969; LERESCU: *Ecaterina Teodoroiu* 1971; COMISEL: *Crossroad* 1974; BRATU: *The Right of Loving* 1975; all at Romanian Opera Bucharest. Awards: Cultural Merit Order 1968; Work Order 1974, Romanian Gvmt. Initiated major policy changes including the realization of perform 33% Romanian works at State Operetta Theater. Mem of Ntl Commtt for Repertories; Commtt of Cult & Socialist Educ, Bucharest. **Res:** 13-15 Apolodor St, Bucharest, Romania.

COERTSE, MIMI; née Maria Sophia Coertse. Coloratura soprano. South African. Resident mem: Staatsoper, Vienna; Cape Town Opera, Johannesburg, Pretoria. Born 12 Jun 1934, Durban, Natal, S Afr. Husband Werner J Ackermann, occupation business exec. One child. Studied: Mme Amée Parkerson, Prof Maria Hittorff; Vienna State Acad, Austria. **Debut:** Königin der Nacht (*Zauberflöte*) Staatsoper, Vienna 1956. Awards: South African Acad Awd for Music 1961; Kammersängerin, Austrian Gvnmt 1966.
Sang with major companies in AUS: Graz, Salzburg Fest, Vienna Staatsoper & Volksoper; CZE: Brno; FRA: Aix-en-Provence Fest; GRE: Athens Fest; FR GER: Cologne, Düsseldorf-Duisburg, Frankfurt, Hamburg, Munich Staatsoper, Stuttgart, Wiesbaden; ITA: Florence Maggio, Milan La Scala, Naples, Palermo Massimo, Trieste, Turin; MON: Monte Carlo; S AFR: Johannesburg; SPA: Barcelona; SWI: Basel, Geneva; UK: Glyndebourne Fest, London Royal. **Roles with these companies incl** BELLINI: Norma; BRITTEN: Tytania (*Midsummer Night*); DONIZETTI: Lucia; EGK: Cathleen (*Irische Legende*);

FLOTOW: Lady Harriet (*Martha*); HANDEL: Alcina, Cleopatra (*Giulio Cesare*); IBERT: Angélique; LEONCAVALLO: Nedda (*Pagliacci*); MASSENET: Manon; MOZART: Fiordiligi★ (*Così fan tutte*), Donna Anna★ (*Don Giovanni*), Konstanze★ (*Entführung aus dem Serail*), Contessa★ (*Nozze di Figaro*), Pamina & Königin der Nacht (*Zauberflöte*); NICOLAI: Frau Fluth (*Lustigen Weiber*); OFFENBACH: Olympia★ & Antonia★ & Giulietta★ (*Contes d'Hoffmann*); ORFF: Solo (*Carmina burana*); PUCCINI: Musetta (*Bohème*), Manon Lescaut, Liù★ (*Turandot*); RAVEL: Concepcion (*Heure espagnole*); SCHOENBERG: Woman (*Erwartung*); STRAUSS, J: Rosalinde★ (*Fledermaus*); STRAUSS, R: Aithra★ (*Aegyptische Helena*), Fiakermilli★‡ (*Arabella*), Zerbinetta (*Ariadne auf Naxos*), Daphne, Aminta★ (*Schweigsame Frau*); VERDI: Alice Ford (*Falstaff*), Gilda★‡ (*Rigoletto*), Violetta (*Traviata*). Also KORNGOLD: (*Ring des Polykrates*). Recorded for: Decca, Vox, Telefunken, Westminster, Eurodisc, Ariola, Turnabout, Saga. Video/Film: Concepcion (*Heure espagnole*). Gives recitals. Appears with symphony orchestra. **Res:** 83 Drakensberg Dr, Pretoria, S Afr.

COLALILLO, MARTHA. Spinto coloratura & lyric soprano. Argentinean. Resident mem: Teatro Colón. Born 6 Dec 1944, Buenos Aires. Husband Dr Adolfo Venturini, occupation anesthetist. Two children. Studied: Inst Superior de Arte, Teatro Colón. **Debut:** Venilia (*Lucrezia Romana*) Teatro Colón 1968. Previous occupations: anesthesia technician. Awards: Mozarteum Purse, Argentina 1968; First Prize Conc Promociones Musicales 1968 and Conc Nacional de Canto 1968.
Sang with major companies in ARG: Buenos Aires; AUS: Vienna Staatsoper. **Roles with these companies incl** BIZET: Micaëla (*Carmen*); MOZART: Fiordiligi (*Così fan tutte*), Donna Anna (*Don Giovanni*), Konstanze (*Entführung aus dem Serail*); PERGOLESI: Serpina (*Serva padrona*); PUCCINI: Mimi (*Bohème*), Cio-Cio-San (*Butterfly*); VERDI: Gilda (*Rigoletto*), Violetta (*Traviata*), Leonora (*Trovatore*). Also RESPIGHI: Venilia (*Lucrezia Romana*); DONIZETTI: Nina (*Giovedi grasso*); VERDI: Fenena (*Nabucco*). Video–TV BA: Fenena (*Nabucco*). **Res:** Valentín Virasoro 1061, Buenos Aires, Argentina.

COLASANTI, VENIERO. Scenic and costume designer for opera, theater, film & television. Is a lighting designer; also an architect. Italian. Born 21 Jul 1910, Rome. Single. **Operatic debut:** Pelléas et Mélisande Teatro dell'Opera, Rome 1937. Theater debut: Elica Film Prod, Rome 1940.
Designed for major companies in AUS: Salzburg Fest; ITA: Florence Maggio & Comunale, Milan La Scala, Naples San Carlo, Palermo Massimo, Rome Opera, Spoleto Fest, Venice, Verona Arena; SWI: Geneva. **Operas designed for these companies incl** BUSONI: *Turandot*; CAVALIERI: *Rappresentazione;* DEBUSSY: *Pelléas et Mélisande;* DONIZETTI: *Fille du régiment;* GLUCK: *Iphigénie en Aulide, Orfeo ed Euridice;* HANDEL: *Acis and Galatea★;* MENOTTI: *Amelia al ballo;* MILHAUD: *Christophe Colomb;* MOZART: *Don Giovanni;* OFFENBACH: *Contes d'Hoffmann;* ORFF: *Carmina burana;*

PONCHIELLI: *Gioconda;* PUCCINI: *Bohème, Butterfly, Rondine, Tosca;* ROSSINI: *Cenerentola, Guillaume Tell;* STRAUSS, R: *Arabella, Rosenkavalier⋆, Salome;* STRAVINSKY: *Perséphone;* VERDI: *Don Carlo, Due Foscari, Otello, Rigoletto, Traviata;* WAGNER: *Lohengrin.* Also MASCAGNI: *Iris;* PACINI: *Saffo;* SCARLATTI: *Mitridate eupatore;* LEONCAVALLO: *Zazà.* **Operatic world premieres:** ROSSELLINI: *Vortice* Teatro S Carlo, Naples 1958; PERAGALLO: *Ginevra degli Almieri* Teatro dell'Opera, Rome 1937. Teaches at Cattedra di Scenografia, Univ Rome. **Res:** V degli Orsini 34, Rome, Italy.

COLLINGE, ROBERT J. American. Gen Mng, Baltimore Opera Co and Eastern Opera Theatre, 11 E Lexington St, Baltimore, MD 21202. In charge of dram & tech matters & finances. Add adm positions til 12/75: Pres, OPERA America, Washington, DC. Born 23 Apr 1928, New Bedford, MA. Single. Studied: Univ of Rhode Island, Providence. Previous occupation: mathematics tchr. Started with present company 1962 as Prod Mng, in present position since 1965. World premieres at theaters under his management: PASATIERI: *Ines de Castro* Baltimore 1976. Mem of Prof Commtt, Central Opera Service; Trustee, National Opera Inst. **Res:** 1101 St Paul St, Baltimore, MD, USA.

COLLINS, ANNE. Contralto. British. Born 29 Aug 1943, Co Durham, UK. Studied: Royal Coll of Music, Oda Slobodskaya, London. **Debut:** Governess *(Pique Dame)* Sadler's Wells, London 1970. **Sang with major companies in** UK: Aldeburgh Fest, London English National. **Roles with these companies incl** BRITTEN: Mrs Herring⋆ *(Albert Herring);* PUCCINI: Suzuki⋆ *(Butterfly);* VERDI: Ulrica⋆ *(Ballo in maschera);* WAGNER: Erda *(Rheingold⋆, Siegfried⋆),* Waltraute⋆ *(Götterdämmerung).* Also HENZE: Beroe⋆ *(Bassariden);* PROKOFIEV: Maria Dimitrevna⋆ *(War and Peace).* Recorded for: EMI. Gives recitals. Appears with symphony orchestra. **Res:** London, UK. Mgmt: IBB/UK.

COLLINS, KENNETH. Lyric & dramatic tenor. British. Resident mem: Welsh National Opera, Cardiff. Born 21 Oct 1935, Birmingham, UK. Wife Valerie. Two sets of twins. Studied: Charles Dean, Ettore Campogalliani. **Debut:** Radames *(Aida)* Welsh National Opera, Cardiff 1971. Previous occupations: optical mechanic. **Sang with major companies in** FRA: Strasbourg; UK: Cardiff Welsh, London English National. **Roles with these companies incl** BIZET: Nadir⋆ *(Pêcheurs de perles);* CILEA: Maurizio *(A. Lecouvreur);* PUCCINI: Rodolfo⋆ *(Bohème),* Pinkerton⋆ *(Butterfly),* Des Grieux⋆ *(Manon Lescaut),* Cavaradossi *(Tosca),* Calaf⋆ *(Turandot);* VERDI: Radames⋆ *(Aida),* Don Carlo⋆, Don Alvaro *(Forza del destino),* Ismaele⋆ *(Nabucco),* Duca di Mantova⋆ *(Rigoletto),* Gabriele⋆ *(Simon Boccanegra),* Alfredo *(Traviata);* WAGNER: Erik⋆ *(Fliegende Holländer).* Also LEONCAVALLO: Marcello *(Bohème).* Gives recitals. Appears with symphony orchestra. Mgmt: AIM/UK.

COLMAGRO, GIANLUIGI. Lyric baritone. Italian. Born 26 Mar 1929, Reggio Emilia, Italy. Wife Antonia Berengan, occupation teacher. Two children. Studied: in Venice, Rome, Siena, Milan. **Debut:** Dott Malatesta *(Don Pasquale)* Tunis 1964. Previous occupations: teacher. **Sang with major companies in** CZE: Prague Smetana; HUN: Budapest; ITA: Bologna, Florence Maggio & Comunale, Genoa, Naples, Palermo, Parma, Spoleto Fest, Trieste, Turin, Venice; SWI: Geneva. **Roles with these companies incl** BIZET: Escamillo⋆ *(Carmen);* CATALANI: Vincenzo Gellner⋆ *(Wally);* DONIZETTI: Dott Malatesta *(Don Pasquale),* Belcore⋆ *(Elisir),* Enrico *(Lucia);* GIORDANO: Carlo Gérard *(Andrea Chénier);* LEONCAVALLO: Tonio *(Pagliacci);* MASCAGNI: Rabbi David *(Amico Fritz),* Alfio *(Cavalleria rusticana);* MENOTTI: John Sorel⋆ *(Consul);* MOZART: Guglielmo *(Così fan tutte);* PERGOLESI: Uberto *(Serva padrona);* PUCCINI: Marcello *(Bohème),* Jack Rance *(Fanciulla del West),* Sharpless *(Butterfly),* Rambaldo *(Rondine),* Scarpia *(Tosca),* Guglielmo Wulf *(Villi);* ROSSINI: Figaro⋆ *(Barbiere di Siviglia),* Dandini⋆ *(Cenerentola);* VERDI: Renato *(Ballo in maschera),* Macbeth⋆, Iago⋆ *(Otello),* Germont⋆ *(Traviata),* Conte di Luna *(Trovatore).* Also DONIZETTI: Cardenio *(Furioso all'isola di San Domingo);* ZANDONAI: Tebaldo *(Giulietta e Romeo);* LEONCAVALLO: Rodolfo⋆ *(Bohème);* MERCADANTE: Manfredo⋆ *(Giuramento);* PUCCINI: Gualtiero⋆ *(Edgar);* MANNINO: Luisella⋆. **World premiere:** PAER: Pizarro *(Leonora)* Teatro Regio, Parma 1974. **Res:** V Calpena 15, Conegliano/Treviso, Italy.

COLOMBO, SCIPIO. Dramatic baritone. Italian. Born 25 May 1910, Vicenza. Married. Two children. Studied: Consv G Verdi, Giuseppe Venturini, Giuseppe De Luca, Milan. **Debut:** Marcello *(Bohème)* Teatro Alessandria 1937. Awards: Order of Merit, Emperor of Japan. **Sang with major companies in** AUS: Bregenz Fest, Graz, Vienna Staatsoper; BEL: Brussels; BRA: Rio de Janeiro; FRA: Aix-en-Provence Fest, Lyon, Marseille, Nice, Strasbourg, Toulouse; FR GER: Hamburg, Hannover, Karlsruhe, Stuttgart; HOL: Amsterdam; ITA: Bologna, Florence Maggio & Comunale, Genoa, Milan La Scala, Naples, Parma, Rome Opera, Trieste, Turin, Venice, Verona Arena; MON: Monte Carlo; POR: Lisbon; SPA: Barcelona; SWI: Basel, Geneva, Zurich; UK: Cardiff Welsh, Edinburgh Fest, London Royal; USA: New York Met. **Roles with these companies incl** d'ALBERT: Sebastiano *(Tiefland);* BARTOK: Bluebeard; BEETHOVEN: Don Pizarro *(Fidelio);* BELLINI: Sir Richard *(Puritani);* BERG: Dr Schön *(Lulu);* BERLIOZ: Balducci *(Benvenuto Cellini);* BIZET: Escamillo *(Carmen),* Zurga *(Pêcheurs de perles);* BORODIN: Prince Igor; BRITTEN: Captain Balstrode *(Peter Grimes);* BUSONI: Matteo⋆ *(Arlecchino);* CATALANI: Vincenzo Gellner; CHARPENTIER: Père *(Louise);* CILEA: Michonnet *(A. Lecouvreur);* DALLAPICCOLA: Prigioniero⋆, Riviere *(Volo di notte);* DONIZETTI: Enrico *(Campanello),* Dott Malatesta⋆‡ *(Don Pasquale),* Belcore *(Elisir),* Alfonse *(Favorite),* Enrico *(Lucia);* FLOTOW: Plunkett *(Martha);* GIORDANO: Carlo Gérard *(Andrea Chénier),* De

Siriex‡ (*Fedora*); HANDEL: Bertaric (*Rode-linda*); HINDEMITH: Mathis; KODALY: Háry János; LEONCAVALLO: Tonio (*Pagliacci*); LORTZING: Peter I★ (*Zar und Zimmermann*); MARTINU: Grigoris (*Griechische Passion*); MASSENET: Hérode (*Hérodiade*), Lescaut (*Manon Lescaut*), Athanaël (*Thaïs*), Albert (*Werther*); MOZART: Guglielmo & Don Alfonso (*Così fan tutte*), Don Giovanni, Conte Almaviva & Figaro (*Nozze di Figaro*); MUSSORGSKY: Shaklovity (*Khovanshchina*); ORFF: Solo (*Carmina burana*); PONCHIELLI: Barnaba (*Gioconda*); PROKO-FIEV: Ruprecht (*Fiery Angel*), Mr Astley★ (*Gambler*); PUCCINI: Jack Rance (*Fanciulla del West*), Gianni Schicchi, Sharpless (*Butterfly*), Lescaut (*Manon Lescaut*), Michele (*Tabarro*), Scarpia★‡ (*Tosca*); ROSSINI: Figaro (*Barbiere di Siviglia*), Dandini (*Cenerentola*), Guillaume Tell, Signor Bruschino, Geronio (*Turco in Italia*); SAINT-SAENS: Grand prêtre (*Samson et Dalila*); STRAUSS, R: Orest (*Elektra*); STRA-VINSKY: Creon (*Oedipus Rex*); VERDI: Amonasro‡ (*Aida*), Renato (*Ballo in maschera*), Rodrigo (*Don Carlo*), Ford (*Falstaff*), Don Carlo (*Forza del destino*), Miller‡ (*Luisa Miller*), Macbeth, Nabucco, Iago (*Otello*), Rigoletto, Germont (*Traviata*), di Luna (*Trovatore*); WAGNER: Wolfram (*Tannhäuser*); WEILL: Trinity Moses (*Aufstieg und Fall der Stadt Mahagonny*); WEIN-BERGER: Schwanda; WOLF-FERRARI: Conte Gil (*Segreto di Susanna*). Also DALLAPIC-COLA: Job; PERSICO: Petruccio (*Bisbetica domata*). **World premieres:** DALLAPICCOLA: Prigioniero, Maggio Mus Florence 1950; PIZ-ZETTI: Cagliostro, Scala Milan 1953; DONATI: Corradino (*Corradino lo svevo*) Comunale Bologna 1948. Recorded for: Westminster, Cetra, MMS. Video/Film—TV: (*Falstaff*); (*Médecin malgré lui*); (*Turco in Italia*). Gives recitals. Appears with symphony orchestra. Teaches voice. On faculty of Staatliche Musikhochschule. **Res:** Jahnstr 11, Karlsruhe, FR Ger.

COLONNELLO, ATTILIO. Scenic and costume designer for opera, theater, film, television; specl in sets. Is a lighting designer, stage director; also a painter & architect. Italian. Born 9 Nov 1931, Milan. Single. Studied: architecture at Polytechnic, Milan. **Operatic debut:** sets & cost, Traviata Maggio Musicale, Florence 1956. Theater debut: Palladio's Teatro Olimpico, Vicenza. Previous occupation: architect. Awards: Commendatore, Cross of Italian Republic.

Designed for major companies in ARG: Buenos Aires; ITA: Bologna, Florence Maggio & Comunale, Milan La Scala, Naples, Palermo, Parma, Rome Opera & Caracalla, Turin, Venice, Verona Arena; SPA: Barcelona; SWI: Zurich; USSR: Leningrad Kirov; USA: Dallas, New York Met. **Operas designed for these companies incl** BELLINI: *Beatrice di Tenda*★†, *Puritani*★†; BOITO: *Mefistofele*★†; DONIZETTI: *Anna Bolena*★, *Don Pasquale*★, *Elisir*★, *Lucia*★, *Roberto Devereux*★; HANDEL: *Giulio Cesare*★†, *Xerxes*★†; MONTE-VERDI: *Incoronazione di Poppea*★†; MOZART: *Così fan tutte*★, *Don Giovanni*★, *Nozze di Figaro*★; PAISIELLO: *Barbiere di Siviglia*★†; PON-CHIELLI: *Gioconda*★; PUCCINI: *Bohème, Gianni Schicchi, Tosca, Turandot*; ROSSINI: *Barbiere di Siviglia, Comte Ory, Guillaume Tell,*

Italiana in Algeri, Signor Bruschino; SPONTINI: *Fernand Cortez*★†; STRAVINSKY: *Oedipus Rex*★†; VERDI: *Aida*★†, *Ballo in maschera*‡, *Due Foscari*★†, *Forza del destino*★†, *Luisa Miller*★†, *Nabucco*★†, *Otello*★†, *Rigoletto*★†, *Traviata*★†, *Trovatore*★†; ZANDONAI: *Francesca da Rimini*★. Also BERLIOZ: *Roméo et Juliette*. **Operatic world premieres:** PIZZETTI: *Clitennestra* La Scala, Milan 1965; ROTA: *Lampada di Aladino* Teatro San Carlo, Naples 1968; ROSSELLINI: *Leggenda del ritorno* La Scala, Milan 1966. Operatic Video/Film—various operas. Exhibitions of stage designs Biennale, Venice 1965; Rizzoli, New York 1969. Teaches at Accad Belle Arti, Rome. **Res:** V Sardegna 48, Rome, Italy.

COLOSIMO, ENRICO. Stages/produces opera, theater & television. Also designs stage-lighting and is an actor & author. Italian. Resident Stage Dir for television in Rome. Born 9 Jan 1924, Catanzaro. Wife Rossana Vedrani, occupation philosophy teacher. Three children. Studied: Consv Cherubini & Univ, Florence; Accad Nazionale d'Arte drammatica, Rome; incl music. Operatic training as asst stage dir at Verona Arena, Florence Maggio Musicale & Venice Fest 1948-52. **Operatic debut:** *Partita a pugni* La Fenice, Venice 1953. Theater debut: Teatro di Corte, Naples 1957. Previous occupation: journalist.

Directed/produced opera for major companies in ITA: Bologna, Florence Comunale, Milan La Scala, Naples, Parma, Rome Opera, Turin, Venice, Verona Arena. **Operas staged with these companies incl** BARTOK: *Bluebeard's Castle*★; BELLINI: *Beatrice di Tenda, Sonnambula;* BIZET: *Pêcheurs de perles;* CILEA: *A. Lecouvreur;* CIMAROSA: *Matrimonio segreto;* DALLAPICCOLA: *Prigioniero*★; DONIZETTI: *Anna Bolena, Don Pasquale*★, *Elisir*★, *Maria di Rohan, Rita;* MASCAGNI: *Cavalleria rusticana;* MASSENET: *Werther;* MENOTTI: *Amelia al ballo;* MOZART: *Don Giovanni;* PUCCINI: *Bohème, Gianni Schicchi, Butterfly*★, *Manon Lescaut, Rondine*★, *Tabarro, Tosca;* ROSSINI: *Barbiere di Siviglia, Cenerentola, Moïse;* VERDI: *Forza del destino, Rigoletto*★, *Trovatore;* WOLF-FERRARI: *Segreto di Susanna*. Also CIMAROSA: *Maestro di cappella;* DALLAPICCOLA: *Job;* DONIZETTI: *Pia de' Tolomei;* GIORDANO: *Mese mariano;* LORENZINI: *Quattro per cinque;* LUALDI: *Furie di Arlecchino;* LUPI: *Danza di Salomè;* RESPIGHI: *Lucrezia Romana;* SCARLATTI: *Cavalier romano;* SORESINA: *Miracolo;* TOSATTI: *Sistema della dolcezza;* VERETTI: *Burlesca*. **Operatic world premieres:** PERAGALLO: *Gita in campagna* La Scala, Milan 1954; CHAILLY: *Ferrovia soprelevata* Teatro Donizetti, Bergamo 1955; PARODI: *Cantata pastorale* San Carlo, Naples 1962. Operatic Video—RAI: *Cenerentola, Barbiere di Siviglia, Testimone indesiderato*. Teaches at Accad Antoniana d'Arte drammatica, Bologna; Consv di Musica, Ferrara. **Res:** V Apollo Pizio 13, Rome, Italy.

COLZANI, ANSELMO. Lyric & dramatic baritone. Italian. Born 28 Mar 1918, Budrio/Bologna, Italy. Wife Ada Bertoni, occupation pianist. Two children. **Debut:** Heerrufer (*Lohengrin*) Teatro Comunale, Bologna 1947. Previous occupations: typewriter mechanic. Awards: Prize, Intl Luigi Illica-Castell' Arquato, Italy 1967; Cavaliere Ufficiale nell'Ordine al Merito della Repubblica Italiana 1971.

Sang with major companies in ARG: Buenos Aires; AUS: Vienna Staatsoper; BRA: Rio de Janeiro; CAN: Toronto; FRA: Aix-en-Provence Fest, Bordeaux, Lyon, Marseille, Nancy, Nice, Paris, Toulouse; FR GER: Munich Staatsoper, Stuttgart, Wiesbaden; ITA: Bologna, Florence Maggio & Comunale, Genoa, Milan La Scala, Naples, Palermo Massimo, Parma, Rome Caracalla & Teatro dell'Opera, Trieste, Turin, Venice, Verona Arena; MEX: Mexico City; MON: Monte Carlo; POR: Lisbon; SPA: Barcelona; USA: Boston, Hartford, Houston, Miami, New York Met, Philadelphia Lyric, San Francisco Opera; YUG: Zagreb. **Roles with these companies incl** BELLINI: Sir Richard (*Puritani*); BIZET: Escamillo (*Carmen*); CILEA: Michonnet (*A. Lecouvreur*); DONIZETTI: Agata★ (*Convenienze/Viva la Mamma*), Alfonse (*Favorite*), Enrico‡ (*Lucia*), Chevreuse (*Maria di Rohan*); FALLA: Tio Sarvaor (*Vida breve*); GIORDANO: Carlo Gérard★ (*Andrea Chénier*), De Siriex (*Fedora*); GLUCK: High Priest (*Alceste*), Thoas (*Iphigénie en Tauride*); LEONCAVALLO: Tonio★ (*Pagliacci*); MASCAGNI: Alfio★ (*Cavalleria rusticana*); PONCHIELLI: Barnaba★‡ (*Gioconda*); PUCCINI: Marcello (*Bohème*), Jack Rance★ (*Fanciulla del West*), Sharpless (*Butterfly*), Michele★ (*Tabarro*), Scarpia★ (*Tosca*); VERDI: Amonasro★ (*Aida*), Renato (*Ballo in maschera*), Don Carlo (*Ernani*), Falstaff★, Don Carlo★‡ (*Forza del destino*), Macbeth, Nabucco, Iago★ (*Otello*), Rigoletto★, Simon Boccanegra, Germont (*Traviata*), Conte di Luna (*Trovatore*); WAGNER: Telramund (*Lohengrin*), Gunther (*Götterdämmerung*), Kurwenal (*Tristan und Isolde*); ZANDONAI: Gianciotto (*Francesca da Rimini*). Also DONIZETTI: Duca d'Alba, Severo (*Poliuto*); GIORDANO: Neri Chiaramantesi (*Cena delle beffe*); GOUNOD: Valentin (*Faust*); SPONTINI: Enrico il Leone (*Agnese di Hohenstaufen*); WALTON: Calcante (*Troilus and Cressida*). **World premieres:** MILHAUD: David, Teatro alla Scala, Milan 1956; CHAILLY: Capitano Marino (*Riva delle Sirti*) Monte Carlo 1959. Recorded for: Urania. Video/Film: Escamillo (*Carmen*). **Res:** V Francesco Albani 58, Milan, Italy. Mgmt: CAM/USA.

COMISSIONA, SERGIU. Conductor of opera and symphony. Israeli. Mus Dir, Baltimore Symph Orch, MD, USA. Born 16 Jun 1928, Bucharest, Romania. Wife Robinne, occupation choreographer. Studied: E Lindenberg, C Silvestri, Bucharest; incl violin, piano, French horn and voice. Operatic training as asst cond at Bucharest Opera 1955-58. **Operatic debut:** CONSTANTINESCO: *Stormy Night* Bucharest Opera 1956. Symphonic debut: Bucharest Symph Radio Orch 1946. Previous occupations: violinist in symph orch, Bucharest 1946-48. Awards: Hon DM Peabody Inst, Baltimore; Golden Medal, City of Göteborg, Sweden; Order of Merit, Romania.

Conducted with major companies in FR GER: Frankfurt; ROM: Bucharest; SWE: Drottningholm Fest, Stockholm; UK: London Royal; USA: Baltimore. **Operas with these companies incl** BEETHOVEN: *Fidelio;* BERLIOZ: *Damnation de*

Faust★; BIZET: *Carmen★;* GOUNOD: *Faust★;* MASSENET: *Manon★;* MOZART: *Così fan tutte★, Entführung aus dem Serail, Nozze di Figaro, Zauberflöte★;* ORFF: *Carmina burana★;* PUCCINI: *Bohème, Butterfly, Tosca;* ROSSINI: *Barbiere di Siviglia★;* SCHOENBERG: *Erwartung;* STRAUSS, J: *Fledermaus★;* STRAUSS, R: *Rosenkavalier★;* TCHAIKOVSKY: *Eugene Onegin;* VERDI: *Aida, Falstaff★, Traviata, Trovatore;* WEBER: *Freischütz.* Video—Swedish TV: *Maestro di cappella.* Conducted major orch in Europe, USA/Canada, Asia, Austrl. Previous positions as Mus Dir with major orch: Haifa Symph Orch, Israel 1959-66; Göteborg Symph Orch, Sweden 1967-72. **Res:** 4000 N Charles St, Baltimore, MD, USA. Mgmt: HUR/USA; IWL/UK.

COMO, FRANCA; née Francesca Como. Dramatic soprano. Italian. Born 4 Dec 1937, Naples. Single. Studied: Iris Adami Corradetti, Padua. **Debut:** Abigaille (*Nabucco*) Teatro Lirico Sperimentale, Spoleto 1960.

Sang with major companies in HUN: Budapest; ITA: Bologna, Naples. **Roles with these companies incl** BELLINI: Norma★; MASCAGNI: Santuzza★ (*Cavalleria rusticana*); PUCCINI: Turandot★; VERDI: Leonora★ (*Forza del destino*), Leonora★ (*Trovatore*). Appears with symphony orchestra. **Res:** V Nomentana 322, Rome, Italy.

CONKLIN, JOHN MARSHALL. Scenic and costume designer for opera, theater. American. Born 22 Jun 1937, Hartford, CT. USA. Single. Studied: Yale Univ. **Operatic debut:** sets, *Dialogues des Carmélites* New York City Op 1966; cost, *Nozze di Figaro* Minnesota Op, Minneapolis 1965. Theater debut: Hartford Stage Co, CT 1962.

Designed for major companies in USA: Baltimore, Houston, Minneapolis, New York City Opera, San Francisco Spring Opera, Santa Fe, Washington DC. **Operas designed for these companies incl** BRITTEN: *Death in Venice★;* MONTEVERDI: *Favola d'Orfeo;* MOZART: *Così fan tutte★, Nozze di Figaro;* POULENC: *Dialogues des Carmélites;* ROSSINI: *Barbiere di Siviglia★;* STRAUSS, R: *Salome.* **Operatic world premieres:** sets, GINASTERA: *Beatrix Cenci* Washington Opera Socy, 1971. **Res:** 253 W 91 St, New York, NY, USA.

CONLON, JAMES. Conductor of opera and symphony. American. Resident Cond, American Opera Center, Juilliard School, New York. Born 1950, New York. Single. Studied: HS of Music & Art, NY; Juilliard School, Jean Morel; incl piano. **Operatic debut:** *Bohème* American Opera Center 1972. Awards: Samuel Chotzinoff Awd, Aspen Music School, CO.

Conducted with major companies in ITA: Spoleto Fest; USA: Philadelphia Grand, Washington DC; et al. **Operas with these companies incl** DONIZETTI: *Don Pasquale;* MUSSORGSKY: *Boris Godunov;* ROSSINI: *Barbiere di Siviglia;* VERDI: *Falstaff, Macbeth;* et al. Also BARBER: *Antony and Cleopatra.* Conducted major orch in USA/Canada. Mgmt: CAM/USA.

CONONOVICI, MAGDALENA; née Stefanov. Dramatic soprano. Romanian. Resident mem: Romanian Opera, Bucharest. Born 25 Jul 1937, Piatra

Neamt. Divorced. Studied: Consv, Prof Mihail Vasilopol, Bucharest. **Debut:** Tosca, Romanian Opera, Cluj 1969. Awards: First Prize, Toulouse 1969; Fr Vinas, Barcelona 1970; Maria Canals, Barcelona 1971; Second Prize, Verviers 1970. **Sang with major companies in** BUL: Sofia; CZE: Prague National; FRA: Toulouse; GER DR: Berlin Staatsoper; ROM: Bucharest. **Roles with these companies incl** GIORDANO: Maddalena★ (*Andrea Chénier*); MASCAGNI: Santuzza (*Cavalleria rusticana*); MOZART: Sesto★ (*Clemenza di Tito*), Donna Anna★ (*Don Giovanni*); PONCHIELLI: Gioconda; PUCCINI: Manon Lescaut★, Tosca★; VERDI: Aida★, Elisabetta★ (*Don Carlo*), Donna Elvira (*Ernani*), Lady Macbeth★‡, Leonora★ (*Trovatore*); WAGNER: Elsa★ (*Lohengrin*), Sieglinde★ (*Walküre*). Also WAGNER: Kundry★ (*Parsifal*). Video/Film: (*Parsifal*), (*Macbeth*), (*Walküre*). Gives recitals. Appears with symphony orchestra. **Res:** 16 Negru Voda St, Bucharest 4, Romania. Mgmt: RIA/ROM; LLP/FRG.

CONSTANTINESCU, NICOLAE. Lyric baritone. Romanian. Resident mem: Romanian Opera, Bucharest. Born 27 Mar 1938, Bucharest. Wife Cecilia, occupation music editor, radio-TV. Studied: Consv, Profs Petre Stefanescu-Goanga, Victoria Costescu-Duca, Bucharest. **Debut:** Enrico (*Lucia*) Romanian Opera 1969.
Sang with major companies in CZE: Prague National; GER DR: Berlin Staatsoper; ROM: Bucharest; SWE: Stockholm. **Roles with these companies incl** BIZET: Escamillo★ (*Carmen*); DONIZETTI: Enrico★ (*Lucia*); MASCAGNI: Alfio★ (*Cavalleria rusticana*); MOZART: Guglielmo★ (*Così fan tutte*); PUCCINI: Marcello (*Bohème*), Sharpless★ (*Butterfly*); VERDI: Rodrigo★ (*Don Carlo*), Germont★ (*Traviata*). Also ENESCU: Theseus★ (*Oedipe*). **World premieres:** TRAILESCU: Negri (*Balcescu*) 1974; BRATU: Officer (*Right for Love*) 1975; both at Romanian Opera. Gives recitals. Appears with symphony orchestra. **Res:** 38A Moise Nicoara St, Bucharest 4, Romania. Mgmt: RIA/ROM.

CONZ, BERNHARD. Conductor of opera and symphony. German. Chief Cond, Städtische Bühnen, Bielefeld, FR Ger; form Gen Mus Dir. Born 1 Jun 1906, Karlsruhe. Studied: Hochschule für Musik, Karlsruhe; Sternsches Konsv, Berlin; incl piano. **Conducted with major companies in** AUS: Salzburg Fest; FR GER: Berlin Deutsche Oper, Bielefeld, Nürnberg, Saarbrücken; ITA: Milan La Scala, Venice; SPA: Barcelona; et al. **Operas with these companies incl** MONTEVERDI: *Favola d'Orfeo;* MOZART: *Così fan tutte, Entführung aus dem Serail, Nozze di Figaro, Zaïde;* STRAUSS, R: *Salome;* WAGNER: *Lohengrin, Parsifal;* et al. Previous positions as Mus Dir with major orch: Pfalz Orch, Ludwigshafen, FR Ger 1947-51.

COOK, DEBORAH. Coloratura soprano. American. Born Philadelphia, PA, USA. Widowed. Husband Dr Robert Kashoff, occupation psychiatrist (deceased). One son. Studied: Miss Irene Williams. **Debut:** Zerbinetta (*Ariadne auf Naxos*) Glyndebourne Touring Opera 1971. Previous occupations: secy, gift shop owner. Awards: Grant,

Hillsberg Fndt, Philadelphia; Winner WGN/Ill Op Guild Awd, Chicago.
Sang with major companies in FR GER: Berlin Deutsche Oper, Essen, Frankfurt, Hamburg Staatsoper, Kassel, Krefeld, Munich Staatsoper & Gärtnerplatz, Stuttgart; UK: Glyndebourne Fest. **Roles with these companies incl** DONIZETTI: Adina★ (*Elisir*), Lucia★‡; MOZART: Konstanze★ (*Entführung aus dem Serail*), Königin der Nacht★ (*Zauberflöte*); OFFENBACH: Olympia★ (*Contes d'Hoffmann*); ORFF: Solo★ (*Carmina burana*); STRAUSS, R: Zerbinetta★ (*Ariadne auf Naxos*); VERDI: Gilda★ (*Rigoletto*). Gives recitals. Appears with symphony orchestra. **Res:** Sigmund Freud Str 76, 6000 Frankfurt 50, FR Ger. Mgmt: MIN/UK.

COOK JEANNE; née Jean Louise Cook. Lyric soprano. American. Born Phoenix, AZ, USA. Single. Studied: Music Acad of the West, Mme Lotte Lehmann, Santa Barbara; William Eddy; Univ of So Calif; UCLA, Dr Jan Popper, Los Angeles, USA; Rudolf Spira, Zurich. **Debut:** Pamina (*Zauberflöte*) Opernhaus Zurich 1960. Awards: Awd for Outstanding Achiev in Perf Arts, Univ of Calif, Santa Barbara 1975; M B Rockefeller Fund, two grants.
Sang with major companies in BEL: Brussels; FRA: Nancy; FR GER: Berlin Deutsche Oper, Bonn, Cologne, Dortmund, Düsseldorf-Duisburg, Essen, Frankfurt, Hamburg, Hannover, Munich Staatsoper, Nürnberg, Stuttgart, Wuppertal; HOL: Amsterdam; ITA: Palermo, Trieste; SPA: Barcelona; SWI: Geneva, Zurich; USA: San Francisco Opera. **Roles with these companies incl** BEETHOVEN: Marzelline (*Fidelio*); BIZET: Micaëla (*Carmen*); BRITTEN: Helena (*Midsummer Night*); GLUCK: Iphigénie★ (*Iphigénie en Tauride*), Euridice; HANDEL: Romilda (*Xerxes*); HONEGGER: Ismene★ (*Antigone*); LEONCAVALLO: Nedda (*Pagliacci*); MOZART: Donna Anna & Donna Elvira★ (*Don Giovanni*), Arminda (*Finta giardiniera*), Contessa (*Nozze di Figaro*), Pamina★ (*Zauberflöte*); PUCCINI: Mimi (*Bohème*), Cio-Cio-San (*Butterfly*); STRAUSS, R: Sophie (*Rosenkavalier*); TCHAIKOVSKY: Lisa (*Pique Dame*); VERDI: Desdemona (*Otello*), Violetta (*Traviata*); WAGNER: Eva (*Meistersinger*), Gutrune★ (*Götterdämmerung*); WEBER: Agathe (*Freischütz*). Also SUTERMEISTER: Sonia (*Raskolnikoff*); PURCELL: Belinda (*Dido and Aeneas*); MARTINU: Lenio (*Griechische Passion*). Recorded for: Decca. Gives recitals. Appears with symphony orchestra. Teaches voice. **Res:** c/o Hay, 22 Foss Court, Walnut Creek, CA 94598, USA. Mgmt: SMN/USA; PAS/FRG.

COOK-MacDONALD, LINDA: neé Linda Lee Cook. Dramatic coloratura soprano. American. Resident mem: Städtische Bühnen, Krefeld, FR Ger; Städtische Bühnen, Dortmund, FR Ger. Born 22 Sep 1947, Twin Falls, ID, USA. Husband Frederick McDonald. Studied: College-Consv of Music, Cincinnati, O, USA; Robert & Lucille Evans; Jan Tamaru, Mainz, FR Ger. **Debut:** Fiordiligi (*Così fan tutte*) Krefeld, FR Ger 1971. Awards: Fulbright Schlshp; Corbett Fndt Fllshp.
Sang with major companies in FR GER: Darmstadt, Dortmund, Essen, Krefeld, Wuppertal; USA: Cincinnati, Memphis, Pittsburgh, Portland.

Roles with these companies incl BIZET: Micaëla (*Carmen*); DONIZETTI: Adina★ (*Elisir*); GOUNOD: Marguerite★ (*Faust*); MOZART: Fiordiligi★ (*Così fan tutte*), Zerlina★ (*Don Giovanni*), Konstanze★ (*Entführung aus dem Serail*), Mme Herz (*Schauspieldirektor*), Pamina★ & Königin der Nacht★ (*Zauberflöte*); PENDERECKI: Philippe★ (*Teufel von Loudun*); PUCCINI: Musetta★ (*Bohème*); STRAUSS, R: Zdenka★ (*Arabella*); VERDI: Alice Ford★ (*Falstaff*); WEBER: Agathe★ (*Freischütz*). Also CAVALLI: Diana★ (*Calisto*); KRENEK: Thamar★ (*Leben des Orestes*). Gives recitals. Appears with symphony orchestra. Res: 1 Freeman Ave, Middleport, NY, USA. Mgmt: SLZ/FRG.

COPLEY, JOHN MICHAEL. Stages/produces opera. Also designs costumes & stage-lighting and is a singer & actor. British. Resident Stage Dir, Royal Opera Covent Garden, London. Born 12 June 1933, Birmingham: Single. Studied: Ntl School of Opera, Joan Cross, London; incl music, piano and voice. Operatic training as asst stage dir at Royal Opera; as stage mng, Sadler's Wells, London. **Operatic debut:** *Nozze di Figaro* Hintlesham Fest, UK.

Directed/produced opera for major companies in AUSTRL: Sydney; BEL: Brussels; CAN: Montreal/Quebec; GRE: Athens Fest; HOL: Amsterdam; POR: Lisbon; SWE: Drottningholm Fest; UK: Aldeburgh Fest, Welsh National, Scottish, London Royal & English National; USA: Chicago, Dallas. **Operas staged for these companies incl** BEETHOVEN: *Fidelio;* BELLINI: *Sonnambula;* BERLIOZ: *Benvenuto Cellini, Troyens★;* BIZET: *Carmen;* BRITTEN: *Midsummer Night★;* DONIZETTI: *Elisir★, Lucia★, Maria Stuarda★;* GLUCK: *Iphigénie en Tauride, Orfeo ed Euridice;* GOUNOD: *Faust★;* HANDEL: *Acis and Galatea;* HAYDN: *Infedeltà delusa;* JANACEK: *Jenufa★;* MOZART: *Clemenza di Tito★, Così fan tutte★, Don Giovanni★, Entführung aus dem Serail, Nozze di Figaro★, Schauspieldirektor, Zauberflöte★;* POULENC: *Mamelles de Tirésias;* PUCCINI: *Bohème★, Butterfly★, Suor Angelica, Tosca, Turandot;* ROSSINI: *Barbiere di Siviglia, Gazza ladra;* STRAUSS, R: *Ariadne auf Naxos★, Elektra★, Rosenkavalier★;* TCHAIKOVSKY: *Eugene Onegin;* VAUGHAN WILLIAMS: *Riders to the Sea;* VERDI: *Ballo in maschera★, Falstaff, Macbeth, Rigoletto★, Traviata★, Trovatore★;* WAGNER: *Lohengrin, Tristan und Isolde.* Teaches at Royal Acad of Music & London Opera Centre. Res: 9D Thistlegrove, London SW10, UK. Mgmt: AIM/UK.

COPPOLA, ANTON. Conductor of opera and symphony; composer. American. Born 21 Mar 1917, New York. Wife Almerinda. Two children. Studied: Gennaro Papi, Fulgenzio Guerrieri, Paul Breisach, Vittorio Giannini; incl oboe, piano, cello and voice. Operatic training as repetiteur, asst cond & chorus master at var small comp in and near New York. **Operatic debut:** *Bohème* San Carlo Opera, San Francisco 1946. Symphonic debut: form Brooklyn Symph, New York 1941. Previous occupations: princ oboist Radio City Music Hall, NY; oboist for radio & records.

Conducted with major companies in USA: Baltimore, Cincinnati, Hartford, Memphis, Newark, New Orleans, New York City Opera, Philadelphia Grand, San Francisco Opera & Spring Opera, Seattle. **Operas with these companies incl** BELLINI: *Norma;* BIZET: *Carmen;* BUSONI: *Arlecchino;* CHERUBINI: *Medea;* DALLAPICCOLA: *Volo di notte;* DELIBES: *Lakmé;* DONIZETTI: *Don Pasquale, Elisir, Lucia;* FLOYD: *Of Mice and Men★;* GIORDANO: *Andrea Chénier;* GOUNOD: *Faust★, Mireille★, Roméo et Juliette★;* GRANADOS: *Goyescas;* HENZE: *Boulevard Solitude;* HUMPERDINCK: *Hänsel und Gretel;* LEONCAVALLO: *Pagliacci★;* MASCAGNI: *Amico Fritz★, Cavalleria rusticana★;* MASSENET: *Cendrillon, Manon★, Thaïs★, Werther★;* MENOTTI: *Medium, Old Maid and the Thief, Telephone;* MILHAUD: *Pauvre matelot;* MONTEMEZZI: *Amore dei tre re;* MONTEVERDI: *Favola d'Orfeo;* MOZART: *Così fan tutte, Don Giovanni, Entführung aus dem Serail, Finta giardiniera, Schauspieldirektor, Lucio Silla, Nozze di Figaro, Zauberflöte;* MUSSORGSKY: *Boris Godunov;* NICOLAI: *Lustigen Weiber;* OFFENBACH: *Contes d'Hoffmann;* ORFF: *Carmina burana;* PERGOLESI: *Maestro di musica, Serva padrona;* PONCHIELLI: *Gioconda;* POULENC: *Dialogues des Carmélites, Mamelles de Tirésias;* PUCCINI: *Bohème★, Fanciulla del West, Gianni Schicchi★, Butterfly★, Manon Lescaut★, Rondine★, Suor Angelica★, Tabarro★, Tosca★, Turandot★, Villi;* PURCELL: *Dido and Aeneas;* RAVEL: *Enfant et les sortilèges, Heure espagnole;* ROSSINI: *Barbiere di Siviglia★, Cenerentola★, Italiana in Algeri★;* SAINT-SAENS: *Samson et Dalila★;* SMETANA: *Bartered Bride;* STRAUSS, J: *Fledermaus;* STRAVINSKY: *Mavra, Rossignol;* THOMAS: *Hamlet, Mignon;* VERDI: *Aida★, Ballo in maschera, Don Carlo★, Falstaff, Forza del destino, Macbeth, Otello, Rigoletto★, Simon Boccanegra, Traviata★, Trovatore★;* WARD: *Crucible★;* WEBER: *Abu Hassan;* WOLF-FERRARI: *Segreto di Susanna.* Also BEESON: *Lizzie Borden‡;* ROSSELLINI: *Guerra.* **World premieres:** BEESON: *Lizzie Borden* New York City Opera 1965; FLOYD: *Of Mice and Men* Seattle, WA 1970; KASTLE: *Deseret* Memphis, TN 1967; FLAGELLO: *Judgment of St Francis* Manhattan School, New York 1966. Video—NET TV: *Lizzie Borden.* Previous positions as Mus Dir with major orch: Westchester Symph, White Plains, NY. **Operas composed:** *Magic Jar.* Teaches at Manhattan School of Music, New York. **Res:** New York, NY, USA.

CORAZZA, RÉMY. Lyric tenor. French. Resident mem: Opéra du Rhin, Strasbourg. Born 16 Apr 1933, Revin, France. Wife Claudette Bigot. Three children. Studied: Consv de Paris, Charles Panzéra, Louis Musy, Gustave Cloez; Marguerite Joye, Paris. **Debut:** Beppe (*Pagliacci*) Opéra Comique, Paris 1959. Previous occupations: double bass player. Awards: First Prize Intl Compt Toulouse, France; Médaille d'Argent, Arts, Sciences, Letters, Society of Paris.

Sang with major companies in BEL: Brussels, Liège; FRA: Bordeaux, Lyon, Marseille, Nancy, Nice, Paris, Rouen, Strasbourg, Toulouse; POR: Lisbon; SWI: Geneva. **Roles with these companies incl** ADAM: Chapelou★ (*Postillon de Lonjumeau*); AUBER: Lorenzo (*Fra Diavolo*); BERLIOZ:

Benvenuto Cellini; BIZET: Captain Silvio★‡ (*Docteur Miracle*), Nadir (*Pêcheurs de perles*); BORODIN: Vladimir (*Prince Igor*); BRITTEN: Lysander (*Midsummer Night*); CHABRIER: Nangis (*Roi malgré lui*); CIMAROSA: Paolino (*Matrimonio segreto*); DALLAPICCOLA: Pellerin & Radio Telegrapher (*Volo di notte*); DELIBES: Gérard (*Lakmé*), Mitou (*Roi l'a dit*); DONIZETTI: Ernesto (*Don Pasquale*), Beppo (*Rita*); EINEM: Camille Desmoulins (*Dantons Tod*); GOUNOD: Vincent★ (*Mireille*), Philémon; HAYDN: Filippo (*Infedeltà delusa*); LECOCQ: Pomponnet★ (*Fille de Madame Angot*); MARTINU: Yannakos★ (*Griechische Passion*); MASSENET: Des Grieux (*Manon*); MENOTTI: Kodanda (*Dernier sauvage*); MILHAUD: Sailor (*Pauvre matelot*); MOZART: Don Ottavio★ (*Don Giovanni*), Belmonte (*Entführung aus dem Serail*), Belfiore (*Finta giardiniera*), Idamante & Idomeneo (*Idomeneo*), Tamino★ (*Zauberflöte*); OFFENBACH: Hoffmann; POULENC: Chevalier de la Force★ (*Dialogues des Carmélites*); PROKOFIEV: Don Jerome★ (*Duenna*); PUCCINI: Rodolfo (*Bohème*), Rinuccio (*Gianni Schicchi*), Pinkerton★ (*Butterfly*), Prunier (*Rondine*), Luigi (*Tabarro*); ROSSINI: Almaviva (*Barbiere di Siviglia*), Don Ramiro (*Cenerentola*), Comte Ory, Neocle (*Assedio di Corinto*), Florville (*Signor Bruschino*); STRAUSS, J: Eisenstein★ & Alfred‡ (*Fledermaus*); STRAUSS, R: Ein Sänger★ (*Rosenkavalier*); STRAVINSKY: Oedipus Rex, Tom Rakewell (*Rake's Progress*); THOMAS: Wilhelm Meister★ (*Mignon*); VERDI: Foresto (*Attila*), Fenton (*Falstaff*), Oronte (*Lombardi*), Rodolfo★ (*Luisa Miller*), Ismaele (*Nabucco*), Alfredo★ (*Traviata*); WAGNER: Walther v d Vogelweide (*Tannhäuser*); WOLF-FERRARI: Filipeto (*Quattro rusteghi*). Also RAMEAU: Zoroastre; RAVEL: Gonzalve★ (*Heure espagnole*); HONNEGER: Cauchon★ (*Jeanne d'arc au bûcher*). World premieres: ROSENTHAL: Adorno (*Hop! Signor*) Toulouse 1962. Recorded for: Pathé-Marconi, Erato. Gives recitals. Appears with symphony orchestra. On faculty of Consv Strasbourg, prof in stage direction. **Res:** 68 r d'Adelshoffen, Schiltigheim 67-300, France. Mgmt: CMW/FRA.

CORBEIL, CLAUDE. Bass-baritone. Canadian. Born 17 Apr 1942, Rimouski, PQ, Canada. Wife Sally. Two children. **Debut:** Don Basilio (*Barbiere di Siviglia*) Montreal 1960.
Sang with major companies in CAN: Montreal/Quebec, Ottawa, Toronto, Vancouver; UK: London Royal Opera & English National; USA: Hartford, Hawaii, New Orleans, New York City Opera, Philadelphia Lyric, Pittsburgh. **Roles with these companies incl** BARTOK: Bluebeard★; DELIBES: Nilakantha (*Lakmé*); MOZART: Guglielmo & Don Alfonso★ (*Così fan tutte*), Don Giovanni★, Figaro★ (*Nozze di Figaro*); PUCCINI: Colline★ (*Bohème*); ROSSINI: Don Basilio★ (*Barbiere di Siviglia*); THOMAS: Lothario★ (*Mignon*); VERDI: Grande Inquisitore (*Don Carlo*), Banquo (*Macbeth*). Also DONIZETTI: Cecil★ (*Maria Stuarda*). Video/Film: Banquo (*Macbeth*); Grande Inquisitore (*Don Carlo*). Gives recitals. Appears with symphony orchestra. **Res:** Montreal, Canada. Mgmt: SAM/USA.

CORDER, BRUCE DERRICK. Canadian. Gen Mng, National Arts Centre/Festival Opera, Confederation Sq, Ottawa, Canada K1P 5W1; also Deputy Dir Gen, National Arts Centre. Adm National Arts Centre Theatre Dept, Music Dept, Dance & Variety Depts. In charge of overall adm matters, tech & finances. Born 16 Sep 1921, London, UK. Wife Colleen, occupation art gallery mng. Two children. Previous positions, primarily adm & theatrical in Toronto: Gen Mng, Bruce Corder Assocs 1966-67; Asst Gen Mng, O'Keefe Centre 1960-65; Prod Mng, CBC TV 1956-60; in London: House & Bus Mng, Royal Opera Covent Garden 1952-56; Mng, Duchess Theatre 1951-52; Asst, Royal Ballet 1947-51. Started with present company in 1967 as Dir of Operations, in present position since 1971. Initiated major policy changes including expansion from one to three operas per festival; expansion of budget. **Res:** 85 Range Rd, Apt 608, Ottawa, Ont, Canada.

CORDES, BARBARA. Lyric soprano. German. Resident mem: Opernhaus Kiel. Born 6 Nov 1948, Landstuhl, Germany. Single. Studied: Henny Schöner, Erika Köth, Munich; Prof Dietger Jakob, Hamburg; M Th Gernot-Heindl, acting, Munich. **Debut:** Bastienne, Münchner Kammeroper 1969.
Sang with major companies in FR GER: Kiel. **Roles with these companies incl** BEETHOVEN: Marzelline★ (*Fidelio*); LORTZING: Marie★ (*Waffenschmied*); ORFF: Solo★ (*Carmina burana*). Also HAYDN: Nerina★ (*Belohnte Treue*); MOZART: Bastienne★. Video/Film - BBC TV London: Bastienne. Gives recitals. Appears with symphony orchestra. **Res:** Dithmarscherstr 15, 23 Kiel, FR Ger. Mgmt: RTB/FRG.

CORELLI, FRANCO. Dramatic tenor. Italian. Born 8 Apr 1923, Ancona. Wife Loretta di Lelio, occupation form soprano. Studied: Pesaro Consv. **Debut:** Don José (*Carmen*) Spoleto 1952. Previous occupation: studied naval engineering, Univ of Bologna; public official. Awards: Winner, Singing Compt Florence 1952.
Sang with major companies in AUS: Salzburg Fest, Vienna Staatsoper; FRA: Paris; FR GER: Hamburg; ITA: Bologna, Florence Maggio, Genoa, Milan La Scala, Naples, Palermo, Rome Opera & Caracalla, Trieste, Venice, Verona Arena; POR: Lisbon; SPA: Barcelona; UK: London Royal; USA: Chicago, Miami, New York Met, Philadelphia Lyric, San Francisco Opera; et al. **Roles with these cos incl** BELLINI: Pollione (*Norma*); CILEA: Maurizio (*A. Lecouvreur*); GIORDANO: Andrea Chénier‡, Loris Ipanov (*Fedora*); GOUNOD: Roméo; HANDEL: Sextus (*Giulio Cesare*); LEONCAVALLO: Canio‡ (*Pagliacci*); MASCAGNI: Turiddu‡ (*Cavalleria rusticana*); MASSENET: Werther; MEYERBEER: Raoul de Nangis (*Huguenots*); PONCHIELLI: Enzo (*Gioconda*); PROKOFIEV: Anatole (*War and Peace*); PUCCINI: Rodolfo (*Bohème*), Dick Johnson (*Fanciulla del West*), Cavaradossi‡ (*Tosca*), Calaf‡ (*Turandot*); SPONTINI: Licinio (*Vestale*); VERDI: Radames‡ (*Aida*), Riccardo (*Ballo in maschera*), Don Carlo, Ernani, Don Alvaro (*Forza del destino*), Rodolfo (*Luisa Miller*), Manrico‡ (*Trovatore*); ZANDONAI: Romeo; et al. Also MUSSORGSKY: Dimitri (*Boris Godunov*); DONIZETTI: Poliuto;

VERDI: Arrigo (*Battaglia di Legnano*). Recorded for: Angel, London, Columbia, Cetra. Video/Film: Cavaradossi (*Tosca*).

CORENA, FERNANDO. Basso-buffo. Swiss. Born 22 Dec 1916, Geneva. Wife Elisabeth. Studied: Mo Enrico Romano, Milan. **Debut:** Dott Bartolo (*Barbiere di Siviglia*) Arena di Verona 1948. Previous occupations: concert & oratorio singer for about 10 yrs. Awards: Grand Prix du Disque.
Sang with major companies in ARG: Buenos Aires; AUS: Salzburg Fest, Vienna Staatsoper; BEL: Brussels; FRA: Nice, Paris, Toulouse; GRE: Athens Fest; FR GER: Berlin Deutsche Oper, Munich Bayerische Staatsoper; GER DR: Berlin Komische Oper; HOL: Amsterdam; ISR: Tel Aviv; ITA: Bologna, Florence Maggio Musicale & Comunale, Genoa, Milan La Scala, Naples, Palermo, Rome Teatro dell'Opera, Trieste, Turin, Venice, Verona Arena; MEX: Mexico City; POR: Lisbon; SPA: Barcelona; SWI: Geneva, Zurich; UK: Edinburgh Fest, London Royal Opera; USA: Chicago, Hartford, Houston, Miami, New Orleans, New York Met, Philadelphia Grand & Lyric, San Francisco Opera, Washington DC. Roles with these companies incl BEETHOVEN: Rocco (*Fidelio*); BELLINI: Rodolfo‡ (*Sonnambula*); BUSONI: Matteo (*Arlecchino*); CIMAROSA: Geronimo (*Matrimonio segreto*); DONIZETTI: Don Pistacchio (*Campanello*), Don Pasquale∗‡, Dott Dulcamara∗‡ (*Elisir*), Sulpice∗ (*Fille du régiment*), Marquis (*Linda di Chamounix*); GALUPPI: Don Tritemio (*Filosofo di campagna*); MASSENET: Lescaut (*Manon*); MENOTTI: Husband (*Amelia al ballo*); MONTEMEZZI: Archibaldo (*Amore dei tre re*); MOZART: Don Alfonso (*Così fan tutte*), Leporello∗‡ (*Don Giovanni*), Osmin∗ (*Entführung aus dem Serail*), Figaro (*Nozze di Figaro*); MUSSORGSKY: Varlaam & Pimen (*Boris Godunov*); OFFENBACH: Coppélius etc (*Contes d'Hoffmann*); PERGOLESI: Tracolino (*Maestro di musica*), Uberto (*Serva padrona*); PONCHIELLI: Alvise‡ (*Gioconda*); PROKOFIEV: Mendoza (*Duenna*), King of Clubs (*Love for Three Oranges*); PUCCINI: Colline (*Bohème*), Gianni Schicchi‡; ROSSINI: Dott Bartolo∗‡ (*Barbiere di Siviglia*), Don Magnifico (*Cenerentola*), Mustafà∗‡ (*Italiana in Algeri*), Geronio (*Turco in Italia*); SMETANA: Kezal (*Bartered Bride*); STRAVINSKY: Empereur de Chine (*Rossignol*); VERDI: Ramfis (*Aida*), Falstaff∗‡, Fra Melitone∗‡ (*Forza del destino*); WAGNER: Daland (*Fliegende Holländer*); WEILL: Trinity Moses (*Aufstieg und Fall der Stadt Mahagonny*); WOLF-FERRARI: Lunardo‡ (*Quattro rusteghi*). Recorded for: Decca, London, RCA, Angel, Cetra, Urania, Richmond, Concert Hall. Video/Film: Dott Bartolo (*Barbiere di Siviglia*); Osmin (*Entführung aus dem Serail*). Gives recitals. Appears with symphony orchestra. Teaches voice. **Res:** V S Giorgio 18, 6976 Castagnola, Switzerland.

CORENNE, RENÉE; née Renée Cornester. Lyric soprano. American. Born 21 Oct 1937, Bucharest, Romania. Husband Amnon Telpasi, occupation cantor. Studied: Bucharest Consv, Stroescu Constantin; Antonio Narducci, Milan; Fausto Cleva, Carlo Moresco, New York. **Debut:** Marie (*Bartered Bride*) Bucharest National Opera 1957.

Sang with major companies in CAN: Toronto; FRA: Paris; ISR: Tel Aviv; ROM: Bucharest; USA: Hartford, Newark, Philadelphia Grand, Pittsburgh. **Roles with these companies incl** BIZET: Micaëla∗ (*Carmen*); GOUNOD: Marguerite∗ (*Faust*); MASSENET: Manon∗; MOZART: Zerlina (*Don Giovanni*); PUCCINI: Mimì∗ & Musetta∗ (*Bohème*); SMETANA: Marie (*Bartered Bride*); TCHAIKOVSKY: Tatiana∗ (*Eugene Onegin*); VERDI: Violetta∗ (*Traviata*). Gives recitals. Teaches voice. **Res:** 324 Lantana Ave, Englewood/Bergen, NJ, USA.

CORMANY, ELAINE; née Faynette Elaine Cormany. Lyric coloratura soprano. American. Resident mem: Hessisches Staatstheater, Wiesbaden, FR Ger. Born 11 May 1944, Clifton, TX, USA. Single. Studied: No Texas St Univ, Vera R Neilson, Denton; Ellen Repp, Julia Drobner, Max Walmer, New York. **Debut:** Violetta (*Traviata*) Shreveport Opera, LA, USA 1967. Awards: First Prize NFMC 1964; Winner Met Op Ntl Counc Awd & Spec Stpd 1965-66; Dallas Civic Op Awd 1967.
Sang with major companies in FR GER: Dortmund, Essen, Saarbrücken, Wiesbaden; ROM: Bucharest; USA: Fort Worth. **Roles with these companies incl** BEETHOVEN: Marzelline∗ (*Fidelio*); BIZET: Micaëla (*Carmen*); DONIZETTI: Norina∗ (*Don Pasquale*), Adina∗ (*Elisir*); HINDEMITH: Helene∗ (*Hin und zurück*); JANACEK: Vixen∗ (*Cunning Little Vixen*); MASSENET: Manon∗; MOZART: Fiordiligi∗ (*Così fan tutte*), Donna Anna (*Don Giovanni*), Konstanze∗‡ (*Entführung aus dem Serail*), Susanna∗ (*Nozze di Figaro*), Pamina∗ (*Zauberflöte*); NICOLAI: Frau Fluth∗ (*Lustigen Weiber*); ORFF: Solo∗ (*Carmina burana*); PFITZNER: Ighino∗ (*Palestrina*); PUCCINI: Mimì∗ (*Bohème*), Lauretta (*Gianni Schicchi*); STRAUSS, J: Adele (*Fledermaus*); THOMAS: Ophélie∗‡ (*Hamlet*); VERDI: Odabella∗ (*Attila*), Nannetta∗‡ (*Falstaff*); Violetta∗‡ (*Traviata*). Also PAGLIASCHWILI: Daissi∗ (*Maro*); TAKTAKASCHWILI: Mindia∗ (*Msia*). Recorded for: Morgen Records. Video−NET TV: Konstanze (*Entführung*). Gives recitals. Appears with symphony orchestra. **Res:** Franz Abt Str 1, 62 Wiesbaden, FR Ger.

CORN, EDWARD. American. Special Asst to the Exec Dir, Metropolitan Opera Assn, Lincoln Center, New York, NY 10023, USA. In charge of admin matters. Born 20 Oct 1932, St Louis, MO, USA. Single. Studied: Yale Univ, New Haven, CT, USA. Previous occupations: journalism; theatrical & concert mgmt; publ rel. Previous positions, primarily administrative: Mng, San Francisco Opera 1972-75 and Western Opera Theater, San Francisco 1970-74; Prod, Gateway Theater, St Louis 1963-66; Mng, August Opera Fest, St Louis 1960-64; Dir of Publicity, Municipal Opera, St Louis 1967; Consultant on Perf Arts, Washington Univ, St Louis 1967-68; Dir Perf Arts Office, Washington Univ, St Louis 1964-67. In present position since 1975. Initiated with Western Opera Theater: Dollar Opera season in San Francisco, street opera pfs, month-long residency throughout State of Alaska. Mem of Opera Advisory Panel, Ntl Endowment for the Arts; Commtt on Gvnmtl Relations, OPERA America. **Res:** 60 W 66 St, New York, NY 10023 USA.

CORNELL, GWYNN; née Sylvia Gwynn Moose. Mezzo-contralto. American. Resident mem: Deutsche Oper am Rhein, Düsseldorf-Duisburg. Born 23 Mar, Concord, NC. Husband Dr Frank Cornell, occupation dentist. Two children. Studied: Acad of Vocal Arts, Sidney Dietsch, Vera McIntyre, Philadelphia; Elsa Seyfert, Armen Boyajian, Risë Stevens, New York. **Debut:** Maddalena (*Rigoletto*) Baltimore Op, USA 1963. Prev occupations: fashion model. Awards: Fulbright Schlshp to Rome; American Opera Aud; First Prize, Baltimore Opera Aud.

Sang with major companies in FR GER: Berlin Deutsche Oper, Cologne, Düsseldorf-Duisburg, Hamburg, Munich Staatsoper, Stuttgart; ITA: Florence Maggio & Comunale, Genoa; POL: Warsaw; SWE: Stockholm; UK: Edinburgh Fest; USA: Baltimore, Hartford, Hawaii, Newark, Philadelphia Grand & Lyric; YUG: Zagreb. **Roles with these companies incl** BIZET: Carmen⋆; DALLAPICCOLA: Circe⋆ (*Ulisse*); DVORAK: Jezibaba⋆ (*Rusalka*); MASCAGNI: Beppe⋆ (*Amico Fritz*); MASSENET: Dulcinée⋆ (*Don Quichotte*); NICOLAI: Frau Reich⋆ (*Lustigen Weiber*); PONCHIELLI: Laura⋆ (*Gioconda*); STRAUSS, R: Klytämnestra⋆ (*Elektra*); STRAVINSKY: Baba the Turk⋆ (*Rake's Progress*); TCHAIKOVSKY: Olga⋆ (*Eugene Onegin*); VERDI: Amneris⋆ (*Aida*), Ulrica⋆ (*Ballo in maschera*), Eboli⋆ (*Don Carlo*), Dame Quickly⋆ (*Falstaff*), Preziosilla⋆ (*Forza del destino*), Azucena⋆ (*Trovatore*); WAGNER: Erda (*Rheingold⋆, Siegfried⋆*), Fricka (*Rheingold⋆, Walküre⋆*), Waltraute (*Götterdämmerung*). Also PUCCINI: Zita (*Gianni Schicchi*). Gives recitals. Appears with symphony orchestra. **Res:** Colonial Rd, Franklin Lakes, NJ, USA; and Bergerstr, Düsseldorf, FR Ger. Mgmt: DSP/USA; SLZ/FRG.

CORRADI, GIAMPAOLO. Dramatic tenor. Italian. Born 7 Nov 1930, Rivarolo Re/Cremona. Wife Eleonora Benaglia. Two children. Studied: Consv A Boito, Parma; Renato Pastorino, Milan. **Debut:** Fritz Kobus (*Amico Fritz*) Teatro Nuovo, Milan 1960. Awards: Gold Medal, Intl Compt Reggio Emilia 1958; Ntl Winner, debut perf 1960.

Sang with major companies in FRA: Orange Fest; FR GER: Hamburg; HOL: Amsterdam; ITA: Bologna, Florence Maggio & Comunale, Milan La Scala, Naples, Palermo, Rome Opera, Turin, Venice. **Roles with these companies incl** DALLAPICCOLA: Jailer/Inquisitor⋆ (*Prigioniero*), Pellerin & Radio Telegrapher (*Volo di notte*); MASCAGNI: Turiddu (*Cavalleria rusticana*); MUSSORGSKY: Vassily Golitsin⋆ (*Khovanshchina*); PETRASSI: Inventore (*Morte dell'aria*); ROSSINI: Aménophis⋆ (*Moïse*); SPONTINI: Cinna‡ (*Vestale*); STRAVINSKY: Vasili‡ (*Mavra*); VERDI: Foresto‡ (*Attila*), Don Carlo‡, Oronte‡ (*Lombardi*), Carlo (*Masnadieri*), Ismaele‡ (*Nabucco*), Duca di Mantova‡ (*Rigoletto*). Also PIZZETTI: Oreste (*Clitennestra*), Straniero; ALLEGRA: Eben (*Ritratto*); LUALDI: Arlecchino (*Furie di Arlecchino*). On records only ROSSINI: Elisero (*Moïse*); VERDI: Riccardo (*Ballo in maschera*). **World premieres:** BETTINELLI: Uomo (*Countdown*) Piccola

Scala, Milan 1969-70. **Res:** V Piero Martinetti 31, Milan, Italy; and V Bruno Visconti 11, Desenzano del Garda/Brescia, Italy.

CORRODI, ANNELIES. Scenic and costume designer for opera, theater. Is a lighting designer; also a painter & specialist in projected scenery. Swiss. Born 26 Apr 1935, Zurich. Studied: Akad der bildenden Künste, Prof Helmut Jürgens, Munich. **Operatic debut:** *Martha* Hessisches Staatstheater, Wiesbaden 1958. Theater debut: Hessisches Staatstheater, Wiesbaden 1958. Awards: Kunstpreis, Lions Club, Basel; Amicus Poloniae, *Polska* Polish magazine, Warsaw.

Designed for major companies in AUS: Graz; DEN: Copenhagen; FRA: Paris; FR GER: Dortmund, Essen, Karlsruhe, Munich Staatsoper & Gärtnerplatz, Nürnberg, Wiesbaden; ITA: Milan La Scala, Rome Caracalla; POL: Warsaw; SWI: Basel, Geneva; USA: Seattle; YUG: Zagreb. **Operas designed for these companies incl** BEETHOVEN: *Fidelio;* BERG: *Lulu, Wozzeck;* BIZET: *Carmen;* BORODIN: *Prince Igor⋆;* BRITTEN: *Albert Herring, Peter Grimes;* BUSONI: *Arlecchino;* DONIZETTI: *Lucia⋆, Lucrezia Borgia;* FLOTOW: *Martha;* GLUCK: *Orfeo ed Euridice⋆;* HENZE: *Boulevard Solitude;* HUMPERDINCK: *Hänsel und Gretel;* JANACEK: *Katya Kabanova;* LORTZING: *Wildschütz;* MOZART: *Così fan tutte, Finta giardiniera, Zauberflöte;* OFFENBACH: *Contes d'Hoffmann;* PUCCINI: *Bohème, Butterfly, Tosca;* ROSSINI: *Guillaume Tell;* STRAUSS, J: *Fledermaus;* STRAUSS, R: *Elektra;* STRAVINSKY: *Rake's Progress⋆;* TCHAIKOVSKY: *Pique Dame;* VERDI: *Aida⋆, Ballo in maschera, Forza del destino, Macbeth, Simon Boccanegra;* WAGNER: *Fliegende Holländer, Lohengrin, Parsifal⋆, Tannhäuser⋆, Tristan und Isolde;* WEBER: *Freischütz;* WOLF-FERRARI: *Quattro rusteghi.* Also HANDEL: *Belshazzar⋆;* PAISIELLO/Wimberger: *Re Teodoro in Venezia⋆.* **Operatic world premieres:** BIALAS: *Aucassin und Nicolette* Staatsoper Munich 1969. **Res:** St Albanring 218, CH-4052 Basel, Switzerland. Mgmt: TAU/SWI; SLZ/FRG.

CORSARO, FRANK ANDREW. Stages/produces opera, theater & television and is an actor & author. American. Resident Stage Dir, New York City Opera. Born 22 Dec 1924, New York. Wife Mary Cross Lueders, occupation singer. One child. Studied: Yale School of Drama, CT; Actors Studio, New York; also music, piano. **Operatic debut:** *Susannah* New York City Opera 1958. Theater debut: New York 1952.

Directed/produced opera for major companies in ITA: Spoleto Fest; USA: Cincinnati, Houston, Lake George, New York City Opera, St Paul, San Francisco Spring, Seattle, Washington DC. **Operas staged for these companies incl** BERG: *Lulu⋆;* BORODIN: *Prince Igor⋆;* CAVALLI: *Ormindo⋆;* CHERUBINI: *Medea⋆;* DEBUSSY: *Pelléas et Mélisande⋆;* DELIUS: *Koanga⋆, Village Romeo and Juliet⋆;* FLOYD: *Susannah;* GOUNOD: *Faust⋆;* HANDEL: *Rinaldo⋆;* JANACEK: *Makropoulos Affair⋆;* JOPLIN: *Treemonisha⋆;* KORNGOLD: *Tote Stadt⋆;* LEONCAVALLO: *Pagliacci⋆;* MASCAGNI: *Cavalleria rusticana⋆;* MONTEVERDI: *In-*

coronazione di Poppea✶; MOZART: *Don Giovanni*✶, *Schauspieldirektor*✶; PROKOFIEV: *Fiery Angel*; PUCCINI: *Bohème*✶, *Butterfly, Manon Lescaut*✶; SALIERI: *Prima la musica*✶; SHOSTAKOVICH: *Katerina Ismailova*; VAUGHAN WILLIAMS: *Hugh the Drover*✶; VERDI: *Rigoletto, Traviata;* WARD: *Crucible.* Also MOORE: *Carry Nation.* **Operatic world premieres:** FLOYD: *Of Mice and Men* Seattle Opera, WA 1970, *Flower and Hawk* Jacksonville Symph, FL 1972; HOIBY: *Summer and Smoke* St Paul Opera, MN 1971; PASATIERI: *Seagull* Houston Opera, TX 1974. Operatic Video—Cincinnati Consv of Music prod *Prince Igor.* Teaches. **Res:** 33 Riverside Dr, New York, USA. Mgmt: CAM/USA.

CORTEZ, VIORICA. Mezzo-soprano & contralto. French. Born 26 Dec 1935, Bucium, Romania. Husband Emmanuel Bondeville, occupation Secy for Life, Acad de Beaux Arts, Paris; composer and Hon Dir Opéra de Paris. One child. **Debut:** Dalila, Toulouse, France 1965. Awards: First Grand Prize Toulouse & Holland; Gold Medal Arena de Verona; Commendatore Ordine Santa Brigida; Municipal Medal of Honor Martina Franca; First Grand Prize with Gold Medal Georges Enesco.

Sang with major companies in AUS: Salzburg Fest, Vienna Staatsoper; BEL: Brussels, Liège; BUL: Sofia; FRA: Aix-en-Provence Fest, Bordeaux, Lyon, Marseille, Nancy, Nice, Orange Fest, Paris, Rouen, Strasbourg, Toulouse; GRE: Athens Fest; FR GER: Berlin Deutsche Oper, Düsseldorf-Duisburg; GER DR: Dresden; HOL: Amsterdam; ITA: Bologna, Milan La Scala, Naples, Rome Opera & Caracalla, Trieste, Turin, Venice, Verona Arena; MON: Monte Carlo; POR: Lisbon; ROM: Bucharest; SPA: Barcelona; UK: London Royal Opera; USA: Chicago, Dallas, Hartford, Houston, New York Met, Philadelphia Grand & Lyric, Pittsburgh, San Antonio, Seattle; YUG: Zagreb, Belgrade. **Roles with these companies incl** BARTOK: Judith (*Bluebeard's Castle*); BELLINI: Adalgisa✶ (*Norma*); BERLIOZ: Béatrice, Marguerite✶ (*Damnation de Faust*), Cassandre & Didon (*Troyens*); BIZET: Carmen✶, Djamileh; BORODIN: Kontchakovna (*Prince Igor*); BRITTEN: Lucretia (*Rape of Lucretia*); CILEA: Princesse de Bouillon (*A. Lecouvreur*); DONIZETTI: Giovanna (*Anna Bolena*), Léonore✶ (*Favorite*), Elisabetta✶ (*Maria Stuarda*), Sara (*Roberto Devereux*); DUKAS: Ariane✶ (*Ariane et Barbe Bleue*); FALLA: Abuela✶ (*Vida breve*); GLINKA: Naina & Ratmir (*Ruslan and Ludmilla*); GLUCK: Clytemnestre✶ (*Iphigénie en Aulide*), Orfeo; HONEGGER: Antigone; JANACEK: Kostelnicka (*Jenufa*); LALO: Margared (*Roi d'Ys*); MASSENET: Dulcinée✶ (*Don Quichotte*), Hérodiade✶, Charlotte✶ (*Werther*); MENOTTI: Mme Flora (*Medium*), Miss Todd (*Old Maid and the Thief*), Lucy (*Telephone*), Mother (*Amahl*); MEYERBEER: Fidès (*Prophète*); MONTEVERDI: Orfeo, Poppea (*Incoronazione di Poppea*); MOZART: Sesto (*Clemenza di Tito*), Dorabella (*Così fan tutte*); MUSSORGSKY: Marina✶ (*Boris Godunov*), Khivria (*Fair at Sorochinsk*), Marfa (*Khovanshchina*); OFFENBACH: Giulietta (*Contes d'Hoffmann*); PONCHIELLI: Laura✶ (*Gioconda*); POU-

LENC: Mère Marie & Prioresse (*Dialogues des Carmélites*); PROKOFIEV: Helene (*War and Peace*); RAVEL: Concepcion✶ (*Heure espagnole*); RIMSKY-KORSAKOV: Ljuba (*Sadko*), Lyoubacha (*Tsar's Bride*); ROSSINI: Sinaïde (*Moïse*), Arsace (*Semiramide*); ROUSSEL: Padmâvati; SAINT-SAENS: Dalila✶; SPONTINI: High Priestess (*Vestale*); STRAUSS, R: Klytämnestra (*Elektra*), Octavian (*Rosenkavalier*), Herodias (*Salome*); STRAVINSKY: Jocasta✶ (*Oedipus Rex*), Baba the Turk (*Rake's Progress*); TCHAIKOVSKY: Pauline (*Pique Dame*); THOMAS: Gertrude (*Hamlet*), Mignon; VERDI: Amneris✶ (*Aida*), Ulrica✶ (*Ballo in maschera*), Eboli✶ (*Don Carlo*), Dame Quickly (*Falstaff*), Azucena✶ (*Trovatore*); WAGNER: Ortrud (*Lohengrin*), Kundry (*Parsifal*), Fricka (*Rheingold, Walküre*), Waltraute (*Götterdämmerung*), Venus (*Tannhäuser*), Brangäne (*Tristan und Isolde*); WEBER: Fatime (*Oberon*). Also ENESCO: Giocasta (*Oedipe*); GLINKA: Vanya (*Life for the Tsar*); GLUCK: Alceste✶, Armide✶, Elena; GOUNOD: Sappho; HONEGGER: Judith; TCHAIKOVSKY: (*Mazeppa*), Iolanthe; VERDI: (*Oberto*). **World premieres:** BONDEVILLE: Cléopatre (*Antoine et Cléopatre*) Opéra Rouen, France 1974. Video/Film—Polytelfilm Hamburg: Maddalena (*Rigoletto*); Azucena (*Trovatore*); (*Cappello di paglia di Firenze*). Gives recitals. Appears with symphony orchestra. **Res:** 25, Quai de Conti, Paris, France.

COSENZA, ARTHUR. Stages/produces opera and is an administrator. American. Gen Dir & Res St Dir, New Orleans Opera Assn, LA 1970- . Born 16 Oct 1924, Philadelphia. Wife Marietta Muhs, occupation form singer. Three children. Studied: Ornstein School of Music, Philadelphia; Berkshire Music Festival, Tanglewood, MA; American Theatre Wing, New York; also music and voice. **Operatic debut:** *Andrea Chénier* New Orleans Op Assn. Previous occupation: singer; professor. Awards: Knight, Order of Star of Italian Solidarity, Italian Gvnmt 1969; Hon Lifetime Mem AGMA 1967; Cultural Awd, Greater No Italian Cultural Socy 1975.

Directed/produced opera for major companies in USA: Hartford, Houston, New Orleans, Philadelphia Lyric, Pittsburgh. **Operas staged with these companies incl** BIZET: *Carmen*✶, *Pêcheurs de perles;* DONIZETTI: *Don Pasquale*✶, *Lucia*✶; GIORDANO: *Andrea Chénier*✶; GOUNOD: *Faust*✶, *Roméo et Juliette*✶; LEONCAVALLO: *Pagliacci*✶; MASCAGNI: *Cavalleria rusticana*✶; MENOTTI: *Amahl, Medium;* PUCCINI: *Bohème*✶, *Gianni Schicchi, Butterfly*✶, *Manon Lescaut, Suor Angelica, Tabarro, Tosca*✶; ROSSINI: *Barbiere di Siviglia*✶; VERDI: *Aida*✶, *Attila*✶, *Ballo in maschera, Macbeth, Rigoletto*✶, *Traviata*✶, *Trovatore*✶; WOLF-FERRARI: *Segreto di Susanna.* Teaches at Loyola Univ of the South, New Orleans. **Res:** 1720 Soniat St, New Orleans, LA 70115, USA.

COSSA, DOMINIC. Baritone. American. Resident mem: Metropolitan Opera, New York; New York City Opera. Born 13 May 1935, Jessup, PA, USA. Wife Janet, occupation travel agent. Two children. Studied: Anthony Marlowe, Detroit, MI; Robert

Weede, Concord, CA, USA. **Debut:** Sharpless (*Madama Butterfly*) New York City Opera 1961. Previous occupations: bartender, schoolteacher, singing waiter, etc. Awards: First Prize Met Op Ntl Counc Aud; American Opera Aud; Liederkranz Awd; Artists Adv Counc Awd.

Sang with major companies in CAN: Montreal/Quebec, Vancouver; ISR: Tel Aviv; ITA: Milan, Spoleto Fest; USA: Cincinnati, Fort Worth, Houston, Kentucky, Lake George, Miami, New Orleans, New York Met & City Opera, Pittsburgh, San Antonio, San Diego, San Francisco Opera & Spring Opera, Washington DC. **Roles with these companies incl** BIZET: Escamillo★ (*Carmen*), Zurga★ (*Pêcheurs de perles*); BRITTEN: Sid (*Albert Herring*); DELIBES: Nilakantha (*Lakmé*); DONIZETTI: Dott Malatesta★ (*Don Pasquale*), Belcore‡ (*Elisir*), Enrico★ (*Lucia*); MASCAGNI: Alfio★ (*Cavalleria rusticana*); MASSENET: Albert★ (*Werther*); MENOTTI: Husband★ (*Tamu-Tamu*); MEYERBEER: Comte de Nevers‡ (*Huguenots*); MOZART: Guglielmo (*Così fan tutte*), Papageno★ (*Zauberflöte*); ORFF: Solo★ (*Carmina burana*); PUCCINI: Marcello★ (*Bohème*), Lescaut★ (*Manon Lescaut*); ROSSINI: Figaro★ (*Barbiere di Siviglia*), Pharaon★ (*Moïse*); VERDI: Rigoletto, Germont★ (*Traviata*). Also GOUNOD: Valentin★ (*Faust*), Mercutio★ (*Roméo et Juliette*); MOZART: Masetto (*Don Giovanni*); STRAUSS, R: Harlekin (*Ariadne auf Naxos*); KORNGOLD: Fritz★ (*Tote Stadt*); MONTEVERDI: Ottone★ (*Incoronazione di Poppea*); HANDEL: Achilla (*Giulio Cesare*). **World premieres:** ELLSTEIN: Isaac (*Golem*) New York City Opera 1962. Recorded for: RCA, London, Columbia. Gives recitals. Appears with symphony orchestra. Teaches voice. Coaches repertoire. **Res:** New Milford, NJ, USA. Mgmt: COL/USA; IWL/UK.

COSSOTTO, FIORENZA. Lyric & dramatic mezzo-soprano. Italian. Born 22 Apr 1935, Crescentino/Vercelli. Husband Ivo Vinco, occupation opera singer. One child. Studied: Turin Consv, Paola della Torre. **Debut:** Musicista (*Manon Lescaut*) La Scala, Milan 1958. Awards: Verdi d'oro, Busseto; Diapason d'oro, Padua; Rosa d'oro, Brescia; Scala d'oro, Milan; First Prizes Illica, Verona, Gonfalone d'oro, Viterbo; Commendatore al Merito della Rep Italiana.

Sang with major companies in ARG: Buenos Aires; AUS: Vienna Staatsoper; BEL: Brussels; CAN: Montreal/Quebec; FRA: Nice, Paris; FR GER: Berlin Deutsche Oper, Cologne, Hamburg, Munich Staatsoper, Stuttgart, Wiesbaden; GER DR: Berlin Komische Oper; ITA: Bologna, Florence Maggio & Comunale, Genoa, Milan La Scala, Naples, Palermo, Rome Opera & Caracalla, Trieste, Turin, Venice, Verona Arena; MON: Monte Carlo; POR: Lisbon; S AFR: Johannesburg; SPA: Barcelona Liceo; SWI: Zurich; UK: Edinburgh Fest, London Royal Opera; USSR: Moscow Bolshoi Theater; USA: Chicago Lyric, Dallas, Miami, New York Met, Seattle. **Roles with these companies incl** BELLINI: Romeo★ (*Capuleti ed i Montecchi*), Adalgisa★‡ (*Norma*); BERLIOZ: Marguerite (*Damnation de Faust*); BIZET: Carmen; CHERUBINI: Neris★‡ (*Medea*); CILEA: Princesse de Bouillon★ (*A. Lecouvreur*); CIMAROSA: Fidalma★ (*Matrimonio segreto*); DONI-

ZETTI: Giovanna★ (*Anna Bolena*), Léonore★‡ (*Favorite*); GLUCK: Orfeo★; GOUNOD: Siebel★ (*Faust*); HANDEL: Amastris★ (*Xerxes*); HUMPERDINCK: Hänsel★; MASCAGNI: Santuzza (*Cavalleria rusticana*); MASSENET: Charlotte★ (*Werther*); MEYERBEER: Urbain★ (*Huguenots*); MONTEVERDI: Orfeo★, Poppea★ (*Incoronazione di Poppea*); MOZART: Dorabella★ (*Così fan tutte*), Cherubino★‡ (*Nozze di Figaro*); MUSSORGSKY: Marina★ (*Boris Godunov*), Marfa★ (*Khovanshchina*); PERGOLESI: Cardella★ (*Frate 'nnamorato*); PONCHIELLI: Laura★‡ (*Gioconda*); PUCCINI: Suzuki★‡ (*Butterfly*), Badessa★ & Principessa★‡ (*Suor Angelica*); ROSSINI: Rosina★ (*Barbiere di Siviglia*), Angelina★ (*Cenerentola*), Isolier★ (*Comte Ory*), Isabella★ (*Italiana in Algeri*), Marchesina Clarice★ (*Pietra del paragone*), Zaida★ (*Turco in Italia*); SAINT-SAENS: Dalila★; SPONTINI: High Priestess★ (*Vestale*); VERDI: Amneris★‡ (*Aida*), Ulrica★‡ (*Ballo in maschera*), Eboli★‡ (*Don Carlo*), Preziosilla★ (*Forza del destino*), Marchesa★ (*Giorno di regno*), Federica★ (*Luisa Miller*), Azucena★‡ (*Trovatore*). Recorded for: RCA, Decca, EMI, Philips, DG, Ricordi, Angelicum. Video/Film: Santuzza (*Cavalleria rusticana*); Favorite; Rosina (*Barbiere*); Amneris (*Aida*); Adalgisa (*Norma*). Gives recitals. Appears with symphony orchestra. **Res:** V E Biondi 1, Milan, Italy.

COSSUTTA, CARLO. Dramatic tenor. Italian. Born 8 May 1932, Trieste, Italy. Wife Nidia. Studied: Mo Manfredo Miselli, Mo Mario Melani, Mo Arturo Wolken, Buenos Aires. **Debut:** Cassio (*Otello*) Teatro Colón, Buenos Aires 1958. Previous occupations: furniture maker. Awards: Sigilo Trecentesco di Trieste.

Sang with major companies in ARG: Buenos Aires; AUS: Vienna Staatsoper; FRA: Marseille, Paris, Rouen; FR GER: Berlin Deutsche Oper, Cologne, Hamburg, Munich Staatsoper, Stuttgart; HUN: Budapest; ITA: Milan La Scala, Spoleto Fest, Trieste, Verona Arena; MEX: Mexico City; MON: Monte Carlo; POR: Lisbon; SPA: Barcelona; UK: London Royal Opera; USSR: Moscow Bolshoi; USA: Boston, Chicago, Houston, New Orleans, New York Met, Philadelphia Lyric, Pittsburgh, San Francisco Opera; YUG: Belgrade. **Roles with these companies incl** BELLINI: Pollione★ (*Norma*); BUSONI: Calaf (*Turandot*); CHERUBINI: Giasone (*Medea*); DONIZETTI: Edgardo (*Lucia*); FALLA: Maese Pedro (*Retablo de Maese Pedro*), Paco‡ (*Vida breve*); MASCAGNI: Turiddu (*Cavalleria rusticana*); MONTEVERDI: Nero (*Incoronazione di Poppea*); PONCHIELLI: Enzo (*Gioconda*); PROKOFIEV: Prince (*Love for Three Oranges*); PUCCINI: Rodolfo (*Bohème*), Dick Johnson★ (*Fanciulla del West*), Pinkerton (*Butterfly*), Des Grieux (*Manon Lescaut*), Luigi (*Tabarro*), Cavaradossi (*Tosca*); STRAUSS, R: Ein Sänger (*Rosenkavalier*); STRAVINSKY: Oedipus Rex; VERDI: Radames★ (*Aida*), Foresto (*Attila*), Riccardo (*Ballo in maschera*), Don Carlo, Don Alvaro (*Forza del destino*), Ismaele (*Nabucco*), Otello★, Duca di Mantova (*Rigoletto*), Gabriele (*Simon Boccanegra*), Alfredo (*Traviata*), Manrico★ (*Trovatore*); WAGNER: Walther v d Vogelweide (*Tannhäuser*). Also VERDI: Macduff (*Macbeth*);

PANIZZA: Fernando (*Aurora*); MUSSORGSKY: Dimitri (*Boris Godunov*). **World premieres:** GINASTERA: Don Rodrigo, Buenos Aires 1964. Recorded for: EMI, DG. Video/Film: Alfredo (*Traviata*). Gives recitals. Appears with symphony orchestra. **Res:** Bristie 8, Santa Croce, Trieste, Italy. Mgmt: GOR/UK.

COSTA, MARY. Lyric coloratura soprano. American. Born Knoxville, TN, USA. Single. Studied: Los Angeles Consv of Music, Mario Chamlee, Ernest St John Metz, CA. **Debut:** Burgundian Lady (*Carmina burana*) San Francisco Opera 1959. Previous occupations: Chrysler TV commercials; filmed voice of Walt Disney's "Sleeping Beauty." Awards: Woman of the Year, Los Angeles 1959; Hon DM Hardin-Simmons Univ, 1973; DAR Honor Medal, 1974.

Sang with major companies in CAN: Vancouver; POR: Lisbon; SWI: Geneva; UK: Glyndebourne, London Royal; USSR: Kiev, Leningrad, Moscow Bolshoi, Tbilisi; USA: Boston, Cincinnati, Hartford, Hawaii, Newark, New York Met, Philadelphia Grand, Pittsburgh, San Antonio, San Francisco Opera, Seattle. **Roles with these companies incl** AUBER: Zerlina (*Fra Diavolo*); BARBER: Vanessa; BELLINI: Norma; BIZET: Micaëla (*Carmen*); BOITO: Margherita (*Mefistofele*); BRITTEN: Tytania (*Midsummer Night*); DONIZETTI: Adina (*Elisir*); GLUCK: Euridice; GOUNOD: Marguerite★ (*Faust*); LEONCAVALLO: Nedda (*Pagliacci*); MASSENET: Manon★; MOZART: Despina (*Così fan tutte*), Pamina (*Zauberflöte*); OFFENBACH: Périchole★; ORFF: Solo (*Carmina burana*); PERGOLESI: Serpina (*Serva padrona*); PUCCINI: Mimi & Musetta★ (*Bohème*), Magda★ (*Rondine*); RAVEL: Concepcion (*Heure espagnole*); ROSSINI: Rosina (*Barbiere di Siviglia*); SMETANA: Marie★ (*Bartered Bride*); STRAUSS, J: Rosalinde (*Fledermaus*); STRAVINSKY: Anne Trulove (*Rake's Progress*); VERDI: Alice Ford★ (*Falstaff*), Desdemona★ (*Otello*), Gilda (*Rigoletto*), Violetta★ (*Traviata*); WOLF-FERRARI: Susanna (*Segreto di Susanna*). **World premieres:** DELLO JOIO: Ninette (*Blood Moon*), San Francisco Opera 1961. Recorded for: RCA. Video – BBC TV London: (*Traviata*); (*Faust*). Appears with symphony orchestra. Affiliated: Vice-Pres, California Inst of the Arts. **Res:** 10450 Wilshire Blvd, Los Angeles, CA, USA. Mgmt: HUR/USA.

COSTA-GREENSPON, MURIEL; née Greenspon. Dramatic alto. American. Resident mem: New York City Opera. Born Detroit, MI, USA. Husband Giorgio Costa, occupation stage technician. Studied: Sam Morgenstern, New York; Univ of Michigan, Josef Blatt, Ann Arbor, USA. **Debut:** Mrs Todd (*Old Maid and the Thief*) Detroit Opera Theater 1960. Awards: three Rockefeller Fndt grants; Grinnell Fndt Awd; var schlshps at Univ of Michigan.

Sang with major companies in ITA: Spoleto Fest; USA: Baltimore, Boston, Chicago, Dallas, Hartford, Houston, New Orleans, New York City Opera, Omaha, Philadelphia Lyric, San Antonio. **Roles with these companies incl** BRITTEN: Mrs Herring★ (*Albert Herring*); CHARPENTIER: Mère (*Louise*); DEBUSSY: Geneviève★ (*Pelléas et Mélisande*); DONIZETTI: Mme Rosa (*Campanello*), Marquise de Birkenfeld★ (*Fille du régiment*); HANDEL: Cornelia★ (*Giulio Cesare*); HENZE: Baronin von Grünwiesel★ (*Junge Lord*); HUMPERDINCK: Hexe (*Hänsel und Gretel*); MENOTTI: Mme Flora★ (*Medium*), Miss Todd★ (*Old Maid and the Thief*); MOORE: Augusta Tabor★ (*Baby Doe*); PROKOFIEV: Clarissa (*Love for Three Oranges*); PUCCINI: Suzuki (*Butterfly*), Badessa★ & Principessa★ (*Suor Angelica*), Frugola★ (*Tabarro*); VERDI: Ulrica★ (*Ballo in maschera*), Dame Quickly★ (*Falstaff*), Azucena★ (*Trovatore*); WAGNER: Erda (*Rheingold*); WEILL: Leocadia Begbick★ (*Aufstieg und Fall der Stadt Mahagonny*). Also GINASTERA: Diana Orsini (*Bomarzo*); BRITTEN: Miss Baggott (*Little Sweep*); BEREZOWSKY: Old Lady (*Babar the Elephant*); PUCCINI: Zita (*Gianni Schicchi*). **World premieres:** HOIBY: Anna Semyonovna (*Natalia Petrovna*) New York City Opera 1964; SCHULLER: Ilsabill (*Fisherman and His Wife*) Boston Opera 1970. Video/Film: Marquise de Birkenfeld (*Fille du régiment*); Ilsabill (*Fisherman and His Wife*). Gives recitals. Appears with symphony orchestra. Mgmt: ACA/USA.

COTRUBAS, ILEANA. Lyric soprano. Rumanian. Resident mem: Royal Opera House, London; Vienna Staatsoper. Born Rumania. Husband Manfred Ramin. Studied: Consv Ciprian Porumbescu, Bucharest; Prof Constantin Stroescu. **Debut:** Yniold (*Pelléas et Mélisande*) Bucharest Opera 1964.

Sang with major companies in AUS: Salzburg Fest, Vienna Staatsoper; BEL: Brussels; FRA: Paris; FR GER: Berlin Deutsche Oper, Frankfurt, Hamburg, Mannheim, Munich Staatsoper; HOL: Amsterdam; ITA: Florence Maggio, Milan La Scala; POR: Lisbon; ROM: Bucharest; UK: Edinburgh Fest, Glyndebourne Fest, London Royal Opera; USA: Chicago; YUG: Zagreb. **Roles with these companies incl** BIZET: Léila (*Pêcheurs de perles*); CAVALLI: Calisto★‡; DEBUSSY: Mélisande★; DONIZETTI: Norina★ (*Don Pasquale*); GLUCK: Euridice★; HUMPERDINCK: Gretel★; MASSENET: Manon★; MOZART: Despina‡ (*Così fan tutte*), Zerlina★ (*Don Giovanni*), Konstanze★ (*Entführung aus dem Serail*), Serpetta‡ (*Finta giardiniera*), Mlle Silberklang★ (*Schauspieldirektor*), Ismene (*Mitridate, re di Ponto*), Susanna★ & Cherubino (*Nozze di Figaro*), Pamina★ (*Zauberflöte*); OFFENBACH: Antonia★ (*Contes d'Hoffmann*); PUCCINI: Mimi★ (*Bohème*), Liù★ (*Turandot*); STRAUSS, R: Sophie★ (*Rosenkavalier*); TCHAIKOVSKY: Tatiana★ (*Eugene Onegin*); VERDI: Oscar (*Ballo in maschera*), Gilda★ (*Rigoletto*), Violetta★ (*Traviata*). Recorded for: Philips, Decca. Gives recitals. Appears with symphony orchestra. **Res:** London, UK.

COURET, GABRIEL. Stages/produces opera & theater. Also designs sets and is a singer & opera translator. French. Adm Dir & Resident Stage Dir, Grand Théâtre, Limoges/Haute-Vienne. Born 12 Apr 1917. Wife Germaine Duminy, occupation architect. Studied: music, piano & voice. Operatic training as asst stage dir at Opéra Comique, Paris. Previous occupation: soloist at Opéra/Opéra Comique. Awards: Chevalier de la Légion d'Honneur; French Mérite sportif. Previous adm positions in opera: Régisseur Général-Dir de la scène, Opéra Comique, Paris 1957-67; Dir de la scène, Théâtre de Monte Carlo 1951-54; Grand Théâtre, Bordeaux 1954-57; Dir Gen, Théâtre de Toulouse 1967-74.

Staged for major companies in BUL: Sofia; FRA: Bordeaux, Marseille, Nice, Orange Fest, Paris, Rouen, Toulouse; SPA: Barcelona; USA: Philadelphia Lyric. **Operas staged with these companies incl** ADAM: *Si j'étais roi;* BECAUD: *Opéra d'Aran;* BERLIOZ: *Benvenuto Cellini, Damnation de Faust, Troyens;* BIZET: *Carmen, Pêcheurs de perles;* CHABRIER: *Roi malgré lui;* CHARPENTIER: *Louise;* DALLAPICCOLA: *Volo di notte;* DEBUSSY: *Pelléas et Mélisande;* DELIBES: *Lakmé;* DONIZETTI: *Elisir, Fille du régiment, Lucia;* FALLA: *Vida breve;* GERSHWIN: *Porgy and Bess;* GLUCK: *Iphigénie en Tauride;* GOUNOD: *Faust, Mireille, Roméo;* IBERT: *Angélique;* LALO: *Roi d'Ys;* LECOCQ: *Fille de Madame Angot;* LEONCAVALLO: *Pagliacci;* MASCAGNI: *Cavalleria rusticana;* MASSENET: *Hérodiade, Jongleur de Notre Dame, Manon, Thaïs, Werther;* MENOTTI: *Dernier sauvage;* MEYERBEER: *Africaine;* MILHAUD: *Médée, Pauvre matelot;* MOZART: *Così fan tutte, Don Giovanni, Entführung aus dem Serail, Nozze di Figaro, Schauspieldirektor, Zauberflöte;* MUSSORGSKY: *Boris Godunov;* OFFENBACH: *Contes d'Hoffmann, Mariage aux lanternes;* PROKOFIEV: *Love for Three Oranges;* PUCCINI: *Bohème, Gianni Schicchi, Butterfly, Suor Angelica, Tabarro, Tosca;* RABAUD: *Mârouf;* RAVEL: *Enfant et les sortilèges, Heure espagnole;* ROSSINI: *Barbiere di Siviglia, Guillaume Tell, Pietra del paragone;* ROUSSEL: *Testament de la Tante Caroline;* SAINT-SAENS: *Samson et Dalila;* STRAUSS, R: *Ariadne auf Naxos, Rosenkavalier, Salome;* VERDI: *Aida, Ballo in maschera, Don Carlo, Forza del destino, Otello, Rigoletto, Traviata, Trovatore;* WAGNER: *Fliegende Holländer, Lohengrin, Parsifal, Tannhäuser, Tristan und Isolde;* WEBER: *Freischütz.* **Operatic world premieres:** BERTHOMIEU: *Königsmark* 1967; DURAND: *Castiglione* 1968; both at Théâtre du Capitole, Toulouse. Teaches. **Res:** Limoges, France.

COUSINS, MICHAEL GENE. Lyric tenor. American. Resident mem: Deutsche Oper am Rhein, Düsseldorf. Born 15 Nov 1940, Evanston, IL. Wife Diane. Two children. Studied: Illinois Wesleyan Univ; Gibner King, Carolina Segrera Holden, New York; Bruno Carmassi, Milan. **Debut:** Fritz (*Amico Fritz*) Mantua, Italy 1969. Awards: Amer Op Aud, Cincinnati; Baltimore Op Aud; Artists Advisory Counc Aud, Chicago; Chicago Musicland Fest; Intl Festival, Vercelli.

Sang with major companies in BEL: Brussels; FRA: Lyon, Paris; FR GER: Cologne, Düsseldorf-Duisburg, Karlsruhe, Munich Staatsoper & Gärtnerplatz. **Roles with these companies incl** BERG: Maler (*Lulu*); DONIZETTI: Ernesto (*Don Pasquale*), Nemorino★ (*Elisir*); MASCAGNI: Fritz (*Amico Fritz*); MASSENET: Des Grieux (*Manon*); MOZART: Ferrando★ (*Così fan tutte*), Don Ottavio★ (*Don Giovanni*), Belmonte★ (*Entführung aus dem Serail*), Tamino★ (*Zauberflöte*); ORFF: Solo★‡ (*Carmina burana*); ROSSINI: Almaviva (*Barbiere di Siviglia*), Don

Ramiro★ (*Cenerentola*), Comte Ory★; STRAUSS, R: Ein Sänger (*Rosenkavalier*); VERDI: Fenton★ (*Falstaff*), Alfredo★ (*Traviata*); WOLF-FERRARI: Florindo (*Donne curiose*). Also SHOSTAKOVICH: Nose. Recorded for: Harmonia Mundi, Cologne Radio. Gives recitals. Appears with symphony orchestra. **Res:** Ambrosiusring 45, 403 Ratingen, FR Ger. Mgmt: IMR/FRA.

COX, JEAN. Heldentenor. American. Resident mem: Nationaltheater Mannheim. Born 16 Jan 1932, Gadsden, AL, USA. Wife Mary Presley. Three children. Studied: Univ of Alabama, William Steven, University, AL, USA; New England Consv of Music, Maria Sundelius, Boston; Wally Kirsamer, Frankfurt; Max Lorenz, Munich. **Debut:** Xerxes, Opernhaus Kiel 1954.

Sang with major companies in AUS: Bregenz, Graz, Vienna Staatsoper & Volksoper; BEL: Brussels; CAN: Ottawa, Toronto; FRA: Aix-en-Provence, Bordeaux, Lyon, Marseille, Nancy, Nice, Paris, Rouen, Strasbourg, Toulouse; FR GER: Bayreuth Fest, Berlin Deutsche Oper, Bielefeld, Bonn, Cologne, Düsseldorf-Duisburg, Essen, Frankfurt, Hamburg, Kassel, Kiel, Mannheim, Munich Staatsoper, Nürnberg, Saarbrücken, Stuttgart, Wiesbaden; GER DR: Berlin Staatsoper; HOL: Amsterdam; ITA: Genoa, Milan La Scala, Naples, Palermo, Trieste; MEX: Mexico City; POR: Lisbon; SPA: Barcelona; SWE: Stockholm; SWI: Geneva, Zurich; USA: Chicago, Hartford, Houston, New Orleans, Pittsburgh, San Antonio, San Diego, Seattle. **Roles with these companies incl** d'ALBERT: Pedro★ (*Tiefland*); AUBER: Fra Diavolo; BEETHOVEN: Florestan★ (*Fidelio*); BERG: Tambourmajor (*Wozzeck*); BIZET: Don José★ (*Carmen*); DONIZETTI: Edgardo (*Lucia*); DVORAK: Prince★ (*Rusalka*); EGK: Christoph (*Verlobung in San Domingo*), Kaspar (*Zaubergeige*); FLOTOW: Lionel (*Martha*); FOSS: Smiley (*Jumping Frog*); GLUCK: Pylade★ (*Iphigénie en Tauride*); HANDEL: Grimwald (*Rodelinda*), Xerxes; HINDEMITH: Charles (*Long Christmas Dinner*), Albrecht v Brandenberg (*Mathis der Maler*); JANACEK: Steva★ (*Jenufa*), Boris (*Katya Kabanova*); LEONCAVALLO: Canio (*Pagliacci*); MOZART: Don Ottavio (*Don Giovanni*); OFFENBACH: Hoffmann★; ORFF: Haemon (*Antigonae*); PUCCINI: Rodolfo (*Bohème*), Dick Johnson (*Fanciulla del West*), Pinkerton★ (*Butterfly*), Des Grieux (*Manon Lescaut*), Cavaradossi★ (*Tosca*), Calaf★ (*Turandot*); ROSSINI: Almaviva (*Barbiere di Siviglia*); SAINT-SAENS: Samson★; SHOSTAKOVICH: Sergei (*Katerina Ismailova*); SMETANA: Hans (*Bartered Bride*); STRAUSS, J: Alfred (*Fledermaus*); STRAUSS, R: Matteo (*Arabella*), Bacchus★ (*Ariadne auf Naxos*), Apollo★ (*Daphne*), Kaiser★ (*Frau ohne Schatten*), Ein Sänger★ (*Rosenkavalier*); STRAVINSKY: Tom Rakewell (*Rake's Progress*); TCHAIKOVSKY: Gherman (*Pique Dame*); VERDI: Radames★ (*Aida*), Riccardo (*Ballo in maschera*), Don Carlo, Don Alvaro★ (*Forza del destino*), Carlo★ (*Masnadieri*), Otello★, Duca di Mantova (*Rigoletto*), Alfredo (*Traviata*), Manrico (*Trovatore*); WAGNER: Erik★ (*Fliegende Holländer*), Lohengrin★, Walther★‡ (*Meistersinger*), Parsifal★, Rienzi, Loge★ (*Rheingold*), Siegmund★ (*Walküre*), Siegfried (*Siegfried★, Götterdämme-*

CRAIG

rung⋆), Tannhäuser⋆, Tristan⋆; WEBER: Max⋆ (*Freischütz*), Hüon (*Oberon*); WEINBERGER: Babinsky (*Schwanda*). Recorded for: Philips. Video/Film: Max (*Freischütz*); Christoph (*Verlobung in San Domingo*). Appears with symphony orchestra. **Res**: Lessingstr 41, 6831 Plankstadt, FR GER. Mgmt: CAM/USA; SLZ/FRG.

COX, JOHN. Stages/produces opera, theater & television. British. Dir of Prod & Resident Stage Dir, Glyndebourne Fest & Glyndebourne Touring Co. Born 12 Mar 1935, Bristol. Single. Studied: Oxford Univ, Nevill Coghill, J Westrup; Glyndebourne, Carl Ebert, Günther Rennert; W Felsenstein, Germany. Operatic training as asst stage dir at Glyndebourne Fest 1959-63. **Operatic debut**: *Ernani* Oxford Univ Opera Club 1957. Theater debut: Oxford Univ 1956. Previous occupation: teacher. Awards: London *Evening Standard* Awd, best opera 1974-75; Fllshp Royal Socy of Arts, London.

Directed/produced opera for major companies in AUSTRL: Sydney; AUS: Vienna Volksoper; FR GER: Frankfurt; UK: Edinburgh Fest, Glyndebourne Fest, London English Ntl; USA: Houston, N Y City Opera, Santa Fe, Washington DC. **Operas staged with these companies incl** CAVALLI: *Egisto⋆;* CHERUBINI: *Medea⋆;* EINEM: *Besuch der alten Dame;* MASSENET: *Werther;* MOZART: *Entführung aus dem Serail⋆, Idomeneo⋆, Zauberflöte;* PUCCINI: *Bohème⋆;* RAVEL: *Enfant et les sortilèges;* ROSSINI: *Barbiere di Siviglia⋆, Turco in Italia;* STRAUSS, R: *Ariadne auf Naxos⋆, Capriccio⋆, Intermezzo⋆, Rosenkavalier⋆;* STRAVINSKY: *Rake's Progress⋆;* WAGNER: *Meistersinger v Nürnberg⋆;* WEBER: *Freischütz*. **Operatic world premieres:** WILLIAMSON: *Lucky Peter's Journey* Engl Ntl Op, London 1969; JONES: *Knife* New Op, Sadler's Wells 1964; TATE: *What D'Ye Call It* New Op, Cheltenham Fest 1966; GOEHR: *Triptych* Music Theatre Ens, London 1967; BIRTWISTLE: *Down by the Greenwood Side* Brighton, UK 1969. **Res**: 7 W Grove, Greenwich/London, UK. Mgmt: AIM/UK.

CRADER, JEANNINE. Dramatic soprano. American. Born 9 May 1934, Jackson, MO, USA. Single. Studied: St Louis Inst of Music, Wm Heyne, MO; San Francisco Opera/Merola Training Prgr, Hans Frohlich, San Francisco; Elda Ercole, New York. **Debut**: First Orphan (*Rosenkavalier*) San Francisco Opera 1955. Previous occupations: stenographer/secy, salesgirl. Awards: Three M B Rockefeller Grants; Winner Merola Debut Aud, San Francisco Opera 1955; American Opera Debut Aud, Cincinnati 1964.

Sang with major companies in CAN: Toronto; ITA: Florence Maggio Musicale, Milan; POR: Lisbon; UK: Cardiff Welsh; USA: Baltimore, Boston, Cincinnati, Fort Worth, Hawaii, Memphis, New York City Opera, Portland, St Paul, San Francisco Opera & Spring Opera. **Roles with these companies incl** BEETHOVEN: Leonore (*Fidelio*); BRITTEN: Female Chorus (*Rape of Lucretia*); GINASTERA: Florinda⋆ (*Don Rodrigo*); MASCAGNI: Santuzza⋆ (*Cavalleria rusticana*); MENOTTI: Magda Sorel (*Consul*); MOZART: Fiordiligi (*Così fan tutte*), Donna Anna & Donna Elvira (*Don Giovanni*), Contessa (*Nozze di Fi-*

garo); PUCCINI: Minnie⋆ (*Fanciulla del West*), Cio-Cio-San (*Butterfly*), Manon Lescaut, Tosca⋆, Turandot⋆; STRAUSS, R: Ariadne⋆ (*Ariadne auf Naxos*), Marschallin (*Rosenkavalier*); VERDI: Desdemona (*Otello*), Violetta (*Traviata*), Leonora (*Trovatore*); WAGNER: Brünnhilde (*Walküre⋆, Siegfried⋆*). Also RAMEAU: Phèdre (*Hippolyte et Aricie*). Gives recitals. Appears with symphony orchestra. Teaches voice. Coaches repertoire. On faculty of No Texas State Univ, Denton. **Res**: 257 W 86 St, New York, NY, USA.

CRAIG, CHARLES JAMES. Dramatic tenor. British. Born 3 Dec 1925, London. Wife Dorothy. Two children. Studied: Sir Thomas Beecham, Dino Borgioli, London. **Debut**: Pinkerton (*Butterfly*) Covent Garden Opera, London 1959.

Sang with major companies in ARG: Buenos Aires; AUS: Salzburg Fest, Vienna Staatsoper; CAN: Vancouver; FRA: Bordeaux, Marseille, Nancy, Paris; FR GER: Berlin Deutsche Oper, Düsseldorf-Duisburg, Hamburg, Munich Staatsoper, Wiesbaden; HOL: Amsterdam; HUN: Budapest; ITA: Bologna, Genoa, Milan La Scala, Naples, Palermo, Parma, Rome Caracalla, Turin, Venice Teatro la Fenice; POR: Lisbon; SPA: Barcelona Liceo; SWI: Geneva, Zurich; UK: Cardiff Welsh, Edinburgh Fest, Glasgow Scottish, London Royal Opera & English National; USA: Boston, Chicago, Houston; YUG: Zagreb. **Roles with these companies incl** BEETHOVEN: Florestan (*Fidelio*); BELLINI: Pollione (*Norma*), Lord Arthur (*Puritani*); BERLIOZ: Benvenuto Cellini, Faust (*Damnation de Faust*); BIZET: Nadir (*Pêcheurs de perles*); BUSONI: Calaf (*Turandot*); DVORAK: Prince (*Rusalka*); GIORDANO: Andrea Chénier⋆; GOUNOD: Faust; LEONCAVALLO: Canio (*Pagliacci*); MASCAGNI: Turiddu (*Cavalleria rusticana*); MOZART: Don Ottavio (*Don Giovanni*); MUSSORGSKY: Vassily Golitsin (*Khovanshchina*); PUCCINI: Rodolfo (*Bohème*), Dick Johnson (*Fanciulla del West*), Pinkerton (*Butterfly*), Des Grieux (*Manon Lescaut*), Luigi (*Tabarro*), Cavaradossi (*Tosca*), Calaf (*Turandot*); SAINT-SAENS: Samson; SHOSTAKOVICH: Sergei (*Katerina Ismailova*); STRAUSS, R: Bacchus (*Ariadne auf Naxos*), Aegisth (*Elektra*); VERDI: Radames (*Aida*), Riccardo (*Ballo in maschera*), Don Carlo, Don Alvaro (*Forza del destino*), Otello, Duca di Mantova (*Rigoletto*), Alfredo (*Traviata*), Manrico (*Trovatore*); WAGNER: Lohengrin, Siegmund (*Walküre*), Siegfried (*Götterdämmerung*); WEBER: Oberon; WEINBERGER: Babinsky (*Schwanda*). Teaches voice. **Res**: Whitfield Brackley, Northampton, UK. Mgmt: GOR/UK.

CRAIG, PATRICIA; née Duncklee. Lirico spinto. American. Resident mem: New York City Opera. Born 21 Jul 1947, New York. Husband Donald E Craig, occupation prof of music. Studied: Ithaca Coll, New York; Don Craig, Mme Marinka Gurewich, New York. **Debut**: Nedda (*Pagliacci*) Milwaukee Florentine Opera 1970. Previous occupations: teacher of classroom music. Awards: Met Ntl Counc Aud Awds.

Sang with major companies in USA: Baltimore, Cincinnati, Fort Worth, Memphis, Milwaukee Florentine, New York City Opera, Omaha, San

Antonio. **Roles with these companies incl** BIZET: Micaëla★ (*Carmen*); BOITO: Margherita (*Mefistofele*); GOUNOD: Marguerite (*Faust*); LEONCAVALLO: Nedda★ (*Pagliacci*); MASSENET: Sophie (*Werther*); MENOTTI: Annina★ (*Saint of Bleecker Street*); MOZART: Fiordiligi★ (*Così fan tutte*), Susanna (*Nozze di Figaro*), Pamina (*Zauberflöte*); OFFENBACH: Antonia (*Contes d'Hoffmann*); PUCCINI: Mimi★ (*Bohème*), Lauretta★ (*Gianni Schicchi*), Cio-Cio-San★ (*Butterfly*), Manon Lescaut★, Magda (*Rondine*), Suor Angelica★, Giorgetta★ (*Tabarro*), Liù (*Turandot*); STRAUSS, J: Rosalinde★ (*Fledermaus*); VERDI: Gilda (*Rigoletto*), Violetta★ (*Traviata*). Video – CBS TV: Gossip (*Questions of Abraham*). Gives recitals. Appears with symphony orchestra. **Res:** 121 W 72 St, New York, NY, USA. Mgmt: LLF/USA; LOM/USA.

CRASNARU, GHEORGHE EMIL. Bass. Romanian. Resident mem: Romanian Opera, Bucharest. Born 30 Aug 1941, Bucharest. Wife Irina, occupation poet. Two children. Studied: Consv, Profs Petre Stefanescu-Goanga, Aurel Alexandrescu, Bucharest. **Debut:** Osmin (*Entführung aus dem Serail*) Romanian Opera 1969. Awards: First Prize, George Enescu Cont 1970 & Montreal Canto Cont 1973; Second Prize J S Bach, Leipzig 1972 & 's Hertogenbosch 1970.
Sang with major companies in ROM: Bucharest. **Roles with these companies incl** BERLIOZ: Méphistophélès★ (*Damnation de Faust*); BORODIN: Galitzky★ (*Prince Igor*); BRITTEN: Theseus (*Midsummer Night*); DELIBES: Nilakantha★ (*Lakmé*); FALLA: Tio Sarvaor★ (*Vida breve*); GOUNOD: Méphistophélès★ (*Faust*); MOZART: Leporello★ & Don Giovanni (*Don Giovanni*), Osmin★ (*Entführung aus dem Serail*); MUSSORGSKY: Boris Godunov; NICOLAI: Falstaff (*Lustigen Weiber*); ROSSINI: Don Basilio★ (*Barbiere di Siviglia*); VERDI: Philip II★ & Grande Inquisitore★ (*Don Carlo*), Silva★ (*Ernani*), Banquo★ (*Macbeth*); WAGNER: König Heinrich★ (*Lohengrin*), Wotan (*Walküre*); WOLF-FERRARI: Lunardo (*Quattro rusteghi*). Also ORFF: Petrus★ (*Mond*); TCHAIKOVSKY: Prince Gremin★ (*Eugene Onegin*). **World premieres:** TRAILESCU: Avram Iancu (*Balcescu*) Romanian Opera 1974. Video/Film: Zamolxe. Gives recitals. Appears with symphony orchestra. **Res:** Bucharest, Romania. Mgmt: RIA/ROM.

CRASS, FRANZ. Bass-baritone. German. Resident mem: Bayerische Staatsoper, Munich; Staatsoper, Vienna. Born 9 Feb 1928, Wipperfürth/Cologne. Studied: Musikhochschule, C Glettenberg, Cologne. **Debut:** Krefeld, Germany, 1954. Previous occupations: actor and impresario of touring company. Awards: Kammersänger, Bayern.
Sang with major companies in ARG: Buenos Aires; AUS: Salzburg Fest, Vienna Staatsoper; FRA: Nancy; FR GER: Bayreuth Fest, Deutsche Oper Berlin, Cologne, Frankfurt, Düsseldorf, Hamburg, Hannover, Krefeld, Mannheim, Munich Staatsoper; ITA: Milan La Scala; SWE: Stockholm; USA: Chicago; et al. **Roles with these companies incl** BEETHOVEN: Rocco (*Fidelio*); HANDEL: Ptolemy‡ (*Giulio Cesare*); MOZART: Commendatore (*Don Giovanni*), Sarastro (*Zauberflöte*); MUSSORGSKY: Pimen (*Boris*

Godunov); NICOLAI: Falstaff‡ (*Lustigen Weiber*); STRAUSS, R: Orest (*Elektra*), Barak (*Frau ohne Schatten*); WAGNER: Holländer‡, König Heinrich (*Lohengrin*), Pogner (*Meistersinger*), Gurnemanz‡ (*Parsifal*), Fafner (*Rheingold*), Landgraf (*Tannhäuser*), König Marke (*Tristan und Isolde*); et al. Recorded for: Philips, DG, Electrola. Gives recitals. Appears with symphony orchestra. **Res:** Maria Eich Str 35, 8032 Gräfeling, FR Ger.

CREA, JOSÉ. Dramatic baritone. Argentinean. Resident mem: Teatro Colón, Buenos Aires. Born 15 Feb 1924. Wife Elena V Rocha. Two children. Studied: Consv Rossini, Pesaro. **Debut:** Amonasro (*Aida*) Teatro San Carlo, Naples.
Sang with major companies in ARG: Buenos Aires; ITA: Naples, Palermo, Rome Caracalla, Turin. **Roles with these companies incl** BARBER: Doctor (*Vanessa*); BEETHOVEN: Don Pizarro (*Fidelio*); BIZET: Escamillo (*Carmen*); FALLA: Tio Sarvaor (*Vida breve*); GIORDANO: Carlo Gérard★ (*Andrea Chénier*); MASCAGNI: Alfio★ (*Cavalleria rusticana*); PUCCINI: Marcello★ (*Bohème*), Gianni Schicchi, Sharpless★ (*Butterfly*), Michele (*Tabarro*); ROSSINI: Figaro (*Barbiere di Siviglia*); VERDI: Amonasro★ (*Aida*), Macbeth, Iago (*Otello*), Simon Boccanegra, Germont★ (*Traviata*), Conte di Luna (*Trovatore*). Also PALMA: Principe Satananda (*Nazdah*). Video/Film: Germont (*Traviata*). Gives recitals. Appears with symphony orchestra. **Res:** Calle Pringles 540, Temperley FNGR, Buenos Aires, Argentina.

CREED, KAY. Dramatic mezzo-soprano. American. Born 19 Aug 1940, Oklahoma City, OK, USA. Husband Carveth Osterhaus, occupation teacher, chmn perf arts, OK City Univ. Studied: OK City Univ, Inez Silberg & Anna Hamlin, OK 1964. **Debut:** Siebel (*Faust*) New York City Opera 1965.
Sang with major companies in SPA: Canary Isl Las Palmas Fest; USA: Cincinnati, Dallas, Fort Worth, Hartford, Hawaii, Houston, Kansas City, Memphis, Miami, New Orleans, New York City Opera, Omaha, Philadelphia Lyric, Pittsburgh, Portland, San Antonio, San Diego. **Roles with these companies incl** BORODIN: Kontchakovna (*Prince Igor*); DONIZETTI: Sara★ (*Roberto Devereux*); GINASTERA: Fortuna★ (*Don Rodrigo*); GOUNOD: Siebel★ (*Faust*); HUMPERDINCK: Hänsel★; MASSENET: Charlotte (*Werther*); MEYERBEER: Urbain (*Huguenots*); MOZART: Dorabella★ (*Così fan tutte*), Cherubino★ (*Nozze di Figaro*); MUSSORGSKY: Marina★ (*Boris Godunov*); OFFENBACH: Giulietta★ (*Contes d'Hoffmann*); PUCCINI: Suzuki★ (*Butterfly*); ROSSINI: Angelina★ (*Cenerentola*); STRAUSS, R: Clairon (*Capriccio*). Also HANDEL: Sextus★ (*Giulio Cesare*); GOUNOD: Stephano★ (*Roméo et Juliette*); BRITTEN: Nancy★ (*Albert Herring*). Gives recitals. Appears with symphony orchestra. Teaches voice. Coaches repertoire. On faculty of Oklahoma City Univ, USA. **Res:** 415 W Eubanks, Oklahoma City, OK, USA. Mgmt: LLF/USA.

CRESPIN, RÉGINE C. Dramatic soprano. French. Born 23 Feb 1927, Marseille. Husband Lou Bruder, occupation prof of German literature. Studied:

Consv National de Musique, 3 first prizes, Paris. **Debut:** Elsa (*Lohengrin*) Mulhouse Opera, France 1951. Awards: Chevalier de la Légion d'Honneur; Commandeur des Arts et Lettres; Chevalier de l'Ordre National du Mérite, French Gvnmt.

Sang with major companies in ARG: Buenos Aires; AUS: Salzburg Fest, Vienna Staatsoper; BEL: Brussels, Liège; CAN: Montreal/Quebec, Ottawa, Toronto; FRA: Aix-en-Provence Fest, Bordeaux, Lyon, Marseille, Nancy, Nice, Orange Fest, Paris, Rouen, Strasbourg, Toulouse; FR GER: Bayreuth Fest, Berlin Deutsche Oper, Cologne, Hamburg; HOL: Amsterdam; ITA: Florence Maggio, Milan La Scala, Naples, Rome Opera, Venice; MEX: Mexico City; MON: Monte Carlo; POR: Lisbon; SPA: Barcelona; SWI: Geneva, Zurich; UK: Edinburgh Fest, Glyndebourne Fest, London Royal; USA: Baltimore, Boston, Chicago, Cincinnati, Dallas, Fort Worth, Hartford, Houston, Miami, Newark, New York Met, Philadelphia Grand, Pittsburgh, Portland, San Antonio, San Francisco Opera, Seattle, Washington DC. **Roles with these companies incl** BEETHOVEN: Leonore (*Fidelio*); BERLIOZ: Béatrice & Hero (*Béatrice et Bénédict*), Marguerite (*Damnation de Faust*), Didon‡ & Cassandre‡ (*Troyens*); BIZET: Carmen‡; BOITO: Margherita (*Mefistofele*); GLUCK: Alceste, Iphigénie (*Iphigénie en Tauride*); GOUNOD: Marguerite (*Faust*); HALEVY: Rachel (*Juive*); HONEGGER: Ismene∗ (*Antigone*); LALO: Margared (*Roi d'Ys*); MASCAGNI: Santuzza (*Cavalleria rusticana*); MASSENET: Salomé (*Hérodiade*), Charlotte (*Werther*); MEYERBEER: Selika (*Africaine*), Valentine (*Huguenots*); MOZART: Fiordiligi (*Così fan tutte*), Donna Anna (*Don Giovanni*); MUSSORGSKY: Marina (*Boris Godunov*); OFFENBACH: Giulietta (*Contes d'Hoffmann*), Périchole; PONCHIELLI: Gioconda; POULENC: Mme Lidoine (*Dialogues des Carmélites*), Femme (*Voix humaine*); PUCCINI: Tosca; PURCELL: Dido; RAVEL: Concepcion (*Heure espagnole*); SPONTINI: Giulia (*Vestale*); STRAUSS, R: Ariadne, Marschallin‡ (*Rosenkavalier*); VERDI: Aida, Amelia (*Ballo in maschera*), Desdemona (*Otello*), Leonora (*Trovatore*); WAGNER: Senta (*Fliegende Holländer*), Elsa (*Lohengrin*), Sieglinde‡ & Brünnhilde‡ (*Walküre*), Gutrune (*Götterdämmerung*), Elisabeth (*Tannhäuser*); WEBER: Rezia (*Oberon*). Also FAURÉ: Pénélope; PIZZETTI: Fedra; MASSENET: Marie-Magdeleine; d'INDY: Etranger. **World premieres:** TOMASI: (*Sampierro Corso*) Bordeaux 1956. Recorded for: EMI, London, Decca, DG, Erato. Gives recitals. Appears with symphony orchestra. **Res:** 3 Ave Frochot, Paris, France. Mgmt: GLZ/FRA; HHB/USA.

CREUZ (SERGE). Scenic and costume designer for opera, theater, film, television. Is a lighting designer; also a painter & illustrator. Belgian. Born 4 May 1924, Brussels. Wife Dounia Sadow, occupation actress. One child. Studied: Brussels and Paris. Prof training: Théâtre Marigny with Jean Louis Barrault, Madeleine Renaud, Paris 1950. **Operatic debut:** Spectacles du Palais, Brussels 1946. Theater debut: St Germain des Prés, Paris 1949-50. Previous occupation: painter. Awards: Prof de Scénographie; past Prof Ecole de la Comédie de l'Est, Strasbourg, France.

Designed for major companies in BEL: Brussels, Liège; FRA: Bordeaux. **Operas designed for these companies incl** BIZET: *Carmen;* BORODIN: *Prince Igor;* DEBUSSY: *Pelléas et Mélisande;* PUCCINI: *Bohème, Butterfly, Tosca;* STRAUSS, J: *Fledermaus;* VERDI: *Ballo in maschera, Macbeth, Nabucco.* Teaches at Ecole Ntl Supér d'architecture et des arts visuels, Brussels, Prof.

CRISTOFOLI, FRANCESCO. Conductor of opera and symphony. Italian. Artistic Dir & Resident Cond, Den Jyske Opera, Aarhus, Denmark. Born 7 Mar 1932, Copenhagen, Denmark. Wife Vibeke Ellinger. Two children. Studied: Consv and Univ, Copenhagen; Accad Chigiana, S Celibidache, Siena; incl piano, cello and voice. Operatic training as repetiteur, asst cond & chorus master at Royal Opera, Copenhagen 1954-57. **Operatic debut:** *Matrimonio segreto* Royal Opera, Copenhagen 1958. Symphonic debut: Danish Radio Symph Orch, Copenhagen 1961. Awards: First Prize, 4th Intl Compt Accad S Cecilia, Rome 1965.

Conducted with major companies in DEN: Copenhagen; FR GER: Dortmund, Essen; ITA: Parma, Rome Opera & Caracalla, Trieste. **Operas conducted with these companies incl** BIBALO: *Lächeln am Fusse der Leiter∗;* BUSONI: *Brautwahl∗;* DONIZETTI: *Don Pasquale, Elisir;* JANACEK: *Cunning Little Vixen;* MASSENET: *Werther;* MONTEVERDI: *Incoronazione di Poppea‡;* MOZART: *Così fan tutte, Don Giovanni∗, Nozze di Figaro;* OFFENBACH: *Contes d'Hoffmann;* PERAGALLO: *Gita in campagna∗;* PETRASSI: *Cordovano∗;* POULENC: *Voix humaine∗;* PUCCINI: *Bohème∗, Gianni Schicchi, Tosca∗;* ROSSINI: *Barbiere di Siviglia, Cenerentola, Turco in Italia∗;* VERDI: *Aida∗, Ballo in maschera, Don Carlo, Falstaff∗, Rigoletto∗, Traviata, Trovatore;* WERLE: *Dream of Thérèse∗.* Also VLAD: *Storia di una Mamma∗;* CHAILLY: *Domanda di matrimonio;* de BANFIELD: *Alissa;* LORENTZEN: *Euridice;* NORHOLM: *Young Park∗;* BERKELEY: *Dinner Engagement.* On records only CAVALLI: *Ormindo;* FALLA: *Retablo de Maese Pedro;* HANDEL: *Giulio Cesare;* HINDEMITH: *Hin und zurück;* MASSENET: *Manon;* STRAVINSKY: *Mavra;* VERDI: *Forza del destino, Simon Boccanegra;* WOLF-FERRARI: *Quattro rusteghi.* **World premieres:** BIBALO: *Miss Julia* Jyske Opera Aarhus, Denmark 1975. Video/Film–Danish TV: *Young Park; Invitation to a Beheading; Hin und zurück; Ende einer Welt.* Conducted major orch in Europe. **Res:** V Zardini 17, 33090 Sequals/Pordenone, Italy; and Rothesgade 4, 2100 Copenhagen, Denmark.

CRIVELLI, FILIPPO. Stages/produces opera, theater, film & television. Also designs stage-lighting and is an author. Italian. Born 27 Mar 1928, Milan. Single. Studied: music, piano. Awards: Luigi Illica Awd 1971.

Directed/produced opera for major companies in ARG: Buenos Aires; AUS: Bregenz Fest; BEL: Brussels; BUL: Sofia; FR GER: Wiesbaden; HOL: Amsterdam; ISR: Tel Aviv; ITA: Bologna, Florence Maggio & Comunale, Genoa, Milan La Scala, Naples, Palermo, Parma, Rome Opera, Spoleto Fest, Trieste, Turin, Venice; MON: Monte

Carlo; SWI: Zurich; UK: Edinburgh Fest; USA: Chicago, Washington DC; YUG: Dubrovnik. **Operas staged with these companies incl** BELLINI: *Norma, Puritani, Sonnambula;* BIZET: *Pêcheurs de perles;* BOITO: *Mefistofele;* CAVALLI: *Giasone;* CIMAROSA: *Matrimonio segreto;* DONIZETTI: *Don Pasquale, Elisir, Fille du régiment★, Rita;* GALUPPI: *Filosofo di campagna;* MASCAGNI: *Cavalleria rusticana★;* MASSENET: *Werther★;* MONTEVERDI: *Combattimento di Tancredi, Favola d'Orfeo;* MOZART: *Così fan tutte★, Don Giovanni, Finta giardiniera★, Schauspieldirektor, Nozze di Figaro;* PERGOLESI: *Frate 'nnamorato, Maestro di musica;* PUCCINI: *Bohème, Gianni Schicchi★, Butterfly, Manon Lescaut, Rondine, Suor Angelica★, Tabarro★, Tosca★;* PURCELL: *Dido and Aeneas;* ROSSINI: *Barbiere di Siviglia, Cenerentola★, Italiana in Algeri★, Scala di seta, Signor Bruschino;* THOMAS: *Mignon;* VERDI: *Aroldo/Stiffelio★, Ernani, Falstaff★, Giorno di regno★, Luisa Miller, Macbeth★, Rigoletto★, Simon Boccanegra, Traviata;* WOLF-FERRARI: *Quattro rusteghi★, Segreto di Susanna.* **Operatic world premieres:** SCIARRINO: *Amore e Psiche* Piccola Scala, Milan 1973; NEGRI: *Giovanni Sebastiano* Teatro Regio, Turin 1970. Operatic Video—RAI TV: *Rita, Scala di seta.* **Res:** Luigi Vitali 2, Milan, Italy.

CROFOOT, ALAN PAUL. Heldentenor & character tenor specialist. Canadian. Resident mem: Canadian Opera Co, Toronto. Born 2 Jun 1929, East York, Ontario, Canada. Wife Dodi Protero, occupation opera singer, soprano. Studied: Univ of Michigan, Chase Baromeo, Josef Blatt, Ann Arbor; Royal Consv of Music, Ernesto Vinci, Aksel Schiotz, Herman Geiger-Torel, Toronto; Krupier Saitger, Lorenz Fehenberger, Munich. **Debut:** Spoletta (*Tosca*) Canadian Opera Co 1956. Previous occupations: psychologist; teacher at Univ of Michigan. Awards: Canada Counc SR Arts Fllshp; Schlshp Royal Consv, Toronto.

Sang with major companies in CAN: Ottawa, Toronto, Vancouver; UK: Glyndebourne Fest, London Eng Ntl; USA: Boston, Cincinnati, Memphis, Milwaukee Florentine, New Orleans, New York City Opera, Pittsburgh, Portland, San Antonio, San Francisco Opera, Washington DC. **Roles with these companies incl** BRITTEN: Nebuchadnezzar★ (*Burning Fiery Furnace*); DALLAPICCOLA: Jailer/Inquisitor (*Prigioniero*); EINEM: Bürgermeister★ (*Besuch der alten Dame*); LEONCAVALLO: Canio (*Pagliacci*); MUSSORGSKY: Shuisky★ (*Boris Godunov*); PROKOFIEV: Truffaldino (*Love for Three Oranges*); PURCELL: Aeneas (*Dido and Aeneas*); SMETANA: Wenzel (*Bartered Bride*); STRAUSS, J: Alfred★ (*Fledermaus*); STRAUSS, R: Aegisth (*Elektra*), Ein Sänger★ (*Rosenkavalier*), Herodes★ (*Salome*); STRAVINSKY: Pêcheur (*Rossignol*); WEILL: Fatty (*Aufstieg und Fall der Stadt Mahagonny*). Also SCHULLER: Angelo Pulisa (*Visitation*); WEILL: Der Geliebte von Morgen (*Royal Palace*). **World premieres:** FLOYD: Josiah Creech (*Markheim*) New Orleans Opera 1966; BEESON: Ben Alexander (*My Heart's in the Highlands*) NET TV 1970; HENZE: Senator Eduardo (*Rachel, la Cubana*) NET TV 1972; WILSON: The Minstrel (*Heloise and Abelard*) Canadian Opera 1973. Recorded for:

HMV. Video—CBC TV: Boles (*Peter Grimes*); NET TV: Ben Alexander (*My Heart's in the Highlands*); Senator Eduardo (*Rachel*); CBC TV: Nebuchadnezzar (*Burning Fiery Furnace*). Gives recitals. Appears with symphony orchestra. Teaches voice. On faculty of Banff Centre for the Arts, Alta, Canada. **Res:** Toronto, Canada. **Mgmt:** SAM/USA.

CROOK, PAUL. Lyric tenor & spinto. British. Resident mem: English National Opera, London. Born 17 Apr 1936, Blackburn, UK. Wife Lorna Haywood, occupation opera singer, soprano. Four children. Studied: Herbert Caesari, London; Herbert Graf & Lotfi Mansouri, dramatics, Intl Opera Centre, Geneva. **Debut:** Spoletta (*Tosca*) Geneva Opera 1969. Previous occupations: coal miner.

Sang with major companies in BEL: Brussels; ITA: Naples, Palermo; SWI: Geneva; UK: London Royal Opera & English National; USA: St Paul, San Diego, Seattle. **Roles with these companies incl** BRITTEN: Albert Herring; MOZART: Pedrillo★ (*Entführung aus dem Serail*); MUSSORGSKY: Shuisky (*Boris Godunov*); PENDERECKI: de Laubardemont★ (*Teufel von Loudun*); PROKOFIEV: Anatole★ (*War and Peace*); STRAUSS, J: Alfred (*Fledermaus*); WAGNER: Mime (*Rheingold★, Siegfried★*). Video/Film: Simpleton (*Boris Godunov*). Gives recitals. **Res:** 64 Tavistock Crt, Tavistock Sq, London, UK. **Mgmt:** SLA/UK; BAR/USA.

CROSBY, JOHN O. American. Founder, Gen Dir & Chief Conductor, Santa Fe Opera/Opera Assn of New Mexico, POB 2408, Santa Fe, NM 87501, 1957-. In charge of overall adm matters, art policy & finances. Conducts var perfs annually at Santa Fe; guest conds. Add adm positions: Pres OPERA America after 1/76. Born 12 July 1926, New York. Single. Studied: Yale Univ, New Haven, CT. Plays the piano. Previous occupations: accompanist. Background primarily musical. Awards: Hon DM, Cleveland Inst of Music 1974, Coll of Santa Fe 1969; Hon DL, Univ of New Mexico 1967. Mem of Bd & Trustee, Manhattan School of Music, NY. **Res:** Santa Fe, NM & New York, USA.

CROSS, RICHARD BRUCE. Bass-baritone. American. Resident mem: Städtische Bühnen, Frankfurt. Born 7 Dec 1935, Faribault, MN, USA. Wife Doris Yarick, occupation opera singer, soprano. Two children. Studied: Cornell Coll, Mt Vernon, IA, USA. **Debut:** Postman (*Scarf*) Spoleto Fest 1958. Awards: Promising Personality, *Theater World* magazine.

Sang with major companies in: CAN: Vancouver; FR GER: Berlin Deutsche Oper, Dortmund, Frankfurt, Hamburg, Stuttgart; HUN: Budapest; ITA: Spoleto Fest, Trieste; MEX: Mexico City; USA: Baltimore, Boston, Hartford, Miami, New York City Opera, Philadelphia Lyric, San Francisco Opera, Santa Fe, Seattle, Washington DC. **Roles with these companies incl** BARTOK: Bluebeard; BELLINI: Oroveso‡ (*Norma*), Sir Richard (*Puritani*), Rodolfo (*Sonnambula*); BERG: Dr Schön★ (*Lulu*); BERLIOZ: Méphistophélès (*Damnation de Faust*); BIZET: Escamillo★ (*Carmen*); BORODIN: Prince Igor; DEBUSSY: Arkel★ (*Pelléas et Mélisande*); GOUNOD: Méphistophélès★ (*Faust*); HALEVY:

Brogny★ (*Juive*); MASSENET: Don Quichotte★; MOZART: Don Giovanni★, Conte Almaviva★ & Figaro (*Nozze di Figaro*); MUSSORGSKY: Boris Godunov★ & Varlaam (*Boris Godunov*); OFFENBACH: Coppélius★ etc (*Contes d'Hoffmann*); PENDERECKI: Barré★ (*Teufel von Loudun*); PROKOFIEV: Ruprecht★ (*Fiery Angel*); PUCCINI: Colline★ (*Bohème*), Scarpia★ (*Tosca*); ROSSINI: Don Basilio★ (*Barbiere di Siviglia*), Assur (*Semiramide*); STRAUSS, R: Orest★ (*Elektra*), Barak★ (*Frau ohne Schatten*), Jochanaan (*Salome*); STRAVINSKY: Nick Shadow★ (*Rake's Progress*); TCHAIKOVSKY: Eugene Onegin; VERDI: Ramfis★ (*Aida*), Philip II★ (*Don Carlo*), Falstaff★, Padre Guardiano★ (*Forza del destino*), Banquo (*Macbeth*); WAGNER: Daland★ (*Fliegende Holländer*), König Heinrich★ (*Lohengrin*), Amfortas★ (*Parsifal*), Orsini★ (*Rienzi*), Wotan★ (*Rheingold*), Hunding (*Walküre*); WARD: John Proctor (*Crucible*). World premieres: MENOTTI: Donato (*Maria Golovin*) Brussels World's Fair 1958; HOIBY: Rakitin (*Natalia Petrovna*) New York City Opera 1964; Postman (*Scarf*) Spoleto Fest 1958. Recorded for: Decca, Westminster, RCA. Gives recitals. Appears with symphony orchestra. **Res:** Frankfurt/Main, FR Ger. Mgmt: DSP/USA; SLZ/FRG.

CRUZ-ROMO, GILDA. Spinto. Mexican. Born 12 February, Guadalajara, Mexico. Husband Robert B Romo, occupation personal mgr. Studied: Consv Nacional de Musica, Mo Angel R Esquivel, Mexico, DF. **Debut:** Ortlinde (*Walküre*) Bellas Artes Opera Intl, Mexico 1962. Awards: First Prize Met Op Ntl Counc Aud.
Sang with major companies in AUS: Vienna Staatsoper; FRA: Paris; ITA: Milan La Scala, Rome Opera, Turin, Venice, Verona Arena; MEX: Mexico City; POR: Lisbon; SPA: Barcelona; UK: London Royal Opera; USSR: Moscow Bolshoi; USA: Baltimore, Chicago, Cincinnati, Dallas, Fort Worth, Hartford, Houston, Memphis, Miami, New Orleans, New York Met & City Opera, Philadelphia Grand, Pittsburgh, San Antonio, San Diego. **Roles with these companies incl** BIZET: Micaëla (*Carmen*); BOITO: Margherita★ (*Mefistofele*); DONIZETTI: Anna Bolena★; FALLA: Salud (*Vida breve*); GIORDANO: Maddalena★ (*Andrea Chénier*); GOUNOD: Marguerite★ (*Faust*); LEONCAVALLO: Nedda★ (*Pagliacci*); OFFENBACH: Antonia★ (*Contes d'Hoffmann*); PUCCINI: Mimi★ & Musetta★ (*Bohème*), Cio-Cio-San★ (*Butterfly*), Manon Lescaut, Suor Angelica★, Giorgetta★ (*Tabarro*), Tosca★, Liù★ (*Turandot*); VERDI: Aida★, Amelia★ (*Ballo in maschera*), Donna Elvira★ (*Ernani*), Leonora★ (*Forza del destino*), Luisa Miller★, Desdemona★ (*Otello*), Violetta★ (*Traviata*), Leonora★ (*Trovatore*); WAGNER: Venus★ (*Tannhäuser*). Recorded for: RAI. Gives recitals. Appears with symphony orchestra. **Res:** 397 Warwick Ave, Teaneck, NJ, USA. Mgmt: HUR/USA; CST/UK.

CSÁNYI, JÁNOS. Heldentenor. Hungarian. Resident mem: Hungarian Opera, Budapest. Born 28 Oct 1931, Nagykörös, Hungary. Wife Irén Tajnay. One child. Studied: Music School Ferenc Erkel; Emmilia Possert, Kálmán Hetényi. **Debut:** Sergei (*Katerina Ismailova*) 1964. Awards: Prize Winner Hungarian Opera 1969, 1971, 1972.

Sang with major companies in HUN: Budapest. **Roles with these companies incl** BEETHOVEN: Florestan (*Fidelio*); ERKEL: Bánk Bán★; GERSHWIN: Sportin' Life (*Porgy and Bess*); JANACEK: Laca★ (*Jenufa*); MUSSORGSKY: Shuisky (*Boris Godunov*); PUCCINI: Pinkerton (*Butterfly*); SHOSTAKOVICH: Sergei (*Katerina Ismailova*); VERDI: Otello★; WAGNER: Siegmund (*Walküre*), Siegfried (*Siegfried★, Götterdämmerung★*); WEBER: Max (*Freischütz*). World premieres: SZOKOLAY: Jefte (*Samson*) Hungarian Opera, Budapest 1972. Video: Sergei (*Katerina Ismailova*). Gives recitals. **Res:** 13-15 Hajós st, 1065 Budapest, Hungary.

CUCCARO, COSTANZA; née Constance Jean Cucare. Lyric coloratura soprano. American. Resident mem: Deutsche Oper, Berlin. Born 16 Mar, Toledo, O, USA. Husband Edwin Penhorwood, occupation composer, accompanist. Studied: Univ of Iowa, Prof Herald Stark, Iowa City, USA; Luigi Ricci, Rome. **Debut:** Scolatella (*König Hirsch*) Zurich Opera 1969. Awards: First Place Met Op Ntl Counc Aud 1967; Fulbright Schlshp to Rome 1968.
Sang with major companies in AUS: Vienna Staatsoper; FRA: Aix-en-Provence Fest; FR GER: Berlin Deutsche Oper, Bonn, Cologne, Frankfurt, Munich Staatsoper, Stuttgart; SWI: Zurich; YUG: Belgrade; USA: New York Met. **Roles with these companies incl** HENZE: Scolatella (*König Hirsch/Re Cervo*); MOZART: Despina★ (*Così fan tutte*), Zerlina★ (*Don Giovanni*), Konstanze★ (*Entführung aus dem Serail*), Mme Herz★ (*Schauspieldirektor*), Königin der Nacht★ (*Zauberflöte*); OFFENBACH: Olympia★ (*Contes d'Hoffmann*); PERGOLESI: Serpina★ (*Serva padrona*); PUCCINI: Lauretta★ (*Gianni Schicchi*); ROSSINI: Rosina★ (*Barbiere di Siviglia*), Fiorilla★ (*Turco in Italia*); STRAUSS, R: Zerbinetta★ (*Ariadne auf Naxos*), Sophie★ (*Rosenkavalier*); VERDI: Oscar★ (*Ballo in maschera*), Gilda★ (*Rigoletto*). Also ROSSINI: Isabella★ (*Italiana in Algeri*); HANDEL: Poppea (*Agrippina*); WOLF-FERRARI: Rosaura★ (*Vedova scaltra*). Video/Film: Mme Herz (*Schauspieldirektor*); Serpina (*Serva padrona*). Gives recitals. Appears with symphony orchestra. **Res:** Berlin, FR Ger. Mgmt: COL/USA; CMW/FRA; SLZ/FRG; IWL/UK.

CUMMINGS, CLAUDIA; née Claudia Jean Colburn. Coloratura soprano. American. Born 12 Nov 1941, Santa Barbara, CA, USA. Husband Jack Aranson, occupation actor, theater mgr. Five children. Studied: San Francisco State Univ, Rue Knapp, San Francisco. **Debut:** Rosina (*Barbiere di Siviglia*) Kansas City Lyric 1971.
Sang with major companies in USA: Kansas City, Miami, San Diego, Seattle. **Roles with these companies incl** DONIZETTI: Marie★ (*Fille du régiment*), Lucia★; GIANNINI: Bianca★ (*Taming of the Shrew*); GOUNOD: Juliette★; ROSSINI: Rosina★ (*Barbiere di Siviglia*). Gives recitals. Appears with symphony orchestra. **Res:** POB 812, Mill Valley, CA 94941, USA.

CURPHEY, MARGARET. Spinto. British. Resident mem: English National Opera, London. Born 27 Feb 1938, Douglas, Isle of Man, UK. Husband

Philip Summerscales, occupation singer. One daughter. Studied: Birmingham School of Music, John Carol Case; David Galiver, Joan Cross, UK. **Debut:** Micaëla (*Carmen*) Sadler's Wells Opera 1965. Previous occupations: dressmaker. Awards: Bronze Medal & Diploma, Bulg Compt for Young Opera Singers, Sofia 1970.

Sang with major companies in BUL: Sofia; UK: Glyndebourne Fest, London English National. **Roles with these companies incl** BERLIOZ: Marguerite★ (*Damnation de Faust*); BIZET: Micaëla★ (*Carmen*); BRITTEN: Ellen Orford (*Peter Grimes*); DONIZETTI: Maria Stuarda★; GIORDANO: Maddalena (*Andrea Chénier*); MASCAGNI: Santuzza★ (*Cavalleria rusticana*); MOZART: Contessa★(*Nozze di Figaro*), Pamina★ (*Zauberflöte*); PUCCINI: Mimi★ & Musetta (*Bohème*); VERDI: Elisabetta★ (*Don Carlo*), Violetta★ (*Traviata*), Leonora★ (*Trovatore*); WAGNER: Elsa★ (*Lohengrin*), Eva★ (*Meistersinger*), Sieglinde★ (*Walküre*), Gutrune★ (*Götterdämmerung*). Gives recitals. Appears with symphony orchestra. **Res:** 9 Thames St, Walton on Thames/Surrey, UK.

CVEJIC, BISERKA. Dramatic mezzo-soprano. Yugoslavian. Resident mem: Staatsoper, Vienna. Born 5 Nov 1928, Split. Husband Dusan, occupation physician. Studied: Josip Rijavec, Zagreb/Berlin. **Debut:** Charlotte (*Werther*) Belgrade Opera 1954. Awards: First Prize, Intl Conc de Chant Verviers, Belgium 1954 and Compt of Operatic Music, Zagreb 1953.

Sang with major companies in ARG: Buenos Aires; AUS: Graz, Vienna Staatsoper; BEL: Brussels, Liège; CZE: Brno, Prague National & Smetana; FRA: Aix-en-Provence Fest, Bordeaux, Marseille, Nice, Paris; FR GER: Berlin Deutsche Oper, Munich Staatsoper, Wiesbaden; GER DR: Berlin Komische Oper & Staatsoper, Dresden; HUN: Budapest; ITA: Milan La Scala, Naples, Palermo, Turin, Verona Arena; MEX: Mexico City; MON: Monte Carlo; POL: Lodz, Warsaw; SPA: Barcelona; UK: Edinburgh Fest, London Royal; USSR: Kiev, Leningrad Kirov, Moscow Bolshoi; USA: Chicago, Dallas, New York Met, Seattle; YUG: Dubrovnik, Zagreb, Belgrade. **Roles with these companies incl** BELLINI: Adalgisa (*Norma*); BERLIOZ: Marguerite (*Damnation de Faust*); BIZET: Carmen★; BRITTEN: Hippolita (*Midsummer Night*); CILEA: Princesse de Bouillon (*A. Lecouvreur*); DONIZETTI: Giovanna (*Anna Bolena*), Léonore (*Favorite*); FALLA: Abuela (*Vida breve*); GLUCK: Clytemnestre (*Iphigénie en Aulide*), Orfeo★; GOUNOD: Siebel (*Faust*); HONEGGER: Antigone; JANACEK: Kabanikha (*Katya Kabanova*); MASSENET: Dulcinée (*Don Quichotte*), Charlotte★ (*Werther*); MONTEVERDI: Poppea (*Incoronazione di Poppea*); MOZART: Cherubino (*Nozze di Figaro*); MUSSORGSKY: Marina★ (*Boris Godunov*), Marfa (*Khovanshchina*); OFFENBACH: Giulietta (*Contes d'Hoffmann*); PONCHIELLI: Laura★ (*Gioconda*); PROKOFIEV: Smeraldina (*Love for Three Oranges*), Helene (*War and Peace*); ROSSINI: Rosina (*Barbiere di Siviglia*); SAINT-SAENS: Dalila★; STRAUSS, R: Herodias★ (*Salome*); STRAVINSKY: Jocasta★ (*Oedipus Rex*); TCHAIKOV-

SKY: Mme Larina & Olga (*Eugene Onegin*), Comtesse (*Pique Dame*); VERDI: Amneris★ (*Aida*), Ulrica★ (*Ballo in maschera*), Eboli★ (*Don Carlo*), Preziosilla★ (*Forza del destino*), Federica★ (*Luisa Miller*), Azucena★ (*Trovatore*); WAGNER: Fricka★ (*Walküre*), Brangäne★ (*Tristan und Isolde*). Recorded for: Decca, Electrola, Jugoton. Gives recitals. Appears with symphony orchestra. **Res:** Puskinova 3, Belgrade, Yugoslavia; and Dorotheerg 22, Vienna, Austria. Mgmt: YGL/YUG.

CZERWENKA, OSKAR. Bass. Austrian. Resident mem: Staatsoper, Vienna. Born 5 Jul 1924, Linz, Austria. Wife Bernadette Grabowsky. Two children. Studied: Prof Otto Iro, Wilhelm Felden. **Debut:** Eremit (*Freischütz*) Graz Oper 1947. Previous occupations: studied painting and ntl economy. Awards: Austrian Kammersänger 1962; Cross of Merit Litteris et Artibus, Pres of Austria.

Sang with major companies in AUS: Bregenz Fest, Graz, Salzburg Fest, Vienna Staatsoper & Volksoper; BEL: Brussels; CAN: Montreal/Quebec; CZE: Prague National; FR GER: Berlin Deutsche Oper, Cologne, Frankfurt, Hamburg, Munich Staatsoper & Gärtnerplatz, Stuttgart, Wiesbaden; HUN: Budapest; POR: Lisbon; SWI: Zurich; UK: Edinburgh Fest, Glyndebourne Fest; USA: New York Met. **Roles with these companies incl** BEETHOVEN: Rocco★ (*Fidelio*); CORNELIUS: Abul Hassan‡ (*Barbier von Bagdad*); DONIZETTI: Don Pasquale, Dott Dulcamara (*Elisir*), Sulpice★ (*Fille du régiment*); FLOTOW: Plunkett (*Martha*); GOTOVAC: Sima (*Ero der Schelm*); HANDEL: Ptolemy (*Giulio Cesare*); HAYDN: Buonafede (*Mondo della luna*); JANACEK: Harasta (*Cunning Little Vixen*), Dikoy★ (*Katya Kabanova*); KLEBE: Jakobowsky (*Jakobowsky und der Oberst*); LORTZING: Van Bett★ (*Zar und Zimmermann*); MOZART: Don Alfonso (*Così fan tutte*), Leporello (*Don Giovanni*), Osmin★ (*Entführung aus dem Serail*), Figaro (*Nozze di Figaro*), Sarastro★ (*Zauberflöte*); MUSSORGSKY: Varlaam (*Boris Godunov*); NICOLAI: Falstaff (*Lustigen Weiber*); ORFF: Solo (*Carmina burana*), Bauer (*Mond*); PERGOLESI: Uberto (*Serva padrona*); PUCCINI: Colline (*Bohème*); RAVEL: Ramiro (*Heure espagnole*); ROSSINI: Don Basilio★ (*Barbiere di Siviglia*), Don Magnifico (*Cenerentola*), Mustafà★ (*Italiana in Algeri*); SHOSTAKOVICH: Boris (*Katerina Ismailova*); SMETANA: Kezal★ (*Bartered Bride*), Peter (*Two Widows*); STRAUSS, R: Orest (*Elektra*), Baron Ochs★ (*Rosenkavalier*), Sir Morosus★ (*Schweigsame Frau*); STRAVINSKY: Creon (*Oedipus Rex*); VERDI: Ramfis (*Aida*), Philip II (*Don Carlo*), Fra Melitone & Padre Guardiano (*Forza del destino*), Banquo (*Macbeth*); WAGNER: Daland★ (*Fliegende Holländer*), Fasolt (*Rheingold*), Hunding (*Walküre*), Landgraf (*Tannhäuser*), König Marke (*Tristan und Isolde*). Also WEINBERGER: Teufel (*Schwanda*); SALMHOFER: Veitinger (*Werbekleid*), Pope (*Ivan Tarassenko*); STRAUSS, R: Waldner★ (*Arabella*). **World premieres:** KLEBE: Jakobowsky (*Jakobowsky und der Oberst*) Hamburg Staatsoper 1965. Recorded for: Philips, Angel, RCA. Video/Film: Uberto (*Serva padrona*); Geronimo (*Matrimonio segreto*); Ramiro (*Heure* *espagnole*); Kezal (*Bartered Bride*); Osmin (*Entführung*); Don Basilio (*Barbiere di Siviglia*); Waldner (*Arabella*); Geronio (*Turco in Italia*); Don Pasquale. Gives recitals. Appears with symphony orchestra. **Res:** Schererstr, Vöcklabruck, Austria. Mgmt: SWZ/SWI.

D

DALBERG, EVELYN; née Evelyn Brigitte Dalrymple. Dramatic mezzo-soprano. South African. Resident mem: Capab Opera, Cape Town. Born 23 May 1939, Leipzig, Germany. Divorced. Two children. Studied: Guildhall School, Parry Jones, London; Hochschule für Musik, Annelies Kupper, Munich; Frederick Dalberg, Cape Town; Mannheim Opera School. **Debut:** Venus (*Tannhäuser*) Koblenz 1964. Awards: Nederburg Prize for Opera, Cape Province.

Sang with major companies in S AFR: Johannesburg. **Roles with these companies incl** BARTOK: Judith (*Bluebeard's Castle*); FLOTOW: Nancy (*Martha*); HUMPERDINCK: Hexe★ (*Hänsel und Gretel*); OFFENBACH: Giulietta★ (*Contes d'Hoffmann*); PUCCINI: Suzuki★ (*Madama Butterfly*); STRAUSS, J: Prinz Orlovsky★ (*Fledermaus*); VERDI: Amneris★ (*Aida*), Ulrica★ (*Ballo in maschera*), Eboli★ (*Don Carlo*), Dame Quickly★ (*Falstaff*); WALTON: Mme Popova (*Bear*); WOLF-FERRARI: Beatrice (*Donne curiose*). Gives recitals. Appears with symphony orchestra. Teaches voice. On faculty of School of Music, Univ of Cape Town. **Res:** Cape Town, S Afr. Mgmt: CAP/SAF.

DALIS, IRENE; née Yvonne Patricia Dalis. Dramatic mezzo-soprano. American. Born 8 Oct 1930, San Jose, CA, USA. Husband George Loinaz, occupation magazine editor. One daughter. Studied: Edyth Walker, Paul Althouse, New York; Dr Otto Müller, Milan. **Debut:** Eboli (*Don Carlo*) Städtische Oper Berlin, FR Ger 1956. Awards: Tower Awd, San Jose State Univ, CA 1974; Distinguished Service Awd, Teachers Coll, Columbia Univ, New York 1961.

Sang with major companies in FR GER: Bayreuth Fest, Berlin Deutsche Oper, Hamburg; ITA: Naples; SPA: Barcelona; UK: London Royal; USA: Chicago, Miami, New York Met, Philadelphia Lyric, San Diego, San Francisco Opera, Seattle. **Roles with these companies incl** CHERUBINI: Neris (*Medea*); CILEA: Princesse de Bouillon (*A. Lecouvreur*); GLUCK: Clytemnestre (*Iphigénie en Aulide*); JANACEK: Kostelnicka (*Jenufa*), Kabanikha (*Katya Kabanova*); MOZART: Dorabella (*Così fan tutte*); MUSSORGSKY: Marina (*Boris Godunov*); PONCHIELLI: Laura (*Gioconda*); PUCCINI: Suzuki (*Butterfly*); SAINT-SAENS: Dalila; STRAUSS, R: Klytämnestra★ (*Elektra*), Amme

(*Frau ohne Schatten*), Herodias (*Salome*); VERDI: Amneris★ (*Aida*), Ulrica★ (*Ballo in maschera*), Eboli (*Don Carlo*), Azucena★ (*Trovatore*); WAGNER: Ortrud (*Lohengrin*), Kundry★‡ (*Parsifal*), Erda (*Rheingold, Siegfried*), Fricka (*Rheingold, Walküre*), Waltraute (*Götterdämmerung*), Venus (*Tannhäuser*), Brangäne★ (*Tristan und Isolde*). Also MASCAGNI: Santuzza★ (*Cavalleria rusticana*); VERDI: Lady Macbeth; WAGNER: Isolde; STRAUSS, R: Gaea (*Daphne*). **World premieres:** DELLO JOIO: Cleo (*Blood Moon*) San Francisco Opera 1961; HENDERSON: Medea, San Diego Opera 1972. Recorded for: Philips. Gives recitals. Appears with symphony orchestra. **Res:** Demarest, NJ, USA. Mgmt: GRA/USA.

DALLA CORTE, DARIO. Stages/produces opera. Designs sets, costumes & stage-lighting and is a painter & fashion designer. Italian. Born 30 Jan 1936, Como. Single. Studied: music & voice. **Operatic debut:** *Lucia* San Remo Fest, Italy 1962 as director/designer. Previous occupation: painter.

Directed/produced opera for major companies in DEN: Copenhagen; FRA: Paris; FR GER: Essen, Wiesbaden; ITA: Bologna, Genoa, Parma, Trieste, Turin; POR: Lisbon Teatro São Carlos; SPA: Barcelona; USA: Dallas, Houston. **Operas staged with these companies incl** BARTOK: *Bluebeard's Castle*‡; BELLINI: *Norma*★‡, *Puritani*★‡; BIZET: *Carmen*★‡; BOITO: *Mefistofele*‡; CILEA: *Adriana Lecouvreur*‡; DONIZETTI: *Don Pasquale*★‡, *Elisir*‡, *Favorite*‡, *Lucia*★‡, *Rita*‡; GIORDANO: *Andrea Chénier*★‡; GOUNOD: *Faust*‡; LEONCAVALLO: *Pagliacci*‡; MASCAGNI: *Cavalleria rusticana*‡; MASSENET: *Manon*★‡, *Werther*★‡; MENOTTI: *Old Maid and the Thief*‡; PONCHIELLI: *Gioconda*‡; PUCCINI: *Bohème*★‡, *Fanciulla del West*★‡, *Butterfly*★‡, *Tosca*★‡; VERDI: *Aida, Ballo in maschera, Due Foscari, Forza del destino, Otello, Rigoletto*★‡, *Traviata, Trovatore*‡. Also DALLAPICCOLA: *Job*★‡. **Operatic world premieres:** CORTESE: *Notti veneziane* Opera House, Genoa 1972. **Res:** V Anfossi 2, Milan, Italy.

DALLAPOZZA, ADOLF. Lyric tenor. Austrian. Resident mem: Staatsoper, Vienna; Volksoper, Vienna. Born 14 Mar 1940, Bozen, Italy. Wife Roswitha. Two children. Studied: Konsv Vienna, Prof Rosa Weissgärber, Prof Elisabeth Radò. **De-**

but: Ernesto (*Don Pasquale*) Volksoper, Vienna 1964. Previous occupations: merchant.

Sang with major companies in ARG: Buenos Aires; AUS: Bregenz Fest, Graz, Vienna Staatsoper & Volksoper; BEL: Brussels; FR GER: Cologne, Hamburg, Munich Staatsoper; ITA: Milan La Scala; MEX: Mexico City; SWI: Basel. **Roles with these companies incl** ADAM: Chapelou (*Postillon de Lonjumeau*); BELLINI: Elvino (*Sonnambula*); CIMAROSA: Paolino (*Matrimonio segreto*); CORNELIUS: Nureddin (*Barbier von Bagdad*); DONIZETTI: Ernesto★ (*Don Pasquale*), Nemorino★ (*Elisir*), Tonio (*Fille du régiment*); EGK: Kaspar (*Zaubergeige*); FLOTOW: Lionel (*Martha*); HAYDN: Nancio (*Infedeltà delusa*); MASSENET: Werther★; MONTEVERDI: Orfeo; MOZART: Ferrando★ (*Così fan tutte*), Belmonte★ (*Entführung aus dem Serail*), Idamante (*Idomeneo*), Tamino★ (*Zauberflöte*); NICOLAI: Fenton (*Lustigen Weiber*); PUCCINI: Rodolfo (*Bohème*), Rinuccio★ (*Gianni Schicchi*); ROSSINI: Almaviva★ (*Barbiere di Siviglia*), Giocondo (*Pietra del paragone*); STRAUSS, J: Alfred★ (*Fledermaus*); STRAUSS, R: Matteo★ (*Arabella*), Ein Sänger (*Rosenkavalier*); STRAVINSKY: Pêcheur (*Rossignol*); VERDI: Alfredo (*Traviata*); WOLF-FERRARI: Filipeto (*Quattro rusteghi*). Also LORTZING: Chateauneuf★ (*Zar und Zimmermann*); WOLF-FERRARI: Zorzeto (*Campiello*); STRAUSS, R: Ital Sänger (*Capriccio*); GOUNOD: Léandre (*Médecin malgré lui*). Recorded for: EMI. Video/Film: (*Turco in Italia*); (*Così fan tutte*). Appears with symphony orchestra. **Res:** Josefstädterstr 57, Vienna, Austria. Mgmt: TAS/AUS.

DALLE MOLLE, GIUSEPPINA. Lyric coloratura mezzo-soprano. Italian. Born 24 Feb 1943, Rome. Husband Tommaso Polese, occupation lawyer. Studied: Mo Cavaniglia, Rome. **Debut:** Fidalma (*Matrimonio segreto*) Teatro Sperimentale, Spoleto 1970. Awards: Winner, Compt Spoleto Fest.

Sang with major companies in ITA: Naples, Rome Opera & Caracalla. **Roles with these companies incl** BELLINI: Adalgisa (*Norma*); BIZET: Carmen; CILEA: Princesse de Bouillon (*A. Lecouvreur*); GOUNOD: Siebel (*Faust*); MOZART: Dorabella (*Così fan tutte*); PUCCINI: Suzuki (*Butterfly*), Principessa (*Suor Angelica*); ROSSINI: Rosina (*Barbiere di Siviglia*), Angelina (*Cenerentola*), Isolier (*Comte Ory*), Pippo (*Gazza ladra*); VERDI: Eboli (*Don Carlo*). **Res:** Rome, Italy.

DAMIANI, LUCIANO. Scenic and costume designer for opera & theater. Is also a painter & sculptor. Italian. Born 14 Jul 1923, Bologna. Studied: Accad di Belle Arti, Bologna.

Designed opera for major companies in ARG: Buenos Aires; AUS: Salzburg Fest, Vienna Staatsoper; FR GER: Berlin Deutsche Oper; HOL: Amsterdam; ITA: Bologna, Florence Maggio, Milan La Scala, Rome Opera, Venice, Verona Arena; USA: Chicago; et al. **Operas designed for these companies incl** BERG: *Wozzeck;* CIMAROSA: *Matrimonio segreto;* LEONCAVALLO: *Pagliacci;* MASCAGNI: *Cavalleria rusticana;* MOZART: *Don Giovanni, Entführung aus dem Serail, Zauberflöte;* PROKOFIEV: *Fiery Angel;* ROSSINI: *Barbiere di Siviglia;* VERDI: *Aida,*

Don Carlo, Luisa Miller, Macbeth, Trovatore; WEILL: *Aufstieg und Fall der Stadt Mahagonny;* et al.

D'AMICO, ACHILLES MATTHEW. American. Gen Adm, State Opera Theater of New Jersey, 141 S Harrison St, East Orange, NJ 07018, USA. In charge of overall adm matters & musical matters and is a musician. Additional adm positions: Orch Personnel Mng, Garden State Arts Center, Holmdel, NJ. Born 11 Aug 1917, Newark, NJ. Wife Antoinette, occupation form musician. Two children. Studied: State Coll, Newark, NJ; New York Univ; Seton Hall Univ, S Orange, NJ. Plays the timpani, piano, trombone. Previous occupation: Supervisor of Music, Newark School System, NJ. Form positions primarily adm & musical. Started with present company 1968 as timpanist, orch personnel mng; in present position since 1974. Initiated major policy changes including expansion of Young Artists Program for schoolchildren throughout New Jersey, presenting concerts, short operas (*La serva padrona, Let's Make an Opera*). Consultant in Musical Affairs, Seton Hall Univ.

DANCUO, MIRJANA. Dramatic soprano. Yugoslavian. Resident mem: Norwegian Opera, Oslo. Born 16 Jan 1929, Karlovac, Yugoslavia. Husband Zdenko Peharda, occupation conductor. One child. Studied: Music Acad of Zagreb, Prof Marija Frankl-Borcic, Yugoslavia. **Debut:** Giannetta (*Elisir*) Opera Zagreb 1953. Previous occupations: ballet dancer.

Sang with major companies in AUS: Vienna Volksoper; BUL: Sofia; CZE: Brno; NOR: Oslo; SPA: Barcelona; YUG: Zagreb, Belgrade. **Roles with these companies incl** BEETHOVEN: Leonore★ (*Fidelio*); BIZET: Micaëla★ (*Carmen*); BOITO: Margherita (*Mefistofele*); BORODIN: Jaroslavna (*Prince Igor*); CILEA: Adriana Lecouvreur; DVORAK: Rusalka; GIORDANO: Maddalena (*Andrea Chénier*); GLUCK: Iphigénie★ (*Iphigénie en Tauride*); GOTOVAC: Djula (*Ero der Schelm*); JANACEK: Kostelnicka★ (*Jenufa*); KODALY: Marie Louise★ (*Háry János*); LEONCAVALLO: Nedda★ (*Pagliacci*); MASCAGNI: Santuzza (*Cavalleria rusticana*); MOZART: Donna Anna★ (*Don Giovanni*), Contessa (*Nozze di Figaro*); MUSSORGSKY: Marina (*Boris Godunov*); OFFENBACH: Giulietta★ (*Contes d'Hoffmann*); PONCHIELLI: Gioconda; PUCCINI: Musetta (*Bohème*), Manon Lescaut, Giorgetta★ (*Tabarro*), Tosca★; RAVEL: Concepcion (*Heure espagnole*); SHOSTAKOVICH: Katerina Ismailova; SMETANA: Marie (*Bartered Bride*); STRAUSS, J: Rosalinde (*Fledermaus*); STRAUSS, R: Marschallin★ (*Rosenkavalier*); TCHAIKOVSKY: Tatiana (*Eugene Onegin*), Lisa★ (*Pique Dame*); VERDI: Amelia (*Ballo in maschera*), Elisabetta★ (*Don Carlo*), Leonora★ (*Trovatore*); WAGNER: Sieglinde★ (*Walküre*), Elisabeth & Venus (*Tannhäuser*); WEILL: Polly (*Dreigroschenoper*). Also VERDI: Amneris (*Aida*); TVEIT: Nille★ (*Jeppe*); MASSENET: Charlotte (*Werther*). Gives recitals. Appears with symphony orchestra. Teaches voice. **Res:** Nedre Kalbakkvei 2 D, Oslo 9, Norway. Mgmt: PGI/NOR.

DANIELI, LUCIA. Dramatic mezzo-soprano & contralto. Italian. Born 4 Feb 1929, Arzignano/Vicenza, Italy. Husband Fernando Cesarei, occupation employee of Amer Embassy. Studied: Mo Arrigo Petrollo, Centro Sperimentale/Teatro Comunale, Florence. **Debut:** Azucena (*Trovatore*) Teatro Sperimentale, Spoleto 1950.

Sang with major companies in AUS: Vienna Staatsoper; BEL: Brussels, Liège; FRA: Marseille, Nancy, Nice, Paris, Strasbourg, Toulouse; FR GER: Berlin Deutsche Oper, Dortmund, Düsseldorf-Duisburg, Hamburg, Mannheim, Munich Staatsoper & Gärtnerplatz; GER DR: Berlin Staatsoper; ITA: Bologna, Florence Maggio & Comunale, Genoa, Milan La Scala, Naples, Palermo, Parma, Rome Opera & Caracalla, Trieste, Turin, Venice, Verona Arena; MON: Monte Carlo; POR: Lisbon; SWI: Geneva, Zurich; UK: Edinburgh Fest; YUG: Dubrovnik, Belgrade. **Roles with these companies incl** BELLINI: Adalgisa (*Norma*); BIZET: Carmen; CIMAROSA: Fidalma (*Matrimonio segreto*); PONCHIELLI: Laura & La Cieca★ (*Gioconda*); PUCCINI: Suzuki (*Butterfly*), Abbadessa★ & Principessa (*Suor Angelica*), Frugola (*Tabarro*); STRAVINSKY: Mère (*Mavra*); TCHAIKOVSKY: Mme Larina (*Eugene Onegin*); VERDI: Amneris (*Aida*), Ulrica★ (*Ballo in maschera*), Dame Quickly (*Falstaff*), Preziosilla (*Forza del destino*), Federica (*Luisa Miller*), Azucena★ (*Trovatore*); WAGNER: Ortrud (*Lohengrin*), Fricka (*Walküre*); WOLF-FERRARI: Margarita★ (*Quattro rusteghi*). Recorded for; Decca, Philips, Columbia, RCA. Video/Film: Ulrica (*Ballo in maschera*); Margarita (*Quattro rusteghi*).

D'ANNA, MARIO. Dramatic baritone. Italian. Born 13 Apr 1940, Palermo, Italy. Wife Claudia Grotz. Studied: Accad Chigiana, Ettore Bastianini, Siena; Adelaide Saraceni, Milan. **Debut:** Giacomo (*Giovanna d'Arco*) As Li Co, Milan 1963. Previous occupations: studied languages.

Sang with major companies in BUL: Sofia; FRA: Nice, Toulouse; FR GER: Berlin Deutsche Oper, Cologne, Munich Staatsoper & Gärtnerplatz, Stuttgart; GER DR: Leipzig; HUN: Budapest State Opera; ITA: Bologna, Florence Maggio & Comunale, Genoa, Naples, Palermo, Trieste, Venice, Verona Arena; SPA: Barcelona, Las Palmas; USA: Cincinnati. **Roles with these companies incl** BIZET: Escamillo (*Carmen*); DONIZETTI: Belcore (*Elisir*), Alfonse★ (*Favorite*), Enrico★ (*Lucia*), Nottingham★ (*Roberto Devereux*); GIORDANO: Carlo Gérard★ (*Andrea Chénier*), De Siriex★ (*Fedora*); HANDEL: Giulio Cesare; LEONCAVALLO: Tonio★ (*Pagliacci*); LORTZING: Peter I (*Zar und Zimmermann*); MASCAGNI: Rabbi David (*Amico Fritz*), Alfio★ (*Cavalleria rusticana*); MEYERBEER: Comte de Nevers★ (*Huguenots*); PERGOLESI: Uberto★ (*Serva padrona*); PONCHIELLI: Barnaba (*Gioconda*); PROKOFIEV: Ruprecht★ (*Fiery Angel*); PUCCINI: Marcello★ (*Bohème*), Sharpless★ (*Butterfly*), Lescaut★ (*Manon Lescaut*), Scarpia★ (*Tosca*); ROSSINI: Figaro★ (*Barbiere di Siviglia*); VERDI: Amonasro★ (*Aida*), Ezio★ (*Attila*), Renato★ (*Ballo in maschera*), Rodrigo (*Don Carlo*), Don Carlo★ (*Forza del destino*), Giacomo★ (*Giovanna d'Arco*), Macbeth, Nabucco, Iago★ (*Otello*), Rigoletto★, Simon Boccanegra★, Germont★ (*Tra-*

viata), Conte di Luna★ (*Trovatore*). **Res:** V Petrarca 22, Milan, Italy.

DANNER, HARRY. Lyric tenor. American. Born Philadelphia, PA, USA. Wife Dorothy Frank, occupation actress, dancer, choreographer. One child. Studied: Beverley Johnson, Sara Lee, New York; Metropolitan Opera Studio; Uta Hagen, dramatics, New York. **Debut:** Almaviva (*Barbiere di Siviglia*) Kansas City Lyric 1967. Awards: Sullivan Fndt Awd.

Sang with major companies in USA: Dallas, Houston, Kansas City, Lake George, San Francisco Spring. **Roles with these companies incl** BERG: Maler (*Lulu*); BRITTEN: Male Chorus (*Rape of Lucretia*); DONIZETTI: Ernesto (*Don Pasquale*); FLOYD: Curley★ (*Of Mice and Men*); GOUNOD: Faust; MENOTTI: Michele★ (*Saint of Bleecker Street*); MOZART: Ferrando (*Così fan tutte*), Don Ottavio (*Don Giovanni*), Belmonte★ (*Entführung aus dem Serail*); PUCCINI: Rodolfo★ (*Bohème*), Pinkerton (*Butterfly*); ROSSINI: Almaviva (*Barbiere di Siviglia*), Lindoro★ (*Italiana in Algeri*); STRAUSS, J: Alfred★ (*Fledermaus*); VERDI: Duca di Mantova★ (*Rigoletto*), Alfredo★ (*Traviata*). **World premieres:** BERNARDO: Pepe (*La Niña*) Lake George Opera, NY 1974. Video—NET TV: Alyosha (*From the House of the Dead*). Gives recitals. Appears with symphony orchestra. **Res:** Englewood, NJ, USA. **Mgmt:** NAP/USA.

DANON, OSCAR. Conductor of opera and symphony; composer. Yugoslavian. Dir & Resident Cond, Belgrade Opera. Born 7 Nov 1913, Sarajevo. Studied: Prague Consv, Josef Suk. Operatic training as asst cond at Prague Opera 1938-41.

Conducted with major companies in AUS: Vienna Staatsoper; ITA: Florence Comunale, Spoleto Fest, Trieste; SPA: Barcelona; YUG: Dubrovnik, Zagreb, Belgrade; et al. **Operas with these companies incl** BORODIN: *Prince Igor‡;* GLINKA: *Life for the Tsar‡;* MUSSORGSKY: *Boris Godunov, Khovanshchina;* PROKOFIEV: *Love for Three Oranges;* RIMSKY-KORSAKOV: *Coq d'or, Maid of Pskov;* SMETANA: *Bartered Bride;* TCHAIKOVSKY: *Eugene Onegin‡, Pique Dame;* WAGNER: *Fliegende Holländer, Lohengrin, Parsifal, Tristan und Isolde;* et al. Recorded for Decca.

DARA, ENZO. Basso-buffo. Italian. Born 13 Oct 1938, Mantua. Wife Ivana Cavallini, occupation singer. Studied: Mo Bruno Sutti, Mantua. **Debut:** Dott Dulcamara (*Elisir*) Reggio Emilia, Italy 1966. Previous occupations: journalist.

Sang with major companies in AUS: Bregenz Fest; BEL: Brussels; CZE: Prague Smetana; FRA: Nice, Orange Fest, Toulouse; FR GER: Hannover, Wiesbaden; GER DR: Leipzig; ISR: Tel Aviv; ITA: Bologna, Genoa, Milan La Scala, Naples, Palermo, Parma, Rome Opera, Spoleto Fest, Venice; MON: Monte Carlo; SPA: Barcelona; USSR: Moscow Bolshoi; YUG: Zagreb. **Roles with these companies incl** CIMAROSA: Geronimo★ (*Matrimonio segreto*); DONIZETTI: Don Pistacchio★ (*Campanello*), Don Pasquale★, Dulcamara★ (*Elisir*), Marquis★ (*Linda di Chamounix*); MOZART: Nardo★ (*Finta giardiniera*); PAISIELLO: Bartolo★ (*Barbiere di Siviglia*);

PUCCINI: Colline (*Bohème*), Gianni Schicchi★; ROSSINI: Dott Bartolo★‡ (*Barbiere di Siviglia*), Tobias Mill★ (*Cambiale di matrimonio*), Dandini★ (*Cenerentola*), Mustafà★ (*Italiana in Algeri*), Geronio★ (*Turco in Italia*); STRAVINSKY: Creon (*Oedipus Rex*); VERDI: Fra Melitone★ (*Forza del destino*), Barone★ (*Giorno di regno*). Also CIMAROSA: Maestro★ (*Maestro di cappella*); MOZART: Colas★ (*Bastien*); ROSSINI: Taddeo★ (*Italiana in Algeri*); DONIZETTI: Sigismondo★ (*Giovedi grasso*); WAGNER: Klingsor★ (*Parsifal*); PAISIELLO: Giorgio (*Nina*). Recorded for: DG. Video/Film: Dott Bartolo (*Barbiere di Siviglia*). Gives recitals. Appears with symphony orchestra. **Res:** V Sacchi 15, Mantua, Italy.

DARLING, ROBERT. Scenic and costume designer opera, ballet & theater; specl in sets. Is lighting designer & stage director. American. Born 1 Oct 1937, Oakland, CA. Wife Ann Farris, occupation arts administrator. Studied: California State Univ, San Francisco; Yale Univ, Donald Oenslager & N Psacharopoulos, New Haven; Bayreuth Master Classes, Wieland Wagner. Also studied piano, double bass, violin, conducting and voice. Prof training: asst to W S Armstrong, Ming Cho Lee, New York 1963-66. **Operatic debut:** *Elisir* San Francisco Opera 1967; as stage dir: *Fliegende Holländer*, Kansas City Lyric, MO. Theater debut: Williamstown Theater Fest, MA 1962. Previous occupation: actor, puppeteer. Previous adm positions in opera: Art Adv, Kansas City Lyric Theater 1973; Art Coord, Spring Opera, San Francisco 1971-72.

Designed for major companies in CAN: Montreal/Quebec, Toronto, Vancouver; USA: Chicago, Hartford, Houston, Kansas City, Kentucky, Portland, San Antonio, San Diego, San Francisco Opera & Spring Opera, Santa Fe, Seattle. **Operas designed for these companies incl** AUBER: *Fra Diavolo;* BIZET: *Carmen;* BRITTEN: *Turn of the Screw★;* DONIZETTI: *Anna Bolena★, Don Pasquale★, Elisir;* EINEM: *Besuch der alten Dame★;* GOUNOD: *Faust★†;* LEONCAVALLO: *Pagliacci;* MENOTTI: *Consul★;* MOZART: *Clemenza di Tito★, Così fan tutte★†, Don Giovanni★†, Entführung aus dem Serail★, Zauberflöte;* ORFF: *Mond;* PROKOFIEV: *War and Peace★;* PUCCINI: *Bohème, Gianni Schicchi, Butterfly★, Rondine, Turandot★;* ROSSINI: *Barbiere di Siviglia;* STRAUSS, R: *Salome★†;* VERDI: *Ballo in maschera★, Don Carlo★, Rigoletto★, Traviata★;* WAGNER: *Fliegende Holländer★†, Parsifal★, Rienzi★†;* WARD: *Crucible★;* WEILL: *Aufstieg und Fall der Stadt Mahagonny★, Dreigroschenoper★.* **Operatic world premieres:** HENDERSON: *Medea* San Diego Opera, CA 1972; ARGENTO: *Col Jonathan and the Saint* Denver Opera, CO 1971. Exhibitions of stage designs ITI US Design 1970; Music Libr Lincoln Center, New York 1975; Museum of Am Crafts, New York 1964; Capricorn Gallery, New York 1968; Ntl Fine Arts Gallery, Washington DC 1975. Teaches at Hidden Valley Music Seminars, Carmel Valley, CA. **Res:** 1211 O St NW, Washington DC 20005, USA. Mgmt: CSA/USA.

DARRENKAMP, JOHN DAVID. Lyric baritone. American. Resident mem: New York City Opera. Born 9 Jul 1935, Lancaster, PA, USA. Wife Joycelyn, occupation empl Bell Telephone. Two children. Studied: Frederick Robinson, Lancaster, PA; Acad of Vocal Arts, Dorothy Di Scala, Philadelphia; Jerry Forderhase, New York. **Debut:** Zuane (*Gioconda*) Philadelphia Lyric 1966. Previous occupations: federal employee, clerk-typist.

Sang with major companies in MEX: Mexico City; SPA: Barcelona; USA: Baltimore, Boston, Cincinnati, Fort Worth, Hartford, Houston, Memphis, Miami, New Orleans, New York City Opera, Philadelphia Lyric, San Antonio, San Diego. **Roles with these companies incl** BIZET: Escamillo (*Carmen*); BORODIN: Prince Igor; DONIZETTI: Dott Malatesta (*Don Pasquale*), Belcore★ (*Elisir*), Enrico★ (*Lucia*), Talbot★ (*Maria Stuarda*); GOUNOD: Valentin (*Faust*); MASCAGNI: Alfio★ (*Cavalleria rusticana*); MASSENET: Lescaut★ (*Manon*); MENOTTI: John Sorel (*Consul*), Dr Stone★ (*Globolinks*); MOZART: Guglielmo★ (*Così fan tutte*), Conte Almaviva★ (*Nozze di Figaro*); OFFENBACH: Coppélius★ etc (*Contes d'Hoffmann*); ORFF: Solo★ (*Carmina burana*); PUCCINI: Marcello★ (*Bohème*), Sharpless★ (*Butterfly*), Lescaut★ (*Manon Lescaut*); ROSSINI: Figaro (*Barbiere di Siviglia*); SHOSTAKOVICH: Boris (*Katerina Ismailova*); STRAUSS, R: Graf (*Capriccio*); VAUGHAN WILLIAMS: John★ (*Hugh the Drover*); VERDI: Germont★ (*Traviata*); WAGNER: Wolfram★ (*Tannhäuser*); WOLF-FERRARI: Conte Gil (*Segreto di Susanna*). Gives recitals. Appears with symphony orchestra. **Res:** 214 Pearl St, Lancaster, PA, USA. Mgmt: CAM/USA.

DAU, KATHARINA. Lyric mezzo-soprano. German. Resident mem: Städtische Bühnen, Münster, FR Ger. Born 25 Jun 1950. Single. **Debut:** Inez (*Trovatore*) Staatsoper, Munich 1972.

Sang with major companies in FR GER: Essen, Munich Staatsoper & Gärtnerplatz. **Roles with these companies incl** HUMPERDINCK: Hänsel★; LORTZING: Gräfin Eberbach★ (*Wildschütz*); MENOTTI: Mrs Nolan★ (*Medium*); MOZART: Dorabella★ (*Così fan tutte*), Ramiro★ (*Finta giardiniera*), Cherubino★ (*Nozze di Figaro*); RAVEL: Concepcion★ (*Heure espagnole*); STRAUSS, R: Octavian★ (*Rosenkavalier*); STRAVINSKY: Jocasta★ (*Oedipus Rex*). Also ENGELMANN: Frau v Damm (*Fall van Damm*). Gives recitals. Appears with symphony orchestra. **Res:** Burchardstr 22, 44 Münster, FR Ger. Mgmt: SLZ/FRG.

DAVIA, FEDERICO. Bass-baritone, bass & basso-buffo. Italian. Born 7 Jul 1933, Genoa, Italy. Wife Amelia Alonge. One daughter. Studied: Piero Magenta, Tristano Illersberg, Genoa. **Debut:** Colline (*Bohème*) As Li Co, 1959. Previous occupations: painter. Awards: Prize, Compt Genoa 1975; Prize City of Busseto; Commend Alexandria Club, Mexico City, and Men of Achievement, Cambridge 1975.

Sang with major companies in BEL: Brussels; DEN: Copenhagen; FRA: Bordeaux, Rouen; FR GER: Kiel; ISR: Tel Aviv; ITA: Bologna, Florence Maggio & Comunale, Genoa, Milan La Scala, Naples, Palermo, Parma, Rome Opera, Trieste, Turin, Venice; MEX: Mexico City; NOR: Oslo; POR: Lisbon; SWE: Drottningholm Fest; UK: Glyndebourne Fest; USA: San Francisco Opera. **Roles with these companies incl** BELLINI: Rodolfo

(*Sonnambula*); BERLIOZ: Méphistophélès (*Damnation de Faust*), Narbal (*Troyens*); CIMAROSA: Count Robinson (*Matrimonio segreto*); DEBUSSY: Arkel★ (*Pelléas et Mélisande*); DONIZETTI: Don Pistacchio (*Campanello*), Don Pasquale★, Dulcamara (*Elisir*), Gasparo★‡ (*Rita*); FALLA: Don Quixote (*Retablo de Maese Pedro*); GLUCK: Cadi (*Cadi dupé*); GOUNOD: Méphistophélès (*Faust*); MOZART: Don Alfonso★ (*Così fan tutte*), Nardo (*Finta giardiniera*), Conte Almaviva (*Nozze di Figaro*); ORFF: Bauer (*Mond*); PERGOLESI: Tracolino (*Maestro di musica*), Uberto (*Serva padrona*); PUCCINI: Colline★ (*Bohème*), Gianni Schicchi★; ROSSINI: Don Basilio (*Barbiere di Siviglia*), Tobias Mill & Slook (*Cambiale di matrimonio*), Don Magnifico (*Cenerentola*), Mustafà★ (*Italiana in Algeri*), Signor Bruschino; SHOSTAKOVICH: Ivan Yakovlevich★ (*Nose*); SMETANA: Kezal★ (*Bartered Bride*); STRAVINSKY: Tiresias (*Oedipus Rex*); VERDI: Ramfis (*Aida*); WOLF-FERRARI: Lunardo (*Quattro rusteghi*). Also PUCCINI: Geronte★ (*Manon Lescaut*). **World premieres:** ROTA: Mago (*Lampada di Aladino*) S Carlo, Naples 1968; CHAILLY: Rebnicov (*Vassilieu*) Genoa 1966; TURCHI: Giudice (*Buon soldato Svajk*) La Scala, Milan 1962; NONO: Premio basso (*Al gran sole carico d'amore*) La Scala, Milan 1975. Recorded for: Arcophone, Argo, Curci, Tono AG, RCA. Video/Film: Gasparo (*Rita*), (*Speziale*); Alidoro (*Cenerentola*). Gives recitals. Appears with symphony orchestra. **Res:** V Tavazzano 16, Milan, Italy.

DAVIDSON, JOY ELAINE; née Joy Elaine Ferguson. Dramatic mezzo-soprano. American. Born 18 Aug 1940, Fort Collins, CO, USA. Husband Dr Robert S, occupation dir psychological research, Veterans Adm Hospital. Three children. Studied: Occidental Coll, Dr Howard S Swan, Los Angeles; Florida State Univ, Mme Elena Nikolaidi, Tallahassee; Mme Irma McDaniels, Dr Daniel Harris, Miami, FL. **Debut:** Angelina (*Cenerentola*) Miami Opera Co 1965. Awards: First Place Compt for Young Opera Singers, Sofia, Bulgaria 1968; Outstanding Young Women of America.
Sang with major companies in AUS: Vienna Staatsoper; BUL: Sofia; CAN: Vancouver; FRA: Lyon; FR GER: Munich Staatsoper; HOL: Amsterdam; ITA: Florence Maggio, Milan La Scala, Spoleto Fest, Turin; POR: Lisbon; SPA: Barcelona; UK: Cardiff Welsh; USA: Dallas, Fort Worth, Houston, Miami, New Orleans, New York City Opera, San Francisco Opera & Spring Opera, Santa Fe. **Roles with these companies incl** BIZET: Carmen★; BORODIN: Kontchakovna (*Prince Igor*); BRITTEN: Lucretia (*Rape of Lucretia*); DONIZETTI: Giovanna★ (*Anna Bolena*); GLUCK: Orfeo; MASSENET: Charlotte★ (*Werther*); MENOTTI: Secretary★ (*Consul*), Desideria★ (*Saint of Bleecker Street*); OFFENBACH: Giulietta★ (*Contes d'Hoffmann*); PONCHIELLI: Laura (*Gioconda*); ROSSINI: Rosina★ (*Barbiere di Siviglia*), Angelina (*Cenerentola*); SAINT-SAENS: Dalila★; STRAVINSKY: Baba the Turk★ (*Rake's Progress*); VERDI: Eboli★ (*Don Carlo*), Preziosilla★ (*Forza del destino*). Also MENOTTI: Mother (*Amahl*); PENDERECKI: Sister Jeanne (*Teufel von Loudun*); SPONTINI:

Ermengarda★ (*Agnese di Hohenstaufen*). Video/Film: Orfeo (*Orfeo ed Euridice*). Gives recitals. Appears with symphony orchestra. **Res:** 5751 SW 74 Ave, Miami, FL, USA. Mgmt: CAM/USA; AIM/UK.

DAVIDSON, MICHAEL. Dramatic baritone. American. Resident mem: Nationaltheater Mannheim. Born 2 May 1935, Long Beach, CA, USA. Wife Marianne. One child. Studied: Vladimir Dubinsky, Los Angeles; Herbert Weiskopf, Hugo Strelitzer, coaching, Los Angeles. **Debut:** Renato (*Ballo in maschera*) Stadttheater Koblenz, FR Ger 1962. Awards: First Place Calif State Music Fed Dennis Awd 1955.
Sang with major companies in AUS: Vienna Staatsoper; CAN: Vancouver; FR GER: Cologne, Dortmund, Düsseldorf-Duisburg, Essen, Frankfurt, Hamburg, Hannover, Karlsruhe, Kiel, Mannheim, Munich Staatsoper, Nürnberg, Stuttgart, Wuppertal; SPA: Barcelona; USA: Portland. **Roles with these companies incl** d'ALBERT: Sebastiano★ (*Tiefland*); BIZET: Escamillo★ (*Carmen*); DONIZETTI: Dott Malatesta (*Don Pasquale*), Belcore (*Elisir*); GIORDANO: Carlo Gérard★ (*Andrea Chénier*); LEONCAVALLO: Tonio★ (*Pagliacci*); MASCAGNI: Alfio★ (*Cavalleria rusticana*); OFFENBACH: Coppélius etc★ (*Contes d'Hoffmann*); ORFF: König★ (*Kluge*); PUCCINI: Marcello★ (*Bohème*), Sharpless★ (*Butterfly*), Lescaut (*Manon Lescaut*), Michele★ (*Tabarro*), Scarpia★ (*Tosca*); RAVEL: Ramiro (*Heure espagnole*); ROSSINI: Sultan Selim (*Turco in Italia*); STRAUSS, R: Musiklehrer★ (*Ariadne auf Naxos*), Graf★ (*Capriccio*); TCHAIKOVSKY: Eugene Onegin; VERDI: Amonasro★ (*Aida*), Renato★ (*Ballo in maschera*), Rodrigo★ (*Don Carlo*), Ford★ (*Falstaff*), Don Carlo★ (*Forza del destino*), Macbeth★, Nabucco★, Iago★ (*Otello*), Rigoletto★, Simon Boccanegra★, Germont★ (*Traviata*), Conte di Luna★ (*Trovatore*); WAGNER: Wolfram (*Tannhäuser*). Also VERDI: Francesco★ (*Masnadieri*); GOUNOD: Valentin★ (*Faust*); STRAUSS, R: Faninal★ (*Rosenkavalier*); HUMPERDINCK: Peter★ (*Hänsel und Gretel*); HANDEL: Terridate (*Radamisto*); LEONCAVALLO: Edipo (*Edipo Re*). **Res:** Am Brunnengarten 28, 68 Mannheim 1, FR Ger. Mgmt: PAS/FRG.

DAVIES, NOEL; né Noel Anthony Hicklin. Conductor of opera and symphony. British. Resident Cond, English National Opera, London. Born 1 Jan 1945, London. Single. Studied: Royal Coll of Music, Sir Adrian Boult, Richard Austin, James Lockhart, London; incl piano, organ, harpsichord, cello and voice. Plays all keyboard instruments. Operatic training as repetiteur & asst cond at English National Opera, London 1967-70. **Operatic debut:** *Zauberflöte,* English National Opera, Bradford, UK 1969. Symphonic debut: Welsh Phil, Llandeilo, UK 1972. Awards: Michael Mudie Awd for Opera, Royal Coll of Music, London.
Conducted with major companies in UK: London English National. **Operas with these companies incl** BIZET: *Carmen★;* DONIZETTI: *Maria Stuarda★;* MASCAGNI: *Cavalleria rusticana;* MENOTTI: *Amahl;* MOZART: *Così fan tutte★, Entführung aus dem Serail★, Idomeneo★, Nozze di Figaro★, Zauberflöte★;* PUCCINI: *Butterfly★;*

PURCELL: *Dido and Aeneas;* ROSSINI: *Barbiere di Siviglia*★, *Signor Bruschino;* STRAUSS, J: *Fledermaus*★; VERDI: *Traviata*★. Conducted major orch in Europe. **Res:** 20, Cricketfield Rd, London E5, UK. Mgmt: MIN/UK.

DAVIES, RYLAND. Lyric tenor. British. Born 9 Feb 1943, Cwm Ebbw Vale, Monmouthshire, Wales, UK. Wife Anne Howells, occupation opera singer, mezzo-soprano. Studied: Royal Manchester Coll of Music, Frederick Cox. **Debut:** Almaviva (*Barbiere di Siviglia*) Welsh National Opera 1964. Awards: Fellow, Royal Manchester Coll of Music; John Christie Awd, Glyndebourne Fest; Imperial League Opera Prize; Boise & Mendelssohn Fndt Schlshp; Ricordi Opera Prize. **Sang with major companies in** AUS: Salzburg Fest; FRA: Bordeaux, Paris; FR GER: Munich Staatsoper; HOL: Amsterdam; UK: Cardiff Welsh, Glasgow Scottish, Glyndebourne Fest, London Royal Opera & English National; USA: Chicago, New York Metropolitan Opera, San Francisco Opera. **Roles with these companies incl** BRITTEN: Robert Devereux (*Gloriana*), Lysander★ (*Midsummer Night*); DONIZETTI: Ernesto★ (*Don Pasquale*), Nemorino (*Elisir*); MOZART: Ferrando★ (*Così fan tutte*), Don Ottavio★ (*Don Giovanni*), Belmonte★‡ (*Entführung aus dem Serail*), Tamino★ (*Zauberflöte*); ROSSINI: Almaviva★ (*Barbiere di Siviglia*); TCHAIKOVSKY: Lenski★ (*Eugene Onegin*); VERDI: Fenton★ (*Falstaff*). Also only on records MASSENET: Armand (*Thérèse*); MOZART: Idamante (*Idomeneo*). Recorded for: Decca, Philips, RCA, EMI. Gives recitals. Appears with symphony orchestra. **Res:** Claygate, Surrey, UK. Mgmt: AIM/UK; CMW/FRA.

DAVIS, COLIN REX. Conductor of opera and symphony. British. Music Dir & Resident Cond, Royal Opera House, Covent Garden, London. Also Music Dir, London Symph Orch, BBC Symph Orch; and Principal guest conductor, Boston Symph Orch. Born 25 Sep 1927, Weybridge, Surrey, UK. Wife Ashraf. Five children. Studied: clarinet, piano, violin. Plays the clarinet. Awards: Commander of the British Empire; Chevalier, Légion d'Honneur. Previous adm positions in opera: Mus Dir, Sadler's Wells Opera, London. **Conducted with major companies in** AUS: Salzburg Fest; FRA: Aix-en-Provence Fest, Paris; GRE: Athens Fest; UK: London Royal & English National; USA: New York Met. **Operas with these companies incl** BEETHOVEN: *Fidelio*★; BENNETT: *Mines of Sulphur;* BERG: *Wozzeck;* BERLIOZ: *Benvenuto Cellini, Damnation de Faust, Troyens;* BIZET: *Carmen;* BRITTEN: *Peter Grimes;* JANACEK: *Cunning Little Vixen;* MOZART: *Clemenza di Tito, Così fan tutte*★, *Don Giovanni*★, *Entführung aus dem Serail*★, *Idomeneo, Nozze di Figaro*★, *Schauspieldirektor, Zauberflöte*★; STRAUSS, R: *Ariadne auf Naxos*★, *Elektra*★; TIPPETT: *Knot Garden*★, *Midsummer Marriage*★; VERDI: *Ballo in maschera*★, *Falstaff*★, *Nabucco*★, *Otello*★, *Traviata*★; WAGNER: *Fliegende Holländer*★, *Rheingold*★, *Walküre*★, *Siegfried*★, *Tannhäuser*★, *Tristan und Isolde*★; WEBER: *Freischütz*★; WEILL: *Aufstieg und Fall der Stadt Mahagonny.* Recorded for Phonogram. Conducted major orch in Europe, USA/Canada.

Res: 7 Highbury Terrace, London, UK. Mgmt: PPM/UK; CAM/USA.

DAVIS, J B; né James Benjamin Davis Jr. Bass. American. Born 6 Aug 1935, Louisville, KY, USA. Wife Barbara Smith-Davis, occupation singer. Two children. Studied: Columbia Univ, drama, New York; Frantz Proschowski, Ruth Pinkerton, John Harris, New York. **Debut:** Enrico (*Lucia*) Kentucky Opera 1961. Previous occupations: actor. Awards: Affiliate Artist; Rockefeller Fndt Grant.

Sang with major companies in USA: Dallas, Fort Worth, Houston, Kansas City, Kentucky, Lake George, Miami, New York City Opera, Omaha, Philadelphia Lyric, St Paul, Seattle. **Roles with these companies incl** DONIZETTI: Enrico (*Lucia*); HANDEL: Ptolemy★ (*Giulio Cesare*); MOZART: Leporello★ & Don Giovanni★ (*Don Giovanni*), Osmin (*Entführung aus dem Serail*), Figaro (*Nozze di Figaro*), Sarastro★ (*Zauberflöte*); NICOLAI: Falstaff (*Lustigen Weiber*); ROSSINI: Don Basilio★ (*Barbiere di Siviglia*); WAGNER: Daland★ (*Fliegende Holländer*); WARD: Rev Hale★ (*Crucible*); WEILL: Mr Peachum★ (*Dreigroschenoper*). Also BRITTEN: Collatinus★ (*Rape of Lucretia*); DONIZETTI: Cecil★ (*Maria Stuarda*); GOUNOD: Frère Laurent (*Roméo et Juliette*). Recorded for: CRI. Gives recitals. **Res:** RDZ Box 600 Sussex, NJ 07461. Mgmt: LLF/USA.

DAYDÉ, BERNARD HÉLIN HENRI. Scenic and costume designer for opera, theater, film, television. Is a lighting designer; also a painter, sculptor & illustrator. French. Resident designer, Théâtre National de l'Opéra, Paris. Born 3 Feb 1921, Paris. Wife Edith Ecker. One child. Studied: through work in theater and ballet. **Operatic debut:** *Orphée aux enfers* Bühnen der Stadt Köln, Cologne 1958. Theater debut: Comédie des Champs-Elysées, Paris 1945. Awards: Chevalier de la Légion d'Honneur 1975; Prix Italia, best TV ballet in Europe 1964; Prix de la Critique Paris 1957; Golden Star for best design, Intl Ballet Fest of Paris 1963 & 1967. Adm position: Dir Gen, Art & Tech Services, Opéra National Paris.

Designed for major companies in AUS: Vienna Volksoper; BEL: Brussels, Liège; CAN: Toronto; DEN: Copenhagen; FRA: Lyon, Marseille, Paris, Toulouse; FR GER: Cologne, Hamburg, Munich Staatsoper, Nürnberg; HOL: Amsterdam; ITA: Milan La Scala, Spoleto Fest, Trieste, Verona Arena; POL: Warsaw; SPA: Barcelona; SWI: Geneva, Zurich; UK: Edinburgh Fest, London English National; USA: Chicago, New York Met; YUG: Belgrade. **Operas designed for these companies incl** BERG: *Lulu;* BIBALO: *Lächeln am Fusse der Leiter;* BIZET: *Carmen;* BRITTEN: *Turn of the Screw;* DONIZETTI: *Don Pasquale;* GLUCK: *Orfeo ed Euridice;* MASSENET: *Werther;* MENOTTI: *Saint of Bleecker Street;* MOZART: *Finta giardiniera;* OHANA: *Syllabaire pour Phèdre;* PENDERECKI: *Teufel von Loudun;* PUCCINI: *Butterfly;* RAVEL: *Enfant et les sortilèges;* WAGNER: *Lohengrin;* WEILL: *Aufstieg und Fall der Stadt Mahagonny.* Also MILHAUD: *Malheurs d'Orphée.* **Operatic world premieres:** PREY: *Coeur révélateur* Théâtre du Capitole, Toulouse 1971; BECAUD: *Opéra* *d'Aran* Théâtre des Champs-Elysées, Paris 1962; SAGUER: *Mariana Pineda* Opéra de Marseille 1969-70; DE PABLO: *Protocolo* Opéra Comique, Paris 1972. Operatic Video/Film — Hamburg Film-TV: *Orphée aux enfers*. Exhibitions of stage designs, paintings, sculptures, var in Paris; designers' ntl and intl exhibitions; Ntl Museum, Lisbon 1949. **Res:** 5 Sq Capitaine Claude Barrès, 92200 Neuilly-sur-Seine, France. Mgmt: LOH/FRA.

DE ALMEIDA, ANTONIO. Conductor of opera and symphony. French. Born 20 Jan 1928, Neuilly-sur-Seine, France. Wife Lynn. Three children. Studied: Yale Univ, USA, Paul Hindemith; Tanglewood, MA, Serge Koussevitzky; Cleveland Orch, George Szell; incl clarinet, piano, cello, bassoon, horn, oboe and voice. Operatic training as asst cond at Teatro São Carlos, Lisbon 1957-59. **Operatic debut:** *Elisir* São Carlos, Lisbon 1958. Symphonic debut: National Symph, Lisbon 1954. Awards: Chevalier des Arts et des Lettres, French Gvnmt.

Conducted with major companies in ARG: Buenos Aires; FRA: Aix-en-Provence Fest, Paris; FR GER: Darmstadt, Frankfurt; HOL: Amsterdam; ITA: Palermo; MON: Monte Carlo; POR: Lisbon; SPA: Barcelona; USA: Cincinnati, Philadelphia Lyric. **Operas with these companies incl** DALLAPICCOLA: *Prigioniero*★; DEBUSSY: *Pelléas et Mélisande;* DONIZETTI: *Don Pasquale, Elisir, Lucia;* FALLA: *Vida breve;* GLUCK: *Iphigénie en Tauride, Orfeo ed Euridice;* GOUNOD: *Faust, Roméo et Juliette;* MASSENET: *Manon, Werther;* MOZART: *Così fan tutte, Don Giovanni, Entführung aus dem Serail, Nozze di Figaro, Zaïde, Zauberflöte;* OFFENBACH: *Contes d'Hoffmann;* PONCHIELLI: *Gioconda;* POULENC: *Mamelles de Tirésias, Voix humaine;* PUCCINI: *Bohème*★, *Gianni Schicchi, Butterfly, Suor Angelica, Tabarro, Tosca*★; ROSSINI: *Barbiere di Siviglia*★, *Comte Ory, Italiana in Algeri;* SAINT-SAENS: *Samson et Dalila;* TCHAIKOVSKY: *Eugene Onegin;* THOMAS: *Mignon;* VERDI: *Aida, Ballo in maschera, Don Carlo, Otello, Rigoletto*★, *Traviata, Trovatore*★; WAGNER: *Fliegende Holländer, Lohengrin, Walküre, Tannhäuser, Tristan und Isolde;* WOLF-FERRARI: *Quattro rusteghi.* Also PETRASSI: *Cordovano;* NEGRI: *Pubblicità ninfa gentile;* GLUCK: *Pélerins de la Mecque.* Only on records HALEVY: *Juive;* BIZET: *Docteur Miracle;* HAYDN: *Infedeltà delusa;* MASSENET: *Navarraise.* Recorded for CBS, RCA, Philips, Barclay, Chant du Monde. Conducted major orch in Europe, USA/Canada, Cent/S America, Africa, Austrl. **Res:** 25 rue des Grands Augustins, Paris, France. Mgmt: GOR/UK.

DEAN, STAFFORD. Lyric bass. British. Born 20 Jun 1937, Surrey, UK. Wife Carolyn Lambourne. Four sons. Studied: Royal Coll of Music, London; Howell Glynne, Otakar Kraus. **Debut:** Zuniga (*Carmen*) Sadler's Wells, London 1964.

Sang with major companies in CZE: Prague National; FRA: Bordeaux, Strasbourg, Toulouse; FR GER: Berlin Deutsche Oper, Cologne, Hamburg, Munich Staatsoper, Stuttgart; HOL: Amsterdam; UK: Aldeburgh Fest, Cardiff Welsh, Glasgow Scottish, Glyndebourne Fest, London Royal & English National; USA: San Francisco Opera. **Roles with these companies incl** BEETHOVEN: Rocco (*Fidelio*); BERLIOZ: Narbal★ (*Troyens*); BRITTEN: Azarias‡ (*Burning Fiery Furnace*), Sir Walter Raleigh (*Gloriana*); DONIZETTI: Don Pasquale; MOZART: Leporello★ (*Don Giovanni*), Figaro★ (*Nozze di Figaro*), Sarastro★ (*Zauberflöte*); PUCCINI: Colline (*Bohème*); ROSSINI: Don Basilio (*Barbiere di Siviglia*); VERDI: Padre Guardiano★ (*Forza del destino*); WAGNER: Daland (*Fliegende Holländer*). Appears with symphony orchestra. **Res:** Rallywood, Munstead, Godalming, Surrey, UK. Mgmt: HPL/UK; SLZ/FRG.

DE ANA, HUGO. Scenic and costume designer for opera, theater. Is a lighting designer; also a painter. Argentinean. Resident designer, Teatro Colón, Buenos Aires. Born 12 May 1949, Buenos Aires. Single. Studied: Ntl Arts School M Belgrano; Ntl Arts Univ P Pueyrredon; Acad of Art E della Carcova; Arts Inst of Teatro Colón, all Argentina. Prof training: Teatro Colón 1969-72. **Operatic debut:** *Serva padrona* Colón 1967. Theater debut: Teatro San Martín, Buenos Aires 1968. Previous occupation: prof of art at high school. Awards: Nehru Gold Medal, Shankar Intl Children's Compt, New Delhi, India 1961.

Designed for major companies in ARG: Buenos Aires. **Operas designed for these companies incl** BELLINI: *Norma*★; BRITTEN: *Albert Herring*★; CIMAROSA: *Matrimonio segreto;* GIORDANO: *Andrea Chénier*★; LEONCAVALLO: *Pagliacci*★; MASCAGNI: *Cavalleria rusticana*★; PERGOLESI: *Serva padrona;* ROSSINI: *Barbiere di Siviglia;* STRAUSS, J: *Fledermaus*★. Also CHERUBINI: *Crescendo.* **Operatic world premieres:** DREI: *Medea* Teatro Colón, Buenos Aires 1973. Operatic TV: *Albert Herring.* Exhibitions of stage designs, paintings Galería de Arte de la Boca 1968; Sala Nacional de Exposiciones 1969, Buenos Aires. **Res:** Tabaré 2046, Buenos Aires, Argentina.

DE BANFIELD, RAFFAELLO. Italian. Art Dir, Teatro Comunale G Verdi, Riva Tre Novembre 1, Trieste 1972- . Is also a composer (*Alissa, Colloquio col tango, Lord Byron's Love Letter, Tombe pour une femme seule*) and stage dir. In charge of musical matters & finances. Additional adm positions: Adm, Generali Ins France, Paris. Born 2 Jun 1922, Newcastle, UK. Single. Plays the piano. Background primarily musical. World premieres at theaters under his management: CHAILLY: *Sogno—ma forse no* Trieste 1975. **Res:** Strd del Friuli 42, Trieste, Italy.

DE BLASIS, JAMES MICHAEL. Stages/produces opera, theater & television. Also designs stage-lighting and is a singer, actor & author. American. Gen Dir & Resident Stage Dir, Cincinnati Opera Assn, 1241 Elm St, Cincinnati, O 45210; also of Young Am Artists Progr & Area Artists-Opera. In charge of overall adm matters, art, mus, dram & tech matters & finances. Additional adm position: Consultant for Opera, Corbett Fndt, Cincinnati. Born 12 Apr 1931, New York. Wife Ruth. One child. Studied: Carnegie Mellon Univ; Karl Kritz, Pittsburgh, PA; incl music, piano, trombone, double bass & voice. Operatic training as asst stage dir at Pittsburgh Opera 1957-62. **Operatic debut:** *Bohème* Florida Symph Orch Opera Guild, Orlando 1962. Theater debut: White Barn Theater, Irwin, PA 1961. Previous occupation: prof of music, head of opera depts, singer, chorus dir. Previous adm positions in opera: asst dir, Pittsburgh Opera 1958-63; op adm, Syracuse Symph, NY 1962-71. Started with present company in 1968 as Prod Dir; in present position since 1973.

Directed/produced opera for major companies in CAN: Toronto; USA: Cincinnati, Fort Worth, Hartford, Hawaii, Houston, Memphis, New York City Opera, Omaha, Philadelphia Lyric, Pittsburgh, Portland, San Antonio, San Diego, San Francisco Spring Opera. **Operas staged with these companies incl** BELLINI: *Norma, Pirata;* BIZET: *Carmen;* DONIZETTI: *Elisir★, Lucia★;* GOUNOD: *Faust★, Roméo et Juliette★;* HUMPERDINCK: *Hänsel und Gretel★;* LEONCAVALLO: *Pagliacci;* MASCAGNI: *Cavalleria rusticana;* MASSENET: *Manon;* MENOTTI: *Amelia al ballo★, Old Maid and the Thief;* MOORE: *Ballad of Baby Doe;* MOZART: *Nozze di Figaro★;* MUSSORGSKY: *Boris Godunov★;* OFFENBACH: *Contes d'Hoffmann★, Périchole;* PUCCINI: *Bohème★, Butterfly★, Manon Lescaut★, Rondine★, Suor Angelica, Tabarro, Tosca★, Turandot★;* ROSSINI: *Barbiere di Siviglia;* STRAUSS, J: *Fledermaus;* VERDI: *Aida★, Ballo in maschera★, Otello, Rigoletto★, Traviata★;* WOLF-FERRARI: *Segreto di Susanna.* Initiated major policy changes including expansion of Syracuse Opera Co season from one opera/one performance to three operas/three to five times; expansion of Cincinnati Opera season from four to six weeks; Young American Artists Program; Opera Previews for ticket holders prior to every performance. Mem of Consortium Commtt, OPERA America; mem of opera panel of NEA. **Res:** One Sherman Square, New York, USA.

DE CARLO, RITA FRANCES. Lyric mezzo-soprano. American. Born 15 Aug 1938. Husband James Sardos, occupation artists mgr. Studied: John Daggett Howell, David Bender, New York. **Debut:** Zita (*Gianni Schicchi*) Chautauqua Opera Fest, NY 1963.
Sang with major companies in CAN: Montreal/Quebec, Toronto, Vancouver; USA: Cincinnati, Hartford, Hawaii, Houston, Milwaukee Florentine, New Orleans, Philadelphia Lyric, Pittsburgh. **Roles with these companies incl** BIZET: Carmen★; DONIZETTI: Marquise de Birkenfeld★ (*Fille du régiment*); GOUNOD: Siebel★ (*Faust*); MENOTTI: Miss Todd (*Old Maid and the Thief*); MOZART: Cherubino★ (*Nozze di Figaro*); MUSSORGSKY: Marina★ (*Boris Godunov*); PONCHIELLI: Laura (*Gioconda*); PUCCINI: Suzuki★ (*Butterfly*), Frugola★ (*Tabarro*); VERDI: Preziosilla★ (*Forza del destino*). Also GIORDANO: Madelon (*Andrea Chénier*). Gives recitals. Appears with symphony orchestra. **Res:** New York, USA. Mgmt: SAM/USA.

DE CECCO, DISMA. Dramatic soprano. Italian. Born Codroipo, Udine. Husband Nicola Benois, occupation scenic designer. Studied: Scuola di Canto, Teatro alla Scala, A Pertile, G Tess, G Bellincioni, Milan; Accad delle Muse, Florence.

Debut: Liù (*Turandot*) La Scala, Milan 1949. Awards: Ambrogino d'oro, Municipality of Milan 1965.
Sang with major companies in ARG: Buenos Aires; BRA: Rio de Janeiro; BUL: Sofia; FRA: Nice; FR GER: Bonn, Cologne; ITA: Milan La Scala, Palermo, Parma, Trieste, Verona Arena; MON: Monte Carlo; SWI: Zurich; UK: Cardiff Welsh, Edinburgh Fest, Glasgow Scottish; USSR: Leningrad Kirov, Moscow Bolshoi, Tbilisi. **Roles with these companies incl** BOITO: Elena★ (*Mefistofele*); GIORDANO: Maddalena (*Andrea Chénier*); MASCAGNI: Santuzza (*Cavalleria rusticana*); MONTEVERDI: Clorinda (*Combattimento di Tancredi*); MUSSORGSKY: Marina (*Boris Godunov*); PUCCINI: Mimi★ (*Bohème*), Manon Lescaut, Tosca★, Liù (*Turandot*); ROSSINI: Mathilde (*Guillaume Tell*); VERDI: Aida★, Elisabetta★ (*Don Carlo*), Abigaille★ (*Nabucco*), Desdemona★ (*Otello*), Leonora (*Trovatore*). Also MILHAUD: (*David*). Recorded for: Cetra. Gives recitals. Appears with symphony orchestra. **Res:** Pza Maria Adelaide 2, Milan, Italy.

DECKER, FRANZ PAUL. Conductor of opera and symphony; composer. German. Resident Cond, Opéra du Québec, Montreal, Canada. Also Music Dir, Montreal Symph Orch 1966- . Born 22 Jun 1923, Cologne. Wife Christa Terka. Two children. Studied: Cologne Consv and Univ; incl piano, violin. Operatic training as asst cond & chorus master at Stadttheater Giessen 1945-46, Opera House Cologne 1945-46. **Operatic debut:** *Butterfly* Opera House Cologne 1946. Symphonic debut: Krefeld Symph, Germany 1946. Awards: Order of Merit 1st Class FR Ger; Herscheppend Schep-Ik Medal, Gvnmt of the Netherlands; Edgar Roquette Pinto Medal, Gvnmt of Brazil; Hon DM Concordia Univ, Montreal. Previous adm positions in opera: Music Dir, Opera House Krefeld 1946-50, State Opera Wiesbaden 1950-53.
Conducted with major companies in CAN: Montreal; FR GER: Bonn, Cologne, Hamburg, Krefeld, Mannheim, Wiesbaden; USA: Dallas. **Operas with these companies incl** d'ALBERT: *Tiefland;* AUBER: *Fra Diavolo;* BEETHOVEN: *Fidelio;* BIZET: *Carmen★;* BRITTEN: *Albert Herring, Billy Budd, Peter Grimes, Rape of Lucretia;* FLOTOW: *Martha;* GAY/Britten: *Beggar's Opera;* GLUCK: *Alceste, Iphigénie en Aulide, Iphigénie en Tauride, Orfeo ed Euridice;* GOUNOD: *Faust;* HINDEMITH: *Mathis der Maler;* HUMPERDINCK: *Hänsel und Gretel;* LEONCAVALLO: *Pagliacci★;* LORTZING: *Waffenschmied, Wildschütz, Zar und Zimmermann;* MASCAGNI: *Cavalleria rusticana★;* MENOTTI: *Amahl, Consul, Telephone;* MOZART: *Così fan tutte: Don Giovanni, Entführung aus dem Serail, Idomeneo, Nozze de Figaro, Zauberflöte;* NICOLAI: *Lustigen Weiber;* OFFENBACH: *Contes d'Hoffmann;* ORFF: *Kluge;* PUCCINI: *Bohème, Fanciulla del West, Gianni Schicchi★, Manon Lescaut★, Suor Angelica★, Tabarro★, Tosca, Turandot;* ROSSINI: *Barbiere di Siviglia;* SMETANA: *Bartered Bride;* STRAUSS, R: *Arabella, Ariadne auf Naxos, Elektra, Frau ohne Schatten, Rosenkavalier, Salome;* VERDI: *Aida, Ballo in maschera, Falstaff★, Nabucco, Otello, Rigoletto, Simon Boccanegra, Traviata, Trovatore;* WAGNER: *Fliegende*

Holländer, Lohengrin, Meistersinger, Rheingold, Walküre, Siegfried, Götterdämmerung, Tannhäuser, Tristan und Isolde*; WEBER: *Freischütz.* Also BRITTEN: *Let's Make an Opera;* KIENZL: *Evangelimann;* MARSCHNER: *Hans Heiling;* LORTZING: *Undine;* MOZART: *Bastien und Bastienne.* **World premieres:** GERHARD: *Dueña* Opera House Wiesbaden 1951. Video—CBC TV: *Tristan und Isolde.* Conducted major orch in Europe, USA/Canada, Cent/S America, & Austrl. Previous positions as Mus Dir with major orch: Wiesbaden Symph 1950-56; Bochum Symph 1956-64; Rotterdam Phil 1962-68. **Operas composed:** *Froschkönig,* no pfs. **Res:** Montreal, PQ, Canada. Mgmt: IWL/UK.

DE FABRITIIS, OLIVIERO. Conductor of opera and symphony. Italian. Born 13 Jun 1904, Rome. Wife Fiore Buonaccorsi. Studied: Sandy Gorlinky, London; incl piano. **Operatic debut:** *Traviata,* Salerno Opera Theater 1925. Symphonic debut: Radio Rome. Previous adm positions in opera: Principal Cond/Music Dir Teatro dell'Opera, Rome; San Carlo, Naples; Teatro Massimo, Palermo; La Fenice, Venice; Teatro Comunale, Bologna; Arena di Verona, etc.

Conducted with major companies in ARG: Buenos Aires; AUS: Vienna Staatsoper; FRA: Paris; FR GER: Berlin Deutsche Oper, Cologne, Dortmund, Frankfurt, Karlsruhe, Mannheim, Munich Staatsoper; ITA: Bologna, Florence Maggio & Comunale, Genoa, Milan La Scala, Naples, Palermo, Rome Opera & Caracalla, Trieste, Turin, Venice, Verona Arena; MEX: Mexico City; MON: Monte Carlo; POR: Lisbon; UK: Edinburgh Fest, London Royal; USA: San Antonio, San Francisco Opera; YUG: Dubrovnik, Zagreb, Belgrade. **Operas with these companies incl** AUBER: *Fra Diavolo;* BELLINI: *Capuleti ed i Montecchi, Norma, Pirata, Puritani, Sonnambula, Straniera;* BERLIOZ: *Damnation de Faust;* BIZET: *Carmen, Jolie Fille de Perth, Pêcheurs de perles;* BOITO: *Mefistofele;* BUSONI: *Turandot;* CATALANI: *Wally;* CHARPENTIER: *Louise;* CHERUBINI: *Medea;* CILEA: *A. Lecouvreur;* CIMAROSA: *Matrimonio segreto;* DEBUSSY: *Pelléas et Mélisande;* DELIBES: *Lakmé;* DONIZETTI: *Anna Bolena, Campanello, Don Pasquale, Elisir, Favorite, Fille du régiment, Linda di Chamounix, Lucia, Lucrezia Borgia, Maria di Rohan, Maria Stuarda;* DUKAS: *Ariane et Barbe Bleue;* FALLA: *Vida breve;* FLOTOW: *Martha;* GIORDANO: *Andrea Chénier‡, Fedora;* GLINKA: *Life for the Tsar;* GLUCK: *Alceste;* GOUNOD: *Faust, Roméo et Juliette;* HANDEL: *Giulio Cesare;* HUMPERDINCK: *Hänsel und Gretel;* JANACEK: *Jenufa;* LEONCAVALLO: *Pagliacci;* MASCAGNI: *Amico Fritz, Cavalleria rusticana, Silvano;* MASSENET: *Cendrillon, Manon, Thaïs, Werther;* MENOTTI: *Amahl, Amelia al ballo, Consul, Medium;* MEYERBEER: *Africaine;* MONTEMEZZI: *Amore dei tre re;* MONTEVERDI: *Combattimento di Tancredi, Incoronazione di Poppea;* MOZART: *Così fan tutte, Don Giovanni, Entführung aus dem Serail, Schauspieldirektor, Nozze di Figaro;* MUSSORGSKY: *Boris Godunov, Khovanshchina;* OFFENBACH: *Contes d'Hoffmann;* ORFF: *Carmina burana;* PAISIELLO: *Barbiere di Siviglia;* PERGOLESI: *Serva padrona;* PON-

CHIELLI: *Gioconda;* POULENC: *Dialogues des Carmélites;* PUCCINI: *Bohème, Fanciulla del West, Gianni Schicchi, Butterfly‡, Manon Lescaut, Rondine, Suor Angelica, Tabarro, Tosca‡, Turandot, Villi;* RIMSKY-KORSAKOV: *Coq d'or, Sadko;* ROSSINI: *Barbiere di Siviglia, Cambiale di matrimonio, Cenerentola‡, Guillaume Tell, Italiana in Algeri, Scala di seta, Turco in Italia;* SAINT-SAENS: *Samson et Dalila;* SPONTINI: *Vestale;* STRAUSS, R: *Ariadne auf Naxos, Rosenkavalier, Salome;* STRAVINSKY: *Mavra, Oedipus Rex;* TCHAIKOVSKY: *Pique Dame;* THOMAS: *Mignon;* VERDI: *Aida, Aroldo, Attila, Ballo in maschera, Corsaro, Don Carlo, Due Foscari, Ernani, Falstaff, Forza del destino, Luisa Miller, Macbeth, Nabucco, Otello, Rigoletto, Simon Boccanegra, Traviata, Trovatore, Vespri;* WAGNER: *Lohengrin, Rienzi, Walküre, Siegfried, Tristan und Isolde;* WEBER: *Oberon;* WOLF-FERRARI: *Donne curiose, Quattro rusteghi, Segreto di Susanna;* ZANDONAI: *Francesca da Rimini, Giulietta e Romeo.* Conducted major orch in Europe, Cent/S America, Asia.

DE FERRA, GIAMPAOLO. Italian. Sovrintendente, Teatro Comunale G Verdi, Riva Tre Novembre 1, Trieste 1969- . In charge of overall adm matters. Additional adm positions: Rector, Univ Studi, Trieste. Born 30 Jun 1929, Trieste. Wife Beatrice Molaro. Studied: Univ of Trieste, laurea jurisprudence. Previous occupation: lawyer. World premieres at theaters under his management: MANNINO: *Speranza* 1970; BUGAMELLI: *Fontana* 1971; VIOZZI: *Elisabetta* 1971; CHAILLY: *Sogno—ma fors e no* 1975, all at Trieste. **Res:** V Ricreatorio 42, Trieste/Opicina, Italy.

DE FILIPPO, EDUARDO. Stages/produces opera, theater, film & television and is an actor & author. Italian. Born 24 May 1900, Naples. Widowed. One son. Studied: Naples, Comps E Scarpetta & V Scarpetta; Comps Altieri, Villani, Carini. **Operatic debut:** *Pietra del paragone* Piccola Scala, Milan 1958. Theater debut: Naples 1922. Previous occupation: actor since 1912; also writer & impresario. Awards: Prize, Teatro dell'Accad del Lincei 1972; *Evening Standard* Awd for Best Play 1973; etc. Previous adm positions in opera: Founder/Dir, Teatro Umoristico De Filippo; Founder/Dir, Teatro di Eduardo.

Directed/produced opera for major companies in FR GER: Berlin Deutsche Oper; ITA: Florence Maggio & Comunale, Milan La Scala, Naples, Rome Opera; UK: Edinburgh Fest; USA: Chicago. **Operas staged with these companies incl** DONIZETTI: *Don Pasquale**; PAISIELLO: *Barbiere di Siviglia;* ROSSINI: *Barbiere di Siviglia, Cenerentola, Pietra del paragone;* SHOSTAKOVICH: *Nose;* VERDI: *Falstaff**, *Rigoletto.* **Opera libretti:** ROTA: *Scoiattolo in gamba* RAI, Venice. **Res:** V Aquileia 16, Rome, Italy. Mgmt: VLO/UK.

DE GROOTE, HILDA MARIA. Lyric coloratura soprano. Belgian. Resident mem: Vienna Staatsoper; Munich Staatsoper. Born 14 Oct 1945, Ghent, Belgium. Husband Reinhold Siegl, occupation mem Vienna Philharmonic Orch. Studied: private teacher, Belgium. **Debut:** Olympia (*Contes d'Hoffmann*) Ghent Opera, Belgium 1961. Previous occupations: chemical student.

Sang with major companies in AUS: Vienna Staatsoper & Volksoper; BEL: Liège; CAN: Montreal/Quebec; FRA: Aix-en-Provence Fest; FR GER: Berlin Deutsche Oper, Munich Staatsoper, Stuttgart, Wiesbaden; GER DR: Berlin Staatsoper; USSR: Moscow Bolshoi. **Roles with these companies incl** BEETHOVEN: Marzelline★ (*Fidelio*); BIZET: Micaëla (*Carmen*); DONIZETTI: Norina★ (*Don Pasquale*); FLOTOW: Lady Harriet★ (*Martha*); GLUCK: Amor★ (*Orfeo ed Euridice*); HUMPERDINCK: Gretel★; MASSENET: Manon★, Sophie★ (*Werther*); MOZART: Zerlina (*Don Giovanni*), Blondchen (*Entführung aus dem Serail*), Susanna★ (*Nozze di Figaro*); NICOLAI: Aennchen★ (*Lustigen Weiber von Windsor*); OFFENBACH: Olympia★ & Antonia★ & Giulietta★ (*Contes d'Hoffmann*); PUCCINI: Musetta (*Bohème*); STRAUSS, J: Adele★ (*Fledermaus*); STRAUSS, R: Fiakermilli★ (*Arabella*), Sophie★ (*Rosenkavalier*); VERDI: Oscar★ (*Ballo in maschera*), Nannetta (*Falstaff*), Gilda (*Rigoletto*); WEBER: Aennchen (*Freischütz*). Also GOUNOD: Siebel★ (*Faust*); ROSSINI: Jemmy (*Guillaume Tell*); d'ALBERT: Nuri★ (*Tiefland*). Gives recitals. Appears with symphony orchestra. **Res:** Theobaldg 15/22, Vienna, Austria 1060. Mgmt: KOA/AUS; SLZ/FRG.

DEHLI, ELSE SYNNOVE. Dramatic soprano. Norwegian. Resident mem: Norwegian Opera, Oslo. Born 20 Nov 1937, Oslo. Husband Thomas MacBone, occupation singer & voice teacher. One daughter. Studied: Oslo, Norway; Musikhochschule Mozarteum, Prof E Thiessen, Salzburg; Akad für Musik und darstellende Kunst, Vienna; with husband Thomas MacBone. **Debut:** Agathe (*Freischütz*) Landestheater Detmold, FR Ger 1961. Previous occupations: private secy. Awards: 5 yrs schlshp Edw Ruuds Fndt; state schlshp for prof singers.

Sang with major company in NOR: Oslo. **Roles with this company incl** BEETHOVEN: Marzelline (*Fidelio*); BERG: Marie★ (*Wozzeck*); BIZET: Micaëla (*Carmen*); DALLAPICCOLA: La Madre★ (*Prigioniero*); GLUCK: Iphigénie (*Iphigénie en Aulide*); KODALY: Örzse (*Háry János*); MOZART: Fiordiligi (*Così fan tutte*), Donna Elvira★ (*Don Giovanni*); OFFENBACH: Antonia & Giulietta★ (*Contes d'Hoffmann*); SHOSTAKOVICH: Katerina Ismailova★; STRAUSS, R: Arabella; VERDI: Alice Ford (*Falstaff*), Leonora (*Forza del destino*), Leonora★ (*Trovatore*); WAGNER: Senta (*Fliegende Holländer*), Eva (*Meistersinger*), Sieglinde★ (*Walküre*), Elisabeth (*Tannhäuser*); WEBER: Agathe (*Freischütz*). Also d'ALBERT: Myrtocle (*Toten Augen*). **World premieres:** JOHNSEN: Maria (*Legend av Svein og Maria*) Norwegian Opera, Oslo 1973. Gives recitals. Appears with symphony orchestra. Teaches voice. On faculty of Univ of Oslo. **Res:** Stjernemyrveien 44, Oslo, Norway. Mgmt: PGI/NOR.

DEIBER, PAUL-EMILE. Stages/produces opera, theater & television. Also designs stage-lighting and is an actor & author. French. Resident Stage Dir for theater & TV in Paris. Born 1 Jan 1925, La Broque. Wife Christa Ludwig, occupation mezzo-

soprano. Two children. Studied: National Drama School, Paris; also music, violin. **Operatic debut:** *Barbiere di Siviglia* Paris 1955. Theater debut: Comédie Française, Paris 1944. Awards: Légion d'honneur. Previous adm positions in opera: Art Dir, Opéra de Paris 1968-71.

Directed/produced opera for major companies in AUS: Vienna Staatsoper; BEL: Brussels; FRA: Aix-en-Provence Fest, Nice, Orange Fest, Paris; GRE: Athens Fest; FR GER: Berlin Deutsche Oper, Munich Gärtnerplatz; ITA: Naples; MEX: Mexico City; POR: Lisbon Teatro São Carlos; SWI: Geneva; USA: Chicago Lyric, New York Met, San Francisco Opera. **Operas staged with these companies incl** BELLINI: Norma★; BERLIOZ: Benvenuto Cellini★, Damnation de Faust; DEBUSSY: Pelléas et Mélisande★; DONIZETTI: Elisir, Favorite★; GOUNOD: Roméo et Juliette★; HONEGGER: Antigone; MASSENET: Manon★, Werther★; MILHAUD: Médée; ORFF: Carmina burana★; PUCCINI: Bohème, Suor Angelica, Tabarro; PURCELL: Dido and Aeneas; VERDI: Luisa Miller★. Previous leading positions with major theater companies: member Comédie Française, Paris 1944-71. **Res:** Rigistr 14, Meggen 6045, Switzerland. Mgmt: LNR/FRA; JUC/SWI.

DELLA CASA, LISA. Lyric soprano & spinto. Swiss. Born 2 Feb 1919, Burgdorf, Switzerland. Husband Dragan Debeljevic. One daughter. Studied: Consvs of Bern & Zurich; Margarethe Haeser, Switzerland. **Debut:** Mimi (*Bohème*) Zurich Opera 1943. Awards: Austrian & Bavarian Kammersängerin; Austrian Cross I Order; Harriet Cohen Medal; Reinhardt Ring.

Sang with major companies in ARG: Buenos Aires; AUSTRL: Sydney; AUS: Bregenz Fest, Graz, Salzburg Fest, Vienna Staatsoper & Volksoper; BEL: Brussels; CAN: Montreal/Quebec, Toronto, Vancouver; FRA: Paris; FR GER: Bayreuth Fest, Berlin Deutsche Oper, Bielefeld, Bonn, Cologne, Dortmund, Düsseldorf-Duisburg, Hamburg Staatsoper, Hannover, Kiel, Munich Staatsoper, Wiesbaden; HOL: Amsterdam; ITA: Milan La Scala, Rome Caracalla, Turin; MON: Monte Carlo; SPA: Barcelona Liceo; SWE: Stockholm; SWI: Basel, Geneva, Zurich; UK: Edinburgh Fest, Glyndebourne Fest, London Royal Opera; USA: Boston, Chicago, Fort Worth, Hawaii, Houston, Miami, New Orleans, New York Met, Philadelphia Grand, San Antonio, San Francisco Opera, Washington DC. **Roles with these companies incl** BEETHOVEN: Marzelline (*Fidelio*); BERLIOZ: Marguerite (*Damnation de Faust*); EINEM: Lucille (*Dantons Tod*), Frl Bürstner (*Prozess*); GERSHWIN: Bess; GLUCK: Euridice; HANDEL: Cleopatra (*Giulio Cesare*), Agrippina★; HINDEMITH: Ursula (*Mathis der Maler*); LEONCAVALLO: Nedda (*Pagliacci*); MOZART: Fiordiligi (*Così fan tutte*), Donna Anna & Donna Elvira★ (*Don Giovanni*), Ilia★ (*Idomeneo*), Contessa★ (*Nozze di Figaro*), Pamina★ & Königin der Nacht (*Zauberflöte*); NICOLAI: Frau Fluth (*Lustigen Weiber*); OFFENBACH: Antonia (*Contes d'Hoffmann*); PUCCINI: Mimi (*Bohème*), Cio-Cio-San (*Butterfly*), Suor Angelica, Tosca; SMETANA: Marie (*Bartered Bride*); STRAUSS, R: Arabella★, Zdenka (*Arabella*), Ariadne★ (*Ariadne auf Naxos*), Gräfin★ (*Capric-*

cio), Chrysothemis (*Elektra*), Marschallin★ & Octavian★ & Sophie (*Rosenkavalier*), Salome; VERDI: Gilda (*Rigoletto*); WAGNER: Elsa★ (*Lohengrin*), Eva★ (*Meistersinger*). **World premieres:** EINEM: three sop parts (*Prozess*) Salzburg Fest 1953. Recorded for: Decca London, RCA, Columbia, DG. Film — Salzburg: Donna Elvira (*Don Giovanni*). Gives recitals. Appears with symphony orchestra. Res: Schloss, Ch-8274 Gottlieben, Switzerland.

DEL MONACO, GIANCARLO. Stages/produces opera. Italian. Oberspielleiter & Resident Stage Dir, Theater Ulm, FR Ger. Born 1945, Italy. Operatic training as asst stage dir in Berlin, Stuttgart & Vienna.

Directed/produced opera for major companies in FR GER: Dortmund; ITA: Naples; et al. **Operas staged with these companies incl** DONIZETTI: *Don Pasquale, Lucia;* HAYDN: *Infedeltà delusa;* OFFENBACH: *Contes d'Hoffmann;* PUCCINI: *Butterfly;* VERDI: *Otello;* WEBER: *Freischütz;* et al. Also GHEDINI: *Pulce d'oro.*

DEL MONACO, MARIO. Dramatic tenor. Italian. Born 27 Jul 1915, Florence. Wife Rina Fedora, occupation form singer. Two sons. Studied: Consv Rossini, Luisa Melai-Palazzini, Arturo Melocchi, Pesaro; Rome Opera Studio. **Debut:** Pinkerton (*Butterfly*) Teatro Puccini, Milan 1941 (while serving in Ital Army). Previous occupation: studied painting and sculpture. Awards: Gold Medal, City of Paris; Academic Order of Lenin, USSR; First Prize Serafin Singing Compt, Rome 1935.

Sang with major companies in ARG: Buenos Aires; AUS: Vienna Staatsoper & Volksoper; BRA: Rio de Janeiro; FRA: Paris; FR GER: Berlin Deutsche Oper, Hamburg; ITA: Bologna, Florence Maggio & Comunale, Milan La Scala, Naples, Palermo, Parma, Rome Opera & Caracalla, Trieste, Turin, Venice, Verona Arena; MEX: Mexico City; POR: Lisbon; SPA: Barcelona; SWE: Stockholm; SWI: Zurich; UK: London Royal; USSR: Moscow Bolshoi; USA: Chicago, New York Met, Philadelphia Grand, Pittsburgh, San Francisco; et al. **Roles with these companies incl** BELLINI: Pollione‡ (*Norma*); BIZET: Don José‡ (*Carmen*); BOITO: Faust‡ (*Mefistofele*); CATALANI: Giuseppe Hagenbach‡ (*Wally*); CILEA: Maurizio‡ (*A. Lecouvreur*); DONIZETTI: Edgardo (*Lucia*); GIORDANO: Andrea Chénier‡, Loris Ipanov‡ (*Fedora*); LEONCAVALLO: Canio‡ (*Pagliacci*); MASCAGNI: Turiddu‡ (*Cavalleria rusticana*); PONCHIELLI: Enzo (*Gioconda*); PUCCINI: Rodolfo‡ (*Bohème*), Dick Johnson‡ (*Fanciulla del West*), Des Grieux‡ (*Manon Lescaut*), Luigi (*Tabarro*), Cavaradossi‡ (*Tosca*), Calaf‡ (*Turandot*); SAINT-SAENS: Samson; VERDI: Radames‡ (*Aida*), Foresto (*Attila*), Don Carlo, Ernani, Don Alvaro‡ (*Forza del destino*), Ismaele (*Nabucco*), Otello‡, Duca di Mantova‡ (*Rigoletto*), Alfredo (*Traviata*), Manrico‡ (*Trovatore*); WAGNER: Lohengrin; et al. Recorded for: Decca/London, HMV. Video/Film: Turiddu (*Cavalleria rusticana*). Mgmt: GOR/UK.

DE LULLO, GIORGIO. Stages/produces opera, theater & television. Also designs sets & stage-lighting and is an actor. Italian. Born 24 Apr 1921,

Rome. Single. Studied: Accad Nazionale dram art, Rome and with Luchino Visconti; incl music and voice. Operatic training as asst stage dir & actor, Rome. **Operatic debut:** *Trovatore* La Scala, Milan 1962-63. Theater debut: Eliseo, Rome 1945. Awards: S Genesio, Nettuno d'oro & other Ital awds.

Directed/produced opera for major companies in FR GER: Munich Staatsoper; ITA: Florence Maggio & Comunale, Milan La Scala, Rome Opera, Spoleto Fest; UK: Edinburgh Fest; USSR: Moscow Bolshoi; USA: Chicago, San Francisco Opera. **Operas staged with these companies incl** DONIZETTI: *Lucia, Maria Stuarda★;* GLUCK: *Alceste;* PUCCINI: *Bohème★;* ROSSINI: *Cenerentola;* STRAVINSKY: *Oedipus Rex★;* VERDI: *Aida★, Due Foscari★, Macbeth, Otello★, Simon Boccanegra★, Traviata★, Vespri★.* Res: V Appia Antica 140, Rome, Italy.

DE MORI, ENRICO. Conductor of opera and symphony; composer. Italian. Born 11 Jun 1930, Roanne, France. Married. Two children. Studied: Roanne, Milan, Verona, Venice, Parma; also piano, violin and voice. Plays the piano. Operatic training as repetiteur, asst cond & chorus master at Teatro alla Scala, Milan. **Operatic debut:** *Barbiere di Siviglia* Milan 1963. Symphonic debut: Sinf di Pomerania, Danzig, Poland 1971. Awards: First Prize, Ntl Compt for pianists 1947.

Conducted with major companies in FR GER: Düsseldorf-Duisburg; ITA: Bologna, Florence Maggio & Comunale, Genoa, Milan La Scala, Parma, Turin, Venice, Verona Arena; POL: Warsaw. **Operas with these companies incl** DONIZETTI: *Don Pasquale, Lucia;* MASSENET: *Portrait de Manon;* MENOTTI: *Amahl;* MONTEVERDI: *Combattimento di Tancredi;* ROSSINI: *Barbiere di Siviglia;* VERDI: *Ballo in maschera, Rigoletto.* **Res:** P Istria 2, Milan, Italy.

DEMPSEY, GREGORY JOHN. Lyric tenor. Australian. Resident mem: English National Opera, London. Born 20 Jul 1931, Melbourne. Wife Anne Marie Smith, occupation singer. Studied: Mavis Kruger; Annie and Heini Portnoj. **Debut:** Don Ottavio (*Don Giovanni*) National Opera of Victoria 1954. Previous occupations: silversmith, welder, truck driver.

Sang with major companies in AUSTRL: Sydney; FR GER: Cologne; UK: Aldeburgh Fest, Cardiff Welsh, Edinburgh Fest, Glasgow Scottish, London Royal & English National; USA: San Francisco Spring Opera. **Roles with these companies incl** d'ALBERT: Pedro (*Tiefland*); BEETHOVEN: Florestan★ (*Fidelio*); BERG: Tambourmajor★ (*Wozzeck*); BERLIOZ: Aeneas★ (*Troyens*); BIZET: Don José★ (*Carmen*); BRITTEN: Albert Herring, Lysander★ (*Midsummer Night*), Peter Grimes, Tempter (*Prodigal Son*), Peter Quint★ (*Turn of the Screw*); HENZE: Dionysus★ (*Bassariden*); JANACEK: Broucek (*Excursions of Mr Broucek*), Steva★ (*Jenufa*), Albert Gregor★ (*Makropoulos Affair*), Skuratoff (*From the House of the Dead*); LEONCAVALLO: Canio★ (*Pagliacci*); MASCAGNI: Turiddu (*Cavalleria rusticana*); MONTEVERDI: Nero (*Incoronazione di Poppea*); MOZART: Don Ottavio (*Don Giovanni*), Tamino (*Zauberflöte*); PENDERECKI: Adam★ (*Teufel von Loudun*);

PROKOFIEV: Prince (*Love for Three Oranges*), Pierre (*War and Peace*); PUCCINI: Rinuccio (*Gianni Schicchi*), Luigi (*Tabarro*); SAINT-SAENS: Samson; SMETANA: Wenzel (*Bartered Bride*); STRAVINSKY: Tom Rakewell (*Rake's Progress*); WAGNER: Erik (*Fliegende Holländer*), David★ (*Meistersinger*), Mime (*Rheingold★, Siegfried★*); WEBER: Max (*Freischütz*); WEILL: Jim Mahoney (*Aufstieg und Fall der Stadt Mahagonny*). **World premieres:** BENNETT: Boconnion (*Mines of Sulphur*) Engl Ntl Op/Sadler's Wells 1965; MUSGRAVE: Wayson (*Decision*) New Opera 1968. Recorded for: EMI. Gives recitals. Appears with symphony orchestra. Mgmt: IWL/UK; EDY/AUSTRL.

DENIC, MIOMIR ALEXANDER. Scenic designer for opera, theater, film, television. Is a lighting designer, stage director; also a painter & architect. Yugoslavian. Resident designer, Narodno Pozoriste, Belgrade. Born 22 Jan 1913, Belgrade. Wife Danica, occupation choreographer. Studied: studio Jovan Bijelic; Art School, Narodno Pozoriste; Tech Univ, Belgrade. Prof training: Belgrade Opera 1933-36. **Operatic debut:** *Tosca* Belgrade Opera 1936. Theater debut: Narodno Pozoriste, Belgrade 1936. Previous occupation: painter. Awards: Greatest Awd, Gvnmt FNRJ 1949; Great Awd of the Republic for 10 yrs of Film 1955; Awds Sterijno Pozorje, Novi Sad, Best Theater Sets 1964, '70, '75; Awd Min of Culture 1970; Awd Assn of Artists of Applied Arts and Designs of Serbia.

Designed for major companies in AUS: Salzburg Fest, Vienna Staatsoper; BEL: Brussels; BUL: Sofia; DEN: Copenhagen; FRA: Nice, Paris; GRE: Athens National & Fest; FR GER: Berlin Deutsche Oper, Frankfurt, Munich Staatsoper, Wiesbaden; GER DR: Berlin Staatsoper, Leipzig; HOL: Amsterdam; ITA: Florence Maggio, Genoa, Palermo, Rome Opera, Trieste, Venice; MON: Monte Carlo; NOR: Oslo; POL: Warsaw; SPA: Barcelona; SWI: Geneva, Zurich; UK: Edinburgh Fest; YUG: Dubrovnik, Zagreb, Belgrade. **Operas designed for these companies incl** d'ALBERT: *Tiefland;* BELLINI: *Norma;* BIZET: *Carmen;* BORODIN: *Prince Igor★;* BRITTEN: *Rape of Lucretia★;* DONIZETTI: *Don Pasquale;* GERSHWIN: *Porgy and Bess★;* GIORDANO: *Andrea Chénier;* GOTOVAC: *Ero der Schelm;* GOUNOD: *Faust;* HUMPERDINCK: *Hänsel und Gretel;* JANACEK: *Katya Kabanova;* LEONCAVALLO: *Pagliacci;* LORTZING: *Wildschütz, Zar und Zimmermann;* MASCAGNI: *Cavalleria rusticana;* MASSENET: *Don Quichotte, Manon, Thaïs, Werther;* MENOTTI: *Consul;* MONIUSZKO: *Halka;* MOZART: *Così fan tutte, Don Giovanni, Entführung aus dem Serail, Nozze di Figaro;* MUSSORGSKY: *Boris Godunov, Fair at Sorochinsk, Khovanshchina;* OFFENBACH: *Contes d'Hoffmann;* PONCHIELLI: *Gioconda;* PROKOFIEV: *Gambler, Love for Three Oranges;* PUCCINI: *Bohème, Fanciulla del West, Gianni Schicchi, Butterfly, Manon Lescaut★, Tosca;* RIMSKY-KORSAKOV: *Coq d'or, Maid of Pskov;* ROSSINI: *Barbiere di Siviglia;* SAINT-SAENS: *Samson et Dalila;* SHOSTAKOVICH: *Katerina Ismailova;* STRAUSS, R: *Salome;* TCHAIKOVSKY: *Eugene Onegin★, Pique*

Dame; VERDI: *Aida, Ballo in maschera, Forza del destino, Macbeth★, Otello, Rigoletto, Traviata, Trovatore;* WAGNER: *Fliegende Holländer;* WEBER: *Freischütz.* Also BINICKI: *At Dawn.* **Operatic world premieres:** LOTRA-KALINSKY: *Analfabeta* 1954; HERCIGONYA: *Mountain Wreath* 1957; LOGAR: *Fortyong* 1966; KONOVIC: *Prince of Zeta* 1968; all at Belgrade Opera. Exhibitions of stage designs & paintings Triennale Novi Sad 1966, 69, 72, 75; Quadrennale Prague 1967, 71, 75. Associated with Avala Film, Belgrade. **Res:** Gospodar Jovanova 42A, Belgrade, Yugoslavia.

DENIZE, NADINE. Dramatic mezzo-soprano. French. Resident mem: Opéra du Rhin, Strasbourg. Born 6 Nov 1943, Rouen, France. Husband Bernard Bovier-Lapierre, occupation assistant executive. One child. Studied: Marie-Louise Christol, Germaine Lubin. **Debut:** Marguerite (*Damnation de Faust*) Opéra de Paris 1967. Awards: First Prize Chant, Art Lyrique, Histoire de la Musique, Consv Natl, Paris.

Sang with major companies in FRA: Aix-en-Provence Fest, Lyon, Marseille, Nice, Orange Fest, Paris, Rouen, Strasbourg; FR GER: Hamburg; HOL: Amsterdam; ITA: Palermo; MON: Monte Carlo; POR: Lisbon. **Roles with these companies incl** BERLIOZ: Béatrice★, Marguerite★ (*Damnation de Faust*), Cassandre★ (*Troyens*); BRITTEN: Hermia★ (*Midsummer Night*); HONEGGER: Antigone★; MASSENET: Hérodiade★, Charlotte★ (*Werther*); MONTEVERDI: Orfeo★; MOZART: Cherubino★ (*Nozze di Figaro*); POULENC: Mère Marie★ (*Dialogues des Carmélites*); RAMEAU: Phèdre★ (*Hippolyte et Aricie*); RAVEL: Enfant★ (*Enfant et les sortilèges*); VERDI: Eboli★ (*Don Carlo*), Federica★ (*Luisa Miller*); WAGNER: Kundry★ (*Parsifal*), Fricka (*Rheingold★, Walküre★*). Also ROUSSEL: Padmavâti★. **World premieres:** DELARUE: L'Enchanteresse (*Médis et Alyssio*) Opéra du Rhin, Strasbourg 1975. Recorded for: Erato. Gives recitals. Appears with symphony orchestra. **Res:** 35 rue François Bonvin, 75015 Paris, France. Mgmt: CMW/FRA.

DE NOBILI, LILA. Scenic and costume designer for opera, theater & film. Is also a painter. Italian. Single.

Designed opera for major companies in FRA: Paris; ITA: Milan La Scala, Rome Opera, Spoleto Fest; UK: London Royal; USA: Cincinnati, Dallas; et al. **Operas designed for these companies incl** BIZET: *Carmen;* PUCCINI: *Bohème, Manon Lescaut;* ROSSINI: *Otello;* VERDI: *Aida, Rigoletto;* et al.

DENYSENKO, WLODZIMIERZ. Bass-baritone. Polish. Resident mem: Teatr Wielki, Warsaw. Born 25 May 1931, Chorzów, Poland. Wife Regina, occupation Vice-Dir, Museum of Technology. Two children. Studied: Prof Waclaw Brzezinski, Warsaw. **Debut:** Don Basilio (*Barbiere di Siviglia*) Bytom Opera, Poland 1952. Previous occupations: construction tech.

Sang with major companies in POL: Warsaw. **Roles with these companies incl** BERG: Wozzeck; BIZET: Escamillo★ (*Carmen*); BORODIN: Prince Igor; DONIZETTI: Don Pasquale;

GERSHWIN: Porgy; GOUNOD: Méphistophélès★ (*Faust*); HALEVY: Brogny (*Juive*); LEONCAVALLO: Tonio (*Pagliacci*); MOZART: Don Alfonso (*Così fan tutte*), Leporello★ (*Don Giovanni*), Figaro★ (*Nozze di Figaro*); MUSSORGSKY: Boris★ (*Boris Godunov*); NICOLAI: Falstaff (*Lustigen Weiber*); PERGOLESI: Tracolino★ (*Maestro di musica*), Uberto (*Serva padrona*); PONCHIELLI: Barnaba (*Gioconda*); PUCCINI: Colline★ (*Bohème*), Scarpia (*Tosca*); ROSSINI: Don Basilio★ (*Barbiere di Siviglia*); SMETANA: Kezal★ (*Bartered Bride*); VERDI: Amonasro & Ramfis (*Aida*), Philip II (*Don Carlo*), Falstaff★, Macbeth, Iago (*Otello*); WAGNER: Landgraf★ (*Tannhäuser*); WEBER: Kaspar★ (*Freischütz*). Recorded for: Polish companies. Gives recitals. Appears with symphony orchestra. **Res:** Molière 8/29, Warsaw, Poland. Mgmt: PAG/POL.

DePAUL, JUDITH; née Giuditta De Paoli. Dramatic soprano. American; Italian res. Born 12 Jul 1944, Florence, Italy. Husband Conte Mario Pinizzotto, occupation painter. Studied: Manhattan School of Music, New York Coll of Music; Kurt Baum, New York; Accad de Santa Cecilia, Rome. **Debut:** Amelia (*Ballo in maschera*) Kansas City Lyric 1966. Previous occupations: 10 yrs ballet with Balanchine and Robbins; 8 yrs American TV starting age 7. Awards: Three times Artist of Year *High Fidelity* magazine; three Gold Medals, Italy; Gonfalona Prize Rome; Premio Shostakovich.

Sang with major companies in AUS: Graz; CZE: Prague National; DEN: Copenhagen; FRA: Paris, Strasbourg, Toulouse; GRE: Athens Fest; GER DR: Dresden, Leipzig; HOL: Amsterdam; ISR: Tel Aviv; ITA: Florence Maggio, Genoa, Palermo, Venice; UK: Edinburgh Fest; USA: Boston, Hartford, Houston, Kansas City, Memphis, Miami, Minneapolis, Newark, New York Met, Omaha, Philadelphia Grand, Pittsburgh, San Diego. **Roles with these companies incl** BARTOK: Judith (*Bluebeard's Castle*); BERG: Marie★ (*Wozzeck*); BERLIOZ: Marguerite (*Damnation de Faust*); BIZET: Carmen★; CHERUBINI: Medea; DEBUSSY: Lia★ (*Enfant prodigue*); DVORAK: Rusalka; GIORDANO: Maddalena★ (*Andrea Chénier*), Fedora★‡; GLUCK: Alceste, Euridice; HALEVY: Rachel (*Juive*); JANACEK: Jenufa, Emilia Marty (*Makropoulos Affair*); LEONCAVALLO: Nedda★ (*Pagliacci*); MASCAGNI: Suzel (*Amico Fritz*), Santuzza★ (*Cavalleria rusticana*); MASSENET: Salomé (*Hérodiade*), Charlotte (*Werther*); MENOTTI: Magda Sorel (*Consul*); MOZART: Donna Anna★ & Donna Elvira★ (*Don Giovanni*), Contessa (*Nozze di Figaro*); OFFENBACH: Giulietta (*Contes d'Hoffmann*); PONCHIELLI: Gioconda★, POULENC: La femme★ (*Voix humaine*); PROKOFIEV: Renata (*Flaming Angel*); PUCCINI: Mimi★ & Musetta★ (*Bohème*), Minnie (*Fanciulla del West*), Cio-Cio-San★ (*Butterfly*), Manon★, Tosca★; SHOSTAKOVICH: Katerina Ismailova★; SPONTINI: Giulia (*Vestale*); STRAUSS, R: Helena (*Aegyptische Helena*), Arabella, Ariadne (*Ariadne auf Naxos*), Chrysothemis★ (*Elektra*), Octavian (*Rosenkavalier*), Salome★‡; TCHAIKOVSKY: Tatiana★ (*Eugene Onegin*), Lisa★ (*Pique Dame*); VERDI: Aida★, Odabella★ (*Attila*), Amelia★‡

(*Ballo in maschera*), Elisabetta (*Don Carlo*), Leonora (*Forza del destino*), Lady Macbeth★, Abigaille★ (*Nabucco*), Desdemona (*Otello*), Amelia (*Simon Boccanegra*), Violetta★ (*Traviata*), Leonora (*Trovatore*); WAGNER: Senta (*Fliegende Holländer*), Elsa (*Lohengrin*), Sieglinde (*Walküre*), Elisabeth & Venus (*Tannhäuser*); WEBER: Rezia (*Oberon*); ZANDONAI: Francesca da Rimini. Also GIORDANO: Mme Sans-Gêne★. Recorded for: ORTF, RAI. Gives recitals. Appears with symphony orchestra. **Res:** V San Pantaleo Campano 24, Rome, Italy. Mgmt: LLF/USA; IMR/FRA; GLZ/FRA; SMD/FRG.

DE PHILIPPE, EDIS. Stages/produces opera. Also designs sets, costumes & stage-lighting and is a singer, actress & author. American. Founder/Director/Producer & Resident Stage Dir, Israel National Opera, Tel Aviv since 1947. Born 21 May 1917, New York. Husband Simha Evan-Zohar, occupation opera dir & administrator. Three children. Studied: NY Univ, Sorbonne Paris, Rome, incl music, piano, violin and voice. Operatic training as asst stage dir. **Operatic debut:** Israel 1945 as sop. Prev occupation: sang leading soprano roles USA, Europe, Central/So America.

Directed/produced op for major cos in ISR: Tel Aviv. **Operas staged for these cos incl** BIZET: *Carmen, Pêcheurs;* CILEA: *A. Lecouvreur;* DELIBES: *Lakmé;* DONIZETTI: *Don Pasquale, Elisir, Lucia;* GIORDANO: *Andrea Chénier;* GOLDMARK: *Königin von Saba★;* GOUNOD: *Faust, Roméo et Juliette;* HUMPERDINCK: *Hänsel und Gretel;* LEONCAVALLO: *Pagliacci;* MASCAGNI: *Amico Fritz, Cavalleria rusticana;* MASSENET: *Manon, Thaïs, Werther;* MOZART: *Don Giovanni, Nozze di Figaro;* MUSSORGSKY: *Khovanshchina;* OFFENBACH: *Contes d'Hoffmann, Périchole;* ORFF: *Carmina burana;* PONCHIELLI: *Gioconda;* PUCCINI: *Bohème, Gianni Schicchi, Butterfly, Manon Lescaut, Tabarro, Tosca, Turandot;* ROSSINI: *Barbiere di Siviglia;* SAINT-SAENS: *Samson et Dalila;* SMETANA: *Bartered Bride;* STRAUSS, J: *Fledermaus;* VERDI: *Aida, Ballo in maschera, Forza del destino, Nabucco, Otello, Rigoletto, Traviata, Trovatore.* **Res:** Tel Aviv, Israel.

DE RIDDER, ANTON. Lyric & dramatic tenor. Dutch. Resident mem: Staatsoper, Karlsruhe; Theater am Gärtnerplatz, Munich. Awards: title of Kammersänger.

Sang with major companies in AUS: Bregenz Fest; FR GER: Düsseldorf-Duisburg, Karlsruhe, Munich Staatsoper & Gärtnerplatz; GER DR: Berlin Komische Oper; HOL: Amsterdam; et al. **Roles with these companies incl** BIZET: Don José (*Carmen*); DONIZETTI: Edgardo (*Lucia*); JANACEK: Steva (*Jenufa*); STRAUSS, J: Alfred (*Fledermaus*); STRAUSS, R: Bacchus (*Ariadne auf Naxos*); VERDI: Alfredo (*Traviata*), Manrico (*Trovatore*); ZIMMERMANN: Desportes (*Soldaten*); et al. Also RAMEAU: Mercure (*Platée*).

DERKSEN, JAN. Dramatic baritone. Dutch. Born 14 Jul 1936, Alkmaar, Holland. Wife Terry Donkers, occupation secy. Studied: Amsterdam Consv of Music. **Debut:** Rigoletto, Trier Opera, FR Ger 1965.

Sang with major companies in AUS: Vienna Staatsoper; FR GER: Bielefeld, Darmstadt, Dortmund, Essen, Hamburg, Hannover, Kassel, Krefeld, Nürnberg; HOL: Amsterdam: ITA: Florence Comunale; UK: Glasgow Scottish; USSR: Kiev, Leningrad Kirov. **Roles with these companies incl** BERG: Wozzeck★; BIZET: Escamillo★ (*Carmen*); DONIZETTI Dott Malatesta★ & Don Pasquale★ (*Don Pasquale*), Belcore★ (*Elisir*), Enrico★ (*Lucia*); GIORDANO: Carlo Gérard (*Andrea Chénier*); PONCHIELLI: Barnaba (*Gioconda*); PUCCINI: Marcello (*Bohème*), Sharpless (*Butterfly*), Scarpia★ (*Tosca*); ROSSINI: Figaro★ (*Barbiere di Siviglia*), Iago★ (*Otello*); VERDI: Amonasro★ (*Aida*), Ezio★ (*Attila*), Renato★ (*Ballo in maschera*), Rodrigo★ (*Don Carlo*), Francesco Foscari★ (*Due Foscari*), Don Carlo★ (*Ernani*), Ford★ (*Falstaff*), Barone★ (*Giorno di regno*), Macbeth★, Nabucco★, Iago★ (*Otello*), Simon Boccanegra★, Germont★ (*Traviata*), Conte di Luna★ (*Trovatore*), Monforte★ (*Vespri*). Gives recitals. Appears with symphony orchestra. Mgmt: HRR/SWI.

DERMOTA, ANTON. Lyric tenor. Austrian. Resident mem: Staatsoper, Vienna. Born 4 Jun 1910, Kropa, Yugosl. Wife Hilda Berger-Weyerwald, occupation pianist. Three children. Studied: State Consv, Ljubljana; Marie Rado, Vienna. **Debut:** Alfredo (*Traviata*) Bratislava 1936. Awards: Ehrenmitglied & Ehrenring, Vienna Staatsoper; Komtur, Papal Gregorius Orden; Ehrenkreuz für Wissenschaft & Kunst l. Klasse, Austria; Goldene Ehrenmedaille, Vienna; Mozart Medal, Mozart Socy. **Sang with major companies in** ARG: Buenos Aires; AUS: Bregenz Fest, Graz, Salzburg Fest, Vienna Staatsoper & Volksoper; BEL: Brussels; CZE: Prague National; DEN: Copenhagen; FRA: Bordeaux, Lyon, Nice, Paris, Strasbourg; GRE: Athens National; FR GER: Bayreuth Fest, Berlin Deutsche Oper, Bielefeld, Cologne, Düsseldorf-Duisburg, Frankfurt, Munich Staatsoper, Stuttgart, Wiesbaden; GER DR: Berlin Komische Oper & Staatsoper, Dresden; HOL: Amsterdam; ITA: Florence Comunale, Milan La Scala, Naples, Rome Opera, Trieste, Turin; MON: Monte Carlo; POR: Lisbon; ROM: Bucharest; SPA: Barcelona; SWI: Geneva, Zurich; UK: Edinburgh Fest, London Royal; YUG: Dubrovnik, Zagreb, Belgrade. **Roles with these companies incl** BEETHOVEN: Florestan (*Fidelio*); BERG: Tambourmajor (*Wozzeck*); BERLIOZ: Faust (*Damnation de Faust*); BIZET: Haroun (*Djamileh*); BORODIN: Vladimir (*Prince Igor*); CORNELIUS: Nureddin (*Barbier von Bagdad*); DONIZETTI: Ernesto (*Don Pasquale*), Nemorino (*Elisir*); FLOTOW: Lionel (*Martha*); GLUCK: Admetos (*Alceste*); HANDEL: Sextus (*Giulio Cesare*), Grimwald (*Rodelinda*); HUMPERDINCK: Königssohn (*Königskinder*); JANACEK: Laca (*Jenufa*); MASSENET: Des Grieux (*Manon*); MOZART: Ferrando‡ (*Così fan tutte*), Don Ottavio‡ (*Don Giovanni*), Belmonte★ (*Entführung aus dem Serail*), Tamino★‡ (*Zauberflöte*); MUSSORGSKY: Shuisky (*Boris Godunov*); NICOLAI: Fenton (*Lustigen Weiber*); OFFENBACH: Hoffmann (*Contes d'Hoffmann*); PFITZNER: Palestrina★; PUCCINI: Rodolfo (*Bohème*), Pinkerton (*Butterfly*); ROSSINI: Almaviva (*Barbiere di Siviglia*); SHOSTAKOVICH: Zinovy (*Katerina Ismailova*);

SMETANA: Hans (*Bartered Bride*), Dalibor★; STRAUSS, J: Alfred‡ (*Fledermaus*); STRAUSS, R: Matteo‡ (*Arabella*), Flamand (*Capriccio*), Leukippos (*Daphne*), Ein Sänger★‡ (*Rosenkavalier*); STRAVINSKY: Oedipus; TCHAIKOVSKY: Lenski (*Eugene Onegin*); VERDI: Fenton (*Falstaff*), Duca di Mantova (*Rigoletto*), Gabriele (*Simon Boccanegra*), Alfredo (*Traviata*); WAGNER: David‡ (*Meistersinger*), Walther v d Vogelweide (*Tannhäuser*); WEBER: Max (*Freischütz*); WOLF-FERRARI: Florindo (*Donne curiose*). Also KIENZL: Mathias★ (*Evangelimann*); STRAUSS, R: Narraboth‡ (*Salome*); HINDEMITH: Hans Schwalb (*Mathis der Maler*). **World premieres:** MARTIN: Ferdinand (*Sturm*) Vienna Staatsoper 1956. Recorded for: Decca, Odeon. Film—Salzburg: Don Ottavio (*Don Giovanni*). Gives recitals. Appears with symphony orchestra. Coaches repertoire. On faculty of Hochschule für Musik, Vienna. **Res:** 36 Hagenbergg, Vienna, Austria.

DERNESCH, HELGA. Dramatic soprano. Austrian. Born 3 Feb 1939, Vienna. Husband Werner Krenn, occupation opera & concert singer. One child. Studied: Consv, Vienna. **Debut:** Marina (*Boris Godunov*) Stadttheater Bern, Switzerland 1961. **Sang with major companies in** AUS: Bregenz Fest, Salzburg Fest, Vienna Staatsoper & Volksoper; BEL: Brussels; FRA: Lyon, Nancy, Paris, Rouen, Toulouse; FR GER: Bayreuth Fest, Berlin Deutsche Oper, Cologne, Düsseldorf-Duisburg, Frankfurt, Hamburg, Hannover, Kiel, Munich Staatsoper, Stuttgart, Wiesbaden; HOL: Amsterdam; HUN: Budapest; ITA: Florence Comunale, Palermo, Trieste; POR: Lisbon; SPA: Barcelona; SWI: Geneva; UK: Edinburgh Fest, Glasgow Scottish, London Royal Opera; USA: Chicago, Dallas. **Roles with these companies incl** BEETHOVEN: Leonore★‡ (*Fidelio*); BERLIOZ: Cassandre★ (*Troyens*); BIZET: Micaëla (*Carmen*); DVORAK: Rusalka; EINEM: Lucille (*Dantons Tod*); LORTZING: Baronin Freimann (*Wildschütz*); MOZART: Fiordiligi (*Così fan tutte*), Donna Anna★ & Donna Elvira (*Don Giovanni*), Contessa (*Nozze di Figaro*); MUSSORGSKY: Marina (*Boris Godunov*); OFFENBACH: Antonia & Giulietta (*Contes d'Hoffmann*); PUCCINI: Mimi (*Bohème*), Manon Lescaut; RIMSKY-KORSAKOV: Fevronia (*Invisible City of Kitezh*); SMETANA: Marie (*Bartered Bride*); STRAUSS, J: Rosalinde (*Fledermaus*); STRAUSS, R: Gräfin (*Capriccio*), Chrysothemis★ (*Elektra*), Färberin★ (*Frau ohne Schatten*), Marschallin★ (*Rosenkavalier*); TCHAIKOVSKY: Lisa (*Pique Dame*); VERDI: Elisabetta (*Don Carlo*), Leonora (*Forza del destino*), Desdemona (*Otello*); WAGNER: Senta (*Fliegende Holländer*), Elsa (*Lohengrin*), Eva (*Meistersinger*), Sieglinde★ (*Walküre*), Brünnhilde (*Walküre★, Siegfried★‡, Götterdämmerung★‡*), Gutrune (*Götterdämmerung*), Elisabeth★‡ (*Tannhäuser*), Isolde★‡; WEBER: Agathe (*Freischütz*). **World premieres:** FORTN 4R: Elisabeth Tudor, Deutsche Oper, Berlin 1972. Recorded for: DG, EMI, Decca. **Res:** Schumannstr 20, Rheinbach, FR Ger. Mgmt: JUC/SWI.

DE ROSIER, G PHILIPPE. Scenic designer for opera, theater & television. Is a lighting designer;

also a painter. American. Resident designer, Starlight Theatre of Kansas City, MO. Born 7 May 1918, Springfield, MA, USA. Single. Studied: Yale Univ Drama School, USA. **Operatic debut:** *Finta giardiniera* Tanglewood, MA 1949. Previous occupation: HS art teacher.

Designed with major companies in USA: Kansas City, St Paul. **Operas with these companies incl** BIZET: *Carmen;* DONIZETTI: *Don Pasquale, Elisir;* FLOYD: *Of Mice and Men;* GIANNINI: *Taming of the Shrew*;* GIORDANO: *Andrea Chénier;* GOUNOD: *Faust;* MOZART: *Don Giovanni, Nozze di Figaro;* OFFENBACH: *Contes d'Hoffmann, Périchole*;* ORFF: *Kluge*;* PUCCINI: *Bohème, Gianni Schicchi*, Tosca*;* ROSSINI: *Barbiere di Siviglia*;* STRAUSS, R: *Ariadne auf Naxos;* VERDI: *Aida, Ballo in maschera, Otello, Trovatore;* WARD: *Crucible.*

DÉRY, GABRIELLA. Dramatic soprano. Hungarian. Resident mem: State Opera, Budapest. Born 12 Oct 1935, Budapest. Husband Andrew Jeszenszky, occupation master of ballet. Studied: Elisabeth Hoor Tempis. **Debut:** Elisabeth Szilágyi *(Hunyadi)* Hungarian State Opera 1958. Previous occupations: lecturer on music. Awards: Merited Artist, Hungarian People's Republic 1971; F Liszt Honor 1967.

Sang with major companies in BUL: Sofia; FIN: Helsinki; FR GER: Wiesbaden; GER DR: Berlin Staatsoper, Leipzig; HUN: Budapest; USSR: Moscow Bolshoi, Tbilisi; YUG: Belgrade. **Roles with these companies incl** BORODIN: Jaroslavna* *(Prince Igor)*, GLUCK: Iphigénie* *(Iphigénie en Tauride);* HANDEL: Rodelinda; JANACEK: Katya Kabanova*; MASCAGNI: Santuzza *(Cavalleria rusticana);* MONTEVERDI: Minerva *(Ritorno d'Ulisse);* MOZART: Fiordiligi* *(Così fan tutte),* Donna Anna* & Donna Elvira* *(Don Giovanni);* OFFENBACH: Giulietta* *(Contes d'Hoffmann);* PUCCINI: Tosca*, Turandot*; ROSSINI: Mathilde* *(Guillaume Tell);* STRAUSS, R: Ariadne* *(Ariadne auf Naxos),* Marschallin *(Rosenkavalier),* Salome*; SUCHON: Katrena* *(Whirlpool);* VERDI: Aida*‡, Amelia *(Ballo in maschera),* Elisabetta *(Don Carlo),* Donna Elvira* *(Ernani),* Alice Ford* *(Falstaff),* Leonora* *(Forza del destino),* Abigaille* *(Nabucco),* Desdemona *(Otello),* Violetta*‡ *(Traviata),* Leonora‡ *(Trovatore);* WOLF-FERRARI: Lucieta* *(Quattro rusteghi).* Also GOLDMARK: Königin von Saba*; ERKEL: Elisabeth* *(Hunyadi László),* sop role *(Brankovics).* Recorded for Hungaroton. Gives recitals. Appears with symphony orchestra. **Res:** Dianastr 33, Budapest, Hungary. **Mgmt:** ICM/HUN.

DE SICA, GENNARO. Lyric tenor. Italian. Born Naples. Studied: Consv U Giordano, Foggia; Accad S Cecilia, Carlo Tagliabue, Rome. **Debut:** Ferrando *(Così fan tutte)* Teatro Sperimentale Spoleto 1963. Previous occupations: bookkeeper at Bank of Naples; official in ministry, Rome. Awards: First Prize, Intl Compt of Voices F Vinas, Barcelona; Prize Intl Singing Compt, Toulouse; Prize, Intl Radio Compt, Munich; Winner, Spoleto Compt.

Sang with major companies in DEN: Copenhagen; FR GER: Bonn, Darmstadt, Frankfurt, Karlsruhe, Kiel, Mannheim, Nürnberg; ITA: Bologna, Florence Comunale, Genoa, Milan. **Roles with these companies incl** ADAM: Chapelou *(Postillon de Lonjumeau);* AUBER: Fra Diavolo* & Lorenzo *(Fra Diavolo);* CIMAROSA: Paolino* *(Matrimonio segreto);* DONIZETTI: Ernesto *(Don Pasquale),* Nemorino *(Elisir),* Tonio *(Fille du régiment);* FLOTOW: Lionel* *(Martha);* GOUNOD: Faust*; HAYDN: Nancio *(Infedeltà delusa);* JANACEK: Alyei *(From the House of the Dead),* Steva *(Jenufa);* MOZART: Ferrando *(Così fan tutte),* Don Ottavio* *(Don Giovanni),* Tamino* *(Zauberflöte);* PUCCINI: Rodolfo* *(Bohème),* Rinuccio* *(Gianni Schicchi),* Pinkerton* *(Butterfly);* ROSSINI: Almaviva* *(Barbiere di Siviglia),* Don Ramiro *(Cenerentola),* Comte Ory, Lindoro* *(Italiana in Algeri),* Narciso* *(Turco in Italia);* STRAUSS, J: Alfred* *(Fledermaus);* STRAUSS, R: Ein Sänger* *(Rosenkavalier);* TCHAIKOVSKY: Lenski* *(Eugene Onegin);* VERDI: Fenton *(Falstaff),* Ismaele* *(Nabucco),* Duca di Mantova* *(Rigoletto),* Alfredo *(Traviata);* WAGNER: David *(Meistersinger);* WOLF-FERRARI: Filipeto *(Quattro rusteghi).* Also CIMAROSA: Valerio* *(Marito disperato);* VERDI: Macduff* *(Macbeth).* Gives recitals. Appears with symphony orchestra. **Res:** Dieburg/Hessen, FR Ger or Naples, Italy.

DESIRON, MARCEL. Conductor of opera. Belgian. Art & Mus Dir, Centre Lyrique de Wallonie, Liège. Born 30 Nov 1913, Amay, Belgium. Widowed. Studied: Salzburg, Paul Bastide; also piano. Operatic training as repetiteur & asst cond at Opéra de Liège 1946-75. **Operatic debut:** Opéra de Liège, Théâtre Royal 1946.

Conducted with major companies in BEL: Liège; FRA: Bordeaux, Nancy; ROM: Bucharest. **Operas with these companies incl** ADAM: *Postillon de Lonjumeau, Si j'étais roi;* d'ALBERT: *Tiefland;* BECAUD: *Opéra d'Aran*;* BEETHOVEN: *Fidelio*;* BERLIOZ: *Damnation de Faust;* BIZET: *Carmen, Pêcheurs de perles;* BOIELDIEU: *Dame blanche;* BORODIN: *Prince Igor*;* CHARPENTIER: *Louise;* DEBUSSY: *Pelléas et Mélisande;* DELIBES: *Lakmé;* DONIZETTI: *Elisir, Favorite, Fille du régiment;* FALLA: *Retablo de Maese Pedro, Vida breve;* FLOTOW: *Martha;* GIORDANO: *Andrea Chénier;* GLUCK: *Iphigénie en Tauride, Orfeo ed Euridice;* GOUNOD: *Faust, Mireille*, Roméo et Juliette*;* IBERT: *Angélique*;* LALO: *Roi d'Ys*;* LEONCAVALLO: *Pagliacci*;* MASCAGNI: *Cavalleria rusticana;* MASSENET: *Don Quichotte, Hérodiade, Jongleur de Notre Dame, Manon, Portrait de Manon, Sappho, Thaïs, Werther*;* MENOTTI: *Consul;* MEYERBEER: *Africaine, Huguenots;* MOZART: *Così fan tutte, Don Giovanni*, Entführung aus dem Serail, Nozze di Figaro, Zauberflöte;* MUSSORGSKY: *Boris Godunov*;* OFFENBACH: *Contes d'Hoffmann*, Périchole, Mariage aux lanternes;* PONCHIELLI: *Gioconda;* POULENC: *Dialogues des Carmélites;* PROKOFIEV: *Love for Three Oranges;* PUCCINI: *Bohème*, Fanciulla del West*, Gianni Schicchi, Butterfly*, Manon Lescaut, Suor Angelica, Tosca, Turandot*;* RABAUD: *Mârouf;* RAVEL: *Enfant et les sortilèges, Heure espagnole;* ROSSINI: *Barbiere di Siviglia*, Guillaume Tell;* SAINT-SAENS: *Samson et Dalila;* SMETANA: *Bartered Bride;* STRAUSS, J: *Fledermaus;* STRAUSS, R: *Rosen-*

kavalier★; TCHAIKOVSKY: *Eugene Onegin, Pique Dame;* THOMAS: *Hamlet, Mignon;* VERDI: *Aida, Ballo in maschera, Don Carlo, Falstaff, Forza del destino, Macbeth, Nabucco, Otello, Rigoletto, Traviata, Trovatore;* WAGNER: *Fliegende Holländer, Lohengrin, Tannhäuser.* **World premieres:** DUBOIS: *Les Suisses* Opéra de Wallonie, Liège 1973. Teaches at Consv Royal de Musique, Liège.

DE STEFANO, FILIPPO JOSEPH. Lyric tenor. American. Resident mem: Israel National Opera, Tel Aviv. Wife Judith Lynn, occupation soprano. Studied: Arturo di Filippi, Miami, FL; Erma Mac Daniel; C Chiesa, Milan. **Debut:** Duca di Mantova (*Rigoletto*) Ferrara Opera, Italy 1965.
Sang with major companies in ISR: Tel Aviv; USA: Hartford, Miami, New York City Opera, Omaha, Philadelphia Grand, Seattle. **Roles with these companies incl** GOUNOD: Faust★; OFFENBACH: Hoffmann★; PUCCINI: Rodolfo★ (*Bohème*), Pinkerton★ (*Butterfly*); VERDI: Don Carlo★, Duca di Mantova★ (*Rigoletto*), Alfredo (*Traviata*), Manrico (*Trovatore*). Video—Teleprompter Cable TV: Alfredo (*Traviata*). Teaches voice. **Res:** Broadway & 73 St, New York, NY, USA.

DE TOMASI, GIUSEPPE. Stages/produces opera, theater & television; is also a writer. Italian. Born 19 Mar 1934, Milan. Single. Studied: Accad and Consv, Milan; incl music and voice. Operatic training as asst stage dir. **Operatic debut:** *Butterfly* Opera Como, Italy 1967. Previous occupation: doctor of chemistry. Awards: Noce d'oro, Lecco 1970; Verdi d'oro, Salsomaggiore Terme 1974.
Directed/produced opera for major companies in AUS: Bregenz Fest, Salzburg Fest; BEL: Brussels; FRA: Strasbourg; GRE: Athens National; FR GER: Essen, Wiesbaden; ITA: Genoa, Milan La Scala, Naples San Carlo, Palermo Massimo, Parma, Spoleto Fest, Trieste, Turin, Venice, Verona Arena; SPA: Barcelona; USA: Newark, Philadelphia Grand, San Francisco Opera. **Operas staged with these companies incl** BELLINI: *Norma★, Sonnambula;* CILEA: *Adriana Lecouvreur★;* DONIZETTI: *Don Pasquale★, Elisir★, Lucrezia Borgia★;* LEONCAVALLO: *Pagliacci★;* MASCAGNI: *Cavalleria rusticana★;* PONCHIELLI: *Gioconda★;* PUCCINI: *Bohème★, Tosca★;* ROSSINI: *Barbiere di Siviglia★, Cenerentola★;* VERDI: *Ballo in maschera★, Don Carlo★, Ernani★, Forza del destino★, Lombardi★, Luisa Miller★, Otello★, Simon Boccanegra★, Traviata★, Trovatore★.* Also GAZZANIGA: *Convitato di pietra.* **Operatic world premieres:** MANNINO: *Notti della paura* Lecco, Italy 1969. Operatic Video/Film—TV: *Life of Giacomo Puccini.* Opera libretti: MANNINO: *Ritratto di Dorian Gray.* **Res:** Mario Pagano 49, Milan, Italy.

DEUTEKOM, CRISTINA; née Stientje Engel. Coloratura soprano. Dutch. Born 28 Aug 1935, Amsterdam. Husband Jacob, occupation ret industrial photographer. One daughter. Studied: Studio of the Netherlands Opera. **Debut:** Königin der Nacht (*Zauberflöte*) Netherlands Opera, Amsterdam 1963. Awards: Knight in the Order of Oranje-Nassau, Queen Juliana; Rigoletto d'Oro, Mantua; Grand Prix du Disque; Singer of the Year, Milan 1973.

Sang with major companies in ARG: Buenos Aires; AUS: Bregenz Fest, Vienna Staatsoper & Volksoper; CAN: Toronto; FRA: Bordeaux, Paris; FR GER: Cologne, Munich Staatsoper, Nürnberg, Saarbrücken, Stuttgart; HOL: Amsterdam; ITA: Bologna, Florence Maggio & Comunale, Genoa, Naples, Parma, Rome Opera, Trieste, Turin, Venice; MEX: Mexico City; SPA: Barcelona; SWI: Zurich; UK: Glasgow Scottish, London Royal; USA: Dallas, Hartford, New Orleans, New York Met, San Francisco Opera. **Roles with these companies incl** BEETHOVEN: Marzelline (*Fidelio*); BELLINI: Norma★, Elvira★ (*Puritani*), Amina★ (*Sonnambula*); DONIZETTI: Lucia★; HANDEL: Alcina★; MENOTTI: Magda Sorel (*Consul*); MOZART: Fiordiligi (*Così fan tutte*), Donna Anna★ (*Don Giovanni*), Konstanze (*Entführung aus dem Serail*), Mme Herz (*Schauspieldirektor*), Königin der Nacht★‡ (*Zauberflöte*); ROSSINI: Anaï★ (*Moïse*); VERDI: Odabella‡ (*Attila*), Amelia★ (*Ballo in maschera*), Giselda‡ (*Lombardi*), Leonora★ (*Trovatore*), Elena★ (*Vespri*). Also ROSSINI: Armida★; WOLF-FERRARI: Marina (*Quattro rusteghi*). Recorded for: Philips, London, Angel/EMI. Video—Hamburg TV: Königin der Nacht (*Zauberflöte*). Gives recitals. Appears with symphony orchestra. **Res:** Amsterdam, Holland. Mgmt: RTB/FRG; CAM/USA.

DE VITA, LUCIANO. Scenic and costume designer for opera, theater. Is a lighting designer; also a painter & sculptor. Italian. Born 24 May 1929, Ancona. Studied: Accad di Belle Arti, Giorgio Morandi, Bologna. **Operatic debut:** sets, cost, *Turandot* Teatro Comunale, Bologna 1969. Awards: Venice Biennale 1960; Biennale d'Arte São Paulo, Brazil 1961; Exposition Intl de Gravure, Ljubljana 1961.
Designed for major companies in HUN: Budapest; ITA: Bologna, Genoa, Naples, Parma; YUG: Zagreb. **Operas designed for these companies incl** PROKOFIEV: *Fiery Angel;* PUCCINI: *Turandot;* VERDI: *Otello.* Also VECCHI: *Veglie di Siena.* Exhibitions of stage designs, paintings sculptures & graphics Rome, Tokyo, New York, Milan, Paris, etc; Galleria d'Arte Moderna, Bologna 1975. Teaches at Accad di Belle Arti di Brera, Milan. **Res:** V Guido Reni 7, Bologna, Italy.

DEVLIN, MICHAEL COLES. Bass-baritone. American. Born 27 Nov 1942, Chicago. Wife Martha, occupation exec secy. One child. Studied: Louisiana State Univ, Baton Rouge, USA; Norman Treigle, Daniel Ferro, USA. **Debut:** Spalanzani (*Contes d'Hoffmann*) New Orleans Opera 1963.
Sang with major companies in UK: Glyndebourne Fest, London Royal Opera; USA: Cincinnati, Fort Worth, Hawaii, Houston, Lake George, New Orleans, New York City Opera, Omaha, San Antonio, San Diego, Santa Fe, Seattle, Washington DC. **Roles with these companies incl** BERLIOZ: Méphistophélès★ (*Damnation de Faust*); BIZET: Escamillo★ (*Carmen*); BOITO: Mefistofele★; CHARPENTIER: Père★ (*Louise*); DEBUSSY: Golaud★ (*Pelléas et Mélisande*); DONIZETTI: Alfonso d'Este★ (*Lucrezia Borgia*); FLOYD: Olin Blitch★ (*Susannah*); GINAS-

TERA: Gian Corrado Orsini★ (*Bomarzo*); GOU-
NOD: Méphistophélès★ (*Faust*); HANDEL:
Giulio Cesare; MASSENET: Don Quichotte★;
MOZART: Don Alfonso★ (*Così fan tutte*), Don
Giovanni★, Conte Almaviva★ & Figaro★ (*Nozze di
Figaro*); MUSSORGSKY: Pimen★ (*Boris Godu-
nov*); OFFENBACH: Coppélius★ etc (*Contes
d'Hoffmann*); PUCCINI: Colline★ (*Bohème*);
RIMSKY-KORSAKOV: Roi Dodon★ (*Coq d'or*);
ROSSINI: Don Basilio★ (*Barbiere di Siviglia*);
STRAVINSKY: Creon (*Oedipus Rex*); TIP-
PETT: Hector★ (*King Priam*); VERDI: Amo-
nasro★ & Ramfis★ (*Aida*). Gives recitals. Appears
with symphony orchestra. Mgmt: CAM/USA;
AIM/UK.

DE WAART, EDO. Conductor of opera and symphony. Dutch. Music Dir, Rotterdam Philhar-
monic, Holland. Born 1 Jun 1941, Amsterdam.
Studied: Amsterdam Muzieklyceum, Haakon Sto-
tijn, Jaap Spaanderman; incl oboe. **Operatic debut:**
Spoleto Fest, Italy 1965. Symphonic debut: Radio
Phil Orch, Amsterdam 1964. Awards: Winner,
Mitropoulos Compt 1964; Edison Record Awds
1969, '71.
   Conducted with major companies in HOL: Am-
sterdam; ITA: Spoleto Fest; MON: Monte Carlo;
USA: Houston, Santa Fe; et al. **Operas with these
companies incl** BARTOK: *Bluebeard's Castle;*
BEETHOVEN: *Fidelio;* BIZET: *Carmen;* ME-
NOTTI: *Saint of Bleecker Street;* MOZART:
Don Giovanni; SCHOENBERG: *Erwartung;*
STRAUSS, R: *Rosenkavalier;* STRAVINSKY:
Rake's Progress; VERDI: *Aida, Falstaff, Tra-
viata;* WAGNER: *Fliegende Holländer, Lohen-
grin;* et al. Conducted major orch in Europe,
USA/Canada.

DEXTER, JOHN. Stages/produces opera, theater,
film & television. British. Dir of Prod, Metropoli-
tan Opera, New York. Also Asst Dir, National
Theatre, London 1963- . Born 2 Aug 1925, Derby,
U.K. Single. **Operatic debut:** Covent Garden, Lon-
don 1966. Previous occupation: theater & film
director.
   Directed/produced opera for major companies in
CZE: Prague National; FRA: Paris; FR GER:
Hamburg; UK: London Royal & English National;
USA: New York Met. **Operas staged with these
companies incl** BRITTEN: *Billy Budd★;* JANA-
CEK: *From the House of the Dead★;* MUS-
SORGSKY: *Boris Godunov★;* PENDERECKI:
Teufel von Loudun★; VERDI: *Ballo in maschera★,
Forza del destino★, Vespri★.* **Res:** New York, NY,
USA.

DIACONESCU, FLORIN. Lyric tenor. Romanian.
Resident mem: Romanian Opera, Bucharest. Born
2 Jul 1942, Busteni. Single. **Debut:** Gérald (*Lakmé*)
Romanian Opera 1970. Previous occupations: mu-
sic teacher.
   Sang with major companies in ITA: Florence
Maggio; ROM: Bucharest; YUG: Belgrade. **Roles
with these companies incl** DELIBES: Gérald★
(*Lakmé*); GOUNOD: Faust★; OFFENBACH:
Hoffmann★; PUCCINI: Rodolfo★ (*Bohème*), Ri-
nuccio★ (*Gianni Schicchi*); RIMSKY-KOR-
SAKOV Prince Vsevolod★ (*Invisible City of
Kitezh*); STRAUSS, J: Alfred★ (*Fledermaus*);
VERDI: Duca di Mantova★ (*Rigoletto*), Alfredo

(*Traviata*). Also DONIZETTI: Edgardo (*Lucia*);
TCHAIKOVSKY: Lenski (*Eugene Onegin*).
World premieres: BENTOIU: Hamlet, Romanian
TV 1972. Video/Film: Hamlet. Gives recitals. Ap-
pears with symphony orchestra. **Res:** 17 Pajurei St,
Bucharest 8, Romania. Mgmt: RIA/ROM.

DIAKOV, ANTON. Bass. Bulgarian. Resident
mem: Basel Opera, Switzerland. Born 9 Dec 1934,
Sofia, Bulgaria. Single. Studied: Prof Assen Dimi-
troff, Sofia; Mo Luigi Ricci, Accad Santa Cecilia,
Rome Opera Studio, Rome. **Debut:** Rangoni (*Boris
Godunov*) Frankfurt Opera 1963. Previous occu-
pations: licensed architect, Sofia & Rome 1958-62.
Awards: First Prize Ntl Music Compt, Sofia 1954,
1956, 1957.
   Sang with major companies in AUS: Salzburg
Fest, Vienna Volksoper; FRA: Marseille; GRE:
Athens Fest; FR GER: Frankfurt, Kiel, Mann-
heim, Stuttgart; ITA: Parma, Turin; POR: Lisbon;
SPA: Barcelona; SWI: Basel, Geneva, Zurich;
USA: New York Met. **Roles with these companies
incl** BARTOK: Bluebeard★; BEETHOVEN: Don
Pizarro★ & Rocco★ (*Fidelio*); BELLINI: Rodolfo
(*Sonnambula*); BIZET: Escamillo (*Carmen*);
BORODIN: Prince Igor & Galitzky (*Prince Igor*);
DALLAPICCOLA: Prigioniero ; DEBUSSY:
Golaud★ & Arkel★ (*Pelléas et Mélisande*); DONI-
ZETTI: Baldassare‡ (*Favorite*); FALLA: Don
Quixote★ (*Retablo de Maese Pedro*); GLINKA:
Ivan Sussanin (*Life for the Tsar*); GOUNOD:
Méphistophélès★ (*Faust*); HINDEMITH: Profes-
sor★ (*Hin und zurück*); JANACEK: Shishkov★
(*From the House of the Dead*); MONTEVERDI:
Orfeo★‡; MOZART: Osmin (*Entführung aus dem
Serail*), Sarastro★ (*Zauberflöte*); MUS-
SORGSKY: Boris★ & Varlaam★‡ & Pimen★ (*Boris
Godunov*), Dosifei (*Khovanshchina*); OFFEN-
BACH: Coppélius etc★ (*Contes d'Hoffmann*);
ORFF: König (*Kluge*); PONCHIELLI: Alvise★‡
(*Gioconda*); PUCCINI: Colline★ (*Bohème*); RIM-
SKY-KORSAKOV: Juri Vsevolodovic (*Invisible
City of Kitezh*); ROSSINI: Don Basilio (*Barbiere
di Siviglia*); VERDI: Ramfis (*Aida*), Philip II★ &
Grande Inquisitore★ (*Don Carlo*), Padre Guar-
diano★ (*Forza del destino*), Banquo (*Macbeth*),
Zaccaria★ (*Nabucco*), Fiesco★ (*Simon Bocca-
negra*), Procida (*Vespri*); WAGNER: Daland
(*Fliegende Holländer*), König Heinrich★ (*Lohen-
grin*), Pogner (*Meistersinger*), Gurnemanz (*Parsi-
fal*), Hunding (*Walküre*), König Marke★ (*Tristan
und Isolde*); WEBER: Kaspar★ (*Freischütz*). Also
CAVALIERI: Consiglio (*Rappresentazione*);
DVORAK: Wassermann (*Rusalka*); TCHAI-
KOVSKY: Kotchubey (*Mazeppa*), Gremin (*Eugene Onegin* EGK: Stadthauptmann (*Revisor*).
World premieres: ORFF: Anachoret (*De temporum fine comedia*) Salzburg Fest 1973. Recorded
for: Decca, Angel, EMI, DG, Pick-Klassik.
Film—Bavaria Cosmotel: Zuniga (*Carmen*). Gives
recitals. Appears with symphony orchestra. **Res:**
Flora Str 3, CH-4057 Basel, Switzerland. Mgmt:
JUC/SWI.

DÍAZ, JUSTINO. Bass. Puerto Rican. Resident
member: Metropolitan Opera, New York. Born 29
January 1940, San Juan, Puerto Rico. Wife Anna
Aragno, occupation ballet dancer. Two children.
Studied: Frederick Jagel, Boris Goldovsky, Au-

gusto Rodriguez. **Debut:** Ben (*Telephone*) Polytech Inst, San German, PR 1957. Awards: Handel Medallion, City of New York 1966; Family of Man Awd.

Sang with major companies in ARG: Buenos Aires; AUS: Salzburg Fest, Vienna Staatsoper; CAN: Ottawa, Toronto, Vancouver; FR GER: Hamburg; ITA: Milan La Scala, Spoleto Fest, Trieste; SPA: Barcelona; USA: Baltimore, Boston, Dallas, Fort Worth, Memphis, Miami, New Orleans, New York Met & City Opera, Pittsburgh, Portland, Washington DC. **Roles with these companies incl** BELLINI: Sir George (*Puritani*), Rodolfo★ (*Sonnambula*); BERLIOZ: Méphistophélès (*Damnation de Faust*); BIZET: Escamillo★ (*Carmen*); BOITO: Mefistofele; CATALANI: Stromminger‡ (*Wally*); CHERUBINI: Creon (*Medea*); DONIZETTI: Raimondo★‡ (*Lucia*); GOUNOD: Méphistophélès★ (*Faust*); HANDEL: Zoroastro (*Orlando furioso*); MEYERBEER: Marcel★ (*Huguenots*); MOZART: Don Alfonso (*Così fan tutte*), Don Giovanni★, Figaro★ (*Nozze di Figaro*), Sarastro (*Zauberflöte*); PAISIELLO: Teodoro (*Re Teodoro in Venezia*); PERGOLESI: Uberto (*Serva padrona*); PONCHIELLI: Alvise (*Gioconda*); PUCCINI: Colline★ (*Bohème*), Scarpia★ (*Tosca*); PURCELL: Aeneas (*Dido and Aeneas*); ROSSINI: Don Basilio★ (*Barbiere di Siviglia*), Maometto II★ (*Assedio di Corinto*); VERDI: Ramfis★ (*Aida*), Attila★, Philip II★ & Grande Inquisitore (*Don Carlo*), Padre Guardiano★ (*Forza del destino*), Conte Walter★ (*Luisa Miller*), Zaccaria★ (*Nabucco*), Procida★ (*Vespri*). Also VERDI: Paolo★ (*Simon Boccanegra*); TCHAIKOVSKY: Gremin (*Eugene Onegin*); BEETHOVEN: Don Fernando★ (*Fidelio*); GOUNOD: Frère Laurent★ (*Roméo et Juliette*); ROSSINI: Pacuvio‡ (*Pietra del paragone*). **World premieres:** BARBER: Antony (*Antony and Cleopatra*) Metropolitan Opera 1966; GINASTERA: Count Cenci (*Beatrix Cenci*) Washington, DC, Opera Society 1971. Recorded for: London, Angel, Vanguard, RCA, ABC. Video/Film: Méphistophélès (*Faust*); Escamillo (*Carmen*); Aeneas (*Dido and Aeneas*). Gives recitals. Appears with symphony orchestra. **Res:** New York, NY, USA. Mgmt: BAR/USA; CAB/SPA.

DICKIE, BRIAN JAMES. British. Opera Mng, Glyndebourne Festival Opera, Lewes, Sussex UK; also Adm of Glyndebourne Touring Opera. Additional adm positions: Casting Adv, National Lyric Centre, Angers, France. Born 23 Jul 1941, Newark, UK. Wife Victoria T S. Three children. Studied: Trinity Coll, Dublin, Ireland. Previous positions, primarily adm & musical: Art Dir, Wexford Festival Opera, Ireland 1967-73. Started with present company 1962 as Adm Asst, in present position since 1967. Initiated major policy changes including expansion of Wexford Festival into present format; planning & organizing Glyndebourne Touring Opera as first administrator. Mem of Opera Coord Commtt, Covent Garden/English National Opera.

DICKIE, MURRAY. Lyric tenor. British. Resident mem: Staatsoper, Vienna. Born 3 Apr 1924, Scotland. Wife Maureen. Four children. Studied: Prof Stefan Pollmann, Vienna & London; Dino Bor-

gioli. **Debut:** Almaviva (*Barbiere di Siviglia*) Cambridge Theatre, London 1947. Awards: Kammersänger, Vienna; Cross of Honor, First Class, Arts and Sciences, Austria.

Sang with major companies in ARG: Buenos Aires; AUS: Bregenz Fest, Graz, Salzburg Fest, Vienna Staatsoper & Volksoper; CAN: Montreal/Quebec; DEN: Copenhagen; FRA: Marseille, Nice, Paris; FR GER: Berlin Deutsche Oper, Bielefeld, Cologne, Düsseldorf-Duisburg, Hamburg, Krefeld, Munich Staatsoper, Wiesbaden; HOL: Amsterdam; HUN: Budapest; ISR: Tel Aviv; ITA: Florence Maggio, Milan La Scala, Rome Opera, Turin, Venice; MON: Monte Carlo; NOR: Oslo; POR: Lisbon; SPA: Barcelona; SWI: Geneva, Zurich; UK: Edinburgh Fest, Glyndebourne Fest, London Royal; USSR: Moscow Bolshoi; USA: Boston, Chicago, Dallas, Fort Worth, New York Met; YUG: Dubrovnik, Zagreb. **Roles with these companies incl** ADAM: Chapelou★ (*Postillon de Lonjumeau*); BEETHOVEN: Florestan (*Fidelio*); BERG: Hauptmann (*Wozzeck*); BERLIOZ: Faust (*Damnation de Faust*); BUSONI: Leandro★ (*Arlecchino*); CORNELIUS: Nureddin (*Barbier von Bagdad*); DONIZETTI: Ernesto★ (*Don Pasquale*), Nemorino★ (*Elisir*); FLOTOW: Lionel (*Martha*); GOUNOD: Faust; HUMPERDINCK: Hexe★ (*Hänsel und Gretel*); LORTZING: Peter Ivanov (*Zar und Zimmermann*); MONTEVERDI: Ulisse (*Ritorno d'Ulisse*); MOZART: Don Ottavio★ (*Don Giovanni*), Pedrillo★ (*Entführung aus dem Serail*), Tamino★ (*Zauberflöte*); NICOLAI: Fenton (*Lustigen Weiber*); ORFF: Solo (*Carmina burana*); POULENC: Chevalier de la Force (*Dialogues des Carmélites*); PUCCINI: Rinuccio (*Gianni Schicchi*), Pinkerton (*Butterfly*); RIMSKY-KORSAKOV: Astrologue (*Coq d'or*); ROSSINI: Almaviva (*Barbiere di Siviglia*), Don Ramiro (*Cenerentola*); SMETANA: Wenzel★ (*Bartered Bride*); STRAUSS, J: Alfred★ (*Fledermaus*); STRAUSS, R: Merkur (*Liebe der Danae*), Ein Sänger (*Rosenkavalier*), Narraboth (*Salome*); VERDI: Fenton (*Falstaff*), Duca di Mantova (*Rigoletto*), Alfredo (*Traviata*); WAGNER: David★ (*Meistersinger*), Walther v d Vogelweide (*Tannhäuser*); WOLF-FERRARI: Filipeto★ (*Quattro rusteghi*). Also MUSSORGSKY: Dimitri (*Boris Godunov*); STRAUSS, R: Ital Sänger (*Capriccio*). **World premieres:** MARTIN: Trinculo (*Sturm*) Vienna 1956; BLISS: Padre (*Olympians*) Covent Garden, London 1949. Recorded for: CBS, HMV, Philips, Decca/London, Westminster. Gives recitals. Appears with symphony orchestra. **Res:** Baden/Vienna, Austria.

DIDIER, LAURA GAMBARDELLA. Dramatic mezzo-soprano. Chilean. Resident mem: Teatro dell'Opera, Caracalla, Rome. Born 9 Jul 1933, Santiago, Chile. Husband Gabriele Gambardella, occupation industrialist. Studied: Margarita Salvi, Chile; Consv Cattolico, Santiago de Chile; Mercedes Llopart, Mo Narducci, Mo Wodnansky, Italy. **Debut:** Fidalma (*Matrimonio segreto*) Teatro Municipale Santiago, Chile 1949.

Sang with major companies in AUS: Salzburg Fest; FIN: Helsinki; FRA: Bordeaux, Lyon, Marseille, Nice; GRE: Athens National; FR GER: Mannheim; ITA: Milan, Naples, Palermo, Rome Opera & Caracalla, Trieste, Turin, Venice; NOR:

Oslo; POR: Lisbon; SPA: Majorca; SWI: Geneva. **Roles with these companies incl** BARTOK: Judith★ (*Bluebeard's Castle*); BELLINI: Adalgisa★ (*Norma*); BIZET: Carmen; BORODIN: Kontchakovna (*Prince Igor*); CIMAROSA: Fidalma (*Matrimonio segreto*); DONIZETTI: Léonore (*Favorite*); MASCAGNI: Beppe★‡ (*Amico Fritz*); MONTEVERDI: Poppea (*Incoronazione di Poppea*); MUSSORGSKY: Marina (*Boris Godunov*), Marfa (*Khovanshchina*); PONCHIELLI: Laura & La Cieca★ (*Gioconda*); ROSSINI: Sinaïde (*Moïse*), Zaida (*Turco in Italia*); SAINT-SAENS: Dalila; SPONTINI: High Priestess (*Vestale*); STRAUSS: Herodias (*Salome*); VERDI: Amneris★‡ (*Aida*), Ulrica (*Ballo in maschera*), Eboli (*Don Carlo*), Preziosilla (*Forza del destino*), Azucena★‡ (*Trovatore*); WAGNER: Ortrud (*Lohengrin*), Waltraute (*Götterdämmerung*), Venus (*Tannhäuser*), Brangäne (*Tristan und Isolde*). Also VIVALDI: Giunone (*Fida ninfa*); MASCAGNI: Santuzza★ (*Cavalleria rusticana*); VERDI: Fenena★ (*Nabucco*). **World premieres:** CHAILLY: Vagabonda (*Riva delle sirti*) Comunale di Treviso 1971. Recorded for: Angel, Decca. Gives recitals. Appears with symphony orchestra. **Res:** V Luigi Capuana 10, Rome, Italy.

DI FRANCO, LORETTA ELIZABETH. Lyric coloratura soprano. American. Resident mem: Mètropolitan Opera, New York. Born 28 Oct 1942, New York. Husband Anthony Martin Pinto, occupation hair stylist. One daughter. Studied: Maud Webber, Walter Taussig, New York. **Debut:** Chloë (*Pique Dame*) Metropolitan Opera 1965. Previous occupations: secy. Awards: First Prize, Met Op Ntl Counc Aud 1965; M B Rockefeller Fund Grant 1963; Kathryn Long Course Schlshp, Met Opera. **Sang with major companies in** USA: New York Met. **Roles with this company incl** DONIZETTI: Lucia; MOZART: Zerlina★ (*Don Giovanni*); PUCCINI: Mimi★ & Musetta★ (*Bohème*), Lauretta★ (*Gianni Schicchi*); VERDI: Oscar★ (*Ballo in maschera*). Gives recitals. Appears with symphony orchestra. **Res:** New York, NY, USA. Mgmt: RAB/AUS.

DIGBY, DESMOND WARD. Scenic and costume designer for opera & theater. Is also a painter & illustrator. Australian. Born 4 Jan 1933, Auckland, New Zealand. Single. Studied: Slade School of Art, London. Prof training: New Zealand Players. **Operatic debut:** Australian Elizabethan Trust Opera Co, Adelaide 1960. Theater debut: Elizabethan Theatre Trust, Brisbane 1961. Previous adm positions in opera: Resident Designer, Australian Opera, Sydney 1967-69. **Designed for major companies in** AUSTRL: Sydney. **Operas designed for these companies incl** BRITTEN: *Rape of Lucretia*★; DELIBES: *Lakmé*★; LEONCAVALLO: *Pagliacci*★; MASCAGNI: *Cavalleria rusticana*★; MOZART: *Così fan tutte*★; PUCCINI: *Fanciulla del West, Gianni Schicchi*★, *Suor Angelica*★, *Tabarro*★; STRAUSS, J: *Fledermaus*; VERDI: *Ballo in maschera, Don Carlo, Traviata;* WOLF-FERRARI: *Quattro rusteghi*. **Operatic world premieres:** FARQUHAR/MARSH: *Unicorn for Christmas* New Zealand Opera, Wellington 1962. Exhibitions of stage designs & paintings Sydney, Melbourne, Brisbane, Perth, Canberra & Newcastle 1959-65.

Res: 67 Carabella St, Kirribilli/Sydney, 2061 NSW, Australia.

DI GIUSEPPE, ENRICO. Lyric tenor. American. Resident mem: Metropolitan Opera, New York; New York City Opera. Born 14 Oct 1938, Philadelphia. Wife Lorna, occupation soprano. Studied: Curtis Inst of Music, Richard Bonelli, Philadelphia; Juilliard School of Music, Hans Heinz, New York. **Debut:** Des Grieux (*Manon*) New Orleans Opera 1959. **Sang with major companies in** CAN: Ottawa, Toronto, Vancouver; MEX: Mexico City; USA: Baltimore, Boston, Cincinnati, Dallas, Fort Worth, Hartford, Houston, Memphis, Milwaukee Florentine, Newark, New Orleans, New York Met & City Opera, Omaha, Philadelphia Grand & Lyric, Pittsburgh, San Antonio, San Francisco Spring, Washington DC. **Roles with these companies incl** BELLINI: Pollione‡ (*Norma*), Lord Arthur★ (*Puritani*), Elvino★ (*Sonnambula*); DONIZETTI: Riccardo★ (*Anna Bolena*), Ernesto★ (*Don Pasquale*), Nemorino★ (*Elisir*), Tonio★ (*Fille du régiment*), Edgardo★ (*Lucia*), Leicester★ (*Maria Stuarda*), Roberto Devereux★; GOUNOD: Faust★, Roméo★; MASCAGNI: Turiddu★ (*Cavalleria rusticana*); MASSENET: Des Grieux★ (*Manon*), Werther★; MENOTTI: Michele (*Saint of Bleecker Street*); MOZART: Ferrando (*Così fan tutte*), Don Ottavio★ (*Don Giovanni*), Tamino (*Zauberflöte*); ORFF: Solo (*Carmina burana*); PUCCINI: Rodolfo★ (*Bohème*), Rinuccio (*Gianni Schicchi*), Pinkerton★ (*Butterfly*), Cavaradossi★ (*Tosca*); RIMSKY-KORSAKOV: Astrologue★ (*Coq d'or*); ROSSINI: Almaviva★ (*Barbiere di Siviglia*), Don Ramiro (*Cenerentola*), Lindoro★ (*Italiana in Algeri*); STRAUSS, R: Flamand (*Capriccio*), Ein Sänger★ (*Rosenkavalier*); VERDI: Riccardo★ (*Ballo in maschera*), Ismaele (*Nabucco*), Duca di Mantova★ (*Rigoletto*), Alfredo★ (*Traviata*). Recorded for: ABC. Video/Film: (*Golden Child*). Gives recitals. Appears with symphony orchestra. **Res:** Pompton Lakes, NJ, USA. Mgmt: CAM/USA.

DILIBERTO, PIETRO. Italian. Secy Gen, Teatro Massimo, Piazza G Verdi, Palermo. Born 21 Jun 1931, Palermo. Wife Ilva Ligabue, occupation opera singer. Studied law, Univ of Palermo. Background primarily adm & theatrical. Started with present company 1955 as head of press office & art secy, in present position since 1961. **Res:** Palermo, Italy.

DIMA, ELENA. Dramatic soprano. Romanian. Resident mem: Romanian Opera, Bucharest. Born Bucharest. Married. Studied: Consv, Profs Constanta Badescu and Petre Stefanescu-Goanga, Bucharest. **Debut:** Contessa (*Nozze di Figaro*) Romanian Opera 1967. **Sang with major companies in** BEL: Liège; BUL: Sofia; CZE: Brno; ROM: Bucharest; USSR: Tbilisi. **Roles with these companies incl** BEETHOVEN: Leonore★ (*Fidelio*); BORODIN: Jaroslavna★ (*Prince Igor*); MASCAGNI: Santuzza★ (*Cavalleria rusticana*); PUCCINI: Tosca★, Turandot★; STRAUSS, R: Marschallin (*Rosenkavalier*); TCHAIKOVSKY: Tatiana (*Eugene Onegin*); VERDI: Aida★, Amelia★ (*Ballo in maschera*), Elisabetta★ (*Don Carlo*), Leonora★

(*Trovatore*); WAGNER: Senta★ (*Fliegende Holländer*), Elsa★ (*Lohengrin*), Eva (*Meistersinger*), Elisabeth (*Tannhäuser*). Recorded for: Electrecord. **Res:** 3 Bucsanesti St, Bucharest 7, Romania. Mgmt: RIA/ROM; GGM/FRG.

DIMITROVA, ANASTASIA ILIEVA. Spinto. Yugoslavian. Resident mem: National Opera House, Skopje, Yugoslavia. Born 16 Nov 1940, Pernik, Bulgaria. Husband Branislav Pop-Gligorov, occupation musicologist. One daughter, one son. Studied: Prof Zvetana Djakovitch, Bulgarian State Consv, Sofia; Prof Miroslav Fritz Lunzer, Zagreb. **Debut:** Abigaille (*Nabucco*) National Opera House, Skopje 1965. Awards: "Mejor voz" Francisco Vinas Compt, Barcelona 1969; Third Prize Voci Verdiane Compt & Golden Mdl, Busseto, Italy 1968.
Sang with major companies in BUL: Sofia; FRA: Strasbourg; FR GER: Karlsruhe, Mannheim, Stuttgart; YUG: Zagreb, Belgrade. **Roles with these companies incl** BELLINI: Norma★; BIZET: Micaëla (*Carmen*); BORODIN: Jaroslavna (*Prince Igor*); DVORAK: Rusalka; GERSHWIN: Bess★; GLUCK: Euridice; GOUNOD: Marguerite (*Faust*); PUCCINI: Mimi★ (*Bohème*), Cio-Cio-San (*Butterfly*), Giorgetta (*Tabarro*); PURCELL: Dido; RIMSKY-KORSAKOV: Olga★ (*Ivan the Terrible*); SMETANA: Marie★ (*Bartered Bride*); TCHAIKOVSKY: Tatiana (*Eugene Onegin*); VERDI: Aida★, Elisabetta (*Don Carlo*), Abigaille★ (*Nabucco*), Leonora (*Trovatore*). Also PROSEV: Magda★ (*Pajazina*). **World premieres:** PROKOPIEV: Simka (*Razdelba*) National Opera Skopje 1971. Gives recitals. Appears with symphony orchestra. Teaches voice. Coaches repertoire. **Res:** ul Rudarska 16 G Petrov, Skopje, Yugoslavia. Mgmt: KAY/USA.

DI PIANDUNI, OSVALDO; né José Osvaldo Di Pianduni. Dramatic tenor & spinto. Uruguayan. Resident mem: Gärtnerplatztheater, Munich. Born 16 Mar 1939, Montevideo, Uruguay. Wife Annette, occupation ballet dancer. Studied: Pasquale Amato, Lotte Bernhard, Montevideo, Uruguay; Clemens Glettenberg, Cologne; Ettore Campogalliani, Mantua, Italy. **Debut:** Lenski (*Eugene Onegin*) Klagenfurt Opera, Austria 1968.
Sang with major companies in FR GER: Bielefeld, Cologne, Munich Gärtnerplatz. **Roles with these companies incl** AUBER: Fra Diavolo★; BIZET: Don José (*Carmen*); DONIZETTI: Edgardo (*Lucia*); GIORDANO: Andrea Chénier; LORTZING: Chateauneuf (*Zar und Zimmermann*); MASCAGNI: Turiddu (*Cavalleria rusticana*); MOZART: Belmonte (*Entführung aus dem Serail*), Tamino (*Zauberflöte*); OFFENBACH: Hoffmann; PUCCINI: Rodolfo (*Bohème*), Pinkerton★ (*Butterfly*), Cavaradossi (*Tosca*), Calaf (*Turandot*); SMETANA: Hans (*Bartered Bride*); STRAUSS, R: Ein Sänger★ (*Rosenkavalier*); TCHAIKOVSKY: Lenski (*Eugene Onegin*); VERDI: Riccardo (*Ballo in maschera*), Duca di Mantova (*Rigoletto*), Alfredo (*Traviata*), Manrico (*Trovatore*). Gives recitals. Appears with symphony orchestra. **Res:** Klenze Str 39, 8 Munich 5, FR Ger. Mgmt: ZFR/FRG.

DI STEFANO, GIUSEPPE. Tenor. Italian. Born 24 Jul 1921, Motta S Anastasia, Sicily, Italy. Wife Maria Girolami. Three children. Studied: Luigi Montesanto, Milan. **Debut:** Des Grieux (*Manon*) Reggio Emilia, Italy 1946. Awards: Commendatore della Repubblica Italiana.
Sang with major companies in ARG: Buenos Aires; AUS: Vienna Staatsoper & Volksoper; BEL: Brussels; BRA: Rio de Janeiro; CZE: Prague National; FRA: Paris; FR GER: Berlin Deutsche Oper; GER DR: Berlin Staatsoper; HOL: Amsterdam; HUN: Budapest; ITA: Bologna, Florence Maggio & Comunale, Genoa, Milan La Scala, Naples, Palermo, Parma, Rome Opera & Caracalla, Trieste, Turin, Venice, Verona Arena; MEX: Mexico City; MON: Monte Carlo; POR: Lisbon; ROM: Bucharest; S AFR: Johannesburg; SPA: Barcelona; SWE: Stockholm; UK: Edinburgh Fest, London Royal Opera; USA: New York Met, San Francisco Opera. **Roles with these companies incl** BELLINI: Elvino‡ (*Sonnambula*); BIZET: Don José★‡ (*Carmen*), Nadir (*Pêcheurs de perles*); BOITO: Faust‡ (*Mefistofele*); CILEA: Maurizio (*A. Lecouvreur*); DONIZETTI: Nemorino★‡ (*Elisir*), Edgardo‡ (*Lucia*); GIORDANO: Andrea Chénier; GOUNOD: Faust; LEONCAVALLO: Canio★‡ (*Pagliacci*); MASCAGNI: Fritz (*Amico Fritz*), Turiddu★‡ (*Cavalleria rusticana*); MASSENET: Des Grieux‡ (*Manon*), Werther; MONTEVERDI: Orfeo; OFFENBACH: Hoffmann; PONCHIELLI: Enzo‡ (*Gioconda*); PUCCINI: Rodolfo★‡ (*Bohème*), Dick Johnson (*Fanciulla del West*), Rinuccio (*Gianni Schicchi*), Pinkerton‡ (*Butterfly*), Des Grieux‡ (*Manon Lescaut*), Luigi★‡ (*Tabarro*), Cavaradossi‡ (*Tosca*), Calaf (*Turandot*); ROSSINI: Almaviva (*Barbiere di Siviglia*); SMETANA: Hans (*Bartered Bride*); TCHAIKOVSKY: Lenski (*Eugene Onegin*); THOMAS: Wilhelm Meister (*Mignon*); VERDI: Radames (*Aida*), Riccardo‡ (*Ballo in maschera*), Fenton (*Falstaff*), Don Alvaro‡ (*Forza del destino*), Rodolfo (*Luisa Miller*), Otello, Duca di Mantova‡ (*Rigoletto*), Alfredo‡ (*Traviata*), Manrico‡ (*Trovatore*); WAGNER: Rienzi. Recorded for: EMI, RCA, London (Decca). Gives recitals. Teaches voice. **Res:** V Omenoni 2, Milan, Italy. Mgmt: GOR/UK.

DITTERT, CARLOS JOÃO. Bass. Brazilian. Resident mem: Teatro Municipal, Rio de Janeiro. Born 5 Nov 1935, Curitiba, Paraná, Brazil. Wife Lucia, occupation music teacher. One child. Studied: Centro Lirico do Paraná, Dulce Odarari; Escola Nacional de Musica, Maria Bezerra; Fernando Araujo, Dra Stani Zawadska. **Debut:** Don Basilio (*Barbiere di Siviglia*) Rio de Janeiro 1969. Awards: First Prize B Gigli; First Prize Carmen Gomes; First Prize Nacional Conc, Rio de Janeiro; Third Prize Vera Janacopulos; Fourth Prize Intl Concours 1969; Hon Causa, Acad Brasileira de Belas Artes.
Sang with major companies in BRA: Rio de Janeiro. **Roles with these companies incl** MOZART: Sarastro★ (*Zauberflöte*); PUCCINI: Colline★ (*Bohème*); ROSSINI: Don Basilio (*Barbiere di Siviglia*). Also GOMES: Don Antonio★ (*Guarany*), Goitacaz★ (*Schiavo*); DONIZETTI: Raimondo (*Lucia*). **World premieres:** SIQUEIRA: Cangaceiro (*Compadecida*) Rio de Janeiro 1965; VILLA-LOBOS: Dr Alex (*Izath*) Rio 1963; MESQUITA: Comte (*Noite do Castelo*) Rio

1963. Video—TV Globo: (*Traviata*); (*Bohème*). Gives recitals. Appears with symphony orchestra. Teaches voice. On faculty of Inst Villa-Lobos. **Res:** rua São Francisco Xavier 121, 306 Tijuca, Rio de Janeiro.

DI VIRGILIO, NICOLAS. Lyric tenor. American. Born North Tonawanda, NY, USA. Wife Gabriella W Dreher, occupation coll academic advisor. Two children. Studied: Eastman School of Music, Rochester, NY; Met Opera Studio & Kathryn Long School, New York; John Howell, Daniel Ferro. **Debut:** Pinkerton (*Butterfly*) Chautauqua Opera, NY 1961. Previous occupations: lumberjack, clothing salesman.
Sang with major companies in BEL: Brussels; FRA: Lyon; HOL: Amsterdam; USA: Baltimore, Cincinnati, Hartford, Houston, Lake George, Miami, Milwaukee Florentine, New Orleans, New York Met & City Opera, Pittsburgh, Portland, St Paul, San Antonio, San Diego, San Francisco Opera, Seattle, Washington DC. **Roles with these companies incl** BERLIOZ: Faust (*Damnation de Faust*); BIZET: Don José★ (*Carmen*); BOITO: Faust★ (*Mefistofele*); DONIZETTI: Ernesto (*Don Pasquale*), Edgardo (*Lucia*), Roberto Devereux★; FLOTOW: Lionel (*Martha*); GOUNOD: Faust★; JANACEK: Laca★ (*Jenufa*); LEONCAVALLO: Canio (*Pagliacci*); MASCAGNI: Turiddu★ (*Cavalleria rusticana*); MENOTTI: Michele★ (*Saint of Bleecker Street*); MOZART: Ferrando (*Così fan tutte*), Don Ottavio (*Don Giovanni*), Idomeneo; OFFENBACH: Hoffmann★; ORFF: Solo★ (*Carmina burana*); PUCCINI: Rodolfo★ (*Bohème*), Rinuccio★ (*Gianni Schicchi*), Pinkerton★ (*Butterfly*), Luigi★ (*Tabarro*), Cavaradossi★ (*Tosca*); ROSSINI: Almaviva (*Barbiere di Siviglia*); SMETANA: Wenzel (*Bartered Bride*); STRAUSS, J: Alfred★ (*Fledermaus*); VERDI: Radames (*Aida*), Riccardo★ (*Ballo in maschera*), Fenton (*Falstaff*), Duca di Mantova★ (*Rigoletto*), Alfredo★ (*Traviata*). Gives recitals. Appears with symphony orchestra. Teaches voice. Stages opera. **Res:** New York, NY, USA. Mgmt: BAR/USA; IMR/FRA; RAB/AUS; TAS/AUS; SLZ/FRG.

DJORDJEVIC, MIRJANA. Dramatic mezzo-soprano. Yugoslavian. Resident mem: Croatian National Theater, Zagreb. Born 24 Nov 1936, Belgrade, Yugoslavia. Divorced. One child. Studied: Prof Anita Mezetova, Belgrade; Prof Zlatko Sir, Zagreb. **Debut:** Maddalena (*Rigoletto*) Opera Belgrade 1966.
Sang with major companies in FR GER: Frankfurt, Stuttgart; ITA: Trieste; POL: Warsaw; SWI: Geneva; UK: Edinburgh Fest; YUG: Zagreb, Belgrade. **Roles with these companies incl** BIZET: Carmen★; GAY/Britten: Mrs Peachum★ (*Beggar's Opera*); MENOTTI: Secretary (*Consul*), Donato's Mother (*Maria Golovin*); PONCHIELLI: La Cieca★ (*Gioconda*); PROKOFIEV: Blanche (*Gambler*), Clarissa★ (*Love for Three Oranges*); PUCCINI: Suzuki (*Butterfly*); SMETANA: Hata (*Bartered Bride*); VERDI: Ulrica★ (*Ballo in maschera*), Azucena (*Trovatore*), WEILL: Leocadia Begbick (*Aufstieg und Fall der Stadt Mahagonny*). Also GOTOVAC: Doma★ (*Ero der Schelm*). Zagreb TV: Mrs Peachum (*Beggar's Opera*). Gives recitals. Appears with symphony orchestra.

Teaches voice. Coaches repertoire. On faculty of Belgrade Consv. **Res:** Marsala Tita, Belgrade, Yugoslavia. Mgmt: CRO/YUG.

DOE, EDWARD NIEL. Bass. American. Resident mem: Opera Repertory Group, Jacksonville, FL, USA. Born 26 Feb 1926, Jacksonville, FL, USA. Single. Studied: Arturo di Filippi, Miami; Virgilio Lazzari, Mo Giuseppe Bamboschek, New York. **Debut:** Il Re (*Aida*) Miami Opera Guild 1949. Previous occupations: Lt JG, US Navy. Awards: Miami Beach Music & Arts League & Miami Opera Guild Schlshp Awd 1966.
Sang with major companies in CAN: Montreal/Quebec; USA: Cincinnati, Hartford, Miami, Philadelphia Grand, San Antonio, San Francisco Spring Opera. **Roles with these companies incl** BELLINI: Oroveso (*Norma*); BIZET: Escamillo (*Carmen*); DONIZETTI: Dott Dulcamara★ (*Elisir*); FLOTOW: Plunkett★ (*Martha*); MOZART: Conte Almaviva (*Nozze di Figaro*), Don Pippo (*Oca del Cairo*), Sarastro (*Zauberflöte*); PUCCINI: Colline★ (*Bohème*), Gianni Schicchi, Sharpless★ (*Butterfly*); ROSSINI: Don Basilio★ (*Barbiere di Siviglia*), Don Magnifico★ (*Cenerentola*); SMETANA: Kezal★ (*Bartered Bride*); VERDI: Ramfis (*Aida*).

DOLL, HANS PETER. German. Gen Int, Württembergisches Staatstheater/Staatsoper Stuttgart, Oberer Schlossgarten 6, D-7000 Stuttgart 1, 1972- ; perf opera, theater, ballet. Is also a stage dir/prod. Born 21 Feb 1925, Offenbach/Main. Wife Peggy. Three children. Studied: Univ Frankfurt/Main, history of theater & literature. Previous positions, primarily adm & theatrical: Dramaturg at opera houses in Frankfurt/Main, Gelsenkirchen, Braunschweig, Bochum, Hannover & Bremen 1946-51; Intendant, Städtische Bühnen Heidelberg, Staatstheater Braunschweig 1961-72. **Res:** Eltinger Str 185, D-7000 Stuttgart 1, FR Ger.

DOMANINSKA, LIBUSE; née Klobaskova. Spinto. Czechoslovakian. Resident mem: National Theater, Prague. Born 4 Jul 1924, Brno, CSSR. Husband Jaroslav Vycichlo, occupation officer. Studied: Consv of Music, Prof Hana Pirkova, Brno; Prof Marie Reznickova, Brno. **Debut:** Blazenka (*Secret*) State Opera, Brno 1945. Awards: Ntl Artist, Pres of CSSR 1974; Merited Artist, Gvnmt of CSSR 1966.
Sang with major companies in ARG: Buenos Aires; AUS: Vienna Volksoper; BEL: Brussels; CZE: Brno, Prague National; FIN: Helsinki; FR GER: Wiesbaden; GER DR: Berlin Staatsoper, Leipzig; HOL: Amsterdam; ITA: Bologna; SPA: Barcelona; SWI: Zurich; UK: Edinburgh Fest; USSR: Moscow Stanislavski. **Roles with these companies incl** BIZET: Micaëla (*Carmen*); BORODIN: Jaroslavna (*Prince Igor*); DVORAK: Kate★ (*Devil and Kate*), Rusalka★; GLINKA: Ludmilla; GLUCK: Euridice; GOUNOD: Marguerite (*Faust*); HANDEL: Galatea; JANACEK: Vixen (*Cunning Little Vixen*), Malinka (*Excursions of Mr Broucek*), Jenufa★†, Katya Kabanova★; MOZART: Fiordiligi★ (*Così fan tutte*), Contessa (*Nozze di Figaro*); OFFENBACH: Giulietta★ (*Contes d'Hoffmann*); PUCCINI: Mimi (*Bohème*), Lauretta (*Gianni Schicchi*), Cio-Cio-

San (*Butterfly*); SMETANA: Marie (*Bartered Bride*), Vendulka★ (*The Kiss*), Blazenka (*Secret*), Carla (*Two Widows*); STRAUSS, R: Chrysothemis (*Elektra*); TCHAIKOVSKY: Tatiana (*Eugene Onegin*), Lisa (*Pique Dame*); VERDI: Aida, Elisabetta★ (*Don Carlo*), Nannetta (*Falstaff*), Abigaille★ (*Nabucco*), Desdemona (*Otello*); WEBER: Agathe (*Freischütz*). Also SMETANA: Jitka★ (*Dalibor*), Krasava★ (*Libuse*), Kate (*Devil's Wall*), Ludise (*Brandenburgers*); RIMSKY-KORSAKOV: Tsarevna (*Tsar Saltan*); DVORAK: Julie★ (*Jakobin*), Xenia (*Dimitrij*); FOERSTER: Eva; KABALEVSKY: Nastja (*Family of Taras*); MOZART: Erste Dame (*Zauberflöte*). **World premieres:** DOUBRAVA: Katherina (*Ballad of Love*) National Theater, Prague 1962. Recorded for: Supraphon. Gives recitals. Appears with symphony orchestra. Teaches voice. Coaches repertoire. On faculty of State Consv Prague. **Res:** Rybna 27, 110 00 Prague 1, CSSR. Mgmt: PRG/CZE.

DOMINGO, PLÁCIDO. Tenor. Spanish. Resident mem: Metropolitan Opera, New York; Royal Opera, London; La Scala, Milan; Hamburg State Opera; Opéra de Paris; Teatro del Liceo, Barcelona. Born 21 Jan 1941, Madrid. Wife Marta, occupation ex-singer. Three children. Studied: Ntl Consv of Music, Mexico City, Mo Carlo Morelli. **Debut:** Alfredo (*Traviata*) Monterrey Opera, Mexico 1961. Previous occupations: pianist, coaching repertoire, TV producer. Awards: Ntl Acad of Recd Arts & Sciences, 4 awds; Orphé d'oro; Edison Awd; Gold Plaque 1972; German Record Prize 1969; Intl Prize Luigi Illica 1971; Prize of the Teatro de España 1972-1973.

Sang with major companies in ARG: Buenos Aires; AUS: Salzburg Fest; CAN: Vancouver, FRA: Marseille, Nice, Paris; FR GER: Berlin Deutsche Oper, Frankfurt, Hamburg, Munich Staatsoper, Stuttgart; HUN: Budapest; ISR: Tel Aviv; ITA: Florence Maggio & Comunale, Milan La Scala, Naples, Rome Opera, Turin, Venice, Verona Arena; MEX: Mexico City; SPA: Barcelona; SWI: Zurich; UK: Edinburgh Fest, London Royal Opera; USSR: Moscow Bolshoi; USA: Baltimore, Boston, Chicago, Cincinnati, Dallas, Fort Worth, Hartford, Houston, Memphis, Miami, Milwaukee Florentine, Newark, New Jersey Opera, New Orleans, New York Met & City Opera, Philadelphia Grand & Lyric, San Antonio, San Diego, San Francisco Opera, Seattle, Washington DC; YUG: Belgrade. **Roles with these companies incl** BELLINI: Pollione‡ (*Norma*); BIZET: Don José★ (*Carmen*), Nadir (*Pêcheurs de perles*); CILEA: Maurizio★ (*A. Lecouvreur*); DONIZETTI: Riccardo (*Anna Bolena*), Edgardo★ (*Lucia*), Roberto Devereux★; GINASTERA: Don Rodrigo; GIORDANO: Andrea Chénier★, Loris Ipanov (*Fedora*); GOUNOD: Faust★, Roméo★; LEONCAVALLO: Canio★‡ (*Pagliacci*); MASCAGNI: Turiddu★ (*Cavalleria rusticana*); MASSENET: Des Grieux (*Manon*); MENOTTI: Lover (*Amelia al ballo*); MEYERBEER: Vasco da Gama★ (*Africaine*); MOZART: Ferrando (*Così fan tutte*), Don Ottavio (*Don Giovanni*); MUSSORGSKY: Shuisky (*Boris Godunov*); OFFENBACH: Hoffmann★‡; PONCHIELLI: Enzo★ (*Gioconda*); PUCCINI: Rodolfo★‡ (*Bohème*), Dick Johnson★ (*Fanciulla del West*), Pinkerton (*Butterfly*), Des Grieux★‡ (*Manon Lescaut*), Luigi★‡ (*Tabarro*), Cavaradossi★‡ (*Tosca*), Calaf★ (*Turandot*); RAMEAU: Hippolyte; ROSSINI: Almaviva (*Barbiere di Siviglia*); SAINT-SAENS: Samson; STRAUSS, R: Ein Sänger‡ (*Rosenkavalier*); TCHAIKOVSKY: Lenski (*Eugene Onegin*); VERDI: Radames★‡ (*Aida*), Riccardo★‡ (*Ballo in maschera*), Don Carlo★‡, Ernani★, Don Alvaro★ (*Forza del destino*), Carlo★‡ (*Giovanna d'Arco*), Rodolfo★ (*Luisa Miller*), Otello★, Duca★ (*Rigoletto*), Alfredo (*Traviata*), Manrico★‡ (*Trovatore*), Arrigo★‡ (*Vespri*); WAGNER: Lohengrin; WEBER: Oberon & Hüon (*Oberon*); ZANDONAI: Paolo★ (*Francesca da Rimini*). Also BOITO: Faust‡ (*Mefistofele*); FALLA: Paco‡ (*Vida breve*); MASSENET: Araquil‡ (*Navarraise*); VERDI: Gabriele‡ (*Simon Boccanegra*), Oronte‡ (*Lombardi*). Recorded for: RCA, EMI, Decca, DG, CBS, Philips, Spanish Columbia. Video/Film: Pinkerton (*Butterfly*). Appears with symphony orchestra. Also conducts opera: New York City Opera; Liceo, Barcelona. Mgmt: SMN/USA; SLA/UK.

DOMINGUEZ, RUBEN; né Aurelio Dominguez Perez. Lyric tenor. Venezuelan. Resident mem: Fundación Teresa Carreño, Caracas. Born 4 Sep 1940, Caracas, Venezuela. Divorced. Two daughters. Studied: Mo Alberto Soresina, Mo Aroldo Fornasari, Milan. **Debut:** Cavaradossi (*Tosca*) Mexico Opera Co 1967. Previous occupations: topographer; merchant. Awards: Silver Medal, Mexico; Trebol d'oro.

Sang with major companies in MEX: Mexico City; USA: Boston, Dallas, Hartford, Miami, New Orleans. **Roles with these companies incl** DONIZETTI: Edgardo (*Lucia*); GIORDANO: Andrea Chénier; PUCCINI: Rodolfo★ (*Bohème*), Cavaradossi★ (*Tosca*); VERDI: Riccardo★ (*Ballo in maschera*), Ismaele (*Nabucco*), Duca di Mantova★ (*Rigoletto*), Alfredo★ (*Traviata*). Gives recitals. Appears with symphony orchestra. Coaches repertoire. **Res:** Caracas, Venezuela. Mgmt: HUR/USA.

DONADIO, GAETANO. Italian. Stage Manager, Teatro dell'Opera, Piazza Beniamino Gigli, Rome, Italy. In charge of tech matters. Born 20 May 1921, Naples. Wife Domenica Micheli. One child. Previous positions primarily theatrical. Started with present company 1938 as technician, in present position since 1971. Awards: The Mayor's Cup of Rome; Campidoglio Prize; Golden Shield of Fiuggi; Felca d'oro, Salerno; Gonfalone d'oro, Viterbo. **Res:** Piazza Re di Roma 3, Rome, Italy.

DONALD, ROBIN; né Donald Robin Smith. Lyric tenor. Australian. Resident mem: Australian Opera, Sydney. Born 26 Mar 1942, Bundaberg, Queensland. Wife Jeni, occupation stenographer. One child. Studied: Queensland Consv of Music, Brisbane; Sadler's Wells/English National Opera, UK. **Debut:** Rodolfo (*Bohème*) Sadler's Wells Opera 1968. Previous occupations: bank clerk; finance officer.

Sang with major companies in AUSTRL: Sydney; BEL: Brussels; FR GER: Munich Gärtnerplatz; UK: Cardiff Welsh, Edinburgh Fest, Glasgow Scottish, London English National. **Roles**

with these companies incl DONIZETTI: Nemorino★ (*Elisir*); JANACEK: Albert Gregor (*Makropoulos Affair*); MASCAGNI: Turiddu★ (*Cavalleria rusticana*); MASSENET: Des Grieux★ (*Manon*); MOZART: Tamino (*Zauberflöte*); PROKOFIEV: Truffaldino (*Love for Three Oranges*); PUCCINI: Rodolfo★ (*Bohème*), Rinuccio★ (*Gianni Schicchi*), Pinkerton★ (*Butterfly*); SMETANA: Lukas (*The Kiss*); STRAUSS, J: Alfred★ (*Fledermaus*); VERDI: Fenton (*Falstaff*), Duca di Mantova (*Rigoletto*), Gabriele★ (*Simon Boccanegra*), Alfredo★ (*Traviata*); WAGNER: Erik (*Fliegende Holländer*), Walther v d Vogelweide★ (*Tannhäuser*). **World premieres:** MURDOCH: Jehingir (*Tamburlaine*) Liverpool Opera 1970. Gives recitals. Appears with symphony orchestra. Mgmt: RDD/AUSTRL; GBN/UK.

DONAT, ZDZISLAWA JÓZEFA. Coloratura soprano. Polish. Resident mem: Teatr Wielki, Warsaw; Staatsoper, Munich. Born 4 Jul, Poznan, Poland. Husband Tadeusz Pajda, occupation journalist. One child. Studied: Prof Zofia Bregy, Warsaw; Mo Ada Sari, Warsaw; Mo Gino Bechi, Siena, Italy. **Debut:** Gilda (*Rigoletto*) Opera Poznan, Poland 1964. Previous occupations: engineer. Awards: Grand Prix Intl Cont for Singers, Toulouse, France; Bronze Medal, Intl Cont for Singers, Helsinki, Finland.
Sang with major companies in AUS: Vienna Staatsoper; BEL: Brussels; CZE: Prague Smetana; FIN: Helsinki; FRA: Toulouse; FR GER: Frankfurt, Munich Gärtnerplatz, Nürnberg, Wiesbaden; GER DR: Berlin Staatsoper, Dresden, Leipzig; ITA: Naples; POL: Lodz, Warsaw. Roles with these companies incl AUBER: Zerlina (*Fra Diavolo*); DONIZETTI: Norina (*Don Pasquale*), Lucia★; HANDEL: Cleopatra (*Giulio Cesare*); HAYDN: Clarissa★ (*Mondo della luna*); MOZART: Konstanze★ & Blondchen (*Entführung aus dem Serail*), Königin der Nacht★ (*Zauberflöte*); NICOLAI: Aennchen★ (*Lustigen Weiber*); OFFENBACH: Olympia (*Contes d'Hoffmann*); PERGOLESI: Serpina★ (*Serva padrona*); ROSSINI: Rosina★ (*Barbiere di Siviglia*); STRAUSS, J: Adele★ (*Fledermaus*); VERDI: Oscar★ (*Ballo in maschera*), Nannetta (*Falstaff*), Gilda★ (*Rigoletto*), Violetta★ (*Traviata*). Also RAVEL: La Princesse/Le Feu (*Enfant et les sortilèges*); LIEBERMANN: Agnes (*Schule der Frauen*). Gives recitals. Appears with symphony orchestra. **Res:** ul Pulawska 111 n 19, 02-595 Warsaw, Poland. Mgmt: PAG/POL; SLZ/FRG.

DONATH, HELEN; née Erwin. Soprano. American. Resident mem: Staatsoper, Vienna; Bayerische Staatsoper, Munich. Born 10 Jul 1940, Corpus Christi, TX. Husband Klaus, occupation conductor & pianist. Studied: Del Mar Coll, Carl Duckwall, Mme Paola Novikova. **Debut:** Inez (*Trovatore*) Cologne Opera 1962.
Sang with major companies in AUS: Salzburg Fest, Vienna Staatsoper; FRA: Paris; FR GER: Berlin Deutsche Oper, Cologne, Frankfurt, Hamburg, Hannover, Munich Staatsoper, Stuttgart; ITA: Milan Scala; SWE: Stockholm; USA: San Francisco Opera; et al. Roles with these companies incl BEETHOVEN: Marzelline (*Fidelio*); BIZET: Micaëla (*Carmen*); BLACHER: Julia; EGK: Jeanne (*Verlobung in San Domingo*); HENZE:

Luise (*Junge Lord*); MARTIN: Branghien (*Vin herbé*); MOZART: Zerlina (*Don Giovanni*), Ilia (*Idomeneo*), Susanna (*Nozze di Figaro*), Pamina (*Zauberflöte*); PUCCINI: Mimi (*Bohème*), Liù (*Turandot*); STRAUSS, R: Sophie (*Rosenkavalier*); VERDI: Oscar‡ (*Ballo in maschera*); WAGNER: Eva‡ (*Meistersinger von Nürnberg*); WEBER: Aennchen (*Freischütz*); et al. Also EGK: Isabella (*Columbus*); RIMSKY-KORSAKOV: Princess (*Tale of Tsar Saltan*); ROSSINI: Donna Fulvia (*Pietra del paragone*). Recorded for: Angel, Philips, London, DG, Nonesuch, Eurodisc. Gives recitals. Appears with symphony orchestra. Mgmt: COL/USA.

DÖNCH, KARL. Bass-baritone & administrator. Austrian. Resident mem: Staatsoper, Vienna; Volksoper, Vienna; since 1972 Gen Mgr & Art Dir of Vienna Volksoper. Born 8 Jan 1915, Hagen, Germany. Divorced. Five children. Studied: Konsv Dresden, Kmsg Lang, Prof Helga Petri, Kurt Striegler. **Debut:** Dott Bartolo (*Barbiere di Siviglia*) Görlitz 1930. Awards: Golden Medal of Honor of Austria; Hon mem Vienna Staatsoper; Professor; Kammersänger; Cross of Honor for Sciences and Arts 1st Class.
Sang with major companies in ARG: Buenos Aires; AUS: Bregenz Fest, Salzburg Fest, Vienna Staatsoper & Volksoper; BEL: Brussels; CAN: Montreal/Quebec; FRA: Bordeaux, Paris; FR GER: Berlin Deutsche Oper, Bonn, Cologne, Düsseldorf-Duisburg, Frankfurt, Munich Staatsoper, Wiesbaden; GER DR: Dresden; HOL: Amsterdam; ITA: Florence Maggio, Genoa, Milan La Scala, Naples, Turin, Venice; MON: Monte Carlo; POR: Lisbon; SWI: Geneva; USA: Boston, New York Met, Philadelphia Grand, Washington DC. Roles with these companies incl ADAM: Bijou (*Postillon de Lonjumeau*); d'ALBERT: Tommaso (*Tiefland*); BERG: Doktor (*Wozzeck*); CIMAROSA: Geronimo (*Matrimonio segreto*); DONIZETTI: Don Pasquale & Malatesta; FLOTOW: Plunkett (*Martha*); GLUCK: Thoas (*Iphigénie en Tauride*); HUMPERDINCK: Hexe (*Hänsel und Gretel*); LORTZING: Baculus★ (*Wildschütz*), Van Bett (*Zar und Zimmermann*); MOZART: Don Alfonso (*Così fan tutte*), Leporello (*Don Giovanni*); NICOLAI: Falstaff & Fluth (*Lustigen Weiber*); OFFENBACH: Coppélius etc (*Contes d'Hoffmann*); ORFF: Bauer (*Kluge*); PUCCINI: Gianni Schicchi, Sharpless (*Butterfly*); ROSSINI: Don Magnifico (*Cenerentola*); SMETANA: Kezal (*Bartered Bride*); STRAUSS, R: Musiklehrer (*Ariadne auf Naxos*); VERDI: Grande Inquisitore (*Don Carlo*), Fra Melitone (*Forza del destino*), Rigoletto; WAGNER: Beckmesser (*Meistersinger*); WOLF-FERRARI: Lunardo (*Quattro rusteghi*). **World premieres:** MARTIN: Roi (*Vin herbé*); LIEBERMANN: (*Penelope*) 1954; EINEM: Simone (*Dantons Tod*) 1947, all at Salzburg Fest. Recorded for: Columbia, London, Decca, CBS. Gives recitals. Appears with symphony orchestra. **Res:** Dr Vogel Gasse 41a, Klosterneuburg/Vienna, Austria.

DOOLEY, WILLIAM E. Bass-baritone. American. Resident mem: Deutsche Oper, Berlin; Metropolitan Opera, New York; Santa Fe Opera, NM, USA. Born 9 Sep 1932, Modesto, CA, USA. Wife

Chardelle H. Studied: Eastman School of Music, Lucy Lee Call, Rochester, NY, USA; Viktoria Vita Prestel, Munich. **Debut:** Rodrigo (*Don Carlo*) Heidelberg Opera, FR Ger 1957. Awards: Kammersänger, Berlin Senate; Kunstpreis, Berlin Senate.

Sang with major companies in AUS: Salzburg Fest; DEN: Copenhagen; FIN: Helsinki; FRA: Nice, Paris; GRE: Athens Fest; FR GER: Berlin Deutsche Oper, Bielefeld, Bonn, Cologne, Düsseldorf-Duisburg, Frankfurt, Hamburg Staatsoper, Kassel, Kiel, Mannheim, Munich Staatsoper, Stuttgart, Wuppertal; MEX: Mexico City; USA: Boston, Houston, New York Metropolitan, San Antonio, San Francisco Opera, Santa Fe. **Roles with these companies incl** BEETHOVEN: Don Pizarro★ (*Fidelio*); BERG: Dr Schön★ (*Lulu*), Wozzeck★; BIZET: Escamillo★ (*Carmen*); GLUCK: Agamemnon (*Iphigénie en Aulide*); HENZE: Mittenhofer (*Elegy for Young Lovers*); JANACEK: Forester★ (*Cunning Little Vixen*); MOZART: Guglielmo★ & Don Alfonso★ (*Così fan tutte*), Don Giovanni★, Conte Almaviva★ (*Nozze di Figaro*); PUCCINI: Marcello★ (*Bohème*), Sharpless (*Butterfly*), Scarpia★ (*Tosca*); ROSSINI: Figaro (*Barbiere di Siviglia*), Sultan Selim★ (*Turco in Italia*); STRAUSS, R: Mandryka★ (*Arabella*), Musiklehrer★ (*Ariadne auf Naxos*), Graf★ (*Capriccio*), Orest★ (*Elektra*), Jochanaan★ (*Salome*); STRAVINSKY: Creon★ (*Oedipus Rex*), Nick Shadow★ (*Rake's Progress*); TCHAIKOVSKY: Eugene Onegin; VERDI: Amonasro★ (*Aida*), Rodrigo★ & Grande Inquisitore (*Don Carlo*), Macbeth★, Iago★ (*Otello*), Germont (*Traviata*), Conte di Luna (*Trovatore*); WAGNER: Holländer★, Telramund★‡ (*Lohengrin*), Amfortas★ (*Parsifal*), Wotan★ (*Rheingold*), Gunther★ (*Götterdämmerung*), Wolfram (*Tannhäuser*), Kurwenal★ (*Tristan und Isolde*); YUN: Ching-Yang (*Traum des Liu-Tung*). **World premieres:** MIHALOVICI: Krapp (*Krapp's Last Tape*) Bielefeld 1963; MILHAUD: Apollo (*Orestie*) Deutsche Oper, Berlin 1963; SESSIONS: Cortez (*Montezuma*) Deutsche Oper, Berlin 1964. Recorded for: RCA. Gives recitals. Appears with symphony orchestra. **Res:** Glockenturmstr 28b, Berlin, FR Ger. Mgmt: CAM/USA.

DORATI, ANTAL. Conductor of opera and symphony; composer. American. Music Dir, National Symph Orch, Washington, DC 1973-76; Chief Cond 1976-79; also Chief Cond, Royal Phil, London. Born 9 Apr 1906, Budapest, Hungary. Wife Ilse v Alpenheim, occupation pianist. One daughter. Studied: Zoltán Kodály, Béla Bartók; Liszt Acad of Music, Budapest; incl piano & cello. Operatic training as asst cond Opera House Budapest 1924-28. **Operatic debut:** State Opera, Budapest 1926. Symphonic debut: Budapest 1925. Awards: Commander of the Order of Vasa, Sweden; Chevalier des Arts et Lettres; var Hon DM; Bruckner & Mahler Medals; 15 recording awds; etc. **Conducted with major companies in** AUS: Vienna Staatsoper & Volksoper; CZE: Brno; FR GER: Frankfurt, Hamburg; HOL: Amsterdam; HUN: Budapest; ITA: Florence Maggio, Rome Opera, Venice; UK: London Royal; USA: Washington DC. **Operas with these companies incl** d'ALBERT: *Tiefland;* BARTOK: *Bluebeard's Castle‡;* BEETHOVEN: *Fidelio;* BERLIOZ: *Benvenuto Cellini;* BIZET: *Carmen;* DALLA-

PICCOLA: *Prigioniero*★‡, *Volo di notte;* DEBUSSY: *Enfant prodigue, Pelléas et Mélisande;* DELIBES: *Lakmé;* HAYDN: *Fedeltà premiata*★; HINDEMITH: *Hin und zurück;* HUMPERDINCK: *Königskinder;* KODALY: *Háry János;* LEONCAVALLO: *Pagliacci;* LORTZING: *Waffenschmied, Wildschütz, Zar und Zimmermann;* MASCAGNI: *Cavalleria rusticana;* MENOTTI: *Amahl, Old Maid and the Thief;* MILHAUD: *Pauvre matelot;* MONTEVERDI: *Combattimento di Tancredi, Orfeo, Incoronazione di Poppea, Ritorno d'Ulisse;* MOZART: *Così fan tutte, Don Giovanni, Entführung aus dem Serail, Nozze di Figaro, Schauspieldirektor★, Zauberflöte;* MUSSORGSKY: *Boris Godunov, Fair at Sorochinsk, Khovanshchina;* NICOLAI: *Lustigen Weiber;* OFFENBACH: *Contes d'Hoffmann, Brigands*★; ORFF: *Carmina burana;* PERGOLESI: *Serva padrona;* PUCCINI: *Bohème, Gianni Schicchi, Butterfly, Manon Lescaut, Suor Angelica, Tabarro, Tosca, Turandot;* RAVEL: *Enfant et les sortilèges, Heure espagnole;* RIMSKY-KORSAKOV: *Coq d'or;* ROSSINI: *Barbiere di Siviglia, Cenerentola, Comte Ory, Italiana in Algeri;* SAINT-SAENS: *Samson et Dalila;* SCHOENBERG: *Erwartung, Glückliche Hand;* SMETANA: *Bartered Bride;* STRAUSS, J: *Fledermaus;* STRAUSS, R: *Aegyptische Helena, Ariadne auf Naxos, Capriccio, Elektra, Rosenkavalier, Salome;* STRAVINSKY: *Mavra, Oedipus Rex;* THOMAS: *Mignon;* VERDI: *Aida, Ballo in maschera, Don Carlo, Falstaff, Forza del destino, Luisa Miller, Macbeth, Otello, Rigoletto, Simon Boccanegra, Traviata, Trovatore;* WAGNER: *Fliegende Holländer‡, Lohengrin, Meistersinger, Parsifal, Rheingold, Walküre★, Siegfried, Götterdämmerung, Tannhäuser, Tristan und Isolde;* WEBER: *Freischütz;* WEINBERGER: *Schwanda;* WOLF-FERRARI: *Sly*. Recorded for Decca/London, RCA, Philips. Conducted major orch in Europe, USA/Canada, Cent/S America, Asia, Africa & Austrl. Previous positions as Mus Dir with major orch: Symph Orch, Minneapolis 1949-60; Symph Orch, Dallas 1945-48. **Res:** Switzerland. Mgmt: HUR/USA; IBB/UK.

D'ORAZI, ATTILIO. Lyric & dramatic baritone. Italian. Born 10 Nov 1929, Rome, Italy. Wife Iole. One daughter. Studied: Armando Piervenanzi, Giuseppe Sorge, Rome. **Debut:** Figaro (*Barbiere di Siviglia*) Teatro Giglio, Lucca 1956. Previous occupations: private employee. Awards: Frescobaldi Prize, Cultural Friends of Music, Ferrara; Cavaliere della Repubblica Italiana.

Sang with major companies in BEL: Brussels; DEN: Copenhagen; FRA: Nancy, Paris, Strasbourg; GRE: Athens National; FR GER: Essen, Wiesbaden; HOL: Amsterdam; HUN: Budapest; ITA: Bologna, Genoa, Milan La Scala, Naples, Palermo, Parma, Rome Opera & Caracalla, Trieste, Turin, Venice; MON: Monte Carlo; POR: Lisbon; SPA: Barcelona; SWI: Geneva; UK: Glyndebourne Fest; YUG: Zagreb. **Roles with these companies incl** BELLINI: Sir Richard★ (*Puritani*); BIZET: Escamillo★ (*Carmen*), Zurga (*Pêcheurs de perles*); CILEA: Michonnet★ (*A. Lecouvreur*); DONIZETTI: Dott Malatesta★ (*Don Pasquale*), Belcore★ (*Elisir*), Alfonse★ (*Favorite*), Enrico★ (*Lucia*); GIORDANO: De Siriex

(*Fedora*); GLUCK: High Priest★ (*Alceste*); LEONCAVALLO: Tonio (*Pagliacci*); MASCAGNI: Rabbi David (*Amico Fritz*), Alfio (*Cavalleria rusticana*); MASSENET: Lescaut (*Manon*); MENOTTI: Husband (*Amelia al ballo*), Bob (*Old Maid and the Thief*); MONTEMEZZI: Manfredo (*Amore dei tre re*); ORFF: Solo (*Carmina burana*); PUCCINI: Marcello★ (*Bohème*), Jack Rance★ (*Fanciulla del West*), Gianni Schicchi★, Sharpless★ (*Butterfly*), Lescaut★ (*Manon Lescaut*), Michele (*Tabarro*), Scarpia★ (*Tosca*); ROSSINI: Figaro★ (*Barbiere di Siviglia*); VERDI: Amonasro★ (*Aida*), Renato★ (*Ballo in maschera*), Falstaff★, Iago★ (*Otello*), Germont★ (*Traviata*), Conte di Luna★ (*Trovatore*). Also PERSICO: Cav di Ripafratta (*Locandiera*); MASCAGNI: Kioto★ (*Iris*). **World premieres:** ROSSELLINI: Comandante (*Campane*) first staged Cairo Opera 1961. Recorded for: Fratelli Fabbri. **Res:** V Padre Semeria 65, Rome, Italy.

DORNYA, MARIA; née Donna Maria Hankla. Dramatic soprano. American. Born 10 Jun, Pulaski, VA, USA. Single. Studied: Ray McDermott, New York. **Debut:** Salome, Wiesbaden 1963. Previous occupations: schoolteacher, model, pianist. Awards: M B Rockefeller Fund Grant; Sullivan Fndt Grants; Winner Ntl Fed Music Clubs.

Sang with major companies in FR GER: Düsseldorf-Duisburg, Hannover, Munich Staatsoper, Nürnberg, Wiesbaden; SWI: Geneva, Zurich; USA: Houston, Kansas City, New York City Opera, Philadelphia Lyric, Washington DC. **Roles with these companies incl** BEETHOVEN: Leonore (*Fidelio*); JANACEK: Katya Kabanova; MOZART: Fiordiligi (*Così fan tutte*), Donna Anna★ (*Don Giovanni*); PUCCINI: Musetta (*Bohème*), Minnie (*Fanciulla del West*), Turandot★; SPONTINI: Giulia (*Vestale*); STRAUSS, J: Rosalinde (*Fledermaus*); STRAUSS, R: Ariadne★ & Komponist (*Ariadne auf Naxos*), Chrysothemis (*Elektra*), Kaiserin★ (*Frau ohne Schatten*), Marschallin & Octavian★ (*Rosenkavalier*), Salome★; VERDI: Amelia (*Ballo in maschera*), Leonora (*Forza del destino*); WAGNER: Senta (*Fliegende Holländer*), Elsa (*Lohengrin*), Sieglinde (*Walküre*), Brünnhilde (*Walküre★, Siegfried★*), Elisabeth★ & Venus★ (*Tannhäuser*), Isolde★. **World premieres:** HOIBY: Natalia (*Natalia Petrovna*) New York City Opera 1964. Gives recitals. Appears with symphony orchestra. Teaches voice. Coaches repertoire. **Res:** Ansonia Hotel, 2109 Broadway, New York, NY 10023, USA. **Mgmt:** MCD/USA; MIN/UK.

DORR, DONALD. Stages/produces opera. Also designs sets, costumes & stage-lighting and is an author. American. Art Dir, Resident Stage Dir & Designer, Opera/South, Jackson, MS. Born 9 Oct 1934, Chicago. Wife Dolores Ardoyno, occupation Gen Mng, Opera/South. Studied: Carroll Coll, Waukesha, WI; Louisiana St Univ, New Orleans; also piano. Operatic training as asst stage dir & designer at New Orleans Opera, LA, 1967-72. **Operatic debut:** *Salome* New Orleans Opera 1971; as designer of sets *Macbeth* New Orleans Op 1967; of costumes *Attila* New Orleans Op 1969. Previous occupation: reporter, Chicago *Daily News.* Previous adm positions in opera: Asst Art Dir, New Orleans Opera 1965-67.

Directed/produced opera for major companies in USA: Jackson Opera/South, New Orleans. **Operas staged with these companies incl** BIZET: *Carmen★†;* DONIZETTI: *Elisir;* KAY: *Juggler of Our Lady★†;* PUCCINI: *Turandot★†;* STILL: *Highway 1, USA★†;* STRAUSS, R: *Salome†;* VERDI: *Aida†, Otello★†;* WAGNER: *Fliegende Holländer★†.* **Operas designed but not staged:** VERDI: *Attila, Macbeth.* **Operatic world premieres:** staged & designed STILL: *Bayou Legend* Opera/South, Jackson 1974. **Opera libretti:** KAY: *Jubilee* Opera/South, Jackson 1976. **Res:** 822 Governor Nicholls, New Orleans, LA, USA.

DÖSE, HELENA ELISABETH ASTRID. Spinto. Swedish. Born 7 Aug, Göteborg, Sweden. Single. Studied: Ingalill Linden, Göteborg; Luigi Ricci, Rome. **Debut:** Aida, Göteborg 1971.

Sang with major companies in AUSTRL: Sydney; DEN: Copenhagen; FRA: Marseille; FR GER: Munich Staatsoper; HUN: Budapest; SWE: Drottningholm Fest, Stockholm; SWI: Geneva; UK: Glyndebourne Fest, London Royal. **Roles with these companies incl** BIZET: Micaëla★.(*Carmen*); JANACEK: Jenufa★; MASCAGNI: Santuzza★ (*Cavalleria rusticana*); MOZART: Fiordiligi★ (*Così fan tutte*), Donna Anna★ (*Don Giovanni*), Cecilio★ (*Lucio Silla*), Contessa★ (*Nozze di Figaro*); PUCCINI: Mimi★ (*Bohème*), Manon Lescaut★, Giorgetta★ (*Tabarro*), Tosca★, Liù★ (*Turandot*); STRAUSS, R: Octavian★ (*Rosenkavalier*); VERDI: Lina★ (*Stiffelio*), Elisabetta★ (*Don Carlo*), Desdemona★ (*Otello*).

DOUGLAS, NIGEL; né Nigel Douglas Leigh-Pemberton. Lyric tenor. British. Born 9 May 1934, Kent, UK. Wife Alexandra Valerie. Studied: Alfred Piccaver, Lily Kundegraber, Vienna; Opera School, Vienna Musikakad; Rupert Bruce-Lockhart, London. **Debut:** Rodolfo (*Bohème*) Vienna Chamber Opera 1959.

Sang with major companies in AUS: Vienna Volksoper; BEL: Brussels; ITA: Venice; SPA: Barcelona; SWI: Basel, Zurich; UK: Aldeburgh Fest, Cardiff Welsh, Edinburgh Fest, Glasgow Scottish, London Royal Opera & English National. **Roles with these companies incl** AUBER: Lorenzo (*Fra Diavolo*); BERG: Alwa★ (*Lulu*), Tambourmajor (*Wozzeck*); BRITTEN: Albert Herring, Edward Fairfax Vere★ (*Billy Budd*), Aschenbach★ (*Death in Venice*), Lysander★ (*Midsummer Night*), Peter Grimes; EINEM: Robespierre★ (*Dantons Tod*); FLOTOW: Lionel (*Martha*); HENZE: Des Grieux (*Boulevard Solitude*); STRAUSS, J: Eisenstein★ (*Fledermaus*); STRAUSS, R: Flamand (*Capriccio*); STRAVINSKY: Tom Rakewell (*Rake's Progress*). Also MARTIN: Antonio★ (*Sturm*). **World premieres:** BRITTEN: Lechmere (*Owen Wingrave*) stg Royal Opera, London 1973; GARDNER: Philip (*The Visitors*) Aldeburgh Fest 1972; SUTERMEISTER: L'Heureux (*Madame Bovary*) Opernhaus Zurich 1967; BURCKHARDT: Jack Worthing (*Bunbury*) Opernhaus Basel 1966. Recorded for: Decca. Video/Film: Beamter (*Julietta*); Lechmere (*Owen Wingrave*). Gives recitals. Appears with symphony orchestra. **Res:** 10 Clonmel Rd, London SW6 5BJ, UK. **Mgmt:** HPL/UK; DSP/USA.

DOUSSANT, HERBERT. Dramatic tenor. American. Born 7 Sep 1931, New York. Divorced. Two children. Studied: Douglas Stanley, Paul Weiner, coaching, New York. **Debut:** Walther (*Meistersinger*) Municipal Opera, Mainz, FR Ger 1958. Previous occupations: purchasing agent.

Sang with major companies in BEL: Liège; GRE: Athens National Opera; FR GER: Bielefeld, Bonn, Cologne, Düsseldorf-Duisburg, Essen, Frankfurt, Hannover, Karlsruhe, Kassel, Kiel, Krefeld, Mannheim, Munich Staatsoper, Nürnberg, Wiesbaden; GER DR: Berlin Komische Oper; ITA: Bologna, Turin; MEX: Mexico City; SPA: Barcelona; USA: Hawaii, Memphis, New York Met, Philadelphia Grand, San Antonio, Seattle. **Roles with these companies incl** BEETHOVEN: Florestan (*Fidelio*); BERG: Alwa (*Lulu*), Tambourmajor (*Wozzeck*); BIZET: Don José (*Carmen*); DESSAU: Lukullus (*Verurteilung des Lukullus*); HINDEMITH: Albrecht v Brandenberg (*Mathis der Maler*); JANACEK: Laca (*Jenufa*), Boris (*Katya Kabanova*); LEONCAVALLO: Canio (*Pagliacci*); MASCAGNI: Turiddu★ (*Cavalleria rusticana*); MOZART: Idomeneo; MUSSORGSKY: Shuisky (*Boris Godunov*); PUCCINI: Dick Johnson (*Fanciulla del West*), Pinkerton (*Butterfly*), Cavaradossi (*Tosca*), Calaf (*Turandot*); SAINT-SAENS: Samson★; SMETANA: Dalibor; STRAUSS, J: Eisenstein & Alfred (*Fledermaus*); STRAUSS, R: Ein Sänger (*Rosenkavalier*), Herodes★ (*Salome*); TCHAIKOVSKY: Lenski (*Eugene Onegin*); VERDI: Radames (*Aida*), Don Alvaro (*Forza del destino*), Ismaele (*Nabucco*), Otello★; WAGNER: Erik★ (*Fliegende Holländer*), Walther (*Meistersinger*), Parsifal, Loge (*Rheingold*), Siegmund (*Walküre*), Siegfried (*Götterdämmerung*), Tannhäuser★ & Walther v d Vogelweide★ (*Tannhäuser*); WEBER: Max (*Freischütz*); WEILL: Jim Mahoney (*Aufstieg und Fall der Stadt Mahagonny*). Also MUSSORGSKY: Dimitri (*Boris Godunov*); PFITZNER: Novagerio (*Palestrina*); HINDEMITH: Hans Schwalb (*Mathis der Maler*). **World premieres:** BENTZON: Mephisto (*Faust III*) Kiel Opera 1964. Recorded for: Westminster. Gives recitals. Appears with symphony orchestra. Teaches voice. **Res:** 2130 Broadway, New York, NY, USA. Mgmt: MJM/USA; PAS/FRG.

DOWNES, EDWARD. Conductor of opera and symphony; translator of operas. British. Resident Cond, Royal Opera Covent Garden, London; Mus Adv & Res Cond, Australian Opera, Sydney. Born 1926, Birmingham, UK. Studied: Univ of Birmingham; Royal Coll of Music, London; incl French horn, piano, violin & organ. Operatic training as repetiteur & prompter at Covent Garden, London 1952-53; asst to H Scherchen 2 yrs. Previous occupations: dept store salesman, waiter, etc; lectured music in Aberdeen. Previous adm positions in opera: Mus Dir & Chief Cond, Sydney Opera, Australia 1972-74.

Conducted with major companies in AUSTRL: Sydney; FRA: Paris; FR GER: Cologne, Düsseldorf-Duisburg, Kiel; ITA: Florence Maggio; UK: Aldeburgh Fest, London Royal & English National; et al. **Operas with these companies incl** BARTOK: *Bluebeard's Castle;* BEETHOVEN: *Fidelio;* BENNETT: *Victory;* BRITTEN: *Peter*

Grimes; BUSONI: *Arlecchino;* HENZE: *Bassariden;* JANACEK: *Excursions of Mr Broucek;* MASCAGNI: *Cavalleria rusticana;* MAXWELL-DAVIES: *Taverner;* MUSSORGSKY: *Boris Godunov, Khovanshchina;* OFFENBACH: *Contes d'Hoffmann;* PROKOFIEV: *War and Peace;* PUCCINI: *Tabarro, Tosca, Turandot;* SEARLE: *Hamlet;* SHOSTAKOVICH: *Katerina Ismailova;* STRAUSS, R: *Rosenkavalier;* VERDI: *Aida, Ballo in maschera, Don Carlo, Falstaff, Forza del destino, Macbeth, Nabucco, Otello, Rigoletto, Traviata, Trovatore;* WAGNER: *Rheingold, Walküre, Siegfried, Götterdämmerung, Tannhäuser, Tristan und Isolde;* WEBER: *Freischütz;* et al. Also STRAUSS, R: *Friedenstag;* BIRTWISTLE: *Punch and Judy.* Conducted major orch in Europe, Asia, Austrl. **Operas translated:** *War and Peace; The Nose.* Mgmt: BAR/USA.

DRAGOVIC, LJILJANA CVETKO. Scenic and costume designer for opera, theater, film, television & ballet; specl in costumes. Is also a fashion designer. Yugoslavian. Resident designer, Belgrade Opera and Ballet and at National Theater, Belgrade. Born 19 Nov 1934, Skoplje. Divorced. One child. Studied: Faculty of Applied Arts, Dusan Ristic, Prof Vladimir Zedrinski, Belgrade. Prof training: National Theater, Belgrade. **Operatic debut:** cost, National Theater, Belgrade 1961. Theater debut: Atelje 212, Belgrade 1960. Previous occupation: painter, fashion designer.

Designed for major companies in YUG: Dubrovnik, Belgrade. **Operas designed for these companies incl** BARTOK: *Bluebeard's Castle;* BORODIN: *Prince Igor;* BRITTEN: *Albert Herring;* DONIZETTI: *Elisir;* EGK: *Zaubergeige;* GOTOVAC: *Ero der Schelm;* HANDEL: *Giulio Cesare;* MASSENET: *Cendrillon, Werther;* OFFENBACH: *Contes d'Hoffmann;* PAISIELLO: *Barbiere di Siviglia;* PUCCINI: *Bohème, Butterfly;* ROSSINI: *Barbiere di Siviglia;* SAINT-SAENS: *Samson et Dalila;* SMETANA: *Bartered Bride;* VERDI: *Aida, Ballo in maschera, Forza del destino, Nabucco, Otello, Rigoletto, Trovatore;* WAGNER: *Fliegende Holländer.* Exhibitions of stage designs Biennale & Triennale, Belgrade, Novi Sad 1972, 73, 74. **Res:** III Bulevar 98/V, Belgrade, Yugoslavia.

DRAKE, ARCHIE ARTHUR. Bass-baritone. American. Resident mem: Seattle Opera, WA, USA. Born 12 Mar 1925, Great Yarmouth, UK. Divorced. Studied: Music Acad of the West, Mme Lotte Lehmann, Santa Barbara, CA, USA; UCLA Opera Theatre, Los Angeles; Univ of So California, William Eddy, Los Angeles. **Debut:** Belcore (*Elisir d'amore*) Los Angeles Grand Opera 1960. Previous occupations: Navigation Officer, British Merchant Navy.

Sang with major companies in USA: Chicago, Cincinnati, Hawaii, Houston, Portland, San Diego, San Francisco & Spring Opera, Seattle. **Roles with these companies incl** BEETHOVEN: Rocco (*Fidelio*); CIMAROSA: Geronimo (*Matrimonio segreto*); DEBUSSY: Arkel (*Pelléas et Mélisande*); DONIZETTI: Dott Malatesta (*Don Pasquale*), Belcore (*Elisir*), Sulpice★ (*Fille du régiment*); FLOYD: George Milton (*Of Mice and Men*); GOUNOD: Méphistophélès★ (*Faust*); MO-

ZART: Don Alfonso★ (*Così fan tutte*), Figaro★ (*Nozze di Figaro*), Papageno (*Zauberflöte*); NICOLAI: Falstaff (*Lustigen Weiber*); OFFENBACH: Coppélius★ etc (*Contes d'Hoffmann*); PUCCINI: Colline★ (*Bohème*), Sharpless★ (*Butterfly*), Rambaldo★ (*Rondine*), Scarpia★ (*Tosca*); ROSSINI: Dott Bartolo★ (*Barbiere di Siviglia*), Don Magnifico (*Cenerentola*); STRAVINSKY: Creon & Tiresias (*Oedipus Rex*); VERDI: Amonasro & Ramfis★ (*Aida*), Philip II★ & Grande Inquisitore★ (*Don Carlo*), Fra Melitone★ & Padre Guardiano★ (*Forza del destino*); WAGNER: Holländer★, Wotan★ (*Walküre*), Wanderer★ (*Siegfried*), Gunther★ (*Götterdämmerung*). Also STRAUSS, R: Graf Waldner (*Arabella*); DONIZETTI: Raimondo (*Lucia*); BRITTEN: Noye (*Noye's Fludde*), Collatinus (*Rape of Lucretia*); PUCCINI: Geronte (*Manon Lescaut*), Timur (*Turandot*). **World premieres:** FLOYD: Candy (*Of Mice and Men*) Seattle Opera 1970; PASATIERI: Lazarus (*Calvary*) Seattle Opera 1971; ARGENTO: Captain Mullikin (*Colonel Jonathan the Saint*) Denver Opera 1971. Gives recitals. Appears with symphony orchestra. **Res:** 805 Warren Ave N, Seattle, WA 98109, USA. Mgmt: WFA/USA.

DRAKE, BRYAN. Lyric baritone. New Zealander. Resident mem: English Opera Group, London. Born 7 Oct 1925, Dunedin, New Zealand. Wife Jean. Three children. Studied: Ernest Drake, New Zealand; Dawson Freer, London. **Debut:** Escamillo (*Carmen*) New Zealand 1948. Awards: LRSM, London.

Sang with major companies in UK: Aldeburgh Fest, Cardiff Welsh, Edinburgh Fest, London Royal & English National. **Roles with these companies incl** BENNETT: Braxton★ (*Mines of Sulphur*); BIZET: Escamillo★ (*Carmen*); BRITTEN: Bottom★ & Theseus★ (*Midsummer Night*), Captain Balstrode (*Peter Grimes*), Father★ (*Prodigal Son*); DONIZETTI: Talbot (*Maria Stuarda*); GAY/Britten: Lockit (*Beggar's Opera*); GOUNOD: Méphistophélès (*Faust*); HANDEL: Polyphemus (*Acis and Galatea*), Garibald★ (*Rodelinda*); LEONCAVALLO: Tonio (*Pagliacci*); MASCAGNI: Alfio (*Cavalleria*); MASSENET: Des Grieux (*Portrait de Manon*); MOZART: Conte Almaviva★ (*Nozze di Figaro*); OFFENBACH: Coppélius etc (*Contes d'Hoffmann*); PUCCINI: Sharpless (*Butterfly*); ROSSINI: Figaro (*Barbiere di Siviglia*); STRAVINSKY: Creon (*Oedipus Rex*); TCHAIKOVSKY: King René (*Iolanthe*); VAUGHAN WILLIAMS: Pilgrim (*Pilgrim's Progress*); VERDI: Pagano (*Lombardi*), Macbeth, Nabucco & Zaccaria (*Nabucco*), Simon Boccanegra, Germont (*Traviata*). Also BRITTEN: Mr Flint★ (*Billy Budd*), Junius★ & Tarquinius★ (*Rape of Lucretia*); CROSSE: Old Man (*Purgatory*); ECCLES: Jupiter★ (*Semele*). **World premieres:** BRITTEN: Donald (*Billy Budd*) Covent Garden 1951; Traveller (*Curlew River*) Aldeburgh Fest 1964; Abbot/Astrologer (*Burning Fiery Furnace*) Aldeburgh Fest 1966; Elder Son (*Prodigal Son*) Aldeburgh Fest 1968; MUSGRAVE: Mr Lamb (*Voice of Ariadne*) Aldeburgh Fest 1974; John Brown (*Decision*) New Opera Co, London 1967. Recorded for: Decca. Video—BBC TV: Balstrode (*Peter Grimes*); Flint (*Billy Budd*). Gives recitals.

Appears with symphony orchestra. Teaches voice. Coaches repertoire. On faculty of Guildhall School of Music & Drama, London. **Res:** 31 Wordsworth Walk, London NW 11, UK.

DRESE, CLAUS HELMUT. German. Gen Int, Bühnen der Stadt Köln, Cologne 1968-75; beginning July 1975 Gen Int, Opernhaus Zurich, Switzerland. In charge of overall adm matters & art policy. Is also a stage dir/prod. Born 25 Dec 1922, Aachen. Wife Helga. Two children. Studied: Univ Cologne; Univ Bonn; Univ Marburg, FR Ger; PhD. Previous positions, primarily theatrical: St Dir: Marburg Theater 1947-50; Osnabrück Stadttheater 1950-52; Nationaltheater Mannheim 1952-59; Dir: Stadttheater Heidelberg 1959-62; Staatstheater Wiesbaden 1962-68. World premieres at theaters under his management: KILLMAYER: *Yolimba* Wiesbaden 1965; SCHOENBACH: *Hysteria* Cologne 1971. Mem of Adm Commtt, Deutscher Bühnenverein; Opernkonferenz. **Res:** after July 1975: Seehaldenstr 16, Kilchberg/Zurich, Switzerland.

DRESSLER, GÜNTER ALBERT. Basso-buffo. German. Resident mem: Staatsoper Dresden, Ger DR. Born 23 Jul 1927, Eibau/Sa. Wife Rosemarie, occupation businesswoman. Two children. Studied: Hochschule für Musik, Prof Adelheid Müller-Hess, Berlin. **Debut:** Magistrate (*Jenufa*) Gerhart Hauptmann Theater, Görlitz 1956. Previous occupations: baker's apprentice, actor, musician in dance orch. Awards: Kammersänger, Ministry of Culture, Ger DR.

Sang with major companies in BUL: Sofia; FR GER: Wiesbaden; GER DR: Berlin Komische Oper, Dresden; USSR: Leningrad Kirov. **Roles with these companies incl** ADAM: Bijou★ (*Postillon de Lonjumeau*); BEETHOVEN: Rocco (*Fidelio*); BERG: Doktor★ (*Wozzeck*); CORNELIUS: Abul Hassan (*Barbier von Bagdad*); DESSAU: Dragon★ (*Lanzelot*); DONIZETTI: Don Pasquale; LEONCAVALLO: Tonio (*Pagliacci*); LORTZING: Baculus★ (*Wildschütz*), Van Bett★ (*Zar und Zimmermann*); MOZART: Leporello★ (*Don Giovanni*), Osmin (*Entführung aus dem Serail*), Figaro (*Nozze di Figaro*); MUSSORGSKY: Varlaam★ (*Boris Godunov*); NICOLAI: Falstaff★ (*Lustigen Weiber*); PAISIELLO: Bartolo★ (*Barbiere di Siviglia*); PROKOFIEV: Mendoza★ (*Duenna*); PUCCINI: Colline★ (*Bohème*); ROSSINI: Don Basilio★ (*Barbiere di Siviglia*); SMETANA: Kezal★ (*Bartered Bride*); VERDI: Fra Melitone★ (*Forza del destino*); WAGNER: Hunding★ (*Walküre*); WEBER: Kaspar★ (*Freischütz*); WEILL: Trinity Moses (*Aufstieg und Fall der Stadt Mahagonny*). Also HANDEL: Radamisto; PAISIELLO: Petronio (*Astrologi*); KURZBACH: Lamme (*Thyl Clans*). **World premieres:** ZIMMERMANN: Habedank (*Levins Mühle*) Staatsoper, Dresden 1973. Video/Film: (*Astrologi*). Appears with symphony orchestra. Coaches repertoire. **Res:** Veilchenweg 25, 8054 Dresden, Ger DR. Mgmt: KDR/GDR.

DREWANZ, HANS. Conductor of opera and symphony. German. Gen Mus Dir & Principal Cond, Staatstheater, Darmstadt, FR Ger since 1963. Also Mus Dir, Orch des Staatstheaters, Darmstadt. Born 2 Dec 1929, Dresden. Wife Christiane. Two children. Studied: Musisches Gymnasium, Prof Kurt Thomas, Sir Georg Solti; incl piano, organ, violin and voice. Plays the piano. Operatic training as asst cond & cond at Städtische Bühnen, Frankfurt 1948-59; Theater der Stadt Wuppertal 1959-63. **Operatic debut:** *Forza del destino* Städtische Bühnen, Frankfurt 1953. Symphonic debut: Orch des Staatstheaters, Braunschweig 1961.

Conducted with major companies in BEL: Brussels; GRE: Athens Fest; FR GER: Cologne, Darmstadt, Düsseldorf-Duisburg, Frankfurt, Munich Staatsoper, Saarbrücken, Stuttgart, Wuppertal. **Operas with these companies incl** BARTOK: *Bluebeard's Castle;* BEETHOVEN: *Fidelio⋆;* BERG: *Lulu;* BERLIOZ: *Damnation de Faust;* BIZET: *Carmen⋆;* CIMAROSA: *Matrimonio segreto;* DESSAU: *Verurteilung des Lukullus⋆;* FORTNER: *Elisabeth Tudor⋆, Don Perlimplin;* GLUCK: *Iphigénie en Tauride, Orfeo ed Euridice;* HINDEMITH: *Hin und zurück;* HUMPERDINCK: *Hänsel und Gretel;* JANACEK: *From the House of the Dead, Jenufa⋆, Katya Kabanova;* LEONCAVALLO: *Pagliacci;* LORTZING: *Wildschütz;* MASCAGNI: *Cavalleria rusticana;* MASSENET: *Cendrillon, Don Quichotte;* MILHAUD: *Abandon d'Ariane, Délivrance de Thésée, Enlèvement d'Europe;* MONTEVERDI: *Combattimento di Tancredi, Favola d'Orfeo, Incoronazione di Poppea, Ritorno d'Ulisse;* MOZART: *Così fan tutte⋆, Don Giovanni⋆, Entführung aus dem Serail⋆, Nozze di Figaro, Zauberflöte⋆;* NICOLAI: *Lustigen Weiber;* PUCCINI: *Bohème⋆, Gianni Schicchi, Tabarro, Tosca⋆, Turandot⋆;* RAVEL: *Enfant et les sortilèges⋆;* REIMANN: *Melusine⋆;* ROSSINI: *Barbiere di Siviglia;* SCHOENBERG: *Moses und Aron⋆;* STRAUSS, J: *Fledermaus;* STRAUSS, R: *Arabella, Ariadne auf Naxos, Elektra, Rosenkavalier, Salome⋆;* STRAVINSKY: *Mavra, Rake's Progress, Rossignol⋆;* TCHAIKOVSKY: *Eugene Onegin, Pique Dame;* VERDI: *Aida, Don Carlo⋆, Falstaff, Forza del destino, Macbeth, Nabucco, Rigoletto, Simon Boccanegra, Traviata;* WAGNER: *Fliegende Holländer⋆, Meistersinger⋆;* WEILL: *Dreigroschenoper.* Also KLEBE: *Räuber;* BLOMDAHL: *Aniara;* SCHOENBERG: *Von heute auf morgen.* Conducted major orch in Europe, Asia. Teaches at Akad für Tonkunst, Darmstadt. **Res:** Darmstadt, FR Ger. **Mgmt:** SMD/FRG.

DRISCOLL, LOREN. Lyric tenor. American. Resident mem: Deutsche Oper, Berlin, FR Ger. Born Midwest, Wyoming, USA. Single. Studied: Boston Univ, David Blair McClosky, USA; Fr Prof von Winterfeldt, Berlin, FR Ger. **Debut:** Dott Caius *(Falstaff)* Boston Opera 1954. Previous occupations: cowboy, radio announcer, swimming instr. Awards: Berliner Kammersänger, Berlin Senate, FR Ger.

Sang with major companies in AUS: Salzburg Fest; BEL: Brussels; FIN: Helsinki; GRE: Athens Fest; FR GER: Berlin Deutsche Oper, Cologne, Essen, Frankfurt, Hamburg; HOL: Amsterdam; ITA: Milan La Scala, Rome Opera; SWE: Drottningholm Fest; UK: Edinburgh Fest, Glyndebourne Fest; USA: Boston, New York Met & City Opera, Santa Fe; YUG: Zagreb, Bel-

grade. **Roles with these companies incl** BERG: Maler⋆*(Lulu),* Andres⋆*(Wozzeck);* BIZET: Don José *(Carmen);* BLACHER: Romeo; CIMAROSA: Paolino⋆ *(Matrimonio segreto);* DONIZETTI: Beppo *(Rita);* EINEM: Camille Desmoulins *(Dantons Tod);* HENZE: Des Grieux *(Boulevard Solitude),* Tony *(Elegy for Young Lovers);* JANACEK: Mazal *(Excursions of Mr Broucek);* MASSENET: Des Grieux *(Manon);* MONTEVERDI: Nero *(Incoronazione di Poppea);* MOZART: Ferrando⋆ *(Così fan tutte),* Don Ottavio⋆ *(Don Giovanni),* Belmonte⋆ & Pedrillo *(Entführung aus dem Serail),* Tamino *(Zauberflöte);* ORFF: Solo⋆ *(Catulli carmina);* PUCCINI: Rodolfo *(Bohème),* Pinkerton⋆ *(Butterfly);* ROSSINI: Almaviva⋆ *(Barbiere di Siviglia),* Don Ramiro *(Cenerentola);* STRAUSS, J: Alfred⋆ *(Fledermaus);* STRAUSS, R: Flamand⋆ *(Capriccio),* Ein Sänger *(Rosenkavalier);* STRAVINSKY: Eumolpe *(Perséphone),* Tom Rakewell⋆ *(Rake's Progress),* Pêcheur *(Rossignol);* SZOKOLAY: Hamlet; VERDI: Fenton *(Falstaff),* Alfredo *(Traviata);* WAGNER: David⋆ *(Meistersinger);* YUN: Pien-Fu *(Traum des Liu-Tung).* **World premieres:** HENZE: Lord Barrat *(Der junge Lord)* Deutsche Oper, Berlin 1965; Dyonisos *(Die Bassariden)* Salzburg Fest 1966. Recorded for: Columbia, DG. Video/Film: Lord Barrat *(Der junge Lord).* Gives recitals. Appears with symphony orchestra. **Res:** Miquel Str 18a, Berlin, FR Ger. **Mgmt:** DSP/USA.

DRIVER, ROBERT BAYLOR. American. Assoc Mng, Kansas City Lyric Theater, 1029 Central, Kansas City, MO 1974-75. In charge of adm matters & finances; also a stage dir/prod. After Nov 1975 Gen Mng, Opera Theatre of Syracuse, NY. Born 26 Aug 1942, São Paulo, Brazil. Wife Monica Macrae, occupation art historian. One child. Studied: Univ of Virginia, Charlottesville; Univ of Munich, FR Ger; Middlebury Summer Language School, VT; Johns Hopkins Univ, Baltimore, MD. Plays the piano. Previous occupations: officer, overseas div, NY First Natl City Bank, 1964-65. Form positions, primarily theatrical: Asst St Dir, Bavarian State Opera, Munich 1965-68; Asst Dir, Kentucky Opera Assn, Louisville 1968-71. Operas staged with above companies incl BIZET: *Carmen;* BRITTEN: *Rape of Lucretia;* DONIZETTI: *Don Pasquale;* PUCCINI: *Butterfly⋆;* ROSSINI: *Barbiere di Siviglia.* **Res:** Kansas City, MO, USA.

DUCKE, RUDOLF. Conductor of opera. German. Resident Cond Staatstheater Kassel since 1940. Born 30 Dec 1912, Neustadt/Aisch, Germany. Wife Annelies. Three children. Studied: Konsv der Musik, Nürnberg, incl piano, oboe, percussion. Plays the piano. Operatic training as repetiteur, asst cond & chorus master at Opera House, Nürnberg 1933-38; Volksoper Berlin 1938-40. **Operatic debut:** *Zar und Zimmermann* Volksoper Berlin 1938.

Conducted with major companies in FR GER: Bayreuth Fest, Kassel, Nürnberg. **Operas with these companies incl** ADAM: *Si j'étais roi;* d'ALBERT: *Tiefland;* AUBER: *Fra Diavolo;* BEETHOVEN: *Fidelio⋆;* BIZET: *Carmen⋆;* CIMAROSA: *Matrimonio segreto;* CORNELIUS: *Barbier von Bagdad;* DESSAU:

Verurteilung des Lukullus; DONIZETTI: *Don Pasquale, Fille du régiment;* EGK: *Zaubergeige;* FLOTOW: *Martha;* GLUCK: *Alceste, Iphigénie en Tauride;* GOUNOD: *Faust;* HANDEL: *Acis and Galatea, Giulio Cesare, Xerxes;* HINDEMITH: *Hin und zurück;* HUMPERDINCK: *Hänsel und Gretel;* LEONCAVALLO: *Pagliacci;* LORTZING: *Waffenschmied★, Wildschütz★, Zar und Zimmermann★;* MARSCHNER: *Hans Heiling;* MASCAGNI: *Cavalleria rusticana;* MENOTTI: *Consul;* MONTEVERDI: *Incoronazione di Poppea;* MOZART: *Così fan tutte★, Don Giovanni, Entführung aus dem Serail, Idomeneo★, Nozze di Figaro★, Zauberflöte★;* NICOLAI: *Lustigen Weiber★;* OFFENBACH: *Contes d'Hoffmann★;* ORFF: *Carmina burana;* PUCCINI: *Bohème, Butterfly★, Turandot;* ROSSINI: *Barbiere di Siviglia★, Cenerentola★;* STRAUSS, J: *Fledermaus★;* TCHAIKOVSKY: *Eugene Onegin;* THOMAS: *Mignon;* VERDI: *Aida★, Ballo in maschera★, Don Carlo★, Falstaff, Forza del destino, Nabucco★, Otello★, Rigoletto★, Traviata★, Trovatore★;* WAGNER: *Fliegende Holländer, Lohengrin★, Meistersinger;* WALTON: *Bear★;* WEBER: *Freischütz★;* WEINBERGER: *Schwanda.* Teaches at Musikakad Kassel. **Res:** Seebergstr 32, Kassel, FR Ger.

DUCREUX, LOUIS. Stages/produces opera & theater and is an actor, administrator, author & composer. French. Dir, Opéra de Nancy. Also Resident Stage Dir for theater in Nancy. Born 22 Sep 1911, Marseille. Divorced. One child. Studied: music and piano. **Operatic debut:** *Manon* Opéra, Marseille 1960. Theater debut: Marseille 1931. Awards: Officier de la Légion d'Honneur; Officier des Arts et Lettres; Prize for Best Stage Dir in Opéra Comique, Paris 1969. Previous adm positions in opera: Opéras de Marseille, Monte Carlo, Nancy 1961-75.
Directed/produced opera for major companies in BEL: Brussels; FRA: Bordeaux, Lyon, Marseille, Nancy, Nice, Paris, Rouen, Strasbourg, Toulouse; ITA: Milan La Scala; MON: Monte Carlo; SWI: Geneva. **Operas staged with these companies incl** ADAM: *Postillon de Lonjumeau★;* BERG: *Lulu;* BIZET: *Carmen★;* CHARPENTIER: *Louise★;* CILEA: *Lecouvreur;* CIMAROSA: *Matrimonio segreto;* GLUCK: *Iphigénie en Aulide, & en Tauride;* LECOCQ: *Fille de Madame Angot;* MASSENET: *Manon, Werther★;* MENOTTI: *Telephone;* MOZART: *Don Giovanni;* POULENC: *Mamelles de Tirésias★;* PUCCINI: *Bohème;* ROSSINI: *Barbiere di Siviglia;* SATIE: *Socrate★;* THOMAS: *Mignon★;* VERDI: *Traviata.* **Operatic world premieres:** DAMASE: *Héritière* Opéra de Nancy 1974; SAGUER: *Mariana Pineda* Opéra de Marseille 1969. **Opera libretti:** DAMASE: *Héritière,* see prem. **Res:** 10 rue Hégésippe-Moreau, 75018 Paris, France.

DUDLEY, JONATHAN. Conductor of opera and symphony. American. Gen Dir & Principal Cond, Omaha Opera Co, NE; Music Adm, Cincinnati Opera, O. Born 1 Sep 1940, Granville, O, USA. Single. Studied: Denison, Boston & Harvard Univs; Sergiu Celibidache; Ntl School of Opera, London; Bayreuth Master Classes; incl flute, cello and voice. Operatic training as repetiteur, asst cond & chorus master at Cincinnati Summer Op-

era, O, 1967; Met Opera Studio, New York 1969-74. **Operatic debut:** *Fra Diavolo* Ntl School of Opera, London 1963. Previous occupations: coaching. Previous adm positions in opera: Music Dir, Met Opera Studio, New York 1969-74.
Conducted with major companies in USA: Cincinnati, Omaha. **Operas with these companies incl** DONIZETTI: *Lucia★;* OFFENBACH: *Périchole★;* PUCCINI: *Bohème★, Gianni Schicchi★;* ROSSINI: *Barbiere di Siviglia★.*

DUDLEY, WILLIAM. Scenic and costume designer for opera, theater, film. Is also a painter. British. Born 4 Mar 1947, London. Single. Studied: St Martin's School of Art, London; Slade School of Art, Nicholas Georgiadis, London. **Operatic debut:** *Billy Budd* Staatsoper, Hamburg 1972. Theater debut: Nottingham Playhouse, UK 1970.
Designed for major companies in FR GER: Hamburg; NOR: Oslo; UK: Welsh National. **Operas designed for these companies incl** BRITTEN: *Billy Budd★;* STRAVINSKY: *Oedipus Rex★;* WAGNER: *Fliegende Holländer.*

DUFFUS, JOHN LOGIE LYALL. British. Asst Gen Adm, Scottish Opera, 39 Elmbank Crescent, Glasgow G2 4PT, Scotland. In charge of overall adm matters. Born 12 Feb 1946, Aberdeen, Scotland. Single. Studied: Aberdeen Univ, Scotland; hon in music. Plays the piano. Previous occupations: Program Asst, BBC, London. Started with present company 1971 as Asst to Gen Adm, in present position since 1973. **Res:** 24 Belmont St, Glasgow, Scotland G12 8EY, UK.

DUGDALE, SANDRA. Coloratura soprano. British. Resident mem: English National Opera, London. Born 4 Jan 1946, Pudsey, Yorkshire, UK. Husband Ewing Ross Sutherland, occupation chartered secy. Studied: Guildhall School of Music and Drama, London; Vera Rosza, Rupert Bruce Lockhart, London. **Debut:** Despina (*Così fan tutte*) Glyndebourne Fest 1970. Awards: Gregory Hast Silver Trophy, Guildhall School of Music & Drama.
Sang with major companies in UK: Glyndebourne Fest, London English National. **Roles with these companies incl** MOZART: *Despina★* (*Così fan tutte*), *Blondchen★* (*Entführung aus dem Serail*); OFFENBACH: *Olympia★* (*Contes d'Hoffmann*); PENDERECKI: *Philippe★* (*Teufel von Loudun*); STRAUSS, J: *Adele★* (*Fledermaus*); STRAUSS, R: *Sophie★* (*Rosenkavalier*); VERDI: *Oscar* (*Ballo in maschera*). Gives recitals. Appears with symphony orchestra. **Res:** 40 Crossway, Welwyn Garden City/Herts, UK. Mgmt: IWL/UK.

DÜGGELIN, WERNER. Stages/produces opera & theater and is an arts administrator. Swiss. Dir & Resident Stage Dir, Stadttheater Basel. Born Switzerland.
Directed/produced opera for major companies in FR GER: Frankfurt, Wiesbaden; SWI: Basel; et al. **Operas staged with these companies incl** JANACEK: *From the House of the Dead;* MOZART: *Entführung aus dem Serail;* STRAUSS, R: *Frau ohne Schatten;* TCHAIKOVSKY: *Eugene Onegin;* et al. Previous leading positions with major theater companies: Prod, Burgtheater, Vienna.

DUNBAR, CLARK DENNIS. Dramatic baritone. American. Resident mem: Musiktheater Gelsenkirchen; Stadttheater Lübeck, FR Ger. Born 25 Jun 1938, Rochester, NY, USA. Wife Jutta Tenor, occupation actress. Studied: Eastman School of Music, Julius Huehn, Rochester, NY; State Univ NY, Richard Sheil, Fredonia; Vienna Acad of Music, Prof Wolfgang Steinbrück, Mo Carlo Zattoni. **Debut:** Rodrigo (*Don Carlo*) Städtische Oper, Bremen 1962. Awards: Fulbright Grant to Vienna 1961; Rockefeller Fndt Grant 1962.

Sang with major companies in AUS: Vienna Volksoper; FR GER: Bonn, Dortmund, Essen, Munich Gärtnerplatz, Saarbrücken; HOL: Amsterdam. **Roles with these companies incl** d'ALBERT: Sebastiano (*Tiefland*); BIZET: Escamillo★ (*Carmen*); CIMAROSA: Count Robinson (*Matrimonio segreto*); DONIZETTI: Dott Malatesta (*Don Pasquale*), Belcore (*Elisir*), Enrico (*Lucia*); GERSHWIN: Crown, (*Porgy and Bess*); GIORDANO: Carlo Gérard (*Andrea Chénier*); LEONCAVALLO: Tonio★ (*Pagliacci*); LORTZING: Graf Eberbach (*Wildschütz*), Peter I (*Zar und Zimmermann*); MOZART: Guglielmo (*Così fan tutte*), Figaro (*Nozze di Figaro*), Papageno (*Zauberflöte*); NICOLAI: Fluth★ (*Lustigen Weiber*); OFFENBACH: Coppélius etc★ (*Contes d'Hoffmann*); ORFF: Kreon (*Antigonae*), Solo (*Carmina burana*); PUCCINI: Marcello★ (*Bohème*), Sharpless★ (*Butterfly*), Lescaut (*Manon Lescaut*); ROSSINI: Figaro★ (*Barbiere di Siviglia*), Robert (*Comte Ory*); STRAUSS, R: Musiklehrer★ (*Ariadne auf Naxos*), Orest (*Elektra*), STRAVINSKY: Empereur de Chine★ (*Rossignol*); VERDI: Renato (*Ballo in maschera*), Rodrigo★ (*Don Carlo*), Ford (*Falstaff*), Don Carlo★ (*Forza del destino*), Germont★ (*Traviata*), Conte di Luna (*Trovatore*); WAGNER: Wolfram (*Tannhäuser*), Kurwenal (*Tristan und Isolde*). Gives recitals. Appears with symphony orchestra. Teaches voice. **Res:** Königsbergerstr 63, 465 Gelsenkirchen, FR Ger. Mgmt: HBM/USA; SLZ/FRG.

DUNLAP, JOHN ROBERT. Dramatic baritone. American. Born 22 Jan 1934, Lancaster, PA, USA. Single. Studied: Amato Opera, New York; Jan Popper, UCLA, CA; Columbia Univ, Rudolph Thomas, New York; Susquehanna Univ, PA, USA; Vienna State Acad for Music and the Performing Arts, Josef Witt, Erik Werba, Austria. **Debut:** Coppélius etc (*Contes d'Hoffmann*) Regensburg Opera, FR Ger 1958. Awards: Ntl Music League Awd; Austrian Gvnmt Grant; M B Rockefeller Fund, two grants.

Sang with major companies in FR GER: Bonn, Frankfurt, Hannover, Wiesbaden, Augsburg; USA: Kansas City, New Orleans, New York Met & City Opera, Portland, St Paul, San Diego, San Francisco Spring Opera. **Roles with these companies incl** BEETHOVEN: Don Pizarro (*Fidelio*); BIZET: Escamillo (*Carmen*); BRITTEN: Traveller (*Curlew River*), Bottom (*Midsummer Night*); DALLAPICCOLA: Prigioniero, Riviere (*Volo di notte*); DONIZETTI: Enrico (*Lucia*); GLUCK: Thoas (*Iphigénie en Tauride*); HANDEL: Giulio Cesare; HINDEMITH: Professor (*Hin und züruck*); LEONCAVALLO: Tonio (*Pagliacci*); MASCAGNI: Alfio (*Cavalleria rusticana*); MOZART: Guglielmo (*Così fan*

tutte), Conte Almaviva (*Nozze di Figaro*); PUCCINI: Marcello (*Bohème*), Sharpless★ (*Butterfly*), Lescaut (*Manon Lescaut*), Michele (*Tabarro*), Scarpia (*Tosca*); SAINT-SAENS: Grand prêtre (*Samson et Dalila*); VERDI: Amonasro (*Aida*), Renato (*Ballo in maschera*), Falstaff, Nabucco, Rigoletto, Germont (*Traviata*), Conte di Luna (*Trovatore*); WAGNER: Holländer, Wotan (*Walküre*), Wolfram (*Tannhäuser*). Also WAGNER: Alberich★ (*Siegfried*). **World premieres:** TRAVIS: Creon (*Passion of Oedipus*) UCLA, CA, USA 1968. **Res:** 57 Westminster Rd, Brooklyn, NY 11218, USA. Mgmt: SMN/USA.

DUNN, MIGNON. Dramatic mezzo-soprano. American. Resident mem: Metropolitan Opera, New York. Born Memphis, TN, USA. Husband Kurt Klippstatter, occupation conductor. Studied: Karin Branzell, New York; American Theatre Wing, acting; Kathryn Turney Long Course, Met Opera; Beverley Johnson, New York. **Debut:** Carmen, New Orleans Opera 1955. Previous occupations: receptionist, tour guide. Awards: Hon DM Southwestern Coll, Memphis, TN, USA.

Sang with major companies in ARG: Buenos Aires; AUS: Vienna Staatsoper; BEL: Brussels; CAN: Montreal/Quebec, Toronto; FIN: Helsinki; FRA: Paris, Strasbourg; FR GER: Berlin Deutsche Oper, Cologne, Düsseldorf-Duisburg, Frankfurt, Hamburg, Karlsruhe; ISR: Tel Aviv; ITA: Verona Arena; MEX: Mexico City; UK: London Royal; USA: Boston, Chicago, Cincinnati, Hartford, Memphis, Newark, New Orleans, New York Met & City Opera, Philadelphia Grand & Lyric, Pittsburgh, Portland, San Francisco Opera. **Roles with these companies incl** BARTOK: Judith (*Bluebeard's Castle*); BERLIOZ: Anna★ (*Troyens*); BIZET: Carmen★; CILEA: Princesse de Bouillon★ (*A. Lecouvreur*); FALLA: Abuela (*Vida breve*); GLUCK: Orfeo★; GOUNOD: Siebel (*Faust*); MASCAGNI: Beppe (*Amico Fritz*); MASSENET: Dulcinée★ (*Don Quichotte*), Hérodiade★; MENOTTI: Desideria (*Saint of Bleecker Street*); MONTEVERDI: Orfeo★, Poppea★ (*Incoronazione di Poppea*); MUSSORGSKY: Marina★ (*Boris Godunov*); OFFENBACH: Giulietta★ (*Contes d'Hoffmann*); PONCHIELLI: Laura★ & La Cieca (*Gioconda*); PUCCINI: Suzuki (*Butterfly*); SAINT-SAENS: Dalila; STRAUSS, R: Klytämnestra (*Elektra*), Amme★ (*Frau ohne Schatten*), Herodias★‡ (*Salome*); TCHAIKOVSKY: Mme Larina (*Eugene Onegin*); VERDI: Amneris (*Aida*), Ulrica (*Ballo in maschera*), Eboli★ (*Don Carlo*), Preziosilla (*Forza del destino*), Federica★ (*Luisa Miller*), Azucena★ (*Trovatore*); WAGNER: Ortrud★ (*Lohengrin*), Magdalene (*Meistersinger*), Erda (*Rheingold, Siegfried*), Fricka (*Rheingold★, Walküre★*), Waltraute★ (*Götterdämmerung*), Venus (*Tannhäuser*), Brangäne★ (*Tristan und Isolde*). Recorded for: DG. Gives recitals. Appears with symphony orchestra. Mgmt: BAR/USA; AIM/UK.

DUNSZT, MARIA. Dramatic soprano. Hungarian. Resident mem: State Opera, Budapest. Born 10 Oct 1936, Budapest. Husband Lenard Czapek, occupation engr. Studied: Acad of Music, Profs Imre Molnar, Oszkar Maleczky, Budapest. **Debut:** Melinda (*Bánk Bán*) State Opera, Budapest 1961. Awards: First Prize & Grand Prix, Intl Compt

Toulouse, France 1960; Second Prize, Intl Compt Erkel, Budapest 1960; Prix Niveau Budapest 1974; Medal CSSR 1974.

Sang with major companies in HUN: Budapest. **Roles with these companies incl** BIZET: Micaëla (*Carmen*); BORODIN: Jaroslavna (*Prince Igor*); ERKEL: Melinda★ (*Bánk Bán*); GOUNOD: Marguerite★ (*Faust*); JANACEK: Kostelnicka (*Jenufa*); MASCAGNI: Santuzza★‡ (*Cavalleria rusticana*); MOZART: Donna Anna★ (*Don Giovanni*); OFFENBACH: Olympia & Antonia & Giulietta (*Contes d'Hoffmann*); ORFF: Kluge; PETROVICS: Sonia (*Crime and Punishment*); PUCCINI: Tosca; ROSSINI: Mathilde (*Guillaume Tell*); SHOSTAKOVICH: Katerina Ismailova★; VERDI: Aida★‡, Elisabetta (*Don Carlo*), Desdemona (*Otello*), Violetta★ (*Traviata*), Leonora★ (*Trovatore*); WAGNER: Elsa★ (*Lohengrin*), Eva★ (*Meistersinger*), Sieglinde★ (*Walküre*), Gutrune (*Götterdämmerung*), Elisabeth★ (*Tannhäuser*). Also GOLDMARK: Sulamit★ (*Königin von Saba*); PETROVICS: Wife (*C'est la guerre*); KACSOTT: King's Daughter (*Johannes Held*); ERKEL: Elisabeth★ (*Hunyadi László*). **World premieres:** PETROVICS: Dressed-up Woman (*Crime and Punishment*) State Opera Budapest 1969-70. Video – Hun TV: Santuzza (*Cavalleria rusticana*); Kostelnicka (*Jenufa*). Appears with symphony orchestra. **Res:** III Arpad Fejedelem utja 59, 1036 Budapest, Hungary.

DU PLESSIS, CHRISTIAN JOHANNES. Lyric baritone. South African. Resident mem: English National Opera, Opera Rara, London. Born 2 Jul 1944, Vryheid, South Africa. Single. Studied: Otakar Kraus, London; Dr Teasdale Griffiths, Esme Webb, South Africa. **Debut:** Yamadori (*Butterfly*) PACT, Johannesburg 1967.

Sang with major companies in S AFR: Johannesburg; SPA: Barcelona; UK: London English National. **Roles with these companies incl** BELLINI: Ernesto★ (*Pirata*); DONIZETTI: Cecil★‡ (*Maria Stuarda*); GLUCK: Oreste★ (*Iphigénie en Tauride*); GOUNOD: Valentin★ (*Faust*); HANDEL: Garibald★ (*Rodelinda*); PUCCINI: Marcello★ (*Bohème*); VERDI: Rodrigo★ (*Don Carlo*), Francesco Foscari★ (*Due Foscari*), Macbeth, Germont★ (*Traviata*). Also MONTEVERDI: Ottone★ (*Incoronazione di Poppea*); STRAUSS, J: Falke (*Fledermaus*); MAYR: Creonte★ (*Medea in Corinto*); PONIATOWSKI: Pascalini★ (*Au travers du mur*). Recorded for: Decca, ABC-Dunhill. Gives recitals. Appears with symphony orchestra. **Res:** c/o Schmid, 8 Haverstock St, London N1, UK.

DU-POND, CARLOS DÍAZ. Stages/produces opera; designs sets & costumes. Mexican. Born 11 Dec 1911, Celaya. Single. Studied: as asst to Armando Agnini, Désiré Defrère, Enrico Frigerio, William von Wymetal, Carlo Maestrini, Tito Capobianco & Renzo Frusca, Mexico City. **Operatic debut:** *Aida* Monterrey 1953. Awards: gold and silver medals; diplomas for best performance of season.

Directed/produced opera for major companies in MEX: Mexico City; USA: Fort Worth. **Operas staged with these companies incl** BELLINI: Sonnambula; BIZET: Carmen; BOITO: Mefistofele; CILEA: Adriana Lecouvreur; DEBUSSY: Enfant prodigue; DONIZETTI: Don Pasquale★, Elisir, Favorite, Lucia★; FALLA: Retablo de Maese Pedro, Vida breve; GIORDANO: Andrea Chénier★; GLUCK: Orfeo ed Euridice; GOUNOD: Faust; HINDEMITH: Hin und zurück; HUMPERDINCK: Hänsel und Gretel; LEONCAVALLO: Pagliacci; MASCAGNI: Amico Fritz, Cavalleria rusticana; MASSENET: Manon, Werther; MENOTTI: Amelia al ballo, Telephone; MONTEVERDI: Combattimento di Tancredi; MOZART: Così fan tutte, Nozze di Figaro, Zauberflöte; OFFENBACH: Contes d'Hoffmann★; PERGOLESI: Serva padrona; PONCHIELLI: Gioconda; POULENC: Dialogues des Carmélites; PUCCINI: Bohème★, Gianni Schicchi, Butterfly★, Manon Lescaut, Suor Angelica, Tabarro, Tosca, Turandot★; PURCELL: Dido and Aeneas; ROSSINI: Barbiere di Siviglia, Cenerentola; STRAUSS, J: Fledermaus; STRAVINSKY: Oedipus Rex; THOMAS: Mignon; VERDI: Aida★, Ballo in maschera★, Don Carlo, Forza del destino, Otello, Rigoletto, Traviata★, Trovatore; WAGNER: Fliegende Holländer★, Lohengrin★, Tannhäuser★; WOLF-FERRARI: Segreto di Susanna. Teaches. **Res:** Copérnico 125, Mexico City, Mexico.

DUPOUY, JEAN. Lyric tenor. French. Resident mem: Opéra de Paris. Born 18 Jul 1938, Pau, France. Married. Studied: Paris Consv Ntl Supérieur de Musique; J Giraudeau, Louis Musy, Paris. **Debut:** Nadir (*Pêcheurs de perles*) Capitole, Toulouse 1968. Awards: First Prize Golden Voice; First Prize in voice and opera, Consv Ntl Sup de Musique, Paris.

Sang with major companies in BEL: Brussels, Liège; FRA: Aix-en-Provence Fest, Bordeaux, Lyon, Marseille, Nice, Paris, Rouen, Toulouse; ITA: Palermo; USA: Miami. **Roles with these companies incl** BERLIOZ: Benvenuto Cellini★, Faust★ (*Damnation de Faust*); BIZET: Nadir★ (*Pêcheurs de perles*); DALLAPICCOLA: Radio Telegrapher (*Volo di notte*); DELIBES: Gérald★ (*Lakmé*); DONIZETTI: Edgardo★ (*Lucia*); GLUCK: Renaud★ (*Armide*); GOUNOD: Faust★, Vincent★ (*Mireille*), Roméo★; MASSENET: Des Grieux★ (*Manon*), Nicias★ (*Thaïs*); PUCCINI: Rodolfo★ (*Bohème*), Pinkerton★ (*Butterfly*); STRAUSS, R: Ein Sänger (*Rosenkavalier*); VERDI: Duca di Mantova★ (*Rigoletto*), Alfredo★ (*Traviata*); WAGNER: Walther v d Vogelweide (*Tannhäuser*). **World premieres:** BONDON: Innocent (*Nuit foudroyée*) Metz Opera 1968. **Res:** Paris, France. Mgmt: IMR/FRA.

DURE, ROBERT. Dramatic tenor. American. Born 25 Nov 1934, Baltimore, MD, USA. Wife Rosemarie, occupation PS music teacher. Two children. Studied: Peabody Consv of Music, Fraser Grange, Felix Brentano, Baltimore, MD; Univ of Maryland, Fague Springman, College Pk, MD; Cecile Jacobson, New York. **Debut:** Villager (*Pagliacci*) Baltimore Civic Opera 1955. Previous occupations: mechanical engineer. Awards: Opera Schlshp Peabody Consv of Music, Baltimore.

Sang with major companies in USA: Baltimore, Hartford, Kentucky, Washington DC. **Roles with these companies incl** BERNSTEIN: Sam (*Trouble in Tahiti*); FLOYD: Sam Polk★ (*Susannah*); HAYDN: Nancio (*Infedeltà delusa*); HINDE-

MITH: Robert (*Hin und zurück*); MOZART: Ferrando (*Così fan tutte*), Don Ottavio★ (*Don Giovanni*); ORFF: Solo (*Carmina burana*); PUCCINI: Rinuccio (*Gianni Schicchi*), Pinkerton (*Butterfly*), Cavaradossi★ (*Tosca*); SMETANA: Hans★ (*Bartered Bride*); STRAUSS, J: Eisenstein★ (*Fledermaus*); VERDI: Alfredo (*Traviata*). Also LIEBERMANN: Horace (*Schule der Frauen*). Video—WJZ TV: Sam Polk (*Susannah*). Gives recitals. Appears with symphony orchestra. Teaches voice. Coaches repertoire. Res: La Porte, IN, USA.

DU TOIT, NELLIE. Spinto. South African. Born 17 Dec 1929, Pietersburg, S Afr. Husband Philip Crouse, occupation translator. Four children. Studied: Cape Town Coll of Music, Adelheid Armhold; Tatiana Makushina, London. **Debut:** Butterfly, National Opera, Cape Town 1957. Awards: Overseas Schlshp for Perf Licenciate, Univ of S Afr; 7th Prize Worldwide Madama Butterfly Compt; Nederburg Prize, Cape Province 1972, Transvaal 1974.

Sang with major companies in S AFR: Johannesburg. **Roles with these companies incl** BELLINI: Norma★; BERLIOZ: Héro (*Béatrice et Bénédict*); BIZET: Micaëla★ (*Carmen*); DONIZETTI: Lucia★; FLOTOW: Lady Harriet (*Martha*); GIORDANO: Maddalena★ (*Andrea Chénier*); LORTZING: Gretchen (*Wildschütz*); MENOTTI: Monica (*Medium*), Lucy (*Telephone*); MOZART: Fiordiligi (*Così fan tutte*), Donna Anna (*Don Giovanni*), Contessa★ & Susanna (*Nozze di Figaro*), Pamina★ & Königin der Nacht (*Zauberflöte*); PERGOLESI: Serpina (*Serva padrona*); PUCCINI: Mimì★ & Musetta (*Bohème*), Lauretta (*Gianni Schicchi*), Cio-Cio-San★ (*Butterfly*), Suor Angelica, Tosca★, Liù★ (*Turandot*); PURCELL: Dido; SMETANA: Marie (*Bartered Bride*); STRAUSS, J: Rosalinde★ (*Fledermaus*); VERDI: Violetta★ (*Traviata*), Leonora (*Trovatore*); WOLF-FERRARI: Susanna (*Segreto di Susanna*). **World premieres:** JOUBERT: Elsie (*Drought*) Johannesburg 1958. Gives recitals. Appears with symphony orchestra. Teaches voice. Coaches repertoire. **Res:** 257 Celliers St Muckleneuk, Pretoria, S Africa.

DUVAL, PIERRE; né Ovide Coutu. Lyric tenor. Canadian. Born Sep 1932, Montreal, Canada. Wife Jacqueline. Two children. Studied: Consv de Musique, Montreal. **Debut:** Pêcheur (*Guillaume Tell*) Teatro dell'Opera, Rome 1961.

Sang with major companies in CAN: Montreal/Quebec, Ottawa, Toronto, Vancouver; ITA: Bologna, Rome Opera; S AFR: Johannesburg; SPA: Barcelona; USA: Fort Worth, Hartford, Hawaii, Milwaukee Florentine, New Orleans, New York City Opera, Philadelphia Grand & Lyric, Pittsburgh. **Roles with these companies incl** BELLINI: Lord Arthur★‡ (*Puritani*), Elvino★ (*Sonnambula*); BIZET: Nadir (*Pêcheurs de perles*); DELIBES: Gérald (*Lakmé*); DONIZETTI: Ernesto★ (*Don Pasquale*), Fernand (*Favorite*), Tonio★ (*Fille du régiment*), Edgardo★ (*Lucia*), Leicester (*Maria Stuarda*); GOUNOD: Faust, Roméo★; MASSENET: Des Grieux★ (*Manon*); MONTEMEZZI: Avito★ (*Amore dei tre re*); MOZART: Don Ottavio★ (*Don Giovanni*); PUCCINI: Rodolfo (*Bohème*), Cavaradossi (*Tosca*); ROSSINI: Almaviva★ (*Barbiere di Siviglia*); VERDI: Fenton★ (*Falstaff*), Duca di Mantova★ (*Rigoletto*). Recorded for: RCA, London, Delphi. Video/Film: Roméo; Macduff (*Macbeth*). Appears with symphony orchestra. **Res:** St Adolphe d'Howard, Canada. Mgmt: SAM/USA.

DVORAKOVA, LUDMILA. Dramatic soprano. Czechoslovakian. Resident mem: Staatsoper, Berlin, German DR. Husband Rudolf Vasata, occupation opera conductor. Studied: State Consv, Prague. **Debut:** Katya Kabanova, Ostrava, CSSR.

Sang with major companies in ARG: Buenos Aires; AUS: Graz, Vienna Staatsoper; BEL: Brussels; CZE: Brno, Prague National & Smetana; DEN: Copenhagen; FIN: Helsinki; FRA: Bordeaux, Marseille, Nice, Paris, Rouen; GRE: Athens Fest; FR GER: Bayreuth Fest, Berlin Deutsche Oper, Bonn, Düsseldorf-Duisburg, Hamburg, Hannover, Karlsruhe, Kiel, Mannheim, Munich Staatsoper, Stuttgart, Wiesbaden; GER DR: Berlin Staatsoper, Dresden, Leipzig; HUN: Budapest; ITA: Genoa, Milan La Scala, Palermo, Rome Opera, Venice; POL: Warsaw; ROM: Bucharest; SPA: Barcelona; SWI: Geneva; UK: London Royal; USSR: Kiev, Leningrad Kirov; USA: New York Met, Philadelphia Grand, San Francisco Opera; YUG: Zagreb. **Roles with these companies incl** BEETHOVEN: Leonore★ (*Fidelio*); DVORAK: Rusalka; MASCAGNI: Santuzza★ (*Cavalleria rusticana*); MOZART: Contessa (*Nozze di Figaro*); PUCCINI: Manon Lescaut, Tosca★, Turandot; SMETANA: Mlada (*Dalibor*), Hedvika (*Devil's Wall*); STRAUSS, R: Ariadne★ (*Ariadne auf Naxos*), Elektra & Chrysothemis (*Elektra*), Färberin (*Frau ohne Schatten*), Marschallin & Octavian (*Rosenkavalier*); VERDI: Aida, Amelia (*Ballo in maschera*), Elisabetta (*Don Carlo*), Leonora (*Trovatore*); WAGNER: Senta★ (*Fliegende Holländer*), Ortrud★ (*Lohengrin*), Brünnhilde (*Walküre★, Siegfried★, Götterdämmerung★*), Gutrune (*Götterdämmerung*), Elisabeth & Venus★ (*Tannhäuser*), Isolde★, Kundry★ (*Parsifal*). Appears with symphony orchestra. **Res:** Na Orechovce 14, Prague, CSSR. Mgmt: PRG/CZE; BAL/FRG.

E

EBERT, PETER. Stages/produces opera & theater and is an actor. British. Intendant & Resident Stage Dir, Staatstheater, Wiesbaden since 1975. Born 6 Apr 1918, Frankfurt/Main. Wife Silvia. Ten children. Operatic training as asst stage dir at Glyndebourne Fest with father, Prof Carl Ebert; New English Opera Co. **Operatic debut:** *Mefistofele* Glasgow Grand Opera, UK 1951. Theater debut: PACT, Johannesburg, S Afr 1966. Previous occupation: film, TV & radio dir. Previous adm positions in opera: Dir of Prod, Scottish Opera, Glasgow 1965-76; Intendant, Stadttheater Augsburg 1968-73; Intendant, Stadttheater Bielefeld 1973-75.

Directed/produced opera for major companies in CAN: Montreal/Quebec, Toronto; DEN: Copenhagen; FR GER: Bielefeld, Düsseldorf-Duisburg, Essen, Hannover, Nürnberg, Wiesbaden; HOL: Amsterdam; ITA: Naples, Rome Opera, Venice; S AFR: Johannesburg; SWI: Basel; UK: Edinburgh Fest, Scottish, Glyndebourne Fest. **Operas staged for these companies incl** ADAM: *Si j'étais roi;* BEETHOVEN: *Fidelio⋆;* BELLINI: *Puritani, Sonnambula;* BERLIOZ: *Troyens⋆;* BIZET: *Carmen⋆;* BOITO: *Mefistofele;* BRITTEN: *Peter Grimes, Rape of Lucretia;* BUSONI: *Arlecchino;* CIMAROSA: *Matrimonio segreto;* DALLAPICCOLA: *Volo di notte;* DEBUSSY: *Pelléas et Mélisande⋆;* DONIZETTI: *Campanello, Don Pasquale⋆, Elisir, Fille du régiment;* EINEM: *Dantons Tod, Prozess;* FLOTOW: *Martha;* GIORDANO: *Andrea Chénier;* GLUCK: *Iphigénie en Aulide, Orfeo ed Euridice;* HANDEL: *Giulio Cesare;* HAYDN: *Mondo della luna;* HUMPERDINCK: *Hänsel und Gretel⋆;* LORTZING: *Wildschütz;* MENOTTI: *Amahl, Medium;* MOZART: *Così fan tutte, Don Giovanni⋆, Entführung aus dem Serail, Finta giardiniera⋆, Idomeneo, Nozze di Figaro⋆, Schauspieldirektor, Zauberflöte⋆;* OFFENBACH: *Contes d'Hoffmann;* PERGOLESI: *Frate 'nnamorato;* PFITZNER: *Palestrina⋆;* PONCHIELLI: *Gioconda;* POULENC: *Dialogues des Carmélites;* PUCCINI: *Bohème⋆, Butterfly⋆, Manon Lescaut, Tabarro;* PURCELL: *Dido and Aeneas;* RAVEL: *Heure espagnole;* ROSSINI: *Barbiere di Siviglia, Cenerentola⋆, Comte Ory⋆, Guillaume Tell, Italiana in Algeri;* SMETANA: *Bartered Bride⋆;* STRAUSS, R: *Ariadne auf Naxos, Daphne, Frau ohne Schatten⋆, Rosenkavalier⋆, Salome;* STRAVINSKY: *Oedipus Rex, Rake's Progress;* VERDI: *Ballo in maschera, Don Carlo⋆, Due Foscari, Ernani, Falstaff⋆, Forza del destino, Nabucco, Otello, Rigoletto⋆, Simon Boccanegra, Traviata, Trovatore;* WAGNER: *Fliegende Holländer, Meistersinger⋆, Rheingold⋆, Walküre⋆, Siegfried⋆, Götterdämmerung⋆;* WEBER: *Freischütz;* WOLF-FERRARI: *Segreto di Susanna.* Operatic Video — BBC TV: *Traviata.* Previous leading positions with major theater companies: Art Dir, Los Angeles Opera, CA 1965. **Res:** Wiesbaden, FR Ger.

ECHARRI, ISABEL. Scenic and costume designer for opera, theater. Is also a painter, sculptor, illustrator & des of tapestry. Spanish. Born 10 Feb 1929, Vera de Bidasoa, Spain. Husband Diégo Etcheverry, occupation designer. Two children. Studied: Ecole Ntl Supérieur des Beaux-Arts, Paris. **Operatic debut:** Grand Théâtre, Nancy, France 1956. Theater debut: Comédie de Paris, 1956.

Designed for major companies in ARG: Buenos Aires; BEL: Brussels, Liège; FRA: Bordeaux, Marseille, Nancy, Paris, Rouen, Toulouse; FR GER: Karlsruhe; POL: Warsaw; SPA: Barcelona. **Operas designed for these companies incl** BIZET: *Carmen⋆;* BOITO: *Mefistofele;* BRITTEN: *Rape of Lucretia⋆;* DEBUSSY: *Pelléas et Mélisande;* GOUNOD: *Mireille;* MASSENET: *Manon⋆, Werther⋆;* MENOTTI: *Consul, Medium;* MOZART: *Così fan tutte, Don Giovanni⋆, Nozze di Figaro⋆, Zauberflöte⋆;* ORFF: *Carmina burana⋆;* PERGOLESI: *Serva padrona⋆;* POULENC: *Dialogues des Carmélites;* PUCCINI: *Tosca⋆, Turandot⋆;* RABAUD: *Mârouf⋆;* STRAUSS, R: *Arabella⋆;* TCHAIKOVSKY: *Pique Dame⋆;* VERDI: *Traviata⋆.* Also LANDOWSKI: *Les Adieux;* FRANCAIX: *Apostrophe;* IBERT-HONEGGER: *Aiglon.* **Operatic world premieres:** CHAILLY: *Thyl* Opéra de Nancy 1963; SEMENOFF: *Don Juan, ou L'amour de la géométrie* Centre Lyrique, Tours 1969; CASANOVA: *Bonheur dans le crime* Capitole, Toulouse 1973; BONDON: *I 330* Opéra de Nantes 1975; SEMENOFF: *Sire Halewyn* Théâtre Graslin, Nantes 1970. Exhibitions of stage designs, paintings, sculptures, graphics and tapestries, Paris 1956; Rome 1958; Aarhus, Denmark 1970; Ibiza 1971; Lausanne 1974; Tokyo 1966; Goltenborg, Denmark 1967; Saint-Etienne 1968; Munich 1964; 12 German museums 1972-73; Paris 1974. **Res:** Paris, France, and Formentera/Balcares, Spain.

ECKER, HEINZ-KLAUS. Bass-baritone & bass. Austrian. Resident mem: Städtische Bühnen, Nürnberg; Gärtnerplatz, Munich. Born 25 Dec 1942, Kiel, FR Ger. Wife Karin. Two children. Studied: Bruckner Konsv, Linz, Austria; Prof Helene Auer, Prof Stefan Zadejan, Prof Tino Halpern, Graz. **Debut:** Alcalde (*Forza del destino*) Stadttheater, Aachen, FR Ger 1964. Previous occupations: technical engineer, Vöst, Linz.

Sang with major companies in AUS: Graz, Vienna Volksoper; FRA: Lyon, Nancy; FR GER: Berlin Deutsche Oper, Bonn, Dortmund, Düsseldorf-Duisburg, Hamburg, Hannover, Munich Staatsoper & Gärtnerplatz, Nürnberg, Stuttgart, Wiesbaden; GER DR: Berlin Staatsoper; NOR: Oslo. Roles with these companies incl BEETHOVEN: Rocco★ (*Fidelio*); DESSAU: Lanzelot★; DONIZETTI: Don Pasquale: EINEM: St Just (*Dantons Tod*); FLOTOW: Plunkett★ (*Martha*); LORTZING: Baculus★ (*Wildschütz*); MOZART: Don Alfonso★ (*Così fan tutte*), Osmin★ (*Entführung aus dem Serail*), Don Pippo (*Oca del Cairo*), Sarastro★ (*Zauberflöte*); MUSSORGSKY: Boris Godunov★; ROSSINI: Don Basilio★ (*Barbiere di Siviglia*); SMETANA: Kezal★ (*Bartered Bride*); STRAUSS, R: Orest★ (*Elektra*), Barak★ (*Frau ohne Schatten*), Baron Ochs★ (*Rosenkavalier*); VERDI: Ramfis (*Aida*), Falstaff★, Fra Melitone (*Forza del destino*), Banquo (*Macbeth*), Zaccaria★ (*Nabucco*); WAGNER: Daland★ (*Fliegende Holländer*), König Heinrich★ (*Lohengrin*), Pogner★ (*Meistersinger*), Fafner★ (*Siegfried*), Landgraf★ (*Tannhäuser*), König Marke (*Tristan und Isolde*); ZIMMERMANN: Wesener★ (*Soldaten*). Video: Nazarene (*Salome*). Gives recitals. Appears with symphony orchestra. **Res:** Lessingstr 4, 8502 Zirndorf, FR Ger. Mgmt: SLZ/FRG.

ECKERT, GERTRAUD. Dramatic mezzo-soprano & soprano. Austrian. Resident mem: Opernhaus, Graz & Innsbruck, Austria. Born 17 Aug 1941, Vienna. Single. Studied: Judith Hellwig; Franz Schuch-Tovini. **Debut:** Cherubino (*Nozze di Figaro*) Théâtre de la Monnaie, Brussels 1963. Previous occupations: secy.

Sang with major companies in AUS: Bregenz Fest, Graz; BEL: Brussels; FR GER: Bonn, Essen. Roles with these companies incl BARTOK: Judith★ (*Bluebeard's Castle*); BIZET: Carmen★; DONIZETTI: Léonore (*Favorite*); EGK: Babekan★ (*Verlobung in San Domingo*); EINEM: Claire★ (*Besuch der alten Dame*); FLOTOW: Nancy★ (*Martha*); GLUCK: Orfeo; HUMPERDINCK: Hänsel; MOZART: Dorabella (*Così fan tutte*), Cherubino (*Nozze di Figaro*); PUCCINI: Suzuki★ (*Butterfly*); ROSSINI: Rosina (*Barbiere di Siviglia*); STRAUSS, J: Prinz Orlovsky★ (*Fledermaus*); STRAUSS, R: Komponist★ (*Ariadne auf Naxos*), Klytämnestra★ (*Elektra*), Octavian★ (*Rosenkavalier*); TCHAIKOVSKY: Olga (*Eugene Onegin*); VERDI: Amneris★ (*Aida*), Ulrica (*Ballo in maschera*), Eboli★ (*Don Carlo*), Preziosilla★ (*Forza del destino*), Azucena★ (*Trovatore*); WAGNER: Ortrud★ (*Lohengrin*), Magdalene★ (*Meistersinger*), Erda★ (*Siegfried*), Fricka (*Rheingold★, Walküre★*), Waltraute★ (*Götterdämmerung*), Venus★ (*Tannhäuser*). Also OFFENBACH: Nicklausse (*Contes d'Hoffmann*); BERG: Marie (*Wozzeck*); FORTNER: Magd (*Bluthochzeit*); MASCAGNI:

Santuzza (*Cavalleria rusticana*); VERDI: Lady Macbeth; SCHMIDT: Esmeralda (*Notre-Dame*). Teaches voice. **Res:** Schirnböckg 3, Vienna 1130, Austria. Mgmt: TAS/AUS; SMD/FRG.

ECKSTEIN, PAVEL. Czechoslovakian. Advisor to the Gen Mng, National Theater Prague, Divadelni 6, Prague 1, CSSR. In charge of adm & artistic matters. Born 27 Apr 1911, Opava, CSR. Wife Anna. One daughter. Studied: Charles Univ Prague; doctorate. Plays the piano & violin. Previous positions, primarily musical: Gen Sec, Intl Music Fest, Prague Spring 1948-52; Sec, Composers Guild of Czechoslovakia 1952-54, 1956-71; Dir, Concert Agency HAU 1954-56; active music critic since 1937. Started in present position in 1964. Awards: Order Polonia Restituta, Pres of Polish Rep; Richard Wagner Gold Medal, Mayor of Bayreuth; Max Reinhardt Silver Medal, Salzburger Festspielfond; Antonin Dvorak Memorial Medal, Guild of Czechoslovak Composers. Mem of board of editors for Czech Music Journal *Hudebni Rozhledy*. **Res:** Srobarova 23, 130 00 Prague 3, CSSR.

EDA-PIERRE, CHRISTIANE. Coloratura soprano. French. Resident mem: Paris Opera. Born Fort de France, Martinique. Husband Pierre Lacaze, occupation Prof Consv de Paris, fencing coach French Olympic Team. One son. Studied: Consv de Paris. **Debut:** Lucia, Paris Opera 1962.

Sang with major companies in FRA: Aix-en-Provence Fest, Bordeaux, Lyon, Marseille, Orange Fest, Paris, Rouen, Strasbourg, Toulouse; FR GER: Berlin Deutsche Oper, Hamburg; HOL: Amsterdam; POR: Lisbon; SPA: Barcelona; UK: Edinburgh Fest; USA: Chicago, Miami. Roles with these companies incl BELLINI: Imogene★ (*Pirata*), Elvira★ (*Puritani*); BERLIOZ: Teresa‡ (*Benvenuto Cellini*); BIZET: Léila (*Pêcheurs de perles*); DELIBES: Lakmé; DONIZETTI: Norina (*Don Pasquale*), Adina (*Elisir*), Lucia★; GLUCK: Amor★ (*Orfeo ed Euridice*); GOUNOD: Juliette; MOZART: Konstanze★ & Blondchen★ (*Entführung aus dem Serail*), Königin der Nacht (*Zauberflöte*); OFFENBACH: Olympia★ & Antonia★ (*Contes d'Hoffmann*); PUCCINI: Musetta (*Bohème*), Lauretta (*Gianni Schicchi*); STRAUSS, J: Adele (*Fledermaus*); STRAUSS, R: Zerbinetta (*Ariadne auf Naxos*); STRAVINSKY: Rossignol; VERDI: Nannetta (*Falstaff*), Gilda★ (*Rigoletto*), Violetta (*Traviata*). Also RAMEAU: (*Indes galantes*). Recorded for: Philips. Video/Film—ORTF TV: Antonia & Olympia (*Contes d'Hoffmann*). Gives recitals. Appears with symphony orchestra. **Res:** Paris, France. Mgmt: BCP/FRA; DBA/USA.

EDDLEMAN, JACK; né Robert Jack Eddleman. Stages/produces opera & theater and is a singer, actor & author. American. Resident Stage Dir, New York City Opera. Born 7 Sep 1933, Millsap, TX. Single. Studied: Univ of Tulsa, OK; Univ of Kansas City, MO; Inst for Advanced Studies in Theatre Arts, NY; incl music, voice and dance. **Operatic debut:** *Yeomen of the Guard* Kansas City Lyric Theater 1972. Theater debut: Theatre 7, Decatur, IL 1965. Previous occupation: performer in Broadway musicals and other productions.

Directed/produced opera for major companies in

USA: Kansas City, Lake George, New York City Opera, St Paul. **Operas staged with these companies incl** LEONCAVALLO: *Pagliacci*★*;* MOZART: *Entführung aus dem Serail*★*, Zauberflöte*★*;* OFFENBACH: *Périchole*★*;* PUCCINI: *Gianni Schicchi*★*;* ROSSINI: *Barbiere di Siviglia*★*;* STRAUSS, J: *Fledermaus*★*.*

EDELMANN, OTTO KARL. Bass-baritone & basso-buffo. Austrian. Resident mem: Staatsoper, Vienna. Born 5 Feb 1917, Vienna. Wife Ilse-Maria, occupation interpreter. Three children. Studied: Akad für Musik und darstellende Kunst, Profs Lierhammer, Gunnar Graarud, Krips, Vienna. **Debut:** Figaro (*Nozze di Figaro*) Gera/Thüringen, Germany. Awards: Medal of Pope John XXIII; Bruckner-Te Deum Awd, Vatican 1959; Dannebrog-Orden Chevalier 1st Class, King of Denmark 1962; Gold Medal of Merit, Gvnmt of Austria 1970; Austrian Kammersänger, Pres of Austria 1960; Max Reinhardt Medal, Fest of Salzburg 1971.

Sang with major companies in AUS: Bregenz Fest, Graz, Salzburg Fest, Vienna Staatsoper & Volksoper; BEL: Brussels, Liège; BRA: Rio de Janeiro; CAN: Montreal/Quebec; DEN: Copenhagen; FRA: Lyon, Marseille, Nancy, Nice, Rouen, Strasbourg; FR GER: Bayreuth Fest, Berlin Deutsche Oper, Cologne, Dortmund, Düsseldorf-Duisburg, Frankfurt, Hamburg, Munich Staatsoper, Nürnberg, Stuttgart, Wiesbaden; ITA: Florence Maggio, Milan La Scala, Turin; MON: Monte Carlo; POR: Lisbon; SWI: Geneva, Zurich; UK: Edinburgh Fest, Glyndebourne Fest; USA: Chicago Lyric, Cincinnati, Dallas Civic, Houston Grand, New York Met, Philadelphia Grand, Pittsburgh, San Antonio, San Diego, San Francisco Opera, Washington DC. **Roles with these companies incl** BEETHOVEN: Don Pizarro‡ & Rocco★ *(Fidelio)*; FLOTOW: Plunkett *(Martha)*; GLUCK: Calchas & Agamemnon *(Iphigénie en Aulide)*; GOUNOD: Méphistophélès *(Faust)*; HINDEMITH: Cardillac; LORTZING: Stadinger *(Waffenschmied)*, Van Bett★ *(Zar und Zimmermann)*; MENOTTI: Husband *(Amelia al ballo)*; MOZART: Leporello★‡ *(Don Giovanni)*, Osmin *(Entführung aus dem Serail)*, Sarastro & Sprecher *(Zauberflöte)*; NICOLAI: Falstaff★ *(Lustigen Weiber)*; ORFF: Petrus★ *(Mond)*; SHOSTAKOVICH: Boris★*(Katerina Ismailova)*; SMETANA: Kezal‡ *(Bartered Bride)*; STRAUSS, R: Graf Waldner‡ *(Arabella)*, Baron Ochs★‡ *(Rosenkavalier)*; VERDI: Ramfis *(Aida)*, Philip II & Grande Inquisitore *(Don Carlo)*, Falstaff‡, Padre Guardiano *(Forza del destino)*; WAGNER: Holländer & Daland‡ *(Fliegende Holländer)*, König Heinrich *(Lohengrin)*, Hans Sachs★‡ & Pogner‡ *(Meistersinger)*, Amfortas & Gurnemanz *(Parsifal)*, Wotan *(Rheingold, Walküre* ‡*)*, Wanderer *(Siegfried)*, Landgraf *(Tannhäuser)*, König Marke *(Tristan und Isolde)*. Also KORNGOLD: *(Kathrin)*. Recorded for: Columbia, His Master's Voice, Philips, Angel. Video/Film: Leporello *(Don Giovanni)*; Baron Ochs *(Rosenkavalier)*; Falstaff; Padre Guardiano *(Forza del destino)*. Gives recitals. Appears with symphony orchestra. Teaches voice. Coaches repertoire. On faculty of Hochschule für Musik und darstellende Kunst, Vienna. Res: Breitenfurterstr 547, 1238 Vienna/Kalksburg, Austria. Mgmt: HJH/USA.

EDER, CLAUDIA. Lyric coloratura mezzo-soprano. German. Resident mem: Hessisches Staatstheater, Wiesbaden; Theater am Gärtnerplatz, Munich. Born 7 Feb 1948, Augsburg, Germany. Husband Prof Dr Lothar Gall, occupation prof of mod history, Univ Frankfurt. Studied: Staatliche Hochschulen für Musik, Munich & Frankfurt; Marianne Schech, Elsa Cavelti. **Debut:** Nicklausse *(Contes d'Hoffmann)* Stadttheater Bielefeld, FR Ger 1973.

Sang with major companies in FR GER: Bielefeld, Munich Gärtnerplatz, Wiesbaden. **Roles with these companies incl** HUMPERDINCK: Hänsel★; MOZART: Dorabella★ *(Così fan tutte)*; PFITZNER: Silla★ *(Palestrina)*; ROSSINI: Angelina★ *(Cenerentola)*. Also OFFENBACH: Nicklausse★ *(Contes d'Hoffmann)*; VERDI: Meg Page★ *(Falstaff)*. Mgmt: RTB/FRG.

EDWARDS, ANNE. Dramatic soprano. British. Born Builth Wells, Wales, UK. Husband Colin Courtney, occupation musician. One son. Studied: Guildhall School of Music, London; Prof Arthur Reckless, Prof Roy Henderson. **Debut:** Frasquita *(Carmen)* Carl Rosa Co, Italy. Awards: Guildhall School Prize; Lord Mayor's Prize, City of London; May Herbut Awd.

Sang with major companies in FR GER: Bielefeld; SPA: Barcelona; UK: Cardiff Welsh, Edinburgh Fest, London Royal Opera & English National. **Roles with these companies incl** BEETHOVEN: Marzelline *(Fidelio)*; BIZET: Micaëla *(Carmen)*; BOITO: Margherita *(Mefistofele)*; BRITTEN: Miss Wingrave★ *(Owen Wingrave)*; GAY/Britten: Lucy *(Beggar's Opera)*; GOUNOD: Marguerite *(Faust)*; HUMPERDINCK: Gretel; LEONCAVALLO: Nedda *(Pagliacci)*; MASCAGNI: Santuzza★ *(Cavalleria rusticana)*; MOZART: Donna Anna & Donna Elvira *(Don Giovanni)*, Konstanze *(Entführung aus dem Serail)*, Elettra *(Idomeneo)*, Contessa *(Nozze di Figaro)*; ORFF: Solo *(Carmina burana)*; PUCCINI: Mimi & Musetta *(Bohème)*, Cio-Cio-San *(Butterfly)*, Manon Lescaut; SMETANA: Marie *(Bartered Bride)*; STRAUSS, J: Rosalinde *(Fledermaus)*; STRAUSS, R: Ariadne *(Ariadne auf Naxos)*, Chrysothemis★ *(Elektra)*, Salome; TCHAIKOVSKY: Lisa *(Pique Dame)*; VERDI: Aida★, Mina *(Aroldo)*, Odabella★ *(Attila)*, Amelia *(Ballo in maschera)*, Elisabetta★ *(Don Carlo)*, Donna Elvira *(Ernani)*, Leonora *(Forza del destino)*, Giselda *(Lombardi)*, Lady Macbeth, Abigaille *(Nabucco)*, Gilda *(Rigoletto)*, Violetta *(Traviata)*, Leonora *(Trovatore)*; WAGNER: Senta *(Fliegende Holländer)*, Elisabeth *(Tannhäuser)*; ZANDONAI: Francesca da Rimini. Also VERDI: Leonora *(Oberto)*. Gives recitals. Appears with symphony orchestra. Mgmt: OEA/UK; LLF/USA.

EHRENSPERGER, GISELA; née Heuzeroth. Lyric soprano. Swiss. Resident mem: Gärtnerplatztheater, Munich. Born 10 Aug 1943, Wiesbaden, Germany. Divorced. Husband Paul, occupation adm director. Two children. Studied: Sofia Husi, Zurich. **Debut:** Musetta *(Bohème)* St Gallen Opera, Switzerland 1965. Awards: Bayerische Kammersängerin, Bayerisches Kultusministerium.

Sang with major companies in FR GER: Berlin Deutsche Oper, Munich Gärtnerplatz, Nürnberg;

GER DR: Berlin Staatsoper; HOL: Amsterdam; ITA: Milan La Scala; SPA: Barcelona. **Roles with these companies incl** BIZET: Micaëla★ (*Carmen*); HENZE: Luise (*Junge Lord*); HUMPERDINCK: Gretel; LEONCAVALLO: Nedda★(*Pagliacci*); LORTZING: Marie (*Waffenschmied*), Gretchen (*Wildschütz*), Marie (*Zar und Zimmermann*); MENOTTI: Monica (*Medium*); MOZART: Konstanze & Blondchen (*Entführung aus dem Serail*), Mlle Silberklang★ (*Schauspieldirektor*), Pamina (*Zauberflöte*); NICOLAI: Aennchen★ (*Lustigen Weiber*); PROKOFIEV: Louisa (*Duenna*); PUCCINI: Mimi & Musetta (*Bohème*); ROSSINI: Rosina (*Barbiere di Siviglia*); STRAUSS, J: Adele (*Fledermaus*). Also PURCELL: all sop roles★ (*Fairy Queen*); d'ALBERT: Nuri★ (*Tiefland*); LOTHAR: Una (*Widerspenstige Heilige*). **World premieres:** WIMBERGER: Imogen (*Lebensregeln*) Gärtnerplatz, Munich 1972; LANG: Dortchen Allgemein (*Alchemist*) Radio Zurich 1969; ROSENBERGER: Elisabeth (*Backside Story*) Bayerischer Rundfunk, Munich 1974. Video/Film−Deutsches Fernsehen: Imogen (*Lebensregeln*); Zurich Radio: Dortchen Allgemein (*Alchemist*). Gives recitals. Appears with symphony orchestra. **Res:** Kempteuerstr 23, 8 Munich, FR GER.

EHRLING, SIXTEN. Conductor of opera and symphony. Swedish. Resident Cond, Metropolitan Opera, New York. Also Resident Cond, Juilliard Orch, New York. Born 3 Apr 1918, Malmö, Sweden. Wife Gunnel Lindgren, occupation form ballerina, Swedish Royal Opera. Two daughters. Studied: Royal Acad of Music, Stockholm; incl piano, violin, cello and voice. Operatic training as repetiteur & asst cond at Royal Opera, Stockholm 1939-44. **Operatic debut:** *Pagliacci* Royal Opera, Stockholm 1942. Symphonic debut: Göteborg Symph, Sweden 1942. Awards: numerous orders and Hon D degrees. Previous adm positions in opera: Mus Dir, Royal Opera, Stockholm 1953-60.

Conducted with major companies in CAN: Montreal/Quebec; FR GER: Hamburg, Wiesbaden; NOR: Oslo; SWE: Drottningholm Fest, Stockholm; UK: Edinburgh Fest, London Royal; USA: New York Met, San Francisco Opera. **Operas with these companies incl** BARTOK: *Bluebeard's Castle★;* BEETHOVEN: *Fidelio;* BERG: *Wozzeck;* BIZET: *Carmen;* BRITTEN: *Peter Grimes★, Rape of Lucretia, Turn of the Screw;* IBERT: *Angélique;* LEONCAVALLO: *Pagliacci;* MASCAGNI: *Cavalleria rusticana;* MASSENET: *Thaïs;* MENOTTI: *Consul;* MOZART: *Zauberflöte;* OFFENBACH: *Contes d'Hoffmann;* PUCCINI: *Bohème, Butterfly, Tosca, Trittico★;* SAINT-SAENS: *Samson et Dalila;* STRAUSS, R: *Rosenkavalier, Salome;* VERDI: *Aida★, Ballo in maschera★, Don Carlo, Falstaff, Otello, Rigoletto, Simon Boccanegra★, Traviata★;* WAGNER: *Fliegende Holländer, Meistersinger, Parsifal, Rheingold★, Walküre★, Siegfried★, Götterdämmerung★, Tannhäuser.* **World premieres:** BLOMDAHL: *Aniara* Royal Opera, Stockholm 1959; ATTERBERG: *Tempest* Royal Opera, Stockholm. Conducted major orch in Europe, USA/Canada, Asia, Austrl. Previous positions as Mus Dir with major orch: Detroit Symph, MI, USA 1963-73. Teaches at Juilliard School, New York. **Res:** 10 W 66 St, New York, USA. Mgmt: CAM/USA.

EICHELBERGER, SUSAN ELAINE. Lyric soprano. American. Resident mem: Israel National Opera, Tel Aviv. Born 4 Aug 1948, Cincinnati, O, USA. Single. Studied: Cincinnati College-Consv of Music, Lucile & Robert Evans; Philadelphia Acad of Vocal Arts, Dorothy Di Scala, PA, USA. **Debut:** Yvette (*Rondine*) Philadelphia Lyric 1972. Awards: Neff Graduate Fllshp, Cincinnati College-Consv of Music, O, USA.

Sang with major companies in ISR: Tel Aviv; USA: Philadelphia Lyric. **Roles with these companies incl** DONIZETTI: Norina★ (*Don Pasquale*); OFFENBACH: Olympia★ & Antonia★ (*Contes d'Hoffmann*), PUCCINI: Mimi★ (*Bohème*), Cio-Cio-San★ (*Butterfly*). Gives recitals. Appears with symphony orchestra. **Res:** 18 Arnon St, Tel Aviv, Israel.

EICKSTAEDT, KARIN. Coloratura soprano. German. Resident mem: Staatsoper Dresden, Staatsoper Berlin, Ger DR. Born 21 Apr 1942, Dessau, Germany. Divorced. Studied: Hochschule für Musik, Weimar, Halle & Leipzig; Profs Helga Forner and Dagmar Freiwald-Lange. **Debut:** Königin der Nacht (*Zauberflöte*) Stadttheater Zeitz, Ger DR 1965. Previous occupations: baby nurse. Awards: Prizewinner Compt Ger DR 1970; Diploma Compt Enescu, Bucharest 1970.

Sang with major companies in CZE: Brno; FR GER: Wiesbaden; GER DR: Berlin Komische Oper & Staatsoper, Dresden, Leipzig; HUN: Budapest; POL: Warsaw; ROM: Bucharest; USSR: Leningrad Kirov. **Roles with these companies incl** ADAM: Madeleine★ (*Postillon de Lonjumeau*); BEETHOVEN: Marzelline★ (*Fidelio*); DESSAU: Elsa★ (*Lanzelot*); HANDEL: Deidamia; HUMPERDINCK: Gretel★; LORTZING: Gretchen (*Wildschütz*); MOZART: Fiordiligi★ & Despina★ (*Così fan tutte*), Konstanze★ & Blondchen★ (*Entführung aus dem Serail*), Mme Herz★ & Mlle Silberklang★ (*Schauspieldirektor*), Cherubino (*Nozze di Figaro*), Königin der Nacht★ (*Zauberflöte*); NICOLAI: Aennchen★ (*Lustigen Weiber*); OFFENBACH: Olympia★ (*Contes d'Hoffmann*); ORFF: Solo★ (*Carmina burana*); PUCCINI: Musetta★ (*Bohème*), Lauretta★ (*Gianni Schicchi*); ROSSINI: Rosina (*Barbiere di Siviglia*); STRAUSS, J: Adele★ (*Fledermaus*); STRAUSS, R: Zerbinetta★ (*Ariadne auf Naxos*), Sophie★ (*Rosenkavalier*); VERDI: Oscar (*Ballo in maschera*), Nannetta★ (*Falstaff*), Gilda★ (*Rigoletto*); WOLF-FERRARI: Lucieta (*Quattro rusteghi*). Also STRAUSS, R: Italienische Sängerin★ (*Capriccio*); LIEBERMANN: Agnes (*Schule der Frauen*); DESSAU: Königin★ (*Lukullus*). **World premieres:** KUNAD: Jeanne (*Maître Pathelin*) Staatsoper Dresden 1969. Recorded for: Eterna. Video−TV: Musetta (*Bohème*); Rosina (*Barbiere di Siviglia*). Gives recitals. Appears with symphony orchestra. Coaches repertoire. **Res:** Spitzwegstr 60, 8020 Dresden, Ger DR. Mgmt: KDR/GDR.

EK, JENS CHRISTIAN. Stages/produces opera & theater. Also designs sets & stage-lighting and is a singer & actor. Norwegian. Dir of Touring Activity & Resident Stage Dir, Norwegian Opera, Oslo. Born 23 Mar 1925, Fredrikstad, Norway. Wife

Merete Nissen, occupation singer. Two children. Operatic training as asst stage dir at Norwegian Opera, Oslo 1962-66. **Operatic debut:** *Serva padrona* Norwegian Opera 1965. Theater debut: Rogaland Theater, Stavanger 1960. Previous occupation: naval officer, actor, singer.

Directed/produced opera for major companies in NOR: Oslo. **Operas staged with these companies incl** BRITTEN: *Rape of Lucretia★;* DONIZETTI: *Elisir★;* MASCAGNI: *Cavalleria rusticana★;* MONTEVERDI: *Incoronazione di Poppea★;* MOZART: *Così fan tutte, Don Giovanni★, Nozze di Figaro★;* PUCCINI: *Bohème★;* ROSSINI: *Barbiere di Siviglia★;* VERDI: *Rigoletto, Traviata★;* WAGNER: *Fliegende Holländer;* WEBER: *Freischütz★.* **Operatic world premieres:** JOHNSEN: *Legenden om Svein og Maria* Norwegian Opera, Oslo 1973. Res: Oskar Braatens V 5B, Oppegard/Sofiemyr 1412, Norway.

ELDER, MARK PHILIP. Conductor of opera and symphony. British. Resident Cond, English National Opera, London. Born 2 Jun 1947, Hexham, Northumberland. Wife Karen Rose Westwood, occupation producer's asst. Studied: Corpus Christi Coll, Cambridge; incl piano, organ, harpsichord, bassoon and voice. Plays the harpsichord, piano. Operatic training as repetiteur, asst cond, chorus master & prompter at Glyndebourne Fest 1970-72; Covent Garden, London 1971-72; Wexford Fest 1968-69. **Operatic debut:** *Rigoletto* Australian Opera, Melbourne 1972. Symphonic debut: Royal Liverpool Phil, UK 1971.

Conducted with major companies in AUSTRL: Sydney; UK: London English National. **Operas with these companies incl** HENZE: *Bassariden★;* MASCAGNI: *Cavalleria rusticana★;* MOZART: *Zauberflöte★;* PROKOFIEV: *War and Peace★;* PUCCINI: *Bohème★, Gianni Schicchi★, Tabarro★;* STRAUSS, R: *Rosenkavalier★;* VERDI: *Ballo in maschera★, Forza del destino★, Nabucco★, Rigoletto★.* Conducted major orch in Europe. **Res:** 108 Eastcombe Ave, London SE7, UK. Mgmt: IWL/UK.

ELIAS, ROSALIND. Lyric mezzo-soprano. American. Resident mem: Metropolitan Opera, New York. Born 13 Mar 1931, Lowell, MA, USA. Husband Zuhayr Moghrabi, occupation lawyer. Studied: New England Consv, Boston; S Cecilia Acad, Rome; Daniel Ferro, New York. **Debut:** Grimgerde (*Walküre*) Metropolitan Opera 1954. Awards: Hon Dr, Merrimack Coll, Andover, MA.

Sang with major companies in ARG: Buenos Aires; AUS: Salzburg Fest, Vienna Staatsoper; CAN: Ottawa; FRA: Aix-en-Provence Fest, Marseille; FR GER: Hamburg; ISR: Tel Aviv; MON: Monte Carlo; POR: Lisbon; SPA: Barcelona; SWI: Geneva; UK: Glasgow Scottish, Glyndebourne Fest; USA: Cincinnati, Hartford, Milwaukee Florentine, New Orleans, New York Met, Philadelphia Lyric, San Francisco Opera. **Roles with these companies incl** BARTOK: Judith‡ (*Bluebeard's Castle*); BARBER: Erika‡ (*Vanessa*); BIZET: Carmen★; CIMAROSA: Fidalma (*Matrimonio segreto*); FLOTOW: Nancy (*Martha*); GOUNOD: Siebel (*Faust*); HANDEL: Orlando (*Orlando furioso*); HUMPERDINCK: Hänsel; MASSENET: Charlotte‡ (*Werther*); MO-

ZART: Dorabella (*Così fan tutte*), Zerlina (*Don Giovanni*), Cherubino‡ (*Nozze di Figaro*); MUSSORGSKY: Marina★ (*Boris Godunov*); OFFENBACH: Giulietta (*Contes d'Hoffmann*); PONCHIELLI: Laura‡ & La Cieca (*Gioconda*); PUCCINI: Suzuki‡ (*Butterfly*); ROSSINI: Rosina★ (*Barbiere di Siviglia*), Angelina (*Cenerentola*), Isolier★ (*Comte Ory*); SAINT-SAENS: Dalila; STRAUSS, R: Octavian (*Rosenkavalier*); STRAVINSKY: Baba the Turk★ (*Rake's Progress*); VERDI: Amneris (*Aida*), Preziosilla‡ (*Forza del destino*), Azucena‡ (*Trovatore*). **World premieres:** BARBER: Erika (*Vanessa*) Metropolitan Opera 1958, Charmian (*Antony and Cleopatra*) Metropolitan Opera 1966. Recorded for: Columbia, RCA. Video—CBS TV: LADERMAN: Bathsheba (*And David Wept*); LEES: Medea (*Medea*). Gives recitals. Appears with symphony orchestra. **Res:** New York, USA. Mgmt: BAR/USA; AIM/UK.

ELIASSON, SVEN OLOF. Dramatic tenor & Jugendl Heldentenor. Swedish. Resident mem: opera companies in Düsseldorf, Frankfurt, Zurich. Born 4 Apr 1933, Boliden, Sweden. Wife Ulla. Three daughters. Studied: Royal Acad of Music, Prof Ragnar Hultén, Stockholm. **Debut:** Don Ottavio (*Don Giovanni*) Oslo Opera, Norway 1962.

Sang with major companies in AUS: Vienna Staatsoper; BEL: Brussels; CAN: Montreal/Quebec; DEN: Copenhagen; FRA: Rouen; FR GER: Berlin Deutsche Oper, Düsseldorf-Duisburg, Hamburg, Kiel, Munich Staatsoper, Stuttgart, Wiesbaden; HOL: Amsterdam; NOR: Oslo; SWE: Drottningholm Fest, Stockholm; SWI: Geneva, Zurich; UK: Edinburgh Fest, Glyndebourne Fest. **Roles with these companies incl** BENNETT: Bonconnion (*Mines of Sulphur*); BIZET: Don José★ (*Carmen*); BRITTEN: Aschenbach★ (*Death in Venice*), Peter Grimes★; BUSONI: Mephisto★ (*Doktor Faust*); DEBUSSY: Pelléas★; GINASTERA: Pier Francesco Orsini★ (*Bomarzo*); GOUNOD: Faust; JANACEK: Albert Gregor★ (*Makropoulos Affair*); MASSENET: Des Grieux★ (*Manon*); MONTEVERDI: Nero★ (*Incoronazione di Poppea*), Ulisse★‡ (*Ritorno d'Ulisse*); MOZART: Tito★ (*Clemenza di Tito*), Ferrando★ (*Così fan tutte*), Don Ottavio (*Don Giovanni*), Belmonte (*Entführung aus dem Serail*); PFITZNER: Palestrina★; PUCCINI: Rodolfo★ (*Bohème*), Pinkerton (*Butterfly*), Luigi (*Tabarro*); ROSSINI: Almaviva (*Barbiere di Siviglia*); SCHOENBERG: Aron★ (*Moses und Aron*); STRAUSS, J: Eisenstein★ & Alfred (*Fledermaus*); STRAUSS, R: Bacchus★ (*Ariadne auf Naxos*); STRAVINSKY: Oedipus★, Tom Rakewell (*Rake's Progress*); TCHAIKOVSKY: Lenski★ (*Eugene Onegin*); VERDI: Riccardo★ (*Ballo in maschera*), Don Carlo, Duca di Mantova (*Rigoletto*), Alfredo★ (*Traviata*), Manrico★ (*Trovatore*); WAGNER: Erik★ (*Fliegende Holländer*), Lohengrin★, Walther★ (*Meistersinger*), Parsifal★; WEBER: Max★ (*Freischütz*). Also MUSSORGSKY: Dimitri (*Boris Godunov*). **World premieres:** KLEBE: Christy (*Wahrer Held*) Opernhaus Zurich 1975. Recorded for: Tele-Dec. Video/Film: Ferrando (*Così fan tutte*). Gives recitals. Appears with symphony orchestra. Teaches voice. Mgmt: NRK/NOR; SLZ/FRG.

ELKINS, MARGRETA. Coloratura & dramatic mezzo-soprano. Australian. Resident mem: Australian Opera, Sydney. Born 16 Oct 1936, Brisbane. Husband Henry James, occupation businessman. One child. Studied: Ruby Dent, Brisbane; Pauline Bindley, Melbourne; Mo Campogalliani, Mantua, Italy; Vera Rozsa, London. **Debut:** Azucena (*Trovatore*) Brisbane Opera Co.

Sang with major companies in AUSTRL: Sydney; CAN: Vancouver; FRA: Lyon, Orange Fest; FR GER: Cologne; HOL: Amsterdam; ITA: Genoa, Naples; POR: Lisbon; SPA: Barcelona; UK: Cardiff Welsh, Edinburgh Fest, London Royal & English National; USA: Boston, Hartford, New Orleans, Philadelphia Lyric. **Roles with these companies incl** BELLINI: Adalgisa★ (*Norma*); BERLIOZ: Ascanio (*Benvenuto Cellini*), Marguerite (*Damnation de Faust*), Didon (*Troyens*); BIZET: Carmen; CILEA: Princesse de Bouillon (*A. Lecouvreur*); DONIZETTI: Léonore (*Favorite*), Sara (*Roberto Devereux*); GLUCK: Clytemnestre (*Iphigénie en Aulide*); GOUNOD: Siebel‡ (*Faust*); HANDEL: Bradamante & Ruggiero (*Alcina*), Giulio Cesare, Bertaric & Hadwig★ (*Rodelinda*); MASSENET: Charlotte (*Werther*); MAYR: Medea★ (*Medea in Corinto*); MEYERBEER: Fidès (*Prophète*); MOZART: Sesto (*Clemenza di Tito*), Dorabella★ (*Così fan tutte*), Cherubino (*Nozze di Figaro*); OFFENBACH: Giulietta (*Contes d'Hoffmann*); PUCCINI: Suzuki (*Butterfly*); ROSSINI: Rosina (*Barbiere di Siviglia*), Sinaïde★ (*Moïse*); SAINT-SAENS: Dalila; STRAUSS, J: Prinz Orlovsky (*Fledermaus*); STRAUSS, R: Komponist★ (*Ariadne auf Naxos*), Amme (*Frau ohne Schatten*), Octavian (*Rosenkavalier*), Herodias★ (*Salome*); VERDI: Amneris★ (*Aida*), Eboli★ (*Don Carlo*), Azucena★ (*Trovatore*); WAGNER: Adriano (*Rienzi*). Also TCHAIKOVSKY: Tatiana (*Eugene Onegin*). **World premieres:** TIPPETT: Helen (*King Priam*) Royal Opera, Coventry, UK 1962. Recorded for: Decca, EMI. Gives recitals. Appears with symphony orchestra. Mgmt: EDY/AUSTRL; IMR/FRA.

ELLIS, BRENT E. Baritone. American. Born 20 Jun 1946, Kansas City, MO, USA. Divorced. Studied: Edna Forsythe, Kansas City, MO; Juilliard School of Music, Marion Freschl, New York; Daniel Ferro, New York; Luigi Ricci, Rome. **Debut:** Maerbale (*Bomarzo*) Washington, DC, Opera Soc 1966. Prev occupations: over two yrs Army service. Awards: Ntl Op Inst Grant; Rockefeller Fndt Grant; Bori Fndt Met Op; Sullivan Grant; Winner WGN Illinois Op Guild Aud of the Air 1972; *Musical America*, Young Artist of the Year 1973.

Sang with major companies in USA: Chicago, Houston, New York City Opera, Omaha, Philadelphia Lyric, San Francisco Spring Opera, Santa Fe, Washington DC. **Roles with these companies incl** BIZET: Escamillo★ (*Carmen*); FLOYD: George Milton★ (*Of Mice and Men*); MASSENET: Lescaut★ (*Manon*); MOZART: Guglielmo★ (*Così fan tutte*), Conte Almaviva & Figaro★ (*Nozze di Figaro*); ROSSINI: Figaro★ (*Barbiere di Siviglia*); TCHAIKOVSKY: King René★ (*Iolanthe*); VERDI: Ford★ (*Falstaff*), Germont★ (*Traviata*), Conte di Luna★ (*Trovatore*). Also MONTEVERDI: Ottone★ (*Incoronazione di Poppea*); WEBER: Cherasmin★ (*Oberon*). **World pre-**

mieres: GINASTERA: Maerbale (*Bomarzo*) Washington, DC, Opera Soc 1967. Gives recitals. Appears with symphony orchestra. Coaches repertoire. **Res:** 251 W 89 St, New York, NY, USA. Mgmt: CAM/USA.

ELMS, LAURIS. Contralto. Australian. Born 20 Oct 1931, Melbourne. Husband Graeme de Graaff, occupation coll principal. One child. Studied: Katherine Wielaert, Melbourne; Dominique Modesti, Paris. **Debut:** Ulrica (*Ballo in maschera*) Royal Opera Covent Garden 1957. Previous occupations: art teacher. Awards: Officer of the British Empire; Medal, Conc Intl of Geneva.

Sang with major companies in AUSTRL: Sydney; UK: London Royal. **Roles with these companies incl** BRITTEN: Lucretia★ (*Rape of Lucretia*); PUCCINI: Principessa★ (*Suor Angelica*), Frugola★ (*Tabarro*); ROSSINI: Arsace (*Semiramide*); TCHAIKOVSKY: Olga (*Eugene Onegin*); VERDI: Amneris★ (*Aida*), Ulrica★ (*Ballo in maschera*), Azucena★ (*Trovatore*). Recorded for: Decca. Video/Film: Dalila; Königin (*Schwanda*). Gives recitals. Appears with symphony orchestra. **Res:** 10 Strathmore Pde Chatswood, 2067 Sydney, Australia.

ELVÍRA, PABLO. Lyric baritone. American. Resident mem: New York City Opera. Born 24 Sep 1938, Santurce, Puerto Rico. Wife Signe Landoe. Studied: Pablo Casals Consv, Puerto Rico. **Debut:** Rigoletto, Indiana Univ Opera Theater, Bloomington, USA 1968. Previous occupations: trumpeter & dir of own dance orch.

Sang with major companies in MEX: Mexico City; USA: Fort Worth, Hartford, Memphis, New Orleans, New York Met & New York City Opera, San Diego, Santa Fe. **Roles with these companies incl** BEETHOVEN: Don Pizarro (*Fidelio*); BELLINI: Sir Richard (*Puritani*); BERG: Wozzeck★; BIZET: Escamillo (*Carmen*), Zurga★ (*Pêcheurs de perles*); DONIZETTI: Dott Malatesta★ (*Don Pasquale*), Belcore (*Elisir*), Alfonse (*Favorite*), Enrico★ (*Lucia*); GIORDANO: Carlo Gérard (*Andrea Chénier*); HENZE: Mittenhofer (*Elegy for Young Lovers*); LEONCAVALLO: Tonio★ (*Pagliacci*); MASCAGNI: Alfio (*Cavalleria rusticana*); MOZART: Don Giovanni, Conte Almaviva★ & Figaro★ (*Nozze di Figaro*), Papageno (*Zauberflöte*); PERGOLESI: Uberto (*Serva padrona*); PONCHIELLI: Barnaba (*Gioconda*); PUCCINI: Marcello (*Bohème*), Gianni Schicchi★, Sharpless★ (*Butterfly*), Michele★ (*Tabarro*), Scarpia★ (*Tosca*); ROSSINI: Figaro★ (*Barbiere di Siviglia*), Conte Asdrubal★ (*Pietra del paragone*); STRAUSS, R: Mandryka★ (*Arabella*); TCHAIKOVSKY: Yeletsky★ (*Pique Dame*); VERDI: Amonasro★ (*Aida*), Renato★ (*Ballo in maschera*), Rodrigo★ (*Don Carlo*), Ford (*Falstaff*), Don Carlo (*Forza del destino*), Iago★ (*Otello*), Rigoletto★, Germont★ (*Traviata*), Conte di Luna★ (*Trovatore*); WOLF-FERRARI; Conte Gil (*Segreto di Susanna*). Also GOUNOD: Valentin★ (*Faust*); ROSSINI: Taddeo (*Italiana in Algeri*); HINES: John the Baptist (*I Am the Way*). **World premieres:** EATON: Heracles, Indiana Univ Opera Theater, Bloomington 1971. Video/Film: Gil (*Segreto di Susanna*); King Melchior (*Amahl*); Uberto (*Serva padrona*). Gives recitals. Appears with symphony orchestra. **Res:** 619 So Tracy, Bozeman, MT, USA. Mgmt: SMN/USA.

EMILI, ROMANO. Lyric tenor. Italian. Resident mem: Deutsche Oper am Rhein, Düsseldorf-Duisburg. Born 7 Nov 1937, Bologna, Italy. Wife Anke Bremen. One daughter. Studied: Mo Armando Grandi, Bologna; Centro Avviamento Lirico, Mo Contini, Florence. **Debut:** Giannetto (*Gazza ladra*) Maggio Musicale, Florence 1965. Previous occupations: merchant. Awards: First Prize Intl Cont, Munich 1965; First Prize Accad Chigiana, Siena 1965.

Sang with major companies in DEN: Copenhagen; FR GER: Cologne, Dortmund, Düsseldorf-Duisburg, Essen, Frankfurt, Hamburg, Mannheim, Munich Staatsoper, Saarbrücken, Stuttgart; HOL: Amsterdam; ITA: Bologna, Florence Maggio & Comunale, Genoa, Rome Opera, Trieste, Turin; MEX: Mexico City; MON: Monte Carlo; UK: Cardiff Welsh; USA: Washington DC. **Roles with these companies incl** ADAM: Chapelou (*Postillon de Lonjumeau*); BIZET: Nadir (*Pêcheurs de perles*); BUSONI: Leandro (*Arlecchino*); CAVALLI: Ormindo; DALLAPICCOLA: Jailer/Inquisitor‡ (*Prigioniero*); DONIZETTI: Riccardo (*Anna Bolena*), Ernesto★ (*Don Pasquale*), Nemorino (*Elisir*), Edgardo★ (*Lucia*); MASSENET: Werther; MOZART: Mitridate★; NICOLAI: Fenton★ (*Lustigen Weiber*); PUCCINI: Rodolfo★ (*Bohème*), Rinuccio (*Gianni Schicchi*), Pinkerton★ (*Butterfly*), Des Grieux (*Manon Lescaut*); ROSSINI: Almaviva★ (*Barbiere di Siviglia*), Giannetto (*Gazza ladra*), Lindoro★ (*Italiana in Algeri*); STRAUSS, R: Ein Sänger★ (*Rosenkavalier*), Henry Morosus (*Schweigsame Frau*); VERDI: Fenton★ (*Falstaff*), Duca di Mantova★ (*Rigoletto*), Alfredo★ (*Traviata*); WOLF-FERRARI: Florindo (*Donne curiose*). Also ROSSINI: Uberto/Giacomo★ (*Donna del lago*). Recorded for: London, Decca. Gives recitals. Appears with symphony orchestra. **Res:** Gemenstr 23, 4044 Kaarst, FR Ger. Mgmt: PAS/FRG; HUR/USA.

ENGEN, KIETH S. Bass. American. Resident mem: Bayerische Staatsoper, Munich. Born 5 Apr 1925, Frazee, MN. Wife Erika, occupation actress, writer. One child. Studied: Mrs O K McMurray, Berkeley, CA; Kmsg Tino Pattiera, Kmsg Pavel Ludikar, Prof Elisabeth Rado, Vienna. **Debut:** Bluebeard (*Bluebeard's Castle*) Munich 1955. Awards: Kammersänger, Bayerische Staatsoper 1963; Order of Merit, Bavaria 1970.

Sang with major companies in ARG: Buenos Aires; AUS: Graz, Salzburg Fest, Vienna Staatsoper & Volksoper; FRA: Paris, Strasbourg; FR GER: Bayreuth Fest, Berlin Deutsche Oper, Cologne, Darmstadt, Dortmund, Düsseldorf-Duisburg, Frankfurt, Hamburg, Hannover, Munich Staatsoper & Gärtnerplatz, Nürnberg, Stuttgart; HOL: Amsterdam; ITA: Florence Maggio, Turin; UK: Edinburgh Fest, London Royal. **Roles with these companies incl** d'ALBERT: Tommaso (*Tiefland*); BARTOK: Bluebeard; BEETHOVEN: Rocco (*Fidelio*); BERG: Doktor★ (*Wozzeck*); BRITTEN: Bottom (*Midsummer Night*); CIKKER: Courvoisier (*Play of Love*); DEBUSSY: Siméon (*Enfant prodigue*); DESSAU: Lanzelot; DONIZETTI: Henry VIII (*Anna Bolena*); FORTNER: Norfolk (*Elisabeth Tudor*);

GLUCK: Thoas (*Iphigénie en Tauride*); GOUNOD: Méphistophélès (*Faust*); HANDEL: Polyphemus (*Acis and Galatea*), Ptolemy (*Giulio Cesare*); HENZE: Mittenhofer (*Elegy for Young Lovers*); JANACEK: Gorianchikov (*From the House of the Dead*); MENOTTI: Husband (*Amelia al ballo*); MEYERBEER: Don Pedro (*Africaine*); MOZART: Publio (*Clemenza di Tito*), Don Alfonso★ (*Così fan tutte*), Don Giovanni, Conte Almaviva★ (*Nozze di Figaro*), Sarastro (*Zauberflöte*); MUSSORGSKY: Varlaam (*Boris Godunov*), Dosifei (*Khovanshchina*); NICOLAI: Falstaff (*Lustigen Weiber*); ORFF: Kreon (*Antigonae*), Solo (*Carmina burana*), König (*Kluge*); PERGOLESI: Marcaniello (*Frate 'nnamorato*); PROKOFIEV: General (*Gambler*); PUCCINI: Colline★ (*Bohème*); ROSSINI: Dott Bartolo★ & Don Basilio★ (*Barbiere di Siviglia*), Conte Asdrubal★ (*Pietra del paragone*), Sultan Selim★ (*Turco in Italia*); SCHOENBERG: Mann (*Glückliche Hand*); STRAUSS, R: Musiklehrer★ (*Ariadne auf Naxos*), La Roche★ (*Capriccio*); STRAVINSKY: Creon (*Oedipus Rex*); VERDI: Ramfis (*Aida*), Philip II★ (*Don Carlo*), Padre Guardiano★ (*Forza del destino*), Banquo (*Macbeth*), Zaccaria★ (*Nabucco*), Fiesco (*Simon Boccanegra*); WAGNER: König Heinrich (*Lohengrin*), Fasolt (*Rheingold*), Hunding (*Walküre*), Landgraf (*Tannhäuser*), König Marke (*Tristan und Isolde*); WEBER: Kaspar (*Freischütz*); ZIMMERMANN: Wesener (*Soldaten*). **World premieres:** ORFF: Prometheus, Stuttgart 1968; HINDEMITH: Kaiser (*Harmonie der Welt*) Munich 1953. Gives recitals. Appears with symphony orchestra. **Res:** Berggeist 16, Murnau, FR Ger.

ENNS, HAROLD R. Bass. American. Born 29 Jul 1930, Fresno, CA, USA. Divorced. Studied: Harry Kohler, Fresno, CA; William Vennard, Ernest St John Metz, Los Angeles. **Debut:** Sparafucile (*Rigoletto*) San Francisco Opera 1954. Awards: San Francisco Opera Aud.

Sang with major companies in USA: Boston, Hawaii, Houston, Kentucky, Milwaukee Florentine, Omaha, Portland, San Diego, San Francisco & Spring Opera, Seattle. **Roles with these companies incl** PUCCINI: Colline★ (*Bohème*); VERDI: Ramfis★ (*Aida*); WAGNER: Daland★ (*Fliegende Holländer*), König Heinrich★ (*Lohengrin*), Landgraf★ (*Tannhäuser*). Also DONIZETTI: Raimondo★ (*Lucia*); MASSENET: Comte des Grieux★ (*Manon*); PUCCINI: Timur★ (*Turandot*); MOZART: Commendatore★ (*Don Giovanni*); GOUNOD: Frère Laurent (*Roméo et Juliette*); MOZART: Sprecher★ (*Zauberflöte*). Gives recitals. Appears with symphony orchestra. **Res:** 5424 Franklin Ave, Los Angeles, CA, USA. Mgmt: CSA/USA.

ENRIQUEZ, FRANCO. Stages/produces opera, theater & television. Also designs stage-lighting. Italian. Resident Stage Dir for theater in Rome. Born 30 Nov 1927, Florence. Divorced. One child. Studied: as asst to Carl Ebert & Herbert Graf at Glyndebourne & Maggio Musicale Fiorentino. Operatic training as asst stage dir. **Operatic debut:** *Khovanshchina* Opera di Roma. Theater debut: Florence 1950.

Directed/produced opera for major companies in ARG: Buenos Aires; FR GER: Düsseldorf-Duisburg, Munich Staatsoper; ITA: Bologna, Florence Maggio & Comunale, Milan La Scala, Naples, Palermo, Rome Opera, Trieste, Turin, Venice, Verona Arena; UK: Glyndebourne Fest; USSR: Moscow Bolshoi. **Operas staged with these companies incl** BELLINI: *Beatrice di Tenda, I Capuleti ed i Montecchi, Norma, Pirata, Puritani;* BERLIOZ: *Damnation de Faust;* BIZET: *Carmen;* CIMAROSA: *Matrimonio segreto;* DONIZETTI: *Anna Bolena, Don Pasquale, Elisir;* FALLA: *Retablo de Maese Pedro;* GIORDANO: *Fedora;* HANDEL: *Xerxes;* LEONCAVALLO: *Pagliacci;* MASCAGNI: *Cavalleria rusticana;* MASSENET: *Manon;* MEYERBEER: *Africaine, Huguenots;* MONTEVERDI: *Incoronazione di Poppea;* MOZART: *Clemenza di Tito, Così fan tutte, Don Giovanni, Entführung aus dem Serail, Nozze di Figaro, Zauberflöte;* MUSSORGSKY. *Boris Godunov, Khovanshchina;* PERGOLESI: *Serva padrona;* POULENC: *Dialogues des Carmélites;* PUCCINI: *Bohème, Gianni Schicchi, Manon Lescaut, Turandot;* PURCELL: *Dido and Aeneas;* ROSSINI: *Barbiere di Siviglia, Cenerentola, Comte Ory, Guillaume Tell, Italiana in Algeri, Turco in Italia;* STRAUSS, R: *Ariadne auf Naxos, Salome;* VERDI: *Aida, Ballo in maschera, Don Carlo, Due Foscari, Luisa Miller, Nabucco, Rigoletto, Simon Boccanegra, Traviata, Trovatore, Vespri;* ZANDONAI: *Francesca da Rimini, Giulietta e Romeo.* Also BUSONI: *Sposa sorteggiata;* CATALANI: *Loreley;* SPONTINI: *Agnese di Hohenstaufen.*

ERBA, GIUSEPPE. Italian. Sovrintendente, Teatro Regio, Piazza Castello 215, Turin 1972- ; also Teatro Alfieri & Teatro Erba, Turin, & var movie theaters. In charge of admin matters, art policy & finances. Born 7 Aug 1916, Turin. Wife Elda Clorico. One child. Studied: Univ of Agriculture, Turin. Previous positions, primarily administrative & theatrical: directed var theaters for 28 years. World premieres at theaters under his management: WEBER: *Die drei Pintos* Turin 1975. Mem and delegate, various Italian arts organizations. **Res:** C Moncalieri 237, Turin, Italy.

ERCSE, MARGIT. Dramatic mezzo-soprano & soprano. Hungarian. Res mem: Hung State Opera, Budapest. Born 26 Jun 1942, Budapest. Husband Dr Béla Sándor, occupation physician. One child. Studied: Ferenc Liszt Acad of Music, Budapest. **Debut:** Cornelia (*Giulio Cesare*) State Opera, Budapest 1966.

Sang with major companies in AUS: Graz; CZE: Prague National; FRA: Marseille; FR GER: Cologne; GER DR: Berlin Staatsoper; HUN: Budapest. **Roles with these companies incl** BARTOK: Judith★ (*Bluebeard's Castle*); HANDEL: Giulio Cesare; MOZART: Dorabella★ (*Così fan tutte*); MUSSORGSKY: Marina★ (*Boris Godunov*); VERDI: Amneris★ (*Aida*), Eboli★ (*Don Carlo*), Preziosilla★ (*Forza del destino*); WAGNER: Fricka★ (*Walküre*), Venus★ (*Tannhäuser*). Also BEETHOVEN: Leonore★ (*Fidelio*); STRAUSS, R: Elektra★; WAGNER: Brünnhilde★ (*Götterdämmerung*). Gives recitals. Appears with symphony orchestra. **Res:** Baba str 7, 1025 Budapest, Hungary. Mgmt: ITK/HUN; TAS/AUS.

EREDE, ALBERTO. Conductor of opera and symphony; operatic stage director. Italian. Born 8 Nov 1908, Genoa. Wife Emilia. Two children. Studied: Bersani, Linari, Barbieri, Genoa; Pozzoli, Milan; Weingartner, Basel; Busch, Dresden; incl piano, cello, organ. Plays the piano. Operatic training as repetiteur, asst cond, chorus master & prompter at Teatro Carlo Felice, Genoa 1926-29. **Operatic debut:** *Ring des Nibelungen* Teatro Regio, Turin 1935. Symphonic debut: Santa Cecilia, Rome 1930. Previous occupations: stud of law, Univ Genoa & Milan. Awards: Grosses Bundesverdienstkreuz, German Gvnmt; Commander, Japanese and Yugoslavian Gvnmts. Previous adm positions in opera: Mus Dir, Salzburg Opera Guild, Vienna 1935-38; New London Opera Co, London 1946-49; Gen Mus Dir, Deutsche Oper am Rhein, Düsseldorf 1958-62.

Conducted with major companies in ARG: Buenos Aires; AUS: Salzburg Fest, Vienna Staatsoper; BEL: Brussels; BRA: Rio de Janeiro; CAN: Montreal/Quebec, Toronto, Vancouver; FRA: Aix-en-Provence Fest, Bordeaux, Paris; FR GER: Bayreuth Fest, Berlin Deutsche Oper, Düsseldorf-Duisburg, Frankfurt, Hamburg, Karlsruhe, Kassel, Munich Staatsoper, Stuttgart, Wiesbaden; HOL: Amsterdam; ITA: Bologna, Florence Comunale, Genoa, Milan La Scala, Naples, Palermo, Parma, Rome Opera & Caracalla, Trieste, Turin, Venice; MON: Monte Carlo; POR: Lisbon; ROM: Bucharest; SWE: Stockholm; SWI: Basel, Geneva, Zurich; UK: Edinburgh, Scottish, Glyndebourne, London Royal; USA: Baltimore, Chicago, New Orleans, New York Met, Pittsburgh, Portland, St Paul, San Antonio, San Diego, Seattle, Washington DC; YUG: Belgrade. **Operas with these companies incl** BEETHOVEN: *Fidelio;* BELLINI: *Norma, Pirata, Puritani, Sonnambula;* BERLIOZ: *Damnation de Faust;* BIZET: *Carmen, Pêcheurs de perles;* BOITO: *Mefistofele;* BORODIN: *Prince Igor;* BUSONI: *Arlecchino, Doktor Faust, Turandot;* CATALANI: *Wally;* CAVALIERI: *Rappresentazione;* CHARPENTIER: *Louise;* CHERUBINI: *Medea;* CILEA: *A. Lecouvreur;* CIMAROSA: *Matrimonio segreto;* DALLAPICCOLA: *Volo di notte;* DEBUSSY: *Pelléas et Mélisande;* DONIZETTI: *Anna Bolena, Campanello, Don Pasquale, Elisir, Favorite‡, Lucia;* FALLA: *Retablo de Maese Pedro;* GIORDANO: *Andrea Chénier;* GLUCK: *Alceste, Iphigénie en Tauride;* GOUNOD: *Faust, Mireille, Roméo et Juliette‡;* HANDEL: *Giulio Cesare;* HAYDN: *Infedeltà delusa;* HUMPERDINCK: *Hänsel und Gretel;* IBERT: *Angélique;* LEONCAVALLO: *Pagliacci‡;* MARTIN: *Vin herbé;* MASCAGNI: *Cavalleria rusticana‡;* MASSENET: *Manon;* MENOTTI: *Consul, Medium;* MEYERBEER: *Huguenots;* MILHAUD: *Pauvre matelot;* MONTEVERDI: *Combattimento di Tancredi;* MOZART: *Clemenza di Tito, Così fan tutte, Don Giovanni, Entführung aus dem Serail, Idomeneo, Nozze di Figaro, Oca del Cairo, Zauberflöte;* MUSSORGSKY: *Boris Godunov;* OFFENBACH: *Contes d'Hoffmann;* ORFF: *Carmina burana;* PERGOLESI: *Serva padrona;* PFITZNER: *Palestrina;* POULENC: *Mamelles de Tirésias;* PROKOFIEV: *Duenna;* PUCCINI: *Bohème‡, Fanciulla del West, Gianni Schicchi, Butterfly‡, Manon Lescaut, Tabarro, Tosca‡, Turandot‡;* PURCELL: *Dido and Aeneas;*

RAMEAU: *Castor et Pollux;* RAVEL: *Heure espagnole;* ROSSINI: *Barbiere di Siviglia‡, Cambiale di matrimonio, Cenerentola, Comte Ory, Guillaume Tell, Italiana in Algeri, Scala di seta;* SCARLATTI: *Trionfo dell'onore;* SHOSTAKOVICH: *Katerina Ismailova;* SMETANA: *Bartered Bride;* SPONTINI: *Vestale;* STRAUSS, R: *Arabella, Ariadne auf Naxos‡, Elektra, Salome;* STRAVINSKY: *Mavra, Rake's Progress;* VERDI: *Aida‡, Attila, Ballo in maschera, Don Carlo, Due Foscari, Falstaff, Forza del destino, Luisa Miller, Macbeth, Nabucco, Otello‡, Rigoletto‡, Simon Boccanegra, Traviata, Trovatore‡, Vespri;* WAGNER: *Lohengrin, Parsifal, Rheingold, Walküre, Siegfried, Götterdämmerung, Tannhäuser, Tristan und Isolde;* WEBER: *Freischütz;* WOLF-FERRARI: *Gioielli della Madonna, Quattro rusteghi, Segreto di Susanna;* ZANDONAI: *Francesca da Rimini.* **World premieres:** MENOTTI: *Old Maid and the Thief* NBC 1939. Recorded for DG, Decca. Video/Film— CBS TV: *Bohème;* RAI: *Don Pasquale;* ORTF: *Clemenza di Tito;* Vienna: *Don Pasquale.* Conducted major orch in Europe, USA/Canada, Cent/S America, Africa. Previous positions as Mus Dir with major orch: RAI Turin 1945-47. **Res:** Turin, Italy.

ERICSON, BARBRO. Dramatic mezzo-soprano. Swedish. Resident mem: Royal Opera, Stockholm. Born 2 Apr 1930, Halmstad, Sweden. Husband Nils Hederén. Studied: Royal Acad of Music, Stockholm; Ragnar Hulthén, Nanny Larsen-Todsen, Käthe Sundström. **Debut:** Eboli (*Don Carlo*) Royal Opera, Stockholm 1956. Awards: Royal Court Singer 1968.

Sang with major companies in AUS: Vienna Staatsoper; DEN: Copenhagen; FIN: Helsinki; FRA: Paris; GRE: Athens Fest; FR GER: Bayreuth Fest, Berlin Deutsche Oper, Cologne, Hamburg, Kiel, Wiesbaden; HOL: Amsterdam; NOR: Oslo; SPA: Barcelona; SWE: Drottningholm Fest; SWI: Zurich; UK: Edinburgh Fest, London Royal; USA: New York Met. **Roles with these companies incl** BERLIOZ: Cassandre & Anna (*Troyens*); BIZET: Carmen⋆; BRITTEN: Hermia (*Midsummer Night*), Miss Jessel (*Turn of Screw*); DEBUSSY: Geneviève (*Pelléas et Mélisande*); GLUCK: Clytemnestre (*Iphigénie en Aulide*), Orfeo⋆; HANDEL: Bradamante⋆ (*Alcina*); MUSSORGSKY: Marina (*Boris Godunov*); PUCCINI: Suzuki⋆ (*Butterfly*), Frugola (*Tabarro*); SCHOENBERG: Woman (*Erwartung*); STRAUSS, R: Klytämnestra⋆ (*Elektra*), Färberin & Amme (*Frau ohne Schatten*), Herodias⋆ (*Salome*); STRAVINSKY: Mère (*Mavra*), Jocasta⋆ (*Oedipus Rex*), Baba the Turk⋆ (*Rake's Progress*); TCHAIKOVSKY: Comtesse⋆ (*Pique Dame*); VERDI: Amneris⋆ (*Aida*), Ulrica⋆ (*Ballo in maschera*), Eboli⋆ (*Don Carlo*), Dame Quickly⋆ (*Falstaff*), Azucena⋆ (*Trovatore*); WAGNER: Ortrud⋆ (*Lohengrin*), Kundry⋆ (*Parsifal*), Erda (*Rheingold⋆, Siegfried⋆*), Fricka (*Rheingold⋆, Walküre*), Waltraute⋆ (*Götterdämmerung*), Venus⋆ (*Tannhäuser*), Brangäne⋆ (*Tristan und Isolde*); WEILL: Leocadia Begbick⋆ (*Aufstieg und Fall der Stadt Mahagonny*). Also BERG: Marie (*Wozzeck*); MASCAGNI: Santuzza (*Cavalleria rusticana*). Recorded for: DG. Video/Film: Frugola (*Tabarro*); Ulrica (*Ballo in maschera*); Miss Jessel

(*Turn of the Screw*). Gives recitals. Appears with symphony orchestra. Mgmt: SVE/SWE.

ERLER, LISELOTTE. Costume designer for opera & theater. German. Resident designer, Deutsche Oper am Rhein, Düsseldorf-Duisburg.

Designed with major companies in AUS: Vienna Volksoper; FR GER: Düsseldorf-Duisburg, Munich Staatsoper; ITA: Milan La Scala; et al. **Operas with these companies incl** BERG: *Wozzeck;* BERLIOZ: *Benvenuto Cellini;* CAVALIERI: *Rappresentazione;* DONIZETTI: *Lucia;* DVORAK: *Rusalka;* JANACEK: *Cunning Little Vixen, Excursions of Mr Broucek, Jenufa, Katya Kabanova, Makropoulos Affair;* MOZART: *Clemenza di Tito, Così fan tutte, Don Giovanni, Entführung aus dem Serail, Idomeneo, Nozze di Figaro, Zauberflöte;* ORFF: *Carmina burana, Kluge;* POULENC: *Mamelles de Tirésias;* STRAVINSKY: *Rake's Progress;* VERDI: *Falstaff, Otello, Trovatore;* WAGNER: *Lohengrin, Rheingold, Tannhäuser, Tristan und Isolde;* WEILL: *Aufstieg und Fall der Stadt Mahagonny;* et al.

ERLO, LOUIS. Stages/produces opera & theater. French. Dir & Resident Stage Dir, Théâtre de l'Opéra, Lyon; Dir, Paris Opera Studio. Born 26 Apr 1929, Lyon. Studied: Ecole de la Martinière; Ecole Ntl Profess de Lyon. Awards: Officier des Arts et des Lettres. Previous adm positions in opera: Gen Mng, Opéra de Lyon 1969-73; Dir, Opéra Comique Paris 1971-73.

Directed/produced opera for major companies in ARG: Buenos Aires; BEL: Brussels; FRA: Lyon, Marseille, Paris, Strasbourg; FR GER: Frankfurt; HOL: Amsterdam; ITA: Venice; POR: Lisbon; SWI: Geneva; USA: San Francisco Opera; et al. **Operas staged with these companies incl** BERG: *Wozzeck;* BERLIOZ: *Troyens;* CHARPENTIER: *Louise;* DEBUSSY: *Pelléas et Mélisande;* GOUNOD: *Faust, Roméo et Juliette;* MARTINU: *Trois souhaites;* MOZART: *Don Giovanni;* OFFENBACH: *Contes d'Hoffmann;* SAINT-SAENS: *Samson et Dalila;* STRAVINSKY: *Rake's Progress;* VERDI: *Macbeth, Simon Boccanegra;* WAGNER: *Walküre;* WEILL: *Aufstieg und Fall der Stadt Mahagonny;* et al. Also FAURE: *Prométhée;* RAMEAU: *Paladins.* Teaches at Studio de l'Opéra, Paris.

ERNANI, FRANCESCO. Italian. Adm Dir, Ente Autonomo Lirico Arena di Verona, Piazza Bra' 28, Verona, Italy. In charge of adm matters & finances. Born 3 Dec 1937, Ancona, Italy. Studied: accounting at Tech Inst A M Lorgna, Verona. Previous positions primarily administrative. In present position since 1971. Awards: Cavaliere Ordine al Merito, Rep of Italy.

ERWEN, KEITH; né Ranald Keith Urwin. Lyric tenor. British. Resident mem: English National Opera, London. Born 6 Oct 1942, Consett, UK. Wife Hazel Mary Ann, occupation singer. One child. Studied: Guildhall School of Music & Drama, Joseph Hislop, London. **Debut:** Duca di Mantova (*Rigoletto*) Welsh National Opera 1969. Awards: Cinzano Ntl Schlshp 1969.

Sang with major companies in FR GER: Cologne; UK: Cardiff Welsh, Glyndebourne Fest,

London Royal & English National. **Roles with these companies incl** AUBER: Fra Diavolo; BIZET: Don José★ (*Carmen*); BRITTEN: Robert Devereux★ (*Gloriana*); DELIUS: Simon Perez★‡ (*Koanga*); DONIZETTI: Ernesto (*Don Pasquale*), Leicester★ (*Maria Stuarda*); FLOTOW: Lionel (*Martha*); GOUNOD: Faust; MASSENET: Des Grieux★ (*Manon*); MOZART: Ferrando (*Così fan tutte*), Tamino★ (*Zauberflöte*); PUCCINI: Rodolfo★ (*Bohème*), Pinkerton★ (*Butterfly*); TCHAIKOVSKY: Lenski (*Eugene Onegin*); VERDI: Corrado (*Corsaro*), Don Carlo★, Jacopo Foscari (*Due Foscari*), Fenton★ (*Falstaff*), Ismaele (*Nabucco*), Duca di Mantova★ (*Rigoletto*), Gabriele★ (*Simon Boccanegra*), Alfredo★ (*Traviata*); WAGNER: Erik★ (*Fliegende Holländer*); WEBER: Abu Hassan. Also VERDI: Macduff★ (*Macbeth*). Recorded for: EMI, Philips. Gives recitals. Appears with symphony orchestra. **Res:** 88 The Avenue, Pinner/Middlesex, UK. Mgmt: SLA/UK.

ESCOFFIER, MARCEL. Scenic and costume designer for opera & theater. Is a lighting designer, stage director; also a painter. French.

Designed opera for major companies in ITA: Palermo, Rome Opera, Venice; UK: Edinburgh Fest; USA: New York Met; et al. **Operas designed for these companies incl** AUBER: *Muette de Portici;* BELLINI: *Straniera;* DONIZETTI: *Fille du régiment;* VERDI: *Giovanna d'Arco;* et al.

ESPOSITO, ANDRÉE. Coloratura soprano. French. Born 7 Feb 1934, Algiers. Husband Julien Haas, occupation opera singer. Studied: Consvs of Algiers & Paris. **Debut:** Violetta (*Traviata*) Opéra de Paris 1959.

Sang with major companies in BEL: Liège; FRA: Bordeaux, Marseille, Nancy, Nice, Paris, Rouen, Strasbourg, Toulouse; GRE: Athens National; FR GER: Karlsruhe; HOL: Amsterdam; MON: Monte Carlo; ROM: Bucharest; SPA: Barcelona; SWI: Geneva. **Roles with these companies incl** BEETHOVEN: Marzelline (*Fidelio*); BELLINI: Giulietta (*Capuleti ed i Montecchi*), Elvira (*Puritani*), Amina (*Sonnambula*); BENNETT: Jenny (*Mines of Sulphur*); BERLIOZ: Hero★ (*Béatrice et Bénédict*), Teresa★ (*Benvenuto Cellini*); BIZET: Micaëla★ (*Carmen*), Léila★ (*Pêcheurs de perles*); BOIELDIEU: Anna★ (*Dame blanche*); CHABRIER: Alexina★ (*Roi malgré lui*); CORNELIUS: Margiana‡ (*Barbier von Bagdad*); DEBUSSY: Mélisande; DONIZETTI: Norina (*Don Pasquale*), Adina (*Elisir*), Lucia★; GLUCK: Euridice; GOUNOD: Marguerite★ (*Faust*), Mireille★, Juliette★; HALEVY: Eudoxie (*Juive*); HONEGGER: Ismene (*Antigone*); LALO: Rozenn (*Roi d'Ys*); MASSENET: Manon★, Thaïs★; MEYERBEER: Inez‡ (*Africaine*), Marguerite de Valois (*Huguenots*); MILHAUD: Créuse (*Médée*), Femme★ (*Pauvre matelot*); MOZART: Fiordiligi (*Così fan tutte*), Donna Anna★ (*Don Giovanni*), Susanna (*Nozze di Figaro*), Pamina★ (*Zauberflöte*); OFFENBACH: Olympia & Antonia & Giulietta (*Contes d'Hoffmann*); PENDERECKI: Philippe★ (*Teufel von Loudun*); POULENC: Blanche (*Dialogues des Carmélites*), Femme (*Voix humaine*); PUCCINI: Mimi (*Bohème*), Lauretta (*Gianni Schicchi*), Liù (*Turandot*); RABAUD: Fille de Sultan (*Mârouf*); ROSSINI: Mathilde (*Guillaume Tell*); STRAUSS, J:

Rosalinde (*Fledermaus*); THOMAS: Philine‡ (*Mignon*); VERDI: Oscar★ (*Ballo in maschera*), Luisa Miller, Gilda★ (*Rigoletto*), Violetta★ (*Traviata*). Also REYER: Hilda (*Sigurd*); BENTOIU: Ophélie (*Hamlet*); ROSENTHAL: Marguerite (*Hop Signor!*); CHERUBINI: Glauce‡ (*Medea*). **World premieres:** LESUR: Lucrèce (*Andréa del Sarto*) Opéra de Marseille 1969. Recorded for: Pathé-Marconi. Video/Film: (*Fledermaus*); Lucrèce (*Andréa del Sarto*). Gives recitals. Appears with symphony orchestra. **Res:** 59 Blvd Voltaire, 75011 Paris, France.

ESSER, HERMIN. Heldentenor. German. Resident mem: Staatsoper, Munich; Staatsoper, Cologne. Born 1 Apr 1928, Rheydt, Germany. Wife Brigitte. Two children. Studied: Schumann Konsv Düsseldorf, Prof Martienssen-Lohmann, FR Ger. **Debut:** Messaggero (*Aida*) Krefeld Opera 1954. Previous occupations: studied graphics & architecture.

Sang with major companies in AUS: Salzburg Fest, Vienna Staatsoper & Volksoper; BEL: Brussels; FRA: Bordeaux, Lyon, Nancy, Nice, Paris, Strasbourg; FR GER: Bayreuth Fest, Berlin Deutsche Oper, Bonn, Cologne, Darmstadt, Dortmund, Düsseldorf-Duisburg, Frankfurt, Hamburg, Hannover, Karlsruhe, Kassel, Kiel, Krefeld, Mannheim, Munich Staatsoper & Gärtnerplatz, Nürnberg, Saarbrücken, Stuttgart, Wiesbaden, Wuppertal; GER DR: Berlin Komische Oper; HOL: Amsterdam; HUN: Budapest; ITA: Bologna, Genoa, Parma, Rome Opera, Turin, Venice; MON: Monte Carlo; POL: Lodz, Warsaw; POR: Lisbon; SWE: Stockholm; SWI: Basel, Geneva, Zurich; UK: Glasgow Scottish; USSR: Moscow Stanislavski; USA: Chicago; YUG: Zagreb. **Roles with these companies incl** d'ALBERT: Pedro★ (*Tiefland*); AUBER: Lorenzo (*Fra Diavolo*); BEETHOVEN: Florestan★ (*Fidelio*); BERG: Tambourmajor★ (*Wozzeck*); BIZET: Don José★ (*Carmen*); DALLAPICCOLA: Jailer/Inquisitor (*Prigioniero*); DONIZETTI: Ernesto (*Don Pasquale*); EINEM: Robespierre (*Dantons Tod*); GLUCK: Pylade (*Iphigénie en Tauride*); LEONCAVALLO: Canio★ (*Pagliacci*); MASCAGNI: Turiddu★ (*Cavalleria rusticana*); MOZART: Ferrando (*Così fan tutte*), Don Ottavio (*Don Giovanni*), Belmonte (*Entführung aus dem Serail*), Idomeneo, Tamino★ (*Zauberflöte*); NICOLAI: Fenton (*Lustigen Weiber*); OFFENBACH: Hoffmann★; PROKOFIEV: Alexis★ (*Gambler*); PUCCINI: Rodolfo (*Bohème*), Rinuccio (*Gianni Schicchi*), Pinkerton★ (*Butterfly*), Des Grieux (*Manon Lescaut*), Luigi★ (*Tabarro*), Cavaradossi (*Tosca*), Calaf★‡ (*Turandot*); SAINT-SAENS: Samson; SHOSTAKOVICH: Sergei★ (*Katerina Ismailova*); SMETANA: Hans (*Bartered Bride*); STRAUSS, J: Alfred★ (*Fledermaus*); STRAUSS, R: Matteo★ (*Arabella*), Bacchus★ (*Ariadne auf Naxos*), Aegisth★ (*Elektra*), Kaiser (*Frau ohne Schatten*), Ein Sänger (*Rosenkavalier*); STRAVINSKY: Tom Rakewell (*Rake's Progress*); TCHAIKOVSKY: Lenski★ (*Eugene Onegin*), Gherman★ (*Pique Dame*); VERDI: Radames★ (*Aida*), Riccardo★ (*Ballo in maschera*), Don Carlo★, Don Alvaro★ (*Forza del destino*), Ismaele (*Nabucco*), Otello★‡, Duca di Mantova (*Rigoletto*), Alfredo (*Traviata*); WAGNER: Erik★‡ (*Fliegende Holländer*), Lohengrin★, Walther ★ &

David★ (*Meistersinger*), Parsifal★, Loge★ (*Rheingold*), Siegmund★ (*Walküre*), Siegfried (*Siegfried★, Götterdämmerung★*), Tannhäuser★ & Walther v d Vogelweide (*Tannhäuser*), Tristan★; WEBER: Max★ (*Freischütz*); WEILL: Jim Mahoney★ (*Aufstieg und Fall der Stadt Mahagonny*). Gives recitals. Appears with symphony orchestra. **Res:** Mittelweg 23, D-6201 Naurod/Taunus, FR Ger. Mgmt: SLZ/FRG.

ETCHEVERRY, DIÉGO. Scenic and costume designer for opera, theater. Is also a painter, sculptor & illustrator. French. Born 20 Mar 1933, Casablanca, Morocco. Wife Isabel, occupation designer. Two children. Studied: Ecole Ntl des Beaux-Arts, Nancy. **Operatic debut:** Opéra de Nancy 1956. Theater debut: Comédie de Paris 1956.

Designed for major companies in ARG: Buenos Aires; BEL: Brussels, Liège; FRA: Bordeaux, Marseille, Nancy, Paris, Rouen, Toulouse; FR GER: Karlsruhe; POL: Warsaw; SPA: Barcelona. **Operas designed for these companies incl** BIZET: *Carmen★;* BOITO: *Mefistofele;* BRITTEN: *Rape of Lucretia★;* DEBUSSY: *Pelléas et Mélisande;* GOUNOD: *Mireille;* MASSENET: *Manon★, Werther★;* MENOTTI: *Consul, Medium;* MOZART: *Così fan tutte, Don Giovanni★, Entführung aus dem Serail, Nozze di Figaro★, Zauberflöte★;* ORFF: *Carmina burana★;* PERGOLESI: *Serva padrona★;* POULENC: *Dialogues des Carmélites;* PUCCINI: *Tosca★, Turandot★;* RABAUD: *Mârouf★;* STRAUSS, R: *Arabella★;* TCHAIKOVSKY: *Pique Dame★;* VERDI: *Traviata★.* Also LANDOWSKI: *Adieux;* SEMENOFF: *Sire Halewyn;* FRANCAIX: *Apostrophe;* IBERT/HONNEGER: *Aiglon.* **Operatic world premieres:** CHAILLY: *Thyl* Opéra Nancy 1963; SEMENOFF: *Don Juan ou L'amour de la géométrie* Centre Lyrique Populaire, St Denis 1969; CASANOVA: *Bonheur dans le crime* Théâtre du Capitole, Toulouse 1973; BONDON: *I 330* Théâtre Graslin, Nantes 1975. Exhibitions of stage designs, sculptures, paintings, graphics Paris 1956, Tokyo 1966, Saint-Etienne 1968, Aarhus 1970, Ibiza 1971, Lausanne 1974, Paris 1974; 1972 tours to German museums. **Res:** 117 Blvd Jourdan, Paris, France.

ETCHEVERRY, JÉSUS. Conductor of opera and symphony. French. Resident Cond, Opéra de Nantes, France 1972- . Married; three children. Plays the violin. **Operatic debut:** Opéra de Casablanca, Morocco. Awards: Légion d'honneur; Palmes Académiques; Mérite artistique. Previous adm positions in opera: Music Dir, Opéra & Opéra Comique, Paris 1957-72; Opéra de Casablanca 1944-47; Nancy, France 1947-57.

Conducted with major companies in BEL: Brussels, Liège; FRA: Bordeaux, Lyon, Marseille, Nancy, Orange Fest, Paris, Rouen, Strasbourg, Toulouse; FR GER: Karlsruhe, Saarbrücken, Wiesbaden; MON: Monte Carlo; SPA: Barcelona. **Operas with these companies incl** AUBER: *Fra Diavolo;* BECAUD: *Opéra d'Aran;* BEETHOVEN: *Fidelio;* BERLIOZ: *Damnation de Faust;* BIZET: *Carmen★‡, Pêcheurs de perles★‡;* BOIELDIEU: *Dame blanche;* BOITO: *Mefistofele;* CHABRIER: *Roi malgré lui;* CIMAROSA: *Matrimonio segreto;* DEBUSSY: *Enfant prodigue, Pelléas et Mélisande;* DELIBES: *Lakmé;* DONIZETTI: *Don Pasquale, Fille du régiment, Lucia;* GLUCK: *Orfeo ed Euridice;* GOUNOD: *Faust★‡, Mireille‡, Philémon et Baucis, Roméo et Juliette★‡;* HALEVY: *Juive;* IBERT: *Angélique;* LALO: *Roi d'Ys;* LECOCQ: *Fille de Madame Angot‡;* LEONCAVALLO: *Pagliacci‡;* MASCAGNI: *Cavalleria rusticana‡;* MASSENET: *Don Quichotte, Hérodiade, Jongleur de Notre Dame, Manon‡, Thaïs‡, Werther‡;* MOZART: *Don Giovanni, Entführung aus dem Serail, Nozze di Figaro, Zauberflöte;* MUSSORGSKY: *Boris Godunov;* OFFENBACH: *Contes d'Hoffmann‡, Périchole;* POULENC: *Dialogues des Carmélites, Voix humaine;* PUCCINI: *Bohème‡, Fanciulla del West, Butterfly‡, Manon Lescaut, Tosca‡;* RABAUD: *Mârouf;* RAVEL: *Heure espagnole;* ROSSINI: *Barbiere di Siviglia, Guillaume Tell;* SAINT-SAENS: *Samson et Dalila;* STRAUSS, J: *Fledermaus;* THOMAS: *Mignon;* VERDI: *Aida, Ballo in maschera, Don Carlo, Falstaff, Otello, Rigoletto‡, Traviata‡, Trovatore;* WAGNER: *Lohengrin.* Video—TV Française: *Louise, Traviata, Manon;* also film. **Res:** 57bis rue Croulebarbe, 75 Paris 13, France.

ETHUIN, PAUL. Conductor of opera and symphony. French. Resident Cond, Théâtre des Arts, Rouen. Also Mus Dir, Orch de Rouen. Born 24 Sep 1924, Bruay sur Escaut, France. Married. One child. Studied: Consv Ntl Supérieur de Musique, Paris; incl flute. Plays the flute. **Operatic debut:** *Faust* Théâtre Municipal, Rheims 1945. Awards: First Prize, Consv de Paris.

Conducted with major companies in BEL: Liège; FRA: Bordeaux, Marseille, Nancy, Nice, Orange Fest, Paris, Rouen, Toulouse; ITA: Naples; SPA: Barcelona. **Operas with these companies incl** ADAM: *Postillon de Lonjumeau★, Si j'étais roi;* BECAUD: *Opéra d'Aran★;* BEETHOVEN: *Fidelio★;* BELLINI: *Norma, Sonnambula★;* BERLIOZ: *Damnation de Faust★;* BIZET: *Carmen★, Pêcheurs de perles★;* BOIELDIEU: *Dame blanche★;* BORODIN: *Prince Igor;* CHARPENTIER: *Louise★;* CILEA: *A. Lecouvreur★;* DEBUSSY: *Pelléas et Mélisande★;* DELIBES: *Lakmé★;* DONIZETTI: *Favorite★, Lucia★;* DUKAS: *Ariane et Barbe Bleue;* GERSHWIN: *Porgy and Bess★;* GIORDANO: *Andrea Chénier★;* GLUCK: *Orfeo ed Euridice;* GOUNOD: *Faust★, Mireille★, Roméo et Juliette★;* HALEVY: *Juive;* LALO: *Roi d'Ys;* LECOCQ: *Fille de Madame Angot★;* LEONCAVALLO: *Pagliacci;* MARTINU: *Griechische Passion★;* MASCAGNI: *Cavalleria rusticana★;* MASSENET: *Don Quichotte★, Hérodiade★, Jongleur de Notre Dame★, Manon★, Thaïs★, Werther★;* MEYERBEER: *Huguenots;* MOZART: *Così fan tutte★, Don Giovanni★, Entführung aus dem Serail★, Nozze di Figaro★, Zauberflöte★;* MUSSORGSKY: *Boris Godunov★;* OFFENBACH: *Contes d'Hoffmann★;* POULENC: *Dialogues des Carmélites★;* PROKOFIEV: *Love for Three Oranges★;* PUCCINI: *Bohème★, Fanciulla del West★, Butterfly★, Manon Lescaut★, Tosca★, Turandot★;* RABAUD: *Mârouf;* ROSSINI: *Barbiere di Siviglia★, Comte Ory, Guillaume Tell;* SAINT-SAENS: *Samson et Dalila;* SMETANA: *Bartered Bride;* STRAUSS, J: *Fledermaus★;* STRAUSS, R: *Rosenkavalier★;* TCHAIKOVSKY: *Eugene*

Onegin★, Pique Dame; THOMAS: *Mignon★;*
VERDI: *Aida★, Ballo in maschera, Don Carlo★,*
Falstaff★, Forza del destino★, Otello★, Rigoletto★,
Traviata★, Trovatore★; WAGNER: *Fliegende*
Holländer★, Lohengrin★, Parsifal★, Rheingold★,
Walküre★, Siegfried★, Götterdämmerung★, Tann-
häuser★, Tristan und Isolde. Also EGK: *Colum-*
bus; LESUR: *Andréa del Sarto★;*
BONDEVILLE: *Mme Bovary;* MESSAGER:
Fortunio, Basoche; HAHN: *Ciboulette;* FAURE:
Pénélope. **World premieres:** BONDEVILLE: *An-*
toine et Cléopâtre 1974; STUBBS: *Hauts de Hur-*
levent 1967, both at Théâtre des Arts, Rouen.
Video—ORTF Paris: *Contes d'Hoffmann; Andréa*
del Sarto. Conducted major orch in Europe, Asia.
Res: 31 Pl des Carmes, Rouen, France.

EVANS, ANNE ELIZABETH. Spinto. British.
Resident mem: English National Opera, London.
Born 20 Aug 1942, London. Husband Heulyn
Jones, occupation civil servant. Studied: Royal
Coll of Music, Ruth Packer, London; Consv de
Musique, Maria Carpi, Herbert Graf, Lotfi Man-
souri, Geneva. **Debut:** Mimi (*Bohème*) Sadler's
Wells Opera 1968. Previous occupations: film libr
recept. Awards: Boise Fndt Music Awd; Sir
Thomas Beecham Operatic Schlshp.
   Sang with major companies in FRA: Rouen;
SWI: Geneva; UK: Cardiff Welsh, London
English National. **Roles with these companies incl**
BEETHOVEN: Marzelline (*Fidelio*); BIZET: Mi-
caëla★ (*Carmen*); BRITTEN: Penelope★ (*Glo-*
riana); LEONCAVALLO: Nedda★ (*Pagliacci*);
MOZART: Servilia (*Clemenza di Tito*), Fiordiligi★
(*Così fan tutte*), Ilia (*Idomeneo*), Contessa★
(*Nozze di Figaro*), Pamina (*Zauberflöte*); OF-
FENBACH: Olympia★ & Antonia★ & Giulietta★
(*Contes d'Hoffmann*); PUCCINI: Mimi★ & Mu-
setta★ (*Bohème*), Tosca★; STRAUSS, J: Rosa-
linde★ (*Fledermaus*); STRAUSS, R: Marschallin★
(*Rosenkavalier*); VERDI: Violetta★ (*Traviata*);
WAGNER: Senta★ (*Fliegende Holländer*), Elsa★
(*Lohengrin*). Gives recitals. Appears with sym-
phony orchestra. **Res:** London, UK. Mgmt:
ASK/UK.

EVANS, SIR GERAINT LLEWELLYN. Bass-baritone. British. Resident mem: Royal Opera, London. Born 16 Feb 1922, Cilfynydd, Wales, UK.
Wive Lady Brenda. Two children. Studied: Guild-
hall School of Music, London; Theo Herrman,
Fernando Carpi. **Debut:** Nachtwächter (*Meister-*
singer von Nürnberg) Royal Opera, London
don 1948. Awards: Knighted, Queen Elizabeth II;
CBE, Queen Elizabeth II; FGSM, Guildhall
School of Music; Hon DM, Wales Univ & Leices-
ter Univ; Hon RAM, Royal Acad of Music; Wor-
shipful Co of Musicians, Sir Charles Santley
Memorial Awd; Harriet Cohen Intl Music Awd;
Opera Medal.
   Sang with major companies in ARG: Buenos
Aires; AUS: Salzburg Fest, Vienna Staatsoper;
FRA: Paris; FR GER: Berlin Deutsche Oper,
Mannheim, Munich Staatsoper; HOL: Amster-
dam; ISR: Tel Aviv; ITA: Genoa, Milan La Scala;
MEX: Mexico City; POL: Warsaw; UK: Al-
deburgh Fest, Cardiff Welsh, Edinburgh Fest,
Glasgow Scottish, Glyndebourne Fest, London
Royal & English National; USA: Chicago, Dallas,
Houston, Miami, New York Met, San Francisco

Opera. **Roles with these companies incl** BARTOK:
Bluebeard; BEETHOVEN: Don Pizarro (*Fi-*
delio); BERG: Wozzeck; BIZET: Escamillo (*Car-*
men); BRITTEN: John Claggart (*Billy Budd*),
Bottom (*Midsummer Night*), Captain Balstrode &
Ned Keene (*Peter Grimes*), Mountjoy (*Gloriana*);
BUSONI: Matteo (*Arlecchino*); DONIZETTI:
Don Pasquale, Dulcamara (*Elisir*), Enrico (*Lucia*);
LEONCAVALLO: Tonio (*Pagliacci*); MASSE-
NET: Lescaut (*Manon*); MOZART: Guglielmo &
Don Alfonso (*Così fan tutte*), Leporello & Masetto
& Don Giovanni (*Don Giovanni*), Conte Almaviva
& Figaro (*Nozze di Figaro*), Papageno (*Zauber-*
flöte); OFFENBACH: Coppélius etc (*Contes*
d'Hoffmann), Don Andres (*Périchole*); PUC-
CINI: Gianni Schicchi, Sharpless (*Butterfly*),
Scarpia (*Tosca*); ROSSINI: Dott Bartolo (*Bar-*
biere di Siviglia); SMETANA: Kezal (*Bartered*
Bride); STRAUSS, R: Musiklehrer (*Ariadne auf*
Naxos); VERDI: Amonasro (*Aida*), Rodrigo (*Don*
Carlo), Falstaff, Fra Melitone (*Forza del destlno*),
WAGNER: Beckmesser (*Meistersinger*). **World**
premieres: HODDINOTT: Trader Case (*Beach of*
Falesa) Welsh National Opera, Cardiff 1974. Re-
corded for: Decca, Angel. Video/Film: Coppélius,
etc (*Contes d'Hoffmann*); Falstaff; HODDI-
NOTT: Sesto (*Murder the Magician*). Govnr,
London Opera Centre. **Directed the following op-**
eras: BRITTEN: *Peter Grimes;* MOZART:
Nozze di Figaro; VERDI: *Falstaff;* also Wales
TV. **Res:** Petts Wood, UK.

EVANS, LLOYD RANNEY. Scenic and costume
designer for opera, television. Is also a painter.
American. Born 2 Nov 1932, Flint, MI. Single.
Studied: Univ of Mich, Ann Arbor; Yale School of
Drama, D Oenslager, CT; F P Bevin. **Operatic**
debut: *Barbiere di Siviglia* L I Arts Fest, NY
1965. Theater debut: CBS TV, New York 1965.
Previous occupation: PS music teacher, Roches-
ter, MI; instructor Hofstra Univ, NY. Awards:
Emmy nomination, Telev Acad 1974.
   Designed for major companies in USA: New
York City Opera, St Paul. **Operas designed for**
these companies incl BRITTEN: *Albert Herring,*
Burning Fiery Furnace, Curlew River, Prodigal
Son; CHERUBINI: *Medea★;* DEBUSSY: *Pel-*
léas et Mélisande; HOIBY: *Summer and Smoke★;*
LEONCAVALLO: *Pagliacci;* MASCAGNI: *Ca-*
valleria rusticana; MENOTTI: *Amahl, Old Maid*
and the Thief; MONTEVERDI: *Incoronazione di*
Poppea★; MOZART: *Don Giovanni, Schauspiel-*
direktor; PUCCINI: *Bohème, Butterfly;* PUR-
CELL: *Dido and Aeneas;* ROSSINI: *Barbiere di*
Siviglia; STRAUSS, J: *Fledermaus★;* STRAUSS,
R: *Ariadne auf Naxos★;* VERDI: *Rigoletto,*
Trovatore. **Operatic world premieres:** HOIBY:
Summer and Smoke St Paul Opera, MN 1971. **Res:**
105 W 72nd St, New York, USA.

EVAN-ZOHAR, SIMHA. Israeli. Founder/Gen Dir
of Adm, Israel National Opera, 1 Allenby St, Tel
Aviv 1947- . In charge of overall adm matters.
Born 5 May 1915, USSR. Wife Edis de Philippe,
occupation Art Dir & Dir/Prod. Three children.
Previous occupation: Gen Secy Israeli Labor Fed-
eration, Histadruth. Background primarily adm.
World premieres at theaters under his manage-
ment: AVIDOM: *Alexandra* Tel Aviv 1959.
Awards: Israeli Gvnmt issued stamp in honor of

company's 25th anniv. Initiated major policy changes including expansion of season from 100 to 300 perfs, and increased opportunities for young singers for opera training and performances. **Res:** 88 Aluf David, Ramat Chen, Israel.

EVERDING, AUGUST. Stages/produces opera, theater, film & television. German. Intendant & Resident Stage Dir, Hamburgische Staatsoper 1973-77; Gen Int designate Bayerische Staatsoper, Munich beginning 1977. Also Resident Stage Dir for theaters in Paris, Bayreuth, NY. Born 31 Oct 1928, Bottrop. Wife Gustava, occupation physician. Three children. Studied: Univ Bonn and Munich, philosophy, theology, Germanics, dramaturgy; also piano, organ & flute. **Operatic debut:** *Traviata* Bayerische Staatsoper, Munich. Theater debut: Münchner Kammerspiele, Munich.

Awards: Prof, Musikhochschule Hamburg; Vice-Pres, Deutscher Bühnenverein; Mem, Intl Theaterinst, Berlin.

Directed/produced opera for major companies in AUS: Salzburg Fest, Vienna Staatsoper; FRA: Paris; FR GER: Bayreuth Fest, Hamburg, Munich Staatsoper; UK: London Royal; USA: New York Met, San Francisco Opera. **Operas staged with these companies incl** MOZART: *Don Giovanni;* MUSSORGSKY: *Boris Godunov, Khovanshchina;* STRAUSS, R: *Elektra, Salome;* VERDI: *Otello;* WAGNER: *Fliegende Holländer, Parsifal, Tristan und Isolde.* **Operatic world premieres:** SEARLE: *Hamlet* Staatsoper, Hamburg 1968. Operatic TV: *Pimpinone.* Previous leading positions with major theater companies: Intendant, Münchner Kammerspiele 1963-73. Teaches at Univ and Musikhochschule, Hamburg. **Res:** Hamburg, FR Ger.

F

FABBRI, FRANCA. Lyric soprano. Italian. Born 28 May 1935, Milan. Single. Studied: Adelina Fiori, Adelaide Saraceni, Giuseppe Pais, Alberto Soresina, Milan. **Debut:** Violetta (*Traviata*) Spoleto Fest 1963. Previous occupations: medical secy. Awards: Winner, Lyric Artist of the Year, Lions Club Milan 1970.

Sang with major companies in BEL: Brussels; FRA: Aix-en-Provence Fest, Toulouse; FR GER: Berlin Deutsche Oper, Cologne, Hamburg, Wiesbaden; HUN: Budapest; ITA: Florence Maggio, Genoa, Milan La Scala, Naples, Palermo, Parma, Rome Opera, Spoleto Fest; POL: Warsaw; SWI: Geneva; USA: San Francisco Spring Opera. **Roles with these companies incl** AUBER: Zerlina (*Fra Diavolo*); BRITTEN: Governess★ (*Turn of the Screw*); DEBUSSY: Lia (*Enfant prodigue*); DONIZETTI: Lucia; GLUCK: Euridice★; GOUNOD: Marguerite (*Faust*); LEONCAVALLO: Nedda★ (*Pagliacci*); MENOTTI: Lucy★ (*Telephone*); MEYERBEER: Marguerite de Valois (*Huguenots*); MONTEVERDI: Euridice (*Favola d'Orfeo*); MOZART: Fiordiligi★ (*Così fan tutte*), Königin der Nacht (*Zauberflöte*); PERGOLESI: Lucrezia (*Frate 'nnamorato*); POULENC: La femme (*Voix humaine*); PUCCINI: Musetta★ (*Bohème*), Giorgetta (*Tabarro*); ROSSINI: Semiramide, Pamira (*Assedio di Corinto*); VERDI: La Marchesa★ (*Giorno di regno*), Desdemona (*Otello*), Gilda (*Rigoletto*), Violetta★ (*Traviata*). Also SHOSTAKOVICH: The Girl★ (*The Nose*); CHABRIER: Hélène★ (*Education manquée*), MALIPIERO: Filomela★ (*Filomela e l'infatuato*); HAZON: Argia (*Agenzia matrimoniale*); MADERNA: Crissida (*Satyricon*). **World premieres:** BETTINELLI: (*Count Down*) 1970; CORTESE: Nastenka (*Notti bianche*) 1973; SAVINIO: Euridice (*Orfeo vedovo*) 1975; NONO: (*Al gran sole carico d'amore*) 1975; all at La Scala, Milan. CHAILLY: Aglaja Ivanovna (*Idiota*) Rome Opera 1970, Vanessa (*Riva delle sirti*) Treviso Opera 1972. Gives recitals. Appears with symphony orchestra. **Res:** V Majocchi 28, Milan, Italy.

FACK, RENATE. Lyric coloratura soprano. German. Resident mem: Hessisches Staatstheater, Wiesbaden, FR Ger. Born 16 Jul 1937, Bremen, Germany. Husband Dr Rolf Ballmann, occupation TV producer. Studied: Hochschule für Musik, Bremen; Annelies Kupper, Munich; Annemarie Leber, Mainz; Karlheinz Jarius, Stuttgart. **Debut:** Papagena (*Zauberflöte*) Opernhaus Hagen, FR Ger 1957.

Sang with major companies in AUS: Vienna Volksoper; FR GER: Cologne, Darmstadt, Dortmund, Düsseldorf-Duisburg, Essen, Hannover, Kassel, Mannheim, Munich Gärtnerplatz, Saarbrücken, Wiesbaden, Wuppertal; SWI: Basel. **Roles with these companies incl** BEETHOVEN: Marzelline (*Fidelio*); CIMAROSA: Elisetta★ (*Matrimonio segreto*); DONIZETTI: Norina (*Don Pasquale*); HUMPERDINCK: Gretel★ (*Hänsel und Gretel*); LORTZING: Marie★ (*Waffenschmied*), Baronin Freimann★ (*Wildschütz*), Marie★ (*Zar und Zimmermann*); MOZART: Despina★(*Così fan tutte*), Blondchen★(*Entführung aus dem Serail*), Cherubino★ (*Nozze di Figaro*); NICOLAI: Aennchen★ (*Lustigen Weiber*); ORFF: Die Kluge★; PUCCINI: Musetta★ (*Bohème*), Lauretta (*Gianni Schicchi*); STRAUSS, J: Adele★ (*Fledermaus*); VERDI: Oscar (*Ballo in maschera*), Nannetta★‡ (*Falstaff*); WEBER: Aennchen★ (*Freischütz*); WOLF-FERRARI: Lucieta★ (*Quattro rusteghi*). Also WEBER: Puck & Droll & Meermädchen (*Oberon*); BRITTEN: Nancy (*Albert Herring*); LORTZING: Hannchen (*Opernprobe*). Recorded for: Tip Recording. Video/Film: Gretel; Adele (*Fledermaus*); Papagena (*Zauberflöte*). Gives recitals. Appears with symphony orchestra. Mgmt: PAS/FRG.

FAGGIONI, PIERO ANTONIO. Stages/produces opera & theater. Also designs sets & stage-lighting and is an actor & author. Italian. Born 12 Aug 1936, Carrara. Single. Studied: Accad Nazionale d'Arte, Rome; asst to Jean Vilar & Luchino Visconti; also music, piano, trumpet & voice. Operatic training as asst stage dir at Teatro la Fenice, Venice 1963-64. **Operatic debut:** *Bohème* Teatro la Fenice 1964. Theater debut: Spoleto 1965. Previous occupation: actor, movie critic. Awards: Golden Nut; Best Young Italian Actor, Ital theater critics 1961.

Directed/produced opera for major companies in FRA: Nice, Paris; FR GER: Berlin Deutsche Oper, Dortmund, Stuttgart; ITA: Florence Maggio, Milan La Scala, Naples San Carlo, Rome Teatro dell'Opera, Venice, Verona Arena; UK: Edinburgh Fest, London Royal Op; USSR: Moscow Bolshoi; USA: San Francisco Opera. **Operas staged with these companies incl** BELLINI: *Capuleti ed i Montecchi★, Puritani*; BIZET: *Carmen;*

DONIZETTI: *Maria Stuarda;* GLUCK: *Alceste*★*;* GOUNOD: *Faust*★*;* MOZART: *Nozze di Figaro*★*;* MUSSORGSKY: *Boris Godunov*★*;* PUCCINI: *Bohème, Fanciulla del West*★, *Tabarro*★, *Tosca*★*;* ROSSINI: *Cambiale di matrimonio*†*;* SAINT-SAENS: *Samson et Dalila*★*;* VERDI: *Ballo in maschera*★, *Don Carlo*★†, *Falstaff, Lombardi, Macbeth, Otello*★★, *Traviata*★†. **Res:** V Massena 21, Milan, Italy. **Mgmt:** SLA/UK.

FALCK, JORMA ANTERO. Dramatic baritone. Finnish. Resident mem: Kansallisooppera, Helsinki. Born 30 Oct 1939, Lappeenranta, Finland. Wife Raija Määttähen-Falck, occupation opera singer. Two children. Studied: Sibelius Akad, Antti Koskinen, Ture Ara, Helsinki; Luigi Ricci, Rome. **Debut:** Narumoff (*Pique Dame*) Kansallisooppera, Helsinki 1963. Previous occupations: post office clerk.

Sang with major companies in FIN: Helsinki. **Roles with these companies incl** BIZET: Escamillo (*Carmen*); BRITTEN: Demetrius★ (*Midsummer Night*); JANACEK: Harasta (*Cunning Little Vixen*); MOZART: Guglielmo★ (*Così fan tutte*), Conte Almaviva★ (*Nozze di Figaro*); PUCCINI: Scarpia (*Tosca*); TCHAIKOVSKY: Eugene Onegin; VERDI: Fra Melitone★ (*Forza del destino*), Germont (*Traviata*); WAGNER: Telramund (*Lohengrin*), Fasolt★ (*Rheingold*). Recorded for: Finnlevy. Gives recitals.

FALEWICZ, MAGDALENA. Lyric soprano. Polish. Resident mem: Komische Oper, Berlin. Born 11 Feb 1946, Lublin, Poland. Husband Ryszard Kula, occupation composer. Studied: Prof Olga Olgina, Dr Maria Kuninska-Opacka, Warsaw; State Coll of Music, Warsaw. **Debut:** Oscar (*Ballo in maschera*) Komische Oper, Berlin, Ger DR 1973. Awards: Fourth Prize, Intl Compt Munich 1970; Second Prize Toulouse 1972.

Sang with major companies in FR GER: Frankfurt; GER DR: Berlin Komische Oper, Leipzig; POL: Warsaw. **Roles with these companies incl** MOZART: Contessa★ & Susanna★ (*Nozze di Figaro*), Pamina★ (*Zauberflöte*); PROKOFIEV: Natasha★ (*War and Peace*); VERDI: Oscar★‡ (*Ballo in maschera*). Video–TV Berlin: Mimi (*Bohème*). Gives recitals. Appears with symphony orchestra. **Mgmt:** PAG/POL; SLZ/FRG.

FANATZEANU, CORNELIU. Lyric tenor. Romanian. Resident mem: Romanian Opera, Bucharest. Born 18 Jan 1933, Cluj. Wife Stela, occupation teacher. Studied: Consv Cluj; Accad S Cecilia, Prof Giorgio Favaretto, Rome. **Debut:** Vladimir (*Prince Igor*) Romanian Opera, Cluj 1955. Awards: Laureate of Intl Conts in Vienna, Prague, Geneva and Bucharest 1960-65.

Sang with major companies in BUL: Sofia; FR GER: Essen, Kassel; ROM: Bucharest; USSR: Kiev, Tbilisi; YUG: Zagreb, Belgrade. **Roles with these companies incl** BERLIOZ: Faust★ (*Damnation de Faust*); DELIBES: Gérald (*Lakmé*); DONIZETTI: Ernesto (*Don Pasquale*), Nemorino★ (*Elisir*), Edgardo★ (*Lucia*); GIORDANO: Andrea Chénier★; GLUCK: Pylade★ (*Iphigénie en Tauride*); GOUNOD: Faust★; JANACEK: Steva★ (*Jenufa*); MASSENET: Des Grieux★ (*Manon*); MOZART: Don Ottavio★ (*Don Giovanni*), Tamino★ (*Zauberflöte*); OFFENBACH: Hoff-

mann★; PUCCINI: Rodolfo★ (*Bohème*), Rinuccio★ (*Gianni Schicchi*), Pinkerton★ (*Butterfly*); ROSSINI: Almaviva (*Barbiere di Siviglia*); SMETANA: Hans★ (*Bartered Bride*); STRAVINSKY: Eumolpe (*Perséphone*); TCHAIKOVSKY: Lenski★ (*Eugene Onegin*); VERDI: Don Carlo★, Fenton★ (*Falstaff*), Ismaele★ (*Nabucco*), Duca di Mantova·(*Rigoletto*), Alfredo★ (*Traviata*); WAGNER: Walther v d Vogelweide★ (*Tannhäuser*); WOLF-FERRARI: Filipeto★ (*Quattro rusteghi*). Also VERDI: Macduff★ (*Macbeth*); RACHMANINOFF: Young Gypsy (*Aleko*). Video/Film: Macduff (*Macbeth*). Gives recitals. Appears with symphony orchestra. Teaches voice. Coaches repertoire. On faculty of J L Caragiale Theater Inst. **Res:** PO 18, Bucharest 1, Romania. **Mgmt:** RIA/ROM; ARM/FRG.

FARCAS, FLORIN. Dramatic tenor. Romanian. Resident mem: Romanian Opera, Bucharest. Born 10 Jul 1937, Bucharest. Wife Valentina, occupation teacher. Two children. Studied: Prof Dinu Badescu, Bucharest. **Debut:** Tonio (*Pagliacci*) Romanian Opera, Cluj 1961.

Sang with major companies in ROM: Bucharest. **Roles with these companies incl** BEETHOVEN: Florestan★ (*Fidelio*); BIZET: Don José★ (*Carmen*); LEONCAVALLO: Canio★ (*Pagliacci*); PUCCINI: Rodolfo★ (*Bohème*), Pinkerton★ (*Butterfly*), Des Grieux (*Manon Lescaut*), Cavaradossi★ (*Tosca*), Calaf★ (*Turandot*); VERDI: Manrico★ (*Trovatore*); WAGNER: Erik★ (*Fliegende Holländer*). Appears with symphony orchestra. **Res:** 27 Mircea Voda St, Bucharest 4, Romania.

FARLEY, CAROLE ANN. Lyric soprano. American. Born 29 Nov 1946, LeMars, IA, USA. Husband José Serebrier, occupation conductor. Studied: Dorothy Barnes, Moscow, IA, USA: William Shriner, Indiana Univ, Bloomington, IN: Marianne Schech, Hochschule für Musik, Munich; Cornelius Reid, New York. **Debut:** Formica (*Ameise*) Landestheater Linz, Austria 1969. Awards: Fulbright Schlshp.

Sang with major companies in BEL: Brussels; FRA: Strasbourg; FR GER: Cologne; UK: Cardiff; USA: New York Met, Philadelphia Lyric. **Roles with these companies incl** BERG: Lulu★; LEONCAVALLO: Nedda (*Pagliacci*); MASSENET: Manon; MOZART: Donna Anna★ (*Don Giovanni*); POULENC: La femme★ (*Voix humaine*); PUCCINI: Mimi★ & Musetta★ (*Bohème*); SMETANA: Marie★ (*Bartered Bride*); STRAUSS, J: Adele★ & Rosalinde★ (*Fledermaus*); TCHAIKOVSKY: Iolanthe★; VERDI: Violetta★ (*Traviata*). Gives recitals. Appears with symphony orchestra. **Res:** 270 Riverside Dr, New York, NY, USA. **Mgmt:** HUR/USA; AIM/UK.

FARMER, ANTHONY ELGAR. Scenic designer for opera, theater, film. Is a lighting designer, stage director; also in advertising. British. Born 7 Jul 1919, Leamington Spa. Single. Studied: London Acad of Dramatic Art. Prof training: Rank Film Studios, London 1946-51. **Operatic debut:** *Traviata* PACT Johannesburg, S Afr 1968. Theater debut: Loft Theatre, Leamington Spa, UK 1937. Previous occupation: mechanical engineer.

Designed for major companies in S AFR: Johannesburg. **Operas designed for these companies incl** BIZET: *Carmen;* DONIZETTI: *Don Pasquale, Lucia di Lammermoor;* JANACEK: *Jenufa;* PUCCINI: *Tosca;* ROSSINI: *Barbiere di Siviglia;* VERDI: *Rigoletto, Traviata.* Exhibitions of stage designs Nico Malan Opera House, Cape Town. **Res:** PO Box 5834, Johannesburg, South Africa.

FAROLFI, RAOUL. Italian. Tech Dir, & Stage Mng, Teatro Comunale/Maggio Musicale Fiorentino, 15 V Solferino, Florence, Italy. In charge of tech matters; is also stage dir/prod. Born 25 Jun 1930, Florence. Wife Elena Mendo, occupation employee. One child. Studied: Accad di Belle Arti Scenografia, Florence. Previous positions primarily theatrical. Started with present company 1965 as Tech Asst Dir; in present position since 1970.

FARRELL, EILEEN. Dramatic soprano. American. Born 13 Feb 1920, Willimantic, CT, USA. Husband Robert V Reagan, occupation retired. Two children. Studied: Merle Alcock, Eleanor McLellan. **Debut:** Santuzza (*Cavalleria rusticana*) San Carlo, Tampa, FL 1956. Awards: Hon Degrs Univ of RI, Loyola, Hartford, Notre Dame Coll (NH), Wagner Coll; Grammy Awd.
Sang with major companies in USA: Chicago, Hartford, Miami, New Orleans, New York Met & City Opera, Pittsburgh, San Antonio, San Francisco Opera, Seattle. **Roles with these companies incl** CHERUBINI: Medea; GIORDANO: Maddalena (*Andrea Chénier*); GLUCK: Alceste; PONCHIELLI: Gioconda; STRAUSS, R: Ariadne (*Ariadne auf Naxos*); VERDI: Leonora (*Forza del destino*), Leonora (*Trovatore*). Also BERG: Marie‡ (*Wozzeck*); DONIZETTI: Elisabetta‡ (*Maria Stuarda*). Recorded for: ABC Dunhill. Gives recitals. Appears with symphony orchestra. Teaches voice. On faculty of Indiana Univ Music School. **Res:** Bloomington, IN, USA. Mgmt: BAR/USA.

FASSBAENDER, BRIGITTE. Mezzo-soprano. German. Resident mem: Bayerische Staatsoper, Munich. Born 3 Jul 1939, Berlin. Divorced. Studied: Städtisches Konsv, Kmsg Willi Domgraf-Fassbaender, Nürnberg. **Debut:** Nicklausse (*Contes d'Hoffmann*) Staatsoper, Munich 1962. Awards: Kammersängerin, Freistaat Bayern, FR Ger 1970.
Sang with major companies in AUS: Salzburg Fest, Vienna Staatsoper; BEL: Brussels; CAN: Toronto; CZE: Prague National; DEN: Copenhagen; FIN: Helsinki; FRA: Bordeaux, Paris; FR GER: Berlin Deutsche Oper, Cologne, Darmstadt, Düsseldorf-Duisburg, Frankfurt, Hamburg, Munich Staatsoper; GER DR: Dresden; HOL: Amsterdam; ITA: Milan La Scala, Naples, Rome Teatro dell'Opera; SWE: Stockholm; SWI: Geneva, Zurich; UK: London Royal; USA: New York Met, Pittsburgh, San Francisco Opera. **Roles with these companies incl** BARTOK: Judith★ (*Bluebeard's Castle*); BIZET: Carmen★‡, Djamileh; DONIZETTI: Elisabetta (*Maria Stuarda*); FLOTOW: Nancy‡ (*Martha*); GLUCK: Orfeo; HANDEL: Amastris (*Xerxes*); HUMPERDINCK: Hänsel; MOZART: Sesto★ & Annio (*Clemenza di Tito*), Dorabella★‡ (*Così fan*

tutte), Ramiro (*Finta giardiniera*), Farnace (*Mitridate, re di Ponto*), Cherubino★ (*Nozze di Figaro*); MUSSORGSKY: Marina★ (*Boris Godunov*); NABOKOV: Princess (*Love's Labour's Lost*); PFITZNER: Silla★‡ (*Palestrina*); PUCCINI: Suzuki (*Butterfly*); ROSSINI: Rosina (*Barbiere di Siviglia*), Marchesina Clarice (*Pietra del paragone*), Zaida (*Turco in Italia*); STRAUSS, J: Prinz Orlovsky★‡ (*Fledermaus*); STRAUSS, R: Octavian★ (*Rosenkavalier*); TCHAIKOVSKY: Olga (*Eugene Onegin*); VERDI: Amneris (*Aida*), Eboli★ (*Don Carlo*), Azucena (*Trovatore*); WAGNER: Magdalene‡ (*Meistersinger*), Adriano‡ (*Rienzi*), Fricka (*Rheingold★, Walküre★*), Waltraute★ (*Götterdämmerung*), Brangäne★ (*Tristan und Isolde*); WEBER: Fatime (*Oberon*). Recorded for: EMI, Polydor, Philips, Eurodisc. Gives recitals. Appears with symphony orchestra. **Res:** c/o: Herbert Melle, Agnesstr 57, 8 Munich 40, FR Ger.

FASSINI, ALBERTO MARIA. Stages/produces opera, theater & television. Also designs stage-lighting. Italian. Born 2 Nov 1938, Palermo. Single. Studied: Accad d'Arte Drammatica, Rome; asst to and collab with Luchino Visconti for ten yrs; also music & voice. **Operatic debut:** *Andrea Chénier* Teatro dell'Opera, Rome 1965.
Directed/produced opera for major companies in CZE: Prague Smetana; FR GER: Frankfurt; GER DR: Berlin Komische Oper; HOL: Amsterdam; ITA: Bologna, Florence Comunale, Genoa, Milan La Scala, Naples, Palermo, Parma, Rome Opera, Spoleto Fest, Trieste, Turin, Venice; USA: Dallas. **Operas staged with these companies incl** AUBER: *Muette di Portici★*; BELLINI: *Norma;* CHERUBINI: *Medea★;* CILEA: *Adriana Lecouvreur;* DONIZETTI: *Caterina Cornaro★, Lucia★, Maria di Rohan★, Roberto Devereux★;* MOZART: *Nozze di Figaro★;* PUCCINI: *Manon Lescaut, Turandot★;* ROSSINI: *Moïse★;* TCHAIKOVSKY: *Pique Dame★;* VERDI: *Corsaro★, Don Carlo, Giovanna d'Arco★, Macbeth★, Otello★, Rigoletto, Traviata.* Also ROSSINI: *Armida;* DONIZETTI: *Gemma di Vergy, Belisario;* ROTA: *Visita meravigliosa;* MERCADANTE: *Elisa e Claudio.* Operatic Video/Film: *Andrea Chénier, Adriana Lecouvreur.* **Res:** Viale Parioli 12, Rome, Italy.

FECHT, JOHANNA-LOTTE. Dramatic soprano, spinto. German. Resident mem: Städtische Bühnen, Nürnberg. Born 15 May, Frankfurt/Main, Germany. Single. Studied: Staatliche Musikhochschule Frankfurt/Main, Prof Schlosshauer. **Debut:** Olympia (*Contes d'Hoffmann*) Staatstheater Saarbrücken 1960.
Sang with major companies in BEL: Brussels; DEN: Copenhagen; FR GER: Berlin Deutsche Oper, Bielefeld, Cologne, Dortmund, Düsseldorf-Duisburg, Hamburg, Hannover, Kassel, Kiel, Krefeld, Nürnberg, Saarbrücken, Stuttgart; USA: Portland. **Roles with these companies incl** BEETHOVEN: Leonore★ (*Fidelio*); DONIZETTI: Norina (*Don Pasquale*); FLOTOW: Lady Harriet (*Martha*); JANACEK: Vixen (*Cunning Little Vixen*), Jenufa★; MONTEVERDI: Euridice‡; MOZART: Fiordiligi★ (*Così fan tutte*), Donna Anna★ (*Don Giovanni*), Konstanze (*Entführung aus dem Serail*), Königin der Nacht (*Zauberflöte*); PUCCINI: Mimi★ (*Bohème*), Cio-Cio-San★ (*But-*

terfly); RAVEL: Concepcion (*Heure espagnole*); ROSSINI: Rosina (*Barbiere di Siviglia*); SMETANA: Marie (*Bartered Bride*); STRAUSS, J: Rosalinde★ (*Fledermaus*); STRAUSS, R: Zdenka & Fiakermilli (*Arabella*), Zerbinetta (*Ariadne auf Naxos*), Chrysothemis★ (*Elektra*), Kaiserin★ (*Frau ohne Schatten*), Sophie (*Rosenkavalier*), Salome★; TCHAIKOVSKY: Lisa★ (*Pique Dame*); VERDI: Aida★, Oscar (*Ballo in maschera*), Gilda (*Rigoletto*), Violetta★ (*Traviata*), Leonora★ (*Trovatore*); WEBER: Agathe★ (*Freischütz*). **World premieres:** BENTZON: Zoe Higgins & Frl Bürstner (*Faust III*) Bühnen Kiel 1964; REIMANN: Sängerin & Edith (*Traumspiel*) Bühnen Kiel 1965. Recorded for: Westdeutscher & Norddeutscher Rundfunk. Gives recitals. Appears with symphony orchestra. Teaches voice. **Res:** Hainstr 25, 85 Nürnberg, FR Ger. Mgmt: PAS/FRG; SLZ/FRG.

FEDOSEYEV, ANDREI ALEKSANDROVICH. Lyric baritone. Russian. Resident mem: Bolshoi Theater, Moscow. Born 1 Feb 1934, Tiraspol. Divorced. Studied: Moscow Consv, A A Solovyova. **Debut:** Eugene Onegin, Novosibirsk Opera 1962. Previous occupations: architect.
Sang with major companies in CZE: Brno, Prague National & Smetana; GER DR: Leipzig; USSR: Leningrad Kirov, Moscow Bolshoi & Stanislavski. **Roles with these companies incl** MOZART: Don Giovanni, Conte Almaviva★ (*Nozze di Figaro*); PROKOFIEV: Prince Andrei Bolkonsky (*War and Peace*); PUCCINI: Marcello (*Bohème*), Sharpless (*Butterfly*); ROSSINI: Figaro (*Barbiere di Siviglia*); TCHAIKOVSKY: Eugene Onegin, Duke Robert★ (*Iolanthe*), Yeletsky (*Pique Dame*); VERDI: Germont (*Traviata*). Recorded for: Melodiya. Gives recitals. Appears with symphony orchestra. **Res:** d 5 kv 65 Malysheva, Moscow, USSR. Mgmt: GOS/USSR.

FELDHOFF, GERD. Dramatic baritone. Resident mem: Deutsche Oper, Berlin. Born 29 Oct 1931, Radevormwald, Germany. Wife Gertrud. Three children. Studied: Prof Husler, Detmold. **Debut:** Figaro (*Nozze di Figaro*) Essen 1959. Awards: Kammersänger, City of Berlin.
Sang with major companies in ARG: Buenos Aires; CAN: Montrea/Quebec; DEN: Copenhagen; FIN: Helsinki; FR GER: Bayreuth Fest, Berlin Deutsche Oper, Cologne, Essen, Frankfurt, Hamburg, Hannover, Kassel, Mannheim, Munich Staatsoper, Stuttgart; HOL: Amsterdam; MEX: Mexico City; USA: New York Met, Washington DC. **Roles with these companies incl** d'ALBERT: Sebastiano‡ (*Tiefland*); BEETHOVEN: Don Pizarro (*Fidelio*); BERG: Zirkusdirektor (*Lulu*); BIZET: Escamillo (*Carmen*); DEBUSSY: Golaud (*Pelléas et Mélisande*); DONIZETTI: Enrico (*Lucia*); EINEM: Ill★ (*Besuch der alten Dame*), St Just (*Dantons Tod*); GIORDANO: Carlo Gérard (*Andrea Chénier*); HUMPERDINCK: Peter (*Hänsel*); MEYERBEER: Nelusco (*Africaine*); MOZART: Don Alfonso★ (*Così*), Figaro★ (*Nozze di Figaro*); PUCCINI: Jack Rance (*Fanciulla del West*), Sharpless (*Butterfly*), Michele (*Tabarro*), Scarpia (*Tosca*); STRAUSS, R: Musiklehrer (*Ariadne auf Naxos*), Graf (*Capriccio*), Orest (*Elektra*), Barak (*Frau ohne Schatten*), Jochanaan (*Salome*); TCHAIKOVSKY: Yeletsky (*Pique Dame*); VERDI: Amonasro (*Aida*), Renato★

(*Ballo*), Grande Inquistore★ & Rodrigo (*Don Carlo*), Falstaff, Don Carlo (*Forza del destino*), Macbeth, Nabucco, Rigoletto, Germont (*Traviata*); WAGNER: Holländer, Telramund (*Lohengrin*), Hans Sachs (*Meistersinger*), Amfortas (*Parsifal*), Wotan (*Rheingold*), Gunther (*Götterdämmerung*), Kurwenal (*Tristan und Isolde*); WEBER: Kaspar (*Freischütz*). **World premieres:** BLACHER: (*200,000 Taler*) Deutsche Oper Berlin 1969. Recorded for: DG, Philips. Video/Film: Sebastiano (*Tiefland*); (*200,000 Taler*). Gives recitals. Appears with symphony orchestra. Mgmt: SLZ/FRG.

FELLER, CARLOS. Basso-buffo. Argentinean. Resident mem: Opernhaus, Cologne. Born 30 Jul 1925, Buenos Aires. Wife Carlota. Two children. Studied: Opera School, Teatro Colón, Editha Fleischer, Buenos Aires. **Debut:** Le Médecin (*Pelléas et Mélisande*) Teatro Colón, Buenos Aires 1946. Previous occupations: studied dentistry, Univ of Montevideo, Uruguay.
Sang with major companies in ARG: Buenos Aires; AUS: Salzburg Fest, Vienna Volksoper; BEL: Brussels; BRA: Rio de Janeiro; FRA: Strasbourg; FR GER: Cologne, Düsseldorf-Duisburg, Frankfurt, Hamburg, Hannover, Kassel, Kiel, Mannheim, Munich Staatsoper, Stuttgart; HOL: Amsterdam; UK: Edinburgh Fest, Glyndebourne Fest. **Roles with these companies incl** BERG: Wozzeck & Doktor★ (*Wozzeck*); BRITTEN: Theseus (*Midsummer Night*); CIMAROSA: Geronimo (*Matrimonio segreto*); CORNELIUS: Abul Hassan★ (*Barbier von Bagdad*); DONIZETTI: Don Pasquale★, Dott Dulcamara★ (*Elisir*); FALLA: Tio Sarvaor (*Vida breve*); GALUPPI: Don Tritemio (*Filosofo di campagna*); GOUNOD: Méphistophélès (*Faust*); HINDEMITH: Professor (*Hin und zurück*); LORTZING: Baculus★ (*Wildschütz*), Van Bett★ (*Zar und Zimmermann*); MOZART: Don Alfonso★ (*Così fan tutte*), Leporello★ (*Don Giovanni*), Osmin★ (*Entführung aus dem Serail*), Nardo (*Finta giardiniera*), Figaro (*Nozze di Figaro*), Don Pippo (*Oca del Cairo*); MUSSORGSKY: Varlaam★ (*Boris Godunov*); NICOLAI: Falstaff (*Lustigen Weiber*); PERGOLESI: Uberto★ (*Serva padrona*); PUCCINI: Colline (*Bohème*), Gianni Schicchi; ROSSINI: Dott Bartolo★ & Don Basilio (*Barbiere di Siviglia*), Tobias Mill (*Cambiale di matrimonio*), Don Magnifico★ (*Cenerentola*), Mustafà (*Italiana in Algeri*), Gaudenzio (*Signor Bruschino*); SMETANA: Kezal★ (*Bartered Bride*), Janus (*The Kiss*); STRAUSS, R: Sir Morosus (*Schweigsame Frau*); STRAVINSKY: Tiresias (*Oedipus Rex*). Also CIMAROSA: Maestro★ (*Maestro di cappella*); BERG: Schigolch★ (*Lulu*); HAYDN: Mastricco (*Pescatrici*). **Res:** Bachemerstr 254, Cologne, FR Ger.

FELSENSTEIN, WALTER. Stages/produces opera, theater & film; is also an actor & writer. Austrian. Intendant & Resident Stage Dir, Komische Oper, Berlin, Ger DR 1947-. Born 30 May 1901, Vienna. Studied: in Vienna & Graz. **Operatic debut:** in Beuthen, Germany. Awards: 5 times Ger DR Ntl Prize; Ger Gold Medal for Merit Service. Mem Deutsche Akad der Künste 1951- ; Hon Dr, Humboldt Univ Berlin & Prague Univ; Hon Mem,

Gesellschaft für Musiktheater, Vienna 1972. Previous adm positions in opera: Oberspielleiter, Oper Basel, Switzerland 1927-34, Frankfurt 1934-38.

Directed/produced opera for major companies in AUS: Salzburg Fest, Vienna Staatsoper; CZE: Prague National; FR GER: Cologne, Frankfurt, Hamburg, Stuttgart; GER DR: Berlin Komische Oper; ITA: Milan La Scala; SWI: Basel, Zurich; USSR: Moscow Bolshoi & Stanislavski; et al. **Operas staged with these companies incl** BARTOK: *Bluebeard's Castle;* BEETHOVEN: *Fidelio;* BIZET: *Carmen;* BRITTEN: *Midsummer Night;* JANACEK: *Cunning Little Vixen, Jenufa;* KODALY: *Háry János;* MASSENET: *Manon;* MOZART: *Così fan tutte, Don Giovanni, Entführung aus dem Serail, Nozze di Figaro, Zauberflöte;* OFFENBACH: *Contes d'Hoffmann;* PAISIELLO: *Barbiere di Siviglia;* PROKOFIEV: *Fiery Angel, Love for Three Oranges;* PUCCINI: *Bohème, Butterfly;* ROSSINI: *Barbiere di Siviglia;* STRAUSS, R: *Ariadne auf Naxos, Elektra, Rosenkavalier, Salome, Schweigsame Frau;* VERDI: *Falstaff, Forza del destino, Otello, Traviata;* WEBER: *Freischütz;* et al. Also SHOSTAKOVICH: *The Nose.* Film: *Otello,, Fidelio;* Komische Oper prod: *Contes d'Hoffmann, Cunning Little Vixen, Bartered Bride;* et al. [† Oct 8, '75.]

FELT, RUTH ALLISON. American. Company Adm, San Francisco Opera, War Memorial Opera House, San Francisco, CA 94102 USA. In charge of adm matters. Born 8 Apr 1939, Willmar, MN, USA. Single. Studied: Univ of California, Los Angeles; BA. Plays the piano. Previous occupations: on staff of Vice Pres of the United States, Hubert H Humphrey. Previous positions primarily administrative: Asst Concert Mng, UCLA Dept of Fine Arts Prods, Los Angeles 1966-71. Started with present company 1971 as Asst Adm, in present position since 1975. **Res:** 1125 Taylor St, San Francisco, CA, USA.

FENN, JEAN DOROTHY. Lyric soprano. American. Husband W T Farwell, occupation theatrical agent. Studied: Amelita Galli-Curci; Homer Samuels; Florence Holtzman; Val Rosing, stage deportment. **Debut:** Elena (*Mefistofele*) San Francisco Opera 1952.

Sang with major companies in USA: Boston, Cincinnati, Fort Worth, Hartford, Hawaii, Houston, Memphis, Miami, Milwaukee Florentine, New Orleans, New York Met & City Opera, Omaha, Philadelphia Grand, Pittsburgh, Portland, St Paul, San Antonio, San Francisco Opera, Seattle. **Roles with these companies incl** BIZET: Micaëla (*Carmen*); FLOTOW: Lady Harriet (*Martha*); GOUNOD: Marguerite★ (*Faust*); LEONCAVALLO: Nedda (*Pagliacci*); MASSENET: Manon, Thaïs; MONTEMEZZI: Fiora (*Amore dei tre re*); MOZART: Contessa★ (*Nozze di Figaro*); OFFENBACH: Antonia (*Contes d'Hoffmann*); PUCCINI: Mimi★ & Musetta (*Bohème*), Lauretta (*Schicchi*), Manon Lescaut, Tosca, Liù (*Turandot*); STRAUSS, J: Rosalinde★ (*Fledermaus*); STRAUSS, R: Zdenka (*Arabella*); VERDI: Desdemona★ (*Otello*), Violetta (*Traviata*); WAGNER: Eva (*Meistersinger*). Gives recitals. Appears with symphony orchestra. **Res:** Bainbridge Is, WN 98110, USA.

FERENCSIK, JANOS. Conductor of opera and symphony. Hungarian. Chief Cond, Hungarian State Opera, Budapest. Also Mus Dir, Hungarian State Symph Orch, Budapest 1952- . Born 18 Jan 1907, Budapest. Single. Studied: form Ntl Consv, Budapest; incl violin, organ. Operatic training as repetiteur at Hungarian State Opera, Budapest 1927-30. **Operatic debut:** *Hänsel und Gretel* Hungarian State Opera, Budapest 1930. Symphonic debut: form Budapest Symph Orch 1931-32. Awards: Kossuth Awd, outstanding artist; hon prof Acad of Liszt. Previous adm positions in opera: Gen Mus Dir, Hungarian State Opera, Budapest 1957-74.

Conducted with major companies in AUS: Vienna Staatsoper; FIN: Helsinki; GER DR: Berlin Staatsoper, Dresden; HUN: Budapest; UK: Edinburgh Fest; USA: San Francisco Opera. **Operas with these companies incl** BARTOK: *Bluebeard's Castle★;* BEETHOVEN: *Fidelio;* BERG: *Wozzeck;* BIZET: *Carmen;* BRITTEN: *Peter Grimes;* DEBUSSY: *Pelléas et Mélisande;* DELIBES: *Lakmé;* ERKEL: *Bánk Bán;* FALLA: *Vida breve;* GLUCK: *Cadi dupé, Orfeo ed Euridice;* GOUNOD: *Faust;* HANDEL: *Rodelinda★;* HUMPERDINCK: *Hänsel und Gretel;* JANACEK: *Katya Kabanova;* KODALY: *Háry János;* LEONCAVALLO: *Pagliacci;* MASCAGNI: *Cavalleria rusticana;* MASSENET: *Manon;* MOZART: *Così fan tutte, Don Giovanni, Entführung aus dem Serail, Nozze di Figaro, Zauberflöte;* MUSSORGSKY: *Boris Godunov, Fair at Sorochinsk, Khovanshchina★;* PUCCINI: *Bohème, Gianni Schicchi, Butterfly, Manon Lescaut, Suor Angelica, Tabarro, Tosca★, Turandot;* ROSSINI: *Barbiere di Siviglia;* STRAUSS, R: *Ariadne auf Naxos, Rosenkavalier, Salome;* TCHAIKOVSKY: *Eugene Onegin;* VERDI: *Aida★, Ballo in maschera★, Don Carlo, Falstaff, Forza del destino, Otello, Rigoletto, Simon Boccanegra, Traviata, Trovatore;* WAGNER: *Fliegende Holländer, Lohengrin, Meistersinger, Parsifal, Rheingold, Walküre, Siegfried, Götterdämmerung, Tannhäuser, Tristan und Isolde;* WEBER: *Freischütz.* Also LEROUX: *Chemineau;* DOHNANYI: *Tante Simona, Tenor;* KODALY: *Spinning Room.* **World premieres:** ZADOR: *Azra* Hungarian State Opera, Budapest 1936. Recorded for Hungaroton. Video—Danish TV: *Xerxes;* Hungarian TV: *Gianni Schicchi.* Conducted major orch in Europe, USA/Canada, Cent/S America, Asia, Austrl. **Res:** Csopaki utca 12, 1022 Budapest, Hungary. Mgmt: ITK/HNG; SUH/USA.

FERGUSON, GENE. Dramatic tenor & Heldentenor. American. Resident mem: Hessisches Staatstheater, Wiesbaden. Born 4 Jun 1940, Windsor, MO. Wife Janet, occupation musician & teacher. Four children. Studied: Helge Roswänge, Munich; Costanzo Gero, New York; Robert Vernon, Kansas City, MO. **Debut:** Pinkerton (*Butterfly*) Teatro Nuovo, Milan 1961. Previous occupations: univ teacher. Awards: Winner American Opera Aud; Winner Met Op Ntl Counc Aud.

Sang with major companies in AUS: Graz; FR GER: Berlin Deutsche Oper, Bielefeld, Cologne, Dortmund, Düsseldorf-Duisburg, Frankfurt, Hamburg, Karlsruhe, Kassel, Krefeld, Mannheim, Stuttgart, Wiesbaden, Wuppertal; ITA: Milan, Palermo. **Roles with these companies incl** BEETHO-VEN: Florestan★ (*Fidelio*); BERLIOZ: Aeneas★ (*Troyens*); BIZET: Don José★ (*Carmen*), Nadir★ (*Pêcheurs de perles*); BORODIN: Vladimir★ (*Prince Igor*); DONIZETTI: Riccardo (*Anna Bolena*); GOUNOD: Faust; MUSSORGSKY: Dimitri (*Boris Godunov*); ORFF: Solo★ (*Carmina burana*); PUCCINI: Pinkerton (*Butterfly*), Luigi★ (*Tabarro*), Cavaradossi★ (*Tosca*), Calaf★ (*Turandot*); ROSSINI: Arnold (*Guillaume Tell*); SAINT-SAENS: Samson; STRAUSS, R: Bacchus★ (*Ariadne auf Naxos*), Kaiser★ (*Frau ohne Schatten*), Ein Sänger★ (*Rosenkavalier*); VERDI: Radames★ (*Aida*), Foresto★ (*Attila*), Riccardo★ (*Ballo in maschera*), Don Carlo★, Don Alvaro (*Forza del destino*), Duca di Mantova (*Rigoletto*), Gabriele (*Simon Boccanegra*), Manrico★ (*Trovatore*), Arrigo (*Vespri*); WAGNER: Erik★ (*Fliegende Holländer*), Lohengrin★, Parsifal★; WEBER: Adolar (*Euryanthe*), Hüon★ (*Oberon*). Gives recitals. Appears with symphony orchestra. Teaches voice. Coaches repertoire. Mgmt: SMN/USA.

FERRANTE, JOHN. Countertenor. American. Born 24 Jan 1925, Hartford, CT, USA. Single. Studied: Rhea Massicotte, Hartt Coll of Music, Hartford; Consv Fontainebleau, France; Lois Albright, New York. **Debut:** Lampionaio (*Manon Lescaut*) Connecticut Opera 1959. Previous occupations: offc mgr, secy, accountant, teacher at Hartt Coll of Music.

Sang with major companies in BEL: Brussels; HOL: Amsterdam; USA: Boston, Minneapolis, San Francisco Opera & Spring Opera. **Roles with these companies incl** STRAVINSKY: Baba the Turk★ (*Rake's Progress*). Also BRITTEN: Oberon★ (*Midsummer Night*); CAVALLI: Alcesta★ (*Erismena*); DONIZETTI: Agata★ (*Convenienze/Viva la Mamma*); ORFF: Solo★ (*Carmina burana*). Recorded for: Vanguard. Gives recitals. Appears with symphony orchestra. **Res:** 2109 Broadway, New York, NY 10023, USA. Mgmt: TPM/USA.

FERRARO, PIERMIRANDA; né Pietro Silvio Ferraro. Dramatic tenor. Italian. Born 30 Oct 1924, Altivole/Treviso. Wife Miranda Boschiero. Four children. Studied: Venice Consv, Mo Bononi; Milan Consv, Mo Aureliano Pertile; Mo De Tura Manrico. **Debut:** Rodolfo (*Bohème*) Teatro Nuovo, Milan 1951. Previous occupations: Naval Acad, Venice. Awards: Commenda of the Italian Republic; Grand Ufficiale and Commendatore, Pres of Italy; Military Order of SS Savior and S Brigida Swede; Verdi Gold Medal, Busseto 1975; Ambrogino d'oro, Comune di Milano 1975.

Sang with major companies in ARG: Buenos Aires; AUS: Vienna Staatsoper; BEL: Brussels, Liège; BRA: Rio de Janeiro; CAN: Montreal/Quebec; FRA: Aix-en-Provence Fest, Bordeaux, Lyon, Marseille, Nancy, Nice, Paris, Rouen, Strasbourg, Toulouse; GRE: Athens National; FR GER: Dortmund, Hamburg, Stuttgart; HUN: Budapest; ITA: Bologna, Florence Maggio & Comunale, Genoa, Milan La Scala, Naples, Palermo, Parma, Rome Opera & Caracalla, Trieste, Turin, Venice; MON: Monte Carlo; POR: Lisbon; SPA: Barcelona; SWI: Basel, Geneva,

Zurich; UK: Aldeburgh Fest, Cardiff Welsh, Edinburgh Fest, Glasgow Scottish, London Royal; USA: Cincinnati, Hartford, Newark, New York City Opera, Philadelphia Lyric, San Francisco Opera, Washington DC; YUG: Zagreb, Belgrade. **Roles with these companies incl** BELLINI: Pollione★ (*Norma*), Gualtiero (*Pirata*), Arturo (*Straniera*); BIZET: Don José★ (*Carmen*); BORODIN: Vladimir (*Prince Igor*); DONIZETTI: Edgardo (*Lucia*); GIORDANO: Andrea Chénier‡; GLUCK: Achille (*Iphigénie en Aulide*); LEONCAVALLO: Canio★ (*Pagliacci*); MASCAGNI: Turiddu (*Cavalleria rusticana*); MUSSORGSKY: Andrei Khovansky (*Khovanshchina*); PONCHIELLI: Enzo‡ (*Gioconda*); PUCCINI: Rodolfo (*Bohème*), Dick Johnson★ (*Fanciulla del West*), Pinkerton (*Butterfly*), Des Grieux (*Manon Lescaut*), Cavaradossi (*Tosca*), Calaf (*Turandot*); ROSSINI: Aménophis (*Moïse*); SAINT-SAENS: Samson★; TCHAIKOVSKY: Gherman (*Pique Dame*); VERDI: Radames★ (*Aida*), Corrado (*Corsaro*), Don Carlo, Ernani, Don Alvaro (*Forza del destino*), Rodolfo (*Luisa Miller*), Ismaele (*Nabucco*), Otello★, Duca di Mantova (*Rigoletto*), Alfredo (*Traviata*), Manrico (*Trovatore*), Arrigo (*Vespri*); WAGNER: Erik (*Fliegende Holländer*), Parsifal, Rienzi, Tannhäuser. Also MASCAGNI: Folco (*Isabeau*), Gugliemo Ratcliff. Recorded for: EMI, HMV. Teaches voice. On faculty of Milan Consv. **Res:** V Piranesi 22, Milan, Italy. Mgmt: GOR/UK; HUR/USA.

FERRIN, AGOSTINO; né Ferin. Bass. Italian. Born 27 Jul 1928, Padua, Italy. Wife Irene Rallo. Two children. Studied: Mo Cesare Chiesa, Milan. **Debut:** Tuteur Ajo (*Comte Ory*) Florence Opera 1957-58.

Sang with major companies in AUS: Vienna Staatsoper; BEL: Brussels; BUL: Sofia; CAN: Montreal/Quebec; DEN: Copenhagen; FRA: Marseille, Nice, Orange Fest, Paris; GRE: Athens Fest; FR GER: Berlin Deutsche Oper, Cologne, Frankfurt, Hamburg, Munich Staatsoper, Wiesbaden; HOL: Amsterdam; ISR: Tel Aviv; ITA: Bologna, Florence Maggio & Comunale, Genoa, Milan La Scala, Naples, Palermo, Parma, Rome Opera, Trieste, Turin, Venice, Verona Arena; MON: Monte Carlo; POR: Lisbon; SPA: Barcelona, Majorca; SWI: Geneva, Zurich; UK: Edinburgh Fest, London Royal; USSR: Moscow Bolshoi; USA: Boston, Chicago Lyric, Dallas, New York Metropolitan, Philadelphia Grand & Lyric; YUG: Dubrovnik. **Roles with these companies incl** BELLINI: Oroveso (*Norma*), Sir George (*Puritani*), Rodolfo (*Sonnambula*); BOITO: Mefistofele; DONIZETTI: Baldassare (*Favorite*), Talbot (*Maria Stuarda*); GOUNOD: Méphistophélès (*Faust*); MEYERBEER: Don Pedro (*Africaine*); PONCHIELLI: Alvise (*Gioconda*); PUCCINI: Colline (*Bohème*); ROSSINI: Don Basilio (*Barbiere di Siviglia*), Moïse; SPONTINI: Pontifex Maximus (*Vestale*); VERDI: Ramfis (*Aida*), Attila, Philip II (*Don Carlo*), Silva (*Ernani*), Padre Guardiano‡ (*Forza del destino*), Banquo (*Macbeth*), Zaccaria (*Nabucco*), Fiesco (*Simon Boccanegra*). Also DONIZETTI: Marino Faliero. Recorded for: His Master's Voice. Video/Film: PAISIELLO: Don Basilio (*Barbiere di Siviglia*). **Res:** V Luigi Gherzi 8, Rome, Italy.

FIASCONARO, GREGORIO. Stages/produces opera. Also designs sets & stage-lighting, conducts and is a baritone. Italian/South African. Art Adv, Cape Town, Performing Arts Board. Born 5 Mar, Palermo. Wife Mabel Marie. One child. Studied: Paganini Consv, Genoa; St Cecilia, Rome; Riccardo Stracciari; Centro Sperimentale; incl music, piano, organ and voice. Operatic training as asst stage dir at var comps Italy, S Afr while solo bar. **Operatic debut as prod:** *Suor Angelica* Cape Town 1951. Awards: Cape Tercentenary for Outstanding Services to Opera Prod; Carnegie Fllshp Awd.

Directed/produced opera for major companies in S AFR: Johannesburg. **Operas staged with these companies incl** BEETHOVEN: *Fidelio;* BERLIOZ: *Troyens;* BERNSTEIN: *Trouble in Tahiti;* BIZET: *Carmen*★*;* DONIZETTI: *Don Pasquale, Lucia di Lammermoor*★*;* GLUCK: *Orfeo ed Euridice*★*;* HUMPERDINCK: *Hänsel und Gretel;* MARTINU: *Comedy on the Bridge;* MASCAGNI: *Cavalleria rusticana;* MENOTTI: *Amahl*★*, Amelia al ballo, Consul*★*, Medium*★*, Old Maid and the Thief*★*, Telephone*★*;* MONTEVERDI: *Combattimento di Tancredi;* MOZART: *Don Giovanni*★*, Entführung aus dem Serail, Nozze di Figaro, Schauspieldirektor*★*;* PERGOLESI: *Serva padrona*★*;* PUCCINI: *Bohème, Gianni Schicchi*★*, Butterfly*★*, Manon Lescaut*★*, Tabarro, Tosca*★*, Turandot*★*;* ROSSINI: *Barbiere di Siviglia, Cenerentola;* STRAUSS, J: *Fledermaus;* VERDI: *Aida*★*, Ballo in maschera*★*, Don Carlo*★*, Falstaff*★*, Otello, Rigoletto*★*, Traviata*★*;* WOLF-FERRARI: *Segreto di Susanna.* Also CHERUBINI: *Osteria portoghese.* **Operatic world premieres:** CHISHOLM: *Dark Sonnet* Cape Town 1952, *Inland Woman* Cape Town 1953; JOUBERT: *Silas Marner* Univ C T Op Co 1961. Teaches at Univ of Cape Town, Dir Opera School. **Res:** 603 Devonshire Hill, Rondebosch/Cape Town, South Africa.

FIFIELD, CHRISTOPHER. Conductor of opera and symphony. British. Resident Cond, Cape Performing Arts Board, Cape Town, S Africa. Born 4 Sep 1945, Croydon, UK. Wife Dr Judith, occupation dental surgeon. One child. Studied: Prof Wolfgang von der Nahmer, Cologne, FR Ger; also piano, organ, viola, clarinet. Operatic training as repetiteur, asst cond & chorus master at Glyndebourne Fest 1971-72. **Operatic debut:** *Amico Fritz* Guildhall School of Music, London 1970. Symphonic debut: Capab Orch, Cape Town 1973. Awards: Conducting Schlshp King Edward VII, UK; German Foundation and British Council.

Conducted with major companies in S AFR: Johannesburg. **Operas staged with these companies incl** BIZET: *Carmen*★*;* DONIZETTI: *Elisir d'amore*★*;* HUMPERDINCK: *Hänsel und Gretel*★*;* MASCAGNI: *Amico Fritz*★*;* MOZART: *Così fan tutte*★*, Nozze di Figaro*★*;* OFFENBACH: *Périchole*★*;* PUCCINI: *Bohème*★*;* ROSSINI: *Barbiere di Siviglia*★*;* VERDI: *Rigoletto*★*.* **World premieres:** HARVEY: *Esther* Sandton Arts, Johannesburg 1975. **Res:** 22 Wargrave Rd, Kenilworth, Cape Town, S Afr.

FINE, WENDY MARION. Spinto. South African. Born Durban. Single. Studied: John van Zyl, Durban; Musik Akad, Profs Christian Moeller, Erik Werba, Vienna; Maria Hittorff. **Debut:** Cio-Cio-San (*Butterfly*) Stadttheater Bern, Switzerland. Awards: Halle Stpd, Natal Eisteddfod, S Africa; Second Prize, Mozart Compt Vienna 1964.

Sang with major companies in AUS: Vienna Volksoper; FRA: Strasbourg; FR GER: Bayreuth Fest, Berlin Deutsche Oper, Cologne, Dortmund, Düsseldorf-Duisburg, Frankfurt, Hamburg, Karlsruhe, Munich Staatsoper, Stuttgart, Wiesbaden; POR: Lisbon; SWI: Geneva; UK: London Royal & English National. **Roles with these companies incl** BERG: Marie★ (*Wozzeck*); BIZET: Micaëla★ (*Carmen*); CORNELIUS: Margiana (*Barbier von Bagdad*); GLUCK: Euridice; GOUNOD: Marguerite (*Faust*); HENZE: Luise (*Junge Lord*); HUMPERDINCK: Gretel★; JANACEK: Jenufa★; ·LEONCAVALLO: Nedda (*Pagliacci*); MOZART: Fiordiligi★ (*Così fan tutte*), Donna Elvira★ (*Don Giovanni*), Ilia (*Idomeneo*), Pamina (*Zauberflöte*); NICOLAI: Frau Fluth (*Lustigen Weiber*); OFFENBACH: Antonia★ & Giulietta★ (*Contes d'Hoffmann*); PUCCINI: Mimi & Musetta★ (*Bohème*); SMETANA: Marie★ (*Bartered Bride*); STRAUSS, J: Rosalinde (*Fledermaus*); STRAUSS, R: Zdenka (*Arabella*), Sophie (*Rosenkavalier*); STRAVINSKY: Anne Trulove (*Rake's Progress*); TCHAIKOVSKY: Tatiana★ (*Eugene Onegin*); VERDI: Desdemona★ (*Otello*); WAGNER: Gutrune★ (*Götterdämmerung*); WARD: Abigail (*Crucible*); WEILL: Jenny★ (*Aufstieg und Fall der Stadt Mahagonny*). Also MARTINU: Maria (*Marienlegende*); SZOKOLAY: Ophelia (*Hamlet*); SUTERMEISTER: Lisbeth (*Roten Stiefel*). Video—ZDF: Marie (*Bartered Bride*), Maria (*Marienlegende*). Recorded for: EMI. **Res:** Prinzregentenstr 54, 8 Munich 22, FR Ger. Mgmt: SLZ/FRG; IWL/UK.

FINEL, PAUL JEAN-MARIE. Dramatic tenor. French. Born 18 Dec 1924, Villeveyrac, Hérault, France. Wife Paulette, occupation prof in fashion design. Three children. Studied: Consv National Montpellier, France; Georges Thill, Mario Podestà. **Debut:** Faust (*Damnation de Faust*) Opéra de Paris 1957. Previous occupations: technician, chemist. Awards: Premier Prix de Chant, Consv de Montpellier, Lauréat Concours de Ténors, Cannes, France.

Sang with major companies in AUS: Vienna Staatsoper; BEL: Liège; FRA: Bordeaux, Lyon, Marseille, Nice, Orange Fest, Paris, Rouen, Strasbourg, Toulouse; GRE: Athens Fest; FR GER: Saarbrücken; ITA: Florence Comunale; POR: Lisbon; SWI: Geneva. **Roles with these companies incl** BEETHOVEN: Florestan★ (*Fidelio*); BERLIOZ: Faust★ (*Damnation de Faust*); Bizet; Don José★ (*Carmen*); CHARPENTIER: Julien (*Louise*); DEBUSSY: Azaël (*Enfant prodigue*); EINEM: Bürgermeister (*Besuch der alten Dame*); GIORDANO: Andrea Chénier★; GLUCK: Pylade (*Iphigénie en Tauride*); GOUNOD: Faust , Roméo; LALO: Mylio (*Roi d'Ys*); LEONCAVALLO: Canio★ (*Pagliacci*); MASCAGNI: Turiddu★ (*Cavalleria rusticana*); MASSENET: Jean le Baptiste (*Hérodiade*), Nicias (*Thaïs*), Werther★; OFFENBACH: Hoffmann; POULENC: Chevalier de la Force (*Dialogues des Carmélites*); PUCCINI: Dick Johnson★ (*Fanciulla del West*), Luigi★ (*Tabarro*), Cavaradossi★ (*Tosca*); SAINT-SAENS: Samson★; STRAUSS, R: Herodes★ (*Sa-*

lome); TCHAIKOVSKY: Gherman★ (*Pique
Dame*); VERDI: Radames★ (*Aida*), Otello★, Al-
fredo (*Traviata*); WAGNER: Erik (*Fliegende
Holländer*), Lohengrin; WEBER: Max★
(*Freischütz*). Also KURKA: Secret Agent & Psy-
choanalyst & Almoner (*Good Soldier Schweik*);
MUSSORGSKY: Dimitri (*Boris Godunov*);
LESUR: Andréa del Sarto. **World premieres:** TO-
MASI: Lt St Avit (*Atlantide*) Opéra de Paris 1958.
Recorded for; Pathé-Marconi, DG.
Video—ORTF: Julien (*Louise*). Gives recitals.
Appears with symphony orchestra. **Res:** 16 Allée
de l'Entente, 93130 Noisy Le Sec, France. Mgmt:
IMR/FRA.

FINNILA, BIRGIT. Contralto. Swedish. Born
1931, Falkenberg. Married. Five children. Studied:
Music Academy, Ingalill Linden, Göteborg; Prof
Roy Henderson, Royal Coll of Music, London.
Debut: Orfeo (*Orfeo ed Euridice*) Göteborg 1967.
Sang with major companies in AUS: Salzburg
Fest; FRA: Orange Fest, Paris; FR GER: Munich
Staatsoper; ITA: Milan La Scala, Turin; SWE:
Stockholm; UK: Edinburgh Fest; USSR: Kiev,
Moscow; USA: Houston Grand Opera. **Roles with
these companies incl** BRITTEN: Lucretia (*Rape of
Lucretia*); VERDI: Azucena (*Trovatore*); WAG-
NER: Erda (*Rheingold, Siegfried*). Also TCHAI-
KOVSKY: Pauline (*Pique Dame*); HANDEL:
Teodata (*Flavio*). Gives recitals. Appears with
symphony orchestra. **Res:** Falkenberg, Sweden.
Mgmt: SVE/SWE.

FISCHER, ADAM. Conductor of opera and symphony. Hungarian. Resident Cond, Finnish National Opera, Helsinki. Also Assistant Cond,
Helsinki Phil. Born 9 Sep 1949, Budapest. Single.
Studied: Bartók Consv, Budapest; Akad für Musik, Vienna, Prof Hans Swarowsky; incl piano,
oboe and voice. Plays the piano. Operatic training
as repetiteur at Vereinigte Bühnen, Graz 1971-72;
Staatsoper, Vienna 1973-74. **Operatic debut:** *Traviata* Stadttheater St Pölten, Austria 1973. Symphonic debut: MÁV Symph Orch, Budapest 1973.
Conducted with major companies in FIN: Hel-
sinki; HUN: Budapest. **Operas with these com-
panies incl** BRITTEN: *Midsummer Night★;*
GOUNOD: *Faust★;* HAYDN: *Infedeltà delusa;*
MOZART: *Così fan tutte★, Schauspieldirektor★,
Nozze di Figaro★;* ROSSINI: *Barbiere di Si-
viglia★;* VERDI: *Don Carlo★, Otello★, Rigoletto★,
Traviata★, Trovatore★.* Video—Hungarian TV:
Mari à la porte. Conducted major orch in Europe.
Res: Ruusulankatu 17/A, 25 Helsinki, Finland.
Mgmt: ITK/HUN; MFZ/FIN.

FISCHER, GEORG. Conductor of opera and sym-
phony. Hungarian. Resident Cond, Opera, Co-
logne. Born 12 Aug 1935, Budapest. Wife Lucia
Popp, occupation opera singer, soprano. Studied:
Salzburg, incl piano & percussion. Plays the piano.
Operatic training as repetiteur at Staatsoper,
Vienna 1960-64. **Operatic debut:** Staatsoper,
Vienna 1963. Symphonic debut: Budapest. Pre-
vious adm positions in opera: Deputy Gen Mus
Dir, Opera, Cologne.
Conducted with major companies in AUS:
Vienna Staatsoper; FR GER: Cologne; HUN:
Budapest; UK: Welsh National. **Operas with these
companies incl** AUBER: *Fra Diavolo★;* DONI-

ZETTI: *Don Pasquale★;* HANDEL: *Rodelinda;*
LORTZING: *Wildschütz★;* MOZART: *Clemenza
di Tito★, Così fan tutte★, Don Giovanni★, Entführung aus dem Serail★, Idomeneo★, Nozze di Fi-
garo★, Zauberflöte★;* ROSSINI: *Barbiere di
Siviglia★, Cenerentola★;* VERDI: *Ballo in maschera, Rigoletto★, Traviata★.* Conducted major
orch in Europe, USA/Canada, Austrl. **Res:** Cologne, FR Ger.

FISCHER-DIESKAU, DIETRICH. Lyric baritone.
German. Born 28 May 1925, Berlin. Married.
Three sons. Studied: George A Walter; Staatliche
Hochschule für Musik, Prof Hermann Weissen-
born, Berlin, FR Ger. **Debut:** Rodrigo (*Don Carlo*)
Städtische Oper Berlin 1948. Awards: Grand Prix
du Disque 1955 & 30 record przs; Bayerischer
Kammersänger 1959; Kammersänger, Berlin
1963; Mozart Medal, Vienna 1962; Golden Gramo-
phone, FR Ger 1975; Naras Awd, USA 1972;
Hon mem: Vienna Konzerthausgesellschaft, Royal
Acad of Music, London, and Royal Swedish Acad,
Stockholm; Grosses Verdienstkreuz, FR Ger;
Golden Orpheus Mantua, Italy; Léonie Sonning
Music Prize, Copenhagen; etc.
Sang with major companies in AUS: Salzburg
Fest, Vienna Staatsoper; FR GER: Bayreuth Fest,
Berlin Deutsche Oper, Munich Staatsoper; HOL:
Amsterdam; UK: Edinburgh Fest, London Royal
Opera. **Roles with these companies incl** BARTOK:
Bluebeard★‡; BEETHOVEN: Don Pizarro‡ (*Fi-
delio*); BERG: Dr Schön‡ (*Lulu*), Wozzeck‡; BU-
SONI: Doktor Faust‡; EINEM: George Danton
(*Dantons Tod*); GLUCK: Agamemnon‡ (*Iphi-
génie en Aulide*); HANDEL: Giulio Cesare‡;
HENZE: Mittenhofer‡ (*Elegy for Young Lovers*);
HINDEMITH: Cardillac‡, Mathis‡; MOZART:
Don Alfonso★‡ (*Così fan tutte*), Don Giovanni‡,
Conte Almaviva★‡ (*Nozze di Figaro*), Papageno‡
(*Zauberflöte*); ORFF: Solo‡ (*Carmina burana*);
PUCCINI: Marcello‡ (*Bohème*), Gianni Schicchi,
Sharpless‡ (*Butterfly*), Scarpia‡ (*Tosca*); ROS-
SINI: Guillaume Tell‡; STRAUSS, R: Man-
dryka★‡ (*Arabella*); Graf‡ & Olivier (*Capriccio*),
Orest‡ (*Elektra*), Barak‡ (*Frau ohne Schatten*),
Jochanaan‡ (*Salome*); TCHAIKOVSKY: Eugene
Onegin‡; VERDI: Renato‡ (*Ballo in maschera*),
Rodrigo★‡ (*Don Carlo*), Falstaff★‡, Don Carlo‡
(*Forza del destino*), Macbeth‡, Iago‡ (*Otello*),
Rigoletto‡, Germont‡ (*Traviata*), Monforte‡ (*Ves-
pri*); WAGNER: Holländer‡ (*Fliegende Hollän-
der*), Telramund‡ (*Lohengrin*), Pogner‡
(*Meistersinger*), Amfortas★‡ (*Parsifal*), Wotan‡
(*Rheingold*), Gunther‡ (*Götterdämmerung*), Wolf-
ram‡ (*Tannhäuser*), Kurwenal‡ (*Tristan und
Isolde*). **World premieres:** HENZE: Mittenhofer
(*Elegy for Young Lovers*) Schwetzingen Fest,
Staatsoper Munich 1961. Recorded for: DG, CBS,
EMI, Decca, Ariola. Gives recitals. Appears with
symphony orchestra. Recently also conducts sym-
phony concerts. **Res:** Lindenallee 22, 1 Berlin 19,
FR Ger.

FISKE, JUNE; née June Rosmond King. Lyric
coloratura soprano. American. Born 4 Feb 1941,
Passaic, NJ, USA. Married. Studied: Menotti
Salta; Evelyn Hertzmann; Daniel Ferro, New
York. **Debut:** Frasquita (*Carmen*) New Jersey Op-
era Festival 1967. Previous occupations: secre-
tary. Awards: Opera America Aud; Philadelphia
Grand Opera Prize.

Sang with major companies in USA: Hartford, Philadelphia Grand, San Antonio. **Roles with these companies incl** BIZET: Micaëla★ (*Carmen*); DONIZETTI: Marie★ (*Fille du régiment*); PUCCINI: Musetta★ (*Bohème*); STRAUSS, J: Adele★ (*Fledermaus*); VERDI: Oscar★ (*Ballo in maschera*). Video/Film: Violetta (*Traviata*). Gives recitals. Appears with symphony orchestra. **Res:** 363 Crescent Dr, Franklin Lakes, NJ 07417, USA. Mgmt: LWI/USA.

FISSORE, ENRICO. Bass-baritone. Italian. Born 23 Jan 1939, Bra/Cuneo. Wife Sylvia Rhys-Thomas, occupation singer. Studied: Consv G Verdi, Mo Michele Accorinti and Mo Alberto Soresina, Turin. **Debut:** Don Giovanni, Teatro Nuovo, Milan 1964.
Sang with major companies in AUS: Bregenz Fest, Salzburg Fest, Vienna Staatsoper; FRA: Bordeaux, Nancy, Rouen, Toulouse; FR GER: Munich Staatsoper, Stuttgart; ITA: Bologna, Genoa, Milan La Scala, Parma, Trieste, Turin, Venice, Verona Arena; SPA: Barcelona; SWI: Geneva; UK: Glyndebourne Fest; USA: Cincinnati; YUG: Dubrovnik, Zagreb. **Roles with these companies incl** DONIZETTI: Dulcamara★ (*Elisir*); MOZART: Guglielmo★ (*Così fan tutte*), Leporello★ (*Don Giovanni*), Figaro★ (*Nozze di Figaro*); PAISIELLO: Bartolo★ (*Barbiere di Siviglia*); PERGOLESI: Uberto★ (*Serva padrona*); PUCCINI: Colline (*Bohème*); ROSSINI: Dott Bartolo★ (*Barbiere di Siviglia*), Slook★ (*Cambiale di matrimonio*), Macrobio (*Pietra del paragone*), Geronio (*Turco in Italia*); SALIERI: Composer★ (*Prima la musica*); VERDI: Fra Melitone★ (*Forza del destino*). Recorded for: Teldec. Video/Film: (*Barbiere di Siviglia*), (*Prima la musica*). Gives recitals. Appears with symphony orchestra. **Res:** Milan, Italy. Mgmt: SLZ/FRG; GBN/UK.

FITÉ, ISABELLA. Lyric soprano. Spanish. Born 14 May 1933, Barcelona. Single. Studied: Consv Municipal de Musica, Mo Fornells, Callao, Bottino, Barcelona; Akad für Musik, Mo Steinbruch, Scholum, Vienna; Accad Chigiana, Gina Cigna, Mo Ammannati, Italy. **Debut:** Leonora (*Trovatore*) Compagnia Lirica Romana 1966. Previous occupations: bookkeeper. Awards: First hon mention, Compt Barcelona and Prize of Merit; Stpd Juan March, Madrid.
Sang with major companies in ITA: Florence Maggio & Comunale, Naples; SPA: Barcelona. **Roles with these companies incl** BIZET: Micaëla (*Carmen*); GALUPPI: Eugenia (*Filosofo di campagna*); GIORDANO: Maddalena★ (*Andrea Chénier*); LEONCAVALLO: Nedda★ (*Pagliacci*); PUCCINI: Mimi★ (*Bohème*); Cio-Cio-San★ (*Butterfly*); VERDI: Leonora★ (*Trovatore*). **World premieres:** SALVADOR: Jacmeta (*Vinatea*) Gran Teatro del Liceo, Barcelona 1972; LUPI: Persefone, Maggio Fiorentino 1970; MALIPIERO: (*Uno dei dieci*) Siena 1971. Gives recitals. Appears with symphony orchestra. **Res:** Pasaje San Ramón Nonato 14, Barcelona, Spain.

FLAGELLO, EZIO DOMENICO. Bass. American. Resident mem: Metropolitan Opera, New York. Born 28 Jan 1933, New York. Wife Anna, occupation PS music teacher. Four children. Studied: Manhattan School of Music, Friedrich Schorr,

New York; Mo Luigi Ricci, Rome. **Debut:** Dulcamara (*Elisir*) Teatro dell'Opera, Rome 1956. Awards: Grammy Awd; First Prize All Army Worldwide Talent; Alumnus of Year Evander Childs HS; Outstanding Alumnus Awd Manhattan School of Music 1973; Fulbright Schlshp for Italy.
Sang with major companies in AUS: Vienna Staatsoper; CAN: Montreal/Quebec, Toronto; CZE: Prague National; FR GER: Berlin Deutsche Oper; GER DR: Berlin Staatsoper; ITA: Florence Maggio & Comunale, Milan La Scala, Rome Opera; USA: Boston, Cincinnati, Dallas, Hartford, Houston Grand Opera, Memphis, Miami, Milwaukee Florentine, New Orleans, New York Metropolitan, Philadelphia Grand & Lyric, Pittsburgh, San Francisco Opera. **Roles with these companies incl** BARBER: Doctor (*Vanessa*); BELLINI: Filippo (*Beatrice di Tenda*), Oroveso (*Norma*), Sir George (*Puritani*), Rodolfo (*Sonnambula*); BERG: Doktor (*Wozzeck*); BERLIOZ: Méphistophélès (*Damnation de Faust*); BOITO: Mefistofele; BORODIN: Prince Igor & Galitzky (*Prince Igor*); BUSONI: Doktor Faust; CHERUBINI: Creon (*Medea*); DALLAPICCOLA: Prigioniero; DONIZETTI: Henry VIII (*Anna Bolena*), Don Pasquale, Dulcamara (*Elisir*), Alfonse & Baldassare (*Favorite*), Enrico (*Lucia*), Alfonso d'Este (*Lucrezia Borgia*); FLOTOW: Plunkett (*Martha*); GOUNOD: Méphistophélès (*Faust*); HALEVY: Brogny (*Juive*); HANDEL: Giulio Cesare; MASCAGNI: Rabbi David (*Amico Fritz*); MASSENET: Sancho & Don Quichotte (*Don Quichotte*); MENOTTI: Husband (*Amelia al ballo*), Maharaja (*Dernier sauvage*); MEYERBEER: Comte de St Bris & Marcel (*Huguenots*); MILHAUD: Créon (*Médée*); MONTEMEZZI: Archibaldo (*Amore dei tre re*); MOZART: Don Alfonso (*Così fan tutte*), Leporello & Don Giovanni (*Don Giovanni*), Figaro★ (*Nozze di Figaro*), Sarastro★ (*Zauberflöte*); MUSSORGSKY: Boris & Varlaam & Pimen (*Boris Godunov*); PUCCINI: Colline★ (*Bohème*), Jack Rance (*Fanciulla del West*), Gianni Schicchi★, Sharpless★ (*Butterfly*), Michele (*Tabarro*), Scarpia (*Tosca*); ROSSINI: Dott Bartolo & Don Basilio★ (*Barbiere di Siviglia*), Dandini & Don Magnifico (*Cenerentola*), Mustafà (*Italiana in Algeri*), Moïse; STRAVINSKY: Creon★ & Tiresias★ (*Oedipus Rex*); VERDI: Ramfis★ (*Aida*), Attila, Philip II★ & Grande Inquisitore (*Don Carlo*), Silva★ (*Ernani*), Falstaff, Fra Melitone & Padre Guardiano★ (*Forza del destino*), Conte Walter (*Luisa Miller*), Banquo (*Macbeth*), Zaccaria (*Nabucco*), Fiesco (*Simon Boccanegra*); WAGNER: Pogner★ (*Meistersinger*), Gurnemanz (*Parsifal*). Also DELLO JOIO: Bull (*The Ruby*). **World premieres:** BARBER: Enobarbus (*Antony and Cleopatra*) Metropolitan Opera, New York 1966. Recorded for: DG, RCA, London, Delphi. Gives recitals. Appears with symphony orchestra. **Res:** Millwood, NY, USA. Mgmt: CAM/USA.

FLEETWOOD, JAMES. Basso-buffo. American. Born 14 Jan 1935, Maryville, MO, USA. Single. Studied: Eastman School of Music, Julius Huehn, Rochester, NY; E J Rehley, Kansas City, MO; Alfredo Valenti, Joseph Pouhe, New York. **Debut:** Osmin (*Entführung aus dem Serail*) Kansas City Lyric 1958. Previous occupations: semi-prof athlete; military service.

Sang with major companies in ITA: Spoleto Fest; USA: Baltimore, Boston, Hartford, Kansas City, Newark, Philadelphia Grand & Lyric Opera, San Antonio. **Roles with these companies incl** CATALANI: Stromminger (*Wally*); DONIZETTI: Don Pasquale★, Dott Dulcamara★(*Elisir*); MOZART: Leporello & Don Giovanni (*Don Giovanni*), Osmin (*Entführung aus dem Serail*); NICOLAI: Falstaff (*Lustigen Weiber*); PERGOLESI: Uberto (*Serva padrona*); PUCCINI: Colline★ (*Bohème*); ROSSINI: Dott Bartolo★ & Don Basilio★ (*Barbiere di Siviglia*). Video—NET TV Opera: Sourin (*Pique Dame*). Gives recitals. Appears with symphony orchestra. Mgmt: LLF/USA.

FLETA, PIERRE; né Anatole Burro-Fleta. French. Stage Dir/Mng, Centre Lyrique de Wallonie, 1 rue des Dominicains, Liège 4000, 1972- . In charge of art policy, musical & tech matters. Is also a stage dir/prod and voice teacher. Born 4 Jul 1925, Villefranche/mer. Wife Claude Portelenelle. One child. Studied: Lycée St Nicolas, Cannes; Consv National de Paris. Plays the piano. Previous occupations: tenor with Paris Opéra; Théâtre Royal de la Monnaie, Brussels; Théâtre Royal, Liège; Bordeaux, Strasbourg, Lyon, Toulouse, Marseille, Nice, Lille, Rouen. **Res:** 3 Bd d'Avroy, Liège, Belgium.

FLETCHER, ROBERT. Scenic and costume designer for opera, theater, film, TV; specl in costumes. American. Born 29 Aug 1923, Cedar Rapids, IA, USA. Single. Studied: Harvard Univ, Cambridge, USA. **Operatic debut:** cost, *Carmen* New England Opera, Boston 1948. Theater debut: Harvard Theatre Wkshp, USA 1945.

Designed for major companies in ITA: Spoleto Fest; USA: Boston, Chicago, New York City Opera, Washington DC. **Operas designed for these companies incl** BIZET: *Carmen;* BRITTEN: *Midsummer Night;* GAY/Britten: *Beggar's Opera;* LEONCAVALLO: *Pagliacci;* MASSENET: *Manon;* MENOTTI: *Unicorn, Gorgon;* MONTEVERDI: *Ballo delle ingrate;* MOZART: *Così fan tutte, Don Giovanni, Entführung aus dem Serail;* MUSSORGSKY: *Boris Godunov;* ORFF: *Catulli carmina;* PIZZETTI: *Assassinio nella cattedrale;* POULENC: *Dialogues des Carmélites;* PROKOFIEV: *War and Peace;* PUCCINI: *Bohème, Suor Angelica, Tosca;* STRAUSS, J: *Fledermaus;* STRAVINSKY: *Rake's Progress, Histoire du soldat;* TCHAIKOVSKY: *Pique Dame;* VERDI: *Don Carlo, Rigoletto, Traviata.* **Operatic world premieres:** GIANNINI: *Servant of Two Masters* New York City Opera 1967. Operatic Video—NBC: *Tosca, Rigoletto, Dialogues des Carmélites, Suor Angelica.* Teaches at Univ of California, Irvine. **Res:** 1314 No Hayworth Ave, Los Angeles, CA 90046, USA.

FLOOD-MURPHY, PIP; né William Frederick Flood-Murphy. British. Tech Dir, Scottish Opera Ltd, Theatre Royal, Hope St, Glasgow, Scotland. In charge of tech matters. Born 17 May 1933, Castlecomen, Cnty Kilkenny, Eire. Wife Marilyn. Two children. Studied: Italia Conti Stage School, London. Previous positions, primarily theatrical: freelance actor, Britain 1948-55; touring tech, Britain 1955-59; St Mng, PACT Pretoria, S Africa

1962-63; St Dir, PACT (ballet) Pretoria 1963-64; freelance st mng, London 1964-67; Guest Tech Adv, Toronto Opera School, Canada 1969. Started with present company 1967 as St Dir, in present position since 1970. **Res:** 34 Belmont St, Glasgow, Scotland, UK.

FLOREI, NICOLAE. Bass. Romanian. Resident mem: Romanian Opera, Bucharest. Born 10 Nov 1927, Vasiova. Wife Nadejdea. Studied: Consv, Prof Petre Stefanescu-Goanga, Bucharest; Prof. **Debut:** Nilakantha (*Lakmé*) Romanian Opera 1955. Awards: Laureate, Intl Conts Bucharest 1955, Warsaw 1955, Geneva 1955.

Sang with major companies in BEL: Liège; BUL: Sofia; CZE: Prague National & Smetana; FRA: Paris, Rouen; FR GER: Mannheim, Munich Staatsoper; HUN: Budapest; ROM: Bucharest; YUG: Zagreb. **Roles with these companies incl** BERLIOZ: Méphistophélès (*Damnation de Faust*); BIZET: Escamillo (*Carmen*); BORODIN: Prince Igor★; DEBUSSY: Arkel★ (*Pelléas et Mélisande*); DELIBES: Nilakantha★ (*Lakmé*); GOUNOD: Méphistophélès★ (*Faust*); MUSSORGSKY: Boris Godunov★; ROSSINI: Don Basilio★ (*Barbiere di Siviglia*); THOMAS: Lothario (*Mignon*); VERDI: Ramfis★ (*Aida*), Philip II★ (*Don Carlo*), Zaccaria★ (*Nabucco*); WAGNER: Holländer★, König Heinrich★ (*Lohengrin*), Hans Sachs (*Meistersinger*), Landgraf★ (*Tannhäuser*). Also ENESCU: Oedipe. **World premieres:** DUMITRESCU: Pandele (*Girl with Carnations*) Romanian Opera 1961. Recorded for: Electrecord. Gives recitals. Appears with symphony orchestra. Teaches voice. Coaches repertoire. **Res:** 9 Magheru Blvd, Bucharest 1, Romania. Mgmt: RIA/ROM; SMD/FRG.

FLORESTA, GABRIELE. Lyric & dramatic baritone. Italian. Born 27 Oct 1936, Castiglione di Sicilia. Single. Studied: Consv G Verdi, Mo Fiorenzo Tasso, Valdomiro Badiali, Alfonso Siliotti, Milan. **Debut:** Amonasro (*Aida*) Teatro Comunale di Adria 1966. Previous occupations: accountant; bldg superintendent. Awards: Winner Conc As Li Co, Teatro Nuovo, Milan.

Sang with major companies in BEL: Brussels; DEN: Copenhagen; FR GER: Frankfurt; ITA: Florence Comunale, Genoa, Naples, Palermo, Trieste, Venice. **Roles with these companies incl** BELLINI: Sir Richard (*Puritani*); BIZET: Escamillo★ (*Carmen*); DONIZETTI: Belcore (*Elisir*), Alfonse★ (*Favorite*), Enrico★ (*Lucia*); GIORDANO: Carlo Gérard★ (*Andrea Chénier*); LEONCAVALLO: Tonio★ (*Pagliacci*); MASCAGNI: Alfio★ (*Cavalleria rusticana*); PUCCINI: Marcello★ (*Bohème*), Sharpless★ (*Butterfly*), Lescaut★ (*Manon Lescaut*), Scarpia (*Tosca*); VERDI: Amonasro★ (*Aida*), Renato★ (*Ballo in maschera*), Don Carlo (*Ernani*), Don Carlo★ (*Forza del destino*), Rigoletto★, Germont★ (*Traviata*), Conte di Luna★ (*Trovatore*). Also GOUNOD: Valentin★ (*Faust*). **Res:** Milan, Italy.

FLORIO, LAWRENCE. Stages/produces opera. Also designs stage-lighting and is a singer. American. Born 20 Nov 1924, Newark, NJ. Wife Ann Florio, occupation singer. One daughter. Studied: Anthony Amato, Anthony Stivanello, New York; also music, piano and voice. Operatic training as asst stage dir & stage mng at Amato Opera Theater, New York 1951-56. **Operatic debut:** *Traviata* Connecticut Opera, Hartford 1957. Previous occupation: salesman. Previous adm positions in opera: Dir, Wagner Opera Co, New York 1957-60.

Directed/produced opera for major companies in USA: Baltimore, Boston, Cincinnati, Hartford, Newark, Philadelphia Grand, Pittsburgh, San Antonio. **Operas staged with these companies incl** BIZET: *Carmen★, Pêcheurs de perles;* DELIBES: *Lakmé;* DONIZETTI: *Lucia;* GOUNOD: *Faust;* LEONCAVALLO: *Pagliacci;* MASCAGNI: *Cavalleria rusticana;* MENOTTI: *Saint of Bleecker Street;* PUCCINI: *Bohème★, Butterfly, Rondine, Tosca★;* ROSSINI: *Barbiere di Siviglia★;* VERDI: *Aida★, Forza del destino, Rigoletto★, Traviata★, Trovatore★.* Teaches privately. **Res:** 63 Bank St, New York 10014, USA.

FLOYD, ALPHA. Lyric spinto. American. Husband Arthur, occupation psychologist. One child. Studied: Juilliard School of Music, New York; Lotte Leonard, Jennie Tourel, Claire Gelda. **Debut:** Königin (*Königin von Saba*) American Opera Society, New York 1970.

Sang with major companies in USA: Houston, Jackson Opera/South, Kentucky, New York City Opera, San Diego. **Roles with these companies incl** JOPLIN: Treemonisha★; PUCCINI: Turandot★; VERDI: Aida★, Leonora★ (*Forza del destino*), Lady Macbeth★. **World premieres:** JOPLIN: Treemonisha, Atlanta Opera, GA, USA 1972. Gives recitals. Appears with symphony orchestra. Mgmt: SHA/USA.

FOLDI, ANDREW HARRY; né András Harry Földi. Bass-baritone & basso-buffo. American. Born 20 Jul 1926, Budapest, Hungary. Wife Leona, occupation accountant. Two children. Studied: Richard de Young, Martial Singher, Chicago; Maria Carpi, Geneva. **Debut:** Biondello (*Taming of the Shrew*) Chicago Lyric Opera 1954. Previous occupations: music critic for the Chicago *Times;* humanities lecturer; Dir of Music Adult Educ Dept, Univ of Chicago; Prof of voice & musicology, De Paul Univ, Chicago; cantor and music dir Temple Isaiah Israel, Chicago; English-speaking Jewish Comm Geneva, Switzerland.

Sang with major companies in AUS: Vienna Staatsoper; BEL: Brussels; FRA: Lyon; FR GER: Munich Staatsoper; HOL: Amsterdam; ITA: Genoa, Milan La Scala, Naples, Spoleto Fest; SWI: Basel, Geneva, Zurich; UK: Aldeburgh Fest; USA: Baltimore, Boston, Chicago, Cincinnati, Hartford, Houston, Miami, New York Met, Philadelphia Lyric, Pittsburgh, Portland, San Diego, San Francisco Opera, Santa Fe, Seattle, Washington DC. **Roles with these companies incl** BEETHOVEN: Don Pizarro & Rocco (*Fidelio*); DONIZETTI: Henry VIII (*Anna Bolena*), Don Pasquale★, Dott Dulcamara★ (*Elisir*), Sulpice★ (*Fille du régiment*); GOUNOD: Méphistophélès (*Faust*); IBERT: Boniface (*Angélique*); LORTZING: Van Bett (*Zar und Zimmermann*); MASSENET: Sancho★ (*Don Quichotte*), Des Grieux (*Portrait de Manon*); MOZART: Don Alfonso★ (*Così fan tutte*), Leporello★ (*Don Giovanni*), Osmin (*Entführung aus dem Serail*), Figaro (*Nozze di Figaro*); NICOLAI: Falstaff (*Lustigen Weiber*); PERGOLESI: Uberto (*Serva padrona*); ROS-

SINI: Dottore Bartolo★‡ (*Barbiere di Siviglia*), Tobias Mill (*Cambiale di matrimonio*), Don Magnifico★‡ (*Cenerentola*), Mustafà‡ (*Italiana in Algeri*), Macrobio★‡ (*Pietra del paragone*); SMETANA: Kezal★ (*Bartered Bride*); STRAUSS, R: Musiklehrer★ (*Ariadne auf Naxos*), Baron Ochs★ (*Rosenkavalier*), Sir Morosus (*Schweigsame Frau*); STRAVINSKY: Tiresias (*Oedipus Rex*), Nick Shadow (*Rake's Progress*); VERDI: Falstaff (*Falstaff*), Fra Melitone★ (*Forza del destino*); WAGNER: Beckmesser★ (*Meistersinger*), Alberich (*Rheingold★, Siegfried, Götterdämmerung★*). Also BERG: Schigolch★ (*Lulu*); VERDI: Paolo (*Simon Boccanegra*); PUCCINI: Colline (*Bohème*), Sacristan★ (*Tosca*); CIMAROSA: Giampaolo (*Astuzie femminili*); HINDEMITH: Baron d'Houdoux (*Neues vom Tage*). **World premieres:** SCHIEBLER: Driller (*Blackwood & Co*) Zurich 1962; APERGHIS: Diderot (*Jacques le fataliste*) Lyon 1974; DELLO JOIO: Theater Director (*Blood Moon*) San Francisco 1961; BARBIER: Savant (*Gulliver*) Brussels 1967. Recorded for: Concert Hall, Columbia, Voix d'Eglise, Vanguard. Video/Film: Bartolo (*Barbiere di Siviglia*). Gives recitals. Appears with symphony orchestra. Teaches voice. Coaches repertoire. **Res:** Geneva, Switzerland, & New York. Mgmt: RAM/AUS; IMR/FRA; DSP/USA.

FOLLEY, LAWRENCE AURELIUS. Lyric baritone. South African. Resident mem: PACT, Pretoria. Born 6 Dec 1929, Benoni/Transvaal. Wife Marie, occupation violinist. Three children. Studied: London Opera School, Dawson Freer, Lucie Manen, London; Franco Ferraris, S Africa. **Debut:** Schaunard (*Bohème*) Sadler's Wells, London 1961. Previous occupations: publ health officer. Awards: First Nederburg Prize for Opera in the Transvaal, Nederburg Trust.

Sang with major opera companies in S AFR: Johannesburg Opera; UK: London English National. **Roles with these companies incl** BIZET: Escamillo★ (*Carmen*); BRITTEN: Captain Balstrode (*Peter Grimes*); DONIZETTI: Don Pasquale★, Enrico★ (*Lucia*), Gasparo (*Rita*); FLOTOW: Plunkett (*Martha*); MASCAGNI: Alfio (*Cavalleria rusticana*); MOZART: Don Giovanni★, Conte Almaviva★ (*Nozze di Figaro*); PUCCINI: Marcello★ (*Bohème*), Sharpless (*Butterfly*), Scarpia★ (*Tosca*); RAVEL: Ramiro (*Heure espagnole*); TCHAIKOVSKY: Yeletsky (*Pique Dame*); VERDI: Amonasro★ (*Aida*), Renato★ (*Ballo in maschera*), Rodrigo★ (*Don Carlo*), Don Carlo★ (*Forza del destino*), Nabucco, Rigoletto★, Germont (*Traviata*), Conte di Luna (*Trovatore*). Also GOUNOD: Valentin (*Faust*); HUMPERDINCK: Peter (*Hänsel und Gretel*). Gives recitals. Appears with symphony orchestra. Teaches voice. **Res:** 98 Alcade Rd, Pretoria, South Africa.

FOMINA, NINA VIKTOROVNA. Lyric-dramatic soprano. Russian. Resident mem: Bolshoi Theater, Moscow. Born 30 Oct 1937, Moscow. Divorced. Studied: Tchaikovsky Moscow State Consv, Prof A E Sveshnikova. **Debut:** Gorislava (*Ruslan and Ludmilla*) Bolshoi Theater, Moscow 1972. Previous occupations: communications engineer. Awards: Laureate, Intl Compt Munich, First Prize.

Sang with major companies in ITA: Milan La Scala; USSR: Moscow Bolshoi. Roles with these cos incl PROKOFIEV: Sofia★ (*Semyon Kotko*); PUCCINI: Mimi★ (*Bohème*); TCHAIKOVSKY: Tatiana★ (*Eugene Onegin*), Lisa★ (*Pique Dame*); VERDI: Aida★, Leonora★ (*Trovatore*). Also TCHAIKOVSKY: Oxana (*Tcherevichki*). Recorded for: Melodiya. Gives recitals. Appears with symphony orchestra. Res: 2 Ulitsa Godovikova, Apt 43, Moscow, USSR.

FONTAGNERE, GUY GASTON. Lyric baritone. French. Resident mem: Opéra de Wallonie, Liège, Belgium. Born 3 May 1924, Bordeaux. Wife Huguette Nadeau. Two children. Studied: René Lapelletrie, Frantz Caruso. Debut: Valentin (*Faust*) Opéra de Bordeaux 1944. Awards: First Prize Opérette, Consv of Bordeaux.

Sang with major companies in BEL: Brussels, Liège; FRA: Bordeaux, Lyon, Marseille, Nancy, Nice, Paris, Rouen, Strasbourg, Toulouse; MON: Monte Carlo; ROM: Bucharest; SWI: Geneva. Roles with these companies incl BECAUD: Mickey★ (*Opéra d'Aran*); BIZET: Escamillo★ (*Carmen*), Zurga (*Pêcheurs de perles*); DEBUSSY: Golaud★ (*Pelléas et Mélisande*); DONIZETTI: Dott Malatesta★ (*Don Pasquale*); GOUNOD: Ourrias★ (*Mireille*); IBERT: Boniface★ (*Angélique*); LEONCAVALLO: Tonio (*Pagliacci*); MASCAGNI: Alfio (*Cavalleria rusticana*); MASSENET: Sancho (*Don Quichotte*), Hérode (*Hérodiade*), Boniface (*Jongleur de Notre Dame*), Lescaut (*Manon*), Athanaël (*Thaïs*), Albert★ (*Werther*); MENOTTI: John Sorel (*Consul*); MONIUSZKO: Janusz (*Halka*); MOZART: Leporello★ & Don Giovanni★ (*Don Giovanni*), Figaro (*Nozze di Figaro*), Papageno★ (*Zauberflöte*); OFFENBACH: Coppélius etc★ (*Contes d'Hoffmann*); PUCCINI: Marcello★ (*Bohème*), Jack Rance★ (*Fanciulla del West*), Gianni Schicchi, Sharpless★ (*Butterfly*), Lescaut (*Manon Lescaut*), Scarpia★ (*Tosca*); RAVEL: Ramiro★ (*Heure espagnole*); ROSSINI: Figaro (*Barbiere di Siviglia*), Iago★ (*Otello*); SAINT-SAENS: Grand prêtre★ (*Samson et Dalila*); TCHAIKOVSKY: Eugene Onegin; THOMAS: Hamlet; VERDI: Amonasro★ (*Aida*), Iago★ (*Otello*), Simon Boccanegra, Germont (*Traviata*). Res: 14 Ave Rogier, Liège, Belgium.

FORRESTER, MAUREEN KATHERINE STEWART. Contralto. Canadian. Resident mem: Metropolitan Opera, New York. Born 25 Jul 1930, Montreal, PQ, Canada. Husband Eugene J Kash, occupation violinist, conductor. Five children. Studied: Mrs Sally Martin, Frank Rowe, Bernard Diamant, Montreal. Debut: Innkeeper (*Boris Godunov*) Pauline Donalda's Opera Co, Montreal 1949-50. Previous occupations: waitress, hat check girl, salesgirl, typist, file clerk, receptionist, telephone operator, etc. Awards: Companion of the Order of Canada, Canadian Gvnmt; Molson Prize; Montreal Critics Awd; Hon DM: St George William Univ, Montreal; St Mary's Univ, Halifax, NS; York Univ, Toronto; Western Univ, London, Ont; Mount Allison Univ, Sask; Wilfred Pelletier Univ, Kitchener, Ont.

Sang with major companies in ARG: Buenos Aires; CAN: Montreal/Quebec, Ottawa, Toronto; USA: Dallas, New York Met & City Opera, San Francisco Opera, Washington DC. Roles with these companies incl GLUCK: Orfeo‡; HANDEL: Cornelia‡ (*Giulio Cesare*), Bertaric‡ (*Rodelinda*), Xerxes; HUMPERDINCK: Hexe★ (*Hänsel und Gretel*); MENOTTI: Mme Flora★ (*Medium*); MONTEVERDI: Poppea★ (*Incoronazione di Poppea*); VERDI: Ulrica★ (*Ballo in maschera*), Dame Quickly★ (*Falstaff*); WAGNER: Erda (*Rheingold★*, *Siegfried★*), Fricka★ (*Walküre*), Brangäne★ (*Tristan und Isolde*). Recorded for: Westminster, RCA, Columbia, DG, Vanguard. Gives recitals. Appears with symphony orchestra. Res: Toronto, Ont, Canada. Mgmt: SHA/USA; SHA/UK.

FORST, JUDITH DORIS. Coloratura mezzo-soprano. Canadian. Born 7 Nov 1943, New Westminster, BC, Canada. Husband Nicol Graham, occupation professor. Two children. Studied: Hans Heinz, Bliss Hebert, New York; French Tickner, Vancouver, BC, Canada; Robert Keyes, Covent Garden, London. Debut: Lola (*Cavalleria rusticana*) Vancouver Opera 1967. Awards: Winner Met Op Ntl Counc Aud 1968; Cross-Canada Talent Fest 1968; Canadian Broadc Co Awd.

Sang with major companies in CAN: Ottawa, Toronto; USA: Fort Worth, New Orleans, New York Met, San Francisco Opera & Spring Opera, Santa Fe. Roles with these companies incl CAVALLI: Clori★ (*Egisto*); GOUNOD: Siebel★ (*Faust*); HUMPERDINCK: Hänsel★; MOZART: Cherubino★ (*Nozze di Figaro*); PUCCINI: Suzuki★ (*Butterfly*); RAVEL: L'Enfant★ (*Enfant et les sortilèges*); TCHAIKOVSKY: Olga★ (*Eugene Onegin*); VERDI: Preziosilla★ (*Forza del destino*). Video—CBC, NET: Hänsel. Gives recitals. Appears with symphony orchestra. Res: Port Moody, BC, Canada. Mgmt: HUR/USA.

FORTES, PAULO. Lyric baritone. Brazilian. Born 7 Feb 1927, Rio de Janeiro. Wife Zilca. Two children. Studied: Gabriella Besanzoni, Murillo de Carvalho, Flaminio Contini, Rio de Janeiro and Florence, Italy. Debut: Germont (*Traviata*) Rio de Janeiro 1948. Awards: Medalha do Mérito Musical, Brazilian Gvnmt; seven Gold Medals, Critics Brazilian Assn; State Theatrical Prize; Schlshp Ministry of Educ; Fourth Century Medal of Rio de Janeiro, etc.

Sang with major companies in ARG: Buenos Aires; BRA: Rio de Janeiro; ITA: Florence Maggio & Comunale, Genoa, Palermo; POR: Lisbon. Roles with these companies incl BIZET: Escamillo★ (*Carmen*), Splendiano (*Djamileh*), Zurga (*Pêcheurs des perles*); BRITTEN: Captain Balstrode (*Peter Grimes*); CILEA: Michonnet★ (*A. Lecouvreur*); DEBUSSY: Siméon (*Enfant prodigue*); DONIZETTI: Enrico★ (*Campanello*), Dott Malatesta★ (*Don Pasquale*), Belcore★ (*Elisir*), Alfonse (*Favorite*), Enrico★ (*Lucia*); GIORDANO: Carlo Gérard★ (*Andrea Chénier*), De Siriex (*Fedora*); GLUCK: Cadi (*Cadi dupé*); GOMES: Colombo, Cambro (*Fosca*); LEONCAVALLO: Tonio★ (*Pagliacci*); MASCAGNI: Rabbi David (*Amico Fritz*), Alfio (*Cavalleria rusticana*); MASSENET: Lescaut (*Manon*), Albert (*Werther*); MENOTTI: Husband★ (*Amelia al ballo*); MOZART: Guglielmo (*Così fan tutte*), Don Giovanni; ORFF: Solo (*Carmina burana*); PONCHIELLI: Barnaba

(*Gioconda*); PUCCINI: Marcello★ (*Bohème*), Jack Rance (*Fanciulla del West*), Gianni Schicchi★, Sharpless (*Butterfly*); RAVEL: Ramiro (*Heure espagnole*); RIMSKY-KORSAKOV: Roi Dodon★ (*Coq d'or*); ROSSINI: Figaro★ (*Barbiere di Siviglia*), Robert (*Comte Ory*); SAINT-SAENS: Grand prêtre (*Samson et Dalila*); VERDI: Amonasro (*Aida*), Renato (*Ballo in maschera*), Ford & Falstaff★ (*Falstaff*), Iago (*Otello*), Rigoletto, Germont★ (*Traviata*), Conte di Luna (*Trovatore*). Also ROSSINI: Taddeo★ (*Italiana in Algeri*); CIMAROSA: Maestro di Cappella★; GOUNOD: Valentin★ (*Faust*); GOMES: Gonzales★ (*Guarany*); LEONCAVALLO: Cascart★ (*Zazà*); MASCAGNI: Kioto (*Iris*); RESPIGHI: Pellegrino (*Maria Egiziaca*); VILLA-LOBOS: Perruche (*Izaht*). **World premieres:** GUARNIERI: Pedro Malazarte (*Malazarte*) Rio de Janeiro 1953; GRAÇA: Don Duardos, Lisboa, Brazil 1971. Video/Film: Marcello (*Bohème*); Melchior (*Amahl*); Ben (*Telephone*); Rigoletto; Falstaff. Gives recitals. Appears with symphony orchestra. **Res:** Rua Barao de Itambi 55, Rio de Janeiro, Brazil. Mgmt: NBA/BRA.

FORTUNE, GEORGE. Dramatic baritone. American. Resident mem: Deutsche Oper Berlin, FR Ger. Born 13 Dec, Boston, MA, USA. Wife Ursula Schroth. One child. Studied: Todd Duncan, Washington, DC; Boston Univ; Georgetown Univ Inst of Languages and Linguistics, Washington, DC. **Debut:** Fluth (*Lustigen Weiber*) Ulm Opera 1960. Awards: Howard Fllshp for postgrad studies abroad, Brown Univ, Providence, RI, USA, 1960; First Prize, Intl Music Cont of FR Ger's Radio 1961; Third Reg Prize, Met Op Ntl Counc Aud, Washington DC, 1959.

Sang with major companies in BEL: Brussels; FRA: Bordeaux, Strasbourg; FR GER: Berlin Deutsche Oper, Bielefeld, Bonn, Düsseldorf-Duisburg, Frankfurt, Hamburg, Munich Staatsoper; ITA: Milan La Scala; SWI: Zurich; UK: Glyndebourne Fest; USA: Santa Fe. **Roles with these companies incl** DONIZETTI: Dott Malatesta (*Don Pasquale*), Enrico★ (*Lucia*); EINEM: Alfred Ill★ (*Besuch der alten Dame*); HANDEL: Giulio Cesare★ (*Boulevard Solitude*); MONTEVERDI: Orfeo; MOZART: Guglielmo (*Così fan tutte*), Conte Almaviva & Figaro (*Nozze di Figaro*); NICOLAI: Fluth (*Lustigen Weiber*); OFFENBACH: Coppélius etc★ (*Contes d'Hoffmann*); ORFF: Solo★ (*Carmina burana*); PONCHIELLI: Barnaba★ (*Gioconda*); PUCCINI: Marcello★ (*Bohème*), Jack Rance★ (*Fanciulla del West*), Sharpless★ (*Butterfly*), Michele★ (*Tabarro*), Scarpia★ (*Tosca*), Guglielmo Wulf (*Villi*); ROSSINI: Figaro (*Barbiere di Siviglia*), Dandini (*Cenerentola*); STRAUSS, R: Graf (*Capriccio*); TCHAIKOVSKY: Yeletsky (*Pique Dame*); VERDI: Amonasro (*Aida*), Ezio (*Attila*), Renato★ (*Ballo in maschera*), Rodrigo★ (*Don Carlo*), Iago★ (*Otello*), Rigoletto, Germont★ (*Traviata*), Conte di Luna★ (*Trovatore*); WAGNER: Wolfram★ (*Tannhäuser*). **World premieres:** NABOKOV: Don Armado (*Love's Labour's Lost*) Deutsche Oper Berlin 1973. Video/Film—NDR: Marcello (*Bohème*). Gives recitals. Appears with symphony orchestra. Teaches voice. Coaches repertoire. On faculty of Berliner Kirchenmusikschule

Johannes Stift, Spandau, Berlin. **Res:** Schreiberring 25, 1 Berlin 42, FR Ger. Mgmt: SLZ/FRG.

FOSS, HARLAN S. Baritone. American. Born 7 Aug 1941, Beverly, MA, USA. Wife Stafford L. Studied: Everett Anderson, Elizabeth Howell, Margaret van der Marck; Jack Clay, acting, USA. **Debut:** Mathieu (*Andrea Chénier*) Fort Worth, TX 1969. Awards: M B Rockefeller Fund Grant; Sullivan Fndt Grant; Reg Finalist Met Op Aud; Finalist San Francisco Op Aud; Gropper Awd, Merola Prgr, San Francisco Op.

Sang with major companies in USA: Ft Worth, Kansas City, Kentucky, St Paul, Washington DC. **Roles with these companies incl** BIZET: Escamillo★ (*Carmen*); MASSENET: Lescaut★ (*Manon*); VERDI: Iago★ (*Otello*), Germont★ (*Traviata*); WARD: John Proctor★ (*Crucible*). **World premieres:** STARER: Innocenti (*Pantagleize*) Brooklyn Coll, NY 1973; SANDOW: Usher (*Fall of the House of Usher*) Music in our Times, NY 1975. Appears with symphony orchestra. **Res:** New York, NY, USA. Mgmt: SFM/USA.

FOSSER, PER E. Stages/produces opera, theater & television. Also designs stage-lighting and is an author. Norwegian. Dramaturg & Resident Stage Dir, Norwegian Opera, Oslo. Born 29 Aug 1939, Oslo. Divorced. One son. Studied: as asst to Lars Rünsten, Copenhagen; Prof Götz Friedrich, Komische Oper, Berlin; incl music & doublebass. Operatic training as asst stage dir. **Operatic debut:** *Butterfly* Norwegian Opera 1971. Theater debut: Norw Brdc Corp, TV Oslo 1974. Awards: Dr of Theatrical Research, Univ of Copenhagen.

Directed/produced opera for major companies in DEN: Copenhagen; NOR: Oslo. **Operas staged with these companies incl** BRITTEN: *Rape of Lucretia★*; DONIZETTI: *Don Pasquale★*; KODALY: *Háry János★*; MENOTTI: *Telephone★*; MOZART: *Nozze di Figaro★*; OFFENBACH: *Contes d'Hoffmann★*; PERGOLESI: *Serva padrona*; PUCCINI: *Schicchi★*, *Butterfly★*, *Tosca*, *Tabarro★*; VERDI: *Trovatore★*; WEILL: *Aufstieg und Fall der Stadt Mahagonny★*. Also GAVEAUX: *Traité nul*; BANQUIERI: *Pazzia senile*; GRETRY: *Amant jaloux*; MARTINU: *Alexandre bis*. **Operatic world premieres:** RYPDAL: *Orpheus Turns and Looks at Eurydice* for Norwegian Opera 1972; EYSER: *Dream of the Man* Vadstena Fest, Sweden 1972. Operatic Video—Norw Brdc TV: *Tivoli*. Opera libretti: RYPDAL: *Orpheus Turns and Looks at Eurydice*, see prem; KOLBERG: *Tivoli*, Norw TV 1974. Teaches at Norw State Opera School. **Res:** Etterstadsletta 83A, Oslo 6, Norway. Mgmt: SLZ/FRG.

FOSTER, LAWRENCE T. Conductor of opera and symphony. American. Music Dir, Houston Symph Orch, TX. Born 23 Oct 1941, Los Angeles. Wife Angela. Studied: Fritz Zweig, Los Angeles. Plays the piano. **Operatic debut:** *Aida* Württembergische Staatsoper, Stuttgart 1964. Symphonic debut: Los Angeles Phil 1965. Awards: Koussevitzky Prize & Eleanor Crane Prize, Tanglewood, Lenox, MA 1966.

Conducted with major companies in FR GER: Stuttgart; UK: Scottish; USA: Houston, Washington DC. **Operas with these companies incl** BERG: *Lulu★*; HANDEL *Rinaldo★*; MASSENET: *Ma-*

non⋆; MOZART: *Don Giovanni*⋆, *Nozze di Figaro*⋆, *Zauberflöte*⋆; VERDI: *Aida*. Conducted major orch in Europe, USA/Canada. **Res:** Houston, TX, USA. Mgmt: CAM/USA; HPL/UK.

FOURNET, JEAN. Conductor of opera and symphony. French. Music Dir, Orch de l'Isle de France, Paris, and Phil of the Dutch Radio, Holland. Born 14 Apr 1913, Rouen. Wife Eude. Two children. Studied: Consv de Paris, Philippe Gaubert; incl flute. Operatic training as repetiteur, asst cond & chorus master at Opéra, Rouen. **Operatic debut:** Théâtre des Arts, Rouen 1935. Symphonic debut: Symph Orch, Rouen. Awards: Chevalier de la Légion d'Honneur, French Gvnmt; Officer in the Royal Order of Orange-Nassau, Holland. Previous adm positions in opera: Mus Dir, Théâtre National de l'Opéra-Comique, Paris.

Conducted with major companies in ARG: Buenos Aires; FRA: Bordeaux, Lyon, Marseille, Nice, Orange Fest, Paris, Rouen, Strasbourg, Toulouse; HOL: Amsterdam; MON: Monte Carlo; POR: Lisbon; SPA: Barcelona; SWE: Stockholm; SWI: Geneva; USA: Chicago, San Francisco Opera. **Operas with these companies incl** BARTOK: *Bluebeard's Castle;* BERLIOZ: *Benvenuto Cellini, Damnation de Faust*⋆; BIZET: *Carmen, Djamileh, Pêcheurs de perles*‡; BOIELDIEU: *Dame blanche;* CHARPENTIER: *Louise*‡; CHERUBINI: *Medea;* DEBUSSY: *Enfant prodigue, Pelléas et Mélisande*⋆; DELIBES: *Lakmé;* DONIZETTI: *Don Pasquale, Favorite;* DUKAS: *Ariane et Barbe Bleue;* GLUCK: *Orfeo ed Euridice*⋆; GOUNOD: *Faust, Mireille, Philémon et Baucis, Roméo et Juliette;* HALEVY: *Juive;* IBERT: *Angélique;* LALO: *Roi d'Ys;* LECOCQ: *Fille de Madame Angot;* LEONCAVALLO: *Pagliacci;* MASCAGNI: *Cavalleria rusticana;* MASSENET: *Don Quichotte, Hérodiade, Jongleur de Notre Dame, Manon*⋆, *Thaïs, Werther*⋆; MENOTTI: *Amahl;* MEYERBEER: *Africaine;* MOZART: *Così fan tutte, Nozze di Figaro;* MUSSORGSKY: *Boris Godunov;* OFFENBACH: *Contes d'Hoffmann;* ORFF: *Carmina burana;* POULENC: *Dialogues des Carmélites, Voix humaine;* PUCCINI: *Bohème, Gianni Schicchi, Butterfly, Tosca;* RABAUD: *Mârouf;* RAVEL: *Enfant et les sortilèges, Heure espagnole*⋆; ROSSINI: *Barbiere di Siviglia;* SAINT-SAENS: *Samson et Dalila;* STRAUSS, R: *Rosenkavalier;* STRAVINSKY: *Mavra, Oedipus Rex, Rossignol;* TCHAIKOVSKY: *Eugene Onegin;* THOMAS: *Hamlet, Mignon;* VERDI: *Aida, Otello, Rigoletto, Traviata;* WAGNER: *Walküre, Tannhäuser, Tristan und Isolde;* WEBER: *Freischütz.* Recorded for Philips, DG. Conducted major orch in Europe, USA/Canada, Cent/S America, Asia. Previous positions as Mus Dir with major orch: Concerts Pasdeloup, Paris; Rotterdam Phil, Holland. Teaches at Ecole Normale de Musique, Paris; Cours Intl Hilversum, Holland. **Res:** rue des Belles Feuilles 62, Paris, France. Mgmt: KSG/FRA; IBK/HOL.

FOWLES, GLENYS RAE. Lyric soprano. Australian. Resident mem: New York City Opera. Born Perth, Australia. Husband Kevin Bleakley, occupation engineer. Studied: Margarita Mayer, Australia; Kurt Adler, New York; Jani Strasser,

London. **Debut:** Oscar (*Ballo in maschera*) Australian Opera, Sydney 1969. Previous occupations: secretary. Awards: Winner Met Op Ntl Counc Aud 1968; Commonwealth Winner Australian Broadc Commss Vocal Compt 1967.

Sang with major companies in AUSTRL: Sydney; UK: Glasgow Scottish, Glyndebourne Fest, London English Natl; USA: New York City Opera. **Roles with these companies incl** BEETHOVEN: Marzelline (*Fidelio*); BIZET: Micaëla⋆ (*Carmen*); BRITTEN: Tytania (*Midsummer Night*), Miss Jessel (*Turn of the Screw*); DONIZETTI: Norina (*Don Pasquale*); GOUNOD: Marguerite (*Faust*); HUMPERDINCK: Gretel; MOZART: Zerlina (*Don Giovanni*), Ilia (*Idomeneo*), Susanna (*Nozze di Figaro*), Pamina (*Zauberflöte*); PUCCINI: Mimi⋆ (*Bohème*), Lauretta⋆ (*Gianni Schicchi*); STRAUSS, R: Sophie (*Rosenkavalier*); STRAVINSKY: Anne Trulove⋆ (*Rake's Progress*); VERDI: Oscar⋆ (*Ballo in maschera*), Nannetta (*Falstaff*), Gilda (*Rigoletto*). Gives recitals. Appears with symphony orchestra. **Res:** 225 W 70 St, New York, NY, USA. Mgmt: LLF/USA; AIM/UK.

FOX, CAROL. American. Gen Mng, Lyric Opera of Chicago, 20 No Wacker Dr, Chicago, IL 60606, USA since 1956. In charge of adm, art policy, tech & finances. Additional administrative positions: Pres, Opera School of Chicago. Born Chicago, IL. Divorced. One child. Studied: Chicago Consv. Previous positions, primarily musical & theatrical: Founder/Pres/Gen Mng, Lyric Theatre of Chicago 1952-56, when company was reorganized as Lyric Op of Chicago. World premieres at theaters under her management: GIANNINI: *The Harvest* 1961; Bicentennial commission PENDERECKI: *Paradise Lost* 1976. Awards: Commendatore nell'Ordine al Merito, Cavaliere al Merito, both Italian Gvnmt; Medal of Merit, City of Chicago; Laureate and Member Lincoln Academy, State of Illinois; Jesse L Rosenberger Medal, Univ Chicago; Hon DL, DH, DFA and DHL from Rosary Coll, Lake Forest Coll, Northwestern Univ, Knox Coll. Initiated major policy changes including extension of season from 16 pfs in 1954 to 52 pfs in 1975 and enlarging budget to $5 million. Instituted American Apprentice Artists Prgm, which in 1974 became the Opera School of Chicago. Also reinstituted own ballet corps under dir Maria Tallchief. Mem of Board of Dir, OPERA America; Opera Panel, Ntl Endowment for the Arts. **Res:** Chicago, IL, USA.

FRANC, TUGOMIR. Bass. Austrian. Resident mem: Staatsoper, Vienna. Born 8 Feb 1935, Zagreb, Yugoslavia. Studied: Prof Zlatko Sir, Prof Lav Vrbanic, Zagreb; Prof Elisabeth Rado, Vienna. **Debut:** Re (*Aida*) Staatsoper, Vienna, 1960. Awards: Third Prize Intl Compt Brussels, 1959.

Sang with major companies in AUS: Graz, Salzburg, Vienna Staats & Volksoper; FRA: Bordeaux, Nancy, Toulouse; FR GER: Bayreuth, Frankfurt, Wiesbaden; ITA: Rome, Turin; SWE: Stockholm; SWI: Geneva; YUG: Dubrovnik, Zagreb, Belgrade. **Roles with these companies incl** BEETHOVEN: Rocco (*Fidelio*); BELLINI: Oroveso (*Norma*); BERLIOZ: Méphistophélès (*Damnation de Faust*); BORODIN: Galitzky (*Prince*

Igor); BRITTEN: Theseus (*Midsummer Night*); DEBUSSY: Arkel (*Pelléas et Mélisande*); DONIZETTI: Henry VIII (*Anna Bolena*); EINEM: St Just (*Dantons Tod*); GLINKA: Ivan (*Life for the Tsar*); GLUCK: Thoas (*Iphigénie en Tauride*); GOUNOD: Méphistophélès (*Faust*); HALEVY: Brogny (*Juive*); HANDEL: Ptolemy (*Giulio Cesare*); JANACEK: Dikoy (*Katya Kabanova*); MASSENET: Des Grieux (*Portrait de Manon*); MEYERBEER: Comte de St Bris (*Huguenots*); MOZART: Publio‡ (*Clemenza di Tito*), Sarastro (*Zauberflöte*); MUSSORGSKY: Pimen (*Boris Godunov*); PONCHIELLI: Alvise (*Gioconda*); PROKOFIEV: Mendoza (*Duenna*); PUCCINI: Colline (*Bohème*); ROSSINI: Don Basilio (*Barbiere di Siviglia*); STRAVINSKY: Tiresias (*Oedipus Rex*); VERDI: Ramfis (*Aida*), Philip II (*Don Carlo*), Padre Guardiano (*Forza del destino*), Conte Walter (*Luisa Miller*), Banquo (*Macbeth*), Fiesco (*Simon Boccanegra*), Procida (*Vespri*); WAGNER: Daland (*Fliegende Holländer*), König Heinrich (*Lohengrin*), Fafner (*Rheingold, Siegfried*), Hunding (*Walküre*), Landgraf (*Tannhäuser*). Also PUCCINI: Timur (*Turandot*); TCHAIKOVSKY: Gremin★ (*Eugene Onegin*); PFITZNER: Madruscht (*Palestrina*); MONTEVERDI: Seneca (*Incoronazione di Poppea*). Recorded for: Concert Hall, Decca. Video/Film: Ivan (*Life for the Tsar*). Gives recitals. Appears with symphony orchestra. Mgmt: RAB/AUS; VIT/SPA.

FRANCESCONI, RENATO. Lyric & dramatic tenor & Heldentenor. Italian. Born 17 Sep 1934, Rome. Wife Maria Grazia Catena. Four daughters. Studied: Mo Armando Piervenanzi, Rome. **Debut:** Manrico (*Trovatore*) Faenza l968. Previous occupations: interior designer.
   Sang with major companies in ARG: Buenos Aires; BEL: Brussels, Liège; FRA: Lyon, Nice, Orange Fest, Strasbourg, Toulouse; FR GER: Düsseldorf-Duisburg; ITA: Palermo, Rome Caracalla, Trieste; SWI: Basel; USA: Hartford, Seattle. **Roles with these companies incl** BELLINI: Pollione★ (*Norma*); BOITO: Faust★ (*Mefistofele*); DONIZETTI: Edgardo★ (*Lucia*); GIORDANO: Andrea Chénier★; LEONCAVALLO: Canio★ (*Pagliacci*); MASCAGNI: Turiddu★ (*Cavalleria rusticana*); MONTEVERDI: Nero★ (*Incoronazione di Poppea*); PUCCINI: Dick Johnson★ (*Fanciulla del West*), Pinkerton★ (*Butterfly*), Des Grieux★ (*Manon Lescaut*), Luigi★ (*Tabarro*), Cavaradossi★ (*Tosca*), Calaf★ (*Turandot*); VERDI: Radames★ (*Aida*), Don Carlo★, Don Alvaro★ (*Forza del destino*), Ismaele★ (*Nabucco*), Otello★, Duca di Mantova★ (*Rigoletto*). Gives recitals. Appears with symphony orchestra. Mgmt: HUR/USA.

FRANCI, CARLO. Conductor of opera and symphony. Italian. Born 18 Jul 1927, Buenos Aires, Argentina. Wife Cabiria Oresti, occupation painter. Two children. Studied: Accad S Cecilia, Rome; incl piano, viola & clavicembalo. **Operatic debut:** *Nabucco* Spoleto 1959. Symphonic debut: Orch Accad S Cecilia, Rome 1957.
   Conducted with major companies in AUS: Bregenz Fest, Vienna Staatsoper; BRA: Rio de Janeiro; FR GER: Berlin Deutsche Oper, Dortmund, Frankfurt, Munich Staatsoper, Wiesba-

den; GER DR: Berlin Komische Oper & Staatsoper; HOL: Amsterdam; HUN: Budapest; ITA: Bologna, Florence Comunale, Genoa, Milan La Scala, Naples, Palermo, Parma, Rome Opera & Caracalla, Spoleto Fest, Trieste, Turin, Venice, Verona Arena; USA: New York Met. **Operas with these companies incl** BARTOK: *Bluebeard's Castle*; BELLINI: *Norma★, Puritani★, Sonnambula*; BOITO: *Mefistofele★*; CAVALIERI: *Rappresentazione*; CHERUBINI: *Medea*; CILEA: *Adriana Lecouvreur★*; CIMAROSA: *Matrimonio segreto★*; DONIZETTI: *Don Pasquale★, Elisir★, Lucia★*; GIORDANO: *Andrea Chénier★, Fedora*; GOUNOD: *Faust*; HANDEL: *Giulio Cesare*; HUMPERDINCK: *Hänsel und Gretel*; MENOTTI: *Dernier sauvage*; MONTEVERDI: *Combattimento di Tancredi, Incoronazione di Poppea*; PUCCINI: *Bohème★, Gianni Schicchi★, Butterfly★, Suor Angelica★, Tabarro★, Tosca★*; ROSSINI: *Barbiere di Siviglia, Cenerentola, Comte Ory, Italiana in Algeri, Otello★*; SMETANA: *Bartered Bride*; SPONTINI: *Fernand Cortez★, Vestale*; VERDI: *Aida★, Ballo in maschera★, Corsaro★, Don Carlo, Ernani, Giovanna d'Arco★, Macbeth★, Rigoletto★, Simon Boccanegra, Traviata★, Trovatore★*; ZANDONAI: *Francesca da Rimini*. Also DONIZETTI: *Belisario*. **World premieres:** ROTA: *Lampada di Aladino* Teatro San Carlo, Naples 1968. Conducted major orch in Europe. Previous positions as Mus Dir with major orch: Radio Eireann Symph, Dublin 1957-58; RAI Symph Orch, Rome 1962-65.

FRANCIS, KENNETH. Bass. British. Born 4 Feb 1936, Tonypandy, Wales, UK. Wife Jacqueline, occupation secy French Embassy. Studied: Welsh Ntl Opera Training Prgr; Redvers Llewellyn, Julia Hilger, John Hargreaves. **Debut:** Dr Grenvil (*Traviata*) PACT, Johannesburg 1971. Previous occupations: civil eng, designer reinforced concrete. Awards: Bronze Medal Conc Intl de Chant, Toulouse 1968.
   Sang with major companies in S AFR: Johannesburg; UK: London English National. **Roles with these companies incl** DONIZETTI: Don Pasquale★, Talbot★ (*Maria Stuarda*); PUCCINI: Colline★ (*Bohème*); STRAVINSKY: Tiresias★ (*Oedipus Rex*); WAGNER: Fasolt★ (*Rheingold*). Appears with symphony orchestra. Mgmt: DOU/UK.

FRANÇOIS, ANDRÉE PAULETTE. Lyric soprano. French. Resident mem: Centre Lyrique de Wallonie, Liège, Belgium. Born 11 Sep 1938, Dombasle, France. Single. Studied: Consv de Nancy, Mme Mairot-Jacquot, France; Ecole Normale de Musique, Jean Giraudeau, acting, Paris; Mo Ettore Campogalliani, Italy. **Debut:** Musetta (*Bohème*) Opéra de Wallonie, Liège 1967. Awards: Second Prize Golden Voice Compt 1964; First Prize Intl Compt of Bel Canto, Liège 1965; Hon Mention Compt UFAM, Paris.
   Sang with major companies in BEL: Brussels, Liège; FRA: Bordeaux, Marseille, Nice, Rouen, Toulouse; GRE: Athens National Opera; FR GER: Karlsruhe; POL: Poznan; ROM: Bucharest. **Roles with these companies incl** BECAUD: Maureen★ (*Opéra d'Aran*); BEETHOVEN: Marzelline★ (*Fidelio*); BIZET: Micaëla★ (*Carmen*); CAVALLI: Sicle★ (*Ormindo*); DEBUSSY:

Mélisande★; GOUNOD: Marguerite★ (*Faust*), Mireille★; MOZART: Donna Elvira★ (*Don Giovanni*), Cherubino★ (*Nozze di Figaro*), Pamina★ (*Zauberflöte*); OFFENBACH: Antonia★ (*Contes d'Hoffmann*); POULENC: Blanche★ (*Dialogues des Carmélites*); PROKOFIEV: Princess★ (*Love for Three Oranges*); PUCCINI: Mimi★ & Musetta (*Bohème*), Lauretta★ (*Gianni Schicchi*), Suor Angelica★, Liù★ (*Turandot*); SMETANA: Marie★ (*Bartered Bride*); STRAUSS, R: Zdenka★ (*Arabella*); TCHAIKOVSKY: Tatiana★ (*Eugene Onegin*); VERDI: Nannetta★ (*Falstaff*), Desdemona (*Otello*). **World premieres:** BONDON: 090 (*I 330*) Opéra de Nantes 1975. Video—Belgian TV: Mireille; (*Bohème*). Mgmt: IMR/FRA.

FRANCY, PAUL; né Gilson. Belgian. Asst to Dir Gen, Centre Lyrique de Wallonie, rue des Dominicains 1, B-4000 Liège. In charge of adm, art policy, mus & dram matters. Is a cond, comp, author, tchr, des. Born 23 Oct 1927, Vaux sous Chèvremont. Wife Marcelle Soeur, occupation adm mgn geriatric hospital. Two children. Studied: Univs Liège, Cambridge, Leyden; Mus High School, Liège; with S Scalais, P Franck, J Leroy, P Gilson, Richard Strauss. Plays the piano. Previous occupations: asst editor, newspaper; cond; comp. Background literary, musical & theatrical. Started with present company in 1967 as Asst Mng. **Res:** Beneden, 10-Bte 181, B-4020 Liège, Belgium.

FRANKLIN, ROGER. Stages/produces opera & theater. Also designs sets & costumes and is a singer, actor & author. American. Born 22 Oct, Boston. Single. Studied: Mme Emilia Ippolito, Boris Goldovsky, Boston; Mass Coll of Art; New York Univ; also music, piano, percussion, guitar & voice. Operatic training as asst stage dir. **Operatic debut:** *Cavalleria rusticana/Pagliacci* Bel Canto Opera, Boston. Theater debut: Theatre Under the Stars, Atlanta, GA. Awards: PhD in music/creative arts, dissertation on Wagner's *Ring,* New York Univ 1975.
Directed/produced opera for major companies in USA: Boston, St Paul. **Operas staged with these companies incl** WAGNER: *Siegfried★, Götterdämmerung★.* **Res:** 174 W 76 St, New York, USA.

FRANZEN, HANS. Bass. German. Resident mem: Opernhaus Zurich; Nationaltheater, Mannheim. Born 5 Feb 1935, Bielefeld, Germany. Wife Elsa Pläser, occupation secy. Three children. Studied, Staatliche Hochschule für Musik, Cologne. **Debut:** Figaro (*Nozze di Figaro*) Opernhaus Cologne 1965. Previous occupations: textile merchant. Awards: First Prize, Compt of German Music Acads.
Sang with major companies in BEL: Brussels, Liège; FRA: Bordeaux, Paris; FR GER: Bayreuth Fest, Bielefeld, Cologne, Darmstadt, Dortmund, Düsseldorf-Duisburg, Essen, Frankfurt, Hamburg, Hannover, Karlsruhe, Kiel, Krefeld, Mannheim, Saarbrücken, Stuttgart, Wiesbaden, Wuppertal; HOL: Amsterdam; ITA: Trieste; SWI: Zurich. **Roles with these companies incl** BEETHOVEN: Rocco (*Fidelio*); DEBUSSY: Arkel (*Pelléas et Mélisande*); MOZART: Publio★ (*Clemenza di Tito*), Leporello (*Don Giovanni*), Osmin★ (*Entführung aus dem Serail*), Figaro★ (*Nozze di Figaro*), Sarastro★ (*Zauberflöte*); MUS-

SORGSKY: Pimen (*Boris Godunov*), Dosifei★ (*Khovanshchina*); PUCCINI: Colline (*Bohème*); ROSSINI: Don Basilio★ (*Barbiere di Siviglia*); SAINT-SAENS: Grand prêtre (*Samson et Dalila*); STRAUSS, R: Sir Morosus (*Schweigsame Frau*); STRAVINSKY: Creon (*Oedipus Rex*); VERDI: Ramfis★ (*Aida*), Philip II (*Don Carlo*), Padre Guardiano★ (*Forza del destino*), Banquo (*Macbeth*), Zaccaria (*Nabucco*), Fiesco★ (*Simon Boccanegra*), Procida★ (*Vespri*); WAGNER: Daland★ (*Fliegende Holländer*), König Heinrich (*Lohengrin*), Pogner★ (*Meistersinger*), Gurnemanz (*Parsifal*), Fasolt★ & Fafner★ (*Rheingold*), Fafner★ (*Siegfried*), Hunding★ (*Walküre*), Hagen★ (*Götterdämmerung*), König Marke (*Tristan und Isolde*). Video—WDR TV: Bartleby. Gives recitals. Appears with symphony orchestra. **Res:** Gartenstr 5, Zurich, Switzerland.

FRAZZONI, GIGLIOLA. Dramatic soprano. Italian. Born 22 Feb 1927, Bologna. Husband Giorgio Vanti, occupation publicity agent. Studied: Mo G Marchesi, Mo O Secchiaroli. **Debut:** Mimi (*Bohème*) Bologna. Previous occupations: painter. Awards: Puccini Gold Medal, Brescia 1966; Silver Medal 1968; Scheriffo d'oro 1975.
Sang with major companies in AUS: Vienna Staatsoper; BEL: Brussels; FRA: Bordeaux; FR GER: Munich Staatsoper, Nürnberg, Stuttgart, Wiesbaden; HOL: Amsterdam; ITA: Bologna, Genoa, Milan La Scala, Naples, Palermo, Parma, Rome Opera & Caracalla, Trieste, Turin, Venice, Verona Arena; POR: Lisbon; S AFR: Johannesburg; SWI: Basel, Geneva, Zurich. **Roles with these companies incl** CILEA: Adriana Lecouvreur; GIORDANO: Maddalena★ (*Andrea Chénier*), Fedora; GOUNOD: Marguerite (*Faust*); LEONCAVALLO: Nedda (*Pagliacci*); MASCAGNI: Santuzza★ (*Cavalleria rusticana*); POULENC: Blanche (*Dialogues des Carmélites*); PUCCINI: Mimi (*Bohème*), Minnie★ (*Fanciulla del West*), Cio-Cio-San (*Butterfly*), Manon Lescaut★, Tosca★; STRAVINSKY: Parasha (*Mavra*); VERDI: Aida, Elisabetta (*Don Carlo*), Leonora (*Trovatore*); WAGNER: Senta (*Fliegende Holländer*); ZANDONAI: Francesca da Rimini. **World premieres:** POULENC: M Marie (*Dialogues des Carmélites*) first stg La Scala 1957. Recorded for: Cetra. Video/Film: (*Fanciulla del West*); (*Butterfly*). **Res:** V Castiglione 162, Bologna, Italy.

FREDRICKS, RICHARD. Dramatic baritone. American. Resident mem: New York City Opera. Born 15 Aug 1933, Los Angeles, CA, USA. Wife Judith Anne. One child. Studied: El Camino Jr Coll, R Neil Hill, CA; Univ of Denver, Florence Lamont Hinman; Carlos Noble, Los Angeles; Beverley Johnson, New York. **Debut:** Schaunard (*Bohème*) New York City Opera 1960. Previous occupations: lab engr in heat transfer.
Sang with major companies in USA: Baltimore, Fort Worth, Hawaii, Houston, Memphis, Miami, Milwaukee Florentine Opera, Newark, New Orleans, New York Met & City Opera, Philadelphia Grand & Lyric, San Antonio, San Diego, San Francisco & Spring Opera. **Roles with these companies incl** BELLINI: Sir Richard★ (*Puritani*); BIZET: Escamillo★ (*Carmen*); BRITTEN: Demetrius (*Midsummer Night*); DONIZETTI: Dott Malatesta★ (*Don Pasquale*), Belcore (*Elisir*),

Enrico★ (*Lucia*), Alfonso d'Este★ (*Lucrezia Borgia*), Talbot★ (*Maria Stuarda*), Nottingham★ (*Roberto Devereux*); GIORDANO: Carlo Gérard (*Andrea Chénier*), LEONCAVALLO: Tonio★ (*Pagliacci*); MASCAGNI: Alfio★ (*Cavalleria rusticana*); MASSENET: Hérode★ (*Hérodiade*), Lescaut★ (*Manon*); MENOTTI: Husband (*Amelia al ballo*), John Sorel (*Consul*); MOORE: Horace Tabor★ (*Baby Doe*); MOZART: Guglielmo (*Così fan tutte*), Don Giovanni★, Conte Almaviva★ & Figaro★ (*Nozze di Figaro*), Papageno (*Zauberflöte*); ORFF: Solo (*Carmina burana*); PUCCINI: Marcello★ (*Bohème*), Jack Rance (*Fanciulla del West*), Gianni Schicchi, Sharpless★ (*Butterfly*), Lescaut★ (*Manon Lescaut*), Michele (*Tabarro*), Scarpia★(*Tosca*); RAVEL: Ramiro★ (*Heure espagnole*); ROSSINI: Figaro★ (*Barbiere di Siviglia*), Dandini★ (*Cenerentola*); VERDI: Renato★ (*Ballo in maschera*), Rodrigo (*Don Carlo*), Rigoletto★, Germont★ (*Traviata*), Conte di Luna (*Trovatore*). Also HENZE: Sekretär (*Junge Lord*); MOORE: Charles (*Carry Nation*). **World premieres:** BEESON: Capt Jason McFarland (*Lizzie Borden*) New York City Opera 1965. Recorded for: Desto, Col. Video/Film: Capt Jason McFarland (*Lizzie Borden*). Gives recitals. Appears with symphony orchestra. Teaches voice. Coaches repertoire. **Res:** New York, NY, USA. Mgmt: CAM/USA; AIM/UK.

FREEDMAN, GERALD. Stages/produces opera, theater, film & television. Also designs sets and is a singer, actor & author. American. Born 25 Jun 1927, Lorain, O. Single. Studied: Northwestern Univ, IL; Mannes School of Music, Alvina Krause, Emmy Joseph, New York; incl music, piano and voice. **Operatic debut:** *Beatrix Cenci* Washington, DC, Opera Socy 1971. Theater debut: New York 1959. Awards: Obie Awd 1959; Northwestern Alumni Awd 1975; Gold Medallion, Amer Coll Theatre Fest 1973, Silver Medallion 1974.

Directed/produced opera for major companies in USA: New York City Opera, San Francisco Spring, Washington DC. **Operas staged for these companies incl** BRITTEN: *Death in Venice★;* FOSS: *Jumping Frog†;* MONTEVERDI: *Favola d'Orfeo★, Incoronazione di Poppea★;* MOZART: *Idomeneo★;* ROSSINI: *Barbiere di Siviglia;* SMETANA: *Bartered Bride;* STRAUSS, J: *Fledermaus★.* Also BACH: *St Matthew Passion★* fully stgd. **Operatic world premieres:** GINASTERA: *Beatrix Cenci* Washington, DC, Opera Socy 1971. Previous leading positions with major theater companies: Art Dir, New York Shakespeare Fest & Public Theatre 1966-71. Teaches at Juilliard School, New York. **Res:** 150 W 87 St, New York, USA. Mgmt: CRB/USA.

FRENI, MIRELLA; née Fregni. Lyric soprano. Italian. Born 27 Feb 1935, Modena. Husband Leone Magiera, occupation conductor & coach. One child. Studied: with uncle, Dante Arcelli; Mo Luigi Bertazzoni; Mo Ettore Campogalliani, Mantua; husband, Mo Leone Magiera. **Debut:** Micaëla (*Carmen*) Teatro Comunale, Modena 1955. Awards: Commendatore della Repubblica Italiana; First Prize, Conc Viotti, Vercelli.

Sang with major companies in AUS: Salzburg Fest, Vienna Staatsoper; FRA: Paris, Rouen; FR

GER: Berlin Deutsche Oper, Hamburg, Munich Staatsoper, Wiesbaden; HOL: Amsterdam; ITA: Bologna, Florence Comunale, Genoa, Milan La Scala, Naples, Palermo, Rome Opera, Trieste, Turin, Venice, Verona Arena; SPA: Barcelona; UK: Glyndebourne Fest, London Royal; USSR: Moscow Bolshoi; USA: Chicago, New York Met, Philadelphia Grand, San Francisco Opera. **Roles with these companies incl** BELLINI: Beatrice di Tenda, Elvira (*Púritani*); BIZET: Micaëla‡ (*Carmen*); BOITO: Margherita (*Mefistofele*); DONIZETTI: Adina‡ (*Elisir*), Marie (*Fille du régiment*); GOUNOD: Marguerite (*Faust*), Juliette‡; HANDEL: Morgana (*Alcina*), Romilda (*Xerxes*); MASCAGNI: Suzel‡ (*Amico Fritz*); MASSENET: Manon‡; MOZART: Zerlina‡ (*Don Giovanni*), Contessa & Susanna‡ (*Nozze di Figaro*); OFFENBACH: Antonia (*Contes d'Hoffmann*); PUCCINI: Mimi‡ (*Bohème*), Liù (*Turandot*); VERDI: Elisabetta (*Don Carlo*), Nannetta (*Falstaff*), Desdemona‡ (*Otello*), Amelia (*Simon Boccanegra*), Violetta‡ (*Traviata*). Recorded for: Angel, RCA, London, Philips, DG, Columbia, Ariola. Video/Film—Italfilm: Mimi (*Bohème*). Mgmt: CST/UK.

FRETWELL, ELIZABETH. Spinto. Australian. Res mem: Australian Opera, Sydney. Born Melbourne. Husband Robert Simmons, occupation businessman. Two children. Studied: National Opera School, Melbourne; Joseph Hislop, London. **Debut:** Tosca, Ntl Opera, Australia l952. Previous occupations: secy.

Sang with major companies in AUSTRL: Sydney; CAN: Toronto; S AFR: Johannesburg; UK: Cardiff Welsh, Edinburgh Fest, Glasgow Scottish, London Royal & English National. **Roles with these companies incl** BEETHOVEN: Leonore★ (*Fidelio*); BRITTEN: Elizabeth (*Gloriana*), Ellen Orford (*Peter Grimes*), Female Chorus★ (*Rape of Lucretia*), Miss Jessel (*Turn of the Screw*); JANACEK: Kostelnicka★ (*Jenufa*); MOZART: Fiordiligi (*Così fan tutte*), Donna Anna (*Don Giovanni*), Contessa & Cherubino (*Nozze di Figaro*); MUSSORGSKY: Marina (*Boris Godunov*); OFFENBACH: Antonia (*Contes d'Hoffmann*); PUCCINI: Musetta★ (*Bohème*), Minnie (*Fanciulla del West*), Cio-Cio-San (*Butterfly*), Suor Angelica, Giorgetta★ (*Tabarro*), Tosca★; STRAUSS, R: Ariadne★ (*Ariadne auf Naxos*); TCHAIKOVSKY: Tatiana (*Eugene Onegin*); VERDI: Aida★, Amelia★ (*Ballo in maschera*), Alice Ford (*Falstaff*), Leonora★ (*Forza del destino*), Violetta (*Traviata*), Leonora (*Trovatore*); WAGNER: Senta (*Fliegende Holländer*), Elsa (*Lohengrin*), Sieglinde (*Walküre*), Venus (*Tannhäuser*). **World premieres:** SITSKY: Mrs Kaufmann (*Lenz*) Australian Opera 1974. **Res:** Sydney, Australia.

FRIEDRICH, GÖTZ. Stages/produces opera, film & television. German. Oberspielleiter, Komische Oper, Berlin, Ger DR. Born 4 Aug 1930, Naumburg/Saale, Germany. Studied: Theater Dipl. Operatic training as asst stage dir at Komische Oper, Berlin, as Dramaturg & Prod Asst since 1953; then Chief Prod Asst & Artistic Asst and wissenschaftlicher Mitarbeiter to Walter Felsenstein. **Operatic debut:** Komische Oper, Berlin 1953-56. Awards: Hochschuldozent, Berlin. Previous adm positions in opera: Chief prod, Hamburg Staatsoper 1973-74, Netherlands Opera Amsterdam 1973-74.

Directed/produced opera for major companies in AUS: Vienna Staatsoper; DEN: Copenhagen; FR GER: Bayreuth Fest, Berlin Deutsche Oper, Hamburg, Munich Staatsoper, Saarbrücken; GER DR: Berlin Komische Oper; HOL: Amsterdam; NOR: Oslo; SWE: Drottningholm Fest, Stockholm; SWI: Zurich; UK: London Royal; et al. **Operas staged with these companies incl** BERG: *Wozzeck;* JANACEK: *Jenufa;* MONTEVERDI: *Ritorno d'Ulisse;* MOZART: *Così fan tutte, Don Giovanni, Zauberflöte;* OFFENBACH: *Contes d'Hoffmann;* PUCCINI: *Bohème;* SCHOENBERG: *Moses und Aron;* STRAUSS, R: *Salome;* VERDI: *Aida, Ballo in maschera, Falstaff, Simon Boccanegra, Trovatore;* WAGNER: *Rheingold, Walküre, Tannhäuser, Tristan und Isolde;* et al. **Operatic world premieres:** MATTHUS: *Der letzte Schuss* Komische Oper, Berlin 1968. Operatic Video—German TV: *Schöne Galatea.*

FRIEND, LIONEL. Conductor of opera and symphony; composer. British. Resident Cond, Staatstheater, Kassel, FR Ger. Also Mus Dir, London Chamber Opera since 1969. Born 13 Mar 1945, London. Wife Jane Hyland, occupation cellist. One child. Studied: Royal Coll of Music, Sir Adrian Boult, London; London Opera Centre; Hans Schmidt-Isserstedt; incl piano, flute. Plays the piano, other keyboard instruments. Operatic training as repetiteur, asst cond & chorus master at Glyndebourne Fest 1969-72. **Operatic debut:** *Traviata* Welsh National Opera, UK 1968. Symphonic debut: London Sinfonietta, Oxford, UK 1972. Awards: Ricordi Prize for Opera Conducting; various cond prizes incl Royal Coll of Music.

Conducted with major companies in FR GER: Kassel; UK: Welsh National. **Operas with these companies incl** BERG: *Lulu★;* BIZET: *Carmen★;* BRITTEN: *Death in Venice★;* DONIZETTI: *Lucia★;* MOZART: *Don Giovanni★, Nozze di Figaro★, Zauberflöte★;* NICOLAI: *Lustigen Weiber★;* PUCCINI: *Bohème;* RAVEL: *Heure espagnole★;* ROSSINI: *Barbiere di Siviglia★;* VERDI: *Traviata;* WALTON: *Bear★.* Conducted major orch in Europe. Mgmt★: MIN/UK; PAS/FRG.

FRIGERIO, EZIO; né Elvezio Frigerio. Scenic and costume designer for opera, theater, film, television. Is a lighting designer. Italian. Born 16 Jul 1930, Erba. Wife Franca, occupation opera costume designer. One child. Studied: Istit Nautico, Savona; Liceo Artistico Brera, Milan. **Operatic debut:** sets, *Amleto* Teatro dell'Opera, Rome 1960; cost, *Matrimonio segreto* La Scala, Milan 1956. Theater debut: Piccolo Teatro di Milano 1955. Previous occupation: naval officer; painter. Awards: twice, San Genesio Prize, Milan; Paladino d'argento, Palermo.

Designed for major companies in FRA: Marseille, Paris; FR GER: Cologne; HOL: Amsterdam; ITA: Florence Maggio & Comunale, Milan La Scala, Naples, Rome Opera, Venice; SWI: Zurich; USA: Chicago. **Operas designed for these companies incl** BEETHOVEN: *Fidelio;* BELLINI: *Capuleti ed i Montecchi;* CHARPENTIER: *Louise;* CIMAROSA: *Matrimonio segreto;* DONIZETTI: *Don Pasquale;* GLUCK:

Iphigénie en Aulide; MONTEVERDI: *Favola d'Orfeo;* MOZART: *Don Giovanni, Nozze di Figaro;* PROKOFIEV: *Fiery Angel;* PUCCINI: *Tosca★;* VERDI: *Otello, Simon Boccanegra★.* Also ZAFRED: *Amleto.* **Operatic world premieres:** PROKOFIEV: *Fiery Angel* La Fenice, Venice 1955. **Res:** 1 Palestro, Rome, Italy.

FRISELL, SONJA BETTIE. Stages/produces opera. Canadian/British. Head of Prod & Resident Stage Dir, La Scala, Milan. Born 5 Aug 1937, Richmond, Surrey, UK. Single. Studied: Guildhall School of Music & Drama, London; with Carl Ebert, Glyndebourne; Deutsche Oper Berlin; incl music, piano, guitar and voice. Operatic training as asst stage dir to Franco Enriquez in Milan, Palermo, Venice 1961-62; to Margherita Wallmann in Milan, Palermo, Naples, Rome, Paris, Monte Carlo 1962-64. **Operatic debut:** *Iphigénie en Tauride* Durham Opera Co, UK 1958. Previous occupation: Asst Box Office & Asst Wardrobe Mng, Sadler's Wells. Awards: Canada Council Arts Schlshp for Italy.

Directed/produced opera for major companies in BEL: Brussels; CAN: Toronto; ITA: Milan La Scala; SWI: Geneva; USA: Chicago, San Francisco Opera. **Operas staged with these companies incl** DONIZETTI: *Lucia★;* MUSSORGSKY: *Khovanshchina;* ROSSINI: *Barbiere di Siviglia, Cambiale di matrimonio;* VERDI: *Simon Boccanegra, Traviata★.* Teaches piano. **Res:** 16 V delle Margherite, Dresano 20077, Italy.

FRYDLEWICZ, MIROSLAV. Heldentenor. Czechoslovakian. Resident mem: National Theater, Prague. Born 23 Feb 1934, Plzen, CSR. Wife Radmila. One daughter. Studied: State Consv, Prof Jan Berlík, Prague. **Debut:** Hans (*Bartered Bride*) Municipal Theater, Opava 1957.

Sang with major companies in CZE: Prague National; GER DR: Berlin Staatsoper, Leipzig; ITA: Naples. **Roles with these companies incl** DVORAK: Jirka★ (*Devil and Kate*), Prince★ (*Rusalka*); JANACEK: Mazal (*Excursions of Mr Broucek*), Steva (*Jenufa*), Boris (*Katya Kabanova*); MASCAGNI: Turiddu (*Cavalleria rusticana*); MOZART: Don Ottavio (*Don Giovanni*); PUCCINI: Rinuccio (*Gianni Schicchi*), Pinkerton (*Butterfly*); ROSSINI: Almaviva (*Barbiere di Siviglia*); SMETANA: Hans (*Bartered Bride*), Jarek (*Devil's Wall*), Lukas★ (*The Kiss*); TCHAIKOVSKY: Lenski (*Eugene Onegin*); VERDI: Riccardo★ (*Ballo in maschera*); WAGNER: Lohengrin★. Also DVORAK: Jirka★ (*Jakobin*); JEREMIAS: Alexej★ (*Brothers Karamazov*); KARMINSKY: Kerensky★ (*Ten Days that Shook the World*). **World premieres:** PAUER: Kleant (*Malade imaginaire*) National Theater, Prague 1970. Gives recitals. Appears with symphony orchestra. **Res:** Chrpová 2252, 10600 Prague 10, CSSR. Mgmt: PRG/CZE.

FULLMER, CHARLES CURTIS. American. Gen Mng, Minnesota Opera Company, 1812 So 6 St, Minneapolis, MN 55454, USA. In charge of adm, art & tech matters & finances. Born 27 Jan 1926, St Paul, MN, USA. Wife Beverly. Three children. Studied: Hamline Univ, St Paul. Previous positions primarily administrative: Vice-Pres, Pryor-

Menz Concerts, Council Bluffs, IA 1961-64; Mng, Minnesota Orch, Minneapolis 1964-72; Exec Dir, Upper Midwest Regional Arts Counc, Minneapolis 1972-74. In present position since 1974. **Res:** St Paul, MN, USA.

FURLAN, LAMBERTO OLINDO. Lyric tenor. Italian. Resident mem: Australian Opera, Sydney. Born 16 Apr 1935, Rovigo. Wife Beryl, occupation opera singer. Studied: Riccardo Zama, Maria Teresa Pediconi, Luigi Malatesta, Rome. **Debut:** Turiddu (*Cavalleria rusticana*) Australian Opera 1972. Previous occupations: tourist guide in Rome.
Sang with major companies in AUSTRL: Sydney. **Roles with these companies incl** MASCAGNI: Turiddu★ (*Cavalleria rusticana*); PUCCINI: Rinuccio★ (*Gianni Schicchi*), Cavaradossi★ (*Tosca*); VERDI: Ismaele★ (*Nabucco*), Duca di Mantova★ (*Rigoletto*). Gives recitals. Appears with symphony orchestra. **Res:** Sydney, Australia.

FURRER, ULRICH. Conductor of opera and symphony; composer. Swiss. Resident Cond, Württembergische Staatstheater, Stuttgart. Born 1 Apr 1942, Berne, Switzerland. Wife Gertraud Kovac. Three children. Studied: Walter Furrer, Liane Furrer, parents; Heinrich Gurtner, Berne; Hans Müller-Kray, Henk Badings, Stuttgart; incl piano, organ, violin, viola, clarinet. Plays the piano, organ. Operatic training as asst cond at Vereinigte Bühnen, Graz 1964-66; Bayreuth Fest 1965. **Operatic debut:** *Italiana in Algeri* Verein Bühnen, Graz 1964. Symphonic debut: Städtisches Orch, Aachen, FR Ger 1973. Awards: Piano & Organ Diplome, Swiss Music Teachers Assn 1962. Previous adm positions in opera: First Cond, Stadttheater Aachen 1971-73.
Conducted with major companies in AUS: Graz; FR GER: Darmstadt, Karlsruhe, Nürnberg, Stuttgart, Wiesbaden; SWI: Basel. **Operas with these companies incl** BEETHOVEN: *Fidelio;* BIZET: *Carmen;* DONIZETTI: *Don Pasquale★, Elisir★;*

FLOTOW: *Martha★;* GIORDANO: *Andrea Chénier;* HAYDN: *Infedeltà delusa;* HUMPERDINCK: *Hänsel und Gretel★;* LEONCAVALLO: *Pagliacci;* LORTZING: *Zar und Zimmermann★;* MASCAGNI: *Cavalleria rusticana;* MOZART: *Don Giovanni, Entführung aus dem Serail★, Nozze di Figaro, Zauberflöte★;* NICOLAI: *Lustigen Weiber;* PUCCINI: *Bohème, Butterfly★, Tosca★;* ROSSINI: *Barbiere di Siviglia, Italiana in Algeri;* STRAUSS, J: *Fledermaus★;* VERDI: *Ballo in maschera, Rigoletto, Traviata★, Trovatore★;* WAGNER: *Fliegende Holländer, Tannhäuser★;* WEBER: *Freischütz.* Also BURKHARD: *Bunbury.* Conducted major orch in Europe. Teaches at Staatliche Hochschule für Musik, Stuttgart. **Res:** Olgastr 8, 7302-Ostfildern 2/Nellingen, FR Ger. **Mgmt:** PAS/FRG.

FÜRSTENBERG, DOROTHEE. Lyric soprano. German. Resident mem: Theater am Gärtnerplatz, Munich. Born 4 Aug 1942, Schwelm, Germany. Single. Studied: Hochschule für Musik, Berlin; Kmsg Elisabeth Grümmer; Felix Dolling, Göttingen. **Debut:** Donna Anna (*Don Giovanni*) Opernhaus Giessen, FR Ger 1967. Awards: Winner of Stipd of German People 1963.
Sang with major companies in FR GER: Essen, Hamburg, Hannover, Munich Gärtnerplatz. **Roles with these companies incl** BEETHOVEN: Marzelline★ (*Fidelio*); LEONCAVALLO: Nedda (*Pagliacci*); LORTZING: Baronin Freimann★ (*Wildschütz*); MARTIN: Iseut★ (*Vin herbé*); MOZART: Donna Anna (*Don Giovanni*); NICOLAI: Frau Fluth★ (*Lustigen Weiber*); OFFENBACH: Antonia & Giulietta (*Contes d'Hoffmann*); SMETANA: Marie (*Bartered Bride*), Blazenka (*Secret*); STRAUSS, J: Rosalinde★ (*Fledermaus*); STRAUSS, R: Arabella; TCHAIKOVSKY: Lisa (*Pique Dame*); VERDI: Desdemona (*Otello*); WEBER: Agathe★ (*Freischütz*); WEILL: Jenny (*Aufstieg und Fall der Stadt Mahagonny*). **Mgmt:** PAS/FRG.

G

GABOR, CONSTANTIN. Basso-buffo. Romanian. Resident mem: Romanian Opera, Bucharest. Born 11 Jul 1929, Brasov. Wife Elisabeta. Studied: Consv Bucharest, Prof Grigore Melnik. **Debut:** Bartolo (*Nozze di Figaro*) Romanian Opera 1956. Awards: Order of Merit, Ministry of Culture.
Sang with major companies in FR GER: Saarbrücken; ROM: Bucharest. **Roles with these companies incl** CIMAROSA: Geronimo (*Matrimonio segreto*); DONIZETTI: Don Pasquale⋆; MOZART: Don Alfonso⋆ (*Così fan tutte*), Leporello⋆ (*Don Giovanni*), Papageno⋆ (*Zauberflöte*); PERGOLESI: Uberto (*Serva padrona*); PROKOFIEV: Mendoza (*Duenna*); ROSSINI: Dott Bartolo⋆ (*Barbiere di Siviglia*); SMETANA: Kezal⋆ (*Bartered Bride*); STRAUSS, R: Baron Ochs (*Rosenkavalier*); VERDI: Fra Melitone (*Forza del destino*). Recorded for: Electrecord. Video/Film: Don Alfonso (*Così fan tutte*), Leporello (*Don Giovanni*), Bartolo (*Barbiere*). Gives recitals. Appears with symphony orchestra. Teaches voice. Coaches repertoire. **Res:** 160 1 May Blvd, Bucharest 8, Romania. Mgmt: RIA/ROM.

GAHMLICH, WILFRIED. Lyric tenor & tenore buffo. German. Resident mem: Niedersächsisches Staatstheater, Hannover. Born 14 Jul 1939, Halle/Saale, Germany. Wife Brigitte. Three children. Studied: Hochschule für Musik, Freiburg, FR Ger; Kmsg Alfred Pfeifle. **Debut:** Pedrillo (*Entführung aus dem Serail*), Giessen, FR Ger 1968. Previous occupations: chemist.
Sang with major companies in FR GER: Düsseldorf-Duisburg, Essen, Hannover, Kiel, Krefeld, Stuttgart, Wiesbaden, Wuppertal. **Roles with these companies incl** BEETHOVEN: Florestan (*Fidelio*); BERG: Tambourmajor (*Wozzeck*); BIZET: Don José (*Carmen*); CIMAROSA: Paolino⋆ (*Matrimonio segreto*); EINEM: Bürgermeister (*Besuch der alten Dame*); GIORDANO: Andrea Chénier; HUMPERDINCK: Königssohn (*Königskinder*); LORTZING: Peter Ivanov⋆ (*Zar und Zimmermann*); MOZART: Pedrillo⋆ (*Entführung aus dem Serail*), Tamino (*Zauberflöte*); SMETANA: Wenzel⋆ (*Bartered Bride*); WAGNER: Erik (*Fliegende Holländer*); WEBER: Max (*Freischütz*). Also LORTZING: Georg (*Waffenschmied*); PERGOLESI: Ascanio (*Frate 'nnamorato*); ZIMMERMANN: Nieswand⋆ (*Levins Mühle*); GEISSLER: Licht⋆ (*Zerbrochene Krug*). **World premieres:** BLACHER: Zyprian (*Yvonne*)

Wuppertal 1973. Gives recitals. Appears with symphony orchestra. Mgmt: PAS/FRG.

GALIN-PERINIC, JASENKA. Dramatic soprano. Yugoslavian. Resident mem: Croatian National Opera, Zagreb. Born 12 Jun 1945, Varazdin. Husband Vinko Perinic, occupation electrical eng. Studied: Zlatko Sir, Lav Vrbanic, Zagreb; Emmy Sittner, Vienna. **Debut:** Leonora (*Forza del destino*) Stadttheater St Gallen, Switzerland 1969. Awards: Third Place, 6th Compt of Music, Yugoslavia 1969.
Sang with major companies in YUG: Zagreb. **Roles with these companies incl** BEETHOVEN: Leonore⋆ (*Fidelio*); GOTOVAC: Djula⋆ (*Ero der Schelm*); HUMPERDINCK: Gretel; MASCAGNI: Santuzza⋆ (*Cavalleria rusticana*); MOZART: Contessa (*Nozze di Figaro*). Also ZAJC: Eva (*Nicola Subic Zrinjski*). Gives recitals. Appears with symphony orchestra. Teaches voice. Coaches repertoire. On faculty of Acad of Music, Zagreb; Hochschule für Musik, Vienna. **Res:** Vinogradska 28, Zagreb, Yugoslavia.

GALL, HUGUES RANDOLPH. French. Assoc Gen Mng, Théâtre National de l'Opéra, 8 rue Scribe, Paris 75009. In charge of overall adm matters & art policy. Born 18 Mar 1940, Honfleur. Single. Studied: political sciences, Paris; German literature, Paris, Münster. Previous occupations: Chargé de mission, Min de l'Agriculture 1966-67; Conseiller tech, Min de l'Education Nationale 1967-68; Min des Affaires Culturelles 1968-69. Background primarily adm. Started with present company in 1969 as Secy Gen; in present position since 1973. Awards: Arts & Lettres/Mérite Agricole/Officier de l'ordre royal du Cambodge. **Res:** Paris, France.

GALLOIS, HENRI. Conductor of opera and symphony. French. Resident Cond, Théâtre du Capitole, Toulouse since 1972. Born 11 May 1944, Algiers. Single. Studied: Algiers, Nice and Paris; incl piano, horn, percussion and voice. Operatic training as chorus master. **Operatic debut:** tour throughout France 1965. Symphonic debut: Toulouse 1972. Awards: Conc Int de Direction d'Orchestre, Besançon, France.
Conducted with major companies in FRA: Bordeaux, Paris, Toulouse; SWI: Geneva. **Operas with these cos** ADAM: *Si j'étais roi;* BEETHOVEN:

Fidelio; BERG: *Wozzeck;* BIZET: *Carmen★, Pêcheurs de perles★;* BOIELDIEU: *Dame blanche★;* DELIBES: *Lakmé;* DONIZETTI: *Don Pasquale, Fille du régiment;* GIORDANO: *Andrea Chénier;* GLUCK: *Alceste;* GOUNOD: *Faust★, Mireille★, Philémon et Baucis, Roméo et Juliette★;* LALO: *Roi d'Ys;* MASCAGNI: *Cavalleria;* MASSENET: *Hérodiade, Manon, Sappho, Werther★;* MENOTTI: *Saint of Bleecker Street★;* MEYERBEER: *Huguenots;* MOZART: *Così fan tutte, Nozze di Figaro, Zauberflöte★;* MUSSORGSKY: *Boris Godunov;* OFFENBACH: *Contes d'Hoffmann★, Périchole★;* ORFF: *Carmina burana★;* POULENC: *Voix humaine★;* PROKOFIEV: *Duenna★;* PUCCINI: *Bohème★, Butterfly★, Manon Lescaut★, Tabarro★, Tosca★, Turandot★;* ROSSINI: *Barbiere di Siviglia★, Guillaume Tell★;* SAINT-SAENS: *Samson et Dalila★;* STRAUSS, J: *Fledermaus★;* TCHAIKOVSKY: *Eugene Onegin;* THOMAS: *Mignon;* VERDI: *Aida, Don Carlo★, Otello, Rigoletto★, Traviata★, Trovatore;* WAGNER: *Fliegende Holländer, Lohengrin, Tannhäuser.* Also NIKIPROWETZKY: *Noces d'ombre;* SAGUER: *Mariana Pineda.* **Res:** rue de l'Esquile 4, Toulouse, France. Mgmt: IMR/FRA.

GALVANY, MARISA; née Myra Beth Genis. Soprano. American. Resident mem: New York City Opera. Born 19 Jun 1936, Paterson, NJ. Husband H G Kornbluth, occupation certified public accountant. Studied: Armen Boyajian. **Debut:** Tosca, Seattle Opera 1968.

Sang with major companies in FRA: Rouen; MEX: Mexico City; SPA: Barcelona; USA: Fort Worth, Hartford, Kentucky, Newark, New Orleans, New York City Opera, Philadelphia Lyric, San Diego, Seattle. **Roles with these companies incl** BELLINI: Norma, Imogene (*Pirata*); CHERUBINI: Medea★; DONIZETTI: Anna Bolena★, Lucia★, Maria Stuarda & Elisabetta★ (*Maria Stuarda*); HALEVY: Rachel★ (*Juive*); MASCAGNI: Santuzza★ (*Cavalleria rusticana*); MASSENET: Salomé★ (*Hérodiade*); MAYR: Medea★‡ (*Medea in Corinto*); MEYERBEER: Valentine★ (*Huguenots*); MOZART: Fiordiligi (*Così fan tutte*), Donna Anna (*Don Giovanni*), Elettra (*Idomeneo*), Contessa (*Nozze di Figaro*); POULENC: Blanche (*Dialogues des Carmélites*); PUCCINI: Musetta (*Bohème*), Cio-Cio-San★ (*Butterfly*), Tosca★, Turandot; PURCELL: Dido; TCHAIKOVSKY: Iolanthe; VERDI: Aida★, Odabella (*Attila*), Amelia★ (*Ballo in maschera*), Donna Elvira (*Ernani*), Lady Macbeth★, Abigaille (*Nabucco*), Desdemona (*Otello*), Violetta★ (*Traviata*), Leonora★ (*Trovatore*), Elena (*Vespri*). Also DONIZETTI: Pauline★ (*Poliuto*). Gives recitals. Appears with symphony orchestra. Mgmt: HUR/USA.

GAMSJÄGER, RUDOLF. Austrian. Director, Wiener Staatsoper, Opernring, A-1010 Vienna. In charge of admin matters. Born 23 Mar 1909, Vienna. Studied: Univ Vienna, philosophy; Akad für Musik, Vienna, incl voice. Plays piano. Previous positions, primarily administrative & musical: Dir & Gen Secy, Gesellschaft der Musikfreunde, Vienna 1946-72. Started with present company 1970 as Dir designate; in present position since 1972, contract till 8/76. Awards:

Max Reinhardt Medal, Salzburg 1970; Commendatore dell'ordine Sancti Silvestri Papae, Vatican 1958; Silver Medals, Austrian Rep; Order of the White Elephant, Thailand 1965; Ehrenring, Vienna Phil Orch 1970. Initiated major policy changes including scheduling series of six to nine performances of an opera retaining the premiere cast within the ten-month repertory season. Mem of advisory panels: Gesellschaft der Musikfreunde; Wiener Männergesangverein; Wiener Beethoven Gesellschaft; NO Tonkünstlerorch; and many more. **Res:** Vienna, Austria.

GANO, DAVID EARL. Scenic designer for opera, theater. Is a stage director. American. Resident designer, New Orleans Opera Assn, LA. Born 9 Jun 1941, Wooster, O. Single. Studied: Mario Cristini, Indiana Univ. Prof training: scenic shop at Starlight Musicals, Kansas City summer 1968. **Operatic debut:** sets, *Trovatore* Bowling Green, O, 1965; cost, *Sonnambula* Memphis Opera, TN 1970. Theater debut: Arena Fair Summer Theater, Wooster 1962. Previous occupation: painter. Previous adm positions in opera: Tech Dir, Memphis Opera Theater 1970-73, New Orleans Opera 1973-75.

Designed for major companies in USA: Cincinnati, Houston, Kansas City, Memphis, New Orleans, Omaha, Philadelphia Lyric, Portland. **Operas designed for these companies incl** BELLINI: *Sonnambula★;* DONIZETTI: *Lucia;* HALEVY: *Juive★;* MASSENET: *Hérodiade★;* MEYERBEER: *Huguenots★;* MOZART: *Don Giovanni★;* PUCCINI: *Butterfly★, Turandot★;* ROSSINI: *Barbiere di Siviglia★;* STRAUSS, R: *Ariadne auf Naxos★;* VERDI: *Aida★, Ballo in maschera★, Macbeth★, Rigoletto★, Traviata★, Trovatore;* WAGNER: *Lohengrin★.* **Res:** New Orleans, LA, USA.

GANZAROLLI, WLADIMIRO. Bass-baritone. Italian. Born 9 Jan 1939, Venice. Studied: Iris Adami Corradetti, Venice. **Debut:** Méphistophélès (*Faust*) Teatro Nuovo, Milan 1958. Previous occupations: physics prof; elem school master.

Sang with major companies in ARG: Buenos Aires; AUS: Vienna Staatsoper & Volksoper; FRA: Aix-en-Provence Fest; FR GER: Wiesbaden; ITA: Bologna, Florence Maggio & Comunale, Genoa, Milan La Scala, Naples, Palermo, Parma, Rome Opera, Spoleto Fest, Trieste, Turin, Venice, Verona Arena; MON: Monte Carlo; POR: Lisbon; SPA: Barcelona; SWI: Geneva, Zurich; UK: London Royal; USA: Boston, Chicago, Philadelphia Lyric. **Roles with these companies incl** BARTOK: Bluebeard; BELLINI: Oroveso (*Norma*), Sir George (*Puritani*), Rodolfo (*Sonnambula*); BERG: Wozzeck; BERLIOZ: Méphistophélès (*Damnation de Faust*); BIZET: Escamillo (*Carmen*); BORODIN: Prince Igor; BRITTEN: Bottom (*Midsummer Night*); CHERUBINI: Creon (*Medea*); CIMAROSA: Count Robinson (*Matrimonio segreto*); CORNELIUS: Abul Hassan (*Barbier von Bagdad*); DEBUSSY: Golaud (*Pelléas et Mélisande*); DONIZETTI: Henry VIII (*Anna Bolena*), Agata (*Convenienze/Viva la Mamma*), Don Pasquale★, Dulcamara (*Elisir*), Sulpice (*Fille du régiment*), Alfonso d'Este (*Lucrezia Borgia*); FALLA: Don Quixote (*Retablo de Maese Pedro*), Tio Sarvaor

185

(*Vida breve*); GLINKA: Ivan (*Life for the Tsar*); GOUNOD: Méphistophélès★ (*Faust*); HINDE-MITH: Cardillac; MASCAGNI: Alfio (*Cavalleria rusticana*); MASSENET: Don Quichotte; MEYERBEER: Comte de Nevers (*Huguenots*); MOZART: Guglielmo★‡ (*Così fan tutte*), Leporello★‡ (*Don Giovanni*), Figaro★‡ (*Nozze di Figaro*), Papageno★ (*Zauberflöte*); MUSSORGSKY: Boris & Varlaam (*Boris Godunov*), Ivan Khovansky (*Khovanshchina*); OFFEN-BACH: Coppélius etc (*Contes d'Hoffmann*); PAISIELLO: Figaro (*Barbiere di Siviglia*); PER-GOLESI: Uberto (*Serva padrona*); PROKO-FIEV: Ruprecht (*Fiery Angel*); PUCCINI: Colline (*Bohème*), Jack Rance (*Fanciulla del West*), Scarpia (*Tosca*); ROSSINI: Don Basilio (*Barbiere di Siviglia*), Dandini & Don Magnifico (*Cenerentola*), Podestà (*Gazza ladra*), Mustafà★ (*Italiana in Algeri*), Assur (*Semiramide*), Maometto (*Assedio di Corinto*), Sultan Selim (*Turco in Italia*); TCHAIKOVSKY: Yeletsky (*Pique Dame*); VERDI: Ramfis (*Aida*), Falstaff★, Barone★‡ (*Giorno di regno*), Pagano (*Lombardi*), Massimiliano Moor (*Masnadieri*), Zaccaria (*Nabucco*); WAGNER: Holländer; WOLF-FERRARI: Lunardo★ (*Quattro rusteghi*). Also PAISIELLO: Conte (*Nina*); MONTEVERDI: Ottone (*Incoronazione di Poppea*); ROSSINI: Parmenione (*Occasione fa il ladro*); PIZZETTI: Arcivescovo (*Assassinio nella cattedrale*); ROSSELLINI: (*Sguardo dal ponte*). **World premieres:** PIZ-ZETTI: Raito (*Calzare d'argento*) La Scala, Milan 1960. **Res:** 4 Viale Legione Romane, Milan, Italy.

GARABEDIAN, EDNA. Dramatic mezzo-soprano. American. Born 28 May 1939, Fresno, CA, USA. Husband Michael Kilijian, occupation prof of health & safety. Two children. Studied: Anna Hamlin, New York; William Vennard, Los Angeles; Lotte Lehmann, Santa Barbara, CA; Rosa Ponselle, Baltimore, MD, USA. **Debut:** Santuzza (*Cavalleria rusticana*) New York City Opera 1965. Previous occupations: prof of vocal studies.
Sang with major companies in USA: Baltimore, Chicago, Houston, Kansas City, New York City Opera, San Diego, San Francisco Opera & Spring Opera, Seattle. **Roles with these companies incl** MASCAGNI: Santuzza★ (*Cavalleria rusticana*); MENOTTI: Desideria (*Saint of Bleecker Street*); MUSSORGSKY: Marina★ (*Boris Godunov*); PUCCINI: Suzuki★ (*Butterfly*), Principessa★ (*Suor Angelica*); ROSSINI: Rosina (*Barbiere di Siviglia*); STRAVINSKY: Jocasta★ (*Oedipus Rex*); TCHAIKOVSKY: Olga★ (*Eugene Onegin*); VERDI: Amneris★ (*Aida*), Ulrica★ (*Ballo in maschera*), Preziosilla★ (*Forza del destino*), Azucena★ (*Trovatore*); WAGNER: Erda★ (*Rheingold*). Gives recitals. Appears with symphony orchestra. Teaches voice. Coaches repertoire. On faculty of San Francisco State Univ. **Res:** 70 De Soto, San Francisco, CA 94127, USA.

GARAVENTA, OTTAVIO. Lyric tenor. Italian. Born 26 Jan 1934, Genoa, Italy. Wife Angela. One daughter. Studied: Rosetta Noli, Vladimiro Badiali. **Debut:** Don Ottavio (*Don Giovanni*) As Li Co, Milan 1954. Awards: Verdi Gold Medal, Compt Busseto; Golden Nut, City of Lecco; Gold Medals, Genoa, Modena, Arenzano, Liguria, etc.

Sang with major companies in ARG: Buenos Aires; AUS: Bregenz Fest, Vienna Staatsoper; BEL: Brussels; CAN: Montreal/Quebec; DEN: Copenhagen; FRA: Aix-en-Provence Fest, Marseille, Toulouse; GRE: Athens National; FR GER: Berlin Deutsche Oper, Frankfurt, Karlsruhe, Wiesbaden; GER DR: Berlin Komische Oper & Staatsoper; HOL: Amsterdam; HUN: Budapest; ITA: Bologna, Florence Maggio & Comunale, Genoa, Milan La Scala, Naples, Palermo, Parma, Rome Opera, Trieste, Turin, Venice, Verona Arena; POR: Lisbon; SPA: Barcelona; SWI: Basel; UK: Edinburgh Fest, Glyndebourne Fest; USA: Chicago, Cincinnati, Philadelphia Grand & Lyric, San Francisco Opera; YUG: Dubrovnik, Zagreb, Belgrade. **Roles with these companies incl** BELLINI: Elvino (*Sonnambula*), Arturo★ (*Straniera*); BOITO: Faust★ (*Mefistofele*); BUSONI: Leandro (*Arlecchino*); CILEA: Maurizio★ (*A. Lecouvreur*); DONIZETTI: Riccardo★ (*Anna Bolena*), Gerardo★ (*Caterina Cornaro*), Ernesto★ (*Don Pasquale*), Nemorino (*Elisir*), Fernand (*Favorite*), Charles★ (*Linda di Chamounix*), Edgardo★ (*Lucia*), Gennaro (*Lucrezia Borgia*), Riccardo (*Maria di Rohan*), Leicester★ (*Maria Stuarda*); MASCAGNI: Turiddu (*Cavalleria rusticana*); MASSENET: Des Grieux★ (*Manon*), Werther★; MOZART: Don Ottavio (*Don Giovanni*), Belfiore (*Finta giardiniera*), Alessandro (*Re pastore*); PONCHIELLI: Enzo★ (*Gioconda*); PUCCINI: Rodolfo★ (*Bohème*), Rinuccio★ (*Gianni Schicchi*), Pinkerton★ (*Butterfly*), Cavaradossi★ (*Tosca*); PURCELL: King Arthur; ROSSINI: Almaviva★ (*Barbiere di Siviglia*), Lindoro★ (*Italiana in Algeri*), Aménophis★ (*Moïse*), Idreno (*Semiramide*); STRAUSS, R: Matteo (*Arabella*), Ein Sänger (*Rosenkavalier*); STRAVINSKY: Pêcheur (*Rossignol*); TCHAIKOVSKY: Lenski★ (*Eugene Onegin*); VERDI: Riccardo★ (*Ballo in maschera*), Fenton★ (*Falstaff*), Carlo (*Giovanna d'Arco*), Oronte★ (*Lombardi*), Rodolfo★ (*Luisa Miller*), Duca di Mantova★ (*Rigoletto*), Alfredo★ (*Traviata*). Also lead ten roles in BUSONI: (*Sposa sorteggiata*); DONIZETTI: (*Belisario*); WOLF-FERRARI: (*Vedova scaltra*); ROTA: (*Cappello di paglia di Firenze*); REFICE: (*Margherita da Cortona*). **World premieres:** MUSCO: Tancredi (*Gattopardo*) Teatro Massimo, Palermo 1967. Video/Film: (*Manon*); (*Arlecchino*). **Res:** Padova 9, Milan, Italy.

GARAZZI, PEYO; né Pierre Etcheverry. Lyric tenor. French. Born 31 Mar 1937, St Jean Pied de Port, France. Wife Martine Liotard, occupation prof of history. Studied: Mme Barsac, Bordeaux; Mme Reiss, Paris. **Debut:** Nadir (*Pêcheurs de perles*) Opéra Royal de Ghent, Brussels 1962.
Sang with major companies in BEL: Liège; FRA: Bordeaux, Paris; FR GER: Munich Staatsoper; GER DR: Berlin Komische Oper. **Roles with these companies incl** BEETHOVEN: Florestan (*Fidelio*); BERLIOZ: Faust (*Damnation de Faust*); BIZET: Nadir★ (*Pêcheurs de perles*); DELIBES: Gérald (*Lakmé*); DONIZETTI: Fernand (*Favorite*), Edgardo★ (*Lucia*); GIORDANO: Andrea Chénier★; GLUCK: Orfeo★; GOUNOD: Faust★, Vincent (*Mireille*), Roméo★; MASCAGNI: Turiddu★ (*Cavalleria rusticana*); MASSENET: Des Grieux★ (*Manon*), Jean (*Sappho*), Nicias (*Thaïs*), Werther★; OFFENBACH: Hoffmann; PUC-

CINI: Rodolfo (*Bohème*), Pinkerton★ (*Butterfly*), Cavaradossi★ (*Tosca*); SCHOENBERG: Aron★; THOMAS: Wilhelm Meister (*Mignon*); VERDI: Duca di Mantova★ (*Rigoletto*), Alfredo (*Traviata*). Appears with symphony orchestra. **Res**: 12 rue des Dames, 75017 Paris, France.

GARCISANZ, ISABEL; née Garcia. Lyric soprano. French. Born 29 Jun 1934, Madrid. Divorced. Studied: Angeles Ottein, Madrid; Erik Werba, Vienna. **Debut:** Comtesse Adèle (*Comte Ory*) Volksoper, Vienna 1964. Previous occupations: studied piano and acting. Awards: First Prize in Voice, Royal Consv Madrid.
  Sang with major companies in FRA: Bordeaux, Lyon, Marseille, Nancy, Nice, Strasbourg, Toulouse; FR GER: Cologne; SPA: Barcelona; UK: Glyndebourne Fest, London English National; USA: Miami. **Roles with these companies incl** BECAUD: Maureen (*Opéra d'Aran*); BEETHOVEN: Marzelline★ (*Fidelio*); CAVALLI: Erisbe★ (*Ormindo*); DONIZETTI: Adina (*Elisir*); FALLA: Salud (*Vida breve*); GRANADOS: Rosario (*Goyescas*); HANDEL: Ruggiero (*Alcina*); MILHAUD: Femme (*Pauvre matelot*); MONTEVERDI: Poppea (*Incoronazione di Poppea*); MOZART: Vitellia (*Clemenza di Tito*), Fiordiligi★ (*Così fan tutte*), Donna Elvira★ & Zerlina (*Don Giovanni*), Arminda & Serpetta (*Finta giardiniera*), Contessa★ & Cherubino (*Nozze di Figaro*); OFFENBACH: Périchole★; POULENC: Blanche (*Dialogues des Carmélites*); PUCCINI: Mimi★ (*Bohème*); RAVEL: Concepcion★ (*Heure espagnole*); ROSSINI: Rosina★ (*Barbiere di Siviglia*), Comtesse Adèle (*Comte Ory*), Desdemona (*Otello*), Zaida (*Turco in Italia*). Also PAER: Gertrude‡ (*Maître de chapelle*). **World premieres:** NIKIPROWETZKY: Jeune fille (*Noces d'ombre*) Toulouse 1974; CASANOVA: Comtesse (*Bonheur dans le crime*) Toulouse 1973; DELERUE: Dara (*Médis et Alyssio*) Strasbourg 1975. Recorded for: ORTF. Gives recitals. Appears with symphony orchestra. **Res**: 3 rue Robert Le Coin, Paris, France. **Mgmt**: RAP/FRA; ASK/UK.

GARD, ROBERT JOSEPH. Lyric tenor. British. Resident mem: Australian Opera, Sydney. Born 7 Mar 1927, Padstow/Cornwall, UK. Wife Doreen Morrow, occupation operatic lyric soprano. Two sons. Studied: Guildhall School of Music and Drama, Prof Walter Hyde, London; Mo Dino Borgioli, London; Prof Fritz Philipsborn, Mme Florence Wiese Norberg, Sydney. **Debut:** Duke (*Rigoletto*) Engl Opera Group, London 1958. Previous occupations: sales clerk in menswear. Awards: Command Perf before HRH Queen Elizabeth II, London Palladium 1954; schlshp Guildhall School of Music, London.
  Sang with major companies in AUSTRL: Sydney; UK: Aldeburgh Fest, Cardiff Welsh. **Roles with these companies incl** BEETHOVEN: Florestan (*Fidelio*); BERLIOZ: Faust (*Damnation de Faust*); BRITTEN: Albert Herring, Male Chorus★ (*Rape of Lucretia*), Peter Quint (*Turn of the Screw*); CHARPENTIER: Julien; DONIZETTI: Ernesto (*Don Pasquale*); HANDEL: Acis; JANACEK: Steva (*Jenufa*); MASSENET: Des Grieux (*Manon*); MOZART: Ferrando (*Così fan tutte*), Don Ottavio (*Don Giovanni*), Tamino (*Zauberflöte*); MUSSORGSKY: Shuisky (*Boris*

Godunov); PROKOFIEV: Anatole (*War and Peace*); ROSSINI: Almaviva (*Barbiere di Siviglia*); STRAUSS, J: Eisenstein & Alfred (*Fledermaus*); STRAUSS, R: Narraboth (*Salome*); STRAVINSKY: Tom Rakewell (*Rake's Progress*); WAGNER: Walther v d Vogelweide (*Tannhäuser*); WEILL: Jim Mahoney (*Aufstieg und Fall der Stadt Mahagonny*). **World premieres:** SUTHERLAND: Goonavil (*Young Kabari*) Elizabethan Trust Opera, Hobart, Australia 1965; WERDER: Sir Reginald (*Affair*) Australian Opera, Sydney 1974. Video—ABC TV Sydney: Julien (*Louise*); Des Grieux (*Manon*); Anatole (*War and Peace*). Gives recitals. Appears with symphony orchestra. **Res**: 26 Campbell St, Balmain Sydney, NSW 2041, Australia.

GARDELLI, LAMBERTO. Conductor of opera and symphony; composer. Italian. Music Dir & Resident Cond, Stadttheater Bern, Switzerland 1968- . Born 1915, Venice. Studied: Liceo Musicale Rossini, Pesaro; Acad Rome; incl piano, double bass. Awards: Orphée d'Or de l'Académie Ntl du Disque Lyrique 1963; Edison Prize 1970; Toscanini Prize 1965.
  Conducted with major companies in DEN: Copenhagen; FIN: Helsinki; FR GER: Berlin Deutsche Oper, Cologne; HOL: Amsterdam; HUN: Budapest; ITA: Bologna, Florence Comunale, Naples, Rome Opera, Trieste; SWE: Drottningholm Fest, Stockholm; UK: Glyndebourne Fest, London Royal; USA: New York Met; et al. **Operas with these companies incl** BELLINI: *Norma;* BIZET: *Carmen;* CHERUBINI: *Medea‡;* DONIZETTI: *Anna Bolena, Don Pasquale, Lucia;* GIORDANO: *Andrea Chénier;* LEONCAVALLO: *Pagliacci;* MASCAGNI: *Cavalleria rusticana;* MOZART: *Clemenza di Tito;* ORFF: *Carmina burana;* PONCHIELLI: *Gioconda‡;* PUCCINI: *Gianni Schicchi‡, Suor Angelica‡, Tabarro‡;* ROSSINI: *Guillaume Tell‡, Moïse;* VERDI: *Aida, Falstaff, Forza del destino‡, Lombardi‡, Macbeth‡, Nabucco‡, Otello, Rigoletto, Traviata, Trovatore;* et al. On records only VERDI: *Attila, Giorno di regno.* Recorded for Decca, HMV-SLS, Philips.

GARNER, LETITIA NORRIS. Dramatic coloratura soprano. American. Resident mem: Hessisches Staatstheater, Wiesbaden. Born 23 Jan 1943, Washington DC. Single. Studied: Univ of Washington, Mary Curtis-Verna, Leon Lishner, Seattle; Univ of Michigan, John McCollum, Ann Arbor; Anna Hamlin, New York.
  Sang with major companies in FR GER: Wiesbaden; ISR: Tel Aviv; POL: Warsaw; USA: Seattle. **Roles with these companies incl** DONIZETTI: Norina★ (*Don Pasquale*), Lucia★; FLOTOW: Lady Harriet (*Martha*); MASSENET: Aurore (*Portrait de Manon*); MENOTTI: Laetitia (*Old Maid and the Thief*); MOZART: Konstanze★ (*Entführung aus dem Serail*), Königin der Nacht★ (*Zauberflöte*); PUCCINI: Mimi★ (*Bohème*), Lauretta★ (*Gianni Schicchi*), Suor Angelica; ROSSINI: Rosina★ (*Barbiere di Siviglia*); SMETANA: Marie★ (*Bartered Bride*); STRAUSS, R: Sophie★ (*Rosenkavalier*). Gives recitals. Appears with symphony orchestra. **Res**: Stiftstr 2, 62 Wiesbaden, FR Ger. Mgmt: SLZ/FRG.

GARRARD, DON; né Donald Edward Burdett Garrard. Bass. Canadian. Born 31 Jul 1931, Vancouver, BC, Canada. Divorced. One daughter. Studied: Consv of Music, Vancouver, BC; Royal Consv of Music, Toronto; Music Acad of the West, Santa Barbara, CA, USA; Luigi Borgonovo, Milan. **Debut:** Sprecher (*Zauberflöte*) Canadian Opera Co, Toronto 1952. Awards: Canada Council Sr Arts Fllshp; CBC Singing Stars of Tomorrow; Best Classical Singer CBC TV; Nos Futures Etoiles, CBC; Prize, Vercelli Concorso, Italy.

Sang with major companies in CAN: Ottawa, Toronto; FR GER: Hamburg; S AFR: Johannesburg; SWE: Drottningholm Fest; UK: Aldeburgh Fest, Cardiff Welsh, Edinburgh Fest, Glasgow Scottish, Glyndebourne Fest, London Royal Opera & English National; USA: Santa Fe, Washington DC. Roles with these companies incl BARTOK: Bluebeard★; BEETHOVEN: Rocco (*Fidelio*); BERLIOZ: Balducci (*Benvenuto Cellini*), Méphistophélès★ (*Damnation de Faust*), Narbal (*Troyens*); BRITTEN: Sir Walter Raleigh (*Gloriana*); DALLAPICCOLA: Riviere (*Volo di notte*); DEBUSSY: Arkel★ (*Pelléas et Mélisande*); DONIZETTI: Talbot★ (*Maria Stuarda*); GOUNOD: Méphistophélès (*Faust*); HANDEL: Zoroastro (*Orlando furioso*); MENOTTI: John Sorel (*Consul*); MOZART: Guglielmo (*Così fan tutte*), Don Giovanni, Sarastro★ (*Zauberflöte*); MUSSORGSKY: Boris★ & Pimen (*Boris Godunov*); PROKOFIEV: King of Clubs (*Love for Three Oranges*); VERDI: Ramfis★ (*Aida*), Attila, Grande Inquisitore (*Don Carlo*), Silva (*Ernani*), Padre Guardiano★ (*Forza del destino*); WAGNER: Daland★ (*Fliegende Holländer*), Wotan (*Rheingold★, Walküre★*), Wanderer★ (*Siegfried*), Hunding★ (*Walküre*). Also PIZZETTI: Becket (*Assassinio nella cattedrale*); HANDEL: King Ernando (*Scipio*); DONIZETTI: Raimondo★ (*Lucia*); STRAVINSKY: Trulove (*Rake's Progress*). World premieres: BRITTEN: Abbot (*Curlew River*) Aldeburgh Fest 1964. Recorded for: Columbia, EMI. Video—CBC TV: Don Giovanni; BBC: Gremin (*Eugene Onegin*). Gives recitals. Appears with symphony orchestra. **Res:** The Bont, Teffont Evias, Wiltshire, UK. Mgmt: AIM/UK; SMN/USA.

GATTO, ARMANDO. Conductor of opera and symphony. Italian. Born 29 Dec 1928, Taranto, Italy. Wife Irene Garifalaki, occupation opera singer. Studied: Maestri Bedini, Calace, Paribeni, Bergamo & Milan; incl piano. Plays the piano. Operatic training as repetiteur & asst cond. **Operatic debut:** *Cappuccin* Fest Novità, Teatro Donizetti, Bergamo, Italy 1958. Symphonic debut: Orch Accad S Cecilia, Rome 1962. Previous adm positions in opera: Art Dir, Arena di Verona 1972-74.

Conducted with major companies in BUL: Sofia; FRA: Toulouse; ITA: Bologna, Genoa, Milan La Scala, Parma, Trieste, Turin, Venice. Operas with these companies incl BELLINI: Puritani★; DALLAPICCOLA: Prigioniero, Volo di notte; DONIZETTI: Lucia★; GIORDANO: Fedora; MASCAGNI: Cavalleria rusticana; MENOTTI: Amelia al ballo; MOZART: Nozze di Figaro; PUCCINI: Bohème★, Gianni Schicchi★, Butterfly★, Turandot★; ROUSSEAU: Devin du village; VERDI: Aida★, Ballo in maschera★, Don Carlo★, Ernani★, Falstaff, Macbeth★ Nabucco, Otello★, Rigoletto★, Traviata★, Trovatore★; WOLF-FERRARI: Segreto di Susanna. World premieres: FERRARI: Cappuccin 1958; BETTINELLI: Pozzo e il pendolo 1967; both at Bergamo. Conducted major orch in Europe, & Cent/S America. **Res:** V Zanella 43, Milan, Italy.

GAVAZZENI, GIANANDREA. Conductor of opera; composer. Italian. Resident Cond, Teatro alla Scala, Milan. Born 25 Jul 1909, Bergamo. Studied: Milan Consv, Pizzetti & Pilati. Previous adm positions in opera: Art Dir, La Scala, Milan 1967-72.

Conducted with major companies in ARG: Buenos Aires; AUS: Salzburg Fest, Vienna Staatsoper; HUN: Budapest; ITA: Florence Maggio, Milan La Scala, Naples, Palermo, Rome Opera, Trieste, Turin, Venice, Verona Arena; MON: Monte Carlo; SWE: Stockholm; SWI: Geneva; USA: Chicago; et al. Operas with these companies incl BELLINI: Norma, Pirata‡; CATALANI: Wally; CILEA: A. Lecouvreur; DONIZETTI: Elisir‡, Favorite, Linda di Chamounix, Lucia, Maria di Rohan; GIORDANO: Andrea Chénier‡; GLUCK: Alceste; GOUNOD: Faust; MEYERBEER: Huguenots‡; MUSSORGSKY: Boris Godunov, Khovanshchina; PONCHIELLI: Gioconda‡; PUCCINI: Bohème, Fanciulla del West, Butterfly‡, Manon Lescaut, Tosca, Turandot; ROSSINI: Elisabetta Regina; STRAVINSKY: Mavra; VERDI: Aida, Ballo in maschera‡, Don Carlo, Falstaff, Forza del destino, Lombardi, Macbeth, Masnadieri, Nabucco, Otello, Rigoletto‡, Simon Boccanegra‡, Traviata, Trovatore, Vespri; et al. Also GHEDINI: Pulce d'oro; DONIZETTI: Belisario; PIZZETTI: Straniero; GIORDANO: Mme Sans-Gêne; on records only MASCAGNI: Amico Fritz. Recorded for DG, Everest-Cetra, RCA, Angel, London.

GAVAZZI, ERNESTO. Lyric tenor (leggero). Italian. Born 7 May 1941, Seregno, Italy. Single. Studied: Civic School, Milan, Mo Bruno Carmassi; School of Teatro alla Scala, Mo Vladimiro Badiali. **Debut:** Nemorino (*Elisir*) Teatro di Treviso 1971. Awards: Stpd, Autunno Musicale Trevigiano.

Sang with major companies in BEL: Brussels; ITA: Genoa, Milan La Scala. Roles with these companies incl BELLINI: Elvino (*Sonnambula*); CIMAROSA: Paolino (*Matrimonio segreto*); DONIZETTI: Nemorino★ (*Elisir*); MONTEVERDI: Ulisse (*Ritorno d'Ulisse*); ROSSINI: Almaviva★ (*Barbiere di Siviglia*), Edward Milfort★ (*Cambiale di matrimonio*), Don Ramiro★ (*Cenerentola*), Giocondo★ (*Pietra del paragone*). Also CIMAROSA: Valerio (*Marito disperato*). **Res:** V Adda 23, Seregno, Italy.

GAYER, CATHERINE. Coloratura soprano. American. Resident mem: Deutsche Oper, Berlin, FR Ger. Born Los Angeles, USA. Husband Abraham Ashkenasi, occupation professor. Two children. Studied: Univ of Cal in Los Angeles & L A City Coll; Tynni Walo Gayer, Prof Leonard Stein, Hugo Strelitzer, Los Angeles; Musikhochschule, Berlin. **Debut:** Companion (*Intolleranza*) La Fenice, Venice 1961. Awards: First Prize, San Francisco Op Aud; Fulbright Schlshp; Kammersängerin, City of Berlin.

Sang with major companies in AUS: Salzburg

Fest, Vienna Staatsoper; FR GER: Berlin Deutsche Oper, Cologne, Düsseldorf-Duisburg, Frankfurt, Hamburg, Mannheim, Munich Staatsoper; HOL: Amsterdam; ITA: Milan La Scala; POR: Lisbon; UK: Edinburgh Fest, Glasgow, London Royal. **Roles with these companies incl** BERG: Lulu⋆; CIMAROSA: Carolina⋆ (*Matrimonio segreto*); DEBUSSY: Mélisande; DONIZETTI: Lucia⋆; GLUCK: Amor (*Orfeo ed Euridice*); HANDEL: Semele; HENZE: Hilda Mack⋆ (*Elegy for Young Lovers*); MOZART: Despina⋆ (*Così fan tutte*), Konstanze⋆ (*Entführung aus dem Serail*), Susanna⋆ & Cherubino⋆ (*Nozze di Figaro*), Königin der Nacht⋆ (*Zauberflöte*); ORFF: Solo⋆ (*Carmina burana*); PUCCINI: Musetta⋆ (*Bohème*); REIMANN: Melusine⋆; RIMSKY-KORSAKOV: Reine de Schemakan⋆ (*Coq d'or*); ROSSINI: Rosina⋆ (*Barbiere di Siviglia*), Fiorilla⋆ (*Turco in Italia*); STRAUSS, R: Zdenka⋆ (*Arabella*), Zerbinetta (*Ariadne auf Naxos*), Sophie⋆ (*Rosenkavalier*), Aminta⋆ (*Schweigsame Frau*); TIPPETT: Jennifer (*Midsummer Marriage*); VERDI: Oscar (*Ballo in maschera*), Nannetta (*Falstaff*), Gilda (*Rigoletto*); YUN: Yu-Chan (*Traum des Liu-Tung*); ZIMMERMANN: Marie⋆ (*Soldaten*). **World premieres:** ORR: Christina (*Hermiston*) Scottish Opera, Edinburgh Fest 1975; DALLAPICCOLA: Nausikaa (*Ulisse*) Berlin 1968; NONO: Companion (*Intolleranza*) Fenice, Venice 1961; HAUBENSTOCK-RAMATI: (*Amerika*) Deutsche Oper Berlin 1966; REIMANN: Melusine, Schwetzingen Fest 1971; HUBER: (*Jot, oder Wann kommt der Herr zurück*) Berlin Fest 1974. Recorded for: DG, Archive. Video/Film: Julietta. Gives recitals. Appears with symphony orchestra. Mgmt: AIM/UK.

GAYLER, WOLFGANG. Conductor of opera and symphony. German. First Cond, Musiktheater, Nürnberg 1965- . Born 19 Dec 1934, Stuttgart. Wife Lelia Doflein. Four children. Studied: Hochschule für Musik, Freiburg, Prof C Ueter; incl piano, double bass and voice. Plays the piano. Operatic training as repetiteur & asst cond at Städt Bühnen Freiburg 1961-65; Bayreuth Fest 1969-71. **Operatic debut:** MONTEVERDI: *Favola d'Orfeo* Städt Bühnen Freiburg, FR Ger 1964. Symphonic debut: Collegium Musicum, Pommersfelden, FR Ger 1966. Previous occupations: pianist. Awards: Kranichsteiner Musikpreis 1958, Music Inst Darmstadt.

Conducted with major companies in FRA: Nancy; FR GER: Frankfurt, Kiel, Nürnberg; ITA: Florence Comunale. **Operas with these companies incl** BARTOK: *Bluebeard's Castle;* BEETHOVEN: *Fidelio;* BERG: *Wozzeck⋆;* BIZET: *Carmen⋆;* BUSONI: *Arlecchino;* DESSAU: *Verurteilung des Lukullus;* DONIZETTI: *Don Pasquale;* EGK: *Verlobung in San Domingo;* GLUCK: *Orfeo ed Euridice;* GOUNOD: *Faust;* HENZE: *Junge Lord;* HINDEMITH: *Mathis der Maler;* HUMPERDINCK: *Hänsel und Gretel⋆;* JANACEK: *From the House of the Dead⋆, Jenufa;* LEONCAVALLO: *Pagliacci;* LORTZING: *Waffenschmied, Wildschütz⋆, Zar und Zimmermann;* MONTEVERDI: *Favola d'Orfeo, Incoronazione di Poppea⋆;* MOZART: *Così fan tutte⋆, Don Giovanni⋆, Entführung aus dem Serail⋆, Nozze di Figaro, Zauberflöte⋆;* MUS-

SORGSKY: *Boris Godunov⋆;* PUCCINI: *Butterfly;* SCHOENBERG: *Moses und Aron⋆;* STRAUSS, J: *Fledermaus;* STRAUSS, R: *Ariadne auf Naxos, Capriccio, Elektra⋆, Frau ohne Schatten⋆, Rosenkavalier, Salome⋆;* TCHAIKOVSKY: *Pique Dame⋆;* THOMAS: *Mignon;* VERDI: *Don Carlo, Falstaff⋆, Forza del destino, Nabucco⋆, Otello, Rigoletto, Traviata, Trovatore⋆;* WAGNER: *Fliegende Holländer, Lohengrin⋆, Meistersinger, Siegfried, Tannhäuser⋆, Tristan und Isolde;* WEBER: *Freischütz;* YUN: *Traum des Liu-Tung⋆, Witwe des Schmetterlings⋆;* ZIMMERMANN: *Soldaten⋆.* Also NONO: *Intolleranza⋆;* HENZE: *Floss der Medusa⋆;* YUN: *Geisterliebe⋆;* HANDEL: *Agrippina.* **Res:** Haimendorfer Str 14, Nürnberg, FR Ger.

GEDDA, NICOLAI H G. Lirico spinto tenor. Swedish. Born 11 Jul 1925, Stockholm. Wife Anastasia. One daughter. Studied: Carl Martin Oehman, Stockholm; Paola Novikova, New York. **Debut:** Chapelou (*Postillon de Lonjumeau*) Royal Opera, Stockholm 1952. Previous occupations: bank clerk. Awards: Litteris et Artibus: 2 Vasa-Order by King Gustav VI Adolph; Dannebrogen (Danish) by King Frederik IX; Royal Court Singer, Swedish Govnmt.

Sang with major companies in ARG: Buenos Aires; AUS: Salzburg Fest, Vienna Staatsoper & Volksoper; CAN: Montreal/Quebec, Toronto; DEN: Copenhagen; FIN: Helsinki; FRA: Aix-en-Provence Fest, Bordeaux, Lyon, Orange Fest, Paris; FR GER: Berlin Deutsche Oper, Frankfurt, Hamburg, Munich Staatsoper, Stuttgart, Wiesbaden; HOL: Amsterdam; HUN: Budapest; ITA: Florence Maggio & Comunale, Milan La Scala, Naples, Rome Opera, Venice; MON: Monte Carlo; POR: Lisbon; SWE: Drottningholm Fest, Stockholm; SWI: Geneva; UK: Cardiff Welsh, Edinburgh Fest, London Royal Opera; USA: Baltimore, Boston, Chicago, Cincinnati Summer Opera, Fort Worth, Hartford, Houston Grand, Newark, New Orleans, New York Metropolitan, Philadelphia Grand & Lyric, Pittsburgh, San Antonio, San Francisco Opera, Washington DC; YUG: Dubrovnik, Zagreb, Belgrade. **Roles with these companies incl** ADAM: Chapelou (*Postillon de Lonjumeau*); AUBER: Fra Diavolo; BARBER: Anatol‡ (*Vanessa*); BELLINI: Tebaldo‡ (*Capuleti ed i Montecchi*), Lord Arthur‡ (*Puritani*), Elvino‡ (*Sonnambula*); BERLIOZ: Benvenuto Cellini‡, Faust‡ (*Damnation de Faust*), Aeneas‡ (*Troyens*); BIZET: Don José⋆‡ (*Carmen*), Nadir‡ (*Pêcheurs de perles*); BOIELDIEU: George Brown (*Dame blanche*); CIMAROSA: Paolino (*Matrimonio segreto*); CORNELIUS: Nurreddin† (*Barbier von Bagdad*); DEBUSSY: Pelléas; DONIZETTI: Nemorino⋆‡, Edgardo (*Lucia*); FLOTOW: Lionel‡ (*Martha*); GLINKA: Sobinin‡ (*Life for the Tsar*); GLUCK: Admetos (*Alceste*), Nuradin‡ (*Cadi dupé*), Pylade‡ (*Iphigénie en Tauride*), Orfeo; GOUNOD: Faust⋆‡, Vincent‡ (*Mireille*), Roméo‡; HANDEL: Acis; HAYDN: Orfeo; MARTIN: Tristan (*Vin herbé*); MASSENET: Des Grieux⋆‡ (*Manon*), Werther‡; MENOTTI: Kodanda (*Dernier sauvage*); MEYERBEER: Raoul de Nangis (*Huguenots*), Jean de Leyde (*Prophète*); MOZART: Tito‡ (*Clemenza di Tito*), Ferrando‡ (*Così fan tutte*), Don Ottavio⋆‡ (*Don Giovanni*), Belmonte‡ (*Entfüh-*

rung aus dem Serail), Idamante & Idomeneo‡ (*Idomeneo*), Tamino‡ (*Zauberflöte*); MUSSORGSKY: Dimitri‡ (*Boris Godunov*); OFFENBACH: Hoffmann∗‡, Guillot (*Mariage aux lanternes*); PFITZNER: Palestrina‡; PUCCINI: Rodolfo (*Bohème*), Pinkerton‡ (*Butterfly*), Cavaradossi (*Tosca*); ROSSINI: Almaviva‡ (*Barbiere di Siviglia*), Arnold∗‡ (*Guillaume Tell*), Narciso‡ (*Turco in Italia*); ROUSSEAU: Colin‡ (*Devin du Village*); STRAUSS, J: Eisenstein‡ (*Fledermaus*); STRAUSS, R: Flamand‡ (*Capriccio*), Ein Sänger‡ (*Rosenkavalier*); STRAVINSKY: Oedipus, Eumolpe‡ (*Perséphone*); TCHAIKOVSKY: Lenski (*Eugene Onegin*), Gherman∗‡ (*Pique Dame*); VERDI: Riccardo (*Ballo in maschera*), Duca di Mantova∗‡ (*Rigoletto*), Alfredo∗‡ (*Traviata*), Arrigo∗‡ (*Vespri*); WAGNER: Lohengrin; WEBER: Abu Hassan‡, Adolar‡ (*Euryanthe*), Max‡ (*Freischütz*), Hüon‡ (*Oberon*). Also ORFF: Sposo (*Trionfo di Afrodite*); LULLY: (*Armide*); LIEBERMANN: (*Schule der Frauen*). **World premieres:** BARBER: Anatol (*Vanessa*) Metropolitan Opera, New York 1958. Recorded for: EMI, Philips, DG. Video/Film: Tamino (*Zauberflöte*); Paolino (*Matrimonio segreto*). Gives recitals. Appears with symphony orchestra. **Res:** Tolochenaz, Switzerland. **Mgmt:** ADL/SWE; HUR/USA; RAB/AUS; GLZ/FRA; SMD/FRG; ASK/UK.

GEIGER-TOREL, HERMAN B; né Geiger. Stages/produces opera, theater, film (Paris 1937) & television. Also designs stage-lighting and is an actor and author. Canadian. Gen Dir & Resident Stage Dir, Canadian Opera Co, Toronto, Ont 1959-76. Born 13 Jul 1907, Frankfurt/M, Germany. Wife Eleonore. Studied: Dr Lothar Wallerstein, Frankfurt/M; Rosy Geiger-Kullmann; Annie Steiger-Betzak; Dr Hoch's Consv, Alfred Auerbach, Frankfurt; incl music, piano & violin. Operatic training as asst stage dir at Opera House, Frankfurt/M 1928-30; Salzburg Fest 1930. **Operatic debut:** *Puppe von Nürnberg* Opera School, Frankfurt/M 1927. Theater debut: Free German Stage, Buenos Aires, Argentina 1940. Previous occupation: teacher Frankfurt/M 1928-30; actor Buenos Aires 1940, Rio de Janeiro 1944. Awards: Hon DL Prince of Wales Coll, Canada; Centennial Medal Gvnmt of Canada 1967; Service Medal of the Order of Canada 1969; Univ of Alberta Ntl Awd. Previous adm positions in opera: Chief Stage Dir, Montevideo 1943-45, Rio de Janeiro 1946-47; Act Art Dir, Rio de Janeiro 1945-47; Art Adv, CBC Radio & TV 1950-59; Art Dir, Canadian Opera Co 1950-58.

Directed/produced opera for major companies in ARG: Buenos Aires; BRA: Rio de Janeiro; CAN: Montreal/Quebec, Toronto, Vancouver; FR GER: Frankfurt; USA: Cincinnati, New York City Opera, Portland. **Operas staged with these companies incl** d'ALBERT: *Tiefland;* BEETHOVEN: *Fidelio;* BELLINI: *Sonnambula;* BIZET: *Carmen∗;* BRITTEN: *Albert Herring, Peter Grimes, Rape of Lucretia;* CHARPENTIER: *Louise;* DONIZETTI: *Don Pasquale∗, Elisir, Lucia;* GIORDANO: *Andrea Chénier;* GLUCK: *Orfeo ed Euridice;* GOUNOD: *Faust, Roméo et Juliette;* HINDEMITH: *Hin und zurück;* HUMPERDINCK: *Hänsel und Gretel;* IBERT: *Angélique;* LEONCAVALLO: *Pagliacci;* MARTINU: *Comedy on the Bridge;* MASCA-

GNI: *Cavalleria rusticana;* MASSENET: *Manon, Werther;* MENOTTI: *Amahl, Consul∗, Medium, Old Maid and the Thief, Telephone;* MILHAUD: *Pauvre matelot;* MONTEVERDI: *Combattimento di Tancredi, Incoronazione di Poppea;* MOZART: *Così fan tutte∗, Don Giovanni∗, Entführung aus dem Serail, Nozze di Figaro, Zauberflöte;* MUSSORGSKY: *Boris Godunov∗;* NICOLAI: *Lustigen Weiber;* OFFENBACH: *Contes d'Hoffmann, Mariage aux lanternes;* ORFF: *Kluge;* PERGOLESI: *Serva padrona;* PUCCINI: *Bohème∗, Fanciulla del West, Gianni Schicchi, Butterfly, Manon Lescaut, Suor Angelica, Tabarro, Tosca;* ROSSINI: *Barbiere di Siviglia;* SAINT-SAENS: *Samson et Dalila;* SMETANA: *Bartered Bride, Secret;* STRAUSS, J: *Fledermaus∗;* STRAUSS, R: *Arabella, Ariadne auf Naxos, Elektra, Rosenkavalier, Salome;* THOMAS: *Mignon;* VAUGHAN WILLIAMS: *Riders to the Sea;* VERDI: *Aida∗, Ballo in maschera, Falstaff, Forza del destino, Macbeth, Otello, Rigoletto, Simon Boccanegra, Traviata, Trovatore;* WAGNER: *Fliegende Holländer∗, Lohengrin, Meistersinger, Parsifal, Rheingold, Walküre∗, Siegfried∗, Götterdämmerung∗, Tannhäuser, Tristan und Isolde;* WEBER: *Oberon;* WEINBERGER: *Schwanda;* WOLF: *Corregidor;* WOLF-FERRARI: *Quattro rusteghi, Segreto di Susanna.* Also KIENZL: *Evangelimann;* WAGNER-REGENY: *Günstling;* REUTTER: *Dr Johannes Faust;* CATALANI: *Loreley;* SCHUBERT: *Weiberverschwörung;* WEILL: *Down in the Valley;* BENJAMIN: *Prima Donna;* d'ALBERT: *Toten Augen;* GOMES: *Schiavo, Guarany, Salvator Rosa, Maria Petrovna.* **Operatic world premieres:** PANNELL: *Luck of Ginger Coffey, Aria da capo;* WILLAN: *Deirdre;* all Canadian Op Co. Operatic Video – CBC: *Don Giovanni, Nozze di Figaro, Tosca, Carmen, Peter Grimes, Eugene Onegin, Telephone, Consul, Gianni Schicchi, Down in the Valley, Fledermaus, Opera Backstage, Barbiere di Siviglia.* **Opera libretti:** CSONKA: *SOS* Cuban Radio, Havana 1949-50; *Opera Backstage* Toronto 1950. Teaches at Opera Dept, Univ of Toronto, Canada 1948. **Res:** 350 Lonsdale Rd, Toronto, Ont M5P 1R6, Canada.

GEIST, GERHARD. Conductor of opera and symphony. German. Resident Cond, Städtische Oper, Frankfurt/Main. Born 16 May 1932, Ansbach. Wife Urszula Koszut, occupation coloratura soprano. One child. Studied: Acad of Music, Munich; incl cond Prof Fritz Lehmann, piano Prof Rosl Schmid. Plays the piano. Operatic training as repetiteur, asst cond & chorus master at Wuppertal Opera 1958-67; Landestheater Linz, Austria 1961-67. **Operatic debut:** Städtische Oper, Frankfurt 1957. Symphonic debut: Landesorch, Linz 1962. Awards: Richard Strauss Prize, City of Munich 1956.

Conducted with major companies in FR GER: Dortmund, Frankfurt, Stuttgart, Wuppertal; POL: Warsaw. **Operas with these companies incl** AUBER: *Fra Diavolo;* CIMAROSA: *Matrimonio segreto∗;* DONIZETTI: *Don Pasquale∗, Elisir;* FLOTOW: *Martha;* GLUCK: *Orfeo ed Euridice∗;* HUMPERDINCK: *Hänsel und Gretel∗;* MONTEVERDI: *Favola d'Orfeo;* MOZART: *Così fan tutte∗, Entführung aus dem Serail∗,*

Nozze di Figaro★*, Zauberflöte*★*;* OFFENBACH: *Contes d'Hoffmann*★*;* PUCCINI: *Bohème*★*, Butterfly*★*, Manon Lescaut, Turandot;* ROSSINI: *Barbiere di Siviglia*★*;* SMETANA: *Bartered Bride*★*;* STRAUSS, J: *Fledermaus*★*;* STRAUSS, R: *Arabella;* VERDI: *Ballo in maschera, Don Carlo, Otello, Rigoletto, Traviata, Trovatore;* WAGNER: *Fliegende Holländer, Meistersinger.* Also HARTMANN: *Simplicius Simplicissimus.* Conducted major orch in Europe. **Res:** Rothschildallee 18, Frankfurt/Main, FR Ger. **Mgmt:** PAS/FRG.

GELIOT, MICHAEL. Stages/produces opera, theater & television and is an author & translator. British. Art Dir & Resident Stage Dir, Welsh National Opera, Cardiff, UK. Born 27 Sep 1933, London. Wife Diana, occupation probation officer. Two children. Studied: Cambridge Univ; also piano. Operatic training as asst stage dir at Sadler's Wells & Glyndebourne Fest 1959-62. **Operatic debut:** BURT: *Volpone* Sadler's Wells, London 1960. Theater debut: English Stage Company, London 1959. Awards: Barcelona Critics Awd, best dir 1974-75.

Directed/produced opera for major companies in CAN: Ottawa; FR GER: Kassel, Munich Staatsoper; HOL: Amsterdam; SPA: Barcelona; SWI: Geneva; UK: Welsh National, Scottish, Glyndebourne Fest, London Royal & English National. **Operas staged with these companies incl** BEETHOVEN: *Fidelio*★*;* BELLINI: *Pirata;* BERG: *Lulu*★*, Wozzeck*★*;* BERLIOZ: *Damnation de Faust;* BIZET: *Carmen*★*, Pêcheurs de perles;* BRITTEN: *Albert Herring, Billy Budd*★*;* DONIZETTI: *Elisir*★*;* GOUNOD: *Faust;* HENZE: *Boulevard Solitude;* HINDEMITH: *Cardillac;* MOZART: *Così fan tutte*★*, Don Giovanni*★*, Entführung aus dem Serail*★*, Idomeneo*★*, Nozze di Figaro*★*, Zauberflöte*★*;* MUSSORGSKY: *Boris Godunov;* PUCCINI: *Turandot*★*;* ROSSINI: *Turco in Italia;* STRAUSS, J: *Fledermaus*★*;* TCHAIKOVSKY: *Eugene Onegin*★*;* VERDI: *Aida*★*, Don Carlo*★*, Giorno di regno, Nabucco*★*, Rigoletto;* WAGNER: *Tristan und Isolde*★*;* WEILL: *Aufstieg und Fall der Stadt Mahagonny.* **Operatic world premieres:** MAXWELL-DAVIES: *Taverner* Covent Garden, London 1972; ORR: *Full Circle* Scottish Opera, Glasgow 1968; JOUBERT: *Under Western Eyes* New Opera Co, London 1969; HODDINOTT: *Beach of Falesa* Welsh National, Cardiff 1974. Operatic Video—Netherlands TV: *Change the World.* Previous leading positions with major theater companies: Art Dir, Welsh Drama Co, Cardiff 1971-75. **Opera libretti:** transl *Zauberflöte, Mahagonny.* **Res:** London/Cardiff, UK. **Mgmt:** HPL/UK; SLZ/FRG.

GENCER, LEYLA. Dramatic coloratura soprano. Turkish. Born 10 Oct 1928, Istanbul. Husband Ibrahim Gencer, occupation bank mng. One child. Studied: Consv of Istanbul and Ankara, Giannina Arangi-Lombardi. **Debut:** Cio-Cio-San (*Butterfly*) Teatro San Carlo, Naples 1954. Awards: 7 gold & 5 silver medals from Italy, Turkey, France, UK, Belgium; spec citations from Dallas, USA, Verona, Naples; intl prizes for recordings; Commendatore della Repubblica Italiana.

Sang with major companies in ARG: Buenos Aires; AUS: Salzburg Fest, Vienna Staatsoper; BEL: Brussels; BRA: Rio de Janeiro; FR GER: Cologne, Munich Staatsoper, Wiesbaden; ITA: Bologna, Florence Maggio & Comunale, Genoa, Milan La Scala, Naples, Palermo, Rome Opera & Caracalla, Spoleto Fest, Trieste, Turin, Venice, Verona Arena; MON: Monte Carlo; NOR: Oslo; POL: Lodz, Warsaw; POR: Lisbon; SPA: Barcelona; SWE: Stockholm; UK: Edinburgh Fest, Glyndebourne Fest, London Royal & English National; USSR: Leningrad Kirov, Moscow Bolshoi; USA: Chicago, Dallas, Newark, New Orleans, Philadelphia Lyric, San Diego, San Francisco Opera; YUG: Belgrade. **Roles with these companies incl** BELLINI: Beatrice di Tenda, Norma, Imogene (*Pirata*), Elvira (*Puritani*), Amina (*Sonnambula*); BOITO: Margherita (*Mefistofele*); CHERUBINI: Medea; CILEA: Adriana Lecouvreur; DONIZETTI: Anna Bolena, Caterina Cornaro★, Lucia, Lucrezia Borgia★, Maria Stuarda★, Elisabetta (*Roberto Devereux*); GLUCK: Alceste★; MASCAGNI: Santuzza★ (*Cavalleria rusticana*); MASSENET: Manon, Charlotte (*Werther*); MENOTTI: Magda Sorel (*Consul*); MONTEVERDI: Ottavia (*Incoronazione di Poppea*); MOZART: Fiordiligi (*Così fan tutte*), Donna Anna & Donna Elvira (*Don Giovanni*), Elettra (*Idomeneo*), Contessa (*Nozze di Figaro*); PONCHIELLI: Gioconda★; PROKOFIEV: Renata (*Fiery Angel*); PUCCINI: Cio-Cio-San (*Madama Butterfly*), Suor Angelica, Giorgetta (*Tabarro*), Tosca, Liù (*Turandot*); ROSSINI: Elisabetta★ (*Elisabetta Regina*), Mathilde (*Guillaume Tell*); SPONTINI: Agnese di Hohenstaufen★; TCHAIKOVSKY: Tatiana (*Eugene Onegin*), Lisa (*Pique Dame*); VERDI: Aida★, Odabella★ (*Attila*), Amelia★ (*Ballo in maschera*), Elisabetta★ (*Don Carlo*), Lucrezia Contarini (*Due Foscari*), Donna Elvira★ (*Ernani*), Leonora (*Forza del destino*), Lady Macbeth★, Desdemona (*Otello*), Gilda (*Rigoletto*), Amelia (*Simon Boccanegra*), Violetta (*Traviata*), Leonora (*Trovatore*), Elena (*Vespri*); ZANDONAI: Francesca da Rimini. Also PACINI: Saffo (*Saffo*); PIZZETTI: Maria (*Straniero*); ROCCA: Edalì (*Monte Ivnor*); DONIZETTI: Antonina★ (*Belisario*), Paolina★ (*Poliuto*); SMAREGLIA: La Falena★; VERDI: Giselda (*Jérusalem*), (*Battaglia di Legnano*). **World premieres:** POULENC: Mère Lidoine (*Dialogues des Carmélites*) La Scala, Milan 1957; PIZZETTI: Prima Corifea (*Assassinio nella cattedrale*) La Scala, Milan 1958. Recorded for: Fonit-Cetra. Video—RAI TV: Leonora (*Trovatore*), Aida, Charlotte (*Werther*), Donna Elvira (*Don Giovanni*). Gives recitals. Appears with symphony orchestra. **Res:** Viale Maino 17/A, Milan, Italy.

GENTILESCA, FRANCO. Stages/produces opera & theater. Also designs stage-lighting and is a prod stage mng. American. Form Assoc Art Dir & Resident Stage Dir, Artists Internationale, Providence, RI. Born 30 May 1943, New York. Single. Studied: as asst to Luchino Visconti, Roman Polanski, Gian Carlo Menotti, Nathaniel Merrill etc; also music, piano and voice. Operatic training as asst stage dir & asst stage mng, St Paul, Cincinnati, Baltimore, Newark, Spoleto, Italy. **Operatic debut:** *Andrea Chénier* Philadelphia Grand Op 1973. Theater debut: Burke Summer Fest, Reading, PA 1975. Previous occupation: elem & HS teacher. **Directed/produced opera for major companies in**

USA: Philadelphia Grand. **Operas staged for these companies incl** GIORDANO: *Andrea Chénier*★; PUCCINI: *Bohème*★. **Res:** 2109 Broadway, New York, USA. Mgmt: ACA/USA.

GEORGE, HAL. Scenic and costume designer for opera; specl in costumes. Is also a painter. American. Single. **Operatic debut:** sets, *Così fan tutte* Amsterdam 1969; cost, *Elegy for Young Lovers* Juilliard School, New York 1965. Theater debut: American Shakespeare Fest, Stratford, CT 1964. Previous occupation: painter; stage dir.
Designed for major companies in HOL: Amsterdam; USA: Boston, Kansas City, New York City Opera, San Diego, San Francisco Opera, Santa Fe. **Operas designed for these companies incl** BENNETT: *Mines of Sulphur;* BOITO: *Mefistofele;* CAVALLI: *Ormindo;* HENZE: *Bassariden, Elegy for Young Lovers;* MASSENET: *Manon;* MOZART: *Clemenza di Tito, Nozze di Figaro, Zauberflöte;* ORFF: *Antigonae, Kluge;* PUCCINI: *Bohème;* PURCELL: *Dido and Aeneas;* ROSSINI: *Barbiere di Siviglia;* VERDI: *Otello;* WEILL: *Dreigroschenoper.* Also SCHOENBERG: *Jakobsleiter* Santa Fe, NM 1968. **Res:** New York, NY, USA. Mgmt: CRB/USA.

GÉRARD, ROLF. Scenic and costume designer for opera, theater, film, television. Is a lighting designer; also a painter, sculptor & illustrator. British. Born 9 Aug 1909, Berlin, Germany. Wife Kyra. Studied: various academies in Berlin & Paris. **Operatic debut:** sets, cost, Sadler's Wells, London 1940. Theater debut: Arts Theater, London 1939. Previous occupation: physician; studied medicine Basel Univ. Awards: Officer of the Légion d'Honneur, French Gvnmt.
Designed for major companies in AUS: Salzburg Fest, Vienna Staatsoper; DEN: Copenhagen; ITA: Florence Maggio, Naples; UK: Edinburgh Fest, Glyndebourne Fest, London Royal; USA: New York Met. **Operas designed for these companies incl** BELLINI: *Sonnambula;* BIZET: *Carmen;* GLUCK: *Orfeo ed Euridice;* GOUNOD: *Faust, Roméo et Juliette;* LEONCAVALLO: *Pagliacci;* MASCAGNI: *Cavalleria rusticana;* MOZART: *Così fan tutte, Don Giovanni, Entführung aus dem Serail, Nozze di Figaro, Oca del Cairo;* OFFENBACH: *Contes d'Hoffmann, Périchole;* PUCCINI: *Bohème;* STRAUSS, R: *Arabella, Rosenkavalier;* STRAUSS, J: *Fledermaus;* TCHAIKOVSKY: *Onegin;* VERDI: *Aida, Don Carlo, Traviata;* WAGNER: *Tannhäuser.* Op Video—NBC & CBS TV: *Bohème, Fledermaus.* Exhibitions of stage designs, paintings, sculptures, & graphics New York, Paris, London. **Res:** 43 Quai Wilson, Geneva, Switzerland.

GERMAIN, JOHN NORMAN. Lyric baritone. Australian. Resident mem: Australian Opera, Sydney. Born 23 Oct 1930, Sydney. Wife Shirley, occupation stage mistress, Australian Opera. One daughter. Studied: NSW Consv of Music, Raymond Beatty; Mr & Mrs H Portnoj, Melbourne and Sydney. **Debut:** Schaunard (*Bohème*) Australian Opera 1957. Previous occupations: schoolteacher.
Sang with major companies in AUSTRL: Sydney. **Roles with these companies incl** BIZET: Escamillo (*Carmen*); DONIZETTI: Dott Malatesta★

(*Don Pasquale*), Belcore (*Elisir*); LEONCAVALLO: Tonio★ (*Pagliacci*); MASCAGNI: Alfio★ (*Cavalleria rusticana*); MOZART: Figaro★ (*Nozze di Figaro*); ORFF: König (*Kluge*); PUCCINI: Jack Rance (*Fanciulla del West*), Sharpless (*Butterfly*); ROSSINI: Figaro & Dott Bartolo★ (*Barbiere di Siviglia*); STRAUSS, R: Musiklehrer (*Ariadne auf Naxos*); STRAVINSKY: Nick Shadow (*Rake's Progress*); VERDI: Rigoletto, Germont (*Traviata*). Also STRAUSS, R: Faninal★ (*Rosenkavalier*); GOUNOD: Valentin (*Faust*); WEILL: Fatty★ (*Aufstieg und Fall der Stadt Mahagonny*). Video—ABC TV Sydney: (*Don Pasquale*). Gives recitals. **Res:** 53 Yule St, Dulwich Hill/Sydney, NSW, Australia.

GESZTY, SYLVIA; née Witkowsky. Coloratura soprano. German. Resident mem: Staatstheater, Stuttgart; Bayerische Staatsoper, Munich. Born 28 Feb 1934, Budapest, Hungary. One child. Studied: Prof Erzsebet Hoor-Tempis, Budapest; Prof Dagmar Freiwald-Lange, Berlin, Ger DR. **Debut:** Amor (*Orfeo ed Euridice*) Staatsoper Berlin, Ger DR 1961. Awards: Kunstpreis der DDR; Kritikerpreis Berlin; Kammersängerin, Berlin.
Sang with major companies in ARG: Buenos Aires; AUS: Salzburg Fest, Vienna Staatsoper; DEN: Copenhagen; FIN: Helsinki; FRA: Lyon, Nancy; FR GER: Berlin Deutsche Oper, Cologne, Düsseldorf-Duisburg, Frankfurt, Hamburg, Hannover, Karlsruhe, Mannheim, Munich Staatsoper, Stuttgart; GER DR: Berlin Komische Oper & Staatsoper, Dresden, Leipzig; HUN: Budapest; ITA: Bologna, Palermo, Rome Opera, Venice; POR: Lisbon; SWE: Drottningholm Fest; SWI: Basel, Geneva; UK: Edinburgh Fest, Glyndebourne Fest, London Royal; USSR: Moscow Stanislavski; USA: New York City Opera. **Roles with these companies incl** BRITTEN: Tytania (*Midsummer Night*); DONIZETTI: Norina‡ (*Don Pasquale*), Lucia‡; GLUCK: Amor (*Orfeo ed Euridice*); HANDEL: Cleopatra (*Giulio Cesare*); HENZE: Manon (*Boulevard Solitude*); LORTZING: Gretchen (*Wildschütz*); MOZART: Fiordiligi & Despina‡ (*Così fan tutte*), Donna Anna (*Don Giovanni*), Konstanze‡ & Blondchen (*Entführung aus dem Serail*), Mme Herz‡ (*Schauspieldirektor*), Susanna‡ (*Nozze di Figaro*), Königin der Nacht‡ (*Zauberflöte*); NICOLAI: Frau Fluth (*Lustigen Weiber*); OFFENBACH: Olympia‡ & Antonia & Giulietta (*Contes d'Hoffmann*); ORFF: Solo (*Carmina burana*); PUCCINI: Mimi & Musetta‡ (*Bohème*); RIMSKY-KORSAKOV: Coq d'or; ROSSINI: Rosina‡ (*Barbiere di Siviglia*); STRAUSS, J: Adele (*Fledermaus*); STRAUSS, R: Fiakermilli (*Arabella*), Zerbinetta (*Ariadne auf Naxos*), Sophie (*Rosenkavalier*); VERDI: Oscar‡ (*Ballo in maschera*), Gilda‡ (*Rigoletto*), Violetta‡ (*Traviata*). Also only on records BELLINI: Elvira (*Puritani*), Amina (*Sonnambula*); CORNELIUS: Margiana (*Barbier von Bagdad*); DELIBES: Lakmé; GOUNOD: Marguerite (*Faust*); LEONCAVALLO: Nedda (*Pagliacci*); PUCCINI: Cio-Cio-San (*Butterfly*); THOMAS: Ophélie (*Hamlet*), Philine (*Mignon*). Recorded for: Ariola-Eurodisc, Telefunken-Decca. Video/Film: Olympia & Antonia & Giulietta (*Contes d'Hoffmann*); Margiana (*Barbier von Bagdad*). Gives recitals. Appears with symphony orchestra. Teaches voice. On faculty of Hoch-

schule für Musik, Stuttgart. **Res:** Felix Dahn Str 9/D, 7 Stuttgart 70, FR Ger. Mgmt: SMD/FRG.

GHAZARIAN, SONA. Coloratura soprano. Lebanese. Resident mem: Staatsoper, Vienna. Born 2 Sep 1945, Beirut, Lebanon. Single. Studied: Ntl Consv, Badia Haddad, Beirut; Accad Chigiana, Giorgio Favaretto, Gino Bechi, Siena; Accad St Cecilia, Rome. **Debut:** Oscar (*Ballo in maschera*) Staatsoper, Vienna 1972. Awards: Hon Diploma Accad Chigiana for Opera & Lieder, Siena; First Prize Intl Compt for Voice, 's Hertogenbosch, Holland; Second Prize Intl Compt, Musikvereins Gesellschaft, Vienna.

Sang with major companies in AUS: Graz, Salzburg Fest, Vienna Staatsoper; BEL: Brussels; FRA: Paris; FR GER: Frankfurt; SWI: Geneva. Roles with these companies incl BELLINI: Amina★ (*Sonnambula*); DONIZETTI: Lucia★; MOZART: Zerlina★(*Don Giovanni*); PUCCINI: Musetta★(*Bohème*); ROSSINI: Rosina★ (*Barbiere di Siviglia*); STRAUSS, R: Fiakermilli★ (*Arabella*); VERDI: Oscar★ (*Ballo in maschera*), Gilda★ (*Rigoletto*), Violetta★ (*Traviata*). Recorded for: BASF. Gives recitals. Appears with symphony orchestra. **Res:** Vienna, Austria. Mgmt: RAB/AUS; IMR/FRA.

GHIAUROV, NICOLAI. Bass. Bulgarian. Resident mem: Staatsoper, Vienna; Staatsoper, Hamburg. Born 13 Sep 1929, Velingrad, Bulgaria. Wife Zlatina, occupation form concert pianist. Two children. Studied: Acad of Music, Sofia; Moscow Consv. **Debut:** Don Basilio (*Barbiere di Siviglia*) Sofia 1955. Awards: First Prize, Intl Singing Cont, Paris 1955.

Sang with major companies in AUS: Salzburg Fest, Vienna Staatsoper; BEL: Brussels, Liège; BUL: Sofia; FRA: Paris; FR GER: Hamburg, Munich Staatsoper, Wiesbaden; ITA: Milan La Scala, Verona Arena; UK: London Royal; USSR: Moscow Bolshoi; USA: Chicago, New York Met, Philadelphia Lyric; et al. Roles with these companies incl BELLINI: Sir George‡ (*Puritani*); BORODIN: Galitzky (*Prince Igor*); CHERUBINI: Creon (*Medea*); DONIZETTI: Baldassare (*Favorite*); GOUNOD: Méphistophélès‡ (*Faust*); MASSENET: Don Quichotte; MEYERBEER: Marcel (*Huguenots*); MOZART: Don Giovanni‡; MUSSORGSKY: Boris‡ & Varlaam & Pimen (*Boris Godunov*), Ivan Khovansky (*Khovanshchina*); PUCCINI: Colline (*Bohème*); ROSSINI: Don Basilio‡ (*Barbiere di Siviglia*); VERDI: Ramfis‡ (*Aida*), Attila, Philip II‡ & Grande Inquisitore (*Don Carlo*), Silva (*Ernani*), Padre Guardiano (*Forza del destino*), Banquo (*Macbeth*), Zaccaria (*Nabucco*), Fiesco (*Simon Boccanegra*); et al. Also PUCCINI: Timur (*Turandot*). DONIZETTI: Raimondo (*Lucia*); TCHAIKOVSKY: Gremin (*Eugene Onegin*); RIMSKY-KORSAKOV: Viking Guest (*Sadko*); BERLIOZ: Frère Laurent (*Roméo et Juliette*). On records only DONIZETTI: Henry VIII (*Anna Bolena*). Recorded for: London, Angel, Decca, Columbia, Supraphon, Balkanton. Gives recitals. Appears with symphony orchestra. Mgmt: GOR/UK.

GHITTI, FRANCO. Lyric tenor. Italian. Born 5 Jan 1932, Iseo/Brescia, Italy. Wife Bruna Archetti,

occupation employee. One son. Studied: Giovanni Inghilleri, Barra Caracciolo Gennaro, Vladimiro Badiali, Domenico Malatesta. **Debut:** Faust, Teatro Sperimentale, Spoleto 1959. Previous occupations: railroad employee. Awards: First Winner, Ntl Compt, Teatro Sperimentale Spoleto 1959.

Sang with major companies in FRA: Marseille, Toulouse; FR GER: Bielefeld, Düsseldorf-Duisburg; HOL: Amsterdam; ITA: Bologna, Genoa, Naples, Trieste, Turin, Venice; SWI: Geneva; USA: New York Met. Roles with these companies incl BERLIOZ: Faust (*Damnation de Faust*); CILEA: Maurizio (*A. Lecouvreur*); DALLAPICCOLA: Radio Telegrapher★ (*Volo di notte*); DONIZETTI: Ernesto (*Don Pasquale*), Edgardo (*Lucia*); GOUNOD: Faust★; JANACEK: Laca★ (*Jenufa*); MASCAGNI: Fritz (*Amico Fritz*); MASSENET: Des Grieux★ (*Manon*); MONTEVERDI: Ulisse (*Ritorno d'Ulisse*); MOZART: Don Ottavio (*Don Giovanni*); PROKOFIEV: Prince (*Love for Three Oranges*); PUCCINI: Rodolfo (*Bohème*), Pinkerton★ (*Butterfly*), Cavaradossi (*Tosca*); VERDI: Alfredo★ (*Traviata*). Also VIOZZI: Giornalista (*Allamistakeo*); GHEDINI: John Claggart (*Billy Budd*). World premieres: BETTINELLI: Edgar (*Pozzo e il pendolo*) Fest Bergamo 1967. Recorded for: Arcophon. **Res:** C Bevilacqua 3, Brescia, Italy.

GHIUSELEV, NICOLA; né Nikola Nikolaev Guzelev. Bass. Bulgarian. Resident mem: National Opera, Sofia. Born 17 Aug 1936, Pavlikeni. Divorced. Two children. Studied: Prof Christo Brambarov, Sofia. **Debut:** Timur (*Turandot*) Ntl Opera, Sofia 1961. Previous occupations: studied painting. Awards: First Prize & Gold Medal, Fest of Youth, Helsinki 1962 and Intl Compt for Young Singers, Sofia 1963; Dimitrov Prize 1965; Artist of the People 1970.

Sang with major companies in AUS: Graz, Salzburg Fest, Vienna Staatsoper; BEL: Brussels; BRA: Rio de Janeiro; BUL: Sofia; CZE: Brno, Prague National & Smetana; FIN: Helsinki; FRA: Bordeaux, Lyon, Marseille, Nice, Paris, Rouen, Toulouse; GRE: Athens National & Fest; FR GER: Hamburg, Munich Staatsoper, Wiesbaden; GER DR: Berlin Staatsoper, Dresden, Leipzig; HOL: Amsterdam; HUN: Budapest; ITA: Milan La Scala, Naples, Parma, Trieste; MON: Monte Carlo; POL: Warsaw; ROM: Bucharest; SPA: Barcelona; SWE: Stockholm; SWI: Geneva; USSR: Kiev, Leningrad Kirov, Moscow Bolshoi, Tbilisi; USA: Chicago, New York Met, Philadelphia Grand, San Francisco Opera; YUG: Dubrovnik, Belgrade. Roles with these companies incl BELLINI: Sir George★ (*Puritani*); BOITO: Mefistofele★; BORODIN: Galitzky★ (*Prince Igor*); CHERUBINI: Creon★ (*Medea*); DONIZETTI: Henry VIII★ (*Anna Bolena*); GOUNOD: Méphistophélès★ (*Faust*); MEYERBEER: Marcel (*Huguenots*); MONTEMEZZI: Archibaldo (*Amore dei tre re*); MOZART: Don Giovanni★, Conte Almaviva★ & Figaro★ (*Nozze di Figaro*); MUSSORGSKY: Boris★ & Varlaam & Pimen (*Boris Godunov*), Ivan Khovansky★ & Dosifei★ (*Khovanshchina*); OFFENBACH: Coppélius etc (*Contes d'Hoffmann*); PONCHIELLI: Alvise (*Gioconda*); PUCCINI: Colline (*Bohème*); ROSSINI: Don Basilio★ (*Barbiere di Siviglia*), Moïse★; TCHAIKOVSKY: King René★ (*Iolanthe*);

VERDI: Ramfis★ (*Aida*), Attila★, Philip II★ & Grande Inquisitore (*Don Carlo*), Silva★ (*Ernani*), Padre Guardiano★ (*Forza del destino*), Banquo★ (*Macbeth*), Zaccaria★ (*Nabucco*), Fiesco★ (*Simon Boccanegra*). Also PIZZETTI: Thomas à Becket (*Assassinio nella cattedrale*); RACHMANINOFF: Aleko. **World premieres:** ILIEV: Padre Gavril (*Master of Boyan*) 1961; PIPKOV: Krumov (*Antigonae 43*) 1963; GOLEMINOV: Zahari (*Legend of the Sinful Love of Zahari Zograf*) 1972; all at Ntl Opera, Sofia. Recorded for: EMI, Decca, Balkanton-Harmonia Mundi. Video/Film: Don Giovanni. Gives recitals. Appears with symphony orchestra. **Res:** Kompl Tchervena Zvezda b1 36, Sofia, Bulgaria. Mgmt: BAA/BUL; CAB/SPA.

GIACOMINI, GIUSEPPE. Lirico spinto tenor. Italian. Born 7 Sep 1940, Padua. Wife Massimiliana. Two children. Studied: Elena Fava Ceriati, Padua; Marcello del Monaco, Treviso; Vladimiro Badiali, Milan. **Debut:** Pinkerton (*Butterfly*) Vercelli 1970. Awards: First Prizes Conc di Adria; San Carlo, Naples; Viotti Compt, Vercelli; Conc della Scala, Milan.
   Sang with major companies in ARG: Buenos Aires; AUS: Graz; BEL: Brussels; CZE: Prague National; FRA: Bordeaux, Paris, Strasbourg; FR GER: Berlin Deutsche Oper, Cologne, Düsseldorf-Duisburg, Frankfurt, Hamburg, Karlsruhe, Mannheim, Munich Staatsoper, Wiesbaden; HUN: Budapest; ITA: Bologna, Milan La Scala, Naples, Parma, Rome Opera, Trieste, Turin; MON: Monte Carlo; POR: Lisbon; SPA: Barcelona, Majorca; SWI: Zurich; USA: Boston, Hartford. **Roles with these companies incl** DONIZETTI: Edgardo★ (*Lucia*); GIORDANO: Loris Ipanov★ (*Fedora*); MASCAGNI: Turiddu★ (*Cavalleria rusticana*); MONTEVERDI: Nero★ (*Incoronazione di Poppea*); PUCCINI: Rodolfo★ (*Bohème*), Dick Johnson★ (*Fanciulla del West*), Pinkerton★ (*Butterfly*), Des Grieux★ (*Manon Lescaut*), Luigi★ (*Tabarro*), Cavaradossi★ (*Tosca*); VERDI: Don Carlo★, Don Alvaro★ (*Forza del destino*), Duca di Mantova★ (*Rigoletto*), Alfredo★ (*Traviata*), Manrico★ (*Trovatore*); WAGNER: Lohengrin★. **Res:** V Brusuglio 19, Milan, Italy. Mgmt: EUM/FRG.

GIACOMOTTI, ALFREDO. Bass-baritone. Italian. Born 18 Oct 1933, Voghera, Italy. Single. Studied: Consv of Milan, Mo Cesare Chiesa, Carmen Melis. **Debut:** Colline (*Bohème*) Italian provinces 1954.
   Sang with major companies in AUS: Bregenz Fest, Vienna Staatsoper; FR GER: Cologne, Munich Staatsoper, Stuttgart; HOL: Amsterdam; ITA: Bologna, Florence Maggio, Genoa, Milan La Scala, Palermo, Venice, Verona Arena; SPA: Barcelona; SWI: Basel; USSR: Moscow Bolshoi. **Roles with these companies incl** BELLINI: Oroveso (*Norma*), Sir George (*Puritani*), Rodolfo★ (*Sonnambula*); BENNETT: Braxton (*Mines of Sulphur*); BERG: Doktor★ (*Wozzeck*); BRITTEN: John Claggart★ (*Billy Budd*); CIMAROSA: Count Robinson★ & Geronimo★ (*Matrimonio segreto*); DONIZETTI: Dulcamara (*Elisir*), Antonio (*Linda di Chamounix*); FALLA: Don Quixote (*Retablo de Maese Pedro*); GOUNOD: Méphistophélès (*Faust*); MOZART: Publio (*Clemenza di Tito*), Don Alfonso★ (*Così fan tutte*),

Leporello★ (*Don Giovanni*), Conte Almaviva★ (*Nozze di Figaro*); MUSSORGSKY: Pimen★ (*Boris Godunov*); PERGOLESI: Uberto (*Serva padrona*); PONCHIELLI: Alvise (*Gioconda*); PROKOFIEV: Faust★ (*Fiery Angel*); PUCCINI: Colline★ (*Bohème*); ROSSINI: Don Basilio★ (*Barbiere di Siviglia*), Macrobio (*Pietra del paragone*), Maometto (*Assedio di Corinto*); STRAVINSKY: Tiresias (*Oedipus Rex*); VERDI: Silva (*Ernani*), Padre Guardiano (*Forza del destino*), Banquo (*Macbeth*), Zaccaria (*Nabucco*), Fiesco (*Simon Boccanegra*), Procida (*Vespri*). **World premieres:** MANZONI: Quartetto Robespierre (*Per Massimiliano Robespierre*) Bologna 1975. Gives recitals. Appears with symphony orchestra. **Res:** V dei Fontanili 39, Milan, Italy.

GIAIOTTI, BONALDO. Bass. Italian. Born 25 Dec 1932, Ziracco, Udine, Italy. Wife Alice. Studied: Ada Crainz, Udine; Bruno Carmassi, Alfredo Strano, Milan, Italy; Dick Marzollo, New York. **Debut:** Colline (*Bohème*) Teatro Nuovo, Milan 1958. Awards: Conc della Assoc Lirico Concertistico, Milan; Conc RAI; Conc Intl Viotti, Vercelli, Italy.
   Sang with major companies in ARG: Buenos Aires; AUS: Vienna Staatsoper; FRA: Bordeaux, Toulouse; FR GER: Hamburg; ITA: Bologna, Florence Maggio, Genoa, Naples, Rome Opera & Caracalla, Trieste, Turin, Venice, Verona Arena; SPA: Barcelona, Madrid, Las Palmas; SWI: Geneva, Zurich; USA: Cincinnati, Miami, Newark, New York Met, Philadelphia Grand & Lyric Operas, San Francisco Opera; YUG: Zagreb, Belgrade. **Roles with these companies incl** BELLINI: Oroveso★ (*Norma*), Sir George★ (*Puritani*), Rodolfo★ (*Sonnambula*); DONIZETTI: Baldassare★ (*Favorite*); GOUNOD: Méphistophélès★ (*Faust*); HALEVY: Brogny (*Juive*); MEYERBEER: Marcel (*Huguenots*); MONTEMEZZI: Archibaldo (*Amore dei tre re*); MOZART: Sarastro★ (*Zauberflöte*); PONCHIELLI: Alvise★ (*Gioconda*); PUCCINI: Colline (*Bohème*); ROSSINI: Don Basilio★ (*Barbiere di Siviglia*), Moïse★; VERDI: Ramfis★‡ (*Aida*), Philip II★ (*Don Carlo*), Silva★ (*Ernani*), Padre Guardiano★ (*Forza del destino*), Conte Walter★ (*Luisa Miller*), Banquo★ (*Macbeth*), Zaccaria★ (*Nabucco*), Fiesco★ (*Simon Boccanegra*), Procida★ (*Vespri*); WAGNER: König Heinrich★ (*Lohengrin*), Gurnemanz (*Parsifal*). Recorded for: Angel, London, RCA. Gives recitals. Appears with symphony orchestra. **Res:** Udine, Italy. Mgmt: CAM/USA.

GIAMMEI, LAMBERTO. Italian. Administrative Director, Teatro dell'Opera, Piazza Beniamino Gigli, Rome, Italy. In charge of adm matters. Born 24 Feb 1910, Subiaco, Italy. Wife Jolanda De Manna, occupation prof in economics & commerce. Two children. Studied: Economics & commerce at Univ of Rome. Previous occupations: Gen Dir, Municipal Dept of the City of Rome. Previous positions primarily administrative. In present position since 1975. **Res:** V Fogliano 31, Rome, Italy.

GIANESELLI, IGINIO. Italian. Secy Gen, Teatro la Fenice, Campo S Fantin, 2519 Venice. In charge of overall adm matters. Born 26 Apr 1938, Venice. Wife Tommasina Pianon. Two children.

Studied: economic & social sciences, Univ Venice. Previous occupations: working in the cinema field and at the Venice Biennale in cinematography. Background primarily adm. Started with present company 1960 as Secy Gen CATL (Center for Intro to Lyric Theater). Mem of Dept of Tourism, Chamber of Commerce, Venice; Hon Commtt to promote Portogruaro Theater Festival, Venice; Hon Commtt, Jazz Festival of Pordenone. **Res:** Dorso Duro 3523, Venice, Italy.

GIBBS, JOHN. Dramatic baritone. British. Born 19 Jun 1937, London. Wife Margaret, occupation pianist & coach. One child. Studied: Royal Acad of Music, London; Domenic Modesti, Paris; Mo Luigi Ricci, Rome; Joan Cross, London. **Debut:** MAW: Joe Blake (*One Man Show*) Phoenix Opera, London 1964. Awards: Martin Schshp, New Philharmonia Orch, London; Arts Counc Awd, London.

Sang with major companies in UK: Aldeburgh Fest, Cardiff Welsh, Glyndebourne Fest, London Royal Opera & English National. **Roles with these companies incl** BIZET: Escamillo (*Carmen*); DONIZETTI: Belcore★ (*Elisir*); LUTYENS: Harold★ (*Time Off? Not a Ghost of a Chance*); MOZART: Guglielmo (*Così fan tutte*), Leporello★ (*Don Giovanni*), Figaro★ (*Nozze di Figaro*), Papageno★ (*Zauberflöte*); ROSSINI: Dott Bartolo★ (*Barbiere di Siviglia*). Also STRAUSS, R: Harlekin★ (*Ariadne auf Naxos*); BRITTEN: Donald★ (*Billy Budd*); TIPPETT: Patroclus (*King Priam*). **World premieres:** MAW: Joe Blake (*One Man Show*) Phoenix Opera, London 1964; BRITTEN: Ananias (*Burning Fiery Furnace*) Aldeburgh Fest 1966; WILLIAMS: Dr Charlton (*Parlour*) Cardiff 1966; MAW: Donal O'Dowd (*Rising of the Moon*) Glyndebourne Fest 1970. Gives recitals. Appears with symphony orchestra. Teaches voice. **Res:** 1 Cleve Rd, London NW6, UK.

GIBBS, RAYMOND DOUGLAS. Lyric tenor, started as baritone. American. Resident mem: Metropolitan Opera, New York. Born 3 Dec, Tucson, AZ, USA. Wife Lee Wilson, occupation actress, singer, dancer. Studied: San Diego State Univ, CA; San Francisco Opera Merola Training Prgr; Manhattan School of Music, New York. **Debut:** as baritone: Wagner (*Faust*) San Diego Opera, CA 1966; as tenor: Roméo, Houston Grand Opera 1972. Awards: Sullivan Fndt Grant.

Sang with major companies in USA: Cincinnati, Fort Worth, Houston, Memphis, New York Met & City Opera, Omaha, Philadelphia Lyric, San Diego, Santa Fe. **Roles with these companies incl** BERG: Maler★ (*Lulu*); DONIZETTI: Nemorino★ (*Elisir*); GOUNOD: Roméo★; MASSENET: Des Grieux★ (*Manon*); MOZART: Tamino★ (*Zauberflöte*); PUCCINI: Rodolfo★ (*Bohème*), Rinuccio★ (*Gianni Schicchi*), Pinkerton★ (*Butterfly*), Cavaradossi★ (*Tosca*); VERDI: Alfredo★ (*Traviata*). Recorded for: DG. Gives recitals. Appears with symphony orchestra. **Res:** New York, NY, USA. Mgmt: HUR/USA; HPL/UK.

GIBSON, ALEXANDER. Conductor of opera and symphony. British. Founder, Art Dir & Princ Cond, Scottish Opera, Glasgow, UK since 1962. Also Mus Dir & Princ Cond, Scottish Ntl Orch & Chorus, Glasgow since 1959. Born 11 Feb 1926,

Motherwell, Scotland, UK. Wife Ann Veronica. Four children. Studied: Glasgow Univ; Royal Coll of Music; Mozarteum, Salzburg; Accad Chigiana, Siena; incl piano, organ. Operatic training as repetiteur & asst cond at Sadler's Wells, London 1951-52 & 1954-57; asst cond Scottish Orch, BBC 1952-54. **Operatic debut:** *Bartered Bride* Sadler's Wells, London 1953. Symphonic debut: BBC Scottish Symph Orch 1953; London Phil Orch, Royal Albert Hall 1953. Awards: Commander of the British Empire; DL Aberdeen Univ; Hon DM Glasgow Univ; DL Stirling Univ; Hon Mem Royal Scottish Acad; Freeman of Motherwell; St Mungo Prize, Glasgow. Previous adm positions in opera: Mus Dir, Sadler's Wells, London 1957-59.

Conducted with major companies in BEL: Brussels; HOL: Amsterdam; UK: Aldeburgh Fest, Edinburgh Fest, Scottish, London Royal & English National; USA: Washington DC. **Operas with these companies incl** BARTOK: *Bluebeard's Castle;* BEETHOVEN: *Fidelio★;* BERLIOZ: *Troyens★;* BIZET: *Carmen★, Pêcheurs de perles;* BRITTEN: *Peter Grimes★;* DALLAPICCOLA: *Volo di notte;* DEBUSSY: *Pelléas et Mélisande★;* DONIZETTI: *Don Pasquale★;* GLUCK: *Alceste★;* GOUNOD: *Faust★;* HENZE: *Elegy for Young Lovers★;* HUMPERDINCK: *Hänsel und Gretel★;* LEONCAVALLO: *Pagliacci;* MASCAGNI: *Cavalleria rusticana;* MENOTTI: *Consul, Telephone;* MILHAUD: *Pauvre matelot;* MONTEVERDI: *Ritorno d'Ulisse★;* MOZART: *Così fan tutte★, Don Giovanni★, Entführung aus dem Serail, Nozze di Figaro★, Zauberflöte★;* MUSSORGSKY: *Boris Godunov★;* PUCCINI: *Bohème, Gianni Schicchi, Butterfly★, Tosca★;* RAVEL: *Heure espagnole;* ROSSINI: *Comte Ory★;* SAINT-SAENS: *Samson et Dalila;* SMETANA: *Bartered Bride;* STRAUSS, J: *Fledermaus★;* STRAUSS, R: *Ariadne auf Naxos★, Rosenkavalier★;* STRAVINSKY: *Rake's Progress★;* TCHAIKOVSKY: *Eugene Onegin★, Pique Dame★;* VAUGHAN WILLIAMS: *Riders to the Sea;* VERDI: *Aida, Ballo in maschera★, Falstaff★, Nabucco, Otello★, Rigoletto, Traviata, Trovatore;* WAGNER: *Fliegende Holländer, Rheingold★, Walküre★, Siegfried★, Götterdämmerung★, Tristan und Isolde★;* WOLF-FERRARI: *Gioielli della Madonna, Quattro rusteghi, Segreto di Susanna.* **World premieres:** HAMILTON: *Catiline Conspiracy* Scotland 1974; PURSER: *Undertaker* Edinburgh Fest 1969; GARDNER: *Moon and Sixpence* Sadler's Wells 1957; ORR: *Full Circle* Scotland 1968, *Hermiston* Scotland 1975; BENNETT: *Ledge* London 1961. Video—BBC¹TV: *Bartered Bride;* BBC²TV: *Traviata.* Conducted major orch in Europe, USA/Canada, Cent/S America. **Res:** 15 Cleveden Gdns, Glasgow G12 OPU, UK. Mgmt: HLT/UK; COL/USA.

GIELEN, MICHAEL ANDREAS. Conductor of opera and symphony; composer. Austrian. Resident Cond, Netherlands Opera, Amsterdam, Holland. Appointed Gen Mus Dir Frankfurt Opera 1977-82. Born 20 Jul 1927, Dresden, Germany. Wife Helga Augsten. Two children. Studied: composition & analysis, Buenos Aires & Vienna; incl piano and cello. Operatic training as repetiteur at Teatro Colón, Buenos Aires 1947-50; Vienna Staatsoper 1951-54. **Operatic debut:** *Jeanne d'Arc au bûcher,* Vienna Staatsoper 1954. Symphonic debut: Chamber Orch, Vienna 1952. Prev adm positions in opera: First Cond, Royal Opera Stockholm 1960-65.

Conducted with major companies in AUS: Vienna Staatsoper & Volksoper; FRA: Aix-en-Provence Fest; GRE: Athens Fest; FR GER: Cologne, Frankfurt, Kiel, Munich Staatsoper, Stuttgart; HOL: Amsterdam; ITA: Florence Maggio; POR: Lisbon; SPA: Barcelona; SWE: Stockholm. Operas with these companies incl BARTOK: *Bluebeard's Castle;* BEETHOVEN: *Fidelio;* BERG: *Wozzeck★;* BIZET: *Carmen;* BORODIN: *Prince Igor;* BRITTEN: *Midsummer Night;* DALLAPICCOLA: *Prigioniero;* DONIZETTI: *Don Pasquale;* EGK: *Revisor;* FLOTOW: *Martha;* GLUCK: *Alceste, Orfeo ed Euridice;* LORTZING: *Waffenschmied;* MENOTTI: *Consul, Medium, Old Maid and the Thief, Telephone;* MOZART: *Così fan tutte, Don Giovanni, Entführung aus dem Serail, Idomeneo, Nozze di Figaro★, Zauberflöte;* OFFENBACH: *Contes d'Hoffmann;* PUCCINI: *Bohème, Butterfly, Turandot;* ROSSINI: *Barbiere di Siviglia;* SCHOENBERG: *Erwartung, Glückliche Hand, Moses und Aron‡;* SMETANA: *Bartered Bride;* STRAUSS, J: *Fledermaus;* STRAUSS, R: *Ariadne auf Naxos, Rosenkavalier, Salome;* STRAVINSKY: *Oedipus Rex, Rake's Progress, Rossignol;* VERDI: *Ballo in maschera, Don Carlo, Falstaff★, Macbeth;* WAGNER: *Fliegende Holländer, Meistersinger, Parsifal, Rheingold, Walküre, Siegfried, Götterdämmerung, Tannhäuser, Tristan und Isolde;* WERLE: *Dream of Thérèse;* ZIMMERMANN: *Soldaten.* Also HINDEMITH: *Neues vom Tage;* ORFF: *Prometheus;* REIMANN: *Traumspiel.*

GIERSTER, HANS. German. Dir of Musiktheater & GMD, Städtische Bühnen Nürnberg, Richard Wagner Platz 2-10, 85 Nürnberg, FR Ger 1965- . In charge of overall adm matters, art policy, mus matters. Is also a conductor. Born 12 Jan 1925, Munich. Wife Gertrud. Studied: Mozarteum, Salzburg; Musikhochschule, Munich. Plays the piano. Previous positions, primarily musical: Cond, Asst to Clemens Krauss, Staatsoper Munich 1942; Cond, Opernhaus Düsseldorf 1945-52; Cond, Staatsoper Munich 1952-56; GMD, Städtische Bühnen Freiburg 1956-65; also permanent Guest Cond, Staatsoper Munich 1956-65. Awards: Bavarian Order of Merit, Bavarian State Gvnmt 1972.

Conducted with major companies in AUS: Vienna Staatsoper; FR GER: Berlin Deutsche Oper, Düsseldorf-Duisburg, Hamburg, Munich Staatsoper, Nürnberg; et al. Operas with these companies incl BERG: *Wozzeck;* MOZART: *Don Giovanni, Nozze di Figaro;* NONO: *Intolleranza;* SCHOENBERG: *Moses und Aron;* STRAUSS, R: *Rosenkavalier;* VERDI: *Aida, Don Carlo, Forza del destino, Otello, Traviata, Trovatore;* WAGNER: *Fliegende Holländer.*

GIETZEN, HERBERT ALFONS. Conductor of opera and symphony; composer. German. Resident Cond, Städtische Bühnen, Bielefeld, FR Ger. Born 28 Oct 1947, Koblenz. Wife Dietlind, occupation teacher. Studied: Prof Herbert Ahlendorf, Franco Ferrara, Herbert von Karajan; also piano, organ, violin and voice. Plays the piano. Operatic training as repetiteur at Städt Bühnen, Bielefeld 1973-75.

Operatic debut: Städt Bühnen, Bielefeld 1974. Symphonic debut: NDR Orch, Hannover 1973. Awards: Winner Concert Compt of Young Artists, Hannover; Third Prize Intl Conductors Compt, Herbert von Karajan Fndt.

Conducted with major companies in FR GER: Bielefeld, Karlsruhe, Wuppertal. Operas with these companies incl d'ALBERT: *Tiefland★;* BEETHOVEN: *Fidelio★;* BIZET: *Carmen★;* MOZART: *Così fan tutte★, Zauberflöte★;* OFFENBACH: *Contes d'Hoffmann★;* SMETANA: *Bartered Bride★;* STRAUSS, J: *Fledermaus★.* Conducted major orch in Europe. Res: Hainteichstr 70, 48 Bielefeld, FR Ger. Mgmt: SLZ/FRG; JUC/SWI.

GILL, RICHARD T. Bass. American. Resident mem: Metropolitan Opera, New York; New York City Opera. Born 30 Nov 1927, Long Branch, NJ, USA. Wife Elizabeth Bjornson, occupation accompanist, editorial assistant. Three children. Studied: Herbert Mayer, Boston, New York. Debut: Ragpicker (*Louise*) Opera Company of Boston 1970. Previous occupations: Master Leverett House, Lecturer on Economics, Harvard Univ; author of 5 books on economics, also short stories, articles. Awards: Phi Beta Kappa, Harvard; summa cum laude, Harvard; Henry Fllshp Oxford; Atlantic Monthly Short Story Prize 1954.

Sang with major companies in USA: Houston, New York Met & City Opera. Roles with these companies incl BELLINI: Sir George★ (*Puritani*); CHERUBINI: Creon★ (*Medea*); DONIZETTI: Henry VIII★ (*Anna Bolena*), Sulpice★ (*Fille du régiment*); MASSENET: Des Grieux★ (*Portrait de Manon*); MOZART: Sarastro★ (*Zauberflöte*); MUSSORGSKY: Varlaam★ & Pimen (*Boris Godunov*); PUCCINI: Colline★ (*Bohème*); STRAVINSKY: Tiresias★ (*Oedipus Rex*). Also MONTEVERDI: Seneca★ (*Incoronazione di Poppea*). Gives recitals. Appears with symphony orchestra. Res: 22 Possum Trail, Upper Saddle River, NJ, USA. Mgmt: CAM/USA.

GILLERI, FULVIO. Italian. Adm Dir, Teatro Comunale G Verdi, Riva Tre Novembre 1, Trieste. Born 14 Feb 1920, Trieste. Wife Luciana Forti. Two children. Studied: business adm. Background primarily adm. Started with present company 1938 as clerk. Initiated major policy changes including founding summer festival of operetta in 1950. Res: V Pozzo del mare 2, Trieste, Italy.

GIMENEZ, EDUARDO GRACÍA. Lyric tenor. Spanish. Born 2 Jun 1940, Mataró/Barcelona. Wife Maria. One daughter. Studied: Carmen Braçons de Colomer, Mo Juan Sabater, Mo Vladimiro Badiali. Debut: Nemorino (*Elisir*) Reggio Emilia, Italy 1967. Previous occupations: textile manufacturing. Awards: Prize Diputación de Barcelona; Prize Achille Peri, Reggio Emilia; Prize Caja de Ahorros de Mataró.

Sang with major companies in BEL: Brussels; FRA: Aix-en-Provence Fest, Bordeaux, Lyon, Nice, Paris, Rouen, Toulouse; HOL: Amsterdam; HUN: Budapest; ISR: Tel Aviv; ITA: Bologna, Genoa, Milan La Scala, Naples, Parma, Turin, Venice; MON: Monte Carlo; SPA: Barcelona, Majorca; USA: Seattle, Washington DC; YUG: Dubrovnik, Zagreb. Roles with these companies incl BELLINI: Elvino‡ (*Sonnambula*); CIMAROSA:

Paolino★ (*Matrimonio segreto*); DONIZETTI: Ernesto★‡ (*Don Pasquale*), Nemorino★ (*Elisir*), Gennaro (*Lucrezia Borgia*), Leicester (*Maria Stuarda*), Beppo★ (*Rita*); GALUPPI: Rinaldo★ (*Filosofo di campagna*); MOZART: Ferrando★ (*Così fan tutte*), Don Ottavio★ (*Don Giovanni*); OFFENBACH: Hoffmann★; PAISIELLO: Almaviva★ (*Barbiere di Siviglia*); PUCCINI: Rinuccio★ (*Gianni Schicchi*); ROSSINI: Almaviva★ (*Barbiere di Siviglia*), Edward Milfort★ (*Cambiale di matrimonio*), Don Ramiro★ (*Cenerentola*), Lindoro★ (*Italiana in Algeri*); VERDI: Fenton★ (*Falstaff*), Alfredo★ (*Traviata*). Also HAYDN: Lindoro (*Fedeltà premiata*); CIMAROSA: Scassaganasce★ (*Mercato di Malmantile*); PAISIELLO: Lindoro (*Osteria di Marechiaro*); RAMEAU: Zoroastre★; DONIZETTI: Ernesto (*Giovedì grasso*); ROSSELLINI: Jacques★ (*Annonce faite à Marie*). Recorded for: Fabbri. Video/Film: Almaviva (*Barbiere di Siviglia*). **Res:** Ave de Sarriá 28, Barcélona, Spain. Mgmt: RMR/SWI; CAM/USA.

GINGRAS, ANDRÉE. Canadian. Festival Adm, National Arts Centre Opera Co, Confederation Square, Ottawa, Ont K1P 5W1. Born Montreal. Single. Studied: Univ of Montreal, Ecole Vincent d'Indy, music & mathematics. Plays the piano. Previous positions, primarily administrative & musical: Music Adm, Stratford Fest, Ont, CAN; Asst Dir, Canadian Broadcasting Corp, TV. Started with present company 1973 as Asst Gen Mng, Programming. Awards: Marly Polydor Awd 1949. **Res:** Ottawa, Canada.

GIOVANINETTI, REYNALD JEAN. Conductor of opera and symphony; operatic stage director. French. Born 11 Mar 1932, Sétif, Algeria. Wife Nicole Poiré. Four children. Studied: Consv Ntl Supérieur de Paris; incl cello. **Operatic debut:** Théâtre Municipal, Besançon, France. Symphonic debut: French Radio & TV 1959. Previous occupations: Prof of Mathematics; researcher and record engineer, French ORTF. Previous adm positions in opera: Music Dir/Gen Dir, Théâtre Municipal, Mulhouse, France 1962-67; Music Dir/Gen Dir, Opéra de Marseille 1968-75. **Conducted with major companies in** AUS: Vienna Staatsoper; FRA: Aix-en-Provence Fest, Marseille, Orange Fest, Paris, Strasbourg; FR GER: Cologne, Düsseldorf-Duisburg, Munich Staatsoper; ITA: Bologna, Palermo, Trieste, Turin, Verona Arena; MON: Monte Carlo; POR: Lisbon; SPA: Barcelona; SWI: Geneva; USA: San Francisco Opera. **Operas with these companies incl** BERG: *Wozzeck★*; BIZET: *Carmen★, Docteur Miracle, Pêcheurs de perles*; BOIELDIEU: *Dame blanche*; BRITTEN: *Curlew River, Peter Grimes★*; CHARPENTIER: *Louise*; CILEA: *A. Lecouvreur*; DEBUSSY: *Pelléas et Mélisande★*; DELIBES: *Lakmé*; DONIZETTI: *Lucia, Lucrezia Borgia, Maria Stuarda*; DUKAS: *Ariane et Barbe Bleue★*; EINEM: *Besuch der alten Dame★*; FALLA: *Retablo de Maese Pedro*; GLUCK: *Alceste, Orfeo ed Euridice*; GOLDMARK: *Königin von Saba*; GOUNOD: *Faust★, Mireille*; KODALY: *Háry János*; LALO: *Roi d'Ys*; LECOCQ: *Fille de Madame Angot*; LEONCAVALLO: *Pagliacci★*; MASCAGNI:

Cavalleria rusticana★; MASSENET: *Don Quichotte, Manon, Werther★*; MENOTTI: *Maria Golovin★, Saint of Bleecker Street★*; MEYERBEER: *Huguenots*; MILHAUD: *Médée*; MOZART: *Clemenza di Tito★, Don Giovanni, Nozze di Figaro★, Zauberflöte★*; MUSSORGSKY: *Boris Godunov*; OFFENBACH: *Contes d'Hoffmann, Périchole*; ORFF: *Kluge*; PENDERECKI: *Teufel von Loudun★*; POULENC: *Dialogues des Carmélites★, Mamelles de Tirésias*; PUCCINI: *Bohème★, Butterfly★, Manon Lescaut★, Tosca★, Turandot*; RABAUD: *Mârouf*; RAVEL: *Heure espagnole★*; ROSSINI: *Barbiere di Siviglia*; SAINT-SAENS: *Samson et Dalila★*; STRAUSS, J: *Fledermaus*; STRAUSS, R: *Salome*; TCHAIKOVSKY: *Eugene Onegin, Pique Dame★*; VERDI: *Aida★, Ballo in maschera★, Don Carlo★, Ernani★, Falstaff, Rigoletto, Simon Boccanegra★, Traviata, Trovatore★*; WAGNER: *Fliegende Holländer★, Lohengrin, Rheingold★, Siegfried, Götterdämmerung★, Tannhäuser, Tristan und Isolde★*; WEBER: *Freischütz*. Also TOMASI: *Miguel Mañara*; ROSENFELD: *Alltägliche Wunder*; RIVIER: *Vénitienne*; EMMANUEL: *Salamine*; LAZZARI: *Tour de feu*. **World premieres:** SEMENOFF: *Evangeline* 1964; TOMASI: *Ulysse* 1965, both at Théâtre Municipal, Mulhouse; SAGUER: *Mariana Pineda* 1970; BENTOIU: *Hamlet* 1974, both at Opéra de Marseille. Video—French TV: *Trovatore*. Conducted major orch in Europe. **Res:** 208 Ave du Fournas, 83700 Saint Raphaël, France. Mgmt: IMR/FRA; GOR/UK; SLZ/FRG.

GIULIANO, GIUSEPPE. Stages/produces opera. Also designs stage-lighting and is a singer & actor. Italian. Asst Art Dir & Resident Stage Dir, Teatro dell'Opera, Rome. Also Resident Stage Dir & Adm for theater in Rome; Art Dir, Teatro Guimera, Santa Cruz, Spain 1974- . Born 19 Jan 1934, Asmara, Eritrea. Wife Gianna Lollini, occupation opera singer, soprano. Studied: Rome, incl music and voice. Operatic training as asst stage dir at var theaters in & outside Italy. **Operatic debut:** *Trovatore* Teatro Siena 1955; as singer: Silvio (*Pagliacci*) Livorno 1952.

Directed/produced opera for major companies in ITA: Naples, Rome Opera; SPA: Barcelona. **Operas staged with these companies incl** BELLINI: *Norma, Pirata, Puritani, Sonnambula*; BIZET: *Carmen*; CILEA: *A. Lecouvreur★*; DONIZETTI: *Anna Bolena★, Don Pasquale★, Elisir, Favorite★, Lucia★*; GIORDANO: *Andrea Chénier, Fedora*; GOUNOD: *Faust*; LEONCAVALLO: *Pagliacci★*; MASCAGNI: *Amico Fritz, Cavalleria rusticana★*; MENOTTI: *Amelia al ballo, Medium, Old Maid and the Thief, Telephone*; PERGOLESI: *Frate 'nnamorato, Serva padrona*; PONCHIELLI: *Gioconda*; PUCCINI: *Bohème, Fanciulla del West, Gianni Schicchi, Butterfly★, Manon Lescaut, Rondine, Suor Angelica, Tabarro★, Tosca★, Turandot*; ROSSINI: *Barbiere di Siviglia, Cenerentola★, Guillaume Tell, Scala di seta*; VERDI: *Aida, Ballo in maschera★, Don Carlo★, Ernani★, Falstaff★, Forza del destino, Luisa Miller★, Nabucco★, Otello, Rigoletto★, Traviata, Trovatore★*. Also ALFANO: *Risurrezione*; GIORDANO: *Cena delle beffe*; MOZART: *Bastien und Bastienne*; ROSSELLINI: *Sguardo dal ponte*. Previous leading positions with major theater companies: Art Consult, Teatro Comunale, L'Aquila 1967-69.

GIULINI, CARLO MARIA. Conductor of opera and symphony. Italian. Music Dir, Vienna Symph Orch, Austria. Born 9 March 1914, Barletta, Italy. Married. Three children. Studied: Accad di S Cecilia, Rome; Chigiana Acad, Siena; A Casella, B Molinari; incl viola. **Operatic debut:** *Traviata* Bergamo 1951. Symph debut: Rome 1944. Awards: Grammy Rec Awd 1971. Prev adm positions in opera: Princ Cond La Scala Milan 1954-58; Princ Cond Rome Opera.

Conducted with major companies in FRA: Aix-en-Provence Fest, Strasbourg; CZE: Prague National; SWI: Zurich; HOL: Amsterdam; ISR: Tel Aviv; ITA: Florence Maggio, Milan La Scala, Rome Opera, Turin, Venice; UK: Edinburgh Fest, Glyndebourne Fest, London Royal; et al. **Operas with these companies incl** GLUCK: *Alceste;* HAYDN: *Mondo della luna;* MOZART: *Nozze di Figaro;* MUSSORGSKY: *Boris Godunov;* ROSSINI: *Cenerentola, Italiana in Algeri;* VERDI: *Attila, Don Carlo‡, Due Foscari, Ernani, Falstaff, Rigoletto, Traviata, Trovatore‡;* WEBER: *Euryanthe;* et al. On records only MOZART: *Don Giovanni.* Recorded for London, Angel, EMI. Conducted major orch in Europe, USA/Canada. Previous positions as Mus Dir with major orch: Orch di Radio Italiana, Turin. **Res:** Bolzano, Italy. Mgmt: CAM/USA; GOR/UK.

GLAZE, GARY. Lyric tenor. American. Resident mem: New York City Opera. Born Pittsburgh, PA, USA. Wife Lorrie Pierce, occupation pianist, teacher. Studied: Univ of Michigan, Ralph Herbert, Ann Arbor, USA; Cornelius Reid, New York. **Debut:** Don Ottavio (*Don Giovanni*) Opera Orch of New York 1969. Previous occupations: secy to dean of music school; two yrs univ instructor. Awards: Outstanding Young Artist, *Musical America,* 1969; Sullivan Fndt Awd; two grants M B Rockefeller Fund.

Sang with major companies in USA: Hawaii, Kansas City, Kentucky, Milwaukee Florentine, New York City Opera, Philadelphia Lyric, San Antonio. **Roles with these companies incl** BRITTEN: Albert Herring★, Peter Quint★ (*Turn of the Screw*); DONIZETTI: Ernesto★ (*Don Pasquale*), Nemorino★ (*Elisir*); GINASTERA: Orsino★ (*Beatrix Cenci*); MENOTTI: Kodanda★ (*Dernier sauvage*); MOZART: Ferrando★ (*Così fan tutte*), Don Ottavio★ (*Don Giovanni*), Belmonte★ (*Entführung aus dem Serail*), Idamante★ (*Idomeneo*), Tamino★ (*Zauberflöte*); ROSSINI: Almaviva★ (*Barbiere di Siviglia*); STRAUSS, J: Alfred★ (*Fledermaus*); WAGNER: David★ (*Meistersinger*). Gives recitals. Appears with symphony orchestra. **Res:** New York, NY, USA. Mgmt: DSP/USA.

GLENN, BONITA LAVADA. Lyric soprano. American. Resident mem: St Gallen Stadttheater, Switzerland. Born 16 Nov 1946, Washington, DC, USA. Single. Studied: Philadelphia Musical Acad, Maureen Forrester, PA; Mme Marinka Gurewich, New York. **Debut:** Musetta (*Bohème*) Pennsylvania Opera Co, Chester, PA, USA 1969. Previous occupations: PS teacher. Awards: three Rockefeller Fndt Grants; Sullivan Fndt Awd.

Sang with major companies in USA: Baltimore, Houston, Lake George, Miami, Philadelphia Grand, Santa Fe. **Roles with these companies incl** BIZET: Léila★ (*Pêcheurs de perles*); DONIZETTI: Adina★ (*Elisir*); MASSENET: Manon★; PUCCINI: Musetta★ (*Bohème*), Liù★ (*Turandot*). Gives recitals. Appears with symphony orchestra. Mgmt: DSP/USA.

GLIGOR, JOVAN; né Jovan Gligorijevic. Dramatic baritone. Yugoslavian. Resident mem: State Opera, Belgrade. Born 16 Oct 1914, Krusevac, Yugoslavia. Wife Olga. Two children. Studied: Consv of Music, Vienna. **Debut:** Silvio (*Pagliacci*) State Opera, Belgrade 1941. Previous occupations: lawyer. Awards: State Order of Labor; Awd of Rep of Serbia; Belgrade Order of Labor, Ntl Theater Awd.

Sang with major companies in AUS: Graz, Vienna Staatsoper & Volksoper; BUL: Sofia; CZE: Brno; DEN: Copenhagen; FRA: Paris; GRE: Athens National & Festival; FR GER: Berlin Deutsche Oper, Wiesbaden; GER DR: Berlin Staatsoper, Dresden; HUN: Budapest; ITA: Palermo, Trieste, Venice; NOR: Oslo; POL: Warsaw; ROM: Bucharest; SPA: Barcelona; SWI: Geneva; UK: Edinburgh Fest; USSR: Leningrad Kirov, Moscow Bolshoi; YUG: Dubrovnik, Zagreb, Belgrade. **Roles with these companies incl** BEETHOVEN: Don Pizarro (*Fidelio*); BIZET: Escamillo★ (*Carmen*); BORODIN: Prince Igor★; DONIZETTI: Dott Malatesta (*Don Pasquale*), Enrico (*Lucia*); GIORDANO: Carlo Gérard (*Andrea Chénier*); GOTOVAC: Sima★ (*Ero der Schelm*); LEONCAVALLO: Tonio★ (*Pagliacci*); MASCAGNI: Alfio★ (*Cavalleria rusticana*); MASSENET: Albert (*Werther*); MUSSORGSKY: Shaklovity★ (*Khovanshchina*); PONCHIELLI: Barnaba★ (*Gioconda*); PUCCINI: Jack Rance (*Fanciulla del West*), Sharpless★‡ (*Butterfly*), Scarpia★ (*Tosca*); ROSSINI: Figaro★ (*Barbiere di Siviglia*); SAINT-SAENS: Grand prêtre (*Samson et Dalila*); TCHAIKOVSKY: Eugene Onegin, Yeletsky★ (*Pique Dame*); VERDI: Amonasro★ (*Aida*), Renato (*Ballo in maschera*), Rodrigo★ (*Don Carlo*), Don Carlo★ (*Forza del destino*), Nabucco★, Iago★ (*Otello*), Rigoletto★, Germont★ (*Traviata*), Conte di Luna★ (*Trovatore*); WAGNER: Holländer. Also PROKOFIEV: Leander★ (*Love for Three Oranges*). Recorded for: Decca, Remington. Gives recitals. Appears with symphony orchestra. Teaches voice. **Res:** Tadeuska Koscuskog 20, Belgrade, Yugoslavia. Mgmt: YGC/YUG.

GLOSSOP, PETER. Baritone. British. Born 6 Jul 1928, Sheffield, UK. Wife Joyce Blackham, occupation opera singer. Studied: Eva Rich, Sheffield; Joseph Hislop, London. **Debut:** Moralès (*Carmen*) Sadler's Wells, London 1953. Previous occupations: bank clerk. Awards: Hon DM, Sheffield Univ 1970; Gold Medal, First Prize Intl Compt Young Opera Singers, Sofia 1961; Gold Medal, Barcelona 1968; Verdi Gold Medal, Parma 1965.

Sang with major companies in ARG: Buenos Aires; AUS: Salzburg Fest, Vienna Staatsoper; BUL: Sofia; CAN: Montreal/Quebec, Toronto; FRA: Lyon, Orange Fest, Paris; FR GER: Berlin Deutsche Oper, Hamburg, Munich Staatsoper; HOL: Amsterdam; HUN: Budapest; ITA: Bologna, Genoa, Milan La Scala, Naples, Palermo, Parma, Spoleto Fest, Trieste, Verona Arena; MEX: Mexico City; POL: Warsaw; SPA: Barcelona; SWI: Zurich; UK: Aldeburgh Fest, Cardiff Welsh, Edinburgh Fest, Glasgow Scottish, London Royal & English National; USA: Boston, Chicago, Dallas Civic Opera, Hartford, Houston, New Orleans, New York Met, Philadelphia Lyric, San Diego, San Francisco Opera; YUG: Dubrovnik. **Roles with these companies incl** BERG: Wozzeck★; BERLIOZ: Choroebus‡ (*Troyens*); BIZET: Escamillo (*Carmen*), Zurga (*Pêcheurs de perles*); BRITTEN: Billy Budd‡, Demetrius (*Midsummer Night*); CATALANI: Vincenzo Gellner (*Wally*); DONIZETTI: Dott Malatesta (*Don Pasquale*), Alfonse (*Favorite*), Nottingham‡ (*Roberto Devereux*); GIORDANO: Carlo Gérard★ (*Andrea Chénier*); HANDEL: Argante (*Rinaldo*); HENZE: Lescaut (*Boulevard Solitude*); LEONCAVALLO: Tonio (*Pagliacci*); MOZART: Guglielmo (*Così fan tutte*), Don Giovanni★; PONCHIELLI: Barnaba (*Gioconda*); PUCCINI: Marcello★ (*Bohème*), Scarpia★ (*Tosca*); PURCELL: Aeneas‡; RAVEL: Ramiro (*Heure espagnole*); ROSSINI: Figaro (*Barbiere di Siviglia*), Guillaume Tell; SAINT-SAENS: Grand prêtre (*Samson et Dalila*); SMETANA: Kezal (*Bartered Bride*); STRAUSS, R: Altair (*Aegyptische Helena*), Jochanaan (*Salome*); TCHAIKOVSKY: Eugene Onegin; THOMAS: Lothario (*Mignon*); VERDI: Amonasro★ (*Aida*), Ezio★ (*Attila*), Renato★ (*Ballo in maschera*), Rodrigo (*Don Carlo*), Don Carlo (*Ernani*), Falstaff★, Don Carlo★ (*Forza del destino*), Miller (*Luisa Miller*), Macbeth, Nabucco★, Iago★ (*Otello*), Simon Boccanegra★, Germont (*Traviata*), Conte di Luna★ (*Trovatore*), Monforte★ (*Vespri*); WAGNER: Wolfram (*Tannhäuser*). Recorded for: Decca, EMI, Westminster. Video/Film: Billy Budd; Rigoletto; Escamillo (*Carmen*); Iago (*Otello*); Tonio (*Pagliacci*); Simon Boccanegra. **Res:** 11 The Bishop's Ave, London, UK. **Mgmt:** GOR/UK.

GOBBATO, ANGELO. Stages/produces opera and is a singer. Italian. Born 5 Jul 1943, Milan. Single. Studied: Prof R Mohr, Mavis Taylor, Cape Town. Incl music, piano and voice: Albina Bini, Adelaide Armholdt, Fred Dalberg, Cape Town; Carlo Tagliabue, Milan. Operatic training as asst stage dir at Cape Town Opera. **Operatic debut:** as bass-baritone, Kezal (*Bartered Bride*) 1965; as stage dir *Matrimonio segreto* 1966; both at CAPAB, Cape Town. Previous occupation: lecturer in chemistry. Awards: First Nederburg Prize for Opera, Stellenbosch Farmers Winery 1972.

Sang with & directed/produced opera for major companies in SOUTH AFR: Cape Town. **Roles with these companies incl** CIMAROSA: Count Robinson (*Matrimonio segreto*); DONIZETTI: Enrico★ (*Campanello*), Don Pasquale★, Enrico★ (*Lucia*); MASCAGNI: Rabbi David★ (*Amico Fritz*); MOZART: Guglielmo★ & Don Alfonso (*Così fan tutte*), Leporello★ (*Don Giovanni*), Figaro★ (*Nozze di Figaro*), Papageno★ (*Zauberflöte*); PUCCINI: Gianni Schicchi★; ROSSINI: Figaro★ & Dott Bartolo★ (*Barbiere di Siviglia*), Dandini★ (*Cenerentola*); SMETANA: Kezal (*Bartered Bride*); VERDI: Ford (*Falstaff*); WOLF-FERRARI: Pantalone (*Donne curiose*), Conte Gil★ (*Segreto di Susanna*). **Operas staged with these**

companies incl BARTOK: *Bluebeard's Castle★;* CIMAROSA: *Matrimonio segreto;* DONIZETTI: *Campanello★, Don Pasquale★, Elisir★;* MASCAGNI: *Amico Fritz★;* MOZART: *Così fan tutte★, Nozze di Figaro★;* NICOLAI: *Lustigen Weiber;* OFFENBACH: *Contes d'Hoffmann★;* PUCCINI: *Bohème★, Butterfly★;* ROSSINI: *Barbiere di Siviglia, Cenerentola★;* STRAUSS, J: *Fledermaus★;* VERDI: *Ballo in maschera★;* WOLF-FERRARI: *Donne curiose, Segreto di Susanna★.* Gives recitals. Appears with symphony orchestra. **Res:** 14 Kohling St, Cape Town, South Africa.

GOBBI, TITO. Dramatic baritone. Italian. Born 24 Oct 1915, Bassano del Grappa, Vicenza, Italy. Wife Matilde de Rensis. One daughter. Studied: Giulio Crimi, Mo Tullio Serafin, Italy. **Debut:** Germont (*Traviata*) Teatro Adriano, Rome 1937.

Sang with major companies in AUS: Salzburg Fest, Vienna Staatsoper; BRA: Rio de Janeiro; CAN: Montreal/Quebec, Ottawa, Toronto; DEN: Copenhagen; FIN: Helsinki; FRA: Lyon, Paris; GRE: Athens Fest; FR GER: Berlin Deutsche Oper, Hamburg, Karlsruhe, Mannheim, Munich Staatsoper, Stuttgart, Wiesbaden; HUN: Budapest; ISR: Tel Aviv; ITA: Bologna, Florence Maggio & Teatro Comunale, Genoa, Milan La Scala, Naples, Palermo, Parma, Rome Opera & Caracalla, Trieste, Turin, Venice, Verona Arena; MON: Monte Carlo; NOR: Oslo; POR: Lisbon; ROM: Bucharest; S AFR: Johannesburg; SWE: Stockholm; SWI: Geneva, Zurich; UK: Cardiff Welsh, Edinburgh Fest, Glasgow Scottish, London Royal Opera; USA: Boston, Chicago Lyric, Hartford, New York Metropolitan, Philadelphia Grand, Pittsburgh, San Antonio, San Diego, San Francisco Opera; YUG: Zagreb, Belgrade. **Roles with these companies incl** BERG: Wozzeck; BERLIOZ: Méphistophélès (*Damnation de Faust*); CILEA: Michonnet (*A. Lecouvreur*); DALLAPICCOLA: Riviere (*Volo di notte*); DONIZETTI: Dott Malatesta (*Don Pasquale*), Belcore (*Elisir*), Enrico (*Lucia*); GIORDANO: Carlo Gérard (*Andrea Chénier*), De Siriex (*Fedora*); HINDEMITH: Professor (*Hin und zurück*); LEONCAVALLO: Tonio (*Pagliacci*); MONTEVERDI: Orfeo; MOZART: Don Giovanni, Conte Almaviva (*Nozze di Figaro*); PUCCINI: Marcello (*Bohème*), Gianni Schicchi, Sharpless (*Butterfly*), Michele (*Tabarro*), Scarpia (*Tosca*); ROSSINI: Figaro (*Barbiere di Siviglia*), Guillaume Tell; SPONTINI: Cinna (*Vestale*); STRAUSS, R: Jochanaan (*Salome*); VERDI: Amonasro (*Aida*), Renato (*Ballo in maschera*), Rodrigo (*Don Carlo*), Ford & Falstaff (*Falstaff*), Macbeth, Nabucco, Iago (*Otello*), Rigoletto, Simon Boccanegra, Germont (*Traviata*); WAGNER: Gunther (*Götterdämmerung*); WOLF-FERRARI: Lelio (*Donne curiose*), Rafaele (*Gioielli della Madonna*). **Directed/produced opera for major companies in** FRA: Paris; ITA: Florence Comunale, Rome Opera, Venice; MON: Monte Carlo; SWI: Zurich; UK: Edinburgh Fest; USA: Chicago. **Operas staged and/or designed with these companies incl** MOZART: *Don Giovanni★;* PUCCINI: *Gianni Schicchi★, Tabarro★, Tosca★;* ROSSINI: *Barbiere di Siviglia★;* VERDI: *Ballo in maschera★, Falstaff★, Otello★, Simon Boccanegra★.* Recorded for: EMI, RCA, Decca, DG. Film: Figaro (*Barbiere di*

Siviglia); Rigoletto; Don Carlo (*Forza del destino*); Belcore (*Elisir*); (*Pagliacci*) etc; total of 26 films. Gives recitals. Appears with symphony orchestra. Teaches voice. **Res:** V Valle della Moletta 47, Rome, Italy. Mgmt: GOR/UK.

GOCKLEY, R DAVID. American. Gen Dir, Houston Grand Opera, Jones Hall for the Performing Arts, 615 Louisiana, Houston, TX 77002; also Texas Opera Theater. In charge of art policy, mus & dram matters & finances. Born 13 Jul 1943, Philadelphia. Wife Patricia Wise, occupation opera singer, soprano. Studied: New England Consv, Boston; Brown Univ, Providence, RI; Columbia Univ, NY. Plays the piano. Previous occupations: opera singer, Santa Fe Opera 1965-67; Dir of Music, Newark Acad 1965-67; Dir of Dram & tchr of Eng, Buckley School, NY 1967-69. Form positions, primarily adm: Box Office/House Mng, Santa Fe Opera 1968; Asst to Mng Dir, Lincoln Center for the Performing Arts, NY 1970. Started with present company in 1970 as Bus Mng; in present position since 1972. World premieres at theaters under his management: PASATIERI: *Seagull* 1974; FLOYD: *Bilby's Doll* 1976, both at Houston. Initiated major policy changes incl: free outdoor Spring Opera Festival of fully staged operas; "American Series" of opera in English, "Young American Series" for students, discount prices; Texas Opera Theater resident touring ensemble; expanded season, subscriptions from 5,000 to 10,000, budget from $600,000 to $2.1 million; hired first guest conductors. Mem of Bd of Dir; OPERA America; Natl Endowment for the Arts Music Advisory Panel, Opera Section; Prof Commtt Central Opera Service. **Res:** Houston, TX, USA.

GODFREY, VICTOR JOHN. Bass-baritone. Canadian. Born Deloraine, Man. Wife Françoise Egberta. Studied: Gladys Whitehead, Winnipeg; Joan Cross CBE, Ntl School of Opera, London; Hans Hotter, Munich; Giovanni Inghilleri, Milan. **Debut:** Dottore (*Macbeth*) Royal Opera, Covent Garden 1960. Previous occupations: studied law. Awards: Winner, Kathleen Ferrier Mem Schlshp, London 1959; Arts Fllshp, Canadian Gvnmt/Canada Council 1959.

Sang with major companies in BEL: Brussels; CAN: Montreal/Quebec; DEN: Copenhagen; FRA: Lyon, Marseille, Nice, Rouen; FR GER: Düsseldorf-Duisburg, Hannover; HOL: Amsterdam; ITA: Florence Comunale, Naples; POR: Lisbon; SWE: Drottningholm Fest; UK: Aldeburgh Fest, Cardiff Welsh, Edinburgh Fest, Glasgow Scottish, London Royal & English National. **Roles with these companies incl** BEETHOVEN: Don Fernando★ (*Fidelio*); BRITTEN: Theseus (*Midsummer Night*); BUSONI: Matteo (*Arlecchino*); DALLAPICCOLA: Antinuo (*Ulisse*); GLUCK: Agamemnon (*Iphigénie en Aulide*); HANDEL: Polyphemus★ (*Acis and Galatea*), Ptolemy (*Giulio Cesare*); HINDEMITH: Mathis; HUMPERDINCK: Peter (*Hänsel und Gretel*); MUSSORGSKY: Varlaam★ (*Boris Godunov*); PUCCINI: Colline (*Bohème*), Scarpia (*Tosca*); STRAUSS, R: Orest (*Elektra*), Jochanaan★ (*Salome*); VERDI: Amonasro (*Aida*), Banquo (*Macbeth*), Zaccaria★ (*Nabucco*), Germont★ (*Traviata*); WAGNER: Amfortas (*Parsifal*), Wotan (*Rheingold★, Walküre★*), Wanderer★ (*Siegfried*), Gunther (*Götterdämmerung*), Wolfram (*Tannhäuser*). Also DONIZETTI: Raimondo (*Lucia*). **World premieres:** TIPPETT: Hector (*King Priam*) Royal Opera, Covent Garden 1962; BRITTEN: Azarias (*Burning Fiery Furnace*) Aldeburgh Fest 1966. Video—CBC TV: Orest (*Elektra*), Colline (*Bohème*), Azarias (*Burning Fiery Furnace*). Gives recitals. Appears with symphony orchestra. **Res:** London, UK & Düsseldorf, FR Ger. Mgmt: CST/UK; SLZ/FRG: RNR/SWI.

GOEKE, LEO. Lyric tenor. American. Born 6 Nov 1936, Kirksville, MO, USA. Wife Margery Ryan, occupation singer. One child. Studied: Louisiana State Univ, Dallas Draper, Baton Rouge; State Univ of Iowa, David Lloyd; Hans Heinz, Margaret Harshaw, New York.

Sang with major companies in FRA: Strasbourg; HOL: Amsterdam; UK: Glyndebourne Fest; USA: Baltimore, New York Met & City Opera, Seattle, Washington DC. **Roles with these companies incl** DONIZETTI: Ernesto (*Don Pasquale*), Edgardo★ (*Lucia*); MASSENET: Des Grieux★ (*Manon*); MOZART: Ferrando★ (*Così fan tutte*), Don Ottavio★ (*Don Giovanni*), Idamante★ (*Idomeneo*), Tamino★ (*Zauberflöte*); PUCCINI: Rodolfo★ (*Bohème*), Ruggero (*Rondine*); ROSSINI: Almaviva★ (*Barbiere di Siviglia*); STRAUSS, J: Alfred★ (*Fledermaus*); STRAUSS, R: Flamand★ (*Capriccio*), Ein Sänger★ (*Rosenkavalier*); STRAVINSKY: Tom Rakewell★ (*Rake's Progress*); VERDI: Fenton (*Falstaff*), Duca di Mantova★ (*Rigoletto*), Alfredo★ (*Traviata*). Recorded for: RCA. Gives recitals. Appears with symphony orchestra. **Res:** New York, NY, USA. Mgmt: KAZ/USA; AIM/UK.

GOLDBERG, REINER. Dramatic tenor. German. Resident mem: Staatsoper Dresden, Staatsoper Berlin, Ger DR. Born 17 Oct 1939, Crostau, Germany. Divorced. Studied: Hochschule für Musik, Prof Arno Schellenberg, Dresden. **Debut:** Luigi (*Tabarro*) Landesbühnen Sachsen, Dresden 1966. Previous occupations: locksmith.

Sang with major companies in FRA: Paris; GER DR: Berlin Staatsoper, Dresden, Leipzig; USSR: Leningrad Kirov. **Roles with these companies incl** d'ALBERT: Pedro★ (*Tiefland*); BEETHOVEN: Florestan★ (*Fidelio*); BERG: Tambourmajor★‡ (*Wozzeck*); GAY/Britten: Macheath (*Beggar's Opera*); MASCAGNI: Turiddu (*Cavalleria rusticana*); MONTEVERDI: Testo★ & Tancredi★ (*Combattimento di Tancredi*); PAISIELLO: Almaviva (*Barbiere di Siviglia*); PUCCINI: Cavaradossi★ (*Tosca*); ROSSINI: Almaviva (*Barbiere di Siviglia*); SCHOENBERG: Aron★; SHOSTAKOVICH: Sergei★ (*Katerina Ismailova*); STRAUSS, J: Eisenstein★ (*Fledermaus*); TCHAIKOVSKY: Gherman★ (*Pique Dame*); VERDI: Fenton★ (*Falstaff*), Manrico (*Trovatore*); WAGNER: Siegmund★ (*Walküre*); WEBER: Max★ (*Freischütz*), Hüon★ (*Oberon*). Also BUZKO: Dreamer★ (*White Nights*); WEINBERGER: Babinsky (*Schwanda*); EGK: Ulysse (*Siebzehn Tage und vier Minuten*); WEILL: Erster Sohn (*Sieben Todessünden*); WAGNER-REGENY: Fabiani (*Günstling*). **World premieres:** MEYER: Mako (*Reiter in der Nacht*) Staatsoper Berlin 1973. Recorded for: Eterna, VEB.

Video/Film: Florestan (*Fidelio*). Gives recitals. Appears with symphony orchestra. Teaches voice. Coaches repertoire. **Res:** Dr Schmincke Allee 4, Radebeul, Ger DR. Mgmt: KDR/GDR.

GOLDSCHMIDT, WALTER. Conductor of opera and symphony; composer; operatic stage director. Austrian. Resident Cond, Opernhaus Graz. Born 16 Mar 1917, Vienna. Wife Sonja, occupation conductor and composer. Two sons, one daughter. Studied: Akad für Musik, Vienna; incl piano, percussion, organ, bassoon and voice. Plays the piano. Operatic training as repetiteur, asst cond, chorus master & opera singer at Opernhaus Graz. **Operatic debut:** Opernhaus Graz 1945. Symphonic debut: Grazer Phil 1948. Awards: Professor 1968.

Conducted with major companies in AUS: Bregenz Fest, Graz, Vienna Volksoper; CAN: Montreal/Quebec, Toronto, Vancouver; FR GER: Bielefeld, Karlsruhe, Krefeld, Mannheim, Munich Staatsoper; ITA: Florencè Maggio, Naples, Rome Caracalla, Trieste, Turin, Venice; SPA: Barcelona, Majorca; SWI: Zurich; USA: Boston, Chicago, Kansas City, Memphis, New Orleans, Philadelphia Grand, Pittsburgh, San Diego, San Francisco Opera, Seattle. **Operas with these companies incl** ADAM: *Postillon de Lonjumeau;* d'ALBERT: *Tiefland;* BEETHOVEN: *Fidelio;* BIZET: *Carmen;* BOIELDIEU: *Dame blanche;* CIMAROSA: *Matrimonio segreto;* DELIBES: *Roi l'a dit;* DVORAK: *Rusalka;* FLOTOW: *Martha;* GERSHWIN: *Porgy and Bess;* GIORDANO: *Andrea Chénier;* GOTOVAC: *Ero der Schelm;* GOUNOD: *Faust;* HALEVY: *Juive;* HINDEMITH: *Cardillac, Hin und zurück;* HUMPERDINCK: *Hänsel und Gretel;* JANACEK: *Jenufa;* KORNGOLD: *Tote Stadt;* LORTZING: *Waffenschmied, Wildschütz, Zar und Zimmermann;* MARSCHNER: *Hans Heiling;* MASCAGNI: *Cavalleria rusticana;* MENOTTI: *Consul, Medium, Telephone;* MOZART: *Bastien und Bastienne, Così fan tutte, Entführung aus dem Serail, Nozze di Figaro, Schauspieldirektor, Zauberflöte;* NICOLAI: *Lustigen Weiber;* OFFENBACH: *Contes d'Hoffmann, Périchole, Mariage aux lanternes;* PERGOLESI: *Serva padrona;* PUCCINI: *Bohème, Gianni Schicchi, Butterfly;* ROSSINI: *Barbiere di Siviglia, Turco in Italia;* SMETANA: *Bartered Bride;* STRAUSS, J: *Fledermaus;* TCHAIKOVSKY: *Eugene Onegin;* VERDI: *Ballo in maschera, Rigoletto, Traviata, Trovatore;* WAGNER: *Fliegende Holländer;* WEBER: *Freischütz;* WEINBERGER: *Schwanda.* Recorded for Livingstone, Preiser. Conducted major orch in Europe, USA/Canada. Previous positions as Mus Dir with major orch: Grazer Phil 1960-69. Teaches at Acad Graz, Prof.

GOMEZ MARTINEZ, MIGUEL ANGEL. Conductor of opera and symphony; composer. Spanish. Resident Cond, Deutsche Oper Berlin, FR Ger. Born 17 Sep 1949, Granada, Spain. Single. Studied: Acad of Music, Vienna, Hans Swarowsky, Karl Österreicher; incl piano, violin and voice. Operatic training as repetiteur & asst cond at Municipal Theater St Pölten, Austria 1970-72; Municipal Theater Lucerne, Switzerland 1972-74. **Operatic debut:** *Fidelio* Deutsche Oper Berlin 1973. Symphonic debut: Acad of Music, Vienna 1970.

Conducted with major companies in AUS: Vienna Staatsoper; FRA: Aix-en-Provence Fest; FR GER: Berlin Deutsche Oper, Frankfurt, Hamburg, Munich Staatsoper; UK: London Royal. **Operas with these companies incl** BEETHOVEN: *Fidelio★;* LEONCAVALLO: *Pagliacci★;* MASCAGNI: *Cavalleria rusticana★;* MOZART: *Don Giovanni, Schauspieldirektor★, Nozze di Figaro★, Oca del Cairo★, Zauberflöte;* PERGOLESI: *Serva padrona★;* PONCHIELLI: *Gioconda★;* PUCCINI: *Bohème, Gianni Schicchi, Tabarro, Tosca;* ROSSINI: *Cambiale di matrimonio★;* VERDI: *Attila, Ballo in maschera★, Don Carlo★, Otello★, Simon Boccanegra★, Trovatore★.* Conducted major orch in Europe. **Res:** Caspar Theyss-Str 11, D-1 Berlin 33, FR Ger. Mgmt: TAU/SWI.

GONZALEZ, CARMEN PAGLIARO; née Vallejo Gonzalez. Lyric mezzo-soprano & contralto. Italian. Born 16 Apr 1939, Valladolid, Spain. Husband Marcello Pagliaro, occupation economist. One child. Studied: Consv Musica, Madrid; Scuola Teatro alla Scala, Milan; Magda Piccarolo, Rodolfo Celletti, Milan. **Debut:** Isolier (*Comte Ory*) Opera da Camera, Milan 1968. Awards: Stipd Ministry of Education, Madrid; Winner Conc La Scala School, Milan.

Sang with major companies in BEL: Brussels; FRA: Aix-en-Provence Fest, Paris, Toulouse; ITA: Bologna, Florence Maggio & Comunale, Genoa, Milan La Scala, Naples, Palermo, Rome Opera & Caracalla, Trieste, Turin, Venice, Verona Arena; MEX: Mexico City; MON: Monte Carlo; POR: Lisbon; SPA: Barcelona; SWI: Zurich; UK: Glyndebourne Fest; USA: New York City Opera, Washington DC; YUG: Dubrovnik, Belgrade. **Roles with these companies incl** BELLINI: Romeo (*Capuleti ed i Montecchi*), Adalgisa (*Norma*); BIZET: Carmen★; CAVALLI: Clori (*Egisto*), Sicle (*Ormindo*); CILEA: Princesse de Bouillon (*A. Lecouvreur*); CIMAROSA: Fidalma (*Matrimonio segreto*); DEBUSSY: Geneviève (*Pelléas et Mélisande*); DONIZETTI: Maffio Orsini (*Lucrezia Borgia*), Sara (*Roberto Devereux*); DUKAS: Ariane & Nourrice (*Ariane et Barbe Bleue*); FALLA: Abuela (*Vida breve*); GLUCK: Orfeo; HANDEL: Bradamante (*Alcina*), Cornelia (*Giulio Cesare*); MASSENET: Charlotte (*Werther*); MONTEVERDI: Poppea (*Incoronazione di Poppea*); MOZART: Dorabella★ (*Così fan tutte*), Cherubino (*Nozze di Figaro*); OFFENBACH: Giulietta (*Contes d'Hoffmann*); PONCHIELLI: Laura (*Gioconda*); PUCCINI: Abbadessa★ (*Suor Angelica*); ROSSINI: Rosina (*Barbiere di Siviglia*), Angelina (*Cenerentola*), Isolier (*Comte Ory*), Isabella (*Italiana in Algeri*); SAINT-SAENS: Dalila; STRAUSS, R: Klytämnestra★ (*Elektra*), Octavian (*Rosenkavalier*); STRAVINSKY: Jocasta (*Oedipus Rex*); TCHAIKOVSKY: Olga (*Eugene Onegin*); VERDI: Amneris (*Aida*), Ulrica (*Ballo in maschera*), Dame Quickly★ (*Falstaff*), Preziosilla (*Forza del destino*). **World premieres:** WEBER/Mahler: (*Drei Pintos*) Turin 1974. Gives recitals. Appears with symphony orchestra. **Res:** V Morgagni 1, Perugia, Italy. Mgmt: CAM/USA.

GONZALEZ, MANUEL. Lyric baritone. Spanish. Resident mem: Théâtre Royal de la Monnaie, Brussels. Born 30 Apr 1944, Madrid. Single. Studied: Royal Consv, Madrid. **Debut:** Ping (*Turandot*) Théâtre Royal, Brussels 1971. Awards: Intl Chamber Awd, Antwerp, Belgium; Prize of Dutch Ministry of Culture.

Sang with major companies in AUS: Vienna Volksoper; BEL: Brussels; FRA: Lyon, Marseille, Nice, Paris; FR GER: Dortmund, Essen, Frankfurt, Hamburg, Hannover, Mannheim, Stuttgart, Wuppertal; ITA: Parma, Turin; POR: Lisbon; SPA: Barcelona; SWI: Geneva. **Roles with these companies incl** BIZET: Escamillo★ (*Carmen*); DEBUSSY: Pelléas; DONIZETTI: Dott Malatesta (*Don Pasquale*), Belcore (*Elisir*), Alfonse (*Favorite*), Enrico (*Lucia*); GIORDANO: Carlo Gérard (*Andrea Chénier*); MASCAGNI: Alfio (*Cavalleria rusticana*); MASSENET: Albert (*Werther*); MOZART: Guglielmo★ (*Così fan tutte*), Leporello & Don Giovanni, Conte Almaviva★ & Figaro★ (*Nozze di Figaro*), Papageno (*Zauberflöte*); PUCCINI: Marcello★ (*Bohème*), Gianni Schicchi★, Sharpless★ (*Butterfly*), Lescaut (*Manon Lescaut*); RAVEL: Ramiro (*Heure espagnole*); ROSSINI: Figaro★ (*Barbiere di Siviglia*), Dandini★ (*Cenerentola*), Robert (*Comte Ory*); SAINT-SAENS: Grand prêtre (*Samson et Dalila*); VERDI: Rodrigo★ (*Don Carlo*), Ford (*Falstaff*), Germont (*Traviata*), Conte di Luna (*Trovatore*); WAGNER: Wolfram (*Tannhäuser*). Also GOUNOD: Valentin (*Faust*); ROSSINI: Taddeo (*Italiana in Algeri*); BRITTEN: Tarquinius (*Rape of Lucretia*); DONIZETTI: Giulio Antiquati (*L'ajo nell'imbarazzo*). Gives recitals. Appears with symphony orchestra. Mgmt: IMR/FRA; SLZ/FRG.

GOODALL, REGINALD. Conductor of opera. British. Resident Cond, English National Opera, London. Born 1905, Lincoln, UK. Studied: Royal Coll of Music, London; also in Munich and Vienna; incl piano, organ, violin. Operatic training as asst cond at Covent Garden, London. Awards: *Evening Standard* Awd, UK. Previous adm positions in opera: Mus Dir, Sadler's Wells, London 1944-46.

Conducted with major companies in UK: Glyndebourne Fest, London Royal & English National; et al. **Operas with these companies incl** BEETHOVEN: *Fidelio;* BERG: *Wozzeck;* BRITTEN: *Gloriana, Peter Grimes, Rape of Lucretia;* MASSENET: *Manon;* PUCCINI: *Gianni Schicchi, Tabarro;* ROSSINI: *Barbiere di Siviglia;* WAGNER: *Fliegende Holländer, Meistersinger, Parsifal, Götterdämmerung, Rheingold, Walküre, Siegfried, Tannhäuser;* et al. **World premieres:** BRITTEN: *Peter Grimes* Sadler's Wells, London 1945.

GOODLOE, ROBERT D. Lyric baritone. American. Resident mem: Metropolitan Opera, New York. Born 5 Oct 1936, St Petersburg, FL, USA. Wife Linda, occupation social worker. Studied: Simpson Coll, Indianola, IA, USA; Harvey Brown, Robert Larsen, Armen Boyajian, USA. **Debut:** Conte Almaviva (*Nozze di Figaro*) Des Moines Civic Opera, IA, USA 1963. Previous occupations: Dir of Public Relations, Simpson Coll, Indianola. Awards: Winner Met Op Ntl Counc Aud 1964.

Sang with major companies in USA: Baltimore, Hartford, Lake George, New York Met, Philadelphia Grand, San Francisco Spring. **Roles with** these companies incl DONIZETTI: Dott Malatesta (*Don Pasquale*), Enrico (*Lucia*); GOUNOD: Mercutio (*Roméo*); LEONCAVALLO: Silvio (*Pagliacci*); MASSENET: Lescaut (*Manon*); MOZART: Conte Almaviva★ (*Nozze di Figaro*); PUCCINI: Marcello★ (*Bohème*), Gianni Schicchi, Sharpless★ (*Butterfly*), Michele (*Tabarro*), Scarpia (*Tosca*); ROSSINI: Figaro (*Barbiere di Siviglia*); TCHAIKOVSKY: Yeletsky (*Pique Dame*); VERDI: Paolo★ (*Simon Boccanegra*), Germont★ (*Traviata*). Gives recitals. Appears with symphony orchestra. **Res:** 205 West End Ave, New York, NY, USA. Mgmt: HUR/USA.

GÖTZ, WERNER. Dramatic tenor. German. Resident mem: Deutsche Oper am Rhein, Düsseldorf. Born 7 Dec 1934, Berlin. Wife Helga. Studied: Prof Schmidtmann, Friedrich Wilcke, Dr W Kelch. **Debut:** Don Alvaro (*Forza del destino*) Oldenburg Opera 1967.

Sang with major companies in CZE: Prague Smetana; GRE: Athens Fest; FR GER: Berlin Deutsche Oper, Bielefeld, Bonn, Cologne, Dortmund, Düsseldorf-Duisburg, Essen, Frankfurt, Hamburg, Hannover, Munich Staatsoper, Stuttgart, Wiesbaden; HOL: Amsterdam; POL: Lodz; SPA: Barcelona; SWI: Zurich; UK: London Royal. **Roles with these companies incl** BEETHOVEN: Florestan★ (*Fidelio*); BERLIOZ: Faust★ (*Damnation de Faust*); DVORAK: Prince★ (*Rusalka*); FLOTOW: Lionel (*Martha*); GIORDANO: Andrea Chénier★; JANACEK: Steva★ (*Jenufa*), Boris★ (*Katya Kabanova*), Albert Gregor★ (*Makropoulos Affair*); KELEMEN: Diego★ (*Belagerungszustand*); MOZART: Belfiore (*Finta giardiniera*), Tamino★ (*Zauberflöte*); MUSSORGSKY: Shuisky (*Boris Godunov*); OFFENBACH: Hoffmann★; PUCCINI: Rodolfo (*Bohème*), Luigi★ (*Tabarro*), Cavaradossi★ (*Tosca*); SMETANA: Hans★ (*Bartered Bride*); STRAUSS, J: Eisenstein (*Fledermaus*); STRAUSS, R: Ein Sänger★ (*Rosenkavalier*); STRAVINSKY: Tom Rakewell (*Rake's Progress*); VERDI: Aroldo (*Stiffelio*), Riccardo (*Ballo in maschera*), Don Carlo★, Don Alvaro★ (*Forza del destino*), Duca di Mantova (*Rigoletto*), Alfredo (*Traviata*); WAGNER: Erik★ (*Fliegende Holländer*), Lohengrin★, Parsifal★; WEILL: Jim Mahoney (*Aufstieg und Fall der Stadt Mahagonny*). Appears with symphony orchestra. Mgmt: SLZ/FRG; PAS/FRG; SMN/USA.

GOUGALOFF, PETER GEORGIEV. Dramatic & spinto tenor. Bulgarian. Resident mem: Deutsche Oper, Berlin; Staatsoper Berlin; Nationaloper Sofia. Born 11 Dec 1929, Velingrade, Bulgaria. Wife Ulrike, occupation teacher. One child. Studied: Prof Brambaroff, Sofia; Helge Rosvänge, Germany; Nikolai Ghiaurov. **Debut:** Turiddu (*Cavalleria rusticana*) Deutsche Oper, Berlin 1961. Previous occupations: Prof State Univ Sofia. Awards: Silver Medal Compt Fest Vienna 1959; Kammersänger, Staatsoper Berlin 1969.

Sang with major companies in BUL: Sofia; CZE: Prague National; DEN: Copenhagen; FRA: Bordeaux, Marseille, Paris, Rouen; FR GER: Berlin Deutsche Oper, Bonn, Cologne, Dortmund, Düsseldorf-Duisburg, Frankfurt, Hamburg, Hannover, Karlsruhe, Kassel, Munich Staatsoper, Nürnberg, Saarbrücken, Stuttgart, Wiesbaden,

Wuppertal; GER DR: Berlin Staatsoper, Dresden, Leipzig; HUN: Budapest; ITA: Florence Maggio; SPA: Barcelona; SWI: Zurich; UK: Edinburgh Fest; USSR: Moscow Bolshoi; USA: San Francisco Opera. **Roles with these companies incl** d'ALBERT: Pedro∗ (*Tiefland*); BELLINI: Lord Arthur (*Puritani*); BIZET: Don José∗ (*Carmen*); BORODIN: Vladimir∗ (*Prince Igor*); DONIZETTI: Fernand (*Favorite*), Edgardo (*Lucia*); GIORDANO: Andrea Chénier∗; HINDEMITH: Apprentice∗ (*Cardillac*); JANACEK: Steva∗ (*Jenufa*), Boris (*Katya Kabanova*); LEONCAVALLO: Canio∗ (*Pagliacci*); MASCAGNI: Turiddu∗ (*Cavalleria rusticana*); MILHAUD: Matelot (*Pauvre matelot*); OFFENBACH: Hoffmann∗; PUCCINI: Rodolfo∗ (*Bohème*), Dick Johnson∗ (*Fanciulla del West*), Pinkerton∗ (*Butterfly*), Des Grieux (*Manon Lescaut*), Cavaradossi∗ (*Tosca*), Calaf∗ (*Turandot*); SHOSTAKOVICH: Sergei∗ (*Katerina Ismailova*); SMETANA: Hans∗ (*Bartered Bride*); STRAUSS, R: Matteo∗ (*Arabella*), Aegisth∗ (*Elektra*), Ein Sänger∗ (*Rosenkavalier*); TCHAIKOVSKY: Count Vodemon∗ (*Iolanthe*), Gherman∗ (*Pique Dame*); VERDI: Radames∗ (*Aida*), Foresto∗ (*Attila*), Riccardo (*Ballo in maschera*), Don Carlo∗, Don Alvaro∗ (*Forza del destino*), Duca di Mantova∗ (*Rigoletto*), Gabriele∗ (*Simon Boccanegra*), Manrico∗ (*Trovatore*); WEBER: Max∗ (*Freischütz*). Also CIKKER: Smelkoff (*Resurrection*); MUSSORGSKY: Dimitri∗ (*Boris Godunov*). Recorded for: Balkanton. Gives recitals. Appears with symphony orchestra. Teaches voice. **Res:** Spandauerstr 41, 1 Berlin 20, FR Ger. Mgmt: PAS/FRG; GRE/FRA.

GRAHAM, COLIN; né Colin Graham-Bonnalie. Stages/produces opera, theater & television. Also designs sets & stg-ltng. British. Art Dir, Eng Mus Theatre Co, London. Born 22 Sep 1931. Hove, UK. Single. Studied: Royal Acad of Dramatic Art, Frederick Ranalow, Phyllis Bedells, London; incl music, piano & voice. Operatic training as asst stage dir at English Opera Group, London 1954-60. **Operatic debut:** *Re pastore* London 1954. Theater debut: Old Vic, London 1961. Previous occupation: stage mng, actor. Awards: Churchill Fllshp 1972; Men of Achievement 1972. Previous adm positions in opera: Dir of Productions, English Opera Group, London 1963-75; Assoc Dir of Prod, Sadler's Wells/English National Opera, London 1968-75.
Directed/produced opera for major companies in BEL: Brussels, Liège; CAN: Montreal/Quebec, Toronto; DEN: Copenhagen; FRA: Bordeaux, Lyon, Paris; HOL: Amsterdam; ITA: Venice; SWE: Drottningholm Fest; SWI: Geneva, Zurich; UK: Aldeburgh Fest, Edinburgh Fest, Scottish, Glyndebourne Fest, London Royal & English National; USA: New York Met, Santa Fe. **Operas staged with these companies incl** BIZET: *Docteur Miracle∗;* BRITTEN: *Albert Herring, Gloriana∗†, Midsummer Night∗, Peter Grimes, Rape of Lucretia∗, Turn of the Screw∗;* CAVALLI: *Ormindo∗;* DEBUSSY: *Pelléas et Mélisande∗;* DONIZETTI: *Don Pasquale;* GAY/Britten: *Beggar's Opera†;* GLUCK: *Orfeo ed Euridice;* HANDEL: *Semele;* HAYDN: *Infedeltà delusa;* HUMPERDINCK: *Hänsel und Gretel;* JANACEK: *Cunning Little Vixen, From the House of the*

Dead; MASSENET: *Manon;* MILHAUD: *Pauvre matelot†;* MONTEVERDI: *Incoronazione di Poppea;* MOZART: *Così fan tutte, Finta giardiniera†, Idomeneo†, Nozze di Figaro;* OFFENBACH: *Contes d'Hoffmann∗, Mariage aux lanternes;* ORFF: *Kluge†;* POULENC: *Mamelles de Tirésias;* PROKOFIEV: *War and Peace∗†;* PUCCINI: *Bohème, Gianni Schicchi†, Butterfly†, Tabarro;* PURCELL: *Dido and Aeneas∗†, King Arthur∗†;* ROSSINI: *Cenerentola∗, Italiana in Algeri, Signor Bruschino;* STRAUSS, J: *Fledermaus;* STRAVINSKY: *Rossignol†;* TCHAIKOVSKY: *Iolanthe∗, Pique Dame∗;* VERDI: *Don Carlo∗, Falstaff∗, Forza del destino, Traviata;* WAGNER: *Lohengrin∗;* WEBER: *Oberon∗;* WOLF-FERRARI: *Quattro rusteghi.* Also CROSSE: *Purgatory∗;* BRITTEN: *Let's Make an Opera.* **Operatic world premieres:** BENNETT: *Mines of Sulphur* 1965, *Penny for a Song* 1967, at Sadler's Wells; *Victory* Royal Op 1969; MAW: *Rising of the Moon* Glyndebourne 1970; BRITTEN: *Burning Fiery Furnace†* 1966, *Curlew River†* 1964, *Death in Venice* 1973, *Golden Vanity* 1967, *Prodigal Son†* 1968, all at Aldeburgh; *Owen Wingrave†* 1971 on BBC TV; WALTON: *Bear* Aldeburgh 1967; CROSSE: *Grace of Todd* 1969; MUSGRAVE: *Voice of Ariadne* 1974, at Aldeburgh. **Operatic Video**—BBC TV: *Tabarro, Histoire du soldat, Hänsel und Gretel.* **Opera libretti:** BENNETT: *Penny for a Song* Sadler's Wells 1967; PURCELL: rev *King Arthur* Engl Op Group 1968; BRITTEN: *Golden Vanity* Aldeburgh 1967. Teaches at London Opera Centre. **Res:** Oxford/London, UK. Mgmt: LMG/UK.

GRAMM, DONALD JOHN. Bass-baritone. American. Resident mem: Metropolitan Opera, New York. Born 26 Feb 1929, Milwaukee, WI, USA. Single. Studied: Chicago Musical Coll, George Graham, IL; Music Acad of the West, Santa Barbara, CA; Ruth Streiter, Boston. **Debut:** Colline (*Bohème*) New York City Opera 1952.
Sang with major companies in FRA: Aix-en-Provence Fest; ITA: Spoleto Fest; MEX: Mexico City; USA: Boston, Chicago, Dallas, Houston, Miami, New Orleans, New York Met & City Opera, Philadelphia Lyric, St Paul, San Antonio, San Francisco Opera, Santa Fe, Seattle, Washington DC. **Roles with these companies incl** BELLINI: Oroveso∗ (*Norma*); BERG: Dr Schön∗ (*Lulu*), Doktor∗ (*Wozzeck*); BRITTEN: Owen Wingrave, Captain Balstrode∗ (*Peter Grimes*); CHARPENTIER: Père (*Louise*); DEBUSSY: Golaud∗ (*Pelléas et Mélisande*); DONIZETTI: Henry VIII (*Anna Bolena*), Talbot∗ (*Maria Stuarda*); FLOTOW: Plunkett (*Martha*); GOUNOD: Méphistophélès (*Faust*); HENZE: Tartaglia (*König Hirsch/Re Cervo*); MASSENET: Sancho∗ (*Don Quichotte*); MILHAUD: Créon (*Médée*); MOZART: Don Alfonso (*Così fan tutte*), Leporello∗‡ (*Don Giovanni*), Osmin (*Entführung aus dem Serail*), Figaro∗ (*Nozze di Figaro*), Papageno∗ (*Zauberflöte*); MUSSORGSKY: Varlaam∗ (*Boris Godunov*); OFFENBACH: Don Andres (*Périchole*); ORFF: Bauer (*Mond*); POULENC: Gendarme (*Mamelles de Tirésias*); PROKOFIEV: Dolokhov∗ (*War and Peace*); PUCCINI: Colline (*Bohème*), Gianni Schicchi∗, Scarpia (*Tosca*); RIMSKY-KORSAKOV: Roi Dodon∗ (*Coq d'or*);

ROSSINI: Dott Bartolo★ & Don Basilio★ (*Barbiere di Siviglia*), Dandini (*Cenerentola*); SCHOENBERG: Moses; SMETANA: Kezal (*Bartered Bride*); STRAVINSKY: Creon‡ & Tiresias (*Oedipus Rex*), Nick Shadow★ (*Rake's Progress*), Empereur de Chine (*Rossignol*); VERDI: Philip II★ (*Don Carlo*), Falstaff★, Banquo (*Macbeth*); WAGNER: Daland (*Fliegende Holländer*). Also PROKOFIEV: Gen Kutuzov (*War and Peace*). **World premieres:** REIF: The Artist (*Artist*) Composers' Showcase Whitney Museum, New York 1972. Recorded for: Columbia, London/Decca. Gives recitals. Appears with symphony orchestra. Teaches voice. Coaches repertoire. On faculty of Yale Univ, New Haven, CN, USA. **Res:** Brookfield, CT, USA. Mgmt: COL/USA; AIM/UK.

GRANT, CLIFFORD SCANTLEBURY. Bass. Australian. Resident mem: English National Opera, London. Born 11 Sep 1930, Randwick, NSW, Australia. Wife Jeanette, occupation pianist. Three children. Studied: Isolde Hill, Annie Portnoj, Australia; Otakar Kraus, UK. **Debut:** Raimondo (*Lucia*) NSW Opera 1952. Previous occupations: commercial artist.

Sang with major companies in AUSTRL: Sydney; UK: Cardiff Welsh, Glasgow Scottish, Glyndebourne Fest, London Royal Opera & English National; USA: San Francisco Opera. **Roles with these companies incl** BELLINI: Oroveso★ (*Norma*); BRITTEN: Sir Walter Raleigh★ (*Gloriana*); MOZART: Sarastro★ (*Zauberflöte*); ROSSINI: Don Basilio★ (*Barbiere di Siviglia*); STRAVINSKY: Tiresias★ (*Oedipus Rex*); VERDI: Ramfis (*Aida*), Philip II★ (*Don Carlo*), Silva (*Ernani*), Padre Guardiano (*Forza del destino*), Zaccaria (*Nabucco*); WAGNER: König Heinrich★ (*Lohengrin*), Pogner (*Meistersinger*), Fasolt★ & Fafner★ (*Rheingold*), Fafner★ (*Siegfried*), Hunding★ (*Walküre*), Hagen★ (*Götterdämmerung*), Landgraf★ (*Tannhäuser*). Also MASSENET: Phorcas★ (*Esclarmonde*). Recorded for: RCA, EMI, Decca, Phonogram, Unicorn. Appears with symphony orchestra. **Res:** 45 Oakleigh Gdns, London, UK. Mgmt: AIM/UK.

GRASSI, PAOLO. Italian. Gen Int (Sovrintendente), Teatro alla Scala & Piccola Scala, V Filodrammatici 2, Milan, Italy. In charge of adm, dram & mus matters; art policy; tech & finance. Add amd positions: Administr Advisor for the Theater Museum of La Scala. Born 30 Oct 1919, Milan. Divorced. One child. Studied: law at Milan Univ. Previous occupations: journalist, critic, dir of theater collections at Einaudi, Feltrinelli and Poligono e Cappelli. Previous positions, primarily theatrical: theater critic with *L'Avanti*, Milan 1945-47; Found & Dir, Piccolo Teatro, Milan 1947-72. Started with present company 1968 as Adm Advisor, in present position since 1972. World premieres at theaters under his management: numerous Italian operas at the Piccola Scala 1947-72; alla Scala: MORTARI: *Specchio a tre luci* 1974; NONO: *Al gran sole carico d'amore* 1975. Awards: Cross 1st Class of Merit, FR Ger; Légion d'Honneur; Order of Arts & Letters; National Order of Merit, France. Initiated major policy changes including the enlargement of public interest, proven by attendance of 55,000 from popular classes, students and juveniles last season; additional productions and performances outside La Scala Theater, e g, at the Palazzo dello Sport, Teatro Lirico, etc; var musical presentations in the city, the province and the region; development of the School for Singers and the School for Ballet. Mem of AGIS, Vice-Pres; ANELS, Pres; Adm Adv of the Theater Museum of La Scala; Commtt mem: Unesco, Italy; the Ballet du XXe Siècle; the Intl Assn of Opera Directors; the House of Culture and Circle of Via de Amicis; and the Recreation and Cultural Department of the City of Milan. **Res:** V Medici 15, Milan, Italy.

GRASSILLI, RAOUL. Stages/produces opera. Also designs stage-lighting and is an actor. Italian. Born 25 Oct 1924, Bologna. Wife Loredana. Two children. Studied: Accad dramm, Silvio d'Amico, Wanda Capodaglio, Rome; incl music. **Operatic debut:** *Rondine* Comunale, Bologna 1971. Awards: Maschera d'oro IDI, Rome.

Directed/produced opera for major companies in ITA: Bologna, Parma, Rome Opera, Turin. **Operas staged with these companies incl** PUCCINI: *Bohème★, Gianni Schicchi, Rondine★;* VERDI: *Aida★, Otello★.* Also GHEDINI: *Billy Budd★;* de BANFIELD: *Lord Byron's Love Letter★;* NEGRI: *Circo Max★.* Teaches at Consv G B Martini, Bologna. **Res:** Audinot 4, Bologna, Italy.

GRATALE, FRANCO. Stages/produces opera, film & television. Also designs sets, costumes & stage-lighting and is an actor. Italian. Resident Stage Dir, New Jersey State Opera, Newark, USA. Born 10 Jun 1933, New York. Wife Tina, occupation music teacher. Four children. Studied: School of Dramatic Arts, Ramon Vinay, New York; incl voice. **Operatic debut:** dir & designer, Paterson Lyric Opera, NJ 1960. Previous occupation: dress designer, Hattie Carnegie.

Directed/produced opera for major companies in GRE: Athens' Fest; FR GER: Saarbrücken; ITA: Trieste; ROM: Bucharest; USA: Hartford, Milwaukee Florentine, Newark, Philadelphia Lyric. **Operas staged with these companies incl** BELLINI: *Norma★†;* BIZET: *Carmen★;* CILEA: *Adriana Lecouvreur★†;* DONIZETTI: *Anna Bolena, Caterina Cornaro★†, Elisir★, Fille du régiment, Lucia★, Lucrezia Borgia;* GIORDANO: *Andrea Chénier★, Fedora★†;* GOUNOD: *Faust★, Roméo et Juliette★†;* HUMPERDINCK: *Hänsel und Gretel★†;* MASCAGNI: *Amico Fritz★, Cavalleria rusticana★†;* MASSENET: *Manon★†, Thaïs†;* MENOTTI: *Amahl★†;* MEYERBEER: *Africaine★;* MOZART: *Così fan tutte★, Don Giovanni★†, Nozze di Figaro★†;* OFFENBACH: *Contes d'Hoffmann;* PONCHIELLI: *Gioconda★†;* PUCCINI: *Bohème★, Fanciulla del West★, Gianni Schicchi★, Butterfly★, Rondine★†, Suor Angelica★, Tabarro★, Tosca★, Turandot★;* RIMSKY-KORSAKOV: *Sadko★;* ROSSINI: *Barbiere di Siviglia★, Turco in Italia★;* SAINT-SAENS: *Samson et Dalila★†;* STRAUSS, R: *Elektra★, Salome★;* VERDI: *Aida★, Attila★†, Ballo in maschera★, Don Carlo★†, Ernani★†, Lombardi★†, Luisa Miller★, Macbeth★†, Nabucco★, Otello★†, Rigoletto★, Traviata★†, Trovatore★;* WAGNER: *Parsifal★;* ZANDONAI: *Francesca da Rimini★.* Teaches privately. Mgmt: LOM/USA.

GREEN, ANNA; née Ann Schneider-Green. Dramatic soprano. British. Born Southampton, UK. Husband Howard Vandenburg, occupation opera singer. Studied: Royal Coll of Music, London. Debut: Amelia (Ballo in maschera) Deutsche Oper am Rhein, Düsseldorf 1961. Previous occupations: concert pianist, artist's model. Awards: ARCM, Royal Coll of Music London.

Sang with major companies in AUS: Graz; CAN: Ottawa, Toronto; FR GER: Bonn, Cologne, Dortmund, Düsseldorf-Duisburg, Essen, Hamburg, Hannover, Karlsruhe, Kassel, Mannheim, Nürnberg, Saarbrücken, Wuppertal; ITA: Bologna; POR: Lisbon; SPA: Barcelona; SWI: Zurich; UK: London Royal Opera; USA: San Diego, Seattle, Washington DC. Roles with these companies incl BEETHOVEN: Leonore (Fidelio); BERG: Marie (Wozzeck); DALLAPICCOLA: Madre (Prigioniero); HINDEMITH: Ursula (Mathis der Maler); MASCAGNI: Santuzza (Cavalleria rusticana); MOZART: Donna Anna (Don Giovanni); OFFENBACH: Giulietta (Contes d'Hoffmann); PROKOFIEV: Fata Morgana (Love for Three Oranges); PUCCINI: Tosca; STRAUSS, R: Ariadne (Ariadne auf Naxos), Elektra, Marschallin (Rosenkavalier); TIPPETT: Hecuba (King Priam); VERDI: Aida★, Amelia (Ballo in maschera), Lucrezia Contarini (Due Foscari), Abigaille (Nabucco), Desdemona (Otello), Amelia (Simon Boccanegra); WAGNER: Senta★ (Fliegende Holländer), Brünnhilde (Walküre★, Siegfried★, Götterdämmerung★), Isolde★; WEBER: Euryanthe. Also d'ALBERT: Marta (Tiefland); FORTNER: Mutter (Bluthochzeit). Gives recitals. Appears with symphony orchestra. Res: Benrather Schlossallee 99, Düsseldorf, FR Ger. Mgmt: IWL/UK; SMN/USA; SLZ/FRG.

GREENWOOD, JANE. Costume designer for opera, theater, television. British. Resident designer, American Shakespeare Fest. Born 30 Apr 1934, Liverpool, UK. Husband Ben Edwards, occupation designer. Two children. Studied: Liverpool Art School; Central School of Arts & Crafts, Ralph Koltai. Operatic debut: Susannah Met Ntl Co on tour, Indianapolis 1965. Theater debut: Oxford Playhouse, UK 1957. Awards: Maharam Awd for Costume Design; nominated for Tony Awd.

Designed for major companies in USA: New York Met, San Francisco Opera, Washington DC. Operas designed for these companies incl DONIZETTI: Favorite★; MONTEVERDI: Ritorno d'Ulisse★; STRAUSS, R: Ariadne auf Naxos★.

GREGER, EMMY. Lyric mezzo-soprano. Dutch. Born 24 Jun 1944, Amsterdam. Single. Studied: Maria Hoving van Driel, Carlo Bino, Amsterdam; Consv Amsterdam. Debut: Hexe (Hänsel und Gretel) Opéra National, Brussels 1968. Previous occupations: window dresser in fur business.

Sang with major companies in BEL: Brussels; FRA: Lyon, Strasbourg, Toulouse; HOL: Amsterdam; POR: Lisbon; SWI: Geneva. Roles with these companies incl BIZET: Carmen★; BRITTEN: Mrs Herring (Albert Herring), Lucretia (Rape of Lucretia); HONEGGER: Antigone★; HUMPERDINCK: Hexe (Hänsel und Gretel); MARTINU: Fairy★ (Trois souhaites); MASSE-

NET: Charlotte★ (Werther); MENOTTI: Mme Flora (Medium); MOZART: Dorabella★ (Così fan tutte); STRAVINSKY: Baba the Turk★ (Rake's Progress); WEILL: Leocadia Begbick★ (Aufstieg und Fall der Stadt Mahagonny). Also RAMEAU: Junon (Platée). World premieres: PRODROMIDES: L'Idole (Passion selon nos doutes) Opéra Lyon 1972; DE KRUYFF: Hendrikje Stoffels (Spinoza) Amsterdam Opera 1971; PREY: Mme de Tourvel (Liaisons dangereuses) Strasbourg 1974. Recorded for: EMI, Pathé-Marconi. Video/Film: Mme Flora (Medium). Gives recitals. Appears with symphony orchestra. Res: Chemin de la Puade 18, 06130 St Jacques, France. Mgmt: IMR/FRA.

GREGOR, BOHUMIL. Conductor of opera and symphony. Czechoslovakian. Chief Cond, National Theater, Prague since 1972. Born 14 Jul 1926, Prague. Wife Blanka. Studied: Zdenek Chalabala, Václav Talích, Prague; incl double bass. Operatic training as asst cond, Opera Fifth of May, Prague 1945-48. Operatic debut: Opera Fifth of May, Prague, 1947. Symphonic debut: Czech Phil Orch, Prague 1952. Previous occupations: double bass player in orch.

Conducted with major companies in BEL: Brussels; BUL: Sofia; CZE: Brno, Prague National; DEN: Copenhagen; FR GER: Cologne, Hamburg, Kiel, Wiesbaden; HOL: Amsterdam; ITA: Venice; SWE: Stockholm; SWI: Zurich; UK: Edinburgh Fest; USSR: Moscow Bolshoi & Stanislavski; USA: San Francisco Opera, Washington DC; YUG: Zagreb, Belgrade. Operas with these companies incl BARTOK: Bluebeard's Castle; BEETHOVEN: Fidelio; BIZET: Carmen★; BORODIN: Prince Igor; DONIZETTI: Don Pasquale★, Elisir, Lucia; DVORAK: Devil and Kate, Rusalka★; GLINKA: Ruslan and Ludmilla★; GOUNOD: Faust; JANACEK: Cunning Little Vixen★‡, Excursions of Mr Broucek★, From the House of the Dead★‡, Jenufa★‡, Katya Kabanova★, Makropoulos Affair★‡; MARTINU: Comedy on the Bridge; MASCAGNI: Cavalleria rusticana★; MONIUSZKO: Halka; MOZART: Così fan tutte, Don Giovanni, Nozze di Figaro; MUSSORGSKY: Boris Godunov; OFFENBACH: Contes d'Hoffmann; ORFF: Kluge; PUCCINI: Bohème★, Gianni Schicchi★, Butterfly★, Manon Lescaut, Tabarro★, Tosca★, Turandot; ROSSINI: Barbiere di Siviglia; SMETANA: Bartered Bride★, Dalibor★, Devil's Wall★, The Kiss, Libuse, Secret★, Two Widows; STRAUSS, R: Ariadne auf Naxos, Rosenkavalier, Salome; STRAVINSKY: Mavra, Rake's Progress; SUCHON: Whirlpool; TCHAIKOVSKY: Eugene Onegin★, Pique Dame; VERDI: Aida, Ballo in maschera, Forza del destino★, Otello, Rigoletto, Traviata★, Trovatore★, Vespri; WAGNER: Fliegende Holländer, Lohengrin, Meistersinger; WEBER: Freischütz. World premieres: KELEMEN: Belagerungszustand Hamburg Staatsoper 1970; KASLIK: Krakatit Ostrava Opera, CSSR 1961; TROJAN: Kolotoc Ostrava Opera 1960. Recorded for Supraphon, Prague. Video—CSSR TV: Krakatit; Danish TV: Katya Kabanova; Swedish TV: Makropoulos Affair. Conducted major orch in Europe. Res: Janáčkovo nábrezí 7, 150 00 Prague 5, CSSR. Mgmt: PGR/CZE; SLZ/FRG.

GREINDL, JOSEF. Bass. German. Resident mem: Deutsche Oper Berlin. Born 23 Dec 1912, Munich. Wife Gertrud Hoebl. Three children. Studied: Music Acad, Paul Bender; Anna Bahr-Mildenburg, Munich. **Debut:** Hunding (*Walküre*) Stadttheater Krefeld 1936.

Sang with major companies in ARG: Buenos Aires; AUS: Salzburg Fest, Vienna Staatsoper; FRA: Paris; FR GER: Bayreuth Fest, Berlin Deutsche Oper, Düsseldorf-Duisburg, Hamburg, Krefeld; GER DR: Berlin Staatsoper; ITA: Milan La Scala, Naples; UK: Edinburgh Fest, London Royal; USA: New York Met; et al. Roles with these companies incl FLÖTOW: Plunkett‡ (*Martha*); MOZART: Osmin‡ (*Entführung aus dem Serail*), Sarastro‡ (*Zauberflöte*); NICOLAI: Falstaff (*Lustigen Weiber*); ROSSINI: Don Basilio (*Barbiere di Siviglia*); STRAUSS, R: Baron Ochs (*Rosenkavalier*); VERDI: Philip II (*Don Carlo*), Padre Guardiano (*Forza del destino*); WAGNER: Daland‡ (*Fliegende Holländer*), König Heinrich (*Lohengrin*), Hans Sachs & Pogner (*Meistersinger*), Gurnemanz (*Parsifal*), Wanderer (*Siegfried*), Fafner (*Rheingold, Siegfried*), Hagen (*Götterdämmerung*), Landgraf (*Tannhäuser*), König Marke (*Tristan und Isolde*); et al. World premieres: ORFF: Prolog & Chorführer (*De Temporum fine comedia*) Salzburg Fest 1973. Recorded for: DG, London, Philips, Seraphim, Urania, Electrola. Video/Film: Rocco (*Fidelio*). Gives recitals. Appears with symphony orchestra. Teaches voice. On faculty of Saarbrücken Opernschule.

GRIFFEL, KAY. Spinto. American. Resident mem: Städtische Bühnen, Cologne. Married. Studied: Northwestern Univ, Evanston, IL, USA; Hochschule für Musik, Berlin, FR Ger; Music Acad of the West, Lotte Lehmann, Santa Barbara, CA. **Debut:** Mercèdes (*Carmen*) Chicago Lyric Opera 1960. Awards: Met Op Ntl Counc Aud Finalist; Singer of the Year, NATS; Rockefeller Fndt Grant; Fulbright Schlshp, Dank stipd DAAD.

Sang with major companies in AUS: Salzburg Fest; BEL: Brussels; FR GER: Berlin Deutsche Oper, Bonn, Cologne, Düsseldorf-Duisburg, Frankfurt, Hamburg, Hannover, Karlsruhe, Krefeld, Munich Staatsoper, Stuttgart; GER DR: Berlin Staatsoper; SPA: Barcelona; UK: Cardiff Welsh; USA: Chicago. Roles with these companies incl BIZET: Micaëla (*Carmen*); GLUCK: Euridice★ (*Faust*); GOUNOD: Marguerite★ (*Faust*); HANDEL: Cleopatra★ (*Giulio Cesare*), Romilda★ (*Xerxes*); MOZART: Fiordiligi★ (*Così fan tutte*), Elettra★(*Idomeneo*), Contessa★(*Nozze di Figaro*); PUCCINI: Mimì★ (*Bohème*), Manon Lescaut★; STRAUSS, J: Rosalinde (*Fledermaus*); STRAUSS, R: Arabella★, Ariadne★ (*Ariadne auf Naxos*), Chrysothemis★ (*Elektra*), Marschallin★ (*Rosenkavalier*); TCHAIKOVSKY: Tatiana (*Eugene Onegin*); VERDI: Elisabetta★ (*Don Carlo*), Alice Ford★ (*Falstaff*), Desdemona★ (*Otello*); WAGNER: Eva★ (*Meistersinger*). World premieres: ORFF: Sybille (*De temporum fine comedia*) Salzburg Fest 1973. Recorded for: DG. Gives recitals. Appears with symphony orchestra. Res: Taunusstr 10, 5303 Rösberg/Cologne, FR Ger. Mgmt: SLZ/FRG; IWL/UK.

GRIFFITH, DAVID. Lyric tenor. American. Resident mem: New York City Opera. Born 17 Sep 1939, Eugene, OR, USA. Wife Elizabeth Lamkin, occupation soprano. Studied: Todd Duncan, Herta Sperber, New York. **Debut:** Camille (*Lustige Witwe*) Dallas Civic Opera 1970.

Sang with major companies in USA: Dallas, New York City Opera, Philadelphia Lyric. Roles with these companies incl DELIUS: Sali★ (*Village Romeo and Juliet*); MONTEVERDI: Nero★ (*Incoronazione di Poppea*); MOZART: Ferrando★ (*Così fan tutte*), Don Ottavio★ (*Don Giovanni*); PUCCINI: Cavaradossi‡ (*Tosca*); STRAUSS, J: Eisenstein★ & Alfred★ (*Fledermaus*). World premieres: BARAB: Jonathan (*Philip Marshall*) Chautauqua Opera, NY 1974. Video/Film: Cavaradossi (*Tosca*). Gives recitals. Appears with symphony orchestra. Res: 736 West End Ave, New York, NY, USA. Mgmt: SCO/USA.

GRIGORESCU, ELENA. Lyric soprano. Romanian. Resident mem: Romanian Opera, Bucharest. Born 20 Apr 1943, Comana. Divorced. Studied: Consv, Prof Elena Saghin, Bucharest. **Debut:** Zerlina (*Don Giovanni*) Romanian Opera 1968.

Sang with major companies in ROM: Bucharest. Roles with these companies incl BEETHOVEN: Marzelline★ (*Fidelio*); DONIZETTI: Norina★ (*Don Pasquale*); MOZART: Despina★ (*Così fan tutte*), Zerlina★ (*Don Giovanni*), Pamina★ (*Zauberflöte*); PERGOLESI: Serpina★ (*Serva padrona*); PUCCINI: Lauretta★ (*Gianni Schicchi*); VERDI: Oscar★ (*Ballo in maschera*). Video/Film: Zerlina (*Don Giovanni*), Norina (*Don Pasquale*), Oscar (*Ballo in maschera*). Gives recitals. Appears with symphony orchestra. Res: 32 Teodosie Rudeanu St, Bucharest 8, Romania. Mgmt: RIA/ROM.

GRILLI, UMBERTO. Tenor. Italian. Born 4 Sep 1934, Pavia, Italy. Wife Fiorella, occupation opera singer. One child. Studied: Adelaide Saraceni. **Debut:** Fritz (*Amico Fritz*) Teatro Nuovo, Milan 1959. Previous occupations: sculptor.

Sang with major companies in ARG: Buenos Aires; AUS: Bregenz Fest, Vienna Staatsoper; BEL: Brussels; FRA: Bordeaux, Nancy, Nice, Rouen, Toulouse; GRE: Athens Fest; FR GER: Cologne, Hamburg, Mannheim, Wiesbaden; HOL: Amsterdam; ITA: Bologna, Florence Maggio & Comunale, Genoa, Milan La Scala, Palermo, Parma, Rome Opera & Caracalla, Trieste, Turin, Venice; MON: Monte Carlo; POL: Warsaw; ROM: Bucharest; SPA: Barcelona; UK: Edinburgh Fest, Glyndebourne Fest; USA: Dallas, Miami, Philadelphia Grand. Roles with these companies incl AUBER: Fra Diavolo, Masaniello★ (*Muette de Portici*); BELLINI: Orombello (*Beatrice di Tenda*), Tebaldo★ (*Capuleti ed i Montecchi*), Lord Arthur★ (*Puritani*), Elvino★ (*Sonnambula*); BOITO: Faust (*Mefistofele*); DONIZETTI: Riccardo★ (*Anna Bolena*), Ernesto★ (*Don Pasquale*), Fernand (*Favorite*), Edgardo★ (*Lucia*), Gennaro (*Lucrezia Borgia*), Riccardo★ (*Maria di Rohan*), Beppo (*Rita*); GOUNOD: Faust★; HAYDN: Nancio (*Infedeltà delusa*); MASCAGNI: Fritz (*Amico Fritz*); MONTEVERDI: Tancredi (*Combattimento di Tancredi*), Orfeo (*Favola d'Orfeo*), Nero (*In-*

coronazione di Poppea); MOZART: Ferrando (*Così fan tutte*); PONCHIELLI: Enzo★ (*Gioconda*); PUCCINI: Rodolfo★ (*Bohème*), Pinkerton★ (*Butterfly*), Ruggero★ (*Rondine*); ROSSINI: Almaviva (*Barbiere di Siviglia*), Comte Ory, Leicester★ (*Elisabetta Regina*), Aménophis★ (*Moïse*), Giocondo (*Pietra del paragone*), Dorvil (*Scala di seta*), Narciso (*Turco in Italia*); STRAUSS, R: Ein Sänger (*Rosenkavalier*); VERDI: Fenton (*Falstaff*), Arvino★ (*Lombardi*), Duca di Mantova★ (*Rigoletto*), Alfredo★ (*Traviata*). Recorded for: Haydn Foundation. **Res:** V Campari 8/E, Pavia, Italy.

GRILLO, JOANN DANIELLE. Dramatic mezzo-soprano. American. Resident mem: Metropolitan Opera, New York. Born 14 May 1939, New York. Husband Richard Kness, occupation opera singer, tenor. One son. Studied: Samuel Margolis, Marinka Gurewich, Anton Guadagno, New York; Clemens Kaiser-Breme, Germany. **Debut:** Amneris (*Aida*) New York Fest 1958.
    Sang with major companies in AUS: Bregenz Fest; CAN: Vancouver; FRA: Marseille, Nice, Paris, Rouen; FR GER: Bielefeld, Düsseldorf-Duisburg, Essen, Frankfurt, Hamburg; ISR: Tel Aviv; ITA: Genoa, Naples; MEX: Mexico City; POR: Lisbon; SPA: Barcelona; SWI: Geneva, Zurich; USA: Cincinnati, Dallas, Fort Worth, Hartford, Miami, Milwaukee Florentine, New Orleans, New York Met & City Opera, Philadelphia Lyric, Pittsburgh, Portland, San Antonio. **Roles with these companies incl** BARTOK: Judith★ (*Bluebeard's Castle*); BELLINI: Adalgisa (*Norma*); BERLIOZ: Marguerite★ (*Damnation de Faust*); BIZET: Carmen★; BRITTEN: Nancy (*Albert Herring*); DONIZETTI: Maffio Orsini★ (*Lucrezia Borgia*); GOUNOD: Siebel (*Faust*); HANDEL: Cornelia (*Giulio Cesare*); MASCAGNI: Santuzza★ (*Cavalleria rusticana*); MASSENET: Charlotte★ (*Werther*); OFFENBACH: Giulietta★ (*Contes d'Hoffmann*); PONCHIELLI: La Cieca (*Gioconda*); PUCCINI: Suzuki (*Butterfly*), Frugola★ (*Tabarro*); ROSSINI: Rosina (*Barbiere di Siviglia*); SAINT-SAENS: Dalila★; STRAVINSKY: Jocasta (*Oedipus Rex*); TCHAIKOVSKY: Olga (*Eugene Onegin*), Pauline (*Pique Dame*); VERDI: Amneris★ (*Aida*), Ulrica (*Ballo in maschera*), Eboli★ (*Don Carlo*), Meg★ (*Falstaff*), Preziosilla★ (*Forza del destino*), Azucena★ (*Trovatore*); WAGNER: Magdalene (*Meistersinger*), Fricka★ (*Walküre*). Gives recitals. Appears with symphony orchestra. **Res:** New York, USA. **Mgmt:** HUR/USA; SLZ/FRG.

GRIMALDI, GIORGIO. Lyric tenor. Italian. Born 25 Feb 1936, Bologna. Wife Carla Chiara, occupation opera singer, soprano. Studied: Mo Ettore Campogalliani. **Debut:** Paolino (*Matrimonio segreto*) Teatro Nuovo, Milan 1962. Previous occupations: clerk.
    Sang with major companies in AUS: Vienna Staatsoper; BEL: Brussels; CZE: Prague National; FRA: Lyon, Strasbourg; FR GER: Essen; HOL: Amsterdam; ITA: Bologna, Florence Maggio & Comunale, Milan La Scala, Naples, Palermo, Parma, Rome Opera, Trieste, Turin, Venice; MEX: Mexico City; POR: Lisbon. **Roles with these companies incl** BELLINI: Elvino★ (*Sonnambula*);

BIZET: Nadir (*Pêcheurs de perles*); CIMAROSA: Paolino★ (*Matrimonio segreto*); DONIZETTI: Ernesto★ (*Don Pasquale*), Nemorino★ (*Elisir*), Edgardo (*Lucia*); HAYDN: Filippo‡ (*Infedeltà delusa*); MASCAGNI: Fritz (*Amico Fritz*); MASSENET: Des Grieux★ (*Manon*), Werther★; MOZART: Ferrando (*Così fan tutte*), Don Ottavio (*Don Giovanni*), Tamino (*Zauberflöte*); PUCCINI: Rodolfo (*Bohème*), Rinuccio (*Gianni Schicchi*), Ruggero (*Rondine*); ROSSINI: Almaviva (*Barbiere di Siviglia*), Aménophis (*Moïse*), Otello, Narciso (*Turco in Italia*); VERDI: Fenton★ (*Falstaff*), Duca di Mantova★ (*Rigoletto*), Alfredo★ (*Traviata*); WOLF-FERRARI: Filipeto (*Quattro rusteghi*). Recorded for: Angelicum, Chant du Monde. Gives recitals. Appears with symphony orchestra. **Res:** V E Duse 20, Bologna, Italy.

GRIPENBERG, THOMAS. Scenic and costume designer for opera, theater. Is a lighting designer. Finnish. Resident designer, Finnish National Opera, Helsinki. Born 26 Nov 1942, Lohja, Finland. Wife Kaarina, occupation interior decorator. One child. Studied: Schauspielseminar Mozarteum, Prof H B Gallée, Salzburg. **Operatic debut:** sets, *Simplicius Simplicissimus* Finnish National Opera 1969; cost, *Nozze di Figaro* Finn Ntl Op 1970. Theater debut: Turku, Finland 1967.
    Designed for major companies in FIN: Helsinki. **Operas designed for these companies incl** BIZET: *Carmen;* EGK: *Verlobung in San Domingo★;* JANACEK: *From the House of the Dead★;* LEONCAVALLO: *Pagliacci★;* MOZART: *Nozze di Figaro;* PUCCINI: *Tabarro★;* STRAUSS, R: *Salome.* Also HARTMANN: *Simplicius Simplicissimus.* **Operatic world premieres:** KUUSISTO: *Mumintroll-Opera* 1974; RAUTAVAARA: *Apollo and Marsyas* 1973; both at Finnish National Opera, Helsinki. Teaches at Taideteollinen Korkeakoulu, Helsinki. **Res:** Vapaaniemi Salmitie, Espoo, Finland.

GRIST, RERI. Lyric coloratura soprano. American. Born New York, USA. Husband Ulf Thomson. One child. Studied: Claire Gelda, New York. **Debut:** Blondchen (*Entführung aus dem Serail*) Santa Fe Opera, NM 1959. Previous occupations: social investigator for Welfare Dept; singer, dancer and actress in Broadway productions as child and teenager. Awards: Alumni Assoc of Queens Coll; LaGuardia Mem Awd; Blanche Thebom Opera Guild Awd; Marian Anderson Awd; YMHA 12th Annual Young Artists Awd; Queens Coll Orch Socy Awd; John Castellini Awd.
    Sang with major companies in ARG: Buenos Aires; AUS: Graz, Salzburg Fest, Vienna Staatsoper & Volksoper; CAN: Montreal/Quebec, Vancouver; FRA: Lyon; FR GER: Berlin Deutsche Oper, Cologne, Munich Staatsoper, Wiesbaden; ITA: Florence Maggio, Milan La Scala, Spoleto Fest; SWI: Geneva, Zurich; UK: Glyndebourne Fest, London Royal; USA: Chicago, Miami, New York Met & City Opera, San Francisco Opera, Santa Fe, Washington DC. **Roles with these companies incl** BIZET: Micaëla (*Carmen*); BRITTEN: Tytania (*Midsummer Night*); DELIBES: Lakmé; DONIZETTI: Norina★ (*Don Pasquale*), Adina★ (*Elisir*), Marie★ (*Fille du régiment*);

GLUCK: Amor (*Orfeo ed Euridice*); HAYDN: Vespina (*Infedeltà delusa*); MOZART: Despina★‡ (*Così fan tutte*), Zerlina★‡ (*Don Giovanni*), Blondchen★‡ (*Entführung aus dem Serail*), Susanna★‡ (*Nozze di Figaro*), Königin der Nacht (*Zauberflöte*); OFFENBACH: Olympia (*Contes d'Hoffmann*); ORFF: Solo (*Carmina burana*); PERGOLESI: Serpina (*Serva padrona*); RIMSKY-KORSAKOV: Coq d'or; ROSSINI: Rosina★ (*Barbiere di Siviglia*), Fanny (*Cambiale di matrimonio*); STRAUSS, J: Adele★ (*Fledermaus*); STRAUSS, R: Zerbinetta★‡ (*Ariadne auf Naxos*), Sophie★ (*Rosenkavalier*), Aminta★ (*Schweigsame Frau*); STRAVINSKY: Rossignol‡; VERDI: Oscar★‡ (*Ballo in maschera*), Nannetta★ (*Falstaff*), Gilda★‡ (*Rigoletto*). Also on records only MOZART: Mme Herz (*Schauspieldirektor*), Aminta (*Re pastore*). Recorded for: DG, EMI, RCA Victor, Vanguard, Polydor, CBS, Oiseau Lyre. Video/Film: Norina (*Don Pasquale*); Aminta (*Schweigsame Frau*); Susanna (*Nozze di Figaro*); Blondchen (*Entführung*); Zerbinetta (*Ariadne auf Naxos*); Rosina (*Barbiere*); Oscar (*Ballo in maschera*); Rossignol. Gives recitals. Appears with symphony orchestra. **Res:** Munich, FR Ger. Mgmt: CAM/USA; RAB/AUS; IWL/UK.

GROBBELAAR, MICHAL J. South African. Gen Mng, Johannesburg Civic Theatre Assn, PO Box 31900, Braamfontein 2017, Rep of South Africa 1962- . In charge of administrative & technical matters, artistic policy & finances. Is also a stage dir/prod. Born 9 Mar 1927, Vereeniging Dist, South Africa. Wife Christine Gertrude, occupation teacher. Previous occupations: actor. Form positions, primarily administrative & theatrical: Company Mng, National Theatre, Pretoria 1952-53; Production Mng 1957-61; Stage Dir, Opera Federation, Johannesburg 1961. Mem of Advisory Bd, Johannesburg School for Art, Ballet & Music; Drama Commtt, Performing Arts Council, Transvaal. **Res:** 26 Roscommon Rd, Parkview/ Johannesburg, South Africa.

GROBE, DONALD ROTH. Lyric tenor. American. Resident mem: Deutsche Oper Berlin; Staatsoper Munich. Born 16 Dec 1929, Ottawa, IL, US. Wife Carol Jean. Three children. Studied: Chicago Musical Coll, grad study; Mannes Coll of Music, New York; Robert Long, Martial Singher, Robert Weede; Fr Prof Margarethe v Winterfeldt. **Debut:** Borsa (*Rigoletto*) Chicago Lyric Opera 1952. Awards: Second Place Chicago Fest 1952; First Place NFMC 1953; Kammersänger, Berlin Senate 1970.

Sang with major companies in AUS: Salzburg Fest, Vienna Staatsoper; FRA: Strasbourg; FR GER: Berlin Deutsche Oper, Bonn, Cologne, Dortmund, Düsseldorf-Duisburg, Frankfurt, Hamburg Staatsoper, Hannover, Krefeld, Mannheim, Munich Staatsoper, Stuttgart, Wiesbaden; HOL: Amsterdam; ITA: Florence Maggio Musicale; MEX: Mexico City; POR: Lisbon; SWE: Stockholm; SWI: Geneva, Zurich; UK: London Royal Opera; USA: Boston, New York Met. **Roles with these companies incl** BERG: Alwa★‡ (*Lulu*); BERLIOZ: Faust (*Damnation de Faust*); BOIELDIEU: George Brown (*Dame blanche*); BRITTEN: Albert Herring★, Aschenbach★ (*Death in Venice*); BUSONI: Leandro (*Arlecchino*); CA-

VALLI: Linfea★ (*Calisto*); CIMAROSA: Paolino★ (*Matrimonio segreto*); DONIZETTI: Ernesto (*Don Pasquale*), Nemorino (*Elisir*); FLOTOW: Lionel (*Martha*); HANDEL: Sextus (*Giulio Cesare*); HAYDN: Cecco (*Mondo della luna*); HENZE: Tony (*Elegy for Young Lovers*); JANACEK: Mazal (*Excursions of Mr Broucek*), Steva (*Jenufa*); LORTZING: Baron Kronthal★ (*Wildschütz*), Peter Ivanov (*Zar und Zimmermann*); MARTIN: Tristan★ (*Vin herbé*); MENOTTI: Michele (*Saint of Bleecker Street*); MONTEVERDI: Orfeo; MOZART: Tito★ (*Clemenza di Tito*), Ferrando★ (*Così fan tutte*), Don Ottavio★ (*Don Giovanni*), Belmonte★ (*Entführung aus dem Serail*), Belfiore (*Finta giardiniera*), Idamante (*Idomeneo*), Lucio Silla, Biondello★ (*Oca del Cairo*), Tamino★ (*Zauberflöte*); OFFENBACH: Hoffmann★; PUCCINI: Rodolfo (*Bohème*), Rinuccio★ (*Gianni Schicchi*), Pinkerton (*Butterfly*), Des Grieux (*Manon Lescaut*); RAMEAU: Castor; ROSSINI: Almaviva★ (*Barbiere di Siviglia*), Edward Milfort★ (*Cambiale di matrimonio*), Don Ramiro★ (*Cenerentola*), Narciso★ (*Turco in Italia*); SMETANA: Hans (*Bartered Bride*); STRAUSS, J: Eisenstein★ & Alfred (*Fledermaus*); STRAUSS, R: Flamand★ (*Capriccio*), Leukippos★ (*Daphne*), Ein Sänger★ (*Rosenkavalier*), Henry Morosus★ (*Schweigsame Frau*); STRAVINSKY: Oedipus Rex★, Tom Rakewell (*Rake's Progress*); SUTERMEISTER: Romeo; VERDI: Don Carlo, Fenton (*Falstaff*), Ismaele (*Nabucco*), Duca di Mantova (*Rigoletto*), Alfredo (*Traviata*); WAGNER: David★ (*Meistersinger*), Walther v d Vogelweide★ (*Tannhäuser*); WEBER: Oberon‡. Also EINEM: Camille Desmoulins (*Dantons Tod*). **World premieres:** HENZE: Wilhelm (*Der junge Lord*) Deutsche Oper Berlin 1965; CIKKER: Camille (*Spiel von Liebe und Tod*) Staatsoper Munich 1969; REIMANN: Oleander (*Melusine*) Deutsche Oper Berlin 1970; FORTNER: Arundel (*Elisabeth Tudor*) Deutsche Oper Berlin 1972. Recorded for: DG, Decca. Video/Film: Henry Morosus (*Schweigsame Frau*); George Brown (*Dame blanche*); Rodolfo (*Bohème*); Lionel (*Martha*); Rinuccio (*Gianni Schicchi*); Wilhelm (*Der junge Lord*); Belmonte (*Entführung aus dem Serail*). Gives recitals. Appears with symphony orchestra. **Res:** Ahrenshooper Zeile 68, 1 Berlin 38, FR Ger. Mgmt: DSP/USA; SLZ/FRG opera; KHA/FRG conc.

GRÖSCHEL, WERNER. Bass. German. Resident mem: Opernhaus Zurich. Born 18 Sep 1940, Nürnberg, Germany. Wife Margot Gröschel-Bacher. One child. Studied: Richard Strauss Konsv, Munich; Kmsg Marcel Cordes, Prof J Metternich. **Debut:** Fiesco (*Simon Boccanegra*) Stadttheater Flensburg, FR Ger 1967. Previous occupations: played cello, rhythm bass, trombone and tuba in dance band.

Sang with major companies in SWI: Zurich. **Roles with these companies incl** BEETHOVEN: Rocco★ (*Fidelio*); CHERUBINI: Creon (*Medea*); DONIZETTI: Don Pasquale; FLOTOW: Plunkett (*Martha*); GOUNOD: Méphistophélès (*Faust*); JANACEK: Dikoy★ (*Katya Kabanova*); MOZART: Don Giovanni, Osmin (*Entführung aus dem Serail*), Conte Almaviva (*Nozze di Figaro*), Sarastro★ (*Zauberflöte*); NICOLAI: Falstaff★ (*Lustigen Weiber*); ROSSINI: Don Basilio★ (*Bar-*

biere di Siviglia); VERDI: Philip II & Grande Inquisitore★ (Don Carlo), Silva★ (Ernani), Zaccaria★ (Nabucco), Fiesco (Simon Boccanegra); WAGNER: Daland (Fliegende Holländer), König Heinrich (Lohengrin), Pogner★ (Meistersinger), Landgraf★ (Tannhäuser); WEILL: Trinity Moses★ (Aufstieg und Fall der Stadt Mahagonny). **World premieres:** KLEBE: Michael James (Wahrer Held) Opernhaus Zurich 1975. Gives recitals. Appears with symphony orchestra. **Res:** Loowiesenstr 28, 8106 Adlikon, Switzerland.

GROSSI, PASQUALE. Scenic and costume designer for opera, theater, film; specl in sets. Is a lighting designer; also an interior designer. Italian. Born 19 May 1942, Rome. Single. Prof training: design studio. **Operatic debut:** sets, Puritani Opéra Municipal, Marseille 1973; cost, Otello Opéra Municipal, Monte Carlo 1970. Theater debut: CIT, Cagliari, Italy 1968.
Designed for major companies in FRA: Marseille; ITA: Palermo, Spoleto Fest, Trieste; JPN: Tokyo; MON: Monte Carlo. **Operas designed for these companies incl** BELLINI: Norma★, Puritani; DONIZETTI: Don Pasquale; MENOTTI: Amelia al ballo, Old Maid and the Thief; PUCCINI: Turandot★; SALIERI: Prima la musica; VERDI: Otello★, Rigoletto★. Also BARBER: Antony and Cleopatra. **Res:** V dei Coronari 226, Rome, Italy.

GRUBER, FERRY. Tenore buffo. Austrian. Resident mem: Staatsoper, Munich. Born 28 Sep 1926, Vienna. Wife Eleonore. Two children. Studied: Musikakad, Prof Hans Swarowsky, Kmsg Herrmann Gallos, Prof Leopold Wlach, clarinet, Prof Czarniawskij, piano, Vienna. **Debut:** Tamino (Zauberflöte) Lucerne Opera, Switzerland 1950. Awards: Bayerischer Kammersänger 1962.
Sang with major companies in AUS: Bregenz Fest, Graz, Salzburg Fest, Vienna Staatsoper & Volksoper; CAN: Ottawa, Vancouver; DEN: Copenhagen; FRA: Strasbourg; FR GER: Cologne, Dortmund, Düsseldorf-Duisburg, Essen, Frankfurt, Hamburg, Hannover, Munich Staatsoper & Gärtnerplatz, Nürnberg, Stuttgart, Wuppertal; GER DR: Berlin Komische Oper; HOL: Amsterdam; ITA: Florence Maggio, Naples; MON: Monte Carlo; POR: Lisbon; SPA: Majorca; SWI: Basel, Zurich; UK: Edinburgh Fest. **Roles with these companies incl** FALLA: Maese Pedro (Retablo de Maese Pedro); FLOTOW: Lionel (Märtha); HANDEL: Acis; HAYDN: Filippo & Nancio (Infedeltà delusa), Cecco (Mondo della luna); HUMPERDINCK: Hexe (Hänsel und Gretel); LORTZING: Baron Kronthal (Wildschütz), Peter Ivanov (Zar und Zimmermann); MASSENET: Des Grieux (Manon); MOZART: Ferrando (Così fan tutte), Don Ottavio (Don Giovanni), Pedrillo (Entführung aus dem Serail), Tamino (Zauberflöte); MUSSORGSKY: Shuisky (Boris Godunov); NICOLAI: Fenton (Lustigen Weiber); OFFENBACH: Hoffmann; ORFF: Solo (Carmina burana); PROKOFIEV: Truffaldino (Love for Three Oranges); PUCCINI: Rinuccio (Gianni Schicchi), Pinkerton (Butterfly); SMETANA: Wenzel & Hans (Bartered Bride); STRAUSS, J: Eisenstein & Alfred (Fledermaus); STRAUSS, R: Baron Lummer (Intermezzo), Ein Sänger (Rosenkavalier); STRAVINSKY: Tom

Rakewell (Rake's Progress); TCHAIKOVSKY: Lenski (Eugene Onegin); VERDI: Duca di Mantova (Rigoletto), Gabriele (Simon Boccanegra), Alfredo (Traviata), Arrigo (Vespri); WAGNER: David (Meistersinger), Walther v d Vogelweide (Tannhäuser); WEILL: Fatty (Aufstieg und Fall der Stadt Mahagonny). Recorded for: Eurodisc-Ariola, Electrola, DG. Gives recitals. Appears with symphony orchestra. **Res:** Planeggerstr 8, 8032 Gräfelting, FR Ger.

GRUBEROVA, EDITA. Coloratura soprano. Austrian. Resident mem: Staatsoper, Vienna. Born 23 Dec 1946, Bratislava, CSSR. Husband Stefan Klimo, occupation musicologist. One child. Studied: Prof Maria Medvecka, Kmsg Ruthilde Boesch. **Debut:** Rosina (Barbiere di Siviglia) National Opera, Bratislava 1968.
Sang with major companies in AUS: Bregenz Fest, Graz, Salzburg Fest, Vienna Staatsoper & Volksoper; FR GER: Cologne, Frankfurt, Hamburg, Munich Staatsoper; UK: Glyndebourne Fest. **Roles with these companies incl** DONIZETTI: Lucia★; MOZART: Konstanze★ & Blondchen★ (Entführung aus dem Serail), Königin der Nacht★ (Zauberflöte); OFFENBACH: Olympia★ & Antonia & Giulietta (Contes d'Hoffmann); ORFF: Solo★ (Carmina burana); ROSSINI: Rosina★ (Barbiere di Siviglia); STRAUSS, J: Adele★ (Fledermaus); STRAUSS, R: Fiakermilli★ (Arabella), Zerbinetta★ (Ariadne auf Naxos), Sophie★ (Rosenkavalier); VERDI: Oscar★ (Ballo in maschera), Gilda★ (Rigoletto), Violetta (Traviata). Gives recitals. Appears with symphony orchestra. Teaches voice. Coaches repertoire. Mgmt: RAB/AUS; TAS/AUS; JUC/SWI; IMR/FRA.

GRÜBLER, EKKEHARD KARL BERNHARD. Scenic and costume designer for opera, theater, film, television. Is a lighting designer; also a painter. German. Resident designer, Opera, Frankfurt am Main. Born 29 Jan 1928, Berlin. Wife Brigitte, occupation artist. Studied: Acad of Fine Arts & Free Univ, Berlin; Yale Univ, Profs Ernst Schütte, Donald Oenslager, Josef Albers, CT. Prof training: asst to Caspar Neher. **Operatic debut:** Fanciulla del West Frankfurt am Main 1958. Theater debut: Renaissance Theater, Berlin 1950.
Designed for major companies in ARG: Buenos Aires; AUS: Bregenz Fest, Graz, Salzburg Fest, Vienna Staatsoper & Volksoper; FR GER: Bonn, Cologne, Darmstadt, Dortmund, Düsseldorf-Duisburg, Essen, Frankfurt, Hamburg, Kassel, Kiel, Mannheim, Munich Staatsoper & Gärtnerplatz, Nürnberg, Wiesbaden; POR: Lisbon; SWI: Geneva, Zurich; USA: Chicago. **Operas designed for these companies incl** AUBER: Fra Diavolo; BEETHOVEN: Fidelio★; BERG: Wozzeck; BERLIOZ: Damnation de Faust★, Troyens★; BRITTEN: Albert Herring, Death in Venice★; CIKKER: Play of Love and Death; CIMAROSA: Matrimonio segreto; DEBUSSY: Pelléas et Mélisande★; DONIZETTI: Anna Bolena, Don Pasquale★, Elisir, Lucia; DVORAK: Rusalka; ElNEM: Besuch der alten Dame★, Prozess; FORTNER: Don Perlimplin; GLUCK: Armide, Iphigénie en Aulide, Orfeo ed Euridice; HAYDN: Mondo della luna; HENZE: Junge Lord★, König Hirsch/Re Cervo; HINDEMITH: Cardillac, Mathis der Maler; JANACEK: Katya Kaba-

nova★, *Makropoulos Affair*★; KELEMEN: *Belagerungszustand;* LIGETI: *Aventures/Nouvelles Aventures;* LORTZING: *Wildschütz;* MASCAGNI: *Cavalleria rusticana*★; MONTEVERDI: *Incoronazione di Poppea, Ritorno d'Ulisse;* MOZART: *Clemenza di Tito*★, *Così fan tutte, Don Giovanni*★, *Entführung aus dem Serail, Idomeneo*★, *Lucio Silla;* MUSSORGSKY: *Boris Godunov*★; NICOLAI: *Lustigen Weiber;* ORFF: *Antigonae;* PROKOFIEV: *Love for Three Oranges*★; PUCCINI: *Bohème*★, *Fanciulla del West, Gianni Schicchi, Tosca, Turandot*★; PURCELL: *Dido and Aeneas;* RAVEL: *Heure espagnole;* ROSSINI: *Barbiere di Siviglia*★, *Cenerentola, Moïse;* SCHOENBERG: *Moses und Aron*★; SMETANA: *Dalibor*★; STRAUSS, J: *Fledermaus*★; STRAUSS, R: *Arabella*★, *Ariadne auf Naxos, Capriccio*★, *Elektra*★, *Frau ohne Schatten, Rosenkavalier*★, *Salome, Schweigsame Frau*★; STRAVINSKY: *Oedipus Rex, Rake's Progress*★; TCHAIKOVSKY: *Eugene Onegin, Maid of Orleans*★; VERDI: *Aida, Ballo in maschera*★, *Don Carlo*★, *Falstaff*★, *Giovanna d'Arco*★, *Nabucco, Otello, Simon Boccanegra, Traviata, Vespri;* WAGNER: *Fliegende Holländer*★, *Meistersinger*★, *Rheingold*★, *Walküre*★, *Siegfried*★, *Götterdämmerung*★, *Tannhäuser*★, *Tristan und Isolde;* WEBER: *Freischütz;* WEILL: *Aufstieg und Fall der Stadt Mahagonny*★, *Dreigroschenoper;* YUN: *Traum des Liu-Tung*★. Also KRENEK: *Karl V, Orpheus.* **Operatic world premieres:** GOEHR: *Arden muss sterben* Staatsoper Hamburg 1967. Operatic Video—TV Hamburg: *Simplicius Simplicissimus;* TV Cologne: *Wozzeck;* TV Munich: *Belshazzar.* Exhibitions of stage designs, paintings & graphics Boston 1950; Berlin 1953. **Res:** Hundertmorgenring 106, D 6083 Walldorf/Hessen, FR Ger.

GRUEBER, ARTHUR. Conductor of opera and symphony; composer; operatic stage director. German. Gen Music Dir & Principal Cond, Badisches Staatstheater, Karlsruhe, FR Ger. Also Music Dir, Badische Staatskapelle, Karlsruhe 1962-76. Born 21 Aug 1910, Essen. Wife Margot Essing. Studied: Hochschule für Musik, Hermann Abendroth, Walter Braunfels, Cologne; incl piano, organ, cembalo, violin and voice. Plays the piano, cembalo. Operatic training as repetiteur, asst cond & chorus master at Opernhaus Frankfurt 1932-38. **Operatic debut:** *Rienzi* Opernhaus Frankfurt 1934. Symphonic debut: Radio-Sinfonie, Frankfurt 1935. Previous adm positions in opera: Musikal Oberleiter, Staatsoper Hamburg, FR Ger 1947-52; Princ Cond, Komische Oper Berlin, Ger DR 1951-55; Gen Mus Dir, Staatstheater Braunschweig, FR Ger 1955-62.

Conducted with major companies in FRA: Nancy, Paris, Strasbourg; FR GER: Berlin Deutsche Oper, Cologne, Düsseldorf-Duisburg, Frankfurt, Hamburg, Karlsruhe, Saarbrücken, Stuttgart, Wuppertal; GER DR: Berlin Komische Oper; ITA: Trieste; POR: Lisbon; YUG: Dubrovnik. Operas with these companies incl d'ALBERT: *Tiefland;* AUBER: *Fra Diavolo;* BEETHOVEN: *Fidelio*★; BERG: *Lulu*★, *Wozzeck*‡; BIZET: *Carmen*★; BUSONI: *Turandot;* EGK: *Verlobung in San Domingo*★‡; EINEM: *Dantons Tod;* FLOTOW: *Martha;* GLUCK: *Iphigénie en Aulide*★‡, *Iphigénie en Tauride, Orfeo*

ed Euridice; HANDEL: *Rodelinda, Xerxes;* HENZE: *Landarzt*★; HINDEMITH: *Hin und zurück*★‡, *Mathis der Maler;* HUMPERDINCK: *Hänsel und Gretel, Königskinder;* JANACEK: *Katya Kabanova;* LEONCAVALLO: *Pagliacci;* LORTZING: *Waffenschmied, Wildschütz, Zar und Zimmermann;* MARTIN: *Vin herbé;* MASCAGNI: *Cavalleria rusticana;* MENOTTI: *Consul;* MILHAUD: *Pauvre matelot;* MONTEVERDI: *Ritorno d'Ulisse;* MOZART: *Così fan tutte, Don Giovanni*★, *Entführung aus dem Serail*★, *Finta giardiniera, Idomeneo, Nozze di Figaro*★, *Zauberflöte*★; MUSSORGSKY: *Boris Godunov;* NICOLAI: *Lustigen Weiber;* OFFENBACH: *Contes d'Hoffmann;* ORFF: *Bernauerin, Kluge;* PERGOLESI: *Serva padrona;* PFITZNER: *Palestrina*★; PUCCINI: *Bohème, Butterfly, Manon Lescaut, Tosca, Turandot*★‡; RAVEL: *Heure espagnole*‡; ROSSINI: *Barbiere di Siviglia, Italiana in Algeri;* SMETANA: *Bartered Bride*‡; STRAUSS, J: *Fledermaus;* STRAUSS, R: *Arabella*★, *Ariadne auf Naxos, Capriccio, Daphne*‡, *Elektra*★, *Intermezzo*★, *Rosenkavalier*‡, *Salome*★, *Schweigsame Frau*★; STRAVINSKY: *Oedipus Rex*‡; SUTERMEISTER: *Raskolnikoff;* TIPPETT: *King Priam, Midsummer Marriage*★‡; VERDI: *Aida*★, *Ballo in maschera, Don Carlo*★, *Falstaff, Forza del destino, Otello*★, *Rigoletto, Simon Boccanegra*★‡, *Traviata, Trovatore;* WAGNER: *Fliegende Holländer*★, *Lohengrin*★, *Meistersinger*★‡, *Parsifal*★‡, *Rienzi, Rheingold*★, *Walküre*★, *Siegfried*★, *Götterdämmerung*★, *Tannhäuser*★, *Tristan und Isolde*★. Also EGK: *Peer Gynt;* RITTER: *Witwe von Ephesus;* BRAUNFELS: *Vögel.* **World premieres:** REUTTER: *Tod des Empedokles* Schwetzingen Fest, FR Ger 1966; FUESSL: *Dybuk* Oper Karlsruhe 1970. Recorded for Radio recds FR Ger, Ger DR and Ireland; Vox. Conducted major orch in Europe. Previous positions as Mus Dir with major orch: Staatsorch Braunschweig 1955-62. **Operas composed:** *Trotz wider Trotz* Staatsoper Hamburg 1948. Teaches at Staatl Hochschule für Musik, Karlsruhe. **Res:** Kantstr 7, Karlsruhe-Eggenstein, FR Ger.

GRUNDHEBER, FRANZ. Lyric & dramatic baritone. German. Resident mem: Staatsoper, Hamburg. Born 27 Sep 1937, Trier, Germany. Wife Maria-Luise, occupation dietitian. One child. Studied: Indiana Univ, Margaret Harshaw, Frank St Leger, Bloomington, USA. **Debut:** Escamillo (*Carmen*) Eutiner Sommerspiele 1967. Previous occupations: officer Ger Air Force 1959-62. Awards: Oberdörffer-Preis, Staatsoper, Hamburg 1970.

Sang with major companies in AUS: Vienna Volksoper; FR GER: Berlin Deutsche Oper, Düsseldorf-Duisburg, Hamburg, Kassel, Stuttgart; ITA: Venice. Roles with these companies incl BIZET: Escamillo★ (*Carmen*); BRITTEN: Mr Redburn★ (*Billy Budd*); CIMAROSA: Count Robinson (*Matrimonio segreto*); DONIZETTI: Belcore★ (*Elisir*); JANACEK: Shishkov★ (*From the House of the Dead*); LEONCAVALLO: Tonio★ (*Pagliacci*); MOZART: Figaro★ (*Nozze di Figaro*), Papageno★ (*Zauberflöte*); MUSSORGSKY: Shaklovity★ (*Khovanshchina*); OFFENBACH: Coppélius, etc★ (*Contes d'Hoffmann*); ORFF: Solo★ (*Carmina burana*); PUCCINI: Marcello★ (*Bohème*); RAVEL: Ramiro★ (*Heure espagnole*); ROSSINI: Dandini★ (*Cenerentola*); SAINT-SAENS: Grand prêtre★ (*Samson et Dalila*); VERDI: Amonasro★ (*Aida*), Iago (*Otello*), Rigoletto★; WEBER: Lysiart★ (*Euryanthe*); ZIMMERMANN: Stolzius★ (*Soldaten*). Also HUMPERDINCK: Peter★ (*Hänsel und Gretel*); MOZART: Sprecher★ (*Zauberflöte*); BUSOTTI: Maffio (*Lorenzaccio*). **World premieres:** TAL: Son of the King (*Ashmedai*) Hamburg Opera 1971. Gives recitals. Appears with symphony orchestra. Teaches voice. **Res:** Grot Sahl 30, 2 Hamburg 56, FR Ger. Mgmt: SLZ/FRG; RAB/AUS.

GRUSELLE, CHRISTIANE. Coloratura soprano. Belgian. Born 8 Feb 1935, Montignies/Sambre-Hainaut, Belgium. Divorced. Studied: Consv Royal Brussels; Mozarteum Salzburg. **Debut:** Micaëla (*Carmen*) Théâtre Royal de Mons, Belgium 1956. Previous occupations: prof for musical education. Awards: Diplôme de Régente, Charleroi; First Prize Voice and Opera, Consv Royal Brussels.
Sang with major companies in BEL: Liège; FRA: Bordeaux, Lyon, Nancy; ROM: Bucharest; YUG: Dubrovnik. **Roles with these companies incl** ADAM: Neméa (*Si j'étais roi*); BIZET: Micaëla (*Carmen*), Léila (*Pêcheurs de perles*); BOIELDIEU: Anna (*Dame blanche*); DELIBES: Lakmé; DONIZETTI: Marie (*Fille du régiment*); GOUNOD: Mireille, Juliette; MASSENET: Manon, Sophie (*Werther*); MENOTTI: Monica (*Medium*); MEYERBEER: Marguerite de Valois (*Huguenots*); MOZART: Susanna (*Nozze di Figaro*); OFFENBACH: Olympia (*Contes d'Hoffmann*); PAISIELLO: Rosina (*Barbiere di Siviglia*); RABAUD: Fille de Sultan (*Mârouf*); ROSSINI: Rosina (*Barbiere di Siviglia*); STRAUSS, J: Adele‡ (*Fledermaus*); STRAUSS, R: Fiakermilli (*Arabella*), Sophie (*Rosenkavalier*); THOMAS: Ophélie (*Hamlet*), Philine (*Mignon*); VERDI: Gilda (*Rigoletto*), Violetta (*Traviata*). Also MOZART: Papagena (*Zauberflöte*); EGK: Maria (*Revisor*); PURCELL: Titania (*Fairy Queen*); POULENC: Constance (*Dialogues des Carmélites*); PAISIELLO: Rosina (*Barbiere di Siviglia*); FIORAVANTI: Rosa (*Cantatrici villane*). Recorded for: Polydor. Video—Télév Paris: (*Fledermaus*), Rosina (*Barbiere di Siviglia*), Rosa (*Cantatrici villane*); Télév RTB: Rosina (*Barbiere di Siviglia*). Gives recitals. Appears with symphony orchestra. Teaches voice. On faculty of Consv Royal. **Res:** Brussels, Belgium.

GUADAGNO, ANTON; né Antonio Guadagno. Conductor of opera and symphony; composer. American. Resident Cond, Staatsoper, Vienna. Born Italy. Wife Dolores Guidone. One child. Studied: Consv Palermo; Consv Santa Cecilia, Rome; Franco Ferrara; B Molinari; Akad Mozarteum, Salzburg, Carlo Zecchi; H von Karajan; A Paumgartner; incl organ, piano. Plays the piano. Operatic training as asst cond at Met Opera, New York 1958-59. **Operatic debut:** *Traviata* Terni/Rome, Italy 1948. Symphonic debut: Mozarteum Orch, Salzburg 1948. Awards: Order of Cavalier, Ital Gvnmt; Gold Medal, Gran Teatro del Liceo, Barcelona; Silver Medal, Peruvian Gvmnt; Grand Prix du Disque, Paris critics; Hon Citizen, City of New Orleans. Previous adm positions in opera: Mus Adm, Philadelphia Lyric Opera 1966-72.
Conducted with major companies in AUS: Bregenz Fest, Vienna Staatsoper; CAN: Montreal/Quebec, Vancouver; FRA: Nice, Orange Fest, Paris; FR GER: Hamburg; HOL: Amsterdam; ITA: Trieste, Turin; MEX: Mexico City; SPA: Barcelona; SWI: Geneva; UK: London Royal; USA: Baltimore, Chicago, Cincinnati, Hartford, Houston Grand Opera, New Orleans, New York City Opera, Philadelphia Lyric Opera, San Francisco Opera & Spring Opera, Seattle, Washington DC; YUG: Belgrade. **Operas with these companies incl** BELLINI: *Capuleti ed i Montecchi, Norma, Pirata, Puritani, Sonnambula, Straniera;* BIZET: *Carmen★, Pêcheurs de perles;* BOITO: *Mefistofele;* DONIZETTI: *Don Pasquale, Elisir, Fille du régiment★, Lucia, Lucrezia Borgia, Maria Stuarda★;* GIORDANO: *Andrea Chénier, Fedora;* GOUNOD: *Faust★, Roméo et Juliette;* HALEVY: *Juive★;* HUMPERDINCK: *Hänsel und Gretel;* LEONCAVALLO: *Pagliacci★;* MASCAGNI: *Cavalleria rusticana★;* MASSENET: *Manon;* MOZART: *Don Giovanni★, Nozze di Figaro;* MUSSORGSKY: *Boris Godunov;* OFFENBACH: *Contes d'Hoffmann★;* PONCHIELLI: *Gioconda;* PUCCINI: *Bohème★, Fanciulla del West, Gianni Schicchi★, Butterfly★, Manon Lescaut★, Rondine★, Suor Angelica★, Tabarro★, Tosca★, Turandot★, Villi★‡;* ROSSINI: *Barbiere di Siviglia★, Cenerentola;* SAINT-SAENS: *Samson et Dalila;* STRAUSS, J: *Fledermaus;* STRAUSS, R: *Salome;* VERDI: *Aida, Attila, Ballo in maschera★, Don Carlo★, Falstaff★, Forza del destino★, Luisa Miller★, Macbeth, Nabucco, Otello★, Rigoletto★, Simon Boccanegra, Traviata★, Trovatore★;* WAGNER: *Meistersinger, Walküre, Tannhäuser, Tristan und Isolde;* ZANDONAI: *Francesca da Rimini.* Recorded for RCA Victor. Conducted major orch in USA/Canada. Mgmt: HUR/UK; AIM/UK.

GUARNERA, GUIDO. Lyric baritone. Italian. Born 20 Apr 1929, Bari. Wife Cristina. Five children. Studied: Giuseppe Borgatti. **Debut:** Germont (*Traviata*) Teatro dell'Opera, Rome 1946. Awards: Commendatore, Rep Italy; Cav, Croce dell'Ordine del Leone di Licarte; Gold Medal, City of Naples.
Sang with major companies in CAN: Toronto; DEN: Copenhagen; FIN: Helsinki; FRA: Bordeaux, Lyon, Toulouse; ITA: Bologna, Florence Maggio & Comunale, Genoa, Naples, Palermo, Rome Opera & Caracalla, Turin; MEX: Mexico City; POR: Lisbon; ROM: Bucharest; SWE: Stockholm; YUG: Zagreb, Belgrade. **Roles with these companies incl** BIZET: Escamillo★ (*Carmen*), Zurga★ (*Pêcheurs de perles*); CILEA: Michonnet★ (*A. Lecouvreur*); DONIZETTI: Dott Malatesta★ (*Don Pasquale*), Belcore★ (*Elisir*), Alfonse★ (*Favorite*), Enrico★ (*Lucia*); GIORDANO: Carlo Gérard★ (*Andrea Chénier*); GLUCK: Ubalde (*Armide*); LEONCAVALLO: Tonio★ (*Pagliacci*); MASCAGNI: Alfio (*Cavalleria rusticana*); PONCHIELLI: Barnaba★ (*Gioconda*); PUCCINI: Marcello★ (*Bohème*), Gianni Schicchi★, Sharpless★ (*Butterfly*), Scarpia★ (*Tosca*); ROSSINI: Figaro★ (*Barbiere di Siviglia*); SPONTINI: Cinna (*Vestale*); VERDI: Amonasro★ (*Aida*), Renato★ (*Ballo in maschera*), Rodrigo★ (*Don Carlo*), Don Carlo

211

(*Ernani*), Falstaff★, Don Carlo★ (*Forza del destino*), Iago★ (*Otello*), Rigoletto★, Germont★ (*Traviata*), Conte di Luna★ (*Trovatore*). Also BUCCHI: Barone (*Gioco del barone*). **Res:** V Val di Zanzo 128, Rome, Italy.

GUARRERA, FRANK; né Francesco Guarrera. Lyric & dramatic baritone. American. Resident mem: Metropolitan Opera, New York. Born 3 Dec 1924, Philadelphia. Wife Adelina. Two children. Studied: Curtis Inst of Music, Richard Bonelli, Philadelphia; Eufemia Gregory, Cornelius L Reid, USA. **Debut:** Fanuel (*Nerone*) La Scala, Milan 1948. Awards: Page One Awd, Newspaper Guild of Greater Philadelphia 1955; Hall of Fame Awd, South Phila H S 1963; Awd of Merit Columbus Italian/American Citizens Assn, Clifton Heights, PA 1971; Anniversary Awd Phila Grand Opera 1968; Citation Consul Gen of Italy 1968; Met Op Silver Clock for 20 yrs; Met Op Silver Cup Awd for 25 yrs.
Sang with major companies in CAN: Montreal/Quebec, Vancouver; ITA: Milan La Scala; USA: Cincinnati Summer Opera; Hartford, Lake George, Miami, New Orleans, New York Met, Philadelphia Grand & Lyric, Pittsburgh, Portland, San Antonio, San Francisco Opera, Seattle. **Roles with these companies incl** BIZET: Escamillo (*Carmen*), Zurga (*Pêcheurs de perles*); BRITTEN: Bottom (*Midsummer Night*); DONIZETTI: Dott Malatesta (*Don Pasquale*), Belcore (*Elisir*), Enrico★‡ (*Lucia*); GIORDANO: Carlo Gérard (*Andrea Chénier*); GOUNOD: Valentin★ (*Faust*); LEONCAVALLO: Tonio★ (*Pagliacci*); MASCAGNI: Alfio★‡ (*Cavalleria rusticana*); MASSENET: Lescaut (*Manon*); MONTEMEZZI: Manfredo (*Amore dei tre re*); MOORE: Horace Tabor (*Baby Doe*); MOZART: Guglielmo‡ & Don Alfonso★ (*Così fan tutte*), Conte Almaviva (*Nozze di Figaro*); MUSSORGSKY: Shaklovity (*Khovanshchina*); ORFF: Solo (*Carmina burana*); PUCCINI: Marcello★ (*Bohème*), Jack Rance (*Fanciulla del West*), Gianni Schicchi★, Sharpless★ (*Butterfly*), Lescaut★ (*Manon Lescaut*), Scarpia (*Tosca*); ROSSINI: Figaro★ (*Barbiere di Siviglia*); TCHAIKOVSKY: Eugene Onegin; VERDI: Amonasro (*Aida*), Rodrigo (*Don Carlo*), Don Carlo (*Ernani*), Ford★ & Falstaff★ (*Falstaff*), Macbeth, Rigoletto★, Simon Boccanegra, Germont★ (*Traviata*), Conte di Luna★ (*Trovatore*). Recorded for: Columbia, RCA. Gives recitals. **Res:** 302 W 86 St, New York, NY, USA. Mgmt: CAM/USA.

GUASTAMACCHIA, NICHY NICOLA. Italian. Adm Dir, Teatro Regio, Piazza Castello 215, Turin 1969- . In charge of admin matters. Born 21 Dec 1934, Cirié/Turin. Wife Giovanna Geninatti, occupation psychologist. Two children. Studied: Turin Univ, hon law degree. Previous occupations: bank employee. Background primarily administrative. Initiated major policy changes including automated accounting and payroll. Mem of Secretariat, Department of Municipal Administration. **Res:** V Susa 42, 10138 Turin, Italy.

GUBISCH, BARBARA; née Schmidt. Dramatic mezzo-soprano. German. Resident mem: Staatsoper Dresden, Ger DR. Born 17 Sep 1938, Eberswalde. Divorced. One child. Studied: Kmsg

Johannes Kemter, Dresden. **Debut:** Eboli (*Don Carlo*) Stadttheater Cottbus, Ger DR 1969. Previous occupations: midwife. Awards: Winner Cont for Young Opera Singers, Ministry of Culture, Ger DR 1970; Winner Enescu Compt, Bucharest 1970.
Sang with major companies in FR GER: Wiesbaden; GER DR: Berlin Staatsoper, Dresden; ROM: Bucharest; USSR: Leningrad Kirov. **Roles with these companies incl** GLUCK: Orfeo★; JANACEK: Kostelnicka★ (*Jenufa*); LORTZING: Gräfin Eberbach★ (*Wildschütz*); MUSSORGSKY: Marina★ (*Boris Godunov*); NICOLAI: Frau Reich (*Lustigen Weiber*); SMETANA: Hata★ (*Bartered Bride*); VERDI: Ulrica (*Ballo in maschera*), Eboli★ (*Don Carlo*), Preziosilla★ (*Forza del destino*), Azucena (*Trovatore*); WAGNER: Erda (*Rheingold*), Fricka★ (*Walküre*), Brangäne★ (*Tristan und Isolde*); WOLF-FERRARI: Margarita★ (*Quattro rusteghi*). Also HANELL: Esther; TCHAIKOVSKY: Pauline (*Pique Dame*). **World premieres:** ZIMMERMANN: Christina (*Levins Mühle*) Staatsoper Dresden 1973; FOREST: Oan (*Odyssee des Mädchen Kin*) Stadtbühnen Erfurt 1975. Gives recitals. Appears with symphony orchestra. Coaches repertoire. **Res:** Rietschelstr 10, 801 Dresden, Ger DR. Mgmt: KDR/GDR.

GUELFI, GIANGIACOMO. Baritone. Italian. Born Rome. Studied: Centro Lirico, Florence. **Debut:** Rigoletto, Spoleto.
Sang with major companies in BRA: Rio de Janeiro; FR GER: Berlin Deutsche Oper, Frankfurt, Hamburg; ITA: Bologna, Florence Comunale, Milan La Scala, Naples, Rome Teatro dell'Opera, Venice, Verona Arena; MON: Monte Carlo; POR: Lisbon; SPA: Barcelona; USA: Chicago, Dallas, New York Met; et al. **Roles with these companies incl** BIZET: Escamillo (*Carmen*); GIORDANO: Carlo Gérard (*Andrea Chénier*); MASCAGNI: Alfio (*Cavalleria rusticana*); MEYERBEER: Nelusco (*Africaine*); PONCHIELLI: Barnaba (*Gioconda*); PUCCINI: Marcello (*Bohème*), Jack Rance (*Fanciulla del West*), Scarpia (*Tosca*); VERDI: Amonasro (*Aida*), Ezio (*Attila*), Renato (*Ballo in maschera*), Rodrigo (*Don Carlo*), Don Carlo (*Forza del destino*), Macbeth, Nabucco, Simon Boccanegra, Germont (*Traviata*), Conte di Luna (*Trovatore*), Monforte (*Vespri*); WAGNER: Telramund (*Lohengrin*); et al.

GUERRA, SANTIAGO. Conductor of opera and symphony. Brazilian. Born 21 Dec 1902, Barcelona, Spain. Wife Stella. Two children. Studied: Consv Dramatico e Musical de São Paulo, Brazil; incl piano. Plays the piano. **Operatic debut:** *Trovatore* Lirica, São Paulo 1928. Symphonic debut: Teatro Municipal, Rio de Janeiro 1936. Previous occupations: dir, operetta comp Lea Candini. Awards: var medals and diplomas.
Conducted with major companies in BRA: Rio de Janeiro. **Operas with these companies incl** AUBER: *Fra Diavolo*; BELLINI: *Norma, Sonnambula*; BIZET: *Carmen*; BOITO: *Mefistofele*; CILEA: *Adriana Lecouvreur*; DEBUSSY: *Enfant prodigue*; DONIZETTI: *Don Pasquale, Elisir★, Lucia★*; GIORDANO: *Andrea Chénier★, Fedora*; GOMES: *Colombo★, Fosca★*; GOUNOD: *Faust*; HUMPERDINCK: *Hänsel und Gretel*; LEONCAVALLO: *Pagliacci★*; MASCAGNI: *Amico*

Fritz, Cavalleria rusticana★; MASSENET: *Manon;* MENOTTI: *Amelia al ballo, Telephone;* MOZART: *Don Giovanni;* PERGOLESI: *Maestro di musica, Serva padrona;* PONCHIELLI: *Gioconda;* PUCCINI: *Bohème*★, *Butterfly*★, *Tosca*★; ROSSINI: *Barbiere di Siviglia*★; VERDI: *Aida*★, *Ballo in maschera, Forza del destino, Otello*★, *Rigoletto*★, *Traviata*★, *Trovatore*★. Also GOMES: *Guarany, Maria Tudor, Schiavo.* Conducted major orch in Cent/S America. Teaches. **Res:** Rua Marques de Abrantes 126, Rio de Janeiro, Brazil.

GUGLIELMI, MARGHERITA. Lyric coloratura soprano. Italian. Born 26 Oct 1938, Portovenere, Italy. Husband Antonio Berini, occupation employee. Studied: Mo Corbellini, Mo Gavarini, La Spezia; Mo Pastorino, Milan. **Debut:** Gilda (*Rigoletto*) Teatro Malibran, Venice 1954. Awards: Gold Medal Lyric Compt, Comune di Chiavari 1955; Golden Nut, Lyric Prize 1969.
  Sang with major companies in AUS: Vienna Staatsoper; BEL: Brussels; BUL: Sofia; CAN: Montreal/Quebec; DEN: Copenhagen; FRA: Bordeaux, Marseille, Nice, Rouen, Toulouse; ITA: Bologna, Florence Maggio & Comunale, Genoa, Milan La Scala, Naples, Palermo, Rome Opera, Trieste, Turin; POR: Lisbon; S AFR: Johannesburg; SPA: Barcelona; SWI: Geneva; UK: Edinburgh Fest; USSR: Kiev, Leningrad Kirov, Moscow Bolshoi & Stanislavski, Tbilisi; USA: Boston, Dallas, Hartford, Philadelphia Grand, Pittsburgh, San Antonio, Washington DC; YUG: Dubrovnik, Zagreb, Belgrade. **Roles with these companies incl** BELLINI: Elvira★ (*Puritani*), Amina★ (*Sonnambula*); CIMAROSA: Carolina★ (*Matrimonio segreto*); DONIZETTI: Norina★ (*Don Pasquale*), Adina★ (*Elisir*), Marie★ (*Fille du régiment*), Lucia★‡; MOZART: Zerlina★ (*Don Giovanni*), Susanna★ (*Nozze di Figaro*); OFFENBACH: Olympia★ (*Contes d'Hoffmann*); PAISIELLO: Rosina★ (*Barbiere di Siviglia*); PUCCINI: Musetta★ (*Bohème*), Lauretta★ (*Gianni Schicchi*); ROSSINI: Rosina★‡ (*Barbiere di Siviglia*), Fanny (*Cambiale di matrimonio*), Elvira★ (*Italiana in Algeri*); STRAUSS, R: Fiakermilli★ (*Arabella*); THOMAS: Philine★ (*Mignon*); VERDI: Oscar★ (*Ballo in maschera*), Nannetta★ (*Falstaff*), Gilda★ (*Rigoletto*). Also ROSSINI: Matilde★ (*Elisabetta Regina*), Matilde de Shabran; WEBER/Mahler: Clarissa (*Drei Pintos*). Recorded for: DG, Supraphon. Gives recitals. Appears with symphony orchestra. **Res:** V Roma 13, 21057 Olgiate Olona/Varese, Italy.

GUILLAUME, EDITH. Lyric mezzo-soprano. Danish. Resident mem: Royal Danish Opera, Copenhagen. Born 14 Jun 1943, Bergerac, France. Husband Niels Hvass. Two children. Studied: Royal Danish Consv, Prof Thyge Thygesen, Prof Monna Ry Andersen, Copenhagen; Mme Janine Michaud, Paris. **Debut:** Thérèse (*Dream of Thérèse*) Jutland Opera 1970. Awards: Carl Nielsen Fllshp 1968; Elisabeth Dons Memorial Fund 1970; Critics' Prize of Hon 1970.
  Sang with major companies in DEN: Copenhagen. **Roles with these companies incl** GOUNOD: Siebel★ (*Faust*); MONTEVERDI: Ottavia★ (*Incoronazione di Poppea*); MOZART: Cherubino★ (*Nozze di Figaro*); ROSSINI: Zaida★ (*Turco in Italia*). Also NORHOLM: B★ (*Young Park*); WERLE: Thérèse★ (*Dream of Thérèse*); POULENC: Femme★ (*Voix humaine*). Gives recitals. Appears with symphony orchestra. **Res:** Ellebakken 2, 2900 Hellerup, Copenhagen, Denmark. Mgmt: WHK/DEN.

GUIOT, ANDRÉA. Spinto. French. Resident mem: Opéra de Paris; Opéra du Rhin, Strasbourg. Born 11 Jan 1928, Garons/Gard, France. Husband Charles Pot, occupation journalist. Studied: Consv Ntl de Paris, Mme Lapeyrette, Mme Michaud; M Noguera, acting, Paris. **Debut:** Antonia (*Contes d'Hoffmann*) Opéra Comique, Paris 1955. Awards: Chevalier des Arts et Lettres, Paris.
  Sang with major companies in ARG: Buenos Aires; AUS: Vienna Staatsoper; BEL: Liège; FRA: Bordeaux, Lyon, Marseille, Nancy, Nice, Orange, Paris, Rouen, Strasbourg, Toulouse; FR GER: Hamburg; HOL: Amsterdam; ITA: Rome Caracalla; MON: Monte Carlo; UK: Edinburgh Fest, Glasgow Scottish; USA: Chicago, Miami, Newark, Philadelphia Lyric, San Antonio. **Roles with these companies incl** BEETHOVEN: Marzelline (*Fidelio*); BERLIOZ: Teresa★ (*Benvenuto Cellini*); BIZET: Micaëla★‡ (*Carmen*), Léila (*Pêcheurs de perles*); BOITO: Margherita★ (*Mefistofele*); CHARPENTIER: Louise★; GIORDANO: Maddalena (*Andrea Chénier*); GLUCK: Alceste, Euridice★; GOUNOD: Marguerite★ (*Faust*), Mireille★, Juliette★; HANDEL: Galatea; LALO: Rozenn (*Roi d'Ys*); LEONCAVALLO: Nedda★ (*Pagliacci*); MASSENET: Salomé (*Hérodiade*), Manon, Fanny (*Sappho*); MOZART: Fiordiligi (*Così fan tutte*), Donna Elvira (*Don Giovanni*), Contessa★ (*Nozze di Figaro*), Pamina (*Zauberflöte*); OFFENBACH: Antonia★ & Giulietta★ (*Contes d'Hoffmann*); POULENC: Mme Lidoine★ (*Dialogues des Carmélites*); PUCCINI: Mimi★ & Musetta (*Bohème*), Cio-Cio-San★ (*Butterfly*), Suor Angelica, Liù★ (*Turandot*); ROSSINI: Mathilde‡ (*Guillaume Tell*); VERDI: Elisabetta★ (*Don Carlo*), Alice Ford★ (*Falstaff*), Desdemona★ (*Otello*), Violetta (*Traviata*). Recorded for: Philips, Pathé-Marconi. Video/Film: Liù (*Turandot*); Alice Ford (*Falstaff*). Appears with symphony orchestra. Teaches voice. Coaches repertoire. On faculty of Consv de Nîmes, Gard, France. **Res:** 59 rue Caulaincourt, 75018 Paris, France. Mgmt: GLZ/FRA; SMN/USA.

GULIN, ANGELES. Dramatic soprano. Spanish. Born 18 Feb, Ribadavia/Orense, Spain. Husband Antonio Blancas, occupation opera singer. One child. Studied: with own father. **Debut:** Königin der Nacht (*Zauberflöte*) Sodre Theater, Montevideo, Uruguay 1963-64. Awards: First Prize, Intl Cont Voci Verdiani, Busseto 1968; Gold Medal, Circulo de Bellas Artes, Madrid 1970; Ntl Theater Awd, Spain 1974.
  Sang with major companies in BEL: Liège; CAN: Montreal/Quebec; CZE: Prague Smetana; FRA: Aix-en-Provence Fest, Marseille, Toulouse; FR GER: Düsseldorf-Duisburg, Hamburg; HOL: Amsterdam; HUN: Budapest; ITA: Bologna, Florence Maggio, Genoa, Naples, Parma, Rome Caracalla, Trieste, Turin, Venice, Verona Arena; MEX: Mexico City; MON: Monte Carlo; SPA: Barcelona; UK: Edinburgh Fest, London Royal; USA: San Francisco Opera. **Roles with these com-**

panies incl BELLINI: Beatrice di Tenda★, Norma; CATALANI: Wally★; DONIZETTI: Lucrezia Borgia★; FALLA: Salud★ (Vida breve); GIORDANO: Maddalena★ (Andrea Chénier); LEONCAVALLO: Nedda (Pagliacci); MEYERBEER: Valentine (Huguenots); MOZART: Donna Anna (Don Giovanni); PONCHIELLI: Gioconda★; PUCCINI: Manon Lescaut★, Tosca★, Turandot★; SPONTINI: Amazily★ (Fernand Cortez); VERDI: Aida★, Mina★ (Stiffelio), Amelia★ (Ballo in maschera), Gulnara★ (Corsaro), Lucrezia Contarini (Due Foscari), Leonora★ (Forza del destino), Luisa Miller★, Lady Macbeth★, Abigaille★ (Nabucco), Gilda (Rigoletto), Amelia (Simon Boccanegra), Violetta★ (Traviata), Leonora★ (Trovatore); WAGNER: Senta (Fliegende Holländer). Also ROSSINI: Elena★ (Donna del lago); VERDI: Alzira★. Gives recitals. Appears with symphony orchestra. Teaches voice. **Res:** Sánchez Barcaiztegui 38, Madrid, Spain.

GULLICKSEN, RICHARD CONRAD. Scenic and costume designer for opera, theater, film, television; specl in sets. Is a lighting designer; also a painter. American. Resident designer, Hawaii Opera Theatre, Honolulu Symph Socy, Hawaii. Born 11 Dec 1931, Chicago. Wife Dorothy, occupation real estate mgr. One child. Studied: Lester Polakov Studio of Stage Design; Roosevelt Univ; Art Inst of Chicago. **Operatic debut:** sets, Carmen Atlanta Opera, GA, USA 1965; cost, Fliegende Holländer Hawaii Opera Theatre 1970. Theater debut: New York Univ 1963. Awards: Atlanta Theatre Awd, Atlanta Theatre Council.

Designed for major companies in USA: Hawaii, San Antonio, Washington DC. **Operas designed for these companies incl** BEETHOVEN: Fidelio; BERLIOZ: Damnation de Faust; BERNSTEIN: Trouble in Tahiti; BIZET: Carmen; DONIZETTI: Elisir; FLOYD: Susannah; GERSHWIN: Porgy and Bess; GOUNOD: Faust; HUMPERDINCK: Hänsel und Gretel; JOPLIN: Treemonisha★; MENOTTI: Amahl, Dernier sauvage; OFFENBACH: Contes d'Hoffmann★; ORFF: Carmina burana; PUCCINI: Bohème, Fanciulla del West, Butterfly, Tosca; PURCELL: King Arthur; RIMSKY-KORSAKOV: Coq d'or; VERDI: Aida, Otello, Rigoletto, Traviata; WAGNER: Fliegende Holländer, Meistersinger; WEILL: Dreigroschenoper. **Operatic world premieres:** JOPLIN: Treemonisha Atlanta Opera Co 1972. Operatic Video—ETV: Trouble in Tahiti. Exhibitions of paintings, collection Univ of Chicago. **Res:** 589 C Kawailoa Rd, Kailua, Hawaii, USA.

GULLINO, WALTER. Lyric tenor. Italian. Born 1 Jun 1933, Dilolo, Congo. Wife Evelyn Utvary. Studied: Beniamino Gigli, Consv G Verdi, Milan. **Debut:** Almaviva (Barbiere di Siviglia) Società del Quartetto, Italy 1958.

Sang with major companies in AUS: Vienna Staatsoper; FRA: Aix-en-Provence Fest; GRE: Athens National; FR GER: Cologne, Wuppertal; ITA: Genoa, Milan La Scala; S AFR: Johannesburg; USSR: Moscow Bolshoi; USA: New Orleans, Philadelphia Grand. **Roles with these companies incl** BELLINI: Elvino★ (Sonnambula); BRITTEN: Peter Quint (Turn of the Screw); CIMAROSA: Paolino (Matrimonio segreto);

DONIZETTI: Ernesto★ (Don Pasquale), Nemorino★ (Elisir); MASCAGNI: Fritz (Amico Fritz); MOZART: Idomeneo; PUCCINI: Rinuccio★ (Gianni Schicchi); ROSSINI: Almaviva★ (Barbiere di Siviglia), Edward Milfort★ (Cambiale di matrimonio); STRAUSS, J: Eisenstein & Alfred (Fledermaus); VERDI: Fenton★ (Falstaff), Duca di Mantova (Rigoletto), Alfredo (Traviata). Also STRAVINSKY: Renard★, Tenor role (Noces); CHABRIER: Gontran★ (Education manquée); MENOTTI: Gaspare★ (Amahl); MOZART: Tenor role★ (Sposo deluso). Gives recitals. **Res:** V Mauro Macchi 93, Milan, Italy.

GUSCHLBAUER, THEODOR. Conductor of opera and symphony. Austrian. Resident Cond, Opéra de Lyon, France; after Sep 1975 Landestheater Linz, Austria. Also Mus Dir, Bruckner Orch, Linz. Born 14 Apr 1939, Vienna. Wife Marie-Christine. One child. Studied: Musik Akad, Hans Swarowsky, Vienna; L von Matacic, H von Karajan, Salzburg; incl cello, piano, viola da gamba. Operatic training as repetiteur & asst cond at Volksoper, Vienna 1964-66. **Operatic debut:** Lustigen Weiber Studio Volksoper, Vienna 1965. Symphonic debut: Barock Ensemble, Vienna 1961. Awards: 5 Grands Prix du Disque, Acad Charles Cros & du Disque Français. Previous adm positions in opera: Mus Dir, Opéra de Lyon, France 1969-75.

Conducted with major companies in AUS: Graz; FRA: Aix-en-Provence Fest, Lyon; FR GER: Cologne; ITA: Florence Maggio: POR: Lisbon; SWI: Geneva. **Operas with these companies incl** BEETHOVEN: Fidelio★; BERG: Wozzeck★; DONIZETTI: Don Pasquale; GLÜCK: Iphigénie en Tauride★; JANACEK: Jenufa★; MONTEVERDI: Favola d'Orfeo★; MOZART: Clemenza di Tito, Così fan tutte★, Don Giovanni★, Entführung aus dem Serail★, Idomeneo, Schauspieldirektor, Nozze di Figaro★, Zauberflöte★; NICOLAI: Lustigen Weiber; PERGOLESI: Serva padrona; PUCCINI: Bohème★, Tosca; PURCELL: Dido and Aeneas; RAVEL: Heure espagnole; ROSSINI: Barbiere di Siviglia, Cenerentola; STRAUSS, R: Rosenkavalier★, Salome★, Schweigsame Frau; WAGNER: Fliegende Holländer★, Lohengrin, Meistersinger★, Walküre★, Siegfried★, Tannhäuser, Tristan und Isolde★; WEILL: Aufstieg und Fall der Stadt Mahagonny. Also BIZET: Carmen; RAMEAU: Platée★. **World premieres:** KOSMA: Hussards 1969; PREY: Jonas 1969; OHANA: Autodafé 1972; all at Opéra de Lyon, France. Conducted major orch in Europe, Asia. **Res:** Rudolfstr 68, A-4020 Linz, Austria. Mgmt: RAB/AUS and others.

GUSELLA, MARIO. Conductor of opera and symphony. Italian. Born 18 Dec 1913, Cesenatico. Wife Giovanna Pasquini. Two children. Studied: Consv G Verdi, Milan; incl cello. Plays the cello. **Operatic debut:** Nabucco La Scala, Milan 1967. Symphonic debut: Orch Radio Lugano, Switzerland 1965. Previous occupations: solo cellist La Scala, Milan and RAI Orch, Turin; cello teacher Consv C Monteverdi, Bolzano.

Conducted with major companies in ITA: Bologna, Florence Maggio & Comunale, Genoa, Milan La Scala, Parma, Rome Opera & Caracalla, Trieste, Turin, Venice. **Operas with these companies incl** CIMAROSA: Matrimonio segreto;

DONIZETTI: *Campanello*★, *Maria di Rohan*, *Maria Stuarda*★; FALLA: *Retablo de Maese Pedro*★; GIORDANO: *Andrea Chénier;* GOUNOD: *Faust*★; HAYDN: *Mondo della luna*★; LEONCAVALLO: *Pagliacci*★; MASCAGNI: *Cavalleria rusticana*★; PAISIELLO: *Barbiere di Siviglia*★; PERGOLESI: *Serva padrona;* PUCCINI: *Bohème, Fanciulla del West, Butterfly, Tosca;* PURCELL: *Dido and Aeneas*★; ROSSINI: *Barbiere di Siviglia*★, *Italiana in Algeri*★, *Pietra del paragone;* STRAVINSKY: *Rossignol*★; VERDI: *Aida*★, *Nabucco*★, *Rigoletto*★, *Trovatore.* Also MANZONI: *Sentenza;* MALIPIERO: *Capitan Spavento;* BETTINELLI: *Pozzo e il pendolo;* BERIO: *Passaggio;* HAZON: *Agenzia matrimoniale.* Conducted major orch in Europe. Teaches at Consv G Verdi, Milan, Head of Orch Cond Class. **Res:** V Biasioli 381, Genoa/Nervi, Italy.

GUSMEROLI, GIOVANNI. Bass. Italian. Born 12 Dec 1937, Lodi/Milan, Italy. Wife Antonella Ferri. Two children. **Debut:** Dulcamara (*Elisir*) Spoleto Fest 1966. Previous occupations: represent of antique furniture dealer. Awards: First Prize Ntl Conc, Spoleto, Italy.

Sang with major companies in AUS: Graz, Vienna Volksoper; FRA: Bordeaux, Marseille, Orange Fest, Rouen; ITA: Bologna, Genoa, Milan La Scala, Rome Opera & Caracalla, Turin; SPA: Barcelona, Majorca; YUG: Dubrovnik. **Roles with these companies incl** BELLINI: Oroveso★ (*Norma*), Sir Richard & Sir George★ (*Puritani*), Rodolfo★ (*Sonnambula*); DONIZETTI: Henry VIII (*Anna Bolena*), Dulcamara (*Elisir*); Baldassare (*Favorite*); FALLA: Don Quixote (*Retablo de Maese Pedro*); PROKOFIEV: King of Clubs (*Love for Three Oranges*); PUCCINI: Colline (*Bohème*); ROSSINI: Don Basilio (*Barbiere di Siviglia*); SPONTINI: Pontifex Maximus (*Vestale*); THOMAS: Lothario (*Mignon*); VERDI: Ramfis (*Aida*), Grande Inquisitore★ (*Don Carlo*), Padre Guardiano★ (*Forza del destino*), Zaccaria (*Nabucco*). Also PUCCINI: Timur★ (*Turandot*); DONIZETTI: Raimondo★(*Lucia*). Gives recitals. Appears with symphony orchestra. Mgmt: TAS/AUS.

GUTHRIE, FREDERICK. Bass. American. Resident mem: Staatsoper, Vienna. Born 31 Mar 1924, Pocatelo, ID, USA. Wife Mary Patricia Doyle. One child. Studied Glynn Ross, Dr Hugo Strelitzer, Los Angeles; Josef Witt, Ludwig Weber, Vienna. **Debut:** Lodovico (*Otello*) Staatsoper, Vienna 1955. Previous occupations: Sergeant US Army in Europe World War II; singer in radio & films, Hollywood 1946-53. Awards: Oesterr Ehrenkreuz für Wissenschaft und Kunst, Pres of Austria 1969; Kammersänger 1975.

Sang with major companies in AUS: Graz, Salzburg Fest, Vienna Staatsoper & Volksoper; BEL: Brussels; CAN: Montreal/Quebec; FRA: Aix-en-Provence Fest; FR GER: Frankfurt, Hamburg, Munich Staatsoper; ITA: Naples, Rome Opera, Trieste, Venice; SWI: Zurich; UK: Edinburgh Fest, Glyndebourne Fest; USA: Seattle. **Roles with these companies incl** BRITTEN: Theseus (*Midsummer Night*); DEBUSSY: Arkel (*Pelléas et Mélisande*); GLUCK: High Priest (*Alceste*); HANDEL: Ptolemy (*Giulio Cesare*); MOZART:

Sarastro★ (*Zauberflöte*); MUSSORGSKY: Pimen (*Boris Godunov*); PUCCINI: Colline★ (*Bohème*); ROSSINI: Don Basilio (*Barbiere di Siviglia*); STRAVINSKY: Tiresias (*Oedipus Rex*); VERDI: Ramfis (*Aida*), Philip II (*Don Carlo*), Padre Guardiano★ (*Forza del destino*), Massimiliano Moor (*Masnadieri*); WAGNER: Daland★ (*Fliegende Holländer*), Gurnemanz (*Parsifal*), Fafner (*Rheingold*★, *Siegfried*★), König Marke★ (*Tristan und Isolde*). Also MOZART: Commendatore★ (*Don Giovanni*); PUCCINI: Timur★ (*Turandot*). **World premieres:** MARTIN: König Alonso (*Sturm*) Staatsoper, Vienna 1956; Siméon (*Mystère de la Nativité*) Salzburg Fest 1960. Recorded for: Westminster, Vanguard. Appears with symphony orchestra. Teaches voice. On faculty of Hochschule für Musik & darst Kunst, Vienna. **Res:** Tanneng 17, A-2384 Breitenfurt, Austria.

GUTSTEIN, ERNST. Dramatic baritone. Austrian. Resident mem: Volksoper, Vienna. Born 15 May 1924, Vienna. Wife Gertrude. Three children. Studied: Musikakad, Prof Kmsg Gustav Fuhsperg, Prof Kmsg Hans Duhan, Prof Kmsg Josef Witt, Vienna. **Debut:** Don Fernando (*Fidelio*) Landestheater, Innsbruck 1948. Awards: Kammersänger, City of Frankfurt/Main 1965; Austrian Kammersänger, Ministry of Culture 1975.

Sang with major companies in AUS: Bregenz Fest, Graz, Salzburg Fest, Vienna Staatsoper & Volksoper; BEL: Brussels; BRA: Rio de Janeiro; CZE: Brno; FRA: Paris, Strasbourg; FR GER: Berlin Deutsche Oper, Bonn, Cologne, Darmstadt, Dortmund, Düsseldorf-Duisburg, Frankfurt, Hamburg, Hannover, Karlsruhe, Kassel, Kiel, Mannheim, Munich Staatsoper, Nürnberg, Saarbrücken, Stuttgart, Wiesbaden; GER DR: Berlin Komische Oper; HUN: Budapest; ITA: Florence Maggio, Rome Opera, Trieste; POR: Lisbon; SPA: Barcelona; SWI: Zurich; UK: London Royal & English National; USSR: Moscow Bolshoi; USA: Chicago. **Roles with these companies incl** d'ALBERT: Sebastiano★ (*Tiefland*); BEETHOVEN: Don Pizarro★ (*Fidelio*); BERG: Dr Schön★ (*Lulu*), Doktor (*Wozzeck*); BERLIOZ: Méphistophélès (*Damnation de Faust*); BIZET: Escamillo (*Carmen*); CILEA: Michonnet (*A. Lecouvreur*); DONIZETTI: Dott Malatesta (*Don Pasquale*), Belcore (*Elisir*), Enrico (*Lucia*); EINEM: Alfred Ill★ (*Besuch der alten Dame*), Priest★ (*Prozess*); FORTNER: Don Perlimplin; GLUCK: Agamemnon (*Iphigénie en Aulide*); HAYDN: Buonafede★ (*Mondo della luna*); HENZE: Landarzt; HINDEMITH: Cardillac★, Mathis★; HUMPERDINCK: Spielmann (*Königskinder*); JANACEK: Sacristan (*Excursions of Mr Broucek*); LEONCAVALLO: Tonio (*Pagliacci*); LORTZING: Graf Eberbach (*Wildschütz*), Peter I★ (*Zar und Zimmermann*); MARTINU: Hans (*Comedy on the Bridge*); MASCAGNI: Alfio (*Cavalleria rusticana*); MASSENET: Lescaut (*Manon*); MONIUSZKO: Janusz (*Halka*); MOZART: Guglielmo (*Così fan tutte*), Don Giovanni, Conte Almaviva★ (*Nozze di Figaro*), Papageno (*Zauberflöte*); OFFENBACH: Coppélius, etc★ (*Contes d'Hoffmann*); ORFF: Solo (*Carmina burana*), König (*Kluge*); PUCCINI: Marcello (*Bohème*), Gianni Schicchi, Sharpless★ (*Butterfly*), Lescaut (*Manon Lescaut*), Michele★ (*Tabarro*), Scarpia (*Tosca*); ROSSINI:

Figaro & Dott Bartolo★ (*Barbiere di Siviglia*); SHOSTAKOVICH: Platon Kusmich Kovalioff (*Nose*); STRAUSS, R: Musiklehrer★ (*Ariadne auf Naxos*), Graf (*Capriccio*), Orest (*Elektra*), Jochanaan (*Salome*); STRAVINSKY: Nick Shadow (*Rake's Progress*); TCHAIKOVSKY: Eugene Onegin; VERDI: Amonasro (*Aida*), Renato (*Ballo in maschera*), Rodrigo (*Don Carlo*), Falstaff, Don Carlo & Fra Melitone (*Forza del destino*), Macbeth, Iago★ (*Otello*), Rigoletto★, Simon Boccanegra, Germont (*Traviata*), Conte di Luna (*Trovatore*); WAGNER: Telramund★ (*Lohengrin*), Amfortas (*Parsifal*), Wotan (*Rheingold*), Wolfram (*Tannhäuser*); WOLF-FERRARI: Conte Gil (*Segreto di Susanna*). Also STRAUSS, R: Faninal★ (*Rosenkavalier*); SCHMIDT: Archidiakon★ (*Notre Dame*); KIENZL: Johannes★ (*Evangelimann*); VERDI: Francesco (*Masnadieri*). **World premieres:** FORTNER: Don Perlimplin (*In seinem Garten liebt Don Perlimplin Belisa*) Opernhaus Cologne/Schwetzingen 1962; WEISHAPPEL: König Nicolo, Volksoper Vienna 1972; KLEBE: Mahon (*Wahrer Held*) Opernhaus Zurich 1975. Recorded for: Electrola, DG, CBS, Concert Hall. Video/Film: Rigoletto; Janusz (*Halka*); Buonafede (*Mondo della luna*). Appears with symphony orchestra. Teaches voice. **Res:** Markt 166, A2851 Krumbach, Austria. Mgmt: TAS/AUS; SLZ/FRG.

GUTTMAN, IRVING ALLEN. Stages/produces opera & television. Also designs stage-lighting. Canadian. Art Dir & Resident Stage Dir, Edmonton Opera Assn, Alta. Born 27 Oct 1928, Chatham, Ont. Single. Studied: Royal Consv of Music, Toronto, Dr Herman Geiger-Torel; also music, piano & voice. Operatic training as asst stage dir at Canadian Opera, Toronto 1947-52. **Operatic debut:** *Faust* CBC TV, Montreal 1954. Awards: Canada Medal, Gvnmt of Canada. Previous adm positions in opera: Art Dir, Vancouver Opera, BC 1960-74.

Directed/produced opera for major companies in CAN: Montreal/Quebec, Toronto, Vancouver; SPA: Barcelona; USA: Baltimore, Fort Worth, Hartford, Hawaii, Houston, New Orleans, Philadelphia Lyric, Pittsburgh, Portland, San Francisco Spring Opera, Santa Fe, Seattle. **Operas staged with these companies incl** BELLINI: *Norma;* BIZET: *Carmen★;* DONIZETTI: *Lucia, Lucrezia Borgia★;* GOUNOD: *Faust★, Roméo et Juliette;* HUMPERDINCK: *Hänsel und Gretel;* LEONCAVALLO: *Pagliacci★;* MASCAGNI: *Cavalleria rusticana★;* MASSENET: *Manon, Werther;* MENOTTI: *Amahl, Consul, Old Maid and the Thief★, Telephone★;* MONTEMEZZI: *Amore dei tre re★;* MOZART: *Don Giovanni, Nozze di Figaro;* MUSSORGSKY: *Boris Godunov;* OFFENBACH: *Contes d'Hoffmann;* PERGOLESI: *Serva padrona;* PUCCINI: *Bohème★, Butterfly★, Manon Lescaut★, Tosca★, Turandot★;* RAVEL: *Heure espagnole;* ROSSINI: *Barbiere di Siviglia★, Cenerentola, Italiana in Algeri;* SAINT-SAENS: *Samson et Dalila;* STRAUSS, R: *Salome;* VERDI: *Aida, Ballo in maschera, Otello, Rigoletto★, Traviata★, Trovatore;* WOLF-FERRARI: *Segreto di Susanna*. **Operatic world premieres:** FLOYD: *Wuthering Heights* Santa Fe, NM, USA 1958. Operatic Video—CBC TV: *Faust, Bohème, Carmen, Prima Donna, Lord Byron's Love Letter, Tabarro*. Teaches at Opera Workshop, Courteney, BC. **Res:** 31-1311 Beach Ave, Vancouver, BC, Canada. Mgmt: SAM/USA; AIM/UK.

H

HAAS, CHRISTOPH LEONHARD. Conductor of opera and symphony. Swiss. Resident Cond, Theater am Gärtnerplatz, Munich. Born 14 Jan 1949, Aaran, Switzerland. Wife Sae Hynn, occupation singer. Studied: Prof Swarowsky, Vienna; also piano, flute, violin & percussion. Plays the piano. Operatic training as repetiteur at Grand Théâtre, Geneva 1971-72; Vienna State Opera 1972-73. **Operatic debut:** *Barbiere di Siviglia* Theater am Gärtnerplatz, Munich 1973.

Conducted with major companies in FR GER: Munich Gärtnerplatz. **Operas with these companies incl** DONIZETTI: *Lucia★; HUMPERDINCK: Hänsel und Gretel★; LORTZING: Zar und Zimmermann★; MENOTTI: Medium★; MOZART: Zauberflöte; ROSSINI: Barbiere di Siviglia★.* Teaches privately. **Res:** Reichenbachstr 33, Munich, FR Ger. Mgmt: ZBV/FRG.

HAAS, JULIEN EMILE. Dramatic baritone. Belgian. Born 29 Mar 1930, Liège. Wife Andrée Esposito, occupation opera singer, soprano. Studied: Consv Liège, Consv Brussels. **Debut:** Valentin (*Faust*) Théâtre de la Monnaie, Brussels 1955.

Sang with major companies in ARG: Buenos Aires; BEL: Brussels, Liège; DEN: Copenhagen; FRA: Bordeaux, Lyon, Marseille, Nice, Paris, Rouen, Strasbourg, Toulouse; GRE: Athens National; FR GER: Berlin Deutsche Oper, Cologne; ITA: Naples, Palermo, Rome Opera, Turin, Venice; MON: Monte Carlo; POR: Lisbon; SWE: Stockholm; SWI: Geneva, Zurich; UK: Edinburgh Fest, Glasgow Scottish; USA: San Francisco Opera. **Roles with these companies incl** BEETHOVEN: Don Pizarro (*Fidelio*); BENNETT: Braxton (*Mines of Sulphur*); BERLIOZ: Méphistophélès (*Damnation de Faust*), Choroebus (*Troyens*); BIZET: Escamillo (*Carmen*), Zurga (*Pêcheurs de perles*); BORODIN: Prince Igor★; DEBUSSY: Golaud★ (*Pelléas et Mélisande*); DONIZETTI: Alfonse (*Favorite*), Enrico★ (*Lucia*); EINEM: Georges Danton (*Dantons Tod*); GOUNOD: Ourrias (*Mireille*); LEONCAVALLO: Tonio (*Pagliacci*); MARTINU: Fotis★ (*Griechische Passion*); MASCAGNI: Alfio (*Cavalleria rusticana*); MASSENET: Hérode (*Hérodiade*), Boniface (*Jongleur de Notre Dame*), Lescaut (*Manon*), Athanaël (*Thaïs*); MEYERBEER: Comte de Nevers (*Huguenots*); MILHAUD: Créon (*Médée*); MONIUSZKO: Janusz (*Halka*); MOZART: Conte Almaviva (*Nozze di Figaro*); MUSSORGSKY: Varlaam (*Boris Godu-*

nov); PAISIELLO: Figaro (*Barbiere di Siviglia*); PENDERECKI: Grandier (*Teufel von Loudun*); PROKOFIEV: Ruprecht (*Fiery Angel*); PUCCINI: Marcello (*Bohème*), Jack Rance (*Fanciulla del West*), Scarpia (*Tosca*); PURCELL: Aeneas; RABAUD: Ali (*Mârouf*); RAVEL: Ramiro (*Heure espagnole*); ROSSELLINI: Pierre de Craon (*Annonce faite à Marie*); SAINT-SAENS: Grand prêtre★ (*Samson et Dalila*); SHOSTAKOVICH: Boris (*Katerina Ismailova*); STRAUSS, R: Mandryka (*Arabella*); TCHAIKOVSKY: Eugene Onegin; VERDI: Amonasro (*Aida*), Renato (*Ballo in maschera*), Rodrigo (*Don Carlo*), Don Carlo (*Forza del destino*), Miller (*Luisa Miller*), Macbeth, Nabucco, Iago (*Otello*), Rigoletto, Germont (*Traviata*), Conte di Luna (*Trovatore*); WAGNER: Telramund (*Lohengrin*), Wolfram (*Tannhäuser*). Also HONEGGER: Créon★ (*Antigone*); MARTIN: Monsieur Pourceaugnac★; GOUNOD: Valentin★ (*Faust*). **World premieres:** ROSENFELD: Ministre (*Miracle à la cour*) Marseille Opera 1975; ROSSELLINI: Armes Vercors (*Annonce faite à Marie*) Opéra Comique Paris 1970, Ministre (*Reine morte*) Monte Carlo 1973. Gives recitals. Appears with symphony orchestra. **Res:** 59 Blvd Voltaire, Paris 11, France.

HABUNEK, VLADO. Stages/produces opera & theater. Yugoslavian. Born 10 Oct 1906, Zagreb. Single. Studied: Zagreb, Paris, incl music & voice. **Operatic debut:** *Semele* Consv of Music, Zagreb 1943. Theater debut: Compagnie des Jeunes, Zagreb 1940. Previous occupation: journalist. Awards: Nazor Awd, Zagreb; City of Zagreb Awd; Officier des Arts et Lettres, Paris.

Directed/produced opera for major companies in HOL: Amsterdam; UK: London Royal; USSR: Leningrad Kirov; USA: New York City Opera; YUG: Dubrovnik, Zagreb. **Operas staged with these companies incl** BIZET: *Carmen★;* BRITTEN: *Curlew River, Midsummer Night, Rape of Lucretia;* BUSONI: *Turandot;* CALDARA: *Dafne★;* GLUCK: *Orfeo ed Euridice★;* IBERT: *Angélique;* JANACEK: *Jenufa★, Makropoulos Affair;* KELEMEN: *Belagerungszustand;* MENOTTI: *Medium;* MOZART: *Così fan tutte, Nozze di Figaro;* MUSSORGSKY: *Boris Godunov, Khovanshchina★;* ORFF: *Antigonae;* POULENC: *Voix humaine;* PUCCINI: *Bohème, Gianni Schicchi;* RAVEL: *Heure espagnole;* SALIERI: *Prima la musica★;* SHOSTAKOVICH:

Katerina Ismailova; STRAUSS, R: *Arabella★, Daphne★;* STRAVINSKY: *Rake's Progress, Rossignol;* TCHAIKOVSKY: *Eugene Onegin;* VERDI: *Don Carlo.* Also ORFF: *Prometheus;* KELEMEN: *Neue Mieter;* ZAJC: *Zrinjski.* **Operatic world premieres:** BRKANOVIC★ *Gold of Zadar* 1954; DEVCIC: *Witch of Labin* 1957; SULEK: *Coriolanus* 1970's, *Tempest* 1970's, all Zagreb; WEISGALL: *Nine Rivers from Jordan* New York City Opera 1963. Previous leading positions with major theater companies: Art Dir, Dubrovnik Fest. **Res:** Mose Pijade 38, Zagreb, Yugoslavia. Mgmt: NAP/USA.

HAEFLIGER, ERNST. Lyric tenor. Swiss. Resident mem: Deutsche Oper, Berlin. Born 6 Jul 1919, Davos. Wife Anna Golin, occupation architect. Three children. Studied: Prof Haefely, Zurich; Fernando Carpi, Prague & Geneva; Julius Patzak, Munich. **Debut:** ORFF: Tiresias (*Antigonae*) Salzburg Fest 1949. Awards: German Critics Prize; Chappel Gold Medal.

Sang with major companies in AUS: Salzburg Fest; BEL: Brussels; FRA: Aix-en-Provence Fest, Bordeaux, Lyon; FR GER: Berlin Deutsche Oper, Hamburg, Munich Staatsoper; ITA: Florence Maggio, Rome Opera; POR: Lisbon; SWI: Basel, Geneva, Zurich; UK: Glyndebourne Fest; USA: Chicago. **Roles with these companies incl** BRITTEN: Aschenbach★ (*Death in Venice*), Male Chorus (*Rape of Lucretia*); BUSONI: Calaf (*Turandot*); CIMAROSA: Paolino (*Matrimonio segreto*); DEBUSSY: Pelléas; DONIZETTI: Ernesto (*Don Pasquale*); GLUCK: Renaud (*Armide*), Pylade (*Iphigénie en Tauride*); HANDEL: Sextus (*Giulio Cesare*), Xerxes; LORTZING: Baron Kronthal (*Wildschütz*); MARTIN: Tristan (*Vin herbé*); MONTEVERDI: Nero (*Incoronazione di Poppea*), Ulisse (*Ritorno d'Ulisse*); MOZART: Ferrando★‡ (*Così fan tutte*), Don Ottavio★‡ (*Don Giovanni*), Belmonte★‡ (*Entführung aus dem Serail*), Idamante & Idomeneo (*Idomeneo*), Tamino★‡ (*Zauberflöte*); NICOLAI: Fenton (*Lustigen Weiber*); PFITZNER: Palestrina★; ROSSINI: Almaviva (*Barbiere di Siviglia*), Comte Ory; SMETANA: Hans (*Bartered Bride*); STRAUSS, R: Flamand (*Capriccio*); VERDI: Fenton (*Falstaff*). Also on records only BEETHOVEN: Florestan (*Fidelio*). **World premieres:** ORFF: Tiresias (*Antigonae*) Salzburg Fest 1949; BLACHER: (*200,000 Taler*) Deutsche Oper Berlin, FR Ger 1969. Recorded for: DG, Polydor Intl. Gives recitals. Appears with symphony orchestra. Teaches voice. On faculty of Hochschule für Musik, Munich. **Res:** Harthauserstr 98, 8 Munich 90, FR Ger. Mgmt: KGZ/SWI.

HAGEGÅRD, ERLAND BÖRJE. Lyric baritone. Swedish. Resident mem: Staatsoper, Hamburg. Born 27 Feb 1944, Brunskog, Sweden. Wife Anne, occupation scenic designer. Studied: Ingesunds Music School, Hans Wihlborg, Sweden; Music Acad, Arne Sunnegård, Stockholm; Akad für Musik, Vienna; Erik Werba, Vienna; Gerald Moore, London. **Debut:** Dionysos, Hippolyte, Pergamon (*Trois opéras minutes*) Vienna Volksoper 1968. Previous occupations: music producer. Awards: Kristina Nilsson stipd, Fröding stipd.

Sang with major companies in AUS: Vienna Staatsoper & Volksoper; FR GER: Frankfurt, Hamburg; SWE: Drottningholm Fest. **Roles with these companies incl** BIZET: Escamillo★ (*Carmen*); DONIZETTI: Belcore (*Elisir*); GOUNOD: Valentin★ (*Faust*); HANDEL: Arsamene★ (*Xerxes*); LORTZING: Graf Eberbach★ (*Wildschütz*), Peter I★ (*Zar und Zimmermann*); MASSENET: Albert★ (*Werther*); MILHAUD: Dionysos (*Abandon d'Ariane*), Hippolyte (*Délivrance de Thésée*), Pergamon (*Enlèvement d'Europe*); MOZART: Don Giovanni★; NICOLAI: Fluth★ (*Lustigen Weiber*); PUCCINI: Marcello★ (*Bohème*); ROSSINI: Dandini★ (*Cenerentola*); TCHAIKOVSKY: Eugene Onegin★; VERDI: Germont★ (*Traviata*). **World premieres:** DEAK: Ur-Fadern (*Fäderna*) Stockholm 1968. Video—TV Denmark: Arsamene (*Xerxes*). Gives recitals. Appears with symphony orchestra. **Res:** Birkenau 5, D-2081 Ellerbek/Hamburg, FR Ger. Mgmt: KBL/SWE; SLZ/FRG.

HAGEGÅRD, HÅKAN. Lyric baritone. Swedish Resident mem: Royal Opera, Stockholm. Born 25 Nov 1945, Karlstad, Sweden. Wife Anna. Two children. Studied: Music Acad, Stockholm; Tito Gobbi, Rome; Gerald Moore, London; Erik Werba, Vienna. **Debut:** Papageno (*Zauberflöte*) Royal Opera, Stockholm 1968.

Sang with major companies in SWE: Drottningholm Fest, Stockholm; UK: Glyndebourne Fest. **Roles with these companies incl** DEBUSSY: Pelléas★; DONIZETTI: Dott Malatesta★ (*Don Pasquale*); MOZART: Guglielmo★ (*Così fan tutte*), Conte Almaviva★ (*Nozze di Figaro*), Papageno★‡ (*Zauberflöte*); ORFF: Solo★ (*Carmina burana*); PUCCINI: Marcello★ (*Bohème*); PURCELL: Aeneas★ (*Dido and Aeneas*); ROSSINI: Figaro★ (*Barbiere di Siviglia*); STRAUSS, R: Graf★ (*Capriccio*); TCHAIKOVSKY: Yeletsky★ (*Pique Dame*); VERDI: Renato★ (*Ballo in maschera*), Rodrigo★ (*Don Carlo*), Rigoletto★. Also BRITTEN: Sid★ (*Albert Herring*). **World premieres:** WERLE: Crispin (*Tintomara*) Royal Opera, Stockholm 1973. Video/Film: Papageno (*Zauberflöte*). Gives recitals. Appears with symphony orchestra. **Res:** Stockholm, Sweden. Mgmt: KBL/SWE; DSP/USA.

HAGEN-WILLIAM, LOUIS; né Louis Williams. Bass-baritone & bass. American. Born 9 Jun 1938, New Orleans, LA, USA. Wife Jacqueline Pilet, occupation interior decorator. One child. Studied: Univ of California, Jan Popper, Los Angeles; Consv de Paris, Maria Braneze; Marguerite Pifteau, Paris. **Debut:** High Priest (*Idomeneo*) Aix-en-Provence Fest 1966. Awards: First Prize, Intl Concs Toulouse, France, and 's Hertogenbosch, Holland.

Sang with major companies in FRA: Aix-en-Provence, Bordeaux, Lyon, Marseille, Nancy, Nice, Paris, Rouen, Strasbourg, Toulouse; POR: Lisbon; SWI: Geneva. **Roles with these companies incl** BERG: Doktor (*Wozzeck*); DELIBES: Nilakantha (*Lakmé*); GOUNOD: Méphistophélès (*Faust*); MOZART: Sarastro (*Zauberflöte*); STRAUSS, R: Orest★ (*Elektra*); WAGNER: Daland (*Fliegende Holländer*), Alberich★ (*Götterdämmerung*), Fasolt★ (*Rheingold*), Fafner (*Rheingold★, Siegfried★*), Hunding★ (*Walküre*), Landgraf (*Tannhäuser*). Also PUCCINI: Timur★

(*Turandot*). **World premieres:** OHANA: (*Autodafé*) Lyon, France 1972. Gives recitals. Appears with symphony orchestra. **Res:** rue Montorgueil 27, Paris, France. Mgmt: CMW/FRA.

HAGER, GHITA F; née Schnessing-Schneeberg. Stages/produces opera. Also designs stage-lighting. German. Born 25 Aug 1929, Tallinn, Estonia. Divorced. One child. Studied: Opera Ballet School, Deutsches Opernhaus Berlin; also music, piano. Operatic training as asst stage dir & choreographer at Stuttgart, Heidelberg, Hamburg, Cologne, Vienna, Milan, Genoa, Zurich, San Francisco. **Operatic debut:** *Barbiere di Siviglia* Western Opera Theater, Grass Valley, CA 1967. Theater debut: dancer, State Opera Munich 1945-53. Previous adm positions in opera: Alaska SW Reg Arts Council/Western Opera Theater, educt work.

Directed/produced opera for major companies in CAN: Vancouver; USA: Portland, San Diego, San Francisco Opera & Spring Opera. **Operas staged with these companies incl** LEON-CAVALLO: *Pagliacci;* MASCAGNI: *Cavalleria rusticana;* MOZART: *Così fan tutte★, Don Giovanni, Nozze di Figaro★;* ORFF: *Carmina burana★;* PUCCINI: *Bohème★, Butterfly★;* STRAUSS, R: *Ariadne auf Naxos;* VERDI: *Rigoletto;* WAGNER: *Parsifal★, Walküre★.* **Operatic world premieres:** HENDERSON: *Medea* San Diego Opera, CA 1972. Teaches. **Res:** Johann Strauss Str 26, 8011 Vaterstetten/Munich, FR Ger. Mgmt: SMT/USA.

HAGER, LEOPOLD. Conductor of opera and symphony; composer; operatic stage director. Austrian. Resident Cond, Staatsoper, Vienna. Also Mus Dir, Mozarteum Orch, Salzburg. Born 6 Oct 1935, Salzburg. Wife Gertrude. One child. Studied: Mozarteum Salzburg, B Paumgartner, G Wimberger, C Bresgen; incl organ, piano, cembalo. Plays the organ, piano, cembalo. Operatic training as repetiteur & asst cond at Stadttheater, Mainz 1957-62; Landestheater, Linz 1962-64. **Operatic debut:** *Italiana in Algeri* Mainz 1957. Symphonic debut: Mozarteum Orch, Salzburg. Awards: Lilli Lehmann Medal, Mozarteum. Previous adm positions in opera: First Cond, Städt Bühnen, Cologne 1964-66; Gen Mus Dir, Städt Bühnen, Freiburg, FR Ger 1965-69.

Conducted with major companies in ARG: Buenos Aires; AUS: Bregenz Fest, Salzburg Fest, Vienna Staatsoper & Volksoper; FRA: Nancy; GRE: Athens Fest; FR GER: Cologne, Darmstadt, Essen, Frankfurt, Hamburg, Hannover, Karlsruhe, Kassel, Kiel, Munich Staatsoper, Stuttgart, Wiesbaden, Wuppertal; HOL: Amsterdam; ITA: Genoa, Naples, Trieste; MEX: Mexico City; SWE: Stockholm; SWI: Basel, Geneva, Zurich; USA: Boston, Chicago, Hartford Connecticut Op, Washington DC; YUG: Zagreb, Belgrade. **Operas with these companies incl** AUBER: *Fra Diavolo;* BEETHOVEN: *Fidelio★;* BERG: *Wozzeck;* BIZET: *Docteur Miracle;* CIMAROSA: *Matrimonio segreto;* DESSAU: *Verurteilung des Lukullus;* HANDEL: *Rodelinda;* HINDEMITH: *Mathis der Maler;* HUMPERDINCK: *Hänsel und Gretel;* JANACEK: *Jenufa;* KODALY: *Háry János★;* LEONCAVALLO: *Pagliacci;* LOR-TZING: *Zar und Zimmermann;* MARTINU: *Griechische Passion;* MASCAGNI: *Cavalleria*

rusticana; MENOTTI: *Amahl;* MOZART: *Così fan tutte★, Don Giovanni★, Entführung aus dem Serail★, Idomeneo, Schauspieldirektor★, Lucio Silla★‡, Mitridate, re di Ponto★‡, Nozze di Figaro★, Re pastore★‡, Zauberflöte★;* MUSSORGSKY: *Boris Godunov, Fair at Sorochinsk;* NICOLAI: *Lustigen Weiber;* OFFENBACH: *Contes d'Hoffmann;* ORFF: *Bernauerin★, Kluge;* PERGOLESI: *Serva padrona;* PFITZNER: *Palestrina★;* PUCCINI: *Bohème★, Gianni Schicchi★, Manon Lescaut, Tosca★, Turandot★;* PURCELL: *King Arthur★;* RAVEL: *Heure espagnole;* ROSSINI: *Barbiere di Siviglia★, Cenerentola, Italiana in Algeri, Turco in Italia★;* STRAUSS, J: *Fledermaus★;* STRAUSS, R: *Arabella★, Ariadne auf Naxos★, Elektra★, Rosenkavalier★, Salome★;* STRAVINSKY: *Rossignol;* VERDI: *Aida★, Ballo in maschera★, Don Carlo★, Falstaff, Forza del destino, Luisa Miller★, Macbeth, Otello, Rigoletto★, Traviata★;* WAGNER: *Fliegende Holländer★, Lohengrin★, Meistersinger, Walküre★, Tannhäuser★;* WEBER: *Freischütz★;* WEINBERGER: *Schwanda.* Also HONEGGER: *Jeanne d'Arc au bûcher★;* MOZART: *Ascanio in Alba★;* MARTINU: *Mirandolina.* Recorded for Harmonia Mundi/BASF. Video—ORF TV: *Bastien und Bastienne.* Conducted major orch in Europe, Cent/S America. Previous positions as Mus Dir with major orch: Phil Orch, Freiburg/Br 1965-69. **Res:** Morzger Str 102, Salzburg, Austria. Mgmt: VLD/AUS; SLZ/FRG; DSP/USA.

HAGER, PAUL. Stages/produces opera & theater. German. Gen Int & Resident Stage Dir, Städtische Bühnen, Dortmund, FR Ger. Born 18 Nov 1925, Germany. Operatic training as asst stage dir at Bayerische Staatsoper, Munich; àsst to Wieland Wagner, Bayreuth. Previous occupation: univ studies in business mngmt.

Directed/produced opera for major companies in ARG: Buenos Aires; AUS. Vienna Staatsoper & Volksoper; FR GER: Bielefeld, Essen, Mannheim, Nürnberg, Stuttgart; GER DR: Dresden; ITA: Naples; USA: San Francisco Opera; et al. **Operas staged with these companies incl** BERG: *Wozzeck;* JANACEK: *Jenufa, Makropoulos Affair;* MOZART: *Don Giovanni, Nozze di Figaro, Zauberflöte;* ORFF: *Antigonae;* PFITZNER: *Palestrina;* PUCCINI: *Tosca, Turandot;* SAINT-SAENS: *Samson et Dalila;* SCHOENBERG: *Erwartung;* SCHULLER: *Visitation;* STRAUSS, R: *Elektra, Rosenkavalier, Salome;* STRAVINSKY: *Rake's Progress;* TCHAIKOVSKY: *Eugene Onegin, Pique Dame;* VERDI: *Don Carlo, Falstaff, Masnadieri, Nabucco, Trovatore;* WAGNER: *Parsifal, Rheingold, Walküre, Siegfried,' Götterdämmerung, Tannhäuser, Tristan und Isolde;* WEBER: *Freischütz;* et al.

HAGGART, MARGARET. Lyric soprano. Australian. Resident mem: English National Opera, London. Born Melbourne, Australia. Husband Michael Foudy, occupation civil engineer. One daughter. Studied: Consv, Antonio Moretti-Pananti, Melbourne Univ. **Debut:** Königin der Nacht (*Zauberflöte*) Welsh National Opera 1972. Previous occupations: receptionist. Awards: Sydney "Sun" Aria, City of Sydney Eisteddfod.

Sang with major companies in UK: Cardiff Welsh, London English National. **Roles with these** companies incl MOZART: Fiordiligi★ (*Così fan tutte*), Königin der Nacht★ (*Zauberflöte*); PUCCINI: Musetta★ (*Bohème*); ROSSINI: Comtesse Adèle★ (*Comte Ory*); STRAUSS, J: Rosalinde★ (*Fledermaus*); VERDI: Gilda★ (*Rigoletto*). Gives recitals. Appears with symphony orchestra. Teaches voice. **Res:** London, UK. Mgmt: IWL/UK.

HALASZ, LÁSZLÓ. Conductor of opera and symphony. American. Mus Dir, Concert Orch & Choir of LI, Inc, New York. Born 6 Jun 1905, Debrecen, Hungary. Wife Suzette Forgues, occupation cellist. Two children. Studied: Liszt Acad, Budapest, Bela Bartok, Ernst von Dohnanyi, Zoltan Kodaly, Leo Weiner; incl piano. Plays the piano. Operatic training as repetiteur & asst cond at State Opera, Budapest 1928-29; Deutsches Theater, Prague 1929-31. **Operatic debut:** *Evangelimann* Volksoper, Vienna 1933. Symphonic debut: Montreal Symph, Que, Canada 1938. Awards: Page One Awd, New York Newspaper Guild; Merit Awd, Ntl Assn Amer Composers & Conductors. Previous adm positions in opera: Mus Dir, St Louis Grand Opera, MO, USA 1938-42; Art & Mus Dir, New York City Opera 1943-51; Mus Dir, German Wing, Teatro del Liceo, Barcelona 1955-58; Mus Dir, Empire State Music Fest, NY 1958-61.

Conducted with major companies in AUS: Vienna Volksoper; BRA: Rio de Janeiro; CAN: Montreal/Quebec; FR GER: Frankfurt; HUN: Budapest; SPA: Barcelona; USA: Baltimore, Chicago, Milwaukee Florentine, New York City Opera, Philadelphia Grand, Washington DC. **Operas with these companies incl** d'ALBERT: *Tiefland*; BIZET: *Carmen, Pêcheurs de perles*; BRITTEN: *Albert Herring*; FLOTOW: *Martha*; GERSHWIN: *Porgy and Bess*★; GIORDANO: *Andrea Chénier*; GLUCK: *Orfeo ed Euridice*★; GOUNOD: *Faust;* JANACEK: *Katya Kabanova;* KODALY: *Háry János;* LEONCAVALLO: *Pagliacci;* MASCAGNI: *Cavalleria rusticana;* MASSENET: *Manon, Werther;* MENOTTI: *Amahl, Amelia al ballo, Old Maid and the Thief;* MOZART: *Don Giovanni*★, *Entführung aus dem Serail, Idomeneo, Schauspieldirektor, Nozze di Figaro, Zauberflöte*★; MUSSORGSKY: *Boris Godunov;* OFFENBACH: *Mariage aux lanternes;* PERGOLESI: *Serva padrona;* PROKOFIEV: *Love for Three Oranges;* PUCCINI: *Bohème, Butterfly*★, *Manon Lescaut, Tosca*★, *Turandot;* ROSSINI: *Barbiere di Siviglia, Turco in Italia;* SAINT-SAENS: *Samson et Dalila*★; SMETANA: *Bartered Bride;* STRAUSS, J: *Fledermaus;* STRAUSS, R: *Ariadne auf Naxos, Elektra, Frau ohne Schatten*★, *Salome;* TCHAIKOVSKY: *Eugene Onegin;* VERDI: *Aida, Ballo in maschera*★, *Falstaff, Otello, Rigoletto, Traviata;* WAGNER: *Fliegende Holländer, Lohengrin, Meistersinger, Walküre, Siegfried, Götterdämmerung, Tristan und Isolde;* WOLF-FERRARI: *Quattro rusteghi.* Also PIZZETTI: *Assassinio nella cattedrale;* TAMKIN: *Dybbuk.* **World premieres:** KAGEN: *Hamlet* Art Theatre, Baltimore 1962; STILL: *Troubled Island* New York City Opera 1949. Recorded for Remington, MGM. Conducted major orch in Europe, USA/Canada, Cent/S America. Teaches at State University NY, Stony Brook. **Res:** 3 Leeds Dr, Port Washington, NY, USA. Mgmt: SMN/USA; SLZ/FRG.

HALÁSZ, MICHAEL. Conductor of opera and symphony; composer. German. Resident Cond, Oper am Gärtnerplatz, Munich; Städtische Oper, Frankfurt. Born 21 May 1938, Kolozsvár, Hungary. Wife Gertraud Kiefel, occupation singer. Studied: Prof Dressel, Essen; incl bassoon, piano. Plays the bassoon. Operatic training as repetiteur & asst cond at Städtische Oper, Gelsenkirchen 1968-70; Oper am Gärtnerplatz, Munich 1972-75. **Operatic debut:** *Trovatore* Städtische Oper, Gelsenkirchen, FR Ger 1970. Symphonic debut: Radio Symph Orch, Berlin, FR Ger 1973. Previous occupations: first bassoonist Philharmonia Hungarica 8 yrs; bassoon teacher Acad of Music, Essen.

Conducted with major companies in FR GER: Darmstadt, Frankfurt, Munich Gärtnerplatz. **Operas with these companies incl** BIZET: *Carmen*★; DONIZETTI: *Don Pasquale*★; LEONCAVALLO: *Pagliacci*★; MARTIN: *Vin herbé;* MASCAGNI: *Cavalleria rusticana*★; MOZART: *Così fan tutte*★, *Entführung aus dem Serail*★, *Zauberflöte*★; PUCCINI: *Bohème*★, *Turandot*★; ROSSINI: *Barbiere di Siviglia*★; SMETANA: *Bartered Bride*★; STRAUSS, J: *Fledermaus*★; STRAUSS, R: *Arabella*★; VERDI: *Forza del destino*★, *Traviata*★, *Trovatore;* WEBER: *Freischütz*★. Also BLACHER: *Flut.* **Res:** Letzter Hasenpfad 13, 6 Frankfurt 70, FR Ger. Mgmt: ZBV/FRG.

HALE, ROBERT. Bass-baritone. American. Resident mem: New York City Opera. Born 22 Aug 1937, San Antonio, Texas, USA. Three sons. Studied: New England Consv of Music, Gladys Miller; Boston Univ, Ludwig Bergmann; Okla Univ, Orcenith Smith; Boris Goldovsky, New York. **Debut:** Figaro (*Nozze di Figaro*) Denver Opera Co 1965. Previous occupations: coll voice teacher. Awards: Ntl Singer of the Year, NATS 1963; Rockefeller Fndt Grant 1967-68; Reg Winner Met Op Ntl Counc Aud 1964; Sullivan Fndt Grant 1967-68.

Sang with major companies in SPA: Canary Isl Las Palmas Fest; USA: New York City Opera, Philadelphia Lyric, Pittsburgh, San Antonio, San Diego, Washington DC. **Roles with these companies incl** BELLINI: Oroveso★ (*Norma*), Sir George★ (*Puritani*); BIZET: Escamillo★ (*Carmen*); BOITO: Mefistofele★; CHARPENTIER: Père★ (*Louise*); DEBUSSY: Golaud★ (*Pelléas et Mélisande*); DONIZETTI: Henry VIII★ (*Anna Bolena*), Dulcamara (*Elisir*), Raimondo★ (*Lucia*); FLOYD: Olin Blitch★ (*Susannah*); GOUNOD: Méphistophélès★ (*Faust*); HANDEL: Polyphemus (*Acis und Galatea*), Giulio Cesare★; MASCAGNI: Alfio (*Cavalleria rusticana*); MOZART: Don Alfonso (*Così fan tutte*), Don Giovanni★, Figaro★ (*Nozze di Figaro*); OFFENBACH: Coppélius etc★ (*Contes d'Hoffmann*); PUCCINI: Colline★ (*Bohème*); ROSSINI: Don Basilio★ (*Barbiere di Siviglia*); VERDI: Banquo★ (*Macbeth*); WAGNER: König Marke★ (*Tristan und Isolde*); WARD: Rev Hale (*Crucible*). Gives recitals. Appears with symphony orchestra. Mgmt: BAR/USA.

HALL, PETER. Stages/produces opera, theater, film & television. Also designs stage-lighting. British. Director, National Theatre of Great Britain. Also Consult Dir, Royal Shakespeare Co, London since 1968. Born 22 Nov 1930, Bury St Edmunds, UK. Wife Jacky. Four children. Studied: Perse School, & St Catharine's, Cambridge, UK. Op debut: *Moon and Sixpence* Sadler's Wells, London 1958. Awards: Commander of British Empire; Chevalier de l'Ordre des Arts et des Lettres; Hon Dr, Univ of York, Univ of Reading, Univ of Liverpool; Hamburg Shakespeare Prize; two Broadway Tony Awds; two London Theatre Critic Awds, etc.

Directed/produced opera for major companies in UK: Glyndebourne Fest, London Royal & English National. Operas staged with these companies incl CAVALLI: *Calisto*★; MONTEVERDI: *Ritorno d'Ulisse*★; MOZART: *Nozze di Figaro*★, *Zauberflöte;* SCHOENBERG: *Moses und Aron;* TCHAIKOVSKY: *Eugene Onegin*★; TIPPETT: *Knot Garden*★; WAGNER: *Tristan und Isolde*★. Previous leading positions with major theater companies: Mng Dir, Royal Shakespeare Co 1960-68; Dir, Arts Theatre, London 1955-57. Assoc Prof of Drama, Warwick Univ.

HALL, PETER JOHN. Scenic and costume designer for opera, theater, film, television; specl in costumes. Is also a painter. British. Resident designer, Dallas Civic Opera, TX, USA. Born 22 Jan 1926, Bristol, UK. Single. Studied: West of England Coll of Art, Bristol, UK. Operatic debut: sets, *Isola dei pazzi* Spoleto Fest 1961; cost, *Puritani* Teatro Massimo, Palermo 1960. Theater debut: National Theatre, London, UK 1959. Previous occupation: fashion designer, interior decoration. Awards: Paladino d'oro; Best Foreign Designer, cost, play *Romeo and Juliet;* sets & cost, ballet *Romeo and Juliet;* Awds from Gvnmt of Italy & Teatro Colón, Argentina.

Designed for major companies in ARG: Buenos Aires; AUS: Bregenz Fest; GRE: Athens Fest; HOL: Amsterdam; ITA: Florence Comunale, Milan La Scala, Palermo, Rome Opera, Spoleto Fest, Trieste, Turin, Venice; UK: London Royal; USA: Boston, Chicago, Dallas, Kansas City, Miami, New York Met. Operas designed for these companies incl BEETHOVEN: *Fidelio*★; BELLINI: *Norma*★, *Puritani;* BIZET: *Carmen, Pêcheurs de perles;* DONIZETTI: *Anna Bolena*★, *Favorite*★, *Lucia*★, *Lucrezia Borgia*★; GIORDANO: *Andrea Chénier*★, *Fedora*★; HANDEL: *Giulio Cesare;* LEONCAVALLO: *Pagliacci;* MASSENET: *Werther*★; MONTEVERDI: *Combattimento di Tancredi, Incoronazione di Poppea;* MOZART: *Don Giovanni, Nozze di Figaro;* MUSSORGSKY: *Boris Godunov*★; PROKOFIEV: *Love for Three Oranges;* PUCCINI: *Bohème, Rondine, Suor Angelica, Tabarro*★, *Tosca;* PURCELL: *Dido and Aeneas;* RIMSKY-KORSAKOV: *Coq d'or*★; ROSSINI: *Barbiere di Siviglia, Cenerentola*★, *Comte Ory, Semiramide;* SAINT-SAENS: *Samson et Dalila;* THOMAS: *Mignon*★; VERDI: *Aida, Falstaff, Forza del destino*★, *Macbeth, Nabucco, Otello*★, *Rigoletto, Traviata.* Res: 210 E 68 St, New York, NY 10021, USA. Mgmt: LTZ/USA; PCK/UK.

HALL, STEPHEN CHARLES. Stages/produces opera. Also designs stage-lighting and is an actor &

author. Australian. General Executive & Resident Stage Dir, Australian Opera, Sydney. Born 7 Nov 1936, Sydney. Single. Studied: in Sydney and London; incl music and voice. Operatic training as stage manager at Royal Opera, Covent Garden, London 1963-65. Operatic debut: *Turandot* Elizabethan Trust Opera, Sydney 1967. Previous occupation: journalist, actor. Previous adm positions in opera: Coord and Adm, Elizabethan Trust Opera, Sydney 1967-69; Artistic Dir, Australian Opera, Sydney 1971-75.

Directed/produced opera for major companies in AUSTRL: Sydney. Operas staged with these companies incl LEONCAVALLO: *Pagliacci*★; MASCAGNI: *Cavalleria rusticana*★; PUCCINI: *Bohème*★, *Fanciulla del West, Tosca*★; VERDI: *Aida*★. Operatic world premieres: SITSKY: *Lenz* 1974; WERDER: *The Affair* 1974; both at Australian Opera, Sydney. Teaches at NSW State Consv of Music, Sydney. Res: 6/24 Tryon Ave, Wollstonecraft 2065, Sydney, Australia. Mgmt: ALL/UK.

HALL, VICKI EILEEN. Coloratura soprano. American. Resident mem: Theater am Gärtnerplatz, Munich. Born 13 Nov 1943, Jefferson, TX, USA. Single. Studied: Willa Stewart, Texas; Elda Ercole, New York; Josef Metternich, Kander Haagen, Germany. Debut: Emily (*Globolinks*) New York City Opera 1970. Previous occupations: choral & stage dir HS and coll.

Sang with major companies in AUS: Bregenz Fest, Vienna Volksoper; FR GER: Cologne, Munich Gärtnerplatz, Wuppertal. Roles with these companies incl BIZET: Lauretta★ (*Docteur Miracle*); CIMAROSA: Carolina★ (*Matrimonio segreto*); HUMPERDINCK: Gretel★; JANACEK: Vixen★ (*Cunning Little Vixen*); LORTZING: Marie★ (*Zar und Zimmermann*); MENOTTI: Lucy★ (*Telephone*); MONTEVERDI: Clorinda★ (*Combattimento di Tancredi*); MOZART: Blondchen★ (*Entführung aus dem Serail*), Susanna★ (*Nozze di Figaro*); NICOLAI: Frau Fluth★ (*Lustigen Weiber*); OFFENBACH: Olympia★ (*Contes d'Hoffmann*); PUCCINI: Musetta★ (*Bohème*); ROSSINI: Rosina★ (*Barbiere di Siviglia*); STRAUSS, J: Adele★ (*Fledermaus*); STRAUSS, R: Sophie★ (*Rosenkavalier*); WEBER: Aennchen (*Freischütz*); YUN: Yu-Chan★ (*Traum des Liu-Tung*). Also MOZART: Rosina★ (*Finta semplice*); GALUPPI: Lesbina★ (*Filosofo di campagna*). Video/Film: Laetitia (*Old Maid and the Thief*). Gives recitals. Appears with symphony orchestra. Res: Munich, FR Ger. Mgmt: PAS/FRG; TAS/AUS.

HALLIN, MARGARETA. Coloratura soprano. Swedish. Resident mem: Royal Opera, Stockholm. Born 22 Feb 1939, Karlskoga, Sweden. Divorced. One child. Studied: Royal Acad of Music, Käthe Sundström, Ragnar Hulén, Sweden. Debut: Rosina (*Barbiere di Siviglia*) Royal Opera, Stockholm 1955. Awards: Royal Court Singer; Kristina Nilsson Awd.

Sang with major companies in AUS: Vienna Staatsoper; BRA: Rio de Janeiro; CAN: Montreal, Quebec; CZE: Prague National; DEN: Copenhagen; FIN: Helsinki; FRA: Paris; FR GER: Hamburg, Munich Staatsoper; ISR: Tel Aviv; ITA: Florence Maggio, Rome Opera; NOR: Oslo;

SWE: Drottningholm Fest, Stockholm; SWI: Zurich; UK: Edinburgh Fest, Glyndebourne Fest, London Royal Opera; USSR: Leningrad Kirov. **Roles with these companies incl** BRITTEN: Lady Billows (*Albert Herring*); DEBUSSY: Mélisande; DONIZETTI: Lucia; HANDEL: Alcina★; HAYDN: Sandrina★ (*Infedeltà delusa*), Clarissa★ (*Mondo della luna*); MASSENET: Manon★; MOZART: Fiordiligi★ (*Così fan tutte*), Donna Anna★ & Zerlina (*Don Giovanni*), Konstanze★ & Blondchen★ (*Entführung aus dem Serail*), Susanna (*Nozze di Figaro*), Königin der Nacht★ (*Zauberflöte*); OFFENBACH: Olympia★ & Antonia★ & Giulietta★ (*Contes d'Hoffmann*); PUCCINI: Mimi★ & Musetta (*Bohème*), Cio-Cio-San (*Butterfly*), Tosca; ROSSINI: Rosina (*Barbiere di Siviglia*); STRAUSS, J: Adele, Rosalinde★ (*Fledermaus*), STRAUSS, R: Marschallin & Sophie★ (*Rosenkavalier*); STRAVINSKY: Anne Trulove (*Rake's Progress*); VERDI: Aida★, Amelia★ (*Ballo in maschera*), Elisabetta★ (*Don Carlo*), Alice Ford (*Falstaff*), Desdemona (*Otello*), Gilda★ (*Rigoletto*), Violetta★ (*Traviata*), Leonora★ (*Trovatore*); WAGNER: Elsa★ (*Lohengrin*). Also HANDEL: Michal (*Saul*). **World premieres:** BLOMDAHL: The Blind Female Poet (*Aniara*) Royal Opera Stockholm 1959; WERLE: Thérèse (*Dream of Thérèse*) Royal Opera 1964, Clara (*Tintomara*) Royal Opera 1973. Gives recitals. Appears with symphony orchestra. Mgmt: ULF/SWE.

HALLIWELL, BRUCE. Lyric & dramatic baritone. S African/British. Resident mem: Israel National Opera, Tel Aviv. Born 10 Aug 1946, Krugersdorp, South Africa. Single. Studied: London Opera Centre, Otakar Kraus, London; Opera Barga, Italy. **Debut:** Charles Blount (*Gloriana*) Haddo House, Scotland 1971. Previous occupations: fine arts student. Awards: Anglo American Awd, South Africa.

Sang with major companies in ISR: Tel Aviv; S AFR: Johannesburg; UK: Glasgow Scottish. **Roles with these companies incl** d'ALBERT: Sebastiano★ (*Tiefland*); BIZET: Escamillo★ (*Carmen*); BRITTEN: Charles Blount★ (*Gloriana*); CAVALLI: Amida★ (*Ormindo*); DONIZETTI: Don Pasquale★, Enrico★ (*Lucia*); GOLDMARK: König Salomon★ (*Königin von Saba*); LEONCAVALLO: Tonio★ (*Pagliacci*); MASCAGNI: Alfio★ (*Cavalleria rusticana*); MOZART: Conte Almaviva★ (*Nozze di Figaro*), OFFENBACH: Coppélius★ etc (*Contes d'Hoffmann*); PUCCINI: Marcello★ (*Bohème*), Sharpless★ (*Butterfly*); ROSSINI: Guillaume Tell★; VERDI: Rigoletto★, Germont★ (*Traviata*). Gives recitals. Appears with symphony orchestra. **Res:** 28 Arba Arotsot, Tel Aviv, Israel. Mgmt: MIN/UK.

HALLSTEIN, INGEBORG. Lyric coloratura soprano. German. Resident mem: Bavarian State Opera, Munich. Born 23 May 1939, Munich. Husband Dr Polanski, occupation physician. One child. Studied: with mother Elisabeth Hallstein & ballet school, Munich. **Debut:** Musetta (*Bohème*) Barock-Theater, Passau, FR Ger. Awards: Kammersängerin, Bavarian State Opera; Golden Screen, German TV; Weltbund für Schutz des Lebens.

Sang with major companies in ARG: Buenos Aires; AUS: Graz, Salzburg Fest, Vienna Staatsoper & Volksoper; BEL: Brussels; CAN: Montreal/Quebec, Ottawa; DEN: Copenhagen; FIN: Helsinki; FRA: Paris, Strasbourg; FR GER: Berlin Deutsche Oper, Cologne, Düsseldorf-Duisburg, Frankfurt, Hamburg, Hannover, Karlsruhe, Kassel, Kiel, Mannheim, Munich Staatsoper & Gärtnerplatz, Nürnberg, Saarbrücken, Stuttgart, Wiesbaden, Wuppertal; GER DR: Dresden, Leipzig; HOL: Amsterdam; ITA: Rome Caracalla, Venice; SWE: Stockholm; SWI: Basel, Geneva, Zurich; UK: Cardiff Welsh, Glasgow Scottish, London Royal. **Roles with these companies incl** BEETHOVEN: Marzelline‡ (*Fidelio*); BENNETT: Lena★ (*Victory*); DONIZETTI: Norina (*Don Pasquale*); FORTNER: Belisa (*Don Perlimplin*); GLUCK: Euridice★ & Amor★ (*Orfeo ed Euridice*); HANDEL: Atalante (*Xerxes*); HAYDN: Clarissa (*Mondo della luna*); HENZE: Luise (*Junge Lord*), Costanze & Scolatella (*König Hirsch/Re Cervo*); HUMPERDINCK: Gretel; LEONCAVALLO: Nedda (*Pagliacci*); LORTZING: Marie (*Waffenschmied*), Gretchen & Baronin Freimann (*Wildschütz*), Marie‡ (*Zar und Zimmermann*); MASSENET: Manon; MOZART: Fiordiligi & Despina★ (*Così fan tutte*), Zerlina★ (*Don Giovanni*), Konstanze (*Entführung aus dem Serail*), Arminda (*Finta giardiniera*), Ilia & Elettra★ (*Idomeneo*), Susanna (*Nozze di Figaro*), Zaïde, Pamina★ & Königin der Nacht★‡ (*Zauberflöte*); NICOLAI: Frau Fluth & Aennchen (*Lustigen Weiber*); OFFENBACH: Olympia (*Contes d'Hoffmann*), Périchole; ORFF: Solo (*Carmina burana*); PAISIELLO: Rosina (*Barbiere di Siviglia*), Lisetta (*Re Teodoro in Venezia*); POULENC: Thérèse (*Mamelles de Tirésias*); PUCCINI: Musetta★ (*Bohème*), Lauretta★ (*Gianni Schicchi*), Liù★ (*Turandot*); ROSSINI: Rosina‡ (*Barbiere di Siviglia*), Elvira (*Italiana in Algeri*), Fiorilla★ & Zaida★ (*Turco in Italia*); STRAUSS, J: Adele★ (*Fledermaus*); STRAUSS, R: Zdenka★ (*Arabella*), Zerbinetta (*Ariadne auf Naxos*), Sophie★ (*Rosenkavalier*), Aminta (*Schweigsame Frau*); VERDI: Gilda★ (*Rigoletto*), Violetta★ (*Traviata*); WEBER: Fatima‡ (*Abu Hassan*), Aennchen (*Freischütz*), Rezia (*Oberon*). Also MAYR: (*Commediante*). Only on records STRAUSS, J: Rosalinde (*Fledermaus*); STRAUSS, R: Kaiserin (*Frau ohne Schatten*). **World premieres:** HENZE: Autonoe (*Bassariden*) Salzburg Fest 1966; BIALAS: Nicolette (*Aucassin et Nicolette*) State Opera, Munich 1969; LOTHAR: (*Westwind*), (*Rappelkopf*) Theater am Gärtnerplatz, Munich. Recorded for: DG, Eurodisc, Columbia, Polydor. Video/Film: (*Love for Three Oranges*); (*Rosenkavalier*); (*Bohème*); (*Turco in Italia*); (*Schweigsame Frau*); Konstanze (*Entführung*); Despina (*Così*); (*Amelia al ballo*); (*Napoleon kommt*); (*Orpheus und Eurydike*). Gives recitals. Appears with symphony orchestra. Teaches voice. On faculty of Elisabeth Hallstein Schule für Musik, Munich. **Res:** Osterwaldstr 73, 8 Munich 40, FR Ger.

HALMEN, PET; né Petre Halmen. Scenic and costume designer for opera, theater, film, television. Is a lighting designer; also a painter, illustrator & fashion designer. German. Born 14 Nov 1942, Talmaciu, Romania. Single. Studied: Michel Raffaeli, Berlin; Jean-Pierre Ponnelle, Munich.

Prof training: Deutsche Oper Berlin. **Operatic debut:** sets, *Salome* Bühnen der Stadt Kiel 1963; cost, *Orfeo* Deutsche Oper am Rhein, Düsseldorf 1967. Theater debut: Theater Tribüne, Berlin 1960. Awards: Awd of German Graphic Society.

Designed for major companies in FR GER: Berlin Deutsche Oper, Bonn, Darmstadt, Düsseldorf-Duisburg, Karlsruhe, Kiel, Munich Staatsoper & Gärtnerplatz, Wiesbaden; ITA: Florence Maggio; POL: Lodz. **Operas designed for these companies incl** BERG: *Lulu★;* BIZET: *Carmen★;* CAVALIERI: *Rappresentazione★;* GLUCK: *Orfeo ed Euridice★;* MENOTTI: *Medium★;* MONTEVERDI: *Favola d'Orfeo★;* MOZART: *Entführung aus dem Serail★;* OFFENBACH: *Contes d'Hoffmann★;* ORFF: *Carmina burana★;* SAINT-SAENS: *Samson et Dalila★;* SCHOENBERG: *Moses und Aron★;* STRAUSS, R: *Salome★.* Also WEILL: *Zar lässt sich photographieren.* **Operatic world premieres:** DALLAPICCOLA: *Ulisse* Berlin 1968. Operatic Video—ZDF: *Carmina burana.* Exhibitions of stage designs, paintings, graphics Milie's Dance Depot Studio, Munich 1975. **Res:** Florastr 56, Düsseldorf, FR Ger.

HAMARI, JULIA. Mezzo-soprano. Resident mem: Deutsche Oper am Rhein, Düsseldorf-Duisburg; Opera Houses, Hannover & Cologne. Born 1942, Budapest, Hungary. Studied: Acad of Music, Budapest; Fatime Martin; Hochschule für Musik, Stuttgart. Awards: First Prize, Intl Compt Erkel, Budapest.

Sang with major companies in FR GER: Cologne, Düsseldorf-Duisburg, Hannover, Stuttgart; et al. **Roles with these companies incl** BELLINI: Adalgisa (*Norma*); BIZET: Carmen; BUSONI: Colombina (*Arlecchino*); GLUCK: Orfeo; HANDEL: Cornelia‡ (*Giulio Cesare*), Amastris (*Xerxes*); MASSENET: Charlotte (*Werther*); MOZART: Sesto (*Clemenza di Tito*), Dorabella (*Così fan tutte*), Farnace (*Mitridate, re di Ponto*), Cherubino (*Nozze di Figaro*); ROSSINI: Rosina (*Barbiere di Siviglia*), Angelina (*Cenerentola*), Isabella (*Italiana in Algeri*); SAINT-SAENS: Dalila; STRAUSS, R: Octavian (*Rosenkavalier*); TCHAIKOVSKY: Olga (*Eugene Onegin*); WEBER: Fatime‡ (*Oberon*); et al. Also HANDEL: David (*Saul*); PURCELL: Dido. Recorded for: DG, Angel. Appears with symphony orchestra. Mgmt: COL/USA.

HAMILTON, CHARLES; né Charles Antony Bennett Hamilton-Groves. Stages/produces opera & theater. Also designs sets and is an actor. British. Resident Stage Dir, Royal Opera House, Covent Garden, London. Born 6 May 1941, Rangoon, Burma. Studied: Royal Coll of Music, Douglas Craig; asst to Dr Günther Rennert. Operatic training as assistant stage director at Glyndebourne Fest Opera, UK 1966-68. **Operatic debut:** *Ormindo* Glyndebourne Touring Co 1968. Theater debut: John Lewis Company, London 1967.

Directed/produced opera for major companies in FRA: Orange Fest; HOL: Amsterdam; UK: Glyndebourne Fest, London Royal. **Operas staged with these companies incl** BEETHOVEN: *Fidelio★;* BIZET: *Carmen;* CAVALLI: *Ormindo★;* DEBUSSY: *Pelléas et Mélisande★;* DONIZETTI: *Don Pasquale★;* PUCCINI: *Turandot★;* STRAUSS, R: *Arabella★, Rosenkavalier★, Salome;* TCHAIKOVSKY: *Eugene Onegin★;* VERDI: *Nabucco★, Rigoletto★, Simon Boccanegra★, Trovatore★;* WAGNER: *Meistersinger.* **Operatic world premieres:** KOX: *Picture of Dorian Gray* Nederlandse Operastichting, Amsterdam 1974. **Res:** Prince of Wales Dr, 6 York Mansions, London SW 11, UK. Mgmt: SRN/HOL; CST/UK.

HAMMOND-STROUD, DEREK. Baritone & basso-buffo. British. Born 10 Jan 1929, London, UK. Single. Studied: Trinity Coll of Music, London; Gerhard Hüsch, Munich; Elena Gerhardt, Roy Henderson, London. **Debut:** Publio (*Clemenza di Tito*) Impresario Society, London 1957. Previous occupations: ophthalmic optician. Awards, Second Prize w Distinction, Intl Vocalist Cont 's Hertogenbosch, Holland; First Prize London Music Fest.

Sang with major companies in FR GER: Munich Gärtnerplatz; SPA: Barcelona; UK: Aldeburgh Fest, Cardiff Welsh, Glyndebourne Fest, London Royal Opera & English National; USA: Houston. **Roles with these companies incl** BRITTEN: Sir Robert Cecil (*Gloriana*); DONIZETTI: Belcore (*Elisir*), Gasparo (*Rita*); LEONCAVALLO: Tonio★ (*Pagliacci*); MOZART: Publio (*Clemenza di Tito*), Guglielmo★ (*Così fan tutte*), Papageno★ (*Zauberflöte*); PUCCINI: Sharpless★ (*Butterfly*); ROSSINI: Dott Bartolo★ (*Barbiere di Siviglia*), Dandini & Don Magnifico★ (*Cenerentola*); VERDI: Falstaff, Fra Melitone★ (*Forza del destino*); WAGNER: Beckmesser★ (*Meistersinger*), Alberich★‡ (*Rheingold, Siegfried, Götterdämmerung*). Also STRAUSS, R: Faninal★ (*Rosenkavalier*); EINEM: Schulmeister★ (*Besuch der alten Dame*); PUCCINI: Sacristan★ (*Tosca*); ROSSINI: Taddeo (*Italiana in Algeri*), Pacuvio (*Pietra del paragone*). **World premieres:** WILLIAMSON: Old Fisherman (*Violins of Saint Jacques*) Sadler's Wells Opera, London 1966. Recorded for: EMI. Gives recitals. Appears with symphony orchestra. Teaches voice. Coaches repertoire. On faculty of Royal Acad of Music, London. **Res:** 18 Sutton Rd, Muswell Hill, London N10, UK. Mgmt: IBB/UK.

HAMPE, CHRISTIANE. Lyric coloratura soprano. German. Resident mem: Basler Theater, Basel, Switzerland. Born 17 Jul 1948, Heidelberg, Germany. Husband Dr Markus Wiebel, occupation judge. Studied: Musikhochschule, Prof Annelies Kupper, Munich. **Debut:** Gilda (*Rigoletto*) Städtische Bühnen, Heidelberg 1971. Awards: var prizes in ntl German compts.

Sang with major companies in AUS: Bregenz Fest; FR GER: Kiel; SWI: Basel. **Roles with these companies incl** HANDEL: Galatea★; HAYDN: Vespina★ (*Infedeltà delusa*), Clarissa★ (*Mondo della luna*); LORTZING: Marie★ (*Zar und Zimmermann*); MOZART: Zerlina★ (*Don Giovanni*), Susanna★ (*Nozze di Figaro*); OFFENBACH: Olympia★ (*Contes d'Hoffmann*), Fanchette★ (*Mariage aux lanternes*); ORFF: Solo★ (*Carmina burana*); ROSSINI: Elvira★ (*Italiana in Algeri*); STRAUSS, J: Adele★ (*Fledermaus*); STRAUSS, R: Sophie★ (*Rosenkavalier*); VERDI: Gilda★ (*Rigoletto*). **World premieres:** HAUPT/ GACKSTETTER: Coloratura Soprano (*Sümtome*) Experimentierbühne, Staatsoper Munich 1970. Gives recitals. Appears with symphony orchestra.

HAMPE, MICHAEL HERMANN. German. Int, Oper der Stadt Köln, Offenbachplatz 5, Cologne 1975- ; also Tanzforum Köln. In charge of overall adm matters, art policy, mus, dram & tech matters & finances. Is also St Dir/prod, actor, cellist. Born 3 Jun 1935, Heidelberg. Wife Sibylle. One child. Studied: Univs Vienna, Munich, Heidelberg, PhD; Otto Falckenberg Schule, Munich. Plays the cello & flute. Background primarily musical & theatrical. Previous positions: Dir, Stadttheater Bern, Switzerland 1961-64; Schauspielhaus Zurich 1965-70; Staatsoper & Staatsschauspiel, Munich 1970-72. Int, Nationaltheater Mannheim 1972-75. World premieres at theaters under his management: SUTERMEISTER: *Madame Bovary* Zurich 1967. **Res:** Thielenbruch Allee 25, Cologne/Delbrück, FR Ger.

HANAK, DORIT. Lyric coloratura soprano. Austrian. Resident mem: Opernhaus Graz. Born 15 Nov 1938, Baden bei Wien, Austria. Husband Dr Tscharré. Studied: Musikakad, Fr Prof Rado, Vienna. **Debut:** Blondchen (*Entführung aus dem Serail*) Opernhaus Graz, Austria 1958. Awards: First Prize Conc Intl de Chant, Belgique. **Sang with major companies in** AUS: Graz, Vienna Staatsoper & Volksoper; BEL: Brussels; FRA: Aix-en-Provence Fest; FR GER: Wiesbaden; ISR: Tel Aviv; SPA: Barcelona; UK: Glyndebourne Fest; USA: Milwaukee Florentine. **Roles with these companies incl** BEETHOVEN: Marzelline (*Fidelio*); BIZET: Micaëla★ (*Carmen*); CIMAROSA: Carolina (*Matrimonio segreto*); DONIZETTI: Norina★ (*Don Pasquale*), Marie (*Fille du régiment*); HAYDN: Vespina (*Infedeltà delusa*); HUMPERDINCK: Gretel (*Hänsel und Gretel*); KODALY: Marie Louise★ (*Háry János*); LORTZING: Baronin Freimann★ (*Wildschütz*), Marie★ (*Zar und Zimmermann*); MENOTTI: Laetitia (*Old Maid and the Thief*); MOZART: Despina★ (*Così fan tutte*), Zerlina★ (*Don Giovanni*), Blondchen (*Entführung aus dem Serail*), Susanna★ (*Nozze di Figaro*), Pamina★ (*Zauberflöte*); NICOLAI: Aennchen★ (*Lustigen Weiber*); OFFENBACH: Olympia (*Contes d'Hoffmann*); PUCCINI: Musetta★ (*Bohème*), Lauretta★ (*Gianni Schicchi*); ROSSINI: Rosina (*Barbiere di Siviglia*); STRAUSS, R: Zdenka (*Arabella*), Sophie★ (*Rosenkavalier*); VERDI: Oscar (*Ballo in maschera*), Gilda (*Rigoletto*); WEBER: Aennchen★ (*Freischütz*); WOLF-FERRARI: Lucieta (*Quattro rusteghi*). Also LIEBERMANN: Agnes (*Schule der Frauen*); EGK: Gretl (*Zaubergeige*). **World premieres:** EINEM: Kathi (*Zerrissene*) Volksoper Vienna 1968. Video/Film: Norina (*Don Pasquale*); Blondchen (*Entführung*); Laetitia (*Old Maid and the Thief*); Salome Pockerl (*Titus Feuerfuchs*); Gretel; Lucieta (*Quattro rusteghi*). Gives recitals. Appears with symphony orchestra. **Res:** Geidorfgürtel 32, A 8010 Graz, Austria. Mgmt: KOA/AUS.

HANKE, FRIEDEMANN. Bass. German. Resident mem: Staatstheater, Darmstadt. Born 4 Jul 1941, Miechowice, Poland. Wife Hedda Andreas, occupation actress. Studied: Prof Franziska Martienssen-Lohmann, Fr Edith Boroschek,

Düsseldorf; Prof Paul Lohmann, Wiesbaden; Kmsg Prof Josef Metternich, Munich. **Debut:** Osmin (*Entführung aus dem Serail*) Osnabrück Opera House 1968.

Sang with major companies in FR GER: Darmstadt, Karlsruhe, Mannheim. **Roles with these companies incl** LORTZING: Baculus★ (*Wildschütz*); MOZART: Don Alfonso★ (*Così fan tutte*); PUCCINI: Colline★ (*Bohème*); ROSSINI: Don Basilio★ (*Barbiere di Siviglia*); STRAVINSKY: Tiresias★ (*Oedipus Rex*); VERDI: Grande Inquisitore★ (*Don Carlo*); WEBER: Kaspar★ (*Freischütz*). Gives recitals. Appears with symphony orchestra. Teaches voice. Coaches repertoire. Mgmt: PAS/FRG.

HANNER, BARRY NEIL. Lyric baritone. American. Resident mem: Städtische Bühnen, Nürnberg. Born 20 Feb 1936, Bloomington, IN, USA. Wife Helga, occupation pianist. Two children. Studied: Curtis Inst of Music, Martial Singher, Dr Herbert Graf, Philadelphia. **Debut:** Belcore (*Elisir*) Badisches Staatstheater, Karlsruhe 1962. Awards: Fulbright Schlshp 1961.

Sang with major companies in AUS: Vienna Volksoper; FR GER: Darmstadt, Karlsruhe, Munich Gärtnerplatz, Nürnberg, Stuttgart, Wiesbaden; HOL: Amsterdam; ITA: Florence Comunale. **Roles with these companies incl** BIZET: Escamillo★ (*Carmen*); CIMAROSA: Count Robinson★ (*Matrimonio segreto*); DONIZETTI: Dott Malatesta★ (*Don Pasquale*), Belcore (*Elisir*); JANACEK: Gorianchikov★ (*From the House of the Dead*); LORTZING: Graf v Liebenau (*Waffenschmied*), Graf Eberbach★ (*Wildschütz*), Peter I★ (*Zar und Zimmermann*); MASSENET: Albert★ (*Werther*); MENOTTI: Dr Stone★ (*Globolinks*); MOZART: Guglielmo★ (*Così fan tutte*), Conte Almaviva (*Nozze di Figaro*), Papageno★ (*Zauberflöte*); ORFF: Solo★ (*Carmina burana*), König★ (*Kluge*); PUCCINI: Marcello (*Bohème*), Sharpless (*Butterfly*); PURCELL: Aeneas★); ROSSINI: Figaro★ (*Barbiere di Siviglia*); TCHAIKOVSKY: Yeletsky (*Pique Dame*); VERDI: Ford★ (*Falstaff*), Germont★ (*Traviata*), Conte di Luna★ (*Trovatore*); WAGNER: Wolfram★ (*Tannhäuser*); YUN: Liu-Tung★ (*Traum des Liu-Tung*); ZIMMERMANN: Stolzius★ (*Soldaten*). Also GOUNOD: Valentin★ (*Faust*); LORTZING: Hans Sachs; GOUNOD: Sganarelle★ (*Médecin malgré lui*); STRAUSS, R: Harlekin (*Ariadne auf Naxos*). **World premieres:** YUN: Prince Fu (*Witwe des Schmetterlings*) Städtische Bühnen, Nürnberg 1969; HENZE: Jean Charles (*Floss der Medusa*) Städtische Bühnen, Nürnberg, first stgd 1972. Gives recitals. Appears with symphony orchestra. Teaches voice. Coaches repertoire. On faculty of Fachakad der Musik, Nürnberg. **Res:** Dörlbach 26, 8501 Burgthann, FR Ger.

HANUS, KAREL. Bass. Czechoslovakian. Resident mem: National Theater, Prague. Born 14 Nov 1929, Jicin, CSR. Wife Hana, occupation nurse. Two children. Studied: Usti nad Labem, Prof Jitka Svabova. **Debut:** Wassermann (*Rusalka*) Liberec Opera 1957.

Sang with major companies in CZE: Brno, Prague National. **Roles with these companies incl** MARTINU: Grigoris★ (*Griechische Passion*);

MOZART: Osmin★ (*Entführung aus dem Serail*), Figaro★ (*Nozze di Figaro*); OFFENBACH: Coppélius etc★ (*Contes d'Hoffmann*); PUCCINI: Colline★ (*Bohème*); SMETANA: Malina★ (*Secret*); STRAVINSKY: Nick Shadow★ (*Rake's Progress*); VERDI: Zaccaria★ (*Nabucco*); WAGNER: König Heinrich★ (*Lohengrin*). Also DVORAK: Burgrave★ (*Jakobin*); SMETANA: Benes★ (*Dalibor*). Video/Film: Rarach (*Devil's Wall*). Gives recitals. Appears with symphony orchestra. **Res**: Pod strojirnami 3, 19000 Prague 9-Vysocany, CSSR. Mgmt: PRG/CZE.

HARASTEANU, POMPEI. Bass. Romanian. Resident mem: Romanian Opera, Bucharest. Born 14 Sep 1935, Gheorghieni. Wife Mioara. Studied: Consv, Profs Constantin Stroescu and George Ionescu, Bucharest. **Debut**: Ferrando (*Trovatore*) Romanian Opera 1967. Awards: First Prize, George Enescu Cont 1967 & Francisco Vinas, Barcelona 1968; Second Prize, Erkel Cont, Budapest 1962 & 's Hertogenbosch 1965.
Sang with major companies in FR GER: Bonn, Cologne, Dortmund; HUN: Budapest; ROM: Bucharest. **Roles with these companies incl** BEETHOVEN: Rocco (*Fidelio*); DELIBES: Nilakantha★ (*Lakmé*); MOZART: Osmin (*Entführung aus dem Serail*), Sarastro★ (*Zauberflöte*); VERDI: Ramfis★ (*Aida*), Grande Inquisitore★ (*Don Carlo*); WAGNER: König Heinrich★ (*Lohengrin*), Landgraf★ (*Tannhäuser*). Also BRITTEN: Budd★ (*Albert Herring*); TCHAIKOVSKY: Prince Gremin (*Eugene Onegin*); PUCCINI: Timur★ (*Turandot*). On records only MOZART: Publio (*Clemenza di Tito*). **World premieres**: TRAILESCU: Kogalniceanu (*Balcescu*) Romanian Opera 1974. Gives recitals. Appears with symphony orchestra. **Res**: Bucharest 5, Romania. Mgmt: RIA/ROM; TAS/AUS.

HARDER, GLENN JOHN. Lyric baritone. Canadian. Resident mem: Stadttheater Bielefeld. Born 22 Apr 1943, Saskatoon, Canada. Wife Kristi Vensand, occupation singer. One child. Studied: Victor Martens, Winnipeg, Canada; Northwestern Univ, Hermanus Baer, Chicago; Nordwestdeutsche Musikakad, Prof Theo Lindenbaum & Gunter Weissenborn, Detmold, FR Ger. **Debut**: Graf Eberbach (*Wildschütz*) Bielefeld Oper 1973. Previous occupations: announcer for Amer & Canad radio & TV. Awards: First Prize, Compt Hochschule Saarbrücken 1971.
Sang with major companies in FR GER: Bielefeld. **Roles with these companies incl** HANDEL: Polyphemus★ (*Acis and Galatea*); LORTZING: Graf Eberbach★ (*Wildschütz*); MOZART: Papageno★ (*Zauberflöte*); ORFF: König★ (*Kluge*); ROSSINI: Dandini★ (*Cenerentola*). Gives recitals. Appears with symphony orchestra. Teaches voice. **Res**: Neustädterstr 6, 48 Bielefeld, FR Ger.

HAREWOOD, LORD GEORGE HENRY HUBERT. British. Mng Dir, English National Opera, The Coliseum, St Martin's Lane, London, UK. In charge of adm & art matters & finances. Born 7 Feb 1923. Wife Patricia. Four children. Studied: Eton College and Cambridge Univ, UK. Previous occupations: wartime soldier. Previous positions primarily administrative: Found/Edit, *Opera* magazine. London 1950-53; Adm, Royal Opera

House, Covent Garden 1953-60; Art Dir, Edinburgh Fest, Scotland 1960-65; Art Dir, Leeds Fest, UK 1958-74; Art Adv, New Philharmonia Orch, London 1965-75. In present position since 1972. World premieres at theaters under his management: CROSSE: *Story of Vasco* Sadler's Wells (now English National), London 1973-74. Awards: Austrian Great Silver Medal of Honor; Order of the Cedars of Lebanon; Hon LLD Leeds Univ and Aberdeen Univ; Hon DM Hull Univ. Mem of BBC Mus Adv Commtt; Arts Counc Touring Commtt; London Opera Centre. **Res**: 3 Clifton Hill, London, UK.

HARNESS, WILLIAM EDWARD. Lyric tenor. American. Born 26 Nov 1940, Pendleton, OR, USA. Wife Marie. Five children. Studied: Mary Curtis-Verna; San Francisco Merola Prgr 1972 & 73; Otto Guth, coach; Robert DeCeunynck, coach. **Debut**: Communicant/tenor arias (*St Matthew Passion*) stgd, San Francisco Spring Opera 1973. Previous occupations: tech svce repair for NCR 12 yrs; civil engr survey for Washington Water Power Co. Awards: Florence Bruce Awd, San Francisco Op Aud; Enrico Caruso Centennial Awd; Kurt Herbert Adler & Rev Dibble Awds; Ntl Op Inst Grant 2 yrs; Schultz Aud Seattle Opera 1972; M B Rockefeller Fund Grant.
Sang with major companies in USA: Boston, Fort Worth, Houston, Memphis, San Francisco Opera & Spring Opera, Seattle. **Roles with these companies incl** DONIZETTI: Nemorino★ (*Elisir*), Tonio★ (*Fille du régiment*); MOZART: Ferrando★ (*Così fan tutte*), Tamino★ (*Zauberflöte*); PUCCINI: Rodolfo★ (*Bohème*), Rinuccio★ (*Gianni Schicchi*), Pinkerton★ (*Butterfly*); VERDI: Alfredo★ (*Traviata*). Gives recitals. Appears with symphony orchestra. **Res**: 22105-39 W, Mountlake Terrace, WA, USA. Mgmt: CAM/USA.

HARPER, HEATHER MARY. Spinto. British. Born 8 May 1930, Belfast, N Ireland, UK. Husband Eduardo J Benarroch, occupation engineer in geophysics. Studied: Trinity Coll of Music, London; Prof Frederic Husler, Switzerland; Helene Isepp, Frederic Jackson, London. **Debut**: Erste Dame (*Zauberflöte*) Glyndebourne Fest 1957. Awards: CBE, Commander British Empire 1965; Worshipful Co of Musicians 1964; Hon DM Queen's Univ Belfast 1966; Hon Mem Royal Acad of Music 1971; Edison Awd 1971.
Sang with major cos in ARG: Buenos Aires; FR GER: Bayreuth, Frankfurt; UK: Aldeburgh, Cardiff Welsh, Edinburgh Fest, Glyndebourne Fest, London Royal Opera & English National; USA: San Antonio, San Francisco Opera. **Roles with these companies incl** BIZET: Micaëla (*Carmen*); BRITTEN: Helena‡ (*Midsummer Night*), Ellen Orford★ (*Peter Grimes*), Female Chorus‡ (*Rape of Lucretia*), Governess★ (*Turn of the Screw*); GAY/Britten: Lucy (*Beggar's Opera*); GOUNOD: Marguerite★ (*Faust*); LORTZING: Gretchen (*Wildschütz*); MOZART: Vitellia (*Clemenza di Tito*), Donna Elvira★‡ (*Don Giovanni*), Ilia★ (*Idomeneo*), Contessa★ (*Nozze di Figaro*); OFFENBACH: Antonia (*Contes d'Hoffmann*); POULENC: Blanche (*Dialogues des Carmélites*); PUCCINI: Mimi (*Bohème*); SCHOENBERG: A Woman (*Erwartung*); STRAUSS, R: Arabella★, Chrysothemis★ (*Elektra*), Kaiserin★ (*Frau ohne*

Schatten); STRAVINSKY: Anne Trulove (Rake's Progress); TIPPETT: Hecuba★ (King Priam); VERDI: Nannetta (Falstaff), Lady Macbeth, Violetta (Traviata); WAGNER: Elsa (Lohengrin). Eva★ (Meistersinger), Gutrune (Götterdämmerung). Also MASSENET: Charlotte★ (Werther); HANDEL: Iphis (Jephtha), Semele; SCHOENBERG: The Friend (Von Heute auf Morgen). Recorded for: EMI, Decca, Philips, CBS. Video/Film: Ellen Orford (Peter Grimes); Mrs Coyle (Owen Wingrave); Lucy Manette (Tale of Two Cities); Violetta (Traviata); Mimi (Bohème); Ilia (Idomeneo); Lucy Lockit (Beggar's Opera). Gives recitals. Appears with symphony orchestra. **Res:** London, UK. Mgmt: PRS/UK; COL/USA.

HÄRTEL, RENATE. Dramatic mezzo-soprano. German. Resident mem: Opernhaus Leipzig. Born 22 Feb 1927, Meerane/Sachsen, Germany. Husband Emil Lang, occupation opera singer. Two sons. Studied: Hochschule für Musik, Prof Annemarie Rauch, Dresden; Elly Doerrer. **Debut:** Fricka (Walküre) Karl-Marx-Stadt, Ger Dr 1955. Previous occupations: teacher. Awards: Kammersängerin, Gvnmt of Ger DR.
  Sang with major companies in GER DR: Berlin Staatsoper, Dresden, Leipzig. **Roles with these companies incl** BIZET: Carmen; DVORAK: Jezibaba★ (Rusalka); JANACEK: Kostelnicka★ (Jenufa); NICOLAI: Frau Reich★ (Lustigen Weiber); PROKOFIEV: Grandmother (Gambler); PUCCINI: Suzuki★ (Butterfly); VERDI: Amneris★ (Aida), Ulrica★ (Ballo in maschera), Eboli★ (Don Carlo), Preziosilla (Forza del destino), Azucena★ (Trovatore); WAGNER: Ortrud★ (Lohengrin), Erda (Rheingold, Siegfried), Fricka (Walküre); WOLF-FERRARI: Beatrice★ (Donne curiose). Also EGK: Aase (Peer Gynt). **World premieres:** MATTHUS: Antonia (Lazarillo vom Tormes) Karl-Marx-Stadt 1964; GEISSLER: Marthe Rull (Zerbrochene Krug) Leipzig 1970. Recorded for: Eterna. Gives recitals. Appears with symphony orchestra. Teaches voice. On faculty of Hochschule für Musik, Leipzig. Mgmt: RBN/FRG.

HARTLEB, HANS. Stages/produces opera, theater & television. Also designs stage-lighting and is an actor. German. Born 3 May 1910, Kassel. Single. Studied: literature, art history; PhD, Univ Munich; also music, piano & voice. Operatic training as asst stage dir at Berlin Opera, Prof C Hagemann. **Operatic debut:** Butterfly Volksoper, Berlin 1937. Theater debut: Staatstheater, Kassel 1964. Awards: Cavaliere and Distinguished Service Cross, Italian Rep; first prize for TV drama. Previous adm positions in opera: Oberspielleiter, Essen 1947-55; Frankfurt 1955-61; Munich 1961-67.
  Directed/produced opera for major companies in ARG: Buenos Aires; AUS: Graz, Salzburg Fest; FRA: Paris; FR GER: Berlin Deutsche Oper, Cologne, Dortmund, Düsseldorf-Duisburg, Essen, Frankfurt, Karlsruhe, Kassel, Kiel, Munich Staatsoper, Wuppertal; GER DR: Leipzig; HOL: Amsterdam; JPN: Tokyo Niki Kai; SWI: Basel, Geneva, Zurich; UK: London English National; USA: Chicago. **Operas staged with these companies incl** d'ALBERT: Tiefland; AUBER: Fra Diavolo; BEETHOVEN: Fidelio★; BERG: Lulu★, Wozzeck★; BIZET: Carmen; BRITTEN: Albert Her-

ring★, Death in Venice★; CIKKER: Play of Love and Death★; CIMAROSA: Matrimonio segreto; CORNELIUS: Barbier von Bagdad; DALLAPICCOLA: Prigioniero; DEBUSSY: Pelléas et Mélisande; DONIZETTI: Anna Bolena, Don Pasquale, Elisir; DVORAK: Rusalka; FLOTOW: Martha; FORTNER: Don Perlimplin; GIORDANO: Fedora; GLUCK: Alceste, Armide, Iphigénie en Aulide, Orfeo ed Euridice; GOUNOD: Faust; HANDEL: Deidamia, Giulio Cesare; HENZE: Junge Lord, König Hirch/Re Cervo; HINDEMITH: Cardillac★, Hin und zurück, Mathis der Maler; HONEGGER: Antigone; LEONCAVALLO: Pagliacci; LORTZING: Waffenschmied, Wildschütz, Zar und Zimmermann; MARTIN: Vin herbé; MASCAGNI: Cavalleria rusticana; MENOTTI: Telephone; MEYERBEER: Africaine★; MILHAUD: Abandon d'Ariane, Délivrance de Thésée, Enlèvement d'Europe; MOZART: Clemenza di Tito★, Così fan tutte★, Don Giovanni, Entführung aus dem Serail, Idomeneo, Nozze di Figaro, Zauberflöte; MUSSORGSKY: Boris Godunov; NICOLAI: Lustigen Weiber; OFFENBACH: Contes d'Hoffmann; OHANA: Syllabaire pour Phèdre; ORFF: Antigonae, Kluge; PFITZNER: Palestrina; POULENC: Dialogues des Carmélites★; PUCCINI: Bohème★, Fanciulla del West, Gianni Schicchi★, Manon Lescaut, Tabarro★, Tosca, Turandot★; ROSSINI: Barbiere di Siviglia, Gazza ladra★, Italiana in Algeri, Moïse★; SCHOENBERG: Erwartung; SMETANA: Bartered Bride; STRAUSS, J: Fledermaus; STRAUSS, R: Arabella, Ariadne auf Naxos, Elektra, Rosenkavalier, Salome, Schweigsame Frau; STRAVINSKY: Oedipus Rex★; TCHAIKOVSKY: Eugene Onegin; THOMAS: Mignon; VERDI: Aida, Ballo in maschera, Don Carlo★, Falstaff★, Forza del destino, Giovanna d'Arco★, Luisa Miller, Macbeth, Masnadieri, Nabucco, Otello, Rigoletto, Simon Boccanegra, Traviata, Trovatore, Vespri★; WAGNER: Fliegende Holländer★, Lohengrin, Meistersinger, Parsifal, Rheingold, Walküre, Siegfried, Götterdämmerung, Tannhäuser, Tristan und Isolde; WEBER: Freischütz; WOLF-FERRARI: Donne curiose, Quattro rusteghi. Also KRENEK: Orpheus★, Karl V; HAYDN: Armida, Pescatrici; EGK: Columbus, Revisor; SCHOENBERG: Von heute auf morgen; WOLF-FERRARI: Vedova scaltra; BRITTEN: Let's Make an Opera; MARTIN: Sturm; LEVY: Mourning Becomes Electra; HONEGGER: Jeanne d'Arc; FORTNER: Wald. **Operatic world premieres:** REUTTER: Brücke von San Luis Rey Opernhaus, Essen 1955. Operatic Video—German TV: Belsazar, Bohème, Wozzeck, Simplicius Simplicissimus, Hänsel und Gretel. Teaches at Mozarteum, Salzburg. **Res:** Romanstr 62a, D 8 Munich 19, FR Ger. Mgmt: SLZ/FRG; SDM/FRG; PAS/FRG; CDA/ARG.

HARTMANN, RUDOLF. Stages/produces opera & theater. German. Born 11 Oct 1900, Ingolstadt, Germany. Studied: Art Acad and Univ, Munich and Bamberg. Previous adm positions in opera: Oberspielleiter, Altenburg 1924-27, Gera 1927-28, Nürnberg 1928-34, Staatsoper Berlin 1934-37, Bayerische Staatsoper Munich 1937-52; Staatsintendant, Bayerische Staatsoper Munich 1952-67.
  Directed/produced opera for major companies in AUS: Salzburg Fest, Vienna Staatsoper & Volks-

oper; FR GER: Bayreuth Fest, Berlin Deutsche Oper, Düsseldorf-Duisburg, Mannheim, Munich Staatsoper, Nürnberg; HOL: Amsterdam; ITA: Milan La Scala; SWE: Stockholm; UK: London Royal; et al. **Operas staged with these companies incl** BARTOK: *Bluebeard's Castle;* BEETHOVEN: *Fidelio;* BERG: *Lulu, Wozzeck;* EGK: *Verlobung in San Domingo, Zaubergeige;* EINEM: *Dantons Tod;* HAYDN: *Infedeltà delusa;* HENZE: *Elegy for Young Lovers;* JANACEK: *Excursions of Mr Broucek, Jenufa;* MONTEVERDI: *Favola d'Orfeo;* MOZART: *Don Giovanni, Entführung aus dem Serail, Zauberflöte;* MUSSORGSKY: *Khovanshchina;* ORFF: *Bernauerin;* STRAUSS, R: *Aegyptische Helena, Arabella, Ariadne auf Naxos, Capriccio, Daphne, Elektra, Frau ohne Schatten, Intermezzo, Liebe der Danae, Rosenkavalier, Salome;* STRAVINSKY: *Rake's Progress;* VERDI: *Otello;* WAGNER: *Fliegende Holländer, Lohengrin, Meistersinger, Rheingold, Walküre, Siegfried, Götterdämmerung, Tristan und Isolde;* WEBER: *Oberon;* et al. **Operatic world premieres:** STRAUSS, R: *Friedenstag* Munich 1938, *Capriccio* Munich 1942, *Liebe der Danae* Salzburg 1952; ORFF: *Der Mond* 1939; TOMASI: *Don Juan de Mañara* 1956; HINDEMITH: *Harmonie der Welt* 1957; last three at Bayerische Staatsoper, Munich.

HARTMANN, RUDOLF A; né Rudolf Gniffke. Bass-baritone, now lyric character baritone. German. Resident mem: Opernhaus Zurich. Born 19 Jan 1937, Bad Windsheim, Germany. Wife Gabriella Patricolo. Two children. Studied: Staatliche Hochschule für Musik, Prof Franz Theo Reuter, Prof Karl Schmitt-Walter, Munich. **Debut:** Masetto (*Don Giovanni*) Städtische Bühnen, Augsburg, FR Ger 1963. Previous occupations: studied law.
   Sang with major companies in FR GER: Nürnberg; SWI: Zurich. **Roles with these companies incl** BUSONI: Matteo (*Arlecchino*); CIMAROSA: Geronimo (*Matrimonio segreto*); LORTZING: Graf Eberbach (*Wildschütz*); MOZART: Guglielmo (*Così fan tutte*), Papageno‡ (*Zauberflöte*); VERDI: Germont (*Traviata*); WAGNER: Beckmesser (*Meistersinger*). Also MOZART: Sprecher (*Zauberflöte*); HANDEL: Otto (*Agrippina*); HUMPERDINCK: Peter (*Hänsel und Gretel*). Recorded for: Concert Hall. Gives recitals. Appears with symphony orchestra. Teaches voice. Mgmt: TAU/SWI; SLZ/FRG.

HARWOOD, ELIZABETH. Lyric coloratura soprano. British. Born 27 May 1938, Kettering, Northants, UK. Husband Julian Royle, occupation publisher & printer. One child. Studied: Royal Acad of Music, Constance Read, London; Royal Manchester Coll of Music, Elsie Thurston; Lucy Manen. **Debut:** Gilda (*Rigoletto*) Sadler's Wells Opera 1961. Awards: Kathleen Ferrier Awd; Verdi Prize, Busseto; Sir Charles Santley Prize, Worshipful Co of Musicians; Fllshp Royal Manchester Coll of Music, LRAM, GRSM.
   Sang with major companies in AUS: Salzburg Fest; BEL: Brussels; DEN: Copenhagen; FRA: Aix-en-Provence Fest, Paris; FR GER: Cologne, Frankfurt, Hamburg, Mannheim, Munich Staatsoper, Stuttgart, Wiesbaden; ITA: Milan La Scala; MON: Monte Carlo; SWI: Geneva; UK: Al-

deburgh Fest, Glasgow Scottish, Glyndebourne Fest, London Royal Opera & English National. **Roles with these companies incl** BEETHOVEN: Marzelline (*Fidelio*); BELLINI: Amina (*Sonnambula*); BRITTEN: Tytania‡ (*Midsummer Night*); DELIUS: Vrenchen‡ (*Village Romeo*); DONIZETTI: Norina⋆ (*Don Pasquale*), Adina (*Elisir*), Lucia⋆; HANDEL: Galatea, Semele; MASSENET: Manon⋆, Sophie (*Werther*); MOZART: Fiordiligi⋆ (*Così fan tutte*), Donna Elvira⋆ (*Don Giovanni*), Konstanze⋆ (*Entführung aus dem Serail*), Contessa⋆ (*Nozze di Figaro*), Pamina (*Zauberflöte*); OFFENBACH: Olympia (*Contes d'Hoffmann*); PUCCINI: Musetta‡ (*Bohème*); ROSSINI: Comtesse Adèle (*Comte Ory*); STRAUSS, R: Fiakermilli (*Arabella*), Zerbinetta (*Ariadne auf Naxos*), Sophie⋆ (*Rosenkavalier*); TIPPETT: Bella (*Midsummer Marriage*); VERDI: Oscar (*Ballo in maschera*), Gilda (*Rigoletto*). Recorded for: Decca. Video/Film—BBC TV: Contessa (*Nozze di Figaro*); three sop roles (*Contes d'Hoffmann*); Violetta (*Traviata*). Gives recitals. On faculty of Royal Manchester Coll of Music, fellow. Mgmt: IBB/UK; SHA/USA.

HAUBOLD, INGRID. Soprano. German. Resident mem: Städtische Bühnen, Bielefeld. Born Berlin, Germany. Single. Studied: Annelies Kupper, Munich; Ellen Repp, New York; Nurit Goren, Kassel. **Debut:** Micaëla (*Carmen*) Opernhaus Detmold 1970. Previous occupations: church music.
   Sang with major companies in FR GER: Bielefeld, Darmstadt, Essen, Kassel, Kiel, Munich Staatsoper. **Roles with these companies incl** BIZET: Micaëla⋆ (*Carmen*); CORNELIUS: Margiana (*Barbier von Bagdad*); GLUCK: Euridice; LORTZING: Baronin Freimann⋆ (*Wildschütz*); MOZART: Donna Anna⋆ & Donna Elvira⋆ (*Don Giovanni*), Contessa Almaviva⋆ (*Nozze di Figaro*), Pamina⋆ (*Zauberflöte*); OFFENBACH: Antonia⋆ & Giulietta⋆ (*Contes d'Hoffmann*); PUCCINI: Mimi⋆ (*Bohème*), Liù⋆ (*Turandot*); SMETANA: Marie⋆ (*Bartered Bride*); STRAUSS, J: Rosalinde⋆ (*Fledermaus*); STRAUSS, R: Arabella⋆, Chrysothemis⋆ (*Elektra*); TCHAIKOVSKY: Lisa⋆ (*Pique Dame*); VERDI: Alice Ford⋆ (*Falstaff*); WAGNER: Elsa⋆ (*Lohengrin*), Eva⋆ (*Meistersinger*); WEBER: Agathe⋆ (*Freischütz*). Gives recitals. Appears with symphony orchestra. Mgmt: SLZ/FRG.

HAUGAN, KRISTINE JUDITH. Scenic and costume designer for opera, theater. Is also a media designer. American. Resident designer, Lake George Opera Fest, Glens Falls, NY. Born 21 Jun 1940, Minneapolis, MN. Single. Studied: Univ of Minnesota, Wendel Josal, R Moulton. **Operatic debut:** sets, *Crucible* St Paul Opera, MN 1969; cost, *Incoronazione di Poppea* Opera Socy of Washington, DC 1973. Theater debut: APA-Phoenix Theater, New York 1965-66.
   Designed for major companies in USA: Lake George, St Paul, Washington DC. **Operas designed for these companies incl** DELIUS: *Village Romeo and Juliet*⋆; FALLA: *Retablo de Maese Pedro*⋆, *Vida breve;* FLOYD: *Of Mice and Men*⋆; MENOTTI: *Medium, Telephone;* MONTEVERDI: *Incoronazione di Poppea*⋆; OFFENBACH: *Périchole*⋆; PERGOLESI: *Serva padrona;* PUCCINI: *Fanciulla del West;* STRAUSS, R: *Ariadne*

auf Naxos; STRAVINSKY: *Rake's Progress*★; VERDI: *Falstaff*★; WARD: *Crucible*★. Also NIELSEN: *Maskarade*★. **Operatic world premieres:** PASATIERI: *Penitentes* Aspen Music Fest, CO 1974. **Res:** 347 W 44th St, New York, USA. Mgmt: SSR/USA.

HAUGK, DIETRICH. Stages/produces opera, theater, film & television and is an actor & author. German/Austrian. Resident Stage Dir for theater & television in Munich. Born 12 May 1925, Ellrich, Germany. Wife Sylvia Lukan, occupation actress. Two children. Studied: theater and piano. **Operatic debut:** *Don Perlimplin* State Opera, Stuttgart 1963. Theater debut: Junges Theater, Hamburg 1954. Previous occupation: actor, quizmaster. Awards: Best Direction of the Year & Golden Nymph for TV directing, Monte Carlo 1965.

Directed/produced opera for major companies in AUS: Vienna Volksoper; FR GER: Munich Staatsoper & Gärtnerplatz, Stuttgart; SWI: Zurich; USA: San Francisco Opera. **Operas staged with these companies incl** AUBER: *Fra Diavolo*★; BARTOK: *Bluebeard's Castle;* BIZET: *Carmen*★; FORTNER: *Elisabeth Tudor*★, *Don Perlimplin*★; PAISIELLO: *Re Teodoro in Venezia;* STRAUSS, R: *Arabella, Ariadne auf Naxos;* STRAVINSKY: *Rossignol;* VERDI: *Ballo in maschera*★; WAGNER: *Parsifal, Tristan und Isolde*★. Also EGK: *Revisor;* OFFENBACH: *Banditen.* **Operatic world premieres:** BIALAS: *Aucassin und Nicolette* Germany 1969; WIMBERGER: *Lebensregeln* Theater am Gärtnerplatz, Munich 1972. Operatic Video—ARD TV, Munich: *Lebensregeln.* Previous leading positions with major theater companies: Thtr Dir, Staatstheater Stuttgart 1957-60. Teaches at Mozarteum, Salzburg; Prof. **Res:** Nelkeng 2/10, A1060 Vienna, Austria.

HAUGLAND, AAGE. Bass-baritone. Norwegian. Resident mem: Royal Opera, Copenhagen. Born 1 Feb 1944, Copenhagen. Wife Anette. One daughter. Studied: Mogens Wöldike and Kristian Riis, Copenhagen. **Debut:** The Brewer (*Comedy on the Bridge*) Oslo Opera 1968. Previous occupations: studied medicine. Awards: Winner, Opera Compt *Aftenposten,* Oslo 1968.

Sang with major companies in DEN: Copenhagen; ITA: Florence Maggio, Venice; NOR: Oslo; UK: London Royal Opera. **Roles with these companies incl** BEETHOVEN: Rocco★ (*Fidelio*); BORODIN: Galitzky★ & Kontchak★ (*Prince Igor*); DUKAS: Barbe Bleue★ (*Ariane*); GLUCK: Thoas★ (*Iphigénie en Tauride*); GOUNOD: Méphistophélès★ (*Faust*); HANDEL: Ptolemy★ (*Giulio Cesare*); MEYERBEER: Cardinal★ (*Prophète*); MOZART: Leporello (*Don Giovanni*), Sarastro★ (*Zauberflöte*); MUSSORGSKY: Boris Godunov & Varlaam★ & Pimen★ (*Boris Godunov*); OFFENBACH: Coppélius, etc★ (*Contes d'Hoffmann*); PUCCINI: Colline (*Bohème*); ROSSINI: Dott Bartolo★ & Don Basilio★ (*Barbiere di Siviglia*); SHOSTAKOVICH: Boris★ (*Katerina Ismailova*); SMETANA: Kezal (*Bartered Bride*); STRAVINSKY: Tiresias (*Oedipus Rex*); VERDI: Ramfis★ (*Aida*), Grande Inquisitore (*Don Carlo*), Falstaff, Banquo★ (*Macbeth*), Zaccaria★ (*Nabucco*); WAGNER: Holländer & Daland★ (*Fliegende Holländer*), Kö-

nig Heinrich★ (*Lohengrin*), Hunding★ (*Walküre*), Landgraf★ (*Tannhäuser*), König Marke (*Tristan und Isolde*); WERLE: Julien★ (*Dream of Thérèse*). Also MONTEVERDI: Seneca★ (*Incoronazione di Poppea*); TCHAIKOVSKY: Gremin (*Eugene Onegin*), Cardinal★ (*Maid of Orleans*). Gives recitals. Teaches voice. On faculty of Univ of Copenhagen. **Res:** Cedervangen 50, 3450 Allerod, Denmark. Mgmt: ASK/UK.

HAUPT-NOLEN, PAULETTE; née Paulette L Houpt. Conductor of opera. American. Born 14 May 1944, Denver, CO. Husband Timothy Nolen, occupation opera singer, baritone. Studied: Denver 16 yrs, incl piano and voice. Plays the piano; concert accompanist. Operatic training as repetiteur & asst cond at various opera companies. **Operatic debut:** *Barbiere di Siviglia* Lake George Opera, NY, 1973. Awards: M B Rockefeller Fund grant for study at Met Op, NY.

Conducted with major companies in USA: Kansas City, Lake George. **Operas with these companies incl** OFFENBACH: *Périchole*★; PUCCINI: *Bohème*★; ROSSINI: *Barbiere di Siviglia*★; STRAUSS, J: *Fledermaus*★; VERDI: *Traviata*★; WARD: *Crucible*★. **Res:** Titusstr 14, Cologne, FR Ger.

HAY, PATRICIA. Lyric soprano. British. Resident mem: Scottish Opera, Glasgow. Born 30 Sep 1944, Ayr, Scotland. Husband John Graham, occupation singer. Studied: Royal Scottish Acad, Winifred Busfield, Glasgow. **Debut:** Cherubino (*Nozze di Figaro*) Scottish Opera Glasgow 1968.

Sang with major companies in HOL: Amsterdam; UK: Edinburgh Fest, Glasgow Scottish. **Roles with these companies incl** BEETHOVEN: Marzelline★ (*Fidelio*); DONIZETTI: Norina★ (*Don Pasquale*); HANDEL: Morgana (*Alcina*); MOZART: Despina★ (*Così fan tutte*), Zerlina★ (*Don Giovanni*), Susanna★ & Cherubino (*Nozze di Figaro*), Pamina★ (*Zauberflöte*); PUCCINI: Musetta★ (*Bohème*); ROSSINI: Rosina★ (*Barbiere di Siviglia*); STRAUSS, J: Adele★ (*Fledermaus*); VERDI: Oscar★ (*Ballo in maschera*). Gives recitals. Appears with symphony orchestra. **Res:** Glasgow, Scotland, UK. Mgmt: IBB/UK.

HAYASHI, YASUKO. Lyric soprano. Italian & Japanese. Born 19 Jul 1948, Kanagawa, Japan. Husband Giannicola Pigliucci, occupation opera singer, bass. One child. Studied: Univ of Arts, Mo Shibata, N Rucci, Tokyo; Consv G Verdi, Mo Campogalliani, Milan; Scuola di Perfez, Teatro alla Scala, Milan; Ma Lia Guarini, Milan. **Debut:** Cio-Cio-San (*Butterfly*) La Scala, Milan 1972. Awards: Conc Voci Rossiniane, Italian TV 1972; Compts in Parma, Vercelli, Busseto, Lonigo, Enna, Montechiani.

Sang with major companies in FRA: Aix-en-Provence Fest; ITA: Florence Comunale, Milan La Scala, Rome Opera, Turin, Venice, Verona Arena; JPN: Tokyo Niki Kai; SPA: Barcelona; UK: London Royal Opera; USA: Chicago. **Roles with these companies incl** CIMAROSA: Carolina★ & Elisetta (*Matrimonio segreto*); DEBUSSY: Lia★ (*Enfant prodigue*); DONIZETTI: Adina★ (*Elisir*), Maria Stuarda★; HALEVY: Rachel★ (*Juive*); MOZART: Servilia★ (*Clemenza di Tito*), Fiordiligi (*Così fan tutte*), Donna Anna★ (*Don*

Giovanni), Serpetta★ (*Finta giardiniera*); PUC-CINI: Cio-Cio-San★ (*Butterfly*), Liù★ (*Turandot*); ROSSINI: Ninetta★ (*Gazza ladra*); STRA-VINSKY: Anne Trulove★ (*Rake's Progress*); VERDI: Luisa Miller★, Desdemona (*Otello*). Also ROSSINI: Sinaïde (*Moïse*). Video/Film—RAI: BELLINI: Bianca (*Bianca e Fernando*); CIMA-ROSA: (*Due Baroni di Rocca Azzurra*). Gives recitals. Appears with symphony orchestra. **Res:** Milan, Italy. Mgmt: GOR/UK; CSA/USA.

HAYWOOD, LORNA MARIE. Lyric soprano. British. Born 29 Jan 1942, Birmingham. Studied: Royal Coll of Music, Mary Parsons, Gordon Clinton, London; Juilliard School of Music, Sergius Kagen, Beverley Johnson, New York. **Debut:** Erste Dame (*Zauberflöte*) Royal Opera, Covent Garden 1966. Awards: Queen's Prize, Royal Coll of Music; Kathleen Ferrier Mem Schlshp, Royal Philharmonic Socy; Saltire Awd, Edinburgh Fest.

Sang with major companies in BEL: Brussels; CZE: Prague National; UK: Cardiff Welsh, Edinburgh Fest, Glyndebourne Fest, London Royal & English National; USA: Chicago, Dallas, Fort Worth, Kentucky, Lake George, St Paul, Seattle, Washington DC. **Roles with these companies incl** BEETHOVEN: Marzelline (*Fidelio*); BIZET: Micaëla★ (*Carmen*); BRITTEN: Lady Billows★ (*Albert Herring*), Female Chorus (*Rape of Lucretia*); HENZE: Elisabeth Zimmer (*Elegy for Young Lovers*); HINDEMITH: Lucia (*Long Christmas Dinner*); JANACEK: Jenufa★, Katya Kabanova★, Emilia Marty★ (*Makropoulos Affair*); LEONCAVALLO: Nedda★ (*Pagliacci*); OF-FENBACH: Giulietta (*Contes d'Hoffmann*); PUCCINI: Mimi★ (*Bohème*), Lauretta★ (*Gianni Schicchi*), Cio-Cio-San★ (*Butterfly*), Manon Lescaut★, Giorgetta★ (*Tabarro*); SMETANA: Marie★ (*Bartered Bride*); STRAUSS, R: Ariadne★ (*Ariadne auf Naxos*), Marschallin★ (*Rosenkavalier*), Sieglinde★ (*Walküre*). Gives recitals. Appears with symphony orchestra. Teaches voice. Coaches repertoire. **Res:** New York, NY, USA. Mgmt: BAR/USA.

HAZY, ERZSEBET. Lyric & dramatic soprano. Hungarian. Resident mem: State Opera, Budapest. Studied: Music Acad, Géza László, Budapest. **Debut:** Oscar (*Ballo in maschera*) State Opera, Budapest 1951.

Sang with major companies in AUSTRL: Sydney; AUS: Vienna Volksoper; BUL: Sofia; CZE: Prague National; FIN: Helsinki; FR GER: Cologne, Dortmund, Wiesbaden; GER DR: Berlin Komische & Staatsoper; HUN: Budapest; ITA: Bologna; POL: Warsaw; ROM: Bucharest; UK: Glyndebourne Fest. **Roles with these companies incl** DEBUSSY: Mélisande★; DONIZETTI: Norina★ (*Don Pasquale*); GERSHWIN: Bess★; GLUCK: Amor★ (*Orfeo ed Euridice*); JANACEK: Katya Kabanova★; KODALY: Örzse★ (*Háry János*); LEONCAVALLO: Nedda★ (*Pagliacci*); ME-NOTTI: Lucy★ (*Telephone*); ·MONTEVERDI: Poppea★ (*Incoronazione di Poppea*); MOZART: Blondchen★ (*Entführung aus dem Serail*), Cherubino★ (*Nozze di Figaro*), Pamina★ (*Zauberflöte*); OFFENBACH: Antonia★ (*Contes d'Hoffmann*); ORFF: Kluge★; PUCCINI: Mimi★ (*Bohème*), Minnie★ (*Fanciulla del West*), Cio-Cio-San★ (*Butterfly*), Manon Lescaut★, Liù★ (*Turandot*);

STRAUSS, J: Adele★ & Rosalinde★(*Fledermaus*); STRAUSS, R: Komponist★ (*Ariadne auf Naxos*), Octavian★ (*Rosenkavalier*), Salome★; SZO-KOLAY: Bride★(*Blood Wedding*); TCHAIKOV-SKY: Tatiana★(*Eugene Onegin*); VERDI: Oscar★ (*Ballo in maschera*); WAGNER: Eva★ (*Meistersinger*). Video/Film: Adele (*Fledermaus*); Bride (*Blood Wedding*). Gives recitals. Appears with symphony orchestra. **Res:** Mátyáshegyi 7/A, Budapest, Hungary.

HEBERT, BLISS. Stages/produces opera. Also designs stage-lighting and is a conductor and author. American. Born 30 Nov 1930, Faust, NY. Single. Studied: Syracuse Univ, Boston Univ; Robert Goldsand, Lélia Gousseau, Pierre Bernac; incl music, piano, flute, saxophone and voice. Operatic training as asst stage dir. at Dallas Civic Opera. **Operatic debut:** *Rake's Progress* Santa Fe Opera 1957. Previous occupation: pianist, accompanist, voice coach. Previous adm positions in opera: Art Adm, Santa Fe Opera 1958, 59; Gen Mng, Washington Opera Socy 1960-63.

Directed/produced opera for major companies in CAN: Ottawa, Toronto, Vancouver; USA: Baltimore, Cincinnati, Fort Worth, Houston, Miami, New Orleans, New York Met & City Opera, Portland, San Diego, San Francisco Spring Opera, Santa Fe, Seattle, Washington DC. **Operas staged with these companies incl** BARTOK: *Bluebeard's Castle*; BIZET: *Carmen★*; BRITTEN: *Burning Fiery Furnace, Curlew River★, Prodigal Son★*; DEBUSSY: *Pelléas et Mélisande★*; DONI-ZETTI: *Elisir, Fille du régiment★, Lucia★*; FALLA: *Vida breve★*; GIORDANO: *Andrea Chénier★*; GOUNOD: *Faust★, Roméo et Juliette*; HENZE: *Boulevard Solitude, König Hirsch/Re Cervo*; LEONCAVALLO: *Pagliacci★*; MASCA-GNI: *Cavalleria rusticana★*; MASSENET: *Manon★, Thaïs★, Werther*; MENOTTI: *Globolinks★, Old Maid and the Thief, Telephone*; MONTE-VERDI: *Combattimento di Tancredi★*; MO-ZART: *Così fan tutte, Don Giovanni★, Entführung aus dem Serail, Idomeneo, Nozze di Figaro★, Schauspieldirektor, Zauberflöte★*; OF-FENBACH: *Contes d'Hoffmann★*; PUCCINI: *Bohème, Gianni Schicchi★, Butterfly★, Manon Lescaut, Suor Angelica, Tabarro★, Tosca★, Turandot*; PURCELL: *Dido and Aeneas★*; RAVEL: *Enfant et les sortilèges★, Heure espagnole*; ROS-SINI: *Barbiere di Siviglia★, Italiana in Algeri*; SAINT-SAENS: *Samson et Dalila*; SCHOEN-BERG: *Erwartung★*; STRAUSS, J: *Fledermaus*; STRAUSS, R: *Ariadne auf Naxos, Capriccio, Rosenkavalier★, Salome★*; STRAVINSKY: *Oedipus Rex, Rossignol★*; TCHAIKOVSKY: *Eugene Onegin★, Pique Dame*; THOMAS: *Mignon*; VERDI: *Aida★, Falstaff, Otello, Rigoletto, Traviata*; WAGNER: *Fliegende Holländer★*. Teaches. **Res:** 11 Riverside Dr, New York, USA.

HEBERT, PAMELA ELIZABETH. Spinto. American. Resident mem: New York City Opera. Born 31 Aug 1946, Los Angeles. Single. Studied: Margaret Hoswell, New York; Maria Callas Master Classes & Tito Capobianco, Juilliard School; Boris Goldovsky. **Debut:** Donna Anna (*Don Giovanni*) New York City Opera 1972. Previous occupations: seamstress. Awards: W M Sullivan Fndt Grant 1972; First Prize, Musician's Club of New York 1972.

Sang with major companies in USA: Lake George, New York City Opera, Washington DC. **Roles with these companies incl** HAYDN: Vespina★ (*Infedeltà delusa*); MONTEVERDI: Poppea★ (*Incoronazione di Poppea*); MOZART: Donna Anna★ (*Don Giovanni*); PUCCINI: Mimi★ (*Bohème*); STRAUSS: Komponist★ (*Ariadne auf Naxos*); WEILL: Jenny★ (*Aufstieg und Fall der Stadt Mahagonny*). **World premieres:** LEICHTLING: Lady (*White Butterfly*) Juilliard School 1971; OVERTON: Aunt (*Huckleberry Finn*) Juilliard School 1971. Videotape: Komponist (*Ariadne auf Naxos*). Gives recitals. Appears with symphony orchestra. **Res:** 121 W 69 St, New York, NY, USA.

HECHT, JOSHUA. Dramatic baritone. American. Born New York, NY, USA. Wife Eve, occupation coach, accompanist. Four children. Studied: Lili Wexberg, New York; Eve Hecht, Walter Cataldi Tassoni, Rome. **Debut:** Comte des Grieux (*Manon*) Baltimore Civic Opera 1953. Previous occupations: grad student Eng Lit, guest lecturer on Irish writers, New York Univ. Awards: Ford Fndt Fllshp 1962; M B Rockefeller Fund Grant.

Sang with major companies in AUS: Graz, Vienna Volksoper; CAN: Vancouver; ISR: Tel Aviv; ITA: Naples, Palermo; MEX: Mexico City; ROM: Bucharest; S AFR: Johannesburg; SPA: Barcelona; USA: Baltimore, Boston, Chicago, Cincinnati, Fort Worth, Hartford, Houston, Miami, Milwaukee Florentine, New Orleans, New York Met & City Opera, Omaha, Philadelphia Grand, Pittsburgh, Portland, San Antonio, San Diego, San Francisco Opera & Spring Opera, Seattle, Washington DC. **Roles with these companies incl** BEETHOVEN: Don Pizarro★ & Rocco (*Fidelio*); BELLINI: Oroveso (*Norma*); BERLIOZ: Méphistophélès (*Damnation de Faust*); BIZET: Escamillo (*Carmen*); BRITTEN: Theseus (*Midsummer Night*); FLOYD: Olin Blitch (*Susannah*); GOUNOD: Méphistophélès (*Faust*); MASSENET: Des Grieux★ (*Portrait de Manon*); MENOTTI: John Sorel★ (*Consul*); MEYERBEER: Comte de St Bris (*Huguenots*); MOZART: Don Alfonso (*Così fan tutte*), Don Giovanni, Figaro (*Nozze di Figaro*), Sarastro (*Zauberflöte*); MUSSORGSKY: Boris Godunov & Pimen (*Boris Godunov*); OFFENBACH: Coppélius, etc★ (*Contes d'Hoffmann*); PONCHIELLI: Alvise (*Gioconda*); PUCCINI: Colline (*Bohème*), Scarpia★ (*Tosca*); ROSSINI: Don Basilio (*Barbiere di Siviglia*); STRAUSS, R: Orest (*Elektra*), Jochanaan★ (*Salome*); STRAVINSKY: Creon & Tiresias (*Oedipus Rex*); VERDI: Amonasro★ & Ramfis (*Aida*), Padre Guardiano (*Forza del destino*), Banquo (*Macbeth*), Zaccaria (*Nabucco*), Iago★ (*Otello*), Rigoletto★, Germont (*Traviata*); WAGNER: Holländer★, König Heinrich (*Lohengrin*), Kurwenal (*Tristan und Isolde*). **World premieres:** WEISGALL: Abe Goldberg (*Nine Rivers from Jordan*) New York City Opera 1968. Recorded for: MGM, Columbia. Gives recitals. Appears with symphony orchestra. **Res:** Rome, Italy. **Mgmt:** LLF/USA; RAB/AUS.

HEDLUND, RONALD. Dram baritone. American. Born 12 May 1937, Minneapolis, MN, USA. Wife Barbara, occupation musician. Studied: Hamline Univ, St Paul, MN; Indiana Univ, Bloomington;

Juilliard School of Music, New York. **Debut:** Wagner (*Faust*) Washington, DC, Opera Society 1966. Previous occupations: naval officer.

Sang with major companies in USA: Boston, Houston, Lake George, New Orleans, New York City Opera, Philadelphia Grand, San Francisco Spring Opera. **Roles with these companies incl** BERLIOZ: Narbal★ (*Troyens*); BRITTEN: Traveller★ (*Death in Venice*); PASATIERI: Juan★ (*Black Widow*), Trigorin★ (*Seagull*); PUCCINI: Marcello (*Bohème*), Scarpia★ (*Tosca*); STRAVINSKY: Nick Shadow (*Rake's Progress*); VERDI: Ford (*Falstaff*), Macbeth★, Rigoletto★, Germont★ (*Traviata*). Also BRITTEN: Tarquinius★ (*Rape of Lucretia*). Gives recitals. Appears with symphony orchestra. **Res:** New York, NY, USA. **Mgmt:** CSA/USA.

HEELEY, DESMOND. Scenic and costume designer for opera, theater, television. Is also a painter. British. Born 1 Jun 1931, W Bromwich, UK. Single. Prof training: Shakespeare Mem Theatre, Stratford, UK 1947-52. **Operatic debut:** *Traviata* Sadler's Wells, London. Theater debut: Shakespeare Mem Theatre, Stratford-on-Avon 1949. Previous occupation: teaching stage design. Awards: two Tony Awds for Britain's Ntl Theatre prod, New York 1968.

Designed for major companies in CAN: Toronto; UK: Glyndebourne Fest, London Royal & English National; USA: New York Met. **Operas designed for these companies incl** BELLINI: *Norma, Puritani;* CIMAROSA: *Matrimonio segreto;* DEBUSSY: *Pelléas et Mélisande;* DONIZETTI: *Maria Stuarda;* GOUNOD: *Faust;* MOZART: *Così fan tutte;* ROSSINI: *Cenerentola;* VERDI: *Traviata.* Exhibitions of stage designs Toronto 1967, London 1969. Teaches at Central School of Arts & Crafts, London. **Res:** London, UK. **Mgmt:** MRR/UK.

HEGGEN, ALMAR GUNVALD. Bass. Norwegian. Resident mem: Norwegian Opera, Oslo. Born 25 May 1933, Valldal, Norway. Wife Aslang. Three children. Studied: Music Consv, Morten Vatn, Oslo; Prof Paul Lohmann, Wiesbaden; Prof C Kaiser-Breme, Essen, FR Ger. **Debut:** Masetto (*Don Giovanni*) Norsk Operaselskap, Oslo 1957.

Sang with major companies in FR GER: Bonn, Frankfurt, Munich Gärtnerplatz, Nürnberg, Stuttgart, Wiesbaden, Wuppertal; NOR: Oslo; SWE: Stockholm. **Roles with these companies incl** d'ALBERT: Tommaso (*Tiefland*); BEETHOVEN: Rocco★ (*Fidelio*); BERG: Doktor★ (*Wozzeck*); CORNELIUS: Abul Hassan (*Barbier von Bagdad*); DONIZETTI: Dott Dulcamara (*Elisir*); EINEM: St Just (*Dantons Tod*); GLUCK: Thoas (*Iphigénie en Tauride*); HANDEL: Ptolemy (*Giulio Cesare*); MOZART: Don Alfonso (*Così fan tutte*), Sarastro★ (*Zauberflöte*); MUSSORGSKY: Pimen★ (*Boris Godunov*); ROSSINI: Don Basilio★ (*Barbiere di Siviglia*); SMETANA: Kezal (*Bartered Bride*); STRAUSS, R: Baron Ochs (*Rosenkavalier*); STRAVINSKY: Tiresias (*Oedipus Rex*); THOMAS: Lothario (*Mignon*); VERDI: Ramfis (*Aida*), Philip II★ & Grande Inquisitore (*Don Carlo*), Padre Guardiano (*Forza del destino*), Banquo (*Macbeth*); WAGNER: Daland★ (*Fliegende Holländer*), König Heinrich (*Lohengrin*), Pogner (*Meistersinger*), Fafner (*Siegfried*),

Hunding★ (*Walküre*), Hagen (*Götterdämmerung*), Landgraf (*Tannhäuser*), König Marke (*Tristan und Isolde*). World premieres: FLIFLET-BRAIN: Absalon (*Anne Pedersdotter*) Norwegian Opera, Oslo 1971; YUN: Liu-Tung (*Traum des Liu-Tung*) Städtische Bühnen, Nürnberg 1969. Video/Film: Rocco (*Fidelio*). Gives recitals. Appears with symphony orchestra. Teaches voice. **Res:** Valhallaveien 53, Kolbotn, Norway. **Mgmt:** NRK/NOR.

HEIKKILÄ, HANNU TAPANI. Bass. Finnish. Resident mem: Finnish National Opera, Helsinki. Born 23 Oct 1922, Helsinki. Wife Anja, occupation secy. Four children. Studied: Heikki Teittinen, Arturo Merlini. **Debut:** Don Basilio (*Barbiere di Siviglia*) Finnish National Opera 1953.

Sang with major companies in FIN: Helsinki; FR GER: Stuttgart; GER DR: Berlin Staatsoper; SWE: Stockholm. **Roles with these companies incl** BARTOK: Bluebeard; BEETHOVEN: Rocco (*Fidelio*); BERG: Doktor (*Wozzeck*); BORODIN: Galitzky (*Prince Igor*); CIMAROSA: Count Robinson (*Matrimonio segreto*); DEBUSSY: Arkel (*Pelléas et Mélisande*); EGK: Cuperus (*Zaubergeige*); GOUNOD: Méphistophélès (*Faust*); MOZART: Don Alfonso (*Così fan tutte*), Figaro★ (*Nozze di Figaro*); MUSSORGSKY: Pimen (*Boris Godunov*); PROKOFIEV: King of Clubs (*Love for Three Oranges*); ROSSINI: Don Basilio (*Barbiere di Siviglia*); STRAVINSKY: Tiresias (*Oedipus Rex*); VERDI: Philip II★ (*Don Carlo*), Padre Guardiano★ (*Forza del destino*); WAGNER: Daland (*Fliegende Holländer*), Hunding (*Walküre*), König Marke★ (*Tristan und Isolde*). Recorded for: Finnlevy. **Res:** Haahkatie 4, Helsinki, Finland.

HEIMALL, LINDA JEANNE. Coloratura mezzosoprano & soprano (Falcon). American. Resident mem: Opernhaus Graz, Austria. Born 21 Jan 1941, E Orange, NJ, USA. Single. Studied: Alfredo Silipigni, Alice Zeppilli, Randolph Mickelson, New York; Franz Schuch-Tovini, Vienna. **Debut:** Musetta (*Bohème*) Italian Lyric, Brooklyn, NY, USA 1963. Previous occupations: bookkeeper. Awards: Maria de Varady Awd, 2 yr contract NY City Opera; Sullivan Fndt Awd; Ntl Socy of Arts & Letters.

Sang with major cos in AUS: Graz; USA: Hartford, Newark, NY City Op. **Mezzo roles with these cos incl** BIZET: Carmen★; BORODIN: Kontchakovna★ (*Prince Igor*); HUMPERDINCK: Hänsel; MOZART: Zerlina (*Don Giovanni*), Cherubino★ (*Nozze di Figaro*); PUCCINI: Frugola★ (*Tabarro*); ROSSINI: Rosina (*Barbiere di Siviglia*), Pippo (*Gazza ladra*). **Soprano roles with these companies incl** BELLINI: Norma★; BIZET: Micaëla★ (*Carmen*); GIORDANO: Fedora★; LEONCAVALLO: Nedda★ (*Pagliacci*); MOZART: Donna Elvira★ & Zerlina★ (*Don Giovanni*); PUCCINI: Mimi & Musetta★ (*Bohème*), Cio-Cio-San★ (*Butterfly*); VERDI: Leonora★ (*Trovatore*). Recorded for: ORF-Rundfunk. Gives recitals. Appears with symphony orchestra. **Res:** Hallerschloss Str 5, Graz, Austria. **Mgmt:** LOM/USA; RAB/AUS.

HEINRICH, PETER. Conductor of opera and symphony. German. Resident Cond, Oper der Landeshauptstadt Kiel, FR Ger. Born 6 Apr 1942,

Berlin. Wife Helgard, occupation teacher. Studied: H Ahlendorf, Berlin; Michael Gielen, Cologne; Franco Ferrara, Venice; George Szell, Cleveland. Incl piano and voice. Plays the piano. Operatic training as repetiteur & chorus master at Opera House, Hagen, FR Ger 1969-70; Opera, Dortmund 1970-72. **Operatic debut:** Lake Erie Opera Co, Cleveland, O, 1968. Awards: conducting flshp to Cleveland.

Conducted with major companies in FR GER: Dortmund, Kiel. **Operas with these companies incl** LORTZING: *Waffenschmied★, Wildschütz★, Zar und Zimmermann★;* MENOTTI: *Telephone;* NICOLAI: *Lustigen Weiber★;* ROSSINI: *Barbiere di Siviglia★;* VERDI: *Simon Boccanegra★.* Conducted major orch in Europe, USA. **Res:** Halberstädter Str 2, 1 Berlin 31, FR Ger.

HEINRICH, RUDOLF. Scenic and costume designer for opera, theater, television. Is a lighting designer, stage director. German Born 10 Feb 1926, Halle. Wife Ursula, occupation pharmacist. One child. Studied: with Max Elten, Paul Pilowski, Walter Felsenstein. Prof training: Leipziger Theater, Ger DR 1948-50. **Operatic debut:** *Hänsel und Gretel* Opera, Leipzig 1949. Theater debut: Städtische Bühnen, Halle, Ger DR 1950. Previous occupation: farmer, 1 yr. Awards: National-Preis Ger DR, Handel Fest 1955, 1960. Previous adm positions in opera: Head of Design, Komische Oper Berlin, Ger DR 1954-61.

Designed for major companies in AUS: Vienna Staatsoper & Volksoper; CAN: Montreal; FR GER: Berlin Deutsche Oper, Cologne, Frankfurt, Hamburg, Mannheim, Munich Staatsoper & Gärtnerplatz, Nürnberg, Stuttgart; GER DR: Berlin Komische Oper & Staatsoper, Leipzig; ITA: Milan La Scala; SWI: Zurich; USA: Boston, New York Met, Santa Fe. **Operas designed for these companies incl** d'ALBERT: *Tiefland;* BEETHOVEN: *Fidelio★;* BERG: *Lulu★, Wozzeck★;* BIZET: *Carmen;* BRITTEN: *Albert Herring★, Midsummer Night;* CIMAROSA: *Matrimonio segreto;* GOUNOD: *Faust;* HANDEL: *Alcina, Ariodante, Deidamia, Giulio Cesare;* HUMPERDINCK: *Hänsel und Gretel;* JANACEK: *Cunning Little Vixen, Katya Kabanova★;* KURKA: *Good Soldier Schweik;* LORTZING: *Zar und Zimmermann;* MASSENET: *Werther★;* MOZART: *Così fan tutte, Don Giovanni★, Entführung aus dem Serail★, Nozze di Figaro★, Zauberflöte★;* MUSSORGSKY: *Boris Godunov;* NICOLAI: *Lustigen Weiber;* OFFENBACH: *Contes d'Hoffmann;* ORFF: *Antigonae★;* PAISIELLO: *Barbiere di Siviglia;* PUCCINI: *Bohème, Manon Lescaut★, Tosca, Turandot;* SCHOENBERG: *Moses und Aron★;* STRAUSS, R: *Arabella, Ariadne auf Naxos, Daphne, Elektra★, Rosenkavalier, Salome★, Schweigsame Frau★;* TCHAIKOVSKY: *Pique Dame;* VERDI: *Aida, Don Carlo★, Forza del destino, Macbeth, Otello, Rigoletto, Simon Boccanegra, Traviata;* WAGNER: *Fliegende Holländer, Lohengrin★, Meistersinger, Parsifal, Rheingold★, Walküre★, Siegfried★, Tannhäuser;* WEBER: *Freischütz★;* WOLF-FERRARI: *Donne curiose, Quattro rusteghi;* ZIMMERMANN: *Soldaten★.* **Operatic world premieres:** FORTNER: *Elisabeth Tudor* Berlin Deutsche Oper, FR Ger 1973. Exhibitions of stage designs, Nationaltheater Mannheim 1973.

Teaches at Akad der bildenden Künste, Munich. **Res:** Munich 40, FR Ger. [†Nov 30 '75]

HEISE, MICHAEL. Conductor of opera and symphony. German. Resident Cond, Deutsche Oper Berlin. Born 22 Jul 1940, Berlin. Wife Angelika, occupation physiotherapist. Two children. Studied: Musikhochschule, Berlin, incl piano, cello, trumpet. Plays the piano. Operatic training as repetiteur & asst cond at Nationaltheater, Mannheim & Braunschweig; Deutsche Oper Berlin 1963-69. **Operatic debut:** Nationaltheater, Mannheim 1966. Symphonic debut: Symph Orch, Berlin 1972. Previous occupations: studies in philosophy; piano soloist. Awards: Third Prize, Piano Comp for Children, Berlin 1954.

Conducted with major companies in FR GER: Berlin Deutsche Oper, Bonn, Cologne, Düsseldorf-Duisburg, Karlsruhe, Kassel, Kiel, Mannheim. **Operas with these companies incl** AUBER: *Fra Diavolo;* BARTOK: *Bluebeard's Castle;* BEETHOVEN: *Fidelio★;* BIZET: *Carmen;* BUSONI: *Arlecchino;* CHARPENTIER: *Louise;* CIMAROSA: *Matrimonio segreto★;* DONIZETTI: *Don Pasquale★;* FLOTOW: *Martha★;* GIORDANO: *Andrea Chénier★;* HENZE: *Junge Lord;* HINDEMITH: *Cardillac★;* LEONCAVALLO: *Pagliacci;* LORTZING: *Zar und Zimmermann;* MASCAGNI: *Cavalleria rusticana;* MOZART: *Clemenza di Tito★, Così fan tutte★, Don Giovanni, Nozze di Figaro★, Zauberflöte;* NICOLAI: *Lustigen Weiber;* OFFENBACH: *Contes d'Hoffmann;* ORFF: *Kluge;* PAISIELLO: *Barbiere di Siviglia;* PERGOLESI: *Serva Padrona;* PUCCINI: *Bohème★, Butterfly, Tosca★;* SMETANA: *Bartered Bride;* STRAUSS, J: *Fledermaus★;* STRAUSS, R: *Ariadne auf Naxos, Capriccio, Elektra, Rosenkavalier, Salome;* TCHAIKOVSKY: *Pique Dame★;* VERDI: *Aida, Ballo in maschera, Don Carlo★, Rigoletto★, Simon Boccanegra★, Traviata, Trovatore;* WAGNER: *Fliegende Holländer★, Meistersinger, Walküre★;* WEBER: *Freischütz★;* WOLF-FERRARI: *Quattro rusteghi.* Also KRENEK: *Karl V★.* Conducted major orch in Europe. **Res:** Wiesenerstr 37, Berlin 42, FR Ger. Mgmt: PAS/FRG; ZBV/FRG.

HELFGOT, DANIEL. Stages/produces opera. Argentinean. Born 24 Dec 1946, Buenos Aires. Single. Studied: Superior Inst of Art, Teatro Colón, Buenos Aires. Operatic training as asst stage dir at Teatro Colón, Lyon, Essen, Milan, San Francisco, Graz. **Operatic debut:** *Rigoletto* Teatro Argentino, La Plata 1972. Previous occupation: journalist, music critic.

Directed/produced opera for major companies in USA: Baltimore, San Francisco Spring Opera. **Operas staged with these companies incl** BIZET: *Pêcheurs de perles★;* DONIZETTI: *Elisir★;* LEONCAVALLO: *Pagliacci★;* MASCAGNI: *Cavalleria rusticana★;* VERDI: *Traviata★.* **Res:** 53 #1127, La Plata, Argentina.

HELIOTIS, MICHAEL. Lyric tenor. Greek. Resident mem: Athens National Opera. Born 10 Nov 1929, Athens. Single. Studied: Marika Kalfopoulo, Athens; Fritz Lunzer, Zagreb; Elisabeth Rado, Vienna. **Debut:** Alfredo (*Traviata*) Athens National Opera 1957. Awards: Gold Medal, Rossini

Celebration, Inst of Culture, Italy 1968; Diplôme d'Honneur, Athens Fest 1966.

Sang with major companies in GRE: Athens National & Fest; FR GER: Saarbrücken; YUG: Dubrovnik, Zagreb. **Roles with these companies incl** CIMAROSA: Paolino (*Matrimonio segreto*); MOZART: Ferrando★ (*Così fan tutte*), Don Ottavio (*Don Giovanni*), Tamino★ (*Zauberflöte*); OFFENBACH: Hoffmann★; ORFF: Solo (*Carmina burana*); PROKOFIEV: Antonio (*Duenna*), Prince (*Love for Three Oranges*); PUCCINI: Rodolfo (*Bohème*), Rinuccio★ (*Gianni Schicchi*); ROSSINI: Almaviva★ (*Barbiere di Siviglia*); STRAUSS, J: Alfred (*Fledermaus*); TCHAIKOVSKY: Lenski★ (*Eugene Onegin*); VERDI: Fenton★ (*Falstaff*), Alfredo (*Traviata*); WAGNER: Erik★ (*Fliegende Holländer*); WEILL: Fatty★ (*Aufstieg und Fall der Stadt Mahagonny*). **World premieres:** GLANVILLE-HICKS: Alcinous (*Nausicaa*) Athens Fest 1961. Gives recitals. Appears with symphony orchestra. **Res:** Tideos 8, Athens, Greece.

HELLMICH, WOLFGANG. Cavalier baritone. German. Resident mem: Staatsoper Dresden, Ger DR. Born 21 May 1935, Dresden. Wife Gisela, occupation employee. Two children. Studied: Carl Maria v Weber Hochschule für Musik, Helga Fischer, Dresden. **Debut:** Ottokar (*Freischütz*) Stadttheater Zittau, Ger DR 1960. Awards: First Prize, Intl Compt Schumann-Wolf, Vienna 1960; Second Prize, Robert Schumann Compt Berlin 1960 and Bach Compt Leipzig 1964; Kammersänger, Ministry of Culture, Ger DR 1972.

Sang with major companies in GER DR: Berlin Staatsoper, Dresden, Leipzig; USSR: Leningrad Kirov. **Roles with these companies incl** DONIZETTI: Dott Malatesta (*Don Pasquale*), Belcore★ (*Elisir*); HANDEL: Giulio Cesare; LORTZING: Graf Eberbach★ (*Wildschütz*); MOZART: Conte Almaviva★ & Figaro★ (*Nozze di Figaro*), Papageno★ (*Zauberflöte*); ORFF: Solo (*Carmina burana*); PUCCINI: Marcello★ (*Bohème*); ROSSINI: Figaro (*Barbiere di Siviglia*); STRAUSS, R: Graf★ (*Capriccio*); VERDI: Rodrigo★ (*Don Carlo*), Germont (*Traviata*). Also HENZE: Sekretär (*Junge Lord*). **World premieres:** ROETTGER: Libero (*Weg nach Palermo*) Landestheater Dessau 1965; ZIMMERMANN: Levin (*Levins Mühle*) Staatsoper Dresden 1973. Recorded for: Eterna, VEB. Gives recitals. Appears with symphony orchestra. Teaches voice. Coaches repertoire. On faculty of Carl Maria v Weber Hochschule für Musik, Dresden. **Res:** Tiergartenstr 86, 8020 Dresden, Ger DR. Mgmt: KDR/GDR.

HELM, HANS. Lyric baritone. German. Resident mem: Staatsoper, Vienna. Born 12 Apr 1934, Passau, Germany. Wife Heidi. Two children. Studied: Else Zeidler, Prof Franz Reuter-Wolf, Munich; Emmi Müller, Krefeld. **Debut:** Shchelkalov (*Boris Godunov*) Opernhaus Graz 1957. Previous occupations: employee in finance dpt.

Sang with major companies in AUS: Bregenz Fest, Graz, Vienna Staatsoper & Volksoper; FR GER: Bielefeld, Cologne, Dortmund, Düsseldorf, Frankfurt, Hannover, Kassel, Munich Gärtnerplatz, Stuttgart, Wuppertal; SPA: Barcelona. **Roles with these companies incl** BERG: Wozzeck★; BIZET: Escamillo (*Carmen*); CIMAROSA: Count

Robinson (*Matrimonio segreto*); DALLAPIC-COLA: Prigioniero; DONIZETTI: Dott Mala-testa★ (*Don Pasquale*), Belcore (*Elisir*), Enrico (*Lucia*), Alfonso d'Este (*Lucrezia Borgia*); EI-NEM: Alfred Ill★ (*Besuch der alten Dame*); LOR-TZING: Graf v Liebenau (*Waffenschmied*), Graf Eberbach★ (*Wildschütz*), Peter I★ (*Zar und Zim-mermann*); MASSENET: Lescaut★ (*Manon*); MENOTTI: Bob (*Old Maid and the Thief*); MO-ZART: Guglielmo★ (*Così fan tutte*), Don Gio-vanni, Conte Almaviva (*Nozze di Figaro*); ORFF: Solo★ (*Carmina burana*); PUCCINI: Marcello★ (*Bohème*), Sharpless★ (*Butterfly*), Lescaut (*Manon Lescaut*); ROSSINI: Figaro★ (*Barbiere di Si-viglia*); STRAUSS, R: Graf★ (*Capriccio*); TCHAIKOVSKY: Eugene Onegin★; VERDI: Rodrigo★ (*Don Carlo*), Don Carlo (*Forza del de-stino*), Germont★ (*Traviata*), Conte di Luna (*Trovatore*); WAGNER: Amfortas (*Parsifal*), Wolfram★ (*Tannhäuser*); ZIMMERMANN: Stolzius (*Soldaten*). Also GOUNOD: Valentin (*Faust*); NICOLAI: Fluth (*Lustigen Weiber*); HENZE: Prinz von Homburg; FORTNER: Leo-nardo (*Bluthochzeit*). Recorded for: Electrola, Decca. Video/Film: (*Mondo della luna*). Appears with symphony orchestra. Mgmt: TAS/AUS; RAB/AUS; SLZ/FRG; PAS/FRG.

HELM, KARL. Bass. German. Resident mem: Bayerische Staatsoper, Munich. Born 3 Oct 1938, Passau, Germany. Wife Erika Leuxner. Two chil-dren. Studied: Else Zeidler, Dresden; Prof Franz Reuter-Wolf, Munich. **Debut:** Don Alfonso (*Così fan tutte*) Stadttheater Bern 1968.
Sang with major companies in FRA: Paris; FR GER: Düsseldorf-Duisburg, Hamburg, Karlsruhe, Munich Staatsoper, Stuttgart; SWI: Basel, Ge-neva. **Roles with these companies incl** BEETHO-VEN: Rocco★ (*Fidelio*); CIKKER: Courvoisier★ (*Play of Love*); DEBUSSY: Arkel★ (*Pelléas et Mélisande*); DONIZETTI: Dulcamara (*Elisir*); MOZART: Publio★ (*Clemenza di Tito*), Don Al-fonso (*Così fan tutte*); MUSSORGSKY: Var-laam★ (*Boris Godunov*); NICOLAI: Falstaff (*Lustigen Weiber*); ORFF: Bauer (*Mond*); ROS-SINI: Moïse; SMETANA: Kezal★ (*Bartered Bride*); VERDI: Philip II★ (*Don Carlo*), Fra Meli-tone (*Forza del destino*), Zaccaria★ (*Nabucco*); WAGNER: Fasolt (*Rheingold*). **World premieres:** BALMER: Ehemann (*Die gefoppten Ehemänner*) Bern, Switzerland 1969. Gives recitals. Appears with symphony orchestra. **Res:** Am Weiher 7, 8021 Strasslach, FR Ger. Mgmt: SLZ/FRG.

HEMMINGS, PETER WILLIAM. British. Gen Adm, Scottish Opera Ltd, Elmbank Crescent, Glasgow; also Scottish Opera Theatre Royal Ltd. In charge of overall adm matters. Born 10 Apr 1934, London. Wife Jane Kearnes. Five children. Studied: Gonville & Caius Coll, Cambridge Univ, UK. Plays the piano & organ. Previous positions, primarily adm: Asst, Harold Holt Ltd 1958-59; Gen Mng, New Opera Co 1957-65; Repertory & Planning Mng, Sadler's Wells Opera 1959-65; all in London. Starfed with present company in 1962 as Adm. World premieres at theaters during his man-agement: HAMILTON: *Catiline Conspiracy* Scottish Opera, Stirling, 1974; ORR: *Full Circle* Perth 1968; PURSER: *Undertaker* Edinburgh 1969. Initiated major policy changes including ex-pansion from 6 to 200 performances, budget in-crease from £6,000 to £1.5 million; initiated company's move to Theatre Royal in Glasgow. Mem of var natl & local commtts. **Res:** Glasgow, Scotland, UK.

HEMSLEY, GILBERT VAUGHN, Jr. Lighting de-signer for opera, theater and ballet; also designs space concepts for opera & theater. Resident light-ing designer, Opera Co of Boston. Born 19 Mar 1936, Bridgeport, CT, USA. Single. Studied: Yale Coll, Drama School; Stanley McCandless, Tharon Musser, Jean Rosenthal. **Operatic debut:** *Lulu* American Ntl Operà on tour, Indianapolis 1967. Theater debut: Theatre on the Green, Wellesley 1958. Previous occupation: restaurateur; grave-digger; sugar shoveler. Awards: *Newsweek* cita-tion as "the Rembrandt of lighting artists." Pre-vious adm positions in opera: Amer Prod Supv, Bolshoi & Stuttgart Ballet at the Met Opera House.
Designed for major companies in FR GER: Stutt-gart; USSR: Moscow Bolshoi; USA: Boston, Dal-las, Houston, Milwaukee Florentine, Washington DC. **Operas designed for these companies incl** BERG: *Lulu;* BERLIOZ: *Béatrice et Bénédict★, Troyens★;* DONIZETTI: *Anna Bolena, Fille du régiment★, Lucrezia Borgia★;* GOUNOD: *Faust★;* HOIBY: *Summer and Smoke★;* LEON-CAVALLO: *Pagliacci★;* MOORE: *Ballad of Baby Doe★;* MOZART: *Così fan tutte★, Nozze di Figaro★;* MUSSORGSKY: *Boris Godunov★;* OF-FENBACH: *Contes d'Hoffmann★;* PROKO-FIEV: *Gambler★, War and Peace★;* PUCCINI: *Bohème★, Butterfly★, Suor Angelica, Tosca★;* ROSSINI: *Barbiere di Siviglia★;* SMETANA: *Bartered Bride★;* STRAUSS, R: *Rosenkavalier★;* TCHAIKOVSKY: *Eugene Onegin★, Pique Dame★;* VERDI: *Falstaff★, Macbeth★, Otello, Traviata★, Trovatore★;* WARD: *Crucible★;* WEILL: *Aufstieg und Fall der Stadt Mahagonny★.* Also MOLCHANOV: *Dawns Are Quiet Here★;* BERNSTEIN: *Mass★.* Exhibitions of lighting slides, Univ of San Diego, CA. Teaches: Prof, Univ of Wisconsin, Madison. **Res:** 602 Stockton Court, Madison, WI, USA. Mgmt: STL/USA.

HENDRICKS, BARBARA. Soprano. American. Born 20 Nov 1948, Stephen, AR, USA. Studied: Jennie Tourel, New York. **Debut:** Erisbe (*Or-mindo*) San Francisco Spring Opera 1974.
Sang with major companies in HOL: Amster-dam; UK: Glyndebourne Fest; USA: Boston, St Paul, San Francisco Opera & Spring Opera, Santa Fe. **Roles with these companies incl** CAVALLI: Calisto★, Erisbe★ (*Ormindo*); EGK: Jeanne★ (*Ver-lobung in San Domingo*); GLUCK: Amor★ (*Orfeo ed Euridice*); JANACEK: Vixen★ (*Cunning Little Vixen*); VERDI: Nannetta★ (*Falstaff*). Gives recit-als. Appears with symphony orchestra. Mgmt: CAM/USA.

HENDRIKX, LODE. Bass. Belgian. Resident mem: Royal Flemish Opera, Antwerp, Belgium. Born 13 Mar 1927, Antwerp, Belgium. Wife Anne Van Den Eynde. Seven children. Studied: Consv of Ant-werp, Willem Ravelli, Belgium. **Debut:** Samuele (*Ballo in maschera*) Royal Flemish Opera, Ant-werp 1963. Previous occupations: salesman.

Sang with major companies in AUS: Salzburg Fest; BEL: Brussels; FRA: Lyon, Toulouse; FR GER: Hamburg, Kassel, Munich Staatsoper; ITA: Genoa, Milan La Scala, Palermo, Rome Opera, Trieste, Venice; MON: Monte Carlo; SWE: Stockholm; SWI: Geneva; UK: Glasgow Scottish, London Royal Opera. Roles with these companies incl d'ALBERT: Tommaso (*Tiefland*); BEETHOVEN: Rocco★ (*Fidelio*); BRITTEN: John Claggart (*Billy Budd*); DEBUSSY: Arkel★ (*Pelléas et Mélisande*); DESSAU: The Dragon (*Lanzelot*); MARTINU: Grigoris★ (*Griechische Passion*); MOZART: Sarastro (*Zauberflöte*); MUSSORGSKY: Pimen★(*Boris Godunov*); ROSSINI: Don Basilio★ (*Barbiere di Siviglia*); STRAVINSKY: Tiresias (*Oedipus Rex*); VERDI: Ramfis★(*Aida*), Grande Inquisitore (*Don Carlo*), Padre Guardiano★ (*Forza del destino*), Zaccaria★ (*Nabucco*), Fiesco (*Simon Boccanegra*); WAGNER: Daland (*Fliegende Holländer*), König Heinrich★ (*Lohengrin*), Pogner★ (*Meistersinger*), Gurnemanz★ (*Parsifal*), Fafner (*Rheingold, Siegfried*), Hunding★ (*Walküre*), Hagen (*Götterdämmerung*), Landgraf (*Tannhäuser*), König Marke★ (*Tristan und Isolde*). Res: Waterloo Str 37, 2600 Berchem, Belgium. Mgmt: SLZ/FRG.

HENZE, HANS WERNER. Conductor of opera and symphony; composer; operatic stage director. German. Born 1 Jul 1925, Gutersloh/Westfalen, Germany. Single. Studied: piano. Operatic training as asst cond at Wiesbaden, FR Ger. **Operatic debut:** Opernhaus Wiesbaden 1958. Symphonic debut: Berlin Phil 1967.
Conducted with major companies in FRA: Aix-en-Provence Fest; FR GER: Berlin Deutsche Oper, Frankfurt, Munich Staatsoper, Wiesbaden; HOL: Amsterdam; ITA: Milan La Scala, Rome Opera, Spoleto Fest; UK: Aldeburgh Fest, Edinburgh Fest, Scottish, Glyndebourne Fest, London Royal; USA: Santa Fe. **Operas with these companies incl** HENZE: *Bassariden★, Boulevard Solitude★, Cimarrón★, Elegy for Young Lovers★, Junge Lord★, König Hirsch/Re Cervo★, Landarzt★, Rachel, la Cubana★.* Conducted major orch in Europe, USA/Canada, Asia. **Operas composed:** all above plus those in COS Contemp Directories 1969 & 1975. Res: Marino/Rome, Italy. Mgmt: SOF/USA.

HERBÉ, MICHÈLE; née Herbé-Fouan. Dramatic soprano. French. Born 17 Feb 1940, Paris. Single. **Debut:** Musetta (*Bohème*) Opéra Comique 1965. Previous occupations: dancer. Awards: two First Prizes, Consv Supérieur de Musique, Paris; Médaille Vermeille Arts-Sciences-Lettres: Prize of Paris Instit.
Sang with major companies in BEL: Brussels, Liège; FRA: Aix-en-Provence Fest, Bordeaux, Lyon, Marseille, Nancy, Nice, Orange Fest, Paris, Rouen, Toulouse; SPA: Barcelona; SWI: Geneva. Roles with these companies incl BEETHOVEN: Leonore★ (*Fidelio*); BERLIOZ: Hero (*Béatrice et Bénédict*); FALLA: Salud★ (*Vida breve*); GIORDANO: Maddalena★ (*Andrea Chénier*); GLUCK: Amor (*Orfeo ed Euridice*); GOUNOD: Marguerite (*Faust*); LEONCAVALLO: Nedda★ (*Pagliacci*); MASCAGNI: Santuzza★ (*Cavalleria rusticana*); MASSENET: Salomé★ (*Hérodiade*); MENOTTI: Magda Sorel★ (*Consul*), Desideria

(*Saint of Bleecker Street*); MUSSORGSKY: Marina★ (*Boris Godunov*); OFFENBACH: Giulietta★ (*Contes d'Hoffmann*), Périchole★; POULENC: Mme Lidoine★ (*Dialogues des Carmélites*); PUCCINI: Musetta★ (*Bohème*), Minnie★ (*Fanciulla del West*), Cio-Cio-San★ (*Butterfly*), Giorgetta★ (*Tabarro*), Tosca★; RAVEL: Concepcion★ (*Heure espagnole*); STRAUSS, J: Rosalinde (*Fledermaus*); STRAUSS, R: Octavian★ (*Rosenkavalier*). Also BERG: Gräfin Geschwitz★ (*Lulu*); RAMEAU: Erinice (*Zoroastre*); HONEGGER: Aiglon★. **World premieres:** BONDON: (*Nuit foudroyée*) ORTF 1966, (*Arbres*) ORTF 1967. Video/Film—ORTF: (*Fille de Mme Angot*); RTB: (*Heure espagnole*). Gives recitals. Appears with symphony orchestra. Mgmt: GRE/FRA.

HERBERT, DORIS. Lyric soprano. German. Resident mem: Opernhaus, Essen. Born 26 Jan 1938, Bamberg, Germany. Husband Franz Neumann, occupation musician. Studied: Marla Vandelinn, Bamberg; Willi Domgraf-Fassbaender, Wilhelm Schoenherr, Nürnberg; Erna Berger, Essen. **Debut:** Lauretta (*Gianni Schicchi*) St Gallen, Switzerland 1961.
Sang with major companies in FR GER: Bielefeld, Dortmund, Düsseldorf-Duisburg, Essen, Krefeld, Mannheim, Wuppertal; SPA: Barcelona. Roles with these companies incl ADAM: Madeleine (*Postillon de Lonjumeau*); AUBER: Zerlina (*Fra Diavolo*); BEETHOVEN: Marzelline (*Fidelio*); DONIZETTI: Norina (*Don Pasquale*); FLOTOW: Lady Harriet (*Martha*); GAY/Britten: Lucy (*Beggar's Opera*); LORTZING: Baronin Freimann (*Wildschütz*), Marie (*Zar und Zimmermann*); MOZART: Despina (*Così fan tutte*), Zerlina (*Don Giovanni*), Blondchen (*Entführung aus dem Serail*), Susanna (*Nozze di Figaro*); OFFENBACH: Olympia (*Contes d'Hoffmann*); ORFF: Solo (*Carmina burana*); PUCCINI: Musetta (*Bohème*), Lauretta (*Gianni Schicchi*); ROSSINI: Rosina (*Barbiere di Siviglia*); STRAUSS, J: Adele (*Fledermaus*); STRAUSS, R: Zerbinetta (*Ariadne auf Naxos*), Sophie (*Rosenkavalier*); VERDI: Oscar (*Ballo in maschera*), Nannetta (*Falstaff*), Gilda (*Rigoletto*); WEBER: Aennchen (*Freischütz*); WEILL: Jenny (*Aufstieg und Fall der Stadt Mahagonny*). Video/Film: (*Gespenst von Canterville*); (*Comte Ory*); (*Schwarzer Peter*). Gives recitals. Appears with symphony orchestra. Mgmt: PAS/FRG.

HERBERT, RALPH. Stages/produces opera and is an actor & singer. American. Born 5 Aug 1909, Vienna, Austria. Wife Ada. Two children. Studied: Neues Wiener Konsv, Vienna; Helene Schemel, Franz Steiner, Ernst Tauber, Robert Weede; incl music, piano and voice. Operatic training as asst stage dir at Metropolitan Opera 1956-57. **Operatic debut:** as dram baritone: Amonasro (*Aida*) Volksoper Vienna 1936; as stage dir: *Bohème* Metropolitan Opera 1957-58. Theater debut: New Opera Co, New York 1945.
Sang with major companies in AUS: Vienna Volksoper; FR GER: Hamburg; MEX: Mexico City; SWI: Zurich; USA: Cincinnati, Fort Worth, Hartford, Houston, Milwaukee Florentine, New Orleans, New York Met & City Opera, Philadelphia Lyric, Pittsburgh, San Francisco Opera,

Seattle, Washington DC. **Roles with these companies incl** d'ALBERT: Sebastiano (*Tiefland*); BEETHOVEN: Don Pizarro (*Figaro*); BERG: Doktor (*Wozzeck*); BIZET: Escamillo (*Carmen*); CHARPENTIER: Père (*Louise*); DONIZETTI: Dulcamara (*Elisir*); GOUNOD: Méphistophélès (*Faust*); LEONCAVALLO: Tonio (*Pagliacci*); LORTZING: Baculus (*Wildschütz*); MASCAGNI: Alfio (*Cavalleria rusticana*); MOZART: Don Alfonso (*Così fan tutte*), Don Giovanni, Conte Almaviva & Figaro (*Nozze di Figaro*), Papageno (*Zauberflöte*); OFFENBACH: Coppélius etc (*Contes d'Hoffmann*), Don Andres (*Périchole*); PERGOLESI: Uberto (*Serva padrona*); PUCCINI: Marcello (*Bohème*), Gianni Schicchi, Sharpless (*Butterfly*), Scarpia (*Tosca*); ROSSINI: Figaro & Dott Bartolo (*Barbiere di Siviglia*), Slook (*Cambiale di matrimonio*), Dandini & Don Magnifico (*Cenerentola*); SMETANA: Kezal (*Bartered Bride*); STRAUSS, R: Musiklehrer (*Ariadne auf Naxos*), Baron Ochs (*Rosenkavalier*), Jochanaan (*Salome*); TCHAIKOVSKY: Eugene Onegin; THOMAS: Lothario (*Mignon*); VERDI: Falstaff, Iago (*Otello*), Rigoletto; WAGNER: Telramund (*Lohengrin*), Beckmesser (*Meistersinger*), Alberich (*Rheingold*, *Götterdämmerung*), Wolfram (*Tannhäuser*), Kurwenal (*Tristan und Isolde*); WOLF-FERRARI: Conte Gil (*Segreto di Susanna*). Also STRAUSS, J: Eisenstein & Falke & Frank (*Fledermaus*); STRAUSS, R: Waldner (*Arabella*), Harlekin (*Ariadne auf Naxos*), Faninal (*Rosenkavalier*); WAGNER: Klingsor (*Parsifal*), Alberich (*Siegfried*). Video–NBC TV: Tomsky (*Pique Dame*), Gianni Schicchi, Figaro (*Barbiere*), Figaro (*Nozze di Figaro*), Ochs (*Rosenkavalier*); NDR TV: Schicchi. **Directed/produced opera for major companies in** USA: Baltimore, Cincinnati, Fort Worth, Hawaii, Houston, Memphis, Milwaukee Florentine, New Orleans, New York Met & City Opera, Pittsburgh, Portland, Seattle, Washington DC. **Operas staged with these companies incl** AUBER: *Fra Diavolo*; BERG: *Wozzeck*; BIZET: *Carmen*; LORTZING: *Wildschütz*; MARTINU: *Comedy on the Bridge*; MASSENET: *Manon*; MENOTTI: *Telephone*; MEYEROWITZ: *Eastward in Eden*; MOZART: *Così fan tutte*, *Don Giovanni*, *Entführung aus dem Serail*, *Nozze di Figaro*, *Schauspieldirektor*, *Zauberflöte*; NICOLAI: *Lustigen Weiber*; OFFENBACH: *Contes d'Hoffmann*, *Périchole*, *Mariage aux lanternes*; PERGOLESI: *Serva padrona*; PUCCINI: *Gianni Schicchi*, *Butterfly*, *Suor Angelica*, *Tosca*; ROREM: *Robbers*; ROSSINI: *Barbiere di Siviglia*; SMETANA: *Bartered Bride*; STRAUSS, J: *Fledermaus*; STRAUSS, R: *Arabella*, *Ariadne auf Naxos**, *Rosenkavalier**, *Salome*; TCHAIKOVSKY: *Eugene Onegin*, *Pique Dame*; VERDI: *Aida*, *Falstaff*, *Rigoletto*, *Traviata*; WAGNER: *Fliegende Holländer**, *Lohengrin*, *Tannhäuser*; WEILL: *Dreigroschenoper*. Recorded for Columbia. Gives recitals. Appears with symphony orchestra. Teaches voice. Coaches repertoire. On faculty of School of Music, Univ of Michigan. **Res:** 580 Riverview Dr, Ann Arbor, MI 48104, USA. **Mgmt:** LLF/USA.

HERBERT, WALTER; né Walter Herbert Seligman. Conductor of opera and symphony. American. Gen Dir & Cond, San Diego Opera, CA 1969-76; Mus Dir, Opera/South, Jackson, MS. Born 18

Feb 1902, Frankfurt/Main. Divorced. One child. Studied: Vienna Akad, Arnold Schoenberg; incl piano, violin,. viola, clarinet. Operatic training as repetiteur at Opera Leipzig, Germany 1924-25. **Operatic debut:** *Carmen* Stadttheater Bern, Switzerland 1925. Previous occupation: mem San Francisco Symph 1939-43. Previous adm positions in opera: Opernchef, Volksoper, Vienna 1931-38; Dir, Opera in English, San Francisco, CA 1940-43; Gen Dir, New Orleans Opera House Assn, LA 1943-54; Gen Dir, Houston Grand Opera, TX 1955-72.

Conducted with major companies in AUS: Vienna Volksoper; FR GER: Düsseldorf-Duisburg, Frankfurt; MEX: Mexico City; POL: Warsaw; SWI: Geneva; USA: Cincinnati, Fort Worth, Houston, Jackson Opera/South, New Orleans, Philadelphia Lyric, San Diego, San Francisco Opera. **Operas with these companies incl** d'ALBERT: *Tiefland*; BEETHOVEN: *Fidelio**; BIZET: *Carmen**, *Djamileh*; CHARPENTIER: *Louise*; CIMAROSA: *Matrimonio segreto*; DELIUS: *Village Romeo and Juliet**; DONIZETTI: *Campanello*, *Don Pasquale*, *Elisir*, *Fille du régiment**, *Lucia*, *Rita*; DVORAK: *Rusalka**; FLOTOW: *Martha*; GIORDANO: *Andrea Chénier*; GLUCK: *Orfeo ed Euridice*; GOUNOD: *Faust*, *Roméo et Juliette*; HALEVY: *Juive*; HENZE: *Junge Lord*; HINDEMITH: *Hin und zurück*; HUMPERDINCK: *Hänsel und Gretel*, *Königskinder*; IBERT: *Angélique*; LEONCAVALLO: *Pagliacci*; LORTZING: *Waffenschmied*, *Wildschütz*, *Zar und Zimmermann*; MASCAGNI: *Cavalleria rusticana*; MASSENET: *Don Quichotte**, *Manon**, *Thaïs*; MENOTTI: *Consul*, *Globolinks**, *Medium**, *Old Maid and the Thief**, *Telephone*; MOORE: *Gallantry*; MOZART: *Così fan tutte*, *Don Giovanni*, *Entführung aus dem Serail*, *Schauspieldirektor*, *Nozze di Figaro*, *Zauberflöte*; MUSSORGSKY: *Boris Godunov*; NICOLAI: *Lustigen Weiber*; OFFENBACH: *Contes d'Hoffmann*; ORFF: *Mond*; PAISIELLO: *Barbiere di Siviglia*; PERGOLESI: *Serva padrona*; PONCHIELLI: *Gioconda*; PUCCINI: *Bohème**, *Gianni Schicchi*, *Butterfly**, *Manon Lescaut*, *Tabarro*, *Tosca**, *Turandot**; RAVEL: *Heure espagnole*; RIMSKY-KORSAKOV: *Coq d'or*; ROSSINI: *Barbiere di Siviglia**, *Cenerentola*, *Signor Bruschino*; SAINT-SAENS: *Samson et Dalila*; SMETANA: *Bartered Bride*; STRAUSS, J: *Fledermaus*; STRAUSS, R: *Elektra*, *Rosenkavalier*, *Salome*; THOMAS: *Mignon*; VERDI: *Aida**, *Ballo in maschera*, *Don Carlo*, *Falstaff*, *Forza del destino*, *Otello**, *Rigoletto*, *Traviata**, *Trovatore**, *Vespri*; WAGNER: *Fliegende Holländer**, *Lohengrin*, *Meistersinger*, *Rheingold**, *Walküre**, *Siegfried**, *Götterdämmerung*, *Tannhäuser*, *Tristan und Isolde*; WEBER: *Freischütz*; WEINBERGER: *Schwanda*; WOLF-FERRARI: *Segreto di Susanna*. Also KIENZL: *Evangelimann*; d'ALBERT: *Golem*. **World premieres:** PETER: *Rutenhof*, Stadttheater Bern, Swi 1931; TCHEREPNIN: *Hochzeit der Sobeïde* Volksoper, Vienna 1933. Conducted major orch in Europe, USA/Canada, Asia. **Res:** 2350 Sixth Ave, San Diego, CA, USA. [†Sep 14, '75]

HERIBAN, JOSEF. Lyric baritone. Czechoslovakian. Resident mem: National Theater, Prague. Born 23 Jul 1922, Trnava, CSR. Wife Dr

Álena Heribanova, occupation surgeon. Two children. Studied: Prof Anny Kornhauserova-Korinska, Rudolf Petrak, Margit Czessany, Bratislava; Tino Pattiera, Lunka Michelova, Prague. **Debut:** Moralès (*Carmen*) Slovak National Theater, Bratislava 1945.

Sang with major companies in CZE: Prague National; HOL: Amsterdam; POL: Warsaw; SPA: Barcelona. **Roles with these companies incl** BIZET: Escamillo (*Carmen*); DONIZETTI: Dott Malatesta (*Don Pasquale*); JANACEK: Harasta★‡ (*Cunning Little Vixen*); LEONCAVALLO: Tonio (*Pagliacci*); MOZART: Guglielmo (*Così fan tutte*); PUCCINI: Marcello★ (*Bohème*), Sharpless★ (*Butterfly*); ROSSINI: Figaro★ (*Barbiere di Siviglia*); TCHAIKOVSKY: Eugene Onegin★, Yeletsky (*Pique Dame*); VERDI: Renato★ (*Ballo in maschera*), Rodrigo★ (*Don Carlo*), Iago (*Otello*), Rigoletto★, Germont (*Traviata*), Conte di Luna (*Trovatore*). Also SMETANA: Tausendmark (*Brandenburgers in Bohemia*); DVORAK: Bohus (*Jakobin*). **World premieres:** CIKKER: Brutus (*Coriolanus*) National Theater, Prague 1974. Recorded for: Supraphon. Gives recitals. **Res:** Puchovska 12, 140 00 Prague 4, CSSR. Mgmt: PRG/CZE.

HERING, KARL-JOSEF. Heldentenor. German. Resident mem: Deutsche Oper, Berlin. Born 14 Feb, Westönnen, Germany. Wife Hedy. Five children. Studied: Franz Völker, Fred Husler, Max Lorenz. **Debut:** Max (*Freischütz*) Opernhaus Hannover 1958. Previous occupations: businessman. Awards: Kammersänger, Berlin Senate.

Sang with major companies in ARG: Buenos Aires; AUS: Bregenz Fest, Graz, Vienna Staatsoper & Volksoper; CAN: Toronto; FRA: Lyon, Marseille, Toulouse; FR GER: Berlin Deutsche Oper, Cologne, Düsseldorf-Duisburg, Frankfurt, Hamburg, Hannover, Karlsruhe, Kassel, Kiel, Krefeld, Mannheim, Saarbrücken, Stuttgart, Wiesbaden Hessisches Staatstheater, Wuppertal; GER DR: Berlin Staatsoper; ITA: Trieste; SPA: Barcelona; UK: London Royal Opera; YUG: Zagreb. **Roles with these companies incl** d'ALBERT: Pedro★ (*Tiefland*); BEETHOVEN: Florestan★ (*Fidelio*); BERG: Tambourmajor★ (*Wozzeck*); HINDEMITH: Robert (*Hin und zurück*); LEONCAVALLO: Canio (*Pagliacci*); MARSCHNER: Konrad‡ (*Hans Heiling*); STRAUSS, J: Alfred★ (*Fledermaus*); STRAUSS, R: Bacchus★ (*Ariadne auf Naxos*), Aegisth★ (*Elektra*); TCHAIKOVSKY: Gherman★ (*Pique Dame*); WAGNER: Erik★ (*Fliegende Holländer*), Walther★ (*Meistersinger*), Parsifal★, Siegmund★ (*Walküre*), Siegfried (*Siegfried★, Götterdämmerung★*), Tristan★; WEBER: Max★‡ (*Freischütz*). Gives recitals. Appears with symphony orchestra. Teaches voice. **Res:** Schopenhauerstr 44, Berlin, FR Ger.

HERLEA, NICOLAE; né Herle. Lyric & dramatic baritone. Romanian. Resident mem: Romanian Opera, Bucharest. Born 28 Aug 1927, Bucharest. Wife Dr Simona, occup physician. One child. Studied: Consv, Prof Aurel Contescu-Duca, Bucharest; Accad S Cecilia, Rome. **Debut:** Silvio (*Pagliacci*) Romanian Opera 1950. Awards: Gold Medals, Prague Spring Fest 1954; Canto Cont, Verviers 1957; Giuseppe Verdi, Milan 1963; Gvnmt of Romania: State Prize 1964, People's

Artist 1962, Cult Merit Order 1968, Rep Star Order 1971, Work Order 1974.

Sang with major companies in AUS: Salzburg Fest, Vienna Staatsoper; BEL: Brussels, Liège; BUL: Sofia;.CZE: Brno, Prague National & Smetana; FIN: Helsinki; FRA: Paris; GRE: Athens National; FR GER: Berlin Deutsche Oper, Hamburg, Stuttgart, Wiesbaden; GER DR: Berlin Staatsoper, Dresden, Leipzig; HUN: Budapest; ITA: Milan La Scala, Naples; POL: Warsaw; ROM: Bucharest; SPA: Barcelona, Majorca; UK: London Royal; USSR: Kiev, Leningrad Kirov, Moscow Bolshoi & Stanislavski, Tbilisi; USA: New York Metropolitan Opera; YUG: Belgrade. **Roles with these companies incl** BIZET: Escamillo★ (*Carmen*); BORODIN: Prince Igor★; DONIZETTI: Enrico★ (*Lucia*); GIORDANO: Carlo Gérard★ (*Andrea Chénier*); LEONCAVALLO: Tonio★‡ (*Pagliacci*); PUCCINI: Scarpia★ (*Tosca*); ROSSINI: Figaro★‡ (*Barbiere di Siviglia*); TCHAIKOVSKY: Eugene Onegin★, Yeletsky★ (*Pique Dame*); VERDI: Amonasro (*Aida*), Renato★ (*Ballo in maschera*), Rodrigo★ (*Don Carlo*), Ford★ (*Falstaff*), Don Carlo★ (*Forza del destino*), Iago★ (*Otello*), Rigoletto★‡, Germont★‡ (*Traviata*), Conte di Luna★ (*Trovatore*). Also GOUNOD: Valentin (*Faust*). **World premieres:** DUMITRESCU: Lazar (*Girl with Carnations*) Romanian Opera 1961. Recorded for: Electrecord, Falcon, Muza. Video/Film: Figaro (*Barbiere*); Renato (*Ballo in maschera*). Gives recitals. Appears with symphony orchestra. **Res:** 32 Dr Lister St, Bucharest 6, Romania. Mgmt: RIA/ROM.

HERLISCHKA, BOHUMIL. Stages/produces opera, theater & television. Czechoslovakian. Resident Stage Dir, Deutsche Oper am Rhein, Düsseldorf, FR Ger. Born 25 Apr 1919, Caslav, CSR. Wife Elfi. Studied: music, piano and voice.

Directed/produced opera for major companies in AUS: Vienna Volksoper; CZE: Prague National & Smetana; FR GER: Berlin Deutsche Oper, Darmstadt, Düsseldorf-Duisburg, Essen, Frankfurt, Hamburg, Kassel, Munich Staatsoper & Gärtnerplatz, Nürnberg, Stuttgart; ITA: Milan La Scala; SWI: Basel, Zurich. **Operas staged with these companies incl** BEETHOVEN: *Fidelio★*; BERLIOZ: *Damnation de Faust★*; BIZET: *Carmen*; BORODIN: *Prince Igor*; DEBUSSY: *Pelléas et Mélisande*; DONIZETTI: *Don Pasquale*; DVORAK: *Rusalka★*; GOUNOD: *Faust★*; HAYDN: *Mondo della luna*; JANACEK: *Cunning Little Vixen★, Excursions of Mr Broucek★, From the House of the Dead★, Jenufa★, Katya Kabanova★, Makropoulos Affair★*; LEONCAVALLO: *Pagliacci*; MASCAGNI: *Cavalleria rusticana*; MEYERBEER: *Prophète*; MOZART: *Don Giovanni★, Nozze di Figaro★, Zauberflöte*; NICOLAI: *Lustigen Weiber*; OFFENBACH: *Contes d'Hoffmann*; ORFF: *Carmina burana★, Kluge★*; POULENC: *Mamelles de Tirésias★*; PROKOFIEV: *Gambler★*; PUCCINI: *Bohème, Butterfly, Tosca★*; ROSSINI: *Barbiere di Siviglia, Guillaume Tell*; SHOSTAKOVICH: *Katerina Ismailova, Nose★*; SMETANA: *Bartered Bride, Dalibor, Secret, Two Widows*; STRAVINSKY: *Oedipus Rex, Rake's Progress*; SUCHON: *Whirlpool*; TCHAIKOVSKY: *Eugene Onegin★, Pique Dame★*; VERDI: *Aida, Ballo in maschera, Don*

Carlo, Otello*, *Rigoletto, Traviata;* WEBER: *Freischütz;* WEILL: *Aufstieg und Fall der Stadt Mahagonny**. Operatic Video/Film—TV: *Jenufa*.

HERMAN, ROBERT. American. Gen Mng, Greater Miami International Opera/Greater Miami Opera Assn, 1200 Coral Way, Miami, FL 1973- ; also Florida Family Opera, Opera Guild of Greater Miami. In charge of overall adm matters, art policy, mus, dram & tech matters & finances. Born 24 Feb 1925, Glendale, CA. Single. Studied: Univ of S California, Los Angeles. Plays the piano. Previous occupations: univ staff; operatic st dir. Form position adm, musical & theatrical: Asst Gen Mng, Metropolitan Opera, New York 1953-72. Awards: Cavaliere, Order of Merit Republic of Italy. Initiated major policy changes including, at Metropolitan Opera, year-round employment, with benefits for principals, chorus; involved in design of art areas of new opera house; Reorganized corporate structure of Opera Guild of Greater Miami, Inc. Mem of Bd of Dir, OPERA America; Music Panel, Fine Arts Council of Florida; Pres, Cultural Exec Council, Miami; Exec Commtt, Fla Advocates. **Res:** 3441 Poinciana Ave, Miami, FL, USA.

HERMANN, ROLAND. Lyric & dramatic baritone. German. Resident mem: Opernhaus Zurich, Switzerland. Born 17 Sep 1936, Bochum, Germany. Wife Eva Hermann-Krüll, occupation sociologist. Studied: Music Acad Frankfurt/Main, Prof Paul Lohmann; Music Acad Freiburg/Breisgau, Prof Margarethe von Winterfeld, FR Ger; Mo Flaminio Contini, Florence, Italy. **Debut:** Conte Almaviva (*Nozze di Figaro*) Opernhaus Trier, FR Ger 1967. Previous occupations: teacher of music and English at German HS. Awards: Prize, Intl Music Compt, Bayerischer Rundfunk 1961; Prize, Compt Music Acad, Stuttgart 1959; Schlshp of the German People's Study Fndt 1956-62.

Sang with major companies in ARG: Buenos Aires; FR GER: Cologne, Munich Staatsoper; SWI: Zurich. **Roles with these companies incl** BIZET: Escamillo* (*Carmen*); BUSONI: Doktor Faust*; DEBUSSY: Golaud* (*Pelléas et Mélisande*); FORTNER: Norfolk* (*Elisabeth Tudor*); GINASTERA: Silvio de Narni (*Bomarzo*); JANACEK: Forester* (*Cunning Little Vixen*); LEONCAVALLO: Tonio* (*Pagliacci*); LORTZING: Graf Eberbach* (*Wildschütz*), Peter I* (*Zar und Zimmermann*); MOZART: Don Alfonso* (*Così fan tutte*), Don Giovanni*, Conte Almaviva* (*Nozze di Figaro*); OFFENBACH: Coppélius etc* (*Contes d'Hoffmann*); ORFF: Solo* (*Carmina burana*); PUCCINI: Marcello* (*Bohème*); REIMANN: Graf von Lusignan* (*Melusine*); STRAUSS, R: Musiklehrer* (*Ariadne auf Naxos*), Graf* (*Capriccio*), Jochanaan* (*Salome*); STRAVINSKY: Empereur de Chine (*Rossignol*); TCHAIKOVSKY: Yeletsky* (*Pique Dame*); VERDI: Germont* (*Traviata*); WAGNER: Amfortas* (*Parsifal*), Gunther* (*Götterdämmerung*), Wolfram* (*Tannhäuser*). Also KRENEK: Karl V*. Recorded for: CBS, Serenus, HM-BASF, EMI, UER. Video/Film—WDR Cologne: Prometheus; (*Carmina burana*); Achill (*Penthesilea*). BR Munich: Lord Ruthven (*Vampyr*); Siegfried (*Genoveva*). SDR Stuttgart: Splendiano (*Djamileh*). SR Saarbrücken: Allazim (*Zaïde*). Gives recitals. Appears with symphony

orchestra. Teaches voice. Coaches repertoire. **Res:** Weinbergstr 68, CH-8006 Zurich, Switzerland, or Grüngürtelstr 50, D-5038 Cologne-Rodenkirchen, FR Ger. Mgmt: KHA/FRG; SLZ/FRG; SMD/FRG; ALL/UK.

HERNDON, THOMAS. Dramatic tenor. American. Resident mem: Staatsoper Hamburg; Staatsoper Stuttgart. Born 23 Jul 1937, Durham, NC, USA. Wife Judith, occupation pianist & organist. Two children. Studied: Westminster Choir Coll, Walter Johnson, NJ, USA; Acad of Vocal Arts, Sidney Dietch, Dorothy Di Scala, Philadelphia; Zurich Intl Opera Center, Dusolina Giannini; Fr Hertha Kalcher, Stuttgart. **Debut:** Ernesto (*Don Pasquale*) Heidelberg, Germany 1964. Awards: M B Rockefeller Fund, 3 grants: Acad of Vocal Arts, 3 yr schlshp.

Sang with major companies in AUS: Vienna Staatsoper; FR GER: Berlin Deutsche Oper, Darmstadt, Düsseldorf-Duisburg, Frankfurt, Hamburg, Hannover, Karlsruhe, Kassel, Mannheim, Munich Staatsoper, Nürnberg, Stuttgart; HOL: Amsterdam; ISR: Tel Aviv; ITA: Florence Maggio; SWI: Zurich. **Roles with these companies incl** DONIZETTI: Ernesto (*Don Pasquale*); EINEM: Hérault de Séchelles* (*Dantons Tod*); GOUNOD: Faust*; JANACEK: Steva*(*Jenufa*); LEONCAVALLO: Canio (*Pagliacci*); LORTZING: Baron Kronthal (*Wildschütz*); MASCAGNI: Turiddu (*Cavalleria rusticana*); MOZART: Belmonte* (*Entführung aus dem Serail*), Tamino* (*Zauberflöte*); MUSSORGSKY: Vassily Golitsin* (*Khovanshchina*); OFFENBACH: Hoffmann*; PUCCINI: Rodolfo* (*Bohème*), Pinkerton* (*Butterfly*), Cavaradossi* (*Tosca*); ROSSINI: Narciso* (*Turco in Italia*); SCHOENBERG: Aron*; SMETANA: Hans* (*Bartered Bride*); STRAUSS, R: Matteo* (*Arabella*), Bacchus*(*Ariadne auf Naxos*), Flamand* (*Capriccio*), Ein Sänger* (*Rosenkavalier*), Henry Morosus* (*Schweigsame Frau*); TCHAIKOVSKY: Lenski* (*Eugene Onegin*); VERDI: Riccardo* (*Ballo in maschera*), Don Carlo*, Ismaele* (*Nabucco*), Duca di Mantova* (*Rigoletto*), Alfredo* (*Traviata*), Manrico* (*Trovatore*); WAGNER: Erik* (*Fliegende Holländer*), Walther v d Vogelweide* (*Tannhäuser*). Gives recitals. Appears with symphony orchestra. Teaches voice. Coaches repertoire. **Res:** Auf der Bojewiese 7/1, 205 Hamburg 80, FR Ger. Mgmt: SLZ/FRG.

HERZ, JOACHIM. German. Op Dir, Städtisches Theater Leipzig, Opernhaus, Karl Marx Platz, 701 Leipzig; also Musikalische Komödie/Oper. In charge of art policy. Is also st dir/prod. Born 15 Jun 1924, Dresden. Wife Charlotte, occupation collaborator in husband's work. Studied: Staatliche Hochschule für Musik u Theater, Dresden; Humboldt Univ, Berlin, Ger DR. Plays the piano & clarinet. Previous occupations: lecturer; coach; st dir; tchr. Form positions primarily musical; St Dir, Landesoper Radebeul, Ger DR 1951-53; Komische Oper Berlin, Ger DR 1953-56; Bühnen der Stadt Köln 1956-57. Started with present company in 1957 as Oberspielleiter, in present position since 1959. World premieres at theaters under his management: BUTTING: *Plautus im Nonnenkloster* 1959; BUSH: *Guayana Johnny* 1966; HANELL: *Griechische Hochzeit* 1969; GEISLER: *Zerbro-*

chene Krug 1971, *Schatten* 1975; all at Leipzig. Awards: Nationalpreis der DDR, 1961 & 1971; Hon Member Bolshoi Theater, Moscow; Order of Merit, Gold; Kunstpreis, Leipzig; Member, Acad of Art, Ger DR. Initiated major policy changes working with Gen Int Karl Kayser since opening of Leipzig Opera; added Experimental Opera, exchange visits with var East European companies; incorporated amateur chorus of 160 into prof chorus of 90; expansion of repertoire incl new or little known works. Mem of Ger DR Center of Intl Theater Institute; at ITI; Head of Dept of Music Theater Members.

Directed/produced opera for major companies in ARG: Buenos Aires; AUS: Vienna Staatsoper; FRA: Paris; FR GER: Cologne, Hamburg; GER DR: Berlin Komische Oper & Staatsoper, Dresden, Leipzig; UK: London Royal; USSR: Moscow Bolshoi. **Operas staged with these companies incl** BORODIN: *Prince Igor;* BRITTEN: *Albert Herring;* DONIZETTI: *Favorite;* EGK: *Zaubergeige;* HANDEL: *Xerxes;* HENZE: *Junge Lord;* JANACEK: *Katya Kabanova;* MEYERBEER: *Huguenots;* MOZART: *Clemenza di Tito, Così fan tutte, Nozze di Figaro;* PROKOFIEV: *War and Peace;* PUCCINI: *Manon Lescaut;* ROSSINI: *Guillaume Tell;* SHOSTAKOVICH: *Katerina Ismailova;* TCHAIKOVSKY: *Maid of Orleans;* VERDI: *Don Carlo, Forza del destino;* WAGNER: *Fliegende Holländer, Rheingold, Meistersinger, Lohengrin, Tannhäuser; etc.* **Operatic world premieres staged:** HANELL: *Griechische Hochzeit* Leipzig, Ger DR 1969; MEYER: *Reiter in der Nacht* Staatsoper Berlin, Ger DR 1973. Video/Film: *Fliegende Holländer.* **Res:** Naunhofer Str 17, Leipzig 7027, Ger DR.

HESS, JOACHIM. Stages/produces opera, theater, film & television and is an author. German. Born 21 Nov 1925, Gelsenkirchen. Wife Brigitte. Studied: Städtische Bühnen, Kiel; also cello. **Operatic debut:** *Schule der Frauen* NDR TV, Hamburg 1958. Theater debut: Jungestheater, Hamburg 1952. Previous occupation: air pilot.

Directed/produced opera for major companies in FR GER: Düsseldorf-Duisburg, Hamburg, Munich Gärtnerplatz; ITA: Naples. **Operas staged with these companies incl** BEETHOVEN: *Fidelio;* BERG: *Wozzeck*★; BRITTEN: *Albert Herring;* LORTZING: *Zar und Zimmermann*★; MENOTTI: *Globolinks*★; MOZART: *Nozze di Figaro, Zauberflöte*★; PENDERECKI: *Teufel von Loudun*★; PUCCINI: *Bohème;* STRAUSS, R: *Arabella*★, *Elektra*★; WAGNER: *Meistersinger*★, *Tristan und Isolde*★. **Operatic world premieres:** KELEMEN: *Belagerungszustand* Staatsoper, Hamburg 1970. **Opera libretti:** *Belagerungszustand,* see prem. Teaches at Falkenbergschule, Munich. **Res:** Wilhelm Keim Str 9a, 8022 Grünwald/Munich, FR Ger. **Mgmt:** TAU/SWI.

HESSE, RUTH MARGOT. Dramatic mezzo-soprano. German. Resident mem: Deutsche Oper, Berlin; Staatsoper, Vienna. Born Wuppertal, Germany. **Debut:** Opernhaus, Lübeck, FR Ger 1960.

Sang with major companies in AUS: Salzburg Fest, Vienna Staatsoper; BEL: Brussels; BRA: Rio de Janeiro; FRA: Bordeaux, Lyon, Marseille, Nice, Orange Fest, Paris, Rouen, Strasbourg, Toulouse; GRE: Athens Fest; FR GER: Bayreuth Fest, Berlin Deutsche Oper, Hamburg Staatsoper, Munich Staatsoper, Stuttgart; HOL: Amsterdam; ITA: Bologna, Milan La Scala, Rome Teatro dell'Opera, Trieste, Turin, Venice; MEX: Mexico City; SPA: Barcelona; SWE: Stockholm; SWI: Geneva; UK: London Royal; USSR: Moscow Bolshoi; USA: Chicago. **Roles with these companies incl** BARTOK: Judith ★ (*Bluebeard's Castle*); BIZET: Carmen★; GLUCK: Orfeo★; MASCAGNI: Santuzza (*Cavalleria rusticana*); MUSSORGSKY: Marina ★ (*Boris Godunov*); OFFENBACH: Giulietta ★ (*Contes d'Hoffmann*); STRAUSS, J: Prinz Orlovsky ★ (*Fledermaus*); STRAUSS, R: Amme ★ (*Frau ohne Schatten*), Herodias ★ (*Salome*); STRAVINSKY: Jocasta ★ (*Oedipus Rex*); VERDI: Amneris ★ (*Aida*), Eboli ★ (*Don Carlo*), Dame Quickly ★ (*Falstaff*), Preziosilla ★ (*Forza del destino*), Federica ★ (*Luisa Miller*), Azucena ★ (*Trovatore*); WAGNER: Ortrud ★ ‡ (*Lohengrin*), Magdalene ★ (*Meistersinger*), Kundry ★ (*Parsifal*), Fricka (*Rheingold* ★ ‡, *Walküre* ★ ‡), Waltraute ★ ‡ (*Götterdämmerung*), Brangäne ★ ‡ (*Tristan und Isolde*). Recorded for: Westminster, Intercord. Gives recitals. Appears with symphony orchestra. Teaches voice. **Res:** Winklerstr 22, Berlin-Grünewald, FR Ger. **Mgmt:** VLA/AUS; HLB/FRA; SFM/USA.

HEYDUCK, PETER. Scenic and costume designer for opera, theater, television. Is a lighting designer; also a painter. German. Resident designer, Städtische Bühnen Nürnberg, FR Ger and at Schweizer Tourné Theater, Basel. Born 27 Nov 1924, Breslau. Wife Brigitta, occupation painter. Two children. Studied: Prof Hans Wildermann, Breslau; Eduard Sturm, Prof Helmut Jürgens, Munich. Prof training: Opernhaus Breslau. **Operatic debut:** sets & cost, *Bartered Bride* Städtische Bühnen Münster, FR Ger 1955. Theater debut: Städtische Bühnen Nürnberg 1955. Awards: Anerkennungspreis Salzburg; Kulturförderungspreis Nürnberg 1960.

Designed for major companies in AUS: Graz, Salzburg Fest, Vienna Volksoper; FR GER: Bonn, Cologne, Frankfurt, Nürnberg; GER DR: Berlin Staatsoper; ITA: Florence Comunale. **Operas designed for these companies incl** ADAM: *Postillon de Lonjumeau;* d'ALBERT: *Tiefland, Toten Augen;* BARTOK: *Bluebeard's Castle;* BEETHOVEN: *Fidelio*★; BIZET: *Carmen, Docteur Miracle;* BLACHER: *Romeo und Julia;* BORODIN: *Prince Igor;* DALLAPICCOLA: *Prigioniero;* DELIBES: *Roi l'a dit;* DESSAU: *Verurteilung des Lukullus;* DONIZETTI: *Don Pasquale, Lucia;* DVORAK: *Rusalka;* EGK: *Verlobung in San Domingo;* FLOTOW: *Martha;* GAY/Britten: *Beggar's Opera;* GLUCK: *Orfeo ed Euridice*★; GOUNOD: *Faust;* HENZE: *Junge Lord;* HINDEMITH: *Cardillac*★, *Mathis der Maler;* HUMPERDINCK: *Hänsel und Gretel, Königskinder;* JANACEK: *Jenufa;* LORTZING: *Wildschütz, Zar und Zimmermann;* MASCAGNI: *Cavalleria rusticana;* MOZART: *Così fan tutte, Entführung aus dem Serail, Finta giardiniera, Idomeneo, Mitridate, re di Ponto*★, *Nozze di Figaro*★, *Zauberflöte;* MUSSORGSKY: *Boris Godunov;* NICOLAI: *Lustigen Weiber*★; ORFF: *Bernauerin, Carmina burana*★, *Kluge;* PFITZNER: *Palestrina;* PONCHIELLI: *Gioconda*★; PROKOFIEV: *Fiery Angel;* PUCCINI: *Bohème, But-*

terfly, Tabarro, Tosca, Turandot;* ROSSINI: *Barbiere di Siviglia;* SMETANA: *Bartered Bride;* STRAUSS, J: *Fledermaus;* STRAUSS, R: *Elektra, Salome;* SUTERMEISTER: *Romeo und Julia;* TCHAIKOVSKY: *Eugene Onegin, Pique Dame;* VERDI: *Don Carlo, Falstaff, Otello, Rigoletto, Traviata;* WAGNER: *Fliegende Holländer, Meistersinger;* WEBER: *Freischütz;* WEILL: *Dreigroschenoper;* YUN: *Sim Tjong*, Traum des Liu-Tung.* Also YUN: *Geisterliebe.* **Operatic world premieres:** YUN: *Witwe des Schmetterlings* 1969; HENZE: *Floss der Medusa* 1972; both at Musiktheater Nürnberg; WOLPERT: *Eingebildete Kranke* Volksoper, Vienna 1975. Exhibitions of stage designs, paintings: Stadttheater Fürth 1972; Haus der Kunst, Munich. **Res:** Hammerwerkstr 16, Schwarzenbruck, FR Ger. **Mgmt:** SLZ/FRG; TAS/AUS.

HEYME, HANSGUENTHER. Stages/produces opera, theater, film & television. German. Born 22 Aug 1935, Bad Mergewtheim. Wife Helga David, occupation actress. Two children. Studied: Erwin Piscator. **Operatic debut:** *Wozzeck* Opernhaus Nürnberg.
   Directed/produced opera for major companies in FR GER: Cologne, Nürnberg. **Operas staged for these companies incl** BERG: *Wozzeck*;* WEILL: *Dreigroschenoper*.* Previous leading positions with major theater companies: Intendant & Thtr Dir, Bühnen des Schauspieles der Stadt Köln, Cologne. Teaches. **Res:** Cologne, FR Ger.

HEYSE, HANS-JOACHIM. German. Gen Int, Theater der Stadt Bonn, Am Böselagerhof 1, 5300 Bonn, FR Ger 1971- . In charge of overall adm matters. Is also a st dir. Born 29 Jun 1929. Wife Elfriede Schimmelschulze, occupation actress. One child. Background primarily theatrical. World premieres at theater under his management: VALDAMBRINI: *Gestiefelte Kater* Bonn 1975.

HICKLIN, TERRY L. American. Tour Dir/Mng, Southern Opera Theatre/Memphis Opera Theatre, Memphis State Univ, TN. In charge of overall adm matters, art policy. Is also a baritone. Born 21 Mar 1949, Springfield, MO. Wife Patricia, occupation singer. Studied: Southwest Missouri State Univ, Springfield; Memphis State Univ. Plays the piano. Started with present company 1971 as grad asst, singer; in present position since 1973. Awards: Natl Opera Inst Grant in Art Adm, 1973-75. Initiated major policy changes including establishment of Southern Opera Theatre, touring 5 states, with 175 performances for Civic Arts Councils, schools, etc; 8 res apprentice artists with nine-month contracts. Mem of Opera Advisory Panel, Tennessee Arts Commission. **Res:** 1701 York, Memphis, TN, USA.

HICKS, DAVID. Stages/produces opera. Also designs stage-lighting and is a singer & author. American. Born 3 Jun 1937, Philadelphia. Single. Studied: Temple University, Philadelphia; Martial Singher, Eleanor Steber; as asst to Tito Capobianco, Frank Corsaro, etc at New York City Opera; including music, piano, violin, clarinet, horn and voice. Operatic training as asst stage dir at New York City Opera 1965-72. **Operatic debut:** *Entführung aus dem Serail* New York City Opera

1967. Previous occupation: teacher, hotel & restaurant mngmt.
   Directed/produced opera for major companies in USA: Cincinnati, Hawaii, New York City Opera, Pittsburgh, Seattle. **Operas staged for these companies incl** BOITO: *Mefistofele*;* DONIZETTI: *Don Pasquale*, Fille du régiment*, Lucia*, Maria Stuarda*, Roberto Devereux*;* GINASTERA: *Bomarzo;* GOUNOD: *Faust;* MASCAGNI: *Cavalleria rusticana*;* MENOTTI: *Medium*, Old Maid and the Thief*;* MOZART: *Entführung aus dem Serail*, Nozze di Figaro*;* OFFENBACH: *Contes d'Hoffmann*;* PUCCINI: *Bohème*, Gianni Schicchi*, Butterfly*, Suor Angelica*, Tabarro*, Tosca;* SAINT-SAENS: *Samson et Dalila;* STRAVINSKY: *Oedipus Rex*;* VERDI: *Ballo in maschera*.* Teaches at Acad of Vocal Arts, Philadelphia. **Res:** 18 W 75 St, New York, USA. **Mgmt:** LLF/USA.

HIDER, RUTH MARIE. American. Asst Dir, New York City Opera, New York State Theater, Lincoln Center, New York. In charge of administrative matters and is a stage dir/prod and form mezzo-soprano. Born 3 Feb, Binghamton, NY. Single. Studied: New York Univ, School of Commerce, accounts and finance. Previous occupations: Dir, Merchandising & Promotion, Station WNBF AM-FM-TV, Binghamton. Form positions, primarily administrative & musical: Bd Mem, Tri-Cities Opera, Binghamton 1952-62. Started with present company 1963 as Adm Intern, Ford Fndt spons; in present position since 1965. Awards: Ford Fndt Fllshp, 3 years. **Res:** New York, NY, USA.

HILLEBRECHT, HILDEGARD. Dramatic soprano. German. Resident mem: Staatsoper Munich; Deutsche Oper Berlin. Husband Karl Robert Stöhr, occupation businessman. Studied: Profs Margarethe v Winterfeldt, Franziska Martienssen-Lohmann, Paul Lohmann. **Debut:** Leonora (*Forza del destino*) Freiburg 1950-51. Awards: Bayerische Kammersängerin, Bayerischer Verdienstorden, Bavarian Gvnmt.
   Sang with major companies in ARG: Buenos Aires; AUS: Salzburg Fest, Vienna Staatsoper; BEL: Brussels; BRA: Rio de Janeiro; CZE: Prague National; DEN: Copenhagen; FIN: Helsinki; FRA: Bordeaux, Nice, Strasbourg; GRE: Athens Fest; FR GER: Bayreuth Fest, Berlin Deutsche Oper, Cologne, Düsseldorf-Duisburg, Essen, Frankfurt, Hamburg, Hannover, Karlsruhe, Mannheim, Munich Staatsoper, Nürnberg, Saarbrücken, Stuttgart, Wiesbaden, Wuppertal; GER DR: Berlin Staatsoper, Dresden; HOL: Amsterdam; ITA: Venice; SPA: Barcelona; SWI: Geneva, Zurich; UK: Edinburgh Fest, London Royal; USA: New York Met, San Diego, San Francisco Opera. **Roles with these companies incl** BEETHOVEN: Leonore* (*Fidelio*); BERLIOZ: Didon (*Troyens*); BUSONI: Herzogin (*Doktor Faust*); DALLAPICCOLA: Madre* (*Prigioniero*), Mrs Fabian (*Volo di notte*); EGK: Cathleen* (*Irische Legende*); FORTNER: Elisabeth Tudor*; GLUCK: Iphigénie (*Iphigénie en Tauride*); HINDEMITH: Tochter des Cardillac, Ursula (*Mathis der Maler*); JANACEK: Jenufa*, Katya Kabanova*, Emilia Marty (*Makropoulos Affair*); MASCAGNI: Santuzza‡ (*Cavalleria rusti-*

càna); MOZART: Fiordiligi (Così fan tutte), Donna Anna & Donna Elvira★ (Don Giovanni), Ilia (Idomeneo), Contessa (Nozze di Figaro); OFFENBACH: Giulietta★ (Contes d'Hoffmann); PUCCINI: Manon Lescaut, Suor Angelica, Giorgetta (Tabarro), Tosca★; PURCELL: Dido; STRAUSS, J: Rosalinde (Fledermaus); STRAUSS, R: Arabella, Ariadne★‡ (Ariadne auf Naxos), Chrysothemis★ (Elektra), Färberin★ & Kaiserin★ (Frau ohne Schatten), Danae (Liebe der Danae), Marschallin★ (Rosenkavalier); TCHAIKOVSKY: Lisa (Pique Dame); VERDI: Aida, Amelia (Ballo in maschera), Elisabetta★ (Don Carlo), Alice Ford (Falstaff), Leonora (Forza del destino), Abigaille (Nabucco), Desdemona★ (Otello), Amelia (Simon Boccanegra), Leonora (Trovatore), Elena★ (Vespri); WAGNER: Senta (Fliegende Holländer), Elsa (Lohengrin), Eva (Meistersinger), Sieglinde★ (Walküre), Gutrune★ (Götterdämmerung), Elisabeth★ (Tannhäuser), Isolde★, Kundry★ (Parsifal); WEBER: Agathe (Freischütz). Recorded for: DG, Eurodisc. Appears with symphony orchestra.

HINDS, ESTHER C. Spinto. West Indian. Born 3 Jan 1943, Barbados, West Indies. Husband Earl S Brown, occupation music teacher, Board of Ed. Two children. Studied: Clyde Burrows, New York; Hartt Coll of Music, Helen Hubbard, Hartford, CT, USA. Debut: Erste Dame (Zauberflöte) New York City Opera 1970. Awards: Finalist Met Op Ntl Counc Aud; NFMC Compt, spons tour of Japan & Korea.

Sang with major companies in USA: Cincinnati, Houston, Jackson Opera/South, New York City Opera, San Diego. Roles with these companies incl BIZET: Micaëla★ (Carmen); MOZART: Donna Elvira★ (Don Giovanni); PUCCINI: Cio-Cio-San (Butterfly), Liù★ (Turandot). Also BARBER: Cleopatra★. Gives recitals. Appears with symphony orchestra. Teaches voice. Coaches repertoire. Res: 218 Tecumseh Ave, Mount Vernon, NY, USA. Mgmt: HUR/USA.

HINES, JEROME; né Jerome Heinz. Bass. American. Resident mem: Metropolitan Opera, New York. Born 8 Nov 1921, Hollywood, CA, USA. Wife Lucia Evangelista, occupation form opera singer. Four children. Studied: Gennaro Curci, Samuel Margolis, New York; Rocco Pandiscio. Debut: Monterone (Rigoletto) San Francisco Opera 1941. Previous occupations: chemist. Awards: Bliss Awd; Caruso Awd.

Sang with major companies in ARG: Buenos Aires; CAN: Montreal/Quebec, Toronto; FR GER: Bayreuth Fest, Munich Staatsoper; HUN: Budapest; ITA: Milan La Scala, Naples, Palermo, Turin; MEX: Mexico City; UK: Edinburgh Fest; USSR: Kiev, Leningrad Kirov, Moscow Bolshoi & Stanislavski, Tbilisi; USA: Cincinnati, Fort Worth, Hartford, Houston, Memphis, Milwaukee Florentine, Newark, New Orleans, New York Met, Philadelphia Grand & Lyric Opera, Pittsburgh, Portland, San Francisco Opera, Seattle. Roles with these companies incl BARTOK: Bluebeard‡; BELLINI: Rodolfo (Sonnambula); BOITO: Mefistofele; BRITTEN: Swallow (Peter Grimes); DEBUSSY: Arkel (Pelléas et Mélisande); DONIZETTI: Baldassare‡ (Favorite); GOUNOD: Méphistophélès★ (Faust); MO-

ZART: Don Giovanni★, Osmin (Entführung aus dem Serail), Sarastro★ (Zauberflöte); MUSSORGSKY: Boris Godunov★ & Varlaam (Boris Godunov), Dosifei (Khovanshchina); OFFENBACH: Coppélius etc (Contes d'Hoffmann); PONCHIELLI: Alvise (Gioconda); PUCCINI: Colline★ (Bohème); ROSSINI: Don Basilio★ (Barbiere di Siviglia); STRAVINSKY: Nick Shadow (Rake's Progress); THOMAS: Lothario (Mignon); VERDI: Ramfis★ (Aida), Attila★, Philip II★ (Don Carlo), Silva (Ernani), Padre Guardiano (Forza del destino), Conte Walter (Luisa Miller), Banquo (Macbeth), Zaccaria (Nabucco), Fiesco (Simon Boccanegra); WAGNER: König Heinrich‡ (Lohengrin), Gurnemanz (Parsifal), Wotan (Rheingold, Walküre), Landgraf (Tannhäuser), König Marke (Tristan und Isolde). Also HANDEL: Ercole; TCHAIKOVSKY: Gremin (Eugene Onegin). World premieres: HINES: Jesus (I Am the Way) So Orange, NJ 1959; BESANZON: Sutter (Golden Childe) NBC TV 1960. Recorded for: RCA, Columbia, London/Decca. Video/Film—CBC TV: Scenes from (Attila), (Mefistofele), (Don Quichotte), (Boris Godùnov). Gives recitals. Appears with symphony orchestra. Composed: I Am the Way. Res: South Orange, NJ, USA. Mgmt: SAM/USA.

HIRATA, KYOKO; née Oda. Dramatic soprano. Japanese. Divorced. Studied: Tokyo Arts Univ; Moscow Ntl Consv; Prof Alexander Kollo, Vienna; Musikhochschule, Prof Bosenius, Cologne; Prof Sonobe, Tokyo. Debut: Tatiana (Eugene Onegin) Consv Opera, Moscow 1967. Awards: Third Place, Intl Conc, Prague 1966; Schumann Prize, Zwickau, Ger DR 1965; First & Fifth Prize, Intl Opera Singer Conc, Sofia 1970.

Sang with major companies in FR GER: Saarbrücken; GER DR: Berlin Staatsoper; JPN: Tokyo Niki Kai; USSR: Leningrad Kirov, Moscow Bolshoi. Roles with these companies incl BEETHOVEN: Leonore (Fidelio); MOZART: Contessa (Nozze di Figaro); PUCCINI: Cio-Cio-San (Butterfly), Tosca; STRAUSS, R: Ariadne (Ariadne auf Naxos); TCHAIKOVSKY: Tatiana (Eugene Onegin); VERDI: Leonora (Forza del destino); WAGNER: Senta (Fliegende Holländer), Sieglinde (Walküre); WEBER: Agathe (Freischütz). Gives recitals. Appears with symphony orchestra. Teaches voice. On faculty of Music School, Tokyo. Res: Bogenstr 6, 56 Wuppertal 2, FR Ger.

HIRST, GRAYSON. Lyric tenor. American. Born 27 Dec 1939, Ojai, CA, USA. Single. Studied: Juilliard School of Music, Jennie Tourel, Christopher West, Tito Capobianco, New York; Music Acad of the West, Martial Singher, Santa Barbara, CA; UCLA Opera Theater, Dr Jan Popper, Los Angeles; Aspen Fest Music School, Jennie Tourel, Dr Elemer Nagy, Aspen, CO. Debut: Ormindo, Opera Socy of Washington, DC 1969. Awards: Ralph Corbett Fndt Intl Opera Fllshp.

Sang with major companies in USA: Boston, Cincinnati, Hartford, Houston, New York City Opera, Philadelphia Lyric, Pittsburgh, San Antonio, San Diego, San Francisco Spring, Washington DC. Roles with these companies incl BIZET: Don José (Carmen); BRITTEN: Peter Quint★ (Turn of the Screw); CAVALLI: Ormindo★;

CIMAROSA: Paolino (*Matrimonio segreto*); DE-BUSSY: Pelléas; DONIZETTI: Ernesto (*Don Pasquale*), Nemorino (*Elisir*), Tonio★ (*Fille du régiment*); FALLA: Maese Pedro (*Retablo de Maese Pedro*); FLOTOW: Lionel (*Martha*); FLOYD: Curley★ (*Of Mice and Men*); GOUNOD: Faust, Roméo★; HAYDN: Nancio (*Infedeltà delusa*); HINDEMITH: Roderick (*Long Christmas Dinner*); MASSENET: Des Grieux (*Manon*), Werther; MONTEVERDI: Nero★ (*Incoronazione di Poppea*); MOZART: Ferrando (*Così fan tutte*), Belmonte (*Entführung aus dem Serail*), Belfiore (*Finta giardiniera*), Alessandro★ (*Re pastore*), Tamino★ (*Zauberflöte*); NICOLAI: Fenton (*Lustigen Weiber*); OFFENBACH: Hoffmann; PUCCINI: Rodolfo (*Bohème*); ROSSINI: Almaviva (*Barbiere di Siviglia*); VERDI: Alfredo★ (*Traviata*). Also JANACEK: Vanya (*Katya Kabanova*); RAVEL: Gonzalve (*Heure espagnole*); MENOTTI: Magician (*Consul*); SEARLE: Poprishchin (*Diary of a Madman*); MOZART: Oebalus★ (*Apollo et Hyacinthus*); WEISGALL: Young Boy (*Purgatory*); BERLIOZ: Iopas★ (*Troyens II*). **World premieres:** PASATIERI: Young Conductor (*Divina*) Juilliard Opera Theater 1966; Guiscardo (*Padrevia*) Brooklyn College Opera 1967; ZADOR: Alfons (*Scarlet Mill*) Brooklyn College Opera 1968; GINASTERA: Orsino (*Beatrix Cenci*) Opera Socy of Washington, DC 1971; THOMSON: Lord Byron, American Opera Center/Juilliard School, NY 1972; STARER: Pantagleize, Brooklyn College Opera 1973; ROREM: Teacher/Barbarian Chief (*Bertha*) Alice Tully Hall/Lincoln Center 1973; AITKEN: First Tenor (*Fables*) New York Chamber Soloists/Library of Congress 1975. Video—NET Opera Theater: Belmonte (*Entführung aus dem Serail*). Gives recitals. Appears with symphony orchestra. Teaches voice. Coaches repertoire. **Res:** 215 W 75 St, New York, NY 10023, USA. Mgmt: HUR/USA.

HIRTE, KLAUS. Character baritone. German. Resident mem: Württembergische Staatsoper, Stuttgart. Born 12 Dec 1937, Berlin. Wife Alice. Three children. Studied: Staatl Hochschule für Musik, Prof Hans Hager, Stuttgart; Thomas Tipton. **Debut:** Dritter Edler (*Lohengrin*) Staatsoper Stuttgart 1964. Previous occupations: toolmaker, soldier & paratrooper. Awards: Max Reinhardt Plaque, Salzburg Fest.
  Sang with major companies in AUS: Salzburg Fest; FR GER: Bayreuth Fest, Bonn, Cologne, Düsseldorf-Duisburg, Frankfurt, Hannover, Karlsruhe, Mannheim, Munich Staatsoper, Nürnberg, Stuttgart; ITA: Venice; POR: Lisbon; USA: Chicago, San Antonio. **Roles with these companies incl** BEETHOVEN: Don Pizarro (*Fidelio*); DONIZETTI: Don Pasquale, Dulcamara (*Elisir*); MOZART: Don Alfonso (*Così fan tutte*), Figaro (*Nozze di Figaro*), Papageno (*Zauberflöte*); WAGNER: Beckmesser (*Meistersinger*), Klingsor (*Parsifal*), Alberich (*Rheingold, Siegfried, Götterdämmerung*), Kurwenal (*Tristan und Isolde*). **Res:** Döringstr 10, 7000 Stuttgart 80, FR Ger. Mgmt: SLZ/FRG; MAA/USA.

HITE, CATHARINE L; née Catharine Farrington Leavey. American. Opera Coord, Hawaii Opera Theatre of the Honolulu Symphony Society, 1000 Bishop St, Honolulu, HI 96813, 1972- . In charge of adm matters. Husband Robert A, occupation trust officer/Asst VP, Hawaiian Trust Co. Three children. Studied: Coll of William & Mary, Williamsburg, VA. Previous occupations: Educt Dept, Honolulu Acad of Arts & National Gallery of Art, Washington DC; Office of Chief Curator, Ntl Gallery. Background primarily adm. Awards: Phi Beta Kappa. **Res:** Honolulu, Hawaii, USA.

HOENE, BARBARA; née Niemann. Lyric soprano. German. Resident mem: Staatsoper Dresden, Ger DR. Born 4 Feb 1944, Cottbus, Germany. Husband Klaus, occupation violinist. One child. Studied: Hochschule für Musik, Leipzig, Prof Seipt, Maria Croonen, Johannes Kemter. **Debut:** Fiordiligi (*Così fan tutte*) Opernhaus Leipzig, Ger DR 1964. Awards: Prizewinner Compt for Opera Singers, Ministry Berlin 1971.
  Sang with major companies in GER DR: Berlin Komische Oper & Staatsoper, Dresden, Leipzig; USSR: Leningrad Kirov. **Roles with these companies incl** BEETHOVEN: Marzelline★ (*Fidelio*); BIZET: Micaëla★ (*Carmen*); CIMAROSA: Carolina★ (*Matrimonio segreto*); GLUCK: Euridice★; HANDEL: Galatea★, Ginevra★ (*Ariodante*), Deidamia★, Romilda★ (*Xerxes*); LEONCAVALLO: Nedda (*Pagliacci*); LORTZING: Baronin Freimann★ (*Wildschütz*), Marie (*Zar und Zimmermann*); MENOTTI: Amelia (*Amelia al ballo*); MOZART: Fiordiligi★ (*Così fan tutte*), Pamina★ (*Zauberflöte*); ORFF: Kluge★; PAISIELLO: Rosina★ (*Barbiere di Siviglia*); STRAUSS, R: Sophie★ (*Rosenkavalier*); VERDI: Nannetta★ (*Falstaff*). Also TCHAIKOVSKY: Nastasja (*Sorceress*). Gives recitals. Appears with symphony orchestra. Coaches repertoire. **Res:** Grundstr 71b, 8054 Dresden, Ger DR. Mgmt: KDR/GDR.

HOFFMAN, GRACE; née Goldie Hoffman. Dramatic mezzo-soprano. American. Resident mem: Württembergische Staatsoper, Stuttgart; Staatsoper, Vienna. Born 14 Jan 1925, Cleveland, O, USA. Single. Studied: Western Reserve Univ, Lila Robeson, Cleveland; Grant Garnell, New York; Manhattan School of Music, Friedrich Schorr, New York; Maria Wetzelsberger, Stuttgart; Mario Basiola, Milan. **Debut:** Mamma Lucia (*Cavalleria rusticana*) Wagner Opera Co, New York, 1951. Previous occupations: schoolteacher, receptionist, salesgirl. Awards: Blanche Thebom Schlshp; Vercelli Prize; Fulbright Schlshp; Kammersängerin.
  Sang with major companies in ARG: Buenos Aires; AUS: Vienna Staatsoper; DEN: Copenhagen; FRA: Bordeaux, Lyon, Marseille, Nancy, Nice, Paris, Strasbourg; GRE: Athens Fest; FR GER: Bayreuth Fest, Berlin Deutsche Oper, Cologne, Darmstadt, Düsseldorf-Duisburg, Frankfurt, Hamburg, Karlsruhe, Mannheim, Munich Staatsoper, Stuttgart, Wiesbaden; GER DR: Dresden; HOL: Amsterdam; ITA: Bologna, Florence Maggio & Comunale, Genoa, Milan La Scala, Naples, Palermo, Rome Opera, Trieste, Venice; POR: Lisbon; SPA: Barcelona; SWI: Basel, Geneva, Zurich; UK: Edinburgh Fest, London Royal; USA: Chicago, Miami, New York Met, Philadelphia Lyric, San Francisco Opera. **Roles with these companies incl** BARTOK: Judith (*Bluebeard's Castle*); BELLINI: Adalgisa★ (*Norma*); BERLIOZ: Cassandre (*Troyens*); BIZET: Car-

men; CILEA: Princesse de Bouillon (*A. Lecouvreur*); DEBUSSY: Geneviève★ (*Pelléas et Mélisande*); DONIZETTI: Elisabetta (*Maria Stuarda*); GLUCK: Orfeo; HANDEL: Cornelia (*Giulio Cesare*); JANACEK: Kostelnicka★ (*Jenufa*), Kabanikha★ (*Katya Kabanova*); MASCAGNI: Santuzza★ (*Cavalleria rusticana*); MOZART: Dorabella (*Così fan tutte*); MUSSORGSKY: Marina (*Boris Godunov*); SMETANA: Hata (*Bartered Bride*); STRAUSS, R: Klytämnestra★ (*Elektra*), Amme★ (*Frau ohne Schatten*), Herodias★ (*Salome*); STRAVINSKY: Jocasta★ (*Oedipus Rex*); VERDI: Amneris★ (*Aida*), Ulrica★ (*Ballo in maschera*), Eboli★ (*Don Carlo*), Dame Quickly (*Falstaff*), Preziosilla (*Forza del destino*), Azucena★ (*Trovatore*); WAGNER: Ortrud★ (*Lohengrin*); Kundry★ (*Parsifal*), Erda (*Rheingold*), Fricka (*Rheingold*★ & *Walküre*★), Waltraute★ (*Götterdämmerung*), Venus★ (*Tannhäuser*), Brangäne★ (*Tristan und Isolde*). Recorded for: various labels. Gives recitals. Appears with symphony orchestra. Res: Bergstr 19, 7441 Neckartailfingen, FR Ger. Mgmt: IBB/UK.

HOFFMANN, HORST. Lyric tenor. German. Resident mem: Staatsoper, Munich; Volksoper, Vienna. Born 13 Jun 1935, Oppeln, Poland. Wife Hannelore. One child. Studied: Musikhochschule, Otto Köhler, Hannover.

Sang with major companies in AUS: Bregenz Fest, Graz, Vienna Staatsoper & Volksoper; FRA: Lyon, Marseille, Rouen, Strasbourg; FR GER: Bayreuth Fest, Berlin Deutsche Oper, Bielefeld, Bonn, Cologne, Darmstadt, Dortmund, Düsseldorf-Duisburg, Frankfurt, Hamburg, Hannover, Kassel, Kiel, Mannheim, Munich Staatsoper & Gärtnerplatz, Nürnberg, Stuttgart, Wuppertal; GER DR: Berlin Staatsoper; HOL: Amsterdam; ITA: Venice; POR: Lisbon; SWI: Basel, Geneva, Zurich. Roles with these companies incl AUBER: Lorenzo (*Fra Diavolo*); BERLIOZ: Faust★ (*Damnation de Faust*); BORODIN: Vladimir (*Prince Igor*); CIKKER: Flüchtling (*Play of Love*); DONIZETTI: Tenor★ (*Convenienze/Viva la Mamma*), Nemorino★ (*Elisir*), Edgardo (*Lucia*); EGK: Christoph★ (*Verlobung in San Domingo*); GLUCK: Pylade (*Iphigénie en Tauride*); JANACEK: Boris★ (*Katya Kabanova*); MOZART: Ferrando★ (*Così fan tutte*), Belmonte★ (*Entführung aus dem Serail*), Idomeneo, Tamino★ (*Zauberflöte*); MUSSORGSKY: Shuisky★ (*Boris Godunov*), Gritzko (*Fair at Sorochinsk*); PUCCINI: Rodolfo★ (*Bohème*), Rinuccio (*Gianni Schicchi*), Pinkerton★ (*Butterfly*); SMETANA: Hans★ (*Bartered Bride*); STRAUSS, J: Eisenstein & Alfred (*Fledermaus*); STRAUSS, R: Matteo★ (*Arabella*), Leukippos (*Daphne*), Ein Sänger (*Rosenkavalier*); VERDI: Alfredo★ (*Traviata*); WAGNER: Walther v d Vogelweide★ (*Tannhäuser*); WEBER: Max★ (*Freischütz*). Also VERDI: Macduff★ (*Macbeth*). Video—ZDF TV: Ritter Huga (*Undine*). Appears with symphony orchestra. Mgmt: SLZ/FRG.

HOFMANN, HUBERT. Bass-baritone. Austrian. Resident mem: Württembergische Staatsoper, Stuttgart.

Sang with major companies in FRA: Paris; FR GER: Bielefeld, Hamburg, Nürnberg, Stuttgart; ITA: Venice; SWI: Zurich; UK: London Royal; USA: Chicago; et al. Roles with these companies incl BORODIN: Prince Igor; ORFF: König (*Kluge*); STRAUSS, R: Orest (*Elektra*), Jochanaan (*Salome*); VERDI: Padre Guardiano (*Forza del destino*); WAGNER: Holländer, Hans Sachs (*Meistersinger*), Amfortas & Gurnemanz (*Parsifal*), Wotan (*Rheingold, Walküre*), Wanderer (*Siegfried*); et al.

HÖISETH, KOLBJÖRN. Dramatic & Heldentenor. Norwegian. Resident mem: Royal Opera, Stockholm. Born 29 Dec 1932, Börsa, Norway. Wife Manol. One daughter. Studied: Egil Nordsjö, Oslo; Ragnar Hultén, Set Svanholm, Stockholm; Kungl Musikhögskolan, Stockholm. Debut: Siegmund (*Walküre*) Royal Opera, Stockholm 1959. Awards: Harriet Cohen Intl Music Awd; The Opera Medal 1966; Set Svanholm Memorial stipd 1974.

Sang with major companies in DEN: Copenhagen; FIN: Helsinki; FRA: Bordeaux, Lyon; FR GER: Berlin Deutsche Oper, Düsseldorf-Duisburg, Hannover, Kassel, Kiel; NOR: Oslo; SWE: Drottningholm Fest, Stockholm; UK: London Royal Opera; USA: New York Met. Roles with these companies incl BERG: Tambourmajor★ (*Wozzeck*); BIZET: Don José (*Carmen*); BUSONI: Mephisto (*Doktor Faust*); GLUCK: Admetos (*Alceste*), Pylade (*Iphigénie en Tauride*); JANACEK: Laca★ (*Jenufa*); LEONCAVALLO: Canio (*Pagliacci*); MUSSORGSKY: Shuisky (*Boris Godunov*); ROSSINI: Arnold (*Guillaume Tell*); STRAUSS, R: Aegisth (*Elektra*), Herodes★ (*Salome*); TCHAIKOVSKY: Gherman★ (*Pique Dame*); VERDI: Radames (*Aida*), Don Carlo★, Ismaele (*Nabucco*), Otello★; WAGNER: Erik (*Fliegende Holländer*), Lohengrin★, Walther (*Meistersinger*), Parsifal★, Loge★ (*Rheingold*), Siegmund★ (*Walküre*), Siegfried (*Siegfried*★, *Götterdämmerung*★), Tannhäuser, Tristan★. Res: Olshammarsgatan 56, Bandhagen, Sweden.

HOLDORF, UDO KARL. Dramatic tenor. German. Resident mem: Deutsche Oper am Rhein, Düsseldorf-Duisburg. Born 10 Jul 1946, Bonn, Germany. Wife Janet Belle Wood, occupation pianist. Studied: Prof Ellen Bosenius, Prof Josef Metternich, Mo Francesco Carrino. Debut: Otello, Stadttheater Würzburg, FR Ger 1971. Awards: Sixth place winner, Intl Compt l'Echo des Travailleurs, Verviers; Fourth place Maria Canals Conc Intl, Barcelona.

Sang with major companies in FR GER: Düsseldorf-Duisburg. Roles with these companies incl BERG: Hauptmann★ (*Wozzeck*); DONIZETTI: Edgardo★ (*Lucia*); GIORDANO: Andrea Chénier★; JANACEK: Broucek★ (*Excursions of Mr Broucek*), Boris★ (*Katya Kabanova*), Albert Gregor★ (*Makropoulos Affair*); LEONCAVALLO: Canio★ (*Pagliacci*); PUCCINI: Des Grieux★ (*Manon Lescaut*), Luigi★ (*Tabarro*), Calaf★ (*Turandot*); STRAUSS, R: Matteo★ (*Arabella*), Herodes★ (*Salome*); VERDI: Otello★; WAGNER: Walther v d Vogelweide★ (*Tannhäuser*). Gives recitals. Appears with symphony orchestra. Teaches voice. **Res:** Nagelsweg 34, Düsseldorf, FR Ger. Mgmt: PAS/FRG.

HOLLEY, WILLIAM; né Cecil William Holley Jr. Dramatic tenor. American. Resident mem: Deutsche Oper am Rhein, Düsseldorf. Born 4 Dec 1930, Bristol, FL, USA. Divorced. Studied: Indiana Univ, Anna Kaskas, Frank St Leger, Paul Mathen, Bloomington, IN; Oklahoma Baptist Univ, Louis Cunningham, USA. **Debut:** Faust, Salzburg Landestheater 1961. Awards: Winner Stud Div NFMC Cont; Winner Chicago Young Artists' Awd.

Sang with major companies in AUS: Salzburg Fest, Vienna Staatsoper & Volksoper; DEN: Copenhagen; FRA: Nice; GRE: Athens Fest; FR GER: Berlin Deutsche Oper, Cologne, Dortmund, Düsseldorf-Duisburg, Essen, Frankfurt, Hamburg, Hannover, Karlsruhe, Kassel, Mannheim, Munich Staatsoper, Stuttgart; HOL: Amsterdam; ITA: Naples; SPA: Barcelona; UK: Edinburgh Fest; USA: San Francisco Opera & Spring Opera. **Roles with these companies incl** BIZET: Don José★ (*Carmen*); GIORDANO: Andrea Chénier★; GOUNOD: Faust; JANACEK: Laca★ (*Jenufa*); MENOTTI: Lover (*Amelia al ballo*); MOZART: Tito★ (*Clemenza di Tito*), Ferrando (*Così fan tutte*), Don Ottavio (*Don Giovanni*), Belmonte (*Entführung aus dem Serail*), Belfiore (*Finta giardiniera*), Tamino★ (*Zauberflöte*); NICOLAI: Fenton (*Lustigen Weiber*); OFFENBACH: Hoffmann★; PUCCINI: Rodolfo★ (*Bohème*), Pinkerton★ (*Butterfly*), Des Grieux★ (*Manon Lescaut*), Ruggero (*Rondine*), Luigi★ (*Tabarro*), Cavaradossi★ (*Tosca*), Calaf★ (*Turandot*); SMETANA: Hans★ (*Bartered Bride*); STRAUSS, R: Ein Sänger★ (*Rosenkavalier*); TCHAIKOVSKY: Lenski (*Eugene Onegin*); VERDI: Riccardo (*Ballo in maschera*), Don Carlo★, Duca di Mantova (*Rigoletto*), Alfredo (*Traviata*). Video/Film: Angelo Custode (*Rappresentazione*). Appears with symphony orchestra. **Res:** Düsseldorf, FR Ger. Mgmt: SLZ/FRG; OSP/USA.

HOLLOWAY, DAVID. Lyric baritone. American. Resident mem: New York City Opera. Born 12 Nov 1942, Grandview, MO, USA. Married. One child. Studied: Univ of Kansas, Robert Baustian, Lawrence, KA; Santa Fe Opera Apprentice Prgr, NM, USA; Luigi Ricci, Rome. **Debut:** Belcore (*Elisir*) Kansas City Lyric Opera 1968. Previous occupations: voice faculty, Univ of Kansas 1966-69. Awards: National Opera Inst Grant 1971-72; M B Rockefeller Fund 1970; prizewinner San Francisco Opera Aud 1968.

Sang with major companies in CAN: Ottawa; USA: Baltimore, Boston, Kansas City, New Orleans, New York City Opera, Omaha, San Diego, Santa Fe, Washington DC. **Roles with these companies incl** DELIUS: Dark Fiddler★ (*Village Romeo and Juliet*); DONIZETTI: Dott Malatesta★ (*Don Pasquale*); FLOYD: George Milton★ (*Of Mice and Men*); MENOTTI: John Sorel (*Consul*), Bob (*Old Maid and the Thief*); MOZART: Guglielmo★ (*Così fan tutte*), Nardo★ (*Finta giardiniera*), Conte Almaviva (*Nozze di Figaro*), Papageno★ (*Zauberflöte*); OFFENBACH: Paquillo★ (*Périchole*); ORFF: Solo★ (*Carmina burana*);

PUCCINI: Marcello★ (*Bohème*), Gianni Schicchi★, Sharpless★ (*Butterfly*), Lescaut★ (*Manon Lescaut*); ROSSINI: Figaro★ (*Barbiere di Siviglia*), Dandini (*Cenerentola*); STRAVINSKY: Nick Shadow (*Rake's Progress*). Also LIGETI: Baritone solo (*Aventures/Nouvelles Aventures*). Gives recitals. Appears with symphony orchestra. **Res:** New York, NY, USA. Mgmt: CAM/USA.

HOLLREISER, HEINRICH. Conductor of opera and symphony. German & Austrian. Born 24 Jun 1913, Munich. Wife Marianne. One child. Studied: Staatl Akad der Tonkunst, Munich; Karl Elmendorff; incl piano, organ, violin, viola. Plays the piano. Operatic training as repetiteur & asst cond at Staatstheater Wiesbaden, Germany 1932-35. **Operatic debut:** Carmen Staatstheater Wiesbaden 1933. Symphonic debut: Orch des Landestheaters Darmstadt 1938. Awards: Hon Prof, by Austrian President 1956; Austrian Cross of Merit first class for Arts & Sciences 1962; Bavarian Order of Merit 1973. Previous adm positions in opera: Gen Mus Dir, Städt Bühnen Düsseldorf 1945-52; First Cond, Staatsoper Vienna 1952-61; Chief Cond, Deutsche Oper Berlin, FR Ger 1961-64.

Conducted with major companies in AUS: Bregenz Fest, Vienna Staatsoper & Volksoper; BEL: Brussels; CAN: Montreal/Quebec; DEN: Copenhagen; FIN: Helsinki; FRA: Marseille; GRE: Athens Fest; FR GER: Bayreuth Fest, Berlin Deutsche Oper, Cologne, Düsseldorf-Duisburg, Hamburg, Kiel, Mannheim, Munich Staatsoper, Stuttgart, Wiesbaden; GER DR: Berlin Staatsoper; HOL: Amsterdam; ITA: Florence Maggio, Palermo; NOR: Oslo; SPA: Barcelona; SWE: Stockholm Royal; SWI: Geneva; UK: Edinburgh Fest, London Royal Opera; USA: New York Metropolitan Opera; YUG: Zagreb, Belgrade. **Operas with these companies incl** d'ALBERT: *Tiefland;* AUBER: *Fra Diavolo;* BARTOK: *Bluebeard's Castle;* BEETHOVEN: *Fidelio★;* BERG: *Lulu★, Wozzeck;* BIZET: *Carmen;* BRITTEN: *Albert Herring, Peter Grimes;* CORNELIUS: *Barbier von Bagdad‡;* EINEM: *Dantons Tod, Prozess;* GLUCK: *Alceste;* GOTOVAC: *Ero der Schelm;* HANDEL: *Giulio Cesare;* HAYDN: *Mondo della luna;* HINDEMITH: *Mathis der Maler;* HONEGGER: *Antigone★;* HUMPERDINCK: *Hänsel und Gretel★;* JANACEK: *Jenufa;* LEONCAVALLO: *Pagliacci;* LORTZING: *Waffenschmied, Wildschütz, Zar und Zimmermann;* MASCAGNI: *Cavalleria rusticana‡;* MENOTTI: *Saint of Bleecker Street;* MEYERBEER: *Prophète;* MOZART: *Così fan tutte★, Don Giovanni★, Entführung aus dem Serail★, Schauspieldirektor, Nozze di Figaro★, Zauberflöte★;* MUSSORGSKY: *Boris Godunov;* OFFENBACH: *Contes d'Hoffmann;* ORFF: *Antigonae, Bernauerin, Carmina burana★;* PFITZNER: *Palestrina★;* POULENC: *Dialogues des Carmélites;* PUCCINI: *Bohème, Butterfly, Tosca, Turandot;* SMETANA: *Bartered Bride, The Kiss;* STRAUSS, J: *Fledermaus;* STRAUSS, R: *Arabella★, Ariadne auf Naxos★, Capriccio★, Elektra★, Frau ohne Schatten★, Rosenkavalier★, Salome★;* STRAVINSKY: *Oedipus Rex★, Rake's Progress;* VERDI: *Aida★, Don Carlo★, Forza del destino, Otello, Traviata, Trovatore;* WAGNER: *Fliegende Holländer★, Lohengrin★, Meistersin-*

ger★, Parsifal★, Rheingold★, Walküre★, Siegfried★, Götterdämmerung★, Tannhäuser★, Tristan und Isolde★; WEBER: Freischütz★, Oberon; WOLF-FERRARI: Segreto di Susanna. **World premieres:** MILHAUD: Orestie Part III, Deutsche Oper Berlin 1963; SESSIONS: Montezuma Deutsche Oper Berlin 1964; BLACHER: 200,000 Taler Deutsche Oper Berlin 1969. Recorded for Eurodisc, Ariola, EMI. Video—ZDF TV: 200,000 Taler, Barbier von Bagdad. Conducted major orch in Europe, Cent/S America, Asia, Africa. **Res:** Rohdestr 3, 8 Munich 60, FR Ger. Mgmt: SLZ/FRG; conc: KHA/FRG.

HOLLWEG, WERNER FRIEDRICH. Lyric tenor. German. Born 13 Sep 1936, Solingen, FR Ger. Wife Constance Daucha, occupation secy. One child. Studied: Nordwestdeutsche Musikakad, Prof Husler, Detmold. **Debut:** Chamber Opera, Vienna 1962. Previous occupations: banking clerk. **Sang with major companies in** AUS: Salzburg Fest, Vienna Staatsoper; CZE: Prague National; FRA: Bordeaux, Nancy; FR GER: Berlin Deutsche Oper, Bonn, Cologne, Darmstadt, Dortmund, Düsseldorf-Duisburg, Hamburg, Hannover, Kiel, Munich Staatsoper, Nürnberg, Stuttgart, Wuppertal; HUN: Budapest; ITA: Florence Maggio & Comunale, Spoleto Fest; SWI: Basel, Geneva, Zurich; UK: Edinburgh Fest. **Roles with these companies incl** ADAM: Chapelou (Postillon de Lonjumeau), Zephoris (Si j'étais roi); BERLIOZ: Faust (Damnation de Faust); CIMAROSA: Paolino (Matrimonio segreto); DONIZETTI: Ernesto (Don Pasquale); GLUCK: Pylade (Iphigénie en Tauride); HANDEL: Acis, Sextus (Giulio Cesare), Xerxes; HENZE: Des Grieux (Boulevard Solitude); LORTZING: Baron Kronthal★ (Wildschütz); MOZART: Tito (Clemenza di Tito), Don Ottavio★ (Don Giovanni), Belmonte★ (Entführung aus dem Serail), Belfiore★‡ (Finta giardiniera), Idomeneo, Alessandro (Re pastore), Tamino★ (Zauberflöte); PROKOFIEV: Anatole (War and Peace); PURCELL: Aeneas; ROSSINI: Almaviva★ (Barbiere di Siviglia), Giocondo (Pietra del paragone), Florville (Signor Bruschino); STRAUSS, J: Alfred★ (Fledermaus); STRAUSS, R: Flamand (Capriccio); STRAVINSKY: Oedipus; TCHAIKOVSKY: Lenski (Eugene Onegin); WAGNER: Walther (Meistersinger), Walther v d Vogelweide‡ (Tannhäuser); WEBER: Max (Freischütz), Oberon. Recorded for: Philips, Decca, EMI. Gives recitals. Appears with symphony orchestra. Teaches voice. Coaches repertoire. **Res:** Eichenstr 71, D-565 Solingen, FR Ger. Mgmt: SLZ/FRG; JUC/SWI.

HOLM, RENATE. Lyric coloratura soprano. German. Resident mem: Vienna Staatsoper; Deutsche Oper, Berlin. Born 10 Aug 1931, Berlin. Divorced. Studied: Maria Ivogün, Munich; Waltraud Waldeck, Berlin; Swana Egilsdottir, Vienna. **Debut:** Helene (Walzertraum) Vienna Volksoper 1957. Awards: Österreichische Kammersängerin, Vienna Staatsoper. **Sang with major companies in** ARG: Buenos Aires; AUS: Bregenz Fest, Graz, Salzburg Fest, Vienna Staatsoper & Volksoper; BEL: Brussels; CZE: Brno; FR GER: Berlin Deutsche Oper, Frankfurt, Hamburg, Munich; SWE: Stockholm;

SWI: St Gallen; UK: London English National; USSR: Moscow Bolshoi. **Roles with these companies incl** BEETHOVEN: Marzelline★ (Fidelio); DONIZETTI: Norina (Don Pasquale); LORTZING: Gretchen (Wildschütz), Marie (Zar und Zimmermann); MOZART: Despina★ (Così fan tutte), Zerlina★ (Don Giovanni), Blondchen★ (Entführung aus dem Serail), Susanna★ (Nozze di Figaro), Pamina (Zauberflöte); NICOLAI: Frau Fluth (Lustigen Weiber); OFFENBACH: Olympia (Contes d'Hoffmann); PUCCINI: Mimi★ & Musetta★(Bohème); ROSSINI: Rosina★(Barbiere di Siviglia); SMETANA: Marie★(Bartered Bride); STRAUSS, J. Adele★‡ (Fledermaus); STRAUSS, R: Zerbinetta (Ariadne auf Naxos), Sophie★ (Rosenkavalier); WEBER: Aennchen★ (Freischütz). Also GOUNOD: Lucinde (Médecin malgré lui); MOZART: Papagena★ (Zauberflöte); WOLF-FERRARI: Gasparina (Campiello). Gives recitals. Appears with symphony orchestra. Teaches voice. Coaches repertoire. **Res:** Cottagegasse 82, A-1190, Vienna, Austria.

HOLM, RICHARD. Lyric tenor. German. Resident mem: Bayerische Staatsoper, Munich. Born 3 Aug 1921, Stuttgart. Wife Elfi, occupation ballerina. Three children. Studied: Hochschule für Musik, Kmsg Rudolf Ritter, Stuttgart. **Debut:** Almaviva (Barbiere di Siviglia) Nürnberg. Awards: Bayerischer Kammersänger 1954; Bayerischer Verdienstorden 1967; Prof & Vice Pres, Staatliche Hochschule für Musik, Munich 1967. **Sang with major companies in** AUS: Graz, Salzburg Fest, Vienna Staatsoper; BEL: Brussels; FRA: Aix-en-Provence Fest, Bordeaux, Lyon, Marseille, Paris, Rouen, Strasbourg; FR GER: Berlin Deutsche Oper, Cologne, Düsseldorf-Duisburg, Frankfurt, Hamburg, Hannover, Kiel, Munich Staatsoper, Nürnberg, Stuttgart, Wiesbaden; GER DR: Berlin Komische Oper; HOL: Amsterdam; ITA: Bologna, Florence Maggio & Comunale, Genoa, Milan La Scala, Naples, Palermo, Turin, Venice; MON: Monte Carlo; POR: Lisbon; SPA: Barcelona; SWE: Stockholm; SWI: Geneva, Zurich; UK: Edinburgh Fest, Glyndebourne Fest, London Royal; USA: Chicago, New York Met, San Francisco Opera. **Roles with these companies incl** BERG: Alwa (Lulu); BLACHER: Romeo; BRITTEN: Aschenbach★ (Death in Venice); CORNELIUS: Nureddin (Barbier von Bagdad); DONIZETTI: Ernesto (Don Pasquale), Edgardo (Lucia); EGK: Christoph (Verlobung in San Domingo); EINEM: Camille Desmoulins & Robespierre★ (Dantons Tod); FLOTOW: Lionel (Martha); GLUCK: Achille (Iphigénie en Aulide), Pylade (Iphigénie en Tauride); HANDEL: Xerxes★; HINDEMITH: Apprentice (Cardillac), Albrecht v Brandenberg (Mathis der Maler); HUMPERDINCK: Königssohn (Königskinder); JANACEK: Alyei (From the House of the Dead), Steva (Jenufa); KORNGOLD: Paul (Tote Stadt); LORTZING: Baron Kronthal (Wildschütz); MASCAGNI: Turiddu (Cavalleria rusticana); MASSENET: Des Grieux (Manon); MONTEVERDI: Nero (Incoronazione di Poppea), Ulisse★ (Ritorno d'Ulisse); MOZART: Tito & Annio (Clemenza di Tito), Ferrando (Così fan tutte), Don Ottavio (Don Giovanni), Belmonte (Entführung aus dem Serail), Belfiore (Finta giardiniera), Idamante & Idomeneo (Idomeneo), Tamino (Zauberflöte); MUS-

SORGSKY: Shuisky★ (*Boris Godunov*), Vassily Golitsin (*Khovanshchina*); NICOLAI: Fenton (*Lustigen Weiber*); OFFENBACH: Hoffmann; ORFF: Tiresias (*Antigonae*), Solo (*Carmina burana*); PENDERECKI: de Laubardemont & Adam‡ (*Teufel von Loudun*); PFITZNER: Palestrina★; PROKOFIEV: Marquis★ (*Gambler*); PUCCINI: Rodolfo (*Bohème*), Rinuccio (*Gianni Schicchi*), Pinkerton (*Butterfly*); PURCELL: Aeneas; ROSSINI: Almaviva★ (*Barbiere di Siviglia*), Lindoro (*Italiana in Algeri*); SCHOENBERG: Aron; SMETANA: Hans (*Bartered Bride*); STRAUSS, J: Eisenstein (*Fledermaus*); STRAUSS, R: Flamand (*Capriccio*), Leukippos (*Daphne*), Aegisth (*Elektra*), Merkur (*Liebe der Danae*), Ein Sänger (*Rosenkavalier*); STRAVINSKY: Tom Rakewell (*Rake's Progress*); TCHAIKOVSKY: Lenski (*Eugene Onegin*); THOMAS: Wilhelm Meister (*Mignon*); VERDI: Riccardo (*Ballo in maschera*), Don Carlo, Fenton (*Falstaff*), Duca di Mantova (*Rigoletto*), Alfredo (*Traviata*); WEBER: Max★ (*Freischütz*), Oberon; WOLF-FERRARI: Florindo (*Donne curiose*), Filipeto (*Quattro rusteghi*). **World premieres:** HINDEMITH: Wallenstein (*Harmonie der Welt*) Munich 1957. Recorded for: DG, Electrola. Gives recitals. Appears with symphony orchestra. Teaches voice. On faculty of Staatl Hochschule für Musik, Munich. **Res:** Richard Strauss Str 111, Munich, FR Ger. Mgmt: SLZ/FRG; TAU/SWI.

HOLMES, EUGENE. Dramatic baritone. American. Resident mem: Deutsche Oper am Rhein, Düsseldorf. Born 7 Mar 1934, Brownsville, TN, USA. Single. Studied: Wirt D Walton, St Louis, MO; Indiana Univ, Frank St Leger, Bloomington, IN; Dorothy Ziegler, Miami, FL. **Debut:** John Proctor (*Crucible*) Goldovsky Opera 1963. Previous occupations: teacher, PS and Univ of Miami. Awards: Performers' Certif, Indiana Univ.
    Sang with major companies in AUS: Graz, Vienna Staatsoper; FR GER: Düsseldorf-Duisburg; UK: Cardiff Welsh, London English National; USA: New York City Opera, San Diego, San Francisco Opera, Seattle, Washington DC. **Roles with these companies incl** DELIUS: Koanga★‡; GERSHWIN: Porgy★‡; GIORDANO: Carlo Gérard★ (*Andrea Chénier*); GLUCK: Thoas (*Iphigénie en Tauride*); LEONCAVALLO: Tonio★ (*Pagliacci*); MOZART: Figaro (*Nozze di Figaro*); PUCCINI: Marcello★ (*Bohème*), Sharpless★ (*Butterfly*), Lescaut★ (*Manon Lescaut*), Michele★ (*Tabarro*), Scarpia★ (*Tosca*); STRAUSS, R: Jochanaan (*Salome*); STRAVINSKY: Creon (*Oedipus Rex*); VERDI: Amonasro★ (*Aida*), Rodrigo★ (*Don Carlo*), Macbeth, Iago (*Otello*), Rigoletto, Simon Boccanegra, Germont★ (*Traviata*), Conte di Luna★ (*Trovatore*); WAGNER: Amfortas (*Parsifal*); WARD: John Proctor (*Crucible*). **World premieres:** MENOTTI: Ukamba (*Most Important Man*) New York City Opera 1971. Recorded for: Angel. Gives recitals. Appears with symphony orchestra. Coaches repertoire. Mgmt: HBM/USA; RAB/AUS.

HOLT, HENRY. Conductor of opera and symphony; also composer. American. Music Dir, Education Dir & Resident Cond, Seattle Opera, WA. Born 11 Apr 1934, Vienna. Wife Dolores Strazicich, occupation opera singer, soprano. Studied: Los Angeles City Coll, Hugo Strelitzer; Univ So Calif, Ingolf Dahl, Los Angeles; Wolfgang Martin; incl piano, clarinet, viola, harpsichord & voice. Plays the piano, harpsichord, clarinet. Operatic training as repetiteur, asst cond, chorus master and tech assist, Koblenz, FR Ger 1962-64; var companies in Calif 1953-61. **Operatic debut:** *Rigoletto* American Opera Co, Los Angeles 1961. Symphonic debut: Seattle Symph, WA 1971. Previous occupations: auto mechanic, instrumentalist, teacher, music arranger & copyist. Previous adm positions in opera: Gen Dir, Portland Opera, OR 1964-66.
    Conducted with major companies in CAN: Vancouver; USA: Portland, Seattle. **Operas with these companies incl** BEETHOVEN: *Fidelio;* BIZET: *Carmen★;* DONIZETTI: *Elisir, Fille du régiment, Lucia;* FLOYD: *Of Mice and Men;* GIORDANO: *Andrea Chénier;* GOUNOD: *Faust★, Roméo et Juliette;* MASCAGNI: *Cavalleria rusticana;* MASSENET: *Manon;* MOZART: *Così fan tutte★, Don Giovanni, Nozze di Figaro, Zauberflöte;* OFFENBACH: *Contes d'Hoffmann★, Périchole;* PASATIERI: *Calvary★, Black Widow★, Seagull★;* PERGOLESI: *Serva padrona;* PUCCINI: *Bohème, Gianni Schicchi★, Butterfly★, Manon Lescaut★, Tosca★, Turandot★;* ROSSINI: *Barbiere di Siviglia★;* SMETANA: *Bartered Bride;* STRAUSS, J: *Fledermaus;* STRAUSS, R: *Rosenkavalier★, Salome★;* TCHAIKOVSKY: *Eugene Onegin★;* VERDI: *Aida★, Ballo in maschera★, Don Carlo★, Forza del destino, Otello, Rigoletto, Traviata, Trovatore;* WAGNER: *Fliegende Holländer, Rheingold★, Walküre★, Siegfried★, Götterdämmerung★;* WARD: *Crucible.* **World premieres:** PASATIERI: *Black Widow* 1972, *Calvary* 1972, both at Seattle Opera. Conducted major orch in USA/Canada. Teaches privately. **Res:** 1526 E Olin Place, Seattle, WA, USA. Mgmt: DIS/USA.

HOLTENAU, RUDOLF HEINRICH. Dramatic baritone. Austrian. Resident mem: Vienna Staatsoper. Born Salzburg, Austria. Married. Studied: Prof Fritz Worff, Vienna. Awards: First Prize Intl Cont for Singing, Vienna.
    Sang with major companies in AUS: Graz, Vienna Staatsoper; BEL: Brussels; CZE: Prague National; FRA: Lyon, Nice; FR GER: Bielefeld, Cologne, Darmstadt, Düsseldorf-Duisburg, Essen, Hannover, Mannheim; ITA: Genoa, Rome Opera & Caracalla, Trieste; MON: Monte Carlo; POR: Lisbon; SPA: Barcelona; SWE: Stockholm; SWI: Zurich; USA: Kentucky. **Roles with these companies incl** BORODIN: Prince Igor★; GOUNOD: Méphistophélès★ (*Faust*); HANDEL: Giulio Cesare★; MOZART: Don Giovanni★, Figaro (*Nozze di Figaro*); MUSSORGSKY: Boris★ & Pimen★ (*Boris Godunov*); OFFENBACH: Coppélius, etc★ (*Contes d'Hoffmann*); ORFF: König★ (*Kluge*); PUCCINI: Scarpia★ (*Tosca*); STRAUSS, R: Orest★ (*Elektra*), Jochanaan★ (*Salome*); VERDI: Amonasro★ (*Aida*), Philip II★ & Grande Inquisitore★ (*Don Carlo*), Falstaff★, Macbeth★, Simon Boccanegra★; WAGNER: Holländer★ (*Fliegende Holländer*), König Heinrich★ (*Lohengrin*), Hans Sachs★ (*Meistersinger*), Amfortas★ (*Parsifal*), Wotan (*Rheingold★, Walküre★*), Wanderer★ (*Siegfried*), Kurwenal★ (*Tristan und Isolde*); WEBER: Kaspar★ (*Freischütz*). Gives recitals.

Appears with symphony orchestra. Teaches voice. **Res:** Rummelhardtstr 6, Vienna, Austria. Mgmt: VLD/AUS; SLZ/FRG.

HOOD, ANN. Mezzo-soprano. British. Resident member: English National Opera, London. Born 21 May 1940, Middleton, Manchester, UK. Studied: Royal Academy of Music, Dame Eva Turner, London; Audrey Langford, Eduardo Asquez. **Debut:** Zweiter Knabe (*Zauberflöte*) Royal Opera Covent Garden 1961. Awards: Regional Awd Cinzano Compt.

Sang with major companies in UK: London English National. **Roles with these companies incl** MONTEVERDI: Poppea★ (*Incoronazione di Poppea*); MOZART: Dorabella★ (*Così fan tutte*); OFFENBACH: Giulietta★ (*Contes d'Hoffmann*); PROKOFIEV: Helene★ (*War and Peace*); STRAUSS, J: Prinz Orlovsky (*Fledermaus*); STRAVINSKY: Jocasta★ (*Oedipus Rex*). Gives recitals. Appears with symphony orchestra. Mgmt: MIN/UK; PAS/FRG.

HOOK, WALTER E. Lyric & dramatic baritone. American. Born 7 Apr 1941, Kansas City, MO, USA. Divorced. Two children. Studied: Univ of Missouri Consv of Music, Kansas City; Metropolitan Opera Studio; Cornelius Reid, Daniel Ferro, New York. **Debut:** Colline (*Bohème*) Kansas City Lyric Theater 1958. Awards: Ntl Opera Inst Grant.

Sang with major companies in USA: Baltimore, Kansas City. **Roles with these companies incl** BARBER: Doctor (*Vanessa*); BIZET: Escamillo (*Carmen*); DEBUSSY: Siméon (*Enfant prodigue*); DONIZETTI: Enrico★ (*Campanello*), Don Pasquale, Belcore★ (*Elisir*); FLOYD: Olin Blitch (*Susannah*); MASCAGNI: Alfio (*Cavalleria rusticana*); MENOTTI: Bob★ (*Old Maid and the Thief*); MOZART: Figaro★ (*Nozze di Figaro*); NICOLAI: Falstaff (*Lustigen Weiber*); OFFENBACH: Coppélius etc (*Contes d'Hoffmann*); PERGOLESI: Uberto (*Serva padrona*); PUCCINI: Colline & Marcello (*Bohème*), Gianni Schicchi★, Sharpless★ (*Butterfly*), Scarpia (*Tosca*); VERDI: Germont (*Traviata*). Also SALIERI: Falstaff; GAY/Britten: Macheath (*Beggar's Opera*); GIANNINI: Hortensio (*Taming of the Shrew*); HOIBY: Postman (*Scarf*); ECCLES: Jupiter (*Semele*); BEESON: Bro' Smiley (*Sweet Bye and Bye*). **World premieres:** THOMSON: Hobhouse (*Lord Byron*) Juilliard American Opera Center, New York 1972; BEESON: Papa Belliart (*Captain Jinks and the Horse Marines*) Kansas City Lyric 1975. Recorded for: CRI, Desto. Video–Cable TV: Uberto (*Serva padrona*). Gives recitals. Appears with symphony orchestra. Teaches voice. Coaches repertoire. **Res:** 312 W 20 St, New York, NY, USA.

HOPF, HANS. Heldentenor. German. Resident mem: Bayerische Staatsoper, Munich. Born 2 Aug 1920, Nürnberg, Germany. Married. Three children. Studied: Paul Bender, Munich; Ragnvald Bjerne, Oslo. **Debut:** Pinkerton (*Butterfly*) Munich 1939. Awards: Bayerischer Kammersänger; Bavarian Order of Merit.

Sang with major companies in ARG: Buenos Aires; AUS: Graz, Salzburg Fest, Vienna Staatso-

per; BRA: Rio de Janeiro; FRA: Bordeaux, Marseille, Nice, Paris, Rouen, Strasbourg; FR GER: Bayreuth Fest, Berlin Deutsche Oper, Cologne, Dortmund, Düsseldorf-Duisburg, Frankfurt, Hamburg, Hannover, Karlsruhe, Kassel, Kiel, Mannheim, Munich Staatsoper & Gärtnerplatz, Nürnberg, Saarbrücken, Stuttgart, Wiesbaden, Wuppertal; GER DR: Berlin Komische Oper & Staatsoper, Dresden, Leipzig; HOL: Amsterdam; ITA: Bologna, Florence Maggio & Comunale, Genoa, Milan La Scala, Naples, Parma, Rome Opera & Caracalla, Trieste, Turin, Venice, Verona Arena; MEX: Mexico City; MON: Monte Carlo; NOR: Oslo; POR: Lisbon; SPA: Barcelona; SWE: Stockholm; SWI: Basel, Geneva, Zurich; UK: London Royal Opera; USSR: Moscow Bolshoi; USA: Chicago, New York Met, Philadelphia Grand, San Francisco Opera. **Roles with these companies incl** ADAM: Chapelou (*Postillon de Lonjumeau*); d'ALBERT: Pedro (*Tiefland*); AUBER: Fra Diavolo & Lorenzo (*Fra Diavolo*); BEETHOVEN: Florestan★‡ (*Fidelio*); BERG: Tambourmajor★ (*Wozzeck*); BIZET: Don José★‡ (*Carmen*); BOIELDIEU: George Brown (*Dame blanche*); CORNELIUS: Nureddin (*Barbier von Bagdad*); DONIZETTI: Edgardo (*Lucia*); EINEM: Bürgermeister★ (*Besuch der alten Dame*); FLOTOW: Lionel (*Martha*); GIORDANO: Andrea Chénier‡; GLUCK: Admetos (*Alceste*); GOUNOD: Faust; HUMPERDINCK: Königssohn (*Königskinder*); KORNGOLD: Paul (*Tote Stadt*); LEONCAVALLO: Canio★‡ (*Pagliacci*); LORTZING: Baron Kronthal (*Wildschütz*), Peter Ivanov (*Zar und Zimmermann*); MASCAGNI: Turiddu★‡ (*Cavalleria rusticana*); MASSENET: Jean‡ (*Jongleur de Notre Dame*), Des Grieux (*Manon*); MEYERBEER: Vasco da Gama (*Africaine*); MOZART: Tito (*Clemenza di Tito*), Ferrando (*Così fan tutte*), Don Ottavio‡ (*Don Giovanni*), Belmonte (*Entführung aus dem Serail*), Tamino (*Zauberflöte*); MUSSORGSKY: Dimitri (*Boris Godunov*), Andrei (*Khovanshchina*); NICOLAI: Fenton (*Lustigen Weiber*); OFFENBACH: Hoffmann; PUCCINI: Rodolfo (*Bohème*), Dick Johnson (*Fanciulla del West*), Rinuccio (*Gianni Schicchi*), Pinkerton (*Butterfly*), Des Grieux‡ (*Manon Lescaut*), Luigi★ (*Tabarro*), Cavaradossi★ (*Tosca*), Calaf‡ (*Turandot*); RIMSKY-KORSAKOV: Sadko (*Barbiere di Siviglia*); SMETANA: Hans‡ (*Bartered Bride*); STRAUSS, J: Eisenstein★ & Alfred★ (*Fledermaus*); STRAUSS, R: Bacchus★‡ (*Ariadne auf Naxos*), Leukippos & Apollo (*Daphne*), Aegisth (*Elektra*), Kaiser★‡ (*Frau ohne Schatten*), Midas (*Liebe der Danae*), Ein Sänger★ (*Rosenkavalier*), Herodes★ (*Salome*); TCHAIKOVSKY: Lenski (*Eugene Onegin*), Gherman (*Pique Dame*); VERDI: Radames★ (*Aida*), Riccardo (*Ballo in maschera*), Don Carlo, Don Alvaro (*Forza del destino*), Rodolfo‡ (*Luisa Miller*), Otello★‡, Duca di Mantova‡ (*Rigoletto*), Gabriele‡ (*Simon Boccanegra*), Alfredo (*Traviata*), Manrico★‡ (*Trovatore*), Arrigo‡ (*Vespri*); WAGNER: Erik★‡ (*Fliegende Holländer*), Lohengrin★‡, Walther★‡ (*Meistersinger*), Parsifal★‡, Rienzi, Siegmund★‡ (*Walküre*), Siegfried (*Siegfried*★‡, *Götterdämmerung*★‡), Tannhäuser★‡, Tristan★‡; WEBER: Adolar (*Euryanthe*), Max‡ (*Freischütz*), Hüon (*Oberon*). Also SCHMIDT, F: (*Notre Dame*);

STRAUSS, R: Narraboth (*Salome*). Teaches voice. **Res**: Etterschlagerstr 16, 8031 Steinebach/Wörthsee, FR Ger, and St Gallerstr 127, Jona, Switzerland. Mgmt: SLZ/FRG.

HORACEK, JAROSLAV. Bass. Czechoslovakian. Resident mem: National Theater, Prague. Born 29 Apr 1926, Dehylov, CSR. Wife Dagmar. Four children. Studied: Prof Rudolf Vasek, Karel Kügler, Peter Burja, Ostrava; Apollo Granforte. **Debut:** Kezal (*Bartered Bride*) Municipal Theater, Opava 1945.

Sang with major companies in BUL: Sofia; CZE: Prague National; HOL: Amsterdam; ITA: Naples; POL: Warsaw; SPA: Barcelona; SWI: Zurich; UK: Edinburgh Fest; USA: Boston. **Roles with these companies incl** BEETHOVEN: Don Pizarro (*Fidelio*); GOUNOD: Méphistophélès★ (*Faust*); MARTINU: Grigoris★ (*Griechische Passion*); MASSENET: Don Quichotte; MOZART: Don Alfonso★ (*Così fan tutte*), Don Giovanni★, Figaro★ (*Nozze di Figaro*); MUSSORGSKY: Boris Godunov★; OFFENBACH: Coppélius etc★ (*Contes d'Hoffmann*); PROKOFIEV: Michael★ (*War and Peace*); PUCCINI: Colline (*Bohème*); ROSSINI: Dott Bartolo★ (*Barbiere di Siviglia*); SMETANA: Kezal★ (*Bartered Bride*), Rarach★ (*Devil's Wall*), Janus★ (*The Kiss*), Malina★ (*Secret*), Peter★ (*Two Widows*); VERDI: Philip II (*Don Carlo*), Fiesco★ (*Simon Boccanegra*); WAGNER: König Heinrich (*Lohengrin*), Hunding★ (*Walküre*); WEBER: Kaspar (*Freischütz*). Also SMETANA: Benes★ (*Dalibor*), Chrudos★ (*Libuse*); DVORAK: Wassermann★ (*Rusalka*), Burgrave★ (*Jakobin*); JEREMIAS: Fjodor Karamazov★ (*Brothers Karamazov*); TCHAIKOVSKY: Gremin★ (*Eugene Onegin*); STRAUSS, R: Graf Waldner★ (*Arabella*). **World premieres:** PAUER: Pourgon (*Malade imaginaire*) National Theater, Prague 1970; MARTINU: Forlimpopoli (*Mirandolina*) National Theater, Prague 1959. Recorded for: Supraphon. Gives recitals. Appears with symphony orchestra. Teaches voice. Coaches repertoire. On faculty of Consv of Music, Prague. **Res:** Podleskova 18, 100 00 Prague 10, CSSR. Mgmt: PRG/CZE; ASK/UK.

HORNE, MARILYN. Mezzo-soprano & soprano. American. Born 16 Jan 1934, Bradford, PA. Husband Henry Lewis, occupation conductor. One child. Studied: Univ of So California, William Vennard, Los Angeles. **Debut:** Hata (*Bartered Bride*) Los Angeles Guild Opera 1954. Awards: DM Rutgers Univ, NJ; DLitt St Peter's Coll, NJ; DM Jersey City State Coll.

Sang with major companies in CAN: Montreal/Quebec, Toronto, Vancouver; FR GER: Frankfurt; ITA: Florence Comunale, Milan La Scala; UK: London Royal; USA: Boston, Chicago, Dallas, Houston, New York Met, Philadelphia Lyric, San Antonio, San Francisco Opera & Spring Opera. **Roles with these companies incl** BELLINI: Adalgisa★ (*Norma*); BIZET: Carmen★; BRITTEN: Hermia (*Midsummer Night*); GLUCK: Orfeo★; HANDEL: Rinaldo★; MUSSORGSKY: Marina (*Boris Godunov*); ROSSINI: Rosina★ (*Barbiere di Siviglia*), Isabella★ (*Italiana in Algeri*), Arsace★ (*Semiramide*), Neocle★ (*Assedio di Corinto*); STRAVINSKY: Jocasta (*Oedipus Rex*); THOMAS: Mignon★; VERDI:

Amneris★ (*Aida*), Eboli★ (*Don Carlo*), Azucena (*Trovatore*). Also PUCCINI: Musetta (*Bohème*), Minnie (*Fanciulla del West*); BEETHOVEN: Marzelline (*Fidelio*); DONIZETTI: Marie (*Fille du régiment*); BERG: Marie (*Wozzeck*). **World premieres:** GIANNINI: Laura (*Harvest*) Chicago Lyric Opera 1961. Recorded for: DG, London, RCA. Gives recitals. Appears with symphony orchestra. **Res:** Orange, NJ, USA. Mgmt: CAM/USA.

HORRES, KURT. Stages/produces opera. German. Resident Stage Dir, Wuppertal. Born 28 Nov 1932, Düsseldorf. Studied: Univ of Cologne. Operatic training as asst stage dir at Komische Oper, Berlin, Ger DR 1954-57. Previous adm positions in opera: 1.Spielleiter, Bonn 1957-60; Oberspielleiter, Städtische Oper Lübeck 1960-64; Dir, Wuppertaler Bühnen 1964-69.

Directed/produced opera for major companies in FR GER: Bonn, Frankfurt, Hamburg, Kassel, Wuppertal; et al. **Operas staged with these companies incl** BEETHOVEN: *Fidelio;* BERG: *Lulu, Wozzeck;* BIZET: *Carmen;* CIKKER: *Play of Love and Death;* DALLAPICCOLA: *Prigioniero, Volo di notte;* DESSAU: *Verurteilung des Lukullus;* EINEM: *Besuch der alten Dame;* IBERT: *Angélique;* KLEBE: *Jakobowsky und der Oberst;* MILHAUD: *Christophe Colomb, Médée;* PENDERECKI: *Teufel von Loudun;* PETROVICS: *Crime and Punishment;* PUCCINI: *Gianni Schicchi;* SCHULLER: *Visitation;* STRAUSS, R: *Schweigsame Frau;* STRAVINSKY: *Oedipus Rex, Rake's Progress;* SZOKOLAY: *Blood Wedding;* WERLE: *Dream of Thérèse;* et al. Also CIKKER: *Resurrection;* PIZZETTI: *Assassinio nella cattedrale;* BURIAN: *The War, Marysa.* **Operatic world premieres:** STEFFENS: *Unter dem Milchwald* Staatsoper Hamburg 1973; BLACHER: *Yvonne, Prinzessin von Burgund* Wuppertal 1973. Teaches at consv.

HORYSA, INGHILD. Dramatic mezzo-soprano. German. Resident mem: Städtische Bühnen, Nürnberg. Born 2 Jan 1944, Bielitz/Oberschlesien, Germany. Husband Jörg Butschek, occupation engineer. Studied: Kmsg Helena Braun, Germany. **Debut:** Hänsel, Bayerische Staatsoper, Munich 1966.

Sang with major companies in AUS: Vienna Volksoper; FR GER: Bielefeld, Darmstadt, Dortmund, Düsseldorf-Duisburg, Essen, Frankfurt, Hamburg, Hannover, Kiel, Mannheim, Munich Staatsoper, Nürnberg, Stuttgart. **Roles with these companies incl** BIZET: Carmen; DONIZETTI: Maffio Orsini (*Lucrezia Borgia*); HUMPERDINCK: Hänsel★; MOZART: Dorabella (*Così fan tutte*), Cherubino★ (*Nozze di Figaro*); MUSSORGSKY: Marina (*Boris Godunov*); NICOLAI: Frau Reich (*Lustigen Weiber*); PROKOFIEV: Clarissa★ (*Love for Three Oranges*); PUCCINI: Suzuki (*Butterfly*); STRAUSS, R: Komponist★ (*Ariadne auf Naxos*), Octavian★ (*Rosenkavalier*); STRAVINSKY: Jocasta (*Oedipus Rex*), Baba the Turk (*Rake's Progress*); VERDI: Amneris★ (*Aida*), Eboli (*Don Carlo*), Preziosilla★ (*Forza del destino*); WAGNER: Fricka (*Walküre*), Venus (*Tannhäuser*), Brangäne (*Tristan und Isolde*). **World premieres:** CIKKER: Lodoiska (*Spiel von Liebe und Tod*) Bayerische Staatsoper,

Munich 1969. Gives recitals. Appears with symphony orchestra. **Res:** Klosterweg 9, 85 Nürnberg, FR Ger. Mgmt: SMD/FRG.

HOSE, ANTHONY PAUL. Conductor of opera. British. Head of Music Staff & Resident Cond, Welsh National Opera, Cardiff. Born 24 May 1944, London. Studied: Royal Coll of Music, London; Rafael Kubelik, Munich; incl piano, clarinet, double bass. Plays the piano & harpsichord. Operatic training as repetiteur, asst cond & chorus master at Glyndebourne Fest; Stadttheater Bremen. **Operatic debut:** *Rake's Progress* Stadttheater Bremen 1969.

Conducted with major companies in UK: Welsh National. **Operas with these companies incl** BIZET: *Pêcheurs de perles*★; DONIZETTI: *Elisir*★; MOZART: *Don Giovanni*★, *Nozze di Figaro*★, *Zauberflöte*★; PUCCINI: *Bohème*★, *Butterfly*★; ROSSINI: *Barbiere di Siviglia*★; STRAUSS, J: *Fledermaus*; STRAVINSKY: *Rake's Progress*; VERDI: *Aida, Nabucco, Rigoletto*★, *Simon Boccanegra*★, *Traviata*★; WAGNER: *Fliegende Holländer*★. **Res:** Cardiff, Wales, UK.

HOUSEMAN, JOHN. Stages/produces opera, theater, film & television. American. Resident Stage Dir & Administr for theater in New York. Born 22 Sep 1902, Bucharest, Romania. Wife Joan. Two children. **Prof operatic debut:** *Otello* Dallas Civic Opera 1963.

Directed/produced opera for major companies in USA: Dallas, Washington DC. **Operas staged with these companies incl** BENNETT: *Mines of Sulphur;* HONEGGER: *Antigone;* PUCCINI: *Tosca*★; THOMSON: *Lord Byron*★; VERDI: *Falstaff.* Also BLOCH: *Macbeth.* **Operatic world premieres:** THOMSON: *Four Saints in Three Acts* Hartford, CT 1934; FARBERMAN: *Losers* Am Op Center, Juilliard, New York 1971. Previous leading positions with major theater companies: Art Dir, American Shakespeare Festival, USA 1956-59; Art Dir, City Center Acting Co, New York 1971-75. Teaches at Drama Div, Juilliard School. **Res:** 565 So Mountain Rd, New City, NY 10956, USA.

HOWARD, ANN; née Ann Pauline Swadling. Dramatic mezzo-soprano. British. Born 22 Jul 1936, London. Husband Keith Giles, occupation travel busin exec. One child. Studied: Mo D Modesti, Paris. **Debut:** Kate Pinkerton (*Butterfly*) Covent Garden, London 1961. Awards: Awd Royal Opera House, Covent Garden, to study in Paris 1962.

Sang with major companies in CAN: Toronto; FRA: Nancy, Rouen; FR GER: Saarbrücken; UK: Cardiff Welsh, Edinburgh Fest, Glasgow Scottish, London Royal Opera & English National; USA: Milwaukee Florentine, New Orleans, New York City Opera, San Diego, Santa Fe. **Roles with these companies incl** BERLIOZ: Cassandre★ (*Troyens*); BIZET: Carmen★; HUMPERDINCK: Hexe★‡ (*Hänsel und Gretel*); SAINT-SAENS: Dalila★; STRAUSS, R: Komponist★ (*Ariadne auf Naxos*); STRAVINSKY: Jocasta★ (*Oedipus Rex*), Baba the Turk★ (*Rake's Progress*); VERDI: Amneris★ (*Aida*), Azucena (*Trovatore*); WAGNER: Ortrud★ (*Lohengrin*), Fricka (*Rheingold*★, *Walküre*), Brangäne★ (*Tristan und Isolde*). Also

RAVEL: Concepcion (*Heure espagnole*); PUCCINI: Musetta (*Bohème*); GOEHR: Alice Arden (*Arden muss sterben*); LALO: Margared (*Roi d'Ys*). **World premieres:** BENNETT: Madam Leda (*Mines of Sulphur*) Sadler's Wells, London 1965. Recorded for: EMI. Video—BBC TV: Hexe (*Hänsel und Gretel*); Prinz Orlovsky (*Fledermaus*). Gives recitals. Appears with symphony orchestra. **Res:** Surbiton/Surrey, UK. Mgmt: SLA/UK; SMN/USA.

HOWELL, GWYNNE RICHARD. Bass. British. Resident mem: Royal Opera, London. Born 13 Jun 1938, Gorseinon, South Wales, UK. Wife Mary. Two sons. Studied: Royal Manchester Coll of Music, Gwilym Jones, UK; Otakar Kraus, London. **Debut:** Monterone (*Rigoletto*) Sadler's Wells, London 1968. Previous occupations: senior planning officer Manchester Corp.

Sang with major companies in FRA: Aix-en-Provence Fest, Orange Fest; SPA: Barcelona; UK: Cardiff Welsh, London Royal & English National. **Roles with these companies incl** BELLINI: Oroveso★ (*Norma*); BRITTEN: Sir Walter Raleigh (*Gloriana*); DONIZETTI: Mocenigo★ (*Caterina Cornaro*), Talbot★ (*Maria Stuarda*); MOZART: Sarastro (*Zauberflöte*); MUSSORGSKY: Pimen★ (*Boris Godunov*); PUCCINI: Colline★ (*Bohème*); VERDI: Ramfis★ (*Aida*), Philip II★ (*Don Carlo*), Padre Guardiano★ (*Forza del destino*); WAGNER: Pogner★ (*Meistersinger*), Landgraf★ (*Tannhäuser*). **World premieres:** MAXWELL-DAVIES: Richard Taverner (*Taverner*) Royal Opera, London 1972. Recorded for: EMI. Appears with symphony orchestra. **Res:** 197 Fox Lane, London N 13, UK. Mgmt: AIM/UK.

HOWELLS, ANNE ELIZABETH. Lyric coloratura mezzo-soprano. British. Born 12 Jan 1941, Southport, Lancashire, UK. Husband Ryland Davies, occupation opera singer. Studied: Royal Manchester Coll of Music, Frederick Cox; Vera Rozsa. **Debut:** Flora (*Traviata*) Welsh National Opera 1964. Awards: Fellow, Royal Manchester Coll of Music.

Sang with major companies in FRA: Lyon, Paris; SWI: Geneva; UK: Glasgow Scottish, Glyndebourne Fest, London Royal & Eng Natl; USA: Chicago, New York Met. **Roles with these cos incl** BRITTEN: Hermia★ (*Midsummer Night*); CAVALLI: Diana★ (*Calisto*); DEBUSSY: Mélisande★; GOUNOD: Siebel★ (*Faust*); MONTEVERDI: Poppea★ (*Incoronazione di Poppea*); MOZART: Annio★ (*Clemenza di Tito*), Dorabella★ (*Così fan tutte*), Zerlina★ (*Don Giovanni*), Cherubino★ (*Nozze di Figaro*); ROSSINI: Rosina★ (*Barbiere di Siviglia*); SEARLE: Ophelia★ (*Hamlet*); STRAUSS, R: Komponist★ (*Ariadne auf Naxos*), Octavian★ (*Rosenkavalier*). Also CAVALLI: Erisbe‡ (*Ormindo*); MONTEVERDI: Minerva★ (*Ritorno d'Ulisse*); PROKOFIEV: Paulina★ (*Gambler*). **World premieres:** BENNETT: Lena (*Victory*) Royal Opera, Glyndebourne Fest 1969 & 1970; MAW: Cathleen Sweeney (*Rising of the Moon*) Glyndebourne Fest 1970. Recorded for: Argo, Decca, Philips. Gives recitals. Appears with symphony orchestra. **Res:**

Claygate, Surrey, UK. Mgmt: AIM/UK; COL/USA.

HOWERY, ROBERT RAY. Scenic designer for opera, theater, television. Is a lighting designer; also a painter & decorator. American. Resident designer, Robert Howery Studios, Houston, TX. Born 4 Nov 1932, Welborn, KA. Divorced. Three children. Studied: Univ of Iowa, Arnold Gillede; Univ of Kansas. **Operatic debut:** *Walküre* Houston Grand Opera, TX 1959. Theater debut: Fiesta Musicals, McAllen, TX 1964. Previous occupation: teacher of scenic design, Univs of St Thomas & Houston, TX.

Designed for major companies in USA: Fort Worth, Houston, New Orleans, Philadelphia Lyric, Pittsburgh. **Operas designed for these companies incl** BIZET: *Carmen*★; DONIZETTI: *Don Pasquale, Elisir;* MENOTTI: *Medium*★; MOZART: *Nozze di Figaro*★; PAISIELLO: *Barbiere di Siviglia;* PUCCINI: *Butterfly, Rondine*★, *Tabarro;* ROSSINI: *Barbiere di Siviglia;* STRAUSS, R: *Salome;* WAGNER: *Walküre.* Exhibitions of stage designs & paintings, Houston. **Res:** 6315 Atwell, Houston, TX, USA.

HOWLETT, NEIL. Baritone. British. Resident mem: English National Opera, London. Born 24 Jul 1934, Mitcham, UK. Wife Elizabeth Robson, occupation opera singer. Two children. Studied: Tino Pattiera, Vienna; Hochschule für Musik, Stuttgart; Otakar Kraus, London; Ettore Campogalliani, Mantua. **Debut:** Ferryman (*Curlew River*) English Opera Group 1964. Previous occupations: studied archeology & anthropology at Cambridge Univ. Awards: Kathleen Ferrier Awd.

Sang with major companies in FRA: Aix-en-Provence Fest, Bordeaux, Marseille, Nice, Rouen, Toulouse; FR GER: Hamburg, Bremen; UK: Aldeburgh Fest, Edinburgh Fest, Glasgow Scottish, London Royal & English National. **Roles with these companies incl** BRITTEN: Ferryman (*Curlew River*); CAVALLI: Amida (*Ormindo*); DEBUSSY: Golaud★ (*Pelléas et Mélisande*); DONIZETTI: Dott Malatesta (*Don Pasquale*); GLUCK: High Priest & Apollo (*Alceste*); HANDEL: Polyphemus (*Acis and Galatea*); LEONCAVALLO: Tonio★ (*Pagliacci*); MASSENET: Des Grieux (*Portrait de Manon*); MOZART: Guglielmo★ (*Così fan tutte*), Nardo (*Finta giardiniera*), Allazim (*Zaïde*); ORFF: Solo (*Carmina burana*); PUCCINI: Marcello★ (*Bohème*), Sharpless★ (*Butterfly*), Scarpia★ (*Tosca*); PURCELL: Aeneas★ (*Dido and Aeneas*); SHOSTAKOVICH: Ivan Yakovlevich (*The Nose*); STRAUSS, R: Robert Storch (*Intermezzo*), Jochanaan★ (*Salome*); STRAVINSKY: Creon (*Oedipus Rex*); TCHAIKOVSKY: Eugene Onegin★; VERDI: Renato★ (*Ballo in maschera*), Rodrigo★ (*Don Carlo*), Ford★ (*Falstaff*), Macbeth, Germont (*Traviata*); WAGNER: Orsini (*Rienzi*). Also PROKOFIEV: Leandro (*Love for Three Oranges*); MOZART: Sprecher (*Zauberflöte*); GOUNOD: Valentin★ (*Faust*). **World premieres:** BRITTEN: Ferryman (*Curlew River*) English Opera Group, Aldeburgh Fest 1964; CROSSE: Mirador (*Story of Vasco*) English National Opera, London 1974. Gives recitals. Appears with symphony orchestra. Teaches voice. On faculty of Guildhall School, London. **Res:** London, UK. Mgmt: ASK/UK.

HOYEM, ROBERT. Lyric tenor. Also stage director. American. Resident mem: Deutsche Oper am Rhein, Düsseldorf. Born 23 Sep 1930, Lewistown, MT, USA. One son. Studied: Montana Univ, John Lester; Manhattan School of Music, Herta Glaz, New York; Max Lorenz, Munich; Margarethe Düren-Herrmann, Cologne. **Debut:** Ferrando (*Così fan tutte*) Städtische Bühnen, Heidelberg 1961. Previous occupations: US Air Force officer; teacher; dir Brooklyn Coll Opera Guild. Awards: Hon grad Montana Univ; Third Prize Intl Schumann-Wolf Cont Vienna 1960; Third Prize Intl Cont Munich 1960.

Sang with major companies in FR GER: Berlin Deutsche Oper, Düsseldorf-Duisburg, Essen, Frankfurt, Hamburg, Karlsruhe, Kiel, Munich Gärtnerplatz, Wuppertal; SWI: Zurich; UK: Glyndebourne Fest. **Roles with these companies incl** BRITTEN: Albert Herring; EINEM: Camille Desmoulins (*Dantons Tod*); FLOTOW: Lionel (*Martha*); GOUNOD: Faust; HANDEL: Ulysses★ (*Deidamia*); HENZE: Des Grieux (*Boulevard Solitude*); JANACEK: Fox★ (*Cunning Little Vixen*), Kudrijash (*Katya Kabanova*); LORTZING: Chateauneuf★ (*Zar und Zimmermann*); MOZART: Tito & Annio★ (*Clemenza di Tito*), Ferrando★ (*Così fan tutte*), Don Ottavio (*Don Giovanni*), Belmonte★ (*Entführung aus dem Serail*), Idomeneo, Marzio★ (*Mitridate, re di Ponto*), Tamino★ (*Zauberflöte*); OFFENBACH: Hoffmann; RAMEAU: Mercure★ (*Platée*); TCHAIKOVSKY: Lenski★ (*Eugene Onegin*). Also KAUFMANN: Junger Mann (*Perlenhemd*); HINDEMITH: Kavalier (*Cardillac*); CAVALIERI: Intelletto★ (*Rappresentazione*). **World premieres:** LOTHAR: Marquis de Malasombra (*Widerspenstige Heilige*) Gärtnerplatztheater, Munich 1968. Appears with symphony orchestra. Teaches voice. Coaches repertoire. Also stages opera: Heidelberg, Bremerhaven. **Res:** Wittelsbachstr 23, Düsseldorf, FR Ger. Mgmt: PAS/FRG; SLZ/FRG; IWL/UK.

HRUSCHKA, WILHELM. Dramatic baritone. German. Resident mem: Oper der Landeshauptstadt Kiel, FR Ger. Born 21 May 1912, Vienna. Wife Liselotte. Studied: Staatsakad, Prof Hans Duhan, Fritz Krauss, Vienna. **Debut:** Amonasro (*Aida*) Allenstein/Ostpreussen, Germany 1937.

Sang with major cos in DEN: Copenhagen; FR GER: Cologne, Darmstadt, Dortmund, Essen, Hamburg, Karlsruhe, Kiel, Mannheim, Stuttgart, Wiesbaden; GER DR: Dresden. **Roles with these companies incl** d'ALBERT: Sebastiano (*Tiefland*); BEETHOVEN: Don Pizarro★ (*Fidelio*); BERG: Wozzeck; BIZET: Escamillo (*Carmen*); DONIZETTI: Dott Malatesta (*Don Pasquale*); EGK: Cuperus (*Zaubergeige*); EINEM: Alfred Ill★ (*Besuch der alten Dame*), George Danton (*Dantons Tod*), Priest (*Prozess*); GIORDANO: Carlo Gérard (*Andrea Chénier*); GLUCK: Agamemnon (*Iphigénie en Aulide*); GOTOVAC: Sima (*Ero der Schelm*); HINDEMITH: Cardillac, Mathis; HUMPERDINCK: Spielmann (*Königskinder*); LEONCAVALLO: Tonio (*Pagliacci*); LOR-

TZING: Grav v Liebenau (*Waffenschmied*), Graf Eberbach (*Wildschütz*), Peter I (*Zar und Zimmermann*); MASCAGNI: Alfio (*Cavalleria rusticana*); MENOTTI: John Sorel (*Consul*); MOZART: Guglielmo (*Così fan tutte*), Don Giovanni, Figaro (*Nozze di Figaro*), Papageno (*Zauberflöte*); MUSSORGSKY: Boris Godunov, Tcherevik (*Fair at Sorochinsk*); OFFENBACH: Coppélius etc (*Contes d'Hoffmann*); ORFF: König (*Kluge*); PUCCINI: Marcello (*Bohème*), Jack Rance (*Fanciulla del West*), Gianni Schicchi, Sharpless (*Butterfly*), Scarpia★ (*Tosca*); STRAUSS, R: Mandryka (*Arabella*), Musiklehrer (*Ariadne auf Naxos*), Baron Ochs (*Rosenkavalier*), Jochanaan★ (*Salome*); STRAVINSKY: Nick Shadow (*Rake's Progress*); TCHAIKOVSKY: Eugene Onegin; VERDI: Amonasro★ (*Aida*), Grande Inquisitore (*Don Carlo*), Falstaff, Don Carlo (*Forza del destino*), Rigoletto, Germont (*Traviata*), Conte di Luna (*Trovatore*); WAGNER: Holländer★, Telramund (*Lohengrin*), Hans Sachs (*Meistersinger*), Amfortas (*Parsifal*), Wotan★ (*Rheingold & Walküre*), Wanderer★ (*Siegfried*), Gunther★ (*Götterdämmerung*), Kurwenal (*Tristan und Isolde*); WEBER: Kaspar (*Freischütz*); WOLF: Tio Lukas (*Corregidor*). Also FUESSEL: Sender (*Dybbuk*) Staatstheater Karlsruhe 1970; BENTZON: (*Faust III*) Kiel 1964; SCHÖNBACH: (*Geschichte von einem Feuer*) Kiel 1968. Appears with symphony orchestra. Teaches voice. **Res:** Holtenauerstr 85, Kiel, FR Ger. Mgmt: TAS/AUS; SLZ/FRG.

HRUZA, LUBOS; né Lubomír Hruza. Scenic and costume designer for opera, theater, film, television. Is a lighting designer; also a painter & illustrator. Czech/Norwegian. Resident designer at National Theater, Oslo. Born 28 Mar 1933, Jihlava, CSR. Wife Marie, occupation designer. One child. Studied: Pedagogical Faculty, Dept Visual Arts, Brno; Acad of Musical Arts, Prague, Dept of Stage Design, Prof Tröster. Prof training: Theater Disk, Prague 1956-59; Divaldo Petra Bezruce, Ostrava 1959-65. **Operatic debut:** *Dame blanche* Hamu, Prague 1958. Theater debut: Theater Jihlava, CSSR 1955. Previous occupation: actor, teacher. Awards: Silver Medal, Prague Quadrennial 1967.

Designed for major companies in DEN: Copenhagen; NOR: Oslo. **Operas designed for these companies incl** DONIZETTI: *Don Pasquale★;* KODALY: *Háry János★;* LECOCQ: *Fille de Madame Angot★;* LEONCAVALLO: *Pagliacci★;* PUCCINI: *Gianni Schicchi★, Tabarro★*. **Operatic world premieres:** KOLBERG: *After the Fair* Norwegian Opera Co, Oslo 1974. Operatic Video—Norw TV: *After the Fair*. Exhibitions of paintings, Ostrava 1961; Berlin 1961; Amsterdam, Krakow, Prague, Oslo. **Res:** Lillevannsveien 15, Oslo, Norway.

HUDSON, PAUL. Bass. British. Born 24 Jun 1945, Barnsley, Yorkshire, UK. Wife Joan Pamela. Two children. Studied: Huddersfield Music Coll, Eugene Everest; Royal Coll of Music, Redfers Llewellyn, London; London Opera Centre, Peggy Troman. **Debut:** WILLIAMSON: Stafan (*Lucky Peter's Journey*) Sadler's Wells Opera 1969. Awards: Peter Stuyvesant Schlshp, London Opera Centre; schlshp & Dr Saleeby Prize, Royal Coll of Music.

Sang with major companies in UK: Cardiff Welsh, London Royal Opera & English National. **Roles with these companies incl** BRITTEN: Sir Walter Raleigh★ (*Gloriana*), Theseus★ (*Midsummer Night*); MOZART: Publio★ (*Clemenza di Tito*), Sarastro★ (*Zauberflöte*); PUCCINI: Colline★ (*Bohème*); ROSSINI: Don Basilio★ (*Barbiere di Siviglia*); SMETANA: Kezal★ (*Bartered Bride*); VERDI: Grande Inquisitore★(*Don Carlo*), Fiesco★ (*Simon Boccanegra*). Also HANDEL: Manoah★ (*Samson*); WILLIAMSON: seven bass parts (*English Eccentrics*); MONTEVERDI: Seneca (*Incoronazione di Poppea*); MAXWELL-DAVIES: Henry VIII (*Taverner*); BERG: Athlet (*Lulu*); WAGNER: Gernot (*Feen*). Recorded for: Philips, BBC. Video/Film: Count de Horn (*Ballo in maschera*). Gives recitals. Appears with symphony orchestra. **Res:** Vissitt Manor, Hemsworth, Yorkshire, UK. Mgmt: HPM/UK.

HUISMAN, MAURICE. Belgian. Dir, Opéra National de Belgique, Théâtre Royal de la Monnaie, 4 rue Léopold, 1000 Brussels. In charge of administrative matters & artistic policy; and is a stage dir/prod. Born 1912, Belgium. Studied: Univ Libre, Brussels; Belgian-Amer Fndt, USA. Previous occupations: Dr in chemistry. Previous positions, primarily administrative & theatrical: Co-Dir, Comédiens Routiers/Théâtre National, Belgium 1945; Dir, Centre Belge des Echanges Culturels Intl 1948; Founder, Centre Culturel du Congo Belge 1956; Co-Founder, Ballet du XX Siècle, Brussels 1960; Dir, Netherlands Opera, Amsterdam 1965-70. In present position since 1959. Mem of Intl Assn of Opera Directors, Pres.

HUNT, ALEXANDRA. Soprano. American. Married. **Debut:** Marie (*Wozzeck*) Tanglewood Fest, MA, USA 1969.

Sang with major companies in FRA: Nancy; FR GER: Hamburg; ITA: Milan La Scala; USA: Newark, Omaha, St Paul, San Francisco Spring. **Roles with these companies incl** BERG: Lulu★, Marie★ (*Wozzeck*); BIZET: Carmen★; FLOYD: Curley's Wife (*Of Mice and Men*); JANACEK: Jenufa★, Katya★ (*Katya Kabanova*); MENOTTI: Monica★ (*Medium*); STRAUSS, J: Rosalinde (*Fledermaus*). Gives recitals. Appears with symphony orchestra. **Res:** New York, USA. Mgmt: NAP/USA; SLZ/FRG.

HUNTER, RITA NELLIE. Dramatic soprano. British. Born 15 Aug 1933, Wallasey, Cheshire, UK. Husband John Thomas, occupation manager. One child. Studied: Edwin Francis, Eva Turner, Redfers Llewellyn, England. **Debut:** Inez (*Trovatore*) Carl Rosa Opera Co 1956. Awards: Countess of Munster Trust Awd.

Sang with major companies in FRA: Strasbourg; FR GER: Munich Staatsoper; UK: London Royal Opera & English National; USA: New York Met, San Francisco Opera. **Roles with these companies incl** BELLINI: Norma; HUMPERDINCK: Gretel; JANACEK: Vixen (*Cunning Little Vixen*); MASCAGNI: Santuzza (*Cavalleria rusticana*); MOZART: Donna Anna (*Don Giovanni*), Elettra (*Idomeneo*); PUCCINI: Musetta (*Bohème*); ROS-

SINI: Pamira (*Assedio di Corinto*); VERDI: Aida, Odabella (*Attila*), Amelia (*Ballo in maschera*), Elisabetta (*Don Carlo*), Abigaille (*Nabucco*), Leonora (*Trovatore*); WAGNER: Senta (*Fliegende Holländer*), Elsa (*Lohengrin*), Brünnhilde (*Walküre, Siegfried‡, Götterdämmerung*). Also WEBER: Eglantine (*Euryanthe*). Recorded for: EMI, Unicorn, Classics for Pleasure. Gives recitals. Appears with symphony orchestra. **Res:** 70 Ember Court Rd, Thames-Ditton, UK. Mgmt: SLA/UK; BAR/USA.

HURTEAU, JEAN-PIERRE. Bass. Canadian. Born 5 Dec 1924, Montreal. Single. Studied: Consv of Music, Montreal; Prof Martial Singher. **Debut:** Frère Laurent (*Roméo et Juliette*) Festival de Montréal 1950. Awards: First Prize, Consv of Music, Montreal; Canada Counc Grant.

Sang with major companies in CAN: Montreal/Quebec, Ottawa, Toronto; FRA: Lyon, Marseille, Paris; ITA: Rome Opera; MON: Monte Carlo; SWI: Geneva; USA: Washington DC. **Roles with these companies incl** BERLIOZ: Méphistophélès★ (*Damnation de Faust*); GOUNOD: Méphistophélès★ (*Faust*), Ramon★ (*Mireille*); HANDEL: Polyphemus (*Acis and Galatea*); MOZART: Don Alfonso★ (*Così fan tutte*), Figaro (*Nozze di Figaro*); MUSSORGSKY: Pimen (*Boris Godunov*); PENDERECKI: Rangier★ (*Teufel von Loudun*); PUCCINI: Colline (*Bohème*); ROSSINI: Don Basilio (*Barbiere di Siviglia*); STRAUSS, R: La Roche (*Capriccio*); VERDI: Ramfis (*Aida*), Padre Guardiano (*Forza del destino*). Also MOZART: Commendatore★ (*Don Giovanni*). Gives recitals. Appears with symphony orchestra. **Res:** 30 Ave du Pres Kennedy, Paris, France.

HVOROV, IOAN. Bass. Romanian. Resident mem: Romanian Opera, Bucharest. Born 4 Jan 1928, Ismail, USSR. Divorced. Studied: Consv Cluj. **Debut:** Kontchak (*Prince Igor*) Romanian Opera, Cluj 1950. Awards: Order of Merit, Cultural Ministry.

Sang with major companies in BEL: Liège; BUL: Sofia; FRA: Paris; GRE: Athens National; FR GER: Stuttgart, Wiesbaden; ROM: Bucharest; USSR: Moscow Bolshoi & Stanislavski. **Roles with these companies incl** BORODIN: Galitzky★ (*Prince Igor*); DONIZETTI: Don Pasquale★; GOUNOD: Méphistophélès★ (*Faust*); MOZART: Sarastro★ (*Zauberflöte*); MUSSORGSKY: Boris★ & Varlaam★ (*Boris Godunov*); ROSSINI: Don Basilio★ (*Barbiere di Siviglia*); STRAUSS, R: Baron Ochs (*Rosenkavalier*); VERDI: Grande Inquisitore★ (*Don Carlo*); WAGNER: Daland★ (*Fliegende Holländer*), Pogner (*Meistersinger*); WEBER: Kaspar (*Freischütz*). Also TCHAIKOVSKY: Prince Gremin (*Eugene Onegin*); ENESCU: Tiresias★ (*Oedipe*); PUCCINI: Timur★ (*Turandot*); DARGOMIZHSKI: Miller (*Russalka*). **World premieres:** LERESCU: Stavrat (*Ecaterina Teodoroiu*) Romanian Opera 1971. Recorded for: Electrecord. Video/Film: Tiresias and High Priest (*Oedipe*); (*Don Pasquale*). Gives recitals. Appears with symphony orchestra. **Res:** 122 Victoriei St, Bucharest 1, Romania. Mgmt: RIA/ROM.

HYNNINEN, JORMA KALERVO. Lyric baritone. Finnish. Resident mem: Finnish National Opera, Helsinki. Born 3 Apr 1941, Leppavirta, Finland. Wife Reetta. Two children. Studied: Sibelius Acad, Matti Tuloisela, Antti Koskinen, Helsinki; Luigi Ricci, Rome; Clemens Kaiser-Breme, Essen. **Debut:** Silvio (*Pagliacci*) Finnish National Opera 1969. Previous occupations: elementary school teacher.

Sang with major companies in FIN: Helsinki; SWE: Stockholm. **Roles with these companies incl** DEBUSSY: Pelléas★; MOZART: Guglielmo★ (*Così fan tutte*), Papageno (*Zauberflöte*); PUCCINI: Marcello (*Bohème*); ROSSINI: Figaro★ (*Barbiere di Siviglia*); VERDI: Rodrigo★ (*Don Carlo*), Don Carlo★ (*Forza del destino*); WAGNER: Wolfram (*Tannhäuser*). Also MADETOJA: Jussi★ (*Ostrobothnians*). Recorded for: Finnlevy. Gives recitals. Appears with symphony orchestra **Res:** Laajavuorent 3 AS 13, Vantaa, Finland.

I

IANCULESCU, MAGDA. Dramatic soprano. Romanian. Resident mem: Romanian Opera, Bucharest. Born 30 Mar 1929, Iassy. Husband Mircea Ionescu-Muscel, occupation engineer. Studied: Consv, Prof Livia Vrabiescu-Vatianu, Bucharest. **Debut:** Rosina (*Barbiere di Siviglia*) Romanian Opera 1952. Awards: Merited Artist, Rep of Romania 1962; Laureate of Intl Contests Bucharest 1953, Prague 1954 and Warsaw 1955.

Sang with major companies in BEL: Liège; BUL: Sofia; CZE: Brno, Prague National; FRA: Lyon, Rouen; POL: Warsaw; ROM: Bucharest; USSR: Kiev, Leningrad Kirov, Moscow Bolshoi, Tbilisi; YUG: Zagreb, Belgrade. **Roles with these companies incl** BORODIN: Jaroslavna⋆ (*Prince Igor*); DEBUSSY: Mélisande⋆; DELIBES: Lakmé; DONIZETTI: Norina (*Don Pasquale*),, Lucia; MASSENET: Manon; MOZART: Fiordiligi⋆ (*Così fan tutte*), Donna Elvira⋆ (*Don Giovanni*), Blondchen (*Entführung aus dem Serail*), Susanna (*Nozze di Figaro*); OFFENBACH: Giulietta⋆ (*Contes d'Hoffmann*); PUCCINI: Mimi & Musetta⋆ (*Bohème*), Manon Lescaut, Tosca⋆; RAVEL: Concepcion (*Heure espagnole*); ROSSINI: Rosina‡ (*Barbiere di Siviglia*); STRAUSS, J: Rosalinde⋆ (*Fledermaus*); STRAUSS, R: Marschallin & Sophie (*Rosenkavalier*); VERDI: Aida⋆, Nannetta (*Falstaff*), Desdemona⋆ (*Otello*), Gilda‡ (*Rigoletto*), Violetta (*Traviata*), Leonora⋆ (*Trovatore*). **World premieres:** TRAILESCU: Puss (*Puss in Boots*) Romanian Opera, Bucharest. Recorded for: Electrecord. Gives recitals. Appears with symphony orchestra. Teaches voice. Coaches repertoire. On faculty of Consv, Bucharest. **Res:** 12 Grigore Mora St, Bucharest 1, Romania. Mgmt: RIA/ROM; SMD/FRG.

IGESZ, BODO. Stages/produces opera and is a translator. Dutch. Resident Stage Dir, Metropolitan Opera, New York; Central City Opera, CO, USA. Born 7 Feb 1935, Amsterdam. Single. Studied: Juilliard School of Music, Frederic Cohen, New York; incl music & piano. Operatic training as asst stage dir at Netherlands Opera, Amsterdam 1961-63. **Operatic debut:** FIORAVANTI: *Cantatrici villane* Juilliard Opera Theater 1960. Previous occupation: language instructor.

Directed/produced opera for major companies in CAN: Montreal/Quebec; FR GER: Frankfurt; HOL: Amsterdam; USA: Baltimore, Cincinnati, Fort Worth, Houston, Memphis, New Orleans, New York Met, Philadelphia Lyric, Portland, San Diego, Santa Fe. **Operas staged with these companies incl** BARTOK: *Bluebeard's Castle⋆;* BEETHOVEN: *Fidelio;* BELLINI: *Puritani, Sonnambula;* BERG: *Wozzeck;* BERLIOZ: *Benvenuto Cellini;* BIZET: *Carmen⋆;* BRITTEN: *Midsummer Night⋆, Peter Grimes;* DALLAPICCOLA: *Prigioniero;* DONIZETTI: *Don Pasquale⋆, Elisir;* FLOTOW: *Martha;* GOUNOD: *Faust;* HALEVY: *Juive⋆;* HAYDN: *Infedeltà delusa;* HENZE: *Bassariden, Junge Lord⋆;* HINDEMITH: *Cardillac;* HUMPERDINCK: *Hänsel und Gretel;* JANACEK: *Jenufa;* KODALY: *Háry János;* MASSENET: *Hérodiade⋆, Manon;* MEYERBEER: *Huguenots⋆;* MONTEVERDI: *Favola d'Orfeo, Ritorno d'Ulisse;* MOZART: *Così fan tutte, Don Giovanni⋆, Nozze di Figaro⋆, Zauberflöte;* OFFENBACH: *Contes d'Hoffmann;* PUCCINI: *Bohème⋆, Tosca⋆, Turandot⋆;* RAVEL: *Heure espagnole;* REIMANN: *Melusine⋆;* ROSSINI: *Comte Ory;* STRAUSS, J: *Fledermaus;* STRAUSS, R: *Ariadne auf Naxos⋆, Elektra, Rosenkavalier, Salome⋆;* TCHAIKOVSKY: *Eugene Onegin;* VERDI: *Ballo in maschera, Don Carlo, Falstaff⋆, Forza del destino⋆, Macbeth⋆, Rigoletto⋆, Simon Boccanegra⋆, Traviata;* WAGNER: *Fliegende Holländer⋆, Lohengrin, Tannhäuser⋆, Tristan und Isolde.* Also ANDRIESSEN: *Kalchas;* CAVALLI: *Scipio Africanus;* MARTIN: *M de Pourceaugnac.* **Operatic world premieres:** SCHOENBERG: *Jakobsleiter* first stg Santa Fe Opera, NM 1968; de KRUIJF: *Spinoza* Netherlands Opera 1971. Teaches. **Res:** 33 E 65 St, New York 10021, USA. Mgmt: DSP/USA.

IHLOFF, JUTTA-RENATE. Lyric soprano. German. Resident mem: var comps in Germany and Austria. Born 1 Nov 1944, Winterberg. Husband Wolfgang Westrup, occupation violinist in HH Phil Orch. Studied: Staatliche Hochschule für Musik, Fr Prof Maja Stein, Hamburg; Giorgio Favaretto, Rome & Siena. **Debut:** Zerlina (*Don Giovanni*) Staatsoper, Hamburg 1973.

Sang with major companies in AUS: Salzburg Fest, Vienna Staatsoper; FR GER: Berlin Deutsche Oper, Düsseldorf-Duisburg, Munich Staatsoper. **Roles with these companies incl** BEETHOVEN: Marzelline⋆ (*Fidelio*); BIBALO: Anni⋆ (*Lächeln am Fusse der Leiter*); BIZET: Lauretta (*Docteur Miracle*); EGK: Gretl⋆ (*Zaubergeige*); HANDEL: Galatea⋆, Cleopatra⋆ (*Giulio Cesare*); HAYDN: Vespina⋆ (*Infedeltà delusa*); HENZE:

Luise★ (*Junge Lord*); HUMPERDINCK: Gretel★; LORTZING: Marie★ (*Waffenschmied*), Gretchen★ (*Wildschütz*), Marie★ (*Zar und Zimmermann*); MONTEVERDI: Poppea★ (*Incoronazione di Poppea*); MOZART: Despina★ (*Così fan tutte*), Zerlina★ (*Don Giovanni*), Blondchen★ (*Entführung aus dem Serail*), Susanna★ (*Nozze di Figaro*), Pamina★ (*Zauberflöte*); NICOLAI: Aennchen★ (*Lustigen Weiber*); OFFENBACH: Antonia★ (*Contes d'Hoffmann*); ORFF: Solo★ (*Carmina burana*), Kluge★; PERGOLESI: Serpina★ (*Serva padrona*); PUCCINI: Mimì★ & Musetta★ (*Bohème*), Lauretta★ (*Gianni Schicchi*); STRAUSS, J: Adele★ (*Fledermaus*); STRAUSS, R: Zdenka★ (*Arabella*), Sophie★ (*Rosenkavalier*); VERDI: Nannetta★ (*Falstaff*); WEBER: Aennchen★ (*Freischütz*); WOLF-FERRARI: Lucieta★ (*Quattro rusteghi*), Susanna★ (*Segreto di Susanna*). Teaches voice. On faculty of Musikhochschule, Hamburg. **Res:** Milchstr, Hamburg, FR Ger.

IIMORI, TAIJIRO. Conductor of opera and symphony. Japanese. Resident Cond, Staatsoper, Hamburg. Also Resident Cond, Yomiuri Nippon Symph Orch, Tokyo. Born 30 Sep 1940, Manchuria, China. Wife Delreen. Studied: Toho Gakuen School of Music, Prof Hidoe Saito; Manhattan School of Music, J Perlea; incl piano, flute, violin, French horn and voice. Plays the piano. Operatic training as repetiteur, asst cond & chorus master at Fujiwara Opera, Tokyo 1961-64; Opernhaus Bremen 1967-70; Nationaltheater Mannheim 1970-73; Bayreuther Fest 1971-72. **Operatic debut:** *Suor Angelica* Fujiwara, Tokyo 1962. Symphonic debut: Yomiuri Nippon Symph Orch, Tokyo 1965. Awards: Fourth Prize, Mitropoulos Compt 1966; Fourth Prize, Karajan Compt 1969; Musician of the Year, Japanese Cultural Min, 1973; Cond of the Year, Barcelona 1972.
Conducted with major companies in FR GER: Hamburg, Kiel, Mannheim; ITA: Bologna; JPN: Tokyo Fujiwara & Niki Kai; SPA: Barcelona. **Operas with these companies incl** GLUCK: *Orfeo ed Euridice;* HUMPERDINCK: *Hänsel und Gretel★;* MOZART: *Così fan tutte★, Nozze di Figaro★, Zauberflöte★;* PUCCINI: *Butterfly★, Suor Angelica;* ROSSINI: *Barbiere di Siviglia;* VERDI: *Aida, Falstaff★, Simon Boccanegra★, Traviata;* WAGNER: *Fliegende Holländer, Walküre★;* WEBER: *Freischütz.* Video—NHK TV: *Freischütz* Niki Kai Tokyo prod. Conducted major orch in Europe, Asia. **Res:** Hamburg, FR Ger. Mgmt: KJM/JPN; PAS/FRG.

ILLES, EVA. Dramatic soprano. Hungarian. Resident mem: Opernhaus, Zurich; Württembergische Staatsoper, Stuttgart. Born Hungary.
Sang with major companies in FR GER: Hamburg, Hannover, Nürnberg, Stuttgart; SWI: Zurich; UK: London Royal; et al. **Roles with these companies incl** BEETHOVEN: Leonore (*Fidelio*); BUSONI: Herzogin (*Doktor Faust*); GIORDANO: Maddalena (*Andrea Chénier*); VERDI: Elena (*Vespri*); WAGNER: Senta (*Fliegende Holländer*), Gutrune (*Götterdämmerung*), Elisabeth & Venus (*Tannhäuser*); et al.

ILOSFALVY, ROBERT. Dramatic tenor. Hungarian. Resident mem: Bayerische Staatsoper, Mu-

nich; Opera House, Cologne. Born 18 Jun 1927, Hódmezövásárhely, Hungary. Wife Ilona Nyulaszi, occupation ballet dancer. Two children. Studied: Hungarian Acad of Music, Profs Andor Lendvay & Zoltán Kodály, Budapest. **Debut:** Laszlo Hunyadi, Hungarian National Opera, Budapest 1954. Awards: Intl Singing Compt Bucharest 1953; Liszt Prize 1962; Budapest Kossuth Awd, Hungarian Gvnmt 1965.
Sang with major companies in AUS: Bregenz Fest, Vienna Staatsoper; DEN: Copenhagen; FRA: Nancy; FR GER: Berlin Deutsche Oper, Cologne, Dortmund, Hamburg, Hannover, Mannheim, Munich Staatsoper, Stuttgart, Wiesbaden; HOL: Amsterdam; HUN: Budapest; ITA: Genoa; UK: London Royal; USSR: Leningrad Kirov, Moscow Bolshoi, Tbilisi; USA: San Francisco Opera. **Roles with these companies incl** AUBER: Fra Diavolo; BEETHOVEN: Florestan (*Fidelio*); BIZET: Don José★ (*Carmen*); DONIZETTI: Edgardo (*Lucia*); GOUNOD: Faust; MOZART: Belmonte (*Entführung aus dem Serail*); OFFENBACH: Hoffmann; PUCCINI: Rodolfo★ (*Bohème*), Dick Johnson★ (*Fanciulla del West*), Des Grieux★ (*Manon Lescaut*), Luigi★ (*Tabarro*), Cavaradossi (*Tosca*); ROSSINI: Arnold (*Guillaume Tell*); SMETANA: Hans (*Bartered Bride*); STRAUSS, J: Alfred (*Fledermaus*); STRAUSS, R: Ein Sänger★ (*Rosenkavalier*); TCHAIKOVSKY: Lenski (*Eugene Onegin*); VERDI: Riccardo★ (*Ballo in maschera*), Don Carlo, Don Alvaro★ (*Forza del destino*), Duca di Mantova‡ (*Rigoletto*), Gabriele (*Simon Boccanegra*), Alfredo★‡ (*Traviata*), Manrico (*Trovatore*), Arrigo (*Vespri*); WAGNER: Walther v d Vogelweide (*Tannhäuser*). Also ERKEL: Hunyadi. Only on records DONIZETTI: Roberto Devereux. Recorded for: Decca, Electrola, Qualiton. Appears with symphony orchestra. **Res:** Dürenerstr 182, Cologne, FR Ger. Mgmt: SLZ/FRG; LLF/USA.

IMALSKA, ALEKSANDRA. Dramatic mezzo-soprano. Polish. Resident mem: State Opera, Poznan, Poland. Born 10 Feb 1933, Kalisz. Husband Roman Jankowiak, occupation conductor. Studied: Prof Cyganska, Prof Zielinska, Poznan; State School of Music, Poland. **Debut:** Jadwiga (*Haunted Castle*) Poznan Opera 1960. Awards: Third Prize Bel Canto Compt, Liège, Queen Elizabeth, Brussels.
Sang with major companies in BEL: Liège; GER DR: Berlin Komische Oper; ITA: Genoa; POL: Lodz, Warsaw; YUG: Zagreb, Belgrade. **Roles with these companies incl** BIZET: Carmen; MENOTTI: Secretary (*Consul*); MUSSORGSKY: Marina (*Boris Godunov*), Marfa (*Khovanshchina*); PONCHIELLI: Laura (*Gioconda*); SZOKOLAY: Mother of Bridegroom (*Blood Wedding*); TCHAIKOVSKY: Comtesse (*Pique Dame*); VERDI: Amneris★ (*Aida*), Ulrica★ (*Ballo in maschera*), Eboli★ (*Don Carlo*), Preziosilla★ (*Forza del destino*), Azucena★ (*Trovatore*); WAGNER: Venus★ (*Tannhäuser*), Brangäne (*Tristan und Isolde*). **World premieres:** RUDZINSKI: Delagia (*Komendant Paryza*) Poznan Opera 1960. Recorded for: Polskie Nagrania. Video/Film: Azucena (*Trovatore*). Gives recitals. Appears with symphony orchestra. Mgmt: PAG/POL.

IMDAHL, HEINZ. Bass-baritone. German. Resident mem: Bayerische Staatsoper, Munich. Born 6 Aug 1924, Düsseldorf. Wife Johanna, occupation hotel mng. Two children. Studied: Kmsg Berthold Pütz, Düsseldorf; Prof Gustav Gründgens, Kmsg Max Lorenz. **Debut:** Moralès (*Carmen*) Düsseldorf 1948. Previous occupations: butcher; army serv. Awards: Bayerischer Kammersänger, Ministry of Culture.

Sang with major companies in AUS: Graz, Vienna Staatsoper & Volksoper; BEL: Brussels, Liège; BRA: Rio de Janeiro; FRA: Bordeaux, Lyon, Marseille, Nancy, Paris, Rouen, Strasbourg, Toulouse; FR GER: Berlin Deutsche Oper, Bonn, Cologne, Darmstadt, Dortmund, Düsseldorf-Duisburg, Essen, Frankfurt, Hamburg, Hannover, Karlsruhe, Kassel, Kiel, Krefeld, Mannheim, Munich Staatsoper, Nürnberg, Saarbrücken, Stuttgart, Wiesbaden, Wuppertal; GER DR: Berlin Staatsoper, Leipzig; HOL: Amsterdam; ITA: Bologna, Florence Maggio, Genoa, Naples, Palermo, Parma, Rome Opera & Caracalla, Trieste, Turin, Venice; MEX: Mexico City; NOR: Oslo; POR: Lisbon; ROM: Bucharest; SPA: Barcelona; SWI: Basel, Geneva, Zurich; UK: London Royal; USA: Philadelphia Grand, San Francisco Opera. **Roles with these companies incl** BEETHOVEN: Don Pizarro★ (*Fidelio*); BIZET: Escamillo (*Carmen*); DALLAPICCOLA: Prigioniero; DONIZETTI: Belcore (*Elisir*); EINEM: Alfred Ill★ (*Besuch der alten Dame*); GLUCK: Oreste (*Iphigénie en Tauride*); HUMPERDINCK: Spielmann (*Königskinder*); LORTZING: Graf v Liebenau (*Waffenschmied*), Graf Eberbach (*Wildschütz*), Peter I (*Zar und Zimmermann*); MASCAGNI: Alfio★ (*Cavalleria rusticana*); MEYERBEER: Nelusco (*Africaine*); MUSSORGSKY: Boris Godunov; OFFENBACH: Coppélius★ etc (*Contes d'Hoffmann*); PUCCINI: Sharpless★ (*Butterfly*); Scarpia★ (*Tosca*); STRAUSS, R: Altair (*Aegyptische Helena*), Musiklehrer★ (*Ariadne auf Naxos*), Olivier (*Capriccio*), Orest★ (*Elektra*), Baron Ochs★ (*Rosenkavalier*), Jochanaan★ (*Salome*); TCHAIKOVSKY: Eugene Onegin; VERDI: Amonasro★ (*Aida*), Rodrigo & Grande Inquisitore (*Don Carlo*), Ford★ & Falstaff★ (*Falstaff*), Macbeth, Nabucco, Rigoletto, Germont (*Traviata*); WAGNER: Holländer★, Friedrich★ (*Liebesverbot*), Telramund★ (*Lohengrin*), Hans Sachs★ (*Meistersinger*), Amfortas★ (*Parsifal*), Alberich (*Rheingold*, *Götterdämmerung*), Wotan (*Rheingold★*, *Walküre★*), Wanderer★ (*Siegfried*), Wolfram★ (*Tannhäuser*), Kurwenal★ (*Tristan und Isolde*); WEBER: Lysiart (*Euryanthe*). Gives recitals. Appears with symphony orchestra. Teaches voice. Mgmt: SLZ/FRG; SMD/FRG.

INBAL, ELIAHU. Conductor of opera and symphony. British & Israeli. Resident Cond, Sinfonie Orch, Hessischer Rundfunk, Frankfurt, FR Ger 1974- . Born 16 Feb 1936, Jerusalem. Wife Helga. One child. Studied: Acad of Music, Jerusalem; Consv Ntl Sup de Musique, Paris; Accad Chigiana, Siena, Italy, with Ferrara, Celibidache; incl violin, clarinet, piano. Plays the violin. **Operatic debut:** *Elektra* Teatro Comunale, Bologna 1968. Symphonic debut: Gadna Orch, Naharia, Israel 1956. Previous occupations: orch violinist & concert master, music & violin teacher. Awards: First Prize, Guido Cantelli Intl Cond Compt.

Conducted with major companies in FR GER: Cologne, Munich Staatsoper, Stuttgart; ITA: Bologna, Florence Comunale, Turin, Verona Arena. **Operas with these companies incl** BERLIOZ: *Béatrice et Bénédict;* MOZART: *Così fan tutte★, Idomeneo★;* STRAUSS, R: *Ariadne auf Naxos★, Elektra;* VERDI: *Don Carlo, Forza del destino★, Traviata★.* Also CHERUBINI: *Anacréon.* Conducted major orchestras in Europe, USA/Canada & Asia. **Res:** Frankfurt/M, FR Ger. Mgmt: WND/FRG; CAM/USA.

INGEBRETSEN, KJELL. Conductor of opera and symphony; composer. Norwegian. Resident Cond, Royal Opera, Stockholm. Born 28 May 1943, Skien. Wife Elisabeth, occupation music teacher. One child. Studied: Music Acad, Mo Kurt Bendix and Herbert Blomstedt, Stockholm; incl piano, organ, violin & clarinet. Plays the piano. Operatic training as repetiteur, asst cond & cond of ballet at Royal Opera, Stockholm. **Operatic debut:** Royal Opera, Stockholm 1969. Symphonic debut: Oslo Phil 1970. Awards: Knight of Dannebrog, Denmark.

Conducted with major companies in NOR: Oslo; POL: Warsaw; SWE: Drottningholm Fest, Stockholm. **Operas with these companies incl** BIZET: *Carmen★;* BRITTEN: *Rape of Lucretia;* DONIZETTI: *Don Pasquale★;* MOZART: *Don Giovanni★, Nozze di Figaro★, Zauberflöte★;* OFFENBACH: *Contes d'Hoffmann★;* PUCCINI: *Bohème★, Butterfly★, Tosca★;* ROSSINI: *Barbiere di Siviglia★;* VERDI: *Ballo in maschera★, Rigoletto★, Trovatore★;* WEILL: *Aufstieg und Fall der Stadt Mahagonny.* Also HALLBERG: *Experiment X, Evakueringen.* Video — Swed TV: *Don Pasquale.* Conducted major orch in Europe. **Res:** Karlbergsv 40, Stockholm, Sweden. Mgmt: PGI/NOR.

INGLE, WILLIAM EARL. Lyric tenor. American. Resident mem: Landestheater Linz, Austria. Born 17 Dec 1934, Texhoma, TX, USA. Wife Sylvia Keene. One child. Studied: Acad of Vocal Arts, Dorothy Di Scala, Philadelphia; Sidney Dietsch, New York; Luigi Ricci, Rome. **Debut:** Tamino (*Zauberflöte*) Flensburg Opera, FR Ger 1965. Previous occupations: music teacher & choral cond. Awards: Fulbright Grant to study in Rome, 2 yrs; NBC TV Op Aud, Philadelphia.

Sang with major companies in AUS: Graz, Vienna Volksoper; FR GER: Düsseldorf-Duisburg, Frankfurt, Hannover, Kassel. **Roles with these companies incl** DONIZETTI: Ernesto (*Don Pasquale*); LORTZING: Baron Kronthal★ (*Wildschütz*); MOZART: Ferrando (*Così fan tutte*), Don Ottavio★ (*Don Giovanni*), Tamino★ (*Zauberflöte*); PUCCINI: Rodolfo (*Bohème*), Pinkerton (*Butterfly*); ROSSINI: Almaviva★ (*Barbiere di Siviglia*); STRAUSS, J: Alfred★ (*Fledermaus*); STRAUSS, R: Flamand (*Capriccio*), Ein Sänger★ (*Rosenkavalier*); VERDI: Fenton (*Falstaff*), Duca di Mantova★ (*Rigoletto*), Alfredo (*Traviata*). Gives recitals. Appears with symphony orchestra. **Res:** Breitwiesergutstr 50, Linz, Austria. Mgmt: RAB/AUS; PAS/FRG.

INGPEN, JOAN; née Joan Mary Eileen Williams. British. Tech Adv for Programing, Théâtre National de l'Opéra, 8 rue Scribe, Paris 9e 1971- .

Born 3 Jan 1916, London. Husband Sebastian Shaw, occupation actor & author. Studied: Royal Acad of Music, London. Plays the piano. Previous occupations: artist's representative. Form position, primarily adm: Controller of Opera Planning, Royal Opera House Covent Garden, London 1962-71. **Res:** 35 rue Parent de Rosan, Paris, France.

IONESCU, GEORGE. Dramatic baritone. Romanian. Resident mem: Komische Oper, Berlin, Ger DR; Städtische Bühnen, Bielefeld. Born 29 May 1934, Limanul, Romania. Wife Svetlana, occupation opera singer. Studied: Prof Nicolae Luca, Constanta, Romania; Prof Elsa Chioreanu, Bucharest. **Debut:** Scarpia (*Tosca*) Opera House, Constanta 1960. Previous occupations: actor.
Sang with major companies in AUS: Vienna Volksoper; FR GER: Bielefeld, Munich Gärtnerplatz; ROM: Bucharest. **Roles with these companies incl** d'ALBERT: Sebastiano★ (*Tiefland*); BEETHOVEN: Don Pizarro★ (*Fidelio*); BIZET: Escamillo★ (*Carmen*); CIMAROSA: Count Robinson (*Matrimonio segreto*); DONIZETTI: Dott Malatesta (*Don Pasquale*); LEONCAVALLO: Tonio (*Pagliacci*); MASCAGNI: Alfio★ (*Cavalleria rusticana*); MASSENET: Lescaut (*Manon*); MOZART: Don Giovanni★; OFFENBACH: Coppélius, etc★ (*Contes d'Hoffmann*); PUCCINI: Marcello★ (*Bohème*), Sharpless★ (*Butterfly*), Scarpia★ (*Tosca*); ROSSINI: Figaro (*Barbiere di Siviglia*); VERDI: Amonasro★ (*Aida*), Renato★ (*Ballo in maschera*), Rodrigo★ (*Don Carlo*), Don Carlo (*Forza del destino*), Nabucco★, Iago★ (*Otello*), Germont★ (*Traviata*), Conte di Luna★ (*Trovatore*); WAGNER: Kurwenal★ (*Tristan und Isolde*). **Res:** Mesterul Manole 11, Sect IV, 4 Bucharest, Romania. Mgmt: TAS/AUS; RIA/ROM.

IROSCH, MIRJANA. Lyric soprano. German. Resident mem: Volksoper, Vienna. Born 24 Oct 1939, Zagreb, Yugoslavia. Divorced. One daughter. Studied: Consv, Prof Fritz Lunzer, Zagreb. **Debut:** Mercedes (*Carmen*) Landestheater Linz, Austria 1962.
Sang with major companies in AUS: Bregenz Fest, Graz, Vienna Staatsoper; BEL: Brussels; FR GER: Frankfurt; SWI: Basel, Zurich. **Roles with these companies incl** BARTOK: Judith (*Bluebeard's Castle*); BIZET: Micaëla★‡ (*Carmen*); DONIZETTI: Anna Bolena; KODALY: Örzse (*Háry János*); MOZART: Fiordiligi (*Così fan tutte*), Donna Elvira (*Don Giovanni*), Cherubino (*Nozze di Figaro*); OFFENBACH: Antonia & Giulietta★ (*Contes d'Hoffmann*); PAISIELLO: Rosina (*Barbiere di Siviglia*); RAVEL: Concepcion★ (*Heure espagnole*); ROSSINI: Rosina (*Barbiere di Siviglia*); SMETANA: Marie★ (*Bartered Bride*); STRAUSS, J: Rosalinde★ (*Fledermaus*); WEILL: Jenny (*Aufstieg und Fall der Stadt Mahagonny*). **World premieres:** EINEM: Mme Schleyer (*Der Zerrissene*) rev vers, Volksoper, Vienna 1968. Gives recitals. Appears with orchestra. **Res:** Wallrisstr 60/1, 1180 Vienna,

Austria. Mgmt: RAB/AUS; TAS/AUS; MIN/UK.

ISRAEL, ROBERT. Scenic and costume designer for opera, theater, television. Is a lighting designer; also a sculptor. American. Born 17 Sep 1939, Detroit, MI. Single. Studied: painting, art history, philosophy. **Operatic debut:** sets & cost, *Good Soldier Schweik* Minnesota Opera Co, Minneapolis 1967. Theater debut: National Educational TV, New York 1970. Previous occupation: Prof of Art History, Cooper Union, New York.
Designed for major companies in BEL: Brussels; HOL: Amsterdam; USA: Kansas City, Minneapolis. **Operas designed for these cos incl** BRITTEN: *Midsummer Night★;* KURKA: *Good Soldier Schweik★;* MAXWELL-DAVIES: *Eight Songs for a Mad King★;* MILHAUD: *Abandon d'Ariane, Délivrance de Thésée, Enlèvement d'Europe;* MOZART: *Entführung aus dem Serail, Zauberflöte★;* PROKOFIEV: *Love for Three Oranges★;* SATIE: *Socrate;* VERDI: *Macbeth★.* **Operatic world premieres:** BEESON: *Sweet Bye and Bye* Kansas City Lyric 1973; ULLMAN: *Kaiser of Atlantis* Ntl Op of the Netherlands 1975; BLITZSTEIN: *Harpies* 1968; STOKES: *Horspfal* 1969; SUSA: *Transformations* 1973; BLACKWOOD: *Gulliver* 1975 all at Minnesota Opera. Operatic Video—NET: *Entführung aus dem Serail.* Exhibitions of stage designs, paintings, sculptures, graphics Whitney Museum, New York 1970; Museum of Modern Art, New York 1974; Walker Art Center, Minneapolis 1975. **Res:** c/o A. Turner, 196 Bowery, New York, USA and Nederlandse Operastichting, Amsterdam, Netherlands.

ITO, KYOKO; née Kyo Hasegawa. Lyric soprano. Japanese. Resident mem: Niki Kai, Tokyo. Born 22 Feb 1927, Kakegawa, Japan. Divorced. One child. Studied: Nobuko Hara, Nobuko Tanaka, Tokyo. **Debut:** Liù (*Turandot*) Tokyo Opera Co 1950. Awards: Art Prize, Ministry of Educt; Mainichi Art Prize, Mainichi Press; First Prize Music Compt NHK Broadcasting Co.
Sang with major companies in JPN: Tokyo Niki Kai. **Roles with these companies incl** BIZET: Micaëla (*Carmen*); FLOTOW: Lady Harriet (*Martha*); HANDEL: Cleopatra (*Giulio Cesare*); MOZART: Despina (*Così fan tutte*), Zerlina★ (*Don Giovanni*), Blondchen (*Entführung aus dem Serail*), Susanna★ (*Nozze di Figaro*), Pamina★ (*Zauberflöte*); POULENC: La femme★ (*Voix humaine*); PUCCINI: Mimi (*Bohème*), Cjo-Cio-San★ (*Butterfly*), Liù (*Turandot*); ROSSELLINI: Violaine (*Annonce faite à Marie*); SMETANA: Marie (*Bartered Bride*); STRAUSS, J: Rosalinde★ (*Fledermaus*); STRAUSS, R: Sophie (*Rosenkavalier*); VERDI: Desdemona (*Otello*), Violetta (*Traviata*). Also DAN: Tsu★ (*Yuzuru*); SHIMIZU: Katsura (*Shuzenji-monogatari*). Recorded for: Nippon Victor. Gives recitals. Appears with symphony orchestra. Teaches voice. On faculty of Kunitachi Music Coll, Prof. **Res:** Jingumae 2-30-25, 405 Shibuyaku, Tokyo, Japan.

J

JACKSON, DAVID. British. Mng, Scottish Opera Theatre Royal, Hope St, Glasgow 1975- . In charge of theater adm matters. Additional adm positions: Box Office Adv, Ntl Theatre of Great Britain, London 1975- . Born 24 Mar 1935, Glasgow. Wife Marlene, occupation children's dance teacher. Three children. Previous positions, primarily adm: st tech, Alhambra Theatre, Glasgow 1955-56, & Saville Theatre, London 1956-57; cinema/theater mng, Granada Theatres, London 1957-63; box office mng/marketing, Royal Opera House Covent Garden 1963-74. Initiated major policy changes including reorganization of box office and booking services at Covent Garden, Paris Opéra, Old Vic Theatre & South Bank Theatre Complex, London. Mem of Computer Booking Commtt, Arts Council of Great Britain; Ticket Selling Commtt, Society of West End Theatre Mng; Theatrical Mng Assn; var commtt Scottish Opera Theatre Royal Ltd. **Res:** Rutherglen, Glasgow, Scotland, UK.

JACOBSSON, JOHN-ERIC. Lyric tenor. Swedish. Resident mem: Royal Opera, Stockholm. Born 6 Oct 1931, Gotland, Sweden. Wife Liv Almaas. Three children. Studied: Toivo Ek, Arne Sunnegårdh, Sweden. **Debut:** Turiddu (*Cavalleria rusticana*) Royal Opera, Stockholm 1964. Previous occupations: clothier. Awards: Jussi Björling & Kristina Nilsson Awds.

Sang with major companies in DEN: Copenhagen; NOR: Oslo; SWE: Drottningholm Fest. **Roles** with these companies incl BERG: Alwa (*Lulu*); BRITTEN: Albert Herring★; MASCAGNI: Turiddu★ (*Cavalleria rusticana*); MOZART: Pedrillo★ (*Entführung aus dem Serail*); PUCCINI: Cavaradossi★ (*Tosca*); STRAUSS, J: Eisenstein★ (*Fledermaus*); VERDI: Ismaele★ (*Nabucco*); WEILL: Jim Mahoney★ (*Aufstieg und Fall der Stadt Mahagonny*). Gives recitals. Appears with symphony orchestra.

JACQUILLAT, JEAN-PIERRE. Conductor of opera and symphony. French. Also Music Dir, Concerts Lamoureux, Paris. Born 13 Jul 1935, Versailles. Wife Cécile Cerrano, occupation violinist. Studied: Pierre Dervaux, André Cluytens, Charles Munch, Paris; incl piano, percussion. Plays the piano, percussion. **Operatic debut:** *Traviata* Opéra de Lyon 1967. Symphonic debut: Concerts Pasdeloup. Previous adm positions in opera: Adm, Opéra de Lyon.

Conducted with major companies in BEL: Brussels; FRA: Aix-en-Provence Fest, Lyon, Marseille, Nice, Paris, Strasbourg; ITA: Rome Caracalla. **Operas with these companies incl** BERG: *Wozzeck★*; BERLIOZ: *Damnation de Faust★*; BIZET: *Carmen★*; DEBUSSY: *Pelléas et Mélisande;* DUKAS: *Ariane et Barbe Bleue;* GOUNOD: *Faust;* KODALY: *Háry János;* MARTINU: *Trois souhaites;* MOZART: *Nozze di Figaro;* OFFENBACH: *Contes d'Hoffmann;* PUCCINI: *Bohème, Tosca;* RAVEL: *Enfant et les sortilèges★, Heure espagnole;* ROSSINI: *Barbiere di Siviglia;* VERDI: *Don Carlo, Rigoletto, Traviata★;* WAGNER: *Tristan und Isolde;* WEILL: *Aufstieg und Fall der Stadt Mahagonny★, Dreigroschenoper★.* Also MOZART: *Apollo ed Hyacinthus;* TELEMANN: *Pimpinone.* Recorded for Pathé-Marconi. Previous positions as Mus Dir with major orch: Angers, France 1968-70. **Res:** 5 rue Biscornet, Paris 75012. Mgmt: IMR/FRA.

JAFFE, MONTE. Bass. American. Studied: Curtis Inst of Music, Philadelphia; Univ of Tennessee, Knoxville, TN; Giorgio Tozzi, New York. **Debut:** Junius (*Rape of Lucretia*) Lake George Opera Fest 1972. Awards: Affiliate Artist; Grace Moore Schlshp, Univ of Tennessee.

Sang with major companies in USA: Lake George, Washington DC. **Roles with these companies incl** BRITTEN: Azarias (*Burning Fiery Furnace*), Junius★ (*Rape of Lucretia*); GOUNOD: Méphistophélès (*Faust*); MOZART: Figaro★ (*Nozze di Figaro*), Sarastro★ (*Zauberflöte*); PUCCINI: Colline★ (*Bohème*); ROSSINI: Don Basilio★ (*Barbiere di Siviglia*), Mustafà★ (*Italiana in Algeri*); SALIERI: Poeta★ (*Prima la musica poi le parole*); THOMAS: Lothario★ (*Mignon*); VERDI: Ramfis★ (*Aida*); WAGNER: Hunding★ (*Walküre*). Gives recitals. Appears with symphony orchestra. **Res:** New York, NY, USA. Mgmt: DSP/USA.

JAHN, GERTRUDE. Lyric & dramatic mezzo-soprano. Austrian. Resident mem: Staatsoper, Vienna. Born 13 Aug 1940, Zagreb, Yugoslavia. Single. Studied: Akad für Musik, Vienna; Elisabeth Rado, Prof Lily Kolar; Prof Erik Werba, coaching, Prof Josef Witt, opera rep, Vienna. **Debut:** GLUCK: Orfeo, Stadttheater Basel 1963.

Sang with major companies in AUS: Salzburg Fest, Vienna Staatsoper & Volksoper; CAN: Montreal/Quebec; FR GER: Berlin Deutsche Oper, Düsseldorf-Duisburg, Hamburg, Munich

Staatsoper, Stuttgart, Wuppertal; ITA: Trieste; SWI: Basel, Zurich; UK: Glyndebourne Fest; USSR: Moscow Bolshoi. **Roles with these companies incl** BIZET: Carmen; CILEA: Princesse de Bouillon★ (*A. Lecouvreur*); FLOTOW: Nancy (*Martha*); GLUCK: Orfeo; HUMPERDINCK: Hänsel; MARTIN: Mère d'Iseut (*Vin herbé*); MENOTTI: Miss Todd (*Old Maid and the Thief*); MOZART: Dorabella★ (*Così fan tutte*), Cherubino★ (*Nozze di Figaro*); OFFENBACH: Giulietta★ (*Contes d'Hoffmann*); PFITZNER: Silla★ (*Palestrina*); PUCCINI: Suzuki★ (*Butterfly*); SMETANA: Hata★ (*Bartered Bride*); STRAUSS, R: Komponist★ (*Ariadne auf Naxos*), Clairon★ (*Capriccio*), Octavian★ (*Rosenkavalier*); TCHAIKOVSKY: Olga★ (*Eugene Onegin*); VERDI: Eboli★ (*Don Carlo*), Preziosilla★ (*Forza del destino*); WAGNER: Magdalene★ (*Meistersinger*), Fricka★ (*Rheingold*); WEBER: Fatime (*Oberon*); WOLF-FERRARI: Margarita (*Quattro rusteghi*). Gives recitals. Appears with symphony orchestra. **Res:** Barmherzigeng 1, A-1030 Vienna, Austria. Mgmt: SLZ/FRG.

JAIA, GIANNI; né Giambattista Jaia. Lyric & dramatic tenor. Italian. Born 12 Oct 1930, Brindisi, Italy. One daughter. Studied: Raoul Frazzi, Florence; Tullio Serafin, Rome. **Debut:** Duca di Mantova (*Rigoletto*) Florence 1950. Previous occupations: pianist. Awards: Gold Medal, Teatro Regio Parma & Ente Turismo Tratani.
Sang with major companies in AUS: Vienna Staatsoper; CAN: Montreal/Quebec; DEN: Copenhagen; FRA: Lyon, Nice, Paris, Rouen, Toulouse; GRE: Athens National; FR GER: Berlin Deutsche Oper, Cologne, Essen, Hamburg, Kiel, Munich Staatsoper, Stuttgart; HOL: Amsterdam; HUN: Budapest; ISR: Tel Aviv; ITA: Bologna, Florence Comunale, Milan La Scala, Naples, Palermo Massimo, Parma, Rome Teatro dell'Opera & Caracalla, Trieste, Turin, Venice, Verona Arena; NOR: Oslo; POR: Lisbon; SPA: Barcelona; SWI: Basel, Geneva, Zurich; UK: Cardiff Welsh, London Royal; USA: Hartford, New York City Opera, Pittsburgh. **Roles with these companies incl** BELLINI: Lord Arthur (*Puritani*); BIZET: Don José (*Carmen*); BOITO: Faust (*Mefistofele*); CILEA: Maurizio★ (*A. Lecouvreur*); DONIZETTI: Riccardo★ (*Anna Bolena*), Nemorino (*Elisir*), Fernand (*Favorite*), Edgardo★ (*Lucia*); HALEVY: Eléazar★ (*Juive*); LEONCAVALLO: Canio★ (*Pagliacci*); MASCAGNI: Fritz (*Amico Fritz*), Turiddu★ (*Cavalleria rusticana*); MASSENET: Des Grieux (*Manon*); MEYERBEER: Raoul de Nangis (*Huguenots*); PONCHIELLI: Enzo (*Gioconda*); PUCCINI: Rodolfo★ (*Bohème*), Pinkerton★ (*Butterfly*), Cavaradossi★ (*Tosca*), Calaf★ (*Turandot*); ROSSINI: Almaviva (*Barbiere di Siviglia*), Arnold (*Guillaume Tell*), Aménophis (*Moïse*); VERDI: Radames (*Aida*), Riccardo★ (*Ballo in maschera*), Don Alvaro (*Forza del destino*), Rodolfo★ (*Luisa Miller*), Duca di Mantova (*Rigoletto*), Manrico★ (*Trovatore*). Recorded for: Angelicum-Ricordi. Video/Film: (*Puritani*); (*Rigoletto*); (*Favorite*); (*Bohème*); (*Traviata*). Gives recitals. Appears with symphony orchestra.

JALAS, ARMAS VEIKKO; né Blomstedt. Conductor of opera, ballet and symphony; composer.
Finnish. Born 23 Jun 1908, Jyväskylä, Finland. Wife Margareta. Three children. Studied: Univ Consv, Helsinki/Paris, I Krohn, Rhené-Baton, Pierre Monteux; incl piano, oboe, organ. Plays the piano. **Operatic debut:** *Tannhäuser* National Opera, Helsinki 1945. Symphonic debut: Helsinki City Orch, Finland 1935. Previous occupations: conc accomp; musical advis & cond Ntl Theater Helsinki; cond Helsinki Theater Orch; head symph orch and cond class Sibelius Acad. Awards: Prof HC, Commander White Rose, Finland; Lion Finn, Dannebrog Danish, Vasa Sweden, Hawk Iceland; officer Arts et Lettres, France. Previous adm positions in opera: Gen Mus Dir, Städtische Bühnen, Lübeck, FR Ger 1956; Res Cond, then Chief Cond, Finnish Ntl Opera, Helsinki 1945-73.
Conducted with major companies in CZE: Prague National; FIN: Helsinki; GRE: Athens Fest; FR GER: Stuttgart; GER DR: Berlin Staatsoper; HUN: Budapest; NOR: Oslo; SWE: Stockholm. **Operas with these companies incl** AUBER: *Fra Diavolo*; BARTOK: *Bluebeard's Castle*; BEETHOVEN: *Fidelio*; BERG: *Lulu*; BERLIOZ: *Damnation de Faust*; BIZET: *Carmen*; BORODIN: *Prince Igor*; BRITTEN: *Peter Grimes, Rape of Lucretia*; DEBUSSY: *Pelléas et Mélisande*; GOUNOD: *Faust*; HUMPERDINCK: *Hänsel und Gretel*; JANACEK: *Katya Kabanova*; KODALY: *Háry János*; LEONCAVALLO: *Pagliacci*; MARTINU: *Comedy on the Bridge*; MASCAGNI: *Cavalleria rusticana*; MASSENET: *Manon*; MENOTTI: *Amahl*; MONTEVERDI: *Incoronazione di Poppea*; MOZART: *Così fan tutte, Don Giovanni, Entführung aus dem Serail, Nozze di Figaro★, Zauberflöte*; MUSSORGSKY: *Boris Godunov*; OFFENBACH: *Contes d'Hoffmann*; ORFF: *Kluge*; PERGOLESI: *Maestro di musica, Serva padrona*; PETROVICS: *Crime and Punishment★*; PROKOFIEV: *Love for Three Oranges*; PUCCINI: *Bohème★, Butterfly, Tosca★, Turandot*; RABAUD: *Mârouf*; RAVEL: *Heure espagnole*; ROSSINI: *Barbiere di Siviglia★*; SAINT-SAENS: *Samson et Dalila*; SHOSTAKOVICH: *Katerina Ismailova*; STRAUSS, R: *Elektra, Rosenkavalier★, Salome*; STRAVINSKY: *Perséphone*; SZOKOLAY: *Blood Wedding★*; TCHAIKOVSKY: *Eugene Onegin, Pique Dame*; VERDI: *Aida, Don Carlo★, Falstaff, Otello, Rigoletto★, Traviata, Trovatore*; WAGNER: *Fliegende Holländer, Lohengrin, Meistersinger, Parsifal, Rheingold★, Walküre, Tannhäuser, Tristan und Isolde*. Also HONEGGER: *Jeanne d'Arc*; LEFLEM: *Aucassin et Nicolette*; NIELSEN: *Maskarade*; eleven Finnish operas. **World premieres:** PYLKKANEN: *Opri ja Oleksi; Tuntematon Sotilas*; Finnish Ntl Opera, Helsinki 1947-67; SONNINEN: *Haavruuva* Opera Comp Tampere, Finland 1975. Video—Finnish TV; *The Prisoner*. Conducted major orch in Europe, USA/Canada, Asia, Africa. **Res:** Tiirasaaren Tie 8D, Helsinki, Finland. Mgmt: MFZ/FIN; SUH/USA.

JAMERSON, THOMAS H. Lyric baritone. American. Resident mem: New York City Opera. Born 3 Jul 1942, New Orleans, LA, USA. Wife Madeleine Mines, occupation singer. Two children, from prev marriage. Studied: Louisiana State Univ, Loren Davidson, Baton Rouge, LA, USA; Cornelius

Reid, New York. **Debut:** Count Almaviva (*Nozze di Figaro*) Metropolitan Opera National Co 1967. Awards: Met Op Ntl Counc Aud Finalist.

Sang with major companies in USA: Baltimore, Boston, New York City Opera, Santa Fe. **Roles with these companies incl** BRITTEN: Demetrius⋆ (*Midsummer Night*); DELIUS: Dark Fiddler⋆ (*Village Romeo and Juliet*); MOZART: Conte Almaviva (*Nozze di Figaro*), Papageno⋆ (*Zauberflöte*); PUCCINI: Marcello⋆ (*Bohème*), Sharpless⋆ (*Butterfly*); ROSSINI: Dandini⋆ (*Cenerentola*); VERDI: Ford (*Falstaff*). Also HANDEL: Achilla⋆ (*Giulio Cesare*); HENZE: Secretary⋆ (*Junge Lord*); MONTEVERDI: Ottone⋆(*Incoronazione di Poppea*); GOUNOD: Valentin⋆ (*Faust*); STRAUSS, R: Faninal⋆ (*Rosenkavalier*). Recorded for: RCA. Gives recitals. Appears with symphony orchestra. Teaches voice. **Res:** New York, NY, USA. Mgmt: LLP/USA.

JAMES, CAROLYNE F. Dramatic mezzo-soprano. American. Born 27 Apr 1945, Wheatland, WY, USA. Single. Studied: Univ of Wyoming, Laramie, USA; Indiana Univ, Bloomington; Daniel Ferro, Margaret Harshaw, Michael Trimble, USA. **Debut:** Mme Flora (*Medium*) St Paul Opera 1970. Previous occupations: asst prof of voice, Univ of Iowa, Iowa City. Awards: Young Artist Awd, NFMC; M B Rockefeller Fund Grant; Lillian Garabedian Awd, Santa Fe, NM, USA.

Sang with major companies in USA: Boston, Cincinnati, Fort Worth, Houston, Kansas City, Lake George, Minneapolis, New York City Opera, St Paul. **Roles with these companies incl** DONIZETTI: Marquise de Birkenfeld⋆ (*Fille du régiment*); FALLA: Abuela (*Vida breve*); HENZE: Baronin von Grünwiesel⋆ (*Junge Lord*); HUMPERDINCK: Hexe (*Hänsel und Gretel*); MENOTTI: Mme Flora⋆ (*Medium*), Miss Todd (*Old Maid and the Thief*); PUCCINI: Frugola⋆ (*Tabarro*); VERDI: Ulrica⋆ (*Ballo in maschera*), Dame Quickly⋆ (*Falstaff*), Azucena⋆ (*Trovatore*); WAGNER: Erda⋆ (*Siegfried*), Fricka⋆ (*Walküre*); WEILL: Leocadia Begbick⋆ (*Aufstieg und Fall der Stadt Mahagonny*). Also PUCCINI: Zita (*Gianni Schicchi*); BEESON: Mother Rainey (*Sweet Bye and Bye*). Recorded for: Desto. Gives recitals. Appears with symphony orchestra. **Res:** New York, NY. Mgmt: CAM/USA.

JAMPOLIS, NEIL PETER. Scenic and costume designer for opera, theater; specl in sets. Is a lighting designer. American. Born 14 Mar 1943, Brooklyn. Wife Jane Reisman, occupation lighting designer. Studied: Goodman Theater, Art Inst of Chicago. **Operatic debut:** sets, *Purgatory* Juilliard School, New York 1966; cost, *Bohème* Netherlands Opera, Amsterdam 1970. Theater debut: Living Arts Theater, Philadelphia 1965. Awards: Tony Awd 1974-75.

Designed for major companies in CAN: Montreal/Quebec; HOL: Amsterdam; USA: Houston, Memphis, New Orleans, New York Met, Philadelphia Lyric, St Paul, Santa Fe, Washington DC. **Operas designed for these companies incl** BEETHOVEN: *Fidelio;* BIZET: *Carmen;* BRITTEN: *Rape of Lucretia;* DEBUSSY: *Pelléas et Mélisande;* DONIZETTI: *Don Pasquale, Elisir;* HALEVY: *Juive⋆;* HENZE: *Junge Lord⋆;* HIN-

DEMITH: *Cardillac;* MASSENET: *Hérodiade⋆;* MENOTTI: *Amahl;* MEYERBEER: *Huguenots⋆;* MONTEVERDI: *Incoronazione di Poppea⋆;* MOZART: *Così fan tutte⋆, Don Giovanni⋆;* PUCCINI: *Bohème⋆, Butterfly⋆, Tosca⋆;* REIMANN: *Melusine⋆;* ROSSINI: *Barbiere di Siviglia⋆, Signor Bruschino⋆;* STRAUSS, R: *Rosenkavalier⋆, Salome⋆;* STRAVINSKY: *Oedipus Rex, Perséphone, Rake's Progress⋆;* VERDI: *Forza del destino⋆, Macbeth⋆, Rigoletto⋆;* WAGNER: *Fliegende Holländer⋆, Lohengrin⋆, Tannhäuser⋆;* WEILL: *Dreigroschenoper.* **Operatic world premieres:** DE KRUYF: *Spinoza* Netherlands Opera, Amsterdam 1971; SCHOENBERG: *Jakobsleiter* Santa Fe Opera, first stgd 1968. **Res:** 130 W 57th St, New York, USA. Mgmt: SSR/USA.

JAMROZ, KRYSTYNA. Dramatic soprano. Polish. Resident mem: Great Theater, Warsaw. Born 29 Aug 1928, Busko-Zdroj, Poland. Husband Mikulicz, occupation dir Foreign Relations, Dept of Polish Radio-TV. One daughter. Studied: Prof Irene Bardy, Wroclaw, Poland; Prof Wanda Werminiska, Warsaw. **Debut:** Santuzza (*Cavalleria rusticana*) State Opera, Wroclaw, Poland 1949. Awards: Order of Polonia Restituta V Class, Counc of State, Poland; Golden Cross of Merit.

Sang with major companies in BRA: Rio de Janeiro; BUL: Sofia; FRA: Rouen; FR GER: Hannover, Karlsruhe, Wiesbaden; POL: Lodz, Warsaw; ROM: Bucharest; USSR: Kiev; YUG: Zagreb, Belgrade. **Roles with these companies incl** BERG: Marie (*Wozzeck*); DALLAPICCOLA: Madre (*Prigioniero*); JANACEK: Jenufa; MASCAGNI: Santuzza⋆ (*Cavalleria rusticana*); MENOTTI: Magda Sorel⋆ (*Consul*); MONIUSZKO: Halka; MOZART: Donna Elvira (*Don Giovanni*), Contessa (*Nozze di Figaro*); PENDERECKI: Jeanne⋆ (*Teufel von Loudun*); PONCHIELLI: Gioconda; PUCCINI: Musetta (*Bohème*), Tosca⋆, Turandot⋆; SMETANA: Marie (*Bartered Bride*); STRAUSS, R: Marschallin (*Rosenkavalier*); SUCHON: Katrena (*Whirlpool*); TCHAIKOVSKY: Tatiana⋆ (*Eugene Onegin*); VERDI: Aida⋆, Amelia (*Ballo in maschera*), Elisabetta⋆ (*Don Carlo*), Desdemona⋆ (*Otello*), Leonora⋆ (*Trovatore*); WAGNER: Senta (*Fliegende Holländer*), Elisabeth (*Tannhäuser*). Recorded for: Polskie Nagrania. Video/Film: Leonora (*Trovatore*); Turandot; Lisa (*Pique Dame*). Appears with symphony orchestra. **Res:** ul Moliera 8 m41, Warsaw, Poland. Mgmt: PAG/POL; IAA/USA.

JANKU, HANNA. Dramatic soprano. Czechoslovakian. Resident mem: Deutsche Oper Berlin; Deutsche Oper am Rhein, Düsseldorf.

Sang with major companies in AUS: Vienna Staatsoper; CZE: Prague National; FR GER: Berlin Deutsche Oper, Düsseldorf-Duisburg, Hamburg, Mannheim, Wuppertal; ITA: Florence Comunale, Rome Opera & Caracalla, Verona Arena; MEX: Mexico City; UK: London Royal; USA: San Francisco Opera; et al. **Roles with these companies incl** PONCHIELLI: Gioconda; PUCCINI: Tosca, Turandot; SMETANA: Mlada (*Dalibor*); STRAUSS, R: Ariadne (*Ariadne auf Naxos*); VERDI: Elisabetta (*Don Carlo*), Leonora

(*Forza del destino*); et al. Also WAGNER: Kundry (*Parsifal*).

JANOUS, JOSEF. Czechoslovakian. Deputy Head Opera Co, National Theater Prague, Divadelní 6, 112 30 Prague 1, 1971- . In charge of overall adm & mus matters. Is also a clarinetist. Born 9 Aug 1927, Méricourt-Corons, France. Wife Eva, occupation painter. Two children. Studied: Music Acad, Brno, CSSR. Previous occupations: orch member, National Theater Prague 1951-71; Prof, State Consv Prague. **Res:** Na dlouhé mezi 15/61, Prague 4/Bráník, CSSR.

JANOWITZ, GUNDULA. Lyric & dramatic soprano. Austrian. Resident mem: Staatsoper, Vienna; Deutsche Oper Berlin. Born 2 Aug 1937, Berlin. Husband Wolfgang Zonner, occupation physician. One child. Studied: Landeskonsv Graz, Hubert Thöny, Austria. **Debut:** Barbarina (*Nozze di Figaro*) Staatsoper, Vienna 1959. Awards: Österr Kammersängerin, 1970.

Sang with major companies in AUS: Graz, Salzburg Fest, Vienna Staatsoper; FRA: Aix-en-Provence Fest; FR GER: Bayreuth Fest, Berlin Deutsche Oper, Frankfurt, Hamburg, Mannheim, Munich Staatsoper; UK: Edinburgh Fest, Glyndebourne Fest; USA: New York Met; et al. **Roles with these companies incl** BEETHOVEN: Marzelline (*Fidelio*); GLUCK: Euridice‡; MOZART: Fiordiligi (*Così fan tutte*), Donna Anna (*Don Giovanni*), Contessa (*Nozze di Figaro*), Pamina (*Zauberflöte*); ORFF: Solo‡ (*Carmina burana*); PFITZNER: Ighino (*Palestrina*); STRAUSS, J: Rosalinde (*Fledermaus*); STRAUSS, R: Arabella, Gräfin‡ (*Capriccio*), Kaiserin (*Frau ohne Schatten*); VERDI: Aida, Odabella (*Attila*), Elisabetta (*Don Carlo*), Amelia (*Simon Boccanegra*); WAGNER: Elsa (*Lohengrin*), Sieglinde‡ (*Walküre*), Gutrune (*Götterdämmerung*); WEBER: Agathe‡ (*Freischütz*); et al. Recorded for: DG, BASF, Angel, Columbia. Appears with symphony orchestra. Mgmt: COL/USA; ASK/UK.

JANOWSKI, MAREK. Conductor of opera and symphony. German. Gen Mus Dir & Resident Cond, Städt Bühnen, Freiburg 1974-75; as of 1975-76 Städt Bühnen, Dortmund. Born 18 Feb 1939, Warsaw, Poland. Wife Marina. One child. Studied: Musikhochschule Cologne, Prof Wolfgang v d Nahmer, Prof Wolfgang Sawallisch; incl violin, piano. Operatic training as repetiteur at Städt Bühnen, Aachen 1961-62; Städt Bühnen, Cologne 1962-64. Previous adm positions in opera: Deputy Gen Mus Dir, Staatsoper Hamburg 1972-73.

Conducted with major companies in FRA: Paris; FR GER: Cologne, Dortmund, Düsseldorf-Duisburg, Hamburg, Munich Staatsoper, Stuttgart, Wiesbaden. **Operas with these companies incl** BEETHOVEN: *Fidelio*; BELLINI: *Norma*; BERG: *Lulu*, *Wozzeck*; BIZET: *Carmen*; BORODIN: *Prince Igor*; CIMAROSA: *Matrimonio segreto*; DEBUSSY: *Pelléas et Mélisande*; DESSAU: *Lanzelot*; DONIZETTI: *Don Pasquale*, *Elisir*; FLOTOW: *Martha*; HAYDN: *Infedeltà delusa*; HENZE: *Junge Lord*; HINDEMITH: *Mathis der Maler*; HUMPERDINCK: *Hänsel und Gretel*; JANACEK: *Cunning Little Vixen*, *From the House of the*

Dead, *Jenufa*; LEONCAVALLO: *Pagliacci*; LORTZING: *Wildschütz, Zar und Zimmermann*; MASCAGNI: *Cavalleria rusticana*; MOZART: *Clemenza di Tito*, *Così fan tutte*, *Entführung aus dem Serail*, *Zauberflöte*; MUSSORGSKY: *Boris Godunov*; NICOLAI: *Lustigen Weiber*; OFFENBACH: *Contes d'Hoffmann*; ORFF: *Kluge*; PENDERECKI: *Teufel von Loudun*‡; POULENC: *Dialogues des Carmélites, Mamelles de Tirésias*; PUCCINI: *Bohème*, *Gianni Schicchi*, *Butterfly*, *Tabarro*, *Tosca*; RAVEL: *Heure espagnole*; ROSSINI: *Barbiere di Siviglia*, *Italiana in Algeri*; STRAUSS, J: *Fledermaus*; STRAUSS, R: *Arabella*, *Ariadne auf Naxos*, *Capriccio*, *Frau ohne Schatten*, *Rosenkavalier*, *Salome*, *Schweigsame Frau*; TCHAIKOVSKY: *Pique Dame*; VERDI: *Ballo in maschera, Don Carlo, Falstaff, Forza del destino, Nabucco*, *Rigoletto*, *Traviata, Trovatore*; WAGNER: *Fliegende Holländer, Lohengrin*, *Meistersinger*, *Götterdämmerung*, *Tannhäuser*, *Tristan und Isolde*; WEBER: *Freischütz*; WEILL: *Aufstieg und Fall der Stadt Mahagonny*; WOLF-FERRARI: *Quattro rusteghi*; ZIMMERMANN: *Soldaten*. Also WEBER: *Euryanthe* on records. **World premieres:** STEFFENS: *Unter Milchwald* Staatsoper Hamburg 1973. Recorded for Philips, EMI. Video/Film—TV Staatsoper Hamburg: *Teufel von Loudun, Orphée aux enfers*. Conducted major orch in Europe. **Res:** Dortmund, FR Ger.

JANSSENS, CHARLES ROMAIN. Stages/produces opera, theater & television. Also designs sets, costumes & stage-lighting and is an actor. Belgian. Born 25 Jul 1932, Ghent. Single. Studied: Royal Inst for Dramatic Art, Ghent; also music, violin & voice. **Operatic debut:** *Let's Make an Opera* Royal Opera, Ghent 1960. Theater debut: drama co, Univ of Ghent 1954. Previous occupation: language teacher.

Directed/produced opera with major companies in BEL: Liège; CAN: Toronto; USA: Pittsburgh. **Operas staged with these companies incl** BEETHOVEN: *Fidelio*‡; BELLINI: *Norma, Puritani*‡; BIZET: *Carmen*‡; BRITTEN: *Peter Grimes*‡; DELIBES: *Lakmé*‡; DONIZETTI: *Lucia*‡, *Lucrezia Borgia*‡, *Rita*‡; FLOTOW: *Martha*‡; GLUCK: *Orfeo ed Euridice*‡; GOUNOD: *Faust*‡, *Roméo et Juliette*‡; JANACEK: *Katya Kabanova*‡; KORNGOLD: *Tote Stadt*‡; LEONCAVALLO: *Pagliacci*‡; MASCAGNI: *Cavalleria rusticana*‡; MASSENET: *Werther*‡; MENOTTI: *Amahl*‡, *Consul*‡; MOZART: *Zauberflöte*‡; NICOLAI: *Lustigen Weiber*‡; OFFENBACH: *Contes d'Hoffmann*‡; ORFF: *Carmina burana*‡, *Mond*; PUCCINI: *Fanciulla del West*‡, *Butterfly*‡, *Suor Angelica*‡; STRAUSS, J: *Fledermaus*‡; STRAUSS, R: *Salome*‡; TCHAIKOVSKY: *Eugene Onegin*‡, *Pique Dame*‡; THOMAS: *Hamlet*‡; VERDI: *Aida*‡, *Ballo in maschera*‡, *Ernani*‡, *Luisa Miller*‡, *Macbeth*‡, *Nabucco*‡, *Otello*‡, *Simon Boccanegra*‡, *Traviata*‡, *Trovatore*‡, *Vespri*‡; WAGNER: *Fliegende Holländer*‡, *Walküre*‡, *Tannhäuser*‡. Also KORNGOLD: *Wunder der Heliane*‡; LEONCAVALLO: *Edipo re*‡; LIEBERMANN: *Penelope*‡; MASCAGNI: *Iris*‡; ORFF: *Catulli carmina*‡, *Trionfo di Afrodite*‡. **Operatic world premieres:** DI VITO: *Trittico*

Royal Opera, Ghent 1965. Teaches at Higher Inst for Drama & Culture, Brussels. **Res:** Baudelostraat 36, Ghent, Belgium. Mgmt: MCD/USA.

JANULAKO, WASSILI; né Wassilios Giannoulakos. Dramatic baritone. Greek. Resident mem: Städtische Bühnen, Cologne; Staatsoper, Stuttgart. Born 14 Sep 1933, Athens, Greece. Wife Ursula. Studied: Athens Consv, Ntl Consv, Greece. **Debut:** High Priest (*Alceste*) Athens Fest 1959. Previous occupations: studies in polit economics Athens Univ. Awards: First Place Intl Opera Compt Decca, Vienna 1961.

Sang with major companies in AUS: Graz, Vienna Staatsoper; CAN: Edmonton; FRA: Toulouse; GRE: Athens National, Athens Fest; FR GER: Berlin Deutsche Oper, Bielefeld, Bonn, Cologne, Dortmund, Düsseldorf-Duisburg, Essen, Frankfurt, Hamburg, Hannover, Karlsruhe, Kiel, Munich Staatsoper & Gärtnerplatz, Nürnberg, Saarbrücken, Stuttgart, Wuppertal; SPA: Barcelona; SWI: Basel, Zurich, Bern; USA: San Francisco Opera. **Roles with these companies incl** BEETHOVEN: Don Pizarro★ (*Fidelio*); BIZET: Escamillo★ (*Carmen*), Zurga★ (*Pêcheurs de perles*); DONIZETTI: Malatesta (*Don Pasquale*), Alfonse (*Favorite*); GIORDANO: Carlo Gérard★ (*Andrea Chénier*); GLUCK: High Priest (*Alceste*), Agamemnon (*Iphigénie en Aulide*); LEON-CAVALLO: Tonio★ (*Pagliacci*); MASCAGNI: Alfio★ (*Cavalleria rusticana*); MILHAUD: Christophe Colomb; MOZART: Don Giovanni★, Conte Almaviva (*Nozze di Figaro*); OFFENBACH: Coppélius★ etc (*Contes d'Hoffmann*); PONCHIELLI: Barnaba★ (*Gioconda*); PUCCINI: Marcello★ (*Bohème*), Jack Rance★ (*Fanciulla del West*), Sharpless★ (*Butterfly*), Michele (*Tabarro*), Scarpia★(*Tosca*); SAINT-SAENS: Grand prêtre★ (*Samson et Dalila*); STRAUSS, R: Mandryka★ (*Arabella*), Jochanaan (*Salome*); VERDI: Amonasro★ (*Aida*), Renato (*Ballo in maschera*), Rodrigo★ (*Don Carlo*), Ford★ (*Falstaff*), Don Carlo★ (*Forza del destino*), Macbeth★, Nabucco★, Iago★ (*Otello*), Rigoletto★, Germont★ (*Traviata*), Conte di Luna★ (*Trovatore*), Monforte★ (*Vespri*); WAGNER: Holländer, Telramund (*Lohengrin*), Amfortas★ (*Parsifal*). Also GOUNOD: Valentin★ (*Faust*); VERDI: Padre (*Stiffelio*). Video/Film: (*Andrea Chénier*); (*Otello*). Gives recitals. Appears with symphony orchestra. Teaches voice. **Res:** Am Alten Posthof 4-6, Cologne, FR Ger. Mgmt: SMD/FRG.

JASPER, BELLA. Coloratura soprano. Hungarian. Resident mem: Deutsche Oper, Berlin. Born 18 Feb 1933, Szöny, Hungary. Divorced. Studied: Prof Olga Révhegyi, Budapest. **Debut:** Gilda (*Rigoletto*) Budapest State Opera 1958. Previous occupations: harp player in orch; conct pianist; voice pedagogue. Awards: Kammersängerin, Deutsche Oper, Berlin 1969.

Sang with major companies in ARG: Buenos Aires; AUS: Bregenz Fest, Vienna Staatsoper & Volksoper; BUL: Sofia; FRA: Paris, Strasbourg, Toulouse; FR GER: Berlin Deutsche Oper, Bonn, Cologne, Düsseldorf-Duisburg, Frankfurt, Hamburg, Hannover, Karlsruhe, Kassel, Kiel, Munich Staatsoper & Gärtnerplatz, Nürnberg, Stuttgart, Wiesbaden, Wuppertal; GER DR: Berlin Staatso-per, Dresden, Leipzig; HOL: Amsterdam; HUN: Budapest; ITA: Genoa, Trieste, Turin, Venice; POL: Warsaw Teatr Wielki; POR: Lisbon; SPA: Madrid; SWI: Basel, Geneva, Zurich; UK: Edinburgh Fest, London English National; USSR: Leningrad Kirov, Moscow Bolshoi; YUG: Zagreb, Belgrade. **Roles with these companies incl** ADAM: Neméa (*Si j'étais roi*); BEETHOVEN: Marzelline (*Fidelio*); BOIELDIEU: Anna (*Dame blanche*); CALDARA: Dafne; CIMAROSA: Elisetta★ (*Matrimonio segreto*); DELIBES: Lakmé; DONIZETTI: Norina (*Don Pasquale*), Linda di Chamounix, Lucia★; DVORAK: Rusalka; ERKEL: Melinda (*Bánk Bán*); GLUCK: Amor (*Orfeo ed Euridice*); GOUNOD: Marguerite (*Faust*), Juliette; HANDEL: Galatea, Atalante (*Xerxes*); HENZE: Ida & Louisa (*Junge Lord*); KODALY: Marie Louise (*Háry János*); LEONCAVALLO: Nedda (*Pagliacci*); MONIUSZKO: Halka; MOZART: Konstanze★ & Blondchen (*Entführung aus dem Serail*), Mme Herz & Mlle Silberklang (*Schauspieldirektor*), Königin der Nacht★ (*Zauberflöte*); OFFENBACH: Olympia★ & Antonia★ & Giulietta★ (*Contes d'Hoffmann*); PROKOFIEV: Fata Morgana (*Love for Three Oranges*); PUCCINI: Musetta★ (*Bohème*), Lauretta (*Gianni Schicchi*); RIMSKY-KORSAKOV: Reine de Schemakan (*Coq d'or*); ROSSINI: Rosina★ (*Barbiere di Siviglia*), Comtesse Adèle (*Comte Ory*); STRAUSS, J: Adele★ (*Fledermaus*); STRAUSS, R: Fiakermilli★ (*Arabella*), Zerbinetta★ (*Ariadne auf Naxos*), Ital Sängerin★, (*Capriccio*), Sophie (*Rosenkavalier*); STRAVINSKY: Rossignol; THOMAS: Philine (*Mignon*); VERDI: Oscar★ (*Ballo in maschera*), Gilda★ (*Rigoletto*), Violetta (*Traviata*); WEBER: Aennchen (*Freischütz*). Also HAYDN: Griletta (*Speziale*). **World premieres:** HENZE: Ida (*Junge Lord*) Deutsche Oper, Berlin 1965. Recorded for: DG. Video/Film: (*Dame blanche*). Appears with symphony orchestra. Teaches voice. Coaches repertoire. On faculty of Hochschule für Musik, Berlin. **Res:** Auguste-Viktoria Str 5, 1 Berlin 33, FR Ger.

JEDLICKA, DALIBOR. Bass-baritone. Czechoslovakian. Resident mem: National Theater, Prague. Born 23 May 1929, Svojanov, CSR. Wife Jirina. Two daughters. Studied: Prof Rudolf Vasek, Ostrava. **Debut:** Mumlal (*Two Widows*) Municipal Theater, Opava 1953.

Sang with major companies in CZE: Brno, Prague National; FRA: Bordeaux; FR GER: Wiesbaden; HOL: Amsterdam; ITA: Bologna, Venice; POL: Warsaw; SWI: Zurich; UK: Edinburgh Fest; YUG: Zagreb, Belgrade. **Roles with these companies incl** BEETHOVEN: Rocco (*Fidelio*); BERLIOZ: Méphisthophélès (*Damnation de Faust*); DVORAK: Marbuel★ (*Devil and Kate*); GOUNOD: Méphisthophélès (*Faust*); JANACEK: Sacristan★ (*Excursions of Mr Broucek*), Gorianchikov★ (*From the House of the Dead*), Dikoy★ (*Katya Kabanova*); MARTINU: Fotis★ (*Griechische Passion*); MASSENET: Sancho (*Don Quichotte*); MOZART: Don Alfonso★ (*Così fan tutte*), Figaro★ (*Nozze di Figaro*), Papageno (*Zauberflöte*); MUSSORGSKY: Boris Godunov; PROKOFIEV: Vassili Denisov★ (*War and Peace*); PUCCINI: Colline★ (*Bohème*); ROSSINI: Don Basilio (*Barbiere di Siviglia*); SME-

TANA: Kezal★(*Bartered Bride*), Rarach★(*Devil's Wall*), Malina★ (*Secret*), Peter★ (*Two Widows*); STRAUSS, R: Orest (*Elektra*); VERDI: Grande Inquisitore★ (*Don Carlo*); WEBER: Kaspar★ (*Freischütz*). Also DVORAK: Wassermann (*Rusalka*), Purkrabi (*Jakobin*); SMETANA: Chrudos (*Libuse*). Recorded for: Supraphon. Video/Film: Figaro (*Nozze di Figaro*); Guglielmo (*Così fan tutte*); Gorianchikov (*From the House of the Dead*); Tamerlano (*Tamerlano*). Gives recitals. Appears with symphony orchestra. Res: Zatecka 8, 110 00 Prague 1, CSSR. Mgmt: PRG/CZE.

JEFFREYS, CELIA. Coloratura soprano. British. Resident mem: Opernhaus Kassel & Darmstadt. Born 20 Jan 1948, Southampton, UK. Single. Studied: Royal Coll of Music, Gordon Clinton, Miss Meriel St Clair, London; Prof Georges Cunelli, London. **Debut:** Adele (*Fledermaus*) Welsh National 1970. Awards: Assoc of the Royal Coll of Music, London.
Sang with major companies in FR GER: Kassel; UK: Cardiff Welsh. **Roles with these companies incl** CIMAROSA: Carolina★ (*Matrimonio segreto*); DONIZETTI: Luigia★ (*Convenienze*); HANDEL: Galatea; MOZART: Zerlina★ (*Don Giovanni*), Ilia★ (*Idomeneo*), Susanna★ (*Nozze di Figaro*); NICOLAI: Aennchen★ (*Lustigen Weiber*); OFFENBACH: Olympia★ (*Contes d'Hoffmann*); PUCCINI: Musetta (*Bohème*); STRAUSS, J: Adele★ (*Fledermaus*); WEBER: Aennchen★ (*Freischütz*). Gives recitals. Appears with symphony orchestra. Res: Fuldatalstr 159, Kassel, FR Ger. Mgmt: SLZ/FRG.

JENNINGS, JERRY. Lyric tenor. American. Born 23 Oct 1936, Carbondale, IL, USA. Wife Nancy Wyckoff. Two children. Studied: Todd Duncan, Washington, DC; Louis Nicholas, Nashville, TN; Sergei Radamsky, Italy; William Reimer, Germany. **Debut:** Hoffmann, Städtische Bühnen, Bielefeld 1964. Awards: Three grants M B Rockefeller Fund.
Sang with major companies in BEL: Brussels; FR GER: Berlin Deutsche Oper, Bielefeld, Bonn, Darmstadt, Düsseldorf-Duisburg, Hamburg, Hannover, Mannheim, Stuttgart, Wuppertal; SWI: Basel; UK: Glyndebourne Fest; USA: New York City Opera. **Roles with these companies incl** ADAM: Chapelou (*Postillon de Lonjumeau*); BERLIOZ: Bénédict★, Faust★ (*Damnation de Faust*); DONIZETTI: Ernesto (*Don Pasquale*), Nemorino (*Elisir*); FLOTOW: Lionel (*Martha*); GOUNOD: Faust; HANDEL: Xerxes; HENZE: Lord Barrat (*Junge Lord*); LORTZING: Baron Kronthal (*Wildschütz*); MOZART: Ferrando★ (*Così fan tutte*), Don Ottavio (*Don Giovanni*), Belmonte★ (*Entführung aus dem Serail*), Belfiore (*Finta giardiniera*), Tamino (*Zauberflöte*); OFFENBACH: Hoffmann; PUCCINI: Rodolfo (*Bohème*), Rinuccio (*Gianni Schicchi*), Pinkerton (*Butterfly*), Cavaradossi (*Tosca*); ROSSINI: Almaviva★ (*Barbiere di Siviglia*), Don Ramiro★ (*Cenerentola*); SMETANA: Hans (*Bartered Bride*); STRAVINSKY: Pêcheur★ (*Rossignol*); TCHAIKOVSKY: Lenski (*Eugene Onegin*); VERDI: Alfredo★ (*Traviata*). Recorded for: Eurodisc. Video/Film—ZBF Ger: Pinkerton (*But-*

terfly). Gives recitals. Teaches voice. Coaches repertoire. Res: 4218 Granny White Pk, Nashville, TN 37204, USA. Mgmt: CAM/USA.

JERNEK, KAREL. Stages/produces opera, theater & television and is an author. Czechoslovakian. Resident Stage Dir, National Theater, Prague. Born 31 Mar 1910, Prague. Wife Olga Jernek-Filipi, occupation costume desgn. One daughter. Studied: Univ of Prague, incl music, violin & piano. **Operatic debut:** *Bartered Bride* Smetana State Theater, Brno 1939. Theater debut: National Theater, Prague 1938. Awards: Merited Artist, Gvnmt CSSR 1966.
Directed/produced opera for major companies in ARG: Buenos Aires; AUS: Vienna Staatsoper & Volksoper; CZE: Brno, Prague National & Smetana; HOL: Amsterdam; ITA: Milan La Scala; SPA: Barcelona; UK: Edinburgh Fest; USSR: Moscow Bolshoi; YUG: Zagreb, Belgrade. **Operas staged for these companies incl** d'ALBERT: *Tiefland★;* AUBER: *Muette de Portici;* BEETHOVEN: *Fidelio;* BERG: *Wozzeck★;* BERLIOZ: *Troyens;* BIZET: *Carmen;* BORODIN: *Prince Igor★;* CHARPENTIER: *Louise;* DVORAK: *Devil and Kate, Rusalka★;* GAY/Britten: *Beggar's Opera;* GIORDANO: *Andrea Chénier★;* GLUCK: *Iphigénie en Tauride, Orfeo ed Euridice;* GOUNOD: *Faust, Roméo et Juliette★;* HALEVY: *Juive;* HINDEMITH: *Mathis der Maler;* HONEGGER: *Antigone;* JANACEK: *Cunning Little Vixen, Excursions of Mr Broucek, From the House of the Dead★, Jenufa, Katya Kabanova★, Makropoulos Affair★;* LEONCAVALLO: *Pagliacci;* LORTZING: *Zar und Zimmermann;* MARTINU: *Comedy on the Bridge, Griechische Passion★;* MASCAGNI: *Cavalleria rusticana;* MASSENET: *Don Quichotte, Manon, Werther;* MONTEVERDI: *Ritorno d'Ulisse;* MOZART: *Così fan tutte★, Don Giovanni★, Idomeneo, Nozze di Figaro★, Zauberflöte;* MUSSORGSKY: *Boris Godunov★, Fair at Sorochinsk;* NICOLAI: *Lustigen Weiber;* OFFENBACH: *Contes d'Hoffmann;* ORFF: *Kluge;* PROKOFIEV: *Fiery Angel, War and Peace★;* PUCCINI: *Bohème★, Gianni Schicchi, Butterfly, Manon Lescaut, Tosca, Turandot★;* ROSSINI: *Barbiere di Siviglia;* SCHOENBERG: *Erwartung;* SHOSTAKOVICH: *Katerina Ismailova★;* SMETANA: *Bartered Bride, Dalibor, Devil's Wall★, The Kiss★, Libuse, Secret, Two Widows★;* STRAUSS, J: *Fledermaus;* STRAUSS, R: *Arabella★, Elektra, Rosenkavalier, Salome★, Schweigsame Frau;* STRAVINSKY: *Rake's Progress;* TCHAIKOVSKY: *Eugene Onegin★, Maid of Orleans, Pique Dame;* VERDI: *Aida, Ballo in maschera, Don Carlo★, Falstaff★, Luisa Miller, Macbeth, Nabucco★, Otello, Rigoletto, Simon Boccanegra★, Traviata, Trovatore;* WAGNER: *Fliegende Holländer, Lohengrin★, Tannhäuser;* WEBER: *Freischütz★;* WEILL: *Dreigroschenoper;* WEINBERGER: *Schwanda;* ZANDONAI: *Francesca da Rimini.* Also DVORAK: *Jakobin★.*
Operatic world premieres: SUCHON: *Katrena* National Theater, Bratislava 1949; CIKKER: *Resurrection* Ntl Thtr Prague 1962, *Christmas Carol* Ntl Thtr Prague 1962. Operatic Video—Prague TV: *Jakobin.* Previous leading positions with major theater companies: Dir of

Drama, Municipal Theater Liberec 1950-52, Olomouc 1952-56, Pardubice 1956-57. **Opera libretti:** VOSTRAK: *Broken Jug* Munic Thtr Usti 1962. Teaches at Acad of Musical Art, Bratislava; Consv, Prague. **Res:** Sporilov 981, Prague 4, CSSR.

JÍLEK, FRANTISEK. Czechoslovakian. Opera Dir, State Theater Brno, Dvorákova 11, Brno. In charge of mus & dram matters. Is also a conductor & composer. Born 22 May 1913, Brno. Wife Lenka. One child. Studied: Master School of Composition, Prague; Brno Consv. Plays the piano. Positions, primarily musical & theatrical: Cond, State Opera Ostrava, CSR 1939-48; Prof, Janácek Acad of Music, Brno—current. Started with present company in 1948 as cond; in present position since 1952. World premieres at theaters under his management; five operas by Czech composers. **Res:** Tábor 42b, Brno, CSSR.

JINDRAK, JINDRICH. Character baritone. Czechoslovakian. Resident mem: National Theater, Prague. Born 4 Nov 1931, Strakonice, CSR. Wife Jana, occupation teacher. Two children. Studied: Music Acad, Kamila Ungrova, Bronislav Chorovic, Prague. **Debut:** Tomas (*The Kiss*) National Theater, Prague 1958. Awards: Artist of Merit, National Theater, Prague, Ministry of Culture CSSR 1973.

Sang with major companies in AUS: Vienna Volksoper; BEL: Brussels; BUL: Sofia; CZE: Brno, Prague National; DEN: Copenhagen; FRA: Bordeaux; FR GER: Kiel; HOL: Amsterdam; ITA: Bologna, Naples; POL: Warsaw; SWI: Zurich; UK: Edinburgh Fest; USSR: Moscow Bolshoi. **Roles with these companies incl** DVORAK: Marbuel★ (*Devil and Kate*); GOTOVAC: Sima (*Ero der Schelm*); JANACEK: Forester★ (*Cunning Little Vixen*); LORTZING: Graf Eberbach (*Wildschütz*); MARTINU: Hans★ (*Comedy on the Bridge*); MASCAGNI: Alfio (*Cavalleria rusticana*); MOZART: Guglielmo★ (*Così fan tutte*), Conte Almaviva★ (*Nozze di Figaro*); ORFF: König (*Kluge*); PUCCINI: Gianni Schicchi; RAVEL: Ramiro★ (*Heure espagnole*); SMETANA: Vok★(*Devil's Wall*), Tomas★(*The Kiss*), Premysl★ (*Libuse*), Kalina★ (*Secret*); TCHAIKOVSKY: Yeletsky (*Pique Dame*); VERDI: Rodrigo (*Don Carlo*), Simon Boccanegra★, Germont (*Traviata*). Also DVORAK: Bohus★(*Jakobin*); DALLAPICCOLA: Prigioniero‡; HENZE: Landarzt‡; KLEBE: Jakobowsky‡; PROKOFIEV: Prince Andrei (*War and Peace*); TCHAIKOVSKY: Eugene Onegin. Recorded for: Supraphon. Video/Film: Tomas (*The Kiss*); Cavaliere (*Mirandolina*); Bohus (*Jakobin*); Vok (*Devil's Wall*); Dott Malatesta (*Don Pasquale*); Marbuel (*Devil and Kate*); Conte Almaviva (*Nozze di Figaro*). Gives recitals. Appears with symphony orchestra. Teaches voice. Coaches repertoire. On faculty of Consv of Music, Prague; AMU School, Prague. **Res:** Jeremenkova 96, Prague, CSSR. **Mgmt:** PRG/CZE.

JIROUS, JIRI. Conductor of opera and symphony; composer. Czechoslovakian. Resident Cond, National Theater, Prague. Born 4 Aug 1923, Prague. Wife Vlasta Urbanová, occupation soprano. Studied: Dir Václav Talich, Prague; incl violin, piano.

Operatic training as asst cond at National Theater, Prague 1942-45. **Operatic debut:** National Theater, Prague 1942. Symphonic debut: Concertgebouw Orch, Amsterdam 1946. Previous occupations: piano & violin soloist 1933-45.

Conducted with major companies in BEL: Brussels, Liège; CZE: Brno, Prague National & Smetana; FRA: Bordeaux; HOL: Amsterdam; ITA: Florence Maggio, Genoa, Naples, Trieste, Turin, Venice; SWI: Basel, Zurich. **Operas with these companies incl** BELLINI: *Norma*; BIZET: *Carmen★*; DEBUSSY: *Pelléas et Mélisande*; DONIZETTI: *Don Pasquale*; DVORAK: *Rusalka*; GLUCK: *Orfeo ed Euridice*; GOUNOD: *Faust*; HANDEL: *Acis and Galatea*; LEONCAVALLO: *Pagliacci*; MASCAGNI: *Cavalleria rusticana*; MASSENET: *Don Quichotte, Manon*; MOZART: *Entführung aus dem Serail*; PUCCINI: *Bohème, Gianni Schicchi, Butterfly★, Tosca, Turandot★*; ROSSINI: *Barbiere di Siviglia★*; SMETANA: *Bartered Bride, Dalibor, Devil's Wall, The Kiss, Secret*; STRAVINSKY: *Rake's Progress★*; TCHAIKOVSKY: *Eugene Onegin, Pique Dame*; THOMAS: *Mignon*; VERDI: *Aida, Ballo in maschera, Don Carlo, Forza del destino, Nabucco★, Otello, Rigoletto★, Simon Boccanegra★, Traviata, Trovatore*. Also HABA, A: *Mother*; MARTINU: *Ariadne*. Recorded for Supraphon. Conducted major orch in Europe. **Res:** Ruská Trida 58/804, Prague 10, CSSR. Mgmt: PRG/CZE.

JOCHUM, EUGEN. Conductor of opera and symphony. German. Resident Cond, Deutsche Oper Berlin, FR Ger. Born 1 Nov 1902, Babenhausen, Bavaria. Wife Maria Moutz. Two daughters. Studied: Akad der Tonkunst, v Hausegger, v Waltershausen, Munich; incl piano, organ. Operatic training as repetiteur & chorus master at State Opera, Munich 1922-25. **Operatic debut:** *Fliegende Holländer* Stadttheater Kiel 1926. Symphonic debut: Munich Phil 1926. Awards: Brahms Medal; Bruckner Medal; hon mem Graz, Mannheim, S Cecilia Rome; Bundesverdienstkreuz 1 Kl; Bayerischer Verdienstorden; Commendatore San Gregorio, Vatican; Professor, Staatskapellmeister.

Conducted with major companies in FR GER: Bayreuth Fest, Berlin Deutsche Oper, Hamburg, Kiel, Mannheim, Munich Staatsoper; GER DR: Berlin Staatsoper; ITA: Florence Maggio & Comunale, Naples, Rome Opera; SPA: Barcelona; UK: Edinburgh Fest; USA: Chicago. **Operas with these companies incl** BEETHOVEN: *Fidelio*; BIZET: *Carmen*; BUSONI: *Turandot*; CORNELIUS: *Barbier von Bagdad*; GIANNINI: *Adúltera*; GLUCK: *Iphigénie en Aulide, Iphigénie en Tauride, Orfeo ed Euridice*; HALEVY: *Juive*; HANDEL: *Giulio Cesare*; MOZART: *Clemenza di Tito, Così fan tutte★, Don Giovanni, Entführung aus dem Serail★, Nozze di Figaro, Zauberflöte*; MUSSORGSKY: *Boris Godunov*; NICOLAI: *Lustigen Weiber*; ORFF: *Carmina burana, Catulli carmina, Trionfo di Afrodite*; PUCCINI: *Rondine, Turandot*; SMETANA: *Bartered Bride*; STRAUSS, J: *Fledermaus*; STRAUSS, R: *Ariadne auf Naxos, Daphne, Elektra, Rosenkavalier, Salome*; VERDI: *Aida, Ballo in maschera, Don Carlo, Falstaff, Otello*; WAGNER: *Fliegende Holländer, Lohengrin★, Meistersinger, Parsifal, Rheingold, Walküre, Siegfried, Göt-*

terdämmerung, Tannhäuser, Tristan und Isolde; WEBER: Euryanthe, Freischütz★; WOLF: Corregidor. Also FALLA: Atlantida; PFITZNER: Christelflein; KRENEK: Jonny spielt auf; SCHILLING: Mona Lisa. Recorded for DG. Conducted major orch in Europe, USA/Canada. Previous positions as Mus Dir with major orch: Städt Orch Kiel 1926-30; Staatsorchester Hamburg 1934-49; Bayerischer Rundfunk 1949-61; Concertgebouw, Amsterdam 1960-62. Teaches at Tanglewood, MA, USA. **Res:** Brunhildenstr 2, 8 Munich 19, FR Ger. Mgmt: LES/UK.

JOHANSSON, HANS. Dramatic tenor. Swedish. Resident mem: Royal Opera, Stockholm. Born 15 Mar 1944, Göteborg, Sweden. Wife Kerstin, occupation teacher. Two children. Studied: Royal Acad of Music, Stockholm. **Debut:** Calaf (Turandot) Royal Opera, Stockholm 1969. Awards: Jussi Björling Schlshp, Swedish State Cultural Dept.

Sang with major companies in FR GER: Kiel; NOR: Oslo; UK: Cardiff Welsh. **Roles with these companies incl** PUCCINI: Pinkerton★ (Butterfly), Calaf★ (Turandot); STRAUSS, J: Alfred★ (Fledermaus); VERDI: Otello★, Manrico★ (Trovatore). Also VOGLER: de la Gardie (Gustav Adolf und Ebba Brahe); STRAUSS, R: Narraboth (Salome). Video/Film: Tamino (Zauberflöte). Gives recitals. Appears with symphony orchestra.

JOHNSON, JAMES. Bass-baritone. American. Resident mem: Städtische Oper, Cologne. Born 15 Feb 1946, Louisiana, USA. Wife Sharon Moore, occupation singer: One child. Studied: Curtis Inst of Music, Martial Singher, Philadelphia. **Debut:** Philip II (Don Carlo) Staatstheater Braunschweig 1972. Awards: First Prize, WGN-Ill Opera Guild Aud of the Air; Rosoff & Fisher Awds, Met Op Ntl Counc Aud.

Sang with major companies in FR GER: Cologne, Hannover, Karlsruhe, Kassel, Munich Staatsoper; USA: Baltimore. **Roles with these companies incl** BEETHOVEN: Rocco★ (Fidelio); DEBUSSY: Arkel★ (Pelléas et Mélisande); MOZART: Conte Almaviva★ (Nozze di Figaro), Sarastro★ (Zauberflöte); PUCCINI: Colline★ (Bohème); SCHOENBERG: Mann★‡ (Glückliche Hand); STRAUSS, R: Orest★ (Elektra); VERDI: Philip II★ & Grande Inquisitore★ (Don Carlo), Padre Guardiano★ (Forza del destino), Zaccaria★ (Nabucco); WAGNER: Daland★ (Fliegende Holländer), König Heinrich★ (Lohengrin). Also MOZART: Sprecher★ (Zauberflöte); TCHAIKOVSKY: Gremin (Eugene Onegin). Recorded for: RAI. Gives recitals. Appears with symphony orchestra. **Res:** Zuckerberg 20, 5039 Hochkirchen, FR Ger. Mgmt: SLZ/FRG; DSP/USA.

JOHNSON, PATRICIA MARION. Dramatic coloratura mezzo-soprano. British. Resident mem: Deutsche Oper, Berlin. Born London. Single. Studied: Maria Linker, Audrey Langford, Dr Schütt. **Debut:** Dritte Magd (Elektra) Royal Opera, Covent Garden, London. Awards: Kammersängerin, Berlin Senate, FR Ger.

Sang with major companies in AUS: Salzburg Fest, Vienna Staatsoper; FRA: Aix-en-Provence Fest, Strasbourg; FR GER: Berlin Deutsche, Hamburg, Munich Staatsoper; UK: Glyndebourne Fest, London Royal Opera & English National;

USA: Santa Fe. **Roles with these companies incl** BERG: Gräfin Geschwitz★‡ (Lulu); BIZET: Carmen; BUSONI: Colombina (Arlecchino); CAVALLI: Diana (Calisto); CIMAROSA: Fidalma (Matrimonio segreto); DONIZETTI: Giovanna (Anna Bolena); EINEM: Claire★ (Besuch der alten Dame); FLOTOW: Nancy (Martha); HENZE: Baron von Grünwiesel★‡ (Junge Lord); HUMPERDINCK: Hexe★ (Hänsel und Gretel); MOZART: Dorabella★ (Così fan tutte); MUSSORGSKY: Marina (Boris Godunov); NABOKOV: Princess★ (Love's Labour's Lost); PUCCINI: Suzuki (Butterfly), Principessa★ (Suor Angelica); ROSSINI: Rosina★ (Barbiere di Siviglia), Angelina★ (Cenerentola), Zaida★ (Turco in Italia); SAINT-SAENS: Dalila; SMETANA: Hata (Bartered Bride); STRAUSS, J: Prinz Orlovsky (Fledermaus); STRAUSS, R: Komponist (Ariadne auf Naxos), Octavian (Rosenkavalier); STRAVINSKY: Jocasta★‡ (Oedipus Rex); TCHAIKOVSKY: Comtesse (Pique Dame); VERDI: Eboli★ (Don Carlo), Dame Quickly (Falstaff), Federica (Luisa Miller), Azucena★ (Trovatore); WAGNER: Fricka (Rheingold★, Walküre★). Also TIPPETT: Andromache★ (King Priam). **World premieres:** HENZE: Baronin Grünwiesel (Junge Lord) Deutsche Oper, Berlin 1965; NABOKOV: Princess (Love's Labour's Lost) Deutsche Oper, Brussels & Berlin 1973. Recorded for: DG, HMV. Appears with symphony orchestra. **Res:** Berlin, FR Ger.

JOHNSON, ROBERT D. Lyric tenor. American. Born 10 Dec 1940, Moline, IL, USA. Wife June. Two children. Studied: Northwestern Univ, Norman Gulbrandsen, Evanston, IL; Dr Edward J Dwyer, Richard Fredricks, New York. **Debut:** Almaviva (Barbiere di Siviglia) New York City Opera 1971. Previous occupations: var industrial adm positions. Awards: Sullivan Fndt Grant.

Sang with major companies in USA: Baltimore, Chicago, Houston, New Orleans, New York City Opera, St Paul, Washington DC. **Roles with these companies incl** DELIUS: Sali★ (Village Romeo and Juliet); DONIZETTI: Ernesto★ (Don Pasquale), Beppo★ (Rita); HANDEL: Acis★; HAYDN: Osmin★ (Incontro improvviso); MASSENET: Des Grieux★ (Manon), Nicias★ (Thaïs); MENOTTI: Lover★ (Amelia al ballo); MONTEVERDI: Tancredi★; MOZART: Ferrando★ (Così fan tutte), Belmonte★ (Entführung aus dem Serail), Tamino★ (Zauberflöte); OFFENBACH: Hoffmann★; ORFF: Solo★ (Carmina burana); PUCCINI: Rodolfo★ (Bohème); ROSSINI: Almaviva★ (Barbiere di Siviglia); SMETANA: Wenzel★ (Bartered Bride); STRAVINSKY: Tom Rakewell★ (Rake's Progress); VERDI: Fenton★ (Falstaff), Alfredo★ (Traviata). Gives recitals. Appears with symphony orchestra. **Res:** New York, NY, USA. Mgmt: SCO/USA.

JONASOVA, JANA; née Ruzková. Coloratura soprano. Czechoslovakian. Resident mem: National Theater, Prague. Born 28 Apr 1943, Plzen, CSR. Husband Petr Jonas, occupation conductor. One daughter. Studied: State Consv, Prof Bendlová, Prague; Music Acad Prague. **Debut:** Konstanze (Entführung aus dem Serail) Municipal Theater, Liberec, CSSR.

Sang with major companies in CZE: Prague National; FRA: Bordeaux; GER DR: Berlin Staatsoper; HOL: Amsterdam; ITA: Palermo; SWI: Geneva; YUG: Zagreb, Belgrade. **Roles with these companies incl** GLUCK: Amor (*Orfeo ed Euridice*); HANDEL: Galatea; MOZART: Fiordiligi★ (*Così fan tutte*), Konstanze★ (*Entführung aus dem Serail*), Pamina & Königin der Nacht (*Zauberflöte*); OFFENBACH: Olympia (*Contes d'Hoffmann*); PERGOLESI: Serpina (*Serva padrona*); PUCCINI: Mimi (*Bohème*); ROSSINI: Rosina★ (*Barbiere di Siviglia*); SMETANA: Barce★ (*The Kiss*); STRAUSS, J: Adele (*Fledermaus*); STRAUSS, R: Fiakermilli★ (*Arabella*), Aminta (*Schweigsame Frau*); VERDI: Oscar (*Ballo in maschera*), Gilda★ (*Rigoletto*), Violetta (*Traviata*). Gives recitals. Appears with symphony orchestra. **Res:** Londynská 54, 120 00 Prague 2, CSSR. Mgmt: PRG/CZE.

JONCHEVA, GALIA MITOVA. Lyric soprano. Bulgarian. Resident mem: Opera House, Sofia. Born 21 Apr 1946, Sofia. Divorced. One child. Studied: Music Consv, Prof Spiliopoulou, Athens; Prof Brambarov, Bulgaria; Prof Maria Brand, Vienna. **Debut:** Tatiana (*Eugene Onegin*) Opera Sofia 1969. Previous occupations: store front designer. Awards: Gold Medal Intl Compt for Young Singers, Sofia.
Sang with major companies in BUL: Sofia; CZE: Prague Smetana; POL: Warsaw; YUG: Belgrade. **Roles with these companies incl** BIZET: Micaëla (*Carmen*); DEBUSSY: Lia (*Enfant prodigue*); DVORAK: Rusalka; GOUNOD: Marguerite (*Faust*); MASSENET: Manon; MOZART: Donna Elvira (*Don Giovanni*), Contessa & Susanna (*Nozze di Figaro*); POULENC: La femme (*Voix humaine*); PUCCINI: Mimi & Musetta (*Bohème*), Cio-Cio-San (*Butterfly*), Liù (*Turandot*); RIMSKY-KORSAKOV: Volkova (*Sadko*); TCHAIKOVSKY: Tatiana (*Eugene Onegin*), Iolanthe, Lisa (*Pique Dame*); VERDI: Desdemona (*Otello*). Also HADJIEV: Albena; Milkana (*Maïstori*); Sevina (*Summer 893*). Teaches voice. Coaches repertoire. **Res:** 6 September 28, Sofia, Bulgaria. Mgmt: ADZ/AUS; SOF/YUG.

JONES, BETTY. Spinto. American. Resident mem: New York City Opera. Born Plainfield, NJ, USA. Husband Eugene D, occupation engineer, senior vice pres. Two children. Studied: Sarah Lawrence Coll, Bronxville, NY; Mannes Coll of Music, New York. **Debut:** Balayeur (*Louise*) Boston Opera 1971. Awards: Concert Artists Guild Awd, New York; Kathryn Turney Long Schlshp, Met Op.
Sang with major companies in ITA: Spoleto Fest; USA: Boston, Chicago, Jackson Opera/South, New York City Opera, San Francisco Opera, Seattle, Washington, DC. **Roles with these companies incl** GERSHWIN: Bess★; MENOTTI: Magda Sorel (*Consul*); MOZART: Donna Anna (*Don Giovanni*); ORFF: Solo★ (*Carmina burana*); PUCCINI: Liù★ (*Turandot*); VERDI: Aida★, Amelia★ (*Ballo in maschera*); WAGNER: Senta★ (*Fliegende Holländer*), Gutrune (*Götterdämmerung*). Gives recitals. Appears with symphony orchestra. **Res:** 146 Westport Rd, Wilton, CT 06097, USA. Mgmt: HJH/USA.

JONES, GWYNETH. Dramatic soprano. Swiss/British. Resident mem: Staatsoper Vienna. Born 7 Nov 1936, Pontnewynydd, Wales, UK. Husband Till Haberfeld, occupation company director. One child. Studied: Royal Coll of Music, Ruth Packer, London; Accad Chigiana, Siena, Italy; Intl Opernstudio, Zurich; Maria Carpi, Geneva. **Debut:** Annina (*Rosenkavalier*) Opernhaus Zürich 1962. Previous occupations: secretary. Awards: ARCM Royal Coll of Music; Hon Fellow Royal Coll of Music, London; first prize for contemp music, Harriet Cohen Int'l Music Awd; Hon DM Univ of Wales, Cardiff.
Sang with major companies in ARG: Buenos Aires; AUS: Vienna Staatsoper; FRA: Marseille, Paris; FR GER: Bayreuth Fest, Berlin Deutsche Oper, Düsseldorf-Duisburg, Frankfurt, Hamburg, Karlsruhe, Munich Staatsoper, Stuttgart; ITA: Florence Maggio, Milan La Scala, Parma, Rome Opera; MON: Monte Carlo Opera; SWI: Geneva, Zurich; UK: Cardiff Welsh, Edinburgh Fest, London Royal Opera; USA: Dallas, New York Met, San Francisco Opera. **Roles with these companies incl** BEETHOVEN: Leonore★‡ (*Fidelio*); BIZET: Carmen (*Carmen*); CHERUBINI: Medea‡; MASCAGNI: Santuzza (*Cavalleria rusticana*); MOZART: Donna Anna★ (*Don Giovanni*); PUCCINI: Cio-Cio-San★ (*Butterfly*), Tosca★; STRAUSS, R: Helena★ (*Aegyptische Helena*), Marschallin★ & Octavian‡ (*Rosenkavalier*), Salome★‡; VERDI: Aida★, Amelia★ (*Ballo in maschera*), Elisabetta★ (*Don Carlo*), Lady Macbeth★ (*Macbeth*), Desdemona★‡ (*Otello*), Leonora★ (*Trovatore*); WAGNER: Senta★‡ (*Fliegende Holländer*), Ortrud‡ (*Lohengrin*), Eva (*Meistersinger*), Sieglinde★ (*Walküre*), Brünnhilde★ (*Walküre, Siegfried, Götterdämmerung*), Gutrune (*Götterdämmerung*), Elisabeth★ & Venus★ (*Tannhäuser*), Kundry‡ (*Pasifal*). Also GLUCK: Orfeo. Recorded for: Decca, DG, CBS, EMI. Video/Film: Leonore (*Fidelio*); Senta (*Fliegende Holländer*). Gives recitals. Appears with symphony orchestra. **Res:** Zürich CH 8040, Switzerland. Mgmt: SLZ/FRG; GOR/UK.

JONSSON, BUSK MARGIT. Lyric soprano. Swedish. Resident mem: Royal Opera, Stockholm. Born 10 Sep 1929, Malung, Sweden. Husband Helge Shoog, occupation actor. Two children. Studied: Musikhögskolan, Stockholm; Musikhochschule, Vienna. **Debut:** La Poupée (*Poupée de Nuremberg*) Stockholm Opera 1954. Awards: Kopparbergstans Kulturstip 1967.
Sang with major companies in FR GER: Hamburg; UK: Edinburgh Fest; USA: Seattle. **Roles with these companies incl** DONIZETTI: Norina★ (*Don Pasquale*); GLUCK: Amor (*Orfeo ed Euridice*); MOZART: Despina★ (*Così fan tutte*), Zerlina (*Don Giovanni*), Blondchen (*Entführung aus dem Serail*), Susanna★ & Cherubino (*Nozze di Figaro*); OFFENBACH: Olympia★ (*Contes d'Hoffmann*); STRAUSS, J: Adele★ (*Fledermaus*); STRAVINSKY: Anne Trulove (*Rake's Progress*); VERDI: Oscar★ (*Ballo in maschera*), Nannetta (*Falstaff*). Gives recitals. Appears with symphony orchestra.

JORAN, JIRI. Bass-baritone. Czechoslovakian. Resident mem: National Theater, Prague. Born 20

Jun 1920, Prague. Wife Vera, occupation travel agency guide. Two children. Studied: Consv of Prague, Prof Hilbert Vavra; Apollo Granforte, Milan; Robert Rosner, Bronislav Chorovic, Prague. Debut: King Vladislav (*Dalibor*) National Theater, Prague 1941. Awards: Artist of Merit, National Theater Prague, Ministry of Culture CSSR.

Sang with major companies in CZE: Prague National; GER DR: Dresden. Roles with these companies incl JANACEK: Harasta★‡ (*Cunning Little Vixen*), Sacristan★ (*Excursions of Mr Broucek*), Jaroslav Prus (*Makropoulos Affair*); MOZART: Don Giovanni; PROKOFIEV: Dolokhov★ (*War and Peace*); PUCCINI: Sharpless★ (*Butterfly*); ROSSINI: Don Basilio★ (*Barbiere di Siviglia*); SMETANA: Tomas (*The Kiss*); TCHAIKOVSKY: Yeletsky (*Pique Dame*); VERDI: Germont (*Traviata*). Recorded for: Supraphon. Gives recitals. Appears with symphony orchestra. Teaches voice. Res: Na Kvetnici 6, Pragŭe 4, CSSR. Mgmt: PRG/CZE.

JORGENSEN, PAUL. Conductor of opera and symphony. Danish. Resident Cond, Royal Opera, Copenhagen. Born 26 Oct 1934, Copenhagen. Wife Marianne, occupation doctor of medicine. One child. Studied: Univ and Royal Consv, Copenhagen; incl violin, viola, piano, organ and voice. Operatic training as asst cond at Royal Opera, Copenhagen 1959-60. Operatic debut: Royal Opera, Copenhagen. Symphonic debut: Sealand Symph Orch, Denmark 1959. Previous occupations: singer, teacher. Awards: First Prize compts Besançon 1960 & Stockholm 1964.

Conducted with major companies in DEN: Copenhagen; NOR: Oslo. Operas with these companies incl BRITTEN: *Rape of Lucretia;* DALLAPICCOLA: *Prigioniero;* DONIZETTI: *Elisir★;* GLUCK: *Iphigénie en Tauride;* GOUNOD: *Faust★;* HENZE: *Elegy for Young Lovers;* HUMPERDINCK: *Hänsel und Gretel;* JANACEK: *Cunning Little Vixen;* MONTEVERDI: *Ritorno d'Ulisse★;* MOZART: *Così fan tutte★, Entführung aus dem Serail, Zauberflöte★;* MUSSORGSKY: *Boris Godunov;* PERGOLESI: *Serva padrona;* PUCCINI: *Gianni Schicchi, Butterfly★, Tosca;* PURCELL: *Dido and Aeneas;* ROSSINI: *Barbiere di Siviglia★;* STRAUSS, J: *Fledermaus★‡;* STRAUSS, R: *Salome★;* STRAVINSKY: *Oedipus Rex, Rake's Progress★;* VERDI: *Aida, Otello★, Rigoletto★.* Also NIELSEN: *Maskarade‡.* World premieres: OLSEN: *Belisa* Royal Opera, Copenhagen 1966; NORGAARD: *Labyrinten* Royal Opera, Copenhagen 1967. Conducted major orch in Europe. Teaches at Copenhagen Univ. Res: Aufikelvej 18, Copenhagen, Denmark. Mgmt: SVE/SWE.

JÖRIS, HANS HERBERT. Conductor of opera and symphony; composer. German. First Cond, Opera House, Hannover 1966- . also Resident Cond, Youth Symph Orch of Lower Saxony. Born 15 May 1925, Viersen, Germany. Wife Hildegard. Three sons, three daughters. Studied: Hochschule für Musik, Cologne, G Wand, Ph Jarnach; incl piano, organ, cello. Plays the piano. Operatic training as asst cond at Dortmund & Cologne 1951-59. Operatic debut: Städtische Bühnen, Dortmund 1959. Symphonic debut: Gürzenich Orch, Cologne

1955. Previous adm positions in opera: First Cond, Opera Dortmund 1959-66.

Conducted with major companies in FR GER: Dortmund, Hannover; ITA: Bologna. Operas with these companies incl d'ALBERT: *Tiefland;* AUBER: *Fra Diavolo;* BEETHOVEN: *Fidelio★;* BIZET: *Carmen★;* BRITTEN: *Albert Herring, Owen Wingrave;* BUSONI: *Doktor Faust;* DONIZETTI: *Lucia;* DVORAK: *Rusalka;* EINEM: *Dantons Tod;* FORTNER: *Don Perlimplin;* GERSHWIN: *Porgy and Bess★;* GLUCK: *Orfeo ed Euridice;* GOUNOD: *Faust★;* HANDEL: *Acis and Galatea, Xerxes;* HAYDN: *Mondo della luna;·* HENZE: *Elegy for Young Lovers;* HINDEMITH: *Mathis der Maler;* HUMPERDINCK: *Hänsel und Gretel, Königskinder;* LEONCAVALLO: *Pagliacci★;* LORTZING: *Zar und Zimmermann,·Undine;* MASCAGNI: *Cavalleria rusticana★;* MOZART: *Così fan tutte★, Don Giovanni, Entführung aus dem Serail★, Idomeneo, Schauspieldirektor, Nozze di Figaro★, Oca del Cairo, Re pastore, Zauberflöte★;* NICOLAI: *Lustigen Weiber★;* OFFENBACH: *Contes d'Hoffmann;* ORFF: *Carmina burana;* PROKOFIEV: *Gambler;* PUCCINI: *Bohème★, Gianni Schicchi★, Butterfly★, Tabarro★, Tosca★;* PURCELL: *Dido and Aeneas;* SMETANA: *Bartered Bride;* STRAUSS, J: *Fledermaus★;* STRAUSS, R: *Arabella★, Capriccio, Rosenkavalier★;* STRAVINSKY: *Oedipus Rex, Perséphone;* TCHAIKOVSKY: *Pique Dame★;* VERDI: *Aida, Ballo in maschera★, Don Carlo, Forza del destino, Nabucco, Otello, Rigoletto★, Simon Boccanegra, Traviata★, Trovatore★;* WAGNER: *Fliegende Holländer★, Meistersinger, Rheingold, Walküre, Tannhäuser, Tristan und Isolde★;* WEBER: *Freischütz;* WOLF-FERRARI: *Quattro rusteghi.* Also KLEBE: *Tödliche Wünsche★.* Res: Geveker Kamp 12, 3 Hannover 91, FR Ger.

JUHRKE, WERNER. Scenic and costume designer for opera, theater, film & television. Is also an illustrator & fashion designer. German. Born 18 Jun 1932, Berlin. Single. Studied: Hochschule für bildende Künste, Profs Ernst Schütte, Alexander Camaro, Willi Schmidt, Berlin. Operatic debut: *Médecin malgré lui* Theater am Gärtnerplatz, Munich 1964. Theater debut: Berliner Ballett 1957.

Designed for major companies in FR GER: Berlin Deutsche Oper, Düsseldorf-Duisburg, Frankfurt, Munich Gärtnerplatz; SWE: Stockholm. Operas designed for these companies incl BIZET: *Carmen★;* PUCCINI: *Turandot★.* Exhibitions of stage designs. Res: Roscher Str 2a, Berlin 12, FR Ger.

JUNE, AVA; née Ava June Wiggins. Lyric soprano. British. Resident mem: English National Opera, London. Born 23 Jul 1934, London. Husband David Charles Cooper, occupation company dir. Studied: Kate Opperman, Clive Carey, Joan Cross, London. Debut: Léila (*Pêcheurs de perles*) Sadler's Wells Opera 1959. Previous occupations: dressmaker. Awards: Queen's Prize Royal Coll of Music 1954; Prize & Gold Medal Intl Compt for Young Opera Singers, Sofia 1963.

Sang with major companies in AUS: Vienna Volksoper; BUL: Sofia; FRA: Aix-en-Provence Fest, Paris; FR GER: Berlin Deutsche Oper, Düsseldorf-Duisburg, Munich Gärtnerplatz; S

AFR: Johannesburg; UK: Cardiff Welsh, Glasgow Scottish, London Royal Opera & English National; USA: San Francisco Opera; YUG: Dubrovnik, Zagreb. **Roles with these companies incl** BARTOK: Judith★ (*Bluebeard's Castle*); BEETHOVEN: Leonore★ & Marzelline (*Fidelio*); BIZET: Micaëla (*Carmen*), Léila (*Pêcheurs de perles*); BRITTEN: Elizabeth★ (*Gloriana*), Ellen Orford★ (*Peter Grimes*); DONIZETTI: Norina (*Don Pasquale*), Elisabetta★ (*Maria Stuarda*); GIORDANO: Maddalena (*Andrea Chénier*); GOUNOD: Marguerite (*Faust*); JANACEK: Katya Kabanova★; MASCAGNI: Santuzza (*Cavalleria rusticana*); MOZART: Donna Anna & Donna Elvira (*Don Giovanni*), Ilia (*Idomeneo*), Contessa★ (*Nozze di Figaro*), Pamina (*Zauberflöte*); PUCCINI: Mimi & Musetta (*Bohème*), Cio-Cio-San★ (*Butterfly*), Tosca; PURCELL: Dido★; SMETANA: Marie (*Bartered Bride*); STRAUSS, J: Rosalinde (*Fledermaus*); STRAUSS, R: Marschallin★ (*Rosenkavalier*); TCHAIKOVSKY: Tatiana (*Eugene Onegin*), Lisa (*Pique Dame*); VERDI: Aida★, Violetta (*Traviata*); WAGNER: Eva (*Meistersinger*), Sieglinde★ (*Walküre*); WEBER: Agathe (*Freischütz*). **World premieres:** BENNETT: Frau Shomberg (*Victory*) Aldeburgh Fest & Royal Opera House 1969. Gives recitals. Appears with symphony orchestra. **Res:** 20 Ladbroke Gardens, London, UK. Mgmt: SLA/UK.

JUNG, DORIS: née Crittenden. Dramatic soprano. American. Resident mem: New York City Opera. Born Centralia, IL, USA. Husband Felix Popper, occupation music adm New York City Opera. One son. Studied: Julius Cohen, Urbana, IL; Emma Zador, New York; Luise Helletsgruber, Vienna; Winifred Cecil, New York. **Debut:** Vitellia (*Clemenza di Tito*) Zurich Opera 1955.

Sang with major companies in AUS: Vienna Staatsoper; CAN: Vancouver; DEN: Copenhagen; FRA: Marseille, Strasbourg; FR GER: Cologne, Dortmund, Frankfurt, Hamburg, Kassel, Munich Staatsoper, Nürnberg, Stuttgart; ITA: Naples; SPA: Barcelona; SWI: Zurich; USA: Minneapolis, New York Met & City Opera, Portland, Washington DC. **Roles with these companies incl** BEETHOVEN: Leonore (*Fidelio*); DALLAPICCOLA: La Madre (*Prigioniero*); GLUCK: Euridice (*Giulio Cesare*); HANDEL: Cleopatra (*Giulio Cesare*); MASCAGNI: Santuzza (*Cavalleria rusticana*); MOZART: Vitellia (*Clemenza di Tito*), Fiordiligi (*Così fan tutte*), Donna Anna★ (*Don Giovanni*), Contessa★ (*Nozze di Figaro*); PUCCINI: Suor Angelica, Tosca; STRAUSS, R: Ariadne★ (*Ariadne auf Naxos*), Gräfin (*Capriccio*), Chrysothemis (*Elektra*), Marschallin★ (*Rosenkavalier*); VERDI: Aida, Amelia (*Ballo in maschera*), Elisabetta (*Don Carlo*), Lady Macbeth (*Macbeth*); WAGNER: Senta (*Fliegende Holländer*), Elsa (*Lohengrin*), Irene (*Rienzi*), Sieglinde★ (*Walküre*), Gutrune (*Götterdämmerung*), Elisabeth★ & Venus★ (*Tannhäuser*), Isolde. Also MOORE: Mary (*Devil and Daniel Webster*); WEISGALL: Helen (*The Tenor*). Recorded for: Westminster. Gives recitals. Appears with symphony orchestra. **Res:** New York, NY, USA. Mgmt: DSP/USA.

JUNGWIRTH, MANFRED. Basso-buffo. Austrian. Resident mem: Vienna Staatsoper. Born 4 Jun 1919, St Pölten, Austria. Wife Lieselotte. Studied: Alice Goldberg, Emilie Auer-Weissgärber, Vienna; Albert d'Andrée, Bucharest; Josef Burgwinkel, Berlin; Rudolf Grossmann, Munich. **Debut:** Méphistophélès (*Faust*) Staatsoper, Bucharest 1941. Previous occupations: prof in music.

Sang with major companies in AUS: Graz, Vienna Staatsoper & Volksoper; BEL: Liège; CAN: Montreal/Quebec; CZE: Prague Smetana; FRA: Bordeaux, Nice, Paris; GRE: Athens Fest; FR GER: Berlin Deutsche Oper, Bonn, Cologne, Darmstadt, Düsseldorf-Duisburg, Frankfurt, Hamburg, Hannover, Kassel, Mannheim, Munich Staatsoper & Gärtnerplatz, Saarbrücken, Stuttgart, Wiesbaden; GER DR: Berlin Komische Oper; HOL: Amsterdam; ITA: Rome Opera, Trieste; POR: Lisbon; ROM: Bucharest; SWI: Basel, Zurich; UK: London Eng Ntl; USSR: Moscow Bolshoi; USA: New York Met, San Francisco Opera; YUG: Dubrovnik. **Roles with these companies incl** BEETHOVEN: Rocco★ (*Fidelio*); BIZET: Escamillo (*Carmen*); CIMAROSA: Geronimo (*Matrimonio segreto*); CORNELIUS: Abul Hassan (*Barbier von Bagdad*); DEBUSSY: Arkel (*Pelléas et Mélisande*); DONIZETTI: Don Pasquale; DVORAK: Marbuel (*Devil and Kate*); GERSHWIN: Porgy; GLUCK: High Priest & Apollo (*Alceste*), Thoas★ (*Iphigénie en Tauride*); GOUNOD: Méphistophélès (*Faust*); LORTZING: Stadinger (*Waffenschmied*), Baculus★ (*Wildschütz*), Van Bett★ (*Zar und Zimmermann*); MOZART: Don Alfonso★ (*Così fan tutte*), Osmin★ (*Entführung aus dem Serail*), Figaro★ (*Nozze di Figaro*), Sarastro (*Zauberflöte*); MUSSORGSKY: Varlaam (*Boris Godunov*); NICOLAI: Falstaff★ (*Lustigen Weiber*); ORFF: Bauer (*Mond*); PUCCINI: Colline (*Bohème*); ROSSINI: Dott Bartolo★ & Don Basilio (*Barbiere di Siviglia*); SMETANA: Kezal★ (*Bartered Bride*); STRAUSS, R: Altair (*Aegyptische Helena*), La Roche★ (*Capriccio*), Baron Ochs★ (*Rosenkavalier*); THOMAS: Lothario (*Mignon*); VERDI: Ramfis (*Aida*), Grande Inquisitore (*Don Carlo*), Silva (*Ernani*), Fra Melitone & Padre Guardiano (*Forza del destino*), Zaccaria (*Nabucco*), Procida (*Vespri*); WAGNER: Holländer & Daland★ (*Fliegende Holländer*), König Heinrich (*Lohengrin*), Pogner★ (*Meistersinger*), Fasolt (*Rheingold*), Fafner (*Rheingold, Siegfried*), Landgraf (*Tannhäuser*), König Marke (*Tristan und Isolde*); WEBER: Kaspar★ (*Freischütz*). Recorded for: Decca. Gives recitals. Appears with symphony orchestra. **Res:** Rienösslg 16, 1040 Vienna, Austria.

JUPITHER, ROLF. Dramatic baritone. Swedish. Resident mem: Royal Opera, Stockholm. Born 11 Jan 1932, Visby, Sweden. Wife Sissel, occupation boutique owner. Three children. Studied: Royal Acad of Music, Käthy Sundström, Sweden. **Debut:** Rigoletto, Norwegian Opera, Oslo 1962. Previous occupations: instrument maker. Awards: Kristina Nilsson Awd.

Sang with major companies in CAN: Montreal/Quebec, Vancouver; DEN: Copenhagen; FR GER: Berlin Deutsche Oper, Kiel; NOR: Oslo; SWE: Drottningholm Fest. **Roles with these companies incl** BEETHOVEN: Don Pizarro★ (*Fidelio*); BIZET: Escamillo★ (*Carmen*); GLUCK: Agamemnon★ (*Iphigénie en Aulide*); HAYDN: Nanni★ (*Infedeltà delusa*); MASCAGNI: Alfio★

(*Cavalleria rusticana*); MASSENET: Des Grieux★ (*Portrait de Manon*); MOZART: Conte Almaviva★ (*Nozze di Figaro*); OFFENBACH: Coppélius★ (*Contes d'Hoffmann*); PUCCINI: Marcello★ (*Bohème*), Sharpless★ (*Butterfly*), Scarpia★ (*Tosca*); ROSSINI: Don Basilio★ (*Barbiere di Siviglia*), Guillaume Tell★; STRAUSS, R: Barak★ (*Frau ohne Schatten*), Jochanaan★ (*Salome*); VERDI: Amonasro★ (*Aida*), Renato★ (*Ballo in maschera*), Rodrigo★ (*Don Carlo*), Don Carlo★ (*Forza del destino*), Nabucco★, Iago★ (*Otello*), Rigoletto★, Germont★ (*Traviata*), Conte di Luna★ (*Trovatore*); WAGNER: Telramund★ (*Lohengrin*), Fasolt★ (*Rheingold*), Gunther★ (*Götterdämmerung*), Kurwenal★ (*Tristan und Isolde*). Gives recitals. Appears with symphony orchestra. Mgmt: KBL/SWE.

JURI, CONSTANTINO GABRIEL. Stages/ produces opera & theater, and is an actor. Argentinean. Resident Stage Dir, Teatro Colón, Buenos Aires. Born 29 Oct 1923, Cordoba, Argentina. Single. Studied: School of Dramatic Arts, Argentina; Accad S Cecilia, Rome; incl music, piano & voice. Operatic training as asst stage dir at Teatro dell'Opera, Rome 1963-66. **Operatic debut:** *Serva padrona* Teatro Colón, Buenos Aires 1967. Theater debut: Teatro Antorcha, Cordoba 1960. Previous occupation: Prof, Univ of Cordoba. Awards: Becado, Fondo Nacional de las Artes, Argentino & Italiano; Cavaliere, Rep of Italy.

Directed/produced opera for major companies in ARG: Buenos Aires; AUS: Vienna Staatsoper; BRA: Rio de Janeiro; USA: Washington DC. **Operas staged with these companies incl** BELLINI: *Norma;* CIMAROSA: *Matrimonio segreto;* DONIZETTI: *Lucia★, Rita★;* GIORDANO: *Andrea Chénier;* MASCAGNI: *Cavalleria rusticana;* MENOTTI: *Amahl;* PAISIELLO: *Barbiere di Siviglia;* PERGOLESI: *Frate 'nnamorato★, Serva padrona★;* PUCCINI: *Bohème, Butterfly★, Tosca★;* ROSSINI: *Barbiere di Siviglia★, Cambiale di matrimonio, Scala di seta★, Signor Bruschino;* SAINT-SAENS: *Samson et Dalila;* VERDI: *Aida★, Don Carlo, Falstaff★, Macbeth, Otello, Rigoletto★, Simon Boccanegra, Traviata★, Trovatore.* Also CHERUBINI: *Crescendo;* FIORAVANTI: *Cantatrice villane;* MOZART: *Bastien und Bastienne;* SALIERI: *Arlecchinata;* GUARNIERI: *Pedro Malazartes.* **Operatic world premieres:** GUIDI-DREI: *Medea* Teatro Colón, Buenos Aires 1973. Teaches at Inst Superior de Arte, Teatro Colón. **Res:** Perú 1121, Buenos Aires, Argentina. Mgmt: QUE/SPA.

JURINAC, SENA; née Srebrenka Jurinac. Lyric & dramatic soprano. Austrian. Resident mem: Staatsoper, Vienna. Born 24 Oct 1921, Travnik, Yugoslavia. Husband Dr Josef Lederle, occupation surgeon. Studied: Milka Kostrencic, Music Acad, Zagreb; Mozarteum, Anna Bahr-Mildenburg, Salzburg. **Debut:** Mimi (*Bohème*) National Opera, Zagreb 1942. Awards: Cross of Honor, Austrian Gvnmt; Cross "Litteris et Artibus" First Class, Austrian Gvnmt; Honorary Mem Staatsoper, Vienna; Austrian Kammersängerin; Mozart Medal, Ring of Honor, Staatsoper, Vienna.

Sang with major companies in ARG: Buenos Aires; AUSTRL: Sydney; AUS: Graz, Salzburg

Fest, Vienna Staatsoper & Volksoper; BEL: Brussels; CZE: Prague National & Smetana; FRA: Paris, Strasbourg; FR GER: Bayreuth Fest, Berlin Deutsche Oper, Cologne, Dortmund, Hamburg, Mannheim, Munich Staatsoper, Stuttgart, Wiesbaden; ITA: Florence Maggio & Comunale, Milan La Scala, Naples, Rome Opera, Venice; MON: Monte Carlo; POR: Lisbon; SWI: Zurich; UK: Edinburgh Fest, Glyndebourne Fest, London Royal; USA: Chicago, San Francisco Opera; YUG: Dubrovnik, Zagreb. **Roles with these companies incl** BEETHOVEN: Leonore & Marzelline (*Fidelio*); BERG: Marie (*Wozzeck*); BIZET: Micaëla (*Carmen*); CORNELIUS: Margiana (*Barbier von Bagdad*); GLUCK: Iphigénie★ (*Iphigénie en Tauride*), Euridice & Amor (*Orfeo ed Euridice*); GOUNOD: Marguerite (*Faust*); JANACEK: Jenufa★; LEONCAVALLO: Nedda (*Pagliacci*); MASSENET: Manon; MONTEVERDI: Poppea (*Incoronazione di Poppea*); MOZART: Fiordiligi (*Così fan tutte*), Donna Anna & Donna Elvira★ (*Don Giovanni*), Ilia & Elettra (*Idomeneo*), Contessa & Cherubino (*Nozze di Figaro*), Pamina (*Zauberflöte*); MUSSORGSKY: Marina (*Boris Godunov*); OFFENBACH: Antonia & Giulietta (*Contes d'Hoffmann*); PFITZNER: Ighino (*Palestrina*); PUCCINI: Mimi (*Bohème*), Cio-Cio-San (*Butterfly*), Suor Angelica, Tosca★; SMETANA: Marie (*Bartered Bride*); STRAUSS, J: Rosalinde (*Fledermaus*); STRAUSS, R: Komponist★ (*Ariadne auf Naxos*), Marschallin★ & Octavian (*Rosenkavalier*); TCHAIKOVSKY: Tatiana (*Eugene Onegin*), Lisa (*Pique Dame*); VERDI: Amelia (*Ballo in maschera*), Elisabetta★ (*Don Carlo*), Leonora (*Forza del destino*), Desdemona (*Otello*); WAGNER: Senta (*Fliegende Holländer*), Eva (*Meistersinger*), Elisabeth (*Tannhäuser*); WEBER: Agathe (*Freischütz*); WOLF-FERRARI: Rosaura (*Donne curiose*). Also MOZART: Dorabella (*Così fan tutte*); EGK: Isabella (*Columbus*); SALMHOFER: Kordula (*Werbekleid*). Recorded for: Angel, Columbia, Electrola, Philips, DG, Seraphim, Westminster, Decca. Video/Film: Suor Angelica; Octavian (*Rosenkavalier*); Marie (*Wozzeck*); Desdemona (*Otello*). Gives recitals. Appears with symphony orchestra. **Res:** Augsburg, FR Ger. Mgmt: URT/AUS.

JUSTUS, WILLIAM. Spinto baritone. American. Resident mem: New York City Opera. Born 12 Nov 1936, Kansas City, MO, USA. Wife Barbara, occupation adm assist, Metropolitan Museum, New York. Studied: E J Remley, Kansas City; Joseph Pouhe, New York. Debut: Figaro (*Barbiere di Siviglia*) Kansas City Lyric 1962.

Sang with major companies in FR GER: Berlin Deutsche Oper, Düsseldorf-Duisburg; SWI: Zurich; USA: Boston, Cincinnati, Hawaii, Kansas City, New Orleans, New York City Opera, Portland, San Francisco Spring Opera, Santa Fe. **Roles with these companies incl** BIZET: Escamillo★ (*Carmen*); DONIZETTI: Dott Malatesta (*Don Pasquale*), Enrico (*Lucia*); GIORDANO: Carlo Gérard (*Andrea Chénier*); MASCAGNI: Alfio★ (*Cavalleria rusticana*); MASSENET: Lescaut (*Manon*); MONTEVERDI: Orfeo; MOZART: Guglielmo (*Così fan tutte*), Don Giovanni, Conte Almaviva (*Nozze di Figaro*); PUCCINI: Marcello★ (*Bohème*), Sharpless★ (*Butterfly*), Scarpia★

(*Tosca*); ROSSINI: Figaro (*Barbiere di Siviglia*); STRAUSS, R: Musiklehrer★ (*Ariadne auf Naxos*), Jochanaan★ (*Salome*); VERDI: Rodrigo (*Don Carlo*), Ford★ (*Falstaff*), Germont★ (*Traviata*), Conte di Luna★ (*Trovatore*). Appears with symphony orchestra. Mgmt: HJH/USA.

K

KABAIVANSKA, RAINA. Lyric soprano. Italian. Born 15 Dec 1934, Burgass, Bulgaria. Divorced. One daughter. Studied: Ntl Consv, Sofia, Bulgaria; Liceo Musicale Viotti, Vercelli, Italy; Teatro alla Scala School, Milan. **Debut:** Giorgetta (*Tabarro*) Vercelli, Italy 1959. Awards: Bellini Awd, Catania 1966; Viotti d'oro, Vercelli 1970.

Sang with major companies in ARG: Buenos Aires; AUS: Vienna Staatsoper; BUL: Sofia; FRA: Paris; FR GER: Hamburg Staatsoper, Mannheim; HUN: Budapest; ITA: Bologna, Genoa, Milan La Scala, Naples, Palermo Massimo, Parma, Trieste, Turin, Verona Arena; SPA: Barcelona; UK: London Royal Opera; USSR: Leningrad Kirov, Moscow Bolshoi; USA: Baltimore, Chicago, Dallas, Fort Worth, Houston, New Orleans, New York Met, San Antonio, San Francisco Opera, Washington DC. **Roles with these companies incl** BELLINI: Beatrice di Tenda & Agnese (*Beatrice di Tenda*), Imogene (*Pirata*); BERLIOZ: Teresa (*Benvenuto Cellini*); BOITO: Margherita (*Mefistofele*); BUSONI: Turandot; CATALANI: Wally*; CILEA: Adriana Lecouvreur*; GIORDANO: Maddalena* (*Andrea Chénier*); GOUNOD: Marguerite* (*Faust*); LEONCAVALLO: Nedda* (*Pagliacci*); MASSENET: Thaïs; PUCCINI: Mimi* (*Bohème*), Cio-Cio-San*‡ (*Butterfly*), Manon Lescaut*, Suor Angelica, Giorgetta (*Tabarro*), Tosca*, Liù (*Turandot*); ROSSINI: Mathilde (*Guillaume Tell*); TCHAIKOVSKY: Lisa* (*Pique Dame*); VERDI: Elisabetta* (*Don Carlo*), Donna Elvira (*Ernani*), Alice Ford (*Falstaff*), Leonora* (*Forza del destino*), Desdemona (*Otello*), Violetta* (*Traviata*), Leonora (*Trovatore*), Elena* (*Vespri*); WAGNER: Irene (*Rienzi*); ZANDONAI: Francesca da Rimini*. Video/Film: Nedda (*Pagliacci*). Gives recitals. **Res:** Piazza Vesuvio 8, 20144 Milan, Italy. Mgmt: EUM/FRG.

KAHANA, MICHAEL; né Mirel Kahana. Lyric tenor. Israeli. Resident mem: Israel National Opera, Tel Aviv. Born 18 Mar 1948, Bucharest. Wife Hen, occupation business mgr. Studied: Joseph Kahana, Music Acad, Israel; Viorica Cosokariu, Romania. **Debut:** Remendado (*Carmen*) Israel National Opera 1971.

Sang with major companies in ISR: Tel Aviv; ROM: Bucharest. **Roles with these companies incl** HUMPERDINCK: Hexe* (*Hänsel und Gretel*); PUCCINI: Luigi (*Tabarro*); SMETANA: Wen-

zel* & Hans* (*Bartered Bride*); STRAUSS, J: Eisenstein* & Alfred* (*Fledermaus*). Gives recitals. Appears with symphony orchestra. **Res:** Iodfat St 1, Tel Aviv, Israel.

KAHMANN, SIEGLINDE. Lyric soprano. German. Resident mem: Opernhaus, Graz; Theater am Gärtnerplatz, Munich. Born 28 Nov 1937, Dresden, Germany. Husband Sigurdur Björnsson, occupation opera singer, tenor. Two children. Studied: Staatliche Hochschule für Musik, Stuttgart. **Debut:** Aennchen (*Lustigen Weiber*) Stuttgart Oper 1959.

Sang with major companies in AUS: Graz, Salzburg Fest, Vienna Staatsoper; FRA: Strasbourg; FR GER: Essen, Hamburg, Karlsruhe, Kassel, Munich Staatsoper & Gärtnerplatz, Stuttgart; GER DR: Leipzig; POR: Lisbon; ROM: Bucharest; SWI: Zurich; UK: Edinburgh Fest. **Roles with these companies incl** AUBER: Zerlina* (*Fra Diavolo*); BEETHOVEN: Marzelline (*Fidelio*); BIZET: Micaëla* (*Carmen*); FLOTOW: Lady Harriet* (*Martha*); GLUCK: Amor* (*Orfeo ed Euridice*); HANDEL: Atalante* (*Xerxes*); HAYDN: Baucis* (*Philemon*); LEONCAVALLO: Nedda* (*Pagliacci*); LORTZING: Marie* (*Waffenschmied*), Gretchen* & Baronin Freimann* (*Wildschütz*), Marie* (*Zar und Zimmermann*); MOZART: Donna Elvira* (*Don Giovanni*), Contessa* & Cherubino* (*Nozze di Figaro*), Pamina* (*Zauberflöte*); NICOLAI: Aennchen* (*Lustigen Weiber*); ORFF: Solo* (*Carmina burana*); PUCCINI: Musetta* (*Bohème*), Lauretta* (*Gianni Schicchi*); SMETANA: Marie* (*Bartered Bride*); STRAUSS, J: Adele* & Rosalinde* (*Fledermaus*); TCHAIKOVSKY: Lisa* (*Pique Dame*); WEBER: Aennchen* (*Freischütz*). Also SUTERMEISTER: Mutter (*Schwarze Spinne*). Gives recitals. Appears with symphony orchestra. **Res:** Ursbergerstr 21, Munich, FR Ger. Mgmt: PAS/FRG; TAS/AUS.

KAHRY, GERHARD. Lyric tenor. Austrian. Resident mem: Stadttheater St Gallen, Switzerland. Born 2 May 1941, Vienna. Wife Elisabeth, occupation graphic designer. Studied: Delia Marion, Tino Pattiera, Prof Paula Köhler, Vienna; Max Lorenz, Munich. **Debut:** Fenton (*Lustigen Weiber*) Volksoper Vienna 1966. Previous occupations: technician, teacher. Awards: Second Prize Intl Conc de Musique, Geneva 1972.

Sang with major companies in AUS: Vienna Volksoper; BRA: Rio de Janeiro; FR GER: Saarbrücken. **Roles with these companies incl** BRITTEN: Male Chorus (*Rape of Lucretia*); DONIZETTI: Ernesto★ (*Don Pasquale*), Nemorino (*Elisir*); GOUNOD: Faust★; MONTEVERDI: Nero (*Incoronazione di Poppea*); MOZART: Ferrando★ (*Così fan tutte*), Belfiore (*Finta giardiniera*), Tamino★ (*Zauberflöte*); NICOLAI: Fenton (*Lustigen Weiber*); PUCCINI: Rodolfo (*Bohème*), Rinuccio (*Gianni Schicchi*); ROSSINI: Florville (*Signor Bruschino*); STRAUSS, J: Eisenstein & Alfred (*Fledermaus*); VERDI: Duca di Mantova★ (*Rigoletto*), Alfredo (*Traviata*); WEBER: Max (*Freischütz*). Also MARTINU: Conte d'Albanfiorita (*Mirandolina*); FARKAS: Schreinermeister (*Wunderschrank*). Video/Film: (*Olympiade*). Gives recitals. Appears with symphony orchestra. **Res:** Rosagasse 11, Vienna 120, Austria. Mgmt: KOA/AUS.

KAISER, ALBERT E. Conductor of opera and symphony. Swiss. Resident Cond, Collegium Musicum Basel. Born 11 Aug 1920, Zurich. Wife Sonja. Two children. Studied: Volkmar Andreae, Silvia Kind, Max Egger, Paul Müller, Zurich; Clemens Krauss, Joseph Marx, Salzburg; also piano, violin, clarinet, trumpet and voice. Plays the piano. Operatic training as repetiteur & asst cond at Opera House, Zurich 1942-45. **Operatic debut:** *Traviata* Opera House, Basel 1945. Symphonic debut: Tonhalleorchester Zurich 1944. Awards: Golden Key from Interlaken.

Conducted with major companies in AUS: Vienna Volksoper; ITA: Palermo; SWI: Basel, Zurich. **Operas with these companies incl** CIMAROSA: *Matrimonio segreto*★; DONIZETTI: *Campanello*★, *Don Pasquale*★; GERSHWIN: *Porgy and Bess*★; HAYDN: *Mondo della luna*★; LORTZING: *Zar und Zimmermann*★; MONTEVERDI: *Combattimento di Tancredi*★; MOZART: *Così fan tutte*★, *Don Giovanni*★, *Entführung aus dem Serail*★, *Finta giardiniera*★, *Nozze di Figaro*★, *Zauberflöte*★; NICOLAI: *Lustigen Weiber*★; OFFENBACH: *Contes d'Hoffmann*★, *Mariage aux lanternes*★; ORFF: *Carmina burana*★; PERGOLESI: *Serva padrona*★; PUCCINI: *Butterfly*★, *Tosca*★; ROSSINI: *Barbiere di Siviglia*★; STRAUSS, J: *Fledermaus*★; VERDI: *Otello*★, *Simon Boccanegra*★, *Traviata*★, *Trovatore*★; WOLF-FERRARI: *Segreto di Susanna*★. Also SUTERMEISTER: *Schwarze Spinne, Rote Stiefel*; STRAVINSKY: *Histoire du soldat*. Video—Swiss TV: *Schwarze Spinne; Rote Stiefel; Histoire du soldat; Yvrogne corrigé*. Conducted major orch in Europe. Teaches at Musikakad Basel. **Res:** Weinbergstr 47, 4102 Binningen, Switzerland. Mgmt: PIO/SWI; CLN/AUS.

KAISER, CARL WILLIAM. Lyric tenor. American. Resident mem: Niedersächsisches Staatstheater, Hannover. Born 28 Jun 1933, Mishawaka, IN, USA. Wife Helen Westra, occupation English teacher. Two children. Studied: Indiana Univ, Maurice Ivins, Eugene Bayless, Bloomington, USA; Catholic Univ of America, Rev Russell Woollen, Washington, DC; Hochschule für Musik, Prof Helmut Melchert, Hamburg. **Debut:** Luigi (*Tabarro*) New Orleans Opera, LA 1960. Previous

occupations: soldier, US Army chorus. Awards: Fulbright Schlshp; Best Male Singer, Chicagoland Music Fest, WGN Radio.

Sang with major companies in AUS: Vienna Volksoper; FR GER: Bielefeld, Cologne, Düsseldorf-Duisburg, Essen, Hamburg, Hannover, Kassel, Krefeld, Mannheim, Wiesbaden, Wuppertal; USA: New Orleans. **Roles with these companies incl** AUBER: Fra Diavolo★; BRITTEN: Lysander (*Midsummer Night*); DONIZETTI: Nemorino★ (*Elisir*); FLOTOW: Lionel★ (*Martha*); GOUNOD: Faust★; LORTZING: Baron Kronthal (*Wildschütz*); MASSENET: Des Grieux★ (*Manon*); MOZART: Ferrando★ (*Così fan tutte*), Don Ottavio★ (*Don Giovanni*), Belmonte★ (*Entführung aus dem Serail*), Tamino★ (*Zauberflöte*); MUSSORGSKY: Shuisky★ (*Boris Godunov*); NICOLAI: Fenton★ (*Lustigen Weiber*); PROKOFIEV: Marquis (*Gambler*); PUCCINI: Rodolfo★ (*Bohème*), Rinuccio★ (*Gianni Schicchi*), Pinkerton★ (*Butterfly*), Luigi (*Tabarro*), Cavaradossi (*Tosca*); ROSSINI: Almaviva★ (*Barbiere di Siviglia*), Don Ramiro★ (*Cenerentola*), Comte Ory★ (*Cenerentola*), Comte Ory; SMETANA: Hans★ (*Bartered Bride*); STRAUSS, J: Alfred (*Fledermaus*); STRAUSS, R: Matteo★ (*Arabella*), Flamand★ (*Capriccio*), Ein Sänger★ (*Rosenkavalier*); STRAVINSKY: Tom Rakewell (*Rake's Progress*); TCHAIKOVSKY: Lenski (*Eugene Onegin*); THOMAS: Wilhelm Meister (*Mignon*); VERDI: Foresto (*Attila*), Riccardo (*Ballo in maschera*), Don Carlo★, Duca di Mantova★ (*Rigoletto*), Alfredo★ (*Traviata*); WAGNER: Walther v d Vogelweide★ (*Tannhäuser*); WEBER: Max (*Freischütz*); WOLF-FERRARI: Florindo★ (*Donne curiose*). Also JANACEK: Fox (*Cunning Little Vixen*); LORTZING: Chateauneuf★ (*Zar und Zimmermann*), Hugo (*Undine*). Recorded for: Columbia. Appears with symphony orchestra. Teaches voice. **Res:** Auf dem Kampe 19a, 3000 Hannover 91, FR Ger. Mgmt: SLZ/FRG.

KALEF, BREDA AVRAM. Contralto. Yugoslavian. Resident mem: National Opera, Belgrade. Born 7 Dec 1936, Belgrade. Husband Branislav Simonovic, occupation architect. One child. Studied: Musical Acad, Prof Zlata Gjungenac, Belgrade; Consv Benedetto Marcello, Prof Maria Carbone, Venice. **Debut:** Mercedès (*Carmen*) Belgrade Opera 1960. Previous occupations: table tennis champion. Awards: 3 prizes, Compt 's Hertogenbosch, Holland.

Sang with major companies in AUS: Vienna Staatsoper; DEN: Copenhagen; FRA: Bordeaux; GRE: Athens Fest; FR GER: Berlin Deutsche Oper; GER DR: Berlin Staatsoper, Leipzig; HUN: Budapest; ISR: Tel Aviv; ITA: Naples, Palermo, Rome Opera, Venice; NOR: Oslo; SPA: Barcelona; YUG: Dubrovnik, Zagreb, Belgrade. **Roles with these companies incl** BELLINI: Adalgisa (*Norma*); BIZET: Carmen★; BORODIN: Kontchakovna★ (*Prince Igor*); BRITTEN: Lucretia★ (*Rape of Lucretia*); MASSENET: Dulcinée‡ (*Don Quichotte*), Charlotte★ (*Werther*); MUSSORGSKY: Marina★ (*Boris Godunov*), Khivria (*Fair at Sorochinsk*), Marfa (*Khovanshchina*); PONCHIELLI: La Cieca★ (*Gioconda*); PROKOFIEV: Smeraldina★ (*Love for Three Oranges*); PUCCINI: Suzuki★ (*Butterfly*); SAINT-SAENS: Dalila; TCHAIKOVSKY: Olga★ (*Eugene One-*

gin); VERDI: Amneris (*Aida*), Ulrica★ (*Ballo in maschera*), Preziosilla★ (*Forza del destino*), Azucena★ (*Trovatore*). Also LOGAR: Mina (*41*); BINICKI: Anda (*At Dawn*). **World premieres:** RADIC: Nerina (*Love Is the Most Important Thing*) Belgrade Opera 1962. Video/Film—Radio TV Belgrade: Carmen; Dulcinée (*Don Quichotte*). Gives recitals. Appears with symphony orchestra. Mgmt: YGC/YUG; SMN/USA.

KAMU, OKKO. Conductor of opera and symphony. Finnish. Resident Cond & Mus Dir, Helsinki Radio; Oslo Phil. Born 7 Mar 1946, Helsinki. Wife Arja Nieminen, occupation ballerina. Three children. Studied: Sibelius Acad, incl violin, piano, chamber music. Plays the violin. Operatic training at Finnish Ntl Opera, Helsinki 1966-69. **Operatic debut:** *Turn of the Screw* Finnish Ntl Opera 1968. Symphonic debut: Helsinki Phil, Finland 1968. Previous occupations: played second violin, Helsinki Phil; concertmaster, Finnish Ntl Opera Orch. Awards: von Karajan Awd, Berlin 1968. **Conducted with major companies in** FIN: Helsinki; SWE: Stockholm. **Operas with these companies incl** BRITTEN: *Turn of the Screw;* CIMAROSA: *Matrimonio segreto;* MOZART: *Così fan tutte, Don Giovanni, Nozze di Figaro, Zauberflöte;* PUCCINI: *Bohème, Tosca;* STRAUSS, J: *Fledermaus;* VERDI: *Aida, Rigoletto, Traviata.* Video—Finnish TV: *Rigoletto.* Conducted major orch in Europe, USA/Canada, Asia, Africa, Austrl. **Res:** Nötö, Finland. Mgmt: CAM/USA; SVE/SWE.

KAPPLMÜLLER, HERBERT. Scenic and costume designer for opera, theater. Is a lighting designer. Austrian. Resident designer, Staatstheater, Kassel, FR Ger. Born 28 Oct 1941, Linz, Austria. Single. Studied: Akad der bildenden Künste, Profs Böckl, Wotruba, Auramidis, Egg, Vienna. **Operatic debut:** *Heure espagnole* Staatstheater Kassel 1975. Theater debut: Landestheater Linz, Austria 1967. **Designed for major company in** FR GER: Kassel. **Operas designed for this company incl** RAVEL: *Enfant et les sortilèges, Heure espagnole★;* STRAUSS, R: *Ariadne auf Naxos★;* WALTON: *Bear★.* Exhibitions of stage designs, paintings, Vienna 1967, Salzburg 1968. **Res:** Landgraf Philipps Pl 2, Kassel, FR Ger.

KARIZS, BÉLA. Heldentenor. Hungarian. Resident mem: Hungarian State Opera, Budapest. Born 28 Aug 1931, Budapest. Divorced. Two children. Studied: Theatrical Art School, Budapest; Prof Dr Jenö Sipos, Budapest. **Debut:** Calaf (*Turandot*) Hungarian State Opera, Budapest 1959. **Sang with major companies in** BUL: Sofia; CZE: Prague Smetana; FR GER: Cologne; GER DR: Berlin Staatsoper; POL: Warsaw; USSR: Moscow Bolshoi. **Roles with these companies incl** MASCAGNI: Turiddu★ (*Cavalleria rusticana*); MONTEVERDI: Nero★ (*Incoronazione di Poppea*); PUCCINI: Pinkerton (*Butterfly*), Des Grieux (*Manon Lescaut*), Cavaradossi★ (*Tosca*), Calaf (*Turandot*); SAINT-SAENS: Samson; VERDI: Radames★ (*Aida*), Don Alvaro (*Forza del destino*), Arvino (*Lombardi*), Gabriele (*Simon Boccanegra*), Manrico★ (*Trovatore*). Recorded for: Hungarian State Rec Co, Budapest. Gives recitals. Appears

with symphony orchestra. **Res:** V Garibaldi u 4, Budapest, Hungary.

KARLSRUD, EDMOND. Bass-baritone. American. Resident mem: Metropolitan Opera, New York. Born 10 Jun 1927, Scobey, MT, USA. Wife Carolyn, occupation prof musician. Three children. Studied: Univ of Minnesota, Earle G Killeen, Minneapolis; Juilliard School of Music, Mack Harrell, New York; Gibner King, New York. **Debut:** Baron Douphol (*Traviata*) Atlanta Opera, GA, 1962. **Sang with major companies in** USA: New Orleans, New York Met. **Roles with these companies incl** MOZART: Figaro★ (*Nozze di Figaro*), Sarastro★ (*Zauberflöte*); STRAVINSKY: Tiresias (*Oedipus Rex*); WAGNER: Landgraf★ (*Tannhäuser*). Also DONIZETTI: Raimondo★ (*Lucia*); BEETHOVEN: Don Fernando★ (*Fidelio*). Gives recitals. Appears with symphony orchestra. Teaches voice. **Res:** Marmaroneck, NY, USA.

KARP, RICHARD. Conductor of opera and symphony. American. Gen Director & Music Dir, Pittsburgh Opera, PA 1942- . Also Music Dir, Westmoreland Symph Orch, Greensburg, PA. Born 5 Mar 1907, Vienna, Austria. Wife Ilse, occupation pianist & organist. Two children. Studied: Royal Consv, Fritz Busch, Fritz Reiner, Dresden; incl piano, violin, viola & voice. Plays the viola. Operatic training as repetiteur & chorus master at Staatstheater and Residenz Theater, Dresden. **Operatic debut:** *Trovatore* Düsseldorf, Germany 1927. Symphonic debut: Dresden Phil Orch 1925. Previous occupations: solo & quartet violist; prof of music and theater. Awards: Cavaliere, Italian Rep; Verdienstkreuz Erster Kl, FR Ger; Dr Hum, Seton Hill Univ/Mus D, StVC. **Conducted with major companies in** FR GER: Düsseldorf-Duisburg, Saarbrücken, Stuttgart; ITA: Milan La Scala; MEX: Mexico City; USA: Baltimore, Cincinnati, New Orleans, Philadelphia Lyric, Pittsburgh, San Francisco Opera. **Operas with these companies incl** BEETHOVEN: *Fidelio★;* BELLINI: *Norma, Sonnambula★;* BERNSTEIN: *Trouble in Tahiti;* BIZET: *Carmen★;* BRITTEN: *Albert Herring;* CIMAROSA: *Matrimonio segreto;* CORNELIUS: *Barbier von Bagdad;* DELIBES: *Lakmé★;* DONIZETTI: *Don Pasquale★, Elisir★, Fille du régiment★, Lucia★;* FLOYD: *Susannah;* GIORDANO: *Andrea Chénier★;* GLUCK: *Iphigénie en Aulide, Orfeo ed Euridice;* GOUNOD: *Faust★, Roméo et Juliette★;* HUMPERDINCK: *Hänsel und Gretel;* LEONCAVALLO: *Pagliacci★;* LORTZING: *Waffenschmied, Wildschütz, Zar und Zimmermann;* MASCAGNI: *Cavalleria rusticana★;* MASSENET: *Manon;* MENOTTI: *Amahl, Amelia al ballo, Medium, Old Maid and the Thief, Telephone;* MONTEMEZZI: *Amore dei tre re★‡;* MONTEVERDI: *Combattimento di Tancredi;* MOZART: *Così fan tutte★, Don Giovanni★, Entführung aus dem Serail, Finta giardiniera★, Nozze di Figaro★, Zauberflöte;* MUSSORGSKY: *Boris Godunov★;* NICOLAI: *Lustigen Weiber;* OFFENBACH: *Contes d'Hoffmann★;* PONCHIELLI: *Gioconda;* PUCCINI: *Bohème★, Gianni Schicchi, Butterfly★, Manon Lescaut★, Suor Angelica, Tabarro★, Tosca★, Turandot;* ROSSINI: *Barbiere di Siviglia★;* SAINT-SAENS: *Samson et Dalila;* SMETANA: *Bartered*

Bride; STRAUSS, J: *Fledermaus;* STRAUSS, R: *Ariadne auf Naxos;* TCHAIKOVSKY: *Eugene Onegin;* THOMAS: *Mignon;* VERDI: *Aida★, Ballo in maschera★, Don Carlo, Forza del destino, Nabucco★, Otello★, Rigoletto★, Traviata★, Trovatore★;* WAGNER: *Fliegende Holländer★, Lohengrin★, Tannhäuser★, Tristan und Isolde;* WARD: *Crucible;* WEBER: *Freischütz, Oberon;* WOLF-FERRARI: *Segreto di Susanna.* Recorded for RCA-Delta. Conducted major orch in Europe, USA/Canada, Cent/S America. Previous positions as Mus Dir with orchestras: Adirondack Symph Orch, Saranac Lake, NY 1940-60. Teaches at Univ of Pittsburgh. Member Prof Commtt Central Opera Service. **Res:** 5467 Bartlett St, Pittsburgh, PA, USA. Mgmt: HUR/USA; PAS/FRG.

KASLIK, VÁCLAV. Stages/produces opera, film & television; is also a conductor & composer. Czechoslovakian. Resident Stage Dir, National Theater, Prague. Born 28 Sep 1917, Policna, CSR. Wife Ruzena. Three children. Studied: Prague Consv of Music; incl piano. Operatic training as asst stage dir at National Theater, Prague. **Operatic debut:** *Orfeo ed Euridice* Brno, CSSR 1943. Theater debut: Laterna Magica, Prague 1958. Awards: Artist of Merit; Laureate State Prize, Gvnmt Awd. Previous adm positions in opera: Mng, Opera of the 5th May, Prague 1945-48; First Dir & Cond, Smetana Theater, Prague 1954-65.

Directed/produced opera for major companies in AUS: Bregenz Fest, Vienna Staatsoper & Volksoper; CZE: Brno, Prague National; DEN: Copenhagen; GRE: Athens Fest; FR GER: Berlin Deutsche Oper, Frankfurt, Hannover, Mannheim, Munich Staatsoper & Gärtnerplatz, Stuttgart, Wiesbaden; GER DR: Dresden; ITA: Milan La Scala, Venice; SWE: Stockholm; SWI: Geneva, Zurich; UK: Edinburgh Fest, London Royal. **Operas staged with these companies incl** BEETHOVEN: *Fidelio★;* BIZET: *Carmen★;* BORODIN: *Prince Igor;* DEBUSSY: *Pelléas et Mélisande★;* DESSAU: *Lanzelot★;* DVORAK: *Devil and Kate, Rusalka★;* HINDEMITH: *Cardillac;* JANACEK: *Cunning Little Vixen★, Excursions of Mr Broucek, From the House of the Dead, Jenufa, Katya Kabanova★, Makropoulos Affair;* MARTINU: *Griechische Passion;* MOZART: *Così fan tutte, Don Giovanni★, Idomeneo★, Nozze di Figaro, Zauberflöte★;* MUSSORGSKY: *Boris Godunov★;* OFFENBACH: *Contes d'Hoffmann★;* ORFF: *Bernauerin;* SCHOENBERG: *Moses und Aron★;* SMETANA: *Bartered Bride, Dalibor, Devil's Wall★;* VERDI: *Aida, Simon Boccanegra★;* WAGNER: *Fliegende Holländer.* Also MARTINU: *Julietta;* CIKKER: *Beg Bajazid.* **Operatic world premieres:** NONO: *Intolleranza* La Fenice, Venice 1961; MARTINU: *Mirandolina* National Theater, Prague 1959. Operatic Video/Film: numerous prod in Milan, Copenhagen, Prague, Munich, Mainz. **Res:** Skretova 10, Prague, CSSR. Mgmt: PRG/CZE.

KASRASHSVILI, MAKVALA FILIMONOVNA. Lyric-dramatic soprano. Russian. Resident mem: Bolshoi Theater, Moscow. Born 13 Mar 1942, Kutaisi. Studied: Tbilisi, Mrs Davidova. **Debut:** Contessa (*Nozze di Figaro*) Bolshoi Theater, Moscow 1968. Awards: First Prize, Trans-Caucasian Compt 1965; Silver Medal, Second Prize in Sofia,

Bulgaria 1968; Grand Prix, Montreal, Canada 1973.

Sang with major companies in BUL: Sofia; CZE: Brno, Prague National; POL: Warsaw; USSR: Moscow Bolshoi. **Roles with these companies incl** BIZET: Micaëla★ (*Carmen*); GOUNOD: Marguerite★ (*Faust*); MOZART: Contessa★ (*Nozze di Figaro*); PROKOFIEV: Natasha★ (*War and Peace*); PUCCINI: Mimi★ (*Bohème*), Minnie★ (*Fanciulla del West*), Lauretta★ (*Gianni Schicchi*), Cio-Cio-San★ (*Butterfly*), Tosca★, Liù★ (*Turandot*); RIMSKY-KORSAKOV: Olga★ (*Maid of Pskov*); STRAVINSKY: Parasha★ (*Mavra*); TCHAIKOVSKY: Tatiana★ (*Eugene Onegin*), Lisa★ (*Pique Dame*); VERDI: Aida★, Leonora★ (*Trovatore*). Also PROKOFIEV: Pauline (*Gambler*); RACHMANINOFF: Francesca da Rimini. Recorded for: Melodiya. Gives recitals. Appears with symphony orchestra. **Res:** d 40 kv 164 Pr Kalinina, Moscow, USSR. Mgmt: GOS/USSR.

KATONA, SANDOR TIBOR. French. Mng, Opéra de Monte Carlo, Monaco 1966- . In charge of overall adm matters & finances. Additional adm position: Mng, Natl Symph Orch, Monaço. Born 8 May 1915, Budapest, Hungary. Divorced. One child. Studied: Univs Budapest, Siena. Previous positions, primarily adm: Asst & Adm Opéra de Paris 1960-66, Aix-en-Provence Fest 1960-66. World premieres at theaters under his management: ROSSELLINI: *Avventuriero* 1968, *Reine morte* 1973; DAMASE: *Madame de* 1970, all at Monte Carlo. Mem of Commtt of Monte Carlo Opera. **Res:** Monte Carlo, Monaco.

KATZ, EBERHARD. Heldentenor. German. Resident mem: Städtische Oper, Cologne; Oper Dortmund. Born 19 Oct 1928, Krombach/Siegen, Germany. Wife Lilli. Two children. Studied: Profs C Glettenberg, J Metternich. **Debut:** Erik (*Fliegende Holländer*) Städtische Oper, Cologne 1963. Previous occupations: beer brewmaster.

Sang with major companies in AUS: Vienna Volksoper; FRA: Lyon, Nice, Rouen, Toulouse; FR GER: Berlin Deutsche Oper, Cologne, Dortmund, Düsseldorf-Duisburg, Essen, Frankfurt, Hannover, Kassel, Krefeld, Munich Staatsoper, Nürnberg, Stuttgart, Wiesbaden, Wuppertal; UK: London English National. **Roles with these companies incl** d'ALBERT: Pedro★ (*Tiefland*); BEETHOVEN: Florestan★ (*Fidelio*); BUSONI: Calaf (*Turandot*); EINEM: Bürgermeister★ (*Besuch der alten Dame*); HANDEL: Grimwald (*Rodelinda*); HINDEMITH: Apprentice‡ (*Cardillac*); MARTIN: Tristan (*Vin herbé*); MASCAGNI: Turiddu (*Cavalleria rusticana*); MUSSORGSKY: Shuisky★ (*Boris Godunov*), Vassily Golitsin (*Khovanshchina*); RIMSKY-KORSAKOV: Prince Vsevolod (*Invisible City of Kitezh*); STRAUSS, R: Bacchus★ (*Ariadne auf Naxos*), Herodes★ (*Salome*); STRAVINSKY: Oedipus; TCHAIKOVSKY: Gherman (*Pique Dame*); WAGNER: Erik★ (*Fliegende Holländer*), Lohengrin, Parsifal, Siegmund★ (*Walküre*), Tannhäuser, Tristan★; WEBER: Max (*Freischütz*); WEILL: Jack★ (*Aufstieg und Fall der Stadt Mahagonny*). Recorded for: DG. Appears with symphony orchestra. Teaches voice. Coaches repertoire. **Res:** Lindenweg 11, 5064 Rösrath/Cologne, FR Ger. Mgmt: PAS/FRG; RNR/SWI.

KATZBÖCK, RUDOLF. Lyric baritone. Austrian. Resident mem: Volksoper, Vienna. Born 4 Nov 1936, Linz, Austria. Wife Rose. Studied: Acad of Music, Kmsg Josef Witt, Vienna; Prof Wolfgang Steinbrück, Prof Christl Mardayn, Vienna. **Debut:** Graf Eberbach (*Wildschütz*) Opernhaus Dortmund 1969. Previous occupations: teacher.

Sang with major companies in AUS: Graz, Vienna Volksoper; FR GER: Dortmund. **Roles with these companies incl** DONIZETTI: Dott Malatesta★ (*Don Pasquale*); LORTZING: Graf Eberbach★ (*Wildschütz*), Peter I (*Zar und Zimmermann*); MOZART: Guglielmo★ (*Così fan tutte*), Figaro★ (*Nozze di Figaro*), Papageno★ (*Zauberflöte*); ROSSINI: Figaro★ (*Barbiere di Siviglia*); VERDI: Rodrigo★ (*Don Carlo*); WAGNER: Wolfram★ (*Tannhäuser*). Also COSMA: Antoine (*Elektronische Liebe*); SCHULZE: Spielmann (*Schwarzer Peter*). **World premieres:** RUBIN: Stanislaus (*Kleider machen Leute*) Volksoper Vienna 1974. Gives recitals. Appears with symphony orchestra. **Res:** Rudolf von Altplatz 4, Vienna 3, Austria. Mgmt: TAS/AUS.

KAUFMANN, REINHARD HERMANN. Conductor of opera. German. Resident Cond, Städtische Bühnen, Dortmund. Also resident cond Philharmonisches Orchester, Dortmund. Born 26 July 1936, Celle, Germany. Wife Sieglinde. Three children. Studied: Staatliche Hochschule für Musik, Prof Wolfgang von der Nahmer, Cologne; incl piano, violin, organ and voice. Plays the piano. Operatic training as repetiteur & asst cond at Stadttheater Aachen 1962-63; Stadttheater Hagen 1963-67; Musical Asst, Bayreuth Fest 1966-68, 1971. **Operatic debut:** *Samson et Dalila* Stadttheater Aachen, FR Ger 1963. **Symphonic debut:** Symphonieorchester, Hagen, Germany 1966. Previous adm positions in opera: Studienleiter, Stadttheater Aachen, FR Ger 1967-70.

Conducted with major companies in FR GER: Dortmund. **Operas with these companies incl** GOUNOD: *Faust★;* MOZART: *Zauberflöte★;* PUCCINI: *Turandot★;* SAINT-SAENS: *Samson et Dalila;* SMETANA: *Bartered Bride★;* STRAUSS, R: *Salome★;* VERDI: *Don Carlo★, Nabucco★;* WAGNER: *Rheingold★.* **Res:** Olpe 8-10, 46 Dortmund, FR Ger. Mgmt: SLZ/FRG.

KAWACHI, SHOZO. Japanese. Adm Dir, Niki Kai Opera, 1-58-13 Yoyogi Shibuya-ku, Tokyo. In charge of overall adm matters. Additional adm positions: Exec Dir, Japan Federation of Musicians, Tokyo. Born 17 Jan 1926, Amagasaki. Wife Setsuko, occupation teacher. Three children. Studied: Yokohama Commercial Coll. Previous position, primarily adm: staff Toho Musical Assn, Tokyo 1947-51. Started with present company as Secy Gen. **Res:** 1-13-9 Shinden, Ichikawa, Japan.

KAWAHARA, YOKO. Lyric soprano. Japanese. Resident mem: Niki Kai, Tokyo; Staatsoper, Hamburg. Born Tokyo, Japan. Studied: Prof Toshiko Toda, Tokyo; Fr Prof Ellen Bosenius, Cologne, FR Ger. **Debut:** Fiordiligi (*Così fan tutte*) Niki Kai, Tokyo. Awards: Mainichi Music Concours, Japan.

Sang with major companies in FR GER: Bayreuth Fest, Bonn, Cologne, Frankfurt, Hamburg, Hannover, Munich Staatsoper, Stuttgart; JPN: Tokyo Niki Kai. **Roles with these companies incl**

BEETHOVEN: Marzelline★ (*Fidelio*); GLUCK: Euridice★; MOZART: Fiordiligi (*Così fan tutte*), Pamina★ (*Zauberflöte*); NICOLAI: Aennchen★ (*Lustigen Weiber*); PUCCINI: Liù★ (*Turandot*); STRAUSS, R: Sophie★ (*Rosenkavalier*); VERDI: Desdemona★ (*Otello*). Gives recitals. Appears with symphony orchestra. **Res:** Colonnaden 54, 2 Hamburg 36, FR Ger. Mgmt: ARM/FRG; conc: KHA/FRG.

KEATING, RODERIC MAURICE. Lyric & buffo tenor. British. Resident mem: Staatstheater der Saar, Saarbrücken. Born 14 Dec 1941, Maidenhead, UK. Wife Martha Kathryn Post. One child. Studied: Cambridge Univ; Royal Acad of Music, Eric Greene, London; Yale Univ, Benjamin de Loache, New Haven, CT; Univ of Texas, Willa Stewart, Austin, USA. **Debut:** Nathanael (*Contes d'Hoffmann*) Houston Grand Opera, TX 1970. Previous occupations: teacher, radio announcer. Awards: DMA Univ of Texas; Ford Intl Fllshp, Ford Fndt.

Sang with major companies in FR GER: Saarbrücken; UK: Glyndebourne Fest; USA: Houston. **Roles with these companies incl** LORTZING: Baron Kronthal★ (*Wildschütz*); MOZART: Don Ottavio★ (*Don Giovanni*), Idamante★ (*Idomeneo*), Tamino★ (*Zauberflöte*); ROSSINI: Almaviva★ (*Barbiere di Siviglia*); STRAUSS, J: Eisenstein★ (*Fledermaus*); WEILL: Fatty★ (*Aufstieg und Fall der Stadt Mahagonny*). Appears with symphony orchestra. **Res:** Finkenweg 2, 6604 Brebach-Fechingen, FR Ger. Mgmt: ARM/FRG; IBB/UK.

KEENE, CHRISTOPHER ANTHONY. Conductor of opera and symphony; operatic stage director. American. Resident Cond, New York City Opera. Also Mus Dir, Syracuse Symph Orch, NY, USA 1975-78 and Mus Dir, Artpark, Lewiston, NY 1974-77. Born 21 Dec 1946, Berkeley, CA, USA. Wife Sara. Two children. Studied: Univ of Calif, Berkeley; incl piano & cello. Operatic training as repetiteur & asst cond at San Francisco Opera 1965-66; San Diego Opera 1967; New York City Opera 1970. **Operatic debut:** *Rape of Lucretia*, Student Opera Theatre, Berkeley 1965. **Symphonic debut:** Rochester Phil, Rochester, NY 1973. Awards: Julius Rudel Awd 1970-71. Previous adm positions in opera: Spoleto Fest, Mus Dir 1973-75, Gen Dir 1974-75.

Conducted with major companies in AUS: Vienna Volksoper; FR GER: Berlin, Hamburg; HOL: Amsterdam Netherlands Opera; ITA: Spoleto Fest, Trieste; UK: London Royal; USA: Milwaukee Florentine, New York Metropolitan & City Opera, Santa Fe. **Operas with these companies incl** BELLINI: *Puritani★;* BERG: *Lulu★;* BIZET: *Carmen★;* CHERUBINI: *Medea★;* DONIZETTI: *Don Pasquale★;* FLOYD: *Susannah★;* GINASTERA: *Beatrix Cenci★, Don Rodrigo★;* GOUNOD: *Faust★;* JANACEK: *Makropoulos Affair★;* LEONCAVALLO: *Pagliacci★;* MASCAGNI: *Cavalleria rusticana★;* MENOTTI: *Amahl, Consul★, Maria Golovin★, Tamu-Tamu★;* MONTEVERDI: *Incoronazione di Poppea★;* MOZART: *Don Giovanni★, Nozze di Figaro★, Zauberflöte★;* MUSSORGSKY: *Boris Godunov★;* PUCCINI: *Butterfly★, Manon Lescaut★, Tosca★;* REIMANN: *Melusine★;* STRAUSS, R: *Ariadne auf Naxos★, Salome★;* VERDI: *Traviata★;*

WEILL: *Aufstieg und Fall der Stadt Mahagonny*. Also BRITTEN: *Turn of the Screw;* DELIUS: *Village Romeo and Juliet;* MENOTTI: *Saint of Bleecker Street.* **World premieres:** FLOYD: *Bilby's Doll* Houston 1976; PASATIERI: *Inez de Castro* Baltimore 1976; MENOTTI: *Most Important Man* New York City Opera 1971, *Tamu-Tamu* Chicago 1973; VILLA-LOBOS: *Yerma* Santa Fe Opera, NM, 1971. Conducted major orch in USA/Canada. **Res:** 650 West End Ave, New York, NY, USA. Mgmt: CAM/USA; AIM/UK.

KEENON, EDGAR ALLEN. Dramatic baritone & bass-baritone. American. Resident mem: Staatstheater Kassel. Born Cincinnati, O, USA. Divorced. One child. Studied: Louis John Johnen, Cincinnati; Cincinnati Coll of Music, O, USA: State Schl of Music, Stuttgart; Hubert Giessen, Stuttgart. **Debut:** Moralès (*Carmen*) Cincinnati Opera 1956. Previous occupations: locomotive engr.

Sang with major companies in BEL: Brussels, Liège; FR GER: Dortmund, Düsseldorf-Duisburg, Essen, Karlsruhe, Kassel, Munich Staatsoper, Saarbrücken, Stuttgart, Wiesbaden, Wuppertal; S AFR: Johannesburg; SWE: Stockholm; USA: Cincinnati. **Roles with these companies incl** d'ALBERT: Sebastiano (*Tiefland*); BEETHOVEN: Don Pizarro (*Fidelio*); BERG: Wozzeck; DEBUSSY: Golaud (*Pelléas et Mélisande*); DONIZETTI: Enrico★ (*Lucia*); EINEM: George Danton (*Dantons Tod*); GIORDANO: Carlo Gérard★ (*Andrea Chénier*); GLUCK: Agamemnon (*Iphigénie en Aulide*); JANACEK: Shishkov★ (*From the House of the Dead*); LEONCAVALLO: Tonio (*Pagliacci*); MASCAGNI: Alfio (*Cavalleria rusticana*); MOZART: Don Alfonso (*Così fan tutte*); OFFENBACH: Coppélius, etc★ (*Contes d'Hoffmann*); ORFF: König (*Kluge*); PUCCINI: Schicchi, Sharpless (*Butterfly*), Scarpia (*Tosca*); RIMSKY-KORSAKOV: Roi Dodon (*Coq d'or*); ROSSINI: Mustafà (*Italiana in Algeri*); STRAUSS, R: Musiklehrer (*Ariadne auf Naxos*), Jochanaan (*Salome*); STRAVINSKY: Creon (*Oedipus Rex*), Nick Shadow (*Rake's Progress*), Empereur de Chine (*Rossignol*); TCHAIKOVSKY: Yeletsky (*Pique Dame*); VERDI: Amonasro★ (*Aida*), Renato★ (*Ballo in maschera*), Rodrigo & Grande Inquisitore★ (*Don Carlo*), Falstaff, Nabucco, Iago★ (*Otello*), Rigoletto★, Germont (*Traviata*); WAGNER: Holländer★, Telramund★ (*Lohengrin*), Hans Sachs★ & Pogner (*Meistersinger*), Amfortas (*Parsifal*), Wotan (*Rheingold★, Walküre★*), Wanderer★ (*Siegfried*), Kurwenal (*Tristan und Isolde*); WALTON: Smirnov★ (*The Bear*); WEBER: Kaspar★ (*Freischütz*); WEILL: Trinity Moses (*Aufstieg und Fall der Stadt Mahagonny*). Also TCHAIKOVSKY: Dunois (*Maid of Orleans*); DESSAU: Judge (*Lukullus*); ZIMMERMANN: Haudy★ (*Soldaten*); LORTZING: Kühleborn (*Undine*); MOZART: Sprecher (*Zauberflöte*). Gives recitals. Teaches voice. **Res:** Amalienstr 12, Kassel, FR Ger.

KEHL, SIGRID. Dramatic soprano & dramatic mezzo-soprano. German, DR. Resident mem: Städtisches Theater, Leipzig; Staatsoper, Berlin. Born 23 Nov 1932, Berlin, Germany. Husband Friedhelm Eberle, occupation actor. One child.

Studied: Hochschule für Musik, Prof Dagmar Freiwald-Lange, Berlin; Mme Maria Carpi, Geneva. **Debut:** Annina (*Rosenkavalier*) Operntheater Leipzig 1957. Awards: Kammersängerin, Minister for Culture, Berlin; Kunstpreis der DDR; Nationalpreis der DDR; Intl Schumann-Preis.

Sang with major companies in AUS: Graz, Vienna Staatsoper; CZE: Brno, Prague National; GER DR: Berlin Komische Oper & Staatsoper, Dresden, Leipzig; ITA: Bologna, Naples, Venice; POL: Warsaw; ROM: Bucharest; SWI: Basel, Geneva; USSR: Tbilisi. **Roles with these companies incl** BARTOK: Judith (*Bluebeard's Castle*); BEETHOVEN: Leonore★‡ (*Fidelio*); JANACEK: Kostelnicka★‡ (*Jenufa*); MASCAGNI: Santuzza★ (*Cavalleria rusticana*); MOZART: Sesto★ (*Clemenza di Tito*); ORFF: Antigonae; PROKOFIEV: Clara (*Duenna*); STRAUSS, R: Ariadne★ (*Ariadne auf Naxos*), Octavian (*Rosenkavalier*), Amme★‡ (*Frau ohne Schatten*), Herodias (*Salome*); TCHAIKOVSKY: Joan of Arc (*Maid of Orleans*); WAGNER: Ortrud★‡ (*Lohengrin*), Sieglinde (*Walküre*), Brünnhilde (*Walküre★‡, Siegfried, Götterdämmerung*), Venus‡ (*Tannhäuser*), Brangäne★ (*Tristan und Isolde*); Magdalene (*Meistersinger*), Fricka (*Rheingold*); BIZET: Carmen; BORODIN: Kontchakovna (*Prince Igor*); JANACEK: Kabanikha (*Katya Kabanova*); MONTEVERDI: Penelope (*Ritorno d'Ulisse*); MUSSORGSKY: Marina (*Boris Godunov*); PROKOFIEV: Helene (*War and Peace*); PUCCINI: Suzuki (*Butterfly*); TCHAIKOVSKY: Mme Larina (*Eugene Onegin*), La Comtesse (*Pique Dame*); VERDI: Amneris (*Aida*), Ulrica (*Ballo in maschera*), Eboli★‡ (*Don Carlo*), Dame Quickly (*Falstaff*), Preziosilla (*Forza del destino*), Azucena (*Trovatore*). Gives recitals. Appears with symphony orchestra. Teaches voice. Coaches repertoire. **Res:** Gohliserstr 1, 7022 Leipzig, Ger DR. Mgmt: KDR/GDR; RAB/AUS.

KÉLEMEN, ZOLTÁN. Bass. Resident mem: Städtische Oper, Cologne; Bayerische Staatsoper, Munich. Born Hungary. Studied: Franz Liszt Acad, Budapest; Accad di S Cecilia, Rome. **Debut:** Städtisches Theater, Augsburg.

Sang with major companies in ARG: Buenos Aires; AUS: Salzburg Fest; FR GER: Bayreuth Fest, Cologne, Darmstadt, Düsseldorf-Duisburg, Hamburg, Munich Staatsoper, Wuppertal; ITA: Naples, Turin; USA: New York Met; et al. **Roles with these companies incl** BARTOK: Bluebeard; BEETHOVEN: Don Pizarro‡ (*Fidelio*); DONIZETTI: Don Pasquale; GLUCK: Thoas (*Iphigénie en Tauride*); MOZART: Don Alfonso (*Così fan tutte*), Leporello (*Don Giovanni*), Osmin (*Entführung aus dem Serail*); NICOLAI: Falstaff (*Lustigen Weiber*); PUCCINI: Gianni Schicchi; SMETANA: Kezal (*Bartered Bride*); STRAUSS, R: Musiklehrer (*Ariadne auf Naxos*); VERDI: Grande Inquisitore (*Don Carlo*), Falstaff; WAGNER: Alberich (*Rheingold‡, Götterdämmerung‡*); et al. Also WAGNER: Klingsor‡ (*Parsifal*). Recorded for: DG, Decca, Angel. **Res:** Schwabenstr 3, 5038 Rodenkirchen, FR Ger.

KELLEY, NORMAN D. Lyric tenor. American. Born 27 Aug 1917, Eddington, ME, USA. Divorced. Two sons. Studied: New England Consv, Boston; Leland Powers Theatre School; Eastman

School of Music, Rochester, NY; Mario B Pagano. **Debut:** Cavaradossi (*Tosca*) Philadelphia La Scala 1947. Previous occupations: Captain US Army, 5 yrs.

Sang with major companies in BEL: Brussels; CAN: Montreal/Quebec, Toronto, Vancouver; FRA: Lyon, Marseille, Nancy, Nice, Paris, Rouen, Toulouse; MEX: Mexico City; POR: Lisbon; USA: Baltimore, Boston, Cincinnati Summer Opera, Fort Worth, Houston, Miami, New Orleans, New York Met & City Opera, Philadelphia Grand & Lyric, Pittsburgh, San Antonio, San Diego, San Francisco Opera. **Roles with these cos incl** BIZET: Don José (*Carmen*); BOITO: Faust (*Mefistofele*); EINEM: (*Besuch der alten Dame*); HUMPERDINCK: Hexe★ (*Hänsel und Gretel*); MASCAGNI: Turiddu (*Cavalleria rusticana*); MENOTTI: Lover (*Amelia al ballo*); MOZART: Pedrillo (*Entführung aus dem Serail*); MUSSORGSKY: Shuisky★ (*Boris Godunov*); ORFF: Erzähler (*Mond*); PROKOFIEV: Mephistopheles (*Fiery Angel*); PUCCINI: Pinkerton★ (*Butterfly*), Cavaradossi (*Tosca*); STRAUSS, J: Eisenstein (*Fledermaus*); STRAUSS, R: Aegisth (*Elektra*), Herodes (*Salome*); VERDI: Alfredo (*Traviata*); WAGNER: Mime★ (*Rheingold, Siegfried*); WOLF: Eugenio de Zuniga (*Corregidor*). Also MENOTTI: Magician (*Consul*). **World premieres:** MOORE: Lord Mark (*Wings of the Dove*) 1961; FLOYD: Eli Pratt (*Passion of Jonathan Wade*) 1962; KURKA: Joseph Schweik (*Good Soldier Schweik*) 1958; WARD: Rev Parris (*Crucible*) 1961; all at New York City Opera. Video/Film — Paramount & BBC TV: Magician (*Consul*). Gives recitals. Appears with symphony orchestra. Teaches voice. Coaches repertoire. **Res:** 50 W 67 St, New York, NY 10023, USA. **Mgmt:** HJH/USA; CST/UK.

KEMPE, RUDOLF. Conductor of opera and symphony. German. Music Dir, Münchner Philharmoniker & BBC Symph Orch, London. Born 14 Jun 1910, Dresden, Wife Cordula, occupation violinist. Three children. Conducted while studying under Fritz Busch, Otto Klemperer, Bruno Walter, Wilhelm Furtwängler, Profs König, Bachmann & Kreissig; incl oboe, piano & violin. Plays the piano & harpsichord. Operatic training as repetiteur & asst cond at Städt Oper, Leipzig 1935-37. **Operatic debut:** *Wildschütz* Städt Oper, Leipzig 1935. Symphonic debut: Städt Orch, Chemnitz 1942. Previous occupations: solo oboist in Gewandhaus Orch, Leipzig. Awards: Bayer Verdienstorden; Naegeli Medal, Zurich; Gold Medal, Munich. Previous adm positions in opera: Chief Cond, Ntl Opera Weimar; Gen Music Dir, Opera Chemnitz 1946-48, Staatsoper Dresden 1949-53 and Bayerische Staatsoper Munich 1952-54.

Conducted with major companies in ARG: Buenos Aires; AUS: Salzburg Fest, Vienna Staatsoper; FRA: Orange Fest; GRE: Athens Fest; FR GER: Bayreuth Fest, Berlin Deutsche Oper, Munich Staatsoper; GER DR: Berlin Komische Oper & Staatsoper, Dresden, Leipzig; SPA: Barcelona; SWE: Stockholm; SWI: Zurich; UK: Edinburgh Fest, London Royal; USA: New York Met. **Operas with these companies incl** d'ALBERT: *Tiefland;* BEETHOVEN: *Fidelio★;* BIZET: *Carmen★;* DONIZETTI: *Don Pasquale, Elisir;*

FLOTOW: *Martha;* GLUCK: *Orfeo ed Euridice;* GOTOVAC: *Ero der Schelm;* HUMPERDINCK: *Hänsel und Gretel, Königskinder;* LEONCAVALLO: *Pagliacci;* LORTZING: *Waffenschmied;* MASCAGNI: *Cavalleria rusticana;* MOZART: *Così fan tutte, Don Giovanni, Entführung aus dem Serail, Finta giardiniera, Nozze di Figaro, Re pastore, Zauberflöte;* NICOLAI: *Lustigen Weiber;* OFFENBACH: *Contes d'Hoffmann;* ORFF: *Bernauerin, Kluge;* PFITZNER: *Palestrina;* PUCCINI: *Bohème, Gianni Schicchi, Butterfly, Tabarro, Tosca, Turandot;* ROSSINI: *Barbiere di Siviglia;* SMETANA: *Bartered Bride‡;* STRAUSS, J: *Fledermaus;* STRAUSS, R: *Arabella, Ariadne auf Naxos‡, Capriccio, Daphne, Elektra★, Frau ohne Schatten, Liebe der Danae, Rosenkavalier★‡, Salome★, Schweigsame Frau;* SUTERMEISTER: *Romeo und Julia;* TCHAIKOVSKY: *Eugene Onegin, Pique Dame;* THOMAS: *Mignon;* VERDI: *Aida★, Ballo in maschera, Don Carlo★, Falstaff, Otello, Rigoletto, Simon Boccanegra, Traviata, Trovatore;* WAGNER: *Fliegende Holländer, Lohengrin‡, Meistersinger‡, Parsifal, Rheingold★, Walküre★, Siegfried★, Götterdämmerung★, Tannhäuser‡, Tristan und Isolde;* WEBER: *Freischütz‡;* WOLF-FERRARI: *Segreto di Susanna.* Also ALFANO: *Cyrano de Bergerac;* DA CAPUA: *Cinesi;* EGK: *Revisor;* GERSTER: *Hexe von Passau;* HONEGGER: *Jeanne d'Arc;* KIENZL: *Evangelimann;* LUALDI: *Granceola;* LORTZING: *Hans Sachs;* MOZART: *Bastien und Bastienne;* OBOUSSIER: *Amphytrion;* TRANTOW: *Antje;* WAGNER: *Feen;* WOLF-FERRARI: *Sly.* Recorded for EMI, Electrola, Decca. Conducted major orch in Europe, USA/Canada, Cent/S America. Previous positions as Mus Dir with major orch: Staatskapelle, Dresden 1949-53; Art Dir Royal Phil Orch, London 1961-75; Chief Cond Tonhalle Orch, Zurich 1965-71. Teaches in Montreux. **Res:** Munich, FR Ger. **Mgmt:** KRG/FRG; IWL/UK; OOC/FRA; ADZ/AUS.

KEMTER, JOHANNES RICHARD. Tenore buffo. German. Resident mem: Staatstheater, Dresden. Born 20 Sep 1918, Chemnitz. Wife Emilie. Two children. Studied: Musikakad, Profs Fussperg, Duhau and Witt, Vienna. **Debut:** Junker Spärlich (*Lustigen Weiber*) Staatsoper, Dresden 1945. Previous occupations: orchestra musician. Awards: Kammersänger.

Sang with major companies in FR GER: Wiesbaden; GER DR: Berlin Komische Oper & Staatsoper, Dresden; USSR: Leningrad Kirov. **Roles with these companies incl** HUMPERDINCK: Hexe★ (*Hänsel und Gretel*); MOZART: Pedrillo (*Entführung aus dem Serail*); ORFF: Tiresias (*Antigonae*), Solo★ (*Carmina burana*), Erzähler (*Mond*); SMETANA: Wenzel★ (*Bartered Bride*); WAGNER: Mime★ (*Rheingold*). **World premieres:** KUNAD: Maître Pathelin, Staatsoper Dresden 1969; ZIMMERMANN: Nieswandt (*Levins Mühle*) Staatsoper Dresden 1973. Recorded for: Eterna, EMI. Video/Film: Nieswandt (*Levins Mühle*). Gives recitals. Appears with symphony orchestra. Teaches voice. Coaches repertoire. On faculty of Konsv-Hochschule für Musik, Dresden. **Res:** Roquettestr 47, Dresden, Ger DR. **Mgmt:** KDR/GDR.

KERNS, ROBERT DOUGLAS. Lyric & dramatic baritone. American. Born Detroit, MI, USA. Single. Studied: Univ of Michigan, Ann Arbor; M del Monaco, coaching. **Debut:** Sharpless (*Butterfly*) Toledo, O, USA 1955.

Sang with major companies in AUS: Salzburg Fest, Vienna Staatsoper & Volksoper; FRA: Paris; FR GER: Berlin Deutsche Oper; UK: London Royal Opera; USA: San Francisco Opera. **Roles with these companies incl** BERLIOZ: Choroebus★ (*Troyens*); BRITTEN: Billy Budd; DONIZETTI: Belcore★ (*Elisir*), Enrico★ (*Lucia*); MOZART: Guglielmo★ (*Così fan tutte*), Don Giovanni★, Conte Almaviva★ (*Nozze di Figaro*); PUCCINI: Marcello★ (*Bohème*), Sharpless★ (*Butterfly*), Lescaut★ (*Manon Lescaut*); STRAUSS, R: Graf★ (*Capriccio*); TCHAIKOVSKY: Eugene Onegin★; VERDI: Rodrigo★ (*Don Carlo*), Ford★ (*Falstaff*), Iago★ (*Otello*), Conte di Luna★ (*Trovatore*); WAGNER: Amfortas★ (*Parsifal*). Recorded for: DG, Decca. Video/Film: Sharpless (*Butterfly*). Gives recitals. Appears with symphony orchestra. **Res:** Italy. **Mgmt:** JUC/SWI.

KERTÉSZ-GABRY, EDITH. née Gáncs. Lyric soprano. German. Resident mem: Städtische Bühnen, Cologne. Born 18 Jul 1927, Budapest. Widowed. Husband István Kertész, occupation conductor (deceased). Three children. Studied: Franz Liszt Akad, Budapest; Fr Molnár, C Pál. **Debut:** Marzelline (*Fidelio*) Budapest State Opera 1953.

Sang with major companies in AUS: Graz, Salzburg Fest; FR GER: Berlin Deutsche Oper, Bielefeld, Bonn, Cologne, Dortmund, Düsseldorf-Duisburg, Frankfurt, Hamburg, Hannover, Kassel, Kiel, Munich Staatsoper, Saarbrücken, Stuttgart; HUN: Budapest. **Roles with these companies incl** AUBER: Zerlina★ (*Fra Diavolo*); BEETHOVEN: Marzelline★ (*Fidelio*); BIZET: Micaëla★ (*Carmen*); DONIZETTI: Norina (*Don Pasquale*); GLUCK: Euridice; HANDEL: Ginevra (*Ariodante*); HENZE: Luise (*Junge Lord*); HINDEMITH: Tochter des Cardillac★ (*Cardillac*), Ursula★ (*Mathis der Maler*); JANACEK: Vixen (*Cunning Little Vixen*); LEONCAVALLO: Nedda (*Pagliacci*); LORTZING: Baronin Freimann★ (*Wildschütz*); MOZART: Servilia★ (*Clemenza di Tito*), Fiordiligi (*Così fan tutte*), Zerlina (*Don Giovanni*), Konstanze (*Entführung aus dem Serail*), Sifare (*Mitridate re di Ponto*), Susanna (*Nozze di Figaro*), Pamina (*Zauberflöte*); NICOLAI: Frau Fluth★ (*Lustigen Weiber*); OFFENBACH: Antonia★ (*Contes d'Hoffmann*); ORFF: Solo (*Carmina burana*), Kluge; PUCCINI: Mimi & Musetta (*Bohème*), Lauretta (*Gianni Schicchi*), Cio-Cio-San (*Butterfly*), Liù (*Turandot*); SMETANA: Marie★ (*Bartered Bride*); STRAUSS, R: Sophie★ (*Rosenkavalier*); VERDI: Nannetta (*Falstaff*), Desdemona (*Otello*), Violetta (*Traviata*). **World premieres:** ZIMMERMANN: Marie (*Soldaten*) Cologne Opera 1965. Gives recitals. Appears with symphony orchestra. Teaches voice. On faculty of Musikhochschule Cologne. **Res:** Franz Seiwert Str 15, 5 Cologne, FR Ger. **Mgmt:** KHA/FRG.

KERTZ, PETER. German. Chefdramaturg, Staatstheater am Gärtnerplatz, Gärtnerplatz 3, D-8 Munich 5, 1967- . In charge of art policy & dram matters. Is also st dir/prod, bass. Born 4 Jun 1934, Nürnberg. Single. Studied: Städtisches Konsv, Nürnberg; Städtische Hochschule fur Musik, Munich; Friedrich Alexander Univ, Erlangen, FR Ger. Plays the piano & flute. Previous positions, primarily musical: Opernhaus, Nürnberg 1959-62; Folkwanghochschule für Musik, Essen 1962-63; Hessisches Staatstheater, Wiesbaden 1963-67. **Res:** Kirchweg 6c, Munich, FR Ger.

KHANZADIAN, VAHAN. Lirico spinto tenor. American. Born 23 Jan 1942, Syracuse, NY, USA. Wife Lynda, occupation model. Studied: Curtis Inst of Music, Martial Singher, Philadelphia. **Debut:** Parpignol (*Bohème*) Chautauqua Opera Co, NY 1960. Awards: Rockefeller Fndt Grant; Sullivan Grant.

Sang with major companies in CAN: Montreal/Quebec, Vancouver; USA: Baltimore, Hartford, Hawaii, Houston, New Orleans, New York City Opera, Portland, St Paul, San Antonio, San Francisco Opera & Spring Opera. **Roles with these companies incl** AUBER: Fra Diavolo; DONIZETTI: Edgardo★ (*Lucia*); FALLA: Paco (*Vida breve*); GIORDANO: Andrea Chénier★; MASCAGNI: Turiddu (*Cavalleria rusticana*); PUCCINI: Rodolfo★ (*Bohème*), Rinuccio★ (*Gianni Schicchi*), Pinkerton (*Butterfly*), Des Grieux (*Manon Lescaut*), Ruggero (*Rondine*); STRAUSS, J: Alfred★ (*Fledermaus*); VERDI: Duca di Mantova★ (*Rigoletto*), Alfredo (*Traviata*). Video—NET TV: Gherman (*Pique Dame*). Gives recitals. Appears with symphony orchestra. Coaches repertoire. **Res:** New York, NY, USA. **Mgmt:** CAM/USA.

KILLEBREW, GWENDOLYN. Dramatic mezzosoprano. American. Born Philadelphia, PA, USA. Studied: Temple Univ, Else Fink, Philadelphia; James A Bostwick, Philadelphia; Juilliard School, Hans J Heinz, Christopher West, New York. **Debut:** Waltraute (*Walküre*) Metropolitan Opera, New York 1967. Previous occupations: music teacher; social worker, music therapist. Awards: Outstanding Alumna, Temple Univ, Philadelphia.

Sang with major companies in AUS: Salzburg Fest; FRA: Bordeaux, Nancy, Nice; FR GER: Bremen, Cologne, Munich Gärtnerplatz; SWI: Geneva; USA: Hartford, New York City Opera, St Paul, San Francisco Opera, Santa Fe, Washington DC; YUG: Zagreb. **Roles with these companies incl** BIZET: Carmen★; BRITTEN: Lucretia★ (*Rape of Lucretia*); DEBUSSY: Geneviève★ (*Pelléas et Mélisande*); DONIZETTI: Léonore★ (*Favorite*); GINASTERA: Lucrecia★ (*Beatrix Cenci*); HANDEL: Cornelia★ (*Giulio Cesare*); MUSSORGSKY: Marina★ (*Boris Godunov*); STRAUSS, R: Klytämnestra★ (*Elektra*); STRAVINSKY: Jocasta (*Oedipus Rex*), Baba the Turk★ (*Rake's Progress*); VERDI: Amneris★ (*Aida*), Ulrica★ (*Ballo in maschera*), Azucena★ (*Trovatore*); WAGNER: Erda★ (*Rheingold*), Fricka (*Rheingold★, Walküre★*). Also MONTEVERDI: Ottavia★ (*Incoronazione di Poppea*). **World premieres:** ORFF: Fourth singer (*De temporum fine comedia*) Salzburg Fest 1973; PASATIERI: Maid (*Divina*) Juilliard School, New York 1966. Recorded for: Cambridge. Gives recitals. Appears with symphony orchestra. **Mgmt:** CAM/USA.

KINDERMAN, WIESLAW. Polish. Tech Dir, Teatr Wielki/Grand Theater, Plac Dabrowskiego, Lódz. In charge of technical matters. Born 8 Jun 1934, Lódz. Married. One child. Studied: engineering, Polytechnic Lódz. Previous occupation: chief engineer. Background primarily theatrical. Started with present company in 1966 as chief engineer; in present position since 1973. World premieres at theaters during his employment: TWARDOWSKI: *Tragedy of St John and Herod* 1969, *Lord Jim* 1975; KURPINSKI: *King Henry VI at Hunting* 1972; all at Lódz. Awards: Medal of Honor, City of Lódz; Medal of 30th Anniv Polish Rep. Res: Obornicka 8/16, Lódz, Poland.

KING, JAMES AMBROS. Heldentenor. American. Resident mem: Bayerische Staatsoper, Munich; Staatsoper, Vienna. Born 22 May 1925, Dodge City, KS. Wife Marie-Luise Nagel, occupation actress. Five children. Studied: Univ of Louisiana, Prof D Draper, Baton Rouge; Univ of Kansas City, MO; Martial Singher, Ralph Errolle, Max Lorenz, Oren Brown, William Hughes, New York. Debut: Don José (*Carmen*) San Francisco Opera 1961. Previous occupations: prof of music; vocal & choral cond, Univ of KY, 9 yrs. Awards: ODK; Kammersänger, German Gvnmt; Grammy Awd; Grand Prix du Disque, twice; mem Phi Mu Alpha Sinfonia. Sang with major companies in ARG: Buenos Aires; AUS: Graz, Salzburg Fest, Vienna Staatsoper; BEL: Brussels; FRA: Lyon, Paris, Strasbourg; FR GER: Bayreuth Fest, Berlin Deutsche Oper, Frankfurt, Hamburg, Hannover, Mannheim, Munich Staatsoper, Wiesbaden; ITA: Florence Maggio, Milan La Scala; SWI: Zurich; UK: London Royal; USA: Cincinnati Summer Opera, New York Metropolitan Opera, Philadelphia Lyric, San Francisco Opera. Roles with these cos incl BEETHOVEN: Florestan⋆ (*Fidelio*); BIZET: Don José⋆ (*Carmen*); DEBUSSY: Azaël (*Enfant prodigue*); GLUCK: Achille (*Iphigénie en Aulide*); LEONCAVALLO: Canio⋆ (*Pagliacci*); MASCAGNI: Turiddu (*Cavalleria rusticana*); ORFF: Solo (*Carmina burana*); PUCCINI: Rodolfo (*Bohème*), Pinkerton (*Butterfly*), Des Grieux⋆ (*Manon Lescaut*), Cavaradossi⋆ (*Tosca*), Calaf⋆ (*Turandot*); SAINT-SAENS: Samson; STRAUSS, R: Bacchus⋆ (*Ariadne auf Naxos*), Apollo (*Daphne*), Aegisth⋆ (*Elektra*), Kaiser⋆ (*Frau ohne Schatten*), Ein Sänger⋆ (*Rosenkavalier*); VERDI: Rádames⋆ (*Aida*), Riccardo (*Ballo in maschera*), Don Carlo, Macduff (*Macbeth*), Otello⋆, Manrico⋆ (*Trovatore*); WAGNER: Erik⋆ (*Fliegende Holländer*), Lohengrin⋆, Walther⋆ (*Meistersinger*), Parsifal⋆, Siegmund⋆ (*Walküre*); WEBER: Max⋆ (*Freischütz*). Recorded for: Eurodisc, RCA, DG, Decca, Electrola. Video/Film: Don Carlo; Apollo (*Daphne*); Florestan (*Fidelio*). Gives recitals. Appears with symphony orchestra. Teaches voice. Coaches repertoire. Res: near Munich, FR Ger. Mgmt: CAM/USA; RAB/AUS.

KING, LIZ. Scenic designer for opera, theater. Is also a painter. British. Born 21 Apr 1951, West Ham, UK. Single. Studied: Southend School of Art. Prof training: Palace Theatre, Westcliff. Operatic debut: *Barbiere di Siviglia* Welsh Ntl Opera, Cardiff 1974. Theater debut: Palace Theatre, Westcliff 1971. Previous occupation: laboratory asst. Designed for major companies in UK: Welsh National. Operas designed for these companies incl MOZART: *Così fan tutte⋆;* ROSSINI: *Barbiere di Siviglia⋆*. Res: 16 Cowbridge Rd, Brynsadler/Pontyclun, Wales, UK.

KINGSLEY, MARGARET; née Polkinghorne. Dramatic soprano. British. Born 20 Feb 1939, Cornwall. Husband William Newcombe, occupation civil eng. Studied: Royal Coll of Music, London. Debut: Erste Dame (*Zauberflöte*) Glyndebourne 1966. Awards: Clara Butt Awd, Royal Coll of Music. Sang with major companies in AUS: Vienna Staatsoper; BEL: Brussels; CZE: Prague National; FRA: Lyon, Paris; FR GER: Hamburg, Hannover, Karlsruhe, Munich Staatsoper, Stuttgart, Wiesbaden; ITA: Naples; SWE: Stockholm; UK: Edinburgh Fest, Glasgow Scottish, Glyndebourne Fest, London Royal & English National; USA: Miami, Washington DC. Roles with these companies incl BEETHOVEN: Leonore⋆ (*Fidelio*); BERLIOZ: Cassandre⋆ (*Troyens*); GLUCK: Euridice; MENOTTI: Mother (*Amahl*); MOZART: Fiordiligi (*Così fan tutte*), Donna Elvira (*Don Giovanni*), Elettra (*Idomeneo*), Contessa (*Nozze di Figaro*); PUCCINI: Musetta (*Bohème*), Giorgetta (*Tabarro*); PURCELL: Dido; STRAUSS, R: Ariadne⋆ (*Ariadne auf Naxos*); TCHAIKOVSKY: Lisa (*Pique Dame*); VERDI: Amelia⋆ (*Ballo in maschera*), Lady Macbeth⋆, Violetta (*Traviata*); WAGNER: Brünnhilde (*Walküre⋆, Siegfried⋆, Götterdämmerung⋆*), Gutrune⋆ (*Götterdämmerung*); WEBER: Rezia (*Oberon*). Appears with symphony orchestra. Res: East Horsley, Surrey, UK. Mgmt: SLA/UK.

KIRCHNER, KLAUS. Lyric baritone. German. Resident mem: Badisches Staatstheater, Karlsruhe. Born 7 Nov 1927, Essen, Germany. Wife Dr Rita, occupation teacher. One child. Studied: Prof Clemens Glettenberg, Cologne, FR Ger; Dr Müller, Milan. Debut: Herr Fluth (*Lustigen Weiber*) Landestheater Detmold 1954. Previous occupations: businessman. Awards: Kammersänger, Ministry of Culture, Baden-Württemberg, FR Ger. Sang with major companies in AUS: Vienna Staatsoper & Volksoper; FRA: Nancy, Strasbourg; FR GER: Berlin Deutsche Oper, Bonn, Cologne, Darmstadt, Dortmund, Düsseldorf-Duisburg, Essen, Frankfurt, Hamburg, Hannover, Karlsruhe, Kassel, Mannheim, Munich Staatsoper, Nürnberg, Stuttgart, Wiesbaden, Wuppertal; HOL: Amsterdam; ITA: Turin, POR: Lisbon; SWI: Geneva, Zurich. Roles with these companies incl BERG: Dr Schön⋆ (*Lulu*); BIZET: Escamillo⋆ (*Carmen*); GLUCK: Oreste (*Iphigénie en Tauride*); HANDEL: Giulio Cesare, Arsamene⋆ (*Xerxes*); HENZE: Landarzt⋆; HINDEMITH: Mathis⋆; LEONCAVALLO: Tonio⋆ (*Pagliacci*); LORTZING: Graf v Liebenau (*Waffenschmied*), Graf Eberbach⋆ (*Wildschütz*), Peter I⋆ (*Zar und Zimmermann*); MOZART: Guglielmo & Don Alfonso⋆ (*Così fan tutte*), Don Giovanni⋆, Conte Almaviva⋆ & Figaro (*Nozze di Figaro*), Papageno (*Zauberflöte*); OFFENBACH: Coppélius⋆ etc (*Contes d'Hoffmann*); ORFF: Solo⋆ (*Carmina burana*), König (*Kluge*); PUCCINI:

Marcello★ (*Bohème*), Gianni Schicchi★, Sharpless★ (*Butterfly*); ROSSINI: Figaro (*Barbiere di Siviglia*), Dandini (*Cenerentola*); SMETANA: Tomas (*The Kiss*); STRAUSS, R: Mandryka★ (*Arabella*), Robert Storch (*Intermezzo*), Jochanaan★ (*Salome*); TCHAIKOVSKY: Eugene Onegin★; THOMAS: Lothario★ (*Mignon*); VERDI: Renato★ (*Ballo in maschera*), Rodrigo (*Don Carlo*), Ford (*Falstaff*), Don Carlo (*Forza del destino*), Rigoletto★, Germont★ (*Traviata*), Conte di Luna★ (*Trovatore*); WAGNER: Amfortas★ (*Parsifal*), Wolfram★ (*Tannhäuser*); WEINBERGER: Schwanda; WOLF-FERRARI: Pantalone (*Donne curiose*). Also EGK: Kaspar (*Zaubergeige*); HENZE: Prinz von Homburg; STRAUSS, R: Faninal (*Rosenkavalier*), Barbier (*Schweigsame Frau*); GLUCK: Orpheus. **World premieres:** FUESSEL: Meschullach (*Dybbuk*) Badisches Staatstheater, Karlsruhe 1970. Gives recitals. Appears with symphony orchestra. Teaches voice. On faculty of Staatliche Hochschule für Musik, Karlsruhe. **Res:** Albert-Schweitzer Str 41, Karlsruhe, FR Ger. Mgmt: SMD/FRG.

KIRSCHSTEIN, LEONORE. Lyric soprano. German. Resident mem: Bayerische Staatsoper, Munich. Born 29 Mar 1936, Stettin, Germany. Husband Ernst Grathwol, occupation opera singer. One child. Studied: Prof Franziska Martienssen-Lohmann, Robt Schumann Konsv, Düsseldorf; Kmsg Irma Bęilke, Berlin. **Debut:** Freia (*Rheingold*) Städt Oper Berlin 1960. Awards: Bayerische Kammersängerin, Bavarian Senate 1974.

Sang with major companies in AUS: Salzburg Fest, Vienna Staatsoper; BEL: Brussels; CZE: Prague National; FRA: Strasbourg; FR GER: Berlin Deutsche Oper, Cologne, Dortmund, Düsseldorf-Duisburg, Frankfurt, Hamburg, Hannover, Karlsruhe, Kiel, Mannheim, Munich Staatsoper, Stuttgart; GER DR: Berlin Staatsoper, Dresden; SWI: Zurich; UK: Edinburgh Fest, Glasgow Scottish; USA: Pittsburgh. **Roles with these companies incl** BIZET: Micaëla★ (*Carmen*); EGK: Jeanne (*Verlobung in San Domingo*); GLUCK: Euridice; HANDEL: Galatea; HINDEMITH: Tochter des Cardillac‡; KORNGOLD: Marietta (*Tote Stadt*); LEONCAVALLO: Nedda (*Pagliacci*); MARSCHNER: Anna‡ (*Hans Heiling*); MOZART: Fiordiligi★ (*Così fan tutte*), Donna Elvira★ (*Don Giovanni*), Contessa★ (*Nozze di Figaro*), Pamina★ & Erste Dame★‡ (*Zauberflöte*); NICOLAI: Frau Fluth (*Lustigen Weiber*); OFFENBACH: Antonia★ (*Contes d'Hoffmann*); PUCCINI: Mimi★ (*Bohème*), Cio-Cio-San★ (*Butterfly*); SMETANA: Marie★ (*Bartered Bride*); STRAUSS, J: Rosalinde★ (*Fledermaus*); STRAUSS, R: Arabella★, Kaiserin★ (*Frau ohne Schatten*); TCHAIKOVSKY: Tatiana★ (*Eugene Onegin*); VERDI: Elisabetta★ (*Don Carlo*), Desdemona★ (*Otello*); WAGNER: Elsa★ (*Lohengrin*), Eva★ (*Meistersinger*), Sieglinde★ (*Walküre*), Gutrune★ (*Götterdämmerung*), Elisabeth★ (*Tannhäuser*); WEBER: Euryanthe★, Agathe★ (*Freischütz*); WEINBERGER: Dorota (*Schwanda*). **World premieres:** YUN: Irdische und himmlische Mutter (*Sim Tjong*) Staatsoper, Munich 1972. Recorded for: DG, EMI, Electrola. Video/Film—ZDF: Agathe (*Freischütz*); NDR-ARD: Erste Dame (*Zauberflöte*). Gives recitals. Appears with symphony or-

chestra. **Res:** Denningerstr 212, 8 Munich, FR Ger. Mgmt: SLZ/FRG; LSM/UK.

KIRSTEN, DOROTHY. Lyric soprano. American. Resident mem: Metropolitan Opera, New York; San Francisco Opera. Born 6 Jul 1917, New Jersey, USA. Husband John Douglas French, occupation Dir Brain Research Inst, UCLA, CA. Studied: Ludwig Fabri, Jose Ruben, Ruth Moltke, Antonietta Stabile. **Debut:** Mimi (*Bohème*) Metropolitan Op 1945. Awards: Handel Medal, Mayor John Lindsay, City of New York; Hon DFA Santa Clara Univ, CA; Hon DM Ithaca Coll; etc.

Sang with major companies in CAN: Montreal/Quebec, Vancouver; MEX: Mexico City; SWE: Stockholm Royal; USSR: Leningrad Kirov, Moscow Bolshoi, Tbilisi; USA: Chicago, Cincinnati, Dallas, Hartford, Hawaii, Miami, Newark, New Orleans, New York Met, Omaha, Philadelphia Grand & Lyric, Pittsburgh, San Antonio, San Francisco Opera, Seattle. **Roles with these companies incl** BIZET: Micaëla (*Carmen*); CHARPENTIER: Louise; GOUNOD: Marguerite (*Faust*), Juliette; LEONCAVALLO: Nedda (*Pagliacci*); MASSENET: Manon; MONTEMEZZI: Fiora (*Amore dei tre re*); POULENC: Blanche (*Dialogues des Carmélites*); PUCCINI: Mimi★ & Musetta (*Bohème*), Minnie★ (*Fanciulla del West*), Cio-Cio-San★‡ (*Butterfly*), Manon Lescaut, Tosca★‡; STRAUSS, J: Rosalinde (*Fledermaus*); TCHAIKOVSKY: Lisa (*Pique Dame*); VERDI: Violetta (*Traviata*). Also WALTON: Cressida (*Troilus and Cressida*). Recorded for: Columbia. Gives recitals. Appears with symphony orchestra. Mgmt: CAM/USA.

KITCHINER, JOHN. Lyric baritone. British. Resident mem: English National Opera, London. Born 2 Dec 1933. Divorced. Studied: London Opera Centre, Joan Cross. **Debut:** Conte Almaviva (*Nozze di Figaro*) Glyndebourne Fest 1965. Previous occupations: carpenter; housing mgr.

Sang with major companies in UK: Cardiff Welsh, Glasgow Scottish, Glyndebourne Fest, London Eng Natl. **Roles with these companies incl** BIZET: Escamillo★ (*Carmen*); HENZE: Pentheus★ (*Bassariden*); LORTZING: Graf Eberbach (*Wildschütz*); MOZART: Guglielmo★ & Don Alfonso★ (*Così fan tutte*), Don Giovanni, Conte Almaviva (*Nozze di Figaro*); POULENC: Gendarme (*Mamelles de Tirésias*); PROKOFIEV: Prince Andrei Bolkonsky★ (*War and Peace*); PUCCINI: Marcello★ (*Bohème*), Sharpless★ (*Butterfly*); ROSSINI: Figaro★ & Dott Bartolo★ (*Barbiere di Siviglia*), Robert★ (*Comte Ory*); TCHAIKOVSKY: Yeletsky (*Pique Dame*); VERDI: Renato (*Ballo in maschera*), Don Carlo★ (*Forza del destino*), Macbeth★, Conte di Luna★ (*Trovatore*). Gives recitals. Appears with symphony orchestra. **Res:** 52 Highams Rd, Hockley/Essex, UK.

KITSOPOULOS, ANTONIA; née Mitsakou. Mezzo-soprano & contralto. American. Born Athens, Greece. Studied: Ntl Consv Athens; Mme Elvira de Hidalgo, Athens. **Debut:** Lola (*Cavalleria rusticana*) Athens National Opera 1954. Awards: M B Rockefeller Fund Grant; schlshps for all studies.

Sang with major companies in GRE: Athens National; USA: Dallas, Memphis, Newark, New York City Opera. **Roles with these companies incl** BELLINI: Adalgisa⋆ (*Norma*); HUMPERDINCK: Hänsel⋆; PONCHIELLI: La Cieca⋆ (*Gioconda*); PUCCINI: Suzuki⋆ (*Butterfly*), Frugola⋆ (*Tabarro*); STRAUSS, J: Prinz Orlovsky⋆ (*Fledermaus*); VERDI: Azucena (*Trovatore*); WEILL: Leocadia Begbick⋆ (*Aufstieg und Fall der Stadt Mahagonny*). Gives recitals. Appears with symphony orchestra. Teaches voice. Coaches repertoire. On faculty of Fairleigh Dickinson Univ, Madison, NJ, USA. **Res:** 11 Robin Hood Rd, Summit, NJ 07901, USA.

KLAIBER, JOACHIM. Stages/produces opera & theater. German. Generalintendant & Stage Dir, Bühnen der Landeshauptstadt Kiel, FR Ger 1963-76. Born 7 Mar 1908, Stuttgart. Wife Carla Henius, occupation singer. Three children. Studied: Univ Freiburg; Theaterwissenschaftliches Inst, Berlin, Richard Weichert, Carl Hagemann, Ernst Legal; also music, piano. **Operatic debut:** *Quattro rusteghi* Stadttheater Lübeck 1933. Previous adm positions in opera: Intendant Städt Bühnen Kaiserslautern 1946-47; Oberspielleiter Hannover 1950-51, Mannheim 1951-58; Intendant Bielefeld 1958-63.

Directed/produced opera for major companies in DEN: Copenhagen; FRA: Strasbourg; FR GER: Bielefeld, Darmstadt, Dortmund, Essen, Hamburg, Hannover, Karlsruhe, Kiel, Mannheim, Saarbrücken, Stuttgart; HOL: Amsterdam; ITA: Trieste; SWI: Zurich. **Operas staged with these companies incl** d'ALBERT: *Tiefland;* BEETHOVEN: *Fidelio;* BERG: *Wozzeck;* BIZET: *Carmen;* BRITTEN: *Albert Herring, Death in Venice⋆, Rape of Lucretia;* CORNELIUS: *Barbier von Bagdad⋆;* DEBUSSY: *Pelléas et Mélisande;* DONIZETTI: *Don Pasquale;* EGK: *Verlobung in San Domingo, Zaubergeige;* EINEM: *Besuch der alten Dame⋆, Prozess;* FLOTOW: *Martha;* FORTNER: *Elisabeth Tudor⋆;* GLUCK: *Iphigénie en Aulide, Iphigénie en Tauride, Orfeo ed Euridice;* GOUNOD: *Faust;* HANDEL: *Xerxes;* HENZE: *Boulevard Solitude, Elegy for Young Lovers, König Hirsch/Re Cervo;* HINDEMITH: *Mathis der Maler;* HUMPERDINCK: *Hänsel und Gretel;* IBERT: *Angélique;* JANACEK: *Jenufa, Katya Kabanova;* LEONCAVALLO: *Pagliacci;* LORTZING: *Wildschütz;* MARSCHNER: *Hans Heiling;* MARTIN: *Vin herbé;* MARTINU: *Griechische Passion;* MASCAGNI: *Cavalleria rusticana;* MENOTTI: *Consul;* MILHAUD: *Abandon d'Ariane, Délivrance de Thésée, Enlèvement d'Europe;* MOZART: *Così fan tutte⋆, Don Giovanni, Entführung aus dem Serail⋆, Nozze di Figaro⋆, Zauberflöte⋆;* NICOLAI: *Lustigen Weiber;* OFFENBACH: *Contes d'Hoffmann;* ORFF: *Kluge, Mond;* PUCCINI: *Bohème, Gianni Schicchi, Tosca, Turandot⋆;* ROSSINI: *Barbiere di Siviglia;* SMETANA: *Bartered Bride;* STRAUSS, J: *Fledermaus;* STRAUSS, R: *Arabella, Ariadne auf Naxos, Elektra, Rosenkavalier, Salome;* STRAVINSKY: *Oedipus Rex, Rake's Progress;* TCHAIKOVSKY: *Eugene Onegin, Pique Dame;* THOMAS: *Mignon;* VERDI: *Aida, Ballo in maschera, Don Carlo, Falstaff⋆, Forza del destino, Macbeth, Otello, Rigoletto, Traviata,*

Trovatorè; WAGNER: *Fliegende Holländer, Lohengrin, Meistersinger, Parsifal, Rheingold, Walküre, Siegfried, Götterdämmerung, Tannhäuser, Tristan und Isolde;* WEBER: *Freischütz;* WOLF: *Corregidor;* WOLF-FERRARI: *Quattro rusteghi.* **Operatic world premieres:** BRESGEN: *Dornröschen* 1943; KAUFFMANN: *Perlenhemd* 1944, both at Strasbourg, France; WIMBERGER: *Schaubudengeschichte* Mannheim 1954; REIMANN: *Traumspiel* 1965; LORENTZEN: *Die Musik kommt mir äusserst bekannt vor* 1974, both Städt Bühnen Kiel; MIHALOVICI: *Krapp's Last Tape* 1961; ZILLIG: *Verlobung in San Domingo* 1961, both Stadttheater Bielefeld. While Intendant at Bielefeld and Kiel a total of 20 operas were performed in world premieres, 1960-74. **Res:** Charles Ross Ring 47, Kiel, FR Ger.

KLARIC, MIRKA. Spinto. Croatian/Yugoslavian. Resident mem: Opera H N K, Zagreb. Born 10 Apr 1934, Donji Vidovec, Yugoslavia. Husband Dalibor Klanjscek, occupation chem eng. Studied: Prof Lea Vomacka, Prof Lav Vrbanic, Zagreb; Studio della Scala, Milan. **Debut:** Santuzza (*Cavalleria rusticana*) Opera H N K, Zagreb 1954. Awards: Vladimir Nazor Awd, Repub of Croatia; Milka Ternina Awd, Assn of Musical Artists of Croatia; Town of Zagreb Awd.

Sang with major companies in AUS: Graz, Vienna Volksoper; BUL: Sofia; CZE: Brno, Prague National; DEN: Copenhagen; FR GER: Frankfurt, Wiesbaden; GER DR: Berlin Staatsoper; HOL: Amsterdam; ITA: Bologna, Genoa, Naples, Trieste, Venice; NOR: Oslo; ROM: Bucharest; SWI: Basel, Geneva; YUG: Dubrovnik, Zagreb, Belgrade. **Roles with these companies incl** BORODIN: Jaroslavna (*Prince Igor*); GAY: Lucy⋆ (*Beggar's Opera*); GIORDANO: Maddalena (*Andrea Chénier*); GOTOVAC: Djula⋆ (*Ero der Schelm*); IBERT: Angélique; LEONCAVALLO: Nedda⋆ (*Pagliacci*); MASCAGNI: Santuzza (*Cavalleria rusticana*); MONTEVERDI: Poppea (*Incoronazione di Poppea*); MOZART: Donna Elvira (*Don Giovanni*); ORFF: Kluge; PROKOFIEV: Renata⋆ (*Flaming Angel*), Fata Morgana⋆ (*Love for Three Oranges*), Natasha (*War and Peace*); PUCCINI: Mimi⋆ (*Bohème*), Cio-Cio-San⋆ (*Butterfly*), Manon Lescaut, Tosca⋆; SHOSTAKOVICH: Katerina Ismailova; SMETANA: Marie⋆ (*Bartered Bride*); STRAUSS, J: Rosalinde (*Fledermaus*); STRAUSS, R: Salome; SZOKOLAY: Braut (*Blood Wedding*); TCHAIKOVSKY: Tatiana (*Eugene Onegin*), Lisa (*Pique Dame*); VERDI: Desdemona (*Otello*). Also KELEMEN: Secretary⋆ (*Kuga la peste*); ZAJC: Jelena⋆ (*Nikola subic zrinjski*). Video/Film: Lisa (*Pique Dame*); Salome. Gives recitals. Appears with symphony orchestra. **Res:** Sailijeva 18, 41000 Zagreb, Yugoslavia.

KLEE, BERNHARD. Conductor of opera and symphony. German. Gen Music Dir, Bühnen der Hansestadt Lübeck, FR Ger. Born 19 Apr 1936, Schleiz/Thüringen. Studied: Consv of Music, Cologne; incl piano. Operatic training as repetiteur at Cologne 1957; Stadttheater Bern 1958.

Conducted with major companies in FR GER: Berlin Deutsche Oper, Cologne, Hamburg, Hannover; UK: London Royal; et al. **Operas with these**

companies incl BEETHOVEN: *Fidelio;* JANA-CEK: *Excursions of Mr Broucek;* MOZART: *Così fan tutte, Don Giovanni, Entführung aus dem Serail, Nozze di Figaro, Zauberflöte;* WAGNER: *Fliegende Holländer, Tannhäuser;* et al. Recorded for DG.

KLEIBER, CARLOS. Conductor of opera and symphony. German. Resident Cond, Württembergische Staatsoper, Stuttgart. Born 3 Jul 1930, Berlin. Studied: privately in Buenos Aires. Operatic training as repetiteur at Oper am Gärtnerplatz, Munich 1953. **Operatic debut:** operetta, Potsdam 1954. Previous occupations: studied chemistry in Zurich.

Conducted with major companies in AUS: Vienna Staatsoper; CZE: Prague National; FRA: Paris; FR GER: Bayreuth Fest, Düsseldorf-Duisburg, Hamburg, Munich Staatsoper, Stuttgart, Wuppertal; SWE: Zurich; UK: London Royal; et al. **Operas with these companies incl** BERG: *Wozzeck;* STRAUSS, J: *Fledermaus;* STRAUSS, R: *Elektra, Rosenkavalier;* VERDI: *Otello, Traviata;* WAGNER: *Meistersinger, Tristan und Isolde;* WEBER: *Freischütz‡;* et al. Recorded for DG.

KLEIMERT, DORRIT. Lyric soprano. Swedish. Resident mem: Royal Opera, Stockholm. Born 23 May 1938, Stockholm. Husband Krister Ljungquist, occupation economist. One child. Studied: Musikhochschule, music teacher education & soloist diploma, Stockholm. **Debut:** Micaëla (*Carmen*) Royal Opera, Stockholm 1966. Awards: Kristina Nilsson stipd; Jussi Björling stipd for Oslo, Norway.

Sang with major companies in DEN: Copenhagen; SWE: Drottningholm Fest. **Roles with these companies incl** BIZET: Micaëla (*Carmen*); GLUCK: Euridice★; MOZART: Pamina★ (*Zauberflöte*); OFFENBACH: Antonia★ (*Contes d'Hoffmann*); PUCCINI: Liù★ (*Turandot*). **World premieres:** WERLE: Amanda (*Tintomara*) Royal Opera, Stockholm 1973. Gives recitals. Appears with symphony orchestra.

KLEIN, ALLEN CHARLES. Scenic and costume designer for opera, theater. Is a lighting designer; also a painter. American. Born 11 Aug 1940, New York. Single. Studied: Boston Univ, Horace Armistead, Raymond Sovey. **Operatic debut:** sets, *Don Giovanni* Houston Grand Op, TX 1964; cost, *Italiana in Algeri* San Francisco Opera 1964. Theater debut: Dallas Summer Musicals, TX 1966.

Designed for major companies in CAN: Vancouver; USA: Baltimore, Houston, New Orleans, New York Met, St Paul, San Diego, San Francisco Spring Opera, Santa Fe, Seattle, Washington DC. **Operas designed for these companies incl** CAVALLI: *Egisto★;* DEBUSSY: *Pelléas et Mélisande★;* DONIZETTI: *Elisir;* GOUNOD: *Roméo et Juliette;* HENZE: *Junge Lord;* LEONCAVALLO: *Pagliacci★;* MASCAGNI: *Cavalleria rusticana★;* MASSENET: *Manon★, Thaïs★;* MOZART: *Don Giovanni, Nozze di Figaro, Zauberflöte;* OFFENBACH: *Contes d'Hoffmann★, Grande Duchesse de Gérolstein★;* PUCCINI: *Tosca★;* RAVEL: *Enfant et les sortilèges★;* ROSSINI: *Italiana in Algeri;* STRAVINSKY: *Rake's Progress;* VERDI: *Falstaff★;* WAGNER: *Fliegende Holländer.* **Operatic world premieres:**

VILLA-LOBOS: *Yerma* Santa Fe Op, NM 1971; PASATIERI: *Seagull* Houston Grand Opera, TX 1974; FLOYD: *Of Mice and Men* Seattle Opera, WA 1970. Teaches at Santa Fe Opera Apprentice Prgr, NM. **Res:** 2109 Broadway, New York, USA. Mgmt: AIM/UK.

KLEIN, ALLEN EDWARD. Scenic and costume designer for opera, theater, television; specl in sets. American. Born 26 Apr 1938, New York. Wife Ellen. One child. Studied: Yale Drama School, New Haven, CT; Lester Polakov School, New York. Prof training: Nolan Scenic Shop, CBS Television, New York. **Operatic debut:** Turnau Opera Players, Woodstock, NY 1955. Theater debut: CBS TV, New York 1961.

Designed for major companies in USA: Lake George, St Paul. **Operas designed for these companies incl** BRITTEN: *Albert Herring, Midsummer Night;* DONIZETTI: *Don Pasquale;* GOUNOD: *Roméo et Juliette;* NICOLAI: *Lustigen Weiber;* OFFENBACH: *Contes d'Hoffmann★;* PUCCINI: *Gianni Schicchi;* RAVEL: *Heure espagnole;* ROSSINI: *Otello;* STRAUSS, J: *Fledermaus★;* STRAUSS, R: *Ariadne auf Naxos.* **Operatic world premieres:** AMRAM: *Twelfth Night* Lake George Op, Glens Falls, NY 1968. **Res:** 1034 Page St, San Francisco, CA, USA.

KLEIN, FRIEDER. Scenic designer for opera, theater. Is a lighting designer, stage director; also a painter. Austrian. Resident designer, Vereinigte Bühnen Graz. Born 20 May 1943, Vienna. Wife Christiana. Two children. Studied: Akad der bildenden Künste, Vienna; asst to Schneider-Siemssen, Vienna. Prof training: Staatsoper Vienna 1967-70. **Operatic debut:** *Tosca* Landestheater Linz, Austria 1970. Theater debut: same as above.

Designed for major companies in AUS: Graz, Salzburg; FR GER: Nürnberg. **Operas designed for these companies incl** NICOLAI: *Lustigen Weiber★;* PUCCINI: *Tosca;* ROSSINI: *Gazza ladra★;* VERDI: *Rigoletto★.* Exhibitions of stage designs, Prague Quadrennial 1971. **Res:** Karl Maria von Weber Gasse 10, Graz, Austria.

KLIMEK, ZDZISLAW. Lyric baritone. Polish. Resident mem: Teatr Wielki, Warsaw. Born 2 Sep 1930, Sosnowiec, Poland. Wife Anna Kwaszczynska, occupation physicist. Two children. Studied: Grzegorz Orlow, Lodz; Margherita Carosio, Venice. **Debut:** Germont (*Traviata*) Lodz Opera Co 1953. Previous occupations: engineer. Awards: Cross of Merit, Polish Gvnmt; Second Prize at World Youth Fest, Warsaw 1955; Second Prize Ntl Singerfest 1954.

Sang with major companies in BUL: Sofia; CZE: Prague National & Smetana; FR GER: Berlin Deutsche Oper, Essen, Wiesbaden; GER DR: Berlin Staatsoper, Dresden, Leipzig; HUN: Budapest; POL: Lodz, Warsaw; ROM: Bucharest; SWI: Geneva; USSR: Moscow Bolshoi, Tbilisi. **Roles with these companies incl** BERG: Wozzeck; BIZET: Escamillo★ (*Carmen*); BORODIN: Prince Igor; DALLAPICCOLA: Prigioniero; DEBUSSY: Siméon★ (*Enfant prodigue*); DONIZETTI: Dott Malatesta (*Don Pasquale*), Enrico (*Lucia*); GIORDANO: Carlo Gérard (*Andrea Chénier*); GLINKA: Ruslan; GLUCK: Oreste

(*Iphigénie en Tauride*); HANDEL: Giulio Cesare; MENOTTI: John Sorel★ (*Consul*); MONIUSZKO: Janusz★ (*Halka*); MOZART: Don Giovanni; PUCCINI: Marcello★ (*Bohème*), Sharpless★ (*Butterfly*), Scarpia (*Tosca*); STRAUSS, R: Orest★ (*Elektra*); STRAVINSKY: Creon★ (*Oedipus Rex*); TCHAIKOVSKY: Eugene Onegin★, Yeletsky (*Pique Dame*); VERDI: Rodrigo★ (*Don Carlo*), Rigoletto, Germont (*Traviata*), Conte di Luna★ (*Trovatore*); WAGNER: Wolfram (*Tannhäuser*). **World premieres:** CZYZ: Robert (*Biakow Losa*) Teatr Wielki, Warsaw 1962. Recorded for: Polskie Nagrania. Gives recitals. Appears with symphony orchestra. Teaches voice. Coaches repertoire. **Res:** ul Moliera 8 m 53, Warsaw, Poland.

KLIPPSTATTER, KURT. Conductor of opera and symphony. Austrian. Resident Cond, Memphis Opera Theatre, TN. Also Music Dir, Arkansas Orch Socy, Little Rock, AR. Born 17 Dec 1934, Graz, Austria. Wife Mignon Dunn, occupation opera singer, mezzo-soprano. Studied: Consv Graz, v Matacic, v Zallinger; Sommerakademie Salzburg; incl violin, viola, piano and voice. Plays the piano. **Operatic debut:** ballet, Opernhaus Graz 1956. Symphonic debut: Graz 1957. Previous occupations: coach and operetta conductor.

Conducted with major companies in AUS: Graz; FRA: Strasbourg; FR GER: Dortmund, Krefeld, Saarbrücken; USA: Memphis. **Operas with these companies incl** BELLINI: *Norma;* BIZET: *Carmen★;* DONIZETTI: *Elisir, Lucia★;* FLOYD: *Susannah★;* JANACEK: *Jenufa;* LORTZING: *Wildschütz, Zar und Zimmermann;* MONIUSZKO: *Halka;* MOZART: *Così fan tutte★, Entführung aus dem Serail, Nozze di Figaro, Zauberflöte;* MUSSORGSKY: *Boris Godunov;* OFFENBACH: *Contes d'Hoffmann★;* PAISIELLO: *Barbiere di Siviglia;* PUCCINI: *Bohème, Gianni Schicchi, Butterfly, Tabarro, Tosca;* PURCELL: *Dido and Aeneas;* ROSSINI: *Barbiere di Siviglia;* STRAUSS, J: *Fledermaus;* STRAUSS, R: *Ariadne auf Naxos, Salome;* THOMAS: *Mignon;* VERDI: *Aida, Ballo in maschera, Forza del destino, Rigoletto, Traviata★, Trovatore;* WAGNER: *Fliegende Holländer.* Conducted major orch in Europe, USA/Canada. Teaches at Memphis State Univ. **Res:** 6605 Granada Dr, Little Rock, AR, USA. Mgmt: BAR/USA; HLB/FRA.

KLOBUCAR, BERISLAV. Conductor of opera and symphony. Yugoslavian. Mus Dir & Resident Cond Royal Opera, Stockholm. Born 28 Aug 1924, Zagreb. Wife Natalie. One child. Studied: Prof Lovro v Matacic, Zagreb; Mo Clemens Krauss, Salzburg; also piano. Operatic training as asst cond at Opera, Zagreb 1943-51. **Operatic debut:** Opera House, Zagreb 1943. Symphonic debut: Fiume Symph Orch, Yugoslavia 1946. Awards: title of Professor.

Conducted with major companies in ARG: Buenos Aires; AUS: Bregenz Fest, Graz, Vienna Staatsoper & Volksoper; BEL: Brussels; CAN: Montreal/Quebec; DEN: Copenhagen; FRA: Lyon, Marseille, Nice, Paris, Toulouse; FR GER: Bayreuth Fest, Berlin Deutsche Oper, Bonn, Hamburg, Munich Staatsoper; ITA: Genoa, Milan La Scala, Naples, Palermo, Turin; SPA: Barcelona; SWE: Stockholm; SWI: Geneva; UK: Edinburgh Fest; USSR: Moscow Bolshoi; USA: Chicago, New York Met; YUG: Zagreb. **Operas with these companies incl** BEETHOVEN: *Fidelio;* BERG: *Wozzeck★;* BERLIOZ: *Damnation de Faust;* BIZET: *Carmen★;* BOITO: *Mefistofele★;* BORODIN: *Prince Igor;* BRITTEN: *Rape of Lucretia;* BUSONI: *Doktor Faust;* CHERUBINI: *Medea★;* DEBUSSY: *Pelléas et Mélisande;* DONIZETTI: *Don Pasquale, Elisir, Lucia;* DVORAK: *Rusalka, Dimitrij;* EINEM: *Besuch der alten Dame★;* FLOTOW: *Martha;* GIORDANO: *Andrea Chénier;* GLINKA: *Life for the Tsar;* GLUCK: *Iphigénie in Tauride;* GOTOVAC: *Ero der Schelm;* GOUNOD: *Faust;* HANDEL: *Giulio Cesare;* HUMPERDINCK: *Hänsel und Gretel;* JANACEK: *Jenufa, Katya Kabanova, Makropoulos Affair;* LEONCAVALLO: *Pagliacci★;* MASCAGNI: *Cavalleria rusticana★;* MASSENET: *Manon★, Werther;* MENOTTI: *Saint of Bleecker Street;* MILHAUD: *Christophe Colomb;* MOZART: *Così fan tutte, Don Giovanni, Entführung aus dem Serail★, Nozze di Figaro, Zauberflöte;* MUSSORGSKY: *Boris Godunov, Khovanshchina;* OFFENBACH: *Contes d'Hoffmann;* ORFF: *Carmina burana, Mond;* PENDERECKI: *Teufel von Loudun★;* PFITZNER: *Palestrina;* POULENC: *Dialogues des Carmélites;* PROKOFIEV: *Fiery Angel;* PUCCINI: *Bohème★, Gianni Schicchi, Butterfly★, Manon Lescaut, Tosca★, Turandot★;* RIMSKY-KORSAKOV: *Invisible City of Kitezh;* ROSSINI: *Barbiere di Siviglia;* SMETANA: *Bartered Bride, Dalibor, Two Widows;* STRAUSS, J: *Fledermaus;* STRAUSS, R: *Arabella★, Ariadne auf Naxos★, Capriccio, Elektra★, Frau ohne Schatten★, Intermezzo, Liebe der Danae, Rosenkavalier★, Salome★;* TCHAIKOVSKY: *Eugene Onegin★, Pique Dame;* VERDI: *Aida★, Ballo in maschera★, Don Carlo★, Falstaff, Forza del destino★, Macbeth★, Nabucco, Otello★, Rigoletto★, Simon Boccanegra, Traviata★, Trovatore★;* WAGNER: *Fliegende Holländer★, Lohengrin★, Meistersinger★, Parsifal★, Rienzi, Rheingold★, Walküre★, Siegfried★, Götterdämmerung★, Tannhäuser★, Tristan und Isolde★;* WEBER: *Freischütz.* Conducted major orch in Europe. Previous positions as Mus Dir with major orch: Graz Phil, Austria 1962-72.

KMENTT, WALDEMAR. Lyric tenor. Austrian. Resident mem: Staatsoper, Vienna. Born 2 Feb 1929. Wife Rosemarie. Two children. **Debut:** Prince (*Love for Three Oranges*) Staatsoper, Vienna 1951. Awards: Austrian Kammersänger; Austrian Ehrenkreuz für Kunst und Wissenschaft.

Sang with major companies in ARG: Buenos Aires; AUS: Bregenz Fest, Graz, Salzburg Fest, Vienna Staatsoper & Volksoper; BEL: Brussels; FRA: Aix-en-Provence Fest; GRE: Athens Fest; FR GER: Bayreuth Fest, Berlin Deutsche Oper, Bielefeld, Dortmund, Düsseldorf-Duisburg, Frankfurt, Hamburg, Munich Staatsoper, Stuttgart; ITA: Milan La Scala; POR: Lisbon; SWE: Drottningholm Fest; UK: Edinburgh Fest. **Roles with these companies incl** AUBER: Lorenzo (*Fra Diavolo*); BEETHOVEN: Florestan★ (*Fidelio*); BERG: Alwa★ (*Lulu*); BIZET: Don José★ (*Carmen*); DONIZETTI: Ernesto (*Don Pasquale*); DVORAK: Prince (*Rusalka*); FLOTOW: Lionel (*Martha*); GLUCK: Pylade★ (*Iphigénie en Tau-*

ride); GOUNOD: Faust★;JANACEK: Laca★(Je-nufa); LORTZING: Baron Kronthal (Wildschütz); MOZART: Ferrando (Così fan tutte), Don Ottavio (Don Giovanni), Belmonte (Entführung aus dem Serail), Idamante & Idomeneo★ (Idomeneo), Tamino★ (Zauberflöte); MUSSORGSKY: Gritzko (Fair at Sorochinsk); NICOLAI: Fenton (Lustigen Weiber); OFFENBACH: Hoffmann★; ORFF: Haemon (Antigonae); PROKOFIEV: Prince (Love for Three Oranges); PUCCINI: Rodolfo★ (Bohème), Pinkerton (Butterfly), Cavaradossi★ (Tosca); PURCELL: Aeneas; ROSSINI: Almaviva (Barbiere di Siviglia), Don Ramiro (Cenerentola); SMETANA: Hans★ (Bartered Bride); STRAUSS, J: Eisenstein★ & Alfred★ (Fledermaus); STRAUSS, R: Bacchus★ (Ariadne auf Naxos), Flamand★ (Capriccio), Kaiser★ (Frau ohne Schatten), Midas (Liebe der Danae), Ein Sänger★ (Rosenkavalier); STRAVINSKY: Oedipus, Eumolpe (Perséphone), Tom Rakewell (Rake's Progress); TCHAIKOVSKY: Lenski★ (Eugene Onegin); WAGNER: Erik★ (Fliegende Holländer), Walther (Meistersinger), Walther v d Vogelweide (Tannhäuser); WEBER: Max★ (Freischütz); WEINBERGER: Babinsky (Schwanda). Recorded for: Philips, Decca. Video/Film: Orfeo (Orfeo ed Euridice); Alfred (Fledermaus). Gives recitals. Appears with symphony orchestra. Res: Prinz Eugenstr 28, Vienna 1040, Austria.

KNESS, RICHARD M; né Kniess. Dramatic tenor & Heldentenor. American. Resident mem: New York City Opera. Born 23 Jul 1937, Rockford, IL, USA. Wife Joann Grillo, occupation opera singer, mezzo-soprano. Three children. Studied: Prof Clemens Kaiser-Breme, Essen, FR Ger; Martial Singher, Philadelphia; Frederick Wilkerson, Washington, DC; Mme Marinka Gurewich, New York. Debut: Duca di Mantova (Rigoletto) St Louis Opera, MO, USA 1966. Previous occupations: owned two art galleries, Washington, DC. Awards: Grammy Awd for Best Classical Recording 1967.
Sang with major companies in FRA: Nancy; FR GER: Dortmund, Düsseldorf-Duisburg, Essen, Hamburg, Krefeld; ISR: Tel Aviv; MEX: Mexico City; USA: Boston, Cincinnati, Hartford, Hawaii, Houston, Kansas City, Memphis, Milwaukee Florentine, New York City Opera, San Antonio, San Diego, San Francisco Opera & Spring Opera. Roles with these companies incl BEETHOVEN: Florestan★ (Fidelio); BERLIOZ: Faust★ (Damnation de Faust); BIZET: Don José★ (Carmen); FLOYD: Sam Polk (Susannah); KORNGOLD: Paul★ (Tote Stadt); LEONCAVALLO: Canio★ (Pagliacci); MASCAGNI: Turiddu★ (Cavalleria rusticana); MUSSORGSKY: Vassily Golitsin★ (Khovanshchina); OFFENBACH: Hoffmann; PUCCINI: Rodolfo (Bohème), Pinkerton★ (Butterfly), Cavaradossi (Tosca), Calaf★ (Turandot); STRAUSS, R: Bacchus★ (Ariadne auf Naxos), Apollo★ (Daphne); STRAVINSKY: Oedipus Rex★; TCHAIKOVSKY: Gherman★ (Pique Dame); VERDI: Radames★ (Aida), Riccardo (Ballo in maschera), Don Alvaro★ (Forza del destino), Duca di Mantova (Rigoletto), Manrico★ (Trovatore); WAGNER: Erik★(Fliegende Holländer); WEILL: Jim Mahoney★ (Aufstieg und Fall der Stadt Mahagonny). Also MUSSORGSKY:

Dimitri★ (Boris Godunov); HANSON: 2 ten roles (Merry Mount); ORFF: (Catulli carmina). Gives recitals. Res: 1550 75 St, Brooklyn, NY, USA. Mgmt: HUR/USA; SLZ/FRG.

KNIE, ROBERTA JOY. Dramatic soprano. American. Born 13 Mar 1938, Cordell, OK, USA. Single. Studied: Univ of Oklahoma, Norman, OK; Elisabeth Parham, Dame Eva Turner, Judy Bounds-Coleman. Debut: Elisabeth (Tannhäuser) Städtische Bühnen, Hagen/Westfalen, FR Ger 1964. Awards: Sigma Alpha Iota, Hon Schlstics.
Sang with major companies in ARG: Buenos Aires; AUS: Bregenz Fest, Graz, Vienna Staatsoper; BEL: Brussels; CAN: Montreal/Quebec; FRA: Lyon, Strasbourg; FR GER: Bayreuth Fest, Berlin Deutsche Oper, Bonn, Cologne, Düsseldorf-Duisburg, Hamburg, Kassel, Mannheim, Munich Staatsoper, Nürnberg, Stuttgart; ITA: Bologna, Parma; POR: Lisbon; SPA: Barcelona; SWE: Stockholm; UK: Cardiff Welsh; USA: Dallas, New York Met. Roles with these companies incl BEETHOVEN: Leonore★ (Fidelio); HINDEMITH: Ursula★ (Mathis der Maler); JANACEK: Emilia Marty★ (Makropoulos Affair); MEYERBEER: Selika★ (Africaine); MOZART: Fiordiligi (Così fan tutte), Donna Anna (Don Giovanni), Elettra (Idomeneo), Contessa (Nozze di Figaro); PUCCINI: Minnie★ (Fanciulla del West), Manon Lescaut, Tosca★; STRAUSS, R: Chrysothemis★ (Elektra), Marschallin★ (Rosenkavalier), Salome★; TCHAIKOVSKY: Lisa (Pique Dame); VERDI: Elisabetta★ (Don Carlo), Leonora (Forza del destino), Desdemona★ (Otello), Leonora (Trovatore); WAGNER: Senta★ (Fliegende Holländer), Elsa★ (Lohengrin), Sieglinde★ (Walküre), Brünnhilde (Walküre★, Siegfried★), Elisabeth★ (Tannhäuser), Isolde★. Video−CBC TV: Isolde. Appears with symphony orchestra. Res: Sonnenvilla, A-8301 Lassnitzhöhe, Austria. Mgmt: SLZ/FRG; COL/USA.

KNIGHT, GILLIAN ROSEMARY. Lyric coloratura mezzo-soprano. British. Resident mem: Royal Opera, Covent Garden, London. Born Redditch, UK. Husband Trevor Morrison, occupation TV technician. One child. Studied: Royal Acad of Music, London; D'Oyly Carte Opera Co. Debut: Ragonde (Comte Ory) Sadler's Wells 1968. Awards: LRAM, Royal Acad of Music.
Sang with major companies in CAN: Montreal/Quebec, Ottawa, Toronto, Vancouver; FRA: Nice, Rouen; UK: Cardiff Welsh, Glasgow Scottish, London Royal & English National. Roles with these companies incl BIZET: Carmen★; BRITTEN: Hippolita★ (Midsummer Night); DEBUSSY: Geneviève (Pelléas et Mélisande); HANDEL: Amastris (Xerxes); LALO: Margared★ (Roi d'Ys); MASSENET: Dulcinée★ (Don Quichotte); MENOTTI: Secretary (Consul); PUCCINI: Suzuki (Butterfly); ROSSINI: Rosina (Barbiere di Siviglia), Isabella (Italiana in Algeri); SAINT-SAENS: Dalila; STRAVINSKY: Baba the Turk (Rake's Progress); TCHAIKOVSKY: Olga★ (Eugene Onegin); VERDI: Ulrica (Ballo in maschera), Preziosilla★ (Forza del destino); WAGNER: Magdalene (Meistersinger), Waltraute (Götterdämmerung). Also TIPPETT: Helen★ (King Priam); VERDI: Fenena (Nabucco), Meg Page (Falstaff); GILBERT: Woman (Scene Machine).

World premieres: MAXWELL-DAVIES: Rose (*Taverner*) Covent Garden 1972; BONDON: I 330 (*I 330*) Nantes 1975. Recorded for: Decca, Philips, CBS. Gives recitals. Appears with symphony orchestra. **Res:** London, UK. **Mgmt:** ASK/UK.

KNIPLOVÁ, NADEZDA. Dramatic soprano. Czechoslovakian. Resident mem: National Opera, Prague; Württembergische Staatsoper, Stuttgart.

Sang with major companies in CZE: Prague National; FR GER: Düsseldorf-Duisburg, Hamburg, Hannover; MEX: Mexico City; SWI: Zurich; et al. **Roles with these companies incl** BEETHOVEN: Leonore (*Fidelio*); JANACEK: Kostelnicka (*Jenufa*); WAGNER: Ortrud (*Lohengrin*), Brünnhilde (*Walküre, Siegfried, Götterdämmerung*); et al. Also FIBICH: Sarka. Recorded for: Westminster.

KNOBLICH, HANS GEORG. Basso-buffo. German. Resident mem: Staatstheater Kassel. Born 30 Sep 1933, Bruehl/Cologne, FR Ger. Single. Studied: Staatliche Hochschule für Musik, Prof Glettenberg, Cologne. **Debut:** Masetto (*Don Giovanni*) Cologne 1959.

Sang with major companies in BEL: Brussels; FR GER: Cologne, Düsseldorf-Duisburg, Kassel, Kiel, Saarbrücken, Wiesbaden; NOR: Oslo. **Roles with these companies incl** ADAM: Bijou (*Postillon de Lonjumeau*); BEETHOVEN: Rocco★ (*Fidelio*); BERG: Doktor (*Wozzeck*); CIMAROSA: Geronimo★ (*Matrimonio segreto*); DONIZETTI: Poet★ (*Convenienze*), Don Pasquale★; FLOTOW: Plunkett★ (*Martha*); GOUNOD: Méphistophélès (*Faust*); LORTZING: Stadinger (*Waffenschmied*), Baculus★ (*Wildschütz*), Van Bett★ (*Zar und Zimmermann*); MOZART: Leporello★ (*Don Giovanni*), Osmin★ (*Entführung aus dem Serail*), Figaro★ (*Nozze di Figaro*), Papageno★ (*Zauberflöte*); NICOLAI: Falstaff★ (*Lustigen Weiber*); PAISIELLO: Bartolo★ (*Barbiere di Siviglia*); PERGOLESI: Uberto (*Serva padrona*); PROKOFIEV: King of Clubs (*Love for Three Oranges*); PUCCINI: Gianni Schicchi; ROSSINI: Dott Bartolo★ (*Barbiere di Siviglia*), Mustafà★ (*Italiana in Algeri*), Macrobio (*Pietra del paragone*); SMETANA: Kezal★ (*Bartered Bride*); STRAUSS, R: Baron Ochs★ (*Rosenkavalier*); VERDI: Ramfis★ (*Aida*), Fra Melitone★ (*Forza del destino*); WAGNER: Alberich (*Rheingold★, Götterdämmerung★*); WEBER: Kaspar (*Freischütz*); ZIMMERMANN: Wesener (*Soldaten*). Gives recitals. Appears with symphony orchestra. **Res:** Alte Breite 22, D-35 Kassel, FR Ger.

KOCH, WILFRIED. Conductor of opera and symphony. German. Resident Cond & chorus master, Oper am Gärtnerplatz, Munich. Also Resident Cond, Munich Phil; Munich Chamber Orch. Born 28 May 1937, Bremen. Wife Ulrike, occupation bookkeeper. Studied: Prof Hans Swarowsky, Vienna; incl piano & voice. Plays the piano, cembalo. Operatic training as repetiteur, asst cond & chorus master at Landestheater Linz, Austria 1962-69. **Operatic debut:** Landestheater Linz, Austria. Symphonic debut: Bruckner Orch, Linz 1967.

Conducted with major companies in FR GER: Darmstadt, Karlsruhe, Munich Gärtnerplatz, Saarbrücken. **Operas with these companies incl** AUBER: *Fra Diavolo★*; BIZET: *Carmen★*; DONIZETTI: *Don Pasquale★*; FLOTOW: *Martha★*; GIORDANO: *Andrea Chénier★*; HUMPERDINCK: *Hänsel und Gretel★*; LORTZING: *Zar und Zimmermann★*; MOZART: *Così fan tutte, Don Giovanni, Zauberflöte★*; PERGOLESI: *Frate 'nnamorato;* PUCCINI: *Bohème, Butterfly;* RAMEAU: *Platée★;* ROSSINI: *Barbiere di Siviglia;* SMETANA: *Bartered Bride★;* VERDI: *Falstaff, Forza del destino, Traviata, Trovatore;* WAGNER: *Fliegende Holländer;* WEILL: *Dreigroschenoper.* Also RONNEFELD: *Ameise;* GOUNOD: *Médecin malgré lui.* Conducted major orch in Europe. Teaches at Staatliche Hochschule für Musik, Prof, Munich. **Res:** Ravensburger Ring 6, 8 Munich 60, FR Ger.

KOCI, PREMYSL. Stages/produces opera and is a baritone and actor. Czechoslovakian. Gen Mng & Resident Stage Dir, National Theater, Prague. Born 1 Jun 1917, Rychvald, CSR. Wife Milena, occupation librarian. Studied: Prof Rudolf Vasek, Ostrava; Profs Václav Talich, Zdenek Chalabala, Prague. **Operatic debut as prod:** Devil and Kate National Theater, Prague 1966. Previous occupation: elem school teacher, opera singer. Awards: Merited Artist & Order for Construction, Gvnmt CSSR.

Directed/produced opera for major companies in CZE: Prague National; HOL: Amsterdam. **Operas staged with these companies incl** JANACEK: *Jenufa★, Makropoulos Affair★;* MOZART: *Entführung aus dem serail★;* SMETANA: *Bartered Bride★, Secret★, Two Widows.* **Operatic world prem:** CIKKER: *Coriolanus* Ntl Theater, Prague 1974. **Sang with major cos in** AUS: Vienna Staatsoper; CZE: Prague National; ITA: Florence Maggio, Venice; YUG: Dubrovnik. **Roles with these companies incl** BEETHOVEN: Don Pizarro (*Fidelio*); BIZET: Escamillo (*Carmen*); DEBUSSY: Golaud (*Pelléas et Mélisande*); DVORAK: Marbuel‡ (*Devil and Kate*); JANACEK: Forester (*Cunning Little Vixen*), Sacristan‡ (*Excursions of Mr Broucek*), Shishkov‡ (*From the House of the Dead*), Jaroslav Prus‡ (*Makropoulos Affair*); LORTZING: Peter I (*Zar und Zimmermann*); MOZART: Don Giovanni, Conte Almaviva (*Nozze di Figaro*); MUSSORGSKY: Boris Godunov; ORFF: König (*Kluge*); PUCCINI: Marcello (*Bohème*), Sharpless (*Butterfly*), Scarpia (*Tosca*); ROSSINI: Figaro★ (*Barbiere di Siviglia*); SMETANA: Vok (*Devil's Wall*), Tomas★ (*Kiss*), Premysl (*Libuse*), Kalina★‡ (*Secret*); STRAUSS, R: Orest (*Elektra*); TCHAIKOVSKY: Eugene Onegin, Yeletsky (*Pique Dame*); VERDI: Amonasro (*Aida*), Iago (*Otello*), Germont (*Traviata*); WAGNER: Telramund (*Lohengrin*), Wolfram (*Tannhäuser*); WEBER: Kaspar (*Freischütz*). Also MOZART: Sprecher (*Zauberflöte*); BRITTEN: Sid (*Albert Herring*); DVORAK: Shuisky (*Dimitrij*), Bohus (*Jakobin*); PROKOFIEV: Alexej (*Story of a Real Man*); SHEBALIN: Petruchio (*Taming of the Shrew*); SUCHON: Mojmir (*Svatopluk*). **World premieres:** HANUS: Prometheus (*Torch of Prometheus*) National Theater, Prague 1965. Recorded for: Supraphon. Gives recitals. Appears with symphony orchestra. Teaches voice. Coaches repertoire. On faculty of Music

Acad, Prague. **Res:** Krocinova 5, Prague, CSSR. Mgmt: PRG/CZE.

KOGEL, RICHARD. Bass-baritone & basso-buffo. German. Resident mem: Theater am Gärtnerplatz, Munich. Born 15 Jan 1927, Munich. Wife Isa. One child. Studied: Staatliche Hochschule für Musik, Munich; Profs Reuther, Eichhorn, Fr Prof Fichtmüller. **Debut:** Figaro (*Nozze di Figaro*) Stadttheater Bern, Switzerland 1952.

Sang with major companies in AUS: Vienna Staatsoper; BRA: Rio de Janeiro; FR GER: Bonn, Dortmund, Düsseldorf-Duisburg, Essen, Frankfurt, Hamburg, Hannover, Karlsruhe, Kassel, Mannheim, Munich Gärtnerplatz, Saarbrücken, Stuttgart, Wiesbaden; GER DR: Berlin Komische Oper; HOL: Amsterdam; ITA: Venice. **Roles with these companies incl** d'ALBERT: Tommaso★ (*Tiefland*); BIZET: Zurga★ (*Pêcheurs de perles*); DONIZETTI: Don Pasquale★; FLOTOW: Plunkett (*Martha*); LEONCAVALLO: Tonio‡ (*Pagliacci*); LORTZING: Stadinger (*Waffenschmied*), Baculus‡ (*Wildschütz*), Van Bett★‡ (*Zar und Zimmermann*); MOZART: Don Alfonso (*Così fan tutte*), Leporello (*Don Giovanni*), Osmin★ (*Entführung aus dem Serail*), Nardo (*Finta giardiniera*), Figaro‡ (*Nozze di Figaro*), Papageno★‡ (*Zauberflöte*); NICOLAI: Falstaff‡ (*Lustigen Weiber*); OFFENBACH: Coppélius, etc‡ (*Contes d'Hoffmann*); PUCCINI: Gianni Schicchi, Sharpless (*Butterfly*); ROSSINI: Dott Bartolo★‡ (*Barbiere di Siviglia*); SMETANA: Kezal★‡ (*Bartered Bride*); STRAUSS, R: La Roche (*Capriccio*); VERDI: Falstaff, Fra Melitone (*Forza del destino*); WAGNER: Alberich (*Rheingold‡, Götterdämmerung‡*). Recorded for: DG, Ariola/Eurodisc. **Res:** Bortenhofstr 17, 8 Munich 70, FR Ger. Mgmt: SLZ/FRG.

KÖHLER, SIEGFRIED. Conductor of opera and symphony. German. Mus Dir & Resident Cond, Hessisches Staatstheater, Wiesbaden, FR Ger. Previous adm positions in opera: Mus Dir, Opernhaus Saarbrücken, FR Ger, until 1974. **Conducted with major companies in** FR GER: Cologne, Saarbrücken, Stuttgart, Wiesbaden; et al. **Operas with these companies incl** BEETHOVEN: *Fidelio;* BERG: *Wozzeck;* MOZART: *Entführung aus dem Serail;* STRAUSS, R: *Arabella, Elektra;* WAGNER: *Fliegende Holländer, Meistersinger, Tannhäuser, Tristan und Isolde;* et al. Also PALIASCHWILI: *Daissi.*

KOHN, KARL-CHRISTIAN. Bass. German. Resident mem: Bayerische Staatsoper, Munich. Born 21 May 1928, Losheim-Saar, Germany. Wife Anne Oehms, occupation music teacher. Two children. Studied: Musikhochschule Saarbrücken, Prof Hans Karolus, Prof Irene Eden, Germany. **Debut:** Figaro (*Nozze di Figaro*) Deutsche Oper Berlin 1955. Awards: Bayerischer Kammersänger, Bayerischer Senat 1962; Spanish Critics Prize, Radio Barcelona & Liceo 1968.

Sang with major companies in AUS: Graz, Vienna Staatsoper; BEL: Brussels; DEN: Copenhagen; FRA: Nancy, Paris, Strasbourg; FR GER: Berlin Deutsche, Bielefeld, Cologne, Darmstadt, Düsseldorf-Duisburg, Frankfurt, Hamburg, Karlsruhe, Kiel, Krefeld, Mannheim, Munich Staatsoper, Nürnberg, Saarbrücken, Stuttgart,

Wiesbaden; GER DR: Dresden; HOL: Amsterdam; ITA: Naples, Palermo, Rome Opera & Caracalla, Turin, Venice; SPA: Barcelona; SWI: Basel, Zurich. **Roles with these companies incl** d'ALBERT: Tommaso (*Tiefland*); BEETHOVEN: Rocco★ (*Fidelio*); BERG: Doktor★ (*Wozzeck*); BIZET: Escamillo (*Carmen*); CORNELIUS: Abul Hassan (*Barbier von Bagdad*); DONIZETTI: Don Pasquale★; FLOTOW: Plunkett (*Martha*); GOUNOD: Méphistophélès (*Faust*); HANDEL: Polyphemus★ (*Acis and Galatea*), Ptolemy (*Giulio Cesare*); LORTZING: Stadinger & Graf v Liebenau (*Waffenschmied*), Baculus (*Wildschütz*), Van Bett (*Zar und Zimmermann*); MEYERBEER: Don Pedro (*Africaine*); MOZART: Don Alfonso (*Così fan tutte*), Leporello (*Don Giovanni*), Osmin★ (*Entführung aus dem Serail*), Figaro (*Nozze di Figaro*), Sarastro★ (*Zauberflöte*); MUSSORGSKY: Pimen★ (*Boris Godunov*); ORFF: Kreon★ (*Antigonae*), Solo (*Carmina burana*); PUCCINI: Colline★ (*Bohème*), Gianni Schicchi; SMETANA: Kezal (*Bartered Bride*); STRAUSS, R: La Roche (*Capriccio*), Orest (*Elektra*), Baron Ochs (*Rosenkavalier*), Sir Morosus (*Schweigsame Frau*); STRAVINSKY: Creon★ (*Oedipus Rex*); THOMAS: Lothario (*Mignon*); VERDI: Ramfis★ (*Aida*), Philip II★ & Grande Inquisitore (*Don Carlo*), Padre Guardiano★ (*Forza del destino*), Banquo★ (*Macbeth*), Fiesco (*Simon Boccanegra*), Procida (*Vespri*); WAGNER: Daland★ (*Fliegende Holländer*), Gurnemanz★ (*Parsifal*), Steffano Colonna (*Rienzi*), Fafner (*Rheingold★, Siegfried★*), Hunding★ (*Walküre*), Landgraf★ (*Tannhäuser*), König Marke★ (*Tristan und Isolde*); WEBER: Kaspar (*Freischütz*); WOLF-FERRARI: Lunardo (*Quattro rusteghi*). Also STRAUSS, R: Peneios (*Daphne*), Graf Waldner★ (*Arabella*); MOZART: Commendatore (*Don Giovanni*); HENZE: Dr Reischmann (*Elegy for Young Lovers*). **World premieres:** EGK: Herr Weiss (*Verlobung in San Domingo*) Bayerische Staatsoper, Munich 1963; BIALAS: Cte Beaucaire (*Aucassin und Nicolette*) Bayerische Staatsoper, Munich 1969. Recorded for: EMI, Electrola, DG. Video/Film: Doktor (*Wozzeck*); Plunkett (*Martha*); Graf Waldner (*Arabella*); Kalender (*Pilger von Mekka*); Gottfried von Ried (*Verlobung in San Domingo*). Gives recitals. Appears with symphony orchestra. Teaches voice. Coaches repertoire. **Res:** Hochkönigstr 12, 8 Munich 82, FR Ger. Mgmt: SLZ/FRG; IMR/FRA.

KOK, GEORGE CHRISTIAAN. Character & buffo tenor. South African. Resident mem: Performing Arts Council of Transvaal, Pretoria. Born 18 Aug 1945. Single. Studied: Toonkuns Akad, Univ of Pretoria, Xander Haagen, Nellie du Toit. **Debut:** Pedrillo (*Entführung aus dem Serail*) PACT, S Afr 1967. Previous occupations: lecturer on singing, Pretoria Coll of Music; opera producer.

Sang with major companies in S AFR: Johannesburg Opera. **Roles with these companies incl** DONIZETTI: Ernesto★ (*Don Pasquale*); HUMPERDINCK: Hexe★ (*Hänsel und Gretel*); JANACEK: Steva★ (*Jenufa*); MOZART: Belmonte★ & Pedrillo★ (*Entführung aus dem Serail*); PUCCINI: Rinuccio★ (*Gianni Schicchi*); ROSSINI: Almaviva★ (*Barbiere di Siviglia*); STRAUSS, J: Eisenstein★ (*Fledermaus*); WAGNER: David★ (*Meistersinger*), Mime★ (*Siegfried*). Also BRIT-

TEN: Bob Boles★ (*Peter Grimes*). Gives recitals. Appears with symphony orchestra. Teaches voice. Coaches repertoire. **Res:** 130 Louis Botha Ave, Pretoria, S Afr.

KOLK, STANLEY. Lyric tenor. American. Resident mem: Städtische Oper, Frankfurt. Born 6 Apr 1935, Fremont, MI, USA. Divorced. One child. Studied: Calvin Coll, Prof James DeJong, Grand Rapids, MI; Mme Elda Ercole, New York. **Debut:** Alfredo (*Traviata*) Washington, DC, Opera Socy 1962. Awards: Ford Fndt Grant.

Sang with major companies in AUS: Salzburg Fest, Vienna Volksoper; CAN: Ottawa; FR GER: Berlin Deutsche Oper, Bonn, Cologne, Frankfurt, Karlsruhe, Munich Staatsoper, Wuppertal; HOL: Amsterdam; POR: Lisbon; SWI: Basel, Geneva; USA: Baltimore, Cincinnati, Hartford, Houston, Kansas City, Miami, Milwaukee Florentine, New Orleans, Philadelphia Lyric, San Antonio, San Francisco Spring, Santa Fe, Seattle, Washington DC. **Roles with these companies incl** BARBER: Anatol (*Vanessa*); BERG: Maler★ (*Lulu*); BIZET: Nadir (*Pêcheurs de perles*); CIMAROSA: Paolino★ (*Matrimonio segreto*); DELIBES: Gérald (*Lakmé*); DONIZETTI: Ernesto★ (*Don Pasquale*), Nemorino (*Elisir*), Tonio★ (*Fille du régiment*); GOUNOD: Faust★, Roméo★; HALEVY: Léopold★ (*Juive*); HANDEL: Xerxes★; HENZE: Lord Barrat★ (*Junge Lord*); LORTZING: Baron Kronthal★ (*Wildschütz*); MASSENET: Des Grieux (*Manon*); MOZART: Tito★ (*Clemenza di Tito*), Ferrando★ (*Così fan tutte*), Don Ottavio★ (*Don Giovanni*), Belmonte★ (*Entführung aus dem Serail*), Mitridate★, Tamino★ (*Zauberflöte*); OFFENBACH: Hoffmann; PUCCINI: Rodolfo★ (*Bohème*), Rinuccio (*Gianni Schicchi*), Pinkerton (*Butterfly*); ROSSINI: Almaviva★ (*Barbiere di Siviglia*), Don Ramiro★ (*Cenerentola*), Lindoro (*Italiana in Algeri*); STRAUSS, J: Alfred (*Fledermaus*); STRAUSS, R: Ein Sänger★ (*Rosenkavalier*); STRAVINSKY: Vasili‡ (*Mavra*), Pêcheur (*Rossignol*); VERDI: Fenton★ (*Falstaff*), Duca di Mantova★ (*Rigoletto*), Alfredo★ (*Traviata*); WAGNER: David★ (*Meistersinger*). Gives recitals. Appears with symphony orchestra. **Res:** Bahn Str 30, 6231 Sulzbach/Ts, FR Ger. Mgmt: SMN/USA; SLZ/FRG.

KOLLO, RENÉ; né Kollodzieyski. Heldentenor. German. Born 20 Nov 1937, Berlin. Wife Dorthe Kollo-Larsen. One child. Studied: Elsa Varena, Berlin. **Debut:** triple bill (*Oedipus Rex*), (*Mavra*), (*Renard*) Staatstheater Braunschweig, FR Ger 1965. Previous occupations: pop singer.

Sang with major companies in AUS: Salzburg Fest, Vienna Staatsoper; BEL: Brussels; FRA: Paris; FR GER: Bayreuth Fest, Berlin Deutsche Oper, Cologne, Düsseldorf-Duisburg, Frankfurt, Hamburg, Hannover, Mannheim, Munich Staatsoper, Stuttgart; ITA: Milan La Scala, Palermo, Venice; POR: Lisbon; SPA: Barcelona; SWI: Geneva. **Roles with these companies incl** BORODIN: Vladimir★ (*Prince Igor*); JANACEK: Laca (*Jenufa*); MOZART: Tito (*Clemenza di Tito*), Tamino★ (*Zauberflöte*); PUCCINI: Pinkerton (*Butterfly*); SMETANA: Hans★‡ (*Bartered Bride*); STRAUSS, J: Eisenstein★‡ (*Fledermaus*); STRAUSS, R: Matteo★‡ (*Arabella*), Ein Sänger★‡

(*Rosenkavalier*); STRAVINSKY: Vasili (*Mavra*), Oedipus Rex; WAGNER: Erik‡ (*Fliegende Holländer*), Lohengrin★, Walther★‡ (*Meistersinger*), Parsifal★‡, Loge★ (*Rheingold*), Siegmund★ (*Walküre*), Tannhäuser★. Recorded for: EMI, Decca, Ariola. Gives recitals. Appears with symphony orchestra. **Res:** Hübschstr 8, Bayreuth, FR Ger. Mgmt: JUC/SWI.

KOMLÓSSY, ERZSÉBET. Dramatic mezzo-soprano & contralto. Hungarian. Resident mem: Hungarian State Opera, Budapest. Born 9 Jul 1933, Salgotarjan, Hungary. Divorced. Two children. Studied: Zene Konsv, Budapest; Dr Laszlo Geza, H Tempis Erzsebet. **Debut:** Haziasszony (*Spinning Room*) Opera House, Szeged 1955. Awards: First Prize Ferenc Liszt; Kossuth Prize, Hungarian Govnmt.

Sang with major companies in AUS: Graz, Vienna Volksoper; BUL: Sofia; CZE: Prague National; GRE: Athens Festival; FR GER: Hamburg, Wiesbaden; GER DR: Berlin Staatsoper, Leipzig; HUN: Budapest; ITA: Bologna, Milan La Scala; POL: Warsaw; ROM: Bucharest; UK: London Royal; USSR: Kiev, Leningrad Kirov, Moscow Bolshoi, Tbilisi; YUG: Zagreb. **Roles with these companies incl** BIZET: Carmen★; BORODIN: Kontchakovna★ (*Prince Igor*); BRITTEN: Mrs Herring★ (*Albert Herring*); DEBUSSY: Geneviève★ (*Pelléas et Mélisande*); FALLA: Abuela★ (*Vida breve*); GLUCK: Orfeo★; KODALY: Örzse★ (*Háry János*); MONTEVERDI: Poppea★ (*Incoronazione di Poppea*); MUSSORGSKY: Marfa★ (*Khovanshchina*); PUCCINI: Suzuki★ (*Madama Butterfly*); SAINT-SAENS: Dalila★; TCHAIKOVSKY: Olga★ (*Eugene Onegin*); VERDI: Amneris★ (*Aida*), Ulrica★ (*Ballo in maschera*), Dame Quickly★ (*Falstaff*), Preziosilla★ (*Forza del destino*), Azucena★ (*Trovatore*); WAGNER: Erda★ (*Rheingold★, Siegfried★*). Also WEILL: Mrs Peachum★ (*Dreigroschenoper*); ERKEL: Gertrude★ (*Bánk Bán*); PUCCINI: Zita (*Gianni Schicchi*). **World premieres:** SZOKOLAY: Gertrudis (*Hamlet*) State Opera, Budapest 1968; Mother of the Groom (*Blood Wedding*) State Opera, Budapest 1964. Recorded for: various. Video/Film: (*Blood Wedding*); (*Spinning Room*); (*Bánk Bán*); (*Gianni Schicchi*). Gives recitals. Appears with symphony orchestra. **Res:** Csanady u 28, 1132 Budapest, Hungary. Mgmt: ITK/HUN.

KONDRASHIN, KIRIL. Conductor of opera and symphony. Russian. Resident Cond, Bolshoi Opera, Moscow. Born 1914, Moscow. Studied: Moscow Consv, incl piano.

Conducted with major companies in USSR: Moscow Bolshoi; USA: Chicago; et al. **Operas with these companies incl** MUSSORGSKY: *Boris Godunov, Khovanshchina;* PUCCINI: *Fanciulla del West, Butterfly, Tosca;* RIMSKY-KORSAKOV: *Coq d'or, Invisible City of Kitezh, Sadko;* SMETANA: *Bartered Bride;* TCHAIKOVSKY: *Eugene Onegin, Iolanthe, Pique Dame;* VERDI: *Rigoletto;* et al. Also PASHCHENKO: *Pompadour;* CHEREMUKHIN: *Kalinka;* SEREV: *Foes of Power.*

KÓNYA, SÁNDOR. Lyric & dramatic tenor. German. Resident mem: Metropolitan Opera, New

York. Born 23 Sep 1923, Sarkad, Hungary. Wife Anneliese. Studied: Franz Liszt Acad, Budapest; Nordwestdeutsche Musikakad, Prof Fred Husler, Detmold; Mo Rico Lani, Milan. **Debut:** Turiddu (*Cavalleria rusticana*) Städtische Oper, Bielefeld 1951.

Sang with major companies in ARG: Buenos Aires; AUS: Vienna Staatsoper; FIN: Helsinki; FRA: Bordeaux, Lyon, Paris, Strasbourg, Toulouse; FR GER: Bayreuth Fest, Berlin Deutsche Oper, Bielefeld, Bonn, Cologne, Darmstadt, Düsseldorf-Duisburg, Hamburg, Hannover, Kassel, Krefeld, Munich Staatsoper, Stuttgart, Wiesbaden; GER DR: Dresden, Leipzig; HUN: Budapest; ITA: Florence Maggio & Comunale, Milan La Scala, Palermo, Rome Opera & Caracalla, Venice, Verona Arena; POR: Lisbon; SPA: Barcelona; SWI: Basel, Zurich; UK: Edinburgh Fest, London Royal; USA: Baltimore, Boston, Chicago Lyric, Dallas Civic, Memphis, Miami, New Orleans, New York Met, Philadelphia Grand & Lyric, Portland, San Diego, San Francisco Opera, Seattle, Washington DC. **Roles with these companies incl** AUBER: Fra Diavolo; BIZET: Don José★ (*Carmen*); BOITO: Faust (*Mefistofele*); CHERUBINI: Giasone (*Medea*); CIMAROSA: Paolino (*Matrimonio segreto*); CORNELIUS: Nureddin (*Barbier von Bagdad*); DONIZETTI: Edgardo★ (*Lucia*); FLOTOW: Lionel (*Martha*); JANACEK: Laca★ & Steva★ (*Jenufa*), Boris (*Katya Kabanova*); LEONCAVALLO: Canio‡ (*Pagliacci*); LORTZING: Peter Ivanov (*Zar und Zimmermann*); MARTIN: Tristan (*Vin herbé*); MASCAGNI: Turiddu★‡ (*Cavalleria rusticana*); MENOTTI: Michele (*Saint of Bleecker Street*); MOZART: Ferrando (*Così fan tutte*); OFFENBACH: Hoffmann‡; PUCCINI: Rodolfo★‡ (*Bohème*), Dick Johnson★ (*Fanciulla del West*), Pinkerton★‡ (*Butterfly*), Des Grieux (*Manon Lescaut*), Cavaradossi★‡ (*Tosca*), Calaf★ (*Turandot*); SMETANA: Dalibor‡; STRAUSS, J: Eisenstein‡ & Alfred‡ (*Fledermaus*); STRAUSS, R: Bacchus (*Ariadne auf Naxos*), Ein Sänger (*Rosenkavalier*); VERDI: Radames‡ (*Aida*), Riccardo (*Ballo in maschera*), Don Carlo★, Don Alvaro★ (*Forza del destino*), Ismaele‡ (*Nabucco*), Otello★, Duca di Mantova‡ (*Rigoletto*), Alfredo (*Traviata*), Manrico‡ (*Trovatore*), Macduff (*Macbeth*); WAGNER: Erik★ (*Fliegende Holländer*), Lohengrin★‡, Walther★ (*Meistersinger*), Parsifal★, Siegmund (*Walküre*); WEBER: Max★ (*Freischütz*), Hüon (*Oberon*); WEINBERGER: Babinsky (*Schwanda*); WOLF-FERRARI: Filipeto (*Quattro rusteghi*). Also TCHAIKOVSKY: Monk (*Sorceress*), German (*Pique Dame*); WAGNER: David (*Meistersinger*). **World premieres:** HENZE: Leandro (*König Hirsch*) Städtische Oper Berlin 1956. **Recorded for:** DG, RCA Victor. Video/Film: Riccardo (*Ballo in maschera*); DOHNANYI: Tenor. Gives recitals. Appears with symphony orchestra. Teaches voice. Coaches repertoire. **Res:** c/o Weihs, 87-11 35 Ave, Jackson Heights, NY 11372, USA; and Bahnhofstr 7, 3053 Steinhude, FR Ger. Mgmt: GOR/UK; NAP/USA.

KOPACKI, TADEUSZ. Dramatic tenor. Polish. Resident mem: Grand Theater, Lódz. Born 3 Mar 1930, Tarnopol, Poland. Wife Delfina Ambroziak, occupation opera singer. Studied: State School of Music, Lódz, Poland 1960; Scuola di Canto, Milan. **Debut:** Jontek (*Halka*) Lódz Opera Co 1960. Awards: Gold Cross of Merit, Polish Council of State.

Sang with major companies in FR GER: Dortmund, Düsseldorf-Duisburg; GER DR: Leipzig; HOL: Amsterdam; POL: Lódz, Warsaw; USSR: Moscow Stanislavski, Tbilisi; YUG: Belgrade. **Roles with these companies incl** BIZET: Don José★ (*Carmen*); BORODIN: Vladimir★ (*Prince Igor*); DONIZETTI: Edgardo★ (*Lucia*); GOUNOD: Faust★; MASSENET: Des Grieux★ (*Manon*); MONIUSZKO: Jontek★ (*Halka*), Stefan★ (*Haunted Castle*); OFFENBACH: Hoffmann★; PUCCINI: Rodolfo★ (*Bohème*), Dick Johnson★ (*Fanciulla del West*), Pinkerton★ (*Butterfly*), Cavaradossi★ (*Tosca*); SMETANA: Hans★ (*Bartered Bride*); TCHAIKOVSKY: Gherman★ (*Pique Dame*); VERDI: Riccardo★ (*Ballo in maschera*), Duca di Mantova★ (*Rigoletto*), Alfredo★ (*Traviata*); WAGNER: Lohengrin★. Gives recitals. Appears with symphony orchestra. Teaches voice. Coaches repertoire. On faculty of State School of Music, Lódz Consv. **Res:** Swierczewskiego 4A, Lódz, Poland. Mgmt: PAG/POL.

KOPP, LEO LÁSZLÓ. Conductor of opera and symphony; composer. American. Mus Dir, Lincoln Symph, NE, USA. Born 7 Oct 1906, Budapest. Wife Hazel. Studied: Leo Weiner, Budapest; Vincent d'Indy, Paris; Paul Gräner, Leipzig; incl piano, violin and voice. Plays the piano. Operatic training as asst cond at var comps in Europe. **Operatic debut:** *Wildschütz* Oldenburg Opera, Germany 1926. Symphonic debut: Königsberger Rundfunk, Germany 1928. Awards: Hon DM Univ of the Pacific, Stockton, CA 1967; Hon mem, Lincoln Musician Assn.

Conducted with major companies in USA: Chicago, Cincinnati Summer, Milwaukee Florentine, Omaha, St Paul. **Operas with these cos incl** ADAM: *Postillon de Lonjumeau*; d'ALBERT: *Tiefland*; BEETHOVEN: *Fidelio*; BIZET: *Carmen*; BOIELDIEU: *Dame blanche*; CORNELIUS: *Barbier von Bagdad*; DEBUSSY: *Pelléas et Mélisande*; DONIZETTI: *Don Pasquale, Elisir★*; FLOTOW: *Martha*; GOUNOD: *Faust*; HALEVY: *Juive*; HINDEMITH: *Cardillac*; HUMPERDINCK: *Hänsel und Gretel*; KORNGOLD: *Tote Stadt*; LEONCAVALLO: *Pagliacci★*; LORTZING: *Wildschütz*; MASCAGNI: *Cavalleria rusticana★*; MASSENET: *Manon*; MENOTTI: *Amelia al ballo, Medium, Old Maid and the Thief, Telephone*; MOZART: *Don Giovanni, Nozze di Figaro, Zauberflöte*; MUSSORGSKY: *Fair at Sorochinsk*; NICOLAI: *Lustigen Weiber*; OFFENBACH: *Contes d'Hoffmann, Périchole, Mariage aux lanternes*; ORFF: *Carmina burana*; PERGOLESI: *Serva padrona*; PONCHIELLI: *Gioconda*; PUCCINI: *Bohème, Fanciulla del West, Gianni Schicchi, Butterfly★, Manon Lescaut, Tosca★, Turandot*; RAVEL: *Heure espagnole*; ROSSINI: *Barbiere di Siviglia*; SAINT-SAENS: *Samson et Dalila*; SMETANA: *Bartered Bride*; STRAUSS, J: *Fledermaus★*; STRAUSS, R: *Rosenkavalier, Salome*; THOMAS: *Mignon*; VERDI: *Aida★, Ballo in maschera★, Falstaff, Forza del destino, Otello, Rigoletto★, Traviata, Trovatore*; WAGNER: *Fliegende Holländer, Lohengrin, Meistersinger, Walküre, Tannhäuser*;

WEBER: *Freischütz*. Also DAMROSCH: *Man Without a Country;* WOLF-FERRARI: *Sly;* GRUENBERG: *Jack and the Beanstalk.* **Res:** 938 N Lombard Ave, Oak Park, IL, USA.

KORAL, CAN. Baritone. French. Born 28 May 1945, Istanbul, Turkey. Wife Hélia T'Hézan, occupation opera singer, soprano. Studied: Istanbul Opera Studio; Consv Ntl de Musique de Paris; École Normale de Musique de Paris. **Debut:** Sharpless *(Butterfly)* Istanbul City Opera 1965. Awards: First Prize of Lyric Art, École Normale de Musique de Paris.
　Sang with major companies in FRA: Lyon, Marseille, Nancy, Nice, Rouen, Toulouse. **Roles with these companies incl** BECAUD: Sean★ *(Opéra d'Aran);* BIZET: Escamillo★ *(Carmen);* DALLA-PICCOLA: Robineau★ *(Volo di notte);* GIORDANO: Carlo Gérard★ *(Andrea Chénier);* MASCAGNI: Alfio★ *(Cavalleria rusticana);* MENOTTI: Husband★ *(Amelia al ballo);* PUCCINI: Marcello★ *(Bohème),* Sharpless★ *(Butterfly);* SCHOENBERG: Der Mann★ *(Glückliche Hand).* **Res:** Choisy-le-Roi, France. **Mgmt:** GRE/FRA.

KORD, KAZIMIERZ. Conductor ·of opera and symphony. Polish. Music Dir, Grand Theater/Teatr Wielki, Warsaw. Also Music Dir, Polish National Television & Radio Orch, Warsaw. Born Silesia. Studied: Acad of Music, Leningrad; School of Music, Cracow; incl piano. Plays the piano. Operatic training as chorus master. **Operatic debut:** Grand Theater, Warsaw 1960. Previous adm positions in opera: Chief Cond, Cracow Opera 1960-68.
　Conducted with major companies in AUS: Vienna Staatsoper; DEN: Copenhagen; FR GER: Düsseldorf-Duisburg, Munich Staatsoper & Gärtnerplatz, Stuttgart; POL: Warsaw; USA: Chicago, New York Met, San Francisco Opera; et al. **Operas with these companies incl** BIZET: *Carmen;* MOZART: *Così fan tutte;* MUSSORGSKY: *Boris Godunov;* SHOSTAKOVICH: *Katerina Ismailova;* STRAVINSKY: *Rake's Progress;* TCHAIKOVSKY: *Eugene Onegin, Pique Dame;* VERDI: *Falstaff, Rigoletto;* et al. Conducted major orch in Europe.

KORDA, JANOS. Lyric & dramatic tenor. German. Resident mem: Staatstheater Kassel. Born 9 May 1929, Szeged, Hungary. Divorced. One child. Studied: Consv, Szeged; Hochschule für Musik, Berlin, FR Ger. **Debut:** Pinkerton *(Butterfly)* Staatstheater Kassel 1962. Previous occupations: long-distance truck driver.
　Sang with major companies in DEN: Copenhagen; GRE: Athens Fest; FR GER: Berlin Deutsche Oper, Bielefeld, Bonn, Cologne, Darmstadt, Dortmund, Düsseldorf-Duisburg, Essen, Frankfurt, Hamburg, Hannover, Karlsruhe, Kassel, Mannheim, Munich Gärtnerplatz, Stuttgart, Wiesbaden, Wuppertal; GER DR: Berlin Staatsoper; HUN: Budapest. **Roles with these companies incl** ADAM: Zephoris *(Si j'étais roi);* AUBER: Fra Diavolo; BIZET: Don José★ *(Carmen);* CHARPENTIER: Julien *(Louise);* DONIZETTI: Edgardo★ *(Lucia);* FLOTOW: Lionel *(Martha);* GIORDANO: Andrea Chénier★; JANACEK: Laca★ & Steva *(Jenufa),* Boris *(Katya*

Kabanova); MASCAGNI: Turiddu *(Cavalleria rusticana);* MOZART: Ferrando *(Così fan tutte),* Don Ottavio *(Don Giovanni);* NICOLAI: Fenton *(Lustigen Weiber);* OFFENBACH: Hoffmann★; PUCCINI: Rodolfo★ *(Bohème),* Pinkerton★ *(Butterfly),* Des Grieux★ *(Manon Lescaut),* Cavaradossi★ *(Tosca);* ROSSINI: Almaviva *(Barbiere di Siviglia);* SMETANA: Hans★ *(Bartered Bride);* STRAUSS, J: Alfred★ *(Fledermaus);* STRAUSS, R: Ein Sänger★ *(Rosenkavalier);* TCHAIKOVSKY: Lenski *(Eugene Onegin),* Gherman★ *(Pique Dame);* VERDI: Radames★ *(Aida),* Riccardo★ *(Ballo in maschera),* Don Carlo★, Don Alvaro★ *(Forza del destino),* Ismaele★ *(Nabucco),* Duca di Mantova★ *(Rigoletto),* Alfredo★ *(Traviata),* Manrico★ *(Trovatore).* Gives recitals. Appears with symphony orchestra. **Res:** Ahnabreite 47, 35 Kassel, FR Ger. **Mgmt:** SLZ/FRG.

KOROLYOV, DENIS ALEKSANDROVICH. Lyric tenor. Russian. Resident mem: Bolshoi Theater, Moscow. Born 24 Dec 1938, Moscow. Studied: Tchaikovsky Moscow Consv, Prof G I Tits. **Debut:** Lenski *(Eugene Onegin)* Stanislavski Theater, Moscow 1964. Awards: First Prize, Intl Compt Munich 1966; Second Prize, Schubert Intl Compt Vienna 1967.
　Sang with major companies in BUL: Sofia; GER DR: Leipzig; POL: Warsaw; USSR: Kiev, Leningrad Kirov, Moscow Bolshoi & Stanislavski. **Roles with these companies incl** BORODIN: Vladimir★ *(Prince Igor);* CIMAROSA: Paolino *(Matrimonio segreto);* DONIZETTI: Nemorino *(Elisir);* GOUNOD: Roméo *(Così fan tutte);* PROKOFIEV: Antonio *(Duenna),* Marquis★ *(Gambler),* Anatole★ *(War and Peace);* PUCCINI: Rodolfo *(Bohème);* RACHMANINOFF: Albert *(Miserly Knight);* RIMSKY-KORSAKOV: Levko *(May Night),* Boyar Lykov★ *(Tsar's Bride);* ROSSINI: Almaviva *(Barbiere di Siviglia);* TCHAIKOVSKY: Lenski‡ *(Eugene Onegin);* VERDI: Duca di Mantova *(Rigoletto),* Alfredo *(Traviata).* Recorded for: Melodiya. Video/Film: Lenski *(Eugene Onegin).* Gives recitals. Appears with symphony orchestra. Teaches voice. Coaches repertoire. On faculty of Music School, Tchaikovsky Moscow Consv. **Res:** d 17 kv 96 ul Gor'kogo, Moscow, USSR. **Mgmt:** GOS/USSR.

KOROLYOVA, GLAFIRA SERAFIMOVNA; née Koslova. Contralto. Russian. Resident mem: Bolshoi Theater, Moscow. Born 27 Dec 1936, Perm, USSR. Husband Y V Korolev, occupation singer with Bolshoi Opera. Studied: Moscow Consv, R Y Alpert, E K Levinson, F S Petrova. **Debut:** Olga *(Eugene Onegin)* Bolshoi Theater 1963.
　Sang with major company in USSR: Moscow Bolshoi. **Roles with this company incl** BORODIN: Kontchakovna *(Prince Igor);* BRITTEN: Oberon *(Midsummer Night);* GLINKA: Banja *(Life for the Tsar);* GOUNOD: Siebel *(Faust);* RIMSKY-KORSAKOV: Nejata *(Sadko);* TCHAIKOVSKY: Olga *(Eugene Onegin).* Gives recitals. Appears with symphony orchestra. **Res:** 12-124 Malaya Gruzinskay, Moscow, USSR.

KORSTEN, GÉRARD. Lirico spinto tenor. South African. Born 6 Dec 1930, Rotterdam, Holland.

Wife Elna. Five children. Studied: Judith Hellwig, Vienna; Coll of Music, Armholt, S Afr; N Du Toit, Pretoria. **Debut:** Rodolfo (*Bohème*) National Opera Co, S Afr 1958. Previous occupations: electr engineer. Awards: Midem Trophy, France; Gold Medal for popular music & ballads.

Sang with major companies in S AFR: Johannesburg. **Roles with these companies incl** BELLINI: Pollione (*Norma*); BIZET: Don José★ (*Carmen*); DONIZETTI: Edgardo★ (*Lucia di Lammermoor*); GIORDANO: Andrea Chénier★; GOUNOD: Faust; JANACEK: Laca (*Jenufa*); LEONCAVALLO: Canio (*Pagliacci*); MASCAGNI: Turiddu (*Cavalleria rusticana*); MOZART: Tamino (*Zauberflöte*); OFFENBACH: Hoffmann; PUCCINI: Rodolfo★ (*Bohème*), Pinkerton (*Butterfly*), Des Grieux (*Manon Lescaut*), Cavaradossi★ (*Tosca*), Calaf★ (*Turandot*); SMETANA: Hans (*Bartered Bride*); STRAUSS, J: Eisenstein★ & Alfred★ (*Fledermaus*); STRAUSS, R: Bacchus★ (*Ariadne auf Naxos*); VERDI: Radames (*Aida*), Alfredo (*Traviata*). Gives recitals. Appears with symphony orchestra. **Res:** 1038 Arcadia Str, Pretoria, S Afr. Mgmt: PBC/SAF.

KOSSOWSKI, EDMUND. Basso cantante. Polish. Resident mem: Teatr Wielki, Warsaw. Born 25 Oct 1920, Osiek, Poland. Wife Marie Jesarz. One child. Studied: Prof B Romaniszyh. **Debut:** Pantler (*Halka*) Poland 1945. Awards: Third Prize Vocal Compt Toulouse, France; Officer, Cross of Polonia Restituta; Badge of Merit, Ministry of Art and Culture.

Sang with major companies in POL: Warsaw. **Roles with these companies incl** BARTOK: Bluebeard; BORODIN: Prince Igor; DONIZETTI: Enrico (*Lucia*); GOUNOD: Méphistophélès (*Faust*); HANDEL: Giulio Cesare, Arsamene (*Xerxes*); MASSENET: Don Quichotte; MONIUSZKO: Janusz (*Halka*); MOZART: Guglielmo (*Così fan tutte*), Leporello & Don Giovanni (*Don Giovanni*); MUSSORGSKY: Boris & Pimen (*Boris Godunov*); OFFENBACH: Coppélius etc (*Contes d'Hoffmann*); PUCCINI: Colline (*Bohème*), Sharpless (*Butterfly*), Scarpia (*Tosca*); RAVEL: Ramiro (*Heure espagnole*); ROSSINI: Figaro (*Barbiere di Siviglia*), Don Magnifico (*Cenerentola*); SMETANA: Kezal (*Bartered Bride*); STRAUSS, R: Baron Ochs (*Rosenkavalier*); STRAVINSKY: Creon (*Oedipus Rex*); TCHAIKOVSKY: Eugene Onegin, Duke Robert & King René (*Iolanthe*); VERDI: Amonasro (*Aida*), Philip II & Grande Inquisitore (*Don Carlo*), Padre Guardiano (*Forza del destino*), Zaccaria (*Nabucco*), Iago (*Otello*), Germont (*Traviata*), Conte di Luna (*Trovatore*); WAGNER: Holländer, König Heinrich (*Lohengrin*), Hans Sachs (*Meistersinger*), Landgraf (*Tannhäuser*). Also DONIZETTI: Raimondo (*Lucia*); MONTEVERDI: Seneca (*Incoronazione di Poppea*). Recorded for: Polish companies. Gives recitals. Appears with symphony orchestra. Teaches voice. On faculty of High School of Music, Warsaw. **Res:** Nowomiyski 7 d 4, 00-271, Warsaw, Poland.

KOSZUT, URSZULA LUCIA. Lyric coloratura soprano. Polish. Resident mem: Staatsoper Vienna; State Opera Frankfurt; State Opera Warsaw. Born 13 Dec 1940, Pszczyna, Poland. Husband Gerhard Geist, occupation opera conductor. One

child. Studied: Maria Eichler-Cholewa, Katowice, Poland; Bogdan Ruskiewicz, Warsaw. **Debut:** Lucia, Stuttgart Opera 1967.

Sang with major companies in AUS: Bregenz Fest, Vienna Staatsoper; CAN: Ottawa, Toronto; FRA: Aix-en-Provence Fest, Toulouse; FR GER: Berlin Deutsche Oper, Cologne, Düsseldorf-Duisburg, Frankfurt, Hamburg, Munich Staatsoper, Nürnberg, Stuttgart; GER DR: Berlin Staatsoper; HOL: Amsterdam; ITA: Genoa; POL: Warsaw; POR: Lisbon; SWI: Basel, Geneva, Zurich; UK: Edinburgh Fest, Glasgow Scottish, Glyndebourne Fest; USA: Chicago, Houston, New Orleans, Portland. **Roles with these companies incl** BELLINI: Imogene★ (*Pirata*); DEBUSSY: Mélisande★ (*Pélléas et Mélisande*); DONIZETTI: Anna Bolena★, Norina (*Don Pasquale*), Lucia; GOUNOD: Marguerite (*Faust*); HINDEMITH: Regina (*Mathis der Maler*); MOZART: Despina (*Così fan tutte*), Konstanze (*Entführung aus dem Serail*), Königin der Nacht (*Zauberflöte*); NICOLAI: Frau Fluth (*Lustigen Weiber*); OFFENBACH: Olympia & Antonia & Giulietta (*Contes d'Hoffmann*); ORFF: Solo (*Carmina burana*); PENDERECKI: Philippe (*Teufel von Loudun*); PUCCINI: Mimi & Musetta (*Bohème*); STRAUSS, R: Fiakermilli (*Arabella*), Zerbinetta (*Ariadne auf Naxos*); VERDI: Oscar (*Ballo in maschera*), Donna Elvira★ (*Ernani*), Nannetta (*Falstaff*), Gilda (*Rigoletto*), Violetta (*Traviata*), Elena★ (*Vespri*). **World premieres:** BURKHARD: Thamar (*Ein Stern geht auf aus Jaakob*) Hamburg Opera 1970; KAGEL: Italienische & Koloratura Soprano (*Staatstheater*) Hamburg Opera 1971; STEFFENS: Miss Price (*Unter Milchwald*) Hamburg Opera 1973. Video/Film: Thamar (*Stern geht auf aus Jaakob*). Gives recitals. Appears with symphony orchestra. Teaches voice. Coaches repertoire. **Res:** Rothschildallee 18, 6 Frankfurt/M, FR Ger. Mgmt: SLZ/FRG; RAB/AUS.

KOTCHER, JAY H. Scenic designer for opera, theater. Is also a painter. American. Born 23 Dec 1946, Brooklyn, NY. Single. Studied: State Univ of NY, Binghamton 1964-68. Prof training: Feller Scenery Studios, New York 1967-68; Metropolitan Opera 1968-69. Operatic debut: Lake George Opera Fest, Glens Falls, NY 1971. Theater debut: Playhouse on the Green, Columbus, O, 1968.

Designed for major companies in USA: Kansas City, Lake George. **Operas designed for these companies incl** BRITTEN: *Rape of Lucretia★*; DONIZETTI: *Convenienze/Viva la Mamma★*; PASATIERI: *Black Widow★*; PUCCINI: *Tosca★*; ROSSINI: *Barbiere di Siviglia★*; STRAUSS, J: *Fledermaus★*; VERDI: *Rigoletto★*; WARD: *Crucible★*; WEILL: *Dreigroschenoper★*. **Res:** New York, NY, USA.

KÖTH, ERIKA. Lyric coloratura soprano. German. Resident mem: Deutsche Oper, Berlin; Bayerische Staatsoper, Munich. Born 15 Sep 1925, Darmstadt, Germany. Husband Ernst Dorn. Studied: Kmsg Else Blank, Karlsruhe, FR Ger. **Debut:** Philine (*Mignon*) Pfalzoper Kaiserslautern, FR Ger 1949. Awards: Bavarian Order of Merit, State Cross of Merit, Heinrich Merck Prize, Gold Mozart Medal.

Sang with major companies in FIN: Helsinki; FRA: Aix-en-Provence Fest, Bordeaux, Paris; FR

GER: Bayreuth Fest, Berlin Deutsche Oper, Bielefeld, Cologne, Darmstadt, Dortmund, Düsseldorf-Duisburg, Frankfurt, Hamburg, Karlsruhe, Kiel, Mannheim, Munich Staatsoper & Gärtnerplatz, Nürnberg, Saarbrücken, Stuttgart, Wiesbaden; GER DR: Berlin Komische Oper, Dresden; HOL: Amsterdam; HUN: Budapest; ITA: Florence Maggio Musicale & Comunale, Milan La Scala, Rome Teatro dell'Opera; MEX: Mexico City; UK: Edinburgh Fest, Glyndebourne Fest, London Royal Opera; USSR: Leningrad Kirov, Moscow Bolshoi; USA: Washington DC. **Roles with these companies incl** BIZET: Micaëla★ (*Carmen*); CIMAROSA: Carolina★ (*Matrimonio segreto*); DELIBES: Lakmé; DONIZETTI: Norina (*Don Pasquale*), Lucia★; EGK: Gretl (*Zaubergeige*); FLOTOW: Lady Harriet (*Martha*); GLUCK: Amor (*Orfeo ed Euridice*); GOUNOD: Marguerite (*Faust*); HAYDN: Vespina★ (*Infedeltà delusa*); HUMPERDINCK: Gretel★; LEONCAVALLO: Nedda (*Pagliacci*); LORTZING: Baronin Freimann★ (*Wildschütz*); MOZART: Fiordiligi★ & Despina (*Così fan tutte*), Donna Elvira★ & Zerlina (*Don Giovanni*), Konstanze (*Entführung aus dem Serail*), Ilia (*Idomeneo*), Susanna★ & Cherubino (*Nozze di Figaro*), Pamina★ & Königin der Nacht (*Zauberflöte*); NICOLAI: Frau Fluth (*Lustigen Weiber*); OFFENBACH: Olympia & Antonia★ (*Contes d'Hoffmann*); PUCCINI: Mimi★ & Musetta (*Bohème*), Liù★ (*Turandot*); ROSSINI: Rosina (*Barbiere di Siviglia*); STRAUSS, J: Adele★ (*Fledermaus*); STRAUSS, R: Fiakermilli★ (*Arabella*), Zerbinetta (*Ariadne auf Naxos*), Sophie★ (*Rosenkavalier*); STRAVINSKY: Anne Trulove★ (*Rake's Progress*); THOMAS: Philine★ (*Mignon*); VERDI: Oscar★ (*Ballo in maschera*), Donna Elvira★ (*Ernani*), Gilda★ (*Rigoletto*), Violetta (*Traviata*); WEBER: Aennchen★ (*Freischütz*). Recorded for: Electrola, DG, EMI, Teldec. Teaches voice. On faculty of Hochschule für Musik, Cologne. **Res:** Erika Köthstr 6, 8011 Baldham/Munich, FR Ger.

KOUBA, MARIA. Soprano. Resident mem: Städtische Oper, Frankfurt/M, FR Ger. Born Altenmarkt, Austria. Studied: Consv Graz, Austria. **Debut:** Salome, Summer Fest, Graz 1957. Awards: State Prize of Austria 1957; Winner Intl Compt, Brussels 1957; Grand Prix des Nations, Paris 1962. **Sang with major companies in** AUS: Graz, Vienna Staatsoper; BEL: Brussels; CAN: Vancouver; FRA: Paris; FR GER: Berlin Deutsche Oper, Düsseldorf-Duisburg, Frankfurt, Hamburg, Munich Staatsoper, Stuttgart; ITA: Naples; UK: London Royal; USA: Fort Worth, Milwaukee Florentine, New Orleans, New York Met, Santa Fe; et al. **Roles with these companies incl** JANACEK: Jenufa; PUCCINI: Cio-Cio-San (*Butterfly*), Tosca, Liù (*Turandot*); SMETANA: Marie (*Bartered Bride*); STRAUSS, R: Komponist (*Ariadne auf Naxos*), Octavian (*Rosenkavalier*); VERDI: Amelia (*Ballo in maschera*), Alice Ford (*Falstaff*), Leonora (*Forza del destino*), Leonora (*Trovatore*); WAGNER: Senta (*Fliegende Holländer*), Eva (*Meistersinger*); et al. Mgmt: HJH/USA.

KOUT, JIRI. Conductor of opera and symphony. Czechoslovakian. Resident Cond, National Theater, Prague. Also Resident Cond, Prague Symph Orch. Born 26 Dec 1937, Nové Dvory u Kutné Hory, CSR. Wife Kvèta, occupation singer. Studied: Music Acad Prague, Prof Karel Ancerl, Alois Klíma, Robert Brock; incl piano, violin, organ. Plays the piano. Operatic training as repetiteur at Tyl Theater, Plzen, CSSR 1964-66. **Operatic debut:** Prague 1963. Symphonic debut: Prague Symph Orch 1964. Awards: Winner Intl Compt Besançon 1965, Brussels 1969. **Conducted with major companies in** CZE: Prague National; YUG: Zagreb, Belgrade. **Operas with these companies incl** AUBER: *Fra Diavolo;* BIZET: *Carmen;* DONIZETTI: *Don Pasquale;* DVORAK: *Rusalka★,* GOUNOD: *Faust;* JANACEK: *Katya Kabanova★;* LORTZING: *Zar und Zimmermann;* MARTINU: *Comedy on the Bridge★;* MOZART: *Nozze di Figaro★;* PUCCINI: *Bohème, Manon Lescaut★;* SMETANA: *Bartered Bride★, Devil's Wall★, Secret★, Two Widows★;* TCHAIKOVSKY: *Eugene Onegin★, Pique Dame★;* VERDI: *Ballo in maschera★, Nabucco, Rigoletto★, Traviata;* WAGNER: *Tannhäuser.* Video–TV CSSR: *Eugene Onegin, Pique Dame.* Conducted major orch in Europe. Mgmt: PRG/CZE.

KOVACS, ESZTER. Dramatic soprano. Hungarian. Resident mem: State Opera, Budapest. Born 18 May 1939, Tiszanana, Hungary. Husband Laszlo Szabo. One child. Studied: Franz Liszt Acad of Music, Budapest. **Debut:** Budapest State Opera 1965. Awards: Franz Liszt Prize for Outstanding Artistry, Hungarian Gvnmt. **Sang with major companies in** CZE: Prague National; FR GER: Düsseldorf-Duisburg; GER DR: Berlin Staatsoper; HUN: Budapest; POL: Warsaw; ROM: Bucharest; SWI: Geneva; USSR: Moscow Bolshoi; USA: Washington DC. **Roles with these companies incl** BARTOK: Judith★ (*Bluebeard's Castle*); MASCAGNI: Santuzza★ (*Cavalleria rusticana*); PROKOFIEV: Fata Morgana★ (*Love for Three Oranges*); STRAUSS, R: Chrysothemis★ (*Elektra*); WAGNER: Senta★ (*Fliegende Holländer*), Sieglinde★ (*Walküre*), Brünnhilde (*Walküre★, Siegfried★, Götterdämmerung★*), Elisabeth★ & Venus★ (*Tannhäuser*). Gives recitals. Appears with symphony orchestra. **Res:** Budapest, Hungary. Mgmt: ITK/HNG; LSM/UK.

KOVÁTS, KOLOS. Bass. Hungarian. Resident mem: Budapest State Opera. Born 31 Jan 1948, Mohács, Hungary. Wife Ildikó Kovács, occupation teacher. One child. Studied: Mrs Ferenc Révhegyi, Hungary. **Debut:** Padre Guardiano (*Forza del destino*) Budapest State Opera 1970. Awards: First Prize Caruso Singing Compt, Rio de Janeiro 1973; Second Prize Tchaikovsky Singing Compt, Moscow 1974; First Prize Ferenc Erkel Singing Compt, Budapest 1970. **Sang with major companies in** FR GER: Frankfurt, Wiesbaden; HUN: Budapest. **Roles with these companies incl** MOZART: Sarastro★ (*Zauberflöte*); MUSSORGSKY: Dosifei★ (*Khovanschchina*); PROKOFIEV: King of Clubs★ (*Love for Three Oranges*); PUCCINI: Colline★ (*Bohème*); ROSSINI: Guillaume Tell★‡; VERDI: Philip II★ (*Don Carlo*), Don Carlo★ & Padre Guardiano★ (*Forza del destino*), Pagano★ (*Lombardi*); WAGNER: Fafner★ (*Siegfried*). Also RANKI: The

King★ (*King Pomadé's New Suit*). Recorded for: EMI, Qualiton. Gives recitals. Appears with symphony orchestra. **Res:** 1144 Ond vezpr u 5/7, Budapest, Hungary. Mgmt: ITK/HUN; ALL/UK; SMN/USA.

KRAAK, MEINARD. Lyric baritone. Dutch. Resident mem: Netherlands Opera, Amsterdam. Born 29 Dec 1938, Winschoten, Holland. Single. Studied: Amsterdam Consv, Jan Keizer; Pierre Bernac, Paris. **Debut:** Junius (*Rape of Lucretia*) 1966. Awards: First Prize Concours Ravel, Paris 1964.
Sang with major companies in HOL: Amsterdam. **Roles with these companies incl** DEBUSSY: Pelléas★; DONIZETTI: Belcore (*Elisir*); FORTNER: Don Perlimplin; HENZE: Landarzt★; MOZART: Guglielmo★ (*Così fan tutte*); PERGOLESI: Uberto★ (*Serva padrona*); THOMAS: Hamlet★. **World premieres:** DE KRUYF: Spinoza (*Spinoza*) The Hague 1971. Gives recitals. Appears with symphony orchestra. Teaches voice. Coaches repertoire. On faculty of Koninklyk Consv, The Hague. **Res:** Palestrinastr 4, Amsterdam, Holland. Mgmt: SLL/HOL.

KRACHMALNICK, SAMUEL. Conductor of opera and symphony. American. Born 1 Sep 1928, St Louis, MO. Wife Gloria Lane, occupation opera singer. Two children. Studied: Juilliard School of Music, Mo Jean Morel, NY; incl piano & Fr horn. **Operatic debut:** *Saint of Bleecker Street* Broadway, New York 1954. Symphonic debut: Boston Pops Orch, Des Moines, IA 1951. Previous occupations: horn player, Ntl Symph Orch, Washington DC. Awards: Koussevitzky Mem Prize; Frederic Mann Prize; both Tanglewood Fest, MA.
Conducted at major companies in CAN: Montreal/Quebec, Ottawa, Toronto, Vancouver; ITA: Genoa, Rome Opera; MEX: Mexico City; SWI: Zurich; USA: Cincinnati, New York City Opera, Portland, Seattle. **Operas conducted with these companies incl** BERNSTEIN: *Trouble in Tahiti;* BIZET: *Carmen★;* BRITTEN: *Peter Grimes, Rape of Lucretia;* DALLAPICCOLA: *Prigioniero;* DEBUSSY: *Enfant prodigue, Pelléas et Mélisande★;* DONIZETTI: *Don Pasquale;* FLOYD: *Markheim★, Susannah;* GAY/Britten: *Beggar's Opera;* GOUNOD: *Faust★;* HINDEMITH: *Hin und zurück;* IBERT: *Angélique;* LEONCAVALLO: *Pagliacci★;* MASCAGNI: *Cavalleria rusticana★;* MASSENET: *Manon★;* MENOTTI: *Amelia al ballo, Consul★, Old Maid and the Thief★;* MEYERBEER: *Prophète;* MOZART: *Nozze di Figaro;* OFFENBACH: *Contes d'Hoffmann★;* PUCCINI: *Bohème, Gianni Schicchi★, Butterfly, Tosca★;* PURCELL: *Dido and Aeneas;* ROSSINI: *Barbiere di Siviglia, Cenerentola, Comte Ory★;* SAINT-SAENS: *Samson et Dalila;* STRAUSS, J: *Fledermaus;* STRAUSS, R: *Salome★;* STRAVINSKY: *Mavra;* VERDI: *Otello, Rigoletto, Traviata★, Trovatore;* WAGNER: *Fliegende Holländer;* WARD: *Crucible.* Also MOORE: *Carry Nation;* BLITZSTEIN: *Regina;* GOUNOD: *Médecin malgré lui.* **World premieres:** PANNELL: *Luck of Ginger Coffey* Canadian Opera Co, Toronto 1967. Recorded for Columbia, Desto. Conducted major orch in Europe, USA/Canada, Cent/S America. Teaches at School of Music, Univ of Washington,

Seattle. **Res:** 901-129th Pl NE, Bellevue 98005, WA, USA.

KRAEMER, HANS; né Franz Krämer. Bass. German, DR. Resident mem: Städtisches Opernhaus Leipzig. Born 20 May 1906, Mainz, Germany. Wife Hannelore. Studied: Prof Otto Iro, Vienna. **Debut:** Ferrando (*Trovatore*) Hanau, Germany 1936. Previous occupations: sculptor. Awards: Kammersänger, Hon Mem, Städtische Oper Leipzig; NPT Art Prize, Gvnmt Ger DR.
Sang with major companies in CZE: Brno, Prague National; FRA: Paris; FR GER: Berlin Deutsche Oper; GER DR: Berlin Komische Oper & Staatsoper, Dresden, Leipzig; USSR: Moscow Bolshoi; YUG: Zagreb, Belgrade. **Roles with these companies incl** BIZET: Zurga (*Pêcheurs de perles*); EGK: Cuperus★ (*Zaubergeige*); FLOTOW: Plunkett (*Martha*); GOUNOD: Méphistophélès (*Faust*); HANDEL: Bertaric (*Rodelinda*); HINDEMITH: Professor (*Hin und zurück*); LEONCAVALLO: Tonio (*Pagliacci*); LORTZING: Stadinger★‡ (*Waffenschmied*); MOZART: Don Alfonso (*Così fan tutte*), Don Giovanni★, Sarastro★ (*Zauberflöte*); MUSSORGSKY: Pimen★ (*Boris Godunov*); NICOLAI: Falstaff‡ (*Lustigen Weiber*); PUCCINI: Colline (*Bohème*); ROSSINI: Don Basilio (*Barbiere di Siviglia*); STRAUSS, R: Baron Ochs (*Rosenkavalier*); SUCHON: Stelina (*Whirlpool*); TCHAIKOVSKY: Eugene Onegin; VERDI: Ramfis★ (*Aida*), Philip II★ (*Don Carlo*), Padre Guardiano★ (*Forza del destino*), Banquo (*Macbeth*), Nabucco★ & Zaccaria★ (*Nabucco*); WAGNER: Daland★ (*Fliegende Holländer*), König Heinrich★ (*Lohengrin*), Pogner★ (*Meistersinger*), Steffano Colonna (*Rienzi*), Fafner (*Rheingold*), Hunding (*Walküre*), Landgraf★ (*Tannhäuser*), König Marke (*Tristan und Isolde*); WEBER: Kaspar (*Freischütz*), WOLF-FERRARI: Lunardo (*Quattro rusteghi*). Recorded for: Eterna u Amiga DDR. Video/Film: Falstaff (*Lustigen Weiber*). Gives recitals. Appears with symphony orchestra. Teaches voice. Coaches repertoire. On faculty of Hochschule für Musik, Leipzig. **Res:** Grassistr 8, Leipzig, Ger DR.

KRAFT, JEAN MARIE. Dramatic mezzo-soprano. American. Resident mem: Metropolitan Opera, New York. Born 9 Jan, Menasha, WI, USA. Husband Richard N Elias, occupation violinist Met Op Orch. Studied: Curtis Inst of Music, Mme Giannini Gregory, Philadelphia; Theodore Harrison, Chicago; William Ernst Vedal, Munich; Felix Wolfes, coach, Boston; Mme Povla Frijsch, New York. **Debut:** Mother (*Six Characters in Search of an Author*) New York City Opera 1963. Previous occupations: started age 4 with piano, later clarinet and trumpet. Awards: Beebe Schlshp New England Consv, Boston.
Sang with major companies in USA: Boston, Fort Worth, Houston, New Orleans, New York Met & City Opera, St Paul, Santa Fe. **Roles with these companies incl** BERG: Gräfin Geschwitz★ (*Lulu*); BRITTEN: Kate Julian★ (*Owen Wingrave*), Miss Jessel (*Turn of the Screw*); DONIZETTI: Marquise de Birkenfeld★ (*Fille du régiment*); MENOTTI: Mme Flora (*Medium*), Miss Todd (*Old Maid and the Thief*); MOORE:

Augusta Tabor (*Baby Doe*); MOZART: Ramiro (*Finta giardiniera*), Cherubino (*Nozze di Figaro*); PENDERECKI: Ninon★ (*Teufel von Loudun*); POULENC: Prioresse★ (*Dialogues des Carmélites*); PROKOFIEV: Clarissa (*Love for Three Oranges*); PUCCINI: Suzuki★ (*Butterfly*); STRAUSS, J: Prinz Orlovsky (*Fledermaus*); STRAUSS, R: Herodias★(*Salome*); VERDI: Amneris★ (*Aida*), Ulrica★ (*Ballo in maschera*), Federica★(*Luisa Miller*). Also PUCCINI: Zita (*Gianni Schicchi*). **World premieres:** BUCCI: Laura (*Tale for a Deaf Ear*) Berkshire Fest, MA, USA 1957. Video/Film: Ramiro (*Finta giardiniera*). Gives recitals. Appears with symphony orchestra. Teaches voice. **Res:** 124 W 79 St, New York, USA. **Mgmt:** LLF/USA.

KRAINIK, ARDIS. American. Asst Mng, Lyric Opera of Chicago & The Opera School of Chicago, 20 No Wacker Dr, Chicago, IL 60606, USA. In charge of adm, art & educ matters; is a form singer. Born 8 Mar 1929, Manitowoc, WI. Single. Studied: Northwestern Univ, Evanston, IL. Plays the piano. Previous occupations: teacher of drama & publ speaking, Racine, WI; mezzo-soprano Lyric Opera of Chicago. Started in adm with present co 1954 as Exec Secy; in present position since 1960. Mem of & Consult, Virginia Opera Assn. **Res:** Chicago, IL, USA.

KRAM, DAVID IAN. Conductor of opera and symphony; composer. British. Resident Cond, Nationaltheater Mannheim, FR Ger. Born 17 Mar 1948, London. Wife Toni Ann, occupation physiotherapist. One child. Studied: Royal Coll of Music, London; Prof Luigi Ricci, Rome; incl piano, violin and voice. Plays the piano. Operatic training as repetiteur & asst cond at Centre Lyrique, Grand Théâtre, Geneva 1969-70; Stadttheater Basel, Switzerland 1970-71. **Operatic debut:** *Retablo de Maese Pedro* Spoleto Fest, Italy 1969. Symphonic debut: Basler Orchestergesellschaft, Switzerland 1971. Previous adm positions in opera: Resident Cond, Stadttheater Basel 1971-75.

Conducted with major companies in FR GER: Mannheim; ITA: Spoleto Fest; SWI: Basel, Geneva. **Operas with these companies incl** AUBER: *Fra Diavolo★;* BRITTEN: *Albert Herring;* DONIZETTI: *Elisir;* FALLA: *Retablo de Maese Pedro;* GLUCK: *Orfeo ed Euridice★;* MOZART: *Così fan tutte, Nozze di Figaro★, Zauberflöte★;* PUCCINI: *Bohème★, Fanciulla del West★, Tosca★;* RAVEL: *Heure espagnole;* ROSSINI: *Barbiere di Siviglia★;* STRAUSS, J: *Fledermaus★;* TCHAIKOVSKY: *Eugene Onegin★.* Conducted major orch in Europe. **Res:** Mannheim, FR Ger.

KRAMPEN, ELKE. Lyric soprano, deutsche Soubrette. German. Resident mem: Nationaltheater, Mannheim. Born 31 May 1948, Wuppertal. Single. Studied: Folkwang-Hochschule Essen, Prof Hilde Wesselmann, FR Ger. **Debut:** Erster Knabe (*Zauberflöte*) Staatsoper Stuttgart 1969.

Sang with major companies in FR GER: Cologne, Karlsruhe, Kassel, Mannheim, Munich Staatsoper, Nürnberg, Stuttgart. **Roles with these companies incl** BRITTEN: Helena★ (*Midsummer Night*); HUMPERDINCK: Gretel★; LORTZING: Gretchen★ (*Wildschütz*); MOZART: Despina★ (*Così fan tutte*); ROSSINI: Elvira★

(*Italiana in Algeri*); WEBER: Aennchen★ (*Freischütz*). Gives recitals. Appears with symphony orchestra. **Mgmt:** PAS/FRG; SLZ/FRG; ARM/FRG.

KRAUS, ALFREDO; né Alfredo Kraus Trujillo. Lyric tenor. Spanish. Born 24 Nov 1927, Las Palmas, Canary Islands, Spain. Wife Rosa Blanca Ley Bird. Four children. Studied: Gali Marcof, Barcelona; Francisco Andrés, Valencia; Mercedes Llopart, Milan. **Debut:** Duca di Mantova (*Rigoletto*) Royal Theater, Cairo 1956. Previous occupations: indust techn engineer. Awards: First Silver Medal, Conc Intl Geneva 1956; Orden Santiago de Espadas, Repub de Portugal; Encomienda de Isabel la Catolica, Spain.

Sang with major companies in ARG: Buenos Aires; AUS: Salzburg Fest, Vienna Staatsoper; FRA: Marseille; FR GER: Wiesbaden Opera; ITA: Bologna, Florence Comunale, Genoa, Milan La Scala, Naples, Palermo, Parma, Rome Opera & Caracalla, Trieste, Turin, Venice; MEX: Mexico City; POR: Lisbon; SPA: Barcelona, Canary Isl Las Palmas Fest; SWI: Geneva; UK: Edinburgh Fest, London Royal; USA: Chicago, Dallas, Hartford, New York Metropolitan Opera, Philadelphia Lyric, San Francisco Opera. **Roles with these companies incl** BELLINI: Lord Arthur★ (*Puritani*), Elvino (*Sonnambula*); BIZET: Nadir★‡ (*Pêcheurs de perles*); BOITO: Faust (*Mefistofele*); DONIZETTI: Ernesto★ (*Don Pasquale*), Nemorino (*Elisir*), Fernand (*Favorite*), Tonio★ (*Fille du régiment*), Charles★ (*Linda di Chamounix*), Edgardo★ (*Lucia*), Gennaro‡ (*Lucrezia Borgia*); FALLA: Paco (*Vida breve*); GOUNOD: Faust; MASSENET: Des Grieux★ (*Manon*), Werther; MOZART: Ferrando‡ (*Così fan tutte*), Don Ottavio (*Don Giovanni*); ORFF: Solo (*Carmina burana*); POULENC: Chevalier de la Force★ (*Dialogues des Carmélites*); PUCCINI: Rodolfo★ (*Bohème*), Rinuccio★ (*Gianni Schicchi*), Pinkerton★(*Butterfly*), Cavaradossi★(*Tosca*); ROSSINI: Almaviva★ (*Barbiere di Siviglia*); VERDI: Fenton★‡ (*Falstaff*), Duca di Mantova★ (*Rigoletto*), Alfredo (*Traviata*). Also CHERUBINI: Nadir (*Ali Baba*); RAVEL: Gonzalve (*Heure espagnole*); ARRIETA: Jorge (*Marina*); OFFENBACH: Hoffmann. Recorded for: EMI, RCA, Ricordi, Carillon. Gives recitals. **Res:** c/o Laureano Irazazabal, Eresma 12, Madrid, Spain.

KRAUSE, TOM. Baritone. Finnish. Born Helsinki. Wife Jean. Studied: Akad für Musik, Margot Skoda, Sergio Nazor, Rudolf Bautz, Vienna. **Debut:** Escamillo (*Carmen*) Städtische Oper, Berlin 1959. Previous occupations: studied medicine. Awards: Kammersänger; Bach Medal, Hamburg; hon mem Delta Omicron.

Sang with major companies in ARG: Buenos Aires; AUS: Salzburg Fest, Vienna Staatsoper; BEL: Brussels; FIN: Helsinki; FRA: Bordeaux, Paris, Toulouse; FR GER: Bayreuth Fest, Berlin Deutsche Oper, Cologne, Hamburg, Hannover, Mannheim, Munich Staatsoper; HOL: Amsterdam; ITA: Bologna, Milan La Scala, Rome Opera, Verona Arena; UK: Glyndebourne Fest, London English National; USA: Chicago, New York Met. **Roles with these companies incl** BEETHOVEN: Don Pizarro★‡ (*Fidelio*); BIZET: Escamillo★‡ (*Carmen*); BRITTEN: Demetrius (*Midsummer*

Night); DONIZETTI: Dott Malatesta★‡ (*Don Pasquale*), Enrico★ (*Lucia*); GLUCK: Thoas (*Iphigénie en Tauride*); HANDEL: Ptolemy★ (*Giulio Cesare*); HAYDN: Nanni (*Infedeltà delusa*); JANACEK: Gorianchikov★ (*From the House of the Dead*); MASCAGNI: Alfio (*Cavalleria rusticana*); MOZART: Guglielmo★‡ (*Così fan tutte*), Don Giovanni★, Conte Almaviva★ & Figaro★ (*Nozze di Figaro*); OFFENBACH: Coppélius etc★ (*Contes d'Hoffmann*); PUCCINI: Marcello★ (*Bohème*), Sharpless★ (*Butterfly*); ROSSINI: Conte Asdrubal (*Pietra del paragone*), Sultan Selim (*Turco in Italia*); SEARLE: Hamlet; STRAUSS, R: Graf (*Capriccio*), Orest★‡ (*Elektra*); STRAVINSKY: Creon★‡ (*Oedipus Rex*), Nick Shadow (*Rake's Progress*); VERDI: Amonasro★ (*Aida*), Rodrigo★ (*Don Carlo*), Ford★ (*Falstaff*), Don Carlo★ (*Forza del destino*), Iago (*Otello*), Germont (*Traviata*); WAGNER: Amfortas★ (*Parsifal*), Wolfram★ (*Tannhäuser*). Also on records only WAGNER: Kurwenal (*Tristan und Isolde*). World premieres: KRENEK: Jason (*Goldene Bock*) 1964; EINEM: Herr von Lipps (*Zerrissene*) 1964; SEARLE: Hamlet 1968; all at Hamburg. Recorded for: Decca-London, DG, EMI. Video/Film: Almaviva (*Nozze di Figaro*), Alfio (*Cavalleria rusticana*). Gives recitals. Appears with symphony orchestra. **Res:** Hamburg, FR Ger. Mgmt: GLZ/FRA; HUR/USA.

KREMIN, INGRID; née Hofmann. Lyric soprano & soubrette. German. Born 19 Aug 1944, Danzig, Germany. Husband Klaus Kremin, occupation certif engr. One child. Studied: Prof Dürr, Tonio Larisch, Hannover; Margot Müller, Hagen, FR Ger. **Debut:** Marie (*Waffenschmied*) Stadttheater Hagen 1968. Previous occupations: perf in musical comedy.
  Sang with major companies in FR GER: Hannover, Kassel. **Roles with these companies incl** BIZET: Micaëla (*Carmen*); DONIZETTI: Norina (*Don Pasquale*); DVORAK: Rusalka; GLUCK: Euridice & Amor (*Orfeo ed Euridice*); HAYDN: Sandrina (*Infedeltà delusa*); LEONCAVALLO: Nedda (*Pagliacci*); LORTZING: Marie (*Waffenschmied*), Gretchen★ (*Wildschütz*); MONTEVERDI: Euridice (*Favola d'Orfeo*); MOZART: Zerlina★ (*Don Giovanni*), Susanna★ (*Nozze di Figaro*), Pamina (*Zauberflöte*); NICOLAI: Aennchen★ (*Lustigen Weiber*); PUCCINI: Lauretta (*Gianni Schicchi*); SMETANA: Marie (*Bartered Bride*); STRAUSS, J: Adele (*Fledermaus*); WEBER: Aennchen★ (*Freischütz*); WOLF-FERRARI: Rosaura (*Donne curiose*), Lucieta (*Quattro rusteghi*). Also MOZART: Papagena★ (*Zauberflöte*). Gives recitals. Appears with symphony orchestra. Mgmt: PAS/FRG.

KRILOVICI, MARINA. Spinto soprano. German. Born 11 Jun 1942, Bucharest, Romania. Husband Kostas Paskalis, occupation opera singer, baritone. One child. Studied: Lidia Vrabiescu-Vatianu, Bucharest; Maria Caniglia, Italy; Mo Luigi Ricci, Rome. **Debut:** Donna Anna (*Don Giovanni*) Opera Bucharest 1967. Awards: First Prize & Gold Medal, Intl Compt G Enesco 1964; First Prize Intl Compt Brussels 1966; First Prize 's Hertogenbosch; First Prize Montreal Compt 1967.
  Sang with major companies in AUS: Vienna Staatsoper; **CAN:** Montreal/Quebec, Toronto; **FRA:** Strasbourg; **GRE:** Athens Fest; **FR GER:** Berlin Deutsche Oper, Hamburg, Karlsruhe, Munich Staatsoper, Saarbrücken, Wiesbaden; **HOL:** Amsterdam; **ITA:** Venice; **POR:** Lisbon; **ROM:** Bucharest; **UK:** London Royal; **USA:** Chicago, Dallas, Houston, New Orleans, New York Met, San Francisco Opera. **Roles with these companies incl** BERLIOZ: Marguerite★ (*Damnation de Faust*); BIZET: Micaëla★ (*Carmen*); BOITO: Margherita★ (*Mefistofele*); CILEA: Adriana Lecouvreur★; GIORDANO: Maddalena★ (*Andrea Chénier*), Fedora★; GOUNOD: Marguerite★ (*Faust*); MASCAGNI: Santuzza★‡ (*Cavalleria rusticana*); MOZART: Donna Anna★ (*Don Giovanni*); PUCCINI: Mimi★ (*Bohème*), Cio-Cio-San★ (*Butterfly*), Manon Lescaut★, Giorgetta★ (*Tabarro*), Tosca★, Liù★ (*Turandot*); PURCELL: Dido★; TCHAIKOVSKY: Tatiana★ (*Eugene Onegin*), Lisa★ (*Pique Dame*); VERDI: Aida★, Amelia★ (*Ballo in maschera*), Elisabetta★ (*Don Carlo*), Alice Ford★ (*Falstaff*), Leonora★ (*Forza del destino*), Desdemona★ (*Otello*), Amelia★ (*Simon Boccanegra*), Leonora★ (*Trovatore*). **World premieres:** POPOVICI: Mariana Pineda, Television Bucharest 1968. Recorded for: Electrecord Romania. Video – BBC London: Micaëla (*Carmen*). Gives recitals. Appears with symphony orchestra. **Res:** Schwedenplatz 3, Vienna, Austria; or Athens, Greece. Mgmt: EUM/FRA; CAM/USA.

KROGH, YNGVAR RONALD. Lyric & dramatic baritone. Norwegian. Resident mem: Norwegian Opera, Oslo. Born 20 Mar 1934, Oslo. Wife Jorunn Guldahl, occupation nurse. Studied: Haldis Ingebjart Isene, Philip Krömer, Oslo; Joel Berglund, Stockholm; Mo Luigi Ricci, Rome. **Debut:** Page (*Amahl*) Det Nye Teater, Oslo 1955. Previous occupations: student of art hist. Awards: finalist, Aftenposten Compt 1961; Italian State Schlshp 1962-63.
  Sang with major companies in FRA: Nancy; **FR GER:** Bielefeld, Mannheim, Saarbrücken; **NOR:** Oslo; **SPA:** Barcelona; **SWI:** Zurich. **Roles with these companies incl** BEETHOVEN: Don Pizarro★ (*Fidelio*); BIZET: Escamillo★ (*Carmen*); BORODIN: Prince Igor; DONIZETTI: Enrico (*Lucia*); GIORDANO: Carlo Gérard (*Andrea Chénier*); GLUCK: Agamemnon (*Iphigénie en Aulide*), Thoas (*Iphigénie en Tauride*); HINDEMITH: Professor (*Hin und zurück*); LEONCAVALLO: Tonio★ (*Pagliacci*); LORTZING: Peter I (*Zar und Zimmermann*); MARTIN: Marc (*Vin herbé*); MASCAGNI: Alfio★ (*Cavalleria rusticana*); MILHAUD: Dionysos (*Abandon d'Ariane*), Hippolyte (*Délivrance de Thésée*), Pergamon (*Enlèvement d'Europe*); MOZART: Conte Almaviva★ & Figaro (*Nozze di Figaro*); ORFF: Solo (*Carmina burana*); PUCCINI: Sharpless★ (*Butterfly*), Scarpia★ (*Tosca*); ROSSINI: Figaro (*Barbiere di Siviglia*); STRAUSS, R: Mandryka (*Arabella*), Jochanaan (*Salome*); VERDI: Amonasro★ (*Aida*), Rodrigo (*Don Carlo*), Nabucco, Iago (*Otello*), Rigoletto★, Germont (*Traviata*), Conte di Luna★ (*Trovatore*); WAGNER: Telramund (*Lohengrin*), Gunther (*Götterdämmerung*). Also GOUNOD: Valentin (*Faust*); LORTZING: Kühleborn (*Undine*); STRAUSS, R: Faninal (*Rosenkavalier*); TCHAIKOVSKY: Dunois (*Maid of Orleans*). **World pre-**

mieres: LEHMANN: Nachrichtensprecher (*Wette*) Stadttheater Saarbrücken 1966. Gives recitals. Appears with symphony orchestra. **Res:** Michelet 38 K, Oslo, Norway. Mgmt: NRK/NOR.

KROMBHOLC, JAROSLAV. Conductor of opera and symphony; composer. Czechoslovakian. Resident Cond, National Theater, Prague. Also Music Dir, Czechoslovak Broadcast Symph Orch, Prague since 1973. Born 30 Jan 1918, Prague. Wife Maria Tauberová, occupation singer. Studied: Vítezslav Novák, Václav Talich; incl piano, violin. Operatic training as repetiteur & asst cond at National Theater, Prague 1940-43. **Operatic debut:** National Theater, Prague 1944. Symphonic debut: Czech Phil Orch, Prague 1941. Awards: Ntl Artist, President of CSSR 1966; Laureate of the State, President of CSSR 1955.

Conducted with major companies in AUS: Bregenz Fest, Vienna Staatsoper & Volksoper; BRA: Rio de Janeiro; BUL: Sofia; CZE: Brno, Prague National; FIN: Helsinki; FR GER: Hamburg, Hannover; GER DR: Berlin Staatsoper, Dresden; HOL: Amsterdam; ITA: Bologna, Naples; POR: Lisbon; ROM: Bucharest; SPA: Barcelona; SWI: Geneva, Zurich; UK: Edinburgh Fest, London Royal; USSR: Moscow Bolshoi & Stanislavski, **Operas with these companies incl** BERG: *Wozzeck;* BRITTEN: *Albert Herring;* DVORAK: *Rusalka*⋆‡; GOUNOD: *Faust;* JANACEK: *Excursions of Mr Broucek*⋆, *Jenufa*⋆, *Katya Kabanova*⋆; MOZART: *Don Giovanni*⋆, *Idomeneo*⋆, *Nozze di Figaro, Zauberflöte;* MUSSORGSKY: *Boris Godunov;* ORFF: *Carmina burana;* PROKOFIEV: *Love for Three Oranges, War and Peace;* SHOSTAKOVICH: *Katerina Ismailova;* SMETANA: *Bartered Bride*⋆‡, *Dalibor*⋆‡, *The Kiss, Libuse*⋆‡, *Secret*‡, *Two Widows*⋆‡; STRAUSS, R: *Elektra, Salome*⋆; SUCHON: *Whirlpool;* TCHAIKOVSKY: *Eugene Onegin, Pique Dame*⋆; WAGNER: *Walküre*⋆. Also MARTINU: *Julietta;* RIMSKY-KORSAKOV: *Snow Maiden;* FOERSTER: *Eva, Jessica;* OSTRCIL: *Johnny's Kingdom;* FIBICH: *Sarka, Bride of Messina;* KUBELIK: *Veronica.* **World premieres:** CIKKER: *Resurrection* National Theater, Prague 1962. Recorded for Supraphon, Prague; Ariola Eurodisc, FR Ger. Video/Film – ZDF TV Munich; CSSR TV; Bavarian Films; CSSR Films: *Bartered Bride.* Conducted major orch in Europe, Cent/S America. **Res:** Pravá 13, R 147 00 Prague 4, CSSR. Mgmt PRG/CZE; SLZ/FRG.

KRUGER, RUDOLF. Conductor of opera and symphony. American. Gen Mng & Mus Dir, Fort Worth Opera Assn, TX, USA. Born 30 Oct, Berlin, Germany. Wife Ruth Elizabeth, occupation singer. One son, one daughter. Studied: State Acad of Music, Vienna, Felix von Weingartner, Erich Zeisl, Josef Krips; Julius Pruwer, Berthold Goldschmidt, Berlin; incl violin, Max Rostal, B Schwarz, and piano, Bruno Eisner. Plays the violin and piano. Operatic training as repetiteur, asst cond & chorus master at New Orleans Opera House Assn, LA 1942-44. **Operatic debut:** *Trovatore* Jackson Opera Guild MS, USA 1948. Symphonic debut: New Orleans Symph Orch 1942. Previous occupations: violinist, pianist. Awards: Certif of recognition, TX Fed of Music Clubs; hon for contribution to Texan culture 1968; Hon citi-

zen of Dallas; Key to City, New Orleans. Previous adm positions in opera: Mus Dir, Jackson Op Guild & Mobile Op Guild 1948-55.

Conducted with major companies in FR GER: Hannover; USA: Cincinnati, Fort Worth, New Orleans. **Operas with these companies incl** BIZET: *Carmen;* DELIBES: *Lakmé;* DONIZETTI: *Don Pasquale, Elisir*⋆, *Fille du régiment*⋆, *Lucia*⋆; FLOTOW: *Martha;* GIORDANO: *Andrea Chénier;* GOUNOD: *Faust*⋆, *Roméo et Juliette;* HUMPERDINCK: *Hänsel und Gretel*⋆; LEONCAVALLO: *Pagliacci*⋆; MASCAGNI: *Cavalleria rusticana*⋆; MASSENET: *Manon;* MOZART: *Don Giovanni, Entführung aus dem Serail, Nozze di Figaro*⋆, *Zauberflöte;* MUSSORGSKY: *Boris Godunov;* OFFENBACH: *Contes d'Hoffmann*⋆; PUCCINI: *Bohème, Gianni Schicchi*⋆, *Butterfly*⋆, *Manon Lescaut, Rondine*⋆, *Tabarro*⋆, *Tosca, Turandot;* RAVEL: *Enfant et les sortilèges;* ROSSINI: *Barbiere di Siviglia*⋆; SAINT-SAENS: *Samson et Dalila*⋆; SMETANA: *Bartered Bride;* STRAUSS, J: *Fledermaus;* STRAUSS, R: *Salome*⋆; VERDI: *Aida, Ballo in maschera, Otello, Rigoletto*⋆, *Traviata*⋆, *Trovatore*⋆; WAGNER: *Lohengrin.* **World premieres:** SMITH, J: *Shepherdess and the Chimneysweep* Ft Worth Opera 1966. Conducted major orchestras in USA. Previous positions as Mus Dir with major orch: Music Dir, Ft Worth Symph, TX 1963-65. **Res:** 5732 Wessex, Fort Worth, TX, USA.

KRZYWICKI, ZDZISLAW. Bass-baritone. Polish. Resident mem: Grand Theater, Lódz, Poland. Born 8 Aug 1938, Warsaw. Single. Studied: High School of Music, Warsaw, Prof Magdalena Halfter. **Debut:** Méphistophélès (*Faust*) Opera Lódz 1967. Awards: Second Prize Intl Compt for Singers, Toulouse 1967.

Sang with major companies in BUL: Sofia; POL: Lódz. **Roles with these companies incl** BEETHOVEN: Rocco (*Fidelio*); BIZET: Escamillo (*Carmen*); BORODIN: Galitzky (*Prince Igor*); GOUNOD: Méphistophélès (*Faust*); MOZART: Don Alfonso (*Così fan tutte*), Papageno (*Zauberflöte*); OFFENBACH: Coppélius etc (*Contes d'Hoffmann*); ROSSINI: Dott Bartolo (*Barbiere di Siviglia*); VERDI: Ramfis (*Aida*), Philip II & Grande Inquisitore (*Don Carlo*). **World premieres:** TWARDOWSKI: King Herod (*Tragedy of King Herod and John the Baptist*) Grand Theater, Lódz 1969. Gives recitals. Appears with symphony orchestra. Teaches voice. Coaches repertoire. **Res:** 34 Mackiewicza St, Lódz, Poland.

KUBELIK, RAFAEL JERONYM. Conductor of opera and symphony; composer. Swiss. Mus Dir, Symph Orch Bavarian Radio, Munich. Born 29 Jun 1914, Bychory/Prague, Czechoslovakia. Wife Elsie Morison, occupation singer. One child. Studied: Consv Prague; incl violin, piano. Plays the piano. **Operatic debut:** *Bartered Bride* State Opera, Brno 1939. Symphonic debut: Czech Phil, Prague 1934. Awards: Hon mem Royal Acad Stockholm & London; Bundesverdienstkreuz Germany; Bavarian Verdienstorden; Portuguese Komturorden; Ritterorden Dannebrog; Golden Mahler Medal; Italian Bruckner Medal; Hon DM Acad Chicago. Previous adm positions in opera: State Opera, Brno, CSR 1939-41; Royal Opera House Covent Garden, London 1955-58; Metropolitan Opera, New York 1973-74.

Conducted with major companies in AUS: Salzburg Fest, Vienna Staatsoper; CZE: Brno; FR GER: Hamburg, Munich Staatsoper; HOL: Amsterdam; ITA: Milan La Scala; SWI: Geneva; UK: Glyndebourne Fest, London Royal; USA: New York Met. Operas with these companies incl BERLIOZ: Troyens*; BIZET: Carmen: BRITTEN: Peter Grimes; DVORAK: Rusalka; JANACEK: From the House of the Dead*, Jenufa*, Katya Kabanova; MOZART: Don Giovanni, Idomeneo, Zauberflöte*; MUSSORGSKY: Boris Godunov*; POULENC: Dialogues des Carmélites; PUCCINI: Bohème; SMETANA: Bartered Bride, Dalibor, The Kiss; TCHAIKOVSKY: Pique Dame; VERDI: Aida, Otello; WAGNER: Meistersinger‡, Götterdämmerung, Tristan und Isolde. Also DVORAK: Jakobin. Only on records ORFF: Oedipus Rex; PFITZNER: Palestrina; VERDI: Rigoletto; WAGNER: Lohengrin; WEBER: Oberon. World premieres: KUBELIK: Veronica State Opera Brno 1947; Cornelia Faroli State Opera Augsburg 1972. Recorded for Polydor. Conducted major orch in Europe, USA/Canada, Cent/S America, Asia, Austrl. Previous positions as Mus Dir with major orch: Czech Phil, Prague 1936-48; Chicago Sym 1950-52. Operas composed: Veronica & Cornelia Faroli, see prem; also Emperor's New Clothes, Flowers of Little Ida, Break of Day. Res: Haus im Sand, Kastanienbaum/Lucerne, Switzerland.

KUBIAK, TERESA; neé Wojtaszek. Spinto. Polish. Resident mem: Teatr Wielki, Lodz, Poland. Born 26 Dec 1937, Ldzan, Poland. Husband Janusz, occupation violoncellist. Two children. Studied: Acad of Music, Prof Olga Olgina, Lodz, Poland. Debut: Micaëla (Carmen) Teatr Wielki, Lodz 1967.

Sang with major companies in AUS: Vienna Staatsoper; CZE: Prague National; GER DR: Leipzig; ITA: Venice; POL: Lodz, Warsaw; POR: Lisbon; SPA: Barcelona; UK: Glyndebourne Fest, London Royal Opera; USSR: Tbilisi; USA: Chicago, Houston, Miami, New York Met, San Francisco Opera. Roles with these companies incl BIZET: Micaëla (Carmen); BORODIN: Jaroslavna (Prince Igor); BRITTEN: Ellen Orford* (Peter Grimes); CAVALLI: Calisto*‡; JANACEK: Jenufa*; MENOTTI: Amelia* (Amelia al ballo); MONIUSZKO: Halka*; PUCCINI: Cio-Cio-San* (Butterfly), Manon*, Giorgetta* (Tabarro), Tosca*; STRAUSS, R: Chrysothemis* (Elektra); TCHAIKOVSKY: Tatiana*‡ (Eugene Onegin), Lisa* (Pique Dame); VERDI: Aida*, Amelia* (Ballo in maschera), Leonora (Forza del destino); WAGNER: Senta* (Fliegende Holländer), Elsa* (Lohengrin); WEBER: Euryanthe*. World premieres: TWARDOWSKI: Herodiade (Tragedy of John and Herod) Teatr Wielki, Lodz 1969. Recorded for: Decca, Argo, Polskie Nagrania. Gives recitals. Appears with symphony orchestra. Teaches voice. Coaches repertoire. Affiliated: Acad of Music, Lodz. Res: Narutowicza 75E/18, Lodz 90-132, Poland. Mgmt: PAG/POL; CAM/USA.

KUCHARSKY, ANDREJ. Dramatic tenor. Czechoslovakian. Resident mem: Opera House, Dortmund; State Opera, Bratislava, Czechoslovakia. Born 6 Jan 1932, Zilina, CSR. Wife Petra, occupation opera producer. Three children. Studied: Emerich von Godin, Tito Schipa. Debut: Lenski (Eugene Onegin) Bratislava State Opera 1956. Previous occupations: veterinary surgeon. Awards: Intl Singer Compt Prague 1954, Warsaw 1955, Geneva 1956, Moscow 1957; Tchaikovsky Prize 1961.

Sang with major companies in AUS: Bregenz Fest; BUL: Sofia; CZE: Brno, Prague National & Smetana; FR GER: Berlin Deutsche Oper, Cologne, Dortmund, Düsseldorf-Duisburg, Frankfurt, Hamburg, Hannover, Karlsruhe, Krefeld, Mannheim, Munich Staatsoper, Nürnberg, Stuttgart, Wiesbaden; GER DR: Dresden, Leipzig; HUN: Budapest State Opera; ITA: Naples; POL: Lódz, Warsaw; SPA: Barcelona Liceo; SWI: Basel, Geneva; USSR: Kiev, Leningrad Kirov, Moscow Bolshoi; YUG: Belgrade. Roles with these companies incl AUBER: Fra Diavolo & Lorenzo (Fra Diavolo); BERG: Hauptmann* & Tambourmajor* (Wozzeck); BIZET: Don José* (Carmen); BORODIN: Vladimir (Prince Igor); DEBUSSY: Pelléas; DVORAK: Prince (Rusalka); FLOTOW: Lionel (Martha); GOUNOD: Faust; HALEVY: Eléazar (Juive); HINDEMITH: Apprentice (Cardillac); JANACEK: Laca* (Jenufa); LEONCAVALLO: Canio* (Pagliacci); MASCAGNI: Turiddu (Cavalleria rusticana); MOZART: Don Ottavio (Don Giovanni), Idomeneo, Tamino (Zauberflöte); MUSSORGSKY: Gritzko (Fair at Sorochinsk); PUCCINI: Rodolfo (Bohème), Rinuccio (Gianni Schicchi), Pinkerton* (Butterfly), Des Grieux (Manon Lescaut), Cavaradossi* (Tosca), Calaf* (Turandot); RIMSKY-KORSAKOV: Levko (May Night), Sadko; ROSSINI: Almaviva (Barbiere di Siviglia); SMETANA: Hans* (Bartered Bride), Dalibor, Vitek (Secret); STRAUSS, R: Ein Sänger (Rosenkavalier); SUCHON: Andrew* (Whirlpool); TCHAIKOVSKY: Lenski (Eugene Onegin), Gherman* (Pique Dame); VERDI: Radames* (Aida), Don Carlo*, Don Alvaro* (Forza del destino), Ismaele* (Nabucco), Otello*, Duca di Mantova (Rigoletto), Alfredo (Traviata), Manrico* (Trovatore), Arrigo* (Vespri); WEBER: Max (Freischütz). World premieres: CIKKER: Bajazid (Bajazid) Bratislava Opera 1957. Recorded for: Supraphon. Appears with symphony orchestra. Res: Notweg 76, 46 Dortmund-Kirchhörde, FR Ger. Mgmt: SMD/FRG; SLK/CZE.

KUCHTA, GLADYS. Dramatic soprano. American. Resident mem: Deutsche Oper Berlin. Born 16 Jun 1923, Chicopee, MA. Husband Friedrich Paasch, occupation concert agent. Studied: Consv Giuseppe Verdi, Milan; Mannes School of Music; Juilliard School of Music; Columbia Opera Workshop, Zinaida Lisichkina, New York. Debut: Donna Elvira (Don Giovanni) Florence 1951. Awards: Fulbright Schlshp 1951-52; Kammersängerin, 1963.

Sang with major companies in ARG: Buenos Aires; AUS: Vienna Staatsoper; FRA: Paris; FR GER: Bayreuth Fest, Berlin Deutsche Oper,

Düsseldorf-Duisburg, Hamburg, Kassel, Stuttgart; ITA: Florence Maggio, Genoa, Milan La Scala; UK: London Royal; USA: New York Met; et al. **Roles with these companies incl** BEETHOVEN: Leonore‡ (*Fidelio*); MASCAGNI: Santuzza (*Cavalleria rusticana*); PUCCINI: Tosca; STRAUSS, R: Elektra & Chrysothemis (*Elektra*); VERDI: Leonore (*Forza del destino*), Abigaille (*Nabucco*), Desdemona (*Otello*); WAGNER: Elsa (*Lohengrin*), Sieglinde & Brünnhilde (*Walküre*), Brünnhilde (*Siegfried*), Brünnhilde & Gutrune (*Götterdämmerung*), Isolde; et al. Also STRAUSS, R: Färberin (*Frau ohne Schatten*). Recorded for: Nonesuch. Appears with symphony orchestra. **Res:** Berlin and Düsseldorf, FR Ger.

KUEBLER, DAVID KENNETH. Lyric tenor. American. Resident mem: Stadttheater Bern, Switzerland. Born 23 Jul 1947, Detroit. Wife Elinore R, occupation bookkeeper. Studied: Thomas Peck, Chicago; Audrey Field, London. **Debut:** Tamino (*Zauberflöte*) Stadttheater Bern 1974. Awards: Ntl Opera Inst Grant 1974-75; Ntl winner WGN Aud of the Air, Ill Opera Guild 1973. **Sang with major companies in** FR GER: Karlsruhe. **Roles with these companies incl** MOZART: Ferrando★ (*Così fan tutte*), Don Ottavio★ (*Don Giovanni*), Tamino★ (*Zauberflöte*); PUCCINI: Rodolfo★ (*Bohème*), Pinkerton★ (*Butterfly*); SMETANA: Hans★ (*Bartered Bride*); STRAUSS, R: Ein Sänger★ (*Rosenkavalier*). Gives recitals. Appears with symphony orchestra. **Res:** Längenbühlstr 11, CH-3302 Moosseedorf, Switzerland. **Mgmt:** CAM/USA; RAB/AUS.

KUHN, ALFRED. Bass & basso-buffo. German. Resident mem: Staatstheater, Darmstadt. Born 2 Nov 1938, Ober-Roden, Germany. Wife Ruth, occupation gymnastics teacher. Studied: Staatl Hochschule für Musik, Prof Paul Lohmann, Frankfurt. **Debut:** Trulove (*Rake's Progress*) Staatstheater, Darmstadt 1963. **Sang with major companies in** FR GER: Darmstadt, Düsseldorf-Duisburg, Frankfurt, Krefeld, Wiesbaden, Wuppertal. **Roles with these companies incl** BEETHOVEN: Rocco★ (*Fidelio*); CIMAROSA: Geronimo (*Matrimonio segreto*); CORNELIUS: Abul Hassan★ (*Barbier von Bagdad*); DONIZETTI: Don Pasquale, Dulcamara (*Elisir*); FLOTOW: Plunkett (*Martha*); GLUCK: Thoas (*Iphigénie en Tauride*); HINDEMITH: Professor (*Hin und zurück*); LORTZING: Stadinger (*Waffenschmied*), Baculus (*Wildschütz*), Van Bett (*Zar und Zimmermann*); MASSENET: Sancho (*Don Quichotte*); MILHAUD: Pergamon★ (*Enlèvement d'Europe*); MOZART: Osmin★ (*Entführung aus dem Serail*), Nardo (*Finta giardiniera*), Don Pippo (*Oca del Cairo*), Osmin (*Zaïde*), Sarastro (*Zauberflöte*); NICOLAI: Falstaff (*Lustigen Weiber*); PAISIELLO: Bartolo (*Barbiere di Siviglia*); PERGOLESI: Uberto (*Serva padrona*); PUCCINI: Colline (*Bohème*); ROSSINI: Dott Bartolo★ & Don Basilio (*Barbiere di Siviglia*), Signor Bruschino; SMETANA: Kezal★ (*Bartered Bride*); VERDI: Philip II★ & Grande Inquisitore★ (*Don Carlo*), Fiesco (*Simon Boccanegra*); WAGNER: Daland★ (*Fliegende Holländer*), Pogner★ (*Meister-singer*), Landgraf (*Tannhäuser*); WEBER: Kaspar★ (*Freischütz*). Gives recitals. Appears with symphony orchestra. **Res:** Heidelberger Str 7, 6051 Nieder-Roden, FR Ger. **Mgmt:** SLZ/FRG.

KUHN, GUSTAV FRIEDRICH. Conductor of opera and symphony; composer. Austrian. Resident Cond, Städtische Bühnen, Dortmund. Born 28 Aug 1946, Salzburg. Married. Studied: Bruno Maderna, Hans Swarowsky, Gerhardt Wimberger; incl piano, violin, trombone, timpani. **Operatic debut:** *Fidelio* State Opera Istanbul, Turkey 1970. Symphonic debut: Mozarteum Orch, Salzburg 1969. Awards: First Prize Conductors Cont ORF, France 1969; Lilli Lehmann Medal, Mozarteum, Salzburg; Grosse Reinhardt Medaille. **Conducted with major companies in** FR GER: Dortmund, Frankfurt, Mannheim, Saarbrücken, Wuppertal; HOL: Amsterdam; ITA: Palermo. **Operas with these companies incl** BEETHOVEN: *Fidelio;* BELLINI: *Norma;* DONIZETTI: *Anna Bolena, Don Pasquale, Lucia;* GERSHWIN: *Porgy and Bess★;* GLUCK: *Orfeo ed Euridice★;* JANACEK: *Jenufa★;* KURKA: *Good Soldier Schweik★;* MOZART: *Così fan tutte, Don Giovanni★, Entführung aus dem Serail★, Nozze di Figaro★, Zauberflöte★;* OFFENBACH: *Contes d'Hoffmann★;* ORFF: *Carmina burana★;* PUCCINI: *Bohème★, Fanciulla del West, Butterfly★, Tosca★, Turandot★;* ROSSINI: *Barbiere di Siviglia;* VERDI: *Don Carlo, Nabucco, Rigoletto★, Traviata, Trovatore★.* **World premieres:** BRESGEN: *Christi Urstaend* Mozarteum Orch, Austria 1970. Conducted major orch in Europe, Asia. **Res:** Elsbethen, Salzburg A-5061, Austria. **Mgmt:** SLZ/FRG; TAU/SWI.

KÜHNE, ROLF. Dramatic baritone. German. Resident mem: Deutsche Oper Berlin; Hessisches Staatstheater, Wiesbaden. Born 11 Jun 1932, Aschersleben, Germany. Wife Gudrun. Studied: Hochschule für Musik, Berlin; Hochschule für Musik, Weimar; Hans Broermann, Berlin. **Debut:** Sarastro (*Zauberflöte*) Opernhaus Karl-Marx-Stadt, Ger DR 1956. Awards: Kammersänger, Berlin Staatsoper. **Sang with major companies in** ARG: Buenos Aires; AUS: Vienna Staatsoper; CZE: Prague Smetana; FIN: Helsinki; FRA: Nice; FR GER: Bayreuth Fest, Berlin Deutsche Oper, Bielefeld, Bonn, Cologne, Düsseldorf-Duisburg, Frankfurt, Hamburg, Hannover, Karlsruhe, Kassel, Kiel, Mannheim, Munich Staatsoper, Stuttgart, Wiesbaden; GER DR: Berlin Komische Oper & Staatsoper, Dresden, Leipzig; HOL: Amsterdam; HUN: Budapest; ITA: Bologna, Milan La Scala, Trieste, Turin; MEX: Mexico City; POL: Warsaw; SPA: Barcelona; SWE: Stockholm; SWI: Zurich; USSR: Moscow Bolshoi; USA: Chicago; YUG: Zagreb. **Roles with these companies incl** d'ALBERT: Sebastiano (*Tiefland*); BEETHOVEN: Don Pizarro★ (*Fidelio*); BERG: Doktor★ (*Wozzeck*); BIZET: Escamillo★ (*Carmen*); BORODIN: Prince Igor; BRITTEN: Traveller/etc (*Death in Venice*); GAY/Britten: Lockit (*Beggar's Opera*); LEONCAVALLO: Tonio (*Pagliacci*); MASCAGNI: Alfio★ (*Cavalleria rusticana*); MO-

ZART: Don Alfonso (*Così fan tutte*), Don Giovanni★, Conte Almaviva (*Nozze di Figaro*); ORFF: König★ (*Kluge*); PENDERECKI: Grandier (*Teufel von Loudun*); PUCCINI: Marcello★ (*Bohème*), Gianni Schicchi, Scarpia (*Tosca*); ROSSINI: Sultan Selim (*Turco in Italia*); STRAUSS, R: Mandryka (*Arabella*), Jochanaan (*Salome*); TCHAIKOVSKY: Eugene Onegin★; VERDI: Amonasro★ (*Aida*), Attila, Rodrigo & Philip II & Grande Inquisitore★ (*Don Carlo*), Don Carlo (*Forza del destino*), Macbeth & Banquo (*Macbeth*), Nabucco★, Iago (*Otello*), Rigoletto, Germont (*Traviata*); WAGNER: Holländer★ & Daland (*Fliegende Holländer*), Telramund★ (*Lohengrin*), Amfortas (*Parsifal*), Alberich (*Rheingold★, Götterdämmerung★*), Wotan (*Rheingold★, Walküre★*), Wanderer★ (*Siegfried*), Gunther (*Götterdämmerung*), Wolfram (*Tannhäuser*), Kurwenal (*Tristan und Isolde*); WEBER: Lysiart (*Euryanthe*), Kaspar★ (*Freischütz*). Also PROKOFIEV: Meressjew (*Story of a Real Man*). Gives recitals. Appears with symphony orchestra. Teaches voice.

KÜHNEL, DIETMAR. Lyric & dramatic tenor. German. Resident mem: Staatstheater Saarbrücken, FR Ger. Born 11 Nov 1942, Berlin. Wife Dietlind. One child. Studied: Hochschule für Musik, Profs Irma Beilke, Bärwinkel, Günther Wilhelms, Berlin. **Debut:** Tamino (*Zauberflöte*) Stadttheater Hildesheim, FR Ger 1969-70.
Sang with major companies in FR GER: Saarbrücken. **Roles with these companies incl** BIZET: Don José★ (*Carmen*); BRITTEN: Albert Herring; CIMAROSA: Paolino (*Matrimonio segreto*); DONIZETTI: Ernesto (*Don Pasquale*), Tonio (*Fille du régiment*); JANACEK: Steva★ (*Jenufa*); MASCAGNI: Turiddu★ (*Cavalleria rusticana*); MASSENET: Des Grieux★ (*Manon*); MOZART: Tamino (*Zauberflöte*); PUCCINI: Rodolfo (*Bohème*); SMETANA: Hans★ (*Bartered Bride*); STRAUSS, J: Eisenstein (*Fledermaus*); STRAUSS, R: Bacchus★ (*Ariadne auf Naxos*); VERDI: Duca di Mantova★ (*Rigoletto*). Gives recitals. Appears with symphony orchestra. On faculty of Hochschule für Musik, Berlin. **Res:** Berlin, FR Ger.

KUHSE, HANNE-LORE. Soprano. German. Born 1925, Schwaan/Mecklenburg. Studied: Rostock Konsv, Charlotte Menzel; Sternschen Konsv, Helene Schlusnus, Berlin; Hans Hagen. **Debut:** Städtische Bühnen, Gera 1952. Awards: Kammersängerin, 1954; Nationalpreis, Ger DR 1962.
Sang with major companies in AUS: Vienna Staatsoper; BUL: Sofia; CZE: Brno, Prague National; FRA: Paris; FR GER: Bayreuth Fest, Cologne, Hamburg; GER DR: Berlin Komische Oper & Staatsoper, Dresden, Leipzig; HUN: Budapest; ITA: Bologna, Venice; POL: Warsaw; ROM: Bucharest; USSR: Leningrad Kirov, Moscow Bolshoi; USA: Philadelphia Grand; YUG: Belgrade; et al. **Roles with these companies incl** BEETHOVEN: Leonore (*Fidelio*); BERG: Marie (*Wozzeck*); BORODIN: Jaroslavna (*Prince Igor*); BUSONI: Turandot; GLUCK: Iphigénie (*Iphigénie en Tauride*); MASCAGNI: Santuzza (*Cavalleria rusticana*); MOZART: Donna Anna (*Don Giovanni*), Königin der Nacht (*Zauberflöte*); MUSSORGSKY: Marina (*Boris Godunov*);

PUCCINI: Tosca, Turandot; SCHOENBERG: Woman (*Erwartung*); STRAUSS, R: Marschallin (*Rosenkavalier*); VERDI: Amelia (*Ballo in maschera*), Elisabetta (*Don Carlo*), Leonora (*Forza del destino*), Lady Macbeth, Abigaille (*Nabucco*), Leonora (*Trovatore*); WAGNER: Senta (*Fliegende Holländer*), Ortrud (*Lohengrin*), Irene (*Rienzi*), Brünnhilde (*Walküre, Siegfried, Götterdämmerung*), Venus (*Tannhäuser*), Isolde; et al. Also HANDEL: Polissena (*Radamisto*); EGK: Isabella (*Columbus*); d'ALBERT: Marta (*Tiefland*). Recorded for: RCA. Gives recitals. Appears with symphony orchestra. Mgmt: KDR/GDR; KAZ/USA.

KULKA, JANOS. Conductor of opera and symphony; composer. German. Resident Cond, Opera, Wuppertal 1964-76; after 1975-76 State Cond, Stuttgart Opera. Born 11 Dec 1929, Budapest. Wife Vera Mazányi. One son. Studied: Acad of Music, Kodaly, Viski, Ferencsik, Somogyi, Budapest; incl piano, double bass, percussion. Plays the piano. Operatic training as repetiteur, asst cond & asst chorus master at State Opera, Budapest 1950-56. **Operatic debut:** State Opera, Budapest 1949. Symphonic debut: State Symph Orch, Budapest 1948. Awards: Critics' Prize Teatro del Liceo, Barcelona 1973.
Conducted with major companies in ARG: Buenos Aires; AUS: Vienna Staatsoper; BEL: Brussels; DEN: Copenhagen; FR GER: Berlin Deutsche Oper, Cologne, Frankfurt, Hamburg, Kassel, Mannheim, Munich Staatsoper, Saarbrücken, Stuttgart, Wiesbaden, Wuppertal; GER DR: Leipzig; HUN: Budapest; ITA: Genoa; SPA: Barcelona; SWI: Geneva, Zurich; USA: Boston. **Operas with these companies incl** BARTOK: *Bluebeard's Castle;* BEETHOVEN: *Fidelio★;* BERG: *Lulu, Wozzeck;* BERLIOZ: *Damnation de Faust;* BIBALO: *Lächeln am Fusse der Leiter;* BIZET: *Carmen★;* CIKKER: *Play of Love and Death, Resurrection;* DALLAPICCOLA: *Prigioniero;* DONIZETTI: *Lucia★;* EINEM: *Besuch der alten Dame;* GIORDANO: *Andrea Chénier;* GLUCK: *Orfeo ed Euridice;* GOUNOD: *Faust;* HUMPERDINCK: *Hänsel und Gretel;* IBERT: *Angélique;* JANACEK: *Jenufa★, Katya Kabanova;* KLEBE: *Jakobowsky und der Oberst;* LEONCAVALLO: *Pagliacci;* LORTZING: *Wildschütz, Zar und Zimmermann;* MASCAGNI: *Cavalleria rusticana;* MILHAUD: *Médée;* MONTEVERDI: *Incoronazione di Poppea;* MOZART: *Così fan tutte, Don Giovanni★, Entführung aus dem Serail, Nozze di Figaro★, Zauberflöte★;* MUSSORGSKY: *Khovanshchina;* OFFENBACH: *Contes d'Hoffmann★;* ORFF: *Kluge;* PENDERECKI: *Teufel von Loudun★;* PERGOLESI: *Frate 'nnamorato;* PETROVICS: *Crime and Punishment;* PUCCINI: *Bohème★, Gianni Schicchi, Butterfly★, Tosca★, Turandot★;* ROSSINI: *Barbiere di Siviglia, Cenerentola;* SCHOENBERG: *Moses und Aron;* SCHULLER: *Visitation;* SMETANA: *Bartered Bride★;* STRAUSS, J: *Fledermaus;* STRAUSS, R: *Arabella, Ariadne auf Naxos, Elektra, Rosenkavalier★, Salome★, Schweigsame Frau★;* STRAVINSKY: *Oedipus Rex★;* SZOKOLAY: *Blood Wedding;* VERDI: *Aida, Ballo in maschera, Don Carlo, Due Foscari, Falstaff, Forza del destino★, Nabucco, Otello★, Rigoletto★, Simon Boccanegra, Tra-*

viata★*, Trovatore*★*;* WAGNER: *Fliegende Holländer*★*, Lohengrin*★*, Meistersinger, Walküre, Götterdämmerung, Tannhäuser;* WEILL: *Aufstieg und Fall der Stadt Mahagonny;* WERLE: *Dream of Thérèse.* Also DESSAU: *Puntila;* CAMPRA: *Carnaval de Venise;* KODALY: *Spinning Room;* SACCHINI: *Oedipe à Colone.* **World premieres:** BLACHER: *Yvonne, Prinzessin von Burgund* Opera, Wuppertal 1973; KOPPEL: *Macbeth* Royal Opera, Copenhagen 1970; PLATEN: *In the Shadow of the Mountain* Bavarian Radio & TV. Video/Film — Stuttgart prod: CIKKER: *Resurrection.* Conducted major orch in Europe, USA/Canada, S America. **Res:** Stuttgart, FR Ger.

KULLENBO, LARS BERTIL. Lyric baritone. Swedish. Resident mem: Royal Opera, Stockholm. Born 2 May 1942, Aseda, Sweden. Married. Studied: Royal Acad of Music, Stockholm; Acad of Music, Vienna; Elisabeth Rado, Vienna; Tito Gobbi, Florence. **Debut:** Silvio (*Pagliacci*) Royal Opera, Stockholm 1964. Awards: Kristina Nilsson and Jussi Björling Schlshps.
Sang with major companies in SWE: Stockholm. **Roles with these companies incl** DONIZETTI: Dott Malatesta★ (*Don Pasquale*); MOZART: Guglielmo (*Così fan tutte*), Figaro★ (*Nozze di Figaro*); PUCCINI: Marcello★ (*Bohème*); ROSSINI: Figaro★ (*Barbiere di Siviglia*); VERDI: Rigoletto★, Germont (*Traviata*).

KUNTNER, RUDOLF. Lighting designer & technician. American. Dir of Stage Operations & resident lighting designer and technician, Metropolitan Opera, New York 1951- . Born Vienna, Austria. Married. Prof training: at electr shops, Brisma Specialities, for Ziegfeld Theater; Kliegl Bros, New York, etc. Previous adm positions: lighting chief, var Broadway theaters.
Lighting at New York Met **the following operas** BARTOK: *Bluebeard's Castle;* BARBER: *Vanessa;* BEETHOVEN: *Fidelio;* BELLINI: *Norma, Sonnambula;* BERG: *Wozzeck;* BERLIOZ: *Troyens;* BIZET: *Carmen;* BRITTEN: *Peter Grimes;* CHARPENTIER: *Louise;* CILEA: *A. Lecouvreur;* DEBUSSY: *Pelléas et Mélisande;* DONIZETTI: *Elisir, Fille du régiment, Lucia;* FLOTOW: *Martha;* GIORDANO: *Andrea Chénier;* GLUCK: *Alceste;* GOUNOD: *Faust;* JANACEK: *Jenufa;* LEONCAVALLO: *Pagliacci;* MASCAGNI: *Cavalleria rusticana;* MOZART: *Così fan tutte, Don Giovanni, Nozze di Figaro, Zauberflöte;* MUSSORGSKY: *Boris Godunov;* OFFENBACH: *Contes d'Hoffmann, Périchole;* PONCHIELLI: *Gioconda;* PUCCINI: *Bohème, Fanciulla del West, Gianni Schicchi, Butterfly, Manon Lescaut, Tosca, Turandot;* ROSSINI: *Barbiere di Siviglia, Italiana in Algeri, Assedio di Corinto;* SAINT-SAENS: *Samson et Dalila;* STRAUSS, R: *Arabella, Ariadne auf Naxos, Elektra, Frau ohne Schatten, Rosenkavalier, Salome;* STRAVINSKY: *Rake's Progress;* TCHAIKOVSKY: *Eugene Onegin, Pique Dame;* VERDI: *Aida, Ballo in maschera, Don Carlo, Ernani, Forza del destino, Luisa Miller, Macbeth, Nabucco, Otello, Rigoletto, Simon Boccanegra, Traviata, Trovatore;* WAGNER: *Fliegende Holländer, Lohengrin, Meistersinger, Parsifal, Rheingold, Walküre, Siegfried, Götterdämmerung,*

Tannhäuser, Tristan und Isolde; WEBER: *Freischütz.*

KUNZ, ERICH. Basso-buffo. Austrian. Resident mem: Staatsoper, Vienna. Born 20 May 1909, Vienna. Wife Friedl. Two children. Studied: Acad for Music, Theo Lierhammer, Vienna. **Debut:** Beckmesser (*Meistersinger*) Vienna Staatsoper 1941. Awards: Mozart Medal; Austrian Order 1st Class for Arts & Sciences; Gold Medal, City of Vienna; Hon Mem, Vienna Staatsoper.
Sang with major companies in ARG: Buenos Aires; AUS: Bregenz Fest, Salzburg Fest, Vienna Staatsoper & Volksoper; BEL: Brussels; BUL: Sofia; CZE: Prague National; DEN: Copenhagen; FRA: Aix-en-Provence Fest, Paris; FR GER: Bayreuth, Berlin Deutsche Oper, Frankfurt, Hamburg, Munich Staatsoper, Wiesbaden; HUN: Budapest; ITA: Florence Maggio & Comunale, Genoa, Milan La Scala, Naples, Rome Opera, Trieste, Venice; MON: Monte Carlo; NOR: Oslo; POR: Lisbon; SWE: Stockholm; SWI: Geneva, Zurich; UK: Edinburgh Fest, Glyndebourne Fest, London Royal & English National; USSR: Moscow Bolshoi; USA: Chicago, New York Met, San Antonio. **Roles with these companies incl** DONIZETTI: Dott Malatesta (*Don Pasquale*); LORTZING: Baculus (*Wildschütz*), Van Bett (*Zar und Zimmermann*); MOZART: Guglielmo★ (*Così fan tutte*), Don Giovanni★, Figaro★ (*Nozze di Figaro*), Papageno★ (*Zauberflöte*); MUSSORGSKY: Varlaam★ (*Boris Godunov*); PUCCINI: Gianni Schicchi★; ROSSINI: Dott Bartolo★ (*Barbiere di Siviglia*); SMETANA: Kezal★ (*Bartered Bride*); STRAUSS, R: Musiklehrer★ (*Ariadne auf Naxos*); VERDI: Fra Melitone★ (*Forza del destino*); WAGNER: Beckmesser★ (*Meistersinger*). Recorded for: His Master's Voice/Columbia. Appears with symphony orchestra. Teaches voice. **Res:** Grinzingerstr 35, A-1190 Vienna, Austria.

KUPFER, HARRY. Stages/produces opera & theater. German. Director of Theater & Chief Stage Director at Staatsoper Dresden, Ger DR. Born 12 Aug 1935, Berlin. Wife Marianne Fischer. One child. Studied: Hochschule für Theaterwissenschaft, Leipzig; incl music. Operatic training as asst stage dir at Halle Operntheater. **Operatic debut:** Nationaltheater Weimar, Ger DR 1967. Awards: Kunstpreis, Ministry of Culture, Ger DR. Previous adm positions in opera: Gen Dir, Nationaltheater Weimar 1967-72.
Directed/produced opera for major companies in AUS: Graz; DEN: Copenhagen; GER DR: Berlin Staatsoper, Dresden. **Operas staged with these companies incl** d'ALBERT: *Tiefland;* BARTOK: *Bluebeard's Castle;* BEETHOVEN: *Fidelio;* BERG: *Wozzeck;* BORODIN: *Prince Igor;* DONIZETTI: *Campanello, Rita;* DVORAK: *Rusalka;* HANDEL: *Alcina;* KLEBE: *Jakobowsky und der Oberst;* MOZART: *Così fan tutte, Don Giovanni, Entführung aus dem Serail*★*, Nozze di Figaro, Zauberflöte*★*;* OFFENBACH: *Contes d'Hoffmann, Périchole;* ORFF: *Kluge;* PAISIELLO: *Barbiere di Siviglia;* PUCCINI: *Butterfly, Turandot;* SCHOENBERG: *Moses und Aron;* STRAUSS, R: *Arabella, Elektra, Frau ohne Schatten, Rosenkavalier, Salome, Schweigsame Frau;* STRAVINSKY: *Mavra;* VERDI: *Ballo in*

maschera, Don Carlo, Falstaff*, Forza del destino, Nabucco, Otello; WAGNER: *Fliegende Holländer, Lohengrin, Tannhäuser, Tristan und Isolde;* WEBER: *Freischütz*;* WEINBERGER: *Schwanda.* Also HANDEL: *Radamisto, Ottone;* MATTHUS: *Letzte Schuss;* RIMSKY-KORSAKOV: *Tsar Saltan.* **Operatic world premieres:** FOREST: *Blumen von Hiroschima* Nationaltheater Weimar 1967; ZIMMERMANN: *Levins Mühle* Staatsoper Dresden 1973. Mgmt: KDR/GDR.

KURIBAYASHI, YOSHINOBU. Lyric baritone. Japanese. Resident mem: Niki Kai Opera, Tokyo. Born 15 Aug 1933, Saga, Japan. Wife Machiko. Two children. Studied: Keikichi Yatabe, Nicola Rucci, Tokyo; Giuseppe Paoletti, Rome; Ettore Campogalliani, Milan. **Debut:** Scarpia (*Tosca*) Fujiwara Opera Co 1958. Awards: First Prize Music Compt, Mainichi Press & NHK Japan Broadc Co; Gold Medal Intl Gianbattista Viotti Music Compt; Mainichi Art Prize.
  Sang with major companies in ARG: Buenos Aires; JPN: Tokyo Fujiwara & Niki Kai; USSR: Kiev, Leningrad Kirov. **Roles with these companies** incl BERLIOZ: Méphistophélès* (*Damnation de Faust*); BIZET: Escamillo* (*Carmen*); DALLAPICCOLA: Riviere (*Volo di notte*); DONIZETTI: Enrico* (*Lucia*); LEONCAVALLO: Tonio* (*Pagliacci*); MASCAGNI: Alfio (*Cavalleria rusticana*); PUCCINI: Marcello* (*Bohème*), Sharpless* (*Butterfly*), Lescaut (*Manon Lescaut*), Michele (*Tabarro*), Scarpia* (*Tosca*).

KURZ, SIEGFRIED ALFRED. Conductor of opera and symphony; composer. German. Gen Music Dir & Resident Cond, Staatsoper Dresden, Ger DR. Also Music Dir, Staatskapelle, Dresden. Born 18 Jul 1930, Dresden. Wife Margot King. One child. Studied: Profs Ernst Hintze and F Finke, Dresden; also piano & trumpet. Operatic training as cond at Dresden Staatstheater 1949- . **Operatic debut:** *Trovatore* Staatsoper, Dresden 1957. Symphonic debut: Staatskapelle, Dresden. Awards: Kunstpreis of the Ger DR.
  Conducted with major companies in FR GER: Wiesbaden; GER DR: Berlin Staatsoper, Dresden, Leipzig; ROM: Bucharest; USSR: Leningrad Kirov. **Operas with these companies** incl ADAM: *Postillon de Lonjumeau*;* d'ALBERT: *Tiefland;* BARTOK: *Bluebeard's Castle*;* BERG: *Wozzeck*;* DESSAU: *Lanzelot*, Verurteilung des Lukullus;* DONIZETTI: *Don Pasquale;* HUMPERDINCK: *Hänsel und Gretel*;* LORTZING: *Waffenschmied, Zar und Zimmermann;* MOZART: *Così fan tutte*, Don Giovanni, Entführung aus dem Serail, Nozze di Figaro*, Zauberflöte*;* MUSSORGSKY: *Boris Godunov*;* NICOLAI: *Lustigen Weiber;* ORFF: *Kluge*;* PUCCINI: *Bohème, Butterfly, Tosca;* ROSSINI: *Barbiere di Siviglia;* SCHOENBERG: *Moses und Aron*;* SMETANA: *Bartered Bride*;* STRAUSS, R: *Ariadne auf Naxos, Rosenkavalier*, Salome;* VERDI: *Falstaff*, Forza del destino*, Rigoletto*, Traviata;* WAGNER: *Fliegende Holländer*, Meistersinger*;* WEBER: *Freischütz*.* **World premieres:** ZIMMERMANN: *Levins Mühle* Staatsoper, Dresden 1973. Conducted major orch in Europe, Cent/S America. **Res:** Dr Rudolf Friedrichstr 38, Radebeul/Dresden, Ger DR. Mgmt: KDR/GDR.

KUSCHE, BENNO. Bass-baritone. German. Resident mem: Bayerische Staatsoper, Munich. Born 30 Jan 1916, Freiburg/Br, Germany. Wife Christine Goerner, occupation singer. Two children. **Debut:** Fra Melitone (*Forza del destino*) Koblenz 1938. Awards: Bavarian Order of Merit; Bayerischer Kammersänger.
  Sang with major companies in ARG: Buenos Aires; AUS: Bregenz Fest, Graz, Salzburg Fest, Vienna Staatsoper & Volksoper; BEL: Brussels; DEN: Copenhagen; FIN: Helsinki; FRA: Bordeaux, Lyon, Marseille, Nice, Paris, Strasbourg, Toulouse; FR GER: Bayreuth Fest, Berlin Deutsche Oper, Cologne, Dortmund, Düsseldorf-Duisburg, Frankfurt, Hamburg, Karlsruhe, Munich Staatsoper & Gärtnerplatz, Stuttgart, Wiesbaden; GER DR: Berlin Komische Oper; HOL: Amsterdam; ITA: Florence Maggio, Naples, Rome Opera; SWI: Zurich; UK: Glyndebourne Fest, London Royal; USA: New York Met, Philadelphia Lyric. **Roles with these companies** incl DONIZETTI: Don Pasquale*, Dulcamara (*Elisir*); EGK: Cuperus (*Zaubergeige*); FALLA: Don Quixote (*Retablo de Maese Pedro*); HANDEL: Ptolemy (*Giulio Cesare*); KODALY: Háry János; LORTZING: Baculus* (*Wildschütz*), Van Bett* (*Zar und Zimmermann*); MOZART: Don Alfonso* (*Così fan tutte*), Leporello* (*Don Giovanni*), Figaro (*Nozze di Figaro*), Papageno (*Zauberflöte*); NICOLAI: Falstaff (*Lustigen Weiber*); ORFF: König (*Kluge*); POULENC: Gendarme (*Mamelles de Tirésias*); PROKOFIEV: King of Clubs (*Love for Three Oranges*); PUCCINI: Colline (*Bohème*), Gianni Schicchi*; RAVEL: Ramiro (*Heure espagnole*); ROSSINI: Dott Bartolo* (*Barbiere di Siviglia*), Don Magnifico* (*Cenerentola*), Macrobio (*Pietra del paragone*); SMETANA: Kezal* (*Bartered Bride*); STRAUSS, R: La Roche* (*Capriccio*); STRAVINSKY: Nick Shadow (*Rake's Progress*); VERDI: Falstaff*, Fra Melitone* (*Forza del destino*); WAGNER: Beckmesser*‡ (*Meistersinger*), Alberich (*Rheingold*‡, Götterdämmerung**). Recorded for: Decca, Telefunken, Ariola, Eurodisc.

KUUSOJA, MAIJU. Contralto. Finnish. Resident mem: Finnish National Opera, Helsinki. Born 25 Nov 1925, Tampere, Finland. Divorced. One child. Studied: Prof Maria Gerhardt, Kmsg Elsa Larsen, Lahja Linko, Aulikki Rautawaara. **Debut:** Marcellina (*Nozze di Figaro*) Finnish National Opera, Helsinki 1949. Awards: Pro Finlandia 1957; Golden Medal Finnish Actors Assn 1971; Silver Medal Assn of Finnish Stages 1971.
  Sang with major companies in CZE: Brno, Prague National; DEN: Copenhagen; FIN: Helsinki; FR GER: Berlin Deutsche Oper, Stuttgart; GER DR: Berlin Komische Oper & Staatsoper; HUN: Budapest; NOR: Oslo; SWE: Stockholm; USSR: Leningrad Kirov, Moscow Bolshoi, Tbilisi; USA: San Antonio. **Roles with these companies** incl BARTOK: Judith (*Bluebeard's Castle*); BERG: Gräfin Geschwitz* (*Lulu*); BIZET: Carmen; BORODIN: Kontchakovna (*Prince Igor*); BRITTEN: Hippolita (*Midsummer Night*), Auntie (*Peter Grimes*); CIMAROSA: Fidalma (*Matrimonio*

segreto); DEBUSSY: Geneviève (*Pelléas et Mélisande*); HUMPERDINCK: Hänsel & Hexe (*Hänsel und Gretel*); JANACEK: Kabanikha (*Katya Kabanova*); MENOTTI: Donato's Mother (*Maria Golovin*); MOZART: Dorabella (*Così fan tutte*); MUSSORGSKY: Khivria★ (*Fair at Sorochinsk*); PUCCINI: Suzuki (*Butterfly*), Frugola★ (*Tabarro*); SAINT-SAENS: Dalila; SMETANA: Hata (*Bartered Bride*); STRAUSS, R: Klytämnestra (*Elektra*), Herodias (*Salome*); STRAVINSKY: Jocasta (*Oedipus Rex*), Baba the Turk (*Rake's Progress*); SZOKOLAY: Mother of the Groom (*Blood Wedding*); TCHAIKOVSKY: Comtesse (*Pique Dame*); VERDI: Amneris (*Aida*), Ulrica (*Ballo in maschera*), Eboli (*Don Carlo*), Dame Quickly (*Falstaff*), Azucena (*Trovatore*); WAGNER: Magdalene (*Meistersinger*), Erda (*Rheingold*), Fricka (*Walküre*); WEILL: Leocadia Begbick★ (*Aufstieg und Fall der Stadt Mahagonny*). **World premieres:** SAIKKOLA: Ristin (*Ristin*) Finnish National Opera, Helsinki 1959; PYLKKANEN: Opri (*Opri and Oleski*) Finnish National Opera 1958; KUUSISTO: Muumi-Mother (*Muumi-Opera*) Finnish National Opera 1974. Recorded for: Fndt for the Promotion of Finnish Music. Video/Film: Azucena (*Trovatore*); Carmen. Appears with symphony orchestra. Teaches voice. Coaches repertoire. **Res:** Apollonkatu 13, Helsinki, Finland.

KYRIAKI, MARGARITA. Lyric soprano. Austrian/Greek. Resident mem: Vienna Staatsoper; Vienna Volksoper. Born 23 September, Athens, Greece. Husband Peter Wagner, occupation bank clerk. One child. Studied: Prof Miltiadis Vithinos, Athens; Hochschule für Musik, Prof Berti Mandl, Prof Kmsg Josef Witt, Vienna; Kmsg Hilde Zadek, Vienna. **Debut:** Pamina (*Zauberflöte*) Klagenfurt, Austria 1964. Awards: prizewinner, Conc for Lied, Akad of Vienna.

Sang with major companies in AUS: Graz, Vienna Staatsoper & Volksoper; GRE: Athens National; FR GER: Bayreuth Fest, Essen, Kassel, Mannheim, Wiesbaden; ITA: Trieste; SPA: Barcelona; SWI: Basel, Zurich; USA: Seattle. **Roles with these companies incl** BEETHOVEN: Marzelline★ (*Fidelio*); BIZET: Micaëla★ (*Carmen*); GLUCK: Euridice; GOUNOD: Marguerite★ (*Faust*); HANDEL: Galatea; LEONCAVALLO: Nedda (*Pagliacci*); LORTZING: Baronin Freimann★ (*Wildschütz*); MEYERBEER: Inez (*Africaine*); MOZART: Vitellia (*Clemenza di Tito*), Fiordiligi★ (*Così fan tutte*), Donna Elvira (*Don Giovanni*), Contessa★ & Susanna (*Nozze di Figaro*), Pamina★ (*Zauberflöte*); OFFENBACH: Antonia & Giulietta★ (*Contes d'Hoffmann*); PENDERECKI: Jeanne (*Teufel von Loudun*); PUCCINI: Mimi★ (*Bohème*); RIMSKY-KORSAKOV: Fevronia (*Invisible City of Kitezh*); SMETANA: Marie★ (*Bartered Bride*); STRAUSS, J: Rosalinde★ (*Fledermaus*); STRAUSS, R: Zdenka (*Arabella*), Octavian★ (*Rosenkavalier*); STRAVINSKY: Anne Trulove (*Rake's Progress*); VERDI: Alice Ford (*Falstaff*); Desdemona★ (*Otello*); WAGNER: Eva (*Meistersinger*). Also BURT: Celia (*Volpone*); KIENZL: Martha (*Evangelimann*); KRENEK: Isabella (*Karl V*); MARTINU: Maria (*Marienlegende*); WOLF-FERRARI: Marina (*Quattro rusteghi*). **World premieres:** WEISHAPPEL: Tochter (*Lederköpfe*) Graz Oper, Austria 1970. Gives recitals. Appears with symphony orchestra. **Res:** Billrothstr 27, 1190 Vienna, Austria. Mgmt: RAB/AUS.

L

LAAKMANN, WILLEM. Dramatic baritone. German. Resident mem: Vereinigte Bühnen, Krefeld & Mönchengladbach, FR Ger. Born Aachen, Germany. Wife Marie-Louise. One son, one daughter. Studied: Leo Ketelaars, Holland; Prof Josef Metternich, Cologne. **Debut:** Lord Tristram (*Martha*) Holland 1969.

Sang with major companies in FR GER: Düsseldorf-Duisburg, Krefeld; HOL: Amsterdam. **Roles with these companies incl** d'ALBERT: Sebastiano (*Tiefland*); BEETHOVEN: Don Pizarro (*Fidelio*); BERG: Dr Schön (*Lulu*), Wozzeck; BIZET: Escamillo★ (*Carmen*), Zurga (*Pêcheurs de perles*); DONIZETTI: Enrico (*Campanello*), Enrico (*Lucia*); LEONCAVALLO: Tonio (*Pagliacci*); MASCAGNI: Alfio★ (*Cavalleria rusticana*); MILHAUD: Agenor (*Enlèvement d'Europe*); MOZART: Leporello (*Don Giovanni*), Papageno★ (*Zauberflöte*); OFFENBACH: Coppélius etc★ (*Contes d'Hoffmann*); ORFF: König (*Kluge*); PUCCINI: Sharpless (*Butterfly*), Scarpia★ (*Tosca*); PURCELL: Aeneas; ROSSINI: Tobias Mill (*Cambiale di matrimonio*); STRAUSS, R: Musiklehrer (*Ariadne auf Naxos*), Jochanaan (*Salome*); TCHAIKOVSKY: Eugene Onegin; VERDI: Amonasro (*Aida*), Don Carlo★ (*Ernani*), Falstaff, Don Carlo★ (*Forza del destino*), Macbeth, Nabucco, Rigoletto★, Germont★ (*Traviata*); WAGNER: Wolfram (*Tannhäuser*); WEBER: Kaspar★ (*Freischütz*); WOLF-FERRARI: Lunardo (*Quattro rusteghi*).

LABÓ, FLAVIANO MARIO. Dramatic tenor. Italian. Born 1 Feb 1927, Borgonovo, Italy. Single. Studied: Mo Ettore Campogalliani, Parma; Mo Renato Pastorino, Milan; Mo Valentino Metti, Piacenza. **Debut:** Cavaradossi (*Tosca*) Teatro Municipale, Piacenza 1954. Previous occupations: railroad employee. Awards: Viotti d'oro, Vercelli 1967; Verdi d'oro, Busseto 1970; Prix de la Ville S Vincent 1969; Gonfalone d'oro, Viterbo 1974; Medaglia d'oro, Piacenza 1969, etc.

Sang with major companies in ARG: Buenos Aires; AUS: Vienna Staatsoper; BEL: Brussels; BRA: Rio de Janeiro; BUL: Sofia; CAN: Montreal/Quebec; CZE: Prague National; FRA: Bordeaux, Marseille, Nice, Paris, Rouen, Strasbourg, Toulouse; FR GER: Berlin Deutsche Oper, Cologne, Düsseldorf-Duisburg, Frankfurt, Hamburg, Hannover, Kiel, Munich Staatsoper, Nürnberg, Stuttgart, Wiesbaden, Wuppertal; GER DR: Berlin Staatsoper; HOL: Amsterdam; HUN: Budapest; ITA: Bologna, Florence Maggio & Comunale, Genoa, Milan La Scala, Naples, Palermo, Parma, Rome Opera & Caracalla, Trieste, Turin, Venice, Verona Arena; MEX: Mexico City; MON: Monte Carlo; NOR: Oslo; POR: Lisbon; SPA: Barcelona; SWI: Zurich; UK: London Royal; USA: Baltimore, Fort Worth, Hartford, Houston, Memphis, Miami, Newark, New Orleans, New York Met & City Opera, Philadelphia Grand & Lyric, San Francisco & Spring Opera, Seattle; YUG: Zagreb, Belgrade. **Roles with these companies incl** BELLINI: Gualtiero (*Pirata*); BIZET: Don José (*Carmen*); BOITO: Faust (*Mefistofele*); DONIZETTI: Edgardo★ (*Lucia*); GIORDANO: Andrea Chénier★; GOUNOD: Faust; LEONCAVALLO: Canio (*Pagliacci*); MASCAGNI: Turiddu★ (*Cavalleria rusticana*); PONCHIELLI: Enzo★ (*Gioconda*); PUCCINI: Rodolfo★ (*Bohème*), Pinkerton★ (*Butterfly*), Des Grieux (*Manon Lescaut*), Cavaradossi★ (*Tosca*), Calaf★ (*Turandot*); VERDI: Radames★ (*Aida*), Riccardo★ (*Ballo in maschera*), Don Carlo★‡ Ernani★, Don Alvaro★ (*Forza del destino*), Carlo (*Giovanna d'Arco*), Rodolfo (*Luisa Miller*), Duca di Mantova★ (*Rigoletto*), Gabriele★ (*Simon Boccanegra*), Alfredo★ (*Traviata*), Manrico★ (*Trovatore*). Also GIORDANO: Vassilij (*Siberia*). Recorded for: RCA, Decca, DG. **Res:** V Maddalena 12, Piacenza, Italy. Mgmt: CAM/USA.

LACKOVIC, OLGA GAVRO; née Milosevic. Dramatic mezzo-soprano. Yugoslavian. Resident mem: Opera of the Ntl Theater, Belgrade. Born 3 Apr 1937, Cetinje, Yugoslavia. Husband Stanislav, occupation mechanical eng. One child. Studied: Mrs Zdenka Zika, Gino Bechi. **Debut:** Kontchakovna (*Prince Igor*) 1964.

Sang with major companies in ROM: Bucharest; YUG: Belgrade. **Roles with these companies incl** BIZET: Carmen★; BORODIN: Kontchakovna★ (*Prince Igor*); GOUNOD: Siebel (*Faust*); MASSENET: Dulcinée (*Don Quichotte*), Charlotte★ (*Werther*); MOZART: Cherubino (*Nozze di Figaro*); OFFENBACH: Giulietta (*Contes d'Hoffmann*); SMETANA: Hata (*Bartered Bride*); STRAUSS, J: Prinz Orlovsky (*Fledermaus*); VERDI: Amneris★ (*Aida*), Eboli (*Don Carlo*), Azucena★ (*Trovatore*). Gives recitals. Appears with symphony orchestra. Teaches voice. Coaches repertoire. Mgmt: YGC/YUG.

LA FERLA, SANDRO. Scenic and costume designer for opera, theater, film, television; specl in sets. Is also a painter. Italian. Born 23 May 1941, Turin, Italy. Wife Ruth, occupation editor. Studied: Acad of Fine Arts, Rome; Mischa Scandella, Rome; Univ of Oklahoma, Norman, USA. **Operatic debut:** *Tamu-Tamu* Intl Congress of Anthropol Sciences, Chicago 1973. Theater debut: Teatro Quirino, Rome 1968. Awards: Fulbright Grant for scenic design study.

Designed for major companies in ITA: Spoleto Fest, Trieste. **Operas designed for these companies incl** MENOTTI: *Consul★, Medium★, Tamu-Tamu★;* RIMSKY-KORSAKOV: *Coq d'or★.* Exhibitions of stage designs, Contemp Stage Design — USA, Lincoln Center New York 1974-75; Ntl Exhib of Stage Design, Venice 1965. **Res:** 345 E 80th St, New York, USA.

LAGGER, PETER. Bass. Swiss. Resident mem: Deutsche Oper, Berlin. Born 7 Sep 1930, Buchs, Switzerland. Wife Liva, occupation actress. Two children. Studied: Consv & Acad of Music, Zurich, Vienna and Italy. **Debut:** Eremit (*Freischütz*) Graz Oper 1953. Previous occupations: pianist, student of literature. Awards: Kammersänger, Senate of Berlin; Critics Awd, Barcelona 1968.

Sang with major companies in AUS: Graz, Salzburg Fest, Vienna Staatsoper; BEL: Brussels; FIN: Helsinki; FRA: Aix-en-Provence Fest, Lyon, Nancy, Nice, Orange Fest, Paris, Strasbourg; GRE: Athens Fest; FR GER: Berlin Deutsche Oper, Frankfurt, Hamburg Staatsoper, Karlsruhe, Kassel, Kiel, Munich Bayerische Staatsoper, Nürnberg, Saarbrücken, Stuttgart, Wiesbaden; HOL: Amsterdam; ISR: Tel Aviv; ITA: Genoa, Milan, Naples, Trieste; POR: Lisbon; SPA: Barcelona; SWI: Basel, Geneva, Zurich; UK: Edinburgh Fest, Glyndebourne Fest; USA: New York City Opera, San Francisco Opera, Washington DC. **Roles with these companies incl** BARTOK: Bluebeard★; BEETHOVEN: Rocco★ (*Fidelio*); GOUNOD: Méphistophélès (*Faust*); HANDEL: Polyphemus (*Acis and Galatea*), Ptolemy (*Giulio Cesare*); LORTZING: Stadinger (*Waffenschmied*), Baculus (*Wildschütz*), Van Bett (*Zar und Zimmermann*); MOZART: Don Alfonso★ (*Così fan tutte*), Leporello (*Don Giovanni*), Osmin★ (*Entführung aus dem Serail*), Figaro (*Nozze di Figaro*), Sarastro★ (*Zauberflöte*); MUSSORGSKY: Boris★ & Varlaam (*Boris Godunov*); NICOLAI: Falstaff★ (*Lustigen Weiber*); PUCCINI: Colline★ (*Bohème*); ROSSINI: Don Basilio★ (*Barbiere di Siviglia*); SMETANA: Kezal (*Bartered Bride*); STRAUSS, R: Orest (*Elektra*), Baron Ochs★ (*Rosenkavalier*); VERDI: Ramfis★ (*Aida*), Philip II★ (*Don Carlo*), Silva★ (*Ernani*), Padre Guardiano★ (*Forza del destino*), Banquo★ (*Macbeth*), Zaccaria★ (*Nabucco*), Fiesco (*Simon Boccanegra*); WAGNER: Daland★ (*Fliegende Holländer*), König Heinrich★ (*Lohengrin*), Pogner★ (*Meistersinger*), Gurnemanz★ (*Parsifal*), Fasolt (*Rheingold*), Fafner (*Rheingold★*, *Siegfried★*), Hunding★ (*Walküre*), Hagen★ (*Götterdämmerung*), Landgraf★ (*Tannhäuser*), König Marke★ (*Tristan und Isolde*); WEBER: Kaspar★ (*Freischütz*). Also HENZE: Cadmos (*Bassariden*). Recorded for: DG. Video/Film: Gremin (*Eugene Onegin*). Gives recitals. Appears with symphony orchestra. **Res:** Rauschenerallee 4, 1 Berlin 19, FR Ger.

LAGHEZZA, ROSA. Dramatic mezzo-soprano. Italian. Born 11 Jun 1939, Trieste. Husband Elio Manni, occupation business exec. One child. Studied: Profs Donassio, Corradetti, Trieste. **Debut:** Mignon, Teatro Nuovo, Milan 1960.

Sang with major companies in AUS: Bregenz Fest; DEN: Copenhagen; FRA: Paris, Toulouse; FR GER: Dortmund, Stuttgart; ITA: Bologna, Florence Maggio & Comunale, Genoa, Milan La Scala, Naples, Palermo, Rome Opera & Caracalla, Spoleto Fest, Trieste, Turin, Venice, Verona Arena; MON: Monte Carlo; NOR: Oslo; SWE: Drottningholm Fest, Stockholm; SWI: Geneva; UK: Glyndebourne Fest; USSR: Leningrad Kirov. **Roles with these companies incl** BELLINI: Adalgisa (*Norma*); BIZET: Carmen; CHARPENTIER: Mère (*Louise*);· CILEA: Princesse de Bouillon (*A. Lecouvreur*); CIMAROSA: Fidalma (*Matrimonio segreto*); DONIZETTI: Marquise de Birkenfeld (*Fille du régiment*); JANACEK: Kostelnicka (*Jenufa*); MENOTTI: Secretary (*Consul*); PONCHIELLI: Laura (*Gioconda*); PROKOFIEV: Clarissa (*Love for Three Oranges*); PUCCINI: Principessa (*Suor Angelica*); ROSSINI: Isabella (*Italiana in Algeri*), Marchesina Clarice (*Pietra del paragone*), Arsace (*Semiramide*); SAINT-SAENS: Dalila; STRAVINSKY: Mère (*Mavra*); VERDI: Amneris (*Aida*), Ulrica (*Ballo in maschera*), Eboli (*Don Carlo*), Dame Quickly (*Falstaff*), Preziosilla (*Forza del destino*), Federica (*Luisa Miller*), Azucena (*Trovatore*); WOLF-FERRARI: Margarita (*Quattro rusteghi*). Video/Film: Clarice (*Pietra del paragone*). **Res:** Segrate Res del Campo 722, Milan, Italy.

LAMARCHE, GÉRARD. Canadian. Exec Dir, L'Opéra du Québec, 175 St Catherine St West, Montreal, Canada. Also of S Wilfrid Pelletier Theatre; Théâtre Maisonneuve; Théâtre Port-Royal, all at Place des Arts, Montreal. In charge of adm, musical, dram matters & artistic policy. Additional administrative positions: Dir Gen, Place des Arts, Montreal. Born 1918, Montreal, Que, Canada. Wife Thérèse. Two children. Studied: Jean de Brébeuf Coll, Montreal; Univ of Montreal. Previous positions, primarily administrative & musical: Dir, French network of CBC Montreal, for 23 yrs. Started in present position in 1964.

LaMARCHINA, ROBERT A. Conductor of opera and symphony; operatic stage director. American. Art & Mus Dir, Hawaii Opera Theatre, Honolulu, USA. Also Resident Cond & Mus Dir, Honolulu Symph Orch, Hawaii since 1967. Born 3 Sep 1928, New York. Single. Studied: Curtis Institute of Music, Philadelphia; incl cello. Plays the cello. Operatic training as asst cond at Baltimore Opera Co, MD. **Operatic debut:** *Butterfly* Fujiwara Opera, Tokyo. Symphonic debut: National Symph Orch, Washington DC. Previous adm positions in opera: Mus Dir, Met Opera National Co, New York and tour USA 1965-67.

Conducted with major companies in ARG: Buenos Aires; ITA: Naples, Spoleto Fest; JPN: Tokyo Fujiwara; MEX: Mexico City; SWI: Zurich; USA: Baltimore, Chicago, Hawaii, New York Met & City Opera, Santa Fe. **Operas with these companies incl** AUBER: *Fra Diavolo;* BERNSTEIN: *Trouble in Tahiti;* BIZET: *Carmen★;* BOITO:

Mefistofele★*;* BRITTEN: *Rape of Lucretia;* DONIZETTI: *Elisir;* FALLA: *Retablo de Maese Pedro;* FLOYD: *Susannah*★*;* FOSS: *Jumping Frog;* GERSHWIN: *Porgy and Bess;* GIORDANO: *Andrea Chénier;* GOUNOD: *Faust*★*;* HUMPERDINCK: *Hänsel und Gretel;* LEONCAVALLO: *Pagliacci;* MASCAGNI: *Cavalleria rusticana;* MASSENET: *Manon, Werther;* MENOTTI: *Amahl*★*, Consul*★*, Dernier sauvage*★*, Medium*★*, Telephone*★*;* MOZART: *Così fan tutte, Entführung aus dem Serail, Nozze di Figaro;* ORFF: *Carmina burana*★*;* PUCCINI: *Bohème*★*, Fanciulla del West*★*, Gianni Schicchi, Butterfly*★*, Tosca*★*, Turandot*★*;* ROSSINI: *Barbiere di Siviglia, Cenerentola*★*;* VERDI: *Aida*★*, Otello*★*, Rigoletto*★*, Traviata;* WAGNER: *Fliegende Holländer*★. Conducted major orch in Europe, USA/Canada, Cent/S America, Asia. **Res:** Honolulu, Hawaii, USA. **Mgmt:** HUR/USA; PAS/FRG.

LAMBRACHE, GEORGE. Dramatic tenor. Romanian. Resident mem: Romanian Opera, Bucharest. Born 19 Sep 1937, Turnu Magurele. Wife Viorica Cojocaru, occupation pianist. One child. Studied: Profs Grigore Melnik, Petre Stefanescu-Goanga, Constantin Stroescu and Viorica Cojocaru. **Debut:** Cavaradossi (*Tosca*) Musical Theater, Galati 1968. Previous occupations: mechanical engineer. **Sang with major companies in** ROM: Bucharest. **Roles with these companies incl** BIZET: Don José★ (*Carmen*); GOUNOD: Faust★; PUCCINI: Rodolfo★ (*Bohème*), Rinuccio★ (*Gianni Schicchi*), Pinkerton★ (*Butterfly*), Cavaradossi★ (*Tosca*); STRAUSS, J: Alfred★ (*Fledermaus*); VERDI: Radames★ (*Aida*), Alfredo★ (*Traviata*), Manrico★ (*Trovatore*); WAGNER: Erik★ (*Fliegende Holländer*), Lohengrin★. **World premieres:** TRAILESCU: Lipan (*Balcescu*) Romanian Opera 1974. Gives recitals. Appears with symphony orchestra. **Res:** 21 Stefan Furtuna St, Bucharest 7, Romania. **Mgmt:** RIA/ROM.

LAMPROPULOS, ATHENA. Dramatic soprano. American. Born Klamath Falls, OR, USA. Husband Raphael Bochbot, occupation librarian. Studied: Teatro dell'Opera, Luigi Ricci, Rome; Ettore Campogalliani, Italy. **Debut:** Suor Angelica, Reggio Emilia, Italy 1962. Awards: Gold Medal, Reggio Emilia, Italy; Teatro Regio, Vercelli; 2 yr Fulbright Grant to Italy. **Sang with major companies in** FRA: Nice; ISR: Tel Aviv; ITA: Palermo, Parma; USA: Houston, Jackson, Kansas City Lyric Theater, Memphis, New Orleans, New York City Opera, Philadelphia Lyric, Portland, Seattle. **Roles with these companies incl** BOITO: Margherita (*Mefistofele*); CILEA: Adriana Lecouvreur; GIORDANO: Maddalena★ (*Andrea Chénier*); MASCAGNI: Santuzza★ (*Cavalleria rusticana*); MOZART: Donna Anna (*Don Giovanni*); PONCHIELLI: Gioconda; PUCCINI: Minnie (*Fanciulla del West*), Manon Lescaut, Suor Angelica, Giorgetta★ (*Tabarro*), Tosca★, Turandot; VERDI: Aida★, Amelia (*Ballo in maschera*), Lady Macbeth, Desdemona (*Otello*), Leonora (*Trovatore*). **Res:** New York, NY, USA.

LANCE, ALBERT; né Lancelot Albert Ingram. Dramatic tenor. French. Born 12 Jul 1925, Adelaide, Australia. Divorced. One child. Studied: Univ Consv, Melbourne; Adelaide Coll of Music; Prof Dominique Modesti, Paris. **Debut:** Cavaradossi (*Tosca*) Victorian Theatre Trust, Australia 1952. **Sang with major companies in** ARG: Buenos Aires; AUSTRL: Sydney; AUS: Vienna Staatsoper; BEL: Liège; BRA: Rio de Janeiro; FRA: Aix-en-Provence Fest, Bordeaux, Lyon, Marseille, Nancy, Nice, Orange Fest, Paris, Rouen, Strasbourg, Toulouse; FR GER: Karlsruhe, Saarbrücken, Stuttgart; HOL: Amsterdam; MON: Monte Carlo; POR: Lisbon; SPA: Barcelona; SWI: Geneva; UK: London Royal Opera; USSR: Kiev, Leningrad Kirov, Moscow Bolshoi; USA: Miami, New Orleans, Philadelphia Grand & Lyric, San Diego, San Francisco Opera. **Roles with these companies incl** BERLIOZ: Faust★ (*Damnation de Faust*); BIZET: Don José★ (*Carmen*); CHERUBINI: Giasone (*Medea*); DEBUSSY: Azaël (*Enfant prodigue*); GOUNOD: Faust, Roméo; LEONCAVALLO: Canio★ (*Pagliacci*); MASSENET: Jean le Baptiste★ (*Hérodiade*), Werther★‡; MILHAUD: Jason (*Médée*); OFFENBACH: Hoffmann★; PUCCINI: Rodolfo (*Bohème*), Pinkerton★‡ (*Butterfly*), Luigi (*Tabarro*), Cavaradossi★‡ (*Tosca*); STRAUSS, R: Aegisth (*Elektra*); VERDI: Riccardo (*Ballo in maschera*), Duca di Mantova (*Rigoletto*); WAGNER: Erik★ (*Fliegende Holländer*). Also DELLO JOIO: (*Blood Moon*); ROUSSEL: (*Padmâvati*). Recorded for: Pathé-Marconi, Philips, Decca, AZ. Gives recitals. Teaches voice. Coaches repertoire. On faculty of Consv de Nice, France. **Res:** c/o Conserv, 5 rue Dr Fougeroux, Le Perreux 94170, France.

LANDY, TONNY; né Tonny Landy Nuppenau. Lyric tenor. Danish. Resident mem: Royal Opera, Copenhagen; Stora Theater, Göteborg, Sweden. Born 30 Jul 1937, Copenhagen. Wife Tove Hyldgaard, occupation opera singer. One child. Studied: Royal Music Consv, Prof Holger Byrding, Copenhagen; Mo Luigi Ricci, Rome; Kmsg Karl Schmitt-Walter, Munich; Prof Vagn Thordal, Copenhagen. **Debut:** Alfredo (*Traviata*) Royal Opera, Copenhagen 1966. Previous occupations: automobile salesman. **Sang with major companies in** DEN: Copenhagen; NOR: Oslo; SWE: Drottningholm Fest, Stockholm. **Roles with these companies incl** DONIZETTI: Nemorino★ (*Elisir*), Edgardo★ (*Lucia*); GOUNOD: Faust★; LECOCQ: Pomponnet★ (*Fille de Madame Angot*); MOZART: Tito★ (*Clemenza di Tito*), Ferrando (*Così fan tutte*), Belmonte (*Entführung aus dem Serail*), Tamino★ (*Zauberflöte*); PUCCINI: Rodolfo★ (*Bohème*), Pinkerton★ (*Butterfly*), Cavaradossi★ (*Tosca*); ROSSINI: Almaviva★ (*Barbiere di Siviglia*); SMETANA: Hans (*Bartered Bride*); STRAUSS, J: Alfred (*Fledermaus*); TCHAIKOVSKY: Lenski★ (*Eugene Onegin*); VERDI: Fenton★ (*Falstaff*); Duca di Mantova★ (*Rigoletto*), Alfredo (*Traviata*). Also BAECK: Yohyo (*Crane Feathers*). Recorded for: Philips. Gives recitals. Appears with symphony orchestra. **Mgmt:** GSI/DEN; SVE/SWE.

LANE, GLORIA; née Siet. Dramatic mezzo-soprano & dramatic soprano. American. Born 6 Jun

1930, Trenton, NJ. Husband Samuel Krachmalnick, occupation conductor. Studied: Elizabeth Westmoreland, Philadelphia. **Debut:** Secretary (*Consul*) 1950; as sop: Santuzza (*Cavalleria rusticana*) 1971. Previous occupations: secy, NJ Dpt of Agriculture. Awards: Clarence Derwent Awd 1949-50; Donaldson Awd 1950.

Sang with major companies in AUS: Graz, Vienna Staatsoper; BEL: Brussels; CAN: Montreal/Quebec, Toronto, Vancouver; DEN: Copenhagen; FRA: Bordeaux, Lyon, Paris; FR GER: Berlin Deutsche Oper; ITA: Bologna, Florence Maggio, Milan La Scala, Naples, Palermo, Parma, Rome Opera & Caracalla, Trieste, Turin, Venice; SPA: Barcelona; UK: Glyndebourne Fest, London Royal; USA: Boston, Chicago, Cincinnati, Hartford, Hawaii, Kansas City, Milwaukee Florentine, Minneapolis, New Orleans, New York City Opera, Philadelphia Grand & Lyric, Pittsburgh, San Diego, San Francisco Opera, Seattle; YUG: Zagreb. **Roles with these companies incl** BARTOK: Judith★ (*Bluebeard's Castle*); BENNETT: Rosalind★ (*Mines of Sulphur*); BIZET: Carmen★; BUSONI: Herzogin★ (*Doktor Faust*); MASCAGNI: Santuzza★ (*Cavalleria rusticana*); MASSENET: Charlotte★ (*Werther*); MENOTTI: Mother of Amahl (*Amahl*); MONTEVERDI: Poppea★ (*Incoronazione di Poppea*); MOZART: Dorabella★ (*Così fan tutte*); MUSSORGSKY: Marina★ (*Boris Godunov*); NICOLAI: Frau Reich (*Lustigen Weiber*); PONCHIELLI: Laura & La Cieca (*Gioconda*); PROKOFIEV: Renata★ (*Flaming Angel*); SAINT-SAENS: Dalila; STRAUSS, R: Ariadne★ (*Ariadne auf Naxos*), Herodias★ (*Salome*); STRAVINSKY: Baba the Turk★ (*Rake's Progress*); VERDI: Amneris★ (*Aida*), Ulrica★ (*Ballo in maschera*), Eboli★ (*Don Carlo*), Preziosilla★ (*Forza del destino*), Federica★ (*Luisa Miller*), Lady Macbeth★, Desdemona★ (*Otello*), Azucena★ (*Trovatore*); WEILL: Leocadia Begbick★ (*Aufstieg und Fall der Stadt Mahagonny*). Also ROSSELLINI: Beatrice (*Sguardo dal ponte*). **World premieres:** MENOTTI: Secretary (*Consul*) 1950, Desideria (*Saint of Bleecker Street*) 1954; both Broadway, New York. Recorded for: Decca, Victor. Video/Film: Marina (*Boris Godunov*). Gives recitals. Appears with symphony orchestra. Teaches voice. **Res:** Seattle, WA, USA.

LANGDON, MICHAEL. Bass. British. Resident mem: Royal Opera, Covent Garden, London. Born 12 Nov 1920, Wolverhampton, UK. Wife Vera, occupation secy. Two children. Studied: Alfred Jerger, Vienna; Maria Carpi, Geneva; Otakar Kraus, London. **Debut:** Night Watchman (*Olympians*) Royal Opera 1950. Previous occupations: clerk; WW II, gunner in Royal Air Force. Awards: Commander of the British Empire, HM Queen Elizabeth II; Hon GSM, Guildhall School of Music.

Sang with major companies in ARG: Buenos Aires; AUS: Vienna Staatsoper; BEL: Brussels; FRA: Aix-en-Provence Fest, Marseille, Nice, Paris; FR GER: Berlin Deutsche Oper, Cologne, Stuttgart, Wiesbaden; HUN: Budapest; ISR: Tel Aviv; MON: Monte Carlo; POR: Lisbon; SWI: Geneva, Zurich; UK: Aldeburgh Fest, Cardiff Welsh, Edinburgh Fest, Glasgow Scottish, Glyndebourne Fest, London Royal & English National; USA: Houston, New York Met & City Opera, San Diego, San Francisco Opera, Seattle. **Roles with these companies incl** BEETHOVEN: Rocco (*Fidelio*); BERG: Doktor★ (*Wozzeck*); BERLIOZ: Narbal (*Troyens*); BRITTEN: John Claggart‡ (*Billy Budd*), Bottom (*Midsummer Night*); DONIZETTI: Don Pasquale★; GOUNOD: Méphistophélès (*Faust*); MOZART: Osmin★ (*Entführung aus dem Serail*), Sarastro (*Zauberflöte*); MUSSORGSKY: Varlaam★ (*Boris*); NICOLAI: Falstaff (*Lustigen Weiber*); PUCCINI: Colline (*Bohème*); ROSSINI: Don Basilio (*Barbiere di Siviglia*), Moïse (*Moïse*); SMETANA: Kezal (*Bartered Bride*); STRAUSS, R: Baron Ochs★ (*Rosenkavalier*); STRAVINSKY: Tiresias (*Oedipus Rex*); VERDI: Ramfis (*Aida*), Grande Inquisitore★ (*Don Carlo*), Banquo (*Macbeth*); WAGNER: Daland★ (*Fliegende Holländer*), Fafner (*Rheingold, Siegfried*), Hunding★ (*Walküre*), Hagen (*Götterdämmerung*), Landgraf (*Tannhäuser*), König Marke (*Tristan und Isolde*); WEBER: Kaspar (*Freischütz*). Also HOLST: Father Philippe★‡ (*Wandering Scholar*); STRAUSS, R: Waldner (*Arabella*); MOZART: Commendatore (*Don Giovanni*); BEETHOVEN: Don Fernando (*Fidelio*); BRITTEN: Swallow (*Peter Grimes*), Quince (*Midsummer Night*). **World premieres:** ORR: Lord Hermiston (*Hermiston*) Scottish Opera 1975. Recorded for: EMI, Decca. Video/Film: Méphistophélès (*Faust*); Claggart (*Billy Budd*). Gives recitals. Appears with symphony orchestra. Teaches voice. Coaches repertoire. **Res:** Hove, Sussex, UK. Mgmt: CST/UK.

LANTIERI, MARTA. Stages/produces opera. Also designs sets, costumes, stage-lighting, and is a singer. Italian. Asst Stage Dir, Staatsoper, Vienna. Also Administr for Teatro G Verdi, Trieste 1972-75. Born 25 Apr 1924, Trieste. Husband Spartaco, occupation builder. One child. Studied: Gilda Dalla Rizza and Curelich, Trieste; Danilo Svara, Ljubljana; incl music and voice. Operatic training as asst stage dir at Staatsoper, Vienna. **Operatic debut:** *Don Pasquale* Teatro Verdi, Trieste 1969. Theater debut: Teatro Sperimentale del Consv, Trieste 1958. Previous occupation: opera singer; prof of scenic design; voice teacher. Awards: Diploma, Accad Tiberina, Rome.

Directed/produced opera for major companies in AUS: Vienna Staatsoper; ITA: Parma, Trieste; SPA: Barcelona. **Operas staged with these companies incl** BELLINI: *Sonnambula;* CAVALIERI: *Rappresentazione;* CIMAROSA: *Matrimonio segreto;* DEBUSSY: *Enfant prodigue†;* DONIZETTI: *Campanello†,* Don Pasquale★, *Elisir★, Lucia;* GLUCK: *Cadi dupé†;* HUMPERDINCK: *Hänsel und Gretel;* MENOTTI: *Telephone†;* MONTEVERDI: *Combattimento di Tancredi;* MOZART: *Così fan tutte, Oca del Cairo;* PERGOLESI: *Serva padrona;* POULENC: *Voix humaine;* PUCCINI: *Bohème★, Butterfly★, Suor Angelica, Tosca★;* ROSSINI: *Barbiere di Siviglia★;* STRAUSS, R: *Ariadne auf Naxos;* VERDI: *Attila, Falstaff, Forza del destino★, Rigoletto★, Traviata★, Trovatore★;* WEILL: *Jasager;* WOLF-FERRARI: *Segreto di Susanna.* Also HAYDN: *Canterina;* ROSSELLINI: *Sguardo dal ponte.* **Operatic world premieres:** VIOZZI: *Elisabetta* Teatro G Verdi, Trieste 1971. Teaches at Consv Tartini, Trieste.

Res: Galleria Protti 2, Trieste, Italy. **Mgmt:** SLZ/FRG.

LANTIERI, RITA. Lyric soprano. Italian. Born 11 Sep 1940, Gorizia. Married. Studied: Consv G Tartini, Trieste; Corso di Perfezionamento, Consv Trieste & S Vincent; Scuola di Canto, Mo Marcello del Monaco, Treviso. **Debut:** Desdemona (*Otello*) Bern Stadttheater, Switzerland 1970. Awards: G B Viotti Prize, Vercelli; Intl Conc, Merano.
Sang with major companies in FRA: Nancy; FR GER: Nürnberg; ITA: Bologna, Trieste, Venice; SWI: Zurich; YUG: Zagreb. **Roles with these companies incl** BIZET: Micaëla (*Carmen*); LEONCAVALLO: Nedda (*Pagliacci*); OFFENBACH: Antonia (*Contes d'Hoffmann*); PUCCINI: Mimi (*Bohème*), Cio-Cio-San (*Butterfly*), Liù (*Turandot*); VERDI: Giovanna d'Arco, Leonora★ (*Trovatore*). Also MANZONI: Carlotta (*Per Massimiliano Robespierre*). **Res:** Viale Monza 355, Milan, Italy.

LANZA TOMASI, GIOACCHINO. Italian. Art Dir, Teatro Massimo, Piazza Verdi, Palermo. In charge of art policy, mus matters. Additional adm position: Art Dir, Accad Filarmonica Romana, Rome. Born 11 Feb 1934, Rome. Wife Mirella. Two children. Plays the piano. Previous occupations: univ prof, music history; Dir, Settimana di Monreale; music critic, Palermo, Venice, Milan. Started with present company in 1972 as Art Adv, in present position since 1974. **Res:** V Butera 28, Palermo, Italy.

LANZILLOTTI, LEONORE AGATHA. Lyric mezzo-soprano. American. Born 24 Jun, New York. Married. One child. Studied: Mme Karin Branzell; Marienka Michna; Mo Carlo Moresco, coaching, USA. **Debut:** Prinz Orlovsky (*Fledermaus*) Honolulu Opera 1964. Previous occupations: insurance repres. Awards: Maria de Varady schlshp, New York City Opera 1968; Mme Karin Branzell schlshp 1969 & 1970; Sullivan Fndt Grants 1969 & 1971.
Sang with major companies in USA: Hartford, Hawaii, Miami, Newark, Philadelphia Grand, San Antonio. **Roles with these companies incl** BIZET: Carmen; GOUNOD: Siebel★ (*Faust*); MASCAGNI: Beppe★ (*Amico Fritz*); PUCCINI: Suzuki★ (*Butterfly*); STRAUSS, J: Prinz Orlovsky★ (*Fledermaus*); VERDI: Amneris (*Aida*), Ulrica★ (*Ballo in maschera*), Azucena★ (*Trovatore*). Also MASCAGNI: Lola (*Cavalleria rusticana*); GIORDANO: Countess & Madelon (*Andrea Chénier*). **Mgmt:** JBF/USA.

LAUBENTHAL, HORST R; né Horst R Neumaier. Lyric tenor. German. Resident mem: Deutsche Oper Berlin, FR Ger; Staatsoper, Vienna. Born 8 Mar 1939, Eisfeld/Thüringen, Germany. Wife Marga Schiml, occupation opera singer, mezzo-soprano. One child. Studied: Rudolf Laubenthal. **Debut:** Don Ottavio (*Don Giovanni*) Würzburg, FR Ger 1967.
Sang with major companies in ARG: Buenos Aires; AUS: Salzburg Fest, Vienna Staatsoper; BEL: Brussels; FRA: Aix-en-Provence Fest, Bordeaux, Orange Fest, Paris; FR GER: Bayreuth, Berlin Deutsche Oper, Bonn, Cologne, Frankfurt, Hamburg, Hannover, Karlsruhe, Munich, Stuttgart; HOL: Amsterdam; ITA: Bologna, Genoa, Milan, Naples, Turin, Venice; POR: Lisbon; SWI: Basel, Zurich; UK: Glyndebourne Fest. **Roles with these companies incl** BUSONI: Leandro (*Arlecchino*); CORNELIUS: Nureddin★ (*Barbier von Bagdad*); DONIZETTI: Edgardo (*Lucia*); HANDEL: Acis, Xerxes★; MOZART: Tito★ (*Clemenza di Tito*), Ferrando★ (*Così fan tutte*), Don Ottavio★ (*Don Giovanni*), Belmonte★ (*Entführung aus dem Serail*), Tamino★ (*Zauberflöte*); PFITZNER: Palestrina★; PUCCINI: Rinuccio (*Gianni Schicchi*); ROSSINI: Lindoro★ (*Italiana in Algeri*), Narciso★ (*Turco in Italia*); SMETANA: Hans (*Bartered Bride*); STRAUSS, R: Ein Sänger★ (*Rosenkavalier*); TCHAIKOVSKY: Lenski★ (*Eugene Onegin*); VERDI: Fenton★ (*Falstaff*); WAGNER: Lohengrin, Walther v d Vogelweide (*Tannhäuser*); WOLF: Corregidor★. Recorded for: DG, Philips, EMI, Eurodisc. **Res:** Heinrich Knote Str 15, 8134 Pöcking, FR Ger. **Mgmt:** OOC/FRA.

LAUFER, MURRAY. Scenic and costume designer for opera, theater, television; specl in sets. Is also a painter. Canadian. Resident designer at St Lawrence Centre for the Arts, Toronto. Born 26 Oct 1929, Toronto. Wife Marie Day, occupation designer. Two children. Studied: Ontario Coll of Art. **Operatic debut:** *Love for Three Oranges* Canadian Opera Co, Toronto 1959. Awards: Centennial Medal, Gvnmt of Canada 1967; Mem, Royal Canadian Acad of Art.
Designed for major companies in CAN: Montreal/Quebec, Ottawa, Toronto. **Operas designed for these companies incl** BARTOK: *Bluebeard's Castle★;* BEETHOVEN: *Fidelio★;* MENOTTI: *Old Maid and the Thief;* MOZART: *Così fan tutte;* PROKOFIEV: *Love for Three Oranges;* PUCCINI: *Turandot;* SMETANA: *Bartered Bride;* STRAUSS, R: *Ariadne auf Naxos;* TCHAIKOVSKY: *Eugene Onegin;* VERDI: *Aida, Forza del destino, Rigoletto, Traviata★;* WAGNER: *Holländer★, Siegfried★, Götterdämmerung★;* WOLF-FERRARI: *Segreto di Susanna.* **Operatic world premieres:** WILSON: *Heloise and Abelard* 1973; SOMERS: *Louis Riel* 1967; both at Canadian Opera Co, Toronto. Exhibitions of stage designs, Toronto Public Libr 1973. **Res:** Toronto, Ont, Canada.

LAURENTI, FRANCO MATTIA. Scenic and costume designer for opera, theater, film & television. Is a lighting designer; also a painter. Italian. Born 22 Mar 1928, Arezzo. Single. Studied: Liceo Artistico, Florence; Accad di Belle Arti, Rome. Prof training: Studio Enrico Prampolini, Rome; Studio Cassandre, Paris. **Operatic debut:** *Ciaccona* Opera, Rome 1956. Theater debut: Teatro Greco, Syracuse, Italy 1956. Awards: Prize for Ballet Scenery & Costumes, Positano 1971.
Designed for major companies in FRA: Paris; FR GER: Wiesbaden; ITA: Florence Maggio & Comunale, Milan La Scala, Naples, Palermo, Rome Opera & Caracalla, Trieste, Venice; MON: Monte Carlo. **Operas designed for these companies incl** CILEA: *Adriana Lecouvreur;* DONIZETTI: *Campanello;* MENOTTI: *Dernier sauvage;* MONTEVERDI: *Favola d'Orfeo;* PAISIELLO: *Re Teodoro in Venezia;* PUCCINI: *Turandot;*

RAVEL: *Enfant et les sortilèges*★*;* ROSSINI: *Cambiale di matrimonio, Cenerentola;* VERDI: *Traviata, Trovatore;* WOLF-FERRARI: *Donne curiose, Quattro rusteghi.* **Operatic world premieres:** MALIPIERO: *Don Tartufo Bacchettone* La Fenice, Venice 1969; PENDERECKI: *Ode for Hiroshima* Teatro Comunale, Florence 1972. Exhibitions of stage designs & paintings Rome 1953, Zurich 1965 and Paris 1974. **Res:** V Eleonora Duse 5/g, Rome, Italy.

LAVANI, CARMEN. Coloratura soprano. Italian. Born 8 May 1942, Privas, France. Single. Studied: Maria Teresa Pediconi, Jolanda Magnoni, Rome. **Debut:** Lauretta (*Gianni Schicchi*) Teatro Sperimentale, Spoleto 1968. Previous occupations: secy. Awards: Diploma di Merito, Accad Chigiana, Siena 1966-67; First Prize, Conc Teatro S Carlo, Naples 1967.
  Sang with major companies in FRA: Aix-en-Provence Fest; ITA: Bologna, Genoa, Milan La Scala, Naples, Palermo, Parma, Turin; USA: Washington DC. **Roles with these companies incl** MONTEVERDI: Clorinda★ (*Combattimento di Tancredi*); MOZART: Despina★ (*Così fan tutte*), Zerlina★ (*Don Giovanni*), Susanna★ (*Nozze di Figaro*); PERGOLESI: Serpina★ (*Serva padrona*); PUCCINI: Lauretta★ (*Gianni Schicchi*); ROSSINI: Fanny★ (*Cambiale di matrimonio*), Comtesse Adèle★ (*Comte Ory*), Elvira★ (*Italiana in Algeri*), Giulia★ (*Scala di seta*), Sofia★ (*Signor Bruschino*); STRAUSS, R: Sophie★ (*Rosenkavalier*); VERDI: Nannetta★ (*Falstaff*). Also PURCELL: Belinda (*Dido and Aeneas*); SALIERI: Colombina (*Arlecchinata*); GAZZANIGA: Donna Elvira (*Convitato di pietra*); SCARLATTI: Costanza (*Griselda*). Gives recitals. Appears with symphony orchestra. **Res:** V 25 Aprile 4, 20091 Bresso/Milan, Italy.

LAVIRGEN, PEDRO. Dramatic tenor. Spanish. Born 31 Jul 1930, Bujalance, Spain. Wife Paquita. Five children. Studied: Don Miguel Barrosa, Madrid. **Debut:** Radames (*Aida*) Mexico City 1964. Previous occupations: elementary & middle school teacher. Awards: Ntl Prize for Operatic Interp, Spain 1964, 1972; Gold Medal Liceo, Barcelona; Gold Medal, Mexico.
  Sang with major companies in ARG: Buenos Aires; AUS: Vienna Staatsoper; CAN: Montreal/Quebec, Ottawa, Toronto; FRA: Nice, Paris; GRE: Athens National; FR GER: Berlin Deutsche Oper, Hamburg, Munich Staatsoper; HUN: Budapest; ITA: Bologna, Genoa, Milan La Scala, Naples, Palermo, Rome Caracalla, Turin, Verona Arena; MEX: Mexico City; POR: Lisbon; SPA: Barcelona Teatro del Líceo, Majorca, Canary Isl Las Palmas Fest; UK: London Royal Opera; USA: Baltimore, Cincinnati, Hartford, Houston, Memphis, Miami, New Orleans, New York Met, Philadelphia Grand & Lyric, Pittsburgh, Seattle; YUG: Belgrade. **Roles with these companies incl** BELLINI: Pollione (*Norma*); BIZET: Don José★ (*Carmen*); CILEA: Maurizio (*A. Lecouvreur*); DONIZETTI: Edgardo (*Lucia*); FALLA: Maese Pedro‡ (*Retablo de Maese Pedro*), Paco (*Vida breve*); GIORDANO: Andrea Chénier; LEONCAVALLO: Canio★ (*Pagliacci*); MASCAGNI: Turiddu (*Cavalleria rusticana*); PUCCINI: Rodolfo★ (*Bohème*), Pinkerton (*But-*

terfly), Luigi (*Tabarro*), Cavaradossi (*Tosca*), Calaf (*Turandot*); SAINT-SAENS: Samson; VERDI: Radames (*Aida*), Riccardo (*Ballo in maschera*), Don Carlo★, Don Alvaro (*Forza del destino*), Otello, Duca di Mantova (*Rigoletto*), Gabriele (*Simon Boccanegra*), Manrico★ (*Trovatore*), Arrigo (*Vespri*); WAGNER: Lohengrin. Also BRETON: Lazaro (*Dolores*); ARRIETA: Jorge (*Marina*). Gives recitals. Appears with symphony orchestra. Teaches voice. **Res:** Arturo Soria 303, Madrid, Spain. **Mgmt:** CAM/USA.

LAWRENCE, DOUGLAS HOWARD. Lyric baritone. American. Born 26 Sep 1942, Los Angeles. Wife Darlene, occupation accompanist. Two children. Studied: Univ of So California, William Vennard, Gwenolyn Koldofsky, Esther Andreas, Ernest St John Metz, Los Angeles. **Debut:** Christ (*St Matthew Passion*) staged, San Francisco Spring Opera 1973. Previous occupations: teacher, El Camino Coll, CA. Awards: National Opera Inst Grant.
  Sang with major companies in USA: San Diego, San Francisco Opera & Spring Opera, Washington DC. **Roles with these companies incl** MASSENET: Lescaut★ (*Manon*); PUCCINI: Colline★ & Marcello★ (*Bohème*); STRAVINSKY: Creon★ (*Oedipus Rex*); VERDI: Germont★ (*Traviata*). Also MONTEVERDI: Ottone★ (*Incoronazione di Poppea*). Gives recitals. Appears with symphony orchestra. Teaches voice. On faculty of Univ of So California, Los Angeles. **Res:** 23142 Dolorosa St, Woodland Hills, CA 91364, USA. **Mgmt:** HUR/USA.

LAYER, FRIEDEMANN. Conductor of opera and symphony. Austrian. Resident Cond, Deutsche Oper am Rhein, Düsseldorf, FR Ger. Born 30 Oct 1941, Vienna. Wife Maria Teresa, occupation singer. Studied: Prof H Swarowsky, Vienna; also piano, flute. Plays the piano. Operatic training as repetiteur & asst cond at Volksoper Vienna; Opera Ulm, FR Ger; Salzburg Fest. **Operatic debut:** Opera Ulm 1964. Symphonic debut: Mozarteum Orch, Salzburg 1970. Previous adm positions in opera: Chief Cond, Landestheater Salzburg 1967-74.
  Conducted with major companies in AUS: Salzburg Fest, Vienna Volksoper; FR GER: Düsseldorf-Duisburg; MEX: Mexico City. **Operas with these companies incl** ADAM: *Si j'étais roi;* AUBER: *Fra Diavolo★;* BIZET: *Carmen;* BRITTEN: *Albert Herring, Death in Venice★, Rape of Lucretia;* DONIZETTI: *Don Pasquale★, Elisir;* DVORAK: *Rusalka★;* GIORDANO: *Andrea Chénier;* GLUCK: *Iphigénie en Aulide, Orfeo ed Euridice;* HUMPERDINCK: *Hänsel und Gretel;* JANACEK: *Excursions of Mr Broucek★;* LORTZING: *Zar und Zimmermann★;* MOZART: *Clemenza di Tito★, Così fan tutte★, Don Giovanni★, Nozze di Figaro★, Zauberflöte; NICOLAI: Lustigen Weiber★;* OFFENBACH: *Contes d'Hoffmann;* ORFF: *Carmina burana★, Kluge★;* POULENC: *Mamelles de Tirésias;* PUCCINI: *Bohème★, Butterfly, Tosca★, Turandot★;* ROSSINI: *Barbiere di Siviglia★, Cenerentola★, Comte Ory★;* SMETANA: *Bartered Bride★;* STRAUSS, J: *Fledermaus;* STRAUSS, R: *Ariadne auf Naxos, Rosenkavalier★;* STRAVINSKY: *Rake's Progress★;* TCHAIKOVSKY: *Eugene Onegin;*

VERDI: *Don Carlo, Falstaff★, Trovatore★;* WAGNER: *Fliegende Holländer;* WOLF-FERRARI: *Donne curiose★.* **Res:** Graf Adolfstr 78, Düsseldorf, FR Ger. Mgmt: TAS/AUS.

LAZAREV, ALEXANDER. Conductor of opera and symphony. Russian. Resident Cond, Bolshoi Opera, Moscow. Born USSR. Studied: Leningrad Consv; Moscow Consv, Prof Ginsberg. **Operatic debut:** *Don Carlo* Bolshoi Opera 1973. Awards: Winner, Third All-Union Cond Compt 1971; First Prize, von Karajan Intl Compt, Berlin 1972.
Conducted with major companies in USSR: Moscow Bolshoi; et al. **Operas with these companies incl** BORODIN: *Prince Igor;* PROKOFIEV: *Gambler;* RIMSKY-KORSAKOV: *Invisible City of Kitezh, Sadko, Tsar's Bride;* TCHAIKOVSKY: *Eugene Onegin;* et al.

LAZARIDIS, STEFANOS. Scenic and costume designer for opera, theater. British. Born 28 Jul 1942, Ethiopia. Single. Studied: in England. **Operatic debut:** Sadler's Wells/English National Opera, London 1970. Theater debut: Yvonne Arnaud Theatre, Guildford, UK 1967.
Designed for major companies in UK: London Royal & English National. **Operas designed for these companies incl** BIZET: *Carmen;* JANACEK: *Katya Kabanova★;* MOZART: *Don Giovanni★, Entführung aus dem Serail★, Nozze di Figaro★;* VERDI: *Trovatore★.* Exhibitions of stage designs: one-man shows London 1969, 1972; British Theatre Museum 1969. Teaches. **Res:** London, UK. Mgmt: AIM/UK.

LAZARO, FRANCISCO. Dramatic tenor. Spanish. Born 14 Mar 1932, Barcelona, Spain. Wife Marie-Luise. One child. Studied: Consv del Liceo, Mme Gali Markoff, Barcelona. **Debut:** Gaspare (*Favorite*) Teatro del Liceo, Barcelona 1960. Previous occupations: designer of toys. Awards: Gold Medal Consv del Liceo, Singing Compt, Barcelona.
Sang with major companies in ARG: Buenos Aires; AUS: Salzburg Fest, Vienna Staatsoper; BEL: Brussels; CAN: Toronto, Vancouver; CZE: Prague National; DEN: Copenhagen; FRA: Lyon; FR GER: Berlin Deutsche Oper, Bielefeld, Cologne, Dortmund, Düsseldorf-Duisburg, Frankfurt, Hamburg, Hannover, Karlsruhe, Kiel, Mannheim, Munich Staatsoper, Stuttgart; GER DR: Leipzig; HUN: Budapest; ITA: Bologna, Parma; NOR: Oslo; SPA: Barcelona; SWE: Stockholm; SWI: Zurich; USA: Pittsburgh; YUG: Zagreb. **Roles with these companies incl** BIZET: Don José★ (*Carmen*); DONIZETTI: Edgardo★ (*Lucia*); LEONCAVALLO: Canio★ (*Pagliacci*); MASCAGNI: Turiddu★ (*Cavalleria rusticana*); PUCCINI: Rodolfo★ (*Bohème*), Rinuccio (*Gianni Schicchi*), Pinkerton★ (*Butterfly*), Des Grieux★ (*Manon Lescaut*), Cavaradossi★ (*Tosca*), Calaf★ (*Turandot*); VERDI: Radames★ (*Aida*), Riccardo★ (*Ballo in maschera*), Don Carlo★, Don Alvaro★ (*Forza del destino*), Ismaele (*Nabucco*), Duca di Mantova★ (*Rigoletto*), Gabriele★ (*Simon Boccanegra*), Manrico★ (*Trovatore*). **Res:** La Torre 3, San Cugat Barcelona, Spain. Mgmt: SMD/FRG.

LAZARUS, ROY. Stages/produces opera, theater & television. Also designs stage-lighting and is a singer, actor & author. American. Born 23 May 1930, Brooklyn, NY. Divorced. Two children. Studied: Syracuse Univ, NY; Juilliard School; incl music & voice. **Operatic debut:** *Ormindo* Juilliard Opera, New York 1968. Previous occupation: on faculty Indiana Univ School of Music, Juilliard School, Oberlin Consv. Awards: Distinguished Alumnus Awd in Recog of Conspicuous Achievement in Field of Music, Syracuse Univ 1972. Previous adm positions in opera: Founder/Art Dir, Oberlin Music Theater 1968-72.
Directed/produced opera for major companies in USA: Kansas City, Kentucky. **Operas staged for these companies incl** MOZART: *Nozze di Figaro★;* PUCCINI: *Tosca★.* Teaches. **Res:** 500 E 85 St, New York, USA.

LAZZARI, AGOSTINO ORLANDO. Lyric tenor. Italian. Born 17 Nov 1919, Genoa/Borzoli. Wife Elsa Iberti. One daughter. Studied: Mo Dino Giacobini, Mo Angelo Costaguta, Genoa; Mo Vincenzo Marini, Rome. **Debut:** Almaviva (*Barbiere di Siviglia*) Compagnia di Milano 1945. Awards: Caravella d'oro, City of Genoa; Cavalieri Commendatore Grand Uff, Ord Milit S Salvator-S Brigida di Svezia.
Sang with major companies in BEL: Brussels; DEN: Copenhagen; FRA: Bordeaux, Marseille, Nice, Paris; FR GER: Berlin Deutsche Oper, Bielefeld, Cologne, Düsseldorf-Duisburg, Essen, Frankfurt, Hamburg, Hannover, Mannheim, Munich Staatsoper, Nürnberg, Saarbrücken, Stuttgart, Wiesbaden; HUN: Budapest; ITA: Bologna, Florence Maggio & Comunale, Genoa, Milan La Scala, Naples, Palermo, Parma, Rome Opera & Caracalla, Trieste, Turin, Venice; MEX: Mexico City; MON: Monte Carlo; NOR: Oslo; POR: Lisbon; SPA: Barcelona; SWI: Basel, Geneva, Zurich; UK: London Royal. **Roles with these companies incl** AUBER: Fra Diavolo; BELLINI: Elvino (*Sonnambula*); BERLIOZ: Faust (*Damnation de Faust*); BIZET: Nadir (*Pêcheurs de perles*); BOITO: Faust (*Mefistofele*); CILEA: Maurizio (*A. Lecouvreur*); CIMAROSA: Paolino (*Matrimonio segreto*); DONIZETTI: Ernesto‡ (*Don Pasquale*), Nemorino (*Elisir*), Fernand (*Favorite*), Charles (*Linda di Chamounix*), Edgardo (*Lucia*); FLOTOW: Lionel (*Martha*); GIORDANO: Loris Ipanov (*Fedora*); GLUCK: Nuradin (*Cadi dupé*); GOUNOD: Faust; HENZE: Des Grieux (*Boulevard Solitude*); HONEGGER: Créon (*Antigone*); MASCAGNI: Fritz (*Amico Fritz*); MASSENET: Des Grieux (*Manon*), Werther; MENOTTI: Lover (*Amelia al ballo*); MILHAUD: Thésée (*Abandon d'Ariane, Délivrance de Thésée*), Jupiter (*Enlèvement d'Europe*); MONTEVERDI: Orfeo; MOZART: Tito (*Clemenza di Tito*), Ferrando (*Così fan tutte*), Don Ottavio (*Don Giovanni*), Belmonte (*Entführung aus dem Serail*); MUSSORGSKY: Shuisky (*Boris Godunov*), Gritzko (*Fair at Sorochinsk*); OFFENBACH: Hoffmann; PAISIELLO: Almaviva (*Barbiere di Siviglia*), Marquis (*Re Teodoro in Venezia*); PERAGALLO: Mario (*Gita in campagna*); POULENC: Chevalier de la Force (*Dialogues des Carmélites*); PROKOFIEV: Antonio (*Duenna*), Prince & Truffaldino (*Love for Three Oranges*); PUCCINI: Rodolfo (*Bohème*), Rinuccio‡ (*Gianni Schicchi*), Pinkerton (*Butterfly*), Ruggero (*Rondine*), Cavaradossi (*Tosca*); ROSSINI: Don Ra-

miro (*Cenerentola*), Lindoro (*Italiana in Algeri*), Otello, Florville (*Signor Bruschino*), Narciso (*Turco in Italia*); SMETANA: Wenzel (*Bartered Bride*); STRAUSS, J: Eisenstein (*Fledermaus*); STRAUSS, R: Merkur (*Liebe der Danae*); STRA-VINSKY: Pêcheur (*Rossignol*); THOMAS: Wilhelm Meister (*Mignon*); VERDI: Riccardo (*Ballo in maschera*), Fenton (*Falstaff*), Rodolfo (*Luisa Miller*), Duca di Mantova (*Rigoletto*), Alfredo (*Traviata*); WAGNER: Lohengrin; WEBER: Abu Hassan, Oberon; WOLF-FERRARI: Filipeto (*Quattro rusteghi*). Also CILEA: Federico (*Arlesiana*); WOLF-FERRARI: Clitandro (*Amore medico*); BONTEMPI: Paride; STRADELLA: Selenco (*Forza dell'amor paterno*); RESPIGHI: Bruto (*Lucrezia*). Recorded for: Philips, Decca, Cetra, Urania. Video/Film: Rodolfo (*Bohème*); Basconero (*Vedova scaltra*); Nemorino (*Elisir*). Gives recitals. Appears with symphony orchestra. Teaches voice. Coaches repertoire. **Res:** V Nino Ronco 39, Genoa/Sampierdarena, Italy.

LEAR, EVELYN. Lyric soprano. American. Born 8 Jan 1930, Brooklyn, New York. Husband Thomas Stewart, occupation singer, baritone. Two children. Studied: Juilliard School, Sergius Kagen, New York; Maria Ivogün, Irma Beilke, Berlin; Daniel Ferro, New York. **Debut:** Komponist (*Ariadne auf Naxos*) Deutsche Oper, Berlin 1959. Awards: Kammersängerin, Deutsche Oper, Berlin; Max Reinhardt Award, Salzburg; Concert Artists Guild, Town Hall recital, New York.
Sang with major companies in ARG: Buenos Aires; AUS: Bregenz Fest, Salzburg Fest, Vienna Staatsoper; BEL: Brussels; FRA: Paris; FR GER: Berlin Deutsche Oper, Frankfurt, Hamburg, Hannover, Munich Staatsoper, Stuttgart, Wiesbaden; HOL: Amsterdam; HUN: Budapest; ITA: Milan La Scala; MEX: Mexico City; MON: Monte Carlo; POR: Lisbon; SWI: Geneva; UK: Cardiff Welsh, Edinburgh Fest, London Royal Opera; USA: Baltimore, Chicago, Dallas, Houston, Kansas City, New Orleans, New York Met, Pittsburgh, San Francisco Opera, Washington DC. **Roles with these companies incl** BARTOK: Judith★ (*Bluebeard's Castle*); BERG: Lulu★‡, Marie★‡ (*Wozzeck*); BERLIOZ: Marguerite (*Damnation de Faust*), Didon★ (*Troyens*); BIZET: Micaëla (*Carmen*); GLUCK: Euridice & Amor (*Orfeo ed Euridice*); HANDEL: Cleopatra (*Giulio Cesare*); MASSENET: Manon; MENOTTI: Monica (*Medium*), Annina (*Saint of Bleecker Street*), Lucy (*Telephone*); MONTEVERDI: Poppea (*Incoronazione di Poppea*); MOZART: Fiordiligi★ & Despina (*Così fan tutte*), Donna Elvira★ (*Don Giovanni*), Mlle Silberklang (*Schauspieldirektor*), Contessa & Cherubino (*Nozze di Figaro*), Pamina‡ (*Zauberflöte*); MUSSORGSKY: Marina‡ (*Boris Godunov*); OFFENBACH: Giulietta (*Contes d'Hoffmann*); ORFF: Kluge; PUCCINI: Mimi★ (*Bohème*), Tosca; PURCELL: Dido; ROSSINI: Fiorilla (*Turco in Italia*); SCHOENBERG: A Woman (*Erwartung*); STRAUSS, R: Komponist★ (*Ariadne auf Naxos*), Gräfin★ (*Capriccio*), Marschallin & Octavian & Sophie (*Rosenkavalier*); TCHAIKOVSKY: Tatiana (*Eugene Onegin*); VERDI: Oscar‡ (*Ballo in maschera*), Alice Ford★ (*Falstaff*), Desdemona (*Otello*); WAGNER: Senta‡ (*Fliegende Holländer*). **World premieres:** KLEBE: Alkmene (*Alkmene*) Berlin 1961; LEVY:

Lavinia (*Mourning Becomes Electra*) Metropolitan Opera, New York 1967; EGK: Jeanne (*Verlobung in San Domingo*) Munich 1963; PASATIERI: Irina (*Seagull*) Houston Grand Opera 1974. Recorded for: Angel, DG. Video/Film: Mimi (*Bohème*); Cherubino (*Nozze di Figaro*); Lulu; Susanna (*Segreto di Susanna*). Gives recitals. Appears with symphony orchestra. **Res:** Losone, Switzerland. Mgmt: CAM/USA; HPL/UK.

LEBEDEVA, NELYA ALEKSANDROVNA. Lyric soprano. Russian. Resident mem: Bolshoi Theater, Moscow. Born 11 Feb 1939, Krasnoyarsk. Husband Shestakov, occupation orchestra musician. One child. Studied: Moscow Consv, N L Dorliak; Gnesin Moscow State Music Pedagog Inst, G A Malytseva. **Debut:** Cherubino (*Nozze di Figaro*) Bolshoi Theater, Moscow. Previous occupations: technologist at machinery constr factory.
Sang with major companies in BUL: Sofia; FR GER: Berlin Deutsche Oper, Dortmund, Munich Gärtnerplatz, Wiesbaden; GER DR: Berlin Komische Oper; HUN: Budapest; ITA: Milan La Scala; POL: Warsaw; USSR: Moscow Bolshoi. **Roles with these companies incl** MOZART: Cherubino★ (*Nozze di Figaro*); PROKOFIEV: Sofia★ (*Semyon Kotko*), Natasha★ (*War and Peace*); RIMSKY-KORSAKOV: Olga★ (*Maid of Pskov*); TCHAIKOVSKY: Iolanthe★. Gives recitals. Appears with symphony orchestra. **Res:** 11-23 ul Iyakovskogo, Moscow, USSR.

LEBEDEVA, NINA ALEKSANDROVNA. Lyric-dramatic soprano. Russian. Resident mem: Bolshoi Theater, Moscow. Born 18 Jul 1939, Moscow. Husband Vladimirov, occupation engineer. Studied: Moscow Consv, E V Shumskaya, O Lebedeva. **Debut:** Micaëla (*Carmen*) Bolshoi Theater, Moscow 1967. Previous occupations: accompanist. Awards: Laureate First Prize Gold Medal, Villa-Lobos Compt Rio de Janeiro.
Sang with major companies in BRA: Rio de Janeiro; USSR: Moscow Bolshoi. **Roles with these companies incl** BIZET: Micaëla★ (*Carmen*); BORODIN: Jaroslavna★ (*Prince Igor*); GOUNOD: Marguerite (*Faust*); LEONCAVALLO: Nedda (*Pagliacci*); MOZART: Contessa (*Nozze di Figaro*); PROKOFIEV: Pauline★ (*Gambler*); PUCCINI: Mimi (*Bohème*), Cio-Cio-San (*Butterfly*), Tosca; TCHAIKOVSKY: Tatiana★ (*Eugene Onegin*), Lisa★ (*Pique Dame*); VERDI: Aida, Leonora★ (*Trovatore*). Recorded for: Melodiya. Gives recitals. Appears with symphony orchestra. **Res:** 20/1-12 ul Chernyshevskogo, Moscow, USSR. Mgmt: GOS/USSR.

LEBERG, JOHN RAOUL. Stages/produces opera. Also designs stage-lighting and is a production mng. Canadian. Prod Mng, Canadian Opera Co, Toronto since 1974. Born 9 Jan 1938, Winnipeg, Man. Wife Margaret, occupation teacher. One child. Studied: Opera Dept, Royal Consv of Music, Toronto; incl music, piano & clarinet. Operatic training as asst stage dir & stage mng, Canadian Opera Co, Toronto 1968-73. **Operatic debut:** *Fledermaus* Hamilton Opera Co, Ont 1971. Previous occupation: teacher of music; composer. Awards: Royal Consv Schlshp, RCM; Canada Council study grant. Previous adm positions in opera: Dir, Hamilton Opera Co 1971-72.

Directed/produced opera for major companies in CAN: Ottawa, Toronto. **Operas staged for these companies incl** BARTOK: *Bluebeard's Castle*★*;* DONIZETTI: *Rita*★*;* GOUNOD: *Faust*★*;* MENOTTI: *Old Maid and the Thief*★*;* MOZART: *Così fan tutte*★*, Nozze di Figaro*★*;* PUCCINI: *Bohème*★*;* ROSSINI: *Barbiere di Siviglia*★*;* SMETANA: *Bartered Bride*★*;* STRAUSS, J: *Fledermaus*★. **Operatic world premieres:** REA: *Prisoners' Play* Univ Toronto 1973; WILSON: *Selfish Giant* Can Op Children's Chorus, Toronto 1973. Teaches at Univ of Toronto Opera Dept, Ont. **Res:** 5 Massey Sq, Apt 1019, Toronto, Can.

LEBRUN, LOUISE. Coloratura soprano. Canadian. Born 9 Jan 1940, Montreal. Husband Marcel Bousquet, occupation impresario. One child. Studied: Vincent d'Indy School of Music, Canada. **Debut:** Feu, Princesse & Rossignol (*Enfant et les sortilèges*) Sadler's Wells, London 1965. Awards: First Prize CBC Ntl Talent Fest.

Sang with major companies in AUS: Salzburg Fest; CAN: Montreal/Quebec, Ottawa; FR GER: Wuppertal; MEX: Mexico City; UK: Glyndebourne Fest, London English National; USA: Hartford, New Orleans, New York City Opera, Philadelphia Lyric, Santa Fe; YUG: Belgrade. **Roles with these companies incl** BEETHOVEN: Marzelline (*Fidelio*); DONIZETTI: Marie★ (*Fille du régiment*), Lucia★; GOUNOD: Juliette★; MOZART: Konstanze★ (*Entführung aus dem Serail*), Susanna★ (*Nozze di Figaro*), Königin der Nacht★ (*Zauberflöte*); OFFENBACH: Olympia (*Contes d'Hoffmann*); ROSSINI: Rosina (*Barbiere di Siviglia*); STRAUSS, R: Sophie (*Rosenkavalier*); VERDI: Oscar★ (*Ballo in maschera*), Nannetta★ (*Falstaff*), Gilda★ (*Rigoletto*), Violetta★ (*Traviata*). Recorded for: Canadian Record Co. Video/Film: Juliette; Susanna (*Segreto di Susanna*). Gives recitals. Appears with symphony orchestra. **Res:** Montreal, PQ, Canada. Mgmt: ARS/CAN.

LEE, MING CHO. Scenic designer for opera, theater. American. Born 3 Oct 1930, Shanghai, China. Wife Elizabeth. Three children. Studied: Occidental Coll, Univ of Calif, Los Angeles. Prof training: under Jo Mielziner, New York 1954-58. **Operatic debut:** *Turco in Italia* Peabody Arts Theater & School of Music, Baltimore MD, 1959. Theater debut: Phoenix Theater, New York 1958. Awards: DHL, Occidental Coll 1975; Tony Awd nomination 1970; Joseph Maharam Awd, Electra 1965, Ergo 1968; Show Business Off-Broadway Awd 1969.

Designed for major companies in ARG: Buenos Aires; FR GER: Hamburg; USA: Baltimore, Boston, Dallas, New York Met & City Opera, San Francisco Opera & Spring Opera, Washington DC. **Operas designed for these companies incl** DONIZETTI: *Anna Bolena*★*, Favorite*★*, Lucia*★*, Maria Stuarda*★*, Roberto Devereux*★*;* FLOYD: *Susannah*★*;* GINASTERA: *Don Rodrigo*★*;* GOUNOD: *Faust;* HANDEL: *Ariodante*★*, Giulio Cesare;* MENOTTI: *Globolinks;* MOZART: *Idomeneo*★*, Nozze di Figaro;* MUSSORGSKY: *Boris Godunov*★*;* OFFENBACH: *Contes d'Hoffmann*★*;* OHANA: *Syllabaire pour Phèdre*★*;* PUCCINI: *Butterfly;* PURCELL: *Dido and Aeneas*★*;* RIMSKY-KORSAKOV: *Coq d'or*★*;* THOMSON: *Four Saints in Three Acts*★*;*

WAGNER: *Tristan und Isolde.* **Operatic world premieres:** GINASTERA: *Bomarzo* Opera Soc of Washington, DC 1967. Exhibitions of stage designs Library & Museum of Perf Arts, Lincoln Center, New York 1969; Museum of City of New York. Teaches at Yale Drama School, New Haven, CT. **Res:** New York, NY, USA.

LEGA, LUIGI MAURIZIO. Dramatic tenor. Italian. Born 7 Apr 1940, Bordighera, Italy. Wife Anna. Studied: Salvatore Salvati, San Remo & Basel; Prof Leni Neuenschwander, Mannheim, FR Ger. **Debut:** Pinkerton (*Butterfly*) Oberhausen Opera, FR Ger 1961.

Sang with major companies in AUS: Graz, Vienna Staatsoper; BRA: Rio de Janeiro; CZE: Brno; FR GER: Berlin Deutsche Oper, Bielefeld, Bonn, Cologne, Düsseldorf-Duisburg, Essen, Frankfurt, Hamburg, Hannover, Karlsruhe, Kassel, Kiel, Krefeld, Mannheim, Munich Staatsoper, Nürnberg, Saarbrücken, Stuttgart, Wiesbaden, Wuppertal; HOL: Amsterdam; ITA: Palermo, Trieste; SPA: Barcelona. **Roles with these companies incl** d'ALBERT: Pedro (*Tiefland*); BEETHOVEN: Florestan (*Fidelio*); BIZET: Don José (*Carmen*); DONIZETTI: Edgardo (*Lucia*); FLOTOW: Lionel (*Martha*); GIORDANO: Andrea Chénier; GLUCK: Pylade (*Iphigénie en Tauride*); LEONCAVALLO: Canio★ (*Pagliacci*); MASCAGNI: Turiddu★ (*Cavalleria rusticana*); OFFENBACH: Hoffmann; PUCCINI: Rodolfo★ (*Bohème*), Pinkerton★ (*Butterfly*), Des Grieux★ (*Manon Lescaut*), Cavaradossi★ (*Tosca*), Calaf★ (*Turandot*); SMETANA: Hans (*Bartered Bride*); STRAUSS, J: Alfred (*Fledermaus*); STRAUSS, R: Ein Sänger (*Rosenkavalier*), Herodes (*Salome*); TCHAIKOVSKY: Gherman (*Pique Dame*); VERDI: Radames★ (*Aida*), Riccardo★ (*Ballo in maschera*), Don Carlo★, Jacopo Foscari (*Due Foscari*), Don Alvaro★ (*Forza del destino*), Ismaele (*Nabucco*), Duca di Mantova (*Rigoletto*), Alfredo (*Traviata*), Manrico★ (*Trovatore*); WAGNER: Erik (*Fliegende Holländer*), Lohengrin, Walther (*Meistersinger*), Walther v d Vogelweide★ (*Tannhäuser*). Gives recitals. Appears with symphony orchestra. Teaches voice. **Res:** Roonstr 65, D 56 Wuppertal 1, FR Ger. Mgmt: VEB/USA.

LEHMANN, HANS PETER. Stages/produces opera. Also designs stage-lighting. German. Oberspielleiter & Resident Stage Dir, Städtische Oper Nürnberg, FR Ger. Studied: music, incl voice. Operatic training as asst stage dir to Wieland Wagner, Bayreuth.

Directed/produced opera for major companies in FR GER: Bayreuth Fest, Nürnberg, Stuttgart, Wuppertal; HOL: Amsterdam; SWI: Zurich; USA: Chicago, New York Met; et al. **Operas staged with these companies incl** BUSONI: *Doktor Faust;* MOZART: *Così fan tutte, Entführung aus dem Serail;* STRAUSS, R: *Elektra, Salome;* TCHAIKOVSKY: *Pique Dame;* VERDI: *Luisa Miller, Otello;* WAGNER: *Lohengrin, Parsifal, Rheingold, Walküre, Siegfried, Götterdämmerung, Tannhäuser, Tristan und Isolde;* et al.

LEHMEYER, JOHN JAY. Costume designer for opera & theater. Is also a stage dir. American. Resident designer & since 1975 Asst Gen Mgr, Baltimore Opera Co, MD. Born 10 Feb 1940,

Baltimore. Single. Studied: Maryland Inst of Art. **Operatic debut:** *Rosenkavalier* Baltimore Opera 1974. Theater debut: Centre Stage, Baltimore 1963. Prev adm positions w Trinity Sq Theatre, Providence, RI; Milwaukee Rep Theatre. **Designed for major companies in** USA: Baltimore, Boston. **Operas designed for these companies incl** MOZART: *Così fan tutte*⋆; PUCCINI: *Tosca*⋆; STRAUSS, R: *Rosenkavalier*⋆; VERDI: *Falstaff*⋆. **Res:** 1101 N Calvert St, Baltimore, MD, USA.

LEHNOFF, NIKOLAUS. Stages/produces opera, film & television. Also designs sets, costumes & stage-lighting. German. Born 20 May 1939, Hannover. Single. Studied: theater history, Univs of Vienna & Munich; also music & piano. Operatic training as asst stage dir at Deutsche Oper Berlin, Bayreuth Fest, Met Opera 1963-71. **Operatic debut:** *Frau ohne Schatten* Opéra, Paris 1972. Awards: PhD, Univ of Vienna.

Directed/produced opera for major companies in ARG: Buenos Aires; FRA: Aix-en-Provence Fest, Orange Fest, Paris, Strasbourg; FR GER: Wuppertal; SWE: Stockholm; USA: Chicago, New York Met, San Francisco Opera. **Operas staged with these companies incl** BEETHOVEN: *Fidelio*⋆; MOZART: *Nozze di Figaro*⋆; STRAUSS, R: *Ariadne auf Naxos*⋆, *Elektra*⋆, *Salome*⋆, *Frau*⋆; VERDI: *Luisa Miller*⋆; WAGNER: *Fliegende Holländer*⋆, *Parsifal*⋆, *Tristan und Isolde*⋆. **Res:** Leopoldstr 96, 8 Munich 40, FR Ger. Mgmt: SLZ/FRG; OOC/FRA.

LEHRBERGER, THOMAS HEINRICH. Lyric tenor. German. Resident mem: Nationaltheater, Mannheim. Born 4 Aug 1934, Reit im Winkl, Germany. Single. Studied: Richard Strauss Konsv, Munich, Prof Esther Mühlbauer. **Debut:** Belmonte (*Entführung aus dem Serail*) Ulmer Theater 1963. Previous occupations: employee at post office. **Sang with major companies in** AUS: Salzburg Fest, Vienna Volksoper; FRA: Lyon, Strasbourg; FR GER: Berlin Deutsche Oper, Bielefeld, Cologne, Frankfurt, Hamburg, Hannover, Karlsruhe, Mannheim, Munich Staatsoper & Gärtnerplatz, Nürnberg, Saarbrücken, Stuttgart; ITA: Florence Comunale; SPA: Barcelona; SWI: Zurich. **Roles with these companies incl** ADAM: Zephoris (*Si j'étais roi*); BRITTEN: Madwoman⋆ (*Curlew River*); CIMAROSA: Paolino⋆ (*Matrimonio segreto*); DONIZETTI: Ernesto⋆ (*Don Pasquale*), Nemorino⋆ (*Elisir*); FLOTOW: Lionel⋆ (*Martha*); HAYDN: Nancio⋆ (*Infedeltà delusa*); LORTZING: Baron Kronthal⋆ (*Wildschütz*); MOZART: Ferrando⋆ (*Così fan tutte*), Don Ottavio⋆ (*Don Giovanni*), Belmonte⋆ (*Entführung aus dem Serail*), Mitridate, Tamino⋆ (*Zauberflöte*); NICOLAI: Fenton⋆ (*Lustigen Weiber*); OFFENBACH: Hoffmann⋆; ORFF: Haemon⋆ (*Antigonae*); PROKOFIEV: Truffaldino⋆ (*Love for Three Oranges*); PUCCINI: Rodolfo (*Bohème*); ROSSINI: Almaviva⋆ (*Barbiere di Siviglia*), Don Ramiro⋆ (*Cenerentola*), Comte Ory; SMETANA: Hans (*Bartered Bride*); STRAUSS, J: Alfred⋆ (*Fledermaus*); STRAVINSKY: Vasili (*Mavra*); SUTERMEISTER: Romeo; VERDI: Fenton (*Falstaff*); WAGNER: David⋆ (*Meistersinger*), Walther v d Vogelweide⋆ (*Tannhäuser*); WEILL: Jim Mahoney (*Aufstieg und Fall der*

Stadt Mahagonny); WOLF-FERRARI: Filipeto (*Quattro rusteghi*). Also HAYDN: Fileno⋆ (*Fedeltà premiata*). **World premieres:** ZAFRED: Laertes (*Hamlet*) Ulmer Theater 1974; SCHWERTZIG: Bänkelsänger (*Langer Weg zur grossen Mauer*) Ulmer Theater 1975. Gives recitals. Appears with symphony orchestra. Teaches voice. Coaches repertoire. Mgmt: SLZ/FRG.

LEIB, GÜNTHER. Lyric baritone. German. Resident mem: Deutsche Staatsoper, Berlin; Staatsoper Dresden, Ger DR. Born 12 Apr 1927, Gotha, Germany. Widowed. One child. Studied: Musikhochschule, Prof Alfred Brockhaus, Weimar. Ger DR. **Debut:** Dott Bartolo (*Barbiere di Siviglia*) Stadttheater Köthen, Ger DR 1952. Previous occupations: violinist. Awards: Kammersänger, Nationalpreisträger, Prof for Voice, Ministry for Culture, Ger DR; Schumann-Preis, City of Zwickau.

Sang with major companies in AUS: Salzburg Fest; CZE: Prague Smetana; FRA: Paris; FR GER: Hamburg, Nürnberg; GER DR: Berlin Staatsoper, Dresden, Leipzig; HUN: Budapest; POL: Warsaw; SWE: Drottningholm Fest; USSR: Moscow Bolshoi. **Roles with these companies incl** DONIZETTI: Dott Malatesta⋆ & Don Pasquale⋆ (*Don Pasquale*); LORTZING: Graf v. Liebenau (*Waffenschmied*), Peter I & Van Bett (*Zar und Zimmermann*); MOZART: Guglielmo⋆‡ & Don Alfonso (*Così fan tutte*), Leporello (*Don Giovanni*), Conte Almaviva & Figaro (*Nozze di Figaro*), Papageno⋆‡ (*Zauberflöte*); PUCCINI: Marcello⋆ (*Bohème*), Sharpless⋆ (*Butterfly*); ROSSINI: Dott Bartolo (*Barbiere di Siviglia*); STRAUSS, R: Musiklehrer⋆(*Ariadne auf Naxos*), Olivier⋆ (*Capriccio*); VERDI: Fra Melitone⋆ (*Forza del destino*); WAGNER: Beckmesser⋆ (*Meistersinger*), Wolfram⋆ (*Tannhäuser*). Also HANDEL: Poro‡, Admeto, Medoro (*Orlando*), Adalberto (*Ottone*), Alexander, Achilla (*Giulio Cesare*); STRAUSS, R: Faninal⋆ (*Rosenkavalier*). **World premieres:** FRIEDRICH: Tartüff (*Tartüff*) Staatsoper Dresden 1962. Recorded for: Eterna. Gives recitals. Appears with symphony orchestra. Teaches voice. Coaches repertoire. On faculty of Carl Maria von Weber Hochschule für Musik, Dresden. **Res:** Barfussweg 6b, Dresden, Ger DR. Mgmt: KDR/GDR; WLS/USA.

LEINSDORF, ERICH. Conductor of opera and symphony. American. Born 4 Feb 1912, Vienna. Wife Vera. Five children, from prev marriage. Studied: Vienna State Acad of Music, Paul Pisk; incl piano, Paul Emerich, cello, Lilly Kosz. Operatic training as repetiteur, asst cond & chorus master at Salzburg Fest 1934-37; var Ital stagioni; Met Opera, New York. **Operatic debut:** *Walküre* Met Opera 1938. Symphonic debut: Vienna Acad 1933. Previous adm positions in opera: Music Consultant & Resident Cond, Met Opera 1957-62.

Conducted with major companies in ARG: Buenos Aires; AUS: Vienna Staatsoper & Volksoper; FR GER: Bayreuth Fest; HOL: Amsterdam; USA: New York Met & City Opera, San Francisco Opera. **Operas with these companies incl** BEETHOVEN: *Fidelio;* BERG: *Wozzeck;* BIZET: *Carmen;* DEBUSSY: *Pelléas et Mélisande;* FLOYD: *Susannah;* GLUCK: *Alceste, Orfeo ed Euridice;* MOZART: *Così fan tutte‡, Don Gio-*

vanni‡, *Entführung aus dem Serail, Nozze di Figaro*‡, *Zauberflöte;* MUSSORGSKY: *Boris Godunov;* POULENC: *Dialogues des Carmélites;* PUCCINI: *Gianni Schicchi, Butterfly*‡, *Tosca*‡; RIMSKY-KORSAKOV: *Coq d'or;* SCHOEN-BERG: *Glückliche Hand;* STRAUSS, J: *Fledermaus;* STRAUSS, R: *Arabella, Ariadne auf Naxos*‡, *Elektra, Rosenkavalier, Salome*‡; STRA-VINSKY: *Rake's Progress;* VERDI: *Macbeth*‡, *Otello, Rigoletto, Simon Boccanegra, Traviata;* WAGNER: *Fliegende Holländer, Lohengrin*‡, *Meistersinger, Parsifal, Rheingold**, *Walküre**‡, *Siegfried**, *Götterdämmerung, Tannhäuser**, *Tristan und Isolde**; WEINBERGER: *Schwanda.* Also WALTON: *Troilus and Cressida;* MARTIN: *Sturm.* Rec only: CORNELIUS: *Barbier von Bagdad;* DONIZETTI: *Lucia;* PUCCINI: *Bohème, Tabarro, Turandot;* ROSSINI: *Barbiere;* VERDI: *Aida, Ballo in maschera.* Recorded for EMI, RCA. Conducted major orch in Europe, USA/Canada, Cent/S America, Asia, Austrl. Previous positions as Mus Dir with major orch: Cleveland Orch, O, USA 1943-45; Rochester Phil, NY 1947-56; Boston Symph Orch 1962-69. **Addr:** c/o: Musil Inc, 320 W 56 St, New York, NY 10019, USA. Mgmt: HUR/USA.

LEITNER, FERDINAND. Conductor of opera and symphony. German. Mus Dir & Principal Cond, Opernhaus Zurich 1969- . Born Berlin, Germany. Wife Gisela Büsing. One child. Studied: Staatliche Hochschule für Musik, Berlin. Previous adm positions in opera: Gen Dir, Bayerische Staatsoper, Munich 1946-47; Gen Dir, Staatsoper, and head of symph concerts, Stuttgart 1947-69.
Conducted with major companies in ARG: Buenos Aires; AUS: Bregenz Fest, Vienna Staatsoper; FIN: Helsinki; FRA: Bordeaux, Lyon, Paris, Strasbourg; FR GER: Bayreuth Fest, Berlin Deutsche Oper, Cologne, Frankfurt, Hamburg, Munich Staatsoper, Nürnberg, Stuttgart; GER DR: Leipzig; HOL: Amsterdam; ITA: Milan La Scala, Naples San Carlo, Palermo Massimo, Rome Teatro dell'Opera, Venice; MEX: Mexico City; MON: Monte Carlo; ROM: Bucharest; SWI: Basel, Zurich; UK: Edinburgh Fest, London Royal; USA: Chicago, San Diego, San Francisco Opera. **Operas with these companies incl** BEETHOVEN: *Fidelio**; BERG: *Lulu**, *Wozzeck;* BIZET: *Carmen;* BUSONI: *Doktor Faust**; CORNELIUS: *Barbier von Bagdad**; DEBUSSY: *Pelléas et Mélisande**; EGK: *Zaubergeige;* EINEM: *Besuch der alten Dame**, *Dantons Tod;* FLOTOW: *Martha;* FORTNER: *Elisabeth Tudor**; GINA-STERA: *Bomarzo**; GLUCK: *Alceste, Iphigénie en Tauride, Orfeo ed Euridice**; HANDEL: *Alcina, Giulio Cesare, Orlando furioso;* HENZE: *Junge Lord;* HINDEMITH: *Mathis der Maler;* JANACEK: *Jenufa;* LORTZING: *Wildschütz**, *Zar und Zimmermann;* MOZART: *Clemenza di Tito**, *Cosi fan tutte**, *Don Giovanni**, *Entführung aus dem Serail**, *Finta giardiniera, Nozze di Figaro**, *Zaïde, Zauberflöte**; NICOLAI: *Lustigen Weiber;* OFFENBACH: *Contes d'Hoffmann;* ORFF: *Antigonae, Bernauerin**, *Carmina burana**, *Kluge**, *Mond;* PUCCINI: *Gianni Schicchi, Butterfly, Tabarro, Toscà;* REIMANN: *Melusine**; ROSSINI: *Barbiere di Siviglia, Turco in Italia;* SMETANA: *Bartered Bride;* STRAUSS, J: *Fledermaus;* STRAUSS, R: *Ara-*

bella*, *Ariadne auf Naxos**, *Capriccio**, *Daphne, Elektra**, *Frau ohne Schatten, Rosenkavalier**, *Salome**; STRAVINSKY: *Oedipus Rex, Rake's Progress;* TCHAIKOVSKY: *Eugene Onegin;* VERDI: *Aida, Don Carlo, Due Foscari, Falstaff**, *Forza del destino, Macbeth, Nabucco, Otello, Trovatore;* WAGNER: *Fliegende Holländer, Lohengrin**, *Meistersinger**, *Parsifal**, *Rheingold**, *Walküre**, *Siegfried**, *Götterdämmerung**, *Tannhäuser**, *Tristan und Isolde**; WEBER: *Euryanthe, Freischütz**, *Oberon;* WEILL: *Aufstieg und Fall der Stadt Mahagonny.* Conducted major orch in Europe, USA/Canada, Cent/S America, Asia, Africa, Austrl. Teaches at Konsv Zurich. **Res:** Zurich, Switzerland. **Mgmt:** KGZ/SWI; IBA/HOL.

LENHART, RENATE. Lyric soprano. Austrian. Resident mem: Zurich Opera, Switzerland. Born 15 Feb, Hohenau, Austria. Divorced. Studied: Vienna Consv, Kmsg Peter Klein, Prof K Hudec; E Phillipp, Kmsg Hilde Zadek, Zoe Prasch von Formacher, Vienna. **Debut:** Cherubino (*Nozze di Figaro*) Bern Opera, Switzerland 1962.
Sang with major companies in AUS: Bregenz Fest, Vienna Staatsoper & Volksoper; BRA: Rio de Janeiro; FRA: Bordeaux, Paris; FR GER: Cologne, Hannover, Munich Staatsoper; SWI: Basel, Zurich. **Roles with these companies incl** BEETHO-VEN: Marzelline* (*Fidelio*); BIZET: Micaëla* (*Carmen*); CHERUBINI: Glauce* (*Medea*); FLOTOW: Lady Harriet* (*Martha*); GINA-STERA: Julia Farnese* (*Bomarzo*); HAYDN: Clarissa (*Mondo della luna*); HENZE: Costanza* (*König Hirsch*/*Re Cervo*); HUM-PERDINCK: Gretel*; LORTZING: Baronin Freimann* (*Wildschütz*); MOZART: Servilia (*Clemenza di Tito*), Zerlina* (*Don Giovanni*), Violante (*Finta giardiniera*), Susanna* & Cherubino (*Nozze di Figaro*), Pamina* (*Zauberflöte*); NICOLAI: Aennchen (*Lustigen Weiber*); OFFENBACH: Antonia* (*Contes d'Hoffmann*); PUCCINI: Lauretta* (*Gianni Schicchi*), Liù* (*Turandot*); ROS-SINI: Elvira* (*Italiana in Algeri*); SMETANA: Marie* (*Bartered Bride*); STRAUSS, J: Adele* (*Fledermaus*); STRAUSS, R: Sophie* (*Rosenkavalier*); WEBER: Aennchen* (*Freischütz*). Also MARTIN: Miranda* (*Sturm*); BURKHARDT: Maria (*Stern geht auf aus Jakob*). Video/Film—ORF Prod Bregenz Fest: Vespina (*Infedeltà delusa*). **Res:** Zurich, Switzerland.

LEON, MAX M. American. Gen Mng/Co-Founder, Opera Company of Philadelphia, 1518 Walnut St, Philadelphia, PA 19102, 1975- . In charge of overall adm matters. Is also a conductor. Additional adm positions: Pres, WDAS Broadcasting Co, Philadelphia. Born 10 Oct 1904, Poland. Widowed. Three children. Plays the violin, saxophone & clarinet. Previous positions, primarily adm & musical: Fndr & Cond, Philadelphia Pops Orch; Assoc Cond, Philadelphia Police & Fireman's Band; Mus Dir, Hageman String Band; Pres, Gen Mng, Philadelphia Grand Opera Co. World premieres at theaters under his management: ARIA: *Jericho Road* Philadelphia 1969. Initiated major policy changes including starting the Educ Dept of Philadelphia Grand Opera, presenting excerpts of operas to schools in Philadelphia area. Mem of Membership Commtt, OP-

ERA America. **Res:** 6041 Drexel Rd, Philadelphia, PA, USA.

LÉON, PIERRE CAMILLE. Stages/produces opera, theater & television. Belgian. Oberspielleiter & Resident Stage Dir, Theater der Stadt Bonn, FR Ger. Born 8 Jan 1924, Brussels. Single. **Operatic debut:** *Don Pasquale* Theater der Stadt Bonn 1967. Theater debut: Volksbühne, Berlin, FR Ger 1963. Previous occupation: art gallery owner. Awards: Prix Plantin, Comité Plantin & City of Antwerp.
    Directed/produced opera for major companies in FR GER: Bonn, Essen, Hannover, Krefeld; SWI: Zurich. **Operas staged with these companies incl** BERG: *Wozzeck;* DONIZETTI: *Anna Bolena, Lucia★, Maria di Rohan, Roberto Devereux;* GERSHWIN: *Porgy and Bess;* MOZART: *Così fan tutte, Don Giovanni, Nozze di Figaro;* OFFENBACH: *Contes d'Hoffmann;* PUCCINI: *Tosca;* RAVEL: *Heure espagnole;* ROSSINI: *Cenerentola;* STRAUSS, R: *Ariadne auf Naxos;* VERDI: *Forza del destino, Otello, Traviata;* WEILL: *Dreigroschenoper;* WOLF-FERRARI: *Quattro rusteghi.* Mgmt: PAS/FRG; SMN/USA.

LEPPARD, RAYMOND JOHN. Conductor of opera and symphony; composer. British. Resident cond, BBC Northern Symph Orch, Manchester, UK. Born 11 Aug 1927, London. Single. Studied: Cambridge Univ, UK; incl viola, piano & harpsichord. Plays the harpsichord. Operatic training as répetiteur & asst cond at Glyndebourne Fest, UK 1953-55. **Operatic debut:** *Nozze di Figaro* Covent Garden, London 1957.
    Conducted with major companies in ARG: Buenos Aires; BEL: Brussels; DEN: Copenhagen; NOR: Oslo; SWE: Drottningholm Fest; UK: Aldeburgh Fest, Scottish, Glyndebourne Fest, London Royal & English National; USA: San Francisco Opera, Santa Fe. **Operas with these companies incl** BRITTEN: *Albert Herring;* CAVALLI: *Calisto★‡, Egisto, Ormindo★‡;* JANACEK: *Cunning Little Vixen★;* MONTEVERDI: *Favola d'Orfeo, Incoronazione di Poppea★, Ritorno d'Ulisse★;* MOZART: *Così fan tutte★, Don Giovanni★, Nozze di Figaro★;* ROSSINI: *Barbiere di Siviglia.* Also MONTEVERDI: *Combattimento di Tancredi* on records. **World premieres:** MAW: *Rising of the Moon* Glyndebourne Fest 1970. Recorded for Argo. As composer he made musical adaptations of var operas by Cavalli and Monteverdi. **Res:** 16 Hamilton Terrace, London NW8, UK.

LEVEUGLE, DANIEL. Stages/produces opera, theater & film and is an actor & author. French. Born 25 Nov 1924, Paris. Wife Georgette, occupation Dr dental surgery. One child. Studied: Charles Dullin, Pierre Renoir. **Operatic debut:** *Nozze di Figaro* Glyndebourne Fest 1965. Theater debut: Comp Daniel Leveugle, Paris 1948.
    Directed/produced opera for major companies in FRA: Aix-en-Provence Fest, Strasbourg, Toulouse; UK: Glyndebourne Fest. **Operas staged for these companies incl** MOZART: *Così fan tutte★, Don Giovanni★, Nozze di Figaro★;* ROSSINI: *Comte Ory★.* Teaches at INSAS, Brussels. **Res:** 8 rue Thérésienne, Brussels 1000, Belgium.

LEVINE, JAMES LAWRENCE. Conductor of opera and symphony. American. Principal Cond, Metropolitan Opera, New York; Music Dir Designate Metropolitan Opera 1976-81. Also Music Dir, Chicago Symph Ravinia Fest; Cincinnati Symph May Fest, USA. Born 23 June 1943, Cincinnati, O, USA. Single. Studied: Aspen Fest School, Wolfgang Vacano, CO; Juilliard School, Jean Morel, New York; Ford Fndt Cond Project, Fausto Cleva, Max Rudolf; George Szell, Cleveland; all conducting. Also piano Marlboro Fest, Rudolf Serkin; Juilliard School, Rosina Lhévinne. Voice & vocal rept Jennie Tourel, Adele Addison, Mack Harrell, Hans Hotter. Plays the piano. **Operatic debut:** *Pêcheurs de perles* Aspen Music Fest, CO 1962. Symphonic debut: Aspen Fest Orch 1961. Awards: Hon DM, Univ of Cincinnati. Previous adm positions in opera: Music Dir, Cleveland Concert Assoc, O 1968-72.
    Conducted with major companies in UK: Welsh National; USA: Cincinnati, New York Met, San Francisco Opera. **Operas with these companies incl** BEETHOVEN: *Fidelio;* BELLINI: *Norma★‡;* BERG: *Wozzeck★;* BERLIOZ: *Damnation de Faust★;* BERNSTEIN: *Trouble in Tahiti★;* BIZET: *Pêcheurs de perles;* BRITTEN: *Albert Herring;* DEBUSSY: *Pelléas et Mélisande;* MOZART: *Così fan tutte★, Don Giovanni★, Entführung aus dem Serail★, Nozze di Figaro★, Zauberflöte★;* PUCCINI: *Gianni Schicchi, Butterfly★, Tosca★;* ROSSINI: *Barbiere di Siviglia★‡, Cambiale di matrimonio;* STRAUSS, R: *Ariadne auf Naxos, Salome★;* STRAVINSKY: *Mavra;* VERDI: *Aida★, Don Carlo, Ernani★, Falstaff★, Forza del destino★, Giovanna d'Arco★‡, Luisa Miller★, Otello★, Rigoletto★, Simon Boccanegra, Traviata★, Trovatore★, Vespri★‡;* WAGNER: *Lohengrin★, Tannhäuser★.* Recorded for RCA, EMI/Angel, ABC Audio Treas. Conducted major orch in Europe, USA/Canada. **Res:** New York, USA. Mgmt: CAM/USA.

LEVINE, JOSEPH. Conductor of opera, ballet and symphony. American. Assoc Cond, Hawaii Opera Theatre, Honolulu, USA 1973- . Also Assoc Cond, Honolulu Symph, Hawaii. Born 14 Aug 1912, Philadelphia. Wife Mary, occupation musician, writer. Two children. Studied: Curtis Inst of Music, Philadelphia; Josef Hofmann, piano; Wanda Landowska, harpsichord; Hans Wohlmuth, Ernst Lert, opera; Fritz Reiner, Artur Rodzinski, cond. **Debut:** *Don Giovanni* Philadelphia Chamber Opera 1947. Symph debut: New Center of Music Orch, Philadelphia 1940. Awards: Achievement Recognition Inst, Lib of Congress; Mercian Medal, College of St Mary, Omaha, NE; Disting Citizen Citation Awd, Creighton Univ, Omaha. Previous adm positions in opera: Art Dir, Omaha Civic Opera, USA 1958-69; Art Dir, Phila Co-Opera, USA 1946-50.
    Conducted with major companies in ARG: Buenos Aires; AUS: Vienna Volksoper; BEL: Brussels; BRA: Rio de Janeiro; CAN: Montreal/Quebec, Ottawa, Toronto, Vancouver; FRA: Paris; GRE: Athens Fest; FR GER: Bonn, Cologne, Düsseldorf-Duisburg, Essen, Frankfurt, Hamburg, Munich Staatsoper, Stuttgart, Wiesbaden; HOL: Amsterdam; ITA: Florence Maggio & Comunale, Genoa, Milan La Scala, Naples, Rome Opera, Trieste, Turin, Venice; MEX: Mexico

City; MON: Monte Carlo; POR: Lisbon; SWI: Geneva, Zurich; UK: Edinburgh Fest, London Royal; USA: Baltimore, Boston, Chicago, Cincinnati, Dallas, Fort Worth, Hartford, Hawaii, Houston, Kansas City, Lake George, Memphis, Miami, Minneapolis, Newark, New Orleans, New York Met, Omaha, Philadelphia Grand, Pittsburgh, Portland, St Paul, San Antonio, San Diego, Seattle, Washington DC; YUG: Zagreb, Belgrade. **Operas with these companies incl** BIZET: *Carmen;* DEBUSSY: *Enfant prodigue;* FALLA: *Vida breve;* GAY/Britten: *Beggar's Opera;* HUMPERDINCK: *Hänsel und Gretel;* LEONCAVALLO: *Pagliacci;* MARTINU: *Comedy on the Bridge;* MENOTTI: *Amahl, Amelia al ballo, Medium*, Old Maid and the Thief, Telephone*;* MOORE: *Ballad of Baby Doe;* MOZART: *Don Giovanni, Nozze di Figaro;* OFFENBACH: *Périchole;* ORFF: *Carmina burana;* PERGOLESI: *Serva padrona;* PUCCINI: *Bohème, Gianni Schicchi, Butterfly, Suor Angelica, Tabarro, Tosca;* RAVEL: *Enfant et les sortilèges;* ROSSINI: *Barbiere di Siviglia;* STRAUSS, J: *Fledermaus;* THOMSON: *Four Saints in Three Acts;* VAUGHAN WILLIAMS: *Riders to the Sea;* VERDI: *Aida, Rigoletto, Traviata*, Trovatore;* WEILL: *Dreigroschenoper;* WOLFFERRARI: *Segreto di Susanna.* Conducted major orch in Europe, USA/Canada, Cent/S America, Asia. Previous positions as Mus Dir with major orch: Omaha Symph, NE, USA 1958-69; Ballet Theatre Orch, New York 1950-58. Teaches. **Res:** 1515 Nuuanu Ave, QT 98, Honolulu, Hawaii, USA. Mgmt: APA/USA.

LEVINE, RHODA JANE. Stages/produces opera, theater & television and is a choreographer and author. American. Born 15 Jun 1932, New York. Single. Studied: Bard Coll, Sarah Lawrence Coll, Max Adrian, Hanya Holm, Martha Graham, Ben Harkarvy, NY; incl piano, guitar. Operatic training as asst stage dir at New York City Opera 1960's. **Operatic debut:** BRITTEN: *Abraham and Isaac* Spoleto Fest 1965. Theater debut: as choreogr, Broadway thtr 1958. Previous occupation: writer, teacher. Awards: Fulbright grant; Jr Literary Guild selection for children's bks.
    Directed/produced opera for major companies in BEL: Brussels; HOL: Amsterdam; ITA: Spoleto Fest; UK: Edinburgh Fest; USA: Kansas City. **Operas staged with these companies incl** DONIZETTI: *Don Pasquale*;* GLUCK: *Orfeo ed Euridice*;* HAYDN: *Mondo della luna*;* JANACEK: *From the House of the Dead*;* KURKA: *Good Soldier Schweik*;* LECOCQ: *Fille de Madame Angot*;* MOZART: *Nozze di Figaro*;* PUCCINI: *Tosca*.* Also SMETANA: *Bartered Bride*.* **Operatic world premieres:** WHITE: *Metamorphosis* Thtr Living Arts, Philadelphia 1969; AUDEN: *Ballad of Barnaby* Edinburgh Fest 1971. Operatic Video—NET TV: *Abraham and Isaac, My Heart's in the Highlands, Pique Dame.* Teaches at Curtis Inst, Philadelphia; Yale Univ, New Haven; Bard Coll, NY. **Res:** 18 E 8 St, New York, USA.

LEVKO, VALENTINA NIKOLAEVNA; née Bichkova. Contralto. Russian. Resident mem: Bolshoi Theater, Moscow. Born 13 Aug 1926, Moscow. Husband Levko, occupation retired pilot; adminis-

trator. One son. Studied: M L Maksakova, T D Zhemchuzhinaya; Gnesin Musical Pedagog Inst; incl violin. **Debut:** Helene (*War and Peace*) Stanislavski Theater, Moscow 1957.
    Sang with major companies in BUL: Sofia; CAN: Montreal/Quebec; FRA: Paris; GER DR: Berlin Staatsoper, Leipzig; ITA: Milan La Scala; POL: Warsaw Teatr Wielki; USSR: Kiev, Leningrad Kirov, Moscow Bolshoi & Stanislavski. **Roles with these companies incl** BORODIN: Kontchakovna*(*Prince Igor*); GLINKA: Ratmir*(*Ruslan and Ludmilla*); MUSSORGSKY: Marfa* (*Khovanshchina*); PROKOFIEV: Duenna*, Helene* (*War and Peace*); RIMSKY-KORSAKOV: Nejata* (*Sadko*), Lyoubacha* (*Tsar's Bride*); SAINT-SAENS: Dalila*; TCHAIKOVSKY: Comtesse*(*Pique Dame*); VERDI: Ulrica*(*Ballo in maschera*), Dame Quickly* (*Falstaff*), Azucena*(*Trovatore*). Recorded for: Melodiya. Gives recitals. Appears with symphony orchestra. Teaches voice. Coaches repertoire. On faculty of Gnesin Musical Pedagog Inst, Moscow. **Res:** 271 Kutuzovskiy Prospekt kv 90, Moscow, USSR.

LEWIS, HENRY. Conductor of opera and symphony. American. Music Dir, New Jersey Symphony, Newark. Born Los Angeles. Wife Marilyn Horne, occupation opera singer. One child. Studied: piano, double bass. Plays the double bass. Previous adm positions in opera: Art Dir, Los Angeles Opera Co 1965.
    Conducted with major companies in CAN: Montreal/Quebec, Vancouver; ITA: Turin; USA: New York Met, San Francisco Opera & Spring Opera; et al. **Operas with these companies incl** BIZET: *Carmen;* DONIZETTI: *Anna Bolena, Don Pasquale;* GLUCK: *Iphigénie en Tauride;* GOUNOD: *Roméo et Juliette;* MASSENET: *Navarraise‡;* MEYERBEER: *Prophète;* MOZART: *Don Giovanni, Zauberflöte;* PUCCINI: *Bohème, Butterfly, Tosca;* ROSSINI: *Barbiere di Siviglia, Italiana in Algeri;* VERDI: *Ballo in maschera, Traviata, Trovatore;* et al. Recorded for Decca. Conducted major orch in Europe, USA/Canada.

LEWIS, RICHARD. Lyric tenor. British. Born Manchester, UK. Wife Elizabeth Muir, occupation concert singer. Two children. Studied: Royal Manchester Coll of Music; Royal Acad of Music, London. **Debut:** Male Chorus (*Rape of Lucretia*) Glyndebourne Fest 1947. Awards: Commander of the British Empire, Queen Elizabeth II; FRAM, Royal Acad of Music, London; FRMCM, Royal Manchester Coll of Music; LRAM, Royal Acad of Music.
    Sang with major companies in ARG: Buenos Aires; AUSTRL: Sydney; AUS: Vienna Staatsoper; FRA: Paris, Strasbourg; FR GER: Berlin Deutsche Oper; SWE: Drottningholm Fest; SWI: Geneva; UK: Edinburgh Fest, Glyndebourne Fest, London Royal; USA: Boston, Chicago, San Francisco Opera. **Roles with these companies incl** BEETHOVEN: Florestan (*Fidelio*); BERG: Alwa (*Lulu*), Hauptmann (*Wozzeck*); BIZET: Don José (*Carmen*); BOITO: Faust (*Mefistofele*); BRITTEN: Albert Herring, Edward Fairfax Vere (*Billy Budd*), Peter Grimes, Male Chorus (*Rape of Lucretia*); BUSONI: Mephisto (*Doktor Faust*); CHERUBINI: Giasone (*Medea*); GLUCK: Ad-

metos (*Alceste*); JANACEK: Steva (*Jenufa*); MASSENET: Des Grieux (*Manon*); MONTE-VERDI: Nero (*Incoronazione di Poppea*); MOZART: Ferrando (*Così fan tutte*), Don Ottavio (*Don Giovanni*), Belmonte (*Entführung aus dem Serail*), Idomeneo*, Tamino (*Zauberflöte*); OFFENBACH: Hoffmann; PUCCINI: Pinkerton (*Butterfly*); SCHOENBERG: Aron*; STRAUSS, J: Eisenstein (*Fledermaus*); STRAUSS, R: Bacchus (*Ariadne auf Naxos*), Aegisth* (*Elektra*), Herodes (*Salome*); STRAVINSKY: Tom Rakewell (*Rake's Progress*); VERDI: Alfredo (*Traviata*). **World premieres:** WALTON: Troilus (*Troilus and Cressida*) Royal Opera 1954; TIPPETT: Mark (*Midsummer Marriage*) Royal Opera 1955, Achilles (*King Priam*) Royal Opera 1962. Recorded for: EMI. Gives recitals. Appears with symphony orchestra. Teaches voice. **Res:** Forest Row, Sussex, UK. Mgmt: IBB/UK; BAR/USA.

LEWIS, WILLIAM. Dramatic tenor. American. Resident mem: Metropolitan Opera, New York. Born 23 Nov 1935, Tulsa, OK, USA. Wife Daphne, occupation opera & concert singer, soprano. Three children. Studied: Karl Kritz, Arthur Faguy-Côté, Fort Worth, TX; Max Klein, Susan Seton, Hulda & Luigi Rossini, New York. **Debut:** Rinuccio (*Gianni Schicchi*) Fort Worth Opera 1953. Previous occupations: athlete, writer. Awards: Winner Met Op Ntl Counc Aud 1955; Winner NATS, Oklahoma City, OK, 1953.
Sang with major companies in CAN: Toronto; ITA: Spoleto Fest; USA: Cincinnati, Dallas, Fort Worth, Hawaii, Milwaukee Florentine Opera, Newark, New York Met & City Opera, Pittsburgh, San Francisco Opera, Santa Fe. **Roles with these companies incl** BELLINI: Pollione (*Norma*); BERG: Alwa* (*Lulu*), Tambourmajor* (*Wozzeck*); BERLIOZ: Bénédict*, Aeneas* (*Troyens*); BIZET: Don José* (*Carmen*); DELIBES: Gérald (*Lakmé*); DONIZETTI: Ernesto (*Don Pasquale*), Nemorino (*Elisir*), Edgardo (*Lucia*); FLOTOW: Lionel (*Martha*); GALUPPI: Rinaldo (*Filosofo di campagna*); GOUNOD: Faust*, Roméo*; JANACEK: Steva* (*Jenufa*); LEONCAVALLO: Canio* (*Pagliacci*); MASCAGNI: Turiddu* (*Cavalleria rusticana*); MASSENET: Des Grieux (*Manon*); MOZART: Don Ottavio (*Don Giovanni*), Belmonte (*Entführung aus dem Serail*), Tamino (*Zauberflöte*); MUSSORGSKY: Dimitri* (*Boris Godunov*); OFFENBACH: Hoffmann*; ORFF: Haemon (*Antigonae*); PUCCINI: Rodolfo* (*Bohème*), Rinuccio (*Gianni Schicchi*), Pinkerton* (*Butterfly*), Des Grieux (*Manon Lescaut*), Luigi* (*Tabarro*), Cavaradossi* (*Tosca*); ROSSINI: Almaviva (*Barbiere di Siviglia*); STRAUSS, J: Eisenstein* & Alfred* (*Fledermaus*); STRAUSS, R: Aegisth (*Elektra*), Kaiser (*Frau ohne Schatten*), Baron Lummer* (*Intermezzo*), Narraboth* (*Salome*); TCHAIKOVSKY: Gherman* (*Pique Dame*); VERDI: Radames (*Aida*), Riccardo (*Ballo in maschera*), Carlo* (*Masnadieri*), Duca di Mantova (*Rigoletto*), Gabriele* (*Simon Boccanegra*), Alfredo* (*Traviata*), Manrico (*Trovatore*), Arrigo* (*Vespri*); WAGNER: Erik* (*Fliegende Holländer*); WEBER: Adolar (*Euryanthe*). Also KORNGOLD: Der Fremde* (*Wunder der Heliane*); ORFF: Hermes (*Prometheus*); HOLST: Prince Hal (*Boar's Head*). **World premieres:** WEISGALL: Mattan

(*Athalia*) New York Concert Opera 1964; BARBER: Bill (*Hand of Bridge*) Spoleto Fest 1959; WILD: St John (*Revelations*) ABC TV 1962. Recorded for: RCA, Vanguard. Video – ABC TV: St John (*Revelations*). Gives recitals. Appears with symphony orchestra. Teaches voice. Coaches repertoire. Composes and directs opera. **Res:** Palm Springs, CA, USA. Mgmt: LOM/USA.

LICCIONI, GEORGES. Lyric tenor. French. Resident mem: Opéra de Paris. Wife Caroline Dumas, occupation lyric soprano. Two children. Studied: Music Consv, Marseille. **Debut:** Vincent (*Mireille*) Marseille Opera. Awards: Chevalier des Arts et Lettres 1971; Chevalier du Mérite National 1973.
Sang with major companies in AUS: Vienna Staatsoper; BEL: Brussels, Liège; BRA: Rio de Janeiro; CAN: Montreal/Quebec; FRA: Aix-en-Provence, Bordeaux, Lyon, Marseille, Nancy, Nice, Orange Fest, Paris, Rouen, Strasbourg, Toulouse; FR GER: Karlsruhe; HOL: Amsterdam; ITA: Rome Caracalla; MON: Monte Carlo; SWI: Geneva; USA: Boston, Miami, New York City Opera. **Roles with these companies incl** BERLIOZ: Benvenuto Cellini, Faust (*Damnation de Faust*); BIZET: Don José (*Carmen*); BOITO: Faust (*Mefistofele*); BORODIN: Vladimir (*Prince Igor*); CHARPENTIER: Julien (*Louise*); DONIZETTI: Edgardo (*Lucia*), Gennaro (*Lucrezia Borgia*); FALLA: Paco (*Vida breve*); GLUCK: Achille (*Iphigénie en Aulide*), Pylade (*Iphigénie en Tauride*); GOUNOD: Faust, Vincent (*Mireille*), Roméo; HALEVY: Léopold (*Juive*); LALO: Mylio (*Roi d'Ys*); MASCAGNI: Turiddu (*Cavalleria rusticana*); MASSENET: Des Grieux (*Manon*), Nicias (*Thaïs*), Werther; MILHAUD: Matelot (*Pauvre matelot*); OFFENBACH: Hoffmann; POULENC: Chevalier de la Force (*Dialogues des Carmélites*); PROKOFIEV: Pierre (*War and Peace*); PUCCINI: Rodolfo (*Bohème*), Dick Johnson (*Fanciulla del West*), Rinuccio (*Gianni Schicchi*), Pinkerton (*Butterfly*), Des Grieux (*Manon Lescaut*), Cavaradossi (*Tosca*), Calaf (*Turandot*); TCHAIKOVSKY: Lenski (*Eugene Onegin*), Gherman (*Pique Dame*); VERDI: Riccardo (*Ballo in maschera*), Don Carlo, Rodolfo (*Luisa Miller*), Duca di Mantova (*Rigoletto*), Alfredo (*Traviata*). Recorded for: Vega. Gives recitals. **Res:** 22 rue des Peupliers, 92500 Rueil-Malmaison, France. Mgmt: GLZ/FRA.

LIEBERMANN, ROLF. Swiss. Adm, Opéra de Paris, 8 rue Scribe, 75009 Paris, France 1973- . In charge of overall adm matters, art policy, mus, dram & tech matters, finances. Is also a composer. Born 14 Sep 1910, Zurich. Wife Gioconda. One child. Studied: Univ of Zurich, Dr of Law; Jose Berr, Consv Zurich; cond with Hermann Scherchen; comp with Wladimir Vogel. Plays the piano. Previous occupations: Mus Dir, Radio Zurich and Norddeutscher Rundfunk, Hamburg. Form position, primarily adm & musical: Gen Int, Staatsoper, Hamburg 1959-73. World premieres at theaters under his management: HENZE: *Prinz von Homburg* 1960; KLEBE, *Figaro lässt sich scheiden* 1963; KRENEK: *Goldene Bock* 1964; EINEM: *Zerrissene* 1964; BIBALO: *Lächeln am Fusse der Leiter* 1965; KLEBE: *Jakobowsky und der Oberst* 1965; BLACHER: *Zwischenfälle bei einer Notlandung* 1966; SCHULLER: *Visitation*

1966; GOEHR: *Arden muss sterben* 1967; SEARLE: *Hamlet* 1968; MENOTTI: *Help, Help, the Globolinks!* 1968; BIBALO: *Pinocchio* 1969; WERLE: *Reise* 1969; PENDERECKI: *Teufel von Loudun* 1969; KELEMEN: *Belagerungszustand* 1970; KRENEK: *Das kommt davon oder Wenn Sardakai auf Reisen geht* 1970; CONSTANT: *Candide* 1971; TAL: *Ashmedai* 1971; KAGEL: *Staatstheater* 1971; HENRY: *Kyldex I* 1973, all in Hamburg. Awards: Hon DM, Spokane Univ, WA; Prof, City of Hamburg; Conrad Ferdinand Meyer Prize; Arts Prize, Zurich; Mozart Prize, Bremen; Reinhardt Ring for activity in musical theater; Comman, Légion d'Honneur; Grosses Bundesverdienst Kreuz, FR Ger. Mem Acad of Fine Arts, Berlin & Hamburg; Hon Mem Royal Socy of Arts, London. **Operas composed:** *Leonore 40/45* Basel 1952; *Penelope* Salzburg 1954; *Schule der Frauen* Louisville, KY 1956. **Res:** Paris, France.

LIEBMAN, MARCIA. Lirico-spinto. American. Resident mem: Musiktheater im Revier, Gelsenkirchen, FR Ger. Born 20 May 1947, New York. Husband Carlos Montané, occupation opera singer. Studied: Brooklyn Coll, New York; Gibner King, New York & Portland, OR; Jerome Lo Monaco, Düsseldorf & Los Angeles. **Debut:** Micaëla (*Carmen*) Gelsenkirchen, FR Ger 1972. Awards: Best Upcoming Female Singer for 1972-73, *Orpheus* Ger opera magazine.
Sang with major companies in FR GER: Cologne, Dortmund, Essen; SPA: Barcelona. **Roles with these companies incl** BIZET: Micaëla★ (*Carmen*); GOUNOD: Marguerite★ (*Faust*); MOZART: Fiordiligi★ (*Così fan tutte*), Donna Elvira★ (*Don Giovanni*); OFFENBACH: Antonia★ (*Contes d'Hoffmann*); PUCCINI: Liù★ (*Turandot*); STRAUSS, J: Rosalinde★ (*Fledermaus*); STRAUSS, R: Arabella★; WEBER: Agathe★ (*Freischütz*). Gives recitals. Appears with symphony orchestra. **Res:** Hotel Maritim, 465 Gelsenkirchen, FR Ger. Mgmt: CAB/SPA.

LIE-HANSEN, BJORN. Bass-baritone. Norwegian. Resident mem: Norwegian Opera, Oslo. Born 26 Mar 1937, Oslo. Single. Studied: Oskar Raaum, Oslo; Joel Berglund, Stockholm; Prof Clemens Glettenberg, Munich; Prof Clemens Kaiser-Breme, Essen. **Debut:** Masetto (*Don Giovanni*) Norwegian Opera 1962. Previous occupations: actor.
Sang with major companies in NOR: Oslo. **Roles with this company incl** BEETHOVEN: Rocco (*Fidelio*); BIZET: Escamillo (*Carmen*); MOZART: Don Alfonso★ (*Così fan tutte*), Leporello★ (*Don Giovanni*); PAISIELLO: Figaro (*Barbiere di Siviglia*); ROSSINI: Dott Bartolo★ (*Barbiere di Siviglia*), Don Magnifico★ (*Cenerentola*); WAGNER: Landgraf (*Tannhäuser*). Also CIMAROSA: Romualdo (*Astuzie femminili*); HAYDN: Apotheker★. Video/Film: Budd (*Albert Herring*); PAISIELLO: Figaro (*Barbiere di Siviglia*). Gives recitals. Appears with symphony orchestra. Teaches voice. Coaches repertoire. **Res:** Oscarsgate 88 IV, Oslo, Norway. Mgmt: PGI/NOR.

LIGABUE, ILVA PALMINA. Dramatic soprano. Italian. Born 23 May 1932, Reggio Emilia. Husband Pietro Diliberto, occupation secy gen, Teatro Massimo Palermo. Studied: Consv G Verdi, Milan; School of Perfez, Teatro alla Scala, Mo Ettore Campogalliani, Giulio Confalonieri, Milan. **Debut:** Marina (*Quattro rusteghi*) Teatro alla Scala, Milan 1957.
Sang with major companies in ARG: Buenos Aires; AUS: Bregenz Fest, Vienna Staatsoper; BEL: Brussels; BRA: Rio de Janeiro; FRA: Aix-en-Provence Fest, Marseille; GRE: Athens Fest; FR GER: Berlin Deutsche Oper, Hamburg, Kiel, Stuttgart, Wiesbaden; HOL: Amsterdam; ISR: Tel Aviv; ITA: Bologna, Florence Maggio & Comunale, Genoa, Milan La Scala, Naples, Palermo, Parma, Rome Opera, Trieste, Turin, Venice, Verona Arena; MEX: Mexico City; MON: Monte Carlo; POR: Lisbon; SWI: Geneva; UK: Edinburgh Fest, Glyndebourne Fest, London Royal; USA: Chicago, Dallas, Philadelphia Lyric; YUG: Dubrovnik, Belgrade. **Roles with these companies incl** BELLINI: Agnese (*Beatrice di Tenda*); BOITO: Margherita (*Mefistofele*); CHERUBINI: Leonora (*Osteria portoghese*); DONIZETTI: Maria di Rohan, Rita; GIORDANO: Maddalena★ (*Andrea Chénier*); GOUNOD: Marguerite (*Faust*); MOZART: Fiordiligi (*Così fan tutte*), Donna Elvira & Zerlina (*Don Giovanni*), Contessa (*Nozze di Figaro*); PERGOLESI: Serpina (*Serva padrona*); PUCCINI: Mimì★ (*Bohème*), Manon Lescaut, Suor Angelica, Tosca★, Liù (*Turandot*); ROSSINI: Mathilde (*Guillaume Tell*); VERDI: Elisabetta★ (*Don Carlo*), Donna Elvira (*Ernani*), Alice Ford★‡ (*Falstaff*), Leonora (*Forza del destino*), Amelia★ (*Masnadieri*), Desdemona (*Otello*), Amelia (*Simon Boccanegra*), Leonora (*Trovatore*); WAGNER: Eva (*Meistersinger*), Elisabeth (*Tannhäuser*); WEBER: Agathe (*Freischütz*); WOLF-FERRARI: Marina★ (*Quattro rusteghi*); ZANDONAI: Francesca da Rimini. Recorded for: Decca, RCA. **Res:** Palermo, Italy.

LIGENDZA, CATERINA. Dramatic soprano. Swedish. Resident mem: Staatsoper, Vienna. Born Stockholm. Studied: Josef Greindl, Vienna. **Debut:** Linz, Austria.
Sang with major companies in AUS: Salzburg Fest, Vienna Staatsoper; BEL: Brussels; FR GER: Bayreuth Fest, Berlin Deutsche Oper, Düsseldorf-Duisburg, Hamburg, Mannheim, Saarbrücken, Stuttgart, Wiesbaden; ITA: Milan La Scala, Trieste; SWI: Geneva; UK: London Royal; USA: New York Met; et al. **Roles with these companies incl** BEETHOVEN: Leonore (*Fidelio*); BORODIN: Jaroslavna (*Prince Igor*); MOZART: Contessa (*Nozze di Figaro*); STRAUSS, R: Arabella, Ariadne (*Ariadne auf Naxos*), Chrysothemis (*Elektra*), Marschallin (*Rosenkavalier*); VERDI: Elisabetta (*Don Carlo*), Desdemona (*Otello*); WAGNER: Senta (*Fliegende Holländer*), Elsa (*Lohengrin*), Brünnhilde (*Walküre, Siegfried, Götterdämmerung*), Elisabeth (*Tannhäuser*), Isolde; WEBER: Agathe (*Freischütz*); et al. Recorded for: DG.

LIGHT, ALAN. Bass-baritone, bass & basso-buffo. British. Resident mem: Australian Opera, Sydney. Born 15 Jul 1916, Sydney. Wife Janice Hill, occupation opera singer. One child. Studied: Mme Marianne Mathy, Sydney. **Debut:** Don Pizarro (*Fidelio*) National Theatre Opera Co, Melbourne 1949. Previous occupations: radio announcer.

Sang with major companies in AUSTRL: Sydney. **Roles with these companies incl** BARTOK: Bluebeard; BEETHOVEN: Don Pizarro★ (*Fidelio*); BIZET: Escamillo (*Carmen*); DONIZETTI: Don Pasquale, Dulcamara★ (*Elisir*); GOUNOD: Méphistophélès (*Faust*); LEONCAVALLO: Tonio (*Pagliacci*); MASCAGNI: Alfio (*Cavalleria rusticana*); MOZART: Osmin★ (*Entführung aus dem Serail*), Sarastro (*Zauberflöte*); MUSSORGSKY: Varlaam (*Boris Godunov*); NICOLAI: Falstaff★ (*Lustigen Weiber*); OFFENBACH: Coppélius etc (*Contes d'Hoffmann*); PERGOLESI: Uberto (*Serva padrona*); PUCCINI: Marcello (*Bohème*), Jack Rance (*Fanciulla del West*), Sharpless (*Butterfly*), Scarpia (*Tosca*); ROSSINI: Dott Bartolo★ & Don Basilio (*Barbiere di Siviglia*); STRAVINSKY: Nick Shadow (*Rake's Progress*); VERDI: Renato (*Ballo in maschera*), Grande Inquisitore (*Don Carlo*), Ford (*Falstaff*), Fra Melitone★ (*Forza del destino*), Simon Boccanegra, Conte di Luna (*Trovatore*); WAGNER: Holländer & Daland (*Fliegende Holländer*), Telramund (*Lohengrin*); WOLF-FERRARI: Conte Gil (*Segreto di Susanna*). Also BRITTEN: Swallow (*Peter Grimes*); Collatinus★ (*Lucretia*); HUMPERDINCK: Peter (*Hänsel und Gretel*); MOZART: Commendatore (*Don Giovanni*). **World premieres:** GROSS: Judge Adam (*Amorous Judge*) Pro Musica Opera Co, Sydney 1962. Video/Film: Tonio (*Pagliacci*); Count (*Prima Donna*); Doctor (*Devil Take Her*); Alidoro (*Cenerentola*). Gives recitals. Appears with symphony orchestra. Teaches voice & staging. Coaches repertoire. Mgmt: GLN/AUSTRL.

LIGI, JOSELLA. Spinto. Italian. Born 10 Nov 1948, Imperia, Italy. Husband Gianfranco Brizio, occupation merchant. **Debut:** Mimi (*Bohème*) Teatro d'Imperia 1972. Awards: First Prize Intl Compt Viotti, Vercelli 1972; Golden Nut, Lecco 1973; Winner Lions Club, Milan 1973; Gold Medal, Mantua 1975; etc. **Sang with major companies in** ARG: Buenos Aires; AUS: Graz; FRA: Toulouse; FR GER: Munich Staatsoper; ITA: Florence Maggio, Milan La Scala, Trieste, Turin, Venice, Verona Arena; USSR: Moscow Bolshoi; USA: San Francisco. **Roles with these companies incl** BOITO: Margherita & Elena‡ (*Mefistofele*); GIORDANO: Maddalena (*Andrea Chénier*); GLUCK: Alceste & Ismene (*Alceste*); PUCCINI: Mimi★ (*Bohème*); TCHAIKOVSKY: Tatiana★ (*Eugene Onegin*); VERDI: Aida★, Amelia★ (*Ballo in maschera*), Elisabetta★ (*Don Carlo*), Leonora★ (*Forza del destino*), Desdemona★ (*Otello*), Amelia★ (*Simon Boccanegra*), Leonora★ (*Trovatore*). Also CHERUBINI: Corinne‡ (*Anacréon*). Mgmt: CAM/USA.

LILOVA, MARGARITA SLATEVA. Dramatic mezzo-soprano & contralto. Bulgarian. Resident mem: Staatsoper, Vienna. Born 26 Jul 1935, Tschervenbrjag, Bulgaria. Husband Peter Angelov Slatev, occupation actor, director. One daughter. Studied: Musik Akad, Prof Maria Zibulke, Sofia; Prof Maria Brand, Vienna. **Debut:** Maddalena (*Rigoletto*) Varna, Bulgaria 1959. Awards: Laureat, Compt for Young Singers, Sofia 1961. **Sang with major companies in** ARG: Buenos Aires; AUS: Bregenz Fest, Salzburg Fest, Vienna Staatsoper & Volksoper; BUL: Sofia; FRA: Paris; FR GER: Berlin Deutsche Oper, Hamburg, Wiesbaden; DR GER: Berlin Komische Oper; HUN: Budapest; ITA: Florence Maggio, Milan La Scala, Rome Opera; POL: Warsaw; UK: London Royal Opera; USA: San Francisco Opera; YUG: Belgrade. **Roles with these companies incl** BARTOK: Judith (*Bluebeard's Castle*); BERLIOZ: Anna★ (*Troyens*); BIZET: Carmen; BORODIN: Kontchakovna (*Prince Igor*); CHERUBINI: Neris★ (*Medea*); DEBUSSY: Geneviève★ (*Pelléas et Mélisande*); GLUCK: Orfeo★; HANDEL: Amastris★ (*Xerxes*); MASSENET: Charlotte (*Werther*); MUSSORGSKY: Marina (*Boris Godunov*), Marfa (*Khovanshchina*); PUCCINI: Suzuki★ (*Butterfly*); SAINT-SAENS: Dalila; TCHAIKOVSKY: Comtesse (*Pique Dame*); VERDI: Amneris★ (*Aida*), Ulrica★ (*Ballo in maschera*), Eboli (*Don Carlo*), Federica★ (*Luisa Miller*), Azucena★ (*Trovatore*); WAGNER: Erda (*Rheingold★*, *Siegfried★*), Fricka (*Rheingold★*, *Walküre★*), Waltraute (*Götterdämmerung*). Also MONTEVERDI/Kraak: Ottavia (*Incoronazione di Poppea*). Gives recitals. Appears with symphony orchestra. **Res:** D Polianov 26, Sofia, Bulgaria. Mgmt: SOF/YUG; RAB/AUS.

LILTVED, ÖYSTEIN. Bass. Norwegian. Born 20 Jan 1934, Arendal. Wife Virginia Oosthuizen, occupation opera singer. Three children. Studied: Maria Hittorff, Vienna; Luciano Donaggio, Trieste; Fred Dalberg, Cape Town. **Debut:** Kontchak (*Prince Igor*) Basel, Switzerland 1959. **Sang with major companies in** FR GER: Düsseldorf-Duisburg, Kassel; NOR: Oslo; S AFR: Johannesburg; SPA: Barcelona Liceo; SWE: Stockholm; SWI: Basel. **Roles with these companies incl** BEETHOVEN: Rocco (*Fidelio*); BELLINI: Oroveso★ (*Norma*); GOUNOD: Méphistophélès (*Faust*); MOZART: Don Alfonso (*Così fan tutte*), Osmin★ (*Entführung aus dem Serail*), Sarastro★ (*Zauberflöte*); MUSSORGSKY: Varlaam & Pimen (*Boris Godunov*); NICOLAI: Falstaff★ (*Lustigen Weiber*); PUCCINI: Colline★ (*Bohème*); ROSSINI: Don Basilio★ (*Barbiere di Siviglia*); SMETANA: Kezal★ (*Bartered Bride*); STRAUSS, R: Orest★ (*Elektra*); VERDI: Ramfis★ (*Aida*); Philip II & Grande Inquisitore★ (*Don Carlo*), Padre Guardiano (*Forza del destino*), Banquo (*Macbeth*), Fiesco (*Simon Boccanegra*); WAGNER: Daland★ (*Fliegende Holländer*), Fafner (*Rheingold, Siegfried*), Hunding (*Walküre*), Hagen★ (*Götterdämmerung*), Landgraf (*Tannhäuser*). Also DONIZETTI: Raimondo★ (*Lucia*); BRITTEN: Swallow (*Peter Grimes*); BORODIN: Kontchak★ (*Prince Igor*); CALDARA: Peneo★ (*Dafne*). Gives recitals. Appears with symphony orchestra. **Res:** 45 Burnside Rd, Tamboerskloof, Cape Town, South Africa. Mgmt: VLD/AUS.

LINDENSTRAND, SYLVIA. Lyric coloratura mezzo-soprano. Swedish. Resident mem: Royal Opera, Stockholm. Born 24 Jun 1942, Stockholm. Single. Studied: Royal Acad of Music, Isobel Ghasal-Öhman, Hjördis Schymberg, Stockholm. **Debut:** Olga (*Eugene Onegin*) Royal Opera, Stockholm 1962. Previous occupations: illustrator. **Sang with major companies in** DEN: Copenhagen; FR GER: Bayreuth Fest, Wiesbaden; SWE:

Drottningholm Fest, Stockholm; UK: Edinburgh Fest, Glyndebourne Fest; USSR: Moscow Bolshoi. **Roles with these companies incl** BRITTEN: Miss Jessel (*Turn of the Screw*); MOZART: Dorabella★ (*Così fan tutte*), Zerlina★ (*Don Giovanni*), Idamante★ (*Idomeneo*), Cherubino★ (*Nozze di Figaro*); MUSSORGSKY: Marina (*Boris Godunov*); PUCCINI: Suzuki★ (*Butterfly*); STRAUSS, R: Octavian★ (*Rosenkavalier*); WAGNER: Fricka★ (*Rheingold*), Brangäne (*Tristan und Isolde*). Also CAVALLI: Prince Luceius (*Scipio Africanus*); HANDEL: Dorinda (*Pastor fido*). Video/Film: (*Carmen*); (*Idomeneo*). Gives recitals. Appears with symphony orchestra. Mgmt: KBL/SWE; ASK/UK.

LINDHJEM, THORBJORN. Dramatic baritone. Norwegian. Resident mem: Norwegian Opera, Oslo. Born 14 May 1933, Sandar, Norway. Wife Kari, occupation teacher. One child. Studied: Joseph Stzereniy, Prof Paul Lohmann, Wiesbaden; Mo Arturo Merlini, Milan. **Debut:** Figaro (*Barbiere di Siviglia*) Norwegian Opera, Oslo 1967. Previous occupations: training schl teacher, Oslo; music teacher at Musikkonsv Opera School, Oslo, 2 yrs. Awards: stipd Norwegian Gvnmt; honors from Mayor of Oslo.
Sang with major companies in NOR: Oslo; SWE: Stockholm. **Roles with these companies incl** BEETHOVEN: Don Pizarro★ (*Fidelio*); BERG: Wozzeck★; DONIZETTI: Dott Malastesta★ (*Don Pasquale*), Belcore★ (*Elisir*); LEONCAVALLO: Tonio★ (*Pagliacci*); MASCAGNI: Alfio★ (*Cavalleria rusticana*); MOZART: Leporello★ (*Don Giovanni*), Figaro★ (*Nozze di Figaro*); OFFENBACH: Coppélius etc★ (*Contes d'Hoffmann*); PERGOLESI: Uberto★ (*Serva padrona*); PUCCINI: Gianni Schicchi★, Sharpless★ (*Butterfly*); ROSSINI: Figaro★ & Dott Bartolo★ (*Barbiere di Siviglia*); STRAVINSKY: Creon★ (*Oedipus Rex*); VERDI: Ford★ (*Falstaff*), Rigoletto★, Germont★ (*Traviata*). **World premieres:** JANSSON: Westmoe (*Et fjelleventyr*) Norwegian Opera 1973. Video/Film: Uberto (*Serva padrona*). Gives recitals. Appears with symphony orchestra. Teaches voice. **Res:** Platåveien 2 B, Oslo 4, Norway.

LINDHOLM, BERIT; née Berit Maria Jonsson. Dramatic soprano. Swedish. Born 14 Oct 1934, Stockholm. Husband Hans, occupation physician. Two children. Studied: Britta von Vegesack, Käthe Sundström, Stockholm. **Debut:** Contessa (*Nozze di Figaro*) Royal Opera, Stockholm 1963. Previous occupations: elementary school teacher.
Sang with major companies in AUS: Vienna Staatsoper; CAN: Montreal/Quebec; CZE: Prague National; FRA: Marseille, Paris; FR GER: Bayreuth Fest, Berlin Deutsche Oper, Düsseldorf-Duisburg, Hamburg, Munich Staatsoper; HOL: Amsterdam; ITA: Naples; SPA: Barcelona; SWE: Stockholm; SWI: Geneva; UK: Edinburgh Fest, Glasgow Scottish, London Royal; USSR: Moscow Bolshoi; USA: Chicago, New York Met, Portland, San Francisco Opera. **Roles with these companies incl** BEETHOVEN: Leonore★ (*Fidelio*); BERLIOZ: Cassandre‡ (*Troyens*); MOZART: Contessa (*Nozze di Figaro*); PUCCINI: Tosca★, Turandot★; STRAUSS, R: Chrysothemis★ (*Elektra*); VERDI: Aida, Amelia★

(*Ballo in maschera*), Abigaille (*Nabucco*); WAGNER: Elsa★ (*Lohengrin*), Sieglinde★ (*Walküre*), Brünnhilde (*Walküre★, Siegfried★, Götterdämmerung★*), Elisabeth★ & Venus (*Tannhäuser*), Isolde★. Recorded for: Decca, EMI, Philips. Gives recitals. Appears with symphony orchestra. **Res:** Stockholm, Sweden. Mgmt: ULF/SWE.

LIND-OQUENDO, ABRAHAM; né Abraham Lind. Dramatic baritone. American. Resident mem: Bremen Opera, FR Ger. Born 1 Aug 1933, New York. Single. Studied: Mr & Mrs Rolf Gérard, New York; Manhattan School of Music, Mrs Friedrich Schorr, New York; Emory K Taylor, New York. **Debut:** Figaro (*Barbiere di Siviglia*) Cincinnati Summer Opera 1960. Previous occupations: printer. Awards: Fulbright Grant for Italy; First Place Intl Compt Enna, Sicily; Rockefeller Fndt Awd; Marie Bauer Awd, Liederkranz Fndt.
Sang with major companies in ISR: Tel Aviv; USA: Cincinnati, Lake George. **Roles with these companies incl** BIZET: Escamillo (*Carmen*), Zurga (*Pêcheurs de perles*); DONIZETTI: Dott Malatesta (*Don Pasquale*), Enrico★ (*Lucia*); GERSHWIN: Porgy★; LEONCAVALLO: Tonio (*Pagliacci*); MOZART: Figaro (*Nozze di Figaro*); OFFENBACH: Coppélius etc.★ (*Contes d'Hoffmann*); PUCCINI: Marcello★ (*Bohème*), Lescaut★ (*Manon Lescaut*), Michele (*Tabarro*), Scarpia (*Tosca*); ROSSINI: Figaro (*Barbiere di Siviglia*); STRAUSS, R: Orest★ (*Elektra*); VERDI: Amonasro★ (*Aida*), Nabucco★, Rigoletto★, Germont (*Traviata*). Gives recitals. Appears with symphony orchestra. Teaches voice. Mgmt: LCA/USA; PAS/FRG.

LINDROOS, PAUL PETER CHRISTER. Heldentenor. Finnish. Resident mem: Royal Theater, Copenhagen. Born 26 Feb 1944, Pojo, Finland. Wife Anja Hillevi, occupation arts, science candidate. Four children. Studied: Sibelius Acad of Finland, Jolanda di Maria Petris, Helsinki; Luigi Ricci, Rome; M del Monaco, Treviso, Italy. **Debut:** Rodolfo (*Bohème*) National Opera, Helsinki 1968. Previous occupations: organist, music teacher. Awards: stipd, Cultural Fund of Finland; stipd, Swedish Fund of Finland.
Sang with major companies in AUS: Vienna Staatsoper; DEN: Copenhagen; FIN: Helsinki; FR GER: Kiel, Munich Staatsoper, Stuttgart; NOR: Oslo. **Roles with these companies incl** BIZET: Don José★ (*Carmen*); JANACEK: Laca (*Jenufa*), Boris (*Katya Kabanova*); MONTEVERDI: Nero (*Incoronazione di Poppea*); PUCCINI: Rodolfo★ (*Bohème*), Des Grieux (*Manon Lescaut*), Cavaradossi★ (*Tosca*); SHOSTAKOVICH: Sergei (*Katerina Ismailova*); STRAUSS, R: Ein Sänger (*Rosenkavalier*); VERDI: Otello, Gabriele★ (*Simon Boccanegra*), Manrico★ (*Trovatore*). Also NIELSEN: David★ (*Saul og David*).

LINDSEY, CLAUDIA. Lyric soprano. American. Husband François Scott, occupation sociologist. Studied: Anna Hamlin, Otto Guth, New York. **Debut:** Clara (*Porgy and Bess*) New York City Opera 1965. Previous occupations: sociologist, editor. Awards: Winner Met Op Natl Counc Aud; Affiliate Artist, 3 yrs; Whitney Fndt Honorarium; Marian Anderson Schlshp; Milton Cross Schlshp; Liederkranz Fndt; 2 Sullivan Fndt Awds.

Sang with major companies in USA: Newark, New York City Opera, San Francisco Spring, Washington DC. Roles with these companies incl BRITTEN: Female Chorus (Rape of Lucretia); DELIUS: Palmyra★‡ (Koanga); MOZART: Fiordiligi (Così fan tutte), Contessa (Nozze di Figaro); PUCCINI: Mimi★ (Bohème); SCHULLER: Teena (Visitation); SMETANA: Marie★ (Bartered Bride); THOMSON: Saint Teresa I★ (Four Saints in Three Acts); VERDI: Aida★, Desdemona (Otello). Recorded for: EMI/Angel. Video/Film—WNET: Saint Teresa I (Four Saints in Three Acts). Gives recitals. Appears with symphony orchestra. Res: New York, NY, USA. Mgmt: DBA/USA.

LINDSTRÖM, SOLWEIG; née Solweig Ethel Elisabeth Larsson. Lyric soprano. Swedish. Resident mem: Royal Opera, Stockholm. Born 25 Oct 1945, Järnamo, Sweden. Husband Hans-Börje, occupation music director. Studied: Musik Hochschule Malmö, Sweden; Musik Hochschule Vienna; Prof Ferdinand Grossmann, Prof Josef Witt, Prof Erik Werba, Vienna. Debut: Desdemona (Otello) Royal Opera, Stockholm 1970.
Sang with major companies in SWE: Drottningholm Fest, Stockholm; UK: Edinburgh Fest. Roles with these companies incl BEETHOVEN: Marzelline★ (Fidelio); BIZET: Micaëla★ (Carmen); GLUCK: Amor★ (Orfeo ed Euridice); PUCCINI: Mimi★ (Bohème); VERDI: Nannetta (Falstaff), Desdemona (Otello). World premieres: LUNDQUIST: Eva (Second of Eternity) Stockholm 1974; WERLE: Gustaf IV (Tintomara) Royal Opera, Stockholm 1973. Video/Film: Micaëla (Carmen). Gives recitals. Appears with symphony orchestra. Mgmt: OEA/UK.

LINGE, RUTH; née Leerstang. Lyric soprano. Norwegian. Resident mem: Norwegian Opera, Oslo. Born 13 Oct, Porsgrunn, Norway. Husband Tormod, occupation pianist. Studied: Mme Andrejewa von Skilondy, Stockholm; Karl Aagaard Östvig, Maria Rajdl, Oslo; Prof Ernst Tempele, Vienna. Debut: Norina (Don Pasquale) Norwegian Opera, Oslo 1951.
Sang with major companies in NOR: Oslo. Roles with these companies incl DONIZETTI: Norina (Don Pasquale), Adina (Elisir); GLUCK: Amor★ (Orfeo ed Euridice); MOZART: Donna Anna★ & Donna Elvira★ & Zerlina (Don Giovanni), Blondchen (Entführung aus dem Serail), Mme Herz★ (Schauspieldirektor), Cherubino (Nozze di Figaro); OFFENBACH: Olympia★ (Contes d'Hoffmann); ORFF: Solo (Carmina burana); PUCCINI: Musetta★ (Bohème), Cio-Cio-San (Butterfly); ROSSINI: Rosina★ (Barbiere di Siviglia); VERDI: Gilda★ (Rigoletto); WEBER: Aennchen (Freischütz). Also CIMAROSA: Ersilia★ (Astuzie femminili); WERLE: Françoise (Dream of Thérèse). World premieres: BRAEIN: Pernille (Den Stundeslose) Norwegian Opera, Oslo 1975. Video/Film: (Schauspieldirektor); (Astuzie femminili). Gives recitals. Appears with symphony orchestra.

LINGWOOD, TOM. Scenic and costume designer for opera, theater, film & television. Is a lighting designer & stage director. British. Resident designer, Australian Opera, Sydney. Born 15 Sep 1927, Guildford, UK. Single. Operatic debut: sets, Agrippina Opera '61, London 1965; cost, Cosa rara Opera '61, London 1968. Theater debut: London Fest Ballet 1952.
Designed for major companies in AUSTRL: Sydney; UK: London Royal. Operas designed for these companies incl PROKOFIEV: War and Peace★†; PUCCINI: Bohème†, Manon Lescaut†; STRAUSS, R: Rosenkavalier★†, Salome★†; VERDI: Aida★†, Forza del destino★†, Nabucco★†. Operatic Video—Assoc TV London: Contes d'Hoffmann. Exhibitions of stage designs Wright-Hepburn Gal, London 1968; Bonython Gal, Sydney 1971. Res: 38 Walter St, Sydney, Australia.

LINKE, FRITZ. Bass & basso-buffo. German. Resident mem: Staatsoper, Stuttgart. Born 15 May 1923, Claussnitz/Sachsen, Germany. Wife Lena. Three children. Debut: Vierter Edler (Lohengrin) Chemnitz Oper, Karl-Marx-Stadt, Ger DR 1950. Previous occupations: baker; athlete. Awards: Kammersänger, Land Baden-Württemberg 1970; Richard Wagner Medal, Bayreuth 1963; Silver Mattias Claudius Medal 1973.
Sang with major companies in ARG: Buenos Aires; AUS: Graz, Vienna Staatsoper; FIN: Helsinki; FRA: Paris; FR GER: Bayreuth Fest, Berlin Deutsche Oper, Bielefeld, Bonn, Cologne, Essen, Frankfurt, Hamburg, Hannover, Karlsruhe, Kassel, Krefeld, Mannheim, Munich Staatsoper & Gärtnerplatz, Nürnberg, Stuttgart; GER DR: Dresden, Leipzig; ITA: Bologna, Rome Opera & Caracalla, Trieste, Venice; POR: Lisbon; ROM: Bucharest; SPA: Barcelona, Madrid; SWI: Zurich; UK: Edinburgh Fest. Roles with these companies incl BEETHOVEN: Rocco (Fidelio); BERG: Doktor (Wozzeck); CIKKER: Bass role (Resurrection); CORNELIUS: Abul Hassan (Barbier von Bagdad); EGK: Cuperus (Zaubergeige); FLOTOW: Plunkett (Martha); JANACEK: Dikoy (Katya Kabanova); LORTZING: Stadinger (Waffenschmied), Baculus (Wildschütz), Van Bett (Zar und Zimmermann); MOZART: Osmin (Entführung aus dem Serail), Osmin (Zaïde), Sarastro (Zauberflöte); MUSSORGSKY: Varlaam (Boris Godunov), Tcherevik (Fair at Sorochinsk); NICOLAI: Falstaff (Lustigen Weiber); ORFF: Bauer (Mond); PENDERECKI: Rangier (Teufel von Loudun); PUCCINI: Colline (Bohème); ROSSINI: Don Basilio (Barbiere di Siviglia), Taddeo (Italiana in Algeri), Geronio (Turco in Italia); SMETANA: Kezal (Bartered Bride); STRAUSS, R: Baron Ochs (Rosenkavalier); VERDI: Ramfis (Aida), Philip II & Grande Inquisitore (Don Carlo), Padre Guardiano (Forza del destino), Fiesco (Simon Boccanegra), Procida (Vespri); WAGNER: Daland (Fliegende Holländer), Pogner (Meistersinger), Fafner (Rheingold, Siegfried), Hunding (Walküre), Landgraf (Tannhäuser); WEBER: Kaspar (Freischütz). Res: Nettelbeckstr 24, 714 Ludwigsburg, FR Ger.

LI-PAZ, MICHAEL. Bass & basso-buffo. Israeli. Resident mem: New York City Opera. Born 11 Sep 1938, Tel Aviv. Widowed. Three children. Studied: Juilliard Schl Amer Op Cnt, Giorgio Tozzi, Alexander Kipnis, New York; Curtis Inst of Music, Max Rudolf, Philadelphia; Haifa Op Studio, Dr Metzger, Dr Theo Bloch, Israel. Debut:

Don Basilio (*Barbiere di Siviglia*) Israel 1970. Awards: full schlshp Juilliard Schl; full schlshp Curtis Inst; America-Israel Cult Fndt Awd; Flagler Museum Awd; Philadelphia Grand Opera Compt Awd; Morton Baum Awd; Bagby Music & Sullivan Fndt Awds.

Sang with major companies in ISR: Tel Aviv; USA: New York City Opera, Philadelphia Grand & Lyric Opera. Roles with these companies incl DONIZETTI: Don Pasquale★; MOZART: Don Alfonso★ (*Così fan tutte*), Leporello★ (*Don Giovanni*), Osmin★ (*Entführung aus dem Serail*), Sarastro (*Zauberflöte*); ROSSINI: Dott Bartolo★ & Don Basilio (*Barbiere di Siviglia*); SMETANA: Kezal (*Bartered Bride*); STRAUSS, R: Baron Ochs★ (*Rosenkavalier*); VERDI: Ramfis★ (*Aida*). Gives recitals. Appears with symphony orchestra. Res: 142 Covington Rd, Philadelphia, PA, USA. Mgmt: KAZ/USA.

LIPP, WILMA. Coloratura & lyric soprano. Austrian. Resident mem: Staatsoper, Vienna; Opernhaus, Zurich. Born 26 Apr 1925, Vienna. Studied: Friedel Sindel, Paola Novikova, Vienna; Toti dal Monte, Milan. Debut: Staatsoper, Vienna 1945.

Sang with major companies in ARG: Buenos Aires; AUS: Bregenz Fest, Salzburg Fest, Vienna Staatsoper & Volksoper; BEL: Brussels; DEN: Copenhagen; FRA: Paris; FR GER: Bayreuth Fest, Berlin Deutsche Oper, Hamburg, Munich Staatsoper, Stuttgart, Wiesbaden; ITA: Milan La Scala, Rome Opera, Turin; SWI: Geneva, Zurich; UK: Glyndebourne Fest, London Royal; et al. Roles with these companies incl BEETHOVEN: Marzelline (*Fidelio*); MOZART: Donna Elvira (*Don Giovanni*), Konstanze‡ (*Entführung aus dem Serail*), Contessa (*Nozze di Figaro*), Pamina & Königin der Nacht‡ (*Zauberflöte*); OFFENBACH: Antonia (*Contes d'Hoffmann*); STRAUSS, J: Adele & Rosalinde‡ (*Fledermaus*); STRAUSS, R: Sophie (*Rosenkavalier*); WAGNER: Eva (*Meistersinger*); et al. Recorded for: DGG, Decca, Philips, Vox, Ariola. Mgmt: GOR/UK.

LIPPERT, MARION ANNA-MARIA. Dramatic soprano & spinto. German. Resident mem: Staatsoper, Stuttgart. Born 24 Sep 1936, Munich. Married. Studied: Kmsg Irma Koboth, Kmsg Prof Hedwig Fichtmüller, Kmsg Prof Annelies Kupper, Munich; Mo Giuseppe Pais, Milan. Debut: Aida, Stadttheater Augsburg 1959. Awards: Kammersängerin, Württembergisches Staatstheater, Stuttgart.

Sang with major companies in ARG: Buenos Aires; AUS: Vienna Staatsoper & Volksoper; CAN: Montreal/Quebec, Toronto, Vancouver; FRA: Marseille, Paris; GRE: Athens Fest; FR GER: Berlin Deutsche Oper, Cologne, Dortmund, Düsseldorf-Duisburg, Essen, Frankfurt, Hamburg, Hannover, Karlsruhe, Munich Staatsoper, Nürnberg, Stuttgart; GER DR: Dresden; ITA: Bologna, Florence Maggio, Naples, Parma, Turin, Venice, Verona Arena; POR: Lisbon; SPA: Barcelona; SWI: Zurich; USA: Baltimore, Chicago, Milwaukee Florentine, New Orleans, New York Metropolitan, Pittsburgh, San Francisco Opera. Roles with these companies incl BEETHOVEN: Leonore★ (*Fidelio*); BELLINI: Norma★; HANDEL: Rodelinda; MASCAGNI: Santuzza (*Cavalleria rusticana*); MOZART: Donna Anna (*Don Giovanni*); PUCCINI: Minnie (*Fanciulla del West*), Manon Lescaut, Suor Angelica, Giorgetta (*Tabarro*), Tosca★, Turandot★; STRAUSS, R: Arabella, Ariadne (*Ariadne auf Naxos*), Chrysothemis★ (*Elektra*), Kaiserin (*Frau ohne Schatten*), Marschallin★ (*Rosenkavalier*), Salome; VERDI: Aida★, Amelia★ (*Ballo in maschera*), Elisabetta (*Don Carlo*), Leonora (*Forza del destino*), Lady Macbeth★, Abigaille★ (*Nabucco*), Desdemona (*Otello*), Amelia (*Simon Boccanegra*), Leonora★ (*Trovatore*); WAGNER: Senta★ (*Fliegende Holländer*), Elsa (*Lohengrin*), Sieglinde★ (*Walküre*), Brünnhilde★ (*Siegfried*), Venus★ (*Tannhäuser*); WEBER: Rezia (*Oberon*). Gives recitals. Appears with symphony orchestra. Res: Stuttgart, FR Ger. Mgmt: CAM/USA.

LISHNER, LEON. Bass. American. Born 4 Jul 1913, New York. Wife Ann, occupation dancer and dance teacher. Five children. Studied: Juilliard Grad School of Music, New York; Trinity Coll of Music, London. Debut: Dott Bartolo (*Nozze di Figaro*) Philadelphia Opera 1942.

Sang with major companies in CAN: Montreal/Quebec, Vancouver; ISR: Tel Aviv; USA: Baltimore, Boston, Chicago, Cincinnati, Hartford, New York City Opera, Philadelphia Lyric, Pittsburgh, Portland, St Paul, San Francisco Opera, Santa Fe, Seattle. Roles with these companies incl BEETHOVEN: Rocco★ (*Fidelio*); BRITTEN: John Claggart (*Billy Budd*); DEBUSSY: Golaud★ & Arkel (*Pelléas et Mélisande*); DONIZETTI: Don Pasquale, Dulcamara (*Elisir*); FLOYD: Markheim; GOUNOD: Méphistophélès (*Faust*); MOZART: Don Alfonso (*Così fan tutte*), Leporello (*Don Giovanni*), Osmin (*Entführung aus dem Serail*), Osmin (*Zaïde*), Sarastro (*Zauberflöte*); OFFENBACH: Coppélius etc (*Contes d'Hoffmann*); PUCCINI: Colline (*Bohème*), Rambaldo★ (*Rondine*); ROSSINI: Dott Bartolo & Don Basilio (*Barbiere di Siviglia*), Don Magnifico (*Cenerentola*); STRAUSS, R: Sir Morosus (*Schweigsame Frau*); STRAVINSKY: Creon (*Oedipus Rex*); VERDI: Banquo (*Macbeth*), Fiesco (*Simon Boccanegra*); WAGNER: Daland (*Fliegende Holländer*), Fafner★ (*Siegfried*), Hunding★ (*Walküre*); WARD: Rev Hale (*Crucible*); WEILL: Mr Peachum (*Dreigroschenoper*). World premieres: MENOTTI: Police Chief (*Consul*) Broadway production 1950; Balthazar (*Amahl*) NBC TV Opera 1951; Don Marco (*Saint of Bleecker Street*) Broadway prod 1954; Death (*Labyrinth*) NBC TV Opera 1963. Recorded for: RCA, Decca. Video—NBC TV: Balthazar (*Amahl*); Death (*Labyrinth*); Markheim (*Markheim*). Gives recitals. Appears with symphony orchestra. Teaches voice. Coaches repertoire. On faculty of Univ of Washington, Seattle, USA. Res: 2114 E Galer, Seattle, WA, USA.

LISOWSKA, HANNA. Spinto soprano. Polish. Resident mem: Teatr Wielki, Warsaw. Born 15 Sep 1939, Warsaw. Husband Antoni Wicherek, occupation conductor. Studied: Middle School of Music, Warsaw; High School of Music, Prof Victor Bregy, Warsaw; Prof Zofia Fedyczkowska, Warsaw. Debut: Tatiana (*Eugene Onegin*) Teatr Wielki, Warsaw.

Sang with major companies in FR GER: Wiesbaden; MEX: Mexico City; POL: Lodz, Warsaw. Roles with these companies incl BIZET: Micaëla (*Carmen*); GOUNOD: Marguerite (*Faust*); MONIUSZKO: Halka★; MOZART: Donna Anna & Donna Elvira (*Don Giovanni*), Contessa★ (*Nozze di Figaro*); PUCCINI: Tosca; STRAUSS, R: Chrysothemis★ (*Elektra*); TCHAIKOVSKY: Tatiana (*Eugene Onegin*); VERDI: Aida★, Elisabetta★ (*Don Carlo*), Alice Ford (*Falstaff*); WAGNER: Elisabeth★ & Venus (*Tannhäuser*). Also RUDZINSKI: Kassandra (*Dismissal of Greek Envoys*). Gives recitals. Appears with symphony orchestra. Mgmt: PAG/POL; SMD/FRG.

LITTLE, FRANK; né Francis E Little. Lyric tenor. American. Born 22 Apr 1936, Greeneville, TN, USA. Wife Carolyn Sauter. Four children. Studied: East Tenn State Univ, Lillian Rhea Hunter; Cincinnati Consv, Robert Powell; Northwestern Univ, Walter Carringer; Clemens Glettenberg, Munich. **Debut:** Normanno (*Lucia*) Chicago Lyric Opera 1970. Previous occupations: univ prof; arts administr; army officer. Awards: Ntl Opera Inst Grant 1972; Hon Citation Washington Coll Acad; Met Op Ntl Counc Aud Reg Winner. Sang with major companies in CAN: Vancouver; ITA: Florence Comunale; SPA: Canary Isl Las Palmas Fest; USA: Chicago, Milwaukee Florentine, Philadelphia Lyric, San Antonio, Washington DC. Roles with these companies incl BERG: Tambourmajor★ (*Wozzeck*); DONIZETTI: Leicester★ (*Maria Stuarda*); PUCCINI: Luigi★ (*Tabarro*); STRAUSS, R: Aegisth★ (*Elektra*); STRAVINSKY: Tom Rakewell★ (*Rake's Progress*); VERDI: Alfredo★ (*Traviata*), Macduff★ (*Macbeth*). Also STRAUSS, R: Narraboth (*Salome*). Gives recitals. Appears with symphony orchestra. Teaches voice. Coaches repertoire. On faculty of DePaul Univ, Chicago; Chmn Voice Dept. **Res:** 150 Thackeray La, Northfield, IL, USA. Mgmt: COL/USA.

LITTLE, GWENLYNN LOIS. Lyric coloratura soprano. Canadian. Husband Richard Davidson, actor. Two children. Studied: Royal Consv of Music, George Lambert, Louis Quilico, Toronto; Boris Goldovsky, Brookline, MA, USA; Otto Guth, New York. **Debut:** Gilda (*Rigoletto*) Canadian Opera, Toronto 1963. Awards: Four Canada Counc Grants for aud & study in Europe & USA; Sir Tyrone Guthrie Awd, Stratford Fest, Ont, Canada. Sang with major companies in CAN: Montreal/Quebec, Ottawa, Toronto, Vancouver; USA: New York City Opera, Portland, Washington DC. Roles with these companies incl BERLIOZ: Héro★ (*Béatrice et Bénédict*); DONIZETTI: Norina (*Don Pasquale*), Rita; GOUNOD: Juliette; HANDEL: Rodelinda; HUMPERDINCK: Gretel; MASSENET: Sophie (*Werther*); MENOTTI: Monica (*Medium*), Laetitia (*Old Maid and the Thief*); MOORE: Baby Doe; MOZART: Despina★ (*Così fan tutte*), Zerlina★ (*Don Giovanni*), Susanna★ (*Nozze di Figaro*), Pamina (*Zauberflöte*); PAISIELLO: Lisetta (*Re Teodoro in Venezia*); PERGOLESI: Lauretta (*Maestro di Musica*), Serpina★ (*Serva padrona*); PUCCINI: Musetta (*Bohème*), Lauretta (*Gianni Schicchi*); RAVEL: Concepcion★ (*Heure espagnole*); ROS-

SINI: Rosina (*Barbiere di Siviglia*); SMETANA: Marie (*Bartered Bride*); STRAUSS, J; Adele★ (*Fledermaus*); VERDI: Oscar (*Ballo in maschera*), Nannetta (*Falstaff*), Gilda (*Rigoletto*); WEBER: Aennchen★ (*Freischütz*); WOLF-FERRARI: Susanna★ (*Segreto di Susanna*). Video/Film – CBC TV: Serpina (*Serva padrona*). Gives recitals. Appears with symphony orchestra. **Res:** 225 W 70 St, #3b, New York, NY 10023, USA. Mgmt: ACA/USA.

LITTLE, VERA PEARL. Dramatic mezzo-soprano & contralto. American. Born 10 Dec, Memphis, TN, USA. Husband Prof Dr S S Augustithis, occupation scientist. Studied: Talladega Coll, Mr Harrison, AL, USA; Consv of Paris, M Jouatte, France; Prof Bärwinkel, Prof Sängerleitner, Germany. **Debut:** Carmen, Berlin 1958-59. Previous occupations: telephonist, nurse & doctor's asst; attendant in children's shelter. Awards: Fulbright Grant; Winner Intl Singing Cont, Munich; Cont Verrière, Belgium. Sang with major companies in AUS: Vienna Staatsoper; FR GER: Berlin Deutsche Oper, Bonn, Cologne, Dortmund, Frankfurt, Hamburg, Kassel, Mannheim Nationaltheater, Munich Staatsoper, Nürnberg, Stuttgart; ISR: Tel Aviv; ITA: Genoa, Milan La Scala; USA: Memphis. Roles with these companies incl BIZET: Carmen‡; DALLAPICCOLA: Circe (*Ulisse*); HENZE: Agave (*Bassariden*), Baronin von Grünwiesel (*Junge Lord*); MONTEVERDI: Poppea★ (*Incoronazione di Poppea*); MUSSORGSKY: Marina★ (*Boris Godunov*); OFFENBACH: Giulietta★ (*Contes d'Hoffmann*); PONCHIELLI: La Cieca★ (*Gioconda*); PUCCINI: Badessa★ (*Suor Angelica*); STRAVINSKY: Jocasta (*Oedipus Rex*), Baba the Turk (*Rake's Progress*); TCHAIKOVSKY: Comtesse★ (*Pique Dame*); VERDI: Amneris★ (*Aida*), Ulrica★ (*Ballo in maschera*), Eboli★ (*Don Carlo*), Dame Quickly★ (*Falstaff*), Preziosilla★ (*Forza del destino*); WAGNER: Erda (*Rheingold★, Siegfried★*), Venus★ (*Tannhäuser*). **World premieres:** HENZE: Begonia (*Junge Lord*) Berlin 1965. Recorded for: DG, Decca. Video/Film: Begonia (*Junge Lord*). Gives recitals. Appears with symphony orchestra.

LIUKKO-VAARA, EINI INKERI. Dramatic soprano, Finnish. Resident mem: Finnish Ntl Opera, Helsinki. Born 8 Jul 1930, Viipuri. Husband Kai Vaara, occupation mng dir. One child. Studied: Sibelius Academy, Ester Rask, Jolanda di Maria Petris, Helsinki; Luigi Ricci, Rome. **Debut:** Aida, Helsinki 1963. Previous occupations: businesswoman. Awards: awds from Suomen Kulttuurirahasto; grants for study trips to Bayreuth, Salzburg and Rome. Sang with major companies in FIN: Helsinki; HUN: Budapest; NOR: Oslo; SWE: Stockholm. Roles with these companies incl BEETHOVEN: Leonore‡ (*Fidelio*); BERG: Marie (*Wozzeck*); BRITTEN: Mrs Grose (*Turn of the Screw*); MOZART: Fiordiligi★ (*Così fan tutte*), Donna Anna (*Don Giovanni*); OFFENBACH: Antonia (*Contes d'Hoffmann*); PUCCINI: Minnie★ (*Fanciulla del West*), Tosca★; STRAVINSKY: Anne Trulove (*Rake's Progress*); VERDI: Aida‡, Amelia (*Ballo in maschera*), Elisabetta★ (*Don Carlo*), Abigaille (*Nabucco*), Desdemona★

(*Otello*). Also records only POULENC: Femme (*Voix humaine*). **World premieres:** KUUSISTO: Vilijonkka (*Muumi-opera*) 1974; KOKKONEN: Daughter (*Last Temptations*) 1975; both at Finnish Ntl Opera, Helsinki. Video/Film: Leonore (*Fidelio*). Gives recitals. Appears with symphony orchestra. Teaches voice. Coaches repertoire. On faculty of Sibelius Akad, Helsinki. **Res:** Runeberginkatu 48 B 31, 00260 Helsinki 26, Finland.

LIVIERO, ANTONIO. Dramatic tenor. Italian. Born 10 Jun 1939, Cittadella/Padua, Italy. Wife Harriet. Two children. Studied: Mo Paoletti and Giaidina, Rome; Mo Leo Mueller and Dick Marzollo, New York; Manhattan School of Music, New York. **Debut:** Alfredo (*Traviata*) Monmouth Opera, Asbury Park, NJ 1965. Awards: Winner, Amer Op Aud, Cincinnati, debut in Milan; schlshp Met Op, for private study in New York.
Sang with major companies in FRA: Toulouse; FR GER: Bonn; ITA: Genoa, Trieste, Venice; USA: Cincinnati. **Roles with these companies incl** BELLINI: Tebaldo★ (*Capuleti ed i Montecchi*); GIORDANO: Andrea Chénier★; MASCAGNI: Turiddu★ (*Cavalleria rusticana*); MEYERBEER: Raoul de Nangis★ (*Huguenots*); PUCCINI: Rodolfo (*Bohème*); STRAUSS, R: Ein Sänger (*Rosenkavalier*); VERDI: Riccardo★ (*Ballo in maschera*), Ismaele★ (*Nabucco*), Gabriele★ (*Simon Boccanegra*), Manrico★ (*Trovatore*). Also MERCADANTE: Armando de Foix (*Due illustri rivali*); MUSSORGSKY: Dimitri (*Boris Godunov*). Recorded for: RAI. **Res:** V Canazei 36, Casal Palocco/Rome, Italy.

LIVINGS, GEORGE. Tenor. American. Born 21 Jul 1945, Dallas, TX, USA. Wife Laurens McMaster, occupation singer, voice teacher. One child. Studied: Austin Coll, Bruce Lunkley, Sherman, TX; Juilliard School, Hans Heinz, New York. **Debut:** Belfiore (*Finta giardiniera*) Opera Co of Boston 1971. Awards: Lucrezia Bori Awd, Met Opera.
Sang with major companies in USA: Boston, Kansas City, Kentucky, Lake George, New York Met & City Opera. **Roles with these companies incl** GOUNOD: Faust★; MOZART: Don Ottavio★ (*Don Giovanni*), Graf Belfiore★ (*Finta giardiniera*), Idamante★ (*Idomeneo*); NICOLAI: Fenton (*Lustigen Weiber*); PUCCINI: Rodolfo★ (*Bohème*); ROSSINI: Almaviva★ (*Barbiere di Siviglia*). Gives recitals. Appears with symphony orchestra. **Res:** 412 West End Ave, New York, NY, USA. Mgmt: LCA/USA.

LLOVERAS, JUAN. Dramatic tenor. Spanish. Resident mem: Staatsoper Hamburg. Born Spain.
Sang with major companies in FR GER: Essen, Hamburg, Hannover, Krefeld; SPA: Barcelona; et al. **Roles with these companies incl** DONIZETTI: Edgardo (*Lucia*); MASSENET: Werther; MONIUSZKO: Stefan (*Haunted Castle*); PUCCINI: Rodolfo (*Bohème*), Pinkerton (*Butterfly*), Cavaradossi (*Tosca*); VERDI: Riccardo (*Ballo in maschera*), Don Carlo, Alfredo (*Traviata*), Manrico (*Trovatore*); et al.

LLOYD, ROBERT. Bass. British. Resident mem: Royal Opera, London. Born 2 Mar 1940, South-

end-on-Sea, UK. Wife Sandra, occupation dance therapist. Four children. Studied: London Opera Centre; Otakar Kraus, London. **Debut:** Fernando (*Leonore/Fidelio*) Univ Coll Opera Soc, UK 1969. Previous occupations: naval officer 1963-66; lecturer in politics. Awards: BA, Oxford Univ, UK.
Sang with major companies in FRA: Aix-en-Provence Fest, Paris; UK: Cardiff Welsh, Glasgow Scottish, Glyndebourne Fest, London Royal & English National; USA: San Francisco Opera. **Roles with these companies incl** DEBUSSY: Arkel★ (*Pelléas et Mélisande*); DONIZETTI: Raimondo★ (*Lucia*); MOZART: Publio★ (*Clemenza di Tito*), Sarastro★ (*Zauberflöte*); PROKOFIEV: King of Clubs (*Love for Three Oranges*); PUCCINI: Colline★ (*Bohème*); WAGNER: Fasolt★ (*Rheingold*). Also MOZART: Commendatore & Masetto (*Don Giovanni*); CAVALLI: Jove (*Calisto*). **World premieres:** JOUBERT: Mikulin (*Under Western Eyes*) New Opera Co, London 1969. Recorded for: Decca, EMI, RCA, Phonogram. Video/Film: Neptune (*Ritorno d'Ulisse*). Gives recitals. Appears with symphony orchestra. Teaches voice. **Res:** 41 Birley Rd, London N20, UK. Mgmt: HPL/UK.

LOCKHART, JAMES. Conductor of opera and symphony. British. Gen Music Dir & Resident Cond, Staatstheater Kassel, FR Ger. Music Dir, Symph Orch, Kassel. Previous adm positions in opera: Mus Dir, Welsh Ntl Opera, Cardiff till 1973.
Conducted with major companies in FR GER: Hamburg, Kassel; UK: Cardiff Welsh; et al. **Operas with these companies incl** BERG: *Lulu;* BIZET: *Carmen;* BRITTEN: *Billy Budd;* MOZART: *Don Giovanni, Idomeneo, Nozze di Figaro, Zauberflöte;* PUCCINI: *Butterfly, Turandot;* VERDI: *Falstaff, Rigoletto, Vespri;* WAGNER: *Rheingold, Walküre, Siegfried, Götterdämmerung.* Video — BBC TV: *Falstaff.*

LÖFFLER, PETER. Swiss. Int, Staatstheater Kassel, D35 Kassel, FR Ger 1972-75. In charge of overall adm matters, art policy, dram matters. Is also a st dir/prod. Born 3 Sep 1926, Zurich. Wife Margret, occupation physician. Studied: Univ, Zurich PhD; Schauspielakad, Zurich. Previous positions, primarily theatrical: Presidial Secy, Akad der Künste, Berlin; Dramaturg, Schauspielhaus Zurich 1949-64; Prod 1959-64; Art Dir 1969-70. **Res:** Am Schanzengraben 27, Zurich, Switzerland.

LOFORESE, ANGELO. Dramatic tenor. Italian. Born 27 Mar 1920, Milan. Wife Emilia Sarri. Two children. Studied: Aureliano Pertile, Emilio Ghirardini, Vladimiro Badiali, Alessandro Ziliani. **Debut:** Manrico (*Trovatore*) 1952. Previous occupations: employee. Awards: Commendation, Emperor of Japan.
Sang with major companies in ARG: Buenos Aires; AUS: Vienna Staatsoper; BEL: Brussels; BRA: Rio de Janeiro; FIN: Helsinki; FRA: Aix-en-Provence Fest, Bordeaux, Lyon, Marseille, Nancy, Nice, Rouen, Strasbourg, Toulouse; GRE: Athens National & Fest; FR GER: Berlin Deutsche Oper, Dortmund, Frankfurt, Hamburg, Kiel, Mannheim, Stuttgart; HUN: Budapest; ITA: Bologna, Florence Maggio & Comunale, Genoa, Milan La Scala, Naples, Palermo, Parma, Rome

Opera & Caracalla, Trieste, Turin, Venice; MON: Monte Carlo; NOR: Oslo; POR: Lisbon; S AFR: Johannesburg; SPA: Barcelona, Majorca; SWI: Basel, Zurich; USA: Philadelphia Grand & Lyric; YUG: Zagreb, Belgrade. **Roles with these companies incl** BELLINI: Pollione★ (*Norma*); BERLIOZ: Faust (*Damnation de Faust*); BIZET: Don José (*Carmen*); BOITO: Faust (*Mefistofele*); BORODIN: Vladimir (*Prince Igor*); CATALANI: Giuseppe Hagenbach (*Wally*); CHARPENTIER: Julien (*Louise*); CHERUBINI: Giasone (*Medea*); CILEA: Maurizio (*A. Lecouvreur*); DALLAPICCOLA: Jailer/Inquisitor★ (*Prigioniero*); DONIZETTI: Nemorino (*Elisir*), Edgardo (*Lucia*); GIORDANO: Andrea Chénier★, Loris Ipanov★ (*Fedora*); GLUCK: Admetos (*Alceste*); GOUNOD: Faust; LEONCAVALLO: Canio★‡ (*Pagliacci*); MASCAGNI: Turiddu★ (*Cavalleria rusticana*); MEYERBEER: Raoul de Nangis★ (*Huguenots*); MUSSORGSKY: Vassily Golitsin (*Khovanshchina*); PONCHIELLI: Enzo (*Gioconda*); PUCCINI: Rodolfo★ (*Bohème*), Pinkerton★ (*Butterfly*), Des Grieux★ (*Manon Lescaut*), Luigi★ (*Tabarro*), Cavaradossi★ (*Tosca*), Calaf (*Turandot*); ROSSINI: Arnold (*Guillaume Tell*), Neocle (*Assedio di Corinto*); STRAUSS, R: Leukippos (*Daphne*); STRAVINSKY: Oedipus; VERDI: Radames (*Aida*), Riccardo (*Ballo in maschera*), Don Carlo, Don Alvaro (*Forza del destino*), Rodolfo (*Luisa Miller*), Ismaele (*Nabucco*), Otello★, Duca di Mantova (*Rigoletto*), Gabriele (*Simon Boccanegra*), Alfredo (*Traviata*), Manrico★ (*Trovatore*); WAGNER: Erik (*Fliegende Holländer*); ZANDONAI: Paolo (*Francesca da Rimini*), Romeo‡. Also VERDI: Macduff★ (*Macbeth*); FIUME: Vecchio (*Tamburo di panno*); LEONCAVALLO: Marcello (*Bohème*); PIZZETTI: Aligi (*Figlia di Jorio*); ZANDONAI: Mateo (*Conchita*). Recorded for: Cetra Fonit, Flli Fabbri. Video/Film: ZANDONAI: Romeo. Teaches voice. On faculty of Consv Benedetto Marcello, Venice. **Res:** V M Gioia 78, Milan, Italy.

LOMBARD, ALAIN. Conductor of opera and symphony. French. Music Dir & Resident Cond, Opéra du Rhin, Strasbourg. Born 4 Oct 1940, Paris. Studied: Gaston Poulet, Suzanne Désmarques, Paris; also piano & violin. Operatic training: child prodigy, cond first concert 9 yrs old. **Operatic debut:** *Faust* Lyon 1961. Symphonic debut: Salle Gaveau, Paris 1956. Awards: Winner, Mitropoulos Cond Compt, New York. Previous adm positions in opera: Principal Cond, Opéra de Lyon 1962-64.
Conducted with major companies in AUS: Salzburg Fest; FRA: Aix-en-Provence Fest, Lyon, Paris, Strasbourg; FR GER: Hamburg; USA: Chicago, Miami, New York Met & City Opera; et al. **Operas with these companies incl** BIZET: *Carmen;* GOUNOD: *Roméo et Juliette‡;* MASSENET: *Hérodiade, Werther;* MUSSORGSKY: *Boris Godunov;* POULENC: *Dialogues des Carmélites;* PUCCINI: *Butterfly;* STRAUSS, R: *Elektra;* VERDI: *Don Carlo, Luisa Miller, Otello;* WAGNER: *Walküre;* et al. Recorded for Angel. Conducted major orch in Europe, USA/Canada. Previous positions as Mus Dir with major orch: Miami Phil Orch, FL, USA 1966-74.

LONDON, GEORGE. Bass-baritone, Stage Dir and Administrator. American. Gen Dir, Opera Society of Washington DC beginning 1975; Exec Dir, National Opera Inst, Washington DC. Previous adm position: Art Adm, J F Kennedy Center, Washington DC; Pres, AGMA. Born 30 May 1920, Montreal. Wife Nora. Two children. Studied: Dr Hugo Strelitzer, Nathan Stewart, Los Angeles; Enrico Rosati, Paola Novikova, New York. **Debut:** as singer, Dr Grenvil (*Traviata*) Hollywood Bowl, CA 1941; as stage dir, *Die Zauberflöte* Juilliard American Opera Center, New York 1971. Awards: Kammersänger, Vienna Staatsoper; Mozart Medal, City of Vienna.
Sang with major companies in AUS: Salzburg Fest, Vienna Staatsoper & Volksoper; CAN: Montreal/Quebec; FRA: Paris; FR GER: Bayreuth Fest, Berlin Deutsche Oper, Cologne, Munich Staatsoper; ITA: Milan La Scala, Venice; UK: Edinburgh Fest, Glyndebourne Fest; USSR: Leningrad Kirov, Moscow Bolshoi; USA: Boston, Miami, New York Metropolitan Opera, San Francisco Opera; YUG: Zagreb, Belgrade. **Roles with these companies incl** BIZET: Escamillo (*Carmen*); DEBUSSY: Golaud‡ (*Pelléas et Mélisande*); GOUNOD: Méphistophélès (*Faust*); MENOTTI: Abdul (*Dernier sauvage*); MOZART: Don Giovanni★‡, Conte Almaviva★‡ & Figaro (*Nozze di Figaro*), Sprecher (*Zauberflöte*); MUSSORGSKY: Boris Godunov★‡; OFFENBACH: Coppélius etc★‡ (*Contes d'Hoffmann*); PUCCINI: Scarpia★‡ (*Tosca*); STRAUSS, R: Mandryka‡ (*Arabella*); TCHAIKOVSKY: Eugene Onegin★; VERDI: Amonasro★ (*Aida*); WAGNER: Holländer‡, Amfortas‡ (*Parsifal*), Wotan (*Rheingold★‡, Walküre★‡*), Wanderer (*Siegfried*), Wolfram (*Tannhäuser*). **Staged opera for major companies in** USA: Dallas, San Diego, Seattle, Washington DC. **Operas staged with these companies incl** MOZART: *Così fan tutte★, Nozze di Figaro★;* PUCCINI: *Tosca★;* WAGNER: *Rheingold★, Walküre★, Siegfried★, Götterdämmerung.* Recorded for: Columbia, Angel, London, RCA. Is member of Opera Advisory Panel, Ntl Endowment for the Arts; Bd of Dir, New York City Center of Music & Drama. **Res:** 8000 Glengalen Lane, Chevy Chase, MD, USA.

LÓPEZ COBOS, JESÚS. Conductor of opera and symphony. Spanish. Resident Cond, Deutsche Oper Berlin. Born 25 Feb 1940, Toro, Zamora, Spain. Wife Gloria, occupation singer. One child. Studied: Madrid; Profs Swarowsky, Oesterreicher, Schmid, Vienna; incl piano, violin and voice. Operatic training as asst cond & chorus master at Madrid 1964-66; Teatro Colón, Buenos Aires 1970. **Operatic debut:** *Zauberflöte* La Fenice, Venice 1970. Symphonic debut: Young Phil Orch, Prague, CSSR 1969. Previous occupations: Doctor of Philosophy, taught 2 yrs in Madrid. Awards: Third Prize Nicolai Malko Compt Copenhagen 1968; First Prize Intl Compt Besançon, France 1968.
Conducted with major companies in FRA: Paris; FR GER: Berlin Deutsche Oper, Cologne, Hamburg, Munich Staatsoper; ITA: Bologna, Palermo, Trieste, Venice; USA: Chicago, San Francisco Opera. **Operas with these companies incl** BIZET: *Carmen★;* CAVALLI: *Calisto★;* DONIZETTI: *Convenienze/Viva la Mamma★, Lucia★;* LEONCAVALLO: *Pagliacci★;* MASCAGNI: *Cavalle-*

ria rusticana★; MOZART: *Entführung aus dem Serail★, Nozze di Figaro★, Zauberflöte★;* PUCCINI: *Bohème★, Butterfly★, Tosca★;* ROSSINI: *Cenerentola★, Italiana in Algeri★, Turco in Italia★;* SPONTINI: *Vestale★;* VERDI: *Aida★, Aroldo★, Attila★, Ballo in maschera★, Corsaro★, Forza del destino★, Luisa Miller★, Nabucco★, Otello★, Rigoletto★, Simon Boccanegra★, Traviata★, Trovatore★, Vespri★.* Conducted major orch in Europe, Cent/S America. **Res:** Königsallee 12a, D-1 Berlin 33, FR Ger. Mgmt: TAU/SWI.

LORAND, COLETTE; née Grauaug. Dramatic soprano. Swiss. Resident mem: Bayerische Staatsoper, Munich; Deutsche Oper Berlin, FR Ger. Born 7 Jan, Zurich. Husband Fred Doetterl, occupation businessman. Studied: Prof Hirtzel, Zurich. **Debut:** Marguerite (*Faust*) Basel. Awards: numerous awds.

Sang with major companies in AUS: Bregenz Fest, Graz, Salzburg Fest, Vienna Staatsoper & Volksoper; BEL: Brussels; BRA: Rio de Janeiro; CZE: Prague National; DEN: Copenhagen; FRA: Paris, Strasbourg; FR GER: Berlin Deutsche Oper, Bonn, Darmstadt, Dortmund, Düsseldorf-Duisburg, Frankfurt, Hamburg, Hannover, Karlsruhe, Kassel, Mannheim, Munich Staatsoper, Nürnberg, Stuttgart, Wuppertal; HOL: Amsterdam; ITA: Florence Maggio & Comunale, Milan La Scala, Naples, Palermo, Rome Opera; POR: Lisbon; SWI: Basel, Geneva, Zurich; UK: Cardiff Welsh, Edinburgh Fest, Glasgow Scottish, London Royal & English National; USA: New York Met, St Paul, San Diego. **Roles with these companies incl** BEETHOVEN: Leonore★ (*Fidelio*); BRITTEN: Lady Billows★ (*Albert Herring*), Female Chorus (*Rape of Lucretia*); CORNELIUS: Margiana (*Barbier von Bagdad*); DALLAPICCOLA: Madre (*Prigioniero*); DONIZETTI: Anna Bolena, Lucia; GLUCK: Iphigénie en Tauride), Euridice; JANACEK: Emilia Marty★ (*Makropoulos Affair*); MARTIN: Branghien (*Vin herbé*); MENOTTI: Mme Euterpova★ (*Globolinks*); MOZART: Fiordiligi (*Così fan tutte*), Donna Anna★ (*Don Giovanni*), Konstanze (*Entführung aus dem Serail*), Elettra (*Idomeneo*), Contessa★ (*Nozze di Figaro*), Pamina & Königin der Nacht (*Zauberflöte*); NICOLAI: Frau Fluth★ (*Lustigen Weiber*); OFFENBACH: Olympia & Antonia & Giulietta★ (*Contes d'Hoffmann*); ORFF: Antigonae★; PENDERECKI: Jeanne★ (*Teufel von Loudun*); PROKOFIEV: Fata Morgana (*Love for Three Oranges*); PUCCINI: Mimi (*Bohème*), Giorgetta★ (*Tabarro*), Tosca★; RIMSKY-KORSAKOV: Coq d'or; SCHOENBERG: Woman★ (*Erwartung*); STRAUSS, J: Rosalinde★ (*Fledermaus*); STRAUSS, R: Komponist (*Ariadne auf Naxos*), Salome★; STRAVINSKY: Anne Trulove (*Rake's Progress*); VERDI: Elisabetta (*Don Carlo*), Lady Macbeth, Desdemona (*Otello*), Gilda (*Rigoletto*), Violetta★ (*Traviata*), Leonora★ (*Trovatore*); WAGNER: Senta★ (*Fliegende Holländer*), Elsa (*Lohengrin*), Eva★ (*Meistersinger*), Elisabeth (*Tannhäuser*); WEBER: Agathe (*Freischütz*), Rezia★ (*Oberon*). Also BLACHER: Primadonna (*Zwischenfälle bei einer Notlandung*); ORFF: Io (*Prometheus*), Sibylle (*De temporum fine comedia*); MOZART: Erste Dame (*Zauberflöte*); SCHOENBERG: Freundin (*Glückliche Hand*); LIEBERMANN: Penelope; HENZE:

Natalie (*Prinz von Homburg*); LEVY: Lavinia (*Mourning Becomes Electra*). **World premieres:** FORTNER: Maria Stuart (*Elisabeth Tudor*) Deutsche Oper Berlin 1972. **Res:** 8026 Ebenhausen, FR Ger.

LORD, WILLIAM UMBACH. Scenic and costume designer for opera, theater. Canadian. Born Red Deer, Alta. Divorced. Studied: Ontario Coll of Art; Univ of Toronto. Prof training: Canadian Opera Co, Toronto. **Operatic debut:** *Cavalleria rusticana* Canadian Op Co, Toronto. Theater debut: Hart House Theatre, Toronto 1960. Previous occupation: company mng, Canadian Op Co. Awards: Canada Council Travel Awd.

Designed for major companies in CAN: Toronto. **Operas designed for these companies incl** BIZET: *Carmen;* BRITTEN: *Burning Fiery Furnace, Prodigal Son, Rape of Lucretia;* PUCCINI: *Bohème;* ROSSINI: *Barbiere di Siviglia;* STRAUSS, J: *Fledermaus.* Also BRITTEN: *Noye's Fludde.* **Operatic world premieres:** WILSON: *Selfish Giant* St Lawrence Cntr & Can Children's Opera, Toronto 1973. Teaches at York Univ, Toronto. **Res:** 400 Avenue Rd, Toronto, Ont, Canada.

LORENGAR, PILAR. Lyric soprano, started as mezzo-soprano. Spanish. Resident mem: Deutsche Oper Berlin. Born 16 Jan 1928, Saragossa, Spain. Husband Jürgen Schaaf, occupation physician. Studied: Consv Barcelona; Carl Ebert, Hertha Klust, Berlin. **Debut:** Barcelona, Spain 1949. Awards: Kammersängerin, City of Berlin, FR Ger; Winner Natl Singing Cont Barcelona 1951.

Sang with major companies in ARG: Buenos Aires; AUS: Salzburg Fest, Vienna Staatsoper; FRA: Aix-en-Provence Fest, Paris; FR GER: Berlin Deutsche Oper, Munich Staatsoper; ITA: Milan La Scala; SPA: Barcelona, Madrid; UK: Glyndebourne Fest, London Royal; USA: Chicago, New York Met, Philadelphia Lyric, San Francisco Opera; et al. **Roles with these companies incl** BEETHOVEN: Marzelline (*Fidelio*); BIZET: Micaëla (*Carmen*); DEBUSSY: Mélisande; GLUCK: Euridice‡; GOUNOD: Marguerite (*Faust*); GRANADOS: Rosario (*Goyescas*); HINDEMITH: Ursula (*Mathis der Maler*); JANACEK: Jenufa; LEONCAVALLO: Nedda‡ (*Pagliacci*); MASSENET: Manon‡; MOZART: Fiordiligi‡ (*Così fan tutte*), Donna Elvira‡ (*Don Giovanni*), Ilia (*Idomeneo*), Contessa & Cherubino‡ (*Nozze di Figaro*), Pamina‡ (*Zauberflöte*); OFFENBACH: Antonia (*Contes d'Hoffmann*); ORFF: Solo (*Carmina burana*); PUCCINI: Mimi‡ (*Bohème*), Cio-Cio-San (*Butterfly*), Manon Lescaut, Suor Angelica, Giorgetta (*Tabarro*), Tosca, Liù (*Turandot*); SMETANA: Marie‡ (*Bartered Bride*); TCHAIKOVSKY: Tatiana (*Eugene Onegin*); VERDI: Elisabetta (*Don Carlo*), Alice Ford (*Falstaff*), Desdemona (*Otello*), Violetta‡ (*Traviata*); WAGNER: Elsa (*Lohengrin*), Eva (*Meistersinger*), Elisabeth (*Tannhäuser*); WEBER: Agathe (*Freischütz*); et al. Also SPONTINI: Olimpia. Recorded for: London, Angel, Pathé, DG, HMV. Gives recitals. Appears with symphony orchestra. Mgmt: COL/USA.

LOREY, FORREST PATRICK. Lyric baritone. American. Born Oklahoma City, OK, USA. Wife

Maury H, occupation flutist, artist. Studied: Cornelius Reid, New York; Manhattan School of Music, Met Opera Studio, New York. **Debut:** Silvio (*Pagliacci*) Syracuse Opera 1971. Awards: Winner Baltimore Opera Compt 1972; Winner SW Young Artists Compt 1963.

Sang with major companies in USA: Baltimore, Cincinnati, Fort Worth, Hawaii, Kentucky, Memphis, Miami, New Orleans, Pittsburgh. **Roles with these companies incl** DONIZETTI: Dott Malatesta★ (*Don Pasquale*), Belcore★ (*Elisir*), Gasparo★ (*Rita*); MOZART: Guglielmo★ (*Così fan tutte*); PUCCINI: Marcello★ (*Bohème*). Also GOUNOD: Valentin★ (*Faust*). Gives recitals. Appears with symphony orchestra. **Res:** New York, USA. Mgmt: SCO/USA.

LORMI, GIORGIO; né Loreto. Lyric baritone. Italian. Born 16 Jun 1941, Milan. Wife Laura Scotti, occupation bookkeeper. Two children. Studied: Maestri Soresina, Llopart, Vedovelli; Centro di perfez, Teatro alla Scala, Milan. **Debut:** Seid (*Corsaro*) Parma, Italy 1972. Previous occupations: head of a printing office. Awards: First Prize, Busseto Competition; Golden Nut, Lecco; Citat Lions Club Milan.

Sang with major companies in ITA: Milan La Scala, Parma, Turin, Venice; USA: Washington DC. **Roles with these companies incl** BRITTEN: Noye★ (*Noye's fludde*); CIMAROSA: Count Robinson★‡ (*Matrimonio segreto*); DONIZETTI: Malatesta★ (*Don Pasquale*); LEONCAVALLO: Edipo Re, Tonio★ (*Pagliacci*); MASSENET: Des Grieux★ (*Portrait de Manon*), Albert★ (*Werther*); PUCCINI: Marcello★ (*Bohème*), Sharpless★ (*Butterfly*); ROSSINI: Figaro★ (*Barbiere di Siviglia*), Slook★ (*Cambiale di matrimonio*); SCHOENBERG: Moses★; VERDI: Ezio★ (*Attila*), Germont★ (*Traviata*). Also GALUPPI: Nardo (*Filosofo di campagna*); LEONCAVALLO: Edipo★ (*Edipo Re*); WEILL: Maestro★ (*Jasager*). Gives recitals. **Res:** V Vallisneri 11/b, Milan, Italy.

LOVE, SHIRLEY. Dramatic mezzo-soprano. American. Resident mem: Metropolitan Opera, New York. Born 6 Jan 1940, Detroit, MI, USA. Single. Studied: Avery Crew, Detroit; Marinka Gurewich, Margaret Harshaw, New York. **Debut:** Zweite Dame (*Zauberflöte*) Metropolitan Opera 1964. Awards: American Opera Aud.

Sang with major companies in HOL: Amsterdam; ITA: Bologna, Florence Comunale; USA: Baltimore, Chicago, Cincinnati, Lake George, Miami, New York Met, Philadelphia Grand & Lyric. **Roles with these companies incl** BERNSTEIN: Dinah (*Trouble in Tahiti*); BIZET: Carmen; BRITTEN: Hermia & Hippolita★ (*Midsummer Night*), Lucretia★ (*Rape of Lucretia*); GLUCK: Orfeo; GOUNOD: Siebel (*Faust*); MENOTTI: Secretary (*Consul*), Mme Flora (*Medium*); MOZART: Dorabella★ (*Così fan tutte*), Cherubino (*Nozze di Figaro*); NICOLAI: Frau Reich★ (*Lustigen Weiber*); PUCCINI: Suzuki★ (*Butterfly*); RAVEL: Enfant★ (*Enfant et les sortilèges*); ROSSINI: Rosina (*Barbiere di Siviglia*), Angelina (*Cenerentola*); STRAVINSKY: Jocasta★ (*Oedipus Rex*); TCHAIKOVSKY: Pauline (*Pique Dame*); WAGNER: Magdalene★ (*Meistersinger*). **World premieres:** KAGEN: Gertrude (*Hamlet*) Baltimore Opera, MD, USA 1962. Gives recitals. Appears with symphony orchestra.

LÖWLEIN, HANS. Conductor of opera and symphony; composer. German. Born 24 Jun 1909, Ingolstadt, Germany. Wife Charlotte Gerbitz. Studied: Akad der Tonkunst, Munich; S von Hausegger, Hans Pfitzner, Dr Knappe, E Bach; incl piano, violin. Plays the piano. Operatic training as repetiteur at Staatsoper, Munich 1933-34. **Operatic debut:** Stadttheater Stettin, Germany 1935. Symphonic debut: Opern und Konzert Orch, Stettin 1936. Previous adm positions in opera: Mus Dir, Stadttheater Stralssund, Germany 1945-46; First Cond, Staatsoper Dresden 1946-49; Mus Oberleiter, Komische Oper Berlin, Ger DR 1949-50; First State Cond, Staatsoper Berlin, Ger DR 1950-61; Deputy Gen Mus Dir, Opernhaus Frankfurt, FR Ger 1961-65; Mus Oberleiter, Stadttheater Basel, Switzerland 1965-72.

Conducted with major companies in CZE: Brno, Prague National; FRA: Paris; FR GER: Berlin Deutsche Oper, Darmstadt, Essen, Frankfurt, Hamburg; GER DR: Berlin Komische Oper & Staatsoper, Dresden, Leipzig; ITA: Turin; SPA: Barcelona; SWI: Basel; UK: London English National. **Operas with these companies incl** ADAM: *Si j'étais roi*; d'ALBERT: *Tiefland*; AUBER: *Fra Diavolo*; BARTOK: *Bluebeard's Castle★*; BEETHOVEN: *Fidelio★*; BIZET: *Carmen*; BRITTEN: *Peter Grimes*; CORNELIUS: *Barbier von Bagdad*; DESSAU: *Verurteilung des Lukullus*; DONIZETTI: *Don Pasquale, Elisir, Fille du régiment*; FLOTOW: *Martha*; FORTNER: *Don Perlimplin*; GLUCK: *Alceste, Iphigénie en Aulide*; GOUNOD: *Faust*; HANDEL: *Ariodante*; HENZE: *Boulevard Solitude*; HINDEMITH: *Mathis der Maler*; HUMPERDINCK: *Hänsel und Gretel★*; JANACEK: *Jenufa★, Katya Kabanova*; LEONCAVALLO: *Pagliacci*; LORTZING: *Waffenschmied, Wildschütz★, Zar und Zimmermann*; MASCAGNI: *Cavalleria rusticana*; MASSENET: *Manon*; MOZART: *Così fan tutte, Don Giovanni★, Entführung aus dem Serail★, Finta giardiniera, Idomeneo, Schauspieldirektor, Nozze di Figaro★, Zauberflöte★*; NICOLAI: *Lustigen Weiber*; OFFENBACH: *Contes d'Hoffmann*; ORFF: *Kluge*; PROKOFIEV: *Duenna, Love for Three Oranges★*; PUCCINI: *Bohème★, Gianni Schicchi, Butterfly, Manon Lescaut, Tabarro, Tosca★*; RAVEL: *Heure espagnole*; ROSSINI: *Barbiere di Siviglia*; SMETANA: *Bartered Bride★*; STRAUSS, J: *Fledermaus*; STRAUSS, R: *Arabella, Ariadne auf Naxos, Elektra, Rosenkavalier, Salome*; STRAVINSKY: *Rake's Progress★*; TCHAIKOVSKY: *Eugene Onegin, Pique Dame*; THOMAS: *Mignon*; VERDI: *Aida, Ballo in maschera★, Don Carlo★, Falstaff★, Forza del destino★, Macbeth, Otello, Rigoletto★, Simon Boccanegra★, Traviata★, Trovatore★*; WAGNER: *Fliegende Holländer, Lohengrin★, Meistersinger, Parsifal★, Rheingold, Walküre, Tannhäuser*; WEBER: *Abu Hassan, Freischütz★*; WEINBERGER: *Schwanda*; WOLF-FERRARI: *Donne curiose, Quattro rusteghi, Segreto di Susanna*. Video/Film—TV: *Freischütz, Schwanda, Butterfly, Barbiere di Siviglia, Heure espagnole*. Film: *Zar und Zimmermann*. Conducted major orch in Europe,

Asia. Teaches at Staatl Musikhochschule, Frankfurt.

LUCACIU, TEODORA. Lirico spinto. Romanian. Resident mem: Romanian Opera, Bucharest. Born Vulcan, Romania. Single. Studied: Ciprian Porumbescu Consv, Prof Constantin Stroescu, Bucharest. **Debut:** Marguerite (*Faust*) Bucharest 1959. Awards: Second Grand Prix, Intl Vocal Conts Geneva 1956 & Toulouse 1957; Gold Medal First Prize, Intl Conts Moscow 1957 & Sofia 1961.

Sang with major companies in ARG: Buenos Aires; AUS: Graz, Vienna Volksoper; BEL: Brussels; BUL: Sofia; CZE: Brno, Prague National & Smetana; FRA: Lyon, Nancy, Strasbourg, Toulouse; GRE: Athens Opera; FR GER: Berlin Deutsche Oper, Düsseldorf-Duisburg, Frankfurt, Karlsruhe, Stuttgart, Wiesbaden; GER DR: Berlin Staatsoper; HUN: Budapest; POL: Lodz, Warsaw; ROM: Bucharest; SWI: Geneva, Zurich; USSR: Kiev, Leningrad Kirov, Moscow Bolshoi, Tbilisi; YUG: Dubrovnik, Zagreb, Belgrade. **Roles with these companies incl** BIZET: Micaëla★ (*Carmen*), Léila (*Pêcheurs de perles*); DEBUSSY: Lia (*Enfant prodigue*), Mélisande★; FALLA: Salud★ (*Vida breve*); GOUNOD: Marguerite★ (*Faust*); HUMPERDINCK: Gretel★; LEONCAVALLO: Nedda★ (*Pagliacci*); MASSENET: Manon★; MOZART: Contessa & Susanna & Cherubino★ (*Nozze di Figaro*); POULENC: Femme★ (*Voix humaine*); PUCCINI: Mimi★ & Musetta★ (*Bohème*), Cio-Cio-San★ (*Butterfly*), Manon Lescaut★, Liù★ (*Turandot*); SCHOENBERG: Woman★ (*Erwartung*); SMETANA: Marie (*Bartered Bride*); STRAUSS, R: Marschallin (*Rosenkavalier*); TCHAIKOVSKY: Tatiana★ (*Eugene Onegin*), Iolanthe, Lisa (*Pique Dame*); VERDI: Elisabetta (*Don Carlo*), Desdemona★ (*Otello*), Violetta (*Traviata*). Gives recitals. Appears with symphony orchestra. Teaches voice. **Res:** Alexandru Sahia St 17, 7 Bucharest, Romania. Mgmt: RIA/ROM.

LUCAS, JAMES. Stages/produces opera, theater. Also designs stage-lighting and is a conductor, actor & author. American. Born 15 Mar 1933, San Antonio, TX. Single. Studied: Juilliard School, Frederic Cohen, Boris Goldovsky, New York; incl music, piano & voice. Operatic training as asst stage dir at Metropolitan Opera, New York 1960-62. **Operatic debut:** *Bohème* New York Opera Theater 1956.

Directed/produced opera for major companies in CAN: Vancouver; USA: Baltimore, Boston, Chicago, Cincinnati, Dallas, Fort Worth, Houston, Kansas City, Lake George, Memphis, Miami, Milwaukee Florentine, Minneapolis, Newark, New York Met & City Opera, Omaha, Philadelphia Grand, Pittsburgh, Portland, San Antonio, San Francisco Spring Opera, Seattle. **Operas staged with these companies incl** BEETHOVEN: *Fidelio★;* BIZET: *Carmen★;* BRITTEN: *Albert Herring;* BUSONI: *Arlecchino★;* CIMAROSA: *Matrimonio segreto;* DEBUSSY: *Enfant prodigue;* DONIZETTI: *Don Pasquale★, Elisir★, Fille du régiment★, Lucia★, Rita★;* FLOTOW: *Martha;* GIORDANO: *Andrea Chénier;* GOUNOD: *Faust★, Roméo et Juliette★;* HUMPERDINCK: *Hänsel und Gretel;* LEONCAVALLO: *Pagliacci★;* MASCAGNI:

Amico Fritz★, Cavalleria rusticana★; MASSENET: *Cendrillon★, Manon★, Navarraise, Werther;* MENOTTI: *Consul, Medium★, Old Maid and the Thief★;* MILHAUD: *Pauvre matelot★;* MOORE: *Ballad of Baby Doe;* MOZART: *Così fan tutte★, Don Giovanni★, Entführung aus dem Serail★, Nozze di Figaro★, Schauspieldirektor, Zauberflöte★;* NICOLAI: *Lustigen Weiber;* OFFENBACH: *Contes d'Hoffmann★, Périchole★;* ORFF: *Kluge, Mond;* PERGOLESI: *Serva padrona;* PONCHIELLI: *Gioconda;* PUCCINI: *Bohème★, Gianni Schicchi★, Butterfly★, Manon Lescaut★, Rondine★, Suor Angelica★, Tabarro★, Tosca★, Turandot★;* PURCELL: *Dido and Aeneas;* RAVEL: *Enfant et les sortilèges;* ROSSINI: *Barbiere di Siviglia★, Cenerentola★, Italiana in Algeri★;* SAINT-SAENS: *Samson et Dalila;* SMETANA: *The Kiss★;* STRAUSS, J: *Fledermaus;* STRAUSS, R: *Ariadne auf Naxos, Salome★;* VAUGHAN WILLIAMS: *Riders to the Sea;* VERDI: *Aida★, Ballo in maschera★, Don Carlo★, Falstaff★, Macbeth, Nabucco, Otello★, Rigoletto★, Simon Boccanegra, Traviata★, Trovatore★;* WAGNER: *Fliegende Holländer★, Lohengrin★;* WARD: *Crucible★;* WEBER: *Freischütz;* WEINBERGER: *Schwanda★;* WOLF-FERRARI: *Segreto di Susanna.* Teaches at Manhattan School of Music, New York. **Res:** 201 W 85 St, New York, NY, USA. Mgmt: HUR/USA.

LUCCARDI, GIANCARLO. Bass. Italian. Born 2 Jul 1939, Cusano Milanino/Milan. Wife Graziella Farina. Four children. Studied: Fiorenzo Tasso, Milan. **Debut:** Don Pasquale, As Li Co, Milan 1963. Previous occupations: mgr of excavating and construction firm.

Sang with major companies in CZE: Prague Smetana; ITA: Bologna, Genoa, Milan, Parma, Verona Arena; UK: Cardiff Welsh. **Roles with these companies incl** BEETHOVEN: Rocco (*Fidelio*); DONIZETTI: Don Pasquale, Dott Dulcamara (*Elisir*); PAISIELLO: Basilio (*Barbiere di Siviglia*); PUCCINI: Colline (*Bohème*); ROSSINI: Don Magnifico (*Cenerentola*); VERDI: Ramfis (*Aida*), Banquo (*Macbeth*); WEBER: Kaspar (*Freischütz*). Also PETRASSI: Cannizares (*Cordovano*); PUCCINI: Timur (*Turandot*). Recorded for: Teldec, Seneca. **Res:** V Acacie 1, Cusano Milanino/Milan, Italy.

LUCHETTI, VERIANO. Lyric tenor. Italian. Born 12 Mar 1939, Tuscania. Wife Mietta Sighele, occupation opera singer, soprano. Two children. Studied: Mo Enrico Piazza, Mo Capuana, Mo Miller, Milan; Mo Picozzi, Rome. **Debut:** Loris Ipanov (*Fedora*) Spoleto Fest 1967. Previous occupations: air force pilot. Awards: Diapason Siracusa; Palcoscenico d'oro; Noce d'oro.

Sang with major companies in AUS: Vienna Staatsoper; BEL: Brussels; BRA: Rio de Janeiro; DEN: Copenhagen; FRA: Aix-en-Provence Fest, Marseille, Paris; FR GER: Berlin Deutsche Oper, Frankfurt, Hamburg, Munich Staatsoper; GER DR: Leipzig; HOL: Amsterdam; HUN: Budapest; ITA: Florence Maggio & Comunale, Milan La Scala, Naples, Palermo, Parma, Spoleto Fest, Trieste, Venice; MEX: Mexico City; MON: Monte Carlo; POR: Lisbon; S AFR: Johannesburg; UK: London Royal; USA: Baltimore, Cincinnati, Dallas, Houston, Philadelphia Lyric. **Roles**

with these companies incl BELLINI: Tebaldo⋆ & Romeo (*Capuleti ed i Montecchi*), Arturo (*Straniera*); BIZET: Don José (*Carmen*); BOITO: Faust (*Mefistofele*); CHARPENTIER: Julien (*Louise*); CHERUBINI: Giasone⋆ (*Medea*); CILEA: Maurizio (*A. Lecouvreur*); DONIZETTI: Nemorino (*Elisir*), Edgardo⋆ (*Lucia*), Roberto Devereux; GOUNOD: Roméo⋆; MASSENET: Des Grieux (*Manon*), Werther; MENOTTI: Lover (*Amelia al ballo*); MEYERBEER: Vasco da Gama⋆ (*Africaine*); MUSSORGSKY: Andrei Khovansky⋆ (*Khovanshchina*); PUCCINI: Rodolfo⋆ (*Bohème*), Pinkerton⋆ (*Butterfly*), Cavaradossi⋆ (*Tosca*), Roberto⋆ (*Villi*); ROSSINI: Aménophis⋆ (*Moïse*); TCHAIKOVSKY: Lenski⋆ (*Eugene Onegin*); VERDI: Foresto⋆ (*Attila*), Riccardo⋆ (*Ballo in maschera*), Don Carlo⋆, Fenton (*Falstaff*), Don Alvaro⋆ (*Forza del destino*), Duca di Mantova (*Rigoletto*), Gabriele⋆ (*Simon Boccanegra*), Alfredo⋆ (*Traviata*); ZANDONAI: Paolo (*Francesca da Rimini*). Also PUCCINI: Edgar⋆; SPONTINI: Enrico⋆ (*Agnese di Hohenstaufen*). **World premieres:** HAZON: (*Donna uccisa con dolcezza*) Parma 1968. Gives recitals. Appears with symphony orchestra. **Res:** 83 Colle Romano, Riano/Rome, Italy.

LÜDEKE, RAINER. Bass-baritone. German. Resident mem: Opernhaus Leipzig. Born 7 Nov 1927, Essen, Germany. Wife Christa-Maria Ziese, occupation singer. Two children. Studied: Erwin Roettgen, Essen; Christa-Maria Ziese, Leipzig. **Debut:** Commendatore (*Don Giovanni*) Volkstheater Halberstadt, Germany 1951. Awards: Kammersänger, Gvnmt Ger DR; Kunstpreis Ger DR, Gvnmt Ger DR.
Sang with major companies in CZE: Brno; GER DR: Berlin Staatsoper, Dresden, Leipzig; POL: Lodz; USSR: Moscow Bolshoi; YUG: Belgrade. Roles with these companies incl d'ALBERT: Sebastiano (*Tiefland*); BEETHOVEN: Don Pizarro⋆ (*Fidelio*); BIZET: Escamillo⋆ (*Carmen*); BORODIN: Prince Igor; GERSHWIN: Porgy⋆; HINDEMITH: Cardillac; LORTZING: Stadinger (*Waffenschmied*); MOZART: Don Alfonso (*Così fan tutte*), Don Giovanni⋆, Osmin (*Entführung aus dem Serail*), Conte Almaviva⋆ & Figaro (*Nozze di Figaro*), Sarastro (*Zauberflöte*); OFFENBACH: Coppélius etc⋆ (*Contes d'Hoffmann*); PUCCINI: Scarpia⋆ (*Tosca*); STRAUSS, R: Mandryka (*Arabella*), Musiklehrer⋆ (*Ariadne*), Barak⋆ (*Frau ohne Schatten*), Jochanaan (*Salome*); VERDI: Amonasro & Ramfis (*Aida*), Philip II⋆ (*Don Carlo*), Padre Guardiano (*Forza del destino*), Iago (*Otello*); WAGNER: Holländer⋆, Telramund⋆ (*Lohengrin*), Wotan (*Rheingold⋆, Walküre⋆*), Wanderer⋆(*Siegfried*), Landgraf (*Tannhäuser*), Kurwenal & König Marke (*Tristan und Isolde*); WEBER: Kaspar⋆ (*Freischütz*). **World premieres:** MASANETZ: Bettler (*Wundervogel*) Landesoper Dresden 1955. Recorded for: Radio DDR, Berliner Rundfunk. Video/Film: (*Fliegende Holländer*). Gives recitals. Appears with symphony orchestra. **Res:** Haussmannstr 7, Leipzig, Ger DR. **Mgmt:** KDR/GDR; SLZ/FRG.

LUDGIN, CHESTER. Baritone. American. Born 20 May 1925, New York. Single. Studied: William S Brady, New York; Amer Theatre Wing, prof training prgr, New York. **Debut:** Scarpia (*Tosca*) Experimental Opera Thtr of Amer, New Orleans, USA 1956. Previous occupations: repres of printing firm.
Sang with major companies in CAN: Montreal/Quebec, Toronto, Vancouver; MEX: Mexico City; USA: Baltimore, Boston, Cincinnati, Fort Worth, Hartford, Hawaii, Houston, Kentucky, Memphis, Miami, Milwaukee Florentine, New Orleans, New York City Opera, Omaha, Philadelphia Grand, Pittsburgh, Portland, St Paul, San Antonio, San Diego, San Francisco & Spring Opera, Santa Fe, Seattle, Washington DC. Roles with these companies incl BEETHOVEN: Don Pizarro (*Fidelio*); BIZET: Escamillo (*Carmen*), Zurga (*Pêcheurs de perles*); DONIZETTI: Belcore (*Elisir*), Enrico (*Lucia*); FLOTOW: Plunkett (*Martha*); FLOYD: Olin Blitch⋆ (*Susannah*); GIORDANO: Carlo Gérard (*Andrea Chénier*); GLUCK: Oreste (*Iphigénie en Tauride*); GOUNOD: Méphistophélès (*Faust*); JANACEK: Jaroslav Prus⋆ (*Makropoulos Affair*); LEONCAVALLO: Tonio⋆ (*Pagliacci*); MASCAGNI: Alfio⋆ (*Cavalleria rusticana*); MASSENET: Lescaut (*Manon*); MENOTTI: John Sorel (*Consul*); MOORE: Horace Tabor (*Baby Doe*); MOZART: Don Giovanni, Conte Almaviva & Figaro (*Nozze di Figaro*); MUSSORGSKY: Boris Godunov; ORFF: Solo (*Carmina burana*); PONCHIELLI: Barnaba (*Gioconda*); PUCCINI: Marcello (*Bohème*), Jack Rance (*Fanciulla del West*), Gianni Schicchi, Sharpless (*Butterfly*), Michele (*Tabarro*), Scarpia⋆ (*Tosca*); ROSSINI: Figaro (*Barbiere di Siviglia*); SAINT-SAENS: Grand prêtre⋆ (*Samson et Dalila*); SHOSTAKOVICH: Boris (*Katerina Ismailova*); STRAUSS, R: Orest (*Elektra*), Jochanaan (*Salome*); VERDI: Amonasro (*Aida*), Renato⋆ (*Ballo in maschera*), Grande Inquisitore (*Don Carlo*), Don Carlo⋆ (*Forza del destino*), Macbeth, Iago (*Otello*), Rigoletto, Germont (*Traviata*), Conte di Luna (*Trovatore*); WAGNER: Holländer⋆, Telramund (*Lohengrin*), Hans Sachs (*Meistersinger*), Kurwenal (*Tristan und Isolde*). Also HANSON: Wrestling Bradford (*Merry Mount*); HOIBY: Postman (*Scarf*). **World premieres:** WARD: John Proctor (*Crucible*) New York City Opera 1961; ELLSTEIN: Golem (*The Golem*) New York City Opera 1962; LaMONTAINE: Joseph (*Novellis, Novellis*) Washington, DC, Opera Soc at National Cathedral 1961; MOORE: Per Hansa (*Giants in the Earth*) rev vers, Univ of ND, USA 1974. Recorded for: Westminster, CRI. Video/Film: Prisoner (*Maria Golovin*); Alfio (*Cavalleria rusticana*); John Sorel (*Consul*). Gives recitals. Appears with symphony orchestra. **Res:** 205 West End Ave, New York, NY, USA. **Mgmt:** LLL/USA.

LUDWIG, CHRISTA. Dramatic mezzo-soprano. Austrian. Resident mem: Staatsoper, Vienna. Born 16 Mar, Berlin. Husband Paul-Emile Deiber, occupation actor & stage dir. One son. Studied: Eugenie Besalla-Ludwig (mother). **Debut:** Prinz Orlovsky (*Fledermaus*) Städtische Bühnen, Frankfurt 1946. Awards: Kammersängerin; First Class Cross of Honor, Arts & Science; Prix des Affaires Culturelles; Grammy Awds; Orphée d'or, German Record Awd; Mozart Medal.
Sang with major companies in ARG: Buenos Aires; AUS: Salzburg Fest, Vienna Staatsoper;

CAN: Montreal/Quebec; FRA: Paris; FR GER: Bayreuth Fest, Berlin Deutsche Oper, Darmstadt, Frankfurt, Hamburg, Hannover, Munich Staatsoper, Wiesbaden; ITA: Milan La Scala; SWE: Drottningholm Fest; UK: London Royal; USSR: Moscow Bolshoi; USA: Chicago, New York Met, San Francisco Opera. **Roles with these companies incl** BARTOK: Judith‡ (*Bluebeard's Castle*); BERLIOZ: Didon★ (*Troyens*); BIZET: Carmen★‡; FLOTOW: Nancy (*Martha*); GLUCK: Orfeo; HANDEL: Cornelia (*Giulio Cesare*); MASSENET: Charlotte (*Werther*); MOZART: Sesto (*Clemenza di Tito*), Dorabella‡ (*Così fan tutte*), Cherubino‡ (*Nozze di Figaro*); MUSSORGSKY: Marina (*Boris Godunov*), Marfa★ (*Khovanshchina*); NICOLAI: Frau Reich (*Lustigen Weiber*); PFITZNER: Silla★ (*Palestrina*); PUCCINI: Suzuki‡ (*Butterfly*); ROSSINI: Rosina (*Barbiere di Siviglia*), Angelina (*Cenerentola*); STRAUSS, J: Prinz Orlovsky★ (*Fledermaus*); STRAUSS, R: Komponist (*Ariadne auf Naxos*), Clairon‡ (*Capriccio*), Klytämnestra★ (*Elektra*), Färberin★ (*Frau ohne Schatten*), Octavian‡ (*Rosenkavalier*); TCHAIKOVSKY: Olga (*Eugene Onegin*); VERDI: Amneris★ (*Aida*), Eboli★ (*Don Carlo*), Preziosilla (*Forza del destino*), Federica★ (*Luisa Miller*); WAGNER: Ortrud★‡ (*Lohengrin*), Magdalene (*Meistersinger*), Kundry‡ (*Parsifal*), Fricka (*Rheingold★, Walküre★‡*), Waltraute★‡ (*Götterdämmerung*), Venus‡ (*Tannhäuser*), Brangäne★‡ (*Tristan und Isolde*). Also GLUCK: Iphigénie (*Iphigénie en Aulide*); STRAUSS, R: Ariadne (*Ariadne auf Naxos*), Marschallin★ (*Rosenkavalier*). Only on records BELLINI: Adalgisa‡ (*Norma*); HUMPERDINCK: Hexe‡ (*Hänsel und Gretel*); SAINT-SAENS: Dalila‡. **World premieres:** EINEM: Claire (*Besuch der alten Dame*) Staatsoper, Vienna 1971. Recorded for: Decca, Polydor, DG, EMI, CBS. Video/Film: Dorabella (*Così fan tutte*); Suzuki (*Butterfly*). Gives recitals. Appears with symphony orchestra. **Res:** Rigistr 14, CH-6045 Meggen, Switzerland Mgmt: JUC/SWI.

LUDWIG, ILSE. Lyric mezzo-soprano. German. Resident mem: Staatsoper Dresden, Ger DR. Born 22 Feb 1929, Bautzen. Husband Wilfried Jahns, occupation opera singer. One child. Studied: Marianne Rau-Hoeglauer, Käte Heine Mitzschke, Prof Annemarie Rauch, Dresden. **Debut:** Pastore (*Tosca*) Staatsoper Dresden 1954. Previous occupations: furn carpenter; draftsman; chorus singer. Awards: Kammersängerin, Ministry of Culture, Ger DR 1969.
　　Sang with major companies in FR GER: Wiesbaden; GER DR: Berlin Staatsoper, Dresden; USSR: Leningrad Kirov. **Roles with these companies incl** BIZET: Carmen; CIMAROSA: Fidalma (*Matrimonio segreto*); GAY/Britten: Polly (*Beggar's Opera*); GLUCK: Orfeo★; HUMPERDINCK: Hänsel★; LORTZING: Gräfin Eberbach★ (*Wildschütz*); MONTEVERDI: Penelope★ (*Ritorno d'Ulisse*); MOZART: Dorabella (*Così fan tutte*); NICOLAI: Frau Reich (*Lustigen Weiber*); PUCCINI: Suzuki★ (*Butterfly*); STRAUSS, R: Clairon★ (*Capriccio*); TCHAIKOVSKY: Olga (*Eugene Onegin*); VERDI: Dame Quickly★ (*Falstaff*), Preziosilla (*Forza del destino*); WAGNER: Erda (*Rheingold*); WEBER: Fatime (*Oberon*); WOLF-FERRARI: Margarita

(*Quattro rusteghi*). Also PAISIELLO: Cassandra (*Astrologi*). Recorded for: VEB, Eterna. Video/Film: Annina (*Rosenkavalier*); (*Matrimonio segreto*). Gives recitals. Appears with symphony orchestra. Coaches repertoire. **Res:** Küntzelmannstr 6, 8051 Dresden, Ger DR. Mgmt: KDR/GDR.

LUDWIG, JOHN McKAY. American. Art Adm, San Francisco Opera Assn, War Memorial Opera House, San Francisco, CA 94102; also of Spring Opera Theater; Western Opera Theater; Merola Opera Program. In charge of admin matters. Born 14 Aug 1935, New Orleans, LA, USA. Divorced. Two daughters. Studied: Yale Univ, Grad Drama Schl. New Haven; Univ of North Carolina, Chapel Hill, USA. Previous occupations: dir of conc series and perf arts fest; dir/mng summer theater; officer US Navy. Previous positions, primarily administrative & theatrical: Co-ordinator of Perf Arts, Walker Art Center, Minneapolis, MN 1963-69; Gen Mng, Minnesota Opera Company, Minneapolis 1963-73; Gen Dir, Wolf Trap Foundation, Vienna, VA, USA 1973-75. Started in present position in 1975. World premieres at theaters under his management: STOKES/GREENBERG: *Horspfal* 1969; BOESING: *Wanderer* 1969; MARSHALL/BALK: *Oedipus and the Sphinx* 1969; GESSNER: *Faust Counter Faust* 1969; MARSHALL: *Business of Good Government* 1970; ARGENTO: *Postcard from Morocco* 1971; SUSA, C: *Transformations* 1972; all at Minnesota Op, Minneapolis. Awards: Admin Internship Ford Fndt, NY; Gen Fllshp Yale Univ; Order of the Golden Fleece, Univ of No Carolina. Initiated major policy changes including founding of Minnesota Op Co, development into art & financially stable repertoire ensbl, spec in premieres of new works & innov prod from stand rep. Season expansion from 8 pfs & 2 prods to 30 pfs and 6 prods, incl national tours in USA. Budget growth from $100,000 per annum to $350,000. Developed Wolf Trap Co from youth summer school to prof trng prgm for opera singer. Mem of OPERA America, Vice-Pres; Prof Comm Central Op Svc; Music Panel/Opera Ntl Endowment for the Arts, Washington; and Visual Arts in Perf Arts Panel, NEA. **Res:** San Francisco, CA, USA.

LUDWIG, LEOPOLD. Conductor of opera and symphony. German. Resident Cond, Hamburg Staatsoper. Born 12 Jan 1908, Witkowitz, CSR. Studied: Consv of Music, Emil Paur, Austria; incl piano & organ. Awards: Prof, Hamburg Senate 1968. Previous adm positions in opera: Mus Dir, Hamburg Staatsoper 1950-70 and Oldenburg Staatsoper 1936-39; Chief Cond, Staatsoper Berlin 1934-50.
　　Conducted with major companies in AUS: Salzburg Fest, Vienna Staatsoper & Volksoper; CZE: Brno; FRA: Paris; FR GER: Berlin Deutsche Oper, Düsseldorf-Duisburg, Hamburg, Munich Staatsoper, Stuttgart; HOL: Amsterdam; ITA: Milan La Scala, Naples; SPA: Barcelona; SWE: Stockholm; UK: Edinburgh Fest, Glyndebourne Fest; USA: New York Met, San Francisco Opera; et al. **Operas with these companies incl** BEETHOVEN: *Fidelio;* BERG: *Lulu‡, Wozzeck;* BIZET: *Carmen;* GLUCK: *Orfeo ed Euridice;* HINDEMITH: *Mathis der Maler;* JANACEK: *Jenufa;*

LEONCAVALLO: *Pagliacci;* MASCAGNI: *Cavalleria rusticana;* MOZART: *Così fan tutte, Don Giovanni, Nozze di Figaro, Zauberflöte;* OFFENBACH: *Contes d'Hoffmann;* SMETANA: *Bartered Bride;* STRAUSS, J: *Fledermaus;* STRAUSS, R: *Arabella, Ariadne auf Naxos, Elektra, Frau ohne Schatten, Rosenkavalier, Salome;* VERDI: *Nabucco, Trovatore;* WAGNER: *Fliegende Holländer, Lohengrin, Meistersinger, Parsifal, Rheingold, Walküre, Siegfried, Götterdämmerung, Tannhäuser;* WEBER: *Freischütz;* et al. Also WERLE: *Resan.* Recorded for HMV-Electrola. Video/Film—Hamburg Opera: *Freischütz.* Conducted major orch in Europe.

LUDWIG, WOLF-DIETER. Stages/produces opera, theater & television. Also designs sets & stagelighting. German. Intendant & Resident Stage Dir, Städtische Bühnen, Mainz. Born 31 Jan 1928, Liegnitz. Wife Erika Brunner. Four children. Studied: Acad Wiesbaden, Theater Düsseldorf, Gründgens; incl music, violin and voice. Operatic training as asst stage dir at Städtische Bühnen, Düsseldorf 1951-53. **Operatic debut:** *Butterfly* Düsseldorf 1953. Previous adm positions in opera: Chief Prod, Theater Basel, Switzerland 1954-55; Chief Prod, Netherlands Op, Amsterdam 1956-64. **Directed/produced opera for major companies in** AUS: Vienna Staatsoper; BEL: Brussels; FRA: Lyon, Marseille, Nancy, Nice; FR GER: Bonn, Essen, Krefeld, Munich Gärtnerplatz, Saarbrücken, Wiesbaden; HOL: Amsterdam; ITA: Milan La Scala; MON: Monte Carlo; SPA: Barcelona; SWI: Basel. **Operas staged with these companies incl** BEETHOVEN: *Fidelio★†;* BIZET: *Carmen★;* DONIZETTI: *Don Pasquale, Lucia★;* GIORDANO: *Andrea Chénier;* GOUNOD: *Faust★;* HENZE: *Boulevard Solitude;* HUMPERDINCK: *Hänsel und Gretel;* JANACEK: *Makropoulos Affair;* LORTZING: *Wildschütz, Zar und Zimmermann;* MASCAGNI: *Cavalleria rusticana;* MENOTTI: *Consul;* MOZART: *Così fan tutte, Don Giovanni, Entführung aus dem Serail, Nozze di Figaro★, Zauberflöte★;* NICOLAI: *Lustigen Weiber;* OFFENBACH: *Contes d'Hoffmann★;* ORFF: *Carmina burana, Kluge;* POULENC: *Voix humaine★;* PUCCINI: *Bohème★, Gianni Schicchi, Manon Lescaut, Suor Angelica, Tabarro, Tosca, Turandot;* RAVEL: *Heure espagnole;* ROSSINI: *Barbiere di Siviglia;* STRAUSS, J: *Fledermaus;* STRAUSS, R: *Arabella, Ariadne auf Naxos, Elektra, Rosenkavalier;* STRAVINSKY: *Rake's Progress;* TCHAIKOVSKY: *Eugene Onegin, Pique Dame;* VERDI: *Aida, Ballo in maschera, Don Carlo★, Forza del destino, Otello★, Rigoletto, Traviata★, Trovatore;* WAGNER: *Fliegende Holländer★, Lohengrin★, Ring★, Tannhäuser★, Tristan und Isolde;* WEBER: *Freischütz;* WEINBERGER: *Schwanda;* WOLF-FERRARI: *Quattro rusteghi.* **Operatic world premieres:** BURKHARD: *Schwarze Spinne* Stadttheater Basel 1953; DRESDEN: *François Villon* 1960; BADINGS: *Josef K* 1961, both at Netherl Op, Amsterdam. Operatic Video—KRO TV Hilversum: *Entführung aus dem Serail.* **Res:** Fasanenweg 4, D8201 Reischenhart, Bavaria, FR Ger.

LUEDERS, MARY CROSS. Mezzo-soprano & contralto. American. Born 5 Jun 1942, Philadelphia, USA. Husband Frank Corsaro, occupation stage director. One child. Studied: Esther Andreas; Curtis Inst of Music, Philadelphia, PA; Acad of Vocal Arts, Dorothy Di Scala, Martial Singher, Philadelphia. **Debut:** Pantasilea (*Bomarzo*) New York City Opera 1968. **Sang with major companies in** MEX: Mexico City; USA: Houston, Milwaukee Florentine, New York City Opera, Philadelphia Lyric, St Paul, Seattle, Washington DC. **Roles with these companies incl** BORODIN: Kontchakovna (*Prince Igor*); FALLA: Abuela★ (*Vida breve*); GINASTERA: Fortuna (*Don Rodrigo*); HUMPERDINCK: Hänsel; MASSENET: Charlotte (*Werther*); MOZART: Cherubino (*Nozze di Figaro*); PONCHIELLI: Laura & La Cieca (*Gioconda*); PUCCINI: Suzuki (*Butterfly*); VERDI: Ulrica (*Ballo in maschera*); WARD: Elizabeth Proctor (*Crucible*). Also MONTEVERDI: Ottavia (*Incoronazione di Poppea*); GINASTERA: Pantasilea (*Bomarzo*). **World premieres:** HOIBY: Rosa Gonzales (*Summer and Smoke*) St Paul Opera, MN 1971. **Res:** 33 Riverside Dr, New York, NY, USA. Mgmt: FLC/USA.

LUIKEN, CAROL. Scenic and costume designer for opera, theater, film; specl in costumes. Is also a painter, illustrator & fashion designer. American. Born 6 Sep 1945, Paterson, NJ. Single. Studied: Columbia Univ, New York. Prof training: asst at Santa Fe Opera, NM 1969. **Operatic debut:** *Arlecchino* & *Guerra* Manhattan School of Music, New York 1971. Theater debut: Off Broadway, New York 1970. Awards: National Opera Inst Grant. **Designed for major companies in** ITA: Spoleto Fest; USA: Baltimore, Santa Fe. **Operas designed for these companies incl** BIZET: *Carmen★;* CIMAROSA: *Matrimonio segreto★;* DONIZETTI: *Don Pasquale★, Elisir★, Rita★;* GIORDANO: *Andrea Chénier★;* HENZE: *Boulevard Solitude★;* LEONCAVALLO: *Pagliacci★;* MASCAGNI: *Cavalleria rusticana★;* MASSENET: *Cendrillon★;* MENOTTI: *Saint of Bleecker Street★;* SMETANA: *The Kiss★;* VERDI: *Aida★, Ballo in maschera★;* WARD: *Crucible★;* WEINBERGER: *Schwanda★.* Also BUSONI: *Arlecchino★;* ROSSELLINI: *Guerra★.* **Operatic world premieres:** LLOYD: *Letter for Queen Victoria* Spoleto Fest, Italy 1974. Exhibitions of paintings. Teaches. **Res:** 400 W 119th St, New York, USA.

LUKÁCS, ERVIN. Conductor of opera and symphony. Hungarian. Resident Cond, State Opera, Budapest. Born 9 Aug 1928, Budapest. Wife Rózsa Szabó, occupation singer. One daughter. Studied: Liszt Acad, Prof L Somogyi, Budapest; Cònsv S Cecilia, Prof F Ferrara, Rome; incl piano, double bass, timpani and voice. **Operatic debut:** State Opera, Budapest 1959. Symphonic debut: Hungarian State Symph, Budapest 1957. Previous occupations: physician. Awards: Hon Artist, Hungarian Gvnmt; Liszt Prize first categ, Hungarian Gvnmt; First Prize Intl Conductors Compt, Acad S Cecilia, Rome 1962. **Conducted with major companies in** GER DR: Berlin Staatsoper; HUN: Budapest; ROM: Bucharest; YUG: Belgrade. **Operas with these companies incl** BIZET: *Carmen★;* BRITTEN: *Midsummer Night★;* DEBUSSY: *Pelléas et Mélisande;* DONIZETTI: *Fille du régiment, Lucia;*

GLUCK: *Orfeo ed Euridice;* GOUNOD: *Faust★;* HANDEL: *Acis and Galatea, Rodelinda★;* HAYDN: *Infedeltà delusa;* LEONCAVALLO: *Pagliacci;* MASCAGNI: *Cavalleria rusticana;* MOZART: *Così fan tutte, Don Giovanni, Entführung aus dem Serail, Zauberflöte★;* MUSSORGSKY: *Boris Godunov;* ORFF: *Kluge;* PETROVICS: *Crime and Punishment★;* PROKOFIEV: *Love for Three Oranges★;* PUCCINI: *Butterfly★, Turandot★;* PURCELL: *Dido and Aeneas★;* RAVEL: *Enfant et les sortilèges;* ROSSINI: *Barbiere di Siviglia★, Cenerentola★, Italiana in Algeri★;* STRAUSS, J: *Fledermaus★;* STRAUSS, R: *Ariadne auf Naxos, Rosenkavalier★;* VERDI: *Aida★, Ballo in maschera★, Don Carlo★, Macbeth★, Nabucco★, Rigoletto;* WAGNER: *Tannhäuser★.* Conducted major orch in Europe, USA/Canada, Asia, Austrl. **Res:** 1026 II Hermann O, u 45, Budapest, Hungary. **Mgmt:** ITK/HUN.

LUKÁCS, MIKLÓS. Hungarian. Dir, Hungarian State Opera, Nepkoatarsasag u 22, 1062 Budapest, Hungary; also of Erkel Szinhaz Theater. In charge of adm, artistic & musical matters; and is also a conductor. Born 4 Feb 1905, Gyula, Hungary. Wife Maria Benigni. Studied: Akad für Musik Berlin, Germany. Plays the piano. Previous occupations: gen secy; opera conductor with var German opera comps 1930-43. Started with present company 1943 as cond, in present position since 1966. World premieres at theaters under his management: SZOKOLAY: *Hamlet* 1968; MIHALY: *Together and Alone* 1967; PETROVICS: *Crime and Punishment* 1970, *Lysistrata* 1972; all at Hungarian State Opera, Budapest. Awards: Kossuth Prize, Merited Artist, Hungarian State. **Res:** 1014 Uria u, Budapest, Hungary.

LUNIN, HANNO. German. Gen Int, Wuppertaler Bühnen, Wuppertal, FR Ger since 1975. In charge of adm, mus & dram matters & finances; is also stage dir/prod. Born 19 Sep 1934, Dorpat, Estonia. Wife Karin Rasenack, occupation actress. Studied: Univs Göttingen and Cologne. Previous positions, primarily theatrical: Chief Dramaturg: Pforzheim Stadttheater 1959-62; Staatstheater Braunschweig 1962-64; Staatstheater Wiesbaden 1964-68; Bühnen der Stadt Köln 1968-70; Thalia Theater Hamburg 1970-75; all FR Ger. **Res:** Wuppertal, FR Ger.

LUXON, BENJAMIN. Lyric baritone. British. Born 11 Jun 1937, Camborne, UK. Wife Shiela Amit, occupation singer. Three children. Studied: Guildhall School of Music, London; Prof Walter Gruner. Debut: English Opera Group 1965. Previous occupations: studied teaching. Awards: Second Prize, Intl Singing Compt Munich 1965; Gulbenkian Awd London 1966-69.

Sang with major companies in SWI: Geneva; UK: Aldeburgh Fest, Edinburgh Fest, Glyndebourne Fest, London Royal & English National; USA: Houston. Roles with these companies incl BRITTEN: Traveller (*Curlew River*), Demetrius (*Midsummer Night*), Elder Son (*Prodigal Son*); JANACEK: Forester★ (*Cunning Little Vixen*); MOZART: Don Giovanni★, Conte Almaviva★ (*Nozze di Figaro*); PUCCINI: Marcello (*Bohème*); PURCELL: Aeneas; TCHAIKOV-

SKY: Eugene Onegin★; VERDI: Rodrigo★ (*Don Carlo*); Ford★ (*Falstaff*); WAGNER: Wolfram (*Tannhäuser*). Also MONTEVERDI: Ulisse★ (*Ritorno d'Ulisse*); BRITTEN: Tarquinius (*Rape of Lucretia*); WALTON: (*Troilus and Cressida*). World premieres: BRITTEN: Owen Wingrave, Covent Garden 1973; MAXWELL-DAVIES: John Taverner (*Taverner*) Covent Garden 1972. Recorded for: Decca, Philips. Video/Film: Owen Wingrave. Gives recitals. Appears with symphony orchestra. **Res:** London, UK. **Mgmt:** HLT/UK; CAM/USA.

LUZZATI, EMANUELE. Scenic and costume designer for opera, theater, television. Is also a painter & illustrator. Italian. Born 3 Jun 1921, Genoa, Italy. Studied: School of Fine Arts, Lausanne. **Operatic debut:** *Diavolessa* Teatro la Fenice, Venice 1952. Theater debut: Teatro Nuovo, Milan 1947. Previous occupation: potter; illustrator. Awards: Prize S Genesio for best scenography, Italy 1962; Nomination for Oscar for *Gazza ladra* film 1966 & *Pulcinella* 1974. Mem Acad of Motion Picture Arts & Sciences, Hollywood, CA.

Designed for major companies in AUS: Vienna Staatsoper; FR GER: Munich Staatsoper; ITA: Bologna, Florence Maggio & Comunale, Genoa, Milan La Scala, Naples, Palermo, Turin; POR: Lisbon; SWI: Geneva; UK: Aldeburgh Fest, Scottish, Glyndebourne Fest; USA: Chicago. **Operas designed for these companies incl** BELLINI: *Capuleti ed i Montecchi;* BERLIOZ: *Damnation de Faust;* BOITO: *Mefistofele;* BRITTEN: *Midsummer Night;* BUSONI: *Arlecchino;* DALLAPICCOLA: *Prigioniero;* DONIZETTI: *Elisir★;* HANDEL: *Alcina;* JANACEK: *Jenufa;* MOZART: *Così fan tutte, Don Giovanni, Entführung aus dem Serail, Zauberflöte;* OFFENBACH: *Périchole;* ORFF: *Bernauerin, Mond;* POULENC: *Voix humaine;* RAVEL: *Heure espagnole;* ROSSINI: *Cenerentola, Gazza ladra, Italiana in Algeri, Turco in Italia;* STRAUSS, R: *Arabella, Elektra★;* STRAVINSKY: *Mavra, Rake's Progress★, Rossignol;* VERDI: *Macbeth, Nabucco.* Also ROSSINI: *Matilde de Shabran;* MONTEVERDI: *Ballo delle ingrate;* BERIO: *Allez-Hop;* DALLAPICCOLA: *Job;* MALIPIERO: *Sette canzoni.* **Operatic world premieres:** RIVIERE: *Per un Don Chisciotte* La Scala 1961; CHAILLY: *Vassiliev* Genoa 1967; DE BELLIS: *Maria Stuarda* Naples 1974. Operatic Film – Bavarian Film Co: *Turco in Italia.* Exhibitions: one-man show Turin 1975. **Res:** V Caffaro 12A, Genoa, Italy.

LUZZATTO, LIVIO. Stages/produces opera. Also designs stage-lighting. Italian. Born 24 Mar 1897, Trieste. Wife Fulvia Cimadori, occupation pianist. Studied: with Ildebrando Pizzetti, Florence; Ottorino Respighi, Rome; incl music & piano. **Operatic debut:** *Tristan und Isolde* Teatro Regio, Turin 1936. Previous occupation: piano teacher, concert manager, musicologist.

Directed/produced opera in major international opera houses. Operas staged with these companies incl BELLINI: *Norma★, Sonnambula★;* BIZET: *Carmen★, Pêcheurs de perles★;* BOITO: *Mefistofele★;* CATALANI: *Wally;* CILEA: *A. Lecou-*

vreur★; CIMAROSA: *Matrimonio segreto★, Mercato di Malmantile;* DONIZETTI: *Don Pasquale★, Elisir★, Favorite★, Fille du régiment★, Lucia★;* GIORDANO: *Andrea Chénier★, Fedora★;* GLUCK: *Alceste★, Orfeo ed Euridice★;* GOUNOD: *Faust★;* LEONCAVALLO: *Pagliacci★;* MASCAGNI: *Amico Fritz★, Cavalleria rusticana★, Isabeau, Piccolo Marat;* MASSENET: *Manon★, Werther★;* MENOTTI: *Amelia al ballo, Consul, Medium;* MONTEMEZZI: *Amore dei tre re;* MONTEVERDI: *Combattimento di Tancredi;* MOZART: *Nozze di Figaro;* MUSSORGSKY: *Boris Godunov★, Khovanshchina;* OFFENBACH: *Contes d'Hoffmann;* PERGOLESI: *Serva padrona;* PONCHIELLI: *Gioconda★;* PUCCINI: *Bohème★, Fanciulla del West★, Gianni Schicchi★, Butterfly★, Manon Lescaut★, Rondine★, Suor Angelica★, Tabarro★, Tosca★, Turandot★;* ROSSINI: *Barbiere di Siviglia★, Cambiale di matrimonio★, Guillaume Tell★, Italiana in Algeri★;* SAINT-SAENS: *Samson et Dalila;* SPONTINI: *Fernand Cortez;* STRAUSS, R: *Arabella, Elektra, Rosenkavalier, Salome;* VERDI: *Aida★, Ballo in maschera★, Forza del destino★, Nabucco, Otello★, Rigoletto, Simon Boccanegra, Traviata★, Trovatore★, Vespri;* WAGNER: *Lohengrin, Meistersinger, Parsifal, Walküre;* WEBER: *Freischütz;* WOLF-FERRARI: *Quattro rusteghi;* ZANDONAI:

Francesca da Rimini. Also ALFANO: *Risurrezione, Sakuntala;* BLOCH: *Macbeth;* CORTESE: *Prometeo;* LUALDI: *Granceola;* ROCCA: *Dibuk, Monte Ivnor;* SANTOLIQUIDO: *Porta verde;* etc. **Opera libretti:** *Judith Bersabea* Freiburg, Germany 1931. Teaches at Consv G Tartini, Trieste. **Res:** V Volturno 2, Rome, Italy.

LYNN, JUDITH. Coloratura soprano. American. Resident mem: Israel National Opera, Tel Aviv. Born Chicago, IL, USA. Husband Filippo De Stefano, occupation tenor. Studied: Filippo De Stefano, New York; Ruth & Mario Chamlee, Los Angeles; Lina Pagliughi, Giuseppe Pais, Milan. **Debut:** Lucia, Teatro della Pergola, Florence 1965. Awards: Schlshp, Ebell Club of Los Angeles; Winner American Opera Aud for Italy 1965.

Sang with major companies in ISR: Tel Aviv; USA: New York City Opera, Philadelphia Grand. **Roles with these companies incl** BIZET: Micaëla★ (*Carmen*); DELIBES: Lakmé★; MOZART: Königin der Nacht★ (*Zauberflöte*); PUCCINI: Musetta★ (*Bohème*); ROSSINI: Rosina★ (*Barbiere di Siviglia*); VERDI: Gilda★ (*Rigoletto*). Video – Teleprompter TV, New York: Violetta (*Traviata*). Gives recitals. Appears with symphony orchestra. Teaches voice. **Res:** New York, NY, USA.

M

MAAG, PETER E. Conductor of opera and symphony; composer; operatic stage director. Swiss. Principal Cond, Teatro Regio Turin & Parma. Born 10 May 1919, St Gallen, Switzerland. Wife Yasmine, occupation stage designer. One child. Studied: asst to Furtwängler & Ansermet, pupil of Alfred Cortot; incl piano, violin. Plays the piano. Operatic training as repetiteur, asst cond, chorus master & chief conductor at Bonn Opera 1956-59, Vienna Volksoper 1964-67. **Operatic debut:** Theater, Biel, Switzerland 1949. Symphonic debut: Orch de la Suisse Romande, Geneva 1953. Previous occupations: grad Univ Zurich & Geneva in philosophy, theology. Awards: Toscanini Medal, City of Parma.

   Conducted with major companies in ARG: Buenos Aires; AUS: Salzburg Fest, Vienna Volksoper; CZE: Prague National; FRA: Aix-en-Provence Fest, Bordeaux, Marseille, Nice, Paris; GRE: Athens Fest; FR GER: Berlin Deutsche Oper, Bonn, Cologne, Darmstadt, Düsseldorf-Duisburg, Frankfurt, Hamburg, Munich Staatsoper; HOL: Amsterdam; ITA: Bologna, Florence Maggio & Comunale, Genoa, Milan La Scala, Naples, Palermo, Parma, Rome Opera, Trieste, Turin, Venice, Verona Arena; MON: Monte Carlo; SWI: Basel, Geneva, Zurich; UK: Glyndebourne, London Royal; USA: Chicago, Minneapolis, New York Met; YUG: Belgrade. **Operas with these companies incl** ADAM: *Postillon de Lonjumeau;* d'ALBERT: *Tiefland;* AUBER: *Fra Diavolo;* BARTOK: *Bluebeard's Castle;* BEETHOVEN: *Fidelio;* BELLINI: *Norma;* BERLIOZ: *Benvenuto Cellini, Damnation de Faust;* BIZET: *Carmen, Pêcheurs de perles;* BRITTEN: *Albert Herring;* BUSONI: *Arlecchino;* CAVALIERI: *Rappresentazione;* CIMAROSA: *Matrimonio segreto;* CORNELIUS: *Barbier von Bagdad;* DEBUSSY: *Enfant prodigue★, Pelléas et Mélisande★;* DELIBES: *Lakmé;* DONIZETTI: *Don Pasquale, Elisir, Fille du régiment, Lucia;* DVORAK: *Rusalka;* FALLA: *Retablo de Maese Pedro★, Vida breve★;* FLOTOW: *Martha;* FOSS: *Jumping Frog;* GLUCK: *Iphigénie en Aulide, Orfeo ed Euridice;* GOUNOD: *Faust, Roméo et Juliette;* HANDEL: *Giulio Cesare;* HINDEMITH: *Hin und zurück;* HUMPERDINCK: *Hänsel und Gretel;* JANACEK: *Jenufa, Katya Kabanova;* LEONCAVALLO: *Pagliacci;* LORTZING: *Waffenschmied, Wildschütz, Zar und Zimmermann;* MARTIN: *Vin herbé;* MARTINU: *Com-*edy on the Bridge; MASCAGNI: *Cavalleria rusticana;* MASSENET: *Don Quichotte, Hérodiade, Manon, Werther;* MENOTTI: *Medium, Telephone;* MILHAUD: *Enlèvement d'Europe;* MONTEVERDI: *Incoronazione di Poppea;* MOZART: *Clemenza di Tito★, Così fan tutte, Don Giovanni★, Entführung aus dem Serail★, Idomeneo, Schauspieldirektor, Nozze di Figaro★, Re pastore, Zauberflöte★;* MUSSORGSKY: *Boris Godunov;* NICOLAI: *Lustigen Weiber;* OFFENBACH: *Contes d'Hoffmann★, Périchole, Mariage aux lanternes;* ORFF: *Kluge, Mond;* PROKOFIEV: *Love for Three Oranges;* PUCCINI: *Bohème★, Gianni Schicchi, Butterfly, Tosca, Turandot;* RAVEL: *Enfant et les sortilèges★, Heure espagnole;* ROSSINI: *Barbiere di Siviglia, Cenerentola, Italiana in Algeri, Signor Bruschino;* SAINT-SAENS: *Samson et Dalila★;* SMETANA: *Bartered Bride, Libuse;* STRAUSS, R: *Arabella, Ariadne, Intermezzo, Salome, Rosenkavalier;* STRAVINSKY: *Rossignol;* TCHAIKOVSKY: *Eugene Onegin, Pique Dame★;* THOMAS: *Mignon;* VERDI: *Aida★, Aroldo/Stiffelio, Attila, Ballo in maschera, Corsaro, Don Carlo, Falstaff★, Forza del destino, Luisa Miller★, Otello, Rigoletto, Traviata★, Trovatore;* WAGNER: *Lohengrin, Parsifal, Tannhäuser;* WEBER: *Freischütz★.* Also CHERUBINI: *Abencérages;* HONEGGER: *Jeanne d'Arc au bûcher;* PAER: *Leonora;* SCHUMANN: *Genoveva.* Video—Vienna TV: *Heure espagnole.* Conducted major orch in Europe, USA/Canada, Cent/S America, Asia. Teaches at Accad Chigiana, Siena, Italy. **Res:** Casa Maag, 7504 Pontresina, Switzerland. Mgmt: GOR/UK; HUR/USA.

MAAZEL, LORIN. Conductor of opera and symphony; composer. American. Music Dir, Cleveland Orch, O 1972- . Born 6 Mar 1930, Neuilly, France. Wife Israela Margalit, occupation pianist. Four children. Studied: Fulbright Fllshp Italy; Berkshire Music Center, Tanglewood, MA; Vladimir Bakaleinikoff, Pittsburgh; incl violin. Plays the violin. **Operatic debut:** *Lohengrin* Bayreuth Festival 1960. Symphonic debut: as child prodigy National Music Camp Orch, Interlochen, MI 1939; as adult Catania Orch, Sicily 1953. Awards: six Grand Prix du Disque; twice Edison Prize; Sibelius Medal, Finland; ASCAP Awd 1975; Hon D degrees, Univ Pittsburgh & Beaver Coll; Hon Mem for Life, Deutsche Oper Berlin; Hon Citizen

Puebla, Mexico. Previous adm positions in opera: Mus Dir, Deutsche Oper Berlin, FR Ger 1965-71.

Conducted with major companies in AUS: Salzburg Fest, Vienna Staatsoper; FRA: Orange Fest; FR GER: Bayreuth Fest, Berlin Deutsche Oper; ITA: Florence, Milan La Scala, Rome; UK: Edinburgh Fest; USA: New York Met. **Operas with these companies incl** BEETHOVEN: *Fidelio*★‡; BIZET: *Carmen*★‡; CIMAROSA: *Matrimonio segreto;* MOZART: *Don Giovanni*★, *Nozze di Figaro;* MUSSORGSKY: *Boris Godunov*★; PUCCINI: *Manon Lescaut*★, *Tosca*★‡; STRAUSS, R: *Elektra*★, *Rosenkavalier;* TCHAIKOVSKY: *Eugene Onegin;* VERDI: *Ballo in maschera*★, *Falstaff, Forza del destino*★, *Otello*★, *Simon Boccanegra*★, *Traviata*★‡; WAGNER: *Fliegende Holländer*★, *Lohengrin*★, *Rheingold, Walküre, Siegfried, Götterdämmerung, Tristan und Isolde.* **World premieres:** DALLAPICCOLA: *Ulisse* Berlin 1968. Conducted major orch in Europe, USA/Canada, Cent/S America, Asia, Austrl. Previous positions as Mus Dir with major orch: Berlin Radio Symph Orch, FR Ger 1965-75. **Res:** Cleveland, O, USA.

MACCIANTI, ANNA. Coloratura soprano. Italian. Born 26 Jun 1930, Fiesole/Florence, Italy. Single. Studied: Maestri Campogalliani, Contini, Angelini. **Debut:** Rosina (*Barbiere di Siviglia*) Teatro Nuovo, Milan 1953. Previous occupations: painter in glass and mosaic. Awards: Winner Conc Teatro Nuovo, Milan 1952, Spoleto 1953, La Scala Milan 1954.

Sang with major companies in AUS: Vienna Volksoper; BEL: Liège; GRE: Athens National; FR GER: Berlin Deutsche Oper, Munich Staatsoper; HOL: Amsterdam; ITA: Florence Maggio & Comunale, Genoa, Naples, Trieste, Turin; POR: Lisbon; S AFR: Johannesburg; SPA: Barcelona, Majorca; SWI: Basel; UK: Edinburgh Fest. **Roles with these companies incl** BELLINI: Elvira★ (*Puritani*), Amina★ (*Sonnambula*); BIZET: Micaëla (*Carmen*), Léila (*Pêcheurs de perles*); DONIZETTI: Norina★‡ (*Don Pasquale*), Adina★ (*Elisir*), Marie★‡ (*Fille du régiment*), Lucia★; GLUCK: Zelmire (*Cadi dupé*); MOZART: Zerlina (*Don Giovanni*), Königin der Nacht (*Zauberflöte*); PUCCINI: Musetta★ (*Bohème*), Liù (*Turandot*); ROSSINI: Rosina★ (*Barbiere di Siviglia*); VERDI: Oscar★ (*Ballo in maschera*), Gilda★‡ (*Rigoletto*), Violetta★ (*Traviata*). Also WOLF-FERRARI: Marionette (*Vedova scaltra*), Gnese (*Campiello*); MOZART: (*Sposo deluso*); TRECATE: Aldina (*Buricchio*). Recorded for: DG, Concert Hall, Club Orpheus. Video/Film: Aldina (*Buricchio*); Marionette (*Vedova scaltra*). **Res:** V G Sercambi 36, Florence, Italy.

MacFARLAND, PAMELA DASHIELL. Lyric & dramatic mezzo-soprano. American. Resident mem: Städtische Bühnen, Mainz. Born 1 May 1947, Washington DC, USA. Single. Studied: Catholic Univ of America, Todd Duncan, Washington, DC; Karl Liebl, Mainz, FR Ger. **Debut:** Liang-Kung (*Geisterliebe*) Kiel Opera 1971. Awards: Ntl Arts & Letters, Washington DC 1969; Corbett Fndt Schlshp 1969.

Sang with major companies in FR GER: Kiel. **Roles with these companies incl** DEBUSSY: Geneviève★ (*Pelléas et Mélisande*); MOZART: Dorabella★ (*Così fan tutte*), Cherubino★ (*Nozze di*

Figaro); PERGOLESI: Cardella★ & Nina (*Frate 'nnamorato*); VERDI: Amneris★ (*Aida*). **World premieres:** YUN: Liang-Kung (*Geisterliebe*) Kiel Opera 1971. Gives recitals. **Res:** Hintere Bleiche 43, Mainz, FR Ger. Mgmt: ARM/FRG.

MACHADO, DAVID. Conductor of opera and symphony; composer. Brazilian. Resident Cond, Teatro Massimo, Palermo, Italy. Born 16 Apr 1938, Cabo Verde/MG, Brazil. Wife Helena, occupation singer. One child. Studied: Staatl Hochschule, Cologne & Freiburg; Accad Musicale Chigiana, Siena; Carl Ueter, Sawallisch, Celibidache, Franco Ferrara; incl piano, bassoon, harpsichord, violin and voice. Plays the piano, bassoon. Operatic training as repetiteur at Teatro Massimo, Palermo 1966-68. **Operatic debut:** *Ballo in maschera* Accad Chigiana, Siena 1966. Symphonic debut: Teatro Municipal, São Paulo, Brazil 1963. Previous occupations: Mus Dir, Cantoria Ars Sacra, São Paulo; Cantor, Freiburger Markuskirche; bassoonist at Orch Sinf, São Paulo. Awards: Second Place, Cantelli Intl Compt 1967; Florence AIDEM Prize 1966; Diploma of Hon & Merit, Accad Chigiana 1966; Arts Prize for conducting, São Paulo 1974.

Conducted with major companies in BUL: Sofia; ITA: Palermo; POR: Lisbon. **Operas with these companies incl** DONIZETTI: *Don Pasquale*★; LEONCAVALLO: *Pagliacci;* MASCAGNI: *Cavalleria rusticana*★; MENOTTI: *Telephone;* MONTEVERDI: *Favola d'Orfeo;* PERGOLESI: *Serva padrona;* PUCCINI: *Bohème*★, *Gianni Schicchi*★, *Butterfly*★, *Suor Angelica*★, *Tabarro*★; ROSSINI: *Barbiere di Siviglia*★; SCHOENBERG: *Glückliche Hand;* TCHAIKOVSKY: *Eugene Onegin*★; VERDI: *Ballo in maschera;* WOLF-FERRARI: *Segreto di Susanna.* Also ROSSINI: *Inganno felice;* COELHO: *Rosas de todo ano*★; CIMAROSA: *Maestro di cappella;* MONTEVERDI-MADERNA: *Orfeo.* **World premieres:** De MEESTER: *2-Pocchi 3-Troppi* Teatro Massimo, Palermo 1969. Video–Op Sofia TV: *Gianni Schicchi, Tabarro, Suor Angelica;* Lisbon TV: *Segreto di Susanna.* Conducted major orch in Europe, S America. **Res:** V Manin 4/A, Palermo, Italy. Mgmt: TAU/SWI.

MACHOTKOVA, MARCELA; née Johnova. Lyric soprano. Czechoslovakian. Resident mem: National Theater, Prague. Born 12 Oct 1931, Turnov, CSR. Husband Dr Zdenek Machotka, occupation surgeon. One daughter. Studied: State Consv, Prof A Penickova, Olga Borova-Valouskova, Prof Zdenek Otava, Prague. **Debut:** DVORAK: Countess (*Peasant a Rogue*) Liberec 1960. Awards: Merited Artist, Gvnmt of Czechoslovakia 1975.

Sang with major companies in CZE: Brno, Prague National; HOL: Amsterdam; ITA: Bologna; POL: Warsaw; SPA: Barcelona; UK: Edinburgh Fest. **Roles with these companies incl** BEETHOVEN: Leonore (*Fidelio*); DVORAK: Princess★ (*Devil and Kate*), Rusalka★; KLEBE: Marianne (*Jakobowsky und der Oberst*); MARTINU: Zenio★ (*Griechische Passion*); MOZART: Donna Elvira★ (*Don Giovanni*), Pamina (*Zauberflöte*); PUCCINI: Mimi★ & Musetta (*Bohème*); SMETANA: Marie★ (*Bartered Bride*), Vendulka★ (*The Kiss*), Libuse★; STRAUSS, R: Arabella★; TCHAIKOVSKY: Tatiana (*Eugene Onegin*), Lisa★ (*Pique Dame*); VERDI: Amelia★ (*Ballo in* *maschera*), Desdemona (*Otello*), Amelia★ (*Simon Boccanegra*); WAGNER: Irene (*Rienzi*). Also DVORAK: Julie★ (*Jakobin*); MOZART: Dorabella (*Così fan tutte*); FIBICH: Sarka. Video/Film: Donna Elvira (*Don Giovanni*); Julie (*Jakobin*). Gives recitals. Appears with symphony orchestra. **Res:** Blatovska 5, 100 00 Prague 10, Czechoslovakia. Mgmt: PRG/CZE.

MACKERRAS, CHARLES; né Alan Charles Mackerras. Conductor of opera and symphony. British. Music Dir & Principal Cond, English National Opera, London. Born 17 Nov 1925, Schenectady, NY, USA. Wife Helena Judith, occupation musician. Two daughters. Studied: New South Wales Consv of Music, Sydney; Prague Acad of Music, Vaclav Talich; incl oboe, piano. Operatic training as repetiteur & asst cond at Sadler's Wells Opera, London 1947-54. **Operatic debut:** *Fledermaus* Sadler's Wells Opera 1948. Symphonic debut: Sydney Symph Orch, Austrl 1946. Previous occupations: princ oboe Sydney Symph; Prof of oboe NSW Consv of Music. Awards: Commander of the British Empire; Hon LRAM Royal Acad of Music. Previous adm positions in opera: First Cond, Hamburg Staatsoper 1966-69.

Conducted with major companies in AUSTRL: Sydney; AUS: Vienna Staatsoper & Volksoper; CZE: Brno, Prague Smetana; DEN: Copenhagen; FRA: Aix-en-Provence Fest, Orange Fest, Paris; FR GER: Hamburg, Munich Gärtnerplatz; GER DR: Berlin Staatsoper; HOL: Amsterdam; ITA: Florence Maggio & Comunale, Rome Opera, Venice; SWI: Geneva; UK: Aldeburgh Fest, Welsh National, Edinburgh Fest, London Royal & English National; USA: Dallas, New York Met, San Francisco Opera; YUG: Zagreb. **Operas with these companies incl** BARTOK: *Bluebeard's Castle★;* BEETHOVEN: *Fidelio★;* BELLINI: *Norma★;* BERLIOZ: *Damnation de Faust★;* BIZET: *Carmen★;* BRITTEN: *Albert Herring, Billy Budd★, Gloriana★, Midsummer Night★, Peter Grimes, Rape of Lucretia, Turn of the Screw;* CAVALIERI: *Rappresentazione★‡;* CIMAROSA: *Matrimonio segreto;* DONIZETTI: *Anna Bolena, Don Pasquale, Elisir, Maria Stuarda★, Roberto Devereux‡;* GALUPPI: *Filosofo di campagna;* GLINKA: *Ruslan and Ludmilla;* GLUCK: *Orfeo ed Euridice★;* GOUNOD: *Faust★;* HINDEMITH: *Hin und zurück, Mathis der Maler;* HOLST: *Savitri;* HUMPERDINCK: *Hänsel und Gretel;* JANACEK: *From the House of the Dead, Jenufa★, Katya Kabanova★, Makropoulos Affair★;* LEONCAVALLO: *Pagliacci;* LORTZING: *Zar und Zimmermann;* MASCAGNI: *Cavalleria rusticana;* MASSENET: *Manon★, Werther;* MENOTTI: *Consul;* MOZART: *Clemenza di Tito★, Così fan tutte★, Don Giovanni★, Entführung aus dem Serail★, Idomeneo★, Nozze di Figaro★, Zauberflöte★;* MUSSORGSKY: *Boris Godunov;* NICOLAI: *Lustigen Weiber;* OFFENBACH: *Contes d'Hoffmann★;* POULENC: *Mamelles de Tirésias;* PUCCINI: *Bohème, Gianni Schicchi, Butterfly★, Tabarro, Tosca★, Turandot★;* PURCELL: *Dido and Aeneas‡;* RIMSKY-KORSAKOV: *Coq d'or, May Night;* ROSSINI: *Barbiere di Siviglia, Cenerentola, Gazza ladra;* SHOSTAKOVICH: *Katerina Ismailova;* SMETANA: *Bartered Bride,*

Dalibor; STRAUSS, J: *Fledermaus★;* STRAUSS, R: *Arabella, Ariadne auf Naxos, Elektra★, Rosenkavalier★, Salome★;* STRAVINSKY: *Oedipus Rex★, Rake's Progress★;* TCHAIKOVSKY: *Eugene Onegin★;* VERDI: *Aida, Aroldo/Stiffelio, Ballo in maschera★, Don Carlo★, Due Foscari, Falstaff, Luisa Miller, Nabucco★, Otello★, Rigoletto, Simon Boccanegra, Traviata★, Trovatore★;* WAGNER: *Fliegende Holländer, Lohengrin★, Meistersinger★, Rheingold★, Walküre★, Siegfried★, Götterdämmerung★;* WEBER: *Freischütz;* WEINBERGER: *Schwanda;* WOLF-FERRARI: *Quattro rusteghi.* Also HANDEL: *Semele★;* CIMAROSA: *Maestro di cappella;* BLOW: *Venus and Adonis;* SZYMANOWSKI: *King Roger★.* **World premieres:** BRITTEN: *Noye's Fludde* Engl Op Grp, Aldeburgh Fest 1958; GOEHR: *Arden muss sterben* Hamburg State Op 1967; LENNOX: *Ruth* Engl Op Grp, Aldeburgh Fest 1956. Recorded for DG, Westminster. Video–Hamburg TV: *Zar und Zimmermann;* CBC & Danish TV: *Turn of the Screw;* BBC TV: *Temistocle, Clemenza di Scipione, Amadigi, Buona figliuola, Alexander, Fledermaus, Pagliacci, Bohème, Carmen, Rigoletto, Otello, Nozze di Figaro, Faust, Contes d'Hoffmann.* Conducted major orch in Europe, USA/Canada, Africa, Austrl. **Res:** 10 Hamilton Terrace, London NW8 9UG, UK. Mgmt: GOR/UK; CAM/USA.

MacLANE, ARMAND RALPH; né McLane. Dramatic baritone. American. Resident mem: Opéra du Rhin, Strasbourg, Fra; Staatstheater Karlsruhe, FR Ger. Born 26 May 1936, New York. Studied: Donald W Johnston, New York; Manhattan School of Music, John Brownlee, New York; Mariano Stabile, Milan; Helge Roswaenge, Munich. **Debut:** Guglielmo (*Così fan tutte*) Metropolitan Opera Studio 1961. Previous occupations: cofounder & co-prod of Lake George Opera Fest, NY. Awards: Loftus Awd, Met Op Ntl Counc Aud 1962; Reg Winner Met Op Aud 1961; Philadelphia Young Artists Awd 1961; Commencement Awd Peabody Consv 1957; M B Rockefeller and Sullivan Fndt Grants.

Sang with major companies in FRA: Aix-en-Provence Fest, Strasbourg; FR GER: Bielefeld, Frankfurt, Karlsruhe, Kassel, Nürnberg, Wiesbaden; ISR: Tel Aviv; SWI: Basel; USA: Lake George. **Roles with these companies incl** BIZET: Escamillo★ (*Carmen*); DONIZETTI: Dott Malatesta (*Don Pasquale*), Belcore (*Elisir*), Enrico (*Lucia*); GIORDANO: Carlo Gérard (*Andrea Chénier*); GLUCK: Agamemnon★ (*Iphigénie en Aulide*); LEONCAVALLO: Tonio★ (*Pagliacci*); MARTIN: Marc (*Vin herbé*); MOZART: Guglielmo (*Così fan tutte*), Conte Almaviva (*Nozze di Figaro*); OFFENBACH: Coppélius etc (*Contes d'Hoffmann*); ORFF: Solo (*Carmina burana*), König (*Kluge*); PUCCINI: Marcello (*Bohème*), Sharpless★ (*Butterfly*), Scarpia (*Tosca*); ROSSINI: Figaro (*Barbiere di Siviglia*); STRAUSS, R: Musiklehrer (*Ariadne auf Naxos*); STRAVINSKY: Nick Shadow (*Rake's Progress*); TCHAIKOVSKY: Yeletsky (*Pique Dame*); VERDI: Amonasro (*Aida*), Renato★ (*Ballo in maschera*), Rodrigo★ (*Don Carlo*), Ford★ (*Falstaff*), Don Carlo (*Forza del destino*), Miller★ (*Luisa Miller*), Macbeth, Nabucco★, Iago (*Otello*), Rigoletto, Germont (*Traviata*), Conte di Luna (*Trova-*

tore); WAGNER: Holländer★, Amfortas★ (*Parsifal*), Kurwenal (*Tristan und Isolde*). Also EGK: Peer Gynt; PFITZNER: Morone (*Palestrina*). **World premieres:** DELERUE: Rubeck (*Médis et Alyssio*) Opéra du Rhin, Strasbourg 1975; LUDWIG: Der Fremde (*Rashomon*) Stadttheater Augsburg 1972. Gives recitals. Appears with symphony orchestra. Teaches voice. **Res:** Rotenfelserstr 40, 7554 Kuppenheim-2 Baden, FR Ger. Mgmt: SLZ/FRG.

MacNEIL, CORNELL HILL. Dramatic baritone. American. Born 24 Sep 1922, Minneapolis, MN, USA. Wife Tania, occupation violinist. Five children. Studied: Hartt School of Music, Friedrich Schorr, Hartford, CT, USA; Virgilio Lazzari, Dick Marzollo, Otto Guth, New York. **Debut:** Germont (*Traviata*) New York City Opera 1953. Previous occupations: machinist.

Sang with major companies in ARG: Buenos Aires; AUS: Vienna Staatsoper; BRA: Rio de Janeiro; FRA: Paris; ITA: Bologna, Florence Maggio & Comunale, Genoa, Milan La Scala, Naples, Palermo, Parma, Rome Opera & Caracalla, Turin, Venice, Verona Arena; MEX: Mexico City; SPA: Barcelona; UK: London Royal Opera; USA: Chicago, Fort Worth, Hartford, Houston, Miami, New Orleans, New York Met & City Opera, Philadelphia Grand & Lyric, Pittsburgh, San Antonio, San Francisco Opera, Seattle. **Roles with these companies incl** BELLINI: Sir Richard (*Puritani*); BIZET: Escamillo (*Carmen*); DONIZETTI: Enrico (*Lucia*); GIORDANO: Carlo Gérard (*Andrea Chénier*); LEONCAVALLO: Tonio★‡ (*Pagliacci*); MASCAGNI: Alfio‡ (*Cavalleria rusticana*); MENOTTI: John Sorel‡ (*Consul*); PONCHIELLI: Barnaba★ (*Gioconda*); PUCCINI: Marcello★ (*Bohème*), Jack Rance‡ (*Fanciulla del West*), Sharpless (*Butterfly*), Lescaut (*Manon Lescaut*), Michele (*Tabarro*), Scarpia (*Tosca*); VERDI: Amonasro★‡ (*Aida*), Renato★‡ (*Ballo in maschera*), Rodrigo★ (*Don Carlo*), Don Carlo (*Ernani*), Ford & Falstaff (*Falstaff*), Don Carlo (*Forza del destino*), Miller★‡ (*Luisa Miller*), Macbeth, Nabucco★, Iago★ (*Otello*), Rigoletto★‡, Simon Boccanegra, Germont★ (*Traviata*), Conte di Luna★ (*Trovatore*), Monforte★ (*Vespri*); WAGNER: Holländer★. Also VERDI: Gusmano (*Alzira*); GOUNOD: Valentin (*Faust*). **World premieres:** MENOTTI: John Sorel (*The Consul*) Philadelphia 1950. Recorded for: RCA, London, Angel, Decca. Gives recitals. **Res:** New York, NY, USA. Mgmt: CAM/USA; CST/UK.

MACONAGHIE, RONALD DERECK. Lyric baritone. Australian. Resident mem: Australian Opera, Sydney. Born 18 Nov 1931, Auckland, New Zealand. Wife Georgina Mary, occupation pre-school teacher. Four children. Studied: James Leighton, New Zealand; London Opera School, Joan Cross; Prof Roy Henderson, Dawson Freer, London. **Debut:** Schaunard (*Bohème*) Sadler's Wells Opera 1956. Awards: New Zealand Gvnmt Scholar 1952,53,54; Joan Hammond Schlshp for study at London Opera School.

Sang with major companies in AUSTRL: Sydney; UK: London English National. **Roles with these companies incl** DONIZETTI: Dott Malatesta (*Don Pasquale*), Belcore★ (*Elisir*); MOZART: Guglielmo & Don Alfonso (*Così fan tutte*),

Leporello (*Don Giovanni*), Figaro★ (*Nozze di Figaro*), Papageno★ (*Zauberflöte*); PUCCINI: Marcello★ (*Bohème*), Sharpless (*Butterfly*); ROSSINI: Figaro★ (*Barbiere di Siviglia*); STRAUSS, R: Musiklehrer★ (*Ariadne auf Naxos*); VERDI: Falstaff, Fra Melitone★ (*Forza del destino*); WAGNER: Wolfram (*Tannhäuser*). Gives recitals. Appears with symphony orchestra. Teaches voice.

MACURDY, JOHN; né John Edward McCurdy. Bass. American. Resident mem: Metropolitan Opera, New York. Born 18 Mar 1929, Detroit, MI, USA. Wife Justine Votypka, occupation musician. Two children. Studied: Avery Crew, Detroit; Elizabeth Wood, New Orleans; Boris Goldovsky, New York. **Debut:** Vieux Hébreu (*Samson et Dalila*) New Orleans 1952. Previous occupations: model die maker.

Sang with major companies in FRA: Aix-en-Provence Fest, Marseille, Nice, Orange Fest, Strasbourg; ITA: Milan La Scala; SWI: Geneva; UK: Glasgow Scottish; USA: Baltimore, Houston, Miami, New Orleans, New York Met & City Opera, Philadelphia Lyric, San Francisco Opera & Spring Opera, Santa Fe. **Roles with these companies incl** BEETHOVEN: Rocco★ (*Fidelio*); BELLINI: Oroveso★ (*Norma*), Rodolfo★ (*Sonnambula*); BERLIOZ: Méphistophélès (*Damnation de Faust*), Narbal (*Troyens*); CHERUBINI: Creon (*Medea*); DEBUSSY: Arkel (*Pelléas et Mélisande*); GOUNOD: Méphistophélès (*Faust*); MOZART: Figaro (*Nozze di Figaro*), Sarastro (*Zauberflöte*); MUSSORGSKY: Pimen (*Boris Godunov*); PONCHIELLI: Alvise (*Gioconda*); PUCCINI: Colline (*Bohème*), Timur★ (*Turandot*); ROSSINI: Don Basilio (*Barbiere di Siviglia*); STRAVINSKY: Creon & Tiresias (*Oedipus Rex*); VERDI: Ramfis★ (*Aida*), Philip II & Grande Inquisitore★ (*Don Carlo*), Silva (*Ernani*), Padre Guardiano★ (*Forza del destino*), Conte Walter★ (*Luisa Miller*), Banquo★ (*Macbeth*), Fiesco★ (*Simon Boccanegra*), Procida★ (*Vespri*); WAGNER: Daland★ (*Fliegende Holländer*), König Heinrich (*Lohengrin*), Pogner★ (*Meistersinger*), Gurnemanz★ (*Parsifal*), Fasolt★ (*Rheingold*), Fafner (*Rheingold★, Siegfried*), Hunding★ (*Walküre*), Hagen★ (*Götterdämmerung*), Landgraf (*Tannhäuser*), König Marke★ (*Tristan und Isolde*); WARD: Rev Hale‡ (*Crucible*). Also DONIZETTI: Raimondo (*Lucia*); MASSENET: Comte Des Grieux (*Manon*); TCHAIKOVSKY: Gremin (*Eugene Onegin*). Gives recitals. Appears with symphony orchestra.

MacWHERTER, ROD; né Rodney McWherter. Dramatic tenor. American. Born 24 Jun 1936, Philadelphia. Wife Eunice Mobley, occupation soprano. One child. Studied: New York Univ; Acad of Vocal Arts, Philadelphia. **Debut:** Froh (*Rheingold*) San Francisco Opera 1967.

Sang with major companies in CAN: Vancouver; FR GER: Dortmund, Düsseldorf-Duisburg, Saarbrücken; USA: Chicago, New Orleans, New York Met, Pittsburgh, San Francisco Opera. **Roles with these companies incl** PUCCINI: Calaf★ (*Turandot*); STRAUSS, R: Bacchus★ (*Ariadne auf Naxos*); VERDI: Radames★ (*Aida*), Ismaele★ (*Nabucco*), Otello★; WAGNER: Erik★ (*Fliegende Holländer*), Siegmund★ (*Walküre*); WEBER:

Max★ (*Freischütz*). Gives recitals. Appears with symphony orchestra.

MADANES, CECILIO. Stages/produces opera, theater, film & television. Also designs sets, costumes & stg-lighting and is an actor. Argentinean. Resident Stage Dir, Teatro Colón, Buenos Aires. Also Resident Stage Dir for TV C9. Born 2 Dec 1923, Buenos Aires. Single. Studied: Paris 1947-54, Rome 1972-73.
Directed/produced opera for major companies in ARG: Buenos Aires. **Operas staged with these companies incl** MENOTTI: *Consul★;* PUCCINI: *Manon Lescaut★;* STRAUSS, J: *Fledermaus★;* VERDI: *Traviata★.* Also BRETON: *Verbena de la paloma;* CASTRO: *Zapatera prodigiosa;* FLORE: *Pergola de las flores;* TORROBA: *Luisa Fernanda.* Operatic Video—TV C9: *Verbena de la paloma.* Previous leading positions with major theater companies: Teatro Caminito, Buenos Aires. **Res:** Rivadavia 2774, Buenos Aires, Argentina.

MADAU DIAZ, ANTONELLO; né Antonio Madau. Stages/produces opera & television. Also designs sets; and is an author & librettist. Italian. Collab Art Dir & Resident Stage Dir, La Scala, Milan since 1974. Born 21 Mar 1931, Perugia, Italy. Wife Lorenza. Three children. Studied: Scenografia Teatrale Vagnetti-Caliterna, Florence; staging: Fersen, Gründgens, Germany. Administration: Luigi Oldani, Milan; also music. Operatic training as asst stage dir at Maggio Musicale, Florence 1954-58; Opera House, Perugia 1955-59. **Operatic debut:** *Hänsel und Gretel* Teatro Carlo Felice, Genoa 1956. Previous adm positions in opera: Prgm Coordin, Arena Verona 1955-65; Prod Mng, Genoa 1957-61.
Directed/prod opera for major companies in FRA: Nancy; GRE: Athens Opera; GER DR: Berlin Komische Oper; ITA: Bologna, Florence Maggio, Genoa, Milan La Scala, Rome Opera, Trieste, Turin, Venice; SPA: Barcelona; UK: Edinburgh Fest; USA: Philadelphia Lyric. **Operas directed for these companies incl** BELLINI: *Capuleti ed i Montecchi, Puritani;* DONIZETTI: *Maria di Rohan, Rita;* GOUNOD: *Faust;* HUMPERDINCK: *Hänsel und Gretel;* MOZART: *Nozze di Figaro;* PETRASSI: *Morte dell'aria;* PROKOFIEV: *Fiery Angel;* PUCCINI: *Butterfly;* ROSSINI: *Barbiere di Siviglia;* SHOSTAKOVICH: *Katerina Ismailova;* STRAVINSKY: *Mavra;* VERDI: *Falstaff;* WOLF-FERRARI: *Segreto di Susanna.* Also NONO: *Fabbrica illuminata;* MALIPIERO: *Capitan Spavento;* MASCAGNI: *Isabeau★;* SMAREGLIA: *Nozze istriane★;* TRECATE: *Buricchio;* BUGAMELLI: *Una domenica;* PORRINO: *Organo di bambù;* SORESINA: *Tre sogni;* HAZON: *Agenzia matrimoniale;* FIUME: *Tamburo di panno;* CHAILLY: *Riva delle sirti;* MORINI: *Vindice;* DONIZETTI: *Marin Faliero;* ZANDONAI: *Via della finestra, Una partita;* MAYER: *Rosa rossa e la bianca;* ROSSELLINI: *Vortice.* **Operatic world premieres:** BETTINELLI: *Count Down* 1970; RENOSTO: *Camera degli sposi* 1972, both Piccola Scala, Milan; FIORDA: *Margot* 1966; STRANO: *Sulla via maestra* 1966; BETTINELLI: *Pozze e il pendolo* 1967; ZANONI: *Ultimo porto* 1968; ZANON: *Leggenda di Giulietta* 1969; ZANETTOVICH: *Celine★* 1971; VAVOLO: *Canto del cigno★‡* 1971; MANENTI: *La*

galla 1971; all at Teatro delle Novità, Bergamo; FERRARI: *Lord Savile* Teatro Comunale, Treviso 1970. Video/Film—RAI TV Turin: *Buricchio;* DDR TV: *Bohème.* **Operatic libretti:** BETTINELLI: *Count Down* Piccola Scala, Milan 1970; ZANON: *Un po' d'arsenico* Teatro Morlacchi, Perugia 1972. Teaches at Consv Musica Morlacchi, Perugia; As Li Co Milan. **Res:** V Pr C di Cavento 21, Milan, Italy.

MADEY, BOGUSLAW. Conductor of opera and symphony; composer. Polish. Art Dir & Principal Cond, Teatr Wielki, Lodz since 1972. Born 31 May 1932, Sosnowiec, Poland. Wife Anna Malewicz, occupation singer, mezzo-soprano. Studied: Music Acad Poznan, S B Poradowski, S Wislocki & B Wodiczko; Guildhall School of Mus, London, R Jones, N Del Mar & W Braithwaite; incl piano W Lewandowski, violin, percussion and voice. Plays the piano. **Operatic debut:** *Don Pasquale* Teatr Wielki, Warsaw 1961. Symphonic debut: Phil Orch, Poznan 1958. Previous occupations; piano teacher at Music Acad, Poznan. Prof & Hon Chair of Cond, Acad, Warsaw. Awards: Composer's Awd, Union of Polish Comp 1955; Medal 30 Yrs of Poland 1974; Gold Cross of Merit 1975.
ꞏ **Conducted with major companies in** FR GER: Dortmund, Düsseldorf-Duisburg, Kiel, Wiesbaden; POL: Lodz, Warsaw. **Operas with these companies incl** BARTOK: *Bluebeard's Castle;* BIZET: *Carmen;* CIMAROSA: *Matrimonio segreto;* DALLAPICCOLA: *Prigioniero;* DONIZETTI: *Don Pasquale;* GIORDANO: *Andrea Chénier;* GLUCK: *Cadi dupé, Iphigénie en Tauride;* GOUNOD: *Faust;* MONIUSZKO: *Halka★, Haunted Castle;* MONTEVERDI: *Favola d'Orfeo;* MOZART: *Don Giovanni, Schauspieldirektor, Zauberflöte;* PERGOLESI: *Maestro di musica;* PUCCINI: *Butterfly, Manon Lescaut, Tosca★;* RAVEL: *Heure espagnole;* ROSSINI: *Barbiere di Siviglia;* SMETANA: *Bartered Bride;* STRAUSS, R: *Rosenkavalier, Salome;* STRAVINSKY: *Oedipus Rex, Perséphone;* TCHAIKOVSKY: *Eugene Onegin;* VERDI: *Aida, Otello, Rigoletto;* WEBER: *Freischütz.* Also MONIUSZKO: *Verbum Nobile, Rafter;* PADEREWSKI: *Manru;* PACIORKIEWICZ: *Usziko.* Video—Polish TV: KAMIENSKI: *Happy Destitution.* Conducted major orch in Europe. Teaches at Acad of Music, Warsaw, Prof & Dean of Faculty. **Res:** ul Slowackiego 27/33 m 36/37, 01-592 Warsaw, Poland. Mgmt: PAG/POL/SLZ/FRG.

MAESTRINI, CARLO. Stages/produces opera, theater & television. Also designs sets. Italian. Born 4 May 1920, Florence. Wife Cesarina Riso, occupation pianist. Two children. Studied: Herbert Graf, Gustav Gründgens, Anton Giulio Bragaglia, Florence; also music & architect. Opera training as asst stage dir at San Carlo Naples, Verona Arena, Maggio Mus Florence 1949-53. **Operatic debut:** PAISIELLO: *Barbiere di Siviglia* Maggio Mus Florence 1953. Theater debut: fest, Venice 1951. Awards: Intl Awd Luigi Illica 1962; Hon D, Univ Montreal 1972.
Directed/produced opera for major companies in ARG: Buenos Aires; AUS: Bregenz Fest; BRA: Rio de Janeiro; CAN: Montreal/Quebec, Ottawa; CZE: Prague National; GRE: Athens Fest; FR GER: Düsseldorf-Duisburg, Frankfurt, Munich

Staatsoper, Stuttgart, Wiesbaden; HOL: Amsterdam; HUN: Budapest; ITA: Bologna, Florence Maggio & Comunale, Genoa, Milan La Scala, Naples, Palermo, Rome Opera & Caracalla, Trieste, Turin, Venice, Verona Arena; MEX: Mexico City; MON: Monte Carlo; POR: Lisbon; SWI: Geneva; USA: Chicago, Dallas, Houston, San Francisco Opera; YUG: Zagreb, Belgrade. **Operas staged with these companies incl** BELLINI: *Norma*★, *Pirata, Puritani, Sonnambula;* BERG: *Wozzeck;* BERLIOZ: *Damnation de Faust;* BIZET: *Carmen*★, *Djamileh;* BOITO: *Mefistofele*★; BORODIN: *Prince Igor;* BUSONI: *Doktor Faust;* CATALANI: *Wally*★; CHERUBINI: *Medea*★; CILEA: *Adriana Lecouvreur;* CIMAROSA: *Matrimonio segreto;* DONIZETTI: *Anna Bolena*★, *Campanello, Don Pasquale*★, *Elisir, Favorite, Fille du régiment, Linda di Chamounix, Lucia†;* GIORDANO: *Andrea Chénier*★, *Fedora*★; GLINKA: *Life for the Tsar;* GLUCK: *Iphigénie en Aulide, Orfeo ed Euridice;* GOUNOD: *Faust;* HUMPERDINCK: *Hänsel und Gretel;* JANACEK: *Jenufa;* LEONCAVALLO: *Pagliacci*★; MASCAGNI: *Cavalleria rusticana*★, *Silvano;* MASSENET: *Manon, Werther;* MENOTTI: *Amahl;* MOZART: *Così fan tutte, Don Giovanni*★, *Nozze di Figaro;* MUSSORGSKY: *Boris Godunov, Fair at Sorochinsk, Khovanshchina;* ORFF: *Mond;* PERGOLESI: *Maestro di musica;* PONCHIELLI: *Gioconda;* POULENC: *Voix humaine;* PROKOFIEV: *War and Peace;* PUCCINI: *Bohème*★†, *Fanciulla del West, Gianni Schicchi*★, *Butterfly, Manon Lescaut*★, *Suor Angelica*★, *Tabarro*★, *Tosca*★, *Turandot;* ROSSINI: *Barbiere di Siviglia, Cambiale di matrimonio, Cenerentola, Comte Ory*★, *Gazza ladra, Guillaume Tell, Italiana in Algeri, Moïse, Pietra del paragone, Scala di seta, Semiramide, Signor Bruschino, Turco in Italia;* SAINT-SAENS: *Samson et Dalila*★; SMETANA: *Bartered Bride;* TCHAIKOVSKY: *Eugene Onegin, Pique Dame;* VERDI: *Aida*★, *Aroldo/Stiffelio, Ballo in maschera*★, *Don Carlo, Ernani, Falstaff*★, *Forza del destino*★, *Lombardi*★, *Luisa Miller, Macbeth*★, *Nabucco*★, *Otello*★, *Rigoletto*★, *Simon Boccanegra, Traviata*★, *Trovatore*★, *Vespri;* WAGNER: *Lohengrin, Meistersinger, Parsifal, Walküre, Tristan und Isolde;* WEBER: *Abu Hassan, Freischütz, Oberon;* ZANDONAI: *Francesca da Rimini.* Also CAVALLI: *Didone;* PIZZETTI: *Fedra, Figlia di Jorio;* MASCAGNI: *Iris, Maschere.* **Operatic world premieres:** TESTI: *Celestina* Maggio Musicale Fiorentino 1963. Teaches at School of Fine Arts, Banff, Alta, Canada. **Res:** V Orcagna 16, Florence, Italy.

MAFFEO, GIANNI. Dramatic baritone. Italian. Born 30 Mar 1936, Vigevano, Italy. Wife Franca Zema, occupation employee. One child. Studied: Liceo Musicale Viotti, Zita Fumagalli, Vercelli. **Debut:** Tonio (*Pagliacci*) As Li Co 1961. Previous occupations: locksmith. Awards: Winner Conc As Li Co 1961; Golden slipper, Comune Vigevano 1964.

Sang with major companies in AUS: Vienna Staatsoper; CZE: Brno, Prague National; FRA: Bordeaux, Nice, Rouen, Toulouse; FR GER: Frankfurt, Munich Staatsoper; ITA: Genoa, Milan La Scala, Naples, Palermo, Turin, Verona Arena; MON: Monte Carlo; POL: Warsaw; POR: Lis-

bon; SPA: Majorca; USA: New York City Opera. **Roles with these companies incl** BELLINI: Sir Richard (*Puritani*); DONIZETTI: Belcore★‡ (*Elisir*), Enrico★ (*Lucia*), Gasparo★ (*Rita*); GIORDANO: Carlo Gérard (*Andrea Chénier*); LEONCAVALLO: Tonio★‡ (*Pagliacci*); MASCAGNI: Rabbi David (*Amico Fritz*); MASSENET: Lescaut (*Manon*); MOZART: Leporello‡ (*Don Giovanni*); PAISIELLO: Figaro (*Barbiere di Siviglia*); PUCCINI: Marcello★‡ (*Bohème*), Sharpless★‡ (*Butterfly*), Lescaut★ (*Manon Lescaut*); VERDI: Amonasro★‡ (*Aida*), Renato (*Ballo in maschera*), Don Carlo★‡ (*Forza del destino*), Nabucco, Rigoletto★, Germont★ (*Traviata*), Conte di Luna★ (*Trovatore*); WOLF-FERRARI: Conte Gil (*Segreto di Susanna*). Recorded for: Decca, Supraphon, Fratelli Fabbri. Film: (*Bohème*). **Res:** V Parini 14, 27029 Vigevano, Italy.

MAHLKE, KNUT. Conductor of opera and symphony. German. Resident Cond, Staatsoper Hamburg. Born 30 Jan 1943, Berlin. Wife Ursula, occupation music teacher. Studied: Jan Koetsier, Kurt Eichhorn, Munich; incl piano, timpani & voice. Operatic training as repetiteur, asst cond & chorus master at Oper am Gärtnerplatz, Munich. **Operatic debut:** *Lustigen Weiber* Gärtnerplatz, Munich 1968. Symphonic debut: Symph Orch, Munich 1972. Awards: Richard Strauss Preis, Hochschule für Musik, Munich.

Conducted with major companies in FR GER: Hamburg, Kassel, Munich Gärtnerplatz. **Operas with these companies incl** BIZET: *Carmen*★; DONIZETTI: *Don Pasquale*★, *Lucia*★; HUMPERDINCK: *Hänsel und Gretel*★; LORTZING: *Waffenschmied, Wildschütz*★, *Zar und Zimmermann*★; MOZART: *Entführung aus dem Serail*★, *Zauberflöte*★; NICOLAI: *Lustigen Weiber*★; SMETANA: *Bartered Bride*★; STRAUSS, J: *Fledermaus;* VERDI: *Trovatore*★; WEBER: *Freischütz*★. Conducted major orch in Europe. **Res:** Hamburg, FR Ger.

MAI, WOLFGANG CHRISTOPH. Scenic and costume designer for opera, theater. Is also a painter. German. Resident designer, Basler Theater, Basel, Switzerland. Born 28 Mar 1942, Trier. Single. Studied: Stuttgarter Akad der bildenden Künste. Prof training: Staatsoper Vienna; Frankfurter Theater. **Operatic debut:** sets, cost, *Entführung aus dem Serail* Basler Theater 1969. Previous adm positions in opera: Dir of Scenery and Properties, Basler Theater.

Designed for major companies in AUS: Vienna Staatsoper; FRA: Strasbourg; FR GER: Darmstadt, Frankfurt; HOL: Amsterdam; SWI: Basel, Zurich. **Operas designed for these companies incl** DEBUSSY: *Pelléas et Mélisande*★; DONIZETTI: *Don Pasquale*★, *Elisir*★; MONTEVERDI: *Incoronazione di Poppea*★; MOZART: *Così fan tutte*★, *Entführung aus dem Serail*★; OFFENBACH: *Mariage aux lanternes*★; PUCCINI: *Bohème*★; SCARLATTI: *Trionfo dell'onore*★; SMETANA: *Bartered Bride*★; STRAUSS, J: *Fledermaus*★; VERDI: *Don Carlo*★, *Traviata*★; WAGNER: *Parsifal*★, *Tristan und Isolde*★; WEILL: *Aufstieg und Fall der Stadt Mahagonny*★, *Dreigroschenoper*★; YUN: *Traum des Liu-Tung*★. **Operatic world premieres:** HOLLIGER: *Magischer Tänzer* Basel 1970. Exhibitions of stage de-

signs Basel 1970, 1972, 1973. Teaches at Arts and Crafts School, Basel. **Res:** Steinengraben 16, Basel, Switzerland.

MAIER, HANNS. German. Dir, Nationaltheater Mannheim, Mozartstr 9, Mannheim 1969- . In charge of overall adm matters & finances. Additional adm position: Dir, Intl Film Week, Mannheim. Born 27 Dec 1924, Mannheim. Wife Marianne. Two children. Background primarily adm. **Res:** Wilhelmstr 2b, 68 Mannheim 51, FR Ger.

MAJEWSKI, ANDRZEJ. Scenic and costume designer for opera, theater; specl in sets. Is a lighting designer, stage director; also a painter. Polish. Resident designer, Teatr Wielki, Warsaw and at Teatr Nowy, Lodz. Born 15 Jun 1936, Warsaw. Single. Studied: Cracow Acad of Fine Arts, Prof Karol Frycz. **Operatic debut:** Opera, Cracow. Theater debut: National Theater, Cracow 1959.

Designed for major companies in AUS: Salzburg Fest; FRA: Paris; FR GER: Cologne, Hamburg, Munich Gärtnerplatz, Wiesbaden; HOL: Amsterdam; ITA: Genoa, Verona; MEX: Mexico City; POL: Lodz, Warsaw; UK: London Royal; YUG: Zagreb. **Operas designed for these companies incl** DEBUSSY: *Enfant prodigue;* DONIZETTI: *Lucia*★*;* JANACEK: *Jenufa;* KELEMEN: *Belagerungszustand;* LEONCAVALLO: *Pagliacci;* MONIUSZKO: *Halka*★*;* MOZART: *Don Giovanni, Zauberflöte*★*;* MUSSORGSKY: *Boris Godunov*★*, Khovanshchina*★*;* OFFENBACH: *Contes d'Hoffmann*★*;* PENDERECKI: *Teufel von Loudun*★*;* SAINT-SAENS: *Samson et Dalila;* STRAUSS, R: *Elektra, Salome;* TCHAIKOVSKY: *Eugene Onegin;* VERDI: *Otello.* **Operatic world premieres:** ORFF: *De Temporum fine comoedia* Salzburg Fest 1973. Exhibitions of stage designs & paintings, Wright Hepburn Gallery, London 1970. **Res:** Potocka 60/5, Warsaw, Poland.

MAKAI, PETER. Scenic and costume designer for opera, theater & television. Is a lighting designer, stage director; also an illustrator. Hungarian. Resident designer & stage director, Hungarian State Opera, Budapest, and as guest designer at Madách Theater & Thália Theater, Budapest. Born 4 Dec 1932, Hódmezövásárhely. Single. Studied: theater, music and piano. Prof training: Hungarian State Opera, Budapest, and as guest designer at Madách 1957-59. **Operatic debut:** Ntl Theater of Szeged 1960. Theater debut: Petöfi Theater, Budapest 1962. Awards: Ferenc Erkel Awd, Ministry of Hung Culture.

Designed for major companies in DEN: Copenhagen; HUN: Budapest; YUG: Belgrade. **Operas designed for these companies incl** BERG: *Lulu;* CIKKER: *Bajazid*★†*;* GAY/Britten: *Beggar's Opera*★†*;* GERSHWIN: *Porgy and Bess*★†*;* HANDEL: *Rodelinda*★†*;* HENZE: *Undine;* JANACEK: *Jenufa;* MENOTTI: *Telephone;* MONTEVERDI: *Incoronazione di Poppea;* MOZART: *Entführung aus dem Serail*†*;* ORFF: *Kluge, Mond*★†*;* PROKOFIEV: *Duenna*★†*, Love for Three Oranges;* RAVEL: *Heure espagnole*★†*;* STRAUSS, R: *Ariadne auf Naxos*★†*;* VERDI: *Falstaff, Lombardi;* WEILL: *Aufstieg und Fall der Stadt Mahagonny;* WOLF-FERRARI: *Quattro*

rusteghi★†. Exhibitions of stage designs Open-Air Place Exhibit, Szeged 1973; Theater Inst, Budapest 1973. Mgmt: ITK/HUN.

MALAGÙ, STEFANIA. Lyric mezzo-soprano. Italian. Born 11 Oct 1933, Milan. Husband Ferrari, occupation businessman. One child. Studied: Mo Arturo Merlini, Scuola Piccola Scala, Mo Giulio Confalonieri, Milan. **Debut:** Guecha (*Iris*) La Scala, Milan 1956. Previous occupations: business secy.

Sang with major companies in AUS: Salzburg Fest, Vienna Staatsoper; FRA: Nancy; FR GER: Berlin Deutsche Oper, Cologne, Munich Staatsoper, Stuttgart, Wiesbaden; HOL: Amsterdam; ISR: Tel Aviv; ITA: Bologna, Florence Maggio & Comunale, Genoa, Milan La Scala, Naples, Palermo, Parma, Rome Opera & Caracalla, Spoleto Fest, Trieste, Turin, Venice; MON: Monte Carlo; POR: Lisbon; SWI: Geneva; USSR: Moscow Bolshoi; USA: Chicago, Dallas. **Roles with these companies incl** BRITTEN: Mrs Grose (*Turn of the Screw*); CIMAROSA: Fidalma★ (*Matrimonio segreto*); DONIZETTI: Giovanna (*Anna Bolena*), Marquise de Birkenfeld★ (*Fille du régiment*), Pierrot (*Linda di Chamounix*), Maffio Orsini★ (*Lucrezia Borgia*); GOUNOD: Siebel★ (*Faust*); HAYDN: Lisetta (*Mondo della luna*); HUMPERDINCK: Hänsel; MASCAGNI: Beppe (*Amico Fritz*); MASSENET: Charlotte (*Werther*); MENOTTI: Secretary (*Consul*); MOZART: Dorabella★ (*Così fan tutte*), Ramiro★ (*Finta giardiniera*), Cherubino★ (*Nozze di Figaro*); PERGOLESI: Cardella★ (*Frate 'nnamorato*); PUCCINI: Suzuki★ (*Butterfly*), Badessa★ (*Suor Angelica*), Frugola★ (*Tabarro*); ROSSINI: Isolier★ (*Comte Ory*), Marchesina Clarice★ (*Pietra del paragone*), Zaida★ (*Turco in Italia*); STRAUSS, R: Komponist (*Ariadne auf Naxos*), Octavian (*Rosenkavalier*); TCHAIKOVSKY: Comtesse (*Pique Dame*); VERDI: Preziosilla★ (*Forza del destino*); ZANDONAI: Samaritana (*Francesca da Rimini*). Also MEYERBEER: (*Robert le diable*). **World premieres:** operas by Rossellini, Dallapiccola, Mortari, Pizzetti. Recorded for: Decca, DG, EMI, Ricordi. Video/Film: Badessa (*Suor Angelica*); Berta (*Barbiere di Siviglia*); Emilia (*Otello*); (*Linguaggio dei fiori*). **Res:** V Pietro Colletta 73, Milan, Italy.

MALAS, SPIRO. Bass-baritone & basso-buffo. American. Resident mem: New York City Opera. Born 28 Jan 1933, Baltimore, MD, USA. Wife Marlena, occupation singer, voice teacher. Two sons. Studied: Peabody Consv, Dr Elemer Nagy, Baltimore; Elsa Baklor, Daniel Ferro, USA. **Debut:** Marco (*Gianni Schicchi*) Baltimore Civic Opera 1959. Previous occupations: auto mechanic, lifeguard, schoolteacher. Awards: American Opera Aud Awd, debut in Milan; Met Op Ntl Counc Aud Study Grant.

Sang with major companies in AUS: Vienna Volksoper, Salzburg Fest; ITA: Florence Maggio, Naples, Rome; USA: Baltimore, Boston, Chicago, Cincinnati, Fort Worth, Hartford, Houston, Miami, Milwaukee Florentine Opera, New York City Opera, Omaha, Philadelphia Grand Opera, Pittsburgh, San Diego, San Francisco Opera, Santa Fe, Washington DC. **Roles with these companies incl**

BEETHOVEN: Rocco (*Fidelio*); BELLINI: Rodolfo (*Sonnambula*); BRITTEN: Bottom (*Midsummer Night*); DONIZETTI: Henry VIII (*Anna Bolena*), Don Pasquale, Dott Dulcamara (*Elisir*), Sulpice (*Fille du régiment*); GINASTERA: Teudiselo (*Don Rodrigo*); HANDEL: Ptolemy (*Giulio Cesare*); HAYDN: Nanni (*Infedeltà delusa*); MOZART: Don Alfonso (*Così fan tutte*), Leporello (*Don Giovanni*), Osmin (*Entführung aus dem Serail*), Figaro (*Nozze di Figaro*); MUSSORGSKY: Varlaam & Pimen (*Boris Godunov*); PUCCINI: Colline (*Bohème*), Gianni Schicchi; RIMSKY-KORSAKOV: Roi Dodon (*Coq d'or*); ROSSINI: Dott Bartolo (*Barbiere di Siviglia*), Don Magnifico (*Cenerentola*), Podestà (*Gazza ladra*), Mustafà (*Italiana in Algeri*), Assur (*Semiramide*); STRAUSS, R: La Roche (*Capriccio*); VERDI: Padre Guardiano (*Forza del destino*); WAGNER: Daland (*Fliegende Holländer*). Recorded for: Decca. Video/Film: (*Fille du régiment*).

MALASPINA, MASSIMILIANO. Bass. Italian. Born 17 Jun 1925, Fara Novarese. Wife Rita Orlandi, occupation opera singer. One child. Studied: Lina Pagliughi. **Debut:** Colline (*Bohème*) Lupi-Guggia-Rola 1959. Previous occupations: antiquarian.

Sang with major companies in BEL: Brussels; BRA: Rio de Janeiro; CAN: Montreal/Quebec; FRA: Paris, Toulouse; FR GER: Frankfurt, Munich Staatsoper, Wiesbaden; GER DR: Berlin Komische Oper; ITA: Genoa, Milan La Scala, Naples, Parma, Rome Opera & Caracalla, Trieste, Turin, Venice; SPA: Barcelona; USA: Miami. **Roles with these companies incl** BELLINI: Oroveso (*Norma*), Sir George (*Puritani*); HANDEL: Ptolemy (*Giulio Cesare*); MOZART: Sarastro (*Zauberflöte*); VERDI: Ramfis (*Aida*), Padre Guardiano (*Forza del destino*), Banquo (*Macbeth*). Teaches voice. **Res:** V Benedetto Spinoza 2, Milan, Italy.

MALASPINA, RITA ORLANDI; née Orlandi. Dramatic soprano. Italian. Resident mem: La Scala, Milan. Born 28 Dec 1937, Bologna, Italy. Husband Massimiliano, occupation lyric singer. One child. **Debut:** Giovanna (*Giovanna d'Arco*) Teatro Nuovo, Milan 1963.

Sang with major companies in ARG: Buenos Aires; AUS: Vienna Staatsoper; BEL: Brussels; BRA: Rio de Janeiro; CAN: Montreal/Quebec; FRA: Nice, Paris, Toulouse; FR GER: Hamburg, Munich Staatsoper, Wiesbaden; HUN: Budapest; ITA: Bologna, Genoa, Milan La Scala, Naples, Palermo, Parma, Rome Opera & Caracalla, Trieste, Turin, Venice, Verona Arena; SPA: Barcelona; UK: London Royal; USA: Miami, New York Met, Philadelphia Lyric. **Roles with these companies incl** GIORDANO: Maddalena★ (*Andrea Chénier*); PUCCINI: Suor Angelica, Tosca★; ROSSINI: Anaï★ (*Moïse*); VERDI: Aida★, Mina★ (*Aroldo/Stiffelio*), Odabella★ (*Attila*), Amelia★ (*Ballo in maschera*), Elisabetta★ (*Don Carlo*), Lucrezia Contarini★ (*Due Foscari*), Donna Elvira★ (*Ernani*), Alice Ford★ (*Falstaff*), Leonora★ (*Forza del destino*), Giovanna d'Arco★, Luisa Miller★, Amelia★ (*Masnadieri*), Abigaille★ (*Nabucco*), Desdemona★ (*Otello*), Amelia★ (*Simon Boccanegra*), Leonora★ (*Trovatore*), Elena★ (*Vespri*); WAG-

NER: Elsa★ (*Lohengrin*). Gives recitals. Appears with symphony orchestra.

MALAVAL, JULIO. Conductor of opera and symphony. Argentinean. Resident Cond, Opernhaus Zurich. Born 19 Jan 1939, Buenos Aires. Wife Gioconda, occupation exec secy. Two children. Studied: Wiener Musikhochschule, Hans Swarowsky, Jelinek-Kedra, Vienna; incl piano. Plays the piano. Operatic training as repetiteur & asst cond at Opernhaus Zurich 1970-75. **Operatic debut:** *Don Carlo* Opernhaus Zurich 1970. Symphonic debut: Buenos Aires Radio Orch 1961.

Conducted with major companies in ARG: Buenos Aires; FR GER: Munich Staatsoper, Stuttgart; SPA: Barcelona; SWI: Zurich. **Operas with these companies incl** BUSONI: *Doktor Faust★;* GINASTERA: *Bomarzo★;* LEONCAVALLO: *Pagliacci★;* MASCAGNI: *Cavalleria rusticana★;* MOZART: *Entführung aus dem Serail★*, *Zauberflöte★;* PUCCINI: *Bohème★*, *Tosca★;* VERDI: *Don Carlo★*, *Ernani★*, *Nabucco★*, *Rigoletto★*, *Traviata★*, *Vespri★*. Conducted major orch in Europe, Cent/S America. Previous positions as Mus Dir with major orch: Orquesta Sinf, Mendoza, Argentina 1962-68. **Res:** Am Brunnenbächli 16/Zollikerberg, Zurich, Switzerland. Mgmt: CDA/ARG; SLZ/FRG.

MALCHENKO, VLADIMIR AFANASIEVICH. Lyric baritone. Russian. Resident mem: Bolshoi Theater, Moscow. Born 20 July 1945, Smolensk. Wife Tamara, occupation physician. One son. Studied: Leningrad Consv, V G Sopina. **Debut:** Yeletsky (*Pique Dame*) Bolshoi Theater, Moscow 1971. Previous occupations: student of engineering. Awards: Laureate, Second Prize, Glinka All-Union Compt; Third Prize Intl Vocalists Compt Montreal, Canada, and Tchaikovsky Compt.

Sang with major companies in USSR: Leningrad Kirov, Moscow Bolshoi. **Roles with these companies incl** PUCCINI: Sharpless★ (*Butterfly*); ROSSINI: Figaro★ (*Barbiere di Siviglia*); TCHAIKOVSKY: Eugene Onegin★, Duke Robert★ (*Iolanthe*), Yeletsky★ (*Pique Dame*); VERDI: Germont★ (*Traviata*). Gives recitals. Appears with symphony orchestra. **Res:** 10-54 M Pereyaslavskaya, Moscow, USSR. Mgmt: SOY/USSR; GOS/USSR.

MALEWICZ-MADEY, ANNA; née Anna Ligia Malewicz. Lyric mezzo-soprano. Polish. Resident mem: Teatr Wielki, Warsaw. Born 13 Feb 1937, Pinsk, Poland. Husband Boguslaw Madey, occupation conductor, Art Dir, Grand Theater, Lodz. Studied: Music Secondary School, Warsaw, M Zbijewska, piano; Music High School F Chopin, Prof Brègy, Warsaw; Accad Chigiana, Prof Favaretto, Siena, Italy. **Debut:** Mercèdes (*Carmen*) Warsaw Opera 1959. Previous occupations: announcer Polish Radio Warsaw 1958. Awards: Laureate Second Prize and Special Hon for Youngest Singer, Ntl Moniuszko Vocal Compt, Warsaw 1958; Second Prize, Intl Vocal Compt, 's Hertogenbosch, Holland 1964.

Sang with major companies in AUS: Graz, Salzburg Fest, Vienna Volksoper; CZE: Prague National; GER DR: Berlin Komische Oper; ITA: Florence Comunale; POL: Lodz, Warsaw; USSR: Moscow Bolshoi. **Roles with these companies incl**

BIZET: Carmen★; GOUNOD: Siebel (*Faust*); HAYDN: Lisetta (*Mondo della luna*); HONEGGER: Judith★; MASSENET: Charlotte★ (*Werther*); MONIUSZKO: Jadwiga (*Haunted Castle*); MOZART: Cherubino (*Nozze di Figaro*); MUSSORGSKY: Marina (*Boris Godunov*); PUCCINI: Suzuki (*Butterfly*); RAVEL: Concepcion★ (*Heure espagnole*); ROSSINI: Rosina (*Barbiere di Siviglia*); STRAUSS, R: Octavian (*Rosenkavalier*). Also MONIUSZKO: Bronia (*Countess*); PADEREWSKI: Aza (*Manru*). World premieres: BARTOLOZZI: Vegliarda (*Tutto ciò che accade ti riguarda*) Maggio Musicale, Florence 1972. Video/Film—Studio RSI Lugano; Sulamite; Polskie Nagrania Muza: Zofia (*Halka*). Gives recitals. Appears with symphony orchestra. Res: ul Moliera 8 m 61, 00-076 Warsaw, Poland. Mgmt: PAG/POL; RAB/AUS.

MALFITANO, CATHERINE. Lyric coloratura soprano. American. Resident mem: New York City Opera. Born 18 Apr 1948, New York. Single. Studied: Joseph Malfitano, New York; Manhattan School of Music, New York; Frank Corsaro & Herbert Berghof Studio, stage deportment, Alfredo Corvino & Berghof Studio, dance, New York. Debut: Nannetta (*Falstaff*) Central City Opera Fest, CO 1972. Awards: National Opera Inst Awd 1973 & 1974; *Daily News* Awd, New York 1966. Sang with major companies in HOL: Amsterdam; USA: Chicago, Houston, Lake George, Minneapolis, New York City Opera, Philadelphia Lyric, Portland, San Diego, San Francisco Spring, Santa Fe, Washington DC. Roles with these companies incl BIZET: Micaëla★ (*Carmen*); CAVALLI: Erisbe★ (*Ormindo*); GLUCK: Euridice★; HENZE: Manon★ (*Boulevard Solitude*); MASCAGNI: Suzel★ (*Amico Fritz*); MASSENET: Manon★; MENOTTI: Annina★ (*Saint of Bleecker Street*); MOZART: Zerlina★ (*Don Giovanni*), Susanna★ (*Nozze di Figaro*), Pamina★ (*Zauberflöte*); OFFENBACH: Périchole★; PASATIERI: Berta★ (*Black Widow*); PUCCINI: Mimi★ (*Bohème*), Lauretta★ (*Gianni Schicchi*), Liù★ (*Turandot*); ROSSINI: Rosina★ (*Barbiere di Siviglia*); STRAUSS, R: Sophie★ (*Rosenkavalier*); VERDI: Nannetta★(*Falstaff*); WARD: Abigail★(*Crucible*); WEILL: Polly★ (*Dreigroschenoper*); WOLF-FERRARI: Susanna★ (*Segreto di Susanna*). Also ARGENTO: Lady with Hand Mirror★ (*Postcard from Morocco*); PASATIERI: Masha★ (*Seagull*). World premieres: SUSA: Princess (*Transformations*) Minnesota Opera, Minneapolis 1973; FLOYD: Doll (*Bilby's Doll*) Houston Grand Opera 1976; PASATIERI: Catherine Sloper (*Washington Square*) Michigan Opera, Detroit 1976. Gives recitals. Appears with symphony orchestra. Res: 500 West End Ave, New York, USA. Mgmt: CAM/USA; HPL/UK.

MALIPONTE, ADRIANA. Lyric soprano. Italian. Born 26 Dec 1942, Italy. Single. Studied: Carmen Melis, Italy; Prof Suzanne Stappen, France. Debut: Micaëla (*Carmen*) Paris Opera 1963. Awards: Grand Prix Intl du Disque, Paris 1965; Orphée d'Or 1973; RAI Trofeo Primavera, Rome 1961; DG 1960, Prix Intl Concours Genève 1973; First Prize Conc Intl Teatro alla Scala 1958; Rosa d'Oro 1975, Teatro Grande Brescia, Italy.

Sang with major companies in ARG: Buenos Aires; AUS: Vienna Staatsoper; BEL: Brussels; BUL: Sofia; FRA: Bordeaux, Marseille, Nice, Paris, Rouen, Strasbourg, Toulouse; FR GER: Dortmund, Düsseldorf-Duisburg, Hamburg; ITA: Genoa, Milan La Scala, Naples, Spoleto Fest, Trieste, Turin, Venice, Verona Arena; MON: Monte Carlo; POR: Lisbon; SPA: Barcelona; SWI: Geneva; UK: Glyndebourne Fest, London Royal Opera; USA: Baltimore, Boston, Chicago, Cincinnati, Hartford, Miami, Milwaukee Florentine, New Orleans, New York Met, Philadelphia Grand & Lyric. Roles with these companies incl BECAUD: Maureen★ (*Opéra d'Aran*), BELLINI: Beatrice di Tenda, Giulietta (*Capuleti ed i Montecchi*), Elvira★ (*Puritani*); BIZET: Micaëla★‡ (*Carmen*), Léila (*Pêcheurs de perles*); CHARPENTIER: Louise★; CHERUBINI: Medea; DONIZETTI: Norina★ (*Don Pasquale*), Adina★ (*Elisir*); GLINKA: Antonida★ (*Life for the Tsar*); GLUCK: Euridice★; GOUNOD: Marguerite★ (*Faust*), Mireille, Juliette★; HANDEL: Cleopatra (*Giulio Cesare*); LEONCAVALLO: Nedda★ (*Pagliacci*); MASCAGNI: Suzel★ (*Amico Fritz*); MASSENET: Manon★, Thäis; MONTEMEZZI: Fiora (*Amore dei tre re*); MOZART: Fiordiligi (*Così fan tutte*), Donna Elvira & Zerlina (*Don Giovanni*), Contessa★ & Susanna (*Nozze di Figaro*), Aminta (*Re pastore*), Pamina★ (*Zauberflöte*); OFFENBACH: Antonia★ (*Contes d'Hoffmann*); ORFF: Solo (*Carmina burana*); PUCCINI: Mimi★ (*Bohème*), Lauretta (*Gianni Schicchi*), Magda (*Rondine*), Suor Angelica, Liù★ (*Turandot*), Anna★‡ (*Villi*); ROSSINI: Rosina★ (*Barbiere di Siviglia*), Anaï (*Moïse*); STRAUSS, R: Zdenka★ (*Arabella*); TCHAIKOVSKY: Tatiana★ (*Eugene Onegin*), Lisa (*Pique Dame*); VERDI: Nannetta (*Falstaff*), Giovanna d'Arco, Luisa Miller, Desdemona★ (*Otello*), Amelia (*Simon Boccanegra*), Violetta★ (*Traviata*), Elena (*Vespri*). Also ROSSELLINI: Dona Rosita (*Dona Rosita nubile*). World premieres: MENOTTI: Sardule (*Dernier sauvage*) Paris Opera 1963. Recorded for: RCA, DG, Carillon. Video/Film—CBS TV: Violetta (*Traviata*). Gives recitals. Appears with symphony orchestra. Res: V Macchi 75, Milan, Italy. Mgmt: HUR/USA.

MALONE, CAROL. Lyric coloratura soprano. American. Resident mem: Deutsche Oper, Berlin. Born 16 Jul, Grayson, KY, USA. Husband John E Parker, occupation physician. Studied: Indiana Univ, Bloomington, USA; Hochschule für Musik, Hamburg; Hochschule für Musik, Cologne; Josef Metternich, Cologne. Debut: Aennchen (*Freischütz*) State Opera, Cologne 1966. Previous occupations: PS music teacher. Awards: Fulbright Schlshp; M B Rockefeller Fund, 2 grants; German Gvnmt Grant.

Sang with major companies in AUS: Salzburg Fest, Vienna Volksoper; BEL: Brussels; FRA: Aix-en-Provence, Lyon, Rouen; FR GER: Berlin Deutsche Oper, Bonn, Cologne, Düsseldorf-Duisburg, Frankfurt, Hamburg, Mannheim, Munich Staatsoper, Stuttgart; HOL: Amsterdam; ITA: Milan La Scala, Venice; UK: Edinburgh Fest; USA: San Francisco Opera; YUG: Belgrade. Roles with these companies incl BEETHOVEN: Marzelline★ (*Fidelio*); DONIZETTI: Adina★ (*Elisir*); HUMPERDINCK: Gretel★; LORTZING:

Gretchen★ (*Wildschütz*); MASSENET: Sophie★ (*Werther*); MOZART: Despina★ (*Così fan tutte*), Zerlina★ (*Don Giovanni*), Blondchen★ (*Entführung aus dem Serail*), Susanna★ (*Nozze di Figaro*); NICOLAI: Aennchen (*Lustigen Weiber*); ORFF: Solo★ (*Carmina burana*); PUCCINI: Lauretta★ (*Gianni Schicchi*); ROSSINI: Fanny★ (*Cambiale di matrimonio*), Fiorilla★ (*Turco in Italia*); STRAUSS, J: Adele★ (*Fledermaus*); STRAUSS, R: Sophie★ (*Rosenkavalier*); VERDI: Nannetta (*Falstaff*); WEBER: Aennchen★ (*Freischütz*). Also BLACHER: Adelaide (*Preussisches Märchen*); MOZART: Auretta (*Oca del Cairo*), Papagena (*Zauberflöte*). **World premieres:** NABOKOV: Jacquenetta (*Love's Labour's Lost*) Deutsche Oper Berlin 1973. Video/Film: Papagena (*Zauberflöte*); Adelaide (*Preussisches Märchen*). Gives recitals. Appears with symphony orchestra.

MALTA, ALEXANDER; né Lagger. Bass. Swiss. Born 28 Sep 1942, Visp, Switzerland. Wife Janet Perry, occupation opera singer. Studied: Desider Kovács, Zurich; Barra-Carracciolo, Milan; Enzo Mascherini, Florence; Accad Chigiana, Siena, Italy. **Debut:** Frate (*Don Carlo*) Staatstheater Stuttgart 1962.
Sang with major companies in AUS: Vienna Volksoper; FR GER: Berlin Deutsche Oper, Bonn, Cologne, Dortmund, Frankfurt, Hamburg, Munich Gärtnerplatz, Stuttgart; ITA: Trieste, Venice; SWI: Geneva, Zurich. **Roles with these companies incl** BARTOK: Bluebeard★ (*Fidelio*); BEETHOVEN: Rocco★ (*Fidelio*); BIZET: Escamillo★ (*Carmen*); BORODIN: Galitzky (*Prince Igor*); CIMAROSA: Geronimo (*Matrimonio segreto*); DONIZETTI: Don Pasquale★; GLUCK: Apollo (*Alceste*); GOUNOD: Méphistophélès★ (*Faust*); HANDEL: Ptolemy (*Giulio Cesare*); LORTZING: Stadinger (*Waffenschmied*), Baculus★ (*Wildschütz*); MOZART: Don Alfonso (*Così fan tutte*), Leporello & Don Giovanni (*Don Giovanni*), Osmin★ (*Entführung aus dem Serail*), Sarastro★ (*Zauberflöte*); NICOLAI: Falstaff★ (*Lustigen Weiber*); PAISIELLO: Bartolo (*Barbiere di Siviglia*); PROKOFIEV: Mendoza★ (*Duenna*); ROSSINI: Don Basilio★ (*Barbiere di Siviglia*), Podestà (*Gazza ladra*); SMETANA: Kezal★ (*Bartered Bride*); VERDI: Banquo (*Macbeth*), Zaccaria (*Nabucco*); WAGNER: Daland (*Fliegende Holländer*); WEILL: Trinity Moses★ (*Aufstieg und Fall der Stadt Mahagonny*). Also DVORAK: Wassermann (*Rusalka*). **World premieres:** VALDAMBRINI: Kater (*Gestiefelte Kater*) Opernhaus Bonn 1975. Recorded for: DG (Archiv), Ariola-Eurodisc. Gives recitals. Appears with symphony orchestra.

MANCHET, ELIANE; née Schaaf. Coloratura soprano. French. Born 26 May 1937, Bamako, Mali, Fr Sudan. Husband Pierre Médecin, occupation stage director/producer. Two children. Studied: Consv de Strasbourg, Marcelle Bunlet. **Debut:** Gilda (*Rigoletto*) Opéra de Lyon 1966. Previous occupations: surgeon's asst.
Sang with major companies in BEL: Brussels; FRA: Bordeaux, Lyon, Marseille, Nancy, Nice, Paris, Rouen, Strasbourg, Toulouse; FR GER: Cologne, Düsseldorf-Duisburg, Frankfurt, Munich Staatsoper, Stuttgart; HOL: Amsterdam; ITA:

Florence Maggio, Milan La Scala, Naples, Rome Opera, Turin, Venice; MON: Monte Carlo; POR: Lisbon; ROM: Bucharest; SWI: Geneva. **Roles with these companies incl** BEETHOVEN: Marzelline (*Fidelio*); BELLINI: Elvira (*Puritani*), Amina (*Sonnambula*); BIZET: Lauretta (*Docteur Miracle*), Catherine (*Jolie Fille de Perth*), Léila★ (*Pêcheurs de perles*); BRITTEN: Tytania (*Midsummer Night*); DEBUSSY: Mélisande★; DONIZETTI: Norina★ (*Don Pasquale*), Adina (*Elisir*), Lucia; GOUNOD: Marguerite (*Faust*), Juliette★; HANDEL: Alcina; MASSENET: Manon★, Sophie (*Werther*); MOZART: Fiordiligi★ (*Così fan tutte*), Donna Anna (*Don Giovanni*), Konstanze★ (*Entführung aus dem Serail*), Violante (*Finta giardiniera*), Ilia (*Idomeneo*), Susanna★ (*Nozze di Figaro*), Königin der Nacht★ (*Zauberflöte*); OFFENBACH: Olympia & Antonia & Giulietta (*Contes d'Hoffmann*); POULENC: Blanche (*Dialogues des Carmélites*); ROSSINI: Rosina★ (*Barbiere di Siviglia*), Comtesse Adèle★ (*Comte Ory*); STRAUSS, J: Rosalinde★ (*Fledermaus*); STRAUSS, R: Zdenka★ (*Arabella*), Zerbinetta★ (*Ariadne auf Naxos*), Sophie★ (*Rosenkavalier*); STRAVINSKY: Rossignol★; VERDI: Oscar (*Ballo in maschera*), Nannetta (*Falstaff*), Gilda (*Rigoletto*), Violetta (*Traviata*). **World premieres:** ROSSELLINI: Violaine (*Annonce faite à Marie*) Opéra Comique, Paris 1970. Recorded for: RAI. Gives recitals. Appears with symphony orchestra. Teaches voice. **Res:** rue Léon Cogniet 13, Paris 17, France. Mgmt: CMW/FRA; SLZ/FRG.

MANDAC, EVELYN. Lyric soprano. Filipino. Resident mem: Metropolitan Opera, New York. Born 16 Aug, Philippines. Husband Sanjoy Bhattacharya, occupation investment banker. Studied: Aurelio Estanislao, Philippines; Hans Heinz, Daniel Ferro, New York. **Debut:** Mimi (*Bohème*) Washington Opera, DC 1969. Awards: Met Op Ntl Counc Aud Prize 1965; Rockefeller Fndt Schlshp; Fulbright Schlshp at Juilliard; Brussels Compt Winner 1965.
Sang with major companies in AUS: Salzburg Fest; CAN: Vancouver; FRA: Toulouse; HOL: Amsterdam; ITA: Rome Opera, Turin; SWI: Geneva; UK: Glyndebourne Fest; USA: Baltimore, Houston, Miami, Minneapolis, New York Met, St Paul, San Antonio, San Francisco Opera, Santa Fe, Seattle, Washington DC. **Roles with these companies incl** BEETHOVEN: Marzelline★ (*Fidelio*); BENNETT: Jenny★ (*Mines of Sulphur*); BIZET: Micaëla★ (*Carmen*), Léila★ (*Pêcheurs de perles*); DEBUSSY: Mélisande★; DONIZETTI: Norina★ (*Don Pasquale*), Adina★ (*Elisir*); FALLA: Salud★ (*Vida breve*); GOUNOD: Juliette★; HANDEL: Galatea★, Almirena★ (*Rinaldo*); HENZE: Luise★ (*Junge Lord*); HUMPERDINCK: Gretel★; MASSENET: Manon★; MEYERBEER: Inez★ (*Africaine*); MONTEVERDI: Clorinda★ (*Combattimento di Tancredi*); MOZART: Despina★ (*Così fan tutte*), Zerlina★ (*Don Giovanni*), Susanna★ (*Nozze di Figaro*), Pamina★ (*Zauberflöte*); ORFF: Solo★ (*Carmina burana*); PUCCINI: Mimi★ (*Bohème*), Lauretta★ (*Gianni Schicchi*), Liù★ (*Turandot*); STRAUSS, R: Sophie★ (*Rosenkavalier*); STRAVINSKY: Anne Trulove★ (*Rake's Progress*); TCHAIKOVSKY: Lisa★ (*Pique Dame*); VERDI: Nannetta★ (*Falstaff*), Gilda★ (*Rigoletto*). Also CAVALLI: Sicle

(*Ormindo*). **World premieres:** PASATIERI: Berta (*Black Widow*) Seattle Opera 1972; Inez (*Inez de Castro*) Baltimore Opera 1976. Recorded for: Philips. Video/Film — NET TV: Lisa (*Pique Dame*). Gives recitals. Appears with symphony orchestra. **Res:** New York, NY, USA. Mgmt: CAM/USA; AIM/UK.

MANNINI, ELENA. Costume designer for opera, theater, film & television. Is a lighting designer; also a painter & fashion designer. Italian. Resident designer, Teatro di Roma/Argentina, Rome. Born 22 Jul 1937, Florence. One child. Studied: Ist Statale d'Arte, Prof Onofrio Martinelli, Florence. **Operatic debut:** *Bohème* Teatro Municipale, Reggio Emilia 1966. Theater debut: film, Italy 1955-56.
Designed for major companies in ITA: Florence Maggio, Rome Opera. **Operas designed for these companies incl** VERDI: *Macbeth, Masnadieri*⋆. Exhibitions of stage designs & paintings Marlborough, Zurich 1972; Sestante, Milan 1973; Société Suisse du Théâtre, Berne. Teaches at art school. **Res:** Erta Canina 29, Florence, Italy.

MANSOURI, LOTFI; né Lotfollah Mansouri. Stages/produces opera & television. Also designs stage-lighting. American. Art Adv, Tehran Opera, Iran 1974-75; Gen Dir Designate Canadian Op Co, Toronto. Born 15 Jun 1929, Tehran, Iran. Wife Marjorie. One child. Studied: Univ of Calif, Dr Jan Popper, Los Angeles; Music Acad of West, Lotte Lehmann, Herbert Graf, Santa Barbara, CA; incl music, piano and voice. Operatic training as asst stage dir & singer at Music Acad of West 1959, Venice Fest 1960, Salzburg Fest 1961, 62. **Operatic debut:** *Tosca* Lós Angeles Grand Op 1959. Theater debut: Marymount Coll, Los Angeles 1957. Previous adm positions in opera: Chief Stage Director, Grand Théâtre de Genève, Switzerland.
Directed/produced opera for major companies in AUS: Vienna Volksoper; CAN: Vancouver; FR GER: Dortmund, Kassel, Nürnberg; HOL: Amsterdam; ITA: Genoa, Milan La Scala, Naples, Palermo, Rome Opera, Turin, Venice; SWI: Geneva, Zurich; USA: Chicago, Dallas, Houston, New Orleans, Philadelphia Lyric, San Diego, San Francisco, Santa Fe, Seattle. **Operas staged with these companies incl** AUBER: *Fra Diavolo;* BARTOK: *Bluebeard's Castle*⋆*;* BARBER: *Vanessa;* BELLINI: *Puritani*⋆*, Sonnambula;* BERG: *Lulu*⋆*, Wozzeck;* BERNSTEIN: *Trouble in Tahiti*⋆*;* BIZET: *Carmen*⋆*;* BOITO: *Mefistofele;* BRITTEN: *Albert Herring*⋆*, Turn of the Screw;* CHARPENTIER: *Louise;* DEBUSSY: *Pelléas et Mélisande;* DONIZETTI: *Anna Bolena*⋆*, Don Pasquale, Elisir*⋆*, Fille du régiment*⋆*, Lucia*⋆*, Lucrezia Borgia*⋆*;* GIORDANO: *Andrea Chénier;* GLUCK: *Orfeo ed Euridice;* GOUNOD: *Faust;* HINDEMITH: *Hin und zurück;* JANACEK: *Jenufa;* LEONCAVALLO: *Pagliacci;* MASCAGNI: *Cavalleria rusticana;* MASSENET: *Don Quichotte, Esclarmonde*⋆*, Manon*⋆*, Werther*⋆*;* MENOTTI: *Amahl, Consul, Medium, Old Maid and the Thief, Telephone;* MEYERBEER: *Africaine*⋆*, Huguenots*⋆*, Prophète;* MONTEVERDI: *Incoronazione di Poppea;* MOORE: *Gallantry;* MOZART: *Così fan tutte*⋆*, Entführung aus dem Serail, Idomeneo*⋆*, Nozze di Figaro, Zauberflöte;* MUSSORGSKY: *Boris Godunov;* NICOLAI: *Lustigen Weiber;*

OFFENBACH: *Contes d'Hoffmann*⋆*;* PONCHIELLI: *Gioconda;* POULENC: *Dialogues des Carmélites;* PUCCINI: *Bohème, Fanciulla del West, Gianni Schicchi, Butterfly, Manon Lescaut*⋆*, Suor Angelica, Tabarro, Turandot*⋆*;* RAVEL: *Heure espagnole*⋆*;* ROSSINI: *Barbiere di Siviglia, Cenerentola*⋆*, Italiana in Algeri*⋆*;* SAINT-SAENS: *Samson et Dalila*⋆*;* SMETANA: *Bartered Bride;* STRAUSS, J: *Fledermaus;* STRAUSS, R: *Ariadne auf Naxos*⋆*, Capriccio*⋆*, Elektra*⋆*, Rosenkavalier*⋆*, Salome;* TCHAIKOVSKY: *Pique Dame;* VERDI: *Aida, Don Carlo*⋆*, Ernani*⋆*, Falstaff*⋆*, Nabucco, Otello, Rigoletto, Simon Boccanegra, Traviata, Trovatore;* WAGNER: *Walküre;* WEILL: *Aufstieg und Fall der Stadt Mahagonny*⋆. Also BLOCH: *Macbeth*. **Operatic world premieres:** PASATIERI: *Black Widow* Seattle Op, WA 1972; SCHIBLER: *Blackwood & Co* Zurich Op, Switzerland 1962. Operatic Video — Zurich TV: *Schule der Frauen*. **Res:** 1261 Genolier/Vaud, Switzerland. Mgmt: CAM/USA.

MANUGUERRA, MATTEO. Lyric baritone. French. Born 5 Oct 1924, Tunisia. Wife Michèle Boutrois. One child. Studied: Umberto Landi; Inst Lirico Teatro Colón, Mo Mobilia, Buenos Aires. **Debut:** Valentin (*Faust*) Opéra de Lyon 1962. Previous occupations: cabinetmaker, house painter, truck driver.
Sang with major companies in ARG: Buenos Aires; AUS: Vienna Staatsoper; BEL: Liège; FRA: Bordeaux, Lyon, Marseille, Nancy, Nice, Paris, Toulouse; GRE: Athens National; FR GER: Frankfurt; ITA: Florence Comunale, Parma, Turin; SPA: Barcelona; SWI: Geneva Grand Théâtre; USA: Chicago Lyric, Cincinnati, Dallas Civic, Hartford, Miami, New Orleans, New York Met, Philadelphia Grand & Lyric, Seattle. **Roles with these companies incl** BECAUD: Sean (*Opéra d'Aran*); BERLIOZ: Balducci (*Benvenuto Cellini*), Choroebus (*Troyens*); BIZET: Escamillo (*Carmen*), Zurga (*Pêcheurs de perles*); DONIZETTI: Belcore (*Elisir*), Enrico (*Lucia*), Alfonso d'Este⋆ (*Lucrezia Borgia*); GIORDANO: Carlo Gérard (*Andrea Chénier*); GOUNOD: Ourrias (*Mireille*); MASCAGNI: Alfio (*Cavalleria rusticana*); MASSENET: Lescaut (*Manon*), Athanaël (*Thaïs*); MEYERBEER: Nelusco (*Africaine*); OFFENBACH: Coppélius etc (*Contes d'Hoffmann*); PONCHIELLI: Barnaba (*Gioconda*); PUCCINI: Marcello (*Bohème*), Gianni Schicchi, Michele (*Tabarro*), Scarpia (*Tosca*), Guglielmo Wulf⋆ (*Villi*); ROSSINI: Figaro (*Barbiere di Siviglia*); SAINT-SAENS: Grand prêtre (*Samson et Dalila*); VERDI: Amonasro⋆ (*Aida*), Renato (*Ballo in maschera*), Rodrigo (*Don Carlo*), Don Carlo⋆ (*Ernani*), Ford (*Falstaff*), Don Carlo⋆ (*Forza del destino*), Pagano (*Lombardi*), Miller (*Luisa Miller*), Nabucco, Iago (*Otello*), Rigoletto⋆, Simon Boccanegra, Germont (*Traviata*), Conte di Luna (*Trovatore*), Monforte⋆ (*Vespri*); ZANDONAI: Gianciotto (*Francesca da Rimini*). **Recorded for:** RCA, Pathé-Marconi. Video — ORTF Paris: Rigoletto, Ford (*Falstaff*). TV Argent: Conte di Luna (*Trovatore*). Gives recitals. Teaches voice. **Res:** Ave Clemenceau 9, Montpellier, France.

MARACINEANU, MICAELA. Coloratura & dramatic mezzo-soprano. Romanian. Resident mem:

Romanian Opera, Bucharest. Born 20 Mar 1942, Bucharest. Single. Studied. Consv, Bucharest. **Debut:** Dorabella (*Così fan tutte*) Romanian Opera 1971.

Sang with major companies in ROM: Bucharest. **Roles with these companies incl** BIZET: Carmen★; DEBUSSY: Geneviève★ (*Pelléas et Mélisande*); MUSSORGSKY: Marina★ (*Boris Godunov*); STRAUSS, J: Prinz Orlovsky★ (*Fledermaus*); VERDI: Eboli★ (*Don Carlo*). Also BRITTEN: Nancy (*Albert Herring*); on records only MOZART: Sesto (*Clemenza di Tito*). **World premieres:** BARBERIS: Kera Duduca, TV 1970. TV: Kera Duduca. Gives recitals. Appears with symphony orchestra. **Res:** 61 Popa Soare St, Bucharest 3, Romania. Mgmt: RIA/ROM.

MARANGONI, BRUNO LUIGI. Bass & basso-buffo. Italian. Resident mem: Teatro la Fenice, Venice; Teatro Carlo Felice, Genoa. Born 13 Apr 1935, Calto/Rovigo. Wife Franca Zapparoli, occupation formerly pianist. Six children. Studied: Mo Campogalliani, Brunelli, Ferraris, Bononi, Bagnoli, Wolf-Ferrari, Amendola, Venice. **Debut:** PICCINNI: Anselmo (*Molinarella*) La Fenice, Venice 1960. Previous occupations: coach for popular music. Awards: NHK Awd, Tokyo 1963.

Sang with major companies in FRA: Aix-en-Provence Fest; ITA: Genoa, Naples, Palermo, Rome Caracalla, Trieste, Turin, Venice, Verona Arena; POR: Lisbon; SPA: Barcelona; UK: Glyndebourne Fest; USA: Chicago; YUG: Belgrade. **Roles with these companies incl** BELLINI: Capellio (*Capuleti ed i Montecchi*), Rodolfo (*Sonnambula*); CIMAROSA: Geronimo (*Matrimonio segreto*); DONIZETTI: Dulcamara (*Elisir*); HANDEL: Giulio Cesare; MEYERBEER: Marcel (*Huguenots*); MOZART: Leporello (*Don Giovanni*), Osmin (*Entführung aus dem Serail*), Sarastro (*Zauberflöte*); PAISIELLO: Bartolo (*Barbiere di Siviglia*); PERGOLESI: Uberto (*Serva padrona*); PONCHIELLI: Alvise (*Gioconda*); PUCCINI: Colline (*Bohème*); ROSSINI: Dott Bartolo & Don Basilio (*Barbiere di Siviglia*), Tobias Mill (*Cambiale di matrimonio*), Conte Asdrubal (*Pietra del paragone*); VERDI: Ramfis (*Aida*), Grande Inquisitore (*Don Carlo*), Jacopo Loredano (*Due Foscari*), Silva (*Ernani*), Padre Guardiano (*Forza del destino*), Pagano (*Lombardi*), Banquo (*Macbeth*), Zaccaria (*Nabucco*), Fiesco (*Simon Boccanegra*), Procida (*Vespri*); WAGNER: Daland (*Fliegende Holländer*), Pogner (*Meistersinger*), Hunding (*Walküre*). Also PUCCINI: Geronte (*Manon Lescaut*); DONIZETTI: Raimondo (*Lucia*); HANDEL: Achilla (*Giulio Cesare*); PUCCINI: Timur (*Turandot*); MOZART: Commendatore (*Don Giovanni*); PIZZETTI: Egisto (*Clitennestra*); MALIPIERO: Creonte (*Mondi celesti*). **World premieres:** ROTA: Re (*Lampada di Aladino*) San Carlo Opera, Naples 1968. Video—RAI: (*Nozze di Figaro*); (*Don Carlo*); (*Elisir*); (*Trovatore*); (*Aida*); (*Guillaume Tell*); (*Pietra del paragone*). Gives recitals. Appears with symphony orchestra. Teaches voice. Coaches repertoire. On faculty of music school, Rome. **Res:** V di Mezzo 100, Castelmassa/Rome, Italy.

MARCOPOULOS, MATA; née Stamatia Zacharopoulou. Dramatic soprano. Greek. Born 23 Jul 1940, Athens. Husband Chris, occupation executive. Studied: Ntl Consv Athens; Mario Natarini, Naples; Tito Gobbi, Florence; Riccardo Moresco, New York. **Debut:** Tosca, National Opera of Greece 1960. Awards: First Prize with Honors, Natl Consv of Greece.

Sang with major companies in BUL: Sofia; GRE: Athens National; USA: Philadelphia Grand. **Roles with these companies incl** MASCAGNI: Santuzza★ (*Cavalleria rusticana*); PONCHIELLI: Gioconda★; PUCCINI: Cio-Cio-San★ (*Butterfly*), Giorgetta (*Tabarro*), Tosca★; VERDI: Leonora (*Forza del destino*), Lady Macbeth, Leonora★ (*Trovatore*). Gives recitals. Appears with symphony orchestra. **Res:** 100 W 57 St, New York, NY 10019, USA. Mgmt: SAM/USA.

MARELLI, MARCO ARTURO. Scenic and costume designer for opera, theater & ballet. Is a lighting designer, stage director; also a painter, illustrator & fashion designer. Swiss. Resident designer, Staatsoper Hamburg and at Atelier Theater, Zurich. Born 21 Aug 1949, Zurich. Single. Studied: Acad for Graphics and Design, Zurich; Akad Salzburg. Prof training: Volksoper & Staatsoper, Vienna 1971-72; Hamburg Staatsoper 1973; Salzburg Fest 1972. **Operatic debut:** *Lustige Witwe* Theater Hagen, FR Ger 1974. Theater debut: Atelier Theater, Zurich 1965. Previous occupation: graphic and poster designer. Awards: Honor Prize, City of Salzburg; Zurich Acad Prize.

Designed for major companies in AUS: Salzburg Fest, Vienna Staatsoper & Volksoper; FR GER: Hamburg. **Operas designed for these companies incl** CHERUBINI: *Medea★*; MASSENET: *Don Quichotte★*; MOZART: *Don Giovanni★, Idomeneo★, Zauberflöte*; RIMSKY-KORSAKOV: *Coq d'or★*; ROSSINI: *Barbiere di Siviglia★*; VERDI: *Aida★, Don Carlo★, Otello★, Trovatore★*. **Operatic world premieres:** BANCHIERI: *Barca* Staatsoper Hamburg 1975. Exhibitions of stage designs & costumes, Salzburg Mus 1973. **Res:** Hohlstr 333, CH-8004 Zurich, Switzerland and Johnsallee 7, D-2000 Hamburg 13, FR Ger.

MARENIC, VLADIMIR IVAN. Scenic and costume designer for opera, theater; specl in sets. Is a lighting designer, stage director; also a painter, illustrator & graphic designer. Yugoslavian. Resident designer, Opera of the National Theater, Belgrade and at the National Theater. Born 31 Aug 1921, Slavonska Pozega. Wife Slavija, occupation physician. One child. Studied: Acad of Applied Arts, Belgrade. **Operatic debut:** sets, *Pagliacci* Novi Sad 1950. Theater debut: Narodno pozoriste, Belgrade 1948. Awards: Golden Medal, Fourth Intl Triennale 1975; Sterija Prize 1957; October Prize 1966.

Designed for major companies in YUG: Belgrade. **Operas designed for these companies incl** BELLINI: *Capuleti ed i Montecchi, Norma★*; BIZET: *Carmen, Pêcheurs de perles★*; BORODIN: *Prince Igor★*; BRITTEN: *Albert Herring★*; DELIBES: *Lakmé*; DONIZETTI: *Don Pasquale, Elisir★, Lucia*; DVORAK: *Rusalka*; GERSHWIN: *Porgy and Bess*; GIORDANO: *Andrea Chénier★*; GLINKA: *Life for the Tsar★*; GLUCK: *Iphigénie en Tauride, Orfeo ed Euridice*; GOTOVAC: *Ero der Schelm★*; GOUNOD: *Faust, Roméo et Juliette;* MASCAGNI: *Cavalleria rusti-*

cana; MASSENET: *Manon, Werther;* ME-NOTTI: *Amelia al ballo;* MOZART: *Don Giovanni, Nozze di Figaro, Zauberflöte;* ORFF: *Carmina burana*;* PAISIELLO: *Barbiere di Siviglia;* PONCHIELLI: *Gioconda;* PROKOFIEV: *Love for Three Oranges;* PUCCINI: *Bohème, Butterfly, Tosca*, Turandot*;* ROSSINI: *Barbiere di Siviglia;* SMETANA: *Bartered Bride;* STRAUSS, J: *Fledermaus;* STRAVINSKY: *Oedipus Rex;* TCHAIKOVSKY: *Eugene Onegin, Pique Dame;* VERDI: *Aida, Ballo in maschera*, Falstaff, Nabucco, Rigoletto*, Traviata, Trovatore;* WAGNER: *Fliegende Holländer;* WEBER: *Freischütz.* **Operatic world premieres:** KALINSKI: *Clerk Comedies* Opera Belgrade 1972; LOGAR: *Conceited Pumpkin* Opera Belgrade 1973. Exhibitions of stage designs, paintings: 7 one-man shows; Novi Sad 1970, Belgrade 1971, Macerata 1972, The Hague 1973. Teaches at Univ of Belgrade. **Res:** Palmoticeva 31, Belgrade, Yugoslavia.

MARES, ROLF. German. Staatsoperndirektor, Hamburgische Staatsoper AG, Dammtorstr, 2 Hamburg 36, FR Ger 1974- . In charge of overall adm matters. Born 16 Jun 1930, Travemünde, Germany. Wife Brigitte. Two children. Previous occupations: Gvnmt Chief Inspector in Finance Dept. Form positions, primarily administrative: Chief Adm, Deutsches Schauspielhaus Hamburg 1964-66; Adm Dir, Thalia Theater Hamburg 1966-73. Mem of Deutscher Bühnenverein: Tarifausschuss & Verwaltungsrat.

MARESCA, BENITO. Dramatic tenor & lirico spinto. Brazilian. Born 14 Jul 1940, São Paulo, Brazil. Wife Isabel, occupation pianist. One child. Studied: Marcel Klass, São Paulo. **Debut:** Turiddu (*Cavalleria rusticana*) São Paulo, Brazil 1965.
Sang with major companies in AUS: Graz, Vienna Staatsoper; BRA: Rio de Janeiro; FR GER: Berlin Deutsche Oper, Frankfurt, Mannheim, Munich Staatsoper, Stuttgart; ITA: Naples, Palermo. **Roles with these companies incl** BELLINI: Pollione* (*Norma*); BIZET: Don José (*Carmen*); DONIZETTI: Nemorino (*Elisir*), Edgardo* (*Lucia*); GOMES: Fernando (*Colombo*), Paolo (*Fosca*); LEONCAVALLO: Canio* (*Pagliacci*); MASCAGNI: Turiddu* (*Cavalleria rusticana*); OFFENBACH: Hoffmann; PUCCINI: Rodolfo* (*Bohème*), Pinkerton* (*Butterfly*), Cavaradossi* (*Tosca*), Calaf* (*Turandot*); VERDI: Radames (*Aida*), Foresto* (*Attila*), Riccardo (*Ballo in maschera*), Don Carlo, Don Alvaro* (*Forza del destino*), Duca di Mantova* (*Rigoletto*), Alfredo* (*Traviata*), Manrico* (*Trovatore*), Arrigo (*Vespri*). Also GOMES: Pery* (*Guarany*), Americo* (*Schiavo*). Appears with symphony orchestra. **Res:** rua Inacio Arruda 206, São Paulo, Brazil. **Mgmt:** SMD/FRG.

MARIANI, FIORELLA. Scenic and costume designer for opera, theater, film. Italian. Born 27 Apr 1933, Rome. Single. Studied: Accad di Belle Arti, Rome. Prof training: as asst to Lila de Nobili & Franco Zeffirelli. **Operatic debut:** *Giovedi grasso* Music Fest Siena 1960. Theater debut: Spoleto Fest 1960. Previous adm positions in opera; Head of Prod Dept, Spoleto Fest 1959-70.

Designed for major companies in FRA: Orange Fest; HOL: Amsterdam; ITA: Florence Maggio & Comunale, Palermo, Rome Opera, Spoleto Fest, Venice. **Operas designed for these companies incl** BELLINI: *Norma*, Sonnambula;* HENZE: *Elegy for Young Lovers*;* MENOTTI: *Amelia al ballo*;* MEYERBEER: *Africaine*;* MONTEVERDI: *Combattimento di Tancredi;* MOZART: *Don Giovanni, Nozze di Figaro;* PAISIELLO: *Barbiere di Siviglia;* PUCCINI: *Manon Lescaut;* ROSSINI: *Cambiale di matrimonio, Signor Bruschino;* STRAUSS, R: *Salome*;* VERDI: *Ballo in maschera*, Luisa Miller.* Operatic Video—TV, Orange Fest: *Norma.* **Res:** V Panama 16, 00198 Rome, Italy.

MARICONDA, VALERIA. Coloratura soprano. Italian. Born 29 Sep 1939, Siena. Husband Dino Asciolla, occupation musician. Studied: Maria Consoli, Giorgio Favaretto, Rome. **Debut:** Xenia (*Boris Godunov*) Rome Opera 1962. Previous occupations: pianist. Awards: Prize Accad Chigiana, Siena 1960.
Sang with major companies in ARG: Buenos Aires; CZE: Prague National; FRA: Paris; FR GER: Stuttgart; ITA: Florence Comunale, Milan La Scala, Naples, Palermo, Rome Opera, Spoleto Fest, Trieste, Turin; MON: Monte Carlo; USSR: Leningrad Kirov, Moscow Bolshoi. **Roles with these companies incl** BELLINI: Amina (*Sonnambula*); DONIZETTI: Norina (*Don Pasquale*), Adina (*Elisir*); GALUPPI: Eugenia (*Filosofo di campagna*); GLUCK: Euridice; MONTEVERDI: Euridice (*Favola d'Orfeo*); MOZART: Zerlina (*Don Giovanni*), Blondchen (*Entführung aus dem Serail*), Violante (*Finta giardiniera*); PAISIELLO: Rosina (*Barbiere di Siviglia*), Lisetta (*Re Teodoro in Venezia*); PERGOLESI: Serpina (*Serva padrona*); PUCCINI: Musetta (*Bohème*), Lauretta (*Gianni Schicchi*); ROSSINI: Rosina* (*Barbiere di Siviglia*), Fanny* (*Cambiale di matrimonio*), Elvira* (*Italiana in Algeri*), Giulia (*Scala di seta*), Sofia (*Signor Bruschino*), Fiorilla* (*Turco in Italia*); VERDI: Oscar* (*Ballo in maschera*). Also ROSSELLINI: Caterina (*Sguardo dal ponte*); MOZART: Papagena* (*Zauberflöte*); GLUCK: Amore* (*Paride e Elena*). **World premieres:** ROSSELLINI: (*Avventuriero*) Monte Carlo Opera 1968. Video/Film: (*Orfeo*); (*Buona figliola*); (*Elisir*); (*Barbiere*); (*Bruschino*); (*Esels Schatten*). Gives recitals. Appears with symphony orchestra. **Res:** V Montanelli 11a, Rome, Italy.

MARILLIER, JACQUES. Scenic and costume designer for opera, theater. Is also a painter, illustrator & architect. French. Resident designer, Théâtre de l'Athénée, Paris. Wife Marie Kant, occupation costume designer for theater. Three children. Studied: Ecole Ntl Supér des Arts décoratifs, Paris. **Operatic debut:** sets, *Nozze di Figaro* Liège, Belgium 1960. Theater debut: Enghien-Casino, France 1950.
Designed for major companies in FRA: Bordeaux, Strasbourg. **Operas designed for these companies incl** BOIELDIEU: *Dame blanche*;* DONIZETTI: *Lucia;* MOZART: *Nozze di Figaro;* PUCCINI: *Manon Lescaut, Tosca, Turandot*;* RAVEL: *Heure espagnole;* VERDI: *Forza del destino, Trovatore.* Exhibitions of paintings & graphics; Dominique Gal, Paris 1961. **Res:** 20 rue de Thorigny, Paris 3, France.

MARINACCI, GLORIA; née Cutsforth. Lyric coloratura soprano. American. Born 12 June 1938, Tacoma, WA, USA. Single. Studied: Evelene Calbreath, Gibner King, Ivan Rasmussen, Luigi Ricci. **Debut:** Musetta (*Bohème*) Portland Opera 1969. Awards: San Francisco Opera Aud; Met Op Ntl Counc Aud, Reg Winner; Petri Awd.

Sang with major companies in CAN: Vancouver; USA: Chicago, Cincinnati, Hawaii, Omaha, Portland, Seattle. **Roles with these companies incl** DONIZETTI: Norina★ (*Don Pasquale*), Lucia★; GOUNOD: Marguerite★ (*Faust*); LEONCAVALLO: Nedda★ (*Pagliacci*); MASSENET: Manon★; MENOTTI: Lucy★ (*Telephone*); MOZART: Despina★ (*Così fan tutte*), Zerlina★ (*Don Giovanni*), Konstanze★ (*Entführung aus dem Serail*), Susanna★ (*Nozze di Figaro*), Pamina★ (*Zauberflöte*); OFFENBACH: Olympia★ (*Contes d'Hoffmann*); ORFF: Solo★ (*Carmina burana*); PASATIERI: Berta (*Black Widow*); PERGOLESI: Serpina (*Serva padrona*); POULENC: La femme (*Voix humaine*); PUCCINI: Mimi & Musetta★ (*Bohème*), Lauretta★ (*Gianni Schicchi*), Lisette★ (*Rondine*), Liù (*Turandot*); ROSSINI: Rosina★ (*Barbiere di Siviglia*); STRAUSS, J: Adele★ (*Fledermaus*); VERDI: Oscar★ (*Ballo in maschera*), Gilda★ (*Rigoletto*), Violetta★ (*Traviata*); WARD: Abigail (*Crucible*). Gives recitals. Appears with symphony orchestra. Teaches voice. Coaches repertoire. **Res:** Rome, Italy and Portland, OR, USA. Mgmt: AOD/USA; DSP/USA.

MARKUN, MARTIN. Swiss. Chief Prgm Dir of Opera (Oberspielleiter), Basler Theater, Basel, Switzerland. In charge of artistic policy, of mus matters, and is also a stage dir/prod. Born 4 Jul 1942, Zurich. Single. Studied: Intl Opernstudio Zurich; Musikakad Zurich. Plays the piano, bassoon. Previous positions, primarily musical & theatrical: Res Stge Dir, Städtische Bühnen Heidelberg, FR Ger 1968-69; Chief Prgm Dir, Opernhaus Zurich, Switzerland 1969-72. In present position since 1972. **Res:** Mühleg 26, Biel-Benken, Switzerland.

MARONEK, JAMES. Scenic designer for opera, theater, television. Is a lighting designer. American. Born 4 Dec 1931, Milwaukee, WI. Wife Carole, occupation drama teacher. Two sons, one daughter. Studied: Goodman School of Drama; Art Inst of Chicago, Otto Benesch; Lyric Opera of Chicago. **Operatic debut:** *Medium & Telephone* Weseley Opera Guild, Chicago 1950. Theater debut: Peninsula Players, Door County, USA 1950. Awards: Joseph Jefferson Awd, best scenic design, Chicago 1973-74.

Designed for major companies in USA: Cincinnati. **Operas designed for these companies incl** DONIZETTI: *Don Pasquale;* MENOTTI: *Medium, Telephone;* MOZART: *Entführung aus dem Serail, Nozze di Figaro★;* PUCCINI: *Tosca;* RAVEL: *Heure espagnole;* VAUGHAN WILLIAMS: *Riders to the Sea;* WEILL: *Dreigroschenoper★*. Exhibitions of stage designs Hull House Chicago 1964; Goodman Theater Chicago 1965; NY Libr/Museum of Perf Arts, Lincoln Center: Contemp Stage Design—USA 1974-75; Prague Quadrennial, CSSR 1975. Teaches at Goodman School of Drama, Chicago. **Res:** 2113 Park Lane, Highland Pk, IL 60035, USA. Mgmt: USC/USA.

MAROVA, LIBUSE. Dramatic mezzo-soprano. Czechoslovakian. Resident mem: National Theater, Prague. Born 24 Dec 1943, Susice, CSR. Husband Norbert Snítil, occupation opera dir. Studied: Music Acad, Premysl Kocí, Prague; Josef Frydl; Stepánka Stepánová; Michael Zabejda. **Debut:** Azucena (*Trovatore*) Tyl Theater, Plzen, CSSR 1965.

Sang with major companies in BEL: Brussels; CZE: Prague National; FRA: Bordeaux; GER DR: Berlin Komische Oper; NOR: Oslo; UK: Edinburgh Fest. **Roles with these companies incl** BIZET: Carmen★; DVORAK: Kate (*Devil and Kate*), Jezibaba★ (*Rusalka*); MARTINU: Nancy★ (*Comedy on the Bridge*); MASSENET: Dulcinée★ (*Don Quichotte*); MOZART: Cherubino★ (*Nozze di Figaro*); MUSSORGSKY: Marina★ (*Boris Godunov*); PROKOFIEV: Helene★ (*War and Peace*); PUCCINI: Suzuki★ (*Butterfly*); SMETANA: Roza★ (*Secret*); STRAVINSKY: Baba the Turk★ (*Rake's Progress*); TCHAIKOVSKY: Olga★ (*Eugene Onegin*); VERDI: Ulrica★ (*Ballo in maschera*), Eboli★ (*Don Carlo*), Azucena (*Trovatore*); WAGNER: Fricka★ (*Walküre*). Also SMETANA: Závis★ (*Devil's Wall*); TCHAIKOVSKY: Pauline★ (*Pique Dame*); FIBICH: Vlasta★ (*Sarka*); PROKOFIEV: Sonia★ (*War and Peace*); DVORAK: Marfa (*Dimitrij*). Recorded for: Supraphon. Gives recitals. Appears with symphony orchestra. **Res:** Trída SNB 9, Prague 10, CSSR. Mgmt: PRG/CZE.

MARQUES, ZACCARIA; né Zacharias Cyrilo Marques. Lyric & spinto tenor. Brazilian. Born 4 Nov 1937, Minas Gerais, Brazil. Wife Eunice Facin, occupation singer. One child. Studied: Domenico Silvestro. **Debut:** Rodolfo (*Bohème*) Rio de Janeiro 1958. Awards: Best Tenor, Acad of Music, Brazil 1972; Best Tenor, Verdi Socy of Music, Brazil 1973.

Sang with major companies in ARG: Buenos Aires; BRA: Rio de Janeiro; ITA: Palermo. **Roles with these companies incl** BIZET: Don José★ (*Carmen*); DONIZETTI: Fernand (*Favorite*), Edgardo (*Lucia*); GOMES: Paolo★ (*Fosca*); LEONCAVALLO: Canio★ (*Pagliacci*); MASCAGNI: Turiddu★ (*Cavalleria rusticana*); MASSENET: Werther; PUCCINI: Rodolfo★ (*Bohème*), Rinuccio (*Gianni Schicchi*), Pinkerton★ (*Butterfly*), Cavaradossi (*Tosca*); RIMSKY-KORSAKOV: Astrologue★ (*Coq d'or*); STRAUSS, R: Ein Sänger (*Rosenkavalier*); VERDI: Radames (*Aida*), Don Carlo★, Fenton (*Falstaff*), Otello★, Duca di Mantova (*Rigoletto*), Alfredo (*Traviata*), Manrico★ (*Trovatore*). Also GOMES: Guarany★, Conte Americo★ (*Schiavo*); MASCAGNI: Osaka (*Iris*); ROCCA: Hanan (*Dibuk*). Video/Film: Paolo (*Fosca*). Gives recitals. Appears with symphony orchestra. **Res:** Augusto Severo 202, Rio de Janeiro, Brazil. Mgmt: QUE/SPA.

MARSEE, SUSANNE; née Susan Irene Dowell. Lyric coloratura mezzo-soprano. American. Resident mem: New York City Opera. Born 26 Nov 1944, San Diego, CA, USA. Husband Brett Hamilton, occupation singer; Dr in educational psychology. Studied: Nadine Conner, CA, USA; Univ of Los Angeles; Richard Fredricks, New York. **Debut:** Sara (*Roberto Devereux*) New York City Opera 1970. Previous occupations: elem school teacher. Awards: Rockefeller Grant; Corbett Fndt Grant; Second Place, Met Op Ntl Counc Aud, reg finalist.

Sang with major companies in MEX: Mexico City; USA: Cincinnati, Fort Worth, Houston, Memphis, Milwaukee Florentine, New York City Opera, Omaha, Philadelphia Lyric, San Diego. Roles with these companies incl DONIZETTI: Giovanna★ (*Anna Bolena*), Maffio Orsini★ (*Lucrezia Borgia*), Sara★ (*Roberto Devereux* ; GOUNOD: Siebel★ (*Faust*); HENZE: Lucile★ (*Rachel, la Cubana*); HUMPERDINCK: Hänsel★; MASSENET: Dulcinée★ (*Don Quichotte*); MEYERBEER: Urbain★ (*Huguenots*); MOZART: Dorabella★ (*Così fan tutte*), Cherubino★ (*Nozze di Figaro*); OFFENBACH: Giulietta★ (*Contes d'Hoffmann*), Périchole★; ROSSINI: Rosina★ (*Barbiere di Siviglia*), Angelina★ (*Cenerentola*); STRAUSS, R: Komponist★ (*Ariadne auf Naxos*), Octavian★ (*Rosenkavalier*); VERDI: Preziosilla★ (*Forza del destino*). Also HANDEL: Sesto (*Giulio Cesare*); OFFENBACH: Nicklausse (*Contes d'Hoffmann*). Recorded for: ABC/Dunhill. Video—NET TV: Lucile (*Rachel, la Cubana*). Gives recitals. Appears with symphony orchestra. Res: 659 W 162 St, New York, NY 10032, USA. Mgmt: HUR/USA; CST/UK.

MARSH, JANE. Dramatic coloratura soprano & spinto soprano. American. Resident mem: Deutsche Oper am Rhein, Düsseldorf. Born 25 Jun 1945, San Francisco. Single. Studied: Oberlin Coll, Ellen Repp, O; Lili Wexberg, Otto Guth, New York; Merola Training Prgr, San Francisco. Debut: Desdemona (*Otello*) Spoleto Fest, Italy 1965. Awards: Met Op Ntl Counc Aud; M B Rockefeller grant; Gold Handel Medallion of New York City; Merit Awd, *Mademoiselle* magazine; Gold Medal, First Prize Tchaikovsky Compt, Moscow USSR.

Sang with major companies in AUS: Salzburg Fest; CZE: Prague National; FR GER: Düsseldorf-Duisburg, Essen, Hamburg; ITA: Naples, Parma, Spoleto, Trieste; S AFR: Johannesburg; USSR: Moscow Bolshoi; USA: Pittsburgh, San Antonio, San Francisco Opera. Roles with these companies incl BIZET: Micaëla (*Carmen*); HANDEL: Achilles★ (*Deidamia*); MOZART: Vitellia★‡ (*Clemenza di Tito*), Fiordiligi★ (*Così fan tutte*), Donna Elvira★ (*Don Giovanni*), Konstanze★‡ (*Entführung aus dem Serail*), Ismene★ (*Mitridate, re di Ponto*), Zaïde★, Pamina★ & Königin der Nacht★ (*Zauberflöte*); OFFENBACH: Antonia★ (*Contes d'Hoffmann*); PUCCINI: Mimi★ & Musetta★ (*Bohème*), Liù★ (*Turandot*); RIMSKY-KORSAKOV: Fevronia★‡ (*Invisible City of Kitezh*); STRAUSS, R: Daphne★; STRAVINSKY: Anne Trulove★ (*Rake's Progress*); TCHAIKOVSKY: Tatiana★ (*Eugene Onegin*); VERDI: Desdemona (*Otello*), Gilda (*Rigoletto*), Violetta★(*Traviata*). Also DONIZETTI: Lucia di Lammermoor; PAER: Leonora. Only on records TCHAIKOVSKY: Agnes (*Maid of Orleans*); GLUCK: Armide. World premieres: ORFF: Sybille (*De Temporum fine comedia*) Salzburg Fest 1973. Recorded for: DG, Polydor, RAI, VARA. Gives recitals. Appears with symphony orchestra. Res: Vienna, Austria. Mgmt: CAM/USA; AIM/UK.

MARTELLI, EDITH. Lyric soprano. Italian. Born 10 Apr 1937, Palvareto/Cremona, Italy. Husband F Guarnieri, occupation orch conductor. One child. Studied: Consv, Parma and Milan; Mo Ettore Campogalliani. Debut: Musica (*Favola d'Orfeo*) Piccola Scala, Milan.

Sang with major companies in AUS: Salzburg Fest; CAN: Montreal/Quebec; FRA: Marseille, Nice, Rouen; FR GER: Munich Staatsoper; GER DR: Berlin Staatsoper; HOL: Amsterdam; ITA: Florence Maggio & Comunale, Genoa, Milan La Scala, Naples, Palermo, Parma, Rome Opera, Spoleto Fest, Trieste, Turin, Venice; MEX: Mexico City; MON: Monte Carlo; SPA: Barcelona; UK: Edinburgh Fest; USA: Chicago. Roles with these companies incl AUBER: Zerlina (*Fra Diavolo*); BEETHOVEN: Marzelline (*Fidelio*); BELLINI: Giulietta (*Capuleti ed i Montecchi*); BIBALO: Anni (*Lächeln am Fuss der Leiter*); BIZET: Micaëla (*Carmen*); DONIZETTI: Serafina★ (*Campanello*), Norina★ (*Don Pasquale*), Adina (*Elisir*), Rita; GOUNOD: Marguerite (*Faust*); HUMPERDINCK: Gretel; MASSENET: Manon, Sophie (*Werther*); MENOTTI: Amelia (*Amelia al ballo*), Monica (*Medium*); MONTEVERDI: Clorinda (*Combattimento di Tancredi*); MOZART: Despina★ (*Così fan tutte*), Violante★ & Serpetta★ (*Finta giardiniera*), Susanna (*Nozze di Figaro*); ORFF: Solo (*Carmina burana*); PERAGALLO: Ornella (*Gita in campagna*); PERGOLESI: Serpina (*Serva padrona*); POULENC: Blanche (*Dialogues des Carmélites*); PUCCINI: Mimi & Musetta★ (*Bohème*), Lauretta★ (*Gianni Schicchi*), Magda★ (*Rondine*), Liù (*Turandot*); ROSSINI: Ninetta (*Gazza ladra*), Elvira (*Italiana in Algeri*), Sofia★ (*Signor Bruschino*), Fiorilla (*Turco in Italia*); STRAUSS, J: Adele (*Fledermaus*); STRAUSS, R: Komponist (*Ariadne auf Naxos*); VERDI: Oscar (*Ballo in maschera*), Nannetta (*Falstaff*), Desdemona (*Otello*), Gilda (*Rigoletto*), Violetta (*Traviata*); WOLF-FERRARI: Lucieta (*Quattro rusteghi*), Susanna (*Segreto di Susanna*). Also HAYDN: Grilletta (*Speziale*); ROTA: Anaïde (*Cappello di paglia di Firenze*). Recorded for: Ricordi, Cetra. Gives recitals. Appears with symphony orchestra. Res: V Archimede 129, Milan, Italy.

MARTÌ, BERNABÉ. Dramatic tenor. Spanish. Wife Montserrat Caballé, occupation opera singer. Studied: Consv Real de Musica, Madrid; Accad di S Cecilia, Rome. Debut: Deutsche Oper am Rhein, Düsseldorf-Duisburg.

Sang with major companies in ARG: Buenos Aires; BEL: Brussels; CAN: Vancouver; FRA: Marseille, Toulouse; FR GER: Cologne, Düsseldorf-Duisburg, Frankfurt, Hannover, Karlsruhe, Stuttgart; MEX: Mexico City; SPA: Barcelona; UK: Edinburgh Fest; USA: Baltimore, Chicago, Cincinnati, Hartford, Miami, New Orleans, New York City Opera, Philadelphia Lyric, Pittsburgh, San Antonio; et al. Roles with these companies incl BELLINI: Pollione (*Norma*), Gualtiero‡ (*Pirata*); BIZET: Don José (*Carmen*); GOUNOD: Faust; LEONCAVALLO: Canio (*Pagliacci*); PUCCINI: Rodolfo (*Bohème*), Pinkerton (*Butterfly*), Des Grieux (*Manon Lescaut*), Luigi (*Tabarro*), Cavaradossi (*Tosca*), Calaf (*Turandot*); STRAUSS, R: Ein Sänger (*Rosenkavalier*);

VERDI: Radames (*Aida*), Riccardo (*Ballo in maschera*), Duca di Mantova (*Rigoletto*), Gabriele (*Simon Boccanegra*), Alfredo (*Traviata*), Manrico (*Trovatore*); et al. Also VERDI: Macduff (*Macbeth*). Recorded for: Angel. Mgmt: CAM/USA.

MARTIKKE, SIGRID. Lyric soprano. Austrian. Resident mem: Vienna Volksoper. Born 8 Oct 1936, Magdeburg, Germany. Divorced. Studied: Rosenberg-Taubenreuther, Berlin; Karg-Bebenburg, Vienna. **Debut:** Contessa (*Nozze di Figaro*) Opernhaus Graz 1971. Previous occupations: dental assistant.
    Sang with major companies in AUS: Graz, Vienna Staatsoper & Volksoper; BEL: Brussels; FR GER: Hamburg, Munich Staatsoper, Wiesbaden; GER DR: Berlin Komische Oper; ISR: Tel Aviv; MON: Monte Carlo; SPA: Majorca; SWI: Basel, Zurich; USA: Omaha. **Roles with these companies incl** MOZART: Contessa★ (*Nozze di Figaro*), Pamina★ (*Zauberflöte*); NICOLAI: Frau Fluth★ (*Lustigen Weiber*); OFFENBACH: Antonia (*Contes d'Hoffmann*); PUCCINI: Musetta★ (*Bohème*); SMETANA: Marie★ (*Bartered Bride*); STRAUSS, J: Rosalinde★ (*Fledermaus*). **World premieres:** RUBIN: Nettchen (*Kleider machen Leute*) Vienna Volksoper 1973. Gives recitals. Appears with symphony orchestra. **Res:** Hermineng 2-4, A-3420 Kritzendorf, Austria. Mgmt: RAB/AUS.

MARTIN, JANIS. Spinto (Jugendlich Dramatische). American. Resident mem: Deutsche Oper, Berlin, FR Ger. Born 16 Aug 1939, Sacramento, CA. Husband Gerhard Hellwig, occupation Intendant, Radio Symph Orch, W Berlin. One child. Studied: Julia Monroe, Sacramento, CA; Lili Wexberg, Otto Guth, New York. **Debut:** Annina (*Traviata*) San Francisco Opera 1960. Awards: Met Op Ntl Counc Aud 1962, 3 yr contract and cash prize.
    Sang with major companies in AUS: Vienna Staatsoper; FRA: Bordeaux, Lyon, Nancy, Nice, Paris, Rouen; FR GER: Bayreuth Fest, Berlin Deutsche Oper, Cologne, Düsseldorf-Duisburg, Frankfurt, Hamburg, Karlsruhe, Mannheim, Munich Staatsoper, Nürnberg, Stuttgart; HOL: Amsterdam; ITA: Milan La Scala; MON: Monte Carlo; SWI: Zurich; UK: London Royal; USA: Chicago, New York Met & City Opera, Philadelphia Grand, San Diego, San Francisco Opera & Spring Opera. **Roles with these companies incl** BARTOK: Judith★ (*Bluebeard's Castle*); BERG: Marie★ (*Wozzeck*); BORODIN: Jaroslavna (*Prince Igor*); BRITTEN: Mrs Grose (*Turn of the Screw*); MOZART: Donna Elvira★ (*Don Giovanni*), Contessa★ & Cherubino (*Nozze di Figaro*); MUSSORGSKY: Marina★ (*Boris Godunov*); OFFENBACH: Giulietta (*Contes d'Hoffmann*); PUCCINI: Tosca★; STRAUSS, R: Ariadne★ & Komponist★ (*Ariadne auf Naxos*), Octavian (*Rosenkavalier*); WAGNER: Senta★ (*Fliegende Holländer*), Eva★ (*Meistersinger*), Sieglinde★ (*Walküre*), Gutrune★ (*Götterdämmerung*), Venus★ (*Tannhäuser*), Brangäne★ (*Tristan und Isolde*), Kundry★ (*Parsifal*). Gives recitals. Appears with symphony orchestra. **Res:** Budapester Str 43, 1 Berlin 30, FR Ger. Mgmt: SLZ/FRG.

MARTINOIU, VASILE CONSTANTIN. Dramatic baritone. Romanian. Resident mem: Romanian Opera, Bucharest. Born 2 Apr 1934, Tirgu-Jiu. Wife Sanda. Studied: Prof Carlo Tagliabue, Italy. **Debut:** Conte di Luna (*Trovatore*) Musical Theater, Galati 1959. Awards: Awd, Erkel Cont Budapest 1966; Maria Canals, Barcelona 1966; Tchaikovsky Cont, Moscow 1966; Voci Verdiane, Busseto 1968.
    Sang with major companies in BEL: Liège; BUL: Sofia; CZE: Prague National; FR GER: Stuttgart; GER DR: Berlin Komische Oper, Dresden, Leipzig; HUN: Budapest; ITA: Parma; POL: Warsaw; ROM: Bucharest; USA: Baltimore, New York City Opera, Philadelphia Grand, Washington DC; YUG: Belgrade. **Roles with these companies incl** BIZET: Escamillo★ (*Carmen*); LEONCAVALLO: Tonio★ (*Pagliacci*); MASCAGNI: Alfio (*Cavalleria rusticana*); PUCCINI: Marcello★ (*Bohème*), Sharpless★ (*Butterfly*), Scarpia★ (*Tosca*); ROSSINI: Figaro★ (*Barbiere di Siviglia*); VERDI: Amonasro★ (*Aida*), Egberto (*Aroldo/Stiffelio*), Renato★ (*Ballo in maschera*), Rodrigo★ (*Don Carlo*), Don Carlo★ (*Forza del destino*), Rigoletto★, Germont★ (*Traviata*), Conte di Luna★ (*Trovatore*). **World premieres:** LERESCU: Col Dobre (*Ecaterina Teodoroiu*) Romanian Opera 1971. Gives recitals. Appears with symphony orchestra. **Res:** 3 Simonide St, Bucharest 6, Romania. Mgmt: RIA/ROM; DSP/USA.

MARTINUCCI, NICOLA. Lyric & dramatic tenor. Italian. Born 28 Mar 1941, Taranto, Italy. Wife Marcellina Scognamiglio. Studied: Ma Sara Sforni Corti. **Debut:** Manrico (*Trovatore*) As Li Co, Milan 1966.
    Sang with major companies in AUS: Graz; FR GER: Düsseldorf-Duisburg; ITA: Florence Maggio & Comunale, Milan La Scala, Venice. **Roles with these companies incl** BIZET: Don José★ (*Carmen*); LEONCAVALLO: Canio★ (*Pagliacci*); MASCAGNI: Turiddu★ (*Cavalleria rusticana*); PUCCINI: Pinkerton★ (*Butterfly*), Cavaradossi★ (*Tosca*), Calaf★ (*Turandot*); VERDI: Radames★ (*Aida*), Foresto★ (*Attila*), Riccardo★ (*Ballo in maschera*), Corrado (*Corsaro*), Don Alvaro★ (*Forza del destino*), Duca di Mantova (*Rigoletto*), Gabriele★ (*Simon Boccanegra*), Manrico★ (*Trovatore*). Also SPONTINI: Filippo★ (*Agnese di Hohenstaufen*). Recorded for: EMI. **Res:** V Tuliparu 3, Milan, Italy. Mgmt: VLD/AUS.

MARTON, EVA; née Eva Heinrich. Spinto. Hungarian. Resident mem: Städtische Oper, Frankfurt/Main; Staatsoper, Vienna. Born 18 Jun 1943, Budapest. Husband Dr Zoltán, occupation surgeon. Two children. Studied: Franz Liszt Music Acad, Budapest. **Debut:** Reine de Schemakan (*Coq d'or*) Budapest Opera 1968.
    Sang with major companies in AUS: Vienna Staatsoper; BEL: Brussels; FRA: Paris; FR GER: Berlin Deutsche Oper, Bielefeld, Frankfurt, Munich Staatsoper; HUN: Budapest; ITA: Florence Maggio; USSR: Moscow Bolshoi. **Roles with these companies incl** BEETHOVEN: Leonore (*Fidelio*); GIORDANO: Maddalena (*Andrea Chénier*); HANDEL: Rodelinda; KODALY: Marie Louise (*Háry János*); MOZART: Donna Anna (*Don Giovanni*), Contessa (*Nozze di Figaro*); PUCCINI: Manon Lescaut, Tosca; PURCELL: Dido; RIMSKY-KORSAKOV: Reine de Schemakan (*Coq d'or*); ROSSINI: Mathilde (*Guillaume Tell*);

STRAUSS, J: Rosalinde (*Fledermaus*); STRAUSS, R: Kaiserin (*Frau ohne Schatten*); TCHAIKOVSKY: Tatiana (*Eugene Onegin*); VERDI: Odabella (*Attila*), Elisabetta (*Don Carlo*), Alice Ford (*Falstaff*), Leonora (*Forza del destino*), Amelia (*Simon Boccanegra*); WAGNER: Eva (*Meistersinger*). Gives recitals. Appears with symphony orchestra. **Res:** Im Sachsenlager 13, 6000 Frankfurt/Main 1, FR Ger. Mgmt: ICM/HUN.

MARX, PETER HELMUT. Conductor of opera and symphony; composer. German. Resident Cond, Städtische Bühnen Bielefeld, FR Ger. Born 10 Nov 1936, Munich. Wife Elsa. One child. Studied: State Acads in Berlin, Stuttgart, Munich; Ernest Bour; incl piano, viola, trombone. Operatic training as repetiteur & chorus master at Opera House, Passau, FR Ger 1964-67. **Operatic debut:** *Nozze di Figaro* Städtisches Theater, Passau 1965. Symphonic debut: Schwäbisches Symph Orch Reutlingen, FR Ger 1966. Previous adm positions in opera: Mus Dir, Südostbayerisches Städtetheater, Passau 1965-67.

Conducted with major companies in FR GER: Bielefeld, Krefeld. **Operas with these companies incl** AUBER: *Fra Diavolo★*; BEETHOVEN: *Fidelio★*; BIZET: *Carmen★*; CIMAROSA: *Matrimonio segreto★*; DONIZETTI: *Don Pasquale*; FLOTOW: *Martha*; HUMPERDINCK: *Hänsel und Gretel, Königskinder*; LORTZING: *Waffenschmied, Wildschütz★, Zar und Zimmermann*; MOZART: *Così fan tutte★, Entführung aus dem Serail, Finta giardiniera, Nozze di Figaro*; OFFENBACH: *Périchole★*; ORFF: *Kluge★*; PUCCINI: *Bohème★, Butterfly★, Tosca★*; ROSSINI: *Barbiere di Siviglia*; STRAUSS, J: *Fledermaus*; VERDI: *Forza del destino, Rigoletto★, Traviata*; WAGNER: *Fliegende Holländer★*; WEBER: *Freischütz★*. Also BLACHER: *Flut*; MAYR: *Commedianti★*. **Res:** Hofacker 10, D-48 Bielefeld, FR Ger.

MÄRZENDORFER, ERNST. Conductor of opera and symphony. Austrian. Resident Cond, Staatsoper, Vienna. Born 26 May 1921, Oberndorf, Salzburg. Wife Lynne Forrester, occupation actress. Studied: Mozarteum, Clemens Krauss, Salzburg; incl piano, violin, viola. Plays the piano. Operatic training as repetiteur, asst cond & chorus master at Vereinigte Bühnen, Graz 1940-50; Teatro Colón, Buenos Aires 1951-52. **Operatic debut:** Vereinigte Bühnen, Graz 1942. Symphonic debut: Phil Orch, Graz 1945. Awards: Prof, President of Austrian Republic.

Conducted with major companies in ARG: Buenos Aires; AUS: Bregenz Fest, Graz, Salzburg Fest, Vienna Staatsoper & Volksoper; DEN: Copenhagen; FR GER: Berlin Deutsche Oper, Darmstadt, Dortmund, Frankfurt, Hamburg; GER DR: Berlin Staatsoper, Dresden; ITA: Naples, Palermo, Rome Opera, Trieste; ROM: Bucharest; USA: New York City Opera, Philadelphia Lyric; YUG: Dubrovnik, Zagreb. **Operas with these companies incl** ADAM: *Si j'étais roi‡*; BARTOK: *Bluebeard's Castle*; BEETHOVEN: *Fidelio★*; BERG: *Lulu*; BIZET: *Carmen★, Djamileh, Pêcheurs de perles*; BRITTEN: *Peter Grimes, Rape of Lucretia*; BUSONI: *Turandot*; CAVALIERI: *Rappresentazione★*; CHERUBINI: *Medea★*; DONIZETTI: *Don Pasquale★, Elisir‡, Lucia★*; DVORAK: *Rusalka*; EINEM: *Dantons Tod★,*

Prozess; FALLA: *Retablo de Maese Pedro★*; GLUCK: *Orfeo ed Euridice;* GOUNOD: *Faust★;* HALEVY: *Juive;* HANDEL: *Acis and Galatea;* HAYDN: *Mondo della luna;* HINDEMITH: *Cardillac, Hin und zurück, Mathis der Maler;* HUMPERDINCK: *Hänsel und Gretel;* JANACEK: *Jenufa★;* KODALY: *Háry János;* LEONCAVALLO: *Pagliacci★;* LORTZING: *Waffenschmied, Wildschütz★, Zar und Zimmermann;* MARTIN: *Vin herbé;* MASCAGNI: *Cavalleria rusticana★;* MASSENET: *Manon;* MEYERBEER: *Huguenots★;* MOZART: *Clemenza di Tito, Così fan tutte★, Don Giovanni★, Entführung aus dem Serail★, Nozze di Figaro★, Zauberflöte★;* MUSSORGSKY: *Boris Godunov;* NICOLAI: *Lustigen Weiber;* OFFENBACH: *Contes d'Hoffmann★, Mariage aux lanternes;* ORFF: *Carmina burana★, Kluge, Mond;* PERGOLESI: *Serva padrona;* PUCCINI: *Bohème★, Fanciulla del West, Gianni Schicchi★, Butterfly★, Suor Angelica, Tabarro, Tosca★;* ROSSINI: *Barbiere di Siviglia★, Cenerentola, Moïse, Otello;* SMETANA: *Bartered Bride★;* STRAUSS, J: *Fledermaus;* STRAUSS, R: *Aegyptische Helena, Arabella, Ariadne auf Naxos★, Capriccio★, Elektra★, Intermezzo★, Rosenkavalier★, Salome★, Schweigsame Frau;* STRAVINSKY: *Mavra, Oedipus Rex, Perséphone, Rossignol;* TCHAIKOVSKY: *Eugene Onegin;* VERDI: *Aida★, Ballo in maschera★, Don Carlo★, Falstaff, Forza del destino★, Nabucco★, Otello★, Rigoletto★, Traviata★, Trovatore★, Vespri;* WAGNER: *Fliegende Holländer★, Lohengrin★, Meistersinger, Rheingold★, Walküre★, Siegfried★, Götterdämmerung, Tannhäuser★, Tristan und Isolde;* WEBER: *Freischütz★;* WEINBERGER: *Schwanda;* WOLF: *Corregidor;* WOLF-FERRARI: *Quattro rusteghi.* Also GLUCK: *Maienkönigin;* IBERT: *Gonzague;* LEONCAVALLO: *Bohème;* MILHAUD: *Maximilien;* PFITZNER: *Christelflein;* RIMSKY-KORSAKOV: *Kashchei the Immortal;* SCHMIDT: *Fredigundis;* STRAUSS, R: *Feuersnot;* TOCH: *Prinzessin auf der Erbse;* WEBER: *Peter Schmoll.* **World premieres:** WEISHAPPEL: *Elga* Operntheater Linz, Austria 1966; *König Nicolo* Volksoper, Vienna 1972; PAUMGARTNER: *Heisse Eisen,* Salzburg. Recorded for Eurodisc, BASF. Video/Film: *Háry János, Gonzague, Elisir, Rappresentazione.* Conducted major orch in Europe, USA/Canada, Cent/S America, Asia. **Res:** Dominikanerbastei 21, Vienna, Austria.

MARZOLFF, SERGE. Scenic and costume designer for opera, theater, television. Is a lighting designer. French. Resident designer, Grand Théâtre, Geneva, and at Théâtre de la Reprise, Lyon, France. Born 22 Jan 1940, Talence/Gironde, France. Married. One child. Studied: Ecole Ntl Supérieur d'Art Dramatique, Strasbourg; Profs Serge Creuz, Hubert Gignoux, Roland Deville. **Operatic debut:** *Butterfly* Opéra du Rhin, Strasbourg 1969. Theater debut: Théâtre des Drapiers, Strasbourg 1968. Previous occupation: art hist teacher, Univ de Strasbourg. Awards: Cinquième Biennale de Paris 1967. Previous adm positions in opera: Chief Designer, Opéra de Nancy, France 1970-73.

Designed for major companies in FRA: Nancy, Strasbourg; SWI: Geneva. **Operas designed for**

these companies incl BRITTEN: *Billy Budd;* EI-NEM: *Besuch der alten Dame★;* LECOCQ: *Fille de Madame Angot★;* MOZART: *Don Giovanni★, Entführung aus dem Serail;* PUCCINI: *Butterfly★, Manon Lescaut★, Turandot★;* RAVEL: *Heure espagnole★;* SAINT-SAENS: *Samson et Dalila★;* STRAUSS, J: *Fledermaus;* STRAUSS, R: *Salome★;* VERDI: *Aida★, Don Carlo★, Otello★, Traviata★;* WAGNER: *Walküre★, Siegfried★, Tristan und Isolde★;* WEILL: *Aufstieg und Fall der Stadt Mahagonny★.* Also NONO: *Intolleranza.* Exhibitions of paintings, Strasbourg 1965; Paris 1966. **Res:** Geneva, Switzerland.

MARZOT, VERA. Costume designer for opera, theater, film & television. Italian. Born 22 Jun 1931, Milan. Single. Prof training: asst to & collaborator with Piero Tosi, Luchino Visconti, Pier Luigi Pizzi, Beni Montresor and Piero Zuffi.
Designed for major companies in ITA: Rome Opera; UK: London Royal. **Operas designed for these companies incl** PURCELL: *Dido and Aeneas;* STRAUSS, R: *Rosenkavalier★;* VERDI: *Don Carlo, Traviata★.* Exhibitions of costume designs Wright Hepburn Gal, London 1967; Museum of Modern Art, New York. **Res:** Corso Vittorio 87, Rome, Italy.

MASCHDRAKOVA, RUMIANA. Soprano. Bulgarian. Resident mem: Krefeld Opera, FR Ger. Born 8 May 1941, Vidin, Bulgaria. Husband Dimitar Rustscheff, occupation conductor. One child. Studied: Musikhochschule Sofia, Prof G Tcherkin; Prof Maria Brand, Vienna. **Debut:** Leonora (*Trovatore*) Leipzig, Ger DR 1967. Awards: Third Prize, Dvorak Compt, Karlovy Vary, CSSR 1966.
Sang with major companies in BUL: Sofia; FR GER: Krefeld; GER DR: Leipzig. **Roles with these companies incl** MASCAGNI: Santuzza (*Cavalleria rusticana*); OFFENBACH: Antonia★ (*Contes d'Hoffmann*); PUCCINI: Tosca★; STRAUSS, R: Salome★; VERDI: Amelia (*Ballo in maschera*), Alice Ford★ (*Falstaff*), Leonora★ (*Trovatore*); WAGNER: Senta★ (*Fliegende Holländer*). Gives recitals. Appears with symphony orchestra. Teaches voice. **Res:** Awizena 1, Sofia, Bulgaria. Mgmt: CDK/YUG; RAB/AUS.

MASINI, GIANFRANCO. Conductor of opera and symphony. Italian. Born 26 Nov 1937, Reggio Emilia, Italy. Wife Mariarosa. Two children. Studied: Consvs Parma and Bologna; Hermann Scherchen; incl piano & voice. Plays the piano. Operatic training as repetiteur, asst cond & chorus master at Teatri Emiliani, Italy. **Operatic debut:** *Bohème* ATER Reggio Emilia 1963. Symphonic debut: Orch Bologna 1968. Previous occupations: teacher at consv.
Conducted with major companies in BUL: Sofia; CZE: Prague National; FRA: Aix-en-Provence Fest, Marseille, Nice, Paris, Toulouse; ITA: Bologna, Parma, Trieste, Turin; SPA: Barcelona Liceo; USA: New York Metropolitan Opera. **Operas with these companies incl** BELLINI: *Beatrice di Tenda★, Norma★, Puritani★, Sonnambula★;* CILEA: *A. Lecouvreur★;* DONIZETTI: *Anna Bolena★, Caterina Cornaro★, Elisir★, Lucia★;* GIORDANO: *Andrea Chénier;* PUCCINI: *Bohème★, Manon Lescaut★, Tosca★, Turandot★;* ROSSINI: *Elisabetta Regina★, Italiana in Algeri★,*

Otello★; VERDI: *Aida★, Forza del destino★, Macbeth★, Rigoletto★, Traviata★, Trovatore★;* ZANDONAI: *Francesca da Rimini★.* Recorded for EMI, Columbia, Philips. Conducted major orch in Europe. Teaches at consv. **Res:** Piazza Vallisneri 3, Reggio Emilia, Italy.

MASLENNIKOV, ALEXEI. Lyric tenor. Russian. Resident mem: Bolshoi Opera, Moscow. Born Leningrad. Studied: Moscow Consv, Ileana Katulskaya. **Debut:** Lenski (*Eugene Onegin*) USSR 1956.
Sang with major companies in USSR: Moscow Bolshoi; et al. **Roles with these companies incl** GLINKA: Finn (*Ruslan and Ludmilla*); MUSSORGSKY: Shuisky‡ (*Boris Godunov*); PROKOFIEV: Alexis (*Gambler*), Anatole‡ (*War and Peace*); et al. Also MUSSORGSKY: Simpleton (*Boris Godunov*). Recorded for. Decca, HMV.

MASSAD, WILLIAM. American. Asst Gen Mng & PR Dir, Fort Worth Opera Assn, 3505 W Lancaster, Fort Worth, TX 76107. In charge of business office & finances. Born 3 Aug 1932, Drumright, OK. Single. Studied: Univ of Oklahoma, Norman. Previous occupations: Acct Exec, PR/adv agency; officer, Intelligence Corps, US Army. Form positions, primarily adm: Exec Dir, Arts Council of Greater Fort Worth 1963-74; PR Dir, Wm Edrington Scott Theater, Fort Worth 1966-73; PR Dir, Fort Worth Art Center-Museum 1965-72. Started with present company in 1962 as PR Dir; in present position since 1970. World premieres at theaters during his engagement: SMITH: *Shepherdess and the Chimneysweep* Ft Worth 1966. Awards: McMahon Fndt Journalism Schlshp, Univ of Oklahoma. Mem of Bd of Dir, Natl Assembly of Community Arts Agencies 1972-74. **Res:** 603 Westview, Fort Worth, TX 76107, USA.

MASTERSON, VALERIE MARGARET. Lyric soprano. British. Resident mem: English National Opera, London. Married. Two children. Studied: Gordon Clinton, Edwardo Asguez, London; Ma Saraceni, Milan. **Debut:** Frasquita (*Carmen*) Landestheater Salzburg 1963. Previous occupations: radiographer. Awards: Countess of Munster Awd.
Sang with major companies in FRA: Toulouse; UK: Glyndebourne Fest, London Royal & English National. **Roles with these companies incl** BIZET: Micaëla★ (*Carmen*); MASSENET: Manon★; MOZART: Konstanze★ (*Entführung aus dem Serail*), Mme Herz★ (*Schauspieldirektor*), Susanna★ (*Nozze di Figaro*); ROSSINI: Comtesse Adèle★ (*Comte Ory*); STRAUSS, J: Adele★ (*Fledermaus*); STRAUSS, R: Sophie★ (*Rosenkavalier*); VERDI: Oscar★ (*Ballo in maschera*), Violetta★ (*Traviata*). Recorded for: EMI. Gives recitals. Appears with symphony orchestra. **Res:** London, UK. Mgmt: MIN/UK.

MASTILOVIC, DANICA. Dramatic soprano. German. Resident mem: Opernhaus Frankfurt; Staatsoper Munich. Born Negotin, Yugoslavia. Husband Klaus Schöll, occupation head of dept, music publ Schott, Mainz. Studied: Musikakad Belgrade, Prof Nikola Cvejic. **Debut:** Tosca, Frankfurt Opera 1959. Awards: First Opera Prize, City of Frankfurt.

Sang with major companies in ARG: Buenos Aires; AUS: Graz, Vienna Staatsoper; BEL: Brussels; DEN: Copenhagen; FRA: Paris; FR GER: Bayreuth Fest, Berlin Deutsche Oper, Cologne, Düsseldorf-Duisburg, Frankfurt, Hamburg, Hannover, Karlsruhe, Kassel, Kiel, Mannheim, Munich Staatsoper, Nürnberg, Saarbrücken, Stuttgart; GER DR: Dresden; ITA: Bologna, Florence Maggio & Comunale, Milan La Scala, Rome Opera, Verona Arena; MEX: Mexico City; POR: Lisbon; SPA: Barcelona; SWE: Stockholm; SWI: Basel, Geneva, Zurich; UK: Edinburgh Fest, London Royal; USA: Chicago, New York Met, Philadelphia, Pittsburgh; YUG: Zagreb, Belgrade. **Roles with these cos incl** BEETHOVEN: Leonore (*Fidelio*); BORODIN: Jaroslavna (*Prince Igor*); MUSSORGSKY: Marina (*Boris Godunov*); PUCCINI: Tosca, Turandot⋆; STRAUSS, R: Elektra⋆, Färberin⋆ (*Frau ohne Schatten*), Herodias (*Salome*); VERDI: Aida⋆, Amelia (*Ballo in maschera*), Elisabetta (*Don Carlo*), Leonora (*Forza del destino*), Abigaille⋆ (*Nabucco*), Desdemona (*Otello*), Amelia (*Simon Boccanegra*), Leonora (*Trovatore*); WAGNER: Senta⋆ (*Fliegende Holländer*), Ortrud (*Lohengrin*), Brünnhilde (*Siegfried, Götterdämmerung*), Elisabeth⋆ & Venus⋆ (*Tannhäuser*), Kundry⋆ (*Parsifal*). Appears with symphony orchestra. **Res:** Frankenwaldstr 2, 65 Mainz 42, FR Ger.

MASTROMEI, GIAN PIERO. Dramatic baritone. Italian. Born 1 Nov 1932, Camaiore, Italy. Wife Silvia Baleani, occupation opera singer. Studied: Scuola di Perfez Arte Lirico, Teatro Colón, Buenos Aires; Mo Mario Melani, Ma Hina Spani, Mo Arturo Wolken. **Debut:** Enrico (*Lucia*) Teatro Colón 1959. Awards: Gold Medal for best interpret, Mexico 1970.

Sang with major companies in ARG: Buenos Aires; AUS: Vienna Staatsoper; BRA: Rio de Janeiro; FRA: Marseille; FR GER: Berlin Deutsche Oper, Frankfurt, Hamburg, Munich Staatsoper; HUN: Budapest; ITA: Florence Maggio & Comunale, Milan La Scala, Naples, Palermo, Parma, Trieste, Turin, Verona Arena; MEX: Mexico City; MON: Monte Carlo; POR: Lisbon; SPA: Barcelona, Majorca; SWI: Zurich; UK: London Royal; USSR: Moscow Bolshoi; USA: Dallas, Houston, Philadelphia Lyric, San Francisco Opera; YUG: Zagreb. **Roles with these companies incl** BELLINI: Sir Richard⋆ (*Puritani*); BIZET: Escamillo⋆ (*Carmen*); CIMAROSA: Geronimo (*Matrimonio segreto*); DALLAPICCOLA: Riviere (*Volo di notte*); DONIZETTI: Don Pistacchio (*Campanello*), Dulcamara (*Elisir*), Alfonse (*Favorite*), Enrico⋆ (*Lucia*); LEONCAVALLO: Tonio⋆ (*Pagliacci*); MASCAGNI: Alfio⋆ (*Cavalleria rusticana*); MASSENET: Lescaut⋆ (*Manon*); MOZART: Figaro (*Nozze di Figaro*); MUSSORGSKY: Varlaam (*Boris Godunov*), Shaklovity (*Khovanshchina*); PAISIELLO: Figaro (*Barbiere di Siviglia*); PERGOLESI: Uberto (*Serva padrona*); PONCHIELLI: Barnaba⋆ (*Gioconda*); PUCCINI: Marcello⋆ (*Bohème*), Jack Rance (*Fanciulla del West*), Gianni Schicchi⋆, Sharpless⋆ (*Butterfly*), Lescaut (*Manon Lescaut*), Michele⋆ (*Tabarro*), Scarpia⋆ (*Tosca*), Gugliemo Wulf (*Villi*); ROSSINI: Figaro (*Barbiere di Siviglia*), Tobias Mill (*Cambiale di matrimonio*); VERDI: Amonasro⋆ (*Aida*), Renato⋆ (*Ballo in*

maschera), Rodrigo⋆ (*Don Carlo*), Ford⋆ (*Falstaff*), Don Carlo⋆ (*Forza del destino*), Macbeth⋆, Nabucco⋆, Iago⋆ (*Otello*), Rigoletto⋆, Simon Boccanegra⋆, Germont⋆ (*Traviata*), Conte di Luna⋆ (*Trovatore*); WAGNER: Wolfram⋆ (*Tannhäuser*). Also SALIERI: Brighella (*Arlecchinata*); PICCINI: Mengotto (*Cecchina*); SCARLATTI: Erminio (*Trionfo dell'onore*). Recorded for: RCA. **Res:** V Renato Fucini 14, Milan, Italy. Mgmt: CST/UK.

MATHES, RACHEL. Spinto soprano. American. Resident mem: Metropolitan Opera, New York. Born 14 Mar 1941, Atlanta, GA, USA. Single. Studied: Prof Andrew Gainey, Birmingham, AL, USA; Akad für Musik und darstellende Kunst, Vienna; Fr Edith Boroschek, Düsseldorf, FR Ger. **Debut:** Aida, Stadttheater Basel 1965. Awards: Fulbright Schlshp for Vienna 1962; First Prize Friday Morning Music Club, Washington DC 1962; First Prize Baltimore Opera Aud 1965.

Sang with major companies in CZE: Prague Smetana; FIN: Helsinki; FR GER: Bonn, Cologne, Dortmund, Düsseldorf-Duisburg, Essen, Hannover, Karlsruhe, Kassel, Kiel, Mannheim, Munich Staatsoper, Nürnberg, Stuttgart; POR: Lisbon; SWI: Basel, Geneva, Zurich; UK: Glasgow Scottish; USA: New York Met & City Opera, Pittsburgh, San Diego. **Roles with these companies incl** BRITTEN: Lady Billows (*Albert Herring*); CAVALLI: Medea⋆ (*Giasone*); HINDEMITH: Ursula⋆ (*Mathis der Maler*); MASCAGNI: Santuzza⋆ (*Cavalleria rusticana*); MOZART: Vitellia⋆ (*Clemenza di Tito*), Donna Anna⋆ (*Don Giovanni*), Elettra⋆ (*Idomeneo*); OFFENBACH: Giulietta⋆ (*Contes d'Hoffmann*); PUCCINI: Cio-Cio-San (*Butterfly*), Giorgetta (*Tabarro*), Tosca⋆, Turandot⋆; STRAUSS, R: Ariadne (*Ariadne auf Naxos*), Marschallin⋆ (*Rosenkavalier*); VERDI: Aida⋆, Amelia (*Ballo in maschera*), Leonora⋆ (*Forza del destino*), Abigaille⋆ (*Nabucco*), Desdemona⋆ (*Otello*), Amelia (*Simon Boccanegra*), Leonora⋆ (*Trovatore*); WAGNER: Senta⋆ (*Fliegende Holländer*), Elsa⋆ (*Lohengrin*), Gutrune (*Götterdämmerung*), Elisabeth⋆ & Venus⋆ (*Tannhäuser*). Also HONEGGER: Magd (*Judith*). **World premieres:** VALDAMBRINI: Agave (*Pentheus*) Bonn Opera, FR Ger 1971; KLEBE: Die Frau (*Märchen von der schönen Lilie*) Schwetzingen, FR Ger 1969. Gives recitals. Appears with symphony orchestra. **Res:** New York, NY, USA. Mgmt: SMN/USA.

MATHESON, JOHN; né Henry John Parke Matheson. Conductor of opera and symphony; operatic stage director. New Zealander. Resident Cond, Royal Opera House, Covent Garden, London. Born 14 May 1928, Dunedin, New Zealand. Wife Margaret Sheryll, occupation singer. Two daughters from previous marriage. Studied: Otago Univ, Dunedin; Royal Coll of Music, London; incl violin, piano and voice. Plays the piano. Operatic training as repetiteur, asst cond & chorus master at Sadler's Wells, London 1952-53, 1960-66; Royal Opera, Covent Garden 1953-60, 1970-75. **Operatic debut:** *Nozze di Figaro* Sadler's Wells, London 1953. Symphonic debut: BBC Northern Orch, Manchester, UK 1964.

Conducted with major companies in FRA: Nice; FR GER: Frankfurt, Hamburg, Munich Staatsoper; HOL: Amsterdam; UK: Welsh National, London Royal & English National. **Operas with these companies incl** BEETHOVEN: *Fidelio★;* BERG: *Wozzeck★;* BERLIOZ: *Damnation de Faust★,* Troyens; BIZET: *Carmen;* BRITTEN: *Albert Herring;* DONIZETTI: *Don Pasquale★, Lucia★;* GOUNOD: *Faust★;* HENZE: *Boulevard Solitude;* LEONCAVALLO: *Pagliacci★;* MASCAGNI: *Cavalleria rusticana★;* MOZART: *Così fan tutte, Don Giovanni★, Entführung aus dem Serail, Nozze di Figaro;* POULENC: *Dialogues des Carmélites;* PUCCINI: *Bohème, Butterfly★, Tosca;* RAVEL: *Enfant et les sortilèges;* ROSSINI: *Barbiere di Siviglia, Guillaume Tell, Moïse, Scala di seta;* SAINT-SAENS: *Samson et Dalila;* SMETANA: *Bartered Bride;* STRAUSS, J: *Fledermaus;* STRAUSS, R: *Ariadne auf Naxos;* TCHAIKOVSKY: *Eugene Onegin, Pique Dame;* VAUGHAN WILLIAMS: *Riders to the Sea;* VERDI: *Aida★, Attila, Ballo in·maschera★, Don Carlo‡, Falstaff★, Rigoletto, Simon Boccanegra★‡, Traviata★, Trovatore;* WAGNER: *Fliegende Holländer★.* Conducted major orch in Europe, Asia, Austrl. **Res:** 112 Harley St, London W1, UK. **Mgmt:** AIM/UK; RAP/FRA.

MATHIS, EDITH. Lyric soprano. Swiss. Born 11 Feb 1938, Lucerne, Switzerland. Husband Bernhard Klee, occupation conductor. Two children. Studied: Elisabeth Bosshart, Zurich. **Debut:** Zweiter Knabe (*Zauberflöte*) Stadttheater Luzern 1956. Awards: Prix Edison, German record prize; Grand Prix du Disque; Wiener Flötenuhr.
Sang with major companies in AUS: Salzburg Fest, Vienna Staatsoper; FR GER: Berlin Deutsche Oper, Cologne, Hamburg, Hannover, Munich Staatsoper; HOL: Amsterdam; SWI: Zurich; UK: Glyndebourne Fest, London Royal Opera; USA: New York Met. **Roles with these companies incl** BEETHOVEN: Marzelline★‡ (*Fidelio*); BERLIOZ: Marguerite‡ (*Damnation de Faust*); CIMAROSA: Elisetta (*Matrimonio segreto*); DEBUSSY: Mélisande★; EGK: Gretl (*Zaubergeige*); GLUCK: Amor (*Orfeo ed Euridice*); HANDEL: Deidamia; HINDEMITH: Regina (*Mathis der Maler*); LORTZING: Marie (*Waffenschmied*), Gretchen (*Wildschütz*), Marie (*Zar und Zimmermann*); MENOTTI: Emily (*Globolinks*); MOZART: Despina★ (*Così fan tutte*), Zerlina★ (*Don Giovanni*), Blondchen (*Entführung aus dem Serail*), Ilia★ (*Idomeneo*), Cinna‡ (*Lucio Silla*), Susanna★ & Cherubino‡ (*Nozze di Figaro*), Aminta‡ (*Re pastore*), Zaïde‡, Pamina★‡ (*Zauberflöte*); NICOLAI: Aennchen‡ (*Lustigen Weiber*); PUCCINI: Lauretta (*Gianni Schicchi*); RAVEL: Child (*Enfant et les sortilèges*); ROSSINI: Rosina (*Barbiere di Siviglia*); STRAUSS, R: Zdenka★ (*Arabella*), Sophie★ (*Rosenkavalier*); VERDI: Nannetta (*Falstaff*); WEBER: Aennchen★‡ (*Freischütz*); WOLF-FERRARI: Lucieta (*Quattro rusteghi*). **World premieres:** EINEM: Kathi (*Zerrissene*) Hamburg Opera 1964; HENZE: Luise (*Junge Lord*) Deutsche Oper, Berlin 1965. Recorded for: DG, Electrola, EMI, BASF. Video/Film: Pamina (*Zauberflöte*); Aennchen (*Freischütz*); Susanna (*Nozze di Figaro*); Zdenka (*Arabella*). Gives recitals. Appears with symphony orchestra. **Res:** Thurbergstr 11, Weinfelden, Switzerland. **Mgmt:** HUS/FRG; DSP/USA.

MATIAS; né Charles Henrioud. Scenic and costume designer for opera, theater, film, television. Is a lighting designer, stage director. Swiss. Born 22 Nov 1926, Yverdon, Switzerland. Single. **Operatic debut:** sets, cost, *Italiana in Algeri* Aix-en-Provence Fest 1970. Theater debut: Renaud-Barrault Comp, Paris 1968.
Designed for major companies in FRA: Aix-en-Provence Fest, Paris, Strasbourg. **Operas designed for these companies incl** MASSENET: *Manon★;* ROSSINI: *Comte Ory★, Italiana in Algeri★;* WEBER: *Freischütz★.* Exhibitions of stage designs, Galerie Proscenium 1970. **Res:** 72 rue Mazarine, Paris 6, France.

MATSUMOTO, SHIGEMI EVE. Lyric soprano. American. Born Denver, CO, USA. Husband Martin J Stark, occupation repres Columbia Artists Mngt. Studied: Kathleen Darragh, Natalie Limonick, Dr David Scott, Los Angeles; Otto Guth, San Francisco; Daniel Ferro, New York. **Debut:** Gerhilde (*Walküre*) San Francisco Opera 1968. Awards: First Prize San Francisco Opera Ntl Aud; Reg Winner Met Op Ntl Counc Aud; 2 yr Grant National Opera Inst; Japanese Woman of the Year for So California.
Sang with major companies in USA: Portland, San Francisco Opera & Spring Opera. **Roles with these companies incl** BIZET: Micaëla★ (*Carmen*); DONIZETTI: Norina★ (*Don Pasquale*); MOZART: Despina★ (*Così fan tutte*); ORFF: Solo★ (*Carmina burana*); PUCCINI: Mimi★ (*Bohème*); ROSSINI: Rosina★ (*Barbiere di Siviglia*). Gives recitals. Appears with symphony orchestra. Affiliated: recitals, master classes, lectures at various coll and univ. **Mgmt:** CAM/USA.

MATTIOTTI, MARIO. Bass. Italian. Born 7 Jun 1933, Genoa. Single. Studied: Liceo Musicale N Paganini, Genoa; Mo Marcello Cortis, Nino Scattolini, Milan. **Debut:** Geronimo (*Matrimonio segreto*) As Li Co, Milan 1962. Previous occupations: officer in merchant marine.
Sang with major companies in CZE: Prague Smetana; FRA: Rouen; ITA: Florence Comunale, Genoa, Milan La Scala; MON: Monte Carlo; SPA: Majorca; YUG: Belgrade. **Roles with these companies incl** BELLINI: Rodolfo (*Sonnambula*); CIMAROSA: Geronimo★ (*Matrimonio segreto*); DONIZETTI: Don Pasquale★, Marquis★ (*Linda di Chamounix*); MUSSORGSKY: Varlaam★ (*Boris Godunov*); ROSSINI: Dott Bartolo★ (*Barbiere di Siviglia*). **World premieres:** LORENZINI: Direttore Centro (*Quattro per cinque*) Teatro delle Novità, Bergamo 1970. Gives recitals. Appears with symphony orchestra. **Res:** Corso S Gottardo 11, Milan, Italy.

MÁTYÁS, MÁRIA. Dramatic soprano. Hungarian. Resident mem: Hungarian Ntl Opera, Budapest. Born 13 Sep 1927, Hajdudorog, Hungary. Married. Studied: Consv, Debrecen, Hungary; Acad of Music, Budapest; Singing Coll, M Polvenesi, Rome. **Debut:** Gretel (*Hänsel und Gretel*) Hungarian Ntl Opera 1947. Previous occupations: teacher. Awards: Kossuth Prize, and other cultural prizes from Hungarian Republic.
Sang with major companies in BUL: Sofia; CZE: Brno, Prague National & Smetana; GER DR: Leipzig; HUN: Budapest; ROM: Bucharest;

USSR: Leningrad Kirov, Moscow Bolshoi, Tbilisi; YUG: Dubrovnik, Zagreb, Belgrade. **Roles with these companies incl** BEETHOVEN: Leonore★ & Marzelline (*Fidelio*); BERG: Marie (*Wozzeck*); BIZET: Micaëla (*Carmen*); BRITTEN: Ellen Orford (*Peter Grimes*); ERKEL: Melinda (*Bánk Bán*); GLINKA: Ludmilla; GOUNOD: Marguerite‡ (*Faust*); HUMPERDINCK: Gretel‡; KODALY: Örzse★‡ (*Háry János*); MASCAGNI: Santuzza★ (*Cavalleria rusticana*); MOZART: Fiordiligi (*Così fan tutte*), Donna Anna (*Don Giovanni*), Konstanze (*Entführung aus dem Serail*), Pamina & Königin der Nacht (*Zauberflöte*); OFFENBACH: Olympia & Giulietta (*Contes d' Hoffmann*); PUCCINI: Mimi‡ (*Bohème*), Lauretta (*Gianni Schicchi*), Tosca★‡; SHOSTAKOVICH: Katerina Ismailova★; SMETANA: Marinka (*The Kiss*); SUCHON: Katrena (*Whirlpool*); TCHAIKOVSKY: Tatiana★‡ (*Eugene Onegin*); VERDI: Elisabetta★ (*Don Carlo*), Leonora★‡ (*Forza del destino*), Lady Macbeth★‡ (*Macbeth*), Desdemona★ (*Otello*), Amelia★ (*Simon Boccanegra*), Violetta‡ (*Traviata*); WAGNER: Senta★ (*Fliegende Holländer*), Elsa★ (*Lohengrin*), Elisabeth★ (*Tannhäuser*). **World premieres:** PETROVICS: Wife (*C'est la guerre*) Hungarian Ntl Opera 1960; KOZMA: Wife (*Electronic Love*) Hungarian Ntl Opera 1962. Recorded for: Hungarian Record Co. Video/Film: Örzse (*Háry János*); Wife (*C'est la guerre*). Appears with symphony orchestra. Teaches voice. Coaches repertoire. **Res:** II Csalán u 33, Budapest, Hungary.

MAUCERI, JOHN. Conductor of opera and symphony; composer. American. Born 12 Sep 1945, New York. Wife Betty. Studied: Yale Univ, Gustav Meier, CT, USA; Berkshire Music Cnt, B Maderna, C Davis, S Ozawa, L Bernstein, in Lenox, MA; incl piano, violin, trumpet, oboe and voice. Operatic training as repetiteur, asst cond & chorus master at New Haven Opera, CT 1966-68; tv prod *Carmen* 1972; asst to Bernstein, Met 1974. **Operatic debut:** *Curlew River* Yale Opera Co, United Nations, New York 1967. Symphonic debut: Yale Symph, New Haven, CT 1968. Previous adm positions in opera: Prod and Art Dir, Spec Yale Opera Co, CT 1966-75. **Conducted with major companies in** ITA: Spoleto Fest; UK: Welsh National; USA: San Francisco Spring Opera, Santa Fe, New York Metropolitan Opera. **Operas with these companies incl** BEETHOVEN: Fidelio★; BERG: *Lulu*★; BRITTEN: *Death in Venice*★; MENOTTI: *Tamu-Tamu*★; MOZART: *Così fan tutte*★; ROSSINI: *Barbiere di Siviglia*★; VERDI: *Don Carlo*★. Video—WNET/PBS, BBC and ORTF/Austria; Bernstein *Mass*. Conducted major orch in Europe, USA/Canada, Cent/S America. Previous positions as Mus Dir with major orch: Yale Symph, New Haven, CT 1968-75. **Operas composed:** *Escalibor*, unproduced; *Sette Piani*, in progress. Teaches at Yale Univ, New Haven. **Res:** New Haven, CT, USA. Mgmt: CAM/USA.

MAURO, ERMANNO. Lirico spinto tenor. Canadian. Born 20 Jan 1939, Trieste, Italy. Wife Dolores. Three children. Studied: Univ of Toronto; Canadian Opera Co, Dr Herman Geiger-Torel, Toronto. **Debut:** Manrico (*Trovatore*) Canadian Opera Co, Toronto 1964. Awards: Canada Counc

Fllshp 1968; Beta Sigma Phi 3 yr schlshp to Toronto Consv; Conc Voci Verdiane, Busseto, Italy 1964.

Sang with major companies in AUS: Vienna Staatsoper; CAN: Ottawa, Toronto, Vancouver; FRA: Lyon; GRE: Athens National Opera; FR GER: Frankfurt; HOL: Amsterdam; UK: Cardiff Welsh, Glasgow Scottish, Glyndebourne Fest, London Royal Opera; USA: New York City Opera, San Diego. **Roles with these companies incl** BIZET: Don José★ (*Carmen*); BOITO: Faust (*Mefistofele*); BRITTEN: Male Chorus (*Rape of Lucretia*); CILEA: Maurizio (*A. Lecouvreur*); DONIZETTI: Edgardo★ (*Lucia*); FALLA: Paco★ (*Vida breve*); GIORDANO: Andrea Chénier★ (*Vida breve*); GOUNOD: Faust★, Roméo★; LEONCAVALLO: Canio★ (*Pagliacci*); MASCAGNI: Turiddu★ (*Cavalleria rusticana*); MASSENET: Werther★; MOZART: Biondello (*Oca del Cairo*); PONCHIELLI: Enzo (*Gioconda*); POULENC: Chevalier de la Force (*Dialogues des Carmélites*); PROKOFIEV: Prince (*Love for Three Oranges*); PUCCINI: Rodolfo★ (*Bohème*), Dick Johnson★ (*Fanciulla del West*), Pinkerton★ (*Butterfly*), Des Grieux★ (*Manon Lescaut*), Luigi (*Tabarro*), Cavaradossi★ (*Tosca*), Calaf★ (*Turandot*); STRAUSS, R: Ein Sänger (*Rosenkavalier*); VERDI: Radames★ (*Aida*), Riccardo★ (*Ballo in maschera*), Don Alvaro★ (*Forza del destino*), Ismaele★ (*Nabucco*), Gabriele★ (*Simon Boccanegra*), Alfredo★ (*Traviata*), Manrico★ (*Trovatore*). Video—BBC TV: Paco (*Vida breve*); CBC TV: (*Tabarro*). **Res:** London, UK. Mgmt: AIM/UK; BAR/USA.

MAUTI NUNZIATA, ELENA. Lyric soprano. Italian. Born 28 Aug 1946, Palma Campania, Italy. Husband Romano Mauti. Studied: Consv S Pietro a Maiella Naples; Ines Alfani Tellini, Gina Cigna. **Debut:** Liù (*Turandot*) Teatro Massimo Palermo 1965. Awards: First Class Certif Compt New Voices RAI/Rome 1969; First Prize Viotti Compt 1970; Gold Medal Rotary Club; First Dante Lari, Reggio Emilia 1967.

Sang with major companies in BUL: Sofia; FRA: Aix-en-Provence Fest, Nice; FR GER: Hamburg; ITA; Genoa, Milan La Scala, Palermo, Trieste, Turin, Venice, Verona Arena; SPA: Barcelona, Majorca; USA: Dallas. **Roles with these companies incl** BELLINI: Elvira★ (*Puritani*); BIZET: Micaëla★ (*Carmen*), Léila (*Pêcheurs de perles*); DONIZETTI: Norina★ (*Don Pasquale*); GOUNOD: Marguerite (*Faust*); LEONCAVALLO: Nedda★ (*Pagliacci*); MASSENET: Manon★; MOZART: Fiordiligi★ (*Così fan tutte*), Donna Elvira★ (*Don Giovanni*); PERGOLESI: Serpina★ (*Serva padrona*); PUCCINI: Mimi★ (*Bohème*), Cio-Cio-San★ (*Butterfly*), Suor Angelica★, Liù★ (*Turandot*); VERDI: Desdemona★ (*Otello*), Violetta★ (*Traviata*). Also BUSONI: Colombina★ (*Arlecchino*); ROSSINI: (*Gazzetta*), (*Inganno felice*); SALIERI: Colombina (*Arlecchinata*). **Res:** V Croce Rossa 8, Palermo, Italy. Mgmt: EUM/FRG; SLA/UK.

MAXIMOWNA, ITA. Scenic and costume designer for opera, theater, film & television. Is a lighting designer, stage director; also a painter. German. Resident designer, San Francisco Opera, USA. Born 31 Oct, Pskov, Russia. Divorced. Studied: Paris; Berlin Acad, Karl Heinz Martin. **Operatic**

debut: Deutsche Oper Berlin, FR Ger 1953. Theater debut: Renaissance Theater, Berlin 1945. Previous occupation: illustrator of books. Awards: Kunstpreis, Berlin 1953; Prize, Teatro la Fenice, Venice 1970.

Designed for major companies in ARG: Buenos Aires; AUS: Graz, Salzburg Fest, Vienna Staatsoper & Volksoper; BEL: Brussels; CAN: Vancouver; FRA: Paris; FR GER: Berlin Deutsche Oper, Cologne, Dortmund, Düsseldorf-Duisburg, Frankfurt, Hamburg, Munich Staatsoper & Gärtnerplatz, Stuttgart, Wiesbaden; HOL: Amsterdam; ITA: Milan La Scala, Palermo, Rome Caracalla, Venice; SPA: Barcelona; SWI: Geneva, Zurich; UK: Edinburgh Fest, Glyndebourne Fest; USA: New York Met, San Francisco Opera. **Operas designed and directed for these companies, some in three to five diff prod, incl** ADAM: *Si j'étais roi;* BEETHOVEN: *Fidelio;* BIZET: *Carmen;* BLACHER: *Romeo und Julia;* BRITTEN: *Albert Herring, Death in Venice;* CIKKER: *Play of Love and Death;* DALLAPICCOLA: *Prigioniero;* DEBUSSY: *Pelléas et Mélisande;* DONIZETTI: *Convenienze/Viva la Mamma;* DVORAK: *Dimitri;* EINEM: *Prozess;* GLUCK: *Armide;* HANDEL: *Xerxes;* HAYDN: *Infedeltà delusa;* KLEBE: *Jakobowsky und der Oberst;* LORTZING: *Wildschütz, Zar und Zimmermann;* MASSENET: *Manon;* MONTEVERDI: *Incoronazione di Poppea;* MOZART: *Clemenza di Tito, Così fan tutte, Don Giovanni, Idomeneo, Nozze di Figaro, Zauberflöte;* ORFF: *Kluge*★*;* PROKOFIEV: *Duenna;* PUCCINI: *Gianni Schicchi, Manon Lescaut, Tabarro;* ROSSINI: *Barbiere di Siviglia, Cenerentola, Comte Ory, Turco in Italia;* SCHOENBERG: *Erwartung;* SCHULLER: *Visitation;* STRAUSS, J: *Fledermaus;* STRAUSS, R: *Ariadne auf Naxos, Capriccio, Rosenkavalier, Salome;* TCHAIKOVSKY: *Pique Dame;* VERDI: *Ballo in maschera, Forza del destino, Otello;* WEILL: *Dreigroschenoper.* Also BLACHER: *Lysistrata, Preussisches Märchen, 200,000 Taler.* **Operatic world premieres:** several operas. Operatic Video/Film—Tech Berlin: *Si j'étais roi, Revisor, Comte Ory, Nozze di Figaro.* Exhibitions of stage designs Berlin 1975. **Res:** Lyckallee 40, Berlin 19, FR Ger.

MAXWELL, LINN. Lyric mezzo-soprano. American. Born 1945, Washington DC, USA. Studied: John Bullock, Washington DC; Margaret van der Marck, New York.

Sang with major companies in FRA: Lyon, Strasbourg; FR GER: Essen. **Roles with these companies incl** GOUNOD: Siebel★ (*Faust*); MASSENET: Charlotte (*Werther*); MOZART: Dorabella★ (*Così fan tutte*), Cherubino★ (*Nozze di Figaro*); OFFENBACH: Nicklausse★ (*Contes d'Hoffmann*); ROSSINI: Rosina★ (*Barbiere di Siviglia*), Isabella★ (*Italiana in Algeri*); STRAUSS, J: Prinz Orlovsky★ (*Fledermaus*); STRAUSS, R: Octavian★ (*Rosenkavalier*); WAGNER: Fricka (*Walküre*). Also PUCCINI: Zita (*Gianni Schicchi*); PURCELL: Sorceress (*Dido and Aeneas*); RAMEAU: (*Zoroastre*); MONTEVERDI: Ottavia & Arnalta★ (*Incoronazione di Poppea*). **World premieres:** SILVERMAN: Ragtime Lady (*Elephant Steps*) Berkshire Fest, Lenox, MA 1968. Gives recitals. Appears with

symphony orchestra. **Res:** New York, NY, USA. Mgmt: SFM/USA; SLZ/FRG.

MAY-CZYZOWSKA, TERESA. Dramatic coloratura soprano. Polish. **Resident mem:** Lodz Opera. Born 22 Jan 1935, Luck, Poland. Widowed. Studied: Prof Wiktor Brégy, Warsaw; Prof Olga Olgina, Lodz; Prof Hilde Rössel-Majdan, Graz/Vienna. **Debut:** Micaëla (*Carmen*) Warsaw Opera 1960. Awards: Musikakad Graz, 1970; First Prize Intl Compt Budapest 1965; First Prize Graz Intl Compt (oratorio); City of Toulouse Médaille 1962.

Sang with major companies in AUS: Graz; CZE: Prague National; GER DR: Dresden, Leipzig; HUN: Budapest; POL: Lodz, Warsaw; USSR: Tbilisi. **Roles with these companies incl** BIZET: Micaëla★ (*Carmen*); DELIBES: Lakmé; GOUNOD: Marguerite★ (*Faust*); LEONCAVALLO: Nedda (*Pagliacci*); MARTIN: Iseut (*Vin herbé*); MONIUSZKO: Halka★; MOZART: Fiordiligi★ (*Così fan tutte*), Konstanze★ (*Entführung aus dem Serail*), Königin der Nacht★ (*Zauberflöte*); PUCCINI: Mimi & Musetta (*Bohème*); ROSSINI: Rosina★ (*Barbiere di Siviglia*); SMETANA: Marie★ (*Bartered Bride*); VERDI: Gilda★ (*Rigoletto*), Violetta★ (*Traviata*). Gives recitals. Appears with symphony orchestra. **Res:** Radomska 16/14, Warsaw, Poland. Mgmt: PAG/POL.

MAYER, FREDERIC DAVID. Lyric tenor. American. **Resident mem:** Gärtnerplatztheater, Munich. Born 21 Apr 1931, Lincoln, NE, USA. Wife Rosemarie, occupation ballet dancer. Three children. Studied: Edgar Schofield, New York; Rocco Pandiscio, Munich. **Debut:** Ferrando (*Così fan tutte*) Ulm, FR Ger 1964. Previous occupations: Prof of music, Columbia Univ, New York. Awards: Bayerischer Kammersänger, Bavarian Gvnmt.

Sang with major companies in AUS: Bregenz Fest, Salzburg Fest, Vienna Staatsoper; FR GER: Berlin Deutsche Oper, Frankfurt, Mannheim, Munich Gärtnerplatz, Nürnberg, Stuttgart; USA: Baltimore, Chicago. **Roles with these companies incl** ADAM DE LA HALLE/Milhaud: Robin; AUBER: Fra Diavolo★ (*Don Pasquale*); HANDEL: Acis★, Sextus (*Giulio Cesare*); HAYDN: Nancio★ (*Infedeltà delusa*); LORTZING: Chateauneuf★ (*Zar und Zimmermann*); MOZART: Ferrando★ (*Così fan tutte*), Pedrillo★ (*Entführung aus dem Serail*), Tamino★ (*Zauberflöte*); NICOLAI: Fenton★ (*Lustigen Weiber*); ORFF: Solo★ (*Carmina burana*); PROKOFIEV: Antonio★ (*Duenna*); ROSSINI: Almaviva★ (*Barbiere di Siviglia*); SHOSTAKOVICH: Zinovy★ (*Katerina Ismailova*), Police Commissioner★ (*The Nose*); STRAUSS, J: Eisenstein★ (*Fledermaus*); STRAVINSKY: Oedipus Rex; VERDI: Alfredo★ (*Traviata*). Also HENZE: Rezensent (*Rachel, la Cubana*). Gives recitals. Appears with symphony orchestra. Teaches voice. **Res:** Munich, FR Ger. Mgmt: SLZ/FRG.

MAZURA, FRANZ. Bass-baritone. German. **Resident mem:** Staatsoper, Hamburg.

Sang with major companies in AUS: Salzburg Fest; BEL: Brussels; FRA: Paris, Strasbourg; FR GER: Bayreuth Fest, Berlin Deutsche Oper, Düsseldorf-Duisburg, Hamburg, Mannheim; USA: San Francisco Opera; et al. **Roles with these**

companies incl BEETHOVEN: Don Pizarro (*Fidelio*); MOZART: Sarastro (*Zauberflöte*); SCHOENBERG: Moses; STRAUSS, R: Baron Ochs (*Rosenkavalier*), Jochanaan (*Salome*); WAGNER: Holländer, Gurnemanz (*Parsifal*), Alberich (*Rheingold, Götterdämmerung*), Wotan (*Rheingold, Walküre*), Gunther (*Götterdämmerung*), Kurwenal (*Tristan und Isolde*); WEBER: Kaspar (*Freischütz*); et al. Mgmt: MAA/USA.

MAZUROK, YURI ANTONOVICH. Lyric baritone. Russian. Resident mem: Bolshoi Theater, Moscow. Born 18 Jul 1931, Krasnik, USSR. Wife Maia. One child. Studied: Consv, Moscow. **Debut:** Eugene Onegin, Bolshoi Theater 1963. Previous occupations: engineer. Awards: People's Artist of the USSR; Winner of Compts Montreal 1967, Bucharest 1963, Prague 1960.

Sang with major companies in AUS: Vienna Staatsoper; BUL: Sofia; CZE: Prague National; FIN: Helsinki; FR GER: Hamburg, Wiesbaden; GER DR: Berlin Staatsoper, Dresden, Leipzig; HUN: Budapest; POL: Warsaw; USSR: Kiev, Leningrad Kirov, Moscow Bolshoi & Stanislavski, Tbilisi. **Roles with these companies incl** PROKOFIEV: Prince Andrei Bolkonsky★ (*War and Peace*); PUCCINI: Marcello★ (*Bohème*), Sharpless★ (*Butterfly*), Scarpia★ (*Tosca*); ROSSINI: Figaro★ (*Barbiere di Siviglia*); VERDI: Amonasro★ (*Aida*), Renato★ (*Ballo in maschera*), Rodrigo★ (*Don Carlo*), Germont★ (*Traviata*), Conte di Luna★ (*Trovatore*); WAGNER: Wolfram★ (*Tannhäuser*). Gives recitals. Appears with symphony orchestra. **Res:** Moscow, USSR.

MAZZINI, GUIDO. Lyric baritone. Italian. Born 16 Aug 1923, Rome. Wife Maria Bianca. Three children. Studied: Manfredi Polverosi, Riccardo Stracciari. **Debut:** Silvio (*Pagliacci*) Teatro San Carlo, Naples 1969. Awards: Cavaliere, Rep of Italy.

Sang with major companies in AUS: Vienna Staatsoper; BEL: Brussels; BUL: Sofia; FIN: Helsinki; FR GER: Wiesbaden; ITA: Bologna, Florence Maggio & Comunale, Genoa, Milan La Scala, Naples, Palermo, Parma, Rome Opera & Caracalla, Spoleto Fest, Trieste, Turin, Venice, Verona Arena; S AFR: Johannesburg; SPA: Barcelona; SWI: Basel, Geneva; UK: Edinburgh Fest, Glasgow Scottish; YUG: Dubrovnik. **Roles with these companies incl** BIZET: Escamillo (*Carmen*), Zurga (*Pêcheurs de perles*); BRITTEN: Mr Redburn★ (*Billy Budd*); CILEA: Michonnet★ (*A. Lecouvreur*); DONIZETTI: Enrico★ (*Campanello*), Dott Malatesta (*Don Pasquale*), Belcore★ (*Elisir*), Enrico (*Lucia*); GIORDANO: Carlo Gérard (*Andrea Chénier*), De Siriex★ (*Fedora*); HENZE: Lescaut (*Boulevard Solitude*); HINDEMITH: Professor (*Hin und zurück*); JANACEK: Jaroslav Prus (*Makropoulos Affair*); LEONCAVALLO: Tonio (*Pagliacci*); MASCAGNI: Rabbi David★ (*Amico Fritz*), Alfio★ (*Cavalleria rusticana*); MASSENET: Albert (*Werther*); MENOTTI: Husband★ (*Amelia al ballo*); MUSSORGSKY: Shaklovity (*Khovanshchina*); OFFENBACH: Coppélius etc★ (*Contes d'Hoffmann*); ORFF: Solo★ (*Carmina burana*); PAISIELLO: Figaro (*Barbiere di Siviglia*); PUCCINI: Marcello★ (*Bohème*), Gianni Schicchi★, Sharpless★ (*Butterfly*), Lescaut★ (*Manon Lescaut*), Rambaldo★

(*Rondine*), Scarpia (*Tosca*); ROSSINI: Figaro (*Barbiere di Siviglia*), Tobias Mill★ (*Cambiale di matrimonio*), Dandini (*Cenerentola*); VERDI: Amonasro (*Aida*), Renato (*Ballo in maschera*), Ford★ (*Falstaff*), Fra Melitone★ (*Forza del destino*), Rigoletto, Germont (*Traviata*), Conte di Luna (*Trovatore*); WAGNER: Beckmesser (*Meistersinger*); WOLF-FERRARI: Conte Gil (*Segreto di Susanna*). Also LEONCAVALLO: Rodolfo (*Bohème*). **World premieres:** MUSCO: Calogero Sedara (*Gattopardo*) Teatro Massimo, Palermo 1967; CHAILLY: Markheim, Spoleto Fest 1967. Recorded for: EMI, His Master's Voice, Cetra, Philips. Video/Film: CHERUBINI: (*Intermezzo*).

MAZZOLI, FERRUCCIO. Bass. Italian. Born 31 Apr 1931, Bologna. Wife Silvana Gozzi, occupation teacher. One child. Studied: Consv G B Martini, Antonio Melandri, Bologna; Consv Abbaco, Prof Rina Malatrasi, Verona. **Debut:** Palemon (*Thaïs*) Teatro Comunale, Bologna 1954. Awards: Personal Medal from Pope John XXIII after RAI concert at Vatican.

Sang with major companies in ARG: Buenos Aires; AUS: Vienna Staatsoper; BUL: Sofia; GRE: Athens National; FR GER: Berlin Deutsche Oper; HUN: Budapest; ITA: Bologna, Florence Maggio & Comunale, Milan La Scala, Naples, Palermo, Parma, Rome Opera & Caracalla, Spoleto Fest, Trieste, Turin, Venice, Verona Arena; MEX: Mexico City; POR: Lisbon; SPA: Barcelona; SWI: Zurich; USA: Chicago, San Diego, San Francisco Opera & Spring Opera; YUG: Zagreb. **Roles with these companies incl** BELLINI: Oroveso★ (*Norma*), Sir George★ (*Puritani*), Rodolfo★ (*Sonnambula*); CATALANI: Stromminger (*Wally*); CHERUBINI: Creon (*Medea*); GOUNOD: Méphistophélès (*Faust*); MASSENET: Des Grieux (*Portrait de Manon*); MOZART: Sarastro★ (*Zauberflöte*); MUSSORGSKY: Pimen★ (*Boris Godunov*); PUCCINI: Colline‡ (*Bohème*); RIMSKY-KORSAKOV: Juri Vsevolodovic (*Invisible City of Kitezh*); ROSSINI: Don Basilio (*Barbiere di Siviglia*), Moïse; STRAUSS, R: Orest (*Elektra*); STRAVINSKY: Tiresias (*Oedipus Rex*); THOMAS: Lothario (*Mignon*); VERDI: Ramfis★ (*Aida*), Philip II & Grande Inquisitore (*Don Carlo*), Padre Guardiano★ (*Forza del destino*), Banquo★ (*Macbeth*), Zaccaria (*Nabucco*), Fiesco★ (*Simon Boccanegra*), Procida (*Vespri*); WAGNER: Pogner (*Meistersinger*), König Marke★ (*Tristan und Isolde*). **World premieres:** PORRINO: Gonnario (*Sardana*) San Carlo Opera, Naples 1964. Recorded for: Cetra, MCA. Video/Film: (*Lucia di Lammermoor*). Coaches repertoire. **Res:** V Pascal 4, Parma, Italy.

MAZZUCATO, DANIELA; née Mazzucato-Meneghini. Coloratura soprano. Italian. Born 1 Dec 1946, Venice. Husband Sergio Tedesco, occupation opera singer, tenor. Studied: Consv B Marcello, Mo Paolo Mirko Bononi, Venice. **Debut:** Gilda (*Rigoletto*) La Fenice, Venice 1966. Previous occupations: ballet student. Awards: Consv Diploma with spec honors 1966; Winner Intl Singing Conc Busseto 1967; First Class Certif Intl Conc Parma 1968 & Apollo Musagete 1970; Miss Melodramma; Verdi d'oro, Salsomaggiore 1974.

Sang with major companies in AUS: Bregenz Fest; CZE: Prague National; FR GER: Düsseldorf-Duisburg; ITA: Bologna, Milan La Scala, Naples, Palermo, Trieste, Venice, Verona Arena. Roles with these companies incl DONIZETTI: Prima Donna★ (Convenienze/Viva la Mamma), Norina★ (Don Pasquale); GIORDANO: Olga★ (Fedora); GLUCK: Amor★ (Orfeo ed Euridice); MASSENET: Sophie★ (Werther); MOZART: Despina★ (Così fan tutte), Violante (Finta giardiniera), Susanna★ (Nozze di Figaro); PUCCINI: Musetta★ (Bohème), Lauretta (Gianni Schicchi), Lisette★ (Rondine); ROSSINI: Rosina★ (Barbiere di Siviglia), Elvira★ (Italiana in Algeri); VERDI: Oscar★ (Ballo in maschera), Nannetta★ (Falstaff), Gilda★ (Rigoletto); WOLF-FERRARI: Lucieta★ (Quattro rusteghi), Susanna★ (Segreto di Susanna). Also ROTA: Elena (Cappello di paglia di Firenze); NEGRI: Woman-Idea (Pubblicità ninfa gentile); CIMAROSA: Béllina (Astuzie femminili); CHERUBINI: Glauce (Medea); PETRASSI: Cristina (Cordovano). Video/Film: Elena (Cappello di paglia); Cristina (Cordovano). Gives recitals. Res: V Monte Altore 10, Abano Terme (PD), Italy.

McARTHUR, EDWIN DOUGLAS. Conductor of opera and symphony; composer. American. Born 24 Sep 1907, Denver, CO, USA. Wife Blanche. Studied: Juilliard School of Music, incl piano, organ. Plays the piano, organ. Operatic debut: Lohengrin Chicago Opera Co 1938. Symphonic debut: Sydney Symph Orch, NSW, Australia 1938. Awards: Hon DM Univ of Denver & Elizabethtown Coll; Spec Awd ASCAP and NAACC. Previous adm positions in opera: Mus Dir, St Louis Municipal Opera, MO, 23 seasons.
Conducted with major companies in USA: Miami, St Paul. Operas with these companies incl BRITTEN: Midsummer Night★; JANACEK: Katya Kabanova★; MOZART: Nozze di Figaro★; OFFENBACH: Contes d'Hoffmann★; POULENC: Dialogues des Carmélites★; PROKOFIEV: Love for Three Oranges★; PUCCINI: Bohème★, Fanciulla del West★, Gianni Schicchi★, Butterfly★, Suor Angelica★, Tosca★; PURCELL: Dido and Aeneas★; RAVEL: Heure espagnole★; ROSSINI: Barbiere di Siviglia★; STRAUSS, R: Schweigsame Frau★; WAGNER: Walküre★, Siegfried★.

McCOLLUM, JOHN MORRIS. Lyric tenor. American. Born 21 Feb 1922, Coalinga, CA. Wife Mary Wilson. Two children. Studied: Mynard Jones, Oakland, CA; Edgar Schofield, New York; American Theatre Wing, New York; Berkshire Music Center, Goldovsky Opera, Lenox, MA. Debut: Fenton (Falstaff) New England Opera Theater 1953. Previous occupations: Editor, News Bulletin, Univ of Calif, Berkeley; City Editor, newspaper, Coalinga, CA; US Naval Aviator WWII. Awards: Atwater Kent Awd, Los Angeles 1950; American Theatre Wing Conct Awd, Town Hall debut recital 1952.
Sang with major companies in CAN: Toronto, Vancouver; ITA: Spoleto Fest; USA: Boston, Cincinnati, Fort Worth, New York City Opera, Santa Fe, Seattle, Washington DC. Roles with these companies incl BERLIOZ: Faust (Damnation de Faust); BRITTEN: Male Chorus (Rape of Lucre-

tia); CIMAROSA: Paolino (Matrimonio segreto); DEBUSSY: Azaël (Enfant prodigue), Pelléas; DONIZETTI: Ernesto (Don Pasquale); GOUNOD: Faust; HANDEL: Acis, Grimwald (Rodelinda); MASSENET: Des Grieux (Manon); MILHAUD: Jason (Médée); MONTEVERDI: Nero (Incoronazione di Poppea); MOZART: Tito (Clemenza di Tito), Ferrando (Così fan tutte), Don Ottavio (Don Giovanni), Belmonte (Entführung aus dem Serail), Belfiore (Finta giardiniera), Idamante (Idomeneo), Tamino (Zauberflöte); MUSSORGSKY: Shuisky (Boris Godunov); PUCCINI: Rodolfo (Bohème); RAMEAU: Hippolyte; ROSSINI: Almaviva (Barbiere di Siviglia), Comte Ory; SMETANA: Wenzel & Hans (Bartered Bride); SPONTINI: Licinio (Vestale); STRAUSS, J: Alfred (Fledermaus); STRAVINSKY: Oedipus, Pêcheur (Rossignol); VERDI: Fenton (Falstaff), Alfredo (Traviata). Also GRETRY: Blondel (Richard Coeur de Lion).
World premieres: HOIBY: Reuel (Scarf) Spoleto Fest 1958; Arkady (Natalia Petrovna) New York City Opera 1964. Gives recitals. Appears with symphony orchestra. Teaches voice. Coaches repertoire. On faculty of Univ of Michigan, Ann Arbor, MI. Res: 2117 Brockman Blvd, Ann Arbor, MI, USA. Mgmt: CAM/USA.

McCRACKEN, JAMES. Dramatic tenor. American. Resident mem: Metropolitan Opera, New York, USA. Born 16 Dec 1926, Gary, IN, USA. Wife Sandra Warfield, occupation opera singer, mezzo-soprano. Two children. Studied: Eulah Winter, Gary, IN; Mario Pagano, New York; Marcello Conati, Milan; Elsa Seyfert, New York/Konstanz, Switz. Debut: Rodolfo (Bohème) Central City Fest, CO. Previous occupations: Roxy Glee Club; Broadway shows. Awards: Hon DM Indiana Univ, Bloomington, IN; Whitbread Awd, best perf Covent Garden, London.
Sang with major companies in ARG: Buenos Aires; AUS: Salzburg Fest, Vienna Staatsoper; FRA: Nice, Paris; GRE: Athens Fest; FR GER: Berlin Deutsche Oper, Bielefeld, Bonn, Cologne, Hamburg, Munich Staatsoper, Wiesbaden; ISR: Tel Aviv; ITA: Palermo, Rome Opera, Trieste; MEX: Mexico City; POR: Lisbon; SPA: Barcelona; SWI: Geneva, Zurich; UK: Aldeburgh Fest, Edinburgh Fest, London Royal Opera; USA: Fort Worth, Hartford Connecticut Opera, Houston, Memphis, Miami, Milwaukee Florentine, New Orleans, New York Met, Philadelphia Grand & Lyric, Pittsburgh, Portland, St Paul, San Antonio, San Diego, San Francisco Opera, Seattle, Washington DC. Roles with these companies incl BEETHOVEN: Florestan★‡ (Fidelio); BIZET: Don José★‡ (Carmen); LEONCAVALLO: Canio★‡ (Pagliacci); MEYERBEER: Jean de Leyde (Prophète); PUCCINI: Calaf★ (Turandot); SAINT-SAENS: Samson★; STRAUSS, R: Bacchus (Ariadne auf Naxos); VERDI: Radames★ (Aida), Don Alvaro (Forza del destino), Otello★‡, Manrico★ (Trovatore); WEBER: Max (Freischütz). Recorded for: London, EMI, DG. Gives recitals. Appears with symphony orchestra. Res: Zurich, Switzerland. Mgmt: CAM/USA; GOR/UK.

McCRAY, JAMES JOSEPH. Heldentenor. American. Born 21 Feb 1939, Warren, O, USA. Wife

Simona, occupation account exec, CBS Radio.
Two children. Studied: Raymond Buckingham. **Debut:** Jim Mahoney (*Aufstieg und Fall der Stadt Mahagonny*) Stratford Fest, Canada 1965. Awards: Met Op Ntl Counc Aud Winner; Met Op Schoen-René Awd.

Sang with major companies in ISR: Tel Aviv; USA: Hawaii, Kansas City Lyric Th, Miami, Newark, New York City Opera, Omaha, St Paul, San Francisco Opera, Seattle. **Roles with these companies incl** BIZET: Don José★ (*Carmen*); BORODIN: Vladimir★ (*Prince Igor*); LEON-CAVALLO: Canio★ (*Pagliacci*); PONCHIELLI: Enzo (*Gioconda*); PUCCINI: Dick Johnson★ (*Fanciulla del West*), Pinkerton (*Butterfly*), Luigi (*Tabarro*), Cavaradossi★ (*Tosca*), Calaf (*Turandot*); SAINT-SAENS: Samson; VERDI: Radames★ (*Aida*), Riccardo (*Ballo in maschera*), Ismaele (*Nabucco*), Manrico★ (*Trovatore*); WAGNER: Erik★ (*Fliegende Holländer*), Siegmund★ (*Walküre*), Siegfried★ (*Siegfried, Götterdämmerung*). Appears with symphony orchestra. Mgmt: LLF/USA.

McDANIEL, BARRY. Lyric baritone. American. Resident mem: Deutsche Oper, Berlin. Born 18 Oct 1930, Topeka, KS, USA. Divorced. Three children. Studied: Juilliard School, Mack Harrell, New York; Consv of Music, Alfred Paulus, Stuttgart; Margarethe von Winterfeld, Berlin. **Debut:** Homonay (*Zigeunerbaron*) Mainz, FR Ger 1954. Awards: Kammersänger, Deutsche Oper Berlin.

Sang with major companies in AUS: Salzburg Fest, Vienna Staatsoper; FRA: Bordeaux, Marseille; FR GER: Bayreuth Fest, Berlin Deutsche Oper, Frankfurt, Hamburg, Karlsruhe, Mannheim, Munich Staatsoper, Stuttgart, Wiesbaden; HOL: Amsterdam; SWI: Geneva; USA: New York Met. **Roles with these companies incl** CIMAROSA: Count Robinson★ (*Matrimonio segreto*); DE-BUSSY: Pelléas★; GLUCK: Oreste★ (*Iphigénie en Tauride*); HANDEL: Giulio Cesare; LEON-CAVALLO: Silvio‡ (*Pagliacci*); LORTZING: Graf Eberbach★ (*Wildschütz*), Peter (*Zar und Zimmermann*); MARTINU: Hans (*Comedy on the Bridge*); MONTEVERDI: Orfeo; MOZART: Guglielmo★ (*Così fan tutte*), Conte Almaviva (*Nozze di Figaro*), Allazim (*Zaïde*), Papageno★ (*Zauberflöte*); ORFF: Solo★ (*Carmina burana*); POULENC: Mari de Tirésias★ (*Mamelles de Tirésias*); PUCCINI: Sharpless (*Butterfly*); PURCELL: Aeneas‡ (*Dido and Aeneas*); ROSSINI: Figaro★ (*Barbiere di Siviglia*), Dandini★ (*Cenerentola*), Poeta★ (*Turco in Italia*); SCHOENBERG: Der Mann (*Glückliche Hand*); STRAUSS, R: Harlekin★ (*Ariadne auf Naxos*), Olivier★ (*Capriccio*), Barbier★ (*Schweigsame Frau*); VERDI: Germont (*Traviata*); WAGNER: Wolfram★ (*Tannhäuser*); WOLF-FERRARI: Conte Gil (*Segreto di Susanna*); YUN: Liu-Tung★ (*Traum des Liu-Tung*). **World premieres:** HENZE: Sekretär (*Junge Lord*) Deutsche Oper Berlin 1965; REI-MANN: Graf (*Melusine*) Deutsche Oper Berlin 1970; NABOKOV: Berowne (*Love's Labour's Lost*) Deutsche Oper Berlin 1973. Recorded for: RCA, DG, Archive. Video/Film: Sekretär (*Junge Lord*); Sharpless (*Butterfly*); Selim (*Turco in Italia*). Gives recitals. Appears with symphony orchestra. **Res:** Schopenhauerstr 31, Berlin 38, FR Ger. Mgmt: CAM/USA; KHA/FRG.

McDONALL, LOIS JEANETTE. Lyric soprano. Canadian. Resident mem: English National Opera, London. Born Larkspur, Alta, Canada. Divorced. Two children. Studied: Eileen Turner, Edmonton, Alta; Glyndwr Jones, Vancouver, BC; Irene Jessner, Toronto; Otakar Kraus, London. **Debut:** Susanna (*Segreto di Susanna*) Canadian Opera Co, Toronto 1969. Previous occupations: medical technician.

Sang with major companies in CAN: Ottawa, Toronto; UK: London English National. **Roles with these companies incl** BENNETT: Jenny★ (*Mines of Sulphur*); MASSENET: Manon; MOZART: Fiordiligi★ (*Così fan tutte*), Konstanze★ (*Entführung aus dem Serail*), Mme Herz (*Schauspieldirektor*), Contessa★ (*Nozze di Figaro*); OF-FENBACH: Antonia★ (*Contes d'Hoffmann*); ORFF: Solo (*Carmina burana*); PUCCINI: Tosca; ROSSINI: Fiorilla (*Turco in Italia*); STRAUSS, J: Rosalinde★ (*Fledermaus*); STRAUSS, R: Arabella, Marschallin★ (*Rosenkavalier*); WAGNER: Elsa (*Lohengrin*); WOLF-FERRARI: Susanna (*Segreto di Susanna*). Also HANDEL: Semele★, Atalanta★. Gives recitals. Appears with symphony orchestra. **Res:** London, UK. Mgmt: MIN/UK.

McDONNELL, THOMAS ANTHONY. Lyric baritone. Australian. Born 27 Apr 1940, Melbourne, Australia. Wife Mary Jennifer, occupation teacher of English. Two children. Studied: Melba Consv, Lennox Brewer, Melbourne. **Debut:** Belcore (*Elisir*) Sutherland-Williamson Opera Co, Australia 1965.

Sang with major companies in AUSTRL: Sydney; UK: London English National. **Roles with these companies incl** BIZET: Escamillo (*Carmen*); MOZART: Almaviva★ & Figaro (*Nozze di Figaro*), Papageno★ (*Zauberflöte*); PROKOFIEV: Prince Andrei Bolkonsky (*War and Peace*); VERDI: Germont (*Traviata*); WAGNER: Wolfram (*Tannhäuser*). Also MONTEVERDI: Ottone★ (*Incoronazione di Poppea*). **World premieres:** CROSSE: Lt September (*Story of Vasco*) English National Opera 1974. Video/Film: Figaro (*Barbiere di Siviglia*). Gives recitals. Appears with symphony orchestra. **Res:** 25 Talbot Rd, London N6, UK. Mgmt: MIN/UK.

McGOWEN, ADAIR; né Roy Adair McGowen. Dramatic baritone. American. Born Houston, TX, USA. Widowed. Studied: Carrol Ault, Houston, TX; Mme Lotte Lehmann, Santa Barbara, CA; Joseph Pouhé, New York; Hermann Firchow, Bielefeld, FR Ger. **Debut:** Monterone (*Rigoletto*) Houston Grand Opera 1959. Previous occupations: engineer, salesman, longshoreman. Awards: Met Op Ntl Counc Aud, Reg Winner.

Sang with major companies in FR GER: Bielefeld, Essen, Hannover, Wuppertal; USA: Houston, Kansas City, Kentucky, Seattle. **Roles with these companies incl** BIZET: Escamillo (*Carmen*); GERSHWIN: Porgy★; GIANNINI: Petruchio‡ (*Taming of the Shrew*); IBERT: Boniface (*Angélique*); MOZART: Almaviva★ (*Nozze di Figaro*); OFFENBACH: Coppélius etc★ (*Contes d'Hoffmann*); RAVEL: Ramiro (*Heure espagnole*); TCHAIKOVSKY: Eugene Onegin★; VERDI: Renato★ (*Ballo in maschera*), Iago★ (*Otello*), Rigoletto★, Germont★ (*Traviata*), Conte di Luna★ (*Trovatore*); WARD: John Proctor (*Crucible*). Also CIKKER: Prince Nechludov★ (*Resurrection*); GOUNOD: Valentin (*Faust*); MONTEVERDI: Ulisse★ (*Ritorno d'Ulisse*). Recorded for: CRI. Gives recitals. Appears with symphony orchestra. **Res:** 513 Genoa-Red Bluff Rd, Houston, TX 77034, USA. Mgmt: NAP/USA; PAS/FRG.

McINTYRE, DONALD CONROY. Bass-baritone. New Zealander. Born 22 Oct 1934, Auckland, New Zealand. Wife Jill. Three children. Studied: Guildhall School, Ellis Keeler, London; Hubert Milverton-Carta, Teachers Training Coll, Auckland; Kaiser-Breme, Bayreuth & London. **Debut:** Zaccaria (*Nabucco*) Welsh National Opera 1959. Previous occupations: schoolteacher.

Sang with major companies in ARG: Buenos Aires; AUS: Vienna Staatsoper; BEL: Brussels; CAN: Montreal/Quebec; CZE: Prague; FR GER: Bayreuth Fest, Berlin Deutsche Oper, Düsseldorf-Duisburg, Hamburg, Hannover, Munich Staatsoper, Stuttgart, Wiesbaden; FRA: Paris; HOL: Amsterdam; ITA: Milan La Scala, Spoleto; SWI: Basel; UK: Cardiff Welsh, Edinburgh Fest, London Royal & English National; USA: Chicago, New York Met. **Roles with these companies incl** BEETHOVEN: Don Pizarro (*Fidelio*); BERLIOZ: Méphistophélès (*Damnation de Faust*); BIZET: Escamillo (*Carmen*); DEBUSSY: Golaud (*Pelléas et Mélisande*); GOUNOD: Méphistophélès (*Faust*); HANDEL: Polyphemus (*Acis*), King of Scotland (*Ariodante*); MOZART: Guglielmo (*Così fan tutte*), Figaro (*Nozze. di Figaro*), Sarastro (*Zauberflöte*); MUSSORGSKY: Varlaam (*Boris Godunov*), Shaklovity (*Khovanshchina*); PUCCINI: Colline (*Bohème*); STRAUSS, R: Orest (*Elektra*), Barak (*Frau ohne Schatten*), Jochanaan (*Salome*); STRAVINSKY: Creon (*Oedipus Rex*); VERDI: Attila; WAGNER: Holländer, Telramund (*Lohengrin*), Amfortas (*Parsifal*), Wotan (*Rheingold, Walküre*), Wanderer (*Siegfried*), Hunding (*Walküre*), Gunther (*Götterdämmerung*), Kurwenal (*Tristan und Isolde*); WEBER: Kaspar (*Freischütz*). Also BRITTEN: Swallow (*Peter Grimes*); MENOTTI: Stranger (*Martin's Lie*); WEILL: Bill (*Mahagonny*); WAGNER: Klingsor (*Parsifal*)★‡; HANDEL: Saul‡. **World premieres:** BENNETT: Heyst (*Victory*) Covent Garden, London 1970. Recorded for: DG, Columbia. Video—Munich TV/Unitel: Holländer. Gives recitals. Appears with symphony orchestra. Mgmt: BAR/USA; IWL/UK.

McINTYRE, JOY. Dramatic soprano. American. Resident mem: Städtische Bühnen, Dortmund. Born 24 Sep 1938, Kinsley, KA, USA. Husband Hansjörg Trefny, occupation architectural engineer. Studied: Oberlin Coll, Ellen Repp, O, USA; New England Consv, Gladys Miller, Boris Goldovsky, Boston; Mozarteum, Salzburg; Edith Boroschek, Düsseldorf, FR Ger.

Sang with major companies in AUS: Graz, Vienna Staatsoper; FRA: Lyon, Strasbourg; FR GER: Berlin Deutsche Oper, Bielefeld, Bonn, Dortmund, Düsseldorf-Duisburg, Essen, Frankfurt, Hamburg, Hannover, Kassel, Munich Staatsoper, Nürnberg, Saarbrücken, Stuttgart, Wiesbaden, Wuppertal; SWI: Basel; UK: Glasgow. **Roles with these companies incl** BARTOK:

Judith (*Bluebeard's Castle*); BEETHOVEN: Leonore★ (*Fidelio*); BERG: Marie★ (*Wozzeck*); JANACEK: Kostelnicka (*Jenufa*); MASCAGNI: Santuzza★ (*Cavalleria rusticana*); OFFENBACH: Giulietta (*Contes d'Hoffmann*); OHANA: Phèdre (*Syllabaire pour Phèdre*); PUCCINI: Turandot★; PURCELL: Dido; STRAUSS, R: Färberin★ (*Frau ohne Schatten*); VERDI: Lady Macbeth, Abigaille★ (*Nabucco*); WAGNER: Ortrud (*Lohengrin*), Brünnhilde (*Walküre★ & Siegfried★ & Götterdämmerung★*), Venus★ (*Tannhäuser*), Brangäne★ (*Tristan und Isolde*). Also LEVY: Christine (*Mourning Becomes Electra*); EINEM: Claire★ (*Besuch der alten Dame*). **World premieres:** STEFFENS: Bäckerin (*Eli*) Dortmund Opera 1967. Video/Film - NET TV: Dido (*Dido and Aeneas*). Gives recitals. **Res:** Schneider Str 9, Dortmund, FR Ger. Mgmt: SMD/FRG; SLZ/FRG.

McKEE, RICHARD. Bass-baritone. American. Resident mem: New York City Opera. Born 28 Dec 1941, Hagerstown, MD, USA. Wife Francine, occupation pediatric nurse. Two children. Studied: Yale Univ, Blake Stern, New Haven, CT; Univ of Illinois, Bruce Foote, Paul Ulanowsky, Urbana, IL; Oren Brown, New York. **Debut:** Leporello (*Don Giovanni*) Goldovsky Opera 1971. Previous occupations: hardware wholesaler. Awards: NATS Awd; Corbett Fndt Grant; Baltimore Opera Aud; Connecticut Opera Awd; Sullivan Fndt Grant.

Sang with major companies in USA: New York City Opera, Portland, Washington DC. **Roles with these companies incl** CORNELIUS: Abul Hassan★ (*Barbier von Bagdad*); DONIZETTI: Sulpice★ (*Fille du régiment*); MOZART: Leporello★ (*Don Giovanni*); ROSSINI: Dott Bartolo★ (*Barbiere di Siviglia*). Also DONIZETTI: Don Gregorio★ (*Ajo nell'imbarazzo*). Gives recitals. **Res:** 182 Daniel Rd, Hamden, CO 06517, USA. Mgmt: TOR/USA.

McKINNEY, THOMAS. Lyric baritone. American. Born 5 May 1946, Lufkin, TX, USA. Single. Studied: Jay Froman, Houston; William Schahn, Lufkin, TX; Seth Riggs, Hollywood; Keith Davis, New York, USA. **Debut:** Shchelkalov (*Boris Godunov*) Houston Grand Opera 1971. Previous occupations: music school teacher, salesman, newspaper reporter. Awards: Winner Met Op Ntl Counc Aud 1971; Ntl Opera Inst Grant 1971-75; Finalist WGN Illinois Opera Guild 1971.

Sang with major companies in AUS: Vienna Volksoper; BEL: Brussels; USA: Cincinnati, Houston, Omaha, San Diego, San Francisco Spring Opera. **Roles with these companies incl** DEBUSSY: Pelléas★; DONIZETTI: Stefano★ (*Convenienze/Viva la Mamma*), Belcore★ (*Elisir*); GAY/Britten: Mr Peachum★ (*Beggar's Opera*); MASSENET: Hérode★ (*Hérodiade*), Athanaël★‡ (*Thaïs*); MENOTTI: Dr Stone★ & Tony★ (*Globolinks*); MOZART: Guglielmo★ (*Così fan tutte*), Don Giovanni★, Conte Almaviva★ (*Nozze di Figaro*), Papageno★ (*Zauberflöte*); ORFF: Solo★ (*Carmina burana*); PUCCINI: Marcello★ (*Bohème*), Gianni Schicchi★; ROSSINI: Figaro★ (*Barbiere di Siviglia*); TCHAIKOVSKY: Eugene Onegin★; THOMAS: Hamlet★; VERDI: Rodrigo★ (*Don Carlo*), Ford★ (*Falstaff*); WOLF-

FERRARI: Conte Gil★ (*Segreto di Susanna*). Also OFFENBACH: Paquillo (*Périchole*). **World premieres:** HENDERSON: Tutor (*Medea*) San Diego Opera 1972. Video/Film—Wexford Fest: Athanaël (*Thaïs*). Gives recitals. Appears with symphony orchestra. **Res:** 141 E 55 St, New York, NY 10022, USA. Mgmt: LLF/USA; RAB/AUS.

McPHERSON, ALEXANDER. Scenic and costume designer for opera, theater. Is also a painter & illustrator. British. Born 16 Sep 1937, London. Wife Valerie Myra. Four children. Prof training: in a scenic shop. **Operatic debut:** *Turandot* Welsh Ntl Opera, Cardiff, UK 1972. Theater debut: Little Theatre, Bristol Old Vic, UK.

Designed for major companies in UK: Welsh National. **Operas designed for these companies incl** FALLA: *Retablo de Maese Pedro★;* PUCCINI: *Turandot;* WEILL: *Dreigroschenoper★.* **Operatic world premieres:** HODDINOTT: *Beach of Falesa* Welsh Ntl Opera 1974. Operatic Video—HTV: *Beach of Falesa.* **Res:** 16 Robinson Dr, Easton/Bristol, UK. Mgmt: PLR/UK.

MÉDECIN, PIERRE. Stages/produces opera, theater & television. French. Born 1 Oct 1935, Nice. Wife Eliane Manchet, occupation opera singer, soprano. Two children. Studied: music, flute and voice. **Operatic debut:** *Walküre* Fest Cimiez, Nice 1957.

Directed/produced opera for major companies in AUS: Graz; BEL: Brussels; FRA: Bordeaux, Lyon, Marseille, Nancy, Nice, Paris, Rouen, Toulouse; HOL: Amsterdam; ITA: Bologna, Genoa, Palermo; POR: Lisbon; ROM: Bucharest; UK: Glyndebourne Fest; YUG: Dubrovnik, Belgrade. **Operas staged for these companies incl** BARTOK: *Bluebeard's Castle;* BEETHOVEN: *Fidelio★;* BELLINI: *Norma;* BERG: *Lulu, Wozzeck;* BERLIOZ: *Béatrice et Bénédict, Damnation de Faust★;* BIZET: *Carmen★;* BOITO: *Mefistofele;* BORODIN: *Prince Igor;* BUSONI: *Doktor Faust;* CHARPENTIER: *Louise;* DEBUSSY: *Pelléas et Mélisande;* DONIZETTI: *Lucia;* FALLA: *Vida breve;* GINASTERA: *Beatrix Cenci;* GLUCK: *Orfeo ed Euridice★;* GOUNOD: *Faust, Roméo et Juliette★;* HENZE: *Elegy for Young Lovers★;* JANACEK: *From the House of the Dead, Katya Kabanova;* LALO: *Roi d'Ys;* LEONCAVALLO: *Pagliacci★;* MASCAGNI: *Cavalleria rusticana★;* MASSENET: *Don Quichotte, Hérodiade, Manon, Thaïs, Werther★;* MENOTTI: *Consul;* MEYERBEER: *Africaine;* MILHAUD: *Pauvre matelot;* MOZART: *Così fan tutte, Don Giovanni★, Nozze di Figaro★, Zauberflöte;* MUSSORGSKY: *Boris Godunov★, Fair at Sorochinsk★, Khovanshchina★;* OFFENBACH: *Contes d'Hoffmann;* POULENC: *Dialogues des Carmélites★;* PUCCINI: *Bohème, Fanciulla del West, Tosca★, Turandot;* RABAUD: *Mârouf;* ROSSELLINI: *Annonce faite à Marie;* SAINT-SAENS: *Samson et Dalila★;* SHOSTAKOVICH: *Katerina Ismailova;* STRAUSS, J: *Fledermaus;* STRAUSS, R: *Elektra, Rosenkavalier, Salome;* TCHAIKOVSKY: *Eugene Onegin;* VERDI: *Aida★, Don Carlo★, Falstaff, Macbeth, Otello, Rigoletto, Traviata, Trovatore;* WAGNER: *Fliegende Holländer★, Lohengrin★, Meistersinger★, Parsifal★, Rheingold★, Walküre★, Siegfried★, Götterdämmerung★,*

Tannhäuser★, Tristan und Isolde★; WOLF-FERRARI: *Quattro rusteghi.* Also TANSMAN: *Serment.* **Operatic world premieres:** TANSMAN: *Rossignol de Boboli* Opéra de Nice 1965. Previous leading positions with major theater companies: Art Adv, Opéra de Nice 1959-67. Teaches. **Res:** rue Léon Cogniet 13, 75017 Paris, France. Mgmt: CMW/FRA.

MEGHOR, CAMILLO; né Camille Van Peteghem. Dramatic baritone & Italian character baritone. Belgian. Resident mem: Opernhaus, Cologne. Born 27 Jul 1935, Antwerp, Belgium. Wife Erika. Two children. Studied: Tino Pattiera, Helge Roswänge. **Debut:** Marcello (*Bohème*) Oper Linz, Austria 1958.

Sang with major companies in AUS: Vienna Staatsoper; Opéra du Rhin; FRA: Strasbourg; FR GER: Berlin Deutsche Oper, Bielefeld, Bonn, Cologne, Darmstadt, Dortmund, Düsseldorf-Duisburg, Essen, Frankfurt, Hamburg, Hannover, Karlsruhe, Kassel, Munich Staatsoper, Saarbrücken, Stuttgart, Wiesbaden; GER DR: Berlin Komische Oper; HOL: Amsterdam; HUN: Budapest; ISR: Tel Aviv; UK: London English National; USA: Chicago. **Roles with these companies incl** BEETHOVEN: Don Pizarro (*Fidelio*); BERLIOZ: Méphistophélès★ (*Damnation de Faust*); BIZET: Escamillo★ (*Carmen*); BUSONI: Doktor Faust; DONIZETTI: Belcore★ (*Elisir*); FORTNER: Norfolk (*Elisabeth Tudor*); GOUNOD: Méphistophélès★ (*Faust*); HAYDN: Buonafede★ (*Mondo della luna*); HINDEMITH: Cardillac; LEONCAVALLO: Tonio★ (*Pagliacci*); LORTZING: Graf Eberbach★ (*Wildschütz*), Peter I★ (*Zar und Zimmermann*); MASCAGNI: Alfio (*Cavalleria rusticana*); MILHAUD: Dionysos (*Abandon d'Ariane*); MOZART: Don Alfonso★ (*Così fan tutte*), Don Giovanni★, Figaro (*Nozze di Figaro*), Papageno★ (*Zauberflöte*); MUSSORGSKY: Boris Godunov; NICOLAI: Falstaff (*Lustigen Weiber*); OFFENBACH: Coppélius etc★ (*Contes d'Hoffmann*); ORFF: Solo (*Carmina burana*), König (*Kluge*), Bauer (*Mond*); PUCCINI: Colline & Marcello★ (*Bohème*), Jack Rance★ (*Fanciulla del West*), Sharpless★ (*Butterfly*), Lescaut★ (*Manon Lescaut*), Michele★ (*Tabarro*), Scarpia★ (*Tosca*); ROSSINI: Figaro★ (*Barbiere di Siviglia*); STRAUSS, R: Mandryka (*Arabella*), Musiklehrer★ (*Ariadne auf Naxos*), Olivier★ (*Capriccio*), Orest★ (*Elektra*), Jochanaan (*Salome*); TCHAIKOVSKY: Yeletsky (*Pique Dame*); VERDI: Amonasro★ & Ramfis★ (*Aida*), Egberto★ (*Aroldo*), Renato★ (*Ballo in maschera*), Rodrigo★ (*Don Carlo*), Ford★ (*Falstaff*), Don Carlo★ (*Forza del destino*), Iago★ (*Otello*), Rigoletto★, Simon Boccanegra, Germont★ (*Traviata*), Conte di Luna★ (*Trovatore*), Monforte★ (*Vespri*); WAGNER: Telramund (*Lohengrin*), Pogner★ (*Meistersinger*), Amfortas (*Parsifal*), Wotan (*Rheingold*), Gunther (*Götterdämmerung*), Wolfram★ (*Tannhäuser*); ZIMMERMANN: Stolzius (*Soldaten*). **World premieres:** ZIMMERMANN: Lt Mary (*Soldaten*) Opernhaus Cologne 1965. Recorded for: Wergo. Video—WDR Cologne: (*Soldaten*). Gives recitals. Appears with symphony orchestra. Teaches voice. Coaches repertoire. On faculty of Eupen Consv, Belgium. **Res:** Rosenweg 25, 4700 Eupen, Belgium. Mgmt: PAS/FRG; SLZ/FRG.

MEHTA, ZUBIN. Conductor of opera and symphony. Indian. Music Dir & Resident Cond, Los Angeles Phil Orch, Los Angeles; Israel Phil Orch, Tel Aviv. Born 29 Apr 1936, Bombay. Wife Nancy. Two children. Studied: with Prof Hans Swarowsky, Vienna; also double bass. Symphonic debut: Liverpool Symph Orch, UK 1960.

Conducted with major companies in AUS: Vienna Staatsoper; CAN: Montreal/Quebec; FR GER: Berlin Deutsche Oper; USA: New York Met. **Operas with these companies incl** BIZET: *Carmen**; MUSSORGSKY: *Boris Godunov*; PUCCINI: *Turandot‡*; VERDI: *Aida*‡, Trovatore*‡*; WAGNER: *Lohengrin, Tristan und Isolde*. Recorded for Decca. Conducted major orch in Europe, USA/Canada, & Asia. Prev positions as Mus Dir with major orch: Montreal Symph.

MEIER, JOHANNA. Spinto. American. Resident mem: New York City Opera. Born Chicago, IL, USA. Husband Guido Della Vecchia, occupation singer. Studied: Univ of Miami, Arturo di Filippi; Manhattan School of Music, John Brownlee, New York. **Debut:** Siebel (*Faust*) Miami Opera Guild, FL, USA. Previous occupations; actress with parents' prod of Black Hills Passion Play. Awards: Pan American Music Fest Schlshp, City of Miami; Young Artist's Awd, Ntl Fed Music Clubs.

Sang with major companies in CAN: Ottawa; USA: Cincinnati, Kentucky, Lake George, New York Met & City Opera, Philadelphia Lyric, Portland, San Diego, Seattle, Washington DC. **Roles with these companies incl** BRITTEN: Governess* (*Turn of the Screw*); CHARPENTIER: Louise*; FLOYD: Susannah*; GOUNOD: Marguerite* (*Faust*); MOZART: Fiordiligi* (*Così fan tutte*), Donna Anna* (*Don Giovanni*), Contessa* (*Nozze di Figaro*), Pamina* (*Zauberflöte*); OFFENBACH: Antonia & Giulietta* (*Contes d'Hoffmann*); PUCCINI: Musetta* (*Bohème*), Tosca*; STRAUSS, J: Rosalinde* (*Fledermaus*); STRAUSS, R: Ariadne* (*Ariadne auf Naxos*), Gräfin* (*Capriccio*), Marschallin* (*Rosenkavalier*); VERDI: Amelia* (*Ballo in maschera*); WAGNER: Senta* (*Fliegende Holländer*), Eva* (*Meistersinger*), Sieglinde* (*Walküre*); WEBER: Agathe (*Freischütz*). **World premieres:** FLAGELLO: Hester (*Sisters*) Manhattan School, 1960; BARAB: Blanche (*Maletroit Door*) Manhattan School, New York 1959. Recorded for: CRI. Video/Film: (*Questions of Abraham*). Gives recitals. Appears with symphony orchestra. **Res:** Glen Rock, NJ, USA. Mgmt: LLF/USA; AIM/UK.

MEISWINKEL, FRANK. Conductor of opera and symphony. German. Resident Cond, Städtische Bühnen, Wuppertal, FR Ger. Born 3 Feb 1938, Düsseldorf. Wife Bernadette, occupation kindergarten teacher. Two children. Studied: Staatl Hochschule für Musik, Cologne, Prof Wolfgang von der Nahmer; incl piano, organ, clarinet and voice. Plays the piano, organ. Operatic training as repetiteur, asst cond & chorus master at Deutsche Oper am Rhein, Düsseldorf 1961-70; Wuppertal Bühnen 1970-72. **Operatic debut:** Bartered Bride Deutsche Oper am Rhein, Düsseldorf-Duisburg 1969. Symphonic debut: Städt Orch, Düsseldorf 1958. Previous occupations: teacher Robert Schu-

mann Consv; pianist, accompanist, chorus master, organist. Awards: Second Prize, piano cont, German Music Fair 1952.

Conducted with major companies in FR GER: Düsseldorf-Duisburg, Wuppertal. **Operas with these companies incl** d'ALBERT: *Tiefland**; BIZET: *Carmen*; BRITTEN: *Albert Herring*; BUSONI: *Arlecchino*; CIMAROSA: *Matrimonio segreto*; DONIZETTI: *Convenienze/Viva la Mamma**; FORTNER: *Don Perlimplin*; GIORDANO: *Andrea Chénier**; GLUCK: *Iphigénie en Tauride**; HINDEMITH: *Hin und zurück*; JANACEK: *From the House of the Dead*; LEONCAVALLO: *Pagliacci*; LORTZING: *Waffenschmied*, Wildschütz**; MASCAGNI: *Cavalleria rusticana*; MILHAUD: *Médée**; MOZART: *Così fan tutte, Entführung aus dem Serail, Zauberflöte*; NICOLAI: *Lustigen Weiber*; OFFENBACH: *Contes d'Hoffmann**; PUCCINI: *Tosca*; ROSSINI: *Barbiere di Siviglia, Turco in Italia**; SMETANA: *Bartered Bride*; STRAUSS, J: *Fledermaus**; TCHAIKOVSKY: *Pique Dame*; VERDI: *Rigoletto**; WEBER: *Freischütz*; WOLF-FERRARI: *Quattro rusteghi**. Also GEISSLER: *Zerbrochene Krug*. **Res:** Degerstr 52, Düsseldorf, FR Ger.

MELANO, FABRIZIO. Stages/produces opera; and is an author. American. Resident Stage Dir, Metropolitan Opera, New York. Born 3 Apr 1938, New York. Single. Studied: Circle in the Square Actor & Director's Wkshp, William Ball, New York; also music. Operatic training as asst stage dir at Santa Fe, NM 1966. **Operatic debut:** *Elisir* San Francisco Opera 1969. Previous occupation: instructor in English, Columbia Univ 1964-65. Awards: Austin Olbrini Travelling Fllshp, Columbia Univ 1961. Previous adm positions in opera: Exec Stage Dir, Santa Fe Opera 1967.

Directed with major companies in USA: Cincinnati, Dallas, Hawaii, Miami, New York Met, Portland, San Francisco Opera. **Operas with these companies incl** BIZET: *Pêcheurs de perles**; DONIZETTI: *Lucia**; GOUNOD: *Roméo et Juliette**; LEONCAVALLO: *Pagliacci**; MASCAGNI: *Cavalleria rusticana**; MASSENET: *Werther**; MOZART: *Nozze di Figaro*; PUCCINI: *Gianni Schicchi*, Rondine*, Suor Angelica*, Tabarro*, Tosca*; VERDI: *Otello*, Rigoletto*, Traviata**. **Res:** 100 W 74 St, New York, NY, USA. Mgmt: CAM/USA; HPL/UK.

MELCHINGER, ULRICH. Stages/produces opera. German. Oberspielleiter & Resident Stage Dir, Staatstheater Kassel. Born 19 May 1937, Frankfurt/M. Wife Dr Christa. Four children. Studied: music, piano. Operatic training as asst stage dir at Staatsoper Vienna, Herb v Karajan; Staatsoper Hamburg, R Liebermann. **Operatic debut:** *Orfeo ed Euridice* Ulm, FR Ger 1960. Previous adm positions in opera: Oberspielleiter, Stadttheater Lübeck 2 yrs.

Directed/produced opera for major companies in FR GER: Karlsruhe, Kassel, Nürnberg; SWI: Basel. **Operas staged with these companies incl** BEETHOVEN: *Fidelio*; BERG: *Wozzeck*; BIZET: *Carmen*; BRITTEN: *Death in Venice, Midsummer Night*; DEBUSSY: *Pelléas et Mélisande*; DONIZETTI: *Lucia**; FALLA: *Vida breve*; FLOTOW: *Martha*; FORTNER: *Don Perlimplin*;

GIORDANO: *Andrea Chénier*★; JANACEK: *From the House of the Dead*★; LEON-CAVALLO: *Pagliacci*; LORTZING: *Wildschütz*; MASCAGNI: *Cavalleria rusticana;* MASSENET: *Don Quichotte*★; MOZART: *Idomeneo*★, *Nozze di Figaro*★; OFFENBACH: *Contes d'Hoffmann*★; PUCCINI: *Bohème, Gianni Schicchi, Manon Lescaut*★, *Tosca;* RAVEL: *Heure espagnole*★; RIMSKY-KORSAKOV: *Coq d'or*★; ROSSINI: *Barbiere di Siviglia;* STRAUSS, R: *Elektra, Rosenkavalier;* TCHAIKOVSKY: *Maid of Orleans;* VERDI: *Ballo in maschera, Don Carlo, Falstaff, Forza del destino, Trovatore;* WAGNER: *Fliegende Holländer*★, *Lohengrin, Meistersinger, Parsifal, Rheingold, Walküre*★, *Siegfried*★, *Götterdämmerung*★; WALTON: *Bear*★. **Operatic world premieres:** STROES: *Ça n'aura pas le prix Nobel* Kassel 1971. **Opera libretti:** GILBERT: *Popgeheuer* Kassel 1971. **Res:** Stiegelwiesen 5, Kassel, FR Ger.

MENIPPO, CARLO. Dramatic tenor. Italian. Born 23 Aug 1933, Piacenza. Wife Esterina Arata. Studied: Ettore Campogalliani, Carlo Tagliabue. **Debut:** Canio (*Pagliacci*) Teatro Nuovo, Milan 1961. Previous occupations: mechanical designer. Awards: First Prize, Reggio Emilia; First Prize for debut, As Li Co.
  Sang with major companies in AUS: Vienna Staatsoper; FRA: Toulouse; GRE: Athens National; ITA: Bologna, Naples, Palermo; SWI: Basel. **Roles with these companies incl** BELLINI: Pollione (*Norma*); BIZET: Don José (*Carmen*); DONIZETTI: Edgardo (*Lucia*); GIORDANO: Andrea Chénier★; LEONCAVALLO: Canio★ (*Pagliacci*); MASCAGNI: Turiddu (*Cavalleria rusticana*); MEYERBEER: Vasco da Gama (*Africaine*); PUCCINI: Rodolfo (*Bohème*), Dick Johnson (*Fanciulla del West*), Pinkerton (*Butterfly*), Cavaradossi★ (*Tosca*), Calaf★ (*Turandot*); SAINT-SAENS: Samson; VERDI: Radames (*Aida*), Don Alvaro★ (*Forza del destino*), Rodolfo (*Luisa Miller*), Otello, Gabriele (*Simon Boccanegra*), Manrico (*Trovatore*), Arrigo (*Vespri*); ZANDONAI: Paolo (*Francesca da Rimini*). Also VERDI: Macduff★ (*Macbeth*). Video/Film: Don Alvaro (*Forza del destino*).

MENOTTI, GIAN CARLO. Stages/produces opera & television and is a composer & author. Italian. Founder/Pres, Festival of Two Worlds, Spoleto 1958- . Born 7 Jul 1911, Cadegliano. Single. Studied: Verdi Consv, Milan; Curtis Inst of Music, Rosario Scalero, Philadelphia; incl music & piano. **Operatic debut:** *Medium* Columbia Univ, New York 1946. Awards: Alice Ditson Fund; two Pulitzer Prizes; NY Drama Critics Awd; var citations.
  Directed/produced opera for major companies in FRA: Paris; FR GER: Hamburg Staatsoper; ITA: Spoleto Fest; USA: New York Metropolitan Opera & City Opera. **Operas staged with these companies incl** BARBER: *Vanessa;* BIZET: *Carmen;* DEBUSSY: *Pelléas et Mélisande;* MENOTTI: *Amahl, Amelia al ballo, Consul, Dernier sauvage, Globolinks, Maria Golovin, Old Maid and the Thief, Saint of Bleecker Street, Tamu-Tamu, Telephone;* MOZART: *Don Giovanni;* PUCCINI: *Bohème;* STRAVINSKY: *Rake's Progress;* WAGNER: *Tristan und Isolde.* Operatic

Video/Film — *Medium, Amahl, Labyrinth.* **Opera libretti:** libretto only BARBER: *Vanessa* Met 1958, rev *Antony & Cleopatra, Hand of Bridge;* FOSS: *Introductions and Goodbyes.* Composed and wrote libretti for all own ops except: *Amelia Goes to the Ball* Philadelphia 1937, *Old Maid and the Thief* NBC 1939, *Island God* Met 1942, *Medium* Columbia Univ 1946, *Telephone* Brdw NY 1947, *Consul* Brdw NY 1950, *Amahl* NBC TV 1951, *Saint of Bleecker St* Brdw NY 1954, *Unicorn* Washington 1965, *Maria Golovin* Brussels 1958, *Labyrinth* NBC TV 1963, *Dernier sauvage* Paris 1963, *Globolinks* Hamburg 1968, *Most Important Man* NY City Op 1970, *Tamu-Tamu* Chicago 1972. **Res:** Gifford, Scotland, UK. **Mgmt:** DSP/USA.

MEREDITH, MORLEY. Dramatic baritone. Canadian. Born Winnipeg, Man, Canada. Wife Erlene. Studied: W H Anderson, Canada; Boris Goldovsky, Tanglewood, MA; Alfredo Martino, Melchiore Luise, USA. **Debut:** Escamillo (*Carmen*) New York City Opera 1957. Awards: Singing Stars of Tomorrow, Canadian Aud of the Air.
  Sang with major companies in CAN: Toronto; SWI: Geneva; UK: Glasgow Scottish; USA: Chicago, Fort Worth, Kansas City, Milwaukee Florentine, New Orleans, New York Met & City Opera, Philadelphia Lyric, St Paul, San Antonio, San Francisco Opera, Washington DC. **Roles with these companies incl** BARTOK: Bluebeard★; BEETHOVEN: Don Pizarro★ (*Fidelio*); BERG: Wozzeck & Doktor★ (*Wozzeck*); BIZET: Escamillo (*Carmen*); BRITTEN: Captain Balstrode★ (*Peter Grimes*); CHERUBINI: Creon (*Medea*); DONIZETTI: Dott Malatesta (*Don Pasquale*); GOUNOD: Méphistophélès★ (*Faust*); MASCAGNI: Alfio★ (*Cavalleria rusticana*); MENOTTI: Maharaja (*Dernier sauvage*); MOZART: Don Alfonso (*Così fan tutte*); OFFENBACH: Coppélius etc★ (*Contes d'Hoffmann*); ORFF: Solo (*Carmina burana*); PROKOFIEV: Prince Andrei (*War and Peace*); PUCCINI: Marcello (*Bohème*), Scarpia★ (*Tosca*); STRAUSS, R: Orest★ (*Elektra*), Jochanaan★ (*Salome*); TCHAIKOVSKY: Eugene Onegin; VERDI: Amonasro★ (*Aida*), Iago★ (*Otello*), Germont (*Traviata*); WAGNER: Holländer★. Also WAGNER: Klingsor (*Parsifal*); STRAUSS, R: Faninal (*Rosenkavalier*); MENOTTI: Mr Scattergood (*Dernier sauvage*). Recorded for: Vanguard. Gives recitals. Appears with symphony orchestra. **Mgmt:** BAR/USA.

MERIGGIOLI, ILEANA. Spinto. Italian. Born 30 June, Trieste, Italy. Single. Studied: Consv G Tartini, Trieste; Luciano Donaggio, Mariano Stabile, Trieste; Mo Giorgio Favaretto, Siena. **Debut:** Elsa (*Lohengrin*) Teatro Verdi, Trieste 1968. Awards: Gold Medal Viotti Intl Cont Vercelli, Italy; Awd Intl Compt Geneva; Schlshp Accad Chigiana, Siena.
  Sang with major companies in AUS: Graz, Vienna Staatsoper; FRA: Toulouse; ITA: Genoa, Milan La Scala, Parma, Trieste, Turin, Venice, Verona Arena; SPA: Barcelona; SWI: Geneva. **Roles with these companies incl** BELLINI: Agnese★ (*Beatrice di Tenda*); DEBUSSY: Lia (*Enfant prodigue*); FALLA: Salud (*Vida breve*); GIORDANO: Maddalena (*Andrea Chénier*); GOUNOD: Marguerite (*Faust*); LEON-

CAVALLO: Nedda (*Pagliacci*); MONTE-MEZZI: Fiora★ (*Amore dei tre re*); MOZART: Donna Anna (*Don Giovanni*); PROKOFIEV: Fata Morgana (*Love for Three Oranges*); PUC-CINI: Mimi (*Bohème*), Manon Lescaut★, Suor Angelica, Giorgetta (*Tabarro*), Liù (*Turandot*); ROSSINI: Mathilde (*Guillaume Tell*), Anaï★ (*Moïse*); VERDI: Aida★, Odabella (*Attila*), Amelia★ (*Ballo in maschera*), Elisabetta★ (*Don Carlo*), Leonora★ (*Forza del destino*), Desde-mona★ (*Otello*), Amelia★ (*Simon Boccanegra*), Leonora★ (*Trovatore*), Elena (*Vespri*); WAGNER: Senta★ (*Fliegende Holländer*), Elsa★ (*Lohengrin*), Eva★ (*Meistersinger*). Also GIORDANO: (*Siberia*); DONIZETTI: (*Belisario*). Gives recitals. Appears with symphony orchestra. **Res**: Trieste, Italy. Mgmt: MAU/USA.

MERIGHI, GIORGIO. Dramatic tenor. Ital. Born 20 Feb 1939, Ferrara. Wife Angela. Two children. Studied: Consv G Rossini, Mo Melocchi, Mme Raggi Valentini, Mo Leodino Ferri, Pesaro. **Debut:** Riccardo (*Ballo in maschera*) Spoleto Fest 1962. Awards: Ntl Schlshp Awd ENAL, three yrs; First Prize, Intl Conc Bilbao, Spain 1968; Diapason d'oro; First Prize, Castrocaro Terme, etc. **Sang with major companies in** AUS: Vienna Staatsoper; BEL: Brussels; FRA: Bordeaux, Lyon, Marseille, Nice; GRE: Athens National; FR GER: Berlin Deutsche Oper, Düsseldorf-Duisburg, Frankfurt, Hamburg, Mannheim, Stuttgart, Wiesbaden; HOL: Amsterdam; ITA: Florence Maggio, Genoa, Milan La Scala, Naples, Palermo, Rome Opera & Caracalla, Trieste, Turin, Venice, Verona Arena; MON: Monte Carlo; POR: Lisbon; SPA: Barcelona, Majorca; SWI: Geneva. **Roles with these companies incl** BELLINI: Tebaldo★ (*Capuleti ed i Montecchi*); BOITO: Faust★ (*Mefistofele*); CILEA: Maurizio★ (*A. Lecouvreur*); GIORDANO: Andrea Chénier★; PONCHIELLI: Enzo★ (*Gioconda*); PUCCINI: Rodolfo★ (*Bohème*), Dick Johnson★ (*Fanciulla del West*), Pinkerton★ (*Butterfly*), Des Grieux★ (*Manon Lescaut*), Luigi★ (*Tabarro*), Cavaradossi★ (*Tosca*), Calaf★ (*Turandot*); VERDI: Riccardo★ (*Ballo in maschera*), Don Alvaro★ (*Forza del destino*), Rodolfo★ (*Luisa Miller*), Duca di Mantova★ (*Rigoletto*), Gabriele★ (*Simon Boccanegra*), Manrico★ (*Trovatore*); ZANDONAI: Paolo (*Francesca da Rimini*). Video—RAI TV: Pinkerton (*Butterfly*). Gives recitals.

MERRILL, NATHANIEL. Stages/produces opera & television. Also designs stage-lighting and is an author. American. Resident Stage Dir, Metropolitan Opera, New York. Also Gen Dir Tech Services & Res Stage Dir, Opéra du Rhin, Strasbourg, France. Born 8 Feb 1927, Newton, MA. Wife Louise Sherman, occupation asst cond Met Opera; Chef de chant, Opéra du Rhin. Three children. Studied: Boris Goldovsky, New England Opera, Boston; also music & piano, clarinet, cello. Operatic training as asst stage dir at Salzburg Fest, Hamburg Staatsoper, Hessian State Opera Wiesbaden, with Graf, Rennert & Schramm. **Operatic debut:** LULLY: *Amadis* Boston 1952. **Directed/produced opera for major companies in** ARG: Buenos Aires; AUS: Bregenz Fest, Salzburg Fest, Vienna Staatsoper & Volksoper; CAN: Montreal/Quebec, Vancouver; FRA: Strasbourg;

FR GER: Frankfurt, Hamburg; ITA: Verona Arena; USA: Baltimore, Chicago, Cincinnati, Fort Worth, Houston, Miami, Milwaukee Florentine, New York Met, Philadelphia Lyric, San Francisco Opera, Washington DC. **Operas staged with these companies incl** BARBER: *Vanessa;* BERLIOZ: *Troyens★;* BIZET: *Carmen★;* BRITTEN: *Burning Fiery Furnace★, Curlew River★, Prodigal Son★;* CILEA: *Adriana Lecouvreur;* DEBUSSY: *Pelléas et Mélisande;* DONIZETTI: *Don Pasquale, Elisir★, Fille du régiment★, Lucia★, Maria Stuarda★;* FLOTOW: *Martha;* GERSHWIN: *Porgy and Bess★;* GIORDANO: *Andrea Chénier;* GLUCK: *Orfeo ed Euridice;* GOUNOD: *Faust★, Roméo et Juliette;* HUMPERDINCK: *Hänsel und Gretel★;* LEONCAVALLO: *Pagliacci;* MOORE: *Ballad of Baby Doe;* MOZART: *Don Giovanni★, Nozze di Figaro★, Zauberflöte;* MUSSORGSKY: *Boris Godunov;* PONCHIELLI: *Gioconda;* POULENC: *Voix humaine★;* PUCCINI: *Bohème★, Fanciulla del West, Gianni Schicchi★, Butterfly, Manon Lescaut★, Tosca, Turandot;* ROSSINI: *Barbiere di Siviglia★;* SAINT-SAENS: *Samson et Dalila;* SMETANA: *Bartered Bride;* STRAUSS, J: *Fledermaus;* STRAUSS, R: *Ariadne auf Naxos, Elektra, Frau ohne Schatten, Rosenkavalier★, Salome★;* VERDI: *Aida★, Don Carlo★, Falstaff★, Luisa Miller, Macbeth, Otello, Rigoletto, Simon Boccanegra★, Traviata★, Trovatore★;* WAGNER: *Fliegende Holländer★, Lohengrin, Meistersinger★, Parsifal★, Rheingold, Walküre, Siegfried, Götterdämmerung, Tannhäuser, Tristan und Isolde.* Previous leading positions with major theater companies: Art Dir, Central City Opera Fest, CO 1972. **Res:** 321 W 78 St, New York, USA. Mgmt: AIM/UK.

MERRILL, ROBERT; né Morris Miller. Lyric & dramatic baritone. American. Resident mem: Metropolitan Opera, New York. Born 4 Jun 1919, Brooklyn, NY, USA. Wife Marion Machno, occupation pianist. Two children. Studied: Samuel Margolis, New York. **Debut:** Germont (*Traviata*) Detroit Opera Co 1944. Previous occupations: sang on radio and at resort hotels. Awards: Hon DM Gustavus Adolphus Coll; Winner Met Aud of the Air 1945; Harriet Cohen Intl Music Awd 1961; Handel Medallion, City of New York 1970; Best Record Awds 1946, 1962, 1964; mem Ntl Council of the Arts 1968-74. **Sang with major companies in** ARG: Buenos Aires; ISR: Tel Aviv; ITA: Venice; MEX: Mexico City; UK: London Royal Opera; USA: Chicago, Cincinnati Summer Opera, Hartford, Miami, Newark, New Orleans, New York Met, Philadelphia Grand, Pittsburgh, San Francisco Opera, Seattle. **Roles with these companies incl** BIZET: Escamillo★‡ (*Carmen*); DONIZETTI: Dott Malatesta (*Don Pasquale*), Enrico (*Lucia*); GIORDANO: Carlo Gérard (*Andrea Chénier*); GOUNOD: Valentin (*Faust*); LEONCAVALLO: Tonio‡ (*Pagliacci*); MASCAGNI: Alfio‡ (*Cavalleria rusticana*); PONCHIELLI: Barnaba‡ (*Gioconda*); PUCCINI: Marcello‡ (*Bohème*), Lescaut‡ (*Manon Lescaut*), Michele‡ (*Tabarro*), Scarpia★ (*Tosca*); ROSSINI: Figaro‡ (*Barbiere di Siviglia*); SAINT-SAENS: Grand prêtre (*Samson et Dalila*); VERDI: Amonasro★‡ (*Aida*), Renato★‡ (*Ballo in maschera*), Rodrigo★ (*Don Carlo*), Ford‡ (*Falstaff*), Don Carlo★‡ (*Forza* *del destino*), Iago (*Otello*), Rigoletto★‡, Germont★‡ (*Traviata*), Conte di Luna★‡ (*Trovatore*). Recorded for: RCA, London, Angel. Video/Film: Escamillo (*Carmen*); Rigoletto. Gives recitals. Appears with symphony orchestra. **Res:** New Rochelle, NY, USA. Mgmt: CAM/USA; AIM/UK.

MESPLÉ, MADY; née Magdeleine Andrée Mesplé. Coloratura soprano. French. Born 7 Mar 1931, Toulouse, France. Divorced. One child. Studied: Consv Ntl de Musique, Mme Izar-Lasson, Toulouse; Georges Jouatte, Janine Micheau, Paris. **Debut:** Lakmé, Opéra de Liège 1952. Previous occupations: jazz pianist; accomp for classical music. Awards: Ntl Order of Merit; Officier des Arts et Lettres.

Sang with major companies in ARG: Buenos Aires; AUS: Vienna Volksoper; BEL: Brussels, Liège; BRA: Rio de Janeiro; FRA: Aix-en-Provence Fest, Bordeaux, Lyon, Marseille, Nancy, Nice, Paris, Rouen, Strasbourg, Toulouse; FR GER: Munich Gärtnerplatz; HUN: Budapest; ITA: Florence Maggio, Naples; MON: Monte Carlo; POR: Lisbon; ROM: Bucharest; SPA: Barcelona; SWI: Geneva; UK: Edinburgh Fest; USSR: Moscow Bolshoi; USA: Chicago, Dallas, Miami, New York Met, Seattle, Washington DC. **Roles with these companies incl** ADAM: Neméa (*Si j'étais roi*); BELLINI: Amina★ (*Sonnambula*); BIZET: Léila (*Pêcheurs de perles*); BRITTEN: Tytania (*Midsummer Night*); DELIBES: Lakmé★‡; DONIZETTI: Norina★ (*Don Pasquale*), Lucia★; GLUCK: Amor★ (*Orfeo ed Euridice*); GOUNOD: Mireille, Juliette★; HANDEL: Morgana (*Alcina*); HENZE: Hilda Mack (*Elegy for Young Lovers*); MASSENET: Sophie‡ (*Werther*); MENOTTI: Kitty (*Dernier sauvage*), Lucy (*Telephone*); MILHAUD: Isabella★‡ (*Christophe Colomb*); MOZART: Konstanze★ & Blondchen (*Entführung aus dem Serail*), Mme Herz★‡ (*Schauspieldirektor*), Cherubino (*Nozze di Figaro*), Königin der Nacht★ (*Zauberflöte*); OFFENBACH: Olympia★ (*Contes d'Hoffmann*); POULENC: Thérèse (*Mamelles de Tirésias*); RABAUD: Fille de Sultan (*Mârouf*); RIMSKY-KORSAKOV: Reine de Schemakan★ (*Coq d'or*); ROSSINI: Rosina★‡ (*Barbiere di Siviglia*), Comtesse Adèle★ (*Comte Ory*); ROUSSEAU: Colette (*Devin du village*); STRAUSS, J: Adele★ (*Fledermaus*), STRAUSS, R: Fiakermilli (*Arabella*), Zerbinetta (*Ariadne auf Naxos*), Sophie (*Rosenkavalier*); STRAVINSKY: Rossignol; THOMAS: Ophélie (*Hamlet*), Philine (*Mignon*); VERDI: Oscar (*Ballo in maschera*), Gilda★ (*Rigoletto*). Also POULENC: Constance (*Dialogues des Carmélites*); RAMEAU: Fatime (*Indes galantes*); RAVEL: Feu/Princesse/Rossignol (*Enfant et les sortilèges*). **World premieres:** MENOTTI: Kitty (*Dernier sauvage*) Paris 1963; OHANA: La voix (*Syllabaire pour Phèdre*) Paris 1970. Gives recitals. Appears with symphony orchestra. Teaches voice. On faculty of Acad Internationale, Nice. **Res:** Blvd de Cimiez, Nice, France. Mgmt: GLZ/FRA: CAM/USA.

MESS, SUZANNE. Costume designer for opera, theater, ballet & television. Canadian. Resident designer, Canadian Opera Co, Canadian Broadcasting Co and at Malabar Ltd, Toronto. Born 2 Aug, Toronto. Single. Studied: Ontario Coll of Art.

Prof training: Helene Pons Studio, New York. **Operatic debut:** *Quattro rusteghi* Canadian Opera Co, Toronto. Theater debut: National Ballet of Canada, Toronto 1951. Awards: Canadian Centennial Medal, Gvnmt of Canada. Previous adm positions in opera: wardrobe supervisor, Canadian Op Co, Toronto 1952-72.

Designed for major companies in CAN: Montreal/Quebec, Ottawa, Toronto, Vancouver; USA: Boston, Cincinnati, Fort Worth, Houston, Milwaukee Florentine, New Orleans, Omaha, San Diego, Santa Fe, Seattle, Washington DC. **Operas designed for these companies incl** BELLINI: *Norma;* BERLIOZ: *Troyens★;* BIZET: *Carmen★;* DONIZETTI: *Elisir★, Lucia★;* GIORDANO: *Andrea Chénier;* GOUNOD: *Faust, Roméo et Juliette★;* HALEVY: *Juive★;* LEONCAVALLO: *Pagliacci;* MASCAGNI: *Cavalleria rusticana;* MASSENET: *Manon★, Thaïs★, Werther;* MENOTTI: *Consul;* MOZART: *Don Giovanni★, Finta giardiniera, Nozze di Figaro★;* MUSSORGSKY: *Boris Godunov★;* NICOLAI: *Lustigen Weiber;* OFFENBACH: *Contes d'Hoffmann★, Périchole★;* PUCCINI: *Bohème★, Fanciulla del West, Butterfly★, Tosca★;* ROSSINI: *Barbiere di Siviglia, Italiana in Algeri;* STRAUSS, R: *Salome;* STRAVINSKY: *Mavra, Rake's Progress;* TCHAIKOVSKY: *Eugene Onegin★;* VERDI: *Aida, Ballo in maschera, Don Carlo★, Falstaff★, Forza del destino★, Otello, Rigoletto★, Traviata★, Trovatore;* WAGNER: *Fliegende Holländer★, Walküre★;* WOLF-FERRARI: *Quattro rusteghi.* **Operatic world premieres:** WILSON: *Heloise and Abelard* Canadian Op Co, Toronto 1973. Operatic Video—CBC TV: *Turn of the Screw, Peter Grimes, Zauberflöte, Otello, Rigoletto, Hänsel und Gretel, Rondine.* Exhibitions of costume designs, Toronto Heliconian Club 1973. **Res:** 1 Warren Rd, Toronto, Ont, Canada.

MESSEL, OLIVER. Scenic and costume designer for opera & theater. Is also a painter. British. Born 13 Jan 1905, London. Theater debut: revue, UK 1926. Awards: CBE, Commander of the British Empire.

Designed opera for major companies in UK: Glyndebourne Fest, London Royal; USA: New York Met; et al. **Operas designed for these companies incl** MOZART: *Entführung aus dem Serail, Idomeneo, Nozze di Figaro, Zauberflöte;* ROSSINI: *Barbiere di Siviglia, Cenerentola, Comte Ory;* SAINT-SAENS: *Samson et Dalila;* STRAUSS, R: *Ariadne auf Naxos, Rosenkavalier;* TCHAIKOVSKY: *Pique Dame;* et al.

METCALF, WILLIAM. Lyric baritone. American. Born 12 Jan 1934, New Bedford, MA, USA. Single. Studied: New England Consv, Boston; Juilliard School of Music, New York. **Debut:** Singer (*Trouble in Tahiti*) New York City Opera 1963.

Sang with major companies in USA: Baltimore, Cincinnati, Fort Worth, Miami, New Orleans, New York City Opera, Philadelphia Grand, Santa Fe, Washington DC. **Roles with these companies incl** BIZET: Escamillo (*Carmen*), Zurga (*Pêcheurs de perles*); BRITTEN: Ananias & Azarias (*Burning Fiery Furnace*), Ferryman & Traveller (*Curlew River*), Demetrius (*Midsummer Night*), Father &

Elder Son (*Prodigal Son*); DEBUSSY: Siméon (*Enfant prodigue*); DONIZETTI: Dott Malatesta (*Don Pasquale*), Belcore★ (*Elisir*); MASSENET: Lescaut★ (*Manon*); MENOTTI: John Sorel (*Consul*), Bob (*Old Maid and the Thief*); MOZART: Guglielmo★ (*Così fan tutte*), Figaro★ (*Nozze di Figaro*), Papageno (*Zauberflöte*); ORFF: Solo★ (*Carmina burana*); PUCCINI: Marcello★ (*Bohème*), Sharpless (*Butterfly*), Lescaut (*Manon Lescaut*); RAMEAU: Pollux; ROSSINI: Figaro (*Barbiere di Siviglia*), Robert★ (*Comte Ory*); STRAUSS, R: Graf & Olivier★ (*Capriccio*), Robert Storch (*Intermezzo*); VERDI: Germont (*Traviata*). Gives recitals. Appears with symphony orchestra. Teaches voice. On faculty of Hartt Coll of Music, Hartford, CT. **Res:** New York, NY, USA. Mgmt: DSP/USA.

MEVEN, FRANZ PETER. Bass. German. Resident mem: Deutsche Oper am Rhein, Düsseldorf; Staatstheater Stuttgart. Born 1 Oct 1929, Cologne, Germany. Wife Erika Klöcker. Studied: Staatliche Hochschule für Musik, Robert Blasius, Cologne. **Debut:** Ferrando (*Trovatore*) Hagen Opera, FR Ger 1957.
Sang with major companies in AUS: Salzburg Fest, Vienna Staatsoper & Volksoper; BEL: Brussels; CAN: Montreal/Quebec; DEN: Copenhagen; FIN: Helsinki; FRA: Marseille, Nancy; FR GER: Bayreuth Fest, Berlin Deutsche Oper, Bonn, Cologne, Düsseldorf-Duisburg, Essen, Frankfurt, Hamburg, Hannover, Karlsruhe, Kiel, Mannheim, Munich Staatsoper & Gärtnerplatz, Nürnberg, Saarbrücken, Stuttgart, Wiesbaden, Wuppertal; HOL: Amsterdam; ITA: Florence Maggio; POR: Lisbon; SPA: Barcelona; SWE: Stockholm; SWI: Basel, Geneva, Zurich; UK: London Royal Opera; USSR: Moscow Bolshoi; USA: San Francisco Opera. **Roles with these companies incl** BEETHOVEN: Rocco★ (*Fidelio*); BRITTEN: Theseus (*Midsummer Night*); DEBUSSY: Arkel (*Pelléas et Mélisande*); DONIZETTI: Sulpice (*Fille du régiment*); GLUCK: Thoas (*Iphigénie en Tauride*); GOUNOD: Méphistophélès (*Faust*); HANDEL: Polyphemus (*Acis and Galatea*), Ptolemy (*Giulio Cesare*); MOZART: Publio (*Clemenza di Tito*), Don Alfonso (*Così fan tutte*), Osmin★ (*Entführung aus dem Serail*), Figaro (*Nozze di Figaro*), Osmin (*Zaïde*), Sarastro★ (*Zauberflöte*); MUSSORGSKY: Boris Godunov★ & Pimen★ (*Boris Godunov*); OFFENBACH: Coppélius, etc (*Contes d'Hoffmann*); ORFF: Bauer★ (*Mond*); PUCCINI: Colline★ (*Bohème*); ROSSINI: Don Basilio (*Barbiere di Siviglia*); SCHOENBERG: Moses★; SMETANA: Kezal (*Bartered Bride*); STRAUSS, R: Orest (*Elektra*), Baron Ochs (*Rosenkavalier*); STRAVINSKY: Creon & Tiresias★ (*Oedipus Rex*); VERDI: Ramfis (*Aida*), Philip II★ & Grande Inquisitore (*Don Carlo*), Padre Guardiano★ (*Forza del destino*), Conte Walter (*Luisa Miller*), Banquo (*Macbeth*), Zaccaria (*Nabucco*), Fiesco (*Simon Boccanegra*); WAGNER: Daland★ (*Fliegende Holländer*), König Heinrich (*Lohengrin*), Hans Sachs★ & Pogner (*Meistersinger*), Gurnemanz★ (*Parsifal*), Fasolt★ & Fafner (*Rheingold*), Fafner★ (*Siegfried*), Hunding★ (*Walküre*), Hagen★ (*Götterdämmerung*), Landgraf★ (*Tannhäuser*), König Marke★ (*Tristan und Isolde*); WEBER: Kaspar★ (*Freischütz*). Recorded for: DG. Appears with

symphony orchestra. **Res:** Post Str 7, 4 Düsseldorf, FR Ger. Mgmt: SLZ/FRG; VLD/AUS.

MEYER, KERSTIN MARGARETA. Mezzo-soprano. Swedish. Resident mem: Royal Opera, Stockholm. Born 3 Apr 1928, Stockholm. Husband Björn Bexelius, occupation theater admin. Studied: Arne Sunnegårdh, Andrejewa von Skilondz, Stockholm; Paola Novikova, New York; Giorgio Favaretto, Rome. **Debut:** Azucena (*Trovatore*) Royal Opera, Stockholm 1952.. Awards: Mem Royal Acad of Music, Stockholm; Swedish Court Singer; Swedish Wasa Order; Medal Litteris et Artibus.
Sang with major companies in ARG: Buenos Aires; AUS: Salzburg Fest, Vienna Staatsoper; BEL: Brussels; CAN: Montreal/Quebec, Vancouver; DEN: Copenhagen; FIN: Helsinki; FRA: Bordeaux, Lyon, Paris, Strasbourg; FR GER: Bayreuth Fest, Berlin Deutsche Oper, Hamburg Staatsoper, Munich Staatsoper, Wiesbaden; ITA: Milan La Scala, Rome Teatro dell'Opera, Turin, Venice; MEX: Mexico City; NOR: Oslo; SPA: Barcelona; SWE: Drottingholm Fest, Stockholm; SWI: Geneva; UK: Edinburgh Fest, Glyndebourne Fest, London Royal; USSR: Moscow Bolshoi; USA: New York Met, San Francisco Opera. **Roles with these companies incl** BERG: Gräfin Geschwitz★‡ (*Lulu*); BERLIOZ: Cassandre & Didon (*Troyens*); BIZET: Carmen★; BRITTEN: Lucretia (*Rape of Lucretia*); CHARPENTIER: Mère (*Louise*); CIMAROSA: Fidalma★ (*Matrimonio segreto*); DEBUSSY: Geneviève (*Pelléas et Mélisande*); EINEM: Claire★ (*Besuch der alten Dame*); GLUCK: Orfeo★; GOUNOD: Siebel (*Faust*); HANDEL: Bradamante & Ruggiero★ (*Alcina*); HENZE: Carolina (*Elegy for Young Lovers*); JANACEK: Kostelnicka★ (*Jenufa*); MONTEVERDI: Penelope (*Ritorno d'Ulisse*); MOZART: Dorabella★ (*Così fan tutte*); SAINT-SAENS: Dalila; STRAUSS, J: Prinz Orlovsky (*Fledermaus*); STRAUSS, R: Komponist (*Ariadne auf Naxos*), Clairon★ (*Capriccio*), Klytämnestra★ (*Elektra*), Amme★ (*Frau ohne Schatten*), Octavian★ (*Rosenkavalier*), Herodias★ (*Salome*); STRAVINSKY: Jocasta (*Oedipus Rex*), Baba the Turk★ (*Rake's Progress*); TCHAIKOVSKY: Comtesse (*Pique Dame*); VERDI: Amneris★ (*Aida*), Ulrica★ (*Ballo in maschera*), Eboli★ (*Don Carlo*), Dame Quickly★ (*Falstaff*), Preziosilla★ (*Forza del destino*), Azucena★ (*Trovatore*); WAGNER: Ortrud★ (*Lohengrin*), Magdalene★ (*Meistersinger*), Kundry★ (*Parsifal*), Erda (*Rheingold★*, *Siegfried★*), Fricka (*Rheingold★*, *Walküre★*), Waltraute★ (*Götterdämmerung*), Brangäne★ (*Tristan und Isolde*). Also MENOTTI: Mother (*Amahl*); MONTEVERDI: Ottavia (*Incoronazione di Poppea*); SEARLE: Queen (*Hamlet*). **World premieres:** MAW: Elisabeth (*Rising of the Moon*) Glyndebourne Fest 1970; GOEHR: Frau Arden (*Arden muss sterben*) Hamburg Opera 1967; HENZE: Agave (*Bassariden*) Salzburg Fest 1966. Gives recitals. Appears with symphony orchestra. **Res:** Valhallavägen 46, Stockholm, Sweden. Mgmt: DSP/USA.

MEYER, OTTOWERNER. Scenic and costume designer for opera & theater. Is a lighting designer. German.

Designed opera for major companies in FR GER: Bonn, Düsseldorf-Duisburg, Hannover; SPA: Barcelona; et al. **Operas designed for these companies incl** DONIZETTI: *Lucia, Roberto Devereux;* FLOTOW: *Martha;* HENZE: *Boulevard Solitude;* MASSENET: *Manon;* MOZART: *Don Giovanni;* STRAUSS, R: *Elektra, Salome;* WOLF-FERRARI: *Quattro rusteghi;* YUN: *Traum des Liu-Tung;* et al. **Operatic world premieres:** ENGELMANN: *Revue* Theater der Stadt Bonn 1973.

MEYER-HANNO, ANDREAS. Stages/produces opera and is an actor & author-translator. German. Dir & Resident Stage Dir, Braunschweiger Staatstheater, FR Ger. Born 18 Feb 1932, Berlin. Single. Studied: music, piano, recorder & voice. Operatic training as asst stage dir at Wuppertaler Bühnen. **Operatic debut:** *Rigoletto* Wuppertaler Bühnen 1959. Previous adm positions in opera: Oberspielleitung, Staatstheater Karlsruhe.
    Directed/produced opera for major companies in FR GER: Darmstadt, Düsseldorf-Duisburg, Karlsruhe, Kiel, Wuppertal; POR: Lisbon. **Operas staged with these companies incl** ADAM: *Postillon de Lonjumeau;* BERG: *Lulu, Wozzeck*★; CIMAROSA: *Matrimonio segreto;* DALLAPICCOLA: *Prigioniero;* DONIZETTI: *Convenienze/Viva la Mamma*★, *Don Pasquale;* DVORAK: *Rusalka;* GAY/Britten: *Beggar's Opera;* GLUCK: *Orfeo ed Euridice;* HENZE: *Boulevard Solitude*★; HUMPERDINCK: *Hänsel und Gretel*★; JANACEK: *Katya Kabanova;* LEONCAVALLO: *Pagliacci;* LORTZING: *Waffenschmied, Wildschütz;* MASCAGNI: *Cavalleria rusticana;* MOZART: *Così fan tutte*★, *Entführung aus dem Serail*★, *Idomeneo, Nozze di Figaro*★, *Zaïde, Zauberflöte*★; NICOLAI: *Lustigen Weiber;* ORFF: *Bernauerin;* PFITZNER: *Palestrina;* PUCCINI: *Bohème, Fanciulla del West*★, *Gianni Schicchi, Madama Butterfly, Manon Lescaut, Tosca;* REIMANN: *Melusine;* ROSSINI: *Barbiere di Siviglia, Comte Ory;* STRAUSS: *Arabella*★, *Ariadne auf Naxos, Elektra*★, *Intermezzo, Salome, Schweigsame Frau;* STRAVINSKY: *Rake's Progress;* TCHAIKOVSKY: *Eugene Onegin*★; VERDI: *Aida, Ballo in maschera, Don Carlo*★, *Otello*★, *Traviata*★, *Trovatore;* WAGNER: *Fliegende Holländer*★, *Parsifal;* WOLF-FERRARI: *Donne curiose.* Also HAYDN: *Fedeltà premiata;* EGK: *Peer Gynt;* BRAUNFELS: *Vögel;* HANDEL: *Agrippina;* DVORAK: *Jakobiner;* KAUFMANN: *Perlenhemd.* **Operatic world premieres:** FUESSEL: *Dybbuk* Karlsruhe 1970; KELTERBORN: *Kaiser Jovian* Karlsruhe 1967. Teaches at Mozarteum, Salzburg. **Res:** Jasperallee 77, Braunschweig, FR Ger. Mgmt: SLZ/FRG.

MEYER-WOLFF, FRIDO. Bass-baritone & bassobuffo. German. Resident mem: Opernhaus Kiel; Grand Théâtre, Nancy. Born 22 Apr 1934, Potsdam, Germany. Single. Studied: Städtisches Konsv, Berlin; Wolf Völker, Carl Ebert; Jean Cocteau, Paris; Hildegarde Scharff, Hamburg. **Debut:** Figaro (*Nozze di Figaro*) Opernhaus Stralsund, Ger DR 1955. Previous occupations: Waganovas Russian Dance Sch, actor, radio announcer, French interp. Awards: Winner Llangollen Int Musical Eisteddfod, N Wales, UK 1954 & 1956; Music Critics Prize, Brussels 1965.

Sang with major companies in BEL: Brussels; DEN: Copenhagen; FRA: Aix-en-Provence Fest, Marseille, Nancy, Nice, Paris; FR GER: Berlin Deutsche Oper, Hamburg, Kassel, Kiel; ITA: Rome Opera, Spoleto Fest; MON: Monte Carlo. **Roles with these companies incl** ADAM: Bijou (*Postillon de Lonjumeau*); BEETHOVEN: Don Pizarro★ & Rocco★ (*Fidelio*); BERG: Dr Schön★ (*Lulu*), Doktor (*Wozzeck*); CHARPENTIER: Père (*Louise*); CIMAROSA: Count Robinson & Geronimo (*Matrimonio segreto*); DEBUSSY: Golaud★ & Arkel (*Pelléas et Mélisande*); DONIZETTI: Don Pistacchio (*Campanello*), Don Pasquale★; EGK: Cuperus (*Zaubergeige*); FLOTOW: Plunkett (*Martha*); GERSHWIN: Porgy★; GOUNOD: Méphistophélès (*Faust*); HALEVY: Brogny (*Juive*); HANDEL: Ptolemy (*Giulio Cesare*); LORTZING: Stadinger★ (*Waffenschmied*), Baculus★ (*Wildschütz*), Van Bett (*Zar und Zimmermann*); MARTIN: Marc (*Vin herbé*); MASSENET: Des Grieux (*Portrait de Manon*); MENOTTI: Maharaja (*Dernier sauvage*); MILHAUD: Créon (*Médée*); MOZART: Don Alfonso★ (*Così fan tutte*), Leporello★ & Don Giovanni★ (*Don Giovanni*), Osmin★ (*Entführung aus dem Serail*), Conte Almaviva★ & Figaro★ (*Nozze di Figaro*), Osmin★ (*Zaïde*), Sarastro★ (*Zauberflöte*); MUSSORGSKY: Boris Godunov & Pimen★ (*Boris Godunov*); NICOLAI: Falstaff★ (*Lustigen Weiber*); ORFF: König★ (*Kluge*), Bauer★ (*Mond*); PERGOLESI: Marcaniello★ (*Frate 'nnamorato*), Uberto (*Serva padrona*); PROKOFIEV: Mendoza★ (*Duenna*); PUCCINI: Colline★ (*Bohème*), Sharpless★ (*Butterfly*), Scarpia★ (*Tosca*); ROSSINI: Dott Bartolo★ & Don Basilio★ (*Barbiere di Siviglia*); SMETANA: Kezal★ (*Bartered Bride*); STRAUSS, R: Orest★ (*Elektra*), Baron Ochs★ (*Rosenkavalier*); VERDI: Ramfis★ (*Aida*), Philip II★ & Grande Inquisitore (*Don Carlo*); Padre Guardiano★ (*Forza del destino*); WAGNER: Daland★ (*Fliegende Holländer*), König Heinrich★ (*Lohengrin*), Beckmesser (*Meistersinger*), Alberich★ (*Götterdämmerung*), Landgraf★ (*Tannhäuser*); WEBER: Kaspar (*Freischütz*). Also EGK: Guldensack (*Zaubergeige*); WAGNER: Alberich★ (*Siegfried*); CZYC: Kynologe (*Kynologe*); MOZART: Commendatore★ (*Don Giovanni*). **World premieres:** MENOTTI: (*Dernier sauvage*) Opéra Comique, Paris 1963; LORENTZEN: Don Alfonso (*Die Musik kommt mir äusserst bekannt vor*) Kiel Opera 1974. Gives recitals. Appears with symphony orchestra. Teaches voice. Coaches repertoire. **Res:** Scharnhorststr 26, 23 Kiel, FR Ger. Mgmt: PAS/FRG.

MICHALSKI, RAYMOND CHARLES. Bass. American. Resident mem: Metropolitan Opera, New York. Born 8 Jun 1933, Bayonne, NJ, USA. Wife Nadine, occupation accompanist, coach & singer. Two children. Studied: Mannes School of Music, Rosalie Miller, New York. **Debut:** Nourabad (*Pêcheurs de perles*) Philadelphia Grand 1959. Awards: Sullivan Fndt Awd; 2 Rockefeller Grants; Ford Fndt Grant; prize winner Intl Compt Munich.
    Sang with major companies in MEX: Mexico City; USA: Boston, Chicago, Fort Worth, Hartford, Miami, Milwaukee Florentine, Newark, New Orleans, New York Met, Philadelphia Grand, San

Diego, San Francisco Opera, Washington DC.
Roles with these companies incl BELLINI: Oroveso★ (*Norma*); BERLIOZ: Méphistophélès
(*Damnation de Faust*); BRITTEN: Claggart (*Billy Budd*); DELIBES: Nilakantha (*Lakmé*); DONIZETTI: Talbot (*Maria Stuarda*); HANDEL: Ptolemy (*Giulio Cesare*), Argante‡ (*Rinaldo*);
MASSENET: Garrido & Remigo (*Navarraise*);
MOZART: Leporello (*Don Giovanni*), Osmin
(*Entführung aus dem Serail*), Sarastro (*Zauberflöte*); MUSSORGSKY: Varlaam★ (*Boris Godunov*); PONCHIELLI: Alvise (*Gioconda*);
PUCCINI: Colline★ (*Bohème*); RAMEAU: Pollux & Jupiter (*Castor et Pollux*); ROSSINI: Don
Basilio (*Barbiere di Siviglia*); SAINT-SAENS:
Grand prêtre (*Samson et Dalila*); SMETANA:
Kezal (*Bartered Bride*); STRAVINSKY: Creon
(*Oedipus Rex*); VERDI: Ramfis★ (*Aïda*), Philip II
& Grande Inquisitore★ (*Don Carlo*), Padre Guardiano (*Forza del destino*), Banquo (*Macbeth*),
Fiesco (*Simon Boccanegra*); WAGNER: Daland★
(*Fliegende Holländer*), König Heinrich★ (*Lohengrin*), Landgraf★ (*Tannhäuser*). Also DONIZETTI: Raimondo★ (*Lucia*); GOUNOD: Frère
Laurent★ (*Roméo et Juliette*); HOIBY: Rakitin
(*Natalia Petrovna*). Recorded for: RCA. Gives
recitals. Appears with symphony orchestra. **Res:**
125 Lincoln Ave, Elizabeth, NJ, USA. **Mgmt:**
LWI/USA.

MICULS, MELITA LUIZE. Dramatic mezzo-soprano. Latvian. Resident mem: Israel Ntl Opera,
Tel Aviv. Born 1 Aug 1945, Latvia. Single. Studied: Coll-Consv of Cincinnati, O; Acad of Vocal
Arts, Philadelphia. **Debut:** Principessa (*Suor Angelica*) Teatro del Liceo, Barcelona 1972. Awards:
Corbett Schlshp to Consv of Cincinnati & Germany 1969; Baltimore Opera Aud 1974.
Sang with major companies in ISR: Tel Aviv;
SPA: Barcelona; USA: Philadelphia Lyric. **Roles
with these companies incl** BIZET: Carmen; BRITTEN: Hippolita★ (*Midsummer Night*); DONIZETTI: Marquise de Birkenfeld★ (*Fille du
régiment*); OFFENBACH: Giulietta★ (*Contes
d'Hoffmann*); PUCCINI: Suzuki★ (*Butterfly*),
Principessa★ (*Suor Angelica*). Also PUCCINI:
Zita (*Gianni Schicchi*); GIORDANO: Madelon
(*Andrea Chénier*). **Res:** 1453 Balfour, Grosse
Pointe, MI, USA.

MICUNIS, GORDON. Scenic and costume designer for opera, theater. Is also an interior designer. American. Born 16 Jun 1933, Lynn, MA.
Single. Studied: Yale Univ, Donald Oenslager,
CT. **Operatic debut:** sets, *Pique Dame* Opera Socy
of Washington, DC 1961; cost, *Butterfly* New
York City Opera 1962. Theater debut: summer
theater, NY 1959. Awards: Permanent Collection
Lincoln Center; Mem ASID, Trustee USA.
Designed for major companies in USA: Baltimore, Boston, Cincinnati, Fort Worth, New Orleans, New York City Opera, San Francisco
Opera, Washington DC. **Operas designed for these
companies incl** BERNSTEIN: *Trouble in Tahiti★;*
BIZET: *Carmen;* CHARPENTIER: *Louise★;*
DONIZETTI: *Don Pasquale;* LEONCAVALLO: *Pagliacci;* MASCAGNI: *Cavalleria
rusticana;* MOZART: *Così fan tutte, Entführung
aus dem Serail, Nozze di Figaro;* PUCCINI:
Gianni Schicchi, Butterfly, Tosca; RAVEL: *En-*

fant et les sortilèges; ROSSINI: *Barbiere di Siviglia;* SCHOENBERG: *Erwartung;* STRAUSS,
R: *Ariadne auf Naxos, Rosenkavalier;* STRAVINSKY: *Rossignol;* TCHAIKOVSKY: *Pique
Dame;* VERDI: *Aida, Rigoletto, Traviata.* Exhibitions of stage designs Wright Hepburn Gallery
1961; ITI Touring Show, Kennedy Center Washington, Lincoln Center New York and Prague,
CSSR: 1975-76. Teaches at Barnard Coll, New
York. **Res:** 490 West End Ave, New York, USA.

MIEDEL, RAINER. Conductor of opera and symphony; composer. German. Also Mus Dir, Gavleborg Symph, Gavle, Sweden 1968-76. Mus Dir
designate, Seattle Symph, WA, USA. Born 1 June
1939, Regensburg, Germany. Divorced. Studied:
Musikhochschule, Berlin; Istvan Kertesz, Franco
Ferrara, Rome; incl cello, piano. Plays the cello.
Operatic debut: *Carmen,* Gavle City Opera, Sweden. Symphonic debut: Stockholm Phil, Sweden
1966. Previous occupations: princ cellist, Stockholm Phil. Awards: Deutsche Studienstiftung
Awd. Previous adm positions in opera: permanent
guest, Stockholm Royal Opera 1973-75; Music Dir
Gavle City Opera 1968-75; permanent guest, Oldenburg State Opera, FR Ger.
Conducted with major companies in BUL: Sofia;
FRA: Nice; SWE: Stockholm; SWI: Basel. **Operas
with these companies incl** BIZET: *Carmen★;*
GERSHWIN: *Porgy and Bess★;* HAYDN:
Mondo della luna; HUMPERDINCK: *Hänsel
und Gretel;* MOZART: *Nozze di Figaro;* ORFF:
Carmina burana; PUCCINI: *Bohème★, Gianni
Schicchi★, Tosca★;* ROSSINI: *Barbiere di Siviglia★;* STRAUSS, J: *Fledermaus★;* VERDI:
Luisa Miller★, Simon Boccanegra★, Traviata★.
Video—Swedish Broadc Corp: *Bohème.* Conducted major orch in Europe, USA/Canada. Previous positions with major orch: assoc cond Baltimore Symph. **Res:** Varbergsvägen 183, Stockholm,
Sweden. **Mgmt:** KBL/SWE; SHA/USA.

MIKÓ, ANDRÁS. Stages/produces opera & television. Hungarian. Chief Prod & Resident Stage Dir,
Allami Opera House, Budapest. Born 30 Jun 1922,
Budapest. Wife Eva Rehák, occupation singer.
Studied: Opera Budapest, Kálmán Nádasdy; also
music, violin & voice. Operatic training as asst
stage dir at Allami Opera House, Budapest 1946-
50. **Operatic debut:** *Così fan tutte* Opera Studio,
Budapest 1948. Theater debut: Television Budapest 1957. Awards: Kossuth Prize 1975; Hon Artist, Hungarian Gvnmt 1964.
Directed/produced opera for major companies in
BEL: Brussels; DEN: Copenhagen; FIN: Helsinki; FR GER: Cologne, Karlsruhe, Wuppertal;
GER DR: Berlin Staatsoper; HUN: Budapest;
ITA: Bologna, Rome Opera; POL: Warsaw; UK:
Edinburgh Fest, London Royal. **Operas staged with
these companies incl** d'ALBERT: *Tiefland;* BARTOK: *Bluebeard's Castle★;* BEETHOVEN: *Fidelio;* BERG: *Lulu★, Wozzeck;* BIZET: *Carmen;*
BOITO: *Mefistofele★;* BRITTEN: *Albert Herring;* DEBUSSY: *Pelléas et Mélisande;* DONIZETTI: *Don Pasquale, Lucia;* ERKEL: *Bánk
Bán;* GAY/Britten: *Beggar's Opera★;* GERSHWIN: *Porgy and Bess★;* GLUCK: *Iphigénie en
Aulide★, Orfeo ed Euridice★;* GOUNOD: *Faust;*
LEONCAVALLO: *Pagliacci;* MASCAGNI: *Cavalleria rusticana;* MENOTTI: *Telephone★;*

MONTEVERDI: *Incoronazione di Poppea*★, *Ritorno d'Ulisse*★; MOZART: *Don Giovanni, Entführung aus dem Serail, Nozze di Figaro, Zauberflöte;* MUSSORGSKY: *Boris Godunov*★; OFFENBACH: *Contes d'Hoffmann;* ORFF: *Kluge;* PUCCINI: *Fanciulla del West, Manon Lescaut, Turandot;* ROSSINI: *Barbiere di Siviglia, Guillaume Tell;* STRAUSS, R: *Rosenkavalier*★, *Salome;* SZOKOLAY: *Blood Wedding*★; VERDI: *Aida*★, *Don Carlo*★, *Falstaff*★, *Lombardi*★, *Macbeth, Otello*★, *Rigoletto, Trovatore;* WAGNER: *Meistersinger*★, *Siegfried, Tannhäuser;* WEILL: *Aufstieg und Fall der Stadt Mahagonny.* Also ERKEL: *Hunyadi László;* PETROVICS: *Lysistrata;* KODALY: *Spinning Room.* **Operatic world premieres:** SZOKOLAY: *Blood Wedding* 1964, *Hamlet* 1968, *Samson* 1973; PETROVICS: *Crime and Punishment* 1969; all at Budapest Op. Operatic Video—TV Budapest: *Bluebeard's Castle, Blood Wedding.* Teaches at Acad of Music, Budapest **Res:** Uri-Utca 44-46, Budapest, Hungary. Mgmt: ITK/HUN; SLZ/FRG.

MIKOVA, ALENA. Dramatic soprano. Czechoslovakian. Resident mem: National Theater, Prague. Born 21 Nov 1928, Prague. Husband Jiri Stilec, occupation musicologist. Studied: Mrs Fassati. **Debut:** Senta (*Fliegende Holländer*) Opera Theater, Usti nad Labem 1954. Previous occupations: Czech monitor, Radio of Prague. Awards: Merited Artist, Gvnmt of Czechoslovakia.

Sang with major companies in AUS: Vienna Staatsoper; BUL: Sofia; CZE: Brno, Prague National; FRA: Marseille; FR GER: Karlsruhe; GER DR: Berlin Staatsoper; POL: Warsaw. **Roles with these companies incl** BEETHOVEN: Leonore★ (*Fidelio*); BRITTEN: Lady Billows (*Albert Herring*); DALLAPICCOLA: La Madre‡ (*Prigioniero*); JANACEK: Vixen★ (*Cunning Little Vixen*), Jenufa & Kostelnicka★ (*Jenufa*), Katya Kabanova, Emilia Marty (*Makropoulos Affair*); LEONCAVALLO: Nedda (*Pagliacci*); MOZART: Donna Anna (*Don Giovanni*), Contessa (*Nozze di Figaro*); OFFENBACH: Giulietta (*Contes d'Hoffmann*); POULENC: La femme★ (*Voix humaine*); PUCCINI: Musetta★ (*Bohème*), Tosca, Turandot★; SCHOENBERG: A Woman★ (*Erwartung*); SHOSTAKOVICH: Katerina Ismailova★; SMETANA: Mlada★ (*Dalibor*), Libuse★; STRAUSS, R: Elektra★, Marschallin★ (*Rosenkavalier*), Salome★; SUCHON: Katrena (*Whirlpool*); VERDI: Aida; WAGNER: Senta (*Fliegende Holländer*), Brünnhilde★ (*Walküre*). Also FIBICH: Sarka; BURIAN: Marysa. **World premieres:** CIKKER: Katusa (*Resurrection*) Ntl Theater, Prague 1962; Katka (*Beg Bajazid*) Bratislava 1957; BORKOVEC: Zdena (*Palecek*) National Theater, Prague 1958; BURGHAUSER: Alena (*Most*) National Theater, Prague 1967. Recorded for: Supraphon. Gives recitals. Appears with symphony orchestra. **Res:** Janackovo nabrezi 5, Prague, Czechoslovakia. Mgmt: PRG/CZE.

MILADINOVITCH, DEJAN DUSAN. Stages/produces opera, theater & television. Also designs sets & stage-lighting and is an author. Yugoslavian. Resident Stage Dir, Serbian National Opera, Novi Sad. Also Resident Stage Dir for theater & television in Novi Sad. Born 2 Dec 1948, Belgrade. Wife Vesna. Studied: Acad for theater, film, radio and TV, Belgrade; incl music & piano. Operatic training as asst stage dir at Ntl Opera Theater, Belgrade 1969-70. **Operatic debut:** *Puss in Boots* Ntl Op Thtr, Belgrade 1971. Theater debut: Ntl Theater, Belgrade 1971. Awards: 2 First Awds for directing.

Directed/produced opera for major companies in YUG: Belgrade. **Operas staged with these companies incl** BIZET: *Carmen*★; BORODIN: *Prince Igor*★; ERKEL: *Bánk Bán*★; GOTOVAC: *Ero der Schelm*★; HAYDN: *Mondo della luna*★; PUCCINI: *Bohème*, *Butterfly*★; VERDI: *Rigoletto*, *Trovatore*★. Also BRITTEN: *Let's Make an Opera*★; KALINSKY: *Analfabeth*★, *Authority*★; KOVATCH: *Master of the Sea.* **Operatic world premieres:** HERCIGONJA: *Grave Pit* Serb Ntl Thtr, Novi Sad 1975. **Res:** Georgi Dimitrova 39, Belgrade, Yugoslavia. Mgmt: YGC/YUG.

MILADINOVITCH, DUSAN SLOBODAN. Conductor of opera and symphony; composer. Yugoslavian. Resident Cond, National Opera, Belgrade. Born 20 Feb 1924, Belgrade. Wife Milica, occupation opera singer. One child. Studied: Acad for Music Arts, Belgrade; incl piano and voice. Plays the piano. Operatic training as repetiteur & asst cond at National Opera, Belgrade 1943-49. **Operatic debut:** *Elisir d'amore* National Opera, Belgrade 1949. Symphonic debut: Belgrade Phil Orch 1951. Awards: Awd National Theater, Belgrade. Previous adm positions in opera: General Dir, National Opera, Belgrade 1969-73.

Conducted with major companies in AUS: Vienna Staatsoper & Volksoper; BUL: Sofia; DEN: Copenhagen; GRE: Athens Fest; GER DR: Berlin Staatsoper, Leipzig; ITA: Palermo, Venice; NOR: Oslo; POL: Warsaw; ROM: Bucharest; SPA: Barcelona; UK: Edinburgh Fest; YUG: Dubrovnik, Zagreb, Belgrade. **Operas with these companies incl** BARTOK: *Bluebeard's Castle*★; BELLINI: *Norma*★; BIZET: *Carmen*★; BORODIN: *Prince Igor*★; CIMAROSA: *Matrimonio segreto*★; DONIZETTI: *Don Pasquale, Elisir;* GOTOVAC: *Ero der Schelm*★; GOUNOD: *Faust*★; HANDEL: *Giulio Cesare;* LEONCAVALLO: *Pagliacci*★; MASCAGNI: *Cavalleria rusticana*★; MASSENET: *Don Quichotte*★, *Werther;* MOZART: *Entführung aus dem Serail*★, *Nozze di Figaro*★, *Zauberflöte*★; MUSSORGSKY: *Boris Godunov*★, *Fair at Sorochinsk*★, *Khovanshchina*★; PONCHIELLI: *Gioconda*★; PUCCINI: *Bohème*★, *Butterfly*★, *Tosca*★, *Turandot*★; ROSSINI: *Barbiere di Siviglia*★; SAINT-SAENS: *Samson et Dalila;* SMETANA: *Bartered Bride*★; TCHAIKOVSKY: *Eugene Onegin*★, *Pique Dame*★; VERDI: *Aida*★, *Don Carlo*★, *Ernani*★, *Forza del destino*★, *Nabucco*★, *Otello*★, *Rigoletto*★, *Traviata*★, *Trovatore*★; WAGNER: *Fliegende Holländer.* Also KONIOVITCH: *Prince of Zeta;* RAJICIC: *Simonida.* **World premieres:** RADITCH: *Monsieur Pourceaugnac* National Opera, Belgrade 1966; LOGAR: *Vain Pumpkin* 1957. Video—TV Belgrade: *Vain Pumpkin, M Pourceaugnac, Prince of Zeta.* Conducted major orch in Europe, Africa. Previous positions as Mus Dir with major orch: Symph Orch Cairo, Egypt 1960-64. Teaches at Music Consv, Belgrade. **Res:** Georgi Dimitrova 39, Belgrade, Yugoslavia. Mgmt: YGC/YUG.

MILADINOVITCH, MILICA DUSAN; née Troja-novitch. Dramatic mezzo-soprano. Yugoslavian. Resident mem: National Opera, Belgrade. Born 21 Feb 1930, Belgrade. Husband Dusan, occupation conductor. One child. Studied: Acad for Musical Arts, Belgrade. **Debut:** Pauline (*Pique Dame*) National Opera, Belgrade 1950. Awards: Awd National Theater, Belgrade; Intl Conc, Geneva; Intl Conc for Singers, Sofia, twice winner.

Sang with major companies in AUS: Vienna Staatsoper & Volksoper; BUL: Sofia; DEN: Copenhagen; FRA: Paris; GRE: Athens National; FR GER: Wiesbaden; GER DR: Berlin Staatsoper; ITA: Venice; NOR: Oslo; POL: Warsaw; SWI: Basel, Geneva, Zurich; UK: Edinburgh Fest; YUG: Dubrovnik, Zagreb, Belgrade. **Roles with these companies incl** BERLIOZ: Marguerite (*Damnation de Faust*); BIZET: Carmen*; BORODIN: Kontchakovna* (*Prince Igor*); BRITTEN: Lucretia (*Rape of Lucretia*); GLUCK: Orfeo; HANDEL: Cornelia (*Giulio Cesare*); MASSENET: Dulcinée* (*Don Quichotte*), Charlotte* (*Werther*); MENOTTI: Secretary (*Consul*); MUSSORGSKY: Marina* (*Boris Godunov*), Khivria (*Fair at Sorochinsk*), Marfa* (*Khovanshchina*); NICOLAI: Frau Reich (*Lustigen Weiber*); PONCHIELLI: Laura & La Cieca* (*Gioconda*); PROKOFIEV: Blanche (*Gambler*), Clarissa* (*Love for Three Oranges*), Helene‡ (*War and Peace*); PUCCINI: Suzuki* (*Butterfly*); SAINT-SAENS: Dalila*; SMETANA: Hata* (*Bartered Bride*); STRAUSS, J: Prinz Orlovsky (*Fledermaus*); STRAVINSKY: Jocasta (*Oedipus Rex*); TCHAIKOVSKY: Olga* (*Eugene Onegin*), Comtesse* (*Pique Dame*); VERDI: Amneris* (*Aida*), Eboli (*Don Carlo*), Preziosilla* (*Forza del destino*), Azucena* (*Trovatore*). Also GLINKA: Vanya‡ (*Life for the Tsar*); RIMSKY-KORSAKOV: Lel‡ (*Snow Maiden*); GOTOVAC: Doma* (*Ero der Schelm*); KONIOVITCH: Yevrossima* (*Prince of Zeta*); VERDI: Fenena* (*Nabucco*). **World premieres:** LOGAR: Fema (*Vain Pumpkin*) National Opera Belgrade 1957; RAJICIC: Theodora (*Simonida*) Ntl Op Belgrade 1957; KONIOVITCH: Petra (*Peasants*) Ntl Op Belgrade 1952. Recorded for: Decca, MGM, Yugoton. Video—Bayerische TV: Carmen; Belgrade TV: Yevrossima (*Prince of Zeta*); Fema (*Vain Pumpkin*). Gives recitals. Appears with symphony orchestra. **Res:** Georgi Dimitrova 39, Belgrade, Yugoslavia. Mgmt: YGC/YUG.

MILASHKINA, TAMARA. Lyric & dramatic soprano. Russian. Resident mem: Bolshoi Opera, Moscow. Born USSR. Studied: in Moscow and Milan.

Sang with major companies in AUS: Vienna Staatsoper; CZE: Prague National; FIN: Helsinki; FRA: Paris; FR GER: Wiesbaden, Wuppertal; ITA: Milan La Scala; USSR: Moscow Bolshoi; et al. **Roles with these companies incl** PROKOFIEV: Natasha (*War and Peace*); PUCCINI: Tosca; RIMSKY-KORSAKOV: Fevronia (*Invisible City of Kitezh*) ; TCHAIKOVSKY: Tatiana (*Eugene Onegin*), Lisa‡ (*Pique Dame*): VERDI: Aida, Leonora (*Trovatore*); et al. Also VERDI: Lida (*Battaglia di Legnano*). Recorded for: Melodiya/Angel.

MILCHEVA-NONOVA, ALEXANDRINA. Mezzo-soprano. Bulgarian. Resident mem: National Opera, Sofia. Born 27 Nov 1936, Shoumen, Bulgaria. Husband Christo Nonov, occupation lawyer. One child. Studied: Bulgarian Consv, Prof G Cherkin, Sofia. **Debut:** Carmen, Varna Opera, Bulgaria 1961. Awards: First Prize, Thirteenth Intl Compt, Toulouse, France 1966.

Sang with major companies in AUS: Vienna Staatsoper; BEL: Brussels; BUL: Sofia; CZE: Prague Ntl, Brno; DEN: Copenhagen; FRA: Lyon, Paris, Rouen, Toulouse; GRE: Athens Fest; FR GER: Wiesbaden; GER DR: Berlin Komische Oper; HOL: Amsterdam; HUN: Budapest; ITA: Florence Maggio, Palermo; POL: Lodz, Warsaw; ROM: Bucharest; SWI: Geneva Grand Théâtre, Zurich; UK: Glyndebourne Fest; USSR: Moscow Bolshoi; YUG: Belgrade. **Roles with these companies incl** BARTOK: Judith* (*Bluebeard's Castle*); BIZET: Carmen*‡; BORODIN: Kontchakovna* (*Prince Igor*); CILEA: Princesse de Boullion (*Adriana Lecouvreur*); MOZART: Dorabella* (*Così fan tutte*), Cherubino* (*Nozze di Figaro*); MUSSORGSKY: Marina*‡ (*Boris Godunov*), Marfa*‡ (*Khovanshchina*); PROKOFIEV: Clarissa* (*Love for Three Oranges*); PUCCINI: Suzuki* (*Butterfly*); ROSSINI: Angelina* (*Cenerentola*); SAINT-SAENS: Dalila*; STRAUSS, R: Octavian* (*Rosenkavalier*); TCHAIKOVSKY: Olga* (*Eugene Onegin*); VERDI: Amneris* (*Aida*), Preziosilla* (*Forza del destino*), Azucena* (*Trovatore*). Recorded for: Balkanton. Gives recitals. Appears with symphony orchestra. Teaches voice. **Res:** k Mladost bl 99/E, 1156 Sofia, Bulgaria. Mgmt: BAA/BUL; VLD/AUS.

MILJAKOVIC, OLIVERA. Lyric soprano. Austrian/Yugoslavian. Resident mem: Staatsoper, Vienna. Born 26 Apr 1939, Belgrade, Yugoslavia. Divorced. One child. Studied: Josef Rijavec, Belgrade; Gina Cigna, Italy; Ludwig Weber, Vienna. **Debut:** Despina (*Così fan tutte*) Staatsoper Vienna 1962. Previous occupations: actress.

Sang with major companies in ARG: Buenos Aires; AUS: Salzburg Fest, Vienna Staatsoper; BEL: Brussels; CAN: Montreal/Quebec; DEN: Copenhagen; FRA: Bordeaux, Lyon, Toulouse; FR GER: Bayreuth Fest, Berlin Deutsche Oper, Hamburg, Mannheim, Munich Staatsoper, Wiesbaden; HOL: Amsterdam; ITA: Florence Maggio, Naples, Trieste, Turin; MON: Monte Carlo; SWI: Zurich; USA: Chicago, Seattle; YUG: Dubrovnik, Zagreb, Belgrade. **Roles with these companies incl** BEETHOVEN: Marzelline* (*Fidelio*); CALDARA: Dafne* & Venus* (*Dafne*); HANDEL: Romilda* (*Xerxes*); MOZART: Despina* (*Così fan tutte*), Zerlina* (*Don Giovanni*), Blondchen (*Entführung aus dem Serail*), Ilia* (*Idomeneo*), Susanna* & Cherubino (*Nozze di Figaro*), Pamina* (*Zauberflöte*); ORFF: Solo (*Carmina burana*); PERGOLESI: Serpina‡ (*Serva padrona*); PFITZNER: Ighino* (*Palestrina*); STRAUSS, R: Zdenka* (*Arabella*), Sophie* (*Rosenkavalier*); VERDI: Oscar* (*Ballo in maschera*), Nannetta (*Falstaff*); WEBER: Aennchen* (*Freischütz*). Also NASTASIJEVIC: Radojka (*Zacarana Vodenica*). Recorded for: Decca, EMI, Eterna, Concert Hall. Video/Film: Marzelline (*Fidelio*); Despina (*Così fan tutte*). Gives recitals. Appears with symphony orchestra. **Res:** Neulingg 37, Vienna, Austria. Mgmt: RAB/AUS; SLZ/FRG.

MILLER, JONATHAN. Stages/produces opera, theater, film & television and is an actor & author. British. Born 1934, London. Wife Rachel, occupation med doctor. Three children. **Operatic debut:** *Arden muss sterben* New Op Co/Sadler's Wells, London 1974. Previous occupation: co-author of & actor in *Beyond the Fringe,* revue; taught Yale Drama School, USA; med doctor.

Directed/produced opera for major companies in UK: Glyndebourne Fest, London English National. **Operas staged with these companies incl** JANACEK: *Cunning Little Vixen★;* MOZART: *Così fan tutte★;* VERDI: *Rigoletto★.* Previous leading positions with major theater companies: Assoc Dir, Ntl Th, London. **Res:** 63 Gloucester Crescent, London NW1, UK. **Mgmt:** HLT/UK; SHA/USA.

MILLER, LAJOS. Dramatic baritone. Hungarian. Resident mem: State Opera, Budapest. Born 23 Jan 1940, Szombathely, Hungary. Wife Susanna Dobranszky, occupation opera singer, soprano. One child. Studied: Akad of Music, Budapest. **Debut:** SZOKOLAY: Horatio (*Hamlet*) Budapest Opera 1968. Awards: Third Prize Erkel Cont; Second Prize Kodály Cont; Great Prize Paris Fauré Cont; First Prize Ferenc Liszt, Culture Ministerium.

Sang with major companies in CZE: Prague National & Smetana; FRA: Aix-en-Provence Fest; FR GER: Bonn, Cologne, Munich Staatsoper, Wiesbaden. **Roles with these companies incl** BRITTEN: Demetrius★ (*Midsummer Night*); HAYDN: Eclittico (*Mondo della luna*); MOZART: Don Giovanni★; ORFF: Solo★ (*Carmina burana*); TCHAIKOVSKY: Eugene Onegin★; VERDI: Renato★ (*Ballo in maschera*), Rodrigo★ (*Don Carlo*), Don Carlo★ (*Forza del destino*), Macbeth★, Conte di Luna★ (*Trovatore*); WAGNER: Wolfram★ (*Tannhäuser*). Also RANKI: Adam (*Tragedy of Man*). Recorded for: Hungarian Magna. Mgmt: ITK/HUN; CMW/FRG: SLZ/FRG.

MILLER, TERREL W. American. Houston Grand Opera Assn, 615 Louisiana/Jones Hall, Houston, TX; Mng, Texas Opera Theater, 1974- . In charge of overall adm matters, tech & finances. Is also a scenic and lighting designer. Born Enid, Oklahoma. Single. Studied: Univ of Oklahoma, Norman. Previous positions adm, musical & theatrical: Asst Gen Mng, Baltimore Opera Co 1972-74; Mng, Bar Harbor Music Fest, ME 1972; St Mng, Santa Fe Opera 1971; St Mng, Central City Opera, CO 1970. Operatic debut as designer: *Rita* Baltimore Opera 1972.

Designed for major companies in USA: Baltimore, Houston. **Operas designed for these companies incl** BRITTEN: *Turn of the Screw★;* DONIZETTI: *Rita★;* HUMPERDINCK: *Hänsel und Gretel★;* MENOTTI: *Amahl★, Old Maid and the Thief★;* MOZART: *Così fan tutte★;* ROSSINI: *Barbiere di Siviglia★;* SOUSA: *El Capitan★.* Initiated major policy changes including founding Eastern Opera Theater of the Baltimore Opera Co, using videotaped orch with live singers on stage. **Res:** Houston, TX, USA.

MILNE, PETER JAMES. Bass-baritone. Canadian. Born 16 Feb 1934, Smiths Falls, Ont, Canada. Divorced. Studied: Univ of Toronto; Mary Rezza;

George Lambert, Toronto; Elliot Lake Summer School, Arthur Schoep, Ont, Canada. **Debut:** Vicar George (*Albert Herring*) Stratford Opera, Ont, Canada 1967. Previous occupations: chemical operator for 9 yrs. Awards: Canada Counc Schlshp for study in Europe.

Sang with major companies in CAN: Toronto. **Roles with these companies incl** BRITTEN: Azarias★ (*Burning Fiery Furnace*); MOZART: Don Alfonso★ (*Così fan tutte*); ROSSINI: Dott Bartolo★ (*Barbiere di Siviglia*); STRAVINSKY: Creon★ (*Oedipus Rex*); VERDI: Fra Melitone★ (*Forza*), Germont (*Traviata*). **World premieres:** SOMERS: Dr Schultz (*Louis Riel*) Canadian Opera, Toronto 1967. Video–CBC TV: Dr Schultz (*Louis Riel*). Gives recitals. Appears with symphony orchestra. **Res:** 150 Brockville St, Smiths Falls, Ont, Canada.

MILNES, SHERRILL EUSTACE. Dramatic baritone. American. Resident mem: Metropolitan Opera, New York. Born 10 Jan 1935, Downers Grove, IL. Wife Nancy Stokes. Three children. Studied: Rosa Ponselle, Boris Goldovsky, Andrew White. **Debut:** Valentin (*Faust*) Metropolitan Opera 1965. Awards: two Hon D; Chairman of Board, Affiliate Artists.

Sang with major companies in ARG: Buenos Aires; AUS: Vienna Staatsoper; FRA: Paris; FR GER: Berlin Deutsche Oper, Hamburg, Munich Staatsoper; GER DR: Berlin Staatsoper; UK: London Royal; USA: Baltimore, Chicago, Cincinnati, Houston, New Orleans, New York Met & City Opera, Pittsburgh, San Antonio. **Roles with these companies incl** BELLINI: Sir Richard★‡ (*Puritani*); DONIZETTI: Enrico★‡ (*Lucia*); GIORDANO: Carlo Gérard (*Andrea Chénier*); GOUNOD: Méphistophélès (*Faust*); LEON-CAVALLO: Tonio★‡ (*Pagliacci*); MASSENET: Remigo★ (*Navarraise*); MOZART: Don Giovanni★; PONCHIELLI: Barnaba (*Gioconda*); PROKOFIEV: King of Clubs (*Love for Three Oranges*); PUCCINI: Jack Rance (*Fanciulla del West*), Michele‡ (*Tabarro*), Scarpia★‡ (*Tosca*); ROSSINI: Figaro★‡ (*Barbiere di Siviglia*); THOMAS: Hamlet★‡; VERDI: Amonasro‡ (*Aida*), Ezio‡ (*Attila*), Renato★‡ (*Ballo in maschera*), Rodrigo★‡ (*Don Carlo*), Don Carlo★ (*Forza del destino*), Giacomo★‡ (*Giovanna d'Arco*), Miller★‡ (*Luisa Miller*), Macbeth★, Iago★ (*Otello*), Rigoletto★‡, Germont★‡ (*Traviata*), Conte di Luna★‡ (*Trovatore*), Monforte★‡ (*Vespri*); WAGNER: König Heinrich (*Lohengrin*). Also on records only MOZART: Guglielmo (*Così fan tutte*); ORFF: Solo (*Carmina burana*); PUCCINI: Marcello (*Bohème*); STRAUSS, R: Jochanaan (*Salome*). **World premieres:** LEVY: Adam Brant (*Mourning Becomes Electra*) Met Opera 1967. Recorded for: RCA, Angel, EMI, London-Decca, Philips. Gives recitals. Appears with symphony orchestra. **Res:** New York and London. Mgmt: BAR/USA.

MINDE, STEFAN PAUL. Conductor of opera and symphony; operatic stage director. German. Gen Dir & Cond, Portland Opera Co, Portland, OR, USA. Born 12 Apr 1936, Leipzig, Germany. Wife Edith. Two children. Studied: Mozarteum, Profs Paumgartner & Wimberger, Salzburg; incl piano, cello, bassoon, percussion. Operatic training as repetiteur, Studienleiter & Cond, Wiesbaden Opera, FR Ger 1959-62; Trier Opera, FR Ger 1962-68. **Operatic debut:** *Leben des Orest* Staatstheater Wiesbaden, FR Ger 1961. **Symphonic debut:** Oregon Symph, Portland, USA 1972. **Awards:** C D Jackson Prize, Berkshire Music Fest, MA, USA.

Conducted with major companies in CAN: Toronto, Vancouver; FR GER: Cologne, Düsseldorf-Duisburg, Saarbrücken, Wiesbaden; USA: Cincinnati, Portland. **Operas with these companies incl** BEETHOVEN: *Fidelio;* BIZET: *Carmen;* BRITTEN: *Rape of Lucretia;* BUSONI: *Arlecchino;* CIMAROSA: *Matrimonio segreto;* DONIZETTI: *Don Pasquale, Elisir, Lucia;* FLOTOW: *Martha;* GIORDANO: *Andrea Chénier;* GLUCK: *Iphigénie en Aulide, Iphigénie en Tauride, Orfeo ed Euridice;* HANDEL: *Giulio Cesare;* HUMPERDINCK: *Hänsel und Gretel;* IBERT: *Angélique;* JANACEK: *Cunning Little Vixen, Jenufa, Makropoulos Affair;* LEONCAVALLO: *Pagliacci;* LORTZING: *Waffenschmied, Wildschütz, Zar und Zimmermann;* MASCAGNI: *Cavalleria rusticana;* MOZART: *Così fan tutte, Don Giovanni, Entführung aus dem Serail, Schauspieldirektor, Nozze di Figaro, Zauberflöte;* MUSSORGSKY: *Fair at Sorochinsk;* NICOLAI: *Lustigen Weiber;* OFFENBACH: *Contes d'Hoffmann;* ORFF: *Carmina burana, Kluge;* PUCCINI: *Bohème, Butterfly, Rondine, Tosca;* ROSSINI: *Barbiere di Siviglia;* SCHOENBERG: *Glückliche Hand;* SMETANA: *Bartered Bride;* STRAUSS, J: *Fledermaus;* STRAUSS, R: *Arabella, Ariadne auf Naxos, Rosenkavalier, Salome;* TCHAIKOVSKY: *Eugene Onegin;* VERDI: *Ballo in maschera, Forza del destino, Otello, Rigoletto, Simon Boccanegra, Traviata, Trovatore;* WAGNER: *Fliegende Holländer, Lohengrin, Tristan und Isolde;* WEBER: *Freischütz;* WEILL: *Aufstieg und Fall der Stadt Mahagonny;* WOLF: *Corregidor;* WOLF-FERRARI: *Quattro rusteghi, Segreto di Susanna.* Also d'ALBERT: *Abreise;* SUTERMEISTER: *Titus Feuerfuchs;* EGK: *Revisor;* ROSSINI: *Pietra del paragone;* REUTTER: *Brücke von San Luis Rey.* Conducted major orch in Europe, USA/Canada. **Res:** Portland, OR, USA. **Mgmt:** DSP/USA; PAS/FRG.

MINTON, YVONNE FAY. Lyric mezzo-soprano. Australian. Born Sydney, Australia. Husband William Barclay, occupation company dir. Two children. **Studied:** Sydney Consv, Marjorie Walker. **Debut:** Maggie (*One Man Show*) London County Council 1964. **Awards:** Hon RAM, London.

Sang with major companies in AUSTRL: Sydney; AUS: Vienna Staatsoper; FR GER: Bayreuth Festival, Cologne, Frankfurt, Hamburg; HOL: Amsterdam; ISR: Tel Aviv; SWI: Geneva; UK: London Royal; USA: Chicago, New York Met, San Francisco Opera. **Roles with these companies incl** BERLIOZ: Ascanio (*Benvenuto Cellini*); DEBUSSY: Geneviève★‡ (*Pelléas et Mélisande*); GLUCK: Orfeo★; MOZART: Sesto★ (*Clemenza di Tito*), Dorabella★‡ (*Così fan tutte*), Cherubino★‡ (*Nozze di Figaro*); MUSSORGSKY: Marina★ (*Boris Godunov*), Marfa★ (*Khovanshchina*); SAINT-SAENS: Dalila★; STRAUSS, R: Octavian★‡ (*Rosenkavalier*); TCHAIKOVSKY: Olga★ (*Eugene Onegin*); TIPPETT: Thea★‡ (*Knot Garden*); WAGNER: Brangäne★ (*Tristan und Isolde*). Also TIPPETT:

Helen★ (*King Priam*). **World premieres:** MAW: Maggie (*One Man Show*) London County Council 1964. Recorded for: Decca, EMI, RCA, Philips. Gives recitals. Appears with symphony orchestra. **Res:** London, UK. **Mgmt:** IWL/UK; COL/USA.

MIRANDA, ANA-MARIA; née Anne-Marie. Coloratura soprano. French/Argentinean. Born 9 Sep 1937, Paris. Husband Hector Garcia, occupation painter & musician. **Studied:** Mario Podestà; Ecole Normale de Musique, Paris. **Debut:** Despina (*Così fan tutte*) Théâtre des Champs-Elysées, Paris 1968. Previous occupations: translator UNESCO, Paris. **Awards:** First Prize Conc Intl de Paris; Second Prize Conc 's Hertogenbosch, Netherlands.

Sang with major companies in AUS: Vienna Volksoper; BEL: Brussels, Liège; FRA: Aix-en-Provence Fest, Bordeaux, Lyon, Marseille, Nancy, Nice, Paris, Rouen, Strasbourg; HOL: Amsterdam; ITA: Spoleto Fest, Trieste; SPA: Barcelona; SWI: Geneva; USA: Chicago. **Roles with these companies incl** BIZET: Micaëla (*Carmen*), Léila★ (*Pêcheurs de perles*); DONIZETTI: Norina★ (*Don Pasquale*); GLUCK: Amor (*Orfeo ed Euridice*); HALEVY: Eudoxie★ (*Juive*); MASSENET: Sophie★ (*Werther*); MENOTTI: Annina★ (*Saint of Bleecker Street*); MOZART: Despina★ (*Così fan tutte*), Zerlina★ (*Don Giovanni*), Blondchen★ (*Entführung aus dem Serail*); OHANA: Phèdre (*Syllabaire pour Phèdre*); PURCELL: Belinda★ (*Dido and Aeneas*); RAMEAU: Aricie★; STRAUSS, J: Adele★ (*Fledermaus*); STRAUSS, R: Sophie★ (*Rosenkavalier*); VERDI: Oscar (*Ballo in maschera*), Gilda★ (*Rigoletto*). Also GRETRY: Zémire★; HONEGGER: Vierge (*Jeanne d'Arc au bûcher*). Only on records ROUSSEAU: Colette (*Devin du village*). Recorded for: Arion, CBS. Gives recitals. Appears with symphony orchestra. **Res:** Paris, France.

MIRDITA, FEDERIK. Stages/produces opera, theater & television. Also designs sets & stage-lighting and is an actor. Austrian. Born 26 Jan 1931, Tirana, Albania. Married. Two children. **Studied:** Vienna, incl music. **Operatic debut:** *Bohème* Stadttheater Bonn. **Theater debut:** Salzburg, Austria. Previous adm positions in opera: Oberspielleiter, Staatstheater Braunschweig 1964-67; Operndirektor, Landestheater Linz 1967-70.

Directed/produced opera for major companies in AUS: Graz, Salzburg Fest; FRA: Bordeaux; FR GER: Bonn, Darmstadt, Frankfurt, Kiel, Krefeld, Saarbrücken, Wiesbaden; HOL: Amsterdam; SWI: Zurich; YUG: Zagreb. **Operas staged with these companies incl** ADAM: *Si j'étais roi;* BARTOK: *Bluebeard's Castle;* BELLINI: *Puritani;* BERG: *Wozzeck;* BIZET: *Carmen;* BORODIN: *Prince Igor;* BRITTEN: *Prodigal Son;* CIMAROSA: *Matrimonio segreto;* DALLAPICCOLA: *Volo di notte;* DONIZETTI: *Don Pasquale, Elisir;* HANDEL: *Giulio Cesare;* JANACEK: *Jenufa, Katya Kabanova;* MENOTTI: *Amahl, Globolinks;* MONTEVERDI: *Ritorno d'Ulisse;* MOZART: *Clemenza di Tito, Così fan tutte, Don Giovanni, Entführung aus dem Serail;* NICOLAI: *Lustigen Weiber;* PUCCINI: *Butterfly, Manon Lescaut, Tosca;* PURCELL: *Dido and Aeneas;* ROSSINI: *Barbiere di Siviglia;* SALIERI: *Prima la musica;* SMETANA: *Bartered Bride;*

STRAUSS, R: *Capriccio, Elektra;* TCHAIKOV-SKY: *Eugene Onegin, Pique Dame;* VERDI: *Ballo in maschera, Otello, Traviata, Trovatore;* WAGNER: *Fliegende Holländer.* Also RONNE-FELD: *Ameise;* ORFF: *Osterspiel;* HANDEL: *Saul.* Teaches at Bruckner Consv, Linz. **Res:** Lessing 35, Linz, Austria. Mgmt: SLZ/FRG.

MIREA, MARINA. Lyric coloratura soprano. Romanian. Resident mem: Romanian Opera, Bucharest. Born Bucharest. Husband Nicolae Mateescu, occupation physician. Studied: Consv, Prof Ana Talmaceanu, Bucharest. **Debut:** Konstanze (*Entführung aus dem Serail*) Romanian Opera 1969. Awards: Prize Interpodium, Bratislava 1974.

Sang with major companies in ROM: Bucharest. **Roles with these companies incl** DELIBES: Lakmé⋆; DONIZETTI: Norina⋆ (*Don Pasquale*), Lucia⋆; MOZART: Konstanze⋆ (*Entführung aus dem Serail*); ROSSINI: Rosina⋆ (*Barbiere di Siviglia*); VERDI: Gilda⋆ (*Rigoletto*); Violetta⋆ (*Traviata*). Gives recitals. Appears with symphony orchestra. **Res:** 16 Blanari St, Bucharest 4, Romania. Mgmt: RIA/ROM; RAP/FRA.

MISCIANO, ALVINIO. Lyric tenor. Italian. Born 29 Aug 1915, Narni/Terni, Italy. Wife Simone Nussbaum. One daughter. Studied: Accad di S Cecilia, Mo Gino Scolari, Rome; Mario Basiola; School of the Rome Opera. **Debut:** Edgardo (*Lucia*) Teatro dell'Opera, Rome 1945. Previous occupations: officer Ital Army. Awards: stpd, Studio of the Rome Opera.

Sang with major companies in ARG: Buenos Aires; AUSTRL: Sydney; AUS: Vienna Volksoper; BEL: Brussels; BRA: Rio de Janeiro; CZE: Prague National; DEN: Copenhagen; FRA: Bordeaux, Marseille, Nice, Paris, Toulouse; GRE: Athens National; FR GER: Karlsruhe, Stuttgart, Wiesbaden; HOL: Amsterdam; HUN: Budapest; ITA: Bologna, Florence Maggio & Comunale, Genoa, Milan La Scala, Naples, Palermo, Rome Opera, Spoleto Fest, Trieste, Turin, Venice; MON: Monte Carlo; POR: Lisbon; S AFR: Johannesburg; SPA: Barcelona; SWI: Zurich; USA: Chicago, Dallas; YUG: Zagreb. **Roles with these companies incl** BARBER: Anatol (*Vanessa*); BEETHOVEN: Florestan (*Fidelio*); BELLINI: Elvino (*Sonnambula*); BERG: Alwa⋆ (*Lulu*); BORODIN: Vladimir (*Prince Igor*); BRITTEN: Lysander (*Midsummer Night*); CILEA: Maurizio (*A. Lecouvreur*); DALLAPICCOLA: Jailer/Inquisitor⋆ (*Prigioniero*); DONIZETTI: Ernesto (*Don Pasquale*), Nemorino (*Elisir d'amore*), Tonio (*Fille du régiment*), Charles (*Linda di Chamounix*), Edgardo (*Lucia*); GIORDANO: Loris Ipanov (*Fedora*); GOUNOD: Faust, Philémon; MASCAGNI: Fritz (*Amico Fritz*); MASSENET: Des Grieux (*Manon*), Werther; MENOTTI: Lover (*Amelia al ballo*); MOZART: Don Ottavio (*Don Giovanni*); MUSSORGSKY: Gritzko (*Fair at Sorochinsk*); PAISIELLO: Almaviva⋆ (*Barbiere di Siviglia*); PERAGALLO: Mario⋆ (*Gita in campagna*); PROKOFIEV: Mephistopheles⋆ (*Fiery Angel*), Marquis⋆ (*Gambler*); PUCCINI: Rodolfo (*Bohème*), Rinuccio (*Gianni Schicchi*), Pinkerton (*Butterfly*), Ruggero & Prunier (*Rondine*), Cavaradossi (*Tosca*); ROSSINI: Almaviva⋆‡ (*Barbiere di Siviglia*), Edward

Milfort⋆ (*Cambiale di matrimonio*), Don Ramiro (*Cenerentola*), Lindoro (*Italiana in Algeri*), Giocondo (*Pietra del paragone*); SMETANA: Hans (*Bartered Bride*); STRAUSS, J: Eisenstein (*Fledermaus*); STRAVINSKY: Vasili (*Mavra*); THOMAS: Wilhelm Meister (*Mignon*); VERDI: Fenton (*Falstaff*), Duca di Mantova (*Rigoletto*), Alfredo (*Traviata*); WEBER: Abu Hassan⋆; WEILL: Jim Mahoney⋆ (*Aufstieg und Fall der Stadt Mahagonny*); WOLF-FERRARI: Filipeto (*Quattro rusteghi*); ZANDONAI: Paolo (*Francesca da Rimini*), Romeo. Also CASTEL-NUOVO-TEDESCO: Jack/John Worthing⋆ (*Importance of Being Earnest*); ROTA: Fadinard (*Cappello di paglia di Firenze*); MALIPIERO: Tireno⋆ (*Minnie la candida*); ALFANO: Dimitri (*Risurrezione*); FRAZZI: Sancho Panza⋆ (*Don Chisciotte*); MOZART: Sesto (*Clemenza di Tito*), Bastien; PAISIELLO: Caloandro (*Molinara*). **World premieres:** BECAUD: Angelo‡ (*Opéra d'Aran*) Théâtre des Champs Elysées, Paris 1962; ROSSELLINI: Cugino (*Linguaggio dei fiori*) Piccola Scala, Milan 1963; TESTI: Vaska (*Albergo dei poveri*) Piccola Scala 1966; CHAILLY: Grigori (*Vassiliev*) Teatro Comunale, Genoa 1966. Recorded for: Pathé-Marconi, Decca. Video/Film: Cavaradossi (*Tosca*), Lindoro (*Italiana in Algeri*), Fadinard (*Cappello di paglia di Firenze*), Vasili (*Mavra*), Raimondo (*Due timidi*), Bob Cratchit (*Canto di natale*). Teaches voice. **Res:** V Roma 187A, Lido di Camaiore/Lucca, Italy.

MITCHELL, DAVID IRA. Scenic and costume designer for opera, theater, film, television; specl in sets. Is a lighting designer. American. Resident designer at NY Shakespeare Fest, Lincoln Center, Public Theater. Born 12 May 1932, Honesdale, PA, USA. Wife Emily, occupation copy editor, Time Inc. Two children. Studied: School of Fine & Applied Arts, Boston Univ, Horace Armistead. **Operatic debut:** *Butterfly* Juilliard School, New York 1966. Theater debut: NY Shakespeare Fest 1965. Awards: NY Drama Desk Awd 1974.

Designed for major companies in CAN: Toronto; FRA: Paris; FR GER: Berlin Deutsche Oper; USA: Cincinnati, Houston, New York City Opera, Philadelphia Lyric, San Francisco Opera, Washington DC. **Operas designed for these companies incl** BOITO: Mefistofele; MASSENET: *Manon*⋆; MUSSORGSKY: *Boris Godunov*⋆; VERDI: *Aida*⋆, *Macbeth*⋆, *Trovatore*⋆.

MITCHELL, LEONA. Soprano. American. Born 13 Oct 1949. Single. Studied: Oklahoma City Univ, USA; San Francisco Merola Prgr; Santa Fe Apprentice Prgr, NM, USA. **Debut:** Micaëla (*Carmen*) San Francisco Opera 1972.

Sang with major companies in FR GER: Stuttgart; SPA: Barcelona; USA: Houston, New York Met, San Francisco Opera, Washington DC. **Roles with these companies incl** BIZET: Micaëla (*Carmen*); GERSHWIN: Bess⋆; MOZART: Donna Elvira (*Don Giovanni*), Susanna⋆ (*Nozze di Figaro*); PUCCINI: Mimi⋆ & Musetta⋆ (*Bohème*), Lauretta (*Gianni Schicchi*), Liù (*Turandot*); ROSSINI: Mathilde (*Guillaume Tell*); TCHAIKOVSKY: Tatiana (*Eugene Onegin*); VERDI: Nannetta (*Falstaff*). Gives recitals. Appears with symphony orchestra. **Res:** 4524 N

Clybourn Ave, Burbank, CA, USA. Mgmt: CAM/USA; AIM/UK.

MITCHINSON, JOHN. Heldentenor. British. Wife Maureen Guy, occupation opera/concert singer, mezzo-soprano. Two children. Studied: Manchester Coll of Music, UK. **Debut:** Oedipus Rex, Sadler's Wells Opera 1969.
Sang with major companies in ISR: Tel Aviv; UK: Edinburgh Fest, Glasgow Scottish, London Royal Opera & Eng Ntl. **Roles with these companies incl** BEETHOVEN: Florestan* (*Fidelio*); BERLIOZ: Bénédict*, Faust* (*Damnation de Faust*); STRAVINSKY: Oedipus Rex*; WAGNER: Siegmund* (*Walküre*). **World premieres:** TAL: Leading ten (*Masada 967*) Israel Opera, Tel Aviv 1973. Recorded for: Philips, Lelio. Gives recitals. Appears with symphony orchestra. **Res:** Gloucestershire, UK. Mgmt: DBA/USA.

MITTELMANN, NORMAN. Dramatic baritone. Canadian. Resident mem: Staatsoper, Hamburg; Opernhaus, Zurich. Born 25 May 1932, Winnipeg, Man, Canada. Wife Roberta, occupation harpist, pianist. Two children. Studied: Curtis Inst of Music, Martial Singher, Philadelphia; Music Acad of West, Santa Barbara, CA, USA; Enzo Mascherini. **Debut:** Marcello (*Bohème*) Canadian Opera Co, Toronto 1958. **Awards:** Singing Stars Awd, Canada; Met Op Ntl Counc Aud Fisher Awd; Rockefeller Fndt Grant.
Sang with major companies in ARG: Buenos Aires; AUS: Vienna Staatsoper; CAN: Montreal/Quebec, Toronto; FRA: Paris; FR GER: Berlin Deutsche Oper, Düsseldorf-Duisburg, Essen, Frankfurt, Hamburg, Karlsruhe, Munich Staatsoper, Stuttgart; ITA: Florence Maggio & Comunale, Milan La Scala, Palermo; SWI: Zurich; UK: London Royal; USA: Chicago, New York Met, Philadelphia Lyric, San Francisco Opera. **Roles with these companies incl** BERLIOZ: Méphistophélès (*Damnation de Faust*); BIZET: Escamillo* (*Carmen*); BORODIN: Prince Igor; DONIZETTI: Enrico* (*Lucia*); EINEM: George Danton* (*Dantons Tod*); GIORDANO: Carlo Gérard* (*Andrea Chénier*); GOUNOD: Méphistophélès (*Faust*); JANACEK: Shishkov (*From the House of the Dead*); MEYERBEER: Nelusco* (*Africaine*); MUSSORGSKY: Shaklovity* (*Khovanshchina*); PROKOFIEV: Ruprecht* (*Fiery Angel*); PUCCINI: Marcello* (*Bohème*), Jack Rance* (*Fanciulla del West*), Gianni Schicchi*, Scarpia (*Tosca*); RAVEL: Ramiro* (*Heure espagnole*); ROSSINI: Guillaume Tell; SAINT-SAENS: Grand prêtre* (*Samson et Dalila*); STRAUSS, R: Mandryka* (*Arabella*), Jochanaan* (*Salome*); TCHAIKOVSKY: Eugene Onegin*; VERDI: Amonasro* (*Aida*), Ezio (*Attila*), Renato* (*Ballo in maschera*), Rodrigo* (*Don Carlo*), Ford* & Falstaff* (*Falstaff*), Don Carlo* (*Forza del destino*), Macbeth, Nabucco*, Iago* (*Otello*), Rigoletto*, Simon Boccanegra, Germont* (*Traviata*), Conte di Luna* (*Trovatore*); WAGNER: Amfortas* (*Parsifal*), Gunther* (*Götterdämmerung*), Wolfram* (*Tannhäuser*), Kurwenal (*Tristan und Isolde*). **World premieres:** BURKHARD: Daniel (*Ein Stern geht auf aus Jakob*) Staatsoper, Hamburg 1970. Video/Film: Daniel (*Stern geht auf*); Iago (*Otello*); Tonio (*Pa-*

gliacci). Gives recitals. Appears with symphony orchestra. **Res:** Aussichtsstr 17, Herrliberg, Switzerland. Mgmt: CSA/USA; SLA/UK; TAS/AUS; SLZ/FRG.

MIXOVA, IVANA HILDEGARDA. Lyric mezzosoprano. Czechoslovakian. Resident mem: National Theater, Prague. Born 2 Dec 1930, Vienna. Husband Ivo Svitavsky, occupation pensioner. One daughter. Studied: Consv Brno, G Redlichová, Bohumil Sobesky; Konstantin Karenin. **Debut:** Berta (*Barbiere di Siviglia*) State Theater, Olomouc 1950. Previous occupations: medical assistant. **Awards:** Merited Artist, Govnmt of Czechoslovakia.
Sang with major companies in BUL: Sofia; CZE: Brno, Prague National; FIN: Helsinki; FR GER: Frankfurt, Hannover, Mannheim, Nürnberg; GER DR: Berlin Staatsoper; HOL: Amsterdam; HUN: Budapest; ITA: Bologna; ROM: Bucharest; SWI: Zurich. **Roles with these companies incl** BIZET: Carmen*; DVORAK: Kate (*Devil and Kate*), Jezibaba* (*Rusalka*); GLUCK: Orfeo; JANACEK: Kabanikha* (*Katya Kabanova*); MASSENET: Dulcinée (*Don Quichotte*); PROKOFIEV: Clarissa (*Love for Three Oranges*); PUCCINI: Suzuki (*Butterfly*); SMETANA: Hata* (*Bartered Bride*), Roza (*Secret*); STRAUSS, R: Klytämnestra (*Elektra*), Octavian (*Rosenkavalier*), Herodias* (*Salome*); STRAVINSKY: Baba the Turk* (*Rake's Progress*); TCHAIKOVSKY: Olga* (*Eugene Onegin*), Comtesse* (*Pique Dame*); VERDI: Eboli* (*Don Carlo*); WAGNER: Fricka* (*Walküre*). Also SMETANA: Martinka (*The Kiss*), Radmila (*Libuse*); VERDI: Meg Page (*Falstaff*); FOERSTER: Portia (*Merchant of Venice*). **World premieres:** CIKKER: Volumnia (*Coriolanus*) National Theater, Prague 1974; PAUER: Toinetta (*Malade imaginaire*) National Theater, Prague 1970. Gives recitals. Appears with symphony orchestra. **Res:** Spanelská 6, 120 00 Prague 2, CSSR. Mgmt: PRG/CZE.

MODENOS, JOHN PHILIP; né Ioannis Philip Modinos. Dramatic baritone. American. Resident mem: Theater der Hansestadt Bremen; Opernhaus Zurich; National Opera, Athens. Born 16 Jun 1930, Omodhos-Limassol, Cyprus. Wife Mary Psicholis. One son. Studied: Estelle Liebling, Thanos Mellos, Otto Herz, New York; Manhattan School of Music; American Theater Wing, New York. **Debut:** Moralès (*Carmen*) New York City Opera 1956. Previous occupations: choir dir Greek churches; Cantor Greek Orth Church. **Awards:** American Theater Wing Conct Awd 1957; Winner American Opera Aud, Cincinnati, USA 1961; Winner Vercelli Singing Cont, Italy 1961.
Sang with major companies in AUS: Vienna Staatsoper; CZE: Brno, Prague National & Smetana; GRE: Athens National & Fest; FR GER: Berlin Deutsche Oper, Hamburg, Kassel, Kiel, Munich Staatsoper, Stuttgart, Bremen; HOL: Amsterdam; ISR: Tel Aviv; ITA: Genoa; SWI: Basel, Geneva, Zurich; UK: Cardiff Welsh, Glyndebourne Fest, London Royal Opera; USA: Cincinnati, Hartford, New York City Opera, Pittsburgh, San Francisco Opera. **Roles with these companies incl** BEETHOVEN: Don Pizarro (*Fidelio*);

BERG: Dr Schön★ (*Lulu*); BIZET: Escamillo★ (*Carmen*), Zurga★ (*Pêcheurs de perles*); BUSONI: Matteo★ (*Arlecchino*); CILEA: Michonnet★ (*A. Lecouvreur*); GIORDANO: Carlo Gérard★ (*Andrea Chénier*); GLUCK: Agamemnon★ (*Iphigénie en Aulide*), Thoas (*Iphigénie en Tauride*); GOUNOD: Valentin (*Faust*); HINDEMITH: Cardillac; MASCAGNI: Alfio (*Cavalleria rusticana*); MOZART: Conte Almaviva & Figaro (*Nozze di Figaro*), Papageno (*Zauberflöte*); ORFF: Solo★ (*Carmina burana*); PUCCINI: Marcello★ (*Bohème*), Jack Rance (*Fanciulla del West*), Sharpless★ (*Butterfly*), Lescaut★ (*Manon Lescaut*), Michele★ (*Tabarro*), Scarpia★ (*Tosca*); ROSSINI: Figaro★ (*Barbiere di Siviglia*), Taddeo (*Italiana in Algeri*); STRAVINSKY: Nick Shadow★ (*Rake's Progress*); VERDI: Amonasro★ (*Aida*), Renato★ (*Ballo in maschera*), Rodrigo (*Don Carlo*), Don Carlo (*Ernani*), Ford (*Falstaff*), Don Carlo★ (*Forza del destino*), Macbeth★, Nabucco★, Iago★ (*Otello*), Rigoletto★, Simon Boccanegra★, Germont★ (*Traviata*), Conte di Luna★ (*Trovatore*); WAGNER: Klingsor (*Parsifal*), Alberich (*Rheingold*★, *Götterdämmerung*★), Wolfram★ (*Tannhäuser*), Kurwenal★ (*Tristan und Isolde*). **World premieres:** GLANVILLE-HICKS: Odysseus/Thoas (*Nausicaa*) Athens Fest 1961; KALOMIRIS: Harkousis (*Paleologos*) Athens Fest 1961. Recorded for: CBS, Joker, Tono AG. Video—BBC TV: bar role (*Arlecchino*). Gives recitals. Appears with symphony orchestra. Teaches voice. **Res:** Alte Landstr 37, 8803 Ruschlikon-Zurich, Switzerland. Mgmt: SAM/USA; ARM/FRG.

MÖDL, MARTHA. Dramatic soprano & mezzosoprano; started as contralto. German. Resident mem: Bayerische Staatsoper, Munich. Born 22 Mar 1912, Nürnberg. Studied: Nürnberg Consv. **Debut:** Hänsel, Stadttheater Remscheid 1942. Previous occupations: bookkeeper. Awards: Kammersängerin.
Sang with major companies in AUS: Salzburg Fest, Vienna Staatsoper; FRA: Paris; FR GER: Bayreuth Fest, Berlin Deutsche Oper, Bielefeld, Cologne, Düsseldorf-Duisburg, Hamburg, Hannover, Kiel, Munich Staatsoper, Nürnberg, Stuttgart; ITA: Milan La Scala; UK: London Royal; USA: New York Met; et al. **Roles with these companies incl** BEETHOVEN: Leonore‡ (*Fidelio*); JANACEK: Kostelnicka (*Jenufa*); MOZART: Cherubino (*Nozze di Figaro*); STRAUSS, R: Elektra‡; STRAVINSKY: Sop Solo (*Oedipus Rex*); WAGNER: Kundry (*Parsifal*), Sieglinde & Brünnhilde‡ (*Walküre*), Brünnhilde‡ (*Siegfried*), Brünnhilde‡ & Gutrune (*Götterdämmerung*), Isolde; et al. Also STRAUSS, R: Kytämnestra (*Elektra*), Amme (*Frau ohne Schatten*), Herodias (*Salome*); WAGNER: Kundry (*Parsifal*); PUCCINI: Zita (*Gianni Schicchi*); TCHAIKOVSKY: Comtesse (*Pique Dame*); GIORDANO: Madelon (*Andrea Chénier*); WAGNER: Waltraute (*Götterdämmerung*); SZOKOLAY: (*Bluthochzeit*). Recorded for: Seraphim-Capitol, Richmond-London, HMV, Cetra, Decca, Telefunken, Philips, Columbia, DG. **Res:** Perlacherstr 19, 8022 Grünwald, FR Ger.

MOFFATT, JOYCE A. American. Mng, Symphony Society of San Antonio/San Antonio Opera, 109 Lexington Ave, San Antonio, TX, USA. In charge of adm & tech matters & finances, and is also a lighting designer. Born 3 Jan 1936, Grand Rapids, MI, USA. Single. Studied: Univ of Michigan, Ann Arbor. Previous positions primarily theatrical: Dir ticket sales, City Center of Music & Drama, New York 1967-72; Asst House Mng, New York State Theater, New York 1969-72; Subscription Mng, Phoenix Theater, New York 1963-66; Stage Mng & Lighting Designer, Off Broadway theaters and summer stock 1955-63. Consultant, New York State Council on the Arts, J F Kennedy Center for the Performing Arts, Theater Inc, Phoenix Theater. Started with present company 1972 as Prod Mng, in present position since 1975. **Res:** San Antonio, TX, USA.

MOFFO, ANNA. Lyric coloratura soprano. Italian. Resident mem: Metropolitan Opera, New York. Born 27 Jun 1935, Wayne, PA, USA. Husband Robert Sarnoff, occupation form Chmn of Board, RCA Records. Studied: Mme Eufemia Giannini-Gregory, Philadelphia; Fulbright Schlshp to Italy. **Debut:** Cio-Cio-San (*Butterfly*) Italian TV production. Awards: Commendatore of the Order of Merit, Republic of Italy; Italy's "Silver Griffo" Awd for film; Grand Prix du Disque; Orfée d'or; *Stereo Review*'s "Record of the Year."
Sang with major companies in AUS: Salzburg Fest, Vienna Staatsoper; FRA: Nice; FR GER: Frankfurt, Hamburg, Munich Staatsoper, Wiesbaden; GER DR: Berlin Komische Oper & Staatsoper; HUN: Budapest; ITA: Florence Maggio & Comunale, Milan La Scala, Naples, Rome Opera, Venice; SWE: Stockholm; UK: London Royal; USA: Chicago, Hartford, Miami, Milwaukee Florentine, New York Met, Philadelphia Grand & Lyric, Pittsburgh, Portland, San Antonio, San Francisco Opera, Seattle. **Roles with these companies incl** DONIZETTI: Norina★ (*Don Pasquale*), Adina★ (*Elisir*), Marie★ (*Fille du régiment*), Lucia★‡; GOUNOD: Marguerite (*Faust*), Juliette; LEONCAVALLO: Nedda★ (*Pagliacci*); MASSENET: Manon; MOZART: Pamina (*Zauberflöte*); OFFENBACH: Olympia & Antonia & Giulietta (*Contes d'Hoffmann*), Périchole; PUCCINI: Mimi★‡ (*Bohème*), Cio-Cio-San★‡ (*Butterfly*), Magda★‡ (*Rondine*), Liù (*Turandot*); ROSSINI: Rosina (*Barbiere di Siviglia*); STRAUSS, J: Rosalinde★ (*Fledermaus*); THOMAS: Philine (*Mignon*); VERDI: Nannetta★‡ (*Falstaff*), Luisa Miller‡, Gilda★‡ (*Rigoletto*), Violetta★‡ (*Traviata*). On records only: BIZET: Micaëla (*Carmen*); GLUCK: Euridice; HALEVY: Eudoxie (*Juive*); HUMPERDINCK: Hänsel; MASSENET: Thaïs; MOZART: Zerlina (*Don Giovanni*), Susanna (*Nozze di Figaro*); PERGOLESI: Serpina (*Serva padrona*); PUCCINI: Musetta (*Bohème*). Recorded for: RCA, Vox, Angel, Ariola-Eurodisc. Video/Film—Italfilm: Violetta (*Traviata*); Lucia; non-operatic films. TV: Cio-Cio-San (*Butterfly*); "The Anna Moffo Show." Gives recitals. Appears with symphony orchestra. Mgmt: VIN/USA; CAM/USA.

MOISEIWITSCH, TANYA. Scenic and costume designer for opera & theater. British. Resident designer, Royal Opera, London. Born 3 Dec 1914, London. Widowed. Studied: Central School of Arts and Crafts, London. Theater debut: Westminster Theatre, London 1934.

Designed opera for major companies in UK: London Royal & English National; USA: New York Met; et al. **Operas designed for these companies incl** BRITTEN: *Peter Grimes;* GAY/Britten: *Beggar's Opera;* MOZART: *Don Giovanni;* ROSSINI: *Barbiere di Siviglia;* et al.

MOLDOVAN, STEFANIA. Dramatic soprano. Hungarian. Resident mem: State Opera House, Budapest. Born 24 Aug 1931, Sajoudvarhely, Romania. Husband Miklos Révész, occupation film dir. One child. Studied: Acad of Music, Budapest. **Debut:** Mimi *(Bohème)* National Theater, Szeged, Hungary 1954. Awards: Liszt Prize 1960; Artist of Merit, Erdemes Müvész 1974.

Sang with major companies in BUL: Sofia; CZE: Brno, Prague National; GER DR: Berlin Komische Oper & Staatsoper; HUN: Budapest; ITA: Bologna; POL: Warsaw; ROM: Bucharest; UK: Edinburgh Fest; USSR: Leningrad Kirov, Moscow Bolshoi. **Roles with these companies incl** BEETHOVEN: Leonore *(Fidelio)*; ERKEL: Melinda *(Bánk Bán)*; KODALY: Örzse *(Háry János)*; MASCAGNI: Santuzza *(Cavalleria rusticana)*; MOZART: Donna Elvira *(Don Giovanni)*; OFFENBACH: Giulietta *(Contes d'Hoffmann)*; PUCCINI: Mimi & Musetta *(Bohème)*, Minnie *(Fanciulla del West)*, Manon Lescaut, Giorgetta *(Tabarro)*, Tosca; STRAUSS, J: Rosalinde *(Fledermaus)*; STRAUSS, R: Ariadne *(Ariadne auf Naxos)*; TCHAIKOVSKY: Tatiana *(Eugene Onegin)*; VERDI: Aida, Amelia *(Ballo in maschera)*, Elisabetta *(Don Carlo)*, Leonora *(Forza del destino)*, Desdemona *(Otello)*, Leonora *(Trovatore)*; WAGNER: Senta *(Fliegende Holländer)*; WEBER: Agathe *(Freischütz)*; WOLF-FERRARI: Lucieta *(Quattro rusteghi)*. Also KODALY: Girl *(Spinning Room)*. **World premieres:** SZOKOLAY: Wife *(Blood Wedding)* State Opera, Budapest 1964. Recorded for: Hungaroton. Videotape: Wife *(Blood Wedding)*. Gives recitals. Appears with symphony orchestra.

MOLDOVEANU, EUGENIA. Lirico spinto. Romanian. Resident mem: Romanian Opera, Bucharest. Born 19 Mar 1944, Busteni, Romania. Husband Constantin Iacob, occupation engineer. Studied: Ciprian Porumbescu Consv, Mme Arta Florescu, Bucharest. **Debut:** Donna Anna *(Don Giovanni)* Bucharest 1968. Awards: First Prize World Youth Fest Sofia 1968, Enescu Fest Bucharest 1970 & Intl Singing Cont Toulouse 1970; Grand Prix, Madama Butterfly Cont, Nagasaki 1973.

Sang with major companies in BUL: Sofia; CZE: Prague Smetana; FRA: Toulouse; GRE: Athens National; FR GER: Stuttgart, Wiesbaden; GER DR: Berlin Staatsoper, Dresden; HOL: Amsterdam; ITA: Trieste; ROM: Bucharest; YUG: Belgrade. **Roles with these companies incl** BIZET: Micaëla★ *(Carmen)*; MASSENET: Manon; MOZART: Fiordiligi★ *(Così fan tutte)*, Donna Anna★ & Donna Elvira *(Don Giovanni)*, Contessa *(Nozze di Figaro)*, Pamina *(Zauberflöte)*; OFFENBACH: Antonia★ & Giulietta★ *(Contes d'Hoffmann)*; PUCCINI: Mimi★ & Musetta★ *(Bohème)*, Cio-Cio-San★ *(Butterfly)*, Manon Lescaut, Tosca, Liù★ *(Turandot)*; STRAUSS, J: Rosalinde★ *(Fledermaus)*; VERDI: Elisabetta *(Don Carlo)*, Donna Elvira★ *(Ernani)*, Leonora *(Forza del destino)*, Desdemona★ *(Otello)*, Violetta★ *(Traviata)*,

Leonora★ *(Trovatore)*, Elena *(Vespri)*. Gives recitals. Appears with symphony orchestra. Teaches voice. **Res:** 13 Decembrie St 31, Bucharest 5, Romania. Mgmt: RIA/ROM.

MOLDOVEANU, VASILE. Lirico spinto tenor. Romanian. Resident mem: Württembergische Staatsoper, Stuttgart. Born 6 Oct 1935, Konstanza, Romania. Wife Maria, occupation ballerina. Studied: Consv Ciprian Porumbescu, Bucharest; Constantin Badescu, Fr Costescu, Bucharest. **Debut:** Alfredo *(Traviata)* Bucharest Opera 1966. Previous occupations: studied medicine.

Sang with major companies in BEL: Liège; FIN: Helsinki; GRE: Athens Fest; FR GER: Frankfurt, Stuttgart; GER DR: Dresden; HOL: Amsterdam; ROM: Bucharest; SPA: Barcelona; SWI: Geneva. **Roles with these companies incl** BORODIN: Vladimir *(Prince Igor)*; DALLAPICCOLA: Radio Telegrapher *(Volo di notte)*; DONIZETTI: Ernesto *(Don Pasquale)*, Edgardo★ *(Lucia)*; FALLA: Paco *(Vida breve)*; HANDEL: Sextus *(Giulio Cesare)*; MOZART: Don Ottavio *(Don Giovanni)*, Pedrillo *(Entführung aus dem Serail)*, Tamino *(Zauberflöte)*; PUCCINI: Rodolfo★ *(Bohème)*, Rinuccio *(Gianni Schicchi)*, Cavaradossi *(Tosca)*; STRAUSS, J: Alfred *(Fledermaus)*; VERDI: Don Carlo, Don Alvaro★ *(Forza del destino)*, Duca di Mantova★ *(Rigoletto)*, Alfredo★ *(Traviata)*, Manrico★ *(Trovatore)*, Arrigo★ *(Vespri)*. Also BENTOIU★: Médecin *(Amour médecin)*; NEGREA: *(Marin Pescarul)*; DUMITRESCU: Ardalus *(Decebal)*. Video—Româna TV: *(Marin Pescarul)*. **Res:** Wintersteinstr 5, 8 Munich 45, FR Ger, or Einkornstr 30, 7 Stuttgart 1, FR Ger. Mgmt: SLZ/FRG.

MOLESE, MICHELE. Dramatic tenor. American. Born 29 Aug 1936, New York. Wife Zoe Papadaki, occupation mezzo-soprano. Studied: Consv, Milan; Mo Emilio Piccoli, Francesco Merli, Milan. **Debut:** Fritz *(Amico Fritz)* Piccola Scala, Milan 1956.

Sang with major companies in AUS: Vienna Staatsoper; BEL: Brussels; BUL: Sofia; CAN: Montreal/Quebec, Vancouver; CZE: Prague National; FRA: Bordeaux, Marseille, Nancy, Nice, Paris, Rouen, Strasbourg; GRE: Athens National Opera & Festival; FR GER: Berlin Deutsche Oper; HOL: Amsterdam; HUN: Budapest; ISR: Tel Aviv; ITA: Bologna, Genoa, Milan La Scala, Naples, Palermo, Spoleto Fest, Trieste, Turin; MEX: Mexico City; MON: Monte Carlo; POR: Lisbon; S AFR: Johannesburg; SPA: Barcelona; USA: Chicago, Hawaii, Houston, Miami, Milwaukee Florentine, New Orleans, New York City Opera, Philadelphia Grand & Lyric, Washington DC; YUG: Dubrovnik, Zagreb, Belgrade. **Roles with these companies incl** BELLINI: Tebaldo *(Capuleti ed i Montecchi)*, Pollione★ *(Norma)*; BERLIOZ: Faust *(Damnation de Faust)*; BIZET: Don José★‡ *(Carmen)*, Nadir *(Pêcheurs de perles)*; BOITO: Faust★ *(Mefistofele)*; CILEA: Maurizio *(A. Lecouvreur)*; DELIBES: Gérald *(Lakmé)*; DONIZETTI: Ernesto *(Don Pasquale)*, Nemorino *(Elisir)*, Edgardo★ *(Lucia)*, Beppo *(Rita)*; GIORDANO: Andrea Chénier★, Loris Ipanov★ *(Fedora)*; GLUCK: Admetos★‡ *(Alceste)*, Achille★ *(Iphigénie en Aulide)*; GOUNOD: Faust★, Roméo★; LEONCAVALLO: Canio★ *(Pa-*

gliacci); MASCAGNI: Fritz★ (*Amico Fritz*), Turiddu★‡ (*Cavalleria rusticana*); MASSENET: Des Grieux★ (*Manon*), Werther★; MEYERBEER: Raoul de Nangis★ (*Huguenots*); MOZART: Tamino (*Zauberflöte*); OFFENBACH: Hoffmann★‡; PONCHIELLI: Enzo★ (*Gioconda*); PROKOFIEV: Prince★ (*Love for Three Oranges*); PUCCINI: Rodolfo★ (*Bohème*), Dick Johnson★ (*Fanciulla del West*), Pinkerton★‡ (*Butterfly*), Des Grieux★ (*Manon Lescaut*), Ruggero (*Rondine*), Luigi★ (*Tabarro*), Cavaradossi★‡ (*Tosca*), Calaf★ (*Turandot*); ROSSINI: Almaviva (*Barbiere di Siviglia*), Arnold★ (*Guillaume Tell*), Florville (*Signor Bruschino*); SAINT-SAENS: Samson; STRAUSS, R: Ein Sänger★ (*Rosenkavalier*); STRAVINSKY: Eumolpe‡ (*Perséphone*); TCHAIKOVSKY: Lenski (*Eugene Onegin*); VERDI: Radames★ (*Aida*), Riccardo★ (*Ballo in maschera*), Ernani, Don Alvaro★ (*Forza del destino*), Duca di Mantova‡ (*Rigoletto*), Alfredo (*Traviata*), Manrico★‡ (*Trovatore*), Arrigo (*Vespri*); ZANDONAI: Paolo (*Francesca da Rimini*). **World premieres:** MENOTTI: Kodanda (*Dernier sauvage*) Paris Opéra Comique 1963. Recorded for: Columbia, Decca, Concert Hall. Video— CBC TV: Hoffmann; Faust; Cavaradossi (*Tosca*); Turiddu (*Cavalleria rusticana*). **Res:** V Sismondi 36, Milan, Italy. Mgmt: ACA/USA.

MOLINARI-PRADELLI, FRANCESCO. Conductor of opera and symphony. Italian. Born 4 Jul 1911, Bologna. Married. Studied: Bologna; Accad di S Cecilia, Bernardino Molinari, Rome. **Operatic debut:** La Scala, Milan 1946. Symphonic debut: 1938.

Conducted with major companies in ARG: Buenos Aires; AUS: Vienna Staatsoper; ITA: Bologna, Florence Maggio & Comunale, Genoa, Milan La Scala, Naples, Palermo, Parma, Rome Opera, Trieste, Turin, Venice, Verona Arena; UK: London Royal; USA: New York Met, San Francisco Opera; et al. **Operas with these companies incl** BELLINI: *Norma, Puritani;* BIZET: *Carmen;* CILEA: *A. Lecouvreur;* DONIZETTI: *Don Pasquale, Elisir‡, Favorite, Fille du régiment, Lucia, Lucrezia Borgia, Maria Stuarda;* FLOTOW: *Martha‡;* GIORDANO: *Andrea Chénier;* GOUNOD: *Faust, Roméo et Juliette;* LEONCAVALLO: *Pagliacci;* MASCAGNI: *Cavalleria rusticana;* MASSENET: *Manon, Werther‡;* PONCHIELLI: *Gioconda;* PUCCINI: *Bohème, Fanciulla del West, Butterfly, Manon Lescaut‡, Rondine‡, Tosca, Turandot‡;* ROSSINI: *Barbiere di Siviglia, Cenerentola, Moïse, Turco in Italia;* VERDI: *Aida, Ballo in maschera, Corsaro, Don Carlo, Ernani, Falstaff, Forza del destino‡, Luisa Miller, Macbeth, Nabucco, Otello, Rigoletto‡, Simon Boccanegra‡, Traviata, Trovatore, Vespri;* WAGNER: *Fliegende Holländer, Lohengrin, Meistersinger, Tannhäuser;* WOLF-FERRARI: *Quattro rusteghi;* et al. Recorded for Philips, Cetra, Angel, Decca, RCA.

MOLL, KURT KONRAD. Bass. German. Resident mem: Staatsoper Hamburg; Bayerische Staatsoper, Munich. Born 11 Apr 1938, Buir, Germany. Wife Ursula, occupation teacher. One child. Studied: Emmy Müller, Krefeld; Musikhochschule, Cologne. **Debut:** Lodovico (*Otello*) Aachen Opera, FR Ger 1961.

Sang with major companies in AUS: Salzburg Fest, Vienna Staatsoper; BEL: Brussels; FRA: Lyon, Paris, Rouen, Toulouse; FR GER: Bayreuth Fest, Bielefeld, Cologne, Dortmund, Essen, Frankfurt, Hamburg, Krefeld, Munich Gärtnerplatz, Nürnberg, Saarbrücken, Stuttgart, Wuppertal; GER DR: Berlin Staatsoper; HUN: Budapest; ITA: Milan La Scala; SWE: Stockholm; SWI: Geneva, Zurich; USSR: Moscow Bolshoi; USA: Chicago, Miami, San Francisco Opera. **Roles with these companies incl** BEETHOVEN: Rocco★ (*Fidelio*); CIKKER: Courvoisier (*Play of Love*); CORNELIUS: Abul Hassan (*Barbier von Bagdad*); EINEM: St Just (*Dantons Tod*); FLOTOW: Plunkett (*Martha*); GOUNOD: Méphistophélès‡ (*Faust*); LORTZING: Stadinger (*Waffenschmied*), Baculus (*Wildschütz*), Van Bett (*Zar und Zimmermann*); MASSENET: Don Quichotte, Des Grieux (*Portrait de Manon*); MOZART: Don Alfonso★ (*Così fan tutte*), Osmin★‡ (*Entführung aus dem Serail*), Allazim (*Zaïde*), Sarastro★‡ (*Zauberflöte*); MUSSORGSKY: Boris Godunov★ & Pimen★ (*Boris Godunov*); NICOLAI: Falstaff★ (*Lustigen Weiber*); PENDERECKI: Barré (*Teufel von Loudun*); PERGOLESI: Uberto (*Serva padrona*); PUCCINI: Colline★ (*Bohème*); ROSSINI: Don Basilio★ (*Barbiere di Siviglia*); SMETANA: Kezal★ (*Bartered Bride*); STRAUSS, R: Sir Morosus★ (*Schweigsame Frau*); VERDI: Ramfis★ (*Aida*), Grande Inquisitore (*Don Carlo*), Padre Guardiano★ (*Forza del destino*); WAGNER: Daland★ (*Fliegende Holländer*), König Heinrich★ (*Lohengrin*), Pogner★ (*Meistersinger*), Gurnemanz★ (*Parsifal*), Fasolt★ (*Rheingold*), Fafner (*Rheingold★, Siegfried★*), Hunding★ (*Walküre*), König Marke★ (*Tristan und Isolde*); WEBER: Kaspar★ (*Freischütz*); ZIMMERMANN: Wesener★ (*Soldaten*). **World premieres:** BIALAS: König (*Gestiefelte Kater*) Staatsoper Hamburg 1975; KAGEL: Bass Partie (*Staatstheater*) Staatsoper Hamburg 1971. Recorded for: EMI, DG. Video/Film: Morosus (*Schweigsame Frau*). Gives recitals. Appears with symphony orchestra. Teaches voice. Coaches repertoire. **Res:** Billwerder Billdeich 500, Hamburg, FR Ger. Mgmt: SLZ/FRG; MAA/USA.

MÖLLERSTRÖM, BRITTA. Lyric coloratura soprano. Swedish. Resident mem: Malmö Stadsteater, Sweden; Stockholm Opera House. Born 30 Apr 1942, Landskrona, Sweden. Husband Jan-Olov Hjelm, occupation musician. One child. Studied: Brigitta Gylling, Sweden. **Debut:** Susanna (*Nozze di Figaro*) Malmö Stadsteater 1966.

Sang with major companies in SWE: Stockholm; UK: Glyndebourne Fest. **Roles with these companies incl** BIZET: Micaëla★ (*Carmen*); BRITTEN: Governess★ (*Turn of the Screw*); GOUNOD: Marguerite★ (*Faust*); MOZART: Despina★ (*Così fan tutte*), Konstanze★ (*Entführung aus dem Serail*), Susanna★ (*Nozze di Figaro*), Königin der Nacht★ (*Zauberflöte*); PUCCINI: Cio-Cio-San★ (*Butterfly*); ROSSINI: Rosina★ (*Barbiere di Siviglia*); STRAUSS, J: Adele★ (*Fledermaus*); STRAUSS, R: Zerbinetta★ (*Ariadne auf Naxos*); VERDI: Oscar★ (*Ballo in maschera*), Gilda★ (*Rigoletto*), Violetta★ (*Traviata*). Also TELEMANN: Vespetta★ (*Pimpinone*). Gives recitals. Appears with symphony orchestra. **Res:** Östra Hyllieväg 6, 21621 Malmö, Sweden. Mgmt: SVE/SWE.

MOLNAR, EVAMARIA. Spinto. Hungarian. Resident mem: Nationaltheater, Mannheim, FR Ger. Born 10 Oct 1929, Hejöcsaba, Hungary. Divorced. One child. Studied: Acad of Music, Budapest, Prof Alice Molnar; Kmsg Prof Domgraf-Fassbaender, Nürnberg. **Debut:** Pamina (*Zauberflöte*) State Opera House, Budapest 1957. Previous occupations: Prof of singing, State Theater Budapest. Awards: Second Prize, Intl Prague Spring Fest; Third Prize, Opera Fest, Vercelli. **Sang with major companies in** AUS: Graz, Vienna Volksoper; FRA: Paris, Strasbourg; FR GER: Düsseldorf-Duisburg, Frankfurt, Hamburg, Hannover, Karlsruhe, Kiel, Mannheim, Munich Staatsoper, Nürnberg, Stuttgart; HUN: Budapest; SPA: Barcelona; USA: Santa Fe, Seattle. **Roles with these companies incl** BEETHOVEN: Marzelline (*Fidelio*); BIZET: Micaëla★(*Carmen*); GIORDANO: Maddalena (*Andrea Chénier*); GLUCK: Euridice; HANDEL: Galatea, Cleopatra (*Giulio Cesare*); JANACEK: Jenufa★; LORTZING: Baronin Freimann (*Wildschütz*); MASCAGNI: Santuzza (*Cavalleria rusticana*); MILHAUD: Phèdre (*Abandon d'Ariane, Délivrance de Thésée*); MOZART: Fiordiligi★ (*Così fan tutte*), Donna Anna★ (*Don Giovanni*), Konstanze★ (*Entführung aus dem Serail*), Contessa★ (*Nozze di Figaro*), Pamina★ (*Zauberflöte*); NICOLAI: Frau Fluth (*Lustigen Weiber*); OFFENBACH: Antonia★ (*Contes d'Hoffmann*); PROKOFIEV: Fata Morgana (*Love for Three Oranges*); PUCCINI: Mimi★ (*Bohème*), Cio-Cio-San★ (*Butterfly*), Giorgetta★ (*Tabarro*), Tosca★, Liù★ (*Turandot*); SMETANA: Marie (*Bartered Bride*); STRAUSS, J: Rosalinde★ (*Fledermaus*); STRAUSS, R: Ariadne (*Ariadne auf Naxos*), Gräfin (*Capriccio*), Daphne, Kaiserin★ (*Frau ohne Schatten*), Salome★; STRAVINSKY: Anne Trulove (*Rake's Progress*); SUCHON: Katrena (*Whirlpool*); TCHAIKOVSKY: Tatiana (*Eugene Onegin*); VERDI: Aida★, Elisabetta (*Don Carlo*), Alice Ford★ (*Falstaff*), Leonora★ (*Forza del destino*), Amelia (*Masnadieri*), Abigaille★ (*Nabucco*), Desdemona★ (*Otello*), Amelia★ (*Simon Boccanegra*), Violetta★ (*Traviata*), Leonora★ (*Trovatore*); WAGNER: Senta★ (*Fliegende Holländer*), Elsa (*Lohengrin*), Eva★ (*Meistersinger*), Gutrune★ (*Götterdämmerung*); WEBER: Agathe (*Freischütz*); WEINBERGER: Dorota (*Schwanda*). Also TRAETTA: Antigone. **World premieres:** HINDEMITH: Lucia (*Long Christmas Dinner*) Mannheim 1961. Appears with symphony orchestra. Teaches voice. Coaches repertoire. **Res:** Breslauer Str 21, 6834 Ketsch, FR Ger.

MOLNAR-TALAJIC, LILIANA. Dramatic soprano. Yugoslavian. Resident mem: Staatsoper, Vienna. Born Sarajevo, Yugoslavia. **Debut:** Contessa (*Nozze di Figaro*) Sarajevo. Previous occupations: chemist. **Sang with major companies in** AUS: Vienna Staatsoper; FR GER: Hamburg, Stuttgart; ITA: Naples, Parma, Turin, Verona Arena; UK: London Royal; USA: Philadelphia Lyric, San Francisco Opera; YUG: Zagreb; et al. **Roles with these companies incl** VERDI: Aida, Amelia (*Ballo in maschera*), Elisabetta (*Don Carlo*), Leonora

(*Forza del destino*), Desdemona (*Otello*), Leonora (*Trovatore*); et al.

MONACHESI, WALTER. Lyric baritone. Italian. Born 19 Jun 1922, Macerata. Wife Grazia Calaresu. Two children. Studied: Mo Gino Berardi, Tullio Serafin. **Debut:** Rabbi David (*Amico Fritz*) Teatro dell'Opera, Rome 1946. Previous occupations: studied medicine. Awards: First Prize, OND Compt and Spoleto Compt; Schlshp Studio of Rome Opera; Cavalierato della Repubblica Italiana. **Sang with major companies in** AUS: Graz, Vienna Staatsoper; BEL: Brussels; BRA: Rio de Janeiro; DEN: Copenhagen; FRA: Lyon, Paris; FR GER: Dortmund, Düsseldorf-Duisburg, Essen, Hamburg, Hannover, Mannheim, Wiesbaden, Wuppertal; HOL: Amsterdam; ISR: Tel Aviv; ITA: Bologna, Florence Maggio & Comunale, Genoa, Milan La Scala, Naples, Palermo, Parma, Rome Opera & Caracalla, Spoleto Fest, Trieste, Turin, Venice; NOR: Oslo; POR: Lisbon; ROM: Bucharest; SPA: Barcelona; SWI: Basel, Geneva, Zurich; UK: Edinburgh Fest, Glyndebourne Fest; USA: Washington DC; YUG: Dubrovnik, Zagreb. **Roles with these companies incl** BELLINI: Ernesto (*Pirata*); BIZET: Zurga (*Pêcheurs de perles*); CILEA: Michonnet (*A. Lecouvreur*); CIMAROSA: Count Robinson (*Matrimonio segreto*); DONIZETTI: Enrico (*Campanello*), Dott Malatesta★ (*Don Pasquale*), Belcore (*Elisir*), Alfonse (*Favorite*), Enrico (*Lucia*); GALUPPI: Don Tritemio (*Filosofo di campagna*); GIORDANO: Carlo Gérard (*Andrea Chénier*), De Siriex (*Fedora*); LEONCAVALLO: Tonio★ (*Pagliacci*); MASCAGNI: Alfio (*Cavalleria rusticana*); MASSENET: Sancho (*Don Quichotte*), Lescaut (*Manon*), Des Grieux (*Portrait de Manon*); MOZART: Guglielmo (*Così fan tutte*), Figaro★ (*Nozze di Figaro*); ORFF: Solo (*Carmina burana*); PERGOLESI: Marcaniello (*Frate 'nnamorato*); PUCCINI: Marcello (*Bohème*), Gianni Schicchi★, Sharpless★ (*Butterfly*), Lescaut (*Manon Lescaut*), Scarpia (*Tosca*); ROSSINI: Figaro★ (*Barbiere di Siviglia*), Dandini (*Cenerentola*); STRAVINSKY: Creon (*Oedipus Rex*); VERDI: Amonasro★ (*Aida*), Renato (*Ballo in maschera*), Rodrigo★ (*Don Carlo*), Ford (*Falstaff*), Don Carlo & Fra Melitone (*Forza del destino*), Macbeth, Rigoletto★, Simon Boccanegra, Germont (*Traviata*), Conte di Luna★ (*Trovatore*). Also SPONTINI: Milton; CIMAROSA: Sempronio (*Mercato di Malmantile*), Conte Fanfaluchi (*Marito disperato*). Recorded for: His Master's Voice, Fabbri, Allegro Royale. **Res:** V Comano 95, Rome, Italy.

MONK, ALLAN JAMES. Bass-baritone. Canadian. Born 19 Aug 1942, Mission City, BC, Canada. Wife Marlene. Two children. Studied: Elgar Higgin, Calgary, Alta, Canada; Boris Goldovsky, USA. **Debut:** Bob (*Old Maid and the Thief*) Western Opera Theater, San Francisco 1967. Previous occupations: dpt store clerk. **Sang with major companies in** CAN: Ottawa, Toronto; USA: Hawaii, Portland, San Francisco Opera & Spring Opera. **Roles with these companies incl** BIZET: Escamillo★ (*Carmen*), Zurga★ (*Pêcheurs de perles*); DONIZETTI: Belcore (*Elisir*), Enrico★ (*Lucia*); MASSENET: Lescaut★ (*Ma-*

non); MENOTTI: John Sorel (*Consul*), Bob (*Old Maid and the Thief*); MOZART: Publio★ (*Clemenza di Tito*), Guglielmo★ (*Così fan tutte*), Don Giovanni★, Conte Almaviva★ & Figaro (*Nozze di Figaro*); STRAUSS, R: Musiklehrer (*Ariadne auf Naxos*). Also EINEM: Musiklehrer (*Besuch der alten Dame*). **World premieres**: WILSON: Abelard (*Heloise and Abelard*) Canadian Opera Co, Toronto 1973. Gives recitals. Appears with symphony orchestra. **Res**: 80 Bralorne Cresc, Calgary, Alta, Canada. Mgmt: SMT/USA.

MONTAL, ANDRÉ. Lyric tenor. American. Born 18 Nov 1940, Baltimore, MD. Single. Studied: Univ of Rochester, Eastman School, NY; Music Acad of the West, Santa Barbara, CA; Curtis Inst of Music, Philadelphia; Catholic Univ of America, Washington DC; Martial Singher, Herbert Graf, Luigi Ricci, Otto Guth, Vladimir Sokoloff, Richard Bonynge. **Debut**: Tebaldo (*Capuleti ed i Montecchi*) American Opera Socy, New York 1964. Awards: Phila Orch Young Artists Awd 1962; Artist Advisory Counc Awd, Chicago 1961; Rockefeller Fndt Grants; Inst of Intl Education stpd.

Sang with major companies in AUSTRL: Sydney; CAN: Vancouver; USA: Boston, Chicago, Kentucky, New York Met, Philadelphia Lyric, San Francisco Opera & Spring Opera. **Roles with these companies incl** BELLINI: Tebaldo (*Capuleti ed i Montecchi*), Elvino (*Sonnambula*); DONIZETTI: Ernesto (*Don Pasquale*), Nemorino (*Elisir*), Tonio (*Fille du régiment*), Edgardo (*Lucia*), Beppo (*Rita*); GOUNOD: Roméo; HANDEL: Oronte (*Alcina*); MONTEVERDI: Nero (*Incoronazione di Poppea*); MOZART: Ferrando (*Così fan tutte*), Don Ottavio (*Don Giovanni*), Belmonte (*Entführung aus dem Serail*); NICOLAI: Fenton (*Lustigen Weiber*); ORFF: Solo (*Carmina burana*); PROKOFIEV: Mephistopheles (*Fiery Angel*); PUCCINI: Pinkerton (*Butterfly*); ROSSINI: Almaviva (*Barbiere di Siviglia*), Lindoro (*Italiana in Algeri*), Idreno (*Semiramide*); STRAUSS, R: Ein Sänger (*Rosenkavalier*); STRAVINSKY: Oedipus; VERDI: Duca di Mantova (*Rigoletto*), Alfredo (*Traviata*). Gives recitals. Appears with symphony orchestra. Teaches voice. Coaches repertoire. **Res**: Washington DC, USA. Mgmt: TOR/USA.

MONTANÉ, CARLOS; né Carlos Eligio-Gabriel Hevia-Montané. Lyric tenor. American. Born 1 Dec 1941, Havana, Cuba. Wife Marcia Liebman-Montané, occupation opera singer. Four children. Studied: New England Consv, Frederick Jagel, Boston; Gibner King, New York/Portland, OR; Jerome Lo Monaco, New York. **Debut**: Alfredo (*Traviata*) New York City Opera 1970. Awards: Met Op Reg Aud, New England 1963; Sullivan Fndt Grant; Diploma of Honor Lincoln-Marti 1971, Dept of HEW, Washington, DC; M B Rockefeller Fund Grant; Artist Advisory Counc, Chicago.

Sang with major companies in FR GER: Berlin Deutsche Oper, Dortmund, Düsseldorf-Duisburg, Frankfurt, Stuttgart; ITA: Turin; USA: Houston, Milwaukee Florentine, New York Met & City Opera, Philadelphia Lyric, Pittsburgh, Seattle. **Roles with these companies incl** BIZET: Don José★ (*Carmen*); DONIZETTI: Edgardo★ (*Lucia*); PUCCINI: Rodolfo★ (*Bohème*), Des Grieux★ (*Manon Lescaut*), Cavaradossi★ (*Tosca*);

STRAUSS, R: Ein Sänger★ (*Rosenkavalier*); VERDI: Riccardo★ (*Ballo in maschera*), Duca di Mantova★ (*Rigoletto*), Alfredo★ (*Traviata*). Appears with symphony orchestra. **Res**: FR Ger. Mgmt: LLF/USA; OEA/UK.

MONTARSOLO, PAOLO. Basso-buffo. Italian. Resident mem: La Sala, Milan. Born 16 Mar 1925, Portici/Naples, Italy. Wife Maria Cecchini, occupation Dir, Special School for Singers at La Scala. One child. Studied: E Conti, B Vingiani, Naples; Schulz, Munich. **Debut**: Lunardo (*Quattro rusteghi*) Teatro Comunale, Bologna 1956. Previous occupations: bookkeeper; studied economy & commerce. Awards: Hon distinct Grande Ufficiale della Repubblica Italiana 1968; Hon distinct from the Emperor of Japan 1961; Gold Prize Viotti 1973 & Santa Margherita 1975; Prize San Remo 1975.

Sang with major companies in AUS: Salzburg Fest, Vienna Volksoper; BRA: Rio de Janeiro; FRA: Bordeaux, Marseille, Nice, Paris, Strasbourg; FR GER: Düsseldorf-Duisburg, Hamburg, Wiesbaden; HOL: Amsterdam; ISR: Tel Aviv; ITA: Bologna, Florence Maggio & Comunale, Genoa, Milan La Scala, Naples, Palermo, Parma, Rome Teatro dell'Opera, Spoleto Fest, Trieste, Turin, Venice Teatro la Fenice, Verona Arena; MON: Monte Carlo; NOR: Oslo; POR: Lisbon; SPA: Barcelona; SWE: Drottningholm Fest; SWI: Geneva; UK: Edinburgh Fest, Glyndebourne Fest; USSR: Moscow Bolshoi; USA: Chicago, Dallas, Houston, New York Met, San Francisco Opera, Washington DC; YUG: Dubrovnik. **Roles with these companies incl** BEETHOVEN: Rocco (*Fidelio*); BERG: Doktor★ (*Wozzeck*); BRITTEN: Bottom (*Midsummer Night*); CIMAROSA: Count Robinson★ & Geronimo★ (*Matrimonio segreto*); DONIZETTI: Don Pistacchio (*Campanello*), Maestro & Agata (*Convenienze/Viva la Mamma*), Don Pasquale★, Dulcamara★ (*Elisir*), Sulpice (*Fille du régiment*), Gasparo‡ (*Rita*); GALUPPI: Don Tritemio (*Filosofo di campagna*); MASSENET: Don Quichotte; MOZART: Don Alfonso★ (*Così fan tutte*), Leporello★ (*Don Giovanni*), Osmin★ (*Entführung aus dem Serail*), Conte Almaviva & Figaro (*Nozze di Figaro*); MUSSORGSKY: Varlaam★ (*Boris Godunov*); OFFENBACH: Coppélius, etc (*Contes d'Hoffmann*); PAISIELLO: Basilio (*Barbiere di Siviglia*); PERGOLESI: Marcaniello (*Frate 'nnamorato*), Uberto‡ (*Serva padrona*); PROKOFIEV: Mendoza (*Duenna*); PUCCINI: Colline (*Bohème*); ROSSINI: Dott Bartolo & Don Basilio★‡ (*Barbiere di Siviglia*), Tobias Mill★ & Slook (*Cambiale di matrimonio*), Don Magnifico★‡ (*Cenerentola*), Podestà (*Gazza ladra*), Mustafà★ (*Italiana in Algeri*), Conte Asdrubal★ & Macrobio (*Pietra del paragone*), Bruschino & Gaudenzio (*Signor Bruschino*), Sultan Selim★ & Geronio★ (*Turco in Italia*); STRAUSS, R: Baron Ochs★ (*Rosenkavalier*); VERDI: Barone (*Giorno di regno*); WOLF-FERRARI: Lunardo (*Quattro rusteghi*). Also CHERUBINI: Oste (*Osteria portoghese*), Brigante (*Ali Baba*), Maggiore Frankestein (*Crescendo*); CIMAROSA: Pulcinella (*Baronessa stramba*), Polidoro (*Italiana in Londra*), Don Catapazio (*Credulo*), Giampolo (*Astuzie femminili*), Pulcinella (*Sposi per accidenti*); FIORAVANTI: Don Mazzone (*Nozze per pun-

tiglio); MOZART: Masetto‡ (*Don Giovanni*); PERGOLESI: Maestro di musica; SACCHINI: Don Anselmo (*Amore soldato*); SCARLATTI: Varrone (*Varrone e Perricca*); PAISIELLO: Notaio (*Molinara*), Petronio (*Astrologi immaginari*). **World premieres:** MAGGIONI: Omar (*Gioco di Soleima*) Bergamo 1955; RIGACCI: King (*Prof King*) Bergamo 1956; ROTA: Nevrastenico (*Notte di un nevrastenico*) Milan/Turin 1959-60; TOSATTI: Marcopulos (*Fiera delle meraviglie*) Rome 1963; HAZON: Lord Frank Ford (*Donna uccisa con dolcezza*) Parma 1967; BUCCHI: Proprietario (*Il coccodrillo*) Bologna 1970; FERRARI: Winckelhoff (*Lord Savile*) Treviso/Catania 1971. Recorded for: RCA, Decca, DG, Columbia, Cetra. Video/Film: Don Basilio (*Barbiere di Siviglia*); Uberto (*Serva padrona*). Teaches voice. **Res:** Piazza Napoli 38, Milan, Italy.

MONTEFUSCO, LICINIO. Dramatic baritone. Italian. Born 30 Oct 1936, Milan. Wife Ilgar Evin. Studied: Rhea Toniolo, Milan. **Debut:** Zurga (*Pêcheurs de perles*) Teatro Nuovo, Milan 1961. Previous occupations: lab technician.

Sang with major companies in AUS: Vienna Staatsoper; BEL: Brussels; BUL: Sofia; FRA: Nice, Paris, Strasbourg, Toulouse; FR GER: Berlin Deutsche Oper, Munich Staatsoper, Stuttgart, Wiesbaden; HOL: Amsterdam; ITA: Bologna, Florence Maggio & Comunale, Genoa, Milan La Scala, Naples, Palermo, Rome Opera, Trieste, Turin, Venice, Verona Arena; MON: Monte Carlo; POR: Lisbon; SPA: Majorca; SWI: Geneva; USA: Philadelphia Grand, San Antonio; YUG: Belgrade. **Roles with these companies incl** BELLINI: Filippo★ (*Beatrice di Tenda*), Ernesto (*Pirata*), Sir Richard★ (*Puritani*); BIZET: Escamillo★ (*Carmen*), Zurga (*Pêcheurs de perles*); DONIZETTI: Lusignano★ (*Caterina Cornaro*), Alfonse (*Favorite*), Enrico (*Lucia*); GIORDANO: Carlo Gérard (*Andrea Chénier*); GOUNOD: Valentin (*Faust*); LEONCAVALLO: Tonio (*Pagliacci*); MASCAGNI: Alfio (*Cavalleria rusticana*); PUCCINI: Marcello (*Bohème*); TCHAIKOVSKY: Eugene Onegin; VERDI: Amonasro (*Aida*), Egberto (*Aroldo*), Renato (*Ballo in maschera*), Rodrigo (*Don Carlo*), Don Carlo (*Ernani*), Ford (*Falstaff*), Don Carlo (*Forza del destino*), Macbeth, Francesco (*Masnadieri*), Nabucco, Iago (*Otello*), Rigoletto, Germont (*Traviata*), Conte di Luna (*Trovatore*), Monforte (*Vespri*); WAGNER: Orsini (*Rienzi*). Also MERCADANTE: Duke Hamilton (*Reggente*); CHAILLY: Capitano Marino★ (*Riva delle Sirti*). Gives recitals. **Res:** V Bruzzes 37, Milan, Italy.

MONTEVERDE, MAURIZIO. Scenic and costume designer for opera, theater, film, television. Italian. Born 20 Sep 1933, Rome. Single. **Operatic debut:** *Mayerling* Teatro San Carlo, Naples 1960. Theater debut: Teatro San Erasmo, Milan 1958.

Designed for major companies in ITA: Bologna, Florence Comunale, Naples, Palermo, Rome Opera, Trieste; POR: Lisbon. **Operas designed for these companies incl** BOITO: *Mefistofele;* CIMAROSA: *Matrimonio segreto;* DONIZETTI: *Elisir, Lucia, Rita;* MOZART: *Nozze di Figaro;* PUCCINI: *Bohème, Rondine★;* ROSSINI: *Barbiere di Siviglia★, Cenerentola, Scala di seta;* SAINT-SAENS: *Samson et Dalila★;* STRAUSS,

J: *Fledermaus;* VERDI: *Aida;* ZANDONAI: *Francesca da Rimini.* Also MERCADANTE: *Elisa e Claudio.* **Operatic world premieres:** GIURANNA: *Mayerling* Teatro San Carlo, Naples 1960; VIOZZI: *Elisabetta* Teatro G Verdi, Trieste 1971. Operatic Video/Film — RAI TV: *Rigoletto;* PAISIELLO: *Mondo della luna;* BLvision-BHE Film: *Traviata.* **Res:** 12 V Timavo, Rome, Italy.

MONTGOMERY, KENNETH MERVYN. Conductor of opera and symphony. British. Mus Dir & Resident Cond, Glyndebourne Touring Opera, UK since 1974. Also Resident Cond & Mus Dir, Bournemouth Sinfonietta, UK; Hilversum Orch, Holland. Born 28 Oct 1943, Belfast, Ireland. Single. Studied: Royal Coll of Music, Sir Adrian Boult, John Pritchard, Hans Schmidt-Isserstedt, London; incl piano, bassoon. Plays the harpsichord. Operatic training as repetiteur, asst cond & chorus master at Glyndebourne Fest 1964-68. **Operatic debut:** *Elisir d'amore* Sadler's Wells, Coventry, UK 1966. Symphonic debut: BBC Northern Symph Orch, Manchester 1966. Awards: Tagore Gold Medal, Royal Coll of Music; Silver Medal, Worshipful Co of Musicians.

Conducted with major companies in HOL: Amsterdam; UK: Welsh National, Glyndebourne Fest, London Royal & English National. **Operas with these companies incl** BRITTEN: *Turn of the Screw★;* CAVALLI: *Calisto★, Ormindo★;* DONIZETTI: *Don Pasquale, Elisir;* MOZART: *Così fan tutte★, Entführung aus dem Serail, Nozze di Figaro★, Re pastore;* PUCCINI: *Bohème, Butterfly;* ROSSINI: *Barbiere di Siviglia;* STRAUSS, R: *Ariadne auf Naxos★, Capriccio★;* STRAVINSKY: *Rake's Progress★;* VERDI: *Falstaff★, Rigoletto, Simon Boccanegra★, Traviata;* WEBER: *Freischütz★, Oberon★.* Video — NOS TV Holland. BOYCE: *Secular Masque.* Conducted major orch in Europe. Mgmt: AIM/UK; BAR/USA.

MONTRESOR, BENI. Scenic and costume designer for opera, theater & film. Is a lighting designer, stage director; also an illustrator & film director. Italian. Born 31 Mar 1926, Bussolengo/Verona. Single. Studied: Accad di Belle Arti, Venice; Centro Sperimentale Cinematografico, Rome. **Operatic debut:** *Vanessa* Spoleto Fest 1962. Non-operatic debut: films, Rome 1952. Awards: decorated Knight, Italian Gvnmt.

Designed for major companies in ITA: Milan La Scala, Spoleto Fest, Venice, Verona Arena; UK: Glyndebourne Fest, London Royal; USA: Hawaii, Houston, New York Met & City Opera, San Francisco Opera, Washington DC. **Operas designed for these companies incl** BERLIOZ: *Benvenuto Cellini;* CATALANI: *Wally;* DEBUSSY: *Pelléas et Mélisande;* DONIZETTI: *Don Pasquale★, Fille du régiment★;* MASSENET: *Esclarmonde★;* MENOTTI: *Amahl, Dernier sauvage, Medium;* MOZART: *Zauberflöte;* PUCCINI: *Turandot★;* PONCHIELLI: *Gioconda;* RAMEAU: *Hippolyte et Aricie★;* ROSSINI: *Cenerentola.* Exhib of stage designs Knoedler Gal, NY 1965; Théâtre Oblique, Paris 1975. **Res:** 31 W 12 St, New York, NY 10011, USA and Bussolengo/Verona, Italy.

MOORE, JOHN RALPH. Scenic and costume designer for opera & film. Is a lighting designer; also a sculptor & author. American. Born 20 Jan 1924, Tryon, NC. Single. Studied: Accad di Belle Arti, Rome, Italy. **Operatic debut:** *Otello* Teatro Comunale, Florence. Awards: Academy Awd nomination 1963.

Designed for major companies in AUS: Salzburg Fest; FR GER: Düsseldorf-Duisburg; ITA: Milan La Scala, Palermo, Rome Opera, Spoleto Fest, Venice; SWI: Geneva. **Operas designed for these companies incl** CAVALIERI: *Rappresentazione;* DONIZETTI: *Fille du régiment;* HANDEL: *Acis and Galatea;* MENOTTI: *Amelia al ballo;* MILHAUD: *Christophe Colomb;* MOZART: *Don Giovanni;* OFFENBACH: *Contes d'Hoffmann;* ORFF: *Carmina burana;* PONCHIELLI: *Gioconda;* PUCCINI: *Bohème, Butterfly, Turandot;* ROSSINI: *Cenerentola, Guillaume Tell;* STRAUSS, R: *Arabella, Rosenkavalier, Salome;* STRAVINSKY: *Perséphone;* VERDI: *Due Foscari, Rigoletto, Traviata;* WAGNER: *Lohengrin.* Exhibitions of stage designs Victoria and Albert Museum, London 1963. **Res:** V degli Orsini 34, Rome, Italy.

MOREIRA, MAURA. Dramatic mezzo-soprano. Brazilian. Resident mem: Cologne Opera. Born Belo Horizonte, Brazil. Single. Studied: Mo Max Hellmann, Profs Wolfgang Steinbrück, Erik Werba, Josef Witt. **Debut:** Santuzza (*Cavalleria rusticana*) Ulmer Theater 1959. Previous occupations: teacher and office worker. Awards: Prize, Voice Cont in Vercelli, Italy; Reis e Silva and Pro Arte, Brazil.

Sang with major companies in BRA: Rio de Janeiro; FR GER: Bielefeld, Bonn, Cologne, Darmstadt, Düsseldorf-Duisburg, Essen, Frankfurt, Hamburg, Hannover, Krefeld, Mannheim, Munich Staatsoper, Stuttgart, Wiesbaden; ITA: Rome Opera; SWI: Basel. **Roles with these companies incl** BELLINI: Adalgisa (*Norma*); MUSSORGSKY: Marfa (*Khovanshchina*); PUCCINI: Suzuki★ (*Butterfly*); SAINT-SAENS: Dalila; SMETANA: Hata★ (*Bartered Bride*); TCHAIKOVSKY: Mme Larina★ (*Eugene Onegin*); VERDI: Amneris★ (*Aida*), Ulrica (*Ballo in maschera*), Eboli (*Don Carlo*), Dame Quickly (*Falstaff*), Azucena★ (*Trovatore*); WAGNER: Venus★ (*Tannhäuser*). Also MASCAGNI: Santuzza (*Cavalleria rusticana*); PROKOFIEV: Fata Morgana (*Love for Three Oranges*); BENNETT: (*Mines of Sulphur*); WARD: Tituba (*Crucible*). **World premieres:** ZIMMERMANN: Weseners Mutter (*Soldaten*) Bühnen der Stadt Köln, Cologne 1965. Recorded for: Vox, Vergo. Gives recitals. Appears with symphony orchestra. **Res:** An der alten Post 22, 5 Cologne 40, FR Ger.

MORELAND, MARGARET ELIZABETH; née Cooksley. British. Secy/Dir, Welsh National Opera and Drama Co Ltd, John St, Cardiff CF1 4SP, UK. In charge of admin matters. Born in Cardiff, UK. Husband Alan Giles. Plays the piano. Previous positions primarily administrative. Started with present company 1948, as administrator. World premieres at theater during her management: HUGHES: *Menna* 1953, *Serch yr Doctor* 1960; WILLIAMS: *The Parlour* 1966; HODDINOTT: *Beach of Falesa* 1974; all at Welsh Ntl Op, Cardiff. Awards: M B E, Queen's Honours List. Mem of Board of Governors, Welsh Coll of Music & Drama. **Res:** Cardiff, UK.

MORELL, BARRY. Lirico spinto tenor. American. Born 30 Mar 1927, New York. Wife Joan, occupation former ballerina. Five children. Studied: Mo Giuseppe Danise, Mo Pasquale Rescigno, New York. **Debut:** Pinkerton (*Butterfly*) New York City Opera 1955. Previous occupations: wool merchant. Awards: Gold Medal of Honor, Corp Lyrica de Arte, Santiago, Chile.

Sang with major companies in ARG: Buenos Aires; AUS: Graz, Vienna Staatsoper; BEL: Liège; FR GER: Berlin Deutsche Oper, Saarbrücken, Stuttgart; HOL: Amsterdam; ITA: Naples, Palermo, Rome Opera; MEX: Mexico City; POL: Warsaw; SPA: Barcelona; SWI: Zurich; UK: London Royal Opera; USA: Baltimore, Chicago, Cincinnati, Fort Worth, Hartford, Hawaii, Houston, Miami, Milwaukee Florentine, New Orleans, New York Met & City Opera, Omaha, Philadelphia Grand & Lyric, Pittsburgh, Portland, San Antonio, San Francisco Opera, Seattle; YUG: Zagreb. **Roles with these companies incl** BIZET: Don José (*Carmen*); CILEA: Maurizio (*A. Lecouvreur*); DONIZETTI: Fernand★ (*Favorite*), Edgardo★ (*Lucia*); GOUNOD: Faust; LEONCAVALLO: Canio★ (*Pagliacci*); MASCAGNI: Turiddu★ (*Cavalleria rusticana*); MASSENET: Des Grieux (*Manon*); OFFENBACH: Hoffmann; PONCHIELLI: Enzo★ (*Gioconda*); PUCCINI: Rodolfo★ (*Bohème*), Pinkerton★ (*Butterfly*), Cavaradossi★ (*Tosca*), Roberto‡ (*Villi*); STRAUSS, R: Matteo (*Arabella*), Ein Sänger★ (*Rosenkavalier*); TCHAIKOVSKY: Lenski (*Eugene Onegin*); VERDI: Radames★ (*Aida*), Riccardo★ (*Ballo in maschera*), Don Carlo★, Don Alvaro★ (*Forza del destino*), Duca di Mantova★ (*Rigoletto*), Gabriele (*Simon Boccanegra*), Alfredo★ (*Traviata*), Manrico★ (*Trovatore*). Also HANDEL: Judas Maccabaeus. **World premieres:** GIANNINI: Mark (*Harvest*) Chicago Lyric Opera 1961. Recorded for: RCA. Gives recitals. Appears with symphony orchestra. **Res:** V Almese 10, Rome, Italy. Mgmt: CAM/USA.

MORELLE, MAUREEN; née Maureen Nina Fullam. Lyric mezzo-soprano. British. Born 16 Aug 1934, Aldershot, Hants, UK. Husband Michael Thomson, occupation tech mng, Royal Opera, Covent Garden. One child. Studied: Royal Coll of Music, London; Andrew Field, Audrey Langford. **Debut:** Rosina (*Barbiere di Siviglia*) Welsh National Opera 1964. Awards: Clara Butt Awd, RCM London 1961; Winner, Queen's Prize for Women Singers 1963; Commendation, Royal Liverpool Compt 1960.

Sang with major companies in UK: Aldeburgh Fest, Cardiff Welsh, Edinburgh Fest, Glyndebourne Fest, London Royal & English National. **Roles with these companies incl** BRITTEN: Hermia (*Midsummer Night*); DEBUSSY: Geneviève (*Pelléas et Mélisande*); HUMPERDINCK: Hänsel; MOZART: Dorabella★ (*Così fan tutte*), Cherubino (*Nozze di Figaro*); PUCCINI: Suzuki (*Butterfly*); ROSSINI: Rosina★ (*Barbiere di Siviglia*), Isolier★ (*Comte Ory*), Pippo (*Gazza ladra*); STRAUSS, J: Prinz Orlovsky★ (*Fledermaus*); TCHAIKOVSKY: Mme Larina★ (*Eugene Onegin*); WAG-

NER: Fricka★ (*Rheingold*). Also DONIZETTI: Smeton (*Anna Bolena*). **World premieres:** BIRT-WISTLE: Judy (*Punch and Judy*) English Opera Grp, Aldeburgh 1968. Gives recitals. Appears with symphony orchestra. **Res:** 33 Boileau Rd, London W 5, UK. Mgmt: MIN/UK.

MORESCO, CARLO. Conductor of opera and symphony; composer; operatic stage director. American. Resident Cond, Connecticut Opera, Hartford; Philadelphia Grand Op; Tulsa Opera Co, OK, USA. Born 20 May 1905, Genoa, Italy. Wife Egle. One child. Plays the violin, piano. Operatic training as repetiteur, asst cond & chorus master at Teatro Carlo Felice, Genoa 1922-30. **Operatic debut:** *Traviata* Carlo Felice, Genoa 1923.
   Conducted with major companies in ARG: Buenos Aires; CAN: Montreal/Quebec, Toronto; ITA: Bologna, Florence Comunale, Genoa, Milan, Naples San Carlo, Parma, Triéste, Turin, Venice, Verona Arena; SWI: Basel; USA: Baltimore, Boston, Chicago, Cincinnati, Fort Worth, Hartford, Memphis, Miami, Milwaukee Florentine, Newark, New Orleans, Omaha, Philadelphia Grand & Lyric, Pittsburgh, San Antonio, San Diego, San Francisco Opera, Washington DC. **Operas with these companies incl** AUBER: *Fra Diavolo;* BELLINI: *Norma★, Puritani★, S nnambula★;* BIZET: *Carmen, Pêcheurs de perles;* BOITO: *Mefistofele;* CATALANI: *Wally;* CILEA: *A. Lecouvreur★;* CIMAROSA: *Matrimonio segreto;* DONIZETTI: *Don Pasquale★, Elisir★, Favorite, Fille du régiment★, Linda di Chamounix, Lucia★;* GIORDANO: *Andrea Chénier, Fedora;* GOUNOD: *Faust★, Roméo et Juliette★;* HUMPERDINCK: *Hänsel und Gretel★;* LEONCAVALLO: *Pagliacci★;* MASCAGNI: *Amico Fritz★, Cavalleria rusticana★;* MASSENET: *Manon, Werther;* MEYERBEER: *Africaine, Huguenots;* MOZART: *Don Giovanni, Nozze di Figaro;* PONCHIELLI: *Gioconda;* PUCCINI: *Bohème★, Fanciulla del West, Gianni Schicchi, Butterfly★, Manon Lescaut★, Rondine, Suor Angelica, Tabarro, Tosca★, Turandot★;* ROSSINI: *Barbiere di Siviglia★, Guillaume Tell, Italiana in Algeri, Moïse;* SAINT-SAENS: *Samson et Dalila★;* STRAUSS, J: *Fledermaus★;* VERDI: *Aida★, Ballo in maschera★, Don Carlo, Ernani, Falstaff, Forza del destino★, Macbeth, Nabucco, Otello★, Rigoletto★, Traviata★, Trovatore★;* WAGNER: *Lohengrin, Tannhäuser;* ZANDONAI: *Francesca da Rimini.* Also MASCAGNI: *Isabeau, Piccolo Marat.* Teaches. **Res:** Hotel Ansonia, 73 St & Broadway, New York, NY, USA.

MORET, COSTANTE. Lirico-spinto tenor. Brazilian. Born 15 Nov 1931, Pordenone, Italy. Wife Edméa de Mello, occupation teacher. Studied: Mo Silvio Piergilli, Mo Santiago Guerra, Rio de Janeiro. **Debut:** Turiddu (*Cavalleria rusticana*) Teatro Municipal, Rio de Janeiro 1957. Previous occupations: officer Secretariat of Educ & Culture, State Gvnmt.
   Sang with major companies in BRA: Rio de Janeiro. **Roles with these companies incl** BEETHOVEN: Florestan (*Fidelio*); BIZET: Don José★ (*Carmen*); CILEA: Maurizio (*A. Lecouvreur*); DONIZETTI: Edgardo (*Lucia*); GIORDANO:

Andrea Chénier; GOMES: Fernando★ (*Colombo*); GOUNOD: Faust; LEONCAVALLO: Canio (*Pagliacci*); MASCAGNI: Fritz★ (*Amico Fritz*), Turiddu★ (*Cavalleria rusticana*); MASSENET: Des Grieux (*Manon*), Nicias (*Thaïs*), Werther; OFFENBACH: Hoffmann; PONCHIELLI: Enzo (*Gioconda*); PUCCINI: Rodolfo★ (*Bohème*), Pinkerton★ (*Butterfly*), Des Grieux (*Manon Lescaut*), Luigi (*Tabarro*), Cavaradossi★ (*Tosca*), Calaf (*Turandot*); SAINT-SAENS: Samson; VERDI: Radames (*Aida*), Riccardo (*Ballo in maschera*), Duca di Mantova★ (*Rigoletto*), Alfredo★ (*Traviata*), Manrico (*Trovatore*). Also BRAGA: Carlito (*Jupira*); GOMES: Americo★ (*Schiavo*). Gives recitals. Appears with symphony orchestra. **Res:** rua Ancora 45, Rio de Janeiro, Brazil.

MORI, ANGELO. Lyric tenor. Italian. Born 27 Nov 1934, Toulouse, France. Wife Augusta Zilli. One child. Studied: Scuola La Fenice, Venice; Mo Marcello Del Monaco. **Debut:** Duca (*Rigoletto*) La Fenice, Venice 1962.
   Sang with major companies in AUS: Vienna Staatsoper; FIN: Helsinki; FRA: Orange Fest; FR GER: Berlin Deutsche Oper, Dortmund, Düsseldorf-Duisburg, Karlsruhe, Stuttgart, Wiesbaden; HOL: Amsterdam; HUN: Budapest; ITA: Bologna, Florence Comunale, Genoa, Milan La Scala, Naples, Palermo, Parma, Rome Opera & Caracalla, Trieste, Turin, Venice; SPA: Barcelona; YUG: Zagreb, Belgrade. **Roles with these companies incl** BELLINI: Pollione★ (*Norma*), BIZET: Don José (*Carmen*); BUSONI: Calaf★ (*Turandot*); DONIZETTI: Riccardo★ (*Anna Bolena*), Fernand (*Favorite*), Edgardo (*Lucia di Lammermoor*), Gennaro (*Lucrezia Borgia*); GIORDANO: Andrea Chénier★, Loris Ipanov (*Fedora*); GOUNOD: Faust; MASCAGNI: Turiddu★ (*Cavalleria rusticana*); MASSENET: Des Grieux (*Manon*); PONCHIELLI: Enzo★ (*Gioconda*); PUCCINI: Rodolfo★ (*Bohème*), Dick Johnson (*Fanciulla del West*), Pinkerton★ (*Butterfly*), Des Grieux★ (*Manon Lescaut*), Luigi (*Tabarro*), Cavaradossi★ (*Tosca*); ROSSINI: Aménophis★ (*Moïse*); SPONTINI: Licinio★ (*Vestale*); VERDI: Radames★ (*Aida*), Riccardo★ (*Ballo in maschera*), Ernani, Don Alvaro‡ (*Forza del destino*), Carlo (*Giovanna d'Arco*), Rodolfo (*Luisa Miller*), Ismaele★ (*Nabucco*), Duca di Mantova★‡ (*Rigoletto*), Gabriele (*Simon Boccanegra*), Alfredo‡ (*Traviata*), Manrico★ (*Trovatore*).

MOROZOV, BORIS MIKHAILOVICH. Bass. Russian. Resident mem: Bolshoi Theater, Moscow. Born 11 Nov 1931, St Kanevskaya. Wife Valentina, occupation ballerina. One son. Studied: Donetsk, Ukraine; Mr Korobeichenko. **Debut:** Kontchak (*Prince Igor*) Odessa Theater 1960. Previous occupations: miner.
   Sang with major companies in USSR: Moscow Bolshoi. **Roles with these companies incl** GLINKA: Farlaf (*Ruslan and Ludmilla*); MUSSORGSKY: Varlaam (*Boris Godunov*), Ivan Khovansky (*Khovanshchina*); RIMSKY-KORSAKOV: Juri Vsevolodovic (*Invisible City of Kitezh*); VERDI: Philip II (*Don Carlo*). Recorded for: Melodiya. **Res:** 29 B Pirogovskaya, Moscow, USSR.

MORPURGO, NELLY; née Pieternella Morpurgo. Dramatic soprano. Dutch. Born 3 Mar 1940, Amsterdam. Divorced. One child. Studied: Muziek Lyceum, Amsterdam, Boris Pelsky; Mo Lastotsjkin, Coby Riemensma. **Debut:** Zweiter Knabe (*Zauberflöte*) Amsterdam 1961.

Sang with major companies in BEL: Brussels; HOL: Amsterdam. **Roles with these companies incl** BARTOK: Judith★ (*Bluebeard's Castle*); BIZET: Micaëla (*Carmen*); BRITTEN: Female Chorus (*Rape of Lucretia*); MENOTTI: Lucy (*Telephone*); MOZART: Fiordiligi (*Così fan tutte*), Contessa (*Nozze di Figaro*); PUCCINI: Musetta★ (*Bohème*). Also MOZART: Erste Dame★ (*Zauberflöte*); BUSONI: Colombina★ (*Arlecchino*); VERDI: Fenena★(*Nabucco*); RAMEAU: Clarine (*Platée*); MENOTTI: Secretary (*Consul*). Video: (*Consul*). Appears with symphony orchestra. **Res:** Hemonystraat 27, Amsterdam, Holland. Mgmt: ALF/HOL.

MORRIS, JAMES. Bass-baritone. American. Resident mem: Metropolitan Opera, New York. Born 10 Jan 1947, Baltimore, MD, USA. Wife Joanne. Studied: Rosa Ponselle, Peabody Consv of Music, Baltimore; Frank Valentino, Nicola Moscona, Anton Guadagno, coach, New York. **Debut:** Crespel (*Contes d'Hoffmann*) Baltimore Civic Opera 1967. Awards: First Prize Baltimore Opera Aud; voice schlshp to Univ of Maryland.

Sang with major companies in CAN: Vancouver; SPA: Barcelona; UK: Glyndebourne Fest; USA: Baltimore, Cincinnati, Houston, Miami, Newark, New Orleans, New York Met, Philadelphia Lyric. **Roles with these companies incl** BELLINI: Oroveso★ (*Norma*); DONIZETTI: Baldassare (*Favorite*); GOUNOD: Méphistophélès★ (*Faust*); MOZART: Don Giovanni★; PUCCINI: Colline★ (*Bohème*); ROSSINI: Don Basilio★ (*Barbiere di Siviglia*), Assur★ (*Semiramide*); VERDI: Ramfis★ (*Aida*), Grande Inquisitore★ (*Don Carlo*), Padre Guardiano★ (*Forza del destino*), Banquo★ (*Macbeth*), Procida★ (*Vespri*). Also DONIZETTI: Raimondo (*Lucia*). Recorded for: RCA, London/Decca. Video: Banquo (*Macbeth*). Gives recitals. Appears with symphony orchestra. **Res:** New York, NY, USA. Mgmt: COL/USA; AIM/UK.

MOSER, EDDA ELISABETH. Dramatic coloratura soprano. German. Resident mem: Vienna Staatsoper; Metropolitan Opera, New York. Born 27 Oct 1941, Berlin, Germany. Husband Peter Csobadi, occupation head of Music Dept, Radio "Voice of Germany", Cologne. Studied: Music Consv of Berlin; Gerty König, Berlin. **Debut:** Konstanze (*Entführung aus dem Serail*) Münster, FR Ger 1967. Previous occupations: medical assistant. Awards: Grand Prix du Disque, France; Grand Prix Lyrique, Prix Lily Pons 1974; Wiener Flötenuhr.

Sang with major companies in AUS: Salzburg Fest, Vienna Staatsoper; BEL: Brussels, Liège; BRA: Rio de Janeiro; FRA: Aix-en-Provence Fest, Lyon, Nancy, Orange Fest, Paris; FR GER: Berlin Deutsche Oper, Bonn, Cologne, Düsseldorf-Duisburg, Frankfurt, Hamburg, Hannover, Munich Staatsoper, Nürnberg, Stuttgart; GER DR: Berlin Staatsoper, Dresden; HUN: Budapest; ITA: Milan La Scala, Venice; SWI: Geneva, Zurich; UK: Edinburgh Fest; USSR: Kiev, Moscow Bolshoi; USA: New York Met; YUG: Belgrade. **Roles with these companies incl** BIZET: Micaëla (*Carmen*); BLACHER: Julia; CAVALIERI: Deidamia★ (*Rappresentazione*); DONIZETTI: Norina★ (*Don Pasquale*), Lucia★; GLUCK: Euridice & Amor (*Orfeo ed Euridice*); GOUNOD: Marguerite★ (*Faust*); HUMPERDINCK: Gretel★; LEONCAVALLO: Nedda★ (*Pagliacci*); LORTZING: Marie (*Waffenschmied*), Baronin Freimann (*Wildschütz*); MOZART: Fiordiligi (*Così fan tutte*), Donna Anna★ & Donna Elvira★ (*Don Giovanni*), Aspasia★ (*Mitridate, re di Ponto*), Königin der Nacht★ (*Zauberflöte*); OFFENBACH: Olympia (*Contes d'Hoffmann*); PUCCINI: Musetta★ (*Bohème*), Liù★ (*Turandot*); SMETANA: Marie★ (*Bartered Bride*); STRAUSS, J: Rosalinde★ (*Fledermaus*), STRAUSS, R: Christine (*Intermezzo*); STRAVINSKY: Rossignol★; VERDI: Gilda★ (*Rigoletto*), Violetta★ (*Traviata*); WAGNER: Eva★ (*Meistersinger*). Also HAYDN: Armida★. **World premieres:** HENZE: Mme la Mort (*Floss der Medusa*) Norddeutscher Rundfunk, Hamburg 1968. Recorded for: DG, EMI/Angel, EMI/Electrola. Video/Film—NDR TV: Lucia di Lammermoor. Gives recitals. Appears with symphony orchestra. **Res:** Elsenborner Str 191, D5, Cologne 41, FR Ger. Mgmt: OOC/FRA; CAM/USA.

MOSLEY, ROBERT. Dramatic baritone. American. Born 22 Jun 1935, Coulder, PA, USA. Divorced. Studied: Wm Bretz, Westchester, PA, USA; Giuseppe Danise, Pasquale Rescignio, New York. **Debut:** Valentin (*Faust*) New York City Opera 1966. Previous occupations: TV performer, church soloist, operetta singer. Awards: Marian Anderson Awd; Met Op Ntl Counc Aud Weyerhaeuser Awd; John Hay Whitney and Rockefeller Fndt Awds.

Sang with major companies in USA: Boston, Fort Worth, Jackson, Memphis, New York City Opera, San Francisco Opera & Spring Opera, Santa Fe, Seattle. **Roles with these companies incl** GERSHWIN: Porgy★; JOPLIN: Father (*Treemonisha*); ORFF: Solo (*Carmina burana*); PUCCINI: Scarpia (*Tosca*); ROSSINI: Iago (*Otello*); VERDI: Amonasro★ (*Aida*), Ford (*Falstaff*), Iago★ (*Otello*), Rigoletto★, Germont (*Traviata*); WAGNER: Holländer★; WEILL: Trinity Moses★ (*Aufstieg und Fall der Stadt Mahagonny*). **World premieres:** STILL: Leonce (*Bayou Legend*) Opera/South, Jackson, MS 1974. Gives recitals. Appears with symphony orchestra. Teaches voice. Coaches repertoire. Mgmt: HJH/USA.

MOSZKOWICZ, IMO. Stages/produces opera, theater, film & television and is an author. German. Born 27 July 1925, Ahlen/Westf, Germany. Wife Renate. Two children. Operatic training as asst stage dir to Gustaf Gründgens, Städtische Bühnen, Düsseldorf. **Operatic debut:** *Entführung aus dem Serail* Wuppertaler Bühnen, FR Ger 1967. Theater debut: Städtische Bühnen, Bielefeld 1955.

Directed/produced opera for major companies in FR GER: Frankfurt, Munich Gärtnerplatz, Wuppertal; SWI: Zurich. **Operas staged for these companies incl** FORTNER: *Elisabeth Tudor★*; GINASTERA: *Bomarzo;* HENZE: *Rachel la Cubana★;* KODALY: *Háry János;* MOZART: *Entführung aus dem Serail★;* ORFF: *Bernauerin★;* ROSSINI: *Barbiere di Siviglia.* Also KRENEK: *Karl V;* KLEBE: *Figaro lässt sich scheiden★.* **Op-**

eratic world premieres: KLEBE: *Wahrer Held* Opernhaus Zurich 1975. Operatic Video—TV WDR/ORF: *Háry János*. Previous leading positions with major theater companies: Art Dir, Künstlertheater, São Paulo, Brazil 1955. Teaches at Mozarteum, Salzburg. **Res:** Uhlandstr 40, 8012 Ottobrunn, FR Ger.

MOTLEY; firm originally composed of Audrey Sophia Harris (deceased), Margaret F Harris (deceased) and **MONTGOMERY, ELIZABETH.** Scenic and costume designer for opera & theater. British. Born 15 Feb 1904, Kidlington/Oxfordshire, UK. Husband Pat Wilmot, occupation writer. One child. Studied: Westminster School of Art, London. Previous occupation: illustrator. **Designed opera for major companies in UK:** Glyndebourne Fest, London English National; USA: New York Met; et al. **Operas designed for these companies incl** FLOTOW: *Martha;* GOUNOD: *Faust;* MOZART: *Così fan tutte, Idomeneo, Zauberflöte;* PUCCINI: *Bohème;* STRAVINSKY: *Rake's Progress;* TCHAIKOVSKY: *Eugene Onegin;* VERDI: *Ballo in maschera, Simon Boccanegra, Trovatore;* WAGNER: *Meistersinger;* et al. **Operatic world premieres:** BERKELEY: *Nelson* London 1954.

MOULSON, ROBERT LEWIS. Lyric tenor. American. Born 26 Nov 1932, Cleveland, O, USA. Wife Darlene. Two children. Studied: Frederick Jagel, Samuel Margolis, New York. **Debut:** Sam (*Susannah*) New York City Opera 1958. Awards: Sullivan Fndt, Ford Fndt, Rockefeller Fndt Grants; Friday Morn Music Club, Washington DC; Geneva Intl Cont. **Sang with major companies in CAN:** Vancouver; FR GER: Bonn, Cologne, Düsseldorf-Duisburg, Frankfurt, Hamburg, Hannover, Stuttgart; USA: Boston, Cincinnati, Houston, New York City Opera, Pittsburgh, Portland, San Francisco Opera & Spring Opera, Seattle. **Roles with these companies incl** BELLINI: Elvino (*Sonnambula*); BERLIOZ: Faust★(*Damnation de Faust*); BIZET: Don José★ (*Carmen*); BORODIN: Vladimir (*Prince Igor*); DONIZETTI: Fernand (*Favorite*), Edgardo (*Lucia*); EGK: Christoph (*Verlobung in San Domingo*); FLOYD: Sam Polk★ (*Susannah*); GOUNOD: Faust; LEONCAVALLO: Canio★ (*Pagliacci*); MASCAGNI: Turiddu★ (*Cavalleria rusticana*); OFFENBACH: Hoffmann★; PUCCINI: Rodolfo (*Bohème*), Dick Johnson (*Fanciulla del West*), Rinuccio (*Gianni Schicchi*), Pinkerton (*Butterfly*), Ruggero (*Rondine*), Cavaradossi★ (*Tosca*); SAINT-SAENS: Samson★; STRAUSS, J: Eisenstein & Alfred (*Fledermaus*); STRAUSS, R: Aegisth (*Elektra*); STRAVINSKY: Oedipus Rex★; VERDI: Radames★ (*Aida*), Don Carlo★, Carlo (*Masnadieri*), Duca di Mantova★ (*Rigoletto*), Alfredo (*Traviata*). **World premieres:** FLOYD: Lennie (*Of Mice and Men*) Seattle Opera 1970. Gives recitals. Appears with symphony orchestra. **Res:** 1100 Old Forge Dr, Roswell, GA 30075, USA. Mgmt: SAM/USA.

MOYLE, JULIAN KERR SCOTT. Lyric baritone. Australian. Resident mem: Welsh National Opera, Cardiff. Born 4 Feb 1927, Melbourne. Single. Studied: Thomas Leslie Middleton, Melbourne; Arnold Matters, Mme Boriska Gereb, London;

Gerald Davies, Cardiff. **Debut:** Dott Malatesta (*Don Pasquale*) Opera for All, Annan, Scotland 1956. Previous occupations: farm laborer, dairy farmer, salesman. **Sang with major companies in UK:** Cardiff Welsh, London Eng Ntl. **Roles with these companies incl** BRITTEN: Mr Redburn★ (*Billy Budd*); DONIZETTI: Dott Malatesta (*Don Pasquale*); JANACEK: Harasta (*Cunning Little Vixen*); MOZART: Don Alfonso★ (*Così fan tutte*), Conte Almaviva & Figaro★ (*Nozze di Figaro*), Papageno★ (*Zauberflöte*); PUCCINI: Marcello (*Bohème*), Sharpless★ (*Butterfly*); ROSSINI: Figaro★ (*Barbiere di Siviglia*), Dandini (*Cenerentola*), Robert (*Comte Ory*); VERDI: Ford★ (*Falstaff*), Germont (*Traviata*). Also ROSSINI: Taddeo (*Italiana in Algeri*); BURT: Bonario (*Volpone*); STRAUSS, R: Harlekin (*Ariadne auf Naxos*). Gives recitals. **Res:** Cardiff, Wales, UK.

MROZ, LEONARD ANDRZEJ. Bass. Polish. Resident mem: Teatr Wielki, Warsaw. Born 19 Jan 1947, Miedzyrzec, Poland. Wife Renata Humen, occupation pianist. Studied: Warsaw State Coll of Music; Zofia Bregy, Jerzy Czaplicki, Warsaw. **Debut:** Pimen (*Boris Godunov*) Teatr Wielki, Warsaw 1972. Awards: Second Prize Geneva Intl Compt 1971. **Sang with major companies in AUS:** Vienna Staatsoper; FR GER: Hamburg, Wiesbaden; MEX: Mexico City; POL: Warsaw. **Roles with these companies incl** MOZART: Don Giovanni★; MUSSORGSKY: Varlaam★ & Pimen★ (*Boris Godunov*); ROSSINI: Don Basilio★ (*Barbiere di Siviglia*); VERDI: Ramfis★ (*Aida*), Philip II★ (*Don Carlo*), Padre Guardiano★ (*Forza del destino*). Also MONIUSZKO: Zbigniew (*Haunted Manor*); DONIZETTI: Raimondo (*Lucia*). Gives recitals. Appears with symphony orchestra. **Res:** Komarowa 70/64, Warsaw, Poland. Mgmt: WLS/USA.

MÜLLER, HAJO. Bass-baritone. German. Resident mem: Staatsoper Dresden, Ger DR. Born 24 Feb 1931, Döbeln. Wife Hiltgund, occupation court employee. Three children. Studied: Kmsg Rudolf Dittrich, Hannes Kemter. **Debut:** Tommaso (*Tiefland*) Karl Marx Stadt, Ger DR 1951. Awards: Kammersänger 1965; Verdienstmedaille, Gvnmt Ger DR 1969; Awd Martin Andersen Nexö 1971. **Sang with major companies in CZE:** Brno; FR GER: Wiesbaden; GER DR: Berlin Staatsoper, Dresden, Leipzig; ROM: Bucharest; USSR: Leningrad Kirov. **Roles with these companies incl** BEETHOVEN: Don Pizarro★ & Rocco (*Fidelio*); BIZET: Escamillo★ (*Carmen*); DESSAU: Lanzelot★; DONIZETTI: Gasparo (*Rita*); FLOTOW: Plunkett (*Martha*); GLUCK: Thoas (*Iphigénie en Tauride*); LEONCAVALLO: Tonio★ (*Pagliacci*); LORTZING: Baculus (*Wildschütz*), Van Bett (*Zar und Zimmermann*); MOZART: Don Alfonso (*Così fan tutte*), Don Giovanni, Sarastro★ (*Zauberflöte*); MUSSORGSKY: Boris★ & Pimen (*Boris Godunov*); ORFF: Solo (*Carmina burana*); PUCCINI: Colline (*Bohème*), Scarpia (*Tosca*); ROSSINI: Don Basilio (*Barbiere di Siviglia*); STRAUSS, R: Jochanaan (*Salome*), Sir Morosus★ (*Schweigsame Frau*); TCHAIKOVSKY: Eugene Onegin★; VERDI: Amonasro & Ramfis (*Aida*),

Philip II★ & Grande Inquisitore★ (*Don Carlo*), Padre Guardiano (*Forza del destino*); WAGNER: Holländer★ & Daland (*Fliegende Holländer*), Telramund★ & König Heinrich (*Lohengrin*), Hans Sachs★ & Beckmesser (*Meistersinger*), Wotan★ (*Walküre*), Fafner (*Rheingold*), Landgraf (*Tannhäuser*), Kurwenal★ & König Marke (*Tristan und Isolde*); WEBER: Kaspar★ (*Freischütz*); WOLF-FERRARI: Lunardo (*Quattro rusteghi*). Also HANDEL: Radamisto; DESSAU: Totenrichter★ (*Verurteilung des Lukullus*); MATTHUS: Jewsjukow (*Letzter Schuss*); HUMPERDINCK: Peter★ (*Hänsel und Gretel*); PUCCINI: Timur★ (*Turandot*). World premieres: ZIMMERMANN: Johann (*Levins Mühle*) Staatsoper Dresden 1973. Recorded for: VEB, Eterna. Video/Film: (*Tannhäuser*). Gives recitals. Appears with symphony orchestra. Teaches voice. Coaches repertoire. **Res:** Weissenberger Str 3b, 8051 Dresden, Ger DR. Mgmt: KDR/GDR.

MUND, UWE CLAUS. Conductor of opera and symphony; composer. Austrian. First Cond, Städtische Bühnen, Frankfurt/Main. Born 30 Mar 1941, Vienna. Wife Gunda. One child. Studied: Prof Hans Swarowsky, Lovro von Matacic, H von Karajan, Ferdinand Grossmann, Leopold Hager; also piano, trumpet, cello and voice. Plays the piano. Operatic training as repetiteur, asst cond & chorus master at Vienna, Freiburg, Munich. **Operatic debut:** Freiburg/Breisgau. Symphonic debut: Wiener Symph, Vienna 1964.
    Conducted with major companies in FRA: Nice; FR GER: Essen, Frankfurt, Kiel, Mannheim, Munich Gärtnerplatz, Stuttgart, Wuppertal; USA: San Francisco Opera. Operas with these companies incl BIZET: *Carmen;* BRITTEN: *Death in Venice;* GOUNOD: *Faust;* HAYDN: *Infedeltà delusa;* HENZE: *Junge Lord;* LEONCAVALLO: *Pagliacci;* MASCAGNI: *Cavalleria rusticana;* MOZART: *Così fan tutte, Don Giovanni, Entführung aus dem Serail, Idomeneo, Nozze di Figaro, Zauberflöte;* NICOLAI: *Lustigen Weiber;* OFFENBACH: *Mariage aux lanternes;* PERGOLESI: *Serva padrona;* PROKOFIEV: *Love for Three Oranges;* PUCCINI: *Bohème, Manon Lescaut, Tosca;* ROSSINI: *Barbiere di Siviglia, Comte Ory;* SHOSTAKOVICH: *Nose;* SMETANA: *Bartered Bride;* STRAUSS, J: *Fledermaus;* VERDI: *Aida, Don Carlo, Macbeth, Rigoletto, Simon Boccanegra, Traviata;* WAGNER: *Fliegende Holländer, Lohengrin;* WEBER: *Freischütz,* WEILL: *Aufstieg und Fall der Stadt Mahagonny;* WERLE: *Dream of Thérèse.* Conducted major orch in Europe, USA/Canada. Teaches. **Res:** Wolfgangstr 24, Frankfurt/Main, FR Ger. Mgmt: ARM/FRG.

MUNDT, RICHARD. Bass. American. Born 8 Sep 1936, Chicago. Single. Studied: Alfredo Gandolfi, New York; Acad of Music, Prof Hitz, Vienna; Agnate Mundt (mother), Woodstock, NY, USA. **Debut:** Commendatore (*Don Giovanni*) Saarbrücken Opera 1962. Previous occupations: real estate; hotel-restaurant mgr.
    Sang with major companies in AUS: Graz; BEL: Liège; CAN: Montreal/Quebec, Ottawa, Toronto; DEN: Copenhagen; FR GER: Darmstadt, Dortmund, Kiel, Saarbrücken; ITA: Spoleto Fest; USA: Chicago, Cincinnati, New York City Opera,

Portland, San Francisco Opera & Spring Opera. **Roles with these companies incl** BEETHOVEN: Rocco (*Fidelio*); DEBUSSY: Arkel (*Pelléas et Mélisande*); MOZART: Don Giovanni★, Osmin★ (*Entführung aus dem Serail*), Figaro★ (*Nozze di Figaro*), Don Pippo★ (*Oca del Cairo*), Sarastro★ (*Zauberflöte*); PUCCINI: Colline★ (*Bohème*); ROSSINI: Don Basilio★ (*Barbiere di Siviglia*), Macrobio (*Pietra del paragone*); SMETANA: Kezal★ (*Bartered Bride*); STRAUSS, R: Orest (*Elektra*); VERDI: Ramfis (*Aida*), Philip II★ (*Don Carlo*), Padre Guardiano (*Forza del destino*); WAGNER: Daland (*Fliegende Holländer*), König Heinrich (*Lohengrin*), Pogner (*Meistersinger*), Fasolt (*Rheingold*), Hunding (*Walküre*), Landgraf (*Tannhäuser*), König Marke (*Tristan und Isolde*). Appears with symphony orchestra. **Res:** c/o Ernst Rieser, PO Box 2872, New York, NY 10001, USA.

MUNN, THOMAS JOHN. Scenic designer for opera, theater & ballet. Is a lighting designer; also a media designer. American. Resident designer, Mary Anthony Dance Theatre. Born 24 Mar 1944, New Britain, CT. Wife Susan Patton, occupation mgr, Lake George Opera Fest. Studied: Boston Univ School Fine & Applied Arts, Horace Armistead, Raymond Sovey. **Operatic debut:** *Zauberflöte* Lake George Fest, Glens Falls, NY 1974. Theater debut: Golden Theater, New York 1970. Previous occupation: tech dir & electrician; taught Columbia Univ 1969-72.
    Designed for major companies in HOL: Amsterdam; USA: Kansas City, Lake George, Minneapolis. **Operas designed for these companies incl** MOZART: *Zauberflöte★;* PUCCINI: *Tosca★;* ROSSINI: *Barbiere di Siviglia★;* STRAUSS, J: *Fledermaus★;* VERDI: *Macbeth★, Rigoletto★, Traviata★;* WARD: *Crucible★.* Operatic world premieres: lighting, BERNARDO: *Child* Lake George Opera Fest 1974. **Res:** 250 W 85 St, New York 10024, USA.

MURRAY, MATTHEW H. Lyric baritone. American. Born Minneapolis, MN, USA. Married. Studied: Manhattan School of Music, John Brownlee, New York; Carmine Gagliardi, New York. **Debut:** Escamillo (*Carmen*) Minnesota Opera Co 1964. Awards: Reg Winner, Singer of the Year, NATS; Schubert Club Awd, Minneapolis, USA.
    Sang with major companies in USA: Boston, Dallas, Minneapolis, New York City Opera, Omaha, St Paul. **Roles with these companies incl** DONIZETTI: Dott Malatesta★ (*Don Pasquale*); MENOTTI: Bob★ (*Old Maid and the Thief*); MOZART: Guglielmo★ (*Così fan tutte*), Conte Almaviva★ (*Nozze di Figaro*), Papageno★ (*Zauberflöte*); PUCCINI: Marcello★ (*Bohème*), Sharpless★ (*Butterfly*); ROSSINI: Figaro★ & Dott Bartolo★ (*Barbiere di Siviglia*); VERDI: Germont★ (*Traviata*). Also NIELSEN: Leonard (*Maskarade*); BAKSA: The Father (*Red Carnations*); MORGENSTERN: Doc Stayer (*Haircut*). Appears with symphony orchestra. Gives recitals. Teaches voice. Coaches repertoire. Mgmt: LCA/USA.

MURRAY, WILLIAM BRUCE. Lyric baritone. American. Resident mem: Deutsche Oper, Berlin; Bayerische Staatsoper, Munich. Born 13 Mar 1935, Schenectady, NY, USA. Wife Nancy Lee, occupation teacher. Three children. Studied: Adelphi Univ, Mme Karin Branzell, New York; L Ricci, S Bertelli, Rome: Fr Herta Kalcher, Stuttgart. **Debut:** Scarpia (*Tosca*) Detmold Landestheater, FR Ger 1960. Previous occupations: music teacher. Awards: Fulbright Fllshp for Rome.

Sang with major companies in AUS: Vienna Staatsoper; BEL: Brussels; FR GER: Berlin Deutsche Oper, Bonn, Cologne, Dortmund, Düsseldorf-Duisburg, Frankfurt, Hamburg, Hannover, Mannheim, Munich Staatsoper, Stuttgart; HOL: Amsterdam; ITA: Milan La Scala; SPA: Barcelona; SWI: Geneva; USA: New York City Opera. **Roles with these companies incl** BIZET: Escamillo (*Carmen*), Zurga (*Pêcheurs de perles*); CIMAROSA: Count Robinson (*Matrimonio segreto*); DALLAPICCOLA: Ulisse; DEBUSSY: Siméon (*Enfant prodigue*); DONIZETTI: Dott Malatesta (*Don Pasquale*), Belcore (*Elisir*), Enrico (*Lucia*); GLUCK: Agamemnon (*Iphigénie en Aulide*); LEONCAVALLO: Tonio★ (*Pagliacci*); MENOTTI: Bob (*Old Maid and the Thief*); MOZART: Guglielmo (*Così fan tutte*), Don Giovanni★, Conte Almaviva★ & Figaro (*Nozze di Figaro*); NICOLAI: Fluth (*Lustigen Weiber*); ORFF: Kreon★ (*Antigonae*); PAISIELLO: Teodoro★ (*Re Teodoro in Venezia*); PONCHIELLI: Barnaba (*Gioconda*); PUCCINI: Marcello★ (*Bohème*), Sharpless (*Butterfly*), Lescaut★ (*Manon Lescaut*), Scarpia (*Tosca*); ROSSINI: Figaro★ (*Barbiere di Siviglia*), Slook★ (*Cambiale di matrimonio*), Conte Asdrubal (*Pietra del paragone*), Poeta★ (*Turco in Italia*); STRAUSS, R: Olivier (*Capriccio*); TCHAIKOVSKY: Yeletsky (*Pique Dame*); VERDI: Renato★ (*Ballo in maschera*), Rodrigo★ (*Don Carlo*), Ford★ (*Falstaff*), Don Carlo★ (*Forza del destino*), Macbeth, Rigoletto★, Germont★ (*Traviata*), Conte di Luna★ (*Trovatore*), Monforte (*Vespri*); WAGNER: Amfortas★ (*Parsifal*), Wolfram★ (*Tannhäuser*); WOLF-FERRARI: Conte Gil (*Segreto di Susanna*). Also d'ALBERT: Arcesius (*Toten Augen*); EGK: Peer Gynt; FORTNER: Leonardo (*Bluthochzeit*); GOUNOD: Valentin (*Faust*); HAYDN: Lindoro (*Pescatrici*), Ernesto (*Mondo della luna*); ORFF: Prometheus; SCHUMANN: Siegfried (*Genoveva*); STRAUSS, R: Harlekin (*Ariadne auf Naxos*). **World premieres:** NABOKOV: King (*Love's Labour's Lost*) Deutsche Oper Berlin in Brussels 1973; MIHALOVICI: Zwillinge (*Jumeaux*) Braunschweig, FR Ger 1963; YUN: Sim (*Sim Tjong*) Bayerische Staatsoper, Munich 1972. Gives recitals. Appears with symphony orchestra. **Res:** Hilsst_ig 27, 1 Berlin 37, FR Ger. Mgmt: SMD/FRG.

MUSSER, THARON. Lighting designer for opera, theater & ballet; she is also a theater & audit lighting consultant. American. Staff Lighting Designer, Dallas Civic Opera, TX; Greater Miami Opera Co, FL and at Mark Taper Forum, Center Theatre Group, Los Angeles. Born 8 Jan 1925, Roanoke, VA. Single. Studied: Berea Coll, KY; Yale Drama School, CT. **Operatic debut:** *Trouble in Tahiti* Brandeis Arts Fest, Waltham, MA 1952. Theater debut: Broadway theater, New York 1956. Awards: two Los Angeles Drama Critics Awds 1970, '72; Tony Awd 1971; three Tony

Awd nominations; Disting Alumnus Awd, Berea Coll 1973.

Designed for major companies in USA: Dallas, Miami. **Operas designed for these companies incl** BEETHOVEN: *Fidelio★*; BERNSTEIN: *Trouble in Tahiti*; BIZET: *Pêcheurs de perles★*; BRITTEN: *Turn of the Screw*; DONIZETTI: *Lucia★, Lucrezia Borgia★*; GIORDANO: *Andrea Chénier★, Fedora*; ORFF: *Carmina burana*; PUCCINI: *Butterfly, Tabarro*; STRAUSS, R: *Ariadne auf Naxos*; THOMAS: *Mignon★*; WAGNER: *Fliegende Holländer★*. Also PIZZETTI: *Assassinio nella cattedrale*. **Operatic world premieres:** BERNSTEIN: *Trouble in Tahiti* Brandeis Arts Fest, Waltham, USA 1952. **Res:** 21 Cornelia St, New York, USA.

MUTI, RICCARDO. Conductor of opera and symphony. Italian. Resident Cond, Maggio Musicale Fiorentino, Florence. Also Principal Cond, New Philharmonia Orchestra, London. Born 28 Jul 1941, Naples. Wife Maria Cristina. Two children. Studied: Consv San Pietro a Maiella, Naples; Consv Giuseppe Verdi, Milan; incl piano, violin. Plays the piano. **Operatic debut:** *Masnadieri* Maggio Musicale, Florence 1969. Symphonic debut: RAI, Milan 1967. Awards: Guido Cantelli Intl Compt 1967; Golden Tuning Fork 1969; Illica-Giacosa Prize 1971; Citation Accad di S Cecilia Rome 1974.

Conducted with major companies in AUS: Salzburg Fest, Vienna Staatsoper; ITA: Florence Maggio & Comunale, Naples. **Operas with these companies incl** BELLINI: *Puritani*; DONIZETTI: *Don Pasquale★, Rita*; LEONCAVALLO: *Pagliacci★*; MASCAGNI: *Cavalleria rusticana★*; MEYERBEER: *Africaine★*; ROSSINI: *Guillaume Tell★*; SPONTINI: *Agnese di Hohenstaufen★*; VERDI: *Aida★‡*, Attila★, *Ballo in maschera‡, Forza del destino★, Macbeth★, Masnadieri★*. Recorded for HMV. Conducted major orch in Europe, USA/Canada, Asia. **Res:** Ravenna, Italy. Mgmt: CAM/USA.

MÜTZEL, MANFRED. Stages/produces opera, theater. German. Intendant & Resident Stage Dir, Theater & Oper, Trier. Born 20 May 1943, Darmstadt. Wife Gertie Charlent, occupation opera & concert singer. Studied: music. **Operatic debut:** FORTNER: *Don Perlimplin* Städt Bühnen Münster, FR Ger 1974.

Directed/produced opera for major companies in FR GER: Darmstadt, Frankfurt, Hannover. **Operas staged with these companies incl** LEONCAVALLO: *Pagliacci★*; LORTZING: *Wildschütz★*; MOZART: *Finta giardiniera★*; NICOLAI: *Lustigen Weiber★*; OFFENBACH: *Contes d'Hoffmann★*; ORFF: *Kluge★*; RAVEL: *Heure espagnole★*.

MYERS, RAYMOND. Dramatic baritone. Australian. Resident mem: Australian Opera, Sydney. Born 1 Jul 1938, Sydney. Wife Renée Goossens. One son. Studied: Florence Taylor, Sydney; Luigi Ricci, Rome. **Debut:** Fernando (*Fidelio*) Australian Opera 1963. Awards: Verdi d'oro, Parma, Italy; Sun Aria Awd, Melbourne; Shell Aria Awd, Canberra.

Sang with major companies in AUSTRL: Sydney; BEL: Brussels; ITA: Milan La Scala, Parma,

Spoleto Fest; UK: Cardiff Welsh, Edinburgh Fest, Glasgow Scottish, Glyndebourne Fest, London English National; USA: New York City Opera. **Roles with these companies incl** BEETHOVEN: Don Pizarro★ (*Fidelio*); BERG: Wozzeck; BERLIOZ: Balducci (*Benvenuto Cellini*); BIZET: Escamillo★ (*Carmen*); GOUNOD: Méphistophélès (*Faust*); LEONCAVALLO: Tonio★ (*Pagliacci*); MASSENET: Albert (*Werther*); MOZART: Figaro (*Nozze di Figaro*); OFFENBACH: Coppélius etc (*Contes d'Hoffmann*); PAISIELLO: Figaro (*Barbiere di Siviglia*); PUCCINI: Marcello (*Bohème*), Gianni Schicchi, Sharpless (*Butterfly*), Scarpia★ (*Tosca*); RAVEL: Ramiro (*Heure espagnole*); ROSSINI: Figaro★ (*Barbiere di Siviglia*), Assur (*Semiramide*); SAINT-SAENS: Grand prêtre (*Samson et Dalila*); VERDI: Amonasro★ (*Aida*), Renato★ (*Ballo in maschera*), Rodrigo★ (*Don Carlo*), Don Carlo (*Forza del destino*), Nabucco, Rigoletto★, Germont (*Traviata*), Conte di Luna (*Trovatore*); WAGNER: Holländer, Alberich (*Rheingold*★, *Götterdämmerung*★), Wolfram★ (*Tannhäuser*). **World premieres:** GIANNINI: Truffaldino (*Servant of Two Masters*) New York City Opera 1967. Recorded for: Decca. Video/Film: Count Agenor (*Violins of St Jacques*); Napoleon (*War and Peace*). Gives recitals. Appears with symphony orchestra. Teaches voice. Coaches repertoire. On faculty of Consv of Music, Sydney. **Res:** Sydney, Australia and London, UK. Mgmt: AIM/UK.

N

NACCARATO, JOHN THOMAS. Scenic and costume designer for opera, theater, film, television. Is a lighting designer, stage director; also a painter, illustrator, architect & fashion designer. American. Born 11 Nov 1938, Los Angeles, CA, USA. Single. Studied: Pasadena Playhouse, CA; UCLA; Polakov Studio, Art Students League, New York. Prof training: R L Grosh & Sons, Los Angeles, design studio. **Operatic debut:** sets & cost, *Rigoletto* Pasadena Op 1963. Theater debut: Pasadena Playhouse 1960. Previous occupation: interior designer, fashion designer. Previous adm positions in opera: Head of Prod, Seattle Opera & Pasadena Opera.

Designed for major companies in CAN: Montreal/Quebec, Toronto, Vancouver; USA: Cincinnati, Dallas, Fort Worth, Hawaii, Houston, Lake George, Minneapolis, Omaha, Pittsburgh, Portland, St Paul, San Antonio, San Diego, Seattle, Washington DC. **Operas designed for these companies incl** BIZET: *Carmen;* BOITO: *Mefistofele;* DONIZETTI: *Fille du régiment, Lucia;* GOUNOD: *Roméo et Juliette;* LEONCAVALLO: *Pagliacci;* MASCAGNI: *Cavalleria rusticana;* MASSENET: *Werther;* MENOTTI: *Consul, Medium;* MOZART: *Così fan tutte, Don Giovanni, Schauspieldirektor, Zauberflöte;* MUSSORGSKY: *Boris Godunov;* OFFENBACH: *Contes d'Hoffmann, Périchole;* PUCCINI: *Bohème, Gianni Schicchi, Butterfly, Manon Lescaut, Tosca;* ROSSINI: *Barbiere di Siviglia;* STRAUSS, J: *Fledermaus;* STRAVINSKY: *Rake's Progress;* TCHAIKOVSKY: *Eugene Onegin;* VERDI: *Aida, Ballo in maschera, Don Carlo, Otello, Rigoletto, Traviata;* WAGNER: *Meistersinger, Rheingold, Walküre, Siegfried, Götterdämmerung, Tannhäuser.* **Operatic world premieres:** PASATIERI: *Black Widow* Seattle Opera, WA 1972. Exhibitions of stage designs & costumes Seattle 1974; Los Angeles 1965. Teaches. **Res:** 901 Sylvanoak Dr, Glendale, CA 91206, USA.

NAGANO, YONAKO. Lyric mezzo-soprano. Japanese. Resident mem: Niki Kai Opera, Tokyo. Born 17 Jul 1933, Tokyo. Husband Hiroshi Wakasugi, occupation conductor. Studied: Ryosuke Hatanaka, Tokyo; Herbert Brauer, Mrs Michi Kowa, Berlin. **Debut:** Athène (*Orestie*) Deutsche Oper, Berlin 1962. Awards: Grand Prix of Arts Festival, Ministry of Culture.

Sang with major companies in FR GER: Berlin Deutsche Oper; JPN: Tokyo Niki Kai. **Roles with these companies incl** HANDEL: Cornelia⋆ (*Giulio Cesare*); MOZART: Dorabella (*Così fan tutte*), Cherubino (*Nozze di Figaro*); PUCCINI: Suzuki (*Butterfly*); STRAUSS, J: Prinz Orlovsky (*Fledermaus*); STRAUSS, R: Komponist⋆ (*Ariadne auf Naxos*); WAGNER: Kundry⋆ (*Parsifal*), Fricka (*Rheingold⋆, Walküre⋆*). Also BEETHOVEN: Leonore (*Fidelio*). **World premieres:** MILHAUD: Athène (*Orestie*) Deutsche Oper, Berlin 1963. Gives recitals. Appears with symphony orchestra. Teaches voice. On faculty of Toho-gakuen Univ, assoc prof; Tokyo Univ of Arts, lecturer. **Res:** Kakinokizaka 2-26-17 Meguroku, Tokyo, Japan.

NAGY, ROBERT DAVID. Dramatic tenor & Heldentenor. American. Resident mem: Metropolitan Opera, New York. Born 3 Mar 1929, Lorain, O, USA. Wife Vincenza. Three children. Studied: Cleveland Inst of Music, O, USA. **Debut:** Giuseppe (*Traviata*) Metropolitan Opera 1957. Awards: Weyerhaeuser Awd, Met Op Ntl Counc Aud 1956.

Sang with major companies in CAN: Montreal/Quebec; SWI: Geneva; USA: Baltimore, Cincinnati, Fort Worth, New Orleans, New York Met & City Opera, Omaha, Philadelphia Lyric, Portland, San Diego, San Francisco Opera, Seattle. **Roles with these companies incl** BEETHOVEN: Florestan (*Fidelio*); BERG: Tambourmajor (*Wozzeck*); BIZET: Don José (*Carmen*); BOITO: Faust (*Mefistofele*); BRITTEN: Peter Grimes; FLOYD: Sam Polk (*Susannah*); GIORDANO: Andrea Chénier; GOUNOD: Faust; HALEVY: Eléazar (*Juive*); LEONCAVALLO: Canio (*Pagliacci*); MUSSORGSKY: Shuisky (*Boris Godunov*); PUCCINI: Dick Johnson (*Fanciulla del West*), Pinkerton (*Butterfly*), Ruggero (*Rondine*), Luigi (*Tabarro*), Cavaradossi (*Tosca*), Calaf (*Turandot*); SAINT-SAENS: Samson; STRAUSS, J: Alfred (*Fledermaus*); STRAUSS, R: Matteo (*Arabella*), Bacchus (*Ariadne auf Naxos*), Leukippos & Apollo (*Daphne*), Aegisth (*Elektra*), Kaiser (*Frau ohne Schatten*), Ein Sänger (*Rosenkavalier*), Herodes (*Salome*); TCHAIKOVSKY: Gherman (*Pique Dame*); VERDI: Radames (*Aida*), Otello, Duca di Mantova (*Rigoletto*), Alfredo (*Traviata*), Manrico (*Trovatore*); WAGNER: Erik (*Fliegende*

Holländer), Lohengrin, Siegmund (*Walküre*); WE-BER: Max (*Freischütz*). Mgmt: LLF/USA.

NAKAYAMA, TEIICHI. Japanese. Gen Dir, Niki Kai Opera, 1-58-13 Yoyogi Shibuya-ku, Tokyo. In charge of art policy. Is also a baritone. Additional administrative position: Exec Dir, Japan Federation of Musicians, Tokyo. Born 6 Feb 1920, Oita. Wife Yasuko, occupation prof. Studied: Tokyo Music Coll; Musikhochschule, Munich. Plays the piano. Previous occupations: Prof, Tokyo Univ of Arts. Started with present company as Bd Chmn. Awards: Arts Festival Awd, Japanese Gvnmt; Mainichi Music Prize, Mainichi Newspaper Co. **Res:** 1-25-12 Sendagaya Shibuya-ku, Tokyo, Japan.

NAKAZAWA, KATSURA. Lyric soprano. Japanese. Resident mem: Niki Kai, Tokyo. Born 23 Nov 1933, Halpin, China. Husband Yotsuo Koyama, occupation mandolin player. Studied: Matabe Kita, Mutsumu Shibata, Tokyo. **Debut:** Gilda (*Rigoletto*) Niki Kai, Tokyo 1959. Awards: Third Prize Prague Spring Intl Compt 1956.
Sang with major companies in JPN: Tokyo Niki Kai. **Roles with these companies incl** BIZET: Micaëla* (*Carmen*); DVORAK: Rusalka; MOZART: Donna Anna (*Don Giovanni*), Susanna (*Nozze di Figaro*), Königin der Nacht (*Zauberflöte*); OFFENBACH: Antonia* (*Contes d'Hoffmann*); PUCCINI: Cio-Cio-San* (*Butterfly*), Tosca*; STRAUSS, J: Adele* (*Fledermaus*); STRAVINSKY: Anne Trulove (*Rake's Progress*); VERDI: Gilda* (*Rigoletto*), Violetta (*Traviata*); WAGNER: Venus (*Tannhäuser*). Also SHIMIZU: Kaede (*Shuzenji-monogatari*); DAN: Tsu (*Yuzuru*). Gives recitals. Appears with symphony orchestra. Teaches voice. On faculty of Tokyo Music Coll, assoc prof. **Res:** Nakameguro l-l-i7, 1002, Meguroku, Tokyo, Japan.

NANNI, FIORAVANTI DOMENICO. Italian. Gen Secy, Teatro alla Scala, V Filodrammatici 2, Milan, Italy. In charge of adm matters. Born 21 May 1934, Nardò/Lecce, Italy. Wife Giannina, occupation teacher. Three children. Studied: law in Bari, Italy. Previous positions primarily administrative. In present position since 1973. **Res:** V Osoppo 3, Milan, Italy.

NAPIER, MARITA; née Jacobs. Dramatic soprano. South African/German. Resident mem: Hamburg Staatsoper. Born Johannesburg, S Afr. Husband Wolfram Assmann, occupation tenor. Studied: Northwest German Music Acad, Prof Th Lindenbaum, Hamburg. **Debut:** Venus (*Tannhäuser*) Bielefeld Opera 1969. Previous occupations: computer programmer.
Sang with major companies in AUS: Vienna Staatsoper; FRA: Bordeaux, Nancy, Rouen; FR GER: Bayreuth Fest, Berlin Deutsche Oper, Bielefeld, Essen, Frankfurt, Hamburg, Hannover, Kassel, Munich Staatsoper, Wuppertal; HOL: Amsterdam; ITA: Milan La Scala; SWI: Geneva; UK: London Royal Opera; USA: Chicago, San Francisco Opera. **Roles with these companies incl** BEETHOVEN: Leonore* (*Fidelio*); GLUCK: Alceste; HANDEL: Romilda* (*Xerxes*); MARTIN: Iseut* (*Vin herbé*); MASCAGNI: Santuzza*

(*Cavalleria rusticana*); MOZART: Fiordiligi* (*Così fan tutte*), Donna Anna* (*Don Giovanni*); PUCCINI: Mimi* (*Bohème*); STRAUSS, R: Ariadne* (*Ariadne auf Naxos*), Chrysothemis* (*Elektra*); TCHAIKOVSKY: Lisa* (*Pique Dame*); VERDI: Aida*, Amelia* (*Ballo in maschera*), Elisabetta* (*Don Carlo*), Leonora* (*Forza del destino*), Lady Macbeth* (*Macbeth*), Abigaille* (*Nabucco*), Leonora* (*Trovatore*); WAGNER: Senta* (*Fliegende Holländer*), Elsa* (*Lohengrin*), Eva* (*Meistersinger*), Sieglinde* & Brünnhilde* (*Walküre*), Gutrune* (*Götterdämmerung*), Elisabeth* & Venus* (*Tannhäuser*); WEBER: Agathe* (*Freischütz*). Also d'ALBERT: Marta (*Tiefland*). Gives recitals. Appears with symphony orchestra. Mgmt: SLZ/FRG; CAM/USA.

NAPOLI, JACOPO. Italian. Artistic Director, Teatro dell'Opera, Piazza Beniamino Gigli, Rome, Italy. In charge of mus matters, and is also a composer. Additional administrative positions: Dir, Consv di Musica di S Cecilia, Rome. Born 26 Aug 1911, Naples. Wife Angela Franco. Three children. Studied: Consv S Pietro a Maiella, Naples. Plays the piano & organ. Previous positions primarily musical: Dir, Consv S Pietro a Maiella, Naples 1954-62; Dir, Consv G Verdi, Milan 1962-72. In present position since 1974. Composed *Dubrowsky II*, Naples 1973; *Masaniello*, La Scala, Milan 1953, and eight other operas. Awards: Naples Prize 1955; Marzotto Prize 1962; Second Prize, Intl Conc G Verdi. Mem of Adm Commtt, Teatro dell'Opera, Rome. **Res:** V dei Graci 18, Rome, Italy.

NAVE, MARIA LUISA. Dramatic coloratura soprano. Italian. Born 28 Jan 1939, Padua, Italy. Single. Studied: Consv B Marcello, Giulietta Simionato, Venice. **Debut:** Fidalma (*Matrimonio segreto*) Teatro Nuovo, Milan 1962.
Sang with major companies in AUS: Vienna Staatsoper; BEL: Brussels; FR GER: Cologne, Frankfurt, Hamburg, Munich Staatsoper; HUN: Budapest; ITA: Bologna, Florence Comunale, Genoa, Naples, Palermo, Parma, Trieste, Turin, Venice, Verona Arena; SPA: Barcelona; SWI: Zurich; USA: Philadelphia Grand, San Francisco Opera. **Roles with these companies incl** BIZET: Carmen*; CILEA: Princesse de Bouillon* (*A. Lecouvreur*); DONIZETTI: Léonore* (*Favorite*); FALLA: Abuela (*Vida breve*); MASSENET: Charlotte (*Werther*); MUSSORGSKY: Marina* (*Boris Godunov*); PONCHIELLI: Laura* (*Gioconda*); ROSSINI: Rosina (*Barbiere di Siviglia*), Angelina* (*Cenerentola*); SAINT-SAENS: Dalila*; VERDI: Amneris* (*Aida*), Eboli* (*Don Carlo*), Preziosilla* (*Forza del destino*), Azucena* (*Trovatore*); WAGNER: Venus (*Tannhäuser*). Gives recitals. Appears with symphony orchestra. **Res:** V Noale 8, Padua, Italy.

NAWE, IZABELLA; née Binek. Coloratura soprano. Polish. Resident mem: Deutsche Staatsoper, Berlin. Born 27 May 1943, Czestochowa, Poland. Husband R Spychalski, occupation singer. Studied: Prof Jadwiga Jezioranska, Katowice, Poland. **Debut:** Gilda (*Rigoletto*) Teatr Wielki, Lodz 1967. Previous occupations: pianist. Awards: Kammersängerin, Deutsche Staatsoper Berlin.

Sang with major companies in AUS: Vienna Staatsoper; BEL: Brussels; FR GER: Hamburg, Munich, Wiesbaden; GER DR: Berlin Staatsoper, Dresden; POL: Lodz, Warsaw; POR: Lisbon; USSR: Tbilisi; USA: San Francisco Opera. Roles with these companies incl DONIZETTI: Norina (*Don Pasquale*); GOUNOD: Marguerite (*Faust*); MOZART: Despina (*Così fan tutte*); Blondchen★ (*Entführung aus dem Serail*), Königin der Nacht★ (*Zauberflöte*); OFFENBACH: Olympia★ (*Contes d'Hoffmann*); ROSSINI: Rosina★ (*Barbiere di Siviglia*); STRAUSS, J: Adele (*Fledermaus*); STRAUSS, R: Zerbinetta★ (*Ariadne auf Naxos*), Sophie★ (*Rosenkavalier*); VERDI: Nannetta (*Falstaff*), Gilda★ (*Rigoletto*). Recorded for: Eterna. Gives recitals. Appears with symphony orchestra. Teaches voice. Coaches repertoire. Res: Pariser Kommune 17, Berlin 1017, Ger DR. Mgmt: PAG/POL; SLZ/FRG.

NEAGU, AURELIAN. Bass. Romanian/Swiss residency. Resident mem: Opernhaus, Zurich. Born 28 Jun 1929, Bucharest. Wife Karin Bannwarth. Studied: Royal Music Acad, Bucharest; Prof Costesco Duca, Romania. Debut: Méphistophélès (*Faust*) Bucharest State Opera 1951. Awards: First Prize, Bel Canto Compt Bucharest, Prague, Sofia & Geneva 1952-55.

Sang with major companies in CZE: Prague National; FR GER: Berlin Deutsche Oper, Cologne, Düsseldorf-Duisburg, Essen, Hamburg, Krefeld, Munich Staatsoper & Gärtnerplatz; ITA: Bologna, Florence Maggio & Comunale, Naples, Palermo; ROM: Bucharest; SWI: Zurich; USSR: Kiev, Moscow Bolshoi; USA: Chicago, New York City Opera. Roles with these companies incl BEETHOVEN: Rocco★ (*Fidelio*); BOITO: Mefistofele; CHERUBINI: Creon★ (*Medea*); FLOTOW: Plunkett (*Martha*); GLINKA: Ivan (*Life for the Tsar*); GOUNOD: Méphistophélès★ (*Faust*); HALEVY: Brogny (*Juive*); MEYERBEER: Marcel (*Huguenots*); MOZART: Leporello (*Don Giovanni*), Figaro (*Nozze di Figaro*); MUSSORGSKY: Boris & Pimen (*Boris Godunov*), Ivan Khovansky & Dosifei (*Khovanshchina*); PUCCINI: Colline (*Bohème*); ROSSINI: Don Basilio (*Barbiere di Siviglia*), Mustafà (*Italiana in Algeri*), Moïse; SMETANA: Kezal (*Bartered Bride*); STRAVINSKY: Tiresias (*Oedipus Rex*); VERDI: Ramfis (*Aida*), Philip II★ (*Don Carlo*), Jacopo Loredano (*Due Foscari*), Silva★ (*Ernani*), Padre Guardiano (*Forza del destino*), Macbeth & Banquo (*Macbeth*), Zaccaria★ (*Nabucco*), Fiesco (*Simon Boccanegra*), Procida★ (*Vespri*); WAGNER: Daland (*Fliegende Holländer*), König Heinrich (*Lohengrin*), Pogner★ (*Meistersinger*), Gurnemanz (*Parsifal*), Fasolt★ (*Rheingold*), Landgraf (*Tannhäuser*), König Marke (*Tristan und Isolde*). Also PUCCINI: Timur (*Turandot*), Geronte (*Manon Lescaut*); MOZART: Commendatore★ (*Don Giovanni*); BORODIN: Kontchak (*Prince Igor*). Appears with symphony orchestra. Res: Seestr 233, Küsnacht/Zurich, Switzerland. Mgmt: TAU/SWI.

NEBLETT, CAROL. Lyric & dramatic soprano. American. Resident mem: New York City Opera. Born 1 Feb 1946, Modesto, CA, USA. Husband Kenneth Schermerhorn, occupation composer, conductor, Music Dir Milwaukee Symph. One son.

Studied: William Vennard, Esther Andreas, Ernest St John Metz, Los Angeles; Lotte Lehmann, Santa Barbara, CA. Debut: Musetta (*Bohème*) New York City Opera 1969. Awards: Young Musicians Fndt, Voice Schlshp.

Sang with major companies in ITA: Turin; SPA: Barcelona; USSR: Kiev, Leningrad, Tbilisi; USA: Baltimore, Boston, Chicago, Cincinnati, Dallas, Fort Worth, Hartford, Houston, Milwaukee Florentine, New Orleans, New York City Opera, Omaha, Philadelphia Grand & Lyric, San Antonio, Washington DC; YUG: Dubrovnik, Zagreb, Belgrade. Roles with these companies incl BEETHOVEN: Leonore (*Fidelio*); BIZET: Micaëla (*Carmen*); BOITO: Margherita★ & Elena (*Mefistofele*); BORODIN: Jaroslavna★ (*Prince Igor*); CHARPENTIER: Louise★; GLUCK: Euridice; GOUNOD: Marguerite (*Faust*); KORNGOLD: Marietta★‡ (*Tote Stadt*); MASSENET: Manon, Thaïs; MONTEVERDI: Poppea★ (*Incoronazione di Poppea*); MOZART: Fiordiligi (*Così fan tutte*), Donna Anna & Donna Elvira (*Don Giovanni*); OFFENBACH: Antonia (*Contes d'Hoffmann*); PUCCINI: Mimi & Musetta (*Bohème*), Minnie (*Fanciulla del West*), Manon Lescaut, Magda (*Rondine*); RIMSKY-KORSAKOV: Reine de Schemakan (*Coq d'or*); ROSSINI: Mathilde (*Guillaume Tell*); STRAUSS, J: Rosalinde (*Fledermaus*); STRAUSS, R: Ariadne★ (*Ariadne auf Naxos*), Chrysothemis (*Elektra*); VERDI: Gilda (*Rigoletto*), Violetta (*Traviata*), Leonora (*Trovatore*); WAGNER: Senta (*Fliegende Holländer*). Recorded for: RCA. Gives recitals. Appears with symphony orchestra. Teaches voice. Coaches repertoire. Res: Milwaukee, WI, USA. Mgmt: CAM/USA; AIM/UK.

NEGRI, ADELAIDA GRACIELA. Spinto & coloratura soprano. Argentinean. Resident mem: Teatro Colón, Buenos Aires. Born 12 Dec 1943, Buenos Aires. Single. Studied: Inst Superior del Teatro Colón, Prof Bernardo Toscano, Buenos Aires; Prof Maria Teresa Pediconi, Rome; London Opera Centre. Debut: Violetta (*Traviata*) La Salle Theatre 1972. Previous occupations: lawyer. Awards: Shell Prize, Teatro Colón School 1971; British Counc Schlshp 1974.

Sang with major companies in ARG: Buenos Aires. Roles with these companies incl BEETHOVEN: Leonore★ (*Fidelio*); DONIZETTI: Rita★‡; MOZART: Donna Anna★ & Donna Elvira★ (*Don Giovanni*); PUCCINI: Cio-Cio-San★ (*Butterfly*), Liù★ (*Turandot*); VERDI: Elisabetta★ (*Don Carlo*), Violetta★ (*Traviata*), Leonora★ (*Trovatore*). Video/Film: Rita. Gives recitals. Appears with symphony orchestra. Res: Isabel la Católica 389, Buenos Aires, Argentina. Mgmt: IWL/UK.

NEGRI, GIUSEPPE. Italian. Pres, Teatro Regio, Via Garibaldi, Parma, Italy; also of Orch Sinfonica Stabile Regionale Emilia-Romagna. In charge of admin & artistic matters. Born 29 Feb 1920, Parma. Married. Studied: Univ of Parma; chemistry & pharmacology. Started in present position in 1956. Res: V Paggeria 22, Parma, Italy.

NEILL, WILLIAM: né John William Neill. Tenor. American. Wife Dixie Ross, occupation coach-accomp, rehearsal pianist Met Opera. One child. Studied: Univ of Texas, Prof Willa Stewart, Austin; Joseph Frank Pouhe, New York. **Debut:** Steuermann (*Fliegende Holländer*) Bühnen der Stadt Essen 1968. Awards: San Francisco Opera Aud, Gropper Awd; Met Op Southwest Reg Aud, First Place; Friday Morning Music Club, Washington DC, Intl Compt, First Place; Singer of the Year, Second Place; Shreveport, LA, Symph Young Artist Compt, First Place; M B Rockefeller Fund Grant, 2 yrs.

Sang with major companies in BEL: Brussels; FR GER: Essen; HOL: Amsterdam; USA: Boston, Houston, Lake George, Minneapolis, New York City Opera, Portland, St Paul, San Francisco Opera & Spring Opera, Washington DC. **Roles with these companies incl** BIZET: Don José★ (*Carmen*); FLOYD: Lennie★ (*Of Mice and Men*); GOUNOD: Faust★; JANACEK: Albert Gregor (*Makropoulos Affair*); KORNGOLD: Paul★ (*Tote Stadt*); MONTEVERDI: Nero★ (*Incoronazione di Poppea*); MOZART: Tamino (*Zauberflöte*); OFFENBACH: Hoffmann★; PROKOFIEV: Pierre★ (*War and Peace*); PUCCINI: Pinkerton★ (*Butterfly*), Cavaradossi★ (*Tosca*); STRAUSS, R: Herodes★ (*Salome*); VERDI: Alfredo★ (*Traviata*); WAGNER: Walther v d Vogelweide★ (*Tannhäuser*); WEILL: Jim Mahoney★ (*Aufstieg und Fall der Stadt Mahagonny*). Also MUSSORGSKY: Dimitri (*Boris Godunov*). **World premieres:** MADERNA: Trimalchio (*Satyricon*) Amsterdam Opera 1973; GESSNER/BALK: Henri Faust (*Faust Counter Faust*) Minneapolis Opera 1971. Video — Netherlands TV: Trimalchio (*Satyricon*). Gives recitals. Appears with symphony orchestra. **Res:** 780 Riverside Dr, New York, NY, USA. Mgmt: SHA/USA.

NELSON, HOWARD D. Lyric baritone. American. Resident mem: Opernhaus Zurich. Born 31 Mar 1930, Devils Lake, ND, USA. Wife Hazel. Studied: Fresno State Coll, Vern Delaney, CA; Univ of Washington, August Werner, Dr Stanley Chapple, Seattle, WA; William Miller, Urbana, IL, USA. **Debut:** Valentin (*Faust*) Opernhaus Zurich 1967. Previous occupations: professional portrait photographer; univ and coll music prof. Awards: First Place San Francisco Op Aud 1960; First Prize American Op Aud, Chicago.

Sang with major companies in FRA: Bordeaux; FR GER: Cologne; SWI: Basel, Geneva, Zurich; USA: Seattle. **Roles with these companies incl** DONIZETTI: Nottingham★ (*Roberto Devereux*); HENZE: Tartaglia (*König Hirsch*); JANACEK: Harasta (*Cunning Little Vixen*); LORTZING: Graf Eberbach (*Wildschütz*); MASSENET: Lescaut (*Manon*); MOZART: Guglielmo★ (*Così fan tutte*), Don Giovanni★, Conte Almaviva★ (*Nozze di Figaro*); PUCCINI: Marcello (*Bohème*), Sharpless★ (*Butterfly*), Lescaut★ (*Manon Lescaut*); STRAUSS, R: Olivier (*Capriccio*); TCHAIKOVSKY: Yeletsky★ (*Pique Dame*); VERDI: Germont★ (*Traviata*); WAGNER: Wolfram★ (*Tannhäuser*); WOLF: Tio Lukas★ (*Corregidor*). Also BEETHOVEN: Don Fernando (*Fidelio*); FORTNER: Leicester★ (*Elisabeth Tudor*); GOUNOD: Valentin (*Faust*); HANDEL: Otto (*Agrippina*); KLEBE: Count Almaviva★ (*Figaro lässt sich scheiden*); STRAUSS, R: Harlekin (*Ariadne auf Naxos*), Faninal★ (*Rosenkavalier*); WOLF-FERRARI: Mylord Runebif★ (*Vedova scaltra*). Gives recitals. Appears with symphony orchestra.

Teaches voice. **Res:** Gorwiden 14, Zurich 8057, Switzerland. Mgmt: SLZ/FRG.

NELSON, JANE; née M Jane Wright. Coloratura soprano. American. Resident mem: Nationaltheater, Mannheim. Born 20 May, Pittsburgh, PA, USA. Single. Studied: Carolina Segrera Holden, New York; Stadttheater Koblenz, FR Ger. **Debut:** Cenerentola, sop vers, Koblenz 1970. Awards: Finalist Met Op Ntl Counc Aud 1972; First Prize Viotti Compt, Italy 1974; Rockefeller & Sullivan Fndts Awds.

Sang with major companies in FR GER: Mannheim. **Roles with these companies incl** DONIZETTI: Lucia, Norina (*Don Pasquale*); FLOTOW: Lady Harriet★ (*Martha*); JANACEK: Vixen★ (*Cunning Little Vixen*); LORTZING: Baronin Freimann★ (*Wildschütz*); MOZART: Zerlina★ (*Don Giovanni*), Konstanze & Blondchen★ (*Entführung aus dem Serail*), Susanna★ (*Nozze di Figaro*), Königin der Nacht★ (*Zauberflöte*); PUCCINI: Musetta★ (*Bohème*); STRAUSS, R: Zerbinetta (*Ariadne auf Naxos*), Sophie (*Rosenkavalier*); VERDI: Nannetta★ (*Falstaff*), Gilda (*Rigoletto*); WEBER: Aennchen★ (*Freischütz*). Gives recitals. Appears with symphony orchestra. **Res:** 220 E 63 St, New York, NY 10021. Mgmt: NAP/USA; SLZ/FRG.

NELSON, JOHN. Conductor of opera and symphony; composer. American. Mus Dir, Nashville Symph, TN, USA. Born 6 Dec 1941, San José, Costa Rica. Wife Anita. Two children. Studied: Wheaton Coll, Consv of Music, IL; Juilliard School, Jean Morel, New York; Julius Herford; incl piano and voice. Plays the piano. Operatic training as asst cond & chorus master at American Opera Center, Juilliard 1965-68. **Operatic debut:** *Don Pasquale* Juilliard Opera Theater, New York 1968. Symphonic debut: Mostly Mozart Fest, New York 1967. Awards: Irving Berlin Conducting Awd, Juilliard School. Previous adm positions: Mus Dir, Greenwich Philharmonic Orch 1966-75, Pro Arte Chorale 1965-75; Founder/Dir, Aspen Choral Inst 1968-73.

Conducted with major companies in SWI: Geneva; USA: Miami, New York Met & City Opera, Santa Fe. **Operas with these companies incl** BEETHOVEN: Fidelio★; BERLIOZ: Damnation de Faust★, Troyens★; BRITTEN: Owen Wingrave★; DONIZETTI: Don Pasquale, Rita; FALLA: Vida breve; JANACEK: Jenufa; LEONCAVALLO: Pagliacci★; MASCAGNI: Cavalleria rusticana★; MONTEVERDI: Incoronazione di Poppea★; MOZART: Idomeneo★; MUSSORGSKY: Boris Godunov★; ORFF: Carmina burana★; PUCCINI: Bohème★, Tosca★; ROSSINI: Barbiere di Siviglia★. Conducted major orch in Europe, USA/Canada, Cent/S America. **Res:** Bogota, NJ, USA. Mgmt: CAM/USA; HLT/UK.

NEMETH, CARL. Austrian. Int, Vereinigte Bühnen Graz/Opernhaus Graz, Kaiser Josef Platz 10, A 8010 Graz 1972-80; also Schauspielhaus. In charge of overall adm matters, art policy, mus, dram & tech matters, finances. Is also a st dir for opera & theater. Born 11 Jan 1926, Vienna. Wife Christa Maurer von Kronegg. Studied: Univ, Vienna. Plays the violin. Previous occupation: asst tchr, Univ of Vienna. Form position adm, musical & theatrical: Dir, Art Dept, Volksoper, Vienna 1963-72. Awards: Theodor Körner Prize. Mem of Dir, Steirischer Herbst Festival. **Res:** Straucherg 12a, 8020 Graz, Austria.

NENTWIG, FRANZ FERDINAND. Dramatic baritone & bass-baritone. German. Resident mem: Staatstheater, Hannover; Staatstheater, Darmstadt; Volksoper, Vienna. Born 23 Aug 1929, Duisburg. Divorced. Two children. **Debut:** Ottokar (*Freischütz*) Stadttheater, Bielefeld 1962. Previous occupations: sculptor; asst stage dir.
  Sang with major companies in AUS: Graz, Vienna Volksoper; FR GER: Bielefeld, Cologne, Darmstadt, Düsseldorf, Frankfurt, Essen, Hamburg, Hannover, Karlsruhe, Krefeld, Mannheim, Stuttgart, Wuppertal; GER DR: Berlin Komische Oper. **Roles with these companies incl** BARTOK: Bluebeard★; BEETHOVEN: Don Pizarro★ (*Fidelio*); BIZET: Escamillo★ (*Carmen*); KODALY: Háry János★; LEONCAVALLO: Tonio★ (*Pagliacci*); MASCAGNI: Alfio★ (*Cavalleria rusticana*); MOZART: Don Alfonso★ (*Così fan tutte*), Conte Almaviva★ (*Nozze di Figaro*); PUCCINI: Scarpia★ (*Tosca*); STRAUSS, R: Mandryka★ (*Arabella*), Jochanaan★ (*Salome*); VERDI: Amonasro★ (*Aida*), Nabucco★, Rigoletto★; WAGNER: Holländer★, Wotan (*Rheingold★, Walküre★*), Wanderer★ (*Siegfried*), Gunther★ (*Götterdämmerung*). Also FUESSEL: Chanaan (*Dybbuk*); BRAUNFELS: Prometheus (*Vögel*). Teaches voice. **Res:** Bergstr 25, Ronnenberg 3, FR Ger. Mgmt: ARM/FRG; RAB/AUS.

NERALIC, TOMISLAV. Bass-baritone. Yugoslavian. Resident mem: Deutsche Oper, Berlin. Born 9 Dec 1917, Karlovac, Yugoslavia. Wife Ada. One child. Studied: Prof Lav Vrbanic, Zagreb. **Debut:** Frate (*Don Carlo*) Zagreb Opera 1939. Awards: Kammersänger, Berlin 1963; Critics Awd, Berlin; National Prize, Yugoslavia.
  Sang with major companies in AUS: Graz, Vienna Staatsoper & Volksoper; BEL: Brussels; CZE: Brno, Prague Smetana; FRA: Bordeaux, Strasbourg, Toulouse; GRE: Athens Fest; FR GER: Berlin Deutsche Oper, Cologne, Düsseldorf-Duisburg, Frankfurt, Hamburg, Hannover, Munich Staatsoper, Stuttgart, Wiesbaden; GER DR: Berlin Staatsoper; HOL: Amsterdam; ITA: Bologna, Florence Maggio & Comunale, Genoa, Milan La Scala, Naples, Palermo, Parma, Rome Opera, Trieste, Turin, Venice; MEX: Mexico City, MON: Monte Carlo; POR: Lisbon; SPA: Barcelona; SWI: Basel, Geneva, Zurich; USA: Chicago, Washington DC; YUG: Dubrovnik, Zagreb, Belgrade. **Roles with these companies incl** d'ALBERT: Sebastiano & Tommaso (*Tiefland*); BARTOK: Bluebeard★; BEETHOVEN: Don Pizarro★ & Rocco★ (*Fidelio*); BERLIOZ: Méphistophélès (*Damnation de Faust*); BORODIN: Prince Igor★ & Galitzky★ (*Prince Igor*); CHERUBINI: Creon (*Medea*); DELIBES: Nilakantha (*Lakmé*); DONIZETTI: Dulcamara (*Elisir*); FLOTOW: Plunkett (*Martha*); GLINKA: Ivan (*Life for the Tsar*); GOUNOD: Méphistophélès (*Faust*); HANDEL: Ptolemy (*Giulio Cesare*); HENZE: Tartaglia (*König Hirsch/Re Cervo*); MOZART: Don Giovanni; MUSSORGSKY: Boris & Varlaam★ & Pimen★ (*Boris Godunov*); OFFENBACH: Coppélius etc★

(*Contes d'Hoffmann*); PONCHIELLI: Alvise★ (*Gioconda*); PUCCINI: Colline (*Bohème*), Scarpia★ (*Tosca*); ROSSINI: Don Basilio (*Barbiere di Siviglia*); SHOSTAKOVICH: Boris (*Katerina Ismailova*); SMETANA: Kezal (*Bartered Bride*); STRAUSS, R: Orest (*Elektra*), Barak (*Frau ohne Schatten*), Baron Ochs (*Rosenkavalier*), Jochanaan (*Salome*); STRAVINSKY: Creon★ (*Oedipus Rex*), Nick Shadow (*Rake's Progress*); VERDI: Amonasro★ & Ramfis★ (*Aida*), Philip II★ & Grande Inquisitore★ (*Don Carlo*), Falstaff, Zaccaria★ (*Nabucco*), Iago (*Otello*); WAGNER: Holländer★, König Heinrich (*Lohengrin*), Hans Sachs (*Meistersinger*), Amfortas (*Parsifal*), Wotan (*Rheingold, Walküre*), Wanderer★ (*Siegfried*), Fasolt (*Rheingold*), Gunther (*Götterdämmerung*), Kurwenal★ (*Tristan und Isolde*). Appears with symphony orchestra. **Res:** Carmerstr 18, Berlin, FR Ger.

NESTERENKO, YEVGENI YEVGENIEVICH. Bass. Russian. Resident mem: Bolshoi Theater, Moscow. Born 8 Jan 1938, Moscow. Wife Ekaterina Dmitrievna, occupation geometry teacher, Moscow Tech Inst. Studied: Rimsky-Korsakov Leningrad Consv, Prof Vasilij Lukanin. **Debut:** Gremin (*Eugene Onegin*) Leningrad Maly Opera Theater 1963. Previous occupations: civil engineer. Awards: Second Prize and Silver Medal, Intl Compt of Young Opera Singers, Sofia, Bulgaria 1967; First Prize and Gold Medal, Tchaikovsky Intl Compt Moscow 1970; Honored Artist USSR.
  Sang with major companies in AUS: Vienna Staatsoper; BUL: Sofia; FRA: Nice; FR GER: Wiesbaden; HUN: Budapest; ITA: Milan La Scala; POL: Lodz, Warsaw Teatr Wielki; USSR: Leningrad Kirov, Moscow Bolshoi. **Roles with these companies incl** BOITO: Mefistofele★; BORODIN: Prince Igor★; GLINKA: Ruslan★‡; GOUNOD: Méphistophélès★ (*Faust*); MUSSORGSKY: Boris★ & Varlaam★ (*Boris Godunov*), Dosifei★ (*Khovanshchina*); PROKOFIEV: King of Clubs★ (*Love for Three Oranges*); PUCCINI: Colline★ (*Bohème*); RIMSKY-KORSAKOV: Vassily Sobakin★‡ (*Tsar's Bride*); ROSSINI: Don Basilio★ (*Barbiere di Siviglia*); TCHAIKOVSKY: King René★‡ (*Iolanthe*); VERDI: Ramfis★ (*Aida*), Philip II★ (*Don Carlo*). Also BORODIN: Kontchak (*Prince Igor*); PROKOFIEV: Kutuzov★ (*War and Peace*); RACHMANINOFF: Malatesta★‡ (*Francesca da Rimini*). Recorded for: Melodiya. Film: Kontchak (*Prince Igor*) Lenfilm. Gives recitals. Appears with symphony orchestra. Teaches voice. Coaches repertoire. On faculty of Tchaikovsky Moscow Consv, Dir Dept of Solo Singing. **Res:** val 24 kv 110 ul Frunzenskiy, Moscow, USSR. Mgmt: SOY/USSR; GOS/USSR.

NEUGEBAUER, HANS. Stages/produces opera. Also designs sets & costumes. German. Head of Prod & Resident Stage Dir, Städtische Bühnen, Cologne. Born 17 Nov 1923, Karlsruhe. Wife Martina. Two children. Studied: Akad Henselmann, Mannheim; Kmsg Josef Degler, Hamburg; incl music, piano and voice. Operatic training as asst stage dir at Städt Bühnen, Frankfurt/M 1956-59. **Operatic debut:** *Cavalleria rusticana* Frankfurt/M 1959. Previous occupation: opera singer, bassbaritone. Previous adm positions in opera: Head of Prod, Staatstheater Kassel 1962-64.

Directed/produced opera for major companies in AUS: Graz; FR GER: Cologne, Düsseldorf-Duisburg, Frankfurt, Karlsruhe, Kassel, Kiel, Krefeld, Mannheim, Nürnberg, Wiesbaden Hessisches Staatstheater; ITA: Trieste; SWI: Basel; UK: Glyndebourne Fest; USA: Chicago. **Operas staged with these companies incl** AUBER: *Fra Diavolo,* BEETHOVEN: *Fidelio;* BENNETT: *Mines of Sulphur;* BERG: *Lulu★, Wozzeck★;* BERLIOZ: *Damnation de Faust★;* BIZET: *Carmen★†;* BRITTEN: *Albert Herring;* DEBUSSY: *Pelléas et Mélisande;* DONIZETTI: *Don Pasquale★, Elisir;* FORTNER: *Elisabeth Tudor★;* GLUCK: *Orfeo ed Euridice;* HAYDN: *Mondo della luna;* HENZE: *Junge Lord, Landarzt;* HINDEMITH: *Cardillac★;* KODALY: *Háry János;* LIGETI: *Aventures/Nouvelles Aventures;* LORTZING: *Wildschütz★;* MASSENET: *Don Quichotte;* MOZART: *Così fan tutte, Entführung aus dem Serail, Nozze di Figaro;* MUSSORGSKY: *Boris Godunov;* NICOLAI: *Lustigen Weiber;* OFFENBACH: *Périchole;* ORFF: *Carmina burana, Kluge, Mond;* PROKOFIEV: *Love for Three Oranges★;* PUCCINI: *Bohème, Fanciulla del West★, Gianni Schicchi, Manon Lescaut, Tosca;* RIMSKY-KORSAKOV: *Invisible City of Kitezh;* ROSSINI: *Barbiere di Siviglia;* STRAUSS, R: *Elektra, Frau ohne Schatten, Rosenkavalier★, Salome;* TCHAIKOVSKY: *Eugene Onegin★;* VERDI: *Aroldo/Stiffelio★, Ballo in maschera, Don Carlo★, Falstaff, Macbeth★, Otello, Vespri;* WAGNER: *Fliegende Holländer★, Meistersinger, Rheingold†, Walküre†, Siegfried★†, Götterdämmerung★†, Tannhäuser★†;* WEBER: *Freischütz;* WEILL: *Aufstieg und Fall der Stadt Mahagonny.* Also HENZE: *Ende einer Welt, Wundertheater;* SEARLE: *Photo of the Colonel;* SZOKOLAY: *Hamlet.* **Operatic world premieres:** ZIMMERMANN: *Soldaten* Cologne 1965. Teaches at Studio of Cologne Opera. **Res:** Voigtelstr 23, Cologne, FR Ger.

NEUHAUS, RUDOLF. Conductor of opera and symphony. German. Resident Cond, Staatsoper Dresden, Ger DR. Born 3 Jan 1914, Cologne. Wife Christel. Seven children. Studied: Hochschule für Musik, Prof Abendroth, Cologne; incl piano & violin. Operatic training as repetiteur & second cond at Landestheater, Neustrelitz 1934-44. **Operatic debut:** *Waffenschmied* Landestheater, Neustrelitz 1934. Symphonic debut: Theater Orch, Neustrelitz 1936. Awards: Prof & Kunstpreis, Ministry of Culture, Ger DR. Previous adm positions in opera: Gen Music Dir, Staatstheater Schwerin & Landesregierung Mecklenburg, Ger DR 1950-53.
Conducted with major companies in CZE: Brno; GER DR: Berlin Komische Oper & Staatsoper, Dresden, Leipzig; USSR: Leningrad Kirov. Operas with these companies incl ADAM: *Si j'étais roi;* d'ALBERT: *Tiefland;* AUBER: *Fra Diavolo;* BEETHOVEN: *Fidelio★;* BIZET: *Carmen★;* BRITTEN: *Albert Herring, Peter Grimes;* CIMAROSA: *Matrimonio segreto;* CORNELIUS: *Barbier von Bagdad;* DONIZETTI: *Don Pasquale, Elisir★;* EGK: *Zaubergeige★;* FLOTOW: *Martha;* GAY/Pepusch: *Beggar's Opera;* GLUCK: *Orfeo ed Euridice;* HENZE: *Junge Lord;* HUMPERDINCK: *Hänsel und Gretel★ Königskinder;* JANACEK: *Jenufa;* KURKA: *Good Soldier*

Schweik; LEONCAVALLO: *Pagliacci★;* LORTZING: *Wildschütz★, Zar und Zimmermann;* MASCAGNI: *Cavalleria rusticana;* MONTEVERDI: *Ritorno d'Ulisse★;* MOZART: *Così fan tutte, Don Giovanni★, Entführung aus dem Serail, Lucio Silla, Nozze di Figaro★, Zauberflöte★;* MUSSORGSKY: *Boris Godunov;* NICOLAI: *Lustigen Weiber;* OFFENBACH: *Contes d'Hoffmann;* ORFF: *Carmina burana, Kluge;* PAISIELLO: *Barbiere di Siviglia★;* PERGOLESI: *Serva padrona;* PROKOFIEV: *Duenna★, Love for Three Oranges, Semyon Kotko;* PUCCINI: *Bohème, Gianni Schicchi, Butterfly★, Manon Lescaut, Tabarro, Tosca★, Turandot★;* ROSSINI: *Barbiere di Siviglia;* SMETANA: *Bartered Bride;* STRAUSS, J: *Fledermaus★;* STRAUSS, R: *Arabella, Capriccio★, Daphne, Liebe der Danae, Rosenkavalier★, Salome;* TCHAIKOVSKY: *Eugene Onegin★;* VERDI: *Aida, Ballo in maschera, Don Carlo★, Forza del destino, Nabucco, Otello, Rigoletto, Traviata, Trovatore;* WAGNER: *Fliegende Holländer★, Lohengrin★, Meistersinger, Rheingold★, Walküre★, Siegfried, Tannhäuser, Tristan und Isolde★;* WEBER: *Freischütz, Oberon★;* WOLF-FERRARI: *Segreto di Susanna.* Also HANDEL: *Alexander;* EGK: *Revisor;* CIKKER: *Beg Bajazid.* **World premieres:** KUNAD: *Maître Pathelin* Staatsoper, Dresden 1969; SCHWAEN: *Leonce und Lena* Staatsoper Berlin, Ger DR 1961. Conducted major orch in Europe. Teaches at Hochschule für Musik, Dresden. **Res:** Schillerstr 19, Dresden, Ger DR. **Mgmt:** KDR/GDR.

NEUMANN, VÁCLAV. Conductor of opera and symphony. Czechoslovakian. Music Dir, Czech Phil Orch, Prague 1968- . Born 29 Sep 1920, Prague. Wife Marta. Three children. Studied: Consv of Music, Prague; incl violin. **Operatic debut:** *Cunning Little Vixen* Komische Oper, Berlin 1956. Symphonic debut: Czech Phil, Prague 1948. Previous occupations: mem of Smetana Quartet. Previous adm positions in opera: Chief Cond, Komische Oper Berlin 1956-64; Gen Mus Dir, Leipzig Opera House 1964-68 and Stuttgart Opera 1970-73.
Conducted with major companies in FR GER: Munich Staatsoper, Stuttgart; GER DR: Berlin Komische Oper, Leipzig. **Operas with these companies incl** AUBER: *Fra Diavolo;* BEETHOVEN: *Fidelio★;* BIZET: *Carmen;* DVORAK: *Rusalka;* GLUCK: *Orfeo ed Euridice;* JANACEK: *Excursions of Mr Broucek, From the House of the Dead, Jenufa, Katya Kabanova★, Makropoulos Affair★;* MOZART: *Don Giovanni★, Nozze di Figaro, Zauberflöte;* MUSSORGSKY: *Boris Godunov;* OFFENBACH: *Contes d'Hoffmann;* PUCCINI: *Bohème, Turandot;* ROSSINI: *Barbiere di Siviglia;* SCHOENBERG: *Erwartung;* SHOSTAKOVICH: *Katerina Ismailova;* SMETANA: *Bartered Bride;* STRAVINSKY: *Oedipus Rex;* TCHAIKOVSKY: *Eugene Onegin;* VERDI: *Nabucco, Otello;* WAGNER: *Fliegende Holländer★, Tristan und Isolde.* **World premieres:** CIKKER: *Spiel von Liebe und Tod* Munich Staatsoper 1969. Recorded for Supraphon, EMI. Video/Film—Bavaria-Film: *Makropoulos Affair; Eugene Onegin.* Conducted major orch in Europe, USA/Canada, & Asia. Previous positions as Mus Dir with major orch: Prague Symph Orch 1956-64;

Gewandhaus Orch, Leipzig 1964-68. Teaches at Acad of Music, Prague. **Res:** Smetanovo nábrezí 12, Prague, CSSR. Mgmt: PRG/CZE; KRG/FRG.

NEUMANN, WOLFGANG. Heldentenor. German. Resident mem: Städtische Bühnen, Bielefeld. Born 20 Jun 1945, Waiern, Austria. Single. Studied: Erwin Röttgen, Essen; Konsv Duisburg, Friedrich Brenn, Ulrich Rapp, Wolfgang Bständig. **Debut:** Max (*Freischütz*) Bielefeld 1973. Previous occupations: computer work.

Sang with major companies in FR GER: Bielefeld. **Roles with these companies incl** d'ALBERT: Pedro★ (*Tiefland*); BEETHOVEN: Florestan★ (*Fidelio*); MUSSORGSKY: Vassily Golitsin★ (*Khovanshchina*); STRAUSS, R: Aegisth★ (*Elektra*); WAGNER: Erik★ (*Fliegende Holländer*); WEBER: Max★ (*Freischütz*). **World premieres:** SMITH: Cuchulain (*Cuchulains Tod*) Bielefeld 1975. Res: Heeper Str 52a, 48 Bielefeld, FR Ger.

NEUMANN-SPALLART, GOTTFRIED. Scenic and costume designer for opera, theater & television; specl in sets. Is also a painter & illustrator. Austrian. Resident Designer, Theater in der Josefstadt, Vienna. Born 29 Mar 1920, Vienna. Wife Bettina, occupation cellist. One child. Studied: Univ of Technology, Prof Stefan Hlawa, Vienna. **Operatic debut:** Staatsoper, Vienna 1946. Theater debut: Burgtheater, Vienna 1947. Awards: Austrian Cross I Class, Science and Art; Prof, Dr.

Designed opera for major companies in AUS: Bregenz Fest, Graz, Salzburg Fest, Vienna Staatsoper & Volksoper; FR GER: Munich Theater am Gärtnerplatz; ISR: Tel Aviv; ITA: Florence Maggio & Comunale, Naples, Rome Opera, Turin; JPN: Tokyo Fujiwara; S AFR: Johannesburg. **Operas designed for these companies incl** BEETHOVEN: *Fidelio;* BIZET: *Carmen;* CIMAROSA: *Matrimonio segreto;* DONIZETTI: *Campanello, Elisir;* HINDEMITH: *Cardillac;* JANACEK: *Jenufa;* MENOTTI: *Old Maid and the Thief;* MOZART: *Don Giovanni, Nozze di Figaro, Zauberflöte;* MUSSORGSKY: *Boris Godunov;* PUCCINI: *Bohème, Tosca;* ROSSINI: *Barbiere di Siviglia, Cenerentola, Italiana in Algeri, Turco in Italia;* STRAUSS, J: *Fledermaus;* STRAUSS, R: *Ariadne auf Naxos, Rosenkavalier;* VERDI: *Aida, Rigoletto, Trovatore;* WAGNER: *Parsifal, Tannhäuser, Tristan und Isolde;* WEILL: *Dreigroschenoper.* **Operatic world premieres:** WEISHAPPEL: *Lederköpfe* Opernhaus, Graz 1970. Exhibitions of stage designs, graphics & paintings Wiener Theaterausstellung 1955, São Paulo Theater Biennale 1958; Theater Museum, Vienna; Wallraf Richards Museum, Cologne. Teaches at Inst für Theaterwissenschaft, Vienna Univ. **Res:** Neuer Markt 9, Vienna A 1010, Austria.

NEVILLE, MARGARET; née Smith. Lyric soprano. British. Resident mem: Städtische Bühnen, Cologne. Born Southampton, UK. Husband John Mould, occupation teacher. Studied: Olive Groves, London; Maria Carpi, Geneva; Ruth Packer, London. **Debut:** Erster Knabe (*Zauberflöte*) Covent Garden 1961. Awards: ARAM, Royal Acad of Music, London 1963; Mozart Memorial Prize, Haydn-Mozart Society, UK 1961.

Sang with major companies in FRA: Aix-en-Provence Fest; FR GER: Berlin Deutsche Oper, Bonn, Cologne, Düsseldorf-Duisburg Deutsche Op am Rhein, Hamburg, Stuttgart; SPA: Barcelona; SWE: Drottningholm Fest; UK: Cardiff Welsh, Edinburgh Fest, Glasgow Scottish, Glyndebourne Fest, London Royal & English National. **Roles with these companies incl** BIZET: Léila★ (*Pêcheurs de perles*); DONIZETTI: Norina★ (*Don Pasquale*); GLUCK: Amor (*Orfeo ed Euridice*); HUMPERDINCK: Gretel★‡; MONTEVERDI: Euridice (*Favola d'Orfeo*); MOZART: Despina★ (*Così fan tutte*), Zerlina★ (*Don Giovanni*), Blondchen (*Entführung aus dem Serail*), Ilia★ (*Idomeneo*), Susanna★ & Cherubino (*Nozze di Figaro*), Pamina★ (*Zauberflöte*); PUCCINI: Mimi (*Bohème*); STRAUSS, J: Adele (*Fledermaus*); STRAVINSKY: Anne Trulove (*Rake's Progress*); VERDI: Oscar★ (*Ballo in maschera*), Nannetta★ (*Falstaff*), Gilda★ (*Rigoletto*). Also HANDEL: Semele. **World premieres:** BENNETT: (*Penny for a Song*) Sadler's Wells, London 1967. Recorded for: EMI. Gives recitals. Appears with symphony orchestra. Teaches voice. **Res:** Ehrenstr 46, Cologne, FR Ger; 15 The Avenue, London W4, UK. Mgmt: ASK/UK; SLZ/FRG.

NEVISON, HOWARD S. Baritone. American. Born 13 Feb 1941, Philadelphia. Wife Fern, occupation office mngr. Studied: Settlement Music School, Tilly Barmach, Philadelphia; Curtis Inst of Music, Eufemia Gregory, Martial Singher, Philadelphia; Nicola Moscona, Giulio Gari, New York. **Debut:** Germont (*Traviata*) Israel National Opera, Tel Aviv 1969. Awards: First Prize Welsh Fest Eisteddfod Compt, UK.

Sang with major companies in ISR: Tel Aviv; USA: New York City Opera, Philadelphia Grand & Lyric, Pittsburgh. **Roles with these companies incl** DONIZETTI: Dott Malatesta★ (*Don Pasquale*), Enrico★ (*Lucia*); GIORDANO: Carlo Gérard (*Andrea Chénier*); LEONCAVALLO: Tonio (*Pagliacci*); MASCAGNI: Rabbi David (*Amico Fritz*), Alfio (*Cavalleria rusticana*); MASSENET: Lescaut (*Manon*); MENOTTI: John Sorel (*Consul*); MEYERBEER: Nelusco (*Africaine*); MOZART: Guglielmo & Don Alfonso (*Così fan tutte*), Leporello (*Don Giovanni*), Conte Almaviva & Figaro (*Nozze di Figaro*), Papageno (*Zauberflöte*); PAISIELLO: Figaro★ & Bartolo (*Barbiere di Siviglia*); PONCHIELLI: Barnaba (*Gioconda*); PUCCINI: Marcello (*Bohème*), Jack Rance (*Fanciulla del West*), Sharpless★ (*Butterfly*), Lescaut (*Manon Lescaut*), Michele★ (*Tabarro*), Guglielmo Wulf (*Villi*); ROSSINI: Figaro★ (*Barbiere di Siviglia*); STRAUSS, R: Mandryka (*Arabella*); TCHAIKOVSKY: Eugene Onegin, Yeletsky (*Pique Dame*); VERDI: Amonasro (*Aida*), Renato★ (*Ballo in maschera*), Rodrigo (*Don Carlo*), Ford (*Falstaff*), Don Carlo (*Forza del destino*), Nabucco, Rigoletto★, Germont (*Traviata*), Conte di Luna (*Trovatore*); WAGNER: Wolfram (*Tannhäuser*); WOLF-FERRARI: Rafaele (*Gioielli della Madonna*). Also GOUNOD: Mercutio (*Roméo et Juliette*); DREYFUS: Narrator (*Garni Sands*). Gives recitals. Appears with symphony orchestra. Teaches voice. **Res:** Brooklyn, NY, USA. Mgmt: WLS/USA.

NEWMAN, DANNY. American. Pub Rel Dir, Lyrić Opera of Chicago, 20 No Wacker Dr, Chicago, IL 60606, USA since 1954. In charge of publicity, promotion & audience development. Additional administrative positions: Consultant in Audience Development, Ford Foundation/Office of the Arts, Theatre Communications Group and The Canada Council. Born 24 Jan 1919, Chicago, IL. Wife Dina, occupation actress. Studied: Wright Coll, Chicago. Previous positions, primarily administrative, in wide range of theatrical and arts enterprises. Awards: Golden Baton, Houston & Cincinnati Symph Orchs; Awd of Merit, Royal Winnipeg Ballet and Cliff Dwellers Club, Chicago; National Theatre Awd, San Diego Old Globe Theatre; Scroll of Honor, San Diego Opera; Awd of Merit, Oregon Symph Orch; Eskimo Awd, Centaur Theatre, Montreal. Initiated major policy changes including expansion of season by enlarging subscription series; accomplished major rise in attendance for var organizations in the performing arts through consultant work, incl New York City Opera, San Francisco Opera, Houston Opera, San Diego Opera, Canadian Opera Company (Toronto). **Res:** 3270 N Lake Shore Dr, Chicago, IL, USA.

NEWTON, NORMA; née Norma Simmons. Spinto soprano. American. Born 20 May, USA. Husband Robert, occupation marine geologist. One child. Studied: Syracuse Univ, Ruth Pinnell, NY; Univ of Texas, Willa Stewart, Austin; Jay Pouhe, Otto Guth, New York. **Debut:** Donna Elvira (*Don Giovanni*) New York City Opera 1964. Previous occupations: voice teacher, Univ of Texas and San Antonio Coll, TX. Awards: Ntl Finalist, Met Op Ntl Counc Aud; Ntl Opera Inst Awd; three M B Rockefeller Fund Awds; Fulbright Awd, US Grant; Ntl Finalist, NATS Awd.
Sang with major companies in AUS: Graz; FR GER: Essen, Hannover, Kiel, Wuppertal; UK: Cardiff Welsh; USA: Dallas, New York City Opera. Roles with these companies incl BEETHOVEN: Marzelline (*Fidelio*); BERG: Marie★ (*Wozzeck*); BIZET: Micaëla★ (*Carmen*); DEBUSSY: Mélisande★; GLUCK: Euridice; GOUNOD: Marguerite (*Faust*), Mireille; JANACEK: Katya Kabanova; MASSENET: Manon, Thaïs; MENOTTI: Mother (*Amahl*); MOZART: Sesto★ (*Clemenza di Tito*), Fiordiligi (*Così fan tutte*), Donna Elvira (*Don Giovanni*), Ilia (*Idomeneo*), Contessa Almaviva & Susanna★ (*Nozze di Figaro*), Pamina★ (*Zauberflöte*); OFFENBACH: Antonia (*Contes d'Hoffmann*); ORFF: Kluge; PUCCINI: Mimi & Musetta (*Bohème*), Cio-Cio-San★ (*Butterfly*), Tosca; RAVEL: Concepcion (*Heure espagnole*); RIMSKY-KORSAKOV: Coq d'or; SMETANA: Marie★ (*Bartered Bride*); STRAUSS, R: Zdenka (*Arabella*); STRAVINSKY: Anne Trulove (*Rake's Progress*); VERDI: Amelia★ (*Ballo in maschera*), Desdemona (*Otello*), Violetta★ (*Traviata*), Leonora (*Trovatore*). Gives recitals. Appears with symphony orchestra. Teaches voice. On faculty of Amer Inst of Musical Studies, Graz, Austria & Dallas, TX, USA. Mgmt: RAB/AUS.

NEYTCHEVA-MILANOVA, LILIANA. Lyric mezzo-soprano. Bulgarian. Resident mem: Bayerische Staatsoper, Munich. Born 5 July 1945, Silistra, Bulgaria. Husband Michail Milanov, occupation opera singer. Studied: Ntl Consv Sofia. **Debut:** Kontchakovna (*Prince Igor*) Opernhaus Leipzig, Ger DR 1969.
Sang with major companies in AUS: Vienna Volksoper; BUL: Sofia; FRA: Nice; FR GER: Munich Bayerische Staatsoper; GER DR: Berlin Komische Oper, Leipzig. Roles with these companies incl AUBER: Pamela★ (*Fra Diavolo*); BARTOK: Judith★ (*Bluebeard's Castle*); BIZET: Carmen★; BORODIN: Kontchakovna (*Prince Igor*); CIMAROSA: Fidalma★ (*Matrimonio segreto*); HANDEL: Amastris★ (*Xerxes*); MOZART: Cherubino★ (*Nozze di Figaro*); MUSSORGSKY: Marina★ (*Boris Godunov*); PUCCINI: Suzuki★ (*Butterfly*); VERDI: Ulrica★ (*Ballo in maschera*), Preziosilla★ (*Forza del destino*). Gives recitals. Appears with symphony orchestra. **Res:** Schleissheimerstr 198, 8 Munich 40, FR Ger. Mgmt: SOF/YUG; SLZ/FRG.

NICOLAI, CLAUDIO. Lyric baritone. German. Resident mem: Opernhaus, Cologne. Born 7 Mar 1929, Kiel, Germany. Wife Carmen. Two children. Studied: Folkwang Hochschule für Musik, Essen; Prof Clemens Kaiser-Breme; Prof Serge Radamsky, Vienna. **Debut:** Kühleborn (*Undine*) Oper am Gärtnerplatz, Munich 1959. Awards: First Prize Phonograph Compt 1956.
Sang with major companies in AUS: Bregenz Fest, Graz, Vienna Staatsoper & Volksoper; BEL: Brussels, Liège; FRA: Strasbourg; FR GER: Bonn, Cologne, Düsseldorf-Duisburg, Frankfurt, Hamburg, Munich Gärtnerplatz, Stuttgart; HOL: Amsterdam; NOR: Oslo; SWI: Basel, Zurich; UK: London English National. Roles with these companies incl BENNETT: Braxton (*Mines of Sulphur*); BIZET: Escamillo★ (*Carmen*); BRITTEN: Billy Budd; CIMAROSA: Count Robinson★ (*Matrimonio segreto*); DONIZETTI: Dott Malatesta★ (*Don Pasquale*), Belcore★ (*Elisir*); HANDEL: Giulio Cesare; HINDEMITH: Mathis★; LORTZING: Graf v Liebenau (*Waffenschmied*), Graf Eberbach★ (*Wildschütz*), Peter I★ (*Zar und Zimmermann*); MOZART: Guglielmo★ (*Così fan tutte*), Don Giovanni★, Conte Almaviva★ (*Nozze di Figaro*), Papageno★ (*Zauberflöte*); PUCCINI: Sharpless (*Butterfly*); ROSSINI: Figaro★ (*Barbiere di Siviglia*), Dandini★ (*Cenerentola*); STRAUSS, R: Olivier★ (*Capriccio*); STRAVINSKY: Nick Shadow (*Rake's Progress*); TCHAIKOVSKY: Eugene Onegin★; THOMAS: Lothario (*Mignon*); VERDI: Rodrigo★ (*Don Carlo*), Germont (*Traviata*); WOLF-FERRARI: Pantalone (*Donne curiose*); ZIMMERMANN: Stolzius (*Soldaten*). Also RIMSKY-KORSAKOV: Lel (*Snow Maiden*); HENZE: Sekretär (*Junge Lord*); GOUNOD: Valentin (*Faust*). Recorded for: Eurodisc. Gives recitals. Appears with symphony orchestra. Teaches voice. **Res:** Meisenweg 24, D-5021 Königsdorf, FR Ger. Mgmt: SLZ/FRG: TAS/AUS.

NICOLESCU, ANTONIUS. Lyric tenor. Romanian. Resident mem: Romanian Opera, Bucharest. Born 17 Aug 1946. Married. One child. Studied: Consv, Prof Mihail Stirbei, Bucharest. **Debut:** Vladimir (*Prince Igor*) Romanian Opera 1971. Awards: Diploma, Cont Vienna 1972; Second Prize, 's Hertogenbosch 1973.

Sang with major companies in GRE: Athens National; GER DR: Berlin Staatsoper; ROM: Bucharest. Roles with these companies incl BIZET: Nadir★ (*Pêcheurs de perles*); DELIBES: Gérald★ (*Lakmé*): DONIZETTI: Ernesto★ (*Don Pasquale*), Edgardo★ (*Lucia*); GOUNOD: Faust★; HANDEL: Acis★; MASSENET: Werther★; MOZART: Ferrando★ (*Così fan tutte*), Don Ottavio★ (*Don Giovanni*), Belmonte★ & Pedrillo★ (*Entführung aus dem Serail*), Tamino★ (*Zauberflöte*); NICOLAI: Fenton★ (*Lustigen Weiber*); PUCCINI: Rodolfo★ (*Bohème*), Pinkerton★ (*Butterfly*); ROSSINI: Almaviva★ (*Barbiere di Siviglia*); STRAUSS, J: Alfred★ (*Fledermaus*); TCHAIKOVSKY: Lenski★ (*Eugene Onegin*); VERDI: Duca di Mantova★ (*Rigoletto*), Alfredo★ (*Traviata*). Video/Film: Fenton (*Lustigen Weiber*). Gives recitals. Appears with symphony orchestra. Res: 6 Delinesti St, Bucharest 7, Romania. Mgmt: RIA/ROM.

NIDETZKY, FRIEDRICH. Bass-baritone. Austrian. Resident mem: Volksoper, Vienna. Born 25 May 1920, Vienna. Wife Margarethe. Studied: Hochschule für Musik & darst Kunst, Profs Maria and Elisabeth Rado, Vienna. Debut: Conte Almaviva (*Nozze di Figaro*) Städt Theater, Biel-Solothurn, Switzerland 1951. Awards: Österr Ehrenkreuz f Wissenschaft u Kunst 1970: Winner, Intl Cont Geneva 1950.

Sang with major companies in AUS: Bregenz Fest, Graz, Salzburg Fest, Vienna Volksoper; BEL: Brussels; MON: Monte Carlo. Roles with these companies incl d'ALBERT: Tommaso (*Tiefland*); BEETHOVEN: Don Pizarro (*Fidelio*); CIMAROSA: Geronimo (*Matrimonio segreto*); DONIZETTI: Dott Malatesta (*Don Pasquale*), Dulcamara (*Elisir*); FLOTOW: Plunkett (*Martha*); IBERT: Boniface (*Angélique*); LORTZING: Stadinger & Graf v Liebenau (*Waffenschmied*), Van Bett (*Zar und Zimmermann*); MOZART: Don Alfonso (*Così fan tutte*), Leporello (*Don Giovanni*), Osmin (*Entführung aus dem Serail*), Papageno (*Zauberflöte*); NICOLAI: Falstaff (*Lustigen Weiber*); ORFF: Bauer (*Mond*); PUCCINI: Gianni Schicchi; ROSSINI: Dott Bartolo (*Barbiere di Siviglia*); SMETANA: Kezal (*Bartered Bride*); VERDI: Fra Melitone (*Forza del destino*); WOLF-FERRARI: Conte Gil (*Segreto di Susanna*). World premieres: WOLPERT: Dr Diaforus (*Eingebildete Kranke*) 1975; RUBIN: (*Kleider machen Leute*) 1973; both at Volksoper, Vienna. Recorded for: ORF. Teaches voice. On faculty of Bruckner Konsv, Linz; Prof. Res: Wildbergstr 18, Linz-Urfahr, Austria.

NIENSTEDT, GERD. Bass-baritone. German & Hon Austrian. Resident mem: Hessisches Staatstheater, Wiesbaden. Born 10 Jul 1932, Hannover. Separated. Two children. Studied: Otto Köhler, Hannover. Debut: Ramfis (*Aida*) Bremerhaven Opera, FR Ger 1954. Previous occupations: businessman. Adm positions: since 1973 Adv to Dir, Bielefeld; since 1975 same in Wiesbaden.

Sang with major companies in ARG: Buenos Aires; AUS: Vienna Staatsoper; BEL: Brussels; CAN: Montreal/Quebec; FRA: Bordeaux, Lyon, Marseille, Nancy, Nice, Paris, Rouen, Toulouse; FR GER: Bayreuth Fest, Bremen, Berlin Deutsche Oper, Bielefeld, Bonn, Cologne, Darmstadt, Dortmund, Düsseldorf-Duisburg, Essen, Frankfurt, Hamburg, Hannover, Karlsruhe, Kassel, Kiel, Krefeld, Mannheim, Munich Staatsoper, Nürnberg, Saarbrücken, Stuttgart, Wiesbaden, Wuppertal; ITA: Milan La Scala, Palermo, Rome Opera & Caracalla, Trieste, Venice; SWI: Geneva, Zurich; USA: Chicago, San Francisco Opera. Roles with these companies incl d'ALBERT: Sebastiano (*Tiefland*); BEETHOVEN: Don Pizarro★ (*Fidelio*); BERG: Wozzeck; BRITTEN: John Claggart (*Billy Budd*); EGK: Cuperus (*Zaubergeige*); EINEM: Lehrer (*Besuch der alten Dame*), St Just (*Dantons Tod*); FLOTOW: Plunkett (*Martha*); GLUCK: Thoas (*Iphigénie en Tauride*); HANDEL: Ptolemy (*Giulio Cesare*); JANACEK: Forester (*Cunning Little Vixen*); LORTZING: Stadinger (*Waffenschmied*); MASCAGNI: Alfio (*Cavalleria rusticana*); MOZART: Sarastro (*Zauberflöte*); MUSSORGSKY: Boris Godunov & Pimen (*Boris Godunov*); Ivan Khovansky★ (*Khovanshchina*); PUCCINI: Colline & Marcello (*Bohème*); STRAUSS, R: Mandryka★ (*Arabella*), Orest★ (*Elektra*), Jochanaan★ (*Salome*); STRAVINSKY: Tiresias (*Oedipus Rex*); VERDI: Ramfis (*Aida*), Philip II & Grande Inquisitore★ (*Don Carlo*), Falstaff★, Padre Guardiano (*Forza del destino*), Zaccaria (*Nabucco*), Simon Boccanegra & Fiesco (*Simon Boccanegra*); WAGNER: Holländer & Daland (*Fliegende Holländer*), König Heinrich (*Lohengrin*), Pogner (*Meistersinger*), Gurnemanz (*Parsifal*), Wotan & Fasolt & Fafner (*Rheingold*), Fafner (*Siegfried*), Hunding (*Walküre*), Gunther★ & Hagen (*Götterdämmerung*), Landgraf (*Tannhäuser*), König Marke★ (*Tristan und Isolde*); WEBER: Kaspar (*Freischütz*). Recorded for: Philips, Phonogram, Grammophon, Decca. Appears with symphony orchestra. Res: Bierstadter Str 36, Wiesbaden, FR Ger. Mgmt: SLZ/FRG.

NIKKONEN, HARRI OLAVI. Bass-baritone. Finnish. Resident mem: Finnish National Opera, Helsinki. Born 26 Jan 1933, Viipuri. Wife Anneli Tuula, occupation dancer. Two children. Studied: Profs Oiva Soini, Clemens Glettenberg; Mo Merlini. Debut: Don Bartolo (*Barbiere di Siviglia*) Finnish Ntl Opera 1959. Awards: State's Award of Finland 1961; Wihuri Awd 1965; Awd City of Helsinki.

Sang with major companies in FIN: Helsinki; GER DR: Berlin Staatsoper; HUN: Budapest; NOR: Oslo; SWE: Stockholm. Roles with these companies incl BERG: Wozzeck; BRITTEN: Bottom (*Midsummer Night*); GERSHWIN: Crown (*Porgy and Bess*); KODALY: Háry János; LEONCAVALLO: Tonio (*Pagliacci*); MENOTTI: Donato★ (*Maria Golovin*); MOZART: Leporello (*Don Giovanni*); MUSSORGSKY: Varlaam★ (*Boris Godunov*), Tcherevik★ (*Fair at Sorochinsk*); PERGOLESI: Uberto★ (*Serva padrona*); PUCCINI: Jack Rance (*Fanciulla del West*), Gianni Schicchi, Michele (*Tabarro*); ROSSINI: Dott Bartolo (*Barbiere di Siviglia*), Mustafà★ (*Italiana in Algeri*); SHOSTAKOVICH: Platon Kusmich Kovalioff (*Nose*); VERDI: Amonasro★ (*Aida*), Falstaff★, Nabucco★, Iago★ (*Otello*). World premieres: RAUTAWAARA: Marsyas (*Apollo and Marsyas*) Finnish Ntl Opera 1973. Gives recitals. Appears with symphony orchestra.

NIKOLIC, MIOMIR. Bass. Yugoslavian. Resident mem: Deutsche Oper, Berlin. Born 10 Mar 1944, Nis, Yugoslavia. Single. Studied: Prof Branko Pivnicki, Prof Anita Mezetova, Belgrade; Prof Octav Enigarescu, Bucharest. **Debut:** Celio (*Love for Three Oranges*) Belgrade Opera 1973. Awards: Second Prize Yugoslav Compt for Young Musicians, Zagreb 1973.

Sang with major companies in FR GER: Berlin Deutsche Oper; YUG: Belgrade. **Roles with these companies incl** BELLINI: Oroveso★ (*Norma*); CIMAROSA: Count Robinson★ (*Matrimonio segreto*); DONIZETTI: Don Pasquale★; MUSSORGSKY: Pimen★ (*Boris Godunov*); PUCCINI: Colline★ (*Bohème*). Gives recitals. Appears with symphony orchestra. **Res:** Hadzi-Milentijeva 23, Belgrade, Yugoslavia. Mgmt: YGC/YUG.

NILSSON, BIRGIT; née Märta Birgit Svensson. Dramatic soprano. Swedish. Born 17 May 1918, Vastra Karup, Sweden. Husband Bertil Niklasson, occupation businessman. Studied: Royal Music Acad, Stockholm. **Debut:** Agathe (*Freischütz*) Royal Opera, Stockholm 1946. Awards: Hovsängerska/Swedish Court Singer; Kammersängerin and Life Member, Vienna Staatsoper.

Sang with major companies in ARG: Buenos Aires; AUSTRL: Sydney; AUS: Vienna Staatsoper; FRA: Orange Fest, Paris; FR GER: Bayreuth Fest, Berlin Deutsche Oper, Düsseldorf-Duisburg, Hamburg, Mannheim, Munich Staatsoper, Wiesbaden; ITA: Milan La Scala; NOR: Oslo; SWE: Stockholm; SWI: Zurich; UK: Glyndebourne Fest, London Royal; USA: Chicago, Newark, New York Met, Philadelphia Grand, Pittsburgh, San Antonio, San Francisco Opera; et al. **Roles with these companies incl** BEETHOVEN: Leonore‡ (*Fidelio*); MOZART: Donna Anna‡ (*Don Giovanni*), Elettra (*Idomeneo*); PUCCINI: Minnie‡ (*Fanciulla del West*), Tosca‡, Turandot‡; STRAUSS, R: Elektra‡, Marschallin (*Rosenkavalier*), Salome‡; VERDI: Aida‡, Amelia‡ (*Ballo in maschera*), Lady Macbeth‡; WAGNER: Senta (*Fliegende Holländer*), Elsa (*Lohengrin*), Sieglinde & Brünnhilde‡ (*Walküre*), Brünnhilde (*Siegfried‡, Götterdämmerung‡*), Elisabeth‡ & Venus‡ (*Tannhäuser*), Isolde‡; et al. Also STRAUSS, R: Färberin (*Frau ohne Schatten*). Recorded for: London, RCA, DG, HMV, Decca, Columbia. Gives recitals. Appears with symphony orchestra.

NIMSGERN, SIEGMUND. Dramatic baritone & bass-baritone. German. Resident mem: Vienna Staatsoper. Born 14 Jan 1940, St Wendel/Saar, Germany. Wife Mechthild. Two children. Studied: Musik Hochschule Saarbrücken, Jakob Stämpfli; Paul Lohmann, Wiesbaden, FR Ger. **Debut:** TCHAIKOVSKY: Lionel (*Maid of Orleans*) Saarbrücken Staatstheater 1967. Awards: First Prize 's Hertogenbosch Compt, Holland 1965; Cologne German Compt 1965; Second Prize ARD Compt Munich 1966; Mendelssohn Prize, Berlin 1967.

Sang with major companies in AUS: Salzburg Fest, Vienna Staatsoper; CAN: Montreal/Quebec; FRA: Nancy, Paris; FR GER: Düsseldorf-Duisburg, Frankfurt, Saarbrücken; ITA: Milan La Scala; SPA: Madrid; SWI: Geneva; UK: London Royal; USA: San Francisco Opera. **Roles with**

these companies incl BEETHOVEN: Don Pizarro (*Fidelio*); BERG: Dr Schön (*Lulu*); BERLIOZ: Méphistophélès (*Damnation de Faust*); BIZET: Escamillo (*Carmen*); BUSONI: Doktor Faust; GLUCK: Ubalde (*Armide*); MOZART: Don Giovanni★; OFFENBACH: Coppélius★ etc (*Contes d'Hoffmann*); PUCCINI: Lescaut★ (*Manon Lescaut*); STRAUSS, R: Orest★ (*Elektra*), Jochanaan★ (*Salome*); VERDI: Rodrigo★ (*Don Carlo*), Iago★ (*Otello*), Simon Boccanegra★; WAGNER: Holländer★, Telramund★ (*Lohengrin*), Amfortas★ (*Parsifal*), Wotan★ (*Rheingold*), Gunther★ (*Götterdämmerung*), Wolfram★ (*Tannhäuser*), Kurwenal★ (*Tristan und Isolde*); WEBER: Kaspar★ (*Freischütz*). Also ENESCU: Oedipe★; TELEMANN: Pimpinone. Recorded for EMI, Teldec, RAI. Video/Film — RAI: Doktor Faust; Leonhard (*Brautwahl*); Hidroat & Ubalde (*Armide*); Telramund (*Lohengrin*); Uberto (*Serva padrona*); Mandryka (*Arabella*); Jochanaan (*Salome*); Kurwenal (*Tristan*); Pagano (*Lombardi*); Siegfried (*Genoveva*); Duca d'Ordow (*Torvaldo e Dorlisca*); Kunrad der Ebner (*Feuersnot*). Israel Brdcst: Iago (*Otello*); Conte di Luna (*Trovatore*). Gives recitals. Appears with symphony orchestra. **Res:** Winnweg 37, St Ingbert/Saar, FR Ger.

NISKA, MARALIN FAE; née Dice. Soprano. American. Resident mem: New York City Opera. Born 16 Nov, San Pedro, CA, USA. Husband William P Mullen, occupation executive, Rockefeller Fund for Music. Two stepchildren. Studied: Louise Mansfield, San Pedro, CA; Ernest St John Metz, No Hollywood, CA; UCLA, Jan Popper, Los Angeles; USC, Walter Ducloux, Los Angeles. **Debut:** Manon, Los Angeles Opera Co 1959. Previous occupations: elementary school teacher. Awards: Woman of the Year, Los Angeles *Times*.

Sang with major companies in HOL: Amsterdam; USA: Boston, Cincinnati, Fort Worth, Hawaii, Houston, Miami, Milwaukee Florentine, New York Met & City Opera, Philadelphia Lyric Opera, San Antonio, San Diego, Santa Fe, Washington DC. **Roles with these companies incl** BERG: Marie★ (*Wozzeck*); BERLIOZ: Cassandre★ (*Troyens*); BIZET: Micaëla (*Carmen*); BORODIN: Jaroslavna★ (*Prince Igor*); BRITTEN: Female Chorus (*Rape of Lucretia*), Governess★ (*Turn of the Screw*); CHERUBINI: Medea★; FLOYD: Susannah★; GOUNOD: Marguerite★ (*Faust*); HANDEL: Cleopatra (*Giulio Cesare*); JANACEK: Emilia Marty★ (*Makropoulos Affair*); LEONCAVALLO: Nedda★ (*Pagliacci*); MASSENET: Manon; MOZART: Donna Anna★ & Donna Elvira★ (*Don Giovanni*), Elettra★ (*Idomeneo*), Contessa★ (*Nozze di Figaro*); OFFENBACH: Giulietta (*Contes d'Hoffmann*); ORFF: Solo (*Carmina burana*); PUCCINI: Mimi★ & Musetta★ (*Bohème*), Cio-Cio-San★ (*Butterfly*), Suor Angelica★, Tosca★; STRAUSS, J: Adele (*Fledermaus*); STRAUSS, R: Komponist★ (*Ariadne auf Naxos*), Salome★; VERDI: Violetta★ (*Traviata*), Elena★ (*Vespri*). Gives recitals. Appears with symphony orchestra. Teaches voice. Coaches repertoire. Mgmt: CAM/USA; AIM/UK.

NIWA, KATSUUMI. Dramatic tenor. Japanese. Resident mem: Niki Kai, Tokyo. Born 2 Aug 1938, Yokohama, Japan. Wife Mie. Two children. Studied: Takeshi Isogaya, Yoshiko Fukuzawa, Tokyo; UCLA, Jan Popper, Los Angeles; Lotte Lehmann, CA, USA. **Debut:** Pinkerton (*Butterfly*) Niki Kai, Tokyo 1967. Awards: First Prize Min-on Music Conc 1967; Prize for Young Artists, Los Angeles Westside Comm Cnt 1963.

Sang with major companies in JPN: Tokyo Niki Kai. **Roles with these companies incl** BEETHO-VEN: Florestan★ (*Fidelio*); BERLIOZ: Faust★ (*Damnation de Faust*), Aeneas★ (*Troyens*); BI-ZET: Don José★ (*Carmen*); HINDEMITH: Charles★ (*Long Christmas Dinner*); MASCAGNI: Turiddu (*Cavalleria rusticana*); ORFF: Solo (*Carmina burana*); PUCCINI: Pinkerton★ (*Butterfly*), Luigi★ (*Tabarro*), Cavaradossi★ (*Tosca*); ROS-SINI: Almaviva (*Barbiere di Siviglia*), Don Ramiro (*Cenerentola*); SHOSTAKOVICH: Sergei★ (*Katerina Ismailova*); STRAUSS, J: Eisenstein (*Fledermaus*); VERDI: Duca di Mantova★ (*Rigoletto*), Alfredo★ (*Traviata*); WAGNER: Siegmund★ (*Walküre*). Video/Film: Nippon Victor. Gives recitals. Appears with symphony orchestra. Teaches voice. On faculty of Nippon Univ, assoc prof. **Res:** 102 Shinjukuku, Tokyo, Japan.

NÖCKER, HANS GÜNTER. Bass-baritone. German. Resident mem: Bayerische Staatsoper, Munich; Deutsche Oper, Berlin. Born 22 Jan 1927, Hagen, Germany. Wife Monika, occupation conductor. Studied: Carl Momberg, Braunschweig, FR Ger; Hans-Hermann Nissen, Willi Domgraf-Fassbänder, Munich. **Debut:** Alfio (*Cavalleria rusticana*) Städtische Bühnen Münster, FR Ger 1952. Awards: Bundesverdienstkreuz, Bundespräsident; Bayerischer Kammersänger, Bavarian Senate; Berliner Kammersänger, Berlin Senate.

Sang with major companies in AUS: Vienna Staatsoper; BEL: Brussels; FR GER: Bayreuth Fest, Berlin Deutsche Oper, Bonn, Cologne, Darmstadt, Düsseldorf-Duisburg, Frankfurt, Hamburg, Hannover, Kassel, Krefeld, Mannheim, Munich Staatsoper, Nürnberg, Stuttgart, Wiesbaden; ITA: Florence Maggio, Palermo, Venice; UK: Edinburgh Fest, London Royal Opera & English National. **Roles with these companies incl** d'ALBERT: Sebastiano★ (*Tiefland*); BEETHO-VEN: Don Pizarro★ (*Fidelio*); BERG: Dr Schön★ (*Lulu*); BIZET: Escamillo★ (*Carmen*); CIKKER: Coriolanus★ (*Coriolanus*); EINEM: George Danton★ (*Dantons Tod*); HENZE: Tartaglia (*König Hirsch/Re Cervo*); HINDEMITH: Mathis; MENOTTI: Bob (*Old Maid and the Thief*); MOZART: Guglielmo (*Così fan tutte*), Conte Almaviva (*Nozze di Figaro*); OFFENBACH: Coppélius★ etc (*Contes d'Hoffmann*); PUCCINI: Scarpia (*Tosca*); STRAUSS, R: Altair (*Aegyptische Helena*), Mandryka★ (*Arabella*), Graf★ (*Capriccio*), Orest★ (*Elektra*), Jupiter (*Liebe der Danae*), Jochanaan★ (*Salome*); STRAVINSKY: Nick Shadow (*Rake's Progress*); TCHAIKOVSKY: Eugene Onegin★; VERDI: Rodrigo (*Don Carlo*), Iago★ (*Otello*); WAGNER: Holländer★, Telramund★ (*Lohengrin*), Hans Sachs (*Meistersinger*), Orsini (*Rienzi*), Wotan★ (*Rheingold*), Gunther★ (*Götterdämmerung*), Kurwenal★ (*Tristan und Isolde*). Also FORTNER: Leonardo (*Bluthochzeit*). **World premieres:** FORTNER: Norfolk (*Elisabeth Tudor*) Deutsche Oper, Berlin 1972; EGK: Hoango (*Verlobung in San Domingo*) Bayerische Staatsoper,

Munich 1963; KUBELIK: Tizian (*Cornelia Faroli*) Augsburg Opera 1971. Video/Film: Graf (*Capriccio*); Hoango (*Verlobung in San Domingo*). Appears with symphony orchestra. **Res:** Warthestr 13, 8 Munich 81, Fr Ger. Mgmt: SMD/FRG.

NOEL, RITA; née Ella Marguerite Noel. Lyric coloratura mezzo-soprano. American. Resident mem: Theater am Gärtnerplatz, Munich. Born 21 Nov 1943, Lancaster, SC, USA. Husband Frank Martin, MD, occupation laryngologist. Studied: Fr Prof Eugenie Ludwig, Vienna; Cornelius Reid, New York; Queens Coll, Albert May, Charlotte, NC; Eastman School of Music, including violin/viola, Rochester, NY, USA. **Debut:** Flora (*Traviata*) Metropolitan Opera Ntl Co 1966. Previous occupations: coll teacher of violin & viola; orch mem Vienna Chamber Orch, Berlin Symph Orch.

Sang with major companies in FR GER: Bielefeld, Munich Gärtnerplatz; HOL: Amsterdam; USA: Miami. **Roles with these companies incl** AU-BER: Pamela (*Fra Diavolo*); BIZET: Carmen★; HANDEL: Cornelia (*Giulio Cesare*); HUM-PERDINCK: Hänsel★; MOZART: Sesto★ (*Clemenza di Tito*), Cherubino★ (*Nozze di Figaro*); NICOLAI: Frau Reich (*Lustigen Weiber*); ROS-SINI: Rosina★ (*Barbiere di Siviglia*); STRAUSS, J: Prinz Orlovsky★ (*Fledermaus*); STRAUSS, R: Octavian★ (*Rosenkavalier*); VERDI: Azucena (*Trovatore*). Also OFFENBACH: Nicklausse★ (*Contes d'Hoffmann*); MASCAGNI: Santuzza★ (*Cavalleria rusticana*). Gives recitals. Appears with symphony orchestra. **Res:** 82 Sexauerstr 3a, Munich, FR Ger. Mgmt: KAY/USA; PAS/FRG.

NOLEN, TIMOTHY. Lyric baritone. American. Resident mem: Bühnen der Stadt Köln, Cologne. Born 9 Jul 1941, Rotan, TX, USA. Wife Paulette Haupt, occupation recital accomp, coach, conductor. One child. Studied: Manhattan School of Music, New York; Walter Blazer, Richard Fredricks, New York. **Debut:** Figaro (*Barbiere di Siviglia*) New Jersey Opera, Newark 1968. Previous occupations: PS teacher. Awards: M B Rockefeller Fund Grant.

Sang with major companies in FRA: Aix-en-Provence Fest, Bordeaux, Nancy, Paris, Rouen; FR GER: Cologne; HOL: Amsterdam; USA: Boston, Chicago, Houston, Lake George, Minneapolis, Newark, Portland, San Francisco Opera & Spring Opera. **Roles with these companies incl** BI-ZET: Escamillo (*Carmen*); CHERUBINI: Creon (*Medea*); DEBUSSY: Pelléas; DONIZETTI: Dott Malatesta★ (*Don Pasquale*), Belcore (*Elisir*), Gasparo (*Rita*); MENOTTI: Bob (*Old Maid and the Thief*); MILHAUD: Créon (*Médée*); MON-TEVERDI: Orfeo; MOZART: Guglielmo★ (*Così fan tutte*), Conte Almaviva & Figaro (*Nozze di Figaro*), Papageno (*Zauberflöte*); ORFF: Solo★ (*Carmina burana*); PUCCINI: Marcello (*Bohème*), Gianni Schicchi, Sharpless (*Butterfly*), Rambaldo (*Rondine*); RAVEL: Ramiro (*Heure espagnole*); ROSSINI: Figaro★ (*Barbiere di Siviglia*), Dandini★ (*Cenerentola*); STRAUSS, R: Olivier (*Capriccio*); STRAVINSKY: Empereur de Chine (*Rossignol*); THOMAS: Hamlet, Lothario (*Mignon*); VERDI: Ford (*Falstaff*); WEILL: Macheath (*Dreigroschenoper*). Also STRAUSS, R: Harlekin★ (*Ariadne auf Naxos*);

MONTEVERDI: Ottone★ (*Incoronazione di Poppea*); ARGENTO: Christopher Sly. **World premieres:** KOX: Lord Henry Wotton (*Portrait of Dorian Gray*) Amsterdam 1974; SELIG: Chocorua, Tanglewood, MA, USA 1972. Gives recitals. Appears with symphony orchestra. Teaches voice. **Res:** Titusstr 14, Cologne, FR Ger. **Mgmt:** CMW/FRA.

NORDIN, BIRGIT. Lyric soprano. Swedish. Resident mem: Royal Opera, Stockholm. Born 22 Feb 1934, Neder Kalix, Sweden. Husband B Stenström, occupation librarian. Studied: Royal Acad of Music, Brita von Vegesack, Stockholm. **Debut:** Oscar (*Ballo in maschera*) Royal Opera, Stockholm 1958. Awards: Royal Court Singer; Kristina Nilsson, Jussi Björling Awds.

Sang with major companies in CAN: Montreal/Quebec; DEN: Copenhagen; FIN: Helsinki; FRA: Paris; FR GER: Berlin ' Deutsche Oper, Hamburg, Hannover, Karlsruhe, Kiel; NOR: Oslo; SWE: Drottningholm Fest; UK: Edinburgh Fest, Glyndebourne Fest, London Royal. **Roles with these companies incl** BERG: Lulu; BRITTEN: Tytania (*Midsummer Night*); DEBUSSY: Mélisande; DONIZETTI: Norina (*Don Pasquale*), Adina (*Elisir*); GLUCK: Amor (*Orfeo ed Euridice*); HANDEL: Alcina & Morgana (*Alcina*); HAYDN: Sandrina (*Infedeltà delusa*), Clarissa (*Mondo della luna*); MASSENET: Manon; MOZART: Fiordiligi★ & Despina★ (*Così fan tutte*), Donna Elvira★ & Zerlina★ (*Don Giovanni*), Konstanze★ & Blondchen (*Entführung aus dem Serail*), Serpetta (*Finta giardiniera*), Susanna★ & Cherubino★ (*Nozze di Figaro*), Mlle Silberklang (*Schauspieldirektor*), Pamina★ & Königin der Nacht (*Zauberflöte*); OFFENBACH: Olympia★ & Antonia★ & Giulietta★ (*Contes d'Hoffmann*); ROSSINI: Rosina★ (*Barbiere di Siviglia*), Anaï (*Moïse*), Sofia★ (*Signor Bruschino*); STRAUSS, J: Adele★ (*Fledermaus*); STRAUSS, R: Komponist★ (*Ariadne auf Naxos*), Sophie★ (*Rosenkavalier*); VERDI: Oscar★ (*Ballo in maschera*), Nannetta★ (*Falstaff*), Gilda★ (*Rigoletto*); WEILL: Jenny (*Aufstieg und Fall der Stadt Mahagonny*). Video: Königin (*Zauberflöte*); Lulu; Oscar (*Ballo in maschera*); Nedda (*Pagliacci*). Gives recitals. Appears with symphony orchestra. **Mgmt:** KBL/SWE.

NORMAN, JESSYE. "Jugendlich" dramatic soprano. American. Born 15 Sep 1945, Augusta, GA, USA. Single. Studied: Howard Univ, Prof C V Grant, Washington, DC; Peabody Consv, Mme Alice Duschak, Baltimore; Univ of Michigan, Ann Arbor, USA; Pierre Bernac, Prof Elizabeth Mannion. **Debut:** Elisabeth (*Tannhäuser*) Deutsche Oper, Berlin 1969.

Sang with major companies in FR GER: Berlin Deutsche Oper; ITA: Florence Maggio & Comunale, Milan La Scala; UK: London Royal. **Roles with these companies incl** BERLIOZ: Cassandre★ (*Troyens*); MEYERBEER: Selika★ (*Africaine*); MOZART: Arminda‡ (*Finta giardiniera*), Contessa★‡ (*Nozze di Figaro*); VERDI: Aida★; WAGNER: Elisabeth★ (*Tannhäuser*). Recorded for: Philips, EMI. Gives recitals. Appears with symphony orchestra. **Res:** London, UK. **Mgmt:** HBM/USA; IWL/UK.

NORRENBROCK, PAUL ANTHONY. Scenic and costume designer for opera, theater, television. Is a lighting designer; also a painter. American. Born 31 Aug 1947, Louisville, KY. Single. Studied: Indiana Univ, Mario Cristini, Andreas Nomikos, R Scammon, L Brauner, Bloomington. **Operatic debut:** *Bohème* Kentucky Op Assn, Louisville 1973. Theater debut: Indiana Univ Theater, Bloomington 1969. Previous occupation: prof. Awards: Best Scenic Design for Community Theater, IN 1971.

Designed for major company in USA: Kentucky. **Operas designed for this company incl** ORFF: *Carmina burana★;* PUCCINI: *Bohème★, Tabarro★.* Exhibitions of stage designs & paintings, Morgan Gallery, Lexington, KY 1971. Teaches at Illinois Wesleyan Univ, Bloomington. **Res:** 1401½ Park St, Bloomington, IL, USA.

NORUP, BENT. Dramatic baritone. Danish. Resident mem: Staatstheater, Braunschweig; Royal Opera, Copenhagen. Born 7 Dec 1936, Hobro, Denmark. Wife Hanne. Two children. Studied: Kristian Riis, Copenhagen; Kmsg Karl Schmitt-Walter, Munich. **Debut:** Kurwenal (*Tristan und Isolde*) Royal Opera, Copenhagen 1970. Previous occupations: bank clerk. Awards: Art Prize of Copenhagen music critics.

Sang with major companies in DEN: Copenhagen; FR GER: Bonn, Dortmund, Essen, Mannheim. **Roles with these companies incl** BEETHOVEN: Don Pizarro★ (*Fidelio*); BERG: Doktor★ (*Wozzeck*); BORODIN: Prince Igor★; BRITTEN: Chorus leader★ (*Curlew River*); GERSHWIN: Crown★ (*Porgy and Bess*); GOUNOD: Méphistophélès★ (*Faust*); MASSENET: Don Quichotte★; PUCCINI: Colline★ (*Bohème*), Sharpless★ (*Butterfly*), Scarpia★ (*Tosca*); SHOSTAKOVICH: Boris★ (*Katerina Ismailova*); STRAUSS, R: Jochanaan★ (*Salome*); STRAVINSKY: Creon★ (*Oedipus Rex*), Nick Shadow★ (*Rake's Progress*); TCHAIKOVSKY: Eugene Onegin★; VERDI: Ford★ (*Falstaff*), Nabucco★, Iago★ (*Otello*); WAGNER: Holländer★, Wotan★ (*Rheingold*), Kurwenal★ (*Tristan und Isolde*). **World premieres:** KOPPEL: Banquo (*Macbeth*) Royal Opera, Copenhagen 1970. Video/Film: Tod (*Junge Park*). Gives recitals. Appears with symphony orchestra. **Res:** Steintorwall 12, Braunschweig, FR Ger. **Mgmt:** GSI/DEN; SLZ/FRG.

NOVELLI, ANNA. Lyric soprano. Italian. Born 2 Jun 1938, Rome. Married. Studied: Advanced School of La Scala, Mo Enrico Piazza, Milan. **Debut:** MASSENET: Manon, Teatro Nuovo, Milan 1960. Previous occupations: studied languages. Awards: winner of 10 opera compts in Italy; 3 ENAL Schlshps, Teatro Comunale, Bologna.

Sang with major companies in AUS: Vienna Staatsoper; CAN: Montreal/Quebec; FRA: Bordeaux, Paris, Rouen, Strasbourg; FR GER: Munich Staatsoper, Nürnberg, Stuttgart; HUN: Budapest; ITA: Bologna, Milan La Scala, Naples, Palermo, Turin, Verona Arena; MON: Monte Carlo; SPA: Majorca; USSR: Moscow Bolshoi. **Roles with these companies incl** BOITO: Margherita (*Mefistofele*); CHARPENTIER: Louise; CILEA: Adriana Lecouvreur; GLUCK: Iphigénie (*Iphigénie en Aulide*); GOUNOD: Marguerite★ (*Faust*); LEONCAVALLO: Nedda★ (*Pagliacci*);

MOZART: Donna Elvira★ (*Don Giovanni*), Contessa (*Nozze di Figaro*); PUCCINI: Mimi★ (*Bohème*), Lauretta (*Gianni Schicchi*), Manon Lescaut, Giorgetta (*Tabarro*), Liù★ (*Turandot*); ROSSINI: Anaï (*Moïse*); VERDI: Odabella (*Attila*), Alice Ford (*Falstaff*), Desdemona★ (*Otello*), Amelia (*Simon Boccanegra*), Elena (*Vespri*); WAGNER: Elsa (*Lohengrin*). Gives recitals. Appears with symphony orchestra. **Res:** V M Novaro 6, Milan, Italy. Mgmt: ABA/FRA.

NOVOA, SALVADOR ANTONIO. Dramatic tenor. Mexican. Born 30 Oct 1937. Mexico City, Mexico. Wife Audrey. Three children. Studied: Mo Felipe Aguilera, Mexico City; Kurt Baum, New York. **Debut:** Pinkerton (*Butterfly*) Mexican Opera Co 1960. Awards: Second Prize Met Op Reg Aud, Mexico 1959.

Sang with major companies in ARG: Buenos Aires; CAN: Toronto, Vancouver; FRA: Marseille; FR GER: Stuttgart; MEX: Mexico City; USA: Boston, Chicago, Cincinnati, Fort Worth, Houston Grand, New York City Opera, Omaha, Philadelphia Lyric, Portland, San Diego, Washington DC. **Roles with these companies incl** BIZET: Don José★ (*Carmen*); BOITO: Faust★ (*Mefistofele*); DONIZETTI: Edgardo★ (*Lucia*); GINASTERA: Don Rodrigo; GIORDANO: Andrea Chénier; GOUNOD: Faust★; LEONCAVALLO: Canio (*Pagliacci*); MASCAGNI: Turiddu★ (*Cavalleria rusticana*); PUCCINI: Rinuccio (*Gianni Schicchi*), Pinkerton (*Butterfly*), Ruggero (*Rondine*), Luigi★ (*Tabarro*), Cavaradossi★ (*Tosca*); VERDI: Radames★ (*Aida*), Riccardo★ (*Ballo in maschera*), Don Alvaro★ (*Forza del destino*), Ismaele (*Nabucco*), Duca di Mantova★ (*Rigoletto*), Alfredo (*Traviata*), Manrico★ (*Trovatore*); WAGNER: Erik (*Fliegende Holländer*). Also BENTOIU: Hamlet; VERDI: Macduff (*Macbeth*). **World premieres:** GINASTERA: Pier Francesco Orsini (*Bomarzo*) Washington, DC, Opera Socy 1967. Recorded for: Columbia. Gives recitals. Appears with symphony orchestra. **Res:** New York, NY, USA. Mgmt: LLF/USA.

NUOTIO, PEKKA. Dramatic tenor. Finnish. Resident mem: Finnish National Opera, Helsinki. Born 21 Feb 1929, Vyburg, Finland. Wife Helena. Two children. Studied: Olavi Nyberg, Helsinki; Clemens Glettenberg, Munich. **Debut:** Duca di Mantova (*Rigoletto*) Finnish National Opera, Helsinki 1958. Awards: Pro Finlandia Medal, Pres of Republic of Finland.

Sang with major companies in AUSTRL: Sydney; CZE: Prague National; FIN: Helsinki; FR GER: Düsseldorf-Duisburg, Hamburg, Stuttgart; GER DR: Berlin Staatsoper; HOL: Amsterdam; HUN: Budapest; NOR: Oslo; SWE: Drottningholm Fest, Stockholm; UK: Glasgow Scottish, London Royal & English National; USA: New York Met. **Roles with these companies incl** BEETHOVEN: Florestan (*Fidelio*); BERG: Hauptmann (*Wozzeck*); BIZET: Don José (*Carmen*); JANACEK: Boris (*Katya Kabanova*); LEONCAVALLO: Canio★ (*Pagliacci*); MASCAGNI: Turiddu (*Cavalleria rusticana*); PUCCINI: Pinkerton (*Butterfly*), Calaf (*Turandot*); SAINT-SAENS: Samson; SHOSTAKOVICH: Sergei (*Katerina Ismailova*); SMETANA: Hans (*Bartered Bride*); STRAUSS, J: Alfred (*Fledermaus*);

STRAVINSKY: Eumolpe (*Perséphone*); SZOKOLAY: Bridegroom (*Blood Wedding*); TCHAIKOVSKY: Gherman (*Pique Dame*); VERDI: Radames★ (*Aida*), Don Carlo★, Fenton (*Falstaff*), Otello★, Duca di Mantova★ (*Rigoletto*), Manrico★ (*Trovatore*); WAGNER: Erik (*Fliegende Holländer*), Loge★ (*Rheingold*), Tannhäuser★, Tristan★. Also MADETOJA: Antti (*Ostrobothnians*); PYLKKANEN: Schneider (*Prisoners*); MUSSORGSKY: Dimitri (*Boris Godunov*). Gives recitals. Appears with symphony orchestra. Teaches voice. **Res:** Arhotie 24 D 24, Helsinki 90, Finland. Mgmt: SLZ/FRG.

NURMELA, KARI. Dramatic baritone. Finnish. Resident mem: Opernhaus Zurich. Born 26 May 1937, Viipuri, Finland. Wife Ranée, occupation photographer. Four children. Studied: Prof O Nyberg, Helsinki; Prof S Radamsky, Vienna; Arturo Meriini, Milan. **Debut:** Conte di Luna (*Trovatore*) Helsinki 1961. Previous occupations: grad Univ of Commerce, Helsinki. Awards: First & Mozart Prize, Conc Intl de Chant de Belgique 1962.

Sang with major companies in CZE: Prague National & Smetana; FIN: Helsinki; FRA: Marseille, Nancy, Orange Fest; FR GER: Düsseldorf-Duisburg, Frankfurt, Hamburg, Hannover, Karlsruhe, Kassel, Kiel, Mannheim, Munich Staatsoper, Stuttgart, Wiesbaden; ITA: Bologna, Florence Maggio & Teatro Comunale, Genoa, Palermo, Venice; POR: Lisbon; SWI: Basel, Geneva, Zurich, USA: Seattle. **Roles with these companies incl** BRITTEN: Traveller (*Curlew River*); CIMAROSA: Count Robinson (*Matrimonio segreto*), DONIZETTI: Dott Malatesta (*Don Pasquale*), Nottingham★ (*Roberto Devereux*); LEONCAVALLO: Tonio★ (*Pagliacci*); LORTZING: Graf v Liebenau (*Waffenschmied*), Graf Eberbach (*Wildschütz*); MASCAGNI: Alfio★ (*Cavalleria rusticana*); MONTEVERDI: Orfeo; MOZART: Don Giovanni★, Nardo (*Finta giardiniera*), Conte Almaviva★ (*Nozze di Figaro*); ORFF: König (*Kluge*); PUCCINI: Marcello (*Bohème*), Sharpless★ (*Butterfly*), Lescaut★ (*Manon Lescaut*), Michele★ (*Tabarro*), Scarpia★ (*Tosca*); ROSSINI: Figaro (*Barbiere di Siviglia*); STRAUSS, R: Mandryka (*Arabella*), Orest★ (*Elektra*); VERDI: Renato★ (*Ballo in maschera*), Rodrigo★ (*Don Carlo*), Don Carlo★ (*Ernani*), Ford (*Falstaff*), Don Carlo★ (*Forza del destino*), Nabucco★, Iago★ (*Otello*), Rigoletto★, Germont (*Traviata*), Conte di Luna★ (*Trovatore*), Monforte (*Vespri*); WAGNER: Beckmesser (*Meistersinger*), Wolfram (*Tannhäuser*); WEINBERGER: Schwanda. Gives recitals. Appears with symphony orchestra. Teaches voice. **Res:** Zurich, Switzerland. Mgmt: GOR/UK.

NURMIMAA, SEPPO UOLEVI. Scenic and costume designer for opera, theater & ballet. Is a lighting designer. Finnish. Resident designer, Finnish National Opera, Helsinki. Born 19 Apr 1931, Helsinki. Wife Outi Rahi, occupation dancer. Two children. **Operatic debut:** *Let's Make an Opera* Finnish Ntl Opera 1958. Theater debut: Student Theater Group, Helsinki 1957. Awards: Pro Finlandia 1970, Gvnmt of Finland.

Designed for major companies in FIN: Helsinki; NOR: Oslo; POR: Lisbon; SWI: Zurich; USA: San Francisco Opera. **Operas designed for these companies incl** BEETHOVEN: *Fidelio;* BERG:

Wozzeck; BIZET: *Carmen;* BRITTEN: *Midsummer Night★, Turn of the Screw;* DONIZETTI: *Don Pasquale;* GERSHWIN: *Porgy and Bess;* GLUCK: *Orfeo ed Euridice★;* HENZE: *König Hirsch/Re Cervo;* JANACEK: *Cunning Little Vixen;* LEONCAVALLO: *Pagliacci;* MASCAGNI: *Cavalleria rusticana;* MOZART: *Così fan tutte★, Zauberflöte;* PUCCINI: *Bohème, Gianni Schicchi, Tosca★;* ROSSINI: *Barbiere di Siviglia★;* SAINT-SAENS: *Samson et Dalila;* SHOSTAKOVICH: *Katerina Ismailova;* STRAUSS, J: *Fledermaus;* STRAUSS, R: *Rosenkavalier;* STRAVINSKY: *Oedipus Rex;* VERDI: *Aida, Otello★, Rigoletto, Traviata, Trovatore.* **Operatic world premieres:** PYLKKANEN: *Ikaros* 1961; SAIKKOLA: *Ristin* 1959; both at Finnish Ntl Opera, Helsinki. Operatic Video/Film — cost, *Rigoletto.* **Res:** Fredrikinkatu 60, Helsinki, Finland.

NYBORG, ANNE KRISTINE. Lyric soprano. Norwegian. Resident mem: Norwegian Opera, Oslo. Born 27 Feb 1938, Oslo. Husband Finn Aberg, occupation teacher. One child. Studied: Anne Brown, Oslo; Paul Lohmann, Wiesbaden, FR Ger; Joan Cross, London. **Debut:** Clara (*Porgy and Bess*) Oslo Opera 1967. Previous occupations: teacher.

Sang with major companies in NOR: Oslo. **Roles with this company incl** MOZART: Despina (*Così fan tutte*), Cherubino★ (*Nozze di Figaro*), Pamina★ (*Zauberflöte*); PUCCINI: Mimi★ (*Bohème*), Cio-Cio-San★ (*Butterfly*); SMETANA: Marie (*Bartered Bride*); STRAUSS, R: Sophie★ (*Rosenkavalier*); VERDI: Nannetta (*Falstaff*); WERLE: Thérèse (*Dream of Thérèse*).

O

OBRAZTSOVA, ELENA VASILIEVNA. Mezzo-soprano. Russian. Resident mem: Bolshoi Opera, Moscow. Born 7 Jul 1939, Leningrad. Husband Makarov, occupation theoretical physicist. Studied: Leningrad Consv, Prof Grigoryve. **Debut:** Marina (*Boris Godunov*) Bolshoi Opera 1965.

Sang with major companies in BUL: Sofia; CZE: Brno, Prague National & Smetana; FRA: Marseille, Paris; FR GER: Wiesbaden; GER DR: Berlin Komische Oper & Staatsoper; HUN: Budapest; ITA: Milan La Scala, Rome Caracalla; MON: Monte Carlo; ROM: Bucharest; SPA: Barcelona, Majorca; USSR: Kiev, Leningrad Kirov, Moscow Bolshoi & Stanislavski, Tbilisi. **Roles with these companies incl** BIZET: Carmen; DONIZETTI: Léonore (*Favorite*); MASSENET: Charlotte‡ (*Werther*); MOZART: Cherubino‡ (*Nozze di Figaro*); MUSSORGSKY: Marina‡ (*Boris Godunov*), Marfa‡ (*Khovanshchina*); PROKOFIEV: Helene‡ (*War and Peace*); SAINT-SAENS: Dalila; STRAVINSKY: Jocasta (*Oedipus Rex*); TCHAIKOVSKY: Comtesse‡ (*Pique Dame*); VERDI: Amneris‡ (*Aida*), Ulrica‡ (*Ballo in maschera*), Eboli‡ (*Don Carlo*), Azucena‡ (*Trovatore*). Gives recitals. Appears with symphony orchestra. Teaches voice. Coaches repertoire. On faculty of Moscow Conservatory. **Res:** Bolshaya Dorogomilovshaya 21, Moscow. Mgmt: GOS/USSR; HUR/USA.

OCHMAN, WIESLAW. Lirico spinto tenor. Polish. Resident mem: Warsaw Opera; Staatsoper, Hamburg. Born 6 Feb 1937, Warsaw, Poland. Wife Krystyna, occupation master's degree Eng. Two children. Studied: Prof Gustaw Serafin, Krakow; Prof Maria Szlapak, Bytom, Poland; Prof Sergiusz Nadgryzowski, Warsaw. **Debut:** Edgardo (*Lucia*) Opera Bytom, Poland. Awards: Awd, Ministry of Culture, Gvnmt of Poland.

Sang with major companies in AUS: Salzburg Fest, Vienna Staatsoper & Volksoper; BUL: Sofia; CZE: Prague National; FRA: Paris; FR GER: Berlin Deutsche Oper, Frankfurt, Hamburg, Hannover, Munich Staatsoper; GER DR: Berlin Staatsoper; HUN: Budapest; POL: Lodz, Warsaw; SPA: Majorca; SWI: Geneva; UK: Glyndebourne Fest; USSR: Moscow Bolshoi; USA: Chicago, New York Met, San Francisco Opera. **Roles with these companies incl** BIZET: Don José★ (*Carmen*), Nadir (*Pêcheurs de perles*); DEBUSSY: Azaël (*Enfant prodigue*); DONIZETTI:

Ernesto (*Don Pasquale*), Edgardo★ (*Lucia*); FLOTOW: Lionel (*Martha*); GIORDANO: Andrea Chénier★; GOUNOD: Faust‡; MASCAGNI: Turiddu★ (*Cavalleria rusticana*); MASSENET: Werther; MONIUSZKO: Jontek★‡ (*Halka*), Stefan★ (*Haunted Castle*); MOZART: Don Ottavio★ (*Don Giovanni*), Idomeneo★, Tamino (*Zauberflöte*); MUSSORGSKY: Andrei Khovansky★ (*Khovanshchina*); PUCCINI: Rodolfo (*Bohème*), Cavaradossi★ (*Tosca*); ROSSINI: Almaviva (*Barbiere di Siviglia*); STRAUSS, J: Alfred★ (*Fledermaus*); STRAUSS, R: Ein Sänger (*Rosenkavalier*); TCHAIKOVSKY: Lenski★ (*Eugene Onegin*); VERDI: Riccardo★ (*Ballo in maschera*), Don Carlo★, Duca di Mantova★ (*Rigoletto*), Alfredo★ (*Traviata*), Arrigo★ (*Vespri*); WEBER: Max (*Freischütz*); WOLF-FERRARI: Florindo (*Donne curiose*). Also MUSSORGSKY: Dimitri★ (*Boris Godunov*); SZYMANOWSKI: Shepherd (*King Roger*); DARGOMYZSKI: Prinz (*Rusalka*). Recorded for: DG, Polydor, Polskie Nagrania. Video/Film: Lenski (*Eugene Onegin*); Don Ottavio (*Don Giovanni*); Narraboth (*Salome*). Gives recitals. Appears with symphony orchestra. **Res:** Miaczynska 46B, Warsaw, Poland. Mgmt: PAG/POL; SLZ/FRG; RAB/AUS; CAM/USA.

OGNIVTSEV, ALEXANDER. Bass. Russian. Resident mem: Bolshoi Opera, Moscow. Born Ukraine, USSR. Married.

Sang with major companies in USSR: Moscow Bolshoi; et al. **Roles with these companies incl** BORODIN: Galitzky (*Prince Igor*); MASSENET: Don Quichotte; MUSSORGSKY: Boris Godunov, Dosifei (*Khovanshchina*); PROKOFIEV: General (*Gambler*); TCHAIKOVSKY: Yeletsky (*Pique Dame*), Gremin (*Eugene Onegin*); et al.

OHANESIAN, DAVID. Dramatic baritone. Romanian. Resident mem: Romanian Opera, Bucharest; Staatsoper, Hamburg. Born 6 Jan 1927, Bucharest. Wife Theodora. Studied: Consv, Prof Aurel Costescu-Duca, Bucharest. **Debut:** Tonio (*Pagliacci*) Romanian Opera, Cluj 1950. Awards: State Prize, Merited Artist 1952; Rameau Medal, Dijon 1964; Grand Prix du Disque, Paris 1974.

Sang with major companies in AUS: Vienna Staatsoper; BEL: Liège; BUL: Sofia; CZE: Brno, Prague National & Smetana; FRA: Lyon, Orange

Fest, Paris, Rouen, Toulouse; GRE: Athens National & Fest; FR GER: Berlin Deutsche Oper, Hamburg, Karlsruhe, Kassel, Munich Staatsoper, Wiesbaden; GER DR: Berlin Staatsoper; HUN: Budapest; ISR: Tel Aviv; POL: Warsaw; ROM: Bucharest; SPA: Barcelona; SWE: Stockholm; SWI: Zurich; USSR: Kiev, Leningrad Kirov, Moscow Bolshoi & Stanislavski, Tbilisi. **Roles with these companies incl** BIZET: Escamillo★ (*Carmen*); BORODIN: Prince Igor & Galitzky★ (*Prince Igor*); DONIZETTI: Enrico★ (*Lucia*); GIORDANO: Carlo Gérard★ (*Andrea Chénier*); GOUNOD: Méphistophélès★ (*Faust*); LEONCAVALLO: Tonio★ (*Pagliacci*); MASCAGNI: Alfio★ (*Cavalleria rusticana*); MONIUSZKO: Janusz (*Halka*); MUSSORGSKY: Boris Godunov★, Tcherevik‡ (*Fair at Sorochinsk*); PUCCINI: Marcello★ (*Bohème*), Scarpia★ (*Tosca*); ROSSINI: Figaro★ (*Barbiere di Siviglia*); SAINT-SAENS: Grand prêtre★ (*Samson et Dalila*); TCHAIKOVSKY: Eugene Onegin★, Amonasro★ (*Aida*), Renato★ (*Ballo in maschera*), Rodrigo★ (*Don Carlo*), Iago★ (*Otello*), Rigoletto★, Germont★ (*Traviata*), Conte di Luna★ (*Trovatore*), Monforte★ (*Vespri*); WAGNER: Telramund★ (*Lohengrin*), Wolfram (*Tannhäuser*), WEBER: Kaspar (*Freischütz*). Also TCHAIKOVSKY: Mazeppa; GOUNOD: Valentin (*Faust*); RACHMANINOFF: Aleko. **World premieres:** CONSTANTINESCU: (*Pana Lesnea Rusalim*), Cluj 1956; POPOVICI: Prometeu 1964; ENESCU: Oedipe 1958; both Romanian Opera. Recorded for: Electrecord. Video/Film: Oedipe, Aleko, Conte di Luna (*Trovatore*). **Res:** 13 Cimpinita St, Bucharest 1, Romania. Mgmt: RIA/ROM; SLZ/FRG; TAS/AUS.

O'HEARN, ROBERT. Scenic and costume designer for opera, theater & ballet; specl in sets. Is a lighting designer. American. Born 19 Jul 1921, Elkhart, IN. Single. Studied: Indiana Univ, Bloomington. **Operatic debut:** sets, *Rake's Progress* Boston Univ 1953; costumes, *Elisir* Metropolitan Opera 1960. Theater debut: Brattle Theatre Co, Cambridge, MA 1948.

Designed for major cos in AUS: Bregenz Fest, Vienna Staatsoper & Volksoper; FRA: Strasbourg; FR GER: Hamburg, Karlsruhe; USA: Boston, Miami, New York Met, Santa Fe, Washington DC. **Operas designed for these companies incl** BIZET: *Carmen★*; BRITTEN: *Midsummer Night★*; DONIZETTI: *Don Pasquale★, Elisir, Lucia;* FALLA: *Retablo de Maese Pedro;* FOSS: *Griffelkin;* GAY/Britten: *Beggar's Opera;* GERSHWIN: *Porgy and Bess★*; HUMPERDINCK: *Hänsel und Gretel;* IBERT: *Angélique;* MOZART: *Don Giovanni, Idomeneo, Nozze di Figaro★, Zauberflöte;* MUSSORGSKY: *Boris Godunov;* PUCCINI: *Bohème, Fanciulla del West★, Gianni Schicchi★, Tabarro;* ROSSINI: *Barbiere di Siviglia★;* SAINT-SAENS: *Samson et Dalila;* STRAUSS, J: *Fledermaus;* STRAUSS, R: *Ariadne auf Naxos, Frau ohne Schatten, Rosenkavalier;* STRAVINSKY: *Rake's Progress;* TCHAIKOVSKY: *Pique Dame;* VERDI: *Aida, Falstaff★, Forza del destino★, Otello, Traviata, Trovatore;* WAGNER: *Meistersinger★, Parsifal.* Also CAVALLI: *Scipio Africanus.* Exhibitions of stage designs Lincoln Cnt Library-Museum of Perf Arts, New York 1974. Teaches at Studio and

Forum of Stage Design, New York. **Res:** 59 Fifth Ave, New York, USA.

OKAMURA, TAKAO. Bass. Japanese. Resident mem: Opernhaus, Cologne, FR Ger. Born 25 Oct 1931, Tokyo. Wife Kazuko. One child. Studied: Consv, Profs Pediconi, Favaretto, Rome: Musikakad, Prof Werba, Vienna. **Debut:** Montano (*Otello*) Italian opera troupe in Tokyo 1959. Awards: First Prize, Intl Cont, Toulouse; Gold Medal, Intl Cont Viotti.

Sang with major companies in FRA: Strasbourg; FR GER: Berlin Deutsche Oper, Cologne, Düsseldorf-Duisburg, Kiel, Munich Staatsoper; ITA: Verona Arena; JPN: Tokyo Fujiwara & Niki Kai; SPA: Barcelona; SWI: Basel, Zurich. **Roles with these companies incl** d'ALBERT: Tommaso (*Tiefland*); BEETHOVEN: Rocco★ (*Fidelio*); DONIZETTI: Don Pasquale; GOUNOD: Méphistophélès★ (*Faust*); HANDEL: Ptolemy (*Giulio Cesare*); MOZART: Publio (*Clemenza di Tito*), Sarastro★ (*Zauberflöte*); MUSSORGSKY: Boris Godunov★; PUCCINI: Colline (*Bohème*); ROSSINI: Don Basilio★ (*Barbiere di Siviglia*); VERDI: Ramfis★ (*Aida*), Philip II & Grande Inquisitore (*Don Carlo*), Padre Guardiano★ (*Forza del destino*), Banquo (*Macbeth*); WAGNER: Daland★ (*Fliegende Holländer*), Fasolt (*Rheingold*), Fafner (*Rheingold‡, Siegfried‡*), Hunding (*Walküre*), König Marke★ (*Tristan und Isolde*). Also PUCCINI: Timur (*Turandot*). **World premieres:** YUN: Son-long (*Geisterliebe*) Kiel 1971; ISHII: Gyoja (*En no Gyoja*) Tokyo-NHK 1961; KOYAMA: Yajiro (*Yamashiro kuniikki*) Tokyo-Roon 1962. Recorded for: Fratelli Fabbri, Westminster. Gives recitals. Appears with symphony orchestra. **Res:** Lothringerstr 23, 5 Cologne 1, FR Ger. Mgmt: MIC/JPN; SLZ/FRG.

OLDANI, LUIGI. Italian. European Representative, Metropolitan Opera, Lincoln Center, New York, NY 10023, USA. Born 31 Dec 1909, San Donato/Milan, Italy. Married. Previous positions primarily administrative & theatrical: Chief Adm 1932-41, Gen Secy 1942-72, Prod Dir & Advisor 1973-74, all at Teatro alla Scala, Milan. In present position since 1975. Awards: Commendatore, Rep of Italy; Artist of Merit, Rep of France; Medal of Merit, City of Milan; Gold Medal, La Scala. **Res:** V dei Gracchi 9, Milan, Italy.

O'LEARY, THOMAS JAMES. Bass. American. Born 3 Sep 1924, Punxsutawney, PA, USA. Wife Dorothy, occupation businesswoman. One child. Studied: Dr E A Thormodsgaard, El Paso, TX; Alexander Kipnis, New York; Mo L d'Angelo, Rome. **Debut:** Kezal (*Bartered Bride*) San Jose Grand Opera 1947.

Sang with major companies in AUS: Graz, Vienna Staatsoper & Volksoper; CAN: Ottawa, Toronto; CZE: Brno; FRA: Lyon, Marseille; FR GER: Berlin Deutsche Oper, Cologne, Düsseldorf-Duisburg, Frankfurt, Hamburg, Hannover, Mannheim, Munich Staatsoper, Nürnberg; ITA: Bologna, Rome Opera, Trieste; SPA: Barcelona, Majorca; SWI: Basel, Geneva, Zurich; USA: Baltimore, Boston, Houston, New Orleans, San Diego, San Francisco Opera. **Roles with these companies incl** BEETHOVEN: Rocco (*Fidelio*); BELLINI: Sir George★ (*Puritani*); BOITO:

Mefistofele; DEBUSSY: Arkel (*Pelléas et Mélisande*); EGK: Cuperus (*Zaubergeige*); GOUNOD: Méphistophélès (*Faust*); MOZART: Sarastro ★ (*Zauberflöte*); MUSSORGSKY: Boris & Varlaam & Pimen (*Boris Godunov*); ORFF: Bauer ★ (*Mond*); PUCCINI: Colline (*Bohème*); SMETANA: Kezal (*Bartered Bride*); STRAUSS, R: Orest (*Elektra*); VERDI: Ramfis ★ (*Aida*), Philip II (*Don Carlo*), Padre Guardiano (*Forza del destino*), Massimiliano Moor ★ (*Masnadieri*), Zaccaria (*Nabucco*), Fiesco (*Simon Boccanegra*); WAGNER: Daland ★ (*Fliegende Holländer*), König Heinrich ★ (*Lohengrin*), Pogner (*Meistersinger*), Gurnemanz (*Parsifal*), Fasolt & Fafner ★ (*Rheingold*), Fafner (*Siegfried*), Hunding ★ (*Walküre*), Hagen ★ (*Götterdämmerung*), Landgraf (*Tannhäuser*), König Marke (*Tristan und Isolde*). Gives recitals. Appears with symphony orchestra. Teaches voice. **Res:** 4249 Westwood Ct, Concord, CA 94521, USA. Mgmt: SAM/USA.

OLIVERO, MAGDA; née Maria Maddalena Olivero. Lyric soprano. Italian. Born 25 Mar 1916, Saluzzo/Turin, Italy. Husband Busch. Studied: travelling companies. **Debut:** Lauretta (*Gianni Schicchi*) Turin 1933.
Sang with major companies in AUS: Vienna Staatsoper; BRA: Rio de Janeiro; FIN: Helsinki; FRA: Paris; FR GER: Berlin Deutsche Oper, Frankfurt, Stuttgart, Wiesbaden; GER DR: Berlin Staatsoper; HOL: Amsterdam; ITA: Bologna, Florence Maggio & Comunale, Genoa, Milan La Scala, Naples, Palermo, Parma, Rome Opera & Caracalla, Trieste, Turin, Venice, Verona Arena; MON: Monte Carlo; POR: Lisbon; SPA: Barcelona; SWI: Geneva, Zurich; UK: Edinburgh Fest; USA: Dallas, Hartford, Kansas City, Newark, New York Met; YUG: Zagreb. **Roles with these companies incl** BIZET: Micaëla (*Carmen*); BOITO: Margherita (*Mefistofele*); CATALANI: Wally; CHERUBINI: Medea; CILEA: Adriana Lecouvreur; GIORDANO: Fedora; GOUNOD: Marguerite (*Faust*); JANACEK: Kostelnicka (*Jenufa*); MASCAGNI: Suzel (*Amico Fritz*), Santuzza (*Cavalleria rusticana*); MASSENET: Manon, Charlotte (*Werther*); MENOTTI: Magda Sorel (*Consul*), Monica (*Medium*); MOZART: Zerlina (*Don Giovanni*); POULENC: Blanche (*Dialogues des Carmélites*), Femme (*Voix humaine*); PUCCINI: Mimi (*Bohème*), Minnie (*Fanciulla del West*), Lauretta (*Gianni Schicchi*), Cio-Cio-San (*Butterfly*), Manon Lescaut, Suor Angelica, Giorgetta (*Tabarro*), Tosca, Liù (*Turandot*); STRAUSS, R: Sophie (*Rosenkavalier*); THOMAS: Philine (*Mignon*); VERDI: Alice Ford & Nannetta (*Falstaff*), Gilda (*Rigoletto*), Violetta (*Traviata*); WAGNER: Elsa (*Lohengrin*); ZANDONAI: Francesca da Rimini, Giulietta. Also ALFANO: Katiusha (*Risurrezione*), Rossana (*Cyrano di Bergerac*), Sakuntala; HONEGGER: Aiglon; LANGELLA: Assunta Spina; GIORDANO: Carmela (*Mese mariano*), Marcella; MALIPIERO: Sette personaggi (*Mondi celesti e infernali, Sette canzoni*); POULENC: Mère Lidoine (*Dialogues des Carmélites*); SAUGUET: Voyante; WOLF-FERRARI: Lucieta & Sora Felice (*Quattro rusteghi*), Vedova (*Vedova scaltra*), Agnese (*Amor medico*), Lucieta (*Campiello*); TCHAIKOVSKY: Maria (*Mazeppa*), Comtesse (*Pique Dame*); MASCAGNI: Iris.

World premieres: TESTI: Melibea (*Celestina*) Maggio Musicale, Florence 1963; ROSSELLINI: Mother (*Guerra*) San Carlo Opera, Naples 1956. Recorded for: Decca, Cetra. Gives recitals. Teaches voice. Coaches repertoire. **Res:** V Politecnico 5, Milan, Italy. Mgmt: NAP/USA.

OLLENDORFF, FRITZ. Basso-buffo. Swiss. Resident mem: Deutsche Oper am Rhein, Düsseldorf-Duisburg. Born 29 Mar 1912, Darmstadt, Germany. Wife Gertrud Nihues. Studied: Vittorino Moratti, Milan. **Debut:** Leporello (*Don Giovanni*) Germany 1937. Awards: First Prize, Intl Voice Compt Geneva 1939.
Sang with major companies in AUS: Bregenz Fest; FRA: Aix-en-Provence Fest, Bordeaux, Paris; FR GER: Düsseldorf-Duisburg, Stuttgart; HOL: Amsterdam; ITA: Florence Maggio, Turin; SPA: Barcelona; SWI: Basel, Geneva, Zurich; UK: Glyndebourne Fest; USA: San Antonio. **Roles with these companies incl** ADAM: Bijou (*Postillon de Lonjumeau*); BEETHOVEN: Rocco (*Fidelio*); CIMAROSA: Geronimo (*Matrimonio segreto*); CORNELIUS: Abul Hassan (*Barbier von Bagdad*); DONIZETTI: Don Pasquale, Dulcamara (*Elisir*), Sulpice (*Fille du régiment*); LORTZING: Stadinger & Graf v Liebenau (*Waffenschmied*), Baculus (*Wildschütz*), Van Bett ★ (*Zar und Zimmermann*); MOZART: Don Alfonso (*Così fan tutte*), Leporello ★ (*Don Giovanni*), Osmin (*Entführung aus dem Serail*), Figaro (*Nozze di Figaro*); MUSSORGSKY: Varlaam (*Boris Godunov*); NICOLAI: Falstaff ★ (*Lustigen Weiber*); PROKOFIEV: Mendoza (*Duenna*); PUCCINI: Gianni Schicchi; ROSSINI: Dott Bartolo ★ (*Barbiere di Siviglia*), Mustafà (*Italiana in Algeri*); SMETANA: Kezal (*Bartered Bride*); STRAUSS, R: Baron Ochs (*Rosenkavalier*); VERDI: Fra Melitone (*Forza del destino*); WAGNER: Daland (*Fliegende Holländer*), Beckmesser (*Meistersinger*), Alberich (*Götterdämmerung*); WOLF-FERRARI: Lunardo (*Quattro rusteghi*). **World premieres:** EGK: Stadthauptmann (*Der Revisor*) Stuttgart, Schwetzingen Fest 1957. **Res:** Graf Reckestr 71, Düsseldorf, FR Ger.

OMAN, JULIA TREVELYAN. Scenic and costume designer for opera, theater, film, television. Is also a painter, illustrator, photographer, author and lecturer. British. Born 11 Jul 1930, Kensington, UK. Husband Dr Roy Strong, occupation Dir, Victoria & Albert Museum, London. Studied: Royal Coll of Art, London. **Operatic debut:** sets, cost, *Mefistofele* Welsh National Op, Cardiff 1957. Theater debut: BBC TV London 1955. Awards: Silver Medal & Royal Scholar, Royal Coll of Art; Designer of the Year Awd 1969.
Designed for major companies in FR GER: Hamburg; UK: London Royal. **Operas designed for these companies incl** PUCCINI: *Bohème ★;* TCHAIKOVSKY: *Eugene Onegin ★;* VERDI: *Ballo in maschera ★*. Exhibitions of stage designs Victoria & Albert Museum, London. **Res:** 2E Morpeth Terrace, London, UK. Mgmt: LMG/UK; LTZ/USA.

ONCINA, JUAN. Lyric & dramatic tenor. Spanish. Resident mem: Staatsoper, Vienna. Born 15 Apr 1925, Barcelona. Wife Tatiana. Studied: Mercedes Capsir, Mme J Campredon, Augusta Oltrabella.

Debut: Almaviva (*Barbiere di Siviglia*) Bologna Opera 1955.

Sang with major companies in ARG: Buenos Aires; AUS: Bregenz Fest, Vienna Staatsoper; BEL: Brussels; BRA: Rio de Janeiro; CAN: Montreal/Quebec; FRA: Aix-en Provence Fest, Bordeaux, Lyon, Marseille, Nancy, Nice, Paris, Rouen, Strasbourg, Toulouse; GRE: Athens Fest; FR GER: Berlin Deutsche Oper, Hamburg, Munich Staatsoper, Saarbrücken, Wiesbaden; GER DR: Berlin Staatsoper; HOL: Amsterdam; HUN: Budapest; ISR: Tel Aviv; ITA: Bologna, Florence Maggio & Comunale, Genoa, Milan La Scala, Naples, Palermo, Rome Opera, Trieste, Turin, Venice; MON: Monte Carlo; POR: Lisbon; SPA: Barcelona; SWI: Basel, Geneva, Zurich; UK: Edinburgh Fest, Glasgow Scottish, Glyndebourne Fest, London Royal; USA: Miami; YUG: Zagreb, Belgrade. **Roles with these companies incl** BEETHOVEN: Florestan (*Fidelio*); BELLINI: Orombello (*Beatrice di Tenda*), Elvino (*Sonnambula*); BIZET: Don José* (*Carmen*), Nadir (*Pêcheurs de perles*); BOIELDIEU: George Brown (*Dame blanche*); BOITO: Faust* (*Mefistofele*); BUSONI: Mephisto (*Doktor Faust*); CHERUBINI: Giasone (*Medea*); CILEA: Maurizio (*A. Lecouvreur*); CIMAROSA: Paolino (*Matrimonio segreto*); DEBUSSY: Pelléas; DONIZETTI: Riccardo (*Anna Bolena*), Ernesto (*Don Pasquale*), Nemorino (*Elisir*), Tonio (*Fille du régiment*), Edgardo* (*Lucia*), Leicester (*Maria Stuarda*), Beppo (*Rita*), Roberto Devereux; FALLA: Maese Pedro (*Retablo de Maese Pedro*); GIORDANO: Andrea Chénier, Loris Ipanov (*Fedora*); GOUNOD: Faust; GRANADOS: Fernando (*Goyescas*); HANDEL: Acis; MASCAGNI: Fritz (*Amico Fritz*); MASSENET: Des Grieux* (*Manon*), Werther*; MONTEVERDI: Nero* (*Incoronazione di Poppea*); MOZART: Ferrando (*Così fan tutte*), Don Ottavio (*Don Giovanni*), Belmonte (*Entführung aus dem Serail*), Alessandro (*Re pastore*), Tamino (*Zauberflöte*); PAISIELLO: Almaviva (*Barbiere di Siviglia*); PROKOFIEV: Prince (*Love for Three Oranges*); PUCCINI: Rodolfo* (*Bohème*), Rinuccio (*Gianni Schicchi*), Pinkerton* (*Butterfly*), Des Grieux* (*Manon Lescaut*), Cavaradossi* (*Tosca*); ROSSINI: Almaviva (*Barbiere di Siviglia*), Don Ramiro (*Cenerentola*), Comte Ory, Lindoro (*Italiana in Algeri*); STRAUSS, J: Eisenstein (*Fledermaus*); THOMAS: Wilhelm Meister (*Mignon*); VERDI: Riccardo* (*Ballo in maschera*), Don Carlo*, Fenton (*Falstaff*), Don Alvaro* (*Forza del destino*), Edoardo (*Giorno di regno*), Rodolfo* (*Luisa Miller*), Duca di Mantova (*Rigoletto*), Alfredo* (*Traviata*); WOLF-FERRARI: Florindo (*Donne curiose*). **World premieres:** RIVIERE: Don Quichotte (*Pour un Don Quichotte*) La Scala, Milan 1961. Recorded for: Westminster, HMV, Decca. Gives recitals. Appears with symphony orchestra. Teaches voice. Coaches repertoire.

O'NEILL, CHARLES EDWARD. Dramatic tenor. American. Resident mem: Theater am Gärtnerplatz, Munich. Born 22 Sep 1930, Ridgefield Park, NJ, USA. Wife Georgette. Six children. Studied: Sidney Dietch, USA. **Debut:** Radames (*Aida*) Fort Worth Opera, TX, USA 1958. **Awards:** Winner Leonard Warren Schlshp 1953; Winner Met Op Aud of the Air 1957.

Sang with major companies in CAN: Toronto, Vancouver; FR GER: Berlin Deutsche Oper, Bonn, Cologne, Darmstadt, Düsseldorf-Duisburg, Essen, Frankfurt, Hamburg, Hannover, Kassel, Kiel, Krefeld, Mannheim, Munich Gärtnerplatz, Stuttgart, Wiesbaden; SWI: Basel, Zurich; USA: Baltimore, Cincinnati Summer Opera, Fort Worth, San Antonio, Santa Fe; YUG: Belgrade. **Roles with these companies incl** BEETHOVEN: Florestan (*Fidelio*); BIZET: Don José* (*Carmen*); GIORDANO: Andrea Chénier; GOUNOD: Faust; HALEVY: Eléazar (*Juive*); LEONCAVALLO: Canio (*Pagliacci*); MASCAGNI: Turiddu (*Cavalleria rusticana*); PUCCINI: Rodolfo (*Bohème*), Pinkerton (*Butterfly*), Des Grieux (*Manon Lescaut*), Cavaradossi (*Tosca*), Calaf* (*Turandot*); SAINT-SAENS: Samson*; STRAUSS, J: Alfred* (*Fledermaus*); STRAUSS, R: Bacchus (*Ariadne auf Naxos*), Ein Sänger (*Rosenkavalier*); STRAVINSKY: Oedipus Rex; TCHAIKOVSKY: Gherman* (*Pique Dame*); VERDI: Radames* (*Aida*), Don Carlo, Don Alvaro* (*Forza del destino*), Otello*, Manrico* (*Trovatore*); WAGNER: Erik* (*Fliegende Holländer*), Siegmund (*Walküre*); WEILL: Jim Mahoney* (*Aufstieg und Fall der Stadt Mahagonny*). **Res:** Duisbergstr 9, Frankfurt, FR Ger.

ONOFREI, MATILDA. Coloratura soprano. Romanian. Resident mem: Romanian Opera, Bucharest. Born 19 Feb 1932, Cluj. Husband Nicolae Voiculetz, occupation scientist. Studied: Profs Constantin Stroescu, Margareta Metaxa, Janine Michaud; Dimitri Onofrei, San Francisco. **Debut:** Konstanze (*Entführung aus dem Serail*) Romanian Opera 1957.

Sang with major companies in ROM: Bucharest. **Roles with these companies incl** DELIBES: Lakmé; DONIZETTI: Lucia*; MOZART: Despina* (*Così fan tutte*), Zerlina* (*Don Giovanni*), Konstanze* & Blondchen (*Entführung aus dem Serail*); PUCCINI: Musetta* (*Bohème*); ROSSINI: Rosina (*Barbiere di Siviglia*); STRAUSS, J: Adele* (*Fledermaus*); STRAUSS, R: Sophie (*Rosenkavalier*); VERDI: Oscar* (*Ballo in maschera*), Gilda (*Rigoletto*). Gives recitals. Appears with symphony orchestra. Teaches voice. Coaches repertoire. **Res:** 15 Baiculesti St, Bucharest, Romania. Mgmt: RIA/ROM.

OPIE, ALAN JOHN. Lyric baritone. British. Resident mem: English National Opera, London. Born 22 Mar 1945, Redruth, UK. Wife Kathleen Smales, occupation opera singer, mezzo-soprano. Studied: Guildhall School of Music & Drama, Arthur Reckless, London; London Opera Centre; Mme Vera Rozsa. **Debut:** Papageno (*Zauberflöte*) Sadler's Wells Opera 1969. **Awards:** AGSM, Guildhall School of Music, London; Cinzano Opera Compt, Schlshp for London Opera Centre.

Sang with major companies in UK: Aldeburgh Fest, Cardiff Welsh, London Eng Natl; USA: Santa Fe. **Roles with these companies incl** BRITTEN: Charles Blount* (*Gloriana*), Demetrius* (*Midsummer Night*); MASSENET: Lescaut* (*Manon*); MENOTTI: Tony (*Globolinks*); MOZART: Guglielmo* (*Così fan tutte*), Papageno* (*Zauberflöte*); ROSSINI: Figaro* (*Barbiere di Siviglia*), Robert (*Comte Ory*); VERDI: Germont*

(*Traviata*). Gives recitals. Appears with symphony orchestra. **Res:** London, UK. **Mgmt:** AIM/UK.

OPTHOF, CORNELIS. Dramatic baritone. Canadian. Resident mem: Canadian Opera Co, Toronto; Metropolitan Opera, New York. Born 10 Feb 1932, Rotterdam, Holland. Wife Natalie. Three children. Studied: Consv of Toronto, Herman Geiger-Torel, Canada. **Debut:** Silvio (*Pagliacci*) Canadian Opera Co, Toronto.

Sang with major companies in AUSTRL: Sydney; CAN: Ottawa, Toronto, Vancouver; SPA: Majorca; UK: London English National; USA: Fort Worth, Hartford, Miami, Milwaukee Florentine, New Orleans, New York Met, Philadelphia Lyric, Pittsburgh, San Francisco Opera, Seattle. **Roles with these companies incl** BELLINI: Sir Richard★ (*Puritani*); DONIZETTI: Dott Malatesta (*Don Pasquale*), Belcore★ (*Elisir*), Enrico★ (*Lucia*), Talbot★ (*Maria Stuarda*); MASCAGNI: Alfio (*Cavalleria rusticana*); MOZART: Guglielmo★ (*Così fan tutte*), Conte Almaviva★ (*Nozze di Figaro*), PUCCINI: Marcello★ (*Bohème*), Sharpless★ (*Butterfly*), Lescaut★ (*Manon Lescaut*), Rambaldo★ (*Rondine*); ROSSINI: Figaro★ (*Barbiere di Siviglia*), Robert★ (*Comte Ory*); VERDI: Amonasro★ (*Aida*), Rodrigo★ (*Don Carlo*), Ford★ (*Falstaff*), Germont★ (*Traviata*), Conte di Luna★ (*Trovatore*). Also HUMPERDINCK: Peter (*Hänsel und Gretel*). **World premieres:** SOMERS: MacDonald (*Louis Riel*) Canadian Opera Co, Toronto 1967. Recorded for: London. Video/Film: Peter (*Hänsel und Gretel*); Rambaldo (*Rondine*). Appears with symphony orchestra. **Res:** Toronto, Ont, Canada. **Mgmt:** SAM/USA.

OROFINO, RUGGERO. Lyric & dramatic tenor. Italian. Resident mem: Staatsoper, Berlin, Ger DR. Born 28 Sep 1932, Barletta/Bari, Italy. Wife Monica. One child. **Debut:** Turiddu (*Cavalleria rusticana*) Teatro Bonci, Cesena, Italy. Previous occupations: stationmaster, mechanic, chorister. Awards: Gold Medal, Teatro dell'Opera, Rome.

Sang with major companies in AUS: Vienna Staatsoper; BEL: Brussels; FIN: Helsinki; FRA: Aix-en-Provence, Paris, Strasbourg; FR GER: Berlin Deutsche Oper, Cologne, Dortmund, Düsseldorf-Duisburg, Frankfurt, Hamburg, Karlsruhe, Munich Staatsoper, Nürnberg, Stuttgart; GER DR: Berlin Komische Oper & Staatsoper, Dresden, Leipzig; HOL: Amsterdam; HUN: Budapest; ITA: Bologna, Florence Comunale, Genoa, Milan La Scala, Parma, Rome Opera & Caracalla, Turin, Venice; USA: Portland. **Roles with these companies incl** BELLINI: Pollione★ (*Norma*); BIZET: Don José (*Carmen*); BOITO: Faust (*Mefistofele*); CHERUBINI: Giasone (*Medea*); CILEA: Maurizio (*A. Lecouvreur*); DONIZETTI: Nemorino (*Elisir*), Edgardo (*Lucia*); GIORDANO: Andrea Chénier★ (*A. Chénier*); GLUCK: Admetos (*Alceste*); HANDEL: Xerxes; JANACEK: Laca★ & Steva★ (*Jenufa*); LEONCAVALLO: Canio (*Pagliacci*); MASCAGNI: Fritz (*Amico Fritz*), Turiddu★ (*Cavalleria rusticana*); MASSENET: Des Grieux (*Manon*); MONTEVERDI: Ulisse (*Ritorno d'Ulisse*); PONCHIELLI: Enzo (*Gioconda*); PUCCINI: Rodolfo★ (*Bohème*), Dick Johnson (*Fanciulla del West*), Pinkerton★ (*Butterfly*), Des Grieux (*Manon Lescaut*), Cavaradossi★ (*Tosca*), Calaf★ (*Turan-*

dot); STRAUSS, J: Alfred★ (*Fledermaus*); STRAUSS, R: Ein Sänger★ (*Rosenkavalier*); VERDI: Radames★ (*Aida*), Riccardo★ (*Ballo in maschera*), Don Carlo★, Ernani, Don Alvaro (*Forza del destino*), Rodolfo★ (*Luisa Miller*), Duca di Mantova★ (*Rigoletto*), Gabriele (*Simon Boccanegra*), Alfredo (*Traviata*), Manrico★ (*Trovatore*), Arrigo (*Vespri*); WAGNER: Lohengrin★; ZANDONAI: Paolo (*Francesca da Rimini*). Gives recitals. Appears with symphony orchestra. Teaches voice. **Mgmt:** SMD/FRG.

OSBORNE, GEORGE. Stages/produces opera & theater. Also designs stage-lighting and is a conductor, singer & college teacher. American. Gen Dir & Resident Stage Dir, Memphis Opera Theatre & Southern Opera Theatre, TN. Born 25 Aug 1938, Ft Worth, TX. Wife Jennifer Johnson, occupation singer. One child. Studied: Oklahoma Univ, Okla City; Riccardo Picozzi, Rome; Indiana Univ, Ross Allen, Hans Busch, Bloomington; incl music, piano & voice. **Operatic debut:** *Orfeo ed Euridice* SW Missouri Op, Springfield 1964. Theater debut: Lyric Theatre, Memphis 1972. Previous adm positions in opera: Assoc Dir, SW Missouri Op, Springfield 1964-66.

Directed/produced opera for major companies in USA: Memphis. **Operas staged with these companies incl** BRITTEN: *Albert Herring★;* DEBUSSY: *Enfant prodigue★;* DONIZETTI: *Don Pasquale★, Elisir★;* MENOTTI: *Amahl★, Consul★;* MOZART: *Don Giovanni★, Zauberflöte★;* MUSSORGSKY: *Boris Godunov★;* PUCCINI: *Butterfly★;* ROSSINI: *Barbiere di Siviglia★;* SAINT-SAENS: *Samson et Dalila★;* STRAUSS, R: *Salome;* VERDI: *Rigoletto.* Previous leading positions with major theater companies: Art Dir, Lyric Theatre, Memphis, TN 1972-74. Teaches at Memphis State Univ. **Res:** 1674 Central, Memphis, TN, USA.

OSTAPIUK, JERZY. Bass. Polish. Resident mem: Teatr Wielki, Warsaw. Born 21 Jun 1936, Uscimów, Poland. Married. Wife's occupation ballet dancer. One child. Studied: Warsaw State School of Music, Prof G Orlow, Warsaw; W Filipowicz, Warsaw. **Debut:** Zbigniew (*Haunted Manor*) Warsaw Opera 1968.

Sang with major companies in FR GER: Essen, Hamburg, Wiesbaden; POL: Warsaw. **Roles with these companies incl** MOZART: Osmin★ (*Entführung aus dem Serail*), Sarastro★ (*Zauberflöte*); MUSSORGSKY: Boris Godunov★ & Varlaam★ (*Boris Godunov*); PENDERECKI: Barré (*Teufel von Loudun*); PUCCINI: Colline (*Bohème*); ROSSINI: Don Basilio★ (*Barbiere di Siviglia*); VERDI: Ramfis★ (*Aida*), Philip II★ & Grande Inquisitore★ (*Don Carlo*); WAGNER: Landgraf★ (*Tannhäuser*). Gives recitals. Appears with symphony orchestra. **Res:** Chtodna 11, apt 1516, Warsaw, Poland. **Mgmt:** PAG/POL; SLZ/FRG.

OSTENDORF, JOHN DANIEL. Bass-baritone. American. Born 1 Nov 1945, New York. Single. Studied: Oberlin Coll, Ohio; Margaret Harshaw, Julia Drobner, Daniel Ferro, New York. **Debut:** Commendatore (*Don Giovanni*) Chautauqua Summer Opera, NY 1969. Awards: Distr Winner Met Op Reg Aud, Cleveland 1967; First Place, Connecticut Opera Aud 1967.

Sang with major companies in USA: Baltimore, Houston, Newark. **Roles with these companies incl** BRITTEN: Ferryman★ & Chorus leader★ (*Curlew River*); MENOTTI: Tony★ (*Globolinks*); MOZART: Don Alfonso★ (*Così fan tutte*); ROSSINI: Don Basilio★ (*Barbiere di Siviglia*); VERDI: Ramfis★ (*Aida*). Gives recitals. Appears with symphony orchestra. Teaches voice. Mgmt: NAP/USA.

OTTO, HANNSKARL. German. Art Adm, Staatstheater am Gärtnerplatz, Munich, FR Ger. In charge of artistic policy. Born 24 Sep 1918, Duisburg, Germany. Wife Christa Heinke, occupation radio announcer. One child. Studied: Univs Munich & Cologne, PhD. Previous occupations: reporter, journalist, critic and editor with German newspapers and magazines, film studios and TV stations. Previous positions primarily theatrical: Dramaturg, Osnabrücker Theater, FR Ger 1952-53; Chief Dramaturg & stge dir, Städtische Bühnen, Augsburg 1953-58; Head of Cultural Dept *Touropa*, Munich 1958-59; Author & TV Editor, Süddeutscher Rundfunk, Stuttgart 1966. In present position since 1967. **Res:** Klingsorstr 10/88, Munich 81, FR Ger.

OTTOLINI, LUIGI. Dramatic tenor. Ital. Born 23 Aug 1928, Milan. Single. Studied: Mo Arturo Merlini, Milan. **Debut:** Pinkerton (*Butterfly*) 1958. Previous occupations: mng, Banco di Roma. Awards: First Prize, Conc G Verdi, Busseto 1959; First Prize, Conc Intl Bel Canto, Radio Brussels, Belgium.
Sang with major companies in ARG: Buenos Aires; AUS: Bregenz Fest, Vienna Staatsoper; BEL: Brussels; FRA: Bordeaux, Lyon, Marseille, Nice, Paris, Rouen, Strasbourg, Toulouse; GRE: Athens National; FR GER: Berlin Deutsche Oper, Bonn, Cologne, Frankfurt, Hamburg, Munich Staatsoper, Nürnberg, Wiesbaden; HOL: Amsterdam; HUN: Budapest; ITA: Bologna, Florence Maggio & Comunale, Milan La Scala, Naples, Palermo, Parma, Rome Opera & Caracalla, Trieste, Turin, Venice; MON: Monte Carlo; POR: Lisbon; SPA: Barcelona, Majorca; SWI: Geneva Grand Théâtre, Zurich; UK: Cardiff Welsh, Edinburg Festival, Glasgow Scottish, London Royal Opera; USSR: Kiev, Leningrad Kirov, Moscow Bolshoi; USA: Chicago, Philadelphia Lyric; YUG: Dubrovnik, Zagreb, Belgrade. **Roles with these companies incl** ADAM DE LA HALLE: Robin; BELLINI: Pollione★ (*Norma*); BERLIOZ: Faust (*Damnation de Faust*); BIZET: Don José (*Carmen*); BOITO: Faust (*Mefistofele*); DONIZETTI: Ernesto (*Don Pasquale*), Nemorino (*Elisir*), Fernand★ (*Favorite*), Edgardo (*Lucia*); GIORDANO: Andrea Chénier; GOUNOD: Faust; LEONCAVALLO: Canio★ (*Pagliacci*); MASCAGNI: Fritz (*Amico Fritz*), Turiddu★ (*Cavalleria rusticana*); MASSENET: Des Grieux (*Manon*), Werther; MEYERBEER: Vasco de Gama (*Africaine*); MONTEVERDI: Nero (*Incoronazione di Poppea*); PONCHIELLI: Enzo (*Gioconda*); PUCCINI: Rodolfo (*Bohème*), Rinuccio (*Gianni Schicchi*), Des Grieux (*Manon Lescaut*), Cavaradossi (*Tosca*), Calaf★ (*Turandot*); ROSSINI: Almaviva (*Barbiere di Siviglia*), Arnold★ (*Guillaume Tell*); VERDI: Radames★ (*Aida*), Foresto (*Attila*), Riccardo★ (*Ballo in maschera*), Don Carlo★, Jacopo Foscari (*Due*

Foscari*), Ernani★, Don Alvaro★ (*Forza del destino*), Ismaele★ (*Nabucco*), Duca di Mantova (*Rigoletto*), Gabriele (*Simon Boccanegra*), Alfredo★ (*Traviata*), Manrico★ (*Trovatore*). Also MASCAGNI: Osaka (*Iris*). Video–RAI: (*Guillaume Tell*); (*Nabucco*). Gives recitals. Appears with symphony orchestra. **Res:** V Fogazzaro 31, Milan, Italy.

ÖTVÖS, CSABA. Lyric baritone. Hungarian. Resident mem: Budapest State Opera. Born 6 Feb 1943, Budapest. Studied: Music Acad Budapest, Mrs Rèvhegyi. **Debut:** Silvio (*Pagliacci*) Budapest State Opera 1970. Previous occupations: chemist.
Sang with major companies in HUN: Budapest. **Roles with these companies incl** DONIZETTI: Enrico★ (*Campanello*), Enrico★ (*Lucia*); PUCCINI: Marcello★ (*Bohème*), Lescaut (*Manon Lescaut*); ROSSINI: Figaro★ (*Barbiere di Siviglia*); VERDI: Don Carlo★ (*Forza del destino*). Gives recitals. Appears with symphony orchestra. **Res:** Màtyàshegyi 7/A, Budapest, Hungary.

ÖTVÖS, GABOR. Conductor of opera and symphony. German. Gen Mus Dir & Resident Cond, Städtische Bühnen Augsburg, FR Ger; also Mus Dir, Philh Orch, Augsburg. Born 21 Sep 1935. Budapest. Wife Heidi, occupation psychologist. Two children. Studied: Budapest State Consv; Franz Liszt Music Acad; Somogyi, Kodály, Budapest; Ligeti, Capuana, Venice, Italy; incl piano, violin and voice. Plays the piano. Operatic training as asst cond Teatro Verdi, Trieste 1958-59; La Fenice, Venice 1959-60. **Operatic debut:** Teatro Verdi, Trieste 1959. Symphonic debut: Orch Fil, Trieste 1958. Previous adm positions in opera: Mus Dir, Teatro Verdi, Trieste 1960-61; Assoc Mus Dir, Städtische Oper, Frankfurt 1967-72.
Conducted with major companies in AUS: Vienna Staatsoper; CAN: Toronto; FR GER: Cologne, Darmstadt, Frankfurt, Hamburg, Hannover, Kiel, Munich Staatsoper; HOL: Amsterdam; HUN: Budapest; ITA: Florence Comunale, Genoa, Milan La Scala, Naples, Palermo, Rome Caracalla, Trieste, Turin, Venice; USA: Boston, Dallas, Minneapolis, New York Met & City Opera, Washington DC. **Operas with these companies incl** BARTOK: *Bluebeard's Castle★;* BEETHOVEN: *Fidelio★;* BELLINI: *Sonnambula;* BERG: *Wozzeck;* BERLIOZ: *Damnation de Faust;* BIZET: *Carmen★;* BORODIN: *Prince Igor★;* CORNELIUS: *Barbier von Bagdad★;* DONIZETTI: *Don Pasquale, Lucia, Rita;* EGK: *Irische Legende★;* ERKEL: *Bánk Bán;* GLINKA: *Life for the Tsar★;* GLUCK: *Orfeo ed Euridice;* GOUNOD: *Faust;* HENZE: *Junge Lord;* HINDEMITH: *Mathis der Maler;* HUMPERDINCK: *Hänsel und Gretel;* JANACEK: *Jenufa, Katya Kabanova, Makropoulos Affair;* KELEMEN: *Belagerungszustand;* KODALY: *Háry János;* LEONCAVALLO: *Pagliacci;* LORTZING: *Wildschütz;* MASCAGNI: *Cavalleria rusticana;* MASSENET: *Manon, Werther★;* MENOTTI: *Consul, Telephone;* MONTEVERDI: *Combattimento di Tancredi;* MOZART: *Così fan tutte, Don Giovanni★, Entführung aus dem Serail★, Nozze di Figaro★, Zauberflöte★;* MUSSORGSKY: *Boris Godunov, Khovanshchina;* ORFF: *Carmina burana★, Kluge, Mond;* PERGOLESI: *Maestro di musica, Serva padrona;*

PROKOFIEV: *Fiery Angel, Love for Three Oranges*★; PUCCINI: *Bohème*★, *Butterfly, Manon Lescaut, Tabarro, Tosca*★, *Turandot*★; ROSSINI: *Barbiere di Siviglia*★, *Cenerentola, Italiana in Algeri*★; SCHOENBERG: *Moses und Aron;* SHOSTAKOVICH: *Katerina Ismailova*★; SMETANA: *Bartered Bride*★; STRAUSS, R: *Arabella*★, *Capriccio, Elektra*★, *Frau ohne Schatten*★, *Rosenkavalier*★, *Salome;* STRAVINSKY: *Oedipus Rex, Rossignol;* VERDI: *Aida, Ballo in maschera*★, *Don Carlo*★, *Due Foscari, Falstaff, Macbeth, Otello, Rigoletto, Traviata*★, *Trovatore;* WAGNER: *Fliegende Holländer*★, *Lohengrin*★, *Tannhäuser*★, *Tristan und Isolde*★; WEBER: *Freischütz;* WOLF-FERRARI: *Quattro rusteghi, Segreto di Susanna.* Previous positions as Mus Dir with orch: Philh Orch, Trieste 1959-61; Hamburg Symph 1961-67. **Res:** Höfats Str 24, 8901 Königsbrunn, FR Ger. Mgmt: WIN/FRG; CAM/USA.

OWEN, LYNN; née Dorothy Lynn Rasmussen. Spinto. American. Born Kenosha, WI, USA. Husband Richard, occupation US Distr Judge and composer. Three children. Studied: Vienna Akad of Music; Juilliard School of Music, New York; Northwestern Univ, Evanston, IL; Salzburg Mozarteum, Austria. **Debut:** Konstanze (*Entführung aus dem Serail*) New Orleans Opera 1958. Previous occupations: office work, farm work, waitress. Awards: Fulbright Fllshp, US and Austrian Gvnmt 1958-1960; M B Rockefeller Awd; Sullivan Fndt Awd; Schlshps to Juilliard, Northwestern, Berkshire Music Fest.

Sang with major companies in FR GER: Cologne, Hamburg, Krefeld; SWI: Zurich; USA: Hartford, New York Met. **Roles with these companies incl** BEETHOVEN: Leonore★ (*Fidelio*); BORODIN: Jaroslavna (*Prince Igor*); PUCCINI: Mimi (*Bohème*), Minnie★ (*Fanciulla del West*), Tosca★, Turandot★; VERDI: Elisabetta★ (*Don Carlo*), Leonora★ (*Forza del destino*), Leonora★ (*Trovatore*); WAGNER: Senta★ (*Fliegende Holländer*). Also WELLESZ: Alkestis. **World premieres:** OWEN: Deborah (*Fisherman Called Peter*) Drew Church, Carmel, NY 1965. Recorded for: Serenus. Gives recitals. Appears with symphony orchestra. Teaches voice. Coaches repertoire. **Res:** 21 Claremont Ave, New York, NY 10027, USA. Mgmt: NAP/USA.

OXENBOULD, MOFFATT BENJAMIN. Stages/produces opera. Australian. Art Admin, Australian Opera, Sydney. Born 18 Nov 1943, Sydney. Single. Studied: Ntl Inst of Dramatic Art, Univ NSW; incl music, piano. Operatic training as asst stage dir at Australian Opera 1964-65, 1967-69. **Operatic debut:** *Turandot* Australian Opera, Adelaide 1970. Previous adm positions in opera: Stg Mng, Sutherland-Williamson Opera, Austrl 1965; Deputy Stg Mng, Sadler's Wells Opera, London 1966-67; Prod Stg Mng, Elizabethan Trust Opera 1967-69.

Directed/produced opera for major companies in AUSTRL: Sydney. **Operas staged with these companies incl** BRITTEN: *Rape of Lucretia*★; PUCCINI: *Gianni Schicchi*★, *Butterfly, Suor Angelica*★, *Tabarro*★. **Res:** 14 Spofforth St, Cremorne/Sydney, Australia.

P

PACHECO, ASSIS; né Armando De Assis Pacheco. Lirico spinto tenor. Brazilian. Born 5 Oct 1914, Itú, S Paulo, Brazil. Wife Marisa Mariz, occupation opera singer. Two children. Studied: Consv Dramático e Musical, Mo Francisco Murino, S Paulo, Brazil. **Debut:** Rodolfo (*Bohème*) Associacão Lyrico Musical Brasileira 1938. Previous occupations: mem "Coral Paulistrano Madrigalista" S Paulo; painter. Awards: Hon Citizen of Rio de Janeiro; S Paulo Trophy and Awd for Best Opera Singer of the Year 1951; Gold Medal Dipl and Awd 1960; Gold Lyre, newspaper *Diario*.

Sang with major companies in ARG: Buenos Aires; BRA: Rio de Janeiro; ITA: Naples, Palermo. **Roles with these companies incl** BIZET: Don José★ (*Carmen*); BOITO: Faust (*Mefistofele*); BRITTEN: Peter Grimes; CILEA: Maurizio (*A. Lecouvreur*); DONIZETTI: Edgardo (*Lucia*); GIORDANO: Andrea Chénier; GOMES: Fernando★ (*Colombo*), Paolo (*Fosca*); GOUNOD: Roméo; LEONCAVALLO: Canio★ (*Pagliacci*); MASCAGNI: Fritz (*Amico Fritz*), Turiddu★ (*Cavalleria rusticana*); MASSENET: Des Grieux (*Manon*), Werther★; PUCCINI: Rodolfo (*Bohème*), Rinuccio (*Gianni Schicchi*), Pinkerton (*Butterfly*), Cavaradossi★ (*Tosca*); ROSSINI: Almaviva (*Barbiere di Siviglia*); VERDI: Radames (*Aida*), Riccardo (*Ballo in maschera*), Otello★, Duca di Mantova★ (*Rigoletto*), Alfredo★ (*Traviata*), Manrico (*Trovatore*); WAGNER: Walther (*Meistersinger*), Tannhäuser. Also GOMES: Peri★ (*Guarany*); Americo (*Schiavo*); MASCAGNI: Osaka (*Iris*); VILLA-LOBOS: Makian (*Izath*). **World premieres:** NEGLIA: Marco (*Zelia*) Catania Opera 1951; VILLA-LOBOS: Corisco (*A Menina das Nuvens*) Rio de Janeiro 1959; GUARNIERI: O Alemão (*Pedro Malazarte*) Rio de Janeiro 1952; SIQUEIRA: João Grillo (*A Compadecida*) Rio de Janeiro 1961. Gives recitals. **Res:** R Marquês de Olinda 61, Rio de Janeiro ZC-02, Brazil.

PADOVANI, GIANFRANCO. Scenic and costume designer for opera, theater & television. Is a lighting designer. Italian. Resident designer, Teatro Stabile di Genova, Italy. Born 20 Jun 1928, Venice. Wife Penelope Baker. One child. Studied: Accad di Belle Arti Brera, Milan. Theater debut: Teatro Stabile, Bolzano 1952.

Designed for major companies in ITA: Genoa, Milan La Scala, Rome Opera, Turin. **Operas de-** signed for these companies incl GOUNOD: *Faust;* MASSENET: *Manon;* PUCCINI: *Manon Lescaut;* ROSSINI: *Gazza ladra;* VERDI: *Lombardi, Luisa Miller, Nabucco, Trovatore*. **Res:** V Bettolo 137/5, Genoa, Italy.

PAGE, PAULA VIVIAN. Lyric soprano. American. Resident mem: Wuppertaler Oper, Wuppertal, FR Ger. Born Corinth, MS, USA. Husband Michel Singher, occupation conductor. One child. Studied: Indiana Univ, Margaret Harshaw, Bloomington; Staatliche Hochschule für Musik, Clara Ebers, Hamburg. **Debut:** Inez (*Trovatore*) Staatsoper Hamburg 1968. Awards: Third Prize, Met Op Ntl Counc Aud; Dr Wilhelm Oberdörffer-Preis, Hamburgische Staatsoper; Second Prize WGN Ill Op Guild Aud of the Air, Chicago; Prizes in Intl Compts Geneva and s' Hertogenbosch.

Sang with major companies in FR GER: Darmstadt, Essen, Hamburg, Hannover, Karlsruhe, Wuppertal. **Roles with these companies incl** BIZET: Micaëla★ (*Carmen*); FORTNER: Belisa★ (*Don Perlimplin*); GLUCK: Euridice★; LEONCAVALLO: Nedda★ (*Pagliacci*); MILHAUD: Créuse★ (*Médée*); MOZART: Cherubino★ (*Nozze di Figaro*), Pamina★ (*Zauberflöte*); NICOLAI: Aennchen (*Lustigen Weiber*); OFFENBACH: Antonia★ (*Contes d'Hoffmann*); PUCCINI: Mimi★ (*Bohème*); STRAUSS, J: Rosalinde★ (*Fledermaus*); VERDI: Gilda★ (*Rigoletto*). Also ZIMMERMANN, U: Marie★ (*Levins Mühle*). **World premieres:** KAGEL: Jugend dram sopr (*Staatstheater*) Staatsoper Hamburg 1971. Recorded for: DG. Gives recitals. Appears with symphony orchestra. **Res:** Wuppertal, FR Ger. Mgmt: SLZ/FRG.

PAIGE, NORMAN; né Norman Murray Seltzer. Lyric character tenor. American. Born 20 Jun 1935, New York. Wife Inci Bashar, occupation opera & concert soprano. One daughter. Studied: Juilliard School of Music, Lucius Metz, New York; American Theatre Wing, Will Lee, acting, New York; Prof Wolfgang Steinbrück, Vienna; Cornelius L Reid, New York. **Debut:** Matteo (*Arabella*) Landestheater Linz, Austria 1958. Previous occupations: leading tenor American Savoyards 1953-56. Awards: Full Schlshp Mozarteum, Salzburg, summers 1959-60.

Sang with major companies in AUS: Salzburg Fest, Vienna Staatsoper; FR GER: Cologne,

Düsseldorf-Duisburg, Hamburg; SPA: Barcelona; USA: Baltimore, Boston, Chicago, Cincinnati, Dallas, Hawaii, Houston, Miami, New York City Opera, Omaha, Portland, San Francisco Opera, Seattle. **Roles with these companies incl** BRITTEN: Male Chorus (*Rape of Lucretia*); CIMAROSA: Paolino★ (*Matrimonio segreto*); DONIZETTI: Ernesto (*Don Pasquale*); EINEM: Robespierre (*Dantons Tod*); HUMPERDINCK: Hexe (*Hänsel und Gretel*); LORTZING: Peter Ivanov (*Zar und Zimmermann*); MASCAGNI: Turiddu (*Cavalleria rusticana*); MASSENET: Nicias (*Thaïs*); MOZART: Ferrando (*Così fan tutte*), Don Ottavio (*Don Giovanni*), Belmonte & Pedrillo★(*Entführung aus dem Serail*), Tamino (*Zauberflöte*); ORFF: Tiresias★ (*Antigonae*); PROKOFIEV: Prince (*Love for Three Oranges*); PUCCINI: Rodolfo (*Bohème*), Rinuccio (*Gianni Schicchi*), Pinkerton (*Butterfly*); ROSSINI: Almaviva (*Barbiere di Siviglia*), Don Ramiro (*Cenerentola*); SMETANA: Wenzel★ (*Bartered Bride*); STRAUSS, R: Matteo (*Arabella*); STRAVINSKY: Tom Rakewell (*Rake's Progress*); SUTERMEISTER: Romeo; VERDI: Alfredo (*Traviata*); WAGNER: Mime★ (*Rheingold*). Also WARD: Rev Parris★ (*Crucible*); MASSENET: Juan★ (*Don Quichotte*). **World premieres:** EDER: Male Chorus (*Oedipus Rex*) Landestheater Linz 1960; ZIMMERMANN: Erster Offizier (*Soldaten*) Opera Cologne 1965. Recorded for: Wergo GMBH. Gives recitals. Appears with symphony orchestra. Teaches voice. Coaches repertoire. On faculty of Univ of Kansas, Lawrence, USA. **Res:** 2006 Quail Creek Dr, Lawrence, KS 66044, USA. Mgmt: SCO/USA.

PALACIO, ERNESTO. Light lyric tenor. Peruvian. Born 19 Oct 1946, Lima, Peru. Single. **Debut:** Lindoro (*Italiana in Algeri*) RAI TV 1972. Previous occupations: Jesuit Order; hon vice-consul of Peru to Milan. Awards: Winner Voci Nuove Rossiniane RAI TV 1972; Winner Peri Voice Compt Reggio Emilia 1971.
Sang with major companies in FRA: Aix-en-Provence, Marseille; ITA: Genoa, Milan La Scala, Naples, Palermo, Rome Opera, Spoleto Fest, Trieste, Turin; UK: London Royal Opera. **Roles with these companies incl** BELLINI: Elvino★ (*Sonnambula*); BERG: Maler★ (*Lulu*); DONIZETTI: Ernesto★ (*Don Pasquale*), Nemorino★ (*Elisir*); MOZART: Ferrando★(*Così fan tutte*); ROSSINI: Almaviva★(*Barbiere di Siviglia*), Edward Milfort★ (*Cambiale di matrimonio*), Don Ramiro★ (*Cenerentola*), Giannetto★(*Gazza ladra*), Lindoro★ (*Italiana in Algeri*), Dorvil★ (*Scala di seta*), Narciso★ (*Turco in Italia*); VERDI: Fenton★ (*Falstaff*). Also CIMAROSA: Franchetto★ (*Due baroni*), Filandro★ (*Astuzie femminili*); ROSSINI: Corradino★ (*Matilde di Shabran*); SALIERI: Artemidoro★ (*Grotta di Trofonio*); RAVEL: Gonzalve★ (*Heure espagnole*). Gives recitals. Appears with symphony orchestra. **Res:** Viale Aretusa 30, 20147 Milan, Italy.

PALAY, ELLIOT JOHN. Heldentenor. American. Resident mem: Städtische Bühnen Freiburg, FR Ger. Born 18 Dec 1948, Milwaukee, WI, USA. Wife Susan W. Studied: Indiana Univ, Charles Kullman, Bloomington, USA; Prof Kaiser-Breme,

Essen, FR Ger. **Debut:** Matteo (*Arabella*) Bühnen der Hansestadt Lübeck, FR Ger 1972.
Sang with major companies in FR GER: Darmstadt, Düsseldorf-Duisburg, Frankfurt, Kiel, Munich Staatsoper, Stuttgart, Wuppertal; USA: New York City Opera. **Roles with these companies incl** BERG: Tambourmajor (*Wozzeck*); JANACEK: Boris★ (*Katya Kabanova*); LEONCAVALLO: Canio★(*Pagliacci*); SMETANA: Hans★(*Bartered Bride*); STRAUSS, R: Matteo★ (*Arabella*); VERDI: Radames★ (*Aida*), Ismaele★ (*Nabucco*); WAGNER: Walther★ (*Meistersinger*), Tristan★; WEILL: Jim Mahoney★ (*Aufstieg und Fall der Stadt Mahagonny*). **Res:** Schiffstr 5, 78 Freiburg i Br, FR Ger. Mgmt: WLS/USA; SLZ/FRG.

PALEVODA, WALTER. American. Asst Mng & Dir of Adm, Greater Miami Opera Assn, 1200 Coral Way, Miami, FL 33145, 1965- . In charge of adm and publicity. Additional administrative position: coordinator and adm, Concert/Opera Series, So Florida. Born 2 Aug 1927, Bronx, NY. Wife Barbara. Three children. Studied: Univ of Miami, Coral Gables, FL. Previous occupation: editor, Intl News Service, New York. Form positions, primarily adm: Pres, Miami Beach Music and Arts League 1968-70; Asst Mng, Univ of Miami Symph, Coral Gables 1958-65. Awards: Mayor's Awd, Key to City of Miami Beach 1970; Top 10 Editor, Univ of Miami Alumni Bulletin 1961. Mem of Fine Arts Council of Florida; Chmn, Theater Panel & Public Media Panel, Fine Arts Council; Florida Alliance for Arts Education; Secy, Men's Opera Club of Greater Miami. **Res:** 7840 SW 32 Terrace, Miami, FL, USA.

PALMER, THOMAS MOYER. Lyric baritone. American. Born 2 Dec 1934, Harrisburg, PA, USA. Wife Martha, occupation real estate broker. Studied: Juilliard School of Music, New York. **Debut:** Valentin (*Faust*) Kansas City Lyric Theatre, MO 1966. Awards: First Prize, National Arts Club, New York.
Sang with major companies in FRA: Aix-en-Provence Fest; SWI: Geneva; USA: Hawaii, Houston, Kansas City, Kentucky, Miami, New York Met, San Diego, San Francisco Spring Opera. **Roles with these companies incl** BERG: Wozzeck; BERLIOZ: Méphistophélès★ (*Damnation de Faust*); BIZET: Escamillo★ (*Carmen*); DONIZETTI: Malatesta★ (*Don Pasquale*), Belcore (*Elisir*); HANDEL: Polyphemus (*Acis and Galatea*); MOZART: Guglielmo (*Così fan tutte*), Conte Almaviva★ (*Nozze di Figaro*), Papageno★ (*Zauberflöte*); PUCCINI: Marcello★ (*Bohème*); ROSSINI: Figaro★ (*Barbiere di Siviglia*); VERDI: Ford★ (*Falstaff*), Iago (*Otello*), Germont★ (*Traviata*). Recorded for: Vanguard. Video/Film: (*Nozze di Figaro*). Gives recitals. Appears with symphony orchestra. Teaches voice. Coaches repertoire. On faculty of Univ of Bridgeport, CT. **Res:** 48 Cobblers Green, New Canaan, CT, USA. Mgmt: DSP/USA.

PÁLOS, IMRE; né Paikert. Dramatic tenor. Hungarian. Resident mem: Hungarian State Opera, Budapest. Born 15 Oct 1917, Budapest. Wife Erzsébet Földiák, occupation music prof. Two children. Studied: Sefcsik Magda Balassáné, Budapest.

Sang with major companies in HUN: Budapest. Roles with these companies incl BEETHOVEN: Florestan★ (*Fidelio*); DALLAPICCOLA: Radio Telegrapher‡ (*Volo di notte*); GOLDMARK: Assad★ (*Königin von Saba*); PUCCINI: Pinkerton★ (*Butterfly*), Cavaradossi★ (*Tosca*), Calaf★ (*Turandot*); SAINT-SAENS: Samson★; SHOSTAKO-VICH: Zinovy★ (*Katerina Ismailova*); SMETANA: Hans★(*Bartered Bride*); STRAUSS, R: Herodes‡ & Narraboth (*Salome*); VERDI: Radames★ (*Aida*), Riccardo★ (*Ballo*), Don Carlo★, Don Alvaro★(*Forza del destino*), Ismaele★ (*Nabucco*), Duca di Mantova★ (*Rigoletto*), Manrico★ (*Trovatore*); WAGNER: Erik★ (*Fliegende Holländer*), Walther‡ (*Meistersinger*). Also VERDI: Macduff (*Macbeth*); ERKEL: Hunyadi László. Res: Erömü 8, Budapest 1117, Hungary.

PANE, TULLIO; né Pasquale Tullio Pane. Lyric tenor. Italian. Resident mem: New York City Opera; Teatro Comunale, Bologna. Born 16 Jun 1935, Naples, Italy. Wife Tosca Borri Niver, occupation actress. Two children. Studied: Studio alla Scala, Milan, with stipd. Debut: Tonio (*Fille du régiment*) Teatro Comunale, Bologna. Awards: Silver Microphone, RAI.

Sang with major companies in ITA: Bologna, Florence Maggio & Comunale, Naples, Parma; SWI: Basel; USA: New York City Opera, Washington DC. Roles with these companies incl BELLINI: Orombello★ (*Beatrice di Tenda*), Elvino★ (*Sonnambula*); BIZET: Nadir (*Pêcheurs de perles*); DONIZETTI: Ernesto★ (*Don Pasquale*), Nemorino★ (*Elisir*), Tonio★ (*Fille du régiment*), Edgardo★ (*Lucia*), Leicester★ (*Maria Stuarda*), Roberto Devereux★; GOUNOD: Faust★; MASSENET: Des Grieux★ (*Manon*), Werther★; MOZART: Don Ottavio★ (*Don Giovanni*), Idomeneo★; PUCCINI: Rodolfo★ (*Bohème*), Rinuccio★ (*Gianni Schicchi*), Pinkerton★ (*Butterfly*); ROSSINI: Almaviva★ (*Barbiere di Siviglia*); VERDI: Duca di Mantova★ (*Rigoletto*), Alfredo★ (*Traviata*). Also ROTA: Fadinard (*Cappello di paglia di Firenze*); MANZONI: Contadino (*Sentenza*). Recorded for: Cetra. Gives recitals. Appears with symphony orchestra. Teaches voice. Res: V Ricci Curbastro 34, Rome, Italy.

PANERAI, ROLANDO. Lyric baritone. Italian. Born 17 Oct 1924, Campi Bisenzio/Florence. Wife Isabella Galardi. Two children. Studied: Mo Raoul Frazzi, Florence; Mo Contini. Debut: Enrico (*Lucia*) Teatro Dante, Campi Bisenzio 1946.

Sang with major companies in AUS: Salzburg Fest, Vienna Staatsoper; BEL: Brussels; BRA: Rio de Janeiro; CAN: Montreal/Quebec; FRA: Aix-en-Provence Fest, Marseille, Nancy, Paris; GRE: Athens National; FR GER: Berlin Deutsche Oper, Munich Staatsoper, Stuttgart, Wiesbaden; HOL: Amsterdam; ISR: Tel Aviv; ITA: Bologna, Florence Maggio & Comunale, Genoa, Milan La Scala, Naples, Palermo, Rome Opera & Caracalla, Spoleto Fest, Trieste, Turin, Venice; MON: Monte Carlo; POR: Lisbon; S AFR: Johannesburg; SPA: Barcelona; SWI: Zurich; UK: London Royal; USSR: Moscow Bolshoi; USA: New York Met, San Francisco Opera; YUG: Zagreb. Roles with these companies incl BELLINI: Sir Richard‡ (*Puritani*); BERLIOZ:

Méphistophélès (*Damnation de Faust*); BIZET: Escamillo (*Carmen*); BORODIN: Prince Igor; BUSONI: Matteo (*Arlecchino*); CATALANI: Vincenzo Gellner (*Wally*); CIMAROSA: Count Robinson★ (*Matrimonio segreto*); DONIZETTI: Enrico★ (*Campanello*), Dott Malatesta★ (*Don Pasquale*), Belcore★‡ (*Elisir*), Alfonse (*Favorite*); GALUPPI: Nardo & Don Tritemio‡ (*Filosofo di campagna*); GIORDANO: De Siriex (*Fedora*); GLUCK: Apollo (*Alceste*); GOUNOD: Jupiter (*Philémon et Baucis*); HINDEMITH: Mathis; LEONCAVALLO: Tonio (*Pagliacci*); MASCAGNI: Rabbi David (*Amico Fritz*), Alfio‡ (*Cavalleria rusticana*); MASSENET: Lescaut (*Manon*), Athanaël (*Thaïs*), Albert (*Werther*); MENOTTI: Husband‡ (*Amelia al ballo*), John Sorel (*Consul*); MONTEMEZZI: Manfredo (*Amore dei tre re*); MONTEVERDI: Orfeo; MOZART: Guglielmo★‡ & Don Alfonso★‡ (*Così fan tutte*), Leporello (*Don Giovanni*), Figaro★‡ (*Nozze di Figaro*), Papageno★ (*Zauberflöte*); ORFF: Kreon (*Antigonae*), Solo (*Carmina burana*); PAISIELLO: Figaro‡ (*Barbiere di Siviglia*); PUCCINI: Marcello★‡ (*Bohème*), Jack Rance★ (*Fanciulla del West*), Gianni Schicchi★, Sharpless‡ (*Butterfly*), Lescaut★ (*Manon Lescaut*), Rambaldo (*Rondine*), Scarpia★ (*Tosca*); ROSSINI: Figaro★ (*Barbiere di Siviglia*), Tobias Mill‡ (*Cambiale di matrimonio*), Dandini (*Cenerentola*), Robert (*Comte Ory*), Guillaume Tell; SAINT-SAENS: Grand prêtre (*Samson et Dalila*); VERDI: Amonasro‡ (*Aida*), Renato (*Ballo in maschera*), Rodrigo (*Don Carlo*), Ford‡ & Falstaff (*Falstaff*), Don Carlo (*Forza del destino*), Giacomo (*Giovanna d'Arco*), Rigoletto, Germont★‡ (*Traviata*), Conte di Luna‡ (*Trovatore*); WAGNER: Holländer, Amfortas (*Parsifal*). Also STRAUSS, R: Filippides (*Esels Schatten*). World premieres: TOSATTI: Palletta (*Partita a pugni*) Fenice, Venice 1953; PROKOFIEV: Ruprecht (*Fiery Angel*) Fenice, Venice 1955; ROSSELLINI: Comandante (*Campane*) RAI 1959; TURCHI: Sveyk (*Soldato Sveyk*) Scala, Milan 1962; ROSSELLINI: Zio (*Linguaggio dei fiori*) Piccola Scala, Milan 1963. Recorded for: His Master's Voice, Cetra Fonit, Ricordi, Decca, DG. Video/Film: (*Barbiere*), (*Rigoletto*), (*Ballo in maschera*), (*Bohème*), (*Cecchina*), (*Frate 'nnamorato*). Res: V de' Cioli 70, Florence, Italy.

PANNI, MARCELLO. Conductor of opera and symphony & composer. Italian. Born 24 Jan 1940, Rome. Wife Jane. One daughter. Studied: Franco Ferrara, Rome; Manuel Rosenthal, Paris; incl piano. Operatic debut: *Mavra* San Carlo Opera, Naples 1971. Symphonic debut: RAI Orch, Rome 1967.

Conducted with major companies in ITA: Bologna, Florence Maggio, Genoa, Milan La Scala, Naples, Palermo, Rome Opera. Operas with these companies incl ADAM DE LA HALLE: *Robin et Marion;* CAVALLI: *Giasone★;* MONTE-VERDI: *Combattimento di Tancredi★;* PER-GOLESI: *Maestro di musica★;* POULENC: *Voix humaine★;* STRAVINSKY: *Mavra★.* Also BERIO: *Laborintus II★;* STRAVINSKY: *Renard★;* BUSSOTTI: *Passion selon Sade★.* World premieres: MANZONI: *Per Massimiliano Robespierre* Teatro Comunale, Bologna 1975. Conducted major orch in Europe. Res: Piazza Borghese 3, Rome, Italy.

PANNI, NICOLETTA. Lyric soprano. Italian. Born 27 Aug 1933, Rome. Husband Mauro Ferrante, occupation businessman. One daughter. Studied: Consv S Cecilia, Rome. **Debut:** Blanche (*Dialogues des Carmélites*) Teatro Verdi, Trieste 1957. Awards: Intl Conc Geneva; Second Prize, Conc ENAL.

Sang with major companies in FRA: Aix-en-Provence Fest, Nice; ITA: Bologna, Florence Maggio & Comunale, Genoa, Milan La Scala, Naples, Palermo, Parma, Rome Opera & Caracalla, Trieste, Turin, Venice; POR: Lisbon; SPA: Barcelona; SWI: Geneva; USA: Baltimore, Chicago, New York Met, Philadelphia Lyric. **Roles with these companies incl** BIZET: Micaëla★ (*Carmen*); BOITO: Margherita (*Mefistofele*); BRITTEN: Miss Jessel (*Turn of the Screw*); DEBUSSY: Mélisande; GLUCK: Euridice; GOUNOD: Marguerite (*Faust*); LEONCAVALLO: Nedda★ (*Pagliacci*); MASCAGNI: Suzel (*Amico Fritz*); MASSENET: Manon, Sophie (*Werther*); MONTEVERDI: Euridice (*Favola d'Orfeo*); MOZART: Zerlina (*Don Giovanni*), Ilia (*Idomeneo*), Contessa★ (*Nozze di Figaro*), Susanna (*Nozze di Figaro*); OFFENBACH: Giulietta★ (*Contes d'Hoffmann*); PUCCINI: Mimi★ (*Bohème*), Lauretta (*Gianni Schicchi*), Liù★ (*Turandot*); RIMSKY-KORSAKOV: Olga★ (*Maid of Pskov*); ROSSINI: Ninetta (*Gazza ladra*); VERDI: Nannetta (*Falstaff*), Desdemona (*Otello*); WOLF-FERRARI: Susanna (*Segreto di Susanna*). Gives recitals. Appears with symphony orchestra. **Res:** V Sebastiano Conca 8, Rome, Italy.

PAOLETTI, ALBERTO. Conductor of opera. Italian. Born 15 Dec 1905, Rome. Wife Gabriella. Four children. Studied: Consv S Cecilia, Maestri Casella, Respighi and Bustini, Rome; incl piano, organ. Plays the piano. Operatic training as repetiteur & asst cond at RAI; S Carlo, Naples; Carlo Felice, Genoa; Teatro dell'Opera, Rome 1945-71. **Operatic debut:** Teatro S Carlo, Naples 1937.

Conducted with major companies in FIN: Helsinki; FRA: Bordeaux, Nice, Rouen; ITA: Genoa, Naples, Rome Opera & Caracalla. **Operas conducted with these companies incl** BELLINI: *Norma, Puritani, Sonnambula;* BIZET: *Carmen, Pêcheurs de perles;* BOITO: *Mefistofele;* CATALANI: *Wally;* CILEA: *Adriana Lecouvreur;* CIMAROSA: *Matrimonio segreto;* DEBUSSY: *Enfant prodigue;* DONIZETTI: *Don Pasquale★, Elisir★, Favorite★, Fille du régiment, Lucia★‡, Roberto Devereux;* GIORDANO: *Andrea Chénier★‡, Fedora★;* GOUNOD: *Faust;* HUMPERDINCK: *Hänsel und Gretel;* LEONCAVALLO: *Pagliacci★;* MASCAGNI: *Amico Fritz, Cavalleria rusticana★;* MASSENET: *Manon★, Werther★;* MONTEMEZZI: *Amore dei tre re;* MUSSORGSKY: *Boris Godunov, Khovanshchina;* PERGOLESI: *Serva padrona;* PONCHIELLI: *Gioconda★;* PUCCINI: *Bohème★‡, Fanciulla del West, Gianni Schicchi★, Butterfly★, Manon Lescaut, Suor Angelica★, Tabarro★, Tosca★, Turandot★;* ROSSINI: *Barbiere di Siviglia★, Comte Ory, Otello;* SAINT-SAENS: *Samson et Dalila;* SPONTINI: *Vestale;* VERDI: *Aida★‡, Ballo in maschera★, Don Carlo, Due Foscari, Forza del destino★, Nabucco★, Otello‡, Rigoletto★, Simon Boccanegra, Traviata★, Trova-*

tore★; WAGNER: *Lohengrin, Meistersinger, Tannhäuser;* WOLF-FERRARI: *Segreto di Susanna.* Recorded for Urania, Capitol, Remington. Teaches privately. **Res:** Piazza Euclide 2, Rome, Italy.

PAPULKAS, SOTO; né Sotirios Papoulkas. Lyric tenor. Greek. Resident mem: Gärtnerplatztheater, Munich; Städtische Bühnen, Nürnberg. Born 3 Feb 1943, Florina, Greece. Wife Gisela Lobinski, occupation interpreter. One child. Studied: Prof Josef Metternich, Cologne. **Debut:** Alfredo (*Traviata*) Städtische Bühnen, Flensburg, FR Ger 1968. Awards: prizewinner Intl Voice Compts Vienna, 's Hertogenbosch and Barcelona.

Sang with major companies in AUS: Vienna Volksoper; FRA: Strasbourg; GRE: Athens National; FR GER: Dortmund, Munich Gärtnerplatz, Nürnberg. **Roles with these companies incl** DONIZETTI: Ernesto★ (*Don Pasquale*), Nemorino★ (*Elisir*), Edgardo★ (*Lucia*); LORTZING: Baron Kronthal★ (*Wildschütz*); MOZART: Ferrando★ (*Così fan tutte*), Don Ottavio★ (*Don Giovanni*), Belmonte★ (*Entführung aus dem Serail*), Idamante★ (*Idomeneo*), Tamino★ (*Zauberflöte*); NICOLAI: Fenton★ (*Lustigen Weiber*); PUCCINI: Rinuccio★ (*Gianni Schicchi*); ROSSINI: Almaviva★ (*Barbiere di Siviglia*), Lindoro★ (*Italiana in Algeri*); STRAUSS, J: Alfred★ (*Fledermaus*); STRAUSS, R: Ein Sänger★ (*Rosenkavalier*); TCHAIKOVSKY: Lenski★ (*Eugene Onegin*); VERDI: Alfredo★ (*Traviata*). Gives recitals. Appears with symphony orchestra. **Res:** Kapellenstr 40, 8031 Eichenau, FR Ger.

PAPVOCKI, BOGDAN. Lirico spinto tenor. Polish. Resident member: Teatr Wielki, Warsaw. Born Tormi, Poland. Single. One child. Studied: Prof Ignacy Dygas. **Debut:** Alfredo (*Traviata*) Silesian Opera, Wroclaw 1946. Awards: Gold Cross of Merit; Knight, Officer and Commander Cross of Polonia Restituta; Ntl Artist of Great Merit; Opera Medal, Harriet Cohen Intl Music Awd, London.

Sang with major companies in BUL: Sofia; CZE; Prague National; FIN: Helsinki; FR GER: Essen, Wiesbaden; GER DR: Berlin Staatsoper, Dresden, Leipzig; HUN: Budapest; ISR: Tel Aviv; MEX: Mexico City; POL: Lodz, Warsaw; ROM: Bucharest; USSR: Kiev, Leningrad Kirov, Moscow Bolshoi, Tbilisi; USA: Chicago; YUG: Zagreb, Belgrade. **Roles with these companies incl** AUBER: Fra Diavolo; BEETHOVEN: Florestan (*Fidelio*); BIZET: Don José (*Carmen*); DALLAPICCOLA: Jailer/Inquisitor (*Prigioniero*); DEBUSSY: Azaël (*Enfant prodigue*); DELIBES: Gérald (*Lakmé*); DONIZETTI: Ernesto (*Don Pasquale*), Nemorino (*Elisir*), Edgardo (*Lucia*); GIORDANO: Andrea Chénier; GLUCK: Pylade (*Iphigénie en Tauride*); GOUNOD: Faust; MONIUSZKO: Jontek★ (*Halka*), Stefan★ (*Haunted Castle*); MOZART: Don Ottavio (*Don Giovanni*), Belmonte (*Entführung aus dem Serail*), Tamino (*Zauberflöte*); MUSSORGSKY: Shuisky (*Boris Godunov*); OFFENBACH: Hoffmann (*Contes d'Hoffmann*); PENDERECKI: Adam (*Teufel von Loudun*); PUCCINI: Rodolfo (*Bohème*), Pinkerton★ (*Butterfly*), Cavaradossi★ (*Tosca*); ROSSINI: Almaviva (*Barbiere di Siviglia*); STRAUSS, R: Ein Sänger (*Rosenkavalier*); STRAVINSKY: Oe-

PARADA

dipus★, Eumolpe (*Perséphone*); TCHAIKOV-
SKY: Lenski★ (*Eugene Onegin*); VERDI:
Riccardo (*Ballo in maschera*), Don Carlo★, Duca
di Mantova★ (*Rigoletto*), Alfredo★ (*Traviata*),
Manrico (*Trovatore*). Also MUSSORGSKY: Di-
mitri (*Boris Godunov*). Video/Film: (*Haunted
Castle*); (*Flis*); (*Dismissal of Greek Envoys*).
Gives recitals. Appears with symphony orchestra.
Res: Moliera 8 d 39, Warsaw, Poland.

PARADA, CLAUDIA OLINFA. Dramatic soprano.
Chilean. Born 11 Sep 1933, Santiago, Chile. Hus-
band Fabbri, occupation gentleman farmer. Stud-
ied: Consv Santiago, Chile. **Debut:** Contessa
(*Nozze di Figaro*) Santiago, Chile 1954. Previous
occupations: violinist, classical dance. Awards:
municipal hon from var Italian cities; Cavaliere
dell'Impero del Sole, Japan.
Sang with major companies in ARG: Buenos
Aires; AUS: Vienna Staatsoper; BEL: Brussels;
BUL: Sofia; DEN: Copenhagen; FRA: Marseille,
Rouen, Toulouse; FR GER: Berlin Deutsche
Oper, Hamburg, Karlsruhe, Munich Staatsoper;
GER DR: Leipzig; HOL: Amsterdam; HUN: Bu-
dapest; ITA: Bologna, Florence Maggio & Comu-
nale, Genoa, Milan La Scala, Naples, Palermo,
Parma, Rome Opera & Caracalla, Trieste, Turin,
Venice, Verona Arena; JPN: Tokyo Fujiwara;
NOR: Oslo; POR: Lisbon; ROM: Bucharest;
SPA: Barcelona, Majorca; SWI: Geneva; UK:
Edinburgh Fest; USA: New York Met; YUG:
Zagreb, Belgrade. **Roles with these companies incl**
BELLINI: Norma★; BERG: Marie★ (*Wozzeck*);
BRITTEN: Ellen Orford★ (*Peter Grimes*); DAL-
LAPICCOLA: Madre★ (*Prigioniero*); DE-
BUSSY: Lia (*Enfant prodigue*); DONIZETTI:
Anna Bolena★, Maria Stuarda★; FALLA: Salud
(*Vida breve*); GIORDANO: Maddalena★ (*Andrea
Chénier*), Fedora★; GOUNOD: Marguerite
(*Faust*); JANACEK: Jenufa★; LEON-
CAVALLO: Nedda★ (*Pagliacci*); MASCAGNI:
Santuzza★ (*Cavalleria rusticana*); MEYERBEER:
Selika★ (*Africaine*); MONTEVERDI: Poppea (*In-
coronazione di Poppea*); MOZART: Donna
Anna★ (*Don Giovanni*), Contessa (*Nozze di Fi-
garo*); PUCCINI: Mimi (*Bohème*), Cio-Cio-San★
(*Butterfly*), Manon Lescaut★, Suor Angelica, Gior-
getta★ (*Tabarro*), Tosca★; ROSSINI: Anaï
(*Moïse*); SHOSTAKOVICH: Katerina Ismai-
lova★; STRAUSS, R: Salome; STRAVINSKY:
Anne Trulove★ (*Rake's Progress*); VERDI:
Aida★, Amelia★ (*Ballo in maschera*), Elisabetta★
(*Don Carlo*), Donna Elvira★ (*Ernani*), Alice Ford★
(*Falstaff*), Leonora (*Forza del destino*), Abigaille
(*Nabucco*), Desdemona (*Otello*), Amelia★ (*Simon
Boccanegra*), Leonora★ (*Trovatore*). Also MER-
CADANTE: Bianca (*Due illustri rivali*); MASSE-
NET: Charlotte (*Werther*). Gives recitals.
Appears with symphony orchestra. Res: V Sar-
degna 44, Milan, Italy.

PARAZZINI, MARIA. Spinto. Italian. Born 18
Dec 1940, Italy. Single. Studied: Consv G Rossini,
Pesaro; Accad Chigiana, Siena; Vacanze-Musicali,
Venice; Centro Lirico, Teatro Massimo, Palermo.
Debut: Violetta (*Traviata*) Palermo Opera 1973.
Awards: Prize Viotti Compt, Vercelli; Winner G
Verdi Compt, Parma.
Sang with major companies in BUL: Sofia; FR
GER: Frankfurt; ITA: Bologna, Florence Maggio

& Comunale, Milan La Scala, Palermo, Turin,
Venice; UK: Edinburgh Fest. **Roles with these
companies incl** BARTOK: Judith★ (*Bluebeard's
Castle*); GIORDANO: Maddalena★ (*Andrea
Chénier*); LEONCAVALLO: Nedda (*Pagliacci*);
MONTEVERDI: Euridice★; PAISIELLO: Ro-
sina★ (*Barbiere di Siviglia*); PUCCINI: Mimi★
(*Bohème*), Suor Angelica, Giorgetta★ (*Tabarro*);
ROSSINI: Anaï (*Moïse*); VERDI: Odabella (*At-
tila*), Violetta (*Traviata*). Also ALFANO: sop role
(*Risurrezione*). **Res:** V Macanno 56, Catto-
lica/Forlì, Italy.

PARKER, ANNETTE. Lyric soprano. American.
Born Charleston, SC. Single. Studied: Margaret
van der Marck, Eleanor Steber, New York; Phyllis
Curtin, Tanglewood; Josephine Antoine, Chau-
tauqua, NY. **Debut:** Suor Angelica, Ambler Fest,
PA 1971. Awards: Winner Concert Artists Guild
Recital Compt 1975; Winner Met Op Reg Aud;
Schlshp Sullivan Fndt.
Sang with major companies in BEL: Brussels;
USA: Fort Worth, New Orleans, St Paul. **Roles
with these companies incl** BIZET: Micaëla (*Car-
men*); FLOYD: Susannah; GLUCK: Euridice;
HANDEL: Galatea★; MOZART: Susanna
(*Nozze di Figaro*), Pamina (*Zauberflöte*); OF-
FENBACH: Antonia★ & Giulietta★ (*Contes
d'Hoffmann*); PUCCINI: Mimi★ & Musetta★
(*Bohème*), Lauretta (*Gianni Schicchi*), Cio-Cio-
San (*Butterfly*); PURCELL: Dido. Gives recitals.
Appears with symphony orchestra. Res: 41 W 86
St, New York 10023, USA. Mgmt: SFM/USA;
IMR/FRA.

PARKER, WILLIAM. Lyric baritone. American.
Born 5 Aug 1943, Butler, PA, USA. Single. Stud-
ied: Frederick Wilkerson, John Bullock, Washing-
ton DC; Rosa Ponselle, Baltimore, USA. **Debut:**
Fiorello (*Barbiere di Siviglia*) No Virginia Opera,
Arlington, USA 1968. Awards: First Prize Balti-
more Opera Aud 1970; First Prize Munich Intl
Compt 1970; First Grand Prize Toulouse Intl
Compt 1970; First Prize Paris Intl Compt 1971;
Singer of the Year NATS 1970, USA.
Sang with major companies in AUS: Vienna
Volksoper; FRA: Strasbourg; USA: Baltimore,
Boston, Philadelphia Lyric, San Francisco Spring
Opera, Santa Fe, Washington DC. **Roles with these
companies incl** DONIZETTI: Dott Malatesta★
(*Don Pasquale*), Gasparo (*Rita*); JANACEK: Ha-
rasta★ (*Cunning Little Vixen*); LORTZING: Graf
v Liebenau★ (*Waffenschmied*), Graf Eberbach★
(*Wildschütz*); MASSENET: Albert★ (*Werther*);
MOZART: Guglielmo★ (*Così fan tutte*), Conte
Almaviva (*Nozze di Figaro*), Papageno★ (*Zauber-
flöte*); PUCCINI: Marcello★, Sharpless (*But-
terfly*). Gives recitals. Appears with symphony
orchestra. Res: 530 No Main St, Butler, PA, USA.
Mgmt: COL/USA.

PARLY, TICHO; né Ticho Parly Frederik Chris-
tiansen. Heldentenor. American. Born 16 Jul 1928,
Copenhagen. Wife Azilda Tirone. Three children.
Studied: Hertha Bjoervig, Copenhagen; Gabrielle
Dauly, Paris; William Herman, New York;
Charles Paddock, New Orleans, LA. **Debut:** Graf
(*Nacht in Venedig*) New Orleans Opera 1958.
Previous occupations: travel agent. Awards: Mem-
bership card number one, Cercle Wagnérien, Paris;
Commen Medal, Wagner Fest, Bayreuth, FR Ger.

Sang with major companies in ARG: Buenos Aires; AUS: Salzburg Fest, Vienna Staatsoper; BEL: Brussels; DEN: Copenhagen; FRA: Nancy, Nice, Paris, Strasbourg; GRE: Athens National; FR GER: Bayreuth Fest, Berlin Deutsche Oper, Cologne, Darmstadt, Dortmund, Düsseldorf-Duisburg, Essen, Frankfurt, Hamburg, Hannover, Kassel, Kiel, Krefeld, Mannheim, Munich Staatsoper, Saarbrücken, Stuttgart, Wuppertal; GER DR: Berlin Staatsoper, Dresden; HUN: Budapest; ITA: Genoa, Milan La Scala, Palermo, Trieste; MEX: Mexico City; NOR: Oslo; POR: Lisbon; SPA: Barcelona, Madrid; SWE: Stockholm; SWI: Basel, Zurich; UK: Edinburgh Fest, Glasgow Scottish, London Royal; USA: Houston, New Orleans, New York Met, San Diego, San Francisco Opera, Seattle. Roles with these companies incl BEETHOVEN: Florestan★ (Fidelio); BERG: Alwa★ (Lulu), Tambourmajor★ (Wozzeck); BIZET: Don José (Carmen); BRITTEN: Peter Grimes★; BUSONI: Mephisto★ (Doktor Faust); EINEM: Bürgermeister★ (Besuch der alten Dame), Camille Desmoulins★ (Dantons Tod); GOUNOD: Roméo★; HINDEMITH: Albrecht v Brandenberg★ (Mathis der Maler); JANACEK: Laca★ & Steva★ (Jenufa); LEONCAVALLO: Canio★ (Pagliacci); MEYERBEER: Vasco da Gama★ (Africaine); MONTEVERDI: Nero (Incoronazione di Poppea); MUSSORGSKY: Dimitri★ (Boris Godunov); OFFENBACH: Hoffmann★; PUCCINI: Rinuccio★ (Gianni Schicchi), Calaf★ (Turandot); SAINT-SAENS: Samson★; STRAUSS, J: Eisenstein★ & Alfred★ (Fledermaus); STRAUSS, R: Bacchus★ (Ariadne auf Naxos), Aegisth★ (Elektra), Kaiser★ (Frau ohne Schatten), Ein Sänger★ (Rosenkavalier), Herodes★ (Salome); STRAVINSKY: Oedipus★; VERDI: Radames★ (Aida), Otello★, Gabriele★ (Simon Boccanegra); WAGNER: Erik★ (Fliegende Holländer), Lohengrin★, Parsifal★, Loge★ (Rheingold), Siegmund★ (Walküre), Siegfried (Siegfried★, Götterdämmerung★), Tannhäuser★, Tristan★; WEBER: Max★ (Freischütz); WEILL: Jim Mahoney★ (Aufstieg und Fall der Stadt Mahagonny). Also EGK: Der Revisor; FORTNER: Murray (Elisabeth Tudor). World premieres: HENZE: Leonardo (Re Cervo) new vers, Staatsoper, Kassel 1963. Recorded for: DG. Res: Zurich, Switzerland.

PASCAN, BORISLAV SVETOLIK. Conductor of opera and symphony. Yugoslavian. Resident Cond, Belgrade Opera. Born 11 Jun 1924, Novi Sad, Yugoslavia. Wife Josepha. Studied: with father, Prof Svetolik; Belgrade Music Acad, Prof K Baranovic; Prof H Swarowsky, Vienna; incl piano. Operatic training as repetiteur & asst cond at Belgrade Opera. **Operatic debut:** Traviata Opera House, Subotica, Yugoslavia 1951. Symphonic debut: Phil of Subotica 1951.

Conducted with major companies in YUG: Belgrade. Operas with these companies incl BIZET: Carmen; BRITTEN: Rape of Lucretia★; DONIZETTI: Don Pasquale; GOUNOD: Faust★; MASSENET: Don Quichotte; MOZART: Nozze di Figaro; PROKOFIEV: Love for Three Oranges★; PUCCINI: Tosca; RIMSKY-KORSAKOV: Maid of Pskov★; ROSSINI: Barbiere di Siviglia; SMETANA: Bartered Bride; STRAUSS, J: Fledermaus; VERDI: Aida★, Ballo in maschera, Don Carlo★, Rigoletto★, Traviata,

Trovatore; WAGNER: Fliegende Holländer. Conducted major orch in Europe. **Res:** Banjicki Put 10, Belgrade, Yugoslavia.

PASHLEY, ANNE. Lyric soprano. British. Born 5 June 1937, Skegness, UK. Husband Jack Irons, occupation singer, voice teacher. Two children. Studied: Guildhall School of Music, Norman Walker, London; Lucie Manen, Zurich. **Debut:** Barbarina (Nozze di Figaro) Covent Garden 1964. Previous occupations: Olympic athlete, sprinter at Melbourne Olympics.

Sang with major companies in UK: Aldeburgh Fest, Cardiff Welsh, Edinburgh Fest, Glasgow Scottish, Glyndebourne Fest, London Royal Opera & English National. **Roles with these companies incl** BEETHOVEN: Marzelline★ (Fidelio); BIZET: Micaëla (Carmen); BRITTEN: Nancy★ (Albert Herring); GAY: Lucy (Beggar's Opera); GLUCK: Amor★ (Orfeo ed Euridice); HUMPERDINCK: Gretel; MOZART: Zerlina★ (Don Giovanni), Susanna★ & Cherubino★ (Nozze di Figaro), Idamante★ (Idomeneo); ORFF: Solo (Carmina burana). Also HANDEL: Iole★ (Hercules); GOUNOD: Siebel★ (Faust); MONTEVERDI: Nerone★ (Incoronazione di Poppea). **World premieres:** MACONCHY: The Girl (Jesse Tree) Dorchester Fest, UK 1970; Daughter (The Parlor) Welsh National 1970; EASTWOOD: Daughter (Rebel) BBC TV 1971. Recorded for: Decca. Video/Film: Jenny (Aufstieg und Fall der Stadt Mahagonny); Adele (Fledermaus); Siebel (Faust); Idamante (Idomeneo); Daughter (Rebel). Gives recitals. Appears with symphony orchestra. **Res:** 289 Goldhawk Rd, London W12, UK.

PASKALIS, KOSTAS. Dramatic baritone. Greek. Resident mem: Staatsoper, Vienna; Bayerische Staatsoper, Munich. Born Athens. Wife Marina Krilovici, occupation opera singer. One daughter. Studied: Athens Consv. **Debut:** Rigoletto, Athens Opera 1954.

Sang with major companies in AUS: Salzburg Fest, Vienna Staatsoper; FRA: Paris; GRE: Athens National; FR GER: Berlin Deutsche Oper, Frankfurt, Hamburg, Mannheim, Munich Staatsoper; ITA: Milan La Scala, Rome Opera; UK: Glyndebourne Fest, London Royal; USA: Boston, Cincinnati, Houston, Miami, New Orleans, New York Met, San Francisco Opera; et al. **Roles with these companies incl** BIZET: Escamillo‡ (Carmen); GIORDANO: Carlo Gérard (Andrea Chénier); GLUCK: Oreste (Iphigénie en Tauride); HENZE: Pentheus (Bassarids); MASSENET: Athanaël (Thaïs); MOZART: Don Giovanni; PONCHIELLI: Barnaba (Gioconda); PUCCINI: Marcello (Bohème), Michele (Tabarro), Scarpia (Tosca); ROSSINI: Figaro (Barbiere di Siviglia); TCHAIKOVSKY: Eugene Onegin; VERDI: Amonasro (Aida), Renato (Ballo in maschera), Rodrigo (Don Carlo), Don Carlo (Ernani), Ford (Falstaff), Don Carlo (Forza del destino), Macbeth, Nabucco, Iago (Otello), Simon Boccanegra, Germont (Traviata), Conte di Luna (Trovatore), Monforte (Vespri); et al. Also GOUNOD: Valentin (Faust). Recorded for: Angel. **Res:** Athens and Vienna. Mgmt: CAM/USA.

PASTINE, GIANFRANCO. Lyric tenor. Italian. Born 1 Feb 1937, Santa Margherita Ligure, Italy.

Wife Maria Dina Marenco, occupation business-woman. One child. **Debut:** MASCAGNI: Silvano, Teatro Nuovo, Milan 1963. Previous occupations: hotel mng. Awards: Winner, Ntl Conc As Li Co.

Sang with major companies in ITA: Bologna, Genoa, Naples, Parma, Rome Opera, Turin; SPA: Barcelona; USA: Cincinnati, Hartford, Philadelphia Grand; YUG: Belgrade. **Roles with these companies** incl BOITO: Faust (*Mefistofele*); DONIZETTI: Ernesto★ (*Don Pasquale*), Nemorino★ (*Elisir*), Fernand★ (*Favorite*), Edgardo★ (*Lucia*), Riccardo★ (*Maria di Rohan*); MASCAGNI: Fritz★ (*Amico Fritz*); MASSENET: Des Grieux★ (*Manon*); MONTEVERDI: Nero★ (*Incoronazione di Poppea*); PUCCINI: Rodolfo★ (*Bohème*), Rinuccio★ (*Gianni Schicchi*), Pinkerton★ (*Butterfly*), Ruggero★ (*Rondine*), Cavaradossi★ (*Tosca*), Roberto★ (*Villi*); ROSSINI: Almaviva★ (*Barbiere di Siviglia*); VERDI: Riccardo★ (*Ballo in maschera*), Fenton★ (*Falstaff*), Duca di Mantova★ (*Rigoletto*), Alfredo★ (*Traviata*). Gives recitals. **Res:** V P Pastine 23, Santa Margherita Ligure, Italy.

PATANÉ, GIUSEPPE. Conductor of opera and symphony. Italian. Born 1 Jan 1932, Naples. Wife Rita Saponaro, occupation form soprano. Two children. Studied: Consv S Pietro a Maiella, Naples; F Cilea, A Savasta, A Longo, T Gargiulo; incl piano, violin, clarinet, trombone, cello. Plays the piano. Operatic training as repetiteur, asst cond & chorus master. **Operatic debut:** *Traviata* San Carlo Opera, Naples 1951. Symphonic debut: San Carlo Orch, Naples 1955. Awards: Cavaliere della Repubblica Italiana; Commendatore dell'Ordine Militare, SS Salvatore & Brigida di Svecia.

Conducted with major companies in AUS: Vienna Staatsoper; BEL: Brussels Monnaie; DEN: Copenhagen; FRA: Orange Fest, Paris, Toulouse; FR GER: Berlin Deutsche Oper, Düsseldorf-Duisburg, Essen, Hamburg, Kiel, Mannheim, Munich Staatsoper, Wiesbaden; GER DR: Berlin Staatsoper, Dresden, Leipzig; ITA: Bologna, Florence Maggio & Comunale, Genoa, Milan La Scala, Naples, Palermo, Parma, Rome Opera & Caracalla, Trieste, Turin, Verona Arena; SWI: Geneva, Zurich; UK: Edinburgh Fest, London Royal; USA: Chicago, S Francisco Op, New York Met. **Operas with these cos** incl ADAM: *Si j'étais roi*; d'ALBERT: *Tiefland*; AUBER: *Fra Diavolo, Muette de Portici*; BARTOK: *Bluebeard's Castle*; BEETHOVEN: *Fidelio*; BELLINI: *Beatrice di Tenda, Capuleti ed i Montecchi, Norma, Pirata, Puritani, Sonnambula, Straniera*; BERG: *Wozzeck*; BERLIOZ: *Béatrice et Bénédict, Benvenuto Cellini, Damnation de Faust, Troyens*; BIZET: *Carmen, Pêcheurs de perles*; BOITO: *Mefistofele*; BORODIN: *Prince Igor*; BUSONI: *Arlecchino, Turandot*; CATALANI: *Wally*; CHARPENTIER: *Louise*; CHERUBINI: *Medea*; CILEA: *A. Lecouvreur*; CIMAROSA: *Matrimonio segreto*; CORNELIUS: *Barbier von Bagdad*; DALLAPICCOLA: *Prigioniero*; DEBUSSY: *Enfant prodigue, Pelléas et Mélisande*; DELIBES: *Lakmé*; DONIZETTI: *Anna Bolena, Campanello, Convenienze/Viva la Mamma, Don Pasquale, Elisir, Favorite, Fille du régiment, Linda di Chamounix, Lucia, Lucrezia Borgia, Maria di Rohan, Maria Stuarda, Rita, Roberto Devereux*; DUKAS: *Ariane et Barbe Bleue*; DVORAK: *Ru-*

salka; FALLA: *Vida breve;* FLOTOW: *Martha;* GERSHWIN: *Porgy and Bess;* GIORDANO: *Andrea Chénier, Fedora;* GLINKA: *Life for the Tsar;* GLUCK: *Alceste, Orfeo ed Euridice;* GOUNOD: *Faust;* HANDEL: *Giulio Cesare, Xerxes;* HUMPERDINCK: *Hänsel und Gretel;* JANACEK: *Jenufa;* LEONCAVALLO: *Pagliacci;* MASCAGNI: *Amico Fritz, Cavalleria rusticana;* MASSENET: *Manon, Thaïs, Werther;* MENOTTI: *Consul, Medium, Telephone;* MEYERBEER: *Africaine, Huguenots, Prophète;* MONTEMEZZI: *Amore dei tre re;* MOZART: *Clemenza di Tito, Così fan tutte, Don Giovanni, Entführung aus dem Serail, Idomeneo, Nozze di Figaro, Zauberflöte;* MUSSORGSKY: *Boris Godunov, Khovanshchina;* NICOLAI: *Lustigen Weiber;* OFFENBACH: *Contes d'Hoffmann;* ORFF: *Carmina burana;* PAISIELLO: *Barbiere di Siviglia;* PERGOLESI: *Serva padrona;* PFITZNER: *Palestrina;* PONCHIELLI: *Gioconda;* PUCCINI: *Bohème, Fanciulla del West, Gianni Schicchi, Butterfly, Manon Lescaut, Rondine, Suor Angelica, Tabarro, Tosca, Turandot;* RAVEL: *Heure espagnole;* RIMSKY-KORSAKOV: *Coq d'or, Invisible City of Kitezh, May Night, Sadko, Tsar's Bride, Christmas Eve;* ROSSINI: *Barbiere di Siviglia, Cambiale di matrimonio, Cenerentola, Guillaume Tell, Italiana in Algeri, Moïse, Scala di seta, Semiramide, Assedio di Corinto, Signor Bruschino, Turco in Italia;* SAINT-SAENS: *Samson et Dalila;* SMETANA: *Bartered Bride;* STRAUSS, J: *Fledermaus;* STRAUSS, R: *Ariadne auf Naxos, Daphne, Elektra, Rosenkavalier, Salome;* STRAVINSKY: *Mavra, Rake's Progress, Rossignol;* TCHAIKOVSKY: *Eugene Onegin, Pique Dame;* THOMAS: *Mignon;* VERDI: *Aida, Aroldo/Stiffelio, Attila, Ballo in maschera, Corsaro, Don Carlo, Due Foscari, Ernani, Falstaff, Forza del destino, Giovanna d'Arco, Lombardi, Luisa Miller, Macbeth, Masnadieri, Nabucco, Otello, Rigoletto, Simon Boccanegra, Traviata, Trovatore, Vespri;* WAGNER: *Fliegende Holländer, Lohengrin, Meistersinger, Parsifal, Rienzi, Rheingold, Walküre, Siegfried, Götterdämmerung, Tannhäuser, Tristan und Isolde;* WEBER: *Freischütz;* WOLF: *Corregidor;* WOLF-FERRARI: *Quattro rusteghi, Segreto di Susanna;* ZANDONAI: *Francesca da Rimini, Giulietta e Romeo.* Also SCHUMANN: *Genoveva;* MEYEROWITZ: *Barrier.* Recorded for Decca, EMI, Eurodisc, DG. Video/Film—TV: *Arlecchino, Turandot, Adriana Lecouvreur, Tosca, Tabarro, Turco in Italia, Otello.* Film: *Traviata.* Conducted major orch in Europe, USA/Canada. **Res:** Viale Bligny 23A, Milan, Italy. Mgmt: JUC/SWI.

PATANÉ, VITTORIO. Stages/produces opera & television. Also designs sets, costumes & stage-lighting and is an author. Italian. Born 18 Apr 1933, Naples. Wife Annamaria Gasparini, occupation soprano. One child. Studied: Univ of Naples, Profs Caccioppoli & Giordani; incl music & piano. Operatic training as asst at var theaters to J P Ponnelle. **Operatic debut:** CIMAROSA: *Pittor Parigino* Genoa 1962. Previous occupation: dir of research in merchandising.

Directed/produced opera for major companies in FRA: Lyon, Marseille, Nice, Paris, Rouen,

Strasbourg, Toulouse; ITA: Genoa, Naples, Parma, Turin; MON: Monte Carlo; POR: Lisbon; SPA: Barcelona. **Operas staged with these companies incl** AUBER: *Fra Diavolo;* BELLINI: *Norma★, Sonnambula;* BIZET: *Carmen, Pêcheurs de perles;* CILEA: *A. Lecouvreur;* CIMAROSA: *Matrimonio segreto★;* DONIZETTI: *Campanello★, Don Pasquale★, Elisir, Lucia;* FALLA: *Retablo de Maese Pedro★;* GALUPPI: *Filosofo di campagna;* GIORDANO: *Andrea Chénier, Fedora;* GLUCK: *Orfeo ed Euridice;* HENZE: *Junge Lord;* LEONCAVALLO: *Pagliacci;* MASCAGNI: *Amico Fritz, Cavalleria rusticana★;* MASSENET: *Manon, Werther;* MENOTTI: *Consul, Telephone★;* MONTEVERDI: *Combattimento di Tancredi★;* MOZART: *Così fan tutte★, Don Giovanni★, Entführung aus dem Serail★, Nozze di Figaro★, Zauberflöte;* PAISIELLO: *Barbiere di Siviglia;* PERGOLESI: *Frate 'nnamorato, Serva padrona★;* PROKOFIEV: *Love for Three Oranges;* PUCCINI: *Bohème, Gianni Schicchi★, Butterfly, Manon Lescaut, Suor Angelica★, Tabarro★, Tosca;* ROSSINI: *Barbiere di Siviglia, Cambiale di matrimonio, Italiana in Algeri★, Scala di seta★, Signor Bruschino★;* STRAUSS, R: *Rosenkavalier;* STRAVINSKY: *Mavra★, Rake's Progress;* VERDI: *Attila, Ballo in maschera, Ernani, Falstaff★, Forza del destino, Nabucco, Otello★, Rigoletto, Simon Boccanegra, Traviata, Trovatore★;* WOLF-FERRARI: *Segreto di Susanna.* Also FUGA: *Otto Schnaffs★†;* MALIPIERO: *Capitan Spavento★†;* MANNINO: *Luisella★;* MUSSORGSKY: *Marriage★†;* PERSICO: *Locandiera★†;* RIMSKY-KORSAKOV: *Mozart and Salieri★†;* ROTA: *Cappello di paglia di Firenze★†.* **Operatic world premieres:** MEYEROWITZ: *Mulatto* first prof stg San Carlo, Naples 1971. Operatic Video—Teheran TV: *Campanello, Adriana Lecouvreur, Retablo de Maese Pedro.* Teaches at Consv Statale di Musica. **Res:** Brescia, Italy.

PATENAUDE, JOAN. Soprano. Canadian. Born 12 Sep 1941, Canada. Widowed. Husband Bruce Yarnell, occupation baritone (deceased). Studied: Bernard Diamant, Montreal; Opera School, Toronto; Kathryn Turney Long School, Met Opera, New York. **Debut:** Micaëla (*Carmen*) New York City Opera 1966. Awards: Four Canada Counc Grants; Rockefeller Fndt Grant; Winner Met Op Ntl Counc Aud; Sullivan Fndt Grant; CBC Talent Fest, Ntl winner.

Sang with major companies in CAN: Toronto; USA: Fort Worth, Kansas City, Lake George, New York City Opera, Pittsburgh, Portland, San Francisco Opera & Spring Opera. **Roles with these companies incl** BIZET: Micaëla★ (*Carmen*); DVORAK: Rusalka★; GOUNOD: Juliette★; LEONCAVALLO: Nedda★ (*Pagliacci*); MASSENET: Manon★; MAYR: Medea★; MENOTTI: Laetitia★ (*Old Maid and the Thief*), Annina★ (*Saint of Bleecker Street*), Lucy★ (*Telephone*); MOZART: Donna Anna★ (*Don Giovanni*), Contessa★ & Susanna & Cherubino (*Nozze di Figaro*), Pamina★ (*Zauberflöte*); NICOLAI: Frau Fluth★ (*Lustigen Weiber*); PUCCINI: Mimi★ (*Bohème*), Suor Angelica, Giorgetta (*Tabarro*), Liù★ (*Turandot*); STRAUSS, R: Arabella★; THOMAS: Ophélie (*Hamlet*); VERDI: Gilda★ (*Rigoletto*),

Violetta★ (*Traviata*). **World premieres:** BERNARDO: Marie (*Child*) Lake George Opera 1974. Recorded for: Vanguard. Gives recitals. Appears with symphony orchestra. **Res:** 11133 Sylvan St, No Hollywood, CA 91606, USA. Mgmt: HUR/USA.

PATRICK, JULIAN. Baritone. American. Born 26 Oct 1927, Meridian, MS, USA. Single. Studied: Cornelius Reid, New York. **Debut:** Germont (*Traviata*) Mobile Opera Co, AL 1950.

Sang with major companies in FRA: Strasbourg; USA: Boston, Chicago, Cincinnati, Dallas, Hawaii, Houston, Jackson Opera/South, New Orleans, New York City Opera, Omaha, Pittsburgh, Portland, San Diego, San Francisco Opera & Spring Opera, Santa Fe, Seattle, Washington DC. **Roles with these companies incl** BELLINI: Ernesto (*Pirata*); BIZET: Escamillo★ (*Carmen*); BORODIN: Prince Igor; DONIZETTI: Dott Malatesta★ (*Don Pasquale*), Belcore★ (*Elisir*), Enrico (*Lucia*); GIORDANO: De Siriex (*Fedora*); LEONCAVALLO: Tonio★ (*Pagliacci*); MASCAGNI: Alfio★ (*Cavalleria rusticana*); MASSENET: Lescaut★ (*Manon*), Athanaël★ (*Thaïs*), Albert★ (*Werther*); MENOTTI: Husband★ (*Amelia al ballo*); MOZART: Guglielmo (*Così fan tutte*), Nardo (*Finta giardiniera*), Conte Almaviva★ & Figaro (*Nozze di Figaro*); PUCCINI: Marcello★ (*Bohème*), Gianni Schicchi★, Sharpless★ (*Butterfly*), Lescaut★ (*Manon Lescaut*), Michele★ (*Tabarro*), Scarpia (*Tosca*); RAVEL: Ramiro (*Heure espagnole*); ROSSINI: Figaro★ (*Barbiere di Siviglia*), Dandini (*Cenerentola*); SAINT-SAENS: Grand prêtre★ (*Samson et Dalila*); STRAUSS, R: Olivier (*Capriccio*), Orest★ (*Elektra*); VERDI: Renato★ (*Ballo in maschera*), Germont (*Traviata*); WAGNER: Holländer★; WARD: John Proctor★ (*Crucible*). Also MOORE: Husband (*Carry Nation*); BERG: Athlet (*Lulu*). **World premieres:** FLOYD: George (*Of Mice and Men*) Seattle Opera 1970; WEISGALL: Don (*Nine Rivers from Jordan*) New York City Opera 1968; IMBRIE: Troll (*Three Against Christmas*) Berkeley, CA 1964. Recorded for: Columbia, Desto. Video/Film: Sam (*Trouble in Tahiti*). Gives recitals. Appears with symphony orchestra. **Res:** Upper Black Eddy, PA, USA. Mgmt: SCO/USA.

PATTERSON, RUSSELL. Conductor of opera and symphony. American. Gen Dir & Principal Cond, Kansas City Lyric Theater, MO, USA 1958- . Born 31 Aug 1928, Greenville, MS, USA. Divorced. Two children. Studied: Louisiana State Univ, Baton Rouge; New England Consv, Boston; Berkshire Music Cnt, MA; Kansas City Consv of Music; Staatl Hochschule, Munich; incl Fr horn. Plays the Fr horn. Operatic training as asst cond & chorus master at European opera houses; New Orleans Opera, LA. **Operatic debut:** *Bohème* Kansas City Lyric Theater 1958. Symphonic debut: Kansas City Phil 1961. Previous occupations: horn player Kansas City Phil etc; orchestrator and arranger; Prof of Music. Awards: Music Man of the Year, Phi Mu Alpha Sinfonia 1969; Fulbright Awd 1952; Kansas City Mayor's Awd of Merit 1957; Certif of Merit, Netherlands Radio 1958. Mem: Prof Cmmtt, Central Opera Service; Board of Dir, OPERA America; Music Panel, NEA; Opera Cmmtt, MO State Arts Council; Univ Assocts.

Conducted with major companies in USA: Kansas City, Lake George. **Operas with these companies incl** BARBER: *Vanessa;* BEETHOVEN: *Fidelio;* BIZET: *Carmen;* DONIZETTI: *Don Pasquale, Elisir, Lucia;* FLOYD: *Of Mice and Men*;* GIANNINI: *Taming of the Shrew*‡;* GIORDANO: *Andrea Chénier;* GOUNOD: *Faust;* HUMPERDINCK: *Hänsel und Gretel*;* LEONCAVALLO: *Pagliacci*;* MASCAGNI: *Cavalleria rusticana*;* MENOTTI: *Amahl, Medium, Saint of Bleecker Street*, Telephone;* MOZART: *Così fan tutte, Don Giovanni, Entführung aus dem Serail*, Finta giardiniera, Schauspieldirektor, Nozze di Figaro*, Zauberflöte;* NICOLAI: *Lustigen Weiber;* OFFENBACH: *Contes d'Hoffmann, Périchole*;* ORFF: *Kluge*;* PERGOLESI: *Maestro di musica, Serva padrona;* POULENC: *Mamelles de Tirésias;* PUCCINI: *Bohème*, Gianni Schicchi*, Butterfly*, Tosca*;* ROSSINI: *Barbiere di Siviglia*;* STRAUSS, J: *Fledermaus*;* STRAUSS, R: *Ariadne auf Naxos;* VERDI: *Aida*, Ballo in maschera, Forza del destino, Otello*, Rigoletto, Traviata*, Trovatore;* WAGNER: *Fliegende Holländer*;* WARD: *Crucible*;* WEBER: *Freischütz;* WOLF-FERRARI: *Segreto di Susanna.* Also BEESON: *Sweet Bye and Bye*‡;* MOORE: *Devil and Daniel Webster.* **World premieres:** BEESON: *Capt Jinks of the Horse Marines,* Kansas City Lyric 1975. Recorded for Desto, RCA, CRI. Cond major orch in Europe, USA/Canada. Taught at Consv of Music, Kansas City. **Res:** 4928 Wornall Rd, Kansas City, MO, 64112 USA.

PATZSCHKE, CHRISTEL. Lyric soprano. German. Resident mem: Stadttheater, Bremerhaven, FR Ger. Born 10 Jul, Mannheim, Germany. Single. Studied: Guildhall School of Music and Drama, Oda Slobodskaya, London; Staatliche Hochschule für Musik, Prof Clara Ebers, Hamburg; Musikakad Detmold, Prof Günther Weissenborn. **Debut:** Mimi *(Bohème)* Landestheater Detmold, FR Ger 1966. Previous occupations: foreign correspondent. Awards: Third Prize Intl Singing Compt Francisco Viñas, Barcelona. **Sang with major companies in** FR GER: Dortmund, Krefeld. **Roles with these companies incl** BEETHOVEN: Marzelline *(Fidelio);* BRITTEN: Helena *(Midsummer Night);* DEBUSSY: Mélisande; EGK: Gretl* *(Zaubergeige);* EINEM: Frl Bürstner* *(Prozess);* FLOTOW: Lady Harriet *(Martha);* GLUCK: Iphigénie* *(Iphigénie en Aulide),* Euridice; GOUNOD: Marguerite *(Faust);* HAYDN: Sandrina *(Infedeltà delusa),* Clarissa *(Mondo della luna);* HUMPERDINCK: Gretel; LEONCAVALLO: Nedda *(Pagliacci);* MOZART: Fiordiligi *(Così fan tutte),* Arminda* *(Finta giardiniera),* Ilia *(Idomeneo),* Pamina* *(Zauberflöte);* OFFENBACH: Antonia* *(Contes d'Hoffmann);* ORFF: Kluge; PUCCINI: Mimi* *(Bohème),* Liù *(Turandot);* SMETANA: Marie* *(Bartered Bride);* STRAUSS, J: Rosalinde *(Fledermaus);* STRAUSS, R: Komponist *(Ariadne auf Naxos);* TCHAIKOVSKY: Tatiana* *(Eugene Onegin);* VERDI: Alice Ford* *(Falstaff),* Desdemona* *(Otello),* Violetta* *(Traviata);* WAGNER: Eva *(Meistersinger),* Gutrune* *(Götterdämmerung).* Also RIMSKY-KORSAKOV: Swan Princess *(Tsar Saltan);* TCHAIKOVSKY: Maria *(Mazeppa);* WOLF-FERRARI: Felice *(Quattro*

rusteghi). Gives recitals. Appears with symphony orchestra. **Res:** Hohenstaufenstr 42, 285 Bremerhaven, FR Ger. Mgmt: ZBV/FRG.

PAUL, ROBERT; né Robert Abelson. Lyric & dramatic baritone. American. Resident mem: New York City Opera. Born 16 Nov, Brooklyn, New York. Wife Helen, occupation singer. Two children. Studied: Edna Beatrice Bloom, School of Sacred Music, Hebrew Univ. **Debut:** Guglielmo *(Così fan tutte)* New England Opera Theatre 1960. Previous occupations: accountant.

Sang with major companies in USA: Lake George, Memphis, New York City Opera, St Paul, Seattle, Washington DC. **Roles with these companies incl** DONIZETTI: Belcore *(Elisir);* FLOYD: George Milton* *(Of Mice and Men);* LEONCAVALLO: Tonio* *(Pagliacci);* MOORE: Horace Tabor* *(Baby Doe);* MOZART: Guglielmo* *(Così fan tutte),* Papageno *(Zauberflöte);* PUCCINI: Marcello* *(Bohème),* Sharpless* *(Butterfly),* Scarpia* *(Tosca);* ROSSINI: Figaro *(Barbiere di Siviglia);* VERDI: Renato* *(Ballo in maschera),* Rigoletto*, Germont *(Traviata);* WARD: John Proctor* *(Crucible).* **World premieres:** KASTLE: Brigham Young *(Deseret)* stgd Memphis Opera 1967. Gives recitals. Appears with symphony orchestra. Teaches voice. **Res:** 108 Sugar Tom's La, East Norwich, NY, USA. Mgmt: SFM/USA.

PAUL, THOMAS. Bass. American. Born 22 Feb 1934, Chicago. Wife Esther, occupation pianist. Four children. Studied: Juilliard School, Hans Heinz, & grad stud conducting, New York; Beverly Johnson, Gibner King, Cornelius Reid, New York. **Debut:** Sparafucile *(Rigoletto)* New York City Opera 1962. Awards: Ford Fndt Grant; First Prize Liederkranz Fndt, New York 1962.

Sang with major companies in CAN: Montreal/Quebec, Vancouver; USA: Baltimore, Cincinnati, Houston, New Orleans, New York City Opera, Philadelphia Lyric, Pittsburgh, St Paul, San Francisco Spring Opera, Washington DC. **Roles with these companies incl** BARTOK: Bluebeard; BEETHOVEN: Rocco *(Fidelio);* BELLINI: Sir George *(Puritani);* BOITO: Mefistofele; CHARPENTIER: Père *(Louise);* GOUNOD: Méphistophélès *(Faust);* HANDEL: Ptolemy* *(Giulio Cesare);* MENOTTI: Don Marco *(Saint of Bleecker Street);* MOZART: Figaro *(Nozze di Figaro),* Sarastro *(Zauberflöte);* MUSSORGSKY: Pimen *(Boris Godunov);* PUCCINI: Colline* *(Bohème);* STRAVINSKY: Tiresias *(Oedipus Rex);* THOMSON: Webster *(Mother of Us All);* VERDI: Ramfis *(Aida),* Padre Guardiano *(Forza del destino);* WAGNER: Pogner *(Meistersinger).* Also GOUNOD: Frère Laurent* *(Roméo et Juliette);* MONTEVERDI: Seneca* *(Incoronazione di Poppea);* DONIZETTI: Raimondo* *(Lucia di Lammermoor);* MASSENET: Comte des Grieux* *(Manon).* **World premieres:** WARD: Jack Spaniard *(Lady from Colorado)* Central City Fest, USA 1964. Gives recitals. Appears with symphony orchestra. Teaches voice. Coaches repertoire. On faculty of Eastman School of Music, Rochester, NY; Aspen School & Festival, Aspen, CO, USA. **Res:** Webster, NY, USA. Mgmt: COL/USA.

PAVAROTTI, LUCIANO. Lyric tenor. Italian. Born 12 Oct 1935, Modena, Italy. Wife Adua Veroni, occupation former teacher. Three children. Studied: Arrigo Pola, Modena; Ettore Campogalliani, Mantua, Italy. **Debut:** Rodolfo (*Bohème*) Teatro Municipale, Reggio Emilia 1961. Previous occupations: schoolteacher. Awards: Medaglia d'oro Giuseppe Verdi, Brescia ·1966; Premio Nazionale Numeri Uno, Florence 1969; Medaglia d'oro Club de la Opera, Mexico City 1969; Targa d'argento Amici della Lirica Italiana, Bilbao 1970; Orfeo d'oro dell'Accademia del Disco Lirico di Francia, Paris 1971; Diploma Lyric Society of Fine Arts, New York & New Jersey 1972; Medaglia d'oro Centenario Enrico Caruso, Naples 1973; etc. **Sang with major companies in** AUS: Salzburg Fest, Vienna Staatsoper; FRA: Paris; FR GER: Berlin Deutsche Oper, Hamburg; HOL: Amsterdam; ITA: Bologna, Genoa, Milan La Scala, Naples, Palermo, Parma, Rome Opera & Caracalla, Venice, Verona Arena; MEX: Mexico City; SPA: Barcelona, Las Palmas Fest; SWI: Geneva, Zurich; UK: Edinburgh Fest, Glyndebourne Fest, London Royal Opera; USA: Chicago, Hartford, Miami, New York Met, Philadelphia Lyric, San Francisco Opera. **Roles with these companies incl** BELLINI: Orombello‡ (*Beatrice di Tenda*), Tebaldo (*Capuleti ed i Montecchi*), Lord Arthur★‡ (*Puritani*), Elvino (*Sonnambula*); DONIZETTI: Nemorino★‡ (*Elisir*), Fernand★‡ (*Favorite*), Tonio★‡ (*Fille du régiment*), Edgardo★‡ (*Lucia*); MASSENET: Des Grieux (*Manon*); MOZART: Idamante (*Idomeneo*); PUCCINI: Rodolfo★‡ (*Bohème*), Pinkerton‡ (*Butterfly*); VERDI: Riccardo★‡ (*Ballo in maschera*), Oronte (*Lombardi*), Rodolfo★ (*Luisa Miller*), Duca di Mantova★‡ (*Rigoletto*), Alfredo (*Traviata*), Manrico (*Trovatore*). Also MASCAGNI: Fritz‡ (*Amico Fritz*); STRAUSS, R: Ein Sänger‡ (*Rosenkavalier*); PUCCINI: Calaf‡ (*Turandot*); VERDI: Macduff‡ (*Macbeth*). Recorded for: Decca, EMI. Gives recitals. Appears with symphony orchestra. **Res:** V Lombroso 12, 4100 Modena, Italy. Mgmt: EUM/FRG; HHB/USA.

PAWASSAR, KLAUS. Conductor of opera and symphony. German. Born 19 Jun 1926, Riga, Latvia. Wife Lilly. Three children. Studied: Profs Gmeindl, Berlin; A Knapp, Lodz; Richter-Haaser, Detmold; Pastuchoff, Riga; incl piano, horn, violin, organ. Plays the piano. Operatic training as repetiteur & asst cond at Stadttheater Hagen 1950-54; Stadttheater Augsburg 1954-64. **Operatic debut:** *Butterfly* Stadttheater Hagen, FR Ger 1952. Symphonic debut: Phil Hungarica, Marl, FR Ger 1971. Previous adm positions in opera: Studienleiter & Cond, Opernhaus Cologne 1964-72. **Conducted with major companies in** AUS: Salzburg Fest; FR GER: Cologne, Saarbrücken, Wiesbaden. **Operas with these companies incl** d'ALBERT: *Tiefland;* BIZET: *Docteur Miracle;* BRITTEN: *Rape of Lucretia★;* DONIZETTI: *Don Pasquale, Elisir;* FLOTOW: *Martha;* GLUCK: *Orfeo ed Euridice;* HUMPERDINCK: *Hänsel und Gretel★, Königskinder;* JANACEK: *Jenufa;* LEONCAVALLO: *Pagliacci;* LORTZING: *Waffenschmied, Wildschütz★, Zar und Zimmermann;* MARSCHNER: *Hans Heiling;* MASCAGNI: *Cavalleria rusticana;* MOZART:

Così fan tutte, Don Giovanni, Entführung aus dem Serail★, Nozze di Figaro★, Zauberflöte; NICOLAI: *Lustigen Weiber★;* OFFENBACH: *Contes d'Hoffmann;* POULENC: *Dialogues des Carmélites;* PUCCINI: *Bohème, Butterfly★;* ROSSINI: *Barbiere di Siviglia;* SAINT-SAENS: *Samson et Dalila★;* SMETANA: *Bartered Bride;* STRAUSS, J: *Fledermaus;* STRAUSS, R: *Salome;* TCHAIKOVSKY: *Pique Dame;* VERDI: *Don Carlo, Nabucco, Traviata, Trovatore;* WAGNER: *Fliegende Holländer, Lohengrin;* WEBER: *Freischütz.* **World premieres:** HAENTJES: *Gesucht werden Tote* Opernhaus Cologne 1966. Teaches at Staatliche Hochschule für Musik, Cologne; Prof. **Res:** Lotharstr 32, Cologne, FR Ger.

PEARL, LOUISE. Dramatic mezzo-soprano. American. Born 22 Mar 1937, New York. Husband Howard Greenwald, occupation private investor. Studied: Grete Stückgold, New York; Kurt Adler, coach, New York. **Debut:** Amneris (*Aida*) Kiel Opera 1964. Previous occupations: musical comedy, Broadway. **Sang with major companies in** AUS: Graz, Vienna Staatsoper; FR GER: Bonn, Düsseldorf-Duisburg, Frankfurt, Hamburg, Kassel, Kiel, Wuppertal; MEX: Mexico City; SWI: Zurich; USA: Cincinnati, Hawaii, Houston, New Orleans, New York Met, Omaha, Washington DC. **Roles with these companies incl** BERG: Gräfin Geschwitz (*Lulu*); BIZET: Carmen★; BRITTEN: Hermia (*Midsummer Night*), Auntie (*Peter Grimes*); CIMAROSA: Fidalma (*Matrimonio segreto*); GOUNOD: Siebel (*Faust*); MOZART: Dorabella (*Così fan tutte*), Cherubino (*Nozze di Figaro*); OFFENBACH: Giulietta (*Contes d'Hoffmann*); STRAUSS, J: Prinz Orlovsky (*Fledermaus*); STRAUSS, R: Komponist★ (*Ariadne auf Naxos*), Octavian★ (*Rosenkavalier*); TCHAIKOVSKY: Olga (*Eugene Onegin*); VERDI: Amneris★ (*Aida*), Ulrica (*Ballo in maschera*), Eboli★ (*Don Carlo*), Preziosilla (*Forza del destino*), Federica (*Luisa Miller*); WAGNER: Magdalene (*Meistersinger*), Venus (*Tannhäuser*); WARD: Elizabeth Proctor★ (*Crucible*). Also STRAUSS, R: Salome★. Gives recitals. Appears with symphony orchestra. **Res:** 165 West End Ave, New York, NY 10023, USA. Mgmt: LWI/USA; PAS/FRG.

PEARLMAN, RICHARD LOUIS. Stages/produces opera, theater & film. Also designs stage-lighting and is an author. American. Born 17 Jul 1937, Norwalk, CT. Single. Studied: as asst to Franco Zeffirelli, Luchino Visconti, Gian Carlo Menotti & Sir Tyrone Guthrie in USA, Italy, UK & Belgium; also music and piano. Operatic training as asst stage dir at Met Opera, New York 1964-67. **Operatic debut:** *Béatrice et Bénédict* Washington, DC, Opera Socy 1964. Theater debut: rock musical, Seattle Opera, WA 1971. Previous occupation: stage mng. Previous adm positions in opera: Gen Mng, Washington, DC, Opera Socy 1968-70.

Directed/produced opera for major companies in USA: Kansas City, S n Francisco Spring, Santa Fe, Seattle, Washing* n DC. **Operas staged for these companies incl** BARBER: *Vanessa;* BERLIOZ: *Béatrice et Bénédict;* BIZET: *Carmen★;* BRITTEN: *Turn of the Screw;* CAVALLI: *Ormindo★;* DONIZETTI: *Don Pasquale★;* MOZART: *Così fan tutte★, Nozze di Figaro★,*

Zauberflöte; PUCCINI: *Bohème*, *Manon Lescaut;* ROSSINI: *Barbiere di Siviglia*; WARD: *Crucible*. Also HOIBY: *Natalia Petrovna*. Teaches. **Res:** 163 W 10 St, New York, USA. Mgmt: CAM/USA.

PEARS, PETER. Tenor. British. Born 22 Jun 1910, Farnham. Single. Studied: Royal Coll of Music, London; Dawson Freer, Clytie Hine Mundy, New York; Julius Guttmann, Lucie Manen, London. **Debut:** Hoffmann, New Opera Co, London 1942. Previous occupations: music teacher 1929-33. Awards: Commander of the British Empire; Hon DM, Cambridge Univ, York Univ, Sussex Univ; FRAM, FRCM, London; Member Royal Swedish Acad.

Sang with major companies in SWI: Zurich; UK: Aldeburgh Fest, Edinburgh Fest, Glyndebourne Fest, London Royal & English National; USA: New York Met. **Roles with these companies incl** BRITTEN: Albert Herring (*Albert Herring*), Edward Fairfax Vere (*Billy Budd*), Nebuchadnezzar (*Burning Fiery Furnace*), Madwoman★ (*Curlew River*), Aschenbach★ (*Death in Venice*), Essex (*Gloriana*), Sir Philip Wingrave★ (*Owen Wingrave*), Peter Grimes, Tempter (*Prodigal Son*), Male Chorus (*Rape of Lucretia*), Peter Quint★ (*Turn of the Screw*); GAY/Britten: Macheath (*Beggar's Opera*); MONTEVERDI: Testo (*Combattimento di Tancredi*); MOZART: Ferrando (*Così fan tutte*), Idomeneo★, Tamino (*Zauberflöte*); PURCELL: Aeneas; ROSSINI: Almaviva (*Barbiere di Siviglia*); SMETANA: Hans (*Bartered Bride*); VERDI: Duca di Mantova (*Rigoletto*), Alfredo (*Traviata*); WAGNER: David (*Meistersinger*). Also BERKELEY: Boaz (*Ruth*). **World premieres:** twelve operas by Benjamin Britten 1945-73 (see list). Recorded for: Decca. Gives recitals. Appears with symphony orchestra. **Res:** Red House, Aldeburgh, UK. Mgmt: PPM/UK; SHA/USA.

PECILE, MIRNA. Dramatic mezzo-soprano. Italian. Born 15 Mar 1943, S Daniele del Friuli. Single. Studied: Mo Piccimini & Ma Giulia Tess, Milan; Ilsebil Bertkau, Germany. **Debut:** Irene (*Belisario*) Teatro la Fenice, Venice 1969. Previous occupations: interpreter. Awards: Winner, Compt G Verdi voices, RAI TV 1971; Third Prize Viotti Compt, Vercelli 1968.

Sang with major companies in AUS: Graz; BEL: Brussels; FRA: Bordeaux, Marseille, Nice, Rouen, Strasbourg, Toulouse; HUN: Budapest; ITA: Bologna, Genoa, Milan La Scala, Parma, Turin, Venice; S AFR: Johannesburg; UK: London Royal; USSR: Moscow Bolshoi. **Roles with these companies incl** BELLINI: Adalgisa★ (*Norma*); MUSSORGSKY: Marina★ (*Boris Godunov*); PONCHIELLI: Laura★ & La Cieca★ (*Gioconda*); VERDI: Amneris★ (*Aida*), Ulrica★ (*Ballo in maschera*), Eboli★ (*Don Carlo*), Preziosilla★ (*Forza del destino*), Azucena★ (*Trovatore*). Appears with symphony orchestra. **Res:** V Massarenti 24, Milan, Italy. Mgmt: GOR/UK.

PEHARDA, ZDENKO. Conductor of opera and symphony; composer. Yugoslavian. Art Adm & Resident Cond, Norwegian Opera, Oslo. Born 2 Mar 1923, Zagreb. Wife Mirjana, occupation opera singer. Three children. Studied: Music Acads, Za-

greb and Ljubljana, Lovro v Matacic, Boris Papandopulo, Danilo Svara, Yugoslavia; incl piano, trombone, trumpet, flute, double bass, timpani and voice. Plays the piano. Operatic training as repetiteur, chorus master & theater mng at var companies. **Operatic debut:** Opera I Zajc, Rijeka, Yugoslavia 1946. Symphonic debut: State Phil Orch, Zagreb 1944. Previous occupations: orch mem; arranger; accompanist; leader of dance & revue orch. Previous adm positions in opera: Secy, Opera I Zajc, Rijeka 1947-55; Art Dir, Narodno Kazaliste, Varazdin, Yugoslavia 1959-60; Dir, State Opera School, Oslo 1964-72.

Conducted with major companies in AUS: Graz; BUL: Sofia; CZE: Brno; FIN: Helsinki; FR GER: Bielefeld, Dortmund, Kiel; ITA: Trieste, Venice; NOR: Oslo; USA: Memphis; YUG: Zagreb, Belgrade. **Operas with these companies incl** d'ALBERT: *Tiefland;* AUBER: *Fra Diavolo;* BEETHOVEN: *Fidelio;* BIZET: *Carmen*★, *Docteur Miracle;* BOITO: *Mefistofele;* BORODIN: *Prince Igor*★; BRITTEN: *Peter Grimes;* CATALANI: *Wally;* CHARPENTIER: *Louise;* CILEA: *A. Lecouvreur;* CIMAROSA: *Matrimonio segreto;* DONIZETTI: *Campanello*★, *Don Pasquale, Elisir*★, *Rita*★; DVORAK: *Rusalka;* FALLA: *Vida breve;* GERSHWIN: *Porgy and Bess*★; GIORDANO: *Andrea Chénier, Fedora;* GLUCK: *Iphigénie en Tauride, Orfeo ed Euridice;* GOTOVAC: *Ero der Schelm;* GOUNOD: *Faust;* GRANADOS: *Goyescas;* HAYDN: *Mondo della luna;* HUMPERDINCK: *Hänsel und Gretel;* JANACEK: *Jenufa*★, *Katya Kabanova;* KODALY: *Háry János*★; LEONCAVALLO: *Pagliacci*★; MARTINU: *Comedy on the Bridge;* MASCAGNI: *Amico Fritz, Cavalleria rusticana;* MASSENET: *Manon, Werther;* MENOTTI: *Amelia al ballo, Consul*★, *Medium;* MOZART: *Don Giovanni*★, *Nozze di Figaro, Oca del Cairo, Zauberflöte*★; MUSSORGSKY: *Boris Godunov;* NICOLAI: *Lustigen Weiber;* OFFENBACH: *Contes d'Hoffmann*★; ORFF: *Carmina burana, Kluge*★; PAISIELLO: *Barbiere di Siviglia;* PERGOLESI: *Serva padrona;* PONCHIELLI: *Gioconda*★; PROKOFIEV: *Duenna, Love for Three Oranges;* PUCCINI: *Bohème*★, *Fanciulla del West, Gianni Schicchi, Butterfly*★, *Manon Lescaut, Tabarro, Tosca*★, *Turandot;* RAVEL: *Heure espagnole;* ROSSINI: *Barbiere di Siviglia*★; SAINT-SAENS: *Samson et Dalila;* SHOSTAKOVICH: *Katerina Ismailova*★; SMETANA: *Bartered Bride;* STRAUSS, J: *Fledermaus*★; STRAUSS, R: *Capriccio, Intermezzo, Rosenkavalier*★; STRAVINSKY: *Mavra;* TCHAIKOVSKY: *Eugene Onegin, Pique Dame*★; VERDI: *Aida, Ballo in maschera, Don Carlo*★, *Forza del destino, Rigoletto*★, *Traviata*★, *Trovatore*★; WAGNER: *Walküre, Tannhäuser;* WEILL: *Aufstieg und Fall der Stadt Mahagonny*★, *Driegroschenoper;* WOLF-FERRARI: *Gioielli della Madonna, Segreto di Susanna.* Also TIJARDOVIC: *Dimnjaci na Jadranu;* GOTOVAC: *Morana;* LHOTKA-KALINSKI: *Pomet;* LISINSKI: *Porin;* BRAEIN: *Anne Pedersdotter;* MARTINU: *Zweimal Alexander;* ODAK: *Dorica Plese;* ZAJC: *Nikola Subic Zrinjski.* **World premieres:** DOBRONIC: *Pokladna Noc* Opera Rijeka, Yugoslavia 1951; PARAC: *Adel and Mara* Opera Rijeka 1952; GOTOVAC: *Derdan* Comedy Theater, Zagreb 1955. Conducted major orch in Europe. Teaches at Music Consv, Oslo. **Res:** Nedre Kalbakkvei 2D, Oslo, Norway. Mgmt: PGI/NOR.

PELLEGRINI, MARIA. Lyric soprano. Canadian. Born Pretoro, Italy. Husband Steven Thomas, occupation stage dir. One child. Studied: Royal Consv of Music, Dr Ernesto Vinci, Toronto. **Debut:** Gilda (*Rigoletto*) Canadian Opera Co, Toronto 1963. Awards: Medaglia d'oro, Genoa Opera, Italy.

Sang with major companies in CAN: Montreal/Quebec, Toronto, Vancouver; ITA: Bologna, Genoa, Parma, Trieste; UK: Cardiff Welsh, London Royal Opera & English National; USA: Fort Worth, Pittsburgh, San Antonio. Roles with these companies incl BELLINI: Amina (*Sonnambula*); DONIZETTI: Adina (*Elisir*); LEON-CAVALLO: Nedda★ (*Pagliacci*); MOZART: Fiordiligi (*Così fan tutte*); PUCCINI: Mimi★ & Musetta★ (*Bohème*), Cio-Cio-San (*Butterfly*), Manon Lescaut, Liù★ (*Turandot*); STRAUSS, R: Chrysothemis (*Elektra*); VERDI: Aida★, Nannetta (*Falstaff*), Amelia★ (*Masnadieri*), Desdemona★ (*Otello*), Gilda★ (*Rigoletto*), Violetta★ (*Traviata*). **Res:** Ennismore, Canada. Mgmt: HUR/USA.

PENKOVA, RENI TODOROVA. Lyric mezzo-soprano. Bulgarian. Resident mem: National Opera, Sofia. Born 28 Oct 1935, V Tarnovo, Bulgaria. Single. Studied: Nadya Aladjem, Elena Doskova-Ricardi. **Debut:** Olga (*Eugene Onegin*) Burgass, Bulgaria 1960.

Sang with major companies in BUL: Sofia; HOL: Amsterdam; UK: Glyndebourne Fest. **Roles with these companies incl** BARTOK: Judith (*Bluebeard's Castle*); BORODIN: Kontchakovna★‡ (*Prince Igor*); GLUCK: Orfeo; GOUNOD: Siebel★ (*Faust*); MOZART: Dorabella (*Così fan tutte*), Cherubino (*Nozze di Figaro*); PUCCINI: Suzuki★ (*Butterfly*); RIMSKY-KORSAKOV: Nejata (*Sadko*); ROSSINI: Angelina (*Cenerentola*); STRAUSS, R: Octavian★ (*Rosenkavalier*); TCHAIKOVSKY: Olga (*Eugene Onegin*); VERDI: Amneris★(*Aida*). Gives recitals. Appears with symphony orchestra.

PERDACHER, WALTER. Scenic and costume designer for opera, theater. Is a lighting designer; also a painter. Austrian. Resident designer, Oper des Staatstheaters Kassel, FR Ger and at Staatstheater Kassel, FR Ger. Born 11 Apr 1930, Graz. Wife Ingrid. Studied: Akad Graz; Akad der schönen Künste, Vienna. Prof training: Opera, Graz; Burgtheater, Vienna 1948-52. **Operatic debut:** Stadttheater Bonn 1954. Theater debut: Stadttheater Bonn 1954. Previous adm positions in opera: Head Designer Bonn, Bremerhaven, Nürnberg, Linz/Austria, Kassel 1954-75.

Designed for major companies in FR GER: Bonn, Kassel, Kiel, Nürnberg; POR: Lisbon. **Operas designed for these companies incl** ADAM: *Si j'étais roi;* d'ALBERT: *Tiefland;* AUBER: *Fra Diavolo;* BARTOK: *Bluebeard's Castle;* BEET-HOVEN: *Fidelio;* BERG: *Lulu;* BIZET: *Carmen;* BRITTEN: *Albert Herring, Death in Venice, Midsummer Night;* BUSONI: *Arlecchino;* CA-VALIERI: *Rappresentazione;* CORNELIUS: *Barbier von Bagdad;* DEBUSSY: *Pelléas et Mélisande;* DONIZETTI: *Campanello, Don Pa-*

squale; DVORAK: *Rusalka;* FLOTOW: *Martha;* GAY/Britten: *Beggar's Opera;* GLUCK: *Iphigénie en Tauride, Orfeo ed Euridice;* HINDE-MITH: *Cardillac, Mathis der Maler;* HUMPERDINCK: *Hänsel und Gretel;* JANA-CEK: *Jenufa;* LORTZING: *Waffenschmied, Wildschütz, Zar und Zimmermann;* MARTIN: *Vin herbé;* MARTINU: *Griechische Passion;* MASCAGNI: *Cavalleria rusticana;* MENOTTI: *Consul, Telephone;* MOZART: *Così fan tutte, Don Giovanni, Entführung aus dem Serail, Finta giardiniera, Nozze di Figaro, Zauberflöte;* MUS-SORGSKY: *Boris Godunov;* NICOLAI: *Lustigen Weiber;* OFFENBACH: *Contes d'Hoffmann;* PERGOLESI: *Serva padrona;* PUCCINI: *Bohème, Fanciulla del West, Gianni Schicchi, Butterfly, Tosca, Turandot;* ROSSINI: *Barbiere di Siviglia;* SMETANA: *Bartered Bride;* STRAUSS, J: *Fledermaus;* STRAUSS, R: *Ariadne auf Naxos, Daphne, Elektra, Liebe der Danae, Rosenkavalier, Salome;* STRAVINSKY: *Oedipus Rex;* VERDI: *Aida, Ballo in maschera, Don Carlo, Falstaff, Forza del destino, Macbeth, Nabucco, Otello, Rigoletto, Traviata, Trovatore;* WAGNER: *Fliegende Holländer, Lohengrin, Meistersinger, Rheingold, Walküre, Tannhäuser, Tristan und Isolde;* WEBER: *Freischütz;* WEILL: *Dreigroschenoper;* WEINBERGER: *Schwanda.* Exhibitions of stage designs, paintings & graphics Bonn 1954; Nürnberg 1965; Vienna 1950. Teaches at Univ Erlangen, FR Ger. **Res:** Fuldablick 43, Kassel, FR Ger. Mgmt: KNL/FRG.

PÉRISSON, JEAN MARIE. Conductor of opera; composer. French. Born 6 Jul 1924, Arcachon, France. Wife Denise Waudby.. Three children. Studied: Coll St Joseph-de-Tivoli, Bordeaux; Consv Ntl Supér de Musique. Awards: First Prize, Conc Intl de Chef d'orch, Fest de Besançon 1952. Previous adm positions in opera: Mus Dir, Opéra de Nice 1956-65.

Conducted with major companies in FRA: Marseille, Nice, Paris; ITA: Naples; USA: Chicago, San Francisco Opera; et al. **Operas with these companies incl** BERLIOZ: *Troyens;* BIZET: *Carmen;* BRITTEN: *Midsummer Night;* CHAR-PENTIER: *Louise;* DEBUSSY: *Pelléas et Mélisande;* GOUNOD: *Faust, Mireille;* JANA-CEK: *Katya Kabanova;* MASSENET: *Don Quichotte, Manon;* MEYERBEER: *Africaine;* PUCCINI: *Bohème, Butterfly, Tosca;* ROSSINI: *Barbiere di Siviglia;* STRAUSS, R: *Rosenkavalier;* VERDI: *Aida, Traviata;* WAGNER: *Tannhäuser;* et al. Conducted major orch in Europe, USA/Canada. **Res:** 111 Ave de Verdun, 92 Issy-les-Moulineaux, France.

PERRIER, CLAUDE. Scenic and costume designer for opera, theater, film, television. Is a lighting designer; also a painter, sculptor, illustrator & architect. French. Resident designer, Bordeaux Grand Théâtre; Liceo, Barcelona. Born 25 Jan 1918, Gannat, France. Wife Simone Sabatier, occupation concert pianist. Studied: Consv Ntl Supérieur, Paris; École Ntl des Beaux Arts & Décoration; Ecole Sup Travaux Publics et Architecture, Paris; Inst des Hautes Etudes Cinématographique, Paris. Prof training: Opéra de Lyon, France. **Operatic debut:** Opéra de Lyon. Theater debut: Art Dir, Reuzillance Film, Montreal; Fiat Film, Paris. Previous occupation: Prof, Consv Ntl de la Région Toulouse. Awards: Grand Prix de la Critique, France; Gold Medal, City of Bordeaux.

Designed for major companies in CAN: Montreal/Quebec; FRA: Bordeaux, Lyon, Marseille, Nancy, Nice, Paris, Rouen, Strasbourg, Toulouse; FR GER: Wiesbaden; HOL: Amsterdam; SPA: Barcelona; SWI: Zurich. **Operas designed for these companies incl** ADAM: *Si j'étais roi;* BEETHOVEN: *Fidelio;* BELLINI: *Puritani;* BERLIOZ: *Benvenuto Cellini, Damnation de Faust;* BIZET: *Carmen, Pêcheurs de perles;* BOITO: *Mefistofele;* BORODIN: *Prince Igor;* CHABRIER: *Roi malgré lui;* CHARPENTIER: *Louise;* DALLAPICCOLA: *Volo di notte;* DEBUSSY: *Pelléas et Mélisande;* DELIBES: *Lakmé, Roi l'a dit;* DONIZETTI: *Lucia;* DUKAS: *Ariane et Barbe Bleue;* EGK: *Verlobung in San Domingo;* EINEM: *Dantons Tod;* FALLA: *Vida breve;* GERSHWIN: *Porgy and Bess;* GIORDANO: *Andrea Chénier;* GLUCK: *Orfeo ed Euridice;* GOLDMARK: *Königin von Saba;* GOUNOD: *Faust, Mireille, Roméo et Juliette;* HINDEMITH: *Mathis der Maler;* LALO: *Roi d'Ys;* LECOCQ: *Fille de Madame Angot;* LEONCAVALLO: *Pagliacci;* MASCAGNI: *Cavalleria rusticana;* MASSENET: *Hérodiade, Manon, Thaïs;* MENOTTI: *Amahl, Consul, Medium;* MEYERBEER: *Huguenots;* MOZART: *Don Giovanni, Nozze di Figaro, Zauberflöte;* MUSSORGSKY: *Boris Godunov;* PROKOFIEV: *Love for Three Oranges;* PUCCINI: *Bohème, Manon Lescaut, Tosca;* RABAUD: *Mârouf;* RAVEL: *Enfant et les sortilèges;* ROSSINI: *Barbiere di Siviglia, Guillaume Tell;* SAINT-SAENS: *Samson et Dalila;* SMETANA: *Bartered Bride;* STRAUSS, J: *Fledermaus;* STRAUSS, R: *Salome;* STRAVINSKY: *Rake's Progress;* THOMAS: *Hamlet, Mignon;* VERDI: *Aida, Ballo in maschera, Don Carlo, Falstaff, Forza del destino, Otello, Rigoletto, Traviata, Trovatore;* WAGNER: *Fliegende Holländer, Lohengrin, Parsifal, Rheingold, Walküre, Siegfried, Götterdämmerung, Tannhäuser.* Also BERTHOMIEU: *Königsmark;* CAPEDEVILLE: *Fille de l'homme;* FAURE: *Pénélope;* FORTNER: *Bluthochzeit;* LULLY: *Armide;* REYER: *Sigurd;* ROSSELLINI: *Sguardo dal ponte;* SANCAN: *Ondine;* RESPIGHI: *Maria Egiziaca;* SCARLATTI: *Mitridate Eupatore.* Operatic Video/Film—TV Toulouse; Radio Pyrénées. Exhibitions of stage designs, Paris, Bordeaux, Lyon. Teaches at Consv de la Région Toulouse. **Res:** 6 rue Mirabeau, 31500 Toulouse, France.

PERRIERS, DANIÈLE BERNADETTE. Light lyric soprano. French. Born 24 Jun 1945, Beaumont-le-Roger, France. Single. Studied: Consv Ntl de Musique, Janine Micheau, Jeanine Rueff, Roger Bourdin (opera), Fanely Revoil (operetta), Paris. **Debut:** Sophie (*Werther*) Marseille Opera 1968. Awards: First Prize in Voice, in Opera, in Operetta, Consv Ntl de Musique, Paris.

Sang with major companies in BEL: Brussels, Liège; DEN: Copenhagen; FRA: Aix-en-Provence Fest, Bordeaux, Lyon, Marseille, Nancy, Nice, Paris, Rouen, Strasbourg, Toulouse; ISR: Tel Aviv; MON: Monte Carlo; SWI: Geneva; UK: Edinburgh Fest, Glyndebourne Fest. **Roles**

with these companies incl ADAM: Neméa (*Si j'étais roi*); BIZET: Léila (*Pêcheurs de perles*); BOIELDIEU: Anna (*Dame blanche*); DONIZETTI: Norina (*Don Pasquale*); LECOCQ: Clairette (*Fille de Madame Angot*); MASSENET: Manon, Sophie (*Werther*); MENOTTI: Emily (*Globolinks*); MOZART: Despina (*Così fan tutte*), Zerlina (*Don Giovanni*), Blondchen (*Entführung aus dem Serail*), Susanna (*Nozze di Figaro*); OFFENBACH: Olympia (*Contes d'Hoffmann*); PERGOLESI: Serpina (*Serva padrona*); PUCCINI: Lauretta (*Gianni Schicchi*); ROSSINI: Rosina (*Barbiere di Siviglia*); STRAUSS, J: Adele (*Fledermaus*); STRAUSS, R: Sophie (*Rosenkavalier*); WEBER: Aennchen (*Freischütz*). **World premieres:** LESUR: Spinette (*Andréa del Sarto*) Opéra de Marseille 1969. Film—Opéra de Genève: Manon; Opéra de Rouen: (*Andréa del Sarto*). **Res:** 109 Bvld de Grenelle, Paris, France. Mgmt: IMR/FRA.

PERRY, JANET. Coloratura soprano. American; Swiss by marriage. Resident mem: Bayerische Staatsoper, Munich. Born 27 Dec 1947, Minneapolis, MN, USA. Husband Alexander Malta, occupation opera singer. Studied: Curtis Inst of Music, Eufemia Gregory, Philadelphia. **Debut:** Zerlina (*Don Giovanni*) Linz Opera, Austria 1969.

Sang with major companies in AUS: Vienna Staatsoper; FRA: Aix-en-Provence Fest; FR GER: Cologne, Frankfurt, Munich Staatsoper & Gärtnerplatz, Stuttgart. **Roles with these companies incl** AUBER: Zerlina★ (*Fra Diavolo*); DONIZETTI: Norina★(*Don Pasquale*), Adina★ (*Elisir*); MOZART: Zerlina★(*Don Giovanni*), Blondchen★ (*Entführung aus dem Serail*), Mme Herz★ (*Schauspieldirektor*), Pamina★ (*Zauberflöte*); NICOLAI: Aennchen★ (*Lustigen Weiber*); OFFENBACH: Olympia★ (*Contes d'Hoffmann*); PUCCINI: Musetta★ (*Bohème*), Lauretta★ (*Gianni Schicchi*); ROSSINI: Rosina★ (*Barbiere di Siviglia*); STRAUSS, J: Adele★ (*Fledermaus*); STRAUSS, R: Zerbinetta★ (*Ariadne auf Naxos*); VERDI: Oscar★ (*Ballo in maschera*), Nannetta★ (*Falstaff*). Video/Film—German TV: operettas. Gives recitals. Appears with symphony orchestra. **Res:** Munich, FR Ger.

PESKÓ, ZOLTÁN. Conductor of opera and symphony; composer. Hungarian. Principal Cond, Teatro Comunale, Bologna, Italy. Born 15 Feb 1937, Budapest, Hungary. Married. Studied: Accad di S Cecilia, Goffredo Petrassi, Rome; Franco Ferrara, Rome, Pierre Boulez, Basel; incl piano, cello, organ. Operatic training as asst cond & asst to GMD, Deutsche Oper Berlin, FR Ger 1968-69; RSO Berlin, FR Ger 1966-68. **Operatic debut:** *Maria Egiziaca* Consv S Cecilia, Rome 1965. Symphonic debut: Radio Italiana, Rome 1965. Previous occupations: Hungarian TV 1960-64; Prof, Hochschule für Musik, Berlin, FR Ger 1970-72. Awards: Nicola d'Atri Prize Accad S Cecilia, Rome 1965; Prize of Ital critics 1972.

Conducted with major companies in FR GER: Berlin Deutsche Oper, Stuttgart; ITA: Bologna, Genoa, Milan La Scala, Parma, Turin, Venice. **Operas with these companies incl** BIZET: *Carmen★;* BRITTEN: *Billy Budd★;* DALLAPICCOLA: *Ulisse★;* JANACEK: *Excursions of Mr Broucek;* MOZART: *Don Giovanni, Entführung* *aus dem Serail, Finta giardiniera★, Nozze di Figaro★;* PROKOFIEV: *Fiery Angel★;* PUCCINI: *Bohème★, Tosca★;* SCHOENBERG: *Glückliche Hand★;* STRAVINSKY: *Rake's Progress;* VERDI: *Don Carlo, Falstaff, Simon Boccanegra★, Trovatore;* WEILL: *Dreigroschenoper.* Also CHAILLY: *Idiota★‡.* Conducted major orch in Europe. Mgmt: JUD/USA; JUC/SWI.

PETERS, REINHARD. Conductor of opera and symphony. German. Gen Mus Dir & Resident Cond, Deutsche Oper Berlin. Also Mus Dir, Philharmonia Hungarica, Marl, Germany. Born 2 Apr 1926, Magdeburg, Germany. Wife Marie-Rose, occupation violinist. Three children. Studied: Hochschule für Musik, Berlin; incl violin, piano. Plays the violin, piano. Operatic training as repetiteur at Staatsoper Berlin 1946-49. **Operatic debut:** *Rigoletto* Staatsoper Berlin 1952. Symphonic debut: Berlin Phil 1952. Previous occupations: violin and piano soloist. Awards: First Prize Intl Cont Besançon 1951; Kulturpreis Rheinland/Westfalen 1960; German Critics Awd 1962. Previous adm positions in opera: First Cond, Deutsche Oper am Rhein, Düsseldorf 1957-61; Gen Mus Dir, Münster, FR Ger 1961-70.

Conducted with major companies in ARG: Buenos Aires; AUS: Salzburg Fest, Vienna Staatsoper & Volksoper; BEL: Brussels; FRA: Bordeaux, Lyon, Marseille, Paris, Rouen, Strasbourg; FR GER: Berlin Deutsche Oper, Bonn, Cologne, Darmstadt, Düsseldorf-Duisburg, Essen, Frankfurt, Hamburg, Hannover, Kassel, Kiel, Mannheim, Munich Staatsoper, Nürnberg, Saarbrücken, Stuttgart, Wiesbaden, Wuppertal; HOL: Amsterdam; ITA: Genoa, Naples, Palermo, Rome Opera & Caracalla, Spoleto Fest, Trieste, Turin; MON: Monte Carlo; POR: Lisbon; SWI: Basel, Geneva, Zurich; UK: Edinburgh Fest, Glyndebourne Fest; USA: Miami. **Operas with these companies incl** ADAM: *Postillon de Lonjumeau;* AUBER: *Fra Diavolo;* BEETHOVEN: *Fidelio★;* BERG: *Lulu★;* BIZET: *Carmen★;* BORODIN: *Prince Igor;* BRITTEN: *Death in Venice★, Gloriana;* DEBUSSY: *Pelléas et Mélisande;* DONIZETTI: *Don Pasquale;* EGK: *Zaubergeige;* EINEM: *Dantons Tod★;* GAY/Britten: *Beggar's Opera;* GLUCK: *Iphigénie en Tauride;* HENZE: *Elegy for Young Lovers, Junge Lord★;* HINDEMITH: *Cardillac, Mathis der Maler;* HUMPERDINCK: *Hänsel und Gretel;* JANACEK: *Excursions of Mr Broucek;* LEONCAVALLO: *Pagliacci;* LORTZING: *Zar und Zimmermann;* MENOTTI: *Saint of Bleecker Street;* MONTEVERDI: *Incoronazione di Poppea★;* MOZART: *Così fan tutte★, Don Giovanni★, Entführung aus dem Serail★, Nozze di Figaro★, Zauberflöte★;* OFFENBACH: *Contes d'Hoffmann★;* ORFF: *Carmina burana;* PAISIELLO: *Barbiere di Siviglia★;* PUCCINI: *Gianni Schicchi, Butterfly, Tosca;* PURCELL: *King Arthur;* ROSSINI: *Barbiere di Siviglia★, Cenerentola★;* SAINT-SAENS: *Samson et Dalila;* SHOSTAKOVICH: *Katerina Ismailova;* SMETANA: *Bartered Bride;* STRAUSS, R: *Arabella, Ariadne auf Naxos, Capriccio★, Elektra, Rosenkavalier★, Salome★;* VERDI: *Aida, Don Carlo, Falstaff, Macbeth, Nabucco, Rigoletto, Traviata, Trovatore;* WAGNER: *Fliegende Holländer★, Rheingold★, Siegfried★, Götterdämmerung★, Tannhäuser★, Tristan und Isolde★;* WE-

BER: *Freischütz★.* Also KELEMEN: *Neue Mieter;* EGK: *Revisor.* **World premieres:** KLEBE: *Räuber* Düsseldorf 1957, *Tödlichen Wünsche* Düsseldorf 1959; LUDWIG: *Rashomon* Augsburg 1972; REIMANN: *Melusine* Deutsche Oper Berlin 1973; NABOKOV: *Love's Labour's Lost* Deutsche Oper Berlin 1973. Conducted major orch in Europe, USA/Canada, Cent/S America, Asia. Previous positions as Mus Dir with major orch: Städtisches Orch Münster, FR Ger 1961-70. **Res:** Im Dol 66, 1 Berlin 33, FR Ger. Mgmt: KRG/FRG; IMR/FRA.

PETERS, ROBERTA; née Roberta Peterman. Coloratura soprano. American. Resident mem: Metropolitan Opera, New York. Born 4 May 1930, New York. Husband Bertram Fields, occupation real estate investor. Two children. Studied: William Hermann, New York. **Debut:** Zerlina (*Don Giovanni*) Metropolitan Opera 1950. Awards: Hon DL Elmira Coll; Hon DH Westminster Coll; Hon DM Ithaca Coll; Woman of the Year, Fed Women's Clubs.

Sang with major companies in AUS: Salzburg Fest, Vienna Staatsoper & Volksoper; FR GER: Berlin Deutsche Oper, Munich Staatsoper & Gärtnerplatz; UK: London Royal Opera; USSR: Leningrad Kirov, Moscow Bolshoi; USA: Baltimore, Cincinnati, Hartford, Hawaii, Newark, New York Met, Philadelphia Grand, Pittsburgh, San Antonio, Seattle. **Roles with these companies incl** BELLINI: Amina (*Sonnambula*); DELIBES: Lakmé; DONIZETTI: Norina★ (*Don Pasquale*), Adina★ (*Elisir*), Lucia★‡; FLOTOW: Lady Harriet (*Martha*); GLUCK: Amor‡ (*Orfeo ed Euridice*); GOUNOD: Juliette★; MENOTTI: Kitty (*Dernier sauvage*); MOZART: Despina‡ (*Così fan tutte*), Zerlina★ (*Don Giovanni*), Susanna★‡ (*Nozze di Figaro*), Königin der Nacht‡ (*Zauberflöte*); PUCCINI: Mimi (*Bohème*), Lauretta (*Schicchi*); ROSSINI: Rosina★‡ (*Barbiere*); STRAUSS, J: Adele★ (*Fledermaus*); STRAUSS, R: Fiakermilli (*Arabella*), Zerbinetta★‡ (*Ariadne auf Naxos*), Sophie (*Rosenkavalier*); VERDI: Oscar★‡ (*Ballo in maschera*), Nannetta★ (*Falstaff*), Gilda★‡ (*Rigoletto*), Violetta★ (*Traviata*). Recorded for: RCA, Columbia, DG. Video/Film: Rosina (*Barbiere di Siviglia*). Gives recitals. Appears with symphony orchestra. **Res:** 64 Garden Rd, Scarsdale, NY, USA. Mgmt: HUR/USA.

PETERSEN, REINHARD. Conductor of opera and symphony. German. First Cond, Staatsoper Hamburg. Born 20 Jan 1943, Hamburg. Wife Marlene. Studied: Music School, Hamburg, Prof Wilhelm Brückner-Rüggeberg; incl piano, trombone. Operatic training as repetiteur & asst cond at Staatsoper Hannover 1965-67. **Operatic debut:** *Barbiere di Siviglia* Staatsoper Hannover 1966. Symphonic debut: Hamburger Sinfoniker 1966. Previous adm positions in opera: Principal Cond, Wuppertaler Bühnen 1972-75.

Conducted with major companies in FR GER: Frankfurt, Hamburg, Hannover, Wuppertal. **Operas with these companies incl** BEETHOVEN: *Fidelio;* BERG: *Lulu★, Wozzeck★;* BIBALO: *Lächeln am Fusse der Leiter★;* BIZET: *Carmen★;* DELIBES: *Roi l'a dit★;* DONIZETTI: *Elisir★;* FORTNER: *Don Perlimplin★;* GIORDANO: *Andrea Chénier★;* GLUCK: *Iphigénie en Aulide,*

Iphigénie en Tauride; HUMPERDINCK: *Königskinder*; LORTZING: *Wildschütz*, *Zar und Zimmermann*; MASCAGNI: *Cavalleria rusticana*; MILHAUD: *Médée*; MOZART: *Entführung aus dem Serail, Zauberflöte*; OFFENBACH: *Contes d'Hoffmann*; PFITZNER: *Palestrina*; PUCCINI: *Bohème, Butterfly*, *Tabarro*, *Tosca*; ROSSINI: *Barbiere di Siviglia*, *Cenerentola*, *Turco in Italia*; STRAUSS, J: *Fledermaus*; STRAUSS, R: *Arabella*; VERDI: *Ballo in maschera*, *Don Carlo*, *Forza del destino*, *Macbeth, Nabucco, Rigoletto*, *Trovatore*; WAGNER: *Fliegende Holländer*, *Walküre*, *Tannhäuser*; WEBER: *Freischütz*. **World premieres:** MEYEROWITZ: *Doppelgängerin* Staatsoper Hannover 1967; EINFELDT: *Palast-Hotel Thanatos* Staatsoper Hannover 1972. Conducted major orch in Europe. **Res:** Kroneweg 18, 2 Hamburg 72, FR Ger.

PETERSEN, ROBERT JAMES. Lyric baritone. American. Resident mem: Seattle Opera Assn, WA, USA. Born 27 Apr 1934, Brainerd, MN, USA. Wife Phyllis Allen, occupation voice teacher. Studied: Dr Fritz Zweig, Tilly de Garmo-Zweig; UCLA Op Wkshp, Dr Jan Popper, Los Angeles; Los Angeles City Coll, Dr Hugo Strelitzer. **Debut:** Germont (*Traviata*), Los Angeles Grand Opera 1959. Previous occupations: diamond core driller; US Army-Aircraft plant worker. Awards: Fulbright Schlshp, Germany 1960; M B Rockefeller Fund Grant 1963.

Sang with major companies in USA: Boston, Hawaii, Seattle. **Roles with these companies incl** d'ALBERT: Sebastiano (*Tiefland*); BARBER: Doctor (*Vanessa*); BIZET: Escamillo (*Carmen*); DONIZETTI: Dott Malatesta (*Don Pasquale*), Enrico★ (*Lucia*); GLUCK: Agamemnon (*Iphigénie en Aulide*); GOUNOD: Valentin★ (*Faust*); LEONCAVALLO: Tonio★ (*Pagliacci*); MASSENET: Lescaut★ (*Manon*); MOZART: Guglielmo★ (*Così fan tutte*), Nardo (*Finta giardiniera*), Conte Almaviva (*Nozze di Figaro*); OFFENBACH: Don Andres★ (*Périchole*); ORFF: König (*Kluge*); PUCCINI: Marcello★ (*Bohème*), Gianni Schicchi, Sharpless★ (*Butterfly*), Lescaut★ (*Manon Lescaut*), Scarpia★ (*Tosca*); PURCELL: Aeneas (*Dido and Aeneas*); ROSSINI: Figaro★ (*Barbiere di Siviglia*); STRAVINSKY: Creon (*Oedipus Rex*); TCHAIKOVSKY: Eugene Onegin; VERDI: Amonasro★ (*Aida*), Renato★ (*Ballo in maschera*), Rodrigo (*Don Carlo*), Falstaff★, Iago★ (*Otello*), Rigoletto★, Germont★ (*Traviata*), Conte di Luna★ (*Trovatore*); WAGNER: Alberich★ (*Götterdämmerung*), Kurwenal★ (*Tristan und Isolde*). Also WAGNER: Alberich★ (*Siegfried*); STRAUSS, R: Faninal★ (*Rosenkavalier*). Gives recitals. Appears with symphony orchestra. Coaches repertoire. **Res:** 1605 E Madison St, Seattle, WA, USA. Mgmt: SMN/USA.

PETERSON, BARR EDWARD. Bass. American. Resident mem: Niedersächsische Staatsoper, Hannover. Born 3 Apr 1924, Mason City, IA. Wife Eva, occupation physician. Two children. Studied: Ruth Streeter, Boston; Franz Karl, Munich. **Debut:** Osmin (*Entführung*) Münster/Westfalen 1955. Previous occupations: asst controller, dept store.

Sang with major companies in FR GER: Dortmund, Düsseldorf-Duisburg, Essen, Hannover,

Kiel, Wuppertal. **Roles with these companies incl** d'ALBERT: Tommaso (*Tiefland*); BEETHOVEN: Rocco★ (*Fidelio*); EGK: Cuperus (*Zaubergeige*); JANACEK: Harasta (*Cunning Little Vixen*); MOZART: Osmin★ (*Entführung aus dem Serail*), Sarastro★ (*Zauberflöte*); MUSSORGSKY: Varlaam★ & Pimen★ (*Boris Godunov*); NICOLAI: Falstaff (*Lustigen Weiber*); ORFF: Bauer (*Kluge*); PROKOFIEV: General (*Gambler*); PUCCINI: Colline★ (*Bohème*); ROSSINI: Don Basilio★ (*Barbiere di Siviglia*); VERDI: Ramfis★ (*Aida*), Philip II★ (*Don Carlo*), Padre Guardiano★ (*Forza del destino*), Banquo (*Macbeth*), Massimiliano Moor (*Masnadieri*), Zaccaria★ (*Nabucco*), Fiesco (*Simon Boccanegra*); WAGNER: Daland★ (*Fliegende Holländer*), König Heinrich★ (*Lohengrin*), Pogner★ (*Meistersinger*), Fasolt★ (*Rheingold*), Fafner★ (*Siegfried*), Hunding★ (*Walküre*), Hagen★ (*Götterdämmerung*), Landgraf★ (*Tannhäuser*), König Marke★ (*Tristan und Isolde*); WEBER: Kaspar (*Freischütz*). **World premieres:** MEYEROWITZ: Arne (*Doppelgängerin*) Hannover 1967. Recorded for: Radio Beromünster. Gives recitals. Appears with symphony orchestra. **Res:** Nienstedter Stadtweg 7G, 3013 Barsinghausen 2, FR Ger.

PETERSON, BENGT OLOF. Stages/produces opera & television. Also designs stage-lighting. Swedish. First Stage Dir/Prod, Royal Opera, Stockholm. Born 16 Sep 1923, Visby. Wife Rose Marie Mengarelli, form occupation dancer. Five children. Studied: Issay Dobrowen, Stockholm; Georg Hartmann, Munich; Carl Ebert, Glyndebourne; Günther Rennert, Hamburg; incl music, piano & violin. Operatic training as asst stage dir at Royal Opera, Stockholm 1948-51. **Operatic debut:** *Kluge* Royal Opera, Stockholm 1951. Awards: Vasa Order, King Gustaf VI Adolf; stpd from ITI.

Directed/produced opera for major companies in DEN: Copenhagen; FR GER: Hamburg, Wiesbaden; NOR: Oslo; SWE: Drottningholm Fest, Stockholm; UK: Edinburgh Fest, London Royal. **Operas staged with these companies incl** BEETHOVEN: *Fidelio*; BIZET: *Carmen*; BRITTEN: *Midsummer Night, Rape of Lucretia*; DONIZETTI: *Don Pasquale, Elisir, Lucia*; GLUCK: *Iphigénie en Aulide, Orfeo ed Euridice*; HANDEL: *Alcina, Orlando furioso*; LEONCAVALLO: *Pagliacci*; MASCAGNI: *Cavalleria rusticana*; MENOTTI: *Amelia al ballo, Telephone*; MOZART: *Entführung aus dem Serail, Zauberflöte*; NICOLAI: *Lustigen Weiber*; OFFENBACH: *Contes d'Hoffmann*; PUCCINI: *Bohème, Tosca, Turandot*; ROSSINI: *Barbiere di Siviglia*; STRAVINSKY: *Oedipus Rex*; TCHAIKOVSKY: *Eugene Onegin*; VERDI: *Aida, Falstaff, Nabucco, Rigoletto*, *Traviata, Trovatore*; WAGNER: *Fliegende Holländer, Meistersinger, Parsifal, Walküre, Tannhäuser*. Also HANDEL: *Pastor fido*; LIEBERMANN: *Penelope, Schule der Frauen*; LULLY: *Carnaval*; NIELSEN: *Maskarade*. **Operatic world premieres:** SUTERMEISTER: *Roten Stiefel* Royal Opera, Stockholm 1951. Teaches at Music Dramatic School, Stockholm. **Res:** Plogvägen 8a, Stockholm/Täby 18351, Sweden.

PETERSON, GLADE. Dramatic tenor. American. Resident mem: Opernhaus Zurich. Born 17 Dec 1928, Fairview, UT, USA. Wife Mardean. Three children. Studied: Ingenuus Bentzar, Carlos Alexander, Salt Lake City, UT; Enrico Rosati, Ettore Verna, New York. **Debut:** Pinkerton (*Butterfly*) NBC Opera 1957. Previous occupations: farmer, coal miner, truck driver.

Sang with major companies in AUS: Salzburg Fest, Vienna Staatsoper; BEL: Brussels; CAN: Toronto; FRA: Bordeaux, Toulouse; FR GER: Berlin Deutsche Oper, Bonn, Düsseldorf-Duisburg, Frankfurt, Hamburg, Munich Staatsoper, Stuttgart; HOL: Amsterdam; ITA: Milan La Scala, Spoleto Fest; SWI: Basel, Geneva, Zurich; USA: Baltimore, Boston, Dallas, Houston, New York Met, Philadelphia Grand, Pittsburgh, Portland, San Diego, San Francisco Opera, Santa Fe. **Roles with these companies incl** BEETHOVEN: Florestan★ (*Fidelio*); BIZET: Don José★ (*Carmen*), Nadir (*Pêcheurs de perles*); CHERUBINI: Giasone★ (*Medea*); DALLAPICCOLA: Pellerin (*Volo di notte*); DONIZETTI: Riccardo (*Anna Bolena*), Tonio (*Fille du régiment*), Edgardo (*Lucia*), Roberto Devereux★; GIORDANO: Andrea Chénier★; GOUNOD: Faust; JANACEK: Laca & Steva (*Jenufa*); LEONCAVALLO: Canio★ (*Pagliacci*); MARTINU: Manolios (*Griechische Passion*); MASCAGNI: Turiddu (*Cavalleria rusticana*); MASSENET: Des Grieux (*Manon*); MOZART: Ferrando (*Così fan tutte*), Don Ottavio (*Don Giovanni*), Belmonte (*Entführung aus dem Serail*), Tamino (*Zauberflöte*); NICOLAI: Fenton (*Lustigen Weiber*); PFITZNER: Palestrina; PROKOFIEV: Prince (*Love for Three Oranges*); PUCCINI: Rodolfo★ (*Bohème*), Dick Johnson (*Fanciulla del West*), Rinuccio (*Gianni Schicchi*), Pinkerton★ (*Butterfly*), Des Grieux★ (*Manon Lescaut*), Luigi★ (*Tabarro*), Cavaradossi★ (*Tosca*), Calaf★ (*Turandot*); SMETANA: Hans (*Bartered Bride*); STRAUSS, R: Bacchus★ (*Ariadne auf Naxos*), Leukippos (*Daphne*), Ein Sänger★ (*Rosenkavalier*); STRAVINSKY: Pêcheur (*Rossignol*); TCHAIKOVSKY: Gherman★ (*Pique Dame*); VERDI: Riccardo★ (*Ballo in maschera*), Don Carlo★, Ernani★, Fenton (*Falstaff*), Don Alvaro★ (*Forza del destino*), Alfredo★ (*Traviata*); WAGNER: Walther (*Meistersinger*), Loge★ (*Rheingold*); WEBER: Adolar★ (*Euryanthe*). Gives recitals. Appears with symphony orchestra. Mgmt: SHA/USA.

PETERSON, ILEANA MARIJA; née Tepfers. Dramatic mezzo-soprano. Swedish. Resident mem: Royal Opera, Stockholm. Born 23 Nov 1934, Riga, Latvia. Husband Paul, occupation law candidate. Studied: Royal Acad of Music, Käthe Sundström, Stockholm. **Debut:** Maddalena (*Rigoletto*) Royal Opera, Stockholm 1964. Awards: Kristina Nilsson Schlshp.

Sang with major companies in DEN: Copenhagen; FR GER: Wiesbaden; NOR: Oslo; SWE: Drottningholm Fest, Stockholm; UK: Edinburgh Fest; USSR: Moscow Bolshoi. **Roles with these companies incl** VERDI: Dame Quickly★ (*Falstaff*), Azucena★ (*Trovatore*); WAGNER: Ortrud★ (*Lohengrin*), Erda (*Rheingold★, Siegfried★*). Also HANDEL: Eurilla★ (*Pastor fido*); CAVALLI: King Syfax★ (*Scipio Africanus*). Gives recitals. Appears with symphony orchestra. Mgmt: KBL/SWE.

PETERSON, ROBERT A. American. Adm & Devlp Dir, Cincinnati Opera Assn, 1241 Elm St, Cincinnati, O 45210; also of educt program/Opera Guild. In charge of adm matters & fund raising. Born 20 Mar 1936, Harvey, IL. Wife Nadene, occupation counselor. Studied: Indiana Univ, Bloomington; Univ of Washington, Seattle. Plays the organ. Previous occupation: Prof of Music. Form position: Adm Asst, Seattle Opera 1970-73. Started with present company in 1974 as Mng. **Res:** 933 Paradrome, Cincinnati, Ohio, USA.

PETKOV, DIMITER. Bass. Bulgarian. Born 5 Mar 1938, Sofia, Bulgaria. Wife Annelise. Studied: Acad of Music, Prof Christo Brumbarov, Sofia. **Debut:** Il Re (*Aida*) National Opera, Sofia 1964. Awards: Grand Prix de Sofia, Intl Compt for Young Opera Singers, Gold Ring & Gold Medal 1967.

Sang with major companies in AUS: Vienna Staatsoper; BEL: Brussels; BUL: Sofia; CZE: Brno, Prague National & Smetana; DEN: Copenhagen; FRA: Bordeaux, Lyon, Marseille, Nice, Paris, Rouen; GRE: Athens Fest; FR GER: Berlin Deutsche Oper, Cologne, Frankfurt, Hamburg, Kiel, Wiesbaden; GER DR: Berlin Staatsoper; HOL: Amsterdam; HUN: Budapest; ITA: Bologna, Florence Maggio, Naples, Palermo, Parma, Rome Teatro dell'Opera, Verona Arena; POL: Warsaw; ROM: Bucharest; SPA: Barcelona, Majorca; SWI: Geneva, Zurich; UK: Glyndebourne Fest; USSR: Leningrad Kirov, Moscow Bolshoi; YUG: Belgrade. **Roles with these companies incl** BELLINI: Oroveso (*Norma*), Rodolfo (*Sonnambula*); CHERUBINI: Creon (*Medea*); DONIZETTI: Henry VIII★ (*Anna Bolena*); GLINKA: Ivan★ (*Life for the Tsar*); GOUNOD: Méphistophélès★ (*Faust*); MEYERBEER: Comte de St Bris (*Huguenots*); MONTEMEZZI: Archibaldo★ (*Amore dei tre re*); MOZART: Leporello (*Don Giovanni*), Osmin (*Entführung aus dem Serail*), Sarastro (*Zauberflöte*); MUSSORGSKY: Boris★ & Varlaam★ & Pimen (*Boris Godunov*), Tcherevik (*Fair at Sorochinsk*), Ivan Khovansky★ (*Khovanshchina*); RIMSKY-KORSAKOV: Tsar Ivan★ (*Maid of Pskov*); ROSSINI: Don Basilio★ (*Barbiere di Siviglia*); SMETANA: Kezal (*Bartered Bride*); VERDI: Ramfis★ (*Aida*), Attila★, Philip II★ & Grande Inquisitore (*Don Carlo*), Silva★ (*Ernani*), Padre Guardiano★ (*Forza del destino*), Banquo★ (*Macbeth*), Zaccaria★ (*Nabucco*), Fiesco★ (*Simon Boccanegra*), Procida★ (*Vespri*). Also PROKOFIEV: Kutuzov★ (*War and Peace*); BORODIN: Kontchak★ (*Prince Igor*); TCHAIKOVSKY: Gremin★ (*Eugene Onegin*); RACHMANINOV: Old Gypsy★ (*Aleko*). Recorded for: EMI, Balcanton/Harmonia Mundi. Video/Film: *Boris Godunov, Khovanshchina*. Teaches voice. **Res:** Switzerland. Mgmt: VLD/AUS; SMN/USA; IMR/FRA; SLZ/FRG.

PETRAKIS, THANOS. Lirico spinto tenor. Greek. Resident mem: Gärtnerplatztheater, Munich; National Opera, Athens. Born 11 Feb 1939, Athens. Single. Studied: Ntl Consv, Athens; Acad of Music, Vienna; Consv Verdi, Milan; Prof Norbert Hitz, Vienna; Alecos Souflas, Athens; Ma Lia Guarini, Milan; Mo Rocco Pandiscio, Munich. **Debut:** Rodolfo (*Bohème*) Athens National Opera 1966. Previous occupations: studied law at Athens Univ, acting at Dramatic School of Ntl Theater, Athens. Awards: Maria Callas Schlshp 1965-67;

Medal of Honor for Exceptional Achievement, Ntl Consv Athens.

Sang with major companies in GRE: Athens National & Fest; FR GER: Kassel, Munich Gärtnerplatz; ITA: Parma. **Roles with these companies incl** BEETHOVEN: Florestan★ (*Fidelio*); BERLIOZ: Faust★ (*Damnation de Faust*); BIZET: Don José★ (*Carmen*); DONIZETTI: Riccardo★ (*Anna Bolena*), Ernesto★ (*Don Pasquale*), Edgardo★ (*Lucia*); GIORDANO: Andrea Chénier★; GOUNOD: Faust★; HINDEMITH: Apprentice★ (*Cardillac*); LEONCAVALLO: Canio★ (*Pagliacci*); MASCAGNI: Turiddu★ (*Cavalleria rusticana*); MONTEVERDI: Nero★ (*Incoronazione di Poppea*); MOZART: Don Ottavio★ (*Don Giovanni*); NICOLAI: Fenton★ (*Lustigen Weiber*); ORFF: Solo★ (*Carmina burana*); PUCCINI: Rodolfo★ (*Bohème*), Pinkerton★ (*Butterfly*), Des Grieux★ (*Manon Lescaut*), Cavaradossi★ (*Tosca*); SHOSTAKOVICH: Sergei★ (*Katerina Ismailova*); STRAUSS, J: Eisenstein★ & Alfred★ (*Fledermaus*); STRAUSS, R: Ein Sänger★ (*Rosenkavalier*); TCHAIKOVSKY: Lenski★ (*Eugene Onegin*); VERDI: Riccardo★ (*Ballo in maschera*), Don Carlo★, Don Alvaro★ (*Forza del destino*), Ismaele★ (*Nabucco*), Duca di Mantova★ (*Rigoletto*), Gabriele★ (*Simon Boccanegra*), Alfredo★ (*Traviata*), Manrico★ (*Trovatore*); WEBER: Max★ (*Freischütz*). Gives recitals. Appears with symphony orchestra. Teaches voice. Coaches repertoire. **Res:** Jagdstr 7, Munich, FR Ger. Mgmt: RAB/AUS.

PÉTRI, FRANTZ. Bass-baritone. French. Born 14 Jan 1935, Paris. Divorced. Two children. Studied: Emma Leblanc, Mario Podesta, Ugo Ugaro, Paris. **Debut:** Scarpia (*Tosca*) Mulhouse, France 1963. Previous occupations: medical student. Awards: First Prize and Honors, Acad Intl de Théâtre Lyrique de Vichy 1962.

Sang with major companies in AUS: Salzburg Fest; BEL: Brussels, Liège; FRA: Bordeaux, Lyon, Marseille, Nancy, Nice, Paris, Rouen, Strasbourg, Toulouse; HOL: Amsterdam; ITA: Rome Opera; MON: Monte Carlo; POR: Lisbon; SWI: Geneva; UK: Glyndebourne Fest; USA: Chicago, San Francisco Opera. **Roles with these companies incl** BARTOK: Bluebeard; BEETHOVEN: Don Pizarro★ (*Fidelio*); BERLIOZ: Méphistophélès★ (*Damnation de Faust*), Narbal (*Troyens*); BIZET: Escamillo (*Carmen*), Zurga (*Pêcheurs de perles*); BORODIN: Prince Igor; DALLAPICCOLA: Ulisse; DEBUSSY: Golaud★ (*Pelléas et Mélisande*); DELIBES: Nilakantha (*Lakmé*); DVORAK: Marbuel (*Devil and Kate*); EINEM: Alfred Ill★ (*Besuch der alten Dame*); GAY/Britten: Mr Peachum★ (*Beggar's Opera*); GLUCK: High Priest (*Alceste*); GOUNOD: Méphistophélès (*Faust*), Ourrias (*Mireille*); JANACEK: Gorianchikov (*From the House of the Dead*); MARTINU: Hans (*Comedy on the Bridge*); MASSENET: Lescaut (*Manon*), Athanaël (*Thaïs*), Albert (*Werther*); MENOTTI: John Sorel (*Consul*); MOZART: Don Alfonso★ (*Così fan tutte*), Conte Almaviva★ (*Nozze di Figaro*), Osmin★ (*Zaïde*); MUSSORGSKY: Varlaam (*Boris Godunov*); OFFENBACH: Coppélius etc (*Contes d'Hoffmann*), Don Andres (*Périchole*); PERGOLESI: Uberto★ (*Serva padrona*); PROKOFIEV: Mendoza★ (*Duenna*); PUCCINI:

Gianni Schicchi, Scarpia★ (*Tosca*); RAVEL: Ramiro★ (*Heure espagnole*); ROSSINI: Dott Bartolo★ (*Barbiere di Siviglia*); SAINT-SAENS: Grand prêtre★ (*Samson et Dalila*); STRAUSS, R: Jochanaan (*Salome*); STRAVINSKY: Nick Shadow★ (*Rake's Progress*); THOMAS: Lothario★ (*Mignon*); VERDI: Ramfis (*Aida*), Falstaff★, Germont (*Traviata*); WAGNER: Wotan (*Rheingold★, Walküre★*), Wanderer★ (*Siegfried*), Fasolt★ (*Rheingold*), Gunther★ (*Götterdämmerung*), Wolfram★ (*Tannhäuser*), Kurwenal (*Tristan und Isolde*); WEILL: Trinity Moses★ (*Aufstieg und Fall der Stadt Mahagonny*). Also CAVALIERI: Consiglio (*Rappresentazione*). Video/Film – Glyndebourne: Don Alfonso (*Così fan tutte*). Appears with symphony orchestra. **Res:** Echandens, Switzerland. Mgmt: RNR/SWI.

PETROV, VLADIMIR NICOLAEVIC. Dramatic tenor. Russian. Resident mem: Bolshoi Theater, Moscow. Born 6 Feb 1926, Moscow. Wife `Svetlana, occupation magazine editor. One son. Studied: Moscow Consv, S P Yudin, USSR; School of La Scala Theater, Mo Vacca, Milan. **Debut:** (*Sadko*) Bolshoi Theater, Moscow 1963. Previous occupations: served in army. Awards: First Place, Compt of Opera Singers, Moscow 1960.

Sang with major companies in FRA: Paris Opera; GER DR: Berlin Staatsoper; HUN: Budapest State Opera; ITA: Florence Maggio & Comunale, Milan La Scala; POL: Warsaw; USSR: Moscow Bolshoi. **Roles with these companies incl** GLINKA: Finn★ (*Ruslan and Ludmilla*); MUSSORGSKY: Vassily Golitsin★‡ (*Khovanshchina*); PROKOFIEV: Pierre★‡ (*War and Peace*); RIMSKY-KORSAKOV: Grishka Kouterma‡ (*Invisible City of Kitezh*), Sadko★‡, Boyar Lykov★ (*Tsar's Bride*); VERDI: Don Carlo‡. Also TCHAIKOVSKY: Andrei (*Mazeppa*). Video/Film: Golitsin (*Khovanshchina*). Gives recitals. Appears with symphony orchestra. Coaches repertoire. **Res:** Sadovo-Sukharevskaya, Moscow, USSR. Mgmt: Ministry of Culture, USSR.

PETROVIC, MILIVOJ. Lyric tenor. Yugoslavian. Resident mem: National Theater, Belgrade. Born 7 Jul 1938, Belgrade. Wife Dolores, occupation French teacher. One child. Studied: Secondary Music School, Belgrade; Prof Zdenka Zikova, Prof Stanoje Jankovic, Yugoslavia; Consv Benedetto Marcello, Prof Paolo M Bononi, Venice, Italy. **Debut:** Alfredo (*Traviata*) National Theater, Belgrade 1970.

Sang with major companies in YUG: Belgrade. **Roles with these companies incl** BORODIN: Vladimir★ (*Prince Igor*); DONIZETTI: Nemorino★ (*Elisir*), Edgardo★ (*Lucia*); SMETANA: Wenzel★ (*Bartered Bride*); TCHAIKOVSKY: Lenski★ (*Eugene Onegin*); VERDI: Alfredo★ (*Traviata*). Also LOGAR: Vasa★ (*Pokondirena tikva*). Video/Film: Kanjos (*Pastrovski vitez*). Gives recitals. Appears with symphony orchestra. **Res:** Beogradski put 24, Belgrade, Yugoslavia.

PETRUSANEC, FRANJO. Bass-baritone. Yugoslavian. Resident mem: Croatian National Opera, Zagreb. Born 27 Jan 1938, Poljanec. Single. Studied: Varazdin Music School, Prof Opolski; Acad of Music Zagreb, Prof Lhotka; Prof Tagliabue, Palermo, Italy. **Debut:** Kutuzov (*War and Peace*)

National Opera Zagreb 1961. Awards: Laureate, Intl Compt Geneva 1968.

Sang with major companies in GRE: Athens Fest; YUG: Dubrovnik, Zagreb, Belgrade. Roles with these companies incl MOZART: Osmin★ (*Entführung aus dem Serail*); ROSSINI: Don Basilio (*Barbiere di Siviglia*); SAINT-SAENS: Grand prêtre★ (*Samson et Dalila*); SMETANA: Kezal★ (*Bartered Bride*); VERDI: Ramfis★ (*Aida*), Grande Inquisitore (*Don Carlo*); WAGNER: Daland★ (*Fliegende Holländer*), Pogner★ (*Meistersinger*), Hunding★ (*Walküre*), König Marke★ (*Tristan und Isolde*). Also BORODIN: Kontchak★ (*Prince Igor*); DONIZETTI: Raimondo★ (*Lucia di Lammermoor*); ZAJC: Sulejman★ (*Nikola Subic Zrinjski*). Gives recitals. Appears with symphony orchestra. Res: Baburicina 22, Zagreb, Yugoslavia.

PETTERSSON, ANN-MARGRET. Stages/produces opera. Also designs stage-lighting. Swedish. Resident Stage Dir, Stockholm Royal Opera. Born 18 Sep 1938, Stockholm. Single. Studied: music, piano and voice. Operatic training as asst stage dir to Göran Gentele, Ingmar Bergman and Rudolf Hartmann at Stockholm Royal Opera 1964-67. Operatic debut: *Lohengrin* Stockholm Royal Opera 1966. Theater debut: Göteborg Theater, Sweden 1972.

Directed/produced opera for major companies in SWE: Drottningholm Fest, Stockholm. Operas staged for these companies incl BRITTEN: *Albert Herring★;* MASSENET: *Manon;* MOZART: *Entführung aus dem Serail, Nozze di Figaro★;* OFFENBACH: *Contes d'Hoffmann;* PERGOLESI: *Serva padrona★;* ROSSINI: *Barbiere di Siviglia;* STRAUSS, R: *Ariadne auf Naxos★;* WAGNER: *Lohengrin.* Also SACCHINI: *Oedipe à Colone;* ROTA: *Cappello di paglia★.* Operatic world premieres: BERWALD: *Drottningen av Golconda* Stockholm Royal Opera 1968. Teaches at Opera School, Stockholm.

PEZZETTI, SERGIO. Basso-buffo. Italian. Born 10 Mar 1934, Perugia. Wife Emilia Cundari, occupation opera singer. One child. Studied: Mo Roberto d'Alessio, Florence; Mo Aldo Zeetti, Perugia. Debut: Zaccarià (*Nabucco*) Teatro Sperimentale, Spoleto 1960. Previous occupations: lawyer. Awards: Winner, Conc Spoleto and two Conc ENAL.

Sang with major companies in DEN: Copenhagen; ITA: Bologna, Florence Maggio & Comunale, Milan La Scala, Naples, Palermo, Rome Opera & Caracalla, Spoleto Fest, Trieste, Turin; USA: New York Met. Roles with these companies incl CIMAROSA: Geronimo★ (*Matrimonio segreto*); DONIZETTI: Don Pistacchio★ (*Campanello*), Don Pasquale★, Dulcamara★ (*Elisir*), Nottingham★ (*Roberto Devereux*); GALUPPI: Don Tritemio (*Filosofo di campagna*); MOZART: Don Alfonso★ (*Così fan tutte*), Leporello★ (*Don Giovanni*); PAISIELLO: Bartolo★ (*Barbiere di Siviglia*); PERGOLESI: Uberto★ (*Serva padrona*); PUCCINI: Gianni Schicchi★; ROSSINI: Dott Bartolo★ (*Barbiere di Siviglia*), Don Magnifico★ (*Cenerentola*), Mustafà★ (*Italiana in Algeri*); VERDI: Fra Melitone★ (*Forza del destino*). World premieres: SONZOGNO: Vecchio (*Boule de suif*) Teatro Donizetti, Bergamo 1969. Recorded for: Angelicum. Film: Giacomo (*Fra Diavolo*).

Teaches voice. Coaches repertoire. On faculty of Wayne State Univ, MI. Res: 18231 Westland Ave, Southfield, MI, USA, and Macello 3, Perugia, Italy. Mgmt: SMN/USA.

PFRETZSCHNER, BRIGITTE. Contralto. German. Resident mem: Staatsoper Dresden, Staatsoper Berlin, Ger DR. Born 6 Jan 1936, Dresden. Husband Berthold Schmidt, occupation opera singer. Four children. Studied: Carl Maria v Weber Hochschule, Frau Intran, Dresden; Marga Seidel, Senta Kutzschbach, Dresden. Debut: Marcellina (*Nozze di Figaro*) Staatsoper, Dresden 1959.

Sang with major companies in FR GER: Wiesbaden; GER DR: Berlin Staatsoper, Dresden, Leipzig; HUN: Budapest, USSR: Leningrad Kirov. Roles with these companies incl CIMAROSA: Fidalma (*Matrimonio segreto*); NICOLAI: Frau Reich★ (*Lustigen Weiber*); PROKOFIEV: Duenna★; STRAVINSKY: Mère★ (*Mavra*); TCHAIKOVSKY: Comtesse (*Pique Dame*); VERDI: Ulrica (*Ballo in maschera*); WAGNER: Magdalene★ (*Meistersinger*), Erda (*Rheingold★, Siegfried★*), Fricka (*Rheingold, Walküre*), Brangäne (*Tristan und Isolde*); WOLF-FERRARI: Margarita (*Quattro rusteghi*). Also STRAUSS, R: Gaea (*Daphne*); on records only FLOTOW: Nancy (*Martha*); GAY/Britten: Mrs Peachum (*Beggar's Opera*); HUMPERDINCK: Hänsel; MOZART: Dorabella (*Così fan tutte*), Cherubino (*Nozze di Figaro*); PUCCINI: Suzuki (*Butterfly*); ROSSINI: Rosina (*Barbiere di Siviglia*); VERDI: Dame Quickly (*Falstaff*). World premieres: ZIMMERMANN: Tante Huse (*Levins Mühle*) Staatsoper, Dresden 1973. Recorded for: VEB, Eterna. Video/Film: (*Levins Mühle*). Gives recitals. Appears with symphony orchestra. Coaches repertoire. Res: An der Berglehne 11, 8051 Dresden, Ger DR. Mgmt: KDR/GDR.

PHILLIPS, LINDA JEANNE. Lyric soprano. American. Born 13 Feb 1946, Hastings, NE, USA. Husband Brent Ellis, occupation opera singer. Studied: Indiana Univ, Margaret Harshaw, Bloomington, USA. Debut: Olympia (*Contes d'Hoffmann*) Kansas City Lyric, MO 1968.

Sang with major companies in MEX: Mexico City; USA: Kansas City, St Paul. Roles with these companies incl BIZET: Micaëla★ (*Carmen*); BRITTEN: Female Chorus★ (*Rape of Lucretia*); CAVALIERI: Nerea (*Rappresentazione*); DONIZETTI: Norina★ (*Don Pasquale*); MENOTTI: Monica★ (*Medium*); OFFENBACH: Olympia (*Contes d'Hoffmann*); PERGOLESI: Serpina★ (*Serva padrona*). World premieres: FERRARI: Moglie (*Mantici*) Barga, Italy 1973; CARMINES: Theodoria Burr (*Duel*) Met Studio, New York 1974. Gives recitals. Appears with symphony orchestra.

PHILLIPS, VAN; né Ivan Keith Phillips. Scenic designer for opera, theater, television. Is a lighting designer; also a painter & sculptor. American. Dir of Design & Techn, Purdue Univ Theater. Born 19 Sep 1943, Pasadena, CA. Wife Bronwen, occupation social worker. One daughter. Studied: Dallas Theater Ctr 1962-63; Southwestern Univ 1963-67; Univ of Texas, Austin 1967-69. Operatic debut: *Trouble in Tahiti* San Antonio Opera, TX 1965. Theater debut: Southwestern Univ, Georgetown,

TX 1963. Previous occupation: actor, adv man on prof circuit, tech dir. Awards: USITT/OISTT, US Scenographic Commission, 1973; USITT Commendation; USITT Board of Dir 1974-76; Chmn, American Theater Assn, Design & Technol Prgrm 1975.

Designed for major companies in USA: San Antonio. **Operas designed for these companies incl** BERNSTEIN: *Trouble in Tahiti;* LEONCAVALLO: *Pagliacci;* MENOTTI: *Medium, Telephone*;* MOZART: *Nozze di Figaro*;* POULENC: *Voix humaine;* PUCCINI: *Gianni Schicchi*;* STRAUSS, R: *Rosenkavalier, Salome*;* VERDI: *Traviata.* Exhibitions of stage designs Tampa Bay Arts Center 1971; Temple Terrace Publ Libr 1972. Teaches at Purdue Univ, West Lafayette, IN. **Res:** 3871 Rome Dr, Lafayette, IN. Mgmt: USC/USA.

PIAVKO, VLADISLAV IVANOVICH. Dramatic tenor. Russian. Resident mem: Bolshoi Theater, Moscow. Born 4 Feb 1941, Krasnaiarsk. Wife Irina Arkhipova, occupation singer. One child. Studied: S Y Rebrikov, Moscow; Renato Pastorino, Milan. **Debut:** Pinkerton (*Butterfly*) Bolshoi Theater 1966. Previous occupations: chauffeur; Army. Awards: First Prize tenor & Third Grand Prix, Intl Singers Compt Belgium 1969; Second Prize, Tchaikovsky Compt Moscow 1970.

Sang with major companies in ARG: Buenos Aires; BUL: Sofia; CZE: Prague National & Smetana; FIN: Helsinki; FR GER: Wiesbaden; ITA: Florence Comunale; ROM: Bucharest; SPA: Majorca; USSR: Kiev, Moscow Bolshoi & Stanislavski Theater, Tbilisi; YUG: Zagreb, Belgrade National Opera. **Roles with these companies incl** BIZET: Don José* (*Carmen*); MUSSORGSKY: Andrei Khovansky*‡ (*Khovanshchina*); PUCCINI: Pinkerton* (*Butterfly*), Cavaradossi* (*Tosca*); RIMSKY-KORSAKOV: Toucha* (*Maid of Pskov*); TCHAIKOVSKY: Count Vodemon* (*Iolanthe*), Gherman* (*Pique Dame*); VERDI: Radames* (*Aida*), Manrico* (*Trovatore*). Also MUSSORGSKY: Dimitri (*Boris Godunov*). Recorded for: Melodiya. Gives recitals. Appears with symphony orchestra. **Res:** d 7 kv 16 ul Nezhdanovoi, Moscow, USSR. Mgmt: GOS/USSR.

PICCHI, MIRTO. Dramatic tenor. Italian. Born 15 Mar 1915, Florence, Italy. Single. Studied: Giulia Tess, Giacomo Armani, Florence. **Debut:** Radames (*Aida*) Teatro alla Scala, summer season 1946. Previous occupations: studied economics & commerce. Awards: Apollo Musagete Talla; Prize of the Rome Capitol.

Sang with major companies in AUS: Vienna Staatsoper & Volksoper; BRA: Rio de Janeiro; FRA: Paris; HOL: Amsterdam; ITA: Bologna, Florence Maggio & Comunale, Genoa, Milan La Scala, Naples, Palermo, Parma, Rome Opera, Trieste, Turin, Venice, Verona Arena; MON: Monte Carlo, POR: Lisbon; SPA: Barcelona; SWI: Zurich; UK: Edinburgh Fest, Glyndebourne Fest, London Royal; USA: Chicago. **Roles with these companies incl** BEETHOVEN: Florestan (*Fidelio*); BELLINI: Pollione (*Norma*), Gualtiero (*Pirata*); BERG: Hauptmann* & Tambourmajor (*Wozzeck*); BERLIOZ: Faust (*Damnation de Faust*); BIZET: Don José (*Carmen*); BRITTEN: Edward Fairfax Vere* (*Billy Budd*), Peter Grimes;

CATALANI: Giuseppe Hagenbach (*Wally*); CHERUBINI: Giasone‡ (*Medea*); DALLAPICCOLA: Jailer/Inquisitor* (*Prigioniero*), Radio Telegrapher (*Volo di notte*); DONIZETTI: Gennaro (*Lucrezia Borgia*); GIORDANO: Andrea Chénier; GLUCK: Admetos (*Alceste*), Renaud (*Armide*); JANACEK: Laca (*Jenufa*); MONTEMEZZI: Avito (*Amore dei tre re*); MONTEVERDI: Nero (*Incoronazione di Poppea*); MOZART: Idomeneo; MUSSORGSKY: Vassily Golitsin* (*Khovanshchina*); PETRASSI: Inventore* (*Morte dell'aria*); PROKOFIEV: Don Jerome (*Duenna*), Anatole (*War and Peace*); PUCCINI: Rodolfo (*Bohème*), Dick Johnson (*Fanciulla del West*), Luigi (*Tabarro*), Cavaradossi (*Tosca*); SPONTINI: Cinna (*Vestale*); STRAUSS, R: Aegisth (*Elektra*), Herodes (*Salome*); STRAVINSKY: Oedipus*, Tom Rakewell* (*Rake's Progress*); TCHAIKOVSKY: Gherman (*Pique Dame*); VERDI: Radames (*Aida*), Riccardo (*Ballo in maschera*), Don Carlo‡, Jacopo Foscari (*Due Foscari*), Ismaele (*Nabucco*), Duca di Mantova (*Rigoletto*), Gabriele (*Simon Boccanegra*); WAGNER: Erik (*Fliegende Holländer*), Walther (*Meistersinger*); WEBER: Max (*Freischütz*), Oberon; ZANDONAI: Paolo (*Francesca da Rimini*). Also LUALDI: Ariuna (*Figlia del re*); VERETTI: Aladino (*Burlesca*); ROCCA: Hanan (*Dibuk*); MULE: Dafni; MUSSORGSKY: Dimitri (*Boris Godunov*); TRAETTA: Creonte (*Antigone*); ROSSINI: Cleomene (*Assedio di Corinto*); SCARLATTI: Corrado (*Griselda*); SUTERMEISTER: Raskolnikoff; ZANDONAI: Josta Boerling (*Cavalieri di Ekebu*); BOITO: Nerone; PIZZETTI: Fra Gherardo, Ippolito (*Fedra*), Straniero, Oreste (*Clitennestra*); VERDI: Macduff (*Macbeth*); BUSONI: Thusman (*Brautwahl*); MALIPIERO: Poeta (*Capricci di Callot*); HENZE: Tiresias (*Bassariden*); MOZART: Don Basilio (*Nozze di Figaro*). **World premieres:** CASTRO: Quiroga (*Proserpina e lo straniero*) 1952; PIZZETTI: Cagliostro 1953, both at Teatro alla Scala; PIZZETTI: Aligi (*Figlia di Jorio*) Teatro San Carlo, Naples 1954; LIZZI: Senocrate (*Pantea*) Teatro Massimo, Palermo 1956, Aci (*Amori di Galatea*) Teatro Massimo, Palermo 1964; TESTI: Calisto (*Celestina*) Florence Maggio Musicale 1963; BUSSOTTI: Stato e Chiesa (*Lorenzaccio*) La Fenice, Venice 1972; GIURANNA: Rodolfo d'Ausburgo (*Mayerling*) Teatro Massimo, Palermo 1962. Recorded for: Cetra, Ricordi. **Res:** Piazza S Felicità 1, Florence, Italy.

PICCINATO, CARLO FERDINANDO. Stages/produces opera & theater. Also designs sets, costumes & stage-lighting and is an actor & author. Italian. Born 16 Nov 1907, Legnago. Wife Idalia Busechian, occupation costumer. Studied: Accad di S Cecilia, Mo Corti & Mo Setaccioli, Rome; incl violin & piano. Operatic training as asst stage dir in Germany. **Operatic debut:** *Meistersinger* Teatro dell'Opera, Rome 1930. Theater debut: own theater company, Trieste 1929.

Directed/produced opera for major companies in ARG: Buenos Aires; AUS: Bregenz Fest; BRA: Rio de Janeiro; BUL: Sofia; FRA: Paris; FR GER: Cologne, Munich Staatsoper & Gärtnerplatz, Stuttgart; ISR: Tel Aviv; ITA: Bologna, Florence Maggio & Comunale, Genoa, Milan La

Scala, Naples, Palermo, Parma, Rome Opera & Caracalla, Spoleto Fest, Trieste, Turin, Venice, Verona Arena; MON: Monte Carlo; SPA: Barcelona; USA: Chicago, San Francisco Opera; YUG: Dubrovnik, Zagreb, Belgrade. **Operas staged with these companies incl** AUBER: *Fra Diavolo;* BARTOK: *Bluebeard's Castle;* BEETHOVEN: *Fidelio;* BELLINI: *Beatrice di Tenda★, Capuleti ed i Montecchi★, Norma★, Pirata, Puritani, Sonnambula, Straniera;* BERLIOZ: *Damnation de Faust;* BIZET: *Carmen, Pêcheurs de perles;* BOITO: *Mefistofele†;* BORODIN: *Prince Igor;* BRITTEN: *Peter Grimes;* BUSONI: *Arlecchino;* CATALANI: *Wally★;* CAVALIERI: *Rappresentazione;* CHARPENTIER: *Louise;* CHERUBINI: *Medea;* CILEA: *A. Lecouvreur;* CIMAROSA: *Matrimonio segreto★;* DALLA-PICCOLA: *Prigioniero;* DEBUSSY: *Pelléas et Mélisande;* DONIZETTI: *Anna Bolena, Convenienze/Viva la Mamma, Don Pasquale★, Elisir★, Favorite, Fille du régiment, Linda di Chamounix★, Lucia, Lucrezia Borgia;* DVORAK: *Rusalka;* FALLA: *Retablo de Maese Pedro;* GIORDANO: *Andrea Chénier, Fedora;* GLUCK: *Alceste, Orfeo ed Euridice★;* GOUNOD: *Faust★†, Roméo et Juliette;* HINDEMITH: *Hin und zurück;* HUMPERDINCK: *Hänsel und Gretel†;* LEONCAVALLO: *Pagliacci;* MASCAGNI: *Amico Fritz★, Cavalleria rusticana;* MASSENET: *Manon, Thaïs, Werther;* MENOTTI: *Amelia al ballo, Consul, Medium, Telephone;* MILHAUD: *Christophe Colomb;* MONTEMEZZI: *Amore dei tre re;* MONTEVERDI: *Combattimento di Tancredi, Favola d'Orfeo, Incoronazione di Poppea;* MOZART: *Così fan tutte, Don Giovanni★†, Entführung aus dem Serail, Nozze di Figaro★, Oca del Cairo★, Zauberflöte†;* MUSSORGSKY: *Boris Godunov, Khovanshchina;* OFFENBACH: *Contes d'Hoffmann;* PAISIELLO: *Barbiere di Siviglia;* PERAGALLO: *Gita in campagna;* PERGOLESI: *Serva padrona;* PONCHIELLI: *Gioconda;* PROKOFIEV: *Love for Three Oranges;* PUCCINI: *Bohème, Fanciulla del West, Gianni Schicchi★, Butterfly, Manon Lescaut, Rondine★, Suor Angelica★, Tabarro, Tosca★, Turandot;* RAMEAU: *Castor et Pollux;* RIMSKY-KORSAKOV: *Coq d'or, Invisible City of Kitezh;* ROSSINI: *Barbiere di Siviglia★, Cambiale di matrimonio, Cenerentola★, Comte Ory, Italiana in Algeri★, Moïse★†, Scala di seta, Signor Bruschino, Turco in Italia★;* SAINT-SAENS: *Samson et Dalila†;* SCARLATTI: *Trionfo dell'onore†;* SPONTINI: *Vestale;* STRAUSS, J: *Fledermaus;* STRAUSS, R: *Elektra, Frau ohne Schatten, Rosenkavalier;* STRAVINSKY: *Rossignol;* TCHAIKOVSKY: *Pique Dame;* THOMAS: *Hamlet, Mignon;* VERDI: *Aida, Ballo in maschera, Corsaro, Don Carlo, Due Foscari, Ernani, Falstaff★, Forza del destino, Giovanna d'Arco, Lombardi, Luisa Miller, Macbeth†, Masnadieri, Nabucco, Otello, Rigoletto★, Simon Boccanegra†, Traviata★, Trovatore, Vespri;* WAGNER: *Fliegende Holländer†, Lohengrin, Parsifal, Rheingold, Walküre, Siegfried, Götterdämmerung, Tannhäuser★†, Tristan und Isolde;* WEBER: *Freischütz, Oberon;* WOLF-FERRARI: *Donne curiose, Gioielli della Madonna, Quattro rusteghi†, Segreto di Susanna†;* ZANDONAI: *Francesca da Rimini★, Giulietta e Romeo★.* Also ALFANO: *Risurrezione, Sakuntala;* BOITO: *Ne-*

rone; FERRARI-TRECATE: *Buricchio, Orso Re;* FIUME: *Tamburo di panno;* GOMES: *Guarany, Schiavo;* GHEDINI: *Baccanti, Ipocrita felice, Pulce d'oro;* DARGOMIZHSKI: *Stone Guest;* MALIPIERO: *Allegra brigata, Capt Spavento, Don Giovanni, Donna Urraca, Favola del figlio cambiato, Mondi celesti e infernali, Passione, Festa della quaresima, Torneo notturno, Venere prigioniera;* MASCAGNI: *Maschere, Piccolo Marat, Iris, Nerone, Isabeau;* MONTEMEZZI: *Nave;* MORTARI: *Figlia del Diavolo;* NABOKOV: *Morte di Rasputin;* PANNAIN: *Mme Bovary;* PICK-MANGIAGALLI: *Basi e botte;* PIZZETTI: *Assassinio nella cattedrale, Debora e Jaele, Figlia di Jorio, Fra Gherardo, Oro, Straniero;* RESPIGHI: *Fiamma, Lucrezia, Maria Egiziaca;* ROCCA: *Dibuk, Monte Ivnor, Terra di leggenda, Morte di Frine, Uragano;* ROTA: *Cappello di paglia;* ROSSINI: *Gazzetta;* TOSATTI: *Giudizio universale, Partita a pugni, Sistema della dolcezza;* ROSSELLINI: *Campane, Guerra, Leggenda del ritorno, Linguaggio dei fiori, Sguardo dal ponte, Vortice;* VIOZZI: *Alamistakeo, Intervento notturno, Sasso pagano;* ZANDONAI: *Cavalieri di Ekebù, Conchita;* ZAFRED: *Amleto, Wallenstein.* **Operatic world premieres:** ALFANO: *Cyrano di Bergerac* Teatro dell'Opera, Rome 1936; BUGAMELLI: *Domenica.* VIOZZI: *Giacca dannata,* both Teatro Verdi, Trieste 1967. Teaches at Centro Avviamento, Palermo. **Res:** V Amendola 7, Trieste, Italy.

PICK-HIERONIMI, MONICA. Lyric coloratura soprano. German, FR Ger. Resident mem: Theater am Gärtnerplatz, Munich. Born 14 Dec 1943, Olpe, Germany. Husband Otto, occupation voice teacher. One child. Studied: Musikhochschule, Prof Dietger Jakob, Cologne. **Debut:** Aennchen (*Lustigen Weiber*) Oberhausen, Germany 1970.

Sang with major companies in AUS: Graz; FR GER: Dortmund Städt Oper, Munich Gärtnerplatz. **Roles with these companies incl** ADAM: Madeleine (*Postillon de Lonjumeau*); DONIZETTI: Norina (*Don Pasquale*); HINDEMITH: Tochter des Cardillac; LORTZING: Baronin Freimann (*Wildschütz*); MOZART: Königin der Nacht (*Zauberflöte*); NICOLAI: Aennchen (*Lustigen Weiber*); ORFF: Solo (*Carmina burana*); SMETANA: Marie (*Bartered Bride*); STRAUSS, J: Rosalinde (*Fledermaus*); VERDI: Violetta (*Traviata*). Gives recitals. Appears with symphony orchestra. **Res:** Parkstr 2, 8007 Anzing/Munich, FR Ger. **Mgmt:** PAS/FRG; SMD/FRG; TAS/AUS.

PIERANTI, DIVA FRANCISCA E. Lyric coloratura soprano. Brazilian. Resident mem: Municipal Opera, Rio de Janeiro. Born 18 Mar 1931, Rio de Janeiro. Married. One daughter. Studied: Pina Monaco, Nonelli Barbastefano, Rio de Janeiro. **Debut:** Musetta (*Bohème*) Municipal Opera, Rio de Janeiro, Brazil 1948. Awards: Order of Santa Brigida, Naples, Italy; Three Gold Medals, Brazilian Critcs Socy; Commendation Carlos Gomes; etc.

Sang with major companies in BRA: Rio de Janeiro; FRA: Nice; ITA: Naples, Palermo; MON: Monte Carlo; POR: Lisbon; ROM: Bucharest. **Roles with these companies incl** BERG: Lulu; CIMAROSA: Carolina (*Matrimonio segreto*);

DEBUSSY: Lia (*Enfant prodigue*); DONI-ZETTI: Serafina (*Campanello*), Norina* (*Don Pasquale*), Adina*(*Elisir*); GLUCK: Amor (*Orfeo ed Euridice*); GOMES: Isabella (*Colombo*); LEONCAVALLO: Nedda (*Pagliacci*); MASSE-NET: Manon, Sophie (*Werther*), MENOTTI: Amelia (*Amelia al ballo*), Lucy (*Telephone*); MO-ZART: Fiordiligi (*Così fan tutte*), Zerlina (*Don Giovanni*); PERGOLESI: Lauretta (*Maestro di musica*), Serpina (*Serva padrona*); POULENC: La femme* (*Voix humaine*); PUCCINI: Mimi* & Musetta (*Bohème*), Lauretta (*Gianni Schicchi*), Cio-Cio-San (*Butterfly*); RIMSKY-KORSAKOV: Coq d'or*; ROSSINI: Rosina* (*Barbiere di Siviglia*); VERDI: Oscar (*Ballo in maschera*), Gilda (*Rigoletto*), Violetta* (*Traviata*). Also GOMES: Cecilia (*Guarany*); FERNANDES: Dionisia (*Malazarte*). Gives recitals. Appears with symphony orchestra. Teaches voice. Mgmt: NBA/BRA.

PIERSON, EDWARD. Bass-baritone. American. Resident mem: New York City Opera. Born 4 Jan 1931, Chicago. Wife Myrtle, occupation artist, art teacher. Two children. Studied: Blanche Branche, Chicago. **Debut:** Creon (*Oedipus Rex*) New York City Opera 1966. Previous occupations: taught music in Chicago PS for twelve yrs.

Sang with major companies in USA: Hartford, Jackson Opera/South, Newark, New York City Opera, Washington DC. **Roles with these companies incl** BEETHOVEN: Don Pizarro (*Fidelio*); BI-ZET: Escamillo* (*Carmen*); BOITO: Mefistofele; BORODIN: Prince Igor*; BRITTEN: Astrologer (*Burning Fiery Furnace*), Ferryman (*Curlew River*); CHARPENTIER: Père (*Louise*); DE-BUSSY: Golaud (*Pelléas et Mélisande*); DELIUS: Koanga; FLOTOW: Plunkett (*Martha*); FLOYD: Olin Blitch (*Susannah*); GERSH-WIN: Porgy* & Crown* (*Porgy and Bess*); GINASTERA: Count Cenci* (*Beatrix Cenci*), Don Julian* (*Don Rodrigo*); GOUNOD: Méphistophélès (*Faust*); HANDEL: Giulio Cesare & Ptolemy* (*Giulio Cesare*); JOPLIN: Father (*Treemonisha*); LEONCAVALLO: Tonio (*Pagliacci*); MOZART: Don Giovanni, Conte Almaviva & Figaro (*Nozze di Figaro*); MUS-SORGSKY: Boris Godunov; OFFENBACH: Coppélius, etc (*Contes d'Hoffmann*); PROKO-FIEV: King of Clubs (*Love for Three Oranges*); PUCCINI: Colline (*Bohème*), Jack Rance (*Fanciulla del West*), Gianni Schicchi, Scarpia* (*Tosca*); RIMSKY-KORSAKOV: Roi Dodon (*Coq d'or*); ROSSINI: Don Basilio (*Barbiere di Siviglia*); SAINT-SAENS: Grand prêtre (*Samson et Dalila*); SHOSTAKOVICH: Boris (*Katerina Ismailova*); STRAUSS, R: Jochanaan (*Salome*); STRAVINSKY: Creon (*Oedipus Rex*); THOM-SON: St Ignatius (*Four Saints in Three Acts*); VERDI: Amonasro (*Aida*); WAGNER: Holländer*, Hans Sachs (*Meistersinger*), Wotan (*Rheingold, Walküre*), Wanderer (*Siegfried*), Gunther (*Götterdämmerung*). **World premieres:** STARER: Bamboola (*Pantagleize*) Brooklyn Coll, New York 1973; HENZE: El Cimarrón (*Rachel, la Cubana*) NET Opera, New York 1973; PANNELL: Pierrot (*Exiles*) Stratford Fest, Ont, Canada 1973. Recorded for: Desto. Video—NET-TV: El Cimarrón (*Rachel, la Cubana*). Gives recitals. Appears with symphony orchestra. Teaches voice.

Coaches repertoire. **Res:** 72 Summit Rd, Elizabeth, NJ 07208, USA. Mgmt: DSP/USA.

PIETARINEN, RIITTA ANNIKKI; née Virintie. Lyric soprano. Finnish. Resident mem: Finnish National Opera, Helsinki. Born 27 Aug 1939, Saarijärvi, Finland. Husband Vilho, occupation voice teacher. One child. Studied: Antti Koskinen, Finland; Ferdinand Grossmann, Austria; Luigi Ricci, Italy; Clemens Kaiser-Breme, Germany. **Debut:** Pamina (*Zauberflöte*) Finnish National Opera, Helsinki 1965.

Sang with major companies in BUL: Sofia; HUN: Budapest; ROM: Bucharest; SWE: Drottningholm Fest. **Roles with these companies incl** BIZET: Micaëla (*Carmen*); BRITTEN: Helena (*Midsummer Night*); ERKEL: Melinda (*Bánk Bán*); GLUCK: Amor (*Orfeo ed Euridice*); LEONCAVALLO: Nedda (*Pagliacci*); MO-ZART: Despina (*Così fan tutte*), Zerlina (*Don Giovanni*), Susanna (*Nozze di Figaro*), Pamina (*Zauberflöte*); PUCCINI: Mimi (*Bohème*), Liù (*Turandot*); ROSSINI: Rosina (*Barbiere di Siviglia*); STRAUSS, J: Adele (*Fledermaus*); SZO-KOLAY: Braut (*Blood Wedding*); VERDI: Oscar (*Ballo in maschera*), Gilda (*Rigoletto*). Also MUS-SORGSKY: Parassia (*Fair at Sorochinsk*). **World premieres:** KUUSISTO: Niiskuneiti (*Muumi*) Finnish National Opera, Helsinki 1974; RAUTA-VAARA: First Lady (*Apollo and Marsyas*) Finnish National Opera 1973. Video/Film: Nedda (*Pagliacci*). Gives recitals. Appears with symphony orchestra. Coaches repertoire. **Res:** Pajupillintie 28 A 6, Helsinki, Finland.

PILOU, JEANNETTE. Lyric soprano. Greek. Born Jul 1937, Fayoum, Egypt. Divorced. Studied: Carla Castellani, Milan. **Debut:** Violetta (*Traviata*) Teatro Smeraldo, Milan 1960.

Sang with major companies in ARG: Buenos Aires; AUS: Salzburg Fest, Vienna Staatsoper; BEL: Brussels; FRA: Aix-en-Provence Fest, Marseille, Paris, Strasbourg; GRE: Athens Fest; FR GER: Bonn, Cologne, Essen, Hamburg, Hannover, Mannheim, Wiesbaden; HOL: Amsterdam; HUN: Budapest; ITA: Bologna, Genoa, Milan La Scala, Naples, Palermo, Parma, Rome Opera, Turin, Venice; MON: Monte Carlo; POR: Lisbon; SPA: Barcelona; UK: Edinburgh Fest, Glasgow Scottish, London Royal; USA: Chicago, Cincinnati, Hartford, Houston, Miami, New Orleans, New York Met, Philadelphia Lyric, Pittsburgh, San Francisco Opera. **Roles with these companies incl** BEETHOVEN: Marzelline (*Fidelio*); BIZET: Micaëla*‡ (*Carmen*); DEBUSSY: Mélisande; DONIZETTI: Adina* (*Elisir*); EINEM: Frl Bürstner (*Prozess*); GLUCK: Euridice; GOU-NOD: Marguerite* (*Faust*), Juliette*; LEON-CAVALLO: Nedda* (*Pagliacci*); MASCAGNI: Suzel (*Amico Fritz*); MASSENET: Manon*, Thaïs; MENOTTI: Lucy (*Telephone*); MO-ZART: Zerlina* (*Don Giovanni*), Susanna* (*Nozze di Figaro*); PUCCINI: Mimi* (*Bohème*), Cio-Cio-San* (*Butterfly*), Manon Lescaut, Magda (*Rondine*), Liù* (*Turandot*); TCHAIKOVSKY: Tatiana (*Eugene Onegin*); VERDI: Nannetta* (*Falstaff*), Violetta* (*Traviata*); WOLF-FERRARI: Susanna (*Segreto di Susanna*). **World premieres:** ROSSELLINI: Ines de Castro (*La reine morte*) Opéra de Monte Carlo 1973;

EROED: Oda (*Die Seidenraupen*) Theater a/d Wien, Vienna 1968. Recorded for: Erato. Gives recitals. **Res:** Milan, Italy. **Mgmt:** CAM/USA.

PINTGEN, HANS-WERNER. Conductor of opera and symphony. German. Principal Cond, Bühnen der Stadt Essen, FR Ger. Born 15 Jan 1940, Neuss, FR Ger. Wife Ingrid Charall, occupation dancer. Two children. Studied: Staatl Hochschule für Musik, Cologne, Prof W von der Nahmer, Jean Martinon; incl piano, organ, violin and voice. Operatic training as repetiteur, asst cond & Studienleiter at Städt Bühnen, Oberhausen 1964-66; Bühnen der Hansestadt Lübeck 1966-72. **Operatic debut:** *Finta giardiniera* Städt Bühnen, Oberhausen, FR Ger 1965. Symphonic debut: Rundfunkorch Hannover 1969. Previous adm positions in opera: Deputy Gen Music Dir, Bühnen der Stadt Lübeck 1972-74.
Conducted with major companies in FR GER: Essen, Kiel, Nürnberg. **Operas with these companies incl** BEETHOVEN: *Fidelio*★; BERG: *Lulu*★; DONIZETTI: *Don Pasquale, Lucia, Rita;* EGK: *Zaubergeige;* FLOTOW: *Martha;* GOUNOD: *Faust;* HAYDN: *Infedeltà delusa*★; HENZE: *Junge Lord*★; HUMPERDINCK: *Hänsel und Gretel;* LORTZING: *Waffenschmied;* MONTEVERDI: *Incoronazione di Poppea*★; MOZART: *Don Giovanni*★, *Nozze di Figaro*★, *Zauberflöte*★; OFFENBACH: *Contes d'Hoffmann;* PUCCINI: *Bohème, Butterfly, Tosca;* RAVEL: *Enfant et les sortilèges, Heure espagnole*★; ROSSINI: *Pietra del paragone;* STRAUSS, J: *Fledermaus*★; STRAUSS, R: *Arabella*★, *Rosenkavalier*★; VERDI: *Aida*★, *Falstaff*★, *Rigoletto*★, *Traviata*★; WAGNER: *Fliegende Holländer*★, *Tannhäuser;* WEILL: *Aufstieg und Fall der Stadt Mahagonny*★. Also CIKKER: *Resurrection;* FORTNER: *Bluthochzeit.* Conducted major orch in Europe. Teaches. **Res:** Bismarckstr 33, 4300 Essen-Kettwig, FR Ger. **Mgmt:** PAS/FRG.

PIZZI, PIER LUIGI. Scenic and costume designer for opera, theater, film, television. Is a lighting designer. Italian. Born 15 Jun 1930, Milan. Single. Studied: Polytechnic, School of Architecture, Milan. **Operatic debut:** *Don Giovanni* Teatro Comunale, Genoa 1952. Theater debut: Piccolo Teatro della Città, Genoa 1951. Awards: San Genesio Prize 1965; Golden Neptune, etc.
Designed for major companies in ARG: Buenos Aires; AUS: Vienna Staatsoper; BEL: Brussels; FR GER: Frankfurt; ITA: Bologna, Florence Maggio & Comunale, Genoa, Milan La Scala, Naples, Palermo, Parma, Rome Opera, Spoleto Fest, Trieste, Turin, Venice, Verona Arena; SWI: Zurich; UK: Glyndebourne Fest, London Royal; USA: Chicago. **Operas designed for these companies incl** BELLINI: *Norma;* BIZET: *Carmen;* CHERUBINI: *Medea;* DONIZETTI: *Don Pasquale, Lucia, Maria Stuarda*★, *Roberto Devereux*★; GLUCK: *Alceste;* GOUNOD: *Faust*★; HANDEL: *Orlando furioso;* HENZE: *Junge Lord*★; MOZART: *Don Giovanni;* MUSSORGSKY: *Boris Godunov*★; PERGOLESI: *Frate 'nnamorato, Serva padrona;* PUCCINI: *Bohème*★, *Gianni Schicchi*★, *Butterfly, Tabarro*★, *Tosca*★, *Turandot*★; ROSSINI: *Barbiere di Siviglia, Cenerentola, Guillaume Tell*★, *Moïse, Si-*

gnor Bruschino, Turco in Italia; STRAVINSKY: *Oedipus Rex;* TCHAIKOVSKY: *Eugene Onegin, Pique Dame*★; VERDI: *Aida*★, *Attila*★, *Corsaro, Don Carlo*★, *Due Foscari, Ernani, Forza del destino*★, *Lombardi, Luisa Miller, Macbeth, Otello*★, *Rigoletto, Simon Boccanegra*★, *Traviata*★, *Trovatore, Vespri;* WAGNER: *Walküre*★, *Siegfried*★; WOLF-FERRARI: *Quattro rusteghi.* **Res:** 51 V del Babuino, Rome, Italy.

PLASSON, MICHEL. Conductor of opera. French. Théâtre du Capitole, Toulouse, France.
Conducted with major companies in FRA: Strasbourg, Toulouse; USA: New York City Opera; et al. **Operas with these companies incl** BERLIOZ: *Benvenuto Cellini;* BIZET: *Carmen;* GOUNOD: *Faust;* MASSENET: *Manon;* OFFENBACH: *Contes d'Hoffmann;* PROKOFIEV: *Duenna, Love for Three Oranges;* PUCCINI: *Tosca;* ROSSINI: *Barbiere di Siviglia, Pietra del paragone;* et al. Also GOUNOD: *Reine de Saba.* **World premieres:** BONDON: *Nuit foudroyée* Metz 1968.

PLATE, WILFRIED. Lyric tenor & tenore buffo. German. Resident mem: Staatstheater Darmstadt. Born 29 May 1937, Hamburg. Wife Heike Wähling. One daughter. Studied: H F Radbert, Hamburg. **Debut:** Fenton (*Falstaff*) Staatsoper Hamburg 1965.
Sang with major companies in FR GER: Darmstadt, Hamburg; UK: Edinburgh Fest. **Roles with these companies incl** BIZET: Don José★ (*Carmen*); CIMAROSA: Paolino★ (*Matrimonio segreto*); DONIZETTI: Ernesto★ (*Don Pasquale*); HAYDN: Filippo (*Infedeltà delusa*); LORTZING: Peter Ivanov★ (*Zar und Zimmermann*); MOZART: Pedrillo★(*Entführung aus dem Serail*); MUSSORGSKY: Gritzko★ (*Fair at Sorochinsk*); NICOLAI: Fenton★ (*Lustigen Weiber*); ORFF: Solo★ (*Carmina burana*); PUCCINI: Rinuccio★ (*Gianni Schicchi*); ROSSINI: Almaviva★ (*Barbiere di Siviglia*), Rodrigo★ (*Otello*); SMETANA: Wenzel★ (*Bartered Bride*); STRAUSS, J: Alfred★ (*Fledermaus*); STRAUSS, R: Ein Sänger★(*Rosenkavalier*); VERDI: Duca di Mantova★ (*Rigoletto*), Alfredo (*Traviata*); WAGNER: David★ (*Meistersinger*), Mime★ (*Rheingold*), Walther v d Vogelweide★(*Tannhäuser*).

PLISHKA, PAUL PETER. Bass. American. Resident mem: Metropolitan Opera, New York. Born 28 Aug 1941, Old Forge, PA, USA. Wife Judith. Three children. Studied: Armen Boyajian, NJ; Montclair State Coll, NJ, USA. **Debut:** Colline (*Bohème*) Met Op National Co 1966. Awards: Winner, Baltimore Opera Aud.
Sang with major companies in CAN: Ottawa, Vancouver; ITA: Spoleto Fest; USA: Hartford, Newark, New Orleans, New York Met, Philadelphia Lyric Opera, Pittsburgh. **Roles with these companies incl** BELLINI: Oroveso★ (*Norma*), Sir George★ (*Puritani*); MOZART: Leporello★ (*Don Giovanni*), Figaro★ (*Nozze di Figaro*); MUSSORGSKY: Pimen★ (*Boris Godunov*); PUCCINI: Colline★ (*Bohème*); VERDI: Ramfis (*Aida*), Banquo★ (*Macbeth*), Procida★ (*Vespri*); WAGNER: Daland★ (*Fliegende Holländer*), König Marke★ (*Tristan und Isolde*). Recorded for: ABC. **Res:** 10 Totem Rd, Freehold, NJ 07728, USA.

PLUMMER, SUSAN JENNIFER. Scenic and costume designer for opera, theater. British. Born 20 Jan 1943, London. Single. Studied: St Martin's School of Art. **Operatic debut:** cost, *Rigoletto* Welsh National Opera, Cardiff 1972.

Designed for major companies in UK: Welsh National. **Operas designed for these companies incl** BIZET: *Pêcheurs de perles*★; SMETANA: *Secret*★; VERDI: *Rigoletto*★. Exhibitions of stage designs. **Res:** 23A Nelson Rd, Greenwich, UK.

POHL, GISELA; née Oschatz. Lyric & dramatic mezzo-soprano. German. Resident mem: Staatsoper & Komische Oper, Berlin; Opernhaus Leipzig, Ger DR. Born 18 Oct 1937, Leipzig, Germany. Husband Reinhart, occupation conductor. Three daughters. Studied: Deutsche Hoshschule für Musik, Prof Friedrich Trommler, Berlin. **Debut:** Azucena (*Trovatore*) Hans-Otto-Theater, Potsdam Ger DR 1967. Awards: Diploma First Class, Prague Spring 1967.

Sang with major companies in GER DR: Berlin Komische Oper & Staatsoper, Leipzig. **Roles with these companies incl** HANDEL: Amastris★ (*Xerxes*); MOZART: Sesto★ (*Clemenza di Tito*), Cherubino★ (*Nozze di Figaro*); PROKOFIEV: Smeraldina★ (*Love for Three Oranges*); ROSSINI: Rosina★ (*Barbiere di Siviglia*); VERDI: Amneris★ (*Aida*). **World premieres:** MATTHUS: Miss Dodd (*Noch einen Löffel Gift, Liebling*) Komische Oper Berlin 1972; MEYER: Sarie Claasen (*Reiter in der Nacht*) Staatsoper Berlin, Ger DR, 1973. Gives recitals. Appears with symphony orchestra. **Res:** August-Bebel-Str 61, 703 Leipzig, Ger DR. **Mgmt:** KDR/GDR.

POKROVSKY, BORIS. Stages/produces opera. Russian. Resident Stage Dir, Bolshoi Opera, Moscow. Born USSR.

Directed/produced opera for major companies in BUL: Sofia; USSR: Moscow Bolshoi; et al. **Operas staged with these companies incl** GLINKA: *Ruslan and Ludmilla;* MUSSORGSKY: *Khovanshchina;* PROKOFIEV: *Fiery Angel, Gambler, Love for Three Oranges, War and Peace;* PUCCINI: *Tosca;* RIMSKY-KORSAKOV: *Invisible City of Kitezh, Sadko, Tsar's Bride;* SHOSTAKOVICH: *Katerina Ismailova, Nose;* TCHAIKOVSKY: *Eugene Onegin, Pique Dame;* et al. **Operatic world premieres:** SHCHEDRIN: *Not Only Love* Chamber Music Theater, Moscow 1972; KHRENNIKOV: *Much Ado from the Heart* Moscow 1972.

POLA, BRUNO. Lyric & dramatic baritone. Italian. Resident mem: Opernhaus, Cologne; from 1975 Opernhaus, Zurich. Born 23 Oct 1943, Rovereto, Italy. Single. Studied: Prof v Kovotszy, Konsv Berlin. **Debut:** Escamillo (*Carmen*) Pfalztheater Kaiserslautern, FR Ger 1968.

Sang with major companies in DEN: Copenhagen; FR GER: Cologne, Dortmund, Düsseldorf-Duisburg, Frankfurt, Hannover, Karlsruhe, Kiel, Nürnberg, Stuttgart; HOL: Amsterdam; SWI: Zurich. **Roles with these companies incl** BARTOK: Bluebeard; BEETHOVEN: Don Pizarro (*Fidelio*); BIZET: Escamillo★ (*Carmen*); DONIZETTI: Dott Malatesta★ (*Don Pasquale*), Enrico★ (*Lucia*); LEONCAVALLO: Tonio★ (*Pagliacci*); MASCAGNI: Alfio★ (*Cavalleria rusticana*);

ORFF: Solo★ (*Carmina burana*), König (*Kluge*); PUCCINI: Marcello★ (*Bohème*), Sharpless★ (*Butterfly*), Michele★ (*Tabarro*), Scarpia★ (*Tosca*); ROSSINI: Figaro★ (*Barbiere di Siviglia*); VERDI: Rodrigo★ (*Don Carlo*), Don Carlo★ (*Forza del destino*), Rigoletto★, Simon Boccanegra★, Germont★ (*Traviata*), Conte di Luna★ (*Trovatore*); WEILL: Trinity Moses (*Aufstieg und Fall der Stadt Mahagonny*). Recorded for: Electrola. Appears with symphony orchestra. **Mgmt:** SLZ/FRG; VLD/AUS.

POLAKOFF, ABE. Dramatic baritone. American. Born Bucharest, Romania. Wife Ethel. Three children. Studied: Nora Bosler, New York; Amer Theater Wing, acting, Op Wkshp, sight reading, New York; Rudolf Schaar, coaching, New York. **Debut:** Conte di Luna (*Trovatore*) Opernhaus Zurich. Previous occupations: engr designer for oil refineries and chemical plants. Awards: Amer Op Aud Awd, perfs in Milan & Florence 1960; Rockefeller Fndt Grants 1961 & 1962; Silver Medal, Vercelli Singing Cont 1960; Amer Theater Wing Schlshp.

Sang with major companies in CAN: Toronto; FR GER: Berlin Deutsche Oper, Bielefeld, Düsseldorf-Duisburg, Frankfurt, Hamburg, Mannheim, Munich Staatsoper, Stuttgart; HOL: Amsterdam; SWI: Zurich; USA: Cincinnati, Kansas City, New York Met & City Opera, Philadelphia Lyric, Pittsburgh, Seattle. **Roles with these companies incl** BIZET: Escamillo (*Carmen*); DONIZETTI: Enrico (*Lucia*); LEONCAVALLO: Tonio★ (*Pagliacci*); MASCAGNI: Alfio★ (*Cavalleria rusticana*); MOZART: Conte Almaviva★ (*Nozze di Figaro*); OFFENBACH: Coppélius etc (*Contes d'Hoffmann*); PUCCINI: Marcello★ (*Bohème*), Sharpless★ (*Butterfly*), Scarpia (*Tosca*); ROSSINI: Figaro (*Barbiere di Siviglia*); VERDI: Amonasro (*Aida*), Renato (*Ballo in maschera*), Francesco Foscari (*Due Foscari*), Don Carlo (*Forza del destino*), Iago (*Otello*), Rigoletto★, Germont★ (*Traviata*), Conte di Luna (*Trovatore*). Also MENOTTI: King Melchior (*Amahl*); GOUNOD: Valentin (*Faust*). **World premieres:** KELTERBORN: Der Soldat (*Errettung Thebens*) Opernhaus Zurich 1963. Gives recitals. Appears with symphony orchestra. **Res:** 134-45 166 Place, Jamaica, NY 11434, USA. **Mgmt:** LWI/USA; JUC/SWI.

POLL, MELVYN. Lyric tenor. American. Resident mem: New York City Opera. Born 15 Jul 1941, Seattle, WA. Wife Rosalind Benaroya. Two children. Studied: Mmes Marinka Gurewich, Elsa Seyfert, New York: Mo Martin Rich, New York; Mo Gustave Stern, Seattle. **Debut:** Rodolfo (*Bohème*) Pfalztheater, Kaiserslautern, FR Ger 1971. Previous occupations: lawyer, grad School of Law, Univ Wash.

Sang with major companies in ISR: Tel Aviv; USA: New York City Opera. **Roles with these companies incl** DONIZETTI: Edgardo* (*Lucia*); GOUNOD: Faust* PUCCINI: Rodolfo* (*Bohème*), Pinkerton* (*Butterfly*); VERDI: Alfredo* (*Traviata*). Gives recitals. Appears with symphony orchestras. **Res:** Larchmont, NY.

POND, HELEN BARBARA. Scenic designer for opera, theater. Collaborates with Herbert Senn.

American. Resident principal designer, Opera Co of Boston and at Cape Playhouse, Dennis, MA. Born 26 Jun 1924, Cleveland, O. Single. Studied: Columbia Univ, Milton Smith, Woodman Thompson, New York. **Operatic professional debut:** Opera Co of Boston 1964. Theater debut: Gate Repertory Co, New York 1955.

Designed for major companies in USA: Boston, New York City Opera. **Operas designed for these companies incl** BELLINI: *Norma★;* BERLIOZ: *Benvenuto Cellini★, Troyens★;* BRITTEN: *Albert Herring;* CHARPENTIER: *Louise;* DONIZETTI: *Elisir, Fille du régiment, Lucia;* GAY/Britten: *Beggar's Opera;* HENZE: *Junge Lord★;* KURKA: *Good Soldier Schweik;* MASSENET: *Don Quichotte★;* MOZART: *Così fan tutte★, Entführung aus dem Serail;* PROKOFIEV: *War and Peace★;* PUCCINI: *Tosca;* RAMEAU: *Hippolyte et Aricie;* ROSSINI: *Barbiere di Siviglia★, Semiramide;* STRAUSS, R: *Ariadne auf Naxos★;* STRAVINSKY: *Rake's Progress;* VERDI: *Falstaff★, Rigoletto, Traviata★;* WAGNER: *Fliegende Holländer;* WEILL: *Aufstieg und Fall der Stadt Mahagonny★.* **Operatic world premieres:** CHAVEZ: *Panfilo and Lauretta* Columbia Univ Op Wrkshp, New York 1957; SCHULLER: *Fisherman and His Wife* Opera Co of Boston 1970. Res: 316 W 51 St, New York 10019, USA.

PONNELLE, JEAN-PIERRE. Stages/produces opera, theater, film & television. Also designs sets, costumes & stage-lighting. French. Born 19 Feb 1932, Paris. Wife Margit Saad, occupation actress. One child. Studied: music, piano. **Operatic debut:** as designer/dir *Tristan und Isolde* Düsseldorf, FR Ger 1962.

Directed/produced opera for major companies in AUS: Graz, Salzburg Fest, Vienna Staatsoper & Volksoper; FRA: Marseille, Paris, Rouen, Strasbourg; FR GER: Cologne, Düsseldorf-Duisburg, Frankfurt, Munich Staatsoper & Gärtnerplatz; HOL: Amsterdam; ITA: Florence Maggio & Comunale, Milan La Scala, Naples; SWE: Stockholm; SWI: Zurich; UK: Edinburgh Fest, London Royal; USA: Chicago, New York Met, San Francisco Opera. **Operas staged with these companies incl** BIZET: *Carmen★†;* BRITTEN: *Midsummer Night†;* DEBUSSY: *Pelléas et Mélisande★†;* DONIZETTI: *Don Pasquale★†;* HAYDN: *Infedeltà delusa†;* HENZE: *Boulevard Solitude★†, Junge Lord†, König Hirsch/Re Cervo★†;* MASSENET: *Manon★†;* MOZART: *Clemenza di Tito★†, Così fan tutte★†, Don Giovanni★†, Entführung aus dem Serail★†, Idomeneo★†, Nozze di Figaro★†, Zauberflöte★†;* MUSSORGSKY: *Boris Godunov★†;* ORFF: *Carmina burana★†;* PUCCINI: *Gianni Schicchi★†, Butterfly★†, Tosca★†;* ROSSINI: *Barbiere di Siviglia★†, Cenerentola★†, Comte Ory★†, Italiana in Algeri★†;* STRAUSS, R: *Ariadne auf Naxos★†;* VERDI: *Don Carlo★†, Otello★†, Rigoletto★†, Simon Boccanegra†, Trovatore†;* WAGNER: *Rheingold★†.* **Operas designed but not staged incl** BELLINI: *Sonnambula;* GOUNOD: *Faust;* LEONCAVALLO: *Pagliacci;* MOZART: *Finta giardiniera;* ORFF: *Kluge;* PUCCINI: *Bohème;* RAMEAU: *Castor et Pollux;* RAVEL: *Heure espagnole;* STRAUSS, R: *Frau ohne Schatten, Intermezzo, Liebe der Danae, Rosenkavalier;* VERDI: *Aida;* WEBER: *Oberon.* Also PUR-

CELL: *Fairy Queen★†.* **Res:** Beethovenstr 12, 8023 Munich/Pullach, FR Ger. Mgmt: JUC/SWI.

POOT, SONJA. Lyric coloratura soprano. British. Resident mem: Württembergische Staatsoper, Stuttgart. Born Netherlands. Single. Studied: Consv, The Hague; Acad of Music, Vienna. **Debut:** Konstanze (*Entführung aus dem Serail*) Bonn Opera 1964. Awards: Second Prize, DG Cont for Opera 1963.

Sang with major companies in AUS: Vienna Staatsoper & Volksoper; CAN: Ottawa; FRA: Bordeaux, Nancy; FR GER: Berlin Deutsche Oper, Bonn, Düsseldorf-Duisburg, Essen, Frankfurt, Hamburg, Hannover, Mannheim, Nürnberg, Stuttgart; HOL: Amsterdam; ITA: Rome Opera; S AFR: Johannesburg; SPA: Barcelona, Canary Isl Las Palmas Fest; SWI: Basel, Geneva. **Roles with these companies incl** ADAM: Neméa (*Si j'étais roi*); DONIZETTI: Anna Bolena, Norina (*Don Pasquale*), Lucia★, Lucrezia Borgia, Maria di Rohan, Elisabetta (*Roberto Devereux*); FLOTOW: Lady Harriet (*Martha*); GLUCK: Euridice; GOUNOD: Marguerite (*Faust*); MOZART: Fiordiligi★ (*Così fan tutte*), Donna Anna (*Don Giovanni*), Konstanze★ (*Entführung aus dem Serail*), Elettra (*Idomeneo*), Contessa (*Nozze di Figaro*), Pamina & Königin der Nacht (*Zauberflöte*); OFFENBACH: Olympia & Antonia & Giulietta (*Contes d'Hoffmann*); PUCCINI: Mimi (*Bohème*); ROSSINI: Rosina (*Barbiere di Siviglia*); VERDI: Alice Ford (*Falstaff*), Violetta★ (*Traviata*), Elena (*Vespri*); WAGNER: Elsa (*Lohengrin*); WEBER: Agathe (*Freischütz*). Gives recitals. Appears with symphony orchestra. **Res:** Dietzenbach, FR Ger. Mgmt: SLZ/FRG.

POPOV, STOJAN. Dramatic baritone. Bulgarian. Resident mem: Nationaloper, Sofia; Vereinigte Bühnen, Graz. Born Sheljaskovo, Bulgaria. Studied: Prof Christov Brambarov, Bulgaria. Awards: First Prize Intl Fest Compt, Helsinki.

Sang with major companies in AUS: Graz, Vienna Staatsoper; BEL: Brussels, Liège; BUL: Sofia; CZE: Brno, Prague National; FRA: Bordeaux, Lyon, Paris; GRE: Athens Fest; FR GER: Berlin Deutsche Oper, Munich Staatsoper, Wiesbaden; GER DR: Berlin Staatsoper; HOL: Amsterdam; HUN: Budapest; ITA: Florence Maggio, Naples; POL: Warsaw; ROM: Bucharest; SPA: Barcelona, Majorca; USSR: Kiev, Leningrad Kirov, Moscow Bolshoi; YUG: Zagreb, Belgrade. **Roles with these companies incl** BIZET: Escamillo★ (*Carmen*), Zurga★ (*Pêcheurs de perles*); BORODIN: Prince Igor★ & Galitzky★ (*Prince Igor*); MUSSORGSKY: Shaklovity★‡ (*Khovanshchina*); PUCCINI: Marcello★ (*Bohème*), Scarpia★ (*Tosca*); ROSSINI: Figaro★ (*Barbiere di Siviglia*); VERDI: Amonasro★ (*Aida*), Don Carlo★ (*Ernani*), Macbeth★, Nabucco★, Iago★ (*Otello*), Rigoletto★, Germont (*Traviata*), Conte di Luna★ (*Trovatore*); WAGNER: Telramund★ (*Lohengrin*). Recorded for: Balcanrecord. Gives recitals. Appears with symphony orchestra. Teaches voice. **Res:** Sofia, Bulgaria. Mgmt: VLD/AUS.

POPOVIC-GORDAN, DUSAN. Dramatic baritone & bass-baritone. Yugoslavian. Resident mem: National Opera, Belgrade. Born 28 Oct 1927, Prilep, Yugoslavia. Wife Gordana, occupation professor.

One child. **Debut:** Germont (*Traviata*) National Opera, Belgrade 1949.

Sang with major companies in AUS: Graz, Vienna Staatsoper; BEL: Brussels; BUL: Sofia; CAN: Montreal/Quebec; CZE: Brno, Prague National; DEN: Copenhagen; FRA: Bordeaux, Lyon, Marseille, Nice, Paris, Strasbourg, Toulouse; GRE: Athens National; FR GER: Bayreuth Fest, Berlin Deutsche Oper, Dortmund, Düsseldorf-Duisburg, Frankfurt, Hannover, Munich Staatsoper & Gärtnerplatz, Saarbrücken, Wiesbaden; GER DR: Berlin Staatsoper, Leipzig; HUN: Budapest; ITA: Bologna, Florence Maggio, Milan La Scala, Palermo, Rome Opera, Trieste, Turin, Venice; MON: Monte Carlo; NOR: Oslo; POL: Warsaw; ROM: Bucharest; SPA: Barcelona; SWE: Stockholm; SWI: Basel, Geneva, Zurich; UK: Edinburgh Fest; USSR: Kiev, Leningrad Kirov, Moscow Bolshoi, Tbilisi; USA: Chicago; YUG: Dubrovnik, Zagreb, Belgrade. **Roles with these companies incl** BEETHOVEN: Don Pizarro★ (*Fidelio*); BELLINI: Sir Richard★ (*Puritani*); BERG: Dr Schön★ (*Lulu*); BIZET: Escamillo★ (*Carmen*); BORODIN: Prince Igor★; EINEM: Georges Danton★ (*Dantons Tod*); FALLA: Don Quixote★ (*Retablo de Maese Pedro*); GERSHWIN: Porgy★; GIORDANO: Carlo Gérard★ (*Andrea Chénier*); GOTOVAC: Sima★ (*Ero der Schelm*); GOUNOD: Méphistophélès★ (*Faust*); JANACEK: Dikoy★ (*Katya Kabanova*); KLEBE: Jakobowsky★ (*Jakobowsky und der Oberst*); LEONCAVALLO: Tonio★ (*Pagliacci*); LORTZING: Baculus★ (*Wildschütz*), Van Bett★ (*Zar und Zimmermann*); MASCAGNI: Alfio★ (*Cavalleria rusticana*); MASSENET: Lescaut★ (*Manon*); MENOTTI: John Sorel★ (*Consul*); MUSSORGSKY: Boris★ & Pimen★ (*Boris Godunov*), Shaklovity★ & Ivan Khovansky★ (*Khovanshchina*); OFFENBACH: Coppélius, etc★ (*Contes d'Hoffmann*); ORFF: Solo★ (*Carmina burana*); PENDERECKI: Grandier★ (*Teufel von Loudun*); PROKOFIEV: Prince Andrei★ (*War and Peace*); PUCCINI: Marcello★ (*Bohème*), Jack Rance★ (*Fanciulla del West*), Lescaut★ (*Manon Lescaut*), Scarpia★ (*Tosca*); ROSSINI: Don Basilio★ (*Barbiere di Siviglia*); SHOSTAKOVICH: Boris★ (*Katerina Ismailova*); SMETANA: Kezal★ (*Bartered Bride*); STRAUSS, R: Mandryka★ (*Arabella*), Musiklehrer★ (*Ariadne auf Naxos*), Orest★ (*Elektra*), Baron Ochs★ (*Rosenkavalier*), Jochanaan★ (*Salome*); STRAVINSKY: Creon★ (*Oedipus Rex*); TCHAIKOVSKY: Eugene Onegin★, Yeletsky★ (*Pique Dame*); VERDI: Amonasro★ (*Aida*), Attila★, Renato★ (*Ballo in maschera*), Rodrigo★ (*Don Carlo*), Falstaff★, Fra Melitone★ (*Forza del destino*), Macbeth★, Nabucco★, Iago★ (*Otello*), Rigoletto★, Simon Boccanegra★, Germont★ (*Traviata*), Conte di Luna★ (*Trovatore*); WAGNER: Holländer★, Telramund★ (*Lohengrin*), Hans Sachs★ (*Meistersinger*), Amfortas★ (*Parsifal*), Wotan★ (*Walküre*), Wanderer★ (*Siegfried*). Recorded for: Decca, MGM. Gives recitals. Appears with symphony orchestra. On faculty of Consv, Belgrade. **Res:** Am Wickersberg 16/Eusheim, Saarbrücken, FR Ger. Mgmt: PAS/FRG.

POPP, LUCIA. Coloratura soprano. Austrian. Resident mem: Cologne Opera; Vienna Staatsoper. Husband Georg Fischer, occupation conductor. Studied: Mrs Anna Prosenc-Hrusovska,

Vienna. **Debut:** Königin der Nacht (*Zauberflöte*) Bratislava, Czechoslovakia 1963.

Sang with major companies in AUS: Graz, Vienna Staatsoper & Volksoper; FRA: Paris; FR GER: Bonn, Cologne, Frankfurt, Hamburg, Karlsruhe, Mannheim, Munich Staatsoper, Stuttgart; ITA: Florence Maggio; UK: London Royal Opera; USA: New York Met. **Roles with these companies incl** AUBER: Zerlina★ (*Fra Diavolo*); BEETHOVEN: Marzelline (*Fidelio*); DONIZETTI: Norina★ (*Don Pasquale*); MOZART: Servilia★ (*Clemenza di Tito*), Despina★ (*Così fan tutte*), Zerlina★ (*Don Giovanni*), Konstanze★ & Blondchen (*Entführung aus dem Serail*), Ilia★ (*Idomèneo*), Susanna★ (*Nozze di Figaro*), Pamina★ & Königin der Nacht (*Zauberflöte*); NICOLAI: Frau Fluth★ (*Lustigen Weiber*); OFFENBACH: Olympia (*Contes d'Hoffmann*); ORFF: Solo (*Carmina burana*), Kluge; ROSSINI: Rosina★ (*Barbiere di Siviglia*); STRAUSS, J: Adele (*Fledermaus*), Sophie★ (*Rosenkavalier*); STRAVINSKY: Anne Trulove (*Rake's Progress*); VERDI: Oscar★ (*Ballo in maschera*), Gilda★ (*Rigoletto*). Recorded for: Decca, CBS, EMI. Video/Film: Marzelline (*Fidelio*); Marie (*Zar und Zimmermann*). Gives recitals. Appears with symphony orchestra.

POPPER, FELIX. Conductor of opera. American. Music Administrator, New York City Opera, Lincoln Center; started w co 1949. Born 12 Dec 1908, Vienna. Wife Doris Jung, occupation opera singer. One son. Repetiteur & asst cond at Montreal Opera 1949-53; San Francisco Opera 1958. **Operatic debut:** *Revisor* New York City Opera 1957. Previous occupations: recital accompanist; music teacher in private schools. Previous adm positions in opera: assoc cond NBC TV Opera, New York 1954-74.

Conducted with major companies in USA: New York City Opera. **Operas with these companies incl** BIZET: *Carmen;* DONIZETTI: *Don Pasquale;* MENOTTI: *Amahl, Amelia al ballo, Consul;* MOZART: *Don Giovanni, Nozze di Figaro, Zauberflöte;* PUCCINI: *Bohème, Butterfly, Tabarro, Tosca;* ROSSINI: *Barbiere di Siviglia★;* STRAUSS, J: *Fledermaus;* STRAUSS, R: *Ariadne auf Naxos★, Capriccio★;* VERDI: *Traviata.* **Res:** New York, NY, USA.

PORCHER, NANANNE. Lighting designer for opera, theater and ballet; also theater consultant. American. Resident designer, American Ballet Theatre, New York. Born 14 Dec 1922, La Grange, GA. Single. Studied: Univ North Carolina, Chapel Hill. Prof training: asst to Jean Rosenthal. **Operatic debut:** *Traviata* Dallas Civic Opera, TX 1959. Theater debut: Civic Light Opera, Los Angeles 1957. Previous occupation: Prod Stage Mng.

Designed for major companies in USA: Boston, Chicago, Dallas, Houston, New York Met & City Opera, Philadelphia Lyric, San Diego, Seattle, Washington DC. **Operas designed for these companies incl** BARTOK: *Bluebeard's Castle;* BEETHOVEN: *Fidelio;* BELLINI: *Puritani;* BERG: *Lulu★, Wozzeck;* BERLIOZ: *Damnation de Faust;* BIZET: *Carmen, Pêcheurs de perles;* BOITO: *Mefistofele;* BORODIN: *Prince Igor;* BRITTEN: *Turn of the Screw;* CAVALLI: *Or-*

mindo; CHERUBINI: *Medea;* DELIBES: *Lakmé;* DELIUS: *Koanga, Village Romeo and Juliet*★*;* DONIZETTI: *Don Pasquale*★*, Elisir, Favorite, Lucia;* GERSHWIN: *Porgy and Bess;* GIORDANO: *Andréa Chenier;* GLUCK: *Orfeo ed Euridice;* GOUNOD: *Faust, Roméo et Juliette;* HANDEL: *Alcina;* KORNGOLD: *Tote Stadt*★*;* KURKA: *Good Soldier Schweik;* LEONCAVALLO: *Pagliacci;* MASCAGNI: *Cavalleria rusticana;* MASSENET: *Manon, Thaïs;* MENOTTI: *Consul, Saint of Bleecker Street*★*, Telephone;* MONTEVERDI: *Incoronazione di Poppea;* MOZART: *Così fan tutte, Don Giovanni, Nozze di Figaro, Zauberflöte;* MUSSORGSKY: *Boris Godunov;* OFFENBACH: *Contes d'Hoffmann;* ORFF: *Carmina burana;* PONCHIELLI: *Gioconda;* PROKOFIEV: *Fiery Angel;* PUCCINI: *Bohème, Butterfly, Suor Angelica, Tosca;* PURCELL: *King Arthur;* RAVEL: *Heure espagnole;* ROSSINI: *Barbiere di Siviglia, Comte Ory, Italiana in Algeri;* SAINT-SAENS: *Samson et Dalila;* SCHULLER: *Visitation;* STRAUSS, J: *Fledermaus;* STRAUSS, R: *Ariadne auf Naxos, Salome;* VERDI: *Aida, Ballo in maschera, Don Carlo, Falstaff, Forza del destino, Nabucco, Otello, Rigoletto, Simon Boccanegra, Traviata, Trovatore;* WAGNER: *Lohengrin.* **Operatic world premieres:** GINASTERA: *Beatrix Cenci* Opera Socy of Washington 1971; BARBER: *Antony and Cleopatra* Metropolitan Opera 1966. **Addr:** 49 W 96th St, New York 10025, USA.

POTTER, RAESCHELLE JULIAN. Spinto. American. Resident mem: Opernhaus Graz. Born 9 Sep 1946, Gulfport, MS, USA. Single. Studied: Univ of Southern Illinois, Marjorie Lawrence, Carbondale; Mo Kurt Adler, Richard Fredricks, New York. **Debut:** Aida, Opernhaus Lübeck, FR Ger 1973. Previous occupations: voice teacher & coach. Awards: American Opera Aud Grant, Cincinnati; WGN winner, Chicago; Met Op Ntl Counc finalist & several grants; Fulbright Schlshp to Vienna 1972-73.
 Sang with major companies in AUS: Graz. **Roles with these companies incl** BIZET: Micaëla★ *(Carmen);* MOZART: Zerlina★*(Don Giovanni);* PUCCINI: Mimi★ *(Bohème),* Lauretta★ *(Gianni Schicchi);* VERDI: Aida★. Gives recitals. Appears with symphony orchestra. **Res:** Rosenberggürtel 35/20, A-8010 Graz, Austria. **Mgmt:** WLS/USA; SLZ/FRG.

PÖTTGEN, ERNST. Stages/produces opera & theater. Also designs stage-lighting. German.
 Directed/produced opera for major companies in ARG: Buenos Aires; AUS: Vienna Staatsoper; DEN: Copenhagen; FIN: Helsinki; FR GER: Berlin Deutsche Oper, Düsseldorf-Duisburg, Munich Staatsoper, Stuttgart; SWI: Zurich; et al. **Operas staged with these companies incl** BEETHOVEN: *Fidelio;* BERLIOZ: *Troyens;* BIZET: *Carmen;* CHERUBINI: *Medea;* DONIZETTI: *Anna Bolena, Elisir;* GAY/Britten: *Beggar's Opera;* HANDEL: *Deidamia, Giulio Cesare;* HAYDN: *Infedeltà delusa;* JANACEK: *Katya Kabanova;* LIGETI: *Aventures/Nouvelles Aventures;* MOZART: *Mitridate re di Ponto, Zauberflöte;* MUSSORGSKY: *Boris Godunov;* PFITZNER: *Palestrina;* PUCCINI: *Turandot;* SCHOENBERG: *Moses und Aron;* STRAUSS,

R: *Rosenkavalier, Schweigsame Frau;* VERDI: *Ballo in maschera, Don Carlo, Forza del destino, Luisa Miller, Rigoletto, Simon Boccanegra, Trovatore;* WAGNER: *Rheingold, Walküre, Siegfried, Götterdämmerung;* WEBER: *Freischütz;* et al. **Operatic world premieres:** GRUENAUER: *Walfischbauch* Württembergisches Staatstheater, Stuttgart 1974.

POWERS, WILLIAM; né William P Powers Jr. Bass-baritone. American. Born 22 Sep 1941, Chicago. Wife Adrienne, occupation interior designer. Studied: Illinois Wesleyan Univ, Lewis E Whikehart, Bloomington, IN; American Consv of Music, David Austin, Chicago; Frederick D Wilkerson, Washington, DC, USA. **Debut:** Frate *(Don Carlo)* Chicago Lyric Opera 1964. Previous occupations: salesman, truck driver, pharmaceutical represent, soldier. Awards: Rockefeller Study Grant; Sullivan Fndt Fllshp; Baltimore Opera Aud winner; Met Op Natl Counc Aud semi-finalist.
 Sang with major companies in USA: Baltimore, Cincinnati, Fort Worth, Hartford, Hawaii, Kansas City, Kentucky, Memphis, Newark, New York City Opera, Omaha, Philadelphia Lyric Opera, Pittsburgh, Portland, San Antonio, San Diego, San Francisco Spring Opera, Washington DC. **Roles with these companies incl** DONIZETTI: Don Pasquale★; FLOYD: Olin Blitch *(Susannah);* GOUNOD: Méphistophélès *(Faust);* MOZART: Leporello★ *(Don Giovanni);* MUSSORGSKY: Varlaam★*(Boris Godunov);* OFFENBACH: Coppélius etc★ *(Contes d'Hoffmann),* Don Andres★ *(Périchole);* PUCCINI: Colline★ *(Bohème);* ROSSINI: Dott Bartolo★ & Don Basilio★ *(Barbiere di Siviglia);* SMETANA: Kezal *(Bartered Bride);* WARD: Rev Hale★ *(Crucible).* Also FLOYD: Candy *(Of Mice and Men);* TCHAIKOVSKY: Gremin *(Eugene Onegin).* Recorded for: CRI. Gives recitals. Appears with symphony orchestra. **Res:** 1871 Kirby Rd, McLean, VA, USA. **Mgmt:** LLF/USA.

PRACHT, MARY ELLEN. Lyric soprano. American. Resident mem: Metropolitan Opera, New York. Born 4 Feb 1936, Bellaire, O, USA. Husband Jascha Silberstein, occupation cellist. One child. Studied: Cincinnati Coll of Music; Ohio State Univ, piano, Columbus; Emmy Joseph, Daniel Ferro, New York. **Debut:** Annina *(Traviata)* Metropolitan Opera, New York 1961.
 Sang with major companies in CAN: Toronto; USA: Cincinnati, Newark, New Orleans, New York Met, Pittsburgh, San Francisco Spring. **Roles with these companies incl** BEETHOVEN: Marzelline *(Fidelio);* BIZET: Micaëla★ *(Carmen),* Léila *(Pêcheurs de perles);* BRITTEN: Helena★ *(Midsummer Night);* DONIZETTI: Adina *(Elisir);* GOUNOD: Marguerite★ *(Faust),* Juliette★*;* LEONCAVALLO: Nedda★ *(Pagliacci);* MOZART: Fiordiligi *(Così fan tutte),* Donna Elvira *(Don Giovanni),* Konstanze *(Entführung aus dem Serail),* Pamina *(Zauberflöte);* OFFENBACH: Périchole; PUCCINI: Liù *(Turandot);* ROSSINI: Rosina *(Barbiere di Siviglia);* SMETANA: Marie *(Bartered Bride);* STRAUSS, J: Rosalinde *(Fledermaus);* STRAVINSKY: Anne Trulove *(Rake's Progress);* VERDI: Nannetta *(Falstaff),* Violetta *(Traviata);* WAGNER: Gutrune★ *(Götterdämmerung).* **World premieres:** WARD: Katie

(*Lady from Colorado*) Central City Fest 1964; BARBER: Octavia (*Antony and Cleopatra*) Met Opera 1966. Gives recitals. Appears with symphony orchestra. **Res:** 245 W 107 St, New York, NY, USA. Mgmt: HJH/USA.

PRÊTRE, GEORGES. Conductor of opera and symphony; composer. French. Born 14 Aug 1924, Douai. Married. Two children. Studied: Consv National, Paris; incl piano, trumpet and voice. **Operatic debut:** Opéra de Marseille 1946. Symphonic debut: Société des Concerts, Paris. Awards: Chevalier Légion d'Honneur 1971.

Conducted with major companies in ARG: Buenos Aires; AUS: Graz, Salzburg Fest, Vienna Staatsoper; BEL: Brussels; CAN: Montreal/Quebec; CZE: Brno, Prague National; DEN: Copenhagen; FRA: aix-en-Provence Fest, Fordeaux, Lyon, Marseille, Orange Fest, Paris, Strasbourg, Toulouse; FR GER: Bonn, Cologne, Düsseldorf-Duisburg, Frankfurt, Hamburg, Hannover, Karlsruhe, Munich Staatsoper; HOL: Amsterdam; ISR: Tel Aviv; ITA: Florence Maggio & Comunale, Milan La Scala, Naples, Rome Opera, Turin, Venice; MON: Monte Carlo; POR: Lisbon; ROM: Bucharest; SPA: Barcelona, Majorca; SWI: Geneva Grand Théâtre; UK: London Royal; USSR: Kiev, Leningrad Kirov; USA: Chicago Lyric, Memphis, Miami, New York Met, San Francisco Opera. Operas with these companies incl ADAM: *Postillon de Lonjumeau, Si j'étais roi;* BEETHOVEN: *Fidelio;* BELLINI: *Norma, Puritani, Sonnambula;* BERG: *Wozzeck;* BERLIOZ: *Béatrice et Bénédict★, Benvenuto Cellini★, Damnation de Faust★, Troyens★;* BIZET: *Carmen★, Jolie Fille de Perth, Pêcheurs de perles;* BOIELDIEU: *Dame blanche;* BOITO: *Mefistofele;* BORODIN: *Prince Igor;* CHABRIER: *Roi malgré lui;* CHARPENTIER: *Louise;* CHERUBINI: *Medea★;* CILEA: *A. Lecouvreur;* DALLA-PICCOLA: *Volo di notte;* DEBUSSY: *Enfant prodigue★, Pelléas et Mélisande★;* DELIBES: *Lakmé★, Roi l'a dit★;* DONIZETTI: *Anna Bolena, Elisir, Favorite, Lucia, Maria Stuarda;* DUKAS: *Ariane et Barbe Bleue;* FALLA: *Retablo de Maese Pedro, Vica breve;* GERSHWIN: *Porgy and Bess;* GIORDANO: *Andrea Chénier;* GLUCK: *Alceste, Armide, Iphigénie en Aulide, Iphigénie en Tauride, Orfeo ed Euridice★;* GOUNOD: *Faust★, Mireille★, Roméo et Juliette★;* HALEVY: *Juive;* HAYDN: *Philemon und Baucis;* HINDEMITH: *Mathis der Maler;* HONEGGER: *Antigone;* HUMPERDINCK: *Hänsel und Gretel;* IBERT: *Angélique;* LALO: *Roi d'Ys★;* LECOCQ: *Fille de Madame Angot;* LEONCAVALLO: *Pagliacci;* MASCAGNI: *Cavalleria rusticana★;* MASSENET: *Don Quichotte★, Hérodiade★, Jongleur de Notre Dame, Manon★, Navarraise, Portrait de Manon★, Sappho, Thaïs, Werther★;* MEYERBEER: *Africaine, Huguenots, Prophète;* MONTEVERDI: *Incoronazione di Poppea;* MOZART: *Così fan tutte, Don Giovanni, Idomeneo, Nozze di Figaro, Zauberflöte;* MUSSORGSKY: *Boris Godunov, Khovanshchina★;* OFFENBACH: *Contes d'Hoffmann★, Périchole;* PONCHIELLI: *Gioconda;* POULENC: *Dialogues des Carmélites★, Mamelles de Tirésias★;* PROKOFIEV: *Fiery Angel;* PUCCINI: *Bohème★, Fanciulla del West, Gianni Schicchi, Butterfly, Manon Lescaut, Tosca★, Tu-*randot★; RABAUD: *Mârouf;* RAMEAU: *Castor et Pollux;* RAVEL: *Enfant et les sortilèges★, Heure espagnole★;* RIMSKY-KORSAKOV: *Coq d'or;* ROSSINI: *Barbiere di Siviglia, Cenerentola, Gazza ladra, Guillaume Tell, Italiana in Algeri, Moïse, Otello, Scala di seta, Semiramide;* SAINT-SAENS: *Samson et Dalila★;* SCHOENBERG: *Erwartung;* SMETANA: *Bartered Bride;* STRAUSS, J: *Fledermaus;* STRAUSS, R: *Arabella, Ariadne auf Naxos, Capriccio★, Elektra, Rosenkavalier★, Salome;* STRAVINSKY: *Oedipus Rex, Perséphone★;* TCHAIKOVSKY: *Eugene Onegin, Pique Dame;* VERDI: *Aida★, Attila, Ballo in maschera, Don Carlo★, Ernani, Falstaff, Luisa Miller, Macbeth, Nabucco, Otello★, Rigoletto, Traviata★, Trovatore, Vespri;* WAGNER: *Fliegende Holländer★, Lohengrin, Meistersinger, Parsifal, Rheingold, Walküre, Siegfried, Tannhäuser, Tristan und Isolde;* WEBER: *Oberon.* **World premieres:** POULENC: *Voix humaine* Paris 1959; BECAUD: *Opéra d'Aran* Paris 1962; ROSSELLINI: *Reine morte* Monte Carlo 1973. Conducted major orch in Europe, USA/Canada. **Res:** Louveciennes, France. Mgmt: GLZ/FRA; CAM/USA.

PREVEDI, BRUNO. Dramatic tenor. Italian. Born 21 Dec 1928, Revere, Mantua. Wife Iride. One child. Studied: Mo Vladimiro Badiali, Mo Alberto Soresina. **Debut:** Turiddu (*Cavalleria rusticana*) Teatro Nuovo, Milan 1959. Previous occupations: technical examiner, Fiat, Milan. Awards: Hon Admiral, State of Texas; Hon Texas Citizen.

Sang with major companies in ARG: Buenos Aires; AUS: Vienna Staatsoper; CAN: Montreal/Quebec; FRA: Paris, Strasbourg; GRE: Athens Fest; FR GER: Berlin Deutsche Oper, Frankfurt, Hamburg, Munich Staatsoper, Wiesbaden; HUN: Budapest; ITA: Bologna, Florence Maggio & Comunale, Genoa, Milan La Scala, Naples, Palermo, Parma, Rome Opera & Caracalla, Turin, Venice, Verona Arena; MEX: Mexico City; S AFR: Johannesburg; SPA: Barcelona; SWI: Zurich; UK: Edinburgh Fest, London Royal; USSR: Moscow; USA: Boston, Dallas, Miami, New York Met, Philadelphia Grand & Lyric; YUG: Dubrovnik, Belgrade. Roles with these companies incl BELLINI: Pollione★ (*Norma*); CHERUBINI: Giasone★‡ (*Medea*); CILEA: Maurizio (*A. Lecouvreur*); GIORDANO: Andrea Chénier★, Loris Ipanov (*Fedora*); GLUCK: Admetos (*Alceste*); LEONCAVALLO: Canio★ (*Pagliacci*); MASCAGNI: Turiddu★ (*Cavalleria rusticana*); PUCCINI: Dick Johnson (*Fanciulla del West*), Pinkerton (*Butterfly*), Cavaradossi (*Tosca*), Calaf (*Turandot*); SPONTINI: Fernand Cortez★; VERDI: Radames★ (*Aida*), Foresto★ (*Attila*), Riccardo (*Ballo in maschera*), Don Carlo★, Jacopo Foscari★ (*Due Foscari*), Ernani★, Don Alvaro★ (*Forza del destino*), Ismaele‡ (*Nabucco*), Gabriele★ (*Simon Boccanegra*), Alfredo (*Traviata*), Manrico★ (*Trovatore*). Also VERDI: Macduff (*Macbeth*); BOITO: Nerone; RACHMANINOFF: Paolo (*Francesca da Rimini*); MUSSORGSKY: Dimitri (*Boris Godunov*); SPONTINI: Filippo (*Agnese di Hohenstaufen*). Recorded for: London/Decca. Video/Film: Cavaradossi (*Tosca*).

PREVIN, ANDRÉ. Conductor of opera and symphony; composer. American. Mus Dir, London

Symph Orch, UK 1968- ; Pittsburgh Symph, PA, USA 1976- . Born 6 Apr 1930, Berlin, Germany. Wife Mia Farrow, occupation actress. Five children. Studied: Berlin Consv; Pierre Monteux, Mario Castelnuovo-Tedesco; incl piano. Plays the piano. Symphonic debut: St Louis Symph, MO, USA 1960. **Conducted with major companies in** AUS: Salzburg Fest; BEL: Brussels; CZE: Prague National; DEN: Copenhagen; UK: Aldeburgh Fest, Edinburgh Fest, London Royal. **Operas with these companies incl** BEETHOVEN: *Fidelio*; BERLIOZ: *Béatrice et Bénédict*; BRITTEN: *Owen Wingrave*; GERSHWIN: *Porgy and Bess*; HINDEMITH: *Hin und zurück*; MOZART: *Schauspieldirektor*, *Re pastore*; ORFF: *Carmina burana*; POULENC: *Voix humaine*; RAVEL: *Enfant et les sortilèges*; STRAUSS, R: *Salome*. Also WALTON: *Troilus and Cressida*. Recorded for EMI, RCA. Conducted major orch in Europe, USA/Canada, Asia. Previous positions as Mus Dir with major orch: Houston Symph, TX, USA 1966-68. **Res:** Leigh/Surrey, UK. **Mgmt:** HPL/UK; CAM/USA.

PREVITALI, FERNANDO. Conductor of opera and symphony; composer. Italian. Art Dir & Resident Cond, Teatro Carlo Felice, Genoa; Res Cond, San Carlo Opera, Naples. Also Mus Dir, Orch di Santa Cecilia, Rome 1953- . Born 16 Feb 1907, Adria, Italy. Studied: Consv of Turin, Franco Alfano; incl piano, cello & organ. Awards: Commdr of the Order of Cedar, Lebanon. Previous adm positions in opera: Dir, Maggio Musicale, Florence 1928-36; Chief Cond, La Scala, Milan 1942-43, 1946-48; Music Dir, Teatro Regio, Turin 1971-73. **Conducted with major companies in** ARG: Buenos Aires; ITA: Florence Maggio & Comunale, Genoa, Milan La Scala, Naples, Palermo, Rome Opera, Trieste, Turin, Venice, Verona Arena; et al. **Operas with these companies incl** BELLINI: *Norma;* BERLIOZ: *Benvenuto Cellini;* BIZET: *Carmen;* BUSONI: *Doktor Faust, Turandot;* CHERUBINI: *Medea;* CILEA: *A. Lecouvreur;* DONIZETTI: *Don Pasquale, Elisir, Favorite, Lucia;* LEONCAVALLO: *Pagliacci;* MASCAGNI: *Cavalleria rusticana;* MOZART: *Nozze di Figaro‡;* PONCHIELLI: *Gioconda;* PUCCINI: *Bohème, Fanciulla del West, Gianni Schicchi, Butterfly, Manon Lescaut, Suor Angelica, Tabarro, Tosca, Turandot;* ROSSINI: *Barbiere di Siviglia‡, Cenerentola, Guillaume Tell, Italiana in Algeri;* VERDI: *Aida, Ballo in maschera, Don Carlo‡, Ernani, Falstaff, Forza del destino, Luisa Miller, Macbeth, Nabucco, Otello, Rigoletto, Simon Boccanegra, Traviata‡, Trovatore‡, Vespri;* et al. Also VERDI: *Battaglia di Legnano;* ROTA: *Visita meravigliosa;* BUSONI: *Brautwahl;* PAISIELLO: *Osteria di Marechiaro.* **World premieres:** NAPOLI: *Dubrowsky II* San Carlo, Naples 1973; DALLAPICCOLA: *Volo di notte* Florence 1940; GHEDINI: *Re Hassan* Venice 1939, *Le baccanti* La Scala, Milan 1948. Conducted major orch in Europe, USA/Canada. Previous positions as Mus Dir with major orch: RAI Symph Orch, Rome 1935-53.

PREY, HERMANN. Lyric baritone. German. Born 11 Jul 1929, Berlin. Wife Barbara Pniok. Three children. Studied: Hochschule für Musik, Prof Günter Baum, Berlin; Harry Gottschalk, Berlin. **Debut:** Moruccio (*Tiefland*) Hessische Oper, Wiesbaden 1952. Awards: First Prize Meistersinger Contest, Nürnberg 1952; Bundesverdienstkreuz, FR Ger 1974. **Sang with major companies in** ARG: Buenos Aires; AUS: Bregenz Fest, Graz, Salzburg Fest, Vienna Staatsoper; FRA: Aix-en-Provence Fest; FR GER: Bayreuth Fest, Berlin Deutsche Oper, Cologne. Düsseldorf-Duisburg, Frankfurt, Hamburg, Munich Staatsoper, Stuttgart, Wiesbaden; ITA: Milan La Scala; UK: London Royal; USA: Boston, Chicago, Houston, New York Met, San Francisco Opera. **Roles with these companies incl** DALLAPICCOLA: Il Prigioniero; DONIZETTI: Dott Malatesta‡ (*Don Pasquale*); GLUCK: Agamemnon (*Iphigénie en Aulide*), Oreste (*Iphigénie en Tauride*); LORTZING: Graf Eberbach‡ (*Wildschütz*), Peter I*‡ (*Zar und Zimmermann*); MOZART: Guglielmo*‡ (*Così fan tutte*), Don Giovanni, Conte Almaviva* & Figaro‡ (*Nozze di Figaro*), Papageno*‡ (*Zauberflöte*); OFFENBACH: Don Andres (*Périchole*); ORFF: Solo*‡ (*Carmina burana*); PUCCINI: Marcello (*Bohème*), Sharpless‡ (*Butterfly*); ROSSINI: Figaro*‡ (*Barbiere di Siviglia*); STRAUSS, R: Olivier‡ (*Capriccio*), Robert Storch (*Intermezzo*); TCHAIKOVSKY: Eugene Onegin‡; VERDI: Renato (*Ballo in maschera*), Rodrigo (*Don Carlo*), Ford (*Falstaff*), Don Carlo (*Forza del destino*), Germont* (*Traviata*); WAGNER: Wolfram* (*Tannhäuser*). Also MOZART: Nardo‡ (*Finta giardiniera*). Recorded for: Decca, DG, EMI, RCA, Philips, Ariola-Eurodisc, BASF. Video/Film: Figaro (*Barbiere di Siviglia*); (*Turco in Italia*); Graf Eberbach (*Wildschütz*); Peter (*Zar und Zimmermann*); Eugene Onegin; (*Carmina burana*); Dott Malatesta (*Don Pasquale*); Guglielmo (*Così fan tutte*). Gives recitals. Appears with symphony orchestra. **Res:** Fichtenstr 14, D-8033 Krailling, FR Ger. **Mgmt:** LNG/FRG; JMH/POR.

PRICE, HENRY PASCHAL. Lyric tenor. American. Born 18 Oct 1945, Oakland, CA, USA. Wife Martha. One child. Studied: No Texas State Univ, Eugene Conley, Denton, TX; Oren Brown, Boris Goldovsky, New York. **Debut:** Alfredo (*Traviata*) Goldovsky Opera Theater 1970. Awards: Ntl Opera Inst, Young Singer Grant 1972-73. **Sang with major companies in** USA: Kansas City, Lake George. **Roles with these companies incl** MOZART: Tamino* (*Zauberflöte*); ROSSINI: Almaviva* (*Barbiere di Siviglia*); STRAUSS, J: Alfred* (*Fledermaus*); VERDI: Fenton* (*Falstaff*), Duca di Mantova* (*Rigoletto*). Gives recitals. Appears with symphony orchestra. **Res:** 54 W 71 St, New York, NY, USA.

PRICE, LEONTYNE; née Mary Leontyne Price. Lirico spinto soprano. American. Resident mem: Metropolitan Opera, New York. Born 10 Feb 1927, Laurel, MS, USA. Divorced. Studied: Mme Florence Page Kimball, Juilliard School. **Debut:** Mme Lidoine (*Dialogues des Carmélites*) San Francisco Opera 1957. Awards: Presidential Medal of Freedom, President of the United States; Spingarn Medal, NAACP; 15 Grammy Awds, Ntl

Acad Recording Arts & Sciences; Leontyne Price Library, Rust Coll, Holly Springs, MS.

Sang with major companies in ARG: Buenos Aires; AUS: Salzburg Fest, Vienna Staatsoper & Volksoper; FRA: Paris; FR GER: Berlin Deutsche Oper, Hamburg; ITA: Milan La Scala, Rome Opera, Verona Arena; UK: London Royal; USA: Chicago, New York Met, Philadelphia Lyric, San Francisco Opera. **Roles with these companies incl** GERSHWIN: Bess; MASSENET: Thaïs; MOZART: Fiordiligi‡ (*Così fan tutte*), Donna Anna★ & Donna Elvira‡ (*Don Giovanni*), Pamina (*Zauberflöte*); ORFF: Kluge; POULENC: Mme Lidoine (*Dialogues des Carmélites*); PUCCINI: Minnie (*Fanciulla del West*), Cio-Cio-San★‡ (*Butterfly*), Manon Lescaut★, Giorgetta★‡ (*Tabarro*), Tosca‡, Liù (*Turandot*); TCHAIKOVSKY: Tatiana (*Eugene Onegin*); VERDI: Aida★‡, Amelia‡ (*Ballo in maschera*), Donna Elvira‡ (*Ernani*), Leonora★‡ (*Forza del destino*), Leonora‡ (*Trovatore*). **World premieres:** BARBER: Cleopatra (*Antony and Cleopatra*) Metropolitan Opera 1966. Recorded for: RCA. Rec only: Carmen. Gives recitals. Appears with symphony orchestra. Mgmt: DIL/USA.

PRICE, MARGARET BERENICE. Lyric soprano. British. Born 13 Apr 1941, Blackwood, Wales, UK. Single. Studied: Trinity Coll of Music, London. **Debut:** Cherubino (*Nozze di Figaro*) Welsh National Opera. Awards: Elisabeth Schumann Prize for Lieder; Silver Medal, Worshipful Co of Musicians; Ricordi Opera Prize; Hon Fllshp & Kennedy Scott Schlshp, Trinity Coll of Music. **Sang with major companies in** AUS: Salzburg Fest, Vienna Staatsoper; BEL: Brussels; CAN: Montreal/Quebec; CZE: Prague National; FRA: Paris; FR GER: Cologne, Hamburg, Munich Staatsoper; ITA: Milan La Scala; POR: Lisbon; SPA: Barcelona; UK: Aldeburgh Fest, Cardiff Welsh, Glasgow Scottish, Glyndebourne Fest, London Royal; USA: Chicago, San Francisco Opera. **Roles with these companies incl** BEETHOVEN: Marzelline (*Fidelio*); BRITTEN: Tytania (*Midsummer Night*); FALLA: Salud (*Vida breve*); HANDEL: Galatea, Semele; MASSENET: Cendrillon; MOZART: Servilia (*Clemenza di Tito*), Fiordiligi‡ (*Così fan tutte*), Donna Anna & Zerlina (*Don Giovanni*), Konstanze (*Entführung aus dem Serail*), Mlle Silberklang (*Schauspieldirektor*), Contessa & Cherubino (*Nozze di Figaro*), Pamina (*Zauberflöte*); PUCCINI: Mimi (*Bohème*); TCHAIKOVSKY: Tatiana (*Eugene Onegin*); VERDI: Nannetta (*Falstaff*), Desdemona (*Otello*), Amelia (*Simon Boccanegra*); WEBER: Agathe (*Freischütz*). Recorded for: EMI. Gives recitals. Appears with symphony orchestra. **Res:** 24 Marylebone High Str, London, UK.

PRICE, PERRY. Lyric tenor. American. Resident mem: Städtische Bühnen, Augsburg, FR Ger. Born 13 Oct 1942, York, PA, USA. Wife Heather Thomson, occupation opera singer, soprano. One child. Studied: Univ of Houston, John Druary, TX; Otakar Kraus, London; Ester Andreas, Richard Fredricks, Otto Guth, New York. **Debut:** Des Grieux (*Manon*) San Francisco Op Merola Prgr 1964. Previous occupations: boat manufacturing; grain elevator construction; music teacher. Awards: First Gropper Awd, San Francisco Op

Merola Prgr; Finalist Prize Winner Met Op Ntl Counc Aud 1969; Ntl Opera Inst Grant 1973-74.

Sang with major companies in CAN: Montreal/Quebec, Toronto, Vancouver; POR: Lisbon; USA: Fort Worth, Houston, Kentucky, New York City Opera, Philadelphia Lyric, Portland, San Diego, S Francisco Spr Op. **Roles with these cos incl** BEETHOVEN: Jacquino (*Fidelio*); CORNELIUS: Nureddin★ (*Barbier von Bagdad*); DONIZETTI: Nemorino (*Elisir*), Edgardo (*Lucia*); FLOYD: Ballad Singer (*Of Mice and Men*); GLINKA: Bogdan (*Life for the Tsar*); GOUNOD: Faust; LEONCAVALLO: Beppe★ (*Pagliacci*); MASSENET: Des Grieux★ (*Manon*), Werther★; MOZART: Ferrando (*Così fan tutte*), Don Ottavio (*Don Giovanni*), Tamino★ (*Zauberflöte*); OFFENBACH: Hoffmann★; PUCCINI: Prunier & Ruggero★ (*Rondine*); ROSSINI: Almaviva★ (*Barbiere di Siviglia*), Lindoro★ (*Italiana in Algeri*); STRAUSS, J: Alfred (*Fledermaus*); VERDI: Duca di Mantova (*Rigoletto*), Alfredo★ (*Traviata*); WAGNER: Walther v d Vogelweide★ (*Tannhäuser*). Gives recitals. Appears with symphony orchestra. Teaches voice. **Res:** Ludwigstr 23, 89 Augsburg, FR Ger; or 20 Washington Ave, Danbury, CT, USA. Mgmt: LLF/USA; SLZ/FRG.

PRIEST, JOHN; né John Walter Kotschnig. American. Tech Dir, San Francisco Opera Assn & Spring Opera Theater, War Memorial Opera House, San Francisco, CA 94102, USA. In charge of technical matters. Born 17 Aug 1931, Geneva, Switzerland. Wife Mary, occupation actress. Three children. Studied: Cornell Univ, Ithaca, NY, USA; Royal Acad of Dram Art, London. Previous occupations: actor. Previous positions, primarily theatrical: Asst Tech Dir, Olney Theatre, MD, USA 1958-65; Founder/Dir, John Priest Assoc, Scenic Studio, Washington, DC 1960-66. In present position since 1966. **Res:** Mill Valley, CA, USA.

PRIKOPA, HERBERT. Tenore buffo. Austrian. Resident mem: Volksoper, Vienna. Born 30 Nov 1935, Vienna. Divorced. Studied: Prof Elisabeth Rado. **Debut:** Frantz (*Contes d'Hoffmann*) Volksoper, Vienna 1958. Previous occupations: pianist, conductor.

Sang with major companies in AUS: Bregenz Fest, Graz, Vienna Staatsoper & Volksoper; SWI: Zurich. **Roles with these companies incl** ADAM: Marquis de Corcy (*Postillon de Lonjumeau*); HAYDN: Cecco★ (*Mondo della luna*); HUMPERDINCK: Hexe★ (*Hänsel und Gretel*). Also WEILL: Jack★ (*Aufstieg und Fall der Stadt Mahagonny*); WOLF-FERRARI: Donna Pasqua★ (*Campiello*); MOZART: Podestà★ (*Finta giardiniera*); SALMHOFER: Koljie (*Iwan Tarassenko*). **World premieres:** WEISHAPPEL: Theaterdirektor (*König Nicolo*) Volksoper, Vienna 1972. Recorded for: Westminster. Video/Film: Cecco (*Mondo della luna*). Appears with symphony orchestra. Teaches voice. Coaches repertoire. **Res:** Conte Cortistr 1, A3021 Pressbaum bei Wien, Austria.

PRING, KATHERINE. Dramatic mezzo-soprano. British. Resident mem; English National Opera, London. Born 4 Jun 1940, Brighton, UK. Husband

R Adams, occupation cellist, London Symphony Orch. Studied: Royal Coll of Music, Ruth Packer, London; Consv de Musique, Maria Carpi, Geneva, Switzerland; Luigi Ricci, Rome; Prof Kaiser-Breme, Essen, FR Ger. Debut: Flora (*Traviata*) Grand Théâtre, Geneva 1966.

Sang with major companies in FR GER: Bayreuth Fest; SWI: Geneva; UK: London Royal Opera & English National. Roles with these companies incl BIZET: Carmen; BRITTEN; Kate Julian (*Owen Wingrave*); CHERUBINI: Neris (*Medea*); HENZE: Agave (*Bassariden*); MONTEVERDI: Poppea (*Incoronazione di Poppea*); MOZART: Dorabella (*Così fan tutte*); PUCCINI: Suzuki (*Butterfly*); STRAUSS, J: Prinz Orlovsky (*Fledermaus*); STRAVINSKY: Jocasta (*Oedipus Rex*); TIPPETT: Thea (*Knot Garden*); VERDI: Eboli (*Don Carlo*), Preziosilla (*Forza del destino*), Azucena; WAGNER: Fricka (*Rheingold‡, Walküre*), Waltraute (*Götterdämmerung*). Recorded for: EMI. Gives recitals. Appears with symphony orchestra. Res: London, UK. Mgmt: ASK/UK; PAS/FRG.

PRINGLE, JOHN DAVID. Lyric baritone. Australian. Resident mem: Australian Opera, Sydney. Born 17 Oct 1938, Melbourne. Wife Marian. Two children. Studied: Anni Portnoj, Melbourne; Luigi Ricci, Rome. Debut: Frank (*Fledermaus*) Australian Opera 1967. Previous occupations: pharmacist. Awards: *Sun* Aria Awd, Melbourne 1967; runner-up Pan-Pacific Reg Met Aud 1967; Adelaide Aria Awd 1966; Schlshp Italian Inst of Cultural Affairs.

Sang with major companies in AUSTRL: Sydney. Roles with these companies incl DONIZETTI: Belcore (*Elisir*); MOZART: Don Giovanni⋆, Conte Almaviva⋆ (*Nozze di Figaro*), Papageno⋆ (*Zauberflöte*); PROKOFIEV: Prince Andrei Bolkonsky⋆ (*War and Peace*); PUCCINI: Marcello⋆ (*Bohème*); ROSSINI: Figaro⋆ (*Barbiere di Siviglia*); STRAVINSKY: Nick Shadow (*Rake's Progress*); VERDI: Renato (*Ballo in maschera*), Rodrigo (*Don Carlo*), Ford (*Falstaff*), Don Carlo⋆ (*Forza del destino*). Also BRITTEN: Tarquinius⋆ (*Rape of Lucretia*); STRAUSS, R: Harlekin⋆ (*Ariadne auf Naxos*); MOZART: Sprecher (*Zauberflöte*). Gives recitals. Appears with symphony orchestra. Res: 45 Matlock St, Canterbury/Victoria, 3126 Melbourne, Australia. Mgmt: AIM/UK.

PRITCHARD, JOHN MICHAEL. Conductor of opera and symphony. British. Music Dir & Resident Cond, Glyndebourne Fest Opera, Lewes/Sussex. Born 5 Feb 1921, London. Single. Studied: var music establishments; Fritz Busch; incl piano & viola. Plays the piano & harpsichord. Operatic training as repetiteur, asst cond & chorus master at Glyndebourne Fest Opera 1949-53. Operatic debut: *Bohème* Carl Rosa Op Co, Bradford 1948. Symphonic debut: Jacques String Orch, London 1946. Previous occupations: wartime work in insurance. Awards: Commander of the British Empire 1962, HRH Queen Elizabeth II; Shakespeare Prize for Spec Distinction in Cultural Affairs 1975; FVS Institute, Hamburg. Previous adm positions in opera; Art Advisor & Principal Cond, Glynde-

bourne Opera 1963-68; Conseiller Artistique, Opéra de Marseille, France 1969-71.

Conducted with major companies in ARG: Buenos Aires; AUSTRL: Sydney; AUS: Salzburg Fest, Vienna Staatsoper; FRA: Aix-en-Provence Fest, Marseille; FR GER: Berlin Deutsche Oper, Cologne, Munich Staatsoper; ITA: Naples; SWI: Geneva; UK: Edinburgh Fest, Glyndebourne Fest, London Royal; USA: Chicago, New York Met, San Francisco Opera. Operas with these companies incl BELLINI: *Norma, Puritani*; BERG: *Wozzeck*; BERLIOZ: *Benvenuto Cellini, Damnation de Faust, Troyens*; BIZET: *Carmen, Docteur Miracle*; BRITTEN: *Gloriana, Peter Grimes⋆*; BUSONI: *Arlecchino*; CIMAROSA: *Matrimonio segreto*; DEBUSSY: *Pelléas et Mélisande*; DONIZETTI: *Don Pasquale⋆, Elisir, Lucia‡*; EINEM: *Besuch der alten Dame⋆*; FALLA: *Retablo de Maese Pedro*; GLUCK: *Alceste, Iphigénie en Aulide, Iphigénie en Tauride, Orfeo ed Euridice*; GOUNOD: *Faust*; HAYDN: *Mondo della luna*; HENZE: *Elegy for Young Lovers*; HUMPERDINCK: *Hänsel und Gretel*; IBERT: *Angélique*; LEONCAVALLO: *Pagliacci*; MARTINU: *Comedy on the Bridge*; MASCAGNI: *Cavalleria rusticana*; MASSENET: *Manon*; MILHAUD: *Pauvre matelot*; MONTEVERDI: *Incoronazione di Poppea‡*; MOZART: *Clemenza di Tito⋆, Così fan tutte⋆, Don Giovanni⋆, Entführung aus dem Serail⋆, Idomeneo⋆‡, Nozze di Figaro⋆, Schauspieldirektor, Zauberflöte⋆*; OFFENBACH: *Contes d'Hoffmann*; ORFF: *Carmina burana⋆*; PERGOLESI: *Serva padrona*; POULENC: *Voix humaine*; PUCCINI: *Bohème, Gianni Schicchi, Butterfly, Suor Angelica, Tabarro, Tosca, Turandot*; PURCELL: *Dido and Aeneas*; RAVEL: *Heure espagnole*; RIMSKY-KORSAKOV: *Coq d'or*; ROSSINI: *Barbiere di Siviglia⋆, Cenerentola, Comte Ory, Gazza ladra, Italiana in Algeri, Pietra del paragone, Scala di seta*; SCHOENBERG: *Erwartung*; STRAUSS, J: *Fledermaus*; STRAUSS, R: *Ariadne auf Naxos⋆, Capriccio⋆, Intermezzo⋆, Rosenkavalier*; STRAVINSKY: *Perséphone, Rake's Progress*; TCHAIKOVSKY: *Eugene Onegin, Pique Dame*; VAUGHAN WILLIAMS: *Hugh the Drover, Riders to the Sea*; VERDI: *Aida, Attila, Ballo in maschera, Don Carlo⋆, Falstaff, Forza del destino, Macbeth⋆, Nabucco, Rigoletto, Traviata⋆, Trovatore*; WAGNER: *Lohengrin*; WEBER: *Oberon*; WOLF-FERRARI: *Segreto di Susanna*. World premieres: BRITTEN: *Gloriana* 1953; TIPPETT: *Midsummer Marriage* 1955, *King Priam* 1962; all at Royal Opera Covent Garden, London. Recorded for EMI/Angel; Decca/London. Conducted major orch in Europe, USA/Canada, Cent/S America, Asia, Africa, Austrl. Previous positions as Mus Dir with major orch: Royal Liverpool Phil, UK 1956-62; London Phil 1962-66. Mgmt: AIM/UK; CAM/USA.

PROTERO, DODI; née Dorothy Ann McIlraith. Lyric coloratura soprano. Canadian. Born 13 Mar 1937, Toronto. Husband Alan P Crofoot, occupation opera singer. Studied: James Rosselino, Toronto; Toti Dal Monte, Venice; Lorenz Fehenberger, Munich; Ferdinand Grossmann, Vienna. Debut: Zweiter Knabe (*Zauberflöte*) San Carlo Opera, Naples 1956. Awards: Canada

Counc Fllshps 1967, 1968, 1973; Schlshp Awd Mozarteum Salzburg 1956-57; Schlshp Awd Accad Chigiana, Siena, Italy 1955.

Sang with major companies in AUS: Salzburg Fest; CAN: Toronto, Vancouver; FR GER: Bielefeld, Cologne, Wuppertal; ITA: Naples, Palermo, Rome; UK: Glyndebourne Fest, London English National; USA: Hartford, New Orleans, Pittsburgh, San Antonio. Roles with these companies incl BEETHOVEN: Marzelline* (Fidelio); BIZET: Micaëla (Carmen); DONIZETTI: Norina* (Don Pasquale), Adina (Elisir), Lucia, Rita; FLOTOW: Lady Harriet (Martha); HAYDN: Clarissa (Mondo della luna); HUMPERDINCK: Gretel; MASSENET: Sophie (Werther); MENOTTI: Lucy (Telephone); MOZART: Despina* (Così fan tutte), Zerlina (Don Giovanni), Violante‡ & Arminda & Serpetta (Finta giardiniera), Susanna (Nozze di Figaro); NICOLAI: Frau Fluth & Aennchen (Lustigen Weiber); PERGOLESI: Serpina‡ (Serva padrona); PUCCINI: Mimi & Musetta* (Bohème), Lauretta (Gianni Schicchi); ROSSINI: Rosina* (Barbiere di Siviglia), Elvira (Italiana in Algeri); STRAUSS, J: Adele* (Fledermaus); STRAVINSKY: Parasha (Mavra); VERDI: Oscar (Ballo in maschera), Gilda (Rigoletto), Violetta (Traviata); WOLF-FERRARI: Susanna (Segreto di Susanna). Also MOZART: Silvia (Ascanio in Alba); d'ALBERT: Nuri‡ (Tiefland). World premieres: SORESINA: La Cameriera (L'Amuleto) Accademia Chigiana, Siena, Italy 1954; LIZZI: Pispoletta (Pantea) Massimo, Palermo 1956; PANNELL: Oona (Luck of Ginger Coffey) Canadian Opera Co, Toronto 1967. Recorded for: Philips. Video/Film: Susanna (Nozze di Figaro); Clarissa (Mondo della luna); Esmeralda (Bartered Bride). Gives recitals. Appears with symphony orchestra. Teaches voice. On faculty of School of Fine Arts, Banff, Alta, Canada. Res: 1306 Second Ave, New York, NY 10021, USA. Mgmt: SAM/USA.

PROTIC, PREDRAG ZIVOJIN. Lyric tenor. Yugoslavian. Resident mem: Belgrade Opera. Born 15 Oct 1945, Belgrade, Yugoslavia. Divorced. One child. Studjed: Prof Nikola Cvejic, Belgrade. Debut: Rodolfo (Bohème) Belgrade Opera. Awards: Hon Diploma, Conc Intl Sofia 1973.

Sang with major companies in BUL: Sofia. Roles with these companies incl BORODIN: Vladimir* (Prince Igor); BRITTEN: Albert Herring*; DONIZETTI: Nemorino* (Elisir); GOUNOD: Faust*; MASSENET: Werther*; MOZART: Tamino* (Zauberflöte); ORFF: Solo* (Carmina burana); PUCCINI: Rodolfo* (Bohème); ROSSINI: Almaviva* (Barbiere di Siviglia); STRAUSS, R: Ein Sänger* (Rosenkavalier); VERDI: Riccardo* (Ballo in maschera), Duca di Mantova* (Rigoletto), Alfredo* (Traviata). Also RAVEL: Gonzalve (Heure espagnole); KUSSER: Daliso (Erindo). Gives recitals. Appears with symphony orchestra. Res: Jurija Gagarina 263, Belgrade, Yugoslavia.

PROTTI, ALDO. Italian baritone. Italian. Born 19 Jul 1920, Cremona, Italy. Wife Adriana Verzellesi. One daughter. Studied: Consv di Parma. Debut: Figaro (Barbiere di Siviglia) Teatro Pergolesi, Iesi, Italy 1948. Previous occupations: marble worker; asst machinist for Italian State Railroad. Awards:

two Japanese honors 1959, 1961; Cavaliere della Repubblica Ital 1969; Viotti d'oro 1960; Intl Prize Vercelli 1961; Palcoscenico d'oro, Mantua 1967; Conc: Teatro alla Scala, ENAL Bologna, RAI Milan.

Sang with major companies in ARG: Buenos Aires; AUS: Bregenz Fest, Graz, Vienna Staatsoper; BEL: Brussels, Liège; CAN: Montreal/Quebec; CZE: Prague National; DEN: Copenhagen; FRA: Bordeaux, Marseille, Nice, Paris, Rouen, Toulouse; GRE: Athens National & Festival; FR GER: Berlin Deutsche Oper, Cologne, Frankfurt, Hannover, Kassel, Munich Staatsoper & Gärtnerplatz, Nürnberg, Stuttgart, Wiesbaden; HOL: Amsterdam; HUN: Budapest; ITA: Bologna, Florence Maggio & Comunale, Genoa, Milan La Scala, Naples, Palermo, Parma, Rome Opera & Caracalla, Trieste, Turin, Venice, Verona; JPN: Tokyo Fujiwara & Niki Kai; MEX: Mexico City; MON: Monte Carlo; POR: Lisbon; ROM: Bucharest; S AFR: Johannesburg; SPA: Barcelona; SWI: Basel, Zurich; USA: Chicago, New York City Opera, Philadelphia Lyric. Roles with these companies incl BEETHOVEN: Don Pizarro* (Fidelio); BELLINI: Sir Richard (Puritani); BIZET: Escamillo* (Carmen); CATALANI: Vincenzo Gellner (Wally); DONIZETTI: Alfonse (Favorite), Antonio (Linda di Chamounix), Enrico* (Lucia); GIORDANO: Carlo Gérard* (Andrea Chénier); GOUNOD: Valentin (Faust); LEONCAVALLO: Tonio* (Pagliacci); MASCAGNI: Alfio* (Cavalleria rusticana); MEYERBEER: Nelusco (Africaine); PONCHIELLI: Barnaba* (Gioconda); PUCCINI: Marcello* (Bohème), Sharpless* (Butterfly), Scarpia* (Tosca); ROSSINI: Figaro* (Barbiere di Siviglia); VERDI: Amonasro* (Aida), Egberto (Aroldo), Renato* (Ballo in maschera), Rodrigo (Don Carlo), Don Carlo* (Ernani), Ford & Falstaff (Falstaff), Don Carlo (Forza del destino), Miller* (Luisa Miller), Nabucco*, Iago* (Otello), Rigoletto*, Simon Boccanegra, Germont* (Traviata), Conte di Luna* (Trovatore), Monforte (Vespri); WAGNER: Holländer, Telramund* (Lohengrin); ZANDONAI: Gianciotto* (Francesca da Rimini). Also CILEA: Baldassare (Arlesiana); SPONTINI: Telasco (Fernand Cortez); ALFANO: Simonson (Risurrezione). World premieres: TRECCATE: Buricchio (Buricchio) Regio di Parma 1949. Recorded for: Decca, Philips. Video/Film: (Fliegende Holländer); (Lohengrin); (Ballo in maschera); (Forza del destino); (Sposa di Corinto); (Dantons Tod); Ford (Falstaff); (Genoveva); (Rigoletto). Gives recitals. Appears with symphony orchestra.

PRUETT, JEROME. Lyric tenor. American. Resident mem: Volksoper, Vienna. Born 22 Nov 1941, Poplar Bluff, MO. Wife Jacquelyn. Two children. Studied: Thorwald Olsen, St Louis; Univ of Colorado, Berton Coffin, CO; Oglebay Inst, Boris Goldovsky, WV. Debut: Ugo (Parisina d'Este) New York Opera Orch 1974. Previous occupations: prof of voice, Iowa St Univ.

Sang with major companies in AUS: Vienna Volksoper; USA: Lake George. Roles with these companies incl DONIZETTI: Ernesto* (Don Pasquale), Tonio* (Fille du régiment); MOZART: Belmonte* (Entführung aus dem Serail), Tamino* (Zauberflöte); NICOLAI: Fenton* (Lustigen Wei-

ber). Also WARD: Rev Parris★ (*Crucible*). **World premieres:** WOLPERT: Cleantes (*Eingebildete Kranke*) Volksoper, Vienna 1975. Gives recitals. Appears with symphony orchestra. **Res:** Vienna, Austria. Mgmt: HUR/USA; RAB/AUS; HPL/UK.

PRYCE-JONES, JOHN. Conductor of opera and symphony; composer. British. Born 11 May 1946, Wellington, UK. Wife Hilary Thomas, occupation soprano. Studied: Corpus Christi Coll, Cambridge, UK; George Hurst, Rafael Kubelik; incl piano, organ, violin. Plays the piano. Operatic training as repetiteur, asst cond & chorus master at Welsh National Opera, Cardiff 1969-71. **Operatic debut:** *Nozze di Figaro* Welsh National Opera, Llandudno, Wales 1970. Symphonic debut: BBC Training Orch, Brighton, UK 1969. Awards: Assoc Royal Coll of Organists. Previous adm positions in opera: Asst Chorus Master, Welsh National Opera, Cardiff 1969-71; Asst to Mus Dir, Perf Arts Council, Johannesburg, S Afr 1972-74.
Conducted with major companies in S AFR: Johannesburg; UK: Welsh National. **Operas with these companies incl** BIZET: *Carmen★;* DONIZETTI: *Elisir★;* MOZART: *Nozze di Figaro★;* ROSSINI: *Barbiere di Siviglia★;* STRAUSS, J: *Fledermaus★;* STRAUSS, R: *Ariadne auf Naxos★;* VERDI: *Aida★, Rigoletto★, Traviata★.* Conducted major orch in Africa. **Res:** Cardiff, Wales, UK. Mgmt: GBN/UK.

PSCHERER, KURT. German. Staatsintendant & Resident Stage Dir, Staatstheater am Gärtnerplatz, 8 Munich 5, FR Ger. Also stages theater and is an actor. Born 3 Jun 1915, Bensen, form Austria, now CSSR. Wife Ursula Heimerer, occupation solo dancer. Two children. Studied: music in Prague; theater in Aussig, Prof Huttig; also piano. Previous occupation: actor. Prev adm positions: Oberspielleiter Kassel & Wiesbaden. In present position since 1964. Awards: Hon Citizen of Alzenau, Bavaria; Bavarian Order of Merit.
Directed/produced opera for major companies in AUS: Bregenz Fest, Graz, Vienna; FR GER: Hamburg, Kassel, Kiel, Munich Gärtnerplatz, Dortmund, Essen, Düsseldorf-Duisburg, Cologne, Nürnberg, Wuppertal; FIN: Helsinki; HOL: Amsterdam; SWI: Basel, Zürich. **Operas staged with these companies incl** BIZET: *Carmen;* DONIZETTI: *Lucia;* GOUNOD: *Faust;* HENZE: *Junge Lord;* JANACEK: *Cunning Little Vixen;* LORTZING: *Zar und Zimmermann;* MOZART: *Entführung aus dem Serail, Zauberflöte;* ROSSINI: *Barbiere di Siviglia;* STRAUSS, J: *Fledermaus;* VERDI: *Traviata.* Also DVORAK: *Rusalka;* PROKOFIEV: *Betrothal in a Monastery;* SHOSTAKOVICH: *Katerina Ismailova, The Nose;* RAMEAU: *Platée;* PURCELL: *Fairy Queen.* **Operatic world premieres:** KILLMAYER: *Jolimba* Munich 1970, WIMBERGER: *Lebensregeln* 1972, HENZE: *Rachel, la Cubana* 1975 stgd, LOTHAR: *Widerspenstige Heilige* 1968, all at Theater am Gärtnerplatz, Munich. Mem: Pres, Bavarian Theater Assn; mem theater jury.

PUECHER, VIRGINIO. Stages/produces opera, theater. Also designs sets, costumes & stage-lighting and is an author & librettist. Italian.

Directed/produced opera for major companies in ITA: Bologna, Florence Maggio, Genoa, Milan La Scala, Naples, Rome Opera, Turin, Venice; USA: Chicago; et al. **Operas staged with these companies incl** BERG: *Wozzeck†;* BRITTEN: *Turn of the Screw;* MASSENET: *Manon†;* PROKOFIEV: *Fiery Angel;* PUCCINI: *Gianni Schicchi†;* STRAUSS, R: *Salome;* STRAVINSKY: *Rake's Progress;* VERDI: *Luisa Miller;* WEILL: *Aufstieg und Fall der Stadt Mahagonny†;* et al. Also MEYEROWITZ: *Mulatto;* PICCINI: *Buona figliola;* BELLI: *Orfeo dolente.* **Operatic world premieres:** MADERNA: *Hyperion* Venice 1964; VALDAMBRINI: *Pentheus* Bonn, FR Ger 1971; BUCCHI: *Coccodrillo* Maggio Musicale, Florence & Bologna 1970. **Opera libretti:** *Pentheus* see prem.

PUGGELLI, LAMBERTO. Stages/produces opera & theater. Italian. Res St Dir, Piccolo Teatro & Teatro San Babila, Milan. Born 11 Apr 1938, Milan. Wife Marisa Minelli, occupation actress. One son. Studied: Accad Filodramm, Milan. Operatic training as asst stage dir at Spoleto Fest with Menotti 1964-67 and asst stage dir with G Strehler 1969-1974. **Operatic debut:** *Oedipus Rex* La Fenice, Venice 1964. Theater debut: Spoleto Fest 1964. Previous occupation: salesman, actor. Awards: St Vincent, Best Prod in Thtr 1973; Golden Nut, Best Op Prod Young Dir 1971.
Directed/produced opera for major companies in ITA: Florence Comunale, Genoa, Milan La Scala, Palermo, Parma, Trieste, Venice. **Operas staged with these companies incl** BARTOK: *Bluebeard's Castle★;* DEBUSSY: *Pelléas et Mélisande;* DESSAU: *Verurteilung des Lukullus★;* DONIZETTI: *Campanello;* LEONCAVALLO: *Pagliacci;* MASCAGNI: *Cavalleria rusticana;* MONTEVERDI: *Incoronazione di Poppea★;* PERAGALLO: *Gita in campagna;* PUCCINI: *Tabarro★;* ROSSINI: *Barbiere di Siviglia;* STRAVINSKY: *Oedipus Rex†;* VERDI: *Attila★.* Also VLAD: *Storia di una Mamma, Dott di vetro;* PETRASSI: *Cordovano.* **Res:** V Sismondi 5, Milan, Italy.

PUMA, SALVATORE. Dramatic tenor. Italian. Born 6 May 1920, Racalmuto/Agrigento. Wife Guadalupe Flores. Studied in Parma and Milan. **Debut:** Radames (*Aida*) Teatro Rossini, Pesaro 1949. Awards: Gold Medals of the cities of Milan, Salsomaggiore and Viterbo; Silver Medal, Gela.
Sang with major companies in BEL: Brussels; BRA: Rio de Janeiro; BUL: Sofia; DEN: Copenhagen; FRA: Paris, Strasbourg; GRE: Athens National; FR GER: Berlin Deutsche Oper, Hamburg, Munich Staatsoper; GER DR: Berlin Staatsoper; HOL: Amsterdam; HUN: Budapest; ITA: Bologna, Florence Maggio & Comunale, Genoa, Milan La Scala, Naples, Palermo, Parma, Rome Opera & Caracalla, Trieste, Turin, Venice, Verona Arena; MEX: Mexico City; ROM: Bucharest; SPA: Majorca; SWI: Zurich; USA: Hartford, Miami, New Orleans, Philadelphia Grand & Lyric; YUG: Belgrade. **Roles with these companies incl** BELLINI: Pollione (*Norma*); BIZET: Don José (*Carmen*); DALLAPICCOLA: Jailer/Inquisitor (*Prigioniero*); DONIZETTI: Fernand (*Favorite*), Edgardo (*Lucia*); GIORDANO: Andrea Chénier; HANDEL: Sextus (*Giulio Cesare*); LEON-

CAVALLO: Canio (*Pagliacci*); MASCAGNI: Turiddu (*Cavalleria rusticana*); PONCHIELLI: Enzo (*Gioconda*); PUCCINI: Rodolfo (*Bohème*), Dick Johnson (*Fanciulla del West*), Rinuccio (*Gianni Schicchi*), Pinkerton (*Butterfly*), Des Grieux (*Manon Lescaut*), Luigi (*Tabarro*), Cavaradossi (*Tosca*), Calaf (*Turandot*); ROSSINI: Aménophis (*Moïse*); SAINT-SAENS: Samson; VERDI: Riccardo (*Ballo in maschera*), Ernani, Don Alvaro (*Forza del destino*), Carlo (*Giovanna d'Arco*), Ismaele (*Nabucco*), Otello, Duca di Mantova (*Rigoletto*), Alfredo (*Traviata*), Manrico (*Trovatore*); WAGNER: Lohengrin; ZANDONAI: Paolo (*Francesca da Rimini*). Also MASCAGNI: (*Iris*), (*Isabeau*), (*Piccolo Marat*), (*Amica*); PIZZETTI: (*Fedra*); SMAREGLIA: (*Nozze istriane*). World premieres: DEL CORONA: Giuliano de Medici, Livorno 1955. Recorded for: Cetra. Gives recitals. Appears with symphony orchestra. Teaches voice. Res: V Jacopone da Todi 25, Rome, Italy.

PUSTELAK, KAZIMIERZ. Lyric tenor. Polish. Resident mem: Teatr Wielki, Warsaw. Born 14 Feb 1930, Nowa-Wies, Poland. Wife Kristine, occupation dental surgeon. One child. Studied: Prof Czeskaw Zaremba, Krakow, Poland; Prof Gennaro Barra, Italy. Debut: Lenski (*Eugene Onegin*) Krakow, Poland 1957. Previous occupations: agricultural engineer. Awards: Polonia Restituta, Polish People's Republic.

Sang with major companies in CZE: Prague National; FR GER: Wiesbaden; HUN: Budapest; POL: Lodz, Warsaw; ROM: Bucharest; SWE: Stockholm; USSR: Moscow Bolshoi, Tbilisi. Roles with these companies incl BERLIOZ: Faust‡ (*Damnation de Faust*); DONIZETTI: Ernesto (*Don Pasquale*), Edgardo (*Lucia*), Beppo‡ (*Rita*); GLUCK: Pylade (*Iphigénie en Tauride*); GOUNOD: Faust; HANDEL: Sextus (*Giulio Cesare*); HAYDN: Ernesto (*Mondo della luna*); MONIUSZKO: Jontek‡ (*Halka*), Stefan∗‡ (*Haunted Castle*); MOZART: Don Ottavio (*Don Giovanni*); OFFENBACH: Hoffmann; PUCCINI: Rodolfo∗ (*Bohème*), Pinkerton∗ (*Butterfly*); ROSSINI: Almaviva∗ (*Barbiere di Siviglia*); SMETANA: Jarek (*Devil's Wall*); STRAUSS, R: Ein Sänger (*Rosenkavalier*); STRAVINSKY: Oedipus, Eumolpe (*Perséphone*); TCHAIKOVSKY: Lenski∗ (*Eugene Onegin*); VERDI: Fenton (*Falstaff*), Duca di Mantova∗ (*Rigoletto*), Alfredo∗ (*Traviata*); WEBER: Max∗ (*Freischütz*). World premieres: RUDZINSKI: Alexander (*Odprawa Postow Greckich*) Krakow 1966. Video/Film: Max (*Freischütz*). Gives recitals. Appears with symphony orchestra. Teaches voice. Coaches repertoire. On faculty of Consv, Warsaw. Res: Okolnik Str N 2, Warsaw, Poland. Mgmt: PAG/POL.

PUTTAR-GOLD, NADA. Dramatic mezzo-soprano. Yugoslavian. Resident mem: Croatian National Opera, Zagreb; Staatsoper, Berlin. Born 5 Nov 1923, Varazdin, Yugoslavia. Husband Ervin Gold, occupation veterinarian. Studied: Prof Lav Vrbanic, Zagreb. Debut: Vanja (*Life for the Tsar*) Croat Ntl Opera, Zagreb 1949. Awards: First Prize, Compts Belgrade 1948 and Verviers, Belgium 1950; Milka Ternina Awd.

Sang with major companies in AUS: Graz, Salzburg Fest, Vienna Staatsoper; BEL: Liège; CZE: Brno; FRA: Paris, Strasbourg; GRE: Athens Fest; FR GER: Berlin Deutsche Oper, Cologne, Darmstadt, Frankfurt, Hamburg, Kassel, Munich Staatsoper, Wiesbaden; GER DR: Berlin Staatsoper; ITA: Naples, Palermo, Trieste, Turin, Venice; SWI: Basel, Geneva, Zurich; UK: London English National; USSR: Leningrad Kirov, Tbilisi; YUG: Dubrovnik, Zagreb, Belgrade. Roles with these companies incl BIZET: Carmen, Djamileh; BORODIN: Kontchakovna∗ (*Prince Igor*); BRITTEN: Lucretia (*Rape of Lucretia*); CHERUBINI: Neris (*Medea*); FALLA: Abuela (*Vida breve*); GLUCK: Orfeo; JANACEK: Kostelnicka (*Jenufa*); MASSENET: Charlotte (*Werther*); MENOTTI: Desideria (*Saint of Bleecker Street*); MUSSORGSKY: Marina (*Boris Godunov*); PONCHIELLI: Laura∗ (*Gioconda*); PROKOFIEV: Smeraldina (*Love for Three Oranges*); PUCCINI: Suzuki (*Butterfly*); SAINT-SAENS: Dalila; STRAUSS, R: Clairon (*Capriccio*), Herodias (*Salome*); VERDI: Amneris∗ (*Aida*), Ulrica (*Ballo in maschera*), Eboli∗ (*Don Carlo*), .Dame Quickly (*Falstaff*), Preziosilla (*Forza del destino*), Azucena∗ (*Trovatore*); WAGNER: Ortrud (*Lohengrin*), Kundry (*Parsifal*), Erda (*Siegfried*), Fricka (*Rheingold, Walküre*), Waltraute (*Götterdämmerung*). Gives recitals. Appears with symphony orchestra. Teaches voice. Coaches repertoire. On faculty of Music School, Zagreb. Res: Leskovacka 6, Zagreb, Yugoslavia. Mgmt: CRO/YUG; PAS/FRG.

PÜTZ, RUTH-MARGRET; née Doerkes. Lyric coloratura soprano. German. Resident mem: Württembergische Staatsoper, Stuttgart. Born 26 Feb 1932, Krefeld, Germany. Husband Michael C Leitner, occupation marketing mgr. Two children. Studied: Otto Köhler, Cologne. Debut: Gretchen (*Wildschütz*) Cologne Opera 1951. Awards: Soviet Cult Awd, Gvnmt USSR 1961; Kammersängerin, Ministry of Culture Baden-Württemberg 1962.

Sang with major companies in ARG: Buenos Aires; AUS: Salzburg Fest, Vienna Staatsoper; FIN: Helsinki; FRA: Lyon, Nice, Strasbourg; FR GER: Bayreuth Fest, Berlin Deutsche Oper, Cologne, Düsseldorf-Duisburg, Essen, Frankfurt, Hamburg, Hannover, Karlsruhe, Kassel, Kiel, Munich Staatsoper, Stuttgart, Wiesbaden, Wuppertal; GER DR: Berlin Staatsoper; ITA: Florence Comunale, Naples, Rome Opera, Venice; POR: Lisbon; SPA: Barcelona; SWI: Geneva, Zurich; UK: Edinburgh Fest. Roles with these companies incl ADAM: Madeleine (*Postillon de Lonjumeau*); BEETHOVEN: Marzelline∗ (*Fidelio*); BIZET: Micaëla∗ (*Carmen*); CIMAROSA: Carolina∗ & Elisetta (*Matrimonio segreto*); DONIZETTI: Serafina (*Campanello*), Norina∗ (*Don Pasquale*), Adina∗ (*Elisir*), Lucia; DVORAK: Rusalka; GLUCK: Euridice & Amor∗‡ (*Orfeo ed Euridice*); HANDEL: Alcina, Ginevra (*Ariodante*), Cleopatra∗ (*Giulio Cesare*); HAYDN: Vespina (*Infedeltà delusa*); HUMPERDINCK: Gretel; LORTZING: Gretchen & Baronin Freimann∗‡ (*Wildschütz*); MOZART: Despina∗ (*Così fan tutte*), Zerlina∗ (*Don Giovanni*), Konstanze∗‡ & Blondchen (*Entführung aus dem Serail*), Ilia (*Idomeneo*), Mlle Silberklang (*Schauspieldirektor*), Susanna⋆ & Cherubino⋆ (*Nozze di Figaro*), Aminta (*Re pastore*), Pamina⋆ & Königin der Nacht (*Zauberflöte*); NICOLAI: Frau Fluth⋆‡ & Aennchen (*Lustigen Weiber*); OFFENBACH: Olympia‡ (*Contes d'Hoffmann*); ORFF: Solo⋆‡ (*Carmina burana*); PAISIELLO: Rosina (*Barbiere di Siviglia*); PERGOLESI: Serpina (*Serva padrona*); PFITZNER: Ighino (*Palestrina*); PUCCINI: Musetta⋆‡ (*Bohème*), Lauretta⋆ (*Gianni Schicchi*), Liù⋆(*Turandot*); RAVEL: Concepcion (*Heure espagnole*); ROSSINI: Rosina‡ (*Barbiere di Siviglia*), Fiorilla⋆ (*Turco in Italia*); STRAUSS, J: Adele⋆ & Rosalinde⋆ (*Fledermaus*); STRAUSS, R: Zdenka⋆ & Fiakermilli (*Arabella*), Zerbinetta (*Ariadne auf Naxos*), Sophie⋆ (*Rosenkavalier*), Aminta (*Schweigsame Frau*); THOMAS: Philine‡ (*Mignon*); VERDI: Oscar⋆ (*Ballo in maschera*), Gilda⋆ (*Rigoletto*), Violetta (*Traviata*); WEBER: Aennchen (*Freischütz*); WOLF-FERRARI: Lucieta (*Quattro rusteghi*). Also d'ALBERT: Nuri (*Tiefland*); BUSONI: Colombina (*Arlecchino*); GAY/Britten: Polly⋆ (*Beggar's Opera*); HANDEL: Emilia (*Flavio*), Iphis (*Jephtha*); LIEBERMANN: Agnes (*Schule der Frauen*); LORTZING: Berthalda⋆‡ (*Undine*); MONTEVERDI: Amore (*Ballo delle ingrate*); MOZART: Papagena⋆‡ & Erste Dame (*Zauberflöte*); ROSSINI: Isabella (*Italiana in Algeri*); SCARLATTI: Carità (*Giardino di rose*); WOLF-FERRARI: Felice (*Quattro rusteghi*); LOTHAR: Mariechen (*Schneider Wibbel*); ORFF: Solo (*Trionfo di Afrodite*). **World premieres:** BIBALO: Anni (*Lächeln am Fuss der Leiter*) Staatsoper, Hamburg 1965; EGK: Circe (*17 Tage und 4 Minuten*) Württembergische Staatsoper, Stuttgart 1966. Recorded for: Columbia, Electrola, Decca, Eurodisc, Eterna, Ariola, Baccarola. Video: Norina (*Don Pasquale*); Lucia; Ighino (*Palestrina*); Berthalda (*Undine*); Ginevra (*Ariodante*); Vespina (*Infedeltà delusa*); Felice (*Quattro rusteghi*); Susanna (*Nozze di Figaro*); Frau Fluth (*Lustigen Weiber*). Gives recitals. Appears with symphony orchestra. Teaches voice. **Res:** Ob Bughalde 35, D-7250 Leonberg, FR Ger. Mgmt: WLS/USA; CDA/ARG.

PY, GILBERT. Dramatic tenor. French. Born 9 Dec 1933, Sète, France. Wife Janine Arcangiou. **Debut:** Pinkerton (*Butterfly*) Verviers, Belgium 1964. Previous occupations: ballet.

Sang with major companies in AUS: Vienna Staatsoper; BEL: Liège; FRA: Bordeaux, Lyon, Marseille, Nice, Paris, Rouen, Strasbourg, Toulouse; FR GER: Düsseldorf-Duisburg, Frankfurt, Hamburg, Karlsruhe, Kiel, Munich Staatsoper, Saarbrücken, Stuttgart; HUN: Budapest; ITA: Florence Maggio & Comunale, Genoa, Milan La Scala, Naples, Palermo, Verona Arena; SPA: Barcelona; USA: Miami, New Orleans. **Roles with these companies incl** BEETHOVEN: Florestan⋆ (*Fidelio*); BERLIOZ: Faust⋆ (*Damnation de Faust*), Aeneas⋆ (*Troyens*); BIZET: Don José⋆‡ (*Carmen*); GOUNOD: Faust⋆; MASSENET: Jean le Baptiste⋆ (*Hérodiade*), Werther⋆; OFFENBACH: Hoffmann⋆; PUCCINI: Pinkerton⋆ (*Butterfly*), Cavaradossi⋆ (*Tosca*), Calaf⋆ (*Turandot*); SAINT-SAENS: Samson⋆; SUTERMEISTER: Raskolnikoff⋆; VERDI: Radames⋆ (*Aida*), Ernani⋆, Otello⋆, Manrico⋆ (*Trovatore*); WAGNER: Lohengrin⋆, Tannhäuser⋆. Recorded for: Erato. Teaches voice. Coaches repertoire. **Res:** 135 rue Ordener, Paris, France. Mgmt: CAM/USA.

Q

QUAYLE, LEO GORDON. Conductor of opera and symphony; composer. South African. Dir of Music & Opera, PACT, Pretoria, S Africa. Also Resident Cond & Mus Dir, PACT Orch, Pretoria. Born 11 Dec 1918, Pretoria. Wife Joan. Two children. Studied: Royal Coll of Music, London; incl piano, violin, viola, oboe, clarinet, timpani and voice. Plays the piano. Operatic training as repetiteur, chorus master & cond at Sadler's Wells, London 1948-58; Welsh Ntl Opera, Cardiff 1951-52; Glyndebourne Fest 1953. **Operatic debut:** *Faust* Sadler's Wells 1948. Symphonic debut: S African Broadcast Symph, Johannesburg 1939. Previous occupations: Dir of Music, SA Entertainment Corp; Union Defence Force 1941-46; Prof, Univ OFS, SA 1958-64. Awards: Fellow, Royal Coll of Music, London ARCM; Hopkinson Gold Medal for Piano, RCM; Nederburg Prize for Opera, S Africa; Stier Prize for conducting, RCM. Previous adm positions in opera: Principal Cond, Sadler's Wells 1948-58; Mus Dir, Welsh Ntl Opera, Cardiff 1952-53.
Conducted with major companies in S AFR: Johannesburg; UK: Welsh National, Scottish, London English National. **Operas with these companies incl** BELLINI: *Norma;* BIZET: *Carmen, Pêcheurs de perles;* BRITTEN: *Peter Grimes;* DONIZETTI: *Don Pasquale★, Lucia;* FLOTOW: *Martha;* GOUNOD: *Faust;* HUMPERDINCK: *Hänsel und Gretel;* LEONCAVALLO: *Pagliacci;* MASCAGNI: *Cavalleria rusticana;* MENOTTI: *Amahl;* MOZART: *Così fan tutte★, Don Giovanni, Entführung aus dem Serail, Nozze di Figaro, Zauberflöte;* NICOLAI: *Lustigen Weiber;* PUCCINI: *Bohème, Gianni Schicchi, Butterfly, Suor Angelica, Tabarro, Tosca;* PURCELL: *Dido and Aeneas;* ROSSINI: *Barbiere di Siviglia, Cenerentola;* SMETANA: *Bartered Bride;* STRAUSS, J: *Fledermaus★;* VAUGHAN WILLIAMS: *Hugh the Drover;* VERDI: *Aida, Don Carlo, Forza del destino, Luisa Miller, Macbeth, Nabucco, Rigoletto, Simon Boccanegra, Traviata★, Trovatore★;* WAGNER: *Fliegende Holländer★.* Video—BBC TV: *Cenerentola.* Conducted major orch in Europe, Africa.

QUEIROZ, GLORIA. Mezzo-soprano. Brazilian. Resident mem: Teatro Municipal, Rio de Janeiro. Born 27 May 1930, Rio de Janeiro. Husband Italo F Da Costa. One child. Studied: Reis E Silva, Ernest Tempele, Ntl School of Music, Fed Univ of Brazil, Roberto Miranda. **Debut:** Lola (*Cavalleria rusticana*) Teatro Municipal, Rio de Janeiro 1954. Awards: Gold Medal & Certificate, Braz Theater Assn; Medal & Merit Diploma Carlos Gomes, Gvnmt of Rio de Janeiro; Alberto Nepomuceno Prize, Braz Assn of Lyric Artists.
Sang with major companies in BRA: Rio de Janeiro. **Roles with these companies incl** BIZET: Carmen★; CILEA: Princesse de Bouillon (*A. Lecouvreur*); CIMAROSA: Fidalma (*Matrimonio segreto*); DONIZETTI: Mme Rosa★ (*Campanello*); HUMPERDINCK: Hexe (*Hänsel und Gretel*); MASSENET: Charlotte (*Werther*); MENOTTI: Secretary (*Consul*); PUCCINI: Suzuki (*Butterfly*), Frugola (*Tabarro*); ROSSINI: Rosina★ (*Barbiere di Siviglia*), Isabella★ (*Italiana in Algeri*); VERDI: Amneris (*Aida*), Dame Quickly (*Falstaff*), Preziosilla (*Forza del destino*); WAGNER: Waltraute (*Götterdämmerung*). Also MASCAGNI: Santuzza (*Cavalleria rusticana*); MOZART: Donna Elvira (*Don Giovanni*); GUARNIERI: Baiana (*Pedro Malazarte*); VILLA-LOBOS: Rainha (*Menina das Nuvens*); BRAGA: Rosália (*Jupyra*); MIGNONE: Irene (*Innocente*); FERNANDEZ: Militina (*Malazarte*); MENOTTI: Mother★ (*Amahl*). **World premieres:** VILLA-LOBOS: Queen (*Young Girl of the Clouds*) Teatro Municipal, Rio 1960's; GEYER: Maria da Gloria (*Anita Garibaldi*) Teatro Municipal, São Paulo 1957. Video/Film: Mother (*Amahl*). Gives recitals. Appears with symphony orchestra. **Res:** Av Delfim Moreira 710/901, Rio de Janeiro, Brazil. Mgmt: PMC/BRA.

QUELER, EVE. Conductor of opera and symphony. American. Music Dir & Cond, Opera Orch of New York. Married. Studied: Carl Bamberger, Joseph Rosenstock, New York; also piano, French horn. Plays the piano. Operatic training as repetiteur & asst cond at Metropolitan Opera Ntl Co 1965; New York City Opera 1965-70. **Operatic debut:** *Bohème* Opera Orch of New York 1968. Symphonic debut: St Louis Symph, MO, 1970. Awards: Musician of the Month, *Musical America* mag 1971; Woman of the Year, NY Business & Professional Women's Club.
Conducted with major companies in SPA: Barcelona; USA: Hartford, Lake George. **Operas with these companies incl** BELLINI: *Puritani★;* BER-

LIOZ: *Damnation de Faust*; BIZET: *Carmen*, *Pêcheurs de perles*; DONIZETTI: *Favorite*; GIORDANO: *Fedora;* GOUNOD: *Faust;* LEONCAVALLO: *Pagliacci;* MASCAGNI: *Cavalleria rusticana*; MEYERBEER: *Africaine;* MONTEVERDI: *Incoronazione di Poppea;* MOZART: *Don Giovanni, Entführung aus dem Serail, Schauspieldirektor, Nozze di Figaro*, Zauberflöte;* OFFENBACH: *Contes d'Hoffmann;* PUCCINI: *Bohème, Butterfly, Suor Angelica*, Tosca*;* RAVEL: *Heure espagnole*; ROSSINI: *Barbiere di Siviglia, Guillaume Tell;* VERDI *Aida*, Lombardi*, Masnadieri*, Rigoletto, Traviata*, Vespri*;* ZANDONAI: *Francesca da Rimini*.

QUILICO, LOUIS. Dramatic baritone. Canadian. Resident mem: Metropolitan Opera, New York. Born 14 Jan 1930, Montreal, PQ, Canada. Wife Lina, occupation concert pianist. Two children. Studied: Martial Singher, New York; Walter Brunelli, Lina Pizzolongo, Rome. **Debut:** Germont *(Traviata)* New York City Opera 1956. Previous occupations: bicycle & motorcycle dealer. Awards: Compagnon de l'Ordre du Canada, Gouverneur Général du Canada.

Sang with major companies in ARG: Buenos Aires; AUS: Vienna Staatsoper; BEL: Brussels; CAN: Montreal/Quebec, Toronto, Vancouver; FRA: Bordeaux, Lyon, Nice, Orange Fest, Paris, Rouen, Strasbourg, Toulouse; FR GER: Wiesbaden; ITA: Florence Maggio, Naples, Palermo, Parma, Rome Caracalla, Spoleto Fest, Turin, Venice; MEX: Mexico City; POR: Lisbon; ROM: Bucharest; SPA: Barcelona, Majorca; UK: Edinburgh Fest, London Royal Opera; USSR: Kiev, Leningrad Kirov, Moscow Bolshoi & Stanislavski, Tbilisi; USA: Baltimore, Boston, Cincinnati, Fort Worth, Hartford, Hawaii, Houston, Miami, Milwaukee Florentine, New Orleans, New York Met & City Opera, Omaha, Philadelphia Lyric, Pittsburgh, San Antonio, San Diego, San Francisco Opera, Seattle, Washington DC. **Roles with these companies incl** BERG: Wozzeck; BERLIOZ: Choroebus* *(Troyens);* BIZET: Escamillo *(Carmen),* Zurga *(Pêcheurs de perles);* BORODIN: Prince Igor; BRITTEN: Demetrius *(Midsummer Night);* DEBUSSY: Golaud *(Pelléas et Mélisande);* DONIZETTI: Belcore *(Elisir),* Alfonse *(Favorite),* Enrico *(Lucia),* Talbot *(Maria Stuarda),* Nottingham *(Roberto Devereux);* GIORDANO: Carlo Gérard *(Andrea Chénier);* GLUCK: Thoas *(Iphigénie en Tauride);* HANDEL: Giulio Cesare; LEONCAVALLO: Tonio *(Pagliacci);* MASCAGNI: Alfio *(Cavalleria rusticana);* MASSENET: Hérode* *(Hérodiade),* Lescaut *(Manon);* MOZART: Publio *(Clemenza di Tito);* OFFENBACH: Coppélius etc *(Contes d'Hoffmann);* PUCCINI: Marcello *(Bohème),* Jack Rance *(Fanciulla del West),* Sharpless *(Butterfly),* Lescaut *(Manon Lescaut),* Michele *(Tabarro),* Scarpia *(Tosca);* ROSSINI: Guillaume Tell; SAINT-SAENS: Grand prêtre *(Samson et Dalila);* STRAVINSKY: Creon *(Oedipus Rex);* TCHAIKOVSKY: Yeletsky *(Pique Dame);* VERDI: Amonasro *(Aida),* Renato *(Ballo in maschera),* Rodrigo *(Don Carlo),* Don Carlo *(Forza del destino),* Miller *(Luisa Miller),* Macbeth, Iago *(Otello),* Rigoletto, Simon Boccanegra, Germont *(Traviata),* Conte di Luna *(Trovatore);* WAGNER: Wolfram *(Tannhäuser).* **World premieres:** MILHAUD: Comte *(La mère coupable)* Geneva Opera 1966. Recorded for: ABC, Decca, DG. Video/Film: Michele *(Tabarro);* Falstaff; Rigoletto; Comte *(La mère coupable).* Gives recitals. Appears with symphony orchestra. Teaches voice. Coaches repertoire. On faculty of Toronto Univ, Dept of Music. **Res:** 152 Dalemount Ave, Toronto, Ont, Canada. Mgmt: HUR/USA; AIM/UK.

R

RADNAY, GEORGE. Baritone. Hungarian. Resident mem: Hungarian State Opera, Budapest. Born 7 Aug 1920, Szurdokpüspöki, Hungary. Wife Margaret Denhof. One child. Studied: Prof Géza László, Budapest. **Debut:** Tonio (*Pagliacci*) Hungarian State Opera 1948. Previous occupations: official. Awards: First Prize Intl Vocal Compt Geneva; Kossuth Prize, Gvnmt of Hungary.

Sang with major companies in BUL: Sofia; CZE: Prague National; HUN: Budapest; ROM: Bucharest; YUG: Belgrade. **Roles with these companies incl** d'ALBERT: Sebastiano (*Tiefland*); BERG: Dr Schön★ (*Lulu*), Wozzeck★; BIZET: Escamillo (*Carmen*); DALLAPICCOLA: Riviere (*Volo di notte*); DELIBES: Nilakantha (*Lakmé*); DONIZETTI: Dott Malatesta (*Don Pasquale*), Enrico (*Lucia*); GAY/Britten; Lockit★ (*Beggar's Opera*); GERSHWIN: Porgy★; HUMPERDINCK: Spielmann (*Königskinder*); KODALY: Háry János; LEONCAVALLO: Tonio (*Pagliacci*); MASCAGNI: Alfio (*Cavalleria rusticana*); MASSENET: Lescaut (*Manon*); MOZART: Papageno (*Zauberflöte*); OFFENBACH: Coppélius etc (*Contes d'Hoffmann*); ORFF: König (*Kluge*); PUCCINI: Marcello (*Bohème*), Jack Rance (*Fanciulla del West*), Gianni Schicchi, Sharpless★ (*Butterfly*), Lescaut (*Manon Lescaut*), Scarpia (*Tosca*); RIMSKY-KORSAKOV: Roi Dodon (*Coq d'or*); ROSSINI: Figaro (*Barbiere di Siviglia*), Don Magnifico (*Cenerentola*); TCHAIKOVSKY: Yeletsky (*Pique Dame*); VERDI: Amonasro★ (*Aida*), Renato (*Ballo in maschera*), Rodrigo★ (*Don Carlo*), Ford & Falstaff (*Falstaff*), Don Carlo (*Forza del destino*), Macbeth, Iago (*Otello*), Rigoletto, Simon Boccanegra, Germont (*Traviata*), Conte di Luna (*Trovatore*); WAGNER: Hans Sachs★ (*Meistersinger*), Kurwenal (*Tristan und Isolde*). Recorded for: Hungaroton. Gives recitals. Appears with symphony orchestra. Coaches repertoire. **Res:** Jászai Mari Sq 4a, Budapest, Hungary.

RADOVAN, FERDINAND. Dramatic baritone. Yugoslavian. Resident mem: Städtische Bühnen Dortmund. Born 26 Jan 1938, Rijeka, Yugoslavia. Wife Lela. Three children. Studied: Prof Julije Pejnovic, Prof Zdenka Zikova, Belgrade. **Debut:** Germont (*Traviata*) Belgrade Opera. Awards: First Prize Conc de Ljubljana 1966.

Sang with major companies in AUS: Graz, Vienna Volksoper; CZE: Prague National; FRA: Bordeaux; FR GER: Dortmund, Düsseldorf-Duis-

burg, Essen, Munich Staatsoper, Stuttgart; ITA: Turin; SPA: Majorca; YUG: Dubrovnik, Zagreb, Belgrade. **Roles with these companies incl** BELLINI: Sir Richard★ (*Puritani*); BIZET: Escamillo★ (*Carmen*); BORODIN: Prince Igor★; DONIZETTI: Dott Malatesta★ (*Don Pasquale*), Enrico★ (*Lucia*); GIORDANO: Carlo Gérard★ (*Andrea Chénier*); LEONCAVALLO: Tonio★ (*Pagliacci*); MASCAGNI: Alfio★ (*Cavalleria rusticana*); MEYERBEER: Nelusco★ (*Africaine*); MILHAUD: Christophe Colombe★; MOZART: Don Giovanni★, Conte Almaviva★ (*Nozze di Figaro*); PONCHIELLI: Barnaba★ (*Gioconda*); PUCCINI: Marcello★ (*Bohème*), Scarpia★ (*Tosca*); ROSSINI: Figaro★ (*Barbiere di Siviglia*); STRAUSS, R: Jochanaan★ (*Salome*); VERDI: Amonasro★ (*Aida*), Renato★ (*Ballo in maschera*), Rodrigo★ (*Don Carlo*), Ford★ (*Falstaff*), Macbeth★, Nabucco★, Iago★ (*Otello*), Rigoletto★, Germont★ (*Traviata*), Conte di Luna★ (*Trovatore*). Gives recitals. Appears with symphony orchestra. **Res:** Wambel-Gesslerstr 14, Dortmund, FR Ger. Mgmt: VLD/AUS; SLZ/FRG.

RAFANELLI, FLORA. Dramatic mezzo-soprano. Italian. Born 30 Sep 1930, Florence. Single. Studied: Profs Nella del Vivo and Rossini; Mo Edoardo Müller. **Debut:** Laura (*Elisa e Claudio*) Maggio Musicale 1960. Previous occupations: voice teacher for choir. Awards: First Prize, Conc As Li Co, 1959; First Prize for television broadcasting.

Sang with major companies in CAN: Montreal/Quebec; FR GER: Munich Staatsoper; GER DR: Dresden; ITA: Bologna, Florence Maggio & Comunale, Genoa, Milan La Scala, Naples, Parma, Rome Opera, Turin, Venice; UK: Edinburgh Fest. **Roles with these companies incl** DONIZETTI: Mme Rosa‡ (*Campanello*), Marquise de Birkenfeld‡ (*Fille du régiment*); HANDEL: Giulio Cesare; HUMPERDINCK: Hänsel; MASCAGNI: Beppe (*Amico Fritz*); MENOTTI: Secretary★ (*Consul*); MOZART: Dorabella★ (*Così fan tutte*), Cherubino (*Nozze di Figaro*); PUCCINI: Suzuki★ (*Butterfly*), Frugola★ (*Tabarro*); SPONTINI: High Priestess★ (*Vestale*); TCHAIKOVSKY: Comtesse★ (*Pique Dame*); VERDI: Meg & Dame Quickly (*Falstaff*), Preziosilla★ (*Forza del destino*), Federica (*Luisa Miller*); ZANDONAI: Samaritana (*Francesca da Rimini*). Also VERDI: Fenena★ (*Nabucco*); PUCCINI: Zita★ (*Gianni Schicchi*); SHOSTAKO-

VICH: Katerina Ismailova; PERI: Euridice (*Euridice*). Recorded for: DG. Video/Film: Mme Rosa (*Campanello*); Marquise (*Fille du régiment*). Gives recitals. Appears with symphony orchestra. **Res:** Corso Italia 32, Florence, Italy.

RAIMONDI, GIANNI. Lyric & dramatic tenor. Italian. Resident mem: La Scala, Milan. Born 17 Apr 1923, Bologna, Italy. Wife Gianna, occupation opera singer. Studied: Antonio Melandri, Bologna; Mario Basiola, Gennaro Barra, Milan. **Debut:** Duca di Mantova (*Rigoletto*) 1947. Awards: Cavaliere & Commendatore, Italian Gvnmt; Diapason d'Oro; Maschera d'Argento; Palma d'Oro; Riccione Prize.

Sang with major companies in ARG: Buenos Aires; AUS: Vienna Staatsoper; BRA: Rio de Janeiro; CAN: Montreal/Quebec; FIN: Helsinki; FRA: Marseille, Nice, Paris, Toulouse; FR GER: Berlin Deutsche Oper, Cologne, Hamburg, Mannheim, Munich Staatsoper, Stuttgart, Wiesbaden; ITA: Bologna, Florence Maggio & Comunale, Genoa, Milan La Scala, Naples, Palermo, Parma, Rome Opera & Caracalla, Trieste, Turin, Venice, Verona Arena; MEX: Mexico City; MON: Monte Carlo; POR: Lisbon; SPA: Barcelona, Majorca; SWI: Geneva, Zurich; UK: Cardiff Welsh, Edinburgh Fest, Glasgow Scottish, Glyndebourne Fest; USSR: Moscow Bolshoi; USA: Cincinnati, Dallas Civic, Houston Grand, Miami, New York Met, Philadelphia Grand, San Francisco Opera. **Roles with these companies incl** BELLINI: Pollione★ (*Norma*), Lord Arthur (*Puritani*); DONIZETTI: Riccardo (*Anna Bolena*), Ernesto (*Don Pasquale*), Charles (*Linda di Chamounix*), Edgardo★ (*Lucia*), Gennaro★ (*Lucrezia Borgia*), Riccardo★ (*Maria di Rohan*), Roberto Devereux★; GLINKA: Bogdan (*Life for the Tsar*); GOUNOD: Faust; MASCAGNI: Fritz (*Amico Fritz*); MENOTTI: Lover (*Amelia al ballo*); PONCHIELLI: Enzo★ (*Gioconda*); PUCCINI: Rodolfo★ (*Bohème*), Rinuccio (*Gianni Schicchi*), Pinkerton★ (*Butterfly*), Cavaradossi★ (*Tosca*); ROSSINI: Arnold★ (*Guillaume Tell*), Aménophis (*Moïse*), Giocondo (*Pietra del paragone*), Idreno (*Semiramide*); VERDI: Riccardo★ (*Ballo in maschera*), Carlo★ (*Masnadieri*), Ismaele★ (*Nabucco*), Duca di Mantova★ (*Rigoletto*), Gabriele★ (*Simon Boccanegra*), Alfredo★ (*Traviata*), Arrigo★ (*Vespri*). Also VERDI: Macduff (*Macbeth*); ROSSINI: (*Armida*). **World premieres:** PANNAIN: (*Madame Bovary*) Teatro San Carlo, Naples 1955; BUCCHI: (*Contrabbasso*) Maggio Musicale, Florence 1954. Recorded for: Cetra, DG, Ricordi. Film: Rodolfo (*Bohème*). **Res:** V Abruzzi 89, Riccione, Italy. Mgmt: EUM/FRG.

RAIMONDI, RUGGERO. Bass-baritone. Italian. Born 3 Oct 1944, Bologna. Wife Vittoria. Two children. Studied: Ghibaudo, Piervenanzi, Daniel Ferro. **Debut:** Colline (*Bohème*) Spoleto Fest 1964.

Sang with major companies in AUS: Salzburg Fest, Vienna Staatsoper; FRA: Paris; FR GER: Berlin Deutsche Oper, Frankfurt, Mannheim, Munich Staatsoper, Wiesbaden; ITA: Bologna, Florence Maggio & Comunale, Genoa, Milan La Scala, Naples, Palermo, Parma, Rome Opera, Trieste, Turin, Venice, Verona Arena; UK: Edinburgh Fest, Glyndebourne Fest, London Royal; USA: Boston, Chicago, Dallas, Memphis, Miami, New Orleans, New York Metropolitan. **Roles with these companies incl** BELLINI: Oroveso★‡ (*Norma*), Sir George (*Puritani*), Rodolfo‡ (*Sonnambula*); CHERUBINI: Creon (*Medea*); DONIZETTI: Baldassare★ (*Favorite*), Alfonso d'Este (*Lucrezia Borgia*); GOUNOD: Méphistophélès★ (*Faust*); MOZART: Don Giovanni★, Figaro (*Nozze di Figaro*), Sarastro (*Zauberflöte*); MUSSORGSKY: Boris Godunov★; PONCHIELLI: Alvise★ (*Gioconda*); PUCCINI: Colline★ (*Bohème*); ROSSINI: Don Basilio★‡ (*Barbiere di Siviglia*), Moïse; STRAVINSKY: Tiresias (*Oedipus Rex*); VERDI: Ramfis★‡ (*Aida*), Attila★‡, Philip II★‡ (*Don Carlo*), Silva★ (*Ernani*), Padre Guardiano★‡ (*Forza del destino*), Pagano‡ (*Lombardi*), Conte Walter★ (*Luisa Miller*), Banquo★ (*Macbeth*), Zaccaria (*Nabucco*), Fiesco★ (*Simon Boccanegra*), Procida★ (*Vespri*). Recorded for: Philips, RCA, EMI, CBS. Mgmt: GOR/UK.

RAITHEL, UTE. Coloratura soprano. German. Resident mem: Städtische Bühnen, Kiel. Born 12 Oct 1944, Fürth/Bayern, Germany. Single. Studied: Consv Nürnberg, Miss Kathryn Harvey; Prof Willy Domgraf-Fassbänder, Prof Peter Markwort, Hamburg. **Debut:** Zerlina (*Fra Diavolo*) Kiel Opera 1969. Previous occupations: state exam in management (Wirtschaftsleiterin); position for 2 yrs. Awards: Förderungspreis für Musik der Stadt Fürth/Bayern, FR Ger 1969.

Sang with major companies in FR GER: Kiel, Nürnberg. **Roles with these companies incl** AUBER: Zerlina (*Fra Diavolo*); HUMPERDINCK: Gretel; LORTZING: Marie★ (*Waffenschmied*), Gretchen★ & Baronin Freimann★ (*Wildschütz*), Marie★ (*Zar und Zimmermann*); MOZART: Despina★ (*Così fan tutte*), Blondchen (*Entführung aus dem Serail*), Cherubino★ (*Nozze di Figaro*); PERGOLESI: Vanella (*Frate 'nnamorato*); ROSSINI: Rosina★ (*Barbiere di Siviglia*); STRAUSS, J: Adele (*Fledermaus*); WEBER: Aennchen (*Freischütz*). Also GERSHWIN: Clara★ (*Porgy and Bess*); LORTZING: Undine★; BIALAS: Nicolette (*Aucassin und Nicolette*). Gives recitals. Appears with symphony orchestra. **Res:** Scharnhorststr 26, Kiel, FR Ger. Mgmt: SLZ/FRG.

RAMELLA, ELVINA. Coloratura soprano. Italian. Born 3 Feb 1931, Biella, Italy. Husband Gennaro Di Miscio, occupation magistrate. Studied: Consv Parma, Mo Italo Brancucci, Elvira De Hidalgo; Consv Milan. **Debut:** Rosina (*Barbiere di Siviglia*) Teatro Nuovo, Milan 1951. Awards: First Prize, Conc G B Viotti, Vercelli; Second Prize, Compt Accad S Cecilia, Rome.

Sang with major companies in FR GER: Bielefeld, Bonn, Cologne, Dortmund, Düsseldorf-Duisburg, Frankfurt, Hamburg, Hannover, Stuttgart; ITA: Bologna, Florence Comunale, Genoa, Milan La Scala, Naples, Palermo, Parma, Rome Opera & Caracalla, Trieste, Turin, Venice, Verona Arena. **Roles with these companies incl** BELLINI: Giulietta‡ (*Capuleti ed i Montecchi*), Elvira‡ (*Puritani*), Amina‡ (*Sonnambula*); CHARPENTIER: Louise; CIMAROSA: Carolina‡ & Elisetta‡ (*Matrimonio segreto*); DONIZETTI: Serafina‡ (*Campanello*), Norina★‡ (*Don Pasquale*), Adina★‡

(*Elisir*), Linda di Chamounix‡, Lucia★‡, Betly‡, Rita‡; MASSENET: Sophie‡ (*Werther*); MEYERBEER: Marguerite de Valois (*Huguenots*); MONTEVERDI: Minerva★‡ (*Ritorno d'Ulisse*); MOZART: Despina (*Così fan tutte*), Zerlina (*Don Giovanni*), Blondchen (*Entführung aus dem Serail*), Mme Herz (*Schauspieldirektor*), Susanna (*Nozze di Figaro*), Königin der Nacht (*Zauberflöte*); OFFENBACH: Olympia (*Contes d'Hoffmann*); PAISIELLO: Rosina (*Barbiere di Siviglia*); PERGOLESI: Serpina★‡ (*Serva padrona*); PUCCINI: Mimi★‡ & Musetta★‡ (*Bohème*); ROSSINI: Rosina‡ (*Barbiere di Siviglia*), Fanny‡ (*Cambiale di matrimonio*), Sofia‡ (*Signor Bruschino*), Fiorilla (*Turco in Italia*); THOMAS: Philine‡ (*Mignon*); VERDI: Oscar★‡ (*Ballo in maschera*), Nannetta (*Falstaff*), Gilda★‡ (*Rigoletto*). Also TELEMANN: Despina (*Pimpinone*); PERGOLESI: Protagonista (*Contadina astuta*); LUALDI: Colombina (*Furie di Arlecchino*). Recorded for: Cetra. Video/Film – Ital TV: (*Linda di Chamounix*). Res: V Bigli 28, Milan, Italy.

RAMEY, SAMUEL E. Bass. American. Resident mem: New York City Opera. Born 28 Mar 1942, Colby, KA, USA. Wife Carrie. Studied: Wichita State Univ, Arthur Newman, Wichita, KA; Armen Boyajian, New York. Debut: Zuniga (*Carmen*) New York City Opera 1973. Awards: Finalist, Met Op Ntl Counc Aud 1972.
Sang with major companies in USA: Milwaukee Florentine, Newark, New York City Opera, Omaha, Philadelphia Lyric Opera, Santa Fe. Roles with these companies incl BIZET: Escamillo★ (*Carmen*); CHERUBINI: Creon★ (*Medea*); DONIZETTI: Henry VIII★ (*Anna Bolena*); GOUNOD: Méphistophélès★ (*Faust*); MOZART: Don Alfonso★ (*Così fan tutte*), Don Giovanni★, Figaro★ (*Nozze di Figaro*); OFFENBACH: Coppélius etc★ (*Contes d'Hoffmann*); PONCHIELLI: Alvise★ (*Gioconda*); PUCCINI: Colline★ (*Bohème*); ROSSINI: Don Basilio★ (*Barbiere di Siviglia*). Also DONIZETTI: Raimondo★ (*Lucia*). Mgmt: CAM/USA.

RANDAZZO, ARLENE CATHERINE; née Hampe. Coloratura soprano. American. Resident mem: New York City Opera. Born Chicago, IL, USA. Husband Salvatore, occupation singer. One daughter. Studied: Lola Urbach, New York; Henry Street Music Settlement, New York; Felix Popper, Kurt Adler, Otto Guth, Carlo Moresco, coaching, New York.
Sang with major companies in ITA: Spoleto Fest; USA: Hartford, Newark, New York City Opera, Philadelphia Grand, Washington DC. Roles with these companies incl BELLINI: Elvira★ (*Puritani*); DONIZETTI: Norina (*Don Pasquale*), Lucia★; GOUNOD: Marguerite (*Faust*), Juliette; LEONCAVALLO: Nedda (*Pagliacci*); MOZART: Königin der Nacht (*Zauberflöte*); PUCCINI: Musetta★ (*Bohème*); RIMSKY-KORSAKOV: Coq d'or; ROSSINI: Rosina★ (*Barbiere di Siviglia*); STRAUSS, J: Adele★ (*Fledermaus*); STRAUSS, R: Sophie (*Rosenkavalier*); VERDI: Oscar (*Ballo in maschera*), Gilda★ (*Rigoletto*), Violetta (*Traviata*); WARD: Abigail (*Crucible*). Gives recitals. Appears with symphony

orchestra. Res: 221 W 82 St, New York, NY 10024, USA. Mgmt: ACA/USA.

RANDOVA, EVA. Mezzo-soprano. Russian. Resident mem: Deutsche Oper Berlin; Deutsche Oper am Rhein, Düsseldorf.
Sang with major companies in CZE: Prague National; FR GER: Bayreuth Fest, Berlin Deutsche Oper, Düsseldorf-Duisburg, Stuttgart; HOL: Amsterdam; SWE: Stockholm; USSR: Moscow Bolshoi; USA: San Francisco Opera; et al. Roles with these companies incl VERDI: Ulrica (*Ballo in maschera*); WAGNER: Ortrud (*Lohengrin*), Kundry (*Parsifal*), Erda (*Rheingold, Siegfried*), Venus (*Tannhäuser*); et al. Also WAGNER: Gutrune (*Götterdämmerung*).

RANKIN, NELL. Dramatic mezzo-soprano. American. Resident mem: Metropolitan Opera, New York. Born 3 Jan 1926, Montgomery, AL. Husband Dr Hugh Clark Davidson, occupation physician for internal medicine. Studied: Mme Jeanne Lorraine, Birmingham, AL; Mme Karin Branzell, New York. Debut: Ortrud (*Lohengrin*) Stadttheater Zurich 1950. Awards: First Prize Intl Conc de Musique, Geneva 1950; Critics Circle Awd, outstanding operatic perf in Spain 1968; placed in American Hall of Fame 1972.
Sang with major companies in ARG: Buenos Aires; AUS: Vienna Staatsoper; CAN: Montreal/Quebec, Vancouver; GRE: Athens Fest; ITA: Bologna, Milan La Scala, Naples; MEX: Mexico City; SPA: Barcelona; SWI: Basel, Zurich; UK: London Royal; USA: Chicago, Cincinnati, Fort Worth, Hartford, Houston, Miami, Milwaukee Florentine, Newark, New Orleans, New York Met, Omaha, Philadelphia Grand, Pittsburgh, San Antonio, San Francisco Opera, Seattle, Washington DC. Roles with these companies incl BELLINI: Adalgisa (*Norma*); BERLIOZ: Cassandre (*Troyens*); BIZET: Carmen; CILEA: Princesse de Bouillon (*A. Lecouvreur*); MASSENET: Charlotte (*Werther*); MOZART: Dorabella (*Così fan tutte*); MUSSORGSKY: Marina (*Boris Godunov*); OFFENBACH: Giulietta (*Contes d'Hoffmann*); PONCHIELLI: Laura★ (*Gioconda*); SAINT-SAENS: Dalila; STRAUSS, R: Herodias★ (*Salome*); VERDI: Amneris★ (*Aida*), Ulrica★ (*Ballo in maschera*), Eboli★ (*Don Carlo*), Azucena★ (*Trovatore*); WAGNER: Ortrud★ (*Lohengrin*), Fricka (*Walküre*), Brangäne★ (*Tristan und Isolde*). Also MASCAGNI: Santuzza★ (*Cavalleria rusticana*); WAGNER: Gutrune★ (*Götterdämmerung*). Gives recitals. Appears with symphony orchestra. Teaches voice. Coaches repertoire. Res: New York, USA. Mgmt: LLF/USA.

RÀPALO, UGO. Conductor of opera and symphony; composer. Italian. Artistic Dir & Resident Cond, San Carlo Opera, Naples. Also Resident Cond, Teatro S Carlo Orch, Naples. Born 25 Feb 1914, Naples. Wife Clara Maresca. Three children. Studied: Consv of Music S Pietro a Maiella, Naples; Profs Cilèa, Gennaro Napoli. Plays the piano. Operatic training as asst cond at var Ital opera comps 1935-46. Operatic debut: *Carmen* Teatro S Carlo, Naples 1935. Symphonic debut: Orch da Camera, Naples 1945. Awards: First Prize SIAE Rome 1941, Conc Socy Scarlatti 1954.

Conducted with major companies in BRA: Rio de Janeiro; FRA: Toulouse; FR GER: Frankfurt; HUN: Budapest; ITA: Bologna, Genoa, Milan La Scala, Naples, Parma, Rome Opera, Trieste, Turin; MON: Monte Carlo; POR: Lisbon; SPA: Barcelona; UK: London Royal. **Operas with these companies incl** BELLINI: *Norma, Sonnambula;* BOITO: *Mefistofele;* CATALANI: *Wally;* CILEA: *A. Lecouvreur*★; CIMAROSA: *Matrimonio segreto;* DONIZETTI: *Anna Bolena, Don Pasquale, Elisir, Favorite*★, *Lucia, Roberto Devereux;* GIORDANO: *Andrea Chénier*★, *Fedora;* GOUNOD: *Faust;* HUMPERDINCK: *Hänsel und Gretel;* LEONCAVALLO: *Pagliacci*★‡; MASCAGNI: *Amico Fritz, Cavalleria rusticana*‡; MASSENET: *Manon, Werther;* MENOTTI: *Medium, Old Maid and the Thief;* MUSSORGSKY: *Boris Godunov;* ORFF: *Carmina burana;* PAISIELLO: *Barbiere di Siviglia;* PERGOLESI: *Frate 'nnamorato;* PONCHIELLI: *Gioconda;* PUCCINI: *Bohème*★‡, *Fanciulla del West*★, *Gianni Schicchi, Manon Lescaut, Suor Angelica, Tabarro, Tosca*★, *Turandot;* ROSSINI: *Barbiere di Siviglia*★, *Cambiale di matrimonio, Guillaume Tell;* SAINT-SAENS: *Samson et Dalila;* VERDI: *Aida, Ballo in maschera*★, *Don Carlo, Falstaff, Forza del destino, Nabucco, Otello*★, *Rigoletto*★, *Simon Boccanegra, Traviata, Trovatore*★; WOLF-FERRARI: *Segreto di Susanna;* ZANDONAI: *Francesca da Rimini.* Also PAISIELLO: *Duello comico;* PERSICO: *Locandiera, Bisbetica donata;* NAPOLI: *Peccatori;* LANGELLA: *Assunta Spina.* Recorded for Philips, RCA, Colosseum, Haydn Soc, BASF, Fabbri, Fontana. Conducted major orch in Europe. **Operas composed:** *Amoroso furfante* Teatro Novità, Bergamo 1941. Teaches at Naples Consv. **Res:** V Andrea d'Isernia 20, Naples, Italy.

RAPP, JACQUES. Scenic and costume designer for opera, theater, television; specl in sets. Is a lighting designer; also a painter, sculptor & illustrator. French. Resident designer, Opéra de Lyon. Born 16 May 1930, Strasbourg. Wife Claude Moussier, occupation dir, theater agency. Two children. Studied: Acad d'Arts décoratifs, Strasbourg. Prof training: at opera companies. **Operatic debut:** Opéra de Strasbourg 1950.

Designed for major companies in ARG: Buenos Aires; FRA: Bordeaux, Lyon, Marseille, Nancy, Paris, Rouen, Strasbourg, Toulouse; FR GER: Berlin; ITA: Venice; POR: Lisbon; SWI: Basel, Geneva. **Operas designed for these companies incl** AUBER: *Fra Diavolo;* BEETHOVEN: *Fidelio*★; BERG: *Wozzeck*★; BERLIOZ: *Damnation de Faust*★; BIZET: *Carmen;* BRITTEN: *Albert Herring*★, *Peter Grimes;* CIMAROSA: *Matrimonio segreto;* DONIZETTI: *Lucia;* DUKAS: *Ariane et Barbe Bleue;* FALLA: *Retablo de Maese Pedro;* GLUCK: *Orfeo ed Euridice;* GOUNOD: *Faust, Mireille, Roméo et Juliette;* HENZE: *Prinz v Homburg;* HINDEMITH: *Hin und zurück;* IBERT: *Angélique;* JANACEK: *Jenufa*★; KODALY: *Háry János;* LALO: *Roi d'Ys;* LECOCQ: *Fille de Madame Angot;* MARTINU: *Trois souhaites*★; MASSENET: *Manon, Thaïs;* MOZART: *Così fan tutte*★, *Don Giovanni*★, *Entführung aus dem Serail*★, *Nozze di Figaro, Schauspieldirektor;* OFFENBACH: *Contes d'Hoffmann, Périchole;* ORFF: *Carmina burana;*

PERGOLESI: *Serva padrona;* PUCCINI: *Bohème, Fanciulla del West, Gianni Schicchi, Tosca;* PURCELL: *Dido and Aeneas;* RAVEL: *Heure espagnole;* ROSSINI: *Barbiere di Siviglia;* SAINT-SAENS: *Samson et Dalila;* STRAUSS, J: *Fledermaus;* STRAVINSKY: *Rake's Progress*★; VERDI: *Aida, Don Carlo, Falstaff, Rigoletto, Simon Boccanegra, Traviata;* WAGNER: *Tristan und Isolde*★; WEILL: *Aufstieg und Fall der Stadt Mahagonny.* Also OHANA: *Autodafé;* PRODOMIDES: *Passion selon nos doutes;* KOSMA: *Hussards;* PREY: *Jonas;* DUHAMEL: *Oiseaux, Rital.* Exhibitions of stage designs, paintings & graphics, Opéra de Lyon. **Res:** Le Sequoia/Charrière Blanche, Ecully, France.

RAVAGLIA, EMILIA. Lyric coloratura soprano. Italian. Born 15 Jan 1936, Padua, Italy. Single. Studied: Adelaide Saraceni, Gilda Dalla Rizza. **Debut:** Gnese (*Campiello*) La Fenice, Venice 1961-62. Previous occupations: piano teacher. Awards: Winner Intl Singing Compt, Teatro la Fenice, Venice.

Sang with major companies in AUS: Salzburg Fest; FR GER: Munich Staatsoper, ISR: Tel Aviv; ITA: Bologna, Florence Maggio, Milan La Scala, Naples, Palermo, Rome Opera, Turin, Venice; USA: New York Met. **Roles with these companies incl** CIMAROSA: Carolina (*Matrimonio segreto*); DONIZETTI: Norina‡ (*Don Pasquale*), Adina (*Elisir*), Rita; GALUPPI: Eugenia (*Filosofo di campagna*); HANDEL: Dalinda‡ (*Ariodante*); HAYDN: Vespina (*Infedeltà delusa*); HUMPERDINCK: Gretel; MASSENET: Sophie (*Werther*); MONTEVERDI: Clorinda (*Combattimento di Tancredi*); MOZART: Despina★ (*Così fan tutte*), Blondchen★ (*Entführung aus dem Serail*), Mme Herz‡ (*Schauspieldirektor*), Königin der Nacht★‡ (*Zauberflöte*); ORFF: Solo★ (*Carmina burana*); PAISIELLO: Rosina‡ (*Barbiere di Siviglia*); PERGOLESI: Serpina★‡ (*Serva padrona*); PUCCINI: Musetta (*Bohème*), Lisette★ (*Rondine*); THOMAS: Philine (*Mignon*); VERDI: Gilda (*Rigoletto*); WOLF-FERRARI: Lucieta (*Quattro rusteghi*), Susanna (*Segreto di Susanna*). Also CIMAROSA: Gismonde★ (*Marito disperato*); RAVEL: Princesse★ (*Enfant et les sortilèges*). **World premieres:** BUCCHI: Moglie (*Coccodrillo*) Teatro Comunale, Bologna 1970; MANNINO: Luisella, Palermo 1969. Recorded for: Chants du Monde. Video/Film: PAISIELLO: (*Barbiere di Siviglia*); PERGOLESI: (*Geloso schernito*). Gives recitals. Appears with symphony orchestra. **Res:** Annia Faustina 5/D, Rome, Italy.

RAVAZZI, GABRIELLA. Lyric soprano. Italian. Born 3 May 1942, Milan. Husband Palumbo Mosca Manlio, occupation musician. Studied: Carla Castellani, Adelina Cambi; Diploma in violin, Consv G Verdi, Milan. **Debut:** Susanna (*Nozze di Figaro*) Teatro Nuovo, Milan 1965. Previous occupations: violinist. Awards: Gold Medal Intl Conc Viotti; Winner Conc Intl Teatro Massimo, Palermo; Ntl Opera Conc, Milan; Golden Nut in Opera, Lecco 1970.

Sang with major companies in BEL: Brussels; ITA: Bologna, Genoa, Milan La Scala, Palermo, Parma, Trieste, Turin, Venice. **Roles with these companies incl** BIZET: Micaëla (*Carmen*); CIMA-

ROSA: Elisetta★ (*Matrimonio segreto*); DALLA-PICCOLA: Mrs Fabian★ (*Volo di notte*); DONIZETTI: Norina★ (*Don Pasquale*), Adina★ (*Elisir*); GALUPPI: Eugenia (*Filosofo di campagna*); LIGETI: Soprano I★ (*Aventures/Nouvelles Aventures*); MENOTTI: Amelia (*Amelia al ballo*), Monica★ (*Medium*), Lucy★ (*Telephone*); MONTEVERDI: Clorinda★ (*Combattimento di Tancredi*); MOZART: Despina (*Così fan tutte*), Zerlina (*Don Giovanni*), Mlle Silberklang (*Schauspieldirektor*), Contessa★ & Susanna (*Nozze di Figaro*), Celidora★ (*Oca del Cairo*); PERGOLESI: Serpina★ (*Serva padrona*); PUCCINI: Musetta★ (*Bohème*), Lisette★ (*Rondine*), Liù (*Turandot*); RIMSKY-KORSAKOV: Reine de Schemakan★ (*Coq d'or*); SALIERI: Tonina★ (*Prima la musica*); VERDI: Oscar (*Ballo in maschera*); WOLF-FERRARI: Susanna (*Segreto di Susanna*). Also PAISIELLO: Spiritillo (*Osteria di marechiaro*); CIMAROSA: Eugenia★ (*Marito disperato*); PETRASSI: Cristina★ (*Cordovano*); BERIO: Ragazzo★ (*Laborintus II*); TESTI: Nastia★ (*Albergo dei poveri*); MADERNA: Scintilla★ (*Satyricon*); WEBER: Clarissa★ (*Drei Pintos*). **World premieres:** MANZONI: Carlotta-Donna 1 (*Per Massimiliano Robespierre*) Teatro Comunale Bologna 1975; CHAILLY: Lei (*Sogno ma forse no*) Teatro Verdi Trieste 1975; RENOSTO: Sposa (*Camera degli sposi*) Piccola Scala Milan 1972; SCIARRINO: Sorella (*Amore e psiche*) La Scala Milan 1973; CORREGGIA: Ayl, Teatro Regio Turin 1973; GASLINI: Soprano (*Colloquio con Malcolm X*) Teatro Comunale Genoa 1970; PACCAGNINI: Soprano (*La misura e il mistero*) La Scala Milan 1970. Recorded for: Fratelli Fabbri. Video – RAI: Mädchen (*Moses und Aron*); Lisetta (*Vera costanza*). Radio Telev Swiss: Brigida (*Sposi per accidente*); Gives recitals. Appears with symphony orchestra. Teaches voice. On faculty of Consv Boito di Parma. **Res:** Strada Fioccardo 51, 10133 Turin, Italy.

RAYAM, CURTIS. Lyric tenor. American. Resident mem: Opera Assn of Greater Miami, FL. Born 4 Feb 1951, Bellville, FL. Single. Studied: Univ of Miami, Mary Henderson Buckley, Coral Gables. **Debut:** Lampanaio (*Manon Lescaut*) Miami Opera 1971. Awards: Met Op Ntl Counc Aud, finalist 1972; Dealey Awd winner Dallas 1974.
Sang with major companies in USA: Houston, Jackson Opera/South, Miami. **Roles with these cos incl** DONIZETTI: Nemorino★ (*Elisir*), Beppe★ (*Rita*), JOPLIN: Remus★ (*Treemonisha*); PUCCINI: Rodolfo★ (*Bohème*), Pinkerton★ (*Butterfly*); VERDI: Cassio★ (*Otello*). Gives recitals. Appears with symphony orchestra. Teaches voice. On faculty of Univ of Miami, Coral Gables, FL. **Res:** Miami, FL, USA.

RAZADOR, JOSÉ Lyric tenor. Italian. Resident mem: Centre Lyrique de Wallonie, Liège, Belgium. Born 15 Mar 1935, Châtelineau, Belgium. Studied: José Lens, Jean Lescanne. **Debut:** Rodolfo (*Bohème*) Liège Opera 1971. Previous occupations: tool mechanic. Awards: First Prize, Royal Consv of Mons, Belgium.
Sang with major companies in BEL: Brussels, Liège; FRA: Nice, Rouen, Toulouse. **Roles with these companies incl** BIZET: Don José★ (*Carmen*), Nadir★ (*Pêcheurs de perles*); BORODIN: Vladi-mir★ (*Prince Igor*); GIORDANO: Andrea Chénier★; GOUNOD: Faust★; LALO: Mylio★ (*Roi d'Ys*); MASSENET: Werther★; MUSSORGSKY: Dimitri★ (*Boris Godunov*); OFFENBACH: Hoffmann★; ORFF: Solo★ (*Carmina burana*); PROKOFIEV: Prince★ (*Love for Three Oranges*); PUCCINI: Rodolfo★ (*Bohème*), Rinuccio★ (*Gianni Schicchi*), Pinkerton★ (*Butterfly*), Cavaradossi★ (*Tosca*), Calaf★ (*Turandot*); SMETANA: Hans★ (*Bartered Bride*); STRAUSS, R: Ein Sänger★ (*Rosenkavalier*); TCHAIKOVSKY: Lenski★ (*Eugene Onegin*); VERDI: Fenton★ (*Falstaff*), Duca di Mantova★ (*Rigoletto*), Alfredo★ (*Traviata*). Video – TV: Rodolfo (*Bohème*). Gives recitals. Teaches voice. On faculty of Music Acad Auvelais. **Res:** 32 rue Sainte-Anne, Auvelais, Belgium. **Mgmt:** IMR/FRA; RAP/FRA.

REALE, MARCELLA. Spinto soprano. American. Born Los Angeles, CA, USA. Studied: Lotte Lehmann, Armand Tokatyan, Santa Barbara; Hochschule für Musik, R Gundlach, Munich. **Debut:** SONZOGNO: (*Passeggeri*) Opera House, Trieste 1961. Awards: Grants from Rockefeller Fndt, M B Rockefeller Fund, Fulbright Schlshp.
Sang with major companies in AUSTRL: Sydney; CAN: Ottawa, Toronto; CZE: Prague National & Smetana; GRE: Athens National; FR GER: Berlin Deutsche Oper, Bonn, Cologne, Düsseldorf-Duisburg, Essen, Hamburg, Hannover, Krefeld, Mannheim, Stuttgart, Wiesbaden, Wuppertal; GER DR: Berlin Staatsoper; ISR: Tel Aviv; ITA: Bologna, Florence Comunale, Genoa, Naples, Parma, Rome Opera, Trieste, Turin; S AFR: Johannesburg; SPA: Barcelona; SWI: Basel, Zurich; UK: Cardiff Welsh, London Royal; USA: Hartford, New York City Opera, Philadelphia Grand, Seattle; YUG: Zagreb, Belgrade. **Roles with these companies incl** BOITO: Margherita (*Mefistofele*); CHARPENTIER: Louise★; CILEA: Adriana Lecouvreur★; CIMAROSA: Carolina (*Matrimonio segreto*); FALLA: Salud (*Vida breve*); GIORDANO: Maddalena★ (*Andrea Chénier*), Fedora★; GOUNOD: Marguerite (*Faust*); JANACEK: Jenufa★; KORNGOLD: Marietta (*Tote Stadt*); LEONCAVALLO: Nedda★ (*Pagliacci*); MASSENET: Manon; MOZART: Fiordiligi (*Così fan tutte*), Donna Anna & Donna Elvira (*Don Giovanni*), Contessa (*Nozze di Figaro*); OFFENBACH: Antonia (*Contes d'Hoffmann*); PUCCINI: Mimi★ (*Bohème*), Minnie★ (*Fanciulla del West*), Lauretta★ (*Gianni Schicchi*), Cio-Cio-San★ (*Butterfly*), Manon Lescaut★, Magda (*Rondine*), Suor Angelica, Giorgetta★ (*Tabarro*), Tosca★, Liù★ (*Turandot*); STRAUSS, R: Chrysothemis (*Elektra*); VERDI: Elisabetta (*Don Carlo*), Leonora (*Forza del destino*), Desdemona★ (*Otello*), Violetta★ (*Traviata*); WAGNER: Senta★ (*Fliegende Holländer*), Elisabeth★ (*Tannhäuser*); ZANDONAI: Francesca da Rimini. Also d'ALBERT: Marta (*Tiefland*); SCARLATTI: Loudice (*Mitridate Eupatore*); BLACHER: Helen (*Flut*); WEILL: Fangele (*Zar lässt sich photographieren*); **World premieres:** SONZOGNO: (*Passeggeri*) Trieste 1967, (*Boule de suif*) Bergamo 1970. Recorded for: EMI, Fonit-Cetra. Video/Film: Manon Lescaut. Gives recitals. Appears with symphony orchestra. **Res:** Lugano, Switzerland, & Milan, Italy. **Mgmt:** MAU/USA; SLA/UK.

REARDON, JOHN. Lyric & dramatic baritone. American. Resident mem: Metropolitan Opera, New York. Born 8 Apr 1930, New York. Single. Studied: Rollins Coll, Ross Rossazza, Winter Park, FL; Margaret Harshaw, Martial Singher, USA. **Debut:** Dr Falke (*Fledermaus*) New York City Opera 1954. Awards: Hon DH, Rollins Coll, Winter Park, FL; Musician of the Month, *Musical America* magazine, USA.

Sang with major companies in CAN: Toronto, Vancouver; ITA: Spoleto Fest, Venice; USA: Baltimore, Boston, Cincinnati, Dallas, Fort Worth, Hawaii, Houston, Miami, New Orleans, New York Met & City Opera, Philadelphia Grand & Lyric, St Paul, San Antonio, San Diego, San Francisco Opera, Santa Fe, Seattle, Washington DC. **Roles with these companies incl** BARBER: Doctor (*Vanessa*); BELLINI: Ernesto (*Pirata*); BERG: Dr Schön★ (*Lulu*); BERLIOZ: Méphistophélès (Damnation de Faust); BIZET: Escamillo★ (*Carmen*); CAVALLI: Amida (*Ormindo*); DEBUSSY: Pelléas; DELIUS: Dark Fiddler★ (*Village Romeo and Juliet*); DONIZETTI: Malatesta (*Don Pasquale*), Belcore★ (*Elisir*); EINEM: George Danton (*Dantons Tod*), Don Quixote (*Retablo de Maese Pedro*); HENZE: Pentheus (*Bassariden*); HINDEMITH: Cardillac; JANACEK: Shishkov★ (*From the House of the Dead*), Starek★ (*Jenufa*); MASSENET: Albert★ (*Werther*); MENOTTI: Husband (*Amelia al ballo*), Abdul★ (*Dernier sauvage*), Dr Stone (*Globolinks*), Donato (*Maria Golovin*), Bob‡ (*Old Maid and the Thief*); MONTEVERDI: Orfeo★; MOORE: Horace Tabor★ (*Baby Doe*); MOZART: Guglielmo (*Così fan tutte*), Don Giovanni★, Conte Almaviva★ (*Nozze di Figaro*), Papageno★ (*Zauberflöte*); OFFENBACH: Coppélius etc (*Contes d'Hoffmann*); ORFF: Solo (*Carmina burana*); PENDERECKI: Grandier (*Teufel von Loudun*); PROKOFIEV: Prince Andrei Bolkonsky★ (*War and Peace*); PUCCINI: Marcello★ (*Bohème*), Gianni Schicchi, Sharpless★ (*Butterfly*), Lescaut (*Manon Lescaut*), Scarpia (*Tosca*); PURCELL: Aeneas (*Dido and Aeneas*); RAVEL: Ramiro (*Heure espagnole*); ROSSINI: Figaro (*Barbiere di Siviglia*), Dandini (*Cenerentola*), Conte Asdrubal★‡ (*Pietra del paragone*); SHOSTAKOVICH: Platon Kusmich Kovalioff (*The Nose*); STRAUSS, J: Eisenstein (*Fledermaus*); STRAUSS, R: Mandryka (*Arabella*), Olivier (*Capriccio*), Jochanaan (*Salome*), Harlekin★ (*Ariadne auf Naxos*); STRAVINSKY: Nick Shadow‡ (*Rake's Progress*); TCHAIKOVSKY: Yeletsky (*Pique Dame*); VERDI: Ford★ (*Falstaff*), Germont (*Traviata*); WAGNER: Wolfram (*Tannhäuser*). Also BERLIOZ: Fieramosca★ (*Benvenuto Cellini*), Somarone (*Béatrice et Bénédict*); FLOYD: Heathcliff (*Wuthering Heights*); GOUNOD: Valentin (*Faust*), Mercutio★ (*Roméo et Juliette*); HUMPERDINCK: Peter (*Hänsel und Gretel*); LIEBERMANN: Poquelin (*Schule der Frauen*); PROKOFIEV: Pantalone (*Love for Three Oranges*); ROSSINI: Taddeo★ (*Italiana in Algeri*). **World premieres:** HOIBY: Belaev (*Natalia Petrovna*) New York City Opera 1964, John Buchanan (*Summer and Smoke*) St Paul Opera, MN 1971; LEVY: Orin (*Mourning Becomes Electra*) Metropolitan Opera, New York 1967; MOORE: Miles Dunster (*Wings of the Dove*) New York City Opera 1961; Charles

(*Carry Nation*) Univ of Kansas, Lawrence 1966; PASATIERI: Trigorin (*Seagull*) Houston Opera 1974; WEISGALL: Yehoyada (*Athaliah*) Concert Opera Assn, New York 1964. Recorded for: Columbia, Mercury, Vanguard, Seraphim, Desto. Video/Film: Groom (*Labyrinth*); Voice of God (*Flood*); Tomsky (*Pique Dame*); Shishkov (*From the House of the Dead*); Masetto (*Don Giovanni*); Papageno (*Zauberflöte*); Jason (*Medea in Corinto*). Gives recitals. Appears with symphony orchestra. Teaches voice. Coaches repertoire. **Res:** New York, NY, USA. Mgmt: HJH/USA.

REBMANN, LISELOTTE. Lyric soprano. German. Resident mem: Staatsoper, Stuttgart. Born 8 Mar 1935, Stuttgart. Husband Karl-Erich Haase, occupation theater agent. Studied: Prof Friedl Mielsch-Nied, Stuttgart; Prof Hermann Reutter, Prof Clara Ebers, Hamburg. **Debut:** Contessa (*Nozze di Figaro*) Staatstheater, Wiesbaden 1959. Awards: Kammersängerin.

Sang with major companies in ARG: Buenos Aires; AUS: Salzburg Fest, Vienna Volksoper; FRA: Strasbourg; GRE: Athens National & Fest; FR GER: Bayreuth Fest, Berlin Deutsche Oper, Bielefeld, Bonn, Cologne, Darmstadt, Dortmund, Düsseldorf-Duisburg, Essen, Frankfurt, Hamburg, Hannover, Karlsruhe, Kassel, Mannheim, Munich Staatsoper, Nürnberg, Saarbrücken, Stuttgart, Wiesbaden, Wuppertal; HOL: Amsterdam; ITA: Turin; NOR: Oslo; SWI: Zurich; UK: Edinburgh Fest; USA: Chicago, New York Met. **Roles with these companies incl** BEETHOVEN: Marzelline★ (*Fidelio*); BERLIOZ: Marguerite★ (*Damnation de Faust*); BIZET: Micaëla★ (*Carmen*); GOUNOD: Marguerite★ (*Faust*); HENZE: Luise★ (*Junge Lord*); MOZART: Vitellia★ (*Clemenza di Tito*), Fiordiligi★ (*Così fan tutte*), Donna Anna★ (*Don Giovanni*), Konstanze (*Entführung aus dem Serail*), Ilia & Elettra★ (*Idomeneo*), Contessa★ & Susanna (*Nozze di Figaro*), Pamina★ (*Zauberflöte*); OFFENBACH: Antonia★ (*Contes d'Hoffmann*); ORFF: Solo (*Carmina burana*), Kluge★ (*Kluge*); PUCCINI: Mimi★ (*Bohème*), Cio-Cio-San★ (*Butterfly*), Liù★ (*Turandot*); SMETANA: Marie (*Bartered Bride*); STRAUSS, R: Arabella★ & Zdenka (*Arabella*), Ariadne★ (*Ariadne auf Naxos*), Daphne★, Kaiserin★ (*Frau ohne Schatten*), Marschallin★ & Sophie (*Rosenkavalier*); TCHAIKOVSKY: Tatiana★ (*Eugene Onegin*); TIPPETT: Jennifer★ (*Midsummer Marriage*); VERDI: Aida★, Elisabetta★ (*Don Carlo*), Alice Ford★ (*Falstaff*), Leonora★ (*Forza del destino*), Luisa Miller★, Desdemona★ (*Otello*), Gilda (*Rigoletto*), Violetta★ (*Traviata*); WAGNER: Eva★ (*Meistersinger*), Elisabeth★ (*Tannhäuser*); WEBER: Agathe★ (*Freischütz*). Recorded for: DG. Gives recitals. Appears with symphony orchestra. **Res:** Solferinoweg 20A, Stuttgart 80, FR Ger. Mgmt: SLZ/FRG; HUS/FRG.

REECE, ARLEY R. Dramatic tenor. American. Born 27 Aug 1945, Yoakum, TX, USA. Divorced. One child. Studied: No Texas St Univ, Eugene Conley; Manhattan School of Music, Daniel Ferro. **Debut:** Assad (*Königin von Saba*) American Opera Society 1970. Previous occupations: manufacturer's rep.

Sang with major companies in BEL: Brussels; FR GER: Karlsruhe; USA: Kentucky, Lake

George, New York City Opera, Washington DC. **Roles with these companies incl** BIZET: Don José★ (*Carmen*); LEONCAVALLO: Canio★ (*Pagliacci*); PUCCINI: Cavaradossi★ (*Tosca*); STRAUSS, R: Bacchus★ (*Ariadne auf Naxos*); VERDI: Macduff★ (*Macbeth*); WEILL: Fatty & Jim Mahoney (*Aufstieg und Fall der Stadt Mahagonny*). Appears with symphony orchestra. **Res:** Lübeck, FR Ger. Mgmt: SLZ/FRG; MIN/UK.

REED, DIANA LaDEAN. Lyric coloratura soprano. American. Born 18 Feb 1947, Akron, O, USA. Married. Studied: Philadelphia Acad of Music, Maureen Forrester; Acad of Vocal Arts, Dorothy Di Scala, Philadelphia. **Debut:** Frasquita (*Carmen*) Philadelphia Lyric 1970. Awards: Outstanding Young Woman of America, Philadelphia Musical Acad; Philadelphia Orch Youth Conct Awd.
Sang with major companies in SPA: Barcelona; USA: Hartford, Philadelphia Lyric. **Roles with these companies incl** BIZET: Micaëla★ (*Carmen*); DONIZETTI: Marie★ (*Fille du régiment*), Lucia★; PUCCINI: Musetta★ (*Bohème*), Lisette★ (*Rondine*); ROSSINI: Rosina★ (*Barbiere di Siviglia*). Gives recitals. Appears with symphony orchestra. **Res:** 111 Sunset Farm Rd, Hartford, CT, USA. Mgmt: HUR/USA.

REICH, GÜNTER. Dramatic baritone. German. Resident mem: Württembergische Staatsoper, Stuttgart. Born Liegnitz, Germany. Wife Judith. Two children. Studied: Staatl Hochschule für Musik, Prof Sengeleitner, Berlin; Dr Unold, Mannheim. **Debut:** Iago (*Otello*) Gelsenkirchen Opera 1961. Previous occupations: farmer, tech drawing. Awards: Kammersänger, State of Württemberg; Siemens-Preis, Senate of Berlin.
Sang with major companies in AUS: Salzburg Fest; BRA: Rio de Janeiro; FR GER: Berlin Deutsche Oper, Bonn, Hamburg, Munich Staatsoper, Stuttgart; GER DR: Leipzig; HOL: Amsterdam; POR: Lisbon; SPA: Barcelona; SWI: Zurich; UK: Edinburgh Fest. **Roles with these companies incl** d'ALBERT: Sebastiano (*Tiefland*); BARTOK: Bluebeard★; BEETHOVEN: Don Pizarro (*Fidelio*); BERG: Wozzeck; BERLIOZ: Méphistophélès (*Damnation de Faust*); BIZET: Escamillo (*Carmen*); DALLAPICCOLA: Ulisse★; DONIZETTI: Don Pasquale★; GLUCK: Hercule (*Alceste*); GOTOVAC: Sima (*Ero der Schelm*); HAYDN: Eclittico (*Mondo della luna*); HENZE: Lescaut (*Boulevard Solitude*); HINDEMITH: Cardillac; JANACEK: Jaroslav Prus (*Makropoulos Affair*); KLEBE: Jakobowsky (*Jakobowsky und der Oberst*); LORTZING: Graf Eberbach (*Wildschütz*), Peter I (*Zar und Zimmermann*); MASCAGNI: Alfio (*Cavalleria rusticana*); MOZART: Guglielmo & Don Alfonso★ (*Così fan tutte*), Leporello★ (*Don Giovanni*), Conte Almaviva (*Nozze di Figaro*), Allazim (*Zaïde*); NICOLAI: Falstaff (*Lustigen Weiber*); OFFENBACH: Coppélius etc (*Contes d'Hoffmann*); ORFF: Solo★ (*Carmina burana*), König★ (*Kluge*); PERGOLESI: Marcaniello (*Frate 'nnamorato*); PUCCINI: Gianni Schicchi, Sharpless (*Butterfly*), Scarpia★ (*Tosca*); ROSSINI: Dott Bartolo★ (*Barbiere di Siviglia*), Mustafà★ (*Italiana in Algeri*), Moïse; SCHOENBERG: Mann★ (*Glückliche Hand*),

Moses★‡; STRAUSS, R: Musiklehrer★ (*Ariadne auf Naxos*), Orest (*Elektra*); STRAVINSKY: Creon & Tiresias (*Oedipus Rex*); VERDI: Amonasro (*Aida*), Renato (*Ballo in maschera*), Nabucco, Iago (*Otello*), Rigoletto, Germont★ (*Traviata*); WAGNER: Telramund★ (*Lohengrin*), Hans Sachs★ & Beckmesser (*Meistersinger*); WOLF: Tio Lukas (*Corregidor*); WOLF-FERRARI: Lunardo★ (*Quattro rusteghi*). Also PFITZNER: Morone (*Palestrina*); STRAUSS, R: Kommandant (*Friedenstag*). **World premieres:** BLACHER: Schimele (*200,000 Taler*) Deutsche Oper Berlin 1969; TAL: Flavius Silva (*Masada 967*) Jerusalem 1973; ZIMMERMANN, B: Stolzius (*Soldaten*) Opera Cologne 1965. Recorded for: Philips, CBS. Video/Film: Moses (*Moses und Aron*). Gives recitals. Appears with symphony orchestra. Teaches voice. **Res:** Hainbuchenweg 41, Stuttgart, FR Ger. Mgmt: SRN/HOL.

REINHARDT, GEORG. Stages/produces opera & theater. German. Operndir & Resident Stage Dir, Deutsche Oper am Rhein, Düsseldorf-Duisburg. Born 27 Mar 1911, Augsburg, Germany. Previous adm positions in opera: Chief Mng, Städtisches Theater Aachen 1941-44 and Städtisches Theater Lübeck 1944-50.
Directed/produced opera for major companies in ARG: Buenos Aires; AUS: Salzburg Fest; BEL: Brussels; FRA: Paris; FR GER: Berlin Deutsche Oper, Cologne, Düsseldorf-Duisburg, Frankfurt, Wiesbaden, Wuppertal; HOL: Amsterdam; ITA: Florence Comunale, Milan La Scala; POR: Lisbon; SWI: Basel, Zurich; et al. **Operas staged with these companies incl** BARTOK: *Bluebeard's Castle;* BEETHOVEN: *Fidelio;* BERG: *Lulu, Wozzeck;* BUSONI: *Arlecchino;* CAVALIERI: *Rappresentazione;* CAVALLI: *Ormindo;* DALLAPICCOLA: *Prigioniero, Ulisse;* GLUCK: *Orfeo ed Euridice;* HINDEMITH: *Cardillac;* JANACEK: *From the House of the Dead;* MOZART: *Clemenza di Tito, Nozze di Figaro, Zauberflöte;* MUSSORGSKY: *Boris Godunov;* SCHOENBERG: *Glückliche Hand, Moses und Aron;* STRAUSS, R: *Ariadne auf Naxos, Rosenkavalier, Schweigsame Frau;* STRAVINSKY: *Rake's Progress;* VERDI: *Ballo in maschera, Don Carlo, Otello;* WAGNER: *Meistersinger, Parsifal, Rheingold, Walküre, Siegfried, Götterdämmerung;* WEBER: *Freischütz;* ZIMMERMANN: *Soldaten;* et al. Also PETRASSI: *Ritratto di Don Chisciotte;* DALLAPICCOLA: *Job;* HANDEL: *Saul.* **Operatic world premieres:** PENDERECKI: *St Luke Passion* first stgd Düsseldorf 1969.

REINKING, WILHELM. Scenic and costume designer for opera, theater, television. Is a lighting designer; also an architect, opera librettist & translator. German. Resident designer, Deutsche Oper Berlin 1954-74. Born 18 Oct 1896, Aachen, Germany. Wife Annelies, occupation costume designer. Two children. Studied: Tech Hochschulen Karlsruhe & Danzig; Univ Munich. **Operatic debut:** sets & cost, Stadttheater Würzburg 1925. Theater debut: Bayerische Landesbühne, Munich 1924. Previous occupation: soldier WW I; student of architecture and philosophy. Awards: Music Prize of German Critics Assn 1959; Hon mem, Board of Deutsche Oper Berlin 1971; Verdienstkreuz am Bande, Pres of FR Ger 1975. Previous adm positions in opera: Head of Design, Hamburgische Staatsoper 1939-41, Staatsoper Vienna 1941-45.

Designed for major companies in AUS: Salzburg Fest, Vienna Staatsoper; BEL: Brussels; CZE: Prague National; FRA: Paris; FR GER: Berlin Deutsche Oper, Darmstadt, Düsseldorf-Duisburg, Frankfurt, Hamburg, Hannover, Mannheim, Munich Staatsoper & Gärtnerplatz, Stuttgart, Wiesbaden; GER DR: Berlin Staatsoper; ITA: Milan La Scala, Rome Opera; ROM: Bucharest; UK: Edinburgh Fest. **Operas designed for these companies incl** d'ALBERT: *Tiefland;* AUBER: *Fra Diavolo, Muette de Portici;* BEETHOVEN: *Fidelio;* BERG: *Wozzeck;* BIZET: *Carmen;* BORODIN: *Prince Igor;* BRITTEN: *Billy Budd, Rape of Lucretia;* CHERUBINI: *Medea;* CIMAROSA: *Matrimonio segreto;* CORNELIUS: *Barbier von Bagdad;* DEBUSSY: *Pelléas et Mélisande;* DONIZETTI: *Fille du régiment, Lucia;* EGK: *Zaubergeige;* EINEM: *Besuch der alten Dame★, Dantons Tod;* GLUCK: *Iphigénie en Tauride, Orfeo ed Euridice;* GOUNOD: *Faust;* HANDEL: *Giulio Cesare, Rodelinda;* HINDEMITH: *Mathis der Maler;* HUMPERDINCK: *Hänsel und Gretel;* JANACEK: *Katya Kabanova;* LEONCAVALLO: *Pagliacci;* LORTZING: *Wildschütz, Zar und Zimmermann;* MARSCHNER: *Hans Heiling;* MASCAGNI: *Cavalleria rusticana;* MENOTTI: *Consul, Saint of Bleecker Street;* MONIUSZKO: *Halka;* MONTEVERDI: *Incoronazione di Poppea;* MOZART: *Così fan tutte, Don Giovanni, Entführung aus dem Serail★, Idomeneo, Nozze di Figaro, Zauberflöte;* MUSSORGSKY: *Boris Godunov;* NICOLAI: *Lustigen Weiber;* OFFENBACH: *Contes d'Hoffmann;* ORFF: *Bernauerin, Kluge;* PERGOLESI: *Serva padrona;* PFITZNER: *Palestrina;* PUCCINI: *Bohème, Fanciulla del West, Gianni Schicchi, Butterfly, Manon Lescaut, Suor Angelica, Tosca★;* PURCELL: *Dido and Aeneas;* RAVEL: *Heure espagnole;* ROSSINI: *Barbiere di Siviglia;* SATIE: *Socrate;* SMETANA: *Bartered Bride;* STRAUSS, J: *Fledermaus;* STRAUSS, R: *Arabella, Ariadne auf Naxos, Capriccio, Daphne, Elektra, Rosenkavalier, Salome;* STRAVINSKY: *Oedipus Rex★, Rake's Progress;* TCHAIKOVSKY: *Eugene Onegin;* THOMAS: *Mignon;* VERDI: *Aida, Ballo in maschera, Don Carlo, Falstaff, Forza del destino, Macbeth, Nabucco, Otello, Rigoletto, Simon Boccanegra, Traviata, Trovatore, Vespri;* WAGNER: *Fliegende Holländer, Lohengrin, Meistersinger, Parsifal, Tannhäuser, Tristan und Isolde;* WEBER: *Abu Hassan, Freischütz, Oberon;* WEINBERGER: *Schwanda;* WOLF-FERRARI: *Quattro rusteghi, Segreto di Susanna.* **Operatic world premieres:** ORFF: *Bernauerin* Staatsoper, Stuttgart 1947; KLEBE: *Alkmene* Deutsche Oper Berlin 1961. Operatic Video/Film—NDR TV 1968: *Fidelio;* UNITEL Film & TV 1969: *Fidelio.* Exhibitions of stage designs in var museums. **Res:** Breisgauerstr 29, Berlin 38, FR Ger.

REISMAN, JANE MARITZA. Lighting designer for opera, theater and dance. American. Born 25 Mar 1937, New York. Husband Neil Peter Jampolis, occupation stage designer. Studied: Vassar Coll, NY 1959; Bayreuth Master Class 1963. Prof training: Polakov Studio of Stage Design 1967-69. **Operatic debut:** *Butterfly* St Paul Opera, MN 1972. Theater debut: York Playhouse, NY 1961. Previous occupation: film prod; teacher Bennington Coll. Awards: fllshp Bayreuth Master Classes, IIE travel grant. Previous adm positions in opera: Prod Coord, Met Opera Ntl Co 1964-65.

Designed for major companies in USA: St Paul, Washington DC. **Operas designed for these companies incl** DELIUS: *Village Romeo and Juliet★;* MONTEVERDI: *Ritorno d'Ulisse★;* PUCCINI: *Bohème★, Gianni Schicchi★, Butterfly★, Tabarro★;* WAGNER: *Walküre★;* WARD: *Crucible★.* **Res:** 130 W 57 St, New York 10019, USA. Mgmt: SSR/USA.

REITER, RONNY. Scenic and costume designer for opera, theater, film, television; specl in costumes. She is a lighting designer; also a painter, sculptor, illustrator, architect & fashion designer. German. Resident designer, Vereinigte Bühnen, Graz, Austria. Born 9 Apr 1939, Würzburg. Divorced. Studied: Prof Helmut Jürgens, Akad der bildenden Künste, Munich. **Operatic debut:** cost, Staatsoper, Vienna 1963. Theater debut: Munich 1964. Awards: Prize for the best costume design, Theater am Gärtnerplatz Munich.

Designed for major companies in AUS: Bregenz Fest, Graz, Salzburg Fest, Vienna Staatsoper & Volksoper; FR GER: Frankfurt, Hamburg, Munich Staatsoper & Gärtnerplatz; HOL: Amsterdam; SWI: Basel, Zurich; UK: London Royal; YUG: Zagreb. **Operas designed for these companies incl** BARTOK: *Bluebeard's Castle;* BELLINI: *Puritani★;* BERLIOZ: *Damnation de Faust;* BIZET: *Carmen★;* BLACHER: *Romeo und Julia;* DEBUSSY: *Pelléas et Mélisande★;* DONIZETTI: *Lucia★;* EINEM: *Dantons Tod;* GOUNOD: *Faust;* JANACEK: *Excursions of Mr Broucek;* MOZART: *Così fan tutte, Don Giovanni, Zauberflöte;* MUSSORGSKY: *Boris Godunov;* OFFENBACH: *Contes d'Hoffmann★;* PFITZNER: *Palestrina;* PUCCINI: *Gianni Schicchi, Butterfly, Tosca;* RAVEL: *Heure espagnole★;* SCHOENBERG: *Erwartung;* SMETANA: *Bartered Bride, Dalibor;* STRAUSS, R: *Daphne, Frau ohne Schatten, Rosenkavalier;* VERDI: *Forza del destino★;* WAGNER: *Fliegende Holländer, Rheingold, Walküre, Siegfried, Götterdämmerung;* WEBER: *Freischütz.* Also WOLF-FERRARI: *Campiello.* Operatic Video/Film—*Heure espagnole, Freischütz.* Exhibitions of stage designs, paintings, Theatermuseum Vienna, Salzburg Festspielhaus Museum. **Res:** Mauerkircherstr 34, Munich, FR Ger.

REMEDIOS, ALBERTO TELISFORO. Heldentenor. British. Resident mem: English National Opera, London. Born 27 Feb 1935, Liverpool, UK. Wife Judith Annette. Three children. Studied: Edwin Francis, Liverpool; Sadler's Wells Opera jr princp, Arnold Matlers, Clive Carey, Joseph Ayslop, London. **Debut:** Tinca (*Tabarro*) Sadler's Wells Opera 1956. Previous occupations: shipyard apprentice welder. Cheshire; Ntl Service, Army. Awards: Queen's Prize, Royal Coll of Music, London 1957; First Prize, Union of Bulgarian Composers, Sofia 1963.

Sang with major companies in BUL: Sofia; FRA: Rouen; FR GER: Frankfurt; S AFR: Johannes-

burg; UK: Cardiff Welsh, London Royal Opera &
English National; USA: San Francisco Opera.
Roles with these companies incl BERLIOZ: Faust★
(*Damnation de Faust*), Aeneas★ (*Troyens*); BI-
ZET: Don José★ (*Carmen*); CILEA: Maurizio★
(*A. Lecouvreur*); DONIZETTI: Edgardo★ (*Lu-
cia*); FLOTOW: Lionel (*Martha*); GOUNOD:
Faust★; MASCAGNI: Turiddu★ (*Cavalleria rusti-
cana*); MASSENET: Des Grieux★‡ (*Manon*),
Araquil★‡ (*Navarraise*), Werther★; MOZART:
Don Ottavio★ (*Don Giovanni*), Idomeneo★, Ta-
mino★ (*Zauberflöte*); MUSSORGSKY: Dimitri‡
(*Boris Godunov*); PUCCINI: Pinkerton★ (*But-
terfly*), Des Grieux★ (*Manon Lescaut*), Luigi★ (*Ta-
barro*), Cavaradossi★ (*Tosca*); RIMSKY-
KORSAKOV: Prince Vsevolod (*Invisible City of
Kitezh*); SAINT-SAENS: Samson★; STRAUSS,
R: Bacchus★ (*Ariadne auf Naxos*), Ein Sänger★
(*Rosenkavalier*); STRAVINSKY: Oedipus Rex★;
TCHAIKOVSKY: Lenski★ (*Eugene Onegin*);
TIPPETT: Mark★‡ (*Midsummer Marriage*);
VERDI: Don Carlo★, Ernani★, Don Alvaro★
(*Forza del destino*), Otello★‡, Duca di Mantova★‡
(*Rigoletto*), Alfredo★ (*Traviata*); WAGNER: Erik
(*Fliegende Holländer*), Lohengrin, Walther (*Mei-
stersinger*), Siegmund★ (*Walküre*), Siegfried (*Sieg-
fried★, Götterdämmerung★*), Walther v d
Vogelweide★ (*Tannhäuser*); WEBER: Max★
(*Freischütz*). Recorded for: EMI. Gives recitals.
Appears with symphony orchestra. Teaches voice.
Res: 27 Ridgeway Southgate, London N14, UK.
Mgmt: AIM/UK.

RENAN, EMILE. Bass-baritone. American. Resi-
dent st dir: Opera Theatre of Rochester, NY,
USA. Born 28 Jun 1913, New York. Wife Doris,
occupation writer. Studied: Eleanor McLellan,
John Daggett Howell, New York. **Debut:** Sacristan
(*Tosca*) New York City Opera 1944.

Sang with major companies in CAN: Mon-
treal/Quebec, Toronto, Vancouver; MEX: Mexico
City; USA: Baltimore, Boston, Chicago, Fort
Worth, Hartford, Houston, Lake George, Mem-
phis, Miami, New Orleans, New York City Opera,
Philadelphia Grand & Lyric Opera, Pittsburgh,
San Antonio. **Roles with these companies incl**
BERG: Doktor (*Wozzeck*); BIZET: Escamillo
(*Carmen*); BRITTEN: Bottom (*Midsummer
Night*); DONIZETTI: Don Pasquale, Dulcamara
(*Elisir*); FLOTOW: Plunkett (*Martha*); GAY: Mr
Peachum‡ (*Beggar's Opera*); LEONCAVALLO:
Tonio (*Pagliacci*); MASCAGNI: Alfio (*Cavalle-
ria rusticana*); MASSENET: Lescaut (*Manon*);
MOZART: Guglielmo & Don Alfonso (*Così fan
tutte*), Leporello (*Don Giovanni*), Figaro (*Nozze di
Figaro*), Papageno (*Zauberflöte*); MUS-
SORGSKY: Varlaam★ (*Boris Godunov*); OF-
FENBACH: Don Andres (*Périchole*);
PERGOLESI: Uberto (*Serva padrona*); PUC-
CINI: Colline & Marcello (*Bohème*), Sharpless
(*Butterfly*); ROSSINI: Figaro★ & Dott Bartolo★ &
Don Basilio (*Barbiere di Siviglia*), Dandini & Don
Magnifico (*Cenerentola*), Bruschino & Gaudenzio
(*Signor Bruschino*); SMETANA: Kezal (*Bartered
Bride*); STRAUSS, R: Graf (*Capriccio*); STRA-
VINSKY: Empereur de Chine★ (*Rossignol*);
WAGNER: Beckmesser (*Meistersinger*), Alberich
(*Rheingold*); WEILL: Mr. Peachum★ (*Dreigro-
schenoper*). Also BLITZSTEIN: Oscar Hubbard
(*Regina*); BRITTEN: Junius (*Rape of Lucretia*);

GOUNOD: Valentin (*Faust*); PROKOFIEV:
Pantalone (*Love for Three Oranges*); STRAUSS,
R: Faninal (*Rosenkavalier*). **World premieres:**
WARD: Baron Regnard (*He Who Gets Slapped*)
New York City Opera, New York 1956; TAM-
KIN: Meyer (*Dybbuk*) New York City Opera
1951; KURKA: Army Doctor & Wolf, a Dog
(*Good Soldier Schweik*) New York City Opera
1958. Recorded for: Columbia, RCA, Desto.
Video – NBC TV: Dott Bartolo (*Barbiere di Si-
viglia*); Dott Malatesta (*Don Pasquale*); Sacristan
(*Tosca*); (*Taming of the Shrew*); NET TV: Em-
pereur (*Rossignol*). Stages opera. Teaches voice.
Coaches repertoire. On faculty of Juilliard School
of Music, NY, USA. **Res:** 360 E 55 St, New York,
NY, USA.

RENICKE, VOLKER. Conductor of opera and
symphony. German. Resident Cond, Opernhaus
Basel, Switzerland. Born 3 Jul 1929, Bremen, Germany. Wife Rey Nishiuchi, occupation opera &
concert singer. Studied: Nordwestdeutsche Musikakad; Eugen Papst, Kurt Thomas, Hans Richter-
Haaser; Paul v Kempen, Siena; incl piano, oboe,
timpani and voice. Plays the piano. Operatic training as repetiteur, asst cond & chorus master at
Landestheater Detmold 1954-57. Städt Bühnen,
Mönchengladbach-Rheydt 1957-61; Städt Bühnen,
Münster 1961-65. **Operatic debut:** Landestheater
Detmold, FR Ger 1954. Symphonic debut: Scarlatti Orch, Siena, Italy 1954.

Conducted with major companies in FR GER:
Cologne, Düsseldorf-Duisburg, Frankfurt, Hanno-
ver, Wiesbaden; ITA: Naples, Palermo; JPN: To-
kyo Fujiwara; SWI: Basel, Zurich. **Operas with
these companies incl** BEETHOVEN: *Fidelio;*
BERG: *Lulu★, Wozzeck★;* BIZET: *Carmen;*
CIMAROSA: *Matrimonio segreto;* DALLAPIC-
COLA: *Prigioniero★;* EGK: *Zaubergeige;*
GLUCK: *Orfeo ed Euridice★;* GOUNOD: *Faust;*
HANDEL: *Xerxes;* HINDEMITH: *Cardillac,
Hin und zurück, Mathis der Maler;* HUM-
PERDINCK: *Hänsel und Gretel★;* JANACEK:
Excursions of Mr Broucek, Jenufa★; LORTZING:
*Waffenschmied, Wildschütz, Zar und Zimmer-
mann;* MASCAGNI: *Cavalleria rusticana;* ME-
NOTTI: *Amelia al ballo★, Medium, Old Maid and
the Thief;* MILHAUD: *Pauvre matelot★;* MON-
TEVERDI: *Incoronazione di Poppea;* MO-
ZART: *Così fan tutte, Don Giovanni★,
Entführung aus dem Serail, Nozze di Figaro★,
Zauberflöte★;* NICOLAI: *Lustigen Weiber;* OF-
FENBACH: *Contes d'Hoffmann★, Mariage aux
lanternes★;* PROKOFIEV: *Love for Three Or-
anges★;* PUCCINI: *Bohème★, Gianni Schicchi,
Butterfly, Manon Lescaut, Tosca★;* ROSSINI:
*Barbiere di Siviglia★, Cambiale di matrimonio,
Italiana in Algeri;* SCARLATTI: *Trionfo
dell'onore;* SMETANA: *Bartered Bride;*
STRAUSS, J: *Fledermaus★;* STRAUSS, R: *Ro-
senkavalier★, Salome★;* STRAVINSKY: *Mavra;*
TCHAIKOVSKY: *Pique Dame;* VERDI: *Aida,
Ballo in maschera, Don Carlo, Forza del destino★,
Rigoletto, Traviata, Trovatore;* WAGNER:
Fliegende Holländer, Tristan und Isolde; WE-
BER: *Freischütz.* Also KLEBE: *Tödlichen
Wünsche;* KELEMEN: *Neue Mieter;* LOR-
TZING: *Undine;* KEISER: *Masaniello furioso;*
CIMAROSA: *Astuzie femminili;* KRENEK:
Schwergewicht; BLACHER: *Flut.* Conducted ma-

jor orch in Europe, Asia. Teaches at Musikhochschule, Zurich. **Res:** c/o Nishiuchi 23-8 Okuzawa 2-Chome Setagaya-Ku, Tokyo, Japan. **Mgmt:** TAU/SWI.

RENNERT, GÜNTHER PETER. Stages/produces opera, theater & television and is an author. German. Gen Mng & Resident Stage Dir, Bayerische Staatsoper, Munich 1967-76. Born 1 Apr 1911, Essen. Wife Elisabeth de Freitas, occupation actress. Four children. Studied: law, music, drama & science, Univs of Munich, Berlin & Halle; incl piano. **Operatic debut:** *Parsifal* Opera House, Frankfurt 1935. Theater debut: Kammerspiele, Hamburg 1947. Previous occupation: asst prod & prod of films. Awards: Prof, DL; Grosses Bundesverdienstkreuz, FR Ger; Austrian Bundesverdienstkreuz für Kunst und Wissenschaft; Bayerischer Verdienstorden; Brahms Medal, City of Hamburg. Previous adm positions in opera: Gen Mng, Staatsoper Hamburg 1946-56.

Directed/produced opera for major companies in ARG: Buenos Aires; AUS: Salzburg Fest, Vienna Staatsoper; CAN: Toronto, Vancouver GRE: Athens Fest; FR GER: Berlin Deutsche Oper, Cologne, Düsseldorf-Duisburg, Frankfurt, Hamburg, Munich Staatsoper, Stuttgart, Wuppertal; GER DR: Berlin Staatsoper; HOL: Amsterdam; ITA: Florence Maggio, Milan La Scala, Naples; SWE: Stockholm; SWI: Zurich; UK: Edinburgh Fest, Glyndebourne Fest, London Royal; USA: New York Met, San Francisco Opera. **Operas staged with these companies incl** d'ALBERT: *Tiefland;* BARTOK: *Bluebeard's Castle;* BEETHOVEN: *Fidelio⋆;* BERG: *Lulu, Wozzeck⋆;* BIZET: *Carmen:* BRITTEN: *Midsummer Night, Peter Grimes, Rape of Lucretia;* CAVALLI: *Ormindo;* CIKKER: *Play of Love and Death;* CORNELIUS: *Barbier von Bagdad;* DALLAPICCOLA: *Prigioniero⋆, Volo di notte;* DONIZETTI: *Don Pasquale;* EGK: *Irische Legende, Verlobung in San Domingo, Revisor;* EINEM: *Dantons Tod, Prozess;* FALLA: *Vida breve;* FLOTOW: *Martha;* FORTNER: *Bluthochzeit;* GAY/Britten: *Beggar's Opera;* GIORDANO: *Andrea Chénier;* GLUCK: *Iphigénie en Aulide, Orfeo ed Euridice;* HANDEL: *Jephtha;* HENZE: *Elegy for Young Lovers;* HINDEMITH: *Cardillac, Mathis der Maler;* HONEGGER: *Antigone;* HUMPERDINCK: *Hänsel und Gretel;* IBERT: *Angélique;* JANACEK: *From the House of the Dead, Jenufa⋆, Makropoulos Affair;* KLEBE: *Jakobowsky und der Oberst;* KODALY: *Spinning Room;* LEONCAVALLO: *Pagliacci;* LORTZING: *Waffenschmied, Wildschütz, Zar und Zimmermann;* MASCAGNI: *Cavalleria rusticana;* MENOTTI: *Consul;* MONTEVERDI: *Incoronazione di Poppea⋆, Ritorno d'Ulisse;* MOZART: *Così fan tutte⋆, Don Giovanni⋆, Entführung aus dem Serail⋆, Nozze di Figaro⋆, Zauberflöte;* MUSSORGSKY: *Boris Godunov;* OFFENBACH: *Contes d'Hoffmann;* ORFF: *Antigonae⋆, Carmina burana, Kluge, Mond;* PENDERECKI: *Teufel von Loudun;* PFITZNER: *Palestrina;* PUCCINI: *Bohème, Gianni Schicchi⋆, Butterfly, Manon Lescaut, Tabarro⋆, Tosca;* RAVEL: *Heure espagnole;* ROSSINI: *Barbiere di Siviglia, Cenerentola, Italiana in Algeri⋆, Pietra del paragone, Turco in Italia⋆;* SCHOENBERG: *Erwartung;* SCHULLER: *Vis-*

itation; SMETANA: *Bartered Bride⋆;* STRAUSS, J: *Fledermaus;* STRAUSS, R: *Arabella, Ariadne auf Naxos, Elektra⋆, Frau ohne Schatten, Rosenkavalier, Salome, Schweigsame Frau⋆;* STRAVINSKY: *Mavra, Histoire, Oedipus, Rake, Renard;* SUTERMEISTER: *Raskolnikoff, Romeo und Julia;* TCHAIKOVSKY: *Pique Dame;* VERDI: *Aida, Aroldo, Ballo in maschera, Don Carlo, Ernani, Falstaff⋆, Forza del destino, Macbeth, Nabucco, Otello, Trovatore, Vespri;* WAGNER: *Fliegende Holländer, Meistersinger, Rheingold⋆, Walküre⋆, Siegfried⋆, Götterdämmerung, Tannhäuser;* WEBER: *Freischütz;* WEILL: *Aufstieg und Fall der Stadt Mahagonny, Dreigroschenoper;* WOLF-FERRARI: *Quattro rusteghi, Segreto di Susanna;* YUN: *Sim Tjong.* Also GERSTER: *Hexe von Passau;* SUTERMEISTER: *Zauberinsel;* BLOMDAHL: *Aniara;* DVORAK: *Dimitri;* HONEGGER: *Jeanne d'Arc au bûcher;* KAUFMANN: *Perlenhemd;* REUTTER: *Saul;* LIEBERMANN: *Schule der Frauen, Leonore 40/45;* SCHOECK: *Penthesilea;* WALTON: *Troilus and Cressida;* BENNETT: *Penny for a Song.* **Operatic world premieres:** WOLF-FERRARI: *Dama Boba* Mainz 1938; MIHALOVICI: *Heimkehr* Hamburg 1947; KRENEK: *Pallas Athene weint* Hamburg 1955; GRUEBER: *Trotz wider Trotz* Hamburg 1948; ORFF: *Oedipus der Tyrann* Stuttgart 1959; BURT: *Volpone* Stuttgart 1960; BIALAS: *Gestiefelte Kater* Schwetzingen/Hamburg 1975; STRAVINSKY: *Flood* first stg, Hamburg 1963. Teaches at consv. Stages classical and modern plays; translates operas into German. **Res:** Schwalbenweg 11a, 8033 Krailling/Munich, FR Ger.

RENNERT, WOLFGANG. Conductor of opera and symphony. German. Resident Cond, Deutsche Staatsoper, Berlin, Ger DR. Born 1 Apr 1928, Cologne. Wife Ulla, occupation actress. One child. Studied: Clemens Krauss, Georg Solti; also piano. Operatic training as repetiteur at Deutsche Oper am Rhein, Düsseldorf, FR Ger 1947-50. **Operatic debut:** Deutsche Oper am Rhein 1948. Symphonic debut: Lübeck Symph Orch, FR Ger 1956.

Conducted with major companies in AUS: Salzburg Fest, Vienna Staatsoper; DEN: Copenhagen; FRA: Lyon, Marseille, Nancy, Paris, Toulouse; GRE: Athens Fest; FR GER: Cologne, Frankfurt, Hamburg, Kiel, Munich Gärtnerplatz, Stuttgart, Wiesbaden; GER DR: Berlin Staatsoper, Dresden; HOL: Amsterdam; ITA: Naples, Palermo, Trieste, Venice; POL: Warsaw; SWI: Geneva; UK: London English National. **Operas with these companies incl** BERG: *Wozzeck⋆;* BERLIOZ: *Damnation de Faust⋆, Troyens;* BIZET: *Carmen⋆;* DONIZETTI: *Don Pasquale;* DVORAK: *Rusalka⋆;* HENZE: *Landarzt;* HUMPERDINCK: *Hänsel und Gretel;* JANACEK: *Cunning Little Vixen⋆, Jenufa⋆;* LEONCAVALLO: *Pagliacci;* LORTZING: *Waffenschmied, Wildschütz;* MASCAGNI: *Cavalleria rusticana;* MENOTTI: *Old Maid and the Thief‡, Telephone‡;* MILHAUD: *Pauvre matelot;* MOZART: *Così fan tutte⋆, Entführung aus dem Serail⋆, Schauspieldirektor⋆, Nozze di Figaro⋆, Zauberflöte⋆;* MUSSORGSKY: *Boris Godunov;* OFFENBACH: *Contes d'Hoffmann⋆;* ORFF: *Kluge;* PENDERECKI: *Teufel von Loudun⋆;* PUCCINI: *Bohème, Fanciulla del West, Gianni*

Schicchi, Manon Lescaut, Tabarro, Tosca, Turandot; ROSSINI: *Barbiere di Siviglia;* SHOSTAKOVICH: *Nose;* SMETANA: *Bartered Bride;* STRAUSS, J: *Fledermaus;* STRAUSS, R: *Arabella*‡, *Ariadne auf Naxos*, *Capriccio, Elektra*, *Rosenkavalier*, *Salome*, *Schweigsame Frau*; TCHAIKOVSKY: *Eugene Onegin, Pique Dame*; VERDI: *Aida*, *Ballo in maschera, Don Carlo, Falstaff*, *Forza del destino, Otello*, *Rigoletto, Simon Boccanegra, Traviata*; WAGNER: *Lohengrin, Rheingold*, *Walküre*, *Siegfried*, *Götterdämmerung*, *Tannhäuser;* WEBER: *Freischütz*; WEILL: *Aufstieg und Fall der Stadt Mahagonny*, *Dreigroschenoper*‡; WOLF-FERRARI: *Quattro rusteghi.* Video—NDR TV: *Simplizissimus;* Austrian TV: *Old Maid, Telephone.* Res: Nonnenstieg 24, Hamburg, FR Ger. Mgmt: SLZ/FRG.

RENZI, EMMA; née Emmerentia Scheepers. Dramatic soprano. So African. Born 8 Apr, Heidelberg, Transvaal, So Africa. Single. Studied: Cape Town Coll of Music; London Opera Centre; Mo Santo Santonocito, Catania; Prof Virginia Borroni, Milan. Debut: Sieglinde (*Walküre*) Karlsruhe Oper 1961.

Sang with major companies in ARG: Buenos Aires; AUS: Graz; FRA: Bordeaux, Nice, Rouen; FR GER: Karlsruhe, Munich Staatsoper; ITA: Bologna, Genoa, Milan La Scala, Naples, Palermo, Parma, Rome Opera; MEX: Mexico City; POR: Lisbon; S AFR: Johannesburg; SPA: Barcelona, Majorca; SWI: Zurich; UK: Edinburgh Fest; USA: Hartford. Roles with these companies incl BELLINI: Norma; BUSONI: Herzogin (*Doktor Faust*); CATALANI: Loreley; GIORDANO: Maddalena (*Andrea Chénier*); MOZART: Contessa (*Nozze di Figaro*); PONCHIELLI: Gioconda*; PUCCINI: Tosca, Turandot*; VERDI: Aida, Amelia* (*Ballo in maschera*), Donna Elvira* (*Ernani*), Leonora* (*Forza del destino*), Lady Macbeth, Abigaille* (*Nabucco*), Leonora (*Trovatore*); WAGNER: Sieglinde (*Walküre*), Elisabeth* (*Tannhäuser*). Gives recitals. Appears with symphony orchestra. Res: V Vipacco 4, Milan, Italy.

REPPA, DAVID. Scenic and costume designer for opera, theater, film, television; specl in sets. Is a lighting designer. American. Resident designer, Metropolitan Opera, New York. Born 2 Nov 1926, Hammond, IN, USA. Wife Mary Ann, occupation artist. Studied: Art Inst of Chicago; Goodman Memorial Theater. Prof training: Metropolitan Opera 1957-58. Operatic debut: sets, *Nozze di Figaro* North Shore Opera, New York 1960; cost, *Bluebeard's Castle* & *Gianni Schicchi* Metropolitan Opera 1974. Theater debut: Goodman Memorial Theater, Chicago 1945. Previous adm positions in opera: Tech Dir, Opera Co of Boston 1964-65.

Designed for major companies in USA: Miami, New York Met. Operas designed for these companies incl BARTOK: *Bluebeard's Castle*; GIANNINI: *Taming of the Shrew;* GOUNOD: *Roméo et Juliette*; MOZART: *Nozze di Figaro;* PUCCINI: *Gianni Schicchi*, *Suor Angelica*, *Tabarro*; VERDI: *Aida*. Res: 173 Riverside Dr, New York, NY, USA.

REPPEL, CARMEN. Dram & lyric soprano. German. Resident mem: Staatstheater Hannover.

Born 27 Apr 1941, Gummersbach, Germany. Husband Herbert Krämer, occupation city manager. Studied: Gisela Aulmann; Staatliche Hochschule für Musik, Hamburg; Master class Prof Erna Berger. Debut: Elisabetta (*Don Carlo*) Städt Bühnen Flensburg 1968.

Sang with major companies in FR GER: Bielefeld, Cologne, Darmstadt, Dortmund, Frankfurt, Hamburg, Hannover, Kassel, Mannheim, Wiesbaden; POL: Lodz, Warsaw. Roles with these companies incl BIZET: Micaëla* (*Carmen*); DEBUSSY: Mélisande*; DONIZETTI: Norina* (*Don Pasquale*); HANDEL: Cleopatra* (*Giulio Cesare*); MOZART: Fiordiligi* (*Così fan tutte*), Donna Anna* & Donna Elvira* (*Don Giovanni*), Elettra* (*Idomeneo*); PUCCINI: Mimi* (*Bohème*), Lauretta* (*Gianni Schicchi*), Liù* (*Turandot*); SMETANA: Marie* (*Bartered Bride*); STRAUSS, J: Rosalinde* (*Fledermaus*); STRAUSS, R: Kaiserin* (*Frau ohne Schatten*), Sophie* (*Rosenkavalier*); STRAVINSKY: Anne Trulove* (*Rake's Progress*); VERDI: Elisabetta* (*Don Carlo*), Desdemona* (*Otello*), Violetta* (*Traviata*), Leonora* (*Trovatore*); WAGNER: Elsa* (*Lohengrin*), Sieglinde* (*Walküre*), Gutrune* (*Götterdämmerung*). Also CIKKER: Katusha (*Resurrection*); FORTNER: Braut (*Bluthochzeit*). Video/Film: Marie (*Bartered Bride*), Pamina (*Zauberflöte*). Res: Waltgerweg 17, 48 Bielefeld 1, FR Ger. Mgmt: SLZ/FRG.

RESCHKE, HEINZ. German. Adm Dir, Bühnen der Landeshauptstadt Kiel, FR Ger 1973- . In charge of overall adm matters. Born 17 Apr 1926, Posen, Poland. Wife Anni. Studied: School for Bus Adm, Kiel. Res: Feldstr 119, Kiel, FR Ger.

RESCIGNO, NICOLA. Conductor of opera. American. Gen Dir & Resident Cond, Dallas Civic Opera, TX, USA. Born New York. Operatic debut: Brooklyn Acad of Music, New York 1943. Previous occupations: degree in law, Italy. Previous adm positions in opera: Co-founder & Dir, Chicago Lyric Opera 1954-56; Co-founder & Mus Dir, Dallas Civic Opera 1957-75.

Conducted with major companies in CAN: Montreal/Quebec; ITA: Naples, Rome Opera, Venice· MEX: Mexico City; POR: Lisbon; UK: London Royal; USA: Chicago Lyric, Cincinnati, Dallas, San Francisco Op; et al. Operas with these companies incl BELLINI: *Norma, Puritani;* BIZET: *Carmen;* CHERUBINI: *Medea;* DONIZETTI: *Anna Bolena, Favorite, Fille du régiment, Lucia, Lucrezia Borgia;* GIORDANO: *Andrea Chénier, Fedora;* GLUCK: *Orfeo ed Euridice;* HANDEL: *Alcina, Giulio Cesare;* IBERT: *Angélique;* LEONCAVALLO: *Pagliacci;* MASSENET: *Thaïs, Werther;* MENOTTI: *Telephone;* MONTEVERDI: *Incoronazione di Poppea;* MOZART: *Don Giovanni, Nozze di Figaro;* ORFF: *Carmina burana;* POULENC: *Voix humaine;* PUCCINI: *Bohème, Butterfly, Suor Angelica, Tabarro, Tosca;* PURCELL: *Dido and Aeneas;* RIMSKY-KORSAKOV: *Coq d'or;* ROSSINI: *Italiana in Algeri;* SAINT-SAENS: *Samson et Dalila;* THOMAS: *Mignon;* VERDI: *Aida, Ballo in maschera, Macbeth, Otello, Rigoletto, Traviata;* ZANDONAI: *Francesca da Rimini*‡; et al. Also CIMAROSA: *Maestro di cappella;* PAISIELLO: *Duello comico;* CHAILLY: *Domanda di matrimonio;* FIUME: *Tamburo di panno.* Recorded for Decca.

RESNIK, REGINA. Dramatic mezzo-soprano, stage dir, form soprano. American. Resident mem: Metropolitan Opera, New York. Born 30 Aug 1924, Bronx, NY, USA. Husband Arbit Blatas, occupation painter, sculptor, scenic designer. One son. Studied: Rosalie Miller, Giuseppe Danise, New York. **Debut:** Lady Macbeth, New Opera Co 1942. Awards: President's Medal, USA; Commander French Acad of Arts, Sciences and Letters; Kammersängerin, Austria.

Sang with major companies in ARG: Buenos Aires; AUS: Salzburg Fest, Vienna Staatsoper & Volksoper; BEL: Brussels; CAN: Montreal/Quebec, Toronto, Vancouver; CZE: Prague National; DEN: Copenhagen; FRA: Marseille, Paris, Strasbourg; GRE: Athens Fest; FR GER: Bayreuth Fest, Berlin Deutsche Oper, Hamburg, Munich Staatsoper, Stuttgart; HOL: Amsterdam; HUN: Budapest; ITA: Milan La Scala, Naples, Rome Opera, Venice; MEX: Mexico City; MON: Monte Carlo; NOR: Oslo; POL: Warsaw; POR: Lisbon; SWE: Drottningholm Fest; UK: Edinburgh Fest, London Royal; USA: Chicago, Cincinnati, Dallas, Fort Worth, Hartford, Houston, Kansas City, Miami, New Orleans, New York Met & City Opera, Philadelphia Grand & Lyric, Pittsburgh, San Antonio, San Francisco Opera, Santa Fe, Seattle, Washington DC. **Roles with these companies incl** BERLIOZ: Cassandre & Didon (*Troyens*); BIZET: Carmen‡; BRITTEN: Lucretia (*Rape of Lucretia*); CILEA: Princesse de Bouillon (*A. Lecouvreur*); DEBUSSY: Geneviève (*Pelléas et Mélisande*); DONIZETTI: Marquise de Birkenfeld★ (*Fille du régiment*); EINEM: Claire★ (*Besuch der alten Dame*); MASSENET: Charlotte (*Werther*); MENOTTI: Mme Flora★‡ (*Medium*); MUSSORGSKY: Marina (*Boris Godunov*); PONCHIELLI: Laura (*Gioconda*); POULENC: Prioresse (*Dialogues des Carmélites*); PUCCINI: Principessa (*Suor Angelica*); STRAUSS, J: Prinz Orlovsky‡ (*Fledermaus*); STRAUSS, R: Klytämnestra★‡ (*Elektra*), Amme (*Frau ohne Schatten*), Herodias★‡ (*Salome*); TCHAIKOVSKY: Comtesse★ (*Pique Dame*); VERDI: Amneris (*Aida*), Ulrica‡ (*Ballo in maschera*), Eboli (*Don Carlo*), Dame Quickly★‡ (*Falstaff*), Azucena (*Trovatore*); WAGNER: Magdalene (*Meistersinger*), Kundry (*Parsifal*), Fricka (*Rheingold, Walküre*), Waltraute (*Götterdämmerung*), Venus (*Tannhäuser*), Brangäne‡ (*Tristan und Isolde*); WALTON: Mme Popova (*Bear*); WEILL: Leocadia Begbick★ (*Aufstieg und Fall der Stadt Mahagonny*). **Soprano roles with these companies incl** BEETHOVEN: Leonore (*Fidelio*); BRITTEN: Ellen Orford (*Peter Grimes*); GIORDANO: Maddalena (*Andrea Chénier*); MASCAGNI: Santuzza (*Cavalleria rusticana*); MOZART: Donna Anna & Donna Elvira (*Don Giovanni*); PUCCINI: Musetta (*Bohème*), Cio-Cio-San (*Butterfly*), Tosca; STRAUSS, J: Rosalinde (*Fledermaus*); STRAUSS, R: Chrysothemis (*Elektra*); VERDI: Aida, Alice Ford (*Falstaff*), Leonora (*Trovatore*); WAGNER: Sieglinde (*Walküre*), Gutrune (*Götterdämmerung*). **World premieres:** ROGERS: Dalila (*Warrior*) Metropolitan Opera 1947. Recorded for: Columbia, RCA, London. Video/Film: (*Bear*); Klytämnestra (*Elek-*

tra): Dame Quickly (*Falstaff*). Gives recitals. Appears with symphony orchestra.

Debut as stage dir: *Carmen* Hamburg State Opera 1971. **Staged/produced opera with major companies in** CAN: Vancouver; FRA: Strasbourg; FR GER: Hamburg; ITA: Venice; POL: Warsaw; POR: Lisbon. **Operas with these companies incl** BIZET: *Carmen★*; MENOTTI: *Medium★, Telephone*; STRAUSS, R: *Elektra★, Salome★*; TCHAIKOVSKY: *Pique Dame★*; VERDI: *Falstaff★*; WALTON: *Bear★*; WEILL: *Mahagonny★*. Gives seminars at New School for Socl Research, New York. **Res:** 50 W 56 St, New York, NY. Mgmt: WLS/USA; CST/UK; KNL/FRG.

REYNOLDS, ANNA. Lyric mezzo-soprano. British. Born Canterbury, UK. Studied: Royal Acad of Music, London; Prof Debora Fambri, Mme Ré Koster, Rome. **Debut:** Geneviève (*Pelléas et Mélisande*) Glyndebourne Fest 1962. Previous occupations: piano teacher. Awards: Fellow of Royal Acad of Music, London.

Sang with major companies in AUS: Salzburg Fest; BEL: Brussels; FRA: Aix-en-Provence, Bordeaux, Nice; FR GER: Bayreuth Fest; ITA: Florence Maggio & Comunale, Genoa, Milan La Scala, Naples, Palermo, Parma, Rome Opera, Spoleto Fest, Trieste, Venice, Verona Arena; POR: Lisbon; UK: Glasgow Scottish, Glyndebourne Fest, London Royal Opera; USA: Chicago, New York Met. **Roles with these companies incl** AUBER: Pamela (*Fra Diavolo*); BARTOK: Judith (*Bluebeard's Castle*); BERLIOZ: Béatrice, Marguerite (*Damnation de Faust*), Anna (*Troyens*); BRITTEN: Mrs Herring (*Albert Herring*); DEBUSSY: Geneviève★ (*Pelléas et Mélisande*); DONIZETTI: Elisabetta (*Maria Stuarda*); HANDEL: Ruggiero (*Alcina*), Silvio★‡ (*Pastor fido*); MARTIN: Mère d'Iseut (*Vin herbé*); MASSENET: Charlotte (*Werther*); MENOTTI: Miss Todd‡ (*Old Maid and the Thief*); MONTEVERDI: Messaggera‡ (*Orfeo*), Ottavia (*Incoronazione di Poppea*); MOZART: Dorabella★ (*Così fan tutte*); PONCHIELLI: La Cieca (*Gioconda*); PUCCINI: Suzuki (*Butterfly*); ROSSINI: Tancredi‡; STRAVINSKY: Jocasta (*Oedipus Rex*); TCHAIKOVSKY: Mme Larina‡ (*Eugene Onegin*); WAGNER: Magdalene★‡ (*Meistersinger*), Fricka (*Rheingold★, Walküre★*), Waltraute★ (*Götterdämmerung*), Brangäne★ (*Tristan und Isolde*). Also TIPPETT: Andromache★ (*King Priam*); HANDEL: Ottone★. Recorded for: DG, Decca, Cetra, EMI, Philips. Gives recitals. Appears with symphony orchestra. **Res:** 37 Chelwood Gardens, Richmond/Surrey, UK. Mgmt: HPL/UK; HUR/USA.

RIBER, JEAN-CLAUDE. Stages/produces opera & theater. Also designs sets, costumes & stage-lighting. French. Gen Mgr & Resident Stage Dir, Grand Théâtre, Geneva, Switzerland. Also Resident Stage Dir & Administr for theater and film, Geneva. Born 14 Sep 1934, Mulhouse. Wife Liliane Meyer. Two children. Studied: Paris, Munich, incl music, piano and voice. **Operatic debut:** *Rigoletto* Théâtre Municipal, Mulhouse 1966. Theater debut: Strasbourg 1967. Awards: Golden Medal, City of Nancy. Previous adm positions in opera: Dir, Théâtre Municipal, Mulhouse 1966-70; Dir, Grand Théâtre, Nancy 1970-73.

Directed/produced opera for major companies in FRA: Bordeaux, Nancy, Strasbourg, Toulouse; FR GER: Saarbrücken; ITA: Genoa, Naples, Trieste; ROM: Bucharest; SWI: Geneva. **Operas staged with these companies incl** BARTOK: *Bluebeard's Castle;* BECAUD: *Opéra d'Aran;* BEETHOVEN: *Fidelio;* BELLINI: *Norma;* BERG: *Lulu*;* BERLIOZ: *Troyens*;* BIZET: *Carmen, Pêcheurs de perles;* BRITTEN: *Curlew River;* DEBUSSY: *Pelléas et Mélisande;* GIORDANO: *Andrea Chénier;* GLUCK: *Orfeo ed Euridice;* LECOCQ: *Fille de Madame Angot;* MASSENET: *Don Quichotte, Manon*;* MENOTTI: *Consul*;* MOZART: *Don Giovanni*, Nozze di Figaro*, Zauberflöte*†;* OFFENBACH: *Contes d'Hoffmann;* ORFF: *Kluge†;* PUCCINI: *Bohème, Butterfly, Tosca, Turandot*;* ROSSINI: *Barbiere di Siviglia;* SAINT-SAENS: *Samson et Dalila;* STRAUSS, J: *Fledermaus;* STRAUSS, R: *Elektra*, Rosenkavalier, Salome*;* TCHAIKOVSKY: *Eugene Onegin*†;* VERDI: *Aida*†, Don Carlo*, Otello*†, Rigoletto*, Traviata*, Trovatore;* WAGNER: *Fliegende Holländer*, Meistersinger, Rheingold*, Walküre*, Siegfried†, Götterdämmerung, Tristan und Isolde*;* WEBER: *Freischütz;* WEILL: *Aufstieg und Fall der Stadt Mahagonny.* Also NONO: *Intolleranza*;* KOVACH: *Rendez-vous*.* **Operatic world premieres:** SEMENOFF: *Contagion* Grand Théâtre, Nancy 1972. Teaches at consv. **Res:** Les Ponsez, 88230 Fraize, France.

RICCIARELLI, KATIA. Lyric soprano. Italian. Born Rovigo, Italy. Studied: Consv Benedetto Marcello, Iris Adami Corradetti, Venice. **Debut:** Mimi (*Bohème*) Mantua Opera 1969. Previous occupations: electrician. Awards: TV Prize Giuseppe Verdi; Premio As Li Co; Premio Delle Muse; Palcoscenico d'oro; Noci d'oro; Verdi Compt, Parma.
Sang with major companies in AUS: Vienna Staatsoper; BEL: Brussels; FRA: Paris; FR GER: Berlin Deutsche Oper, Frankfurt, Hamburg Staatsoper, Munich Staatsoper; ITA: Milan La Scala, Parma, Rome Teatro dell'Opera, Trieste, Turin, Venice, Verona Arena; SPA: Barcelona; UK: London Royal Opera; USSR: Moscow Bolshoi; USA: Chicago, New Orleans, New York Met, San Francisco Opera. **Roles with these companies incl** BELLINI: Giulietta* (*Capuleti ed i Montecchi*), Imogene* (*Pirata*), Alaide* (*Straniera*); BIZET: Micaëla* (*Carmen*); DONIZETTI: Anna Bolena*, Caterina Cornaro*, Lucrezia Borgia*, Maria di Rohan*, Maria Stuarda*; GOUNOD: Marguerite* (*Faust*); MASSENET: Manon*; MOZART: Donna Anna* (*Don Giovanni*), Contessa* (*Nozze di Figaro*), Pamina* (*Zauberflöte*); OFFENBACH: Antonia* & Giulietta* (*Contes d'Hoffmann*); PUCCINI: Mimi* (*Bohème*), Suor Angelica*‡, Liù* (*Turandot*); PURCELL: Dido*; ROSSINI: Elisabetta* (*Elisabetta Regina*), Mathilde* (*Guillaume Tell*), Desdemona* (*Otello*), Pamira* (*Assedio di Corinto*); VERDI: Amelia* (*Ballo in maschera*), Medora* (*Corsaro*), Elisabetta* (*Don Carlo*), Lucrezia Contarini* (*Due Foscari*), Giovanna d'Arco*, Luisa Miller*, Desdemona* (*Otello*), Amelia*‡ (*Simon Boccanegra*), Violetta* (*Traviata*), Leonora* (*Trovatore*); WAGNER: Elsa* (*Lohengrin*). Also CHERUBINI: Corinne

(*Anacréon*); GLUCK: Elena (*Paride ed Elena*). Recorded for: RCA. Mgmt: CAM/USA.

RICH, MARTIN. Conductor of opera and symphony. American. Resident Cond, Metropolitan Opera, New York. Also Music Dir & Cond, Phil Symph of Westchester, Mt Vernon, NY. Born 8 Oct 1908, Breslau, Germany. Wife Maria F, occupation arts adm, author. One daughter. Studied: Hochschule für Musik, Franz Schreker, Julius Prüwer, Berlin; incl piano, Georg Bertram, Artur Schnabel; and voice. Plays the piano. Operatic training as asst cond at Dortmund Opera House, Germany. **Operatic debut:** *Manon* Metropolitan Opera 1955. Symphonic debut: Dortmund Symph, Germany 1930. Previous occupations: faculty mem Curtis Inst of Music, Philadelphia, 5 yrs; lecturer and master classes Howard and Temple Univs.
Conducted with major companies in CAN: Montreal/Quebec, Vancouver; FR GER: Dortmund, Wuppertal; ISR: Tel Aviv; ITA: Bologna; MEX: Mexico City; ROM: Bucharest; USA: Cincinnati, Jackson Opera/South, New York Met, Philadelphia Grand. **Operas with these companies incl** d'ALBERT: *Tiefland;* BELLINI: *Sonnambula;* BIZET: *Carmen;* DONIZETTI: *Elisir, Lucia;* FLOTOW: *Martha;* GOUNOD: *Faust*, Roméo et Juliette*;* HUMPERDINCK: *Königskinder;* LORTZING: *Wildschütz;* MASSENET: *Manon, Werther*;* MOZART: *Don Giovanni, Nozze di Figaro;* NICOLAI: *Lustigen Weiber;* ORFF: *Kluge*;* PUCCINI: *Bohème, Butterfly, Tabarro*, Tosca, Turandot*;* ROSSINI: *Barbiere di Siviglia;* STRAUSS, J: *Fledermaus;* STRAUSS, R: *Ariadne auf Naxos, Elektra, Rosenkavalier, Salome;* TCHAIKOVSKY: *Pique Dame;* VERDI: *Ballo in maschera*, Falstaff, Forza del destino*, Rigoletto, Traviata, Trovatore;* WEBER: *Freischütz.* Recorded for RAI Rome & Milan, NDR Hamburg. Video — CBC TV: *Rosenkavalier.* Conducted major orch in Europe, USA/Canada, Cent America, Asia. Teaches. **Res:** New York, NY, USA.

RICHARDSON, CAROL. Lyric mezzo-soprano. American. Resident mem: Bühnen der Landeshauptstadt, Kiel. Born California, USA. Husband Jeffrey Smith, occupation head coach, Kiel. Studied: Occidental Coll, Los Angeles; Martial Singher, Philadelphia; Harriett Gill. **Debut:** Nicklausse (*Contes d'Hoffmann*) Stadttheater Klagenfurt, Austria 1973. Awards: First Place Winner, San Francisco Opera Reg Aud 1971.
Sang with major companies in FR GER: Hamburg, Kiel. **Roles with these companies incl** MOZART: Dorabella* (*Così fan tutte*), Cherubino* (*Nozze di Figaro*); PUCCINI: Frugola* (*Tabarro*); ROSSINI: Rosina* (*Barbiere di Siviglia*); STRAUSS, J: Prinz Orlovsky* (*Fledermaus*). Gives recitals. Appears with symphony orchestra. **Res:** Kiel, FR Ger. Mgmt: SLZ/FRG.

RICHTER, CASPAR. Conductor of opera and symphony. German. Mus Dir & Resident Cond, RJO-RIAS, Berlin, FR Ger. Born 16 Sep 1944, Lübeck, Germany. Single. Studied: Staatl Hochschule für Musik, Prof Albert Bittner, Hamburg; incl piano, organ, percussion and voice. Plays the piano & organ. Operatic training as repetiteur at

Deutsche Oper Berlin, FR Ger. **Operatic debut:**
Besuch der alten Dame Deutsche Oper Berlin
1972. Symphonic debut: RJO-RIAS, Berlin 1972.
Previous occupations: asst Norddeutscher Rund-
funk 1968. Awards: Kurt Magnus Preis, German
TV Awd 1975.
Conducted with major companies in FR GER:
Berlin Deutsche Oper, Bonn, Essen, Kiel. **Operas
with these companies incl** BARTOK: *Bluebeard's
Castle*★; BEETHOVEN: *Fidelio*★; BERN-
STEIN: *Trouble in Tahiti;* BIZET: *Docteur Mi-
racle;* BLACHER: *Romeo und Julia;* BORODIN:
Prince Igor★; BRITTEN: *Rape of Lucretia;* CA-
VALLI: *Calisto*★; CIMAROSA: *Matrimonio se-
greto*★; DONIZETTI: *Don Pasquale;*
FORTNER: *Elisabeth Tudor*★; GAY/Britten:
Beggar's Opera★; GLUCK: *Cadi dupé;*
HAYDN: *Infedeltà delusa;* HENZE: *Junge
Lord*★, *Landarzt;* HUMPERDINCK: *Hänsel und
Gretel*★; MARTINU: *Comedy on the Bridge;*
MENOTTI: *Telephone;* MILHAUD: *Abandon
d'Ariane, Délivrance de Thésée, Enlèvement
d'Europe;* MONTEVERDI: *Combattimento di
Tancredi;* MOZART: *Clemenza di Tito*★, *Schau-
spieldirektor, Zauberflöte*★; MUSSORGSKY:
Boris Godunov★; OFFENBACH: *Contes
d'Hoffmann*★, *Mariage aux lanternes*★; ORFF:
Kluge★; PURCELL: *Dido and Aeneas;* REI-
MANN: *Melusine*★; ROSSINI: *Barbiere di Si-
viglia*★, *Turco in Italia*★; SCHOENBERG: *Moses
und Aron*★; STRAUSS, J: *Fledermaus*★; STRA-
VINSKY: *Mavra*★, *Oedipus Rex*★. Also HO-
NEGGER: *Roi David;* BLACHER: *Preussisches
Märchen.* Recorded for RIAS. Video—SFB TV:
Preussisches Märchen. Conducted major orch in
Europe, Asia. Teaches at Staatl Hochschule für
Musik, Berlin. **Res:** Königsallee 35, 1 Berlin-West
33, FR Ger.

RIDDERBUSCH, KARL. Bass-baritone & bass.
Born Recklinghausen, Germany. Studied: Folk-
wangschule, Essen.
Sang with major companies in ARG: Buenos
Aires; AUS: Salzburg Fest, Vienna Staatsoper;
FRA: Paris; FR GER: Bayreuth Fest, Berlin
Deutsche Oper, Dortmund, Düsseldorf-Duisburg,
Essen, Hamburg, Mannheim, Munich Staatsoper,
Stuttgart, Wiesbaden; ITA: Milan La Scala, Rome
Opera; UK: London Royal; USA: Chicago, New
York Met; et al. **Roles with these companies incl**
BEETHOVEN: Rocco‡ (*Fidelio*); MOZART: Sa-
rastro (*Zauberflöte*); STRAUSS, R: La Roche
(*Capriccio*), Baron Ochs (*Rosenkavalier*), Sir Mo-
rosus (*Schweigsame Frau*); VERDI: Philip II
(*Don Carlo*); WAGNER: Daland (*Fliegende
Holländer*), König Heinrich‡ (*Lohengrin*), Hans
Sachs‡ & Pogner (*Meistersinger*), Fasolt‡ & Faf-
ner (*Rheingold*), Hunding (*Walküre*), Hagen‡
(*Götterdämmerung*), Landgraf (*Tannhäuser*), Kö-
nig Marke‡ (*Tristan und Isolde*); WEBER: Kaspar
(*Freischütz*); et al. Also TCHAIKOVSKY: Gre-
min (*Eugene Onegin*); MOZART: Commendatore
(*Don Giovanni*). Recorded for: Decca, DG, Angel.

RIECKER, CHARLES J. American. Art Admin,
Metropolitan Opera Assn, Lincoln Center, New
York, NY 10023, USA. In charge of admin &
artistic matters. Born 21 Jul 1934, New York. Wife
Wally Cleva. Plays the piano. Started with present

company 1959 as Tech Asst; in present position
since 1972. **Res:** New York, NY, USA.

RIEGEL, KENNETH. Lyric tenor. American.
Resident mem: Metropolitan Opera, New York.
Born 29 Apr 1938, Womelsdorf, PA, USA. Studied: Wellington Wolf, coach, Reading, PA; Manhattan School of Music, Metropolitan Opera
Studio, New York. **Debut:** Alchemist (*König
Hirsch*) Santa Fe Opera 1965. Previous occupa-
tions: retail exec. Awards: Rockefeller Fndt
Grant; Sullivan Fndt Grant.
Sang with major companies in HOL: Amster-
dam; ITA: Spoleto Fest; USA: Cincinnati, Hous-
ton, New York Met & City Opera, Portland, San
Francisco Opera, Santa Fe, Seattle. **Roles with
these companies incl** BERLIOZ: Faust★ (*Damna-
tion de Faust*); BIZET: Nadir (*Pêcheurs de
perles*); BRITTEN: Nebuchadnezzar (*Burning
Fiery Furnace*), Madwoman (*Curlew River*),
Tempter (*Prodigal Son*), Peter Quint (*Turn of the
Screw*); DONIZETTI: Ernesto★ (*Don Pasquale*),
Nemorino★ (*Elisir*), Tonio (*Fille du régiment*),
Leicester (*Maria Stuarda*), Roberto Devereux;
GOUNOD: Faust★, Roméo; HENZE: Lord Bar-
rat★ (*Junge Lord*), Leandro (*König Hirsch/Re
Cervo*); MASSENET: Jean le Baptiste (*Héro-
diade*), Jean (*Jongleur de Notre Dame*), Des
Grieux (*Manon*), Nicias (*Thaïs*), Werther★; MO-
ZART: Ferrando★ (*Così fan tutte*), Don Ottavio
(*Don Giovanni*), Belmonte & Pedrillo (*Entführung
aus dem Serail*), Idamante & Idomeneo (*Ido-
meneo*), Lucio Silla, Tamino (*Zauberflöte*); MUS-
SORGSKY: Shuisky (*Boris Godunov*);
OFFENBACH: Hoffmann; ORFF: Tenor solo
(*Carmina burana*); PROKOFIEV: Prince (*Love
for Three Oranges*); PUCCINI: Rodolfo
(*Bohème*), Rinuccio (*Gianni Schicchi*), Pinkerton
(*Butterfly*), Ruggero (*Rondine*); RIMSKY-KOR-
SAKOV: Astrologue (*Coq d'or*); ROSSINI: Al-
maviva (*Barbiere di Siviglia*), Don Ramiro
(*Cenerentola*), Comte Ory, Leicester (*Elisabetta
Regina*), Lindoro (*Italiana in Algeri*); SHOSTA-
KOVICH: Police Commissioner (*The Nose*);
STRAUSS, J: Alfred (*Fledermaus*); STRAUSS,
R: Matteo (*Arabella*), Flamand (*Capriccio*),
Aegisth★ (*Elektra*), Ein Sänger★ (*Rosenkavalier*);
STRAVINSKY: Oedipus Rex, Tom Rakewell
(*Rake's Progress*); THOMSON: Lord Byron;
VERDI: Fenton (*Falstaff*), Alfredo (*Traviata*);
WAGNER: David (*Meistersinger*). Also KRE-
NEK: Aegisth (*Leben des Orest*). Gives recitals.
Appears with symphony orchestra. **Res:** 9 Monroe
Pl, Brooklyn Hgts, NY 11201, USA. Mgmt:
DSP/USA.

RIEMER, RUDOLF. Lyric baritone. German.
Resident mem: Städtisches Opernhaus Leipzig,
Ger DR. Born 25 Apr 1935, Pirna, Germany. Wife
Karin. Two children. Studied: Konsv Dresden,
Frau Dorothea Schröder; Hochschule für Musik,
Prof Herbert Winkler, Dresden; Wilhelm Klemm,
Leipzig, Ger DR. **Debut:** Masino (*List und Liebe*)
Städtisches Opernhaus Leipzig 1960. Previous oc-
cupations: carpenter. Awards: Kammersänger,
Ministry of Culture, Ger DR.
Sang with major companies in CZE: Brno,
Prague National; FR GER: Wiesbaden; GER DR:
Berlin Komische Oper & Staatsoper, Dresden,

Leipzig; ITA: Genoa. **Roles with these companies incl** CIMAROSA: Count Robinson★ (*Matrimonio segreto*); DONIZETTI: Dott Malatesta (*Don Pasquale*), Belcore (*Elisir*); GOTOVAC: Sima (*Ero der Schelm*); HANDEL: Arsamene★ (*Xerxes*); LORTZING: Graf v Liebenau★ (*Waffenschmied*), Peter I★ (*Zar und Zimmermann*); MOZART: Guglielmo★ (*Così fan tutte*), Papageno★ (*Zauberflöte*); PUCCINI: Marcello★ (*Bohème*); ROSSINI: Figaro★ (*Barbiere di Siviglia*); VERDI: Renato★ (*Ballo in maschera*), Conte di Luna★ (*Trovatore*); WOLF-FERRARI: Lelio★ (*Donne curiose*). Also TCHAIKOVSKY: Dunois★ (*Maid of Orleans*); STRAUSS, R: Harlekin★ (*Ariadne auf Naxos*); NICOLAI: Fluth★ (*Lustigen Weiber*); BRITTEN: Sid★ (*Albert Herring*); PERGOLESI: Tracollo (*Livietta e Tracollo*). **World premieres:** HANELL: Grigoris (*Griechische Hochzeit*) Leipzig 1969; GEISSLER: Arzt (*Der Schatten*) Leipzig 1975. Video/Film: (*Boccaccio*); Sid (*Albert Herring*); Guglielmo (*Così fan tutte*); Arsamene (*Xerxes*). Gives recitals. Appears with symphony orchestra. Teaches voice. Coaches repertoire. On faculty of Hochschule für Musik, Leipzig. **Res:** Fockestr 11, 703 Leipzig, Ger DR. **Mgmt:** KDR/GDR.

RIGACCI, BRUNO. Conductor of opera and symphony; composer. Italian. Art Dir, Opera Barga Fest, Italy, since 1974. Born 6 Mar 1921, Florence. Wife Ulla Johanssohn, occupation singer. Two children. Studied: Florence, with mother; Alfredo Casella; incl piano, organ and voice. Plays the piano. Operatic training as repetiteur & asst cond at Maggio Musicale, Florence 1951-57; Acad Music Chigiana, Siena 1945-57. **Operatic debut:** RIGACCI: *Prof King* Teatro delle Novità, Bergamo, Italy 1956. Symphonic debut: Maggio Musicale, Florence 1958. Previous occupations: piano soloist since 1929; teacher. Awards: First Prize for opera *Ecuba*, Intl Conc Teatro dell'Opera, Rome 1950; Rificolona d'oro, Amici dell'Opera.

Conducted with major companies in BEL: Brussels; DEN: Copenhagen; FRA: Nancy, Strasbourg; FR GER: Wiesbaden; GER DR: Berlin Staatsoper; ITA: Bologna, Florence Maggio & Comunale, Genoa, Milan La Scala, Naples, Parma, Rome Opera, Trieste, Turin, Venice; SPA: Barcelona, Las Palmas Fest; SWE: Stockholm; SWI: Basel; USA: New York City Opera, San Diego. **Operas with these companies incl** ADAM DE LA HALLE: *Robin et Marion*★; BELLINI: *Norma*★, *Puritani*★; BIZET: *Carmen;* BUSONI: *Arlecchino*★; DONIZETTI: *Convenienze/Viva la Mamma, Don Pasquale*★, *Elisir, Favorite, Lucia;* GIORDANO: *Andrea Chénier, Fedora;* GOUNOD: *Faust;* HANDEL: *Orlando furioso;* LEONCAVALLO: *Pagliacci*★; MASCAGNI: *Cavalleria rusticana;* MENOTTI: *Amelia al ballo, Consul;* MILHAUD: *Pauvre matelot*★; MOZART: *Così fan tutte*★; PAISIELLO: *Barbiere di Siviglia;* PERGOLESI: *Maestro di musica, Serva padrona;* PUCCINI: *Bohème, Gianni Schicchi*★, *Butterfly, Rondine*★, *Suor Angelica, Tabarro*★, *Tosca*★, *Turandot;* ROSSINI: *Barbiere di Siviglia, Italiana in Algeri*★, *Scala di seta;* SALIERI: *Prima la musica*★; SATIE: *Socrate*★; SCARLATTI: *Trionfo dell'onore*★; VERDI: *Aida, Ballo in maschera, Ernani, Macbeth*★, *Nabucco, Otello, Rigoletto, Traviata, Trovatore;* WOLF-

FERRARI: *Segreto di Susanna*. Also ROSSINI: *Equivoco stravagante*★, *Adina;* DONIZETTI: *Giovedi grasso*★, *Parisina d'Este*★, *Pia de' Tolomei*★, *Pigmalione;* LEONCAVALLO: *Edipo Re;* SALIERI: *Falstaff*★; CILEA: *Arlesiana;* ORLANDINI: *Giocatore;* PERI: *Euridice;* DA CAPUA: *Zingara;* TRAETTA: *Antigone;* CIMAROSA: *Due Baroni*★; PAISIELLO: *Astrologi immaginari*★, *Duello comico;* PETRASSI: *Cordovano;* DALLAPICCOLA: *Job;* de BANFIELD: *Alissa;* ROSSELLINI: *Guerra, Campane, Vortice, Sguardo dal ponte;* FIUME: *Tamburo di panno;* FRAZZI: *Don Chisciotte;* MALIPIERO: *Torneo notturno*. **World premieres:** VLAD: *Gabbiano* Settimane Musicali Senesi, Siena 1968. Conducted major orch in Europe, USA/Canada. Previous positions as Mus Dir with major orch: Settimane Musicali Senesi, Siena, Italy 1965-69; Philadelphia Music Theatre, PA, USA 1973- . **Operas composed:** *Ecuba* Teatro dell'Opera, Rome 1951; *Prof King* Teatro delle Novità, Bergamo, Italy 1956. Teaches at Cherubini Consv of Music, Florence. **Res:** V Giambologna 39, Florence 50132, Italy.

RIMINI, RUGGERO. Stages/produces opera & theater and is a writer. Italian. Resident Stage Dir, Summer Opera Festival, Barga. Born 8 Jul 1947, Florence. Single. Studied: theater and music. Operatic training as asst to Italian directors 1968-73. **Operatic debut:** *Puritani* Reggio Emilia, Italy 1971. Theater debut: with own company, Florence 1969.

Directed/produced opera for major companies in ITA: Bologna, Florence Maggio & Comunale, Parma, Trieste; USA: Seattle. **Operas staged with these companies incl** BELLINI: *Norma*★, *Sonnambula*★; DONIZETTI: *Don Pasquale*★, *Stuarda;* HUMPERDINCK: *Hänsel und Gretel*★; LEONCAVALLO: *Pagliacci*★; MASCAGNI: *Cavalleria rusticana*★; MOZART: *Così fan tutte*★; PUCCINI: *Fanciulla del West*★, *Gianni Schicchi*★, *Tabarro*★, *Turandot*★; VERDI: *Falstaff*★, *Trovatore*★. Also BRITTEN: *Little Sweep;* PAISIELLO: *Nina;* ROSSINI: *Barbiere di Siviglia, Italiana in Algeri*. Teaches history of modern theater, Univ of Florence. **Res:** V Lamarmora 53, Florence, Italy.

RINALDI, ALBERTO. Lyric baritone. Italian. Born 6 Jun 1939, Rome. Wife Elvira Lopez. One daughter. Studied: Consv di Santa Cecilia, Mo Piervenanzi, Rome. **Debut:** Simon Boccanegra, Teatro Nuovo, Spoleto 1963. Awards: Rome Maschera d'Argento per la Lirica 1971.

Sang with major companies in AUS: Bregenz Fest; BRA: Rio de Janeiro; CZE: Prague National; FRA: Aix-en-Provence Fest, Paris, Strasbourg; FR GER: Dortmund, Stuttgart; ISR: Tel Aviv; ITA: Bologna, Florence Maggio & Comunale, Genoa, Milan La Scala, Naples, Palermo, Parma, Rome Opera & Caracalla, Spoleto Fest, Trieste, Turin, Venice; MON: Monte Carlo; SWI: Geneva; UK: Edinburgh Fest; USSR: Leningrad Kirov; USA: Chicago, Philadelphia Lyric, San Francisco Opera, Washington DC. **Roles with these companies incl** BIZET: Escamillo (*Carmen*); BRITTEN: Billy Budd; CILEA: Michonnet (*A. Lecouvreur*); CIMAROSA: Count Robinson (*Matrimonio segreto*); DONIZETTI: Enrico (*Campanello*), Dott Malatesta (*Don Pasquale*), Belcore

(*Elisir*), Gasparo (*Rita*); GIORDANO; De Siriex (*Fedora*); MASSENET: Lescaut (*Manon*), Des Grieux (*Portrait de Manon*); MENOTTI: Husband (*Amelia al ballo*), Bob (*Old Maid and the Thief*); MOZART: Guglielmo (*Così fan tutte*), Figaro (*Nozze di Figaro*); PAISIELLO: Figaro (*Barbiere di Siviglia*), Teodoro (*Re Teodoro in Venezia*); PUCCINI: Marcello (*Bohème*), Gianni Schicchi, Sharpless (*Butterfly*), Lescaut (*Manon Lescaut*); PURCELL: Aeneas; ROSSINI: Figaro (*Barbiere di Siviglia*), Tobias Mill & Slook (*Cambiale di matrimonio*), Dandini (*Cenerentola*), Robert (*Comte Ory*), Podestà (*Gazza ladra*), Sultan Selim (*Turco in Italia*); VERDI: Ford (*Falstaff*), Simon Boccanegra, Germont (*Traviata*); WOLF-FERRARI: Lelio (*Donne curiose*), Conte Gil (*Segreto di Susanna*). Recorded for: EMI. Video/Film: (*Il Campanello*). Appears with symphony orchestra. **Res:** V Archimede 35, Rome, Italy.

RINALDI, MARGHERITA. Lyric soprano. Italian.
Sang with major companies in AUS: Bregenz Fest; ITA: Florence Comunale, Genoa, Milan La Scala, Turin; USA: Dallas; et al. **Roles with these companies incl** BELLINI: Amina (*Sonnambula*); CIMAROSA: Carolina (*Matrimonio segreto*); DONIZETTI: Norina (*Don Pasquale*), Marie (*Fille du régiment*), Linda di Chamounix; MEYERBEER: Berthe (*Prophète*); STRAUSS, R: Marschallin & Sophie (*Rosenkavalier*); VERDI: Nannetta (*Falstaff*), Marchesa (*Giorno di regno*), Gilda (*Rigoletto*); et al. Recorded for: Philips.

RINALDI, MAURIZIO. Conductor of opera and symphony. Italian. Born 16 Apr 1937, Rome. Single. Studied: Consv S Cecilia, Mo Ferdinandi, Mo Franco Ferrara, Rome; incl piano. Operatic training as personal asst to Mo Franco Capuana 1966-67. **Operatic debut:** *Traviata* La Fenice Co at Cairo, Egypt 1966. Symphonic debut: Phil Orch Helsinki, Finland 1972.
Conducted with major companies in FIN: Helsinki; HOL: Amsterdam; ITA: Milan La Scala, Rome Opera & Caracalla, Spoleto Fest, Turin, Verona Arena. **Operas conducted with these companies incl** DONIZETTI: *Lucia**; LEONCAVALLO: *Pagliacci**; MASCAGNI: *Cavalleria rusticana**; MENOTTI: *Telephone**; PUCCINI: *Bohème**, *Tosca**; VERDI: *Aroldo**‡, *Corsaro**‡, *Due Foscari**‡, *Rigoletto**, *Traviata*. Also VERDI: *Alzira**, *Battaglia di Legnano**; BETTINELLI: *Pozzo e il pendolo**; VIOZZI: *Allamistakeo**; ROSSELLINI: *Guerra*. Conducted major orch in Europe. **Res:** V Archimede 62, Rome, Italy. **Mgmt:** SMN/USA.

RINAUDO, MARIO. Bass. Italian. Born 25 Sep 1936, Chieti, Italy. Wife Annamaria. Two children. Studied: Nazzareno De Angelis. **Debut:** Fiesco (*Simon Boccanegra*) Teatro Sperimentale, Spoleto 1963.
Sang with major companies in BRA: Rio de Janeiro; FRA: Bordeaux, Nancy; ITA: Bologna, Florence Maggio & Comunale, Genoa, Milan La Scala, Naples, Palermo Massimo, Rome Teatro dell'Opera & Caracalla, Trieste, Turin, Venice; POR: Lisbon; SPA: Barcelona. **Roles with these companies incl** BELLINI: Capellio* (*Capuleti ed i*

Montecchi*), Oroveso (*Norma*), Sir George* (*Puritani*); DONIZETTI: Baldassare* (*Favorite*), Enrico & Raimondo (*Lucia*); MEYERBEER: Don Pedro* (*Africaine*); MONTEMEZZI: Archibaldo* (*Amore dei tre re*); PONCHIELLI: Alvise* (*Gioconda*); PUCCINI: Colline* (*Bohème*); ROSSINI: Don Basilio* (*Barbiere di Siviglia*); STRAVINSKY: Creon & Tiresias (*Oedipus Rex*); VERDI: Ramfis* (*Aida*), Silva* (*Ernani*), Padre Guardiano* (*Forza del destino*), Conte Walter* (*Luisa Miller*), Banquo* (*Macbeth*), Zaccaria (*Nabucco*), Fiesco* (*Simon Boccanegra*). Also GOMES: Gaiolo (*Fosca*); MASSENET: Comte des Grieux (*Manon*); TCHAIKOVSKY: Gremin (*Eugene Onegin*); MONTEVERDI: Seneca (*Incoronazione di Poppea*); MEYERBEER: Bertram (*Robert le Diable*). Gives recitals. Appears with symphony orchestra. **Res:** V Enrico Albanese 235, Rome, Italy.

RINTZLER, MARIUS ADRIAN. Bass. German. Resident mem: Deutsche Oper am Rhein, Düsseldorf. Born 14 Mar 1932, Bucharest, Romania. Wife Sanda, occupation coach, Düsseldorf Opera. Studied: Prof A Alexandrescu, Romania; Sanda Rintzler (wife), Düsseldorf. **Debut:** Don Basilio (*Barbiere di Siviglia*) Bucharest Opera 1964. Previous occupations: composer.
Sang with major companies in BRA: Rio de Janeiro; DEN: Copenhagen; FR GER: Dortmund, Düsseldorf-Duisburg, Hamburg; ITA: Florence Maggio; NOR: Oslo; ROM: Bucharest; SWE: Drottningholm Fest, Stockholm; UK: Edinburgh Fest, Glyndebourne Fest, London Royal Opera; USA: New York Met, San Francisco Opera. **Roles with these companies incl** BARTOK: Bluebeard*; BEETHOVEN: Rocco (*Fidelio*); BERLIOZ: Méphistophélès (*Damnation de Faust*); CIMAROSA: Geronimo (*Matrimonio segreto*); DEBUSSY: Arkel (*Pelléas et Mélisande*); DONIZETTI: Henry VIII (*Anna Bolena*); GOUNOD: Méphistophélès (*Faust*); HANDEL: Polyphemus (*Acis and Galatea*), King of Scotland‡ (*Ariodante*), Zoroastro‡ (*Orlando furioso*); LORTZING: Van Bett (*Zar und Zimmermann*); MASSENET: Sancho* (*Don Quichotte*); MOZART: Leporello* (*Don Giovanni*), Osmin* (*Entführung aus dem Serail*), Sarastro* (*Zauberflöte*); NICOLAI: Falstaff (*Lustigen Weiber*); PERGOLESI: Uberto‡ (*Serva padrona*); PUCCINI: Colline* (*Bohème*); ROSSINI: Don Basilio* (*Barbiere di Siviglia*), Don Magnifico (*Cenerentola*); SMETANA: Kezal (*Bartered Bride*); STRAUSS, R: La Roche (*Capriccio*); Baron Ochs (*Rosenkavalier*), Sir Morosus (*Schweigsame Frau*); STRAVINSKY: Tiresias (*Oedipus Rex*); VERDI: Ramfis* (*Aida*), Philip II (*Don Carlo*); WAGNER: Daland (*Fliegende Holländer*), König Heinrich (*Lohengrin*), Pogner (*Meistersinger*), Alberich (*Rheingold**, Götterdämmerung**); ZIMMERMANN: Wesener* (*Soldaten*). Recorded for: RCA, DG, Electrecord. Gives recitals. Appears with symphony orchestra. **Res:** Düsselkämpchen 10, Düsseldorf, FR Ger. **Mgmt:** DSP/USA.

RIPPON, MICHAEL GEORGE. Bass-baritone. British. Born 10 Dec 1938, Coventry, UK. Wife Josephine Helena, occupation pianist. One child.

Studied: Royal Acad of Music, London; St John's Coll, Cambridge, UK. **Debut:** Leporello (*Don Giovanni*) Welsh National Opera 1969. Awards: MA Cantab, Cambridge, UK; ARAM, Royal Acad of Music, London.

Sang with major companies in SWE: Drottningholm Fest; UK: Aldeburgh Fest, Cardiff Welsh, Glyndebourne Fest, London Royal Opera & English National. **Roles with these companies incl** BERLIOZ: Balducci (*Benvenuto Cellini*); BRITTEN: Ananias★ (*Burning Fiery Furnace*), Traveller★ (*Curlew River*); FALLA: Tio Sarvaor (*Vida breve*); FLOTOW: Plunkett (*Martha*); GAY: Lockit★ (*Beggar's Opera*); HANDEL: Polyphemus★ (*Acis and Galatea*); HENZE: Montejo★ (*Cimarrón*); HOLST: Death★ (*Savitri*); MASSENET: Albert (*Werther*); MOZART: Don Alfonso (*Così fan tutte*), Leporello & Don Giovanni (*Don Giovanni*), Figaro (*Nozze di Figaro*); PUCCINI: Marcello (*Bohème*); PURCELL: Aeneas (*Dido and Aeneas*), Oswald★ (*King Arthur*); ROSSINI: Dott Bartolo★ (*Barbiere di Siviglia*), Slook (*Cambiale di matrimonio*); STRAVINSKY: Nick Shadow (*Rake's Progress*); VAUGHAN WILLIAMS: John (*Hugh the Drover*). Also MOZART: Sprecher★ (*Zauberflöte*). Recorded for: EMI, RCA, Pye. Gives recitals. Appears with symphony orchestra. Teaches voice. **Res:** 31 Coll Dr, Ruislip, Middlesex, UK. Mgmt: IBB/UK.

RISTOW, RODERICK. Dramatic baritone. American. Resident mem: Staatstheater Hannover. Born 10 Aug 1937, Los Angeles. Wife Marilyn. Two children. Studied: Joseph J Klein, Los Angeles; Enzo Mascherini, Rome. **Debut:** Baron Douphol (*Traviata*) Euterpe Opera, Los Angeles 1958. Previous occupations: baseball player.

Sang with major companies in AUS: Graz; FRA: Nancy, Toulouse; FR GER: Cologne, Darmstadt, Düsseldorf-Duisburg, Essen, Hamburg, Hannover, Karlsruhe, Kassel, Mannheim, Munich Gärtnerplatz, Nürnberg, Stuttgart, Wuppertal; POR: Lisbon; SWI: Basel, Zurich; USA: San Francisco Spring Opera, Seattle. **Roles with these companies incl** d'ALBERT: Sebastiano★ (*Tiefland*); BEETHOVEN: Don Pizarro★ (*Fidelio*); BIZET: Escamillo★ (*Carmen*); CIMAROSA: Count Robinson (*Matrimonio segreto*); DEBUSSY: Golaud (*Pelléas et Mélisande*); DONIZETTI: Enrico★ (*Lucia*); GERSHWIN: Crown★ (*Porgy and Bess*); GIORDANO: Carlo Gérard★ (*Andrea Chénier*); LEONCAVALLO: Tonio★ (*Pagliacci*); MASCAGNI: Alfio★ (*Cavalleria rusticana*); MOZART: Conte Almaviva (*Nozze di Figaro*); OFFENBACH: Coppélius etc (*Contes d'Hoffmann*); PUCCINI: Marcello★ (*Bohème*), Scarpia★ (*Tosca*); ROSSINI: Figaro (*Barbiere di Siviglia*); STRAUSS, R: Orest★ (*Elektra*), Jochanaan★ (*Salome*); VERDI: Amonasro★ (*Aida*), Renato★ (*Ballo in maschera*), Rodrigo★ (*Don Carlo*), Don Carlo★ (*Forza del destino*), Nabucco★, Rigoletto★, Germont★ (*Traviata*), Conte di Luna★ (*Trovatore*); WAGNER: Amfortas (*Parsifal*); WALTON: Smirnov★ (*The Bear*). Appears with symphony orchestra. **Res:** Karlsruherstr 17, 3 Hannover, FR Ger.

RITCH, DAVID. Stages/produces opera & theater and is an actor. British. Sr Staff Prod & Resident Stage Dir, English National Opera, London. Born

28 Jul 1932, Johannesburg, S Africa. Single. Studied: Old Vic Theatre Co, Miss Iris Warren, London; incl music, piano and voice. Operatic training as asst stage dir at Sadler's Wells, London 1970-71. **Operatic debut:** *Thomas Bullen* London & tour 1972. Theater debut: London 1969. Previous occupation: diamond sorter, schoolteacher. Acting debut: Old Vic Co 1951.

Directed/produced opera for major companies in UK: London English National. **Operas staged with these companies incl** BEETHOVEN: *Fidelio★;* BENNETT: *Mines of Sulphur★;* BERLIOZ: *Damnation de Faust★;* BIZET: *Carmen★;* BRITTEN: *Gloriana★, Rape of Lucretia;* DONIZETTI: *Maria Stuarda★;* JANACEK: *Katya Kabanova★;* LEONCAVALLO: *Pagliacci★;* MASCAGNI: *Cavalleria rusticana★;* MASSENET: *Manon★;* MOZART: *Entführung aus dem Serail★;* OFFENBACH: *Contes d'Hoffmann★;* PROKOFIEV: *War and Peace★;* STRAVINSKY: *Oedipus Rex★;* VERDI: *Don Carlo★;* WAGNER: *Meistersinger★, Rheingold★, Walküre★, Siegfried★, Götterdämmerung★.* **Operatic world premieres:** HIGGS: *Thomas Bullen* London 1972. Teaches. **Res:** 2 Ormonde Gate, London SW3, UK.

RIVERS, MALCOLM. Dramatic baritone. British. Resident mem: English National Opera, London. Born 19 Apr 1937, Ipswich. Wife Pamela. One daughter. Studied: Royal Coll of Music, Marie Marchant, John Hargreaves, London. **Debut:** Collatinus (*Rape of Lucretia*) English Opera Gp, Aldeburgh 1965. Previous occupations: librarian; Royal Air Force.

Sang with major companies in UK: Aldeburgh Fest, Glyndebourne Fest, London English National; USA: Seattle. **Roles with these companies incl** BIZET: Escamillo★ (*Carmen*); BRITTEN: Astrologer★ (*Burning Fiery Furnace*), Traveller★ (*Curlew River*), Charles Blount★ (*Gloriana*), Theseus★ (*Midsummer Night*), Elder Son★ (*Prodigal Son*); GAY/Britten: Lockit (*Beggar's Opera*); LEONCAVALLO: Tonio★ (*Pagliacci*); MASCAGNI: Alfio★ (*Cavalleria rusticana*); MOZART: Don Alfonso★ (*Così fan tutte*); OFFENBACH: Coppélius etc★ (*Contes d'Hoffmann*); PENDERECKI: Mannoury★ (*Teufel von Loudun*); PROKOFIEV: Dolokhov★ (*War and Peace*); ROSSINI: Dott Bartolo★ (*Barbiere di Siviglia*); STRAVINSKY: Creon★ (*Oedipus Rex*); VERDI: Rigoletto★; WAGNER: Telramund★ (*Lohengrin*), Alberich (*Rheingold★, Siegfried★, Götterdämmerung★*); WALTON: Smirnov (*Bear*). **World premieres:** BERKELEY: Laodomas (*Castaway*) Aldeburgh 1967; CROSSE: Furlong (*Grace of Todd*) Aldeburgh 1969. Video/Film: Tonio (*Pagliacci*), Rigoletto, Bartolo (*Barbiere*), Coppélius etc (*Hoffmann*). Gives recitals. Appears with symphony orchestra. **Res:** 44 Merryhill Mount, Bushey/Herts, UK. Mgmt: MIN/UK.

RIVOLI, GIANFRANCO. Conductor of opera. Italian. Resident Cond, Teatro Regio, Turin 1971-. **Conducted with major companies in** FRA: Aix-en-Provence Fest, Marseille, Paris; FR GER: Düsseldorf-Duisburg; ITA: Milan La Scala, Palermo, Rome Opera, Turin; POR: Lisbon; SWI: Geneva; USA: Cincinnati, Philadelphia Lyric; et al. **Operas with these companies incl** BELLINI: *Puritani;* BRITTEN: *Peter Grimes;* BUSONI:

Arlecchino; DONIZETTI: *Anna Bolena, Elisir;* DVORAK: *Rusalka;* JANACEK: *Jenufa;* MASSENET: *Werther;* MONTEVERDI: *Favola d'Orfeo;* MOZART: *Zauberflöte;* MUSSORGSKY: *Boris Godunov;* OFFENBACH: *Contes d'Hoffmann;* PONCHIELLI: *Gioconda;* PUCCINI: *Bohème, Butterfly;* ROSSINI: *Barbiere di Siviglia, Italiana in Algeri;* STRAVINSKY: *Rake's Progress;* VERDI: *Aida, Rigoletto, Traviata;* WAGNER: *Siegfried;* et al. Also TOSATTI: *Partita a pugni;* HONEGGER: *Jeanne d'Arc au bûcher.* **World premieres:** FUGA: *Confessione* Teatro Regio, Turin 1971.

RIZZO, FRANCIS. Stages/produces opera. American. Artistic Administrator, Wolf Trap Farm Park, Vienna, VA since 1973. Born 8 Nov 1936, New York. Single. Studied: Yale Drama School, Nikos Psacharapoulos, CT; Gian Carlo Menotti. Operatic training as asst stage dir to Gian Carlo Menotti 1964-70. **Operatic debut:** *Medium & Globolinks* Houston Grand Opera, TX 1972.

Directed/produced opera for major companies in FRA: Marseille; ITA: Trieste; USA: Baltimore, Houston, Kansas City, New York City Opera, Santa Fe, Washington DC. **Operas staged for these companies incl** MENOTTI: *Amahl, Consul★, Globolinks★, Maria Golovin★, Medium★, Saint of Bleecker Street★, Telephone★;* MUSSORGSKY: *Boris Godunov★;* PUCCINI: *Butterfly★;* STRAUSS, R: *Salome★.* **Res:** 590 West End Ave, New York 10024, USA. Mgmt: CAM/USA.

ROAR, LEIF. Bass-baritone. Danish. Resident mem: Deutsche Oper am Rhein, Düsseldorf.

Sang with major companies in ARG: Buenos Aires; AUS: Bregenz Fest, Salzburg Fest; BEL: Brussels; DEN: Copenhagen; FR GER: Bonn, Düsseldorf-Duisburg, Hamburg, Mannheim, Munich Staatsoper, Stuttgart; ITA: Milan La Scala; USA: San Francisco Opera; et al. **Roles with these companies incl** BEETHOVEN: Don Pizarro (*Fidelio*); BIZET: Escamillo (*Carmen*); DALLAPICCOLA: Ulisse; HINDEMITH: Mathis; MOZART: Don Giovanni, Conte Almaviva (*Nozze di Figaro*); PUCCINI: Scarpia (*Tosca*); STRAUSS, R: Mandryka (*Arabella*), Jochanaan (*Salome*); STRAVINSKY: Nick Shadow (*Rake's Progress*); WAGNER: Holländer, Telramund (*Lohengrin*), Amfortas (*Parsifal*), Wotan (*Rheingold, Walküre*), Wanderer (*Siegfried*), Wolfram (*Tannhäuser*), Kurwenal (*Tristan und Isolde*); et al. **World premieres:** KLEBE: Mann mit der Lampe (*Märchen von der schönen Lilie*) Schwetzingen 1969. Appears with symphony orchestra.

ROBERTS, BRENDA. Dramatic soprano. American. Resident mem: Staatsoper, Hamburg. Born 16 Mar 1945, Lowell, IN, USA. Husband Johannes Horneber, occupation conductor & coach. Studied: Northwestern Univ, Prof Hermanus Baer, Evanston; Lotte Lehmann & Gerald Moore, master classes; Kmsg Josef Metternich. **Debut:** Sieglinde (*Walküre*) Staatstheater Saarbrücken 1968.

Sang with major companies in FR GER: Bayreuth Fest, Bielefeld, Bonn, Düsseldorf-Duisburg, Essen, Frankfurt, Hamburg, Nürnberg, Saarbrücken, Wiesbaden, Wuppertal; USA: Chicago, San Francisco Opera. **Roles with these companies incl** BERG: Lulu★; GLUCK: Euridice; MASCA-GNI: Santuzza★ (*Cavalleria rusticana*); MOZART: Donna Elvira★ (*Don Giovanni*), Konstanze (*Entführung aus dem Serail*), Contessa★ (*Nozze di Figaro*); OFFENBACH: Olympia & Antonia & Giulietta (*Contes d'Hoffmann*); PUCCINI: Musetta (*Bohème*), Giorgetta★ (*Tabarro*), Tosca★, Turandot★; STRAUSS, R: Ariadne★ (*Ariadne auf Naxos*), Elektra★; VERDI: Aida★, Elisabetta★ (*Don Carlo*), Lady Macbeth★, Desdemona★ (*Otello*), Violetta★ (*Traviata*), Leonora★ (*Trovatore*); WAGNER: Senta★ (*Fliegende Holländer*), Elsa (*Lohengrin*), Sieglinde★ (*Walküre*), Brünnhilde★ (*Siegfried*). Also STRAUSS, R: Färberin★ (*Frau ohne Schatten*). Gives recitals. Appears with symphony orchestra. **Res:** Hamburg, FR Ger. **Mgmt:** CST/UK.

ROBERTS, KATHLEEN. Lyric soprano. American. Resident mem: Staatstheater Darmstadt, FR Ger. Born 9 Oct 1941, Hattiesburg, MS. Husband Dr Klaus Striegler, occupation chemist. One daughter. Studied: Mississippi Coll, Prof Gerald Claxton; Texas Christian Univ, Prof Désiré Ligeti; Intl School of Opera, Zurich; Eva Ambrosius, Darmstadt. **Debut:** Violetta (*Traviata*) St Gallen Opera, Switzerland 1967. Previous occupations: music instr in univ. **Awards:** M B Rockefeller Fnd grnt; Delta Omicron Awd for foreign study; Outstanding Young Women of America 1968.

Sang with major companies in FR GER: Cologne, Darmstadt, Frankfurt; SWI: Geneva, Zurich. **Roles with these companies incl** BEETHOVEN: Marzelline★ (*Fidelio*); BIZET: Micaëla (*Carmen*); CIMAROSA: Carolina★ (*Matrimonio segreto*); CORNELIUS: Margiana★ (*Barbier von Bagdad*); EINEM: Frl Bürstner★ (*Prozess*); FLOTOW: Lady Harriet★ (*Martha*); GOUNOD: Juliette; HENZE: Luise★ (*Junge Lord*); HUMPERDINCK: Gretel★; MENOTTI: Mother (*Amahl*), Laetitia (*Old Maid and the Thief*); MONTEVERDI: Minerva★ (*Ritorno d'Ulisse*); MOZART: Konstanze★ (*Entführung aus dem Serail*), Susanna★ (*Nozze di Figaro*), Pamina★ (*Zauberflöte*); PUCCINI: Mimi★ (*Bohème*), Lauretta (*Gianni Schicchi*); PURCELL: Dido; STRAUSS, R: Sophie★ (*Rosenkavalier*); STRAVINSKY: Parasha★ (*Mavra*); VERDI: Violetta★ (*Traviata*); WEBER: Aennchen★ (*Freischütz*); WOLF-FERRARI: Rosaura★ (*Donne curiose*). Gives recitals. Appears with symphony orchestra. Teaches voice. Coaches repertoire. **Res:** Eulerweg 6, 6103 Griesheim, FR Ger.

ROBERTS, REBECCA. Lyric soprano. American. Resident mem: Opéra du Rhin, Strasbourg. Born 7 Jan 1948, Sendai, Japan. Single. Studied: Mary Henderson Buckley, Miami, FL, USA. **Debut:** Rose (*Street Scene*) Ambler Fest, PA, USA 1970. Awards: NATS Singer of the Year; G B Dealey, *Dallas Morning News* Awd; Palm Beach Civic Opera Aud; District Aud Met Op Awd.

Sang with major companies in FRA: Strasbourg; USA: Miami. **Roles with these companies incl** BERLIOZ: Héro★ (*Béatrice et Bénédict*); BIZET: Micaëla★ (*Carmen*); BRITTEN: Helena★ (*Midsummer Night*); DONIZETTI: Adina★ (*Elisir*); MONTEVERDI: Euridice★ (*Orfeo*); MOORE: Lola★ (*Gallantry*); PUCCINI: Lauretta★ (*Gianni Schicchi*); STRAUSS, J: Adele★

(*Fledermaus*). **World premieres:** DELERUE: Leli (*Médis et Alyssio*) Opéra du Rhin, Strasbourg 1975. Gives recitals. Appears with symphony orchestra. **Res:** Strasbourg, France. Mgmt: IMR/FRA.

ROBINSON, FAYE. Lyric coloratura soprano. American. Resident mem: New York City Opera. Born 2 Nov 1943, Houston, TX. Studied: Texas Southern Univ, Ruth Stewart, Houston; No Texas State Univ, A Lynch, Denton; Ellen Faull, New York City. **Debut:** Micaëla (*Carmen*) New York City Opera 1972. Awards: First Place reg winner Met Op Ntl Counc Aud & semi-finalist, NY 1968; First Prize, San Francisco Opera Aud 1969; Third Prize, Intl Singing Compt, Munich 1970.

Sang with major companies in FRA: Aix-en-Provence Fest; SPA: Barcelona; USA: Houston, Jackson Opera/South, New York City Opera, Washington DC. **Roles with these companies incl** BIZET: Micaëla★ (*Carmen*); DONIZETTI: Norina★ (*Don Pasquale*), Adina★ (*Elisir*), Lucrezia Borgia★; GOUNOD: Juliette★; MOZART: Konstanze★ (*Entführung aus dem Serail*), Mme Silberklang★ (*Schauspieldirektor*); PERGOLESI: Serpina (*Serva padrona*); PUCCINI: Liù★ (*Turandot*); VERDI: Oscar (*Ballo in maschera*), Desdemona (*Otello*). Gives recitals. Appears with symphony orchestra. Mgmt: CAM/USA.

ROBINSON, FORBES. Bass. British. Resident member: Royal Opera, London, UK. Born 21 May 1926, Macclesfield, UK. Wife Marion. Two children. Studied: Harry Shaw, Leicester; Hamilton Harris, Manchester; Scuola di Canto, La Scala, Milan. **Debut:** Monterone (*Rigoletto*) Covent Garden 1954. Previous occupations: schoolteacher in physic educ & geography. Awards: Hon Dipl in Physic Educt, Loughborough, UK: Opera Medal, Harriet Cohen Intl Musical Awd 1963.

Sang with major companies in ARG: Buenos Aires; GER DR: Berlin Staatsoper; SPA: Barcelona; SWI: Zurich; UK: Aldeburgh Fest, Cardiff Welsh, Edinburgh Fest, Glasgow Scottish, London Royal & English National. Roles with these companies incl BEETHOVEN: Don Pizarro (*Fidelio*); BELLINI: Rodolfo★ (*Sonnambula*); BRITTEN: John Claggart★ (*Billy Budd*), Sir Walter Raleigh (*Gloriana*), Bottom & Theseus (*Midsummer Night*); CORNELIUS: Abul Hassan (*Barbier von Bagdad*); DONIZETTI: Dulcamara (*Elisir*); MOZART: Don Giovanni★, Figaro (*Nozze di Figaro*), Sarastro (*Zauberflöte*); MUSSORGSKY: Boris Godunov★, Shaklovity (*Khovanshchina*); OFFENBACH: Coppélius etc (*Contes d'Hoffmann*); PUCCINI: Colline★ (*Bohème*); RIMSKY-KORSAKOV: Roi Dodon (*Coq d'or*); ROSSINI: Don Basilio★ (*Barbiere di Siviglia*); SCHOENBERG: Moses; SMETANA: Kezal (*Bartered Bride*); VERDI: Ramfis★ (*Aida*), Philip II★ (*Don Carlo*), Banquo (*Macbeth*), Fiesco★ (*Simon Boccanegra*); WAGNER: Wotan & Fasolt (*Rheingold*). Also HANDEL: Hercules; PUCCINI: Timur (*Turandot*). **World premieres:** TIPPETT: King Priam (*King Priam*) Covent Garden 1962; BRITTEN: Theseus (*Midsummer Night*) English Opera Group, Aldeburgh Fest 1960. Gives recitals. Appears with symphony orchestra. **Res:** 225 Princes Gardens, London, UK.

ROBINSON. FRANCIS. American. Asst Mng, Metropolitan Opera, Lincoln Center, New York 10023. Is chief of press dept and tour dir. Born 28 Apr 1910, Henderson, KY. Single. Studied: Vanderbilt Univ, Nashville, TN. Previous occupations: staff Radio Station WSM; reporter, then Sunday Editor of *Nashville Banner*. Form positions, primarily administrative: press repres Judith Anderson, USA tour 1948; Berkshire Music Fest Tanglewood, summers 1947, 48; Katharine Cornell 1939-42 and 1946-48; Theatre Incorp 1946-47. Press repres and Comp Mng, Playwrights' Company 1938-39; Cornelia Otis Skinner 1938-39. Started with present company in 1948 as tour dir; 1950-62 also head of box office and subscription; since 1954 head of press dept. Awards: Handel Medallion, City of New York; Cavaliere Order of Merit, Rep of Italy; Hon DL Westminster Choir Coll; Awd of Merit, Lotos Club. Mem of Board of Trustees, Manhattan School of Music, New York. **Res:** 220 Central Park So, New York, USA.

ROBINSON, GAIL. Coloratura soprano. American. Resident mem: Metropolitan Opera, New York. Born 7 Aug 1946, Meridian, MS. Husband Henno Lohmeyer, occupation TV prod, journalist. Studied: Memphis State Univ, Mrs J Norvell Taylor, TN; Robley Lawson, New York. **Debut:** Lucia, Memphis Opera Theatre 1967. Awards: Winner Met Op Ntl Counc Aud 1968; Rockefeller Fndt Grant.

Sang with major companies in CAN: Vancouver; FR GER: Hamburg; SWI: Geneva; USA: Chicago, Kentucky, Memphis, New Orleans, New York Met, Omaha, Philadelphia Grand, San Antonio. **Roles with these companies incl** BELLINI: Amina (*Sonnambula*); BIZET: Léila (*Pêcheurs de perles*); DONIZETTI: Norina (*Don Pasquale*), Marie (*Fille du régiment*), Lucia; GLUCK: Amor (*Orfeo*); GOUNOD: Juliette; HANDEL: Romilda (*Xerxes*); MENOTTI: Lucy (*Telephone*); MOZART: Fiordiligi (*Così fan tutte*), Zerlina (*Don Giovanni*); PUCCINI: Musetta (*Bohème*), Lisette (*Rondine*); ROSSINI: Rosina (*Barbiere di Siviglia*); VERDI: Oscar (*Ballo in maschera*), Gilda (*Rigoletto*). **Res:** New York & Berlin, FR Ger. Mgmt: CAM/USA.

ROBINSON, MARIE; née Marie Elizabeth Hadley. Spinto. American. Resident mem: Vereinigte Bühnen Graz, Austria. Born 2 Dec 1940, Thomasville, GA, USA. Husband Emmett, occupation music teacher. Five children. Studied: Florida State Univ, Yvonne Cianella, Elena Nikolaidi, Tallahassee, FL; Florida A&M Univ, Tallahassee, FL. **Debut:** Aida, Opernhaus Graz 1974. Previous occupations: music teacher, Detroit PS, MI, USA. Awards: The Diuguid Fllshp, Southern Fllshp Fund; 3 yr NDEA Doctoral Fllshp, US Gvnmt grant; Finalist Intl Compt for Bel Canto, Rio de Janeiro.

Sang with major companies in AUS: Graz; FR GER: Munich Staatsoper. **Roles with these companies incl** MOZART: Donna Anna★ (*Don Giovanni*); PUCCINI: Giorgetta★ (*Tabarro*), Tosca★; VERDI: Aida★; WAGNER: Sieglinde★ (*Walküre*). Gives recitals. **Res:** 114 Second Ave, Thomasville, GA, USA. Mgmt: TAS/AUS; SLZ/FRG.

ROBSON, ELIZABETH. Lyric soprano. British. Born 17 Jan 1939, Dundee, Scotland, UK. Husband Neil Howlett, occupation baritone, English National Opera Co. Two children. Studied: Royal Scottish Acad of Music, Margaret Dick, Glasgow; Lala Sarsonska, Florence; Ettore Campogalliani, Mantua; Otakar Kraus, London. Debut: Micaëla (*Carmen*) Sadler's Wells Opera 1962. Awards: Counfrarie dis Eschansoun dou Rei Reinie.

Sang with major companies in FRA: Aix-en-Provence Fest, Bordeaux, Strasbourg, Toulouse; FR GER: Hamburg; ITA: Milan La Scala, Naples; UK: Cardiff Welsh, Edinburgh Fest, Glasgow Scottish, Glyndebourne Fest, London Royal Opera & English National. Roles with these companies incl BEETHOVEN: Marzelline (*Fidelio*); BIZET: Micaëla (*Carmen*); BRITTEN: Helena (*Midsummer Night*); GLUCK: Amor (*Orfeo ed Euridice*); LEONCAVALLO: Nedda★ (*Pagliacci*); MOZART: Vitellia (*Clemenza di Tito*), Fiordiligi★ (*Così fan tutte*), Zerlina★ (*Don Giovanni*), Contessa★ & Susanna★ (*Nozze di Figaro*), Pamina (*Zauberflöte*); OFFENBACH: Antonia★ (*Contes d'Hoffmann*); PUCCINI: Musetta★ (*Bohème*), Lauretta (*Gianni Schicchi*); STRAUSS, J: Rosalinde (*Fledermaus*); STRAUSS, R: Zdenka★ (*Arabella*), Sophie★ (*Rosenkavalier*); STRAVINSKY: Anne Trulove (*Rake's Progress*); VERDI: Nannetta★ (*Falstaff*), Gilda★ (*Rigoletto*); WEILL: Jenny (*Aufstieg und Fall der Stadt Mahagonny*). Also GLUCK: Elena (*Paride ed Elena*). Video/Film: Lauretta (*Gianni Schicchi*). Gives recitals. Appears with symphony orchestra. Res: London, UK. Mgmt: GOR/UK.

ROCCHI, ALDO. Italian. Mus Adm, Teatro Comunale/Maggio Musicale Fiorentino, 15 V Solferino, Florence, Italy. In charge of art policy & mus matters; is also a musicologist. Born 11 Jun 1921, San Casciano dei Bagni/Siena. Wife Adriana Bigliazzi, occupation mng. Three children. Studied: Consv S Cecilia, B Somma, Rome & Consv S Pietro a Maiella, V Frazzi, Naples. Plays the piano & organ. Previous occupations: asst stage dir. Started with present company 1955 as asst stage dir; in present position since 1967.

ROCCHI, MANLIO. Lyric tenor. Italian. Born 23 Nov 1935, Olevano Romano/Rome, Italy. Wife Giuseppina. Two children. Studied: Consv di S Cecilia, Rome, Prof Elena d'Ambrosio. Debut: Prunier (*Rondine*) 1961. Awards: Gold medals Verdi Assn, Assn of S Mercadante; Diploma Lions Club.

Sang with major companies in BEL: Brussels; BUL: Sofia; FRA: Orange Fest; GRE: Athens National; HOL: Amsterdam; ISR: Tel Aviv; ITA: Bologna, Milan La Scala, Naples, Palermo, Rome Opera & Caracalla, Venice; ROM: Bucharest; SWI: Zurich. Roles with these companies incl BELLINI: Lord Arthur★ (*Puritani*), Elvino★ (*Sonnambula*); CIMAROSA: Paolino★ (*Matrimonio segreto*); DONIZETTI: Ernesto★ (*Don Pasquale*), Nemorino★‡ (*Elisir*), Edgardo★ (*Lucia*), Beppo★ (*Rita*); LEONCAVALLO: Canio★ (*Pagliacci*); MASCAGNI: Fritz★ (*Amico Fritz*); MENOTTI: Lover★ (*Amelia al ballo*); MONTEVERDI: Testo★ & Tancredi★ (*Combattimento di Tancredi*); PUCCINI: Rodolfo★ (*Bohème*), Rinuccio★ (*Gianni Schicchi*), Pinkerton★ (*Butterfly*), Prunier★ (*Rondine*), Cavaradossi★ (*Tosca*), Roberto★ (*Villi*); ROSSINI: Almaviva★ (*Barbiere di Siviglia*), Aménophis (*Moïse*), Dorvil★ (*Scala di seta*), Florville★ (*Signor Bruschino*); VERDI: Riccardo★ (*Ballo in maschera*), Fenton★ (*Falstaff*), Ismaele★ (*Nabucco*), Duca di Mantova★‡ (*Rigoletto*), Alfredo★ (*Traviata*). Also CILEA: Federico (*Arlesiana*); ZAFRED: Re (*Amleto*). World premieres: VLAD: Avvocato & Poeta (*Sogno*) Bergamo 1973. Recorded for: RCA Victor, Fratelli Fabbri. Video/Film: (*Ajo nell'imbarazzo*). Res: V Vecchiano 10, Rome, Italy.

RODEN, ANTHONY. Lyric tenor. Australian. Resident mem: English National Opera, London. Born 19 Mar 1937, Adelaide, NSW, Australia. Wife Doreen Cryer, occupation singer. Two children. Studied: Adelaide Consv, Arnold Matters, Donald Munro, Australia; London Opera Centre, Alexander Young. Debut: Lenski (*Eugene Onegin*) Glyndebourne Fest 1971. Previous occupations: worked for fire & accident marine insurance co. Awards: John Christie Awd, Glyndebourne Fest; Winner 's Hertogenbosch Vocal Compt, Holland; Opera Prize Adelaide Consv.

Sang with major companies in FR GER: Krefeld; HOL: Amsterdam; UK: Cardiff Welsh, Glyndebourne Fest, London English National. Roles with these companies incl CAVALLI: Ormindo★; LORTZING: Baron Kronthal★ (*Wildschütz*); MOZART: Ferrando★ (*Così fan tutte*), Don Ottavio★ (*Don Giovanni*), Belmonte★ (*Entführung aus dem Serail*), Idamante★ & Idomeneo★ (*Idomeneo*), Tamino★ (*Zauberflöte*); PUCCINI: Rinuccio★ (*Gianni Schicchi*); ROSSINI: Almaviva★ (*Barbiere di Siviglia*); STRAUSS, J: Alfred★ (*Fledermaus*); STRAUSS, R: Flamand★ (*Capriccio*); TCHAIKOVSKY: Lenski★ (*Eugene Onegin*). Video – ITV London/Glyndebourne: Belmonte (*Entführung*). Gives recitals. Appears with symphony orchestra. Res: 33 Castlebar Rd, London W5, UK. Mgmt: ASK/UK; CMW/FRA.

RÖDIN, MARGOT KERSTIN BIRGITTA. Lyric mezzo-soprano. Swedish. Resident mem: Royal Opera, Stockholm. Born 12 Mar 1935, Stockholm. Divorced. One child. Studied: Ingeborg Berling; Musikaliska Akad, Prof Ragnar Hultén; Operaskolan Stockholm; Wilhelm Freund, Erik Werba, Gerald Moore, coach conc rep. Debut: Oberon (*Midsummer Night*) Royal Opera, Stockholm 1961.

Sang with major companies in SWE: Drottningholm Fest, Stockholm. Roles with these companies incl BRITTEN: Mrs Herring★ (*Albert Herring*), Oberon (*Midsummer Night*); HANDEL: Bradamante & Ruggiero (*Alcina*); MOZART: Dorabella (*Così fan tutte*), Cherubino (*Nozze di Figaro*); PUCCINI: Suzuki (*Butterfly*); ROSSINI: Rosina★ (*Barbiere di Siviglia*), Marchesina Clarice★ (*Pietra del paragone*); STRAUSS, R: Octavian (*Rosenkavalier*); TCHAIKOVSKY: Olga (*Eugene Onegin*). Also HANDEL: Apollo/Mirtillo★ (*Pastor fido*); WERLE: Thérèse★ (*Dream of Thérèse*); CAVALLI: Sofombe★ (*Scipio Africanus*). Gives recitals. Appears with symphony orchestra. Mgmt: KBL/SWE.

RODZINSKI, RICHARD. American. Art Adm, Metropolitan Opera, Lincoln Center, New York, NY 10023, USA. In charge of overall artistic matters, and is also a composer. Born 23 Jan 1945, New York. Single. Studied: Oberlin Coll, Ohio; Columbia Coll and Univ, New York. Plays the piano. Previous positions primarily musical: Stge Mng and Mng Theatrical Div, Festival of Two Worlds, Spoleto, Italy, three seasons; Art Asst to Gen Dir, San Francisco Opera, CA 1969-75. In present position since 1975. **Res:** New York, NY, USA.

ROE, CHARLES RICHARD. Lyric baritone. American. Resident mem: New York City Opera. Born 4 May 1940, Cleveland, O, USA. Divorced. Three children. Studied: Baldwin Wallace Coll, Burton Garlinghouse, Berea, O; Univ of Illinois, Bruce Foote, Urbana, IL; Univ of Michigan, John McCollum, Ann Arbor, MI, USA. **Debut:** Rambaldo (*Rondine*) Michigan Opera Theatre, Detroit 1971. Previous occupations: coll music teacher. Awards: Singer of the Year, NATS 1966.
Sang with major companies in USA: New York City Opera. **Roles with these companies incl** MENOTTI: John Sorel* (*Consul*); MOZART: Guglielmo* (*Così fan tutte*); PUCCINI: Sharpless* (*Butterfly*), Lescaut* (*Manon Lescaut*), Rambaldo* (*Rondine*); ROSSINI: Figaro* (*Barbiere di Siviglia*); VERDI: Ford (*Falstaff*). Also MONTEVERDI: Nero* (*Incoronazione di Poppea*). Gives recitals. Appears with symphony orchestra. Teaches voice. **Res:** 2633 Whitewood, Ann Arbor, MI, USA. Mgmt: ACA/USA.

ROGERS, NOËLLE. Lyric soprano. American. Married. Studied: Univ of Michigan, Ann Arbor, USA; Annette Havens, New York; Boris Goldovsky, coach, New York. **Debut:** Violetta (*Traviata*) Goldovsky Opera Theater 1970. Previous occupations: receptionist. Awards: National Opera Inst grant; Elsa Stanley Gardner grant, Met Op.
Sang with major companies in FRA: Aix-en-Provence Fest, Marseille; HOL: Amsterdam; UK: London Royal Opera; USA: Kansas City, New York City Opera, Philadelphia Lyric, St Paul, Washington DC. **Roles with these companies incl** FLOYD: Susannah*; HANDEL: Rodelinda*; MOZART: Vitellia* (*Clemenza di Tito*), Fiordiligi* (*Così fan tutte*), Donna Anna* (*Don Giovanni*); PUCCINI: Musetta* (*Bohème*); VERDI: Gilda* (*Rigoletto*), Violetta* (*Traviata*); WARD: Abigail* (*Crucible*). Also BEESON: Sister Rose Ora (*Sweet Bye and Bye*). Recorded for: Desto. Video/Film - French TV: Vitellia (*Clemenza di Tito*). Gives recitals. Appears with symphony orchestra. Mgmt: CAM/USA; IWL/UK.

ROHDE, VOLKER. Conductor of opera and symphony. German. Resident Cond, Staatsoper Dresden, Ger DR. Born 4 May 1939, Greifswald. Wife Ingeborg, occupation physiotherapist. One child. Studied: Prof H Förster, Berlin; also piano. Plays the piano. Operatic training as repetiteur & chorus master at Komische Oper Berlin 1963-68; Theater Zwickau/Sa 1968-70. **Operatic debut:** *Così fan tutte* Theater Zwickau, Ger DR 1970. Symphonic debut: Phil Orch, Dresden 1969. Awards: Fourth Place, Intl Cond Compt Budapest 1974; Second Place, Weber Compt Dresden 1969.

Conducted with major companies in GER DR: Berlin Staatsoper, Dresden. **Operas with these companies incl** ADAM: *Postillon de Lonjumeau*; d'ALBERT: *Tiefland*; BEETHOVEN: *Fidelio*; DONIZETTI: *Elisir*; GLUCK: *Iphigénie en Tauride, Orfeo ed Euridice*; HUMPERDINCK: *Hänsel und Gretel*; LEONCAVALLO: *Pagliacci*; LORTZING: *Waffenschmied, Wildschütz, Zar und Zimmermann*; MOZART: *Entführung aus dem Serail, Schauspieldirektor, Nozze di Figaro, Zauberflöte*; ORFF: *Kluge*; PAISIELLO: *Barbiere di Siviglia*; PUCCINI: *Bohème, Butterfly, Tosca*; SMETANA: *Bartered Bride*; STRAUSS, J: *Fledermaus*; STRAVINSKY: *Mavra*; TCHAIKOVSKY: *Eugene Onegin*; VERDI: *Rigoletto, Traviata*; WAGNER: *Fliegende Holländer*; WEBER: *Freischütz*. Also LEONCAVALLO: *Edipo Re*; STRAVINSKY: *Renard*; BUZKO: *White Nights*. Conducted major orch in Europe. Teaches at Hochschule für Musik, Dresden. **Res:** Bachmannstr 2, Dresden, Ger DR. Mgmt: KDR/GDR.

RÖHRL, MANFRED. Bass-buffo. German. Resident mem: Deutsche Oper, Berlin. Born 12 Sep 1935, Augsburg, Germany. Wife Helga, occupation dancer. One child. Studied: Konsv Augsburg, Prof Franz Kelch, Prof Margarete von Winterfeld. **Debut:** Masetto (*Don Giovanni*) Augsburg 1958. Awards: Kammersänger, Berlin Senate.
Sang with major companies in BEL: Brussels; FRA: Nancy, Strasbourg; GRE: Athens Fest; FR GER: Berlin Deutsche Oper, Bonn, Cologne, Düsseldorf-Duisburg Deutsche Oper am Rhein, Hamburg Staatsoper, Karlsruhe, Kiel, Munich Staatsoper; MEX: Mexico City; SWI: Basel, Geneva, Zurich; UK: Edinburgh Fest; YUG: Zagreb, Belgrade. **Roles with these companies incl** BERG: Doktor (*Wozzeck*); BOIELDIEU: Gaveston (*Dame blanche*); BUSONI: Matteo (*Arlecchino*); CIMAROSA: Geronimo* (*Matrimonio segreto*); CORNELIUS: Abul Hassan (*Barbier von Bagdad*); DONIZETTI: Don Pasquale, Belcore (*Elisir*); EGK: Cuperus (*Zaubergeige*); EINEM: St Just* (*Dantons Tod*); HANDEL: Bertaric (*Rodelinda*); JANACEK: Sacristan* (*Excursions of Mr Broucek*); LORTZING: Baculus* (*Wildschütz*), Van Bett (*Zar und Zimmermann*); MARTINU: Hans (*Comedy on the Bridge*); MEYERBEER: Comte Oberthal (*Prophète*); MOZART: Don Alfonso (*Così fan tutte*), Leporello* (*Don Giovanni*), Figaro* (*Nozze di Figaro*), Papageno* (*Zauberflöte*); MUSSORGSKY: Varlaam* (*Boris Godunov*); NABOKOV: Berowne* (*Love's Labour's Lost*); OFFENBACH: Coppélius etc (*Contes d'Hoffmann*); PUCCINI: Marcello (*Bohème*); ROSSINI: Dott Bartolo* (*Barbiere di Siviglia*), Don Magnifico (*Cenerentola*); SMETANA: Kezal (*Bartered Bride*); STRAUSS, R: La Roche (*Capriccio*); VERDI: Grande Inquisitore (*Don Carlo*), Fra Melitone* (*Forza del destino*), Zaccaria (*Nabucco*); WEBER: Kaspar (*Freischütz*). Also BLACHER: Fadenkreutz* (*Preussisches Märchen*); EGK: Guldensack (*Zaubergeige*). **World premieres:** HENZE: Bürgermeister (*Junge Lord*), Deutsche Oper, Berlin 1965; NABOKOV: Boyet (*Love's Labour's Lost*) Deutsche Oper in Brussels 1973. Recorded for: DG, Ariola-Eurodisc, RIAS, SFB. Video/Film: Papageno (*Zauber-*

flöte); Gaveston (*Dame blanche*); Bürgermeister (*Junge Lord*); Fadenkreutz (*Preussisches Märchen*). Gives recitals. Appears with symphony orchestra. Teaches voice. On faculty of Hochschule für Musik, Berlin. **Res:** Fasanen Str 1, Berlin, FR Ger.

RÓKA, ISTVÁN. Lyric tenor. Hungarian. Resident mem: Hungarian State Opera, Budapest. Born 7 Oct 1941, Zalalövö, Hungary. Wife Ilona Dreilinger. Studied: Miss Zsuzsa Szentendrey, Mrs Ivankovics, Miss Maria Ersek, Budapest. **Debut:** Ein Sänger (*Rosenkavalier*) Hungarian State Opera 1971. Previous occupations: soloist with Hungarian Folk Ens.
Sang with major companies in HUN: Budapest. **Roles with these companies incl** BRITTEN: Lysander★ (*Midsummer Night*); DONIZETTI: Edgardo★ (*Lucia*); PROKOFIEV: Prince★ (*Love for Three Oranges*); PUCCINI: Rodolfo★ (*Bohème*); STRAUSS, R: Ein Sänger★ (*Rosenkavalier*). Gives recitals. Appears with symphony orchestra. **Res:** II Csalogány St 13-19, Budapest, Hungary.

ROMANELLA, NELLY. Coloratura soprano. Argentinean. Resident mem: Teatro Colón, Buenos Aires. Born 1 Dec 1938, Capital Federal, Argentina. Studied: Emma Brizzio. **Debut:** Lauretta (*Gianni Schicchi*) Teatro Colón 1965.
Sang with major companies in ARG: Buenos Aires. **Roles with these companies incl** AUBER: Zerlina (*Fra Diavolo*); BIZET: Micaëla (*Carmen*), Lauretta (*Docteur Miracle*); CIMAROSA: Carolina (*Matrimonio segreto*); DONIZETTI: Norina (*Don Pasquale*), Adina (*Elisir*), Linda di Chamounix, Lucia, Rita; GOUNOD: Juliette; LEONCAVALLO: Nedda (*Pagliacci*); MENOTTI: Amelia (*Amelia al ballo*); MOZART: Zerlina (*Don Giovanni*), Serpetta (*Finta giardiniera*); PUCCINI: Musetta (*Bohème*), Lauretta (*Gianni Schicchi*), Lisette (*Rondine*), Liù (*Turandot*); ROSSINI: Rosina (*Barbiere di Siviglia*); STRAUSS. J: Adele (*Fledermaus*); VERDI: Oscar (*Ballo in maschera*), Gilda (*Rigoletto*), Violetta (*Traviata*). **World premieres:** PERUZZO: Desconocida (*Voz del silencio*) Teatro Colón 1969. Gives recitals. Appears with symphony orchestra. Teaches voice. **Res:** Capital Federal/Buenos Aires, Argentina.

ROMERO, ANGELO. Bass-baritone. Italian. Born 30 May 1940, Cagliari, Italy. Wife Maria Teresa Portoghese. Two children. Studied: Prof Elena d'Ambrosio, Rome. **Debut:** MONTEVERDI: Orfeo, Opera da Camera, Rome 1966. Previous occupations: dramatic actor.
Sang with major companies in ARG: Buenos Aires; FRA: Aix-en-Provence Fest; ITA: Bologna, Florence Maggio, Genoa, Milan La Scala, Palermo, Parma, Rome Opera, Spoleto Fest, Turin, Venice; MON: Monte Carlo; SWI: Geneva; USA: Cincinnati. **Roles with these companies incl** DONIZETTI: Dott Malatesta★‡ (*Don Pasquale*); MOZART: Leporello‡ (*Don Giovanni*), Figaro★‡ (*Nozze di Figaro*), Papageno★‡ (*Zauberflöte*); PUCCINI: Marcello★ (*Bohème*), Gianni Schicchi★, Sharpless★‡ (*Butterfly*), Lescaut★‡ (*Manon Lescaut*); ROSSINI: Figaro★ (*Barbiere di Siviglia*), Dandini★ (*Cenerentola*), Robert‡ (*Comte Ory*), Signor Bruschino★‡; TCHAIKOVSKY: Eugene Onegin★‡; VERDI: Rodrigo★‡ (*Don Carlo*). Also VERDI: Stanislao★ (*Finto Stanislao*); GAZZANIGA: Pasquariello★ (*Convitato di pietra*). **Res:** V Susa 5, Rome, Italy. **Mgmt:** HUR/USA.

RONI, LUIGI. Bass. Italian. Resident mem: La Scala, Milan. Born 22 Feb 1942, Vergemoli/Lucca, Italy. Wife Julika Belkova. One child. Studied: Sara Sforni Corti, Milan. **Debut:** Méphistophélès (*Faust*) Spoleto Fest 1966.
Sang with major companies in AUS: Vienna Staatsoper; FRA: Paris; FR GER: Berlin Deutsche Oper, Munich Staatsoper; ITA: Florence Maggio & Teatro Comunale, Genoa, Milan La Scala, Naples, Palermo, Rome Opera & Caracalla, Trieste, Turin, Venice, Verona Arena; MON: Monte Carlo; POR: Lisbon; UK: London Royal Opera; USSR: Moscow Bolshoi; USA: Chicago, Dallas, Houston, New York City Opera, Washington DC; YUG: Zagreb. **Roles with these companies incl** BELLINI: Oroveso★ (*Norma*), Sir George★ (*Puritani*), Rodolfo★ (*Sonnambula*); DONIZETTI: Henry VIII★ (*Anna Bolena*), Baldassare★ (*Favorite*), Alfonso d'Este★ (*Lucrezia Borgia*); GOUNOD: Méphistophélès★ (*Faust*); MOZART: Publio (*Clemenza di Tito*), Sarastro (*Zauberflöte*); MUSSORGSKY: Pimen★ (*Boris Godunov*); PONCHIELLI: Alvise★ (*Gioconda*); ROSSINI: Don Basilio★ (*Barbiere di Siviglia*), Guillaume Tell; SAINT-SAENS: Grand prêtre (*Samson et Dalila*); STRAVINSKY: Creon★ & Tiresias★ (*Oedipus Rex*); VERDI: Ramfis★ (*Aida*), Grande Inquisitore★ (*Don Carlo*), Silva★ (*Ernani*), Padre Guardiano★ (*Forza del destino*), Conte Walter★ (*Luisa Miller*), Banquo★ (*Macbeth*), Zaccaria★ (*Nabucco*), Fiesco★ (*Simon Boccanegra*). Also MOZART: Commendatore★‡ (*Don Giovanni*); PROKOFIEV: Inquisitor (*Fiery Angel*); ROSSINI: Gessler★ (*Guillaume Tell*). Recorded for: EMI, Phonogram. **Res:** Viale Romagna 14, Milan, Italy. **Mgmt:** VLD/AUS.

ROSADA, LUCIANO. Conductor of opera and symphony. Italian. Music Dir & Cond, Pomeriggi Musicali di Milano. Born 19 Feb 1923, Venice. Wife Giuliana. Two children. Studied: Antonio Guarnieri, Siena; Herman Scherchen, Venice; also piano, violin. Plays the piano. Operatic training as repetiteur at La Scala, Milan 1948-53. **Operatic debut:** *Amuleto* Teatro Novità, Bergamo 1954. Symphonic debut: Accad Chigiana, Siena 1947. Previous occupations: violinist in orch.
Conducted with major companies in FRA: Nice, Paris; FR GER: Bielefeld, Stuttgart, Wiesbaden; HUN: Budapest; ITA: Bologna, Florence Maggio & Comunale, Genoa, Milan La Scala, Naples, Palermo, Parma, Spoleto Fest, Turin, Venice; SPA: Barcelona; SWI: Zurich. **Operas with these companies incl** BELLINI: *Puritani;* CIMAROSA: *Matrimonio segreto;* DONIZETTI: *Campanello★, Don Pasquale, Elisir, Lucia, Rita★, Giovedi grasso★;* FALLA: *Retablo de Maese Pedro, Vida breve★;* GALUPPI: *Filosofo di campagna★;* GIORDANO: *Andrea Chénier★;* GLUCK: *Cadi dupé★;* MASCAGNI: *Amico Fritz★, Cavalleria rusticana;* MENOTTI: *Amelia al ballo, Consul;* MONTEVERDI: *Favola d'Orfeo;* MOZART: *Cosi fan tutte, Sposo deluso★;* POULENC: *Voix humaine;* PUCCINI: *Bohème★, Butterfly, Manon Lescaut★, Tosca, Turandot;* ROSSINI: *Barbiere*

461

di Siviglia*, Cambiale di matrimonio, Scala di seta, Signor Bruschino*; SALIERI: Arlecchinata*; VERDI: Aida, Otello, Rigoletto*, Traviata; WOLF-FERRARI: Campiello; ZANDONAI: Giulietta e Romeo. Also LOGROSCINO: Governatore; PETRASSI: Cordovano; PICCINNI: Buona figliola; MALIPIERO: Torneo notturno. **World premieres:** SONZOGNO: Boule de suif Novità, Bergamo 1970; CORTESE: Notti bianche/Veneziani Piccola Scala, Milan 1973. Video/Film: Rigoletto, Signor Bruschino, Cambiale di matrimonio. Conducted major orch in Europe. Teaches at Consv G B Martini, Bologna; Dir d'orch. **Res:** Revere 1, Milan, Italy.

ROSE, JUERGEN. Scenic and costume designer for opera & theater. German.
Designed opera for major companies in AUS: Salzburg Fest, Vienna Staatsoper; FRA: Paris; FR GER: Bayreuth Fest, Berlin Deutsche Oper, Frankfurt, Hamburg, Munich Staatsoper, Stuttgart; ITA: Milan La Scala; et al. **Operas designed for these companies incl** BERG: Lulu, Wozzeck; DONIZETTI: Lucia; MOZART: Così fan tutte, Don Giovanni, Zauberflöte; STRAUSS, R: Salome; VERDI: Don Carlo, Simon Boccanegra; WAGNER: Parsifal, Tannhäuser; et al. **Operatic world premieres:** YUN: Sim Tjong Bayerische Staatsoper, Munich 1972.

ROSEN, ALBERT. Conductor of opera and symphony. Czechoslovakian. Resident Cond, Dublin Grand Opera Socy; National Theater, Prague. Princ Cond, Radio Telefis Eireann, Dublin 1969- . Born 14 Feb 1924, Vienna. Divorced. Two children. Studied: Prague Consv, Alois Klima; Vienna Akad für Musik und darstellende Kunst, H Swarowsky, Josef Marx, Ebenstein; incl piano, violin, horn and voice. Plays the organ. Operatic training as repetiteur, asst cond & chorus master at Plzen Opera, CSSR 1949-59; National Opera, Prague 1960-71; & reptr/cond of ballet. **Operatic debut:** Rusalka Plzen State Opera, CSSR 1949. Symphonic debut: Plzen Phil 1951. Previous adm positions in opera: Princ Cond, Smetana Theater, Prague 1956-57.
Conducted with major companies in CZE: Brno, Prague National & Smetana. **Operas with these companies incl** BEETHOVEN: Fidelio; BERLIOZ: Damnation de Faust; BIZET: Carmen*; CORNELIUS: Barbier von Bagdad*; DONIZETTI: Don Pasquale*, Elisir, Lucia*, Lucrezia Borgia; DVORAK: Devil and Kate, Rusalka; JANACEK: Jenufa*, Katya Kabanova*; LEONCAVALLO: Pagliacci*; MARTINU: Griechische Passion; MASCAGNI: Cavalleria rusticana*; MASSENET: Don Quichotte; MOZART: Don Giovanni*, Nozze di Figaro*; ORFF: Carmina burana*; PROKOFIEV: Gambler*; PUCCINI: Gianni Schicchi*, Butterfly*; ROSSINI: Barbiere di Siviglia, Italiana in Algeri, Otello; SMETANA: Bartered Bride*, Devil's Wall, The Kiss, Secret, Two Widows; STRAUSS, J: Fledermaus; STRAUSS, R: Rosenkavalier; STRAVINSKY: Mavra, Oedipus Rex, Rake's Progress; TCHAIKOVSKY: Pique Dame*; VERDI: Ballo in maschera*, Don Carlo, Rigoletto*, Traviata*; WAGNER: Fliegende Holländer*, Lohengrin; WEBER: Abu Hassan. Also DVORAK: Schelm und die Bauern; CIKKER:

Resurrection; TCHAIKOVSKY: Mazeppa. **World premieres:** BURGHAUSER: Bridge National Theater, Prague 1967. Conducted major orch in Europe. **Res:** 70 Haddington Rd, Dublin, Ireland. **Mgmt:** LAL/UK; PRG/CZE; DBA/USA.

ROSS, ELINOR; née Elinor Marilyn Rosenthal. Dramatic soprano. American. Born 1 Aug 1932, Tampa, FL, USA. Widowed. Husband Jerome A Lewis, occupation attorney (deceased). One son. Studied: William P Herman, Zinka Milanov, Dick Marzollo, New York. **Debut:** Leonora (Trovatore) Cincinnati Opera 1958. Previous occupations: salesperson.
Sang with major companies in ARG: Buenos Aires; AUS: Vienna Staatsoper; CAN: Toronto, Vancouver; GER DR: Berlin Komische Oper; HOL: Amsterdam; HUN: Budapest; ITA: Bologna, Florence Maggio, Milan La Scala, Palermo, Rome Caracalla, Venice, Verona Arena; USA: Baltimore, Boston, Chicago, Cincinnati, Fort Worth, Hartford, Houston, Milwaukee Florentine, New Orleans, New York Metropolitan, Philadelphia Grand, Pittsburgh, San Antonio, San Francisco Opera, Seattle; YUG: Zagreb. **Roles with these companies incl** BELLINI: Norma; BERLIOZ: Marguerite (Damnation de Faust); CHERUBINI: Medea; GIORDANO: Maddalena (Andrea Chénier); MASCAGNI: Santuzza* (Cavalleria rusticana); MOZART: Donna Anna* (Don Giovanni); PONCHIELLI: Gioconda*; PUCCINI: Cio-Cio-San (Butterfly), Tosca*, Turandot*; ROSSINI: Anaï (Moïse); VERDI: Aida*, Amelia* (Ballo in maschera), Elisabetta* (Don Carlo), Donna Elvira (Ernani), Leonora (Forza del destino), Lady Macbeth*, Abigaille (Nabucco), Desdemona (Otello), Leonora* (Trovatore); WAGNER: Elsa (Lohengrin). Gives recitals. Appears with symphony orchestra. **Res:** 336 Central Park West, New York, USA. **Mgmt:** BAR/USA.

ROSS, GLYNN. American. Gen Dir, Seattle Opera Assn, 305 Harrison St, Seattle, WA 98109. In charge of adm matters, artistic policy, dram matters & tech. Born 15 Dec 1914. Wife Angelamaria. Four children. Started with present company as founder/director. For accomplishments see report on Seattle Opera Co. Mem of Bd, OPERA America; Prof Commtt, Central Opera Service. **Res:** Bellevue, WA, USA.

ROSSEL, ROGER; né Vandeputte. Conductor of opera and symphony. Belgian. Resident Cond, Centre Lyrique de Wallonie, Liège. Born 22 Nov 1930, Brussels. Wife Jeannine Berdel, occupation prof of ballet. Studied: Consv of Brussels; incl piano, violin. Plays the violin. Operatic training as asst cond & cond at Théâtre de la Monnaie, Brussels 1964-68. **Operatic debut:** Théâtre de la Monnaie. Symphonic debut: Orch Ntl, Brussels. Previous occupations: concertmaster Opéra Ntl, Brussels.
Conducted with major companies in BEL: Brussels, Liège; CAN: Montreal/Quebec; MEX: Mexico City; ROM: Bucharest. **Operas with these companies incl** BEETHOVEN: Fidelio; BIZET: Carmen*, Pêcheurs de perles*; BORODIN: Prince Igor*; CIMAROSA: Matrimonio segreto*;

DELIBES: *Lakmé;* DONIZETTI: *Elisir*;* FALLA: *Retablo de Maese Pedro*;* GOUNOD: *Faust*, Roméo et Juliette*;* IBERT: *Angélique*;* LALO: *Roi d'Ys*;* LECOCQ: *Fille de Madame Angot*;* MASSENET: *Don Quichotte*, Hérodiade*, Manon*, Werther*;* MENOTTI: *Consul, Telephone*;* MOZART: *Don Giovanni*, Zauberflöte*;* OFFENBACH: *Contes d'Hoffmann*;* ORFF: *Carmina burana*;* POULENC: *Voix humaine*;* PUCCINI: *Bohème*, Butterfly, Tosca, Turandot*;* RABAUD: *Mârouf;* RAVEL: *Heure espagnole*;* SAINT-SAENS: *Samson et Dalila;* STRAUSS, J: *Fledermaus*;* STRAVINSKY: *Mavra*, Rossignol;* TCHAIKOVSKY: *Pique Dame*;* VERDI: *Aida*, Macbeth, Nabucco*, Otello*, Rigoletto*, Traviata*.* Also GRETRY: *Lucile.* Recorded for Alpha. Conducted major orch in Europe, Asia. Previous positions as Mus Dir with major orch: Chamber Orch, Théâtre de la Monnaie, Brussels 1964-67. Teaches at Consv Royal de Mons. Res: 38 rue Charles Lemaire, 1160 Brussels, Belgium.

ROSSELLINI, RENZO. Italian. Pres, Ntl Opera & Orch of Monte Carlo, Palais Heracles, Monaco 1970- . In charge of overall adm matters, art policy, musical matters. Is also a composer. Additional adm positions: Adm Councilor, Società Italiana Autori ed Editori, Rome. Born 2 Feb 1908, Rome. Wife Anita Limongelli. One child. Studied: Consv di Musica S Cecilia, Rome. Plays the piano. Previous occupations: mus critic *Il Messaggero,* Rome. Among his operas are *Guerra, Avventuriero, Sguardo dal ponte, Annonce faite à Marie, Reine morte.* Awards: Cavaliere di Gran Croce al Merito, Rep of Italy; Comman, Order of St Charles; Academician of S Cecilia, Rome and Cherubini Acad, Florence; mem, Philharmonia Acad, Bologna. Res: Monte Carlo, Monaco.

ROSSI, MARIO. Conductor of opera and symphony. Italian. Chief Cond, RAI Orch, Turin 1945- . Born 29 Mar 1902, Rome. Studied: Accad di S Cecilia, Rome.

Conducted with major companies in FR GER: Berlin Deutsche Oper; ITA: Bologna, Florence Maggio, Genoa, Milan La Scala, Naples, Rome Opera, Trieste, Turin, Venice, Verona Arena; USA: Chicago; et al. **Operas with these companies incl** BELLINI: *Norma, Puritani;* BIZET: *Carmen;* BUSONI: *Arlecchino, Doktor Faust, Turandot;* DONIZETTI: *Don Pasquale‡, Elisir, Favorite, Fille du régiment‡, Lucia;* LEONCAVALLO: *Pagliacci;* MASCAGNI: *Cavalleria rusticana;* MOZART: *Don Giovanni, Nozze di Figaro, Zauberflöte;* PERGOLESI: *Serva padrona;* ROSSINI: *Barbiere di Siviglia, Cenerentola‡, Comte Ory, Moïse, Otello, Pietra del paragone;* VERDI: *Aida, Ballo in maschera, Don Carlo, Falstaff‡, Forza del destino, Luisa Miller‡, Macbeth, Nabucco, Otello, Rigoletto, Simon Boccanegra, Traviata, Trovatore, Vespri;* et al. Also PERGOLESI: *Livietta e Tracollo;* PICCINI: *Didone;* ROSSINI: *Tancredi,* on records only *Guillaume Tell.* Recorded for Cetra. Previous positions as Mus Dir with major orch: Chief Cond, Maggio Musicale, Florence 1936-44.

ROSSI, VITTORIO. Scenic and costume designer for opera, theater, film, television; is a lighting designer, stage director; also an architect & writer. Italian. Resident designer & consultant, Arena di Verona, and at Associati Compagnio di Prosa, Italy. Born 4 Nov 1936, Rome. Single. Studied: Univ of Architecture, Rome.

Designed for major companies in DEN: Copenhagen; FRA: Orange Fest, Paris; HOL: Amsterdam; ITA: Milan, Turin, Venice, Verona Arena; USA: Chicago. **Operas designed for these companies incl** BERG: *Wozzeck;* BIZET: *Carmen;* MASSENET: *Manon;* MONTEVERDI: *Combattimento di Tancredi;* PERGOLESI: *Serva padrona;* PUCCINI: *Bohème, Manon Lescaut, Tosca, Turandot;* VERDI: *Macbeth, Otello.* Exhibitions of stage designs in Italy. **Res:** V di Panico 72, Rome, Italy.

ROSSI-LEMENI, NICOLA MAKEDON. Bass. Italian. Born 6 Nov 1920, Constantinople. Wife Virginia Zeani, occupation opera singer. One child. **Debut:** Varlaam (*Boris Godunov*) La Fenice, Venice 1946. Previous occupations: law student; officer in the army. Awards: Great Officer Order of Merit, Italian Rep; Commander Order of Pope S Silvester; Orfeo d'oro, Golden Medal SIAE; Maschera d'argento twice, Luigi Illica Awd, etc.

Sang with major companies in ARG: Buenos Aires; BEL: Brussels; BRA: Rio de Janeiro; FRA: Bordeaux, Marseille, Nancy, Nice, Paris; FR GER: Hamburg; HUN: Budapest; ITA: Bologna, Florence Maggio & Comunale, Genoa, Milan La Scala, Naples, Palermo, Parma, Rome Teatro dell'Opera & Caracalla, Trieste, Turin, Venice, Verona Arena; MEX: Mexico City; MON: Monte Carlo; POR: Lisbon; ROM: Bucharest; S AFR: Johannesburg; SPA: Barcelona; SWI: Basel, Geneva; UK: London Royal; USSR: Leningrad Kirov, Moscow Bolshoi; USA: Chicago, New York Met, Philadelphia Grand, San Francisco Opera & Spring Opera; YUG: Dubrovnik, Zagreb. **Roles with these companies incl** BEETHOVEN: *Don Pizarro* (*Fidelio*); BELLINI: *Oroveso* (*Norma*), Sir Richard* (*Puritani*), Rodolfo* (*Sonnambula*); BERLIOZ: *Méphistophélès* (*Damnation de Faust*); BOITO: *Mefistofele*;* BRITTEN: *John Claggart* (*Billy Budd*); CHARPENTIER: *Père* (*Louise*); CIMAROSA: *Geronimo* (*Matrimonio segreto*); DEBUSSY: *Golaud* (*Pelléas et Mélisande*); DONIZETTI: *Henry VIII* (*Anna Bolena*), Dulcamara* (*Elisir*), Baldassare* (*Favorite*); FALLA: *Don Quixote* (*Retablo de Maese Pedro*); GOUNOD: *Méphistophélès* (*Faust*); HANDEL: *Giulio Cesare*;* MASSENET: *Sancho* & Don Quichotte* (*Don Quichotte*); MOZART: *Leporello & Don Giovanni* (*Don Giovanni*), Figaro* (*Nozze di Figaro*); MUSSORGSKY: *Boris Godunov* & Varlaam (*Boris Godunov*), Ivan Khovansky* (*Khovanshchina*); OFFENBACH: *Coppélius, etc* (*Contes d'Hoffmann*); PONCHIELLI: *Alvise* (*Gioconda*); PUCCINI: *Colline* (*Bohème*); RIMSKY-KORSAKOV: *Tsar Ivan* (*Maid of Pskov*); ROSSELLINI: *Ferrante‡* (*Reine morte*); ROSSINI: *Don Basilio* (*Barbiere di Siviglia*), Guillaume Tell, Moïse, Sultan Selim (*Turco in Italia*); SPONTINI: *Cinna* (*Vestale*); TCHAIKOVSKY: *Eugene Onegin*;* VERDI: *Ramfis* (*Aida*), Philip II* (*Don Carlo*), Silva* (*Ernani*), Falstaff*, Padre Guardiano (*Forza del destino*), Miller* & Conte Walter* (*Luisa Miller*), Zaccaria* (*Nabucco*);

WAGNER: Daland★ (*Fliegende Holländer*), König Heinrich★ (*Lohengrin*), Landgraf (*Tannhäuser*); WEBER: Kaspar★ (*Freischütz*); WOLF-FERRARI: Lunardo★ (*Quattro rusteghi*). Also GRUENBERG: Emperor Jones. **World premieres:** MUSCO: (*Gattopardo*) Palermo 1967; PIZZETTI: (*Assassinio nella cattedrale*) Scala 1958; ROSSELLINI: (*Sguardo dal ponte*) Rome 1961, (*Reine morte*) M Carlo 1973, (*Avventuriero*) M Carlo 1968, (*Legende del ritorno*) La Scala Milan 1966; ROTA: (*Visita mervigliosa*) Palermo 1970; NAPOLI: (*Dubrovski*) Naples 1973; ZAFRED: (*Wallenstein*) Rome 1965; BRAGA SANTOS: (*Trilogia das Barcas*) Lisbon. Recorded for: HMV, Angel, Philips, Cetra. Video/Film: (*Boris Godunov*). Gives recitals. Appears with symphony orchestra. Teaches voice. **Stages opera. Res:** V Nomentana 761, Rome, Italy.

ROSSIUS, RAYMOND. Belgian. Dir Gen, Centre Lyrique de Wallonie, 1 rue des Dominicains, 4000 Liège; perform at Théâtre Royal de Liège and Grand Théâtre de Verviers. In charge of overall adm matters, art policy, finances. Is also a stage director/producer. Born 16 May 1926, Rochefort. Wife Madeleine Lassaux, occupation professor. Three children. Studied: Athénée Royal, Marche; Ecole Tech Commerc & Consv, Brussels; Consv, Namur. Previous occupations: opera singer; stage dir 1954-62, var Belgian theaters, television; Dir of Cultural Services, Province of Namur. Started with present company in 1967 as Dir, Opéra de Wallonie; in present position since 1974. Awards: Chevalier, Ordre de Léopold II; Officier, Ord of Merit, Luxembourg. Initiated major policy changes including expansion of season from 7 months to 12 months; merger of companies from Liège and Verviers. **Res:** rue du Moulin 55, Rochefort, Belgium.

ROSTROPOVICH, MSTISLAV. Conductor of opera and symphony; composer. Russian. Music Dir, Natl Symph Orch, Washington DC, USA, beginning 1976. Born 27 Mar 1927, Baku, USSR. Wife Galina Vishnevskaya, occupation opera singer. Two children. Studied: Moscow Consv, Shebalin, Kozalupov; incl cello. Plays the cello. Other occupations: concert cellist; piano accompanist. Awards: Winner, Russian Cello Compt 1945; Intl Youth & Student Cello Compt, Prague 1947 & Budapest 1949; Intl Cello Compt, Wigan Prize 1950. **Conducted with major companies in** AUS: Vienna Volksoper; USSR: Moscow Bolshoi; USA: San Francisco; et al. **Operas with these companies incl** MOZART: *Nozze di Figaro;* MUSSORGSKY: *Boris Godunov;* PROKOFIEV: *War and Peace;* STRAUSS, J: *Fledermaus;* TCHAIKOVSKY: *Eugene Onegin‡;* et al. Recorded for HMV, Melodiya. Teaches.

ROTH, GÜNTER. Stages/produces opera & theater. German. Generalintendant & Resident Stage Dir, Niedersächsische Staatstheater, Hannover. Born 30 Mar 1925, Hannover. Wife Dora Koschak, occupation singer. One child. Studied: Reinhard Lehmann, Alfred Noller, Hannover. Operatic training as asst stage dir at Landestheater, Hannover 1949. **Operatic debut:** *Tiefland* Landestheater, Hannover 1950. Previous adm positions in opera:

Generalintendant 6 yrs, Musiktheater im Revier, Gelsenkirchen.
Directed/produced opera for major companies in AUS: Vienna Volksoper; FRA: Strasbourg; FR GER: Berlin Deutsche Oper, Bonn, Cologne, Dortmund, Düsseldorf-Duisburg, Essen, Frankfurt, Hamburg, Hannover, Kassel, Kiel, Munich Gärtnerplatz, Wuppertal; HOL: Amsterdam; ITA: Milan La Scala, Naples; POR: Lisbon; SWI: Geneva, Zurich. **Operas staged with these companies incl** ADAM: *Si j'étais roi;* d'ALBERT: *Tiefland★;* AUBER: *Fra Diavolo★;* BARTOK: *Bluebeard's Castle;* BEETHOVEN: *Fidelio;* BIZET: *Carmen;* BORODIN: *Prince Igor;* BRITTEN: *Albert Herring, Owen Wingrave;* CAVALLI: *Calisto;* CHERUBINI: *Medea★;* CIMAROSA: *Matrimonio segreto;* CORNELIUS: *Barbier von Bagdad;* DALLAPICCOLA: *Volo di notte;* DEBUSSY: *Pelléas et Mélisande★;* DONIZETTI: *Don Pasquale, Elisir, Lucia;* DVORAK: *Rusalka;* FLOTOW: *Martha;* GAY/Britten: *Beggar's Opera;* GERSHWIN: *Porgy and Bess;* GLUCK: *Orfeo ed Euridice;* GOUNOD: *Faust;* HANDEL: *Giulio Cesare;* HENZE: *Boulevard Solitude;* HINDEMITH: *Hin und zurück, Mathis der Maler★;* LORTZING: *Zar und Zimmermann;* MARTIN: *Vin herbé;* MASSENET: *Don Quichotte, Manon;* MENOTTI: *Amelia al ballo, Telephone;* MILHAUD: *Pauvre matelot;* MOZART: *Così fan tutte, Don Giovanni, Entführung aus dem Serail, Finta giardiniera, Nozze di Figaro, Zauberflöte;* MUSSORGSKY: *Boris Godunov;* NICOLAI: *Lustigen Weiber;* OFFENBACH: *Contes d'Hoffmann;* ORFF: *Kluge, Mond;* PROKOFIEV: *War and Peace;* PUCCINI: *Bohème, Gianni Schicchi, Butterfly, Manon Lescaut, Tosca★, Turandot;* RAVEL: *Heure espagnole;* ROSSINI: *Barbiere di Siviglia, Comte Ory, Italiana in Algeri, Signor Bruschino;* SMETANA: *Bartered Bride;* STRAUSS, J: *Fledermaus;* STRAUSS, R: *Arabella, Ariadne auf Naxos, Capriccio, Frau ohne Schatten, Rosenkavalier, Salome, Schweigsame Frau;* STRAVINSKY: *Rake's Progress;* SUTERMEISTER: *Romeo und Julia;* TCHAIKOVSKY: *Eugene Onegin;* THOMAS: *Mignon;* VERDI: *Aida, Ballo in maschera, Don Carlo, Due Foscari, Falstaff, Nabucco, Otello, Rigoletto, Traviata, Trovatore;* WAGNER: *Meistersinger, Rheingold, Walküre, Siegfried, Götterdämmerung, Tannhäuser;* WEBER: *Freischütz;* WOLF-FERRARI: *Donne curiose, Quattro rusteghi, Segreto di Susanna.* Also FORTNER: *Bluthochzeit;* HENZE: *Ende einer Welt;* HINDEMITH: *Harmonie der Welt;* KLEBE: *Alkmene;* MARTINU: *Mirandolina;* WOLF-FERRARI: *Vedova scaltra.* **Operatic world premieres:** KLEBE: *Tödlichen Wünsche* 1959, *Räuber* 1957, both at Deutsche Oper am Rhein, Düsseldorf; *Ermordung Cäsars* Bühnen der Stadt Essen 1959. Teaches at Staatl Hochschule für Musik und Theater, Hannover. **Res:** Emmichpl 1, Hannover, FR Ger.

ROTH, WOLFGANG. Scenic and costume designer for opera, theater, film & television. Is a lighting designer; also a painter, illustrator & architect. American. Born 25 Feb 1910, Berlin. Wife Lee. Studied: State Acad of Art, Berlin. Prof training: Piscator Bühne and Kroll Oper, Berlin 1929-

31. **Operatic debut:** Stadttheater Zurich 1934. Theater debut: Piscator Bühne, Berlin 1930. Previous occupation: housepainter trainee. Previous adm positions in opera: Cincinnati Summer Opera, USA 1959-61; Vancouver Opera Fest, Canada 1963.

Designed for major companies in AUS: Salzburg Fest, Vienna Volksoper; CAN: Toronto, Vancouver; GRE: Athens Fest; FR GER: Munich Staatsoper; SWI: Zurich; USA: Boston, Chicago, Cincinnati, Dallas, New York Met & City Opera, San Francisco Spring Opera, Washington DC. **Operas designed for these companies incl** BELLINI: *Sonnambula;* BIZET: *Carmen;* BRITTEN: *Peter Grimes;* CORNELIUS: *Barbier von Bagdad;* DONIZETTI: *Don Pasquale;* EINEM: *Dantons Tod;* FLOYD: *Susannah;* GERSHWIN: *Porgy and Bess;* GIORDANO: *Andrea Chénier;* GOUNOD: *Faust;* HINDEMITH: *Hin und zurück;* HUMPERDINCK: *Hänsel und Gretel;* IBERT: *Angélique;* MENOTTI: *Old Maid and the Thief;* MILHAUD: *Pauvre matelot;* MOZART: *Don Giovanni, Schauspieldirektor;* MUSSORGSKY: *Boris Godunov;* NICOLAI: *Lustigen Weiber;* PERGOLESI: *Serva padrona;* PUCCINI: *Bohème, Fanciulla del West, Butterfly, Manon Lescaut, Tosca;* RAVEL: *Enfant et les sortilèges;* ROSSINI: *Barbiere di Siviglia;* STRAUSS, J: *Fledermaus;* STRAUSS, R: *Salome;* STRAVINSKY: *Histoire du soldat;* VERDI: *Aida, Ballo in maschera, Don Carlo, Macbeth, Nabucco, Otello, Traviata;* WAGNER: *Tristan und Isolde;* WEBER: *Freischütz;* WEILL: *Dreigroschenoper;* WOLF-FERRARI: *Quattro rusteghi.* Also LIEBERMANN: *Schule der Frauen.* **Operatic world premieres:** WEILL: *Down in the Valley* Bloomington IL, USA 1948. Exhibitions of stage designs, paintings & graphics Germany, Austria, Switzerland, US and Canada, 1932-75. **Res:** 405 E 63 St, New York, NY 10021, USA.

ROTHENBERGER, ANNELIESE. Lyric soprano. German. Resident mem: Staatsoper, Vienna. Born 19 Jun 1926, Mannheim, Germany. Husband Gerd W Dieberitz, occupation journalist. Studied: Mannheim Music Consv. **Debut:** Oscar (*Ballo in maschera*) Staatsoper, Hamburg 1949. Awards: Bayerische Kammersängerin, Munich 1963; Oesterreichische Kammersängerin 1967; Cross of Merit First Class, FR Ger; Max Reinhardt Medal, Salzburg; etc.

Sang with major companies in ARG: Buenos Aires; AUS: Salzburg Fest, Vienna Staatsoper & Volksoper; BEL: Brussels; CAN: Montreal/Quebec; DEN: Copenhagen; FRA: Aix-en-Provence Fest; FR GER: Berlin Deutsche Oper, Cologne, Dortmund, Düsseldorf-Duisburg, Hamburg, Karlsruhe, Mannheim, Munich Staatsoper, Stuttgart, Wiesbaden, Wuppertal; ITA: Florence Maggio, Milan La Scala; MON: Monte Carlo; SWI: Basel, Zurich; UK: Edinburgh Fest, Glyndebourne Fest; USA: New York Met, Philadelphia Grand & Lyric. **Roles with these companies incl** AUBER: Zerlina (*Fra Diavolo*); BEETHOVEN: Marzelline (*Fidelio*); BERG: Lulu; BIZET: Micaëla (*Carmen*); DONIZETTI: Norina (*Don Pasquale*); EGK: Gretl (*Zaubergeige*); EINEM: Frl Bürstner (*Prozess*); FLOTOW: Lady Harriet /Martha; GAY/Britten: Lucy (*Beggar's Opera*); GLUCK: Euridice & Amor (*Orfeo ed Euridice*);

HAYDN: Clarissa (*Mondo della luna*); HUMPERDINCK: Gretel; IBERT: Angélique; LORTZING: Gretchen & Baronin Freimann (*Wildschütz*); MENOTTI: Lucy (*Telephone*); MONTEVERDI: Poppea (*Incoronazione di Poppea*); MOZART: Fiordiligi & Despina (*Così fan tutte*), Zerlina (*Don Giovanni*), Konstanze & Blondchen (*Entführung aus dem Serail*), Ilia (*Idomeneo*), Susanna & Cherubino (*Nozze di Figaro*), Pamina & Königin der Nacht (*Zauberflöte*); NICOLAI: Aennchen (*Lustigen Weiber*); OFFENBACH: Olympia & Antonia & Giulietta (*Contes d'Hoffmann*); PUCCINI: Mimi & Musetta (*Bohème*), Lauretta (*Gianni Schicchi*), Cio-Cio-San (*Butterfly*), Liù (*Turandot*); RAVEL: Concepcion (*Heure espagnole*); ROSSINI: Rosina (*Barbiere di Siviglia*); STRAUSS, J: Adele & Rosalinde (*Fledermaus*); STRAUSS, R: Zdenka (*Arabella*), Komponist (*Ariadne auf Naxos*), Sophie (*Rosenkavalier*); STRAVINSKY: Anne Trulove (*Rake's Progress*); VERDI: Oscar (*Ballo in maschera*), Nannetta (*Falstaff*), Gilda (*Rigoletto*), Violetta (*Traviata*); WEBER: Aennchen (*Freischütz*). **World premieres:** SUTERMEISTER: Madame Bovary, Zurich 1967. Gives recitals. Appears with symphony orchestra. **Res:** CH-8268 Salenstein, Switzerland.

ROULEAU, JOSEPH ALFRED. Bass. Canadian. Born 28 Feb 1929, Matane, PQ, Canada. Married. Three children. Studied: Consv de Musique, Montreal; Martial Singher, Ruzena Herlinger; Mario Basiola, Rachaele Mori, Milan. **Debut:** Philip II (*Don Carlo*) Montreal Opera Guild 1955. Previous occupations: studied economics & political science. Awards: Prix Calixa-Lavallée, Société St Jean Baptiste de Montréal 1967.

Sang with major companies in ARG: Buenos Aires; AUSTRL: Sydney; BEL: Brussels; CAN: Montreal/Quebec, Ottawa, Toronto; FRA: Bordeaux, Lyon, Marseille, Nancy, Nice, Paris, Strasbourg, Toulouse; FR GER: Berlin Deutsche Oper, Munich Staatsoper; HOL: Amsterdam; HUN: Budapest State Opera; ISR: Tel Aviv; ITA: Rome Opera; MON: Monte Carlo; ROM: Bucharest; S AFR: Johannesburg; SPA: Barcelona; SWI: Geneva; UK: Aldeburgh Fest, Edinburgh Fest, Glasgow Scottish, London Royal Opera; USSR: Kiev, Leningrad Kirov, Moscow Bolshoi, Tbilisi; USA: Boston, New Orleans, New York City Opera. **Roles with these companies incl** BELLINI: Oroveso★ (*Norma*), Sir George (*Puritani*), Rodolfo (*Sonnambula*); BERLIOZ: Méphistophélès★ (*Damnation de Faust*), Narbal★ (*Troyens*); BOITO: Mefistofele★; CHARPENTIER: Père★ (*Louise*); DEBUSSY: Arkel★ (*Pelléas et Mélisande*); DONIZETTI: Dott Dulcamara (*Elisir*); DUKAS: Barbe Bleue (*Ariane et Barbe Bleue*); FALLA: Don Quixote★ (*Retablo de Maese Pedro*), Tio Sarvaor★ (*Vida breve*); GOUNOD: Méphistophélès★ (*Faust*); MASSENET: Don Quichotte★; MOZART: Don Alfonso (*Così fan tutte*), Osmin★ (*Entführung aus dem Serail*), Sarastro★ (*Zauberflöte*); MUSSORGSKY: Boris Godunov★ & Pimen★ (*Boris Godunov*), Dosifei (*Khovanshchina*); OFFENBACH: Coppélius etc (*Contes d'Hoffmann*); PERGOLESI: Uberto (*Serva padrona*); PROKOFIEV: The General★ (*Gambler*); PUCCINI: Colline (*Bohème*); ROSSINI: Don Basilio★ (*Barbiere* *di Siviglia*), Moïse★, Assur★‡ (*Semiramide*); STRAVINSKY: Tiresias (*Oedipus Rex*); THOMAS: Lothario (*Mignon*); VERDI: Ramfis★ (*Aida*), Philip II★ & Grande Inquisitore (*Don Carlo*), Padre Guardiano (*Forza del destino*), Banquo (*Macbeth*), Fiesco (*Simon Boccanegra*); WAGNER: Daland (*Fliegende Holländer*), Fafner (*Siegfried*). **World premieres:** SOMERS: Bishop Taché (*Louis Riel*) Canadian Opera Co, Toronto 1967. Recorded for: Pathé-Marconi, Decca. Video/Film: Osmin (*Entführung aus dem Serail*); Bishop Taché (*Louis Riel*); Boris Godunov. Gives recitals. Appears with symphony orchestra. **Res:** 2 Laverock, Manor Pk, Chislehurst/Kent, UK. Mgmt: AIM/UK; HUR/USA.

ROUX, MICHEL. Basso-buffo. French. Resident mem: Opéra de Paris. Born 1 Sep 1924, Angoulême, France. Wife Lucienne. Three children. Studied: Consv of Paris. **Debut:** Méphistophélès (*Faust*) Opéra de Paris 1950. Previous occupations: stage director/producer at London City Center Opera. Awards: 3 times First Prize, Paris Consv: voice, opera and opéra comique; Gold Medal Harriet Cohen 1964-65.

Sang with major companies in AUS: Vienna Staatsoper; BEL: Brussels, Liège; CZE: Prague National; FRA: Aix-en-Provence Fest, Bordeaux, Lyon, Marseille, Nancy, Nice, Paris, Rouen, Strasbourg, Toulouse; FR GER: Berlin Deutsche Oper, Karlsruhe, Saarbrücken; HOL: Amsterdam; ITA: Florence Comunale, Genoa, Milan La Scala, Palermo, Parma, Venice; MON: Monte Carlo, NOR: Oslo; POR: Lisbon; SPA: Barcelona; SWI: Geneva; UK: Glyndebourne Fest; USA: Chicago. **Roles with these companies incl** BERLIOZ: Méphistophélès (*Damnation de Faust*); BIZET: Escamillo (*Carmen*); BOIELDIEU: Gaveston (*Dame blanche*); CHARPENTIER: Père (*Louise*); CIMAROSA: Geronimo (*Matrimonio segreto*); DEBUSSY: Golaud (*Pelléas et Mélisande*); DELIBES: Nilakantha (*Lakmé*); DONIZETTI: Don Pasquale, Dott Dulcamara (*Elisir*); GOUNOD: Méphistophélès (*Faust*), Ourrias (*Mireille*), Jupiter (*Philémon et Baucis*); MASSENET: Boniface (*Jongleur de Notre Dame*), Athanaël (*Thaïs*), Albert (*Werther*); MOZART: Don Alfonso (*Così fan tutte*); Leporello & Don Giovanni (*Don Giovanni*), Conte Almaviva & Figaro (*Nozze di Figaro*); OFFENBACH: Coppélius etc (*Contes d'Hoffmann*); PERGOLESI: Uberto (*Serva padrona*); POULENC: Gendarme (*Mamelles de Tirésias*); PUCCINI: Colline & Marcello (*Bohème*), Gianni Schicchi, Sharpless (*Butterfly*), Scarpia (*Tosca*); RAMEAU: Pollux (*Castor et Pollux*); RAVEL: Ramiro (*Heure espagnole*); RIMSKY-KORSAKOV: Roi Dodon (*Coq d'or*); ROSSINI: Dott Bartolo (*Barbiere di Siviglia*), Don Magnifico (*Cenerentola*), Robert (*Comte Ory*), Mustafà (*Italiana in Algeri*), Macrobio (*Pietra del paragone*), Signor Bruschino; ROUSSEAU: Le Devin (*Devin du village*); STRAUSS, R: Musiklehrer (*Ariadne auf Naxos*), Olivier (*Capriccio*); THOMAS: Lothario (*Mignon*); VERDI: Falstaff; WOLF-FERRARI: Conte Gil (*Segreto di Susanna*). Also TOMASI: Morhange (*Atlantide*) Opéra de Paris 1961. Recorded for: DG, Decca, Pathé-Marconi. Gives recitals. Appears with symphony orchestra.

Teaches voice. Coaches repertoire. **Res:** 95 Blvd de Lattre, Suresnes, France. Mgmt: ASK/UK.

ROY, WILL. Bass. American. Resident mem: New York City Opera. Born Schenectady, NY, USA. Wife Nancy Honegger, occupation opera singer, voice teacher. One daughter. Studied: Curtis Inst of Music, Martial Singher, Philadelphia; Manhattan School of Music, John Brownlee, New York. **Debut:** Don Alfonso (*Così fan tutte*) Mozart Fest Opera, New York 1965. Previous occupations: actor; mgr missile & space vehicle dept, Gen Electric. Awards: Winner Met Op Ntl Counc Aud 1965; Winner Conc Verdi, Busseto, Italy 1972.

Sang with major companies in SWI: Geneva; USA: Fort Worth, Hartford, Minneapolis, Newark, New Orleans, New York City Opera, Philadelphia Grand, Washington DC. **Roles with these companies incl** BIZET: Escamillo★ (*Carmen*); DEBUSSY: Arkel★ (*Pelléas et Mélisande*); DELIBES: Nilakantha★ (*Lakmé*); DELIUS: Don José★ (*Koanga*); GOUNOD: Méphistophélès★ (*Faust*); MASSENET: Des Grieux★ (*Portrait de Manon*); MOZART: Don Alfonso★ (*Così fan tutte*), Don Giovanni★, Osmin★ (*Entführung aus dem Serail*), Sarastro★ (*Zauberflöte*); PUCCINI: Colline★(*Bohème*); ROSSINI: Don Basilio★ (*Barbiere di Siviglia*); SMETANA: Kezal★ (*Bartered Bride*); STRAVINSKY: Tiresias★ (*Oedipus Rex*); VERDI: Ramfis★ (*Aida*). Also THOMAS: Claudius (*Hamlet*); DELIUS: Marti (*Village Romeo and Juliet*); BRITTEN: Junius (*Rape of Lucretia*). Gives recitals. Appears with symphony orchestra. Teaches voice. **Res:** Teaneck, NJ, USA. Mgmt: LLF/USA.

ROZHDESTVENSKY, GENNADY NIKOLAEVICH. Conductor of opera and symphony. Russian. Resident Cond, Bolshoi Opera, Moscow. Also Resident Cond, Phil Orch, Stockholm, Sweden. Born 4 May 1930, Moscow. Previous adm positions in opera: Mus Dir, Bolshoi Theater, Moscow until 1970.

Conducted with major companies in POL: Warsaw; UK: London Royal; USSR: Kiev, Moscow Bolshoi & Stanislavski; et al. **Operas with these companies incl** GLINKA: *Life for the Tsar, Ruslan and Ludmilla*; MUSSORGSKY: *Boris Godunov, Khovanshchina*; PROKOFIEV: *Duenna, Fiery Angel, Gambler, Love for Three Oranges*; RACHMANINOFF: *Miserly Knight*‡; RIMSKY-KORSAKOV: *Invisible City of Kitezh, Sadko*; SHOSTAKOVICH: *Katerina Ismailova*; SMETANA: *Bartered Bride*; TCHAIKOVSKY: *Eugene Onegin, Maid of Orleans*‡, *Pique Dame*; et al. Also KHOLMINOV: *Optimistic Tragedy*. Recorded for HMV, Melodiya.

ROZSOS, ISTVAN. Dramatic tenor. Hungarian. Resident mem: State Opera, Budapest. Born 6 Jul 1944, Budapest. Wife Katalin Frank, occupation musician. Studied: Musical Univ, Olga Revhegyi, Eva Kutrucz, Budapest. **Debut:** Scaramuccio (*Ariadne auf Naxos*) State Opera, Budapest 1967.

Sang with major companies in HUN: Budapest. **Roles with these companies incl** BERG: Maler★ (*Lulu*); GERSHWIN: Sportin' Life★ (*Porgy and Bess*); HANDEL: Acis★; HAYDN: Filippo★‡ (*Infedeltà delusa*), Cecco (*Mondo della luna*); JANACEK: Steva★ (*Jenufa*); MONTEVERDI:

Testo (*Combattimento di Tancredi*); MOZART: Pedrillo★ (*Entführung aus dem Serail*); PROKO-FIEV: Prince★ (*Love for Three Oranges*); PUC-CINI: Rinuccio★ (*Gianni Schicchi*), Pinkerton★ (*Butterfly*); VERDI: Don Carlo★; WAGNER: David★ (*Meistersinger*), Walther v d Vogelweide★ (*Tannhäuser*); WEBER: Abu Hassan★. Gives recitals. Appears with symphony orchestra. Coaches repertoire. **Res:** Szalag u 11, H-1011 Budapest, Hungary. **Mgmt:** ITK/HUN.

RUBES, JAN. Bass & director. Canadian. Resident mem: Canadian Opera Company, Toronto; is also Dir of COC Touring and Program Development. Born 6 Jun 1920, Volyne, Czechoslovakia. Wife Susan, occupation theatrical producer. Three children. Studied: Consv of Music & Acad of Musical Arts, Prague; Univ of Toronto, Canada. **Debut:** Don Basilio (*Barbiere di Siviglia*) Prague 1940. Previous occupations: medical student. Awards: Ministry of Educt Awd, CSR; Canadian Centennial Medal, Gvnmt of Canada 1967.

Sang with major companies in CAN: Montreal/Quebec, Ottawa, Toronto, Vancouver; CZE: Prague National & Smetana; FR GER: Frankfurt; USA: Chicago, New Orleans, New York City Opera, Pittsburgh, Seattle, Washington DC. **Roles with these companies** incl BARTOK: Bluebeard; BEETHOVEN: Rocco (*Fidelio*); BRITTEN: Bottom (*Midsummer Night*); CHERUBINI: Creon (*Medea*); DONIZETTI: Don Pistacchio (*Campanello*), Don Pasquale★; DVORAK: Marbuel (*Devil and Kate*); GOUNOD: Méphistophélès (*Faust*); MOZART: Don Alfonso★ (*Così fan tutte*), Leporello★ (*Don Giovanni*), Osmin (*Entführung aus dem Serail*), Figaro (*Nozze di Figaro*), Sarastro (*Zauberflöte*); MUSSORGSKY: Boris Godunov; PERGOLESI: Uberto (*Serva padrona*); PUCCINI: Colline★ (*Bohème*); ROSSINI: Don Basilio (*Barbiere di Siviglia*); SMETANA: Kezal (*Bartered Bride*), Rarach (*Devil's Wall*), Malina (*Secret*); STRAVINSKY: Creon (*Oedipus Rex*); VERDI: Ramfis (*Aida*), Padre Guardiano (*Forza del destino*); WAGNER: Fafner★ (*Siegfried*), Hunding (*Walküre*). Also TCHAIKOVSKY: Gremin (*Eugene Onegin*). **World premieres:** POLGAR: The Man (*The European Lover*) Toronto 1967. Video—CBC TV: Bluebeard; Sparafucile (*Rigoletto*). Gives recitals. Appears with symphony orchestra. Teaches voice. Coaches repertoire and acting. On faculty of York Univ, Toronto. **Res:** 55 Sumner Hts Dr, Willowdale, Ont, Canada. **Mgmt:** HAY/CAN.

RUDEL, JULIUS. Conductor of opera and symphony. American. Dir & Principal Cond, New York City Opera since 1957. Mus Dir, Caramoor Fest, Katonah, NY. Born 6 Mar 1921, Vienna, Austria. Wife Rita, occupation Dr of Psychology. Three children. Studied: Vienna; Mannes School of Music, New York; incl piano. Operatic training as asst cond at New York City Opera 1944-57. **Operatic debut:** *Zigeunerbaron* New York City Opera 1944. Awards: Hon DM, Univ of VT, Pace Coll NY, Univ of MI; Newspaper Gld Page One Awd; Gold Mdl Ntl Arts Club; Ditson Awd Col Univ; Cit ASCAP & Socy of Negro Muscn; NYC Handel Mdl; Hon Insg Austrian Gvnmt; Hon Cross of Merit, FR Ger; Hon Lt Army of Israel;

Awd for Young Cond in Honor of JR, New York City Opera Board of Dir. Previous adm positions in opera: Mus Dir, Kennedy Center, Washington DC 1972-75; Mus Dir, Cincinnati May Fest; Mus Advsr, Wolf Trap Farm Park, Vienna, VA.

Conducted with major companies in AUS: Vienna Volksoper; CAN: Montreal/Quebec; FRA: Paris Opéra; FR GER: Cologne, Hamburg, Munich Staatsoper, Stuttgart; ITA: Spoleto Fest, Venice; USA: Baltimore, Cincinnati, Houston, New Orleans, New York City Opera, Philadelphia Lyric, Washington DC. **Operas with these companies** incl BEETHOVEN: *Fidelio*; BELLINI: *Puritani*★‡; BIZET: *Carmen*★; BOITO: *Mefistofele*★‡; BORODIN: *Prince Igor*; BRITTEN: *Burning Fiery Furnace*★, *Curlew River*★, *Midsummer Night*, *Prodigal Son*, *Rape of Lucretia*★, *Turn of the Screw*★; CAVALLI: *Ormindo*★; CHARPENTIER: *Louise*; CHERUBINI: *Medea*★; DEBUSSY: *Pelléas et Mélisande*; DONIZETTI: *Anna Bolena*★‡, *Roberto Devereux*★; FLOTOW: *Martha*; FLOYD: *Susannah*★; GERSHWIN: *Porgy and Bess*; GIANNINI: *Taming of the Shrew*; GINASTERA: *Don Rodrigo*; GIORDANO: *Andrea Chénier*; GOUNOD: *Faust*★; HANDEL: *Ariodante*★, *Giulio Cesare*★‡; HENZE: *Junge Lord*★; HOIBY: *Summer and Smoke*★; HUMPERDINCK: *Hänsel und Gretel*★; LEONCAVALLO: *Pagliacci*★; MASCAGNI: *Cavalleria rusticana*★; MASSENET: *Manon*★‡, *Thaïs*★‡; MENOTTI: *Amelia al ballo*, *Consul*; MONTEVERDI: *Combattimento di Tancredi*★, *Incoronazione di Poppea*★; MOORE: *Ballad of Baby Doe*; MOZART: *Così fan tutte*★, *Don Giovanni*★, *Entführung aus dem Serail*★, *Idomeneo*★, *Schauspieldirektor*★, *Nozze di Figaro*★, *Zauberflöte*★; OFFENBACH: *Contes d'Hoffmann*★‡; ORFF: *Carmina burana*★, *Kluge*; PROKOFIEV: *Fiery Angel*, *Love for Three Oranges*; PUCCINI: *Bohème*★, *Gianni Schicchi*★, *Butterfly*★, *Manon Lescaut*, *Suor Angelica*★, *Tabarro*★, *Tosca*★, *Turandot*★; PURCELL: *Dido and Aeneas*★; RAVEL: *Heure espagnole*★; RIMSKY-KORSAKOV: *Coq d'or*★; ROSSINI: *Barbiere di Siviglia*★, *Signor Bruschino*; SAINT-SAENS: *Samson et Dalila*; SALIERI: *Prima la musica*★; SHOSTAKOVICH: *Katerina Ismailova*; SMETANA: *Bartered Bride*★; STRAUSS, J: *Fledermaus*; STRAUSS, R: *Ariadne auf Naxos*★, *Capriccio*★, *Rosenkavalier*★, *Salome*★; TCHAIKOVSKY: *Eugene Onegin*; VERDI: *Aida*★, *Ballo in maschera*★, *Forza del destino*★, *Otello*★, *Rigoletto*★, *Traviata*★, *Trovatore*★; WAGNER: *Lohengrin*, *Meistersinger*★, *Walküre*, *Tannhäuser*; WEBER: *Freischütz*. **World premieres:** HOIBY: *Natalia Petrovna* 1964; KURKA: *Good Soldier Schweik* 1958; MOORE: *Wings of the Dove* 1961; ELLSTEIN: *Golem* 1962; FLOYD: *Passion of Jonathan Wade* 1962; GIANNINI: *Servant of Two Masters* 1967, all at New York City Opera; GINASTERA: *Bomarzo*‡ Washington DC 1967, *Beatrix Cenci* Washington DC 1972; FLOYD: *Molly Sinclair* Raleigh, NC 1963. Recorded for: EMI, Angel, Columbia, ABC, RCA. Conducted major orch in Europe, USA/Canada, Asia. **Mgmt:** HUR/USA; DSP/USA.

RUDOLF, MAX. Conductor of opera and symphony. American. Born 15 Jun 1902, Frankfurt/Main, Germany. Wife Liese. Two children.

467

Studied: Consv of Music, Bernhard Sekles, Frankfurt; incl piano, organ, cello, trumpet in high school, and voice. Operatic training as asst cond & chorus master at Stadttheater Freiburg i/B 1922-23; Hessisches Landestheater, Darmstadt 1923-26. **Operatic debut:** *Fledermaus* Stadttheater Freiburg i/B 1923. Symphonic debut: Berlin Phil 1929. Awards: hon degrees Univ of Cincinnati, Miami Univ, Curtis Inst of Music, Baldwin-Wallace Coll, Temple Univ; Alice Ditson Awd. Previous adm positions in opera: Artistic Adm, Metropolitan Opera, New York 1950-58 (Cond Met 1945-58); Princpl Cond, Hess Landestheater, Darmstadt 1927-29; German Opera Co, Prague 1929-35; Head of Opera Dept, Curtis Inst of Music, Philadelphia 1970-73.

Conducted with major companies in CZE: Prague German; FR GER: Darmstadt, Frankfurt; USA: Cincinnati, New York Met. **Operas with these companies incl** ADAM: *Si j'étais roi;* d'ALBERT: *Tiefland;* BEETHOVEN: *Fidelio;* BIZET: *Carmen, Djamileh;* BRITTEN: *Rape of Lucretia;* BUSONI: *Arlecchino;* CIMAROSA: *Matrimonio segreto;* CORNELIUS: *Barbier von Bagdad;* DONIZETTI: *Don Pasquale★, Elisir★;* FLOTOW: *Martha;* GLUCK: *Orfeo ed Euridice;* HINDEMITH: *Hin und zurück;* HUMPERDINCK: *Hänsel und Gretel;* LEONCAVALLO: *Pagliacci;* LORTZING: *Waffenschmied, Wildschütz, Zar und Zimmermann;* MASCAGNI: *Cavalleria rusticana;* MOZART: *Don Giovanni★, Entführung aus dem Serail, Lucio Silla, Nozze di Figaro, Zauberflöte;* MUSSORGSKY: *Boris Godunov;* NICOLAI: *Lustigen Weiber;* OFFENBACH: *Contes d'Hoffmann, Mariage aux lanternes;* PERGOLESI: *Serva padrona;* PUCCINI: *Bohème, Butterfly, Manon Lescaut, Tosca;* ROSSINI: *Barbiere di Siviglia, Cenerentola, Signor Bruschino;* SAINT-SAENS: *Samson et Dalila;* SMETANA: *Two Widows;* STRAUSS, J: *Fledermaus;* STRAUSS, R: *Ariadne auf Naxos, Intermezzo, Rosenkavalier★;* VERDI: *Aida, Ballo in maschera, Falstaff, Otello, Rigoletto, Traviata, Trovatore;* WAGNER: *Fliegende Holländer★, Lohengrin, Meistersinger, Walküre, Siegfried, Tannhäuser, Tristan und Isolde;* WEBER: *Abu Hassan, Freischütz;* WOLF-FERRARI: *Quattro rusteghi.* Also FLOTOW: *Alessandro Stradella;* GOUNOD: *Médecin malgré lui;* DOHNANYI: *Tenor;* REZNICEK: *Spiel oder Ernst;* KRENEK: *Schwergewicht;* SCHUBERT: *Verschworenen, Vierjährige Posten.* **World premieres:** ROGERS: *Warrior* Metropolitan Opera, New York 1947. Recorded for Columbia, Cetra-Everest. Conducted major orch in Europe, USA/Canada. Previous positions as Mus Dir with major orch: Cincinnati Symph Orch, O, USA 1958-70. **Res:** 220 West Rittenhouse Square, Philadelphia, PA, USA. Mgmt: HUR/USA.

RUGTVEDT, UNNI. Contralto. Norwegian. Resident mem: Staatsoper, Vienna. Born 6 Jun 1934, Skien, Norway. Single. Studied: Norsk Musikkonsv, Oslo; Prof Oscar Raum, Oslo; Kmsg Käthe Sundström, Stockholm; Kmsg Max Lorenz, Munich; Prof Kaiser-Breme, Essen, FR Ger. **Debut:** Ulrica *(Ballo in maschera)* Royal Opera, Stockholm 1964. Awards: Prize Winner, Intl Song Cont Verdi Jubilee, Venice 1964; five months' fllshp for

studies in Italy; Fllshp Björnska Fonden, Stockholm 1968.

Sang with major companies in AUS: Graz, Vienna Staatsoper; FRA: Toulouse; FR GER: Bayreuth Festival, Hannover; ITA: Florence Comunale, Naples; NOR: Oslo; SWE: Drottningholm Fest, Stockholm. **Roles with these companies incl** BENNETT: Leda & Rosalind‡ *(Mines of Sulphur);* GLUCK: Orfeo; PONCHIELLI: La Cieca★ *(Gioconda);* PUCCINI: Suzuki★ *(Butterfly);* SMETANA: Hata★ *(Bartered Bride);* TCHAIKOVSKY: Mme Larina★ & Olga *(Eugene Onegin);* VERDI: Ulrica *(Ballo in maschera);* WAGNER: Erda *(Rheingold★, Siegfried),* Fricka *(Walküre).* Also CIMAROSA: Doralba *(Impresario angustie);* SCARLATTI: Rosmira *(Onestà negli amori);* HANDEL: Dalinda *(Ariodante).* **World premieres:** BUCHT: Ingebjörg *(Tronkrävarna)* Royal Opera, Stockholm 1966. Recorded for: DG. Video—TV in Italy, Sweden, Norway. Appears with symphony orchestra. **Res:** Prinz Eugenstr 4/19, 1040 Vienna, Austria.

RUISI, GIUSEPPE FERDINANDO. Conductor of opera, symph; composer; musicologist. Italian. Born 26 Apr 1914, Port Said, Egypt. Married. Three children. Studied: Consv of Music, Palermo and Rome; Mo Gustavo Natale, Mario Pilati and Alessandro Bustini; incl piano, violin and voice. Plays the piano. Operatic training as asst cond at Royal Opera House, Rome 1939-41. **Operatic debut:** *Don Pasquale* Rome 1938. Symphonic debut: RAI Symph Orch, Rome 1945. Awards: Gold Medal, Intl Fest Iesi, Italy; Premio Campidoglio, Intl Cultural Center, Rome 1975.

Conducted with major companies in FRA: Lyon; FR GER: Bonn, Düsseldorf-Duisburg; ITA: Genoa, Naples, Trieste, Turin; SPA: Barcelona; SWI: Basel, Geneva, Zurich. **Operas conducted with these companies incl** BELLINI: *Norma★, Sonnambula;* BIZET: *Carmen, Pêcheurs de perles;* BOITO: *Mefistofele★;* CILEA: *Adriana Lecouvreur★;* CIMAROSA: *Matrimonio segreto★;* DONIZETTI: *Campanello, Don Pasquale, Elisir, Favorite, Lucia★;* GIORDANO: *Andrea Chénier, Fedora;* LEONCAVALLO: *Pagliacci★;* MASCAGNI: *Amico Fritz, Cavalleria rusticana★;* MASSENET: *Manon;* MENOTTI: *Telephone;* PERGOLESI: *Serva padrona;* PONCHIELLI: *Gioconda;* PUCCINI: *Bohème★, Butterfly★, Manon Lescaut★, Tosca★;* ROSSINI: *Barbiere di Siviglia★;* VERDI: *Aida★, Ballo in maschera★, Ernani★, Forza del destino★, Macbeth★, Nabucco★, Otello★, Rigoletto, Traviata★, Trovatore★;* WOLF-FERRARI: *Segreto di Susanna.* Also DONIZETTI: *Furioso all'Isola di S Domingo;* MASCAGNI: *Piccolo Marat;* NAPOLI: *Dubrowsky II.* **World premieres:** MARCACCI: *Evangelina* Rome Opera 1954. Conducted major orch in Europe & Africa. Teaches at Consv S Pietro a Maiella, Naples. **Res:** V Topino 24, 00199 Rome, Italy. Mgmt: ABA/FRA.

RUK-FOCIC, BOZENA. Lirico spinto. Yugoslavian. Res mem: Croatian National Opera, Zagreb. Born 31 Oct 1937, Zagreb. Husband Avdo Focic, occupation engineer. One child. Studied: Prof Zlatko Sir, Zagreb. **Debut:** Micaëla *(Carmen)* Basel, Switzerland 1961. Awards: Milka Ternina Awd, Zagreb.

Sang with major companies in AUS: Graz, Salzburg Fest, Vienna Staatsoper; GRE: Athens Fest; FR GER: Hamburg, Stuttgart; GER DR: Berlin Staatsoper; HUN: Budapest; ITA: Genoa, Rome, Milan La Scala, Naples, Palermo, Trieste, Turin; ROM: Bucharest; SPA: Barcelona; SWI: Basel, Geneva, Zurich; UK: London Royal; USSR: Kiev; USA: Houston, Pittsburgh, Seattle, Washington DC; YUG: Dubrovnik, Zagreb, Belgrade. Roles with these companies incl BIZET: Micaëla★ (Carmen); BORODIN: Jaroslavna★ (Prince Igor); GLUCK: Alceste★, Euridice★; GOTOVAC: Djula★ (Ero der Schelm); MOZART: Contessa (Nozze di Figaro); PUCCINI: Mimì★ (Bohème), Cio-Cio-San★ (Butterfly), Manon Lescaut★, Tosca★; SMETANA: Marie (Bartered Bride); STRAUSS, R: Arabella★, Ariadne★ (Ariadne auf Naxos), Chrysothemis★ (Elektra); TCHAIKOVSKY: Tatiana (Eugene Onegin), Lisa (Pique Dame); VERDI: Aida★, Elisabetta★ (Don Carlo), Leonora★ (Forza del destino), Desdemona★ (Otello), Leonora★ (Trovatore); WAGNER: Elsa (Lohengrin), Eva★ (Meistersinger), Sieglinde★ (Walküre), Gutrune★ (Götterdämmerung), Elisabeth★ (Tannhäuser); WEBER: Agathe★ (Freischütz). Gives recitals. Appears with symphony orchestra. Jurjevska 49, Zagreb, Yugoslavia. Mgmt: CAM/USA.

RUMOWSKO-MACHNIKOWSKA, HANNA. Dramatic soprano. Polish. Resident mem: Teatr Wielki, Warsaw. Husband Bronislaw Machnikowski, occupation manager Polish Airlines. One child. Studied: Prof W Bregy. Debut: Leonora (Trovatore) Warsaw Opera 1959. Awards: Premier Grand Prix, Toulouse; Gold Cross of Merit. Sang with major cos in AUS: Vienna Volksoper & Staatsoper; CZE: Prague; FRA: Toulouse; FR GER: Bayreuth Fest, Berlin Deutsche Oper, Düsseldorf-Duisburg, Frankfurt, Hamburg; GER DR: Berlin Komische Oper; POL: Lodz, Warsaw; SWI: Bern; USSR: Kiev, Moscow Bolshoi. Roles with these companies incl BEETHOVEN: Marzelline (Fidelio); BELLINI: Norma; GIORDANO: Maddalena★ (Andrea Chénier); GLUCK: Alceste, Iphigénie (Iphigénie en Tauride), Euridice; HANDEL: Cleopatra (Giulio Cesare); MASCAGNI: Santuzza (Cavalleria rusticana); MENOTTI: Magda Sorel (Consul); MONIUSZKO: Halka★; MOZART: Donna Anna★ & Donna Elvira★ (Don Giovanni); MUSSORGSKY: Marina★ (Boris Godunov); OFFENBACH: Giulietta (Contes d'Hoffmann); PUCCINI: Cio-Cio-San★ (Butterfly), Manon Lescaut, Tosca★, Turandot & Liù (Turandot); STRAUSS, R: Elektra★, Marschallin (Rosenkavalier); TCHAIKOVSKY: Lisa★ (Pique Dame); VERDI: Aida★, Amelia (Ballo in maschera), Elisabetta★ (Don Carlo), Leonora (Forza del destino), Leonora★ (Trovatore); WAGNER: Elisabeth★ (Tannhäuser). Gives recitals. Appears with symphony orchestra. Res: Moliera 8, Warsaw, Poland.

RUNDGREN, BENGT ERIK. Bass-baritone. Swedish. Resident mem: Deutsche Oper, Berlin. Born 21 Apr 1931, Karlskrona, Sweden. Wife Aina Margareta. One child. Studied: Prof Arne Sunnergård, Sweden. Debut: Commendatore (Don Giovanni) Stockholm Opera 1962.

Sang with major companies in AUS: Vienna Staatsoper; CAN: Montreal/Quebec; FIN: Helsinki; FRA: Orange Fest; FR GER: Bayreuth Fest, Berlin Deutsche Oper, Bielefeld, Hamburg, Hannover, Munich Staatsoper; ITA: Naples; NOR: Oslo; SWE: Drottningholm Fest, Stockholm; SWI: Geneva, Zurich; UK: Edinburgh Fest; USA: Chicago, New York Met. Roles with these companies incl MOZART: Osmin (Entführung aus dem Serail), Sarastro (Zauberflöte); MUSSORGSKY: Pimen (Boris Godunov); ROSSINI: Don Basilio (Barbiere di Siviglia); VERDI: Ramfis (Aida), Grande Inquisitore (Don Carlo), Padre Guardiano (Forza del destino), Zaccaria (Nabucco); WAGNER: Daland (Fliegende Holländer), König Heinrich (Lohengrin), Pogner (Meistersinger), Gurnemanz (Parsifal), Fasolt (Rheingold), Fafner (Rheingold, Siegfried), Hunding (Walküre), Hagen (Götterdämmerung), Landgraf (Tannhäuser), König Marke (Tristan und Isolde). Also TCHAIKOVSKY: Gremin (Eugene Onegin). Video: Daland (Fliegende Holländer). Appears with symphony orchestra. Teaches voice. Coaches repertoire. Res: Landauerstr 4, Berlin, FR Ger. Mgmt: TAU/SWI.

RUNGE, PETER-CHRISTOPH. Lyric baritone. German. Resident mem: Deutsche Oper am Rhein, Düsseldorf. Born 12 Apr 1939, Lübeck. Wife Judith Wilkinson. Studied: Hochschule für Musik, Lilly Schmitt de Giorgi, Hamburg; Edith Boroschek, Düsseldorf. Debut: Guglielmo (Così fan tutte) Opera Flensburg 1958-59. Previous occupations: master degr in bookbinding. Sang with major companies in AUS: Vienna Volksoper; BEL: Brussels; FRA: Lyon; FR GER: Cologne, Düsseldorf-Duisburg, Frankfurt, Hamburg, Karlsruhe, Kassel, Mannheim, Munich Staatsoper, Stuttgart, Wiesbaden, Wuppertal; HOL: Amsterdam; ITA: Florence Maggio; POL: Warsaw; SWE: Stockholm; SWI: Basel; UK: Edinburgh Fest, Glasgow Scottish, Glyndebourne Fest; YUG: Zagreb. Roles with these companies incl BRITTEN: Demetrius (Midsummer Night), Sid (Albert Herring); CAVALLI: Amida★ (Ormindo); CIMAROSA: Count Robinson (Matrimonio segreto); DEBUSSY: Pelléas (Pelléas); DONIZETTI: Dott Malatesta (Don Pasquale), Belcore★ (Elisir); GLUCK: Oreste (Iphigénie en Tauride); KODALY: Suitor (Spinning Room); LORTZING: Graf Eberbach (Wildschütz), Peter I (Zar und Zimmermann); MARSCHNER: Hans Heiling; MONTEVERDI: Orfeo★ (Orfeo); MOZART: Guglielmo★ (Così fan tutte), Nardo★ (Finta giardiniera), Figaro★ (Nozze di Figaro), Papageno★ (Zauberflöte); NICOLAI: Fluth (Lustigen Weiber); ORFF: Solo★ (Carmina burana); PUCCINI: Marcello (Bohème), Sharpless (Butterfly); PURCELL: Aeneas; REIMANN: Graf von Lusignan (Melusine); ROSSINI: Figaro★ (Barbiere di Siviglia), Dandini★ (Cenerentola), Robert★ (Comte Ory); STRAUSS, R: Olivier★ (Capriccio), Barbier★ (Schweigsame Frau); WAGNER: Beckmesser (Meistersinger), Wolfram★ (Tannhäuser); ZIMMERMANN: Stolzius★ (Soldaten). Also STRAUSS, R: Harlekin★ (Ariadne auf Naxos); MONTEVERDI: Ottone★ (Incoronazione di Poppea), Testo (Combattimento di Tancredi); GOUNOD: Valentin (Faust); CAVALIERI: Corpo★ (Rappresentazione di anima). Recorded for: Argo,

London, Decca, EMI. Video—ZDF Germany: Graf (*Wildschütz*); Zurga (*Pêcheurs de perles*). Gives recitals. Appears with symphony orchestra. **Res:** Arnoldstr 23, 4 Düsseldorf 30, FR Ger. Mgmt: SLZ/FRG; NIM/HOL; IMR/FRA.

RUNSTEN, LARS E I. Stages/produces opera. Also designs sets, costumes & stage-lighting and is an author. Swedish. Art Adv & Stage Dir, Norwegian Opera, Oslo 1973- . Born 9 Aug 1931, Stockholm. Wife Nenne Ramstedt, occupation translator. Three children. Studied: Stockholm Univ. Operatic training as asst stage dir at Royal Opera, Stockholm 1956-60. **Operatic debut:** *Orfeo ed Euridice* Royal Opera, Drottningholm Fest 1957; as designer, *Twilight Crane* Royal Opera, Stockholm 1958. Awards: Commander Royal Order of Dannebrog, Denmark. Previous adm positions in opera: Generalintendant, Norwegian Opera, Oslo 1969-73.

Directed/produced opera for major companies in AUS: Graz; DEN: Copenhagen; FIN: Helsinki; FR GER: Hamburg, Hannover; NOR: Oslo; SPA: Barcelona; SWE: Drottningholm Fest, Stockholm; SWI: Basel, Zurich; UK: Edinburgh Fest. **Operas staged with these companies incl** BEETHOVEN: *Fidelio†*; BERG: *Wozzeck∗†*; CHARPENTIER: *Louise*; DALLAPICCOLA: *Prigioniero∗†*; DEBUSSY: *Pelléas et Mélisande†*; GLUCK: *Alceste†*, *Iphigénie en Tauride∗†*; HANDEL: *Ariodante, Rodelinda*; KURKA: *Good Soldier Schweik*; MOZART: *Nozze di Figaro†*; MUSSORGSKY: *Boris Godunov*; PURCELL: *Dido and Aeneas†*; ROSSINI: *Cambiale di matrimonio†*; SHOSTAKOVICH: *Katerina Ismailova∗†*; STRAUSS, R: *Salome*; STRAVINSKY: *Oedipus Rex†*, *Rake's Progress∗*; VERDI: *Aida∗, Don Carlo∗†, Otello∗, Traviata, Trovatore*; WAGNER: *Lohengrin, Walküre∗†, Tannhäuser*; WERLE: *Dream of Thérèse∗*. Also MARTIN: *Sturm∗*; WERLE: *Resan∗*; sev Scandinavian operas. **Operatic world premieres:** 4 Swedish, 3 Danish & 2 Norwegian operas in Stockholm, Copenhagen, Hamburg & Oslo 1958-74. **Opera libretti:** WERLE: *Dream of Thérèse* Royal Opera Stockholm 1964, *Resan* Staatsoper Hamburg 1969. **Res:** Karlsudd, Vaxholm, Sweden. Mgmt: SLZ/FRG.

RUOHONEN, SEPPO JUHANI. Dramatic tenor. Finnish. Resident mem: Finnish National Opera, Helsinki. Born 25 Apr 1946, Turku, Finland. Wife Marja Katrüna, occupation music teacher. One child. Studied: Hochschule für Musik, Ricci, Dermota, Piltti, Kolo, Vienna. **Debut:** Don Alvaro (*Forza del destino*) 1973. Previous occupations: choirmaster & music teacher.

Sang with major companies in FIN: Helsinki. **Roles with these companies incl** BIZET: Don José∗ (*Carmen*); DONIZETTI: Ernesto∗ (*Don Pasquale*); GOUNOD: Faust∗; MOZART: Don Ottavio∗ (*Don Giovanni*); PUCCINI: Rodolfo∗ (*Bohème*), Cavaradossi∗ (*Tosca*); SMETANA: Hans∗ (*Bartered Bride*); VERDI: Riccardo∗ (*Ballo in maschera*), Don Carlo∗, Don Alvaro∗ (*Forza del destino*), Duca di Mantova∗‡ (*Rigoletto*), Alfredo∗‡ (*Traviata*), Manrico∗ (*Trovatore*). Also MUSSORGSKY: Dimitri (*Boris Godunov*). Video—Finnish TV: Duca di Mantova (*Rigoletto*). Gives recitals. Appears with symphony orchestra.

Teaches voice. Coaches repertoire. **Res:** Käärtipolku 1A6, Helsinki, Finland.

RUSSO, SALVATORE. Scenic and costume designer for opera, theater, film & television. Is a lighting designer; also a painter, illustrator & fashion designer. Italian. Born 22 Oct 1940, Palermo. Studied: Accad di Belle Arti, Sezione Scenografia, Rome; Angelo Canevari; Lila de Nobili. **Operatic debut:** *Campanello* Teatro Massimo, Palermo 1967. Theater debut: Gulbenkian Fest, Lisbon 1970. Awards: Positano Prize.

Designed for major companies in BUL: Sofia; FRA: Bordeaux, Nice, Paris, Toulouse; ITA: Florence Comunale, Naples, Palermo Massimo, Rome Teatro dell'Opera, Spoleto Fest, Venice, Verona Arena; POR: Lisbon. **Operas designed for these companies incl** AUBER: *Fra Diavolo*; DONIZETTI: *Don Pasquale, Favorite*; MASSENET: *Thaïs*; ORFF: *Carmina burana*; PERGOLESI: *Serva padrona*; PUCCINI: *Tosca*; VERDI: *Nabucco*. Also MERCADANTE: *Elisa e Claudio*; HAZON: *Agenzia matrimoniale*; NEGRI: *Giorno di nozze*. Operatic Video—RAI TV: *Don Pasquale, Fra Diavolo*. **Res:** Viale Mazzini 134, Rome, Italy.

RUZDJAK, VLADIMIR. Lyric & dramatic baritone. Yugoslavian. Born 21 Sep 1922, Zagreb. Studied: Acad of Music, Zagreb; Prof Milan Reizer. **Debut:** Yeletsky (*Pique Dame*) Croatian Ntl Opera, Zagreb 1947. Awards: Kammersänger, City of Hamburg; First Prize, Intl Compt Geneva 1949; Vladimir Nazor Prize, Zagreb 1963; Milka Ternina Prize, Zagreb.

Sang with major companies in CZE: Prague Smetana; FR GER: Berlin Deutsche Oper, Düsseldorf-Duisburg, Frankfurt, Hamburg, Hannover, Kassel, Munich Staatsoper, Stuttgart; GER DR: Berlin Komische Oper; ITA: Naples, Spoleto Fest; SPA: Barcelona; UK: Aldeburgh Fest, London Royal; USSR: Moscow Bolshoi; USA: New York Met, San Francisco Opera; YUG: Dubrovnik, Zagreb, Belgrade. **Roles with these companies incl** BORODIN: Prince Igor; BRITTEN: Demetrius (*Midsummer Night*); DALLAPICCOLA: Prigioniero; DEBUSSY: Golaud (*Pelléas et Mélisande*); DONIZETTI: Dott Malatesta∗ (*Don Pasquale*), Enrico (*Lucia*); EINEM: Georges Danton (*Dantons Tod*); GIORDANO: Carlo Gérard∗ (*Andrea Chénier*); GOTOVAC: Sima‡ (*Ero der Schelm*); LEONCAVALLO: Tonio∗ (*Pagliacci*); MASSENET: Lescaut (*Manon*); MEYERBEER: Comte de Nevers (*Huguenots*); MONTEVERDI: Orfeo; MOZART: Don Giovanni, Conte Almaviva (*Nozze di Figaro*); ORFF: Solo (*Carmina burana*), König (*Kluge*); PERGOLESI: Uberto∗ (*Serva padrona*); PONCHIELLI: Barnaba∗ (*Gioconda*); PUCCINI: Marcello∗ (*Bohème*), Gianni Schicchi, Sharpless∗ (*Butterfly*); PURCELL: Aeneas; RAVEL: Ramiro (*Heure espagnole*); ROSSINI: Figaro∗ (*Barbiere di Siviglia*), Dandini (*Cenerentola*), Signor Bruschino; SALIERI: Poet∗ (*Prima la musica*); STRAUSS, R: Mandryka∗ (*Arabella*), Jochanaan (*Salome*); TCHAIKOVSKY: Eugene Onegin; VERDI: Amonasro∗ (*Aida*), Renato∗ (*Ballo in maschera*), Rodrigo (*Don Carlo*), Don Carlo (*Ernani*), Ford (*Falstaff*), Don Carlo∗ (*Forza del destino*), Nabucco, Iago (*Otello*), Rigoletto∗,

Germont★ (*Traviata*), Conte di Luna★ (*Trovatore*); WAGNER: Wolfram (*Tannhäuser*). Also ZAJC: Zrinjski (*Nikola Subic Zrinjski*). **World premieres:** HENZE: Prinz von Homburg, 1960; TAL: König (*Ashmedai*) 1971; both at Hamburg Opera. Recorded for: Jugoton. Video/Film: Yeletsky & Tomsky (*Pique Dame*); Zrinjski (*Nikola Subic Zrinjski*). Gives recitals. Appears with symphony orchestra. Coaches repertoire. On faculty of Acad of Music, Zagreb; Prof. **Res:** Galjerova 28, Zagreb, Yugoslavia. Mgmt: CDK/YUG.

RYCHTARIK, RICHARD WASLAV. Scenic and costume designer for opera, film & television; specl in sets. Is a lighting designer; also a painter & architect. American. Born 20 Jul 1894, Chocen, CSR. Wife Gertrude. One daughter. Studied: Univ of Prague, CSR. **Operatic debut:** Cleveland Orch Opera Prod, USA 1934. Theater debut: Prague National Theater 1920. Previous occupation: architect; Fair designer.
Designed opera for major companies in CAN: Montreal/Quebec; CZE: Prague National; ITA: Milan La Scala; SWI: Zurich; USA: Cincinnati, New Orleans, New York Met & City Opera, Philadelphia Grand, San Francisco Opera. **Operas designed for these companies incl** AUBER: *Fra Diavolo;* BERG: *Lulu;* BERLIOZ: *Damnation de Faust;* BIZET: *Carmen;* BRITTEN: *Peter Grimes;* DEBUSSY: *Pelléas et Mélisande;* DONIZETTI: *Don Pasquale, Lucia;* DVORAK: *Rusalka;* GLUCK: *Alceste, Iphigénie en Aulide;* GOUNOD: *Faust;* HANDEL: *Acis and Galatea;* HINDEMITH: *Hin und zurück;* HUMPERDINCK: *Hänsel und Gretel;* IBERT: *Angélique;* LEONCAVALLO: *Pagliacci;* MARTINU: *Comedy on the Bridge;* MASCAGNI: *Cavalleria rusticana;* MASSENET: *Manon, Werther;* MOZART: *Così fan tutte, Don Giovanni, Entführung aus dem Serail, Idomeneo, Nozze di Figaro, Zauberflöte;* PUCCINI: *Bohème, Fanciulla del West, Gianni Schicchi, Manon Lescaut, Tabarro;* RAVEL: *Heure espagnole;* ROSSINI: *Barbiere di Siviglia;* SHOSTAKOVICH: *Katerina Ismailova;* SMETANA: *Bartered Bride, Dalibor, Secret;* STRAUSS, J: *Fledermaus;* STRAUSS, R: *Elektra, Rosenkavalier, Salome;* TCHAIKOVSKY: *Eugene Onegin, Pique Dame;* THOMAS: *Mignon;* VERDI: *Aida, Falstaff, Rigoletto, Traviata;* WAGNER: *Fliegende Holländer, Walküre, Tannhäuser, Tristan und Isolde;* WEINBERGER: *Schwanda;* WOLF-FERRARI: *Segreto di Susanna.* Also RUBINSTEIN: *Sleeping Beauty.* **Operatic world premieres:** MENOTTI: *Island God* Metropolitan Opera 1942. Operatic Video/Film—CBS TV, NY: *Carmen, Traviata;* RAI TV, Milan: *Falstaff.* Exhibitions of stage designs, paintings & model maquettes, various museums & galleries. **Res:** New York, NY, USA.

RYDL, KURT. Bass. Austrian. Resident mem: Staatsoper, Stuttgart. Born 8 Oct 1947, Vienna. Wife Christiane. Studied: Prof Kolo, Vienna; Prof Petkov, Moscow. **Debut:** Daland (*Fliegende Holländer*) Staatsoper, Stuttgart 1973. Awards: First & Third Prize Viñas Compt, Barcelona 1971; Second Prize Barcelona 1974; Second Prize Grand Prix du Chant, Paris 1972.

Sang with major companies in FR GER: Bayreuth Fest, Stuttgart; ITA: Venice; POR: Lisbon; SPA: Barcelona. **Roles with these companies incl** BEETHOVEN: Rocco★ (*Fidelio*); BOITO: Mefistofele★; DONIZETTI: Don Pasquale★; GOUNOD: Méphistophélès★ (*Faust*); MOZART: Sarastro★ (*Zauberflöte*); MUSSORGSKY: Pimen★ (*Boris Godunov*); PUCCINI: Colline★ (*Bohème*); ROSSINI: Don Basilio★ (*Barbiere di Siviglia*); SMETANA: Kezal★ (*Bartered Bride*); STRAUSS, R: Orest★(*Elektra*); VERDI: Ramfis★ (*Aida*), Philip II★ (*Don Carlo*), Padre Guardiano★ (*Forza del destino*), Banquo★ (*Macbeth*), Zaccaria★ (*Nabucco*), Procida★ (*Vespri*); WAGNER: Daland★(*Fliegende Holländer*), Pogner★ (*Meistersinger*), Fafner (*Rheingold★, Siegfried★*), Landgraf★ (*Tannhäuser*), König Marke★ (*Tristan und Isolde*). Also MONTEVERDI: Seneca (*Incoronazione di Poppea*); WEINBERGER: Zauberer (*Schwanda*). Gives recitals. Appears with symphony orchestra. **Res:** Vogelsangstr 123a, Stuttgart, FR Ger. Mgmt: TAS/AUS; VLD/AUS; SLZ/FRG.

RYSANEK, LEONIE. Dramatic soprano. Austrian. Resident mem: Staatsoper, Vienna. Born 14 Nov 1928, Vienna. Husband E L Gausmann, occupation musicologist. Studied: Clothilde Radony v Oltean, Prof Alfred Jerger, Prof Rudolf Grossmann, Vienna. **Debut:** Agathe (*Freischütz*) Landestheater Innsbruck 1949. Awards: Austrian Cross 1st Class for Science & Art; Hon Mem Vienna Staatsoper; Austrian and Bavarian Kammersängerin; Chappel Gold Medal, London; Silver Rose, Vienna Phil.
Sang with major companies in AUS: Graz, Salzburg Fest, Vienna Staatsoper & Volksoper; CAN: Montreal, Toronto; FRA: Aix-en-Provence Fest, Bordeaux, Lyon, Marseille, Nancy, Nice, Orange Fest, Paris, Toulouse; GRE: Athens Fest; FR GER: Bayreuth Fest, Berlin Deutsche Oper, Cologne, Frankfurt, Hamburg, Mannheim, Munich Staatsoper, Saarbrücken, Stuttgart, Wiesbaden, Mainz; HUN: Budapest; ITA: Milan La Scala, Naples, Rome Opera; MON: Monte Carlo; SWI: Zurich; UK: Edinburgh Fest, London Royal; USSR: Moscow Bolshoi; USA: Boston, Chicago, Cincinnati, Dallas, Houston Grand Opera, New York Met, Philadelphia Grand & Lyric, San Antonio, San Diego, San Francisco Opera, Washington DC. **Roles with these companies incl** BEETHOVEN: Leonore★‡ (*Fidelio*); CHARPENTIER: Louise; CHERUBINI: Medea★; GIORDANO: Maddalena (*Andrea Chénier*); HINDEMITH: Ursula (*Mathis der Maler*); MASCAGNI: Santuzza (*Cavalleria rusticana*); MOZART: Donna Anna & Donna Elvira (*Don Giovanni*), Elettra (*Idomeneo*), Contessa (*Nozze di Figaro*); OFFENBACH: Antonia (*Contes d'Hoffmann*); PONCHIELLI: Gioconda★; PUCCINI: Tosca★, Turandot; SMETANA: Mlada★ (*Dalibor*); STRAUSS, R: Helena (*Aegyptische Helena*), Arabella, Ariadne★‡ (*Ariadne auf Naxos*), Chrysothemis★ (*Elektra*), Kaiserin★‡ (*Frau ohne Schatten*), Danae (*Liebe der Danae*), Marschallin★ (*Rosenkavalier*), Salome★; TCHAIKOVSKY: Tatiana (*Eugene Onegin*); VERDI: Aida, Amelia★ (*Ballo in maschera*), Elisabetta★ (*Don Carlo*), Leonora (*Forza del destino*), Lady Macbeth‡, Abigaille (*Nabucco*), Desdemona‡

(*Otello*), Gilda (*Rigoletto*); WAGNER: Senta★‡ (*Holländer*), Elsa★ (*Lohengrin*), Kundry★ (*Parsifal*), Sieglinde★‡ & Brünnhilde (*Walküre*), Gutrune (*Götterdämmerung*), Elisabeth★ (*Tannhäuser*); WEBER: Agathe (*Freischütz*), Rezia (*Oberon*). Also LORTZING: Berthalda (*Undine*); d'ALBERT: Marta (*Tiefland*), Myrthokle (*Toten Augen*); EGK: Solveig & Rothaarige (*Peer Gynt*). Recorded for: RCA, Teldec, London, EMI, Electrola, DG, Philips, Phonogram. Video—TV: Lady Macbeth; Tosca; Aida. Appears with symphony orchestra. **Res:** Eichendorffstr 12, 8201 Altenbeuern, FR Ger. Mgmt: OOC/FRA.

RYSANEK, LOTTE. Lyric soprano. Austrian. Resident mem: Staatsoper, Vienna. Born 18 Mar 1929, Vienna. Husband Herbert Dörler, occupation businessman. Studied: Vienna Consv, Prof Rudolf Grossmann. **Debut:** MASSENET: Manon, Klagenfurt, Austria 1950. Awards: Kammersängerin, Austrian Gvnmt 1968.

Sang with major companies in AUS: Bregenz Fest, Graz, Vienna Staatsoper & Volksoper; FR GER: Berlin Deutsche Oper, Düsseldorf-Duisburg, Hamburg, Karlsruhe, Munich Staatsoper; SWI: Zurich. **Roles with these companies incl** BEETHOVEN: Marzelline (*Fidelio*); BIZET: Micaëla★ (*Carmen*), Léila (*Pêcheurs de perles*); BRITTEN: Lady Billows (*Albert Herring*); DONIZETTI: Adina (*Elisir*); EINEM: Frl Bürstner (*Prozess*); GIORDANO: Maddalena (*Andrea Chénier*); GOUNOD: Marguerite (*Faust*); HUMPERDINCK: Gretel; JANACEK: Jenufa; LEONCAVALLO: Nedda★ (*Pagliacci*); LORTZING: Baronin Freimann (*Wildschütz*); MASSENET: Manon; MOZART: Fiordiligi (*Così fan tutte*), Donna Elvira★ (*Don Giovanni*), Contessa (*Nozze di Figaro*), Pamina & Königin der Nacht (*Zauberflöte*); NICOLAI: Frau Fluth (*Lustigen Weiber*); OFFENBACH: Antonia★ & Giulietta (*Contes d'Hoffmann*); PUCCINI: Mimi & Musetta★ (*Bohème*), Cio-Cio-San★ (*Butterfly*), Manon Lescaut, Liù★ (*Turandot*); SMETANA: Marie★ (*Bartered Bride*); STRAUSS, J: Rosalinde★ (*Fledermaus*); TCHAIKOVSKY: Lisa (*Pique Dame*); VERDI: Aida, Elisabetta (*Don Carlo*), Alice Ford (*Falstaff*), Leonora★ (*Forza del destino*), Luisa Miller, Desdemona (*Otello*), Leonora★ (*Trovatore*); WAGNER: Elsa (*Lohengrin*), Gutrune (*Götterdämmerung*), Elisabeth (*Tannhäuser*); WEBER: Agathe★ (*Freischütz*); WEINBERGER: Dorota (*Schwanda*). Appears with symphony orchestra.

S

SABLJIC, MLADEN. Stages/produces opera. Yugoslavian. Resident Stage Dir, National Opera, Belgrade. Born 6 Apr 1921, Bosanska Gradiska. Wife Olga, occupation producer. One child. Studied: Gitis, Moscow; Belgrade; incl music, violin and voice. **Operatic debut:** *Elisir* Belgrade 1949. Previous adm positions in opera: Dir, Opera Belgrade 1964-69.

Directed/produced opera for major companies in AUS: Graz; FRA: Nice; GRE: Athens National & Fest; FR GER: Hannover, Saarbrücken; ITA: Bologna, Genoa, Palermo, Rome Opera & Caracalla, Trieste; MON: Monte Carlo; SPA: Barcelona; YUG: Belgrade. **Operas staged with these companies incl** BELLINI: *Norma;* BIZET: *Carmen, Pêcheurs de perles;* BORODIN: *Prince Igor*; BRITTEN: *Albert Herring, Rape of Lucretia;* CIMAROSA: *Matrimonio segreto;* DONIZETTI: *Lucia;* FALLA: *Vida breve;* GIORDANO: *Andrea Chénier;* GOTOVAC: *Ero der Schelm*; HANDEL: *Giulio Cesare;* JANACEK: *Katya Kabanova;* MASSENET: *Don Quichotte, Manon, Werther*; MOZART: *Entführung aus dem Serail, Nozze di Figaro;* MUSSORGSKY: *Boris Godunov, Fair at Sorochinsk, Khovanshchina;* PROKOFIEV: *Gambler, Love for Three Oranges;* PUCCINI: *Bohème, Fanciulla del West*, *Butterfly, Tosca;* RIMSKY-KORSAKOV: *Maid of Pskov;* ROSSINI: *Barbiere di Siviglia, Moïse;* SAINT-SAENS: *Samson et Dalila;* SMETANA: *Bartered Bride;* TCHAIKOVSKY: *Eugene Onegin*, *Pique Dame*; THOMAS: *Mignon;* VERDI: *Aida, Ballo in maschera, Don Carlo, Ernani, Forza del destino*, *Macbeth, Nabucco, Otello, Rigoletto, Traviata, Trovatore;* WAGNER: *Fliegende Holländer;* WEBER: *Freischütz.* Teaches at Acad of Music, Belgrade. **Res:** Djure Salaja 7, Belgrade, Yugoslavia. Mgmt: SLZ/FRG.

SACCOMANI, LORENZO. Lyric & dramatic baritone. Italian. Born 9 Jun 1938, Milan. Wife Giuseppina Pallavicini. Two children. Studied: with uncle, Attilio Saccomani, Mo Piazza, Mo Vladimiro Badiali & Mo Alfonso Siliotti, Milan. **Debut:** Silvio (*Pagliacci*) Fest Avignon, France 1964. Previous occupations: industrial designer. Awards: Second Prize, G B Viotti, Vercelli; Fourth Prize, G Verdi, Parma; First Prize, Lions Club Milan.

Sang with major companies in AUS: Vienna Staatsoper; BUL: Sofia; FRA: Bordeaux, Marseille, Nancy, Nice, Rouen, Strasbourg, Toulouse; FR GER: Frankfurt; ITA: Genoa, Milan La Scala, Palermo, Parma, Turin, Venice; MEX: Mexico City; POR: Lisbon; SPA: Barcelona; UK: London Royal; USA: Chicago, Dallas, New York Met. **Roles with these companies incl** BELLINI: Sir Richard* (*Puritani*); BIZET: Escamillo* (*Carmen*); DONIZETTI: Alfonse* (*Favorite*), Enrico* (*Lucia*); LEONCAVALLO: Tonio* (*Pagliacci*); MASSENET: Lescaut* (*Manon*); MUSSORGSKY: Shaklovity* (*Khovanshchina*); PUCCINI: Marcello* (*Bohème*), Sharpless* (*Butterfly*); VERDI: Ezio* (*Attila*), Renato* (*Ballo in maschera*), Rodrigo* (*Don Carlo*), Don Carlo* (*Forza del destino*), Nabucco*, Rigoletto*, Germont* (*Traviata*), Conte di Luna* (*Trovatore*), Monforte* (*Vespri*). Also VERDI: Francesco* (*Masnadieri*); GOUNOD: Valentin* (*Faust*). Video/Film: Valentin (*Faust*). **Res:** V Pasubio 39, Cesano Boscone/Milan, Italy.

SACK, MICHAEL LOUIS. American. Business Admin, San Francisco Opera Assn, War Memorial Opera House, San Francisco, CA 94102, USA; also of Spring Opera & Western Opera Theater, Merola Opera Program. In charge of finances, and is a Cert Publ Acct. Born 8 Dec 1934, Jacksonville, FL, USA. Wife Jeannie. Two children. Studied: Cornell Univ, Ithaca, NY; Univ of Florida, Gainesville, USA. Previous positions, primarily administrative: Mem, Board of Dir and Treas, Civic Music Assn, Jacksonville, FL. Started in present position in 1975. **Res:** 2914 Sacramento St, San Francisco, CA, USA.

SAEDÉN, ERIK. Bass-baritone. Swedish. Resident mem: Royal Opera, Stockholm. Born 3 Sep 1924, Vänersborg, Sweden. Wife Elisabeth, occupation concert soloist. Three children. Studied: Royal Acad of Music, Stockholm. **Debut:** Rangström (*Gilgamesj*) Royal Opera, Stockholm 1952. Awards: Royal Court Singer.

Sang with major companies in FR GER: Bayreuth Fest, Berlin Deutsche Oper; SWE: Drottningholm Fest. **Roles with these companies incl** BERG: Wozzeck; BIZET: Escamillo (*Carmen*); BUSONI: Doktor Faust; CHARPENTIER: Père (*Louise*); DALLAPICCOLA: Il Prigioniero, Ulisse, Riviere (*Volo di notte*); DEBUSSY: Golaud* (*Pelléas et Mélisande*); GLUCK: Oreste (*Iphigénie en Aulide*); JANACEK: Jaroslav Prus* (*Makropoulos Affair*); LEONCAVALLO: Tonio (*Pagliacci*); MASSENET: Lescaut* (*Manon*);

MOZART: Don Alfonso★(*Così fan tutte*), Leporello★ & Don Giovanni (*Don Giovanni*), Conte Almaviva & Figaro★ (*Nozze di Figaro*); MUSSORGSKY: Pimen (*Boris Godunov*); OFFENBACH: Coppélius etc★ (*Contes d'Hoffmann*); PERGOLESI: Uberto (*Serva padrona*); PUCCINI: Sharpless★ (*Butterfly*), Scarpia★ (*Tosca*); ROSSINI: Figaro & Don Basilio★ (*Barbiere di Siviglia*), Guillaume Tell, Conte Asdrubal★ (*Pietra del paragone*); STRAUSS, R: Jochanaan★ (*Salome*); STRAVINSKY: Nick Shadow (*Rake's Progress*); TCHAIKOVSKY: Eugene Onegin, Yeletsky★ (*Pique Dame*); VERDI: Amonasro★ & Ramfis (*Aida*), Renato★ (*Ballo in maschera*), Rodrigo★ (*Don Carlo*), Ford★ (*Falstaff*), Nabucco, Iago★ (*Otello*), Germont (*Traviata*); WAGNER: Holländer, Telramund★ (*Lohengrin*), Hans Sachs & Pogner (*Meistersinger*), Amfortas★ (*Parsifal*), Wotan★ (*Rheingold*), Wanderer★ (*Siegfried*), Gunther★(*Götterdämmerung*), Wolfram (*Tannhäuser*), Kurwenal★(*Tristan und Isolde*). **World premieres:** BLOMDAHL: Mimarobe (*Aniara*) 1959; WERLE: Julien (*Dream of Thérèse*) 1964; BERWALD: S Phar (*Drottningen av Golconda*) 1968; all at Royal Opera, Stockholm. Recorded for: Columbia. Video/Film: (*Zauberflöte*). Gives recitals. Appears with symphony orchestra. Teaches voice. Coaches repertoire. On faculty of Royal Acad of Music, Stockholm. **Res:** Stockholm, Sweden. Mgmt: KBL/SWE.

SALDARI, LUCIANO. Lyric tenor. Italian. Born 9 Dec 1934, Ascoli Piceno, Italy. Wife Maria Luisa Vicinelli. One son. Studied: Consv G B Martini, Mo Antonio Melandri, Bologna. **Debut:** Duca (*Rigoletto*) Teatro Sperimentale, Spoleto 1957. Awards: Viotti Gold Medal, Vercelli; Verdi Gold Medal, Parma; Palcoscenico d'oro and Rigoletto d'oro, Mantua; Targa d'oro, Brescia; Gold Medal, City of Correggio. **Sang with major companies in** AUS: Vienna Staatsoper; BEL: Brussels; BUL: Sofia; CZE: Prague Smetana; FRA: Bordeaux, Marseille, Nancy, Nice, Orange Fest, Paris, Rouen, Toulouse; GRE: Athens National; FR GER: Berlin Deutsche Oper, Cologne, Essen, Nürnberg, Wiesbaden; HOL: Amsterdam; HUN: Budapest; ITA: Bologna, Florence Comunale, Genoa, Milan La Scala, Naples, Palermo, Parma, Trieste, Turin, Venice; ROM: Bucharest; S AFR: Johannesburg; SPA: Barcelona; SWI: Geneva, Zurich; USA: Seattle; YUG: Dubrovnik, Belgrade. **Roles with these companies incl** BELLINI: Gualtiero (*Pirata*), Lord Arthur★ (*Puritani*), Elvino (*Sonnambula*), Arturo (*Straniera*); BOITO: Faust (*Mefistofele*); DONIZETTI: Nemorino (*Elisir*), Fernand (*Favorite*), Edgardo★ (*Lucia*), Gennaro★ (*Lucrezia Borgia*); GOUNOD: Faust; MASCAGNI: Fritz (*Amico Fritz*); MASSENET: Des Grieux (*Manon*); PUCCINI: Rodolfo (*Bohème*), Pinkerton★ (*Butterfly*), Ruggero (*Rondine*); STRAVINSKY: Vasili (*Mavra*); VERDI: Duca di Mantova★ (*Rigoletto*), Alfredo★ (*Traviata*), Manrico (*Trovatore*). **Res:** V Priv Chiappa 17, Pieve Ligure, Italy. Mgmt: EUM/FRG.

SALEMKA, IRENE. Lyric soprano. Canadian. Born 3 Oct 1931, Steinbach, Man, Canada. Divorced. Studied: Mo Ernesto Barbini, Dr Herman Geiger-Torel, Toronto; Hans Löwlein, Frank-

furt/M. **Debut:** Juliette (*Roméo et Juliette*) Montreal Opera 1955. Previous occupations: secy. Awards: Hon DL, Univ of Sask, Regina, Canada 1972.

Sang with major companies in AUS: Vienna Volksoper; CAN: Montreal/Quebec, Toronto, Vancouver; FR GER: Bonn, Cologne, Essen, Frankfurt, Hannover, Munich Staatsoper, Stuttgart, Wuppertal; HOL: Amsterdam; SWI: Basel; UK: Edinburgh Festival, London Royal; USA: New Orleans, Washington DC. **Roles with these companies incl** BIZET: Micaëla (*Carmen*); BRITTEN: Helena★ (*Midsummer Night*); CHARPENTIER: Louise; GOUNOD: Marguerite (*Faust*), Juliette; HANDEL: Cleopatra (*Giulio Cesare*); MENOTTI: Monica (*Medium*); MOZART: Donna Elvira (*Don Giovanni*), Susanna (*Nozze di Figaro*), Pamina★ (*Zauberflöte*); OFFENBACH: Olympia & Antonia★ & Giulietta★ (*Contes d'Hoffmann*); PUCCINI: Mimi★ (*Bohème*), Lauretta (*Gianni Schicchi*), Cio-Cio-San (*Butterfly*), Liù★ (*Turandot*); RAMEAU: Minerva (*Castor et Pollux*); RAVEL: Concepcion (*Heure espagnole*); STRAUSS, R: Sophie (*Rosenkavalier*); VERDI: Violetta (*Traviata*). Recorded for: DG. Video—BBC TV: Marguerite (*Faust*); CBC TV: Monica (*Medium*). Gives recitals. Appears with symphony orchestra. **Res:** Albert Einsteinstr 30, Göttingen, FR Ger; 1364 Argyle St, Regina, Sask, Canada. Mgmt: HOM/FRG.

SALMINEN, MATTI KALERVO. Bass. Finnish. Resident mem: Städtische Bühnen, Cologne; Opernhaus Zurich. Born 7 Jul 1945, Turku, Finland. Wife Leena Grönroos. One child. **Debut:** Philip II (*Don Carlo*) National Opera, Helsinki 1969.

Sang with major companies in FIN: Helsinki; FRA: Nancy; FR GER: Cologne, Düsseldorf-Duisburg, Hamburg, Munich Staatsoper, Nürnberg, Stuttgart; HOL: Amsterdam; HUN: Budapest; SWE: Stockholm; SWI: Zurich; UK: London Royal. **Roles with these companies incl** BEETHOVEN: Rocco★ (*Fidelio*); GLINKA: Ivan★ (*Life for the Tsar*); MOZART: Publio★ (*Clemenza di Tito*), Sarastro★ (*Zauberflöte*); MUSSORGSKY: Pimen (*Boris Godunov*); PUCCINI: Colline★ (*Bohème*); ROSSINI: Don Basilio (*Barbiere di Siviglia*); VERDI: Ramfis★ (*Aida*), Philip II★ & Grande Inquisitore★ (*Don Carlo*), Padre Guardiano (*Forza del destino*); WAGNER: Daland★(*Fliegende Holländer*), König Heinrich★(*Lohengrin*), Pogner★ (*Meistersinger*), Fasolt★ & Fafner★ (*Rheingold*), Fafner★ (*Siegfried*), Hunding★ (*Walküre*), Landgraf★ (*Tannhäuser*), König Marke★ (*Tristan und Isolde*). **World premieres:** SALLINEN: Ratsumies, Savonlinna Opera Fest 1975. Recorded for: Don-Pinto, RCA. Gives recitals. Appears with symphony orchestra. **Res:** Hermann-Lönsstr 17, Cologne, FR Ger. Mgmt: SLZ/FRG; IWL/UK.

SALTA, ANITA MARIA. Spinto. American. Resident mem: Stadttheater, Essen. Born 1 Sep 1937, New York. Single. Studied: Mo Menotti Salta, New York. **Debut:** Aida, Jacksonville, FL, USA 1959. Previous occupations: secy at CBS, New York and California.

Sang with major companies in FRA: Marseille; FR GER: Dortmund, Essen, Hannover, Kassel,

Kiel, Krefeld, Nürnberg, Stuttgart, Wuppertal. **Roles with these companies incl** BERLIOZ: Didon★ (*Troyens*); BIZET: Micaëla (*Carmen*); EGK: Cathleen★(*Irische Legende*); GIORDANO: Maddalena (*Andrea Chénier*); GLINKA: Antonida★ (*Life for the Tsar*); GLUCK: Alceste, Iphigénie (*Iphigénie en Tauride*); GOUNOD: Marguerite (*Faust*); JANACEK: Katya Kabanova; LEONCAVALLO: Nedda (*Pagliacci*); MASCAGNI: Santuzza (*Cavalleria rusticana*); MOZART: Fiordiligi (*Così fan tutte*), Donna Elvira (*Don Giovanni*), Elettra (*Idomeneo*), Contessa★ (*Nozze di Figaro*); MUSSORGSKY: Marina (*Boris Godunov*); OFFENBACH: Giulietta (*Contes d'Hoffmann*); ORFF: Solo (*Carmina burana*); PUCCINI: Mimi (*Bohème*), Cio-Cio-San (*Butterfly*), Manon Lescaut, Tosca★; ROSSINI: Mathilde (*Guillaume Tell*); SHOSTAKOVICH: Katerina★ (*Katerina Ismailova*); SMETANA: Marie (*Bartered Bride*); STRAUSS, J: Rosalinde★ (*Fledermaus*); STRAUSS, R: Ariadne (*Ariadne auf Naxos*), Chrysothemis (*Elektra*), Marschallin★ (*Rosenkavalier*); TCHAIKOVSKY: Tatiana (*Eugene Onegin*); VERDI: Aida★, Odabella (*Attila*), Amelia★ (*Ballo in maschera*), Elisabetta★ (*Don Carlo*), Alice Ford★ (*Falstaff*), Leonora (*Forza del destino*), Desdemona (*Otello*), Gilda (*Rigoletto*), Amelia (*Simon Boccanegra*), Violetta (*Traviata*), Leonora (*Trovatore*), Elena★ (*Vespri*); WAGNER: Elsa★ (*Lohengrin*), Eva (*Meistersinger*), Elisabeth (*Tannhäuser*); WEBER: Agathe (*Freischütz*). Also BIZET: Carmen; EGK: Isabella (*Columbus*). **Res:** Lindenallee 79, Essen, FR Ger. **Mgmt:** PAS/FRG.

SALTER, RICHARD. Lyric baritone. British. **Resident mem:** Hessisches Staatstheater, Darmstadt. Born 12 Nov 1943, Hindhead, Surrey, UK. Wife Deirdre, occupation teacher. Studied: Royal Coll of Music, London; Akad für Musik, Vienna; Prof Christian Moeller, Prof Ilse Rapf, Kmsg Anton Dermota; Mo E Campogalliani, Mantua. **Debut:** Krusina (*Bartered Bride*) Darmstadt Opera 1971. Awards: Richard Tauber Memorial Schlshp, Anglo-Austrian Music Socy, London 1968. **Sang with major companies in FR GER:** Darmstadt, Frankfurt. **Roles with these companies incl** CIMAROSA: Count Robinson★ (*Matrimonio segreto*); MOZART: Guglielmo★ (*Così fan tutte*), Papageno★ (*Zauberflöte*); PUCCINI: Marcello★ (*Bohème*); ROSSINI: Figaro★ (*Barbiere di Siviglia*); STRAVINSKY: Empereur de Chine★ (*Rossignol*); WAGNER: Wolfram★ (*Tannhäuser*); WOLF-FERRARI: Lelio★ (*Donne curiose*). Also MATTHUS: Fletcher★ (*Noch ein Löffel Gift, Liebling*); HENZE: Hauptmann★ (*Bassariden*). Recorded for: Philips. Video/Film: Anderer Mann (*Moses und Aron*). Gives recitals. Appears with symphony orchestra. **Res:** Thylmannweg 9, 61 Darmstadt, FR Ger. **Mgmt:** IBB/UK; ARM/FRG; PAS/FRG; SLZ/FRG.

SALZER, BEEB; né Clarence M Salzer, Jr. Scenic designer for opera, theater, film. Is a lighting dsgn; also a painter. American. Born 8 Jun 1933, Cincinnati, O, USA. Wife Deborah, occupation teacher. Two children. Studied: Yale Univ, School of Drama, Donald Oenslager. Prof training: design studio George Jenkins, New York 1962-67. **Operatic debut:** *Pêcheurs de perles* Manhattan School of

Music, New York 1962. Theater debut: Cincinnati Playhouse, 1956. **Designed for major companies in USA:** Baltimore, Kansas City. **Operas designed for these companies incl** DONIZETTI: *Don Pasquale;* MASSENET: *Thaïs, Werther;* MENOTTI: *Saint of Bleecker Street★;* PUCCINI: *Butterfly★, Rondine.* **Operatic world premieres:** FLAGELLO: *Judgment of St Francis* Manhattan School of Music, New York 1966. Exhibitions of stage designs, paintings Van Bovenkamp Gal, NY 1964-65; Santiago, Chile 1958; Panama 1959; Tucson 1958; Cincinnati 1956; Rye, NY 1974; Contemp Scene Design, Lincoln Center Library & Museum 1975; Museum of Contemp Crafts, New York 1965. Teaches at Lehman Coll, City Univ of New York. **Res:** 25 Hawthorne Ave, Port Chester, NY, USA.

SAMAR, PARI. Lyric mezzo-soprano. Iranian. Resident mem: Städtische Oper, Frankfurt; Oper am Gärtnerplatz, Munich. Born 28 Dec 1937, Teheran, Iran. Husband Dr A A Aryanpour Kachani, occupation repres of Iranian Ministry of Culture in Frankfurt. One child. Studied: Vocal Acad in Vienna, Mrs Ilse Rapf, Kristien Möller, Erik Werba, Vienna. **Debut:** Isolier (*Comte Ory*) Vienna Volksoper 1964. Previous occupations: ballet and dance. **Sang with major companies in AUS:** Vienna Volksoper; FR GER: Cologne, Darmstadt, Essen, Frankfurt, Hamburg, Karlsruhe, Kassel, Munich Staatsoper & Gärtnerplatz. **Roles with these companies incl** BERLIOZ: Marguerite (*Damnation de Faust*); BIZET: Carmen★; BORODIN: Kontchakovna (*Prince Igor*); DVORAK: Jezibaba★ (*Rusalka*); FLOTOW: Nancy (*Martha*); HUMPERDINCK: Hänsel★; MOZART: Dorabella★ (*Così fan tutte*), Cherubino★ (*Nozze di Figaro*); MUSSORGSKY: Marina★ (*Boris Godunov*); OFFENBACH: Giulietta★ (*Contes d'Hoffmann*); PUCCINI: Suzuki (*Butterfly*); ROSSINI: Rosina★ (*Barbiere di Siviglia*), Angelina★ (*Cenerentola*), Isolier (*Comte Ory*), Isabella★ (*Italiana in Algeri*); VERDI: Eboli★ (*Don Carlo*), Preziosilla★ (*Forza del destino*). Also OFFENBACH: Nicklausse★ (*Contes d'Hoffmann*); JANACEK: Barbara★ (*Katya Kabanova*). Gives recitals. **Res:** Inheidenerstr 71, 6 Frankfurt/Main, FR Ger.

SAMARITANI, PIERLUIGI. Scenic and costume designer for opera, theater, film. Is a lighting designer; also a painter. Italian. Born 29 Sep 1942, Novara, Italy. Single. **Operatic debut:** sets & cost, *Manfred* Teatro dell'Opera, Rome 1964. Theater debut: Th du Gymnase, Paris 1962.

Designed for major companies in FRA: Marseille, Paris; FR GER: Hamburg, Munich Gärtnerplatz; ITA: Bologna, Florence Maggio, Milan La Scala, Naples, Palermo, Rome Opera, Spoleto Fest, Trieste, Turin, Venice; SWI: Geneva; USA: Chicago. **Operas designed for these companies incl** BIZET: *Carmen★;* DONIZETTI: *Don Pasquale★, Lucia★, Maria di Rohan★;* FALLA: *Retablo de Maese Pedro★;* GLUCK: *Orfeo ed Euridice★;* MASSENET: *Don Quichotte★;* MENOTTI: *Amahl★, Globolinks★, Maria Golovin★, Medium★;* MONTEVERDI: *Favola d'Orfeo;* MOZART: *Clemenza di Tito;* OFFENBACH: *Contes d'Hoffmann★;* POULENC: *Dialogues des Carmélites★;* PUCCINI: *Bohème★,*

Gianni Schicchi, *Suor Angelica*, *Tabarro*; ROSSINI: *Moïse*, *Semiramide;* SPONTINI: *Vestale;* TCHAIKOVSKY: *Eugene Onegin*; VERDI: *Giovanna d'Arco*, *Otello*; WAGNER: *Tristan und Isolde*. Operatic Video/Film – RAI: MONTEVERDI: *Orfeo*. Exhibitions of stage designs, Spoleto Fest 1972. **Res:** V Nicola Fabrizi 11/A, Rome, Italy.

SAMUELSEN, ROY. Bass-baritone. American. Born 12 Jun 1933, Moss, Norway. Wife Mary Lou, occupation PS teacher. Three children. Studied: Josef Heuler, Würzburg, Germany; Brigham Young Univ, John Halliday, Provo, UT; Indiana Univ, Paul Matthew, Carl van Buskirk, Bloomington, USA. Previous occupations: sheet metal worker. Awards: Lotte Lehmann Awd, Music Acad of the West, Santa Barbara, CA; Met Op Ntl Counc Aud Finalist.
Sang with major companies in NOR: Oslo; USA: Chicago, Kansas City, Kentucky, Memphis. **Roles with these companies incl** BEETHOVEN: Don Pizarro (*Fidelio*); BIZET: Escamillo (*Carmen*); BORODIN: Galitzky (*Prince Igor*); BRITTEN: Captain Balstrode (*Peter Grimes*); BUSONI: Doktor Faust*; DONIZETTI: Dott Malatesta (*Don Pasquale*), Enrico (*Lucia*); FLOTOW: Plunkett (*Martha*); GIORDANO: Carlo Gérard (*Andrea Chénier*); GOUNOD: Méphistophélès* (*Faust*); LEONCAVALLO: Tonio (*Pagliacci*); MOZART: Don Giovanni*, Conte Almaviva* (*Nozze di Figaro*), Sarastro (*Zauberflöte*); MUSSORGSKY: Boris Godunov, Tcherevik (*Fair at Sorochinsk*); NICOLAI: Falstaff & Fluth (*Lustigen Weiber*); OFFENBACH: Coppélius, etc (*Contes d'Hoffmann*); PUCCINI: Colline* & Marcello (*Bohème*), Jack Rance (*Fanciulla del West*), Michele* (*Tabarro*), Scarpia* (*Tosca*); ROSSINI: Figaro (*Barbiere di Siviglia*); STRAUSS, R: Mandryka (*Arabella*), Jochanaan* (*Salome*); STRAVINSKY: Creon (*Oedipus Rex*); TCHAIKOVSKY: Yeletsky (*Pique Dame*); VERDI: Amonasro* & Ramfis (*Aida*), Renato (*Ballo in maschera*), Grande Inquisitore* (*Don Carlo*), Falstaff*, Don Carlo (*Forza del destino*), Macbeth, Rigoletto, Simon Boccanegra, Germont (*Traviata*), Conte di Luna (*Trovatore*); WAGNER: Holländer, Hans Sachs (*Meistersinger*), Amfortas & Gurnemanz* (*Parsifal*), Wotan (*Walküre*), Wolfram (*Tannhäuser*); WEBER: Kaspar (*Freischütz*). Also DONIZETTI: Raimondo* (*Lucia*); PUCCINI: Timur* (*Turandot*); BORODIN: Kontchak (*Prince Igor*); MOZART: Sprecher (*Zauberflöte*). **World premieres:** HEIDEN: Lazarus (*Darkened City*) Indiana Univ Opera 1963; KAUFMANN: Wm Connor (*Hoosier Tale*) Indiana Univ Opera, Bloomington 1966. Gives recitals. Appears with symphony orchestra. Teaches voice. Coaches repertoire. On faculty of Indiana Univ, Prof of Music, Bloomington. **Res:** 2012 Montclair Ave, Bloomington, IN, USA. Mgmt: SMN/FRG.

SANDNER, ARWED ERNST. Bass-baritone & basso-buffo. German. Resident mem: Opernhaus Zurich; Volksoper, Vienna. Born 20 Jul 1929, Königsberg. Wife Rita, occupation secy. Four children. Studied: Michael Bohnen, Harry Gottschalk, Berlin; Emma Wolf-Dengel, Karlsruhe. **Debut:** Zweiter Geharnischter (*Zauberflöte*) Komische

Oper Berlin 1954. Previous occupations: textile merchant.
Sang with major companies in AUS: Vienna Volksoper; BEL: Brussels; FRA: Lyon, Nancy, Nice, Paris, Rouen, Toulouse; FR GER: Cologne, Düsseldorf-Duisburg, Essen, Hannover, Karlsruhe, Stuttgart; GER DR: Berlin Komische Oper; ITA: Turin; SPA: Barcelona; SWI: Zurich; USSR: Moscow Stanislavski. **Roles with these companies incl** ADAM: Bijou (*Postillon de Lonjumeau*); d'ALBERT: Tommaso (*Tiefland*); BEETHOVEN: Rocco* (*Fidelio*); BERG: Doktor (*Wozzeck*); CIMAROSA: Geronimo (*Matrimonio segreto*); DONIZETTI: Don Pasquale*, Dulcamara (*Elisir*), Enrico (*Lucia*); FLOTOW: Plunkett (*Martha*); GAY/Britten: Mr Peachum (*Beggar's Opera*); GLUCK: Hercules (*Alceste*); GOUNOD: Méphistophélès (*Faust*); HANDEL: Giulio Cesare; LORTZING: Stadinger (*Waffenschmied*), Baculus* (*Wildschütz*), Van Bett (*Zar und Zimmermann*); MOZART: Don Alfonso (*Così fan tutte*), Leporello (*Don Giovanni*), Osmin* (*Entführung aus dem Serail*), Figaro (*Nozze di Figaro*), Sarastro (*Zauberflöte*); MUSSORGSKY: Boris & Pimen (*Boris Godunov*); NICOLAI: Falstaff* (*Lustigen Weiber*); OFFENBACH: Don Andres* (*Périchole*); ORFF: König (*Kluge*); PUCCINI: Colline (*Bohème*); ROSSINI: Dott Bartolo & Don Basilio (*Barbiere di Siviglia*), Mustafà (*Italiana in Algeri*); SMETANA: Kezal (*Bartered Bride*); STRAUSS, R: Orest (*Elektra*), Sir Morosus (*Schweigsame Frau*); VERDI: Ramfis (*Aida*), Philip II (*Don Carlo*), Fra Melitone & Padre Guardiano (*Forza del destino*); WAGNER: Daland (*Fliegende Holländer*), Beckmesser* (*Meistersinger*), Alberich (*Rheingold*, *Götterdämmerung*)); WEBER: Kaspar* (*Freischütz*); WOLF: Juan Lopez (*Corregidor*); WOLF-FERRARI: Ottavio (*Donne curiose*). Also WAGNER: Alberich (*Siegfried*), Klingsor (*Parsifal*); HUMPERDINCK: Peter (*Hänsel und Gretel*); KLEBE: Pedrillo (*Figaro lässt sich scheiden*); MARTIN: Caliban (*Sturm*); WOLF-FERRARI: Don Alvaro (*Vedova scaltra*); PUCCINI: Sacristan (*Tosca*). **World premieres:** KLEBE: Jimmy Farell (*Wahrer Held*) Opernhaus Zurich 1975. Gives recitals. Appears with symphony orchestra. **Res:** Maurstr 46, CH 8117 Zurich-Fällanden, Switzerland. Mgmt: SLZ/FRG; PAS/FRG; VLD/AUS.

SANDOR, JOHN CARSON. Lyric tenor. American. Born 27 Mar 1946, Fairmont, WV, USA. Wife Carole. Studied: Oberlin Coll, Richard Miller, O, USA; Juilliard School of Music, Hans Heinz; Manhattan School of Music, Ellen Faull, New York. **Debut:** Rinuccio (*Gianni Schicchi*) Metropolitan Opera Studio 1971. Previous occupations: Dir of Music, East Orange HS, NJ. Awards: Ntl Opera Inst Grant; Inst of Intl Education stipd; Sullivan Fndt Grant; Winner Viotti Compt, Vercelli; opera schlshps in coll.
Sang with major companies in FRA: Paris; SPA: Barcelona; USA: Hartford Connecticut Op, Lake George, Miami, Newark, New Orleans, Philadelphia Lyric, San Francisco Spring, Santa Fe, Washington DC. **Roles with these companies incl** BELLINI: Elvino* (*Sonnambula*); DONIZETTI: Riccardo* (*Anna Bolena*), Gerardo (*Caterina Cornaro*), Ernesto* (*Don Pasquale*), Edgardo*

(*Lucia*), Leicester (*Maria Stuarda*); HENZE: Des Grieux⋆ (*Boulevard Solitude*); PUCCINI: Rinuccio⋆ (*Gianni Schicchi*); SMETANA: Lukas⋆ (*The Kiss*). Recorded for: Philips. Gives recitals. Appears with symphony orchestra. **Res:** 64 Bon Ave Circle, Suffern, NY, USA. Mgmt: CAM/USA; CAB/SPA.

SANDOZ, MAY. Dram coloratura soprano. Swiss. Resident mem: Bühnen der Stadt Köln, Cologne. Born 25 Jun, Lucerne, Switzerland. Divorced. Studied: Musik-Akad, Paul Sandoz (father) Basel, Switzerland. **Debut:** Königin der Nacht (*Zauberflöte*) Interlaken, Switzerland 1963. Previous occupations: medical secy. Awards: Medal, Conc Intl d'Interprétation Musicale, Geneva.
  Sang with major companies in AUS: Vienna Staatsoper; FR GER: Berlin Deutsche Oper, Cologne, Dortmund, Düsseldorf-Duisburg, Essen, Frankfurt, Hannover, Karlsruhe, Mannheim, Munich Staatsoper, Nürnberg, Stuttgart, Wiesbaden, Wuppertal; SWI: Basel. **Roles with these companies incl** ADAM: Madeleine (*Postillon de Lonjumeau*); DONIZETTI: Norina⋆ (*Don Pasquale*), Lucia⋆, Lucrezia Borgia⋆; FLOTOW: Lady Harriet⋆ (*Martha*); FORTNER: Mary Stuart⋆ (*Elisabeth Tudor*); LORTZING: Baronin Freimann⋆ (*Wildschütz*); MOZART: Fiordiligi⋆ (*Così fan tutte*), Konstanze⋆ (*Entführung aus dem Serail*), Ilia⋆ (*Idomeneo*), Contessa⋆ (*Nozze di Figaro*), Pamina & Königin der Nacht (*Zauberflöte*); NICOLAI: Frau Fluth⋆ (*Lustigen Weiber*); ORFF: Solo⋆ (*Carmina burana*); PUCCINI: Musetta⋆ (*Bohème*); ROSSINI: Rosina⋆ (*Barbiere di Siviglia*); STRAUSS, J: Rosalinde (*Fledermaus*); VERDI: Oscar⋆ (*Ballo in maschera*), Alice Ford (*Falstaff*), Gilda⋆ (*Rigoletto*), Violetta⋆ (*Traviata*), Leonora (*Trovatore*). Gives recitals. Appears with symphony orchestra. **Res:** Belvederestr 60, 5 Cologne 41, FR Ger. Mgmt: SLZ/FRG; PAS/FRG; SMD/FRG; ARM/FRG; TAS/AUS.

SANJUST, FILIPPO. Scenic & costume designer and stage director for opera & theater. Is a lighting designer; also a choreographer. Italian. Born Italy. Studied: Princeton Univ, USA.
  Designed and staged opera for major companies in AUS: Salzburg Fest, Vienna Staatsoper; BEL: Brussels; FR GER: Berlin Deutsche Oper, Frankfurt, Hamburg; HOL: Amsterdam; ITA: Florence Maggio & Comunale, Naples, Rome Opera; UK: London Royal & English Ntl. **Operas designed for these cos incl** BERG: *Lulu;* CAVALLI: *Erismena†;* CIMAROSA: *Matrimonio segreto;* DEBUSSY: *Pelléas et Mélisande†;* GLUCK: *Iphigénie en Tauride, Orfeo ed Euridice†;* HENZE: *Bassariden, Junge Lord;* LEONCAVALLO: *Pagliacci;* MASCAGNI: *Cavalleria rusticana;* MONTEVERDI: *Incoronazione di Poppea†;* MOZART: *Idomeneo†, Zauberflöte†;* NABOKOV: *Love's Labour's Lost;* PUCCINI: *Manon Lescaut, Tosca;* ROSSINI: *Barbiere di Siviglia, Cenerentola†;* STRAUSS, R: *Ariadne auf Naxos, Rosenkavalier;* TCHAIKOVSKY: *Eugene Onegin;* VERDI: *Aida†, Don Carlo, Falstaff, Nabucco†, Rigoletto, Trovatore;* WAGNER: *Lohengrin†, Parsifal†;* et al. Also designed and staged HANDEL: *Semele*. **Operatic world premieres:** designed HENZE: *Bassariden* Salzburg Fest 1966; BURKHARD: *Ein Stern geht auf aus Jakob* Staatsoper Hamburg 1970.

SANTELLI, GIOVANNA. Lyric coloratura soprano. Italian. Born 23 Aug 1937, Florence. Single. Studied: Consv L Cherubini, Mo Cremesini, Florence. **Debut:** Zerlina (*Fra Diavolo*) Teatro Nuovo, Milan 1961.
  Sang with major companies in BEL: Brussels; FIN: Helsinki; FRA: Toulouse; FR GER: Bielefeld, Cologne, Düsseldorf-Duisburg, Essen, Frankfurt, Hamburg, Wiesbaden; HOL: Amsterdam; ITA: Florence Maggio & Comunale, Milan La Scala, Palermo, Turin; POR: Lisbon. **Roles with these companies incl** AUBER: Zerlina; BELLINI: Amina (*Sonnambula*); BIZET: Micaëla⋆ (*Carmen*); CIMAROSA: Carolina (*Matrimonio segreto*); DONIZETTI: Norina (*Don Pasquale*), Adina (*Elisir*); GIORDANO: Olga (*Fedora*); MASCAGNI: Suzel⋆ (*Amico Fritz*); PUCCINI: Musetta⋆ (*Bohème*), Lauretta (*Gianni Schicchi*); ROSSINI: Rosina⋆ (*Barbiere di Siviglia*), Fanny (*Cambiale di matrimonio*); VERDI: Oscar⋆ (*Ballo in maschera*), Nannetta (*Falstaff*), Gilda (*Rigoletto*), Violetta (*Traviata*); WOLF-FERRARI: Susanna (*Segreto di Susanna*); ZANDONAI: Francesca da Rimini. Also GASPARINI: Ofelia (*Amleto*); CIMAROSA: Eugenia & Gismonda (*Marito disperato*). Film: Musetta (*Bohème*).

SANTI, NELLO. Conductor of opera. Italian. Born 1931, Adria, Italy. Married. Studied: Music Consv, Venice; Mo Coltro; incl piano. **Operatic debut:** *Rigoletto* Opera House, Padua 1951.
  Conducted with major companies in AUS: Salzburg Fest, Vienna Staatsoper & Volksoper; FRA: Lyon, Marseille, Paris; FR GER: Berlin Deutsche Oper, Cologne, Düsseldorf-Duisburg, Hamburg, Munich Staatsoper; ITA: Bologna, Florence Maggio & Comunale, Milan La Scala, Parma, Venice, Verona Arena; POR: Lisbon; SWI: Geneva, Zurich; UK: London Royal; USA: New York Met, Philadelphia Lyric; et al. **Operas with these companies incl** BELLINI: *Norma, Puritani;* BIZET: *Carmen;* BOITO: *Mefistofele;* BORODIN: *Prince Igor;* DONIZETTI: *Lucia, Maria Stuarda;* GIORDANO: *Andrea Chénier;* LEONCAVALLO: *Pagliacci†;* MASCAGNI: *Cavalleria rusticana;* PONCHIELLI: *Gioconda;* PUCCINI: *Bohème, Fanciulla del West, Gianni Schicchi, Butterfly, Manon Lescaut, Tosca, Turandot;* VERDI: *Aida, Ballo in maschera, Don Carlo, Ernani, Forza del destino, Macbeth, Otello, Simon Boccanegra, Traviata, Trovatore, Vespri;* WAGNER: *Fliegende Holländer, Lohengrin, Meistersinger, Parsifal, Tannhäuser, Tristan und Isolde;* et al. Recorded for RCA.

SANTUNIONE, ORIANNA. Dramatic soprano. Italian. Born 1 Sep 1934, Sassuolo/Modena, Italy. Single. Studied: Ma Carmen Melis, Mo Renato Pastorino, Milan. **Debut:** Fedora, As Li Co, Italy 1960. Awards: Golden Nut, Lecce; Golden Plaque, Brescia and Sassuolo; Gold Medal, Modena; Giulietta Prjze, Verona 1975.
  Sang with major companies in FRA: Nice, Paris, Rouen; FR GER: Hamburg, Munich Staatsoper; HOL: Amsterdam; HUN: Budapest; ITA: Bologna, Florence Maggio & Comunale, Genoa, Milan La Scala, Naples, Palermo, Parma, Rome Teatro dell'Opera, Trieste, Turin, Venice, Verona Arena; SPA: Barcelona Liceo; UK: London Royal; USA: Cincinnati, Dallas, Philadelphia Lyric. **Roles with these companies incl** CHERU-

BINI: Medea★‡; GIORDANO: Maddalena★ (*Andrea Chénier*), Fedora★; LEONCAVALLO: Nedda★ (*Pagliacci*); MASCAGNI: Santuzza★ (*Cavalleria rusticana*); PONCHIELLI: Gioconda★; PUCCINI: Mimi★ (*Bohème*), Minnie★ (*Fanciulla del West*), Cio-Cio-San (*Butterfly*), Manon Lescaut★, Tosca★; ROSSINI: Mathilde★ (*Guillaume Tell*); VERDI: Aida★, Amelia (*Ballo in maschera*)★, Elisabetta★ (*Don Carlo*), Donna Elvira★ (*Ernani*), Leonora★ (*Forza del destino*), Desdemona★ (*Otello*), Amelia★ (*Simon Boccanegra*), Leonora★ (*Trovatore*); WAGNER: Ortrud★ (*Lohengrin*); ZANDONAI: Francesca da Rimini★. Also GIORDANO: Madame Sans-Gêne; GHEDINI: sop role (*Baccanti*). Video—RAI: Desdemona (*Otello*); Elsa (*Lohengrin*). **Res**: V Stoppani 33, Milan, Italy. **Mgmt**: GOR/UK.

SANZOGNO, NINO. Conductor of opera and symphony; composer. Italian. Born 13 Apr 1911, Venice. Studied: Gian Francesco Malipiero & Hermann Scherchen; also violin.
Conducted with major companies in ARG: Buenos Aires; AUS: Bregenz Fest; ITA: Florence Comunale, Milan La Scala, Naples, Palermo, Rome Opera, Turin, Venice, Verona Arena; SWI: Geneva; UK: Edinburgh Fest; USA: Chicago, New York Met, San Francisco Opera; et al. **Operas with these companies incl** BELLINI: *Norma, Sonnambula, Straniera;* BERG: *Lulu, Wozzeck;* CATALANI: *Wally;* DALLAPICCOLA: *Prigioniero;* DONIZETTI: *Fille du régiment, Maria Stuarda;* GIORDANO: *Andrea Chénier, Fedora;* HENZE: *Bassariden;* HINDEMITH: *Cardillac, Mathis der Maler;* JANACEK: *Cunning Little Vixen;* LEONCAVALLO: *Pagliacci;* MASCAGNI: *Cavalleria rusticana;* MOZART: *Così fan tutte;* ORFF: *Carmina burana;* PERAGALLO: *Gita in campagna;* PETRASSI: *Morte dell'aria;* PONCHIELLI: *Gioconda;* POULENC: *Dialogues des Carmélites;* PROKOFIEV: *Fiery Angel;* PUCCINI: *Bohème, Fanciulla del West, Gianni Schicchi, Butterfly, Manon Lescaut, Rondine, Suor Angelica, Tabarro, Tosca, Turandot;* ROSSINI: *Barbiere di Siviglia, Cenerentola, Elisabetta Regina, Italiana in Algeri;* SHOSTAKOVICH: *Katerina Ismailova;* VERDI: *Aida, Ballo in maschera, Don Carlo, Ernani, Falstaff, Forza del destino, Luisa Miller, Macbeth, Nabucco, Otello, Rigoletto, Simon Boccanegra, Traviata, Trovatore, Vespri;* WAGNER: *Fliegende Holländer;* WEILL: *Aufstieg und Fall der Stadt Mahagonny;* ZANDONAI: *Francesca da Rimini;* et al. Also RICCI: *Piedigrotta;* MEYERBEER: *Robert le diable;* WALTON: *Troilus and Cressida;* MILHAUD: *David;* SCARLATTI: *Griselda;* PIZZETTI: *Assassinio nella cattedrale;* MALIPIERO: *Sette canzoni, Allegra brigata, Figliuolo prodigo.* **World premieres:** CHAILLY: *Idiota* Teatro dell'Opera, Rome 1970; BARTOLOZZI: *Tutto ciò che accade ti riguarda* Florence 1972; MALIPIERO: *L'Iscariota* 1972, *Uno dei dieci* 1971, both at Siena.

SARABIA, GUILLERMO. Baritone. American. Resident mem: Deutsche Oper am Rhein, Düsseldorf-Duisburg. Born 1937, Mazatlan, Mexico. Studied: Opera Studio/Consv Zurich, Herbert Graf; Dusolina Giannini; Carl Ebert master classes; Pasadena Playhouse, CA. **Debut:** BUSONI: Doktor Faust, Detmold 1965.
Sang with major companies in FR GER: Cologne, Dortmund, Düsseldorf-Duisburg, Kiel, Munich Staatsoper, Stuttgart; USA: New York Met & City Opera, Philadelphia Lyric, Washington DC; et al. **Roles with these companies incl** BEETHOVEN: Don Pizarro (*Fidelio*); BERG: Wozzeck; BIZET: Escamillo (*Carmen*); DONIZETTI: Alfonso d'Este (*Lucrezia Borgia*); GIORDANO: Carlo Gérard (*Andrea Chénier*); LEONCAVALLO: Tonio (*Pagliacci*); MASCAGNI: Alfio (*Cavalleria rusticana*); MOZART: Don Giovanni, Conte Almaviva (*Nozze di Figaro*); OFFENBACH: Coppélius etc (*Contes d'Hoffmann*); PUCCINI: Sharpless (*Butterfly*), Michele (*Tabarro*); RAVEL: Ramiro (*Heure espagnole*); STRAUSS, R: Jochanaan (*Salome*); TCHAIKOVSKY: Yeletsky (*Pique Dame*); VERDI: Amonasro (*Aida*), Don Carlo (*Ernani*), Macbeth, Nabucco, Iago (*Otello*), Rigoletto, Simon Boccanegra, Germont (*Traviata*), Conte di Luna (*Trovatore*); WAGNER: Holländer, Telramund (*Lohengrin*); et al. Also LEVY: Orin (*Mourning Becomes Electra*); MOZART: Sprecher (*Zauberflöte*). Appears with symphony orchestra. **Mgmt:** HUR/USA.

SARDI, IVAN; né Ivan Szepes. Bass. Italian. Resident mem: Deutsche Oper, Berlin. Born 7 Jul 1930, Budapest. Wife Marie Luise, occupation violinist. Two children. Studied: Antonio Melandri, Bologna. **Debut:** Padre Guardiano (*Forza del destino*) Teatro Grande, Brescia 1951.
Sang with major companies in FRA: Toulouse; FR GER: Berlin Deutsche Oper, Hamburg, Munich Staatsoper; GER DR: Berlin Staatsoper; HUN: Budapest; ISR: Tel Aviv; ITA: Bologna, Florence Maggio, Genoa, Milan La Scala, Parma, Trieste; POR: Lisbon; UK: Glyndebourne Fest. **Roles with these companies incl** ADAM: Bijou (*Postillon de Lonjumeau*); d'ALBERT: Tommaso (*Tiefland*); BEETHOVEN: Rocco★ (*Fidelio*); BELLINI: Rodolfo (*Sonnambula*); DEBUSSY: Arkel (*Pelléas et Mélisande*); MOZART: Don Alfonso★ (*Così fan tutte*), Leporello★ (*Don Giovanni*); MUSSORGSKY: Pimen★ (*Boris Godunov*); PONCHIELLI: Alvise (*Gioconda*); PUCCINI: Colline★ (*Bohème*); STRAUSS, R: Orest (*Elektra*); STRAVINSKY: Creon (*Oedipus Rex*); VERDI: Ramfis★ (*Aida*), Padre Guardiano (*Forza del destino*); WAGNER: Landgraf (*Tannhäuser*). Recorded for: DG, Philips. **Res:** Holstweg 25, 1 Berlin 37, FR Ger.

SARDINERO, VINCENZO; né Sardinero-Puerto. Lyric baritone. Spanish. Born 12 Jan 1937, Barcelona. Wife Teresa Soto. Three children. Studied: Mo Vladimiro Badiali, Milan; Consv of Barcelona, Jaime F Puig, Spain. **Debut:** Germont (*Traviata*) Teatro Liceo, Barcelona 1967. Awards: First Prize Vinas, Barcelona; First Prize Verdi Voices, Parma; Schlshp Fundación March & Dipotación de Barcelona; Bellas Artes Awd; var radio cont.
Sang with major companies in FRA: Aix-en-Provence Fest, Bordeaux, Lyon, Nice, Paris; FR GER: Hamburg, Munich Staatsoper; HOL: Amsterdam; HUN: Budapest; ISR: Tel Aviv; ITA: Milan La Scala, Naples, Palermo, Parma, Rome Opera, Turin; MEX: Mexico City; POR: Lisbon;

SPA: Barcelona, Majorca; SWI: Basel; UK: London Royal Opera; USA: Chicago, Hartford, Miami, New York City Opera, Philadelphia Lyric, Pittsburgh. **Roles with these companies incl** BELLINI: Ernesto★ (*Pirata*); BIZET: Escamillo★ (*Carmen*), Zurga★ (*Pêcheurs de perles*); CILEA: Michonnet★ (*A. Lecouvreur*); DONIZETTI: Dott Malatesta★ & Don Pasquale (*Don Pasquale*), Belcore★ (*Elisir*), Alfonse★ (*Favorite*), Enrico★‡ (*Lucia*), Chevreuse★ (*Maria di Rohan*), Nottingham★ (*Roberto Devereux*); FALLA: Don Quixote★ (*Retablo de Maese Pedro*), Tio Sarvaor★ (*Vida breve*); GIORDANO: Carlo Gérard★ (*Andrea Chénier*); GOUNOD: Méphistophélès★ (*Faust*); GRANADOS: Paquiro★ (*Goyescas*); LEONCAVALLO: Tonio★ (*Pagliacci*); MASCAGNI: Alfio★ (*Cavalleria rusticana*); MASSENET: Lescaut★ (*Manon*), Garrido‡ (*Navarraise*), Albert★ (*Werther*); MOZART: Figaro★ (*Nozze di Figaro*); PUCCINI: Marcello‡ (*Bohème*), Sharpless★ (*Butterfly*), Lescaut★‡ (*Manon Lescaut*); ROSSINI: Figaro★ (*Barbiere di Siviglia*); VERDI: Ezio★ (*Attila*), Renato★ (*Ballo in maschera*), Rodrigo★ (*Don Carlo*), Ford★ (*Falstaff*), Don Carlo★ (*Forza del destino*), Barone★‡ (*Giorno di regno*), Germont★ (*Traviata*), Conte di Luna★ (*Trovatore*). Recorded for: Philips, Angel, CBS, RCA. Gives recitals. Appears with symphony orchestra. Teaches voice. **Res:** Ave Infanta Carlota, Barcelona, Spain.

SARGANT, JAMES EDMUND. British. Tech Adm, English National Opera, The Coliseum, St Martin's Lane, London, UK. In charge of tech matters. Additional administrative positions: Tech Consultant, Barbican Arts Centre, Royal Shakespeare Co, Stratford-upon-Avon, UK. Born 24 Aug 1935, London. Divorced. Studied: economics and law at Trinity Coll, Cambridge, UK. Previous positions primarily administrative & theatrical: Stage Mng/Dir & Staff Prod, Sadler's Wells, London 1958-61; Design & Graphics Adm, ABC TV London 1961-64; Prod Controller, Madame Tussaud's, London 1966-71; Prod Controller, Royal Shakespeare Co, London & Stratford-upon-Avon 1971-74; Mng Dir, Theatre Projects Services, London 1974-75. In present position since 1975. Awards: Hon Mem, Guildhall School of Music and Drama, London. **Res:** London, UK.

SARROCA, SUZANNE; née Negre-Sarroca. Lyric soprano. French. Born 21 Apr 1927, Carcassonne/Aude, France. Widowed. Husband Louis, occupation antiquarian & prof of opera (deceased). One child. Studied: Consv de Toulouse, Louis Negre; Claude Jean, Jeanine Reiss. **Debut:** Tosca, Opéra Comique, Paris 1949-50. Awards: First Prize Consv of Toulouse; Chevalier des Arts et Lettres.
Sang with major companies in ARG: Buenos Aires; AUS: Salzburg Fest, Vienna Staatsoper; BEL: Brussels; BRA: Rio de Janeiro; CAN: Montreal/Quebec; FRA: Bordeaux, Lyon, Marseille, Nancy, Nice, Orange Fest, Paris, Rouen, Strasbourg, Toulouse; FR GER: Hamburg; ITA: Florence Maggio, Rome Caracalla; MON: Monte Carlo; POR: Lisbon; SWI: Geneva; UK: London Royal; USA: New York City Opera. **Roles with these companies incl** BECAUD: Maureen (*Opéra d'Aran*); BEETHOVEN: Leonore (*Fidelio*); BERLIOZ: Marguerite (*Damnation de Faust*), Didon

& Cassandre (*Troyens*); BIZET: Carmen; CAVALIERI: Deidamia★ (*Rappresentazione*); CHARPENTIER: Louise★; CILEA: Adriana Lecouvreur★; GIORDANO: Maddalena (*Andrea Chénier*); GLUCK: Iphigénie (*Iphigénie en Aulide*), Euridice; JANACEK: Emilia Marty (*Makropoulos Affair*); MASCAGNI: Santuzza (*Cavalleria rusticana*); MASSENET: Salomé (*Hérodiade*), Sophie (*Werther*); MENOTTI: Maria Golovin★; MOZART: Donna Anna (*Don Giovanni*), Contessa★ (*Nozze di Figaro*); MUSSORGSKY: Marina (*Boris Godunov*); OFFENBACH: Giulietta★ (*Contes d'Hoffmann*); POULENC: Blanche★ & Mme Lidoine (*Dialogues des Carmélites*); PUCCINI: Mimi & Musetta★ (*Bohème*), Manon Lescaut, Giorgetta (*Tabarro*), Tosca★, Liù (*Turandot*); PURCELL: Dido; RAMEAU: Minerva (*Castor et Pollux*); STRAUSS, R: Marschallin★ & Octavian★ (*Rosenkavalier*); TCHAIKOVSKY: Tatiana (*Eugene Onegin*), Lisa (*Pique Dame*); VERDI: Aida, Amelia (*Ballo in maschera*), Elisabetta★ (*Don Carlo*), Desdemona (*Otello*), Leonora (*Trovatore*); WAGNER: Senta (*Fliegende Holländer*), Elsa (*Lohengrin*), Sieglinde (*Walküre*), Elisabeth (*Tannhäuser*); WEBER: Rezia (*Oberon*). Also MASSENET: Charlotte (*Werther*); HENZE: sop role (*Prinz von Homburg*); BARRAUD: (*Symphonie de Numance*). **World premieres:** DAMASE: (*Madame de*) Monte Carlo 1970; GRUENENWALD: (*Sardanapale*) Monte Carlo 1960. Appears with symphony orchestra. **Res:** 34 rue Notre Dame de Lorette, Paris, France. Mgmt: IMR/FRA.

SASS, SYLVIA. Dramatic soprano Hungarian. Resident mem: Budapest State Opera. Born 12 Jul 1951, Budapest. Husband György Hajdu. Studied: Budapest Music Acad, Mrs Ferenc Révhegyi, Hungary. **Debut:** Frasquita (*Carmen*) Budapest State Opera 1971.
Sang with major companies in AUS: Bregenz Fest, Salzburg Fest, Vienna Staatsoper; BUL: Sofia; FR GER: Frankfurt, Wiesbaden; HUN: Budapest; YUG: Belgrade. **Roles with these companies incl** MOZART: Donna Anna ★ (*Don Giovanni*); PUCCINI: Mimi★ (*Bohème*), Tosca★; VERDI: Giselda★ (*Lombardi*), Desdemona★ (*Otello*), Violetta★ (*Traviata*); WAGNER: Gutrune★ (*Götterdämmerung*). Recorded for: Hungaroton. Video/Film—Hungarian TV: Helene (*Häusliche Krieg*). **Res:** I Jégverem u 8, Budapest, Hungary. Mgmt: ITK/HUN; TAS/AUS; SEN/UK.

SASSOLA, RENATO PABLO CARLOS. Lyric tenor. Argentinean. Resident mem: Teatro Colón, Buenos Aires. Born 7 Jan 1927, Rosario, Argentina. Divorced. Three children. Studied: Hina Spani, Felipe Romito, Juan Martini, Ferruccio Calusio. **Debut:** Rodolfo (*Bohème*) Teatro Colón 1951. Awards: Diploma from Assn of Music Critics 1957.
Sang with major companies in ARG: Buenos Aires; AUS: Vienna Staatsoper; BRA: Rio de Janeiro; MEX: Mexico City; USA: Washington DC. **Roles with these companies incl** BIZET: Nadir (*Pêcheurs de perles*); BUSONI: Mephisto (*Doktor Faust*); DALLAPICCOLA: Pellerin★ (*Volo di notte*); DONIZETTI: Ernesto (*Don Pasquale*), Nemorino (*Elisir d'amore*), Edgardo (*Lucia*),

Beppo★(*Rita*); GOUNOD: Faust★; HAYDN: Ernesto (*Mondo della luna*); LALO: Mylio (*Roi d'Ys*); MASCAGNI: Fritz (*Amico Fritz*); MASSENET: Des Grieux (*Manon*), Werther; MENOTTI: Lover (*Amelia al ballo*); MOZART: Don Ottavio (*Don Giovanni*), Belfiore★ (*Finta giardiniera*), Alessandro★ (*Re pastore*); MUSSORGSKY: Vassily Golitsin (*Khovanshchina*); ORFF: Solo (*Carmina burana*); PAISIELLO: Almaviva★ (*Barbiere di Siviglia*); POULENC: Chevalier de la Force (*Dialogues des Carmélites*); PUCCINI: Rodolfo (*Bohème*), Rinuccio★ (*Gianni Schicchi*), Pinkerton (*Butterfly*), Ruggero (*Rondine*), Cavaradossi (*Tosca*); ROSSINI: Almaviva★ (*Barbiere di Siviglia*), Edward Milfort (*Cambiale di matrimonio*), Dorvil★ (*Scala di seta*), Florville (*Signor Bruschino*); STRAUSS, J: Eisenstein★ (*Fledermaus*); STRAUSS, R: Ein Sänger (*Rosenkavalier*); STRAVINSKY: Oedipus; VERDI: Fenton★ (*Falstaff*), Duca di Mantova (*Rigoletto*), Alfredo★ (*Traviata*); WEINBERGER: Babinsky (*Schwanda*). Also MUSSORGSKY: Dimitri (*Boris Godunov*); STRAUSS, R: Narraboth (*Salome*); BUCHARDO: Erio (*Sueno de alma*). **World premieres:** CASTRO: Novio (*Bodas de sangre*) Teatro Colón 1956. Recorded for: Odeon. Gives recitals. Appears with symphony orchestra. **Res:** Concepcion Arenal 2323, Buenos Aires, Argentina.

SASSU, ALIGI. Scenic and costume designer for opera, theater. Is a lighting designer; also a painter, sculptor & illustrator. Italian. Born 17 Jul 1912, Milan. Wife Maria Helena Olivares, occupation soprano. Studied: Accad di Brera, Milan. **Operatic debut:** *La Giara* La Scala, Milan 1961. Theater debut: Milan 1961. Awards: Accademico di San Luca, Rome.

Designed for major companies in ITA: Milan, Palermo. **Operas designed for these companies incl** BIZET: *Carmen★;* VERDI: *Vespri★.* Also FALLA: *Amor brujo* Teatro Massimo, Palermo. **Operatic world premieres:** NASCIMBENE: *Anch'io sono l'America* Teatro Sociale, Lecco 1969. Exhibitions of stage designs, paintings, sculptures & graphics 1927-75. **Res:** V Sirtori 26, Monticello Brianza/Como, Italy.

SAUNDERS, ARLENE. Spinto; Jugendlich-Dramatische. American. Resident mem: Staatsoper Hamburg. Born Cleveland, O, USA. Single. Studied: Baldwin-Wallace Coll, Berea, O; Florence Barbour, New York. **Debut:** Mimi (*Bohème*) Teatro Nuovo, Milan 1961. Awards: Kammersängerin, State of Hamburg 1967; Mayor's Awd for Outstanding Service to New York City 1962; Gold Medal, Voice Compt Vercelli, Italy.

Sang with major companies in AUS: Vienna Staatsoper; CAN: Toronto; FRA: Paris; FR GER: Berlin Deutsche Oper, Cologne, Dortmund, Düsseldorf-Duisburg, Frankfurt, Hamburg, Hannover, Mannheim, Munich Staatsoper, Stuttgart, Wiesbaden; ITA: Florence Comunale, Milan La Scala, Rome Opera; SWI: Geneva, Bern; UK: Glyndebourne Fest; USA: Baltimore, Boston, Cincinnati, Fort Worth, Hartford, Houston, New York Met & City Opera, Philadelphia Lyric, San Francisco Opera, Seattle, Washington DC. **Roles with these companies incl** BIZET: Micaëla (*Carmen*); CHARPENTIER: Louise★; GLUCK: Eu-

ridice; GOUNOD: Marguerite (*Faust*); LEONCAVALLO: Nedda★(*Pagliacci*); MASSENET: Manon; MENOTTI: Mother (*Amahl*); MOZART: Fiordiligi★(*Così fan tutte*), Donna Elvira★ (*Don Giovanni*), Contessa★(*Nozze di Figaro*), Pamina (*Zauberflöte*); OFFENBACH: Antonia (*Contes d'Hoffmann*); PROKOFIEV: Natasha★ (*War and Peace*); PUCCINI: Mimi★ (*Bohème*), Giorgetta (*Tabarro*), Tosca★, Liù (*Turandot*); SMETANA: Marie★ (*Bartered Bride*); STRAUSS, J: Rosalinde (*Fledermaus*); STRAUSS, R: Arabella★, Ariadne★ (*Ariadne auf Naxos*), Gräfin★ (*Capriccio*), Chrysothemis★ (*Elektra*), Marschallin★ (*Rosenkavalier*); STRAVINSKY: Anne Trulove (*Rake's Progress*); TCHAIKOVSKY: Tatiana (*Eugene Onegin*); WAGNER: Senta★ (*Fliegende Holländer*), Elsa★ (*Lohengrin*), Eva★ (*Meistersinger*), Sieglinde★ (*Walküre*), Elisabeth★ (*Tannhäuser*); WEBER: Agathe★ (*Freischütz*). **World premieres:** GINASTERA: Beatrix Cenci, Op Socy of Washington, DC 1971: MENOTTI: Mme Euterpova (*Help, Help, the Globolinks!*) Hamburg Staatsoper 1968; KLEBE: Marianne (*Jakobowsky und der Oberst*) Hamburg Staatsoper 1965. Recorded for: Philips. Video/Film: Contessa (*Nozze di Figaro*); Agathe (*Freischütz*); Eva (*Meistersinger*); Arabella; Mme Euterpova (*Globolinks*). Gives recitals. Appears with symphony orchestra. **Res:** Leinpfad 31, 2 Hamburg, FR Ger. **Mgmt:** GOR/UK.

SAVOIE, ROBERT. Dramatic baritone. Canadian. Born 21 Apr 1927, Montreal, PQ, Canada. Wife Aline, occupation artist. Two children. Studied: Pauline Donalda, Montreal; Antonio Narducci, Milan. **Debut:** Scarpia (*Tosca*) Teatro Nuovo, Milan 1953. Previous occupations: studied chemical engineering. Awards: Singing Stars of Tomorrow, Winner CBC Compt for debut in Italy.

Sang with major companies in CAN: Montreal/Quebec; FRA: Bordeaux, Lyon, Marseille, Nice, Paris, Rouen, Strasbourg, Toulouse; USA: Dallas, Pittsburgh, Washington DC. **Roles with these companies incl** BIZET: Escamillo (*Carmen*); BRITTEN: Captain Balstrode (*Peter Grimes*); DEBUSSY: Golaud (*Pelléas et Mélisande*); LEONCAVALLO: Tonio (*Pagliacci*); MASSENET: Sancho (*Don Quichotte*), Lescaut (*Manon*), Albert (*Werther*); MENOTTI: John Sorel (*Consul*), Bob (*Old Maid and the Thief*); MOZART: Guglielmo & Don Alfonso (*Così fan tutte*), Leporello & Don Giovanni (*Don Giovanni*), Conte Almaviva & Figaro (*Nozze di Figaro*); PERGOLESI: Uberto (*Serva padrona*); PUCCINI: Marcello (*Bohème*), Gianni Schicchi, Sharpless (*Butterfly*), Lescaut (*Manon Lescaut*), Michele (*Tabarro*), Scarpia (*Tosca*); RAVEL: Ramiro (*Heure espagnole*); ROSSINI: Dandini (*Cenerentola*); SAINT-SAENS: Grand prêtre (*Samson et Dalila*); VERDI: Amonasro (*Aida*), Renato (*Ballo in maschera*), Rodrigo (*Don Carlo*), Ford & Falstaff (*Falstaff*), Fra Melitone (*Forza del destino*), Iago (*Otello*), Rigoletto. Gives recitals. Appears with symphony orchestra. Teaches voice. Coaches repertoire. **Mgmt:** SAM/USA.

SAWALLISCH, WOLFGANG. Conductor of opera and symphony. German. Gen Music Dir & Resident Cond, Bayerische Staatsoper, Munich 1971- . Also Music Dir, Orch de la Suisse Romande,

Geneva. Born 23 Aug 1923, Munich. Wife: Mechthild. One child. Studied: with Hans Sachse, Wolfgang Ruoff; Munich Consv; incl piano & voice. Operatic training as repetiteur at Opera, Augsburg 1947-50. Previous adm positions in opera: Gen Mus Dir, Aachen 1953-57, Wiesbaden 1957-59, and Cologne 1959-63.

Conducted with major companies in AUS: Salzburg Fest, Vienna Staatsoper; FR GER: Bayreuth Fest, Cologne, Hamburg, Munich Staatsoper, Wiesbaden; ITA: Milan La Scala; UK: Edinburgh Fest, London Royal; et al. **Operas with these companies incl** BEETHOVEN: *Fidelio;* MOZART: *Così fan tutte, Don Giovanni, Entführung aus dem Serail, Idomeneo, Nozze di Figaro, Zauberflöte;* PUCCINI: *Gianni Schicchi, Tabarro;* SMETANA: *Bartered Bride;* STRAUSS, R: *Arabella, Ariadne auf Naxos, Capriccio‡, Daphne, Elektra, Frau ohne Schatten, Intermezzo, Rosenkavalier, Salome, Schweigsame Frau;* VERDI: *Falstaff;* WAGNER: *Fliegende Holländer‡, Lohengrin, Meistersinger, Parsifal, Rheingold, Walküre, Siegfried, Götterdämmerung, Tannhäuser‡, Tristan und Isolde;* WEBER: *Freischütz;* et al. **World premieres:** YUN: *Sim Tjong* Bayerische Staatsoper, Munich 1972. Recorded for Philips. Conducted major orch in Europe & USA/Canada. Previous positions as Mus Dir with major orch: Wiener Symphoniker, Austria; et al. Teaches at conservatory.

SCARFIOTTI, FERDINANDO. Scenic and costume designer for opera, theater, film, television; specl in sets. Italian. Born 6 Mar 1941, Potenza Picena, Italy. Single. Studied: Univ of Rome. Prof training: La Scala with F Zeffirelli, Lila de Nobili, Milan; Spoleto with L Visconti. **Operatic debut:** *Falstaff* Staatsoper, Vienna 1966. Theater debut: Teatro Stabile, Rome 1965. Previous occupation: studied architecture. Awards: Film Awd, Socy of Film and Television Arts, London 1971; Nastro d'Argento, Rome 1971.

Designed for major companies in AUS: Vienna Staatsoper; HOL: Amsterdam; ITA: Florence Maggio, Milan La Scala, Rome Opera, Spoleto Fest; UK: London Royal; USA: Dallas. **Operas designed for these companies incl** ROSSINI: *Barbiere di Siviglia;* STRAUSS, R: *Rosenkavalier;* VERDI: *Ballo in maschera, Falstaff, Rigoletto, Simon Boccanegra, Traviata, Trovatore;* WEILL: *Aufstieg und Fall der Stadt Mahagonny.* Exhibitions of stage designs, Victoria & Albert Museum, London. **Res:** Rome, Italy.

SCARPINATI, NICHOLAS JOSEPH. Bass-baritone. American. Resident mem: Israel National Opera, Tel Aviv. Born 16 Jul 1944, New York. Single. Studied: Mannes Coll of Music, Otto Guth, New York; Felix Popper, Adelaide Bishop, Nora Bosler, Robley Lawson, Frank Corsaro (acting), Paul Meyer (coaching), New York. **Debut:** Marquis (*Traviata*) New Jersey State Opera, Newark 1974. Previous occupations: IBM tab supervisor.

Sang with major companies in ISR: Tel Aviv; USA: Newark. **Roles with these companies incl** BIZET: Escamillo⋆ (*Carmen*); DONIZETTI: Don Pasquale⋆; MOZART: Figaro⋆ (*Nozze di Figaro*); OFFENBACH: Coppélius etc⋆ (*Contes d'Hoffmann*); PUCCINI: Colline⋆ (*Bohème*); ROSSINI: Don Basilio⋆ (*Barbiere di Siviglia*). Also DONIZETTI: Raimondo (*Lucia*). Gives re-

citals. Appears with symphony orchestra. **Res:** 148 Throckmorton La, Old Bridge, NJ, USA.

SCHACHTELI, WERNER. Scenic and costume designer for opera, theater. Is a lighting designer; also a painter. German. Born 23 Jul 1927, Cologne. Single. Prof training: Asst Des, Kiel Opera 1945-48. **Operatic debut:** *Fliegende Holländer* Ulm 1960. Theater debut: ballet, Staatsoper Munich 1955. Previous adm positions in opera: Chief Des, Opera Oberhausen, FR Ger 1962-63.

Designed for major companies in AUS: Vienna Staatsoper; FR GER: Berlin Deutsche Oper, Düsseldorf-Duisburg, Frankfurt, Hannover, Kassel, Kiel, Munich Staatsoper & Gärtnerplatz, Stuttgart, Wuppertal; ITA: Florence Maggio. **Operas designed for these companies incl** BIZET: *Carmen⋆;* FLOTOW: *Martha⋆;* GRANADOS: *Goyescas⋆;* MOZART: *Entführung aus dem Serail⋆, Zauberflöte⋆;* STRAUSS, J: *Fledermaus⋆;* STRAUSS, R: *Ariadne auf Naxos⋆;* TCHAIKOVSKY: *Eugene Onegin⋆;* VERDI: *Trovatore⋆;* WAGNER: *Fliegende Holländer⋆.* **Operatic world premieres:** BENTZON: *Faust III* Opera, Kiel 1964. Exhibitions of stage designs Librairie Gay Savoir, Paris 1953. **Res:** Bayerische Str 2, 1 Berlin 15, FR Ger. Mgmt: HUS/FRG.

SCHAEFER, GEORGE McCORD. American. Gen Mng, St Paul Opera Assn, Minnesota Bldg, St Paul, MN, USA 1968-75. In charge of adm, musical & dramatic matters, art policy, tech & finances. Born 16 Mar 1928, Holbrook, AZ. Single. Studied: Univ of Ariz, Tucson, music; Univ of Vienna; Univ of So Calif, Los Angeles; Mills Coll, CA; Städt Akad Basel, Switzerland; Amer Inst for Foreign Trade. Plays the piano. Previous occupations: Arts Council Dir, Charlotte, NC; Fort Wayne, IN; & St Paul, MN. Form positions primarily musical. World premieres at theaters under his management: HOIBY: *Summer and Smoke* St Paul 1971. Initiated major policy changes including removing "civic" from title; created summer rep season; established Artist-in-Residence program; introduced Affiliate Artist program to Minn; raised Opera budget from $150,000 to $750,000; organized Gramma Fisher Club of regional opera companies. Mem of Steering Commtt to form OPERA America; Prof Commtt, Central Opera Service. **Res:** 319 Palos Verdes Blvd, Redondo Beach, CA 90277, USA.

SCHAEFER, HANS JOACHIM. German. Chefdramaturg for opera, operetta, ballet, concerts, plays, Staatstheater Kassel, Am Friedrichsplatz 15, D 3500 Kassel. In charge of overall adm matters, art policy, music & dram matters. Additional adm positions: 1st chair, Goethe Gesellschaft, Kassel. Born 9 Jul 1923, Laasphe/Lahn. Wife Barbara. Three children. Studied: Philipps Univ, Marburg/Lahn. Plays the piano. Started with present company in 1950 as Dramaturg; in present position since 1959. **Res:** Am Hange 39, D 35 Kassel-Ki, FR Ger.

SCHAENEN, LEE. Conductor of opera and symphony. American. Music Dir, Dallas Civic Orchestra, TX. Born 10 Aug 1925, New York. Wife Nell Foster, occupation singer. Studied: Juilliard School of Music, Columbia Univ, New York; Antonia Brico, Jean Morel; incl piano, French horn. Plays the piano. Operatic training as repetiteur & asst cond at New York City Opera 1945-53; La Scala, Milan 1956. **Operatic debut:** *Traviata* New York City Opera 1949. Symphonic debut: Teatro San Carlo Orch, Naples 1954. Previous adm positions in opera: Chief Cond, Stadttheater Bern, Switzerland 1959-65.

Conducted with major companies in AUS: Bregenz Fest, Vienna Volksoper; FRA: Marseille, Nancy, Nice; FR GER: Berlin Deutsche Oper, Frankfurt, Munich Staatsoper, Stuttgart; ITA: Florence Comunale, Palermo; POR: Lisbon; SWI: Geneva; USA: Chicago, New York City Opera. **Operas with these companies incl** AUBER: *Muette de Portici*★; BARTOK: *Bluebeard's Castle;* BEETHOVEN: *Fidelio;* BELLINI: *Puritani;* BIZET: *Carmen*★; BRITTEN: *Albert Herring, Burning Fiery Furnace*★, *Curlew River*★, *Prodigal Son*★, *Turn of the Screw;* CILEA: *Adriana Lecouvreur*★, CIMAROSA: *Matrimonio segreto;* DONIZETTI: *Don Pasquale*★, *Elisir*★, *Lucia*★; GERSHWIN: *Porgy and Bess*★; GLUCK: *Alceste, Orfeo ed Euridice*★; HAYDN: *Infedeltà delusa;* KORNGOLD: *Tote Stadt*★; LEONCAVALLO: *Pagliacci;* MASCAGNI: *Cavalleria rusticana;* MASSENET: *Don Quichotte;* MENOTTI: *Consul*★, *Medium*★; MOZART: *Così fan tutte, Don Giovanni*★, *Entführung aus dem Serail, Nozze di Figaro, Zauberflöte*★; NICOLAI: *Lustigen Weiber;* OFFENBACH: *Contes d'Hoffmann*★; ORFF: *Carmina burana, Kluge;* PUCCINI: *Bohème, Gianni Schicchi*★, *Butterfly*★, *Suor Angelica*★, *Tabarro*★; PURCELL: *Dido and Aeneas*★; ROSSINI: *Barbiere di Siviglia, Cenerentola*★, *Comte Ory;* STRAUSS, R: *Ariadne auf Naxos, Capriccio, Rosenkavalier;* STRAVINSKY: *Mavra;* VERDI: *Aida, Ballo in maschera, Don Carlo, Falstaff, Forza del destino, Macbeth, Otello, Rigoletto, Traviata, Trovatore;* WAGNER: *Fliegende Holländer*★, *Meistersinger, Walküre, Tannhäuser.* Also GAZZANIGA: *Convitato di pietra.* Conducted major orch in Europe, USA/Canada. Teaches at Southern Methodist Univ, Dallas. **Res:** Casella Postale 67, Pescia, Italy. Mgmt: SLZ/FRG.

SCHÄFER, LAWRENCE. Scenic and costume designer for opera, theater & ballet; specl in sets. Canadian. Born 12 Nov 1940, Kitchener, Ont. Single. Studied: Royal Consv of Music, Toronto. Prof training: with H Geiger-Torel, Canadian Opera Co, Toronto. **Operatic debut:** sets, *Albert Herring* Royal Consv Toronto 1964; cost, *Kluge* Royal Consv Toronto 1966. Theater debut: Ntl Ballet of Canada, Toronto 1965. Awards: Tyrone Guthrie Awd, Stratford Shakespearian Fest of Canada; Jean Chalmers Awd, Canadian Opera Co.

Designed for major companies in CAN: Ottawa, Toronto, Vancouver; USA: Portland. **Operas designed for these companies incl** BRITTEN: *Albert Herring, Rape of Lucretia;* DONIZETTI: *Lucia*★; MENOTTI: *Amahl;* MOZART: *Don Giovanni;* ORFF: *Kluge;* POULENC: *Dialogues des Carmélites;* PROKOFIEV: *Love for Three Oranges;* PUCCINI: *Tosca;* STRAUSS, R: *Elektra;* STRAVINSKY: *Oedipus Rex;* VERDI: *Rigoletto*★. Also STRAVINSKY: *Histoire du soldat*★. **Operatic world premieres:** WILLAN: *Deirdre* Royal Consv Opera School, Toronto 1965; PANNELL: *Luck of Ginger Coffey* Canadian Op Co

1967; POLGAR: *Glove* Canadian Op Co 1975. Operatic Video—CBC TV: *Glove.* Exhibitions of stage designs Prague, CSSR 1970; Univ of Waterloo, Ont, Canada 1974. Teaches at Innis Coll, Univ of Toronto. **Res:** 7 Walmer Rd, Toronto, Canada M5R 2W8.

SCHARY, ELKE. Coloratura soprano. German. Born 8 Feb 1947, Beuthen. Husband Herbert Moelle. Studied: Kmsg Prof Erna Berger and Clara Ebers,Hamburg & Maria Reining, Salzburg; Hermann Firchow, Bielefeld. **Debut:** Blondchen (*Entführung*) Nationaltheater, Munich 1971-72.

Sang with major companies in AUS: Salzburg Fest, Vienna Staatsoper & Volksoper; FR GER: Berlin Deutsche Oper, Bielefeld, Dortmund, Essen, Frankfurt, Hannover, Karlsruhe, Kassel, Kiel, Mannheim, Munich Staatsoper, Nürnberg, Saarbrücken, Stuttgart, Wiesbaden; ITA: Milan La Scala; SWI: Geneva; YUG: Zagreb. **Roles with these companies incl** AUBER: Zerlina★ (*Fra Diavolo*); BEETHOVEN: Marzelline★ (*Fidelio*); BIZET: Micaëla★ (*Carmen*); CIMAROSA: Carolina★ (*Matrimonio segreto*); DONIZETTI: Norina★ (*Don Pasquale*); GLUCK: Amor★ (*Orfeo ed Euridice*); HUMPERDINCK: Gretel★; LORTZING: Marie★ (*Waffenschmied*), Gretchen★ & Baronin Freimann★ (*Wildschütz*), Marie★ (*Zar und Zimmermann*); MOZART: Despina★ (*Così fan tutte*), Zerlina★ (*Don Giovanni*), Susanna★ & Cherubino★ (*Nozze di Figaro*); NICOLAI: Aennchen★ (*Lustigen Weiber*); OFFENBACH: Olympia★ (*Contes d'Hoffmann*); PERGOLESI: Serpina★ (*Serva padrona*); PUCCINI: Musetta★ (*Bohème*), Lauretta★ (*Gianni Schicchi*); ROSSINI: Rosina★ (*Barbiere di Siviglia*); STRAUSS, J: Adele★ (*Fledermaus*); STRAUSS, R: Zerbinetta★ (*Ariadne auf Naxos*), Sophie★ (*Rosenkavalier*); VERDI: Oscar★ (*Ballo in maschera*), Nannetta★ (*Falstaff*), Gilda★ (*Rigoletto*); WEBER: Aennchen★ (*Freischütz*). Recorded for: Decca. Video—Bavarian TV: (*Wildschütz*). Mgmt: SLZ/FRG.

SCHAULER, EILEEN. Spinto. American. Resident mem: New York City Opera. Born 1 Jul, Millburn, NJ, USA. Husband Irwin Charone, occupation TV-screen-stage actor. One son. Studied: Juilliard School of Music, Maria Winetskaya, Catherine Aspinall, Alfredo Valenti, Frederick Cohen, New York; Gibner King, New York; also piano, ballet and drama. **Debut:** Tosca, St Paul Opera, MN 1961. Awards: Alice Breen Memorial Awd, Juilliard School; New York Singing Teachers Assn, An Hour of Music Recital Awd; Sullivan Fndt, 2 grants.

Sang with major companies in CAN: Ottawa, Toronto; USA: Baltimore, Fort Worth, New Orleans, New York City Opera, Omaha, Philadelphia Grand, St Paul, San Antonio, San Diego, Seattle. **Roles with these companies incl** BRITTEN: Governess★ (*Turn of the Screw*); GINASTERA: Beatrix Cenci★, Florinda★ (*Don Rodrigo*); MASCAGNI: Santuzza★ (*Cavalleria rusticana*); MOZART: Donna Anna★ & Donna Elvira (*Don Giovanni*); OFFENBACH: Giulietta★ (*Contes d'Hoffmann*); PROKOFIEV: Renata (*Fiery Angel*); PUCCINI: Mimi & Musetta (*Bohème*), Giorgetta (*Tabarro*), Tosca★; SHOSTAKOVICH: Katerina★ (*Katerina Ismailova*); STRAUSS, J: Rosalinde★ (*Fledermaus*); STRAUSS, R: Chrysothemis★ (*Elektra*), Marschallin (*Rosenkavalier*), Salome★; VERDI: Amelia (*Ballo in maschera*), Desdemona (*Otello*). Also BIZET: Carmen★; WEISGALL: Four women‡ (*Nine Rivers from Jordan*); MOORE: Beret (*Giants in the Earth*). **World premieres:** GIANNINI: Beatrice (*Servant of Two Masters*) New York City Opera 1967. Gives recitals. Appears with symphony orchestra. **Res:** New York, NY, USA. Mgmt: LLF/USA.

SCHELLEN, FERNANDO. Dutch. Adm, Netherlands Opera/Nederlandse Operastichting, Stadsschouwburg, Amsterdam 1969- . In charge of overall adm matters, tech & finances. Born 11 Oct 1934, The Hague. Married. Four children. Background adm, musical & theatrical. World premieres at theaters during his engagement: coop three composers: *Reconstructie* Amsterdam 1969; KOX: *Dorian Gray* Scheveningen 1974; de KRUYF: *Spinoza* Amsterdam 1971. Initiated major policy changes including expansion of season from 90 to 165 pfs. Pres, Netherlands Wind Ensemble; mem of commtt mus dram & chamber mus, Amsterdam Arts Council; Treas, Amsterdam Cultural Information Centre; Musica Antiqua Amsterdam. **Res:** Meander 749, Amstelveen, Netherlands.

SCHENK, MANFRED. Bass. German. Resident mem: Städtische Oper, Frankfurt.
Sang with major companies in AUS: Bregenz Fest, Vienna Staatsoper; FR GER: Frankfurt, Munich Gärtnerplatz; ITA: Rome Opera; SPA: Barcelona; UK: Glyndebourne Fest; et al. **Roles with these companies incl** BEETHOVEN: Rocco (*Fidelio*); MEYERBEER: Comte de St Bris (*Huguenots*); MOZART: Osmin (*Entführung aus dem Serail*), Sarastro (*Zauberflöte*); PUCCINI: Colline (*Bohème*); SMETANA: Kezal (*Bartered Bride*); STRAUSS, R: Musiklehrer (*Ariadne auf Naxos*); VERDI: Ramfis (*Aida*), Padre Guardiano (*Forza del destino*); WAGNER: Daland (*Fliegende Holländer*), Pogner (*Meistersinger*), Gurnemanz (*Parsifal*), Fafner (*Siegfried*), Hunding (*Walküre*), Landgraf (*Tannhäuser*), König Marke (*Tristan und Isolde*); et al.

SCHENK, OTTO. Stages/produces opera & theater and is an actor. Austrian. Prod Supervisor & Resident Stage Dir, Staatsoper, Vienna. Born 1930, Vienna. Wife Ruth Michaelis, occupation actress. Three children. Studied: Max Reinhardt Seminar, Vienna.
Directed/produced opera for major companies in AUS: Salzburg Fest, Vienna Staatsoper & Volksoper; FRA: Paris; FR GER: Berlin Deutsche Oper, Frankfurt, Munich Staatsoper, Stuttgart; ITA: Milan La Scala; SWI: Basel, Zurich; USA: New York Met; et al. **Operas staged with these companies incl** AUBER: *Fra Diavolo;* BEETHOVEN: *Fidelio;* BERG: *Lulu;* DONIZETTI: *Don Pasquale;* EINEM: *Besuch der alten Dame, Dantons Tod;* JANACEK: *Jenufa;* MOZART: *Così fan tutte, Don Giovanni, Nozze di Figaro, Zauberflöte;* PUCCINI: *Bohème, Tosca;* SCHOENBERG: *Moses und Aron;* STRAUSS, R: *Rosenkavalier;* VERDI: *Don Carlo, Macbeth, Otello, Rigoletto, Simon Boccanegra, Traviata;* WAGNER: *Meistersinger;* WEBER: *Freischütz;* et al. **Res:** Vienna, Austria.

SCHERLER, BARBARA. Coloratura & lyric mezzo-soprano. German. Resident mem: Deutsche Oper, Berlin. Born 20 Jan 1938, Leipzig, Germany. Single. Studied: Hochschule für Musik, Berlin; Prof Irmgard Reimann-Rühle, Prof Margarete Bärwinkel, Kmsg Josef Greindl. **Debut:** Cherubino (*Nozze di Figaro*) Staatsoper, Hannover 1959. Awards: First Prize Concerts of Young Artists, Hannover 1962.
Sang with major companies in AUS: Vienna Staatsoper; BEL: Brussels; GRE: Athens Fest; FR GER: Berlin Deutsche Oper, Cologne, Darmstadt, Dortmund, Düsseldorf-Duisburg, Frankfurt, Hamburg, Hannover, Kassel, Kiel, Munich Staatsoper, Nürnberg, Stuttgart, Wiesbaden Hessisches Staatstheater; ITA: Venice; MEX: Mexico City; POR: Lisbon; SWE: Drottningholm Fest; SWI: Zurich; UK: Edinburgh Fest, London Royal Opera. **Roles with these companies incl** BENNETT: Rosalind (*Mines of Sulphur*); BIZET: Carmen★; BRITTEN: Hermia (*Midsummer Night*), Lucretia (*Rape of Lucretia*); DONIZETTI: Maffio Orsini (*Lucrezia Borgia*); HANDEL: Rinaldo; HAYDN: Lisetta (*Mondo della luna*); HUMPERDINCK: Hänsel★; LORTZING: Gräfin Eberbach (*Wildschütz*); MOZART: Sesto★ & Annio (*Clemenza di Tito*), Dorabella★ (*Così fan tutte*), Cherubino★ (*Nozze di Figaro*); NICOLAI: Frau Reich★ (*Lustigen Weiber*); PERGOLESI: Cardella (*Frate 'nnamorato*); PFITZNER: Silla★ (*Palestrina*); PUCCINI: Suzuki (*Butterfly*), Principessa★ (*Suor Angelica*), Frugola★ (*Tabarro*); ROSSINI: Rosina (*Barbiere di Siviglia*), Angelina★ (*Cenerentola*); STRAUSS, J: Prinz Orlovsky★ (*Fledermaus*); STRAUSS, R: Komponist★ (*Ariadne auf Naxos*), Clairon★ (*Capriccio*), Octavian★ (*Rosenkavalier*); TCHAIKOVSKY: Olga (*Eugene Onegin*); VERDI: Preziosilla (*Forza del destino*); WAGNER: Magdalene (*Meistersinger*). Recorded for: DG. Gives recitals. Appears with symphony orchestra. Coaches repertoire. **Res:** Angerburger Allee 3, 1 Berlin 19, FR Ger. Mgmt: SMD/FRG; OOC/FRA.

SCHERREIKS, HERBERT THEODOR. Scenic and costume designer for opera, theater. Is a lighting designer; also a painter & architect. American. Resident designer, Opernhaus Essen, FR Ger and at Städtische Bühnen, Essen. Born 27 Feb 1930, New York. Single. Studied: Akad der bildenden Künste, Emil Preetorius, Munich; Bayérische Staatsoper, Helmut Jürgens. Prof training: Bayerische Staatsoper 1956-59. **Operatic debut:** *Schöne Galathée* Hessische Staatsoper, Wiesbaden 1964-65. Theater debut: Schauspielhaus, Bochum, FR Ger 1960. Previous occupation: graphic & advertising artist. Awards: stpd Akad & Bayerische Staatsoper 1954, 1956.
Designed for major companies in FR GER: Bielefeld, Bonn, Essen, Hamburg, Wiesbaden; ITA: Florence Comunale; SWI: Zurich. **Operas designed for these companies incl** AUBER: *Fra Diavolo;* BRITTEN: *Albert Herring;* DONIZETTI: *Don Pasquale;* GERSHWIN: *Porgy and Bess★;* HENZE: *Junge Lord★;* LEONCAVALLO: *Pagliacci★;* LORTZING: *Waffenschmied, Zar und Zimmermann★;* MASCAGNI: *Cavalleria rusticana;* MOZART: *Così fan tutte, Entführung aus dem Serail, Schauspieldirektor, Zauberflöte;* NI-

COLAI: *Lustigen Weiber;* ORFF: *Kluge;* PUC-CINI: *Bohème*★, *Butterfly;* ROSSINI: *Barbiere di Siviglia*★, *Cenerentola;* VERDI: *Aida*★, *Forza del destino, Rigoletto, Trovatore;* WAGNER: *Fliegende Holländer, Tannhäuser.* Also WEILL: *Sieben Todessünden, Zar lässt sich photographieren.* Exhibitions of stage designs Akad Ausstellung, Haus der Kunst, Munich 1965. **Res:** Munich and Essen, FR Ger. Mgmt: HSM/FRG.

SCHIAVI, FELICE ROLANDO. Dramatic baritone. Italian. Born 4 Jul 1931, Vimercate, Italy. Wife Teresa Radaelli. One child. Studied: Riccardo Malipiero, Carlo Tagliabue, Carlo Alfieri, Enrico Pessina, Monza/Milan. Awards: Golden Medal, City of Busseto, best interpret of Verdi operas 1960.
  Sang with major companies in BEL: Liège; CZE: Prague National & Smetana; FRA: Bordeaux, Lyon, Marseille, Nancy, Nice, Paris, Rouen, Strasbourg, Toulouse; FR GER: Mannheim, Munich Staatsoper; ITA: Bologna, Florence Maggio & Comunale, Milan La Scala, Naples, Parma, Rome Opera, Trieste, Turin, Venice; POL: Warsaw; SPA: Barcelona, Majorca; UK: Cardiff, Edinburgh Fest, Glasgow Scottish; USSR: Moscow Bolshoi; YUG: Belgrade. **Roles with these companies incl** BELLINI: Sir Richard★ (*Puritani*); BIZET: Escamillo★ (*Carmen*); DONIZETTI: Alfonse★ (*Favorite*), Enrico (*Lucia*); GIORDANO: Carlo Gérard★ (*Andrea Chénier*); LEON-CAVALLO: Tonio★ (*Pagliacci*); MASCAGNI: Alfio★ (*Cavalleria rusticana*); PONCHIELLI: Barnaba★ (*Gioconda*); PUCCINI: Marcello★ (*Bohème*), Scarpia★ (*Tosca*); ROSSINI: Figaro★ (*Barbiere di Siviglia*); VERDI: Amonasro★ (*Aida*), Renato★ (*Ballo in maschera*), Rodrigo★ (*Don Carlo*), Don Carlo★ (*Ernani*), Don Carlo★ (*Forza del destino*), Macbeth★, Nabucco★, Iago★ (*Otello*), Rigoletto★, Simon Boccanegra★, Germont★ (*Traviata*), Conte di Luna★ (*Trovatore*). Also GOU-NOD: Valentin (*Faust*); MENOTTI: Ben (*Telephone*); MASCAGNI: (*Lodoletta*), (*Piccolo Marat*). **Res:** V Isonzo 10, 20043 Arcore/Milan, Italy.

SCHIML, MARGA. Lyric mezzo-soprano & contralto. German. Born 29 Nov 1945, Weiden/Opf. Husband Horst Laubenthal, occupation opera singer, tenor. One child. Studied: Prof Hanno Blaschke, Munich; Frau Hartmann-Dressler, Berlin. **Debut:** HANDEL: Policare (*Tigrane*) Basel Opera, Switzerland 1967.
  Sang with major companies in AUS: Graz, Salzburg Fest, Vienna Staatsoper; FRA: Orange Fest; FR GER: Munich Staatsoper; SWI: Basel, Zurich. **Roles with these companies incl** BIZET: Carmen; DONIZETTI: Sara (*Roberto Devereux*); HANDEL: Cornelia (*Giulio Cesare*); HUM-PERDINCK: Hänsel★; MOZART: Annio★ (*Clemenza di Tito*), Dorabella (*Così*), Cherubino★ (*Figaro*); STRAUSS, J: Orlovsky (*Fledermaus*); WAGNER: Magdalene (*Meistersinger*), Erda (*Rheingold*★, *Siegfried*★), Fricka (*Walküre*); WE-BER: Puck‡ (*Oberon*). Recorded for: DG. Gives recitals. Appears with symphony orchestra. **Res:** Heinrich Knote Str 15, 8134 Pöcking, FR Ger. Mgmt: OOC/FRA.

SCHIPPERS, THOMAS. Conductor of opera and symphony. American. Music Dir, Cincinnati Symph Orch, O. Born 9 Mar 1930, Portage, MI, USA. Widowed. Studied: Curtis Inst, Philadelphia; Yale Univ, New Haven, CT; incl piano, organ, violin, oboe and voice. Plays the piano & organ. Operatic training as repetiteur & asst cond at New York City Opera 1952-54. **Operatic debut:** *Don Pasquale* Metropolitan Opera, New York 1955. Symphonic debut: Philadelphia Orch, PA 1948. Awards: American Composers Awd of Merit.
  Conducted with major companies in ARG: Buenos Aires Teatro Colón; BEL: Brussels; CAN: Montreal; FIN: Helsinki; FRA: Aix-en-Provence Fest, Lyon, Paris; GRE: Athens Fest; FR GER: Bayreuth Fest, Berlin Deutsche Oper, Munich Staatsoper; HOL: Amsterdam; ISR: Tel Aviv; ITA: Bologna, Florence Maggio & Comunale, Genoa, Milan La Scala, Naples, Palermo, Rome Opera, Spoleto Fest, Trieste, Turin, Venice; MON: Monte Carlo; POR: Lisbon; SWI: Geneva; UK: London Royal; USSR: Kiev, Leningrad, Moscow Stanislavski; USA: Cincinnati, New York Met. **Operas with these companies incl** BEET-HOVEN: *Fidelio;* BERG: *Wozzeck;* BERLIOZ: *Damnation de Faust;* BERNSTEIN: *Trouble in Tahiti;* BIZET: *Carmen*‡, *Pêcheurs de perles;* BRITTEN: *Albert Herring, Billy Budd, Rape of Lucretia;* CHERUBINI: *Medea;* CIMAROSA: *Matrimonio segreto;* DEBUSSY: *Enfant prodigue, Pelléas et Mélisande;* DONIZETTI: *Campanello, Don Pasquale, Elisir, Favorite, Lucia*‡, *Rita;* EINEM: *Dantons Tod, Prozess;* FALLA: *Atlantida;* GLUCK: *Alceste;* HANDEL: *Acis and Galatea, Giulio Cesare;* HAYDN: *Mondo della luna;* HUMPERDINCK: *Hänsel und Gretel;* MASCAGNI: *Cavalleria rusticana;* MASSE-NET: *Manon;* MENOTTI: *Amahl*‡, *Amelia al ballo, Consul, Medium, Old Maid and the Thief, Saint of Bleecker Street*‡, *Telephone;* MONTE-VERDI: *Incoronazione di Poppea;* MOZART: *Così fan tutte, Don Giovanni, Entführung aus dem Serail, Idomeneo, Nozze di Figaro;* MUS-SORGSKY: *Boris Godunov*★; OFFENBACH: *Contes d'Hoffmann;* POULENC: *Voix humaine;* PROKOFIEV: *Fiery Angel, Love for Three Oranges;* PUCCINI: *Bohème*★‡, *Manon Lescaut*★, *Suor Angelica, Tosca;* RAVEL: *Enfant et les sortilèges, Heure espagnole;* RIMSKY-KOR-SAKOV: *Ivan the Terrible;* ROSSINI: *Barbiere di Siviglia*★, *Cenerentola, Comte Ory, Italiana in Algeri, Moïse, Assedio di Corinto*★‡, *Turco in Italia;* SAINT-SAENS: *Samson et Dalila*★; SCHOENBERG: *Erwartung;* SMETANA: *Bartered Bride;* STRAUSS, R: *Aegyptische Helena, Elektra, Rosenkavalier, Salome;* STRAVINSKY: *Oedipus Rex;* TCHAIKOVSKY: *Eugene Onegin, Pique Dame;* THOMSON: *Four Saints in Three Acts;* VERDI: *Aida, Ballo in maschera, Don Carlo*★, *Due Foscari, Ernani*★‡, *Forza del destino*‡, *Lombardi, Luisa Miller, Macbeth*‡, *Masnadieri, Nabucco, Otello*★, *Traviata, Trovatore*‡, *Vespri;* WAGNER: *Fliegende Holländer, Lohengrin, Meistersinger*★, *Walküre;* WOLF-FERRARI: *Quattro rusteghi, Segreto di Susanna.* Also MERCADANTE: *Giuramento;* DONI-ZETTI: *Duca d'Alba.* **World premieres:** BAR-BER: *Antony and Cleopatra* Metropolitan Opera, New York 1966. Recorded for RCA, ABC, London, Angel. Video—NBC TV: *Amahl.* Conducted major orch in Europe, USA/Canada, Cent/S

America, Asia. **Res:** New York, USA. **Mgmt:** CAM/USA; DSP/USA.

SCHIRMER, ASTRID. Dramatic soprano. German. Resident mem: Niedersächsisches Staatstheater, Hannover; Städtische Bühnen Essen; Nationaltheater Mannheim. Born 8 Nov 1942, Berlin. Husband Carl Graf von Pfeil, occupation conductor. One child. Studied: Hochschule für Musik, Prof Elisabeth Grümmer, Berlin; Fr Johanna Rakow, Berlin. **Debut:** Senta (*Fliegende Holländer*) Landestheater Coburg 1967. Awards: Stipd of the German People.

Sang with major companies in FR GER: Berlin Deutsche Oper, Bielefeld, Cologne, Düsseldorf-Duisburg, Essen, Frankfurt, Hannover, Karlsruhe, Kassel, Krefeld, Mannheim, Nürnberg, Saarbrücken, Stuttgart; SPA: Barcelona. **Roles with these companies incl** BEETHOVEN: Leonore★ (*Fidelio*); BRITTEN: Lady Billows★ (*Albert Herring*), Miss Wingrave★ (*Owen Wingrave*); GERSHWIN: Bess★; MASCAGNI: Santuzza★ (*Cavalleria rusticana*); MOZART: Donna Anna★ (*Don Giovanni*); PUCCINI: Giorgetta★ (*Tabarro*), Tosca★, Turandot★; STRAUSS, R: Arabella★, Ariadne★ (*Ariadne auf Naxos*), Gräfin★ (*Capriccio*), Christine★ (*Intermezzo*); VERDI: Aida★, Amelia★ (*Ballo in maschera*), Leonora★ (*Forza del destino*), Desdemona★ (*Otello*); WAGNER: Senta (*Fliegende Holländer*), Sieglinde★ (*Walküre*), Brünnhilde★ (*Siegfried*), Elisabeth★ & Venus★ (*Tannhäuser*). Also d'ALBERT: Marta (*Tiefland*). Gives recitals. Appears with symphony orchestra. **Res:** Steenewark 19, 3053 Steinhude, FR Ger. Mgmt: SLZ/FRG.

SCHMIDT, DOUGLAS WOCHER. Scenic and costume designer for opera, theater, film, television; specializes in sets. American. Born 4 Oct 1942, Cincinnati, Ohio, USA. Single. Studied: Boston Univ, Raymond Sovey, Horace Armistead; Studio and Forum of Stage Design, Lester Polakov, New York. Prof training: design studio Ming Cho Lee, New York 1967-68. **Operatic debut:** sets, *Bohème* Juilliard School, New York 1966; cost, *Segreto di Susanna* Boston Univ, Opera Div 1964. Theater debut: Monmouth Rep Theatre, ME, USA 1961. Awards: Maharam Fndt Awd 1972-73; two NY Drama Desk Awds 1974.

Designed for major companies in HOL: Amsterdam; USA: New York City Opera, Washington DC. **Operas designed for these companies incl** BENNETT: *Mines of Sulphur*; HONEGGER: *Antigone*; LIGETI: *Aventures/Nouvelles Aventures*★; MONTEVERDI: *Incoronazione di Poppea*★, *Ritorno d'Ulisse*★; MOZART: *Nozze di Figaro*; OFFENBACH: *Contes d'Hoffmann*; PUCCINI: *Bohème*; SATIE: *Socrate*★; STRAUSS, R: *Salome*★; VERDI: *Ballo in maschera*; WEILL: *Aufstieg und Fall der Stadt Mahagonny*★; WOLF-FERRARI: *Segreto di Susanna*★. Also OFFENBACH: *Croquefer*; BIRTWISTLE: *Down by the Greenwood Side*; WEILL: *Jasager*. **Operatic world premieres:** SELIG: *Chocorua* Music Th Proj, Tanglewood, MS 1972; MADERNA: *Satyricon* Netherlands Op 1973; FARBERMAN: *The Losers* 1971; OVERTON: *Huckleberry Finn* 1971; both at Amer Op Center, Juilliard School, New York. Exhibitions of stage designs, Libr & Museum of the Perf Arts, Lincoln Center, New York. Teaches at Studio & Forum of Stage Design,

New York. **Res:** 5 W 86 St, New York, NY, USA. Mgmt: HHA/USA.

SCHMIDT, MANFRED. Stages/produces opera, theater, film & television and is a singer. German. Born 27 Jun 1929, Berlin. Wife Gisela, occupation architect. Studied: Hochschule für Musik, Profs Herbert Brauer & Jean Nadolovitch, Berlin; Frida Leider; incl music and voice. Operatic training as asst stage dir at Studio, Staatsoper Berlin 1954-59.

Directed/produced opera for major companies in AUS: Bregenz Fest, Salzburg Fest, Vienna Staatsoper; BEL: Brussels; CZE: Prague National & Smetana; FRA: Paris; GRE: Athens Fest; FR GER: Berlin Deutsche Oper, Bielefeld, Bonn, Cologne, Dortmund, Düsseldorf-Duisburg, Essen, Frankfurt, Hamburg, Hannover, Krefeld, Munich Staatsoper, Saarbrücken, Stuttgart, Wiesbaden, Wuppertal; GER DR: Berlin Komische Oper & Staatsoper; HOL: Amsterdam; ITA: Bologna, Florence Maggio, Genoa, Milan La Scala, Naples, Rome Opera, Venice; SWI: Zurich; UK: London English National. **Operas staged with these companies incl** BEETHOVEN: *Fidelio*; BERG: *Lulu, Wozzeck*; BORODIN: *Prince Igor*; BRITTEN: *Albert Herring*; BUSONI: *Doktor Faust*; CIMAROSA: *Matrimonio segreto*; CORNELIUS: *Barbier von Bagdad*; DONIZETTI: *Don Pasquale, Elisir, Favorite*; DVORAK: *Rusalka*; FLOTOW: *Martha*; GLUCK: *Alceste, Cadi dupé*; GOUNOD: *Faust*; HANDEL: *Xerxes*; HAYDN: *Infedeltà delusa*; HENZE: *Junge Lord*; HINDEMITH: *Cardillac*; KORNGOLD: *Tote Stadt*; LEONCAVALLO: *Pagliacci*; LORTZING: *Wildschütz, Zar und Zimmermann*; MASSENET: *Manon, Werther*; MOZART: *Clemenza di Tito, Così fan tutte, Don Giovanni, Entführung aus dem Serail, Finta giardiniera, Mitridate re di Ponto, Zauberflöte*; MUSSORGSKY: *Khovanshchina*; NICOLAI: *Lustigen Weiber*; ORFF: *Carmina burana, Kluge*; PERGOLESI: *Serva padrona*; PUCCINI: *Gianni Schicchi, Tosca*; RIMSKY-KORSAKOV: *Sadko*; ROSSINI: *Barbiere di Siviglia, Italiana in Algeri*; SMETANA: *Bartered Bride, Two Widows*; STRAUSS, J: *Fledermaus*; STRAUSS, R: *Arabella, Capriccio, Frau ohne Schatten, Rosenkavalier, Salome*; STRAVINSKY: *Oedipus Rex, Rake's Progress*; TCHAIKOVSKY: *Eugene Onegin*; VERDI: *Falstaff, Otello, Traviata*; WAGNER: *Fliegende Holländer, Meistersinger, Tannhäuser, Tristan und Isolde*; WOLF-FERRARI: *Quattro rusteghi*; ZIMMERMANN: *Soldaten*. Also HAYDN: *Speziale*. Operatic Video—Ger TV: *Colin et Colinette, Tosca, Spinning Room*. **Res:** Robert Koch Str 38, 5 Cologne 41, FR Ger. Mgmt: PAS/FRG; SLZ/FRG.

SCHMIDT, TRUDELIESE. Lyric mezzo-soprano. German. Resident mem: Deutsche Oper am Rhein, Düsseldorf. Single. Studied: Hannes Richrath. **Debut:** Hänsel, Saarbrücken 1965.

Sang with major companies in AUS: Vienna Staatsoper; FRA: Nancy; FR GER: Bayreuth Fest, Berlin Deutsche Oper, Bielefeld, Dortmund, Düsseldorf-Duisburg, Essen, Frankfurt, Hamburg, Munich Staatsoper, Nürnberg, Saarbrücken, Stuttgart, Wiesbaden; HOL: Amsterdam; ITA: Florence Maggio; SWI: Zurich; UK: London Royal. **Roles with these companies incl** BERLIOZ: Marguerite★ (*Damnation de Faust*); BUSONI: Colombina (*Arlecchino*); CAVALLI: Sicle★ (*Ormindo*); GOUNOD: Siebel (*Faust*); HANDEL: Amastris (*Xerxes*); HUMPERDINCK: Hänsel★; MOZART: Dorabella★ (*Così fan tutte*), Cherubino★ (*Nozze di Figaro*); PROKOFIEV: Blanche★ (*Gambler*); PUCCINI: Suzuki★ (*Butterfly*); RAVEL: Enfant★ (*Enfant et les sortilèges*); ROSSINI: Isolier★ (*Comte Ory*), Isabella (*Italiana in Algeri*); STRAUSS, J: Prinz Orlovsky (*Fledermaus*); STRAUSS, R: Komponist★ (*Ariadne auf Naxos*), Octavian★ (*Rosenkavalier*); THOMAS: Mignon; VERDI: Preziosilla (*Forza del destino*); YUN: Mme Tian (*Witwe des Schmetterlings*); ZIMMERMANN: Charlotte★ (*Soldaten*). Recorded for: Ariola, Eurodisc. Video/Film: (*Barbier von Bagdad*). **Res:** Vennstr 8, Düsseldorf 22, FR Ger. Mgmt: SLZ/FRG; ASK/UK.

SCHNAPKA, GEORG. Bass. German. Born 27 May 1932, Schlesisch Ostrau, CSR. Wife Elisabeth Schwarzenberg, occupation opera singer. One child. Studied: Bruckner Konsv, Prof Andreas Sotzkow, Linz, Austria. **Debut:** Repela (*Corregidor*) Städtische Bühnen, Heidelberg, FR Ger 1954.

Sang with major companies in AUS: Vienna Staatsoper & Volksoper; FRA: Bordeaux, Strasbourg; FR GER: Berlin Deutsche Oper, Cologne, Dortmund, Düsseldorf-Duisburg, Frankfurt, Hamburg, Hannover, Karlsruhe, Kiel, Mannheim, Munich Staatsoper & Gärtnerplatz, Nürnberg, Saarbrücken, Stuttgart, Wiesbaden, Wuppertal; GER DR: Dresden; HOL: Amsterdam; ITA: Florence Maggio, Trieste, Venice; POR: Lisbon; ROM: Bucharest; SPA: Majorca; SWI: Zurich; USA: Baltimore, New York City Opera, Washington DC. **Roles with these companies incl** d'ALBERT: Tommaso★ (*Tiefland*); BEETHOVEN: Rocco★(*Fidelio*); FLOTOW: Plunkett★ (*Martha*); HALEVY: Brogny (*Juive*); LORTZING: Stadinger (*Waffenschmied*), Baculus★ (*Wildschütz*), Van Bett★ (*Zar und Zimmermann*); MOZART: Don Alfonso (*Così fan tutte*), Leporello★ (*Don Giovanni*), Osmin★ (*Entführung aus dem Serail*), Sarastro★ (*Zauberflöte*); MUSSORGSKY: Varlaam & Pimen★ (*Boris Godunov*); NICOLAI: Falstaff★ (*Lustigen Weiber*); PUCCINI: Colline★ (*Bohème*); ROSSINI: Dott Bartolo★ (*Barbiere di Siviglia*); SHOSTAKOVICH: Ivan Yakovlevich (*Nose*); SMETANA: Kezal★ (*Bartered Bride*); STRAUSS, R: Baron Ochs★ (*Rosenkavalier*); VERDI: Ramfis (*Aida*), Philip II (*Don Carlo*), Banquo (*Macbeth*); WAGNER: Daland★ (*Fliegende Holländer*), Fafner (*Rheingold★, Siegfried★*), Hunding★ (*Walküre*), Landgraf (*Tannhäuser*), König Marke (*Tristan und Isolde*); WEBER: Kaspar★ (*Freischütz*). Video/Film: Teufel (*Schwanda*). Gives recitals. Appears with symphony orchestra. Coaches repertoire. **Res:** Alpspitzstr 6, 8011 Oberpframmern, FR Ger. Mgmt: SLZ/FRG; TAU/SWI; TAS/AUS.

SCHNEIDER, PETER. Conductor of opera and symphony. Austrian. Chief Cond, Deutsche Oper am Rhein, Düsseldorf/Duisburg. Born 26 Mar 1939, Vienna. Wife Dagmar, occupation actress. Three children. Studied: Akad f Musik u darst Kunst, Prof Hans Swarowsky, Vienna; incl piano, accordion, violin and voice. Plays the piano. Operatic training as repetiteur & asst cond at Landes-

theater, Salzburg 1959-61; Städt Bühnen, Heidelberg 1961-68. **Operatic debut:** *Giulio Cesare* Landestheater, Salzburg 1960. Symphonic debut: Städt Orch Heidelberg 1963.

Conducted at major companies in FR GER: Cologne, Dortmund, Düsseldorf-Duisburg, Hamburg; ITA: Florence Maggio. **Operas conducted with these companies incl** ADAM: *Postillon de Lonjumeau*; BEETHOVEN: *Fidelio★*; BERG: *Wozzeck★*; BERLIOZ: *Damnation de Faust★*; BIZET: *Carmen*; CAVALIERI: *Rappresentazione★*; CAVALLI: *Ormindo★*; DALLAPICCOLA: *Ulisse★*; DONIZETTI: *Don Pasquale, Elisir, Lucia★*; DVORAK: *Rusalka★*; FLOTOW: *Martha*; GOUNOD: *Faust*; HANDEL: *Deidamia★*; JANACEK: *Cunning Little Vixen★, Excursions of Mr Broucek★, Katya Kabanova★, Makropoulos Affair★*; LEONCAVALLO: *Pagliacci*; LORTZING: *Wildschütz, Zar und Zimmermann★*; MASCAGNI: *Cavalleria rusticana*; MASSENET: *Don Quichotte★*; MOZART: *Così fan tutte, Don Giovanni★, Idomeneo★, Mitridate re di Ponto★, Nozze di Figaro★, Zauberflöte★*; OFFENBACH: *Contes d'Hoffmann★*; PUCCINI: *Bohème★, Butterfly★, Manon Lescaut★*; ROSSINI: *Barbiere di Siviglia★, Italiana in Algeri★*; SMETANA: *Bartered Bride*; STRAUSS, J: *Fledermaus★*; STRAUSS, R: *Ariadne auf Naxos★, Rosenkavalier★, Salome★*; VERDI: *Ballo in maschera, Falstaff, Forza del destino, Rigoletto, Traviata★, Trovatore★*; WAGNER: *Fliegende Holländer★, Lohengrin★, Parsifal★, Rheingold★, Tannhäuser★*; WOLF-FERRARI: *Quattro rusteghi*. **Res:** Engerstr 73, 4150 Krefeld, FR Ger.

SCHNEIDER-SIEMSSEN, GÜNTHER. Scenic and costume designer for opera, theater, film, television; specl in sets. Is a lighting designer; also a painter. Austrian. Resident designer, Staatsoper & Volksoper, Vienna and at Burgtheater, Vienna. Born 7 Jun 1926, Augsburg, Germany. Wife Eva. Two children. Studied: Akad der bildenden Künste, Prof Preetorius; Akad für angewandte Kunst, Prof Sievert; Theaterwissenschaft Univ, Prof Kutscher; asst to Clemens Krauss, Staatsoper, all in Munich. Prof training: Staatsoper, Munich 1941-44. **Operatic debut:** sets, *Consul* Landestheater Salzburg 1951; cost, *Ariodante* Staatstheater Bremen 1956. Theater debut: Lustspielhaus, Munich. Previous occupation: head of Tourneebühne Junges Theater; film architect.

Designed for major companies in ARG: Buenos Aires; AUS: Salzburg Festival, Vienna Staatsoper & Volksoper; BUL: Sofia; FRA: Paris; FR GER: Berlin Deutsche Oper, Cologne, Düsseldorf-Duisburg, Essen, Frankfurt, Hamburg, Munich Staatsoper & Gärtnerplatz, Nürnberg, Stuttgart; HOL: Amsterdam; ITA: Milan La Scala, Venice; SWI: Geneva, Zurich; UK: London Royal; USSR: Moscow Bolshoi; USA: Chicago, New York Met; YUG: Zagreb. **Operas designed for these companies incl** d'ALBERT: *Tiefland*; AUBER: *Fra Diavolo*; BARTOK: *Bluebeard's Castle*; BEETHOVEN: *Fidelio★*; BERG: *Lulu*; BIZET: *Carmen*; BRITTEN: *Midsummer Night*; DEBUSSY: *Pelléas et Mélisande★*; DONIZETTI: *Elisir*; EINEM: *Besuch der alten Dame★, Dantons Tod*; FLOTOW: *Martha*; GLUCK: *Orfeo ed Euridice*; GOUNOD: *Faust*; HANDEL: *Ariodante*; HINDE-

MITH: *Mathis der Maler;* HUMPERDINCK: *Königskinder;* JANACEK: *Jenufa*;* LOR-TZING: *Waffenschmied, Wildschütz, Zar und Zimmermann;* MENOTTI: *Consul;* MOZART: *Così fan tutte*, Don Giovanni, Entführung aus dem Serail, Schauspieldirektor, Nozze di Figaro, Zauberflöte;* MUSSORGSKY: *Boris Godunov;* OFFENBACH: *Contes d'Hoffmann;* PAI-SIELLO: *Re Teodoro in Venezia*;* PFITZNER: *Palestrina;* PUCCINI: *Tosca;* RAVEL: *Heure espagnole;* ROSSINI: *Barbiere di Siviglia*;* SCHOENBERG: *Erwartung, Glückliche Hand, Moses und Aron*;* SMETANA: *Bartered Bride;* STRAUSS, J: *Fledermaus*;* STRAUSS, R: *Daphne, Elektra, Frau ohne Schatten*, Rosenkavalier, Salome;* STRAVINSKY: *Rake's Progress;* TCHAIKOVSKY: *Eugene Onegin;* VERDI: *Aida*, Don Carlo, Luisa Miller*, Macbeth, Otello*, Rigoletto, Traviata;* WAGNER: *Fliegende Holländer*, Lohengrin, Meistersinger*, Parsifal*, Rheingold*, Walküre*, Siegfried*, Götterdämmerung*, Tannhäuser, Tristan und Isolde*;* WEBER: *Freischütz*;* WOLF-FERRARI: *Segreto di Susanna.* Also HONEGGER: *Jeanne d'Arc au bûcher;* FORTNER: *Bluthochzeit;* HOLTERSDORF: *Gesteinigten;* HINDE-MITH: *Harmonie der Welt;* HANDEL: *Belshazzar;* WOLF-FERRARI: *Campiello.* **Operatic world premieres:** ORFF: *De Temporum fine comoedia* Salzburg Fest 1973; EINEM: *Besuch der alten Dame* Staatsoper, Vienna 1972; WIMBER-GER: *Dame Kobold* Städt Bühnen, Frankfurt 1964; BIALAS: *Aucassin und Nicolette* Staatsoper, Munich 1969-70. Operatic Video—Bayer Rdfk-TV: *Daphne.* Exhibitions of stage designs Vienna 1969; New York 1970; Berlin 1971; Reinhardt Museum, Salzburg 1972. Teaches at Intl Sommerakad für bildende Kunst, Salzburg. **Res:** Schlickg 4, Vienna 9, Austria. Mgmt: DSP/USA.

SCHÖFER, OTTOKAR. Bass. Austrian. Resident mem: Volksoper, Vienna. Born 18 Mar 1930, Feldkirch, Austria. Wife Irene. One child. Studied: Max Lorenz, Elfriede Sindel. **Debut:** Zuniga (*Carmen*) Volksoper, Vienna 1955. Previous occupations: studied medicine.
Sang with major companies in AUS: Vienna Staatsoper & Volksoper; ITA: Naples, Palermo, Rome Opera; SWI: Geneva; USA: Chicago. **Roles with these companies incl** d'ALBERT: Tommaso* (*Tiefland*); BEETHOVEN: Rocco (*Fidelio*); DONIZETTI: Don Pasquale*; EGK: Cuperus (*Zaubergeige*); FLOTOW: Plunkett (*Martha*); MOZART: Osmin (*Entführung aus dem Serail*), Sarastro* (*Zauberflöte*); NICOLAI: Falstaff* (*Lustigen Weiber*); WAGNER: Fafner (*Rheingold*, Siegfried**), Hunding* (*Walküre*), Hagen (*Götterdämmerung*). Also ROTA: Padre (*Cappello di paglia di Firenze*). Recorded for: ORF. Teaches voice. **Res:** Unterach/Attersee, A4866 Austria. Mgmt: TAU/SWI.

SCHOMBERG, MARTIN. Lyric tenor. German. Resident mem: Opernhaus Zurich. Born 7 Nov 1944, Höxter, Germany. Single. Studied: Musikhochschule Hamburg, Prof Maya Stein, Prof Jakob Stämpfli. **Debut:** Lenski (*Eugene Onegin*) Mainz 1972.
Sang with major companies in AUS: Salzburg Fest; FR GER: Cologne, Düsseldorf-Duisburg,

Hamburg; SWI: Basel, Zurich. **Roles with these companies incl** BERG: Maler (*Lulu*); HAYDN: Nancio* (*Infedeltà delusa*); MOZART: Don Ottavio* (*Don Giovanni*), Belmonte* (*Entführung aus dem Serail*), Tamino* (*Zauberflöte*); STRAUSS, J: Alfred* (*Fledermaus*); STRAUSS, R: Ein Sänger* (*Rosenkavalier*); TCHAIKOVSKY: Lenski* (*Eugene Onegin*); WAGNER: Walther v d Vogelweide* (*Tannhäuser*); WOLF-FERRARI: Florindo* (*Donne curiose*). **World premieres:** KLEBE: Shawn Keogh (*Wahrer Held*) Opernhaus Zurich 1975. Gives recitals. Appears with symphony orchestra. **Res:** Uetlibergstr 240, 8045 Zurich, Switzerland. Mgmt: JUC/SWI.

SCHRAMM, ERNST GEROLD. Lyric baritone. German. Born 8 Jul 1938, Steinheim. Wife Elfriede, occupation teacher. Two children. Studied: Profs Martin Grundler, Bruno Vondenhoff, E Arnold; Johann Goethe Univ, Frankfurt/M. **Debut:** Marullo (*Rigoletto*) Staatstheater, Hannover 1966. Previous occupations: chorus master, pianist. Awards: First Prize & Kulturpreis, Intl Compt Geneva 1965.
Sang with major companies in AUS: Bregenz Fest, Salzburg Fest, Vienna Volksoper; FR GER: Berlin Deutsche Oper, Frankfurt, Hannover, Wuppertal. **Roles with these companies incl** BERLIOZ: Méphistophélès‡ (*Damnation de Faust*); FORTNER: Don Perlimplin*; HAYDN: Nanni (*Infedeltà delusa*); HENZE: Mittenhofer‡ (*Elegy for Young Lovers*); HINDEMITH: Mathis; LORTZING: Graf Eberbach* (*Wildschütz*); MASSENET: Lescaut (*Manon*); MOZART: Guglielmo* (*Così fan tutte*), Conte Almaviva* (*Nozze di Figaro*), Don Pippo* (*Oca del Cairo*), Papageno* (*Zauberflöte*); ORFF: König* (*Kluge*); ROSSINI: Figaro‡ (*Barbiere di Siviglia*), Robert (*Comte Ory*); SMETANA: Kalina‡ (*Secret*); WAGNER: Hans Sachs* (*Meistersinger*), Wolfram* (*Tannhäuser*); WOLF-FERRARI: Lelio* (*Donne curiose*). Also MOZART: Cassandro* (*Finta semplice*). Rec for: DG. Video/Film: Achilla (*Giulio Cesare*), Prof (*Hin und zurück*). Gives recitals. Appears with symph orch. Teaches voice. Coaches repertoire. On faculty of Hochschule für Musik, Frankfurt/M. **Res:** Eschersheimerlandstr 33, Frankfurt, FR Ger. Mgmt: SLZ/FRG; TAS/AUS.

SCHREIER, PETER. Lyric tenor. German. Resident mem: Deutsche Staatsoper, Berlin, Ger DR. Born 29 Jul 1935, Meissen. Wife Renate Kupsch, occupation physical therapist. Two children. Studied: Hochschule für Musik, Dresden; Fritz Polster, Leipzig. **Debut:** Erster Gefangener (*Fidelio*) Staatsoper, Dresden 1959. Awards: 2 Nationalpreise, Schumann Preis, Händel Preis, Ger DR; var Grand Prix du Disque.
Sang with major companies in ARG: Buenos Aires; AUS: Salzburg Fest, Vienna Staatsoper; FIN: Helsinki; FRA: Paris; FR GER: Cologne, Frankfurt, Hamburg, Munich Staatsoper; GER DR: Berlin Staatsoper, Dresden; HUN: Budapest; ITA: Milan La Scala, Rome Opera; POL: Warsaw; ROM: Bucharest; SWE: Drottningholm Fest; USSR: Moscow Bolshoi; USA: New York Met. **Roles with these companies incl** CIMAROSA: Paolino (*Matrimonio segreto*); MOZART: Ferrando (*Così fan tutte*), Don Ottavio (*Don Giovanni*), Belmonte (*Entführung aus dem Serail*),

Tamino (*Zauberflöte*); NICOLAI: Fenton (*Lustigen Weiber*); ROSSINI: Almaviva‡ (*Barbiere di Siviglia*); STRAUSS, R: Flamand (*Capriccio*); WAGNER: David (*Meistersinger*), Loge (*Rheingold*). Also LORTZING: Chateauneuf (*Zar und Zimmermann*). **World premieres:** DESSAU: Physiker (*Einstein*) Staatsoper, Berlin 1974. Gives recitals. Appears with symphony orchestra. **Res:** Calberlastr 13, 8054 Dresden, Ger DR. Mgmt: KDR/GDR; MAA/USA.

SCHRÖCK, SOPHIA. Costume designer for opera, theater, television. German. Head of Costume Dépt & Resident Designer, Oper am Gärtnerplatz, Munich. Born 6 Sep 1931, Munich. Single. Studied: Akad der bildenden Künste, Munich; Profs Emil Preetorius, Helmut Jürgens. **Operatic debut:** *Daphne* Staatsoper, Munich 1957. Theater debut: Stadttheater Basel, Switzerland 1956. Previous adm positions in opera: Chief Costume Des, Staatsoper, Munich 1957-64 and Städtische Bühnen, Cologne 1964-69.

Designed for major companies in AUS: Vienna Staatsoper & Volksoper; FR GER: Cologne, Dortmund, Frankfurt, Munich Staatsoper & Gärtnerplatz; HOL: Amsterdam; SWI: Basel; USA: Chicago. **Operas designed for these companies incl** ADAM: *Postillon de Lonjumeau;* BEETHOVEN: *Fidelio;* BENNETT: *Mines of Sulphur;* BIZET: *Carmen*★; BRITTEN: *Billy Budd;* DONIZETTI: *Don Pasquale;* GLUCK: *Iphigénie en Tauride, Orfeo ed Euridice;* HANDEL: *Deidamia, Giulio Cesare;* HENZE: *Elegy for Young Lovers, König Hirsch/Re Cervo;* HINDEMITH: *Mathis der Maler;* MARTIN: *Vin herbé;* MOZART: *Clemenza di Tito, Don Giovanni, Nozze di Figaro, Zauberflöte*★; OFFENBACH: *Contes d'Hoffmann;* ORFF: *Carmina burana, Mond;* PFITZNER: *Palestrina;* RIMSKY-KORSAKOV: *Invisible City of Kitezh;* ROSSINI: *Barbiere di Siviglia, Comte Ory, Italiana in Algeri;* ROUSSEL: *Testament de la Tante Caroline;* SCHOENBERG: *Erwartung;* STRAUSS, J: *Fledermaus;* STRAUSS, R: *Ariadne auf Naxos, Daphne, Frau ohne Schatten, Rosenkavalier*★, *Schweigsame Frau;* STRAVINSKY: *Oedipus Rex;* TCHAIKOVSKY: *Pique Dame;* VERDI: *Aida, Ballo in maschera, Don Carlo, Otello, Traviata;* WAGNER: *Meistersinger, Tannhäuser;* ZIMMERMANN: *Soldaten.* Also EGK: *Columbus;* HARTMANN: *Simplicius Simplicissimus;* KILLMAYER: *Yolimba;* ORFF: *Oedipus der Tyrann, Trionfo di Afrodite, Catulli carmina.* Operatic Video–ZDF: *Hänsel und Gretel; Belshazzar.* **Res:** Kandinskystr 27, Munich, FR Ger.

SCHRÖDER-FEINEN, URSULA. Dramatic soprano. German. Born Gelsenkirchen. Husband: Bernd Feinen. **Debut:** Aida, Gelsenkirchen 1963.

Sang with major companies in AUS: Salzburg Fest, Vienna Staatsoper; CAN: Montreal/Quebec; CZE: Prague National & Smetana; DEN: Copenhagen; FRA: Nancy, Nice, Paris, Strasbourg; FR GER: Bayreuth Fest, Berlin Deutsche Oper, Bonn, Düsseldorf-Duisburg, Essen, Hamburg, Hannover, Karlsruhe, Munich Staatsoper, Nürnberg, Stuttgart; GER DR: Berlin Staatsoper, Leipzig; HOL: Amsterdam; ITA: Milan La Scala, Naples, Rome Caracalla, Trieste; POR: Lisbon; SWI: Geneva; UK: Edinburgh Fest; USA: Chi-

cago, New York Met, San Francisco Opera. **Roles with these companies incl** BEETHOVEN: Leonore★ (*Fidelio*); GERSHWIN: Bess★; GLUCK: Alceste; GOTOVAC: Djula (*Ero der Schelm*); HANDEL: Cleopatra (*Giulio Cesare*); HINDEMITH: Tochter des Cardillac; JANACEK: Jenufa; MOZART: Donna Elvira (*Don Giovanni*); OFFENBACH: Giulietta (*Contes d'Hoffmann*); ORFF: Kluge; PUCCINI: Cio-Cio-San (*Butterfly*), Giorgetta (*Tabarro*), Tosca, Turandot★; SMETANA: Marie★ (*Bartered Bride*); STRAUSS, R: Elektra★ & Chrysothemis★ (*Elektra*), Färberin (*Frau ohne Schatten*), Salome★; VERDI: Aida, Oscar (*Ballo in maschera*), Desdemona (*Otello*); WAGNER: Senta★ (*Fliegende Holländer*), Ortrud (*Lohengrin*), Eva (*Meistersinger*), Kundry (*Parsifal*), Sieglinde★ & Brünnhilde (*Walküre*), Brünnhilde (*Siegfried, Götterdämmerung*), Venus★ (*Tannhäuser*), Isolde. Recorded for EMI. Gives recitals. Appears with symphony orchestra.

SCHUBERT, REINHOLD. Stages/produces opera & theater. Also designs stage-lighting and is an author. German. Administrator for Radio Cologne. Born 13 Mar 1928, Misburg/Hannover. Wife Hannelore, occupation journalist. Three children. Studied: Staatliche Hochschule für Musik, Cologne, incl music, violin & piano. **Operatic debut:** *Flut/Diary of a Madman/Zar lässt sich photographieren* Krefeld 1960. Previous occupation: music critic 1953-56. Previous adm positions in opera: Chefdramaturg, Deutsche Oper am Rhein, Düsseldorf-Duisburg 1956-62; Oberspielleiter, Städtische Bühnen Dortmund 1962-66; Oberspielleiter, Landestheater Linz/Donau 1966-67; Oberspielleiter, Nationaltheater Mannheim 1967-68.

Directed/produced opera for major companies in AUS: Graz; FR GER: Darmstadt, Dortmund, Düsseldorf-Duisburg, Kassel, Krefeld, Mannheim, Munich Gärtnerplatz. **Operas staged for these companies incl** d'ALBERT: *Tiefland*★; BARTOK: *Bluebeard's Castle;* CORNELIUS: *Barbier von Bagdad;* DONIZETTI: *Elisir, Lucia;* EINEM: *Besuch der alten Dame*★, *Prozess;* FORTNER: *Don Perlimplin;* GLUCK: *Orfeo ed Euridice;* GOUNOD: *Faust;* HINDEMITH: *Cardillac, Mathis der Maler;* JANACEK: *Katya Kabanova, Makropoulos Affair*★; LORTZING: *Zar und Zimmermann;* MOZART: *Così fan tutte, Idomeneo, Nozze di Figaro;* NICOLAI: *Lustigen Weiber;* OFFENBACH: *Contes d'Hoffmann;* ORFF: *Kluge, Mond;* PENDERECKI: *Teufel von Loudun;* PUCCINI: *Bohème, Manon Lescaut, Tabarro;* ROSSINI: *Barbiere di Siviglia;* STRAUSS, R: *Ariadne auf Naxos;* VERDI: *Aida, Ballo in maschera, Falstaff*★, *Nabucco, Otello*★, *Rigoletto;* WAGNER: *Tannhäuser;* WOLF-FERRARI: *Donne curiose.* Also HINDEMITH: *Harmonie der Welt;* KLEBE: *Räuber.* **Operatic world premieres:** WEISHAPPEL: *Elga* Landestheater Linz, Austria 1966. Previous leading positions with major theater companies: Intendant, Vereinigte Bühnen, Graz, Austria 1968-72. Teaches at Staatliche Musikhochschule Rheinland. **Res:** Cologne, FR Ger.

SCHUH, OSCAR FRITZ. Stages/produces opera. German. Born 15 Jan 1904, Germany.

Directed/produced opera for major companies in
AUS: Salzburg Fest, Vienna Staatsoper & Volks-
oper; DEN: Copenhagen; FR GER: Berlin
Deutsche Oper, Cologne, Düsseldorf-Duisburg,
Frankfurt, Hamburg, Munich Staatsoper,
Nürnberg; ITA: Milan La Scala, Naples, Rome
Opera, Venice; SWI: Zurich. **Operas staged with
these companies incl** BARBER: *Vanessa;* BEET-
HOVEN: *Fidelio;* BERG: *Wozzeck;* BIZET:
Carmen, Djamileh; BOIELDIEU: *Dame blanche;*
BORODIN: *Prince Igor;* EGK: *Zaubergeige;*
FLOTOW: *Martha;* GLUCK: *Alceste, Orfeo ed
Euridice;* HANDEL: *Giulio Cesare, Rodelinda;*
HINDEMITH: *Cardillac;* HUMPERDINCK:
Hänsel und Gretel, Königskinder; JANACEK:
Jenufa; MILHAUD: *Pauvre matelot;* MOZART:
*Così fan tutte, Don Giovanni, Entführung aus dem
Serail, Idomeneo, Nozze di Figaro, Zauberflöte;*
OFFENBACH: *Contes d'Hoffmann;* ORFF:
Carmina burana; PERGOLESI: *Serva padrona;*
PFITZNER: *Palestrina;* PROKOFIEV: *Love for
Three Oranges;* PUCCINI: *Bohème, Gianni
Schicchi, Butterfly, Manon Lescaut, Tabarro,
Tosca;* SMETANA: *Bartered Bride;* STRAUSS,
J: *Fledermaus;* STRAUSS, R: *Arabella, Ariadne
auf Naxos, Frau ohne Schatten, Rosenkavalier;*
STRAVINSKY: *Oedipus Rex;* TCHAIKOV-
SKY: *Pique Dame;* VERDI: *Aida, Ballo in ma-
schera, Falstaff, Forza del destino, Macbeth,
Masnadieri, Simon Boccanegra, Traviata, Trova-
tore;* WAGNER: *Fliegende Holländer, Meister-
singer, Parsifal, Tannhäuser;* WEBER:
Freischütz, Oberon; WEINBERGER: *Schwanda;*
WOLF-FERRARI: *Donne curiose.* **Operatic
world premieres:** EGK: *Irische Legende;* EINEM:
Dantons Tod, Der Prozess; FORTNER: *Don Perlimplin;* MARTIN: *Le Vin herbé;* ORFF: *Antigonae.* **Res:** 267 Grossgmein, Salzburg, Austria.

SCHULTZ, CARL ALLEN. Bass-baritone & basso-
buffo. American. Resident mem: Staatsoper, Hamburg. Born 14 Mar 1934, Los Angeles. Single.
Studied: Univ of So Cal, Walter Ducloux, Gwendolyn Koldofky, Los Angeles; Kmsg Fritz
Schaetzler, Hollywood; Stuttgart Hochschule,
Kmsg Franz Völker. **Debut:** Commander Joab
(*David*) Israeli prod, NY 1956. Previous occupations: prof accompanist; vocalist and MC with ice
revue. Awards: Fulbright Schlshp to Germany
1959; First Prize Intl Vocal Compt Geneva 1960;
two piano schlshps to Univ of So Cal, Los
Angeles.
Sang with major companies in FR GER: Frank-
furt, Hamburg, Kiel, Mannheim, Stuttgart; ISR:
Tel Aviv; SWI: Zurich. **Roles with these companies
incl** BEETHOVEN: Rocco (*Fidelio*); CIMA-
ROSA: Geronimo ★ (*Matrimonio segreto*);
CORNELIUS: Abul Hassan (*Barbier von Bagdad*); DONIZETTI: Don Pasquale ★, Belcore &
Dulcamara (*Elisir*); GLINKA: Svietozar ★ (*Ruslan
and Ludmilla*); LORTZING: Van Bett (*Zar und
Zimmermann*); MOZART: Don Alfonso (*Così fan
tutte*), Osmin (*Entführung aus dem Serail*), Osmin
(*Zaïde*), Sarastro (*Zauberflöte*); MUSSORGSKY:
Pimen (*Boris Godunov*); PUCCINI: Colline
(*Bohème*); ROSSINI: Don Magnifico ★ (*Ceneren-
tola*); VERDI: Ramfis (*Aida*), Philip II (*Don
Carlo*), Fra Melitone ★ (*Forza del destino*), Zaccaria (*Nabucco*); WAGNER: König Heinrich (*Lo-
hengrin*); WOLF-FERRARI: Lunardo (*Quattro

rusteghi). Also PUCCINI: Timur (*Turandot*). Recorded for: DG. Appears with symphony orchestra. **Res:** An der Alster 31, 2000 Hamburg 1, FR
Ger. Mgmt: PAS/FRG.

SCHWANBECK, BODO. Bass-baritone & basso-
buffo. German. Resident mem: Opernhaus Frank-
furt. Born 20 Jul 1935, Schwerin, Germany. Wife
Christel Hoepping. Two children. Studied: Musik-
hochschule, Munich; Prof Franz-Theo Reuter,
Munich; K H Jarius, Stuttgart. **Debut:** Vaarlam
(*Boris Godunov*) Detmold, FR Ger 1959.
Sang with major companies in FRA: Aix-en-
Provence Fest; FR GER: Bonn, Cologne, Darm-
stadt, Dortmund, Düsseldorf-Duisburg, Frankfurt,
Hamburg, Hannover, Karlsruhe, Kassel, Mann-
heim, Munich Staatsoper & Gärtnerplatz,
Nürnberg, Saarbrücken, Stuttgart; POR: Lisbon;
SPA: Barcelona; SWI: Basel, Zurich; USA: New
York City Opera. **Roles with these companies incl**
BEETHOVEN: Don Pizarro & Rocco (*Fidelio*);
BERG: Wozzeck ★; CIMAROSA: Geronimo ★
(*Matrimonio segreto*); DEBUSSY: Golaud (*Pel-
léas et Mélisande*); DONIZETTI: Don Pas-
quale ★, Dulcamara ★ (*Elisir*); FLOTOW: Plunkett
(*Martha*); GLUCK: Thoas (*Iphigénie en Tau-
ride*); GOUNOD: Méphistophélès ★ (*Faust*);
HAYDN: Buonafede (*Mondo della luna*); LOR-
TZING: Baculus ★ (*Wildschütz*), Van Bett ★ (*Zar
und Zimmermann*); MASSENET: Sancho ★ (*Don
Quichotte*); MEYERBEER: Don Pedro (*Afri-
caine*); MOZART: Don Alfonso ★ (*Così fan tutte*),
Leporello ★ (*Don Giovanni*), Osmin ★ (*Entführung
aus dem Serail*), Figaro ★ (*Nozze di Figaro*), Papa-
geno ★ (*Zauberflöte*); MUSSORGSKY: Varlaam
(*Boris Godunov*); NICOLAI: Falstaff ★ (*Lustigen
Weiber*); OFFENBACH: Don Andres (*Péri-
chole*); PROKOFIEV: King of Clubs (*Love for
Three Oranges*); PUCCINI: Colline ★ (*Bohème*);
ROSSINI: Dott Bartolo ★ (*Barbiere di Siviglia*),
Don Magnifico ★ (*Cenerentola*), Mustafà ★ (*Italiana
in Algeri*); SMETANA: Kezal ★ (*Bartered Bride*);
STRAUSS, R: Baron Ochs ★ (*Rosenkavalier*), Sir
Morosus ★ (*Schweigsame Frau*); VERDI: Fal-
staff ★, Fra Melitone ★ (*Forza del destino*); WAG-
NER: Beckmesser (*Meistersinger*), Alberich
(*Rheingold, Götterdämmerung*). Also BERG: Ro-
drigo (*Lulu*); MOZART: Sprecher (*Zauberflöte*);
STRAUSS, R: Graf Waldner (*Arabella*). **World
premieres:** SUTERMEISTER: Rouault (*Madame
Bovary*) Opernhaus Zurich 1967. Video/Film
—ORTF Paris: Mustafà (*Italiana in Algeri*). Gives
recitals. Appears with symphony orchestra. **Res:**
Parkstr 9, 6464 Waldrode, FR Ger. Mgmt:
SLZ/FRG; SFM/USA.

SCHWARTZMAN, SEYMOUR. Dramatic baritone. American. Resident mem: Philadelphia Opera. Born 7 Dec 1930, New York. Wife Leona,
occupation real estate agent. Two children. Studied: Acad of Vocal Arts & Temple Univ, Philadelphia; Hebrew Union Coll, School of Sacred
Music. **Debut:** Sonora (*Fanciulla del West*) Philadelphia Lyric 1964. Previous occupations: cantor
1954-1966. Awards: First Prize WGN Illinois Opera Guild Aud of the Air 1966; American Opera
Aud, Magro Awd Cincinnati, O, 1966.
Sang with major companies in ISR: Tel Aviv;
POR: Lisbon; SWI: Geneva; USA: Cincinnati,
Fort Worth, Hartford, Houston, Minneapolis,

Newark, New Orleans, New York City Opera, Philadelphia Grand & Lyric, Pittsburgh, St Paul, San Diego, San Francisco Spring Opera. **Roles with these companies incl** BIZET: Escamillo (*Carmen*); DONIZETTI: Enrico (*Lucia*), Talbot★ (*Maria Stuarda*), Nottingham★ (*Roberto Devereux*); GIORDANO: Carlo Gérard (*Andrea Chénier*); LEONCAVALLO: Tonio & Silvio (*Pagliacci*); MASCAGNI: Rabbi David (*Amico Fritz*), Alfio (*Cavalleria rusticana*); MENOTTI: John Sorel (*Consul*); OFFENBACH: Coppélius etc (*Contes d'Hoffmann*); ORFF: Solo (*Carmina burana*); PUCCINI: Marcello (*Bohème*), Sharpless★ (*Butterfly*), Michele (*Tabarro*), Scarpia★ (*Tosca*); SAINT-SAENS: Grand prêtre (*Samson et Dalila*); VERDI: Amonasro★ (*Aida*), Renato★ (*Ballo in maschera*), Don Carlo★ (*Forza del destino*), Rigoletto★, Germont★ (*Traviata*), Conte di Luna (*Trovatore*); WAGNER: Holländer. Also GOUNOD: Valentin (*Faust*). Gives recitals. Appears with symphony orchestra. Teaches voice. Coaches repertoire. **Res:** 400 Lodges La, Elkins Park, PA, USA. **Mgmt:** LLF/USA; TAS/AUS.

SCHWARZENBERG, ELISABETH; née Czernohorsky. Dramatic soprano. Austrian. Resident mem: Volksoper, Vienna. Born 23 Sep 1933, Vienna. Husband Georg Schnapka, occupation opera singer, bass. Studied: Akad für Musik und darstellende Kunst, Vienna. **Debut:** Eva (*Meistersinger*) Deutsche Oper am Rhein, Düsseldorf 1956. Awards: Austrian State Prize; prizes at Geneva and Verviers.

Sang with major companies in AUS: Graz, Salzburg Fest, Vienna Staatsoper & Volksoper; BEL: Brussels; FRA: Bordeaux, Lyon, Marseille, Nancy, Nice, Rouen, Strasbourg, Toulouse; FR GER: Bayreuth Fest, Berlin Deutsche Oper, Cologne, Düsseldorf-Duisburg, Essen, Frankfurt, Hamburg, Kassel, Mannheim, Munich Staatsoper, Nürnberg, Wuppertal; HOL: Amsterdam; ITA: Milan La Scala, Palermo, Trieste, Turin; MON: Monte Carlo; POR: Lisbon; SWI: Basel, Geneva, Zurich; YUG: Dubrovnik. **Roles with these companies incl** BEETHOVEN: Marzelline (*Fidelio*); BIZET: Micaëla (*Carmen*); EINEM: Lucille (*Dantons Tod*); HANDEL: Romilda (*Xerxes*); HUMPERDINCK: Gretel; JANACEK: Emilia Marty (*Makropoulos Affair*); KODALY: Marie Louise (*Háry János*); MARTIN: Branghien★ (*Vin herbé*); MOZART: Fiordiligi (*Così fan tutte*), Donna Elvira★‡ (*Don Giovanni*), Ilia (*Idomeneo*), Contessa (*Nozze di Figaro*), Zaïde, Pamina★ (*Zauberflöte*); PFITZNER: Ighino (*Palestrina*); PUCCINI: Suor Angelica; PURCELL: Dido; RIMSKY-KORSAKOV: Coq d'or; SMETANA: Marie (*Bartered Bride*); STRAUSS, R: Zdenka (*Arabella*), Komponist (*Ariadne auf Naxos*), Chrysothemis★ (*Elektra*), Marschallin★ (*Rosenkavalier*); TCHAIKOVSKY: Tatiana (*Eugene Onegin*); VERDI: Elisabetta★ (*Don Carlo*); WAGNER: Eva (*Meistersinger*), Gutrune★ (*Götterdämmerung*); WEBER: Agathe (*Freischütz*). Also KLEBE: Amalia (*Räuber*). **World premieres:** WAGNER-REGENY: (*Bergwerk zu Falun*) Salzburg Fest 1961. Recorded for: Ariola, Eurodisc. Gives recitals. Appears with symphony orchestra. Teaches voice. Coaches repertoire. **Res:** Alpspitzstr 6, 8011 Oberpframmern/Munich, FR Ger. **Mgmt:** SLZ/FRG; TAU/SWI.

SCHWINGER, WOLFRAM. German. Dir of Opera, Württembergisches Staatstheater, Staatsoper Stuttgart, D 7 Stuttgart, FR Ger. In charge of adm matters & art policy; and is also a musicologist. Born 14 Jul 1928, Dresden, Germany. Wife Margarete. Three children. Studied: Humboldt Univ, Berlin, Germany. Plays the piano. Previous occupation: music edit & critic. In present position since 1975. World premieres at theater under his management: KLEBE: *Mädchen aus Domrémy* Stuttgart 1976. **Res:** Stuttgart, FR Ger.

SCIUTTI, GRAZIELLA. Lyric soprano. Italian. Studied: with father, Rome; Acad di Santa Cecilia, Rome. **Debut:** Lucy (*Telephone*) Aix-en-Provence Fest 1951. Awards: Europremio, Venice; H Cohen Awd, London; Philips Mozart Fest Prize, Salzburg; Microfono d'Argento, Rome.

Sang with major companies in ARG: Buenos Aires; AUS: Salzburg Fest, Vienna Staatsoper & Volksoper; BEL: Brussels, Liège; CAN: Montreal/Quebec; FRA: Aix-en-Provence Fest, Nice, Paris; FR GER: Berlin Deutsche Oper, Frankfurt, Hannover, Munich Staatsoper, Nürnberg, Wiesbaden; HOL: Amsterdam; ITA: Florence Comunale, Genoa, Milan La Scala, Naples, Palermo, Rome Opera, Venice; MON: Monte Carlo; S AFR: Johannesburg; SWE: Drottningholm; SWI: Basel, Geneva; UK: Edinburgh Fest, Glyndebourne Fest, London Royal Op; USA: Dallas, Miami, San Francisco Opera, Washington D C. **Roles with these companies incl** BEETHOVEN: Marzelline★ (*Fidelio*); CIMAROSA: Carolina (*Matrimonio segreto*); DALLAPICCOLA: Mrs Fabian (*Volo di notte*); DONIZETTI: Norina★‡ (*Don Pasquale*), Rita‡; GALUPPI: Eugenia (*Filosofo di campagna*); GLUCK: Amor (*Orfeo ed Euridice*); HANDEL: Morgana‡ (*Alcina*), Ginevra‡ (*Ariodante*), Angelica‡ (*Orlando furioso*); MENOTTI: Monica (*Medium*), Lucy (*Telephone*); MONTEVERDI: Clorinda (*Combattimento di Tancredi*), Poppea; MOZART: Servilia‡ (*Clemenza di Tito*), Despina★‡ (*Così fan tutte*), Zerlina★‡ (*Don Giovanni*), Serpetta (*Finta giardiniera*), Mme Herz‡ & Mlle Silberklang (*Schauspieldirektor*), Susanna‡ (*Nozze di Figaro*), Celidoro‡ (*Oca del Cairo*); PAISIELLO: Rosina★‡ (*Barbiere di Siviglia*); PERGOLESI: Lauretta‡ (*Maestro di musica*), Serpina‡ (*Serva padrona*); ROSSINI: Rosina★ (*Barbiere di Siviglia*), Comtesse Adèle (*Comte Ory*), Elvira‡ (*Italiana in Algeri*), Giulia★‡ (*Scala di seta*), Fiorilla★ (*Turco in Italia*); STRAUSS, J: Adele (*Fledermaus*); STRAVINSKY: Anne Trulove (*Rake's Progress*); VERDI: Oscar (*Ballo in maschera*), Nannetta‡ (*Falstaff*); WEILL: Polly (*Dreigroschenoper*); WOLF-FERRARI: Lucieta★ (*Quattro rusteghi*), Susanna★ (*Segreto di Susanna*). **World premieres:** SAUGUET: Marianne (*Caprices de Marianne*) Aix-en-Provence Fest 1954. Recorded for: EMI, Decca, Philips, Ricordi. Gives recitals. Appears with symphony orchestra. **Res:** Geneva, Switzerland. **Mgmt:** GOR/UK.

SCORSONI, RENZO. Dramatic baritone. Italian. Born 20 Apr 1929, Terni. Wife Flaminia Dante, occupation agency adv. Studied: Consv G Verdi, Mo Benvenuto Franci, Mo Riccardo Zama, Turin. **Debut:** Marcello (*Bohème*) Teatro Sperimentale, Spoleto. Awards: Winner Ntl Cont ENAL, Minis-

try of Culture & Recrea for President of the Republic.
Sang with major companies in ITA: Florence Maggio & Comunale, Naples, Palermo, Rome Opera & Caracalla, Venice. **Roles with these companies incl** BIZET: Escamillo (*Carmen*); DONIZETTI: Enrico★ (*Lucia*); GIORDANO: Carlo Gérard★ (*Andrea Chénier*); LEONCAVALLO: Tonio★ (*Pagliacci*); MASCAGNI: Alfio★ (*Cavalleria rusticana*); MENOTTI: Dr Stone★ (*Globolinks*); PUCCINI: Marcello★ (*Bohème*), Sharpless★ (*Butterfly*), Scarpia★ (*Tosca*), Guglielmo Wulf★‡ (*Villi*); RIMSKY-KORSAKOV: Juri Vsevolodovic (*Invisible City of Kitezh*); VERDI: Amonasro★ (*Aida*), Renato (*Ballo in maschera*), Don Carlo (*Forza del destino*), Nabucco, Rigoletto★, Germont★ (*Traviata*), Conte di Luna★ (*Trovatore*). Also VERDI: Gusmano (*Alzira*); LEONCAVALLO: Tamar (*Zingari*); PUCCINI: Frank (*Edgar*). Video/Film − RAI: Sebastiano★ (*Tiefland*). **Res:** V E Pistelli 4, Rome 00135, Italy.

SCOTTO, RENATA. Lyric soprano. Italian. Born 24 Feb 1935, Savona, Italy. Husband Lorenzo Anselmi, occupation violinist. Two children. Studied: Accad Musicale Savonese; Mercedes Llopart, Milan; Consv Giuseppe Verdi, Milan; Lorenzo Anselmi, husband. **Debut:** Violetta (*Traviata*) Teatro Nuovo, Milan 1954.
Sang with major companies in ARG: Buenos Aires; AUS: Salzburg Fest, Vienna Staatsoper; BEL: Brussels; CAN: Montreal/Quebec; CZE: Prague National; FRA: Marseille, Nice, Paris; GRE: Athens Fest; FR GER: Berlin Deutsche Oper, Frankfurt, Hamburg, Munich Staatsoper, Stuttgart, Wiesbaden; HUN: Budapest; ITA: Bologna, Florence Maggio & Comunale, Genoa, Milan La Scala, Naples, Palermo, Parma, Rome Opera, Trieste, Turin, Venice, Verona Arena; MEX: Mexico City; MON: Monte Carlo; POR: Lisbon; SPA: Barcelona; SWI: Basel, Geneva, Zurich; UK: Edinburgh Fest, London Royal; USSR: Moscow Bolshoi; USA: Chicago, Dallas, Hartford, Miami, Newark, New York Met, Philadelphia Lyric, Pittsburgh, San Francisco Opera; YUG: Belgrade. **Roles with these companies incl** BELLINI: Giulietta (*Capuleti ed i Montecchi*), Norma★, Elvira (*Puritani*), Amina★ (*Sonnambula*), Alaide★ (*Straniera*); BIZET: Micaëla (*Carmen*), Léila (*Pêcheurs de perles*); CATALANI: Walter (*Wally*); CHARPENTIER: Louise; DEBUSSY: Lia (*Enfant prodigue*); DONIZETTI: Anna Bolena★, Norina★ (*Don Pasquale*), Adina★ (*Elisir*), Linda di Chamounix★, Lucia★‡, Maria di Rohan★, Maria Stuarda★; GOUNOD: Marguerite★ (*Faust*); HUMPERDINCK: Gretel; LEONCAVALLO: Nedda★ (*Pagliacci*); MASCAGNI: Suzel (*Amico Fritz*); MASSENET: Manon; MOZART: Fiordiligi (*Così fan tutte*), Donna Elvira (*Don Giovanni*), Contessa (*Nozze di Figaro*); OFFENBACH: Antonia★ & Giulietta★ (*Contes d'Hoffmann*); PERGOLESI: Serpina‡ (*Serva padrona*); PUCCINI: Mimi★‡ (*Bohème*), Lauretta (*Gianni Schicchi*), Cio-Cio-San★‡ (*Butterfly*), Suor Angelica★, Giorgetta★ (*Tabarro*), Liù★‡ (*Turandot*); RIMSKY-KORSAKOV: Fevronia (*Invisible City of Kitezh*); ROSSINI: Fanny‡ (*Cambiale di matrimonio*), Pamira (*Assedio di Corinto*); SMETANA: Marie (*Bartered Bride*); SPONTINI: Giulia★ (*Vestale*); TCHAIKOVSKY: Lisa (*Pique Dame*); VERDI:

Amelia★ (*Ballo in maschera*), Nannetta (*Falstaff*), Giovanna d'Arco, Giselda★ (*Lombardi*), Luisa Miller★, Desdemona★ (*Otello*), Gilda★ (*Rigoletto*), Amelia★ (*Simon Boccanegra*), Violetta★ (*Traviata*), Leonora★ (*Trovatore*), Elena★ (*Vespri*). Also MEYERBEER: Isabelle (*Robert le diable*); BELLINI: Bianca★ (*Bianca e Fernando*). Recorded for: EMI, Cetra, DG, Columbia, Harmonia. Gives recitals. Appears with symphony orchestra. **Res:** Gonzaga/Mantua, Italy. Mgmt: LOM/USA.

SCOVOTTI, JEANETTE LOUISE. Coloratura soprano. American. Resident mem: Staatsoper Hamburg. Born 5 Dec 1936, New York. Husband Klaus Andersen, occupation engineer. Studied: Third Street Music School, Margit Schey, New York; Juilliard Music School, Frederic Cohen, Frederic Waldman; High School of Music and Art, New York. **Debut:** Adele (*Fledermaus*) Metropolitan Opera 1962. Awards: Kammersängerin, State Senate of Hamburg; winner Town Hall recital debut, New York Singing Teachers Assn.
Sang with major companies in ARG: Buenos Aires; AUS: Vienna Staatsoper & Volksoper; CAN: Vancouver; FR GER: Berlin Deutsche Oper, Cologne, Düsseldorf-Duisburg, Hamburg, Munich Staatsoper, Stuttgart; HOL: Amsterdam; ITA: Genoa, Turin; SPA: Barcelona; UK: London Royal Opera; USA: Baltimore, Boston, Chicago, Cincinnati, Dallas, Houston, Lake George, Miami, Newark, New York Met & City Opera, Philadelphia Grand, San Francisco Opera & Spring Opera, Santa Fe, Washington, DC.; YUG: Dubrovnik. **Roles with these companies incl** CIMAROSA: Carolina★ (*Matrimonio segreto*); DONIZETTI: Norina★ (*Don Pasquale*), Adina (*Elisir*), Lucia★; GIORDANO: Olga (*Fedora*); GLINKA: Ludmilla (*Ruslan and Ludmilla*); MASSENET: Sophie (*Werther*); MENOTTI: Monica (*Medium*), Lucy (*Telephone*); MOZART: Despina★ (*Così fan tutte*), Zerlina★ (*Don Giovanni*), Konstanze★ & Blondchen (*Entführung aus dem Serail*), Mlle Silberklang (*Schauspieldirektor*), Giunia (*Lucio Silla*), Susanna★ (*Nozze di Figaro*), Königin der Nacht★ (*Zauberflöte*); NICOLAI: Frau Fluth (*Lustigen Weiber*); OFFENBACH: Olympia★ (*Contes d'Hoffmann*); ORFF: Solo★ (*Carmina burana*); PUCCINI: Musetta★ (*Bohème*), Lauretta (*Gianni Schicchi*); RAMEAU: Minerva‡ (*Castor et Pollux*); RAVEL: Concepcion (*Heure espagnole*); RIMSKY-KORSAKOV: Reine de Schemakan (*Coq d'or*); ROSSINI: Rosina★ (*Barbiere di Siviglia*), Fiorilla (*Turco in Italia*); STRAUSS, J: Adele (*Fledermaus*); STRAUSS, R: Fiakermilli★ (*Arabella*), Zerbinetta★ (*Ariadne auf Naxos*), Sophie (*Rosenkavalier*), Aminta★ (*Schweigsame Frau*); STRAVINSKY: Rossignol★; VERDI: Oscar★ (*Ballo in maschera*), Nannetta★ (*Falstaff*), Gilda★ (*Rigoletto*), Violetta (*Traviata*). Also BIZET: Marie★ (*Ivan IV*); BACH, J C: Arsinda★ (*Clemenza di Scipione*). **World premieres:** KRENEK: Sardekai (*Wenn Sardekai auf Reisen geht*) Hamburg Opera 1970; SCHULLER: Miss Hampton (*Visitation*) Hamburg Opera 1966. Recorded for: Telefunken. Video/Film − Telair: (*Castor et Pollux*). Gives recitals. Appears with symphony orchestra. **Res:** Heimweg 7, Hamburg, FR Ger. Mgmt: LLS/USA; AIM/UK.

SEBASTIAN, GEORGES. Conductor of opera and symphony. Born 17 Aug 1903, Budapest. Studied: with Zoltán Kodály, Leo Weiner, Bruno Walter; incl piano. Operatic training as repetiteur at Bayerische Staatsoper, Munich.

Conducted with major companies in BEL: Brussels; FRA: Aix-en-Provence Fest, Marseille, Paris, Toulouse; FR GER: Berlin Deutsche Oper, Hamburg, Munich Staatsoper; GER DR: Leipzig; SPA: Barcelona; SWI: Geneva; USA: New York Met, San Francisco Opera; et al. Operas with these companies incl BEETHOVEN: *Fidelio;* BIZET: *Carmen;* DONIZETTI: *Lucia;* MASSENET: *Thaïs‡;* MOZART: *Così fan tutte, Don Giovanni, Nozze di Figaro, Zauberflöte;* MUSSORGSKY: *Boris Godunov;* PROKOFIEV: *War and Peace;* PUCCINI: *Bohème, Fanciulla del West, Manon Lescaut, Tosca;* ROSSINI: *Barbiere di Siviglia;* STRAUSS, R: *Ariadne auf Naxos, Elektra, Rosenkavalier, Salome;* THOMAS: *Mignon‡;* VERDI: *Aida, Ballo in maschera, Don Carlo, Falstaff, Forza del destino, Otello, Rigoletto, Traviata, Trovatore;* WAGNER: *Lohengrin, Walküre, Götterdämmerung, Tannhäuser, Tristan und Isolde;* et al. Recorded for Richmond, Decca. Previous positions as Mus Dir with major orch: Phil Orch, Scranton, PA, USA 1940-45; Radio Orch, New York. **Res:** France.

SEBASTIANI, SYLVA; née Sylva Anghelone. Dramatic soprano. Italian. Born 8 Dec 1942, Trieste. Divorced. One son. Studied: Viorica Ursuleac Krauss, Afro Poli. **Debut:** Manon Lescaut, Teatro Reggio Emilia, Italy 1969. Awards: Prize, Compt Barcelona, Spain; First Prizes and Gold Medals Reggio Emilia, Parma, Busseto and Merano.

Sang with major companies in AUS: Salzburg Fest; CZE: Prague National; HUN: Budapest; ITA: Bologna, Parma, Rome Opera, Venice; SPA: Barcelona; YUG: Dubrovnik. **Roles with these companies incl** BELLINI: Norma★; DONIZETTI: Lucrezia Borgia; DVORAK: Rusalka★; GIORDANO: Maddalena★ (*Andrea Chénier*); LEONCAVALLO: Nedda★ (*Pagliacci*); MASCAGNI: Santuzza★ (*Cavalleria rusticana*); PONCHIELLI: Gioconda★; PUCCINI: Mimi★ (*Bohème*), Minnie★ (*Fanciulla del West*), Manon Lescaut★, Suor Angelica★, Tosca★, Turandot★; SPONTINI: Amazily★ (*Fernand Cortez*), Giulia★ (*Vestale*); VERDI: Aida★, Amelia★ (*Ballo in maschera*), Elisabetta★ (*Don Carlo*), Donna Elvira★ (*Ernani*), Leonora★ (*Forza del destino*), Lady Macbeth★, Abigaille★ (*Nabucco*), Violetta★ (*Traviata*), Leonora★ (*Trovatore*); WAGNER: Elsa (*Lohengrin*), Isolde; ZANDONAI: Francesca da Rimini★. Also MANNINO: (*Vivì*). Gives recitals. **Res:** V di Val Cannuta 15, Rome, Italy.

SEEFEHLNER, EGON. Austrian. Gen Int, Deutsche Oper Berlin, Richard Wagner Str; Gen Dir designate, Staatsoper, Vienna 1976- . In charge of overall adm matters. Born 3 Jun 1912, Vienna. Single. Studied: Univ, Konsularakad, Theresianische Akad, Vienna; LLD. Previous positions, primarily adm & musical: Gen Secy, Konzerthausgesellsch, Vienna; Gen Secy, Vienna State Opera 1954-61. Started with present company in 1961 as Deputy Gen Int; in present position since 1972. World premieres at theaters under his management: FORTNER: *Elisabeth Tudor*

Berlin 1972; NABOKOV: *Love's Labour's Lost* Brussels 1973, perf by Deutsche Oper. **Res:** Olympischestr 10, Berlin, FR Ger.

SEEGER, HORST. German. Dir, Staatsoper & Staatstheater Dresden, Hainweg 5, 8051 Dresden 1973- . In charge of overall adm matters, art policy. Is also a st dir/prod. Born 6 Nov 1926, Berlin/Erkner. Wife Traute, occupation teacher. Two children. Studied: Humboldt Univ, Berlin; PhD. Plays the piano & violin. Previous occupations: mus critic Berlin, Ger DR 1957-60. Form position: Dramaturg, Komische Oper Berlin, Ger DR 1960-73. World premieres at theaters under his management: MATTHUS: *Letzte Schuss* Berlin 1968; GEISLER: *Doppelgänger* Berlin 1969; ZIMMERMANN: *Levins Mühle* Dresden 1973. Awards: Lessing-Preis 1972, Min of Culture, Ger DR. **Res:** Dresden, Ger DR.

SEGERSTAM, LEIF SELIM. Conductor of opera and symphony; composer. Finnish. Mus Dir, ORF Symph Orch, Vienna after Aug 1975. Born 2 Mar 1944, Vasa, Finland. Wife Hannele Angervo, occupation violinist. Two children. Studied: Sibelius Acad, Prof Tauno Hannikainen, Helsinki; Prof Jussi Jalas; Juilliard School of Music, New York, Jean Morel; incl violin, piano, recorder, trumpet. Plays the violin, viola, piano. **Operatic debut:** *Barbiere di Siviglia* Opera Socy of Tampere, Finland 1962. Symphonic debut: Helsinki Youth Orch 1961. Previous occupations: concert & orch violinist; awd winning pianist; chamber musician. Previous adm positions in opera: Music Dir, Royal Opera, Stockholm 1971-72; Adm Asst & First Cond, Deutsche Oper Berlin 1972-73; Gen Mng, Finnish National Opera, Helsinki 1973-74.

Conducted with major companies in ARG: Buenos Aires; AUS: Salzburg Fest; DEN: Copenhagen; FIN: Helsinki; FR GER: Berlin Deutsche Oper, Hamburg; ITA: Milan La Scala; SWE: Stockholm; SWI: Geneva; UK: London Royal; USA: New York Met. **Operas with these companies** incl BERG: *Wozzeck★;* BUSONI: *Doktor Faust★;* GERSHWIN: *Porgy and Bess;* JANACEK: *From the House of the Dead★, Makropoulos Affair★;* KODALY: *Háry János;* MOZART: *Don Giovanni★, Entführung aus dem Serail★, Nozze di Figaro★;* PUCCINI: *Bohème★, Manon Lescaut★, Tosca★, Turandot★;* ROSSINI: *Barbiere di Siviglia, Cenerentola★;* STRAUSS, J: *Fledermaus;* STRAUSS, R: *Rosenkavalier★, Salome★;* STRAVINSKY: *Rake's Progress★;* VERDI: *Aida, Don Carlo★, Otello★, Traviata;* WAGNER: *Parsifal★, Tristan und Isolde★.* Also WERLE: *Resan★.* Video—Finnish TV: *Barbiere di Siviglia.* Conducted major orch in Europe & USA/Canada. **Res:** Mäntyviita 3E 35, Tapiola, Finland. Mgmt: JUC/SWI.

SEIBEL, KLAUSPETER. Conductor of opera and symphony. German. Resident Cond, Städt Bühnen Frankfurt; after Aug 1975 Gen Mus Dir, Opera House Freiburg, FR Ger. Also Mus Dir, Phil Orch Freiburg. Born 7 May 1936, Offenbach, Germany. Wife Jutta Reumann, occupation singer. Three children. Studied: Städt Konsv Nürnberg; Staatl Hochschule für Musik, Munich; incl piano. Plays the piano. Operatic training as repetiteur & asst cond at Theater am Gärtnerplatz, Munich 1957-

60. **Operatic debut:** *Périchole* Theater am Gärtnerplatz 1958. Symphonic debut: Phil, Munich 1961. Awards: Richard Strauss Stipd, City of Munich 1957; Third Prize, Nicolai Malko Compt, Copenhagen 1965; Second Prize, Dimitri Mitropoulos Compt, New York 1969.

Conducted with major companies in FR GER: Bielefeld, Düsseldorf-Duisburg, Frankfurt, Hamburg, Kassel, Munich Staatsoper & Gärtnerplatz, Saarbrücken. **Operas with these companies incl** d'ALBERT: *Tiefland;* AUBER: *Fra Diavolo;* BEETHOVEN: *Fidelio*★*;* BERG: *Lulu*★*;* BIZET: *Carmen*★*;* DESSAU: *Verurteilung des Lukullus;* DONIZETTI: *Campanello, Don Pasquale*★*, Fille du régiment;* EGK: *Zaubergeige;* FLOTOW: *Martha;* FORTNER: *Don Perlimplin;* GERSHWIN: *Porgy and Bess*★*;* GLUCK: *Orfeo ed Euridice*★*;* GOUNOD: *Faust*★*;* HENZE: *Bassariden*★*, Junge Lord*★*;* HUMPERDINCK: *Hänsel und Gretel*★*;* JANACEK: *Katya Kabanova*★*;* LEONCAVALLO: *Pagliacci*★*;* LORTZING: *Waffenschmied, Wildschütz, Zar und Zimmermann*★*;* MASCAGNI: *Cavalleria rusticana*★*;* MONTEVERDI: *Incoronazione di Poppea;* MOZART: *Così fan tutte, Don Giovanni*★*, Entführung aus dem Serail*★*, Nozze di Figaro*★*, Oca del Cairo, Zauberflöte*★*;* OFFENBACH: *Contes d'Hoffmann*★*, Périchole;* ORFF: *Kluge, Mond;* PROKOFIEV: *Love for Three Oranges;* PUCCINI: *Bohème*★*, Butterfly*★*, Tosca*★*, Turandot*★*;* ROSSINI: *Barbiere di Siviglia*★*, Comte Ory, Italiana in Algeri;* SCHOENBERG: *Erwartung*★*;* SMETANA: *Bartered Bride;* STRAUSS, J: *Fledermaus*★*;* STRAUSS, R: *Arabella*★*, Ariadne auf Naxos*★*, Elektra*★*, Frau ohne Schatten*★*, Rosenkavalier*★*, Salome*★*;* TCHAIKOVSKY: *Eugene Onegin*★*, Maid of Orleans;* THOMAS: *Mignon;* VERDI: *Aida, Ballo in maschera*★*, Don Carlo*★*, Falstaff*★*, Forza del destino*★*, Otello, Rigoletto*★*, Traviata, Trovatore*★*;* WAGNER: *Lohengrin, Meistersinger, Rheingold;* WEBER: *Freischütz*★*;* WOLF-FERRARI: *Quattro rusteghi.* **World premieres:** GILBERT: *Scene Machine* Staatstheater Kassel, FR Ger 1971. Conducted major orch in Europe, USA/Canada. **Res:** Freiburg, FR Ger.

SELLNER, GUSTAV RUDOLF. Stages/produces opera. German. Born 25 May 1905, Traunstein, Germany. Studied: Munich Univ. Previous adm positions in opera: Intendant, Darmstadt till 1961, Deutsche Oper Berlin 1961-72.

Directed/produced opera for major companies in AUS: Salzburg Fest, Vienna Staatsoper; FR GER: Berlin Deutsche Oper, Darmstadt, Essen, Hamburg, Hannover, Kiel; et al. **Operas staged with these companies incl** BERG: *Lulu, Wozzeck;* BIZET: *Carmen;* CIMAROSA: *Matrimonio segreto;* DALLAPICCOLA: *Ulisse;* EINEM: *Besuch der alten Dame, Dantons Tod;* GLUCK: *Iphigénie en Tauride;* HENZE: *Bassariden, Elegy for Young Lovers, Junge Lord;* MOZART: *Entführung aus dem Serail, Idomeneo;* MUSSORGSKY: *Boris Godunov;* ORFF: *Carmina burana;* REIMANN: *Melusine;* SCHOENBERG: *Moses und Aron;* STRAUSS, R: *Rosenkavalier;* VERDI: *Don Carlo, Otello, Simon Boccanegra;* WAGNER: *Rheingold, Walküre, Siegfried, Götterdämmerung;* et al. Also ORFF: *Prometheus.* **Operatic world premieres:** HENZE: *Junge Lord*

Deutsche Oper Berlin 1965, *Bassariden* Salzburg 1966; DALLAPICCOLA: *Ulisse* 1968; BLACHER: *200,000 Taler* 1969; REIMANN: *Melusine* 1971, all at Deutsche Oper Berlin.

SENN, HERBERT CHARLES. Scenic designer for opera, theater. Collaborates with Helen Pond. American. Resident principal designer, Opera Co of Boston and at Cape Playhouse, Dennis, MA. Born 9 Oct 1924, Ilion, NY. Single. Studied: Columbia Univ, Milton Smith, Woodman Thompson, New York. **Operatic professional debut:** Opera Co of Boston 1964. Theater debut: Gate Repertory Co, New York 1955.

Designed for major companies in USA: Boston, New York City Opera. **Operas designed for these companies incl** BELLINI: *Norma*★*;* BERLIOZ: *Benvenuto Cellini*★*, Troyens*★*;* BRITTEN: *Albert Herring;* CHARPENTIER: *Louise;* DONIZETTI: *Elisir, Fille du régiment, Lucia;* GAY/orig: *Beggar's Opera;* HENZE: *Junge Lord*★*;* KURKA: *Good Soldier Schweik;* MASSENET: *Don Quichotte*★*;* MOZART: *Così fan tutte*★*, Entführung aus dem Serail;* PROKOFIEV: *War and Peace*★*;* PUCCINI: *Tosca;* RAMEAU: *Hippolyte et Aricie;* ROSSINI: *Barbiere di Siviglia*★*, Semiramide;* STRAUSS, R: *Ariadne auf Naxos*★*;* STRAVINSKY: *Rake's Progress;* VERDI: *Falstaff*★*, Rigoletto, Traviata*★*;* WAGNER: *Fliegende Holländer;* WEILL: *Aufstieg und Fall der Stadt Mahagonny*★*.* **Operatic world premieres:** CHAVEZ: *Panfilo and Lauretta* Columbia Univ Opera Wrkshp, New York 1957; SCHULLER: *Fisherman and his Wife* Opera Co of Boston 1970. **Res:** 316 W 51 St, New York 10019, USA.

SEQUI, SANDRO. Stages/produces opera, theater & television. Also designs stage-lighting and is an author. Italian. Born 10 Nov 1935, Rome. Single. Studied: Ntl Acad of Dramatic Arts, Rome; incl music & piano. **Operatic debut:** RESPIGHI: *Lucrezia* La Fenice, Venice 1961. Theater debut: Spoleto Fest 1960.

Directed/produced opera for major companies in ARG: Buenos Aires; BEL: Brussels; FRA: Aix-en-Provence Fest, Orange Fest; GRE: Athens Fest; HOL: Amsterdam; ITA: Bologna, Florence Maggio & Comunale, Genoa, Milan La Scala, Naples, Palermo, Rome Opera, Spoleto Fest, Turin, Venice; POR: Lisbon; UK: Edinburgh Fest, London Royal; USA: Chicago, New York Met. **Operas staged with these companies incl** BELLINI: *Capuleti ed i Montecchi*★*, Norma*★*, Puritani*★*, Sonnambula;* CIMAROSA: *Matrimonio segreto;* DONIZETTI: *Fille du régiment*★*;* FALLA: *Retablo de Maese Pedro;* GLUCK: *Iphigénie en Aulide;* JANACEK: *Jenufa*★*;* MASSENET: *Manon;* MONTEVERDI: *Combattimento di Tancredi, Favola d'Orfeo, Incoronazione di Poppea;* MOZART: *Così fan tutte, Don Giovanni, Nozze di Figaro;* PAISIELLO: *Barbiere di Siviglia;* PUCCINI: *Bohème*★*, Butterfly, Manon Lescaut, Turandot;* ROSSINI: *Guillaume Tell*★*, Otello, Semiramide*★*, Assedio di Corinto*★*, Signor Bruschino;* VERDI: *Attila*★*, Ballo in maschera*★*, Don Carlo*★*, Nabucco, Otello, Rigoletto, Simon Boccanegra, Traviata;* WAGNER: *Lohengrin.* **Operatic world premieres:** CHAILLY: *Idiota* Opera, Rome 1970. **Res:** V Monterone 2, Rome, Italy.

SERBO, RICO FRANK. Lyric tenor. American. Resident mem: Gärtnerplatztheater, Munich. Born 9 May 1940, Stockton, CA, USA. Wife Carol Kirkpatrick, occupation singer. Two children. Studied: Univ of the Pacific, Henry Welton, Stockton, CA; Mabel Riegelman, San Francisco; Robert Weede, Concord, CA. **Debut:** Don Ramiro (*Cenerentola*) San Francisco Opera Merola Prgr 1965. Previous occupations: chemist. Awards: Kirsten Flagstad Awd, New York 1966; M B Rockefeller Fund Grant 1966; Euterpe Opera Awd, Los Angeles 1967; Corbett Fndt Grant, Cincinnati, O, 1969. **Sang with major companies in** FR GER: Essen, Munich Gärtnerplatz; HOL: Amsterdam; USA: San Francisco Opera & Spring Opera, Santa Fe, Seattle. **Roles with these companies incl** BOITO: Faust (*Mefistofele*); DONIZETTI: Ernesto⋆(*Don Pasquale*); FLOTOW: Lionel (*Martha*); HENZE: Tony⋆ (*Elegy for Young Lovers*), Lord Barrat⋆ (*Junge Lord*); MASCAGNI: Turiddu (*Cavalleria*); MOZART: Ferrando (*Così fan tutte*), Tamino⋆ (*Zauberflöte*); NICOLAI: Fenton (*Lustigen Weiber*); PUCCINI: Rodolfo (*Bohème*); ROSSINI: Almaviva (*Barbiere di Siviglia*), Don Ramiro (*Cenerentola*); SHOSTAKOVICH: Zinovy⋆ (*Katerina Ismailova*); STRAUSS, R: Ein Sänger⋆ (*Rosenkavalier*); STRAVINSKY: Tom Rakewell (*Rake's Progress*); SUTERMEISTER: Romeo⋆; VERDI: Fenton⋆ (*Falstaff*), Alfredo⋆ (*Traviata*); WOLF-FERRARI: Filipeto⋆ (*Quattro rusteghi*). **World premieres:** HENZE: Eusebio & Paco & Alberto (*Rachel, la Cubana*) Gärtnerplatztheater, Munich, first stgd 1975. Gives recitals. Appears with symphony orchestra. Teaches voice. Coaches repertoire. Mgmt: VLD/AUS.

SEREBRINSKY, TITO. Stages/produces opera & theater. Argentinean. Resident Stage Dir, Marseille Opera, France. Born 1937, Buenos Aires. Single. Studied: Teatro Colón 1961-63; as asst to Margherita Wallmann 1970. Operatic training as asst stage dir at Geneva Opera 1963-65. **Operatic debut:** *Così fan tutte* Théâtre Municipal de Tours, France 1969. Theater debut: Spanish plays in Geneva 1966-68. **Directed/produced opera for major companies in** ARG: Buenos Aires; FRA: Bordeaux, Marseille, Paris; ITA: Trieste; MON: Monte Carlo. **Operas staged with these companies incl** BELLINI: *Puritani⋆;* DONIZETTI: *Don Pasquale, Elisir⋆;* FALLA: *Vida breve⋆;* GLUCK: *Orfeo ed Euridice;* LECOCQ: *Fille de Madame Angot⋆;* MOZART: *Così fan tutte⋆, Don Giovanni⋆;* VERDI: *Ballo in maschera⋆, Rigoletto⋆.* Also LESUR: *Andrea del Sarto;* HAHN: *Ciboulette.* **Res:** Marseille, France. Mgmt: DBA/USA.

SERENI, MARIO. Lyric & dramatic baritone. Italian. Resident mem: Metropolitan Opera, New York; Staatsoper, Vienna; La Scala, Milan. Born 25 Mar 1928, Perugia. Wife Elsa. Four children. Studied: Accad Chigiana, Siena; Accad S Cecilia, Rome. **Debut:** Wolfram (*Tannhäuser*) Teatro Massimo, Palermo 1956. Previous occupations: precision mechanic. Awards: Arena d'oro, Verona; Verdi Awd, Parma. **Sang with major companies in** ARG: Buenos Aires; AUS: Vienna Staatsoper & Volksoper; CAN: Montreal/Quebec; FRA: Marseille; ITA: Florence Maggio & Comunale, Milan La Scala, Naples, Palermo, Parma, Rome Opera & Caracalla, Trieste, Turin, Venice, Verona Arena; MEX: Mexico City; MON: Monte Carlo; POR: Lisbon; USA: Baltimore, Chicago Lyric, Dallas, Hartford Connecticut Opera, Houston, Miami, New Orleans, New York Met, Philadelphia Grand & Lyric; YUG: Belgrade. **Roles with these companies incl** BIZET: Escamillo⋆ (*Carmen*); CILEA: Michonnet⋆ (*A. Lecouvreur*); DONIZETTI: Dott Malatesta⋆ (*Don Pasquale*), Belcore⋆ (*Elisir*), Enrico⋆ (*Lucia*); GIORDANO: Carlo Gérard⋆ (*Andrea Chénier*); GOUNOD: Méphistophélès (*Faust*); LEONCAVALLO: Tonio⋆ (*Pagliacci*); MASCAGNI: Alfio⋆ (*Cavalleria rusticana*); PONCHIELLI: Barnaba⋆ (*Gioconda*); PUCCINI: Marcello⋆ (*Bohème*), Jack Rance⋆ (*Fanciulla del West*), Sharpless⋆ (*Butterfly*), Lescaut⋆ (*Manon Lescaut*), Rambaldo⋆ (*Rondine*), Michele⋆ (*Tabarro*), Scarpia⋆ (*Tosca*); ROSSINI: Figaro⋆ (*Barbiere di Siviglia*); VERDI: Amonasro⋆ (*Aida*), Renato⋆ (*Ballo in maschera*), Rodrigo⋆ (*Don Carlo*), Don Carlo⋆ (*Ernani*), Ford⋆ (*Falstaff*), Don Carlo⋆ (*Forza del destino*), Giacomo⋆ (*Giovanna d'Arco*), Miller⋆ (*Luisa Miller*), Macbeth⋆, Nabucco⋆, Iago⋆ (*Otello*), Simon Boccanegra⋆, Germont⋆ (*Traviata*), Conte di Luna⋆ (*Trovatore*). Recorded for: RCA, Angel, RAI. Video/Film— Met Opera/NHK: (*Barbiere*). Gives recitals. Appears with symphony orchestra. Teaches voice. **Res:** V Mario Angeloni 1, Perugia, Italy.

SERGI, ARTURO; né Arthur Kagan. Dramatic tenor. American. Born 8 Nov 1927, New York. Wife Leonore, occupation dramatic soprano. One child. Studied: Michael Zetkin, Leon Cortilli, Friedrich Schorr, New York; Sergio Nazor, Rome. **Debut:** Otello, Städtische Oper Wuppertal 1955. **Sang with major companies in** AUS: Vienna Staatsoper; BRA: Rio de Janeiro; FRA: Paris; FR GER: Bayreuth Fest, Berlin Deutsche Oper, Cologne, Dortmund, Düsseldorf-Duisburg, Essen, Frankfurt, Hamburg, Hannover, Karlsruhe, Kassel, Kiel, Krefeld, Mannheim, Munich Staatsoper, Nürnberg, Stuttgart, Wiesbaden, Wuppertal; GER DR: Leipzig; HOL: Amsterdam; HUN: Budapest; ITA: Bologna, Florence Maggio, Genoa, Milan La Scala, Palermo; SPA: Barcelona; UK: London Royal Opera; USA: Hawaii, Houston, New York Met & City Opera, Omaha, San Diego, Seattle. **Roles with these companies incl** BEETHOVEN: Florestan⋆‡ (*Fidelio*); BERG: Maler (*Lulu*), Tambourmajor (*Wozzeck*); BIZET: Don José⋆ (*Carmen*); BOITO: Faust⋆ (*Mefistofele*); BRITTEN: Peter Grimes; DALLAPICCOLA: Jailer/Inquisitor (*Prigioniero*), Pellerin & Radio Telegrapher (*Volo di notte*); DONIZETTI: Ernesto (*Don Pasquale*), Nemorino (*Elisir*), Edgardo⋆ (*Lucia*); EINEM: Joseph K (*Prozess*); GIORDANO: Andrea Chénier; GLUCK: Admetos (*Alceste*), Achille (*Iphigénie en Aulide*); HANDEL: Sextus (*Giulio Cesare*); HINDEMITH: Apprentice (*Cardillac*), Albrecht v Brandenberg (*Mathis der Maler*); LEONCAVALLO: Canio (*Pagliacci*); MASCAGNI: Turiddu (*Cavalleria rusticana*); MASSENET: Werther; MENOTTI: Kodanda (*Dernier sauvage*); MONTEVERDI: Nero (*Incoronazione di Poppea*); MOZART: Tito (*Clemenza di Tito*); OFFENBACH: Hoffmann⋆; PUCCINI: Rodolfo⋆ (*Bohème*), Dick Johnson (*Fanciulla del West*), Pinkerton★ (*Butterfly*), Des Grieux (*Manon Lescaut*), Luigi★ (*Tabarro*), Cavaradossi (*Tosca*), Calaf (*Turandot*); SAINT-SAENS: Samson★; STRAUSS, J: Alfred★ (*Fledermaus*); STRAUSS, R: Bacchus (*Ariadne auf Naxos*), Aegisth (*Elektra*), Ein Sänger (*Rosenkavalier*), Herodes★ (*Salome*); STRAVINSKY: Oedipus Rex; TCHAIKOVSKY: Lenski (*Eugene Onegin*), Gherman (*Pique Dame*); VERDI: Radames★ (*Aida*), Riccardo (*Ballo in maschera*), Don Carlo, Ernani, Don Alvaro (*Forza del destino*), Ismaele (*Nabucco*), Otello★, Duca di Mantova (*Rigoletto*), Gabriele (*Simon Boccanegra*), Alfredo (*Traviata*), Manrico (*Trovatore*), Arrigo (*Vespri*); WAGNER: Erik★ (*Fliegende Holländer*), Lohengrin, Walther (*Meistersinger*), Parsifal, Siegmund (*Walküre*), Tannhäuser, Walther v d Vogelweide (*Tannhäuser*); WEBER: Max (*Freischütz*). Also DVORAK: Dimitrij; STRAUSS, R: Italienischer Sänger (*Capriccio*); MUSSORGSKY: Dimitri (*Boris· Godunov*); KLEBE: Cherubino (*Figaro lässt sich scheiden*). Recorded for: Eurodisc. Gives recitals. Appears with symphony orchestra. Teaches voice. Coaches repertoire. On faculty of Univ of Texas, Austin, USA. **Res:** 3925 Knollwood Dr, Austin, TX, USA. Mgmt: JEN/USA.

SERKOYAN, GÉRARD. Bass. French. Resident mem: Opéra de Paris. Born 14 Jul 1922, Istanbul, Turkey. Wife Lise, occupation professor. Studied: Consv de Paris, Paul Razavet. **Debut:** Sarastro (*Zauberflöte*) Lyon Opera 1950.
Sang with major companies in BEL: Liège; FRA: Bordeaux, Lyon, Marseille, Nancy, Nice, Orange Fest, Paris, Rouen, Strasbourg, Toulouse; ITA: Naples. **Roles with these companies incl** BEETHOVEN: Rocco★ (*Fidelio*); BELLINI: Oroveso★ (*Norma*), Rodolfo★ (*Sonnambula*); BERLIOZ: Méphistophélès (*Damnation de Faust*); CHARPENTIER: Père★ (*Louise*); DEBUSSY: Arkel★ (*Pelléas et Mélisande*); DONIZETTI: Baldassare (*Favorite*); GOUNOD: Méphistophélès★ (*Faust*), Ramon★ (*Mireille*); HALEVY: Brogny (*Juive*); MASSENET: Phanuel★ (*Hérodiade*), Des Grieux★ (*Portrait de Manon*); MEYERBEER: Marcel★ (*Huguenots*); MOZART: Osmin★ (*Entführung aus dem Serail*), Sarastro★ (*Zauberflöte*); MUSSORGSKY: Boris★ & Pimen★ (*Boris Godunov*), Dosifei (*Khovanshchina*); OFFENBACH: Coppélius etc★ (*Contes d'Hoffmann*); PENDERECKI: Barré★ (*Teufel von Loudun*); PROKOFIEV: King of Clubs★ (*Love for Three Oranges*); PUCCINI: Colline (*Bohème*); ROSSINI: Don Basilio★ (*Barbiere di Siviglia*); VERDI: Ramfis★ (*Aida*), Philip II★ (*Don Carlo*), Padre Guardiano (*Forza del destino*), Banquo (*Macbeth*), Zaccaria★ (*Nabucco*), Fiesco (*Simon Boccanegra*), Procida (*Vespri*); WAGNER: Daland★ (*Fliegende Holländer*), König Heinrich (*Lohengrin*), Pogner (*Meistersinger*), Fafner (*Siegfried*), Hunding★ (*Walküre*), Landgraf★ (*Tannhäuser*), König Marke★ (*Tristan und Isolde*). Also PUCCINI: Timur★ (*Turandot*); DONIZETTI: Raimondo★ (*Lucia*); TCHAIKOVSKY: Gremin★ (*Eugene Onegin*); MOZART: Commendatore★ (*Don Giovanni*); GOUNOD: Frère Laurent★· (*Roméo et Juliette*). Gives recitals. Appears with symphony orchestra. **Res:** 27 rue Victor Hugo, Paris 93110, France. Mgmt: CMW/FRA.

SERRANO, MARTA; née Marta Piedad Huerga. Lyric soprano. Argentinean. Resident mem: Teatro Colón, Buenos Aires. Born 16 Nov 1936, Buenos Aires. Husband Hector, occupation advertising. One child. Studied: Inst Superior del Teatro Colón, Hina Spani; Alfred Hollander, Caracas, Venezuela; Elena Hirn, Primavera Sivieri, Buenos Aires. **Debut:** Contessa (*Nozze di Figaro*) 1961.
Sang with major companies in ARG: Buenos Aires. **Roles with these companies incl** BIZET: Micaëla★ (*Carmen*); BOITO: Margherita (*Mefistofele*); CHARPENTIER: Louise; CIMAROSA: Elisetta (*Matrimonio segreto*); DEBUSSY: Lia (*Enfant prodigue*); DONIZETTI: Serafina (*Campanello*), Adina (*Elisir*), Rita; FLOTOW: Lady Harriet (*Martha*); GINASTERA: Florinda (*Don Rodrigo*); GLUCK: Iphigénie (*Iphigénie en Tauride*); GOUNOD: Marguerite (*Faust*); HUMPERDINCK: Gretel★; LEONCAVALLO: Nedda (*Pagliacci*); MASCAGNI: Suzel (*Amico Fritz*); MASSENET: Manon; MOZART: Despina (*Così fan tutte*), Donna Anna & Zerlina★ (*Don Giovanni*), Konstanze (*Entführung aus dem Serail*), Contessa★ & Susanna & Cherubino (*Nozze di Figaro*), Pamina (*Zauberflöte*); OFFENBACH: Antonia (*Contes d'Hoffmann*); PERGOLESI: Lucrezia (*Frate 'nnamorato*), Serpina (*Serva padrona*); PUCCINI: Mimi★ & Musetta★ (*Bohème*), Lauretta★ (*Gianni Schicchi*), Cio-Cio-San★ (*Butterfly*), Magda (*Rondine*), Liù★ (*Turandot*); RAVEL: Concepcion (*Heure espagnole*); ROSSINI: Ninetta (*Gazza ladra*); SMETANA: Marie★ (*Bartered Bride*); STRAUSS, J: Adele★ & Rosalinde (*Fledermaus*); VERDI: Nannetta★ (*Falstaff*), Luisa Miller, Desdemona★ (*Otello*), Amelia (*Simon Boccanegra*), Violetta★ (*Traviata*), Leonora (*Trovatore*); WAGNER: Senta (*Fliegende Holländer*), Elsa (*Lohengrin*), Eva (*Meistersinger*), Elisabeth (*Tannhäuser*); WOLF-FERRARI: Rosaura (*Donne curiose*), Lucieta (*Quattro rusteghi*). Video/Film: (*Campanello*). Gives recitals. Appears with symphony orchestra. **Res:** Rosetti 628-Florida, Buenos Aires, Argentina.

SERRLÝA, SIVIA. Dramatic coloratura soprano. American. Born Baltimore, MD, USA. Single. Studied: Rosa Ponselle, Hugo Weisgall, Baltimore; V Cinque, Milan; Mario Fiorella, Henry Jacobi, New York. **Debut:** Adele (*Fledermaus*) Baltimore Civic Opera 1955. Previous occupations: piano & voice teacher. Awards: Marian Anderson Vocal Awd; Concert Artists Guild; Sullivan Awd; Ntl Fed of Music Clubs Awd; Baltimore Professional Musicians Awd; Studio Club of New York; NATS Awd.
Sang with major companies in AUS: Salzburg Fest; FRA: Aix-en-Provence Fest, Toulouse; FR GER: Cologne Städtische Oper, Karlsruhe, Munich Gärtnerplatz; ITA: Florence Maggio & Comunale, Parma, Rome Caracalla, Turin, Venice, Verona Arena; ROM: Bucharest; SWE: Stockholm; SWI: Zurich; UK: Edinburgh Fest, Glyndebourne Fest; USA: Baltimore. **Roles with these companies incl** BELLINI: Norma★, Elvira (*Puritani*); BOITO: Margherita (*Mefistofele*); DONIZETTI: Anna Bolena★, Lucia, Lucrezia Borgia; HANDEL: Galatea, Alcina; MENOTTI: Mother (*Amahl*), Lucy (*Telephone*); MOZART: Konstanze★ (*Entführung aus dem Serail*), Mme Herz (*Schauspieldirektor*), Pamina★ & Königin der

SERVAES

Nacht★(*Zauberflöte*); ORFF: Solo★ (*Carmina bu-
rana*); POULENC: La femme★ (*Voix humaine*);
PUCCINI: Mimi (*Bohème*), Lauretta (*Gianni
Schicchi*), Suor Angelica★, Tosca; RAMEAU:
Aricie; ROSSINI: Rosina (*Barbiere di Siviglia*),
Mathilde (*Guillaume Tell*), Semiramide;
STRAUSS, J: Adele & Rosalinde (*Fledermaus*);
STRAUSS, R: Zerbinetta (*Ariadne auf Naxos*);
STRAVINSKY: Parasha (*Mavra*), Rossignol;
THOMAS: Ophélie (*Hamlet*), Philine (*Mignon*);
VERDI: Odabella (*Attila*), Amelia (*Ballo in ma-
schera*), Lucrezia Contarini (*Due Foscari*), Donna
Elvira (*Ernani*), Gilda★(*Rigoletto*), Violetta★(*Tra-
viata*), Leonora★ (*Trovatore*); WEBER: Fatima
(*Abu Hassan*), Agathe (*Freischütz*). Also WEIS-
GALL: Coloratura (*Six Characters in Search of
an Author*). Gives recitals. Appears with sym-
phony orchestra. Teaches voice. Coaches reper-
toire. **Res:** 300 W 55 St, New York, NY, USA.
Mgmt: MPC/USA.

SERVAES, WILLIAM REGINALD. British. Gen
Mng, Aldeburgh Festival, Suffolk 1P15 5AX, UK.
In charge of overall adm matters. Born 30 Jun
1921, Bournemouth. Wife Patricia. Five children.

SESTINI-PALLI, TINA. Scenic designer for opera
& theater. Is also a painter, illustrator & fashion
designer. Italian. Born Pinerolo Po/Pavia, Italy.
Husband Dino Sestini, occupation chemist. Two
children. **Operatic debut:** *Butterfly* Teatro Doni-
zetti, Bergamo 1956. Awards: First Prize, Stelle di
Natale, Genoa 1973 and Intl Akad, Vienna.
  Designed for major companies in BEL: Brussels;
FR GER: Frankfurt, Munich Staatsoper; ITA:
Bologna, Florence Maggio & Comunale, Genoa,
Milan La Scala, Naples, Palermo, Parma, Rome
Opera, Spoleto Fest, Turin, Venice. **Operas de-
signed for these companies incl** DONIZETTI:
Maria Stuarda★, Rita★; MENOTTI: *Medium★,
Saint of Bleecker Street★;* MOZART: *Entführung
aus dem Serail★, Zauberflöte;* PERGOLESI:
Maestro di musica★; PUCCINI: *Gianni
Schicchi★, Butterfly★, Manon Lescaut★, Suor An-
gelica★, Tabarro★;* PURCELL: *Dido and
Aeneas★;* ROSSINI: *Barbiere di Siviglia;* WAG-
NER: *Parsifal★;* WOLF-FERRARI: *Segreto di
Susanna.* Also HAYDN: *Speziale;* DONI-
ZETTI: *Betly;* ROSSELLINI: *Campane.* Exhibi-
tions of paintings & graphics Milan 1952, Venice
Biennale 1962. **Res:** Viale Vittorio Emanuele 54,
Bergamo, Italy.

SGOURDA, ANTIGONE. Spinto soprano. Greek.
Born Athens. Studied: National Music Coll, Ma-
nolis Calomiris, Greece; Music Acad, Vienna. **De-
but:** Mimi (*Bohème*) Städtisches Theater, Bonn
1963.
  Sang with major companies in ARG: Buenos
Aires; AUS: Graz, Vienna Staatsoper; GRE:
Athens National & Fest; FR GER: Bonn, Co-
logne, Düsseldorf-Duisburg, Essen, Frankfurt,
Hamburg, Kassel, Munich Staatsoper; HOL: Am-
sterdam; ITA: Venice; SWI: Basel, Zurich; UK:
Edinburgh Fest, Glyndebourne Fest. **Roles with
these companies incl** BELLINI: Beatrice★ &
Agnese★ (*Beatrice di Tenda*); BOITO: Margh-
erita★ (*Mefistofele*); CHERUBINI: Medea★;
DONIZETTI: Elisabetta★ (*Roberto Devereux*);
DVORAK: Rusalka; GLUCK: Euridice★;

HANDEL: Cleopatra★(*Giulio Cesare*); HINDE-
MITH: Ursula★ (*Mathis der Maler*); JANACEK:
Katya Kabanova; LEONCAVALLO: Nedda★
(*Pagliacci*); MASCAGNI: Santuzza★ (*Cavalleria
rusticana*); MASSENET: Manon★; MOZART:
Fiordiligi★ (*Così fan tutte*), Donna Anna★‡ (*Don
Giovanni*), Elettra★ (*Idomeneo*), Contessa★ &
Cherubino★ (*Nozze di Figaro*), Pamina★ (*Zauber-
flöte*); OFFENBACH: Antonia★ & Giulietta★
(*Contes d'Hoffmann*); ORFF: Solo★ (*Carmina bu-
rana*); PONCHIELLI: Gioconda; PUCCINI:
Mimi★ (*Bohème*), Lauretta★ (*Gianni Schicchi*),
Manon Lescaut★, Suor Angelica★, Giorgetta★ (*Ta-
barro*), Tosca★, Liù★ (*Turandot*); PURCELL:
Dido; SMETANA: Marie★ (*Bartered Bride*);
STRAUSS, R: Arabella★, Ariadne★ (*Ariadne auf
Naxos*); TCHAIKOVSKY: Tatiana★ (*Eugene
Onegin*), Lisa (*Pique Dame*); VERDI: Aida,
Amelia★ (*Ballo in maschera*), Elisabetta★ (*Don
Carlo*), Alice Ford★ (*Falstaff*), Leonora★ (*Forza
del destino*), Lady Macbeth★, Abigaille★ (*Na-
bucco*), Amelia★ (*Simon Boccanegra*), Violetta★
(*Traviata*), Leonora (*Trovatore*); WAGNER: Elsa
(*Lohengrin*). Recorded for: EMI. **Res:** Zurich,
Switzerland; Athens, Greece.

SHADE, ELLEN GERTRUDE. Lyric soprano.
American. Born New York. Divorced. Studied:
Juilliard American Opera Center, N.Y., Santa Fe
Apprentice Prgr, NM, USA; Cornelius Reid. **De-
but:** Liù (*Turandot*) Frankfurt Opera 1972.
  Sang with major companies in FR GER: Frank-
furt; ITA: Florence Maggio; USA: New Orleans,
Philadelphia Lyric, Pittsburgh, Santa Fe. Roles
with these companies incl BERLIOZ: Marguerite★
(*Damnation de Faust*); BIZET: Micaëla★ (*Car-
men*); CAVALLI: Climene★ (*Egisto*); FALLA:
Salud★ (*Vida breve*); GLUCK: Euridice★ (*Orfeo
ed Euridice*); GOUNOD: Marguerite★ (*Faust*);
LEONCAVALLO: Nedda (*Pagliacci*); MO-
ZART: Sesto (*Clemenza di Tito*), Fiordiligi★ (*Così
fan tutte*), Donna Elvira (*Don Giovanni*),
Contessa★ & Cherubino (*Nozze di Figaro*), Pa-
mina★ (*Zauberflöte*); PUCCINI: Mimi★
(*Bohème*), Liù★ (*Turandot*); SMETANA: Marie★
(*Bartered Bride*); TCHAIKOVSKY: Iolanthe★;
WAGNER: Eva★ (*Meistersinger*). Gives recitals.
Appears with symphony orchestra. **Res:** New
York, NY, USA. Mgmt: CAM/USA; AIM/UK.

SHADE, NANCY. Spinto soprano. American. Resident mem: New York City Opera. Born Rockford,
IL, USA. Single. Studied: De Pauw Univ, Green-
castle, IN, USA; Indiana Univ, Bloomington;
Vera Scammon. **Debut:** Leonora (*Trovatore*) Kentucky Opera 1969. Awards: First Prize Met Op
Ntl Counc Aud 1968; Concorso per Voce Ver-
diane, Busseto, Italy 1970; WGN Awd, Chicago
1968.
  Sang with major companies in FR GER: Ham-
burg; ITA: Spoleto Fest; USA: Cincinnati, Ha-
waii, Houston, Kansas City, Kentucky, Memphis,
Milwaukee Florentine, New Orleans, New York
City Opera, Philadelphia Lyric, Pittsburgh, St
Paul, San Diego, Seattle. **Roles with these com-
panies incl** BOITO: Margherita★ (*Mefistofele*);
FLOYD: Susannah★; GOUNOD: Juliette;
JANACEK: Jenufa★; KORNGOLD: Marietta★
(*Tote Stadt*); LEONCAVALLO: Nedda★ (*Pa-
gliacci*); MOZART: Contessa★ (*Nozze di Figaro*);

OFFENBACH: Antonia★ & Giulietta★ (*Contes d'Hoffmann*); PUCCINI: Mimi★ & Musetta★ (*Bohème*), Cio-Cio-San★ (*Butterfly*), Manon Lescaut★; VERDI: Desdemona (*Otello*), Leonora (*Trovatore*). Gives recitals. Appears with symphony orchestra. **Res:** Ansonia Hotel, New York, NY, USA. Mgmt: LLF/USA; SLZ/FRG.

SHADUR, LAWRENCE S. Dramatic baritone. American. Resident mem: Metropolitan Opera, New York. Born 13 Aug 1938, New York. Wife Isabelle. Studied: Robert Weede, Herbert Janssen, Olga Ryss, Dick Marzollo, New York. **Debut:** Ford (*Falstaff*) Stadttheater Bern, Switzerland 1965. Previous occupations: at CBS-TV and in musical comedy. Awards: Sullivan Fndt Awd.
Sang with major companies in FR GER: Cologne, Nürnberg; SWI: Geneva; USA: Baltimore, Cincinnati, Milwaukee Florentine, New York Met, San Antonio, Washington DC. **Roles with these companies incl** BIZET: Escamillo★ (*Carmen*); ORFF: Bauer★ (*Mond*); STRAUSS, R: Jochanaan★ (*Salome*); VERDI: Amonasro★ (*Aida*), Macbeth★, Monforte★ (*Vespri*); WAGNER: Holländer★, Wolfram★ (*Tannhäuser*). Appears with symphony orchestra. **Res:** New York, NY, USA. Mgmt: BAR/USA; AIM/UK.

SHANE, RITA FRANCES. Coloratura soprano. American. Resident mem: Metropolitan Opera, New York. Born New York. Husband Daniel F Tritter, occupation advertising. One child. Studied: Beverley Peck Johnson, New York; Bliss Hebert, coach, New York; Santa Fe Opera Apprentice Prgr, NM; Hunter Opera Theater, New York. **Debut:** Olympia (*Contes d'Hoffmann*) Chattanooga Opera, TN, USA 1964. Awards: Rockefeller Fndt Grant; Sullivan Fndt Grant.
Sang with major companies in AUS: Salzburg Festival, Vienna Staatsoper; FRA: Strasbourg; FR GER: Munich Staatsoper; HOL: Amsterdam; ITA: Milan La Scala; SWI: Geneva; USA: Baltimore, Chicago, Kentucky, Lake George, New Orleans, New York Met & City Opera, Philadelphia Lyric, San Diego, Santa Fe. **Roles with these companies incl** BERG: Lulu; BIZET: Micaëla★ (*Carmen*); DONIZETTI: Adina (*Elisir*), Lucia★, Maria Stuarda★; HALEVY: Eudoxie★ (*Juive*); HANDEL: Armida (*Rinaldo*); HENZE: Hilda Mack (*Elegy for Young Lovers*); MASSENET: Manon; MEYERBEER: Marguerite de Valois★ (*Huguenots*), Berthe★ (*Prophète*); MOZART: Donna Anna & Donna Elvira (*Don Giovanni*), Konstanze★ (*Entführung aus dem Serail*), Mme Herz★ (*Schauspieldirektor*), Susanna (*Nozze di Figaro*), Königin der Nacht★ (*Zauberflöte*); NICOLAI: Frau Fluth (*Lustigen Weiber*); OFFENBACH: Olympia (*Contes d'Hoffmann*); ORFF: Solo (*Carmina burana*); POULENC: Mme Lidoine (*Dialogues des Carmélites*); PROKOFIEV: Fata Morgana (*Love for Three Oranges*); PUCCINI: Musetta★ (*Bohème*); ROSSINI: Comtesse Adèle★ (*Comte Ory*), Fiorilla (*Turco in Italia*); SCHOENBERG: A Woman★ (*Erwartung*); SMETANA: Marie★ (*Bartered Bride*); STRAUSS, J: Rosalinde★ (*Fledermaus*), Fiakermilli (*Arabella*), Zerbinetta (*Ariadne auf Naxos*); STRAVINSKY: Rossignol★; VERDI: Oscar★ (*Ballo in maschera*), Gilda★ (*Rigoletto*), Violetta★ (*Tra-*

viata); WOLF-FERRARI: Susanna (*Segreto di Susanna*). Also RAVEL: Feu/Rossignol★ (*Enfant et les sortilèges*). Gives recitals. Appears with symphony orchestra. **Res:** New York, NY, USA. Mgmt: HHB/USA; AIM/UK.

SHARPE, TERENCE. Lyric baritone. British. Resident mem: Welsh National Opera, Cardiff. Born 30 Aug 1933, Sheffield, UK. Wife Audrey. Two children. Studied: Stanley Jepson, Sheffield; Luigi Ricci, Rome; Otakar Kraus, London. **Debut:** Sherasmin (*Oberon*) Cambridge Univ Opera, UK 1967. Previous occupations: architect 1956-67. Awards: First Prize Conc de Bel Canto, Liège, Belgium; Third Prize Conc de Bel Canto Gianbattista Viotti, Vercelli, Italy.
Sang with major companies in FR GER: Munich Gärtnerplatz; SWI: Geneva; UK: Cardiff Welsh, London Eng Ntl. **Roles with these companies incl** BIZET: Escamillo (*Carmen*); BRITTEN: Billy Budd★, Charles Blount★ (*Gloriana*); DONIZETTI: Dott Malatesta (*Don Pasquale*), Belcore★ (*Elisir*), Enrico★ (*Lucia*); GLUCK: Oreste (*Iphigénie en Tauride*); LEONCAVALLO: Tonio★ (*Pagliacci*); MOZART: Guglielmo★ (*Così fan tutte*); PUCCINI: Marcello★ (*Bohème*), Lescaut★ (*Manon Lescaut*); ROSSINI: Figaro★ (*Barbiere di Siviglia*); VERDI: Amonasro★ (*Aida*), Rodrigo★ (*Don Carlo*), Ford★ (*Falstaff*), Don Carlo★ (*Forza del destino*), Miller★ (*Luisa Miller*), Macbeth★, Nabucco★, Rigoletto★, Simon Boccanegra★, Germont★ (*Traviata*), Conte di Luna★ (*Trovatore*). Recorded for: EMI, RCA. Gives recitals. Appears with symphony orchestra. **Res:** 10 Westbourne Rd, Penarth, UK.

SHAW, GLEN BYAM; né Glencairn Alexander Byam Shaw. Stages/produces opera & theater and is an actor. British. Mem of the Directorate & Resident Stage Dir, English National Opera, London. Born 13 Dec 1904, London. Wife Angela Baddeley, occupation actress. Two children. Operatic training as mem of James Bernard Fagan's Oxford Players Co. **Operatic debut:** *Rake's Progress* Sadler's Wells, London 1962. Theater debut: Oxford Univ Dramatic Socy 1936. Previous occupation: actor; military serv WW II. Awards: Commander of the British Empire; Hon DL, Birmingham Univ.
Directed/produced opera for major companies in UK: London English National. **Operas staged with these companies incl** BARTOK: *Bluebeard's Castle★*; GLUCK: *Orfeo ed Euridice*; GOUNOD: *Faust;* MOZART: *Così fan tutte, Idomeneo;* STRAUSS, J: *Fledermaus;* WAGNER: *Meistersinger, Rheingold★, Walküre★, Siegfried★, Götterdämmerung★;* WEBER: *Freischütz.* Previous leading positions with major theater companies: Mem of Directorate, Old Vic Theatre 1946-51; Dir, Old Vic Theatre School; Co-Dir, Shakespeare Mem Thtr, Stratford-upon-Avon 1952-56, Dir 1956-59, Governor 1960-75. Teaches at Old Vic Theatre School, London. **Res:** London, UK.

SHELLE, EILEEN. née Nankin. Lyric soprano. American. Born 23 May, New York. Husband Dr Joel Birnbaum, occupation scientist. Three children. Studied: Ludwig Donath, Erik Thorendahl, Joan Dornemann, New York. **Debut:** Lakmé, Bordeaux Opera 1969. Awards: First Prize, Concorso Intl di Musica G B Viotti, Italy; Corbett Fndt Fllshp.

Sang with major companies in FRA: Bordeaux; SPA: Barcelona; USA: Cincinnati, Fort Worth, Hartford, Hawaii, Houston, Kentucky, Omaha, Philadelphia Lyric, Portland, San Diego. **Roles with these companies incl** DELIBES: Lakmé; DONIZETTI: Norina (*Don Pasquale*), Adina★ (*Elisir*); GOUNOD: Juliette★; HUMPERDINCK: Gretel★; MENOTTI: Lucy (*Telephone*); MOZART: Despina (*Così fan tutte*), Zerlina★ (*Don Giovanni*), Susanna★ (*Nozze di Figaro*); OFFENBACH: Antonia★ (*Contes d'Hoffmann*); PERGOLESI: Serpina (*Serva padrona*); PUCCINI: Mimi★ & Musetta★ (*Bohème*), Lisette★ (*Rondine*); VERDI: Gilda★ (*Rigoletto*). Gives recitals. Appears with symphony orchestra. **Res:** 34 Horseshoe La, Roslyn Hts, NY, USA.

SHERMAN, ENOCH. Lyric tenor. American. Resident mem: Lyric Opera of Chicago. Born 1945, Michigan, USA. Divorced. Two children. Studied: Margaret van der Marck, New York. **Debut:** Canio & Turiddu (*Pagliacci & Cavalleria rusticana*) Orange County Lyric Opera, Los Angeles 1969. Previous occupations: insurance salesman. Awards: Finalist San Francisco Opera Aud 1973.

Sang with major companies in USA: Chicago, St Paul. **Roles with these companies incl** BRITTEN: Male Chorus★ (*Rape of Lucretia*), Peter Quint★ (*Turn of the Screw*); DELIBES: Gérald★ (*Lakmé*); DONIZETTI: Ernesto★ (*Don Pasquale*), Edgardo★ (*Lucia*); MOZART: Ferrando★ (*Così fan tutte*), Don Ottavio★ (*Don Giovanni*), Tamino★ (*Zauberflöte*); PUCCINI: Rodolfo★ (*Bohème*), Pinkerton★ (*Butterfly*); STRAVINSKY: Tom Rakewell (*Rake's Progress*). Gives recitals. Appears with symphony orchestra. **Res:** New York, NY, USA. Mgmt: SFM/USA.

SHILLING, ERIC. Bass-baritone. British. Resident mem: English National Opera, London. Born 12 Oct 1920, London. Wife Erica Johns, occupation soprano. Two children. Studied: Guildhall School of Music & Drama, Walter Hyde, London; Royal Coll of Music, Dorothea Webb, Clive Carey, London; Frank Titterton. **Debut:** Marullo (*Rigoletto*) Sadler's Wells Opera 1945. Awards: ARCM & Hon ARCM, Royal Coll of Music, London.

Sang with major companies in UK: Cardiff Welsh, Edinburgh Fest, London Eng Natl. **Roles with these companies incl** BENNETT: Braxton (*Mines of Sulphur*); BRITTEN: Sir Robert Cecil★ (*Gloriana*); DONIZETTI: Don Pasquale; MOZART: Don Alfonso★ (*Così fan tutte*), Papageno (*Zauberflöte*); ORFF: König (*Kluge*); PENDERECKI: Mannoury★ (*Teufel von Loudun*); ROSSINI: Dott Bartolo★ (*Barbiere di Siviglia*), Don Magnifico (*Cenerentola*), Podestà (*Gazza ladra*); SMETANA: Kezal (*Bartered Bride*); WAGNER: Daland (*Fliegende Holländer*), Beckmesser (*Meistersinger*), Alberich★ (*Götterdämmerung*). Also JANACEK: Dr Kolenaty (*Makropoulos Affair*); WILLIAMSON: Agenor (*Violins of Saint Jacques*); STRAUSS, R: Faninal★ (*Rosenkavalier*). World premieres: BENNETT: Bellboy (*Penny for a Song*) Sadler's Wells Opera 1967; WILLIAMSON: Hawthorne (*Our Man in Havana*) Sadler's Wells 1963; CROSSE: Major

Braun (*Story of Vasco*) Sadler's Wells 1974. Recorded for: EMI, L'Oiseau Lyre, Argo, Saga. Gives recitals. Appears with symphony orchestra. Teaches voice. Coaches repertoire. On faculty of Royal Coll of Music, London. **Res:** London, UK. Mgmt: MIN/UK.

SHINALL, VERN. Dramatic baritone. American. Resident mem: New York City Opera. Born 22 Jun 1936, St Louis, MO, USA. Wife Marilyn Ballard. Three children. Studied: Indiana Univ, Frank St Leger, Charles Kullman, Tibor Kozma, Bloomington, IN; Frank Pandolfi, CT, USA. **Debut:** Scarpia (*Tosca*) Kansas City Lyric 1964.

Sang with major companies in USA: Boston, Cincinnati, Hartford, Houston, Kansas City, Milwaukee Florentine, Newark, New Orleans, New York City Opera, Omaha, Philadelphia Grand, St Paul, San Antonio. **Roles with these companies incl** BEETHOVEN: Don Pizarro (*Fidelio*); BIZET: Escamillo★ (*Carmen*); FLOYD: Olin Blitch (*Susannah*); GIORDANO: Carlo Gérard★ (*Andrea Chénier*); GOUNOD: Méphistophélès (*Faust*); LEONCAVALLO: Tonio★ (*Pagliacci*); MASCAGNI: Alfio★ (*Cavalleria rusticana*); MOZART: Don Giovanni; OFFENBACH: Coppélius etc (*Contes d'Hoffmann*); PONCHIELLI: Barnaba★ (*Gioconda*); PUCCINI: Jack Rance★ (*Fanciulla del West*), Sharpless★ (*Butterfly*), Lescaut★ (*Manon Lescaut*), Michele★ (*Tabarro*), Scarpia★ (*Tosca*); VERDI: Amonasro★ (*Aida*), Rigoletto, Conte di Luna★ (*Trovatore*); WAGNER: Holländer, Telramund★ (*Lohengrin*), Wotan (*Rheingold, Walküre★*), Wanderer★ (*Siegfried*); WARD: John Proctor★ (*Crucible*). Gives recitals. Appears with symphony orchestra. Mgmt: JBF/USA.

SHIRLEY, GEORGE IRVING. Lyric tenor. American. Born 18 Apr 1934, Indianapolis, IN, USA. Wife Gladys, occupation artist and educator. Two children. Studied: Amos Ebersole, Edward Boatner, Detroit, MI; Themy Georgi, Washington, DC; Cornelius Reid, New York. **Debut:** Eisenstein (*Fledermaus*) Turnau Opera Players, New York 1959. Previous occupations: teacher Detroit PS; mem & solo US Army Chorus, Washington DC, 1956-59. Awards: Winner Met Op Ntl Counc Aud; American Opera Aud; Natl Arts Club Awd; Hon DH Wilberforce Univ, O, USA 1967.

Sang with major companies in ARG: Buenos Aires; ITA: Spoleto Fest; UK: Glasgow Scottish, Glyndebourne Fest, London Royal Opera; USA: Memphis, Milwaukee Florentine, New York Met & City Opera, San Francisco Spring Opera, Santa Fe, Washington DC. **Roles with these companies incl** BELLINI: Elvino (*Sonnambula*); BERG: Alwa (*Lulu*); BIZET: Don José★ (*Carmen*); CAVALLI: Egisto (*Egisto*★‡); DEBUSSY: Pelléas★‡; DONIZETTI: Riccardo (*Anna Bolena*), Nemorino (*Elisir*), Edgardo★ (*Lucia*); GOUNOD: Faust★, Roméo★; HENZE: Leandro (*König Hirsch/Re Cervo*); MASSENET: Des Grieux (*Manon*); MOZART: Ferrando‡ (*Così fan tutte*), Don Ottavio★ (*Don Giovanni*), Idomeneo★‡, Tamino★ (*Zauberflöte*); PUCCINI: Rodolfo (*Bohème*), Pinkerton★ (*Butterfly*), Des Grieux (*Manon Lescaut*), Cavaradossi★ (*Tosca*); REIMANN: Oleander★ (*Melusine*); ROSSINI: Almaviva (*Barbiere di Siviglia*); STRAUSS, R: Bacchus (*Ariadne auf Naxos*), Apollo (*Daphne*), Ein Sänger (*Rosenkavalier*), Herodes (*Salome*); STRAVINSKY: Oedipus Rex, Tom Rakewell★ (*Rake's Progress*); VERDI: Fenton (*Falstaff*), Duca di Mantova★ (*Rigoletto*), Gabriele (*Simon Boccanegra*), Alfredo (*Traviata*); WAGNER: Erik (*Fliegende Holländer*), David (*Meistersinger*), Loge★ (*Rheingold*). Also RA- VEL: Gonzalve (*Heure espagnole*). Recorded for: RCA, Philips, Columbia. Video/Film: Tamino (*Zauberflöte*). Gives recitals. Appears with sym- phony orchestra. Teaches voice. Coaches reper- toire. On faculty of Staten Island Community Coll, NY. Artist-in-residence Morgan State Coll, Balti- more, MD. Res: Upper Montclair, NJ, USA. Mgmt: JUD/USA; AIM/UK.

SHIRLEY-QUIRK, JOHN. Bass-baritone. British. Born 28 Aug 1931, Liverpool, UK. Wife Patricia, occupation physician. Two children. Studied: Roy Henderson, London. **Debut:** Docteur (*Pelléas et Mélisande*) Glyndebourne Fest 1961. Previous oc- cupations: lecturer in chemistry, Acton Tech Coll, UK. Awards: Commander of the Order of the British Empire/CBE; Hon Mem Royal Acad of Music, London.
Sang with major companies in UK: Aldeburgh Fest, Glasgow Scottish, London Royal; USA: New York Met. **Roles with these companies incl** BRITTEN: Mr Redburn (*Billy Budd*), Ananias‡ (*Burning Fiery Furnace*), Ferryman‡ (*Curlew River*), Traveller etc★‡ (*Death in Venice*), Father‡ (*Prodigal Son*); DEBUSSY: Golaud★ & Arkel (*Pelléas et Mélisande*); HENZE: Mittenhofer★ (*Elegy for Young Lovers*); HOLST: Death★ (*Sa- vitri*); MOZART: Don Alfonso (*Così fan tutte*), Conte Almaviva★ (*Nozze di Figaro*); PURCELL: Aeneas★‡; TCHAIKOVSKY: Eugene Onegin. Also RAMEAU: Thésée‡ (*Hippolyte et Aricie*); BRITTEN: Theseus‡ (*Midsummer Night*); DELIUS: Dark Fiddler‡ (*Village Romeo and Ju- liet*). World premieres: BRITTEN: all baritone roles in church operas, Aldeburgh Fest 1962-68; Coyle (*Owen Wingrave*) Aldeburgh Fest 1970; Traveller (*Death in Venice*) Aldeburgh Fest 1973. Recorded for: Decca, Philips, EMI, Argo. Video/Film: Redburn (*Billy Budd*); Eugene One- gin; Conte Almaviva (*Nozze di Figaro*); Coyle (*Owen Wingrave*). Gives recitals. Appears with symphony orchestra. **Res:** High Wycombe, UK. Mgmt: HPL/UK; CAM/USA.

SICOT, IRÈNE MARIE-THÉRÈSE. Lyric soprano. French. Resident mem: Opéra de Paris. Born 10 Oct 1930, Angers, France. Husband Henri Bohrer, occupation opera singer, tenor. Studied: Consv Ntl de Musique de Paris, Renée Gilly, Louis Musy, Gustave Cloëz. **Debut:** Micaëla (*Carmen*) Paris Opera 1960. Awards: First Prize in voice, opera and opéra comique, Consv Ntl de Paris.
Sang with major companies in BEL: Liège; FRA: Aix-en-Provence Fest, Bordeaux, Lyon, Marseille, Nice, Paris, Rouen, Toulouse; ISR: Tel Aviv; ROM: Bucharest; SWI: Geneva. **Roles with these companies incl** BECAUD: Maureen★ (*Opéra d'Aran*); BIZET: Micaëla★ (*Carmen*), Léila (*Pê- cheurs de perles*); CHARPENTIER: Louise★; GIORDANO: Maddalena (*Andrea Chénier*); GOUNOD: Marguerite★ (*Faust*), Mireille★, Ju- liette; LEONCAVALLO: Nedda★ (*Pagliacci*); MASCAGNI: Santuzza★ (*Cavalleria rusticana*); MASSENET: Salomé (*Hérodiade*), Manon★,

Thaïs, Sophie★ (*Werther*); MOZART: Donna Anna (*Don Giovanni*); OFFENBACH: Antonia★ & Giulietta★ (*Contes d'Hoffmann*); POULENC: La femme★ (*Voix humaine*); PUCCINI: Mimi★ & Musetta★ (*Bohème*), Manon Lescaut★, Giorgetta (*Tabarro*), Tosca★; SMETANA: Marinka (*The Kiss*); VERDI: Violetta (*Traviata*). Recorded for: Pathé-Marconi. Video/Film—ORTF, TV Bel- gium: Maureen (*Opéra d'Aran*). Gives recitals. Appears with symphony orchestra. Teaches voice. Coaches repertoire.

SIEPI, CESARE. Bass. Italian. Born 10 Feb 1923, Milan. Wife Louellen. Two children. Studied: Ce- sare Chiesa, Italy; Dick Marzollo, New York. **Debut:** Sparafucile (*Rigoletto*) Schio, Italy 1941.
Sang with major companies in AUS: Salzburg Fest, Vienna Staatsoper; BRA: Rio de Janeiro; CAN: Montreal/Quebec, Toronto; CZE: Prague National; FRA: Paris; FR GER: Hamburg, Mu- nich Staatsoper, Wiesbaden; HUN: Budapest; ITA: Bologna, Florence Maggio & Teatro Comu- nale, Genoa, Milan La Scala, Naples, Palermo, Parma, Rome Opera, Trieste, Turin, Venice, Ve- rona Arena; MEX: Mexico City; SPA: Barcelona; SWI: Zurich; UK: Edinburgh Fest, London Royal Opera; USA: Baltimore, Boston, Chicago, Cincin- nati, Fort Worth, Hartford, Houston Grand, Mi- ami, New Orleans Opera House, New York Met- ropolitan, Philadelphia Lyric, Pittsburgh, San Francisco Opera, Washington Opera Society, DC. **Roles with these companies incl** BEETHO- VEN: Don Fernando (*Fidelio*); BELLINI: Oro- veso★ (*Norma*), Sir George (*Puritani*), Rodolfo (*Sonnambula*); BOITO: Mefistofele★; DONI- ZETTI: Henry VIII (*Anna Bolena*), Baldassare (*Favorite*); GOUNOD: Méphistophélès★ (*Faust*); HANDEL: Giulio Cesare; MOZART: Don Gio- vanni★, Figaro★ (*Nozze di Figaro*); MUS- SORGSKY: Boris Godunov, Dosifei★ (*Khovanshchina*); PONCHIELLI: Alvise★ (*Gio- conda*); PUCCINI: Colline★ (*Bohème*); ROS- SINI: Don Basilio★ (*Barbiere di Siviglia*), Moïse; VERDI: Ramfis★ (*Aida*), Philip II★ & Grande Inquisitore (*Don Carlo*), Silva (*Ernani*), Padre Guardiano★ (*Forza del destino*), Zaccaria (*Na- bucco*), Fiesco★ (*Simon Boccanegra*); WAGNER: Pogner (*Meistersinger*), Gurnemanz★ (*Parsifal*); WEBER: Kaspar (*Freischütz*). Recorded for: Co- lumbia, London (Decca), RCA, Cetra. Film: (*Don Giovanni*). Gives recitals. Appears with symphony orchestra. **Res:** Milan, Italy. Mgmt: CAM/USA.

SIGHELE, MIETTA; née Mariantonietta Sighele. Lyric soprano. Italian. Born Rovereto/Trento. Husband Veriano Luchetti, occupation opera singer, tenor. Two children. Studied: Mo Enrico Piazza, Milan; Scuola del Teatro dell'Opera, Rome. **Debut:** Cio-Cio-San (*Butterfly*) Spoleto. Awards: Diapason d'oro, Syracuse; Commendatore.
Sang with major companies in ARG: Buenos Aires; AUS: Vienna Staatsoper; BEL: Brussels; BRA: Rio de Janeiro; CAN: Montreal/Quebec, Toronto, Vancouver; FR GER: Hamburg, Karls- ruhe; ITA: Bologna, Florence Maggio & Comu- nale, Genoa, Milan La Scala, Naples, Palermo, Rome Opera & Caracalla, Spoleto Fest, Trieste, Turin, Venice; MEX: Mexico City; MON: Monte Carlo; POR: Lisbon; S AFR: Johannesburg; SPA:

Barcelona, Majorca; SWI: Geneva; USA: Baltimore, Chicago, Dallas, Houston, New Orleans, Philadelphia Grand & Lyric, Pittsburgh. **Roles with these companies incl** BIZET: Micaëla★ (*Carmen*); CILEA: Adriana Lecouvreur; GOUNOD: Marguerite (*Faust*); JANACEK: Katya Kabanova; LEONCAVALLO: Nedda★ (*Pagliacci*); MASCAGNI: Suzel (*Amico Fritz*); MASSENET: Manon★; MEYERBEER: Inez (*Africaine*); MOZART: Vitellia (*Clemenzo di Tito*), Fiordiligi★ (*Così fan tutte*), Donna Anna (*Don Giovanni*); PUCCINI: Mimi★ (*Bohème*), Lauretta★ (*Gianni Schicchi*), Cio-Cio-San★ (*Butterfly*), Manon Lescaut, Suor Angelica, Giorgetta★ (*Tabarro*), Liù★ (*Turandot*), Anna (*Villi*); TCHAIKOVSKY: Tatiana (*Eugene Onegin*), Lisa (*Pique Dame*); VERDI: Alice Ford (*Falstaff*), Desdemona★ (*Otello*), Amelia★ (*Simon Boccanegra*); WAGNER: Elsa (*Lohengrin*). Also BARBER: Erika (*Vanessa*); PUCCINI: Fidelia (*Edgar*). Video–RAI TV & Yugosl TV: (*Bohème*); NHK TV: (*Butterfly*). Gives recitals. Appears with symphony orchestra. **Res:** 83 Colle Romano, Riano/Rome, Italy.

SILIPIGNI, ALFREDO. Conductor of opera and symphony. American. Art Dir & Cond, New Jersey State Opera, East Orange, USA 1965-75. Born 9 Apr 1931, Atlantic City, NJ. Wife Gloria. Three children. Studied: Westminster Choir Coll, Juilliard School; incl piano, organ, strings and voice. Plays the piano, organ. Operatic training as repetiteur, asst cond & chorus master at Connecticut Opera, Hartford 1958-68. **Operatic debut:** Opera Gala, Lauter Opera Co, Newark, NJ 1949. Symphonic debut: Symph of the Air, New York 1958. Awards: Centennial Medallion, St Peter's Coll; Muncp Hon City of Trenton, NJ; San Remo, Italy. Previous adm positions in opera: Gen Dir, Lauter Opera Co, Newark 1950-55; Art Adm, Connecticut Opera, Hartford 1958-68.

Conducted with major companies in ITA: Turin; MEX: Mexico City; USA: Hartford, Newark. **Operas with these companies incl** BELLINI: *Norma★;* BIZET: *Carmen★;* DONIZETTI: *Caterina Cornaro★, Don Pasquale;* GIORDANO: *Fedora★;* GOUNOD: *Faust;* MASCAGNI: *Cavalleria rusticana★;* MASSENET: *Manon;* MOZART: *Don Giovanni;* PONCHIELLI: *Gioconda★;* PUCCINI: *Bohème★, Gianni Schicchi★, Butterfly★, Manon Lescaut, Tabarro★, Tosca, Turandot★;* ROSSINI: *Barbiere di Siviglia★;* VERDI: *Aida★, Attila★, Ballo in maschera★, Forza del destino, Otello★, Rigoletto★, Traviata★, Trovatore.*

SILJA, ANJA. Dramatic soprano. German. Resident mem: Deutsche Oper Berlin; Staatsoper, Hamburg. Born 3 Apr 1940, Berlin. One child. **Debut:** Rosina (*Barbiere di Siviglia*) Deutsche Oper Berlin 1956; first concert Berlin and Hamburg 1948.

Sang with major companies in AUS: Salzburg Fest, Vienna Staatsoper; BEL: Brussels; DEN: Copenhagen; FRA: Aix-en-Provence Fest, Paris; FR GER: Bayreuth Fest, Berlin Deutsche Oper, Frankfurt, Hamburg, Hannover, Munich Staatsoper, Nürnberg, Stuttgart; ITA: Rome Opera, Trieste; POR: Lisbon; SPA: Barcelona; SWI: Geneva; UK: London Royal; USA: Chicago, New York Met, San Francisco Opera; et al. **Roles with these companies incl** BEETHOVEN: Leonore (*Fidelio*); BERG: Lulu, Marie (*Wozzeck*); BIZET: Micaëla (*Carmen*); JANACEK: Jenufa, Katya Kabanova, Emilia Marty (*Makropoulos Affair*); MASCAGNI: Santuzza (*Cavalleria*); MOZART: Fiordiligi (*Così fan tutte*), Konstanze (*Entführung aus dem Serail*), Königin der Nacht (*Zauberflöte*); OFFENBACH: Olympia & Antonia & Giulietta (*Contes d'Hoffmann*); PROKOFIEV: Renata (*Flaming Angel*); PUCCINI: Tosca, Turandot & Liù (*Turandot*); ROSSINI: Rosina (*Barbiere di Siviglia*); SCHOENBERG: Woman (*Erwartung*); STRAUSS, R: Zerbinetta (*Ariadne auf Naxos*), Salome; VERDI: Lady Macbeth, Desdemona (*Otello*), Violetta (*Traviata*), Leonora (*Trovatore*); WAGNER: Senta‡ (*Fliegende Holländer*), Elsa (*Lohengrin*), Eva (*Meistersinger*), Sieglinde & Brünnhilde (*Walküre*), Brünnhilde (*Siegfried*, *Götterdämmerung*), Elisabeth & Venus (*Tannhäuser*), Isolde; et al. Also BIZET: Carmen. Recorded for: Philips, London. **Res:** Lugano, Switzerland. Mgmt: COL/USA.

SILLS, BEVERLY: née Belle Miriam Silverman. Coloratura soprano. American. Resident mem: New York City Opera; Metropolitan Opera, New York. Born 26 May 1929, New York. Husband Peter B Greenough, occupation newspaper editor, ret. One son, one daughter. Studied: Estelle Liebling, New York. **Debut:** Micaëla (*Carmen*) Philadelphia Opera, abt 1948. Awards: Hon DM: Harvard Univ, Cambridge, MA; New York Univ; Temple Univ, Philadelphia; New England Consv of Music, Boston. Edison Recording Awd; Emmy TV Awd.

Sang with major companies in ARG: Buenos Aires; AUS: Vienna Staatsoper; FR GER: Berlin Deutsche Oper; ITA: Milan La Scala, Naples, Venice; MEX: Mexico City; SWI: Geneva; UK: London Royal Opera; USA: Baltimore, Boston, Cincinnati, Fort Worth, Hartford, Houston, Memphis, Miami, Milwaukee Florentine Opera, Newark, New Orleans, New York Met & City Opera, Philadelphia Grand & Lyric, Pittsburgh, Portland, San Antonio, San Diego, San Francisco Opera, Seattle. **Roles with these companies incl** BELLINI: Giulietta★‡ (*Capuleti ed i Montecchi*), Norma★‡, Imogene (*Pirata*), Elvira★‡ (*Puritani*); BIZET: Micaëla★ (*Carmen*); CHARPENTIER: Louise; DONIZETTI: Anna Bolena★‡, Adina (*Elisir*), Marie★ (*Fille du régiment*), Lucia★‡, Lucrezia Borgia★, Maria Stuarda★‡, Elisabetta★‡ (*Roberto Devereux*); GOUNOD: Marguerite★ (*Faust*); HANDEL: Ginevra★ (*Ariodante*), Cleopatra★‡ (*Giulio Cesare*); HINDEMITH: Helene (*Hin und zurück*); MASSENET: Manon★, Thaïs; MONTEMEZZI: Fiora (*Amore dei tre re*); MOORE: Baby Doe; MOZART: Donna Anna & Donna Elvira (*Don Giovanni*), Konstanze (*Entführung aus dem Serail*), Mme Herz (*Schauspieldirektor*), Contessa (*Nozze di Figaro*), Königin der Nacht (*Zauberflöte*); OFFENBACH: Olympia★ & Antonia★ & Giulietta★ (*Contes d'Hoffmann*); PUCCINI: Mimi & Musetta (*Bohème*), Lauretta (*Gianni Schicchi*), Suor Angelica, Giorgetta (*Tabarro*), Tosca; RAMEAU: Aricie; RIMSKY-KORSAKOV: Reine de Schemakan (*Coq d'or*); ROSSINI: Rosina★ (*Barbiere di Siviglia*), Pamira★‡ (*Assedio di Corinto*); STRAUSS, J: Adele & Rosalinde (*Fledermaus*); STRAUSS, R: Zerbinetta★ (*Ariadne auf Naxos*), Daphne, Sophie (*Ro-

senkavalier); THOMAS: Philine (*Mignon*); VERDI: Aida, Violetta★(*Traviata*). Also NONO: (*Intolleranza*); MOORE: (*Wings of the Dove*). **World premieres:** WEISGALL: Prima Donna (*Six Characters in Search of an Author*) 1959. Recorded for: RCA, ABC, MGM, Angel. Video: Marie (*Fille du régiment*); Elisab∙ 'tt. (*Roberto Devereux*). Gives recitals. Appear with symphony orchestra. Mgmt: LLF/USA.

SILVA, STELLA. Mezzo-soprano & contralto. Italian. Born 6 Jan 1948, Buenos Aires, Argent. Husband Ronaldo Rosa, occupation conductor. Studied: Inst Superior de Arte, Teatro Colón, Buenos Aires; Liceo Musicale G Viotti, Vercelli, Italy. **Debut:** Preziosilla (*Forza del destino*) Opéra de Bordeaux 1969. Previous occupations: elementary teacher. Awards: Stpd Studio del Fondo Nacional de las Artes, Buenos Aires; First Prize, Conc As Li Co of Milan.

Sang with major companies in ARG: Buenos Aires; AUS: Vienna Staatsoper; FRA: Bordeaux, Lyon, Nice, Strasbourg; FR GER: Berlin Deutsche Oper, Hamburg; ITA: Parma, Turin, Verona Arena; S AFR: Johannesburg; SPA: Barcelona; USA: Washington DC. **Roles with these companies incl** BELLINI: Adalgisa★ (*Norma*); BIZET: Carmen★; CILEA: Princesse de Bouillon★ (*A. Lecouvreur*); CIMAROSA: Fidalma★ (*Matrimonio segreto*); DONIZETTI: Léonore★ (*Favorite*); GLUCK: Orfeo★; HUMPERDINCK: Hexe★ (*Hänsel und Gretel*); MASCAGNI: Beppe★ (*Amico Fritz*); MASSENET: Charlotte★ (*Werther*); MENOTTI: Mme Flora★ (*Medium*); MONTEVERDI: Orfeo★; PONCHIELLI: Laura★ & La Cieca (*Gioconda*); PUCCINI: Principessa★ (*Suor Angelica*); SAINT-SAENS: Dalila★; SPONTINI: High Priestess (*Vestale*)★; VERDI: Amneris★ (*Aida*), Ulrica★ (*Ballo in maschera*), Eboli★ (*Don Carlo*), Dame Quickly★ (*Falstaff*), Preziosilla★ (*Forza del destino*), Federica★ (*Luisa Miller*), Azucena★ (*Trovatore*); WAGNER: Ortrud★ (*Lohengrin*); WOLF-FERRARI: Margarita★ (*Quattro rusteghi*). Also MASCAGNI: Santuzza★ (*Cavalleria rusticana*); CILEA: Rosa★ (*Arlesiana*); VIVALDI: Holofernes★ (*Juditha triumphans*). Gives recitals. Appears with symphony orchestra. **Res:** V Cesare Saldini 22, 20133 Milan, Italy.

SILVER, PHILLIP JACK. Scenic designer for opera, theater. Is a lighting designer. Canadian. Resident designer, Citadel Theatre. Born 30 Jun 1943, Edmonton, Alta. Wife Brenda. Two children. Studied: Ntl Theatre School of Canada, Mark Negin, François Barbeau, Robert Prevost, Montreal. **Operatic debut:** *Faust* Edmonton Opera 1967. Theater debut: Center Stage, Baltimore, MD, USA 1967.

Designed for major companies in CAN: Vancouver; USA: Portland. **Operas designed for these companies incl** BELLINI: *Norma★;* BIZET: *Carmen★;* DONIZETTI: *Lucia;* GOUNOD: *Faust;* MENOTTI: *Consul;* MOZART: *Nozze di Figaro★;* PUCCINI: *Bohème★;* PURCELL: *Dido and Aeneas;* ROSSINI: *Barbiere di Siviglia;* VERDI: *Aida★, Rigoletto, Trovatore★.* Exhibitions of stage designs, Toronto Central Library 1971. **Res:** 106 Glenwood Cres, St Albert, Alta, Canada.

SIMACEK, OLDRICH. Scenic and costume designer for opera, theater; specl in sets. Is a lighting designer; also a painter & sculptor. Czechoslovakian. Scenographer, National Theater, Prague. Born 2 Sep 1919, Prague. Wife Sylva Maresová, occupation theater historian. Four children. Studied: Acad for Applied Arts, Prague, Profs Benda, Kratochvil & Kysela. **Operatic debut:** *Entführung aus dem Serail* State Theater Stibor, Olomouc, CSSR 1942. Theater debut: State Theater, Olomouc 1942. Awards: Golden Medal of Prague Quadriennale 1971; Golden Medal of Biennale São Paulo 1973; Artist of Merit, Gvnmt of CSSR 1968.

Designed for major companies in ARG: Buenos Aires; AUS: Vienna Staatsoper & Volksoper; BUL: Sofia; CZE: Brno, Prague National & Smetana; FRA: Lyon, Strasbourg; HOL: Amsterdam; SPA: Barcelona; SWI: Geneva. **Operas designed for these companies incl** d'ALBERT: *Tiefland;* BARTOK: *Bluebeard's Castle;* BEETHOVEN: *Fidelio;* BIZET: *Carmen;* BORODIN: *Prince Igor★;* DONIZETTI: *Don Pasquale;* DVORAK: *Devil and Kate★, Rusalka★;* FLOTOW: *Martha;* GAY/Britten: *Beggar's Opera;* GIORDANO: *Andrea Chénier;* GLUCK: *Orfeo ed Euridice;* GOUNOD: *Faust★, Roméo et Juliette;* HUMPERDINCK: *Hänsel und Gretel;* JANACEK: *Excursions of Mr Broucek, Makropoulos Affair★;* KLEBE: *Jakobowsky und der Oberst;* LEONCAVALLO: *Pagliacci;* LORTZING: *Wildschütz, Zar und Zimmermann;* MARTINU: *Comedy on the Bridge, Griechische Passion;* MASCAGNI: *Cavalleria rusticana;* MASSENET: *Manon;* MONIUSZKO: *Halka;* MONTEVERDI: *Favola d'Orfeo;* MOZART: *Don Giovanni, Entführung aus dem Serail★, Schauspieldirektor, Nozze di Figaro;* MUSSORGSKY: *Boris Godunov★, Khovanshchina;* NICOLAI: *Lustigen Weiber;* OFFENBACH: *Contes d'Hoffmann;* ORFF: *Kluge;* PERGOLESI: *Serva padrona;* PROKOFIEV: *War and Peace★;* PUCCINI: *Bohème, Butterfly★, Tosca;* RAVEL: *Heure espagnole;* RIMSKY-KORSAKOV: *Coq d'or;* ROSSINI: *Barbiere di Siviglia;* SAINT-SAENS: *Samson et Dalila;* SHOSTAKOVICH: *Katerina Ismailova;* SMETANA: *Bartered Bride, Dalibor, Devil's Wall, The Kiss, Libuse, Two Widows★;* STRAUSS, R: *Salome;* SUCHON: *Whirlpool★;* TCHAIKOVSKY: *Eugene Onegin, Pique Dame;* VERDI: *Aida, Ballo in maschera, Don Carlo, Nabucco, Rigoletto★, Simon Boccanegra★, Traviata, Trovatore;* WAGNER: *Fliegende Holländer★, Rheingold★, Walküre★, Siegfried★, Götterdämmerung★;* WEBER: *Freischütz.* Exhibitions of stage designs, Olomouc 1958; São Paulo 1973. **Res:** Laubova 3/1626, Prague, CSSR. Mgmt: PRG/CZE; SLZ/FRG; IMR/FRA.

SIMIONESCU, ELENA. Lyric soprano. Romanian. Resident mem: Romanian Opera, Bucharest. Born 23 Apr 1937, Bucharest. Married. Studied: Consv, Prof Arta Florescu, Bucharest. **Debut:** Gilda (*Rigoletto*) Lyric Theater, Constanta 1964. Awards: Third Prize, Intl Cont George Enescu, Bucharest 1961.

Sang with major companies in BEL: Brussels; FR GER: Saarbrücken; ROM: Bucharest; YUG: Belgrade. **Roles with these companies incl** DONI-

SIMON

ZETTI: Norina★ (*Don Pasquale*); MOZART: Despina★ (*Così fan tutte*), Konstanze★ (*Entführung aus dem Serail*), Pamina★ (*Zauberflöte*); ROSSINI: Rosina★ (*Barbiere di Siviglia*); STRAUSS, J: Adele★ (*Fledermaus*); VERDI: Gilda★ (*Rigoletto*), Violetta★ (*Traviata*). Also TRAILESCU: Puss★(*Puss in Boots*). Gives recitals. Appears with symphony orchestra. **Res:** 29 Costache Aristia St, Bucharest 7, Romania. **Mgmt:** RIA/ROM.

SIMON, JOANNA. Lyric mezzo-soprano. American. Born 20 Oct 1940, New York. Single. Studied: Marion Freschl, Daniel Ferro, New York; Sarah Lawrence Coll, New York, USA. **Debut:** Cherubino (*Nozze di Figaro*) New York City Opera 1962. Awards: Met Op Ntl Counc Aud Finalist 1962; First Prize Marian Anderson Awd.
Sang with major companies in ARG: Buenos Aires; AUS: Salzburg Fest; FRA: Bordeaux; USA: Baltimore, Cincinnati, Fort Worth, Houston, Memphis, Miami, Philadelphia Grand, Seattle. **Roles with these companies incl** BIZET: Carmen★; MASSENET: Charlotte★ (*Werther*); MENOTTI: Desideria★ (*Saint of Bleecker Street*); MOZART: Dorabella★ (*Così fan tutte*), Cherubino (*Nozze di Figaro*); MUSSORGSKY: Marina★ (*Boris Godunov*). **World premieres:** GINASTERA: Pantasilea (*Bomarzo*) Washington, DC, Opera Soc 1967; PASATIERI: Raquel (*Black Widow*) Seattle Opera 1972. Video/Film: Piacere (*Rappresentazione di anima e di corpo*). Gives recitals. Appears with symphony orchestra. **Res:** New York, USA. **Mgmt:** DSP/USA.

SIMONELLA, LIBORIO. Spinto tenor. Argentinean. Resident mem: Teatro Colón, Buenos Aires. Born 10 Jan 1933, Cordoba, Argentina. Wife Maria Leonor Morales. One child. Studied: with Mario Melani, Primavera de Sivieri, Angel Celega. **Debut:** Roberto (*Villi*) Teatro Colón 1967. Previous occupations: engineer.
Sang with major companies in ARG: Buenos Aires; BRA: Rio de Janeiro. **Roles with these companies incl** BIZET: Don José★ (*Carmen*); DONIZETTI: Edgardo (*Lucia*); GIORDANO: Andrea Chénier; LEONCAVALLO: Canio (*Pagliacci*); MASCAGNI: Turiddu★ (*Cavalleria rusticana*); OFFENBACH: Hoffmann★; PUCCINI: Rodolfo★ (*Bohème*), Pinkerton★ (*Butterfly*), Cavaradossi★ (*Tosca*); STRAUSS, R: Aegisth★ (*Elektra*); VERDI: Radames★ (*Aida*), Ismaele★ (*Nabucco*), Duca di Mantova (*Rigoletto*), Alfredo★ (*Traviata*). **World premieres:** GUIDI-DREI: Jason (*Medea*) Teatro Colón 1973. Appears with symphony orchestra. **Res:** Lavalle 1131, Buenos Aires, Argentina. **Mgmt:** CDA/ARG.

SIMONINI, PIERCARLO. Scenic and costume designer for opera, theater, film & television. Is a lighting designer; also a painter. Italian. Born 27 Jan 1927, Reggio Emilia. Wife Luciana Miari. Three children. Studied: Accad di Belle Arti di Brera, Profs Enrico Kaneclin, Atanasio Soldati, Pietro Reina, Eva Tea, Milan. Prof training: Piccolo Teatro di Milano. **Operatic debut:** *Manon Lescaut* Opera, Monte Carlo 1967. Theater debut: Théâtre de l'Oeuvre-Herbert, Paris 1960. Awards: Cavaliere della Repubblica Italiana.

Designed for major companies in BEL: Brussels; FRA: Marseille, Paris, Rouen; ITA: Milan La Scala, Naples, Rome Caracalla, Venice; MON: Monte Carlo. **Operas designed for these companies incl** AUBER: *Fra Diavolo;* PUCCINI: *Manon Lescaut.* Also LESUR: *Andrea del Sarto.* **Operatic world premieres:** ROSSELLINI: *Annonce faite à Marie* Opéra Comique, Paris 1970; *Reine morte* Opéra de Monte Carlo, Monaco 1973. Exhibitions at several group shows in Paris. **Res:** 7 Blvd Beaumarchais, Paris 4, France.

SIMONOV, YURI. Conductor of opera. Russian. Music Dir & Resident Cond, Bolshoi Opera, Moscow. Born 1941, USSR. Studied: Univ of Saratov, USSR; Leningrad Consv, Profs Rabinovich and Mravinsky. **Operatic debut:** DARGOMIZHSKY: *Rusalka* Leningrad Consv Opera Studio.
Conducted with major companies in CZE: Prague National; USSR: Moscow Bolshoi; et al. **Operas with these companies incl** GLINKA: *Ruslan and Ludmilla;* MUSSORGSKY: *Boris Godunov;* PROKOFIEV: *Gambler;* TCHAIKOVSKY: *Pique Dame;* VERDI: *Aida;* et al. Also MOLCHANOV: *Dawns Are Quiet Here.*

SIMONSEN, DAG. Norwegian. Publicity Dir, Den Norske Opera/Norwegian Opera, 23c Storgaten, Oslo 1, 1969- . Is also a musician. Born 6 Apr 1946, Oslo. Single. Studied: Oslo Univ; Royal Acad of Music, London; Franz Liszt Acad, Budapest. Plays the clarinet. Previous occupations: princpl clarinet, Army Staff Band, Oslo 1965-67. Form positions, primarily adm & musical: County Music Supervisor, Hammerfest 1967-69. Mem of Repertory & Cooperation Commtt, Norwegian Opera; Publicity Coord Commtt of Theaters, Oslo. **Res:** 44 Thomas Heftyes Gate, Oslo 2, Norway.

SINDIK, ANKA. Lyric coloratura soprano. Yugoslavian. Resident mem: Staatsoper Kassel. Born 27 Jul 1943, Tivat, Yugoslavia. Husband Dorde Trifkovic, occupation author. Studied: Music Acad, Zagreb; Consv Salzburg, Prof Fritz Lunzer, Austria. **Debut:** Norina (*Don Pasquale*) Zagreb 1967. Previous occupations: secy.
Sang with major companies in FR GER: Kassel; SWI: Basel; YUG: Zagreb. **Roles with these companies incl** BEETHOVEN: Marzelline (*Fidelio*); BRITTEN: Tytania★ (*Midsummer Night*); CIMAROSA: Elisetta★ (*Matrimonio segreto*); DONIZETTI: Norina (*Don Pasquale*), Adina★ (*Elisir*); GOTOVAC: Djula (*Ero der Schelm*); LEONCAVALLO: Nedda★ (*Pagliacci*); MOZART: Despina★ (*Così fan tutte*), Zerlina★ (*Don Giovanni*), Susanna★ (*Nozze di Figaro*), Pamina★ (*Zauberflöte*); NICOLAI: Aennchen★ (*Lustigen Weiber*); PAISIELLO: Rosina★ (*Barbiere di Siviglia*); PERGOLESI: Serpina★ (*Serva padrona*); PUCCINI: Lauretta★ (*Gianni Schicchi*); STRAUSS, J: Adele★ (*Fledermaus*); STRAUSS, R: Sophie (*Rosenkavalier*); VERDI: Nannetta★ (*Falstaff*), Violetta★ (*Traviata*); WEBER: Aennchen★ (*Freischütz*). Video—Swiss TV: Agnes (*Schule der Frauen*). Gives recitals. Appears with symphony orchestra. **Res:** Bannatal Marktstr 10, 3501 Kassel, FR Ger. **Mgmt:** CDK/YUG.

SINDILARU, MARIA; née Vintila. Lyric soprano & spinto. Romanian. Resident mem: Romanian

Opera, Bucharest. Born 18 Sep 1927, Husi. Divorced. One child. Studied: Consv, Prof Arta Florescu, Bucharest; Maria Nevi Cerkaska. **Debut:** Lauretta (*Gianni Schicchi*) Romanian Opera 1954.

Sang with major companies in BUL: Sofia; ROM: Bucharest; USSR: Kiev, Tbilisi. **Roles with these companies incl** BIZET: Micaëla★ (*Carmen*); GLUCK: Euridice; GOUNOD: Marguerite★ (*Faust*); MASSENET: Manon; OFFENBACH: Antonia★ (*Contes d'Hoffmann*); PUCCINI: Mimi★ (*Bohème*), Cio-Cio-San★ (*Butterfly*), Liù★ (*Turandot*); SMETANA: Marie★ (*Bartered Bride*); TCHAIKOVSKY: Tatiana★ (*Eugene Onegin*); VERDI: Aida★. Also ENESCU: Antigona (*Oedipe*). Recorded for: Electrecord. Gives recitals. Appears with symphony orchestra. **Res:** 7 Magheru Blvd, Bucharest 1, Romania. Mgmt: RIA/ROM.

SINNONE, ILEANA. Lyric soprano. Italian. Born 4 Dec, Milan. Divorced. One child. Studied: Mo Wladimiro Badiali, Milan. **Debut:** Norina (*Don Pasquale*) Salò, Italy 1965. **Awards:** First Prize Conc A Peri, Reggio Emilia, Italy 1966.

Sang with major companies in FRA: Strasbourg, FR GER: Berlin Deutsche Oper, Hamburg, Munich Staatsoper; GER DR: Berlin Komische Oper, Leipzig; HUN: Budapest; ITA: Bologna, Genoa, Milan La Scala, Naples, Rome Caracalla, Venice; SPA: Majorca Fest; SWI: Geneva; UK: Cardiff Welsh; USA: Washington DC; YUG: Zagreb. **Roles with these companies incl** BIZET: Micaëla★ (*Carmen*); CIMAROSA: Carolina★ (*Matrimonio segreto*); DONIZETTI: Norina★ (*Don Pasquale*), Adina★ (*Elisir*); GOUNOD: Marguerite★ (*Faust*); HANDEL: Cleopatra★ (*Giulio Cesare*); MASCAGNI: Suzel★ (*Amico Fritz*), Sophie★ (*Werther*); MONTEVERDI: Poppea★ (*Incoronazione di Poppea*); MOZART: Donna Anna★‡ (*Don Giovanni*), Contessa★ (*Nozze di Figaro*); PERGOLESI: Serpina★ (*Serva padrona*); PUCCINI: Mimi★ & Musetta★ (*Bohème*), Liù★ (*Turandot*); VERDI: Alice Ford★ (*Falstaff*), Desdemona★ (*Otello*), Amelia★ (*Simon Boccanegra*). Also MOZART: Bastienne; PERGOLESI: Livietta; DONIZETTI: Stefanina (*Giovedì grasso*); PAISIELLO: (*Osteria di Marechiaro*); PUCCINI: Fidelia★ (*Edgar*). Recorded for: Casa Fabbri. Gives recitals. Appears with symphony orchestra. **Res:** V dell'Allodola 16, Milan, Italy. Mgmt: MAU/USA.

SINYAVSKAYA, TAMARA ILINICHNA. Dramatic mezzo-soprano. Russian. Resident mem: Bolshoi Theater, Moscow. Born 7 June 1943, Moscow. Husband Magomaev, occupation singer. Studied: Moscow Consv, O P Pomerantseva; State Theatrical Inst, D B Belyavskaya; school of La Scala Theater, Milan. **Debut:** Ratmir (*Ruslan and Ludmilla*) Bolshoi Theater, Moscow 1965. Awards: Gold Medal, Sofia 1968; First Prize, Belgium 1969.

Sang with major companies in USSR: Moscow Bolshoi. **Roles with these companies incl** BORODIN: Kontchakovna (*Prince Igor*); GLINKA: Ratmir★ (*Ruslan and Ludmilla*); MUSSORGSKY: Marina★ (*Boris Godunov*); PROKOFIEV: Blanche★ (*Gambler*); RIMSKY-KORSAKOV: Ljuba (*Sadko*), Lyoubacha (*Tsar's Bride*); TCHAIKOVSKY: Olga (*Eugene Onegin*).

Also GLINKA: Vanya (*Life for the Tsar*); MUSSORGSKY: Fedor (*Boris Godunov*); KHOLMINOV: Komissar (*Optimistic Tragedy*). **World premieres:** MOLCHANOV: Zhenka (*Dawns Are Quiet Here*) Bolshoi Theater 1975. Recorded for: Melodiya. Gives recitals. Appears with symphony orchestra. **Res:** Moscow, USSR.

SIRISCEVIC, NADA. Coloratura soprano. Yugoslavian. Resident mem: Croatian National Opera, Zagreb. Born Zagreb. Studied: Lav Vrbanic, Zlatko Sir, Vladimir Ruzdjak, Zagreb. **Debut:** Gilda (*Rigoletto*) Croat Ntl Op 1965. Awards: Milka Ternina Awd, Zagreb.

Sang with major companies in FR GER: Berlin Deutsche Oper; ITA: Palermo; SPA: Majorca; USSR: Moscow Bolshoi; YUG: Dubrovnik, Zagreb, Belgrade. **Roles with these companies incl** BIZET: Micaëla (*Carmen*); DONIZETTI: Lucia★; FLOTOW: Lady Harriet (*Martha*); GLUCK: Amor (*Orfeo ed Euridice*); MOZART: Konstanze★ (*Entführung aus dem Serail*), Mlle Silberklang (*Schauspieldirektor*), Susanna (*Nozze di Figaro*), Königin der Nacht (*Zauberflöte*); ORFF: Solo★ (*Carmina burana*); PERGOLESI: Serpina (*Serva padrona*); PUCCINI: Musetta★ (*Bohème*); ROSSINI: Rosina★ (*Barbiere di Siviglia*); SALIERI: Tonina★ (*Prima la musica*); STRAUSS, J: Adele (*Fledermaus*); STRAUSS, R: Fiakermilli★ (*Arabella*); VERDI: Oscar★ (*Ballo in maschera*), Gilda★ (*Rigoletto*), Violetta★ (*Traviata*). Video/Film — Zagreb: Königin der Nacht (*Zauberflöte*). Gives recitals. Appears with symphony orchestra. Teaches voice. Coaches repertoire. **Res:** Galjerova 28, Zagreb, Yugoslavia. Mgmt: CDK/YUG.

SIVIERI, ENRIQUE CÉSAR MANLIO. Argentinean. Director General Artístico, Teatro Colón, Cerrito 618, Buenos Aires, Argentina; and Opera de Cámara del Teatro Colón. In charge of art policy and is also a conductor & stage dir/prod. Born 16 Jul 1915, Buenos Aires. Wife Primavera Andrian, occupation voice teacher. Two children. Studied: privately with Vicente Scaramuzza. Plays the piano. Previous occupations: concert pianist, conductor, director, set designer, lecturer. Form positions, primarily administrative, musical & theatrical: Dir Gen, Teatro Argentino La Plata 1946-48; Art Dir, Teatro Municipal Santiago, Chile 1948-50. Started with present company 1959 as Art Dir; in present position since 1974. Awards: San Francisco Solano Prize, Unión de Compositores Argentinos, 1968. Initiated major policy changes including change from *stagione* theater to repertory theater, expansion of audiences and activities to encompass other communities in the country. Founder & permanent mem of Centro Argentino de Teatro, since 1957; Commtt, Interamericano de Teatro Musical dependiente de la UNESCO. **Res:** Tucumán 340, Buenos Aires, Argentina.

SKALICKI, AMREI; née Annemarie Scheucher. Costume designer for opera, theater, TV. Is also an architect. Austrian. Born 19 Feb 1935, Graz, Austria. Husband Dr Wolfram Skalicki, occupation stage designer. Two children. Studied: Tech Hochschule, Dipl Eng degree, Prof Weber, Prof Winkler, Graz. **Operatic debut:** *Così fan tutte*

Opernhaus Essen 1970. Theater debut: ORTF TV, Paris, 1973.

Designed for major companies in ARG: Buenos Aires; AUS: Graz; FRA: Lyon, Marseille, Strasbourg; FR GER: Dortmund, Essen, Krefeld; SWI: Geneva; USA: San Francisco Opera. **Operas designed for these companies incl** BARTOK: *Bluebeard's Castle★;* DEBUSSY: *Pelléas et Mélisande★;* GIORDANO: *Andrea Chénier★;* GOUNOD: *Faust★;* MASSENET: *Manon★;* MEYERBEER: *Africaine★;* MOZART: *Così fan tutte★, Idomeneo★, Zauberflöte★;* OFFENBACH: *Contes d'Hoffmann★;* POULENC: *Dialogues des Carmélites★;* PUCCINI: *Gianni Schicchi★, Tosca★;* SAINT-SAENS: *Samson et Dalila★;* STRAUSS, R: *Ariadne auf Naxos★, Elektra★, Rosenkavalier★;* VERDI: *Falstaff★, Macbeth★, Nabucco, Trovatore★;* WAGNER: *Fliegende Holländer★, Walküre★, Götterdämmerung★, Tannhäuser★.* Operatic Video—ORTF TV, Paris: *Manon.* Exhibitions of stage designs, San Francisco Libr 1972; Dortmund 1975. Teaches. **Res:** Ausseerstr 64, A-8940 Liezen, Austria.

SKALICKI, WOLFRAM. Scenic and costume designer for opera & television; specl in sets. Is a lighting designer & stage director. Austrian. Resident designer, Vereinigte Bühnen Graz, Austria. Born 10 Jun 1925, Vienna. Wife Amrei, occupation architect, costume designer. Two children. Studied: Acad of Fine Arts, Prof Emil Pirchan, Vienna; Univ of Vienna, history of art and theater. **Operatic debut:** sets, *Così fan tutte* Music Acad Vienna 1949; cost, *Zauberflöte* Ver Bühnen Graz 1955. Theater debut: Scala Theater Vienna 1950. Awards: Fuger Silver Medal & Masterschool Prize, Acad F Arts, Vienna; PhD, Univ Vienna; Hon Prof Music, Univ Graz.

Designed for major companies in ARG: Buenos Aires; AUS: Graz, Vienna Volksoper; FRA: Lyon, Marseille, Strasbourg; FR GER: Dortmund, Essen, Krefeld, Munich Gärtnerplatz; SPA: Majorca; SWI: Geneva; USA: San Francisco Opera. **Operas designed for these companies incl** d'ALBERT: *Tiefland;* BARTOK: *Bluebeard's Castle;* BEETHOVEN: *Fidelio;* BELLINI: *Puritani★;* BERLIOZ: *Damnation de Faust★, Troyens★;* BIZET: *Carmen★;* BRITTEN: *Rape oj Lucretia;* BUSONI: *Doktor Faust;* CIMAROSA: *Matrimonio segreto;* CORNELIUS: *Barbier von Bagdad;* DALLAPICCOLA: *Prigioniero;* DEBUSSY: *Pelléas et Mélisande★;* DONIZETTI: *Don Pasquale, Favorite, Lucia★;* EINEM: *Besuch der alten Dame★, Dantons Tod;* FLOTOW: *Martha;* GIORDANO: *Andrea Chénier★;* GLUCK: *Iphigénie en Tauride, Orfeo ed Euridice;* GOUNOD: *Faust★;* HINDEMITH: *Cardillac;* JANACEK: *Excursions of Mr Broucek, Katya Kabanova;* KORNGOLD: *Tote Stadt;* LEONCAVALLO: *Pagliacci;* LORTZING: *Waffenschmied;* MASCAGNI: *Cavalleria rusticana;* MASSENET: *Manon★;* MEYERBEER: *Africaine★;* MILHAUD: *Christophe Colomb;* MOZART: *Così fan tutte, Don Giovanni, Entführung aus dem Serail, Idomeneo★, Schauspieldirektor, Nozze di Figaro, Zauberflöte★;* MUSSORGSKY: *Boris Godunov★;* NICOLAI: *Lustigen Weiber;* OFFENBACH: *Contes d'Hoffmann★, Périchole;* ORFF: *Kluge;* PFITZNER: *Palestrina;* POU-

LENC: *Dialogues des Carmélites;* PROKOFIEV: *Fiery Angel;* PUCCINI: *Bohème, Gianni Schicchi, Butterfly, Tabarro★, Tosca★, Turandot;* PURCELL: *Dido and Aeneas;* RIMSKY-KORSAKOV: *Invisible City of Kitezh;* ROSSINI: *Barbiere di Siviglia;* SHOSTAKOVICH: *Katerina Ismailova;* SMETANA: *Bartered Bride;* STRAUSS, J: *Fledermaus★;* STRAUSS, R: *Arabella, Ariadne auf Naxos★, Elektra★, Frau ohne Schatten, Rosenkavalier★, Salome;* STRAVINSKY: *Rake's Progress;* TCHAIKOVSKY: *Pique Dame★;* VERDI: *Aida, Ballo in maschera, Don Carlo, Falstaff★, Forza del destino, Macbeth★, Nabucco★, Rigoletto, Traviata, Trovatore, Vespri;* WAGNER: *Fliegende Holländer★, Lohengrin, Meistersinger, Parsifal, Rienzi★, Rheingold★, Walküre★, Siegfried★, Götterdämmerung★, Tannhäuser, Tristan und Isolde;* WEBER: *Abu Hassan, Freischütz★;* WEILL: *Dreigroschenoper;* WOLF-FERRARI: *Quattro rusteghi.* Also SUTERMEISTER: *Titus Feuerfuchs;* WOLF-FERRARI: *Vedova scaltra;* MONTEVERDI: *Lamento d'Arianna.* Operatic Video—ORTF Paris: *Manon.* Exhibitions of stage designs Vienna 1947; San Francisco 1951; São Paulo 1954; New York 1970; Klagenfurt 1972; Graz 1972. Teaches at Univ of Music and Perf Arts, Graz. **Res:** Ausseerstr 64, A-8940 Liezen, Austria.

SKALICKY, JAN. Costume designer for opera, theater, television. Resident designer, Bühnen der Stadt Köln, Cologne. Born Joliet, IL, USA. Single. Studied: School of Commercial Art, Prague. **Operatic debut:** *Eugene Onegin* State Theater Pilsen, CSSR 1954. Theater debut: National Theater, Prague 1957.

Designed for major companies in AUS: Salzburg Fest, Vienna Staatsoper & Volksoper; CZE: Prague National & Smetana; DEN: Copenhagen; FRA: Paris; FR GER: Berlin Deutsche Oper, Cologne, Düsseldorf-Duisburg, Frankfurt, Hamburg, Munich Staatsoper & Gärtnerplatz, Wiesbaden; GER DR: Berlin Komische Oper; HOL: Amsterdam; ITA: Milan La Scala; NOR: Oslo; POL: Warsaw; SWE: Stockholm; SWI: Basel, Geneva, Zurich; UK: London Royal; USA: Boston, New York Met. **Operas designed for these companies incl** AUBER: *Fra Diavolo★;* DEBUSSY: *Pelléas et Mélisande★;* DESSAU: *Lanzelot★;* DONIZETTI: *Don Pasquale★;* DVORAK: *Devil and Kate★, Rusalka★;* FORTNER: *Elisabeth Tudor★;* GOUNOD: *Faust;* HINDEMITH: *Cardillac★;* JANACEK: *Cunning Little Vixen★, Excursions of Mr Broucek★, From the House of the Dead★, Jenufa★, Katya Kabanova★, Makropoulos Affair;* MARTINU: *Griechische Passion;* MONTEVERDI: *Favola d'Orfeo★;* MOZART: *Così fan tutte★, Don Giovanni★, Idomeneo★, Mitridate, re di Ponto★;* MUSSORGSKY: *Boris Godunov★;* OFFENBACH: *Contes d'Hoffmann★;* PROKOFIEV: *Fiery Angel★;* PUCCINI: *Bohème★, Fanciulla del West★;* SMETANA: *Bartered Bride★;* STRAUSS, R: *Ariadne auf Naxos★, Salome★;* VERDI: *Aida★, Don Carlo★, Falstaff★, Forza del destino★, Macbeth★, Nabucco★, Simon Boccanegra★, Traviata★, Trovatore★, Vespri★;* WAGNER: *Tannhäuser★, Tristan und Isolde★;* WEILL: *Dreigroschenoper★;* ZIMMERMANN: *Soldaten★.*

SKOMRLJ, IKE FRANCISKA. Costume designer for opera, theater, film, television. Also creates cartoon slides for children. Yugoslavian. Resident designer, Croatian Ntl Opera Theater, Zagreb and at Croatian Ntl Theater, Zagreb. Born 13 Jul 1936, Zagreb. Single. Studied: Acad of Drama, Zagreb. **Operatic debut:** *Bartered Bride* Croat Ntl Op, Zagreb 1957. Theater debut: ballet, Varazdin, Yugoslavia 1957. Awards: Festival Awd Novi Sad, Yugoslavia. **Designed for major companies in** YUG: Dubrovnik, Zagreb. **Operas designed for these companies incl** DONIZETTI: *Elisir;* GLUCK: *Orfeo ed Euridice⋆;* SMETANA: *Bartered Bride;* STRAUSS, R: *Daphne⋆;* VERDI: *Ballo in maschera.* **Res:** Kuseviceva 3, Zagreb, Yugoslavia.

SKRAM, KNUT. Lyric baritone. Norwegian. Resident mem: Norwegian Opera, Oslo. Born 18 Dec 1937, Saebö, Norway. Wife Hanne, occupation ballet dancer. Two children. Studied: Montana State Univ, George Buckbee, Bozeman, MT, USA; Prof Paul Lohmann, Wiesbaden, FR Ger; Mo Luigi Ricci, Rome; Prof Kristian Riis, Copenhagen. **Debut:** Amonasro (*Aida*) Norwegian Opera, Oslo 1964. Previous occupations: architecture degree, Montana State Univ, USA 1963; position as architect, 6 months. Awards: First Prize, Intl Music Compt, SD Rundfunk, Munich 1967; First Prize, Nordic Vocal Compt, Scand Ntl Radio & TV, Helsinki 1971. **Sang with major companies in** NOR: Oslo; UK: Glyndebourne Fest. **Roles with these companies incl** BIZET: Escamillo⋆ (*Carmen*); BRITTEN: Captain Balstrode (*Peter Grimes*); DALLAPICCOLA: Il Prigioniero⋆; GLUCK: Oreste⋆ (*Iphigénie en Tauride*); MENOTTI: Bob (*Old Maid and the Thief*); MOZART: Guglielmo⋆ (*Cosi fan tutte*), Don Giovanni⋆, Conte Almaviva & Figaro⋆ (*Nozze di Figaro*), Papageno⋆ (*Zauberflöte*); ORFF: König (*Kluge*); PUCCINI: Marcello⋆ (*Bohème*), Sharpless (*Butterfly*); PURCELL: Aeneas (*Dido and Aeneas*); ROSSINI: Figaro⋆ (*Barbiere di Siviglia*); TCHAIKOVSKY: Eugene Onegin, Yeletsky (*Pique Dame*); VERDI: Amonasro (*Aida*), Rodrigo (*Don Carlo*), Ford (*Falstaff*), Germont (*Traviata*), Conte di Luna⋆ (*Trovatore*). Also BRITTEN: Sid (*Albert Herring*), Tarquinius⋆ (*Rape of Lucretia*); MONTEVERDI: Ottone (*Incoronazione di Poppea*); NIELSEN: Henrik⋆ (*Maskarade*). **World premieres:** RYPDAL: Orfeus (*Orfeus Turns and Looks at Euridike*) Norwegian Opera 1972; TVEITT: Baronen (*Jeppe*) Norwegian Opera 1966. Video/Film: Figaro (*Nozze di Figaro*); Sid (*Albert Herring*); Aeneas (*Dido and Aeneas*). Gives recitals. Appears with symphony orchestra. **Res:** H Tveters Vei 29, Oslo, Norway. Mgmt: AIM/UK.

SKROWACZEWSKI, STANISLAW. Conductor of opera and symphony; composer; operatic stage director. American. Mus Dir, Minnesota Orch, Minneapolis, USA. Born 3 Oct 1923, Lwow, Poland. Wife Krystyna. Three children. Studied: Music Acads Lwow, Krakow; Nadia Boulanger, Paris; incl piano, violin, viola and voice. Plays the piano, violin, viola. **Operatic debut:** State Opera, Wroclaw, Poland 1946. Symphonic debut: Phil Orch, Lwow 1945. Awards: First Prize Intl Conductors Compt, Rome 1956; Hon DL Hamline

Univ, Macalester Coll, St Paul; Second Prize Intl Composers Compt, Belgium 1953; Commanders Cross, Poland 1956. Previous adm positions in opera: Mus Dir & Cond, Wroclaw State Opera. **Conducted with major companies in** ARG: Buenos Aires; AUS: Salzburg Fest, Vienna Staatsoper & Volksoper; CZE: Prague Smetana; FRA: Aix-en-Provence Fest, Nice, Paris; FR GER: Frankfurt; HOL: Amsterdam; HUN: Budapest; ISR: Tel Aviv; ITA: Bologna, Florence Maggio & Comunale, Genoa, Milan, Naples, Palermo, Rome Opera & Caracalla, Trieste, Turin, Venice; MEX: Mexico City; MON: Monte Carlo; NOR: Oslo; POL: Lodz, Warsaw; POR: Lisbon; ROM: Bucharest; SWE: Stockholm; SWI: Basel; USA: Minneapolis, New York Met, Philadelphia Grand & Lyric, St Paul, Santa Fe. **Operas with these companies incl** BARTOK: *Bluebeard's Castle;* BEETHOVEN: *Fidelio⋆;* BERG: *Wozzeck;* BERLIOZ: *Damnation de Faust;* GLUCK: *Orfeo ed Euridice;* MONIUSZKO: *Halka, Haunted Castle;* MOZART: *Cosi fan tutte, Don Giovanni, Entführung aus dem Serail, Nozze di Figaro⋆, Zauberflöte⋆;* MUSSORGSKY: *Boris Godunov;* PENDERECKI: *Teufel von Loudun⋆;* RAVEL: *Enfant et les sortilèges;* ROSSINI: *Barbiere di Siviglia;* STRAUSS, R: *Elektra, Salome;* TCHAIKOVSKY: *Eugene Onegin;* WAGNER: *Fliegende Holländer, Lohengrin, Meistersinger, Tannhäuser⋆, Tristan und Isolde.* Conducted major orch in Europe, USA/Canada, Cent/S America, Austrl. Previous positions as Mus Dir with major orch: Mus Dir & Cond, Katowice Ntl Phil, Krakow Phil Orch, Warsaw Ntl Orch, Poland. **Operas composed:** *The Lion's Inn,* 1956; no pf. **Res:** Minneapolis, MN, USA. Mgmt: HUR/USA; GLZ/FRA.

SLATINARU, MARIA; née Buzurin. Spinto. Romanian. Resident mem: Romanian Opera, Bucharest. Born 25 May 1938, Iassy. Husband Virgil Nistor, occupation TV prod. Studied: Consv, Profs Arta Florescu and Aurel Alexandrescu, Bucharest. **Debut:** Elisabetta (*Don Carlo*) Romanian Opera 1969. Awards: First Prize, 's Hertogenbosch 1969; Second Prize, Toulouse 1968; Third Prize, Fr Vinas, Barcelona. **Sang with major companies in** BEL: Liège; FR GER: Cologne, Düsseldorf-Duisburg, Karlsruhe, Mannheim, Stuttgart, Wiesbaden; ROM: Bucharest; SWI: Zurich. **Roles with these companies incl** GIORDANO: Maddalena⋆ (*Andrea Chénier*); GOUNOD: Marguerite (*Faust*); PUCCINI: Mimi⋆ (*Bohème*), Manon Lescaut⋆, Liù⋆ (*Turandot*); STRAUSS, R: Arabella⋆; TCHAIKOVSKY: Lisa⋆ (*Pique Dame*); VERDI: Elisabetta⋆ (*Don Carlo*), Abigaille⋆ (*Nabucco*), Amelia⋆ (*Simon Boccanegra*), Leonora⋆ (*Trovatore*); WAGNER: Elsa⋆ (*Lohengrin*), Sieglinde⋆ (*Walküre*). Also on records only BOITO: Margherita (*Mefistofele*); PONCHIELLI: Gioconda; PUCCINI: Turandot. Recorded for: Electrecord. Video/Film: Maria (*Marin Pescarul*), (*Negrea*). Gives recitals. Appears with symphony orchestra. **Res:** 3 Gh Dej Blvd, Bucharest 6, Romania. Mgmt: RIA/ROM; SLZ/FRG; PAS/FRG.

SLÄTTEGÅRD, GUNILLA LOVISA; née Wallin. Coloratura soprano. Swedish. Born 29 Mar 1938, Jönköping, Sweden. Husband Staffan Söllcher, occupation stage manager. Studied: Royal Acad of Music, Stockholm; Dagmar Gustafsson, Hjördis Schymberg, Sweden. **Debut:** Blondchen (*Entführung aus dem Serail*) Drottningholm Court Theatre. Awards: Margit Rosengren and Jussi Björling Awds.

Sang with major companies in SWE: Drottningholm Fest, Stockholm. **Roles with these companies incl** DONIZETTI: Norina★ (*Don Pasquale*); GLUCK, Amor★ (*Orfeo ed Euridice*); MOZART: Despina★ (*Così fan tutte*), Blondchen★ (*Entführung aus dem Serail*), Pamina (*Zauberflöte*); OFFENBACH: Olympia★ (*Contes d'Hoffmann*); PERGOLESI: Serpina (*Serva padrona*); ROSSINI: Rosina★ (*Barbiere di Siviglia*). **World premieres:** ROSENBERG: Celia (*Hus med dubbel Ingång*) Royal Opera, Stockholm 1970. Gives recitals. Appears with symphony orchestra.

SLÄTTEGÅRD, TORD. Lyric tenor. Swedish. Resident mem: Royal Opera, Stockholm. Born 3 Aug 1933, Kalmar, Sweden. Wife Cecilia, occupation teacher. Studied: Royal Acad of Music, Hjördis Schymberg, Stockholm. **Debut:** Alfredo (*Traviata*) Royal Opera, Stockholm 1963. Awards: Kristina Nilsson Awd.

Sang with major companies in DEN: Copenhagen; NOR: Oslo; SWE: Drottningholm Fest. **Roles with these companies incl** DONIZETTI: Ernesto★ (*Don Pasquale*); HANDEL: Oronte★ (*Alcina*); MOZART: Ferrando★ (*Così fan tutte*), Don Ottavio★ (*Don Giovanni*), Belmonte★ (*Entführung aus dem Serail*); OFFENBACH: Hoffmann★; ROSSINI: Almaviva★ (*Barbiere di Siviglia*), Florville★ (*Signor Bruschino*); VERDI: Fenton★ (*Falstaff*), Alfredo★ (*Traviata*). Also BERWALD: Nadir (*Drottningen av Golconda*); HANDEL: Silvio (*Pastor fido*), Jonathan (*Saul*). Gives recitals. Appears with symphony orchestra.

SMILJANIĆ, RADMILA. Spinto. Yugoslavian. Resident mem: Narodno Pozoriste, Belgrade, Yugoslavia. Born 25 Jul 1940, Banja Luka, Yugoslavia. Husband Branislav Mijailovic, occupation engineer. One child. Studied: Muzicka Akad, Prof Spiler Bruha, Sarajevo, Yugoslavia. **Debut:** Djula (*Ero der Schelm*) Narodno Pozoriste, Sarajevo 1965. Awards: First Prize Intl Conc, Reggio Emilia, Italy 1965; Third Prize Yugoslav Conc, Ljubljana 1966; Second Prize Yugoslav Conc, Zagreb 1967.

Sang with major companies in ITA: Trieste; SPA: Barcelona; YUG: Dubrovnik, Zagreb, Belgrade. **Roles with these companies incl** BARTOK: Judith (*Bluebeard's Castle*); BIZET: Micaëla★ (*Carmen*); GERSHWIN: Bess; GLINKA: Antonida★ (*Life for the Tsar*); GOTOVAC: Djula (*Ero der Schelm*); GOUNOD: Marguerite (*Faust*); MASCAGNI: Santuzza★ (*Cavalleria rusticana*); MILHAUD: La Femme★ (*Pauvre matelot*); MOZART: Fiordiligi & Despina★ (*Così fan tutte*), Contessa★ (*Nozze di Figaro*); PUCCINI: Mimi★ (*Bohème*), Cio-Cio-San (*Butterfly*), Tosca★, Turandot★ & Liù (*Turandot*); RIMSKY-KORSAKOV: Olga★ (*Maid of Pskov*); SHOSTAKOVICH: Katerina Ismailova; SMETANA: Marie★ (*Bartered Bride*); TCHAIKOVSKY: Tatiana★ (*Eugene Onegin*), Lisa★ (*Pique Dame*); VERDI: Aida, Amelia (*Ballo in maschera*), Desdemona★ (*Otello*),

Leonora★ (*Trovatore*); WEBER: Agathe★ (*Freischütz*).

SMILLIE, THOMSON JOHN. British. Art Dir, Wexford Festival Opera, Theatre Royal, Wexford, Ireland 1972-. In charge of art policy. Add adm posts: Dir of PR, Scottish Opera, Elmbank Crescent, Glasgow 924PT, Scotland; and secy, Scottish Opera Club. Born 29 Sep 1942, Glasgow. Wife Anne Pringle. Four children. Studied: Glasgow Univ. Previous occupations: Trainee Exec, William Collins publisher 1963-65. Started with Scottish Opera in 1966 as Publ Asst. Mem of Wexford Festival Repertoire Subcommtt; Scottish Opera Marketing Commtt, Theatre Royal Campaign Commtt. **Res:** 132 Hyndland Rd, Glasgow, G129PN, Scotland.

SMITH, CAROL. Dramatic mezzo-soprano. American/Swiss. Resident mem: Opernhaus Zurich; Bayerische Staatsoper, Munich. Born 20 Feb 1926, Oakpark, IL, USA. Husband Audinoff Zanforlin, occupation violinist, Tonhalle Orchestra, Zurich. Studied: Lola Fletcher, Chicago; American Consv, Chicago; Mario Cordone, Milan. **Debut:** Moraima (*Re Hassan*) Naples Opera 1961. Awards: Chicago *Tribune* Best Singer 1944; Vera Dougan, NFWC, Woman of the Year Awd 1967.

Sang with major companies in AUS: Salzburg Fest, Vienna Staatsoper; FRA: Aix-en-Provence Fest, Marseille; GRE: Athens Fest; FR GER: Berlin Deutsche Oper, Düsseldorf-Duisburg, Frankfurt, Hamburg, Karlsruhe, Kiel, Munich Staatsoper, Stuttgart, Wiesbaden; ITA: Milan La Scala, Naples; MON: Monte Carlo; SWI: Basel, Geneva, Zurich; USA: Chicago, Cincinnati, Miami, New York City Opera, Washington DC. **Roles with these companies incl** BIZET: Carmen; BORODIN: Kontchakovna (*Prince Igor*); CHERUBINI: Neris (*Medea*); DONIZETTI: Sara★ (*Roberto Devereux*); MASSENET: Charlotte (*Werther*); MONTEVERDI: Orfeo★, Poppea (*Incoronazione di Poppea*); OFFENBACH: Giulietta★ (*Contes d'Hoffmann*); PONCHIELLI: La Cieca (*Gioconda*); PUCCINI: Frugola (*Tabarro*); REIMANN: Pythia★ (*Melusine*); TCHAIKOVSKY: Comtesse★ (*Pique Dame*); VERDI: Amneris★ (*Aida*), Ulrica★ (*Ballo in maschera*), Eboli★ (*Don Carlo*), Dame Quickly★ (*Falstaff*), Azucena★ (*Trovatore*); WAGNER: Brangäne★ (*Tristan und Isolde*). Also GINASTERA: Pantasilea★ (*Bomarzo*); SCHOECK: Penthesilea★; MASCAGNI: Santuzza (*Cavalleria rusticana*); PUCCINI: Zita (*Gianni Schicchi*). **World premieres:** GINASTERA: Lucretia (*Beatrix Cenci*) Washington DC 1971. Recorded for: Harmonia Mundi. Video/Film: Penthesilea. Gives recitals. Appears with symphony orchestra. Teaches voice. **Res:** Apollostr 2, 8032 Zurich, Switzerland. **Mgmt:** SLZ/FRG.

SMITH, DONALD SYDNEY. Dramatic tenor. Australian. Resident mem: Australian Opera Co, Sydney. Born Bundaberg, Australia. Wife Thelma Joyce, occupation secy. Three children. Studied: Mo Les Edye, Brisbane. **Debut:** Faust, Brisbane Opera Co 1948. Previous occupations: farmer. Awards: OBE, Queen's Birthday Honors; Henry Lawson Fest Australian Arts Awd.

Sang with major companies in AUSTRL: Sydney; MEX: Mexico City; UK: Cardiff Welsh,

Edinburgh Fest, Glasgow Scottish, London Royal & English National. **Roles with these companies incl** BIZET: Don José (*Carmen*); GOUNOD: Faust, Roméo; LEONCAVALLO: Canio★ (*Pagliacci*); MASCAGNI: Turiddu★ (*Cavalleria rusticana*); PUCCINI: Rodolfo (*Bohème*), Dick Johnson (*Fanciulla del West*), Pinkerton (*Butterfly*), Des Grieux (*Manon Lescaut*), Luigi★ (*Tabarro*), Cavaradossi★ (*Tosca*), Calaf (*Turandot*); ROSSINI: Almaviva (*Barbiere di Siviglia*); SMETANA: Wenzel (*Bartered Bride*); VERDI: Radames★ (*Aida*), Foresto (*Attila*), Riccardo (*Ballo in maschera*), Corrado (*Corsaro*), Ernani, Don Alvaro★ (*Forza del destino*), Duca di Mantova★ (*Rigoletto*), Alfredo (*Traviata*), Manrico (*Trovatore*). Video/Film: Cavaradossi (*Tosca*). Gives recitals. Teaches voice.

SMITH, JULIAN BRICKNELL. Conductor of opera and symphony. British. Chorus Master & Resident Cond, Welsh National Opera; Cardiff. Born 21 Apr 1944, Worcester Park, UK. Wife Kate, occupation music teacher. Studied: Raymond Leppard, Peter le Huray, Phyllis Palmer, Cambridge; also piano, harpsichord. Plays the piano, harpsichord. Operatic training as repetiteur & chorus master at Welsh National, Cardiff 1973-74. **Operatic debut:** *Rigoletto* Welsh Ntl Op 1973. Symphonic debut: Welsh Phil, Swansea, Wales 1974. Previous occupations: lecturer Nottingham Univ, UK 1969-73.

Conducted with major companies in UK: Welsh National. **Operas with these companies incl** MOZART: *Idomeneo★, Zauberflöte★;* PUCCINI: *Manon Lescaut★;* VERDI: *Otello★, Rigoletto★, Simon Boccanegra★.* Conducted major orch in Europe. **Res:** Cardiff, Wales, UK.

SMITH, MALCOLM SOMMERVILLE. Bass. American. Resident mem: Deutsche Oper am Rhein, Düsseldorf-Duisburg. Born 22 Jun 1933, Rockville Centre, NY, USA. Married. Studied: Oberlin Consv of Music, Prof Harold Bryson, Sidney Dietch, NY, USA; Indiana Univ, Prof Paul Matthen, Frank St Leger, Bloomington, IN; Prof Clemens Kaiser-Breme, Germany. **Debut:** Inquisitor (*Fiery Angel*) New York City Opera 1965. Previous occupations: HS music teacher.

Sang with major companies in AUS: Vienna Staatsoper; FR GER: Bielefeld, Cologne, Düsseldorf-Duisburg, Hamburg, Hannover, Krefeld; ITA: Spoleto Fest, Trieste; USA: Chicago, Cincinnati, Fort Worth, Houston, Lake George, Miami, Milwaukee Florentine, New York Met & City Opera, Philadelphia Lyric, San Antonio, San Francisco Opera & Spring Opera, Seattle. **Roles with these companies incl** BEETHOVEN: Rocco★ (*Fidelio*); BERG: Doktor★ (*Wozzeck*); BRITTEN: Theseus★ (*Midsummer Night*); DEBUSSY: Arkel (*Pelléas et Mélisande*); GOUNOD: Méphistophélès (*Faust*); HANDEL: Polyphemus (*Acis and Galatea*), Ptolemy (*Giulio Cesare*); MASSENET: Des Grieux (*Portrait of Manon*); MEYERBEER: Don Pedro★ (*Africaine*); MOZART: Don Giovanni★, Osmin (*Entführung aus dem Serail*), Sarastro★ (*Zauberflöte*); MUSSORGSKY: Pimen (*Boris Godunov*); PONCHIELLI: Alvise★ (*Gioconda*); PUCCINI: Colline★ (*Bohème*); ROSSINI: Don Basilio★ (*Barbiere di Siviglia*), Moïse; STRAUSS, R: La

Roche★ (*Capriccio*); STRAVINSKY: Tiresias (*Oedipus Rex*); VERDI: Ramfis★ (*Aida*), Philip II★ & Grande Inquisitore★ (*Don Carlo*), Padre Guardiano (*Forza del destino*); WAGNER: Daland★ (*Fliegende Holländer*), König Heinrich★ (*Lohengrin*), Pogner★ (*Meistersinger*), Gurnemanz★ (*Parsifal*), Fasolt★ (*Rheingold*), Hunding★ (*Walküre*), Landgraf★ (*Tannhäuser*), König Marke★ (*Tristan und Isolde*); WOLF-FERRARI: Ottavio★ (*Donne curiose*). Also DVORAK: Wassermann★ (*Rusalka*); HANDEL: Saul★. Gives recitals. Appears with symphony orchestra. **Res:** Düsseldorf, FR Ger and Montvale, NJ, USA. Mgmt: DSP/USA.

SMITH, OLIVER. Scenic designer for opera, theater, film & ballet. American. Co-Dir American Ballet Theatre. Born 13 Feb 1918, Wawpawn, WI, USA. Single. Studied: Penn State Univ, USA. **Operatic debut:** *Traviata* Metropolitan Opera, New York 1958. Theater debut: Ballet Russe de Monte Carlo, New York 1943. Previous occupation: painter. Awards: Handel Medallion, City of New York; Shubert Awd, New York; Distinguished Alumni Awd Penn State; Hon DL Bucknell Univ.

Designed for major companies in USA: Boston, Chicago, Kansas City, New York Met & City Opera, San Francisco Opera, Washington DC. **Operas designed for these companies incl** BIZET: *Carmen;* FLOTOW: *Martha;* GERSHWIN: *Porgy and Bess;* MOZART: *Don Giovanni;* PURCELL: *Dido and Aeneas;* SCHOENBERG: *Moses und Aron;* STRAUSS, J: *Fledermaus★;* VERDI: *Falstaff★, Traviata.* **Operatic world premieres:** MENOTTI: *Most Important Man* New York City Opera 1971. Exhibitions of stage designs, Penn State 1945; Musm Mod Art 1946; NY Libr & Musm of Perf Arts 1975. Teaches at New York Univ. **Res:** Brooklyn, NY, USA. Mgmt: LTZ/USA.

SOCCI, GIANNI; né Giovanni Socci. Basso-buffo. Italian. Born 19 Mar 1939, Rome. Single. Studied: Consv S Cecilia, Rome; Mo Giorgio Favaretto, Mo Armando Piervenanzi, Franca Cavarra, Rome. **Debut:** PAISIELLO: Achmed (*Re Teodoro in Venezia*) Piccolo Teatro Comico 1965. Previous occupations: librarian at Accad S Cecilia, Rome. Awards: Grand Prize, Ital TV Compt for Young Voices 1963-64.

Sang with major companies in BEL: Brussels; CAN: Montreal/Quebec; DEN: Copenhagen; FRA: Paris, Rouen, Strasbourg, Toulouse; FR GER: Cologne, Dortmund, Frankfurt, Nürnberg, Stuttgart; ITA: Genoa, Milan La Scala, Naples, Palermo, Rome Opera, Spoleto Fest, Trieste, Turin, Venice; MON: Monte Carlo; SPA: Barcelona; USSR: Leningrad Kirov; USA: Philadelphia Lyric, Washington DC. **Roles with these companies incl** CIMAROSA: Geronimo★ (*Matrimonio segreto*); DONIZETTI: Don Pistacchio★ (*Campanello*), Mocenigo★ (*Caterina Cornaro*), Don Pasquale★, Dulcamara★ (*Elisir*), Sulpice (*Fille du régiment*); HINDEMITH: Professor (*Hin und zurück*); MOZART: Don Alfonso★ (*Così fan tutte*), Leporello★ (*Don Giovanni*), Osmin (*Entführung aus dem Serail*), Nardo (*Finta giardiniera*), Figaro (*Nozze di Figaro*), Don Pippo (*Oca del Cairo*), Osmin (*Zaïde*), Papageno (*Zauberflöte*); PAISIELLO: Bartolo (*Barbiere di Siviglia*); PERGOLESI: Tracolino (*Maestro di musica*), Uberto

(*Serva padrona*); ROSSINI: Dott Bartolo★ (*Barbiere di Siviglia*), Tobias Mill★ (*Cambiale di matrimonio*), Don Magnifico★ (*Cenerentola*), Podestà (*Gazza ladra*), Mustafà★ (*Italiana in Algeri*), Conte Asdrubal (*Pietra del paragone*), Dormont (*Scala di seta*), Gaudenzio (*Signor Bruschino*), Geronio (*Turco in Italia*). Also TESTI: Magnano★ (*Albergo dei poveri*); PUCCINI: Sacrestano (*Tosca*); ROSSINI: Paccuvio★ (*Pietra del paragone*). World premieres: NONO: Basso (*Gran sole carico d'amore*) Milan 1975. Video—RAI TV: Martino (*Occasione fa il ladro*), Tobias Mill (*Cambiale di matrimonio*). Gives recitals. Appears with symphony orchestra. Res: V della Pietà 10, Rome, Italy. Mgmt: IMR/FRA.

SÖDERBLOM, ULF ARNE. Conductor of opera and symphony. Finnish. Mus Dir & Chief Cond, Finnish National Opera, Helsinki. Born 5 Feb 1930, Turku/Åbo. Wife Karin. Five children. Studied: Akad f Musik u darst Kunst, H Swarowsky, Vienna; incl piano & voice. **Operatic debut:** *Zauberflöte* Turku 1957. Symphonic debut: Radio Symph Orch, Helsinki 1956.

Conducted at major companies in ARG: Buenos Aires; FIN: Helsinki; FR GER: Hamburg; GER DR: Berlin Staatsoper, Leipzig; HUN: Budapest; NOR: Oslo; POL: Warsaw; SWE: Stockholm; SWI: Basel, Geneva. **Operas with these companies incl** BEETHOVEN: *Fidelio;* BERG: *Wozzeck;* BIZET: *Carmen;* BRITTEN: *Albert Herring, Midsummer Night★;* CIMAROSA: *Matrimonio segreto;* DONIZETTI: *Don Pasquale, Elisir, Lucia;* EGK: *Zaubergeige;* GLUCK: *Orfeo ed Euridice;* GOUNOD: *Faust;* HANDEL: *Xerxes;* HENZE: *König Hirsch/Re Cervo★;* JANACEK: *Cunning Little Vixen★;* LEONCAVALLO: *Pagliacci;* MASCAGNI: *Cavalleria rusticana;* MOZART: *Così fan tutte★, Don Giovanni, Nozze di Figaro★, Zauberflöte★;* MUSSORGSKY: *Fair at Sorochinsk★;* OFFENBACH: *Contes d'Hoffmann;* PUCCINI: *Bohème, Gianni Schicchi, Butterfly, Tosca★;* ROSSINI: *Barbiere di Siviglia, Italiana in Algeri;* SHOSTAKOVICH: *Nose★;* SMETANA: *Bartered Bride;* STRAUSS, J: *Fledermaus;* STRAUSS, R: *Rosenkavalier★, Salome;* STRAVINSKY: *Oedipus Rex, Rake's Progress;* VERDI: *Aida, Ballo in maschera★, Don Carlo★, Forza del destino★, Rigoletto, Traviata, Trovatore★;* WAGNER: *Tristan und Isolde★.* Also MERIKANTO: *Juha★;* HARTMANN: *Simplicius Simplicissimus.* **World premieres:** SALLINEN: *The Horseman* Savonlinna Fest, Finland 1975; KOKKONEN: *Last Temptations* National Opera, Helsinki 1975. Res: Riihitie 3, Helsinki 33, Finland.

SÖDERSTRÖM, ELISABETH. Soprano. Swedish. Resident mem: Royal Opera, Stockholm. Born 7 May 1927, Stockholm. Husband Sveker Olow, occupation Captain, RSN. Three children. Studied: Royal Acad of Music, Andrejewa de Skilondz, Stockholm. **Debut:** Bastienne, Drottningholm Court Theatre 1947. Awards: Commander Order of Wasa; "Litteris et Artibus" Singer of the Royal Court of Sweden; mem of the Royal Acad of Music, Stockholm.

Sang with major companies in AUS: Salzburg Fest, Vienna Staatsoper; DEN: Copenhagen; FIN: Helsinki; FRA: Marseille, Paris; FR GER: Düsseldorf-Duisburg, Hamburg, Munich Staatsoper, Nürnberg, Wiesbaden; ITA: Palermo; MON: Monte Carlo; POL: Warsaw; SWE: Drottningholm Fest, Stockholm; SWI: Geneva; UK: Aldeburgh Fest, Edinburgh Fest, Glyndebourne Fest, London Royal Opera; USSR: Leningrad Kirov; USA: New York Met. **Roles with these companies incl** BEETHOVEN: Marzelline (*Fidelio*); BENNETT: Jenny (*Mines of Sulphur*); BERG: Marie (*Wozzeck*); BIZET: Micaëla (*Carmen*); BRITTEN: Helena (*Midsummer Night*), Governess (*Turn of the Screw*); BUSONI: Herzogin (*Doktor Faust*); CHARPENTIER: Louise; DALLAPICCOLA: Mrs Fabian (*Volo di notte*); DEBUSSY: Lia (*Enfant prodigue*), Mélisande; DONIZETTI: Adina (*Elisir*); FLOTOW: Lady Harriet, (*Martha*); GLUCK: Alceste, Iphigénie (*Iphigénie en Aulide*), Euridice; GOUNOD: Marguerite (*Faust*); HANDEL: Morgana (*Alcina*); HENZE: Elisabeth Zimmer (*Elegy for Young Lovers*); HINDEMITH: Regina (*Mathis der Maler*); JANACEK: Jenufa, Katya Kabanova‡, Emilia Marty (*Makropoulos Affair*); LEONCAVALLO: Nedda (*Pagliacci*); MARTIN: Iseut (*Vin herbé*); MASSENET: Thaïs; MENOTTI: Anna Gómez (*Consul*); MEYERBEER: Selika (*Africaine*); MONTEVERDI: Nerone (*Incoronazione di Poppea*); MOZART: Fiordiligi (*Così fan tutte*), Donna Elvira (*Don Giovanni*), Ilia (*Idomeneo*), Contessa & Susanna (*Nozze di Figaro*), Pamina (*Zauberflöte*); OFFENBACH: Olympia & Antonia & Giulietta (*Contes d'Hoffmann*); ORFF: Solo (*Carmina burana*); PERGOLESI: Lauretta (*Maestro di musica*); PFITZNER: Ighino (*Palestrina*); POULENC: La femme (*Voix humaine*); PUCCINI: Mimi & Musetta (*Bohème*), Cio-Cio-San (*Butterfly*), Manon, Giorgetta (*Tabarro*), Liù (*Turandot*); ROSSINI: Sofia (*Signor Bruschino*); STRAUSS, J: Adele & Rosalinde (*Fledermaus*); STRAUSS, R: Ariadne & Komponist (*Ariadne auf Naxos*), Gräfin (*Capriccio*), Christine (*Intermezzo*), Marschallin & Octavian & Sophie (*Rosenkavalier*); TCHAIKOVSKY: Tatiana (*Eugene Onegin*), Iolanthe, Lisa (*Pique Dame*); VERDI: Alice Ford (*Falstaff*), Desdemona (*Otello*), Violetta (*Traviata*); WAGNER: Eva (*Meistersinger*). Also BLOMDAHL: Daisy Doody (*Aniara*); LIEBERMANN: Telemachos (*Penelope*); SUTERMEISTER: Elisabeth (*Rote Stiefel*); BLECH: Else (*Versiegelt*); CAVALLI: Ericlea (*Scipio*); MOZART: Rosina (*Finta semplice*); SCARLATTI: (*Honestà negli amori*); KRAUS: Dido (*Aeneas i Charthago*). **World premieres:** LIDHOLM: Kvinnan (*Holländaren*) Swedish Radio 1967; BERWALD: (*Drottningen av Golconda*) Stockholm 1968; ROSENBERG: Laura (*Hus med dubbel ingång*) Stockholm 1970. Recorded for: EMI, CBS, DG, Teldec. Video/Film—Swedish TV: about ten operas. Gives recitals. Appears with symphony orchestra. Res: Lidingö, Sweden. Mgmt: IWL/UK.

SÖDERSTRÖM, GUNILLA. Dramatic mezzo-soprano. Swedish. Resident mem: Royal Opera, Stockholm. Single. Studied: Royal Acad of Music, Kerstin Thorborg, Käthe Sundström, Stockholm. **Debut:** Lisetta (*Mondo della luna*) Drottningholm Court Theater 1969.

Sang with major companies in SWE: Drottningholm Fest, Stockholm. **Roles with these companies incl** BIZET: Carmen★; BRITTEN: Bianca★

(*Rape of Lucretia*); GLUCK: Orfeo; HAYDN: Lisetta (*Mondo della luna*); MOZART: Cherubino (*Nozze di Figaro*); PROKOFIEV: Smeraldina (*Love for Three Oranges*); PUCCINI: Suzuki★ (*Butterfly*); ROSSINI: Angelina★ (*Cenerentola*); TCHAIKOVSKY: Olga (*Eugene Onegin*); VERDI: Amneris★ (*Aida*), Ulrica★ (*Ballo in maschera*), Eboli★ (*Don Carlo*). **World premieres:** WERLE: Adolfine (*Tintomara*) Royal Opera, Stockholm 1973.

SOHERR, HERMANN H F. Scenic and costume designer for opera, theater, film, television. Is a lighting designer. German. Resident designer, Deutsche Oper am Rhein, Düsseldorf. Born 24 Nov 1924, Mannheim. Wife Ute, occupation Red Cross social worker. One daughter. Studied: Profs L Sievert & W Preetorius, Munich. Prof training: Akad & Staatsoper, Munich 1943. **Operatic debut:** *Martha* Städtische Bühnen, Frankfurt/Main 1947. Theater debut: Städtische Bühnen, Frankfurt 1946. Previous occupation: soldier.

Designed for major companies in ARG: Buenos Aires; FR GER: Bielefeld, Dortmund, Düsseldorf-Duisburg, Frankfurt, Hamburg, Hannover, Mannheim, Munich Gärtnerplatz, Nürnberg, Wuppertal; HOL: Amsterdam. **Operas designed for these companies incl** ADAM: *Postillon de Lonjumeau;* d'ALBERT: *Tiefland★;* BEETHOVEN: *Fidelio★;* BERG: *Lulu, Wozzeck;* BIZET: *Carmen;* BRITTEN: *Rape of Lucretia;* BUSONI: *Arlecchino;* CHABRIER: *Roi malgré lui;* CIMAROSA: *Matrimonio segreto;* DESSAU: *Verurteilung des Lukullus;* DONIZETTI: *Anna Bolena, Don Pasquale, Elisir★, Lucia;* FLOTOW: *Martha;* GIORDANO: *Andrea Chénier★;* HAYDN: *Infedeltà delusa;* HUMPERDINCK: *Hänsel und Gretel★;* JANACEK: *Jenufa★;* LEONCAVALLO: *Pagliacci★;* LORTZING: *Waffenschmied, Wildschütz, Zar und Zimmermann;* MASCAGNI: *Cavalleria rusticana★;* MASSENET: *Don Quichotte, Manon★;* MENOTTI: *Amelia al ballo;* MOZART: *Così fan tutte★, Idomeneo;* NICOLAI: *Lustigen Weiber★;* OFFENBACH: *Contes d'Hoffmann★;* ORFF: *Bernauerin★;* PROKOFIEV: *Love for Three Oranges;* PUCCINI: *Bohème★, Gianni Schicchi★, Butterfly★, Manon Lescaut★, Tosca, Turandot★;* RAVEL: *Heure espagnole★;* ROSSINI: *Barbiere di Siviglia, Cambiale di matrimonio, Comte Ory;* SMETANA: *Bartered Bride, The Kiss;* STRAUSS, J: *Fledermaus★;* STRAUSS, R: *Arabella★, Ariadne auf Naxos, Capriccio★, Elektra, Rosenkavalier, Schweigsame Frau★;* TCHAIKOVSKY: *Maid of Orleans★;* VERDI: *Ballo in maschera, Forza del destino, Macbeth, Rigoletto, Traviata;* WAGNER: *Fliegende Holländer, Lohengrin, Meistersinger;* WEILL: *Aufstieg und Fall der Stadt Mahagonny, Dreigroschenoper★;* WEINBERGER: *Schwanda;* WOLF-FERRARI: *Donne curiose★.* Exhibitions of stage designs, Prague 1973. **Res:** Am Buschhäuschen 37, 56 Wuppertal 1, FR Ger.

SOKORSKA, BOGNA; née Kaczmarska. Coloratura soprano. Polish. Resident mem: Bühnen der Stadt Essen; Warsaw Chamber Opera. Born 6 Apr 1937, Warsaw. Husband Jerzy Sokorski, occupation composer, pianist. One daughter. Studied: Maria Dobrowolska-Gruszczynska, Ada Sari, Warsaw; Dorothy Robson, London; Warsaw State

School of Music. **Debut:** Gilda (*Rigoletto*) Warsaw Objazdowa Opera 1955. Awards: Commander, Cross of Polonia Restituta; Polish Grant.

Sang with major companies in AUS: Vienna Staatsoper; FR GER: Bonn, Cologne, Düsseldorf-Duisburg, Essen, Frankfurt, Hamburg, Karlsruhe, Kiel, Munich Staatsoper, Nürnberg, Stuttgart, Wuppertal; GER DR: Berlin Staatsoper; POL: Warsaw, POR: Lisbon; ROM: Bucharest; SWI: Zurich. **Roles with these companies incl** ADAM: Madeleine★ (*Postillon de Lonjumeau*); BRITTEN: Tytania (*Midsummer Night*); DELIBES: Lakmé; DONIZETTI: Norina★ (*Don Pasquale*); MOZART: Fiordiligi (*Così fan tutte*), Konstanze★ & Blondchen (*Entführung aus dem Serail*), Königin der Nacht★ (*Zauberflöte*); NICOLAI: Frau Fluth★ (*Lustigen Weiber von Windsor*); OFFENBACH: Olympia★ (*Contes d'Hoffmann*); PERGOLESI: Serpina (*Serva padrona*); PUCCINI: Musetta (*Bohème*); ROSSINI: Rosina (*Barbiere di Siviglia*); STRAUSS, J: Adele (*Fledermaus*); STRAUSS, R: Zerbinetta★ (*Ariadne auf Naxos*); VERDI: Oscar★ (*Ballo in maschera*), Gilda★ (*Rigoletto*), Violetta (*Traviata*). Also HAYDN: Griletta (*Speziale*); HENZE: Ida★ (*Junge Lord*); KURPINSKI: Julia★ (*Szarlatan*). **World premieres:** CZYZ: Bialowlosa (*Bialowlosa*) Warsaw Grand Opera 1962. Recorded for: Polskie Nagrania. Gives recitals. Appears with symphony orchestra. Teaches voice. On faculty of Gov Sec School of Music, Warsaw; Intl Music Seminar, Weimar. **Res:** Brandta 2a, 05-820 Piastów, Poland.

SOLLORS, DANIEL MICHAEL. Scenic and costume designer for opera, theater; specl in sets. Is also a painter. American. Resident designer, Memphis Opera Theater, TN. Born 28 Aug 1941, Gary, IN. Single. Studied: Indiana Univ Opera Theater, Mario Cristini, Andreas Nomikos, Bloomington. **Operatic debut:** Indiana Univ Opera 1970. Previous occupation: actor.

Designed for major companies in USA: Memphis. **Operas designed for these companies incl** BIZET: *Carmen★;* DONIZETTI: *Don Pasquale★, Elisir★;* GERSHWIN: *Porgy and Bess★;* MENOTTI: *Amahl★, Consul★;* MOZART: *Così fan tutte★;* PUCCINI: *Tosca★;* STRAUSS, R: *Ariadne auf Naxos★, Salome★;* VERDI: *Falstaff★, Rigoletto★, Traviata★, Trovatore★.* Exhibitions of stage designs, Memphis 1975. **Res:** 3382 Northwood Dr, Memphis, TN, USA.

SOLTI, SIR GEORG. Conductor of opera and symphony. British. Music Dir, Chicago Symph, USA. Born 21 Oct 1912, Budapest. Wife Valerie Pitts. Two children. Studied: Budapest Acad, Ernst von Dohnányi, Zoltán Kodály, Weiner; incl piano. Plays the piano. Operatic training as repetiteur & asst cond at Opera, Budapest. **Operatic debut:** *Nozze di Figaro* Opera, Budapest 1938. Symphonic debut: Budapest Symph 1936. Previous occupations: concert pianist. Awards: Commander of the British Empire; Commandant de la Légion d'Honneur. Previous adm positions in opera: Gen Mus Dir, Bayerische Staatsoper, Munich 1946-52; Gen Mus Dir, Städtische Bühnen, Frankfurt 1952-61; Mus Dir, Royal Opera, Covent Garden, London 1961-71.

Conducted with major companies in AUS: Vienna Staatsoper; CAN: Montreal/Quebec;

FRA: Aix-en-Provence Fest, Paris, Strasbourg; FR GER: Berlin Deutsche Oper, Frankfurt, Hamburg, Munich Staatsoper; ISR: Tel Aviv; ITA: Milan La Scala; UK: Glyndebourne Fest, London Royal; USA: Chicago, Dallas, New York Met, San Francisco Opera. **Operas with these companies incl** BARTOK: *Bluebeard's Castle;* BERG: *Lulu, Wozzeck;* BERLIOZ: *Damnation de Faust;* BIZET: *Carmen★;* BRITTEN: *Billy Budd, Midsummer Night;* GLUCK: *Iphigénie en Tauride, Orfeo ed Euridice;* KODALY: *Háry János;* MOZART: *Così fan tutte, Don Giovanni★, Entführung aus dem Serail, Idomeneo, Nozze di Figaro★, Zauberflöte★;* PUCCINI: *Bohème;* SCHOENBERG: *Moses und Aron★;* SHOSTAKOVICH: *Katerina Ismailova;* STRAUSS, J: *Fledermaus;* STRAUSS, R: *Arabella, Ariadne auf Naxos, Elektra, Frau ohne Schatten, Rosenkavalier, Salome;* TCHAIKOVSKY: *Eugene Onegin;* TIPPETT: *King Priam;* VERDI: *Aida, Don Carlo, Falstaff★, Forza del destino, Otello, Rigoletto, Traviata;* WAGNER: *Fliegende Holländer, Lohengrin, Meistersinger, Parsifal, Rheingold, Walküre, Siegfried, Götterdämmerung, Tannhäuser, Tristan und Isolde;* WEBER: *Freischütz.* Recorded for Decca, RCA. Conducted major orch in Europe, USA/Canada, Cent/S America. **Res:** c/o Mrs E M Blech, 9 Leonard Court, London W8 6NL, UK.

SOLYOM-NAGY, SANDOR; né Sandor Nagy. Dramatic baritone. Hungarian. Resident mem: State Opera of Hungary, Budapest. Born 21 Dec 1941, Siklós, Hungary. Wife Magda Metzger, occupation music teacher. Studied: Eva Kutrucz, Budapest. **Debut:** Scarpia (*Tosca*) Budapest State Opera 1966. Awards: Third Prize Intl Compt Erkel, 1965, 70; First Prize Liszt, Budapest 1972.

Sang with major companies in AUS: Vienna Staatsoper; BUL: Sofia; CZE: Prague National; FR GER: Cologne; HUN: Budapest; USSR: Moscow Bolshoi. **Roles with these companies incl** BIZET: Escamillo★ (*Carmen*); BRITTEN: Bottom★(*Midsummer Night*); DONIZETTI: Enrico★ (*Lucia*); GAY/Britten: Lockit★ (*Beggar's Opera*); GLUCK: Agamemnon‡ (*Iphigénie en Aulide*), Oreste (*Iphigénie en Tauride*); HANDEL: Garibaldo★ (*Rodelinda*); LEONCAVALLO: Tonio★ (*Pagliacci*); MASCAGNI: Alfio (*Cavalleria*); MOZART: Guglielmo★ (*Così fan tutte*), Conte Almaviva★ (*Nozze di Figaro*), Papageno (*Zauberflöte*); PUCCINI: Scarpia★ (*Tosca*); STRAUSS, R: Jochanaan★ (*Salome*); VERDI: Amonasro★ (*Aida*), Grande Inquisitore (*Don Carlo*), Nabucco★, Iago★ (*Otello*); WAGNER: Hans Sachs (*Meistersinger*), Wotan★ (*Rheingold*), Gunther★ (*Götterdämmerung*). Gives recitals. Appears with symphony orchestra. **Res:** Bod P U 1, 1112 Budapest, Hungary. Mgmt: ITK/HUN; SLZ/FRG.

SONDHEIMER, HANS. Lighting designer & tech director of opera; also an architect and theater consultant. American. Technical Dir, New York City Opera. Born 6 Dec 1901, Gelnhausen, Germany. Wife Jane Lily, occupation secy. Studied: Inst of Technology, Munich; Prof Adolf Linnebach, Bavarian State Theater, Munich. Prof training: Bavarian State Theater & Opera, Munich 1922-25. **Operatic debut:** lighting, State Theater Darmstadt, Germany 1927. Previous occupation: mech & electr engineering. Awards: Officers Cross, Order of Merit, FR Ger.

Lighting at FR GER: Darmstadt, Hamburg; USA: Cincinnati, Lake George, New York City Opera, Washington DC **the following operas** BARTOK: *Bluebeard's Castle;* BELLINI: *Puritani;* BERG: *Wozzeck;* BERNSTEIN: *Trouble in Tahiti;* BIZET: *Carmen;* BRITTEN: *Albert Herring, Midsummer Night's Dream, Rape of Lucretia, Turn of the Screw;* CHERUBINI: *Medea;* DALLAPICCOLA: *Prigioniero;* DEBUSSY: *Pelléas et Mélisande;* DELIUS: *Village Romeo and Juliet;* DONIZETTI: *Anna Bolena, Lucia, Lucrezia Borgia, Maria Stuarda, Roberto Devereux;* FALLA: *Vida breve;* FLOTOW: *Martha;* GERSHWIN: *Porgy and Bess;* GIANNINI: *Taming of the Shrew;* GINASTERA: *Beatrix Cenci, Bomarzo, Don Rodrigo;* GIORDANO: *Andrea Chénier;* GLUCK: *Orfeo ed Euridice;* GOUNOD: *Faust;* HANDEL: *Ariodante, Giulio Cesare;* HENZE: *Junge Lord;* HOIBY: *Summer and Smoke;* HUMPERDINCK: *Hänsel und Gretel;* JANACEK: *Makropoulos Affair;* KLEBE: *Jakobowsky und der Oberst;* KURKA: *Good Soldier Schweik;* LEONCAVALLO: *Pagliacci;* MASCAGNI: *Cavalleria rusticana;* MASSENET: *Manon, Werther;* MENOTTI: *Amahl, Amelia al ballo, Consul, Globolinks, Maria Golovin, Médium, Old Maid and the Thief, Saint of Bleecker Street, Telephone;* MONTEVERDI: *Incoronazione di Poppea, Ritorno d'Ulisse;* MOORE: *Ballad of Baby Doe;* MOZART: *Così fan tutte, Don Giovanni, Entführung aus dem Serail, Idomeneo, Nozze di Figaro, Zauberflöte;* MUSSORGSKY: *Boris Godunov;* NICOLAI: *Lustigen Weiber;* OFFENBACH: *Contes d'Hoffmann;* ORFF: *Carmina burana;* PERGOLESI: *Serva padrona;* PROKOFIEV: *Love for Three Oranges;* PUCCINI: *Bohème, Gianni Schicchi, Butterfly, Manon Lescaut, Suor Angelica, Tabarro, Tosca, Turandot;* RAVEL: *Heure espagnole;* RIMSKY-KORSAKOV: *Coq d'or;* ROSSINI: *Barbiere di Siviglia, Cenerentola;* SHOSTAKOVICH: *Katerina Ismailova;* SMETANA: *Bartered Bride;* STRAUSS, J: *Fledermaus;* STRAUSS, R: *Ariadne auf Naxos, Capriccio, Intermezzo, Rosenkavalier, Salome;* STRAVINSKY: *Oedipus Rex, Rossignol;* TCHAIKOVSKY: *Eugene Onegin;* VERDI: *Aida, Ballo in maschera, Falstaff, Macbeth, Rigoletto, Traviata, Trovatore;* WAGNER: *Fliegende Holländer, Meistersinger;* WARD: *Crucible;* WEILL: *Dreigroschenoper;* WOLF-FERRARI: *Quattro rusteghi.* **Res:** New York, NY, USA.

SOOTER, EDWARD. Heldentenor. American. Resident mem: Oper der Landeshauptstadt Kiel. Born 8 Dec 1934, Salina, KA, USA. Wife Sharon Tebbenkamp, occupation English correspondent, Univ of Kiel. Three children. Studied: Friends Univ, Elsa Haury, Wichita, KA; Kansas Univ, Joseph Wilkins, Lawrence, KA; Musikhochschule, Helmut Melchert, Hamburg. **Debut:** Florestan (*Fidelio*) Bremerhaven Opera, 1966. Awards: Met Op Ntl Counc Aud Finalist 1960; DAAD stipd 1964, 1966.

Sang with major companies in FR GER: Bielefeld, Cologne, Essen, Karlsruhe, Kiel, Mannheim, Wiesbaden. **Roles with these cos incl** BEETHOVEN: Florestan★ (*Fidelio*); BERG: Alwa (*Lulu*); BIZET: Don José (*Carmen*); DESSAU: Lukullus★ (*Verurteilung des Lukullus*); GOUNOD: Faust★; LEONCAVALLO: Canio (*Pa-*

gliacci); MOZART: Idomeneo; OFFENBACH: Hoffmann; PUCCINI: Des Grieux★ (*Manon Lescaut*); SAINT-SAENS: Samson★; SMETANA: Hans (*Bartered Bride*); STRAUSS, R: Aegisth★ (*Elektra*); VERDI: Riccardo (*Ballo in maschera*), Ernani, Otello★, Manrico (*Trovatore*); WAGNER: Erik★ (*Fliegende Holländer*), Walther (*Meistersinger*), Parsifal★, Siegmund★ (*Walküre*), Tannhäuser★, Tristan★; WEILL: Jim Mahoney (*Aufstieg und Fall der Stadt Mahagonny*); WEINBERGER: Babinsky (*Schwanda*). Gives recitals. Appears with symphony orchestra. Res: Fleethörn 64, 23 Kiel, FR Ger. Mgmt: SLZ/FRG.

SORDELLO, ENZO. Lyric & dramatic baritone. Italian. Born 20 Apr 1931, Pievebovigliana, Italy. Wife Josette Petrani. Two children. Studied: Mo Campogalliani, Mo Confalonieri, Mo Ruffo, Scuola di perfez, Teatro alla Scala. **Debut:** Enrico (*Lucia*) Teatro Toselli, Cuneo 1952. Previous occupations: PS teacher. Awards: Cavaliere dell'Ordine al Merito della Repubblica Italiana; Winner, Conc di perfez Teatro alla Scala, resulting in debut 1954.
   Sang with major companies in ARG: Buenos Aires; AUS: Bregenz Fest, Vienna Staatsoper; BEL: Brussels; CAN: Montreal/Quebec, Vancouver; FRA: Bordeaux, Lyon, Paris; FR GER: Berlin Deutsche Oper; ITA: Bologna, Florence Maggio & Comunale, Genoa, Milan La Scala, Naples, Palermo, Parma, Rome Opera, Trieste, Turin, Venice; MON: Monte Carlo; POR: Lisbon; SWI: Geneva; UK: Glyndebourne Fest, London English National; USA: Boston, Dallas, Hartford, Houston, Miami, Newark, New Orleans, New York Met, Philadelphia Lyric, Pittsburgh; YUG: Dubrovnik, Zagreb, Belgrade. **Roles with these companies incl** BELLINI: Filippo (*Beatrice di Tenda*), Sir Richard (*Puritani*); BIZET: Escamillo (*Carmen*), Zurga (*Pêcheurs de perles*); BUSONI: Matteo (*Arlecchino*); CATALANI: Vincenzo Gellner (*Wally*); CILEA: Michonnet★ (*A. Lecouvreur*); CIMAROSA: Count Robinson (*Matrimonio segreto*); DONIZETTI: Dott Malatesta★ (*Don Pasquale*), Belcore★ (*Elisir*), Alfonse (*Favorite*), Enrico (*Lucia*), Carlo Gérard (*Andrea Chénier*), De Siriex (*Fedora*); IBERT: Boniface (*Angélique*); LEONCAVALLO: Tonio (*Pagliacci*); MASCAGNI: Rabbi David (*Amico Fritz*), Alfio (*Cavalleria rusticana*); MASSENET: Lescaut★ (*Manon*), Albert★ (*Werther*); MONTEMEZZI: Manfredo (*Amore dei tre re*); MOZART: Allazim (*Zaïde*); PONCHIELLI: Barnaba (*Gioconda*); PUCCINI: Marcello★ (*Bohème*), Gianni Schicchi, Sharpless★ (*Butterfly*), Lescaut★ (*Manon Lescaut*), Michele★ (*Tabarro*), Scarpia (*Tosca*); RAVEL: Ramiro (*Heure espagnole*); ROSSINI: Figaro★ (*Barbiere di Siviglia*), Robert (*Comte Ory*), Guillaume Tell; SAINT-SAENS: Grand prêtre (*Samson et Dalila*); SPONTINI: Cinna (*Vestale*); VERDI: Amonasro★ (*Aida*), Ezio★ (*Attila*), Renato (*Ballo in maschera*), Don Carlo (*Ernani*), Ford★ (*Falstaff*), Don Carlo (*Forza del destino*), Macbeth, Nabucco, Iago (*Otello*), Rigoletto★, Simon Boccanegra, Germont★ (*Traviata*), Conte di Luna (*Trovatore*). Also ROSSINI: Poeta (*Turco in Italia*); MONTEVERDI: Ottone (*Incoronazione di Poppea*); CHERUBINI: Pedrillo (*Osteria portoghese*); GOUNOD: Valentin (*Faust*), Mercutio★ (*Roméo et Juliette*); LIEBERMANN: Arnolph★ (*Schule der Frauen*); PAN-

NAIN: Enrico (*Mme Bovary*); CORTESE: Principe (*Notte veneziana*); CARISSIMI: Storico (*Judicium Salomonis*); MALIPIERO: Socrate (*Morte di Socrate*). Recorded for: Decca/London, His Master's Voice, Delphi. Video/Film: Carlo Gérard (*Andrea Chénier*), Poeta (*Turco in Italia*), Ford (*Falstaff*), Lescaut (*Manon Lescaut*), Albert (*Werther*), Count Robinson (*Matrimonio segreto*), Figaro (*Barbiere di Siviglia*). Gives recitals. Appears with symphony orchestra. **Res:** Villa America, 12018 Roccavione/Cuneo, Italy.

SORELL, CHRISTIANE. Lyric soprano. Austrian. Resident mem: Volksoper, Vienna. Born 13 Jan 1936, Vienna. Married. Studied: Akad für Musik & darstellende Kunst, Prof Ferdinand Grossmann, Vienna; Tino Pattiera, Italy. **Debut:** Gilda (*Rigoletto*) Volksoper, Vienna 1957. Previous occupations: concert violinist. Awards: Kammersängerin, Rep of Austria 1966; Goldenes Verdienstzeichen, City of Vienna 1975.
   Sang with major companies in AUS: Graz, Vienna Staatsoper & Volksoper; FRA: Bordeaux, Lyon, Nice; FR GER: Düsseldorf-Duisburg, Frankfurt, Hamburg, Hannover, Mannheim, Munich Staatsoper, Stuttgart; ITA: Bologna; SWI: Zurich. **Roles with these companies incl** BERLIOZ: Marguerite★ (*Damnation de Faust*); CORNELIUS: Margiana (*Barbier von Bagdad*); DVORAK: Rusalka★‡; GLUCK: Zelmire‡ (*Cadi dupé*); MASSENET: Manon; MONIUSZKO: Halka‡; MOZART: Pamina★ & Königin der Nacht (*Zauberflöte*); OFFENBACH: Antonia★ (*Contes d'Hoffmann*); PUCCINI: Lauretta‡ (*Gianni Schicchi*), Cio-Cio-San (*Butterfly*), Suor Angelica★‡; TCHAIKOVSKY: Lisa (*Pique Dame*); VERDI: Elisabetta (*Don Carlo*), Amelia★ (*Masnadieri*), Leonora (*Trovatore*); WAGNER: Elsa★ (*Lohengrin*), Eva (*Meistersinger*), Elisabeth★ (*Tannhäuser*); WEBER: Agathe★ (*Freischütz*); WEINBERGER: Dorota (*Schwanda*). Also KIENZL: Martha★ (*Evangelimann*); HONEGGER: Marguerite (*Jeanne d'Arc au bûcher*); d'ALBERT: Marta★ (*Tiefland*); SALMHOFER: Kordula★ (*Werbekleid*); ROSSINI: Gemmy (*Guillaume Tell*). **World premieres:** SALMHOFER: Marei (*Dreikönig*) Volksoper, Vienna 1970. Video/Film: (*Suor Angelica*); (*Gianni Schicchi*); (*Werbekleid*); (*Halka*); Zelmire (*Cadi dupé*). Gives recitals. Appears with symphony orchestra. Mgmt: URT/AUS; KOA/AUS; VLD/AUS; SLZ/FRG; IMR/FRA.

SOTIN, HANS. Bass. German. Resident mem: Staatsoper, Hamburg; Staatsoper, Vienna. Born 10 Sep 1939, Dortmund, Germany. Wife Regina. Three children. Studied: Friedrich Wilhelm Hezel, Prof Dieter Jacob. **Debut:** Polizeikomissar (*Rosenkavalier*) Städtische Oper, Essen 1962. Previous occupations: chemical engineer. Awards: Awd of the County Nordshein/Westfalen; Friedrich Oberdörfer Preis.
   Sang with major companies in ARG: Buenos Aires; AUS: Vienna Staatsoper; BEL: Brussels; CAN: Montreal/Quebec; FRA: Paris; FR GER: Bayreuth Fest, Cologne, Düsseldorf-Duisburg, Essen, Frankfurt, Hamburg, Hannover, Kassel, Kiel, Saarbrücken, Stuttgart; ITA: Florence Maggio & Comunale, Milan La Scala, Rome Opera, Venice; POR: Lisbon; SWI: Zurich; UK: Edinburgh Fest, Glyndebourne Fest, London Royal; USA: Chi-

cago, New York Met. **Roles with these companies incl** BERG: Doktor★ (*Wozzeck*); CORNELIUS: Abul Hassan‡ (*Barbier von Bagdad*); GOEHR: Arden (*Arden muss sterben*); HINDEMITH: Lorenz (*Mathis der Maler*); KELEMEN: Plague (*Belagerungszustand*); KLEBE: Jakobowsky (*Jakobowsky und der Oberst*); LORTZING: Van Bett★ (*Zar und Zimmermann*); MOZART: Don Alfonso★ (*Così fan tutte*), Sarastro★ (*Zauberflöte*); MUSSORGSKY: Boris Godunov; PUCCINI: Colline★ (*Bohème*); ROSSINI: Don Basilio★ (*Barbiere di Siviglia*); STRAUSS, R: La Roche★ (*Capriccio*), Baron Ochs★ (*Rosenkavalier*); VERDI: Philip II★ & Grande Inquisitore★ (*Don Carlo*), Padre Guardiano (*Forza del destino*), Procida★ (*Vespri*); WAGNER: König Heinrich★ (*Lohengrin*), Pogner★‡ (*Meistersinger*), Gurnemanz★‡ (*Parsifal*), Wotan (*Rheingold★, Walküre★*), Wanderer★ (*Siegfried*), Fafner (*Rheingold★, Siegfried★*), Hunding★ (*Walküre*), Landgraf★‡ (*Tannhäuser*), König Marke★ (*Tristan und Isolde*). **World premieres:** KELEMEN: Diego (*Belagerungszustand*) 1970; KLEBE: Würfelspieler (*Jakobowsky und der Oberst*) 1965; WERLE: Professor (*Resan*) 1969; all at Hamburg Staatsoper. Recorded for: EMI, Decca, DG, Philips, RCA. Video: Eremit (*Freischütz*); Doktor (*Wozzeck*); Van Bett (*Zar und Zimmermann*); Sarastro (*Zauberflöte*); Minister (*Fidelio*); Orest (*Elektra*). Appears with symphony orchestra. Teaches voice. **Res:** Immenweg 11, 2105 Seevetal 3, FR Ger. Mgmt: HUS/FRG; COL/USA; IMR/FRA; ASK/UK.

SOULIOTIS, ELENA. Dramatic soprano. Italian. Born 28 May 1943, Athens. Husband Marcello Guerrini, occupation pianist. Studied: Alfredo Bontà, Iascha Galperin, Bianca Lietti, Buenos Aires; Mercedes Llopart, Milan. **Debut:** Santuzza (*Cavalleria rusticana*) Teatro San Carlo, Naples 1964. Awards: Montepulciano, Grifo 1972; Florence, Rificolona 1966; Naples, Circolo della Stampa; Bellini d'oro, Catania; Verdi d'oro, Brescia; Palcoscenico d'oro, Mantua; 3rd Fest Madrid; etc. **Sang with major companies in** ARG: Buenos Aires Teatro Colón; AUS: Vienna Staatsoper; BRA: Rio de Janeiro; BUL: Sofia; CAN: Montreal/Quebec; FRA: Paris; GRE: Athens Fest; FR GER: Kiel; HUN: Budapest; ITA: Florence Maggio & Comunale, Genoa, Milan La Scala, Naples, Palermo, Rome Opera, Trieste; MEX: Mexico City; POR: Lisbon; SPA: Madrid; UK: London Royal; USA: Chicago, Dallas, Philadelphia Lyric, San Antonio. **Roles with these companies incl** BELLINI: Norma★‡, Alaide★ (*Straniera*); BOITO: Elena (*Mefistofele*); CATALANI: Loreley; DONIZETTI: Anna Bolena★‡; MASCAGNI: Santuzza★‡ (*Cavalleria rusticana*); PONCHIELLI: Gioconda; PUCCINI: Minnie★ (*Fanciulla del West*), Manon Lescaut, Tosca★; VERDI: Aida, Amelia (*Ballo in maschera*), Leonora (*Forza del destino*), Luisa Miller, Lady Macbeth★‡, Abigaille★‡ (*Nabucco*), Desdemona (*Otello*), Leonora (*Trovatore*); ZANDONAI: Francesca da Rimini★. Recorded for: Decca. **Res:** V Incontri 38/40, 50139 Florence, Italy. Mgmt: HHB/USA.

SOUMAGNAS, JEAN-LOUIS. Bass. French. Resident mem: Opéra, Paris. Born 8 Nov 1938, Rodez, France. Wife Yvette Lassort. Two children. Studied: Consv de Bordeaux. **Debut:** Méphistophélès (*Faust*) Bordeaux 1964. Awards: Voix d'Or 1960; Second Grand Prix, Conc Intl Toulouse.

Sang with major companies in FRA: Bordeaux, Marseille, Nancy, Nice, Orange Fest, Paris, Rouen, Toulouse; ITA: Naples; POR: Lisbon. **Roles with these companies incl** BERLIOZ: Méphistophélès (*Damnation de Faust*); DEBUSSY: Arkel (*Pelléas et Mélisande*); DELIBES: Nilakantha★ (*Lakmé*); DUKAS: Barbe Bleue (*Ariane et Barbe Bleue*); GOUNOD: Méphistophélès★ (*Faust*), Ramon★ (*Mireille*); MASSENET: Phanuel★ (*Hérodiade*); MEYERBEER: Comte de St Bris (*Huguenots*); MONTEVERDI: Orfeo; MOZART: Don Alfonso★ (*Così fan tutte*), Don Giovanni★, Figaro★ (*Nozze di Figaro*); OFFENBACH: Coppélius etc (*Contes d'Hoffmann*); PUCCINI: Colline★ (*Bohème*); ROSSINI: Don Basilio★ (*Barbiere di Siviglia*); VERDI: Ramfis★ (*Aida*), Philip II (*Don Carlo*), Padre Guardiano (*Forza del destino*), Procida★ (*Vespri*). Also MASSENET: Comte des Grieux (*Manon*); RABAUD: Sultan (*Mârouf*); BRITTEN: Collatinus (*Rape of Lucretia*); MASSENET: Frère Laurent (*Roméo et Juliette*). **World premieres:** SANCAN: Le Bucheron (*Ondine*) Bordeaux 1966; CAPDEVIELLE: Colonel Rizzi (*Fille de l'homme*) Bordeaux 1967. Recorded for: GID. Video/Film—ORTF: (*Enfance du Christ*); Crespel (*Contes d'Hoffmann*). Gives recitals. Appears with symphony orchestra. **Res:** 32 rue de Vermandois, 78570 Andresy, France. Mgmt: IMR/FRA; HPL/UK.

SOUNOVA, DANIELA. Lyric soprano. Czechoslovakian. Resident mem: National Theater, Prague. Born 17 May 1943, Prague. Husband Ivan Brouk, occupation singer. One child. Studied: Prof Vlasta Linhartová, Marie Vojtková, Prague. **Debut:** Marie (*Bartered Bride*) Oldrich Stibors Theater, Olomouc, CSSR 1969.

Sang with major companies in CZE: Prague National; ITA: Bologna; UK: Edinburgh Fest. **Roles with these companies incl** BIZET: Micaëla★ (*Carmen*); MOZART: Donna Elvira★ (*Don Giovanni*); OFFENBACH: Antonia★ (*Contes d'Hoffmann*); PROKOFIEV: Natasha★ (*War and Peace*); PUCCINI: Liù★ (*Turandot*); SMETANA: Marie★ (*Bartered Bride*). Also SMETANA: Jitka★ (*Dalibor*). **World premieres:** CIKKER: Virginia (*Coriolanus*) National Theater, Prague 1974. Appears with symphony orchestra. **Res:** Leningradská 32, Prague 10, CSSR. Mgmt: PRG/CZE.

SOUZA, NOEMI. Lyric mezzo-soprano. Argentinean. Resident mem: Teatro Colón, Buenos Aires; Teatro Argentino, La Plata. Born 19 Jun 1929, Bahía Blanca. Single. Studied: Opera School of Teatro Colón, Editha Fleischer, Sergio Tulian. **Debut:** Berta (*Barbiere di Siviglia*) Teatro Colón 1947. Awards: Prize as Best Singer, Municipality of Buenos Aires 1971.

Sang with major companies in ARG: Buenos Aires. **Roles with these companies incl** BERLIOZ: Anna (*Troyens*); BIZET: Carmen; GOUNOD: Siebel (*Faust*); HUMPERDINCK: Hänsel; MARTINU: Nancy (*Comedy on the Bridge*); MENOTTI: Secretary★ (*Consul*); MOZART: Dorabella★ (*Così fan tutte*), Cherubino (*Nozze di Figaro*); PUCCINI: Suzuki★ (*Butterfly*); SME-

TANA: Hata (*Bartered Bride*); STRAUSS, J: Prinz Orlovsky (*Fledermaus*); STRAUSS, R: Herodias★ (*Salome*); STRAVINSKY: Jocasta★ (*Oedipus Rex*); VERDI: Preziosilla (*Forza del destino*). **World premieres:** CASTRO: Marfa (*Proserpina y el extranjero*) Teatro Colón. Gives recitals. Appears with symphony orchestra. Teaches voice. Coaches repertoire. On faculty of Consv Nacional, Buenos Aires & Consv Provincial, La Plata. **Res:** Libertad 1445-Vicente López, Buenos Aires, Argentina.

SOUZAY, GÉRARD; né Tisserand. Dramatic baritone. French. Born 8 Dec 1920, Angers, France. Single. Studied: Consv de Paris, Pierre Bernac, Vanni-Marcoux, Claire Croiza, Lotte Lehmann. **Debut:** MONTEVERDI: Orfeo, New York City Opera 1960. Awards: First Prize in Voice, Consv of Paris; Chevalier de la Légion d'Honneur; Chevalier de l'Ordre des Arts et Lettres.
Sang with major companies in AUS: Vienna Staatsoper; FRA: Aix-en-Provence Fest, Paris; FR GER: Munich Staatsoper; ITA: Florence Maggio & Comunale, Rome Opera; UK: Glyndebourne Fest; USA: New York Met. **Roles with these companies incl** BERLIOZ: Méphistophélès‡ (*Damnation de Faust*); DEBUSSY: Golaud★‡ (*Pelléas et Mélisande*); MOZART: Don Giovanni, Conte Almaviva (*Nozze di Figaro*); PURCELL: Aeneas. Also, on records only MASSENET: Lescaut (*Manon*); Remigo (*Navarraise*); RAMEAU: Pollux. Recorded for: Columbia, Pathé-Marconi, EMI, Telefunken. Gives recitals. Appears with symphony orchestra. Teaches voice. **Res:** Paris, France. Mgmt: CMW/FRA.

SOVIERO, DIANA. née Catani. Lyric soprano. American. Resident mem: New York City Opera. Born Jersey City, NJ, USA. Husband Louis, occupation language teacher. Studied: Mme Marinka Gurewich, Mo Martin Rich, coach, Boris Goldovsky, coach, New York; Caterina Basiola, Milan. **Debut:** Mimi (*Bohème*) Chautauqua Fest, NY, USA. Awards: National Opera Inst Grant; Affiliate Artist Fllshp 1974-75.
Sang with major companies in USA: Fort Worth, Lake George, New York City Opera, St Paul. **Roles with these companies incl** BIZET: Micaëla (*Carmen*); DELIUS: Vrenchen★ (*Village Romeo*); DONIZETTI: Norina (*Don Pasquale*); HAYDN: Sandrina★ (*Infedeltà delusa*); LEONCAVALLO: Nedda★ (*Pagliacci*); MASSENET: Manon★; MOZART: Zerlina★ (*Don Giovanni*); PUCCINI: Lauretta★ (*Gianni Schicchi*). Gives recitals. Appears with symphony orchestra. **Res:** Rosedale, NY, USA. Mgmt: HBM/USA.

SOYER, ROGER. Bass. French. Born 1 Sep 1939, Thiais, France. Wife Anne-Marie Thellière. Two children. Studied: Consv Ntl Supérieur de Musique, Georges Jouatte, Louis Musy, Paris. **Debut:** Colline (*Bohème*) Opéra Comique, Paris 1965. Awards: Chevalier de l'Ordre du Mérite.
Sang with major companies in AUS: Salzburg Fest, Vienna Staatsoper; BEL: Brussels, CZE: Prague National; DEN: Copenhagen; FRA: Aix-en-Provence Fest, Lyon, Marseille, Nice, Orange Fest, Paris, Strasbourg, Toulouse; FR GER: Cologne, Munich Staatsoper, Stuttgart; ISR: Tel Aviv; ITA: Florence Maggio, Milan La Scala, Venice; MON: Monte Carlo; POR: Lisbon; SPA: Barcelona; SWI: Geneva; UK: Edinburgh Fest; USA: Chicago, Miami, New York Met, San Francisco Opera. **Roles with these companies incl** BERLIOZ: Méphistophélès★ (*Damnation de Faust*); DEBUSSY: Arkel★ (*Pelléas et Mélisande*); DONIZETTI: Alfonso d'Este (*Lucrezia Borgia*); GOUNOD: Méphistophélès★ (*Faust*); MOZART: Don Giovanni★‡; PUCCINI: Colline★ (*Bohème*); ROSSINI: Don Basilio (*Barbiere di Siviglia*); VERDI: Germont (*Traviata*), Procida★ (*Vespri*). Also CAMPRA: Léandre & Pluton (*Carnaval de Venise*). **World premieres:** BECAUD: MacCreagh (*Opéra d'Aran*) Théâtre des Champs Elysées 1962. Recorded for: Philips, HMV, EMI. Video—TV: (*Don Giovanni*), (*Pelléas et Mélisande*). Appears with symphony orchestra. **Res:** Sceaux, France. Mgmt: GZL/FRA.

SPIESS, LUDOVIC. Lyric tenor. Romanian. Resident mem: Romanian Opera, Bucharest; Staatsoper, Vienna. Born 13 May 1938, Cluj. Wife Gerda, occupation pianist. One child. Studied: Bucharest and Milan. **Debut:** Duca di Mantova (*Rigoletto*) Musical Theater, Galati 1962. Awards: First Prize, Toulouse 1964 and Rio de Janeiro 1965.
Sang with major companies in ARG: Buenos Aires; AUS: Salzburg Fest, Vienna Staatsoper; BRA: Rio de Janeiro; FRA: Aix-en-Provence Fest, Bordeaux, Lyon, Nancy, Orange Fest, Paris, Rouen, Toulouse; FR GER: Cologne, Munich Staatsoper, Stuttgart, Wiesbaden; GER DR: Berlin Staatsoper; HUN: Budapest; ITA: Milan La Scala, Naples, Palermo, Rome Caracalla, Turin, Verona Arena; ROM: Bucharest; SWI: Basel, Zurich; UK: London Royal; USSR: Leningrad Kirov, Moscow Bolshoi, Tbilisi; USA: Houston Grand, New York Met, Philadelphia Grand, San Francisco Opera; YUG: Zagreb, Belgrade. **Roles with these companies incl** BEETHOVEN: Florestan★‡ (*Fidelio*); GIORDANO: Andrea Chénier★; GLUCK: Achille★‡ (*Iphigénie en Aulide*); LEONCAVALLO: Canio★ (*Pagliacci*); MOZART: Tamino (*Zauberflöte*); MUSSORGSKY: Vassily Golitsin‡ (*Khovanshchina*); PUCCINI: Rodolfo★ (*Bohème*), Pinkerton★ (*Butterfly*), Cavaradossi★ (*Tosca*), Calaf★ (*Turandot*); SAINT-SAENS: Samson★; SMETANA: Dalibor★‡; STRAUSS, R: Ein Sänger★ (*Rosenkavalier*); STRAVINSKY: Oedipus Rex★; VERDI: Radames★ (*Aida*), Riccardo★ (*Ballo in maschera*), Don Carlo★, Don Alvaro★ (*Forza del destino*), Otello★, Manrico★ (*Trovatore*); WAGNER: Lohengrin; WEBER: Hüon (*Oberon*). Also MUSSORGSKY: Dimitri★ (*Boris Godunov*). Recorded for: Electrecord, Decca, Ariola, Electrola. Gives recitals. Appears with symphony orchestra. **Res:** 57 Polona St, Bucharest 1, Romania. Mgmt: RIA/ROM; TAS/AUS.

SQUARZINA, LUIGI. Stages/produces opera, theater & television and is a film actor. Italian. Gen Dir, Teatro Stabile, Genoa. Born 18 Feb 1922, Livorno. Married. One son. Studied: Acad Nazionale d'Arte Drammatica, Rome. **Operatic debut:** Florence Maggio Musicale 1957. Theater debut: Rome 1947. Previous occupation: dir, drama section *Enciclopedia dello spettacolo.* Awards: 4 times S Genesio Prize; Gramsci, St Vincent, Marzotto, Théâtre des Nations Prize; Nastro d'argento, Donatello d'oro, Nettuno d'oro.

Directed/produced opera for major companies in AUS: Vienna Staatsoper; ITA: Florence Maggio & Comunale, Milan La Scala, Palermo Massimo, Rome Opera, Venice La Fenice, Verona Arena. **Operas staged with these companies incl** BRITTEN: *Midsummer Night;* DALLAPICCOLA: *Prigioniero;* MASSENET: *Manon;* MOZART: *Don Giovanni;* PERAGALLO: *Gita in campagna;* PUCCINI: *Turandot*★*;* ROSSINI: *Gazza ladra*★*;* STRAVINSKY: *Oedipus Rex;* VERDI: *Aida*★*, Falstaff, Forza del destino*★*, Lombardi.* Also BLOCH: *Macbeth;* CESTI: *Orontea;* KRENEK: *Jonny spielt auf;* PIZZETTI: *Fedra;* ZAFRED: *Amleto.* **Operatic world premieres:** MUSCO: *Gattopardo* Massimo, Palermo 1967. **Opera libretti:** *Gattopardo,* see prem. Teaches at Univ of Bologna. **Res:** V Fiori Oscuri 9, Milan, Italy.

SRUBAR, TEODOR. Lyric baritone. Czechoslovakian. Resident mem: National Theater, Prague. Born 18 Jul 1917, Ostrava, CSR. Wife Marta. One child. Studied: Music Consv, Brno, Czechoslovakia; Prof Emma Matouskova, Prague; Apollo Granforte, Milan. **Debut:** Silvio (*Pagliacci*) National Theater, Prague 1942. Previous occupations: student of law, Univ Brno. Awards: Merited Artist, Gvnmt of CSSR, Ministry of Culture.
Sang with major companies in AUS: Vienna Staatsoper; CZE: Brno, Prague National; HUN: Budapest; UK: Edinburgh Fest. **Roles with these companies incl** BIZET: Escamillo (*Carmen*); BORODIN: Prince Igor; CHARPENTIER: Père (*Louise*); JANACEK: Gorianchikov (*From the House of the Dead*); LEONCAVALLO: Tonio (*Pagliacci*); LORTZING: Peter I (*Zar und Zimmermann*); MASCAGNI: Alfio (*Cavalleria rusticana*); MONIUSZKO: Janusz (*Halka*); MOZART: Conte Almaviva (*Nozze di Figaro*); ORFF: Solo‡ (*Carmina burana*); PROKOFIEV: Prince Andrei (*War and Peace*); PUCCINI: Sharpless★ (*Butterfly*); SMETANA: Vok★ (*Devil's Wall*), Tomas★ (*Kiss*), Premysl★ (*Libuse*), Kalina★ (*Secret*); STRAUSS, R: Jochanaan (*Salome*); TCHAIKOVSKY: Eugene Onegin, Yeletsky★ (*Pique Dame*); VERDI: Amonasro (*Aida*), Renato★ (*Ballo in maschera*), Rodrigo★ (*Don Carlo*), Nabucco★, Rigoletto★, Simon Boccanegra★, Germont★ (*Traviata*), Conte di Luna (*Trovatore*); WAGNER: Holländer, Telramund★ (*Lohengrin*), Wolfram (*Tannhäuser*). Also SMETANA: King Vladislav★ (*Dalibor*); DVORAK: Bohus★ (*Jakobin*); FIBICH: Premysl★ (*Sarka*). **World premieres:** CIKKER: Nechludov (*Resurrection*) National Theater, Prague 1962; PAUER: Petr Vok (*Zuzana Vojirova*) National Theater 1958; VOMACKA: Boleslav (*Boleslav I*) National Theater 1956. Recorded for: Supraphon. Gives recitals. Appears with symphony orchestra. Teaches voice. On faculty of Acad of Music Arts, Prague. **Res:** Belehradska 96, Prague, CSSR. **Mgmt:** PRG/CZE.

STADLER, IRMGARD. Lyric soprano. Resident mem: Staatsoper, Vienna; Württembergische Staatsoper, Stuttgart.
Sang with major companies in AUS: Vienna Staatsoper; FR GER: Stuttgart; ITA: Bologna; POR: Lisbon; UK: Glyndebourne Fest; et al. **Roles with these companies incl** BIZET: Micaëla (*Carmen*); MUSSORGSKY: Marina (*Boris* *Godunov*); SMETANA: Marie (*Bartered Bride*); STRAUSS, R: Komponist (*Ariadne auf Naxos*); WAGNER: Elsa (*Lohengrin*), Gutrune (*Götterdämmerung*); et al. Also CAVALLI: Juno (*Calisto*). Appears with symphony orchestra.

STAJNC, JAROSLAV. Bass-baritone. Czechoslovakian. Resident mem: Deutsche Oper am Rhein, Düsseldorf. Born 7 May 1943, Prague. Wife Brigitte. One child. Studied: Konsv Prague; Akad für Musik, Vienna. **Debut:** Eremit (*Freischütz*) Volksoper, Vienna 1968. Previous occupations: electro-technician. Awards: First Prize Deutsche Grammophon, Vienna 1966.
Sang with major companies in AUS: Graz, Vienna Volksoper; CAN: Vancouver; CZE: Brno; GRE: Athens Fest; FR GER: Düsseldorf-Duisburg; ITA: Florence Maggio; SWE: Drottningholm Fest. **Roles with these companies incl** BERG: Doktor★ (*Wozzeck*); DONIZETTI: Dott Dulcamara★ (*Elisir*); HANDEL: Polyphemus (*Acis and Galatea*); JANACEK: Dikoy (*Katya Kabanova*); LORTZING: Stadinger (*Waffenschmied*); MOZART: Publio★ (*Clemenza di Tito*); ORFF: Bauer (*Mond*); PUCCINI: Colline★ (*Bohème*); ROSSINI: Don Basilio★ (*Barbiere di Siviglia*), Mustafà (*Italiana in Algeri*); SMETANA: Kezal★ (*Bartered Bride*); STRAUSS, R: Orest★ (*Elektra*); STRAVINSKY: Tiresias (*Oedipus Rex*); WAGNER: Fasolt★ (*Rheingold*), Fafner★ (*Siegfried*), Hunding★ (*Walküre*); WEBER: Omar (*Abu Hassan*), Kaspar★ (*Freischütz*); WOLF-FERRARI: Pantalone★ (*Donne curiose*). **World premieres:** EINEM: Wixer (*Der Zerrissene*) rev vers, Volksoper, Vienna 1968. Gives recitals. Appears with symphony orchestra. **Res:** Freiligrathstr 34, Düsseldorf, FR Ger. **Mgmt:** PAS/FRG; RAB/AUS.

STAMFORD, JOHN SCOTT. Lirico spinto tenor. American. Born 5 Sep 1923, Chicago. Wife Mildred, occupation regist nurse. One child. Studied: Chicago Consv, Dr Edgar Nelson; Manhattan School of Music, Herta Glaz, New York; Albert Sciarretti, New York. **Debut:** Manrico (*Trovatore*) American Opera Co 1952.
Sang with major companies in CAN: Montreal/Quebec; USA: Miami, New York City Opera, St Paul. **Roles with these companies incl** BOITO: Faust★ (*Mefistofele*); FALLA: Paco (*Vida breve*); FLOYD: Sam Polk★ (*Susannah*); GINASTERA: Orsino★ (*Beatrix Cencil*), Don Rodrigo★; JANACEK: Albert Gregor★ (*Makropoulos Affair*); LEONCAVALLO: Canio★ (*Pagliacci*); SHOSTAKOVICH: Sergei (*Katerina Ismailova*); STRAUSS, J: Eisenstein (*Fledermaus*); STRAUSS, R: Flamand (*Capriccio*); STRAVINSKY: Oedipus Rex★. Also WARD: Judge Danforth★ (*Crucible*). Gives recitals. Appears with symphony orchestra. Teaches voice. **Res:** 1533 Wales Ave, Baldwin, NY, USA.

STAMM, HARALD. Bass. German. Resident mem: Staatsoper, Hamburg; Opernhaus, Cologne. Born 29 Apr 1938, Frankfurt. Wife Ute Krähmer. Two children. Studied: Franz Fehringer. **Debut:** Simon (*Quattro rusteghi*) Musiktheater Gelsenkirchen, FR Ger 1968. Previous occupations: studied natural sciences. Awards: Prize Intl Schubert Compt, Vienna 1967; UDMK Opera Compt, Berlin 1968.

Sang with major companies in AUS: Graz, Vienna Staatsoper & Volksoper; FRA: Nice, Rouen; FR GER: Berlin Deutsche Oper, Cologne, Darmstadt, Düsseldorf-Duisburg, Essen, Frankfurt, Hamburg, Hannover, Kassel, Munich Staatsoper; HUN: Budapest; ITA: Rome Opera, Venice; SWI: Geneva, Zurich. Roles with these companies incl d'ALBERT: Tommaso★ (*Tiefland*); BEETHOVEN: Rocco★ (*Fidelio*); CIMAROSA: Geronimo (*Matrimonio segreto*); DONIZETTI: Raimondo★ (*Lucia*); FLOTOW: Plunkett (*Martha*); HANDEL: Ptolemy (*Giulio Cesare*); MASSENET: Don Quichotte★; MOZART: Publio★ (*Clemenza di Tito*), Don Giovanni★, Sarastro★ (*Zauberflöte*); MUSSORGSKY: Pimen★ (*Boris Godunov*); PERGOLESI: Uberto (*Serva padrona*); PUCCINI: Colline★ (*Bohème*); ROSSINI: Don Basilio★ (*Barbiere di Siviglia*); STRAUSS, R: Orest★ (*Elektra*); VERDI: Philip II★ & Grande Inquisitore★ (*Don Carlo*), Padre Guardiano★ (*Forza del destino*), Zaccaria★ (*Nabucco*); WAGNER: Daland★ (*Fliegende Holländer*), König Heinrich★ (*Lohengrin*), Fasolt★ (*Rheingold*), Fafner (*Rheingold★, Siegfried★*), Hunding★ (*Walküre*), König Marke★ (*Tristan und Isolde*). Also MOZART: Commendatore★ (*Don Giovanni*). World premieres: BIALAS: Koch/Wirt (*Gestiefelter Kater*) Hamburg Staatsoper 1975. Gives recitals. Appears with symphony orchestra. Res: Timm-Kröger-Weg 18, 2 Hamburg 63, FR Ger. Mgmt: SLZ/FRG.

STANESCU, LUCIA. Dramatic soprano. Romanian. Resident mem: Romanian Opera, Cluj-Napoca. Born Somesul Rece, Romania. Single. Studied: Ciprian Porumbescu Consv, Profs Constantin Stroescu & Dina Badescu, Bucharest. Debut: Cherubino (*Nozze di Figaro*) Romanian Opera, Cluj 1954. Awards: First Prize, World Youth Fest, Bucharest 1953 & Intl Music Cont, Moscow 1957; State Prize Romanian Gvnmt 1958; Merited Artist, Rep of Rom 1960.
Sang with major companies in BUL: Sofia; CZE: Prague National; FRA: Toulouse; HUN: Budapest; ITA: Rome Opera; ROM: Bucharest; SWE: Stockholm; USSR: Kiev, Leningrad Kirov, Moscow Bolshoi. Roles with these companies incl GOUNOD: Marguerite (*Faust*); LEONCAVALLO: Nedda★ (*Pagliacci*); MASCAGNI: Santuzza★ (*Cavalleria rusticana*); PUCCINI: Mimi★ (*Bohème*), Cio-Cio-San★ (*Butterfly*), Manon Lescaut★, Tosca★; VERDI: Aida★, Desdemona (*Otello*). Gives recitals. Appears with symphony orchestra. Res: Arram Iancu St 3, Cluj-Napoca, Romania. Mgmt: RIA/ROM.

STAPP, OLIVIA; née Brewer. Dramatic mezzo-soprano. American. Resident mem: New York City Opera. Born 31 May 1940, New York. Husband Dr Henry Stapp, occupation theoretical physicist. One child. Studied: Mo Ettore Campogalliani, Mo Rodolfo Ricci, Oren Brown. Debut: Beppe (*Amico Fritz*) Spoleto Fest 1960. Awards: Fulbright Schlshp, 2 yrs.
Sang with major companies in AUS: Vienna Volksoper; FR GER: Berlin Deutsche Oper, Wuppertal; SWI: Basel; USA: New York City Opera, Washington DC. Roles with these companies incl BIZET: Carmen★; CIMAROSA: Fidalma (*Matrimonio segreto*); DONIZETTI: Giovanna★ (*Anna Bolena*), Sara★ (*Roberto Devereux*); HUM-

PERDINCK: Hänsel; MASCAGNI: Beppe (*Amico Fritz*); MOZART: Dorabella★ (*Così fan tutte*); ROSSINI: Rosina (*Barbiere di Siviglia*), Isabella★ (*Italiana in Algeri*); SMETANA: Hata (*Bartered Bride*); STRAUSS, R: Komponist★ (*Ariadne auf Naxos*), Herodias★ (*Salome*); STRAVINSKY: Jocasta★ (*Oedipus Rex*); TCHAIKOVSKY: Olga (*Eugene Onegin*); VERDI: Ulrica (*Ballo in maschera*), Dame Quickly. (*Falstaff*); WOLF-FERRARI: Margarita (*Quattro rusteghi*). Also MASCAGNI: Santuzza (*Cavalleria rusticana*); MENOTTI: Magda Sorel★ (*Consul*); ALFANO: Katiusha (*Risurrezione*). World premieres: EATON: Dejanira (*Heracles*) Indiana Univ Opera, Bloomington, USA 1971. Gives recitals. Appears with symphony orchestra. Res: 1404 Leroy, Berkeley, CA, USA. Mgmt: CAM/USA.

STARK, PHIL; né Philipp Stork. Character tenor & Heldentenor. Canadian. Resident mem: Canadian Opera Co, Toronto. Born 30 Dec 1929, Germany. Wife Hilda, occupation airline passenger agent. Studied: Susanne Horn-Stoll, Darmstadt; Opera School Darmstadt and Frankfurt, FR Ger. Debut: Almaviva (*Barbiere di Siviglia*) Heidelberg, FR Ger 1953. Previous occupations: violinist, at 13 mem of symph orch.
Sang with major companies in AUS: Graz; CAN: Montreal/Quebec, Ottawa, Toronto, Vancouver; FRA: Bordeaux, Strasbourg; FR GER: Cologne, Dortmund, Düsseldorf-Duisburg, Karlsruhe, Mannheim, Nürnberg, Wiesbaden, Wuppertal; SWI: Zurich; USA: Cincinnati, Hartford, New York Met, Portland, Seattle, Washington DC. Roles with these companies incl AUBER: Fra Diavolo & Lorenzo (*Fra Diavolo*); BIZET: Don José (*Carmen*); BRITTEN: Albert Herring; CORNELIUS: Nureddin (*Barbier von Bagdad*); DONIZETTI: Ernesto (*Don Pasquale*); FLOTOW: Lionel (*Martha*); GOUNOD: Faust; HUMPERDINCK: Hexe★ (*Hänsel und Gretel*); LORTZING: Baron Kronthal (*Wildschütz*), Peter Ivanov (*Zar und Zimmermann*); MASCAGNI: Turiddu (*Cavalleria rusticana*); MOZART: Ferrando★ (*Così fan tutte*), Don Ottavio★ (*Don Giovanni*), Tamino★ (*Zauberflöte*); MUSSORGSKY: Shuisky (*Boris Godunov*); NICOLAI: Fenton (*Lustigen Weiber*); OFFENBACH: Hoffmann; ORFF: Solo (*Carmina burana*); PUCCINI: Rodolfo (*Bohème*), Rinuccio (*Gianni Schicchi*), Pinkerton (*Butterfly*); ROSSINI: Almaviva (*Barbiere di Siviglia*), Rodrigo (*Otello*); SMETANA: Hans★ (*Bartered Bride*); STRAUSS, J: Alfred★ (*Fledermaus*); STRAUSS, R: Bacchus (*Ariadne auf Naxos*), Aegisth★ (*Elektra*), Ein Sänger (*Rosenkavalier*), Herodes★ (*Salome*); STRAVINSKY: Tom Rakewell (*Rake's Progress*); THOMAS: Wilhelm Meister (*Mignon*); WAGNER: Mime (*Rheingold★, Siegfried★*), Walther v d Vogelweide (*Tannhäuser*); WEBER: Max (*Freischütz*); WEINBERGER: Babinsky★ (*Schwanda*). Also LIEBERMANN: Alfred (*Leonore 40/45*); SOMERS: André Nault (*Louis Riel*). World premieres: WILSON: Alberic (*Heloise and Abelard*) Canadian Opera Co, Toronto 1973; Devil (*Summoning of Everyman*) Stratford Fest 1974. Gives recitals. Appears with symphony orchestra. Mgmt: LLF/USA.

STAVRU, CORNEL. Dramatic tenor. Romanian. Resident mem: Romanian Opera, Bucharest. Born 31 Aug 1929, Constanta. Wife Teodora. One child. Studied: Profs Aurel Costescu-Duca & Alexandru Colfescu, Bucharest. **Debut:** Manrico (*Trovatore*) Romanian Opera 1958. Previous occupations: building eng. Awards: Merited Artist, Romanian Gvnmt.

Sang with major companies in BEL: Liège; BUL: Sofia; CZE: Prague National; GRE: Athens National & Fest; GER DR: Dresden; HUN: Budapest; ROM: Bucharest; YUG: Belgrade. **Roles with these companies incl** BEETHOVEN: Florestan★ (*Fidelio*); BIZET: Don José★ (*Carmen*); GIORDANO: Andrea Chénier★‡; LEONCAVALLO: Canio★‡ (*Pagliacci*); MASCAGNI: Turiddu★‡ (*Cavalleria rusticana*); PUCCINI: Cavaradossi★ (*Tosca*), Calaf★ (*Turandot*); VERDI: Riccardo★ (*Ballo in maschera*), Don Carlo★, Otello★, Manrico★‡ (*Trovatore*); WAGNER: Walther (*Meistersinger*), Tannhäuser★. Also on records only FALLA: Paco (*Vida breve*); VERDI: Ernani; WEBER: Oberon. **World premieres:** TRAILESCU: Lipan (*Balcescu*) Romanian Opera 1974. Recorded for: Electrecord. Appears with symphony orchestra. **Res:** 1 Av Protopopescu St, Bucharest 1, Romania. **Mgmt:** RIA/ROM.

STEFANOV, IVAN. Bass. Bulgarian. Born 1 Aug 1927, Sofia, Bulgaria. Wife Mariana. One child. Studied: Mariana Radev, Zagreb. **Debut:** Sparafucile (*Rigoletto*) Narodna Opera, Vraca, Bulgaria 1960.

Sang with major companies in AUS: Graz; BUL: Sofia; FRA: Bordeaux; GRE: Athens Fest; ITA: Bologna, Trieste, Turin, Venice; SWI: Geneva; YUG: Dubrovnik, Zagreb, Belgrade. **Roles with these companies incl** BARTOK: Bluebeard; BEETHOVEN: Don Pizarro★ (*Fidelio*); BORODIN: Galitzky★ (*Prince Igor*); DONIZETTI: Dott Dulcamara (*Elisir*); GOUNOD: Méphistophélès (*Faust*); MOZART: Osmin (*Entführung aus dem Serail*); MUSSORGSKY: Ivan Khovansky (*Khovanshchina*); PONCHIELLI: Alvise★ (*Gioconda*); PUCCINI: Colline (*Bohème*); ROSSINI: Don Basilio★ (*Barbiere di Siviglia*); TCHAIKOVSKY: King René★ (*Iolanthe*); VERDI: Ramfis★ (*Aida*), Philip II★ & Grande Inquisitore★ (*Don Carlo*), Padre Guardiano (*Forza del destino*). Recorded for: RAI. Teaches voice. On faculty of Consv Sofia. **Res:** Zagreb, Yugoslavia.

STEFANOVA, NINA. Spinto. Bulgarian. Resident mem: Staatstheater Hessen, Kassel, FR Ger. Born 13 Jun 1943, Varna, Bulgaria. Husband Gerd Fromholz, occupation engineer. Studied: Music School, Varna; Consv Bucharest; Musik Akad, Vienna. **Debut:** Fiordiligi (*Così fan tutte*) Kassel 1969. Previous occupations: schoolteacher, music. Awards: Second Prize Intl Voice Compts Bucharest 1967, Barcelona 1968 & 1969, 's Hertogenbosch 1972; Third Prize Paris 1973.

Sang with major companies in DEN: Copenhagen; FRA: Bordeaux, Paris, Rouen, Toulouse; FR GER: Bielefeld, Essen, Frankfurt, Hamburg, Hannover, Karlsruhe, Kassel, Mannheim, Wiesbaden; SPA: Barcelona; UK: Cardiff Welsh. **Roles with these companies incl** BIZET: Micaëla (*Carmen*); MOZART: Fiordiligi (*Così fan tutte*), Donna Elvira (*Don Giovanni*), Ilia (*Idomeneo*), Contessa

(*Nozze di Figaro*), Pamina (*Zauberflöte*); OFFENBACH: Antonia (*Contes d'Hoffmann*); PUCCINI: Mimi (*Bohème*), Lauretta (*Gianni Schicchi*), Liù★ (*Turandot*); TCHAIKOVSKY: Tatiana (*Eugene Onegin*), Lisa (*Pique Dame*); VERDI: Aida, Desdemona (*Otello*), Gilda (*Rigoletto*), Leonora (*Trovatore*); WEBER: Agathe (*Freischütz*). Gives recitals. Appears with symphony orchestra. **Res:** 3501 Habichtswald Burghasunger Str 7, Kassel, FR Ger. **Mgmt:** SLZ/FRG.

STEFFEK, HANNY. Lyric soprano. Austrian. Resident mem: Volksoper, Vienna. Born 9 Dec 1927, Bielce, Poland. Husband Albert Moser, occupation Gen Secy, Socy of Friends of Music, Vienna. **Debut:** Erster Knabe (*Zauberflöte*) Salzburg Fest 1949. Awards: Kammersängerin, Bayerische Staatsoper; Austrian Medal of Honor, Vienna Staatsoper, Austrian Gvnmt.

Sang with major companies in AUS: Bregenz Fest, Graz, Salzburg Fest, Vienna Staatsoper & Volksoper; BRA: Rio de Janeiro; FRA: Aix-en-Provence Fest, Marseille, Nice, Strasbourg; FR GER: Berlin Deutsche Oper, Cologne, Frankfurt, Munich Staatsoper, Stuttgart, Wiesbaden; HOL: Amsterdam; ITA: Florence Maggio, Naples, Palermo, Rome Opera, Turin, Venice; MON: Monte Carlo; NOR: Oslo; SPA: Barcelona; SWI: Geneva, Zurich; UK: Edinburgh Fest, London Royal; USA: Chicago. **Roles with these companies incl** BEETHOVEN: Marzelline (*Fidelio*); BIZET: Micaëla (*Carmen*); CIMAROSA: Carolina & Elisetta★ (*Matrimonio segreto*); GLUCK: Euridice★ & Amor (*Orfeo ed Euridice*); HAYDN: Vespina★ (*Infedeltà delusa*); LORTZING: Marie (*Zar und Zimmermann*); MOZART: Despina (*Così fan tutte*), Zerlina (*Don Giovanni*), Blondchen (*Entführung aus dem Serail*), Mlle Silberklang (*Schauspieldirektor*), Susanna★ & Cherubino (*Nozze di Figaro*), Pamina (*Zauberflöte*); NICOLAI: Aennchen (*Lustigen Weiber*); OFFENBACH: Antonia (*Contes d'Hoffmann*); ORFF: Kluge★; PFITZNER: Ighino (*Palestrina*); PUCCINI: Lauretta★ (*Gianni Schicchi*), Liù (*Turandot*); ROSSINI: Rosina (*Barbiere di Siviglia*); SMETANA: Marie (*Bartered Bride*); STRAUSS, J: Adele (*Fledermaus*); STRAUSS, R: Zdenka (*Arabella*), Christine (*Intermezzo*), Sophie (*Rosenkavalier*); VERDI: Oscar (*Ballo in maschera*), Nannetta (*Falstaff*), Gilda (*Rigoletto*); WEBER: Aennchen★ (*Freischütz*). Recorded for: EMI, DG. Gives recitals. Appears with symphony orchestra. Teaches voice. Coaches repertoire. **Res:** Buchleiteng 75, Vienna, Austria. **Mgmt:** TAU/SWI.

STEGER, INGRID. Dramatic soprano. German. Born 27 Feb, Roding/Oberpfalz, Germany. Husband Walter Rechl, occupation mathematician. One child. Studied: Kmsg Max Lorenz, Kmsg Hans Hotter, Germany. **Debut:** Achilles (*Deidamia*) Staatstheater Kassel.

Sang with major companies in AUS: Graz, Salzburg Festival, Vienna Staatsoper; FRA: Strasbourg; FR GER: Bielefeld, Darmstadt, Dortmund, Düsseldorf-Duisburg, Essen, Frankfurt, Hamburg, Hannover, Karlsruhe, Kassel, Kiel, Nürnberg, Stuttgart; GER DR: Berlin Staatsoper, Dresden; ITA: Parma, Trieste, Venice; POR: Lisbon; SPA: Majorca; SWI: Basel, Zurich; USA: San Francisco Opera. **Roles with these companies** incl BARTOK: Judith (*Bluebeard's Castle*); BEETHOVEN: Leonore★ (*Fidelio*); GLUCK: Iphigénie★ (*Iphigénie en Tauride*); HANDEL: Achilles (*Deidamia*), Rodelinda; JANACEK: Kostelnicka★ (*Jenufa*); MASCAGNI: Santuzza★ (*Cavalleria rusticana*); MOZART: Cherubino (*Nozze di Figaro*); OFFENBACH: Giulietta (*Contes d'Hoffmann*); ORFF: Antigonae; PUCCINI: Tosca, Turandot★; PURCELL: Dido★; STRAUSS, R: Ariadne★ & Komponist (*Ariadne auf Naxos*), Elektra★; TCHAIKOVSKY: Tatiana (*Eugene Onegin*); VERDI: Amelia★ (*Ballo in maschera*), Lady Macbeth★; WAGNER: Senta★ (*Fliegende Holländer*), Elsa, Ortrud★ (*Lohengrin*), Sieglinde★ (*Walküre*), Brünnhilde★ (*Walküre, Siegfried*), Gutrune (*Götterdämmerung*), Elisabeth & Venus★ (*Tannhäuser*), Isolde★, Kundry★ (*Parsifal*). Gives recitals. Appears with symphony orchestra. Teaches voice. Res: 42 Oberhausen, FR Ger. Mgmt: VLD/AUS.

STEIN, HORST WALTER. Conductor of opera and symphony. German. Gen Mus Dir & Cond, Hamburgische Staatsoper, Hamburg 1972-76. Born 2 May 1928, Elberfeld, Germany. Wife Hannelore Kaiser, occupation art historian. Two children. Studied: Musisches Gymnasium (high school for the arts) Frankfurt/M; Hochschule für Musik, Cologne; incl piano, oboe, percussion and voice. Operatic training as repetiteur at Städtische Bühnen, Wuppertal, Germany. **Operatic debut:** Städtische Bühnen, Wuppertal 1949. Symphonic debut: Staatskapelle Berlin. Awards: Cond emeritus NHK Symph Orch, Tokyo; Mem Freie Akademie der Künste, Hamburg. Previous adm positions in opera: Operndir, Nationaltheater Mannheim, FR Ger 1963-70; Princ Cond, Staatsoper, Vienna 1970-72.

Conducted with major companies in ARG: Buenos Aires; AUS: Salzburg Fest, Vienna Staatsoper; BUL: Sofia; CZE: Brno, Prague Smetana; DEN: Copenhagen; FRA: Lyon, Paris, Toulouse; FR GER: Bayreuth Fest, Düsseldorf-Duisburg, Essen, Frankfurt, Hamburg, Kiel, Mannheim, Nürnberg, Wiesbaden, Wuppertal; GER DR: Berlin Staatsoper, Dresden; ITA: Bologna, Florence Maggio & Comunale, Milan La Scala, Naples, Turin, Venice; UK: London English National; USA: San Francisco Opera. Operas with these companies incl d'ALBERT: *Tiefland;* AUBER: *Fra Diavolo;* BEETHOVEN: *Fidelio★;* BIZET: *Carmen★;* BORODIN: *Prince Igor;* BRITTEN: *Midsummer Night;* CHERUBINI: *Medea★;* CORNELIUS: *Barbier von Bagdad;* DALLAPICCOLA: *Prigioniero;* DONIZETTI: *Don Pasquale;* FLOTOW: *Martha;* GLUCK: *Iphigénie en Tauride, Orfeo ed Euridice;* GOUNOD: *Faust;* HONEGGER: *Antigone;* HUMPERDINCK: *Hänsel und Gretel;* IBERT: *Angélique;* JANACEK: *Jenufa, Katya Kabanova;* LEONCAVALLO: *Pagliacci;* LORTZING: *Waffenschmied, Wildschütz, Zar und Zimmermann;* MASCAGNI: *Cavalleria rusticana;* MONIUSZKO: *Halka;* MOZART: *Così fan tutte★, Don Giovanni★, Entführung aus dem Serail★, Nozze di Figaro★, Zauberflöte★;* MUSSORGSKY: *Boris Godunov★, Khovanshchina★;* NICOLAI: *Lustigen Weiber;* OFFENBACH: *Contes d'Hoffmann;* ORFF: *Carmina burana★;* PFITZNER: *Palestrina;* PUCCINI: *Bohème★, Gianni Schicchi, Butterfly★, Tosca★, Turandot★;*

RAVEL: *Heure espagnole;* ROSSINI: *Barbiere di Siviglia, Cambiale di matrimonio, Cenerentola, Pietra del paragone, Turco in Italia;* SCHOENBERG: *Erwartung★, Moses und Aron★;* SMETANA: *Bartered Bride★;* STRAUSS, J: *Fledermaus★;* STRAUSS, R: *Arabella★, Ariadne auf Naxos★, Capriccio★, Daphne★, Elektra★, Rosenkavalier★, Salome★;* STRAVINSKY: *Oedipus Rex, Rake's Progress;* TCHAIKOVSKY: *Eugene Onegin★;* VERDI: *Aida★, Ballo in maschera★, Don Carlo★, Forza del destino, Nabucco, Otello, Rigoletto, Traviata, Trovatore;* WAGNER: *Fliegende Holländer★, Lohengrin★, Meistersinger★, Parsifal★, Rheingold★, Walküre★, Siegfried★, Götterdämmerung★, Tannhäuser★, Tristan und Isolde★;* WEBER: *Freischütz★.* **World premieres:** FOREST: *Arme Konrad* Staatsoper Berlin 1959; EINEM: *Besuch der alten Dame* Staatsoper, Vienna 1971. Recorded for DG, Electrola, VEB-Berlin. Video—Berlin Ost TV: *Eugene Onegin;* Hamburg TV: *Zauberflöte, Arabella.* Conducted major orch in Europe, USA/Canada, Cent/S America, Asia. Teaches at Hochschule für Musik u darst Kunst, Hamburg. Res: Borchlingweg 38, Hamburg 52, FR Ger. Mgmt: TAU/SWI; MAA/USA.

STEINER, ELISABETH. Lyric mezzo-soprano. German. Resident mem: Staatsoper, Hamburg. Born 17 Mar 1940, Berlin. Husband Reiner Szelinski, occupation author. Two children. Studied: Frida Leider, Richard Sengeleitner, Rudolf Bautz. **Debut:** Schwester Wanda (*Rosamunde Floris*) Deutsche Oper, Berlin 1961. Awards: title of Kammersängerin.

Sang with major companies in AUS: Salzburg Fest; DEN: Copenhagen; FR GER: Bayreuth Fest, Berlin Deutsche Oper, Cologne, Frankfurt, Hamburg, Kassel, Kiel, Munich Staatsoper, Stuttgart, Wuppertal; HOL: Amsterdam; ITA: Florence Maggio, Milan La Scala, Venice; SWE: Stockholm; SWI: Zurich; UK: London English National; USA: New York Met; YUG: Zagreb. Roles with these companies incl BERLIOZ: Ascanio★ (*Benvenuto Cellini*); BIZET: Carmen★; BRITTEN: Nancy (*Albert Herring*), Helena (*Midsummer Night*); FALLA: Salud (*Vida breve*); GLUCK: Euridice; HUMPERDINCK: Hänsel★; LORTZING: Gräfin Eberbach (*Wildschütz*); MASSENET: Dulcinée★ (*Don Quichotte*); MOZART: Sesto & Annio (*Clemenza di Tito*), Dorabella★ (*Così fan tutte*), Cherubino★ (*Nozze di Figaro*); NICOLAI: Frau Reich★ (*Lustigen Weiber*); OFFENBACH: Nicklausse★ (*Contes d'Hoffmann*); PUCCINI: Suzuki★ (*Butterfly*); STRAUSS, J: Prinz Orlovsky★ (*Fledermaus*); STRAUSS, R: Komponist★ (*Ariadne auf Naxos*), Clairon (*Capriccio*), Octavian★ (*Rosenkavalier*); VERDI: Preziosilla★ (*Forza del destino*); WEILL: Jenny (*Aufstieg und Fall der Stadt Mahagonny*). Also WAGNER: Adriano★ (*Rienzi*); MENOTTI: Mother (*Amahl*); RAVEL: Concepcion★ (*Heure espagnole*). **World premieres:** KRENEK: Glaukis (*Goldener Bock*) 1964; EINEM: Mme Schleyer (*Zerrissene*) 1964; BLACHER: Assistentin (*Zwischenfälle bei einer Notlandung*) 1966; PENDERECKI: Ninon (*Teufel von Loudun*) 1969; KELEMEN: Sekretärin (*Belagerungszustand*) 1970; KRENEK: Heloise (*Das kommt davon, oder Wenn Sardakai auf Reisen geht*) 1970;

BURKHARDT: Rachel (*Stern geht auf aus Jakob*) 1970; STEFFENS: Polly Garter (*Unter dem Milchwald*) 1973; all at Hamburg Staatsoper. Recorded for: Philips, Eurodisc, Electrola. Video/Film: Cherubino (*Nozze di Figaro*). Gives recitals. Appears with symphony orchestra. Teaches voice. Mgmt: SLZ/FRG; ARM/FRG.

STELLA, ANTONIETTA; née Maria Antonietta Stella. Lyric & dramatic soprano. Italian. Born 15 Mar 1929, Perugia. Husband Giuseppe Trepiccioni. Studied: Consv Francesco Morlacchi, Aldo Zeeti, Perugia; Accad S Cecilia, Rome. **Debut:** Leonora (*Forza del destino*) Rome Opera 1951. Awards: First Prize, Spoleto Opera Fest 1949.

Sang with major companies in AUS: Salzburg Fest, Vienna Staatsoper; BEL: Brussels; BRA: Rio de Janeiro; FRA: Paris; ITA: Bologna, Florence Comunale & Maggio, Genoa, Milan La Scala, Naples, Palermo, Parma, Rome Opera, Turin, Venice, Verona Arena; POR: Lisbon; UK: London Royal Opera; USA: Chicago, New York Met; et al. **Roles with these companies incl** DONIZETTI: Linda di Chamounix‡; GIORDANO: Maddalena‡ (*Andrea Chénier*); MASCAGNI: Santuzza (*Cavalleria rusticana*); MEYERBEER: Selika (*Africaine*); PUCCINI: Mimì‡ (*Bohème*), Cio-Cio-San (*Butterfly*), Manon Lescaut, Tosca‡, Liù (*Turandot*); VERDI: Aida, Mina (*Aroldo/Stiffelio*), Amelia‡ (*Ballo in maschera*), Elisabetta‡ (*Don Carlo*), Desdemona (*Otello*), Amelia‡ (*Simon Boccanegra*), Violetta‡ (*Traviata*), Leonora‡ (*Trovatore*); et al. Also SPONTINI: Ermengarda (*Agnese di Hohenstaufen*); GARGIULO: Marie Antoinette. **World premieres:** de BELLIS: Maria Stuarda, Naples 1974. Recorded for: Cetra, Philips, DG, HMV, Angel, Capitol, Seraphim. Gives recitals. Appears with symphony orchestra. **Res:** Rome, Italy. Mgmt: GOR/UK.

STENSVOLD, TERJE. Lyric baritone. Norwegian. Resident mem: Norwegian Opera, Oslo. Born 10 Oct 1943, Baerum, Norway. Wife Kari, occupation teacher. Two children. Studied: J Szterenyi, L Sunde, M Isene, C Kaiser-Breme, Oslo. **Debut:** Zuniga (*Carmen*) Norwegian Opera, Oslo 1972. Previous occupations: German & English teacher. Awards: Wallenberg Schlshp, 4 yrs.

Sang with major companies in NOR: Oslo. **Roles with these companies incl** BRITTEN: Tarquinius★ (*Rape of Lucretia*); DONIZETTI: Dott Malatesta★ (*Don Pasquale*); GLUCK: Thoas★ (*Iphigénie en Tauride*); KODALY: Háry János★; MOZART: Papageno★ (*Zauberflöte*); ROSSINI: Slook★ (*Cambiale di matrimonio*). **World premieres:** JANSON: Trommy (*Fjelleventyret*) Norwegian Opera, Oslo 1973. Gives recitals. Appears with symphony orchestra. **Res:** Hegdehaugsvn 14B, Oslo 1, Norway.

STEVENS, JOHN WRIGHT. Scenic and costume designer for opera, theater, television; specl in sets and stage lighting. Is also a teacher of stage design. American. Studied: Yale Drama School, Donald Oenslager, CT; Catholic Univ of America, Washington, DC. Prof training: scenic shop Opera Socy of Washington, DC 1962-64. **Operatic debut:** sets, *Gianni Schicchi* Santa Fe Opera, NM 1964; cost, *Gianni Schicchi* Met Opera Studio 1971. Theater debut: Repertory Theater of St Louis 1966.

Designed for major companies in USA: Cincinnati, Memphis, Omaha, San Francisco Spring Opera, Santa Fe, Washington DC. **Operas designed for these companies incl** BIZET: *Carmen★, Pêcheurs de perles★;* BRITTEN: *Death in Venice★;* CAVALLI: *Ormindo★;* DONIZETTI: *Convenienze/Viva la Mamma★, Don Pasquale★;* FLOYD: *Of Mice and Men★;* MOZART: *Entführung aus dem Serail★;* PUCCINI: *Bohème★, Gianni Schicchi★, Tosca;* ROSSINI: *Barbiere di Siviglia;* STRAUSS, R: *Arabella, Capriccio;* STRAVINSKY: *Rake's Progress;* VERDI: *Rigoletto, Traviata*. Also MADERNA: *Satyricon*. Exhibitions of stage designs Yale Univ Art Gallery 1966; Univ of New Mexico Art Gallery 1974. Teaches at Univ of Alberta, Edmonton, Canada 1975. **Res:** 111 E 88th St, New York 10028, USA.

STEVENS, RON. Lyric & spinto tenor. American. Resident mem: Australian Opera Co, Sydney. Born 18 Sep 1940, Los Angeles. Wife Jennifer, occupation journalist. Studied: Joseph Klein, Glendale, CA; Univ of So Calif, USA. **Debut:** Hans (*Bartered Bride*) Guild Opera, Los Angeles 1970. Previous occupations: company exec vice-pres.

Sang with major companies in AUSTRL: Sydney. **Roles with these companies incl** JANACEK: Laca★ (*Jenufa*); OFFENBACH: Hoffmann★; PROKOFIEV: Pierre (*War and Peace*); PUCCINI: Luigi★ (*Tabarro*); STRAUSS, R: Bacchus★ (*Ariadne auf Naxos*); VERDI: Ismaele★ (*Nabucco*); WEILL: Jim Mahoney★ (*Aufstieg und Fall der Stadt Mahagonny*). **World premieres:** SITZKY: Lenz (*Lenz*) Australian Opera 1974; BANKS: Tenor (*Limbo*) New So Wales Op 1973; DREYFUS: Kane Chapman (*Garni Sands*) Sydney 1975. Gives recitals. Appears with symphony orchestra. **Res:** 35 Riley St, Oatley, NSW 2223, Sydney, Australia.

STEWART, JOHN HARGER. Lyric tenor. American. Resident mem: Städtische Oper Frankfurt. Born 31 Mar 1940, Cleveland, O, USA. Divorced. Studied: Yale Univ, New Haven, CT; Brown Univ, Providence, RI; Cornelius Reid, Frederick Jagel, USA. **Debut:** Pinkerton (*Butterfly*) Santa Fe Opera, NM 1968. Previous occupations: college teaching: theory, voice and choral conducting.

Sang with major companies in CAN: Ottawa; FR GER: Frankfurt; HOL: Amsterdam; SWI: Geneva; USA: Cincinnati, Fort Worth, Houston, Milwaukee Florentine, New York Met & City Opera, Omaha, Philadelphia Lyric, Pittsburgh, San Antonio, San Diego, Santa Fe, Washington DC. **Roles with these companies incl** BIZET: Nadir (*Pêcheurs de perles*); BORODIN: Vladimir (*Prince Igor*); BRITTEN: Albert Herring; DEBUSSY: Azaël (*Enfant prodigue*); DELIBES: Gérald (*Lakmé*); DELIUS: Sali★ (*Village Romeo and Juliet*); DONIZETTI: Ernesto★ (*Don Pasquale*), Nemorino★ (*Elisir*), Leicester (*Maria Stuarda*); GOUNOD: Roméo★; MOZART: Ferrando★ (*Così fan tutte*), Don Ottavio★ (*Don Giovanni*), Belmonte★ (*Entführung aus dem Serail*), Tamino★ (*Zauberflöte*); PENDERECKI: de Laubardemont★ (*Teufel von Loudun*); PUCCINI: Rodolfo★ (*Bohème*), Rinuccio (*Gianni Schicchi*), Pinkerton★ (*Butterfly*), Cavaradossi (*Tosca*); ROSSINI: Almaviva★ (*Barbiere di Siviglia*); STRAUSS, J: Alfred★ (*Fledermaus*); VERDI: Alfredo★ (*Traviata*).

Gives recitals. Appears with symphony orchestra. **Res:** New York, NY, USA. Mgmt: CAM/USA; AIM/UK.

STEWART, THOMAS JAMES Jr. Dramatic baritone. American. Born 29 Aug 1928, San Saba, TX, USA. Wife Evelyn Lear, occupation singer, soprano. Two children. Studied: Baylor Univ, Prof Robert Hopkins, Waco, TX; Juilliard School of Music, Mack Harrell, New York; Hochschule für Musik, Jaro Prohaska, Berlin; Daniel Ferro, New York. **Debut:** Raimondo (*Lucia*) Chicago Lyric Opera 1954. Previous occupations: mathematician, statistical conslt. Awards: Kammersänger, Deutsche Oper Berlin; Richard Wagner Medal, Bayreuth.
Sang with major companies in AUS: Salzburg Fest, Vienna Staatsoper; BEL: Brussels; CZE: Prague National; FIN: Helsinki; FRA: Bordeaux, Lyon, Orange Fest, Paris; FR GER: Bayreuth Fest, Berlin Deutsche Oper, Cologne, Düsseldorf-Duisburg, Frankfurt, Hamburg, Hannover, Mannheim, Munich Staatsoper, Nürnberg, Stuttgart, Wiesbaden; HUN: Budapest; ITA: Florence Maggio; SWI: Basel, Geneva, Zurich; UK: London Royal Opera; USA: Boston, Chicago, New York Met, Pittsburgh, San Francisco Opera. **Roles with these companies incl** d'ALBERT: Tommaso (*Tiefland*); BARTOK: Bluebeard; BEETHOVEN: Don Pizarro★ (*Fidelio*); BIZET: Escamillo (*Carmen*); DEBUSSY: Golaud★ (*Pelléas et Mélisande*); LORTZING: Graf v Liebenau (*Waffenschmied*); MOZART: Don Giovanni★, Conte Almaviva★ (*Nozze di Figaro*); OFFENBACH: Coppélius etc★ (*Contes d'Hoffmann*); ORFF: König‡ (*Kluge*); PUCCINI: Scarpia★ (*Tosca*); PURCELL: Aeneas★ (*Dido and Aeneas*); ROSSINI: Sultan Selim (*Turco in Italia*); STRAUSS, R: Musiklehrer (*Ariadne auf Naxos*), Graf & La Roche (*Capriccio*), Orest★ (*Elektra*), Jochanaan★ (*Salome*); TCHAIKOVSKY: Eugene Onegin★, Yeletsky (*Pique Dame*); VERDI: Amonasro★ (*Aida*), Renato (*Ballo in maschera*), Rodrigo (*Don Carlo*), Ford★ (*Falstaff*), Iago★ (*Otello*), Rigoletto, Germont (*Traviata*), Conte di Luna (*Trovatore*), Monforte (*Vespri*); WAGNER: Holländer★‡, Hans Sachs★ (*Meistersinger*), Amfortas★‡ (*Parsifal*), Wotan (*Rheingold★, Walküre★‡*), Wanderer★‡ (*Siegfried*), Gunther★‡ (*Götterdämmerung*), Wolfram★ (*Tannhäuser*), Kurwenal★ (*Tristan und Isolde*); WOLF-FERRARI: Conte Gil★ (*Segreto di Susanna*). Also WAGNER: Telramund‡ (*Lohengrin*). **World premieres:** BLACHER: William (*Rosamunde Floris*) Berlin 1960; MILHAUD: Oreste (*Oreste d'Eschyle*) Berlin 1963; KLEBE: Zeus (*Alkmene*) Berlin 1961. Recorded for: DG, Eurodisc. Video/Film: Conte Gil (*Segreto di Susanna*); Wotan (*Walküre*). Gives recitals. Appears with symphony orchestra. **Res:** Losone, Switzerland. Mgmt: CAM/USA; IWL/UK.

STILINOVIC, BRANKA. Dramatic soprano. Yugoslavian. Resident mem: Croatian National Opera, Zagreb. Born 24 Oct 1926, Zagreb. Husband Milan, occupation professor. One child. Studied: Prof Nada Pirnat, Zagreb. **Debut:** Santuzza (*Cavalleria rusticana*) National Opera, Rijeka, Yugoslavia 1957. Previous occupations: worked for radio station RTV, Zagreb. Awards: Grada Zagreb Prize; Milka Ternina Prize, Zagreb.

Sang with major companies in AUS: Salzburg Fest; GRE: Athens Fest; FR GER: Cologne; GER DR: Berlin Komische Oper & Staatsoper; HUN: Budapest; ITA: Bologna, Naples; SWI: Basel; YUG: Dubrovnik, Zagreb, Belgrade. **Roles with these companies incl** BEETHOVEN: Leonore★ (*Fidelio*); BIZET: Micaëla (*Carmen*); BORODIN: Jaroslavna★ (*Prince Igor*); GIORDANO: Maddalena (*Andrea Chénier*); GOTOVAC: Djula‡ (*Ero der Schelm*); MASCAGNI: Santuzza★ (*Cavalleria rusticana*); MOZART: Donna Anna★ (*Don Giovanni*); PONCHIELLI: Gioconda★; PROKOFIEV: Natasha (*War and Peace*); PUCCINI: Tosca★; SMETANA: Marie (*Bartered Bride*); TCHAIKOVSKY: Tatiana (*Eugene Onegin*), Lisa★ (*Pique Dame*); VERDI: Aida★, Amelia★ (*Ballo in maschera*), Elisabetta★ (*Don Carlo*), Abigaille★ (*Nabucco*), Leonora★ (*Trovatore*); WAGNER: Senta (*Fliegende Holländer*). Also LISINSKI: Irmengarda (*Porin*); ZAJC: Eva/Jelena‡ (*Nikola Subic Zrinjski*). **World premieres:** GOTOVAC: Dalmaro, Croatian Ntl Opera, Zagreb 1964. Recorded for: Jugoton. Video/Film: (*Ban leget*); (*Zrinjski*); (*Porin*); (*Oganj*); (*Don Carlo*). Gives recitals. Appears with symphony orchestra. Teaches voice. Coaches repertoire. On faculty of Acad of Music, Zagreb. **Res:** Trg Zrtava Fasizma 9, Zagreb, Yugoslavia.

STILWELL, RICHARD D. Lyric baritone. American. Born St Louis, MO, USA. Wife Elizabeth, occupation pianist. Studied: Daniel Ferro, New York; Indiana Univ, Frank St Leger, Paul Mathin, Bloomington, IN, USA. **Debut:** Pelléas, New York City Opera 1971.
Sang with major companies in AUS: Vienna Staatsoper; CAN: Vancouver; FRA: Aix-en-Provence, Marseille, Paris; FR GER: Hamburg; HOL: Amsterdam; ITA: Milan La Scala, Trieste, Turin, Venice; SWI: Geneva; UK: Glyndebourne Fest, London Royal; USA: Boston, Chicago, Houston, New York Met & City Opera, Pittsburgh, San Francisco Opera, Santa Fe, Washington DC. **Roles with these companies incl** BRITTEN: Billy Budd★; DEBUSSY: Pelléas★; GLUCK: Oreste★ (*Iphigénie en Tauride*); HANDEL: Giulio Cesare; MENOTTI: Donato★ (*Maria Golovin*); MOZART: Guglielmo★ (*Così fan tutte*), Don Giovanni★, Conte Almaviva★ (*Nozze di Figaro*), Papageno★ (*Zauberflöte*); ORFF: Solo★ (*Carmina burana*); PUCCINI: Marcello★ (*Bohème*); ROSSINI: Figaro★ (*Barbiere di Siviglia*), Dandini (*Cenerentola*); STRAUSS, R: Olivier★ (*Capriccio*); TCHAIKOVSKY: Eugene Onegin★; VERDI: Ford★ (*Falstaff*), Germont (*Traviata*). Also BRITTEN: Sid★ (*Albert Herring*); GLUCK: Orfeo★; MONTEVERDI: Ulisse★ (*Ritorno d'Ulisse*), Ottone★ (*Incoronazione di Poppea*). **World premieres:** PASATIERI: Constantine (*The Seagull*) Houston Grand Opera 1974. Gives recitals. Appears with symphony orchestra. **Res:** McLean, VA, USA. Mgmt: CAM/USA; HPL/UK.

STODDART, JOHN STEWART. Scenic and costume designer for opera, theater, film. Is also a painter, illustrator & architect. Australian. Born 24 Jan 1936, Sydney. Single. Studied: School of Arch, Univ of Sydney. **Operatic debut:** *Così fan tutte* Scottish Opera, Glasgow 1967. Theater debut:

Oxford Playhouse, UK 1967. Previous occupation: architect.

Designed for major companies in ARG: Buenos Aires; AUSTRL: Sydney; CAN: Ottawa, Toronto; UK: Aldeburgh Fest, Edinburgh Fest, Scottish, London Royal & English National; USA: Washington DC. **Operas designed for these companies incl** BRITTEN: *Turn of the Screw;* CAVALLI: *Ormindo;* DONIZETTI: *Favorite;* GLUCK: *Alceste★;* MOZART: *Clemenza di Tito★, Così fan tutte, Entführung aus dem Serail★, Nozze di Figaro★, Zauberflöte;* PUCCINI: *Butterfly, Rondine;* ROSSINI: *Otello;* SEARLE: *Hamlet;* STRAUSS, R: *Ariadne auf Naxos★, Rosenkavalier★.* Also ROSSINI: *Equivoco stravagante.* **Operatic world premieres:** GARDNER: *Visitors* English Op Group, Aldeburgh Fest 1972. Exhibitions of stage designs. **Res:** 201 Hammersmith Grove, London W 6, UK. Mgmt: AIM/UK.

STOIAN, ION. Lyric tenor. Romanian. Resident mem: Romanian Opera, Bucharest. Born 26 Dec 1927, Constanta. Wife Georgeta. Studied: Consv, Profs Romulus Vrabiescu, Jean Rinzescu, Petre Stefanescu-Goanga & Gheorghe Kulibin, Bucharest. **Debut:** Belmonte (*Entführung aus dem Serail*) Romanian Opera 1958. Awards: Laureate, Ntl Cont 1953.

Sang with major companies in ROM: Bucharest. **Roles with these companies incl** BRITTEN: Albert Herring★; DONIZETTI: Ernesto★ (*Don Pasquale*); MOZART: Ferrando★ (*Così fan tutte*), Don Ottavio★ (*Don Giovanni*), Belmonte★ & Pedrillo★ (*Entführung aus dem Serail*); MUSSORGSKY: Shuisky★ (*Boris Godunov*); ORFF: Erzähler★ (*Mond*); PROKOFIEV: Antonio (*Duenna*); ROSSINI: Almaviva★ (*Barbiere di Siviglia*); SMETANA: Wenzel★ (*Bartered Bride*); STRAUSS, J: Eisenstein★ (*Fledermaus*); TCHAIKOVSKY: Lenski (*Eugene Onegin*); VERDI: Fenton (*Falstaff*), Alfredo★ (*Traviata*); WAGNER: David (*Meistersinger*). **World premieres:** TRAILESCU: Ionica (*Puss in Boots*) Romanian Opera. Gives recitals. Appears with symphony orchestra. Teaches voice. Coaches repertoire. On faculty of Consv, Bucharest. **Res:** 17 D Cantemir Blvd, Bucharest 5, Romania. Mgmt: RIA/ROM.

STOICA, MARIANA; née Iordanescu. Dramatic soprano. Romanian. Resident mem: Romanian Opera, Bucharest. Born 3 Nov 1933, Bucharest. Husband Gheorghe, occupation mechanical engr. Two children. Studied: Consv, Profs Constanta Badescu and Stela Simonetti, Bucharest. **Debut:** Leonora (*Trovatore*) Romanian Opera, Cluj 1961. Awards: Intl Erkel Cont, Budapest; Intl George Enescu Cont, Bucharest.

Sang with major companies in CZE: Prague National; ROM: Bucharest; USSR: Kiev. **Roles with these companies incl** MASCAGNI: Santuzza★ (*Cavalleria rusticana*); PUCCINI: Mimi (*Bohème*), Tosca★, Turandot★; VERDI: Aida★, Amelia★ (*Ballo in maschera*), Desdemona (*Otello*), Leonora★ (*Trovatore*); WAGNER: Senta★ (*Fliegende Holländer*), Elsa★ (*Lohengrin*), Elisabeth★ (*Tannhäuser*). **World premieres:** DUMITRESCU: Drigisa (*Decebal*) Romanian Opera, Bucharest 1969. Video/Film: Elisabeth (*Tannhäuser*). Gives recitals. Appears with symphony orchestra. **Res:** 323 1 May Blvd, Bucharest 8, Romania. Mgmt: RIA/ROM; SLA/UK.

STOJANOV, STOJAN; né Stojan Gancev. Dramatic tenor. Bulgarian. Resident mem: National Opera, Sofia; National Opera, Belgrade. Born 28 Dec 1929. Wife Elena, occupation ballerina. Two children. Studied: Prof Hristo Braubarov. **Debut:** Rodolfo (*Bohème*) Varna, Bulgaria 1960.

Sang with major companies in BUL: Sofia; CZE: Brno, Prague National; FRA: Strasbourg; FR GER: Karlsruhe, Mannheim, Saarbrücken, Stuttgart; HUN: Budapest; ITA: Bologna; SWI: Geneva; USSR: Leningrad Kirov; YUG: Dubrovnik, Zagreb, Belgrade. **Roles with these companies incl** BEETHOVEN: Florestan★ (*Fidelio*); BELLINI: Pollione★ (*Norma*); BIZET: Don José★ (*Carmen*), Nadir (*Pêcheurs de perles*); BORODIN: Vladimir★ (*Prince Igor*); DONIZETTI: Edgardo★ (*Lucia*); GOTOVAC: Mitcha★ (*Ero der Schelm*); GOUNOD: Faust; LEONCAVALLO: Canio (*Pagliacci*); MASCAGNI: Turiddu★ (*Cavalleria rusticana*); MONTEVERDI: Orfeo; PONCHIELLI: Enzo★ (*Gioconda*); PUCCINI: Rodolfo★ (*Bohème*), Pinkerton (*Butterfly*), Luigi (*Tabarro*), Cavaradossi★ (*Tosca*), Calaf★ (*Turandot*); SMETANA: Hans★ (*Bartered Bride*); STRAUSS, R: Matteo (*Arabella*), Herodes★ (*Salome*); TCHAIKOVSKY: Gherman★ (*Pique Dame*); VERDI: Radames★ (*Aida*), Riccardo‡ (*Ballo in maschera*), Don Carlo★, Ismaele★ (*Nabucco*), Duca di Mantova (*Rigoletto*), Alfredo (*Traviata*), Manrico★ (*Trovatore*); WAGNER: Erik (*Fliegende Holländer*). Also MUSSORGSKY: Dimitri (*Boris Godunov*). Gives recitals. Appears with symphony orchestra. Coaches repertoire. On faculty of Music Acad Sofia. **Res:** Sofia, Bulgaria.

STOLZE, GERHARD. Dramatic tenor. Austrian. Resident mem: Staatsoper, Vienna. Born 1 Oct 1926, Dessau/Anhalt, Germany. Married. Two children. Studied: Prof Hermann Weissenborn, Berlin. **Debut:** Yamadori (*Butterfly*) Staatsoper, Dresden 1949. Awards: Kammersänger, Berlin Senate; Kammersänger, Vienna Staatsoper; Ntl Prize of the Ger DR 1958.

Sang with major companies in AUS: Salzburg Fest, Vienna Staatsoper & Volksoper; BEL: Brussels; CAN: Montreal/Quebec; CZE: Prague National; DEN: Copenhagen; FIN: Helsinki; FRA: Bordeaux, Lyon, Paris; GRE: Athens Fest; FR GER: Bayreuth Fest, Berlin Deutsche Oper, Cologne, Frankfurt, Hamburg, Munich Staatsoper, Nürnberg, Stuttgart, Wiesbaden; GER DR: Berlin Komische Oper & Staatsoper, Dresden; ITA: Naples, Venice; SPA: Barcelona; SWE: Stockholm; SWI: Zurich; UK: Edinburgh Fest, London Royal Opera; USA: Chicago, New York Met. **Roles with these companies incl** AUBER: Masaniello (*Muette de Portici*); BERG: Maler★ (*Lulu*), Hauptmann★ (*Wozzeck*); BRITTEN: Oberon (*Midsummer Night*); EINEM: Robespierre★ (*Dantons Tod*), Joseph K★ (*Prozess*); HANDEL: Sextus (*Giulio Cesare*), Xerxes; HENZE: Lord Barrat (*Junge Lord*); HINDEMITH: Apprentice (*Cardillac*); JANACEK: Laca★ (*Jenufa*); KLEBE: Oberst★ (*Jakobowsky und der Oberst*); LORTZING: Peter Ivanov (*Zar und Zimmermann*); MONIUSZKO: Jontek (*Halka*); MONTEVERDI: Nero★ (*In-*

coronazione di Poppea); MOZART: Don Ottavio (*Don Giovanni*), Belmonte & Pedrillo★ (*Entführung aus dem Serail*), Tamino (*Zauberflöte*); MUSSORGSKY: Shuisky★ (*Boris Godunov*), Vassily Golitsin (*Khovanshchina*); ROSSINI: Narciso★ (*Turco in Italia*); SCHOENBERG: Aron★; SHOSTAKOVICH: Sergei (*Katerina Ismailova*); SMETANA: Hans (*Bartered Bride*); STRAUSS, J: Alfred (*Fledermaus*); STRAUSS, R: Aegisth (*Elektra*), Herodes★ (*Salome*); STRAVINSKY: Tom Rakewell★ (*Rake's Progress*); TCHAIKOVSKY: Lenski (*Eugene Onegin*); VERDI: Rodolfo (*Luisa Miller*); WAGNER: David (*Meistersinger*), Loge★ (*Rheingold*), Mime (*Rheingold★, Siegfried★*), Walther v d Vogelweide (*Tannhäuser*); WEBER: Max (*Freischütz*); WEILL: Jim Mahoney★ (*Aufstieg und Fall der Stadt Mahagonny*). **World premieres:** EGK: Chlestakov (*Revisor*) Stuttgart 1957; ORFF: Oedipus (*Oedipus der Tyrann*) Stuttgart 1959; KLEBE: Oberst (*Jakobowsky und der Oberst*) Hamburg 1965. Recorded for: Decca, DG. Video/Film: (*Revisor*); (*Entführung*); (*Mahagonny*); (*Resurrection*). Gives recitals. Appears with symphony orchestra. Teaches voice. Coaches repertoire. **Res:** Statzeng 4, A3400 Klosterneuburg, Austria.

STRASFOGEL, IAN. Stages/produces opera, theater & film and is an author. American. Gen Dir & Res Stage Dir, Opera Socy of Washington, DC 1972-75. Born 5 Apr 1940, New York. Wife Judith Norell, occupation harpsichordist. Studied: Harvard Univ, USA; Walter Felsenstein. Operatic training as asst stage dir at New York City Opera 1962-63. **Operatic debut:** *Don Giovanni* New York City Opera. Awards: Phi Beta Kappa, Harvard Univ. Previous adm positions in opera: Art Adv, Philadelphia Lyric Opera 1973-74; Dir, Augusta Opera, GA; Music Theatre Project Tanglewood, MA 1971-73; Op Dept, New England Consv, Boston 1968-72.

Directed/produced opera for major companies in HOL: Amsterdam; USA: Baltimore, Kansas City, New York City Opera, Philadelphia Lyric, St Paul, Washington DC. **Operas staged with these companies incl** BIZET: *Carmen;* CAVALLI: *Calisto★;* DONIZETTI: *Lucia;* FLOYD: *Of Mice and Men★;* LIGETI: *Aventures/Nouvelles Aventures★;* MAXWELL-DAVIES: *Eight Songs for a Mad King★;* MENOTTI: *Medium;* MONTE-VERDI: *Combattimento di Tancredi, Favola d'Orfeo, Incoronazione di Poppea, Ritorno d'Ulisse★;* MOZART: *Zauberflöte;* OFFEN-BACH: *Contes d'Hoffmann;* PUCCINI: *Gianni Schicchi★, Butterfly, Suor Angelica, Tabarro★, Tosca;* SATIE: *Socrate★;* STRAUSS, R: *Salome★;* STRAVINSKY: *Oedipus Rex, Rake's Progress★, Rossignol;* VERDI: *Macbeth★, Otello★, Traviata;* WEILL: *Aufstieg und Fall der Stadt Mahagonny.* Also BIRTWISTLE: *Down by the Greenwood Side★;* OFFENBACH: *Ba-Ta-Clan★, Croquefer★.* **Operatic world premieres:** MA-DERNA: *Satyricon* Netherlands Opera, Amsterdam 1973. **Res:** 915 West End Ave, New York, NY 10025, USA. **Mgmt:** CAM/USA; HPL/UK.

STRASFOGEL, IGNACE. Conductor of opera and symphony; composer. American. Principal Cond, Opéra du Rhin, Strasbourg. Born 17 Jul 1909,

Warsaw, Poland. Wife Alma Lubin. Two children. Studied: Hochschule für Musik, Berlin; incl piano. Plays the piano. Operatic training as asst cond at Staatsoper, Berlin; Municipal Opera, Düsseldorf. **Operatic debut:** *Eugene Onegin* Metropolitan Opera, New York 1958. Symphonic debut: New York Phil 1945. Previous occupations: accomp and coach; official pianist NY Phil 1935-45. Awards: Mendelssohn State Prize for Composition, Germany; Liberation Medal, King Christian X, Denmark.

Conducted with major companies in FRA: Strasbourg; SWI: Geneva; USA: Cincinnati, New York Met, St Paul. **Operas with these companies incl** BARBER: *Vanessa;* BEETHOVEN: *Fidelio;* BIZET: *Carmen★;* DONIZETTI: *Lucia;* GOU-NOD: *Faust;* MILHAUD: *Abandon d'Ariane;* MOZART: *Così fan tutte, Don Giovanni, Nozze di Figaro, Zauberflöte★;* OFFENBACH: *Périchole;* PUCCINI: *Bohème, Butterfly★, Tosca;* ROSSINI: *Barbiere di Siviglia;* STRAUSS, J: *Fledermaus★;* STRAUSS, R: *Elektra★, Rosenkavalier★;* TCHAIKOVSKY: *Eugene Onegin;* VERDI: *Aida, Luisa Miller★, Rigoletto, Traviata;* WAGNER: *Fliegende Holländer★, Meistersinger★, Rheingold, Tannhäuser.* Also BARBER: *Antony and Cleopatra;* DONIZETTI: *Betly;* GLUCK: *Ivrogne corrigé.* Conducted major orch in USA/Canada, Cent/S America. **Res:** 8 quai Lezay Marnesia, Strasbourg, France.

STRATAS, TERESA. Lyric soprano. Canadian. Born 26 May 1938, Toronto. Studied: Mme Irene Jessner, Toronto; Toronto Consv, Univ of Toronto.

Sang with major companies in AUS: Salzburg Fest, Vienna Staatsoper; CAN: Montreal/Quebec, Ottawa, Toronto, Vancouver; FRA: Paris; FR GER: Berlin Deutsche Oper, Frankfurt, Hamburg, Munich Staatsoper; HOL: Amsterdam; ITA: Milan La Scala; UK: London Royal; USSR: Leningrad Kirov, Moscow Bolshoi; USA: Cincinnati, Houston, New York Met, Philadelphia Grand & Lyric, San Francisco Opera. **Roles with these companies incl** BERG: Lulu; BIZET: Micaëla★ (*Carmen*); DVORAK: Rusalka★; GOUNOD: Marguerite★ (*Faust*); HUMPERDINCK: Gretel★; MENOTTI: Sardule★ (*Dernier sauvage*); MOZART: Despina★ (*Così fan tutte*), Zerlina★ (*Don Giovanni*), Susanna★ & Cherubino★ (*Nozze di Figaro*); OFFENBACH: Antonia★ (*Contes d'Hoffmann*), Périchole★; PUCCINI: Mimi★ (*Bohème*), Lauretta★ (*Gianni Schicchi*), Cio-Cio-San★ (*Butterfly*), Magda★ (*Rondine*), Tosca, Liù★ (*Turandot*); SMETANA: Marie★ (*Bartered Bride*); STRAUSS, R: Komponist★ (*Ariadne auf Naxos*); TCHAIKOVSKY: Tatiana★ (*Eugene Onegin*), Lisa★ (*Pique Dame*); VERDI: Desdemona★ (*Otello*), Violetta★ (*Traviata*). **World premieres:** FALLA: (*Atlantida*) La Scala Milan 1962. Recorded for: Polydor, Eurodisc. Film: Salome; Tatiana (*Eugene Onegin*); (*Rondine*); Marie (*Bartered Bride*). **Mgmt:** HPL/UK.

STREHLER, GIORGIO. Stages/produces opera. Italian. Fest Supervisor & Resident Stage Dir, Salzburg Festival since 1973; Art Consult to Karajan. Born 1921, Italy. **Operatic debut:** *Traviata* La Scala, Milan 1947.

Directed/produced opera for major companies in AUS: Salzburg Fest; FRA: Paris; ITA: Florence

Maggio & Comunale, Milan La Scala, Rome Opera; et al. **Operas staged with these companies incl** BEETHOVEN: *Fidelio;* DESSAU: *Verurteilung des Lukullus;* LEONCAVALLO: *Pagliacci;* MASCAGNI: *Cavalleria rusticana;* MOZART: *Entführung aus dem Serail, Nozze di Figaro, Zauberflöte;* VERDI: *Rigoletto, Simon Boccanegra;* WEILL: *Aufstieg und Fall der Stadt Mahagonny;* et al.

STREICH, RITA. Coloratura soprano. German. Resident mem: Staatsoper, Vienna. Born 18 Dec 1920, Barnaul, Russia. Husband Dieter Berger, occupation theater researcher. One child. Studied: Paula Klötzer, Augsburg; Maria Ivogün, Erna Berger, W Domgraf-Fassbaender, Berlin. **Debut:** Zerbinetta *(Ariadne auf Naxos)* Aussig 1944. Awards: Austrian Kammersängerin; German Bundesverdienstkreuz First Class; Orphée d'Or, Best Singing of the Year; var record awds.

Sang with major companies in ARG: Buenos Aires; AUS: Salzburg Fest, Vienna Staatsoper & Volksoper; FRA: Aix-en-Provence Fest, Paris; FR GER: Bayreuth Fest, Berlin Deutsche Oper, Hamburg, Munich Staatsoper, Stuttgart, Wiesbaden; GER DR: Berlin Komische Oper & Staatsoper; ITA: Milan La Scala, Naples, Rome Teatro dell'Opera, Venice; NOR: Oslo; UK: Glyndebourne Fest; USA: Chicago, San Francisco Opera. **Roles with these companies incl** DONIZETTI: Norina *(Don Pasquale),* Adina *(Elisir);* FLOTOW: Lady Harriet *(Martha);* GLUCK: Amor *(Orfeo ed Euridice);* HUMPERDINCK: Gretel‡; MOZART: Despina‡ *(Così fan tutte),* Zerlina *(Don Giovanni),* Konstanze & Blondchen‡ *(Entführung aus dem Serail),* Serpetta‡ *(Finta giardiniera),* Mlle Silberklang‡ *(Schauspieldirektor),* Susanna*‡ *(Nozze di Figaro),* Zaïde*‡, Königin der Nacht *(Zauberflöte);* NICOLAI: Frau Fluth‡ *(Lustigen Weiber);* OFFENBACH: Olympia‡ & Antonia‡ & Giulietta *(Contes d'Hoffmann);* PERGOLESI: Serpina‡ *(Serva padrona);* ROSSINI: Rosina‡ *(Barbiere di Siviglia);* STRAUSS, J: Adele*‡ *(Fledermaus);* STRAUSS, R: Zerbinetta‡ *(Ariadne auf Naxos),* Sophie‡ *(Rosenkavalier);* VERDI: Oscar *(Ballo in maschera),* Gilda *(Rigoletto),* Violetta*‡ *(Traviata);* WEBER: Aennchen‡ *(Freischütz).* **World premieres:** ERBSE: Marquise von O *(Julietta)* Salzburg Fest 1959; KUESTERER: Olivia *(Was ihr wollt)* 1953. Recorded for: DG, Angel, Philips, EMI. Gives recitals. Appears with symphony orchestra. Teaches voice. On faculty of Sommerakademie Mozarteum, Salzburg; Folkwanghochschule, Essen; Musikakademie Vienna; Prof. **Res:** Kärntnerstr 23, Vienna, Austria. Mgmt: CAM/USA.

STROS, LADISLAV. Stages/produces opera & television. Also designs sets & costumes. Czechoslovakian. Born 22 Aug 1926, Husinek, CSR. Wife Libuse, occupation singer. One child. Studied: music, piano, violin and voice. Operatic training as asst stage dir at National Theater, Prague. **Operatic debut:** *Jan Vyrava* Ustí Nad Labem, CSSR 1950. Previous occupation: sculptor. Awards: First Prize, Fest Wiesbaden 1973; Golden Pen, Music Critics.

Directed/produced opera for major companies in AUS: Salzburg Fest; BEL: Brussels; BUL: Sofia; CZE: Brno, Prague National; FRA: Bordeaux;

FR GER: Bielefeld, Cologne, Dortmund, Frankfurt, Karlsruhe, Kassel, Kiel, Krefeld, Nürnberg, Wiesbaden; HOL: Amsterdam; ITA: Parma, Venice; POL: Warsaw; UK: Edinburgh Fest; YUG: Zagreb. **Operas staged with these companies incl** BEETHOVEN: *Fidelio;* BERLIOZ: *Benvenuto Cellini;* BIZET: *Carmen*†; BORODIN: *Prince Igor;* BRITTEN: *Albert Herring;* CHARPENTIER: *Louise;* DONIZETTI: *Don Pasquale*†; DVORAK: *Rusalka*†; GOUNOD: *Faust;* JANACEK: *Cunning Little Vixen*†, *From the House of the Dead;* LEONCAVALLO: *Pagliacci*†; MASCAGNI: *Cavalleria rusticana*†; MOZART: *Così fan tutte*, *Don Giovanni*†, *Entführung aus dem Serail, Nozze di Figaro, Zauberflöte*†; MUSSORGSKY: *Boris Godunov*†, *Khovanshchina*†; OFFENBACH: *Contes d'Hoffmann*†; PERGOLESI: *Serva padrona*†; PUCCINI: *Tosca*, *Turandot*†; RAVEL: *Heure espagnole;* ROSSINI: *Barbiere di Siviglia*; SMETANA: *Bartered Bride*†, *Libuse*†, *Two Widows*†; VERDI: *Don Carlo, Forza del destino*†, *Rigoletto*, *Trovatore, Vespri*†; WAGNER: *Walküre*†; WEBER: *Freischütz.* Operatic Video—Prague TV: *Nozze di Figaro;* KREJCI: *Uproar in Ephesus.* Teaches at Consv, Prague. **Res:** Na Rejdisti 1, Prague, CSSR. Mgmt: PRG/CZE; PAS/FRG.

STRUMMER, PETER. Bass-baritone. Canadian. Resident mem: Minnesota Opera Co, Minneapolis. Born 8 Sep 1948, Vienna, Austria. Widowed. Studied: Cleveland Inst of Music, Yi Kwei Szi, O, USA; Eleanor Steber; Juilliard School American Opera Center, New York. **Debut:** Leporello *(Don Giovanni)* Minnesota Opera Co 1973. Awards: Cleveland Inst of Music, Juilliard School, schlshps; Goldovsky Awd, Cleveland Inst; M B Rockefeller Fund Grant; New Artists Assoc of BC Awd; Beryl Rubenstein Awd; James C Brooks Awd, Canada.

Sang with major companies in USA: Kansas City, Minneapolis, San Francisco Opera, Santa Fe. **Roles with these companies incl** DONIZETTI: Dulcamara *(Elisir);* JANACEK: Forester* & Harasta* *(Cunning Little Vixen);* MOZART: Guglielmo* *(Così fan tutte),* Leporello* *(Don Giovanni),* Papageno* *(Zauberflöte);* NICOLAI: Falstaff* *(Lustigen Weiber).* Also MONTEVERDI: Tancredi* *(Combattimento di Tancredi e Clorinda).* **World premieres:** SUSA: Neighboring King *(Transformations)* Minnesota Opera 1973; BALK/BRUNELLE: Bass role *(Newest Opera in the World)* Minnesota Opera, Minneapolis 1974. Gives recitals. Appears with symphony orchestra. Mgmt: DBA/USA.

STRYCZEK, KARL-HEINZ. Character baritone. German. Resident mem: Staatsoper Dresden, Staatsoper Berlin, Ger DR. Born 5 May 1937, Nikelsdorf. Wife Gisela Harnapp, occupation ophthalmologist. One child. Studied: Hochschule für Musik, Prof Peter Russ, Leipzig. **Debut:** Germont *(Traviata)* Landesbühnen Sachsen 1964. Awards: First Prize, Schumann Cont, Zwickau, Ministry of Culture Ger DR 1963; Diploma Vienna and Toulouse 1959.

Sang with major companies in FIN: Helsinki; FRA: Paris; FR GER: Wiesbaden; GER DR: Berlin Staatsoper, Dresden; USSR: Leningrad Kirov. **Roles with these companies incl** BEETHO-

VEN: Don Pizarro★ (*Fidelio*); BERG: Wozzeck★; LEONCAVALLO: Tonio★ (*Pagliacci*); MASCAGNI: Alfio★ (*Cavalleria rusticana*); MOZART: Conte Almaviva & Figaro★ (*Nozze di Figaro*); ORFF: Solo★ (*Carmina burana*), König★ (*Kluge*); PUCCINI: Jack Rance (*Fanciulla del West*), Scarpia★ (*Tosca*); VERDI: Amonasro★ (*Aida*), Falstaff★, Don Carlo★ (*Forza del destino*), Iago★ (*Otello*). Also TCHAIKOVSKY: Count (*Sorceress*). **World premieres:** ZIMMERMANN: Weiszmantel (*Levins Mühle*) Staatsoper Dresden 1973; KUNAD: Sabellicus, Staatsoper Berlin 1974. Appears with symphony orchestra. Coaches repertoire. **Res:** Bennostr 11, 8122 Radebeul, Ger DR. Mgmt: KDR/GDR.

STÜCKMANN, WERNER. Bass-baritone & bassobuffo. German. Resident mem: Staatstheater am Gärtnerplatz, Munich. Born 13 Aug 1936, Dortmund, Germany. Wife Doris. One child. Studied: Städt Konsv, Dortmund, FR Ger. **Debut:** Masetto (*Don Giovanni*) Städtische Bühnen Dortmund 1961. Previous occupations: export/import business.
Sang with major companies in FR GER: Darmstadt, Dortmund. **Roles with these companies incl** BEETHOVEN: Rocco★ (*Fidelio*); LORTZING: Baculus★ (*Wildschütz*), Van Bett★ (*Zar und Zimmermann*); MOZART: Don Alfonso★ (*Così fan tutte*), Leporello (*Don Giovanni*), Figaro (*Nozze di Figaro*), Sarastro (*Zauberflöte*); PUCCINI: Colline (*Bohème*); ROSSINI: Dott Bartolo★ (*Barbiere di Siviglia*), Don Magnifico (*Cenerentola*); THOMAS: Lothario (*Mignon*); VERDI: Grande Inquisitore★ (*Don Carlo*), Fra Melitone★ (*Forza del destino*), Banquo★ (*Macbeth*), Zaccaria★ (*Nabucco*); WAGNER: Daland (*Fliegende Holländer*), Landgraf (*Tannhäuser*), König Marke (*Tristan und Isolde*); WEBER: Kaspar★ (*Freischütz*). Appears with symphony orchestra. **Res:** Emmeringer Str 5, 8031 Eichenau, FR Ger.

STUTZMANN, CHRISTIANE. Spinto. French. Born 7 Nov 1939, Pont-à-Mousson, France. Husband Christian Dupuy, occupation singing & acting teacher. One child. Studied: Consv Ntl Supérieur de Musique de Paris, Jean Giraudeau; Consv de Musique de Nancy, piano and organ. **Debut:** Tosca, Opéra de Paris 1969. Awards: First Prize in Voice, Consv Paris 1961; First Prize of Golden Voices 1962; First Prize for Excellence in Song and Opera, Nancy 1960; Chevalier des Arts et Lettres 1974, Ministère des Affaires Culturelles, Paris.
Sang with major companies in BEL: Brussels, Liège; BRA: Rio de Janeiro; FRA: Bordeaux, Lyon, Marseille, Nancy, Nice, Paris, Rouen, Strasbourg, Toulouse; ITA: Naples, Turin, Venice; MON: Monte Carlo. **Roles with these companies incl** BECAUD: Maureen★ (*Opéra d'Aran*); BERLIOZ: Béatrice; BIZET: Micaëla (*Carmen*); BORODIN: Jaroslavna★ (*Prince Igor*); CHABRIER: Alexina★ (*Roi malgré lui*); CHARPENTIER: Louise★; GIORDANO: Maddalena (*Andrea Chénier*); GOUNOD: Marguerite★ (*Faust*), Mireille; LEONCAVALLO: Nedda★ (*Pagliacci*); MARTINU: Katerina★ (*Griechische Passion*); MASCAGNI: Santuzza★ (*Cavalleria rusticana*); MENOTTI: Magda Sorel (*Consul*); MOZART: Contessa★ (*Nozze di Figaro*); PUCCINI: Mimi★ & Musetta (*Bohème*), Cio-Cio-San★ (*But-*

terfly), Manon★, Giorgetta (*Tabarro*), Tosca★; RAVEL: Concepcion★ (*Heure espagnole*); ROSSINI: Mathilde (*Guillaume Tell*); SMETANA: Marinka (*The Kiss*); TCHAIKOVSKY: Tatiana (*Eugene Onegin*), Lisa (*Pique Dame*); VERDI: Aida, Desdemona (*Otello*). Also MASSENET: Grisélidis; SAUGUET: Clélia Conti (*Chartreuse de Parme*); MARTINU: Involende★ (*Trois souhaits*); DE BANFIELD: Alissa★. **World premieres:** ROSSELLINI: Mara (*L'Annonce faite à Marie*) Opéra-Comique Paris 1970; SEMENOFF: Elle (*La Contagion*) Nancy 1972; Purmelande (*Sire Halewyn*) Nantes 1974. Recorded for: Pathé-Marconi, Sonopresse, Vega, Guild Intl du Disque. Video/Film—ORTF TV: Tosca; Marguerite (*Faust*). **Res:** Ave de Joinville 9, 94 Nogent/Marne, France. Mgmt: RNR/SWI; BCP/FRA.

SUITNER, OTMAR. Conductor of opera and symphony. Gen Mus Dir & Princ Cond, Staatsoper Berlin, Ger DR 1964-75; after Aug 1976 Gen Mus Dir, Deutsche Oper, Berlin, FR Ger. Also Resident Cond, Staatskapelle, Berlin, Ger DR. Born 16 May 1922, Innsbruck, Austria. Wife Marita. Studied: Mozarteum Salzburg, Prof Ledwinka, Clemens Krauss; incl piano. Operatic training as repetiteur & asst cond at Landestheater Innsbruck 1942-44. **Operatic debut:** Landestheater Innsbruck 1942. Symphonic debut: Mozarteum Orch, Salzburg 1941. Previous occupations: concert pianist. Awards: Prof, Austrian Gvnmt; Commendatore Gregorius Orden, Pope Paul. Previous adm positions in opera: Gen Music Dir, Staatsoper Dresden, Ger DR 1960-64.
Conducted with major companies in ARG: Buenos Aires; AUS: Bregenz Fest, Vienna Staatsoper; CZE: Prague Smetana; FIN: Helsinki; FRA: Aix-en-Provence Fest, Paris; GRE: Athens Fest; FR GER: Bayreuth Fest, Dortmund, Essen, Hamburg, Kassel; GER DR: Berlin Staatsoper, Dresden; ITA: Bologna, Florence Maggio & Comunale, Genoa, Trieste, Venice; POL: Warsaw; USSR: Moscow Bolshoi; USA: San Francisco Opera. **Operas with these companies incl** BEETHOVEN: *Fidelio★; *BIZET: *Carmen;* GLUCK: *Cadi dupé‡; *HANDEL: *Acis and Galatea;* HUMPERDINCK: *Hänsel und Gretel‡;* LORTZING: *Wildschütz;* MOZART: *Così fan tutte★‡, Don Giovanni★, Entführung aus dem Serail★‡, Nozze di Figaro★‡, Zauberflöte★‡;* NICOLAI: *Lustigen Weiber;* PUCCINI: *Bohème★, Gianni Schicchi, Suor Angelica, Tabarro, Tosca★;* ROSSINI: *Barbiere di Siviglia★;* SMETANA: *Bartered Bride‡;* STRAUSS, J: *Fledermaus★;* STRAUSS, R: *Arabella, Ariadne auf Naxos, Capriccio, Daphne★, Elektra★, Frau ohne Schatten★, Rosenkavalier★, Salome★‡, Schweigsame Frau;* VERDI: *Rigoletto;* WAGNER: *Fliegende Holländer★, Lohengrin★, Meistersinger★, Parsifal, Rheingold★, Walküre★, Siegfried★, Götterdämmerung★, Tannhäuser★, Tristan und Isolde★;* WEBER: *Abu Hassan‡, Freischütz★.* **World premieres:** DESSAU: *Puntila* 1966, *Einstein* 1973, both Staatsoper Berlin, Ger DR. Recorded for Columbia, Philips, Eterna, Teldec, Eurodisc. Conducted major orch in Europe & Asia. Previous positions as Mus Dir with major orch: Staatskapelle Dresden 1960-64. Teaches at Sommerakad Mozarteum, Salzburg. Mgmt: MAA/USA.

SUKIS, LILIAN. Lyric soprano. Canadian. Resident mem: Bayerische Staatsoper, Munich; Staatsoper, Vienna. Born Lithuania. Studied: McMaster Univ, Canada; Royal Consv Toronto, Mme Irene Jessner. Awards: Royal Society of Canada Schlshp 1962.
Sang with major companies in ARG: Buenos Aires; AUS: Vienna Staatsoper; CAN: Toronto; FR GER: Cologne, Frankfurt, Munich Staatsoper; USA: New York Met; et al. **Roles with these companies incl** BIZET: Micaëla (*Carmen*); BRITTEN: Lady Billows (*Albert Herring*); DEBUSSY: Mélisande; GLUCK: Euridice; GOUNOD: Marguerite (*Faust*); MOZART: Fiordiligi (*Così fan tutte*), Contessa (*Nozze di Figaro*), Pamina (*Zauberflöte*); PROKOFIEV: Pauline (*Gambler*); PUCCINI: Mimi (*Bohème*); VERDI: Luisa Miller; et al. **World premieres:** WILLAN: Deirdre, Toronto; YUN: Sim Tjong, Munich Staatsoper 1972. Gives recitals.

SULLIVAN, DAN; né Roger Daniel Sullivan. Bass-baritone. American. Born 13 Feb 1940, Eureka, IL, USA. Wife Maria K, occupation artist. Two children. Studied: Illinois Wesleyan Univ, Bloomington, IL; Northwestern Univ, Evanston, IL; Boris Goldovsky Opera Inst, New York; Hermanus Baer. **Debut:** Valentin (*Faust*) Omaha Opera Co 1970. Previous occupations: asst prof voice & opera. Awards: Gerald Chramer Schlshp, Northwestern Univ, Evanston, IL, USA.
Sang with major companies in USA: Kansas City, Omaha, San Francisco Opera & Spring Opera, Washington DC. **Roles with these companies incl** BIZET: Escamillo (*Carmen*); BUSONI: Doktor Faust★; DONIZETTI: Dott Malatesta & Don Pasquale★ (*Don Pasquale*), Belcore★ & Dulcamara★ (*Elisir*); LEONCAVALLO: Tonio (*Pagliacci*); MOZART: Guglielmo★ & Don Alfonso★ (*Così fan tutte*), Leporello★ & Don Giovanni★ (*Don Giovanni*), Conte Almaviva★ & Figaro★ (*Nozze di Figaro*), Papageno★‡ (*Zauberflöte*); PERGOLESI: Tracolino (*Maestro di musica*); PUCCINI: Marcello (*Bohème*), Gianni Schicchi★, Sharpless★ (*Butterfly*), Scarpia★ (*Tosca*); ROSSINI: Figaro★ & Dott Bartolo★ (*Barbiere di Siviglia*), Don Magnifico★ (*Cenerentola*); VERDI: Amonasro★ (*Aida*), Rigoletto★, Germont★ (*Traviata*); WAGNER: Beckmesser★ (*Meistersinger*). Also STRAUSS, J: Dr Falke (*Fledermaus*); FLOYD: Slim (*Of Mice and Men*); DONIZETTI: Impresario★ (*Convenienze/Viva la Mamma*). Gives recitals. Appears with symphony orchestra. Teaches voice. Mem: Affiliate Artists Inc, New York, and Ottumwa (Iowa) Arts Council.

SULZBERGER, NIKOLAUS. Stages/produces opera. German. Dir of the Opera & Resident Stage Dir, Städtische Bühnen, Essen. Born 19 Dec 1938, Zwickau. Divorced. Two children. Studied: dramaturgy and art history Cologne, Berlin & Vienna; also music & piano. Operatic training as asst stage dir at Deutsche Oper Berlin, FR Ger 1963-71. **Operatic debut:** *Trovatore* Teatro Grande, Brescia, Italy 1970.
Directed/produced opera for major companies in FR GER: Berlin Deutsche Oper, Bielefeld, Darmstadt, Essen, Frankfurt, Kassel; HOL: Amsterdam. **Operas staged with these companies incl** BEETHOVEN: *Fidelio;* BRITTEN: *Rape of Lucretia;* DONIZETTI: *Convenienze/Viva la Mamma, Don Pasquale;* GAY/Britten: *Beggar's Opera;* MASCAGNI: *Cavalleria rusticana;* MOZART: *Don Giovanni, Entführung aus dem Serail;* OFFENBACH: *Contes d'Hoffmann;* PAISIELLO: *Barbiere di Siviglia;* PUCCINI: *Tosca, Turandot;* RAVEL: *Heure espagnole;* ROSSINI: *Barbiere di Siviglia;* STRAUSS, R: *Arabella, Salome;* VERDI: *Rigoletto, Trovatore★;* WEBER: *Freischütz.*

SUPPA, CARL M. American. Art Dir, Opera Company of Philadelphia, 1518 Walnut St, Philadelphia, PA 19102; also of Light Opera Co of Philadelphia. In charge of art policy, mus & dram matters, tech. Is also a conductor. Born 2 Nov 1925, Philadelphia. Wife Veronica, occupation teacher. Three children. Studied: Combs Coll of Music, Philadelphia. Plays the piano. Previous occupations: teacher. Form positions, primarily musical: Cincinnati Opera, Philadelphia Lyric as coach, prompter, chorus master; Gen Mgr, Philadelphia Lyric 1974-75. Started with present company in 1963 as accompanist; in present position since 1974. World premieres at theaters under his management: MENOTTI: *Hero* Philadelphia 1976. Awards: Hon DM, Combs Coll of Music; Finalist, Compt Arturo Toscanini, Rome. Initiated major policy changes including expansion of number of prods and perfs through merger of Philadelphia Lyric and Philadelphia Grand Opera Cos. Mem of OPERA America. **Res:** Springfield, PA, USA.

SUSSKIND, WALTER JAN. Conductor of opera and symphony; composer. British. Mus Dir, St Louis Symph, MO, USA 1968-75. Born 1 May 1913, Prague. Wife Janis. Studied: Prague Consv, George Szell; incl piano, French horn. Plays the piano. Operatic training as repetiteur, asst cond & chorus master at German Opera, Prague 1933-38. **Operatic debut:** *Traviata* German Opera, Prague 1936. Symphonic debut: Royal Liverpool Phil, UK 1945. Previous occupations: concert pianist. Awards: Hon DH So Illinois Univ; Hon DFA Washington Univ; Israel Independence Plaque; Mem Ntl Socy of Literature & the Arts. Previous administr positions in opera: Mus Dir, Carl Rosa Opera, London 1942-45; Principal Guest Cond, Sadler's Wells, London 1945-47 and Ntl Opera of Canada, Toronto 1956-65.
Conducted with major companies in AUSTRL: Sydney; CAN: Montreal/Quebec, Ottawa, Toronto; CZE: Prague Smetana; FR GER: Berlin Deutsche Oper, Düsseldorf-Duisburg, Hamburg; ISR: Tel Aviv; UK: Aldeburgh Fest, Edinburgh Fest, Scottish, Glyndebourne Fest, London English National; USA: New York City Opera, Washington DC. **Operas with these companies incl** BARTOK: *Bluebeard's Castle*‡; BIZET: *Carmen★;* BOITO: *Mefistofele;* FLOTOW: *Martha;* GOUNOD: *Faust;* HUMPERDINCK: *Hänsel und Gretel;* JANACEK: *Makropoulos Affair★;* LEONCAVALLO: *Pagliacci;* MASCAGNI: *Cavalleria rusticana;* MENOTTI: *Telephone;* MOZART: *Così fan tutte, Don Giovanni, Entführung aus dem Serail, Nozze di Figaro★, Zauberflöte;* MUSSORGSKY: *Boris Godunov, Fair at Sorochinsk;* OFFENBACH: *Contes d'Hoffmann;* ORFF: *Carmina burana★;* PROKOFIEV: *Love for Three Oranges;* PUCCINI: *Bohème, Gianni*

Schicchi, Butterfly, Tosca, Turandot; RIMSKY-KORSAKOV: *Coq d'or★;* ROSSINI: *Barbiere di Siviglia, Cenerentola;* SHOSTAKOVICH: *Katerina Ismailova;* SMETANA: *Bartered Bride;* STRAUSS, J: *Fledermaus;* STRAUSS, R: *Ariadne auf Naxos, Elektra, Rosenkavalier, Salome;* STRAVINSKY: *Oedipus Rex★, Rossignol;* TCHAIKOVSKY: *Eugene Onegin;* VERDI: *Aida, Ballo in maschera, Macbeth, Nabucco, Rigoletto, Traviata, Trovatore;* WAGNER: *Fliegende Holländer, Meistersinger, Walküre★.* Recorded for Bartok Records. Video—Toronto CBC TV: *Eugene Onegin, Zauberflöte, Elektra, Peter Grimes.* Conducted major orch in Europe, USA/Canada, Cent/S America, Asia, Africa, Austrl. Previous positions as Mus Dir with major orch: Scottish Ntl Symph, Glasgow 1946-52; Victoria Symph, Melbourne, Australia 1953-55; Toronto Symph, Ont, Canada 1956-65. Teaches at So Illinois Univ, Edwardsville, USA. **Res:** St Louis, MO, USA. Mgmt: CAM/USA; LAL/UK.

SUTEJ, JOSIP. Tenore spinto. Yugoslavian. Resident mem: Croatian National Opera, Zagreb; National Opera, Belgrade. Born 21 Nov 1920, Vinica. Wife Vinka Seroncic, occupation singer in radio chorus. Two children. Studied: Zlatko Sir, Liga Dorogy, Ancica Mitrovic, Zagreb. **Debut:** Hans (*Bartered Bride*) Ntl Opera Zagreb 1946. Awards: Diploma, Conc Treviso, Italy.

Sang with major companies in GER DR: Berlin Komische Oper; ITA: Genoa, Naples, Trieste; USSR: Kiev, Moscow Stanislavski; YUG: Dubrovnik, Zagreb, Belgrade. **Roles with these companies incl** BIZET: Don José (*Carmen*); CILEA: Maurizio (*A. Lecouvreur*); DELIBES: Gérald (*Lakmé*); GOTOVAC: Mitcha★ (*Ero der Schelm*); MASCAGNI: Turiddu★ (*Cavalleria rusticana*); MASSENET: Werther; ORFF: Haemon (*Antigonae*); PUCCINI: Rodolfo★ (*Bohème*), Pinkerton★ (*Butterfly*), Cavaradossi (*Tosca*); SMETANA: Hans★ (*Bartered Bride*); STRAUSS, J: Eisenstein (*Fledermaus*); VERDI: Riccardo (*Ballo in maschera*), Duca di Mantova (*Rigoletto*), Alfredo (*Traviata*), Manrico (*Trovatore*). Also GOTOVAC: Bojan (*Morana*). Gives recitals. Appears with symphony orchestra. Teaches voice. Coaches repertoire. Mgmt: CDK/YUG.

SUTHERLAND, JOAN. Dramatic coloratura soprano. Australian. Born 7 Nov 1926, Sydney. Husband Richard Bonynge, occupation orchestra and opera conductor. One son. Studied: mother, Clive Carey, Richard Bonynge. **Debut:** Erste Dame (*Zauberflöte*) Covent Garden, London 1952. Previous occupations: priv secy. Awards: Commander of the British Empire; Hon D Aberdeen Univ, UK; Hon DA Rider Coll.

Sang with major companies in ARG: Buenos Aires; AUSTRL: Sydney; AUS: Vienna Staatsoper; CAN: Vancouver; DEN: Copenhagen; FRA: Paris; FR GER: Hamburg; HOL: Amsterdam; ITA: Florence Maggio, Genoa, Milan La Scala, Naples, Palermo, Venice; POR: Lisbon; SPA: Barcelona, Canary Isl Las Palmas Fest; UK: Aldeburgh Fest, Edinburgh Fest, Glyndebourne Fest, London Royal; USA: Boston, Chicago, Dallas, Hartford, Houston, Miami, New Orleans, New York Met, Philadelphia Grand & Lyric, San Antonio, San Diego, San Francisco Opera, Seattle. **Roles with these companies incl** BELLINI: Beatrice

di Tenda‡, Norma★‡, Elvira★‡ (*Puritani*), Amina‡ (*Sonnambula*); BIZET: Micaëla‡ (*Carmen*); BRITTEN: Penelope★ (*Gloriana*); DELIBES: Lakmé‡; DONIZETTI: Marie★‡ (*Fille du régiment*), Lucia★‡, Lucrezia Borgia, Maria Stuarda★‡; GOUNOD: Marguerite‡ (*Faust*); HANDEL: Alcina‡, Cleopatra★ (*Giulio Cesare*), Rodelinda★; MASSENET: Esclarmonde★; MEYERBEER: Marguerite de Valois‡ (*Huguenots*); MOZART: Vitellia (*Clemenza di Tito*), Donna Anna★‡ (*Don Giovanni*), Mme Herz (*Schauspieldirektor*), Contessa (*Nozze di Figaro*), Pamina & Königin der Nacht (*Zauberflöte*); OFFENBACH: Olympia★‡ & Antonia★‡ & Giulietta★‡ (*Contes d'Hoffmann*), Périchole; POULENC: Mme Lidoine (*Dialogues des Carmélites*); PURCELL: Dido; ROSSINI: Semiramide★‡; STRAUSS, J: Rosalinde★‡ (*Fledermaus*); SUTERMEISTER: Julia; THOMAS: Philine (*Mignon*); VERDI: Aida, Amelia (*Ballo in maschera*), Desdemona (*Otello*), Gilda★‡ (*Rigoletto*), Violetta★‡ (*Traviata*); WAGNER: Eva (*Meistersinger*); WEBER: Euryanthe, Agathe (*Freischütz*). Also PUCCINI: Turandot‡; DONIZETTI: Adina‡ (*Elisir*); HANDEL: Galatea‡; HAYDN: Orfeo. **World premieres:** TIPPETT: Jennifer (*Midsummer Marriage*) Covent Garden 1955. Recorded for: EMI, Decca/London. Video—Who's Afraid of Opera series. Gives recitals. Appears with symphony orchestra. **Res:** Les Avants, Switzerland. Mgmt: IWL/UK; COL/USA.

SUTTIE, ALAN. Conductor of opera and symphony. British. Resident Cond, Welsh National Opera, Cardiff, UK. Born 25 Feb 1938, Kirucaldy, Fife, Scotland. Wife Ann Caroline, occupation secy. Four children. Studied: Alexander Gibson, UK; also piano, trumpet, timpani, percussion. Plays the timpani, percussion. Operatic training as asst cond at Scottish Opera, Glasgow 1967-71. **Operatic debut:** *Elisir* Opera da Camera, Edinburgh, Scotland 1968. Symphonic debut: Scottish Ntl Symph, Aberdeen 1967. Previous occupations: principal timpanist BBC Symph. Awards: Assoc of Royal Coll of Music, ARCM; Gulbenkian Schlshp; Bulgin Silver Medal, Worshipful Co of Musicians.

Conducted with major companies in UK: Welsh National, Scottish, London Royal. **Operas with these companies incl** BIZET: *Pêcheurs de perles★;* DONIZETTI: *Elisir;* PUCCINI: *Bohème★, Gianni Schicchi★, Butterfly★, Suor Angelica★, Tabarro★, Turandot★;* STRAUSS, J: *Fledermaus★;* VERDI: *Aida★, Ballo in maschera★, Rigoletto★, Simon Boccanegra★.* Conducted major orch in Europe. **Res:** Folkestone, UK. Mgmt: GBN/UK.

SUTTON, VERN: né Everett Lavern Sutton. Lyric & buffo tenor. American. Resident mem: Minnesota Opera, Minneapolis, USA. Born 8 Apr 1938, Oklahoma City, OK, USA. Wife Phyllis. One child. Studied: Ethel Rader, Denison, TX; Roy A Schussler, Minneapolis, MN, USA; Luigi Ricci, Rome, Italy. **Debut:** John (*Masque of Angels*) Center Opera, Minneapolis 1963.

Sang with major companies in USA: Houston, Kansas City, Lake George, Minneapolis, St Paul, San Francisco Spring Opera. **Roles with these companies incl** BRITTEN: Albert Herring★, Male Chorus (*Rape of Lucretia*); KURKA: Schweik★ (*Good Soldier Schweik*); MONTEVERDI: Testo★

(*Combattimento di Tancredi*), Nero (*Incoronazione di Poppea*); MOZART: Ferrando (*Così fan tutte*), Don Ottavio★ (*Don Giovanni*), Pedrillo (*Entführung aus dem Serail*). Also HAYDN: Eclittico (*Mondo della luna*); BIRTWISTLE: Punch (*Punch and Judy*). **World premieres:** ARGENTO: Mr Owen (*Postcard from Morocco*) Center Opera, MN 1971; John (*Masque of Angels*) Center Opera, MN 1964; GESSNER: John Faustus (*Faust Counter Faust*) Center Opera, MN 1971; SUSA: Wizard (*Transformations*) Minnesota Opera, form Center Opera, MN 1973. Recorded for: Desto. Gives recitals. Appears with symphony orchestra. Coaches repertoire. On faculty of Univ of Minnesota. **Res:** 1805 Talmadge SE, Minneapolis, MN, USA.

SVACOV, VLADAN. Stages/produces opera, theater & television. Yugoslavian. Chief Dramaturg & Resident Stage Dir, Croatian National Theater, Zagreb. Born 27 Nov 1930, Zagreb. Divorced. One child. Studied: Acad for Theater and Cinematography, Zagreb. **Operatic debut:** *Rita* Croat Ntl Th, Zagreb 1967. Theater debut: National Theater, Dubrovnik 1961. Previous occupation: high school teacher & univ prof.

Directed/produced opera for major companies in YUG: Zagreb. **Operas staged with these companies incl** DONIZETTI: *Elisir*★*;* HUMPERDINCK: *Hänsel und Gretel*★*;* MOZART: *Nozze di Figaro*★*;* PUCCINI: *Gianni Schicchi;* WEILL: *Aufstieg und Fall der Stadt Mahagonny*★*, Dreigroschenoper.* Teaches at Acad for Theater and Cinematography. **Res:** Trg M Tita 5, Zagreb, Yugoslavia.

SVEHLA, ZDENEK. Lyric tenor. Czechoslovakian. Resident mem: National Theater, Prague. Born 16 Jul 1924, Brno, CSR. Wife Jarmila, occupation teacher, dancer. One child. Studied: Janácek Acad, Prof Sobesky, Brno; Apollo Granforte, Milan; Carlo Pollacco, Venice. **Debut:** Gabriele (*Simon Boccanegra*) Opera Olomouc, CSSR 1951.

Sang with major companies in AUS: Vienna Staatsoper; BEL: Brussels; CZE: Brno, Prague National; GRE: Athens National; FR GER: Wiesbaden, Wuppertal; ITA: Bologna, Milan La Scala, Naples; ROM: Bucharest; SPA: Barcelona; SWI: Basel, Zurich; UK: Edinburgh Fest; YUG: Zagreb, Belgrade. **Roles with these companies incl** AUBER: Alfonso (*Muette de Portici*); CHARPENTIER: Julien (*Louise*); GLUCK: Achille (*Iphigénie en Aulide*); GOLDMARK: Assad (*Königin von Saba*); GOUNOD: Roméo; JANACEK: Mazal (*Excursions of Mr Broucek*), Steva (*Jenufa*); LEONCAVALLO: Canio (*Pagliacci*); MASSENET: Des Grieux (*Manon*); MONIUSZKO: Jontek (*Halka*); MOZART: Tito (*Clemenza di Tito*), Ferrando★ (*Così fan tutte*), Don Ottavio★ (*Don Giovanni*), Belmonte (*Entführung aus dem Serail*), Tamino (*Zauberflöte*); OFFENBACH: Hoffmann; PROKOFIEV: Prince (*Love for Three Oranges*); PUCCINI: Rodolfo (*Bohème*), Pinkerton (*Butterfly*), Des Grieux (*Manon Lescaut*), Cavaradossi (*Tosca*); SMETANA: Hans (*Bartered Bride*), Vitek★ (*Secret*); STRAUSS, J: Eisenstein (*Fledermaus*); STRAUSS, R: Matteo★ (*Arabella*), Ein Sänger (*Rosenkavalier*); TCHAIKOVSKY: Lenski★ (*Eu-*

gene Onegin); VERDI: Radames (*Aida*), Riccardo (*Ballo in maschera*), Don Carlo, Duca di Mantova (*Rigoletto*), Gabriele‡ (*Simon Boccanegra*), Alfredo (*Traviata*). Also JANACEK: Kudrijash★ (*Katya Kabanova*). Recorded for: Supraphon. Film: Prince (*Rusalka*). **Res:** Sevastoposká 17, Prague, CSSR. Mgmt: PRG/CZE; VLD/AUS.

SVEJDA, MIROSLAV. Lyric tenor. Czechoslovakian. Resident mem: National Theater, Prague. Born 7 Dec 1939, Brno, CSR. Wife Jitka, occupation cultural officer. Four children. Studied: Prof Marie Reznícková, Brno; Prof Teodor Srubar, Prof Premysl Kocí, Prague. **Debut:** Pinkerton (*Butterfly*) National Theater, Prague 1970. Previous occupations: construction engineer.

Sang with major companies in CZE: Brno, Prague National; USA: Boston; YUG: Zagreb, Belgrade. **Roles with these companies incl** DONIZETTI: Ernesto★ (*Don Pasquale*), Tonio★ (*Fille du régiment*); JANACEK: Boris★ (*Katya Kabanova*); MOZART: Don Ottavio★ (*Don Giovanni*); PUCCINI: Rodolfo★ (*Bohème*), Pinkerton★ (*Butterfly*); ROSSINI: Almaviva★ (*Barbiere di Siviglia*); SMETANA: Hans★ (*Bartered Bride*), Jarek★ (*Devil's Wall*), Vitek★ (*Secret*), Heinrich★ (*Two Widows*); TCHAIKOVSKY: Lenski★ (*Eugene Onegin*); VERDI: Duca di Mantova★ (*Rigoletto*), Gabriele★ (*Simon Boccanegra*), Alfredo★ (*Traviata*). Also DVORAK: Jirí★ (*Jakobín*); RAVEL: Gonzalve★ (*Heure espagnole*). Video/Film: Ernesto (*Don Pasquale*); Almaviva (*Barbiere di Siviglia*); Lenski (*Eugene Onegin*); Jarek (*Devil's Wall*); Jirí (*Jakobín*); Andrej (*Family of Taras*). Gives recitals. Appears with symphony orchestra. **Res:** Jablonského 7, 170 00 Prague 7, CSSR. Mgmt: PRG/CZE; PAS/FRG.

SVETLEV, MICHAIL. Lirico spinto tenor. Bulgarian. Resident mem: Stadttheater Augsburg; Stadttheater Bremen, FR Ger. Born 6 Mar 1943, Sofia. Single. Studied: Mo Stojan Kisijow, Sofia. **Debut:** Manrico (*Trovatore*) Stadttheater Passau 1971. Previous occupations: theology student and chanson singer. Awards: Winner Ntl Operetta Compt Sofia 1968; Silver Medal, Vercelli, Italy 1974.

Sang with major companies in BUL: Sofia; FR GER: Bielefeld, Bonn, Darmstadt, Düsseldorf-Duisburg, Essen, Munich Gärtnerplatz, Stuttgart. **Roles with these companies incl** BIZET: Don José★ (*Carmen*); DONIZETTI: Edgardo★ (*Lucia*); FLOTOW: Lionel★ (*Martha*); GLINKA: Bogdan★ (*Life for the Tsar*); MASCAGNI: Turiddu (*Cavalleria rusticana*); PUCCINI: Rodolfo★ (*Bohème*), Cavaradossi★ (*Tosca*), Calaf★ (*Turandot*); SHOSTAKOVICH: Sergei★ (*Katerina Ismailova*); SMETANA: Hans★ (*Bartered Bride*); STRAUSS, J: Alfred★ (*Fledermaus*); STRAUSS, R: Matteo★ (*Arabella*), Bacchus★ (*Ariadne auf Naxos*); VERDI: Riccardo★ (*Ballo in maschera*), Don Carlo★, Alfredo★ (*Traviata*), Manrico★ (*Trovatore*), Arrigo★ (*Vespri*). Also SEARLE: Poprischtschin (*Diary of a Madman*). **Res:** Bremen, FR Ger. Mgmt: PAS/FRG; BAA/BUL; SLZ/FRG.

SVOBODA, JOSEF. Scenic and costume designer for opera, theater, film; specl in sets. Is also an architect. Czechoslovakian. Chief designer, National Theater, Prague. Born 10 May 1920, Caslav, CSR. Wife Libuse. One daughter. Studied: Spec School for Architecture, Prague; Acad of Applied Arts, Prague, Prof Smetana. Awards: National Artists, & Laureate of the State Prize, Order of Work, Pres of the CSSR; Gold Medal, Best Foreign Staff Designer, São Paulo 1961; Netherlands' Sikkensprijs 1969; HD Royal Coll of Art, London 1969; LA Drama Critics Awd 1970; Munich Critics' Prize 1970; Kulturpreis, German Photo Socy, Cologne 1971. Also Chief of Laterna Magica, Prague.

Designed for major companies in AUS: Salzburg Fest, Vienna Staatsoper & Volksoper; BEL: Brussels; BRA: Rio de Janeiro; CAN: Montreal/Quebec; CZE: Brno, Prague National; DEN: Copenhagen; FIN: Helsinki; FRA: Paris; GRE: Athens Fest; FR GER: Bayreuth Fest, Berlin Deutsche Oper, Dortmund, Düsseldorf-Duisburg, Frankfurt, Hamburg, Mannheim, Munich Staatsoper, Nürnberg, Stuttgart, Wiesbaden; GER DR: Berlin Komische Oper & Staatsoper; HOL: Amsterdam; HUN: Budapest; ITA: Florence Comunale, Milan La Scala, Rome Opera, Turin, Venice; POL: Warsaw; SWE: Stockholm; SWI: Geneva, Zurich; UK: Edinburgh Fest, London Royal & English National; USSR: Leningrad Kirov, Moscow Bolshoi & Stanislavski; USA: Boston, Chicago, New York Met & City Opera, Washington DC; YUG: Zagreb, Belgrade. **Operas designed for these companies incl** BEETHOVEN: *Fidelio*★; BELLINI: *Sonnambula;* BERG: *Wozzeck;* BERLIOZ: *Troyens*★; BIZET: *Carmen*★; CIKKER: *Coriolanus*★; DEBUSSY: *Pelléas et Mélisande*★; DESSAU: *Lanzelot*★; DVORAK: *Devil and Kate, Rusalka;* GLINKA: *Ruslan and Ludmilla;* GOUNOD: *Faust;* HANDEL: *Acis and Galatea;* HINDEMITH: *Cardillac;* JANACEK: *Excursions of Mr Broucek, From the House of the Dead, Jenufa*★, *Katya Kabanova*★; LEONCAVALLO: *Pagliacci;* MARTINU: *Griechische Passion, Trois souhaites;* MASCAGNI: *Cavalleria rusticana;* MASSENET: *Don Quichotte;* MONIUSZKO: *Halka;* MOZART: *Così fan tutte, Don Giovanni, Entführung aus dem Serail, Idomeneo, Nozze di Figaro, Zauberflöte;* MUSSORGSKY: *Boris Godunov*★; OFFENBACH: *Contes d'Hoffmann;* PROKOFIEV: *Duenna, Fiery Angel, Love for Three Oranges;* PUCCINI: *Bohème, Gianni Schicchi, Tosca;* RIMSKY-KORSAKOV: *Coq d'or;* ROSSINI: *Barbiere di Siviglia, Italiana in Algeri;* SMETANA: *Bartered Bride, Dalibor, Devil's Wall*★, *The Kiss, Libuse, Secret*★; STRAUSS, R: *Ariadne auf Naxos, Frau ohne Schatten, Salome;* STRAVINSKY: *Rake's Progress*★; SUCHON: *Whirlpool*★; TCHAIKOVSKY: *Eugene Onegin, Pique Dame;* VERDI: *Aida, Ballo in maschera, Don Carlo, Forza del destino, Macbeth, Nabucco, Otello, Rigoletto, Simon Boccanegra*★, *Trovatore, Vespri*★; WAGNER: *Fliegende Holländer, Meistersinger, Rheingold*★, *Walküre, Siegfried, Götterdämmerung, Tannhäuser, Tristan und Isolde*★; WEBER: *Freischütz, Oberon;* WEINBERGER: *Schwanda;* ZIMMERMANN: *Soldaten*★. Also KAREL: *Godmother Death;* MARTINU: *Julietta;* KREJCI: *Uproar in Ephesos.* **Operatic world premieres:** HANUS: *Torch of Prometheus* 1965; DOUBRAVA: *Love Ballad* 1962; PAUER: *Zuzana Vostrova* 1958; all at National Theater,

Prague. Operatic Video/Film – Brno; FISCHER: *Romeo, Julie a tma.* Exhibitions of stage designs. Teaches at Acad of Applied Arts, Prague. **Res:** Na Kvetnici 850/6, Prague 4, CSSR.

SVORC, ANTONIN. Bass-baritone. Czechoslovakian. Resident mem: National Theater, Prague; Staatsoper, Berlin. Born 12 Feb 1934, Jaromer, CSR. Married. One child. Studied: Prof Ing Jan Berlik, Prague. **Debut:** Don Pizarro (*Fidelio*) City Theater, Liberec, CSSR 1955. Awards: Merited Artist, Gvnmt of CSSR.

Sang with major companies in AUS: Vienna Staatsoper; BUL: Sofia; CZE: Brno, Prague National & Smetana; FRA: Paris; FR GER: Cologne, Düsseldorf-Duisburg, Frankfurt, Hannover, Karlsruhe, Kassel, Wiesbaden; GER DR: Berlin Staatsoper, Dresden; HUN: Budapest; ITA: Genoa, Spoleto Fest, Trieste, Venice; MON: Monte Carlo; POL: Warsaw; ROM: Bucharest; SPA: Barcelona; SWI: Zurich; UK: Edinburgh Fest. **Roles with these companies incl** BEETHOVEN: Don Pizarro★ (*Fidelio*); GLINKA: Ruslan; JANACEK: Shishkov (*From the House of the Dead*); MARTINU: Fotis (*Griechische Passion*); MASCAGNI: Alfio★ (*Cavalleria rusticana*); MUSSORGSKY: Boris Godunov★; PUCCINI: Scarpia★ (*Tosca*); STRAUSS, R: Orest (*Elektra*), Barak★ (*Frau ohne Schatten*), Jochanaan★ (*Salome*); VERDI: Amonasro★ (*Aida*), Nabucco & Zaccaria (*Nabucco*), Iago (*Otello*), Simon Boccanegra★; WAGNER: Holländer★, Telramund★ (*Lohengrin*), Hans Sachs (*Meistersinger*), Wotan★ (*Walküre*), Kurwenal★ (*Tristan und Isolde*). Also SMETANA: Chrudes★ (*Libuse*); FIBICH: Premysl★ (*Sarka*). **World premieres:** CIKKER: Coriolanus (*Coriolanus*) National Theater, Prague 1974. Recorded for: Supraphon. Video/Film: Méphistophélès (*Faust*). Gives recitals. Appears with symphony orchestra. **Res:** Na Klaudiance 12, 14700 Prague 4, CSSR. Mgmt: PRG/CZE.

SWEENEY, BARBARA B. American. Asst Gen Mng, St Paul Opera Assn, 544 Minn Bldg, St Paul, MN 55101, USA. In charge of adm matters. Born 6 Jan 1937. Husband John Palmer, occupation engineer. Previous positions, primarily administrative: in radio, TV, advert fields. Started with present company 1967 as Office Mng; in present position since 1969. World premieres at theaters during time of employment: HOIBY: *Summer and Smoke* St Paul Opera 1971. Initiated major policy changes: converted all accounting to computer, cutting costs. **Res:** St Paul, MN, USA.

SWIFT, TOM; né Thomas Kneafcy. Dramatic tenor. British. Resident mem: English National Opera, London. Born 2 Oct 1928, Wigan, Lancashire, UK. Wife Amethyst. One son, one daughter. Studied: John Tobin, Liverpool & London; London Opera School, now Opera Centre, London; Gustav Sacher, London. **Debut:** Camille de Rosillion (*Lustige Witwe*) Sadler's Wells Opera, London 1958. Awards: grant for further studies, Arts Counc of Great Britain.

Sang with major companies in FR GER: Dortmund, Kassel, Wuppertal; UK: English National. **Roles with these companies incl** d'ALBERT: Pedro★ (*Tiefland*); BEETHOVEN: Florestan★ (*Fidelio*); BERG: Tambourmajor★ (*Wozzeck*); BI-

ZET: Don José* (*Carmen*); EINEM: Bürgermeister (*Besuch der alten Dame*); LEONCAVALLO: Canio* (*Pagliacci*); MASCAGNI: Turiddu* (*Cavalleria rusticana*); PENDERECKI: de Laubardemont* (*Teufel von Loudun*); PUCCINI: Cavaradossi (*Tosca*); STRAUSS, J: Alfred* (*Fledermaus*); STRAUSS, R: Ein Sänger* (*Rosenkavalier*); TCHAIKOVSKY: Gherman* (*Pique Dame*); VERDI: Riccardo* (*Ballo in maschera*), Don Carlo*, Manrico* (*Trovatore*); WAGNER: Lohengrin. Appears with symphony orchestra. Mgmt: IWL/UK.

SYDNEY, JON; né John Walter Brady. Dramatic tenor. Australian. Resident mem: English National Opera, London. Born 28 Nov 1933, Sydney. Divorced. Two children. Studied: Mme M Mathy, Sydney; John Hargreaves, English National Opera, London. **Debut:** Cavaradossi (*Tosca*) Australian Opera 1967. Previous occupations: real estate; confectionery busn.
Sang with major companies in AUSTRL: Sydney; UK: London English National. **Roles with these companies incl** BIZET: Don José* (*Carmen*); DONIZETTI: Leicester* (*Maria Stuarda*); PENDERECKI: de Laubardemont* (*Teufel von Loudun*); PUCCINI: Pinkerton* (*Butterfly*), Cavaradossi (*Tosca*); VERDI: Riccardo* (*Ballo in maschera*), Manrico* (*Trovatore*). Gives recitals. Appears with symphony orchestra. **Res:** 60 Ridley Ave, London, UK. **Mgmt:** OEA/UK.

SYKORA, PETER NARZISS. Scenic and costume designer for opera & theater. Is a lighting designer, stage director; also an illustrator. German. Resident designer, Staatsoper Dresden, Ger DR and at Staatstheater, Dresden. Born 23 Apr 1944, Reichenberg, CSR. Wife Heidrun, occupation puppeteer. One child. Studied: Hochschule für bildende Künste, Prof Reichard, Dresden. **Operatic debut:** *Traviata* Stadttheater Freiberg, Ger DR 1969. Theater debut: Stadttheater Freiberg 1968. Previous occupation: commercial & theatrical painter.
Designed for major companies in GER DR: Berlin Staatsoper, Dresden. **Operas designed for these companies incl** BARTOK: *Bluebeard's Castle*; MOZART: *Zauberflöte*; STRAVINSKY: *Mavra*; WAGNER: Tristan und Isolde*. **Operatic world premieres:** KUNAD: *Sabellicus* Deutsche Staatsoper Berlin, Ger DR 1974. **Res:** Florastr 15, Berlin 110, Ger DR. **Mgmt:** KDR/GDR.

SYMCOX, PETER JOHN FORTUNE. Stages/produces opera, theater & television. Canadian. Senior Music Prod, Canadian Broadcasting Corporation for French & English networks from Montreal. Born 7 Jun 1925, Chelmsford, UK. Single. Studied: Oxford Univ; Old Vic Theatre School, London; also music & piano. **Operatic debut:** *Telephone* CBC TV, Montreal 1963. Theater debut: Montreal Rep Theatre, CAN 1956. Awards: MA Oxford Univ, UK; Gov, Dominion Drama Fest, CAN.
Directed/produced opera for major companies in Montreal/Quebec, Toronto; USA: Hartford, Milwaukee Florentine Opera, Pittsburgh. **Operas staged with these companies incl** GOUNOD: *Roméo et Juliette*; OFFENBACH: *Contes d'Hoffmann*; PUCCINI: *Bohème, Butterfly*,

Tabarro; VERDI: *Otello*, *Rigoletto*. Video— CBC TV: BERNSTEIN: *Tahiti*; BRITTEN: *Burning Fiery Furnace*; MASSENET: *Don Quichotte*; MENOTTI: *Telephone*; MOZART: *Figaro*; MUSSORGSKY: *Boris*; PUCCINI: *Butterfly*; STRAUSS, J: *Fledermaus*; VERDI: *Macbeth*. **Res:** Habitat 67, Montreal, Canada. **Mgmt:** HUR/USA.

SZABÓ, RÓZSA. Lyric soprano. Hungarian. Resident mem: State Opera, Budapest. Born 17 Mar 1932, Budapest. Husband Dr Ervin Lukács, occupation conductor. One child. Studied: Music Consv, Rezsö Feleki, Jenö Sipos, Budapest. **Debut:** Konstanze (*Entführung aus dem Serail*) State Opera, Budapest 1965.
Sang with major companies in FIN: Helsinki; HUN: Budapest. **Roles with these companies incl** BIZET: Micaëla (*Carmen*); BRITTEN: Helena* (*Midsummer Night*); LEONCAVALLO: Nedda* (*Pagliacci*); MOZART: Konstanze (*Entführung aus dem Serail*); PUCCINI: Musetta (*Bohème*), Lauretta* (*Gianni Schicchi*), Cio-Cio-San* (*Butterfly*), Liù* (*Turandot*); VERDI: Violetta* (*Traviata*); WEILL: Jenny (*Aufstieg und Fall der Stadt Mahagonny*). Appears with symphony orchestra. **Res:** 1026 Hermann O u 45, Budapest, Hungary. **Mgmt:** ITK/HUN.

SZALMA, FERENC JÓZSEF. Bass. Hungarian. Resident mem: State Opera of Hungary, Budapest. Born 19 Mar 1923, Szeged, Hungary. Wife Dr Elisabeth Relowszky, occupation surgeon. One child. Studied: Prof Bruno Kazametz, Nürnberg; Prof Anna Renyé, Szeged; Prof Pál Varga, Budapest. **Debut:** Commendatore (*Don Giovanni*) National Opera, Szeged, Hungary 1954. Previous occupations: medical student. Awards: Franz Liszt Prize, Ministry of Educt, Hungary.
Sang with major companies in BEL: Brussels; FR GER: Wiesbaden; HUN: Budapest; YUG: Belgrade. **Roles with these companies incl** BARTOK: Bluebeard*; BEETHOVEN: Rocco* (*Fidelio*); DONIZETTI: Dulcamara (*Elisir*); FALLA: Don Quixote* (*Retablo de Maese Pedro*); GLINKA: Ivan (*Life for the Tsar*); GOUNOD: Méphistophélès* (*Faust*); HALEVY: Brogny (*Juive*); KODALY: Háry János* (*Háry János*); MOZART: Osmin (*Entführung aus dem Serail*), Sarastro* (*Zauberflöte*); MUSSORGSKY: Varlaam* & Pimen* (*Boris Godunov*), Dosifei* (*Khovanshchina*); NICOLAI: Falstaff (*Lustigen Weiber*); ORFF: Bauer (*Mond*); PROKOFIEV: Mendoza (*Duenna*), King of Clubs* (*Love for Three Oranges*); PUCCINI: Colline* (*Bohème*); ROSSINI: Dott Bartolo* (*Barbiere di Siviglia*); VERDI: Ramfis*‡ (*Aida*), Philip II* & Grande Inquisitore* (*Don Carlo*), Silva (*Ernani*), Padre Guardiano* (*Forza del destino*), Zaccaria* (*Nabucco*), Fiesco (*Simon Boccanegra*), Procida (*Vespri*); WAGNER: Holländer*, König Heinrich (*Lohengrin*), Pogner* (*Meistersinger*), Gurnemanz (*Parsifal*), Fasolt* (*Rheingold*), Hunding (*Walküre*), Hagen* (*Götterdämmerung*), Landgraf* (*Tannhäuser*), König Marke* (*Tristan und Isolde*); WEBER: Kaspar (*Freischütz*); WOLF-FERRARI: Lunardo (*Quattro rusteghi*). Recorded for: Qualiton. Gives recitals. Appears with symphony orchestra. **Res:** 1118 Ménesi ut 39, Budapest, Hungary. **Mgmt:** ITK/HUN.

SZCZEPANSKA, KRYSTYNA. Coloratura mezzosoprano. Polish. Resident mem: Teatr Wielki, Warsaw. Born 25 Jan 1917, Nasielsk, Poland. Divorced. One child. Studied: Warsaw Consv, Prof Belina Skupiewski. **Debut:** Amneris (*Aida*) Schlesische Oper, Wrozlaw 1947. Awards: Gold Cross of Merit; Cross of Knight; Awd of Ministry of Art and Culture.
Sang with major company in POL: Warsaw.
Roles with this company incl BIZET: Carmen★; DONIZETTI: Léonore (*Favorite*); GLUCK: Orfeo; GOUNOD: Siebel (*Faust*); HANDEL: Cornelia (*Giulio Cesare*); MASSENET: Charlotte (*Werther*); MENOTTI: Secretary (*Consul*); MONIUSZKO: Jadwiga (*Haunted Castle*); MONTEVERDI: Orfeo, Poppea (*Incoronazione di Poppea*); MOZART: Dorabella (*Così fan tutte*); MUSSORGSKY: Marina (*Boris Godunov*); OFFENBACH: Giulietta (*Contes d'Hoffmann*); PONCHIELLI: Laura (*Gioconda*); PUCCINI: Suzuki (*Butterfly*); SAINT-SAENS: Dalila; STRAUSS, R: Octavian (*Rosenkavalier*); STRAVINSKY: Jocasta (*Oedipus Rex*); TCHAIKOVSKY: Mme Larina & Olga (*Eugene Onegin*), Comtesse (*Pique Dame*); VERDI: Amneris (*Aida*), Ulrica (*Ballo in maschera*), Eboli (*Don Carlo*), Azucena (*Trovatore*); WAGNER: Venus (*Tannhäuser*). Also HONEGGER: Judith. Recorded for: Polish Records. Gives recitals. Appears with symphony orchestra. Teaches voice. On faculty of High School of Music, Warsaw. **Res:** Moliera 8d 23, Warsaw, Poland.

SZIRTES, GYÖRGY. Hungarian. Adm Mng & Asst to Int, Hungarian State Opera House, Népköztársaság utja 22, 1061 Budapest VI; also Erkel Theater. In charge of overall adm matters & finances. Born 22 Aug 1923, Budapest. Wife Eva Thury, occupation actress. One child. Studied: Acad of Dram Art, Budapest. Previous occupations: actor, Vigszinház, Comedy Theater, Budapest 1947-49. Form position, primarily theatrical: Sec, Mng to the Adm, Operetta Theater, Budapest 1949-62. Started with present company in 1962 as Adm Mng, in present position since 1974. Awards: Medal for Socialist Culture, Ministry of Culture, Budapest; Commem Medallion, Silver & Gold, Presidium Hungarian People's Rep. Initiated major policy changes including developing subscription audience through appearances of internat artists and ensembles; school programs to increase student attendance; originated international tour. Mem of Union of Theater Artists; Art Council; Commtt of Mgmt; Commtt for Culture, Municipal District Commtt. **Res:** Lenin Krt 60, Budapest Hungary.

SZÖNYI, OLGA. Dramatic mezzo-soprano. Hungarian. Resident mem: Hungarian State Opera, Budapest. Born 2 Jul 1936, Budapest. Husband Dr I Russay, occupation pres Oil & Minerals Trading Co, Budapest. Studied: Acad of Music Ferenc Liszt, Budapest; Prof Dr Jenö Sipos, Prof Pál Varga, Budapest. **Debut:** Eboli (*Don Carlo*) Opera Frankfurt/Main 1957. Awards: Ntl Prize Ferenc Liszt, Hungarian State; Merited Artist, Hungarian State.
Sang with major companies in AUS: Salzburg Fest; BUL: Sofia; CAN: Montreal/Quebec; CZE: Brno, Prague National & Smetana Theater; FRA: Paris; FR GER: Cologne, Frankfurt, Wiesbaden; HUN: Budapest; ITA: Rome Opera; POL: Warsaw; ROM: Bucharest; UK: Edinburgh Fest; USA: Boston, Chicago. **Roles with these companies incl** AUBER: Pamela (*Fra Diavolo*); BARTOK: Judith★‡ (*Bluebeard's Castle*); BERG: Gräfin Geschwitz★ (*Lulu*); BIZET: Carmen; GOLDMARK: Königin von Saba★; HUMPERDINCK: Hänsel; KODALY: Marie Louise‡ (*Háry János*); MOZART: Dorabella★ (*Così fan tutte*); MUSSORGSKY: Marina (*Boris Godunov*); STRAUSS, R: Komponist (*Ariadne auf Naxos*), Octavian★ (*Rosenkavalier*); VERDI: Amneris (*Aida*), Eboli (*Don Carlo*), Preziosilla (*Forza del destino*); WAGNER: Magdalene (*Meistersinger*), Venus★ (*Tannhäuser*), Brangäne (*Tristan und Isolde*). Also ERKEL: Gertrudis (*Bánk Bán*); RAVEL: Concepcion (*Heure espagnole*); WAGNER: Brünnhilde (*Walküre*). Also BEETHOVEN: Leonore★ (*Fidelio*); KOZMA: Wife (*Amour électronique*). Recorded for: Mercury, Decca, Hungaroton. Video/Film: Wife (*The Great Dramatist*). Gives recitals. Appears with symphony orchestra. **Res:** Lorántiffy Zsuzsanna u 1, 1022 Budapest, Hungary. Mgmt: ITK/HUN; TAS/AUS.

SZOSTEK-RADKOWA, KRYSTYNA; née Szostek. Dramatic mezzo-soprano. Polish. Resident mem: Teatr Wielki, Warsaw. Born 14 Mar 1936, Katowice, Poland. Divorced. Two children. Studied: Music Acad, Profs Faryaszewska and Lenczewska, Katowice. **Debut:** Azucena (*Trovatore*) Katowice 1960. Awards: Gold Cross of Merit, Polish Gvnmt.
Sang with major companies in AUS: Vienna Staatsoper; BEL: Brussels; BUL: Sofia; CZE: Prague National; FRA: Bordeaux, Strasbourg, Toulouse; FR GER: Hamburg, Wiesbaden; GER DR: Berlin Staatsoper; HUN: Budapest; POL: Lodz, Warsaw; SPA: Majorca; USSR: Kiev, Leningrad Kirov, Moscow Bolshoi, Tbilisi; YUG: Zagreb, Belgrade. **Roles with these companies incl** BARTOK: Judith★ (*Bluebeard's Castle*); BIZET: Carmen★‡; BORODIN: Kontchakovna★‡ (*Prince Igor*); DEBUSSY: Geneviève★‡ (*Pelléas et Mélisande*); FLOTOW: Nancy★‡ (*Martha*); GLUCK: Orfeo★; HANDEL: Cornelia★ (*Giulio Cesare*); MONIUSZKO: Jadwiga★‡ (*Haunted Castle*); MONTEVERDI: Poppea★ (*Incoronazione di Poppea*); MUSSORGSKY: Marina★ (*Boris Godunov*); PENDERECKI: Ninon★ (*Teufel von Loudun*); PONCHIELLI: Laura★ & La Cieca★ (*Gioconda*); PROKOFIEV: Helene★ (*War and Peace*); PUCCINI: Suzuki★ (*Butterfly*); RAVEL: Enfant★ (*Enfant et les sortilèges*); SAINT-SAENS: Dalila★‡; STRAUSS, R: Klytämnestra★ (*Elektra*); STRAVINSKY: Jocasta★ (*Oedipus Rex*); TCHAIKOVSKY: Olga★ (*Eugene Onegin*), Comtesse★ (*Pique Dame*); VERDI: Amneris★ (*Aida*), Ulrica★ (*Ballo in maschera*), Eboli★ (*Don Carlo*), Azucena★‡ (*Trovatore*); WAGNER: Ortrud★ (*Lohengrin*). Recorded for: Polskie Nagrania. Gives recitals. Appears with symphony orchestra. **Res:** Warsaw, Poland. Mgmt: PAG/POL.

T

TACHIKAWA, SUMITO. Lyric baritone. Japanese. Resident mem: Niki Kai Opera, Tokyo. Born 15 Feb 1929, Oita, Japan. Wife Misako. Two children. Studied: Tiichi Nakayama, Tokyo. **Debut:** Germont (*Traviata*) Niki Kai Opera 1952. Awards: Mainichi Music Prize, Mainichi Press 1959.

Sang with major companies in JPN: Tokyo Fujiwara & Niki Kai. **Roles with these companies incl** BIZET: Escamillo★ (*Carmen*); DONIZETTI: Don Pasquale★; MOZART: Guglielmo★ & Don Alfonso (*Così fan tutte*), Leporello & Don Giovanni★ (*Don Giovanni*), Conte Almaviva★ & Figaro (*Nozze di Figaro*), Papageno (*Zauberflöte*); OFFENBACH: Coppélius etc (*Contes d'Hoffmann*); PUCCINI: Sharpless (*Butterfly*); ROSSINI: Figaro (*Barbiere di Siviglia*), Dandini★ (*Cenerentola*); VERDI: Germont★ (*Traviata*). Gives recitals. Appears with symphony orchestra. **Res:** Jingumae 6-16-12, 501 Shibuyaku, Tokyo, Japan.

TADDEI, GINO. Lyric tenor. Italian. Born 4 Jun 1943, Genoa, Italy. Wife Giovanna Savio. Studied: Accad S Agostino, Genoa; School of Teatro alla Scala, Milan. Previous occupations: studied architecture. Awards: First Prize, Intl Singing Compt Florence.

Sang with major companies in BUL: Sofia; CZE: Prague National; FRA: Bordeaux, Nice; ITA: Florence Maggio & Comunale, Milan La Scala, Palermo, Trieste, Venice. **Roles with these companies incl** BELLINI: Orombello★ (*Beatrice di Tenda*); CILEA: Maurizio★ (*A. Lecouvreur*); DONIZETTI: Riccardo (*Anna Bolena*), Fernand★ (*Favorite*), Riccardo★ (*Maria di Rohan*); MOZART: Don Ottavio★ (*Don Giovanni*); PUCCINI: Rodolfo★ (*Bohème*), Rinuccio (*Gianni Schicchi*), Pinkerton★ (*Butterfly*), Cavaradossi (*Tosca*); VERDI: Riccardo★ (*Ballo in maschera*), Jacopo Foscari (*Due Foscari*), Duca di Mantova★ (*Rigoletto*), Alfredo★ (*Traviata*). **World premieres:** BUGAMELLI: (*Fontana*) Trieste 1971. Recorded for: Fabbri, Supraphon, BASF. **Res:** V Ripamonti 193, Milan, Italy.

TADDEI, GIUSEPPE. Baritone & bass. Italian. Born 26 Jun 1916, Genoa, Italy. Wife Maria Antonietta Laureti. **Debut:** Heerrufer (*Lohengrin*) Teatro dell'Opera, Rome 1936.

Sang with major companies in ARG: Buenos Aires; AUS: Bregenz Fest, Graz, Salzburg Fest, Vienna Staatsoper & Volksoper; BEL: Brussels; BRA: Rio de Janeiro; BUL: Sofia; CZE: Prague National; FIN: Helsinki; FRA: Lyon, Marseille, Nancy, Strasbourg; GRE: Athens National; FR GER: Berlin Deutsche Oper, Cologne, Frankfurt, Kassel, Munich Staatsoper, Stuttgart, Wiesbaden; HOL: Amsterdam; HUN: Budapest; ITA: Bologna, Florence Maggio & Comunale, Genoa, Milan La Scala, Naples, Palermo, Parma, Rome Opera & Caracalla, Trieste, Turin, Venice, Verona Arena; MEX: Mexico City; MON: Monte Carlo; POR: Lisbon; ROM: Bucharest; SPA: Barcelona; SWI: Zurich; UK: London Royal; USA: Chicago, Dallas, Fort Worth, Hartford, Miami, Newark, New Orleans, New York City Opera, Philadelphia Lyric, San Francisco Opera. **Roles with these companies incl** BELLINI: Filippo (*Beatrice di Tenda*), Ernesto (*Pirata*), Sir George (*Puritani*); BIZET: Escamillo (*Carmen*); BORODIN: Prince Igor; CATALANI: Vincenzo Gellner (*Wally*); CHARPENTIER: Père (*Louise*); CILEA: Michonnet (*A. Lecouvreur*); DALLAPICCOLA: Robineau (*Volo di notte*); DONIZETTI: Lusignano (*Caterina Cornaro*), Dott Malatesta (*Don Pasquale*), Belcore & Dulcamara (*Elisir*), Sulpice★ (*Fille du régiment*), Antonio‡ (*Linda di Chamounix*), Enrico (*Lucia*); GIORDANO: Carlo Gérard (*Andrea Chénier*), De Siriex (*Fedora*); GLUCK: High Priest (*Alceste*); LEONCAVALLO: Tonio★‡ (*Pagliacci*); MASCAGNI: Rabbi David (*Amico Fritz*), Alfio (*Cavalleria rusticana*); MASSENET: Albert (*Werther*); MENOTTI: Husband (*Amelia al ballo*); MEYERBEER: Comte de Nevers (*Huguenots*); MOZART: Leporello★‡ (*Don Giovanni*), Figaro★ (*Nozze di Figaro*), Papageno (*Zauberflöte*); MUSSORGSKY: Varlaam (*Boris Godunov*), Shaklovity (*Khovanshchina*); OFFENBACH: Coppélius, etc (*Contes d'Hoffmann*); PONCHIELLI: Barnaba★ (*Gioconda*); PUCCINI: Marcello★‡ (*Bohème*), Jack Rance★ (*Fanciulla del West*), Gianni Schicchi★‡, Sharpless (*Butterfly*), Michele★ (*Tabarro*), Scarpia★‡ (*Tosca*); ROSSINI: Figaro★‡ (*Barbiere di Siviglia*), Dandini & Don Magnifico (*Cenerentola*), Guillaume Tell‡, Mustafà (*Italiana in Algeri*), Macrobio (*Pietra del paragone*); SAINT-SAENS: Grand prêtre (*Samson et Dalila*); STRAUSS, R: Barak (*Frau ohne Schatten*); VERDI: Amonasro★ (*Aida*), Renato★ (*Ballo in maschera*), Rodrigo (*Don Carlo*), Don Carlo‡ (*Ernani*), Falstaff★‡, Don Carlo (*Forza del destino*), Barone★ (*Giorno di* *regno*), Miller★ (*Luisa Miller*), Macbeth★‡, Nabucco, Iago★‡ (*Otello*), Rigoletto★‡, Simon Boccanegra★, Germont (*Traviata*), Conte di Luna★ (*Trovatore*), Monforte (*Vespri*); WAGNER: Holländer, Telramund (*Lohengrin*), Alberich (*Götterdämmerung*), Wolfram (*Tannhäuser*). Also DONIZETTI: Belisario. Only on records MOZART: Guglielmo (*Così fan tutte*), Don Giovanni; ROSSINI: Moïse. Recorded for: Columbia, Cetra, Decca, DG, RCA, Philips. Video/Film: Carlo Gérard (*Andrea Chénier*); Dulcamara (*Elisir*); Falstaff. Gives recitals. Appears with symphony orchestra. **Res:** V Trionfale 5675, Rome, Italy.

TADEO, GIORGIO. Basso-buffo. Italian. Born 2 Oct 1929, Verona. Wife Mariella Adani, occupation opera singer. Two children. Studied: Consv Parma, Mo Campogalliani; Perfez School, La Scala, Milan. **Debut:** Méphistophélès (*Faust*) Teatro Massimo, Palermo 1953. Awards: Gold Medal, Compt G Verdi, Parma.

Sang with major companies in ARG: Buenos Aires; AUS: Salzburg Fest, Vienna Staatsoper; FRA: Aix-en-Provence Fest, Paris, Strasbourg; GRE: Athens Fest; FR GER: Berlin Deutsche Oper, Cologne, Düsseldorf-Duisburg, Hamburg, Munich Staatsoper, Wiesbaden; HOL: Amsterdam; ISR: Tel Aviv; ITA: Bologna, Florence Maggio & Comunale, Genoa, Milan La Scala, Naples, Palermo, Parma, Rome Opera & Caracalla, Trieste, Turin, Venice, Verona Arena; MEX: Mexico City; MON: Monte Carlo; POR: Lisbon; SPA: Barcelona; SWI: Basel, Geneva, Zurich; UK: London Royal; USA: Chicago, Dallas, Seattle. **Roles with these companies incl** BELLINI: Capellio (*Capuleti ed i Montecchi*), Rodolfo (*Sonnambula*); BRITTEN: John Claggart★ (*Billy Budd*); BUSONI: Matteo (*Arlecchino*); CIMAROSA: Geronimo★ (*Matrimonio segreto*); DONIZETTI: Don Pistacchio (*Campanello*), Maestro (*Convenienze/Viva la Mamma*), Don Pasquale★, Dulcamara★ (*Elisir*), Gasparo (*Rita*); FALLA: Don Quixote (*Retablo de Maese Pedro*); GALUPPI: Don Tritemio★ (*Filosofo di campagna*); HANDEL: Polyphemus (*Acis and Galatea*), Ptolemy (*Giulio Cesare*); HAYDN: Buonafede (*Mondo della luna*); JANACEK: Gorianchikov (*From the House of the Dead*); MENOTTI: Husband (*Amelia al ballo*); MEYERBEER: Marcel (*Huguenots*); MOZART: Don Alfonso★ (*Così fan tutte*), Leporello★ (*Don Giovanni*), Conte Almaviva★ & Figaro (*Nozze di Figaro*), Sarastro★ (*Zauberflöte*); MUSSORGSKY: Pimen★ (*Boris Godunov*); PAISIELLO: Bartolo (*Barbiere di Siviglia*); PERGOLESI: Marcaniello (*Frate 'nnamorato*), Tracolino (*Maestro di musica*), Uberto★ (*Serva padrona*); PETRASSI: Towerkeeper★ (*Morte dell'aria*); PUCCINI: Colline★ (*Bohème*); ROSSINI: Dott Bartolo★ & Don Basilio★ (*Barbiere di Siviglia*), Tobias Mill★ & Slook★ (*Cambiale di matrimonio*), Don Magnifico★ (*Cenerentola*), Podestà (*Gazza ladra*), Macrobio (*Pietra del paragone*), Gaudenzio★ (*Signor Bruschino*), Sultan Selim★ & Geronio★ (*Turco in Italia*); VERDI: Ramfis★ (*Aida*), Padre Guardiano (*Forza del destino*), Banquo★ (*Macbeth*), Rigoletto; WAGNER: König Heinrich (*Lohengrin*); WEBER: Omar (*Abu Hassan*); WEILL: Trinity Moses (*Aufstieg und Fall der Stadt Mahagonny*); WOLF-FERRARI: Lunardo★ (*Quattro rusteghi*).

Also BUSONI: Manasse (*Brautwahl*); PETRASSI: Cannizares (*Cordovano*); SALIERI: Trofonio (*Grotta di Trofonio*); CIMAROSA: Giampaolo (*Astuzie femminili*). Recorded for: DG, Pathé-Marconi. Video – RAI TV: (*Astuzie femminili*). Gives recitals. Appears with symphony orchestra. Teaches voice. Coaches repertoire. **Res:** V Copernico 59 A, Milan, Italy.

TAGGER, NICOLA. Lyric tenor. Italian. Born 10 May 1930, Pazarjik, Bulgaria. Wife Silvana, occupation former dramatic soprano. One child. Studied: Tel Aviv Consv; Mo Binetti, Milan. **Debut:** Duca di Mantova (*Rigoletto*) Eliseo, Rome 1956. Previous occupations: mem of kibbutz.

Sang with major companies in ARG: Buenos Aires; AUS: Vienna Staatsoper; BEL: Liège; BUL: Sofia; FRA: Nice; FR GER: Berlin Deutsche Oper, Bonn, Düsseldorf-Duisburg, Frankfurt, Hannover, Nürnberg; GER DR: Dresden; HOL: Amsterdam; HUN: Budapest; ISR: Tel Aviv; ITA: Bologna, Florence Maggio & Comunale, Genoa, Milan La Scala, Naples, Palermo, Rome Opera & Caracalla, Trieste, Turin, Verona Arena; MON: Monte Carlo; POL: Warsaw; POR: Lisbon; S AFR: Johannesburg; SPA: Barcelona; SWE: Stockholm; SWI: Zurich; UK: Edinburgh Fest; USA: Chicago; YUG: Zagreb, Belgrade. **Roles with these companies incl** BERG: Tambourmajor★ (*Wozzeck*); BERLIOZ: Benvenuto Cellini; BOITO: Faust★ (*Mefistofele*); BUSONI: Leandro★ (*Arlecchino*), Mephisto★ (*Doktor Faust*); CAVALLI: Ormindo★; CILEA: Maurizio★ (*A. Lecouvreur*); DONIZETTI: Ernesto★ (*Don Pasquale*), Fernand★ (*Favorite*), Edgardo★ (*Lucia*), Riccardo★ (*Maria di Rohan*), Leicester★ (*Maria Stuarda*); GOUNOD: Faust★; HANDEL: Lurcanio★ (*Ariodante*); MASSENET: Des Grieux★ (*Manon*), Nicias★ (*Thaïs*); MILHAUD: Thésée★ (*Abandon d'Ariane*); MONTEVERDI: Orfeo★; MOZART: Don Ottavio★ (*Don Giovanni*), Idamante★ (*Idomeneo*), Mitridate★; POULENC: Chevalier de la Force★ (*Dialogues des Carmélites*); PROKOFIEV: Mephistopheles★ (*Fiery Angel*); PUCCINI: Rodolfo★ (*Bohème*), Pinkerton★ (*Butterfly*), Cavaradossi★ (*Tosca*); ROSSINI: Almaviva★ (*Barbiere di Siviglia*), Arnold★ (*Guillaume Tell*), Otello★; STRAUSS, R: Bacchus (*Ariadne auf Naxos*); TCHAIKOVSKY: Gherman★ (*Pique Dame*); VERDI: Riccardo★ (*Ballo in maschera*), Don Carlo★, Ismaele★ (*Nabucco*), Duca di Mantova★ (*Rigoletto*), Alfredo★ (*Traviata*); WAGNER: Lohengrin★; ZIMMERMANN: Graf★ (*Soldaten*). Gives recitals. Appears with symphony orchestra.

TAGLIAVINI, FRANCO. Lirico spinto tenor. Italian. Born 29 Oct 1934, Novellara, Reggio Emilia, Italy. Wife Eliane Claustre. Studied: Liceo Musicale GB Viotti, Vercelli, Italy; Lita Fumagalli-Riva, Italy. **Debut:** Canio (*Pagliacci*) Teatro Nuovo, Milan 1961.

Sang with major companies in AUS: Vienna Staatsoper; BEL: Brussels; FRA: Lyon, Nice; FR GER: Berlin Deutsche Oper, Dortmund, Karlsruhe, Mannheim, Stuttgart; HUN: Budapest; ITA: Bologna, Florence Maggio & Comunale, Milan La Scala, Naples, Palermo Massimo, Rome Teatro dell'Opera & Caracalla, Turin, Venice; MON: Monte Carlo; S AFR: Johannesburg; SPA: Barce-

Iona, Majorca; SWI: Zurich; UK: Edinburgh Fest, London Royal Opera; USSR: Moscow Bolshoi; USA: Boston, Chicago, Dallas, Houston, Miami, New York Met, Philadelphia Lyric, San Diego, San Francisco Opera; YUG: Zagreb, Belgrade. **Roles with these companies incl** BELLINI: Pollione★ (*Norma*); BIZET: Don José★ (*Carmen*); BOITO: Faust (*Mefistofele*); CILEA: Maurizio (*A. Lecouvreur*); DONIZETTI: Riccardo (*Anna Bolena*), Edgardo★ (*Lucia*), Leicester★ (*Maria Stuarda*); GIORDANO: Andrea Chénier; LEONCAVALLO: Canio (*Pagliacci*); MASCAGNI: Turiddu★ (*Cavalleria rusticana*); PONCHIELLI: Enzo★ (*Gioconda*); PUCCINI: Rodolfo (*Bohème*), Pinkerton (*Butterfly*), Des Grieux (*Manon Lescaut*), Cavaradossi★ (*Tosca*), Calaf★ (*Turandot*); ROSSINI: Aménophis (*Moïse*); SPONTINI: Licinio (*Vestale*); STRAUSS, R: Ein Sänger★ (*Rosenkavalier*); TCHAIKOVSKY: Lenski (*Eugene Onegin*); VERDI: Radames★ (*Aida*), Foresto★ (*Attila*), Riccardo★ (*Ballo in maschera*), Don Carlo★, Jacopo Foscari★ (*Due Foscari*), Ismaele (*Nabucco*), Duca di Mantova (*Rigoletto*), Gabriele★ (*Simon Boccanegra*), Alfredo★ (*Traviata*), Arrigo★ (*Vespri*); WAGNER: Lohengrin★; ZANDONAI: Paolo (*Francesca da Rimini*). Also VERDI: Macduff★ (*Macbeth*); GIORDANO: Lefèvre (*Mme Sans-Gêne*); MUSSORGSKY: Dimitri (*Boris Godunov*). Video: Turiddu (*Cavalleria rustic̀ana*). Appears with symphony orchestra. **Res:** V Maiocchi 23, Milan, Italy. Mgmt: GOR/UK.

TAGUCHI, KOSUKE. Lyric tenor. Japanese. Resident mem: Niki Kai, Tokyo. Born 8 Feb 1941, Tottori, Japan. Single. Studied: Mrs Tsuruyo Takeoka; Takanosuke Watanabe, Tokyo. **Debut:** Beppe (*Pagliacci*) Fujiwara, Tokyo 1969.

Sang with major companies in JPN: Tokyo Fujiwara, Niki Kai. **Roles with these companies incl** MOZART: Ferrando (*Così fan tutte*), Tamino★ (*Zauberflöte*); NICOLAI: Fenton (*Lustigen Weiber*); OFFENBACH: Hoffmann★; PUCCINI: Rodolfo★ (*Bohème*), Pinkerton★ (*Butterfly*); VERDI: Duca di Mantova★ (*Rigoletto*); WEBER: Max (*Freischütz*). Appears with symphony orchestra. Teaches voice. On faculty of Kunutachi Music Coll, lecturer. **Res:** Nishi 2/20/10, 423, Kunutachi, Japan.

TAILLON, JOCELYNE JEANNE. Lyric mezzo-soprano & contralto. French. Resident mem: Opéra de Paris. Born 19 May 1941, Doudeville, France. Single. Studied: Ntl Consv, Grenoble, Suzanne Balguerie, Germaine Lubin. **Debut:** Nourrice (*Ariane et Barbe Bleue*) Bordeaux Fest 1968. Previous occupations: ORTF prod asst, electronic supervisor. Awards: First Prize Ntl Conc Voix d'or 1956; Prix Caruso.

Sang with major companies in BEL: Brussels; FRA: Aix-en-Provence Fest, Bordeaux, Lyon, Marseille, Paris, Rouen, Strasbourg, Toulouse; HOL: Amsterdam; ITA: Rome Opera; POR: Lisbon; SWI: Geneva; UK: Glyndebourne Fest; USA: Chicago, Washington DC. **Roles with these companies incl** DEBUSSY: Geneviève★ (*Pelléas et Mélisande*); GOUNOD: Taven★ (*Mireille*); KODALY: Marie Louise★ (*Háry János*); MUSSORGSKY: Marfa (*Khovanshchina*); PROKOFIEV: Duenna★; PUCCINI: Suzuki★ (*Butterfly*), Principessa (*Suor Angelica*); ROSSINI: Isabella (*Italiana in Algeri*); STRAUSS, R: Klytämnestra (*Elektra*); STRAVINSKY: Baba the Turk (*Rake's Progress*); VERDI: Ulrica★ (*Ballo in maschera*), Dame Quickly★ (*Falstaff*), Azucena★ (*Trovatore*); WAGNER: Erda (*Rheingold★, Siegfried*), Fricka (*Rheingold, Walküre★*), Waltraute (*Götterdämmerung*). Also MONTE-VERDI: Messaggera & Proserpina (*Orfeo*), Arnalta (*Incoronazione di Poppea*). Recorded for: EMI. Gives recitals. Appears with symphony orchestra. **Res:** 48 Ave Suffren, Le Blanc Mesnil, France. Mgmt: IMR/FRA; SFM/USA.

TAJO, ITALO. Bass-baritone and stage director. Italian. Born 25 Apr 1915, Pinerolo. Wife Inelda Meroni, occupation form actress. One child. Studied: voice & violin, Turin. **Debut:** Fafner (*Rheingold*) Teatro Regio, Turin 1935; as stage director: *Mozart and Salieri*, San Carlo Opera, Naples 1954. Previous occupations: studied engineering.

Sang with major companies in AUS: Vienna Staatsoper; BRA: Rio de Janeiro; DEN: Copenhagen; FRA: Paris, Strasbourg; FR GER: Berlin Deutsche Oper; HOL: Amsterdam; ITA: Bologna, Florence Maggio & Comunale, Genoa, Milan La Scala, Naples, Palermo, Parma, Rome Opera & Caracalla, Trieste, Turin, Venice, Verona Arena; MON: Monte Carlo; POR: Lisbon; SPA: Barcelona; SWI: Geneva; UK: Edinburgh Fest, Glyndebourne Fest, London Royal; USA: Baltimore, Boston, Chicago Lyric, Cincinnati, Hartford, Houston Grand Opera, Newark, New Orleans, New York Met, Philadelphia Grand, Pittsburgh, San Antonio, San Francisco Opera, Seattle, Washington DC; YUG: Dubrovnik, Belgrade. **Roles with these companies incl** BELLINI: Oroveso (*Norma*), Sir George (*Puritani*), Rodolfo (*Sonnambula*); BERG: Doktor (*Wozzeck*); BERLIOZ: Narbal (*Troyens*); BORODIN: Galitzky (*Prince Igor*); CATALANI: Stromminger (*Wally*); CIMAROSA: Geronimo (*Matrimonio segreto*); DONIZETTI: Don Pistacchio (*Campanello*), Don Pasquale★, Dulcamara★ (*Elisir*), Baldassare (*Favorita*), Sulpice (*Fille du régiment*), Alfonso d'Este (*Lucrezia Borgia*); DVORAK: Marbuel (*Devil and Kate*); FALLA: Don Quixote (*Retablo de Maese Pedro*); GALUPPI: Don Tritemio (*Filosofo di campagna*); GOUNOD: Méphistophélès (*Faust*); MASSENET: Don Quichotte★; MONTEMEZZI: Archibaldo (*Amore dei tre re*); MOZART: Don Alfonso (*Così fan tutte*), Don Giovanni & Leporello (*Don Giovanni*), Osmin (*Entführung aus dem Serail*), Figaro (*Nozze di Figaro*), Sarastro (*Zauberflöte*); MUSSORGSKY: Boris Godunov, Ivan Khovansky (*Khovanshchina*); PONCHIELLI: Alvise (*Gioconda*); PROKOFIEV: General (*Gambler*); PUCCINI: Colline (*Bohème*), Gianni Schicchi; RIMSKY-KORSAKOV: Roi Dodon (*Coq d'or*); ROSSINI: Dott Bartolo & Don Basilio★ (*Barbiere di Siviglia*), Don Magnifico★ (*Cenerentola*), Moïse, Signor Bruschino; SHOSTAKOVICH: Ivan Yakovlevich (*Nose*); SMETANA: Kezal (*Bartered Bride*); STRAUSS, R: Baron Ochs (*Rosenkavalier*); THOMAS: Lothario (*Mignon*); VERDI: Ramfis (*Aida*), Attila, Philip II (*Don Carlo*), Silva (*Ernani*), Padre Guardiano (*Forza del destino*), Banquo (*Macbeth*), Fiesco (*Simon Boccanegra*); WAGNER: König Marke (*Tristan und Isolde*);

WOLF-FERRARI: Lunardo (*Quattro rusteghi*). Also PIZZETTI: Hanoc (*Straniero*), Eurito d'Ilaco (*Fedra*); ZANDONAI: Sintram (*Cavalieri di Ekebù*); BORODIN: Kontchak (*Prince Igor*); MASCAGNI: Pantalone (*Maschere*), Cieco (*Iris*); RIMSKY-KORSAKOV: Salieri; WOLF-FERRARI: Anzoleto (*Campiello*), Milord (*Vedova scaltra*); BUSONI: Pantalone (*Turandot*); ALFANO: Durvasas (*Sakuntala*); WALTON: Calcante (*Troilus and Cressida*); CAVALLI: Jarba (*Didone*); GOUNOD: Géronte (*Médecin malgré lui*); MOZART: Cola (*Bastien und Bastienne*); PAISIELLO: Conte Padre (*Nina*); PERGOLESI: Tracollo; CIMAROSA: Don Crisobolo (*Impresario in angustie*), Don Demofonte (*Due Baroni di Rocca Azzurra*); ROSSINI: Don Pomponio (*Gazzetta*), Don Pardenione (*Occasione fa il ladro*), Padre (*Gazza ladra*); MASSENET: Comte (*Manon*); PUCCINI: Timur (*Turandot*). **World premieres:** MALIPIERO: Agamennone (*Ecuba*) Rome Opera 1941; PERSICO: Marchese Forlipopoli (*Locandiera*) Rome 1941; PIZZETTI: Mugnaio (*Oro*) Scala, Milan 1947; BUCCHI: Contrabbassista (*Contrabbasso*) Florence Maggio 1954; TOSATTI: Schmuller (*Giudizio universale*) Scala, Milan 1955; ROTA: Nevrastenico (*Notte di un nevrastenico*), RAI Turin 1959; NONO: Torturato (*Intolleranza*) Venice, Int Fest 1961. **Operas staged incl** BRITTEN: *Albert Herring*★; CIMAROSA: *Matrimonio segreto;* DONIZETTI: *Campanello;* HAYDN: *Infedeltà delusa;* MASSENET: *Don Quichotte*★; MILHAUD: *Pauvre matelot;* MOZART: *Don Giovanni, Nozze di Figaro*★, *Schauspieldirektor*★; PUCCINI: *Gianni Schicchi, Tabarro;* ROSSINI: *Barbiere di Siviglia*★, *Cenerentola, Scala di seta;* VERDI: *Falstaff*★, *Trovatore*★. Also HANDEL: *Agrippina;* RIMSKY-KORSAKOV: *Mozart and Salieri;* CIMAROSA: *Sposi per accidenti;* SACCHINI: *Contadina in corte;* BUCCHI: *Notte in paradiso*★; ROSSINI: *Inganno felice*★; DANIEL PURCELL: *Judgment of Paris*★; FERRARI: *Mantici*★. Recorded for: RCA Victor, Cetra. Film: Don Basilio (*Barbiere*), Raimondo (*Lucia*), Dulcamara (*Elisir*), Mephistopheles (*Faust and the Devil*), Don Pasquale. Teaches acting. Coaches repertoire and drama. On faculty of Coll-Consv of Music, Univ of Cincinnati, Prof & Artist-in-Residence. Res: 5541 Penway Court, Cincinnati, O, USA.

TAKALA, AINO SISKO. Dramatic mezzo-soprano. Finnish. Resident mem: Finnish National Opera, Helsinki. Born 30 Apr 1928, Ylihärmä, Finland. Husband Harry Anttila, occupation Major. Studied: Yolanda di Maria Petris, Elsa Larcén, Luigi Ricci, Clemens Glettenberg; Sibelius Acad, Helsinki; Musical Acad, Siena. Debut: Carmen, Finnish National Opera 1963.
Sang with major companies in FIN: Helsinki; HUN: Budapest; NOR: Oslo; SWE: Stockholm. Roles with these companies incl BIZET: Carmen; BRITTEN: Hermia★ (*Midsummer Night*); MONTEVERDI: Poppea (*Incoronazione di Poppea*); MOZART: Dorabella (*Così fan tutte*); MUSSORGSKY: Marina★ (*Boris Godunov*); OFFENBACH: Giulietta★ (*Contes d'Hoffmann*); PUCCINI: Suzuki (*Butterfly*); ROSSINI: Isabella (*Italiana in Algeri*); STRAVINSKY: Jocasta (*Oedipus Rex*); TCHAIKOVSKY: Mme Larina

(*Eugene Onegin*); VERDI: Amneris (*Aida*), Eboli★ (*Don Carlo*), Preziosilla (*Forza del destino*), Azucena (*Trovatore*); WAGNER: Ortrud (*Lohengrin*), Kundry (*Parsifal*), Fricka (*Rheingold*), Venus★ (*Tannhäuser*), Brangäne (*Tristan und Isolde*). Also PUCCINI: Tosca★. Gives recitals. Appears with symphony orchestra. **Res:** Nuolitie 6 C, Helsinki, Finland.

TALARICO, RITA. Lyric soprano. Italian. Born 30 May 1941, Rome. Husband Carlo Liberatori, occupation official, Alitalia airl. Studied: Gabriella Besanzoni; Consv di S Cecilia, Prof Maria Pediconi, Rome. Debut: Eleonora (*Furioso all'isola di San Domingo*) Spoleto Fest 1967. Awards: Winner Intl Cont Teatro Sperimentale Belli, Spoleto, by Rome Opera; Hon, Young Lyrical Revelation of La Scala 1968-69, Lions Club, Milan.
Sang with major companies in CAN: Montreal/Quebec; FRA: Lyon, Rouen; ITA: Bologna, Florence Maggio, Genoa, Milan La Scala, Naples, Palermo, Parma, Rome Opera & Caracalla, Spoleto Fest, Trieste; USA: New York City Opera, Philadelphia Lyric. **Roles with these companies incl** AUBER: Zerlina★ (*Fra Diavolo*); BELLINI: Beatrice di Tenda, Elvira★ (*Puritani*), Amina (*Sonnambula*); BIZET: Micaëla★ (*Carmen*), Léila (*Pêcheurs de perles*); BOITO: Margherita (*Mefistofele*); CATALANI: Anna (*Loreley*); CAVALLI: Climene (*Egisto*); CHERUBINI: Medea; CIMAROSA: Carolina (*Matrimonio segreto*); DONIZETTI: Adina★ (*Elisir*), Marie (*Fille du régiment*); GLUCK: Euridice★; GOUNOD: Marguerite (*Faust*); MARTINU: Popelka (*Comedy on the Bridge*); MASCAGNI: Suzel (*Amico Fritz*); MASSENET: Manon, Aurore (*Portrait de Manon*); MOZART: Donna Anna (*Don Giovanni*), Contessa & Susanna (*Nozze di Figaro*); PUCCINI: Mimi★ (*Bohème*), Cio-Cio-San (*Butterfly*), Suor Angelica★, Liù (*Turandot*); VERDI: Medora (*Corsaro*), Nannetta★ (*Falstaff*), Violetta★ (*Traviata*); WAGNER: Elsa (*Lohengrin*); WEBER: Agathe★ (*Freischütz*); WOLF-FERRARI: Susanna (*Segreto di Susanna*). Also ROSSINI: Amenaïde (*Tancredi*); PIZZETTI: Ifigenia. Gives recitals. Appears with symphony orchestra. **Res:** Viale delle Milizie 15, Rome, Italy.

TALIAFERRO, KERRY. Conductor of opera. American. Second Cond, Wuppertaler Bühnen, FR Ger. Born 24 Mar 1938, Pasco, WA, USA. Wife Dagmar, occupation translator. One child. Studied: Prof Herbert Ahlendorf, Berlin; Peter Maag, Siena; Richard Lert, Orkney Springs, VA, USA; incl keyboard instruments. Plays the piano. Operatic training as repetiteur at New York City Opera 1964-65; rept & asst chorus master Santa Fe Opera 1964-65; rept & asst cond Darmstadt Opera Theater 1966-69; asst cond & assoc chorus master Württembergische Staatsoper, Stuttgart 1969-73. Operatic debut: Pietra del paragone, Darmstadt, Germany 1967. Symphonic debut: symph & radio orchs, South German Radio, Stuttgart 1969-1973. Awards: Fulbright Schlshp 1965-66; Rockefeller grant 1966.
Conducted with major companies in FR GER: Darmstadt, Stuttgart, Wuppertal. **Operas with these companies incl** BIZET: *Carmen*★; FORTNER: *Don Perlimplin*★; GLUCK: *Orfeo ed Euridice*★; HAYDN: *Infedeltà delusa;* HUMPERDINCK:

Hänsel und Gretel★, Königskinder★; JANACEK: *From the House of the Dead;* LORTZING: *Wildschütz★;* MOZART: *Nozze di Figaro★, Zaïde, Zauberflöte★;* NICOLAI: *Lustigen Weiber★;* PUCCINI: *Tosca;* ROSSINI: *Italiana in Algeri★, Pietra del paragone;* STRAUSS, J: *Fledermaus★;* VERDI: *Don Carlo★, Nabucco★, Rigoletto★, Traviata★.* Res: Siegersbusch 57, Wuppertal, Germany. Mgmt: ARM/FRG.

TALVELA, MARTTI OLAVI. Bass. Finnish. Born 4 Feb 1935, Hiitola, Finland. Wife Anna, occupation teacher. Three children. Studied: Music Acad, Lahti, Finland; Martin Öhman, Stockholm. **Debut:** Commendatore (*Don Giovanni*) Royal Opera, Stockholm 1961. Awards: Kammersänger, Deutsche Oper Berlin.

Sang with major companies in AUS: Vienna Staatsoper, Salzburg Fest; FIN: Helsinki; FRA: Paris; FR GER: Bayreuth Fest, Berlin Deutsche Oper, Hamburg, Munich Staatsoper; ITA: Milan La Scala, Rome Opera; SWE: Stockholm; SWI: Zurich; UK: London Royal Opera; USA: Chicago, New York Met, San Francisco Opera. **Roles with these companies incl** MOZART: Sarastro★ (*Zauberflöte*); MUSSORGSKY: Boris Godunov★ & Pimen★ (*Boris Godunov*), Dosifei★ (*Khovanshchina*); VERDI: Ramfis★ (*Aida*), Philip II & Grande Inquisitore (*Don Carlo*), Padre Guardiano★ (*Forza del destino*), Banquo (*Macbeth*), Zaccaria (*Nabucco*), Fiesco★ (*Simon Boccanegra*); WAGNER: Daland★ (*Fliegende Holländer*), König Heinrich (*Lohengrin*), Gurnemanz★ (*Parsifal*), Fasolt★ (*Rheingold*), Hunding★ (*Walküre*), Hagen (*Götterdämmerung*), Landgraf (*Tannhäuser*), König Marke★ (*Tristan und Isolde*). Gives recitals. Appears with symphony orchestra. **Res:** Jatasalmentie 5, Helsinki, Finland. Mgmt: CST/UK.

TAMASSY, EVA. Contralto. German. Resident mem: Städtische Bühnen, Cologne. Born 19 Mar 1937, Budapest. Divorced. Studied: Dr Geza Laszlo, Gerda Gleuer, Kurt Schneider, Xander Hagen. **Debut:** Maddalena (*Rigoletto*) Hungarian State Opera, Budapest 1951. Awards: Third Prize Bach, Budapest; Third Prize Bartók, Budapest; Third Prize Voice Compt, Bucharest; Third Prize Prague Spring 1954.

Sang with major companies in AUS: Vienna Staatsoper & Volksoper; CZE: Prague Smetana; FRA: Marseille, Nancy, Nice, Paris, Toulouse; FR GER: Bielefeld, Bonn, Cologne, Dortmund, Düsseldorf-Duisburg, Frankfurt, Hamburg, Hannover, Kassel, Kiel, Mannheim, Munich Staatsoper & Gärtnerplatz, Nürnberg, Stuttgart, Wiesbaden, Wuppertal; HUN: Budapest; ITA: Bologna, Naples, Parma, Rome Opera, Trieste, Venice; POR: Lisbon; ROM: Bucharest; SWI: Bern. **Roles with these companies incl** BIZET: Carmen★; BORODIN: Kontchakovna (*Prince Igor*); DEBUSSY: Geneviève (*Pelléas et Mélisande*); GLUCK: Orfeo★; HANDEL: Cornelia (*Giulio Cesare*); JANACEK: Kabanikha (*Katya Kabanova*); KODALY: Marie Louise (*Háry János*); MASCAGNI: Lola (*Cavalleria rusticana*); MASSENET: Dulcinée (*Don Quichotte*); MUSSORGSKY: Marina (*Boris Godunov*); PUCCINI: Suzuki★ (*Butterfly*); ROSSINI:

Marchesina Clarice (*Pietra del paragone*); SAINT-SAENS: Dalila★; SMETANA: Hata (*Bartered Bride*); STRAUSS, R: Clairon (*Capriccio*), Klytämnestra (*Elektra*); STRAVINSKY: Baba the Turk (*Rake's Progress*); TCHAIKOVSKY: Mme Larina & Olga (*Eugene Onegin*); VERDI: Amneris (*Aida*), Ulrica★ (*Ballo in maschera*), Eboli (*Don Carlo*), Azucena★ (*Trovatore*); WAGNER: Erda (*Rheingold★, Siegfried★*), Fricka (*Rheingold★, Walküre★*), Waltraute★ (*Götterdämmerung*), Brangäne (*Tristan und Isolde*). Also KODALY: Haziasszony (*Spinning Room*); SZOKOLAY: Queen (*Hamlet*). Gives recitals. Appears with symphony orchestra. **Res:** 51 Cäsarstr, 70 Cologne, FR Ger. Mgmt: SLZ/FRG; CMW/FRA.

TAPPY, ERIC. Lyric tenor. Swiss. Born 19 May 1931, Lausanne, Switzerland. Wife Denise, occupation prof. Two children. Studied: Fernando Carpi, Geneva; Ernst Reichert, Salzburg; Eva Liebenberg, Hilversum. **Debut:** RAMEAU: Zoroastre, Opéra Comique, Paris 1964. Previous occupations: teacher. Awards: Prix Edison, Amsterdam 1968; Gold Medal, Drottningholm, Sweden.

Sang with major companies in BEL: Brussels; FRA: Aix-en-Provence Fest, Bordeaux, Lyon, Marseille, Strasbourg, Toulouse; FR GER: Cologne, Hamburg; HOL: Amsterdam; MON: Monte Carlo; POR: Lisbon; SWE: Drottningholm Fest; SWI: Geneva; UK: London Royal Opera; USA: San Francisco Opera. **Roles with these companies incl** BERG: Alwa (*Lulu*); CAVALLI: Ormindo★; DEBUSSY: Pelléas★; FALLA: Maese Pedro (*Retablo de Maese Pedro*); HANDEL: Acis; MARTIN: Tristan★ (*Vin herbé*); MONTEVERDI: Testo★ & Tancredi (*Combattimento di Tancredi*), Orfeo★‡, Nero★ (*Incoronazione di Poppea*); MOZART: Tito★ (*Clemenza di Tito*), Ferrando★ (*Così fan tutte*), Don Ottavio★ (*Don Giovanni*), Belmonte★ (*Entführung aus dem Serail*), Idomeneo★, Tamino★ (*Zauberflöte*); POULENC: Chevalier de la Force★ (*Dialogues des Carmélites*); PURCELL: Aeneas; RAMEAU: Hippolyte; ROSSINI: Don Ramiro (*Cenerentola*); ROUSSEAU: Colin (*Devin du village*); STRAUSS, J: Eisenstein & Alfred (*Fledermaus*); STRAVINSKY: Oedipus Rex★; TCHAIKOVSKY: Lenski★ (*Eugene Onegin*). Also MARTIN: Ferdinand (*Sturm*); RAMEAU: Zoroastre‡. **World premieres:** MARTIN: Musician & Lawyer (*M de Pourceaugnac*) Opéra de Genève 1963; MILHAUD: Léon (*Mère coupable*) Opéra de Genève 1966. Recorded for: Erato. Gives recitals. Appears with symphony orchestra. Coaches repertoire. On faculty of Opera Studio, Paris. **Res:** Ch de la Mouette, 1092 Belmont, Switzerland. Mgmt: RNR/SWI; IMR/FRA; AIM/UK.

TARNAY, GYULA; né Gyula Tar. Heldentenor. Hungarian. Resident mem: Hungarian National Opera, Budapest. Born 28 Aug 1928, Fehérgyarmat, Hungary. Wife Veronica, occupation teacher. Two children. Studied: Liszt Music Akad, Prof Endre Rösler, Budapest. **Debut:** Florestan (*Fidelio*) Hungarian National Opera 1957. Previous occupations: soloist with company of Hungarian People's Army.

Sang with major companies in AUS: Vienna Volksoper; HUN: Budapest; SWI: Zurich. **Roles with these companies incl** BEETHOVEN: Florestan (*Fidelio*); BERG: Tambourmajor (*Wozzeck*); BIZET: Don José★ (*Carmen*); BRITTEN: Albert Herring; DALLAPICCOLA: Jailer/Inquisitor (*Prigioniero*); ERKEL: Bánk Bán★; MASCAGNI: Turiddu (*Cavalleria rusticana*); PUCCINI: Pinkerton (*Butterfly*); SMETANA: Hans (*Bartered Bride*); STRAUSS, R: Matteo (*Arabella*), Bacchus (*Ariadne auf Naxos*); VERDI: Don Carlo, Alfredo (*Traviata*); WAGNER: Erik★ (*Fliegende Holländer*), Lohengrin, Walther★ (*Meistersinger*), Parsifal, Tannhäuser★. **World premieres:** PETROVICS: Refugié (*Cést la guerre*) Hungarian National Opera, Budapest 1962. Gives recitals. Appears with symphony orchestra. **Res:** Pusztaszeri 29, 1025 Budapest, Hungary. Mgmt: ITK/HUN; KRK/FRG.

TARRÉS, ENRIQUETA. Dramatic soprano. Spanish. Resident mem: Staatsoper, Hamburg; Staatsoper, Stuttgart. Born Spain.

Sang with major companies in AUS: Vienna Staatsoper; FRA: Paris; FR GER: Berlin Deutsche Oper, Cologne, Frankfurt, Hamburg, Stuttgart; MEX: Mexico City; SPA: Barcelona; SWI: Basel; USA: New York Met; et al. **Roles with these companies incl** HINDEMITH: Ursula (*Mathis der Maler*); MEYERBEER: Valentine (*Huguenots*); PUCCINI: Mimi (*Bohème*), Cio-Cio-San (*Butterfly*); STRAUSS, R: Chrysothemis (*Elektra*), Kaiserin (*Frau ohne Schatten*); VERDI: Amelia (*Ballo in maschera*), Desdemona (*Otello*), Leonora (*Trovatore*); et al.

TARSKI, ALEXANDER; né Tabaksblat. Conductor of opera and symphony; composer. Israeli. Resident Cond, National Opera, Tel Aviv. Born 10 Nov 1921, Lodz, Poland. Wife Irena. One child. Studied: Consv Lodz, Warsaw, Leningrad; incl piano & voice. Plays the piano. Operatic training as repetiteur & asst cond at National Opera Tashkent, 1944-45. **Operatic debut:** National Opera, Tashkent, USSR 1944. Symphonic debut: Phil Lodz, Poland 1948.

Conducted with major companies in ISR: Tel Aviv; POL: Lodz, Warsaw. **Operas with these companies incl** BIZET: *Carmen★, Pêcheurs de perles;* BORODIN: *Prince Igor;* CILEA: *A. Lecouvreur;* CIMAROSA: *Matrimonio segreto;* DELIBES: *Lakmé;* DONIZETTI: *Don Pasquale★, Elisir, Lucia★;* DVORAK: *Rusalka;* FLOTOW: *Martha;* GLINKA: *Life for the Tsar, Ruslan and Ludmilla;* GLUCK: *Orfeo ed Euridice;* GOLDMARK: *Königin von Saba★;* GOUNOD: *Faust★, Roméo et Juliette★;* HAYDN: *Mondo della luna;* HUMPERDINCK: *Hänsel und Gretel★;* LEONCAVALLO: *Pagliacci;* LORTZING: *Wildschütz;* MASCAGNI: *Cavalleria rusticana;* MENOTTI: *Telephone;* MONIUSZKO: *Halka, Haunted Castle;* MOZART: *Così fan tutte, Don Giovanni, Entführung aus dem Serail, Nozze di Figaro, Zauberflöte;* MUSSORGSKY: *Boris Godunov;* NICOLAI: *Lustigen Weiber;* OFFENBACH: *Contes d'Hoffmann★, Périchole, Mariage aux lanternes;* PERGOLESI: *Serva padrona;* PONCHIELLI: *Gioconda;* PUCCINI: *Bohème★, Gianni Schicchi, Butterfly★, Manon Lescaut, Tabarro, Tosca★;* RIMSKY-KOR-

SAKOV: *May Night, Tsar's Bride;* ROSSINI: *Barbiere di Siviglia★;* SAINT-SAENS: *Samson et Dalila;* SMETANA: *Bartered Bride;* STRAUSS, J: *Fledermaus★;* STRAUSS, R: *Rosenkavalier, Salome;* TCHAIKOVSKY: *Eugene Onegin, Iolanthe, Pique Dame;* VERDI: *Aida, Ballo in maschera, Forza del destino, Nabucco, Rigoletto★, Traviata★, Trovatore;* WAGNER: *Lohengrin;* WEBER: *Freischütz, Oberon;* WOLF-FERRARI: *Quattro rusteghi, Segreto di Susanna.* Conducted major orch in Europe. Teaches at Tel Aviv Univ & School for Singers. **Res:** 5 Slonimskistr, Bitsaron, Tel Aviv, Israel.

TASKOVA, SLAVKA. Coloratura soprano. Italian/Bulgarian. Born 16 Nov 1940, Sofia. Husband Prof Pier Paolo Paoletti, occupation surgeon. One child. Studied: Accad Chigiana, Gina Cigna, Siena; Lina Pagliughi, Milan. **Debut:** Rosina (*Barbiere di Siviglia*) 1966. Previous occupations: concert pianist. Awards: Prize, Intl Apollo Musagete; Deutscher Schallplattenpreis for Contemp Music 1975; First Prizes in Italy and France for best recordings.

Sang with major companies in AUS: Vienna Volksoper; BUL: Sofia; FRA: Paris; FR GER: Berlin Deutsche Oper, Cologne, Darmstadt, Frankfurt, Hamburg, Munich Staatsoper, Saarbrücken; HOL: Amsterdam; ITA: Bologna, Florence Maggio & Comunale, Genoa, Milan La Scala, Palermo, Spoleto Fest, Venice; POL: Warsaw; YUG: Zagreb. **Roles with these companies incl** BELLINI: Beatrice di Tenda★, Giulietta★ (*Capuleti ed i Montecchi*), Amina★ (*Sonnambula*); BERG: Lulu★, Marie★ (*Wozzeck*); DALLAPICCOLA: Mrs Fabian★ (*Volo di notte*); DELIBES: Lakmé★; DONIZETTI: Norina★ (*Don Pasquale*), Adina★ (*Elisir*), Marie★ (*Fille du régiment*), Lucia★; GLINKA: Ludmilla★; GLUCK: Armide; HANDEL: Rodelinda; HENZE: Manon (*Boulevard Solitude*); LIGETI: Soprano★ (*Aventures/Nouvelles Aventures*); MENOTTI: Amelia★ (*Amelia al ballo*), Lucy★ (*Telephone*); MOZART: Despina★ (*Così fan tutte*), Zerlina★ (*Don Giovanni*), Elettra★ (*Idomeneo*), Königin der Nacht★ (*Zauberflöte*); PUCCINI: Musetta★ (*Bohème*), Lauretta★ (*Gianni Schicchi*); RIMSKY-KORSAKOV: Coq d'or★; ROSSINI: Rosina★ (*Barbiere di Siviglia*), Giulia★ (*Scala di seta*), Sofia★ (*Signor Bruschino*); SCHOENBERG: Woman★ (*Erwartung*); STRAUSS, R: Zerbinetta★ (*Ariadne auf Naxos*), Sophie★ (*Rosenkavalier*); STRAVINSKY: Parasha★ (*Mavra*), Anne Trulove★ (*Rake's Progress*), Rossignol★; VERDI: Oscar★ (*Ballo in maschera*), Nannetta★ (*Falstaff*), Gilda★ (*Rigoletto*), Violetta★ (*Traviata*); YUN: Sim Tjong★; ZIMMERMANN: Marie★ (*Soldaten*). **World premieres:** REIMANN: Melusine, Deutsche Oper, Schwetzingen Fest, FR Ger 1971; NONO: I soprano (*Al gran sole carico d'amore*) Scala, Milan 1975. Recorded for: DG, Vergo. Gives recitals. Appears with symphony orchestra. **Res:** Bagnoro 0575/23882 Arezzo, Italy. Mgmt: SLZ/FRG.

TATTERMUSCHOVA, HELENA. Coloratura soprano/soubrette. Czechoslovakian. Resident mem: National Theater, Prague. Born 28 Jan 1933, Prague. Husband Jaroslav Boda, occupation musician. One child. Studied: State Consv, Prof Vlasta Linhartová, Prague. **Debut:** Musetta (*Bohème*)

State Theater, Ostrava 1955. Awards: Second Prize Intl Cont Prague 1954; Supraphon Prize 1973.

Sang with major companies in BEL: Brussels; BUL: Sofia; CZE: Prague National; FRA: Bordeaux; HOL: Amsterdam; ITA: Naples, Venice; POL: Warsaw; SPA: Barcelona; UK: Edinburgh Fest. Roles with these companies incl BEETHOVEN: Marzelline (Fidelio); BIZET: Micaëla* (Carmen); GLUCK: Amor (Orfeo ed Euridice); JANACEK: Vixen*‡ (Cunning Little Vixen), Malinka (Excursions of Mr Broucek); MOZART: Servilia (Clemenza di Tito), Despina* (Così fan tutte), Zerlina* (Don Giovanni), Blondchen (Entführung aus dem Serail), Susanna* (Nozze di Figaro); PROKOFIEV: Louisa (Duenna); PUCCINI: Musetta* (Bohème), Lauretta (Gianni Schicchi), Cio-Cio-San (Butterfly), Liù* (Turandot); ROSSINI: Rosina*(Barbiere di Siviglia); SMETANA: Blazenka* (Secret), Carla* (Two Widows); STRAUSS, R: Zdenka* (Arabella), Sophie (Rosenkavalier); VERDI: Oscar*(Ballo in maschera), Gilda (Rigoletto); WEBER: Aennchen (Freischütz). Also SMETANA: Jitka* (Dalibor), Barce* (The Kiss), Katuska* (Devil's Wall); JEREMIAS: Grushenka* (Brothers Karamazov); JANACEK: Aljeja* (From the House of the Dead); FIBICH: Ariel (Tempest). Recorded for: Supraphon. Gives recitals. Appears with symphony orchestra. Res: Detská 210/667, 100 00 Prague 10, CSSR. Mgmt: PRG/CZE.

TATUM, NANCY COLTHARP. Dramatic soprano. American. Resident mem: Metropolitan Opera, New York. Born 25 Aug 1937, Memphis, TN, USA. Husband Wiley E, occupation prof of voice, Memphis State Univ. Studied: Zelma Lee Thomas, Memphis; Samuel Margolis, New York; Wiley Tatum, husband. Debut: Aida, Oper Saarbrücken 1963. Previous occupations: secy. Awards: Gold Medallion, Intl Op Compt Sofia, Bulgaria 1963.

Sang with major companies in ARG: Buenos Aires; AUS: Vienna Staatsoper & Volksoper; BEL: Brussels; BUL: Sofia; CAN: Montreal/Quebec, Vancouver; FRA: Bordeaux, Lyon, Marseille, Nancy, Nice, Paris, Rouen, Strasbourg, Toulouse; GRE: Athens National; FR GER: Berlin Deutsche Oper, Bonn, Dortmund, Düsseldorf-Duisburg, Essen, Hamburg, Mannheim, Munich Staatsoper, Saarbrücken, Stuttgart; HOL: Amsterdam; HUN: Budapest; ITA: Milan La Scala, Parma, Spoleto Fest; ROM: Bucharest; SWI: Geneva, Zurich; USA: Cincinnati, Dallas, Hartford, Houston, Memphis, Minneapolis, New York Met & City Opera, Pittsburgh, San Antonio, San Francisco Opera; YUG: Zagreb. Roles with these companies incl BEETHOVEN: Leonore (Fidelio); BELLINI: Norma*; GLUCK: Alceste, Iphigénie (Iphigénie en Aulide); MASCAGNI: Santuzza* (Cavalleria rusticana); MOZART: Donna Anna (Don Giovanni); PONCHIELLI: Gioconda; PUCCINI: Lauretta (Gianni Schicchi), Tosca*, Turandot*; SCHUMANN: Genoveva; STRAUSS, R: Ariadne* (Ariadne auf Naxos), Kaiserin* (Frau ohne Schatten); VERDI: Aida*, Odabella (Attila), Amelia* (Ballo in maschera), Leonora* (Forza del destino), Lady Macbeth*, Abigaille* (Nabucco), Desdemona (Otello); WAGNER: Senta* (Fliegende Holländer), Kundry (Parsifal), Sieglinde* (Walküre)*, Brünnhilde

(Siegfried), Elisabeth* & Venus (Tannhäuser). Video — ORTF TV: Senta (Fliegende Holländer); Turandot; Leonora (Forza del destino); Genoveva. Gives recitals. Appears with symphony orchestra. Res: 1520 Central Ave, Memphis, TN, USA. Mgmt: HUR/USA; IMR/FRA.

TAVERNIA, PATRICK. Stages/produces opera & television. American. Resident Stage Dir, Metropolitan Opera, New York. Born Anaconda, MT. Single. Studied: music, piano and voice. Operatic training as asst stage dir at New York City Opera 1952-54. Operatic debut: Manon Lescaut Met Opera 1958. Awards: Fulbright Schlshp.

Directed/produced opera for major companies in USA: Baltimore, Boston, Chicago, Milwaukee Florentine, New Orleans, New York Met & City Opera, Philadelphia Lyric. Operas staged with these companies incl BIZET: Carmen; DONIZETTI: Don Pasquale, Elisir, Fille du régiment, Lucia; GIORDANO: Andrea Chénier; LEONCAVALLO: Pagliacci; MASCAGNI: Cavalleria rusticana; MENOTTI: Amahl, Dernier sauvage; MONTEVERDI: Incoronazione di Poppea; MOZART: Così fan tutte, Don Giovanni, Nozze di Figaro; PONCHIELLI: Gioconda; PUCCINI: Bohème, Fanciulla del West, Butterfly, Tosca, Turandot; ROSSINI: Barbiere di Siviglia, Cenerentola, Italiana in Algeri; VERDI: Aida, Don Carlo, Ernani, Forza del destino, Rigoletto, Traviata, Trovatore. Res: New York, NY, USA.

TAYLOR, RICHARD V. Lyric tenor. American. Resident mem: New York City Opera. Born 1 Jan 1949, Newburgh, NY, USA. Single. Studied: Tri-Cities Opera Wkshp, Carmen Savoca, Peyton Hibbitt, Binghamton, NY. Debut: Gérald (Lakmé) Tri-Cities Opera, Binghamton, NY 1969. Awards: Sullivan Fndt Awd.

Sang with major companies in USA: Kentucky, Lake George, New York City Opera, Washington DC. Roles with these companies incl BRITTEN: Male Chorus* (Rape of Lucretia); CHERUBINI: Giasone* (Medea); GOUNOD: Faust*; HAYDN: Filippo*(Infedeltà delusa); MOZART: Don Ottavio* (Don Giovanni), Idomeneo*; PUCCINI: Rodolfo* (Bohème); VERDI: Alfredo* (Traviata). Also STRAUSS, R: Narraboth* (Salome). World premiere: BROOKS: Prince (Rapunzel) Tri-Cities Opera, Binghamton, NY 1971. Mgmt: MKA/USA.

TEAR, ROBERT. Lyric tenor. British. Born 8 Mar 1939, Barry, Wales, UK. Wife Hilary. Two children. Studied: Kings Coll, Cambridge; Julian Kimbell, UK. Debut: Madwoman (Curlew River) English Opera Group, Aldeburgh Fest 1964. Awards: Harriet Cohen Medal.

Sang with major companies in FRA: Paris; HOL: Amsterdam; UK: Aldeburgh Fest, Edinburgh Fest, Glasgow Scottish, London Royal. Roles with these companies incl BRITTEN: Madwoman (Curlew River), Lysander* (Midsummer Night), Peter Grimes, Tempter (Prodigal Son), Male Chorus* (Rape of Lucretia), Peter Quint* (Turn of the Screw); DELIUS: Sali‡ (Village Romeo and Juliet); GLUCK: Admetos* (Alceste); HANDEL: Acis; HOLST: Satyavan‡ (Savitri); MONTEVERDI: Nero* (Incoronazione di Poppea); MOZART: Don Ottavio* (Don Giovanni),

Idomeneo★; MUSSORGSKY: Vassily Golitsin★ (*Khovanshchina*); RAMEAU: Hippolyte‡; STRAUSS, R: Matteo★(*Arabella*); TCHAIKOVSKY: Lenski★ (*Eugene Onegin*); VERDI: Alfredo★(*Traviata*); WAGNER: Loge★(*Rheingold*). Also TIPPETT: Paris★ (*King Priam*). **World premieres**: BRITTEN: Misael (*Burning Fiery Furnace*) Engl Op Grp, Aldeburgh 1966; Younger Son (*Prodigal Son*) Engl Op Grp, Aldeburgh 1968; TIPPETT: Dov (*Knot Garden*) Royal Op Covent Garden, London 1970; CROSSE: Todd (*Grace of Todd*) Engl Op Grp, Aldeburgh 1969. Recorded for: EMI, Decca, Philips, Argo. Video/Film: Lenski (*Eugene Onegin*); (*Prodigal Son*); (*Burning Fiery Furnace*). Gives recitals. Appears with symphony orchestra. Teaches voice. Coaches repertoire. On faculty of Royal Coll of Music, Prof, London. **Res**: 101 D Clarendon Rd, London W11, UK. **Mgmt**: HLT/UK.

TEBALDI, RENATA. Lyric & dramatic soprano. Italian. Born 1 Feb 1922, Pesaro. Single. Studied: Parma Consv; Pesaro Consv, Carmen Melis, G Pais. **Debut**: Elena (*Mefistofele*) Teatro Municipale, Rovigo 1943.
Sang with major companies in ARG: Buenos Aires; AUS: Vienna Staatsoper; BRA: Rio de Janeiro; FRA: Paris; FR GER: Berlin Deutsche Oper, Hamburg; HOL: Amsterdam; ITA: Florence Maggio, Milan La Scala, Naples, Palermo, Parma, Rome Opera, Trieste, Venice, Verona Arena; SPA: Barcelona; UK: Edinburgh Fest, London Royal; USA: Boston, Chicago, Dallas, New York Met, Philadelphia Lyric, San Francisco Opera; et al. **Roles with these companies incl** BIZET: Micaëla (*Carmen*); BOITO: Margherita‡ (*Mefistofele*); CATALANI: Wally‡; CILEA: Adriana Lecouvreur★‡; GIORDANO: Maddalena★‡ (*Andrea Chénier*), Fedora; GOUNOD: Marguerite (*Faust*); HANDEL: Cleopatra (*Giulio Cesare*); MASCAGNI: Suzel (*Amico Fritz*); MOZART: Donna Elvira (*Don Giovanni*), Contessa (*Nozze di Figaro*); PONCHIELLI: Gioconda‡; PUCCINI: Mimi‡ (*Bohème*), Minnie‡ (*Fanciulla del West*), Cio-Cio-San★‡ (*Butterfly*), Manon Lescaut‡, Tosca‡; ROSSINI: Mathilde (*Guillaume Tell*), Pamira (*Assedio di Corinto*); SPONTINI: Amazily (*Fernand Cortez*); TCHAIKOVSKY: Tatiana (*Eugene Onegin*); VERDI: Aida‡, Alice Ford★(*Falstaff*), Leonora‡ (*Forza del destino*), Giovanna d'Arco, Desdemona★ (*Otello*), Amelia (*Simon Boccanegra*), Violetta (*Traviata*); WAGNER: Elsa (*Lohengrin*), Eva (*Meistersinger*), Elisabeth (*Tannhäuser*); et al. Also: REFICE: Cecilia; SPONTINI: Olimpia; CASAVOLA: Salammbô. On records MASCAGNI: Santuzza (*Cavalleria rusticana*); PUCCINI: Lauretta (*Gianni Schicchi*), Suor Angelica, Giorgetta (*Tabarro*), Liù (*Turandot*); VERDI: Amelia (*Ballo in maschera*), Elisabetta (*Don Carlo*), Leonora (*Trovatore*). Recorded for Fonit, Cetra, Decca, London, Richmond, RCA. Video/Film: Aida, Elsa (*Lohengrin*); both soundtrack only. Gives recitals. Appears with symphony orchestra. Mgmt: CAM/USA; GOR/UK.

TEDESCO, SERGIO. Lyric & character tenor. Italian. Born 23 Apr 1934, La Spezia, Italy. Wife Daniela Mazzucato, occupation soprano. Studied: Consv S Cecilia, Mo Piervenanzi, Mo Francardi,

Rome. **Debut**: Arlecchino (*Maschere*) Teatro Comunale, Florence 1955-56. Previous occupations: actor of film & stage. Awards: Gold Medal Zandonai; Silver Medal Trieste Lloyd.
Sang with major companies in ITA: Bologna, Milan La Scala, Naples, Palermo, Rome Opera & Caracalla, Trieste, Venice. **Roles with these companies incl** DONIZETTI: Tenor★ (*Convenienze/Viva la Mamma*); EINEM: Camille Desmoulins★ (*Dantons Tod*); HAYDN: Ernesto★ (*Mondo della luna*); MOZART: Pedrillo★(*Entführung aus dem Serail*); MUSSORGSKY: Shuisky★ (*Boris Godunov*), Vassily Golitsin★ (*Khovanshchina*); PROKOFIEV: Truffaldino★ (*Love for Three Oranges*); PUCCINI: Prunier★ (*Rondine*). **World premieres**: VIOZZI: Cpt Tedesco (*Elisabetta*) Trieste Opera 1971. Video/Film − RAI: Scrivano (*Khovanshchina*). Gives recitals. Appears with symphony orchestra. **Res**: V Montealtore 10, Abano Terme, Italy.

TE KANAWA, KIRI. Lyric soprano. New Zealander. Resident mem: Royal Opera House, London. Born Gisborne, New Zealand. Husband Desmond Park, occupation company dir. Studied: Dame Sister Mary Leo, Auckland, New Zealand; London Opera Centre; Mme Vera Rozsa, London. **Debut**: Blumenmädchen (*Parsifal*) Royal Opera House 1971. Awards: Order of the British Empire (OBE).
Sang with major companies in FRA: Aix-en-Provence Fest, Bordeaux, Lyon, Paris; UK: Glasgow Scottish, Glyndebourne Fest, London Royal Opera; USA: New York Met, San Francisco Opera, Santa Fe. **Roles with these companies incl** BIZET: Micaëla★‡ (*Carmen*); GOUNOD: Marguerite★(*Faust*); MOZART: Fiordiligi★(*Così fan tutte*), Donna Elvira★‡ (*Don Giovanni*), Contessa★ (*Nozze di Figaro*), Pamina★ (*Zauberflöte*); PUCCINI: Mimi★ (*Bohème*); VERDI: Desdemona★ (*Otello*), Amelia★ (*Simon Boccanegra*). Recorded for: Philips, Decca. Gives recitals. Appears with symphony orchestra. **Res**: London, UK. Mgmt: AIM/UK; CAM/USA.

TELASKO, RALPH. Bass-baritone. Austrian. Resident mem: Opernhaus Zurich. Born 10 Aug 1911, Vienna. Wife Elisabeth. Studied: Music Acad and Consv, Prof Victor Fuchs, Vienna. **Debut**: Heerrufer (*Lohengrin*) Vienna Volksoper 1934.
Sang with major companies in ARG: Buenos Aires; AUS: Graz, Salzburg Fest, Vienna Staatsoper & Volksoper; BEL: Brussels; BRA: Rio de Janeiro; CZE: Brno, Prague Smetana; FRA: Bordeaux, Lyon, Marseille, Nancy, Nice, Rouen, Toulouse; FR GER: Bayreuth Fest, Cologne, Darmstadt, Düsseldorf-Duisburg, Frankfurt, Mannheim, Saarbrücken, Wiesbaden, Wuppertal; ITA: Florence Comunale, Venice; POR: Lisbon; SPA: Barcelona; SWI: Basel, Geneva, Zurich; USA: Baltimore, Boston, Chicago, Hartford, Houston, Newark, New Orleans, New York City Opera, Philadelphia Lyric, Pittsburgh, Washington DC. **Roles with these companies incl** d'ALBERT: Sebastiano (*Tiefland*); BARTOK: Bluebeard; BEETHOVEN: Don Pizarro (*Fidelio*); BERG: Doktor (*Wozzeck*); BIZET: Escamillo (*Carmen*); BORODIN: Galitzky (*Prince Igor*); DEBUSSY: Golaud (*Pelléas et Mélisande*); GIORDANO:

Carlo Gérard (*Andrea Chénier*); GLUCK: Oreste (*Iphigénie en Tauride*); GOLDMARK: König Salomon (*Königin von Saba*); GOUNOD: Méphistophélès (*Faust*); HINDEMITH: Professor (*Hin und zurück*); HUMPERDINCK: Spielmann (*Königskinder*); LEONCAVALLO: Tonio (*Pagliacci*); LORTZING: Van Bett (*Zar und Zimmermann*); MASCAGNI: Alfio (*Cavalleria rusticana*); MASSENET: Lescaut (*Manon*), Athanaël (*Thaïs*), Albert (*Werther*); MENOTTI: Husband (*Amelia al ballo*); MEYERBEER: Comte Oberthal (*Prophète*); MOZART: Don Alfonso★ (*Così fan tutte*), Leporello & Don Giovanni (*Don Giovanni*), Conte Almaviva & Figaro (*Nozze di Figaro*); MUSSORGSKY: Boris Godunov & Varlaam (*Boris Godunov*); NICOLAI: Fluth (*Lustigen Weiber*); OFFENBACH: Coppélius etc (*Contes d'Hoffmann*); ORFF: Bauer★ (*Kluge*); PUCCINI: Colline★ (*Bohème*), Gianni Schicchi, Sharpless (*Butterfly*), Lescaut (*Manon Lescaut*), Scarpia (*Tosca*); RABAUD: Ali (*Mârouf*); RAVEL: Ramiro (*Heure espagnole*); ROSSINI: Dott Bartolo★ (*Barbiere di Siviglia*), Mustafà (*Italiana in Algeri*); SAINT-SAENS: Grand prêtre (*Samson et Dalila*); STRAUSS, R: Mandryka (*Arabella*), Musiklehrer (*Ariadne auf Naxos*), Graf (*Capriccio*), Orest (*Elektra*), Baron Ochs (*Rosenkavalier*), Jochanaan (*Salome*); STRAVINSKY: Nick Shadow (*Rake's Progress*); VERDI: Amonasro (*Aida*), Philip II & Grande Inquisitore★ (*Don Carlo*), Falstaff, Fra Melitone (*Forza del destino*), Iago (*Otello*); WAGNER: Holländer, Friedrich (*Liebesverbot*), Telramund (*Lohengrin*), Pogner (*Meistersinger*), Amfortas (*Parsifal*), Alberich (*Rheingold*), Wotan (*Rheingold, Walküre*), Wanderer (*Siegfried*), Gunther (*Götterdämmerung*), Wolfram (*Tannhäuser*), Kurwenal★ (*Tristan und Isolde*); WEBER: Kaspar (*Freischütz*); WOLF: Tio Lukas (*Corregidor*). Also BERG: Tierbändiger & Rodrigo★ (*Lulu*); STRAUSS, R: Faninal★ (*Rosenkavalier*); BEETHOVEN: Don Fernando★ (*Fidelio*). Recorded for: Tono AG. Gives recitals. Appears with symphony orchestra. Teaches voice. **Res:** Tödiweg 2, CH-8802 Kilchberg/Zurich, Switzerland.

TENNSTEDT, KLAUS. Conductor of opera and symphony. German. Gen Music Dir & Resident Cond, Oper der Landeshauptstadt Kiel, FR Ger.

Conducted with major companies in FR GER: Berlin Deutsche Oper, Hamburg, Kiel, Munich Staatsoper; GER DR: Dresden; et al. **Operas with these companies incl** DESSAU: *Verurteilung des Lukullus;* EINEM: *Besuch der alten Dame;* HENZE: *Boulevard Solitude;* JANACEK: *Jenufa;* MOZART: *Nozze di Figaro;* PUCCINI: *Turandot;* ROSSINI: *Barbiere di Siviglia;* STRAUSS, R: *Elektra, Salome;* VERDI: *Simon Boccanegra;* WAGNER: *Götterdämmerung;* et al. **Res:** Kiel, FR Ger.

TEODORIAN, VALENTIN. Lyric tenor. Romanian. Resident mem: Romanian Opera, Bucharest. Born 4 Jun 1928, Bucharest. Wife Elena, occupation painter. Studied: with father Constantin Teodorian; Consv, Bucharest. **Debut:** Beppo (*Pagliacci*) Romanian Opera 1949. Awards: Laureate, Spring in Prague Fest 1955; Merited Artist, Romanian Gvnmt.

Sang with major companies in BUL: Sofia; FR GER: Saarbrücken; HUN: Budapest; ROM: Bucharest; USSR: Leningrad Kirov, Moscow Stanislavski, Tbilisi; YUG: Belgrade. **Roles with these companies incl** BORODIN: Vladimir‡ (*Prince Igor*); BRITTEN: Albert Herring★; DEBUSSY: Pelléas★; DELIBES: Gérald (*Lakmé*); DONIZETTI: Ernesto★ (*Don Pasquale*); MASSENET: Des Grieux (*Manon*); MOZART: Ferrando★ (*Così fan tutte*), Belmonte★ (*Entführung aus dem Serail*), Tamino★ (*Zauberflöte*); OFFENBACH: Hoffmann★; ORFF: Erzähler★ (*Mond*); PROKOFIEV: Antonio (*Duenna*); PUCCINI: Rodolfo (*Bohème*), Rinuccio‡ (*Gianni Schicchi*); ROSSINI: Almaviva★ (*Barbiere di Siviglia*); STRAUSS, J: Eisenstein★ (*Fledermaus*); TCHAIKOVSKY: Lenski (*Eugene Onegin*); VERDI: Fenton (*Falstaff*), Alfredo★ (*Traviata*); WAGNER: David (*Meistersinger*). Also on records only BRITTEN: Peter Grimes; DALLAPICCOLA: Radio Telegrapher (*Volo di notte*); MONTEVERDI: Ulisse (*Ritorno d'Ulisse*); PURCELL: King Arthur. **World premieres:** TRAILESCU: Emperor (*Puss in Boots*) Romanian Opera. Recorded for: VEB. Video/Film: Almaviva (*Barbiere di Siviglia*). Gives recitals. Appears with symphony orchestra. Teaches voice. Coaches repertoire. **Res:** 15 Gh Dej Blvd, Bucharest 6, Romania. Mgmt: RIA/ROM.

TER-ARUTUNIAN, ROUBEN. Scenic and costume designer for opera, theater, film, TV. American. Born 24 Jul 1920, Tiflis, Russia. Single. Studied: Reimann Schule, F Wilhelm Univ, Berlin; Univ Vienna; Ecole des Beaux Arts, Paris. **Operatic debut:** sets, *Bluebeard's Castle* & *Heure espagnole* New York City Opera 1952; cost, *Bartered Bride* Volksoper Dresden, Germany 1943. Theater debut: Third Army Spec Serv; dancers of Staatsoper, Berlin 1941. Awards: Antoinette Perry Awd Best Costumes 1958; Outer Critics' Circle Awd Best Scenic Design 1957; Emmy Awd Best Art Dir, NBC TV.

Designed for major companies in AUS: Vienna Volksoper; FR GER: Hamburg; GER DR: Dresden; ITA: Milan La Scala, Rome Opera, Spoleto Fest, Venice; USA: New York City Opera, Santa Fe. **Operas designed for these companies incl** BARTOK: *Bluebeard's Castle;* BIZET: *Carmen★;* DEBUSSY: *Pelléas et Mélisande★;* EINEM: *Prozess;* GLUCK: *Orfeo ed Euridice;* HENZE: *Bassariden;* HOIBY: *Scarf;* HUMPERDINCK: *Hänsel und Gretel;* MENOTTI: *Maria Golovin;* MOORE: *Devil and Daniel Webster;* PENDERECKI: *Teufel von Loudun★;* PUCCINI: *Gianni Schicchi★, Butterfly, Suor Angelica, Tabarro;* RAVEL: *Heure espagnole;* ROSSINI: *Cenerentola;* SMETANA: *Bartered Bride;* STRAUSS, R: *Salome.* **Operatic world premieres:** MENOTTI: *Maria Golovin* 1958; HOIBY: *Scarf* 1958; DELLO JOIO: *Blood Moon* San Francisco 1961; HENZE: *Rachel la Cubana* NET 1975; STRAVINSKY: *Flood* CBS TV 1962; FOSS: *Griffelkin* NBC TV 1955. Operatic Video—NBC TV Opera: *Zauberflöte, Entführung aus dem Serail, Ariadne auf Naxos.* Exhibitions of stage designs Wright-Hepburn-Webster Gal, NY 1968; Canyon Road Art Gal Santa Fe, NM 1968; V Astor Gal, Lib & Musm of Perf Arts, Lincoln Center, NY 1970. **Res:** 360 E 55 St, New York 10022, USA.

TERMER, HELGA ELISABETH. Lyric coloratura soprano. German. Resident mem: Staatstheater Dresden, Ger DR. Born 25 Jun 1938, Berlin. Husband Hans-E Zimmer, occupation conductor. Studied: Rudolf Wille, Kmsg Elisabeth Rose, Prof Rita Meinl-Weise, Berlin. **Debut:** Nannetta (*Falstaff*) Staatstheater Schwerin, Germany 1961. Awards: Diploma Intl Robert Schumann Compt, Zwickau 1969; First Prize, Ntl Compt Ger DR, Berlin 1970; Third Prize, Intl Erkel Compt, Budapest 1970.

Sang with major companies in FR GER: Wiesbaden; GER DR: Berlin Staatsoper, Dresden; USSR: Leningrad Kirov. **Roles with these companies incl** BEETHOVEN: Marzelline★ (*Fidelio*); CIMAROSA: Elisetta (*Matrimonio segreto*); CORNELIUS: Margiana (*Barbier von Bagdad*); DONIZETTI: Adina★ (*Elisir*); FLOTOW: Lady Harriet (*Martha*); GLUCK: Amor (*Orfeo ed Euridice*); HUMPERDINCK: Gretel; LEONCAVALLO: Nedda★ (*Pagliacci*); LORTZING: Baronin Freimann★ (*Wildschütz*), Marie (*Zar und Zimmermann*); MOZART: Zerlina (*Don Giovanni*), Blondchen★ (*Entführung aus dem Serail*), Mlle Silberklang★ (*Schauspieldirektor*), Susanna★ (*Nozze di Figaro*), Königin der Nacht★ (*Zauberflöte*); NICOLAI: Frau Fluth★ & Aennchen (*Lustigen Weiber*); OFFENBACH: Antonia★ (*Contes d'Hoffmann*); ORFF: Solo★ (*Carmina burana*), Kluge; PROKOFIEV: Louisa★ (*Duenna*); PUCCINI: Musetta (*Bohème*); STRAUSS, J: Adele (*Fledermaus*); STRAVINSKY: Parasha★ (*Mavra*); VERDI: Oscar (*Ballo in maschera*); WEBER: Aennchen★ (*Freischütz*). Also on records only AUBER: Zerlina (*Fra Diavolo*). **World premieres:** ZIMMERMANN: Marie (*Levins Mühle*) Staatsoper Dresden 1973. Recorded for: VEB. Gives recitals. Appears with symphony orchestra. Coaches repertoire. Mgmt: KDR/GDR.

TERRANOVA, VITTORIO ANTONIO. Light lyric tenor. Italian. Born 18 Jun 1945, Licata, Italy. Single. Studied: Prof Maria Carbone, Prof Sara Sforni Corti. **Debut:** Lord Arthur (*Puritani*) Theater, Mantua 1970. Previous occupations: salesman for Olivetti.

Sang with major companies in AUS: Bregenz Fest, Graz, Vienna Staatsoper; CZE: Prague Smetana; FRA: Toulouse; FR GER: Düsseldorf-Duisburg, Frankfurt, Hamburg; GER DR: Dresden; HOL: Amsterdam; ITA: Bologna, Florence Maggio & Comunale, Milan La Scala, Palermo, Parma, Rome Caracalla, Spoleto Fest, Trieste, Venice; SPA: Barcelona; USA: Chicago, New York City Opera. **Roles with these companies incl** ADAM: Chapelou (*Postillon de Lonjumeau*); AUBER: Alfonso★ (*Muette de Portici*); BELLINI: Tebaldo (*Capuleti ed i Montecchi*), Lord Arthur★ (*Puritani*), Elvino★ (*Sonnambula*); BIZET: Nadir★ (*Pêcheurs de perles*); CHARPENTIER: Julien (*Louise*); CIMAROSA: Paolino (*Matrimonio segreto*); DONIZETTI: Riccardo★ (*Anna Bolena*), Ernesto★ (*Don Pasquale*), Nemorino★ (*Elisir*), Fernande★ (*Favorite*), Tonio★ (*Fille du régiment*), Charles★ (*Linda di Chamounix*), Leicester★ (*Maria Stuarda*), Roberto Devereux★; FLOTOW: Lionel (*Martha*); GOUNOD: Faust; MASCAGNI: Fritz (*Amico Fritz*); MASSENET: Des Grieux (*Manon*), Werther★; MOZART: Tito (*Clemenza di Tito*), Ferrando★ (*Così fan tutte*), Don Ottavio★

(*Don Giovanni*), Belmonte★ (*Entführung aus dem Serail*), Tamino★ (*Zauberflöte*); ORFF: Solo★ (*Carmina burana*); PAISIELLO: Almaviva★ (*Barbiere di Siviglia*); PUCCINI: Rinuccio★ (*Gianni Schicchi*); ROSSINI: Almaviva★ (*Barbiere di Siviglia*), Don Ramiro★ (*Cenerentola*), Comte Ory★, Leicester★ (*Elisabetta Regina*), Lindoro★ (*Italiana in Algeri*), Idreno★ (*Semiramide*), Florville★ (*Signor Bruschino*), Narciso★ (*Turco in Italia*); STRAUSS, R: Ein Sänger★ (*Rosenkavalier*); THOMAS: Wilhelm Meister (*Mignon*); VERDI: Fenton★ (*Falstaff*), Edoardo★ (*Giorno di regno*), Duca di Mantova★ (*Rigoletto*), Alfredo★ (*Traviata*); WEILL: Jim Mahoney★ (*Aufstieg und Fall der Stadt Mahagonny*). Also CIMAROSA: (*Sposi per accidenti*); ROSSINI: (*Armida*). Video/Film: Lord Arthur (*Puritani*). Gives recitals. Appears with symphony orchestra. Res: V A Tadino 46, Milan, Italy. Mgmt: CAM/USA.

TERRASSON, RENÉ-PIERRE. Stages/produces opera & television. Also designs sets, costumes & stage-lighting and is an author. French. Gen Dir & Resident Stage Dir, Opéra de Nantes. Born 19 May 1924, Valence/Drôme. Wife Arlette Corlet, occupation therapist. One child. Studied: Consv de Dijon, incl music, piano and voice. **Operatic debut:** Opéra de Nantes 1973. Theater debut: Centre Dramatique, Dijon 1948. Previous occupation: singer, comedian. Awards: Grand Prix du Disque, Acad Georges Cros. Previous adm positions in opera: Chief Stage Dir, Théâtre des Arts, Rouen 1971.

Directed/produced opera for major companies in BEL: Brussels, Liège; FRA: Nancy, Paris, Rouen, Strasbourg, Toulouse; ITA: Venice. **Operas staged with these companies incl** ADAM: *Si j'étais roi;* BECAUD: *Opéra d'Aran†;* BERLIOZ: *Damnation de Faust;* BIZET: *Carmen, Pêcheurs de perles†;* CHARPENTIER: *Louise;* CIMAROSA: *Matrimonio segreto;* DEBUSSY: *Pelléas et Mélisande†;* DONIZETTI: *Don Pasquale;* GOUNOD: *Faust, Roméo et Juliette;* IBERT: *Angélique†;* MARTINU: *Griechische Passion;* MASSENET: *Jongleur de Notre Dame, Werther;* MENOTTI: *Consul†;* MOZART: *Così fan tutte, Entführung aus dem Serail†, Nozze di Figaro;* POULENC: *Dialogues des Carmélites;* PUCCINI: *Bohème†, Manon Lescaut, Tosca;* RABAUD: *Mârouf;* RAVEL: *Heure espagnole;* ROSSINI: *Barbiere di Siviglia†;* ROUSSEAU: *Devin du village†;* VERDI: *Falstaff†, Traviata;* WAGNER: *Fliegende Holländer.* **Operatic world premieres:** BONDON: *I 330* Opéra de Nantes 1975, *Ana et l'albatros* Opéra de Metz 1975; SEMENOFF: *Sire Halewyn* Nantes 1970. Operatic Video—ORTF: *Devin du village.* Mgmt: IMR/FRA.

TERZIAN, ANITA. Coloratura mezzo-soprano. American. Resident mem: Opéra du Rhin, Strasbourg. Born 12 Oct 1947. Single. Studied: Juilliard School, Jennie Tourel, New York. **Debut:** Rosina (*Barbiere di Siviglia*) Théâtre de la Monnaie, Brussels 1973. Awards: Ntl Opera Inst Awd; Winner Intl Voice Compt Munich 1971; Rockefeller Fndt Grant; Liederkranz Awd.

Sang with major companies in BEL: Brussels Monnaie, Liège; FRA: Strasbourg; GRE: Athens National; ISR: Tel Aviv; USA: San Francisco

Opera. **Roles with these companies incl** BIZET: Carmen*; BORODIN: Kontchakovna* (*Prince Igor*); CIMAROSA: Elisetta* (*Matrimonio segreto*); MASSENET: Charlotte* (*Werther*); MOZART: Sesto* (*Clemenza di Tito*); OFFENBACH: Périchole*; ROSSINI: Rosina* (*Barbiere di Siviglia*), Isabella* (*Italiana in Algeri*), Sinaïde* (*Moïse*); STRAUSS, J: Prinz Orlovsky* (*Fledermaus*); TCHAIKOVSKY: Olga* (*Eugene Onegin*). Also MONTEVERDI: Ottavia* (*Incoronazione di Poppea*). Gives recitals. **Res:** New York, NY, USA, and Strasbourg, France. **Mgmt:** SHA/USA; IMR/FRA.

TESCHLER, FRED FRITZ. Bass & basso-buffo. German. Resident mem: Staatsoper Dresden, Ger DR. Born 27 Sep 1926, Dresden. Wife Renate, occupation engr. Two children. Studied: Senta Kutzschbach, Dresden. **Debut:** Bauer (*Kluge*) Staatsoper, Dresden 1955. Previous occupations: journalist, merchant. Awards: Kammersänger, Ministry of Culture, Ger DR.

Sang with major companies in AUS: Salzburg Fest; BUL: Sofia; CZE: Brno; FR GER: Stuttgart; GER DR: Berlin Komische Oper & Staatsoper, Dresden, Leipzig; HUN: Budapest; ROM: Bucharest; SWI: Zurich; USA: Baltimore, Boston. **Roles with these companies incl** d'ALBERT: Tommaso (*Tiefland*); BEETHOVEN: Rocco* (*Fidelio*); EGK: Cuperus* (*Zaubergeige*); HANDEL: Polyphemus* (*Acis and Galatea*), King of Scotland* (*Ariodante*); LORTZING: Stadinger (*Waffenschmied*), Van Bett (*Zar und Zimmermann*); MOZART: Don Alfonso* (*Così fan tutte*), Osmin* (*Entführung aus dem Serail*), Sarastro* (*Zauberflöte*); MUSSORGSKY: Pimen* (*Boris Godunov*); NICOLAI: Falstaff* (*Lustigen Weiber*); ORFF: Bauer* (*Mond*); PUCCINI: Colline (*Bohème*); ROSSINI: Don Basilio* (*Barbiere di Siviglia*); SMETANA: Kezal* (*Bartered Bride*); STRAUSS, R: La Roche* (*Capriccio*), Baron Ochs* (*Rosenkavalier*); VERDI: Ramfis (*Aida*), Philip II* & Grande Inquisitore* (*Don Carlo*), Padre Guardiano* (*Forza del destino*), Zaccaria (*Nabucco*); WAGNER: Daland* (*Fliegende Holländer*), König Heinrich (*Lohengrin*), Pogner* (*Meistersinger*), Fasolt* & Fafner* (*Rheingold*), Hunding* (*Walküre*), König Marke* (*Tristan und Isolde*); WEBER: Omar* (*Abu Hassan*), Kaspar* (*Freischütz*); WOLF-FERRARI: Ottavio (*Donne curiose*), Lunardo* (*Quattro rusteghi*). Also HANDEL: Lycomedes* (*Deidamia*). Gives recitals. Appears with symphony orchestra. **Mgmt:** KDR/GDR; LLF/USA.

THALLAUG, EDITH. Coloratura mezzo-soprano. Norwegian. Resident mem: Royal Opera, Stockholm. Born Oslo, Norway. Husband Ulf Björkegren, occupation singer, tenor. Studied: Giurggja Leppée, Joel Berglund. **Debut:** Dorabella (*Così fan tutte*) Göteborg, Sweden 1962. Previous occupations: actress. Awards: Norwegian Critics Awd 1973.

Sang with major companies in DEN: Copenhagen; FIN: Helsinki; NOR: Oslo; SWE: Drottningholm Fest, Stockholm; UK: Glyndebourne Fest; USSR: Moscow Bolshoi. **Roles with these companies incl** BARTOK: Judith (*Bluebeard's Castle*); BENNETT: Rosalind (*Mines of Sulphur*); BIZET: Carmen*; BRITTEN: Hippolita (*Midsum-*

mer Night); HANDEL: Bradamante* (*Alcina*); MONTEVERDI: Penelope (*Ritorno d'Ulisse*); MOZART: Dorabella* (*Così fan tutte*), Cherubino* (*Nozze di Figaro*); PUCCINI: Suzuki (*Butterfly*); ROSSINI: Rosina* (*Barbiere di Siviglia*), Angelina* (*Cenerentola*), Isabella (*Italiana in Algeri*), Arsace (*Semiramide*); SAINT-SAENS: Dalila; STRAUSS, J: Prinz Orlovsky (*Fledermaus*); STRAUSS, R: Komponist* (*Ariadne auf Naxos*), Amme* (*Frau ohne Schatten*), Octavian* (*Rosenkavalier*); TCHAIKOVSKY: Olga (*Eugene Onegin*); VERDI: Amneris* (*Aida*), Eboli* (*Don Carlo*), Azucena* (*Trovatore*); WAGNER: Venus (*Tannhäuser*). Also WERLE: Thérèse* (*Dream of Thérèse*); MONTEVERDI: Ottavia (*Incoronazione di Poppea*). Recorded for: Philips. Video—Swedish TV: (*Carmen*); Norwegian TV: (*Cenerentola*). Gives recitals. Appears with symphony orchestra. **Mgmt:** SVE/SWE.

THAU, PIERRE-EUGÈNE. Bass. French. Resident mem: Opéra du Rhin, Strasbourg. Born 16 Dec 1933, Toulouse, France. Wife Yone, occupation secy. One child. Studied: Consv de Toulouse, Prof Mme Izar. **Debut:** Charles V (*Don Carlo*) Opéra de Paris 1965. Previous occupations: life insurance salesman. Awards: First Prize in Voice, Toulouse Consv; First Prize in Interpret 1962; First Prize Conc de Lyon 1963; First Prize Intl Verdi Compt, Venice 1964.

Sang with major companies in BEL: Liège; BRA: Rio de Janeiro; FRA: Aix-en-Provence Fest, Bordeaux, Lyon, Marseille, Nancy, Nice, Paris, Rouen, Strasbourg, Toulouse; FR GER: Hamburg, Saarbrücken; ITA: Florence Maggio, Milan La Scala, Venice; MON: Monte Carlo; POR: Lisbon; SPA: Barcelona. **Roles with these companies incl** BELLINI: Sir George* (*Puritani*); BERLIOZ: Balducci* (*Benvenuto Cellini*), Méphistophélès* (*Damnation de Faust*), Narbal* (*Troyens*); BRITTEN: Theseus* (*Midsummer Night*); GOUNOD: Méphistophélès* (*Faust*), Ramon (*Mireille*); HALEVY: Brogny* (*Juive*); MASSENET: Phanuel* (*Hérodiade*); MOZART: Publio* (*Clemenza di Tito*), Figaro (*Nozze di Figaro*); PUCCINI: Colline* (*Bohème*); ROSSINI: Don Basilio* (*Barbiere di Siviglia*); THOMAS: Lothario* (*Mignon*); VERDI: Ramfis (*Aida*), Padre Guardiano* (*Forza del destino*), Banquo (*Macbeth*), Fiesco (*Simon Boccanegra*), Procida (*Vespri*). Also GOUNOD: Frère Laurent* (*Roméo et Juliette*); RABAUD: Sultan (*Mârouf*); MONTEVERDI: Seneca* (*Incoronazione di Poppea*); PUCCINI: Timur* (*Turandot*). **World premieres:** MILHAUD: St Louis (*St Louis*) Rio de Janeiro 1973; ROSSELLINI: Prince (*La Reine morte*) Monte Carlo 1973. Recorded for: Philips, Pathé-Marconi, Erato. Video/Film: Timur (*Turandot*). Gives recitals. Appears with symphony orchestra. **Mgmt:** IMR/FRA.

THAW, DAVID MARTIN. Lyric tenor. American. Resident mem: Bayerische Staatsoper, Munich. Born 19 Jun 1928, New York. Wife Claire Watson, occupation opera singer, soprano. One child. Studied: Giovanni Martinelli, Cesare Sturani, New York; Giuseppe Pais, Milan. **Debut:** Vincent (*Mireille*) Vichy, France 1954.

Sang with major companies in AUS: Salzburg Fest, Vienna Staatsoper; BEL: Brussels; FRA:

Aix-en-Provence Fest, Bordeaux, Lyon, Nice, Strasbourg; FR GER: Bayreuth Fest, Berlin Deutsche Oper, Bonn, Cologne, Dortmund, Düsseldorf-Duisburg, Frankfurt, Hamburg, Hannover, Karlsruhe, Munich Staatsoper & Gärtnerplatz, Stuttgart; GER DR: Berlin Komische Oper; HOL: Amsterdam; ITA: Turin; SWI: Zurich; USA: New York City Opera, San Francisco Opera. **Roles with these companies incl** AUBER: Fra Diavolo; BIZET: Nadir (*Pêcheurs de perles*); BRITTEN: Lysander (*Midsummer Night*); DONIZETTI: Nemorino (*Elisir*); GOUNOD: Vincent (*Mireille*); HAYDN: Ernesto (*Mondo della luna*); HINDEMITH: Wolfgang Capito (*Mathis der Maler*); HUMPERDINCK: Hexe* (*Hänsel und Gretel*); MASSENET: Des Grieux (*Manon*), Nicias (*Thaïs*); MENOTTI: Lover (*Amelia al ballo*); MOZART: Ferrando (*Così fan tutte*), Don Ottavio (*Don Giovanni*), Pedrillo (*Entführung aus dem Serail*), Tamino (*Zauberflöte*); MUSSORGSKY: Vassily Golitsin (*Khovanshchina*); NICOLAI: Fenton (*Lustigen Weiber*); PROKOFIEV: Prince (*Love for Three Oranges*); PUCCINI: Pinkerton (*Butterfly*); ROSSINI: Giocondo (*Pietra del paragone*); SMETANA: Wenzel* (*Bartered Bride*); STRAUSS, J: Eisenstein* & Alfred* (*Fledermaus*); STRAUSS, R: Flamand (*Capriccio*); TCHAIKOVSKY: Lenski (*Eugene Onegin*); THOMAS: Wilhelm Meister (*Mignon*); VERDI: Fenton (*Falstaff*), Alfredo* (*Traviata*); WAGNER: David (*Meistersinger*), Walther v d Vogelweide (*Tannhäuser*); WOLF-FERRARI: Filipeto (*Quattro rusteghi*). Also HENZE: Hohenzollern (*Prinz von Homburg*). Recorded for: DG, Eurodisc. Mgmt: SLZ/FRG.

THEYARD, HARRY; né Harry L Theard Jr. Spinto tenor. American. Resident mem: Metropolitan Opera, New York. Born 28 Sep 1939, New Orleans, LA, USA. Wife Maureen Tiongco, occupation actress. Studied: Armen Boyajian, New York. **Debut:** Michele (*Saint of Bleecker Street*) New York City Opera 1965.
Sang with major companies in CAN: Toronto; ITA: Spoleto Fest; MEX: Mexico City; USA: Boston, Chicago, Cincinnati, Hartford, Jackson, Kentucky, Miami, Milwaukee Florentine, Newark, New Orleans, New York Met & City Opera, Philadelphia Lyric, San Francisco Opera, Seattle, Washington DC. **Roles with these companies incl** BELLINI: Pollione (*Norma*); BERLIOZ: Faust* (*Damnation de Faust*); BIZET: Don José* (*Carmen*); BOITO: Faust* (*Mefistofele*); BORODIN: Vladimir (*Prince Igor*); CHARPENTIER: Julien* (*Louise*); DONIZETTI: Edgardo* (*Lucia*); FLOYD: Sam Polk* (*Susannah*); GOUNOD: Roméo*; JANACEK: Albert Gregor* (*Makropoulos Affair*); LEONCAVALLO: Canio* (*Pagliacci*); MASCAGNI: Turiddu* (*Cavalleria rusticana*); MASSENET: Des Grieux* (*Manon*); MENOTTI: Michele* (*Saint of Bleecker Street*); MOZART: Don Ottavio* (*Don Giovanni*); MUSSORGSKY: Dimitri* (*Boris Godunov*), Andrei Khovansky (*Khovanshchina*); OFFENBACH: Hoffmann*; PUCCINI: Rodolfo* (*Bohème*), Rinuccio (*Gianni Schicchi*), Pinkerton* (*Butterfly*), Des Grieux* (*Manon Lescaut*), Cavaradossi* (*Tosca*), Calaf* (*Turandot*); ROSSINI: Cleomene* (*Assedio di Corinto*); VERDI: Radames* (*Aida*), Riccardo* (*Ballo in maschera*), Ernani,

Don Alvaro* (*Forza del destino*), Duca di Mantova (*Rigoletto*), Alfredo (*Traviata*), Manrico (*Trovatore*), Arrigo (*Vespri*). **World premieres:** FLOYD: Curley (*Of Mice and Men*) Seattle Opera 1970; MENOTTI: Dr Arnek (*Most Important Man*) New York City Opera 1971; PANNELL: Ginger Coffey, Canadian Opera Co 1967. Recorded for: Angel. Appears with symphony orchestra. **Res:** Montauk, Long Island, NY, USA. Mgmt: DSP/USA.

T'HEZAN, HELIA; née Arlette C-T'Hezan. Dramatic soprano. French. Resident mem: Opéra de Paris. Born 23 Aug 1934, Rieumes, Hte Garonne, France. Husband Can Koral, occupation opera singer. Studied: Consv de Toulouse; Hochschule für Musik, Berlin. **Debut:** LULLY: Armide, Opéra de Bordeaux. Awards: First Prize in voice, interpret, piano & harp, Consv de Toulouse.
Sang with major companies in BEL: Liège; FRA: Bordeaux, Lyon, Marseille, Nancy, Nice, Paris, Rouen, Strasbourg, Toulouse; ITA: Rome Opera, Trieste, Turin; MON: Monte Carlo; POR: Lisbon; SWI: Geneva; UK: Glyndebourne Fest, London Royal; USA: Philadelphia Lyric. **Roles with these companies incl** BARTOK: Judith* (*Bluebeard's Castle*); BERLIOZ: Béatrice; BIZET: Carmen*; BOITO: Margherita (*Mefistofele*); BRITTEN: Helena (*Midsummer Night*), Ellen Orford* (*Peter Grimes*), Governess (*Turn of the Screw*); DALLAPICCOLA: Mrs Fabian* (*Volo di notte*); GIORDANO: Maddalena* (*Andrea Chénier*); GLUCK: Iphigénie* (*Iphigénie en Aulide*), Iphigénie (*Iphigénie en Tauride*); GOUNOD: Marguerite* (*Faust*); IBERT: Angélique; LEONCAVALLO: Nedda* (*Pagliacci*); MASCAGNI: Santuzza* (*Cavalleria rusticana*); MASSENET: Salomé (*Hérodiade*), Anita (*Navarraise*), Thaïs; MENOTTI: Magda Sorel (*Consul*); MEYERBEER: Valentine* (*Huguenots*); MILHAUD: Médée, Femme* (*Pauvre matelot*); MOZART: Donna Elvira (*Don Giovanni*), Contessa* (*Nozze di Figaro*); OFFENBACH: Giulietta* (*Contes d'Hoffmann*); PENDERECKI: Jeanne* (*Teufel von Loudun*); PROKOFIEV: Fata Morgana* (*Love for Three Oranges*); PUCCINI: Mimi* & Musetta* (*Bohème*), Minnie* (*Fanciulla del West*), Manon Lescaut, Giorgetta (*Tabarro*), Tosca*; VERDI: Leonora* (*Forza del destino*), Desdemona (*Otello*), Amelia* (*Simon Boccanegra*), Leonora (*Trovatore*). Also GOUNOD: Balkis* (*Reine de Saba*); MARTINU: Reine* (*Hamlet*); MASSENET: Charlotte (*Werther*); MILHAUD: Mercédès* (*Fiesta*); RAMEAU: Erinice* (*Zoroastre*). **World premieres:** ROSSELLINI: Infante (*Reine morte*) Opéra de Monte Carlo 1973. Video: Desdemona (*Otello*); Manon Lescaut; (*Contes d'Hoffmann*). Gives recitals. Appears with symphony orchestra. **Res:** 52 E Dolet, Choisy-le-Roi 94600, France. Mgmt: RAP/FRA.

THOMA, HELGE. He stages/produces opera & theater. German. Resident Stage Dir, Staatsoper, Vienna 1975- . Born 30 Oct 1936, Mannheim. Single. Studied: Hochschule für Musik, Prof Friedrich Wührer, Mannheim; Univ of Vienna. **Operatic debut:** Salome Bielefeld 1967. Theater debut: Schiller Theater, Berlin.

Directed/produced opera for major companies in FR GER: Berlin Deutsche Oper, Bielefeld, Karlsruhe, Kassel, Wiesbaden. **Operas staged with these companies incl** CAVALLI: *Giasone*★; CIMAROSA: *Matrimonio segreto*★; DONIZETTI: *Don Pasquale*★. **Res:** Kaiserdamm 25a, Berlin, FR Ger. Mgmt: SLZ/FRG.

THOMAS, JESS. Dramatic tenor & Heldentenor. American. Resident mem: San Francisco Opera; Metropolitan Opera, New York; Staatsoper, Vienna. Born 4 Aug 1927, Hot Springs, SD, USA. Wife Violeta. Two children. Studied: Otto Schulmann, Stanford Univ, CA, & San Francisco. **Debut:** Haushofmeister (*Rosenkavalier*) San Francisco Opera 1957. Previous occupations: school psychologist. Awards: Bavarian Kammersänger 1963; Richard Wagner Medallion, Bayreuth 1963; San Francisco Opera Medallion 1972. **Sang with major companies in** AUS: Salzburg Fest, Vienna Staatsoper; CZE: Prague National & Smetana; FRA: Nancy, Paris; FR GER: Bayreuth Fest, Berlin Deutsche Oper, Frankfurt, Karlsruhe, Munich Staatsoper, Stuttgart, Wiesbaden; ITA: Milan La Scala, Venice; MEX: Mexico City; MON: Monte Carlo; POR: Lisbon; SWI: Basel, Zurich; UK: London Royal; USSR: Moscow Bolshoi; USA: Hartford, Houston, New York Met, Philadelphia Lyric, San Francisco Opera, Seattle. **Roles with these companies incl** d'ALBERT: Pedro (*Tiefland*); BEETHOVEN: Florestan★ (*Fidelio*); BERLIOZ: Aeneas (*Troyens*); BIZET: Don José (*Carmen*); BRITTEN: Peter Grimes★; DEBUSSY: Azaël (*Enfant prodigue*); GIORDANO: Andrea Chénier; GOUNOD: Faust; LEONCAVALLO: Canio (*Pagliacci*); MASCAGNI: Turiddu (*Cavalleria rusticana*); MEYERBEER: Vasco da Gama (*Africaine*); MOZART: Belmonte (*Entführung aus dem Serail*), Tamino (*Zauberflöte*); MUSSORGSKY: Dimitri (*Boris Godunov*); OFFENBACH: Hoffmann★; PONCHIELLI: Enzo (*Gioconda*); PUCCINI: Rodolfo (*Bohème*), Pinkerton (*Butterfly*), Cavaradossi★ (*Tosca*), Calaf★ (*Turandot*); PURCELL: Aeneas; SAINT-SAENS: Samson; SMETANA: Hans (*Bartered Bride*); STRAUSS, R: Menelaus★ (*Aegyptische Helena*), Bacchus★‡ (*Ariadne auf Naxos*), Apollo (*Daphne*), Kaiser‡ (*Frau ohne Schatten*), Ein Sänger (*Rosenkavalier*); TCHAIKOVSKY: Lenski★ (*Eugene Onegin*); VERDI: Radames★ (*Aida*), Riccardo (*Ballo in maschera*), Don Carlo★, Jacopo Foscari (*Due Foscari*), Fenton★ (*Falstaff*), Don Alvaro (*Forza del destino*), Ismaele (*Nabucco*), Gabriele (*Simon Boccanegra*), Alfredo (*Traviata*), Manrico (*Trovatore*), Macduff (*Macbeth*); WAGNER: Lohengrin★‡, Walther★‡ (*Meistersinger*), Parsifal★‡, Rienzi, Loge★ (*Rheingold*), Siegmund★ (*Walküre*), Siegfried (*Siegfried★‡*, *Götterdämmerung*★), Tannhäuser★, Tristan★; WEBER: Oberon. Also FORTNER: Mond (*Bluthochzeit*). **World premieres:** BARBER: Caesar (*Antony and Cleopatra*) Metropolitan Opera, New York 1966. Recorded for: DG, EMI, Philips, Eurodisc/RCA. Video—WDF Cologne: Alvaro (*Forza del destino*). Gives recitals. Appears with symphony orchestra. **Res:** Tiburon, CA, USA. Mgmt: COL/USA; IWL/UK.

THOMAS, ROBERT L. Spinto tenor. American. Born 29 May 1929, Santa Monica, CA. Wife Renate Deppisch, occupation ballerina. One child. Studied: Frank Tavaglione, Riverside, CA; Mo Carrino, Mme Boroschek, Düsseldorf; Rudolf Bautz, Cologne, FR Ger. **Debut:** Foresto (*Attila*) Hessische Oper, Wiesbaden 1957. Previous occupations: machinist, Lockheed Aircraft; theology student. Awards: First Prize Merola Memorial Aud, San Francisco Op 1957.

Sang with major companies in AUS: Graz; BEL: Brussels; FRA: Bordeaux, Marseille, Nancy, Nice, Strasbourg; FR GER: Berlin Deutsche Oper, Bonn, Cologne, Darmstadt, Düsseldorf-Duisburg, Essen, Frankfurt, Hamburg, Hannover, Karlsruhe, Kassel, Kiel, Krefeld, Mannheim, Munich Staatsoper, Nürnberg, Stuttgart, Wiesbaden; GER DR: Dresden, Leipzig; HOL: Amsterdam; ITA: Bologna, Florence Maggio, Genoa, Naples, Palermo, Parma, Trieste, Turin, Venice; SWI: Basel, Geneva, Zurich; USA: Chicago; YUG: Dubrovnik, Zagreb. **Roles with these companies incl** BERLIOZ: Aeneas (*Troyens*); BIZET: Don José★ (*Carmen*); DONIZETTI: Ernesto (*Don Pasquale*), Edgardo★ (*Lucia*); DVORAK: Prince★ (*Rusalka*); EINEM: Bürgermeister★ (*Besuch der alten Dame*); GIORDANO: Andrea Chénier★; GOUNOD: Faust; LEONCAVALLO: Canio★ (*Pagliacci*); MASCAGNI: Turiddu★ (*Cavalleria rusticana*); MONTEMEZZI: Avito (*Amore dei tre re*); MONTEVERDI: Testo & Tancredi (*Combattimento di Tancredi*); MOZART: Ferrando (*Così fan tutte*), Don Ottavio (*Don Giovanni*), Idomeneo, Tamino (*Zauberflöte*); OFFENBACH: Hoffmann★; ORFF: Solo (*Carmina burana*); PUCCINI: Rodolfo★ (*Bohème*), Rinuccio (*Gianni Schicchi*), Pinkerton★ (*Butterfly*), Des Grieux (*Manon Lescaut*), Luigi★ (*Tabarro*), Cavaradossi★ (*Tosca*), Calaf★ (*Turandot*); ROSSINI: Don Ramiro (*Cenerentola*); SMETANA: Hans (*Bartered Bride*); STRAUSS, J: Eisenstein & Alfred (*Fledermaus*); STRAUSS, R: Bacchus★ (*Ariadne auf Naxos*), Kaiser★ (*Frau ohne Schatten*), Ein Sänger (*Rosenkavalier*), Herodes★ (*Salome*); SUTERMEISTER: Raskolnikoff; VERDI: Radames★ (*Aida*), Foresto★ (*Attila*), Riccardo★ (*Ballo in maschera*), Don Carlo★, Ernani, Don Alvaro★ (*Forza del destino*), Duca di Mantova (*Rigoletto*), Gabriele (*Simon Boccanegra*), Alfredo (*Traviata*), Manrico★ (*Trovatore*); WAGNER: Walther v d Vogelweide (*Tannhäuser*); WEBER: Max★ (*Freischütz*). Appears with symphony orchestra. Teaches voice. Coaches repertoire. **Res:** Harnackstr 10, 46 Dortmund, FR Ger.

THOMASCHKE, THOMAS MICHAEL. Bass. German DR. Resident mem: Grosses Opernhaus, Leipzig. Born 2 Aug 1943, Pirna, Germany. Wife Ivana, occupation art historian. Two children. Studied: Hochschule für Musik, Prof Harry Schwikkardi, Dresden, Ger DR. **Debut:** Sacristan (*Tosca*) Stadttheater Freiberg 1966. Previous occupations: gardener; studied French horn. Awards: Kammersänger.

Sang with major companies in CZE: Brno, Prague National & Smetana; FR GER: Wiesbaden; GER DR: Berlin Komische Oper, Dresden, Leipzig; ITA: Milan La Scala, Venice; POL: Lodz. **Roles with these companies incl** BEETHOVEN: Rocco★ (*Fidelio*); CIMAROSA: Geronimo★ (*Matrimonio segreto*); GOUNOD: Méphistophélès★ (*Faust*); HANDEL: Polyphemus★ (*Acis and Galatea*), Giulio Cesare★; JANACEK: Harasta★ (*Cunning Little Vixen*); MEYERBEER: Marcel★ (*Huguenots*); MOZART:. Osmin★ (*Entführung aus dem Serail*), Figaro★ (*Nozze di Figaro*), Sarastro★ (*Zauberflöte*); ORFF: Bauer★ (*Kluge*); ROSSINI: Don Basilio★ (*Barbiere di Siviglia*); SMETANA: Kezal (*Bartered Bride*); WAGNER: Fasolt★ (*Rheingold*), Fafner (*Rheingold*★, *Siegfried*★), Hunding★ (*Walküre*), Hagen★ (*Götterdämmerung*). Also WAGNER-REGENY: Renard★ (*Günstling*). **World premieres:** KUNAD: Thibauld (*Maitre Pathelin*) Staatsoper Dresden 1969. Recorded for: EMI, Philips, VEB, Melodiya, Opus. Gives recitals. Appears with symphony orchestra. Teaches voice. Coaches repertoire. **Res:** Prellerstr 19, 7022 Leipzig, Ger DR. Mgmt: KDR/GDR; SLZ/FRG; SLA/UK.

THOMPSON, HUGH R. Lyric baritone and stage director. American. Born 19 Jun 1915, Tacoma, WA. Single. Studied: Juilliard Graduate School of Music, Anna Schoen-René. Leopold Sachse, New York. **Debut:** Ford (*Falstaff*) Chicago 1942; as stage dir: *Nozze di Figaro*, August Fest St Louis, MO 1955. Previous occupations: journalist, music critic. Awards: Winner Met Op Aud of the Air 1944.

Sang with major companies in CAN: Montreal/Quebec; USA: Boston, Chicago, Cincinnati, Hartford, Kansas City, Miami, Newark, New Orleans, New York Met & City Opera, Philadelphia Lyric, Pittsburgh, San Francisco Opera, Washington DC. **Roles with these companies incl** BIZET: Escamillo (*Carmen*); CHARPENTIER: Père (*Louise*); DONIZETTI: Belcore (*Elisir*), Enrico (*Lucia*); FLOTOW: Plunkett (*Martha*); GIANNINI: Petruchio (*Taming of the Shrew*); GOUNOD: Valentin (*Faust*), Mercutio (*Roméo*); LEONCAVALLO: Tonio (*Pagliacci*); MASSENET: Don Quichotte; MENOTTI: Husband (*Amelia al ballo*); MOZART: Conte Almaviva (*Nozze di Figaro*), Papageno (*Zauberflöte*); MUSSORGSKY: Boris Godunov; PUCCINI: Marcello (*Bohème*), Lescaut (*Manon Lescaut*), Scarpia (*Tosca*); ROSSINI: Don Basilio (*Barbiere di Siviglia*), Dandini (*Cenerentola*); STRAUSS, R: Jochanaan (*Salome*); VERDI: Amonasro (*Aida*), Renato (*Ballo in maschera*), Ford★ (*Falstaff*), Iago (*Otello*); WAGNER: Telramund (*Lohengrin*); WOLF-FERRARI: Conte Gil (*Segreto di Susanna*). **World premieres:** DELLO JOIO: Cochon (*Trial at Rouen*) NBC 1956; HOLLINGSWORTH: Husband (*Grande Bretêche*) NBC 1957. **Operas staged incl** BIZET: *Carmen;* DELIBES: *Lakmé;* DONIZETTI: *Fille du régiment;* GIORDANO: *Andrea Chénier;* GOUNOD: *Faust;* HUMPERDINCK: *Hänsel und Gretel;* LEONCAVALLO: *Pagliacci;* MASCAGNI: *Cavalleria rusticana;* MENOTTI: *Telephone;* MUSSORGSKY: *Boris Godunov;* OFFENBACH: *Contes d'Hoffmann;* PUCCINI: *Bohème, Butterfly, Tosca;* SMETANA: *Bartered Bride;* STRAUSS, J: *Fledermaus;* VERDI: *Aida, Rigoletto, Trovatore.* Recorded for: RCA Victor. Gives recitals. Appears with symphony orchestra. Teaches voice. Coaches repertoire and drama. On faculty of Univ of Miami, FL; previously stage mgr & dir Cincinnati Summer Opera 1959-66. **Res:** Coral Gables, FL, USA.

THOMSON, HEATHER. Lyric soprano. Canadian. Resident mem: Canadian Opera Co, Toronto; New York City Opera. Born 7 Dec 1940, Vancouver, BC, Canada. Husband Perry Price, occupation tenor. One child. Studied: Royal Consv, Herman Geiger-Torel, Irene Jessner, Toronto. **Debut:** Mimi (*Bohème*) Canadian Opera Co, Toronto 1963.

Sang with major companies in CAN: Montreal/Quebec, Ottawa, Toronto, Vancouver; HOL: Amsterdam; UK: Glasgow Scottish, London English National; USA: Boston, Fort Worth, Houston, New Orleans, New York City Opera, Pittsburgh, Portland. **Roles with these companies incl** BEETHOVEN: Marzelline (*Fidelio*); BIZET: Micaëla (*Carmen*); GOUNOD: Marguerite★ (*Faust*); MASSENET: Manon; MOZART: Fiordiligi★ (*Così fan tutte*), Donna Elvira★ (*Don Giovanni*), Contessa★ (*Nozze di Figaro*), Pamina★ (*Zauberflöte*); OFFENBACH: Olympia & Antonia & Giulietta (*Contes d'Hoffmann*); PUCCINI: Mimi★ & Musetta★ (*Bohème*), Cio-Cio-San (*Butterfly*), Giorgetta★ (*Tabarro*), Liù★ (*Turandot*); STRAUSS, J: Rosalinde (*Fledermaus*); STRAVINSKY: Anne Trulove (*Rake's Progress*); TCHAIKOVSKY: Tatiana★ (*Eugene Onegin*); VERDI: Nannetta (*Falstaff*), Violetta★ (*Traviata*). **World premieres:** WILSON: Heloise (*Heloise and Abelard*) Canadian Opera Co 1973. Gives recitals. Appears with symphony orchestra. **Res:** Danbury, CT, USA. Mgmt: SAM/USA.

TICHY, GEORG. Lyric baritone. Austrian. Resident mem: Staatsoper, Vienna. Born 9 Jun 1949, Vienna. Divorced. Three children. Studied: Kmsg Hilde Zadek, Vienna. **Debut:** Seemann (*Tristan und Isolde*) Staatsoper, Vienna 1973. Previous occupations: mech engr.

Sang with major companies in AUS: Vienna Staatsoper & Volksoper. **Roles with these companies incl** BRITTEN: Elder Son★ (*Prodigal Son*); MOZART: Don Giovanni, Conte Almaviva (*Nozze di Figaro*), Papageno (*Zauberflöte*); PUCCINI: Sharpless★ (*Butterfly*); ROSSINI: Figaro★ (*Barbiere di Siviglia*); VERDI: Rigoletto, Germont (*Traviata*). Gives recitals. Appears with symphony orchestra. Teaches voice. **Res:** Burgg 18, Vienna 7, Austria. Mgmt: RAB/AUS.

TIDBOALD, DAVID. Conductor of opera and symphony. British. Resident Cond, CAPAB, Nico Malan Opera House, Cape Town, South Africa. Born 23 Sep 1926, Plymouth, UK. Single. Studied: Leopold Ludwig, Berlin; Richard Glas, London; incl piano, percussion & double bass. Operatic training as repetiteur in London. **Operatic debut:** London 1956. Symphonic debut: London 1953.

Conducted with major companies in S AFR: Johannesburg. **Operas with these companies incl** BARTOK: *Bluebeard's Castle*★; DONIZETTI: *Lucia*★; FOSS: *Jumping Frog;* MOZART: *Don Giovanni*★, *Entführung aus dem Serail;* OFFENBACH: *Contes d'Hoffmann*★; PERGOLESI: *Serva padrona;* PUCCINI: *Bohème*★, *Butterfly*★, *Tosca, Turandot*★; ROSSINI: *Cenerentola*★; SMETANA: *Bartered Bride;* STRAUSS, J: *Fledermaus;* VERDI: *Aida*★, *Ballo in maschera*★, *Falstaff, Otello*★, *Rigoletto*★, *Traviata*★. Conducted major orch in Europe & Africa. Teaches at

Cape Town Univ. **Res:** Mark Rd 5/7, Cape Town, South Africa.

TIGGELER, STEFFEN. Stages/produces opera; also conducts. German. Oberspielleiter, Art Mng & Resident Stage Dir, Staatsoper Hannover. Born 28 Feb 1931, Mönchengladbach. Wife Monica, occupation violinist. Three children. Studied: Musikhochschule Detmold, Kurt Thomas; incl music, violin & piano. Operatic training as asst stage dir at Opera, Krefeld 1953-57. **Operatic debut:** *Telephone* Staatsoper, Hannover 1960. Theater debut: Hannover 1959. Previous occupation: conductor. Awards: Awd, Olympic Committee, Munich 1972.

Directed/produced opera for major companies in FR GER: Bayreuth Fest, Dortmund, Hannover, Krefeld; USA: Fort Worth. **Operas staged with these companies incl** ADAM: *Si j'étais roi;* ADAM DE LA HALLE: *Robin et Marion;* d'ALBERT: *Tiefland;* BEETHOVEN: *Fidelio;* BERG: *Wozzeck;* BIZET: *Carmen;* BORODIN: *Prince Igor;* BRITTEN: *Peter Grimes, Rape of Lucretia;* DELIBES: *Roi l'a dit★;* DONIZETTI: *Elisir★;* EGK: *Verlobung in San Domingo;* EINEM: *Dantons Tod;* FLOTOW: *Martha★;* GLUCK: *Iphigénie en Aulide, Orfeo ed Euridice;* GOUNOD: *Faust;* HANDEL: *Giulio Cesare;* HAYDN: *Mondo della luna;* HENZE: *Elegy for Young Lovers★, Junge Lord;* HINDEMITH: *Hin und zurück;* HONEGGER: *Antigone;* HUMPERDINCK: *Hänsel und Gretel★;* JANACEK: *Cunning Little Vixen, From the House of the Dead, Jenufa, Katya Kabanova;* KODALY: *Háry János, Spinning Room;* LEONCAVALLO: *Pagliacci★;* LORTZING: *Waffenschmied, Wildschütz, Zar und Zimmermann★;* MARTIN: *Vin herbé;* MASCAGNI: *Cavalleria rusticana★;* MENOTTI: *Amahl;* MILHAUD: *Pauvre matelot;* MOZART: *Così fan tutte★, Don Giovanni, Entführung aus dem Serail★, Idomeneo, Nozze di Figaro, Zauberflöte;* MUSSORGSKY: *Boris Godunov;* NICOLAI: *Lustigen Weiber;* OFFENBACH: *Contes d'Hoffmann, Périchole;* ORFF: *Antigonae, Kluge, Mond;* PFITZNER: *Palestrina;* PROKOFIEV: *Gambler;* PUCCINI: *Bohème, Gianni Schicchi, Butterfly, Manon Lescaut, Tabarro, Tosca;* PURCELL: *Dido and Aeneas;* RAVEL: *Heure espagnole;* ROSSINI: *Barbiere di Siviglia, Cenerentola, Comte Ory, Italiana in Algeri, Pietra del paragone;* SAINT-SAENS: *Samson et Dalila★;* SMETANA: *Bartered Bride, Secret;* STRAUSS, J: *Fledermaus;* STRAUSS, R: *Arabella, Ariadne auf Naxos, Daphne, Elektra, Frau ohne Schatten, Rosenkavalier, Salome;* STRAVINSKY: *Oedipus Rex, Rake's Progress, Rossignol;* TCHAIKOVSKY: *Pique Dame★;* VERDI: *Aida, Ballo in maschera, Don Carlo, Falstaff, Forza del destino, Macbeth, Masnadieri, Otello, Rigoletto, Simon Boccanegra, Traviata, Trovatore;* WAGNER: *Fliegende Holländer★, Lohengrin★, Meistersinger★, Rheingold★, Walküre★, Siegfried★, Götterdämmerung, Tannhäuser, Tristan und Isolde;* WEBER: *Freischutz;* WEINBERGER: *Schwanda;* WOLF-FERRARI: *Segreto di Susanna.* Also DITTERSDORF: *Doktor und Apotheker;* GLUCK: *Chinesi;* GOETZ: *Der Widerspenstigen Zähmung;* LORTZING: *Undine;* MARTINU: *Julietta.* **Operatic world premieres:** LUDWIG: *Rashomon* Opera Augsburg 1972; EINFELD: *Palast-Hotel Thanatos* Hanno-

ver 1972; DE LA MOTTE: *Aufsichtsrat* Hannover 1970. Teaches at Schule Schloss Salem b/Baden. **Res:** Maschstr 19, 3 Hannover, FR Ger. Mgmt: SLZ/FRG; SMN/USA.

TILLIUS, SVEN-GUNNAR CARL. Swedish. Financial Dir & Vice Pres, Royal Swedish Opera, Box 16094, S-103 22 Stockholm 16, Sweden. In charge of adm matters & finances. Born 17 Oct 1937, Göteborg, Sweden. Wife Margareta, occupation nurse. Two children. Studied: Commercial Univ Göteborg, economics. Previous positions primarily administrative: Fin Mng, Opera House Göteborg 1964-69; Fin Mng, City Theater Göteborg 1971-73. In present position since 1973. **Res:** Jägarstigen 65, S-18146 Lidingö, Sweden.

TINSLEY, PAULINE CECILIA. Spinto. British. Born Wigan, UK. Husband George M Neighbour, occupation secy, Perf Rght Socy Ltd, London. One son, one daughter. Studied: Northern School of Music, Margaret Dillon, Ellis Keeler, Manchester; The Opera School, Joan Cross, St John's Wood; Roy Henderson, Eva Turner. **Debut:** ROSSINI: Desdemona (*Otello*) Philopera, London 1961. Awards: LRAM, Royal Acad of Music, London.

Sang with major companies in CAN: Vancouver; FR GER: Hamburg; HOL: Amsterdam; SPA: Majorca; SWI: Zurich; UK: Aldeburgh Fest, Cardiff Welsh, London Royal & English National; USA: Houston, New York City Opera, Philadelphia Lyric, Santa Fe, Washington DC. **Roles with these companies incl** BEETHOVEN: Leonore★ (*Fidelio*); BRITTEN: Lady Billows★ (*Albert Herring*); DONIZETTI: Anna Bolena, Elisabetta★ (*Maria Stuarda*); MOZART: Fiordiligi (*Così fan tutte*), Donna Elvira (*Don Giovanni*), Elettra‡ (*Idomeneo*), Contessa & Susanna (*Nozze di Figaro*), Königin der Nacht (*Zauberflöte*); PUCCINI: Tosca★, Turandot★; VERDI: Aida★, Amelia★ (*Ballo in maschera*), Elisabetta★ (*Don Carlo*), Donna Elvira (*Ernani*), Leonora (*Forza del destino*), Lady Macbeth★, Abigaille★ (*Nabucco*), Gilda (*Rigoletto*), Leonora★ (*Trovatore*); WAGNER: Senta★ (*Fliegende Holländer*), Elsa (*Lohengrin*). Also BEETHOVEN: Leonore, orig vers. Recorded for: Philips. Appears with symphony orchestra. **Res:** Altham Rd, Springfield House, Hatch End, Pinner HA54RQ, UK.

TIPTON, THOMAS; né Thomas Max Pointkowski. Dramatic baritone. American. Resident mem: Staatsoper, Munich. Born 18 Nov 1926, Wyandotte, MI. Wife Margret, occupation foreign language secy. Two children. Studied: Herbert Swanson, Michigan State Coll, East Lansing; Bernardo de Muro, Rome; Chase Baromeo, Univ of Mich, Ann Arbor; Lyle Lyons, Wyandotte, USA. **Debut:** Bob (*Old Maid and the Thief*) New York City Opera 1954. Previous occupations: mail carrier, taxi driver, dishwasher, etc. Awards: Detroit Grinnell Schlshp; Second Place, Met Op Ntl Counc Aud.

Sang with major companies in ARG: Buenos Aires; AUS: Graz, Salzburg Fest, Vienna Staatsoper & Volksoper; BEL: Brussels; CZE: Prague National; FRA: Lyon, Nancy; FR GER: Bayreuth Fest, Berlin Deutsche Oper, Düsseldorf-Duisburg, Frankfurt, Hamburg, Hannover, Karlsruhe, Krefeld, Mannheim, Munich Staatsoper, Nürnberg, Saarbrücken, Stuttgart; HOL: Amsterdam; UK: London Royal; USA: Dallas, Houston, Kansas City, Milwaukee Florentine, New York City Opera, Pittsburgh, Portland, San Francisco Opera. **Roles with these companies incl** BEETHOVEN: Don Pizarro★ (*Fidelio*); BERG: Wozzeck; BIZET: Escamillo (*Carmen*); BRITTEN: Traveller etc★ (*Death in Venice*); DONIZETTI: Agata★ (*Convenienze/Viva la Mamma*), Enrico (*Lucia*); GIORDANO: Carlo Gérard (*Andrea Chénier*); GOUNOD: Valentin (*Faust*); HANDEL: Arsamene (*Xerxes*); HUMPERDINCK: Peter (*Hänsel und Gretel*); LEONCAVALLO: Tonio (*Pagliacci*); MASCAGNI: Alfio (*Cavalleria rusticana*); MILHAUD: Christophe Colomb; MOZART: Guglielmo (*Così fan tutte*), Nardo (*Finta giardiniera*), Conte Almaviva (*Nozze di Figaro*); OFFENBACH: Coppélius etc★ (*Contes d'Hoffmann*); ORFF: Kreon (*Antigonae*), König (*Kluge*); PAISIELLO: Teodoro (*Re Teodoro in Venezia*); PUCCINI: Marcello (*Bohème*), Sharpless★ (*Butterfly*), Lescaut (*Manon Lescaut*), Michele★ (*Tabarro*), Scarpia★ (*Tosca*); RAVEL: Ramiro (*Heure espagnole*); ROSSINI: Dott Bartolo★ (*Barbiere di Siviglia*); STRAUSS, R: Faninal (*Rosenkavalier*); STRAVINSKY: Nick Shadow (*Rake's Progress*); VERDI: Amonasro★ (*Aida*), Renato★ (*Ballo in maschera*), Rodrigo (*Don Carlo*), Ford★ & Falstaff★ (*Falstaff*), Don Carlo (*Forza del destino*), Miller (*Luisa Miller*), Macbeth, Nabucco, Iago★ (*Otello*), Rigoletto★, Simon Boccanegra, Germont★ (*Traviata*), Conte di Luna★ (*Trovatore*), Monforte (*Vespri*); WAGNER: Amfortas (*Parsifal*), Gunther (*Götterdämmerung*), Wolfram (*Tannhäuser*). **World premieres:** HINDEMITH: Roderick (*Long Christmas Dinner*) Mannheim 1961. Video – German TV: Coppélius etc (*Contes d'Hoffmann*). Gives recitals. Appears with symphony orchestra. Teaches voice. Coaches repertoire. **Res:** Oneginstr 25, Munich, FR Ger. **Mgmt:** HJH/USA.

TITUS, ALAN WITKOWSKI. Lyric baritone. American. Born 28 Oct 1945, New York. Wife Janet. Studied: Hans Heinz, Daniel Ferro, New York. **Debut:** Marcello (*Bohème*) Washington, DC, Opera Soc 1969. Awards: Sergius Kagen Memorial Schlshp, Juilliard School, New York.
  Sang with major companies in FRA: Aix-en-Provence Fest, Marseille, Strasbourg; HOL: Amsterdam; USA: Boston, Cincinnati, Dallas, Houston, New York City Opera, Philadelphia Lyric, St Paul, San Francisco & Spring Opera, Santa Fe, Seattle, Washington DC. **Roles with these companies incl** BIZET: Escamillo★ (*Carmen*); BRITTEN: Owen Wingrave★; DEBUSSY: Pelléas★; DELIUS: Dark Fiddler★ (*Village Romeo and Juliet*); DONIZETTI: Belcore★ (*Elisir*); MOZART: Papageno★ (*Zauberflöte*); ORFF: Solo★ (*Carmina burana*); PUCCINI: Marcello★ (*Bohème*); REIMANN: Graf von Lusignan★ (*Melusine*); ROSSINI: Figaro★ (*Barbiere di Siviglia*); STRAVINSKY: Nick Shadow (*Rake's Progress*). Also MONTEVERDI: Nero (*Incoronazione di Poppea*). **World premieres:** HENZE: Three Lovers (*Rachel, la Cubana*) WNET Opera Theatre, New York 1974. Recorded for: Philips, Columbia. Video – WNET: Three Lovers (*Rachel, la Cubana*). Gives recitals. Appears with symphony orchestra. **Res:** New York, NY, USA. **Mgmt:** CAM/USA; CMW/FRA.

TOBIN, ROBERT L B. Stages/produces opera & theater. Also designs sets & stage-lighting and is an actor & author. American. Born 12 Mar 1934, San Antonio, TX. Single. Studied: music. Operatic training as asst stage dir at San Antonio Grand Opera. **Operatic debut:** *Boris Godunov* San Antonio Grand Opera 1959. Theater debut: San Antonio Theatre 1957. Awards: Cavaliere ufficiale, Ordine Merito, Repubblica Italiana; Order of Alamo; Kappa Alpha. Previous adm positions in opera: Prod Coord, San Antonio Grand Opera Fest, TX 1951-57; Pres, Festival of Two Worlds, Spoleto, Italy.
  Directed/produced opera for major companies in USA: San Antonio. **Operas staged with these companies incl** FLOYD: *Susannah;* MENOTTI: *Amahl★†;* MOZART: *Così fan tutte†, Don Giovanni★†;* MUSSORGSKY: *Boris Godunov;* POULENC: *Voix humaine†;* STRAUSS, R: *Elektra†.* Natl Chmn, Central Opera Service, New York 1961-71; Hon Ntl Chmn 1971- ; Mem Board of Dir, Santa Fe Opera, Opera Co of Boston, San Antonio Grand Opera. Perf in opera: Sir Edgar (*Junge Lord*) New York City Opera 1974. **Res:** 173 Iralee Rd, San Antonio, TX, USA.

TODISCO, NUNZIO. Lyric & dramatic tenor, Heldentenor. Italian. Born 11 Jun 1942, Torre del Greco, Italy. Wife Anna Dispare. Four children. Studied: Maria Grazia Marchini, Naples. **Debut:** Canio (*Pagliacci*) Spoleto Fest, Italy 1971. Previous occupations: waiter on passenger ship. Awards: Intl Compt cup, Parma; other prizes from Verona, Mantua, Naples, Imperia, Chiaiano, Spoleto.
  Sang with major companies in ITA: Naples, Rome Opera & Caracalla, Trieste. **Roles with these companies incl** BIZET: Don José★ (*Carmen*); DONIZETTI: Edgardo★ (*Lucia*); LEONCAVALLO: Canio★ (*Pagliacci*); MASCAGNI: Turiddu★ (*Cavalleria rusticana*); PONCHIELLI: Enzo★ (*Gioconda*); PUCCINI: Pinkerton★ (*Butterfly*), Luigi★ (*Tabarro*); VERDI: Ismaele★ (*Nabucco*), Manrico★ (*Trovatore*); WAGNER: Erik★ (*Fliegende Holländer*). Also VERDI: Macduff★ (*Macbeth*). **Res:** V Bufale 30, Torre del Greco, NA, Italy.

TOFFOLO, LUIGI. Conductor of opera and symphony. Italian. Born 4 Jun 1909, Trieste. Wife Maria Luzzatti, occupation teacher. Studied: Profs Josef Marx and Edward Steuermann, Trieste & Vienna; also piano & organ. Plays the piano. **Operatic debut:** *Werther* De Rosa-Moraro Opera Co, Trieste 1947. Symphonic debut: Orch da Camera Triestina 1931. Previous adm positions in opera: Reg Orch Dir, Teatro G Verdi, Trieste 1946-56; Art Dir 1968-72.
  Conducted with major companies in FR GER: Nürnberg, Saarbrücken; HUN: Budapest; ITA: Florence Comunale, Genoa, Trieste, Turin; ROM: Bucharest; USA: Cincinnati. **Operas with these companies incl** BUSONI: *Arlecchino;* DONIZETTI: *Don Pasquale, Lucrezia Borgia★;* MASSENET: *Thaïs†, Werther†;* MENOTTI: *Amelia al ballo;* MOZART: *Così fan tutte;* PUCCINI: *Bohème★†, Butterfly★, Turandot★†;* VERDI:

Rigoletto★, *Traviata*★, *Trovatore*★; WAGNER: *Tristan und Isolde*★‡. Also on records only DEBUSSY: *Enfant prodigue;* DONIZETTI: *Campanello;* DVORAK: *Rusalka;* GLUCK: *Cadi dupé;* MOZART: *Nozze di Figaro;* POULENC: *Voix humaine;* SMETANA: *Dalibor.* Conducted major orch in Europe, USA/Canada. Previous positions as Mus Dir with major orch: Filarmonica, Trieste 1946-56. Teaches at Consv Tartini, Trieste. **Res:** Rossetti 39, Trieste, Italy.

TOMASELLI, BRUNO ADAM. Dramatic baritone Argentinean. Resident mem: Teatro Colón, Buenos Aires. Born 8 Jan 1932, Buenos Aires. Wife Perla Emma Barsanti. One son. Studied: Alfredo Barsanti, Thea Vitulli, Mauricio Sorin, Enrique Ricci. **Debut:** Dr Falke (*Fledermaus*) Teatro Colón 1965. Previous occupations: studied construction engineering.

Sang with major companies in ARG: Buenos Aires; BRA: Rio de Janeiro; USA: Washington DC. **Roles with these companies incl** BIZET: Escamillo (*Carmen*); BUSONI: Doktor Faust; CIMAROSA: Count Robinson & Geronimo (*Matrimonio segreto*); DONIZETTI: Enrico (*Campanello*), Dott Malatesta & Don Pasquale (*Don Pasquale*), Belcore (*Elisir*), Enrico (*Lucia*), Gasparo (*Rita*); FALLA: Don Quixote (*Retablo de Maese Pedro*); GINASTERA: Gian Corrado Orsini (*Bomarzo*); GIORDANO: Carlo Gérard (*Andrea Chénier*); HANDEL: Giulio Cesare, Arsamene (*Xerxes*); HAYDN: Eclittico & Buonafede (*Mondo della luna*); LEONCAVALLO: Tonio (*Pagliacci*); MASCAGNI: Rabbi David (*Amico Fritz*), Alfio (*Cavalleria rusticana*); MASSENET: Albert (*Werther*); MENOTTI: Husband (*Amelia al ballo*); MOZART: Leporello (*Don Giovanni*), Nardo (*Finta giardiniera*), Conte Almaviva & Figaro (*Nozze di Figaro*); MUSSORGSKY: Boris & Varlaam (*Boris Godunov*); ORFF: Solo (*Carmina burana*); PAISIELLO: Figaro (*Barbiere di Siviglia*); PERGOLESI: Tracolino (*Maestro di musica*), Uberto (*Serva padrona*), Dott Pietro (*Frate 'nnamorato*); PONCHIELLI: Barnaba (*Gioconda*); PUCCINI: Marcello (*Bohème*), Gianni Schicchi, Sharpless (*Butterfly*), Lescaut (*Manon Lescaut*), Michele (*Tabarro*), Scarpia (*Tosca*), Guglielmo Wulf (*Villi*); RAVEL: Ramiro (*Heure espagnole*); ROSSINI: Figaro (*Barbiere di Siviglia*), Guillaume Tell, Dormont (*Scala di seta*), Gaudenzio (*Signor Bruschino*); SAINT-SAENS: Grand prêtre (*Samson et Dalila*); VERDI: Amonasro (*Aida*), Renato (*Ballo in maschera*), Don Carlo (*Ernani*), Ford & Falstaff (*Falstaff*), Don Carlo (*Forza del destino*), Iago (*Otello*), Rigoletto, Simon Boccanegra, Germont (*Traviata*), Conte di Luna (*Trovatore*). **World premieres:** PERUSSO: Joven (*Voz del silencio*) Teatro Colón 1969. Gives recitals. Appears with symphony orchestra. **Res:** Belgrano 861, Buenos Aires, Argentina.

TOMOWA-SINTOW, ANNA. Spinto. Bulgarian. Resident mem: Staatsoper, Berlin, Ger DR. Born 22 Sep 1941, Stara Zagora, Bulgaria. Husband Awram Sintow, occupation actor. One child. Studied: Prof Zlatev-Tscherkin, Katja Spiridonowa, Sofia. **Debut:** Tatiana (*Eugene Onegin*) Opera House, Stara Zagora, Bulgaria 1965. Previous occupations: pianist. Awards: Ntl Prize of the GDR; Grant of the GDR; Kammersängerin, Ministry of Culture of the GDR: Merited Artist of the Republic of Bulgaria.

Sang with major companies in AUS: Salzburg Fest; BEL: Brussels; BRA: Rio de Janeiro; BUL: Sofia; FIN: Helsinki; FRA: Nancy, Paris; FR GER: Munich Staatsoper; GER DR: Berlin Staatsoper, Dresden, Leipzig; POL: Warsaw; ROM: Bucharest; USSR: Moscow Bolshoi; USA: San Francisco Opera. **Roles with these companies incl** BOITO: Margherita★ (*Mefistofele*); BORODIN: Jaroslavna★‡ (*Prince Igor*); MOZART: Fiordiligi★ (*Così fan tutte*), Donna Anna★ (*Don Giovanni*), Contessa★ (*Nozze di Figaro*); PUCCINI: Lauretta‡ (*Gianni Schicchi*), Cio-Cio-San★ (*Butterfly*), Manon★; STRAUSS, R: Arabella★, Ariadne★; TCHAIKOVSKY: Tatiana★ (*Eugene Onegin*); VERDI: Aida★, Abigaille★ (*Nabucco*), Desdemona★ (*Otello*), Violetta★ (*Traviata*), Leonora★ (*Trovatore*). Recorded for: Eterna, DG. Appears with symphony orchestra. Coaches repertoire. **Res:** Leipziger Str 47/0704, 108 Berlin, Ger DR. **Mgmt:** BAA/BUL; SLZ/FRG.

TOMS, CARL. Scenic and costume designer for opera, theater, film, television. British. Head of Design, Young Vic for Ntl Theatre. Born 29 May 1927, Kirkby-in-Ashfield/Notts, UK. Single. Studied: Mansfield School of Art; Royal Coll of Art, Old Vic School, London. **Operatic debut:** *Segreto di Susanna* Glyndebourne Fest 1958. Theater debut: Royal Court Th, London 1957. Awards: Tony Awd for best set design 1974-75; Officer of British Empire, Queen Elizabeth II.

Designed for major companies in HOL: Amsterdam; SPA: Majorca; UK: Aldeburgh Fest, Welsh National, Edinburgh Fest, Scottish, Glyndebourne Fest, London Royal & English National; USA: Chicago, New York City Opera, San Diego, San Francisco Opera. **Operas designed for these companies incl** BELLINI: *Norma*★, *Puritani*★; BRITTEN: *Midsummer Night*, *Peter Grimes*★; DONIZETTI: *Lucia;* GLUCK: *Iphigénie en Tauride;* ROSSINI: *Barbiere di Siviglia, Cenerentola;* STRAUSS, R: *Frau ohne Schatten;* VERDI: *Ballo in maschera*★, *Falstaff, Macbeth*★; WAGNER: *Meistersinger*★; WOLF-FERRARI: *Segreto di Susanna.* **Operatic world premieres:** WILLIAMSON: *Our Man in Havana* Sadler's Wells, London 1963. Exhibitions of stage designs in one-man shows, UK. **Res:** White House, Beaumont/Broxbourne, UK. Mgmt: TFP/UK.

TÖPPER, HERTHA. Lyric & dramatic mezzo-soprano. Austrian & German. Resident mem: Bayerische Staatsoper, Munich. Born 19 Apr 1924, Graz, Austria. Husband Franz Mixa. Studied: Prof Maria Salmar, Prof Franz Mixa. **Debut:** Ulrica (*Ballo in maschera*) Opernhaus Graz 1946. Awards: Bayerische Kammersängerin 1955; Bavarian Order of Merit 1962; Bayreuth Medal 1962.

Sang with major companies in ARG: Buenos Aires; AUS: Graz, Vienna Staatsoper; BEL: Brussels; FR GER: Bayreuth Fest, Berlin Deutsche Oper; Frankfurt, Hamburg, Mannheim, Munich Staatsoper & Gärtnerplatz, Stuttgart, Wiesbaden Hessisches Staatstheater; GER DR: Berlin Staatsoper, Dresden; ITA: Milan La Scala, Naples, Venice; MON: Monte Carlo; POR: Lisbon; SWI: Zurich; UK: Edinburgh Fest, London Royal Opera; USA: New York Met, San Diego,

San Francisco Opera. **Roles with these companies incl** BARTOK: Judith✶‡ (*Bluebeard's Castle*); BIZET: Carmen✶; BRITTEN: Auntie (*Peter Grimes*); CIMAROSA: Fidalma (*Matrimonio segreto*); DEBUSSY: Geneviève✶ (*Pelléas et Mélisande*); FLOTOW: Nancy (*Martha*); GLUCK: Orfeo✶; HANDEL: Ulisse (*Deidamia*), Cornelia (*Giulio Cesare*), Amastris (*Xerxes*); HUMPERDINCK: Hänsel; MARTIN: Mère d'Iseut (*Vin herbé*); MENOTTI: Secretary (*Consul*); MONTEVERDI: Orfeo‡; MOZART: Sesto (*Clemenza di Tito*), Dorabella (*Così fan tutte*), Cherubino‡ (*Nozze di Figaro*); MUSSORGSKY: Marina (*Boris Godunov*), Marfa (*Khovanshchina*); NICOLAI: Frau Reich (*Lustigen Weiber*); PFITZNER: Silla (*Palestrina*); PUCCINI: Suzuki (*Butterfly*); STRAUSS, J: Prinz Orlovsky (*Fledermaus*); STRAUSS, R: Clairon✶‡ (*Capriccio*), Octavian‡ (*Rosenkavalier*); STRAVINSKY: Jocasta (*Oedipus Rex*); TCHAIKOVSKY: Mme Larina & Olga (*Eugene Onegin*); THOMAS: Mignon; VERDI: Amneris✶ (*Aida*), Ulrica (*Ballo in maschera*), Eboli (*Don Carlo*), Preziosilla (*Forza del destino*), Azucena✶ (*Trovatore*); WAGNER: Magdalene✶ (*Meistersinger*), Fricka (*Rheingold✶, Walküre✶*), Waltraute✶ (*Götterdämmerung*), Brangäne✶(*Tristan und Isolde*); WEINBERGER: Königin (*Schwanda*). Also GLUCK: Paride; HANDEL: Agrippina; VERDI: Lady Macbeth; WOLF: Frasquita (*Corregidor*). **World premieres:** HINDEMITH: Mutter Keppler (*Harmonie der Welt*) Munich 1957; YUN: Paengdok (*Sim Tjong*) Munich 1972. Recorded for: DG, Philips, Electrola, Columbia, Eurodisc, Telefunken, Decca. Video/Film: (*Eugene Onegin*); (*Finta giardiniera*); (*Matrimonio segreto*). Gives recitals. Appears with symphony orchestra. Teaches voice. Coaches repertoire. On faculty of Staatliche Musikhochschule Munich; Prof. **Res:** Aidenbachstr 207, 8 Munich, FR Ger.

TORIGI, RICHARD; né Santo V Tortorigi. Lyric baritone. American. Born 30 Oct 1917, New York. Wife Lorna, occupation nurse. Two children. Studied: American Theatre Wing, Amato Workshop, Eleanor McLellan, Dick Marzollo, New York. **Debut:** Escamillo (*Carmen*) Rochester Opera, NY 1947. Previous occupations: Air Force, 1st Lt radar.
  Sang with major companies in CAN: Vancouver; SPA: Barcelona; USA: Baltimore, Boston, Chicago, Cincinnati, Dallas, Fort Worth, Hartford Connecticut Opera, Houston Grand, Miami, Milwaukee Florentine, New Orleans, New York City Opera, Philadelphia Grand & Lyric, Pittsburgh, St Paul, San Antonio, Seattle, Washington DC. **Roles with these companies incl** BIZET: Escamillo✶ (*Carmen*); DONIZETTI: Dott Malatesta (*Don Pasquale*), Belcore (*Elisir*), Enrico (*Lucia*); FLOTOW: Plunkett (*Martha*); GINASTERA: Silvio de Narni✶‡ (*Bomarzo*); LEONCAVALLO: Tonio (*Pagliacci*); MASSENET: Lescaut (*Manon*); MENOTTI: John Sorel (*Consul*); MOZART: Guglielmo (*Così fan tutte*); PUCCINI: Marcello✶ (*Bohème*), Sharpless✶ (*Butterfly*), Lescaut (*Manon Lescaut*), Scarpia (*Tosca*); ROSSINI: Figaro (*Barbiere di Siviglia*); VERDI: Amonasro (*Aida*), Renato (*Ballo in maschera*), Rodrigo (*Don Carlo*), Ford (*Falstaff*), Iago (*Otello*), Rigoletto, Germont (*Traviata*), Conte di

Luna (*Trovatore*); WOLF-FERRARI: Conte Gil (*Segreto di Susanna*). Also CASTELNUOVO-TEDESCO: Bassanio (*Merchant of Venice*); GOUNOD: Valentin (*Faust*). Video—NBC TV: Manfredo (*Amore dei tre re*); Marcello (*Bohème*). Film: Alfio (*Cavalleria rusticana*).

TOSCANO, CAROL. Lyric soprano. American. Born 12 Aug 1941, Philadelphia, PA. Husband Anthony Squillacote, occupation singer. Studied: Marinka Gurewich, Clare Gelda, Floria Mari. **Debut:** Rosina (*Barbiere di Siviglia*) Teatro Nuovo, Milan 1965. Awards: Phila Youth Conct Awd; Marian Anderson Awd; Met Op Ntl Counc Aud; Rockefeller Fndt Grant; Sullivan Fndt Awd; American Opera Aud.
  Sang with major companies in USA: Chicago, Fort Worth, Houston, New Orleans, St Paul, San Diego, San Francisco Spring Opera, Santa Fe, Washington DC. **Roles with these companies incl** DONIZETTI: Norina (*Don Pasquale*), Adina✶ (*Elisir*); GLUCK: Amor (*Orfeo ed Euridice*); HENZE: Scolatella (*König Hirsch/Re Cervo*); OFFENBACH: Olympia (*Contes d'Hoffmann*); PUCCINI: Mimì✶ (*Bohème*); RAVEL: Concepcion✶ (*Heure espagnole*); ROSSINI: Rosina (*Barbiere di Siviglia*), Fiorilla (*Turco in Italia*); STRAUSS, R: Fiakermilli✶ (*Arabella*); VERDI: Gilda✶ (*Rigoletto*). Also HENZE: Ida (*Junge Lord*); ROSSINI: Gemmy✶ (*Guillaume Tell*). Gives recitals. Appears with symphony orchestra. **Res:** 31 E 12 St, New York, NY 10003, USA. Mgmt: WLS/USA.

TOURANGEAU, HUGUETTE. Contralto. Canadian. Born 12 Aug 1938, Montreal. Husband Barry W Thompson. Studied: Consv de Québec, Mrs Ruzena Herlinger, Montreal; Mo Richard Bonynge. **Debut:** Cherubino (*Nozze di Figaro*) Stratford Fest, Ontario 1964. Previous occupations: studied education. Awards: Canada Counc Grant; Met Op Ntl Counc Reg Auditions: Fisher Fndt Awd 1964.
  Sang with major companies in AUSTRL: Sydney; CAN: Montreal/Quebec, Toronto, Vancouver; FR GER: Hamburg; HOL: Amsterdam; MEX: Mexico City; USA: Boston, Dallas, Fort Worth Opera, Hartford, Houston Grand, New York Metropolitan & City Opera, Philadelphia Lyric, Portland, San Francisco Opera, Santa Fe, Seattle. **Roles with these companies incl** BELLINI: Adalgisa✶ (*Norma*); BIZET: Carmen✶; DONIZETTI: Elisabetta✶‡ (*Maria Stuarda*); GLUCK: Orfeo✶; GOUNOD: Siebel (*Faust*); HANDEL: Giulio Cesare✶, Bertaric✶ (*Rodelinda*); MASSENET: Parseis✶‡ (*Esclarmonde*); MOZART: Dorabella✶ (*Così fan tutte*), Zerlina✶ (*Don Giovanni*), Cherubino✶ (*Nozze di Figaro*); OFFENBACH: Giulietta✶ (*Contes d'Hoffmann*); PUCCINI: Suzuki✶ (*Butterfly*); ROSSINI: Rosina✶ (*Barbiere di Siviglia*), Arsace✶ (*Semiramide*); STRAUSS, J: Prinz Orlovsky✶ (*Fledermaus*); THOMAS: Mignon✶; VERDI: Federica✶ (*Luisa Miller*). Also OFFENBACH: Nicklausse✶ (*Contes d'Hoffmann*); MASSENET: Thérèse✶; BIZET: Djamileh. Recorded for: Decca, London. Video—Dutch TV: Carmen, Mignon; CBC: Mlle Lange (*Fille de Mme Angot*). Gives recitals. Appears with symphony orchestra. **Res:** Vancouver, BC, Canada. Mgmt: COL/USA.

TOZZI, GIORGIO. Bass-baritone. American. Born 8 Jan 1923, Chicago. Wife Monte Amundsen, occupation singer. Two children. Studied: Giacomo Rimini, Rosa Raisa, Chicago; Giulio Lorandi, Milan; De Paul Univ, Chicago; Armen Boyajian, New York. **Debut:** Tarquinius (*Rape of Lucretia*) Lyric Opera of Chicago 1948. Awards: Gold Record RCA; Winner Artists Advis Counc, Chicago.

Sang with major companies in ARG: Buenos Aires; AUS: Salzburg Fest; FRA: Aix-in-Provence Fest, Nice; FR GER: Frankfurt, Hamburg, Munich Staatsoper; ITA: Florence Maggio & Comunale, Genoa, Milan La Scala, Palermo, Parma, Rome Opera, Trieste, Turin, Venice; POR: Lisbon; USA: Boston, Hartford, Houston, Miami, New Orleans, New York Met, Portland, St Paul, San Antonio, San Francisco Opera. **Roles with these companies incl** BEETHOVEN: Rocco★ (*Fidelio*); BELLINI: Oroveso★ (*Norma*), Rodolfo★ (*Sonnambula*); BOITO: Mefistofele; BRITTEN: Billy Budd★ & John Claggart (*Billy Budd*); CATALANI: Stromminger (*Wally*); CHERUBINI: Creon (*Medea*); CIMAROSA: Count Robinson (*Matrimonio segreto*); DEBUSSY: Arkel★ (*Pelléas et Mélisande*); FLOTOW: Plunkett (*Martha*); GOUNOD: Méphistophélès (*Faust*); HANDEL: Giulio Cesare; MENOTTI: Bob (*Old Maid and the Thief*); MEYERBEER: Comte de St Bris (*Huguenots*); MONTEMEZZI: Archibaldo (*Amore dei tre re*); MOZART: Don Giovanni★, Figaro★ (*Nozze di Figaro*), Sarastro (*Zauberflöte*); MUSSORGSKY: Boris★ & Pimen (*Boris Godunov*); PONCHIELLI: Alvise (*Gioconda*); PUCCINI: Colline★ (*Bohème*); ROSSINI: Don Basilio★ (*Barbiere di Siviglia*), Slook (*Cambiale di matrimonio*); SMETANA: Kezal (*Bartered Bride*); VERDI: Ramfis★ (*Aida*), Philip II★ (*Don Carlo*), Silva (*Ernani*), Padre Guardiano (*Forza del destino*), Conte Walter★ (*Luisa Miller*), Banquo★ (*Macbeth*), Zaccaria★ (*Nabucco*), Fiesco★ (*Simon Boccanegra*), Procida (*Vespri*); WAGNER: Daland★ (*Fliegende Holländer*), Hans Sachs★ & Pogner (*Meistersinger*), Gurnemanz★ (*Parsifal*), König Marke★ (*Tristan und Isolde*). **World premieres:** BARBER: Doctor‡ (*Vanessa*) Metropolitan Opera 1958. Recorded for: RCA, London, Cetra. Video/Film: Hans Sachs (*Meistersinger*). Gives recitals. Appears with symphony orchestra. Teaches voice. Coaches repertoire. On faculty of Juilliard School, New York. **Res:** Malibu, CA, USA. Mgmt: CAM/USA; SLZ/FRG.

TRACEY, EDMUND. British. Production Director, English National Opera, London Coliseum, St Martin's Lane, London WC2; also of New Opera Co. In charge of art policy & dram matters. Is also a translator and librettist. Born 14 Nov 1927, Preston. Single. Studied: Lincoln Coll, Oxford; Guildhall School of Music & Drama, London. Plays the piano. Previous occupations: music critic. Started with present company in 1965 as Literary Mng; in present position since 1966. World premieres at theater during his engagement: WILLIAMSON: *Violins of St Jacques* London 1966, *Lucky Peter's Journey* London 1969; BENNETT: *Penny for a Song* London 1967; CROSSE: *Story of Vasco* London 1974. Made the following new translations: *Fledermaus,* dialogue; *Leonore/Fidelio,* dial; *Contes d'Hoffmann;* *Entführung aus dem Serail; Traviata; Manon; Belle Hélène,* dial; *Tosca,* others. Libretto: *Lucky Peter's Journey.* Mem of New Opera Company Commtt. **Res:** London, UK.

TRAMA, UGO. Bass. Italian. Born 4 Aug 1932, Naples. Single. Studied: Emilia Gubitosi, Naples; Accad Chigiana, Accad S Cecilia, Mo Giorgio Favaretto, Siena & Rome. **Debut:** Banquo (*Macbeth*) Spoleto Fest 1958. Previous occupations: teacher.

Sang with major companies in AUS: Bregenz Fest; BEL: Brussels; CZE: Prague National; DEN: Copenhagen; FIN: Helsinki; FRA: Aix-en-Provence Fest, Bordeaux, Marseille, Nancy, Paris, Rouen, Strasbourg; FR GER: Munich Staatsoper; HOL: Amsterdam; ITA: Bologna, Florence Maggio & Comunale, Genoa, Milan La Scala, Naples, Palermo, Parma, Rome Opera, Spoleto Fest, Venice; SPA: Barcelona; SWI: Geneva; UK: Edinburgh Fest, Glyndebourne Fest; USA: Dallas, San Francisco Opera; YUG: Dubrovnik. **Roles with these companies incl** BERLIOZ: Méphistophélès (*Damnation de Faust*); CIMAROSA: Count Robinson★ (*Matrimonio segreto*); DONIZETTI: Don Pasquale; GOUNOD: Méphistophélès (*Faust*); MONTEVERDI: Orfeo; MOZART: Leporello★ & Don Giovanni★ (*Don Giovanni*), Figaro★ (*Nozze di Figaro*); PERGOLESI: Uberto (*Serva padrona*); PUCCINI: Colline (*Bohème*); ROSSINI: Don Basilio★ (*Barbiere di Siviglia*), Conte Asdrubal (*Pietra del paragone*); STRAVINSKY: Tiresias (*Oedipus Rex*); VERDI: Attila, Philip II (*Don Carlo*), Silva (*Ernani*), Padre Guardiano (*Forza del destino*), Zaccaria (*Nabucco*), Simon Boccanegra. Recorded for DG, CAM-RCA, Angelicum, Orpheus, Pathé-Marconi, Argo. Gives recitals. Appears with symphony orchestra. **Res:** V Monterone 2, Rome, Italy. Mgmt: IMR/FRA; ALY/SWI.

TRAWINSKA MOROZ, URSZULA. Coloratura soprano. Polish. Resident mem: Teatr Wielki, Warsaw. Born 4 Oct 1937, Gmezno, Poland. Husband Bohdan, occupation lawyer. One child. Studied: Prof Ada Sazi, Warsaw; Prof Gina Cigna, Italy. **Debut:** Mimi (*Bohème*) Opera House, Warsaw 1962. Awards: Laureate of Vocal Compt, Liège, Belgium 1963.

Sang with major companies in POL: Warsaw. **Roles with these companies incl** BIZET: Micaëla★ (*Carmen*); DONIZETTI: Lucia★; GOUNOD: Marguerite★ (*Faust*); HAYDN: Clarissa★ (*Mondo della luna*); MENOTTI: Magda Sorel (*Consul*); MONTEVERDI: Poppea (*Incoronazione di Poppea*); MOZART: Zerlina★ (*Don Giovanni*), Susanna★ (*Nozze di Figaro*), Königin der Nacht★ (*Zauberflöte*); MUSSORGSKY: Marina (*Boris Godunov*); OFFENBACH: Olympia★ & Antonia★ & Giulietta★ (*Contes d'Hoffmann*); PENDERECKI: Philippe★ (*Teufel von Loudun*); PUCCINI: Mimi★ & Musetta★ (*Bohème*); RAVEL: Concepcion★ (*Heure espagnole*); ROSSINI: Rosina★ (*Barbiere di Siviglia*); VERDI: Nannetta★ (*Falstaff*), Gilda★ (*Rigoletto*), Violetta★ (*Traviata*). Also MONIUSZKO: Hanna (*Haunted Castle*). Video: (*Homeless Swallow*). Gives recitals. Appears with symphony orchestra. **Res:** Moliera 8, Warsaw, Poland.

TREMPONT, MICHEL FERNAND. Lyric baritone & baritono-buffo. Belgian. Born 28 Jul 1928, Boussu, Belgium. Studied: Rogatchewsky, Francis Andrien, Consv Royal de Mons, Belgium. **Debut:** Valentin (*Faust*) Liège Opera 1952. Awards: First Prize & special schlshp for voice & opera, Consv Royal Mons.

Sang with major companies in BEL: Brussels, Liège; FRA: Aix-en-Provence Fest. Bordeaux, Lyon, Marseille, Nancy, Nice, Paris, Rouen, Toulouse; ITA: Venice; MON: Monte Carlo; POR: Lisbon; ROM: Bucharest. **Roles with these companies incl** ADAM: Mossoul (*Si j'étais roi*); BECAUD: Mickey★ (*Opéra d'Aran*); BIZET: Escamillo (*Carmen*), Zurga (*Pêcheurs de perles*); BRITTEN: Captain Balstrode (*Peter Grimes*); CIMAROSA: Count Robinson★ (*Matrimonio segreto*); DONIZETTI: Dott Malatesta★ (*Don Pasquale*), Enrico (*Lucia*); GIORDANO: De Siriex (*Fedora*); GOUNOD: Ourrias (*Mireille*); MARTINU: Hans (*Comedy on the Bridge*); MASCAGNI: Alfio (*Cavalleria rusticana*); MASSENET: Sancho★ (*Don Quichotte*), Boniface★ (*Jongleur de Notre Dame*), Lescaut★ (*Manon*), Albert★ (*Werther*); MENOTTI: John Sorel (*Consul*); MOZART: Guglielmo★ & Don Alfonso★ (*Così fan tutte*), Leporello★ (*Don Giovanni*), Figaro★ (*Nozze di Figaro*), Papageno★ (*Zauberflöte*); OFFENBACH: Don Andres (*Périchole*); ORFF: Solo (*Carmina burana*), König (*Kluge*); PERGOLESI: Uberto (*Serva padrona*); PUCCINI: Marcello★ (*Bohème*), Gianni Schicchi★, Sharpless★ (*Butterfly*), Lescaut★ (*Manon Lescaut*); RABAUD: Ali★ & Mârouf★ (*Mârouf*); RAVEL: Ramiro★ (*Heure espagnole*); ROSSINI: Figaro★ (*Barbiere di Siviglia*), Dandini★ & Don Magnifico★ (*Cenerentola*), Robert (*Comte Ory*), Taddeo★ (*Italiana in Algeri*); ROUSSEL: Ferdinand (*Testament de la Tante Caroline*); THOMAS: Hamlet; VERDI: Ford & Falstaff★ (*Falstaff*), Germont (*Traviata*); WAGNER: Beckmesser (*Meistersinger*); WOLF-FERRARI: Conte Gil★ (*Segreto di Susanna*). Also GOUNOD: Valentin (*Faust*); MILHAUD: Matelot (*Pauvre matelot*). Recorded for: EMI. Mgmt: BCP/FRA; IMR/FRA; DOU/UK.

TRIMARCHI, DOMENICO. Lyric baritone & bass-baritone. Italian. Born 21 Dec 1940, Naples, Italy. Single. Studied: Naples Consv S Pietro; Mo Gino Campese, Italy. **Debut:** Belcore (*Elisir*) Teatro la Fenice, Venice 1964. Previous occupations: scenic artist & tech designer.

Sang with major companies in FR GER: Dortmund, Frankfurt, Stuttgart; ITA: Florence Maggio & Comunale, Genoa, Milan La Scala, Naples, Palermo, Rome Opera, Trieste, Turin, Venice, Verona Arena; UK: Edinburgh Fest, London Royal Opera; USA: Chicago; YUG: Dubrovnik. **Roles with these companies incl** BELLINI: Baron Valdeburgo★ (*Straniera*); BERLIOZ: Balducci (*Benvenuto Cellini*); BIZET: Escamillo★ (*Carmen*), Zurga (*Pêcheurs de perles*); CILEA: Michonnet (*A. Lecouvreur*); CIMAROSA: Count Robinson & Geronimo (*Matrimonio segreto*); DONIZETTI: Enrico (*Campanello*), Dott Malatesta★ (*Don Pasquale*), Belcore★ & Dott Dulcamara★ (*Elisir*), Alfonse★ (*Favorite*), Antonio (*Linda di Chamounix*), Enrico★ (*Lucia*); GLUCK: Apollo★ (*Alceste*); GOUNOD: Valentin★ (*Faust*); HENZE: Pentheus (*Bassariden*); LEON-

CAVALLO: Tonio (*Pagliacci*); MASSENET: Lescaut (*Manon*), Albert★ (*Werther*); MOZART: Guglielmo & Don Alfonso (*Così fan tutte*), Leporello★ (*Don Giovanni*), Conte Almaviva & Figaro (*Nozze di Figaro*); PAISIELLO: Figaro★ (*Barbiere di Siviglia*); PERGOLESI: Marcaniello★ (*Frate 'nnamorato*); PUCCINI: Marcello★ (*Bohème*), Gianni Schicchi★, Sharpless★ (*Butterfly*); ROSSINI: Figaro★ & Dott Bartolo & Don Basilio (*Barbiere di Siviglia*); SPONTINI: Cinna (*Vestale*); VERDI: Ford (*Falstaff*), Fra Melitone★ (*Forza del destino*), Barone★ (*Giorno di regno*), Germont (*Traviata*). **Res:** So Vittorio Emanuele 182, 80121 Naples, Italy.

TRIPP, ALVA. Lyric tenor. American. Resident mem: Deutsche Oper am Rhein, Düsseldorf-Duisburg. Born 11 Nov 1937, Washington, NC. Wife Drusilla Lodge, occupation opera singer. Two children. Studied: Francis German; Mannes Coll of Music, New York; Staatliche Hochschule für Musik, Franz Theo Reuter, Munich; Staatliche Hochschule für Musik, Josef Metternich, Cologne. **Debut:** Ernesto (*Don Pasquale*) Kaiserslautern, FR Ger 1966. Awards: German Acad Exchange stipd; Bavarian Ministry of Culture stipd; Fulbright grant.

Sang with major companies in AUS: Vienna Staatsoper; FR GER: Bonn, Cologne, Düsseldorf, Frankfurt, Hamburg, Wiesbaden. **Roles with these companies incl** BERG: Maler★ (*Lulu*); CAVALLI: Ormindo★; DONIZETTI: Nemorino★ (*Elisir*); MOZART: Don Ottavio★ (*Don Giovanni*), Belmonte★ (*Entführung aus dem Serail*), Idamante★ (*Idomeneo*), Marzio★ (*Mitridate, re di Ponto*); NICOLAI: Fenton★ (*Lustigen Weiber*); OFFENBACH: Hoffmann★; PUCCINI: Rinuccio★ (*Gianni Schicchi*); ROSSINI: Almaviva★ (*Barbiere di Siviglia*); STRAVINSKY: Tom Rakewell★ (*Rake's Progress*); TCHAIKOVSKY: Lenski★ (*Eugene Onegin*); VERDI: Ismaele★ (*Nabucco*); WAGNER: Walther v d Vogelweide★ (*Tannhäuser*); WOLF-FERRARI: Florindo★ (*Donne curiose*). Gives recitals. Appears with symphony orchestra. Mgmt: PAS/FRG.

TROISI, MARIO CARLOS. Stages/produces opera, theater & television. Also designs stage-lighting and is a singer, actor & author. Argentinean. Resident Stage Dir, Teatro Colón, Buenos Aires. Also Resident Stage Dir for theater in Buenos Aires & Santiago, Chile. Born 19 Oct 1910, Córdoba, Argentina. Wife Amalia Carini, occupation teacher. Studied: Eleonora Deise, Mario Sammarco, Alfredo Casella; incl music, piano and voice. **Operatic debut:** *Carmen* Opéra, Rome 1949. Theater debut: Rome 1935. Previous occupation: philosophy student, lecturer, actor. Awards: Arts Club, Asociación Cultural de las Americas; honors for 50 yrs in art.

Directed/produced opera for major companies in ARG: Buenos Aires; BRA: Rio de Janeiro; ITA: Bologna, Florence Comunale, Rome Opera. **Operas staged with these companies incl** BELLINI: *Norma, Sonnambula;* BIZET: *Carmen★;* BOITO: *Mefistofele;* CILEA: *A. Lecouvreur;* CIMAROSA: *Matrimonio segreto;* DONIZETTI: *Don Pasquale, Elisir, Favorite, Lucia;* GIORDANO: *Andrea Chénier;* GLUCK: *Orfeo ed Euridice;* HUMPERDINCK: *Hänsel und Gretel;* LEON-

TROTTER

CAVALLO: *Pagliacci, Zazà;* MASCAGNI: *Cavalleria rusticana;* MASSENET: *Manon, Werther;* MENOTTI: *Amelia al ballo, Consul, Telephone;* MOZART: *Così fan tutte, Nozze di Figaro;* MUSSORGSKY: *Boris Godunov;* PERGOLESI: *Maestro di musica, Serva padrona;* PUCCINI: *Bohème*, Fanciulla del West, Gianni Schicchi, Butterfly, Tosca;* ROSSINI: *Barbiere di Siviglia*;* SAINT-SAENS: *Samson et Dalila;* VERDI: *Aida, Ballo in maschera, Rigoletto, Traviata*, Trovatore*;* WAGNER: *Lohengrin;* WOLF-FERRARI: *Segreto di Susanna.* Also BOERO: *Matrero;* SCHIUMA: *Tabaré.* **Operatic world premieres:** BOERO: *Zincali* 1954; GARCIA-ESTRADA: *Cuarterona* 1951, both at Teatro Colón. Operatic Video – TV Peretti: *Barbiere di Siviglia, Traviata, Bohème, Pagliacci.* Previous leading positions with major theater companies: Tech Dir, Teatro Municipal de Santiago, Chile 1955-63. Teaches at Facultad de. Medicina, Buenos Aires. **Res:** Virses Linieres 121, Buenos Aires, Argentina.

TROTTER, LINDA. Lirico spinto soprano. American. Resident mem: Landestheater Innsbruck, Austria. Born 24 Jul, Los Angeles, USA. Husband Erich Heger, occupation sales dir. Studied: Univ of So Calif, Los Angeles; Intl Opernstudio Zurich, Dr Herbert Graf; Dusolina Giannini, Judy Bounds Coleman. **Debut:** Dorabella (*Così fan tutte*) Opernhaus Gelsenkirchen, FR Ger 1964. Awards: M B Rockefeller Fund Grant.
Sang with major companies in AUS: Graz; **FR GER:** Essen; **SPA:** Majorca. **Mezzo roles with these companies incl** MOZART: Dorabella* (*Così fan tutte*), Ramiro (*Finta giardiniera*), Cherubino (*Nozze di Figaro*); ROSSINI: Isolier (*Comte Ory*); STRAUSS, R: Komponist* (*Ariadne auf Naxos*), Octavian (*Rosenkavalier*). **Soprano roles with these companies incl** MOZART: Donna Elvira* (*Don Giovanni*); PUCCINI: Mimi* (*Bohème*); SMETANA: Marie* (*Bartered Bride*); STRAUSS, R: Ariadne* (*Ariadne auf Naxos*); VERDI: Leonora* (*Forza del destino*), Desdemona* (*Otello*); WAGNER: Elsa* (*Lohengrin*), Sieglinde* (*Walküre*), Gutrune* (*Götterdämmerung*). Video/Film: Ramiro (*Finta giardiniera*). Gives recitals. Appears with symphony orchestra. **Res:** Wopfnerstr 6, Innsbruck, Austria. **Mgmt:** TAS/AUS.

TROYANOS, TATIANA. Dramatic mezzo-soprano. American. Born 12 Sep 1938, New York. Single. Studied: Juilliard School, Hans Heinz, New York. **Debut:** Hippolita (*Midsummer Night*) New York City Opera 1963. Previous occupations: secy. Awards: Alumni Schlshp Juilliard School, NY.
Sang with major companies in AUS: Salzburg Fest, Vienna Staatsoper; **CAN:** Montreal/Quebec, Ottawa, Toronto; **FRA:** Aix-en-Provence, Marseille, Paris, Toulouse; **GRE:** Athens Fest; **FR GER:** Berlin Deutsche Oper, Hamburg, Munich Gärtnerplatz, Stuttgart, Wiesbaden; **HOL:** Amsterdam; **ITA:** Florence Maggio & Comunale, Milan La Scala, Palermo, Rome Opera, Venice; **POR:** Lisbon; **SWE:** Stockholm; **SWI:** Geneva; **UK:** Edinburgh Fest, London Royal Opera; **USA:** Boston, Chicago, Dallas, Kentucky, New York City Opera, Pittsburgh, San Francisco Opera,

Washington DC. **Roles with these companies incl** BELLINI: Romeo* (*Capuleti ed i Montecchi*), Adalgisa* (*Norma*); BERLIOZ: Marguerite (*Damnation de Faust*); BIZET: Carmen*; BRITTEN: Hippolita (*Midsummer Night*); CIMAROSA: Elisetta (*Matrimonio segreto*); DONIZETTI: Giovanna (*Anna Bolena*), Maffio Orsini* (*Lucrezia Borgia*), Sara* (*Roberto Devereux*); GLUCK: Orfeo*; GOUNOD: Siebel (*Faust*); HANDEL: Ariodante*, Cleopatra‡ (*Giulio Cesare*); MASSENET: Charlotte* (*Werther*); MONTEVERDI: Poppea (*Incoronazione di Poppea*); MOZART: Dorabella*‡ (*Così fan tutte*), Cherubino*‡ (*Nozze di Figaro*); MUSSORGSKY: Marina* (*Boris Godunov*); OFFENBACH: Giulietta* (*Contes d'Hoffmann*); PENDERECKI: Ninon (*Teufel von Loudun*); PROKOFIEV: Smeraldina* (*Love for Three Oranges*); PUCCINI: Suzuki (*Butterfly*); SAINT-SAENS: Dalila*; STRAUSS, J: Prinz Orlovsky* (*Fledermaus*); STRAUSS, R: Komponist*‡ (*Ariadne auf Naxos*), Clairon*‡ (*Capriccio*), Octavian* (*Rosenkavalier*); STRAVINSKY: Jocasta* (*Oedipus Rex*), Baba the Turk (*Rake's Progress*); VERDI: Eboli* (*Don Carlo*), Preziosilla* (*Forza del destino*). Also MASCAGNI: Santuzza* (*Cavalleria rusticana*); MOZART: Donna Elvira* (*Don Giovanni*). **World premieres:** PENDERECKI: Jeanne‡ (*Teufel von Loudun*) Hamburg Staatsoper 1969. Recorded for: DG, RCA, Philips. Gives recitals. Appears with symphony orchestra. **Res:** 98 Riverside Dr, New York, NY, USA. Mgmt: CAM/USA; SLZ/FRG.

TRUSSEL, JACK. Lyric tenor. American. Born 7 Apr 1943, San Francisco. Wife Beti Seay, occupation actress. Studied: Ball State Univ, George Newton, Muncie, IN; Cornelius Reid, New York. **Debut:** Pinkerton (*Butterfly*) Oberlin Fest 1970. Awards: Ntl Opera Inst Grant; M B Rockefeller Fund Grant.
Sang with major companies in USA: Boston, Dallas, Houston, Milwaukee Florentine, New Orleans, San Francisco Spring Opera, Santa Fe. **Roles with these companies incl** BERG: Alwa* (*Lulu*); BIZET: Don José* (*Carmen*); PUCCINI: Rodolfo* (*Bohème*), Cavaradossi* (*Tosca*); VAUGHAN WILLIAMS: Hugh* (*Hugh the Drover*). Also STRAUSS, R: Narraboth* (*Salome*). **World premieres:** PASATIERI: Dr Dorn (*Seagull*) Houston Grand Opera 1974. Video – NET TV: Naroumov (*Pique Dame*). Gives recitals. Appears with symphony orchestra. **Res:** New York, USA.

TUCCI, GABRIELLA. Lyric soprano. Italian. Born 4 Aug 1932, Rome. Husband Leonardo Filoni, occupation voice teacher. Two children. Studied: Leonardo Filoni (husband) Rome; also studied piano. **Debut:** Violetta (*Traviata*) Teatro Giglio, Lucca, Italy 1951. Awards: Commendatore of Italian Republic; Commenda from the Empress of Japan; Gran Dama of the Intl Acad of Pontzen of the Order Knights of St Brigida.
Sang with major companies in ARG: Buenos Aires; **AUSTRL:** Sydney; **AUS:** Vienna Staatsoper; **DEN:** Copenhagen; **FR GER:** Berlin Deutsche Oper, Munich Staatsoper, Stuttgart, Wiesbaden; **HUN:** Budapest; **ITA:** Bologna, Florence Maggio & Comunale, Milan La Scala, Naples

San Carlo, Palermo Massimo, Rome Opera & Caracalla, Trieste, Turin, Venice, Verona Arena; MON: Monte Carlo; NOR: Oslo; POR: Lisbon; S AFR: Johannesburg; UK: London Royal Opera; USSR: Moscow Bolshoi; USA: Baltimore, Boston, Chicago Lyric, Cincinnati Summer Opera, Hartford, Houston Grand, Miami, New Orleans, New York Met, Philadelphia Grand, Pittsburgh, San Antonio, San Diego, San Francisco Opera. Roles with these companies incl BELLINI: Elvira (Puritani); BIZET: Micaëla★ (Carmen); BOITO: Margherita (Mefistofele); BRITTEN: Helena (Midsummer Night); CILEA: Adriana Lecouvreur; GIORDANO: Maddalena★ (Andrea Chénier); GLUCK: Euridice; GOUNOD: Marguerite★ (Faust); LEONCAVALLO: Nedda‡ (Pagliacci); MASCAGNI: Suzel (Amico Fritz); MASSENET: Manon, Thaïs; MEYERBEER: Valentine (Huguenots); MOZART: Donna Anna & Donna Elvira (Don Giovanni), Contessa (Nozze di Figaro); ORFF: Solo (Carmina burana); PERGOLESI: Serpina (Serva padrona); POULENC: Blanche (Dialogues des Carmélites); PROKOFIEV: Natasha (War and Peace); PUCCINI: Mimi★ (Bohème), Lauretta (Gianni Schicchi), Cio-Cio-San★ (Butterfly), Manon Lescaut, Suor Angelica, Tosca★, Liù (Turandot); ROSSINI: Mathilde (Guillaume Tell), Anaï★ (Moïse); TCHAIKOVSKY: Lisa (Pique Dame); VERDI: Aida★, Amelia★ (Ballo in maschera), Elisabetta (Don Carlo), Elvira (Ernani), Alice Ford (Falstaff), Leonora★ (Forza del destino), Luisa Miller★, Desdemona (Otello), Gilda (Rigoletto), Amelia (Simon Boccanegra), Violetta★ (Traviata), Leonora‡ (Trovatore); WAGNER: Eva (Meistersinger). Also PIZZETTI: Maria (Straniero); PIZZETTI: Mariola★ (Fra Gherardo); PICCINNI: (Didon); DARGOMIZHSKY: Donna Anna (Stone Guest); DONIZETTI: (Furioso all'isola di San Domingo). Recorded for: Decca, London, Angel. Video/Film: Liù (Turandot); Mathilde (Guillaume Tell). Gives recitals. Appears with symphony orchestra. Res: Largo San Pio V 16, Rome, Italy.

TUGARINOVA, TATIANA FEDOROVNA; née Guseva. Lyric-dramatic soprano. Russian. Resident mem: Bolshoi Theater, Moscow. Born 15 May 1925, Moscow. Husband Andreev, occupation architect. One daughter. Studied: Moscow Consv, Prof N Dorliak. **Debut:** Kupava (Snow Maiden) Bolshoi Theater, Moscow 1956. Previous occupations: economist.

Sang with major companies in AUS: Vienna Staatsoper; FRA: Paris; ITA: Milan La Scala; USSR: Kiev Opera, Leningrad Kirov, Moscow Bolshoi Theater, Tbilisi. Roles with these companies incl BORODIN: Jaroslavna★‡ (Prince Igor); RIMSKY-KORSAKOV: Fevronia★ (Invisible City of Kitezh); TCHAIKOVSKY: Lisa★ (Pique Dame); VERDI: Aida★, Elisabetta★ (Don Carlo), Lady Macbeth‡. Also RIMSKY-KORSAKOV: Tsaritsa Militrisea (Tsar Saltan), Vera Sheloga★ (Maid of Pskov); DARGOMIZHSKY: Natasha★ (Rusalka); TCHAIKOVSKY: Maria (Mazeppa). Recorded for: Melodiya. Gives recitals. Appears with symphony orchestra. Res: 21 B Dorogomilovskaya, Apt 60, Moscow, USSR.

TURGEON, BERNARD. Dramatic baritone. Canadian. Born 20 Oct 1932, Edmonton, Alta, Canada.

Wife Dolores, occupation musician. Three children. Studied: Lamber, Toronto; Grossmann, Rathauser, Vienna. **Debut:** Sergeant (Manon) Canadian Opera Co, Toronto 1951. Awards: Alberta Gvnmt; Toronto Consv; Canada Council; City of Edmonton; Singing Stars of Tomorrow.

Sang with major companies in CAN: Montreal/Quebec, Ottawa, Toronto, Vancouver; UK: Cardiff Welsh, Edinburgh Fest, Glasgow Scottish, Glyndebourne Fest, London Royal & English National; USSR: Kiev, Moscow Bolshoi, Tbilisi; USA: Pittsburgh, San Diego, Seattle, Washington DC. Roles with these companies incl BELLINI: Sir Richard (Puritani); BIZET: Escamillo★ (Carmen); BRITTEN: Astrologer★ (Burning Fiery Furnace); DONIZETTI: Dott Malatesta★ (Don Pasquale); LEONCAVALLO: Tonio★ (Pagliacci); MASCAGNI: Alfio★ (Cavalleria rusticana); MASSENET: Lescaut★ (Manon); MENOTTI: John Sorel (Consul), Bob (Old Maid and the Thief); MOZART: Don Giovanni, Conte Almaviva (Nozze di Figaro); PUCCINI: Marcello★ (Bohème), Gianni Schicchi, Sharpless★ (Butterfly), Lescaut (Manon Lescaut), Michele★ (Tabarro), Scarpia (Tosca); ROSSINI: Dott Bartolo (Barbiere di Siviglia); STRAUSS, R: Musiklehrer (Ariadne auf Naxos); VERDI: Amonasro★ (Aida), Rodrigo★ (Don Carlo), Ford & Falstaff★ (Falstaff), Rigoletto, Germont (Traviata). World premieres: SOMERS: Louis Riel, Canadian Opera Co, Toronto 1967. Gives recitals. Appears with symphony orchestra. Teaches voice. On faculty of Banff School of Fine Arts, Alta, Canada. Res: 14308 59 Ave, Edmonton, Alta, Canada. Mgmt: DBA/USA; CCA/CAN.

TURNER, CLARAMAE; née Claramae Haas. Contralto. American. Born 28 Oct 1920, Dinuba, CA, USA. Husband Frank Hoffmann, occupation engineer. Studied: Nino Comel, Armando Agnini, Giacomo Spadoni, San Francisco; Dick Marzollo, New York. **Debut:** Mother (Contes d'Hoffmann) San Francisco Opera 1945.

Sang with major companies in ARG: Buenos Aires; CAN: Toronto, Vancouver; ITA: Venice; MEX: Mexico City; MON: Monte Carlo; SPA: Barcelona; USA: Baltimore, Boston, Chicago, Cincinnati, Dallas, Fort Worth, Hartford, Houston Grand, Kansas City Lyric Theater, Memphis, Miami, Milwaukee Florentine, Newark NJ Opera, New Orleans, New York Met & City Opera, Omaha, Philadelphia Grand & Lyric, Pittsburgh, Portland, St Paul, San Antonio, San Diego, San Francisco Opera, Seattle, Washington DC. Roles with these companies incl BIZET: Carmen; BRITTEN: Auntie (Peter Grimes); CHARPENTIER: Mère (Louise); CHERUBINI: Neris (Medea); DEBUSSY: Geneviève (Pelléas et Mélisande); DONIZETTI: Marquise de Birkenfeld★ (Fille du régiment); FLOTOW: Nancy (Martha); GLUCK: Orfeo; HENZE: Baronin von Grünwiesel (Junge Lord); HUMPERDINCK: Hexe (Hänsel und Gretel); MENOTTI: Miss Todd (Old Maid and the Thief); MOORE: Augusta Tabor (Baby Doe); MUSSORGSKY: Marina (Boris Godunov); PONCHIELLI: Laura & La Cieca (Gioconda); POULENC: Prioresse (Dialogues des Carmélites); PUCCINI: Suzuki (Butterfly), Principessa★ (Suor Angelica), Frugola★ (Tabarro), Zita★ (Gianni Schicchi); SAINT-SAENS: Dalila;

STRAUSS, J: Prinz Orlovsky (*Fledermaus*); STRAUSS, R: Klytämnestra (*Elektra*), Herodias (*Salome*); STRAVINSKY: Jocasta (*Oedipus Rex*); VERDI: Amneris (*Aida*), Ulrica (*Ballo in maschera*), Dame Quickly (*Falstaff*), Preziosilla (*Forza del destino*), Azucena (*Trovatore*); WAGNER: Magdalene (*Meistersinger*), Erda (*Rheingold, Siegfried*), Fricka (*Walküre*). Also ad BANFIELD: (*Colloquio col Tango*), (*Lord Byron's Love Letter*). **World premieres:** MENOTTI: Madame Flora (*Medium*) Columbia Univ, New York 1946; GINASTERA: Diana Orsini (*Bomarzo*) Washington, DC, Opera Soc 1967; COPLAND: Ma Moss (*Tender Land*) New York City Opera 1954. Recorded for: Columbia, RCA. Video/Film: Madame Flora (*Medium*); Mother (*Hänsel und Gretel*). Gives recitals. Appears with symphony orchestra. Teaches voice. Coaches repertoire. **Res:** Salt Point, New York, USA.

TURNER, MARGARITA JOY. Lyric soprano. Australian. Resident mem: Städtische Bühnen, Essen. Born 11 Mar 1943, Perth, Australia. Husband Jorgos Canacakis-Canàs, occupation lecturer music therapy. Studied: Jorgos Canàs, Prof Th Lindenbaum, Germany; Emelie Hooke, London. **Debut:** Micaëla (*Carmen*) Städtische Bühnen, Krefeld 1969. Previous occupations: secy. **Sang with major companies in** FR GER: Cologne, Essen, Krefeld, Saarbrücken, Wiesbaden, Wuppertal. **Roles with these companies incl** BEETHOVEN: Marzelline★ (*Fidelio*); BIZET: Micaëla★ (*Carmen*); DEBUSSY: Mélisande★; FLOTOW: Lady Harriet★ (*Martha*); GOUNOD: Marguerite★ (*Faust*); HENZE: Luise★ (*Junge Lord*); LEONCAVALLO: Nedda★ (*Pagliacci*); MOZART: Fiordiligi★ (*Così fan tutte*), Pamina★ (*Zauberflöte*); OFFENBACH: Antonia★ (*Contes d'Hoffmann*); PUCCINI: Mimi★ (*Bohème*), Liù★ (*Turandot*); RAVEL: Concepcion★ (*Heure espagnole*); SMETANA: Marie★ (*Bartered Bride*); STRAUSS, J: Rosalinde★ (*Fledermaus*); STRAUSS, R: Sophie★ (*Rosenkavalier*); VERDI: Violetta★ (*Traviata*); WAGNER: Eva★ (*Meistersinger*). Gives recitals. Appears with symphony orchestra. Teaches voice. On faculty of Univ of Essen. **Res:** Essen, FR Ger. **Mgmt:** PAS/FRG.

TURNOVSKY, MARTIN. Czechoslovakian. Mus Dir, Norwegian Opera, Storegaten 23C, Oslo 1, 1975- . In charge of art policy & mus matters. Is also a conductor. Born 29 Sep 1928, Prague. Wife Zdenka. Two children. Studied: Mus Acad, Prague, Prof K Ancerl, G Szell. Plays the piano. Previous positions, primarily musical: Mus Dir, Dresden State Opera 1966-68; Mus Dir with orch: Dresdner Staatskapelle 1967-68; Czech Radio Orch 1963-67. Guest conducting: Deutsche Oper Berlin, Stuttgarter Staatsoper, Volksoper Vienna. **Operas conducted with above companies incl** GLUCK: *Orfeo;* HENZE: *Junge Lord;* DVORAK: *Rusalka;* JANACEK: *Jenufa;* LEONCAVALLO: *Pagliacci;* MOZART: *Nozze di Figaro, Zauberflöte★;* MUSSORGSKY: *Boris;* ROSSINI: *Barbiere;* SMETANA: *Bartered Bride, The Kiss;* TCHAIKOVSKY: *Pique Dame;* VERDI: *Rigoletto.* Awards: First Prize, Int Cond Compt, Besançon; Grand Prix du Disque 1968. **Res:** Ulrichg 4, 1020 Vienna, Austria. **Mgmt:** SVE/SWE.

TUROFSKY, RIKI; née Rita Nan Turofsky. Lyric coloratura soprano. Canadian. Born 20 Feb 1944, Toronto. Husband Robert Sunter, occupation arts administrator. One child. Studied: Vancouver Opera Training Prgr, BC, Canada; Merola Opera Prgr, San Francisco; Univ of Toronto; Music Acad of the West, Santa Barbara, CA, USA. **Debut:** Oscar (*Ballo in maschera*) Vancouver Opera 1970. Awards: Prize winner Montreal Intl Compt; Canada Counc Arts Bursary; Hon grad Univ of Toronto. **Sang with major companies in** CAN: Toronto, Vancouver; USA: Houston, Kansas City. **Roles with these companies incl** DONIZETTI: Marie★ (*Fille du régiment*); MOZART: Zerlina★ (*Don Giovanni*), Susanna★ (*Nozze di Figaro*); OFFENBACH: Olympia (*Contes d'Hoffmann*); PUCCINI: Musetta★ (*Bohème*); VERDI: Oscar (*Ballo in maschera*), Gilda★ (*Rigoletto*). **World premieres:** POLGAR: Princess (*Glove*) Canadian Opera Co 1975. Video/Film: Princess (*Glove*). Gives recitals. Appears with symphony orchestra. **Res:** 35 Bishop St, Toronto, Ont, Canada.

TYL, NOEL. Dramatic baritone. American. Born 31 Dec 1936, West Chester, PA, USA. Divorced. One child. Studied: Gibner King, New York. **Debut:** Don Basilio (*Barbiere di Siviglia*) Teatro della Pergola, Florence 1964. Previous occupations: publ rel exec, Ruder & Finn, NY; real estate adm. Awards: Winner American Opera Aud, Cincinnati, O, 1964. **Sang with major companies in** AUS: Vienna Staatsoper; CAN: Vancouver; FR GER: Düsseldorf-Duisburg, Munich Gärtnerplatz; SPA: Barcelona; USA: Boston, Cincinnati, Houston, New Orleans, New York City Opera, Omaha, Philadelphia Lyric, San Diego, Seattle, Washington DC. **Roles with these companies incl** MASSENET: Don Quichotte★; PROKOFIEV: King of Clubs (*Love for Three Oranges*); PUCCINI: Colline (*Bohème*), Scarpia★ (*Tosca*); RIMSKY-KORSAKOV: Roi Dodon (*Coq d'or*); ROSSINI: Don Basilio★ (*Barbiere di Siviglia*); VERDI: Amonasro★ & Ramfis★ (*Aida*), Grande Inquisitore (*Don Carlo*); WAGNER: Amfortas★ (*Parsifal*), Wotan (*Rheingold★, Walküre★*), Wanderer★ (*Siegfried*). Also HUMPERDINCK: Peter★ (*Hänsel und Gretel*). Gives recitals. **Res:** Washington, DC, USA. **Mgmt:** CAM/USA.

TYNES, MARGARET. Spinto. American. Born 11 Sep 1929, Saluda, VA, USA. Husband Hans von Klier, occupation architect. Studied: Mo Emil Cooper, New York; Mo Tullio Serafin, Giuseppe Pais, Italy; Ma Lola Hayes, New York; Columbia Univ, New York. **Debut:** Lady Macbeth, Montreal 1959. Previous occupations: music & English HS teacher. Awards: Hon D from A & T Univ, Greensboro, NC, USA; Gold Medal G Verdi, Pavia, Italy. **Sang with major companies in** AUS: Vienna Staatsoper; CAN: Montreal/Quebec, Toronto; CZE: Prague National & Smetana; FRA: Lyon; HUN: Budapest; ITA: Bologna, Milan La Scala, Naples, Palermo, Parma, Spoleto Fest, Trieste, Turin; SPA: Barcelona; SWI: Zurich; USA: Baltimore, Milwaukee Florentine, New York Met & City Opera. **Roles with these companies incl** BEL-

LINI: Norma; BERG: Marie (*Wozzeck*); BIZET: Micaëla (*Carmen*); JANACEK: Jenufa★; PRO-KOFIEV: Fata Morgana (*Love for Three Oranges*); PUCCINI: Tosca★; PURCELL: Dido; STRAUSS, R: Salome★; VERDI: Aida★, Lady Macbeth★, Desdemona (*Otello*); WEILL: Jenny★ (*Aufstieg und Fall der Stadt Mahagonny*). Gives recitals. Appears with symphony orchestra. **Res:** Viale Coni Zugna 8, Milan, Italy. Mgmt: NAP/USA.

TYRÉN, ARNE. Bass. Swedish. Resident mem: Royal Opera, Stockholm. Born 27 Feb 1928, Stockholm. Wife Ruth. Two children. Studied: Royal Acad, Prof Ragner Hulthén, Stockholm. **Debut:** Grande Inquisitore (*Don Carlo*) Royal Opera, Stockholm 1956. Previous occupations: travel agent.

Sang with major companies in CZE: Prague National & Smetana; DEN: Copenhagen; FIN: Helsinki; FR GER: Cologne, Hamburg; ISR: Tel Aviv; ITA: Turin; NOR: Oslo; POR: Lisbon; SWE: Drottningholm Fest, Stockholm. **Roles with these companies incl** BARTOK: Bluebeard★; BEETHOVEN: Rocco★ (*Fidelio*); BERG: Doktor★ (*Wozzeck*); BERLIOZ: Narbal★ (*Troyens*); BRITTEN: Bottom (*Midsummer Night*); CHARPENTIER: Père (*Louise*); DALLAPICCOLA: Robineau★ (*Volo di notte*); DONIZETTI: Don Pasquale★; HANDEL: Bertaric (*Rodelinda*); HAYDN: Buonafede (*Mondo della luna*); MO-ZART: Don Alfonso (*Così fan tutte*), Leporello★ (*Don Giovanni*), Osmin★ (*Entführung aus dem Serail*), Nardo (*Finta giardiniera*), Figaro★ (*Nozze di Figaro*), Sarastro★ (*Zauberflöte*); MUSSORGSKY: Boris★ & Varlaam★(*Boris Godunov*); OFFENBACH: Coppélius etc★ (*Contes d'Hoffmann*); PAISIELLO: Bartolo★ (*Barbiere di Siviglia*); PUCCINI: Colline★ (*Bohème*); ROSSINI: Dott Bartolo★ (*Barbiere di Siviglia*), Don Magnifico★ (*Cenerentola*), Signor Bruschino; STRAUSS, R: Baron Ochs★ (*Rosenkavalier*); STRAVINSKY: Creon★ & Tiresias★ (*Oedipus Rex*); VERDI: Ramfis★ (*Aida*), Philip II★ & Grande Inquisitore★ (*Don Carlo*), Falstaff★, Banquo (*Macbeth*), Zaccaria (*Nabucco*), Germont★ (*Traviata*); WAGNER: Holländer★ & Daland (*Fliegende Holländer*), König Heinrich★ (*Lohengrin*), Pogner (*Meistersinger*), Gurnemanz★ (*Parsifal*), Wotan (*Rheingold★, Walküre★*), Wanderer★ (*Siegfried*), Hunding (*Walküre*), Hagen★ (*Götterdämmerung*), Landgraf (*Tannhäuser*), König Marke★ (*Tristan und Isolde*); WEILL: Trinity Moses (*Aufstieg und Fall der Stadt Mahagonny*). Also TCHAIKOVSKY: Gremin (*Eugene Onegin*); HANDEL: Saul; JANACEK: Kolenaty (*Makropoulos Affair*). **World premieres:** WERLE: Reuterholm (*Tintomara*) Royal Opera, Stockholm 1973; BLOMDAHL: Chefone (*Aniara*) Royal Opera, Stockholm 1959; BLOMDAHL: Herrn von Hancken, Royal Opera, Stockholm 1965. Gives recitals. Appears with symphony orchestra. Stages opera. Mgmt: SVE/SWE.

U

UDE, ARMIN. Lyric tenor. German. Resident mem: Staatsoper Dresden, Ger DR. Born 16 Jan 1933, Weissenfels/Saale. Wife Helga Theis, occupation singer, secy. One child. Studied: Erna Hähnel-Zuleger, Leipzig; Prof Dagmar Freiwald-Lange, Berlin. **Debut:** Fenton (*Lustigen Weiber*) Frankfurt/O 1959. Previous occupations: studied philosophy, Leipzig. Awards: Diploma, Intl Bach Compt, Leipzig 1964; Intl Erkel Compt, Budapest 1965.

Sang with major companies in BUL: Sofia; FR GER: Wiesbaden; GER DR: Berlin Komische Oper & Staatsoper, Dresden, Leipzig; USSR: Leningrad Kirov. Roles with these companies incl DONIZETTI: Ernesto (*Don Pasquale*), Nemorino⋆ (*Elisir*); EINEM: Robespierre (*Dantons Tod*); HANDEL: Acis; LORTZING: Baron Kronthal⋆(*Wildschütz*); MEYERBEER: Raoul de Nangis⋆ (*Huguenots*); MOZART: Don Ottavio⋆ (*Don Giovanni*), Belmonte⋆ (*Entführung aus dem Serail*), Tamino⋆ (*Zauberflöte*); NICOLAI: Fenton⋆ (*Lustigen Weiber*); ORFF: Solo⋆ (*Carmina burana*); PAISIELLO: Almaviva⋆ (*Barbiere di Siviglia*); PROKOFIEV: Antonio⋆ (*Duenna*); PUCCINI: Rodolfo (*Bohème*); ROSSINI: Almaviva (*Barbiere di Siviglia*); STRAUSS, J: Alfred⋆ (*Fledermaus*); STRAUSS, R: Flamand⋆ (*Capriccio*), Ein Sänger⋆ (*Rosenkavalier*), Henry Morosus⋆ (*Schweigsame Frau*); TCHAIKOVSKY: Lenski⋆ (*Eugene Onegin*); WEBER: Abu Hassan⋆, Oberon⋆; WOLF-FERRARI: Florindo (*Donne curiose*). Also HANDEL: Tigrane (*Radamisto*), Alexander (*Poro*), Ulysses⋆ (*Deidamia*); BERG: Andres⋆ (*Wozzeck*); HENZE: Wilhelm (*Junge Lord*); WEILL: Tenor (*Seven Deadly Sins*); DESSAU: Heinrich⋆ (*Lanzelot*); STRAUSS, R: Ital Sänger⋆ (*Capriccio*). World premieres: ZIMMERMANN: Wirt Rosinke (*Levins Mühle*) Staatsoper, Dresden 1973. Recorded for: VEB. Gives recitals. Appears with symphony orchestra. Teaches voice. Coaches repertoire. On faculty of Hanns Eisler Hochschule für Musik, Berlin. **Res:** Weg zur Quelle 12, 1162 Berlin/Hirschgarten, Ger DR. Mgmt: KDR/GDR.

UHL, FRITZ; né Friedrich Ludwig Uhl. Dramatic tenor & Heldentenor. Austrian. Resident mem: Bayerische Staatsoper, Munich; Staatsoper, Vienna. Born 2 Apr 1928, Vienna. Wife Erika Stari. One child. Studied: Ferdinand Grossmann, Elisabeth Rado, Josef Witt, Vienna; Hanno Blaschke, Munich. **Debut:** Hüon (*Oberon*) Opera Graz, Austria 1952. Awards: Bayerischer Kammersänger, Ministry of Culture 1962; Richard Wagner Medal, Bayreuth Fest 1964.

Sang with major companies in ARG: Buenos Aires; AUS: Graz, Salzburg Fest, Vienna Staatsoper & Volksoper; BEL: Brussels; CAN: Montreal/Quebec; FRA: Lyon, Marseille, Nancy, Nice, Paris, Rouen, Strasbourg, Toulouse; GRE: Athens National Opera; FR GER: Bayreuth Fest, Berlin Deutsche Oper, Bielefeld, Bonn, Cologne, Dortmund, Düsseldorf-Duisburg, Essen, Frankfurt, Hamburg, Hannover, Karlsruhe, Kiel, Krefeld, Munich Staatsoper, Nürnberg, Saarbrücken, Stuttgart, Wuppertal; HOL: Amsterdam; HUN: Budapest; ITA: Bologna, Florence Maggio Musicale, Naples, Rome Teatro dell'Opera, Trieste, Turin, Venice; MEX: Mexico City; ROM: Bucharest; SPA: Barcelona; SWE: Stockholm; SWI: Basel, Geneva, Zurich; UK: London Royal Opera & English National; USA: San Diego, San Francisco Opera, Los Angeles; YUG: Zagreb. Roles with these companies incl d'ALBERT: Pedro (*Tiefland*); BEETHOVEN: Florestan⋆ (*Fidelio*); BERG: Alwa⋆ (*Lulu*), Tambourmajor⋆‡ (*Wozzeck*); BIZET: Don José (*Carmen*); EINEM: Robespierre (*Dantons Tod*); GOUNOD: Faust; HINDEMITH: Albrecht v Brandenberg⋆ (*Mathis der Maler*); JANACEK: Steva (*Jenufa*); LEONCAVALLO: Canio (*Pagliacci*); MEYERBEER: Vasco da Gama (*Africaine*); MUSSORGSKY: Shuisky⋆ (*Boris Godunov*); ORFF: Haemon‡ (*Antigonae*); SCHOENBERG: Aron⋆; SHOSTAKOVICH: Sergei (*Katerina Ismailova*); STRAUSS, J: Eisenstein⋆ (*Fledermaus*); STRAUSS, R: Menelaus (*Aegyptische Helena*), Bacchus (*Ariadne auf Naxos*), Apollo (*Daphne*), Aegisth⋆‡ (*Elektra*), Ein Sänger (*Rosenkavalier*), Herodes⋆ (*Salome*); VERDI: Radames (*Aida*), Aroldo (*Aroldo/Stiffelio*), Don Alvaro (*Forza del destino*), Otello, Manrico (*Trovatore*); WAGNER: Erik⋆‡ (*Fliegende Holländer*), Lohengrin, Walther⋆ (*Meistersinger*), Parsifal⋆, Loge⋆‡ (*Rheingold*), Siegmund⋆ (*Walküre*), Siegfried (*Götterdämmerung*), Tristan‡; WEBER: Max⋆ (*Freischütz*), Hüon (*Oberon*). Also ORFF: Hermes⋆ (*Prometheus*); KRENEK: Aegisth (*Leben des Orest*); PFITZNER: Novagerio (*Palestrina*); HEGER: Bettler und König (*Bettler Namenlos*). World premieres: KATTNIGG: Casanova (*Donna Miranda*) Opera Graz 1953; CIKKER:

Crapart (*Play of Love*) Staatsoper Munich 1969; KRENEK: Francesco (*Zauberspiegel*) ARD TV Munich 1967; RUBIN: Wirt (*Kleider machen Leute*) Volksoper Vienna 1973. Recorded for: Decca, Philips, DG, CBS, Fabbri, BASF. Video — ARD TV Munich: Francesco (*Zauberspiegel*). Gives recitals. Appears with symphony orchestra. **Res:** Lindauerstr 9, Munich 83, FR Ger. Mgmt: SLZ/FRG; VLD/AUS.

UHRMACHER, HILDEGARD. Coloratura soprano. German. Resident mem: Staatsoper, Hamburg and Munich. Born 15 Dec, Mönchengladbach, Germany. Single. Studied: Prof Glettenberg, Prof Peter Witsch, Cologne; Fr Genot-Heindl, acting, Studio Munich. **Debut:** Vespina (*Infedeltà delusa*) Deutsche Oper am Rhein, Düsseldorf 1964. Previous occupation: elem school teacher.

Sang with major companies in AUS: Vienna Staatsoper; FR GER: Berlin Deutsche Oper, Cologne, Dortmund, Düsseldorf-Duisburg, Frankfurt, Hamburg, Hannover, Karlsruhe, Kassel, Krefeld, Munich Staatsoper, Nürnberg, Stuttgart; HOL: Amsterdam; ITA: Florence Maggio; UK: Cardiff Welsh. **Roles with these companies incl** BERG: Lulu*; BRITTEN: Helena (*Midsummer Night*); CIMAROSA: Carolina (*Matrimonio segreto*); DESSAU: Elsa* (*Lanzelot*); DONIZETTI: Prima Donna* (*Convenienze/Viva la Mamma*), Lucia*; FLOTOW: Lady Harriet (*Martha*); HAYDN: Vespina (*Infedeltà delusa*); HENZE: Manon* (*Boulevard Solitude*); LEONCAVALLO: Nedda (*Pagliacci*); LORTZING: Baronin Freimann* (*Wildschütz*); MOZART: Despina (*Così fan tutte*), Konstanze* (*Entführung aus dem Serail*), Königin der Nacht* (*Zauberflöte*); NICOLAI: Frau Fluth* (*Lustigen Weiber*); OFFENBACH: Olympia* & Antonia* & Giulietta* (*Contes d'Hoffmann*); POULENC: Thérèse* (*Mamelles de Tirésias*); PUCCINI: Musetta* (*Bohème*); STRAUSS, J: Adele & Rosalinde* (*Fledermaus*); STRAUSS, R: Fiakermilli* (*Arabella*), Zerbinetta* (*Ariadne auf Naxos*); VERDI: Gilda* (*Rigoletto*), Violetta* (*Traviata*); WEBER: Agathe (*Freischütz*); WOLF-FERRARI: Felice (*Quattro rusteghi*); ZIMMERMANN: Marie* (*Soldaten*). Also BUSSOTTI: Mara* (*Lorenzaccio*); FLOTOW: Leonore* (*Alessandro Stradella*). Appears with symphony orchestra. Teaches voice. Coaches repertoire. **Res:** Mexikoring 7, Hamburg 60, FR Ger. Mgmt: SLZ/FRG; TAS/AUS.

ULFUNG, RAGNAR SIGURD. Dramatic tenor. Norwegian. Resident mem: Royal Opera, Stockholm. Born 28 Feb 1927, Oslo. Wife Bjoerg. Four children. Studied: Oslo Consv of Music; Milan privately. **Debut:** Magician (*Consul*) Oslo New Theater. Awards: Oslo Critics Awd; Goeran Gentele Awd.

Sang with major companies in AUS: Vienna Staatsoper; CAN: Montreal/Quebec; DEN: Copenhagen; FIN: Helsinki; FRA: Paris; FR GER: Bonn, Frankfurt, Hamburg, Kiel, Mannheim, Stuttgart, Wiesbaden; ITA: Milan La Scala; NOR: Oslo; SWE: Drottningholm Fest, Stockholm; UK: Edinburgh Fest, Glyndebourne Fest, London Royal; USSR: Moscow Bolshoi; USA: Boston, Chicago, New York Met, San Diego, San

Francisco Opera, Santa Fe. **Roles with these companies incl** BERG: Maler* (*Lulu*); BIZET: Don José* (*Carmen*); GOUNOD: Faust; HINDEMITH: Apprentice (*Cardillac*); JANACEK: Broucek (*Excursions of Mr Broucek*), Steva* (*Jenufa*), Albert Gregor* (*Makropoulos Affair*); LEONCAVALLO: Canio (*Pagliacci*); MASCAGNI: Turiddu* (*Cavalleria rusticana*); MONTEVERDI: Nero* (*Incoronazione di Poppea*), Ulisse (*Ritorno d'Ulisse*); MOZART: Don Ottavio (*Don Giovanni*), Tamino (*Zauberflöte*); MUSSORGSKY: Shuisky* (*Boris Godunov*); OFFENBACH: Hoffmann*; PENDERECKI: Adam* (*Teufel von Loudun*); PUCCINI: Rodolfo (*Bohème*), Cavaradossi* (*Tosca*); PURCELL: Aeneas; SCHOENBERG: Aron; SMETANA: Hans (*Bartered Bride*); STRAUSS, J: Eisenstein* & Alfred* (*Fledermaus*); STRAUSS, R: Aegisth* (*Elektra*), Herodes* (*Salome*); STRAVINSKY: Tom Rakewell* (*Rake's Progress*); TCHAIKOVSKY: Lenski* (*Eugene Onegin*); VERDI: Riccardo* (*Ballo in maschera*), Don Carlo*, Ernani, Duca di Mantova (*Rigoletto*), Alfredo* (*Traviata*); WAGNER: Erik (*Fliegende Holländer*), Mime (*Rheingold*, *Siegfried*). Also ROTA: Fadinard* (*Capello di paglia di Firenze*). **World premieres:** WERLE: leading ten (*Resan*) Hamburg Staatsoper 1969; MAXWELL-DAVIES: Taverner, Covent Garden, London 1972. Video — Stockholm TV: (*Ballo in maschera*); (*Makropoulos Affair*). Film: (*Zauberflöte*). Gives recitals. Appears with symph orch. Also stages opera. Teaches voice. Coaches repertoire. On faculty of Santa Fe Apprentice Prgr. **Res:** Stockholm, Sweden. Mgmt: DSP/USA.

UNGER, GERHARD. Lyric & buffo tenor. German. Resident mem: Württembergische Staatsoper, Stuttgart; Staatsoper, Vienna. Born 26 Nov 1916, Bad Salzungen, Germany. Studied: Hochschule für Musik, Berlin. **Debut:** Nationaltheater, Weimar 1947. Previous occupations: concert & oratorio singer. Awards: title of Kammersänger.

Sang with major companies in AUS: Salzburg Fest, Vienna Volksoper; FR GER: Bayreuth Fest, Berlin Deutsche Oper, Düsseldorf-Duisburg, Hamburg, Munich Staatsoper, Stuttgart; GER DR: Berlin Staatsoper, Dresden; et al. **Roles with these companies incl** MOZART: Pedrillo‡ (*Entführung aus dem Serail*); PUCCINI: Pinkerton‡ (*Butterfly*); ROSSINI: Almaviva (*Barbiere di Siviglia*); STRAUSS: Sänger‡ (*Rosenkavalier*); WAGNER: David‡ (*Meistersinger*), Mime (*Rheingold*, *Siegfried*); et al. Also MOZART: Podestà (*Finta giardiniera*). Recorded for: Angel, HMV, DG, Vox, Urania, Electrola. Appears with symphony orchestra.

UNRUH, STAN. Dramatic & Heldentenor. American. Born 1939. Single. Studied: Juilliard School of Music, piano, New York; vocal training France.

Sang with major companies in BEL: Brussels; FRA: Bordeaux, Nancy, Nice, Orange Fest, Rouen, Toulouse; MON: Monte Carlo. **Roles with these companies incl** BEETHOVEN: Florestan* (*Fidelio*); BIZET: Don José* (*Carmen*); MUSSORGSKY: Dimitri* (*Boris Godunov*); PUCCINI: Des Grieux* (*Manon Lescaut*), Calaf* (*Turandot*); SAINT-SAENS: Samson; STRAUSS, R: Bacchus (*Ariadne auf Naxos*); STRAVINSKY: Vasili* (*Mavra*), Oedipus Rex*;

TCHAIKOVSKY: Count Vodemon★ (*Iolanthe*); WAGNER: Lohengrin, Parsifal★, Siegmund★ (*Walküre*), Tristan★. Gives recitals. Appears with symphony orchestra. **Res:** Paris, France. **Mgmt:** CMW/FRA; SFM/UK.

UPHAGEN, ERIKA. Dramatic soprano. German. Born Danzig. Divorced. Studied: Kmsg Prof Erna Berger, Germany. **Debut:** Donna Anna (*Don Giovanni*) Wuppertaler Bühnen 1964.

Sang with major companies in AUS: Graz; FRA: Marseille, Paris; FR GER: Bielefeld, Bonn, Cologne, Dortmund, Essen, Hamburg, Hannover, Kassel, Munich Staatsoper, Nürnberg, Wiesbaden, Wuppertal; GER DR: Leipzig; ITA: Florence Maggio, Milan La Scala; SWI: Zurich; USSR: Tbilisi. **Roles with these companies incl** BEETHOVEN: Leonore★ (*Fidelio*); HINDEMITH: Ursula (*Mathis der Maler*); JANACEK: Jenufa★; MASCAGNI: Santuzza★ (*Cavalleria rusticana*); MOZART: Fiordiligi★ (*Così fan tutte*), Donna Anna★ & Donna Elvira★ (*Don Giovanni*), Contessa★ (*Nozze di Figaro*); OFFENBACH: Giulietta (*Contes d'Hoffmann*); PUCCINI: Tosca; STRAUSS, R: Chrysothemis★ (*Elektra*), Marschallin★ (*Rosenkavalier*); VERDI: Aida★, Amelia★ (*Ballo in maschera*), Elisabetta★ (*Don Carlo*), Desdemona★ (*Otello*), Leonora★ (*Trovatore*), Elena★ (*Vespri*); WAGNER: Senta★ (*Fliegende Holländer*), Elsa★ (*Lohengrin*), Sieglinde★ (*Walküre*), Elisabeth★ (*Tannhäuser*); WEBER: Agathe★ (*Freischütz*). Also EGK: Ninabella (*Zaubergeige*); DVORAK: Anninka (*Schelm und die Bauern*); HANDEL: Deborah. Gives recitals. Appears with symphony orchestra. **Res:** Meissnerstr 32, Hamburg, FR Ger.

UPPMAN, THEODOR. Lyric baritone. American. Resident mem: Metropolitan Opera, New York. Born 12 Jan 1920, Palo Alto, CA, USA. Wife Jean, occupation co-editor, Lincoln Center Programs. Two children. Studied: Curtis Inst of Music, Steuart Wilson, Philadelphia; Univ of So California, Carl Ebert, Los Angeles; Ruth Chamlee, Los Angeles; Herbert Janssen, New York. **Debut:** Pelléas, New York City Opera 1948. Awards: First Prize Atwater Kent Awd 1947; First Prize Gainsborough Awd 1947.

Sang with major companies in FRA: Aix-en-Provence Fest; MEX: Mexico City; UK: London Royal; USA: Baltimore, Chicago, Cincinnati, Fort Worth, Lake George, Memphis, Milwaukee Florentine, New York Met & City Opera, Philadelphia Lyric, San Antonio, San Francisco Opera, Santa Fe, Seattle, Washington DC. **Roles with these companies incl** BIZET: Escamillo (*Carmen*); DEBUSSY: Pelléas; DONIZETTI: Dott Malatesta (*Don Pasquale*), Belcore★ (*Elisir*); MOZART: Guglielmo (*Così fan tutte*), Conte Almaviva★ (*Nozze di Figaro*), Papageno★ (*Zauberflöte*); PUCCINI: Marcello (*Bohème*), Sharpless★ (*Butterfly*); ROSSINI: Robert (*Comte Ory*); STRAUSS, R: Musiklehrer (*Ariadne auf Naxos*), Jochanaan (*Salome*); STRAVINSKY: Creon (*Oedipus Rex*). Also ROSSINI: Taddeo★ (*Italiana in Algeri*); OFFENBACH: Paquillo (*Périchole*); STRAUSS, J: Eisenstein (*Fledermaus*); HINDEMITH: Eduard (*Neues vom Tage*); STRAUSS, R: Harlekin (*Ariadne auf Naxos*). **World premieres:** BRITTEN: Billy (*Billy Budd*) Covent Garden 1951;

FLOYD: Jonathan Wade (*Passion of Jonathan Wade*) New York City Opera 1962; VILLA-LOBOS: Victor (*Yerma*) Santa Fe Opera 1971; PASATIERI: Juan (*Black Widow*) Seattle Opera 1972. Gives recitals. Appears with symphony orchestra. **Res:** New York, NY, USA. **Mgmt:** CAM/USA.

URBINI, PIERLUIGI. Conductor of opera and symphony. Italian. Born 2 Jun 1929, Rome. Studied: Consv and Accad S Cecilia, Rome; incl violin, piano. **Operatic debut:** *Falstaff* Teatro Massimo, Palermo, Italy. Symphonic debut: Orch Accad S Cecilia, Rome. Previous occupations: concert violinist. Awards: Citation, Accad Chigiana, Siena.

Conducted with major companies in FIN: Helsinki; FRA: Nice; FR GER: Dortmund; ITA: Bologna, Florence Maggio, Milan La Scala, Naples, Palermo, Parma, Rome Opera & Caracalla, Trieste, Venice; MON: Monte Carlo; NOR: Oslo. **Operas with these companies incl** BELLINI: *Sonnambula;* CIMAROSA: *Matrimonio segreto;* DONIZETTI: *Campanello, Don Pasquale, Elisir, Rita;* MASCAGNI: *Cavalleria rusticana;* MENOTTI: *Medium, Telephone;* PERGOLESI: *Serva padrona;* PUCCINI: *Bohème, Rondine, Tosca;* ROSSELLINI: *Annonce faite à Marie★;* ROSSINI: *Barbiere di Siviglia, Cenerentola★, Otello, Scala di seta, Signor Bruschino;* STRAVINSKY: *Mavra, Oedipus Rex★;* VERDI: *Falstaff, Rigoletto, Traviata, Trovatore;* WEBER: *Freischütz.* Previous positions as Mus Dir with major orch: Orch Accad S Cecilia, Rome 1965-72. Teaches at Consv S Cecilia, Rome. **Res:** V Dell'Annunziatella 33, Rome, Italy.

URRILA, IRMA KRISTIINA. Lyric soprano. Finnish. Resident mem. The Norwegian Opera, Oslo. Born 29 Jan 1943, Helsinki. Husband Per Ake Andersson, occupation conductor. Studied: Aino Elenius, Finland; Carla Castellani, Milan; Clemens Kaiser-Breme, Germany. **Debut:** Mimi (*Bohème*) Helsinki Opera 1964. Awards: Second Prize Conc Intl Giuseppe Verdi, Parma, Italy 1966; First Prize Conc Intl di Canto, Lonigo, Italy 1965.

Sang with major companies in DEN: Copenhagen; FIN: Helsinki; NOR: Oslo; SWE: Stockholm. **Roles with these companies incl** BEETHOVEN: Marzelline (*Fidelio*); BIZET: Micaëla★ (*Carmen*); BRITTEN: Female Chorus★ (*Rape of Lucretia*); DONIZETTI: Adina (*Elisir*); KODALY: Marie Louise★ (*Háry János*); LEONCAVALLO: Nedda★ (*Pagliacci*); MOZART: Fiordiligi★ (*Così fan tutte*), Zerlina★ (*Don Giovanni*), Contessa★ (*Nozze di Figaro*), Pamina★† (*Zauberflöte*); PUCCINI: Mimi★ (*Bohème*), Lauretta★ (*Gianni Schicchi*), Cio-Cio-San★ (*Butterfly*), Liù (*Turandot*); STRAUSS, R: Sophie★ (*Rosenkavalier*); VERDI: Gilda (*Rigoletto*). Also ROSENBERG: Silvia (*Marionetter*). Recorded for: Sveriges Radio. Video/Film: Marzelline (*Fidelio*); Pamina (*Zauberflöte*). Gives recitals. Appears with symphony orchestra. **Res:** Enebakkveien 164, Oslo, Norway. **Mgmt:** MFZ/FIN.

USTINOV, PETER. Stages/produces opera, theater & film; is also an actor, singer & author. Born 16 Apr 1921, London. Studied: London Theatre Studio, Michel St Denis; incl voice. Theater debut: Squaring the Circle vaudeville theater, London

1941. Awards: FRSA, Fellow of Royal Society of Arts, London; *Evening Standard* Awd for best new play 1957; Emmy TV Awd, New York 1957.

Directed/produced opera for major companies in AUS: Vienna Staatsoper; FRA: Paris; FR GER: Hamburg; UK: Edinburgh Fest, London Royal; et al. **Operas staged with these companies incl** MAS-SENET: *Don Quichotte;* MOZART: *Don Giovanni, Zauberflöte;* PUCCINI: *Gianni Schicchi;* RAVEL: *Heure espagnole;* SCHOENBERG: *Erwartung;* et al. Operatic Video—Ger TV, Hamburg Op prod: *Zauberflöte.*

V

VAJNAR, FRANTISEK. Conductor of opera and symphony. Czechoslovakian. Resident Cond, National Theater, Prague. Born 15 Sep 1930, Strasice, CSR. Wife Veroslava. Two children. Studied: Profs Václav Talich, Alois Klíma, Prague; incl violin, piano and voice. Operatic training as asst cond at Army Opera, Prague 1953-55. **Operatic debut:** *Rusalka* Army Opera, Prague 1953. Symphonic debut: Symph Orch, Karlovy Vary, CSSR 1960. Previous occupations: violinist. Previous adm positions in opera: Opera Mng, State Theater Ustí, CSSR 1962-74.

Conducted with major companies in CZE: Prague National; HOL: Amsterdam. **Operas with these companies incl** BARTOK: *Bluebeard's Castle;* BEETHOVEN: *Fidelio;* BORODIN: *Prince Igor;* DVORAK: *Rusalka★;* LEONCAVALLO: *Pagliacci★;* MARTINU: *Comedy on the Bridge;* MUSSORGSKY: *Boris Godunov★;* SMETANA: *Bartered Bride★, Dalibor★, The Kiss★, Libuse★;* STRAVINSKY: *Mavra, Rake's Progress;* SUCHON: *Whirlpool★;* WAGNER: *Lohengrin★.* Video—TV CSSR: *Two Widows, Devil's Wall, Barbiere di Siviglia, Carmen, Mirandolina.* Conducted major orch in Europe. Teaches at Music Acad, Prague. **Res:** Slezska 27, Prague 3, CSSR. Mgmt: PRG/CZE.

VALAITIS, VLADIMIR ANTONOVICH. Bassbaritone. Russian. Resident mem: Bolshoi Theater, Moscow. Born 23 Apr 1923, Selo Sitkovtsy, Ukraine. Wife Taisiya, occupation teacher, choreographer. One daughter. Studied: Kharkov State Consv, Prof P V Golubev, Ukraine. **Debut:** Gianciotto Malatesta (*Francesca da Rimini*) Bolshoi Theater, Moscow 1957. Previous occupations: Soviet Army officer; soloist of Army Ensemble. Awards: Ntl Artist, USSR.

Sang with major companies in CZE: Brno, Prague National; GER DR: Leipzig; ITA: Milan La Scala; USSR: Leningrad Kirov Opera, Moscow Bolshoi Theater. **Roles with these companies incl** BIZET: Escamillo★ (*Carmen*); BORODIN: Prince Igor★; MOZART: Conte Almaviva★ (*Nozze di Figaro*); MUSSORGSKY: Shaklovity★ (*Khovanshchina*); PUCCINI: Scarpia★ (*Tosca*); RIMSKY-KORSAKOV: Gregory Griaznoi★ (*Tsar's Bride*); TCHAIKOVSKY: Eugene Onegin★, Yeletsky★ (*Pique Dame*); VERDI: Amonasro★ (*Aida*), Rodrigo★ (*Don Carlo*), Ford★ (*Falstaff*), Rigoletto★; WAGNER: Holländer. Recorded for: Melodiya. Film: Ebn-Khakiya (*Io-*

lanthe). Gives recitals. Appears with symphony orchestra. **Res:** dom 10, kv 44 ul Troitskaya, Moscow, USSR. Mgmt: HUR/USA.

VALENTE, BENITA. Lyric soprano. American. Resident mem: Metropolitan Opera, New York. Born Delano, CA, USA. Husband Anthony P Checchia, occupation music administrator. Studied: Chester Hayden, Lotte Lehmann, Martial Singher, Margaret Harshaw, USA. **Debut:** Pamina (*Zauberflöte*) Freiburg, FR Ger 1962. Awards: Met Op Ntl Counc Aud winner 1960; Philadelphia Orch Youth Concerts 1958; Curtis Inst Schlshp, Philadelphia 1955-1960.

Sang with major companies in FRA: Strasbourg; FR GER: Dortmund, Nürnberg; HOL: Amsterdam; ITA: Spoleto Fest; SWI: Zurich; USA: Baltimore, Boston, Kentucky, New York Met, Santa Fe, Washington DC. **Roles with these companies incl** BEETHOVEN: Marzelline (*Fidelio*); BRITTEN: Tytania★ (*Midsummer Night*), Governess★ (*Turn of the Screw*); CAVALLI: Erisbe (*Ormindo*); CHARPENTIER: Louise★; CORNELIUS: Margiana (*Barbier von Bagdad*); DONIZETTI: Serafina (*Campanello*); HANDEL: Alcina★; HINDEMITH: Helene (*Hin und zurück*); HUMPERDINCK: Gretel; MONTEVERDI: Clorinda★ (*Combattimento di Tancredi*), Euridice★ (*Orfeo*); MOZART: Fiordiligi (*Così fan tutte*), Ilia (*Idomeneo*), Susanna★ (*Nozze di Figaro*), Pamina★ (*Zauberflöte*); NICOLAI: Aennchen (*Lustigen Weiber*); PUCCINI: Lauretta (*Gianni Schicchi*), Suor Angelica; PURCELL: Belinda★ (*Dido and Aeneas*); ROSSINI: Elvira (*Italiana in Algeri*); STRAUSS, J: Adele (*Fledermaus*); STRAUSS, R: Zdenka (*Arabella*); STRAVINSKY: Anne Trulove (*Rake's Progress*); VERDI: Nannetta★ (*Falstaff*), Gilda★ (*Rigoletto*). **World premieres:** ROREM: Peony (*Childhood Miracle*) 1955. Video/Film—TV: (*Childhood Miracle*). Gives recitals. Appears with symphony orchestra. **Res:** Philadelphia, PA, USA. Mgmt: DSP/USA.

VALENTINI, LUCIA. Coloratura mezzo-soprano. Italian. Born 28 Aug 1948, Padua, Italy. Husband Alberto Terrani, occupation actor. **Debut:** Rosina (*Barbiere di Siviglia*) Mantua 1970. Awards: First Prize Rossini Voice Cont, RAI, Rome.

Sang with major companies in AUS: Vienna Staatsoper; BEL: Brussels; CZE: Prague National; FRA: Nice, Paris; FR GER: Frankfurt,

Munich Staatsoper, Stuttgart; GER DR: Dresden, Leipzig; ITA: Florence Maggio, Genoa, Milan La Scala, Rome Opera, Turin, Venice; MON: Monte Carlo; SPA: Barcelona; SWI: Geneva; USA: Chicago, New York Met. **Roles with these companies incl** CAVALLI: Sicle★ (*Ormindo*); CILEA: Princesse de Bouillon★ (*A. Lecouvreur*); CIMAROSA: Fidalma★ (*Matrimonio segreto*); HANDEL: Bradamante★ (*Alcina*); MONTEVERDI: Orfeo★; MOZART: Dorabella★ (*Così fan tutte*); ROSSINI: Rosina★ (*Barbiere di Siviglia*), Angelina★ (*Cenerentola*), Isolier★ (*Comte Ory*), Pippo★ (*Gazza ladra*), Isabella★ (*Italiana in Algeri*), Sinaïde (*Moïse*); SCARLATTI: Leonora★ & Doralice★ (*Trionfo dell'onore*); SPONTINI: High Priestess★ (*Vestale*). Also GLUCK: (*Cinesi*). Recorded for: Philips. Video/Film—La Scala prod: Angelina (*Cenerentola*). Gives recitals. Appears with symphony orchestra. **Res:** Padua, Italy. **Mgmt:** LOM/USA.

VALENTOVA, IVONA; née Gedziková. Soubrette. Czechoslovakian. Resident mem: National Theater, Prague. Born 29 Jan 1944, Ostrava, CSR. Husband Jirí Holec, occupation machine designer. Studied: State Consv, Prof Jechová, Ostrava; Prof Premysl Kocí, Marie Veselá, Prague. **Debut:** Blondchen (*Entführung aus dem Serail*) National Theater, Prague 1973.
Sang with major companies in CZE: Prague National. **Roles with these companies incl** MARTINU: Popelka★ (*Comedy on the Bridge*); MOZART: Despina★ (*Così fan tutte*), Zerlina★ (*Don Giovanni*), Blondchen★ (*Entführung aus dem Serail*). Also SMETANA: Barce★ (*The Kiss*). **World premieres:** MOLCHANOV: Kirjanova (*Dawns Are Quiet Here*) Bolshoi Opera, Moscow 1975. **Res:** Rípská 4, 101 00 Prague 10, CSSR. **Mgmt:** PRG/CZE.

VALJAKKA, TARU; née Taru Aura Helena Kumpunen. Spinto soprano. Finnish. Born 16 Sep 1938, Helsinki. Husband Risto, occupation school headmaster. Two children. Studied: Antti Koskinen, Helsinki; Gerald Moore, Stockholm & Helsinki; Erik Werba, Salzburg; Concita Badia, Santiago de Compostela. **Debut:** Donna Anna (*Don Giovanni*) Finnish Ntl Opera, Helsinki 1964. Previous occupations: violin teacher, chorus leader.
Sang with major companies in CZE: Prague National; FIN: Helsinki; GER DR: Berlin Komische Oper; HUN: Budapest; NOR: Oslo. **Roles with these companies incl** BEETHOVEN: Marzelline (*Fidelio*); BERG: Lulu; BIZET: Micaëla‡ (*Carmen*); BRITTEN: Tytania (*Midsummer Night*); CATALANI: Wally; DEBUSSY: Mélisande★; EGK: Jeanne (*Verlobung in San Domingo*); GERSHWIN: Bess; GLUCK: Euridice★; LEONCAVALLO: Nedda★ (*Pagliacci*); MOZART: Fiordiligi (*Così fan tutte*), Donna Anna★ (*Don Giovanni*), Contessa★ (*Nozze di Figaro*), Pamina★ (*Zauberflöte*); OFFENBACH: Antonia (*Contes d'Hoffmann*); ORFF: Solo★ (*Carmina burana*); PUCCINI: Mimi (*Bohème*); SCHOENBERG: Woman (*Erwartung*); VERDI: Aida, Leonora (*Forza del destino*), Desdemona (*Otello*), Leonora (*Trovatore*). **World premieres:** SALLINEN: Anna (*Horseman*) Savonlinna Opera Fest 1975. Recorded for: Finnlevy. Gives recitals. Appears with

symphony orchestra. **Res:** Bulevardi 19A, Helsinki, Finland. Mgmt: MFZ/FIN; RAL/UK.

VALLI, ROMOLO. Italian. Art Dir, Festival of Two Worlds, Spoleto, winter addr: V Margutta 17, Rome, Italy. In charge of dram & mus matters, art policy, and is a stage dir/prod. Additional administrative positions: Dir, Compagnia Romolo Valli. Born 11 Jan 1924, Reggio Emilia, Italy. Single. Studied: Reggio Emilia, BA; Univ of Parma, law. Previous occupations: actor, critic, journalist. Prev positions, primarily theatrical: Mem of Giorgio Strehler's Piccolo Teatro of Milan, 1952-54; Co-fder/dir with De Lullo of Compagnia dei Giovani 1954- . In present position since 1972. **Res:** V Appia Antica 140, Rome, Italy.

VALTASAARI, TAPANI HEIKKI. Lyric and dramatic baritone. Finnish. Resident mem: National Opera, Helsinki. Born 12 Mar 1941, Helsinki. Wife Eeva Mansnérus. Two children. Studied: Onerva Rautiainen, Lauri Lahtinen, Lea Piltti; Prof C Kaiser-Breme. **Debut:** Tartaglia (*König Hirsch*) National Opera, Helsinki 1971. Previous occupations: elem school teacher. Awards: Suomen Kultuurirahasto; Jenny ja Antti Wihurin rahasto; Niilo Helanderin Säätiö; Paulon Säätiö.
Sang with major companies in FIN: Helsinki. **Roles with these companies incl** JANACEK: Gorianchikov★ (*From the House of the Dead*); MOZART: Don Alfonso★ (*Così fan tutte*), Don Giovanni, Conte Almaviva & Figaro★ (*Nozze di Figaro*); PUCCINI: Scarpia★ (*Tosca*); ROSSINI: Figaro★ (*Barbiere di Siviglia*); VERDI: Renato★ (*Ballo in maschera*), Iago★ (*Otello*), Germont (*Traviata*), Conte di Luna★ (*Trovatore*); WAGNER: Wotan★ (*Rheingold*). **World premieres:** MERIKANTO: (*Juha*) Helsinki 1967; MARTTINEN: (*Tulitikkuja lainaamassa*) Helsinki. Video/Film: BLACHER: Fischer (*Flut*). Gives recitals. Appears with symphony orchestra. **Res:** Aapelinkatu 13 B 7, 02230 Espoo, Finland.

VAN ALLAN, RICHARD; né Alan Philip Jones. Bass-baritone. British. Resident mem: Royal Opera, London. Born 28 May 1935, Nottingham, UK. Divorced. One son. Studied: Birmingham School of Music; David Franklin, Jani Strasser, UK. **Debut:** Priester & Geharnischter (*Zauberflöte*) Glyndebourne Fest 1966. Previous occupations: police officer; science school teacher. Awards: John Christie Awd, Glyndebourne, UK.
Sang with major companies in FRA: Bordeaux, Nice, Paris; UK: Cardiff Welsh, Glyndebourne Fest, London Royal & English National. **Roles with these companies incl** BEETHOVEN: Don Pizarro★ (*Fidelio*); BERG: Doktor★ (*Wozzeck*); MOZART: Don Alfonso★‡ (*Così fan tutte*), Leporello★ & Don Giovanni (*Don Giovanni*), Osmin★ (*Entführung aus dem Serail*), Figaro★ (*Nozze di Figaro*); PUCCINI: Colline★ (*Bohème*); ROSSINI: Don Basilio★ (*Barbiere di Siviglia*), Don Magnifico (*Cenerentola*), Dormont (*Scala di seta*), Sultan Selim (*Turco in Italia*); VERDI: Ramfis (*Aida*), Philip II★ & Grande Inquisitore★ (*Don Carlo*), Banquo (*Macbeth*), Zaccaria★ (*Nabucco*); WAGNER: König Heinrich (*Lohengrin*). **World premieres:** MAW: Jowler (*Rising of the Moon*) Glyndebourne Fest 1970. Recorded for: Philips, EMI, Decca. Appears with symphony orchestra.

Res: 343 Essex Rd, N1 London, UK. Mgn ·· CST/UK; CMW/FRA.

VAN DAM, JOSÉ; né Joseph Van Damme. Bass-baritone. Belgian. Res mem: Deutsche Oper, Berlin, FR Ger. Born 25 Aug 1940, Brussels. Married. Studied: Acad de Musique, Brussels; Consv Royal, Frederic Anspach, Brussels. **Debut:** Escamillo (*Carmen*) Paris 1961. Awards: German Critics' Prize 1973; Berliner Kammersänger 1974.

Sang with major companies in AUS: Salzburg Fest, Vienna Staatsoper; BEL: Brussels, Liège; FRA: Aix-en-Provence Fest, Bordeaux, Marseille, Nice, Paris, Rouen, Strasbourg, Toulouse; GRE: Athens Fest; FR GER: Berlin Deutsche Oper, Düsseldorf-Duisburg; HOL: Amsterdam; ITA: Milan La Scala, Venice; MON: Monte Carlo; POR: Lisbon; SWI: Geneva, Zurich; UK: London Royal; USA: New York Met, San Francisco Spring Opera, Santa Fe. **Roles with these companies incl** BERLIOZ: Balducci (*Benvenuto Cellini*), Méphistophélès★ (*Damnation de Faust*); BIZET: Escamillo★‡ (*Carmen*); BORODIN: Prince Igor; CHARPENTIER: Père (*Louise*); DEBUSSY: Golaud (*Pelléas et Mélisande*); DELIBES: Nilakantha (*Lakmé*); DONIZETTI: Alfonso d'Este (*Lucrezia Borgia*); GOUNOD: Méphistophélès★ (*Faust*); MASSENET: Sancho (*Don Quichotte*), Athanaël★ (*Thaïs*); MEYERBEER: Comte de St Bris (*Huguenots*); MOZART: Don Alfonso (*Così fan tutte*), Leporello★ & Don Giovanni (*Don Giovanni*), Figaro★ (*Nozze di Figaro*); MUSSORGSKY: Boris Godunov★; OFFENBACH: Coppélius, etc (*Contes d'Hoffmann*); PUCCINI: Colline★ (*Bohème*); Gianni Schicchi; ROSSINI: Don Basilio★ (*Barbiere di Siviglia*), Dandini (*Cenerentola*); SAINT-SAENS: Grand prêtre (*Samson et Dalila*); STRAUSS, R: Orest (*Elektra*), Jochanaan (*Salome*); VERDI: Attila★, Philip II (*Don Carlo*), Zaccaria (*Nabucco*), Fiesco★ (*Simon Boccanegra*); WAGNER: Amfortas (*Parsifal*). Recorded for: DG, EMI, Erato, Decca. Video/Film: Lodovico (*Otello*). Gives recitals. Appears with symphony orchestra. Mgmt: JUC/SWI.

VAN DEN BERG, PIETER. Bass. Dutch. Resident mem: Netherlands Opera, Amsterdam. Born 6 Oct 1928, Mydrecht, Holland. Wife Helma. Two children. Studied: Eugen Fuchs, Berlin; Jess Walters, London; Ruth Horna, Amsterdam. **Debut:** Guardiano (*Forza del destino*) Koblenz, FR Ger 1954. Awards: First Prize Intl Compt Verviers, 1954.

Sang with major companies in BEL: Brussels; FR GER: Bayreuth Fest, Bielefeld, Düsseldorf-Duisburg, Hamburg; GER DR: Berlin Staatsoper; HOL: Amsterdam; SPA: Barcelona; UK: Glasgow Scottish. **Roles with these companies incl** BEETHOVEN: Rocco (*Fidelio*); BELLINI: Oroveso (*Norma*); BERG: Doktor★ (*Wozzeck*); BERLIOZ: Balducci (*Benvenuto Cellini*); DEBUSSY: Arkel (*Pelléas et Mélisande*); DONIZETTI: Don Pasquale, Baldassare (*Favorite*); EGK: Cuperus (*Zaubergeige*); FALLA: Don Quixote (*Retablo de Maese Pedro*); FLOTOW: Plunkett (*Martha*); GERSHWIN: Porgy; GOUNOD: Méphistophélès (*Faust*); HANDEL: Ptolemy (*Giulio Cesare*), Garibald★ (*Rodelinda*); MENOTTI: Don Marco (*Saint of Bleecker Street*); MOZART: Osmin (*Entführung aus dem Serail*), Sarastro (*Zauberflöte*); MUSSORGSKY: Pimen (*Boris*

Godunov); NICOLAI: Falstaff (*Lustigen Weiber*); PUCCINI: Colline (*Bohème*); ROSSINI: Don Basilio (*Barbiere di Siviglia*), Moïse; STRAVINSKY: Tiresias (*Oedipus Rex*); SUCHON: Stelina (*Whirlpool*); VERDI: Ramfis (*Aida*), Philip II & Grande Inquisitore (*Don Carlo*), Silva (*Ernani*), Padre Guardiano (*Forza del destino*), Zaccaria (*Nabucco*), Fiesco (*Simon Boccanegra*); WAGNER: Daland (*Fliegende Holländer*), König Heinrich (*Lohengrin*), Alberich (*Götterdämmerung*), Fasolt (*Rheingold*), Fafner (*Rheingold, Siegfried*), Hunding (*Walküre*), Landgraf (*Tannhäuser*), König Marke (*Tristan und Isolde*); WOLF-FERRARI: Lunardo (*Quattro rusteghi*). **World premieres:** ANDRIESSEN: (*Reconstruction*) Netherlands Opera, Amsterdam 1969; DE KRUYF: (*Spinoza*) Holland Fest 1971. Recorded for: EMI. Gives recitals. Appears with symphony orchestra. Teaches voice. Coaches repertoire. Mgmt: NIM/HOL.

VAN DER BILT, PETER. Dramatic baritone. Dutch. Resident mem: Deutsche Oper am Rhein, Düsseldorf. Studied: Amsterdam.

Sang with major companies in AUS: Vienna Staatsoper; BEL: Brussels; FR GER: Düsseldorf-Duisburg; HOL: Amsterdam; UK: Glasgow Scottish; et al. **Roles with these companies incl** CAVALLI: Amida (*Ormindo*); DONIZETTI: Dott Malatesta (*Don Pasquale*); GLUCK: High Priest (*Alceste*); JANACEK: Forester (*Cunning Little Vixen*), Shishkov (*From the House of the Dead*), Jaroslav Prus (*Makropoulos Affair*); MASSENET: Don Quichotte; MOZART: Guglielmo & Don Alfonso (*Così fan tutte*), Don Giovanni, Figaro & Conte Almaviva (*Nozze di Figaro*); MUSSORGSKY: Varlaam (*Boris Godunov*); ROSSINI: Don Basilio (*Barbiere di Siviglia*); STRAVINSKY: Nick Shadow (*Rake's Progress*); WAGNER: Beckmesser (*Meistersinger*), Amfortas (*Parsifal*); et al. Appears with symphony orchestra. Mgmt: SLL/HOL.

VAN DER GEEST, SIMON. Lyric tenor. Dutch. Resident mem: Netherlands Opera, Amsterdam. Born 15 Nov 1935, Haarlem, Holland. Studied: Muziek Lyceum and Consv, Amsterdam; Mozarteum Salzburg, Prof Rennert, Julius Patzak, Austria. **Debut:** Tamino (*Zauberflöte*) Netherlands Opera 1968.

Sang with major companies in HOL: Amsterdam. **Roles with these companies incl** BRITTEN: Albert Herring, Male Chorus (*Rape of Lucretia*); DONIZETTI: Ernesto (*Don Pasquale*), Nemorino (*Elisir*); HUMPERDINCK: Hexe (*Hänsel und Gretel*); LORTZING: Peter Ivanov (*Zar und Zimmermann*); MASSENET: Werther; MOZART: Ferrando (*Così fan tutte*), Don Ottavio (*Don Giovanni*), Belmonte (*Entführung aus dem Serail*), Belfiore (*Finta giardiniera*), Idamante (*Idomeneo*), Tamino (*Zauberflöte*); NICOLAI: Fenton (*Lustigen Weiber*); ORFF: Solo (*Carmina burana*); PAISIELLO: Almaviva (*Barbiere di Siviglia*); ROSSINI: Almaviva (*Barbiere di Siviglia*), Lindoro (*Italiana in Algeri*); SCARLATTI: Riccardo (*Trionfo dell'onore*); SMETANA: Wenzel & Hans (*Bartered Bride*); STRAUSS, J: Alfred (*Fledermaus*); STRAUSS, R: Ein Sänger (*Rosenkavalier*); STRAVINSKY: Pêcheur (*Rossignol*); THOMAS: Wilhelm Meister (*Mignon*); VERDI:

Edoardo (*Giorno di regno*). Video/Film: Hoffmann. Appears with symphony orchestra. Teaches voice. Coaches repertoire. **Res:** Jansstraat 61, Haarlem, Holland. Mgmt: NIM/HOL; RTB/FRG.

VAN DER MERWE, JACO; né Jacobus Johannes van der Merwe. Dramatic baritone. South African. Born 7 Jul, Britstown. Wife Hilda. Three children. Studied: Profs David Roode, Alberto Terassi, Arnold Fulton, Isobel McLaren, Bloemfontein & Johannesburg. **Debut:** Don Alfonso (*Così fan tutte*) Volksteater, Pretoria 1953. Awards: var Gold Medals & Stpds, Ntl Eisteddfod/Cambrian Socy. **Sang with major companies in** S AFR: Johannesburg. **Roles with these companies incl** BEETHOVEN: Don Pizarro (*Fidelio*); BIZET: Escamillo (*Carmen*); DONIZETTI: Don Pasquale & Dott Malatesta (*Don Pasquale*); HAYDN: Nanni (*Infedeltà delusa*); LEONCAVALLO: Tonio (*Pagliacci*); MASCAGNI: Alfio (*Cavalleria rusticana*); MENOTTI: Husband (*Amelia al ballo*), John Sorel (*Consul*); MOZART: Don Alfonso★ (*Così fan tutte*), Figaro★ (*Nozze di Figaro*), Papageno★ (*Zauberflöte*); OFFENBACH: Coppélius etc★ (*Contes d'Hoffmann*); PAISIELLO: Figaro★ & Bartolo★ (*Barbiere di Siviglia*); PUCCINI: Marcello★ (*Bohème*), Gianni Schicchi★, Sharpless★ (*Butterfly*), Scarpia (*Tosca*); ROSSINI: Figaro★ & Dott Bartolo (*Barbiere di Siviglia*), Mustafà★ (*Italiana in Algeri*); VERDI: Amonasro (*Aida*), Falstaff, Fra Melitone★ (*Forza del destino*), Macbeth, Nabucco★, Rigoletto★, Germont★ (*Traviata*), Conte di Luna (*Trovatore*); WAGNER: Wolfram (*Tannhäuser*); WOLF-FERRARI: Conte Gil (*Segreto di Susanna*). Also HAYDN: Speziale★; SUTERMEISTER: Priester★ (*Schwarze Spinne*); HUMPERDINCK: Peter★ (*Hänsel und Gretel*). Gives recitals. Appears with symphony orchestra. **Res:** 10 Greenlands Rd, Auckland Park/Johannesburg, South Africa.

VAN GINKEL, PETER. Bass-baritone. Canadian. Resident mem: Opernhaus, Nürnberg. Born 10 Mar 1932, Eindhoven, Holland. Wife Irma, occupation ballet dancer. Studied: Quebec Consv de Musique, Montreal; Merola Opera Prgr, Kurt Herbert Adler, Otto Guth, San Francisco. **Debut:** Colonel (*Peter Ibbetson*) Empire State Music Fest, Woodstock, NY 1960. Previous occupations: construction business. Awards: Best Student of the Year, Quebec Consv; Singing Stars of Tomorrow, First Prize. **Sang with major companies in** CAN: Montreal/Quebec, Ottawa, Toronto, Vancouver; FR GER: Cologne, Dortmund, Düsseldorf-Duisburg, Mannheim, Nürnberg, Stuttgart, Wuppertal; USA: Chicago, San Francisco Opera. **Roles with these companies incl** BERG: Wozzeck★; BIZET: Escamillo★ (*Carmen*); FLOTOW: Plunkett★ (*Martha*); GIORDANO: Carlo Gérard★ (*Andrea Chénier*); HINDEMITH: Cardillac★; JANACEK: Shishkov★ (*From the House of the Dead*); LEONCAVALLO: Tonio★ (*Pagliacci*); MASCAGNI: Alfio★ (*Cavalleria rusticana*); MOZART: Don Alfonso (*Così fan tutte*), Figaro (*Nozze di Figaro*); MUSSORGSKY: Boris Godunov; ORFF: König★ (*Kluge*); PUCCINI: Gianni Schicchi★, Sharpless★ (*Butterfly*); STRAUSS, R: Jochanaan★ (*Salome*); STRAVINSKY: Empereur de Chine

(*Rossignol*); VERDI: Iago★ (*Otello*), Rigoletto★; WAGNER: Holländer★, Alberich★ (*Götterdämmerung*), Wotan★ (*Walküre*); WEBER: Kaspar★ (*Freischütz*). Also HUMPERDINCK: Peter (*Hänsel und Gretel*). Gives recitals. Appears with symphony orchestra. Teaches voice. Mgmt: WLS/USA; PAS/FRG.

VAN JUETEN, GRIT. Lyric coloratura soprano. German. Resident mem: Nationaltheater, Mannheim. Born 17 Apr 1944, Hamburg. Husband Hanno Bauer, occupation architect. Studied: Fr Prof Le Lingemann, Marie-Theres Gernot-Heindl, Annemarie Hanschke, Musikwissenschaft Univ, Munich. **Debut:** Aennchen (*Lustigen Weiber*) Theater am Gärtnerplatz, Munich 1966. **Sang with major companies in** AUS: Vienna Volksoper; FR GER: Bielefeld, Düsseldorf-Duisburg, Essen, Frankfurt, Karlsruhe, Kassel, Kiel, Mannheim, Munich Staatsoper & Gärtnerplatz, Nürnberg, Stuttgart, Wiesbaden; HOL: Amsterdam; SWI: Zurich. **Roles with these companies incl** AUBER: Zerlina (*Fra Diavolo*); BELLINI: Amina (*Sonnambula*); CHABRIER: Laula (*Etoile*); CIMAROSA: Carolina★ (*Matrimonio segreto*); DELIBES: Lakmé; DESSAU: Königin (*Verurteilung des Lukullus*); DONIZETTI: Adina (*Elisir*), Marie★ (*Fille du régiment*), Lucia; FLOTOW: Lady Harriet★ (*Martha*); GERSHWIN: Bess; HANDEL: Agrippina; HUMPERDINCK: Gretel★; JANACEK: Vixen★ (*Cunning Little Vixen*); LEONCAVALLO: Nedda★ (*Pagliacci*); LORTZING: Baronin Freimann (*Wildschütz*); MONTEVERDI: Poppea (*Incoronazione di Poppea*); MOZART: Despina★ (*Così fan tutte*), Zerlina (*Don Giovanni*), Konstanze★ (*Entführung aus dem Serail*), Susanna (*Nozze di Figaro*), Pamina★ & Königin der Nacht★ (*Zauberflöte*); NICOLAI: Frau Fluth & Aennchen (*Lustigen Weiber*); OFFENBACH: Olympia & Antonia (*Contes d'Hoffmann*); ORFF: Solo (*Carmina burana*); PUCCINI: Musetta★ (*Bohème*), Lauretta★ (*Gianni Schicchi*); PURCELL: Fairy Queen; ROSSINI: Rosina★ (*Barbiere di Siviglia*); STRAUSS, J: Adele★ (*Fledermaus*); STRAUSS, R: Sophie (*Rosenkavalier*), Aminta (*Schweigsame Frau*); VERDI: Gilda (*Rigoletto*), Violetta (*Traviata*); WOLF-FERRARI: Marina★ (*Quattro rusteghi*). **World premieres:** KUBELIK: Cornelia Faroli (*Cornelia Faroli*) Augsburg Opera 1972. Video – ARD: Cornelia Faroli. Gives recitals. Appears with symphony orchestra. **Res:** Geraer Ring 10, 68 Mannheim 42, FR Ger. Mgmt: SLZ/FRG.

VAN KESTEREN, JOHN. Lyric tenor. Dutch. Born 4 May 1921, The Hague. Wife Louise. Studied: Royal Consv in The Hague, Lothar Wallerstein; Nadia Boulanger, Paris; Vera Schwarz, Vienna. **Debut:** Ein Sänger (*Rosenkavalier*) Staatsoper, Vienna 1954. Previous occupations: elec engineer. Awards: Knight of the Royal House of Orange Nassau; Kammersänger; var prizes. **Sang with major companies in** ARG: Buenos Aires; AUS: Bregenz Fest, Salzburg Fest, Vienna Staatsoper & Volksoper; BEL: Brussels; BRA: Rio de Janeiro; CAN: Montreal/Quebec, Ottawa; DEN: Copenhagen; FRA: Strasbourg; FR GER: Berlin Deutsche Oper, Cologne, Dortmund, Frankfurt, Hamburg, Karlsruhe, Munich Staatsoper & Gärtnerplatz, Nürnberg, Stuttgart, Wuppertal; GER DR: Berlin Komische Oper; HOL: Amsterdam; ITA: Milan La Scala, Palermo; POL: Warsaw; POR: Lisbon; SWE: Drottningholm Fest, Stockholm; SWI: Basel, Geneva, Zurich; USSR: Moscow Bolshoi; USA: Boston, Cincinnati, Dallas, New York City Opera, Pittsburgh. **Roles with these companies incl** ADAM: Chapelou★ (*Postillon de Lonjumeau*), Zephoris (*Si j'étais roi*); BERLIOZ: Faust (*Damnation de Faust*); BIZET: Nadir (*Pêcheurs de perles*); BOIELDIEU: George Brown (*Dame blanche*); BRITTEN: Aschenbach (*Death in Venice*), Oberon (*Midsummer Night*); CAVALLI: Giasone★, Ormindo★; CIMAROSA: Paolino★ (*Matrimonio segreto*); CORNELIUS: Nureddin (*Barbier von Bagdad*); DELIBES: Gérald (*Lakmé*); DONIZETTI: Ernesto★ (*Don Pasquale*), Nemorino (*Elisir*), Tonio (*Fille du régiment*), Beppo (*Rita*); EGK: Amandus (*Zaubergeige*); FLOTOW: Lionel (*Martha*); GLUCK: Pylade (*Iphigénie en Tauride*); GOUNOD: Faust; HANDEL: Acis★, Sextus (*Giulio Cesare*), Xerxes; HAYDN: Nancio (*Infedeltà delusa*), Ernesto (*Mondo della luna*); LECOCQ: Ange Pitou (*Fille de Madame Angot*); MASSENET: Jean★ (*Jongleur de Notre Dame*); MAYR: Giasone (*Medea in Corinto*); MONTEVERDI: Orfeo★, Ulisse (*Ritorno d'Ulisse*); MOZART: Ferrando (*Così fan tutte*), Don Ottavio★ (*Don Giovanni*), Belmonte★ (*Entführung aus dem Serail*), Belfiore (*Finta giardiniera*), Idamante (*Idomeneo*), Tamino (*Zauberflöte*); NICOLAI: Fenton★ (*Lustigen Weiber*); ORFF: Solo★ (*Carmina burana*), Erzähler★ (*Mond*); PFITZNER: Palestrina; PURCELL: King Arthur; RAMEAU: Castor; RIMSKY-KORSAKOV: Astrologue (*Coq d'or*); ROSSINI: Almaviva★ (*Barbiere di Siviglia*), Comte Ory, Lindoro (*Italiana in Algeri*), Dorvil (*Scala di seta*), Narciso (*Turco in Italia*); SMETANA: Wenzel (*Bartered Bride*); STRAUSS, J: Eisenstein★ & Alfred★ (*Fledermaus*); STRAUSS, R: Flamand★ (*Capriccio*), Ein Sänger★ (*Rosenkavalier*); THOMAS: Wilhelm Meister (*Mignon*); VERDI: Alfredo (*Traviata*); WEBER: Oberon; WOLF-FERRARI: Florindo★ (*Donne curiose*). Also LORTZING: Chateauneuf (*Zar und Zimmermann*); RAMEAU: Platée★; PURCELL: (*Fairy Queen*)★. Recorded for: DG, Eurodisc, Ariola, Telefunken, Philips. Gives recitals. Appears with symphony orchestra.

VAN MILL, ARNOLD. Bass. Dutch. Born 26 Mar 1921, Schiedam, Netherlands. Studied: Consvs Rotterdam and The Hague; Prof Segers de Beyl. **Debut:** Théâtre de la Monnaie, Brussels 1946. **Sang with major companies in** ARG: Buenos Aires; AUS: Vienna Staatsoper; BEL: Brussels; BRA: Rio de Janeiro; FRA: Paris; FR GER: Bayreuth Fest, Hamburg, Wiesbaden; HOL: Amsterdam; ITA: Milan La Scala; POR: Lisbon; UK: Edinburgh Fest; USA: Dallas, San Francisco Opera; et al. **Roles with these companies incl** CORNELIUS: Abul Hassan (*Barbier von Bagdad*); MOZART: Osmin‡ (*Entführung aus dem Serail*), Don Giovanni, Sarastro (*Zauberflöte*); MUSSORGSKY: Boris Godunov; VERDI: Ramfis‡ (*Aida*), Philip II (*Don Carlo*); WAGNER: Daland (*Fliegende Holländer*), Titurel (*Parsifal*), Hunding (*Walküre*), Hagen (*Götterdämmerung*), König

Marke‡ (*Tristan und Isolde*); et al. Also MOZART: Commendatore‡ (*Don Giovanni*). Recorded for: RCA, London.

VANNI, HELEN ELIZABETH; née Spaeth. Soprano, form mezzo-soprano. American. Resident mem: Santa Fe Opera, NM. Born 30 Jan 1924, Davenport, IA, USA. Husband Mario Angelo, occupation industrial engineer. Three children. Studied: Mme Marinka Gurewich, Martin Rich, Edyth Walker, New York. **Debut:** Page (*Rigoletto*) Metropolitan Opera 1956. **Sang with major companies in** CAN: Montreal/Quebec, Toronto; UK: Glyndebourne Fest; USA: Baltimore, Cincinnati, New York Met & City Opera, Pittsburgh, Portland, San Francisco Opera & Spring Opera, Santa Fe, Washington DC. **Sop roles with these companies incl** BERLIOZ: Béatrice (*Béatrice et Bénédict*); MOZART: Donna Elvira★ (*Don Giovanni*), Contessa (*Nozze di Figaro*); ROSSINI: Rosina (*Barbiere di Siviglia*); STRAUSS, R: Ariadne★ & Komponist (*Ariadne auf Naxos*), Gräfin (*Capriccio*), Marschallin★ (*Rosenkavalier*); VERDI: Alice Ford (*Falstaff*). **Mezzo-sop roles with these cos incl** BERLIOZ: Ascanio (*Benvenuto Cellini*); GOUNOD: Siebel (*Faust*); HUMPERDINCK: Hänsel; MOZART: Dorabella (*Così fan tutte*), Idamante (*Idomeneo*), Cherubino (*Nozze di Figaro*); MUSSORGSKY: Marina (*Boris Godunov*); PUCCINI: Suzuki (*Butterfly*); ROSSINI: Rosina (*Barbiere di Siviglia*), Isabella (*Italiana in Algeri*); STRAUSS, J: Prinz Orlovsky (*Fledermaus*); STRAUSS, R: Clairon (*Capriccio*), Octavian (*Rosenkavalier*); STRAVINSKY: Jocasta (*Oedipus Rex*); TCHAIKOVSKY: Mme Larina (*Eugene Onegin*); THOMAS: Mignon; VERDI: Preziosilla (*Forza del destino*). Gives recitals. Appears with symphony orchestra. Teaches voice. Coaches repertoire. On faculty of Cleveland Inst of Music, head of voice dept. **Res:** 970 Washington Ave, Ho-Ho-Kus, NJ, USA. Mgmt: CSA/USA.

VAN QUAILLE, JACQUELINE. Spinto. Belgian. Resident mem: Opéra de Liège. Born 6 Oct 1938, Gentbrugge, Belgium. Husband Gilbert Cornelis, occupation cinematographer. Three children. Studied: Consv Royale de Ghent; Mme Vina Bovy, Ghent; Mo Ettore Campogalliani, Italy. **Debut:** Pamina (*Zauberflöte*) Ghent Opera 1960. Awards: First Prize of Distinction in Voice and Opera, Consv Royal Ghent; Prize of Special Distinction, H M King Baudouin. **Sang with major companies in** AUS: Graz, Vienna Volksoper; BEL: Liège; FR GER: Essen, Frankfurt, Munich Gärtnerplatz, Wuppertal; ROM: Bucharest. **Roles with these companies incl** BEETHOVEN: Leonore (*Fidelio*); BERLIOZ: Marguerite (*Damnation de Faust*); BORODIN: Jaroslavna★ (*Prince Igor*); BRITTEN: Ellen Orford (*Peter Grimes*); BUSONI: Herzogin (*Doktor Faust*); CILEA: Adriana Lecouvreur★; DVORAK: Rusalka; GIORDANO: Maddalena★ (*Andrea Chénier*); GLUCK: Iphigénie (*Iphigénie en Tauride*); GOUNOD: Marguerite★ (*Faust*); KORNGOLD: Marietta★ (*Tote Stadt*); MASCAGNI: Santuzza (*Cavalleria rusticana*); MASSENET: Salomé (*Hérodiade*); MEYERBEER: Valentine★ (*Huguenots*); MONTEVERDI: Poppea (*Incoronazione di Poppea*); MOZART:

Donna Elvira (*Don Giovanni*), Contessa (*Nozze di Figaro*), Pamina (*Zauberflöte*); OFFENBACH: Antonia & Giulietta (*Contes d'Hoffmann*); PUCCINI: Mimi (*Bohème*), Minnie★ (*Fanciulla del West*), Manon Lescaut★, Suor Angelica, Tosca★; ROSSINI: Mathilde (*Guillaume Tell*); STRAUSS, J: Rosalinde★ (*Fledermaus*); STRAUSS, R: Arabella★, Chrysothemis (*Elektra*), Marschallin★ (*Rosenkavalier*); TCHAIKOVSKY: Tatiana (*Eugene Onegin*), Lisa (*Pique Dame*); VERDI: Aida★, Amelia★ (*Ballo in maschera*), Elisabetta (*Don Carlo*), Alice Ford★ (*Falstaff*), Leonora (*Forza del destino*), Lady Macbeth★, Desdemona (*Otello*), Amelia (*Simon Boccanegra*), Violetta★ (*Traviata*), Leonora★ (*Trovatore*); WAGNER: Sieglinde★ (*Walküre*), Elisabeth★ & Venus★ (*Tannhäuser*), Isolde★. **World premieres:** DI VITO-DELVAUX: Reine de la lune (*Spoutnik*) Ghent 1960's; KAUFFMANN: (*Perlenhemd*) Opernhaus Wuppertal 1963. Video/Film: Isolde. Gives recitals. Appears with symphony orchestra. Teaches voice. Coaches repertoire. On faculty of Ecole de Musique de Furnes. **Res:** Ave de la mer 205, 8460 Koksijde, Belgium.

VAN REE, JEAN; né Hendrik Schlösser. Lyric & dramatic tenor. Dutch. Resident mem: Städtische Bühnen, Cologne; Basler Theater, Basel. Born 7 Mar 1943, Kerkrade, Holland. Single. Studied: Else Bischof-Bornes, Aachen, FR Ger; Franzisca Martienssen-Lohmann, Düsseldorf. **Debut:** Marquis de Chateauneuf (*Zar und Zimmermann*) Mainz 1963. Previous occupations: bank officer. Awards: Gaudeamus Compt Modern Music, Utrecht, Holland; Medal Salzburger Fest, Austria. **Sang with major companies in** AUS: Salzburg Fest; FRA: Rouen; FR GER: Berlin Deutsche Oper, Cologne, Frankfurt, Hamburg, Hannover, Krefeld; HOL: Amsterdam; HUN: Budapest; SWI: Basel, Geneva. **Roles with these companies incl** ADAM: Chapelou & Marquis de Corcy (*Postillon de Lonjumeau*); AUBER: Fra Diavolo★; BERG: Alwa★‡ (*Lulu*); BUSONI: Mephisto★‡ (*Doktor Faust*); DONIZETTI: Ernesto (*Don Pasquale*); HANDEL: Acis; HINDEMITH: Apprentice★ (*Cardillac*); MOZART: Don Ottavio (*Don Giovanni*); OFFENBACH: Hoffmann★; PAISIELLO: Almaviva (*Barbiere di Siviglia*); ROSSINI: Almaviva (*Barbiere di Siviglia*); SMETANA: Hans★ (*Bartered Bride*); STRAUSS, J: Alfred★ (*Fledermaus*); STRAVINSKY: Oedipus Rex★‡; WEILL: Jim Mahoney★ (*Aufstieg und Fall der Stadt Mahagonny*). Also SZOKOLAY: Laertes (*Hamlet*). **World premieres:** KUBELIK: Rodrigo (*Cornelia Faroli*) Augsburg 1971. Video/Film: (*Schauspieldirektor*), (*Zaïde*). Gives recitals. Appears with symphony orchestra. Teaches voice. **Res:** Bungalow "Il Trovatore", 5159 Türnich, FR Ger. Mgmt: SLZ/FRG; TAS/AUS.

VAN TASSEL, CHARLES. Lyric & dramatic baritone; character baritone. American. Resident mem: Opernhaus Kassel, FR Ger. Born 25 Aug 1937, New York. Single. Studied: Theodor Schlott, Bremen, FR Ger; Mo Luigi Ricci, Rome; Blake Stern, New Haven, CT, USA. **Debut:** WEISGALL: Old Man (*Purgatory*) Contemporary Chamber Players, Chicago 1967. Previous occupations: Asst Research Dir, Amalgamated Meat Cutters Union, Chicago. Awards: *High Fidelity* Magazine Awd, Gt Barrington, MA, USA 1967; M B Rockefeller Grant 1968. **Sang with major companies in** FR GER: Kassel, Wiesbaden. **Roles with these companies incl** BIZET: Escamillo★ (*Carmen*); BRITTEN: Demetrius★ (*Midsummer Night*); CIMAROSA: Count Robinson★ (*Matrimonio segreto*); DONIZETTI: Maestro★ (*Convenienze*); HENZE: Landarzt★; LORTZING: Graf Eberbach★ (*Wildschütz*); MOZART: Conte Almaviva★ (*Nozze di Figaro*); PUCCINI: Marcello★ (*Bohème*); STRAUSS, R: Jochanaan★ (*Salome*); VERDI: Rodrigo★ (*Don Carlo*). Also NICOLAI: Fluth★ (*Lustigen Weiber*). **World premieres:** STROÉ: "He" (*Nobelpreis wird nicht verliehen!*) Opernhaus Kassel, FR Ger 1971. Gives recitals. Appears with symphony orchestra. **Res:** Fr-Ebert Str 116, Kassel, FR Ger.

VAN VROOMAN, RICHARD CLYDE. Lyric tenor. American. Resident mem: Opernhaus Zurich. Born 29 Jul 1936, Kansas City, MO, USA. Single. Studied: Consv of Music, Kansas City; Salzburger Mozarteum, Austria; Max Lorenz; Enzo Mascherini, Italy. **Debut:** Lorenzo (*Fra Diavolo*) Bregenzer Fest 1962. Awards: Outstanding Young Men of America, US Univ Commtt; Fulbright Schlshp; Intl Inst of Men of Achievement Awd. **Sang with major companies in** AUS: Bregenz Fest, Salzburg Fest; BEL: Brussels; FRA: Aix-en-Provence, Bordeaux, Marseille, Nancy, Paris; FR GER: Düsseldorf-Duisburg, Frankfurt, Hamburg; HOL: Amsterdam; ITA: Rome Opera; NOR: Oslo; POR: Lisbon; SWI: Geneva, Zurich; UK: Glyndebourne Fest; USA: Kansas City. **Roles with these companies incl** AUBER: Lorenzo (*Fra Diavolo*); BIZET: Nadir (*Pêcheurs de perles*); DONIZETTI: Ernesto (*Don Pasquale*), Nemorino (*Elisir*); GLUCK: Pylade★ (*Iphigénie en Tauride*); HANDEL: Acis‡; JANACEK: Alyei (*From the House of the Dead*); LORTZING: Baron Kronthal (*Wildschütz*); MENOTTI: Lover (*Amelia al ballo*); MOZART: Ferrando★ (*Così fan tutte*), Don Ottavio★ (*Don Giovanni*), Belmonte★ & Pedrillo★ (*Entführung aus dem Serail*); Tamino★‡ (*Zauberflöte*); NICOLAI: Fenton (*Lustigen Weiber*); PAISIELLO: Almaviva (*Barbiere di Siviglia*); PROKOFIEV: Truffaldino★ (*Love for Three Oranges*); PUCCINI: Rinuccio (*Gianni Schicchi*); ROSSINI: Almaviva★‡ (*Barbiere di Siviglia*), Lindoro★ (*Italiana in Algeri*), Rodrigo (*Otello*); SMETANA: Wenzel (*Bartered Bride*); STRAUSS, R: Ein Sänger (*Rosenkavalier*); VERDI: Fenton★ (*Falstaff*); WAGNER: David★ (*Meistersinger*); WOLF-FERRARI: Filipeto (*Quattro rusteghi*). Also MOZART: Fauno (*Ascanio in Alba*); BERG: Andres★ (*Wozzeck*); HAYDN: Lindoro★ (*Fedeltà premiata*), Perseus. **World premieres:** EDER: Der Junge (*Der Kardinal*) Austrian TV 1962. Recorded for: CBS, Epic, Philips, Fontana, Concert Hall, Turnabout, Serenus, Intl Guild du Disque. Video/Film: PAISIELLO: Lindoro (*Barbiere di Siviglia*); Junge (*Kardinal*); Fenton (*Falstaff*); Andres (*Wozzeck*); Alyei (*From the House of the Dead*). Gives recitals. Appears with symphony orchestra. Teaches voice. **Res:** 4618 Warwick Blvd, Kansas City, MO, USA. Mgmt: KOA/AUS.

VANZO, ALAIN. Lyric & dramatic tenor. French. Resident mem: Paris Opéra. Born 2 Apr 1928, Monaco. Wife Michaud. One child. **Debut:** Duca di Mantova (*Rigoletto*) Paris Opéra 1958. Previous occupations: sang in musicals and operettas. Awards: Chevalier des Arts et Lettres, Paris.

Sang with major companies in AUS: Vienna Staatsoper; BEL: Brussels, Liège; BUL: Sofia; CAN: Montreal/Quebec; FRA: Aix-en-Provence, Bordeaux, Lyon, Marseille, Nancy, Nice, Orange Fest, Paris, Rouen, Strasbourg, Toulouse; HOL: Amsterdam; HUN: Budapest; ITA: Naples; MEX: Mexico City; MON: Monte Carlo; POR: Lisbon; ROM: Bucharest; SPA: Barcelona; SWI: Geneva, Zurich; UK: Glyndebourne Fest, London Royal Opera & English National; USA: Miami, New York Met & City Opera, San Francisco Opera; YUG: Belgrade. Roles with these companies incl BECAUD: Angelo (*Opéra d'Aran*); BELLINI: Elvino (*Sonnambula*); BERLIOZ: Benvenuto Cellini, Faust (*Damnation de Faust*); BIZET: Don José (*Carmen*), Smith (*Jolie Fille de Perth*), Nadir (*Pêcheurs de perles*); BOITO: Faust (*Mefistofele*); CHARPENTIER: Julien (*Louise*); CILEA: Maurizio (*A. Lecouvreur*); DELIBES: Gérald (*Lakmé*); DONIZETTI: Edgardo (*Lucia*), Gennaro (*Lucrezia Borgia*); GIORDANO: Andrea Chénier; GOUNOD: Faust, Vincent (*Mireille*), Roméo; LALO: Mylio (*Roi d'Ys*); MASCAGNI: Turiddu (*Cavalleria rusticana*); MASSENET: Jean le Baptiste (*Hérodiade*), Jean (*Jongleur de Notre Dame*), Des Grieux (*Manon*), Araquil (*Navarraise*), Werther; OFFENBACH: Hoffmann; POULENC: Chevalier de la Force (*Dialogues des Carmélites*); PUCCINI: Rodolfo (*Bohème*), Dick Johnson (*Fanciulla del West*), Pinkerton (*Butterfly*), Des Grieux (*Manon Lescaut*), Cavaradossi (*Tosca*); STRAUSS, R: Ein Sänger (*Rosenkavalier*); VERDI: Don Carlo, Duca di Mantova (*Rigoletto*), Gabriele (*Simon Boccanegra*), Alfredo (*Traviata*), Manrico (*Trovatore*), Arrigo (*Vespri*). Recorded for: Decca, Pathé, Vega, CBS. Gives recitals. Appears with symphony orchestra. **Res:** 3 Ave Nast, Gournay s/Marne 93460, France. Mgmt: RNR/SWI.

VARADY, JULIA. Soprano. Hungarian. Resident mem: Oper der Stadt Köln, Cologne; Bayerische Staatsoper, Munich. Born Hungary.

Sang with major companies in FR GER: Cologne, Frankfurt, Mannheim, Munich Staatsoper; UK: Aldeburgh Fest, Glyndebourne Fest; USA: San Francisco; et al. Roles with these companies incl BARTOK: Judith (*Bluebeard's Castle*); GLUCK: Alceste, Euridice; GOUNOD: Marguerite (*Faust*); MASCAGNI: Santuzza (*Cavalleria rusticana*); MOZART: Vitellia (*Clemenza di Tito*), Fiordiligi (*Così fan tutte*), Donna Elvira (*Don Giovanni*), Elettra (*Idomeneo*), Contessa (*Nozze di Figaro*); OFFENBACH: Olympia & Antonia & Giulietta (*Contes d'Hoffmann*); PUCCINI: Cio-Cio-San (*Butterfly*), Giorgetta (*Tabarro*), Liù (*Turandot*); ROSSINI: Rosina (*Barbiere di Siviglia*); STRAUSS, R: Arabella, Komponist (*Ariadne auf Naxos*), Chrysothemis (*Elektra*); VERDI: Elisabetta (*Don Carlo*), Leonora (*Forza del destino*), Lady Macbeth, Violetta (*Traviata*), Leonora (*Trovatore*); et al. Appears with symphony orchestra. **Res:** 19 Nymphenburger Str 90, Munich, FR Ger. Mgmt: COL/USA.

VARIADIS, SERGE. Stages/produces opera, theater & television and is an actor. Greek. Resident Stage Dir, National Opera, Athens. Also Resident Stage Dir for theater in Athens. Born 1926, Paris. Wife Sylvia Franc, occupation singer. Two children. Studied: Prof René Simon, Paris; Margherita Wallmann, Riccardo Moresco, Mladen Sablic, Athens; also music and voice. Operatic training as asst stage dir at National Opera, Athens. **Operatic debut:** *Nabucco* National Opera, Athens 1962. Theater debut: Paris 1945.

Directed/produced opera for major companies in GRE: Athens National & Fest; YUG: Belgrade. Operas staged with these companies incl BEETHOVEN: *Fidelio;* BELLINI: *Norma;* BIZET: *Carmen;* BOITO: *Mefistofele;* BORODIN: *Prince Igor;* CIMAROSA: *Matrimonio segreto;* DONIZETTI: *Elisir, Favorite, Lucia;* GIORDANO: *Andrea Chénier;* GOUNOD: *Faust★;* LEONCAVALLO: *Pagliacci★;* MASCAGNI: *Cavalleria rusticana★;* MASSENET: *Manon, Werther;* MOZART: *Così fan tutte, Don Giovanni;* MUSSORGSKY: *Boris Godunov, Fair at Sorochintsk, Khovanshchina;* OFFENBACH: *Contes d'Hoffmann;* ORFF: *Kluge★;* PERGOLESI: *Serva padrona;* PONCHIELLI: *Gioconda★;* POULENC: *Dialogues des Carmélites;* PROKOFIEV: *Love for Three Oranges;* PUCCINI: *Bohème★, Gianni Schicchi, Butterfly, Manon Lescaut★, Suor Angelica, Tabarro, Tosca★;* RAVEL: *Heure espagnole★;* ROSSINI: *Barbiere di Siviglia, Signor Bruschino★;* STRAUSS, J: *Fledermaus;* TCHAIKOVSKY: *Eugene Onegin, Pique Dame;* VERDI: *Aida, Ballo in maschera, Don Carlo, Ernani, Forza del destino, Otello, Rigoletto★, Simon Boccanegra, Traviata★, Trovatore★;* WAGNER: *Lohengrin, Tannhäuser;* WOLF-FERRARI: *Segreto di Susanna★.* Operatic world premieres: NEZERITIS: *Iro and Leandros* National Opera, Athens 1970. Teaches. **Res:** Asklipiu 57, Athens, Greece. Mgmt: KRI/GRE.

VARISCO, TITO. Scenic and costume designer for opera & theater. Is a lighting designer; also a painter, architect & teacher of scenography. Italian. Dir of Stage Design, La Scala, Milan. Born 21 Jan 1915, Milan. Wife Margherita Bellini, occupation teacher of costume design. One child. Studied: Accad di Belle Arti and Facoltà di Architettura, Milan. Prof training: var theaters. **Operatic debut:** *Les Sylphides* ballet at La Scala, Milan 1961. Theater debut: Teatro Filodrammatici, Milan 1936. Awards: Commendatore, Republic of Italy; Medaglia d'oro, Polytechnic Milan; Silver Medal, 5th Triennale Milan.

Designed for major companies in ARG: Buenos Aires; ITA: Milan La Scala, Rome Opera, Trieste, Turin. Operas designed for these companies incl BELLINI: *Capuleti ed i Montecchi★, Puritani★;* BOITO: *Mefistofele★;* DONIZETTI: *Campanello, Favorite★;* GOUNOD: *Faust;* MASSENET: *Werther;* POULENC: *Voix humaine;* PUCCINI: *Butterfly, Turandot;* ROSSINI: *Barbiere di Siviglia;* VERDI: *Rigoletto, Trovatore;* ZANDONAI: *Francesca da Rimini, Giulietta e Romeo.* Also TOSATTI: *Partita a pugni.* Operatic video—RAI TV, Milan: *Werther.* Exhibitions of stage designs & paintings. Teaches at Accad di

Belle Arti di Brera, Milan. **Res:** V Mulino delle Armi 23, Milan, Italy.

VARNAY, ASTRID IBOLYKA. Dramatic soprano and mezzo-soprano. American. Born 25 Apr 1918, Stockholm. Widowed. Husband Hermann O Weigert, occupation opera conductor & Wagner expert (deceased). Studied: Maria Varnay (mother); Paul Althouse, New York; Mo Hermann Weigert, coaching; Dr Lothar Wallerstein, stage direction. **Debut:** Sieglinde (*Walküre*) Metropolitan Opera 1941. Previous occupations: secy & typist in business firm relating to first edition books. Awards: Bayerische Kammersängerin, Munich 1963; Bayerischer Verdienstorden, Munich 1967.

Sang with major companies in ARG: Buenos Aires; AUS: Graz, Salzburg Fest, Vienna Staatsoper; BEL: Brussels; BRA: Rio de Janeiro; CAN: Montreal/Quebec, Toronto; FRA: Lyon, Nancy, Nice, Paris, Strasbourg; GRE: Athens Fest; FR GER: Bayreuth Fest, Berlin Deutsche Oper, Bielefeld, Bonn, Cologne, Darmstadt, Dortmund, Düsseldorf-Duisburg, Essen, Frankfurt, Hamburg, Hannover, Karlsruhe, Kassel, Kiel, Krefeld, Mannheim, Munich Staatsoper, Nürnberg, Saarbrücken, Stuttgart, Wiesbaden, Wuppertal; GER DR: Dresden; HUN: Budapest; ITA: Florence Maggio, Genoa, Milan La Scala, Naples, Palermo, Rome Opera, Trieste; MEX: Mexico City; MON: Monte Carlo; POR: Lisbon; SPA: Barcelona; SWI: Basel, Geneva, Zurich; UK: Edinburgh Fest, Glyndebourne Fest, London Royal Opera; USA: Baltimore, Boston, Chicago, Cincinnati, Dallas, Fort Worth, Houston, Miami, Newark, New Orleans, New York Met, Philadelphia Grand & Lyric, Pittsburgh, St Paul, San Antonio, San Francisco Opera, Santa Fe, Seattle, Washington DC. **Roles with these companies incl** BEETHOVEN: Leonore (*Fidelio*); HUMPERDINCK: Mother★ (*Hänsel und Gretel*); JANACEK: Katya Kabanova★ Kostelnicka (*Jenufa*); MASCAGNI: Santuzza★ (*Cavalleria rusticana*); PONCHIELLI: Gioconda; STRAUSS, R: Elektra‡ & Klytämnestra★ (*Elektra*), Amme★ (*Frau ohne Schatten*), Marschallin (*Rosenkavalier*), Salome & Herodias★ (*Salome*); VERDI: Aida, Leonora (*Forza del destino*), Lady Macbeth, Desdemona (*Otello*), Leonora (*Trovatore*); WAGNER: Senta‡ (*Fliegende Holländer*), Elsa‡ & Ortrud‡ (*Lohengrin*), Sieglinde (*Walküre*), Brünnhilde (*Walküre*★‡, *Siegfried*‡, *Götterdämmerung*★), Gutrune (*Götterdämmerung*), Elisabeth & Venus (*Tannhäuser*), Kundry (*Parsifal*), Isolde; WEILL: Leocadia Begbick★ (*Aufstieg und Fall der Stadt Mahagonny*). Also EINEM: Claire (*Besuch der alten Dame*). **World premieres:** MENOTTI: Telea (*Island God*) Metropolitan Opera 1942; ORFF: Jokasta (*Oedipus der Tyrann*) Stuttgart 1959. Recorded for: DG. Video/Film: Kostelnicka (*Jenufa*); Herodias (*Salome*). Gives recitals. Appears with symphony orchestra. Teaches voice. Coaches repertoire. On faculty of Düsseldorf Consv, master classes. **Res:** Munich, FR Ger. Mgmt: SLZ/FRG.

VARONA, JOSÉ LUCIANO. Scenic and costume designer for opera, theater, film, television. Argentinean. Born 14 Aug 1930, Mendoza, Argentina. Wife Mary M Duzak, occupation artist. Studied: Escuela Superior de Bellas Artes, Ernesto de la Carcova, Rodolfo Franco, Mario Vanarelli, Buenos Aires. **Operatic debut:** *Love for Three Oranges* Teatro Colón, Buenos Aires 1959.

Designed for major companies in ARG: Buenos Aires; AUSTRL: Sydney; CAN: Vancouver; FRA: Paris; FR GER: Berlin Deutsche Oper, Hamburg; HOL: Amsterdam; ITA: Spoleto Fest; USA: Baltimore, Houston, New York City Opera, San Francisco Opera, Washington DC. **Operas designed for these companies incl** BELLINI: *Norma*★; BIZET: *Carmen*★; DONIZETTI: *Anna Bolena*★, *Campanello*, *Lucia*, *Lucrezia Borgia*★, *Maria Stuarda*, *Roberto Devereux*; GLUCK: *Orfeo*★; GOUNOD: *Faust*; HANDEL: *Ariodante*, *Giulio Cesare*, *Rodelinda*★; LEONCAVALLO: *Pagliacci*; MASCAGNI: *Cavalleria rusticana*; MASSENET: *Manon*; MENOTTI: *Saint of Bleecker Street*; MONTEVERDI: *Incoronazione di Poppea*★; MOZART: *Così fan tutte*; MUSSORGSKY: *Boris Godunov*; OFFENBACH: *Contes d'Hoffmann*★; PROKOFIEV: *Love for Three Oranges*★; RIMSKY-KORSAKOV: *Coq d'or*; ROSSINI: *Italiana in Algeri*★; SCARLATTI: *Trionfo dell'onore*★; STRAUSS, R: *Rosenkavalier*; STRAVINSKY: *Mavra*, *Rake's Progress*; VERDI: *Aida*★, *Attila*★, *Ballo in maschera*★, *Macbeth*, *Rigoletto*, *Traviata*★, *Trovatore*. Also CASTRO: *Proserpina y el extranjero*; SCHIAMMARELLA: *Marianita Limena*. **Operatic world premieres:** GINASTERA: *Bomarzo* Washington Opera Socy 1967. Exhibitions of stage designs, Buenos Aires 1953, 1956, 1957. Teaches at Lester Polakov School of Design, New York. **Res:** 130 W 86th St, New York, NY, USA. Mgmt: GOR/UK.

VARVISO, SILVIO. Conductor of opera and symphony. Swiss. Gen Music Dir & Resident Cond, Württembergische Staatsoper, Stuttgart. Also Music Dir, Staatsorch Stuttgart. Born 26 Feb 1924, Zurich. Wife Josiane. Studied: Zurich Consv; incl piano, violin, clarinet, percussion. **Operatic debut:** St Gallen Opera, Switzerland 1947. Symphonic debut: Basel Symph, 1950. Awards: Royal Court Conductor, King Gustav Adolf of Sweden 1971. Previous adm positions in opera: Mus Dir, Basel, Switzerland 1956-62; Mus Dir, Royal Opera, Stockholm 1965-71.

Conducted with major companies in AUS: Vienna Staatsoper; CAN: Montreal/Quebec, Vancouver; FRA: Paris; FR GER: Bayreuth Fest, Hamburg, Munich Staatsoper & Gärtnerplatz, Stuttgart; POR: Lisbon; SWE: Stockholm; SWI: Basel; UK: Glyndebourne Fest; USA: New York Metropolitan Opera, Philadelphia Grand, Portland, San Diego, San Francisco Opera. **Operas with these companies incl** BARTOK: *Bluebeard's Castle*★; BEETHOVEN: *Fidelio*; BELLINI: *Norma*‡, *Sonnambula*; BIZET: *Carmen*★; BRITTEN: *Midsummer Night;* CILEA: *A. Lecouvreur;* DALLAPICCOLA: *Prigioniero;* DEBUSSY: *Pelléas et Mélisande;* DONIZETTI: *Anna Bolena*‡, *Don Pasquale*, *Elisir*, *Lucia;* FALLA: *Vida breve;* GLUCK: *Alceste*, *Orfeo ed Euridice;* GOUNOD: *Faust;* HANDEL: *Alcina*, *Giulio Cesare;* HUMPERDINCK: *Hänsel und Gretel;* MASCAGNI: *Cavalleria rusticana*‡; MASSENET: *Manon;* MOZART: *Così fan tutte*, *Don Giovanni*, *Entführung aus dem Serail*, *Nozze di Figaro*, *Zauberflöte;* MUSSORGSKY: *Boris*

Godunov; NICOLAI: *Lustigen Weiber;* OFFEN-BACH: *Contes d'Hoffmann;* ORFF: *Carmina burana, Kluge;* POULENC: *Mamelles de Tirésias;* PROKOFIEV: *Fiery Angel;* PUCCINI: *Bohème, Gianni Schicchi, Butterfly, Tosca, Turandot;* RAVEL: *Heure espagnole;* ROSSINI: *Barbiere di Siviglia∗‡, Guillaume Tell, Italiana in Algeri‡, Moïse;* STRAUSS, J: *Fledermaus;* STRAUSS, R: *Arabella∗, Ariadne auf Naxos, Rosenkavalier∗, Salome, Schweigsame Frau;* STRAVINSKY: *Rake's Progress;* TCHAIKOVSKY: *Eugene Onegin, Pique Dame;* VERDI: *Aida, Ballo in maschera∗, Don Carlo∗, Falstaff, Forza del destino, Otello, Rigoletto, Traviata, Trovatore, Vespri;* WAGNER: *Fliegende Holländer∗, Lohengrin∗, Meistersinger∗‡, Rheingold∗, Walküre∗, Siegfried∗, Götterdämmerung∗, Tristan und Isolde∗;* WEINBERGER: *Schwanda.* **World premieres:** SUTERMEISTER: *Titus Feuerfuchs* Basel Stadttheater 1958. Recorded for Đecca/London, Philips. Video—Austrian TV: *Barbiere di Siviglia;* ZDF TV: *Don Pasquale.* Conducted major orch in Europe & USA/Canada. **Res:** Stuttgart, FR Germany. Mgmt: COL/USA.

VASSALLO, ALDO MIRABELLA; né Gesualdo Mirabella. Stages/produces opera & theater and is a singer & actor. Italian. Resident Stage Dir, Teatro Massimo, Palermo. Born 6 Jan 1915, Palermo. Wife Gilda Riina. Studied: Italy and Germany, incl music, violin and voice. Operatic training as asst stage dir at var Italian opera houses. **Operatic debut:** *Meistersinger* Teatro la Fenice, Venice 1947. Theater debut: Italy 1950. Previous occupation: violinist, baritone.

   Directed/produced opera for major companies in FRA: Paris; FR GER: Munich Staatsoper, Wiesbaden; ITA: Bologna, Florence Comunale, Genoa, Milan La Scala, Naples, Palermo, Parma, Rome Opera & Caracalla, Trieste, Turin, Venice; UK: Edinburgh Fest, London Royal; USA: Chicago; YUG: Dubrovnik. **Operas staged with these companies incl** BELLINI: *Capuleti ed i Montecchi, Norma, Puritani∗, Sonnambula∗, Straniera;* BIZET: *Carmen;* BOITO: *Mefistofele∗;* CATALANI: *Wally;* CILEA: *A. Lecouvreur∗;* DALLAPICCOLA: *Prigioniero, Volo di notte;* DONIZETTI: *Don Pasquale, Elisir∗, Favorite, Fille du régiment, Lucia∗;* GIORDANO: *Andrea Chénier∗, Fedora∗;* GLINKA: *Life for the Tsar;* GOUNOD: *Faust;* LEONCAVALLO: *Pagliacci∗;* MASCAGNI: *Amico Fritz, Cavalleria rusticana∗;* MASSENET: *Manon, Thaïs, Werther;* MENOTTI: *Consul;* MOZART: *Don Giovanni;* MUSSORGSKY: *Boris Godunov∗;* OFFENBACH: *Contes d'Hoffmann;* PONCHIELLI: *Gioconda∗;* POULENC: *Dialogues des Carmélites;* PUCCINI: *Bohème∗, Fanciulla del West∗, Gianni Schicchi, Butterfly∗, Manon Lescaut∗, Suor Angelica, Tabarro, Tosca∗, Turandot∗, Villi;* ROSSINI: *Barbiere di Siviglia, Guillaume Tell;* SAINT-SAENS: *Samson et Dalila;* STRAUSS, J: *Fledermaus;* STRAUSS, R: *Rosenkavalier;* THOMAS: *Hamlet, Mignon;* VERDI: *Aida∗, Attila∗, Ballo in maschera∗, Don Carlo∗, Ernani∗, Falstaff, Forza del destino∗, Macbeth∗, Nabucco, Otello, Rigoletto, Simon Boccanegra∗, Traviata∗, Trovatore∗, Vespri;* WAGNER: *Fliegende Holländer, Lohengrin, Walküre, Tannhäuser∗;* WOLF-FERRARI: *Segreto di Susanna;*

ZANDONAI: *Francesca da Rimini, Giulietta e Romeo.* Also MASCAGNI: *Isabeau∗, Piccolo Marat∗;* ROSSELLINI: *Guerra;* SANTONE-CITO: *Lupa∗;* TCHAIKOVSKY: *Mazeppa.* Teaches at Centro Avviamento Teatro Lirico, Palermo. **Res:** V Pignatelli Aragona .84, Palermo, Italy.

VAUGHAN, ELIZABETH; née Elizabeth Myfanwy Jones. Spinto. British. Born 12 Mar 1938, Lianfyllin, Wales, UK. Husband Ray Brown, occupation musician. Two children. Studied: Royal Acad of Music, Olive Groves, London; Dame Eva Turner, London. **Debut:** Abigaille (*Nabucco*) Welsh National Opera. Awards: Kathleen Ferrier Awd; FRAM; ARAM; LRAM.

   Sang with major companies in AUSTRL: Sydney; AUS: Vienna Staatsoper; CAN: Montreal/Quebec; FRA: Nancy, Toulouse; FR GER: Berlin Deutsche Oper, Düsseldorf-Duisburg, Hamburg, Munich Staatsoper; S AFR: Johannesburg; UK: Cardiff Welsh, Edinburgh Fest, Glasgow Scottish, London Royal Opera; USA: Miami, New York Met. **Roles with these companies incl** BERLIOZ: Teresa‡ (*Benvenuto Cellini*); BRITTEN: Tytania (*Midsummer Night*); GLUCK: Euridice∗; GOUNOD: Marguerite∗ (*Faust*); MOZART: Donna Elvira∗ (*Don Giovanni*), Konstanze (*Entführung aus dem Serail*), Contessa (*Nozze di Figaro*); PUCCINI: Mimi & Musetta (*Bohème*), Cio-Cio-San∗ (*Butterfly*), Manon Lescaut∗, Liù (*Turandot*); TIPPETT: Hecuba∗ (*King Priam*); VERDI: Aida, Amelia∗ (*Ballo in maschera*), Donna Elvira∗(*Ernani*), Alice Ford∗(*Falstaff*), Abigaille∗ (*Nabucco*), Desdemona (*Otello*), Gilda (*Rigoletto*), Amelia∗ (*Simon Boccanegra*), Violetta∗ (*Traviata*), Leonora (*Trovatore*). Gives recitals. Appears with symphony orchestra. **Res:** Delamere House, Gt Wymondley/Herts, UK. Mgmt: GBN/UK; RAP/FRA.

VEASEY, JOSEPHINE. Dramatic mezzo-soprano. British. Resident mem: Royal Opera, Covent Garden, London. Born 10 Jul 1930, London. Married. Two children. Studied: Audrey Langford; Mme Olczewska, Vienna. **Debut:** Cherubino (*Nozze di Figaro*) Covent Garden 1955. Previous occupations: secretary. Awards: Commander of the British Empire, HM Queen Elizabeth II 1970.

   Sang with major companies in AUS: Salzburg Fest; FRA: Aix-en-Provence Fest, Marseille, Nancy, Nice, Orange Fest, Paris, Rouen, Toulouse; FR GER: Frankfurt, Deutsche Oper Berlin, Munich Staatsoper, Hamburg; ITA: Milan La Scala; POR: Lisbon; SPA: Barcelona; SWI: Geneva; UK: Edinburgh Fest, Glyndebourne Fest, London Royal; USA: New York Met, San Francisco Opera. **Roles with these companies incl** BELLINI: Adalgisa (*Norma*); BERLIOZ: Marguerite (*Damnation de Faust*), Cassandre & Anna & Didon (*Troyens*); BIZET: Carmen; BRITTEN: Hermia (*Midsummer Night*); GLUCK: Orfeo; HANDEL: Bradamante & Ruggiero (*Alcina*); HUMPERDINCK: Hänsel; MASSENET: Charlotte (*Werther*); MOZART: Dorabella (*Così fan tutte*), Cherubino (*Nozze di Figaro*); MUSSORGSKY: Marina (*Boris Godunov*); PUCCINI: Suzuki (*Butterfly*); STRAUSS, R: Octavian (*Rosenkavalier*), Herodias (*Salome*); VERDI: Amneris (*Aida*), Eboli (*Don Carlo*), Preziosilla

(*Forza del destino*); WAGNER: Magdalene (*Meistersinger*), Kundry (*Parsifal*), Fricka (*Rheingold, Walküre* ‡), Waltraute (*Götterdämmerung*), Venus (*Tannhäuser*), Brangäne (*Tristan und Isolde*). Also on records only BERLIOZ: Béatrice, Marguerite (*Damnation de Faust*). Recorded for: Oiseau-Lyre, London, Philips. Appears with symphony orchestra. **Res:** Surrey, UK. **Mgmt:** CST/UK; BAR/USA.

VEDERNIKOV, ALEXANDER FILIPOVICH. Bass. Russian. Resident mem: Bolshoi Theater, Moscow. Born 23 Dec 1927, Kirov, USSR. Wife Natalya Nicolaevna, occupation organist, senior grad, Consv of Moscow. Three children. Studied: Moscow Consv, Alperg-Hasina; La Scala School, Mo Barra, Milan. **Debut:** Ivan Susanin, Moscow 1957. Awards: First Prize, Schumann Compt 1956; Winner State Prize of USSR 1969.
Sang with major companies in AUS: Vienna Staatsoper; BUL: Sofia; CZE: Prague National; FRA: Paris; GER DR: Berlin Staatsoper; HUN: Budapest; ITA: Milan La Scala; POL: Warsaw; USSR: Kiev, Leningrad Kirov, Moscow Bolshoi, Tbilisi. **Roles with these companies incl** BORODIN: Galitzky★ (*Prince Igor*); GLINKA: Ivan★ (*Life for the Tsar*), Ruslan★ & Farlaf★ (*Ruslan and Ludmilla*); GOUNOD: Méphistophélès (*Faust*); MUSSORGSKY: Boris★ & Varlaam★ & Pimen★ (*Boris Godunov*), Ivan Khovansky★ & Dosifei★ (*Khovanshchina*); PROKOFIEV: Michael★ (*War and Peace*); RIMSKY-KORSAKOV: Juri Vsevolodovic★ (*Invisible City of Kitezh*), Vassily Sobakin★ (*Tsar's Bride*); ROSSINI: Don Basilio★ (*Barbiere di Siviglia*); SHOSTAKOVICH: Boris★ (*Katerina Ismailova*); VERDI: Ramfis (*Aida*), Philip II & Grande Inquisitore (*Don Carlo*); WAGNER: Daland (*Fliegende Holländer*). Gives recitals. Appears with symphony orchestra. Teaches voice. **Res:** Moscow, USSR.

VEENINGA, JENNIE JANTINA. Dramatic soprano. Dutch. Resident mem: Netherlands Opera, Amsterdam; Opera Forum, Enschede, Holland. Born 28 Nov 1936, Haarlem, Holland. Single. Studied: Amsterdam Consv, Coby Riemersma, Holland. **Debut:** Desdemona (*Otello*) Royal Flemish Opera, Antwerp, Belgium 1963. Previous occupations: teaching theater costume design.
Sang with major companies in BEL: Brussels; FRA: Paris; FR GER: Kassel; GER DR: Dresden; HOL: Amsterdam; ITA: Milan La Scala; UK: Glyndebourne Fest; YUG: Dubrovnik, Zagreb. **Roles with these companies incl** GERSHWIN: Bess; GOUNOD: Marguerite (*Faust*); MASCAGNI: Santuzza (*Cavalleria rusticana*); MENOTTI: Lucy (*Telephone*); MOZART: Contessa★ (*Nozze di Figaro*); PUCCINI: Tosca★, Liù (*Turandot*); PURCELL: Dido; RIMSKY-KORSAKOV: Coq d'or; STRAUSS, J: Rosalinde★ (*Fledermaus*); VERDI: Aida, Elisabetta★ (*Don Carlo*), Alice Ford★ (*Falstaff*), Leonora★ (*Forza del destino*), Desdemona (*Otello*), Leonora (*Trovatore*); WAGNER: Elsa★ (*Lohengrin*), Eva (*Meistersinger*), Elisabeth (*Tannhäuser*); WEBER: Agathe (*Freischütz*). Gives recitals. Appears with symphony orchestra. **Res:** Burg-Hogguerstraat 709, Amsterdam, Holland.

VELERIS, MABEL. Spinto. Argentinean. Resident mem: Teatro Colón, Buenos Aires. Born 8 Dec

1937, Buenos Aires. Husband Miguel Glujovsky, occupation businessman. One child. Studied: Prof Maria Castagna, Roberto Kinsky; Inst of Art, Teatro Colón. **Debut:** Suor Angelica, Teatro Colón 1964. Previous occupations: teacher.
Sang with major companies in ARG: Buenos Aires; BRA: Rio de Janeiro. **Roles with these companies incl** BEETHOVEN: Leonore★ (*Fidelio*); BELLINI: Norma★; BRITTEN: Lady Billows★ (*Albert Herring*); DALLAPICCOLA: Mrs Fabian★ (*Volo di notte*); GIORDANO: Maddalena (*Andrea Chénier*); GLUCK: Iphigénie (*Iphigénie en Tauride*); MASCAGNI: Santuzza (*Cavalleria rusticana*); MENOTTI: Magda Sorel (*Consul*); MOZART: Donna Anna (*Don Giovanni*); ORFF: Sposa★ (*Trionfo di Afrodite*); PONCHIELLI: Gioconda; PUCCINI: Cio-Cio-San (*Butterfly*), Suor Angelica★, Giorgetta★ (*Tabarro*), Tosca★, Liù★ (*Turandot*); VERDI: Aida★, Odabella (*Attila*), Amelia★ (*Ballo in maschera*), Elisabetta (*Don Carlo*), Donna Elvira (*Ernani*), Leonora (*Forza del destino*), Luisa Miller, Lady Macbeth, Amelia (*Simon Boccanegra*), Violetta (*Traviata*), Leonora (*Trovatore*); WAGNER: Senta (*Fliegende Holländer*), Elisabeth (*Tannhäuser*); ZANDONAI: Francesca da Rimini. Also SCHIUMA: Quilla (*Virgenes del sol*). Video/Film: (*Albert Herring*); (*Ballo in maschera*). Gives recitals. Appears with symphony orchestra. **Res:** Billinghurst 1451, Buenos Aires, Argentina. **Mgmt:** GER/ARG.

VELIS, ANDREA. Lyric tenor. American. Resident mem: Metropolitan Opera, New York. Born 7 Jun 1932, New Kensington, PA, USA. Single. Studied: M Louise Taylor, Pittsburgh and New York; Royal Consv of Music, Santa Cecilia Rome, Italy. **Debut:** Goro (*Butterfly*) Pittsburgh Opera 1955. Awards: Grammy & Orpheus Awds.
Sang with major companies in USA: Chicago, Cincinnati, Hartford, Newark, New York Met, Philadelphia Grand & Lyric, Pittsburgh, San Francisco Opera. **Roles with these companies incl** BERG: Hauptmann★ (*Wozzeck*); BRITTEN: Nebuchadnezzar★ (*Burning Fiery Furnace*), Madwoman★ (*Curlew River*), Tempter★ (*Prodigal Son*); HAYDN: Osmin★ (*Incontro improvviso*); HUMPERDINCK: Hexe (*Hänsel und Gretel*); MONTEVERDI: Testo★ (*Combattimento di Tancredi*); MUSSORGSKY: Shuisky★ (*Boris Godunov*); WAGNER: Mime (*Rheingold*). Also MUSSORGSKY: Simpleton★ (*Boris Godunov*). **World premieres:** BARBER: Mardian (*Antony and Cleopatra*) Metropolitan Opera 1966. Recorded for: Columbia. Gives recitals. Appears with symphony orchestra. Coaches repertoire. **Res:** New York, USA.

VELTRI, MICHELANGELO. Conductor of opera and symphony. Argentinean. Resident Cond, Fest Internazionale, Opera Caracas, Venezuela. Born 18 Aug 1940, Buenos Aires. Wife Maria Esther. Studied: Consv Manuel de Falla, Buenos Aires; incl piano, violin and voice. Plays the piano. Operatic training as repetiteur, asst cond & chorus master at Teatro Colón, Buenos Aires 1960-65. **Operatic debut:** *Trovatore* Teatro Colón 1964. Symphonic debut: Sinfonica Venezuela, Caracas 1972. Previous occupations: medical student. Awards: Gold Medal, Asoc Musica, Buenos Aires 1965; Silver Medal, Opera Mexico 1967.

Conducted with major companies in ARG: Buenos Aires; AUS: Vienna Staatsoper; FRA: Marseille; ITA: Milan La Scala, Trieste; MEX: Mexico City; POR: Lisbon; SPA: Barcelona, Majorca; USA: New York Met, Seattle. **Operas with these companies incl** BELLINI: *Norma**, *Puritani**, *Sonnambula**; BIZET: *Carmen**; CATALANI: *Wally**; CILEA: *A. Lecouvreur**; DONIZETTI: *Lucia**; GIORDANO: *Andrea Chénier**; LEONCAVALLO: *Pagliacci**; MASCAGNI: *Cavalleria rusticana**; PUCCINI: *Bohème**, *Butterfly**, *Manon Lescaut**, *Rondine**, *Tabarro**, *Tosca**, *Turandot**; ROSSINI: *Barbiere di Siviglia**; SAINT-SAENS: *Samson et Dalila**; VERDI: *Aida**, *Ballo in maschera**, *Don Carlo**, *Ernani**, *Falstaff**, *Forza del destino**, *Macbeth**, *Nabucco**, *Otello**, *Rigoletto**, *Simon Boccanegra**, *Traviata**, *Trovatore**, *Vespri**. Video/Film: *Rondine, Tosca, Butterfly, Puritani;* all Teatro Colón prods. Conducted major orch in Cent/S America. Teaches privately. **Res:** V Sangallo 29, Milan, Italy. Mgmt: CDA/ARG.

VENTO, MARC. Bass-baritone. French. Born 30 May 1936, Ollioules, France. Wife Claudie Jacquelin, occupation prof of dance. Studied: Consv de Toulouse, Mme Shauny-Lasson; Consv Ntl de Paris, J Giraudeau, L Noguera, acting. **Debut:** Nilakantha (*Lakmé*) Toulouse Opera 1959. Awards: Grand Prize, Consv de Toulouse 1958; First Prize in Voice, Interpretation and Diction Consv de Paris 1961; First Prize Opéra Comique, Paris.

Sang with major companies in BEL: Brussels, Liège; BRA: Rio de Janeiro; FRA: Aix-en-Provence Fest, Bordeaux, Lyon, Marseille, Nancy, Paris, Rouen, Strasbourg, Toulouse; FR GER: Karlsruhe; ITA: Milan La Scala, Naples, Palermo, Rome Opera; MON: Monte Carlo; POL: Warsaw; POR: Lisbon. **Roles with these companies incl** ADAM: Bijou (*Postillon de Lonjumeau*); BECAUD: MacGreagh (*Opéra d'Aran*); BERLIOZ: Narbal (*Troyens*); BIZET: Escamillo* (*Carmen*); BOIELDIEU: Gaveston (*Dame blanche*); BORODIN: Galitzky (*Prince Igor*); DEBUSSY: Golaud* (*Pelléas et Mélisande*); DELIBES: Nilakantha (*Lakmé*); DONIZETTI: Sulpice (*Fille du régiment*); FALLA: Don Quixote (*Retablo de Maese Pedro*); GLUCK: High Priest (*Alceste*); GOUNOD: Méphistophélès (*Faust*), Ramon* (*Mireille*); MOZART: Don Giovanni, Conte Almaviva (*Nozze di Figaro*); MUSSORGSKY: Boris Godunov, Tzigane (*Fair at Sorochinsk*); OFFENBACH: Coppélius etc* (*Contes d'Hoffmann*); PROKOFIEV: Leandro (*Love for Three Oranges*); PUCCINI: Colline* (*Bohème*); RABAUD: Sultan (*Mârouf*); ROSSELLINI: Pierre de Craon* (*Annonce faite à Marie*); ROSSINI: Don Basilio* (*Barbiere di Siviglia*), Conte Asdrubal* (*Pietra del paragone*); VERDI: Philip II (*Don Carlo*). Also LANDOWSKY: Le Prince (*Le Fou*); DAMASE: Julien (*Colombe*). **World premieres:** SEMENOFF: Cristobal (*Evangeline*) Mulhouse 1963; DUHAMEL: Le Rital (*Lundi Monsieur vous serez riche*) Théâtre de la Renaissance, Paris 1968; CHARPENTIER: L'Avesque (*Béatris*) Aix-en-Provence Fest 1971; DAMASE: Mr Henri (*Eurydice*) Bordeaux Fest 1972; Dr Sloper (*L'Héritière*) Nancy Fest 1974; BENTOIU: Le Roi (*Hamlet*) Marseille 1974. Recorded for: CBS. Video/Film – ORTF TV: L'ami (*Pauvre matelot*). Mgmt: BCP/FRA.

VERCHI, NINO GIOVANNI. Conductor of opera and symphony; composer. Italian. Born 21 Feb 1921, Trieste. Wife Nella. Two children. Studied: Consv Trieste; incl piano. Operatic training as repetiteur & asst cond at var Italian theaters 1937-47; La Scala, Milan 1947-52. **Operatic debut:** *Consul* Teatro Verdi, Trieste 1952.

Conducted with major companies in AUS: Vienna Staatsoper; BRA: Rio de Janeiro; CAN: Toronto; FRA: Nancy; FR GER: Hamburg, Karlsruhe, Mannheim, Wiesbaden; ITA: Bologna, Genoa, Milan La Scala, Naples, Palermo, Rome Opera & Caracalla, Trieste, Turin, Venice, Verona Arena; POR: Lisbon; SPA: Barcelona; USA: New York Met; YUG: Dubrovnik, Belgrade. **Operas with these companies incl** BELLINI: *Norma**, *Puritani**, *Sonnambula*‡; BIZET: *Carmen**; BOITO: *Mefistofele*; BRITTEN: *Peter Grimes;* CILEA: *A. Lecouvreur**; CIMAROSA: *Matrimonio segreto;* DONIZETTI: *Anna Bolena, Don Pasquale**‡, *Elisir**, *Favorite**, *Linda di Chamounix**, *Lucia, Maria Stuarda**, *Rita**; FLOTOW: *Martha;* GIORDANO: *Andrea Chénier, Fedora;* GOUNOD: *Faust;* LEONCAVALLO: *Pagliacci**; MASCAGNI: *Cavalleria rusticana**; MASSENET: *Manon**, *Werther;* MENOTTI: *Amahl, Amelia al ballo, Consul, Medium, Saint of Bleecker Street;* OFFENBACH: *Contes d'Hoffmann;* PONCHIELLI: *Gioconda;* PUCCINI: *Bohème**, *Fanciulla del West**, *Gianni Schicchi, Butterfly**, *Manon Lescaut**, *Rondine, Suor Angelica, Tosca**, *Turandot**; ROSSINI: *Barbiere di Siviglia**, *Cenerentola;* SAINT-SAENS: *Samson et Dalila;* STRAUSS, R: *Arabella;* STRAVINSKY: *Mavra;* VERDI: *Aida**, *Ballo in maschera**, *Don Carlo**, *Ernani**, *Falstaff, Forza del destino**, *Giovanna d'Arco, Luisa Miller, Otello**, *Rigoletto**, *Simon Boccanegra**, *Traviata**, *Trovatore**; WOLF-FERRARI: *Quattro rusteghi**; ZANDONAI: *Francesca da Rimini**. Recorded for Fratelli Fabbri. **Operas composed:** *Dramma della Crocifissione, Lauda della Natività, Pik Badaluk* all at RAI, Italy 1944-68; *Liriche* Teatro Nuovo, Milan 1952. Teaches. **Res:** V Panzeri 5, Milan, Italy.

VERMEERSCH, JEF. Dramatic baritone. Belgian. Resident mem: Deutsche Oper, Berlin. Born 7 Feb 1928, Bruges, Belgium. Wife Ursula Spiller. One child. Studied: Achiel van Beveren, Antwerp; Koninklijk Muziekkonsv, Ghent, Belgium. **Debut:** Wotan (*Rheingold*) Royal Flemish Opera 1961.

Sang with major companies in AUS: Graz, Salzburg Fest, Vienna Staatsoper; BEL: Brussels; CZE: Prague National; FRA: Bordeaux, Lyon, Nancy, Nice, Rouen, Toulouse; GRE: Athens National; FR GER: Berlin Deutsche Oper, Bielefeld, Cologne, Dortmund, Düsseldorf-Duisburg, Frankfurt, Hamburg, Hannover, Karlsruhe, Mannheim, Munich Staatsoper, Stuttgart; GER DR: Berlin Staatsoper; HOL: Amsterdam; ITA: Genoa, Palermo, Venice; POR: Lisbon; SPA: Barcelona; SWE: Stockholm; SWI: Geneva; USA: San Francisco Opera. **Roles with these companies incl** d'ALBERT: Sebastiano* & Tommaso (*Tiefland*); BEETHOVEN: Don Pizarro* (*Fidelio*); BOIELDIEU: Gaveston* (*Dame blanche*);

BORODIN: Prince Igor*; BRITTEN: Theseus (*Midsummer Night*); DEBUSSY: Golaud (*Pelléas et Mélisande*); DELIBES: Nilakantha (*Lakmé*); DONIZETTI: Don Pasquale, Baldassare (*Favorite*); EINEM: St Just (*Dantons Tod*); FALLA: Don Quixote (*Retablo de Maese Pedro*); HANDEL: Giulio Cesare; HINDEMITH: Professor (*Hin und zurück*), Roderick (*Long Christmas Dinner*); LORTZING: Baculus (*Wildschütz*), Van Bett (*Zar und Zimmermann*); MOZART: Leporello (*Don Giovanni*), Figaro (*Nozze di Figaro*); MUSSORGSKY: Boris* & Varlaam (*Boris Godunov*); OFFENBACH: Coppélius etc (*Contes d'Hoffmann*) ; PUCCINI: Gianni Schicchi; ROSSINI: Dott Bartolo (*Barbiere di Siviglia*), Conte Asdrubal (*Pietra del paragone*); SAINT-SAENS: Grand prêtre* (*Samson et Dalila*); STRAUSS, R: Musiklehrer (*Ariadne auf Naxos*), La Roche (*Capriccio*), Orest* (*Elektra*), Jochanaan* (*Salome*); VERDI: Amonasro* (*Aida*), Philip II (*Don Carlo*), Falstaff, Zaccaria (*Nabucco*); WAGNER: Holländer*, König Heinrich (*Lohengrin*), Hans Sachs* (*Meistersinger*), Amfortas* & Gurnemanz (*Parsifal*), Wotan (*Rheingold**, *Walküre**), Wanderer* (*Siegfried*), Hagen (*Götterdämmerung*), Kurwenal* (*Tristan und Isolde*); WEBER: Kaspar* (*Freischütz*). Also HINDEMITH: Keppler (*Harmonie der Welt*); PFITZNER: Carlo Borromeo (*Palestrina*); PIZZETTI: Thomas à Becket (*Assassinio nella cattedrale*); TIPPETT: King Fisher (*Midsummer Marriage*). Gives recitals. Appears with symphony orchestra. **Res:** Kurfürstendamm 59/60, 1 Berlin 15, FR Ger. Mgmt: SLZ/FRG.

VERRETT, SHIRLEY. Lyric & dramatic mezzo-soprano. American. Resident mem: Metropolitan Opera, New York. Born 31 May 1931, New Orleans, LA. Husband Louis LoMonaco, occupation painter; professor. One child. Studied: Anna Fitziu, Hollywood; Juilliard School of Music, Mme Marion Freschl, New York. **Debut:** Zigeunerin (*Rasputins Tod*) Cologne Opera 1959-60. Previous occupations: real estate sales agent. Awards: Naumburg Awd; Marian Anderson Awd; John Hay Whitney Fllshp; Ford Fndt Fllshp; M B Rockefeller Fund grant.
   Sang with major companies in AUS: Vienna Staatsoper; CAN: Montreal/Quebec; FRA: Paris; FR GER: Cologne; ITA: Florence Maggio & Comunale, Milan La Scala, Naples, Spoleto Fest; SPA: Barcelona; SWI: Geneva; UK: London Royal; USSR: Kiev, Moscow Bolshoi; USA: Cincinnati, Dallas, New York Met & City Opera, Philadelphia Grand, Pittsburgh, San Francisco Opera, Washington DC. **Roles with these companies incl** BARTOK: Judith* (*Bluebeard's Castle*); BERLIOZ: Cassandre* & Didon*‡ (*Troyens*); BIZET: Carmen*; BRITTEN: Lucretia (*Rape of Lucretia*); DONIZETTI: Léonore (*Favorite*), Elisabetta (*Maria Stuarda*); GLUCK: Orfeo*‡; ROSSINI: Neocle*‡ (*Assedio di Corinto*); SAINT-SAENS: Dalila*; STRAVINSKY: Jocasta‡ (*Oedipus Rex*); VERDI: Amneris (*Aida*), Ulrica‡ (*Ballo in maschera*), Eboli‡ (*Don Carlo*), Federica‡ (*Luisa Miller*), Azucena (*Trovatore*). Also MEYERBEER: Selika (*Africaine*); VERDI: Lady Macbeth. Recorded for: EMI/Angel, RCA, ABC, Columbia. On records only BELLINI: Adalgisa (*Norma*); DONIZETTI: Giovanna (*Anna Bolena*), Maffio Orsini (*Lucrezia Borgia*);

ROSSINI: Sinaïde (*Moïse*); VERDI: Preziosilla (*Forza del destino*). Gives recitals. Appears with symphony orchestra. **Res:** New York, NY, USA. Mgmt: HUR/USA; AIM/UK.

VESELÁ, MARIE; née Kozousková. Dramatic mezzo-soprano. Czechoslovakian. Resident mem: National Theater, Prague. Born 7 Apr 1935, Polesony, CSR. Husband Ludvík Vesely, occupation officer. Studied: Prof Terezie Blumová; Music Acad, Prof Premysl Kocí, Prague. **Debut:** Ulrica (*Ballo in maschera*) National Theater, Prague 1967.
   Sang with major companies in CZE: Prague National. **Roles with these companies incl** DVORAK: Kate* (*Devil and Kate*), Jezibaba* (*Rusalka*); MOZART: Dorabella* (*Così fan tutte*), Cherubino* (*Nozze di Figaro*); SMETANA: Roza* (*Secret*); TCHAIKOVSKY: Olga* (*Eugene Onegin*); VERDI: Ulrica* (*Ballo in maschera*). Also SMETANA: Zavis* (*Devil's Wall*); OFFENBACH: Nicklausse* (*Contes d'Hoffmann*); TCHAIKOVSKY: Pauline* (*Pique Dame*); FIBICH: Vlasta* (*Sarka*). Gives recitals. Appears with symphony orchestra. Teaches voice. **Res:** Dubecská 18, 100 00 Prague 10, CSSR. Mgmt: PRG/CZE.

VICKERS, JON. Heldentenor. Canadian. Born 29 Oct 1926, Prince Albert, Sask. Married. Five children. Studied: Royal Consv, George Lambert, Toronto. **Debut:** Aeneas (*Troyens*) Royal Opera London 1956. Previous occupations: gen mng, Woolworth's, Winnipeg; sang church music and oratorio.
   Sang with major companies in AUS: Salzburg Fest, Vienna Staatsoper; CAN: Montreal/Quebec, Toronto, Vancouver; FRA: Orange Fest; FR GER: Bayreuth Fest; ITA: Milan La Scala; UK: London Royal; USA: Chicago, Dallas, Houston, New York Met, Philadelphia Lyric, San Francisco Opera; et al. **Roles with these companies incl** BEETHOVEN: Florestan‡ (*Fidelio*); BERLIOZ: Benvenuto Cellini, Aeneas‡ (*Troyens*); BIZET: Don José‡ (*Carmen*); BRITTEN: Peter Grimes, Male Chorus (*Rape of Lucretia*); CHERUBINI: Giasone (*Medea*); GIORDANO: Andrea Chénier; JANACEK: Laca (*Jenufa*); LEONCAVALLO: Canio (*Pagliacci*); MOZART: Don Ottavio (*Don Giovanni*); PURCELL: Aeneas; SAINT-SAENS: Samson‡; STRAUSS, R: Herodes (*Salome*); TCHAIKOVSKY: Gherman (*Pique Dame*); VERDI: Radames‡ (*Aida*), Riccardo (*Ballo in maschera*), Don Carlo, Don Alvaro (*Forza del destino*), Otello‡, Duca di Mantova (*Rigoletto*), Alfredo (*Traviata*); WAGNER: Erik (*Fliegende Holländer*), Lohengrin, Parsifal, Siegmund‡ (*Walküre*), Tristan‡; et al. Recorded for: RCA, Angel, DG, London. Video/Film: Don José (*Carmen*); Otello; Canio (*Pagliacci*). Gives recitals. Appears with symphony orchestra.

VIITANEN, USKO SAMUEL. Dramatic baritone. Finnish. Resident mem: Finnish National Opera, Helsinki. Born 23 Feb 1928, Orimattila, Finland. Wife Laristo Virpi, occupation solo dancer, Ntl Ballet. Studied: Music Acad Lahti, Lea Piltti, Finland; Martin Öhman, Stockholm; Karl Hudez, Vienna; Luigi Ricci, Rome. **Debut:** Arsamene (*Xerxes*) Finnish National Opera, Helsinki 1958.

Previous occupations: played in dance band. Awards: Pro Finlandia, Pres of Finland.

Sang with major companies in BUL: Sofia; FIN: Helsinki; GER DR: Berlin Staatsoper; HUN: Budapest; NOR: Oslo; ROM: Bucharest; SWE: Stockholm. Roles with these companies incl DONIZETTI: Belcore (Elisir); HANDEL: Arsamene (Xerxes); HAYDN: Buonafede (Mondo della luna); LEONCAVALLO: Tonio★ (Pagliacci); MOZART: Papageno (Zauberflöte); PUCCINI: Marcello★ (Bohème), Jack Rance★ (Fanciulla del West), Sharpless (Butterfly), Scarpia★ (Tosca); ROSSINI: Figaro★ (Barbiere di Siviglia); TCHAIKOVSKY: Yeletsky (Pique Dame); VERDI: Renato★ (Ballo in maschera), Rodrigo★ (Don Carlo), Ford (Falstaff), Don Carlo (Forza del destino), Iago★ (Otello), Rigoletto★, Germont (Traviata), Conte di Luna★ (Trovatore); WAGNER: Amfortas (Parsifal), Wolfram (Tannhäuser). Also MADETOJA: Anttj (Ostrobothnians). World premieres: PYLKKANEN: Hietanen (Unknown Soldier) Finnish National Opera, Helsinki 1967. Finnish TV: Rigoletto, Tonio (Pagliacci). Gives recitals. Appears with symphony orchestra. Res: Takametsäntie 2 B, Helsinki, Finland.

VILLAGROSSI, FERRUCCIO FERDINANDO. Scenic and costume designer for opera & theater. Is a lighting designer; also an interior decorator. Italian. Born 14 Apr 1937, Milan. Single. Studied: Liceo Artistico Beato Angelico; Accad Cimabue, Milan. Prof training: asst to Attilio Colonnello. **Operatic debut:** Trovatore Teatro Sociale, Como. Theater debut: Teatro Nuovo, Milan 1970. Awards: Noce d'oro, Lecco 1970.

Designed for major companies in ITA: Genoa, Parma, Rome Teatro dell'Opera, Trieste, Turin, Venice, Verona Arena; SPA: Barcelona; USA: San Francisco Opera. Operas designed for these companies incl BELLINI: Beatrice di Tenda; BIZET: Carmen; CATALANI: Wally; CILEA: Adriana Lecouvreur; DALLAPICCOLA: Volo di notte; DONIZETTI: Fille du régiment, Lucia; MASCAGNI: Amico Fritz; MONTEVERDI: Favola d'Orfeo; MOZART: Nozze di Figaro; PUCCINI: Bohème; ROSSINI: Cenerentola, Italiana in Algeri; SHOSTAKOVICH: Katerina Ismailova; SPONTINI: Vesfale; VERDI: Luisa Miller, Traviata. Operatic world premieres: FERRARI: Lord Savile Treviso, Italy 1970. Res: Corso XXII Marzo 4, Milan, Italy.

VILMA, MICHÈLE. Dramatic mezzo-soprano. French. Single. Studied: Consv de Rouen, France. Debut: Dalila, Rouen Opera 1962.

Sang with major companies in BEL: Brussels, Liège; FRA: Aix-en-Provence, Bordeaux, Lyon, Marseille, Nancy, Nice, Paris, Rouen, Strasbourg, Toulouse; GRE: Athens National; FR GER: Bayreuth Fest, Cologne; MON: Monte Carlo; POR: Lisbon; SWI: Geneva; USA: Boston, New York Met. Roles with these companies incl BELLINI: Adalgisa★ (Norma); BERLIOZ: Marguerite (Damnation de Faust), Cassandre★& Anna★ (Troyens); BIZET: Carmen★; BORODIN: Kontchakovna★ (Prince Igor); CILEA: Princesse de Bouillon★ (A. Lecouvreur); DEBUSSY: Geneviève★ (Pelléas et Mélisande); DONIZETTI: Giovanna★ (Anna Bolena), Léonore★ (Favorite); GLUCK: Clytemnestre★ (Iphigénie en Aulide),

Orfeo★; LALO: Margared★ (Roi d'Ys); MASSENET: Dulcinée★ (Don Quichotte), Hérodiade★, Charlotte★ (Werther); MEYERBEER: Fidès★ (Prophète); MUSSORGSKY: Marina★ (Boris Godunov); PONCHIELLI: Laura★ (Gioconda); POULENC: Mère Marie★ & Prioresse★ (Dialogues des Carmélites); PUCCINI: Principessa★ (Suor Angelica); SAINT-SAENS: Dalila★; TCHAIKOVSKY: Comtesse★ (Pique Dame); VERDI: Amneris★ (Aida), Ulrica★ (Ballo in maschera), Eboli★ (Don Carlo), Preziosilla★ (Forza del destino), Azucena★ (Trovatore); WAGNER: Ortrud (Lohengrin), Kundry★ (Parsifal), Erda (Rheingold★, Siegfried★), Fricka (Rheingold★, Walküre★), Waltraute★ (Götterdämmerung), Venus★ (Tannhäuser), Brangäne★ (Tristan und Isolde). Also MASCAGNI: Santuzza (Cavalleria rusticana); GLUCK: Iphigénie (Iphigénie en Tauride); MEYERBEER: Selika (Africaine); MONTEVERDI: Ottavia & Arnalta (Incoronazione di Poppea); ROUSSEL: Padmâvati. Recorded for: Angel. Res: Paris, France. Mgmt: SFM/USA.

VINCENZI, EDO. Italian. Adm Secy, Ente Autonomo Lirico Arena di Verona, Piazza Bra' 28, Verona, Italy. In charge of adm, art, tech & musical matters. Born 26 Aug 1921, Bigarello/Mantua, Italy. Married. Studied: music and voice. Plays the piano. Previous positions primarily musical & theatrical. Started with present company 1948 as Asst Secy, in present position since 1968. Awards: Cavaliere & Cavaliere Ufficiale al Merito, and Commendatore, Rep of Italy.

VINCO, IVO. Bass. Italian. Born 8 Nov 1927, Verona. Wife Fiorenza Cossotto, occupation opera singer. One child. Studied: Liceo Musicale Verona, Signora Zilotti; Teatro alla Scala, Mo Campogalliani. Debut: Ramfis (Aida) Verona Opera 1954. Awards: Cavaliere and Commendatore, Rep of Italy.

Sang with major companies in ARG: Buenos Aires; AUS: Vienna Staatsoper; BEL: Brussels; CAN: Montreal/Quebec; FRA: Bordeaux, Nice, Paris; FR GER: Berlin Deutsche Oper, Hamburg, Munich Staatsoper, Wiesbaden; GER DR: Berlin Komische Oper; ITA: Bologna, Florence Maggio & Comunale, Genoa, Milan La Scala, Naples, Palermo, Parma, Rome Opera & Caracalla, Trieste, Turin, Venice, Verona Arena; MEX: Mexico City; MON: Monte Carlo; POR: Lisbon; SPA: Barcelona, Majorca; USSR: Moscow Bolshoi; USA: Chicago, Miami, NY Met, Seattle. Roles with these companies incl BELLINI: Oroveso★ (Norma), Sir George★ (Puritani), Rodolfo★ (Sonnambula); BOITO: Mefistofele; DONIZETTI: Henry VIII★ (Anna Bolena), Don Pasquale★, Dulcamara★ (Elisir), Baldassare★ (Favorite), Enrico★‡ (Lucia); MEYERBEER: Don Pedro★ (Africaine); MONTEMEZZI: Archibaldo★ (Amore dei tre re); MOZART: Sarastro★ (Zauberflöte); MUSSORGSKY: Pimen★ (Boris Godunov), Dosifei★ (Khovanshchina); PONCHIELLI: Alvise★‡ (Gioconda); PUCCINI: Colline★ (Bohème); ROSSINI: Don Basilio★ (Barbiere di Siviglia), Don Magnifico★ (Cenerentola), Gaudenzio★ (Signor Bruschino); STRAVINSKY: Creon★ (Oedipus Rex); VERDI: Ramfis★ (Aida), Philip II★ & Grande Inquisitore★‡ (Don Carlo), Silva★ (Ernani), Padre Guardiano★ (Forza del destino), Banquo★ (*Macbeth*), Zaccaria★ (*Nabucco*), Fiesco★ (*Simon Boccanegra*); WAGNER: Daland★ (*Fliegende Holländer*), König Heinrich★ (*Lohengrin*), Pogner★ (*Meistersinger*), Landgraf★ (*Tannhäuser*); WOLF-FERRARI: Lunardo★ (*Quattro rusteghi*). Also PUCCINI: Timur (*Turandot*); ROSSINI: Conte (*Pietra del paragone*); WAGNER: Klingsor (*Parsifal*). Recorded for: EMI, Ricordi, DG. Video/Film: Colline (*Bohème*); Oroveso (*Norma*); Ramfis (*Aida*). Gives recitals. Appears with symphony orchestra. Res: V E Biondi 1, Milan, Italy.

VINZING, UTE. Dramatic soprano. German. Resident mem: Städtische Oper, Wuppertal.
Sang with major companies in AUS: Bregenz Fest; FR GER: Hannover, Nürnberg, Wuppertal; et al. **Roles with these companies incl** BEETHOVEN: Leonore (*Fidelio*); WAGNER: Senta (*Fliegende Holländer*), Elsa (*Lohengrin*), Sieglinde & Brünnhilde (*Walküre*), Brünnhilde (*Siegfried*, *Götterdämmerung*), Elisabeth (*Tannhäuser*), Isolde; et al.

VISCONTI, LUCHINO. Stages/produces opera, theater & film. Also designs sets and is an actor & author. Italian. Born 2 Nov 1906, Italy. Studied: music & cello. Asst to Jean Renoir in films. **Operatic debut:** *Vestale* La Scala, Milan 1954. Film debut: Italy 1943.
Directed/produced opera for major companies in AUS: Vienna Staatsoper; FR GER: Berlin Deutsche Oper, Hamburg; ITA: Milan La Scala, Palermo, Rome Opera, Spoleto Fest; UK: Edinburgh Fest, Glyndebourne Fest, London Royal; et al. **Operas staged with these companies incl** BELLINI: *Sonnambula;* DONIZETTI: *Anna Bolena;* GLUCK: *Iphigénie en Tauride;* MOZART: *Nozze di Figaro;* PUCCINI: *Manon Lescaut;* STRAUSS, R: *Rosenkavalier, Salome;* VERDI: *Don Carlo, Falstaff, Macbeth, Simon Boccanegra†, Traviata, Trovatore;* WAGNER: *Tristan und Isolde;* et al. Also DONIZETTI: *Duca d'Alba.* **Operatic world premieres:** MANNINO: *Diavolo nel giardino* Palermo 1963. **Opera libretti:** *Diavolo nel giardino,* see prem. **Res:** Rome, Italy.

VISHNEVSKAYA, GALINA. Lyric & dramatic soprano. Russian. Born 25 Oct 1926, Leningrad. Husband Mstislav Rostropovich, occupation cellist & conductor. Two children. Studied: Consv Leningrad, Mme Garina. **Debut:** STRELNIKOV: (*Kholopka*) Leningrad 1952. Awards: Grand Prix de l'Académie du disque.
Sang with major companies in AUS: Vienna Staatsoper; FR GER: Berlin Deutsche Oper; UK: London Royal; USSR: Moscow Bolshoi Opera; USA: New York Metropolitan Opera, San Francisco Opera; et al. **Roles with these companies incl** BEETHOVEN: Leonore (*Fidelio*); GOUNOD: Marguerite (*Faust*); MOZART: Cherubino (*Nozze di Figaro*); MUSSORGSKY: Marina‡ (*Boris Godunov*); PROKOFIEV: Natasha‡ (*War and Peace*); PUCCINI: Cio-Cio-San (*Butterfly*), Tosca; RIMSKY-KORSAKOV: Martha‡ (*Tsar's Bride*); SHOSTAKOVICH: Katerina Ismailova; TCHAIKOVSKY: Tatiana (*Eugene Onegin*), Lisa (*Pique Dame*); VERDI: Aida, Alice Ford (*Falstaff*); et al. Recorded for: London, Melodiya.

Video/Film: Katerina Ismailova. Gives recitals. Appears with symphony orchestra. Mgmt: HUR/USA.

VISSER, LIEUWE. Bass. Dutch. Resident mem: Netherlands Opera, Amsterdam. Born 23 Aug 1940, Diemen, Holland. Wife Anneke Uittenbosch, occupation harpsichordist. One child. Studied: Jo van de Meent, Amsterdam; Accad di Santa Cecilia, Giorgio Favaretto, Rome. **Debut:** Don Basilio (*Barbiere di Siviglia*) Netherlands Opera, Amsterdam 1973. Previous occupations: historian. Awards: Gold Medal Intl Voice Compt Toulouse, France.
Sang with major companies in FRA: Toulouse; HOL: Amsterdam. **Roles with these companies incl** DONIZETTI: Dulcamara★ (*Elisir*), Gasparo (*Rita*); GALUPPI: Don Tritemio★ (*Filosofo di campagna*); HANDEL: Ptolemy (*Giulio Cesare*); HOLST: Death★ (*Savitri*); LORTZING: Van Bett (*Zar und Zimmermann*); MOZART: Don Alfonso (*Così fan tutte*); ROSSINI: Don Basilio★ (*Barbiere di Siviglia*); VERDI: Zaccaria★ (*Nabucco*). Also PAISIELLO: Basilio★ (*Barbiere di Siviglia*); MONTEVERDI: Pluto★ (*Ballo delle ingrate*). **World premieres:** KOX: Basil Hallward (*Picture of Dorian Gray*) Netherlands Opera 1974. Gives recitals. Appears with symphony orchestra. Mgmt: NIM/HOL; HBM/USA.

VITKOVÁ, BLANKA. Lyric mezzo-soprano. Czechoslovakian. Resident mem: National Theater, Prague. Born 14 Nov 1948, Prague, CSR. Husband Oldrich Král, occupation singer. One child. Studied: State Consv Prague, Prof Miluse Fidlerová. **Debut:** Jezibaba (*Rusalka*) National Theater, Prague 1972.
Sang with major companies in CZE: Prague National. **Roles with these companies incl** DVORAK: Jezibaba★ (*Rusalka*); MOZART: Cherubino★ (*Nozze di Figaro*); PUCCINI: Suzuki★ (*Butterfly*); SMETANA: Roza★ (*Secret*); TCHAIKOVSKY: Olga★ (*Eugene Onegin*); VERDI: Ulrica★ (*Ballo in maschera*). Also PROKOFIEV: Sonia★ (*War and Peace*). Gives recitals. Appears with symphony orchestra. Res: Komsomolská 16/924, Prague, CSSR. Mgmt: PRG/CZE.

VIVIENNE, HAZEL. Conductor of opera and symphony. British. After fall 1975 Head of Music Staff & Resident Cond, English National Opera, London. Born 14 Jul 1934, Bromborough, Cheshire. Single. Studied: Royal Manchester Coll of Music, Grahame Clifford, voice; Lucy Pierce, piano. Plays the piano, organ, celeste. Ballet rehearsal pianist, Sadler's Wells 1956-58; repetiteur, English Ntl Opera 1959-64; chorus master since 1964. **Dramatic debut:** *Penny for a Song* Sadler's Wells, London 1967. Awards: Fellow Royal Manchester Coll of Music.
Conducted with major companies in UK: London English National. **Operas with these companies incl** BRITTEN: *Gloriana★;* MONTEVERDI: *Favola d'Orfeo, Incoronazione di Poppea★;* ROSSINI: *Comte Ory★, Italiana in Algeri.* Also BENNETT: *Penny for a Song★;* HANDEL: *Semele★.* Res: London, UK.

VOGEL, BARBARA. Lyric soprano. German. Resident mem: Deutsche Oper, Berlin. Born Berlin, Germany. Husband Hans-Ludwig Spohr, occupation physician. Studied: Prof Hugo Diez, Prof Margarete von Winterfeldt, Prof Ira Hartmann. **Debut:** Barbarina (*Nozze di Figaro*) Deutsche Oper, Berlin 1963.

Sang with major companies in ARG: Buenos Aires; BRA: Rio de Janeiro; FRA: Aix-en-Provence Fest, Paris, Strasbourg; FR GER: Berlin Deutsche Oper, Bielefeld, Cologne, Essen, Hannover, Kassel, Mannheim, Nürnberg; POR: Lisbon; SWE: Drottningholm Fest. **Roles with these companies incl** BERG: Lulu★; HENZE: Luise★ (*Junge Lord*); HUMPERDINCK: Gretel★; LORTZING: Gretchen★ (*Wildschütz*), Marie★ (*Zar und Zimmermann*); MENOTTI: Monica★ (*Medium*); MONTEVERDI: Euridice (*Favola d'Orfeo*); MOZART: Despina★ (*Così fan tutte*), Zerlina★ (*Don Giovanni*), Blondchen★ (*Entführung aus dem Serail*), Pamina★ (*Zauberflöte*); WAGNER: Eva★ (*Meistersinger*); WEBER: Aennchen★ (*Freischütz*).

VOGEL, RAYMOND. Stages/produces opera & television and is an actor. French. Resident Stage Dir for theater in Strasbourg. Born 1 Apr 1915, Paris. Wife Marguerite Gaschi, occupation pianist. Studied: Consv National de Paris, incl music and voice. **Operatic debut:** Opéra de Strasbourg 1955.

Directed/produced opera for major companies in FRA: Bordeaux, Lyon, Marseille, Paris, Rouen, Strasbourg, Toulouse; ITA: Naples; SWI: Basel, Geneva. **Operas staged with these companies incl** BIZET: *Carmen, Docteur Miracle;* BOIELDIEU: *Dame blanche★;* BRITTEN: *Albert Herring;* DELIBES: *Lakmé★;* GAY/Britten; *Beggar's Opera★;* GLUCK: *Alceste;* GOUNOD: *Faust, Mireille★;* IBERT: *Angélique;* KODALY: *Háry János;* MASSENET: *Thaïs;* OFFENBACH: *Périchole;* PUCCINI: *Bohème, Fanciulla del West, Butterfly;* STRAUSS, J: *Fledermaus★;* VERDI: *Don Carlo, Falstaff;* WAGNER: *Fliegende Holländer;* WEILL: *Dreigroschenoper★.* Also SEMENOFF: *Evangeline.* **Operatic world premieres:** DUHAMEL: *Lundi, Monsieur, vous serez riche* Strasbourg 1968; SEMENOFF: *Ours* France 1966; TOMASI: *Ulysse* France 1961. **Res:** 7 rue Nicolas Taunay, Paris 14, France. Mgmt: SLZ/FRG.

VOGEL, SIEGFRIED. Bass-baritone. German. Resident mem: Deutsche Staatsoper Berlin, Komische Oper Berlin, Ger DR. Born 6 Mar 1937, Chemnitz. Wife Erika Stahr, occupation opera singer. One child. Studied: Musikhochschule Dresden, Prof Johannes Kemter. **Debut:** Zizell (*Si j'étais roi*) Staatsoper Dresden 1959. Awards: Kammersänger and Nationalpreisträger, Ministry for Culture, Ger DR.

Sang with major companies in AUS: Vienna Volksoper; BEL: Brussels; BUL: Sofia; CZE: Prague National; FIN: Helsinki; FRA: Paris; GER DR: Berlin Komische Oper & Staatsoper, Dresden, Leipzig; HOL: Amsterdam; HUN: Budapest; ITA: Milan La Scala, Rome Opera; POL: Warsaw; ROM: Bucharest; SWE: Drottningholm Fest; USSR: Moscow Bolshoi. **Roles with these companies incl** ADAM: Bijou★ (*Postillon de Lonjumeau*); BEETHOVEN: Rocco★ (*Fidelio*); BIZET: Escamillo★ (*Carmen*); GERSHWIN: Crown★ (*Porgy and Bess*); GOUNOD:

Méphistophélès (*Faust*); HANDEL: Ptolemy★ (*Giulio Cesare*); KODALY: Háry János; LORTZING: Baculus (*Wildschütz*), Van Bett (*Zar und Zimmermann*); MONIUSZKO: Janusz (*Halka*); MOZART: Guglielmo & Don Alfonso★ (*Così fan tutte*), Leporello★ & Don Giovanni★ (*Don Giovanni*), Figaro★ (*Nozze di Figaro*), Papageno & Sarastro★ (*Zauberflöte*); MUSSORGSKY: Varlaam★ & Pimen (*Boris Godunov*); OFFENBACH: Coppélius etc (*Contes d'Hoffmann*); PENDERECKI: Grandier (*Teufel von Loudun*); PUCCINI: Colline★ (*Bohème*); ROSSINI: Don Basilio★ (*Barbiere di Siviglia*); SMETANA: Kezal★ (*Bartered Bride*); STRAUSS, R: Baron Ochs★ (*Rosenkavalier*); VERDI: Ramfis★ (*Aida*), Philip II & Grande Inquisitore (*Don Carlo*); WAGNER: Daland★ (*Fliegende Holländer*), König Heinrich★ (*Lohengrin*), Pogner★ (*Meistersinger*), Gurnemanz★ (*Parsifal*), Wotan★ & Fasolt★ (*Rheingold*), Hunding★ (*Walküre*), Landgraf★ (*Tannhäuser*); WEBER: Omar (*Abu Hassan*), Kaspar★ (*Freischütz*). **World premieres:** DESSAU: Lanzelot (*Lanzelot*) 1969; MEYER: Lanny Swarts (*Reiter in der Nacht*) 1973; both Deutsche Staatsoper Berlin; KOCHAN: Baumann (*Karin Lenz*) Komische Oper Berlin 1971. Gives recitals. Appears with symphony orchestra. Mgmt: KDR/GDR; SLZ/FRG.

VOINEA, SILVIA. Coloratura soprano. Romanian. Resident mem: Romanian Opera, Bucharest. Born 1 Nov 1942, Bacau, Romania. Husband Gabriel Homotescu, occupation engineer. Studied: Ciprian Porumbescu Consv, Mmes Magda Janculescu, Viorica Teisanu, Bucharest. **Debut:** Olympia (*Contes d'Hoffmann*) Bucharest 1968.

Sang with major companies in BUL: Sofia; GER DR: Berlin Staatsoper, Leipzig; ROM: Bucharest. **Roles with these companies incl** DELIBES: Lakmé★; DONIZETTI: Norina★ (*Don Pasquale*), Lucia★; GLUCK: Amor★ (*Orfeo ed Euridice*); MOZART: Despina★ (*Così fan tutte*), Konstanze★ & Blondchen★ (*Entführung aus dem Serail*), Mme Herz (*Schauspieldirektor*), Königin der Nacht★ (*Zauberflöte*); OFFENBACH: Olympia★ (*Contes d'Hoffmann*); ROSSINI: Rosina★ (*Barbiere di Siviglia*); STRAUSS, J: Adele★ & Rosalinde★ (*Fledermaus*); STRAVINSKY: Rossignol★; VERDI: Gilda (*Rigoletto*). **Res:** Tincani St 4, 7 Bucharest, Romania. Mgmt: RIA/ROM.

VOKETAITIS, ARNOLD MATHEW. Bass-baritone. American. Resident mem: Lyric Opera of Chicago; New York City Opera. Born 11 May 1931, East Haven, CT, USA. Wife Nijole, occupation fashion model. Two children. Studied: Mo Francesco Riggio, New Haven, CT; Mme Elda Ercole, Leila Edwards, Kurt Saffir, New York; Yale Univ, theater training, New Haven, CT, USA. **Debut:** Vanuzzi (*Schweigsame Frau*) New York City Opera 1958. Previous occupations: cashier, used car salesman, dance band trumpeter, radio announcer. Awards: Rockefeller Fndt Grant; First Place Connecticut Opera Aud of the Air 1957; First Prize First Army Talent, Second Prize All Army.

Sang with major companies in CAN: Montreal/Quebec, Vancouver; MEX: Mexico City; SPA: Barcelona; USA: Chicago, Houston, Miami, Milwaukee Florentine, Minneapolis, New York

City Opera, Omaha, Pittsburgh, San Antonio. **Roles with these companies incl** BARTOK: Bluebeard★; BEETHOVEN: Rocco★ (Fidelio); BRITTEN: Theseus★ (Midsummer Night); DONIZETTI: Dulcamara★ (Elisir), Sulpice★ (Fille du régiment); FLOYD: Olin Blitch★ (Susannah); GOUNOD: Méphistophélès★ (Faust); MASSENET: Phanuel★ (Hérodiade); MOZART: Don Giovanni★, Figaro★ (Nozze di Figaro); MUSSORGSKY: Pimen★ (Boris Godunov); OFFENBACH: Coppélius etc★ (Contes d'Hoffmann); PONCHIELLI: Alvise★ (Gioconda); PROKOFIEV: King of Clubs★ (Love for Three Oranges); PUCCINI: Colline★ (Bohème); ROSSINI: Don Basilio★ (Barbiere di Siviglia), Don Magnifico★ (Cenerentola); THOMSON: St Ignatius★ (Four Saints in Three Acts); VERDI: Ramfis★ (Aida); Jacopo Loredano★ (Due Foscari), Banquo★ (Macbeth); WAGNER: Hunding★ (Walküre); WARD: Rev Hale★ (Crucible); WEBER: Kaspar★ (Freischütz). Also DONIZETTI: Raimondo★ (Lucia). Recorded for: Desto. Video/Film: Paramt Tele Pay TV: Mr Kofner (Consul). Gives recitals. Appears with symphony orchestra. Teaches voice. Coaches repertoire. **Res:** Chicago, IL, USA. Mgmt: LLF/USA.

VON DOHNÁNYI, CHRISTOPH. Conductor of opera and symphony; composer. German. Gen Dir & Principal Cond, Städt Oper, Frankfurt; after Aug 1976 Gen Mus Dir, Staatsoper Hamburg. Also Mus Dir, Museumsorch, Frankfurt. Born 8 Sep 1929, Berlin. Wife Zillessen, occupation actress. Three children. Studied: Musik Hochschule, Munich; Ernst v Dohnányi, USA; incl piano, flute and voice. Operatic training as repetiteur & asst cond at Opera Houses Munich & Frankfurt 1953-57. **Operatic debut:** Opera House Frankfurt 1955. Symphonic debut: Radio Orch, Hannover. Awards: Richard Strauss Prize, Munich. Previous adm positions in opera: Gen Mus Dir, Opera House Lübeck; Gen Mus Dir, Opera House Kassel.

Conducted with major companies in AUS: Salzburg Fest, Vienna Staatsoper; FRA: Paris; GRE: Athens Fest; FR GER: Berlin Deutsche Oper, Cologne, Frankfurt, Kassel, Munich Staatsoper, Stuttgart; UK: Edinburgh Fest, London Royal; USA: Chicago, New York Met, San Francisco Opera. **Operas with these companies incl** BARTOK: Bluebeard's Castle; BEETHOVEN: Fidelio; BENNETT: Mines of Sulphur; BERG: Lulu, Wozzeck; BIZET: Carmen; BUSONI: Arlecchino; CHERUBINI: Medea; DALLAPICCOLA: Prigioniero; DEBUSSY: Pelléas et Mélisande; EINEM: Dantons Tod; GLUCK: Orfeo ed Euridice; GOUNOD: Faust; HAYDN: Infedeltà delusa; KODALY: Háry János; MOZART: Così fan tutte, Don Giovanni, Entführung aus dem Serail, Nozze di Figaro, Zauberflöte; MUSSORGSKY: Boris Godunov; OFFENBACH: Contes d'Hoffmann; ORFF: Carmina burana; PERGOLESI: Serva padrona; PROKOFIEV: Fiery Angel; PUCCINI: Bohème, Gianni Schicchi, Butterfly, Tabarro, Tosca; SCHOENBERG: Erwartung, Moses und Aron; STRAUSS, J: Fledermaus; STRAUSS, R: Arabella, Ariadne auf Naxos, Elektra, Frau ohne Schatten, Rosenkavalier, Salome; STRAVINSKY: Mavra, Oedipus Rex; TCHAIKOV-

SKY: Eugene Onegin; VERDI: Ballo in maschera, Don Carlo, Falstaff, Forza del destino, Macbeth, Otello, Rigoletto; WAGNER: Fliegende Holländer, Lohengrin, Meistersinger, Parsifal, Götterdämmerung, Tannhäuser, Tristan und Isolde; WEBER: Freischütz. Also CIKKER: Christmas Carol; PIZZETTI: Assassinio nella cattedrale; BENNETT: Victory; KODALY: Spinning Room. **World premieres:** HENZE: Junge Lord‡ Deutsche Oper, Berlin 1965; Bassariden Salzburg Fest 1966. Conducted major orch in Europe, USA/Canada. Previous positions as Mus Dir with major orch: Chief Cond, WDR Orch, Cologne. **Res:** Kuckucksweg 17, Königstein i/Ts, FR Ger. Mgmt: KHA/FRG; LSM/UK.

VON HALEM, VICTOR. Bass. German. Resident mem: Deutsche Oper, Berlin. Born 26 Mar 1940, Berlin. Wife Gabriele. One child. Studied: Prof Else Domberger, Staatliche Hochschule für Musik, Munich. **Debut:** Eremit (Freischütz) Deutsche Oper Berlin 1966.

Sang with major companies in AUS: Salzburg Fest; CAN: Montreal/Quebec; FRA: Nancy, Orange Fest; GRE: Athens Fest; FR GER: Berlin Deutsche Oper, Bonn, Cologne, Hamburg, Munich Staatsoper & Gärtnerplatz, Stuttgart; ITA: Genoa, Rome Opera. **Roles with these companies incl** BEETHOVEN: Rocco★ (Fidelio); HANDEL: Polyphemus (Acis and Galatea); MEYERBEER: Comte Oberthal (Prophète); MOZART: Publio★ (Clemenza di Tito), Osmin (Zaïde), Sarastro★ (Zauberflöte); MUSSORGSKY: Varlaam★ (Boris Godunov); PONCHIELLI: Alvise★ (Gioconda); PUCCINI: Colline (Bohème); ROSSINI: Don Basilio★ (Barbiere di Siviglia), Geronio★ (Turco in Italia); STRAVINSKY: Tiresias★ (Oedipus Rex); VERDI: Ramfis★ (Aida), Grande Inquisitore★ (Don Carlo), Padre Guardiano★ (Forza del destino); WAGNER: Daland★ (Fliegende Holländer), König Heinrich★ (Lohengrin), Pogner★ (Meistersinger), Fasolt★ (Rheingold), Fafner (Rheingold★, Siegfried★). Gives recitals. Appears with symphony orchestra. **Res:** Salzbrunner Str 29, 1 Berlin 33, FR Ger. Mgmt: SLZ/FRG; OOC/FRA.

VON JORDIS, EELCO; né Eelco Voet van Vormizeele. Bass-baritone & bass. German. Born 11 May 1942, Graz, Austria. Single. Studied: Studio della Scala, A Granforte, Milan; Dusolina Giannini, Zurich; Hochschule für Musik, Graz, Austria. **Debut:** Frate (Don Carlo) Graz 1965-66.

Sang with major companies in AUS: Graz; BEL: Brussels; FR GER: Bielefeld, Düsseldorf-Duisburg, Kassel; ITA: Milan La Scala; YUG: Zagreb. **Roles with these companies incl** BEETHOVEN: Don Pizarro (Fidelio); BERG: Doktor (Wozzeck); BIZET: Escamillo★ (Carmen); BORODIN: Galitzky (Prince Igor); BRITTEN: Theseus (Midsummer Night); CORNELIUS: Abul Hassan (Barbier von Bagdad); DONIZETTI: Dulcamara★ (Elisir); EINEM: St Just (Dantons Tod); GOUNOD: Méphistophélès★ (Faust); LORTZING: Stadinger (Waffenschmied), Van Bett (Zar und Zimmermann); MASCAGNI: Alfio (Cavalleria rusticana); MOZART: Don Alfonso (Così fan tutte), Don Giovanni★, Sarastro★ (Zauber-

flöte); MUSSORGSKY: Boris; OFFENBACH: Coppélius etc (*Contes d'Hoffmann*); ORFF: Bauer (*Mond*); PUCCINI: Colline★ (*Bohème*), Scarpia (*Tosca*); RIMSKY-KORSAKOV: Roi Dodon (*Coq d'or*); ROSSINI: Dott Bartolo (*Barbiere di Siviglia*), Mustafà (*Italiana in Algeri*); SMETANA: Kezal (*Bartered Bride*); STRAVINSKY: Empereur de Chine (*Rossignol*); VERDI: Ramfis (*Aida*), Philip II★ & Grande Inquisitore (*Don Carlo*), Padre Guardiano (*Forza del destino*), Procida (*Vespri*); WAGNER: Daland (*Fliegende Holländer*), König Heinrich★ (*Lohengrin*), Landgraf (*Tannhäuser*); WEBER: Kaspar (*Freischütz*); WOLF-FERRARI: Lunardo (*Quattro rusteghi*). Also PUCCINI: Timur (*Turandot*). Gives recitals. Appears with symphony orchestra. Teaches voice. **Res:** Westring 11, Kassel/Vellmar, FR Ger. Mgmt: PAS/FRG.

VON KARAJAN, HERBERT. Conductor of opera and symphony; operatic stage director and lighting designer for own prod. Austrian. Perm Cond & Prod, Salzburger Fest 1962- ; Founder & Gen Dir, Easter Fest, Salzburg 1967- . Also Chief Cond & Art Dir, Berliner Phil, Berlin, FR Ger 1955- ; Dir, Gesellschaft der Musikfreunde, Vienna 1947- ; Princ Cond, La Scala, Milan 1950- . Born 5 Apr 1908, Salzburg. Wife Eliette. Two children. Studied: piano, cembalo and voice. Plays the piano and cembalo. Operatic training as repetiteur, asst cond & chorus master at Salzburger Fest. **Operatic debut:** *Nozze di Figaro* Ulm, Germany 1927. Symphonic debut: Mozarteum Orch, Salzburg. Awards: numerous awds. Previous adm positions in opera: Art & Mus Dir, Ulm 1927-33; Gen Mus Dir, Aachen 1933-38; Staatsoper Berlin 1938-44; Dir, Staatsoper Vienna 1956-64; Art Dir, Salzburger Fest 1956-62.

Conducted with major companies in AUS: Salzburg Fest, Vienna Staatsoper; FR GER: Berlin Deutsche Oper; ITA: Milan La Scala; USA: New York Met. **Operas with these companies incl** BEETHOVEN: *Fidelio*★; BIZET: *Carmen*★; DEBUSSY: *Pelléas et Mélisande;* DONIZETTI: *Lucia;* GLUCK: *Iphigénie en Aulide, Orfeo ed Euridice;* GOUNOD: *Faust;* HUMPERDINCK: *Hänsel und Gretel;* LEONCAVALLO: *Pagliacci;* MASCAGNI: *Cavalleria rusticana;* MEYERBEER: *Huguenots;* MONTEVERDI: *Incoronazione di Poppea;* MOZART: *Così fan tutte, Don Giovanni*★, *Entführung aus dem Serail, Zauberflöte;* MUSSORGSKY: *Boris Godunov;* ORFF: *Carmina burana;* PUCCINI: *Bohème*★, *Fanciulla del West, Gianni Schicchi, Butterfly*★, *Manon Lescaut, Tosca;* ROSSINI: *Barbiere di Siviglia, Cambiale di matrimonio, Cenerentola, Comte Ory, Guillaume Tell;* SMETANA: *Bartered Bride, Dalibor, Devil's Wall;* STRAUSS, J: *Fledermaus;* STRAUSS, R: *Aegyptische Helena, Arabella, Ariadne auf Naxos, Capriccio, Daphne, Elektra, Frau ohne Schatten, Intermezzo, Liebe der Danae, Rosenkavalier, Salome;* STRAVINSKY: *Oedipus Rex, Perséphone;* TCHAIKOVSKY: *Eugene Onegin, Iolanthe, Maid of Orleans, Pique Dame;* VERDI: *Aida, Aroldo/Stiffelio, Attila, Ballo in maschera, Corsaro, Don Carlo*★, *Due Foscari, Ernani, Falstaff, Forza del destino, Giorno di regno, Giovanna d'Arco, Lombardi, Luisa Miller, Macbeth, Masnadieri, Nabucco, Otello, Rigoletto, Simon Bocca-*

negra, Traviata, Trovatore, Vespri; WAGNER: *Fliegende Holländer, Liebesverbot, Lohengrin, Meistersinger, Parsifal, Rienzi, Rheingold, Walküre, Siegfried, Götterdämmerung, Tannhäuser, Tristan und Isolde;* WEBER: *Abu Hassan, Euryanthe, Freischütz, Oberon;* WERLE: *Dream of Thérèse, Tintomara;* WOLF-FERRARI: *Donne curiose, Gioielli della Madonna, Quattro rusteghi, Segreto di Susanna.* **World premieres:** ORFF: *Trionfo di Afrodite* La Scala, Milan 1953; *De temporum fine comedia* Salzburger Fest 1973. Recorded for Polydor, Decca, EMI. Video/Film: *Bohème, Pagliacci, Cavalleria rusticana, Otello, Butterfly.* Conducted major orch in Europe, USA/Canada, Cent/S America. Previous positions as Mus Dir with major orch: Wiener Symphoniker, Wiener Philharmoniker, Orchestre de Paris, Philharmonia Orchestra London. Teaches at Herbert von Karajan Foundation, Berlin and Salzburg. Awards Karajan Prize to winner of Intl Cond Compt, Berlin. **Res:** St Moritz, Switzerland. Mgmt: JUC/SWI; CAM/USA.

VONK, HANS F. Conductor of opera and symphony. Dutch. Resident Cond & Mus Dir designate (1976-80), Netherlands Opera, Amsterdam. Also Resident Cond, Radio Phil, Hilversum, Holland. Born 18 Jun 1942, Amsterdam. Wife Jessie, occupation classical dancer. Studied: Amsterdam; Franco Ferrara, Siena; Hermann Scherchen, Salzburg; also piano, violin. Plays the piano. **Operatic debut:** *Don Perlimplin* Netherlands Opera, Amsterdam 1971. Symphonic debut: Amsterdam Phil 1966. Previous occupations: Cond, Dutch Ntl Ballet.

Conducted with major companies in HOL: Amsterdam. **Operas with these companies incl** DONIZETTI: *Rita*★; FORTNER: *Don Perlimplin*★; GLUCK: *Orfeo ed Euridice*★; HAYDN: *Infedeltà delusa*★; MOZART: *Così fan tutte*★, *Entführung aus dem Serail*★, *Idomeneo*★; PROKOFIEV: *Gambler*★, *Love for Three Oranges*★; ROSSINI: *Cambiale di matrimonio*★; STRAVINSKY: *Rake's Progress*★; TCHAIKOVSKY: *Iolanthe*★; VERDI: *Nabucco*★. Conducted major orch in Europe, USA/Canada. **Res:** Stadionkade 8, Amsterdam, Holland. Mgmt: IBK/HOL; CAM/USA.

VON MAGNUS, PETER. German. Chefdramaturg, Opera, Niedersächsische Staatstheater, Opernplatz 1, Hannover 1971- . In charge of art policy. Also lecturer, Staatliche Hochschule für Musik & Theater, Hannover. Born 13 May 1927, Schwerin/Mecklenburg. Wife Dagmar v Cölln, occupation businesswoman. Studied: Staatliche Schauspielschule Schwerin; PhD Free Univ, Berlin; Univ, Munich. Plays the piano. Previous occupations: actor, director, journalist. Form positions, primarily theatrical: Mecklenburgisches Staatstheater, Schwerin 1950-53; Bühnen der Hansestadt Lübeck 1962-64; Südwestfunk, Baden-Baden 1964-66; Städtische Bühnen, Dortmund 1966-68; Musiktheater im Revier, Gelsenkirchen 1968-71. **Res:** Hauptstr 34, D-3001 Isernhagen FB, Krs Hannover, FR Ger.

VON MATACIC, LOVRO. Conductor of opera and symphony; composer; operatic stage director. Yugoslavian. Chief Cond, Monte Carlo Opera; Art

Dir, Fest of Dubrovnik, Yugoslavia. Also Chief
Cond, Monte Carlo National Symph Orch; Chief
Cond, Zagreb Symph Orch, Yugoslavia; Hon
Cond, NHK Symph, Tokyo, Japan. Born 14 Feb
1899, Susak, Yugoslavia. Married. Studied: Oskar
Nedbal, Vienna 1918-30; incl piano, violin. Oper-
atic training as repetiteur & asst cond at var opera
houses Austria & Germany. **Operatic debut:**
Vienna 1925. Symphonic debut: Dresden 1923.
Awards: Bruckner Medal, Bruckner Society,
Vienna 1964; etc. Previous adm positions in opera:
Dir/Chief Cond Vienna, Dresden, Belgrade,
Frankfurt etc; Gen Mus Dir Staatsoper Berlin,
Ger DR 1956.
Conducted with major companies in AUS:
Vienna Staatsoper; CZE: Prague National; FRA:
Aix-en-Provence, Marseille, Nice, Paris; FR
GER: Berlin Deutsche Oper, Frankfurt, Munich
Staatsoper & Gärtnerplatz; GER DR: Dresden;
HUN: Budapest; ITA: Rome Opera & Caracalla;
MON: Monte Carlo; SWI: Geneva. **Operas with
these companies incl** BEETHOVEN: *Fidelio*;*
BELLINI: *Norma;* BERG: *Lulu, Wozzeck;* BER-
LIOZ: *Damnation de Faust;* BIZET: *Carmen,
Pêcheurs de perles;* BORODIN: *Prince Igor;*
CHARPENTIER: *Louise;* CILEA: *A. Lecou-
vreur;* DEBUSSY: *Pelléas et Mélisande;* DONI-
ZETTI: *Don Pasquale, Elisir;* DVORAK:
Rusalka; FLOTOW: *Martha;* GIORDANO: *An-
drea Chénier;* GLINKA: *Life for the Tsar, Ruslan
and Ludmilla;* GLUCK: *Iphigénie en Aulide, Or-
feo ed Euridice;* HINDEMITH: *Cardillac, Mathis
der Maler;* HONEGGER: *Antigone;* JANACEK:
Jenufa, Katya Kabanova; KODALY: *Háry
János;* LEONCAVALLO: *Pagliacci;* MONTE-
VERDI: *Favola d'Orfeo*, Incoronazione di Pop-
pea*;* MOZART: *Così fan tutte, Don Giovanni,
Entführung aus dem Serail, Nozze di Figaro, Re
pastore, Zauberflöte;* MUSSORGSKY: *Boris
Godunov*, Khovanshchina;* PROKOFIEV: *Love
for Three Oranges;* PUCCINI: *Bohème, Fanciulla del West, Tosca, Turandot;* ROSSINI: *Barbiere di Siviglia, Cenerentola;* SMETANA:
Bartered Bride; STRAUSS, R: *Aegyptische Helena, Arabella, Ariadne auf Naxos, Capriccio,
Elektra, Frau ohne Schatten, Intermezzo, Rosenkavalier, Salome, Schweigsame Frau;* TCHAI-
KOVSKY: *Eugene Onegin, Pique Dame;*
VERDI: *Aida, Ballo in maschera, Falstaff, Forza
del destino, Rigoletto, Simon Boccanegra, Traviata, Trovatore;* WAGNER: *Fliegende Holländer, Lohengrin, Meistersinger, Parsifal*,
Rheingold, Walküre*, Siegfried, Götterdämmerung, Tannhäuser, Tristan und Isolde*;* WEBER:
Euryanthe, Freischütz, Oberon. Conducted major
orch in Europe, USA/Canada, Asia. Previous positions as Mus Dir with major orch: Dresden
Staatskapelle 1956. Teaches. **Res:** Dubrovnik,
Mokosica, Yugoslavia. Mgmt: CMV/FRA.

VON STADE, FREDERICA. Lyric mezzo-soprano.
American. Resident mem: Metropolitan Opera,
New York. Born 1 Jun, Somerville, NJ, USA.
Husband Peter Elkus, occupation singer, bass-bar-
itone. Studied: Mannes Coll of Music, Sebastian
Engelberg, New York. **Debut:** Zweiter Knabe
(*Zauberflöte*) Metropolitan Opera 1970. Prev oc-
cupations: salesgirl, Tiffany; secy, Amer Shake-
speare Fest, Stratford, CT, USA. Awards:

Metropolitan Opera, Frank Chapman Awd; W M
Sullivan Awd; Ntl Arts Club Awd.
Sang with major companies in AUS: Salzburg
Fest; FRA: Paris; ITA: Spoleto Fest; UK: Lon-
don Royal Opera; USA: Boston, Houston, New
York Met, San Francisco Opera & Spring Opera,
Santa Fe, Seattle, Washington DC. **Roles with these
companies incl** BELLINI: Adalgisa* (*Norma*);
BERLIOZ: Béatrice*, Marguerite* (*Damnation
de Faust*); GOUNOD: Siebel* (*Faust*); HUM-
PERDINCK: Hänsel*; MASSENET: Belle-mère
(*Cendrillon*); MOZART: Sesto* (*Clemenza di
Tito*), Dorabella* (*Così fan tutte*), Zerlina* (*Don
Giovanni*), Cherubino* (*Nozze di Figaro*); ROS-
SINI: Rosina* (*Barbiere di Siviglia*), Angelina*
(*Cenerentola*), Isolier* (*Comte Ory*). Also DE-
BUSSY: Mélisande*; MONTEVERDI: Penelope
(*Ritorno d'Ulisse*). **World premieres:** VILLA
LOBOS: Maria (*Yerma*) Santa Fe Opera 1971;
PASATIERI: Nina (*The Seagull*) Houston Grand
Opera 1974. Film: Cherubino (*Nozze di Figaro*).
Gives recitals. Appears with symphony orchestra.
Res: New York, NY, USA. Mgmt: CAM/USA.

VON STROHMER, HERBERT. Austrian. Deputy
Dir, Staatsoper Wien, Opernring 2, 1010 Vienna,
Austria. In charge of artistic policy. Born 26 Sep
1924, Austria. Wife Hannelore, occupation singer.
One child. Previous positions, primarily theatrical:
Art Adm Dir, Staatstheater für Oper Ballett und
Schauspiel, Stuttgart, FR Ger. Started in present
position in 1972. Awards: title of Professor. **Res:**
Rohrerg 5, Vienna, Austria.

VON TOMORY, NANDOR. Bass. Hungarian.
Resident mem: Städtische Bühnen, Nürnberg.
Born 4 Sep 1930, Miskolc, Hungary. Divorced.
Two children. Studied: Bruckner Konsv, Linz,
Austria. **Debut:** Kaspar (*Freischütz*) Landestheater
Linz, Austria 1967. Previous occupations: weaver.
Sang with major companies in FR GER:
Nürnberg; HUN: Budapest. **Roles with these com-
panies incl** ADAM: Bijou (*Postillon de Lon-
jumeau*); d'ALBERT: Tommaso (*Tiefland*);
EINEM: St Just (*Dantons Tod*); FLOTOW: Plun-
kett* (*Martha*); LORTZING: Stadinger (*Waffen-
schmied*); MOZART: Don Alfonso* (*Così fan
tutte*), Osmin (*Entführung aus dem Serail*), Sa-
rastro* (*Zauberflöte*); MUSSORGSKY: Varlaam
(*Boris Godunov*); NICOLAI: Falstaff* (*Lustigen
Weiber*); ORFF: Bauer (*Mond*); PUCCINI: Col-
line (*Bohème*), Jack Rance (*Fanciulla del West*);
ROSSINI: Don Basilio (*Barbiere di Siviglia*);
SMETANA: Kezal (*Bartered Bride*); STRAUSS,
R: Orest (*Elektra*), Baron Ochs (*Rosenkavalier*);
VERDI: Grande Inquisitore* (*Don Carlo*), Ban-
quo (*Macbeth*); WAGNER: Pogner (*Meistersin-
ger*), Alberich (*Götterdämmerung*); WEBER:
Kaspar (*Freischütz*); ZIMMERMANN: Wesener
(*Soldaten*). **Res:** Hummelsteinerweg 71, Nürnberg,
FR Ger.

VOSSBERG, TITUS DIETER. Scenic and costume
designer for opera, theater, film & television. Is
also a painter, illustrator & fashion designer. German. Born 21 Jan 1934, Hamburg. Single. Studied:
Meisterschule für angewandte Kunst, Bernhard
Klein, Mariane Herting, Berlin. **Operatic debut:**

Ariadne auf Naxos Teatro alla Scala, Milan 1963. Theater debut: Renato Rascel Comp, Rome 1955.

Designed for major companies in ARG: Buenos Aires; AUS: Salzburg Fest; FRA: Nice; ITA: Milan La Scala, Naples, Rome Opera & Caracalla. **Operas designed for these companies incl** BELLINI: *Norma;* BIZET: *Carmen;* DONIZETTI: *Anna Bolena, Elisir, Lucia;* PUCCINI: *Turandot;* VERDI: *Ballo in maschera, Vespri;* WOLF-FERRARI: *Quattro rusteghi;* ZANDONAI: *Francesca da Rimini.* Exhibitions of stage designs & paintings Palazzo Reale, Naples 1969. **Res:** V del Governo Vecchio 3, Rome, Italy.

VOTTO, ANTONINO. Conductor of opera and symphony. Italian. Born 30 Oct 1896, Piacenza, Italy. Wife Lina Bordon. Studied: Consv S Pietro a Maiella, Prof Alessandro Longo, Naples; incl piano. Plays the piano. Operatic training as repetiteur & assistant conductor at Teatro alla Scala, Milan. **Operatic debut:** *Pagliacci* Teatro Verdi, Trieste 1920. Symphonic debut: Symph Orch, Teatro alla Scala 1927. Previous occupations: concert pianist. Awards: Cavalieri Uff Corona d'Italia; Commendatore al merito, Repubblica Italiana; Accad di S Cecilia; Commendatore Ord Militare de Santiago da Espada, Portugal.

Conducted with major companies in ARG: Buenos Aires; AUS: Vienna Staatsoper; BEL: Brussels; BRA: Rio de Janeiro; CZE: Prague National; FRA: Bordeaux; GRE: Athens Fest; FR GER: Berlin Deutsche Oper, Cologne, Dortmund, Frankfurt, Hannover; GER DR: Berlin Staatsoper, Dresden; HOL: Amsterdam; HUN: Budapest; ITA: Bologna, Florence Maggio & Comunale, Genoa, Milan La Scala, Palermo, Parma, Rome Opera, Trieste, Turin, Venice, Verona Arena; POR: Lisbon; SPA: Barcelona; SWI: Geneva, Zurich; UK: Edinburgh Fest, London Royal; USA: Chicago. **Operas with these companies incl** AUBER: *Fra Diavolo;* BARTOK: *Bluebeard's Castle;* BELLINI: *Beatrice di Tenda, Norma★, Pirata, Puritani★, Sonnambula★‡;* BI-ZET: *Carmen, Pêcheurs de perles;* BOITO: *Mefistofele;* BUSONI: *Arlecchino;* CATALANI: *Wally;* CHARPENTIER: *Louise;* CILEA: *A. Lecouvreur;* CIMAROSA: *Matrimonio segreto;* DONIZETTI: *Don Pasquale, Elisir, Favorite, Fille du régiment, Lucia;* FALLA: *Retablo de Maese Pedro, Vida breve;* GIORDANO: *Andrea Chénier, Fedora;* GLUCK: *Orfeo ed Euridice;* GOUNOD: *Faust;* HUMPERDINCK: *Hänsel und Gretel;* LEONCAVALLO: *Pagliacci;* MASCAGNI: *Amico Fritz, Cavalleria rusticana, Silvano;* MASSENET: *Manon, Thaïs, Werther;* MENOTTI: *Amelia al ballo;* MEYERBEER: *Huguenots;* MONTEMEZZI: *Amore dei tre re;* MONTEVERDI: *Combattimento di Tancredi;* MOZART: *Entführung aus dem Serail;* MUSSORGSKY: *Boris Godunov, Fair at Sorochinsk, Khovanshchina;* OFFENBACH: *Contes d'Hoffmann;* PERGOLESI: *Serva padrona;* PONCHIELLI: *Gioconda★‡;* PUCCINI: *Bohème‡, Fanciulla del West, Gianni Schicchi, Butterfly, Manon Lescaut, Suor Angelica, Tabarro, Tosca★, Turandot, Villi;* RABAUD: *Mârouf;* ROSSINI: *Barbiere di Siviglia, Italiana in Algeri;* SAINT-SAENS: *Samson et Dalila;* SPONTINI: *Vestale;* STRAUSS, R: *Ariadne auf Naxos, Salome;* THOMAS: *Hamlet, Mignon;* VERDI: *Aida, Ballo in maschera‡, Don Carlo, Ernani, Falstaff, Forza del destino, Luisa Miller, Nabucco, Otello, Rigoletto, Simon Boccanegra, Traviata‡, Trovatore, Vespri;* WAGNER: *Lohengrin, Meistersinger;* WOLF-FERRARI: *Quattro rusteghi;* ZANDONAI: *Francesca da Rimini.* Recorded for His Master's Voice, Cetra, DG. Video—RAI TV: *Gianni Schicchi, Tosca.* Conducted major orch in Europe, USA/Canada. Previous positions as Mus Dir with major orch: RAI—Milan, Rome, Turin; Orch S Cecilia, Rome; Teatro alla Scala, Milan; Chicago Symph Orch, USA; Maggio Musicale, Florence; Orch di Teatro Comunale, Bologna; Teatro Verdi, Trieste; Teatro la Fenice, Venice; Residentie Orch, The Hague, Holland. **Res:** Piazzale Aquileia 10, Milan, Italy.

W

WABER, HUBERT CAROLUS. Basso-buffo.
Dutch. Resident mem: Netherlands Opera, Amsterdam. Born 3 Apr 1938, Heer, Holland. Married. Studied: Leo Ketelaars. **Debut:** Bass role
(*Finta semplice*) Kammeroper, Vienna 1967. Previous occupations: printer. Awards: Grand Prix,
Voice Compt, Verviers 1967; First Prize, Voice
Compt, Montreal 1970; First Prize 's Hertogenbosch, Holland 1969.
Sang with major companies in FR GER: Düsseldorf-Duisburg; HOL: Amsterdam. **Roles with these
companies incl** DONIZETTI: Don Pasquale⋆,
Dulcamara (*Elisir*); FLOTOW: Plunkett (*Martha*); GOUNOD: Méphistophélès (*Faust*); LORTZING: Van Bett (*Zar und Zimmermann*);
MOZART: Don Alfonso⋆ (*Così fan tutte*), Leporello (*Don Giovanni*), Osmin⋆ (*Entführung aus
dem Serail*), Sarastro (*Zauberflöte*); MUS-
SORGSKY: Varlaam (*Boris Godunov*); NI-
COLAI: Falstaff (*Lustigen Weiber*); PUCCINI:
Colline⋆ (*Bohème*); ROSSINI: Dott Bartolo⋆
(*Barbiere di Siviglia*); SMETANA: Kezal⋆ (*Bartered Bride*); VERDI: Ramfis (*Aida*), Philip II⋆
(*Don Carlo*), Silva (*Ernani*), Fra Melitone & Padre
Guardiano (*Forza del destino*), Banquo (*Macbeth*),
Zaccaria (*Nabucco*), Fiesco (*Simon Boccanegra*);
WAGNER: König Heinrich (*Lohengrin*). Gives
recitals. Appears with symphony orchestra. **Res:**
c/o: Sellström, Apollolaan 197, Amsterdam, Holland. Mgmt: SLZ/FRG.

WÄCHTER, EBERHARD. Dramatic baritone.
Austrian. Resident mem: Staatsoper, Vienna. Born
9 Jul 1929, Vienna. Studied: Musikhochschule,
Elisabeth Rado, Vienna; incl piano. **Debut:** Silvio
(*Pagliacci*) Volksoper, Vienna 1953.
Sang with major companies in ARG: Buenos
Aires; AUS: Salzburg Fest, Vienna Staatsoper &
Volksoper; BEL: Brussels; FR GER: Bayreuth
Fest, Berlin Deutsche Oper, Munich Staatsoper,
Stuttgart, Wiesbaden; ITA: Milan La Scala, Rome
Opera; UK: Edinburgh Fest, Glyndebourne Fest,
London Royal; USA: New York Metropolitan
Opera; et al. **Roles with these companies incl** EI-
NEM: Danton (*Dantons Tod*); MARTIN: Prospero (*Sturm*); MOZART: Leporello & Don
Giovanni‡ (*Don Giovanni*), Conte Almaviva‡
(*Nozze di Figaro*); STRAUSS, R: Mandryka (*Arabella*), Graf‡ (*Capriccio*), Storch (*Intermezzo*), Jochanaan‡ (*Salome*); VERDI: Renato (*Ballo in
maschera*), Rodrigo (*Don Carlo*), Simon Bocca-
negra, Conte di Luna (*Trovatore*); WAGNER:
Amfortas (*Parsifal*), Wolfram‡ (*Tannhäuser*), Kurwenal‡ (*Tristan und Isolde*); et al. Also
STRAUSS, R: Faninal‡ (*Rosenkavalier*). Recorded for: Angel, London, DG, Philips, Columbia, RCA. Gives recitals. Appears with symphony
orchestra.

WAGEMANN, ROSE. Dramatic soprano and
mezzo-soprano. German. Born 23 Jul 1940. Grabowce, Poland. Husband Bednorz, occupation
clerk. Two children. Studied: Staatl Hochschule
für Musik, Prof Irma Beilke, Berlin. **Debut:** Carmen, Krefeld/Gladbach Opera 1969. Previous occupations: studied painting & graphics. Awards:
First prize, compt Berlin 1968.
Sang with major companies in AUS: Vienna
Staatsoper; BEL: Brussels; BRA: Rio; FR GER:
Berlin Deutsche Oper, Bielefeld, Düsseldorf, Essen, Karlsruhe, Krefeld, Saarbrücken, Stuttgart,
Wiesbaden; USA: Chicago. **Roles with these companies incl** BARTOK: Judith (*Bluebeard*); BEET-
HOVEN: Leonore (*Fidelio*); BELLINI: Romeo
(*Capuleti*); BIZET: Carmen; HANDEL: Cornelia
(*Giulio Cesare*); HINDEMITH: Dame (*Cardillac*), Ursula (*Mathis der Maler*); MONTE-
VERDI: Ottavia (*Incoronazione di Poppea*);
MOZART: Dorabella (*Così fan tutte*); PUR-
CELL: Dido; STRAUSS, R: Komponist (*Ariadne
auf Naxos*), Octavian (*Rosenkavalier*); VERDI:
Amneris (*Aida*), Eboli (*Don Carlo*), Azucena &
Leonora (*Trovatore*); WAGNER: Ortrud (*Lohengrin*), Brünnhilde (*Siegfried, Götterdämmerung*),
Venus (*Tannhäuser*), Isolde. Recorded for: Eurodisc, BASF, RCA, Phonogram. Gives recitals.
Appears with symphony orchestra. **Res:** Unter
dem Friedhof 1, 4952 Porta Westfalica, FR Ger.
Mgmt: HUS/FRG; RAB/AUS; TAU/SWI;
IWL/UK.

WAGNER, LJUBICA. Scenic and costume designer for opera, theater, film, TV; specl in costumes. Lighting & fashion designer. Yugoslavian.
Res designer, Theater Comedy, Zagreb and at
music theaters in Zagreb & Dubrovnik. Born 30
Oct 1934, Zagreb. Husband Lujo Galic, occupation actor. One child. Studied: Acad of Theater
Art, Zagreb. **Operatic debut:** sets, STRAUSS, R:
Don Juan Croatian Ntl Theater, Zagreb 1956;
cost, Trinaestic Dolls Theater, Zagreb 1956. Theater debut: ballet, Croatian Ntl Theater 1956.

Designed for major companies in YUG: Dubrovnik, Zagreb. **Operas designed for these companies incl** BARTOK: *Bluebeard's Castle;* BORODIN: *Prince Igor;* BUSONI: *Arlecchino;* CHERUBINI: *Medea;* DALLAPICCOLA: *Volo di notte;* DONIZETTI: *Lucia;* LEONCAVALLO: *Pagliacci;* MASCAGNI: *Cavalleria rusticana;* MENOTTI: *Telephone;* MILHAUD: *Pauvre matelot;* MOZART: *Entführung aus dem Serail, Zaïde, Zauberflöte;* ORFF: *Antigonae;* PUCCINI: *Gianni Schicchi, Manon Lescaut;* TCHAIKOVSKY: *Pique Dame;* VERDI: *Ballo in maschera, Don Carlo, Traviata;* WAGNER: *Fliegende Holländer.* **Operatic world premieres:** BERSA: *Mozart's Death* Croat Ntl Th, Osijek, Yugoslavia 1975. Exhibitions of stage designs in 1971, 73, 75 at Zagreb, Novi Sad and Prague. **Res:** Nova Cesta 169, Opatija, Yugoslavia.

WAGNER, WOLFGANG. Stages/produces opera. Also designs sets, costumes. German. Gen Dir & Resident Stage Dir, Bayreuther Festspiele, FR Ger 1966- ; Co-Dir with Wieland Wagner 1951-66. Born 30 Aug 1919, Bayreuth. Operatic training as asst stage dir at Bayreuther Fest; Staatsoper Berlin. **Operatic debut:** Staatsoper Berlin 1944.

Directed/produced opera for major companies in BEL: Brussels; FR GER: Bayreuth Fest, Hamburg, Munich Staatsoper; ITA: Naples, Parma, Rome Opera, Venice; SPA: Barcelona; et al. **Operas staged with these companies incl** MOZART: *Don Giovanni;* WAGNER: *Fliegende Holländer, Lohengrin, Meistersinger, Rheingold, Walküre, Siegfried, Götterdämmerung, Tristan und Isolde;* et al.

WÄHLTE, EDGAR. Lyric tenor. German, DR. Resident mem: Staatsoper, Leipzig. Born 24 Sep 1930, Lauban, Germany. Wife Margret Grund, occupation opera singer. Two children. Studied: Prof Lüttner-Meissner, Prof Laux, Prof Thilmann, Prof Flämig. **Debut:** Nemorino (*Elisir*) Leipzig 1961. Previous occupations: silversmith. Awards: Art Prize, City of Leipzig; Kammersänger, Oper Leipzig.

Sang with major companies in GER DR: Berlin Komische Oper & Staatsoper, Dresden, Leipzig. **Roles with these companies incl** ADAM: Chapelou (*Postillon de Lonjumeau*); AUBER: Lorenzo (*Fra Diavolo*); BRITTEN: Albert Herring; DONIZETTI: Ernesto (*Don Pasquale*), Nemorino (*Elisir*); EINEM: Bürgermeister★ (*Besuch der alten Dame*); GERSHWIN: Sportin' Life (*Porgy and Bess*); HANDEL: Xerxes; JANACEK: Boris (*Katya Kabánova*); KORNGOLD: Paul (*Tote Stadt*); MASCAGNI: Turiddu (*Cavalleria rusticana*); MONIUSZKO: Jontek (*Halka*); MOZART: Ferrando (*Così fan tutte*), Pedrillo (*Entführung aus dem Serail*), Belfiore (*Finta giardiniera*), Tamino (*Zauberflöte*); OFFENBACH: Paquillo (*Périchole*); PUCCINI: Rodolfo★ (*Bohème*), Pinkerton★ (*Butterfly*), Calaf (*Turandot*); RIMSKY-KORSAKOV: Sadko; ROSSINI: Almaviva (*Barbiere di Siviglia*), Rodrigo (*Otello*); SHOSTAKOVICH: Sergei (*Katerina Ismailova*); SMETANA: Wenzel & Hans (*Bartered Bride*); STRAUSS, J: Eisenstein & Alfred (*Fledermaus*); STRAUSS, R: Ein Sänger (*Rosenkavalier*); TCHAIKOVSKY: Lenski (*Eugene Onegin*); VERDI: Fenton (*Falstaff*), Alfredo★ (*Traviata*);

WAGNER: Mime (*Rheingold*★, *Siegfried*), Walther v d Vogelweide (*Tannhäuser*); WEILL: Jim Mahoney★ (*Aufstieg und Fall der Stadt Mahagonny*). Also LORTZING: Baron de Chateauneuf (*Zar und Zimmermann*); MUSSORGSKY: Simpleton (*Boris Godunov*). **World premieres:** HANELL: (*Griechische Hochzeit*) Leipzig 1969; BUSH: Joseph (*Guyana Jonny*) Leipzig 1966. Video/Film: Xerxes; Albert Herring. Gives recitals. Appears with symphony orchestra. **Res:** Poetenweg 45, Leipzig 7022, Ger DR. Mgmt: KDR/GDR.

WAIDELICH, JÜRGEN-DIETER. German. Gen Int, Bühnen der Stadt Essen, II Hagen 4 - 6, Essen 1974- . In charge of overall adm matters, art policy, mus & dram matters, finances. Is also a st dir/prod. Additional adm positions: Administrator, Deutscher Bühnenverein. Born 23 May 1931, Berlin. Wife Marianne Gerstlauer, occupation teacher. Four children. Studied: Univ, Munich; PhD. Plays the cello. Previous occupations: Asst, Univ of Munich. Form positions, primarily adm & theatrical: Dramaturg, Württemberg Staatstheater, Stuttgart 1956-59; Chefdram, Stadttheater Bremerhaven 1959-67, Int 1967-74. **Res:** Grüne Harfe 3, Essen, FR Ger.

WAKASUGI, HIROSHI. Conductor of opera and symphony. Japanese. Music Dir, Tokyo Chamber Opera Socy. Also Music Dir, Yomiuri Nippon Symph Orch, Tokyo 1965-75. Born 31 May 1935, Tokyo. Wife Yonako Nagano, occupation opera & concert singer. Studied: Tokyo Univ of Arts, Profs N Kaneko & H Saito; incl piano, viola, clarinet and voice. Plays the piano. Operatic training as repetiteur, asst cond & chorus master at Fujiwara Opera, Tokyo 1955-57; Niki Kai Opera, Tokyo 1957-61. **Operatic debut:** *Nozze di Figaro* Niki Kai Opera 1958. **Symphonic debut:** Tokyo Symph Orch, 1961. Awards: Ntl Culture Prize, Japanese Cultural Ministry 1967; Mainichi Music Prize, Mainichi Press, Japan 1967-74.

Conducted with major companies in FR GER: Darmstadt; JPN: Tokyo Niki Kai. **Operas with these companies incl** BARTOK: *Bluebeard's Castle*★; BEETHOVEN: *Fidelio;* BERLIOZ: *Damnation de Faust*★, *Troyens*★; BRITTEN: *Albert Herring, Curlew River*★, *Midsummer Night*★; BUSONI: *Arlecchino;* DEBUSSY: *Pelléas et Mélisande*★; GLUCK: *Orfeo ed Euridice*★; HANDEL: *Giulio Cesare;* HENZE: *Landarzt*★; HINDEMITH: *Hin und zurück*★, *Long Christmas Dinner;* LIGETI: *Aventures/Nouvelles Aventures;* MARTIN: *Vin herbé;* MASCAGNI: *Cavalleria rusticana;* MENOTTI: *Amahl, Medium, Telephone;* MILHAUD: *Pauvre matelot*★; MONTEVERDI: *Incoronazione di Poppea;* MOZART: *Così fan tutte, Don Giovanni*★, *Nozze di Figaro, Zauberflöte*★; ORFF: *Carmina burana*★, *Kluge;* PAISIELLO: *Barbiere di Siviglia;* PERGOLESI: *Serva padrona*★; POULENC: *Mamelles de Tirésias*★, *Voix humaine*★; PROKOFIEV: *Love for Three Oranges;* PUCCINI: *Bohème, Gianni Schicchi, Butterfly, Tosca;* PURCELL: *Dido and Aeneas;* RAVEL: *Enfant et les sortilèges, Heure espagnole;* ROSSINI: *Barbiere di Siviglia*★, *Italiana in Algeri*★; SCHOENBERG: *Erwartung*★; STRAUSS, J: *Fledermaus*★; STRAUSS, R: *Ariadne auf Naxos*★;

STRAVINSKY: *Oedipus Rex★;* VERDI: *Otello★, Rigoletto, Traviata, Trovatore★;* WAGNER: *Fliegende Holländer★, Parsifal, Rheingold★;* WEBER: *Freischütz.* Also ANON, Twelfth Cent: *Play of Daniel;* PERI: *Euridice;* TELEMANN: *Pimpinone;* CIMAROSA: *Maestro di cappella;* FORTNER: *Bluthochzeit;* HAUBENSTOCK-RAMATI: *Spiel;* SCHOENBERG: *Von heute auf morgen.* World premieres: var Japanese contemp operas. Video—NHK TV: *Voix humaine, Heure espagnole, Amahl.* Conducted major orch in Europe, Asia. Res: 2-26-17 Kakinokizaka, Megoruku, Tokyo, Japan. Mgmt: HUS/FRG.

WAKEFIELD, JOHN; né John Darling. Lyric tenor. British. Born 21 Jun 1936, Wakefield, UK. Wife Jennifer Ann, occupation writer. One daughter. Studied: Royal Acad of Music, Roy Henderson, London; Mo Ettore Campogalliani, Mantua. Debut: Levko (*May Night*) Welsh National Opera 1961. Previous occupations: grocer. Awards: Fellow of Royal Acad of Music, London; Kathleen Ferrier Schlshp.
　Sang with major companies in ARG: Buenos Aires; BEL: Brussels; FRA: Lyon; FR GER: Munich Gärtnerplatz; SWE: Drottningholm Fest; UK: Aldeburgh Fest, Cardiff Welsh, Glasgow Scottish, Glyndebourne Fest, London Royal & English National; USA: Santa Fe. Roles with these companies incl BIZET: Smith (*Jolie Fille de Perth*); BRITTEN: Robert Devereux★ (*Gloriana*); CAVALLI: Ormindo★‡; DELIUS: Sali★ (*Village Romeo and Juliet*); HANDEL: Acis; MONTEVERDI: Orfeo★, Ulisse (*Ritorno d'Ulisse*); MOZART: Ferrando (*Così fan tutte*), Belmonte (*Entführung aus dem Serail*), Idamante (*Idomeneo*), Tamino★ (*Zauberflöte*); PUCCINI: Rodolfo★ (*Bohème*), Rinuccio (*Gianni Schicchi*); PURCELL: Aeneas★; RIMSKY-KORSAKOV: Levko (*May Night*); STRAUSS, J: Eisenstein★ (*Fledermaus*), VERDI: Fenton★ (*Falstaff*), Ismaele★ (*Nabucco*), Alfredo★ (*Traviata*). Also VERDI: Macduff (*Macbeth*); TIPPETT: Paris (*King Priam*). World premieres: MAW: Cornet Beaumont (*Rising of the Moon*) Glyndebourne Fest 1970; VILLA-LOBOS: Juan (*Yerma*) Santa Fe Opera 1971. Recorded for: Argo, Philips. Video/Film: Alfredo (*Traviata*). Gives recitals. Appears with symphony orchestra. Res: London, UK. Mgmt: SLA/UK.

WAKHEVITCH, GEORGE. Scenic and costume designer for opera, theater, film, television. Is a lighting designer; also a painter, illustrator & architect. French. Resident designer at Salzburg Fest; Opéra Monte-Carlo. Born 18 Aug 1907, Odessa. Wife Jeanne Renucci, occupation costume designer. Four children. Studied: School of Decorative Arts, Paris; Edwin Scott, Paul Tchelitscheff, Christian Bérard. Prof training: Comédie Française, Paris. Operatic debut: Royal Opera, Covent Garden, London 1948. Theater debut: Théâtre de l'Oeuvre, Paris 1931. Awards: Officer, Légion d'Honneur; Knight of Arts and Letters, France.
　Designed for major companies in AUS: Salzburg Fest, Vienna Staatsoper; BRA: Rio de Janeiro; FRA: Aix-en-Provence Fest, Bordeaux, Lyon, Marseille, Nancy, Paris, Rouen, Strasbourg, Toulouse; FR GER: Berlin Deutsche Oper; ITA:

Florence Maggio & Comunale, Milan La Scala, Naples, Palermo, Rome Opera & Caracalla, Venice, Verona Arena; MON: Monte Carlo; SWI: Geneva, Zurich; UK: London Royal; USA: New York Met. Operas designed for these companies incl BEETHOVEN: *Fidelio★;* BIZET: *Carmen★;* GOUNOD: *Roméo et Juliette★;* MENOTTI: *Medium★;* MOZART: *Don Giovanni★;* MUSSORGSKY: *Khovanshchina★;* OFFENBACH: *Contes d'Hoffmann★;* RAVEL: *Heure espagnole★;* ROUSSEAU: *Devin du village★;* TCHAIKOVSKY: *Eugene Onegin★;* VERDI: *Ballo in maschera★, Don Carlo, Falstaff★, Forza del destino★, Macbeth★, Simon Boccanegra;* WAGNER: *Meistersinger, Rheingold, Walküre, Siegfried, Götterdämmerung, Tristan und Isolde.* Operatic world premieres: POULENC: *Dialogues des Carmélites* La Scala, Milan 1957; DAMASE: *L'Héritière* Grand Théâtre, Nancy 1974. Operatic Video/Film—RAI TV: *Otello, Linguaggio dei fiori.* Film: *Medium.* Beta Film Munich: *Pagliacci, Carmen.* Exhibitions of stage designs, paintings, Paris 1962, '70, '73, '75; also Nantes, Casablanca, Saint-Tropez. Teaches at École Beaux-Arts, Marseille. Res: 96 Blvd Latour-Maubourg, Paris 75007, France. Mgmt: GOR/UK.

WALBECK, GÜNTER. Scenic and costume designer for opera, theater, film, television. Is also a painter, illustrator & author. German. Res first designer, Städt Bühnen, Essen, FR Ger. Born 3 Jan 1939, Dresden. Wife Inge Kobelt. Three children. Studied: Kunstakad Düsseldorf, Prof Teo Otto. Prof training: Schauspielhaus Zurich. Operatic debut: sets & cost, *Nozze di Figaro* Staatstheater Kassel, FR Ger 1972. Theater debut: Schauspielhaus Zurich 1966.
　Designed for major companies in FR GER: Berlin Deutsche Oper, Essen, Kassel. Operas designed for these companies incl BEETHOVEN: *Fidelio★;* BIZET: *Carmen★;* DONIZETTI: *Convenienze/Viva la Mamma★;* GAY/Britten: *Beggar's Opera★;* MOZART: *Clemenza di Tito★, Entführung aus dem Serail★, Nozze di Figaro★;* OFFENBACH: *Contes d'Hoffmann★;* PUCCINI: *Tosca★;* RAVEL: *Heure espagnole★;* SMETANA: *The Kiss★;* STRAUSS, R: *Salome★;* VERDI: *Rigoletto★;* WEBER: *Freischütz★.* Res: Glehnerweg 27, 4000 Düsseldorf 11, FR Ger.

WALK, WINFRIED. Basso-buffo. Austrian. Resident mem: Landestheater, Linz. Born 15 May 1931, Steyr, Austria. Wife Eva Maria, occupation opera singer. One child. Studied: Eva Ambrosius, Darmstadt; Julius Patzak, Hans Duhan, Vienna. Debut: Trinity Moses (*Aufstieg und Fall der Stadt Mahagonny*) Opernhaus Kiel 1960. Previous occupations: engineer.
　Sang with major companies in FR GER: Bielefeld, Darmstadt, Dortmund, Kiel, Krefeld, Munich Gärtnerplatz. Roles with these companies incl BEETHOVEN: Rocco (*Fidelio*); CIMAROSA: Geronimo (*Matrimonio segreto*); DONIZETTI: Don Pasquale; FLOTOW: Plunkett (*Martha*); JANACEK: Harasta (*Cunning Little Vixen*); LORTZING: Stadinger (*Waffenschmied*), Baculus★ (*Wildschütz*), Van Bett★ (*Zar und Zimmermann*); MOZART: Leporello★ (*Don Giovanni*), Osmin (*Entführung aus dem Serail*), Nardo (*Finta giardiniera*), Sarastro (*Zauberflöte*); NICOLAI:

Falstaff★ (*Lustigen Weiber*); PUCCINI: Colline (*Bohème*); ROSSINI: Dott Bartolo★ (*Barbiere di Siviglia*), Mustafà (*Italiana in Algeri*); SMETANA: Kezal (*Bartered Bride*); STRAUSS, R: Baron Ochs★ (*Rosenkavalier*); VERDI: Philip II (*Don Carlo*), Fra Melitone (*Forza del destino*); WAGNER: Daland (*Fliegende Holländer*), Fafner (*Rheingold, Siegfried*), Hunding (*Walküre*), Landgraf (*Tannhäuser*). Res: Tauberweg 3, A 4020 Linz, Austria.

WALKER, DAVID. Scenic and costume designer for opera, theater, film, television; specl in costumes. Is also an illustrator. British. Born 18 Jul 1934, Calcutta, India. Single. Studied: Central School of Arts and Crafts, Jeannetta Cochrane. Operatic debut: *Così fan tutte* Dublin Fest, UK 1961-62. Theater debut: Theatre Wrkshp, UK 1960. Previous occupation: costume cutter, prop maker, wig dresser, painter's model. Awards: Emmy Awd, American TV.
Designed for major companies in ITA: Palermo, Venice; POR: Lisbon; SWE: Drottningholm Fest, Stockholm; UK: Aldeburgh Fest, Welsh National, Edinburgh Fest, Glyndebourne Fest, London Royal & English National; USA: New York Met. Operas designed for these companies incl BIZET: *Carmen★;* DONIZETTI: *Lucia★;* GLUCK: *Orfeo ed Euridice;* HANDEL: *Acis and Galatea;* MASSENET: *Werther;* MOZART: *Così fan tutte, Don Giovanni, Entführung aus dem Serail;* PUCCINI: *Bohème, Manon Lescaut, Suor Angelica;* PURCELL: *Fairy Queen;* ROSSINI: *Guillaume Tell;* STRAUSS, R: *Rosenkavalier★;* VERDI: *Traviata★;* WAGNER: *Meistersinger.* Also ROTA: *Visita meravigliosa.* Exhibitions of stage designs, London 1968, 1970; Victoria and Albert Museum, Covent Garden Exhib, London 1970, 1973. Res: Long Barn, Leasgill, Cumbria, UK. Mgmt: DLZ/UK.

WALKER, JOHN EDWARD. Lyric tenor. American. Born 19 Aug 1933, Bushnell, IN, USA. Wife Sandra. Three children. Studied: Univ of Denver, CO; Univ of Illinois, Urbana; Univ of Indiana, Bloomington; Olga Ryss, New York. Debut: Tamino (*Zauberflöte*) Bern Stadttheater, Switzerland 1964. Awards: Mack Harrell Awd, Aspen School of Music; Finalist Met Op Ntl Counc Aud 1964.
Sang with major companies in BEL: Brussels; CAN: Toronto; FR GER: Cologne, Frankfurt, Stuttgart; SWI: Zurich; USA: Chicago, Dallas, Kentucky, Omaha, Portland, San Diego, San Francisco Opera & Spring Opera, Santa Fe, Seattle. Roles with these companies incl BIZET: Nadir (*Pêcheurs de perles*); BRITTEN: Albert Herring, Lysander (*Midsummer Night*); CORNELIUS: Nureddin (*Barbier von Bagdad*); DONIZETTI: Ernesto★ (*Don Pasquale*), Nemorino★ (*Elisir*); GOUNOD: Faust; HOLST: Satyavan (*Savitri*); MASSENET: Werther; MOZART: Ferrando★ (*Così fan tutte*), Don Ottavio★ (*Don Giovanni*), Belmonte★ (*Entführung aus dem Serail*), Idamante (*Idomeneo*), Tamino★ (*Zauberflöte*); NICOLAI: Fenton (*Lustigen Weiber*); PUCCINI: Rodolfo★ (*Bohème*), Rinuccio (*Gianni Schicchi*), Prunier★ (*Rondine*); ROSSINI: Almaviva★ (*Barbiere di Siviglia*); SMETANA: Hans★ (*Bartered Bride*); STRAUSS, J: Eisenstein & Alfred★ (*Fledermaus*); TCHAIKOVSKY: Lenski★ (*Eugene Onegin*); VERDI: Fenton (*Falstaff*), Alfredo (*Traviata*); WAGNER: David★ (*Meistersinger*). Video–CBC TV: Prunier (*Rondine*). Gives recitals. Appears with symphony orchestra. Res: RR #2, Murrayville, IL, USA. Mgmt: CSA/USA.

WALKER, MALLORY ELTON. Lyric tenor. American. Born 22 May 1935, New Orleans, LA, USA. Divorced. Three children. Studied: Occidental Coll, Los Angeles; Met Opera Studio, Mo George Schick; Cornelius Reid, New York. Debut: Tom Rakewell (*Rake's Progress*) Washington, DC, Opera Socy 1959. Awards: Ford Fndt Grant; Rockefeller Fndt Grant.
Sang with major companies in FR GER: Cologne, Stuttgart; ITA: Spoleto Fest; USA: Cincinnati, Houston, Kansas City, Lake George, Miami, San Francisco Spring Opera. Roles with these companies incl BARBER: Anatol (*Vanessa*); BERG: Alwa★ (*Lulu*); BIZET: Nadir★ (*Pêcheurs de perles*); BRITTEN: Albert Herring; DONIZETTI: Nemorino (*Elisir*); GOUNOD: Roméo; HAYDN: Filippo★ (*Infedeltà delusa*); MOZART: Ferrando (*Così fan tutte*), Don Ottavio (*Don Giovanni*), Belmonte (*Entführung aus dem Serail*), Idomeneo, Tamino (*Zauberflöte*); NICOLAI: Fenton (*Lustigen Weiber*); PROKOFIEV: Prince (*Love for Three Oranges*); PUCCINI: Rodolfo★ (*Bohème*), Rinuccio (*Gianni Schicchi*), Prunier★ (*Rondine*); SMETANA: Hans (*Bartered Bride*); STRAUSS, J: Alfred (*Fledermaus*); STRAUSS, R: Ein Sänger (*Rosenkavalier*); STRAVINSKY: Oedipus Rex, Tom Rakewell (*Rake's Progress*); VERDI: Fenton (*Falstaff*), Alfredo (*Traviata*). Gives recitals. Appears with symphony orchestra. Teaches voice. Coaches repertoire. On faculty of Boston Consv of Music. Res: 70 The Fenway, Boston, MA, USA. Mgmt: DSP/USA.

WALKER, ROBERT CHARLES. American. Financial Adm, New York City Opera, New York State Theater, Lincoln Center, New York. In charge of finances. Born 29 Oct 1944, Alameda, CA. Wife Diana Kehrig, occupation singer. Studied: Univ of Calif Berkeley, Calif State Coll San Francisco, Univ of Calif at Los Angeles, MBA. Plays the organ. Previous occupations: Lieutenant, US Navy 1967-71. Background primarily administrative & musical. Started with present company 1972. Mem of OPERA America commtt. Res: 18 W 70th St, New York, NY, USA.

WALKER, SANDRA. Mezzo-soprano. American. Resident mem: New York City Opera. Born 1 Oct 1946, Richmond, VA, USA. Husband Melvin Brown, occupation singer. Studied: Univ of North Carolina; Manhattan School of Music, New York; Oren Brown, New York. Debut: Flosshilde (*Rheingold*) San Francisco Opera 1972. Previous occupations: music teacher.
Sang with major companies in USA: Chicago, New York City Opera, Philadelphia Lyric, San Francisco Opera, Washington DC. Roles with these companies incl BIZET: Carmen; DONIZETTI: Marquise de Birkenfeld (*Fille du régiment*); MENOTTI: Secretary (*Consul*); PUCCINI: Suzuki (*Butterfly*), Frugola (*Tabarro*). Also MADERNA: Fortunata (*Satyricon*). Gives recitals. Appears with symphony orchestra. Res: New York, NY, USA. Mgmt: LLF/USA.

WALKER, SARAH. Lyric and dramatic mezzo-soprano. British. Resident member: English National Opera, London. Born 11 Mar 1945, Cheltenham, UK. Husband Graham Allum, occupation gen mgr, Kent Opera & Unicorn Opera Cos. Studied: Royal Coll of Music, London, violin & cello; Mme Vera Rozsa, voice. **Debut:** Diana/Giove (*Calisto*) Glyndebourne Fest 1970. Awards: Schlshp Martin Musical Trust Fund.

Sang with major companies in UK: Aldeburgh Fest, Glasgow Scottish, Glyndebourne Fest, London Royal Opera & English National. **Roles with these companies incl** BERLIOZ: Marguerite (*Damnation de Faust*), Didon★ (*Troyens*); CAVALLI: Diana★ (*Calisto*); MASSENET: Charlotte★ (*Werther*); MAW: Elizabeth★ (*Rising of the Moon*); MONTEVERDI: Poppea (*Incoronazione di Poppea*); MOZART: Dorabella★ (*Così fan tutte*); PUCCINI: Suzuki★ (*Butterfly*); STRAVINSKY: Baba the Turk (*Rake's Progress*); WAGNER: Magdalene★ (*Meistersinger*). Also MONTEVERDI: Ottavia★ (*Incoronazione di Poppea*); DONIZETTI: Maria Stuarda★; HAYDN: Anna★ (*Ritorno di Tobit in patria*); VERDI: Meg Page★ (*Falstaff*). Gives recitals. Appears with symphony orchestra. **Res:** London, UK.

WALKER, WILLIAM. Lyric baritone. American. Resident mem: Metropolitan Opera, New York. Born 29 Oct 1931, Waco, TX, USA. Wife Marci Martin. Four children. Studied: Texas Christian Univ, John Brigham, San Antonio, TX. **Debut:** Schaunard (*Bohème*) Fort Worth Opera, TX 1955. Awards: Disting Alumnus Texas Christian Univ 1970; Met Op Ntl Counc Aud Winner; Met contract & Weyerhaeuser Awd 1962.

Sang with major companies in CAN: Vancouver; USA: Fort Worth, Miami, Milwaukee Florentine, New Orleans, New York Met, San Antonio, Santa Fe, Washington DC. **Roles with these companies incl** BIZET: Escamillo★ (*Carmen*); DONIZETTI: Dott Malatesta★ (*Don Pasquale*); LEON-CAVALLO: Tonio★ (*Pagliacci*); MASCAGNI: Alfio (*Cavalleria rusticana*); MENOTTI: Bob (*Old Maid and the Thief*); MOZART: Guglielmo (*Così fan tutte*), Conte Almaviva (*Nozze di Figaro*), Papageno (*Zauberflöte*); ORFF: Solo (*Carmina burana*); PUCCINI: Marcello★ (*Bohème*), Sharpless★ (*Butterfly*), Lescaut★ (*Manon Lescaut*); ROSSINI: Figaro★ (*Barbiere di Siviglia*); SAINT-SAENS: Grand prêtre★ (*Samson et Dalila*); VERDI: Amonasro (*Aida*), Ford★ (*Falstaff*), Nabucco, Rigoletto, Germont★ (*Traviata*). Also GOUNOD: Valentin★ (*Faust*). Gives recitals. Appears with symphony orchestra. **Res:** San Antonio, TX, USA. Mgmt: CAM/USA.

WALLAT, HANS. Conductor of opera and symphony. German. Gen Music Dir & Resident Cond, Opernhaus, Nationaltheater Mannheim. Born Berlin. Studied: Musikakad Leipzig; Staatskonsv Schwerin, Germany. Previous occupations: chorus master, Mecklenburg State Theater, Schwerin 1952. Previous adm positions in opera: Gen Mus Dir, Städtische Oper Bremen 1965-69.

Conducted with major companies in AUS: Vienna Staatsoper; FRA: Paris; FR GER: Bayreuth Fest, Berlin Deutsche Oper, Cologne, Mannheim, Stuttgart; GER DR: Leipzig; ITA: Trieste; USA: New York Met; et al. **Operas with these companies incl** BEETHOVEN: *Fidelio;* BIZET: *Carmen;* DONIZETTI: *Don Pasquale;* MOZART: *Don Giovanni, Entführung aus dem Serail, Nozze di Figaro, Zauberflöte;* PUCCINI: *Bohème, Butterfly, Tosca;* ROSSINI: *Barbiere di Siviglia;* STRAUSS, R: *Ariadne auf Naxos, Frau ohne Schatten, Rosenkavalier, Salome;* VERDI: *Aida, Ballo in maschera, Forza del destino, Nabucco, Simon Boccanegra, Traviata, Trovatore;* WAGNER: *Fliegende Holländer, Lohengrin, Meistersinger, Parsifal, Rheingold, Walküre, Siegfried, Götterdämmerung, Tannhäuser, Tristan und Isolde;* WEBER: *Freischütz;* et al. Previous positions as Mus Dir with major orch: Phil Orch, Bremen 1965-69.

WALLBERG, HEINZ. Conductor of opera and symphony. German. Resident Cond, Staatsoper, Vienna; Gen Mus Dir designate Bühnen der Stadt Essen, FR Ger. Also Music Dir, Tonkünstlerorch, Vienna. Born 16 Mar 1923, Herringau-Hamm/Westfalen, Germany. Married. Studied: Dortmund Consv; Musikhochschule, Cologne; incl violin, trumpet. Previous adm positions in opera: Mus Oberleiter, Städtische Bühnen Augsburg 1954; Gen Mus Dir, Hessisches Staatstheater, Wiesbaden until 1974.

Conducted with major companies in AUS: Vienna Staatsoper; FR GER: Berlin Deutsche Oper, Cologne, Düsseldorf-Duisburg, Hamburg, Munich Staatsoper, Wiesbaden; ITA: Rome Opera, Venice; et al. **Operas with these companies incl** BEETHOVEN: *Fidelio;* GLUCK: *Orfeo ed Euridice;* MOZART: *Così fan tutte, Don Giovanni, Entführung aus dem Serail, Idomeneo, Nozze di Figaro, Zauberflöte;* PUCCINI: *Bohème, Gianni Schicchi, Butterfly, Manon Lescaut, Tosca, Turandot;* STRAUSS, R: *Ariadne auf Naxos, Capriccio, Elektra, Rosenkavalier, Salome;* VERDI: *Aida, Don Carlo, Forza del destino, Otello, Rigoletto, Traviata, Trovatore;* WAGNER: *Fliegende Holländer, Lohengrin, Meistersinger, Parsifal, Rheingold, Walküre, Siegfried, Götterdämmerung, Tannhäuser, Tristan und Isolde;* WEBER: *Freischütz;* et al.

WALLER, JUANITA: née Woods. Dramatic soprano. American. Born 29 Mar 1939, Pittsburgh, PA, USA. Divorced. One child. Studied: Carnegie-Mellon Univ, Maria Malpi, Pittsburgh. **Debut:** Salome, Bremen Opera, FR Ger.

Sang with major companies in AUS: Vienna Volksoper; FR GER: Düsseldorf-Duisburg, Wuppertal; ITA: Naples; SWI: Zurich; USA: Jackson Opera/South, San Antonio. **Roles with these companies incl** GERSHWIN: Bess★; MONTEVERDI: Poppea★ (*Incoronazione di Poppea*); STRAUSS, R: Salome★; VERDI: Aida★. **World premieres:** STILL: Aurore (*Bayou Legend*) Opera/South, Jackson 1974. Gives recitals. Appears with symphony orchestra. Teaches voice. Coaches repertoire. Mgmt: HJH/USA.

WALLMANN, MARGARITA. Stages/produces opera, film, & television. Also designs stage-lighting; and is an author. Resident Stage Dir, Opéra de Monte-Carlo. Born 22 Jun 1914, Vienna. Studied: in Berlin, Vienna and Paris; also music. **Operatic debut:** Staatsoper Vienna. Previous occupation: dancer and choreographer. Awards: First Prize for opera staging, Salzburg Fest; Toscanini Medal; Puccini Prize; Max Reinhardt Medal; Intl Prize Luigi Illica; Prize, Italian Società Autori ed Editori; etc.

Directed/produced for major companies in ARG: Buenos Aires; AUS: Salzburg Fest, Vienna Staatsoper; FRA: Bordeaux, Marseille, Nice, Paris, Rouen; GRE: Athens Opera & Fest; FR GER: Berlin Deutsche Oper; ITA: Florence Maggio & Comunale, Milan La Scala, Naples, Rome Opera & Caracalla, Trieste, Turin; MON: Monte Carlo; POR: Lisbon; UK: London Royal Opera; USA: New York Met. **Operas directed for these companies incl** AUBER: *Muette de Portici;* BEETHOVEN: *Fidelio**; BELLINI: *Capuleti ed i Montecchi, Norma, Pirata, Puritani, Sonnambula;* BERG: *Wozzeck;* BERLIOZ: *Damnation de Faust, Troyens;* BIZET: *Carmen;* BOITO: *Mefistofele;* BUSONI: *Doctor Faust;* CHARPENTIER: *Louise;* CHERUBINI: *Medea;* CILEA: *A. Lecouvreur;* CIMAROSA: *Matrimonio segreto;* DEBUSSY: *Enfant prodigue, Pelléas et Mélisande;* DONIZETTI: *Anna Bolena, Campanello, Don Pasquale, Favorite, Fille du régiment, Lucia, Lucrezia Borgia, Maria Stuarda, Rita, Roberto Devereux;* FALLA: *Retablo de Maese Pedro, Vida breve;* GAY/Britten: *Beggar's Opera;* GIORDANO: *Andrea Chénier;* GLUCK: *Alceste, Armide, Iphigénie en Aulide, Iphigénie en Tauride, Orfeo ed Euridice;* GOUNOD: *Faust;* GRANADOS: *Goyescas;* HANDEL: *Giulio Cesare;* HINDEMITH: *Cardillac;* HONEGGER: *Antigone, Jeanne d'Arc au bûcher;* HUMPERDINCK: *Hänsel und Gretel;* JANACEK: *Katya Kabanova;* MASCAGNI: *Cavalleria rusticana;* MASSENET: *Manon;* MENOTTI: *Amelia al ballo, Medium;* MEYERBEER: *Robert le diable;* MONTEVERDI: *Combattimento di Tancredi, Favola d'Orfeo, Incoronazione di Poppea;* MOZART: *Don Giovanni, Finta giardiniera, Zauberflöte;* PENDERECKI: *Teufel von Loudun;* PFITZNER: *Palestrina;* PIZZETTI: *Figlia di Jorio, Debora e Jaele;* PONCHIELLI: *Gioconda;* POULENC: *Dialogues des Carmélites, Voix humaine;* PROKOFIEV: *Fiery Angel;* PUCCINI: *Bohème, Fanciulla del West, Manon Lescaut, Turandot;* PURCELL: *Dido and Aeneas;* RABAUD: *Mârouf;* RESPIGHI: *Fiamma;* RAVEL: *Enfant et les sortilèges, Heure espagnole;* ROSSINI: *Barbiere di Siviglia, Semiramide;* SCARLATTI, A: *Mitridate Eupatore;* STRAUSS, R: *Arabella, Daphne, Liebe der Danae;* STRAVINSKY: *Histoire du soldat, Perséphone;* TCHAIKOVSKY: *Eugene Onegin;* VERDI: *Aida, Ballo in maschera, Don Carlo, Falstaff, Forza del destino, Luisa Miller, Macbeth, Nabucco, Otello, Rigoletto, Traviata, Trovatore;* WEBER: *Euryanthe, Oberon;* WEINBERGER: *Schwanda;* WOLF: *Corregidor;* ZANDONAI: *Francesca da Rimini.* **Operatic world premieres:** PIZZETTI: *Clitennestra* 1965, *Assassinio nella cattedrale* 1958, both La Scala, Milan; MARTIN: *Mystère de la nativité* Salzburg Fest 1960; CASTELNUOVO-TEDESCO: *Mercante di Venezia* Florence Fest 1961; BECAUD: *Opéra d'Aran* Paris 1962; POULENC: *Dialogues des Carmélites* 1st stgd La Scala, Milan 1957; MILHAUD: *David* 1st stgd La Scala, Milan 1955; BENTOIU: *Hamlet* Marseille 1974; LESUR: *Andrea del Sarto* Marseille 1969; BONDEVILLE: *Antoine et Cléopatre* Rouen 1974; ROSSELLINI:

Leggenda del ritorno La Scala, Milan 1966, *La reine morte* Opéra Monte-Carlo 1973; etc. **Res:** 26 Blvd des Moulins, Palais Albany, Monte Carlo, Monaco.

WARD, DAVID. Bass-baritone. British. Born 3 Jul 1922, Dumbarton, Scotland, UK. Wife Susan Eily Vivian. Studied: RCM, Clive Carey, London; Hans Hotter, Germany; Luigi Ricci, Italy. **Debut:** Count Walter (*Luisa Miller*) Sadler's Wells Opera, London 1953. Previous occupations: naval officer, schoolteacher. Awards: CBE Her Majesty Queen Elizabeth II; FRCM, RCM London; RAM London; LLD, Strathclyde Univ, Glasgow.

Sang with major companies in ARG: Buenos Aires; AUS: Vienna Staatsoper; CAN: Toronto, Vancouver; FRA: Bordeaux, Lyon, Marseille, Nice; FR GER: Bayreuth Fest, Cologne, Düsseldorf-Duisburg, Hamburg, Stuttgart; ITA: Milan La Scala, Naples; MEX: Mexico City; POR: Lisbon; UK: Cardiff Welsh, Edinburgh Fest, Glasgow Scottish, Glyndebourne Fest, London Royal & English National; USA: Chicago, Miami, New Orleans, New York Met, San Diego, San Francisco Opera. **Roles with these companies incl** BARTOK: Bluebeard*; BEETHOVEN: Rocco* (*Fidelio*); DEBUSSY: Arkel*‡ (*Pelléas et Mélisande*); FLOTOW: Plunkett (*Martha*); GOUNOD: Méphistophélès (*Faust*); MEYERBEER: Marcel (*Huguenots*); MOZART: Sarastro (*Zauberflöte*); MUSSORGSKY: Boris Godunov*, Ivan Khovansky* (*Khovanshchina*), Colline (*Bohème*); ROSSINI: Don Basilio* (*Barbiere di Siviglia*), Moïse; SMETANA: Kezal (*Bartered Bride*); STRAUSS, R: Sir Morosus (*Schweigsame Frau*); STRAVINSKY: Tiresias (*Oedipus Rex*); VERDI: Philip II* & Grande Inquisitore (*Don Carlo*), Padre Guardiano* (*Forza del destino*), Conte Walter (*Luisa Miller*), Zaccaria* (*Nabucco*), Fiesco (*Simon Boccanegra*); WAGNER: Holländer*, König Heinrich (*Lohengrin*), Pogner* (*Meistersinger*), Wotan (*Rheingold**, *Walküre**), Wanderer* (*Siegfried*), Fasolt (*Rheingold*), Hunding‡ (*Walküre*), Landgraf (*Tannhäuser*), König Marke* (*Tristan und Isolde*). Recorded for: EMI, Decca, Westminster, RCA, CBS. Appears with symphony orchestra. **Res:** 14 Clarence Terrace, London NW1, UK. Mgmt: IWL/UK; COL/USA.

WARDEN, WILLIAM BURNAND. American. Gen Mng & Exec Dir, Connecticut Opera Assn, 15 Lewis St, Hartford, CT 06103, 1974- . In charge of overall adm matters, art policy, mus, dram & tech matters, finances. Born 19 Oct 1922, London, UK. Divorced. Previous occupations: Chmn, Bucks County Bd of Commss, PA; Chmn, Solebury Township Bd of Supervisors, Bucks Cnty. Form positions, primarily adm: Financial Adm, Secy-Treas, Vc Pres, Pres, Co-Chmn, Co-Mng, Philadelphia Lyric Opera 1961-73. Awards: Ufficiale Ordine al Merito della Repubblica Italiana. Initiated major policy changes including building own scenery for at least one new prod per season. Mem of Auditions Commtt, Translation Commtt, OPERA America; Chmn, Music Commtt, Greater Hartford Arts Festival; Prof Commtt, Hartford Arts Council. **Res:** 111 Sunset Farm Rd, West Hartford, CT, USA.

WARE, CLIFTON; né Durward Clifton Ware, Jr. Lyric tenor. American. Born 15 Mar 1937, Newton, MS, USA. Wife Elizabeth Jean Oldham, occupation piano teacher, organist. Three sons. Studied: Northwestern Univ, Evanston, IL, USA. **Debut:** Pinkerton (*Butterfly*) Jackson Opera Guild 1962. Previous occupations: minister of music, choral director, opera director. Awards: MN Deputy Gov NOA; MN Chapter Pres NATS; Fisk Awd vocal compt Northwestern Univ.

Sang with major companies in USA: Minneapolis, New Orleans, St Paul. **Roles with these companies incl** GOUNOD: Faust; MASCAGNI: Turiddu (*Cavalleria rusticana*); MENOTTI: Lover (*Amelia al ballo*); MOZART: Ferrando (*Così fan tutte*), Tamino∗ (*Zauberflöte*); PUCCINI: Rinuccio (*Gianni Schicchi*), Pinkerton (*Butterfly*); STRAUSS, J: Eisenstein (*Fledermaus*); STRAUSS, R: Matteo (*Arabella*); STRAVINSKY: Tom Rakewell∗ (*Rake's Progress*). Also NIELSEN: Leander∗(*Maskarade*); WARD: Rev Parris∗ (*Crucible*); FISHER: Prince∗ (*Happy Prince*); SOUSA: Verrada∗ (*El Capitan*); ARGENTO: John∗ (*Masque of Angels*). **World premieres:** HOIBY: Roger (*Summer and Smoke*) St Paul Opera 1971. Gives recitals. Appears with symphony orchestra. Teaches voice. Coaches repertoire. On faculty of Univ of Minnesota, Minneapolis. **Res:** 3429 Benjamin NE, Minneapolis, MN 55418, USA. **Mgmt:** DBA/USA.

WARFIELD, SANDRA; née Flora-Jean Bornstein. Dramatic mezzo-soprano. American. Born 6 Aug 1929, Kansas City, MO, USA. Husband James McCracken, occupation tenor. One daughter. Studied: Walter Ehrnman, Mr & Mrs van Duzee, Kansas City, MO; Marcello Conati, Milan; Else Seyfert, NY & Konstanz, Ger. **Debut:** Prinz Orlovsky (*Fledermaus*) Chautauqua Opera Fest, NY 1950. Awards: Alumni Achievement Awd, Univ of Missouri.

Sang with major companies in AUS: Vienna Staatsoper; FRA: Marseille, Nice; FR GER: Berlin Deutsche Oper, Bielefeld; ITA: Venice; SPA: Barcelona; SWI: Geneva, Zurich; USA: Cincinnati, Hartford Connecticut Opera, Miami, Milwaukee Florentine, New Orleans, New York Met, St Paul, San Francisco Opera, Seattle. **Roles with these companies incl** BIZET: Carmen∗; DONIZETTI: Léonore (*Favorite*); FLOTOW: Nancy (*Martha*); GLUCK: Orfeo; MARTINU: Katerina (*Griechische Passion*); MASCAGNI: Santuzza∗ (*Cavalleria rusticana*), Dulcinée (*Don Quichotte*); MEYERBEER: Fidès (*Prophète*); MOZART: Dorabella (*Così fan tutte*); PONCHIELLI: La Cieca (*Gioconda*); POULENC: Mère Marie (*Dialogues des Carmélites*); SAINT-SAENS: Dalila∗; STRAUSS, J: Prinz Orlovsky (*Fledermaus*); STRAUSS, R: Octavian (*Rosenkavalier*); STRAVINSKY: Mère‡ (*Mavra*); VERDI: Amneris∗ (*Aida*), Ulrica (*Ballo in maschera*), Eboli (*Don Carlo*), Azucena∗ (*Trovatore*); WAGNER: Erda (*Rheingold, Siegfried*), Fricka (*Rheingold, Walküre*). Also BRITTEN: Oberon (*Midsummer Night's Dream*); SUTERMEISTER: Mother (*Raskolnikoff*). Gives recitals. Appears with symphony orchestra. **Res:** Zurich, Switzerland. **Mgmt:** CAM/USA; GOR/UK.

WARTENEGG, HANNA; née Johanna Warzilek. Scenic and costume designer for opera, theater. Is a lighting designer; also an illustrator. Austrian. Chief Designer, Vereinigte Bühnen Graz and at Schauspielhaus Graz. Born 1 Oct 1939, Vienna. Single. Studied: Hochschule für angewandte Kunst, Prof Arch Otto Niedermoser, Prof Elli Rolf, Vienna. Prof training: Kammeroper, Vienna 1961-62. **Operatic debut:** Fiery Angel Vereinigte Bühnen Graz 1962. Theater debut: Schönbrunner Schlosstheater, Max Reinhardt Seminar, Vienna. Awards: Austrian State Prize for sets & cost 1962; stipd from Akad für angewandte Kunst, Vienna 1961.

Designed for major companies in AUS: Graz; FR GER: Dortmund, Munich Gärtnerplatz, Nürnberg. **Operas designed for these companies incl** BERG: *Lulu;* BERLIOZ: *Damnation de Faust;* BUSONI: *Doktor Faust;* CIMAROSA: *Matrimonio segreto;* DEBUSSY: *Pelléas et Mélisande;* DONIZETTI: *Favorite;* EINEM: *Besuch der alten Dame;* FALLA: *Vida breve;* FLOTOW: *Martha;* GIORDANO: *Andrea Chénier;* GLUCK: *Iphigénie en Tauride;* GOUNOD: *Roméo et Juliette;* JANACEK: *Katya Kabanova;* MASSENET: *Manon;* MEYERBEER: *Africaine;* MONTEVERDI: *Combattimento di Tancredi;* MOZART: *Entführung aus dem Serail∗;* MUSSORGSKY: *Boris Godunov;* NICOLAI: *Lustigen Weiber;* OFFENBACH: *Contes d'Hoffmann;* PROKOFIEV: *Fiery Angel;* PUCCINI: *Bohème, Manon Lescaut, Tosca;* RIMSKY-KORSAKOV: *Invisible City of Kitezh;* ROSSINI: *Barbiere di Siviglia, Gazza ladra∗;* SMETANA: *Bartered Bride;* STRAUSS, J: *Fledermaus;* STRAUSS, R: *Arabella, Rosenkavalier;* STRAVINSKY: *Oedipus Rex;* TCHAIKOVSKY: *Eugene Onegin;* THOMAS: *Hamlet;* VERDI: *Attila, Ballo in maschera, Otello∗, Rigoletto, Trovatore;* WAGNER: *Rienzi;* WEBER: *Freischütz.* Exhibitions of stage designs, Graz 1973. Teaches at Hochschule für Musik und darst Kunst, Graz. **Res:** Richard Wagnerg 33, Graz, Austria.

WASHINGTON, PAOLO. Bass. Italian. Born 24 May 1932, Florence. Wife Eliana Jonnamaria. One child. Studied: Centro Lirico, Teatro Comunale, Florence; Mo Flaminio Contini, Bruno Bartoletti, Italy. **Debut:** Douglas (*Donna del lago*) Teatro Comunale, Florence 1958. Awards: Prizes for artistic merit at conts in Japan, Spain, Portugal, Italy.

Sang with major companies in ARG: Buenos Aires; AUS: Bregenz Fest, Salzburg Fest; BEL: Brussels; CAN: Vancouver; FRA: Marseille, Nice, Toulouse; GRE: Athens National; HUN: Budapest; ITA: Bologna, Florence Maggio & Teatro Comunale, Genoa, Milan La Scala, Naples, Palermo, Parma, Rome Opera & Caracalla, Trieste, Turin, Venice, Verona Arena; MEX: Mexico City; POR: Lisbon; SPA: Barcelona, Majorca; SWI: Geneva; UK: Edinburgh Fest; USA: Chicago. **Roles with these companies incl** BELLINI: Oroveso∗ (*Norma*), Sir George∗ (*Puritani*), Rodolfo∗(*Sonnambula*); BIZET: Zurga (*Pêcheurs de perles*); CHERUBINI: Creon∗ (*Medea*); CIMAROSA: Geronimo (*Matrimonio segreto*); DONIZETTI: Don Pasquale∗, Dott Dulcamara∗ (*Elisir*), Baldassare∗ (*Favorite*), Antonio (*Linda di Chamounix*), Talbot∗(*Maria Stuarda*); HANDEL: Zoroastro (*Orlando furioso*); HENZE: Cadmus (*Bassariden*); MENOTTI: Maharaja (*Dernier sauvage*); MUSSORGSKY: Pimen∗ (*Boris Godu-*

nov), Ivan Khovansky★ & Dosifei★ (*Khovansh-china*); PONCHIELLI: Alvise★ (*Gioconda*); PROKOFIEV: Ruprecht (*Fiery Angel*); PUC-CINI: Colline★ (*Bohème*); RIMSKY-KORSAKOV: Roi Dodon★ (*Coq d'or*), Juri Vsevolodovic (*Invisible City of Kitezh*); ROS-SINI: Don Basilio★ (*Barbiere de Siviglia*), Robert (*Comte Ory*), Podestà (*Gazza ladra*), Mustafà (*Italiana in Algeri*), Moïse; STRAVINSKY: Creon★ & Tiresias★ (*Oedipus Rex*); VERDI: Ram-fis★ (*Aida*), Grande Inquisitore (*Don Carlo*), Silva★ (*Ernani*), Padre Guardiano★ (*Forza del destino*), Conte Walter (*Luisa Miller*), Banquo★ (*Macbeth*), Zaccaria★ (*Nabucco*), Fiesco★ (*Simon Bocca-negra*), Procida★ (*Vespri*); WAGNER: Daland★ (*Fliegende Holländer*), König Heinrich★ (*Lohen-grin*), Wotan (*Walküre*). Also BERLIOZ: Frère Laurent (*Roméo et Juliette*); CHERUBINI: Frate (*Elisa*). Recorded for: Angelicum, DG, Voce del Padrone, Decca. Video/Film: Mustafà (*Italiana in Algeri*); Gualtiero (*Guglielmo Tell*); Raimondo (*Lucia di Lammermoor*). Gives recitals. Appears with symphony orchestra. Coaches repertoire.

WATSON, CLAIRE; née Claire McLamore. Spinto. American. Resident mem: Bayerische Staatsoper, Munich. Born 3 Feb 1927, New York. Husband David M Thaw, occupation singer & stage dir. Five children. Studied: Elisabeth Schu-mann, Sergius Kagen, New York. **Debut**: Desde-mona (*Otello*) Graz Oper, Austria 1951. Awards: Bavarian Order of Merit, Bavarian Gvnmt; Kam-mersängerin, Ministry of Culture.

Sang with major companies in ARG: Buenos Aires; AUS: Graz, Salzburg Fest, Vienna Staatso-per; BEL: Brussels; CAN: Toronto; FR GER: Berlin Deutsche Oper, Cologne, Darmstadt, Dort-mund, Düsseldorf-Duisburg, Frankfurt, Hamburg, Hannover, Mannheim, Munich Staatsoper, Nürnberg, Stuttgart, Wiesbaden; HOL: Amster-dam; ITA: Florence Comunale, Milan La Scala, Naples, Rome Opera, Turin, Venice; POR: Lis-bon; ROM: Bucharest; SPA: Barcelona; SWI: Basel, Zurich; UK: Edinburgh Fest, Glynde-bourne Fest, London Royal Opera; USA: Boston, Chicago, New Orleans, Pittsburgh, San Francisco Opera, Washington DC; YUG: Zagreb. **Roles with these companies incl** BEETHOVEN: Leonore★ (*Fidelio*); BIZET: Micaëla (*Carmen*); BRITTEN: Ellen Orford‡ (*Peter Grimes*); GLUCK: Iphigénie (*Iphigénie en Aulide*); HANDEL: Cleopatra (*Giulio Cesare*); LORTZING: Baronin Freimann (*Wildschütz*); MOZART: Vitellia (*Clemenza di Tito*), Fiordiligi (*Così fan tutte*), Donna Anna★‡ & Donna Elvira (*Don Giovanni*), Elettra (*Idomeneo*), Contessa★ (*Nozze di Figaro*), Pamina (*Zauber-flöte*); OFFENBACH: Giulietta (*Contes d'Hoffmann*); PUCCINI: Mimi (*Bohème*), Cio-Cio-San (*Butterfly*), Tosca, Liù (*Turandot*); PUR-CELL: Dido; STRAUSS, R: Arabella, Ariadne★ (*Ariadne auf Naxos*), Gräfin★ (*Capriccio*), Chryso-themis★ (*Elektra*), Marschallin★ (*Rosenkavalier*); TCHAIKOVSKY: Tatiana (*Eugene Onegin*); VERDI: Aida, Amelia★ (*Ballo in maschera*), Elisabetta★ (*Don Carlo*), Alice Ford (*Falstaff*), Leonora★ (*Forza del destino*), Desdemona★ (*Otello*); WAGNER: Senta★ (*Fliegende Hollän-der*), Elsa★ (*Lohengrin*), Eva★‡ (*Meistersinger*), Sieglinde★ (*Walküre*), Gutrune‡ (*Götterdämme-rung*), Elisabeth★ (*Tannhäuser*); WEBER:

Agathe‡ (*Freischütz*). Recorded for: London (Decca), Electrola, Eurodisc, Intercord. Video/Film: Ariadne (*Ariadne auf Naxos*). Gives recitals. Appears with symphony orchestra. **Res**: Haus 62, 8919 Holzhausen/Ammersee, FR Ger. Mgmt: HUR/USA.

WATSON, LEE; né Leland Hale Watson. Scenic designer for opera, theater. Is a lighting designer. American. Resident designer, New Jersey State Opera, Newark, NJ. Born 18 Feb 1926, Charleston, IL. Single. Studied: State Univ of Iowa, Iowa City; Yale Univ, New Haven, CT. **Operatic debut**: sets, *Carmen* New Jersey State Opera 1975; lighting, *Lost in the Stars* New York City Opera 1958. Theater debut: Playhouse, New York 1954. Previous occupation: teacher, author; CBS TV lighting designer. Awards: Obie for light-ing Off Broadway, 1959.

Designed for major companies in USA: Balti-more, Dallas, Houston, Milwaukee Florentine, Newark, New York City Opera, Philadelphia Grand. **Operas designed for these companies incl** BIZET: *Carmen★*; BRITTEN: *Midsummer Night, Turn of the Screw*; BUSONI: *Turandot*; KURKA: *Good Soldier Schweik*; LEON-CAVALLO: *Pagliacci*; MASCAGNI: *Cavalleria rusticana*; MENOTTI: *Globolinks, Maria Golo-vin*; MOORE: *Ballad of Baby Doe*; MOZART: *Don Giovanni*; OFFENBACH: *Contes d'Hoffmann*; PUCCINI: *Bohème, Gianni Schicchi, Butterfly*; STRAUSS, J: *Fledermaus*; STRAUSS, R: *Rosenkavalier, Salome*; VERDI: *Aida, Rigoletto*. Also designed lights for KURKA: *Good Soldier Schweik*; BRITTEN: *Rape of Lu-cretia*; HOIBY: *Scarf*; MOORE: *Devil and Dan-iel Webster* all at New York City Opera 1958-59; ORFF: *Mond* Houston 1970. Teaches at Purdue Univ, W Lafayette, IN. **Res**: 40-04 215 Pl, Bay-side, NY, USA.

WATT-SMITH, IAN RICHARD. Stages/produces opera, theater & television and is an author. Brit-ish. Dir of Prod & Resident Stage Dir, Welsh National Opera, Cardiff, Wales. Born 17 Apr 1943, Sheffield. Single. Operatic training as asst stage dir at Scottish Opera, Glasgow 1968-70. **Operatic de-but**: ORR: *Full Circle* Scottish Opera 1969. The-ater debut: Hampstead Theatre, London 1966. Previous adm positions in opera: Sr Staff Prod 2 yrs, Scottish Opera, Glasgow.

Directed/produced opera for major companies in UK: Welsh National, Scottish. **Operas staged with these companies incl** BRITTEN: *Albert Herring★, Peter Grimes★*; DONIZETTI: *Don Pasquale*; FLOTOW: *Martha*; MENOTTI: *Telephone*; MOZART: *Don Giovanni*; PUCCINI: *Butterfly*; ROSSINI: *Barbiere di Siviglia★, Cenerentola*; SMETANA: *Secret*; VERDI: *Traviata★*; WAG-NER: *Fliegende Holländer★*. **Operatic world pre-mieres**: PURSER: *Undertaker* Scottish Opera, Edinburgh 1969. Operatic Video—Scottish TV: *Undertaker*. Previous leading positions with major theater companies: Assoc Dir, Perth Theatre, Scotland 1967-68; Asst Dir, Royal Court Theatre, London 1966-67; Asst Dir, Hampstead Theatre, London 1965-66. **Res**: Smithies Ave, Sully/Glamorgan, S Wales, UK.

WAUGH, IRENE. Lyric mezzo-soprano. Austra-lian. Resident mem: Hessisches Staatstheater,

Wiesbaden, FR Ger. Born 29 Jun 1947, Newcastle, NSW, Australia. Single. Studied: Sydney Consv of Music, Ruth E Ladd; Nitsa Anayanni, Vienna; Konsv Stadt Wien, Prof Hudez, Vienna. **Debut:** Nicklausse (*Contes d'Hoffmann*) Volksoper Vienna 1973. Awards: Twice winner of Doris Smith Schlshp, Consv of Music, Newcastle, Australia.
Sang with major companies in AUS: Vienna Volksoper; FR GER: Cologne, Wiesbaden. **Roles with these companies incl** FLOTOW: Nancy* (*Martha*); HUMPERDINCK: Hänsel*; MOZART: Dorabella* (*Così fan tutte*), Cherubino* (*Nozze di Figaro*); ROSSINI: Rosina* (*Barbiere di Siviglia*); WEBER: Fatime* (*Oberon*); YUN: Mme Tian*‡ (*Witwe des Schmetterlings*). Recorded for: WDR, ORF. Gives recitals. Appears with symphony orchestra. **Res:** Geisbergstr 32, 62 Wiesbaden, FR Ger. Mgmt: ARM/FRG; RAB/AUS.

WEATHERS, FELICIA. Dramatic soprano. American. Born 13 Aug 1939, St Louis, MO. Studied: Indiana Univ, Charles Kullman, Dorothee Manski. **Debut:** Zurich. Awards: Second Prize, Met Op Ntl Counc Aud 1957.
Sang with major companies in AUS: Vienna Staatsoper; FR GER: Berlin Deutsche Oper, Düsseldorf-Duisburg, Hamburg, Kiel, Munich Staatsoper, Saarbrücken; SWE: Stockholm; SWI: Zurich; UK: London Royal; USA: Chicago, Cincinnati, Houston, Kansas City, New York Met, Philadelphia Lyric; et al. **Roles with these companies incl** PROKOFIEV: Renata (*Flaming Angel*); PUCCINI: Cio-Cio-San (*Butterfly*); STRAUSS, R: Salome (*Salome*); TCHAIKOVSKY: Lisa (*Pique Dame*); VERDI: Aida, Elisabetta (*Don Carlo*), Leonora (*Trovatore*); et al. **World premieres:** SCHULLER: Teena (*The Visitation*) Hamburg 1967. Recorded for: Decca, London. Gives recitals. Mgmt: CAM/USA.

WEAVING, JON WEYMOUTH. Heldentenor. Australian. Born 23 Feb 1936, Melbourne, Australia. Wife Monique Brynnel, occupation operetta diva. Two children. Studied: Browning Mummery, Melbourne, Australia; Audrey Langford, London; Ken Neate, Munich; Anni Assian-Röhrling, Kiel, FR Ger. **Debut:** Eisenstein (*Fledermaus*) Sadler's Wells Opera, London 1960. Previous occupations: radio announcer.
Sang with major companies in FRA: Lyon; FR GER: Bielefeld, Essen, Hannover, Kiel, Munich Staatsoper, Wiesbaden; UK: Aldeburgh Fest, London English National. **Roles with these companies incl** BEETHOVEN: Florestan (*Fidelio*); BIZET: Don José (*Carmen*); DELIUS: Sali (*Village Romeo and Juliet*); GAY/Britten: Macheath (*Beggar's Opera*); GIORDANO: Andrea Chénier; GOUNOD: Faust; LEONCAVALLO: Canio (*Pagliacci*); OFFENBACH: Hoffmann; PUCCINI: Luigi (*Tabarro*); STRAUSS, J: Eisenstein (*Fledermaus*); STRAUSS, R: Bacchus (*Ariadne auf Naxos*), Ein Sänger (*Rosenkavalier*); TCHAIKOVSKY: Gherman (*Pique Dame*); VERDI: Don Alvaro (*Forza del destino*), Otello; WAGNER: Erik* (*Fliegende Holländer*), Lohengrin, Loge* (*Rheingold*), Siegmund* (*Walküre*), Siegfried (*Siegfried*, *Götterdämmerung*); WEBER: Hüon (*Oberon*). Also MUSSORGSKY: Di-

mitri* (*Boris Godunov*). **World premieres:** SCHOENBACH: Bauernführer (*Geschichte von einem Feuer*) Kiel Opera 1968; NIEHAUS: Der Mann (*Maldoror*) Kiel Opera 1970; LUDWIG: Kaufmann (*Rashomon*) Augsburg Opera, FR Ger 1972. Video—TV: Sosthene (*Violins of Saint Jacques*). Gives recitals. **Res:** Herbrüggenstr 109, 43 Essen 11, FR Ger. Mgmt: SLZ/FRG.

WEBER, WOLFGANG KLAUS. Stages/produces opera & theater. Also designs stage-lighting and is an author. German. Resident Stage Dir & Asst to the Dir, Volksoper, Vienna. Born 2 Dec 1935, Munich. Wife Irmtraud. One daughter. Studied: piano, cembalo, violin, organ. Operatic training as asst stage dir at Opera, Heidelberg; State Opera, Stuttgart; Vienna State Opera with Paul Hager 1956-60, Herbert v Karajan 1960-62. **Operatic debut:** *Norma* Opera, Graz, Austria 1962. Theater debut: Volksoper, Vienna 1968.
Directed/produced opera for major companies in AUS: Bregenz Fest, Graz, Salzburg Fest, Vienna Staatsoper & Volksoper; FR GER: Bielefeld, Dortmund, Krefeld, Nürnberg; ITA: Florence Maggio; USA: Chicago, New York Met, San Francisco Opera. **Operas staged for these companies incl** ADAM: *Postillon de Lonjumeau;* d'ALBERT: *Tiefland;* BARTOK: *Bluebeard's Castle;* BELLINI: *Norma;* CIMAROSA: *Matrimonio segreto;* DALLAPICCOLA: *Prigioniero;* DESSAU: *Verurteilung des Lukullus;* DONIZETTI: *Favorite, Lucia;* EGK: *Verlobung in San Domingo;* EINEM: *Prozess;* FLOTOW: *Martha;* GLUCK: *Orfeo ed Euridice;* HENZE: *Junge Lord;* HINDEMITH: *Cardillac*;* LEONCAVALLO: *Pagliacci;* MASCAGNI: *Cavalleria rusticana;* MOZART: *Don Giovanni, Entführung aus dem Serail, Finta giardiniera, Idomeneo, Mitridate re di Ponto, Nozze di Figaro;* MUSSORGSKY: *Boris Godunov;* NICOLAI: *Lustigen Weiber;* ORFF: *Kluge;* PROKOFIEV: *Duenna;* PUCCINI: *Bohème, Tabarro, Tosca*, Turandot*;* ROSSINI: *Barbiere di Siviglia;* SAINT-SAENS: *Samson et Dalila;* SMETANA: *Bartered Bride;* STRAUSS, R: *Elektra;* VERDI: *Ballo in maschera, Don Carlo, Macbeth, Otello, Rigoletto, Traviata;* WAGNER: *Rheingold*, Walküre*, Siegfried*, Götterdämmerung*, Tristan und Isolde*;* YUN: *Traum des Liu-Tung.* Also NONO: *Intolleranza;* HONEGGER: *Judith;* YUN: *Geisterliebe*.* **Operatic world premieres:** YUN: *Witwe des Schmetterlings* Nürnberg 1969; HENZE: *Floss der Medusa* Nürnberg 1972; WEISHAPPEL: *König Nicolo* Volksoper, Vienna 1972; RUBIN: *Kleider machen Leute* Volksoper 1973; WOLPERT: *Eingebildete Kranke* Volksoper 1975. **Res:** Alleesgasse 7, 3400 Klosterneuburg/Vienna, Austria. Mgmt: TAS/AUS.

WECHSLER, GIL. Lighting designer for opera, theater. American. Resident designer, Lyric Opera of Chicago, USA, and at Stratford Fest, Ont, Canada. Born 5 Feb 1942, New York. Single. Studied: Yale School of Drama, CT. **Operatic debut:** *Due Foscari* Lyric Opera of Chicago 1972. Theater debut: Broadway, New York 1968.
Designed for major companies in USA: Chicago, New York Met. **Operas designed for these companies incl** BERG: *Wozzeck*;* BIZET: *Carmen*;* BRITTEN: *Peter Grimes*;* DEBUSSY: *Pelléas*

et Mélisande; DONIZETTI: *Don Pasquale★, Favorite, Fille du régiment★, Maria Stuarda★;* MASSENET: *Don Quichotte★, Manon★;* MOZART: *Così fan tutte★;* PUCCINI: *Bohème★, Madama Butterfly, Tosca★;* STRAUSS, R: *Rosenkavalier;* VERDI: *Ballo in maschera★, Due Foscari★, Falstaff★, Simon Boccanegra★, Traviata★;* WAGNER: *Walküre, Siegfried, Götterdämmerung.* Teaches at New York Univ; Yale Univ; Ntl Theatre School, Montreal, Canada.

WEDER, ULRICH. Conductor of opera and symphony. German. Resident Cond, Stadttheater, Bremerhaven, FR Ger. Also Resident Cond, Städt Symph Orch, Bremerhaven. Born 9 May 1934, Bremen. Wife Waltraut Winter, occupation singer. Two children. Studied: Prof Kurt Thomas, Prof Bernhard Paumgartner, G Wimberger, Mo Franco Ferrara, Mo F Previtali; incl organ, piano. Plays the piano, cembalo. Operatic training as repetiteur, asst cond & Studienleiter at Salzburger Opernstudio 1957-59; Stadttheater Bonn 1962-65; Deutsche Oper Berlin, FR Ger 1965-68. **Operatic debut:** *Freischütz* Städt Bühnen, Essen 1961. Symphonic debut: Orch Accad di S Cecilia, Rome 1962. Awards: Lilli Lehmann Medal, Intl Compt Mozarteum, Salzburg. Previous adm positions in opera: Oper am Gärtnerplatz, Munich, First Cond 1969-71, Chief Cond 1971-73. Appointed Gen Mus Dir, Stadttheater Bremerhaven 1975-78.

Conducted with major companies in AUS: Salzburg Fest; FR GER: Berlin Deutsche Oper, Bielefeld, Bonn, Essen, Hamburg, Kiel, Munich Staatsoper & Gärtnerplatz, Saarbrücken; HOL: Amsterdam; SWI: Basel. **Operas with these companies incl** AUBER: *Fra Diavolo★;* BARTOK: *Bluebeard's Castle;* BEETHOVEN: *Fidelio★;* BIZET: *Carmen★;* BUSONI: *Arlecchino, Turandot;* CIMAROSA: *Matrimonio segreto;* DONIZETTI: *Don Pasquale★;* DVORAK: *Rusalka★;* FLOTOW: *Martha;* GOUNOD: *Faust;* HENZE: *Boulevard Solitude, Elegy for Young Lovers, Junge Lord★;* JANACEK: *Cunning Little Vixen★;* LEONCAVALLO: *Pagliacci;* LORTZING: *Waffenschmied, Wildschütz, Zar und Zimmermann;* MILHAUD: *Pauvre matelot;* MOZART: *Così fan tutte, Don Giovanni, Entführung aus dem Serail★, Finta giardiniera, Nozze di Figaro, Zauberflöte★;* NICOLAI: *Lustigen Weiber;* OFFENBACH: *Contes d'Hoffmann★;* PROKOFIEV: *Duenna★;* PUCCINI: *Bohème★, Tosca;* ROSSINI: *Barbiere di Siviglia★;* SMETANA: *Bartered Bride★, Two Widows;* STRAUSS, J: *Fledermaus★;* STRAUSS, R: *Ariadne auf Naxos;* TCHAIKOVSKY: *Pique Dame★;* VERDI: *Ballo in maschera, Don Carlo★, Otello, Traviata★, Trovatore;* WEBER: *Freischütz;* WEILL: *Aufstieg und Fall der Stadt Mahagonny.* Also PURCELL: *Fairy Queen★;* DITTERSDORF: *Doktor und Apotheker;* MIHALOVICI: *Krapp's Last Tape;* RAMEAU: *Platée;* WIMBERGER: *Dame Kobold;* LOTHAR: *Widerspenstige Heilige.* **World premieres:** YUN: *Traum des Liu-Tung* Deutsche Oper Berlin 1965. Recorded for Philips. Conducted major orch in Europe. Teaches at Richard Strauss Konsv, Munich. Res: Bismarck Str 60, Bremerhaven, FR Ger.

WEGRZYN, ROMAN. Heldentenor. Polish. Resident mem: Teatr Wielki, Warsaw. Born 27 Jul 1928, Lwow, Poland. Wife Barbara. One child. Studied: PWSM, Anatol Wronski, Wrozlaw; High School of Music, Wrozlaw. **Debut:** Jontek (*Halka*) Opera Krakow, Poland 1960.

Sang with major companies in CZE: Brno, Prague National & Smetana; FRA: Nancy; FR GER: Bonn, Frankfurt, Karlsruhe, Munich Gärtnerplatz, Wiesbaden; GER DR: Berlin Staatsoper; POL: Lodz, Warsaw; USSR: Kiev. **Roles with these companies incl** BEETHOVEN: Florestan (*Fidelio*); BIZET: Don José★ (*Carmen*); DONIZETTI: Edgardo (*Lucia*); LEONCAVALLO: Canio (*Pagliacci*); MASSENET: Werther; MONIUSZKO: Jontek★ (*Halka*); MUSSORGSKY: Dimitri★ (*Boris Godunov*); PENDERECKI: de Laubardemont★ (*Teufel von Loudun*); PUCCINI: Rinuccio (*Gianni Schicchi*), Pinkerton (*Butterfly*), Cavaradossi★ (*Tosca*), Calaf (*Turandot*); SHOSTAKOVICH: Sergei★ (*Katerina Ismailova*); STRAUSS, R: Aegisth (*Elektra*); TCHAIKOVSKY: Gherman (*Pique Dame*); VERDI: Don Carlo★, Otello★, Alfredo (*Traviata*), Manrico★ (*Trovatore*); WAGNER: Tannhäuser★. Video/Film: SZYMANOWSKI: Old King (*Hagith*). Appears with symphony orchestra. Res: ul Potocka 60 m 30, 01-652 Warsaw, Poland.

WEIDINGER, CHRISTINE MARIE. Lyric soprano. American. Resident mem: Metropolitan Opera, New York. Born 31 Mar 1946, Springville, NY, USA. Single. Studied: Grand Canyon Coll, Marlene Delavan, Pax, AZ, Arizona State Univ, Richard Dales, Tempe, AZ, USA; San Fernando State Coll, David Scott, Northridge, CA; Indiana Univ, Margaret Harshaw, Bloomington, USA. **Debut:** Cherubino (*Nozze di Figaro*) Central City Opera, CO, USA 1972. Previous occupations: secy. Awards: First Place Met Op Ntl Counc Aud 1972.

Sang with major companies in USA: New York Met, San Francisco Spring. **Roles with these companies incl** BEETHOVEN: Marzelline (*Fidelio*); HUMPERDINCK: Gretel★; MOZART: Konstanze★ (*Entführung aus dem Serail*); PUCCINI: Musetta★ (*Bohème*); ROSSINI: Elvira★ (*Italiana in Algeri*). Also GOUNOD: Stephano★ (*Roméo et Juliette*). Gives recitals. Appears with symphony orchestra. Res: 155 W 68 St, New York, NY, USA. Mgmt: DSP/USA.

WEIKERT, RALF. Conductor of opera and symphony; composer. Austrian. Mus Dir & Principal Cond, Theater der Stadt Bonn 1968- . Born 10 Nov 1940, St Florian, Austria. Wife Heidemarie. Two children. Studied: Bruckner Konsv, Linz; Acad of Music, Prof Hans Swarowsky, Vienna; incl piano, violin. Operatic training as repetiteur & asst cond at Landestheater Salzburg 1963-66. **Operatic debut:** *Zauberflöte* Landestheater Salzburg 1964. Symphonic debut: ORF Symph Orch, Vienna 1963. Previous occupations: composed music for 3 films. Awards: Mozart Interpret Prize, Ministry for Educ, Vienna 1966; First Prize Nicolai Malko, Radio Denmark 1965; Karl-Böhm-Preis 1975, Ministry for Educt, Salzburg.

Conducted with major companies in AUS: Salzburg Fest, Vienna Staatsoper; DEN: Copenhagen; FR GER: Bonn, Hamburg; ITA: Trieste. **Operas with these companies incl** ADAM: *Si j'étais roi;* BEETHOVEN: *Fidelio★;* BERG: *Wozzeck;* BI-

ZET: *Carmen;* DELIBES: *Roi l'a dit;* DONI-ZETTI: *Anna Bolena★, Campanello★, Don Pasquale, Elisir★, Favorite, Maria di Rohan, Roberto Devereux;* DVORAK: *Rusalka★;* GLUCK: *Alceste;* HINDEMITH: *Hin und zurück★, Mathis der Maler★;* LEONCAVALLO: *Pagliacci★;* MASSENET: *Don Quichotte★;* MOZART: *Così fan tutte★, Don Giovanni★, Idomeneo★, Nozze di Figaro★, Zauberflöte;* MUSSORGSKY: *Boris Godunov★;* OFFENBACH: *Contes d'Hoffmann★;* PROKOFIEV: *Love for Three Oranges★;* PUCCINI: *Bohème, Tosca, Turandot;* RAVEL: *Heure espagnole;* SMETANA: *Bartered Bride;* STRAUSS, J: *Fledermaus★;* STRAUSS, R: *Arabella, Ariadne auf Naxos, Rosenkavalier★, Salome★;* STRAVINSKY: *Rake's Progress;* TCHAIKOVSKY: *Eugene Onegin★;* VERDI: *Aida, Falstaff, Forza del destino, Otello★, Trovatore★;* WAGNER: *Fliegende Holländer★, Lohengrin★, Tannhäuser.* **World premieres:** VALDAMBRINI: *Pentheus* 1971, Gestiefelte Kater 1975; DE GRANDIS: *Il Cieco di Hyuga* 1969; ENGELMANN: *Revue* 1973; all at Theater Bonn. Video–Danish TV: *Campanello.* Conducted major orch in Europe. **Res:** Alte Bonner Str 38, Bonn-Holzlar, FR Ger. **Mgmt:** SLZ/FRG; CMW/FRA.

WEIKL, BERND. Lyric baritone. German. Resident mem: Hamburg Staatsoper; Vienna Staatsoper; Deutsche Oper Berlin. Born 29 Jul 1942, Vienna. Wife Karin. Studied: Hannover Staatl Hochschule für Musik und Theater, Prof Naan Pöld, Prof William Reimer, Hannover. **Debut:** (*Zar und Zimmermann*) Deutsche Oper am Rhein, Düsseldorf 1970. Previous occupations: studied national economics.

Sang with major companies in AUS: Salzburg Fest, Vienna Staatsoper & Volksoper; CZE: Prague National; FRA: Nancy; FR GER: Bayreuth Fest, Berlin Deutsche Oper, Düsseldorf-Duisburg, Essen, Frankfurt, Hamburg, Hannover; GER DR: Berlin Staatsoper; SWI: Geneva; UK: London Royal Opera. **Roles with these companies incl** BIZET: Zurga★‡ (*Pêcheurs de perles*); BUSONI: Matteo★‡ (*Arlecchino*); DONIZETTI: Belcore★ (*Elisir*); GOUNOD: Valentin (*Faust*); LORTZING: Graf Eberbach★ (*Wildschütz*), Peter I★(*Zar und Zimmermann*); MARSCHNER: Hans Heiling★‡; MOZART: Guglielmo★ (*Così fan tutte*), Don Giovanni★, Conte Almaviva★ (*Nozze di Figaro*); MUSSORGSKY: Shaklovity★ (*Khovanshchina*); NICOLAI: Fluth★ (*Lustigen Weiber*); ORFF: Solo★ (*Carmina burana*); ROSSINI: Figaro★ (*Barbiere di Siviglia*); SAINT-SAENS: Grand prêtre★‡ (*Samson et Dalila*); STRAUSS, R: Jochanaan★‡ (*Salome*); TCHAIKOVSKY: Eugene Onegin★‡; VERDI: Ford★ (*Falstaff*), Germont★ (*Traviata*), Conte di Luna (*Trovatore*); WAGNER: Amfortas★ (*Parsifal*), Wolfram★‡ (*Tannhäuser*); WOLF-FERRARI: Lelio (*Donne curiose*). Also PFITZNER: (*Palestrina*)★‡; GOUNOD: Valentin (*Faust*). Recorded for: DG, London (Decca), Eurodisc, Ariola. Video/Film: Jochanaan (*Salome*). Gives recitals. Appears with symphony orchestra. **Res:** Alsterkamp 26, 2 Hamburg 13, FR Ger. Mgmt: SLZ/FRG.

WEIL, ERNÖ S. Stages/produces opera & theater. German. Spielleiter & Resident Stage Dir,

Städtische Bühnen, Bielefeld. Born 27 Mar 1947, Munich. Wife Susanne von Steimker. Studied: music. Operatic training as asst stage dir at Städt Bühnen Augsburg, Bayreuth Fest 1970-73. **Operatic debut:** *Lucia* Städt Bühnen Augsburg 1973.

Directed/produced opera for major companies in FR GER: Bielefeld. **Operas staged with these companies incl** d'ALBERT: *Tiefland★;* DONIZETTI: *Lucia★;* ORFF: *Kluge★;* VERDI: *Ballo in maschera★;* WAGNER: *Fliegende Holländer★.* **Res:** Nikolausbergstr 8, 808 Fürstenfeldbruck b Munich, FR Ger.

WELLER, DIETER. Bass-baritone. German. Resident mem: Städtische Bühnen, Frankfurt. Born 25 May 1937, Essen, Germany. Wife Dörthe, occupation dancer. One child. Studied: Erwin Röttgen, Essen, FR Ger. **Debut:** Padre Guardiano (*Forza del destino*) Städtische Bühnen, Bremerhaven 1963. Previous occupations: industrial businessman.

Sang with major companies in AUS: Vienna Volksoper; BEL: Brussels; FR GER: Berlin Deutsche Oper, Cologne, Dortmund, Düsseldorf-Duisburg, Frankfurt, Munich Gärtnerplatz; SWI: Basel, Zurich; UK: Edinburgh Fest; USA: San Francisco Opera. **Roles with these companies incl** BEETHOVEN: Rocco (*Fidelio*); BERG: Doktor★ (*Wozzeck*); CIMAROSA: Geronimo (*Matrimonio segreto*); FLOTOW: Plunkett‡ (*Martha*); GOUNOD: Méphistophélès★ (*Faust*); LORTZING: Stadinger★ (*Waffenschmied*); MOZART: Don Alfonso (*Così fan tutte*), Leporello (*Don Giovanni*), Osmin (*Entführung aus dem Serail*), Figaro (*Nozze di Figaro*), Osmin (*Zaïde*), Papageno & Sarastro (*Zauberflöte*); PUCCINI: Colline (*Bohème*); ROSSINI: Don Basilio★ (*Barbiere di Siviglia*), Don Magnifico (*Cenerentola*); SMETANA: Kezal (*Bartered Bride*); VERDI: Ramfis (*Aida*), Attila, Philip II & Grande Inquisitore (*Don Carlo*), Fra Melitone & Padre Guardiano (*Forza del destino*), Zaccaria (*Nabucco*); WAGNER: König Heinrich★ (*Lohengrin*), Beckmesser★ (*Meistersinger*), Steffano Colonna (*Rienzi*), Alberich (*Rheingold*), Hagen★ (*Götterdämmerung*), Landgraf (*Tannhäuser*); WOLF-FERRARI: Lunardo (*Quattro rusteghi*). **World premieres:** WOLPERT: Argan (*Der eingebildete Kranke*) Volksoper, Vienna 1975. Recorded for: Electrola. Gives recitals. Appears with symphony orchestra. **Res:** Ferdinandstr 5, Bad Homburg, FR Ger. Mgmt: PAS/FRG; DSP/USA.

WELLS, PATRICIA. Lyric soprano. American. Resident mem: New York City Opera. Born 16 Oct, Ruston, LA, USA. Studied: Juilliard School of Music, Hans Heinz, New York. **Debut:** Mallika (*Lakmé*) Shreveport Civic Opera, LA 1963. Awards: First Prize, Intl Compt Munich 1971.

Sang with major companies in CAN: Ottawa; HOL: Amsterdam; ITA: Spoleto Fest; USA: Boston, Chicago, Dallas, Fort Worth, Hawaii, Houston, Kentucky, Minneapolis, New York City Opera, Omaha, Portland, San Diego, Santa Fe, Washington DC. **Roles with these companies incl** BERLIOZ: Teresa★ (*Benvenuto Cellini*); BIZET: Micaëla★ (*Carmen*); BRITTEN: Female Chorus (*Rape of Lucretia*), Miss Jessel★ (*Turn of the Screw*); CAVALLI: Erisbe (*Ormindo*); DELIUS: Vrenchen★ (*Village Romeo*); FLOYD: Susannah*; MILHAUD: Femme (*Pauvre matelot*); MONTEVERDI: Poppea (*Incoronazione di Poppea*); MOZART: Fiordiligi* (*Così fan tutte*), Donna Anna (*Don Giovanni*), Elettra* (*Idomeneo*), Contessa* (*Nozze di Figaro*), Pamina* (*Zauberflöte*); PUCCINI: Mimi* (*Bohème*); STRAUSS, J: Rosalinde* (*Fledermaus*); STRAUSS, R: Gräfin* (*Capriccio*); VAUGHAN WILLIAMS: Mary* (*Hugh the Drover*); VERDI: Gilda* (*Rigoletto*), Violetta* (*Traviata*), Leonora* (*Trovatore*). **World premieres:** PASATIERI: Masha (*Seagull*) Houston Grand Op 1974. Gives recitals. Appears with symphony orchestra. **Res:** Greenwich, CT, USA. Mgmt: CAM/USA.

WELSBY, NORMAN. Dramatic baritone. British. Resident mem: English National Opera, London. Born 7 Feb 1939, Warrington, Cheshire, UK. Wife Carole Adelin, occupation teacher. One child. Studied: Royal Manchester Coll of Music, Gwilym Jones, London; Otakar Kraus. **Debut:** Masetto (*Don Giovanni*) Sadler's Wells Co 1968. Previous occupations: prod mgr, advertising agy, clerk at tannery. Awards: Curtis Gold Medal, Royal Manchester Coll; Imperial League of Opera Prize; Ricordi Prize.
Sang with major companies in UK: London English National. **Roles with these companies incl** BIZET: Escamillo* (*Carmen*); BRITTEN: Sir Robert Cecil (*Gloriana*); DONIZETTI: Talbot (*Maria Stuarda*); HENZE: Pentheus (*Bassariden*); MASCAGNI: Alfio* (*Cavalleria rusticana*); MOZART: Guglielmo* (*Così fan tutte*), Figaro* (*Nozze di Figaro*); VERDI: Renato (*Ballo in maschera*), Fra Melitone* (*Forza del destino*); WAGNER: Wotan (*Rheingold*), Gunther (*Götterdämmerung*). Gives recitals. Appears with symphony orchestra. **Res:** 37 Arundel Gdns, London N21 3AG, UK. Mgmt: MIN/UK.

WELTING, RUTH LYNN. Coloratura soprano. American. Born 11 May 1949, Memphis, TN, USA. Single. Studied: Mo Luigi Ricci, Rome; Daniel Ferro, New York; Frank Corsaro, dramatics, New York; Jannène Reiss, Paris. **Debut:** Blondchen (*Entführung aus dem Serail*) New York City Opera 1970. Previous occupations: pianist. Awards: Second Place Met Op Ntl Counc Aud; Rockefeller Fndt Grant; Ntl Opera Inst Grant; Ntl Guild of Piano Teachers Paderewski Awd; schlshps to Memphis State Univ & Juilliard School.
Sang with major companies in HOL: Amsterdam; ITA: Spoleto Fest; UK: London Royal; USA: Dallas, Fort Worth, Hawaii, Houston, Memphis, New York City Opera, St Paul, San Antonio, San Francisco Opera, Santa Fe, Washington DC. **Roles with these companies incl** DONIZETTI: Norina* (*Don Pasquale*), Marie* (*Fille du régiment*), Lucia*; HUMPERDINCK: Gretel*; MENOTTI: Kitty* (*Dernier sauvage*); MOZART: Despina* (*Così fan tutte*), Zerlina* (*Don Giovanni*), Blondchen (*Entführung aus dem Serail*), Mme Herz* & Mlle Silberklang* (*Schauspieldirektor*), Königin der Nacht* (*Zauberflöte*); OFFENBACH: Olympia* (*Contes d'Hoffmann*); PUCCINI: Lisette* (*Rondine*); RIMSKY-KORSAKOV: Coq d'or*; ROSSINI: Rosina* (*Barbiere di Siviglia*); SALIERI: Tonina* (*Prima la musica*); STRAUSS, J: Adele* (*Fledermaus*);

STRAUSS, R: Zerbinetta* (*Ariadne auf Naxos*); THOMAS: Philine* (*Mignon*); VERDI: Oscar* (*Ballo in maschera*), Nannetta* (*Falstaff*), Gilda* (*Rigoletto*). Also BRITTEN: Miss Wordsworth* (*Albert Herring*); RAVEL: Feu/Rossignol* (*Enfant et les sortilèges*); HENZE: Ida* (*Junge Lord*). Recorded for: Philips, London. Video/Film: Zerbinetta (*Ariadne auf Naxos*). Gives recitals. **Res:** 407 Amsterdam Ave, New York, NY, USA. Mgmt: CAM/USA; AIM/UK.

WENDEL, HEINRICH. Scenic and costume designer for opera & theater. Is also a painter. German. Born 9 Mar 1915, Germany. Studied: Berlin Acad of Art. Prof training: apprentice in Bremen, Berlin and Hamburg.
Designed opera for major companies in ARG: Buenos Aires; AUS: Vienna Staatsoper; BEL: Brussels; FR GER: Berlin Deutsche Oper, Düsseldorf-Duisburg, Nürnberg, Saarbrücken, Wuppertal; HOL: Amsterdam; ITA: Milan La Scala; et al. **Operas designed for these companies incl** BARTOK: *Bluebeard's Castle*; BERG: *Wozzeck*; BUSONI: *Arlecchino*; CAVALIERI: *Rappresentazione*; DALLAPICCOLA: *Prigioniero, Ulisse*; GLUCK: *Orfeo ed Euridice*; JANACEK: *From the House of the Dead*; MONTEVERDI: *Favola d'Orfeo*; MOZART: *Clemenza di Tito, Zauberflöte*; MUSSORGSKY: *Boris Godunov*; PFITZNER: *Palestrina*; SCHOENBERG: *Glückliche Hand, Moses und Aron*; STRAVINSKY: *Rake's Progress*; VERDI: *Ballo in maschera, Otello*; WAGNER: *Fliegende Holländer, Lohengrin, Parsifal, Tannhäuser, Tristan und Isolde*; WEBER: *Freischütz*; ZIMMERMANN: *Soldaten*; et al. Also HANDEL: *Saul*. **Operatic world premieres:** PETRASSI: *Ritratto di Don Chisciotte* La Scala, Milan 1967; KLEBE: *Märchen von der schönen Lilie* Schwetzingen 1969; PENDERECKI: *St Luke Passion* first stgd Deutsche Oper am Rhein, Düsseldorf 1969.

WENDELKEN-WILSON, CHARLES; né Charles Edwin Wilson. Conductor of opera and symphony. American. Resident Cond & Art Adv, Florentine Opera Co, Milwaukee, WI. Also Mus Dir Dayton Phil, Dayton, O. Born 3 Jan 1938, Jersey City, NJ. Single. Studied: Mannes College of Music, Carl Bamberger, New York; incl piano, organ, harpsichord, violin, flute and voice. Plays the piano, harpsichord, organ. Operatic training as repetiteur & asst cond at New York City Opera 1960-66; chorus master at Philadelphia Lyric Op 1961-63. **Operatic debut:** triple bill of Amer operas, Neway Op Thtr, New York 1960. Symphonic debut: Boston Symph, 1967. Previous adm positions in opera: Mus Dir, Merola Op Prgr, San Francisco Opera 1971-73.
Conducted with major companies in USA: Baltimore, Cincinnati, Milwaukee Florentine, New York City Opera, San Francisco Opera & Spring Opera. **Operas with these companies incl** BIZET: *Carmen*; BRITTEN: *Midsummer Night, Turn of the Screw*; CHARPENTIER: *Louise*; DONIZETTI: *Fille du régiment*, *Lucia*, *Maria Stuarda*, *Rita*, *Roberto Devereux*; GAY/Britten: *Beggar's Opera*; GOUNOD: *Faust*; JANACEK: *Makropoulos Affair*; LEONCAVALLO: *Pagliacci*; MASCAGNI: *Cavalleria rusticana*; MASSENET: *Manon*;

MENOTTI: *Amahl, Consul, Globolinks, Old Maid and the Thief★, Saint of Bleecker Street★;* MOZART: *Così fan tutte★, Don Giovanni★, Entführung aus dem Serail, Nozze di Figaro★, Zauberflöte;* MUSSORGSKY: *Boris Godunov;* OFFENBACH: *Contes d'Hoffmann★;* ORFF: *Carmina burana★;* PUCCINI: *Bohème★, Gianni Schicchi, Butterfly★, Suor Angelica, Tabarro, Tosca★;* STRAUSS, J: *Fledermaus★;* STRAUSS, R: *Rosenkavalier★;* STRAVINSKY: *Oedipus Rex★;* VERDI: *Aida, Ballo in maschera★, Rigoletto★, Traviata★, Trovatore★.* Video—NET TV: *Fille du régiment,* Wolf Trap prod. Conducted major orch in USA/Canada. Res: Dayton & San Francisco, USA. Mgmt: BAR/USA.

WENDT-WALTHER, URSULA; née Wendt. Lyric soprano. German. Resident mem: Opernhaus Nürnberg. Born 13 Mar 1939, Berlin. Husband Wolf Walther, occupation actor. Studied: Musikhochschule, Berlin; Kari Nurmela, Zurich.
Sang with major companies in FR GER: Düsseldorf-Duisburg, Hannover, Kiel, Mannheim, Nürnberg, Wiesbaden; SWI: Basel. **Roles with these companies incl** BEETHOVEN: Marzelline (*Fidelio*); BIZET: Micaëla (*Carmen*); FLOTOW: Lady Harriet★ (*Martha*); HINDEMITH: Tochter des Cardillac★ (*Cardillac*); LEONCAVALLO: Nedda★ (*Pagliacci*); LORTZING: Baronin Freimann★ (*Wildschütz*); MOZART: Fiordiligi★ (*Così fan tutte*), Donna Elvira★ (*Don Giovanni*), Contessa (*Nozze di Figaro*), Pamina★ (*Zauberflöte*); OFFENBACH: Olympia★ & Antonia★ & Giulietta★ (*Contes d'Hoffmann*); ROSSINI: Elvira (*Italiana in Algeri*); SMETANA: Marie (*Bartered Bride*); STRAUSS, J: Rosalinde★ (*Fledermaus*); VERDI: Alice Ford (*Falstaff*), Desdemona (*Otello*), Leonora (*Trovatore*); WAGNER: Eva (*Meistersinger*); WEBER: Agathe (*Freischütz*); WEILL: Jenny★ (*Aufstieg und Fall der Stadt Mahagonny*); ZIMMERMANN: Marie★ (*Soldaten*). Gives recitals. Appears with symphony orchestra. Teaches voice.

WENKEL, ORTRUN. Dramatic mezzo-soprano & contralto. German. Born 25 Oct 1942, Buttstädt/Thur, Germany. Husband Dr Peter Rothe, occupation univ prof, geologist. Studied: Franz Liszt Hochschule, E Kern, Weimar; Staatl Hochschule für Musik, Prof Lohmann, Frankfurt; Prof Elsa Cavelti. **Debut:** GLUCK: Orfeo, Heidelberg Opera House 1971-72.
Sang with major companies in FR GER: Bayreuth Fest, Cologne, Munich Staatsoper, Stuttgart, Wiesbaden; HOL: Amsterdam; SWI: Basel, Geneva. **Roles with these companies incl** GLUCK: Orfeo★; HANDEL: Amastris (*Xerxes*); MONTEVERDI: Penelope★ (*Ritorno d'Ulisse*); ORFF: Ismene★ (*Antigonae*); STRAUSS, R: Clairon★ (*Capriccio*), Octavian★ (*Rosenkavalier*); TCHAIKOVSKY: Olga★ (*Eugene Onegin*); VERDI: Azucena★ (*Trovatore*); WAGNER: Erda (*Rheingold★, Siegfried★*), Waltraute★ (*Götterdämmerung*). Gives recitals. Appears with symphony orchestra. **Res:** D 6902 Sandhausen/Heidelberg, FR Ger. Mgmt: SLZ/FRG.

WENNBERG, SIV ANNA MARGARETHA; née Johansson. Dramatic soprano. Swedish. Resident mem: Staatsoper, Stuttgart. Born 18 Sep 1944, Sundsvall, Sweden. Husband Bengt, occupation

musician. Studied: Royal Acad of Music, Prof Arne Sunnegårdh, Stockholm. **Debut:** Sieglinde (*Walküre*) Royal Opera, Stockholm 1972.
Sang with major companies in AUS: Graz, Vienna Staatsoper; FRA: Nice, Rouen; FR GER: Berlin Deutsche Oper, Düsseldorf-Duisburg, Hamburg, Munich Staatsoper, Stuttgart; SPA: Barcelona; SWE: Stockholm; SWI: Geneva; UK: Cardiff Welsh, London Royal. **Roles with these companies incl** BEETHOVEN: Leonore★ (*Fidelio*); STRAUSS, R: Ariadne★ (*Ariadne auf Naxos*); VERDI: Aida★, Desdemona★ (*Otello*); WAGNER: Senta★ (*Fliegende Holländer*), Elsa (*Lohengrin*), Sieglinde★ (*Walküre*), Elisabeth (*Tannhäuser*). Gives recitals. Appears with symphony orchestra. **Res:** Odengatan 32, Stockholm, Sweden. Mgmt: SLZ/FRG; ASK/UK.

WESSEL-THERHORN, HELMUT. Conductor of opera. German. Resident Cond, Deutsche Oper am Rhein, Düsseldorf-Duisburg. Born 3 May 1927, Münster. Wife Brigitta. Two children. Studied: Nordwestdeutsche Musikakad, Detmold; Profs Kurt Thomas, Jost Michaels and Fritz Huth; incl piano, cembalo, horn, violin. Plays the piano. Operatic training as repetiteur, asst cond & chorus master at Städtische Bühnen, Münster 1952-61. **Operatic debut:** *Zar und Zimmermann* Städtische Bühnen, Münster 1952-53. Symphonic debut: Staatskapelle, Wiesbaden 1961. Awards: Prof, Nordwestdeutsche Musikakad, Detmold. Previous adm positions in opera: First Cond, Hess Staatstheater, Wiesbaden 1961-64; Music Adm, Landestheater Coburg 1964-67; Gen Music Dir, Stadt Mainz 1967-74.
Conducted with major companies in FR GER: Düsseldorf-Duisburg, Hamburg, Kiel, Stuttgart, Wiesbaden; YUG: Zagreb. **Operas with these companies incl** HANDEL: *Giulio Cesare;* HUMPERDINCK: *Hänsel und Gretel, Königskinder;* LORTZING: *Waffenschmied, Wildschütz;* MASCAGNI: *Cavalleria rusticana;* MONTEVERDI: *Incoronazione di Poppea;* MOZART: *Così fan tutte, Don Giovanni, Entführung aus dem Serail, Finta giardiniera, Idomeneo★, Nozze di Figaro★, Zauberflöte★;* MUSSORGSKY: *Boris Godunov;* NICOLAI: *Lustigen Weiber;* ORFF: *Antigonae, Kluge, Mond;* PERGOLESI: *Serva padrona;* PUCCINI: *Bohème, Butterfly★, Manon Lescaut, Tosca★, Turandot;* ROSSINI: *Barbiere di Siviglia;* STRAUSS, J: *Fledermaus★;* STRAUSS, R: *Arabella★, Ariadne auf Naxos, Rosenkavalier, Salome;* STRAVINSKY: *Rake's Progress;* TCHAIKOVSKY: *Eugene Onegin★;* VERDI: *Aida★, Ballo in maschera, Don Carlo★, Falstaff, Forza del destino, Luisa Miller, Otello, Rigoletto, Simon Boccanegra, Traviata, Trovatore;* WAGNER: *Fliegende Holländer★, Lohengrin★, Meistersinger, Parsifal, Rheingold, Walküre, Siegfried, Götterdämmerung, Tannhäuser, Tristan und Isolde★;* WEBER: *Freischütz;* WOLF-FERRARI: *Donne curiose★, Quattro rusteghi★.* **World premieres:** BODO WOLF: *Der Sittenmeister* Städt Bühnen, Münster 1956. Conducted major orch in Europe. Previous positions as Mus Dir with major orch: Orch of Landestheater Coburg 1964-67; Städt Orch, Mainz 1967-74. Teaches at Nordwestdeutsche Musikakad. **Res:** Kasernenstr 25, 4 Düsseldorf and Eschweilerstr 21, 493 Detmold 1, FR Ger. Mgmt: PAS/FRG.

WEST, JOHN. Bass. American. Born 25 Oct 1938, Cleveland, O, USA. Single. Studied: Curtis Inst, Martial Singher, Philadelphia; Beverley Johnson, New York. **Debut:** Sarastro (*Zauberflöte*) San Francisco Spring Opera 1963. Awards: Philadelphia Orch Young Artists Awd; Third Prize Munich Intl Compt; Sixth Prize Tchaikovsky Intl Compt.

Sang with major companies in CAN: Vancouver; FR GER: Hannover; ITA: Spoleto Fest; MEX: Mexico City; USA: Fort Worth, Houston, Lake George, Philadelphia Lyric, Pittsburgh, Portland, San Francisco Spring, Santa Fe, Seattle, Washington DC. Roles with these companies incl BEETHO-VEN: Rocco★ (*Fidelio*); BELLINI: Oroveso (*Norma*); BERLIOZ: Méphistophélès (*Damnation de Faust*); BRITTEN: Chorus leader (*Curlew River*); DEBUSSY: Arkel★ (*Pelléas et Mélisande*); FALLA: Don Quixote (*Retablo de Maese Pedro*); GERSHWIN: Porgy★; GOUNOD: Méphistophélès★ (*Faust*); MOZART: Don Alfonso (*Così fan tutte*), Sarastro (*Zauberflöte*); MUSSORGSKY: Boris Godunov★; PUCCINI: Colline★ (*Bohème*); ROSSINI: Don Basilio (*Barbiere di Siviglia*); STRAUSS, R: La Roche★ (*Capriccio*), Baron Ochs★ (*Rosenkavalier*); STRAVINSKY: Tiresias (*Oedipus Rex*); VERDI: Ramfis★ (*Aida*); WAGNER: Hunding (*Walküre*). Gives recitals. Appears with symphony orchestra. **Res:** New York, NY, USA. **Mgmt:** HUR/USA.

WEWEZOW, GUDRUN; née Hoffmann. Dramatic mezzo-soprano. German. Resident mem: Bayerische Staatsoper, Munich. Born 24 Jun 1936, Heidelberg, Germany. Husband Herbert, occupation manager. Studied: Prof Philomena Herbst-Latour, Heidelberg; Erika Becker, Basel; Gerda Heuer, Wiesbaden; Maud Cunitz, München-Baldham. **Debut:** Sainte Catherine (*Jeanne d'arc au bûcher*) Basel, Switzerland 1959. Previous occupations: secy.

Sang with major companies in AUS: Salzburg Fest; DEN: Copenhagen; FIN: Helsinki; FR GER: Düsseldorf-Duisburg, Hamburg, Karlsruhe, Mannheim, Munich Staatsoper, Nürnberg, Wiesbaden; SWE: Stockholm; SWI: Basel. Roles with these companies incl BRITTEN: Mrs Herring★ (*Albert Herring*); EGK: Babekan★ (*Verlobung in San Domingo*); GLUCK: Orfeo; MOZART: Ramiro (*Finta giardiniera*); NICOLAI: Frau Reich (*Lustigen Weiber*); PERGOLESI: Cardella★ (*Frate 'nnamorato*); PUCCINI: Suzuki★ (*Butterfly*); SMETANA: Hata★‡ (*Bartered Bride*); TCHAIKOVSKY: Mme Larina (*Eugene Onegin*); VERDI: Ulrica (*Ballo in maschera*), Azucena (*Trovatore*); WAGNER: Magdalene (*Meistersinger*), Erda (*Rheingold, Siegfried*), Fricka (*Walküre*), Waltraute★ (*Götterdämmerung*); ZIMMERMANN: Charlotte★ (*Soldaten*). Also HINDEMITH: Gräfin von Helfenstein★ (*Mathis der Maler*); STRAUSS, R: Leda (*Liebe der Danae*); DONIZETTI: Smeton (*Anna Bolena*); VERDI: Fenena★ (*Nabucco*). **World premieres:** YUN: Frau am Brunnen (*Sim Tjong*) Bayerische Staatsoper, Munich 1972. Recorded for: BASF, Ariola/Eurodisc. Video/Film: (*Zar und Zimmermann*). Gives recitals. Appears with symphony orchestra. Teaches voice. **Res:**

Föhrenweg 17, 8011 Pöring, FR Ger. Mgmt: SLZ/FRG.

WEXLER, PETER JOHN. Scenic and costume designer for opera, theater, film, television. Is a lighting designer, stage director; also an architect & spatial/lighting designer of perf arts facilities. American. Born 31 Oct 1936, New York. Wife Constance, occupation costume designer. Studied: Univ of Mich, School of Arch & Des; Art Students League, NY; Yale School of Drama. Prof training: Chautauqua Opera Assn, NY. **Operatic debut:** New York City Opera 1964. Theater debut: American Shakespeare Fest, Stratford, CT 1959. Previous occupation: supernumerary Met Opera. Awards: Drama Critics Circle Awd 1971; nominee, Antoinette Perry Awd 1968; Winner ANTA-ITI Compt 1965; J Maharam Awd, Drama Desk 1968 & 69.

Designed for major companies in USA: Houston, Minneapolis, New York Met & City Opera, San Diego, Washington DC. Operas designed for these companies incl BERLIOZ: *Troyens★;* BERN-STEIN: *Mass★;* BRITTEN: *Burning Fiery Furnace★, Curlew River★, Prodigal Son★;* MEYERBEER: *Prophète★;* MOZART: *Così fan tutte, Zauberflöte;* PUCCINI: *Bohème;* VERDI: *Otello★;* WEILL: *Dreigroschenoper.* Operatic world premieres: ARGENTO: *Masque of Angels* 1964; BLOW: *Venus and Adonis* 1964; both at Center Opera Co, Minneapolis; BEESON: *Lizzie Borden* New York City Opera 1965. Exhibitions of stage designs & paintings Wright-Hepburn-Webster Gal, NY 1967; Museum Mod Art, Paris; Mus Contemp Crafts, NY; Smithsonian, Washington; Lincoln Cnt Libr-Musm, NY; drawings and photos in natl magazines, newspapers, art/text books. **Res:** 277 West End Ave, New York, USA. **Mgmt:** VIN/USA; AIM/UK.

WEYL, ROMAN. Scenic and costume designer for opera, theater, film, television. Is also an illustrator. German. Born 30 Jul 1921, Mainz. Wife Susanne Wiston, occupation actress. Two children. Studied: Staatliche Kunstakad, Dresden. **Operatic debut:** Komische Oper Berlin, Ger DR 1951. Theater debut: Schiffbauerdammtheater, Berlin 1943. Awards: Art Prize, Berlin 1959.

Designed for major companies in AUS: Vienna Staatsoper & Volksoper; FR GER: Munich Staatsoper & Gärtnerplatz, Stuttgart, Wiesbaden; GER DR: Berlin Komische Oper & Staatsoper, Dresden, Leipzig; SWI: Zurich; USA: San Francisco Opera. Operas designed for these companies incl AUBER: *Fra Diavolo;* BIZET: *Carmen;* FORTNER: *Elisabeth Tudor;* MOZART: *Zauberflöte;* NICOLAI: *Lustigen Weiber;* PUCCINI: *Tabarro;* VERDI: *Otello, Trovatore;* WAGNER: *Tristan und Isolde.* Also EGK: *Revisor.* Exhibitions of stage designs & graphics, Kunstamt Berlin 1974; Theater Museum, Munich 1969. Teaches at Mozarteum Salzburg. **Res:** Waldsängerpfad 3, 1 Berlin 38, Ger DR.

WHITE, JOHN S; né Hans Schwarzkopf. American. Mng Dir, New York City Opera, New York State Theater, Lincoln Center, New York. In charge of adm matters & finances. Born 4 Mar 1910, Vienna. Single. Studied: Univ Vienna; Sorbonne, Paris; Univ Perugia, Italy; Univ Besançon,

France. Previous occupations: linguist, writer; faculty mem Schotten Realschule Vienna, New School for Social Research New York, Lycée Français New York. Background primarily administrative. Started with present company 1946 as asst stage dir; in present position since 1968. World premieres at theaters under his co-management: KURKA: *Good Soldier Schweik* 1958; WEISGALL: *Six Characters in Search of an Author* 1959; MOORE: *Wings of the Dove* 1961; ROREM: *Miss Julie* 1965; ELLSTEIN: *Golem* 1962; WEISGALL: *Nine Rivers from Jordan* 1968; FLOYD: *Passion of Jonathan Wade* 1962; BEESON: *Lizzie Borden* 1965; GIANNINI: *Servant of Two Masters* 1967; MENOTTI: *Most Important Man* 1971; all at New York City Opera. Awards: First Prize, Italian Cultural Inst Schlshp. Initiated major policy changes which have caused the New York City Opera to grow to a major intl operatic institution. **Res:** New York, NY, USA.

WHITE, WILLARD WENTWORTH. Bass. Jamaican. Born 10 Oct 1946, Jamaica, WI. Wife Gillian, occupation music teacher. One child. Studied: Juilliard School, Beverley Johnson, Giorgio Tozzi, New York; Erik Thorendahl, New York. **Debut:** Colline (*Bohème*) New York City Opera 1974. Awards: National Opera Inst Grant, 2 yrs; full schlshp Juilliard, 6 yrs; M B Rockefeller Fund Awd.

Sang with major companies in USA: Houston, Lake George, New York City Opera, San Francisco Opera & Spring Opera. **Roles with these companies incl** BELLINI: Sir George★ (*Puritani*); CHERUBINI: Creon★ (*Medea*); JOPLIN: Father★ (*Treemonisha*); MOZART: Osmin★ (*Entführung aus dem Serail*); PUCCINI: Colline★ (*Bohème*). **World premieres:** OVERTON: Jim (*Huckleberry Finn*) Juilliard American Opera Center, New York 1971. Gives recitals. Appears with symphony orchestra. **Res:** 5775 Mosholu Ave, New York, NY, USA. Mgmt: HUR/USA; HPL/UK.

WICH, GÜNTHER. Conductor of opera and symphony. German. Gen Mus Dir & Resident Cond, Deutsche Oper am Rhein, Düsseldorf-Duisburg. Born 23 May 1928, Bamberg. Wife Maria. One child. Studied: Hochschule für Musik, Freiburg/Br; incl flute. **Operatic debut:** Städtische Bühnen, Freiburg/Br. Symphonic debut: Phil Orch, Freiburg/Br.

Conducted with major companies in AUS: Graz, Vienna Staatsoper; FIN: Helsinki; FR GER: Düsseldorf-Duisburg, Hannover, Munich Staatsoper, Stuttgart; HOL: Amsterdam; ITA: Florence Maggio, Venice; POL: Warsaw; SWE: Stockholm; UK: London Royal. **Operas with these companies incl** BEETHOVEN: *Fidelio★*; BERG: *Lulu★, Wozzeck★;* BRITTEN: *Death in Venice★;* DALLAPICCOLA: *Ulisse★;* EINEM: *Dantons Tod;* GLUCK: *Orfeo ed Euridice★;* HANDEL: *Xerxes;* HUMPERDINCK: *Hänsel und Gretel;* KELEMEN: *Belagerungszustand★;* LORTZING: *Waffenschmied;* MARTIN: *Vin herbé;* MONTEVERDI: *Incoronazione di Poppea★;* MOZART: *Clemenza di Tito★, Così fan tutte★, Don Giovanni★, Idomeneo, Mitridate, re di Ponto★, Nozze di Figaro★, Zauberflöte★;* PFITZNER: *Palestrina★;* PURCELL: *Dido and Aeneas★, King Arthur★;* ROSSINI: *Barbiere di Siviglia;* SCHOENBERG: *Erwartung, Glückliche Hand, Moses und Aron★;* SMETANA: *Bartered Bride;* STRAUSS, J: *Fledermaus;* STRAUSS, R: *Arabella, Ariadne auf Naxos★, Daphne, Rosenkavalier★, Salome★, Schweigsame Frau★;* VERDI: *Aida, Ballo in maschera, Falstaff, Nabucco, Otello;* WAGNER: *Fliegende Holländer★, Lohengrin★, Meistersinger★, Parsifal★, Rheingold★, Walküre★, Siegfried★, Götterdämmerung★, Tannhäuser★, Tristan und Isolde★;* WEBER: *Freischütz★;* ZIMMERMANN: *Soldaten★.* Conducted major orch in Europe, Asia.

WICHEREK, ANTONI. Conductor of opera and symphony. Polish. Art Dir & Resident Cond, Great Wielki Theater, Warsaw 1973- . Born 18 Feb 1929, Zory, Poland. Wife Hanna Lisowska, occupation opera singer. One child. Studied: Prof K Wilkomirski, Wrozlaw; Prof W Bierdiajew, Warsaw; Prof Capuano, Venice; incl violin, piano. Operatic training as asst cond at Wrozlaw Opera House. **Operatic debut:** *Coq d'or*, Wrozlaw Opera House, Poland 1954. Symphonic debut: Phil Orchestra, Wrozlaw 1954. Previous occupations: studied law.

Conducted with major companies in FR GER: Bayreuth Fest, Essen, Wiesbaden; GER DR: Berlin Staatsoper; ITA: Venice. **Operas with these companies incl** DONIZETTI: *Don Pasquale;* DVORAK: *Rusalka;* GOUNOD: *Faust;* HUMPERDINCK: *Hänsel und Gretel;* JANACEK: *Jenufa;* MASCAGNI: *Cavalleria rusticana;* MENOTTI: *Consul;* MONIUSZKO: *Halka★, Haunted Castle★;* MONTEVERDI: *Incoronazione di Poppea;* MOZART: *Così fan tutte;* MUSSORGSKY: *Boris Godunov;* ORFF: *Mond;* PERGOLESI: *Serva padrona;* PONCHIELLI: *Gioconda;* PUCCINI: *Bohème, Butterfly, Turandot;* RIMSKY-KORSAKOV: *Coq d'or;* SALIERI: *Prima la musica;* STRAVINSKY: *Oedipus Rex;* TCHAIKOVSKY: *Eugene Onegin;* VERDI: *Aida★, Ballo in maschera, Don Carlo, Falstaff, Otello, Traviata, Trovatore;* WAGNER: *Tannhäuser.* **World premieres:** RUDZINSKI: *Commander of Paris* Poznan 1960; *Dismissal of Greek Envoys* Krakow 1966; *Peasants* Warsaw 1974. Video/Film: *Sulamita, Dismissal of Greek Envoys, Uschiko, Finta polacca, Maestro di cappella.* Conducted major orch in Europe. Previous positions as Mus Dir with major orchs in Poland. Teaches at High School of Music, Warsaw. **Res:** Okólnik str 1, Warsaw, Poland. Mgmt: PAG/POL.

WICKS, DENNIS. Bass. British. Resident mem: English National Opera, London. Born 6 Oct 1928, Ringmer, Sussex, UK. Wife Jean Anne. Two children. Studied: Jani Strasser, David Franklin. **Debut:** Truffaldino (*Ariadne auf Naxos*) Glyndebourne Fest 1961. Previous occupations: carpenter & joiner.

Sang with major companies in UK: Cardiff Welsh, Edinburgh Fest, Glyndebourne Fest, London Royal & English National; USA: Chicago. **Roles with these companies incl** BEETHOVEN: Rocco★ (*Fidelio*); BENNETT: Braxton★ (*Mines of Sulphur*); HENZE: Cadmus★ (*Bassariden*); JANACEK: Dikoy★ (*Katya Kabanova*); MOZART: Osmin★ (*Entführung aus dem Serail*), Sarastro★ (*Zauberflöte*); SMETANA: Kezal

(*Bartered Bride*); STRAUSS, R: Baron Ochs★ (*Rosenkavalier*); VERDI: Grande Inquisitore★ (*Don Carlo*); WAGNER: Fafner★ (*Siegfried*). Also MONTEVERDI: Seneca★(*Incoronazione di Poppea*); STRAUSS, R: Graf Waldner★ (*Arabella*). Recorded for: CBS, Philips. Gives recitals. Appears with symphony orchestra. **Res:** Brighton, UK. Mgmt: SLA/UK.

WIEMANN, ERNST. Bass. German. Resident mem: Staatsoper, Hamburg. Born 21 Dec 1919, Stapelburg, Germany. Wife Maria. Two children. Studied: Philomena Herbst-Latour, Hamburg; Paul Bender, Munich. **Debut:** Daland (*Fliegende Holländer*) Opernhaus Gelsenkirchen, FR Ger 1952. Awards: Kammersänger, State of Hamburg 1965; Mozart Plaque, City of Brussels.

Sang with major companies in AUS: Graz, Vienna Staatsoper; BEL: Brussels; DEN: Copenhagen; FRA: Aix-en-Provence Fest, Bordeaux, Lyon, Marseille, Nice, Paris, Toulouse; FR GER: Berlin Deutsche Oper, Düsseldorf-Duisburg, Frankfurt, Hamburg, Kassel, Kiel, Munich Staatsoper, Nürnberg, Saarbrücken, Stuttgart; GER DR: Berlin Staatsoper; ITA: Bologna, Florence Maggio, Milan La Scala, Rome Opera, Turin, Venice; SPA: Barcelona; SWI: Zurich; UK: Edinburgh Fest, London Royal Opera & English National; USA: Boston, Dallas, New Orleans, New York Met. **Roles with these companies incl** d'ALBERT: Tommaso (*Tiefland*); BEETHOVEN: Rocco★ (*Fidelio*); CIMAROSA: Geronimo (*Matrimonio segreto*); CORNELIUS: Abul Hassan★ (*Barbier von Bagdad*); DEBUSSY: Arkel (*Pelléas et Mélisande*); EGK: Cuperus (*Zaubergeige*); EINEM: St Just (*Dantons Tod*); FLOTOW: Plunkett (*Martha*); HINDEMITH: Lorenz v Pommersfelden (*Mathis der Maler*); LORTZING: Baculus (*Wildschütz*); MEYERBEER: Marcel (*Huguenots*); MOZART: Osmin★(*Entführung aus dem Serail*), Sarastro★ (*Zauberflöte*); MUSSORGSKY: Pimen★ (*Boris Godunov*); PUCCINI: Colline★(*Bohème*); ROSSINI: Don Basilio (*Barbiere di Siviglia*); SMETANA: Kezal (*Bartered Bride*); STRAUSS, R: Orest (*Elektra*), Barak★ (*Frau ohne Schatten*); STRAVINSKY: Tiresias (*Oedipus Rex*); VERDI: Ramfis★ (*Aida*), Philip II★ & Grande Inquisitore (*Don Carlo*), Padre Guardiano★ (*Forza del destino*), Zaccaria★ (*Nabucco*); WAGNER: Daland★ (*Fliegende Holländer*), König Heinrich★ (*Lohengrin*), Hans Sachs★ & Pogner★ (*Meistersinger*), Gurnemanz★ (*Parsifal*), Fasolt★ & Fafner★ (*Rheingold*), Fafner (*Siegfried*), Hunding (*Walküre*), Hagen (*Götterdämmerung*), Landgraf★ (*Tannhäuser*), König Marke★ (*Tristan und Isolde*); WEBER: Kaspar★ (*Freischütz*). Video/Film: Rocco (*Fidelio*); Pogner (*Meistersinger*). Gives recitals. Appears with symphony orchestra. Teaches voice.

WILCOX, CAROL ANN. Lyric coloratura soprano. American. Born 9 Mar 1945, Antioch, CA, USA. Husband Robert Owen Jones, occupation tenor. Studied: Univ of Kansas; Manhattan School of Music, New York; Richard Fredricks, New York. **Debut:** Despina (*Così fan tutte*) Metropolitan Opera Studio 1970.

Sang with major companies in USA: Hartford, Houston, Kansas City, Lake George, Milwaukee Florentine, Minneapolis, New York Met, Pitts-

burgh, Portland, Washington DC. **Roles with these companies incl** DONIZETTI: Adina★ (*Elisir*), Marie★ (*Fille du régiment*); MOZART: Despina★ (*Così fan tutte*), Zerlina★ (*Don Giovanni*), Susanna★ (*Nozze di Figaro*), Pamina★ (*Zauberflöte*); OFFENBACH: Périchole★; STRAUSS, J: Adele★ & Rosalinde★ (*Fledermaus*); VERDI: Oscar★ (*Ballo in maschera*), Gilda★ (*Rigoletto*); WARD: Abigail★ (*Crucible*); WEILL: Polly★ (*Dreigroschenoper*). **World premieres:** BEESON: Aurelia (*Captain Jinks of the Horse Marines*) Kansas City Lyric 1975. Recorded for: RCA. Gives recitals. Appears with symphony orchestra. **Res:** New York, NY, USA.

WILDEN, HENRI. Lyric tenor. Australian. Resident mem: Australian Opera, Sydney. Born 2 Apr 1937, Mauritius, UK. Wife Marie Rose. Four children. Studied: in France. **Debut:** Duke (*Rigoletto*) Australian Opera 1972. Previous occupations: accountant.

Sang with major companies in AUSTRL: Sydney. **Roles with these companies incl** DONIZETTI: Nemorino★ (*Elisir*); OFFENBACH: Hoffmann★; PUCCINI: Rodolfo★ (*Bohème*), Rinuccio★ (*Gianni Schicchi*); ROSSINI: Almaviva★ (*Barbiere di Siviglia*); VERDI: Ismaele★ (*Nabucco*), Duca di Mantova★ (*Rigoletto*). Gives recitals. **Res:** 17 Adamson Ave, Thornleigh, NSW, Australia.

WILDERMANN, WILLIAM. Bass-baritone. American. Born 2 Dec 1919, Stuttgart, Germany. Divorced. One child. Studied Carl Yost. **Debut:** Re (*Aida*) San Carlo Opera, Naples 1946. Previous occupations: longshoreman, landscape gardener.

Sang with major companies in ARG: Buenos Aires; AUS: Vienna Volksoper; BEL: Brussels; CAN: Ottawa, Toronto; FRA: Rouen; FR GER: Bonn, Dortmund, Düsseldorf-Duisburg, Mannheim, Munich Staatsoper, Stuttgart; ITA: Palermo; MEX: Mexico City; SWI: Geneva; USA: Chicago, Cincinnati, Hartford, Miami, Newark, New Orleans, New York Met & City Opera, Philadelphia Grand & Lyric, Pittsburgh, San Antonio, San Francisco Opera, Seattle. **Roles with these companies incl** BEETHOVEN: Rocco★ (*Fidelio*); BELLINI: Oroveso (*Norma*); BUSONI: Matteo (*Arlecchino*); CIMAROSA: Geronimo★ (*Matrimonio segreto*); FLOTOW: Plunkett (*Martha*); GAY/Britten: Lockit★ (*Beggar's Opera*); GOUNOD: Méphistophélès (*Faust*); LORTZING: Stadinger (*Waffenschmied*); MONTEMEZZI: Archibaldo (*Amore dei tre re*); MOZART: Don Alfonso (*Così fan tutte*), Don Giovanni; MUSSORGSKY: Pimen★ (*Boris Godunov*); NICOLAI: Falstaff (*Lustigen Weiber*); PUCCINI: Colline (*Bohème*); ROSSINI: Don Basilio (*Barbiere di Siviglia*), Guillaume Tell; SAINT-SAENS: Grand prêtre (*Samson et Dalila*); STRAUSS, R: Orest★ (*Elektra*), Barak★ (*Frau ohne Schatten*), Baron Ochs (*Rosenkavalier*); THOMAS: Lothario (*Mignon*); VERDI: Ramfis★ (*Aida*), Grande Inquisitore★ (*Don Carlo*), Falstaff, Padre Guardiano★ (*Forza del destino*), Banquo (*Macbeth*), Zaccaria★ (*Nabucco*), Fiesco (*Simon Boccanegra*); WAGNER: Daland★ (*Fliegende Holländer*), König Heinrich (*Lohengrin*), Pogner (*Meistersinger*), Wotan & Fasolt★ (*Rheingold*), Hunding (*Walküre*), Hagen★ (*Götterdämmerung*), Landgraf★ (*Tannhäuser*), König Marke (*Tristan* *und Isolde*); WEBER: Kaspar★ (*Freischütz*). Video/Film: Marke (*Tristan und Isolde*). Mgmt: SAM/USA; CDA/ARG.

WILEY, DARLENE. Lyric soprano. American. Resident mem: Staatstheater, Darmstadt. Born 11 Nov 1945, Joliet, IL, USA. Husband Gale F, occupation journalist. One child. Studied: Coll of Wooster, Dale Moore, MA; Univ of Illinois, Paul Ulanowsky, Bruce Foote, John Wustman, Urbana, USA. **Debut:** Pamina (*Zauberflöte*) Chautauqua Fest, NY 1969. Previous occupations: Prof of Voice, Oberlin Consv. Awards: Phi Kappa Lambda Musical Awd, Theodore Presser Perf Awd, Coll of Wooster.
Sang with major companies in FR GER: Darmstadt. **Roles with these companies incl** BEETHOVEN: Marzelline★ (*Fidelio*); BIZET: Micaëla★ (*Carmen*); CIMAROSA: Carolina★ & Elisetta★ (*Matrimonio segreto*); CORNELIUS: Margiana★ (*Barbier von Bagdad*); MOZART: Pamina (*Zauberflöte*); PUCCINI: Liù★ (*Turandot*); VERDI: Gilda★ (*Rigoletto*); WOLF-FERRARI: Rosaura★ (*Donne curiose*). Gives recitals. Appears with symphony orchestra. Teaches voice. **Res:** Heinrich Heine Str 21, 6103 Griesheim, FR Ger. Mgmt: ARM/FRG.

WILLIAMS, MARY. Spinto soprano. British. Born London, UK. Single. Studied: Royal Acad of Music, Maggie Teyte, London; Edguardo Asquey, London. **Debut:** Leonora (*Fidelio*) Kaiserslautern, FR Ger 1970. Awards: LRAM, Royal Acad, London.
Sang with major companies in FR GER: Kiel. **Roles with these companies incl** MOZART: Contessa★ (*Nozze di Figaro*); PUCCINI: Manon Lescaut★, Tosca★; VERDI: Aida★; WAGNER: Senta★ (*Fliegende Holländer*). Gives recitals. Appears with symphony orchestra. Teaches voice. **Res:** Laburnham Gardens, Cranham-Upminster/Essex, UK. Mgmt: MIN/UK.

WILLIAMS, NANCY. Lyric coloratura mezzo-soprano. American. Born Cleveland, O, USA. Single. Studied: Mme Sylvie Derdeyn, Pittsburgh, PA; Boris Goldovsky, New York, USA. **Debut:** Cherubino (*Nozze di Figaro*) New England Opera Theater 1958.
Sang with major companies in USA: Boston, Cincinnati, Dallas, Fort Worth, Hartford, Hawaii, Houston, Kentucky, Lake George, Miami, New Orleans, New York Met & City Opera, Philadelphia Grand & Lyric, Pittsburgh, St Paul, San Diego, San Francisco Spring Opera. **Roles with these companies incl** BERLIOZ: Ascanio★ (*Benvenuto Cellini*); BERNSTEIN: Dinah★‡ (*Trouble in Tahiti*); BIZET: Carmen★; BRITTEN: Lucretia★ (*Rape of Lucretia*); DUKAS: Nourrice (*Ariane et Barbe Bleue*); FLOTOW: Nancy (*Martha*); GOUNOD: Siebel (*Faust*); HUMPERDINCK: Hänsel★‡ & Hexe (*Hänsel und Gretel*); MASSENET: Anita (*Navarraise*), Charlotte (*Werther*); MOORE: Announcer (*Gallantry*); MOZART: Dorabella★ (*Così fan tutte*), Idamante (*Idomeneo*), Cherubino (*Nozze di Figaro*); OFFENBACH: Périchole★; PASATIERI: Raquel★ (*Black Widow*); PONCHIELLI: Laura (*Gioconda*); PUCCINI: Suzuki★ (*Butterfly*); ROSSINI: Rosina (*Barbiere di Siviglia*), Angelina

(*Cenerentola*), Isolier (*Comte Ory*), Isabella★ (*Italiana in Algeri*); STRAUSS, J: Prinz Orlovsky★ (*Fledermaus*); STRAUSS, R: Komponist★ (*Ariadne auf Naxos*), Octavian (*Rosenkavalier*); STRAVINSKY: Baba the Turk★ (*Rake's Progress*); THOMAS: Gertrude (*Hamlet*), Mignon; VERDI: Preziosilla (*Forza del destino*); WAGNER: Magdalene (*Meistersinger*); WARD: Elizabeth Proctor★ (*Crucible*). Also MASSENET: Jean (*Jongleur de Notre Dame*); RAVEL: Concepcion (*Heure espagnole*); DEBUSSY: Lia★ (*Enfant prodigue*); WAGNER: Sieglinde★ (*Walküre*); OHANA: Phèdre★ (*Syllabaire pour Phèdre*); PURCELL: Dido★; MENOTTI: Mother (*Amahl*); OFFENBACH: Nicklausse★ (*Contes d'Hoffmann*); VERDI: Meg Page★ (*Falstaff*); MUSSORGSKY: Feodor‡ (*Boris Godunov*); BRITTEN: Nancy (*Albert Herring*); DONIZETTI: Smeton★ (*Anna Bolena*). **World premieres:** HOIBY: Mrs Bassett (*Summer and Smoke*) St Paul Opera 1971; BERNARDO: Mother (*The Child*) Lake George Opera 1974. Recorded for Columbia. Video/Film: Dinah (*Trouble in Tahiti*). Gives recitals. Appears with symphony orchestra. **Res:** 31 Parkway Rd, Bronxville, NY 10708, USA. Mgmt: SCO/USA.

WILSING, JOERN W. Lyric baritone. German. Resident mem: Badisches Staatstheater, Karlsruhe. Born 25 Oct 1940, Hamm, Germany. Wife Barb, occupation nurse. Studied: Staatliche Hochschule für Musik, Prof C Glettenberg, Cologne; Mozarteum, Salzburg 1962, 1963; Richard-Strauss-Konsv, Munich. **Debut:** Heerrufer (*Lohengrin*) Coburg Oper, FR Ger 1964. Previous occupations: one-year apprentice in industr mngt of mining.
Sang with major companies in AUS: Salzburg Fest; FRA: Nancy; FR GER: Cologne, Dortmund, Düsseldorf-Duisburg, Essen, Karlsruhe, Munich Staatsoper & Gärtnerplatz, Nürnberg, Stuttgart; GER DR: Berlin Komische Oper & Staatsoper; HOL: Amsterdam; SWI: Basel. **Roles with these companies incl** BIZET: Escamillo★ (*Carmen*); DONIZETTI: Dott Malatesta★ (*Don Pasquale*), Enrico★ (*Lucia*); LORTZING: Graf v Liebenau★ (*Waffenschmied*), Peter I★ (*Zar und Zimmermann*); MOZART: Guglielmo★ (*Così fan tutte*), Don Giovanni, Conte Almaviva★ (*Nozze di Figaro*), Papageno★ (*Zauberflöte*); PROKOFIEV: Ferdinand (*Duenna*); PUCCINI: Marcello★ (*Bohème*); ROSSINI: Figaro★ (*Barbiere di Siviglia*); SMETANA: Tomas (*The Kiss*); TCHAIKOVSKY: Eugene Onegin★, Yeletsky (*Pique Dame*); VERDI: Rodrigo★ (*Don Carlo*), Germont★ (*Traviata*), Conte di Luna (*Trovatore*); WAGNER: Wolfram (*Tannhäuser*). Also PFITZNER: Luna (*Palestrina*); RAMEAU: Kitheron (*Platée*); GOUNOD: Valentin (*Faust*); NICOLAI: Fluth (*Lustigen Weiber*); SHOSTAKOVICH: Doctor (*The Nose*); AUBER: Lord Cockburn (*Fra Diavolo*); HENZE: Secretary (*Junge Lord*); SMETANA: Krusina (*Bartered Bride*); PUCCINI: Timur (*Turandot*). Appears with symphony orchestra. Teaches voice. **Res:** Rheinufer, 7501 Leopoldshafen, FR Ger.

WILSON, CATHERINE JULIA. Lyric soprano. British. Born Glasgow, Scotland, UK. Husband Leonard Hancock, occupation musician. Studied:

Royal Manchester Coll of Music, Elsie Thurston, UK; Ruth Packer, London; Maria Carpi, Geneva. **Debut:** Angelina (*Cenerentola*) Sadler's Wells, London 1960. Previous occupations: secy & teacher. Awards: Hon Fellow Royal Manchester Coll of Music, UK.

Sang with major companies in FR GER: Cologne; SWI: Geneva; UK: Aldeburgh Fest, Cardiff Welsh, Glasgow Scottish, Glyndebourne Fest, London English National; USA: Houston, Santa Fe. **Roles with these companies incl** BRITTEN: Helena★ (*Midsummer Night*), Mrs Julian★ (*Owen Wingrave*), Ellen Orford★ (*Peter Grimes*), Governess★ (*Turn of the Screw*); MENOTTI: Mme Euterpova★ (*Globolinks*); MOZART: Fiordiligi (*Così fan tutte*), Ilia (*Idomeneo*), Contessa★ & Cherubino (*Nozze di Figaro*); PUCCINI: Mimi & Musetta★ (*Bohème*); ROSSINI: Rosina★ (*Barbiere di Siviglia*), Comtesse Adèle (*Comte Ory*), Ninetta (*Gazza ladra*); STRAUSS, J: Rosalinde★ (*Fledermaus*); STRAUSS, R: Marschallin★ (*Rosenkavalier*); TCHAIKOVSKY: Lisa (*Pique Dame*); VERDI: Violetta (*Traviata*); WAGNER: Gutrune★ (*Götterdämmerung*). **World premieres:** BENNETT: Jenny (*Mines of Sulphur*) Sadler's Wells, London 1965; HAMILTON: Fulvia (*Cataline Conspiracy*) Scottish Opera 1974. Recorded for: Decca. Video—BBC TV: Jenny (*Mines of Sulphur*). Gives recitals. Appears with symphony orchestra. **Res:** 18 St Mary's Grove, London N1, UK. Mgmt: AIM/UK.

WIMBERGER, GERHARD. Conductor of opera and symphony; composer; operatic stage director. Austrian. Mem, Board of Dir & Cond, Salzburg Fest. Born 30 Aug 1923, Vienna. Wife Eva. Two children. Studied: Clemens Krauss, Johann Nep David; also piano, organ, oboe, clarinet. Operatic training as repetiteur & asst cond at Volksoper, Vienna 1947-48; Landestheater Salzburg 1948-51. **Operatic debut:** *Lustigen Weiber* Landestheater Salzburg 1949. Awards: Austrian State Prize in Composition 1967.

Conducted with major companies in AUS: Salzburg Fest; FR GER: Berlin Deutsche Oper, Munich Staatsoper & Gärtnerplatz. **Operas with these companies incl** NICOLAI: *Lustigen Weiber;* PAISIELLO: *Re Teodoro in Venezia;* STRAUSS, J: *Fledermaus.* **World premieres:** WIMBERGER: *Lebensregeln* Theater am Gärtnerplatz, Munich 1972. Video—Bavarian TV: *Lebensregeln.* Conducted major orch in Europe. **Operas composed:** *Schaubudengeschichte* Nationaltheater Mannheim 1954; *Battaglia oder Der rote Federbusch* Deutsche Oper am Rhein, Schwetzingen/Duisburg 1960; *Dame Kobold* Städt Bühnen, Frankfurt 1964; *Lebensregeln.* Teaches at Hochschule für Musik & darstellende Kunst, Mozarteum, Salzburg. **Res:** Wallmannweg 13, Salzburg, Austria.

WIMBERGER, PETER. Dramatic baritone & bass. Austrian. Resident mem: Staatsoper, Vienna. Born 14 May 1940, Vienna. Wife Graziella, occupation pianist. Two children. Studied: Musikakad, Vienna; Kmsg Paul Schöffler, Kmsg Adolf Vogel. **Debut:** Pietro (*Simon Boccanegra*) Städtische Oper, Dortmund 1963.

Sang with major companies in AUS: Bregenz Fest, Vienna Staatsoper; DEN: Copenhagen;

FRA: Lyon, Marseille, Nice; FR GER: Bonn, Dortmund, Düsseldorf-Duisburg, Frankfurt, Kassel, Munich Staatsoper; ITA: Florence Maggio; POL: Warsaw; SPA: Barcelona; SWI: Basel. **Roles with these companies incl** BEETHOVEN: Don Pizarro★ (*Fidelio*); BIZET: Escamillo★ (*Carmen*); HINDEMITH: Mathis; MOZART: Sarastro★ (*Zauberflöte*); MUSSORGSKY: Pimen★ (*Boris Godunov*); PUCCINI: Colline (*Bohème*); ROSSINI: Don Basilio★ (*Barbiere di Siviglia*); STRAUSS, R: Orest (*Elektra*), Jochanaan★ (*Salome*); VERDI: Ramfis★ (*Aida*), Philip II (*Don Carlo*), Padre Guardiano★ (*Forza del destino*), Conte Walter★ (*Luisa Miller*); WAGNER: Daland★ (*Fliegende Holländer*), König Heinrich★ (*Lohengrin*), Pogner (*Meistersinger*), Wotan (*Rheingold★, Walküre★*), Gunther★ (*Götterdämmerung*). Appears with symphony orchestra. **Res:** Margaretenstr 91, A-1050 Vienna, Austria. Mgmt: TAS/AUS; SLZ/FRG.

WINBERGH, GÖSTA ANDERS. Lyric tenor. Swedish. Resident mem: Royal Opera, Stockholm. Born 30 Dec 1943, Stockholm. Divorced. One child. Studied: Royal Acad of Music, Martin Oehman, Erik Saedén, Hjördis Schymberg, Stockholm. **Debut:** Rodolfo (*Bohème*) Opera House Göteborg, Sweden 1971. Awards: Jussi Björling and Kristina Nilsson Awds.

Sang with major companies in DEN: Copenhagen; FRA: Aix-en-Provence; USA: San Francisco Opera. **Roles with these companies incl** GOUNOD: Faust★; MOZART: Ferrando★ (*Così fan tutte*), Don Ottavio★ (*Don Giovanni*), Belmonte★ (*Entführung aus dem Serail*); PUCCINI: Rodolfo★ (*Bohème*), Cavaradossi★ (*Tosca*); ROSSINI: Almaviva★ (*Barbiere di Siviglia*), Leicester★ (*Elisabetta Regina*), Giocondo★ (*Pietra del paragone*); STRAUSS, J: Alfred★ (*Fledermaus*); STRAUSS, R: Ein Sänger★ (*Rosenkavalier*); TCHAIKOVSKY: Lenski★ (*Eugene Onegin*); VERDI: Duca di Mantova★ (*Rigoletto*), Alfredo★ (*Traviata*). **World premieres:** LUNDQUIST: Erik (*Sekund av Evighet*) Royal Opera, Stockholm 1974. Video: Rodolfo (*Bohème*). Gives recitals. Appears with symphony orchestra. Mgmt: KBL/SWE.

WINTHER, JOHN. Danish. Gen Mng, Australian Opera, 569 George St, Sydney, 1973- ; and of Australian Opera Studio. In charge of admin matters, art policy & finances. Is also a pianist. Born 20 Aug 1933, Copenhagen. Wife Lone Koppel, occupation opera singer. Three children. Previous occupations: pianist and oboist; Gen Mng, Royal Danish Ballet & Music Fest; Opera Dir, Royal Theater Copenhagen 1961-71. World premieres at theaters under his management: WERDER: *Affair;* SITSKY; *Lenz;* SCULTHORPE: *Rites of Passage;* all at Sydney 1974. OLSEN: *Belisa;* KOPPEL: *Macbeth;* NORGAARD: *Labyrinten;* SCHMIDT: *Udstilling;* all at Copenhagen 1966-70. Mem of Music Bd, Australian Council; Elizabethan Theatre Trust; and Dir, Tasmanian Opera Company. **Res:** Sydney, Australia.

WINTHER, LONE KOPPEL; née Lone Koppel. Spinto. Danish. Resident mem: Australian Opera, Sydney.; Royal Theater, Copenhagen. Born 20

May 1938, Copenhagen. Husband John Winther, occupation Gen Mng, Australian Opera. Three children. Studied: Acad of Music, Copenhagen, Prof Dora Sigurdsson. **Debut:** Musetta (*Bohème*) Royal Theater, Copenhagen 1961.

Sang with major companies in AUSTRL: Sydney; DEN: Copenhagen; FR GER: Bonn, Kiel, Stuttgart. **Roles with these companies incl** BEETHOVEN: Leonore (*Fidelio*); BERG: Marie (*Wozzeck*); JANACEK: Jenufa★, Katya Kabanova; MASCAGNI: Santuzza (*Cavalleria rusticana*); MILHAUD: Femme (*Pauvre matelot*); MOZART: Donna Anna (*Don Giovanni*); PUCCINI: Manon Lescaut, Tosca; SHOSTAKOVICH: Katerina Ismailova; STRAUSS, R: Arabella, Ariadne & Komponist★ (*Ariadne auf Naxos*), Chrysothemis (*Elektra*), Salome★; TCHAIKOVSKY: Tatiana (*Eugene Onegin*), Lisa (*Pique Dame*); VERDI: Elisabetta (*Don Carlo*), Abigaille★ (*Nabucco*), Amelia (*Simon Boccanegra*), Leonora (*Trovatore*); WAGNER: Senta★ (*Fliegende Holländer*), Elisabeth & Venus★ (*Tannhäuser*); WEILL: Jenny★ (*Aufstieg und Fall der Stadt Mahagonny*). **World premieres:** KOPPEL: Mother (*Story of a Mother*) 1965; Lady Macbeth (*Macbeth*) 1970; both at Royal Theater, Copenhagen. Gives recitals. Appears with symphony orchestra. **Res:** 46 Anzac Ave, Sydney, NSW 2027, Australia.

WISE, PATRICIA. Lyric coloratura soprano. American. Resident mem: New York City Opera; Volksoper, Vienna. Born 31 Jul, Wichita, KA, USA. Husband David Gockley, occupation Gen Dir, Houston Opera. Studied: Univ of Kansas, Miriam Stewart Green, MO, USA; Santa Fe Opera, NM, USA; Margaret Harshaw, New York. **Debut:** Susanna (*Nozze di Figaro*) Kansas City Lyric 1966. Awards: M B Rockefeller Fund Grant for two yrs; Sullivan Fndt Grant; Dealey Memorial Awd, Dallas; Naftzger Young Artist Awd, Wichita, KA; Midland Young Artist Awd, TX, USA.

Sang with major companies in AUS: Vienna Volksoper; ISR: Tel Aviv; USA: Baltimore, Fort Worth, Houston, Kansas City, New Orleans, New York City Opera, Omaha, Philadelphia Lyric, Pittsburgh, San Antonio, Santa Fe. **Roles with these companies incl** BIZET: Micaëla (*Carmen*); DONIZETTI: Norina★ (*Don Pasquale*), Marie★ (*Fille du régiment*), Lucia★; GINASTERA: Julia Farnese (*Bomarzo*); GLUCK: Euridice; GOUNOD: Juliette★ (*Roméo*); HANDEL: Dalinda★ (*Ariodante*); HENZE: Luise★ (*Junge Lord*); MOZART: Despina★ (*Così fan tutte*), Zerlina★ (*Don Giovanni*), Blondchen (*Entführung aus dem Serail*), Mme Herz★ (*Schauspieldirektor*), Susanna★ (*Nozze di Figaro*), Königin der Nacht★ (*Zauberflöte*); ORFF: Solo (*Carmina burana*); PUCCINI: Musetta★ (*Bohème*); RIMSKY-KORSAKOV: Coq d'or & Reine de Schemakan (*Coq d'or*); ROSSINI: Rosina★ (*Barbiere di Siviglia*); STRAUSS, J: Adele (*Fledermaus*); STRAUSS, R: Zerbinetta★ (*Ariadne auf Naxos*), Sophie★ (*Rosenkavalier*); VERDI: Oscar★ (*Ballo in maschera*), Gilda★ (*Rigoletto*). **World premieres:** SCHOENBERG: Soul/Dying One (*Jakobsleiter*) stg Santa Fe Opera 1968. Gives recitals. Appears with symphony orchestra. Coaches repertoire. **Res:** Houston, TX, USA. Mgmt: CAM/USA; RAB/AUS.

WIXELL, INGVAR. Lyric baritone. Swedish. Resident mem: Deutsche Oper Berlin; Städtische Oper, Frankfurt. Born 1931, Lulea, Sweden. Wife Margareta, occupation form model. Two children. Studied: Stockholm Consv, Prof Dramstad. **Debut:** Papageno (*Zauberflöte*) Gävle 1955. Awards: title of Kammersänger.

Sang with major companies in AUS: Salzburg Fest; FR GER: Bayreuth Fest, Berlin Deutsche Oper, Frankfurt, Hamburg, Mannheim; SWE: Stockholm; UK: Glyndebourne Fest, London Royal; USA: New York Met, San Francisco Opera; et al. **Roles with these companies incl** BIZET: Escamillo (*Carmen*); DONIZETTI: Belcore (*Elisir*); MOZART: Guglielmo (*Così fan tutte*), Don Giovanni‡, Conte Almaviva‡ & Figaro (*Nozze di Figaro*); PUCCINI: Scarpia (*Tosca*); ROSSINI: Figaro (*Barbiere di Siviglia*); TCHAIKOVSKY: Eugene Onegin; VERDI: Renato (*Ballo in maschera*), Rodrigo (*Don Carlo*), Don Carlo (*Forza del destino*), Rigoletto, Simon Boccanegra; et al. Also GOUNOD: Valentin (*Faust*); on records only VERDI: Barone (*Giorno di regno*). Recorded for: Philips. Gives recitals.

WLASCHIHA, EKKEHARD. Dramatic baritone. German, DR. Resident mem: Städtisches Opernhaus, Leipzig, Ger DR. Born 28 May 1938, Pirna, Germany. Wife Birgit, occupation biochemist. One child. Studied: Franz Liszt Hochschule, Fr Prof Helene Jung, Weimar, Ger DR. **Debut:** Don Fernando (*Fidelio*) Opera House, Gera, Ger DR 1961-62. Awards: Kammersänger, Ministry of Culture 1974.

Sang with major companies in BUL: Sofia; GER DR: Dresden, Leipzig; USSR: Leningrad Kirov. **Roles with these companies incl** BEETHOVEN: Don Pizarro★‡ (*Fidelio*); BIZET: Escamillo★ (*Carmen*); BORODIN: Galitzky (*Prince Igor*); DONIZETTI: Belcore (*Elisir*); GERSHWIN: Crown★‡ (*Porgy and Bess*); JANACEK: Forester (*Cunning Little Vixen*); LEONCAVALLO: Tonio★‡ (*Pagliacci*); MASCAGNI: Alfio★‡ (*Cavalleria rusticana*); MOZART: Conte Almaviva (*Nozze di Figaro*); OFFENBACH: Coppélius etc‡ (*Contes d'Hoffmann*); ORFF: König (*Kluge*); PUCCINI: Jack Rance (*Fanciulla del West*), Lescaut★ (*Manon Lescaut*), Scarpia★‡ (*Tosca*); STRAUSS, R: Jochanaan‡ (*Salome*); STRAVINSKY: Nick Shadow (*Rake's Progress*); VERDI: Amonasro (*Aida*), Renato (*Ballo in maschera*), Germont★ (*Traviata*); WAGNER: Amfortas★ (*Parsifal*). Also GOETZ: Petruchio (*Widerspenstigen Zähmung*); EGK: Kaspar (*Zaubergeige*); MOZART: Sprecher (*Zauberflöte*); NICOLAI: Fluth (*Lustigen Weiber*). **World premieres:** KUNAD: Bill Brook (*Bill Brook*) Landesbühnen Dresden 1965; HANELL: Menelaos (*Griechische Hochzeit*) Nationaltheater Leipzig 1969; GEISSLER: Schatten (*Schatten*) Opernhaus Leipzig 1975. Recorded for: Deutsche Schallplatte. Video/Film - TV Leningrad: (*Fidelio*). Mgmt: KDR/GDR.

WOHLERS, RÜDIGER. Lyric tenor. German. Born 1941, Germany. Married.

Sang with major companies in AUS: Vienna Staatsoper; FR GER: Cologne, Darmstadt, Frankfurt, Hamburg, Munich Staatsoper, Stuttgart; HOL: Amsterdam; SWI: Zurich. **Roles with these companies incl** DONIZETTI: Ernesto★ (*Don Pa-*

squale); MOZART: Tito (*Clemenza di Tito*), Ferrando★ (*Così fan tutte*), Don Ottavio★ (*Don Giovanni*), Belmonte★ (*Entführung aus dem Serail*), Idamante★ (*Idomeneo*), Tamino★ (*Zauberflöte*); ROSSINI: Almaviva★ (*Barbiere di Siviglia*). Gives recitals. Appears with symphony orchestra. Mgmt: SFM/USA.

WOITACH, RICHARD. Conductor of opera and symphony; composer. American. Resident Cond, Metropolitan Opera, New York. Born 27 Jul 1935, Binghamton, NY, USA. Studied: Eastman School of Music, Paul White, Rochester, NY; incl piano with Orazio Frugoni, flute and voice. Plays the piano, organ, harpsichord. Operatic training as repetiteur, asst cond & chorus master: Metropolitan Opera 1959-68; Cincinnati Summer Opera, O 1959-62. **Operatic debut:** *Barbiere di Siviglia* Cincinnati Opera 1961. Symphonic debut: Cosmopolitan Youth Orchestra, New York 1968. Previous adm positions in opera: Music Dir Western Opera Theater, San Francisco 1968-70, 1972.

Conducted with major companies in CAN: Vancouver; USA: Boston, Cincinnati, New York Met, San Francisco Opera & Spring Opera. **Operas with these companies incl** DONIZETTI: *Lucia★; MO-*ZART: *Finta giardiniera;* PUCCINI: *Gianni Schicchi★, Butterfly★, Suor Angelica★, Tabarro★;* ROSSINI: *Barbiere di Siviglia★, Assedio di Corinto★;* VERDI: *Aida, Vespri★.* **Res:** New York, USA.

WOLANSKY, RAYMOND. Lyric baritone & character baritone. American. Resident mem: Württembergische Staatsoper, Stuttgart. Born 15 Feb 1926, Cleveland, O, USA. Wife June. Studied: Cleveland Inst of Music; New England Consv of Music, Boston; Acad of Vocal Arts, Philadelphia. **Debut:** Silvio (*Pagliacci*) Milwaukee Opera Fest 1949-50. Previous occupations: USNR. Awards: Kammersänger, State of Baden-Württemberg.

Sang with major companies in ARG: Buenos Aires; AUS: Bregenz Fest, Graz, Vienna Staatsoper & Volksoper; BEL: Brussels; BRA: Rio de Janeiro; DEN: Copenhagen; FRA: Marseille, Paris, Strasbourg, Toulouse; GRE: Athens Fest; FR GER: Berlin Deutsche Oper, Bonn, Cologne, Düsseldorf-Duisburg, Frankfurt, Hamburg, Hannover, Karlsruhe, Mannheim, Munich Staatsoper, Stuttgart, Wiesbaden; ITA: Naples, Trieste; POR: Lisbon; SWI: Zurich; UK: Edinburgh Fest, Glyndebourne Fest, London Royal Opera; USA: Chicago, San Francisco Opera. **Roles with these companies incl** BELLINI: Sir Richard (*Puritani*); BIZET: Escamillo★ (*Carmen*); CIMAROSA: Count Robinson★ (*Matrimonio segreto*); DONIZETTI: Dott Malatesta★ (*Don Pasquale*), Enrico★ (*Lucia*); EGK: Cuperus (*Zaubergeige*); EINEM: Alfred Ill★ (*Besuch der alten Dame*); GLUCK: Oreste (*Iphigénie en Tauride*); HANDEL: Arsamene (*Xerxes*); HOLST: Death (*Savitri*); LEONCAVALLO: Tonio★ (*Pagliacci*); LORTZING: Graf v Liebenau (*Waffenschmied*), Peter I★ (*Zar und Zimmermann*); MASCAGNI: Alfio (*Cavalleria rusticana*); MASSENET: Lescaut (*Manon*); MONTEMEZZI: Manfredo (*Amore dei tre re*); MONTEVERDI: Orfeo; MOZART: Don Giovanni★, Conte Almaviva★ (*Nozze di Figaro*), Papageno (*Zauberflöte*); OFFENBACH: Coppélius etc★ (*Contes d'Hoffmann*); ORFF: Solo★‡ (*Car-*

mina burana); PUCCINI: Marcello (*Bohème*), Sharpless★ (*Butterfly*); SMETANA: Tomas (*The Kiss*); STRAUSS, R: Mandryka★ (*Arabella*), Olivier (*Capriccio*), Jochanaan★ (*Salome*); TCHAIKOVSKY: Eugene Onegin★, Yeletsky★ (*Pique Dame*); VERDI: Amonasro (*Aida*), Renato★ (*Ballo in maschera*), Rodrigo★ (*Don Carlo*), Francesco Foscari (*Due Foscari*), Don Carlo★ (*Forza del destino*), Nabucco, Iago (*Otello*), Rigoletto★, Germont (*Traviata*), Conte di Luna★ (*Trovatore*); WAGNER: Amfortas★ (*Parsifal*), Wolfram★ (*Tannhäuser*). **World premieres:** MENOTTI: Dr Stone (*Globolinks*) Staatsoper Hamburg 1968; KELEMEN: The Plague (*Belagerungszustand*) Hamburg 1970; KRENEK: Uru-Muru (*Das kommt davon oder Wenn Sardakai auf Reisen geht*) Hamburg 1970. Recorded for: EMI. Video/Film: Cuperus (*Zaubergeige*); Peter I (*Zar und Zimmermann*); Dr Stone (*Globolinks*); Mandryka (*Arabella*). Gives recitals. Appears with symphony orchestra. **Res:** Sindelfingerstr 24, 7251 Warmbronn, FR Ger. Mgmt: SLZ/FRG; HLT/UK.

WOLFF, BEVERLY. Dramatic mezzo-soprano. American. Born 6 Nov 1928, Atlanta, GA. Husband John Dwiggins, occupation stockbroker. Two children. Studied: Gertrude McFarland, Atlanta; Acad of Vocal Arts, Sidney Dietch, Philadelphia; Boris Goldovsky, Tanglewood, MA. **Debut:** Cherubino (*Nozze di Figaro*) New York City Opera 1960.

Sang with major companies in FR GER: Cologne; ITA: Florence Maggio & Comunale, Spoleto Fest, Turin, Venice; MEX: Mexico City; USA: Boston, Houston, Miami, Milwaukee Florentine, New York City Opera, Philadelphia Grand & Lyric, San Antonio, San Francisco Opera & Spring Opera, Santa Fe, Washington DC. **Roles with these companies incl** BARTOK: Judith (*Bluebeard's Castle*); BARBER: Erika (*Vanessa*); BELLINI: Adalgisa★ (*Norma*); BERLIOZ: Marguerite★ (*Damnation de Faust*); BERNSTEIN: Dinah (*Trouble in Tahiti*); BIZET: Carmen; BRITTEN: Lucretia (*Rape of Lucretia*); DONIZETTI: Sara★‡ (*Roberto Devereux*); GOUNOD: Siebel (*Faust*); HANDEL: Sesto‡ (*Giulio Cesare*); MASSENET: Charlotte (*Werther*); MENOTTI: Desideria (*Saint of Bleecker Street*); MONTEVERDI: Poppea★ (*Incoronazione di Poppea*); MOZART: Sesto★ (*Clemenza di Tito*), Cherubino (*Nozze di Figaro*); MUSSORGSKY: Marfa (*Khovanshchina*); OFFENBACH: Giulietta (*Contes d'Hoffmann*); PUCCINI: Suzuki (*Butterfly*); ROSSINI: Marchesina Clarice★‡ (*Pietra del paragone*); SAINT-SAENS: Dalila★; VERDI: Amneris★ (*Aida*), Eboli★ (*Don Carlo*), Dame Quickly (*Falstaff*); WAGNER: Brangäne★ (*Tristan und Isolde*); WARD: Elizabeth Proctor★ (*Crucible*). Also MERCADANTE: Bianca (*Giuramento*). **World premieres:** MENOTTI: Wife (*Most Important Man*) New York City Opera 1970; MOORE: Carry Nation, Univ of Kansas 1966. Recorded for: Westminster, RCA, Desto, CRI. Video—NBC TV: Dinah (*Trouble in Tahiti*), Hotel Clerk (*Labyrinth*). Gives recitals. Appears with symphony orchestra. Coaches repertoire. **Res:** 2215 Nevada Rd, Lakeland, FL, USA. Mgmt: CAM/USA.

WOLLRAD, ROLF. Bass & basso-buffo. German. Resident mem: Staatsoper Dresden, Ger DR. Born 6 Feb 1938, Döbeln. Wife Irmtraud, occupation vineyard owner. Two children. Studied: Hochschule für Musik, Prof Peter Russ, Leipzig; State Consv, Prof Ilia Jossifoff, Sofia. **Debut:** Sarastro (*Zauberflöte*) Landesbühnen Sachsen, Dresden, Ger DR 1964. Awards: Bachpreis, Leipzig 1964.

Sang with major companies in FR GER: Wiesbaden; GER DR: Berlin Staatsoper, Dresden; USSR: Leningrad Kirov. **Roles with these companies incl** BEETHOVEN: Rocco★ (*Fidelio*); CIMAROSA: Geronimo (*Matrimonio segreto*); DONIZETTI: Dulcamara★ (*Elisir*); EGK: Cuperus★ (*Zaubergeige*); LORTZING: Stadinger (*Waffenschmied*), Baculus★ (*Wildschütz*), Van Bett (*Zar und Zimmermann*); MOZART: Leporello (*Don Giovanni*), Osmin (*Entführung aus dem Serail*), Figaro (*Nozze di Figaro*); MUSSORGSKY: Pimen★ (*Boris Godunov*); NICOLAI: Falstaff (*Lustigen Weiber*); ORFF: Bauer (*Mond*); PAISIELLO: Bartolo★ (*Barbiere di Siviglia*); PUCCINI: Gianni Schicchi. Also WAGNER-REGENY: Renard (*Günstling*). **World premieres:** ZIMMERMANN: Korrinth (*Levins Mühle*) Staatsoper, Dresden 1973. Video/Film: (*Fidelio*). Gives recitals. Appears with symphony orchestra. Coaches repertoire. **Res:** Mittlere Bergstr 44, Radebeul, Ger DR. Mgmt: KDR/GDR.

WONG, CAREY GORDON. Scenic and costume designer for opera, theater. Is a stage director; also a graphic designer, filmmaker & illustrator. American. Resident designer, Portland Opera Assn, OR. Born 5 Feb 1950, Portland. Single. Studied: Yale School of Drama, Ming Cho Lee, Jeanne Button, William Warfel, CT. Prof training: Portland Opera 1974-75. **Operatic debut:** sets, *Freischütz* Portland Opera 1974; sets/cost, *Leben des Orestes* Portland Opera 1975. Theater debut: Yale Univ Theater, New Haven, CT 1972. Previous occupation: theater historian. Awards: Phi Beta Kappa, Yale Univ 1970.

Designed for major companies in USA: Portland. **Operas designed for these companies incl** MONTEVERDI: *Favola d'Orfeo★;* MOZART: *Entführung aus dem Serail★;* WEBER: *Freischütz★* Also KRENEK: *Leben des Orestes.* Exhibitions of stage designs, Portland State Univ 1974. Res: Portland, OR, USA.

WOODLAND, RAE. Lyric soprano. British. Born Nottingham, UK. Husband Denis Stanley, occupation engineer. Studied: National Opera School, Prof Roy Henderson, Joan Cross CBE, London. **Debut:** Königin der Nacht (*Zauberflöte*) Sadler's Wells. Previous occupations: secretary, typist. Awards: Ntl Classics Prize, Opera School, London.

Sang with major companies in BEL: Liège; FRA: Aix-en-Provence Fest, Lyon; HOL: Amsterdam; ITA: Rome Caracalla, Venice; UK: Aldeburgh Fest, Cardiff Welsh, Edinburgh Fest, Glasgow Scottish, Glyndebourne Fest, London Royal Opera & English National; USSR: Moscow Stanislavski. **Roles with these companies incl** BELLINI: Elvira (*Puritani*); BERLIOZ: Marguerite (*Damnation de Faust*); BOITO: Margherita (*Mefistofele*); BRITTEN: Lady Billows★ (*Albert Herring*), Female Chorus★ (*Rape of Lucretia*), Miss Jessel★

(*Turn of the Screw*); GOUNOD: Marguerite (*Faust*); HANDEL: Galatea (*Acis and Galatea*); KODALY: Örzse (*Háry János*); MASCAGNI: Santuzza★ (*Cavalleria rusticana*); MOZART: Fiordiligi (*Così fan tutte*), Donna Anna & Donna Elvira★ (*Don Giovanni*), Konstanze (*Entführung aus dem Serail*), Elettra★ (*Idomeneo*), Mme Herz (*Schauspieldirektor*), Contessa (*Nozze di Figaro*), Pamina & Königin der Nacht (*Zauberflöte*); OFFENBACH: Olympia & Antonia & Giulietta (*Contes d'Hoffmann*); ORFF: Solo (*Carmina burana*); PUCCINI: Mimi★ (*Bohème*); SMETANA: Marie (*Bartered Bride*), Carla (*Two Widows*); STRAUSS, J: Rosalinde (*Fledermaus*); TCHAIKOVSKY: Tatiana (*Eugene Onegin*); VAUGHAN WILLIAMS: Mary (*Hugh the Drover*); VERDI: Aida, Odabella (*Attila*), Alice Ford★ (*Falstaff*), Giselda (*Lombardi*), Luisa Miller, Lady Macbeth, Desdemona (*Otello*), Leonora (*Trovatore*); WAGNER: Venus (*Tannhäuser*).

WOOLLAM, KENNETH GEOFFREY. Tenor. British. Resident mem: English National Opera, London. Born 16 Jan 1937, Chester, UK. Wife Phoebe, occupation music teacher. Three children. Studied: Royal Coll of Music, Heddle Nash, Hervey Alan, Ruth Packer, London. **Debut:** Pierre (*War and Peace*) Sadler's Wells, London 1972. Previous occupations: radio & television engineer.

Sang with major companies in UK: London English National. **Roles with these companies incl** JANACEK: Boris★ (*Katya Kabanova*); LEONCAVALLO: Canio★ (*Pagliacci*); MONTEVERDI: Nero★ (*Incoronazione di Poppea*); PROKOFIEV: Pierre★ (*War and Peace*); STRAUSS, J: Alfred★ (*Fledermaus*); STRAVINSKY: Oedipus Rex★; VERDI: Alfredo★ (*Traviata*); WAGNER: Siegmund★ (*Walküre*). Video/Film: Alfredo (*Traviata*); Canio (*Pagliacci*); Hoffmann. Gives recitals. Appears with symphony orchestra. **Res:** 20 Burnaby Gardens, Chiswick, London W4, 3DT, UK. Mgmt: MIN/UK.

WOPMANN, ALFRED. Stages/produces opera. Austrian. Dir, Studio of the Staatsoper, Vienna. Born 23 Nov 1936, Wels. Wife Ingrid, occupation HS teacher. One child. Studied: as asst to Otto Schenk, Luchino Visconti, August Everding, Götz Friedrich; Acad of Music, Vienna; incl music & violin. Operatic training as asst stage dir at Staatsoper, Vienna. **Operatic debut:** *Besuch der alten Dame* Musiktheater, Dortmund 1972. Previous occupation: asst at Burgtheater & TV, Vienna; violinist in Staatsoper orch. Awards: Dr; Körner-Preis 1963, Theodor Körner Fndt, Austrian Gvnmt.

Directed/produced opera for major companies in AUS: Graz; FRA: Orange Fest; FR GER: Dortmund, Wiesbaden; ITA: Milan La Scala, Trieste. **Operas staged with these companies incl** BELLINI: *Sonnambula★;* LEONCAVALLO: *Pagliacci★;* MASCAGNI: *Cavalleria rusticana★;* STRAUSS, R: *Rosenkavalier★, Salome★.* Teaches at Opera Studio, Vienna. Mgmt: TAS/AUS; SLZ/FRG; OOC/FRA.

WORKMAN, WILLIAM. Lyric baritone. American. Resident mem: Städtische Oper, Frankfurt. Born 4 Feb 1940, Valdosta, GA, USA. Wife Elizabeth Parker. Studied: Davidson Coll, Donald Plott; Curtis Inst of Music, Martial Singher, Philadelphia; Music Acad of the West, Martial Singher, Santa Barbara, CA; Hedwig Schilling, Hamburg. **Debut:** Zweiter Gefangene (*Fidelio*) Hamburg Staatsoper 1965. Awards: Oberdorfer Prize, Hamburg Staatsoper.

Sang with major companies in AUS: Vienna Staatsoper; FRA: Aix-en-Provence Fest, Marseille, Paris, Strasbourg; FR GER: Frankfurt, Hamburg, Stuttgart; HOL: Amsterdam; SWI: Geneva; USA: Dallas, Santa Fe. **Roles with these companies incl** BRITTEN: Billy Budd★; CIMAROSA: Count Robinson (*Matrimonio segreto*); DEBUSSY: Pelléas; DONIZETTI: Dott Malatesta★ (*Don Pasquale*); MOZART: Guglielmo★ (*Così fan tutte*), Figaro★ (*Nozze di Figaro*), Papageno★ (*Zauberflöte*); PUCCINI: Marcello★ (*Bohème*); ROSSINI: Figaro★ (*Barbiere di Siviglia*); STRAUSS, R: Olivier★ (*Capriccio*). Also STRAUSS, R: Barbier★ (*Schweigsame Frau*); GOUNOD: Valentin★ (*Faust*). **World premieres:** MENOTTI: Tony (*Globolinks*) Hamburg Staatsoper 1968; PENDERECKI: de Condé (*Teufel von Loudun*) Hamburg Staatsoper 1969. Video/Film: Papageno (*Zauberflöte*); Tony (*Globolinks*). Gives recitals. Appears with symphony orchestra. **Res:** Bad Homburg, FR Ger. Mgmt: DSP/USA; ASK/UK.

WU, WILLIAM; né Wen-Hsiu Wu. Lyric & dramatic tenor. Chinese (Taiwan). Resident mem: Deutsche Oper, Berlin; Niki Kai, Tokyo. Born 8 Nov 1935, Taiwan, China. Wife Yumiko Nagata. One child. Studied: Prof Takeo Ito, Mo Walter Taussig. **Debut:** Canio (*Pagliacci*) Deutsche Oper, Berlin 1973.

Sang with major companies in FR GER: Berlin Deutsche Oper; JPN: Tokyo Niki Kai. **Roles with these companies incl** BERG: Maler★ (*Lulu*); LEONCAVALLO: Canio★ (*Pagliacci*); STRAUSS, R: Ein Sänger (*Rosenkavalier*). Also WAGNER: Steuermann★ (*Fliegende Holländer*); MUSSORGSKY: Dimitri★ (*Boris Godunov*). Gives recitals. Appears with symphony orchestra. **Res:** 19 Angerburger Allee 53, Berlin, FR Ger.

WÜSTEMANN, KARL. Dramatic & Italian tenor. German. Resident mem: Staatsoper Dresden, Ger DR. Born 24 Mar 1929, Laupheim. Wife Evelin, occupation hairdresser. One child. Studied: Studio Komische Oper Berlin, Fr Kmsg Deitil; Studio Staatsoper Berlin, Eva Adamy. **Debut:** Alfredo (*Traviata*) Theater Stralsund, Germany 1961. Previous occupations: turner, smith, builder. Awards: Kammersänger, Ministry of Culture, Ger DR 1972.

Sang with major companies in FR GER: Wiesbaden; GER DR: Berlin Komische Oper & Staatsoper, Dresden, Leipzig; USSR: Leningrad Kirov. **Roles with these companies incl** DESSAU: Lukullus★ (*Verurteilung des Lukullus*); JANACEK: Steva (*Jenufa*); LEONCAVALLO: Canio★ (*Pagliacci*); MASCAGNI: Turiddu (*Cavalleria rusticana*); MOZART: Don Ottavio (*Don Giovanni*), Tamino (*Zauberflöte*); PUCCINI: Rodolfo (*Bohème*), Pinkerton★ (*Butterfly*), Cavaradossi★ (*Tosca*), Calaf★ (*Turandot*); SMETANA: Hans★ (*Bartered Bride*); STRAUSS, J: Alfred★ (*Fledermaus*); STRAUSS, R: Ein Sänger★ (*Rosen-*

kavalier); VERDI: Radames (*Aida*), Don Carlo★, Don Alvaro★ (*Forza del destino*), Ismaele (*Nabucco*), Alfredo★ (*Traviata*), Manrico (*Trovatore*); WAGNER: Lohengrin; WEBER: Hüon★ (*Oberon*). **World premieres:** ZIMMERMANN: Tomaschewski (*Levins Mühle*) Staatsoper, Dresden 1973. Video/Film: (*Tabarro*). Appears with symphony orchestra. Coaches repertoire. **Res:** Forsthausstr 12, 8053 Dresden, Ger DR. Mgmt: KDR/GDR.

WYATT, CAROL. Dramatic mezzo-soprano. American. Resident mem: Staatsoper, Hamburg. Born 20 Oct 1943, Marshall, TX, USA. Single. Studied: Baylor Univ, Tina Piazza, Waco, TX, USA; Mo T Jappelli, Milan. **Debut:** Amneris (*Aida*) Palermo 1969. Previous occupations: schoolteacher.

Sang with major companies in AUS: Graz; FR GER: Dortmund, Frankfurt, Hamburg, Karlsruhe, Kiel, Saarbrücken; ITA: Palermo, Spoleto Fest; SWI: Geneva, Zurich; USA: Cincinnati. **Roles with these companies incl** HUMPERDINCK: Hänsel; MOZART: Sesto (*Clemenza di Tito*), Dorabella (*Così fan tutte*); MUSSORGSKY: Marina (*Boris Godunov*); OFFENBACH: Giulietta (*Contes d'Hoffmann*); TCHAIKOVSKY: Olga (*Eugene Onegin*); VERDI: Amneris (*Aida*), Eboli (*Don Carlo*), Azucena (*Trovatore*); WEBER: Eglantine (*Euryanthe*). Also MASCAGNI: Santuzza★ (*Cavalleria rusticana*); BUSSETTI: George Sand (*Lorenzaccio*). Appears with symphony orchestra. Mgmt: DSP/USA.

WYCKOFF, LOU ANN. Spinto. American. Resident mem: Deutsche Oper, Berlin. Born 20 Jul, Berkeley, CA, USA. Single. Studied: Dr Vivian Long, Los Angeles; Gibner King, New York; Prof Josef Metternich, Berlin; Prof Irmgard Hartmann, Berlin. **Debut:** Donna Elvira (*Don Giovanni*) Spoleto Fest 1967. Previous occupations: exec secy. Awards: four Rockefeller Fndt Grants 1965-69; First Prize Artists Advisory Counc, Chicago 1968; Sullivan Fndt Awd.

Sang with major companies in BEL: Brussels; FRA: Lyon, Marseille; FR GER: Berlin Deutsche Oper, Cologne, Düsseldorf-Duisburg, Hamburg, Munich Staatsoper; ITA: Genoa, Milan La Scala, Spoleto Fest, Venice; USA: Washington DC. **Roles with these companies incl** BERLIOZ: Marguerite (*Damnation de Faust*); DEBUSSY: Lia★ (*Enfant prodigue*); LEONCAVALLO: Nedda★ (*Pagliacci*); MOZART: Vitellia★ (*Clemenza di Tito*), Donna Elvira★ (*Don Giovanni*), Contessa Almaviva★ (*Nozze di Figaro*); MUSSORGSKY: Marina★ (*Boris Godunov*); ORFF: Solo★ (*Carmina burana*); POULENC: Mme Lidoine★ (*Dialogues des Carmélites*); TCHAIKOVSKY: Lisa★ (*Pique Dame*); VERDI: Odabella★ (*Attila*), Amelia★ (*Ballo in maschera*), Alice Ford★ (*Falstaff*), Leonora★ (*Trovatore*); WAGNER: Eva★ (*Meistersinger*); WEBER: Agathe★ (*Freischütz*). **World premieres:** NABOKOV: Rosaline (*Love's Labour's Lost*) Berlin, Deutsche Oper 1973. Gives recitals. Appears with symphony orchestra. **Res:** Kurfürstendamm 59/60, 1 Berlin 15, FR Ger. Mgmt: DSP/USA.

WYSOCZANSKA, JADWIGA. Spinto. Czechoslovakian. Resident mem: National Theater,

Prague. Born 24 May 1927, Prague, Czechoslovakia. Husband Jan Stros, occupation mem Czech Philharmonic. Two children. Studied: Prof V Aim, M Krásová, Prague; J Logacevová, Liberec. **Debut:** Marie (*Bartered Bride*) Smetana Theater, Prague 1947.

Sang with major companies in CZE: Brno, Prague National; HOL: Amsterdam; ITA: Bologna, Florence Comunale, Genoa, Naples, Palermo, Parma, Verona Arena. **Roles with these companies incl** BIZET: Micaëla (*Carmen*); DVORAK: Rusalka★‡; HANDEL: Rodelinda; JANACEK: Vixen (*Cunning Little Vixen*), Malinka (*Excursions of Mr Broucek*), Jenufa; MONIUSZKO: Halka; MOZART: Fiordiligi★ (*Così fan tutte*), Donna Anna★ & Donna Elvira (*Don Giovanni*), Contessa★ (*Nozze di Figaro*), Pamina (*Zauberflöte*); OFFENBACH: Antonia (*Contes d'Hoffmann*); PROKOFIEV: Sofia (*Semyon Kotko*); PUCCINI: Mimi & Musetta (*Bohème*), Cio-Cio-San★ (*Butterfly*); RAVEL: Concepcion (*Heure espagnole*); RIMSKY-KORSAKOV: Martha (*Tsar's Bride*); SMETANA: Marie★ (*Bartered Bride*), Mlada (*Dalibor*), Hedvika (*Devil's Wall*), Marinka & Vendulka★ (*The Kiss*), Libuse, Blazenka (*Secret*), Carla (*Two Widows*); STRAUSS, R: Sophie (*Rosenkavalier*); TCHAIKOVSKY: Tatiana★ (*Eugene Onegin*), Lisa (*Pique Dame*); VERDI: Aida, Amelia★ (*Ballo in maschera*); WAGNER: Elisabeth (*Tannhäuser*); WEBER: Agathe (*Freischütz*). Also SMETANA: Anezka (*Two Widows*), Vlcenka (*Brandenburgers in Bohemia*); DVORAK: Julie (*Jakobin*); MARTINU: Julietta. Recorded for Supraphon. Gives recitals. Appears with symphony orchestra. Teaches voice. **Res:** Svábova 4/394, Prague, CSSR. Mgmt: PRG/CZE.

599

Y

YACHMI, ROHANGIS. Coloratura mezzo-soprano. Austrian. Resident mem: Staatsoper, Vienna. Born 13 Sep 1940, Teheran, Iran. Husband Dr Horst Caucig, occupation physician. One child. Studied: Musikhochschule, Profs Pitzinger & von den Hof, Frankfurt; Mo Toffolo, Trieste. **Debut:** Cherubino (*Nozze di Figaro*) Dortmund 1961.

Sang with major companies in AUS: Vienna Staatsoper & Volksoper; FR GER: Bielefeld, Cologne, Dortmund, Essen, Hamburg, Munich Staatsoper, Nürnberg, Stuttgart, Wiesbaden; GER DR: Berlin Komische Oper; ITA: Genoa; SWI: Basel; USSR: Moscow Bolshoi. **Roles with these companies incl** BIZET: Carmen★; GLUCK: Orfeo★; GOUNOD: Siebel★ (*Faust*); HUMPERDINCK: Hänsel; MOZART: Cherubino★‡ (*Nozze di Figaro*); PUCCINI: Suzuki★ (*Butterfly*); ROSSINI: Rosina★ (*Barbiere di Siviglia*), Isabella★ (*Italiana in Algeri*), Zaida★‡ (*Turco in Italia*); STRAUSS, R: Octavian★‡ (*Rosenkavalier*); VERDI: Preziosilla★ (*Forza del destino*). Also BERG: Gymnasiast★ (*Lulu*); OFFENBACH: Nicklausse★ (*Contes d'Hoffmann*); MARTINU: Sister Pascalina (*Marienlegende*). Recorded for: Concert Hall. Video/Film: (*Contes d'Hoffmann*); (*Turco in Italia*); (*Marienlegende*). Gives recitals. Appears with symphony orchestra. Mgmt: RAB/AUS; SLZ/FRG; HSM/FRG.

YANNOPOULOS, DINO; né Konstantin Yannopoulos. Stages/produces opera & theater. Also designs stage-lighting. American. Dir & Resident Stage Dir, Opera Co of Curtis Inst of Music, Philadelphia, USA. Born Athens, Greece. Wife Marguerite Willauer, occupation soprano. One son. Studied: in Vienna; in Salzburg with Herbert Graf.

Directed/produced opera for major companies in AUS: Vienna Volksoper; GRE: Athens Fest; USA: Cincinnati, New Orleans, New York Met, Philadelphia Lyric, San Francisco Spring Opera, Seattle; et al. **Operas staged with these companies incl** BEETHOVEN: *Fidelio;* BELLINI: *Norma;* BRITTEN: *Rape of Lucretia;* CHERUBINI: *Medea;* DEBUSSY: *Pelléas et Mélisande;* DONIZETTI: *Don Pasquale, Lucia;* GIORDANO: *Andrea Chénier;* GLUCK: *Orfeo ed Euridice;* HANDEL: *Giulio Cesare;* MOZART: *Don Giovanni, Entführung aus dem Serail;* MUSSORGSKY: *Boris Godunov;* PONCHIELLI:

Gioconda; PUCCINI: *Tabarro, Tosca;* STRAUSS, R: *Ariadne auf Naxos, Rosenkavalier, Salome;* VERDI: *Ernani;* WAGNER: *Meistersinger;* et al.

YANNUZZI, WILLIAM A. American. Music Adm, Baltimore Opera Co, 11 E Lexington St, Baltimore, MD 21202. In charge of art policy, mus matters. Born 30 Jul 1933, Baltimore. Single. Studied: Johns Hopkins Univ, Baltimore; St John's Coll, Santa Fe, NM. Plays the piano. Previous occupations: teacher secondary school & coll. Started with present company in 1961 as Asst Cond, in present position since 1973. Awards: Phi Beta Kappa. **Res:** 1136 Baker Ave, Baltimore, MD, USA.

YAUGER, MARGARET; née Sara Margaret Yauger. Lyric mezzo-soprano. American. Born Birmingham, AL, USA. Husband Malcolm Smith, bass. Studied: Converse Coll, Spartanburg, SC; New England Consv of Music, Boston; Daniel Ferro, New York. **Debut:** Meg Page (*Falstaff*) American Ntl Opera Co 1966. Previous occupations: part-time model. Awards: Sullivan Fndt Awd; American Opera Center Schlshp; finalist Miss Alabama Cont.

Sang with major companies in USA: Boston, Lake George, New York City Opera. **Roles with these companies incl** BRITTEN: Lucretia★ (*Rape of Lucretia*); GOUNOD: Siebel★ (*Faust*); VERDI: Meg Page★(*Falstaff*); WARD: Elizabeth Proctor★ (*Crucible*). Also WEILL: Jenny★ (*Dreigroschenoper*). Gives recitals. Appears with symphony orchestra.

YOCKEY, JOANN VIVIAN; née Soab. Lyric soprano. American. Husband Ross Yockey. Studied: Loyola Univ, New Orleans, LA, USA; Juilliard School, New York. **Debut:** Liù (*Turandot*) New Orleans Opera 1972. Awards: Met Gulf-Coast Reg Aud; Opera Co of Boston Aud; New York Youth Symphony Vocal Compt; Liederkranz Fndt; Sullivan Fndt.

Sang with major companies in USA: Boston, Lake George, Newark, New Orleans. **Roles with these companies incl** BIZET: Micaëla (*Carmen*); HUMPERDINCK: Gretel★; LEONCAVALLO: Nedda★ (*Pagliacci*); PROKOFIEV: Natasha★ (*War and Peace*); PUCCINI: Cio-Cio-San★ (*Butterfly*), Magda★ (*Rondine*), Liù★ (*Turandot*);

VERDI: Alice Ford★ (*Falstaff*), Gilda★ (*Rigoletto*). Gives recitals. Appears with symphony orchestra. **Res:** North Bergen, NJ, USA. Mgmt: HUR/USA.

YOUNG, ALEXANDER; né Basil Alexander Youngs. Lyric tenor. British. Born 18 Oct 1920, London. Wife Jean Anne. Two children. Studied: Royal Coll of Music, London; Prof Stefan Pollman. **Debut:** Scaramuccio (*Ariadne auf Naxos*) Glyndebourne Fest 1951. Previous occupations: war service in Army.

Sang with major companies in NOR: Oslo; UK: Aldeburgh Fest, Cardiff Welsh, Edinburgh Fest, Glasgow Scottish, Glyndebourne Fest, London Royal & English National; USA: San Francisco Opera. **Roles with these companies incl** BIZET: Haroun (*Djamileh*), Captain Silvio (*Docteur Miracle*); BRITTEN: Lysander (*Midsummer Night*), Peter Quint (*Turn of the Screw*); CIMAROSA: Paolino (*Matrimonio segreto*); DALLAPICCOLA: Jailer/Inquisitor (*Prigioniero*); FALLA: Maese Pedro; HANDEL: Xerxes; HAYDN: Filippo (*Infedeltà delusa*), Cecco (*Mondo della luna*); HOLST: Satyavan (*Savitri*); MONTEVERDI: Orfeo; MOZART: Ferrando★ (*Così fan tutte*), Don Ottavio (*Don Giovanni*), Belmonte★ (*Entführung aus dem Serail*), Belfiore (*Finta giardiniera*), Idomeneo★, Tamino (*Zauberflöte*); PURCELL: Aeneas; ROSSINI: Almaviva (*Barbiere di Siviglia*), Don Ramiro (*Cenerentola*), Comte Ory; SMETANA: Wenzel (*Bartered Bride*); STRAUSS, J: Eisenstein (*Fledermaus*); STRAUSS, R: Matteo (*Arabella*); STRAVINSKY: Tom Rakewell★‡ (*Rake's Progress*); WAGNER: David (*Meistersinger*); WEBER: Abu Hassan, Oberon. Also HANDEL: Jupiter★ (*Semele*); Jephtha★, Grimwald‡ (*Rodelinda*); GLUCK: Orfeo, 1774 Paris vers; EGK: Chlestakov (*Revisor*). **World premiere:** HAMILTON: Cicero (*Catiline Conspiracy*) Scottish Opera, Glasgow 1974. Recorded for: DG, Westminster, Cambridge, CBS. Gives recitals. Appears with symphony orchestra. Teaches voice. Coaches repertoire. On faculty of Royal Northern Coll of Music, head of School of Vocal Studies, Manchester. **Res:** Spring Bank Start La, Whaley Bridge, Stockport, Cheshire, UK. Mgmt: CVX/UK.

Z

ZACCARIA, NICOLA ANGELO; né Nicolas Angelos Zachariou. Bass. Greek. Born 9 Mar 1923, Piraeus, Greece. Wife Elefteria. Studied: Athens Consv, Miltos Vithinos, Greece. **Debut:** Raimondo (*Lucia*) Athens Opera 1952. Awards: Comman of St Mark Alex ,nder, and other honors from Greek Gvnmt.

Sang with major companies in AUS: Graz, Salzburg Fest, Vienna Staatsoper; BEL: Brussels; BRA: Rio de Janeiro; FRA: Aix-en-Provence Fest, Orange Fest, Paris; GRE: Athens National Opera & Festival; FR GER: Berlin Deutsche Oper, Cologne, Munich Staatsoper & Gärtnerplatz; ITA: Bologna, Florence Maggio & Comunale, Genoa, Milan La Scala, Naples, Palermo, Parma, Rome Opera, Trieste, Turin, Venice; MEX: Mexico City; MON: Monte Carlo; S AFR: Johannesburg; SPA: Barcelona; SWI: Geneva; UK: London Royal Opera; USSR: Moscow Bolshoi; USA: Dallas Civic Opera. **Roles with these companies incl** BEETHOVEN: Rocco (*Fidelio*); BELLINI: Capellio (*Capuleti ed i Montecchi*), Oroveso★ (*Norma*), Sir George★ (*Puritani*), Rodolfo★ (*Sonnambula*); BIZET: Zurga (*Pêcheurs de perles*); CATALANI: Stromminger★ (*Wally*); CHERUBINI: Creon (*Medea*); DEBUSSY: Arkel★ (*Pelléas et Mélisande*); DONIZETTI: Baldassare★ (*Favorite*); GLINKA: Ivan (*Life for the Tsar*); GLUCK: Apollo (*Alceste*), Agamemnon (*Iphigénie · en Aulide*); GOUNOD: Méphistophélès (*Faust*); MARTIN: Marc (*Vin herbé*); MASSENET: Remigo★ (*Navarraise*); MEYERBEER: Marcel★ (*Huguenots*); MOZART: Osmin (*Entführung aus dem Serail*), Sarastro (*Zauberflöte*); MUSSORGSKY: Pimen★ (*Boris Godunov*); PONCHIELLI: Alvise (*Gioconda*); PUCCINI: Colline★ (*Bohème*); ROSSINI: Don Basilio★ (*Barbiere di Siviglia*); SMETANA: Kezal (*Bartered Bride*); STRAVINSKY: Creon & Tiresias (*Oedipus Rex*); TCHAIKOVSKY: Eugene Onegin; THOMAS: Lothario★ (*Mignon*); VERDI: Ramfis★ (*Aida*), Philip II★ & Grande Inquisitore★ (*Don Carlo*), Silva (*Ernani*), Padre Guardiano★ (*Forza del destino*), Miller (*Luisa Miller*), Banquo (*Macbeth*), Zaccaria (*Nabucco*), Fiesco★ (*Simon Boccanegra*), Procida (*Vespri*); WAGNER: Daland (*Fliegende Holländer*), König Heinrich (*Lohengrin*), König Marke★ (*Tristan und Isolde*).

ZAFRED, MARIO. Italian. Art Dir, Teatro dell'Opera, Rome, Italy. Is also a composer of operas: *Amleto* Rome 1961; *Wallenstein* Rome 1965. Res: Rome, Italy.

ZANASI, MARIO. Dramatic baritone. Italian. Born 8 Jan 1927, Bologna, Italy. Married. One child. Studied: Consv G B Martini, Bologna; Scuola di Perfezionamento, Teatro alla Scala, Milan. **Debut:** Germont (*Traviata*) Bologna 1954. Previous occupations: studies in industrial field. Awards: First Prize Winner Compt Il Grande Caruso; MGM, His Master's Voice 1952.

Sang with major companies in AUS: Vienna Staatsoper; CAN: Montreal/Quebec, Toronto; FRA: Lyon, Paris, Toulouse; FR GER: Cologne, Düsseldorf-Duisburg, Hamburg, Wiesbaden; GER DR: Berlin Komische Oper; HUN: Budapest; ISR: Tel Aviv; ITA: Bologna, Florence Maggio & Comunale, Genoa, Milan La Scala, Naples, Palermo, Parma, Rome Opera & Caracalla, Trieste, Turin, Venice, Verona Arena; POR: Lisbon; SPA: Barcelona; SWI: Zurich; UK: Edinburgh Fest, London Royal Opera; USSR: Moscow Bolshoi; USA: Chicago, Dallas, Miami, New York Met, Philadelphia Lyric, San Francisco Opera. **Roles with these companies incl** BELLINI: Filippo★ (*Beatrice di Tenda*), Sir Richard (*Puritani*); BIZET: Escamillo (*Carmen*); DONIZETTI: Belcore (*Elisir*), Alfonse★ (*Favorite*), Enrico★ (*Lucia*), Chevreuse (*Maria di Rohan*); GIORDANO: Carlo Gérard★ (*Andrea Chénier*); LEONCAVALLO: Tonio (*Pagliacci*); MASCAGNI: Alfio (*Cavalleria rusticana*); MUSSORGSKY: Shaklovity (*Khovanshchina*); PONCHIELLI: Barnaba★ (*Gioconda*); PUCCINI: Marcello (*Bohème*), Jack Rance (*Fanciulla del West*), Sharpless (*Butterfly*), Scarpia★ (*Tosca*), Guglielmo Wulf (*Villi*); ROSSINI: Figaro★ (*Barbiere di Siviglia*); VERDI: Amonasro★ (*Aida*), Ezio (*Attila*), Renato★ (*Ballo in maschera*), Rodrigo★ (*Don Carlo*), Francesco Foscari (*Due Foscari*), Don Carlo (*Ernani*), Don Carlo (*Forza del destino*), Giacomo (*Giovanna d'Arco*), Miller (*Luisa Miller*), Macbeth★, Massimiliano Moor (*Masnadieri*), Nabucco★, Iago★ (*Otello*), Rigoletto★, Simon Boccanegra★, Germont (*Traviata*), Conte di Luna (*Trovatore*); WAGNER: Telramund (*Lohengrin*). Also CHERUBINI: Germano (*Elisa*); GIORDANO: Napoleon (*Madame Sans-Gêne*); GOUNOD: Valentin (*Faust*); ZANDONAI: Tebaldo (*Giulietta e Romeo*); SCARLATTI: Ottone (*Griselda*). **Res:** V Dante 2, 40125 Bologna, Italy.

ZANI, GIACOMO. Conductor of opera and symphony. Italian. Born 9 Jul 1934, Casalmaggiore, Italy. Wife Paola Faimali, occupation painter. Studied: Consv of Milan, Paribeni; Consv of Paris, Barzin, Blot, Fourestier; incl piano, Prof Alati. Plays the piano. **Operatic debut:** *Cavalleria rusticana* Giovani Cantanti, Milan 1967. Symphonic debut: Radio Italiana, Milan 1964. Awards: Diploma of Merit, Conc of Florence 1966; Golden Nut 1970. Previous adm positions in opera: Gen Dir, Teatro Massimo, Palermo 1971-73.

Conducted with major companies in FRA: Paris, Toulouse Opera; ITA: Naples San Carlo, Palermo, Parma, Trieste, Turin; MON: Monte Carlo; UK: Edinburgh Fest; YUG: Zagreb, Belgrade. **Operas with these companies incl** AUBER: *Muette de Portici*★; BELLINI: *Puritani*★; DONIZETTI: *Don Pasquale*★, *Elisir*★, *Lucia;* GIORDANO: *Andrea Chénier*★; MASCAGNI: *Cavalleria rusticana;* MENOTTI: *Amelia al ballo*★, *Medium*★, *Telephone;* PERGOLESI: *Serva padrona;* PUCCINI: *Bohème*★, *Gianni Schicchi*★, *Butterfly*★, *Suor Angelica*★, *Tabarro*★, *Tosca*★; ROSSINI: *Barbiere di Siviglia*★‡, *Elisabetta Regina*★, *Italiana in Algeri*★, *Scala di seta, Signor Bruschino;* VERDI: *Aida*★, *Forza del destino*★, *Macbeth*★, *Rigoletto, Traviata*★, *Trovatore;* WOLF-FERRARI: *Segreto di Susanna.* Also ALFANO: *Risurrezione*★; MENOTTI: *Most Important Man*★; CIMAROSA: *Italiana in Londra;* ROSSELLINI: *Guerra;* CHAILLY: *Domanda di matrimonio*★, *Procedura penale.* Recorded for Supraphon Prague. Conducted major orch in Europe. Previous positions as Mus Dir with major orch: Orch del Massimo di Palermo 1971-73. **Res:** Viale Argonne 51, Milan, Italy. Mgmt: GBN/UK.

ZANNINI, LAURA LUDOVICA. Lyric mezzo-soprano. Italian. Born 4 Apr 1937, Trieste. Single. Studied: Consv Benedetto Marcello, Venice, Gilda dalla Rizza; Mo Bruno Maderna. **Debut:** Isabella (*Italiana in Algeri*) Spoleto Fest 1955. Previous occupations: accountant. Awards: First Prize Spoleto Fest; First Prize Teatro Nuovo, Milan.

Sang with major companies in AUS: Vienna Staatsoper; BEL: Brussels; DEN: Copenhagen; FRA: Bordeaux, Paris, Toulouse; FR GER: Dortmund, Munich Staatsoper, Wiesbaden; HUN: Budapest; ISR: Tel Aviv; ITA: Bologna, Florence Maggio & Comunale, Genoa, Milan La Scala, Naples, Palermo, Parma, Spoleto Fest, Trieste, Turin, Venice, Verona Arena; MON: Monte Carlo; POL: Warsaw; POR: Lisbon; SPA: Barcelona; UK: Edinburgh Fest, London Royal; USSR: Moscow Bolshoi. **Roles with these companies incl** AUBER: Pamela (*Fra Diavolo*); BERLIOZ: Marguerite (*Damnation de Faust*); BORODIN: Kontchakovna (*Prince Igor*); BRITTEN: Auntie★ (*Peter Grimes*), Mrs Grose★ (*Turn of the Screw*); BUSONI: Colombina★ (*Arlecchino*); CIMAROSA: Fidalma★ (*Matrimonio segreto*); DONIZETTI: Mme Rosa (*Campanello*), Léonore (*Favorite*), Marquise de Birkenfeld (*Fille du régiment*); FALLA: Abuela (*Vida breve*); GOUNOD: Siebel (*Faust*); HENZE: Agave★ (*Bassariden*); MASCAGNI: Beppe (*Amico Fritz*); MENOTTI: Secretary★ (*Consul*), Mme Flora (*Medium*), Miss Todd★ (*Old Maid and the Thief*); MONTEVERDI: Poppea (*Incoronazione di Poppea*); MOZART: Dorabella★ (*Così fan tutte*), Ramiro (*Finta giardiniera*), Farnace (*Mitridate, re di Ponto*); MUSSORGSKY: Marina (*Boris Godunov*); POULENC: Prioresse (*Dialogues des Carmélites*); PUCCINI: Suzuki★ (*Butterfly*), Frugola★ (*Tabarro*); ROSSINI: Zaida (*Turco in Italia*); SCHOENBERG: Woman (*Erwartung*); STRAUSS, R: Komponist (*Ariadne auf Naxos*); STRAVINSKY: Baba the Turk★ (*Rake's Progress*); VERDI: Preziosilla (*Forza del destino*), Azucena (*Trovatore*); WAGNER: Magdalene (*Meistersinger*); WEILL: Leocadia Begbick (*Aufstieg und Fall der Stadt Mahagonny*); WOLF-FERRARI: Margarita (*Quattro rusteghi*); ZANDONAI: Samaritana (*Francesca da Rimini*). **World premieres:** BUCCHI: Strega (*Notte in paradiso*) Como & Florence 1960; TESTI: Vassilisse (*Albergo dei poveri*) Piccola Scala 1966. Recorded for: DG. Gives recitals. Appears with symphony orchestra. **Res:** V Egadi 5, Milan, Italy.

ZANOLLI, SILVANA. Lyric soprano. Italian. Born 14 Oct 1928, Fiume, Yugoslavia. Husband Otello Borgonovo, occupation opera singer. Studied: Mo Luciano Tomelleri, Mo Tomaso Jappelli, School of the Teatro alla Scala, Milan. **Debut:** Paoluccia (*Buona figliola*) Teatro alla Scala, Milan 1951. Awards: Gold Medals of Tel Aviv and Glyndebourne Fests.

Sang with major companies in ARG: Buenos Aires; AUSTRL: Sydney; AUS: Bregenz Fest, Vienna Staatsoper; BEL: Brussels; BRA: Rio de Janeiro; FRA: Nancy, Nice; FR GER: Bonn, Cologne, Frankfurt, Kiel, Munich Staatsoper, Nürnberg, Stuttgart, Wiesbaden; GER DR: Berlin Komische Oper; ISR: Tel Aviv; ITA: Bologna, Florence Maggio & Comunale, Genoa, Milan La Scala, Naples, Palermo, Parma, Rome Opera, Spoleto Fest, Trieste, Turin, Venice, Verona; MEX: Mexico City; MON: Monte Carlo; POL: Warsaw; POR: Lisbon; SPA: Barcelona; SWI: Geneva, Zurich; UK: Cardiff Welsh, Edinburgh Fest, Glasgow Scottish, Glyndebourne Fest, London Royal; USA: New York Met. **Roles with these companies incl** BIZET: Micaëla (*Carmen*), Léila (*Pêcheurs de perles*); BOITO: Margherita (*Mefistofele*); CIMAROSA: Elisetta‡ (*Matrimonio segreto*); DONIZETTI: Adina (*Elisir*), Rita; FALLA: Salud (*Vida breve*); GIORDANO: Olga (*Fedora*); GOUNOD: Marguerite (*Faust*); HINDEMITH: Helene (*Hin und zurück*); LEONCAVALLO: Nedda★ (*Pagliacci*); MASCAGNI: Suzel (*Amico Fritz*); MASSENET: Sophie (*Werther*); MENOTTI: Amelia (*Amelia al ballo*), Lucy (*Telephone*); MONTEVERDI: Clorinda (*Combattimento di Tancredi*); MOZART: Donna Elvira (*Don Giovanni*), Arminda (*Finta giardiniera*), Susanna (*Nozze di Figaro*); ORFF: Solo (*Carmina burana*); PERGOLESI: Serpina★ (*Serva padrona*); POULENC: Constance (*Dialogues des Carmélites*); PUCCINI: Mimi & Musetta★ (*Bohème*), Cio-Cio-San (*Butterfly*), Liù (*Turandot*); ROSSINI: Clorinda (*Cenerentola*); STRAUSS, R: Komponist (*Ariadne auf Naxos*); VERDI: Alice Ford (*Falstaff*); WOLF-FERRARI: Felice★ (*Quattro rusteghi*), Susanna (*Segreto di Susanna*). Also CIMAROSA: Erlecca (*Sposi per accidente*), Lesbina (*Credulo*); ROTA: Anaïde (*Cappello di paglia*); GIORDANO: Lisabetta (*Cena delle beffe*); CASELLA: Baccante (*Favola d'Orfeo*); SALIERI: Ofelia (*Grotta di*

Trofonio); ROSSINI: Aspasia (*Pietra del paragone*); CILEA: Vivette (*Arlesiana*); CHAILLY: (*Procedura penale*); TCHAIKOVSKY: Mme Larina (*Eugene Onegin*). Recorded for: Philips, Fabbri. Video—Eurovision: (*Cappello di paglia*); (*Cenerentola*). **Res:** V J Kennedy 7, Cologno Monzese/Milan, Italy.

ZANOTELLI, HANS. Conductor of opera and symphony. German. Resident Cond, Phil Orch, Stuttgart. Born 23 Aug 1927, Wuppertal. Studied: Musikhochschule, Cologne. Operatic training as repetiteur at Bühnen Remscheid-Solingen 1945-50. Previous adm positions in opera: Gen Mus Dir, Staatstheater Darmstadt 1957; Mus Dir, Städtische Oper Augsburg until 1972.
   Conducted with major companies in FR GER: Berlin Deutsche Oper, Bonn, Darmstadt, Düsseldorf-Duisburg, Hamburg, Stuttgart; et al. **Operas with these companies incl** BEETHOVEN: *Fidelio;* BERLIOZ: *Troyens;* BIZET: *Carmen;* DONIZETTI: *Lucia;* FLOTOW: *Martha;* GLUCK: *Alceste, Iphigénie en Tauride;* JANACEK: *Jenufa, Katya Kabanova;* MOZART: *Don Giovanni, Finta giardiniera, Idomeneo, Nozze di Figaro, Zauberflöte;* PFITZNER: *Palestrina;* PUCCINI: *Bohème, Butterfly, Manon Lescaut, Tosca;* ROSSINI: *Barbiere di Siviglia;* STRAUSS, R: *Ariadne auf Naxos, Elektra, Rosenkavalier, Salome;* VERDI: *Aida, Ballo in maschera, Don Carlo, Forza del destino, Macbeth, Otello, Rigoletto, Traviata, Trovatore;* WAGNER: *Fliegende Holländer, Lohengrin, Meistersinger, Tannhäuser;* WEBER: *Freischütz;* WOLF-FERRARI: *Quattro rusteghi;* et al. Also EGK: *Peer Gynt.*

ZARA, MEREDITH. Coloratura soprano. American. Resident mem: Deutsche Oper am Rhein, Düsseldorf-Duisburg. Born Atlanta, GA, USA. Studied: Indiana Univ, Bloomington; Manhattan School of Music, New York; Inge Manski-Lundeen, Edith Boroschek. **Debut:** Solo (*Carmina burana*) New York City Opera 1963. Previous occupations: medical secy. Awards: Young Artists Awd, Brevard Music Fndt; Fulbright Schlshp, US Gvnmt; Hon Mention, Intl Compt for Young Opera Singers, Sofia.
   Sang with major companies in AUS: Vienna Staatsoper & Volksoper; CZE: Prague National; FR GER: Bonn, Cologne, Dortmund, Düsseldorf-Duisburg, Essen, Frankfurt, Hamburg, Hannover, Karlsruhe, Kassel, Krefeld, Munich Staatsoper, Nürnberg, Stuttgart; HOL: Amsterdam; ITA: Florence Maggio; USA: New York City Opera. **Roles with these companies incl** DONIZETTI: Adina★(*Elisir*), Lucia★; FLOTOW: Lady Harriet★ (*Martha*); MOZART: Fiordiligi (*Così fan tutte*), Konstanze★ (*Entführung aus dem Serail*), Aspasia★(*Mitridate, re di Ponto*), Königin der Nacht★ (*Zauberflöte*); NICOLAI: Frau Fluth★ (*Lustigen Weiber*); OFFENBACH: Olympia★ (*Contes d'Hoffmann*); ORFF: Solo (*Carmina burana*); PUCCINI: Musetta (*Bohème*); ROSSINI: Rosina★ (*Barbiere di Siviglia*), Comtesse Adèle★ (*Comte Ory*); STRAUSS, R: Fiakermilli★ (*Arabella*), Zerbinetta★ (*Ariadne auf Naxos*), Sophie★ (*Rosenkavalier*), Aminta★ (*Schweigsame Frau*); VERDI: Gilda★ (*Rigoletto*), Violetta★ (*Traviata*). Also HAYDN: Armida; DALLAPICCOLA:

Nausicaa★‡ (*Ulisse*). Gives recitals. Appears with symphony orchestra. **Res:** Düsseldorf, FR Ger.

ZARMAS, PIERIS. Dramatic baritone. Cypriote. Resident mem: Theater der Stadt Bonn, FR Ger. Born 8 Mar 1933, Akanthou/Famagusta, Cyprus. Studied: Guildhall School of Music and Drama, London; Fernando Ferrara, A Soresina, A Narducci, Milan. **Debut:** Sharpless (*Butterfly*) Gran Teatro del Liceo, Barcelona 1962. Previous occupations: teacher of math and Greek; schoolmaster. Awards: Awds ARCM, LGSM and LRAM, London; PhD Univ Bonn.
   Sang with major companies in GRE: Athens National & Fest; FR GER: Bonn, Cologne, Dortmund, Düsseldorf-Duisburg; SPA: Barcelona. **Roles with these companies incl** BEETHOVEN: Don Pizarro★ (*Fidelio*); BIZET: Escamillo (*Carmen*); DALLAPICCOLA: Prigioniero; DONIZETTI: Enrico (*Lucia*), Nottingham★ (*Roberto Devereux*); GERSHWIN: Crown★ (*Porgy and Bess*); GLUCK: Hercules (*Alceste*), Oreste (*Iphigénie en Tauride*); LEONCAVALLO: Tonio★ (*Pagliacci*); MOZART: Leporello★ & Don Giovanni (*Don Giovanni*), Figaro★ (*Nozze di Figaro*), Papageno (*Zauberflöte*); OFFENBACH: Coppélius etc (*Contes d'Hoffmann*); PUCCINI: Marcello (*Bohème*), Scarpia★ (*Tosca*); ROSSINI: Figaro (*Barbiere di Siviglia*); STRAUSS, R: Orest (*Elektra*), Jochanaan★ (*Salome*); VERDI: Amonasro (*Aida*), Renato (*Ballo in maschera*), Falstaff, Don Carlo (*Forza del destino*), Iago★ (*Otello*), Rigoletto★, Germont (*Traviata*), Conte di Luna★ (*Trovatore*); WAGNER: Telramund★ (*Lohengrin*), Alberich (*Rheingold*). Also FORTNER: Leonardo (*Bluthochzeit*). **World premieres:** VALDAMBRINI: Cadmos (*Pentheus*) 1971; Koch (*Gestiefelte Kater*) 1974; both at Bonn, FR Ger. Gives recitals. Appears with symphony orchestra.

ZAROU, JEANNETTE. Lyric soprano. Canadian. Resident mem: Deutsche Oper am Rhein, Düsseldorf; Canadian Opera Co, Toronto. Born Ramallah, Palestine. Single. Studied: Royal Consv of Music, Univ of Toronto, Mme Irene Jessner, John Covgart, coaching, Toronto; Mme Halina Wyszkowski; Leon Major & Dr Herman Geiger-Torel, stage deportment, Toronto. **Debut:** Liù (*Turandot*) Canadian Opera Co Toronto 1965. Previous occupations: auto insurance clerk. Awards: Eaton Graduating Awd, Eaton Co, Toronto Univ Artist Diploma 1964; CBC Talent Festival Aud 1966; Canada Counc Grants 1965-67; var Kiwanis & Canadian Ntl Exhibition Compt Awds 1959-61.
   Sang with major companies in CAN: Toronto; FRA: Bordeaux, Rouen; FR GER: Berlin Deutsche Oper, Bielefeld, Cologne, Düsseldorf-Duisburg, Frankfurt, Hamburg, Karlsruhe, Kiel, Munich Staatsoper, Nürnberg. **Roles with these companies incl** BEETHOVEN: Marzelline★ (*Fidelio*); BIZET: Micaëla★ (*Carmen*); GOUNOD: Marguerite★ (*Faust*); MONTEVERDI: Euridice★ (*Orfeo*); MOZART: Servilia★ (*Clemenza di Tito*), Ilia★ (*Idomeneo*), Sifare★ (*Mitridate, re di Ponto*), Pamina★ (*Zauberflöte*); OFFENBACH: Antonia★ (*Contes d'Hoffmann*); POULENC: Blanche (*Dialogues des Carmélites*); PUCCINI: Mimi & Musetta★ (*Bohème*), Lauretta★ (*Gianni Schicchi*), Liù

(*Turandot*); STRAUSS, R: Zdenka★ (*Arabella*), Sophie★ (*Rosenkavalier*). Also BRITTEN: Miss Wordsworth (*Albert Herring*); WILLAN: Deirdre (*Deirdre*). Gives recitals. Appears with symphony orchestra. Res: Auf der Germarke 25, 4 Düsseldorf 12, FR Ger.

ZEANI, VIRGINIA; née Zehan. Lirico-spinto soprano. Italian. Born 21 Oct 1928, Solovastru, Romania. Husband Nicola Rossi-Lemeni, occupation singer. One child. Studied: Lidia Lipkowska, Bucharest; Aureliano Pertile, Milan. **Debut:** Violetta (*Traviata*) Bologna 1948. Awards: Diapason d'oro; Arena d'oro; Gold Medal for Art Merit, Egypt; Gold Medal Opera Barcelona; Commander Order of Merit, It Rep Gvnmt.
Sang with major companies in AUS: Vienna Staatsoper & Volksoper; BEL: Brussels; BRA: Rio de Janeiro; CAN: Montreal/Quebec, Vancouver; FRA: Bordeaux, Lyon, Marseille, Nancy, Nice, Paris, Strasbourg, Toulouse; GRE: Athens National; FR GER: Berlin Deutsche Oper; HOL: Amsterdam; HUN: Budapest; ITA: Bologna, Florence Maggio & Comunale, Genoa, Milan La Scala, Naples, Palermo, Parma, Rome Opera & Caracalla, Spoleto Fest, Trieste, Turin, Venice; MEX: Mexico City; MON: Monte Carlo; POR: Lisbon; ROM: Bucharest; SPA: Barcelona; SWI: Basel, Geneva, Zurich; USSR: Leningrad Kirov, Moscow Bolshoi; USA: Houston, New Orleans, New York Met, Philadelphia Grand; YUG: Belgrade. **Roles with these companies incl** BELLINI: Elvira (*Puritani*), Amina (*Sonnambula*); BIZET: Micaëla (*Carmen*); BOITO: Margherita★ (*Mefistofele*); BUSONI: Turandot; CILEA: Adriana Lecouvreur★; DONIZETTI: Adina (*Elisir*), Linda di Chamounix, Lucia, Maria di Rohan; GIORDANO: Fedora★; HANDEL: Cleopatra★ (*Giulio Cesare*); LEONCAVALLO: Nedda (*Pagliacci*); MASSENET: Manon★, Thaïs, Charlotte (*Werther*); MENOTTI: Magda Sorel★ (*Consul*); MONTEMEZZI: Fiora★ (*Amore dei tre re*); MOZART: Zerlina (*Don Giovanni*); OFFENBACH: Olympia★ & Antonia★ & Giulietta★ (*Contes d'Hoffmann*); POULENC: Blanche (*Dialogues des Carmélites*), Femme★ (*Voix humaine*); PUCCINI: Mimi★ & Musetta (*Bohème*), Cio-Cio-San★ (*Butterfly*), Manon Lescaut★, Magda★ (*Rondine*), Suor Angelica, Tosca★; RIMSKY-KORSAKOV: Olga (*Maid of Pskov*); ROSSINI: Rosina (*Barbiere di Siviglia*), Desdemona★ (*Otello*); TCHAIKOVSKY: Tatiana★ (*Eugene Onegin*); VERDI: Aida★, Alzira, Elisabetta★ (*Don Carlo*), Desdemona★ (*Otello*), Gilda (*Rigoletto*), Violetta★ (*Traviata*), Elena (*Vespri*); WAGNER: Senta★ (*Fliegende Holländer*), Elsa (*Lohengrin*); WEBER: Agathe★ (*Freischütz*). Also ALFANO: (*Risurrezione*); MASCAGNI: (*Piccolo Marat*)★.
World premieres: POULENC: Blanche (*Dialogues des Carmélites*) La Scala, Milan 1957; GIURANNA: Vetzera (*Mayerling*) Naples; de BANFIELD: Alissa, Geneva 1965. Recorded for: Electrecord, Cetra. Video—TV: (*Rigoletto*). Gives recitals. Res: V Nomentana 761, Rome, Italy.

ZECCHILLO, GIUSEPPE. Lyric baritone. Italian. Born 18 Dec 1929, São Paulo, Brazil. Divorced. One child. Studied: Consv G Verdi, Aureliano Pertile and Carlo Tagliabue, Milan. **Debut:** Ger-

mont (*Traviata*) Teatro Nuovo, Milan 1953. Awards: Oscar della Lirica; Medaglia d'oro Famiglia Meneghina and Città di Milano.
Sang with major companies in AUS: Bregenz Fest; ITA: Bologna, Florence Maggio & Comunale, Genoa, Milan La Scala, Naples, Palermo, Rome Opera & Caracalla, Trieste, Turin, Venice, Verona Arena; MON: Monte Carlo; USA: New York City Opera, San Francisco Opera & Spring Opera. **Roles with these companies incl** BERG: Wozzeck★; BERLIOZ: Mefistofele; BIZET: Zurga★ (*Pêcheurs de perles*); BRITTEN: Billy Budd★; BUSONI: Matteo★ (*Arlecchino*), Doktor Faust★; CHARPENTIER: Père★ (*Louise*); CILEA: Michonnet (*A. Lecouvreur*); CIMAROSA: Count Robinson & Geronimo (*Matrimonio segreto*); DALLAPICCOLA: Prigioniero★, Riviere★ & Robineau★ & Leroux★ (*Volo di notte*); DONIZETTI: Henry VIII★ (*Anna Bolena*), Enrico★ (*Campanello*), Dott Malatesta★ (*Don Pasquale*), Belcore★ (*Elisir*), Alfonse★ & Baldassare★ (*Favorite*), Enrico★ (*Lucia*); GALUPPI: Don Tritemio (*Filosofo di campagna*); GIORDANO: De Siriex★ (*Fedora*); HANDEL: Giulio Cesare; JANACEK: Gorianchikov★ & Shishkov★ (*From the House of the Dead*); LEONCAVALLO: Tonio★ (*Pagliacci*); MASCAGNI: Rabbi David★ (*Amico Fritz*), Alfio★ (*Cavalleria rusticana*); MASSENET: Lescaut★ (*Manon*); MENOTTI: Husband★ (*Amelia al ballo*), Bob★ (*Old Maid and the Thief*); MOZART: Guglielmo★ & Don Alfonso★ (*Così fan tutte*), Leporello★ (*Don Giovanni*), Figaro★ (*Nozze di Figaro*); OFFENBACH: Coppélius etc★ (*Contes d'Hoffmann*); PAISIELLO: Figaro★ (*Barbiere di Siviglia*); PERGOLESI: Marcaniello★ (*Frate 'nnamorato*), Uberto★ (*Serva padrona*); PONCHIELLI: Barnaba★ (*Gioconda*); PROKOFIEV: Faust★ (*Fiery Angel*); PUCCINI: Marcello★ (*Bohème*), Gianni Schicchi★, Sharpless★ (*Butterfly*), Lescaut★ (*Manon Lescaut*), Michele★ (*Tabarro*); ROSSINI: Figaro★ (*Barbiere di Siviglia*), Tobias Mill★ & Slook★ (*Cambiale di matrimonio*), Dandini★ (*Cenerentola*), Bruschino★ & Gaudenzio★ (*Signor Bruschino*); SCHOENBERG: Moses★; THOMAS: Lothario★ (*Mignon*); VERDI: Amonasro★ (*Aida*), Ford★ (*Falstaff*), Fra Melitone★ (*Forza del destino*), Rigoletto★, Germont★ (*Traviata*); WOLF-FERRARI: Lelio★ & Ottavio★ & Pantalone (*Donne curiose*), Lunardo★ (*Quattro rusteghi*), Conte Gil★ (*Segreto di Susanna*). Also PAISIELLO: Giorgio (*Nina*); MONTEVERDI: Storico (*Combattimento di Tancredi*). Recorded for: Cetra. Res: V Fiori Chiari 16, Milan, Italy.

ZEDDA, ALBERTO. Conductor of opera and symphony. Italian. Born 2 Jan 1928, Milan. Wife Graziella Rossi. One child. Studied: Consv of Music, Alceo Galliera, Carlo Maria Giulini, Antonino Votto, Milan; incl piano, organ. **Operatic debut:** *Barbiere di Siviglia* As Li Co, Milan 1956. Symphonic debut: Orch Teatro Massimo, Palermo 1957. Previous occupations: musicologist, essayist, journalist. Awards: First Prize, Primavera Cont for Young Cond, RAI/Rome 1957; Grand Prix du Disque et des Discophiles 1963.
Conducted with major companies in CZE: Prague Smetana; DEN: Copenhagen; FRA: Bordeaux; FR GER: Berlin Deutsche Oper, Wiesbaden; ISR: Tel Aviv; ITA: Genoa, Naples, Parma, Rome

Opera, Trieste, Venice; POL: Warsaw; POR: Lisbon; SPA: Barcelona; UK: London Royal; USA: Cincinnati, New York City Opera. **Operas with these companies incl** BELLINI: *Beatrice di Tenda;* DONIZETTI: *Elisir, Fille du régiment, Rita**‡; LEONCAVALLO: *Pagliacci**; MASCAGNI: *Cavalleria rusticana**; MASSENET: *Manon;* MENOTTI: *Amahl;* PERGOLESI: *Serva padrona*‡; PUCCINI: *Bohème**, *Gianni Schicchi, Butterfly**, *Manon Lescaut**; ROSSINI: *Barbiere di Siviglia**, *Cambiale di matrimonio, Gazza ladra;* VERDI: *Aida, Falstaff**, *Giorno di regno**, *Otello**, *Rigoletto, Traviata**; WOLF-FERRARI: *Quattro rusteghi**. Also ROSSELLINI: *Sguardo dal ponte;* LEONCAVALLO: *Bohème*‡; CIMAROSA: *Maestro di cappella*‡; WOLF-FERRARI: *Vedova scaltra;* MORTARI: *Scuola delle mogli;* HAZON: *Agenzia matrimoniale*‡. **World premieres:** SONZOGNO: *I Passeggeri* 1961; VIOZZI: *La Giacca dannata* 1967; BUGAMELLI: *Una Domenica* 1967, all at Teatro Verdi, Trieste. Recorded for Philips, RCA, Cetra-Fonit, Rifi, Trio Records-Japan. Video/Film — BL Vision TV: *Barbiere di Siviglia;* Cine Lirica Ital: *Rita.* Conducted major orch in Europe, Asia. Co-Editor of Critical Ed of Complete Works of Rossini, appt/Fndt Rossini. Teaches at Consv of Music G Nicolini, Piacenza. **Res:** 12, V Pisacane, 20129 Milan, Italy.

ZEFFIRELLI, FRANCO; né Gian Franco Corsi. Stages/produces opera, theater, film & television. Also designs sets, costumes & stage-lighting and is an actor and author. Italian. Born 12 Feb 1927, Florence. Single. Studied: voice. Operatic training as asst stage dir. **Operatic debut:** *Cenerentola* Teatro alla Scala, Milan 1953-54.

Directed/produced opera for major companies in AUS: Salzburg Fest, Vienna Staatsoper; BEL: Brussels; CAN: Montreal/Quebec; FRA: Paris; FR GER: Berlin Deutsche Oper, Düsseldorf-Duisburg, Munich Staatsoper; HOL: Amsterdam; ISR: Tel Aviv; ITA: Florence Maggio, Genoa, Milan La Scala, Naples, Palermo, Parma, Rome Opera, Spoleto Fest, Trieste, Venice; SPA: Barcelona; SWI: Zurich; UK: Edinburgh Fest, Glyndebourne Fest, London Royal; USSR: Moscow Bolshoi; USA: Chicago, Dallas, Kansas City, New York Met. **Operas staged for these companies incl** BELLINI: *Norma*‡, *Puritani*‡; BIZET: *Carmen;* DONIZETTI: *Don Pasquale*‡, *Elisir*‡, *Fille du régiment*‡, *Linda di Chamounix*‡, *Lucia*‡, *Rita*‡; HANDEL: *Alcina*‡; LEONCAVALLO: *Pagliacci**‡; MASCAGNI: *Cavalleria rusticana**‡; MASSENET: *Thaïs;* MONTEVERDI: *Favola d'Orfeo*‡, *Incoronazione di Poppea*‡; MOZART: *Don Giovanni**‡; MUSSORGSKY: *Boris Godunov*‡; PERAGALLO: *Gita in campagna;* PERGOLESI: *Frate 'nnamorato*‡, *Serva padrona*‡; PUCCINI: *Bohème*‡, *Tosca*‡; ROSSINI: *Barbiere di Siviglia, Cenerentola*‡, *Italiana in Algeri*‡, *Turco in Italia*‡; SCARLATTI: *Trionfo dell'onore;* THOMAS: *Mignon;* VERDI: *Aida, Ballo in maschera, Falstaff**‡, *Otello*‡, *Rigoletto, Traviata*‡, *Trovatore*. Also PERI: *Euridice;* SCARLATTI: *Griselda;* TRAETTA: *Serve rivali;* DONIZETTI: *Giovedì grasso;* CASELLA: *Favola d'Orfeo.* **Operatic world premieres:** BARBER: *Antony and Cleopatra*‡ Met Opera, New York 1966; MANNINO: *Vivì* San Carlo, Naples

1959. **Opera libretti:** *Antony and Cleopatra.* Video/Film: various. **Res:** 448 V Appia Pignatelli, Rome, Italy. Mgmt: MRR/UK.

ZEUMER, GERTI. Lyric soprano. German. Resident mem: Deutsche Oper Berlin. Born 24 Oct, Braunschweig, Germany. One child. Studied: Staatliche Hochschule für Musik, Prof W Dürr, Hannover; Fr Prof Henny Wolf, Hamburg. **Debut:** Staatstheater Braunschweig 1959.

Sang with major companies in AUS: Salzburg Fest, Vienna Staatsoper; BEL: Brussels; FR GER: Berlin Deutsche Oper, Cologne, Düsseldorf-Duisburg, Frankfurt, Hamburg, Hannover, Kassel, Stuttgart; SPA: Barcelona. **Roles with these companies incl** BEETHOVEN: Marzelline* *(Fidelio);* BELLINI: Elvira *(Puritani);* DONIZETTI: Norina *(Don Pasquale),* Adina *(Elisir),* Lucia; EINEM: Lucille* *(Dantons Tod);* FLOTOW: Lady Harriet *(Martha);* GLUCK: Euridice*; HAYDN: Clarissa *(Mondo della luna);* HENZE: Luise* *(Junge Lord);* HUMPERDINCK: Gretel*; KLEBE: Marianne *(Jakobowsky und der Oberst);* LORTZING: Baronin Freimann* *(Wildschütz),* Marie *(Zar und Zimmermann);* MARSCHNER: Anna* *(Hans Heiling);* MOZART: Fiordiligi* & Despina *(Così fan tutte),* Zerlina *(Don Giovanni),* Konstanze *(Entführung aus dem Serail),* Cherubino *(Nozze di Figaro),* Pamina* *(Zauberflöte);* NICOLAI: Frau Fluth *(Lustigen Weiber);* OFFENBACH: Olympia & Antonia *(Contes d'Hoffmann);* PFITZNER: Ighino* *(Palestrina);* PUCCINI: Mimi & Musetta *(Bohème),* Lauretta *(Gianni Schicchi);* ROSSINI: Rosina *(Barbiere di Siviglia);* STRAUSS, J: Rosalinde* *(Fledermaus);* STRAUSS, R: Zdenka* *(Arabella),* Zerbinetta *(Ariadne auf Naxos),* Octavian* *(Rosenkavalier);* VERDI: Nannetta *(Falstaff);* WAGNER: Eva* *(Meistersinger).* **World premieres:** NABOKOV: *(Love's Labour's Lost)* Deutsche Oper Berlin 1973. Recorded for: Eurodisc. Video/Film: Baronin Freimann *(Wildschütz).* Gives recitals. Appears with symphony orchestra. **Res:** Berlin, FR Ger. Mgmt: KHA/FRG.

ZIDEK, IVO. Lyric & dramatic tenor. Czechoslovakian. Resident mem: National Theater, Prague. Born 4 Jun 1926, Kravare, CSR. Wife Libuse. Two sons. Studied: Prof Rudolf Vasek, Ostrava, CSR. **Debut:** Werther, State Theater, Ostrava, CSSR 1946. Awards: State Prize, Pres of CSSR 1952; Merited Artist, Gvnmt of CSSR 1957; Order of Labor, Gvnmt of CSSR 1968.

Sang with major companies in ARG: Buenos Aires; AUS: Vienna Staatsoper & Volksoper; BEL: Brussels; BUL: Sofia; CZE: Brno, Prague National; FR GER: Hamburg, Mannheim, Stuttgart, Wiesbaden; GER DR: Berlin Staatsoper; HOL: Amsterdam; HUN: Budapest; ITA: Bologna, Parma, Venice; MON: Monte Carlo; POL: Warsaw; SPA: Barcelona; SWI: Geneva, Zurich; UK: Edinburgh Fest; USSR: Moscow Bolshoi; YUG: Dubrovnik, Zagreb, Belgrade. **Roles with these companies incl** BEETHOVEN: Florestan *(Fidelio);* DVORAK: Prince*‡ *(Rusalka);* JANACEK: Mazal*‡ *(Excursions of Mr Broucek),* Skurotov* *(From the House of the Dead),* Laca* & Steva*‡ *(Jenufa),* Boris* *(Katya Kabanova),* Albert Gregor*‡ *(Makropoulos Affair);* MARTINU:

Manolios★ (*Griechische Passion*); MO-
NIUSZKO: Jontek (*Halka*); MOZART: Don Ot-
tavio★ (*Don Giovanni*), Tamino (*Zauberflöte*);
OFFENBACH: Hoffmann; PROKOFIEV:
Pierre★ (*War and Peace*); PUCCINI: Calaf★ (*Tu-
randot*), ROSSINI: Almaviva (*Barbiere di Si-
viglia*); SHOSTAKOVICH: Sergei (*Katerina
Ismailova*); SMETANA: Hans★‡ (*Bartered
Bride*), Dalibor★, Jarek★‡ (*Devil's Wall*), Lukas★
(*The Kiss*), Stalav★‡ (*Libuse*), Vitek★‡ (*Secret*),
Heinrich★‡ (*Two Widows*); STRAVINSKY: Tom
Rakewell★ (*Rake's Progress*); TCHAIKOVSKY:
Lenski★ (*Eugene Onegin*), Gherman (*Pique
Dame*); VERDI: Riccardo (*Ballo in maschera*),
Don Carlo★, Duca di Mantova (*Rigoletto*), Alfredo
(*Traviata*); WAGNER: Lohengrin★, Siegmund
(*Walküre*), Walther v d Vogelweide (*Tannhäuser*).
Also JEREMIAS: Alexej★ (*Brothers Karamazov*).
Only on records STRAVINSKY: Oedipus. Re-
corded for: Supraphon, DG. Video/Film: Hoff-
mann; Rodolfo (*Bohème*); Steva (*Jenufa*);
Hans/Jenik (*Bartered Bride*); Ladislav (*Two Wid-
ows*); Böhm (*Julius Fucik*). Gives recitals. Appears
with symphony orchestra. Res: Národní trída 34,
Prague 1, CSSR. Mgmt: PRG/CZE.

ZIESE, CHRISTA-MARIA. Dramatic soprano.
German. Resident mem: Opernhaus, Leipzig, Ger
DR. Born 13 Jul 1924, Ascherleben, Germany.
Husband Rainer Lüdeke, occupation singer. Two
children. Studied: Gottlieb Zeithammer, Josef-
Maria Hausschild, Leipzig. **Debut:** Hänsel, Leipzig
1947. Awards: First Bach Prize, Dresden Bach
Committee of Ger DR; First Prize Prague Spring;
Ntl Prize of Ger DR; Kammersängerin, Ger DR.
    Sang with major companies in CZE: Brno; FRA:
Nice; FR GER: Düsseldorf-Duisburg, Hamburg,
Hannover; GER DR: Berlin Komische Oper &
Staatsoper, Dresden, Leipzig; SWI: Zurich;
USSR: Moscow Bolshoi. **Roles with these com-
panies incl** BEETHOVEN: Leonore★ (*Fidelio*);
MASCAGNI: Santuzza★ (*Cavalleria rusticana*);
OFFENBACH: Giulietta★ (*Contes d'Hoffmann*);
PUCCINI: Tosca, Turandot; STRAUSS, R: Ara-
bella, Kaiserin★ (*Frau ohne Schatten*), Octavian
(*Rosenkavalier*), Salome★; TCHAIKOVSKY:
Lisa (*Pique Dame*); VERDI: Aida, Amelia★ (*Ballo
in maschera*), Elisabetta★ (*Don Carlo*); WAG-
NER: Senta★ (*Fliegende Holländer*), Elsa★ (*Lo-
hengrin*), Eva (*Meistersinger*), Elisabeth & Venus
(*Tannhäuser*), Isolde; WEBER: Agathe
(*Freischütz*), Rezia (*Oberon*). Gives recitals. Ap-
pears with symphony orchestra. Teaches voice.
Res: Haussmannstr 7, Leipzig, Ger DR. Mgmt:
KDR/GDR.

ZIINO, OTTAVIO. Conductor of opera and symphony; composer. Italian. Resident Cond, Orch
Sinfonica Siciliana, Palermo. Born 11 Nov 1909,
Palermo. Wife Giulia Pirrotta. Two children. Stud-
ied: Consv Palermo, Mo Savasta; Accad S Cecilia,
Mo Pizzetti and Molinari, Rome; incl piano, organ,
violin. Plays the piano. Operatic training as repeti-
teur & asst cond at Teatro Carlo Felice, Genoa
1933-36; San Carlo Opera, Naples 1938; Teatro
Massimo, Palermo. **Operatic debut:** *Bohème* Tea-
tro Massimo, Palermo 1932. Symphonic debut:
Orch Accad S Cecilia, Rome 1939. Awards: Verdi
Awd; Polifemo Awd; Gold Medal, Ministry of
Education, Italy. ∙

Conducted with major companies in AUSTRL:
Sydney; AUS: Graz; BEL: Brussels; BRA: Rio de
Janeiro; DEN: Copenhagen; FR GER: Hamburg,
Saarbrücken; ITA: Naples, Palermo, Parma,
Rome Opera & Caracalla, Trieste; NOR: Oslo;
ROM: Bucharest; SPA: Barcelona; USA: Cincin-
nati, Hartford, Philadelphia Grand. **Operas with
these companies incl** BELLINI: *Norma, Puritani,
Sonnambula;* BIZET: *Carmen, Pêcheurs de
perles;* DALLAPICCOLA: *Volo di notte;* DONI-
ZETTI: *Elisir, Favorite, Lucia★;* GIORDANO:
Andrea Chénier, Fedora; GLUCK: *Orfeo ed Eu-
ridice;* GOUNOD: *Faust;* HAYDN: *Mondo della
luna;* LEONCAVALLO: *Pagliacci;* MASCA-
GNI: *Cavalleria rusticana;* MASSENET: *Ma-
non;* MONTEVERDI: *Combattimento di
Tancredi;* PONCHIELLI: *Gioconda;* PUCCINI:
Bohème★, Butterfly★, Tosca, Turandot★; ROS-
SINI: *Barbiere di Siviglia;* SAINT-SAENS: *Sam-
son et Dalila;* VERDI: *Aida★, Ballo in maschera,
Don Carlo, Ernani, Forza del destino, Macbeth,
Nabucco, Otello, Rigoletto★, Traviata, Trovatore;*
ZANDONAI: *Giulietta e Romeo.* Also CILEA:
Arlesiana; MASCAGNI: *Piccolo Marat;* AL-
FANO: *Risurrezione, Madonna Imperia;* PIZ-
ZETTI: *Fra Gherardo;* MALIPIERO: *Sette
canzoni;* LEONCAVALLO: *Zazà.* **World pre-
mieres:** FERRARI-TRECATE: *Capanna dello
Zio Tom* Teatro Regio, Parma 1952. Recorded for
Cetra, Supraphon. Conducted major orch in Eu-
rope. Teaches at and is Dir of Consv S Pietro a
Maiella, Naples. **Res:** V Denza 23, Rome, Italy.

ZIKMUNDOVA, EVA; née Maskova. Spinto.
Czechoslovakian. Resident mem: National The-
ater, Prague. Born 4 May 1932, Kromeriz, Czech-
oslovakia. Divorced. One child. Studied: Consv,
Vera Strelcová, Brno; Acad of Music, Zdenek
Otava, Prague; Premysl Kocí, Marie Vojtková.
Debut: Vendulka (*The Kiss*) State Opera, Ostrava
1957. Awards: Merited Mem of the Ntl Theater,
Ministry of Culture.
    Sang with major companies in BEL: Brussels;
BUL: Sofia; CZE: Brno, Prague National; FR
GER: Hannover, Mannheim; GER DR: Berlin
Staatsoper; HOL: Amsterdam; ITA: Bologna,
Florence Maggio, Genoa, Naples, Venice; POL:
Warsaw; UK: Edinburgh Fest. **Roles with these
companies incl** DVORAK: Princess★ (*Devil and
Kate*), Rusalka★; JANACEK: Vixen★ (*Cunning
Little Vixen*), Jenufa★, Katya Kabanova★; LEON-
CAVALLO: Nedda (*Pagliacci*); MASCAGNI:
Santuzza (*Cavalleria rusticana*); MOZART:
Donna Elvira★ (*Don Giovanni*), Contessa★ (*Nozze
di Figaro*); RAVEL: Concepcion★ (*Heure espa-
gnole*); SMETANA: Marie (*Bartered Bride*); Hed-
vika★ (*Devil's Wall*), Vendulka (*The Kiss*),
Blazenka (*Secret*); STRAUSS, R: Arabella★; SU-
CHON: Katrena (*Whirlpool*); TCHAIKOVSKY:
Tatiana★ (*Eugene Onegin*), Lisa (*Pique Dame*);
VERDI: Elisabetta★ (*Don Carlo*), Amelia★ (*Simon
Boccanegra*); WAGNER: Sieglinde★ (*Walküre*),
Elisabeth (*Tannhäuser*). Also SMETANA: Kra-
sava (*Libuse*); MOZART: Erste Dame (*Zauberflöte*); DVORAK: Julie (*Jakobin*). **World
premieres:** MACHA: Lee (*Lake Ukereve*) National Theater, Prague 1966. Recorded for: Supraphon. Gives recitals. Appears with symphony
orchestra. Teaches voice. Coaches repertoire. On

faculty of State Consv, Prague. **Res:** Mánesova 23, Prague 2, CSSR. Mgmt: PRG/CZE.

ZILIO, ELENA. Lyric coloratura mezzo-soprano. Italian. Born Bolzano, Italy. Husband Attilio Burchiellaro, occupation singer. Studied: Consv C Monteverdi, Mrs Marcucci, Bolzano; Accad Chigiana, Siena, S Cecilia, Rome; Mo G Favaretto. **Debut:** Sofia (*Signor Bruschino*) Spoleto Fest 1963.

Sang with major companies in AUS: Bregenz Fest; BEL: Brussels; CAN: Montreal/Quebec; FRA: Paris; FR GER: Cologne; ISR: Tel Aviv; ITA: Florence Maggio & Comunale, Genoa, Milan La Scala, Naples, Palermo, Rome Opera & Caracalla, Spoleto Fest, Trieste, Turin, Venice, Verona Arena; SWI: Geneva; USA: Boston, Chicago, San Antonio, Washington DC; YUG: Dubrovnik. **Roles with these companies incl** CIMAROSA: Fidalma (*Matrimonio segreto*); DONIZETTI: Pierrot★ (*Linda di Chamounix*); GOUNOD: Siebel (*Faust*); MASCAGNI: Beppe★ (*Amico Fritz*); MENOTTI: Miss Todd (*Old Maid and the Thief*); MOZART: Cherubino (*Nozze di Figaro*); PAISIELLO: Belisa (*Re Teodoro in Venezia*); PONCHIELLI: La Cieca (*Gioconda*); PUCCINI: Suzuki (*Butterfly*); ROSSINI: Rosina (*Barbiere di Siviglia*), Jemmy (*Guillaume Tell*), Zaïda (*Turco in Italia*). Also PUCCINI: Musetta★ (*Bohème*); BELLINI: Isoletta★ (*Straniera*); DONIZETTI: Norina★ (*Don Pasquale*), Armando★ (*Maria di Rohan*); PAISIELLO: Rosina★ (*Barbiere di Siviglia*); ROSSINI: Fanny★ (*Cambiale di matrimonio*); VERDI: Giulietta (*Finto Stanislao*); DARGOMYZHSKY: Laura★ (*Stone Guest*). Gives recitals. Appears with symphony orchestra. **Res:** Fienili Colle Salvia 00049, Velletri/Rome, Italy.

ZIMMERMANN, JÖRG. Scenic and costume designer for opera, theater, television. Is a lighting designer, stage director. Swiss. Resident designer, Basler Theater, Basel and at Kammerspiele, Munich. Born 27 May 1933, Zurich. Wife Petra Fahrnländer, occupation actress. Two children. Studied: Theater, Zurich, Teo Otto. Prof training: Theater, Zurich. **Operatic debut:** sets, cost, Städtische Oper Berlin, FR Ger 1957. Theater debut: Drama Theater, Hamburg 1954.

Designed for major companies in AUS: Salzburg Fest; FRA: Aix-en-Provence Fest, Paris, Rouen; FR GER: Bayreuth Fest, Berlin Deutsche Oper, Frankfurt, Hamburg, Munich Staatsoper, Nürnberg; HOL: Amsterdam; ITA: Milan La Scala; SWE: Stockholm; SWI: Basel, Zurich; UK: Edinburgh Fest. **Operas designed for these companies incl** BARTOK: *Bluebeard's Castle;* BERG: *Lulu;* DEBUSSY: *Pelléas et Mélisande;* DONIZETTI: *Elisir;* DVORAK: *Rusalka;* EGK: *Zaubergeige;* EINEM: *Besuch der alten Dame;* FLOTOW: *Martha;* GLUCK: *Orfeo ed Euridice;* HAYDN: *Infedeltà delusa;* JANACEK: *Excursions of Mr Broucek, From the House of the Dead;* MASSENET: *Portrait de Manon;* MOZART: *Così fan tutte, Entführung aus dem Serail, Idomeneo, Nozze di Figaro, Zauberflöte;* MUSSORGSKY: *Boris Godunov;* OFFENBACH: *Périchole;* ORFF: *Mond;* PUCCINI: *Manon Lescaut, Tosca;* ROSSINI: *Barbiere di Siviglia;* STRAUSS, J: *Fledermaus;* STRAUSS, R: *Frau ohne Schatten, Rosenkavalier, Salome;* VERDI: *Don Carlo, Falstaff, Forza del destino, Luisa Miller, Nabucco, Traviata, Trovatore;* WAGNER: *Fliegende Holländer, Lohengrin, Parsifal, Walküre;* WEBER: *Freischütz, Oberon;* WEILL: *Dreigroschenoper.* **Operatic world premieres:** BIALAS: *Gestiefelte Kater* Hamburg Staatsoper 1975. **Res:** Grenzacherweg 261, Basel/Riehen, Switzerland.

ZINKLER, CHRISTIANE; née Möckl. Contralto. German. Resident mem: Städt Bühnen, Dortmund. Born 23 Nov 1947, Coburg, Germany. Widowed. Husband Björn Loewenstierna, occupation lawyer (deceased). One child. Studied: Kmsg Willy Domgraf-Fassbaender, Prof Clemens Kaiser-Breme. **Debut:** Secondo Messaggero (*Job*) Deutsche Oper Düsseldorf 1968.

Sang with major companies in DEN: Copenhagen; FR GER: Dortmund, Düsseldorf-Duisburg, Essen, Hamburg, Wiesbaden; ITA: Florence Maggio. **Roles with these companies incl** DONIZETTI: Maffio Orsini (*Lucrezia Borgia*); GLUCK: Orfeo; HUMPERDINCK: Hänsel; MONTEVERDI: Poppea (*Incoronazione di Poppea*); MOZART: Dorabella (*Così fan tutte*), Cherubino (*Nozze di Figaro*); NICOLAI: Frau Reich (*Lustigen Weiber*); PUCCINI: Suzuki (*Butterfly*); SMETANA: Hata (*Bartered Bride*); VERDI: Ulrica (*Ballo in maschera*); WAGNER: Erda (*Rheingold, Siegfried*), Fricka (*Rheingold, Walküre*). Also MONTEVERDI: Arnalta (*Incoronazione di Poppea*). Video/Film – BBC: 2 Messaggero (*Job*). Gives recitals. Appears with symphony orchestra. **Res:** Steinbruchg 15, 8631 Niederfüllbach, FR Ger. Mgmt: PAS/FRG.

ZIPPRODT, PATRICIA. Costume designer for opera, theater, film, television & ballet. American. Born Evanston, IL. Single. Studied: Chicago Art Inst; Wellesley Coll; Fashion Inst of Technology, New York. Prof training: with several costume designers. **Operatic debut:** *Bohème* Boston Opera Co 1960. Theater debut: Bijou Theater, New York. Previous occupation: puppeteer, stained glass window cartoonist. Awards: five Tony nominations, two Tony Awds; J P Maharam Awd; three Drama Desk Awds; Emmy Awd; Special Wellesley Achiev Awd 1972.

Designed for major companies in USA: Boston, New York Metropolitan & City Opera. **Operas designed for these companies incl** PROKOFIEV: *Fiery Angel;* PUCCINI: *Bohème, Madama Butterfly;* RAMEAU: *Hippolyte et Aricie;* SHOSTAKOVICH: *Katerina Ismailova;* WEILL: *Aufstieg und Fall der Stadt Mahagonny.* Also THOMSON: *Mother of Us All.* **Operatic world premieres:** THOMSON: *Lord Byron* Juilliard School, New York 1972. Exhibitions of stage designs Wright-Hepburn Gal, London 1968-69; Museum of City of NY; River Run Gal, Edgartown, MA 1974; Toneel Mus, Amsterdam 1975; Univ So Cal, Los Angeles; Sotheby-Parke Bernet, Los Angeles 1970; ITI/USA Intl Travelling Exhibit 1975. Lectures at New York Univ, Yale, Pratt, Univ of R I, Florida State, Wellesley, etc. **Res:** 45 University Pl, New York 10003, USA.

ZITEK, VACLAV. Lyric baritone. Czechoslovakian. Resident mem: National Theater,

Prague. Born 24 Mar 1932, Tisá, CSR. Wife Helena, occupation HS Prof. Studied: Adrian Levicky, Prague. **Debut:** Germont (*Traviata*) Opera Studio, Prague 1957.

Sang with major companies in CZE: Prague National; FRA: Bordeaux; GER DR: Berlin Komische Oper & Staatsoper; ROM: Bucharest; USSR: Moscow Bolshoi. **Roles with these companies incl** BIZET: Escamillo★ (*Carmen*); MONTEVERDI: Orfeo; MOZART: Don Giovanni★, Conte Almaviva★ (*Nozze di Figaro*); MUSSORGSKY: Boris Godunov; ORFF: Solo★ (*Carmina burana*); PROKOFIEV: Prince Andrei★ (*War and Peace*); PUCCINI: Sharpless★ (*Butterfly*); ROSSINI: Figaro★ (*Barbiere di Siviglia*); SMETANA: Vok★ (*Devil's Wall*), Tomas★ (*The Kiss*), Premysl★ (*Libuse*), Kalina★ (*Secret*); STRAUSS, R: Mandryka★ (*Arabella*); TCHAIKOVSKY: Eugene Onegin★, Yeletsky★ (*Pique Dame*); VERDI: Amonasro (*Aida*), Rodrigo (*Don Carlo*), Macbeth, Nabucco★, Rigoletto★, Germont (*Traviata*). Also SMETANA: King Vladislav★ (*Dalibor*), Tausendmark (*Brandenburgers*); MARTINU: Theseus★ (*Ariadne*); DVORAK: Bohus (*Jakobin*); GOUNOD: Valentin (*Faust*); KOVAROVIC: Lomikar (*Dog Heads*); PAUER: Petr Vok (*Susan Vojírová*); FRIEDRICH: Tartuffe; SHEBALIN: Petruchio (*Taming of the Shrew*). Gives recitals. Appears with symphony orchestra. **Res:** Lumírova 9, 120 00 Prague 2, CSSR. Mgmt: PRG/CZE.

ZOBEL, INGEBORG. Dramatic soprano. German. Resident mem: Staatsoper Dresden, Staatsoper Berlin, Ger DR. Born 31 Jul 1928, Görlitz. Husband Heinz Woldt, occupation painter. One child. Studied: Staatl Akad für Musik und Theater, Eduard Plate, Dresden. **Debut:** Amelia (*Ballo in maschera*) Stadttheater Cottbus, Ger DR 1952. Awards: Kammersängerin, Ministry of Culture, Ger DR 1962.

Sang with major companies in FR GER: Wiesbaden; GER DR: Berlin Staatsoper, Dresden, Leipzig; HUN: Budapest; SPA: Barcelona; USSR: Leningrad Kirov. **Roles with these companies incl** BARTOK: Judith★ (*Bluebeard's Castle*); BEETHOVEN: Leonore★ (*Fidelio*); MASCAGNI: Santuzza (*Cavalleria rusticana*); PUCCINI: Tosca★, Turandot★; STRAUSS, R: Marschallin★ (*Rosenkavalier*), Salome; VERDI: Lady Macbeth; WAGNER: Senta★ (*Fliegende Holländer*), Ortrud★ (*Lohengrin*), Brünnhilde★ (*Walküre*), Isolde★. Also STRAUSS, R: Amme★ (*Frau ohne Schatten*); LEONCAVALLO: Jocaste★ (*Edipo Re*). Recorded for: VEB. Gives recitals. Appears with symphony orchestra. Teaches voice. Coaches repertoire. On faculty of Franz Liszt Musikhochschule, Weimar. **Res:** Rote Gasse 16, Meissen, Ger DR. Mgmt: KDR/GDR.

ZSCHAU, MARILYN. Spinto. American. Res mem: Opernhaus, Zurich & Basel. Born 9 Feb 1941, Chicago. Divorced. Studied: Juilliard Opera Theater, Christopher West, New York; John Lester, Missoula, MT, USA. **Debut:** Marietta (*Tote Stadt*) Volksoper, Vienna 1967. Previous occupations: secy in publ, advertising, hospitals.

Sang with major companies in AUS: Vienna Staatsoper & Volksoper; FR GER: Bielefeld, Frankfurt, Hamburg, Stuttgart; HUN: Budapest;

SWI: Basel, Zurich. **Roles with these companies incl** CILEA: Adriana Lecouvreur★; EINEM: Lucille★ (*Dantons Tod*); JANACEK: Vixen (*Cunning Little Vixen*), Malinka★ (*Excursions of Mr Broucek*); KORNGOLD: Marietta (*Tote Stadt*); LEONCAVALLO: Nedda★ (*Pagliacci*); MOZART: Fiordiligi★ (*Così fan tutte*), Donna Elvira★ (*Don Giovanni*), Contessa (*Nozze di Figaro*), Pamina★ (*Zauberflöte*); OFFENBACH: Antonia & Giulietta (*Contes d'Hoffmann*); ORFF: Kluge★; PUCCINI: Mimi★ (*Bohème*), Minnie★ (*Fanciulla del West*), Cio-Cio-San★ (*Butterfly*), Manon Lescaut★, Giorgetta★ (*Tabarro*); STRAUSS, R: Komponist (*Ariadne auf Naxos*), Gräfin★ (*Capriccio*), Marschallin★ & Octavian (*Rosenkavalier*); TCHAIKOVSKY: Tatiana★ (*Eugene Onegin*); VERDI: Desdemona (*Otello*), Violetta★ (*Traviata*); WEILL: Jenny★ (*Mahagonny*). Also HANDEL: Agrippina; HAYDN: Celia★ (*Fedeltà premiata*); WOLF-FERRARI: Marina★ (*Quattro rusteghi*). Appears with symphony orchestra. **Res:** Am Oeschbrig 41, Zurich, Switzerland. Mgmt: SLZ/FRG; TAS/AUS.

ZSOLT, BENDE. Lyric baritone. Hungarian. Resident mem: Hungarian State Opera, Budapest. Born 23 May 1926, Budapest. Single. Studied: Ferenc Liszt Acad of Music, Prof Ferencné Révhegyi, Budapest. **Debut:** Don Giovanni, Opera Co Szeged, Hungary 1956. Previous occupations: studied architecture. Awards: Merited Artist, F Liszt Prize winner.

Sang with major companies in CZE: Prague National; GER DR: Berlin Staatsoper; HUN: Budapest; UK: Glyndebourne Fest; USSR: Moscow Bolshoi. **Roles with these companies incl** BRITTEN: Demetrius★ (*Midsummer Night*); DONIZETTI: Dott Malatesta★ (*Don Pasquale*), Belcore (*Elisir*); FLOTOW: Plunkett (*Martha*); GLUCK: Oreste (*Iphigénie en Tauride*); HANDEL: Bertaric★ (*Rodelinda*); KODALY: Háry János★‡; MOZART: Don Giovanni★, Conte Almaviva★ (*Nozze di Figaro*), Papageno★ (*Zauberflöte*); ORFF: Solo★ (*Carmina burana*); PUCCINI: Marcello★ (*Bohème*), Lescaut★ (*Manon Lescaut*); PURCELL: Aeneas★; ROSSINI: Figaro★ (*Barbiere di Siviglia*), Dandini (*Cenerentola*), Robert (*Comte Ory*), Geronio (*Turco in Italia*); TCHAIKOVSKY: Eugene Onegin★; VERDI: Rodrigo★ (*Don Carlo*), Fra Melitone★ (*Forza del destino*), Germont★ (*Traviata*); WAGNER: Wolfram★ (*Tannhäuser*); WOLF-FERRARI: Conte Gil★ (*Segreto di Susanna*). Also GOUNOD: Valentin★ (*Faust*). **World premieres:** RANKY: Adam (*Tragedy of Men*) Hungarian State Opera 1970-71; SZOKOLAY: Horatio (*Hamlet*) Hung St Op 1968; PETROVICS: Razumihin (*Crime and Punishment*) Hung St Op 1969. Recorded for: Hungaroton, Decca. Video/Film: Don Giovanni; Rodrigo (*Don Carlo*); Figaro (*Barbiere di Siviglia*); Wolfram (*Tannhäuser*). Gives recitals. Appears with symphony orchestra. Teaches voice. Coaches repertoire. On faculty of Ferenc Liszt Acad of Music, Budapest; prof. **Res:** Szenthározság 9, Budapest 1014, Hungary. Mgmt: ITK/HUN.

ZUFFI, PIETRO. Stages/produces opera, theater, film & television. Also designs sets, costumes & stage-lighting and is an author, painter, sculptor, architect and illustrator. Italian. Born 28 Apr 1919,

609

Imola/Bologna. Single. Studied: Accad di Belle Arti, Florence; Piccolo Teatro di Milano, Strehler; La Scala Milan, Visconti, Carena. Film: Art Dir Rossellini, Fellini, Antonioni. **Operatic debut:** sets, cost, *Alceste* La Scala Milan 1954. Theater debut: prod/designer, 36 theater prod and 8 films. Previous occupation: painter; prof of scenic des, Accad Belle Arti, Bari. Awards: Paladino d'argento, Accad Teatro Palermo; Nettuno d'oro, Teatro Comunale Bologna; San Genesio, Accad del Teatro Milan; Leone di San Marco, Fest Venice.

Directed/produced opera for major companies in ARG: Buenos Aires; AUS: Vienna Staatsoper; BRA: Rio de Janeiro; FRA: Paris; FR GER: Düsseldorf-Duisburg; ITA: Bologna, Florence, Genoa, Milan La Scala, Naples, Palermo, Rome Opera, Trieste, Verona Arena; SPA: Barcelona; SWI: Zurich; USSR: Moscow Bolshoi; USA: Chicago, San Francisco Opera. **Operas staged with these companies incl** BELLINI: *Pirata†;* BERLIOZ: *Troyens†;* BIZET: *Carmen†;* DONIZETTI: *Favorite⋆†;* GIORDANO: *Andrea Chénier†;* GLUCK: *Orfeo ed Euridice†;* HANDEL: *Giulio Cesare⋆;* LEONCAVALLO: *Pagliacci†;* MONTEVERDI: *Ritorno d'Ulisse†;* PONCHIELLI: *Gioconda†;* PUCCINI: *Manon Lescaut⋆†;* ROSSELLINI: *Sguardo dal Ponte†;* ROSSINI: *Moïse, Donna del lago⋆†;* SAINT-SAENS: *Samson et Dalila†;* SPONTINI: *Vestale†;* VERDI: *Aida†, Don Carlo†, Nabucco†;* WAGNER: *Lohengrin†.* Also WALTON: *Troilus and Cressida†;* PIZZETTI: *Assassinio nella cattedrale⋆†.* Operatic Video—RAI TV: *Carmen.* Teaches at Accad di Belle Arti, Bari. **Res:** V dei Vecchiarelli 37, Rome, Italy.

ZYLIS-GARA, TERESA GERALDA; née Zylis. Lirico-spinto soprano. Polish. Born 23 Jan 1935, Wilno, Poland. Studied: Prof Olga Olgina, Lodz, Poland. **Debut:** Halka, Krakow, Poland 1957.

Awards: Winner Polish Ntl Compt, Warsaw; Winner Intl Singing Compt, Munich; Mozart Gold Medal, Mexico City; Polish Ntl Awd, Great Distinction for Artistic Achievement.

Sang with major companies in AUS: Vienna Staatsoper; BEL: Brussels; CZE: Prague; FRA: Aix-en-Provence, Bordeaux, Lyon, Marseille, Nancy, Orange Fest, Paris; FR GER: Berlin Deutsche Oper, Cologne, Dortmund, Düsseldorf-Duisburg, Frankfurt, Hamburg, Hannover, Munich Staatsoper; HOL: Amsterdam; HUN: Budapest; ITA: Rome Opera, Venice; MEX: Mexico City; MON: Monte Carlo; SPA: Barcelona; SWI: Geneva; UK: Glyndebourne Fest, London Royal; USA: Boston, Chicago Lyric, Dallas, Hartford Connecticut Opera, Miami, New Orleans, New York Metropolitan, San Francisco Opera. **Roles with these companies incl** BERLIOZ: Teresa (*Benvenuto Cellini*); DONIZETTI: Anna Bolena; DVORAK: Rusalka; GLUCK: Euridice; GOUNOD: Marguerite⋆ (*Faust*), Mireille; MASSENET: Manon; MONIUSZKO: Halka; MONTEVERDI: Poppea‡ (*Incoronazione di Poppea*); MOZART: Fiordiligi⋆ (*Così fan tutte*), Donna Elvira⋆ (*Don Giovanni*), Ilia (*Idomeneo*), Contessa⋆ (*Nozze di Figaro*), Pamina⋆ (*Zauberflöte*); MERCADANTE: Elisa (*Giuramento*); PUCCINI: Mimi⋆ (*Bohème*), Cio-Cio-San⋆ (*Butterfly*), Manon Lescaut⋆, Suor Angelica, Tosca⋆, Liù⋆ (*Turandot*); SMETANA: Marie⋆ (*Bartered Bride*); STRAUSS, R: Komponist‡ (*Ariadne auf Naxos*), Marschallin & Octavian (*Rosenkavalier*); TCHAIKOVSKY: Tatiana⋆ (*Eugene Onegin*), Lisa (*Pique Dame*); VERDI: Elisabetta⋆ (*Don Carlo*), Alice Ford (*Falstaff*), Desdemona⋆ (*Otello*), Violetta⋆ (*Traviata*), Leonora⋆ (*Trovatore*). Also CAVALIERI: Angelo Custode‡ (*Rappresentazione*). Recorded for: EMI, London, DG. Gives recitals. Appears with symphony orchestra. **Res:** Düsseldorf, FR GER. Mgmt: SLZ/FRG; CAM/USA.

Opera Company Profiles

Opera Company Profiles*

ARGENTINA

TEATRO COLÓN, Cerrito no. 618, Buenos Aires, Argentina; tel 35-5414. Founded in 1908. Perf at Teatro Colón since 1908. Built in 1908 as an opera house, seat cap 2,485; incl standing 3,500; avg aud 2,555. Perf also at Teatro Municipal Gral San Martín, Teatro Coliseo, Teatro Municipal Enrique Santos Discépolo and open air theaters. Company owned and operated by City of Buenos Aires, which also manages Teatro Municipal Gral San Martín, Teatro Municipal Enrique Santos Discépolo and summer theaters; Municipal Int José Embrioni; Gen Art Dir Enrique Sivieri; Tech Dir Oscar Lagomarsino; Adm Dir Cristóbal L Juliá.

SEASON	OPENING Day Month		CLOSING Day Month		NO OF PFS	NO OF PROD	NO OF NEW PROD	NO OF NON-OPERA PFS*
1974	8	Feb	15	Dec	213	19	9	131
1975	30	Jan	30	Nov	282	14	7	145

*Operettas, musicals, ballet, etc.

Repertoire 1974 — Boero: *Matrero*; Honegger: *Jeanne d'Arc au bûcher*; Humperdinck: *Hänsel und Gretel*; Leoncavallo: *Pagliacci*; Mascagni: *Cavalleria rusticana*; Puccini: *Bohème, Gianni Schicchi, Butterfly, Suor Angelica, Tabarro*; Rossini: *Barbiere di Siviglia*; Schoenberg: *Moses und Aron*; Strauss, J: *Fledermaus*; Strauss, R: *Salome*; Verdi: *Trovatore*. **Opera de Cámara** — Donizetti: *Campanello, Rita*; Fioravanti: *Cantatrici villane*.
1975 — Boero: *Matrero*; Giordano: *Andrea Chénier*; Mussorgsky: *Boris Godunov*; Pahlen: *Pinocchio*; Panizza: *Bizancio*; Puccini: *Butterfly, Tosca*; Ravel: *Enfant et les sortilèges, Heure espagnole*; Strauss, J: *Fledermaus*; Strauss, R: *Elektra, Salome*; Torroba: *Luisa Fernanda*; Verdi: *Trovatore*.

Company performs all operas in orig language. Pfs broadcast on radio two to three times a week, some live, some taped; one pf of each prod is videotaped. No annual tour; some guest engagements in Latin American countries. Subsidiary company: Opera de Cámara del Teatro Colón, chamber opera at Teatro Colón. Company has training program for conductors/coaches.

Budget for 1975 Arg $250,284,055 (US $25,529,000). Income: 100% government subsidy. Ticket prices: Arg $60-12; 60% subscription, 40% single ticket sale.

Number of persons engaged for opera in 1975: resident solo artists: 134; guest solo artists: 14; chorus members: 136; orchestra members: 137 & 133; musical staff: 32; conductors: 26; stage directors/producers: 11; choreographers: 3; corps de ballet: 132; administrative staff: 163; technical, scenic, costume: 264.

Company maintains two orchs: Orquesta Estable, 137 mem; Orquesta Filarmónica de Buenos Aires, 133 mem; builds all sets & costumes in own workshops.

Policy determined by Gen Art Dir E Sivieri, Tech Dir O Lagomarsino & Adm Dir C Juliá.

*Companies are listed alphabetically by city within country.

AUSTRALIA

THE AUSTRALIAN OPERA, PO Box J194, Brickfield Hill, Sydney, Australia 2000; tel 26 2976. Founded in 1956 as The Elizabethan Trust Opera Co; changed in 1970 to The Australian Opera. Perf at Sydney Opera House since 1973, built in 1973 as an opera house, seat cap 1,500; at Brisbane; at Princess Theatre, Melbourne, planning for completion in 1980, Victorian Arts Center, 2,000-seat State Theatre for opera in Melbourne; at Canberra Theatre, Canberra City; at Adelaide Festival Theatre, Adelaide, built in July 1973 as multipurpose hall; at Hobart. Company first perf at Elizabethan Theatre in Sydney from 1956 to 1964, seat cap 1,520; also at Her Majesty's, Tivoli. Private non-profit organization; Bd Chmn Charles J Berg, OBE; Gen Mng John Winther; Mus Dir Richard Bonynge, beg 1976; Art Adm Moffatt Oxenbould; Co Secy Douglas McLaggan; St Dir Anthony Everingham.

SEASON	OPENING Day Month	CLOSING Day Month	NO OF PFS	NO OF OPERAS	NO OF NEW PROD	NO OF NON-OPERA PFS*
1973	Mar	Dec	178	12	5	—
1974	Jan	Nov	233	17	7	36

*Operettas, musicals, ballet, etc.

World prems during these seasons: Sitsky's *Lenz* 3/74; Werder's *The Affair* 3/74; Sculthorpe's *Rites of Passage* 9/74.

Repertoire 1974 — Janáček: *Jenufa*; Leoncavallo: *Pagliacci*; Mascagni: *Cavalleria rusticana*; Mozart: *Nozze di Figaro, Don Giovanni, Zauberflöte*; Offenbach: *Contes d'Hoffmann*; Prokofiev: *War and Peace*; Puccini: *Bohème, Trittico, Tosca*; Rossini: *Barbiere di Siviglia*; Sculthorpe: *Rites of Passage*; Sitsky: *Lenz*; Verdi: *Nabucco*; Wagner: *Tannhäuser*; Werder: *Affair*.
1975 — Donizetti: *Elisir*; Janáček: *Jenufa*; Mozart: *Zauberflöte*; Offenbach: *Contes d'Hoffmann*; Puccini: *Tosca*; Rossini: *Barbiere di Siviglia*; Verdi: *Aida, Rigoletto*; Weill: *Mahagonny*.

Company performs 50% of all operas in orig language. Six pfs taped and rebroadcast annually. Company performs regularly in Sydney, Melbourne, Brisbane, Canberra, Adelaide, Hobart. It has a training program for 12 singers and one coach per season.

Budget for 1974 Austrl $3,970,000 (US $5,915,000). Income: 58% box office, 40% gvnmt subsidies, 1% private/corp/fndn grants, 1% other. Ticket prices: Austrl $16.50-1.50; 75% subscription, 25% single ticket sale.

Number of persons engaged for 1974: resident solo artists: 40; guest solo artists: 7; chorus members: 49; musical staff: 11; conductors: 4; stage directors/producers: 3; set & costume designers: 3; administrative staff: 11; technical, scenic, costume: 33.

Company uses Elizabethan Trust Sydney and Melbourne Orchs; builds no sets but 90% of its costumes in own workshops.

Board of Directors: Chmn Charles J Berg, OBE; Dep Chmn Maurice C Timbs; Leonard L Amadio; Guilford Bell; Patrick Clancy; Prof Zelman Cowen, CMG; Mrs John Davies; Mrs Marcel Dekyvere, CBE; The Rt Hon The Earl of Harewood; Rex Hobcroft; The Hon Mr Justice Mahoney; John Mostyn; Maurice Parker; Bruce Piggott, CBE; Sir Ian Potter; N R Seddon, CBE; Dale Turnbull; Vincent Warrener.

AUSTRIA

BREGENZER FESTSPIELE, Kornmarktstr 6, A 6900 Bregenz, Austria; tel 22 811. Founded in 1945. Perf at Theater am Kornmarkt since 1955. Built in 1955; seat cap 692, avg aud 600. Other theaters: Schlosshof Hohenems; Seebühne—Theater on the Lake, seat cap 6,400; since 1945. Company is a non-profit organization subsidized by gvnmt; Pres Dr Albert Fuchs; Fest Dir Prof Ernst Bär; Treas Dr Franz Kaiser; Tech Dir Karlheinz Miltner.

SEASON	OPENING Day Month	CLOSING Day Month	NO OF PFS	NO OF OPERAS	NO OF NEW PROD	NO OF NON-OPERA PFS*
1974	19 Jul	20 Aug	51	3	3	30
1975	17 Jul	18 Aug	58	3	3	51

*Operettas, musicals, ballet, concerts, etc.

Repertoire 1974 — Theater on the Lake — Wagner: *Fliegende Holländer*; **Theater am Kornmarkt —** Rossini: *Armida*; **Hohenems —** Haydn: *Pescatrici*.
1975 — Theater on the Lake — Bizet: *Carmen*; **Theater am Kornmarkt —** Verdi: *Finto Stanislao*; **Hohenems —** Haydn: *Mondo della luna*.

Company performs 75% of all operas in orig language. Perfs are broadcast live regularly.

Budget for 1974-75 AS 31,000,000 (US $1,575,000); 100% gvnmt subsidy. Ticket prices: AS400-80; 33% subscription, 67% single ticket sale.

Number of persons engaged in 1975 abt 1,200: guest solo artists: 200; chorus members: 120; orchestra members: 130; musical staff: 250; stage directors/producers: 8; set & costume designers: 8; choreographers: 2; corps de ballet: 80; administrative staff: 18; technical, scenic, costume: 160.

Company uses the Wiener Symphoniker orch; builds 50% of sets and 20% costumes in own workshops.

Policy determined by Board of Directors: Pres Dr Albert Fuchs; Vice-Pres Dr Karl Erschen and Dr Richard Sannwald.

SALZBURGER FESTSPIELE, Hofstallgasse 1, Salzburg, Austria; tel 42 5 41. Founded in 1920. Perf at Grosses Festspielhaus, built in 1960 as an opera house, seat cap 2,170; Kleines Festspielhaus, built in 1924 as an opera house, seat cap 1,383; Felsenreitschule, built in 1933 as an opera house, seat cap 1,549. Perf in each theater since the respective opening year. Company is owned and operated by the Republic of Austria and Province and City of Salzburg, in cooperation with the Foreign Visitors Furtherance Fund (Fremdenverkehrsförderungsfonds); Dir Dr Tassilo Nekola; Directorate — Pres Josef Kaut, Dr Friedrich Gehmacher, Dr Ernst Haeusserman, Herbert von Karajan, Prof Gerhard Wimberger.

SEASON	OPENING Day Month	CLOSING Day Month	NO OF PFS	NO OF OPERAS	NO OF NEW PROD	NO OF NON-OPERA PFS*
1974	26 Jul	30 Aug	104	5	4	80
1975	26 Jul	30 Aug	89	5	3	64

*Operettas, musicals, ballet, etc.

Repertoire 1974 — Mozart: *Così fan tutte, Entführung aus dem Serail, Nozze di Figaro, Zauberflöte*; Strauss, R: *Frau ohne Schatten*.
1975 — Mozart: *Così fan tutte, Entführung aus dem Serail, Nozze di Figaro*; Strauss, R: *Frau ohne Schatten*; Verdi: *Don Carlo*.

Company performs all operas in orig language. Pfs regularly broadcast live on radio.

Budget for 1975 AS 131,100,000 (US $7,735,000). Income: 58% box office, 42% gvnmt subsidies. Ticket prices: AS1,500-50; 97% single ticket sale.

Number of persons engaged by company in 1975: 2,520: resident solo artists: —; guest solo artists: 198; chorus members: 557; orchestra members: 696; musical staff: —; conductors: 19; stage directors/producers: 7; set & costume designers: 6; choreographers: 1; corps de ballet: —; administrative and clerical staff: 44; technical, scenic, costume: 471.

Company uses only guest orch; builds all of its sets and costumes in own workshops.

Trustees: Kmrat Alfred Haidenthaller; Dr Otto Autengruber; DDr Dipl Ing Hans Lechner; Dr Heinz Pruckner; Mayor Heinrich Salfenauer; Gen Sec Dir Robert Jungbluth and the Directorate of the Salzburg Festival, above.

(Above information does not include Easter Festival, which is a separate operation.)

WIENER STAATSOPER, Opernring, A-1010 Vienna, Austria; tel 52 76 36. Founded in 1869 as Court Opera. Pfs were suspended 1945-55, during which time company perf at Theater an der Wien. Perf at Wiener Staatsoper since 1869. Built in 1869 as an opera house. Damaged in WW II. Rebuilt in 1955, seat cap 1,642 plus 567 standing room, avg aud 1,511. Prev theater: Kärntnertortheater until 1869. Perf also at Volksoper, Theater an der Wien, Redoutensaal. Company owned and operated by Austrian State Theater Association (Österr Bundestheaterverband), Ministry of Education and Culture, which also manages Burgtheater, Volksoper and Akademietheater; Gen Secy Robert

Jungbluth; Dir Prof Rudolf Gamsjäger; Vice-Dir Herbert von Strohmer; Art Mng Hubert Deutsch; Tech Mng Hans Langer, Robert Stangl; Prgm & Publ Rel Lothar Knessl. Dir designate Prof Dr Egon Seefehlner 1976.

SEASON	OPENING Day Month	CLOSING Day Month	NO OF PFS	NO OF PROD	NO OF NEW PROD	NO OF NON-OPERA PFS*
73-74	1 Sep	30 Jun	297	45	6	18
74-75	1 Sep	30 Jun	297	46	6	18

*Operettas, ballet.

Repertoire 1973-74 — Beethoven: *Fidelio;* Bizet: *Carmen;* Cherubini: *Medea;* Gounod: *Faust;* Janácek: *Jenufa, Katya Kabanová;* Leoncavallo: *Pagliacci;* Mascagni: *Cavalleria rusticana;* Massenet: *Manon;* Mozart: *Don Giovanni, Entführung aus dem Serail, Nozze di Figaro, Zauberflöte;* Offenbach: *Contes d'Hoffmann;* Puccini: *Bohème, Butterfly, Tosca, Turandot;* Rossini: *Barbiere di Siviglia;* Schoenberg: *Moses und Aron;* Strauss, R: *Arabella, Ariadne auf Naxos, Capriccio, Elektra, Rosenkavalier, Salome;* Tchaikovsky: *Eugene Onegin;* Verdi: *Aida, Ballo in maschera, Don Carlo, Luisa Miller, Otello, Rigoletto, Traviata, Trovatore;* Wagner: *Fliegende Holländer, Lohengrin, Parsifal, Rheingold, Walküre, Siegfried, Götterdämmerung, Tannhäuser, Tristan und Isolde;* Weber: *Freischütz.*
1974-75 — Beethoven: *Fidelio;* Bizet: *Carmen;* Gounod: *Faust;* Janácek: *Katya Kabanová;* Leoncavallo: *Pagliacci;* Mascagni: *Cavalleria rusticana;* Massenet: *Manon;* Mozart: *Così fan tutte, Don Giovanni, Entführung aus dem Serail, Nozze di Figaro, Zauberflöte;* Offenbach: *Contes d'Hoffmann;* Pfitzner: *Palestrina;* Puccini: *Bohème, Butterfly, Tosca, Turandot;* Rossini: *Barbiere di Siviglia;* Strauss, R: *Elektra, Rosenkavalier, Salome;* Tchaikovsky: *Eugene Onegin;* Verdi: *Aida, Ballo in maschera, Don Carlo, Forza del destino, Luisa Miller, Otello, Rigoletto, Traviata, Trovatore;* Wagner: *Fliegende Holländer, Lohengrin, Parsifal, Rheingold, Walküre, Siegfried, Götterdämmerung, Tannhäuser, Tristan und Isolde;* Weber: *Freischütz.*

Company performs 90-95% of all operas in orig language. Abt four pfs are taped and rebroadcast annually. Guest exchange engagements 1971-75 incl USSR: Moscow 7 pfs. Company has a training prgm for singers.

Budget for 1974 AS 375 mill (US $22,125,000). Income: 25% box office; 75% gvnmt. Ticket prices: AS 500-25; 40% subscription, 60% single ticket sale.

Number of persons engaged in 1974-75 is appr 835 without workshops. Workshops for all four State Theaters are handled by the central office of the Austr State Theater Assn. Same applies to the admin staff of the company; resident solo artists: 140; guest solo artists: 30; chorus members: 105; orchestra members: 150; musical staff and art mngmt: 22; conductors: appr 20; stage directors/producers: 5; set & costume designers: 6; choreographers: 2; corps de ballet: 90; administrative staff: 4—see above; technical, scenic, costume: 260—see above.

Company uses the Vienna Phil Orch; builds 80% of sets and costumes in own workshops.

Policy determined by Minister for Educ & Culture, Dr Fred Sinowatz, and Gen Secy of the Austr State Theater Assn, Robert Jungbluth; also by legislation of the Ntl Assembly of the Austr Parliament.

VOLKSOPER WIEN, Währingerstr 78, 1090 Vienna, Austria; tel 34 36 27. Founded in 1898 as Kaiserjubiläums-Stadttheater; in 1906 assumed name Volksoper/Kaiserjubiläums-Stadttheater. Pfs were suspended in 1924-25 and 1928-29. Reopened 1929 as Neues Wiener Schauspielhaus, with pfs suspended during 1932-34. In 1938-44 the company was called Opernhaus der Stadt Wien. Finally, in 1945, the company merged with that of the State Opera. It became a Federal State Theater known as Staatsoper in der Volksoper; in 1955 became the Volksoper. Perf at Volksoper since 1945. Built in 1898 for operas, plays and operettas, seat cap 1,472 plus 114 standing room, avg aud 1,280. Company owned and operated by Austrian State Theater Association (Österr Bundestheaterverband),

Ministry for Education and Culture, which also manages Staatsoper, Burgtheater and Akademietheater; Gen Secy Robert Jungbluth; Dir Kmsg Karl Dönch; Deputy Dir Gandolf Buschbeck, Assts Dr Robert Herzl and Wolfgang Weber; Prgm & Publ Rel Lothar Knessl.

SEASON	OPENING Day Month		CLOSING Day Month		NO OF PFS	NO OF OPERAS	NO OF NEW PROD	NO OF NON-OPERA PFS*
73-74	22	Sep	30	Jun	286	15	7	24
74-75	1	Sep	30	Jun	307	15	4	16

*Operettas, musicals, ballet.

World prems during these seasons: Rubin's *Kleider machen Leute* 12/73; Wolpert's *Eingebildete Kranke* 3/75.

Repertoire 1973-74 — Auber: *Fra Diavolo*; Donizetti: *Fille du régiment*; Humperdinck: *Hänsel und Gretel*; Kienzl: *Evangelimann*; Lortzing: *Wildschütz, Zar und Zimmermann*; Mozart: *Nozze di Figaro, Zauberflöte*; Nicolai: *Lustigen Weiber*; Offenbach: *Contes d'Hoffmann*; Rubin: *Kleider machen Leute*; Smetana: *Bartered Bride*; Strauss, J: *Fledermaus*; Weill: *Aufstieg und Fall der Stadt Mahagonny*; Wolf-Ferrari: *Quattro rusteghi*.
1974-75 — Bizet: *Carmen*; Donizetti: *Don Pasquale, Fille du régiment*; Humperdinck: *Hänsel und Gretel*; Kienzl: *Evangelimann*; Mozart: *Nozze di Figaro, Zauberflöte*; Nicolai: *Lustigen Weiber*; Offenbach: *Contes d'Hoffmann*; Schmidt: *Notre Dame*; Smetana: *Bartered Bride*; Strauss, J: *Fledermaus*; Weill: *Aufstieg und Fall der Stadt Mahagonny*; Wolf-Ferrari: *Quattro rusteghi*; Wolpert: *Eingebildete Kranke*.

Two or three pfs are taped and rebroadcast. Guest exchange engagements 1971-75 incl BEL: Brussels 10 pfs; AUS: Graz 3 pfs.

Budget for 1974 AS 174 mill (US $10,266,000). Income: 22% box office; 78% gvnmt. Ticket prices: AS 220-20; 35% subscription, 65% single ticket sale.

Number of persons engaged in 1974-75 is 500 without workshops. Workshops for all four State Theaters are handled by the central office of the Austr State Theater Assn. There are appr 540 persons. Same applies to the admin staff of the company: resident solo artists: 85; guest solo artists: 15; chorus members: 72; orchestra members: 95; musical staff and art mngmt: 16; conductors: 15; stage dirs/prods: 5; set & costume designers: 9; choreographers: 1; corps de ballet: 41; administrative staff: 3—see above; technical, scenic, costume: 140.

Company uses its own orch; builds 80% of sets and costumes in own workshops.

Policy determined by Minister for Education & Culture, Dr Fred Sinowatz, and Gen Secy of the Austr State Theater Assn, Robert Jungbluth; also by legislation of the Ntl Assembly of the Austr Parliament.

BELGIUM

OPERA NATIONAL DE BELGIQUE, 4, rue Léopold, 1000 Brussels, Belgium; tel 217 22 11. Founded in 1700 as Théâtre Royal de la Monnaie; changed name to Opéra National de Belgique in 1963. Perf at Théâtre Royal de la Monnaie, seat cap 1,100, avg aud 1,000. Co owned and operated by Gvnmt of Belgium; Dir Maurice Huisman since 1959; Art Dir, also for Ballet du XXe Siècle, Maurice Béjart; Adm Dir Anne Lotsy; Dir Opéra-Studio Ida Huisman.

SEASON	OPENING Day Month		CLOSING Day Month		NO OF PFS	NO OF OPERAS	NO OF NEW PROD	NO OF NON-OPERA PFS*
73-74	21	Aug	17	Jul	123	12	—	25
74-75	23	Aug	23	Jun	131	12	—	51

*Ballet

World prem during these seasons: Nabokov's *Love's Labour's Lost* prod by Deutsche Oper Berlin in Brussels 10/73.

Repertoire 1973-74 — Beethoven: *Fidelio;* Britten: *Death in Venice;* Debussy: *Pelléas et Mélisande;* Donizetti: *Don Pasquale;* Mozart: *Zauberflöte;* Puccini: *Butterfly;* Rossini: *Cenerentola;* Tchaikovsky: *Eugene Onegin;* Verdi: *Don Carlo, Traviata;* Wagner: *Fliegende Holländer, Parsifal.*

1974-75 — Bizet: *Carmen;* Cavalli: *Erismena;* Honegger: *Jeanne d'Arc au bûcher;* Mozart: *Così fan tutte, Don Giovanni;* Puccini: *Manon Lescaut;* Schoenberg: *Moses und Aron;* Strauss, R: *Salome;* Verdi: *Ballo in maschera;* Wagner: *Lohengrin;* Weill: *Aufstieg und Fall der Stadt Mahagonny, Sieben Todsünden.*

Company performs all operas in orig language. Guest engagements 1973-75 incl Paris 14 pfs and Vienna 4 pfs. Subsidiary companies incl Opéra-Studio and Ballet du XXe Siècle.

Budget n/a.

Number of persons engaged in 1974-75 n/a. No resident solo artists, guests only. Chorus mems: 32; orch mems 67.

Company engages orch and singers on a seasonal basis.

CENTRE LYRIQUE DE WALLONIE, rue des Dominicains, Liège, Belgium; tel (041) 23 59 10. Founded in 1974; form Opéra de Wallonie. Perf at Théâtre Royal, Liège since 1967. Built in 1820 as an opera house, seat cap 1,260, avg aud 900. Perf also at Grand Théâtre, Verviers. Private non-profit organization; Chmn of Bd Hubert Pirotte; Dir Gen Raymond Rossius; Mus Dir Marcel Desiron; Stg Mng Pierre Fleta; Tech Dir Pierre Pesenti.

As Opéra de Wallonie:

SEASON	OPENING Day Month	CLOSING Day Month	NO OF PFS	NO OF OPERAS	NO OF NEW PROD	NO OF NON-OPERA PFS*
73-74	1 Sep	31 May	165	13	6	8
74-75	5 Sep	31 May	198	9	4	11

*Operettas & musicals.

World prem during these seasons: Dubois' *Les Suisses* 10/73.

Repertoire n/a.

Company performs over 5% of all operas in orig language. No radio broadcasts; 2 videotapings per season. Exchange guest engagements 1971-75 incl FR GER: Aachen; BEL: Brussels, Ghent, Antwerp, Charleroi, Mons, Verviers; LUX: Esch; FRA: Besançon, Nancy; POL: Poznan; ROM: Bucharest.

Budget for 1974-75 B Fr 234,316,492 (US $6,560,000). Income: 26% box office, 74% gvnmt. Ticket prices: B Fr 200-50; 45% subscription, 55% single ticket sale.

Number of persons engaged for 1974-75: resident solo artists: 21; guest solo artists: 14; chorus members: 80; orchestra members: 90; musical staff: 6; conductors: 3; stage directors/producers: 1; set & costume designers: 1; choreographers: 1; corps de ballet: 28; administrative staff: 4; technical, scenic, costume: 94.

Company maintains permanent orch; builds 80% of sets & costumes in own workshops.

CANADA

L'OPÉRA DU QUÉBEC, 175 St Catherine St W, Montreal, Canada; tel 842-2141. Founded in 1970. Perf at Salle Wilfrid Pelletier of Place des Arts since 1970. Built in 1963 as opera house and concert hall, seat cap 3,000, avg aud 2,910. Prev theaters: Salle Louis Fréchette, Quebec City, and Opera Hall, Ottawa, Ontario. Company is a non-profit organization; Pres Judge Jacques Vadboncoeur; Dir Gen & Exec Dir Gérard Lamarche; admin by Place des Arts.

SEASON	OPENING Day Month	CLOSING Day Month	NO OF PFS	NO OF OPERAS	NO OF NEW PROD	NO OF NON-OPERA PFS
73-74	May	Mar	24	3	—	—
74-75	Apr	Mar	27	3	—	—

Repertoire 1973-74 — Massenet: *Manon*; Mozart: *Don Giovanni*; Verdi: *Otello*.
1974-75 — Puccini: *Bohème, Butterfly*; Verdi: *Falstaff*.

Company performs all operas in orig language. Annual tour to Quebec City.

Budget for 1974-75 Can $818,000 (US $825,000). Receives gvnmt subsidies. Ticket prices: Can $15-4; 35% subscription, 65% single ticket sale.

Company uses local symph orch; builds all sets and costumes in own workshops. Activities suspended for 1975-76; to be resumed in 1976-77.

Policy determined by Board of Dir: Pres, Judge Jacques Vadboncoeur; Vice-Pres, J-M Poitras and J C Delorme; Exec Dir, Gérard Lamarche; Members, Guy Beaulne, Lionel Daunais, Dr G Lachance, R Miville des Chênes; Treas, Raymond Dionne.

NATIONAL ARTS CENTRE FESTIVAL OPERA, Box 1534, Stn B, Ottawa, Canada K1P 5W1; tel (613) 996-5051. Founded in 1971. Perf at National Arts Centre since 1971. Built in 1969 as an opera house, seat cap for opera 2,140, avg aud 1,600. Company federally funded, operating under independent board of trustees; head officer G. Hamilton Southam, Director General; Gen Mng Bruce Corder; Mus Dir Mario Bernardi; Adm Andrée Gingras.

SEASON	OPENING Day Month	CLOSING Day Month	NO OF PFS	NO OF OPERAS	NO OF NEW PROD	NO OF NON-OPERA PFS
1974	July	July	13	3	2	—
1975	July	July	12	3	2	—

Repertoire 1974 — Mozart: *Don Giovanni, Entführung aus dem Serail*; Rossini: *Comte Ory*.
1975 — Mozart: *Zauberflöte*; Offenbach: *Belle Hélène*; Verdi: *Traviata*.

Company performs 50% of all operas in orig language. Some pfs broadcast, which are always taped; 1 pf videotaped, beginning 1975.

Budget 1975 Can $1,000,000 (US $1,009,000), excl of rental fees for hall or general services. Ticket prices: Can $8.50-3.75; 10% by subscription, 65% of capacity single ticket sale.

Number of persons engaged for 1975: resident solo artists: —; guest solo artists: 42; chorus members: 62; orchestra members: 52; musical staff: 7; conductors: 2; stage directors/producers: 3; set & costume designers: 4; choreographers: 1; corps de ballet: 2; administrative staff: 3; technical, scenic, costume: 154.

Company uses local symph orch; builds all sets and 90% of costumes in own workshop.

Board of Trustees: François Mercier, QC, David A Golden, Mrs Suzanne Marie Duff, George A Fierheller, Arthur Gelber, OC, Mrs Annette Rothstein, Mrs Helen Coleman, Mrs Yolande Crépeau, Dr Emmanuel M Finkleman, Miss Maureen Forrester, CC, Laurent Picard, André Fortier, Sydney Newman, His Worship Lorry Greenberg, His Worship Gilles Rocheleau.

CANADIAN OPERA COMPANY, 35 Front St E, Toronto, Canada; tel 363-9256. Founded in 1950. Perf at O'Keefe Centre for the Performing Arts since 1961. Built in 1960 as a multi-purpose auditorium, seat cap 3,155, avg aud 2,800. Company first perf at Royal Alexandra Theatre, Toronto, 1950-60. Private non-profit organization; Pres D A Sloan; Gen Dir Herman Geiger-Torel till 1976, then Gen Dir Lotfi Mansouri; Adm Dir B A Chalmers; Dir of Touring & Prog Develpmt Jan Rubes; Dir of Publicity Harvey Chusid.

MAIN SEASON	OPENING Day Month	CLOSING Day Month	NO OF PFS	NO OF PROD	NO OF NEW PROD	NO OF NON-OPERA PFS
1973	7 Sep	13 Oct	36	6	3	—
1974	6 Sep	12 Oct	36	7	5	—

World prem during these seasons: Wilson's *Heloise and Abelard* 9/73.

Repertoire 1973 — Rossini: *Barbiere di Siviglia*; Verdi: *Rigoletto*; Wagner: *Götterdäm-merung*; Beethoven: *Fidelio*; Wilson: *Héloise and Abélard*. Touring Comp — Mozart: *Così fan tutte*; Menotti: *The Old Maid and the Thief*.
1974 — Bartok: *Bluebeard's Castle*; Ravel: *L'Heure espagnole*; Bizet: *Carmen*; Gounod: *Faust*; Mussorgsky: *Boris Godunov*; Verdi: *Traviata*; Wagner: *Fliegende Holländer*. Touring Comp — Puccini: *La Bohème*; Polgar: *The Glove*.

Company performs 75% of all operas in orig language. Guest engagements at National Arts Centre, Ottawa, since 1971-72; 4 pfs each season. Subsidiary company for touring, 14 singers, 23 orch mem, perf throughout Canada and western US 11/73-3/74, 90 pfs of one opera, school tour (Ontario) 2-3/75, 29 pfs of one opera.

Budget for 1974 Can $2,200,000 (US $2,220,000). Income: 54% box office, 36% gvnmt subsidies, 10% private/corp/fndn grants. Ticket prices: Can $15.50-3; 55% by subscription, 45% single ticket sale.

Number of persons engaged by company in 1974: resident solo artists: 44; guest solo artists: 33; chorus members: 54; orchestra members: 56; musical staff: 12; conductors: 5; stage directors/producers: 6; set & costume designers: 4; administrative staff: 7; technical, scenic, costume: 82.

Company uses local symph orch; builds 66% of its sets, none of its costumes in own workshops.

VANCOUVER OPERA ASSOCIATION, 111 Dunsmuir St, Vancouver, BC, Canada; tel (604) 682-2871. Founded in 1959. Perf at Queen Elizabeth Theatre, 649 Cambie St, Vancouver, since 1960. Built in 1957 as a multi-purpose auditorium; seat cap 2,820, avg aud 2,600. Private non-profit organization; Pres William Steen; Gen Mng Brian M Hanson until 1975, succeeded by B Thompson; Art Dir Richard Bonynge; Scenic Dir Harold Laxton; Tech Dir A Barratelli.

SEASON	OPENING Day	Month	CLOSING Day	Month	NO OF PFS	NO OF OPERAS	NO OF NEW PROD	NO OF NON-OPERA PFS*
73-74	25	Oct	4	May	14	3	2	1
74-75	24	Oct	3	May	17	4	3	—

*Operettas, musicals, ballet, etc.

Repertoire 1973-74 — Bizet: *Carmen*; Verdi: *Don Carlo, Traviata*.
1974-75 — Donizetti: *Lucia*; Piccinni: *Buona figliuola*; Handel: *Rodelinda*; Verdi: *Rigoletto*; Wagner: *Walküre*. (Incl workshop.)

Company performs 75% of all operas in orig language. It has a training prgm for 8 singers per season.

Budget for 1973-74 Can $614,773 (US $620,000). Income: 50% box office, 30% gvnmt subsidies, 10% priv/corp/fndn grants, 10% other income. Ticket prices: Can $12-5; 35% by subscription, 65% single ticket sale.

Number of persons engaged by company in 1974-75: resident solo artists: 28; guest solo artists: 22; chorus members: 128; orchestra members: 88; musical staff: 3; conductors: 4; stage directors/producers: 4; set & costume designers: 2; administrative staff: 1; technical, scenic, costume: 83.

Company uses local symph orch; builds all of its sets in own workshop.

Board of Dir: W R Steen, Pres; F G A McCullough, Past Pres; Mrs R W Douglas, Vice-Pres; W M Robson, Hon Sec; D B McNeil, Hon Treas; David Spencer, W Armstrong, D H Bell-Irving, M Duffus, B Hareid, A Aberbach, J R Baker, D Cooke, S Evans, D G Gibbs, J C Gilmer, Mrs C H McLean, N Sarkari, S Waddell, H L Warner.

CZECHOSLOVAKIA

NATIONAL THEATER PRAGUE, Divadelni 6, 112 30 Prague, CSSR; tel 26 97 50. Founded in 1881. Perf at National Theater, Smetana Theater, Tyl Theater. National Theater built in 1883 as an opera house, first used by company in 1883, seat cap 1,159;

Smetana Theater built in 1885 as an opera house (orig had its own company), first used by company in 1948, seat cap 1,076; Tyl Theater built in 1783 as an opera house, first used by company in 1920, seat cap 1,046; avg aud 87.6%. First perf at Provisional Theater Prague, 1862-83. Also perf at Interim Theater, 1939-44, during German occupation. Company is owned and operated by national gvnmt through the Ministry of Culture; Gen Mng Premysl Koci; Deputy Head of Opera Josef Janous; Head of Adm Dept Dr Arnost Berger; Art Adv Pavel Eckstein.

SEASON	OPENING Day	Month	CLOSING Day	Month	NO OF PFS	NO OF OPERAS	NO OF NEW PROD	NO OF NON-OPERA PFS*
73-74	1	Sep	27	Jun	390	31	7	99
74-75	5	Sep	29	Jun	367	31	5	104

*Ballet.

World prem during these seasons: Cikker's *Coriolanus* 4/74.

Repertoire 1971-75 — Beethoven: *Fidelio*; Bizet: *Carmen*; Cikker: *Coriolanus*; Dvorák: *Devil and Kate, Jakobin, Rusalka*; Fibich: *Sarka*; Janácek: *Jenufa, Katya Kabanová, Cunning Little Vixen, From the House of the Dead*; Jeremias: *Brothers Karamazov*; Karminsky: *Ten Days That Shook the World*; Martinu: *Greek Passion, Marienlegende, Comedy on the Bridge, Ariadne*; Molchanov: *Dawns Are Quiet Here*; Mozart: *Cosi fan tutte, Don Giovanni, Nozze di Figaro, Entführung aus dem Serail*; Mussorgsky: *Boris Godunov*; Offenbach: *Contes d'Hoffmann*; Poulenc: *Voix humaine*; Prokofiev: *War and Peace*; Puccini: *Bohème, Madama Butterfly, Turandot*; Ravel: *Heure espagnole*; Rossini: *Barbiere di Siviglia*; Smetana: *Bartered Bride, Dalibor, The Kiss, Libuse, Two Widows, Secret, Devil's Wall*; Strauss, R: *Arabella, Salome*; Stravinsky: *Rake's Progress*; Suchon: *Whirlpool*; Tchaikovsky: *Eugene Onegin, Pique Dame*; Verdi: *Ballo in maschera, Nabucco, Rigoletto, Simon Boccanegra*; Wagner: *Lohengrin, Walküre*.

Company performs 50% of all operas in orig language. Some pfs broadcast on radio, live or taped; 1 or 2 pfs videotaped per season. Annual tour of 2 operas in 2 or 3 pfs to Bratislava & Brno. During last four seasons guest engagements of complete ensemble incl SPA: Barcelona 6 pfs, Madrid 6 pfs; ITA: Bologna 8 pfs, Modena 2 pfs, Parma 1 pf, Piacenza 2 pfs, Ravenna 1 pf, Reggio Emilia 2 pfs, Venice 6 pfs; YUG: Belgrade 2 pfs, Zagreb 2 pfs; BUL: Sofia 6 pfs; USSR: Moscow 8 pfs; FR GER: Schweinfurt 5 pfs; Wiesbaden 4 pfs; GRE: Athens 4 pfs. Of chamber opera incl ITA: Modena 2 pfs, Piacenza 1 pf, Reggio Emilia 4 pfs; FR GER: Bayreuth 2 pfs; SWI: Lausanne 2 pfs, Basel 1 pf, Yverdon 1 pf, La Chaux de Fonds 1 pf, Langenthal 1 pf; AUS: Leoben 1 pf; FRA: Bordeaux 2 pfs; DEN: Copenhagen 3 pfs. Subsidiary company: Komorní opera Náradního divadla, for chamber operas, perf at home and out of town.

Budget n/a. Ticket prices: Kcs 28-12; 40% subscription, 60% single ticket sale.

Number of persons engaged for opera in 1974-75: resident solo artists: 70; chorus members: 160; orchestra members: 234; conductors: 8; stage directors/producers: 4; set & costume designers: 4; choreographers: 4; corps de ballet: 120; administrative staff: *; technical, scenic, costume: *

*Serve all three theaters, info n/a.

Company maintains two orchs; builds all sets & 90% of its costumes in own workshops.

FINLAND

SUOMEN KANSALLISOOPPERA, Finnish National Opera, Albertinkatu 34 8, Helsinki, Finland; tel 90-642 6 1. Founded in 1873, pfs suspended 1879-81, 1915-17. Perf in present theater since 1914. Built in 1879, not as an opera house; seat cap 550, avg aud 500. Private non-profit organization w gvnmt subsidies; Bd Chmn Roger Lindberg; Pres Jaakko Numminen; Gen Dir Juhani Raiskinen; Bus Mng Simo Tavaste; Chief Cond Ulf Söderblom.

SEASON	OPENING Day	Month	CLOSING Day	Month	NO OF PFS	NO OF OPERAS	NO OF NEW PROD	NO OF NON-OPERA PFS*
73-74	30	Sep	30	May	226	n/a	11	106
74-75	3	Sep	6	Jun	320	n/a	7	190

*Operettas, musicals, ballet, etc.

FRANCE

World prems during these seasons: Rautavaara's *Apollo and Marsyas* 9/73; Kuusisto's *Muumin-opera* 12/74.

Repertoire 1973-74 — Bizet: *Carmen*; Janáček: *From the House of the Dead*; Madetoja: *Ostrobosnians*; Merikanto: *Elina's Death*; Mozart: *Nozze di Figaro*; Mussorgsky: *Fair at Sorochinsk*; Puccini: *Bohème, Tosca*; Rautavaara: *Apollo and Marsyas*; Rossini: *Barbiere di Siviglia*; Strauss, J: *Zigeunerbaron*; Szokolay: *Blood Wedding*; Verdi: *Don Carlo, Forza del destino, Rigoletto, Trovatore*; Wagner: *Tristan und Isolde*; Werle: *Journey*; et al.
1974-75 — Britten: *Midsummer Night's Dream*; Janáček: *From the House of the Dead*; Kuusisto: *Muumin-opera*; Madetoja; *Ostrobosnians*; Mozart *Così fan tutte*; Puccini: *Tosca*; Shostakovich: *Nose*; Verdi: *Otello, Rigoletto, Trovatore*; et al.

Company performs 25% of all operas in orig language. Two or three pfs broadcast live on radio per season; 1 pf videotaped. Annual tour of one opera, 4 pfs, to FIN: Kuoplo, Turku, Oulu; SWE: Stockholm; USSR: Minsk. Guest engagement as an exchange with Staatsoper Berlin, 2 pfs. Company has training program for 30 singers per season.

Budget for 1974-75 FMK 12,000,000 (US $3,372,000). Income: 14% box office, 80% gvnmt subsidies, 6% city gvnmt. Ticket prices: FMK 25-5; 30% subscription, 70% single ticket sale.

Number of persons engaged for 1974-75: resident solo artists: 42; guest solo artists: 10; chorus members: 40; orchestra members: 65; musical staff: 3; conductors: 4; stage directors/producers: 2; set & costume designers: 2; choreographers: 2; corps de ballet: 45; administrative staff: 12; technical, scenic, costume: 41.

Company maintains its own orch on a seasonal basis; builds all of its sets & costumes in own workshops.

FRANCE

OPÉRA DE LYON, Hotel de Ville de Lyon, 69001 Lyon, France; tel (78) 28 09 50 and 28 69 60. Founded in 1969. Perf at Opéra de Lyon since 1969. Built in 1831 as an opera house; seat cap 1,350, avg aud 1,050. Company owned and operated by city and state gvnmt under the Ministry of Cultural Affairs, which also operates the Auditorium, Théâtre des Célestins; Gen Dir Louis Erlo.

Season begins in Sept, ends in July, with abt 81 pfs of 6 operas, incl 6 new prods, & 5 non-operatic pfs each season.

World prems 1973-75: Martinu's *Trois souhaits* 5/73; Aperghis' *Jacques, le fataliste* 3/74.

Repertoire 1973-74 — Aperghis: *Jacques, le fataliste*; Beethoven: *Fidelio*; Honegger: *Jeanne d'Arc au bûcher*; Mozart: *Don Giovanni*; Purcell: *Dido and Aeneas*; Verdi: *Aida*.
1974-75 — Borodin: *Prince Igor*; Janáček: *Jenufa*; Kurka: *Good Soldier Schweik*; Mozart: *Così fan tutte, Entführung aus dem Serail*; Rameau: *Zoroastre*; Rossini: *Barbiere di Siviglia*; Wagner: *Tristan und Isolde*.

Company performs all operas in orig language.

Budget for opera & symphony for 1973 Fr 15,353,672 (US $3,002,000). Income: 15% box office; 85% gvnmt. Ticket prices: Fr 30-7; 60% subscription, 40% single ticket sale.

Number of people engaged by company 1974-75: resident solo artists: 9; chorus members: 44; orchestra members: 103; musical staff: 1; conductors: 2; stage directors/producers: 2; set & costume designers: 3; choreographers: 1; corps de ballet: 36; administrative staff: 1; technical, scenic, costume: 53.

Company uses local symph orch; builds all its sets and costumes in own workshops.

OPÉRA DE MARSEILLE, 1 rue Molière, Marseille, France; tel (91) 54 76 70. Perf at Opéra Municipal, built in 1787 as an opera house, seat cap 1,850, avg aud 1,500; pfs suspended 1919-24 for rebuilding of house after fire finished in Art Deco style. Company is owned and operated by city and provincial gvnmt under the Municipal Council of the City of Marseille. Asst to the Mayor Marcel Paoli; Art Dir Jacques Karpo; Mus Dir Diego Masson; Cond Maurice Susan; St Dir Tito Serebrinsky.

SEASON	OPENING Day	Month	CLOSING Day	Month	NO OF PFS	NO OF OPERAS	NO OF NEW PROD	NO OF NON-OPERA PFS*
73-74	12	Oct	9	Jun	95	13	6	48
74-75	11	Oct	8	Jun	99	13	4	49

*Operettas, musicals, ballet, concerts, etc.

World prem during these seasons: Bentoiu's *Hamlet* 5/74.

Repertoire 1973-74 — Bartók: *Bluebeard's Castle*; Bellini: *Puritani*; Bentoiu: *Hamlet*; Falla: *Vida breve*; Lecocq: *Fille de Madame Angot*; Mozart: *Così fan tutte*; Offenbach: *Contes d'Hoffmann*; Puccini: *Bohème*; Rameau: *Hippolyte et Aricie*; Schoenberg: *Erwartung*; Verdi: *Aida*; Wagner: *Götterdämmerung*; Weill: *Dreigroschenoper*.

1974-75 — Bellini: *Norma*; Gounod: *Faust*; Hahn: *Ciboulette*; Massenet: *Werther*; Mozart: *Clemenza di Tito*; Mussorgsky: *Boris Godunov, Khovanshchina*; Puccini: *Tosca*; Rosenfeld: *Miracle à la cour*; Vanzo: *Pêcheur d'étoiles*; Verdi: *Ballo in maschera*; Wagner: *Rheingold*; Weill: *Aufstieg und Fall der Stadt Mahagonny*.

Company performs most operas in orig language, some are repeated in French.

Budget for 1974-75 Fr 18,888,910 (US $4,256,000). Income: 10% box office, 85% City of Marseille, 5% other. Ticket prices: Fr 50-10; over 30% subscription.

Number of persons engaged for opera in 1974-75: resident solo artists: 12; guest solo artists : n/a; chorus members: 44; orchestra members: 70; musical staff: 3; conductors: 3; stage directors/producers: 2; set & costume designers: 1; choreographers: 1; corps de ballet: 22; administrative staff: 20; technical, scenic, costume: 81; in other capacities 1 animatrice culturelle (Pub Rel).

Company maintains its own orch on an annual basis; builds all sets & costumes in own workshops.

Policy and program determined by Art Dir J Karpo.

THÉÂTRE NATIONAL DE L'OPÉRA, Académie Nationale de Musique, 8 rue Scribe, Paris 9e, France; tel 742 2693. Founded in 1669. Perf at Théâtre National de l'Opéra since 1875. Built in 1875 as an opera house, seat cap 1,991. Company first perf at Salle du Jeu de Paume de la Bouteille 1669-71. Also perf at Jeu de Paume du Bel Air; Palais Royal; Menus-Plaisirs; Salle des Machines; Porte Saint-Martin; Montansier; Favart; Louvois; Le Peletier; Ventadour. Company owned and operated by the Gvnmt of France under the Réunion de Théâtres Lyriques Nationaux; Adm Rolf Liebermann; Adjt Adm Hugues R Gall; Tech Adv Joan Ingpen; Tech & Art Dir Bernard Daydé; Dir of Dance Raymond Franchetti.

SEASON	OPENING Day	Month	CLOSING Day	Month	NO OF PFS	NO OF OPERAS	NO OF NEW PROD	NO OF NON-OPERA PFS
73-74	12	Sep	7	Jul	116	12	8	n/a
74-75	24	Sep	26	Jul	116	15	5	n/a

Repertoire 1973-75 — Dukas: *Ariane et Barbe Bleue*; Gluck: *Orfeo ed Euridice*; Gounod: *Faust*; Massenet: *Don Quichotte, Manon*; Mozart: *Così fan tutte, Don Giovanni, Nozze di Figaro*; Offenbach: *Contes d'Hoffmann*; Puccini: *Bohème, Tosca*; Schoenberg: *Moses und Aron*; Saint-Saëns: *Samson et Dalila*; Strauss, R: *Elektra*; Verdi: *Don Carlo, Forza del destino, Trovatore, Vespri*; Wagner: *Parsifal*.

Company performs all operas in orig language. Three pfs broadcast live in 1974-75; no videotapes.

Budget n/a. Income: 20% box office, 80% gvnmt subsidies. Ticket prices: Fr 150-10; 20% subscription, 80% single ticket sale.

Number of persons engaged by company 1974-75: resident solo artists: 12; chorus members: 100; orchestra members: 180; musical staff: 5; conductors: 19; stage directors/producers: 5; set & costume designers: 10; choreographers: 7; corps de ballet: 200; administrative & clerical staff: 139; technical, scenic, costume: 354.

Company maintains its own orch on seasonal basis; builds 80% of its sets and 90% of its costumes in own workshops.

THÉÂTRE DES ARTS, rue Général Leclerc, Rouen, France; tel 70 48 50. Perf at Théâtre des Arts, built in 1962 as an opera house, seat cap 1,380, avg aud 1,000. Company is owned and operated by the city gvnmt (see below) & Gen Dir André Cabourg; Adm Fernand Seligmann; Mus Dir Paul Ethuin; Chief Des Roger Gaujoin.

SEASON	OPENING Day	Month	CLOSING Day	Month	NO OF PFS	NO OF PROD	NO OF NEW PROD	NO OF NON-OPERA PFS*
73-74	6	Oct	12	May	94	14	1	66
74-75	3	Oct	22	May	87	12	2	63

*Operettas, musicals, ballet, etc.

World prem during these seasons: Bondeville's *Antoine et Cléopatre* 3/74.

Repertoire 1973-74 — Boieldieu: *Dame blanche*; Bondeville: *Antoine et Cléopatre*; Charpentier: *Louise*; Debussy: *Pelléas et Mélisande*; Gounod: *Faust, Mireille*; Leoncavallo: *Pagliacci*; Mascagni: *Cavalleria rusticana*; Puccini: *Butterfly, Tosca*; Rossini: *Barbiere di Siviglia*; Strauss, J: *Fledermaus*; Verdi: *Trovatore*; Wagner: *Lohengrin*.

1974-75 — Adam: *Postillon de Lonjumeau*; Lesur: *Andréa del Sarto*; Massenet: *Jongleur de Notre Dame*; Mozart: *Così fan tutte, Zauberflöte*; Mussorgsky: *Boris Godunov*; Puccini: *Bohème*; Saint-Saëns: *Samson et Dalila*; Strauss, R: *Rosenkavalier*; Verdi: *Falstaff*; Wagner: *Walküre*.

Company performs 50% of all operas in orig language. No radio broadcasts, one pf videotaped per season. Guest engagement, 1973-74, Caen, Angers.

Budget and ticket prices n/a.

Number of persons engaged for 1974-75: chorus members: 42; orchestra members: 65; conductors: 2; set & costume designers: 2; choreographers: 1; corps de ballet: 25; administrative staff: 6; technical, scenic, costume: 44.

Company maintains its own orch on seasonal basis; builds 60% of its sets and 30% of costumes in own workshops.

Company policy is determined by Mayor Jean Lecanuet of Rouen and the Municipal Theater Commission: Pres Dr R Rambert, Deputy Mayor in Charge of the Arts; Th Simon; M Beghin; & other members of the Municipal Council.

OPÉRA DU RHIN, 19 Place Broglie, Strasbourg, France. Perf at Théâtre Municipal Strasbourg, seat cap 1,150, avg aud 1,100; Théâtre Municipal Colmar; and Théâtre Municipal Mulhouse. Company is owned and operated by the Province; Pres Joseph Fortmann; Art Dir Alain Lombard; Adm Dir Jean-Pierre Wurtz; Gen Dir of Tech Svces Nathaniel Merrill: Asst Art Dir Jean-Pierre Brossmann.

SEASON	OPENING Day	Month	CLOSING Day	Month	NO OF PFS	NO OF OPERAS	NO OF NEW PROD	NO OF NON-OPERA PFS*
1974-75	4	Oct	25	Jun	145	12	7	30

*Operettas, musicals, ballet, etc.

World prem during these seasons: Delerue's *Médys et Allyssio* 3/75.

Repertoire 1973-74 — Einem: *Besuch der alten Dame*; Hadyn: *Infedeltà delusa*; Lecocq: *Fille de Madame Angot*; Mozart: *Nozze di Figaro*; Prey: *Liaisons dangereuses*; Puccini: *Manon Lescaut*; Rameau: *Hippolyte et Aricie*; Verdi: *Otello*; Wagner: *Walküre*.

1974-75 — Bizet: *Carmen*; Britten: *Midsummer Night*; Delerue: *Médys et Allyssio*; Gounod: *Mireille*; Monteverdi: *Incoronazione di Poppea*; Mozart: *Zauberflöte*; Puccini: *Butterfly*; Strauss, J: *Fledermaus*; Strauss, R: *Elektra*; Verdi: *Don Carlo, Luisa Miller*; Wagner: *Fliegende Holländer*.

Company performs 75% of all operas in orig language. 1 pf per season is videotaped. Guest engagement 1973-75 to FR GER: Landau.

Budget n/a.

Number of persons engaged in 1974-75: resident solo artists: 20; chorus members: 46; orchestra members: 90 and 55*; administrative staff: 7.

Company uses local symph orchs of Strasbourg and Mulhouse*; builds 75% of its sets and costumes in own workshops.

FEDERAL REPUBLIC OF GERMANY

DEUTSCHE OPER BERLIN, Richard Wagner Str 10, 1 Berlin 10, FR Ger; tel 34381. Founded in 1910, pfs suspended 1943-45. Perf at Deutsche Oper Berlin since 1912. Built in 1912 as an opera house, seat cap 1,900, avg aud 1,615. Company owned and operated by city and state gvnmt under the Senate for Sciences and Art, West Berlin, which also manages the Schiller-Theater and Schlossparktheater; Senator Peter Löffler; Gen Int Prof Dr Egon Seefehlner; State Art Dir Heinz Kunze; Art Adm Dir Siegfried Müssig; Chefdram Claus H Henneberg.

SEASON	OPENING Day Month		CLOSING Day Month		NO OF PFS	NO OF OPERAS	NO OF NEW PROD	NO OF NON-OPERA PFS*
73-74	23	Aug	30	Jun	312	67	7	46
74-75	18	Aug	30	Jun	321	69	10	60

*Operettas, musicals, ballet, etc.

World prem during these seasons: Huber's *Jot* 9/73.

Repertoire 1973-74 — Bartók: *Bluebeard's Castle*; Beethoven: *Fidelio*; Berg: *Lulu*; Blacher: *Preussisches Märchen*; Borodin: *Prince Igor*; Cimarosa: *Matrimonio segreto*; Egk: *Revisor*; Einem: *Besuch der alten Dame*; Fioravanti: *Cantatrici villane*; Fortner: *Elisabeth Tudor*; Henze: *Junge Lord*; Huber: *Jot oder Wann kommt der Herr zurück?*; Humperdinck: *Hänsel und Gretel*; Leoncavallo: *Pagliacci*; Lortzing: *Wildschütz*; Mascagni: *Cavalleria rusticana*; Mozart: *Così fan tutte, Don Giovanni, Entführung aus dem Serail, Nozze di Figaro, Zauberflöte*; Mussorgsky: *Boris Godunov*; Nabokov: *Love's Labour's Lost*; Offenbach: *Contes d'Hoffmann*; Orff: *Carmina burana, Catulli carmina*; Paisiello: *Don Chisciotte della Mancia*; Pfitzner: *Palestrina*; Ponchielli: *Gioconda*; Puccini: *Bohème, Butterfly, Manon Lescaut, Tosca, Turandot*; Rossini: *Barbiere di Siviglia, Cenerentola, Turco in Italia*; Schoenberg: *Moses und Aron*; Strauss, J: *Fledermaus*; Strauss, R: *Ariadne auf Naxos, Elektra, Frau ohne Schatten, Rosenkavalier, Salome*; Stravinsky: *Oedipus Rex*; Tchaikovsky: *Eugene Onegin*; Verdi: *Aida, Attila, Don Carlo, Forza del destino, Otello, Rigoletto, Simon Boccanegra, Traviata, Trovatore*; Wagner: *Fliegende Holländer, Lohengrin, Meistersinger, Parsifal, Rheingold, Walküre, Siegfried, Götterdämmerung, Tannhäuser, Tristan und Isolde*; Weber: *Freischütz*.

1974-75 — Bartók: *Bluebeard's Castle*; Beethoven: *Fidelio*; Berg: *Lulu*; Blacher: *Preussisches Märchen*; Borodin: *Prince Igor*; Britten: *Death in Venice*; Cavalli: *Calisto*; Cimarosa: *Matrimonio segreto*; Egk: *Revisor*; Einem: *Besuch der alten Dame*; Fioravanti: *Cantatrici villane*; Humperdinck: *Hänsel und Gretel*; Leoncavallo: *Pagliacci*; Lortzing: *Wildschütz*; Mascagni: *Cavalleria rusticana*; Mozart: *Clemenza di Tito, Così fan tutte, Don Giovanni, Entführung aus dem Serail,*

Oca del Cairo, Nozze di Figaro, Zauberflöte; Mussorgsky: *Boris Godunov*; Nabokov: *Love's Labour's Lost*; Offenbach: *Contes d'Hoffmann*; Orff: *Carmina burana, Catulli carmina*; Pfitzner: *Palestrina*; Ponchielli: *Gioconda*; Puccini: *Bohème, Gianni Schicchi, Butterfly, Manon Lescaut, Suor Angelica, Tabarro, Tosca, Turandot*; Rossini: *Barbiere di Siviglia, Cenerentola, Turco in Italia*; Schoenberg: *Moses und Aron*; Strauss, J: *Fledermaus*; Strauss, R: *Arabella, Ariadne auf Naxos, Elektra, Frau ohne Schatten, Rosenkavalier, Salome*; Tchaikovsky: *Eugene Onegin*; Verdi: *Aida, Attila, Ballo in maschera, Don Carlo, Forza del destino, Otello, Rigoletto, Simon Boccanegra, Traviata, Trovatore*; Wagner: *Fliegende Holländer, Lohengrin, Meistersinger, Rheingold, Walküre, Siegfried, Götterdämmerung, Tannhäuser, Tristan und Isolde*; Weber: *Freischütz*.

Company performs 50% of all operas in orig language. Some pfs taped and rebroadcast on radio. Guest engagements 1973 — BEL: Brussels 5 pfs; FR GER: Schwetzingen 4 pfs, Kiel 1 pf, Bonn 2 pfs, Horchst 1 pf; 1974 — YUG: Belgrade 2 pfs; FR GER: Bonn 3 pfs; 1975 — FR GER: Schwetzingen 3 pfs. Company has training program for 5 singers per season.

Budget for 1975 DM 47,100,000 (US $ 17,050,000). Income: 85% gvnmt subsidies. Ticket prices: DM 36-4; 80% subscription, 20% single ticket sale.

Number of persons engaged for 1975-76: resident solo artists: 53; guest solo artists: 45; chorus members: 112; orchestra members: 142; musical staff: 8; conductors: 15; stage directors/producers: 6; set & costume designers: 8; choreographers: 2; corps de ballet: 56; administrative & clerical staff: 44; technical, scenic, costume: 363.

Company maintains its own orch on a permanent basis; builds all its sets and 80% of its costumes in own workshops.

BÜHNEN DER STADT BIELEFELD, 3 Brunnenstr, D 48 Bielefeld, FR Ger; tel 51 24 89. Founded in 1904, perf since then at Bühnen der Stadt Bielefeld. Built in 1904 as an opera house; seat cap 775, avg aud 620. Company owned and operated by Cultural Dept of the City of Bielefeld, which also manages Theater am Alten Markt; in charge Representative Dr Helmut Aufderheide; Int Peter Ebert until 1975, succeeded by Int Heiner Bruns; Gen Mus Dir George-W Schmöhe; Dram Dir Stavros Doufexis; Adm Dir Paul Gerhard Bohrenkämper.

SEASON	OPENING Day	OPENING Month	CLOSING Day	CLOSING Month	NO OF PFS	NO OF OPERAS	NO OF NEW PROD	NO OF NON-OPERA PFS*
73-74	15	Sep	13	Jul	178	11	9	104
74-75	6	Sep	17	Jul	173	16	8	100

*Operettas, musicals, ballet, etc.

World prem during these seasons: J B Smith's *Cuchulains Tod* 4/75.

Repertoire 1973-74 — Bizet: *Carmen*; Debussy: *Pelléas et Mélisande*; Lortzing: *Wildschütz*; Offenbach: *Contes d'Hoffmann*; Rossini: *Cenerentola*; Strauss, R: *Elektra*; Verdi: *Ballo in maschera, Falstaff*; Wagner: *Fliegende Holländer*. **1974-75** — d'Albert: *Tiefland*; Beethoven: *Fidelio*; Bizet: *Carmen*; Menotti: *Amahl*; Mozart: *Zauberflöte*; Mussorgsky: *Khovanshchina*; Offenbach: *Contes d'Hoffmann*; Schoenberg: *Glückliche Hand*; Smetana: *Bartered Bride*; Smith: *Cuchulains Tod*; Staden: *Seelewig*; Strauss, R: *Elektra*; Verdi: *Ballo in maschera, Simon Boccanegra*; Wagner: *Tristan und Isolde*; Weill: *Kleine Mahagonny*.

Budget n/a.

Number of persons engaged in 1974-75: 360.

Company uses local symph orch; builds 95% of its sets and costumes in own workshops.

THEATER DER STADT BONN, Am Böselagerhof 1, Bonn, FR Ger; tel 650931. Founded in 1953; operetta theater in 1946. Before '53, visits by Cologne Op. Perf at Sparten Theater since 1965. Built in 1965 for opera, theater, ballet; seat cap 896, avg aud 833. Prev theaters: Stadttheater Bonn, destroyed in 1944, seat cap 1,063; 1948-65 Bonner

Bürgerverein. Company owned and operated by City of Bonn, which also manages Stadttheater Bonn-Bad Godesberg GmbH; Chmn Dr Wolfgang Hesse; Gen Int Hans-Joachim Heyse; Chefdram Jochen Jachmann; Mus Dir Ralf Weikert; Oberspiell Opera Pierre Léon; Tech Dir Heinrich Ritter; Adm Mng Fritz Wiesmeier; Adm Albert Neffgen.

SEASON	OPENING Day Month	CLOSING Day Month	NO OF PFS	NO OF OPERAS	NO OF NEW PROD	NO OF NON-OPERA PFS*
73-74	2 Sep	5 Jul	85	8	6	55
74-75	1 Sep	9 Jul	93	7	6	19

*Ballet & theater only.

World prems during these seasons: Engelmann's *Revue* 10/73; Valdambrini's *Der gestiefelte Kater* 3/75.

Repertoire 1973-74 — Engelmann: *Revue*; Gershwin: *Porgy and Bess*; Massenet: *Don Quichotte*; Offenbach: *Banditen*; Prokofiev: *Love for Three Oranges*; Puccini: *Tosca*; Strauss, R: *Arabella, Salome*.
1974-75 — Dvořák: *Rusalka*; Mozart: *Nozze di Figaro*; Valdambrini: *Gestiefelte Kater*; Verdi: *Rigoletto*; Wagner: *Fliegende Holländer*.

Company performs over 5% of all operas in orig language. No radio broadcasts; occasional videotape broadcasts of scenes. Opera guest engagements 1971-75 incl FR GER: Solingen 53 pfs, Recklinghausen 9 pfs, Gummersbach 6 pfs; LUX: 4 pfs.

Budget for 1974-75 DM 21,293,400 (US $8,858,000). Income: 12% box office, 38% city gvnmt, 50% federal gvnmt. Ticket prices: DM 18-5; 79% subscription, 16% single ticket sales, 5% complimentary.

Number of persons engaged for 1974-75: resident solo artists: 19; guest solo artists: 54; chorus members: 39; orchestra members: 99; conductors: 4; stage directors/producers: 7; set & costume designers: 8; choreographers: 3; corps de ballet: 25; administrative and clerical staff: 10; technical, scenic, costume: 160.

Company uses local symph orch; builds all sets & costumes in own workshops.

Policy determined by City Council, Dept of Culture & Chmn Dr Brüse.

OPER DER STADT KÖLN, Offenbachplatz, 5 Cologne 1, FR Ger; tel 2076-1. Perf at Oper der Stadt Köln since 1957. Built in 1957 as an opera house, seat cap 1,346. Company owned and operated by City of Cologne, which also manages Schauspiel and Tanz-Forum; State Cult Representative Dr Kurt Hackenberg; Int Dr Michael Hampe; Deputy Gen Mus Dir Georg Fischer; Dram Dir Hans Neugebauer, Dr Klaus-Peter Kehr; Tech Dir Helmut Grosser, Dr Fritzdieter Gerhards.

SEASON	OPENING Day Month	CLOSING Day Month	NO OF PFS	NO OF OPERAS	NO OF NEW PROD	NO OF NON-OPERA PFS
73-74	14 Sep	20 Jul	—	—	6	—
74-75	21 Sep	19 Jul	—	—	6	—

Repertoire 1973-74 — Auber: *Fra Diavolo*; Fortner: *Elisabeth Tudor*; Haydn: *Mondo della luna*; Mozart: *Entführung aus dem Serail*; Strauss, R: *Ariadne auf Naxos*; Verdi: *Don Carlo, Traviata*; Wagner: *Meistersinger*.
1974-75 — Debussy: *Pelléas et Mélisande*; Mozart: *Idomeneo, Nozze di Figaro*; Puccini: *Bohème*; Tchaikovsky: *Eugene Onegin*.

Company performs 25% of all operas in orig language. It has a training prgm for singers.

Budget n/a.

Number of persons engaged in 1974-75 n/a.

Company uses local symph orch; builds 80% of its sets and all costumes in own workshops.

DEUTSCHE OPER AM RHEIN, Theatergemeinschaft Düsseldorf-Duisburg, Heinrich Heine Allee 16, Düsseldorf, FR Ger; tel 89081. Founded in 1956. Perf at Deutsche Oper am Rhein and at Theater der Stadt Duisburg, König Heinrich Platz, since 1956. Built in 1875, orig not as an opera house, destroyed and rebuilt several times; seat cap 1,342; avg aud 1,288. Company owned and operated by cities of Düsseldorf and Duisburg; Gen Int Prof Dr Grischa Barfuss; Adm Dir Dieter Scheible; Opera Dir Georg Reinhardt; Gen Mus Dir Prof Günther Wich; Dir Scenic Dept Heinrich Wendel.

Season begins in September, with the first performance alternating between Düsseldorf and Duisburg, and terminates in July. In Düsseldorf, 300 pfs; in Duisburg, 150. Repertory approx 50 operas, 20 ballets; 11 new prods each year.

Repertoire 1973-74 — Beethoven: *Fidelio*; Berg: *Wozzeck*; Berlioz: *Damnation de Faust*; Cavalieri: *Rappresentazione di anima*; Cavalli: *Ormindo*; Donizetti: *Elisir*; Handel: *Saul*; Hindemith: *Cardillac*; Humperdinck: *Hänsel und Gretel*; Janácek: *Cunning Little Vixen, Jenufa, Katya Kabanova, Makropoulos Affair*; Kelemen: *Belagerungszustand*; Lortzing: *Zar und Zimmermann*; Mozart: *Entführung aus dem Serail, Mitridate, re di Ponto, Nozze di Figaro, Zauberflöte*; Nicolai: *Lustigen Weiber*; Orff: *Carmina burana, Mond*; Puccini: *Bohème, Gianni Schicchi, Butterfly, Manon Lescaut, Tabarro, Tosca*; Rossini: *Barbiere di Siviglia, Cenerentola, Italiana in Algeri*; Schoenberg: *Moses und Aron*; Smetana: *Bartered Bride*; Strauss, R: *Arabella, Ariadne auf Naxos, Elektra, Rosenkavalier, Salome, Schweigsame Frau*; Tchaikovsky: *Eugene Onegin*; Verdi: *Aida, Don Carlo, Macbeth, Otello*; Wagner: *Fliegende Holländer, Lohengrin, Meistersinger, Parsifal, Rheingold, Walküre, Siegfried, Götterdämmerung*; Weber: *Freischütz*; Zimmermann: *Soldaten*.

1974-75 — Beethoven: *Fidelio*; Berg: *Wozzeck*; Britten: *Death in Venice*; Cavalieri: *Rappresentazione di anima*; Donizetti: *Elisir*; Giordano: *Andrea Chénier*; Handel: *Saul*; Humperdinck: *Hänsel und Gretel*; Janácek: *Cunning Little Vixen, Excursions of Mr Broucek, Jenufa, Katya Kabanová, Makropoulos Affair*; Kelemen: *Belagerungszustand*; Lortzing: *Zar und Zimmermann*; Mozart: *Don Giovanni, Entführung aus dem Serail, Mitridate, re di Ponto, Nozze di Figaro, Zauberflöte*; Nicolai: *Lustigen Weiber*; Orff: *Carmina burana, Kluge*; Puccini: *Bohème, Gianni Schicchi, Butterfly, Manon Lescaut, Tabarro, Tosca, Turandot*; Rossini: *Barbiere di Siviglia, Cenerentola, Comte Ory, Italiana in Algeri*; Schoenberg: *Moses und Aron*; Smetana: *Bartered Bride*; Strauss, R: *Arabella, Ariadne auf Naxos, Elektra, Rosenkavalier, Salome, Schweigsame Frau*; Verdi: *Don Carlo, Otello*; Wagner: *Fliegende Holländer, Lohengrin, Meistersinger, Parsifal, Rheingold, Walküre, Siegfried, Götterdämmerung, Tannhäuser*; Weber: *Freischütz*; Wolf-Ferrari: *Donne curiose*; Zimmermann: *Soldaten*.

Company performs 50% of all operas in orig language. Annual tour; 1973-74 — YUG: Zagreb; BEL: Ghent; SWE: Stockholm; SPA: Barcelona. Subsidiary company: Studio for Young Opera Singers.

Budget n/a.

Number of persons engaged for 1974-75: resident & guest solo artists: 78; chorus members: 85; orchestra members: 102; musical staff: 10; conductors: 10; stage directors/producers: 8; set & costume designers: 13; choreographers: 8; corps de ballet: 71; technical, scenic, costume: 27.

Company performs with Düsseldorf and Duisburg symph orchs, respectively; builds all sets and costumes in own workshops.

BÜHNEN DER STADT ESSEN, Theaterplatz 11, 43 Essen 1, FR Ger; tel 0201 181 4541. Founded in 1892. Perf at Bühnen der Stadt Essen Theater since 1950. Built in 1950 as an opera house; seat cap 786. Prev theater: Opernhaus Essen, used 1892-1944, seat cap 800. Company owned and operated by the City of Essen; Gen Int Dr Jürgen-Dieter Waidelich; Gen Mus Dir Prof Heinz Wallberg; Stage Mng Nikolaus Sulzberger; Chief Des Ekkehard Kröhn; Tech Dir Siegfried Ehrenberg.

SEASON	OPENING Day	Month	CLOSING Day	Month	NO OF PFS	NO OF OPERAS	NO OF NEW PROD	NO OF NON-OPERA PFS*
73-74	8	Sep	11	Jul	190	n/a	8	84
74-75	15	Sep	16	Jul	203	n/a	10	96

*Operettas, musicals, ballet, etc.

Repertoire 1973-74 — Donizetti: *Lucia*; Flotow: *Martha*; Strauss, J: *Fledermaus*; Strauss, R: *Elektra, Rosenkavalier*; Verdi: *Aida*; et al.

1974-75 — Beethoven: *Fidelio*; Donizetti: *Lucia*; Fioravanti: *Cantatrici villane*; Gershwin: *Porgy and Bess*; Henze: *Junge Lord*; Mozart: *Entführung aus dem Serail*; Ravel: *Heure espagnole*; Strauss, R: *Rosenkavalier*; Verdi: *Aida, Rigoletto*.

Company performs 75% of all operas in orig language. Pfs broadcast on radio once a year. Exchange guest engagements 1971-75 incl BEL: Brussels; FR GER: Recklinghausen Ruhrfestspiele.

Budget for 1974-75 DM 19,130,000 (US $7,958,000). Income: 18% box office, 82% city gvnmt. Tickets sold 55% by subscription, 45% single ticket sale.

Number of persons engaged in 1974-75: resident solo artists: 22; guest solo artists: 18; chorus members: 40; conductors: 9; stage directors/producers: 8; set & costume designers: 14; choreographers: 3; administrative staff: n/a.

Company uses local symph orch; builds all sets and costumes in own workshop.

FRANKFURTER OPER, Untermainanlage 11, D 6000 Frankfurt am Main, FR Ger; tel 0611/25621. Perf at Frankfurt Oper, seat cap 1,387. Company owned and operated by City of Frankfurt; Gen Dir Christoph von Dohnányi; Adm Dir Ulrich Schwab; Deputy Dir Gerard Mortier; Tech Dir Max von Vequel.

SEASON	OPENING Day Month	CLOSING Day Month	NO OF PFS	NO OF OPERAS	NO OF NEW PROD	NO OF NON-OPERA PFS*
73-74	15 Aug	1 Jul	n/a	42	5	n/a
74-75	21 Aug	22 Jun	197	38	7	52

*Operettas, musicals, ballet, etc.

Repertoire 1973-74 — Bartók: *Bluebeard's Castle*; Beethoven: *Fidelio*; Berg: *Lulu, Wozzeck*; Bizet: *Carmen*; Debussy: *Pelléas et Mélisande*; Donizetti: *Don Pasquale*; Gluck: *Orfeo ed Euridice*; Gounod: *Faust*; Henze: *Junge Lord*; Humperdinck: *Hänsel und Gretel*; Janácek: *Katya Kabanová*; Lortzing: *Wildschütz*; Mozart: *Don Giovanni, Entführung aus dem Serail, Zauberflöte*; Offenbach: *Contes d'Hoffmann*; Prokofiev: *Fiery Angel*; Puccini: *Bohème, Turandot*; Rossini: *Barbiere di Siviglia*; Schoenberg: *Erwartung, Moses und Aron*; Smetana: *Bartered Bride*; Strauss, J: *Fledermaus*; Strauss, R: *Arabella, Elektra, Frau ohne Schatten, Rosenkavalier, Salome*; Tchaikovsky: *Eugene Onegin*; Verdi: *Ballo in maschera, Don Carlo, Falstaff, Forza del destino, Rigoletto, Traviata*; Wagner: *Lohengrin, Meistersinger, Parsifal, Tannhäuser*; Weber: *Freischütz*.

1974-75 — Bartók: *Bluebeard's Castle*; Berg: *Lulu, Wozzeck*; Bizet: *Carmen*; Donizetti: *Don Pasquale*; Gounod: *Faust*; Henze: *Bassariden*; Humperdinck: *Hänsel und Gretel*; Janácek: *Katya Kabanová*; Lortzing: *Wildschütz*; Mozart: *Così fan tutte, Don Giovanni, Entführung aus dem Serail, Nozze di Figaro, Zauberflöte*; Puccini: *Tosca, Bohème*; Schoenberg: *Erwartung, Moses und Aron*; Smetana: *Bartered Bride*; Strauss, J: *Fledermaus*; Strauss, R: *Arabella, Elektra, Frau ohne Schatten, Rosenkavalier, Salome*; Verdi: *Ballo in maschera, Don Carlo, Falstaff, Forza del destino, Rigoletto, Traviata*; Wagner: *Götterdämmerung, Lohengrin, Meistersinger, Parsifal*; Weber: *Freischütz*.

Company performs 75% of all operas in orig language. Guest engagements incl BEL: Flanders Fest 2 pfs; SWI: Zurich 1 pf; UK: Edinburgh Fest 2 pfs.

Budget n/a. Company income: 10% box office receipts, 90% gvnmt subsidies. Ticket prices: DM 32-3.

Number of persons engaged for 1974-75: resident solo artists: 63; guest solo artists: n/a; chorus members: 66; orchestra members: 104; musical staff: 12; conductors: 7; stage directors/producers: 5; set & costume designers: 10; choreographers: 2; corps de ballet: 30; administrative staff: 19; technical, scenic, costume: n/a.

Company maintains its own orch on seasonal basis; builds all of its sets and costumes in own workshops.

HAMBURGISCHE STAATSOPER, Gr Theaterstr 34, 2 Hamburg 36, FR Ger; tel 35 11 51. Founded in 1678. Pfs were suspended in 17th & 18th centy and in 1945. Perf at Hamburgische Staatsoper since 1926. Built in 1926 as an opera house, rebuilt in 1955; seat cap 1,675, avg aud 1,500. Prev theater: Gänsemarkt, 1678-1825; seat cap abt 2,000. Perf also: Volksoper 1925-1926; Thalia Theater 1944; Schauspielhaus 1946-48; Musikhalle 1944-46; Besenbinderhof 1954-55. Company owned and operated by Freie und Hansestadt Hamburg, which also manages Deutsches Schauspielhaus and Thalia Theater; Mayor Dr Dieter Biallas; Int Prof August Everding; Dir Staatsoper Rolf Mares; Gen Mus Dir Prof Horst Stein.

SEASON	OPENING Day Month	CLOSING Day Month	NO OF PFS	NO OF OPERAS	NO OF NEW PROD	NO OF NON-OPERA PFS*
73-74	14 Aug	30 Jun	317	53	15	49
74-75	29 Aug	22 Jun	301	55	11	65

*Operettas, musicals, ballet, etc.

Repertoire 1973-74 — Beethoven: *Fidelio*; Berg: *Wozzeck*; Britten: *Billy Budd*; Bussotti: *Lorenzaccio*; Cimarosa: *Matrimonio segreto*; Donizetti: *Don Pasquale, Lucia*; Humperdinck: *Hänsel und Gretel*; Janáček: *From the House of the Dead, Jenufa*; Leoncavallo: *Pagliacci*; Lortzing: *Wildschütz, Zar und Zimmermann*; Mascagni: *Cavalleria rusticana*; Mozart: *Così fan tutte, Don Giovanni, Entführung aus dem Serail, Nozze di Figaro, Zauberflöte*; Mussorgsky: *Boris Godunov*; Nicolai: *Lustigen Weiber*; Offenbach: *Contes d'Hoffmann*; Pound: *Testament de Villon*; Puccini: *Bohème, Butterfly, Tosca*; Schoenberg: *Moses und Aron*; Smetana: *Bartered Bride*; Strauss, R: *Arabella, Ariadne auf Naxos, Capriccio, Elektra, Rosenkavalier, Salome, Schweigsame Frau*; Telemann: *Pimpinone*; Verdi: *Aida, Ballo in maschera, Don Carlo, Falstaff, Forza del destino, Nabucco, Rigoletto, Trovatore, Vespri*; Wagner: *Fliegende Holländer, Lohengrin, Rheingold, Walküre, Siegfried, Götterdämmerung, Tristan und Isolde*; Weber: *Freischütz*.

1974-75 — Beethoven: *Fidelio*; Berg: *Wozzeck*; Bialas: *Gestiefelte Kater*; Britten: *Billy Budd*; Donizetti: *Don Pasquale, Lucia*; Humperdinck: *Hänsel und Gretel*; Janáček: *Jenufa*; Leoncavallo: *Pagliacci*; Lortzing: *Wildschütz, Zar und Zimmermann*; Mascagni: *Cavalleria rusticana*; Massenet: *Don Quichotte*; Motte: *So oder so*; Mozart: *Così fan tutte, Don Giovanni, Entführung aus dem Serail, Nozze di Figaro, Zauberflöte*; Mussorgsky: *Boris Godunov, Khovanshchina*; Nicolai: *Lustigen Weiber*; Offenbach: *Contes d'Hoffmann*; Puccini: *Bohème, Butterfly, Tosca*; Rossini: *Cenerentola*; Schoenberg: *Moses und Aron*; Smetana: *Bartered Bride*; Strauss, R: *Arabella, Ariadne auf Naxos, Capriccio, Elektra, Rosenkavalier, Salome, Schweigsame Frau*; Telemann: *Pimpinone*; Verdi: *Aida, Ballo in maschera, Don Carlo, Falstaff, Forza del destino, Nabucco, Rigoletto, Traviata, Trovatore, Vespri*; Wagner: *Fliegende Holländer, Lohengrin, Meistersinger, Rheingold, Walküre, Siegfried, Götterdämmerung*; Weber: *Freischütz*.

Company performs 75% of all operas in orig language. Guest engagements 1971-75 incl HOL: Tilburg/The Hague 5 pfs; FR GER: Kiel 1 pf, Munich 1 pf, Schwetzingen 3 pfs, Wolfsburg 1 pf, Bremerhaven 1 pf; ITA: Florence 3 pfs, Venice 3 pfs; SPA: Granada 3 pfs; ISR: Caesarea, Jerusalem, Tel Aviv 9 pfs.

Budget for 1974-75 estim DM 44,304,800 (US $18,431,000). Income: 16.5% box office; 82% gvnmt; 0.3% priv/corp/fndt grants; 1.2% other income. Ticket prices: DM 50-2; 40% subscription, 60% single ticket sale.

Number of persons engaged in 1974-75: 826; resident solo artists: 75; guest solo artists: 28; chorus members: 83; orchestra members: 134; musical staff: 19; conductors: 6; stage directors/producers: 3; set & costume designers: 5; choreographers: 2; corps de ballet: 56; administrative staff: 12; technical, scenic, costume: 335.

Company uses local symph orch; builds all sets and costumes in own workshops.

Policy determined by Supervisory Commtt: Mayor Dr Dieter Biallas; Int Prof August Everding; Dir Staatsoper Rolf Mares; Dir of Senate Carl Heinrich Bonnet; Walter Matthies; Herbert Samuel; Dr Heinz Liebrecht; Eduard Söring; Dr Alfred C Toepfer; Dr Wolf Wöhler; Dr Fred Eckhard; Rüdiger Köhn; Hans Lederer.

NIEDERSÄCHSISCHE STAATSTHEATER HANNOVER Gmbh, STAATSOPER,

Opernplatz 1, Hannover, FR Ger; tel 0511/168-1. Founded in 1689, perf annually except 1714-86, 1944-45. Perf at Staatsoper since 1852. Built 1845-52 as an opera house; seat cap 1,503, avg aud 1,202. Company first perf at Schlosstheater Hannover 1689-1714. Also perf at Galeriegebäude Hannover-Herrenhausen 1943-50. Company is owned and operated by the city, state and national gvnmts; adm dept also manages the Staats-theater Hannover, Staatsschauspiel. Gen Int Staatsoper Prof Günter Roth; Gen Mus Dir George Alexander Albrecht; Chief Dram Dr Peter von Magnus; Dir of Prgrm & Art Mng Dieter Kreuzer; Choreographer Gise Furtwängler.

SEASON	OPENING Day Month		CLOSING Day Month		NO OF PFS	NO OF OPERAS	NO OF NEW PROD	NO OF NON-OPERA PFS*
73-74	28	Aug	5	Jul	314	41	11	103
74-75	28	Aug	5	Jul	325	34	8	111

*Operettas, musicals, ballets, etc.

Repertoire 1973-74 — Beethoven: *Fidelio*; Bizet: *Carmen*; Britten: *Albert Herring, Owen Wingrave*; Donizetti: *Lucia*; Flotow: *Martha*; Henze: *Elegy for Young Lovers*; Humperdinck: *Hänsel und Gretel*; Klebe: *Tödlichen Wünsche*; Kodály: *Háry János*; Leoncavallo: *Pagliacci*; Mascagni: *Cavalleria rusticana*; Mozart: *Così fan tutte, Don Giovanni, Entführung aus dem Serail, Nozze di Figaro,Zauberflöte*; Mussorgsky: *Boris Godunov*; Nicolai: *Lustigen Weiber*; Pfitzner: *Palestrina*; Puccini: *Bohème, Gianni Schicchi, Butterfly, Tabarro, Tosca*; Rossini: *Barbiere di Siviglia, Cenerentola*; Smetana: *Bartered Bride*; Strauss, J: *Fledermaus*; Strauss, R: *Arabella, Capriccio, Rosenkavalier*; Tchaikovsky: *Pique Dame*; Verdi: *Ballo in maschera, Don Carlo, Rigoletto*; Wagner: *Fliegende Holländer, Meistersinger, Tannhäuser, Tristan und Isolde, Walküre*.

1974-75 — d'Albert: *Tiefland*; Beethoven: *Fidelio*; Bizet: *Carmen*; Britten: *Albert Herring, Owen Wingrave*; Gershwin: *Porgy and Bess*; Humperdinck: *Hänsel und Gretel*; Klebe: *Tödlichen Wünsche*; Leoncavallo: *Pagliacci*; Lortzing: *Zar und Zimmermann*; Mascagni: *Cavalleria rusticana*; Mozart: *Così fan tutte, Don Giovanni, Entführung aus dem Serail, Zauberflöte*; Mussorgsky: *Boris Godunov*; Puccini: *Gianni Schicchi, Butterfly, Tabarro, Tosca*; Rossini: *Barbiere di Siviglia*; Smetana: *Bartered Bride*; Strauss, J: *Fledermaus*; Strauss, R: *Rosenkavalier*; Tchaikovsky: *Pique Dame*; Verdi: *Don Carlo, Rigoletto, Trovatore*; Wagner: *Fliegende Holländer, Meistersinger, Walküre, Siegfried, Götterdämmerung, Tristan und Isolde*.

Company performs 75% of all operas in orig language. Guest engagement: Leverkusen City Theater 2 pfs.

Budget for 1974-75 DM 18,404,000 (US $7,656,000). Income: 13.3% box office, 86.7% gvnmt. Ticket prices: DM 24-9, 60% subscription, 40% single ticket sale.

Number of persons engaged for 1974-75: resident solo artists: 43; guest solo artists: 12; chorus members: 60; orchestra members: 99; musical staff: 4; conductors: 6; stage directors/producers: 3; set & costume designers: 3; choreographers: 3; corps de ballet: 42; administrative staff: 3; technical, scenic, costume: 315.

Company uses local symph orch; builds all its sets and costumes in own workshops.

Company administration: Gen Int Prof G Roth; Adm Dir Wilhelm Homann; Mng Bruno Grigo.

BADISCHES STAATSTHEATER KARLSRUHE, Baumeisterstr 11, Karlsruhe, FR Ger; tel 0721/1521. Founded in 1747. Pfs were suspended in 1944. Perf at Badisches Staats-theater since 1975. Built in 1975 as an opera house, seat cap 1,400. Prev theater: Karlsruhe-Durlach. Company owned and operated by Province Baden-Württemberg; Minister of Culture Prof Hahn; Gen Int Hans-Georg Rudolph; Gen Mus Dir Arthur Grüber; Dram Dir Willi Rohde; Ballet Dir Manfred Taubert.

SEASON	OPENING Day Month		CLOSING Day Month		NO OF PFS	NO OF PROD	NO OF NEW PROD	NO OF NON-OPERA PFS*
73-74	24	Sep	21	Jun	n/a	22	6	9
74-75	29	Sep	29	Jun	n/a	21	4	7

*Operettas, musicals, ballet, etc.

Repertoire 1973-74 — Cavalli: *Giasone*; Mozart: *Nozze di Figaro*; Mussorgsky: *Fair at Sorochinsk*; Offenbach: *Contes d'Hoffmann*; Tippett: *Midsummer Marriage*; Wagner: *Fliegende Holländer*.

1974-75 — Beethoven: *Fidelio*; Gluck: *Iphigénie en Aulide*; Mozart: *Così fan tutte*; Orff: *Kluge*; Puccini: *Turandot*; Smetana: *Bartered Bride*; Stravinsky: *Mavra*; Verdi: *Nabucco, Simon Boccanegra*; Wagner: *Parsifal, Tannhäuser*; Salomon: *Jason and Medea*.

Company performs 5% of all operas in orig language. Several pfs taped and rebroadcast. Annual tour in 1973-74 incl FR GER: Leverkusen, Worms; FRA: Strasbourg; LUX: Esch-sur-Alzette. Company gives exchange engagements.

Budget n/a. Ticket prices: DM 22.50-6.50.

Number of persons engaged in 1974-75: resident solo artists: 75; guest solo artists: 4; chorus members: 44; orchestra members: 80; conductors: 7; stage directors/producers: 13; set & costume designers: 2; choreographers: 2; corps de ballet: 26; administrative staff: 24.

Company maintains its own orch on a seasonal basis; builds all sets and costumes in own workshops.

STAATSTHEATER KASSEL, 35 Kassel, FR Ger; tel 0561/13213. Founded in 1701 and perf annually since then. Perf at Staatstheater Kassel since 1959. Built in 1959 as an opera house, seat cap 954, avg aud 765. Company owned and operated by the City of Kassel and Province of Hessen; Int Dr Peter Löffler; Gen Mus Dir James Lockhart.

SEASON	OPENING Day	Month	CLOSING Day	Month	NO OF PFS	NO OF PROD	NO OF NEW PROD	NO OF NON-OPERA PFS*
73-74		Sep		Jun	223	24	11	92
74-75		Sep		Jun	203	18	10	98

*Operettas, musicals, ballet, etc.

Repertoire 1973-74 — Berg: *Lulu*; Bizet: *Carmen*; Britten: *Midsummer Night*; Donizetti: *Convenienze/Viva la Mamma, Lucia*; Mozart: *Idomeneo, Nozze di Figaro, Zauberflöte*; Offenbach: *Contes d'Hoffmann*; Strauss, R: *Salome*; Wagner: *Rheingold, Walküre, Siegfried, Götterdämmerung*; Weber: *Freischütz*.

1974-75 — Bizet: *Carmen*; Britten: *Death in Venice, Midsummer Night*; Cimarosa: *Matrimonio segreto*; Donizetti: *Convenienze/Viva la Mamma, Lucia*; Giordano: *Andrea Chénier*; Mozart: *Nozze di Figaro, Zauberflöte*; Offenbach: *Contes d'Hoffmann*; Ravel: *Heure espagnole*; Strauss, R: *Ariadne auf Naxos, Salome*; Tchaikovsky: *Pique Dame*; Verdi: *Aida*; Walton: *Bear*; Weber: *Freischütz*.

Company performs 5% of all operas in orig language.

Budget for 1974-75 DM 19,000,000 (US $7,904,000). Income: 15% box office; 85% city gvnmt. Ticket prices: DM 21-4.50; 20% subscription, 80% single ticket sale.

Number of persons engaged in 1974-75: resident solo artists: 32; chorus members: 42; orchestra members: 80; musical staff: 12; conductors: 7; stage directors/producers: 6; set & costume designers: 7; choreographers: 2; corps de ballet: 22; administrative and clerical staff: 41; technical, scenic, costume: 262.

Company uses own orch on a seasonal basis; builds 90% of its sets and 80% of its costumes in own workshops.

BÜHNEN DER LANDESHAUPTSTADT KIEL, Rathausplatz, Kiel, FR Ger; tel 901/28 92. Founded in 1907. Perf at Opernhaus since 1907. Built 1905-7 as an opera house; rebuilt 1950-53; seat cap 984, avg aud 700. Company owned and operated by City of Kiel, which also manages the Schauspielhaus with Studiobühne and Jugendtheater; Gen Int Dr Joachim Klaiber; Gen Mus Dir Klaus Tennstedt; Dram Dir Heinz Lukas-Kindermann; Tech Dir Hans Vietor.

SEASON	OPENING Day	Month	CLOSING Day	Month	NO OF PFS	NO OF OPERAS	NO OF NEW PROD	NO OF NON-OPERA PFS*
73-74	15	Sep	6	Jul	218	12	—	83
74-75	21	Sep	29	Jun	181	12	—	78

*Operettas, musicals, ballet, etc.

World prems during these seasons: Davidsson's *Geparden, impotent* 1/75; Auber/Honolka's *Das Glas Wasser* 3/75.

Repertoire 1973-74 — Britten: *Let's Make an Opera*; Fortner: *Elisabeth Tudor*; Gershwin: *Porgy and Bess*; Haydn: *Infedeltà premiata*; Lortzing: *Waffenschmied*; Mozart: *Così fan tutte, Nozze di Figaro*; Puccini: *Tosca*; Rossini: *Barbiere di Siviglia*; Strauss, R: *Salome*; Verdi: *Aida*; Wagner: *Parsifal*.

1974-75 — Auber/Honolka: *Glas Wasser*; Britten: *Death in Venice*; Dessau: *Verurteilung des Lukullus*; Lortzing: *Undine*; Mozart: *Così fan tutte, Nozze di Figaro, Zauberflöte*; Puccini: *Manon Lescaut, Tosca*; Strauss, R: *Elektra*; Verdi: *Rigoletto*; Wagner: *Parsifal*.

Subsidiary company for experimental works: Opernstudio, 10-15 pfs annually.

Budget, for both opera and theater: 1974 DM 16,752,555 (US $6,064,000). Income: 10% box office; 85.5% gvnmt; 0.2% private, corp & fndn grants; 4.3% other. Ticket prices: DM 16-4.

Number of persons engaged for 1974: resident solo artists: 21; guest solo artists: 9; chorus members: 37; orchestra members: 75; conductors: 6; stage directors/producers: 2; set & costume designers: 5; choreographers: 2; corps de ballet: 19; technical, scenic, costume: 108.

Company maintains own orch on seasonal basis; builds 99% of its sets and costumes in own workshops.

VEREINIGTE STÄDTISCHE BÜHNEN KREFELD-MÖNCHENGLADBACH, Theaterplatz, 415 Krefeld, FR Ger; tel 02151/2 84 84. Perf at Vereinigte Städtische Bühnen Krefeld-Mönchengladbach. Theater in Krefeld built in 1963, seat cap 832; Mönchengladbach in 1965, seat cap 735. Company owned and operated by City; Gen Int Joachim Fontheim; Gen Mus Dir Robert Satanowski; Principal Cond John Bell; Dramatg Dr Paul W Becker, Gert Becker and Hans Ulrich Kaegi.

SEASON	OPENING Day	Month	CLOSING Day	Month	NO OF PFS	NO OF PROD	NO OF NEW PROD	NO OF NON-OPERA PFS*
73-74	20	Sep	11	Jul	220	10	7	3
74-75	19	Sep	10	Jul	220	10	7	3

*Operettas, musicals, ballet, etc.

Repertoire 1973-74 — Lortzing: *Waffenschmied*; Mozart: *Zauberflöte*; Strauss, R: *Elektra*; Weber: *Freischütz*.
1974-75 — Offenbach: *Contes d'Hoffmann*; Penderecki: *Teufel von Loudun*; Puccini: *Tosca*; Verdi: *Falstaff*.

Company performs 5% of all operas in orig language. Several pfs taped and rebroadcast. Guest engagement 1972-73 in Cologne.

Budget n/a. Ticket prices: DM 15-5; 25% subscription.

Number of persons engaged in 1974-75; resident solo artists: 69*; guest solo artists: 4; chorus members: 34; orchestra members: 77; musical staff: 3; conductors: 4; stage directors/producers: 7; set & costume designers: 12; choreographers: 2; corps de ballet: 19; administrative staff: 60; technical, scenic, costume: 103.
*Opera 30, theater 39

Company uses its own orch on a seasonal basis; builds 80% of its sets and costumes in own workshops.

NATIONALTHEATER MANNHEIM, Mozartstr 9, Mannheim, FR Ger; tel 0621/1900-1. Founded in 1779. Pfs were suspended 1943-45. Perf at Nationaltheater Mannheim since 1779. Built in 1779, seat cap 1,200. Destroyed in 1943 and rebuilt 1957; seat cap big theater 1,000, small theater 570, studio 100. Between 1945-56 company perf in var other houses. Company owned and operated by City of Mannheim and Province Baden-Württemberg; Head Cultural Dept, Mayor Manfred David; Int Arnold Petersen; Gen Mus Dir & Dir of Opera Hans Wallat; Prgm Dir Friedrich Meyer-Oertel; Chief Dramatg Alexander de Montléart; Adm Dir Hanns Maier.

SEASON	OPENING Day Month	CLOSING Day Month	NO OF PFS	NO OF OPERAS	NO OF NEW PROD	NO OF NON-OPERA PFS*
73-74	8 Sep	10 Jul	611	21	6	437
74-75	1 Sep	2 Jul	626	37	7	437

*Operettas, musicals, ballet, etc.

Repertoire 1973-74 — d'Albert: *Tiefland*; Berg: *Lulu*; Giordano: *Andrea Chénier*; Janácek: *Cunning Little Vixen*; Leoncavallo: *Edipo Re*; Mozart: *Don Giovanni*; Puccini: *Tosca*; Strauss, R: *Frau ohne Schatten, Schweigsame Frau*; Tchaikovsky: *Maid of Orleans*; Verdi: *Aida, Falstaff, Nabucco, Simon Boccanegra*; Wagner: *Meistersinger, Parsifal, Rheingold, Walküre, Siegfried, Götterdämmerung, Tristan und Isolde*.

1974-75 — d'Albert: *Tiefland*; Cikker: *Coriolanus*; Flotow: *Martha*; Giordano: *Andrea Chénier*; Janácek: *Cunning Little Vixen*; Leoncavallo: *Edipo Re*; Lortzing: *Wildschütz*; Mozart: *Così fan tutte, Don Giovanni, Entführung aus dem Serail, Nozze di Figaro*; Puccini: *Bohème, Gianni Schicchi, Butterfly, Tabarro, Tosca*; Rossini: *Barbiere di Siviglia*; Strauss, R: *Frau ohne Schatten*; Tchaikovsky: *Maid of Orleans*; Verdi: *Aida, Falstaff, Nabucco, Otello, Rigoletto, Simon Boccanegra, Traviata*; Wagner: *Fliegende Holländer, Lohengrin, Meistersinger, Parsifal, Rheingold, Walküre, Siegfried, Götterdämmerung, Tannhäuser, Tristan und Isolde*; Weber: *Freischütz*.

Except for 1 prod, company performs all operas in German. Annual tour 1973-74 incl FR Ger: Landau, Leverkusen, Ludwigshafen/Rhein; LUX: Luxembourg; SPA: Barcelona; 9 pfs, 8 prods. Company also gives guest engagements.

Budget n/a.

Number of persons engaged in 1974-75: resident solo artists: 35; chorus members: 46; orchestra members: 88; conductors: 4; stage directors/producers: 8; set & costume designers: 10; choreographers: 1; corps de ballet: 16; administrative staff: 23; technical, scenic, costume: 201.

Company uses local symph orch.

BAYERISCHE STAATSOPER, Max Joseph Platz 2, 8 Munich 1, FR Ger; tel 21851. Founded in 1818; pfs suspended 1943-45. Perf at Nationaltheater, form Königl Hof- und Nationaltheater, since 1818. Built in 1818; rebuilt in 1825 and again after WW II in 1963; seat cap 2,101, avg aud 1,940. Other theaters: Prinzregententheater, Altes Residenz-theater/Cuvilliés Theater and Theater im Marstall. Company owned and operated by Bavarian State Ministry for Education and Culture, State Minister Prof Hans Maier, also manages Altes Residenztheater/Cuvilliés Theater and Staatstheater am Gärtnerplatz; State Int Prof Dr Günther Rennert; Gen Mus Dir Prof Wolfgang Sawallisch; Asst State Int & Chief Dramaturg Dr Horst Goerges; Prod Dir Herbert List; Tech Dir Walter Huneke. Staat Int designate Prof August Everding 1977.

SEASON	OPENING Day Month	CLOSING Day Month	NO OF PFS	NO OF PROD	NO OF NEW PROD	NO OF NON-OPERA PFS*
73-74	20 Sep	4 Aug	384	46	8	111
74-75	21 Sep	3 Aug	383	51	8	128

*Operettas, musicals, ballet, etc.

Repertoire 1973-74 — Beethoven: *Fidelio*; Berg: *Lulu, Wozzeck*; Bizet: *Carmen*; Debussy: *Pelléas et Mélisande*; Donizetti: *Don Pasquale*; Henze: *Boulevard Solitude*; Humperdinck: *Hänsel und Gretel*; Janácek: *Jenufa*; Mozart: *Don Giovanni, Nozze di Figaro, Zauberflöte*; Mussorgsky: *Boris Godunov*; Offenbach: *Contes d'Hoffmann*; Orff: *Carmina burana*; Prokofiev: *Gambler*; Puccini: *Bohème, Gianni Schicchi, Madama Butterfly, Tabarro, Tosca, Turandot*; Smetana: *Bartered Bride*; Strauss, R: *Ariadne auf Naxos, Elektra, Rosenkavalier, Salome, Schweigsame Frau*; Verdi: *Aida, Don Carlo, Falstaff, Forza del destino, Otello, Simon Boccanegra, Trovatore*; Wagner: *Fliegende Holländer, Parsifal, Tannhäuser, Walküre*; Yun: *Sim Tjong*.

1974-75 — Beethoven: *Fidelio*; Berg: *Lulu, Wozzeck*; Bizet: *Carmen*; Britten: *Death in Venice*; Debussy: *Pelléas et Mélisande*; Henze: *Boulevard Solitude*; Humperdinck: *Hänsel und Gretel*; Mozart: *Don Giovanni, Entführung aus dem Serail, Idomeneo, Nozze di Figaro, Zauberflöte*; Mussorgsky: *Boris Godunov*; Offenbach: *Contes d'Hoffmann*; Orff: *Antigonae*; Puccini: *Bohème, Gianni Schicchi, Madama Butterfly, Tabarro, Tosca*; Rossini: *Barbiere di Siviglia*; Smetana: *Bartered Bride*; Strauss, J: *Fledermaus*; Strauss, R: *Capriccio, Elektra, Rosenkavalier, Salome*; Verdi: *Aida, Don Carlo, Falstaff, Forza del destino, Otello, Traviata, Trovatore*; Wagner: *Fliegende Holländer, Meistersinger, Parsifal, Rheingold, Tannhäuser, Walküre*.

Company performs 75% of all operas in orig language. 6 pfs per season broadcast live, 1 pf videotaped. Annual tour of 1 opera in 5 pfs at Fränkische Festwoche/Bayreuth. Guest engagements 1972-75 — UK: London 4 pfs; AUS: Vienna 3 pfs; JPN: Tokyo and Osaka 22 pfs; MON: Monte Carlo 4 pfs; LUX: Luxembourg 2 pfs; FR GER: Stuttgart 2 pfs, Frankfurt 1 pf, Leverkusen 1 pf, Bayreuth 5 pfs. Subsidiary companies: Experimentierbühne der Bayer Staatsoper, 7 pfs annually in different locations; Opernstudio der Bayer Staatsoper, for junior performers, 2-3 pfs at Theater im Marstall. Company has a training prgm for 8 singers per season.

Budget for 1974 DM 48,462,600 (US $17,543,000). Income: 20.79% box office; 60.65% gvnmt; 13.47% priv/corp/fndt grants; 4.59% other income. Ticket prices: DM 39.50-3.50; 18.92% subscription, 81.08% single ticket sale.

Number of persons engaged in 1974-75 abt 1,450: resident & guest solo artists: 138; chorus members: 96; orchestra members: 139; musical staff: 12; conductors: 21; stage directors/producers: 22; set & costume designers: 36; choreographers: 16; corps de ballet: 59; administrative staff: 12; technical, scenic, costume: 702.

Company maintains own orch on seasonal basis; builds all its sets and costumes in own workshops.

STAATSTHEATER AM GÄRTNERPLATZ, Gärtnerplatz 3, 8 Munich 5, FR Ger; tel 089/263041. Founded in 1937. Preceding & present comp perf at Staatstheater am Gärtnerplatz since 1865. Built in 1865 as theater for opera and drama; seat cap 855, avg aud 812. Perf also at Cuvilliés Theater and Deutsches Theater, Munich. Company owned and operated by Bavarian State Ministry for Educ & Culture, which also manages Bavarian Staatsoper and Bavarian Staatsschauspiel; Minister's Prof H Maier & Dr Walter Keim; State Int Kurt Pscherer; Principal Cond Franz Allers; Chief Dramatg Dr Peter Kertz; Art Mng Dr Hanskarl Otto; Chief Admin Johann M Bouillon.

SEASON	OPENING Day	Month	CLOSING Day	Month	NO OF PFS*	NO OF OPERAS*	NO OF NEW PROD*	NO OF NON-OPERA PFS
73-74	13	Aug	3	Jun	330	35	6	100
74-75	20	Aug	22	Jul	330	35	6	100

*Bavarian Opera ensembles combined.

World prem during these seasons: Henze's *Rachel, la Cubana* first stg pf 5/75.

Repertoire 1973-74 - Donizetti: *Lucia*; Menotti: *Medium*; Shostakovich: *Katerina Ismailova*; Weill: *Zar lässt sich photographieren*.

1974-75 — Henze: *Rachel, la Cubana*; Humperdinck: *Hänsel und Gretel*; Leoncavallo: *Pagliacci*; Mascagni: *Cavalleria rusticana*; Mozart: *Entführung aus dem Serail*.

Company performs all operas in German. Several pfs broadcast. Annual tour of abt 4 operas in 15 pfs to FR GER: Aschaffenburg, Erlangen, Ingolstadt, Kempten, Schweinfurt, Weissenburg; ITA: Bolzano. Also guest engagements 1971-75 incl Deutsche Oper Berlin, Schwetzingen, Leverkusen, Böblingen, Würzburg, Kiel, Milan and Merano, Italy.

Budget for 1974-75 DM 16,256,000 (US $6,732,000). Income: 15-18% box office; 82-85% gvnmt; other income from occas broadcasts. Ticket prices: DM 22-4.50; 40% subscription, 60% single ticket sale.

Number of persons engaged in 1974-75: resident solo artists: 40; guest solo artists: 24; chorus members: 42; orchestra members: 71; musical staff: 9; conductors: 6; stage directors/producers: 3; set & costume designers: 2; choreographers: 1; corps de ballet: 31; administrative and clerical staff: 27; technical, scenic, costume: 107.

Company maintains its own orch; builds all sets and costumes in own workshops.

STÄDTISCHE BÜHNEN NÜRNBERG, MUSIKTHEATER, Richard Wagner Pl 2, 8500 Nürnberg, FR Ger; tel 20 45 85. Founded in 1905. Perf at Städtische Bühnen Nürnberg since 1905, except 1942-45. Built as an opera house in 1905; seat cap 1,456, avg aud 1,000. Company first perf at Opernhaus Nürnberg. Company is owned and operated by the City of Nürnberg and State Gvnmt of Bavaria; Cultural Deputy Dr Hermann Glaser; Dir of Musiktheater Hans Gierster; Bus Dir Willi Eck; First Stage Dir Hans-Peter Lehmann; Tech Dir Max Grünwald.

SEASON	OPENING Day Month		CLOSING Day Month		NO OF PFS	NO OF OPERAS	NO OF NEW PROD	NO OF NON-OPERA PFS*
73-74	3	Sep	21	Jul	244	32	14	128
74-75	9	Sep	20	Jul	230	30	11	120

*Operettas, musicals, ballet, etc.

Repertoire 1973-74 — Bizet: *Carmen*; Burkhard: *Feuerwerk*; Flotow: *Martha*; Henze: *Floss der Medusa*; Hindemith: *Cardillac*; Humperdinck: *Hänsel und Gretel*; Monteverdi: *Incoronazione di Poppea*; Mozart: *Così fan tutte, Don Giovanni, Entführung aus dem Serail, Zauberflöte*; Nono: *Intolleranza*; Offenbach: *Contes d'Hoffmann*; Puccini: *Tosca*; Rossini: *Barbiere di Siviglia*; Schoenberg: *Moses und Aron*; Strauss, J: *Fledermaus*; Strauss, R: *Frau ohne Schatten, Rosenkavalier, Salome*; Verdi: *Falstaff, Macbeth, Nabucco, Rigoletto, Traviata*; Wagner: *Lohengrin, Meistersinger, Tannhäuser*; Weber: *Freischütz*; Yun: *Geisterliebe, Träume*; Zimmermann: *Soldaten*.

1974-75 — Beethoven: *Fidelio*; Berg: *Wozzeck*; Burkhard: *Feuerwerk*; Gounod: *Médecin malgré lui*; Henze: *Floss der Medusa*; Humperdinck: *Hänsel und Gretel*; Janáček: *From the House of the Dead*; Mozart: *Così fan tutte, Don Giovanni, Zauberflöte*; Mussorgsky: *Boris Godunov*; Nono: *Intolleranza*; Orff: *Bernauerin*; Puccini: *Tosca*; Rossini: *Barbiere di Siviglia*; Schoenberg: *Moses und Aron*; Strauss, J: *Fledermaus*; Strauss, R: *Elektra, Frau ohne Schatten, Rosenkavalier, Salome*; Verdi: *Nabucco, Macbeth, Trovatore*; Wagner: *Lohengrin, Meistersinger, Tannhäuser*; Weber: *Freischütz*; Zimmermann: *Soldaten*.

Company performs all operas in German. Only 1 pf broadcast on radio. Guest engagements 1971-75 incl SWI: Zurich 1 pf, Basel 1 pf; ITA: Florence 6 pfs; AUS: Vienna 1 pf; FR Ger: Munich 1 pf.

Budget for 1974 DM 25,200,000 (US $9,122,000). Income: 6% box office, 78% City of Nürnberg, 16% State of Bavaria. Ticket prices: DM 20-4, 80% subscription, 20% single ticket sale.

Number of persons engaged by company 1974-75: resident solo artists: 34; chorus members: 53; orchestra members: 85; conductors: 13; stage directors/producers: 8; set & costume designers: 11; choreographers: 2; corps de ballet: 26; administrative staff: 10; technical, scenic, costume: 213.

Company maintains its own orch on a permanent basis; builds all its sets and costumes in own workshops.

WÜRTTEMBERGISCHE STAATSOPER, Oberer Schlossgarten, Stuttgart, FR Ger; tel 21951. Founded in 1912. Perf at Württembergische Staatstheater since 1912. Built in 1912 as an opera house, seat cap 1,400, avg aud 1,200. Company owned and operated by provincial Gvnmt of Baden-Württemberg and City of Stuttgart, which also manages the Schauspielhaus, Staatstheaterballett, Liederhalle and Kammertheater; Gen Int Hans Peter Doll; Gen Mus Dir Silvio Varviso; Opera Dir Dr Wolfram Schwinger, Ballet Dir Marcia Haydée; Dram Dir Dr H Knorr.

SEASON	OPENING Day Month	CLOSING Day Month	NO OF PFS	NO OF OPERAS	NO OF NEW PROD	NO OF NON-OPERA PFS*
74-75	Sep	Jul	232	36	4	52

*Ballet.

Repertoire 1974-75 — Beethoven: *Fidelio*; Bizet: *Carmen*; Britten: *Albert Herring, Death in Venice*; Dallapiccola: *Prigioniero*; Donizetti: *Elisir, Lucia*; Janácek: *Cunning Little Vixen, Katya Kabanová*; Monteverdi: *Incoronazione di Poppea*; Mozart: *Così fan tutte, Don Giovanni*; Mussorgsky: *Boris Godunov*; Nicolai: *Lustigen Weiber*; Offenbach: *Contes d'Hoffmann*; Orff: *Carmina burana, Kluge, Mond*; Schoenberg: *Moses und Aron*; Strauss, R: *Salome*; Stravinsky: *Oedipus Rex*; Tchaikovsky: *Pique Dame*; Verdi: *Ballo in maschera, Don Carlo, Forza del destino, Otello, Vespri*; Wagner: *Fliegende Holländer, Lohengrin, Meistersinger, Rheingold, Walküre, Siegfried, Götterdämmerung, Tannhäuser, Tristan und Isolde*.

Company performs 25% of all operas in orig language. Gives guest engagements.

Budget n/a for opera alone. income for entire Staatstheater: 25% box office; 75% gvnmt. Ticket prices: DM 33-5; 60% subscription, 40% single ticket sale.

Number of persons engaged in 1974-75: resident and guest solo artists: 75; chorus members: 69; orchestra members: 99; musical staff: 12; conductors: 11; stage directors/producers: 7; set & costume designers: 6; choreographers: 5; corps de ballet: 37 and 24 solo.

Company maintains its own orch; builds 90% of its sets and costumes in own workshops.

WUPPERTALER BÜHNEN, Spinnstr, Wuppertal, FR Ger; tel 0202/593091. Founded in 1946. Perf at Opernhaus since 1956. Rebuilt in 1956 as an opera house, seat cap 851, avg aud 851. Prev theater: old opera house at same location. Company owned and operated by City of Wuppertal; Cultural Advisor Dr Revermann; Gen Int Dr Hanno Lunin; Gen Mus Dir Prof Hanns-Martin Schneidt; Tech Dir Rolf Bachmann; Chief Admin Erich Neumann; Adm Mng Heinz Thiele.

SEASON	OPENING Day Month	CLOSING Day Month	NO OF PFS	NO OF PROD	NO OF NEW PROD	NO OF NON-OPERA PFS
73-74	1 Sep	7 Jul	182	10	10	—
74-75	8 Sep	9 Jul	184	10	10	—

World prem during these seasons: Blacher's *Yvonne, Prinzessin von Burgund* 9/73.

Repertoire 1973-74 — Berg: *Lulu*; Blacher: *Yvonne*; Gluck: *Iphigénie en Tauride*; Humperdinck: *Königskinder*; Offenbach: *Contes d'Hoffmann*; Rossini: *Turco in Italia*; Verdi: *Nabucco*.

1974-75 — Bizet: *Carmen*; Fortner: *Don Perlimplin*; Geissler: *Zerbrochene Krug*; Lortzing: *Wildschütz*; Purcell: *Fairy Queen*; Verdi: *Don Carlo*; Wagner: *Walküre*; Zimmermann: *Levins Mühle*.

Company performs all operas in German. Only excerpts of some pfs are taped and re-broadcast or videotaped. Company gives guest engagements.

Budget for 1974-75 DM 17,200,000 (US $6,226,000). Income: 15.9% box office; 84.1% city gvnmt. Ticket prices: DM 18-5; 82% subscription, 18% single ticket sale.

Number of persons engaged in 1974-75: 356; resident solo artists: 31; chorus members: 40; orchestra members: 83; musical staff: 4; conductors: 5; stage directors/producers: 6 & guests; set & costume designers: 4; choreographers: 1; corps de ballet: 28; administrative staff: *.

*Most admin staff also engaged in drama.

Company uses local symph orch; builds all sets and costumes in own workshops.

GERMAN DEMOCRATIC REPUBLIC

STAATSOPER DRESDEN, Grimau-Allee 27, Dresden, Ger DR; tel 496311. Founded in 1667. Staatsoper Dresden built 1878, destroyed 1945. Perf at Schauspielhaus, seat cap 1,200, avg aud 1,160. First perf at Opernhaus am Taschenberg; from 1719 Opernhaus am Zwinger; from 1841 first Semper-Bau. Since 1945 also perf at Grosses Haus & Kleines

Haus der Staatstheater Dresden; the latter seat cap 500. Company is owned and operated by the State Ministry of Culture & County & City Cult Dept; Gen Mng Opera Dr Horst Seeger; Dir Harry Kupfer; Mus Adm Siegfried Kurz.

SEASON	OPENING Day Month	CLOSING Day Month	NO OF PFS	NO OF OPERAS	NO OF NEW PROD	NO OF NON-OPERA PFS
73-74	18 Aug	21 Jul	253	32	9	—
74-75	5 Sep	28 Jun	249	34	4	—

Repertoire 1973-74 — Buzko: *White Nights*; Donizetti: *Elisir*; Mozart: *Bastien und Bastienne, Schauspieldirektor*; Paisiello: *Barbiere di Siviglia*; Strauss, J: *Fledermaus*; Strauss, R: *Schweigsame Frau*; Stravinsky: *Mavra, Renard*; Verdi: *Falstaff*; plus 23 revivals.

1974-75 — Bartók: *Bluebeard's Castle*; Petrov: *Erschaffung der Welt*; Puccini: *Tosca*; Schoenberg: *Moses und Aron*; plus 30 revivals.

Company perf 5% of all operas in orig language. Guest engagements 1974-75 incl FR GER: Wiesbaden; USSR: Leningrad; YUG: Ljubljana.

Budget n/a. Income: 30% box office, 70% gvnmt subsidies. Ticket prices: Ger DR M 12-3.50; 65% subscription, 35% single ticket sale.

Number of persons engaged in 1974-75: resident solo artists: 33; guest solo artists: 18; chorus members: 80; orchestra members: 126; musical staff: 11; conductors: 3; stage directors/producers: 2; set & costume designers: 3; choreographers: 2; corps de ballet: 36; administrative staff: 8; technical, scenic, costume: 208.

Company maintains its own orch; builds all its sets and costumes in own workshops.

STÄDTISCHE THEATER LEIPZIG, OPER, Operndirektion, Opernhaus am Karl-Marx-Platz, 701 Leipzig, Ger DR; tel 7641. Founded in 1945. Perf at Opernhaus since 1960. Built in 1960 as an opera house, seat cap 1,682, avg aud 1,380. Company first perf at Dreilindenstrasse, form the Variété, 1945-60, seat cap 1,200, which now has its own ensemble for operas, musicals & operettas. Company is owned and operated by the City of Leipzig, Städtische Theater Leipzig, which also manages the Musikalische Komödie, Schauspielhaus, Kammerspiele, Theater der Jungen Welt, Kellertheater; Gen Int Prof Karl Kayser; Dir Opera Joachim Herz; Gen Mus Dir Gert Bahner; Dram Adm Günther Lohse; Tech Dir Helmuth Ernst; Adm Klaus Drescher.

SEASON	OPENING Day Month	CLOSING Day Month	NO OF PFS	NO OF OPERAS	NO OF NEW PROD	NO OF NON-OPERA PFS*
73-74	18 Aug	6 Jul	305	33	4	26
74-75	16 Aug	4 Jul	224**	33	5	33

*Operettas, musicals, at other houses. **Closed for 3 months because of fire damage.

World prem during these seasons: Geissler's *Der Schatten* 8/31/75.

Repertoire 1973-74 — Auber: *Fra Diavolo*; Beethoven: *Fidelio*; Dvorák: *Rusalka*; Egk: *Zaubergeige*; Gershwin: *Porgy and Bess*; Gounod: *Faust*; Handel: *Xerxes*; Humperdinck: *Hänsel und Gretel*; Janácek: *Cunning Little Vixen*; Leoncavallo: *Pagliacci*; Lortzing: *Zar und Zimmermann*; Mascagni: *Cavalleria rusticana*; Mozart: *Così fan tutte, Entführung aus dem Serail, Nozze di Figaro*; Offenbach: *Contes d'Hoffmann*; Puccini: *Butterfly, Manon Lescaut*; Tchaikovsky: *Maid of Orleans*; Verdi: *Ballo in maschera, Don Carlo, Otello, Traviata, Trovatore*; Wagner: *Fliegende Holländer, Lohengrin, Rheingold, Walküre*; Weber: *Freischütz*. **Keller & Komödie** — Cimarosa: *Matrimonio segreto*; Geissler: *Verrückte Jourdain, Zerbrochene Krug*.

1974-75 — Auber: *Fra Diavolo*; Beethoven: *Fidelio*; Bizet: *Carmen*; Dvorák: *Rusalka*; Egk: *Zaubergeige*; Geissler: *Schatten*; Gershwin: *Porgy and Bess*; Gounod: *Faust*; Handel: *Xerxes*; Humperdinck: *Hänsel und Gretel*; Janácek: *Cunning Little Vixen*; Leoncavallo: *Pagliacci*; Mascagni: *Cavalleria rusticana*; Meyerbeer: *Huguenots*; Mozart: *Così fan tutte, Entführung aus dem Serail, Nozze di Figaro, Zauberflöte*; Offenbach: *Contes d'Hoffmann*; Puccini: *Bohème, Manon Lescaut*; Tchaikovsky: *Maid of Orleans*; Verdi: *Ballo in maschera, Otello, Traviata, Trovatore*; Wagner: *Fliegende Holländer, Rheingold, Walküre*; Weber: *Freischütz*. **Keller & Komödie** — Cimarosa: *Matrimonio segreto*; Einem: *Zerrissene*; Geissler: *Zerbrochene Krug*.

Company performs all operas in German.

Some pfs broadcast on radio, live or taped; occasional pfs videotaped. Guest engagements 1971-75 incl POL: Lodz 3 pfs; FR GER: Wiesbaden 2 pfs; GER DR: Berlin 2 pfs; CUBA: Havana 7 pfs; ITA: Genoa 3 pfs; CSSR: Bratislava 1 pf, Brno 1 pf, Prague 1 pf. Company has training program for singers; education program for all members.

Budget is part of State Theater. Income 33% box office, 67% gvnmt subsidies. Ticket prices: Ger DR M 12-5, 40% subscription, 60% single ticket sale.

Number of persons engaged in 1974-75: resident solo artists: 48; guest solo artists: 16; chorus members: 92; musical staff: 10; conductors: 6; stage directors/producers: 2; set & costume designers: *; choreographers: 2; corps de ballet: 56; administrative staff: *; technical, scenic, costume: 116.

*Company uses the adm, clerical & tech staff and stage & costume designers of the Städt Theater.

Company uses Gewandhausorchester for all perf, at home and on tour; builds all its sets and costumes in own workshops.

HOLLAND

DE NEDERLANDSE OPERASTICHTING, Marnixstraat 427, Amsterdam, Netherlands; tel 020-255454. Founded in 1964. Perf at Stadsschouwburg, Amsterdam, since 1966. Built in 1894, not as an opera house, seat cap 950, avg aud 810. Prev theaters: Congreszaal RAI, Amsterdam, 1965-66, seat cap 1,200; Circustheatre Scheveningen, municipal theaters in Rotterdam and Utrecht. Company is owned and operated by city, state and national gvnmts under Minister of Cultural Affairs; Bd Chmn Dr J Wouters; Int Hans de Roo; Mus Dir Hans Vonk; Adm F J A Schellen; Adj Adm Mrs M D Sundermeijer-Kempen; Head Tech Dept Cees List.

SEASON	OPENING Day	Month	CLOSING Day	Month	NO OF PFS	NO OF PROD	NO OF NEW PROD	NO OF NON-OPERA PFS*
73-74	14	Sep	6	Jul	152	18	12	18
74-75	13	Sep	23	Jun	158	20	13	—

*Operettas, musicals, ballet, etc.

World prems during these seasons: Kox's *Dorian Gray* 1974; Maderna's *Satyricon* 1973.

Repertoire 1973-74 — Bellini: *Norma*; Berg: *Wozzeck*; Cavalli: *Ormindo*; Debussy: *Pelléas et Mélisande*; Donizetti: *Don Pasquale*; Kox: *Picture of Dorian Gray*; Lecocq: *Fille de Madame Angot*; Monteverdi: *Combattimento di Tancredi, Orfeo, Incoronazione di Poppea*; Mozart: *Entführung aus dem Serail*; Offenbach: *Contes d'Hoffmann*; Puccini: *Bohème*; Strauss, R: *Ariadne auf Naxos*; Verdi: *Falstaff, Rigoletto*; Wagner: *Tristan und Isolde*.

1974-75 — Bartók: *Bluebeard's Castle*; Cimarosa: *Maestro di cappella*; Handel: *Rodelinda*; Janácek: *Makropoulos Affair*; Kurka: *Good Soldier Schweik*; Mozart: *Così fan tutte*; Puccini: *Butterfly, Tosca*; Rossini: *Cambiale di matrimonio*; Schoenberg: *Erwartung*; Shostakovich: *The Nose*; Strauss, R: *Elektra*; Stravinsky: *Rake's Progress*; Tchaikovsky: *Eugene Onegin*; Verdi: *Ballo in maschera, Nabucco, Traviata*.

Company performs 75% of all operas in orig language. Abt 8 pfs taped and rebroadcast on radio annually. Guest engagement in 1972-73 — BEL: Brussels, 2 prods of contemp operas. Company has training program for abt 10 singers.

Budget for 1974-75 D f 14,087,000 (US $4,930,000). Income: 10% box office; 90% gvnmt subsidies. Ticket prices: D f 19-4.50; 40% by subscription, 60% single ticket sale.

Number of persons engaged for 1974-75: guest solo artists: 140; chorus members: 40; musical staff: 5; administrative staff: 5; technical, scenic, costume: 75; with guest conductors, producers, designers, etc.

Company uses the radio orch and other symph orch; builds 80% of its sets & costumes in own workshops.

HUNGARY

MAGYAR ÁLLAMI OPERAHAZ, Népköztársaság u 22, Budapest, Hungary; tel 312-550. Founded in 1884. Perf at Operahaz since 1884, built in 1884 as an opera house, seat cap 1,200, avg aud 1,080; and at Erkel Szinház since 1951, built in 1905 as an opera house, seat cap 2,400, avg aud 1,800. Company owned and operated by state government under the Ministry of Culture; Gen Dir Miklós Lukács; Asst Dir György Szirtes; Chief Prod András Mikó; First Cond András Kórodi.

Season begins in September, closes in June, over 500 pfs of 60 operas, with 4-6 new prods annually; approx 20 ballets.

World prem 1973-75: Szokolay's *Samson* 10/73.

Repertoire 1971-75 — Bartók: *Bluebeard's Castle*; Beethoven: *Fidelio*; Berg: *Lulu*; Bizet: *Carmen*; Britten: *Midsummer Night*; Donizetti: *Campanello, Don Pasquale, Lucia*; Erkel: *Bánk Bán, Hunyadi László*; Gay/Britten: *Beggar's Opera*; Gershwin: *Porgy and Bess*; Gluck: *Orfeo ed Euridice*; Goldmark: *Königin von Saba*; Gounod: *Faust*; Handel: *Rodelinda*; Janácek: *Jenufa*; Kacsóh: *János Vitéz*; Kodály: *Háry János, Spinning Room*; Leoncavallo: *Pagliacci*; Mascagni: *Cavalleria rusticana*; Monteverdi: *Incoronazione di Poppea, Ritorno d'Ulisse*; Mozart: *Così fan tutte, Don Giovanni, Entführung aus dem Serail, Nozze di Figaro, Zauberflöte*; Mussorgsky: *Khovanshchina*; Petrovics: *Crime and Punishment, Lysistrata*; Prokofiev: *Love for Three Oranges*; Puccini: *Bohème, Fanciulla del West, Gianni Schicchi, Butterfly, Manon Lescaut, Tosca, Turandot*; Ránki: *Tragedy of Man, King Pomade's New Suit*; Rossini: *Barbiere di Siviglia*; Saint-Saëns: *Samson et Dalila*; Strauss, J: *Fledermaus*; Strauss, R: *Rosenkavalier, Salome*; Szokolay: *Blood Wedding, Samson*; Tchaikovsky: *Eugene Onegin*; Verdi: *Aida, Ballo in maschera, Don Carlo, Falstaff, Forza del destino, Lombardi, Macbeth, Nabucco, Otello, Rigoletto, Simon Boccanegra, Traviata, Trovatore*; Wagner: *Fliegende Holländer, Lohengrin, Meistersinger, Rheingold, Walküre, Siegfried, Götterdämmerung, Tannhäuser, Tristan und Isolde*.

Company performs all operas in Hungarian. Some pfs broadcast on radio. Company does not have a regular tour but does guest and exchange engagements.

Budget n/a. Income: 30% box office; 70% gvnmt subsidies. Ticket prices: Hun fl 40-15; spec pfs Hun fl 160-20; 65% subscription, 35% single ticket sale.

Number of persons engaged for opera in 1974-75: resident solo artists: 107; chorus members: 161; orchestra members: 205; musical staff: 10; conductors: 10; stage directors/producers: 4; set & costume designers: 4; choreographers: 2; corps de ballet: 120; administrative and clerical staff: 62; technical, scenic, costume: 380; others: 138.

Company maintains its own orch on a seasonal basis; builds all its sets and costumes in own workshops.

ISRAEL

ISRAEL NATIONAL OPERA, 1 Allenby St, Tel Aviv, Israel; tel 57227. Founded in 1947. Perf at Israel National Opera House since 1958. Built in 1958, not as an opera house; seat cap 990, avg aud 810. First perf at Habima Theater 1947-58, seat cap 1,200. Company is a non-profit organization; Bd Chmn Judge Z Berinson; Pres Dr Y Bader; Gen Dir Edis de Philippe; Adm Simha Evan Zohar; Cond George Singer; Tech Dir Yehezkel Goldman.

Season generally begins in September and ends in August; 20 operas and operettas, 3 or 4 new prods annually.

Repertoire n/a.

Company performs 75% of all operas in orig language. Some pfs broadcast, live or taped. Each new prod is toured to other large Israeli cities, incl Jerusalem, Haifa and Beersheba. Company has training program for 17 or 18 singers and 2 cond/coaches per season.

Budget for 1974-75 Israeli £ 3,000,000 (US $498,000). Income: 30% box office, 60% gvnmt subsidies, 10% other. Ticket prices: £ 40-15.

Number of persons engaged in 1974-75: resident solo artists: 35; guest solo artists: 5; chorus members: 50; orchestra members: 60; musical staff: 8; conductors: 5; stage directors/producers: 1; set & costume designers: 1; choreographers: 3; corps de ballet: 18; administrative staff: 5; technical, scenic, costume: 22.

Company maintains its own orch on a seasonal basis; builds all its sets and costumes in own workshops.

Board of Directors: Dr Y Bader, A Dolzin, Y Groman, Ch Levanon, J Haft, S Evan Zohar, Edis de Philippe, D Ben Arie, Dr M Ashkenazi, Mrs Ch Moses, M Marcus, Y Yeshayahu, B Keshet.

ITALY

MAGGIO MUSICALE FIORENTINO & TEATRO COMUNALE, 15 V Solferino, Florence, Italy; tel 26-28-41. Perf opera at Teatro Comunale di Firenze since 1933. Built in 1928 as an opera house; seat cap 2,100, avg aud 1,900. Other theater: Teatro della Pergola, seat cap 1,100. Company is gvnmt owned and operated; Pres Elio Gabbuggiani; Gen Dir Mo Massimo Bogianckino; Mus Dir Mo Aldo Rocchi; Tech Dir Prof Raoul Farolfi; Adm Dir Gilberto Bambi, Chief of Personnel Walter Boccaccini.

SEASON	OPENING Day Month		CLOSING Day Month		NO OF PFS	NO OF PROD	NO OF NEW PROD	NO OF NON-OPERA PFS*
73-74	6	May	17	Feb	46	7	4	25
74-75	7	May	1	Feb	75	12	7	24

*Operettas, musicals, ballet, etc.

Repertoire 1973-74 — Nono: *Intolleranza*; Puccini: *Fanciulla del West*; Spontini: *Agnese di Hohenstaufen*; Tchaikovsky: *Pique Dame*; Verdi: *Aida, Ballo in maschera*.

1974-75 — Bellini: *Sonnambula*; Busoni: *Arlecchino*; Henze: *Floss der Medusa*; Malipiero: *Torneo notturno*; Puccini: *Bohème*; Tchaikovsky: *Eugene Onegin*; Verdi: *Forza del destino, Macbeth*.

Company performs 75% of all operas in orig language. A few pfs taped or broadcast live.

Budget n/a.

Number of persons engaged in 1974-75: resident & guest solo artists: 60; chorus members: 99; orchestra members: 118; musical staff: 22; conductors: 10; stage directors/producers: 16; set & costume designers: 16; choreographers: 2; corps de ballet: 43; administrative staff: 32; technical, scenic, costume: 124.

Company uses local symph orch; builds 75% of its sets and 10% of costumes in own workshops.

TEATRO COMUNALE DELL'OPERA, V XX Settembre 33/7, Genoa, Italy; tel 010-542 792. Founded in 1936. Perf at Teatro Margherita, V XX Settembre 20, Genoa, since 1963; spring and fall seasons. Built in 1948, not as an opera house; seat cap 2,000, avg aud 1,400. First perf at Teatro Carlo Felice 1936-63, until its demolition. Currently being rebuilt for 1979-80; seat cap 1,600. Concert perf also at Politeama Genovese. Company is owned and operated by the national gvnmt, ANELS; Mayor Fulvio Cerofolini; Gen Int Giovanni A Ugo; Art Dir Fernando Previtali; Gen Sec Dr Alessandro Levrero; Tech Dir Augusto Colombara.

SEASON	OPENING Day Month		CLOSING Day Month		NO OF PFS	NO OF OPERAS	NO OF NEW PROD	NO OF NON-OPERA PFS*
74	27	Mar	25	Jun	46	13	1	80
	18	Oct	2	Dec				
75	1	Apr	25	Jun	30	10	1	80

*Operettas, musicals, ballet, etc.

Repertoire 1974 — Bellini: *Norma*; Donizetti: *Elisir, Lucia*; Malipiero: *Minnie la candida*; Petrassi: *Cordovano*; Puccini: *Butterfly, Manon Lescaut*; Purcell: *Dido and Aeneas*; Rossini: *Matilde di Shabran, Pietra del paragone*; Stravinsky: *Renard*; Verdi: *Traviata*; Wagner: *Walküre*.

1975 — Bizet: *Carmen*; Dallapiccola: *Volo di notte*; Donizetti: *Linda di Chamounix*; Handel: *Xerxes*; Puccini: *Tosca*; Rossini: *Cambiale di matrimonio*; Spontini: *Vestale*; Verdi: *Ernani, Rigoletto, Trovatore*.

Company performs 5% of all operas in orig language. Some pfs videotaped. Guest engagement 6/71 — BUL: Sofia 4 pfs. Exchange visit with Leipzig Opera 11/75 3 pfs. Subsidiary company: Intl Ballet Festival, perf at Park Theater, Nervi, 23 pfs biennially in July.

Budget n/a. Ticket prices: L7,500-500; 70% subscription, 30% single ticket sale.

Number of persons engaged by company April-June 1975: incl 100 guest solo artists, cond, des, etc.; chorus members: 80; orchestra members: 101; musical staff: 8; administrative staff: 25; technical, scenic, costume: 50.

Company maintains its own orch on an annual basis; builds 5% of its sets and costumes in own workshops.

TEATRO ALLA SCALA, V Filodrammatici 2, Milan, Italy; tel 8879. Founded 1778. Perf at Teatro alla Scala since its founding. Built in 1778 as an opera house, seat cap 2,200, avg aud 2,200. Ensemble also perf at Piccola Scala. Public company, co-owned and operated by the Province of Lombardy and the City of Milan; Chmn & Pres Aldo Aniasi; Gen Int Paolo Grassi; Mus Dir Claudio Abbado; Secy Gen Fioravanti Nanni; Adm Tito Varisco.

SEASON	OPENING Day	Month	CLOSING Day	Month	NO OF PFS	NO OF PROD	NO OF NEW PROD	NO OF NON-OPERA PFS*
73-74	7	Dec	29	May	95	16	—	8
74-75	7	Dec	20	May	110	14	1	7

*Operettas, musicals, ballet, etc.

World prems during these seasons: Nono's *Al gran sole carico d'amore* 4/74; Mortari's *Specchio a tre luci* 1974.

Repertoire 1973-74 — Bellini: *Norma*; Bizet: *Carmen*; Cimarosa: *Marito disperato*; Donizetti: *Favorite*; Gazzaniga: *Convitato di pietra*; Hindemith: *Hin und zurück*; Janácek: *Jenufa*; Maderna: *Satyricon*; Mozart: *Nozze di Figaro*; Puccini: *Fanciulla del West*; Rossini: *Cenerentola, Italiana in Algeri*; Strauss, R: *Salome*; Verdi: *Simon Boccanegra*; Wagner: *Walküre*.

1974-75 — Beethoven: *Fidelio*; Bellini: *Norma*; Prokofiev: *Love for Three Oranges*; Puccini: *Bohème, Tosca*; Rossini: *Italiana in Algeri*; Verdi: *Attila, Ballo in maschera*; Wagner: *Siegfried*.

Company performs 90% of all operas in orig language. Annual tour of 3-4 operas in 15 pfs. Guest and exchange engagements 1973-76 incl UK: London Royal; USSR: Moscow Bolshoi. Subsidiary companies incl Piccola Scala for chamber opera and the Museum of the Teatro alla Scala. Company has a training prgm for 15 singers per season and the Intl Cantelli Compt for Young Conductors.

Budget n/a. Income: 15% box office; 80% gvnmt; 5% other income. Ticket prices: L 20,000-500.

Number of persons engaged in 1974-75: resident solo artists: 15; guest solo artists: 250; chorus members: 100; orchestra members: 130; musical staff: 15; conductors: 10; stage directors/producers: 1; set & costume designers: 10; choreographers: 10; corps de ballet: 80; administrative staff: 15; technical, scenic, costume: 225.

Company maintains own orch; builds 40% of its sets and costumes in own workshops.

TEATRO DI SAN CARLO, V San Carlo, Naples, Italy; tel 081-39 07 45. Founded in 1737. Pfs were suspended in 1942-43. Perf at Teatro di San Carlo since 1737. Built in 1737 as an opera house, seat cap 2,000, avg aud 1,650. Company owned and operated jointly by the

Natl Gvnmt of Italy, the Province of Campania and the City of Naples; Gen Int Adriano Falvo; adm staff to be reappointed.

Length of seasons and number of pfs n/a.

Repertoire 1973-74 — Donizetti: *Don Pasquale, Rita*; Leoncavallo: *Pagliacci*; Mascagni: *Cavalleria rusticana*; Mozart: *Zauberflöte*; Ponchielli: *Gioconda*; Puccini: *Bohème, Tosca*; Rimsky-Korsakov: *Coq d'or*; Verdi: *Forza del destino, Otello, Traviata*; Viviani: *Maria Stuart*; Wagner: *Siegfried*.

1974-75 — Alfano: *Risurrezione*; Bizet: *Carmen*; Calbi: *Ritorno*; Donizetti: *Elisir, Lucia*; Milella: *Una storia d'altri tempi*; Mozart: *Nozze di Figaro*; Prokofiev: *Fiery Angel*; Puccini: *Fanciulla del West*; Verdi: *Ballo in maschera, Falstaff*.

Budget n/a.

Number of persons engaged in 1974-75 n/a.

Company builds 90% of its sets and 50% of its costumes in own workshops.

TEATRO MASSIMO, Piazza Verdi, Palermo, Italy; tel 210672. Perf at Teatro Massimo since 1897. Built in 1897 as an opera house; seat cap 1,500, avg aud 1,200. Also perf at Teatro Politeama, Palermo. Company is a public organization; Chmn The Mayor of Palermo; Spec Commissioner Sovrint Dr Piero Cardia; Art Dir Prof Gioacchino Lanza Tomasi; Scenic Dir Antonio Carollo.

SEASON	OPENING Day Month		CLOSING Day Month		NO OF PFS	NO OF PROD	NO OF NEW PROD	NO OF NON-OPERA PFS*
73-74	15	Jan	10	Aug	73	9	1	2
74-75	3	Dec	14	Aug	108	15	3	18

*Operettas, musicals, ballet, etc.

Repertoire 1973-74 — Gomez: *Guarany*; Gounod: *Faust*; Leoncavallo: *Pagliacci*; Mascagni: *Cavalleria rusticana*; Menotti: *Most Important Man*; Puccini: *Butterfly, Turandot*; Verdi: *Forza del destino, Nabucco*.

1974-75 — Dallapiccola: *Prigioniero*; Donizetti: *Don Pasquale, Lucia*; Gluck: *Armide*; Mozart: *Don Giovanni*; Negri: *Pubblicità ninfa gentile*; Piccinni: *Buona figliuola*; Puccini: *Bohème, Butterfly*; Rossini: *Barbiere di Siviglia*; Tchaikovsky: *Eugene Onegin*; Verdi: *Attila, Traviata*.

Company performs 75% of operas in orig language. Guest engagement 1972 — UK: Edinburgh Fest 10 pfs. Company has a training program for singers.

Budget for 1974-75 L 7,468,000,000 (US $11,949,000). Income: 4% box office, 90% gvnmt, 6% priv/corp/fndt grants. Ticket prices: L 10,000-1,000; 90% subscription, 10% single ticket sale.

Number of people engaged 1974-75: resident solo artists: 8; guest solo artists: 90; chorus members: 90; orchestra members: 110; musical staff: 8; conductors: 1; stage directors/producers: 8; set & costume designers: 3; choreographers: 2; corps de ballet: 40; administrative staff: 30; technical, scenic, costume: 200.

Company maintains its own orch on a permanent basis; builds 60% of its sets and 70% costumes in own workshops.

TEATRO REGIO, V Garibaldi, Parma, Italy; tel 35964-30009. Founded in 1829. Perf at Teatro Regio since 1829. Built in 1829 as an opera house; seat cap 1,400, avg aud 1,200. Company owned and operated by the City of Parma; Chairman & Pres Dr Giuseppe Negri.

SEASON	OPENING Day Month		CLOSING Day Month		NO OF PFS	NO OF PROD	NO OF NEW PROD	NO OF NON-OPERA PFS
73-74	26	Dec		Apr	26	9	4	—
74-75	26	Dec		Apr	26	9	4	—

Repertoire 1973-74 — Britten: *Billy Budd*; Massenet: *Werther*; Mozart: *Zauberflöte*; Paer: *Leonora*; Verdi: *Lombardi, Macbeth, Rigoletto*.

Company performs 90% of all operas in orig language. Some pfs taped and rebroadcast on radio and TV. Additional annual tour of 4 operas in 30 pfs at Italian cities, also in Belgium and Hungary.

Budget n/a. Income: 35% box office; 40% gvnmt; 25% other income. Ticket prices: L 6,000-1,000.

Number of persons engaged in 1974-75: guest solo artists: 73; chorus members: 58; orchestra members: 75; musical staff: 6; conductors: 8; stage directors/producers: 2; set & costume designers: 2; choreographers: 1; corps de ballet: 1; administrative staff: 4; technical, scenic, costume: 11.

Company uses the Orchestra Sinfonica Regionale; does not make its own sets or costumes.

TEATRO DELL'OPERA, Piazza Beniamino Gigli, Rome, Italy; tel 463641. Founded in 1946. Perf at Teatro dell'Opera since 1946. Built in 1888 as an opera house under the name Teatro Costanzi, changed its name 1928 to Teatro Reale dell'Opera and 1946 to present name; seat cap 2,000, avg aud 1,800. Opera company operated by the City of Rome; Pres Mayor Clelio Darida; Gen Int Sen Franco Rebecchini; Art Dir Mo Jacopo Napoli; Adm Dir Dr Lamberto Giammei; Asst to Art Dir Mo Fernando Cavaniglia; Stage Mng Gaetano Donadio.

SEASON	OPENING Day	Month	CLOSING Day	Month	NO OF PFS	NO OF OPERAS	NO OF NEW PROD	NO OF NON-OPERA PFS*
73-74	24	Nov	18	Jun	111	14	6	26
74-75	27	Dec	28	Jun	104	12	—	31

*Ballet.

Repertoire 1973-74 — Berg: *Wozzeck*; Debussy: *Pelléas et Mélisande*; Donizetti: *Elisir*; Puccini: *Bohème, Fanciulla del West*; Rossellini: *Reine morte*; Rossini: *Gazza ladra*; Verdi: *Don Carlo, Falstaff, Trovatore*; Wagner: *Parsifal*. **Caracalla** — Mascagni: *Cavalleria rusticana*; Puccini: *Tosca*; Verdi: *Aida*.

1974-75 — Cilea: *Adriana Lecouvreur*; Donizetti: *Don Pasquale*; Giordano: *Andrea Chénier*; Pizzetti: *Assassinio nella cattedrale*; Puccini: *Butterfly, Manon Lescaut*; Rossini: *Otello*; Saint-Saëns: *Samson et Dalila*; Tchaikovsky: *Eugene Onegin*; Wagner: *Parsifal*. **Caracalla** — Bizet: *Carmen*; Verdi: *Aida, Rigoletto*.

Company performs all operas in orig language. For summer fest, company performs at Baths of Caracalla, avg of 30 pfs annually.

Budget for 1974-75 L 8,500,000,000 (US $13,600,000). Income: 7% box office, 93% gvnmt. Ticket prices: L 6,000-1,200, 70% subscription, 30% single ticket sale.

Number of persons engaged in 1974-75 n/a.

Company maintains own orch; builds 90% of sets and costumes in own workshops.

FESTIVAL OF TWO WORLDS, SPOLETO, V Margutta 17, Rome, Italy; tel 679-9346. Founded in 1958. Perf at Teatro Nuovo and Teatro Caio Melisso, Spoleto, Italy, since 1958. Teatro Nuovo built in 18th century, seat cap 850, avg aud 850; Teatro Caio Melisso built in 17th century, seat cap 350, avg aud 350. Company is a private non-profit organization owned and operated by The Festival Foundation, 119 West 57 St, New York, in cooperation with its Italian counterpart; presents also theater, concerts, ballet and visual arts events. Fder/Pres Gian Carlo Menotti; Gen Dir for Italy Raf Ravaioli; Art Dir Romolo Valli; Tech Dir Renato Morozzi; Publ Rel Dir Mario Natale.

SEASON	OPENING Day	Month	CLOSING Day	Month	NO OF PFS	NO OF OPERAS	NO OF NEW PROD	NO OF NON-OPERA PFS
74	14	Jun	7	Jul	24	4	3	n/a
75	20	Jun	13	Jul	17	4	3	n/a

Repertoire 1974 — Berg: *Lulu*; Menotti: *Tamu-Tamu*; Puccini: *Manon Lescaut*; Salieri: *Prima la musica*.

1975 — Bizet: *Docteur Miracle*; Donizetti: *Don Pasquale*; Menotti: *Old Maid and the Thief, Telephone*.

Company performs 25% of all operas in orig language. Some pfs are taped and broadcast; 1 pf per season videotaped.

Budget for 1975 L 520,000,000 (US $780,000). Income: 30% box office, 40% gvnmt, 30% priv/corp/fndt grants. Ticket prices: L 5,000-L 1,500; 100% single ticket sale.

Number of persons engaged in 1975: guest solo artists: 96; chorus members: 81; orchestra members: 102; conductors: 7; stage directors/producers: 4; set & costume designers: 14; choreographers: 5; corps de ballet: 32; administrative staff: 4.

Company assembles orch for each prod; builds 70% of its sets and 80% costumes in own workshops.

TEATRO COMUNALE GIUSEPPE VERDI, Piazza G Verdi, Trieste, Italy; tel 040 62931. Founded in 1801. Perf at Teatro Verdi since 1801. Built in 1795 as an opera house; seat cap 1,200, avg aud 1,000. Company owned and operated by the City of Trieste; Pres, Mayor M Spaccini; Gen Int, Prof G de Ferra; Art Dir Raffaello de Banfield; Adm Dir Fulvio Gilleri.

SEASON	OPENING Day Month	CLOSING Day Month	NO OF PFS	NO OF OPERAS	NO OF NEW PROD	NO OF NON-OPERA PFS*
73-74	6 Nov	13 Apr	56	12	4	21
74-75	7 Nov	27 Apr	60	13	4	21

*Operettas.

World prem during these seasons: Chailly's *Sogno—ma forse no* 1/75.

Repertoire 1973-74 — Bellini: *Capuleti ed i Montecchi*; Giordano: *Andrea Chénier*; Massenet: *Manon*; Menotti: *Maria Golovin*; Penderecki: *Teufel von Loudun*; Puccini: *Tosca*; Rimsky-Korsakov: *Coq d'or*; Smetana: *Bartered Bride*; Verdi: *Macbeth, Rigoletto*; Wagner: *Götterdämmerung*.

1974-75 — Chailly: *Sogno—ma forse no*; Cilea: *Adriana Lecouvreur*; Donizetti: *Elisir*; Puccini: *Gianni Schicchi, Manon Lescaut, Suor Angelica, Tabarro*; Smareglia: *Falena*; Strauss, R: *Rosenkavalier*; Verdi: *Due Foscari, Falstaff*; Tchaikovsky: *Eugene Onegin*; Wagner: *Parsifal*.

Company performs 75% of all operas in orig language. Annual tour incl YUG: Zagreb.

Budget n/a.

Number of persons engaged in 1974-75 n/a.

Company maintains its own orchestra.

TEATRO REGIO, Piazza Castello 215, Turin, Italy; tel 549126. Founded in 1740. Perf at new Teatro Regio since 1973. Built in 1740 as an opera house, rebuilt several times; seat cap 1,788. Company first perf at original Teatro Regio. Also perf at Teatro Lirico & fall season at Palazzo dello Sport, seat cap 9,000; Sept, 12 pfs, 3 prods. Company is a public non-profit organization; Sovrint Giuseppe Erba.

SEASON	OPENING Day Month	CLOSING Day Month	NO OF PFS	NO OF OPERAS	NO OF NEW PROD	NO OF NON-OPERA PFS*
73-74	27 Nov	7 May	54	8	4	1
74-75	26 Nov	6 May	59	7	2	1

*Operettas, musicals, ballet, etc.

World prem during these seasons: Correggia's *Ayl* 10/73.

Repertoire 1973-74 — Bellini: *Norma*; Borodin: *Prince Igor*; Giordano: *Andrea Chénier*; Offenbach: *Contes d'Hoffmann*; Rossini: *Moise*; Verdi: *Ballo in maschera*,

Rigoletto; Zandonai: *Francesca da Rimini.* **Fall season/Palazzo dello Sport —** Donizetti: *Elisir*; Puccini: *Butterfly.*

1974-75 — Gounod: *Faust*; Malipiero: *Capricci di Callot*; Mozart: *Così fan tutte*; Puccini: *Fanciulla del West*; Verdi: *Don Carlo, Forza del destino*; Weber/Mahler: *Drei Pintos.* **Fall season/Palazzo dello Sport —** Donizetti: *Lucia*; Puccini: *Tosca*; Rossini: *Cenerentola.*

Company performs 50% of all operas in orig language. Guest engagements 1972-74 incl FRA: Versailles 3 pfs; Orange Fest 2 pfs.

Budget for 1974 L 4,634,000,000 (US $7,414,000). Income: 10% box office, 78% gvnmt, 12% other. Ticket prices: L 15,000-3,000; 67% subscription, 33% single ticket sale.

Number of persons engaged by company in 1974-75: chorus members: 85; orchestra members: 121; musical staff: 12; conductors: 8; stage directors/producers: 8; set & costume designers: 16; choreographers: 2; corps de ballet: 23; administrative staff: 30; technical, scenic, costume: 90.

Company uses local symph orch; builds 20% of its sets and costumes in own workshops.

TEATRO LA FENICE, Campo S Fantin 2519, Venice, Italy; tel 25191-24473. Founded in 1767; pfs were suspended 1859-64 & 1915-18. Perf at La Fenice since 1792. Built in 1790 as an opera house; seat cap 1,200. Prev theater: Teatro S Benedetto, 1767. Company supported by the State; Chm & Pres Mayor Dr Mario Rigo; Gen Int Comm Mario Pezzutto; Gen Adm Iginio Gianeselli; Adm Dir Achille Pavan; Head of Press Office Dr Giuseppe Pugliese; Tech & Art Adm Mo Arturo Wolf Ferrari; First Cond Mo Eugenio Bagnoli.

SEASON	OPENING Day Month	CLOSING Day Month	NO OF PFS	NO OF OPERAS	NO OF NEW PROD	NO OF NON-OPERA PFS*
73-74	2 Nov	2 Jul	65	11	—	3
74-75	Closed	—	—	—	—	—

*Ballet

Repertoire 1972-73 — Bellini: *Capuleti ed i Montecchi*; Busoni: *Turandot*; Dallapiccola: *Volo di notte*; Donizetti: *Lucia*; Janácek: *From the House of the Dead*; Mussorgsky: *Boris Godunov*; Puccini: *Rondine*; Rossellini: *Annonce faite à Marie*; Verdi: *Nabucco, Traviata*; Wagner: *Meistersinger*; Wolf-Ferrari: *Quattro rusteghi.*

1973-74 — Debussy: *Pelléas et Mélisande*; Donizetti: *Maria di Rohan*; Mozart: *Così fan tutte*; Puccini: *Butterfly, Tosca*; Rossini: *Moïse*; Spontini: *Fernand Cortez*; Testi: *Albergo dei poveri*; Verdi: *Ballo in maschera, Don Carlo*; Weber: *Freischütz.*

Company performs 50% of all operas in orig language. Subsidiary company, Festival Intern Musica Contemporanea, performs contemp music at the Biennale. Company has a training prgm for cond/coaches

Budget n/a.

Number of persons engaged in 1973-74: chorus members: 75; orchestra members: 163; conductors: 14; stage directors/producers: 14; set & costume designers: 14; choreographers: 14; corps de ballet: 15; administrative staff: 34; technical, scenic, costume: 189.

Company uses local symph orch.

LIRICO ARENA, Piazza Brà 28, Verona, Italy; tel 23520. Founded in 1913. Pfs suspended 1915-18 and 1940-45. Perf at Arena, a Roman amphitheater, since 1913. Built in 1st century AD; seat cap abt 20,000, avg aud abt 15,000. Company is a non-profit organization; Gen Int Carlo Alberto Cappelli; Art Dir Luciano Chailly; Adm Dir Francesco Ernani.

SEASON	OPENING Day Month	CLOSING Day Month	NO OF PFS	NO OF OPERAS	NO OF NEW PROD	NO OF NON-OPERA PFS*
74	13 Jul	25 Aug	23	3	3	6
75	12 Jul	26 Aug	26	3	3	3

*Operettas, musicals, ballet, etc.

Repertoire 1974 — Puccini: *Tosca*; Saint-Saëns: *Samson et Dalila*; Verdi: *Aida.*

1975 — Bizet: *Carmen*; Puccini: *Turandot*; Verdi: *Forza del destino.*

Company performs all operas in orig language.

Budget for 1975 L 3,600,000,000 (US $5,400,000). Income: 40% box office; 55% gvnmt; 5% other income. Ticket prices L 20,000-3,000; 2% subscription, 98% single ticket sale.

Number of persons engaged in 1974-75 n/a.

Company assembles orch for each prod; builds all sets in own workshops.

JAPAN

NIKI KAI, 1-58-13 Yoyogi Shibuya-ku, Tokyo, Japan; tel (03) 370-6441. Founded in 1952. Perf at Hibiya Public Hall 1952-61, seat cap 2,500. Other theaters: Sankei Hall; Tokyo Bunka Kaikan. Company is a private non-profit organization; Pres & Gen Dir Teiichi Nakayama; Adm Dir Shozo Kawachi.

SEASON	OPENING Day Month	CLOSING Day Month	NO OF PFS	NO OF OPERAS	NO OF NEW PROD	NO OF NON-OPERA PFS
73-74	Apr	Mar	20	7	4	—
74-75	Apr	Mar	17	6	2	—

Repertoire 1973-74 — Dan: *Yuzuru*; Gluck: *Orfeo ed Euridice*; Mozart: *Nozze di Figaro, Zauberflöte*; Shostakovich: *Katerina Ismailova*; Toda: *Story of Kyara City*; Wagner: *Fliegende Holländer.*

1974-75 — Mozart: *Così fan tutte*; Rossini: *Barbiere di Siviglia*; Strauss, J: *Fledermaus*; Verdi: *Macbeth, Rigoletto*; Weber: *Freischütz.*

Company performs 75% of all operas in orig language. 4 pfs per year taped and rebroadcast on radio and TV. Annual tour, 1973-74 incl 22 pfs in Japanese cities. Company has a training prgm for 5 singers per year.

Budget for 1974-75 Y 114,752,000 (US $340,000). Income: 52% box office; 38% gvnmt; 4% priv grants; 6% other income. Ticket prices: Y 3,500-1,500; 30% subscription, 70% single ticket sale.

Number of persons engaged in 1974-75: resident solo artists: 56; chorus members: 74; orchestra members: 82; musical staff: 6; conductors: 3; stage directors/producers: 3; set & costume designers: 6; choreographers: 2; corps de ballet: 18; administrative staff: 5; technical, scenic, costume: 16.

Company uses local symph orch.

Policy determined by board of dir: Gen Dir Teiichi Nakayama; Adm Dir Shozo Kawachi; Dir Ryosuke Hatanaka, Takanosuke Watanabe and Shigeo Harada.

MONACO

OPÉRA DE MONTE-CARLO, Principality of Monaco; tel 30 69 31. Founded in 1879; company consists entirely of guest artists. Perf at Opéra de Monte-Carlo since 1879. Built in 1879 as an opera house; seat cap 600, avg aud 600. Company is a private non-profit organization subsidized by SBM Company, Monte Carlo; Pres Mo Renzo Rossellini; Principal Cond Lovro von Matacic; Admin Mng Tibor Katona; Art Mng Riccardo Vitale; Principal Stg Dir Margherita Wallmann; Principal Dsgn George Wakhevitch.

SEASON	OPENING Day Month	CLOSING Day Month	NO OF PFS	NO OF PROD	NO OF NEW PROD	NO OF NON-OPERA PFS*
73-74	19 Nov	Easter	18	11	—	7
74-75	19 Nov	Easter	18	11	—	7

*Ballet

NORWAY

Repertoire 1973-74 — Massenet: *Werther*; Mozart: *Così fan tutte*; Puccini: *Manon Lescaut*; Verdi: *Falstaff*, et al.

1974-75 — Donizetti: *Elisir*; Giordano: *Andrea Chénier*; Poulenc: *Voix humaine*; Puccini: *Bohème*; Ravel: *Heure espagnole*; Verdi: *Rigoletto*, et al.

Company performs all operas in orig language.

Budget n/a. Ticket prices: Fr 50-25; 100% single ticket sale.

Number of persons engaged 1974-75: guest solo artists: 24; chorus members: 50; orchestra members: 86; musical staff: 2; conductors: 5; stage directors/producers: 4; set & costume designers: 4; choreographers: 1; administrative staff: 3; technical, scenic, costume: 38.

Company uses National Symph of Monte Carlo; builds 25% of its sets and costumes in own workshops.

Policy determined by Supervisory Commtt: Pres Renzo Rossellini, Admin Mng Tibor Katona, Art Mng Riccardo Vitale.

NORWAY

DEN NORSKE OPERA, 23c Storgaten, Oslo 1, Norway; tel (02) 33 79 85. Founded in 1957. Perf at Den Norske Opera since 1959; seat cap 1,049, avg aud 761; theater not built as an opera house. Company is a private non-profit organization in form of a limited company with the Government, the Municipality of Oslo and the Norwegian Opera Foundation as stockholders; Chm of Board Bjorn Haug; Gen Mng Gunnar Brunvoll; Mus Dir Martin Turnovsky; Prod Dir Arne Neergaard; Tech Dir Charles Nielsen.

SEASON	OPENING Day	OPENING Month	CLOSING Day	CLOSING Month	NO OF PFS	NO OF OPERAS	NO OF NEW PROD	NO OF NON-OPERA PFS*
73-74	1	Aug	16	Jun	196	15	5	104
74-75	31	Jul	15	Jun	191	11	5	74

*Operettas, musicals, ballet, etc.

World prem during these seasons: Johnsen's *Legend of Svein and Maria* 9/73.

Repertoire 1973-74 — Dallapiccola: *Prigioniero*; Donizetti: *Don Pasquale*; Gluck: *Iphigénie en Tauride*; Johnsen: *Legend of Svein and Maria*; Mozart: *Don Giovanni, Nozze di Figaro, Zauberflöte*; Puccini: *Gianni Schicchi, Tabarro*; Rossini: *Barbiere di Siviglia*; Strauss, R: *Rosenkavalier*; Stravinski: *Oedipus Rex*; Verdi: *Rigoletto, Trovatore*; Wagner: *Walküre*.

1974-75 — Donizetti: *Don Pasquale*; Kodály: *Háry János*; Leoncavallo: *Pagliacci*; Mozart: *Don Giovanni, Zauberflöte*; Offenbach: *Contes d'Hoffmann*; Rossini: *Barbiere di Siviglia, Cambiale di matrimonio*; Strauss, R: *Rosenkavalier*; Verdi: *Don Carlo, Trovatore*.

Company performs 5% of all operas in orig language. Two or three pfs taped and rebroadcast on radio and TV. Annual tour, 1973-74 incl 36 pfs in Norwegian cities. Guest engagements 1971-75 incl SWE: Stockholm 3 pfs; FIN: Kuopio 3 pfs; SPA: Barcelona 3 pfs; NOR: Stavanger 3 pfs, Gjovik 1 pf.

Budget for 1975 N Kr 26,300,000 (US $5,050,000). Income: 3.9% box office; 94.4% gvnmt; 1.7% other income. Ticket prices: N Kr 30-5; 74.6% subscription, 25.4% single ticket sale.

Number of persons engaged in 1974-75: 350 on permanent basis; resident solo artists: 28; guest solo artists: 15; chorus members: 40; orchestra members: 64; musical staff excl ballet: 8; conductors: 3; asst stage directors/producers: 3; corps de ballet: 22; administrative staff: 12; technical, scenic, costume: 150.

Company uses its own orch; builds all sets and costumes in own workshops.

Policy determined by Board of Trustees: Bjorn Haug, Aase Bjerkholt, representing Gvnmt; Rolf Stranger, Kjell Bakkelund, repr Municipality of Oslo; Alfredo Gianni, Bjorn Larssen, repr the employees of the company; the Norwegian Opera Foundation.

POLAND

TEATR WIELKI/GRAND THEATER WARSAW, Moliera St 5, Warsaw, Poland; tel 26-30-01. Founded in 1833. Perf at Grand Theater Warsaw since 1965. Built in 1825 as an opera house; seat cap 1,905, avg aud 1,876. Destroyed during WW II and rebuilt in 1965. Prev theater: Opera House Warsaw, Nowogrodzka St. Company owned and operated by the City of Warsaw, Dept of Culture; Gen Dir Zdzislaw Sliwinski; Art Dir Antoni Wicherek; Tech Dir Jerzy Bojar; Adm Dir Harry Anders.

SEASON	OPENING Day Month		CLOSING Day Month		NO OF PFS	NO OF OPERAS	NO OF NEW PROD	NO OF NON-OPERA PFS*
73-74	1	Sep	31	Aug	261	26	5	80
74-75	1	Sep	31	Aug	238	25	4	—

*Operettas, musicals, ballet, etc.

World prems during these seasons: Bloch's *Sleeping Princess* 9/74; Rudzinski's *The Peasants* 9/74.

Repertoire 1971-75 — Bacewicz: *Desire*; Bergman: *Ecce Homo*; Bizet: *Carmen*; Donizetti: *Lucia*; Menotti: *Consul*; Moniuszko: *Halka, Haunted Castle*; Monteverdi: *Incoronazione di Poppea*; Mosolow: $E = MC_2$; Mozart: *Nozze di Figaro*; Mussorgsky: *Boris Godunov*; Penderecki: *Teufel von Loudun*; Puccini: *Butterfly, Tosca*; Rossini: *Barbiere di Siviglia*; Rózycki: *Master Twardowski*; Rudzinski: *Dismissal of Greek Envoys, Peasants*; Tchaikovsky; *Eugene Onegin*; Verdi: *Aida, Don Carlo, Falstaff, Traviata, Trovatore*; Wagner: *Tannhäuser*.

Company performs 25% of all operas in orig language. Pfs of new prods are broadcast twice a year on radio, and one prod is videotaped. Company gives guest engagements and arranges exchange visits; maintains a theater museum.

Budget n/a. Income: 20% box office; 80% city gvnmt. Ticket prices: Zl 70-20; 42% subscription, 58% single ticket sale.

Number of persons engaged in 1974-75: resident solo artists: 56; chorus members: 120; orchestra members: 140; conductors: 6; stage directors/producers: 1; set & costume designers: 5; choreographers: 4; corps de ballet: 120; administrative staff: 18; technical, scenic, costume: 413.

Company builds 99% of its sets and 98% of its costumes in own workshops.

Policy determined by Ministry of Culture and Art, Warsaw.

ROMANIA

OPERA ROMÂNA, Gh Gheorghiu Dej Blv 70-72, Bucharest, Romania; tel 14-69-80. Founded in 1877. Perf at Opera Romȃna since 1954. Built in 1953 as an opera house; seat cap 960, avg aud 825. Prev theater: Teatrul National, 1879-1902; seat cap 1,000. Destroyed in 1944. Perf also: Teatrul Liric, Eforie Theater, Operetta Theater, former Queen Marie Theater. Company owned and operated by Cultural and Socialist Education Committee of Bucharest, which also manages National Theater, Comedy Theater, Bulandra, Nottara, Teatrul Mic, Giulesti, Operetta, Creanga and Tandarica. Pres Prof Amza Saceanu; Gen Dir Petre Codreanu; Dep Dir Constantin Zavaleanu; Principal Cond Cornel Trailescu; Chief Stage Dir Hero Lupescu.

SEASON	OPENING Day Month		CLOSING Day Month		NO OF PFS	NO OF OPERAS	NO OF NEW PROD	NO OF NON-OPERA PFS*
73-74	16	Oct	16	Jun	251	34	6	73
74-75	1	Oct	30	Jun	236	31	7	67

*Operettas, musicals, ballet, etc.

World prems during these seasons: Buicliu's *Doamna Chiajna* 10/73; Trailescu's *Balcescu* 8/74; Bratu's *Right of Loving* 3/75.

SPAIN

Repertoire 1971-75 — Beethoven: *Fidelio*; Bizet: *Carmen*; Borodin: *Prince Igor*; Bratu: *The Right of Loving*; Britten: *Albert Herring*; Buicliu: *Doamna Chiajna*; Constantinescu: *Stormy Night*; Debussy: *Pelléas et Mélisande*; Delibes: *Lakmé*; Donizetti: *Don Pasquale, Lucia*; Dumitrescu: *Decebal, King Ion*; Enesco: *Oedipus*; Gounod: *Faust*; Leoncavallo: *Pagliacci*; Lerescu: *Ecaterina Teodoroiu*; Mascagni: *Cavalleria rusticana*; Mozart: *Così fan tutte, Don Giovanni, Entführung aus dem Serail, Zauberflöte*; Mussorgsky: *Boris Godunov*; Offenbach: *Contes d'Hoffmann*; Orff: *Mond*; Puccini: *Bohème, Gianni Schicchi, Butterfly, Tosca, Turandot*; Rossini: *Barbiere di Siviglia*; Smetana: *Bartered Bride*; Strauss, J: *Fledermaus*; Trailescu: *Balcescu, Puss in Boots*; Verdi: *Aida, Ballo in maschera, Don Carlo, Otello, Rigoletto, Traviata, Trovatore*; Wagner: *Fliegende Holländer, Lohengrin, Tannhäuser*.

Company performs 25% of all operas in orig language. 4-10 pfs per season taped and rebroadcast on radio, 4 pfs videotaped. Occasional tours; 1973-74 Ploiesti, Pitesti, Mamaia, Neptun, Giurgiu and other towns in Romania. Guest engagements 1971-75 incl BUL: Russe 4 pfs; GRE: Thesaloniki 6 pfs; YUG: Belgrade 1 pf; GER DR: Berlin 2 pfs; AUS: Klagenfurt 11 pfs; SWE: Stockholm 3 pfs; and ITA: Piave 12 pfs. Company has training prgm for all its singers.

Budget n/a. Income: 10% box office, 90% gvnmt. Ticket prices: RL 18-4.

Number of persons engaged in 1974-75: resident solo artists: 64; chorus members: 95; orchestra members: 97; musical staff: 19; conductors: 5; stage directors/producers: 2; set & costume designers: 4; choreographers: 2; corps de ballet: 71*; administrative staff: 66; technical, scenic, costume: 192.

*44 solo dancers.

Company maintains own orch; builds all sets and costumes in own workshops.

Policy determined by Supervisory Commtt: Gen Dir Petre Codreanu; Dep Dir Constantin Zavaleanu; singers Valentin Loghin and Valentin Teodorian; dancer Florin Mateescu; cond Cornel Trailescu; stg dir Hero Lupescu; Chorus Master Stelian Olariu and other members of the company.

SPAIN

GRAN TEATRO DEL LICEO, calle San Pablo 1 bis, Barcelona 1, Spain; tel 226 26 03. Founded 1847; formerly Liceo Filarmonico de Montesion. Pfs were suspended 1861-62. Perf at Gran Teatro del Liceo since 1847. Built in 1847 as an opera house; destroyed by fire 1861 and reopened 1862. Prev theater: Teatro Santa Cruz. Private non-profit organization; Gen Int Juan A Pamias.

Lengths of season, number of pfs n/a.

Repertoire 1973-74 — Donizetti: *Caterina Cornaro, Lucia*; Gluck: *Iphigénie en Tauride*; Gounod: *Faust*; Massenet: *Iris*; Montemezzi: *Amore dei tre re*; Mozart: *Così fan tutte*; Puccini: *Bohème*; Rossini: *Barbiere di Siviglia*; Saint-Saëns: *Samson et Dalila*; Salvador: *Vinatea*; Strauss, R: *Rosenkavalier*; Verdi: *Aida, Attila, Traviata, Trovatore*; Wagner: *Walküre*; Weber: *Freischütz*.

1974-75 — Beethoven: *Fidelio*; Bizet: *Carmen*; Cimarosa: *Matrimonio segreto*; Donizetti: *Anna Bolena*; Halévy: *Juive*; Jolivet: *Dolores*; Massenet: *Manon*; Mozart: *Don Giovanni*; Puccini: *Tosca*; Rossini: *Guillaume Tell*; Strauss, R: *Elektra*; Verdi: *Falstaff, Forza del destino, Macbeth, Vespri*; Wagner: *Siegfried*.

Budget n/a. Ticket prices: P 350-40.

Number of persons engaged 1974-75: resident solo artists and chorus members: 126; orchestra members: n/a; musical staff: 7; conductors: 16; stage directors/producers: 13; choreographers: 6; corps de ballet: n/a, 6 solo ballerinas.

Company maintains its own orch.

AMIGOS CANARIOS DE LA OPERA, Festival Las Palmas, Canary Islands, Spain. Founded in 1975. Perf at Teatro Perez Galdos. Private organization under the patronage of the Administration of the Canary Islands, the City of Las Palmas and the Ministry for

Tourism; Pres Alejandro del Castillo y Bravo de Laguna; Gen Dir & Stge Dir Tito Capobianco; Mus Dirs Theo Alcantara, Richard Bonynge, Christopher Keene, Bruno Rigacci; Adm Dir Garcia Campos; Tech Dir Carl Toms and Mario Vanarelli.

First season 29 Apr-30 May 1975; 17 pfs, 5 operas.

Repertoire 1975 — Donizetti: *Maria Stuarda*; Offenbach: *Contes d'Hoffmann*; Puccini: *Tosca*; Verdi: *Macbeth, Otello*.

Budget, income and ticket prices n/a.

Number of persons engaged for the 1975 festival: guest solo artists: 25; chorus members: *; orchestra members: *; musical staff: 4; conductors: 5; stage directors/ producers: 3; set & costume designers: 2; choreographers: n/a; corps de ballet: n/a; administrative staff: n/a; technical, scenic, costume: 9.

*Company used the Symph Orch and Chamber Chorus of the Univ of Michigan, USA.

SWEDEN

ROYAL OPERA STOCKHOLM, Gustav Adolfs torg, Stockholm, Sweden; tel 08-22 17 40. Founded in 1773. Perf at Royal Opera since 1898. Built in 1898 as an opera house; seat cap 1,147, avg aud 1,078. Prev theaters: 1773-82 Slora Bollhuset; 1782-1891 new Opera House, seat cap 948; 1891-98 Nya Teatern and Södra Teatern; Drottningholm Court Theater. Company owned and operated by Gvnmt of Sweden, which also manages Royal Dramatic Theater, Stadsteatern, Södra Teatern; Gen Mng of Opera Bertil Bokstedt; Mus Dir Berislav Klobucar; Tech Dir Sven-Eric Josdal; Prod Dir Bengt Peterson; Financial Dir Sven-Gunnar Tillius.

SEASON	OPENING Day Month	CLOSING Day Month	NO OF PFS	NO OF OPERAS	NO OF NEW PROD	NO OF NON-OPERA PFS*
73-74	1 Sep	14 Jun	300	35	—	138
74-75	Opera house closed for rebuilding. 450 pfs in other theaters in Sweden and abroad.					

*Operettas, musicals, ballet, etc.

World prem during these seasons: Hemberg's *Love Love Love* 10/73.

Repertoire 1973-74 — Berg: *Wozzeck*; Berwald: *Drottningen av Golconda*; Bizet: *Carmen*; Britten: *Albert Herring*; Glaser: *Boy and the Voice*; Gluck: *Orfeo ed Euridice*; Janácek: *Jenufa*; Lundquist: *Sekund av Evighet*; Mozart: *Don Giovanni, Nozze di Figaro, Zauberflöte*; Offenbach: *Contes d'Hoffmann*; Poulenc: *Voix humaine*; Puccini: *Bohème, Tosca*; Rosenberg: *Joseph and his Brothers*; Rossini: *Barbiere di Siviglia*; Schoenberg: *Moses und Aron*; Strauss, J: *Fledermaus*; Strauss, R; *Ariadne auf Naxos, Elektra, Rosenkavalier, Salome*; Tchaikovsky: *Pique Dame*; Verdi: *Ballo in maschera, Don Carlo, Rigoletto, Traviata, Trovatore*; Wagner: *Rheingold, Walküre, Siegfried, Götterdämmerung, Tristan und Isolde*; Zimmermann: *Soldaten*.

1974-75 — no repertoire available. No pfs at Royal Opera House due to alterations; perf in other halls and on tour only.

Company performs 50% of all operas in orig language. Sev pfs broadcast live on radio and 2 pfs videotaped. Annual tour of Swedish cities. Guest engagements 1971-75 incl UK: Edinburgh 9 pfs, Brighton 6 pfs; NOR: Bergen 5 pfs; FIN: Helsinki 2 pfs; FR GER: Kiel 2 pfs, Wiesbaden 4 pfs; Hong Kong 6 pfs. Exchange engagements incl USSR: Moscow 8 pfs, Leningrad 5 pfs.

Budget for 1974-75 Kr 51,000,000 (US $12,495,000). Income: 6% box office; 92% gvnmt; 2% other income. Ticket prices: Kr 35-2; 50% subscription.

Number of persons engaged in 1974-75: 750; resident solo artists: 45; guest solo artists: 15; chorus members: 70; orchestra members: 120; musical staff: 7; conductors: 9; stage directors/producers: 2; set & costume designers: 2; choreographers: 4; corps de ballet: 70; administrative staff: 8; technical, scenic, costume: 190.

Company maintains its own orch on a seasonal basis; builds all sets and costumes in own workshops.

651

SWITZERLAND

Policy determined by Board of Directors: Chmn Roland Palsson; Vice-Chmn Sten Sture Landström; Gen Mng Bertil Bokstedt; mems J Nordensson, Eskil Hemberg, Henrik Sjögren and Karl Ludwig Wiechel.

SWITZERLAND

GRAND THÉÂTRE DE GENÈVE, 11 Blvd du Théâtre, Geneva, Switzerland; tel 21 23 18. Founded in 1879. Pfs were suspended 1951-62. Perf at Grand Théâtre de Genève since 1879. Built in 1879 as an opera house; seat cap, 1,480. Destroyed by fire in 1951 and reopened 1962. Company owned and operated by the Fondation du Grand Théâtre, City of Geneva; Gen Dir Jean-Claude Riber.

SEASON	OPENING Day	Month	CLOSING Day	Month	NO OF PFS	NO OF OPERAS	NO OF NEW PROD	NO OF NON-OPERA PFS*
73-74	13	Sep	17	Jun	93	8	6	46
74-75	17	Sep	12	Jun	91	9	5	38

*Operettas, musicals, ballet, etc.

Repertoire 1973-74 — Britten: *Turn of the Screw*; Donizetti: *Elisir*; Handel: *Xerxes*; Mozart: *Idomeneo*; Saint-Saëns: *Samson et Dalila*; Strauss, J: *Fledermaus*; Strauss, R: *Elektra*; Verdi: *Otello*; Wagner: *Fliegende Holländer*.

1974-75 — Berlioz: *Troyens*; Borodin: *Prince Igor*; Janácek: *Katya Kabanová*; Mozart: *Entführung aus dem Serail*; Prokofiev: *Love for Three Oranges*; Puccini: *Manon Lescaut*; Rossini: *Barbiere di Siviglia*; Strauss, R: *Salome*; Wagner: *Rheingold*.

Company performs all operas in orig language. Every prod is taped and rebroadcast on radio.

Budget for 1974-75 SFr 7,943,900 (US $3,110,000). Income: 35.2% box office; 64.8% gvnmt. Ticket prices: SFr 36-9; 54.4% subscription, 45.6% single ticket sale.

Number of persons engaged in 1974-75: guest solo artists: 125; chorus members: 36; musical staff: 5; stage directors/producers: 6; set & costume designers: 1; choreographers: 1; corps de ballet: 33; administrative and clerical staff: 10; technical, scenic, costume: 75.

Company uses the Orchestre de la Suisse Romande; builds its own sets and costumes.

Policy determined by the Fondation du Grand Théâtre; Pres Jean-Flavien Lalive; Vice-Pres Roger Aubert; Secry Albert Chauffat; City Counsellors Mme Lise Girardin and Claude Ketterer; mems Alfred Borel, Roger de Candolle, Charles Gorgerat, Pierre Jacquet, Willy Kunz, Rolf Zwicky.

THEATER-AKTIENGESELLSCHAFT ZÜRICH, Schillerstr 1, Zurich, Switzerland; tel 32-69-20. Founded in 1891. Perf at Opernhaus Zürich since 1891. Built in 1891 as an opera house; seat cap 1,200, avg aud 900. Company is a non-profit organization; Chmn Hans Sulzer; Dir Dr Claus Helmut Drese; Mus Dir Prof Ferdinand Leitner; Adm Dir Hannes Strasser; Prgm Dir Werner Saladin; Stage Mng Max Roethlisberger.

SEASON	OPENING Day	Month	CLOSING Day	Month	NO OF PFS	NO OF OPERAS	NO OF NEW PROD	NO OF NON-OPERA PFS*
73-74	9	Sep	27	Jun	302	22	12	121
74-75	8	Sep	28	Jun	289	22	10	130

*Operettas, musicals, ballet, etc.

World prem during these seasons: Klebe's *Ein wahrer Held* 1/75.

Repertoire 1973-74 — Beethoven: *Fidelio*; Humperdinck: *Hänsel und Gretel*; Martin: *Sturm*; Mozart: *Così fan tutte, Don Giovanni, Nozze di Figaro*; Offenbach: *Contes d'Hoffmann*; Puccini: *Gianni Schicchi, Tabarro, Tosca*; Reimann: *Melusine*; Strauss, R: *Capriccio, Rosenkavalier*; Verdi: *Ballo in maschera, Ernani, Nabucco, Rigoletto, Traviata*; Wagner: *Lohengrin, Meistersinger, Parsifal, Tannhäuser*.

1974-75 — Haydn: *Fedeltà premiata*; Humperdinck: *Hänsel und Gretel*; Klebe: *Wahrer Held*; Mozart: *Così fan tutte, Don Giovanni, Nozze di Figaro, Zauberflöte*; Orff: *Kluge*; Puccini: *Manon Lescaut*; Strauss, R: *Capriccio, Rosenkavalier*; Tchaikovsky: *Pique Dame*; Verdi: *Ballo in maschera, Ernani, Nabucco, Otello, Rigoletto, Traviata*; Wagner: *Meistersinger, Parsifal, Tannhäuser*; Weber: *Freischütz*.

Company performs 75% of all operas in orig language. Guest engagements 1971-75 incl SWI: Lugano, Lausanne; FRA: Bordeaux. Also operates Internationales Opern Zentrum.

Budget for 1974-75 SFr 29,000,000 (US $11,154,000). Income:12% box office, 83.7% gvnmt, 4.3% other income. Ticket prices: SFr 27-5; 17½% subscription, 82½% single ticket sale.

Number of persons engaged in 1974-75: resident solo artists: 46; guest solo artists: 52; chorus members: 54; orchestra members: 82; musical staff: 11; conductors: 7; stage directors/producers: 7; set & costume designers: 11; choreographers: 4; corps de ballet: 38; administrative staff: 24; technical, scenic, costume: 150.

Company uses local symph orch; builds all sets and costumes in own workshops.

UNION OF SOVIET SOCIALIST REPUBLICS

BOLSHOI OPERA, Sverdlov Square, Moscow, USSR. Founded in 1776. Perf at Bolshoi Opera Theatre since 1856. Built in 1856 as an opera house; seat cap 2,100; avg aud 2,100. Perf also at Palace of Congress; seat cap 6,000. Company first perf private theatres 1776-1780 & 1805-1824; at Petrovsky Theatre 1780-1805; at Bolshoi-Petrovsky Theatre 1825-1853. Company owned and operated by state under USSR Ministry of Culture, Piotr Nilych Demechov, Minister; also manages Stanislavsky Theatre, Filial Theatre, Nemirovich-Danchenko Music Theatre. Opera Dir Kiril Molchanov until summer 1975; Mus Dir Yuri Simonov, Chief St Dir Boris Pokrovsky.

Company has ten-month season of opera and ballet; rep of abt 25 operas, 5 new prods.

World prem during last two seasons: Molchanov's *Dawns Are Quiet Here* 4/75.

Repertoire n/a.

Company performs 65% Russian operas, 35% foreign operas; all in Russian. Gives guest engagements: 1975 in New York. Also sponsors Bolshoi Ballet & Bolshoi Museum. Has a training prgm for young singers.

Budget n/a. Ticket prices: US abt $4-80c.

Number of persons engaged for 1974-75: 2,000; resident solo artists: 80; chorus members: 300; orchestra members: 250; corps de ballet: 300; conductors: 7; technical, scenic, costume: 600.

Company maintains own orchestra; builds all sets and costumes in own workshops.

Policy is determined by Adm Board: Dir & 3 Vice Dirs; Minister & Vice Minister of Culture; Art Board: leading solo artists; Praesidium: Mus Dir, Chief St Dir & Des, Ballet & Chorus Master.

UNITED KINGDOM

WELSH NATIONAL OPERA COMPANY, John St, Cardiff, UK; tel 40541. Founded in 1946. Perf at New Theatre, Park Pl, Cardiff, since 1954. Built in 1906, not as an opera house; seat cap for opera 1,124, avg aud 980. Prev theaters: 1946-51 Prince of Wales Theatre, Cardiff, seat cap 1,000; 1952-53 Sophia Gardens Pavilion, Cardiff. Private non-profit organization; Chmn Lord Davis; Gen Mgr James Mowat; Mus Dir Richard Armstrong; Art Dir Michael Geliot.

SEASON	OPENING Day	Month	CLOSING Day	Month	NO OF PFS	NO OF OPERAS	NO OF NEW PROD	NO OF NON-OPERA PFS
73-74	18	Sep	15	Jun	140	12	4	—
74-75	10	Sep	28	Jun	119	11	4	—

World prem during these seasons: Hoddinott's *The Beach of Falesa* 2/74.

Repertoire 1973-74 — Bizet: *Pêcheurs de perles*; Britten: *Billy Budd*; Donizetti: *Elisir*; Hoddinott: *Beach of Falesa*; Mozart: *Idomeneo, Zauberflöte*; Puccini: *Bohème, Butterfly*; Strauss, J: *Fledermaus*; Verdi: *Don Carlo, Rigoletto, Simon Boccanegra*.

1974-75 — Bizet: *Pêcheurs de perles*; Britten: *Billy Budd*; Donizetti: *Elisir*; Mozart: *Così fan tutte*; Offenbach: *Grande Duchesse de Gérolstein*; Puccini: *Bohème, Manon Lescaut*; Rossini: *Barbiere di Siviglia*; Verdi: *Don Carlo, Simon Boccanegra*; Wagner: *Fliegende Holländer*.

Company performs over 25% of all operas in orig language. One perf is broadcast live and one videotaped per season. Annual tour of abt 11 operas in over 90 pfs at Swansea, Bristol, Oxford, Liverpool, Manchester, Leeds, Birmingham, Norwich, Southampton, Leicester, Peterborough, Haverfordwest, Aberystwyth, Connah's Quay, Southsea, Wolverhampton, Llandudno, Wrexham. Guest engagements 1973-75 incl SWI: Lausanne 1 pf, Zurich 2 pfs; SPA: Barcelona 3 pfs. Sister companies: Welsh Drama Co — 180 pfs annually; Welsh Philharmonia — 43 concerts annually.

Budget for 1974-75 £960,305 (US $2,244,000). Income: 16% box office, 74% gvnmt, 7% local authorities, 3% other. Ticket prices: £2.50-65p; no subscription, only single ticket sale.

Number of persons engaged for 1974-75: resident solo artists: 7; guest solo artists: 40; chorus members: 42-60; orchestra members: 51-120; musical staff: 8; conductors: 8; stage directors/producers: 6; set & costume designers: 7; choreographers: 2; corps de ballet: 6; administrative staff: 13; technical, scenic, costume: 52.

Company maintains own permanent orch, Welsh Philh; builds 90% of its sets & 99% of its costumes in own workshops.

Council of Mngt: Exec Chmn Alfred Francis; Vc Chmn The Lord Davies of Llandinam; Councillor J Allison; D Cantlay; G T Cantlay; Christopher Cory; Raymond Edwards; Idris Evans; Councillor H Ferguson Jones; T Mervyn Jones; David Mansel Lewis; Secy Margaret Moreland; T M Hadyn Rees; Councillor H H Roberts; G H Sylvester; David W Thomas; Wynford Vaughan-Thomas; J Lewis Walters.

GLYNDEBOURNE FESTIVAL OPERA, Lewes/Sussex, UK; tel Ringmer (0273) 81 23 21. Founded in 1934; pfs suspended 1941-45. Perf at Glyndebourne Opera House since 1934. Built in 1934 as an opera house; seat cap 800, avg aud 750. Company is a private non-profit organization; Chmn George W L Christie; Gen Adm Moran Caplat CBE; Mus Dir John Pritchard CBE; Prod Dir John Cox; Mng Brian Dickie.

SEASON	OPENING Day	OPENING Month	CLOSING Day	CLOSING Month	NO OF PFS	NO OF OPERAS	NO OF NEW PROD	NO OF NON-OPERA PFS
74	23	May	4	Aug	65	5	2	—
75	22	May	6	Aug	68	5	2	—

Repertoire 1974 — Cavalli: *Calisto*; Einem: *Besuch der alten Dame*; Mozart: *Idomeneo, Nozze di Figaro*; Strauss, R: *Intermezzo*.

1975 — Janácek: *Cunning Little Vixen*; Mozart: *Così fan tutte*; Strauss, R: *Intermezzo*; Stravinsky: *Rake's Progress*; Tchaikovsky: *Eugene Onegin*.

Company performs 95% of all operas in orig language. Pfs are broadcast live regularly and at least 1 opera videotaped annually. Guest engagements 1971-75 incl BEL: Brussels, Ghent during Flanders Fest; DEN: Copenhagen 4 pfs. Subsidiary companies incl Glyndebourne Touring Opera, with 25-30 pfs annually in major UK cities such as Norwich, Manchester, Bristol, Southampton, Oxford.

Budgets for 1974-75 n/a. Income: 80% box office; 20% other income; no gvnmt subsidies. Ticket prices: £11.90-4.30; 100% single ticket sale.

Number of persons engaged in 1974-75: 348; guest solo artists: 48; chorus members 44; orchestra members: 70; musical staff: 13; mus libr: 3; conductors: 5; stage directors/producers: 4; set & costume designers: 6; choreographers: 2; corps de ballet: 6; administrative staff: 6; technical, scenic, costume: 67.

Company engages London Phil Orch for the Fest and Bournemouth Sinfonietta for the Glyndebourne Touring Opera; builds all sets and costumes in own workshops.

Policy determined by Glyndebourne Productions Ltd: Directors: Chmn G W L Christie Esq, Gerald Coke Esq CBE, Anthony Lloyd Esq QC, E Scott Norman Esq, Miss Gillian Swire; Gen Admin Moran Caplat Esq CBE; Secy Janet Moores; Treas John Barden Esq.

ENGLISH NATIONAL OPERA, form Sadler's Wells Opera, St Martin's Lane, London, UK; tel 836 0111. Founded in 1931. Perf at The Coliseum since 1968. Built in 1904; seat cap 2,354. Prev theaters: Old Vic Theatre; Sadler's Wells Theatre, seat cap 1,500, 1934-68. Company is government owned and operated through the Arts Council of Gt Britain, which also manages Royal Opera House, Covent Garden; National Theatre, South Bank; and Royal Shakespeare Company, Stratford. In charge of Arts Council: The Lord Gibson. Mng Dir Lord Harewood; Mus Dir Charles Mackerras; Adm Dir Glen Byam Shaw until '75, succ Rupert Rhymes; Dram Dir Edmund Tracey; and Tech Adm James Sargant.

SEASON	OPENING Day Month		CLOSING Day Month		NO OF PFS	NO OF OPERAS	NO OF NEW PROD	NO OF NON-OPERA PFS
73-74	31	Jul	8	Jun	282	24	6	—
74-75	3	Aug	14	Jun	259	24	4	—

World prem during these seasons: Crosse's *The Story of Vasco* 3/74.

Repertoire 1971-75 — Bartŏk: *Bluebeard's Castle*; Bennett: *Mines of Sulphur*; Berlioz: *Damnation de Faust*; Bizet: *Carmen*; Britten: *Gloriana*; Crosse: *Story of Vasco*; Donizetti: *Maria Stuarda*; Henze: *Bassariden*; Janáček: *Katya Kabanová, Makropoulos Affair*; Leoncavallo: *Pagliacci*; Mascagni: *Cavalleria rusticana*; Massenet: *Manon*; Monteverdi: *Incoronazione di Poppea*; Mozart: *Così fan tutte, Entführung aus dem Serail, Nozze di Figaro, Zauberflöte*; Offenbach: *Contes d'Hoffmann*; Penderecki: *Teufel von Loudun*; Prokofiev: *War and Peace*; Puccini: *Bohème, Butterfly*; Rossini: *Barbiere di Siviglia, Comte Ory, Italiana in Algeri*; Strauss, J: *Fledermaus*; Strauss, R: *Rosenkavalier*; Stravinsky: *Oedipus Rex*; Verdi: *Ballo in maschera, Don Carlo, Forza del destino, Rigoletto, Traviata, Trovatore*; Wagner: *Lohengrin, Meistersinger, Rheingold, Walküre, Siegfried, Götterdämmerung*.

Company performs all operas in English. A few pfs are broadcast live per season. Annual tour of 12 operas in 120 pfs in UK: Bristol, Manchester, Birmingham, Leeds, Newcastle, Wolverhampton, Liverpool, Bradford, Hull, Norwich, Nottingham, Coventry, Cardiff, Southampton and Eastbourne. Guest engagements 1972-75 incl FR GER: Munich 2 pfs; AUS: Vienna 5 pfs.

Budget n/a. Ticket prices: £3.30-50p; single ticket sale only.

Number of persons engaged in 1974-75: resident solo artists: 45; guest solo artists: 30; chorus members: 75; orchestra members: 91; musical staff: 14; conductors: 7; stage directors/producers: 6; set & costume designers: 1; choreographers: 3; corps de ballet: 18; administrative staff: 20; technical, scenic, costume: 145.

Company maintains own orch on a seasonal basis; does not build sets.

Policy determined by Board of Trustees: Rt Hon Kenneth Robinson; Mrs Iris Bonham; Lord Barnetson; Lord Goodman; Brig K Hargreaves; David Lawman; Prof Sir Anthony Lewis CBE MA; Sir Leslie Scarman; Miss Joanna Smith; Prof Bernard Williams FBA.

ROYAL OPERA, Royal Opera House, London WC2, UK; tel 01 240 1200. Founded in 1946; formerly Royal Opera Covent Garden. Perf at Royal Opera House, Covent Garden since 1946. Built in 1858 as an opera house; seat cap 2,250, avg aud 2,000. Company is a private non-profit organization, which also manages The Royal Ballet; Chm of Board Sir Claus Moser; Patron HRH The Prince of Wales; Gen Adm John Tooley; Mus Dir Colin Davis. Original company founded 1732.

SEASON	OPENING Day Month		CLOSING Day Month		NO OF PFS	NO OF OPERAS	NO OF NEW PROD	NO OF NON-OPERA PFS*
73-74	17	Sep	27	Jul	300	26	2	150
74-75	30	Sep	2	Aug	300	25	4	150

*Ballet.

Repertoire 1973-74 — Beethoven: *Fidelio*; Bizet: *Carmen*; Britten: *Death in Venice, Midsummer Night, Owen Wingrave*; Donizetti: *Don Pasquale*; Gluck: *Iphigénie en Tauride*; Janáček: *Jenufa*; Mozart: *Clemenza di Tito, Don Giovanni*; Mussorgsky: *Boris Godunov*; Puccini: *Bohème, Tosca, Turandot*; Strauss, R: *Elektra, Rosenkavalier, Salome*; Tchaikovsky: *Eugene Onegin*; Verdi: *Aida, Falstaff, Forza del destino, Rigoletto, Otello, Simon Boccanegra, Traviata*; Wagner: *Tannhäuser*.

1974-75 — Berg: *Wozzeck*; Britten: *Death in Venice, Peter Grimes*; Debussy: *Pelléas et Mélisande*; Gounod: *Faust*; Mozart: *Così fan tutte, Clemenza di Tito, Nozze di Figaro*; Mussorgsky: *Boris Godunov*; Puccini: *Bohème, Butterfly, Tosca*; Rossini: *Barbiere di Siviglia*; Strauss, R: *Frau ohne Schatten*; Tchaikovsky: *Eugene Onegin*; Tippett: *King Priam*; Verdi: *Ballo in maschera, Falstaff, Forza del destino, Traviata, Trovatore*; Wagner: *Rheingold, Walküre, Siegfried, Tannhäuser*.

Company performs 75% of all operas in orig language. Approx 8 pfs per season are broadcast on radio, live or taped. Subsidiary companies incl English Opera Group for festival pfs and touring. Training prgm maintained by the company is handled by its associated postgraduate school, the London Opera Centre.

Budget incl ballet comps for 1974-75 £ 4,900,000 (US $11,451,000). Income: 40% box office; 52% gvnmt subs; 5% private grants; 3% other income. Ticket prices: £ 6.50-60p.

Number of persons engaged in 1974-75: resident solo artists: 117; guest solo artists: varies; chorus members: 72; orchestra members: 107; musical staff: 13; conductors: 4 & guests; stage directors/producers & guests: 4; set & costume designers: guests; choreographers: n/a; corps de ballet: n/a; administrative staff: 230; technical, scenic, costume: 268.

Company maintains its own orchestra; builds 75% of its sets and costumes in own workshops.

Policy determined by Board of Directors: Chmn Sir Claus Moser; Secy Robert Armstrong; Directors The Lord Annan, M B Carter, C Clark, The Lord Goodman, The Lord Kissin, P Pavitt, Sir John Pope-Hennessy, The Lord Robbins, J Sainsbury, F Sandilands and J Thorn.

UNITED STATES OF AMERICA

BALTIMORE OPERA COMPANY, INC, 11 E Lexington St, Baltimore, MD 21202, USA; tel (301) 727-0592. Incorporated in 1950; existed as an amateur organization since 1932. Perf at Lyric Theatre, 128 W Mt Royal Ave, Baltimore since 1952. Built in 1894, not as an opera house; seat cap 2,500, avg aud 2,500. Previous theaters: Maryland Casualty Co Auditorium 1950-51, seat cap 1,000; Baltimore Polytechnic Inst Auditorium 1951. Company is a private non-profit organization; Chm Fred I Archibald; Pres Harry B Cummings; Gen Mng Robert Joy Collinge; Asst Gen Mng John J Lehmeyer; Mus Adm William A Yannuzzi.

SEASON	OPENING Day	OPENING Month	CLOSING Day	CLOSING Month	NO OF PFS	NO OF OPERAS	NO OF NEW PROD	NO OF NON-OPERA PFS
73-74	1	Nov	8	Apr	9	3	—	—
74-75	30	Oct	14	Apr	9	4	1	—

Repertoire 1973-74 — Bizet: *Carmen*; Donizetti: *Elisir*; Leoncavallo: *Pagliacci*; Mascagni: *Cavalleria rusticana*.

1974-75 — Massenet: *Thaïs*; Puccini: *Tosca*; Strauss, R: *Rosenkavalier*.

Company performs 75% of all operas in orig language. Subsidiary company: Eastern Opera Theatre touring Maryland schools, abt 40-50 pfs annually.

Budget for 1974-75 $470,000. Income: 55% box office; 13% gvnmt; 32% priv/corp/fndt grants. Ticket prices: $14-5; 100% subscription.

Number of persons engaged in 1974-75: guest solo artists: 37; chorus members: 40; orchestra members: 65; musical staff: 2; conductors: 4; stage directors/producers: 3; set & costume designers: 3; administrative staff: 5; technical, scenic, costume: 22.

Company uses Baltimore Symph Orch.

Policy is determined by board of directors: Chm Fred I Archibald; Pres Harry B Cummings; Vc-Pres Mark Collins, George Harrison, John Wright; Secy/Treas Gideon N Steiff; mems: C C Bruck, S J Campbell, R B Case, W H Daiger, C A Dunning, J H Fetting, C S Garland, F A Gunther, J G Hutzler, J Meyerhoff, M H Miller, J P O'Conor, Rosa Ponselle, C H Peterson, C Ridgely, S M Wolff, C R Zarfoss.

OPERA COMPANY OF BOSTON, 172 Newbury St, Boston, MA 02116, USA; tel (617) 267-8050. Founded in 1958. Perf at Orpheum Theatre, Washington St, since 1970; seat cap 2,500. Prev theaters: Little Theater, Donnelly, Kresge, Shubert, Savoy, Rockwell Cage, Tufts Gymnasium, Cyclorama. Company is a private non-profit organization; Chmn The Hon Senator Edward J Brooke; Pres Laszlo J Bonis; Art Dir Sarah Caldwell; Mng Dir Robert E Reilly; Art Adm Patricia Ryan; Tech Dir George Koraly.

SEASON	OPENING Day Month	CLOSING Day Month	NO OF PFS	NO OF OPERAS	NO OF NEW PROD	NO OF NON-OPERA PFS
74	Feb	Jun	12	4	4	—
75	Feb	Jun	12	4	4	—

Repertoire 1974 — Massenet: *Don Quichotte*; Prokofiev: *War and Peace*; Puccini: *Butterfly*; Rossini: *Barbiere di Siviglia*. **Opera New England** — Foss: *Jumping Frog*; Puccini: *Butterfly*.
1975 — Bellini: *Capuleti ed i Montecchi*; Berlioz: *Benvenuto Cellini*; Mozart: *Così fan tutte*; Verdi: *Falstaff*. **Opera New England** — Offenbach: *Voyage to the Moon*; Rossini: *Barbiere di Siviglia*.

Guest engagement, USA: Vienna, VA, 2 pfs. Subsidiary company, Opera New England, touring cities in New England states, mostly junior performers; 6 operas in 34 pfs annually.

Budget 1975-76 incl subsd co: $1,300,000. Ticket prices: $27-8.

Number of persons engaged in 1974-75: 243.

Company assembles orch for each prod; builds all its sets and 75% of costumes in own workshops.

Policy determined by officers and board of directors: Chmn of the Brd The Hon Edward W Brooke, Sen from Massachusetts; Pres Laszlo J Bonis; Vc Pres Mrs Frederick W Haffenreffer and Robert L B Tobin; Treas Augustin H Parker; Asst Treas Joseph H Bragdon Jr; Secy-Counsel Dean E Nicholson Esq; Art Dir Sarah Caldwell; and 19 mems of the brd of dir.

LYRIC OPERA OF CHICAGO, 20 N Wacker Dr, Chicago, IL 60606, USA; tel (312) 346-6111. Founded in 1954; pfs were suspended during 1967 season due to failure to achieve agreement with musicians' union. Perf at Opera House, Kemper Insurance Bldg, since 1954. Built in 1929 as opera house; seat cap 3,535, avg aud 3,535. Company is a private non-profit organization; Chmn T M Thompson; Pres William S North; Gen Mng Carol Fox; Art Dir Bruno Bartoletti; Asst Mng Ardis Krainik; Busn Mng Donald Britton; PR Dir Danny Newman; Dir of Developm Frank Caleb.

SEASON	OPENING Day Month	CLOSING Day Month	NO OF PFS	NO OF OPERAS	NO OF NEW PROD	NO OF NON-OPERA PFS
74	20 Sep	14 Dec	52	8	3	—
75	19 Sep	13 Dec	52	7	3	—

Repertoire 1974 — Britten: *Peter Grimes*; Donizetti: *Don Pasquale, Favorite*; Massenet: *Don Quichotte*; Puccini: *Butterfly*; Verdi: *Falstaff, Simon Boccanegra*; Wagner: *Götterdämmerung*.
1975 — Beethoven: *Fidelio*; Donizetti: *Lucia di Lammermoor*; Gluck: *Orfeo ed Euridice*; Mozart: *Nozze di Figaro*; Strauss, R: *Elektra*; Verdi: *Otello, Traviata*.

Company performs all operas in orig language. Opening of each opera in season's repertoire broadcast live. Subsidiary company: The Opera School of Chicago, for junior performers; perf at the Civic Theatre Chicago, also concert pfs of operas with Midwestern symph orchs and colls & univs; 12 pfs annually. It has a training prgm for 11 singers and 1 cond/coach per season.

Budget for 1975 $5,368,000. Income: 38% box office, 5% gvnmt, 55% priv/corp/fndt grants, 2% other income. Ticket prices: $19.50-5.75; 81.4% subscription, 18.6% single ticket sale.

Number of persons engaged in 1975: guest solo artists: 51; chorus members: 93*; orchestra members: 90*; musical staff: 15; conductors: 6; stage directors/producers: 6; set & costume designers: 5; choreographers: 2; corps de ballet: 24*; administrative staff: 10; technical, scenic, costume: 70.

*Incl supplemental chorus, orch and ballet.

Company maintains own orch on seasonal basis.

Policy determined by Board of Directors: Hon Chmn Mayor Richard J Daley; Chm T M Thompson; Vice-Chm J W Van Gorkom; Pres William S North; Chm Exec Committ Edward F Blettner; Exec Vice Pres James C Hemphill, Dagget Harvey, William O Beers, George E Johnson; Vice-Pres Edward D Benninghoven, Sidney Epstein, John W Seabury, Archie R Boe, Charles B Stauffacher, Daniel J Terra; Secy Lee A Freeman, Sr; Treas Sam J DiGiovanni; 47 other board members; and Carol Fox, Gen Mng.

THE CINCINNATI OPERA ASSOCIATION, 1241 Elm St, Cincinnati, O, 45210, USA; tel (513) 621-1919. Founded in 1920. Perf at Music Hall since 1972. Built in 1878, refurbished in 1972; seat cap 3,632. Prev theater: Cincinnati Zoo Pavilion, 1920-71; seat cap 2,800. Company is a private non-profit organization; Chm James M E Mixter; Pres Harry H Santen; Gen Dir James de Blasis; Adm Dir Robert Peterson; Tech Dir Roy Hopper.

SEASON	OPENING Day Month	CLOSING Day Month	NO OF PFS	NO OF OPERAS	NO OF NEW PROD	NO OF NON-OPERA PFS
74	26 Jun	3 Aug	14	6	2	—
75	18 Jun	26 Jul	15	6	5	—

Repertoire 1974 — Donizetti: *Roberto Devereux*; Mussorgsky: *Boris Godunov*; Offenbach: *Périchole*; Puccini: *Bohème, Manon Lescaut*; Verdi: *Ballo in maschera*.

1975 — Gounod: *Faust*; Puccini: *Gianni Schicchi, Suor Angelica, Tabarro, Turandot*; Verdi: *Trovatore*; Wagner: *Fliegende Holländer*.

Company performs one-third of all operas in orig language. Subsidiary companies incl opera division of Area Artists, touring nearby towns, 4 pfs annually; educational prgms and classroom presentations in local schools, 60 pfs annually; Young American Artists Program, perf at parks, 21 pfs; experimental programs (*Little Mahagonny*), 6 pfs annually in local cabaret-type setting. Company has a training prgm for 4-5 singers per year.

Budget for 1975 $888,253. Income: 45% box office; 9% gvnmt; 35% priv/corp/fndt grants; 11% other income. Ticket prices: $15-3; 57% subscription, 43% single ticket sale.

Number of persons engaged in 1975: resident solo artists: 6; guest solo artists: 22; chorus members: 46; orchestra members: 60; musical staff: 5; conductors: 5; stage directors/producers: 4; set & costume designers: 5; choreographers: 1; corps de ballet: 12; administrative staff: 3; technical, scenic, costume: 24.

Company uses local orch; builds 50% of sets and 15% of costumes in own workshops.

Policy determined by board of directors: Harry H Santen, G Gibson Carey, John S Hopple, James M E Mixter, Lenwood F Maurer.

DALLAS CIVIC OPERA COMPANY, INC, PO Box 987, Dallas, TX 75221, USA; tel (214) 748-9329. Founded in 1957. Perf at Fair Park Music Hall, Dallas, since 1957. Built in 1925, not as an opera house; seat cap 3,420, avg aud 3,000. Company is a private non-profit organization; Pres Grady Jordan; Gen Dir Nicola Rescigno.

SEASON	OPENING Day Month	CLOSING Day Month	NO OF PFS	NO OF PROD	NO OF NEW PROD	NO OF NON-OPERA PFS
74	1 Nov	10 Dec	16	4	1	—
75	31 Oct	13 Dec	17	4	1	—

Repertoire 1974 — Bellini: *Puritani*; Donizetti: *Lucrezia Borgia*; Puccini: *Tosca*; Thomas: *Mignon*.

1975 — Donizetti: *Anna Bolena*; Offenbach: *Contes d'Hoffmann*; Puccini: *Madama Butterfly*; Wagner: *Tristan und Isolde*.

Company performs 90% of all operas in orig language.

Budget for 1974 $1,115,729. Income: 36% box office; 9% gvnmt; 52% priv/corp/fndt grants; 3% other income. Ticket prices: $19-2.50; 72% subscription, 28% single ticket sale.

Number of persons engaged in 1974: guest solo artists: 26; chorus members: 64; orchestra members: 83; musical staff: 6; conductors: 2; stage directors/producers: 4; set & costume designers: 2; choreographers: 1; corps de ballet: 16; administrative staff: 8; technical, scenic, costume: 46.

Company uses local symph orch; builds 90% of sets and costumes in own workshops.

FORT WORTH OPERA ASSOCIATION, 3505 West Lancaster, Fort Worth, TX 76107, USA; tel (817) 738-0711. Founded in 1946. Perf at Tarrant County Convention Center, John F. Kennedy Theater, 1111 Houston St since 1968. Built in 1968; seat cap 3,054, avg aud 2,000. Prev theater: Will Rogers Memorial Auditorium 1946-68; seat cap 3,000. Company is a private non-profit organization; Pres Rice M Tilley Jr; Gen Mng & Mus Dir Rudolf Kruger; Asst Gen Mng William Massad.

SEASON	OPENING Day	Month	CLOSING Day	Month	NO OF PFS	NO OF OPERAS	NO OF NEW PROD	NO OF NON-OPERA PFS
73-74	30	Nov	24	Apr	11	6	—	—
74-75	17	Oct	13	Apr	13	6	—	—

1973-74 — Donizetti: *Lucia*; Humperdinck: *Hänsel und Gretel*; Leoncavallo: *Pagliacci*; Mascagni: *Cavalleria rusticana*; Mozart: *Nozze di Figaro*; Strauss, R: *Salome*.

1974-75 — Donizetti: *Fille du régiment*; Humperdinck: *Hänsel und Gretel*; Puccini: *Gianni Schicchi, Tabarro*; Saint-Saëns: *Samson et Dalila*; Verdi: *Traviata*.

Company performs 50% of all operas in orig language. Guest engagements 1973-75 incl Shreveport, LA, 1 pf.

Budget for 1974-75 $294,400. Income: 28% box office; 4% gvnmt; 42% priv/corp/fndt grants; 26% other income. Ticket prices: $8.50-3; 60% subscription, 40% single ticket sale.

Number of persons engaged in 1974-75: 232; resident solo artists: 23; guest solo artists: 29; chorus members: 50; orchestra members: 60; musical staff: 3; conductors: 1; stage directors/producers: 4; choreographers: 1; corps de ballet: 25; administrative staff: 2; technical, scenic, costume: 30.

Company maintains its own orch on a seasonal basis.

Policy is determined by Board of Directors: Pres Rice M Tilley Jr; Exec Vice-Pres Lee B Freese; Secy Mrs Ira Butler; Treas Jeff Fraley; Chm Prod Commtt Ernest Allen; Chmn Ticket Commtt Mrs J Ertel & Mrs O Fultz.

CONNECTICUT OPERA ASSOCIATION, INC, 15 Lewis St, Hartford, CT 06103, USA; tel (203) 527-0713. Founded in 1942. Perf at Horace Bushnell Memorial, 166 Capitol Ave, Hartford, since 1943. Built in 1930 as an opera house; seat cap 2,651, avg aud 2,300. Prev theater: Avery Theater, 1942-43; seat cap 299. Company is a private non-profit organization; Chm Mrs Wm Foote; Pres Edward L Hennessy Jr; Gen Mng & Dir William B Warden; Adm Asst Helen G Silansky.

SEASON	OPENING Day	Month	CLOSING Day	Month	NO OF PFS	NO OF PROD	NO OF NEW PROD	NO OF NON-OPERA PFS
73-74		Oct		Apr	9	6	—	—
74-75		Oct		Apr	9	6	—	—

Repertoire 1973-74 — Bellini: *Puritani*; Bizet: *Carmen*; Donizetti: *Fille du régiment, Maria Stuarda*; Verdi: *Ballo in maschera, Trovatore*.

1974-75 — Donizetti: *Elisir*; Puccini: *Bohème, Manon Lescaut*; Verdi: *Aida, Forza del destino*.

Company performs all operas in orig language. 6 pfs broadcast live per season.

Budget $365,000. Ticket prices: $16-5; 54% subscription, 46% single ticket sale.

Number of persons engaged in 1974-75 incl: chorus members: 52; orchestra members: 55; musical staff: 2; conductors: 4; stage directors/producers: 4; administrative staff: 2; technical, scenic, costume: 19.

Company uses local symph orch; builds 20% of sets in own workshops.

Policy is determined by Board of Trustees: Chm Mrs Wm Foote; Vice-Chm Edward L Hennessy Jr; Pres Roger S Bruttomesso; Gen Mng & Dir William B Warden; Vice-Pres Donald Hines, Mrs Christopher Percy, Dr John Basile, David Fineberg, Arthur Silverman, Rolf Bibow, David Chase, Mrs Edward Hennessy, Frederick Worcester, Joseph Spada, Andrew Pinto, George Cook; Secy Mrs Robert Wolin; Asst Secy Mrs John Basile; Admin Asst Mrs Helen Silansky; also 12 Trustees active term ends 1976; 18 Trustees active term ends 1977; 13 Trustees active term ends 1978; and 10 Trustees-Associate.

HAWAII OPERA THEATRE OF THE HONOLULU SYMPHONY SOCIETY, 1000 Bishop Street Ste 303, Honolulu, Hawaii 96813, USA; tel (808) 537-6171. Founded in 1961. Perf at Blaisdell Memorial Center, 777 Ward Ave, Honolulu, since 1964. Built in 1964; seat cap 2,017, avg aud 1,916. Prev theater: 1961-64 McKinley High School Auditorium, seat cap 2,000. Company is a private non-profit organization; Pres Elliott H Brilliant; Gen Mng Gordon T Coats; Mus & Art Dir Robert LaMarchina; Assoc Cond Joseph Levine; Res Dsgn Richard Gullicksen; Asst to Gen Mng Catharine Hite.

SEASON	OPENING Day	Month	CLOSING Day	Month	NO OF PFS	NO OF OPERAS	NO OF NEW PROD	NO OF NON-OPERA PFS
73-74	7	Oct	22	Apr	11	3	—	—
74-75	27	Sep	10	Apr	11	3	—	—

Repertoire 1973-74 — Gounod: *Faust*; Menotti: *Dernier sauvage*; Puccini: *Bohème*.

1974-75 — Boito: *Mefistofele*; Offenbach: *Contes d'Hoffmann*; Verdi: *Otello*.

Company performs 75% of all operas in orig language. Annual tour incl Wailuku, Maui.

Budget for 1974-75 $331,355 est. Income: 67% box office; 10% gvnmt; 8% priv/corp/fndt grants; 15% other income. Ticket prices: $12.50-3.50; 69% subscription, 31% single ticket sale.

Number of persons engaged in 1974-75: resident solo artists: 14; guest solo artists: 14; chorus members: 68; orchestra members: 63; musical staff: 6; conductors: 2; stage directors/producers: 3; set & costume designers: 2; choreographers: 3; corps de ballet: 13; administrative staff: 11; technical, scenic, costume: 32.

Company uses the Honolulu Symph Orch; builds 95% of sets and 5% of costumes in own workshops.

Policy determined by Steering Commtt: Pres Elliott Brilliant; Vice Pres Charles Wichman, Mrs Arthur Sprague, Galen Leong and Mrs Arthur Orvis; Treas Mrs Ronald Loftus; Secy Mrs Joseph Lipinski. In addition there are 35 Council Members on the Commtt.

HOUSTON GRAND OPERA ASSOCIATION, 615 Louisiana, Houston, TX 77002, USA; tel (713) 227-1287. Founded in 1956. Perf at Jones Hall since 1966. Built in 1966 as a multi-purpose auditorium; seat cap 2,893, avg aud 2,800. Prev theater: 1956-66 Music Hall, seat cap 3,100. Company is a private non-profit organization; Chm G C Wakefield; Pres Maurice Aresty; Gen Dir David Gockley; Mng Robert A Buckley; Mng Texas Opera

Theater Terrel Miller; Music Adm Chris Nance. Spring pfs at Miller Pk; free, outdoor pfs; avg aud 7,000.

SEASON	OPENING Day Month	CLOSING Day Month	NO OF PFS	NO OF OPERAS	NO OF NEW PROD	NO OF NON-OPERA PFS
73-74	Oct	Jun	194	11	9	—
74-75	Oct	Jun	190	11	10	—

World prem during these seasons: Pasatieri's *The Seagull* 3/74.

Repertoire 1973-74 — Bizet: *Carmen*; Boito: *Mefistofele*; Mozart: *Entführung aus dem Serail, Nozze di Figaro*; Offenbach: *Périchole*; Pasatieri: *Seagull*; Verdi: *Macbeth, Traviata*; Weill: *Dreigroschenoper*. Texas Opera Theater — Pasatieri: *Calvary*; Weill: *Little Mahagonny*; Mozart: *Così fan tutte*.

1974-75 — Berg: *Lulu*; Donizetti: *Lucrezia Borgia*; Joplin: *Treemonisha*; Massenet: *Manon*; Puccini: *Bohème*; Strauss, R: *Rosenkavalier*; Verdi: *Trovatore*. Texas Opera Theater — Britten: *Turn of the Screw*; Mozart: *Così fan tutte*; Anon: *Play of Herod*.

Company presents all operas in two series: the Intl Series in orig language, the Am Series in English. Subsidiary company: Texas Opera Theater, a touring company of young performers presenting chamber operas in Texas; 140 pfs annually.

Budget for 1974-75 $1,800,000. Income: 50% box office; 10% gvnmt; 30% priv/corp/fndt grants; 10% other income. Ticket prices: $20-1.25; 89% subscription, 11% single ticket sale.

Number of persons engaged in 1974-75: resident solo artists: 8; guest solo artists: 75; chorus members: 60; orchestra members: 65; musical staff: 4; conductors: 6; stage directors/producers: 8; set & costume designers: 23; administrative staff: 17; technical, scenic, costume: 42.

Company uses local symph orch; builds 90% of sets and 10% of costumes in own workshops.

OPERA/SOUTH, Mississippi Inter-Collegiate Opera Guild Inc, Jackson State Univ, Jackson, MS 17055, USA; tel (601) 968-2051. Founded in 1971. Perf at Jackson City Auditorium since 1971. Built in 1968; seat cap 2,420, avg aud 1,500. Company is a private non-profit organization; Chm & Pres J Louis Stokes; Gen Mng Dolores Ardoyno; Art Dir Donald Dorr.

SEASON	OPENING Day Month	CLOSING Day Month	NO OF PFS	NO OF OPERAS	NO OF NEW PROD	NO OF NON-OPERA PFS
73-74	27 Apr	—	1	1	1	—
74-75	15 Nov	19 Apr	3	2	2	—

World prem during these seasons: William Grant Still's *A Bayou Legend* 11/74.

Repertoire 1973-74 — Verdi: *Otello*.

1974-75 — Still: *Bayou Legend*; Wagner: *Fliegende Holländer*.

Company performs all operas in English. Fall pfs taped and rebroadcast on radio.

Budget for 1974-75 $100,150. Income: 10% box office; 25% gvnmt; 25% priv/corp/fndt grants; 40% other income. Ticket prices: $8-2.

Number of persons engaged in 1974-75; guest solo artists: 15; chorus members: 75; orchestra members: 45; musical staff: 1; conductors: 2; stage directors/producers: 1; set & costume designers: 1; administrative staff: 2; technical, scenic, costume: 2.

Company assembles orch for each prod; builds all sets and costumes in own workshops.

Policy is determined by Board Commtt: Pres J Louis Stokes; Secy Rosia L Crisler; Treas Estus Smith; also John A Peoples Jr, Dollye M E Robinson and Mae Helen Thomas.

KANSAS CITY LYRIC THEATER, 1029 Central, Kansas City, MO 64105, USA; tel (816) 471-4933. Founded in 1958. Perf at Lyric Theatre, form Capri Theatre, since 1970; seat cap 1,400, avg aud 1,000. Prev theaters: Rockhill Theater 1958-67, seat cap 700; Uptown Theatre 1968-69. Company is a private non-profit organization; Chm Robert B Snapp Jr;

Pres Charles Hanson; Gen Dir Russell Patterson; Assoc Mng Robert B Driver Jr; Dir
P R Roberta Sue Wedlan; Theater Mng James Sutherland; Exec Secy Melissa Ferrand.

SEASON	OPENING Day	Month	CLOSING Day	Month	NO OF PFS	NO OF OPERAS	NO OF NEW PROD	NO OF NON-OPERA PFS
74	18	Sep	25	Oct	20	4	4	—
75	19	Sep	26	Oct	25	5	5	—

World prem during these seasons: Beeson's *Captain Jinks of the Horse Marines* 9/75.

Repertoire 1974 — Beeson: *Sweet Bye and Bye*; Offenbach: *Périchole*; Puccini: *Tosca*; Wagner: *Fliegende Holländer*.

1975 — Mozart: *Zauberflöte*; Strauss, J: *Fledermaus*; Susa: *Transformations*; Verdi: *Traviata*; Ward: *Crucible*.

Company performs all operas in English. Pfs periodically taped and rebroadcast on radio. Annual tour 1 or 2 operas in 2 to 6 pfs incl Topeka and Manhattan, KS, and Maryville, MO. Subsidiary companies incl Young Audiences Group, 50 pfs annually of chamber opera in schools.

Budget for 1975 $375,000. Income: 25% box office, 10% gvnmt, 50% priv/corp/fndt grants; 15% other income. Ticket prices: $8.50-3; 50% subscription, 50% single ticket sale.

Number of persons engaged in 1975: resident solo artists: 10; guest solo artists: 20; chorus members: 30; orchestra members: 50; musical staff: 5; conductors: 3; stage directors/producers: 3; set & costume designers: 4; choreographers: 1; corps de ballet: 6; administrative staff: 6; technical, scenic, costume: 24.

Company uses local symph orch; builds 60% of sets and 20% of costumes in own workshops. Also exchanges prods with Minnesota Opera and Lake George Festival as part of Co-Opera.

Policy determined by Board of Directors: Chm Robert Snapp Jr; Pres Charles Hanson; Vice-Chm Richard Stern; Legal Adv Landon Rowland; Hon Chms Henry Haskell, Dr Fred Fowler, Louis Sosland.

LAKE GEORGE OPERA FESTIVAL, Box 471, Glens Falls, NY 12801, USA; tel (518) 793-3858. Founded in 1962. Perf at Queensbury Festival Auditorium since 1965. Built in 1965; seat cap 870, avg aud 590. Prev theater: Diamond Point Theatre 1962-65; seat cap 300. Company is a private non-profit organization; Pres H Wayne Judge; Gen Dir David Lloyd; Mus Dir Paul Callaway; Prod Mng David Thomas Lloyd; Business Mng A Nicholas Buttino.

SEASON	OPENING Day	Month	CLOSING Day	Month	NO OF PFS	NO OF OPERAS	NO OF NEW PROD	NO OF NON-OPERA PFS*
74	11	Jul	19	Aug	30	5	4	5
75	13	Jul	23	Aug	29	5	4	7

*Operettas, musicals, ballet, etc.

World prem during these seasons: Bernardo's *The Child* 8/74.

Repertoire 1974 — Bernardo: *The Child*; Mozart: *Zauberflöte*; Rossini: *Barbiere di Siviglia*; Strauss, J: *Fledermaus*; Verdi: *Traviata*.

1975 — Mozart: *Zauberflöte*; Offenbach: *Périchole*; Puccini: *Butterfly*; Stravinsky: *Rake's Progress*; Verdi: *Falstaff*.

Company performs all operas in English. 1 pf broadcast in 1973 and 1975 and 1 pf videotaped in 1975. Guest engagements 1973-75 incl Southern Vermont Arts Center, 1 pf; Lake Placid Center for Music, Art and Drama, NY, 6 pfs in 1973, 6 pfs in 1974. Company has a training prgm for 40 singers and 1 adm per season.

Budget for 1974-75 $350,000. Income: 25% box office, 35% gvnmt, 35% priv/corp/fndt grants, 5% other income. Ticket prices: $8-1; 40% subscription, 60% single ticket sale.

Number of persons engaged in 1975: 175; resident solo artists: 38; chorus members: 17; orchestra members: 33; musical staff: 5; conductors: 3; stage directors/producers: 4; set, cost & lt designers: 6; choreographers: 1; administrative staff: 5; technical, scenic, costume: 21.

Company maintains its own orch on a seasonal basis; builds 75% of sets and 10% of costumes in own workshops.

Policy is determined by Board of Trustees: Pres H Wayne Judge; Vice Pres J Walter Juckett; Treas George R Coughlan; Secy Mrs George F Jones; Asst Secy Mrs Joseph C Palamountain; Pres Opera Guild Mrs S Richard Spitzer; and 13 other trustees.

KENTUCKY OPERA ASSOCIATION, Gardencourt, Alta Vista Rd, Louisville, KY 40205, USA; tel (502) 897-7197. Founded in 1952. Perf at Macauley Theater, Broadway, since 1963. Built in 1921; seat cap 1,437, avg aud 1,437. Prev theater: Columbia Auditorium 1952-63, seat cap 1,200. Company is a private non-profit organization; Pres Clay Morton; Dir Moritz v Bomhard; Asst to the Dir Neil Ryan; Office Mng Dianne Albers; Tech Dir Richard Mix.

SEASON	OPENING Day Month		CLOSING Day Month		NO OF PFS	NO OF OPERAS	NO OF NEW PROD	NO OF NON-OPERA PFS
73-74	25	Sep	2	Mar	14	4	4	—
74-75	27	Sep	2	Mar	12	5	5	—

Repertoire 1973-74 — Floyd: *Susannah*; Mozart: *Entführung aus dem Serail*; Puccini: *Tosca*; Verdi: *Otello*.

1974-75 — Mozart; *Così fan tutte*; Orff: *Carmina burana*; Puccini: *Tabarro*; Verdi: *Traviata*; Wagner: *Fliegende Holländer*.

Company performs 50% of all operas in orig language. Perfs are taped regularly and rebroadcast, each 7 times. Annual tour of one opera in 4 to 6 pfs, partially sponsored by Kentucky State Arts Commission. Pfs mostly at univs. Company has a training prgm in cooperation with Univ of Louisville for 5-15 singers per season.

Budget for 1974-75 $194,000. Income: 52% box office; 11% gvnmt; 12% priv/corp/fndt grants; 25% Louisville Fund. Ticket prices: $8.50-2.50; 64% subscription, 36% single ticket sale.

Number of persons engaged in 1974-75: resident solo artists: 12; guest solo artists: 14; chorus members: 117; orchestra members: 48; musical staff: 1; conductors: 1; stage directors/producers: 3; set & costume designers: 4; choreographers: 1; corps de ballet: 32; administrative staff: 5; technical, scenic, costume: 25.

Company assembles orch for each prod; builds 50% of its sets and 75% of its costumes in own workshops.

Policy determined by Company Dir Moritz v Bomhard and the following Board members: Clay Morton, Janet Graff, James Welch, Jerry Starling and Sophia Harrison.

MEMPHIS OPERA THEATRE, Memphis State Univ, Memphis, TN 38152, USA; tel (901) 454-2706. Founded in 1956. Perf at Auditorium Music Hall, Front at Poplar, Memphis, since 1956, seat cap 2,400, avg aud 2,000. Company is a private non-profit organization; Pres Dr Richard Bicks; Gen Dir George Osborne; Mus Dir Kurt Klippstatter; Tech Adm Daniel Sollors; Aud Devlp Dir Terry Hicklin; P R Dir Reva Cook.

SEASON	OPENING Day Month		CLOSING Day Month		NO OF PFS	NO OF OPERAS	NO OF NEW PROD	NO OF NON-OPERA PFS
73-74	22	Sep	21	Apr	150	9	5	—
74-75	13	Sep	1	May	200	9	6	—

Repertoire 1973-74 — Donizetti: *Elisir*; Menotti: *Consul*; Offenbach: *Contes d'Hoffmann*; Puccini: *Tosca*; Strauss, R: *Salome*; Verdi: *Rigoletto*. Southern Opera Theater — Humperdinck: *Hänsel und Gretel*; Rossini: *Cenerentola*; Gatty: *Rumpelstilzkin*.

1974-75 — Donizetti: *Don Pasquale*; Floyd: *Of Mice and Men*; Puccini: *Bohème*; Verdi: *Forza del destino, Traviata*. Southern Opera Theatre — Barab: *Little Red Riding Hood*; Britten: *Prodigal Son*; Freund: *Bishop's Ghost*; Menotti: *Amahl*.

Company performs 50% of all operas in orig language. Annual tour of 3 to 5 operas in 100 to 150 pfs incl St Louis, Knoxville, Jackson TN, Jackson MS, Atlanta and numerous smaller communities. Subsidiary company: touring group Southern Opera Theatre, 200 pfs annually. Company has training prgm for 8 singers, 2 conds and 2 adms per season.

Budget for 1974-75 $300,000. Income: 45% box office; 10% gvnmt; 15% priv/corp/fndt grants; 30% other income. Ticket prices: $15-5; 35% subscription, 65% single ticket sale.

Number of persons engaged in 1974-75: resident solo artists: 8; guest solo artists: 20; chorus members: 60; orchestra members: 40; musical staff: 2; conductors: 2; stage directors/producers: 3; set & costume designers: 2; choreographers: 1; corps de ballet: 12; administrative staff: 5; technical, scenic, costume: 8.

Company maintains its own orch; builds 80% of its sets and 25% of its costumes in own workshops.

GREATER MIAMI OPERA ASSOCIATION, 1200 Coral Way, Miami, FL 33145, USA; tel (305) 854-1643. Founded in 1941. Perf at Dade County Auditorium, 2901 W Flagler St, Miami, and Miami Beach Theatre of the Performing Arts, 1700 Washington Ave, since 1950. Both theaters built in 1950; seat cap Dade County Aud 2,501; Miami Beach Theatre 2,906; avg aud for both theaters is full capacity. Prev theater: Miami Senior High School Aud 1941-49; seat cap 1,000. Other theaters: War Memorial Auditorium, Ft Lauderdale, FL; seat cap 2,500. Company is a non-profit organization; Chmn George Beebe; Pres Mrs Joseph Crawley; Gen Mng Robert Herman; Art Dir Emerson Buckley; Dir Opera Guild Lee diFilippi; Adm Dir Walter Palevoda.

SEASON	OPENING Day	OPENING Month	CLOSING Day	CLOSING Month	NO OF PFS*	NO OF OPERAS	NO OF NEW PROD	NO OF NON-OPERA PFS**
73-74	3	Nov	7	Apr	16	5	3	64
74-75	18	Jan	13	Apr	19	4	3	70

*Totals incl Miami and Ft Lauderdale pfs.
**Operettas, musicals, ballet, etc.

World prem during these seasons: Julia Smith's *Daisy* 11/73.

Repertoire 1973-74 — Bizet: *Pêcheurs de perles*; Donizetti: *Lucia*; Giordano: *Andrea Chénier*; Ward: *Crucible*. **Florida Family Opera** — Moore: *Gallantry*; Puccini: *Bohème, Gianni Schicchi, Butterfly*; Smith: *Daisy*.

1974-75 — Donizetti: *Elisir*; Gounod: *Roméo et Juliette*; Verdi: *Rigoletto*; Wagner: *Fliegende Holländer*. **Florida Family Opera** — same operas in English.

Company performs all operas in both the orig language and English. 2 pfs videotaped, one each 1965 and 1975. Guest engagements 1973-75 incl Ft Lauderdale 3 pfs per season, Daytona Beach 2 pfs and Ft Myers 1 pf, all Florida. Subsidiary company: Florida Family Opera perf at special events, 5 pfs; at condominiums in 2 counties, 70 pfs; at schools, 60 pfs annually. Company has a training prgm for 45 singers, 2 tech assts and 1 adm per season.

Budget for 1974-75 $1,250,000. Income: 36% box office; 8% gvnmt; 28% priv/corp/ fndt grants; 28% other income. Ticket prices: Intl Series $25-7; Family Opera $5-2.50; 87% subscription, 13% single ticket sale.

Number of persons engaged in 1974-75: 241; resident solo artists: 12; guest solo artists: 18; chorus members: 45; orchestra members: 48; musical staff: 5; conductors: 2; stage directors/producers: 2; set & costume designers: 4; choreographers: 1; corps de ballet: 12; administrative staff: 11; technical, scenic, costume: 55.

Company uses a local symph orch; builds 75% of its sets in own workshops.

Policy determined by Board of Directors: George Beebe, Mrs Joseph Crawley, Mrs Arturo diFilippi, Mrs R R Balfe, H Cordes, R Crane, J M Curtis, Dr R Elias, A Gallagher, Dr L Jacobson, T Keating, Mrs U Menendez, G Miller, Mrs N S Morris, Col R Pentland Jr, R Perry, W Singer, A Vadia.

MILWAUKEE FLORENTINE OPERA COMPANY, 750 N Lincoln Memorial Dr, Milwaukee, WI 53202, USA; tel (414) 273-6444. Founded in 1932. Perf at Performing Arts Center, 929 N Water St, Milwaukee since 1969. Built in 1969; seat cap 2,219, avg aud 2,100. Prev theater: Pabst Theatre 1932-68; seat cap 1,700. Company is a private non-profit organization; Pres Wilbert E Schauer; Gen Mng Alan J Bellamente; Art Adv Charles Wendelken-Wilson; Asst to Gen Mng Joyce Regner; Prod Coord Katherine Koch; Founder Consultant John Anello.

SEASON	OPENING Day Month	CLOSING Day Month	NO OF PFS	NO OF OPERAS	NO OF NEW PROD	NO OF NON-OPERA PFS
73-74	13 Oct	4 May	8	4	—	—
74-75	10 Oct	3 May	10	5	—	—

Repertoire 1973-74 — Leoncavallo: *Pagliacci*; Mascagni: *Cavalleria rusticana*; Puccini: *Tosca*; Verdi: *Otello, Trovatore.*

1974-75 — Donizetti: *Elisir, Lucia*; Offenbach: *Contes d'Hoffmann*; Puccini: *Manon Lescaut*; Verdi: *Aida.* Tour — Menotti: *Medium.*

Subsidiary company: Opera on Wheels, 15 pfs annually at schools.

Budget for 1974-75 $400,000. Income: 50% box office; 25% priv/corp/fndt grants; 25% other income. Ticket prices: $17.50-3; 75% subscription, 25% single ticket sale.

Number of persons engaged in 1974-75: resident solo artists: 20; guest solo artists: 24; chorus members: 65; orchestra members: 85; musical staff: 5; conductors: 4; stage directors/producers: 4; choreographers: 1; corps de ballet: 10; administrative staff: 2; technical, scenic, costume: 60.

Company uses local symph orch; does not maintain scenic or costume workshop.

Policy determined by Board of Trustees: Mrs William Baird, Edwin Bartlett Jr, Courtland R Conlee, Mrs James E Detienne, Mrs Robert Hedrick, Walter E Kroening, Daniel J McLaughlin, F Preston Mottram, Thomas O'Byrne, Mrs Karl Peters, Lawrence Regner Jr, Wilbert E Schauer, Andrew M Spheeris, Mrs Frederick D Usinger, Eckard von Estorff, Mrs John Wermuth, Robert Zigman.

MINNESOTA OPERA COMPANY, 1812 So 6 St, Minneapolis, MN 55454, USA; tel (612) 339-6726. Founded in 1963 as Center Opera Co. Perf at I A O'Shaughnessy Auditorium, Coll of St Catherine, St Paul, since 1975; seat cap 1,750. Prev theaters: Walker Art Center & Guthrie Theater. Company is a private non-profit organization; Pres S R Pflaum; Gen Mng Charles C Fullmer; Stage Dir H Wesley Balk; Mus Dir Philip Brunelle; Tech Dir/Dsgn Bruce Miller; Stage Mng Christine Wopat.

SEASON	OPENING Day Month	CLOSING Day Month	NO OF PFS	NO OF OPERAS	NO OF NEW PROD	NO OF NON-OPERA PFS
73-74	—	—	30	7	2	—
74-75	—	—	35	7	3	—

World prems during these seasons: Brunelle/Balk's *Newest Opera in the World* 5/74 & *Gallimaufry* 12/74; Blackwood/Kaplan/Lewin's *Gulliver* 2/75.

Repertoire 1973-74 — Argento: *Masque of Angels*; Balk/Brunelle: *Newest Opera in the World*; Devin/Hodkin: *Vos Populous*; Monteverdi: *Combattimento di Tancredi*; Mozart: *Don Giovanni*; Sousa: *Capitan*; Susa: *Transformations.*

1974-75 — Balk/Brunelle: *Gallimaufry, Newest Opera in the World*; Blackwood/Kaplan Lewin: *Gulliver*; Britten: *Albert Herring*; Mozart: *Zauberflöte*; Susa: *Transformations*; Williamson: *Growing Castle.*

Company performs all operas in English; gives guest engagements. Company has a training prgm for 14 singers per season.

Budget for 1974-75 $298,500. Ticket prices: $8.50-4.50.

Number of persons engaged in 1974-75: resident solo artists: 7; guest solo artists: 5; chorus members: 14; conductors: 2; stage directors/producers: 2; set & costume designers: 2; choreographers: 2; administrative staff: 3; technical, scenic, costume: 14.

Company assembles orch for each prod; builds all its sets and costumes in own workshops.

Policy determined by Board of Directors: Pres Stephen R Pflaum; Vice Pres Robert H Engels and Morris M Sherman; Secy Thomas M Levis Jr; Treas James R Elsesser; and 42 other board members.

NEW ORLEANS OPERA ASSOCIATION, 333 St Charles Ave, New Orleans, LA 70130, USA; tel (504) 529-2278. Founded in 1943. Perf at New Orleans Theater of Performing Arts, 801 No Rampart St, since 1973. Built in 1973 as a multi-media auditorium/concert hall; seat cap 2,317, avg aud 2,200. Prev theater: Municipal Auditorium 1943-73; seat cap 2,754. Opera in New Orleans dates back to 1796. The French Opera House was destroyed by fire in 1919. In 1943, after an absence of 24 years, opera performances were revived by the present company. Company is a private non-profit organization; Pres James A Noe Jr; Gen Dir Arthur G Cosenza; Mus Dir & Res Cond Knud Andersson; Tech Dir & Res Dsgn David Gano.

SEASON	OPENING Day Month	CLOSING Day Month	NO OF PFS	NO OF OPERAS	NO OF NEW PROD	NO OF NON-OPERA PFS
73-74	18 Oct	4 May	12	6	3	—
74-75	3 Oct	3 May	12	6	3	—

Repertoire 1973-74 — Bizet: *Carmen*; Gounod: *Faust*; Halévy: *Juive*; Strauss, R: *Ariadne auf Naxos*; Verdi: *Rigoletto, Traviata*.

1974-75 — Massenet: *Hérodiade*; Puccini: *Bohème, Manon Lescaut, Tosca*; Verdi: *Aida*; Wagner: *Lohengrin*.

Company performs all operas in orig language.

Budget for 1974-75 $435,000. Income: 50% box office; 10% gvnmt; 35% priv/corp/fndt grants; 5% other income. Ticket prices: $25-4; 80% subscription, 20% single ticket sale.

Number of persons engaged in 1974-75: resident solo artists: 13; guest solo artists: 28; chorus members: 75; orchestra members: 65; musical staff: 3; conductors: 3; stage directors/producers: 3; set & costume designers: 3; choreographers: 1; corps de ballet: 10; administrative staff: 4; technical, scenic, costume: 47.

Company uses local symph orch; builds all sets in own workshops.

Policy determined by Board of Directors: Pres James A Noe Jr; Vice-Pres H Lloyd Hawkins Jr, John W Sims, Edward B Benjamin, John G Panzeca, Mrs Stockton B Jefferson, Mrs James A Noe Jr, Hon Victor H Schiro; Secy Owen Q Niehaus; Treas John G. Panzeca; and 75 board members.

METROPOLITAN OPERA ASSOCIATION, INC, Lincoln Center, New York, NY 10023, USA; tel (212) 799-3100. Founded in 1883. Pfs suspended 1892-1893 because fire destroyed auditorium. Perf at Metropolitan Opera House at Lincoln Center since 1966. Built in 1966 as an opera house; seat cap 3,788, avg aud 3,567. Prev theater: Metropolitan Opera House on Broadway at 39 St, 1883-1966; seat cap 3,612. Company is a private non-profit organization; Chmn George Moore until 1975, succeeded by Langdon Van Norden; Pres William Rockefeller; Exec Dir Anthony A Bliss; Gen Mng Schuyler G Chapin until 1975; Mus Dir, beginning 1976, James Levine; Prod Dir John Dexter; Asst Mng Francis Robinson; Fin Dir Richard J Clavell; Art Adms Charles Riecker and Richard Rodzinski; Tech Adm Michael Bronson.

SEASON	OPENING Day Month	CLOSING Day Month	NO OF PFS	NO OF OPERAS	NO OF NEW PROD	NO OF NON-OPERA PFS*
73-74	17 Sep	20 Apr	238	25	6	5
	27 May	15 Jun				
74-75	23 Sep	19 Apr	210	25	4	5

*Free concert pfs in city parks.

Repertoire 1973-74 — Berlioz: *Troyens*; Bizet: *Carmen*; Donizetti: *Elisir*; Mozart: *Don Giovanni, Zauberflöte*; Offenbach: *Contes d'Hoffmann*; Puccini: *Bohème, Butterfly, Manon Lescaut*; Rossini: *Barbiere di Siviglia, Italiana in Algeri*; Strauss, R: *Rosenkavalier, Salome*; Verdi: *Otello, Rigoletto, Simon Boccanegra, Traviata, Trovatore, Vespri*; Wagner: *Götterdämmerung, Parsifal, Tristan und Isolde*.

1974-75 — Bartók: *Bluebeard's Castle*; Berg: *Wozzeck*; Britten: *Death in Venice*; Donizetti: *Don Pasquale*; Gounod: *Roméo et Juliette*; Janacek: *Jenufa*; Leoncavallo: *Pagliacci*; Mascagni: *Cavalleria rusticana*; Mozart: *Don Giovanni*; Mussorgsky: *Boris Godunov*; Puccini: *Bohème, Gianni Schicchi, Butterfly, Manon Lescaut, Tosca, Turandot*; Rossini: *Italiana in Algeri, Assedio di Corinto*; Verdi: *Falstaff, Forza del destino, Traviata, Vespri*; Wagner: *Rheingold, Walküre, Siegfried, Götterdämmerung*.

Company performs most operas in orig language. 20 matinee pfs broadcast live per season. Annual tour of 7 operas, 49 pfs in Cleveland, Boston, Atlanta, Memphis, Dallas, Minneapolis, Detroit, Wolf Trap / Farm Pk, Vienna, VA. Pfs not included in total above. Guest engagements in 1975: JPN: Tokyo, Nagoya and Osaka; 3 operas, 18 pfs.

Budget for 1974-75 $27,600,000. Income: 54% box office, 5% gvnmt, 26% priv / corp / fndt grants. Ticket prices: $20-4; 60% subscription, 40% single ticket sale.

Number of persons engaged in 1974-75: 910; resident & guest solo artists: 155; chorus members: 78; orchestra members: 92; musical staff: 14; conductors: 15; stage directors / producers: 11; set & costume designers: 7; corps de ballet: 32; administrative staff: 26; technical, scenic, costume: 218.

Company maintains own orch; builds all sets and costumes in own workshops.

Policy is determined by Board of Directors upon recommendation of officers and the exec commtt. Officers: Chm Emeritus Lowell Wadmond; Chm of Board Langdon Van Norden; Pres William Rockefeller; Chm Exec Commtt Laurence D Lovett; Vice Presidents J William Fisher, Michael V Forrestal, Mrs Alexander M Laughlin; Treas James S Smith; Asst Treas James C Hemphill; Secy Alton E Peters; Asst Secy Eva Popper; Legal Counsel Lauterstein & Lauterstein. Board of Dir: Emeritus Dirs Mrs August Belmont and Mrs Lewis W Douglas; and 36 other dirs. Artistic policy is determined by Mus Dir James Levine and Prod Dir John Dexter.

NEW YORK CITY OPERA, NY State Theater, Lincoln Center, New York, NY 10023, USA; tel (212) 877-4700. Founded in 1944. Perf at New York State Theater since 1966. Built in 1964; seat cap 2,737, avg aud 2,600. Prev theater: City Center Theater, 130 W 55 St, 1944-65; seat cap 2,934. Company is a private non-profit organization; Fin Chm David Lloyd-Jacob; Dir Julius Rudel; Mng Dir John S White; Asst Mng Dir Daniel R Rule; Asst Dir Ruth Hider; Mus Adm Felix Popper; Tech Dir Hans Sondheimer; Fin Adm R C Walker.

SEASON	OPENING Day Month		CLOSING Day Month		NO OF PFS	NO OF OPERAS	NO OF NEW PROD	NO OF NON-OPERA PFS
73-74	29	Aug	28	Apr	131	28	5	—
74-75	28	Aug	27	Apr	160	29	6	—

Fall season til late Nov, Spring season begins Feb.

Repertoire 1973-74 — Bellini: *Puritani*; Bizet: *Carmen*; Cherubini: *Medea*; Delius: *Village Romeo and Juliet*; Donizetti: *Anna Bolena, Lucia, Maria Stuarda, Roberto Devereux*; Ginastera: *Beatrix Cenci*; Gounod: *Faust*; Leoncavallo: *Pagliacci*; Mascagni: *Cavalleria rusticana*; Massenet: *Manon*; Menotti: *Consul*; Monteverdi: *Incoronazione di Poppea*; Mozart: *Don Giovanni, Idomeneo, Nozze di Figaro, Zauberflöte*; Offenbach: *Contes d'Hoffmann*; Puccini: *Bohème, Butterfly, Tosca*; Rossini: *Barbiere di Siviglia*; Strauss, R: *Ariadne auf Naxos, Rosenkavalier*; Verdi: *Rigoletto, Traviata*.

1974-75 — Bellini: *Puritani*; Bizet: *Carmen*; Cherubini: *Medea*; Debussy: *Pelléas et Mélisande*; Delius: *Village Romeo and Juliet*; Donizetti: *Anna Bolena, Lucia, Maria Stuarda, Roberto Devereux*; Gounod: *Faust*; Korngold: *Tote Stadt*; Leoncavallo: *Pagliacci*; Mascagni: *Cavalleria rusticana*; Menotti: *Consul*; Monteverdi: *Incoronazione di Poppea*; Mozart: *Don Giovanni, Idomeneo, Nozze di Figaro*; Puccini: *Bohème, Butterfly, Manon Lescaut, Tosca, Turandot*; Rossini: *Barbiere di Siviglia*; Strauss, J: *Fledermaus*; Strauss, R: *Ariadne auf Naxos, Salome*; Verdi: *Ballo in maschera, Traviata*.

Company performs 75% of all operas in orig language. Annual tour of 15 operas, 45 pfs in Los Angeles, CA, and Washington, DC. Subsidiary company, New York City Opera Theater, 25 pfs annually by junior performers in schools and community centers. Company has a training prgm for 1-2 adm per season.

Budget for 1974-75 $6,000,000. Income: 65% box office, 15% gvnmt, 15% priv/corp/fndt grants, 5% other income. Ticket prices: $10.95-2.50; 55% subscription, 45% single ticket sale.

Number of persons engaged in 1974-75: resident & guest solo artists: 120; chorus members: 80; orchestra members: 75; conductors: 19; stage directors/producers: 19; set & costume designers: 21; choreographers: 3; corps de ballet: 14; administrative staff: 14; technical, scenic, costume: 38.

Company maintains own orch; does not have scenic or costume workshop.

OMAHA OPERA COMPANY, 1200 City National Bank Bldg, Omaha, NE 68102, USA; tel (402) 346-4398. Founded in 1957. Perf at Orpheum Theatre, 16 St & Harney, since 1975. Built in 1927; seat cap 2,700, avg aud 2,000. Prev theater: Joslyn Art Museum 1957-63, seat cap 1,200; also Music Hall. Company is a private non-profit organization; Pres Wm S Matthews; Gen Dir Jonathan Dudley.

SEASON	OPENING Day Month	CLOSING Day Month	NO OF PFS	NO OF OPERAS	NO OF NEW PROD	NO OF NON-OPERA PFS
73-74	Nov	Apr	8	3	—	—
74-75	Nov	Apr	9	3	—	—

Repertoire 1973-74 — Donizetti: *Elisir*; Mozart: *Nozze di Figaro*; Puccini: *Tosca*.

1974-75 — Donizetti: *Lucia*; Offenbach: *Périchole*; Puccini: *Bohème*; tour — Rossini: *Barbiere di Siviglia*.

Company performs 50% of all operas in orig language. Annual tour of 1 opera, 12 pfs in small cities in Nebraska and Iowa.

Budget for 1974-75 $255,000. Income: 50% box office, 11% gvnmt, 34% priv/corp/fndt grants, 5% other income. Ticket prices: $14-3; 56% subscription, 44% single ticket sale.

Number of persons engaged in 1974-75: guest solo artists: 30; chorus members: 40; orchestra members: 40; conductors: 1; stage directors/producers: 1; choreographers: 1; corps de ballet: 8; administrative staff: 1; technical, scenic, costume: 35.

Company maintains own orch.

Policy determined by Board of Directors: Pres William S Matthews; Vice Pres F Simon, H Kooper, E Morsman, Mrs A Rimmerman, S Yaffe, Mrs J Jeter; Treas Harold Hoff; Secy Ms Polly Abariotes; Pres Omaha Opera Angels Mrs Paul Euler; Pres Omaha Opera Craftsman's Guild Mrs Herbert Forbes; and 9 other members.

OPERA COMPANY OF PHILADELPHIA, 1518 Walnut St, Philadelphia, PA 19102, USA; tel (215) 732-5814. Founded in 1975 as result of a merger between Philadelphia Grand Opera Co and Philadelphia Lyric Opera Co. Perf since 1975 at Academy of Music, Broad and Locust Sts, where both above companies performed. Built in 1857 as an opera house; seat cap 2,921, avg aud 2,775. Company is a private non-profit organization; Chmn John B Leake; Pres Mrs H Douglas Paxson; Gen Mng Dr Max M Leon; Art Dir Carl Suppa. New co plans 9 operas in 15 pfs for 1975-76.

SEASON	OPENING Day Month	CLOSING Day Month	NO OF PFS	NO OF OPERAS	NO OF NEW PROD	NO OF NON-OPERA PFS
73-74	Oct	Apr	7&6	6&6	—	—
74-75	Oct	Apr	7&7	7&7	—	—

Philadelphia Grand repertoire 1973-74 — Donizetti: *Lucia*; Gounod: *Faust*; Puccini: *Butterfly*; Verdi: *Aida, Rigoletto, Traviata*.

1974-75 — Bizet: *Carmen*; Donizetti: *Elisir*; Puccini: *Bohème, Tosca*; Rossini: *Barbiere di Siviglia*; Strauss, J: *Fledermaus*; Verdi: *Trovatore*.

Philadelphia Lyric repertoire 1973-74 — Donizetti: *Maria Stuarda*; Mozart: *Nozze di Figaro*; Puccini: *Bohème, Gianni Schicchi, Tabarro*; Verdi: *Macbeth*.

1974-75 — Donizetti: *Elisir*; Gounod: *Roméo et Juliette*; Verdi: *Rigoletto, Traviata*. Tour — Menotti: *Telephone*.

Company performs 75% of all operas in orig language. Opening night pf broadcast live. Subsidiary company, Light Opera Co of Philadelphia, a touring group perf chamber opera, approx 15 pfs in English annually. Company has a training prgm for 8 singers per season.

Budget n/a. Income: 60% box office. Ticket prices: $16-3.50; 50% subscription, 50% single ticket sale.

Number of persons engaged in 1975: resident solo artists: 23; guest solo artists: 22; chorus members: 44; orchestra members: 54; musical staff: 1; conductors: 3; stage directors/producers: 3; choreographers: 1; corps de ballet: 12; administrative staff: 3; technical, scenic, costume: 35.

Company maintains its own orch on a seasonal basis.

Policy determined by Exec Commtt of Board of Directors: Co-Chmn John B Leake and Paul R Trichon; Pres Mrs H Douglas Paxson; Exec Vice-Pres & Company Chmn Francesco Leto; Secy Mrs George Chimples; Treas Howard Butcher IV; and Mrs Vincent Micari, James Lewis Griffiths.

PITTSBURGH OPERA, INC, 600 Penn Ave, Pittsburgh, PA 15222, USA. Founded in 1939. Perf at Heinz Hall for the Performing Arts since 1971. Built in 1927 and renovated as a symph hall/opera theater in 1971. Prev theaters: Carnegie Music Hall 1939-42, Foster Memorial, The Syria Mosque 1945-71. Company is a private non-profit organization; Pres Gurdon Flagg; Vice Pres M O Fabiani; Gen & Mus Dir Richard Karp; Art Dir Ms Barbara Karp; Asst to Pres Vincent Artz; Tech Dir Thomas Struthers.

SEASON	OPENING Day	OPENING Month	CLOSING Day	CLOSING Month	NO OF PFS	NO OF OPERAS	NO OF NEW PROD	NO OF NON-OPERA PFS
73-74	18	Oct	30	Mar	12	7	1	—
74-75	10	Oct	1	Mar	14	6	5	—

Repertoire 1973-74 — Beethoven: *Fidelio*; Gounod: *Faust*; Leoncavallo: *Pagliacci*; Mozart: *Don Giovanni*; Puccini: *Tabarro*; Rossini: *Barbiere di Siviglia*; Verdi: *Traviata*.

1974-75 — Donizetti: *Elisir, Fille du régiment*; Puccini: *Bohème, Manon Lescaut*; Verdi: *Otello, Trovatore*.

Company performs 75% of all operas in orig language. Guest engagement in Butler, PA, 1 pf. Company has a training prgm in cooperation with Carnegie-Mellon Univ, 4 singers per season.

Budget for 1974-75 $515,760. Income: 48% box office, 5% gvnmt, 7% priv/corp/fndt grants, 40% other income. Ticket prices: $12-4.50; 68% subscription, 32% single ticket sale.

Number of persons engaged in 1974-75: resident solo artists: 26; guest solo artists: 34; chorus members: 54; orchestra members: 67; musical staff: 4; conductors: 1; stage directors/producers: 6; set & costume designers: 4; choreographers: 1; corps de ballet: 8; administrative staff: 3; technical, scenic, costume: 26.

Company uses local symph orch; builds abt 30% of its sets in own workshops.

Policy determined by Board of Directors: Pres Gurdon Flagg; Vice Pres M O Fabiani; Secy Mrs John Byerly; Treas Joseph Neubauer; and 64 other members.

PORTLAND OPERA ASSOCIATION INC, 922 S W Main, Portland, OR 97207, USA; tel (503) 248-4741. Founded in 1950. Perf at Portland Civic Auditorium, 222 S W Clay St, since 1966. Built in 1917, remodeled in 1968; seat cap 3,000, avg aud 2,760. Prev theaters: Oriental Theatre; Washington Park Amphitheatre, 1957-75, seat cap 5,000, currently used for summer prods. Company is a private non-profit organization; Pres Peter H Koehler; Gen Dir & Cond Stefan Minde.

SEASON	OPENING Day Month	CLOSING Day Month	NO OF PFS	NO OF OPERAS	NO OF NEW PROD	NO OF NON-OPERA PFS
73-74	27 Sep	11 May	10	5	—	—
74-75	26 Sep	20 May	12	5	—	—

Repertoire 1973-74 — Donizetti: *Don Pasquale*; Offenbach: *Contes d'Hoffmann*; Puccini: *Bohème*; Smetana: *Bartered Bride*; Strauss, R: *Ariadne auf Naxos*.

1974-75 — Donizetti: *Elisir*; Strauss, R: *Salome*; Stravinsky: *Rossignol*; Verdi: *Rigoletto*; Weber: *Freischütz*.

Company performs 50% of all operas in orig language. Company has a training prgm for 16-20 singers per season.

Budget n/a. Income: 56% box office, 42% priv/corp/fndt grants, 2% other income. Ticket prices: $22-5; 75% subscription, 25% single ticket sale.

Number of persons engaged in 1974-75: chorus members: 22; musical staff: 1; conductors: 1; stage directors/producers: 4; set & costume designers: 1; administrative staff: 5; costume: 3. (Soloists: n/a.)

Company maintains own orch on seasonal basis; builds 25% of sets and costumes in own workshops.

Policy determined by Executive Commtt.

SAINT PAUL OPERA ASSOCIATION, Minnesota Bldg, St Paul, MN 55101, USA; tel (612) 227-6679. Founded in 1933. Pfs temporarily suspended in 1975. Perf at I A O'Shaughnessy Auditorium, 2004 Randolph Ave, since 1970. Built in 1969; seat cap 1,747. Prev theaters: Saint Paul Auditorium Theatre 1933-69, seat cap 2,687; also Crawford Livingston Theatre — St Paul Arts & Science Center. Company is a private non-profit organization; Pres Sister Alberta Huber; Gen Mng George M Schaefer; Prod Mng Irl Mowery; Mus Dir Igor Buketoff; Asst Gen Mng Barbara B Sweeney (all until 1975); Off Mng Kathleen Y Davis.

SEASON	OPENING Day Month	CLOSING Day Month	NO OF PFS	NO OF OPERAS	NO OF NEW PROD	NO OF NON-OPERA PFS
74	19 Jun	3 Aug	15	6	5	—
75	none					

Repertoire 1973 — Delius: *Village Romeo and Juliet*; Puccini: *Bohème*; Wagner: *Walküre*; Ward: *Crucible*.

1974— Bizet: *Carmen*; Egk: *Verlobung in San Domingo*; Fisher: *Happy Prince*; Massenet: *Manon*; Puccini: *Gianni Schicchi*; Wagner: *Siegfried*.

1975 — no pfs.

Company performs 50% of all operas in orig language. 1 pf broadcast live per season. Company has a training prgm for 25 singers per season.

Budget for 1974 $780,771. Income: 20% box office, 10% gvnmt, 60% priv/corp/fndt grants, 10% other income. Ticket prices: $9-1; 60% subscription, 40% single ticket sale.

Number of persons engaged in 1974: guest solo artists: 34; chorus members: 25; orchestra members: 60; musical staff: 7; conductors: 3; stage directors/producers: 5; set & costume designers: 9; choreographers: 1; corps de ballet: 6; administrative staff: 5; technical, scenic, costume: 51.

Company assembles orch for each prod; builds 80% of sets and 30% of costumes in own workshops.

Policy determined by Board of Directors: Pres Sister Alberta Huber; Vice Pres Calvin Didier, Donald Houpt; Secy W Schoenbohm; Treas Edward Clapp; and 32 other members.

SYMPHONY SOCIETY OF SAN ANTONIO, OPERA FEST, 109 Lexington Ave, San Antonio, TX 78205, USA; tel (512) 225-6161. Subsidiary opera company founded in 1945. Perf at Theater for the Performing Arts since 1969. Built in 1968; seat cap 2,779, avg aud 2,225. Also perf at Municipal Auditorium 1945-74; seat cap 6,000. Company is a private non-profit organization; Chmn James S Calvert; Pres Mrs Louis P Bishop; Mus Dir Victor Alessandro; Mng Joyce A Moffatt; Assoc Cond & Choral Dir Roger Melone; Asst Mng Linda V Moorhouse.

SEASON	OPENING Day Month	CLOSING Day Month	NO OF PFS	NO OF OPERAS	NO OF NEW PROD	NO OF NON-OPERA PFS
74	1 Feb	12 May	8	4	1	—
75	24 Jan	18 May	6	3	—	—

Repertoire 1974 — Donizetti: *Lucia*; Mozart: *Nozze di Figaro*; Verdi: *Traviata*; Wagner: *Meistersinger*.

1975 — Gershwin: *Porgy and Bess*; Offenbach: *Contes d'Hoffmann*; Orff: *Carmina burana*; Puccini: *Butterfly*; Strauss, R: *Salome*.

Company performs 75% of all operas in orig language. Annual tour of 2 operas in 2 pfs at McAllen, TX, and Shreveport, LA. Guest engagements 1973-75: Rio Grande Valley Intl Music Fest, TX.

Budget for opera & symphony for 1974-75 $1,434,400. Income: 28.9% box office; 23.3% gvnmt; 4.3% priv/corp/fndt grants; 43.5% other income. Ticket prices: $12.50-5.50; 60% subscription, 40% single ticket sale.

Number of persons engaged in 1975: guest solo artists: 40; chorus members: 120; orchestra members: 77; conductors: 4; stage directors/producers: 3; administrative staff: 6; technical, scenic, costume: 32.

Company is owned and managed by local orch.

SAN FRANCISCO OPERA ASSOCIATION, War Memorial Opera House, San Francisco, CA 94102, USA; tel (415) 861-4008. Founded in 1923. Perf at War Memorial Opera House since 1932. Built in 1932 as an opera house; seat cap 3,252, avg aud 3,252. Prev theater: Civic Auditorium 1923-31; seat cap 6,000. Other theaters: Sacramento Memorial Theater; Greek Theater, Berkeley; Shrine Auditorium and Dorothy Chandler Pavilion, Los Angeles. Company is a private non-profit organization: Chmn R Gwin Follis; Pres Walter M Baird; Gen Dir Kurt Herbert Adler; Co Adm Ruth Allison Felt; Art Adm John McKay Ludwig; Tech Dir John Priest; Bus Adm Michael L Sack.

SEASON	OPENING Day Month	CLOSING Day Month	NO OF PFS	NO OF OPERAS	NO OF NEW PROD	NO OF NON-OPERA PFS
73-74	7 Sep	25 Nov	57	11	3	—
74-75	13 Sep	1 Dec	60	12	4	—

For subsidiary cos, see below.

Repertoire 1973-74 — Britten: *Peter Grimes*; Donizetti: *Favorite*; Mozart: *Così fan tutte*; Mussorgsky: *Boris Godunov*; Puccini: *Bohème, Fanciulla del West*; Strauss, J: *Fledermaus*; Strauss, R: *Elektra*; Verdi: *Don Carlo, Rigoletto, Traviata*; Wagner: *Tannhäuser*. **Spring Opera** — Cavalli: *Ormindo*; Donizetti: *Don Pasquale*; Floyd: *Of Mice and Men*. **Western Opera** — Bernstein: *Trouble in Tahiti*; Britten: *Turn of the Screw*; Humperdinck: *Hänsel und Gretel*; Krenek: *What Price Confidence*; Rossini: *Barbiere di Siviglia*. **Merola Opera** — Mozart: *Zauberflöte*.

1974-75 — Donizetti: *Fille du régiment*; Massenet: *Esclarmonde*; Mozart: *Don Giovanni*; Puccini: *Butterfly, Manon Lescaut*; Rossini: *Cenerentola*; Strauss, R: *Salome*; Verdi: *Luisa Miller, Otello*; Wagner: *Parsifal, Tristan und Isolde*. **Spring Opera** — Bizet: *Pêcheurs de perles*; Britten: *Death in Venice*; Donizetti: *Convenienze/Viva la Mamma*; Mozart: *Entführung aus dem Serail*. **Western Opera** — Bernstein: *Trouble in Tahiti*; Krenek: *What Price Confidence*; Mozart: *Don Giovanni*; Offenbach: *Contes d'Hoffmann*; Rossini: *Barbiere di Siviglia*; Verdi: *Traviata*. **Merola Opera** — Bizet: *Carmen*; Mozart: *Finta giardiniera*.

Company performs 95% of all operas in orig language. Pfs are broadcast live once a week during season. Subsidiary companies: Spring Opera Theater for experimental & chamber works, 19 pfs annually at Curran Theater in April; Merola Opera Program for junior performers, 3 pfs annually at Paul Masson Vineyards in Saratoga & Stern Grove in San Francisco in summer; Western Opera Theater touring the Western states, 85 pfs annually. Company has a training prgm for 16-20 singers and 2 administrators per season.

Budget abt $6 mill. Income: 63% box office. Ticket prices: $23-6; 76% subscription, 24% single ticket sale.

Number of persons engaged in 1974-75: guest solo artists: 70; chorus members: 69; orchestra members: 82; musical staff: 8; conductors: 9; stage directors/producers: 8; set & costume designers: 11; choreographers: 1; corps de ballet: 12; administrative staff: 18; technical, scenic, costume: 270.

Company maintains own orch on seasonal basis; builds 90% of its sets and 5% of its costumes in own workshops.

Policy determined by Board of Directors: Chmn R Gwin Follis; Pres Walter M Baird; Vice-Pres Richard K Miller; Treas James D Robertson; Secy Robert C Harris; 68 other board members, and Gen Dir K H Adler.

SANTA FE OPERA, PO Box 2408, Sante Fe, NM 87501, USA; tel (505) 982-3851. Founded in 1957. Perf at Santa Fe Opera since 1957; seat cap first 500, enlarged to 1,200; destroyed by fire and rebuilt 1967, seat cap 1,500. Interim theater 1967: Sweeney Gym. Company is a private non-profit organization; Chmn E H Tatum, Jr; Pres Mrs Walter M Mayer; Gen Dir John O Crosby; Art Adm Richard Gaddes; Exec Asst Harriet Kimbro.

SEASON	OPENING Day	OPENING Month	CLOSING Day	CLOSING Month	NO OF PFS	NO OF OPERAS	NO OF NEW PROD	NO OF NON-OPERA PFS
74	5	Jul	24	Aug	30	5	1	—
75	2	Jul	23	Aug	31	6	2	—

Repertoire 1974 — Berg: *Lulu*; Cavalli: *Egisto*; Mozart: *Zauberflöte*; Offenbach: *Grand Duchesse de Gérolstein*; Puccini: *Bohème*.

1975 — Bizet: *Carmen*; Falla: *Vida breve*; Janácek: *Cunning Little Vixen*; Mozart: *Così fan tutte*; Ravel: *Enfant et les sortilèges*; Verdi: *Falstaff*.

Company performs 75% of all operas in orig language. Company has an Apprentice Prgm for 44 singers, 1-2 administrators, and 50 technical personnel per season.

Budget for 1975 $1,000,000. Income: 45% box office, 50.6% gvnmt/priv/corp/fndt grants, 4.4% other income. Ticket prices: $15-5; 7% subscription, 93% single ticket sale.

Number of persons engaged in 1975: resident solo artists: 25; chorus members: 44; orchestra members: 62; musical staff: 10; conductors: 4; stage directors/producers: 3; set & costume designers: 5; choreographers: 2; corps de ballet: 8; administrative staff: 9; technical, scenic, costume: 30*.

*Plus 50 tech apprentices.

Company maintains own orch on seasonal basis; builds all its sets and 35% of costumes in own workshops.

Policy determined by Board of Directors: Chmn Edward H Tatum Jr; Vice-Chmns J I Staley and Robert L B Tobin; Pres Mrs Walter M Mayer; Vice-Pres Thomas B Catron III and Mrs Walter B Driscoll; Treas Mrs David B Hall; Secy Mrs Alan C Vedder; and 37 other members.

SEATTLE OPERA ASSOCIATION, INC, 305 Harrison, Seattle, WA 98109, USA; tel (206) 447-4700. Founded in 1964. Perf at Seattle Opera House, 300 Mercer, since 1964. Built in 1962 for World's Fair; seat cap 3,000, avg aud 2,880. Company is a private non-profit organization; Pres Sheffield Phelps; Gen Dir Glynn Ross; Mus & Educ Dir Henry Holt; Finance & Devlp Dir Lloyd Yunker.

SEASON	OPENING Day Month	CLOSING Day Month	NO OF PFS	NO OF OPERAS	NO OF NEW PROD	NO OF NON-OPERA PFS*
73-74	13 Sep	18 May	56	7	4	72
74-75	11 Sep	18 May	43	6	—	118

*Educt prgms.

Repertoire 1973-74 — Britten: *Noye's Fludde*; Donizetti: *Fille du régiment*; Leoncavallo: *Pagliacci*; Mozart: *Così fan tutte*; Puccini: *Gianni Schicchi*; Verdi: *Rigoletto*; Wagner: *Siegfried*.

1974-75 — Boito: *Mefistofele*; Massenet: *Manon*; Rossini: *Barbiere di Siviglia*; Verdi: *Aida, Trovatore*; Wagner: *Götterdämmerung*.

Company performs an Intl Series in orig language, and the same prods in a Ntl Series in English with different principals. Several pilot prgm pfs broadcast live per season.

Annual tour of one opera in 6-8 pfs to Spokane, Pullman, Olympia and Port Angeles, WA. Guest engagements 1971-75 to Phoenix, AZ, 8 pfs; Spokane, WA, 4 pfs. Exchange engagement to YUG: Sarajevo as part of spec artist exchange prgm, 4 pfs, 1 prod. In 1975 initiated Northwest Summer Festival with two sets of *Ring des Nibelungen*, one orig, other in Eng with diff casts. Company has a training prgm for 3 singers per season.

Budget for 1973-74 $1,215,578. Income: 43.4% box office, 22.4% gvnmt, 10.4% priv/corp/fndt grants, 23.8% other income. Ticket prices: $13.75-2.25; 87% subscription, 13% single ticket sale.

Number of persons engaged in 1974-75: 518, details n/a.

Company uses local symph orch; builds 20% of sets and costumes in own workshops.

Policy determined by the Board of Directors; 60 members.

OPERA SOCIETY OF WASHINGTON, 2401 H St NW, Washington, DC 20037, USA; tel (202) 333-5011. Founded in 1956. Perf at Opera House of the Kennedy Center for the Performing Arts since 1971. Built in 1971 as an opera house; seat cap 2,200, avg aud 2,200. Prev theater: Lisner Auditorium 1956-71; seat cap 1,500. Company is a private non-profit organization; Chmn & Pres Christine Hunter; Dir until 1975 Ian Strasfogel, succeeded by George London; Mng Dir David Baber.

SEASON	OPENING Day Month	CLOSING Day Month	NO OF PFS	NO OF OPERAS	NO OF NEW PROD	NO OF NON-OPERA PFS
73-74	21 Sep	22 Apr	22	6	4	—
74-75	9 Oct	10 Feb	10	3	1	—

Repertoire 1973-74 — Massenet: *Manon*; Monteverdi: *Ritorno d'Ulisse*; Puccini: *Gianni Schicchi, Tabarro*; Rossini: *Barbiere di Siviglia*; Verdi: *Macbeth*.

1974-75 — Monteverdi: *Incoronazione di Poppea*; Strauss, R: *Salome*; Wagner: *Walküre*.

Company performs 75% of all operas in orig language.

Budget for 1974-75 $575,000. Income: 38% box office, 15% gvnmt, 47% priv/corp/fndt grants. Ticket prices: $25-5; 60% subscription, 40% single ticket sale.

Number of persons engaged in 1974-75: guest solo artists: 50; chorus members 9 (max 75); orchestra members: 70; musical staff: 3; conductors: 3; stage directors/producers: 3; set & costume designers: 2; choreographers: 1; administrative staff: 7.

Company assembles orch for each prod; occasionally builds sets or costumes.

Policy determined by Board of Trustees: Pres Christine Hunter; Vice-Pres Col Charles D Daniel; Vice-Pres Carl S Shultz; Sec Edith Martin; Treas Lee Marks; Counsel Perry Ausbrook; Members at Large Col C Haskell Small, Dr Alec Levin.

YUGOSLAVIA

OPERA NARODNOG POZORISTA U BEOGRADU (Belgrade National Opera) Francuska 3, Belgrade, Yugoslavia; tel 625-085. Founded in 1919. Perf at National Theater. Built in 1868; seat cap 891 Company owned and operated by the State and the City; Dir Djordje Djurdjevic; First Cond Dusan Miladinović; Dram Konstantin Vinaver; Gen Secy Vlastimir Stefanović; Tech Dir Dobrilo Nikolić.

SEASON	OPENING		CLOSING		NO OF PFS	NO OF OPERAS	NO OF NEW PROD	NO OF NON-OPERA PFS*
	Day	Month	Day	Month				
73-74	1	Oct	30	Jun	194	28	4	66
74-75	1	Oct	30	Jun	160	25	4	51

*Ballet.

Repertoire 1971-75 — Bellini: *Norma*; Binicki: *Na Uranku*; Bizet: *Carmen*; Borodin: *Prince Igor*; Britten: *Rape of Lucretia*; Glinka: *Ivan Susanin*; Donizetti: *Elisir, Lucia*; Gershwin: *Porgy and Bess*; Gotovac: *Ero der Schelm*; Gounod: *Faust*; Konjovic: *Duke of Zeta*; Logar: *1941*; Massenet: *Werther*; Menotti: *Telephone*; Mozart: *Nozze di Figaro, Zauberflöte*; Mussorgsky: *Boris Godunov, Khovanshchina*; Poulenc: *Voix humaine*; Puccini: *Bohème, Butterfly, Tosca*; Rajicic: *Simonida*; Rimsky-Korsakov: *Maid of Pskov*; Rossini: *Barbiere di Siviglia*; Tchaikovsky: *Mazeppa*; Verdi: *Aida, Ballo in maschera, Don Carlo, Ernani, Forza del destino, Rigoletto, Traviata, Trovatore, Nabucco, Otello*.

Company performs 25% of all operas in orig language. Pfs are broadcast regularly; 1-2 pfs per season videotaped. Annual tour of 4-6 cities. Guest and exchange engagements 1971-75: SPA: Madrid 8 pfs; SWI: Lausanne 8 pfs. Subsidiary company, Krug 101, performs chamber opera, 15-20 pfs annually. Company has a training prgm for 12 singers per season.

Budget n/a. Income: 20% box office, 70% gvnmt, 10% corp grants. Ticket prices: Din 60-10; 30% subscription, 70% single ticket sale.

Number of persons engaged in 1974-75: resident solo artists: 38; guest solo artists: 25; chorus members: 82; orchestra members: 68; conductors: 4; stage directors/producers: 3; set & costume designers: 3; choreographers: 2; corps de ballet: 70; administrative staff: 8; technical, scenic, costume: 180.

Company maintains own orch; builds all its sets and 90% of its costumes in own workshops.

List of Opera Companies

Artists involved with the productions of these companies, selected by the Advisory Panel, were invited to submit biographical information in accordance with the criteria detailed on page ix.

ARGENTINA

Buenos Aires: Teatro Colón*

AUSTRALIA

Sydney: The Australian Opera*

AUSTRIA

Bregenz: Bregenzer Festspiele*
Graz: Vereinigte Bühnen,
   Opernhaus
Salzburg: Salzburger Festspiele
   (Summer)* (& Easter)
Vienna: Wiener Staatsoper*
Vienna: Volksoper Wien*

BELGIUM

Brussels: Opéra National de
   Belgique*

Liège: Centre Lyrique de
   Wallonie*

BRAZIL

Rio de Janeiro: Teatro Municipale

BULGARIA

Sofia: National Opera

CANADA

Montreal/Quebec: L'Opéra de
   Québec*
Ottawa: National Arts Centre
   Festival Opera*
Toronto: Canadian Opera
   Company*
Vancouver: Vancouver Opera
   Association*

*Companies whose profiles appear in the profiles section beginning on page 613.

CZECHOSLOVAKIA

Brno: Janácek Opera House
Prague: Smetana Theatre &
National Theatre*

DENMARK

Copenhagen: Royal Opera House

FINLAND

Helsinki: Suomen Kansallisooppera (Finnish National)*

FRANCE

Aix-en-Provence: Aix-en-
Provence Festival
Bordeaux: Grand Théâtre
Municipal
Lyon: Opéra de Lyon*
Marseille: Opéra de Marseille*
Nancy: Théâtre Municipal
Nice: Théâtre de l'Opéra
Orange: Festival d'Orange
Paris: Théâtre National de
l'Opéra*
Rouen: Théâtre des Arts*
Strasbourg: Opéra du Rhin*
Toulouse: Théâtre du Capitole

FEDERAL REPUBLIC
OF GERMANY

Bayreuth: Bayreuther Festspiele
Berlin: Deutsche Oper Berlin*
Bielefeld: Bühnen der Stadt
Bielefeld*
Bonn: Theater der Stadt Bonn*
Cologne: Oper der Stadt Köln*
Darmstadt: Staatstheater
Dortmund: Städtische Bühnen
Düsseldorf-Duisburg: Deutsche
Oper am Rhein*
Essen: Bühnen der Stadt Essen*

Frankfurt: Frankfurter Oper*
Hamburg: Hamburgische
Staatsoper*
Hannover: Niedersächsisches
Staatstheater Hannover*
Karlsruhe: Badisches Staats-
theater Karlsruhe*
Kassel: Staatstheater Kassel*
Kiel: Bühnen der Landeshaupt-
stadt Kiel*
Krefeld: Vereinigte Städtische
Bühnen Krefeld-Mönchen-
gladbach*
Mannheim: Nationaltheater
Mannheim*
Munich: Bayerische Staatsoper*
Munich: Staatstheater am
Gärtnerplatz*
Nürnberg: Städtische Bühnen
Nürnberg, Musiktheater*
Saarbrücken: Saarländisches
Staatstheater
Stuttgart: Württembergische
Staatsoper Stuttgart*
Wiesbaden: Hessisches Staats-
theater
Wuppertal: Wuppertaler Bühnen*

GERMAN DEMOCRATIC
REPUBLIC

Berlin: Komische Oper
Berlin: Staatsoper Berlin
Dresden: Staatsoper Dresden*
Leipzig: Städtische Theater
Leipzig, Oper*

GREECE

Athens: Athens Festival
Athens: National Opera

HOLLAND

Amsterdam: De Nederlandse
Operastichting (Opera Foundation)*

HUNGARY

Budapest: Magyar Állami
Operház*

ISRAEL

Tel Aviv: Israel National Opera*

ITALY

Bologna: Teatro Comunale
Florence: Maggio Musicale
Fiorentino & Teatro
Comunale*
Genoa: Teatro Comunale
dell'Opera*
Milan: Teatro alla Scala*
Naples: Teatro di San Carlo*
Palermo: Teatro Massimo*
Parma: Teatro Regio*
Rome: Teatro dell'Opera &
Terme di Caracalla*
Spoleto: Festival of Two Worlds*
Trieste: Teatro Comunale
Giuseppe Verdi*
Turin: Teatro Regio*
Venice: Teatro La Fenice*
Verona: Lirico Arena*

JAPAN

Tokyo: Fujiwara Opera
Tokyo: Niki Kai Opera Company*

MEXICO

Mexico City: Palacio de Bellas
Artes, Opera

MONACO

Monte Carlo: Opéra de
Monte-Carlo*

NORWAY

Oslo: Den Norske Opera*

POLAND

Lódz: Wielki Opera Lódz
Warsaw: Teatr Wielki/Grand
Theater Warsaw*

PORTUGAL

Lisbon: Teatro Nacional de San
Carlo

ROMANIA

Bucharest: Opera Româna*

SOUTH AFRICA

Johannesburg: Municipal Opera

SPAIN

Barcelona: Gran Teatro del
Liceo*
Las Palmas: Amigos Canarios
de la Opera*

SWEDEN

Drottningholm: Drottningholm
Festival
Stockholm: Royal Opera
Stockholm*

SWITZERLAND

Basel: Stadttheater Basel
Geneva: Grand Théâtre de
Genève*
Zurich: Theater-Aktiengesell-
schaft Zürich*

UNION OF SOVIET SOCIALIST REPUBLICS

Kiev: Shevchenko State Opera
Leningrad: Kirov Opera Theatre
Moscow: Bolshoi Opera*
Moscow: Stanislavski &
Danchenko Music Theatre
Tbilisi: Paliashvili Opera Theatre

UNITED KINGDOM

Aldeburgh: Aldeburgh Festival
Cardiff: Welsh National Opera*
Edinburgh: Edinburgh Festival
Glasgow: Scottish National
 Opera
Glyndebourne: Glyndebourne
 Festival Opera*
London: English National Opera
 (form Sadler's Wells)*
London: Royal Opera (form
 Covent Garden)*

UNITED STATES OF AMERICA

Baltimore: Baltimore Opera
 Company*
Boston: Opera Company of
 Boston*
Chicago: Lyric Opera of Chicago*
Cincinnati: Cincinnati Opera
 Association*
Dallas: Dallas Civic Opera
 Company*
Fort Worth: Fort Worth Opera
 Association*
Hartford: Connecticut Opera
 Association*
Hawaii: Hawaii Opera Theatre of
 the Honolulu Symphony*
Houston: Houston Grand Opera
 Association*
Jackson: Opera/South*
Kansas City: Kansas City Lyric
 Theater*
Lake George: Lake George Opera
 Festival*
Louisville: Kentucky Opera
 Association*
Memphis: Memphis Opera
 Theatre*
Miami: Greater Miami Opera
 Association*

Milwaukee: Milwaukee
 Florentine Opera Company*
Minneapolis: Minnesota Opera
 Company* (form Center Opera)
Newark: New Jersey State Opera
 Company
New Orleans: New Orleans Opera
 Association*
New York: Metropolitan Opera
 Association*
New York: New York City Opera*
Omaha: Omaha Opera Company*
Philadelphia: Opera Company
 of Philadelphia* (form Phila-
 delphia Grand Opera & Phila-
 delphia Lyric)
Pittsburgh: Pittsburgh Opera,
 Inc*
Portland: Portland Opera
 Association*
St Paul: St Paul Opera
 Association*
San Antonio: Symphony Society
 of San Antonio, Opera
 Festival*
San Diego: San Diego Opera
 Company
San Francisco: San Francisco
 Opera Association & Spring
 Opera Company*
Santa Fe: Santa Fe Opera*
Seattle: Seattle Opera
 Association*
Washington DC: Opera Society
 of Washington*

YUGOSLAVIA

Belgrade: Opera Narodnog
 Pozorista u Beogradu
 (Belgrade National Opera)*
Dubrovnik: Dubrovnik Summer
 Festival
Zagreb: Zagreb/Croatian
 National Opera

Directory of
International Artists' Agents*

ARG	**ARGENTINA**		**BEL**	**BELGIUM**

ARG   **ARGENTINA**

CDA   Conciertos Daniel, Lavalle 1171-3/o, Buenos Aires.

GER   Conciertos Gerard, Ave Corrientes 127, Buenos Aires.

AUSTRL   **AUSTRALIA**

EDY   Jenifer Edy Art Mgmt, 2 Dunlop Ave, Melbourne.

GLN   Gunlan Productions, 12 Glen St/ Wilsons Pt, Sydney.

RDD   Robin Donald Ltd, 4 Bedford St/ Earlwood, Sydney.

AUS   **AUSTRIA**

ADZ   Alfred Diez, Lothringerstr 20, 1030 Vienna.

CLN   Dr Peter Clyne, Hotel im Palais Schwarzenberg, 1030 Vienna.

KOA   Olga Altmann, Jacquingasse 37/55, 1030 Vienna.

RAB   Agentur Raab, Plankengasse 7, A-1010 Vienna.

TAS   Starka-Holender, Mariahilferstr 3, 1060 Vienna.

TRY   Terry AG, Johannessteig 8, 2340 Mödling/Vienna.

VLD   Opera/Lotte Vladarski, Reithlegasse 12, 1190 Vienna.

BEL   **BELGIUM**

GAR   Gaston Arien, 38-40 Huidevetterstraat, Antwerp.

BRA   **BRAZIL**

NBA   Nonelli Barbastetane, rua Barão de Itambi 55, Rio de Janeiro.

PMC   Aulus Promoções Walter Santos Filho, Caixa Portal 1387, ZC:00, Rio de Janeiro.

BUL   **BULGARIA**

BAA   Sofiaconcert/Bulgarian Artistic Agency, Staboliiski St 17, Sofia.

CAN   **CANADA**

ACM   Artists Canada Mgmt, 150 Edlinton Ave E, Toronto, Ont M4P 1E8.

ARS   Ars Musicalis-Canada, Denis Bousquet, 5174 Côte des Neiges, Montreal, PQ H3T 1X8.

CCA   Canadian Concert & Artist, 1822 Sherbrook, W Montreal, PQ H2K 1B3.

CCN   Concerts Canada, 151 Sparks St, Ottawa, Ont K1P 5V8.

HAY   Haysett Ltd, 55 Sumner Hts Dr, Willowdale, Ont M2K 1Y5.

IAR   International Artists, 178 Victoria St, Toronto, Ont M5B 1T7.

*The following agents are listed with their codes and abbreviations of their country in the biographical entries of the artists they represent (CDA/ARG).

INTERNATIONAL AGENTS

| OAC | Ontario Arts Council, 151 Bloor St W, Toronto, Ont M5F 1F4. |
| RMM | Robert Meyer Artist Mgmt, 4493 Emily Carr Dr, Victoria, BC V8X 2N5. |

CZE CZECHOSLOVAKIA

| PRG | Pragokoncert, Maltezske nam 1, Mala Strana/Prague 1. |
| SLK | Slov-Koncert, Bratislava. |

DEN DENMARK

| GSI | Goesta Schwarck, 48 Dalgas Blvd, 2000 Copenhagen F. |
| WHK | Wilhelm Hansen, Gothersgade 9-11, 1123 Copenhagen K. |

FIN FINLAND

| MFZ | Musik Fazer, Aleksanterink 11, 00101 Helsinki. |

FRA FRANCE

ABA	AMILC-Arturo Barosi, 29 rue Pastorelli, 06000 Nice.
BCP	Concerts de Paris-Pontavice, 139 Blvd Magenta, 75010 Paris.
CMW	Concerts, M Werner & Claude Stricker, 74 rue des Cevennes, 75075 Paris.
DAU	Robert Deniau, 23 rue de St Quentin, 75010 Paris.
GLZ	Michel Glotz, 141 Blvd St Michel, 75005 Paris.
GRE	Gisele Ribera, 7 rue Daunou, 75002 Paris.
IMR	Organisation Artistique Intl Rainer, 24 rue d'Artois, F-75008 Paris.
KSG	Kiesgen, 252 rue du Faubourg St Honoré, 75008 Paris.
LNR	Marceline Lenoir, 99 Blvd Malesherbes, 75008 Paris.
LOH	Luc Olivier Houdia, 52 Ave de Breteuil, 75007 Paris.
OOC	Organisation Intl Opéra et Concert, Germinal Hilbert, 5 rue du Faubourg St Honoré, 75008 Paris.
RAP	Agéance Rapicault, 27 Blvd Poissonnière, 75002 Paris.

FRG FEDERAL REPUBLIC OF GERMANY

ARM	Theateragentur Mohr, Rahmhofstr 4, 6 Frankfurt/M.
BAL	Balhausagentur, Martiusstr 3, 8 Munich 40.
EUM	Euromusica-Zellermeyer, Hotel Steinplatz, 1 Berlin.
GGM	Georg Mund, Adelbertg 58, 6 Frankfurt/M.
HOM	Cornelius Hom, Rahmhofstr 4, 6 Frankfurt/M.
HSM	Hans Schmid, Cuvilliésstr 31, 8 Munich.
HUS	Hans Ulrich Schmid, Postfach 1667, 3 Hannover 1.
KHA	Hans Adler, Auguste Viktoriastr 64, 1 Berlin 33.
KRG	Konzertdirektion Goette-Paulsen-Lutz, Collonaden 70, 2 Hamburg 36.
KRK	Konzert R Kollitsch, Geisbergstr 40, 1 Berlin 30.
KRV	R Vedder, Mauerkircherstr 8, 8 Munich 27.
LLP	Louisa Laxer-Petrov, Oberwegstr 28, 6 Frankfurt/M.
LNG	Christian Lange, Sperberweg 18, D-8033 Krailling.
MEL	Herbert Melle, Agnerstr 57, 8 Munich 40.
PAS	Friedrich Paasch, Drakestr 2, Düsseldorf-Oberkassel 4.
RBN	Künstleragentur Röhrbein, Krausenstr 9/10, 108 Berlin.
RTB	H R Rothenberg, Flurweg 26, 1 Berlin 47.
SLZ	Robert Schulz, Martiusstr 3, 8 Munich 40.
SMD	Harry Schmidt, Leopoldstr 44, 8 Munich 40.
WND	Concerto Winderstein-Göhre, Postfach 108 Steinsdorfstr, 8 Munich 1.
ZBV	Zentrale Bühnenvermittlung Rothenberg, Frankfurt/M 6.
ZFR	ZAV-Frankfurt, Feuerbachstr 42-46, Frankfurt/M6.

GDR GERMAN DEMOCRATIC REPUBLIC

| KDR | Künstleragentur der Deutschen Demokratischen Republik, Krausenstr 9/10, 102 Berlin. |

GRE	**GREECE**
BAA	Bureau Artistique d'Athènes Kourakos, Ave de l'Université 39, Athens 132.
KRI	Theodore Kritas, Anthimu Gazi, Athens 9.

HOL	**HOLLAND**
ALF	Pieter Alferink, Apollolaan 81, Amsterdam.
IBK	Interartists Beek/Koning, Koninginnegracht 82, The Hague.
NIM	Nederlands Impresariaat Waveren, Van Breestraat 77, Amsterdam.
SLL	Angela Sellström, Apollolaan 197, Amsterdam.
SRN	Alex Saron, 3 Waluwenwer 11, Bläricum.

HUN	**HUNGARY**
ITK	Interkoncert Mngt, Vörösmartry 1 sz, 1368 Budapest.
NEM	Nemzetközi Koncertiroda, Vörösmarty, Budapest.

ITA	**ITALY (Artistic Consultants)**
	ALCI, V Paolo da Cannobio 2, 20122 Milan.
	Ansaloni, V San Pietro all'Orto 3, 20121 Milan.
	Gabriele d'Averio, Piazza Melozzo da Forlì 4, 00196 Rome.
	Studio M & Esa de Simone, Lungotevere delle Navi 19, 00183 Rome.
	Simonetta Lippi, V San Teodoro 18, 1 00186 Rome.
	Dragon Lissac, Corso P'ta Vigentera 18, 20122 Milan.
	Lirica Toscana, V dell'Oliviera 60, 45485 Florence.
	Musart-Garrasi, V Manzoni 31, 20121 Milan.
	Alfredo Paglione, Galleria 32, V Brera N6, 20121 Milan.
	Propaganda Musicale, V Sicilia, 00187 Rome.
	Segretariato Artistico Italiano, Corso d'Italia 97, 00198 Rome.
	Stageart Ltd, Foro Bonaparte 57, 20121 Milan.
	Ann Summers-Dossena, V Mario dei Fiori 42, 00187 Rome.

JPN	**JAPAN**
JAR	Japan Art Staff Co Ltd/Sasaki, 5-1-20 Yakumo Megaro-ku, Tokyo.
KJM	Kaijimoto Concert Mgmt, Izumo Bldg, 8-8-1 Ginza/Chuo-ku, Tokyo.
MIC	Million Concert Co, Mori Bldg 2, 1-10-8 Nishishinbashi Minato-ku, Tokyo.

MEX	**MEXICO**
DAN	Conciertos Daniel, Jose Maria Marroqui 28-405, Mexico City.

NOR	**NORWAY**
NRK	Norsk Konsert/L Jarner, Klingenberggatan 4, Oslo 1.
PGI	Per Gottschalk Impresario, Tollbogaten 3, Oslo 1.

POL	**POLAND**
PAG	Polish Artists Agency/Pagart, Plac Zwyciestwa 9, Warsaw.

POR	**PORTUGAL**
JMH	Jean-Michel Hubert, Av Eng Duarte Pacheco 3-3, Lisbon.

ROM	**ROMANIA**
RIA	ARIA/V Florea, Blvd N Balcescu 2, 7 Bucharest.

SAF	**SOUTH AFRICA**
CAP	CAPAB/L Steyer, Box 4107, Cape Town.
PBC	PACT Opera/Bel Canto, 1038 Arcadia St, Hatfield/Pretoria.

SPA	**SPAIN**
CAB	Carlos Caballé, V Augusta 59, 4 Barcelona 6.
QUE	Daniel Ricardo de Quesada Conciertos, Los Madrazo 16, Madrid 14.
VIT	Vitoria/F Keller, Alcala 30-5 o, Madrid 14.

INTERNATIONAL AGENTS

SWE   SWEDEN

ADL   Adolfi, Drottninggatan 73A, 11136 Stockholm.

KBL   Konsertbolaget, Vasagatan 15-17, 11120 Stockholm.

SVE   Svensk Konsertdirektion/Lodding, Junigatan 27, 41515 Göteborg.

ULF   Ulf Törnquist, Norrtullsgatan 26, 11345 Stockholm.

SWI   SWITZERLAND

ALY   Artistes Lyriques/Sieber, Postgasse 21, 8750 Glarus.

HRR   H R Rothenberg, Thormanstr 66, 3000 Bern.

JUC   Emil Jucker, Music and Arts SA, Tobelhofstr 2, 8044 Zurich.

KGZ   Konzertgesellschaft Zurich/Payot, Steinwiesstr 2, 8032 Zurich 7.

PIO   Pio Chesini Agentur, Aeschenvorstadt 24, 4000 Basel.

RNR   M Rainer/Darsa, 42 rue de Rumine, 1005 Lausanne.

SWZ   Schweizer Theater Agentur, Eynar Grabowsky, Malzg 18, 4000 Basel.

TAU   Martin Taubmann, Bohl Str 23, 6300 Zug.

UK   UNITED KINGDOM

AIM   AIM/Horsfield, 5 Regents Park Rd, London NW1 7TL.

ALL   Allied Artists/Slotover, 36 Beauchamp Place, London SW3.

ASK   Lies Askonas, 19a Air St, London W1R 6LQ.

CST   John Coast, 1 Park Close/Knightsbridge, London SW1.

CVX   Choveaux Mgmt, Mancroft Towers, Lowestoft, Suffolk.

DLZ   Larry Dalzell Co, 3 Goodwin's Court, St Martin's Lane, London WC2.

DOU   Basil Douglas, 8 St George's Terrace, Regent Park Rd, London NW1.

GBN   Greenan & Brown, 19B Belsize Pk, London NW3.

GOR   S A Gorlinsky Ltd, 35 Dover St, London W1X 4NJ.

HLT   Harold Holt Ltd, 134 Wigmore St, London W1H 0DJ.

HPL   Harrison/Parrott Ltd, 22 Hillgate St, London W8 7SR.

IBB   Ibbs & Tillett, 124 Wigmore St, London W1H 0AX.

IWL   Ingpen & Williams Ltd/H Hartog, 14 Kensington Court, London W8.

LAL   London Artists Ltd, 124 Wigmore St, London W1H 0AX.

LES   Robert Leslie, 53 Bedford Rd, London SW4.

LMG   London Mgmt, 235 Regent St, London W1A 2JT.

LSM   Lotte S Medak Mgmt, 39 Albert Ct, Prince Consort Rd, London SW7 2BH.

MIN   Music International/Dalrymple, 13 Ardilaun Rd, London N5 2QR.

MRR   William Morris Mgmt, 4 Savile Row, London W1.

OEA   Owen Evans Artist's Mgmt Ltd, 38 Wigmore St, London W1H 9DF.

PLR   MLR Representation Ltd, 194 Old Brompton Road, London, SW5 0AS.

PPM   Pears Phipps Mgmt, 8 Halliford St, London N1 3HE.

PRS   Prestissimo Ltd/Buck, 15 Lancaster Grove, London NW3.

SEN   Dido Senger Opera & Concert Artists' Repr, 103 Randolph Ave, London W9 1 DL.

SHA   Shaw/Wright Concerts Ltd, 131c Kensington Church St, London W8 7LP.

SLA   Stafford Law Assocts, 14A Station Ave, Walton-on-Thames/Surrey KT12 1PE.

TFP   Trafalgar Perry, 12a Goodwin's Ct, St Martin's Lane, London WC2.

VLO   Int Cop Agency/van Loewen, 81-83 Shaftesbury Ave, London W1V 8BX.

USA   UNITED STATES OF AMERICA

ABW   Alix B Williamson, 1860 Broadway, New York, NY 10023.

ACA   Assoc Concert Artists, 2109 Broadway, New York, NY 10023.

AMC   American Chamber Concerts Inc, 890 West End Ave, New York, NY 10025.

AOD   Anne J O'Donnell Mgmt, 353 W 57 St, New York, NY 10019.

APA   Associated Pacific Artists, 40 Kenrock Bldg, 1402 Kapiolani Blvd, Honolulu, HI 96814.

ATI   Artists Int'l Mgmt, Irena Arn, 1050 North Point, San Francisco,

CA 94109; and Leo B Ruiz, 663 Fifth Ave, New York, NY 10022.

AWS   Arnold Weissberger, 120 E 56 St, New York, NY 10022.

BAR   Herbert Barrett Mgmt Inc, 1860 Broadway, New York, NY 10023.

BCK   Becker Ltd, 805 Everest Cnt, Mill Valley, CA 94941.

CAM   Columbia Artists Mgmt Inc, 165 W 57 St, New York, NY 10019.

COL   Colbert Artists Mgmt Inc, 111 W 57 St, New York, NY 10019.

CRB   Coleman-Rosenberg, 667 Madison Ave, New York, NY 10022.

CSA   Cone/Susman Artists Reps, 14 E 60 St, New York, NY 10022.

DBA   Dina Bader Associates, 444 E 82 St, New York, NY 10028.

DIL   Hubert Dilworth, 1133 Broadway, New York, NY 10010.

DSP   Thea Dispeker, 59 E 54 St, New York, NY 10022.

DST   De Santi-Meneghetti Theatrical Inc, 312 W 48 St, New York, NY 10036.

FLC   M L Falcone, 155 W 68 St, New York, NY 10023.

FLD   Maurice Feldman, 745 Fifth Ave, New York, NY 10022.

FUL   Richard Fulton Inc, 850 Seventh Ave, New York, NY 10019.

GRA   Peter Gravina, 115 E 92 St, New York, NY 10028.

HBM   Harry Beall Mgmt Inc, 119 W 57 St, New York, NY 10019.

HES   Hesseltine and Baker Assoc, 119 W 57 St, New York, NY 10019.

HHA   Helen Harvey Assocs, 110 W 57 St, New York, NY 10019.

HHB   Herbert H Breslin Inc, 119 W 57 St, New York, NY 10019.

HJH   Hans J Hofmann, 200 W 58 St, New York, NY 10019.

HUR   Hurok Concerts Inc, 540 Madison Ave, New York, NY 10022

IAA   International Artists Agency, 1564 18 Ave, San Francisco, CA 94122.

JBF   John B Fisher Mgmt, 155 W 68 St, New York, NY 10023.

JEN   Helen Jensen Artists Mgmt, 716 Joseph Vance Bldg, Third & Union Ave, Seattle, WA 98101.

JJJ   John Jae Jones, 300 Central Park W, New York, NY 10024.

JLM   Judith Liegner Artists Mgmt, 1860 Broadway, New York, NY 10023.

JRM   Joanne Rile Mgmt, 119 N 18 St, Philadelphia, PA 19103.

JUD   Judd Concert Artist Bureau, 127 W 69 St, New York, NY 10023.

KAY   Albert Kay Assocs Inc, 58 W 58 St, New York, NY 10019.

KAZ   Kazuko Hillyer Intl Inc, 250 W 57 St, New York, NY 10019.

KRT   Harry J Kraut, 1414 Ave of the Americas, New York, NY 10019.

LAN   Robert Lantz Inc, 114 E 55 St, New York, NY 10022.

LCA   Lake & Courtenay Artist Mgmt, 411 E 53 St, New York, NY 10022.

LEI   Jacques Leiser, 155 W 68 St, New York, NY 10023.

LLF   Ludwig Lustig & Florian Ltd, 111 W 57 St, New York, NY 10019.

LOM   Robert J Lombardo, 30 W 60 St, New York, NY 10023.

LWI   Louise Williams Mgmt, 165 W 66 St, New York, NY 10023.

LYR   Lyra Mgmt, 16 W 61 St, New York, NY 10023.

MAA   Mariedi Anders Artists Mgmt Inc, 535 El Camino del Mar, San Francisco, CA 94121.

MAR   Marianne Marshall, 33 66 Place, Long Beach, CA 90803.

MAU   Maurel Enterprises Inc, 225 W 34 St, New York, NY 10001.

MCD   Ray McDermott, 2109 Broadway, New York, NY 10023.

MJM   Mary Jane Matz, 235 W 70 St, New York, NY 10023.

MKR   Mark Kirmayer Artists Mgmt, 100 Manhattan Ave, Union City, NJ 07087.

MMS   Martha Moore Smith Ents, 2109 Broadway, New York, NY 10023.

NAP   Matthews/Napal Ltd, 270 West End Ave, New York, NY 10023.

NYR   New York Recital Assoc Inc, 353 W 57 St, New York, NY 10019.

OTA   Overland Talent Assoc, 210 E 52 St, New York, NY 10022.

PAL   Phyllis Allen, 1605 E Madison St, Seattle, WA 98122.

PDL   Michael Podoli Concert Mgmt, 171 W 71 St, New York, NY 10023.

PMS   PMS Concert Agency, 3200 37 Ave W, Seattle, WA 98199.

RAM   Robert Arrow Music Ents, 130 South 18 St, Philadelphia, PA 19103.

RIV   Riva Mgmt, 260 West End Ave, New York, NY 10023.

RMG   Robert M Gewald Mgmt, 2 W 59 St, New York, NY 10019.

INTERNATIONAL AGENTS

SAM   Sardos Artist Mgmt Corp, 180 West End Ave, New York, NY 10023.

SCO   Jim Scovotti Mgmt, 185 West End Ave, New York, NY 10023.

SFM   David Schiffmann, 57 W 68 St, New York, NY 10023.

SHA   Shaw Concerts Inc, 1995 Broadway, New York, NY 10023.

SIM   Arthur Shafman Int'l Mgmt Ltd, 520 Fifth Ave, New York, NY 10036.

SLD   Sterling Lord Agency, 660 Madison Ave, New York, NY 10022.

SMN   Eric Semon Assocs Inc, 111 W 57 St, New York, NY 10019.

SMT   Dina Smith, 13075 Broadway Terrace, Oakland, CA 94611.

SOF   Sheldon Soffer Mgmt Inc, 130 W 56 St, New York, NY 10019.

SOM   Sommers/Rosen Inc, 1405 Locust St, Philadelphia, PA 19102.

SSR   Smith-Stevens Representation Ltd, 1650 Broadway, New York, NY 10019.

SUH   Andrew Schulhof Mgmt, 260 West End Ave, New York, NY 10023.

TOR   Tornay Mgmt Ltd, 250 W 57 St, New York, NY 10019.

TPM   Torrence/Perrotta Mgmt, 1860 Broadway, New York, NY 10023.

UEB   Ruth Uebel, 205 E 63 St, New York, NY 10021.

USC   United Scenic Artists, 3435 S Dearborn, Chicago, IL.

UTA   Unique Talent Assoc, 297 Lenox Road, Brooklyn, NY 11226.

VAT   Vincent Attractions, 119 W 57 St, New York, NY 10019.

VIN   Edgar Vincent, 156 E 52 St, New York, NY 10022.

WFA   William Felber Agency, 6636 Hollywood Blvd, Los Angeles, CA 90028.

WLS   William L Stein Inc, 111 W 57 St, New York, NY 10019.

WMA   William Morris Agency, 1350 Ave of the Americas, New York, NY 10019.

YCA   Young Concert Artists, 75 E 55 St, New York, NY 10022.

USSR   **UNION OF SOVIET SOCIALIST REPUBLICS**

GOS   Grosconcert, Niglinnaya 15, Moscow.

VEN   **VENEZUELA**

CDV   Conciertos Daniel/Enrique de Quesada, Ave Urdaneta, Caracas.

YUG   **YUGOSLAVIA**

CDK   Concert Direktion/Foglar, Zagreb.

CRO   Croatiakoncert Agency, Trnjanska BB, Zagreb.

YGC   Yugoconcert, Terazije 41, Belgrade.